HANDBOOK OF
CHILD PSYCHOLOGY

HANDBOOK OF CHILD PSYCHOLOGY

FIFTH EDITION

Volume 2:   Cognition, Perception, and Language

Editor-in-Chief

WILLIAM DAMON

Volume Editors

DEANNA KUHN and ROBERT S. SIEGLER

John Wiley & Sons, Inc.

New York • Chichester • Weinheim • Brisbane • Singapore • Toronto

Publisher: Jeffrey W. Brown

Editor: Kelly A. Franklin

Managing Editor: Maureen B. Drexel

Composition
and Management: Publications Development Company of Texas

This text is printed on acid-free paper.

This publication is designed to provide accurate and authoritative
information in regard to the subject matter covered. It is sold
with the understanding that the publisher is not engaged in
rendering professional services. If legal, accounting, medical,
psychological, or any other expert assistance is required, the
services of a competent professional person should be sought.

Library of Congress Cataloging-in-Publication Data:

Handbook of child psychology / William Damon, editor. — 5th ed.
        p.   cm.
      Includes bibliographical references and index.
      Contents: v. 1. Theoretical models of human development /
Richard M. Lerner, volume editor — v. 2. Cognition, perception, and
language / Deanna Kuhn and Robert Siegler, volume editors —
v. 3. Social, emotional, and personality development / Nancy Eisenberg,
volume editor — v. 4. Child psychology in practice / Irving E. Sigel
and K. Ann Renninger, volume editors.
      ISBN #0-471-05730-4 (v. 2 : cloth : alk. paper). —
ISBN 0-471-17893-4 (set : alk. paper)
      1. Child psychology.   I. Damon, William, 1944–
BF721.H242   1997
155.4—dc21   96-49157

Printed in the United States of America

10 9 8 7 6 5 4 3 2 1

Editorial Advisory Board

Contributors

Richard Aslin, Ph.D.
Center for Visual Science & Department of Psychology
University of Rochester
Rochester, New York

Martin S. Banks, Ph.D.
School of Optometry & Department of Psychology
University of California, Berkeley
Berkeley, California

Janette B. Benson, Ph.D.
Department of Psychology
University of Denver
Denver, Colorado

Bennett I. Bertenthal, Ph.D.
Department of Psychology
University of Virginia
Charlottesville, Virginia

David F. Bjorklund, Ph.D.
Department of Psychology
Florida Atlantic University
Boca Raton, Florida

Lois Bloom, Ph.D.
Teachers College
Columbia University
New York, New York

Robbie Case, Ph.D.
Institute of Child Study
University of Toronto
Toronto, Ontario

Rachel K. Clifton, Ph.D.
Department of Psychology
University of Massachusetts
Amherst, Massachusetts

Judy S. DeLoache, Ph.D.
Department of Psychology
University of Illinois—Urbana/Champaign
Champaign, Illinois

Michel Ferrari, Ph.D.
Department of Psychology
University of Pittsburgh
Pittsburgh, Pennsylvania

John H. Flavell, Ph.D.
Department of Psychology
Stanford University
Stanford, California

Rochel Gelman, Ph.D.
Department of Psychology
University of California
Los Angeles, California

Susan A. Gelman, Ph.D.
Department of Psychology
University of Michigan
Ann Arbor, Michigan

Marshall M. Haith, Ph.D.
Department of Psychology
University of Denver
Denver, Colorado

Mark Johnson, Ph.D.
MRC Cognitive Development Unit
London, United Kingdom

Peter W. Jusczyk, Ph.D.
Department of Psychology
Johns Hopkins University
Baltimore, Maryland

Philip J. Kellman, Ph.D.
Department of Psychology
University of California, Los Angeles
Los Angeles, California

David Klahr, Ph.D.
Department of Psychology
Carnegie Mellon University
Pittsburgh, Pennsylvania

Deanna Kuhn, Ph.D.
Department of Developmental and
    Educational Psychology
Teachers College
Columbia University
New York, New York

Brian MacWhinney, Ph.D.
Department of Psychology
Carnegie Mellon University
Pittsburgh, Pennsylvania

Jean M. Mandler, Ph.D.
Department of Cognitive Science
University of California, San Diego and
Cognitive Development Unit
University College London
San Diego, California

Michael Maratsos, Ph.D.
Institute of Child Development
University of Minnesota
Minneapolis, Minnesota

Ellen M. Markman, Ph.D.
Psychology Department
Stanford University
Stanford, California

Kevin F. Miller, Ph.D.
Beckman Institute
University of Illinois—Urbana/Champaign
Urbana, Illinois

Patricia H. Miller, Ph.D.
Department of Psychology
University of Florida
Gainesville, Florida

David Moshman, Ph.D.
Department of Educational Psychology
University of Nebraska
Lincoln, Nebraska

Sophia L. Pierroutsakos, Ph.D.
Department of Psychology
University of Illinois—Urbana/Champaign
Champaign, Illinois

David B. Pisoni, Ph.D.
Department of Psychology
Indiana University
Bloomington, Indiana

Barbara Rogoff, Ph.D.
Department of Psychology
University of California, Santa Cruz
Santa Cruz, California

Wolfgang Schneider, Ph.D.
Department of Psychology
University of Wuerzburg
Wuerzburg, Germany

Robert S. Siegler, Ph.D.
Department of Psychology
Carnegie Mellon University
Pittsburgh, Pennsylvania

Robert J. Sternberg, Ph.D.
Department of Psychology
Yale University
New Haven, Connecticut

Henry M. Wellman, Ph.D.
Department of Psychology
University of Michigan
Ann Arbor, Michigan

Earl M. Williams, Ph.D.
Department of Psychology
University of California
Los Angeles, California

Amanda L. Woodward, Ph.D.
Department of Psychology
University of Chicago
Chicago, Illinois

Foreword

PAUL MUSSEN

This fifth edition of the *Handbook of Child Psychology* belongs to an invaluable scholarly tradition: the presentation, at approximately 15-year intervals, of a well-planned, comprehensive, authoritative account of the current state of the field. Successive editions of the *Handbook* (or *Manual,* as it was called in the first three editions) reflect the history of the study of human development over the past half-century.

The first two editions (the second, a moderately revised version of the first) reported the accomplishments of the field in an earlier era during which there were relatively few developmental psychologists. *Description* and *measurement of changes over time* were the principal goals of research and speculation. Very little attention was paid to explanation, theory, systems, or models.

The years immediately following World War II were a watershed for science, a period marked by an immensely powerful surge in interest and activity in all sciences, including psychology. The number of scientifically trained psychologists proliferated, and fields or subdivisions within the discipline became more clearly defined. A more modern form of developmental psychology began to take shape and became a major field that was linked to other areas of psychology and allied disciplines but had its own agendas of research and theory. Continuities with earlier work were evident in new investigations and conceptualizations of standard topics—that is, topics of enduring interest—such as language, intelligence, moral behavior, the nature–nurture controversy, and social influences on development. Not surprisingly, the new investigations surpassed the earlier ones in breadth, depth, and scientific sophistication.

Most significantly, the scope of the field was immeasurably extended to include numerous new topics; innovative, more adequate methods of investigation were devised, and *explanation*—and therefore theories about mechanisms and processes—was emphasized. And, for many reasons, the new generation of developmental psychologists—many of whom were trained in other areas such as social, experimental, and clinical psychology—were generally more productive than their predecessors.

Among the myriad factors that account for the many significant advances in the field are: a basic quest for knowledge, and the self-perpetuating nature of scientific endeavors—investigations that yield interesting, sometimes unexpected, findings prompt new questions (as well as modifications of theories) and, consequently, further research. In addition, and of equal importance, developmental psychologists are generally sensitive to social issues and technological changes that may have significant impacts on children's health and development. These concerns frequently are sources of novel investigations and theories, further expanding the boundaries of the field.

Because developmental psychology had been transformed since the end of World War II, the third (1970) edition of the *Manual,* which I edited, was inevitably vastly different from the first two. In addition to up-to-date chapters on topics of continued interest, it included several chapters on theory, psycholinguistics, aggression, attachment, behavior genetics, and creativity, all of which still stand as central issues.

Like most productive scientific disciplines, developmental psychology continues to progress ceaselessly, in profound and complex ways, and at an ever-increasing rate. In 1983, the fourth edition of the *Handbook* was published. It was twice the size of the third edition, and it encompassed standard topics (usually handled in more refined and penetrating ways) and many new, fruitful areas.

Like the years following World War II, the period since 1980 has been one of unprecedented growth, change, and specialization in developmental psychology. The many theoretical and empirical developments in the discipline generated the need for this new edition. It is virtually impossible to delineate the numerous factors affecting its structure and contents, but some of the most significant influences—only a small sample, hardly an exhaustive list—can be highlighted. For example, compelling evidence of the variety and complexity of the determinants of all parameters of psychological development (and the interactions among them) cast doubt on the explanatory power of major theories that conceptualized development in terms of very few dimensions. In widely accepted current approaches and models, development is viewed as the product of multiple variables operating at multiple levels. This orientation, most explicit in several chapters of Volume 1, is also apparent in many other sections in which person–context interactions are discussed. The multivariate approach also calls attention to the limitations on generalizations from research; conclusions derived from a study with a particular population and under specified conditions may not be valid for other groups or under other circumstances. As a consequence, many chapters in this new edition include in-depth discussions of patterns of development in ethnic minorities and in diverse familial and peer group contexts. Renewed vigorous and innovative research in critical psychological parameters such as temperament, character, and emotion, reflected in several chapters, has also been significantly influenced by the multivariable approach.

As the search for the processes underlying development continues, the need to involve significant advances in other scientific disciplines accelerates. Thus, the present edition has chapters that incorporate information from the cognitive sciences, information processing, neurology, and the cultural psychology of development. Moreover, the boundaries of the field have been substantially broadened and enhanced by recent empirical work and conceptualization about psychological development throughout the life span, as reflected in several chapters.

Fortunately, in recent years, professional practitioners and policy makers have recognized the actual and potential contributions of developmental psychology to the solution of critical social and educational problems—for example, problems of parenting, childrearing in nontraditional families, effective teaching, school drop-out, and violence in television programs. Because of this recognition and the notable advances in applied research, one of the volumes of this edition is devoted exclusively to child psychology in practice.

To assist him in the extraordinarily difficult and complicated task of selecting and organizing the most prominent and exciting areas of contemporary developmental psychology, William Damon, the general editor, chose six volume editors who are recognized leaders in the field and have considerable experience in editing journals and books. Next, outstanding experts were invited to contribute critical, integrated chapters on the theoretical and substantive accomplishments of their area of expertise.

As a consequence of these authors' impeccable scholarship, intuitive and informed insights, dedication, creativity, and painstaking work, the fifth edition of the *Handbook* fully achieves its purpose: the timely presentation of an accurate and comprehensive report of the current state of developmental psychology. Readers who compare these volumes with earlier editions will be impressed with how much our understanding of human development has been enhanced in recent years, how much more solid information is available, and how much deeper and more relevant conceptualizations in the field have become. But this indispensable publication is more than an encyclopedic report, for it is enriched by thoughtful perceptions of key issues and keen insights about where matters stand and what still needs to be done. It is an invaluable aid in mapping out the future directions of this vital and dynamic field. The editors and authors have done the field of developmental psychology a great service. Everyone who is seriously interested in human development is deeply indebted to them.

Preface to The Handbook of Child Psychology, Fifth Edition

WILLIAM DAMON

THE *HANDBOOK*'S BACK PAGES—AND OURS

Developmental questions may be asked about almost any human endeavor—even about the enterprise of asking developmental questions. We may ask: How has the field of developmental study developed? In a field that has been preoccupied by continuity and change, where are the continuities and where are the changes?

Many of the chapters of this fifth edition of the *Handbook of Child Psychology* address our field's growth and progress in connection with the particular topics that they examine, and the three historical chapters (by Cairns, by Overton, and by Valsiner) present a panoramic view of our profession. As general editor of the *Handbook's* fifth edition, I wish to add a further data point: the history of the *Handbook,* which stands as an indicator of the continuities and changes within our field. The *Handbook* has long and notable credentials as a beacon, organizer, and encyclopedia of developmental study. What does its history tell us about where we have been, what we have learned, and where we are going? What does it tell us about what has changed and what has remained the same in the questions that we ask, in the methods that we use, and in the theoretical ideas that we draw on in our quest to understand human development?

It is tempting to begin with a riddle: What fifth edition has six predecessors but just three prior namesakes? Given the context of the riddle, there is not much mystery to the answer, but the reasons for it will tell us something about the *Handbook* and its history.

Leonard Carmichael was President of Tufts University when he guided Wiley's first edition of the *Handbook.* The book (one volume at that time) was called the *Manual of Child Psychology,* in keeping with Carmichael's intention of producing an "advanced scientific manual to bridge the gap between the excellent and varied elementary textbooks in this field and the scientific periodical literature. . . . "[1]

The publication date was 1946, and Carmichael complained that "this book has been a difficult and expensive one to produce, especially under wartime conditions."[2] Nevertheless, the project was worth the effort. The *Manual* quickly became the bible of graduate training and scholarly work in the field, available virtually everywhere that children's development was studied. Eight years later, now head of the Smithsonian Institution as well as editor of the book's second edition, Carmichael wrote, in the preface: "The favorable reception that the first edition received not only in America but all over the world is indicative of the growing importance of the study of the phenomena of the growth and development of the child."[3]

The second edition had a long life; not until 1970 did Wiley bring out a third edition. Carmichael was retired by then, but he still had a keen interest in the book. At his insistence, his own name became part of the title of the third edition: *Carmichael's Manual of Child Psychology.* Paul Mussen took over as editor, and once again the project flourished. Now a two-volume set, the third edition swept across the social sciences, generating widespread interest in developmental psychology and its related disciplines. Rarely had a scholarly compendium become both so dominant in its own field and so familiar in related disciplines. The set became an essential source for graduate students and advanced scholars alike. Publishers referred to *Carmichael's Manual* as the standard against which other scientific handbooks were compared. The fourth edition, published in 1983, was redesignated by John Wiley & Sons as the *Handbook of Child Psychology.* By then, Carmichael had passed away. The set of books, now expanded to four volumes, became widely referred to in the field as "the Mussen handbook."

Words can have the power to reawaken dusty memories. When John Wiley & Sons replaced the title word *Manual* with *Handbook,* an important piece of scholarly history was inadvertently recalled. Wiley's fourth edition had a long-forgotten ancestor that was unknown to most of the new book's readers. The ancestor was called *A Handbook of Child Psychology,* and it preceded Wiley's own first edition by over 15 years. I quote here from two statements by Leonard Carmichael:

> Both as editor of the *Manual* and as the author of a special chapter, the writer is indebted . . . [for] extensive excerpts and the use of other materials previously published in the *Handbook of Child Psychology, Revised Edition. . . .*[4]

> Both the *Handbook of Child Psychology* and the *Handbook of Child Psychology, Revised Edition,* were edited by Dr. Carl Murchison. I wish to express here my profound appreciation for the pioneer work done by Dr. Murchison in producing these handbooks and other advanced books in psychology. The *Manual* owes much in spirit and content to the foresight and editorial skill of Dr. Murchison.[5]

The first quote comes from Carmichael's preface to the 1946 edition, the second from his preface to the 1954 edition. We shall never know why Carmichael waited until the 1954 edition to add the personal tribute to Carl Murchison. Perhaps a careless typist dropped the laudatory passage from a handwritten version of the 1946 preface, and its omission escaped Carmichael's notice. Perhaps eight years of further adult development increased Carmichael's generosity of spirit; or perhaps Murchison or his family complained. In any case, Carmichael from the start directly acknowledged the roots of his *Manual,* if not their author. Those roots are a revealing part of the *Handbook's* story— and of our own "back pages," as intellectual descendants of the early pioneers in the Murchison and Carmichael handbooks.

Carl Murchison was a scholar/impresario who edited *The Psychological Register;* founded and edited key psychological journals; wrote books on social psychology, politics, and the criminal mind; and compiled an assortment of handbooks, psychology texts, autobiographies of renowned psychologists, and even a book on psychic beliefs (Sir Arthur Conan Doyle and Harry Houdini were among the contributors). Murchison's first *Handbook of Child Psychology* was published by a small university press in 1931,

when the field itself was still in its childhood. Murchison wrote:

> Experimental psychology has had a much older scientific and academic status [than child psychology], but at the present time it is probable that much less money is being spent for pure research in the field of experimental psychology than is being spent in the field of child psychology. In spite of this obvious fact, many experimental psychologists continue to look upon the field of child psychology as a proper field of research for women and for men whose experimental masculinity is not of the maximum. This attitude of patronage is based almost entirely upon a blissful ignorance of what is going on in the tremendously virile field of child behavior.[6]

Murchison's masculine figures of speech, of course, are from another time; they might supply good material for a social history study of gender stereotyping. That aside, Murchison was prescient in the task that he undertook and the way that he went about it. At the time this passage was written, developmental psychology was known only in Europe and in a few American labs and universities. Nevertheless, Murchison predicted the field's impending ascent: "The time is not far distant, if it is not already here, when nearly all competent psychologists will recognize that one-half of the whole field of psychology is involved in the problem of how the infant becomes an adult psychologically."[7]

For his original 1931 *Handbook,* Murchison looked to Europe and to a handful of American centers (or "field stations") for child research (Iowa, Minnesota, University of California at Berkeley, Columbia, Stanford, Yale, Clark). Murchison's Europeans included a young epistemologist named Jean Piaget, who, in an essay on "Children's Philosophies," quoted from verbal interviews of 60 Genevan children between the ages of 4 and 12 years. Piaget's chapter would provide most American readers with their introduction to his initial research program on children's conceptions of the world. Another European, Charlotte Bühler, wrote a chapter on children's social behavior. In this chapter, which still reads freshly today, Bühler described intricate play and communication patterns among toddlers—patterns that developmental psychology would not rediscover until the late 1970s. Bühler also anticipated the critiques of Piaget that would appear during the sociolinguistics heyday of the 1970s: "Piaget, in his studies on children's talk and reasoning, emphasizes that their talk is much more egocentric than social . . . that children from three to seven years accompany all their manipulations with talk which actually is not so much intercourse as monologue . . . [but] the special relationship of the child to each of the different members of the household is distinctly reflected in the respective conversations."[8] Other Europeans included Anna Freud, who wrote on "The Psychoanalysis of the Child," and Kurt Lewin, who wrote on "Environmental Forces in Child Behavior and Development."

The Americans whom Murchison chose were equally distinguished. Arnold Gesell wrote a nativistic account of his twin studies—an enterprise that remains familiar to us today—and Louis Terman wrote a comprehensive account of everything known about the "gifted child." Harold Jones described the developmental effects of birth order, Mary Cover Jones wrote about children's emotions, Florence Goodenough wrote about children's drawings, and Dorothea McCarthy wrote about language development. Vernon Jones's chapter on "children's morals" focused on the growth of *character*, a notion that was to become lost to the field during the cognitive-developmental revolution, but has lately reemerged as a primary concern in the study of moral development.

Murchison's vision of child psychology left room for an examination of cultural differences as well. He included a young anthropologist named Margaret Mead, just back from her tours of Samoa and New Guinea. In this early essay, Mead wrote that her motivation in traveling to the South Seas was to discredit the view that Piaget, Levy-Bruhl, and other nascent structuralists had put forth concerning "animism" in young children's thinking. (Interestingly, about one-third of Piaget's chapter in the same volume was dedicated to showing how it takes Genevan children years to outgrow animism.) Mead reported some data that she called "amazing": "In not one of the 32,000 drawings (by young 'primitive' children) was there a single case of personalization of animals, material phenomena, or inanimate objects."[9] Mead parlayed these data into a tough-minded critique of Western psychology's ethnocentrism, making the point that animism and other beliefs are more likely to be culturally induced than intrinsic to early cognitive development. This is hardly an unfamiliar theme in contemporary psychology. Mead also offered a research guide for developmental field workers in strange cultures, complete with methodological and practical advice, such as: translate questions into native linguistic categories; don't do controlled experiments; don't do studies that require knowing ages of subjects, which are usually unknowable; and live next door to the children whom you are studying.

Despite the imposing roster of authors that Murchison had assembled for the 1931 *Handbook of Child Psychology*, his achievement did not satisfy him for long. Barely two years later, Murchison put out a second edition, of which he wrote: "Within a period of slightly more than two years, this first revision bears scarcely any resemblance to the original *Handbook of Child Psychology*. This is due chiefly to the great expansion in the field during the past three years and partly to the improved insight of the editor."[10]

Murchison also saw fit to provide the following warning in his second edition: "There has been no attempt to simplify, condense, or to appeal to the immature mind. This volume is prepared specifically for the scholar, and its form is for his maximum convenience."[11] It is likely that sales of Murchison's first volume did not approach textbook levels. Perhaps he also received negative comments regarding its accessibility. For the record, though, despite Murchison's continued use of masculine phraseology, 10 of the 24 authors in the second edition were women.

Murchison exaggerated when he wrote that his second edition bore little resemblance to the first. Almost half of the chapters were virtually the same, with minor additions and updating. Moreover, some of the authors whose original chapters were dropped were asked to write about new topics. So, for example, Goodenough wrote about mental testing rather than about children's drawings, and Gesell wrote a more general statement of his maturational theory that went well beyond the twin studies.

But Murchison also made some abrupt changes. Anna Freud was dropped, auguring the marginalization of psychoanalysis within academic psychology. Leonard Carmichael made his first appearance, as author of a major chapter (by far, the longest in the book) on prenatal and perinatal growth. Three other physiologically oriented chapters were added as well: one on neonatal motor behavior, one on visual–manual functions during the first two years of life, and one on physiological "appetites" such as hunger, rest, and sex. Combined with the Goodenough and Gesell shifts in focus, these additions gave the 1933 *Handbook* more of a biological thrust, in keeping with Murchison's long-standing desire to display the hard-science backbone of the emerging field.

Leonard Carmichael took his 1946 *Manual* several steps further in the same direction. First, he appropriated five Murchison chapters on biological or experimental topics such as physiological growth, scientific methods, and mental testing. Second, he added three new biologically oriented chapters on animal infancy, on physical growth, and on motor and behavioral maturation (a *tour de force* by Myrtal McGraw that instantly made Gesell's chapter in the same volume obsolete). Third, he commissioned Wayne Dennis to write an adolescence chapter that focused exclusively on physiological changes associated with puberty. Fourth, Carmichael dropped Piaget and Bühler.

But five Murchison chapters on social and cultural influences in development were retained: two chapters on environmental forces on the child (by Kurt Lewin and by Harold Jones), Dorothea McCarthy's chapter on children's language, Vernon Jones's chapter on children's morality (now entitled "Character Development—An Objective Approach"), and Margaret Mead's chapter on "primitive" children (now enhanced by several spectacular photos of mothers and children from exotic cultures around the world). Carmichael stayed with three other psychologically oriented Murchison topics (emotional development, gifted children, and sex differences), but selected new authors to cover them.

Carmichael's 1954 revision—his second and final edition—was very close in structure and content to the 1946 *Manual*. Carmichael again retained the heart of Murchison's original vision, many of Murchison's original authors and chapter topics, and some of the same material that dated all the way back to the 1931 *Handbook*. Not surprisingly, the chapters that were closest to Carmichael's own interests got the most significant updating. As Murchison had tried to do, Carmichael leaned toward the biological and physiological whenever possible. He clearly favored experimental treatments of psychological processes. Yet Carmichael still kept the social, cultural, and psychological analyses by Lewin, Mead, McCarthy, Terman, Harold Jones, and Vernon Jones, and he even went so far as to add one new chapter on social development by Harold and Gladys Anderson and one new chapter on emotional development by Arthur Jersild.

The Murchison/Carmichael volumes make for fascinating reading, even today. The perennial themes of the field were there from the start: the nature–nurture debate; the generalizations of universalists opposed by the particularizations of contextualists; the alternating emphases on continuities and discontinuities during ontogenesis; and the standard categories of maturation, learning, locomotor activity, perception, cognition, language, emotion, conduct, morality, and culture—all separated for the sake of analysis, yet, as authors throughout each of the volumes acknowledged, all somehow inextricably joined in the dynamic mix of human development.

These things have not changed. Yet much in the early handbooks/manuals is now irrevocably dated. Long lists of children's dietary preferences, sleeping patterns, elimination habits, toys, and somatic types look quaint and pointless through today's lenses. The chapters on children's thought and language were done prior to the great contemporary breakthroughs in neurology and brain/behavior research, and they show it. The chapters on social and emotional development were ignorant of the processes of social influence and self-regulation that soon would be revealed through attribution research and other studies in social psychology. Terms such as *behavior genetics, social cognition, dynamic systems, information processing,* and *developmental psychopathology* were unknown. Even Mead's rendition of the "primitive child" stands as a weak straw in comparison to the wealth of cross-cultural knowledge available today.

Most tellingly, the assortments of odd facts and normative trends were tied together by very little theory throughout the Carmichael chapters. It was as if, in the exhilaration of discovery at the frontiers of a new field, all the facts looked interesting in and of themselves. That, of course, is what makes so much of the material seem odd and arbitrary. It is hard to know what to make of the lists of facts, where to place them, which ones were worth keeping track of and which ones are expendable. Not surprisingly, the bulk of the data presented in the Carmichael manuals seems not only outdated by today's standards but, worse, irrelevant.

By 1970, the importance of theory for understanding human development had become apparent. Looking back on Carmichael's last *Manual,* Paul Mussen wrote: "The 1954 edition of this *Manual* had only one theoretical chapter, and that was concerned with Lewinian theory which, so far as we can see, has not had a significant lasting impact on developmental psychology."[12] The intervening years had seen a turning away from the norm of psychological research once fondly referred to as "dust-bowl empiricism."

The Mussen 1970 handbook—or *Carmichael's Manual,* as it was still called—had an entirely new look. The two-volume set carried only one chapter from the earlier books—Carmichael's updated version of his own long chapter on the "Onset and Early Development of Behavior," which had made its appearance under a different title in Murchison's 1933 edition. Otherwise, as Mussen wrote in his preface, "It should be clear from the outset . . . that the present volumes are not, in any sense, a *revision* of the earlier editions; this is a completely new *Manual.*"[13]

And it was. In comparison to Carmichael's last edition 16 years earlier, the scope, variety, and theoretical depth of the Mussen volumes were astonishing. The field had blossomed, and the new *Manual* showcased many of the new bouquets that were being produced. The biological perspective was still strong, grounded by chapters on physical growth (by J. M. Tanner) and physiological development (by Dorothy Eichorn), and by Carmichael's revised chapter (now made more elegant by some excerpts from Greek philosophy and modern poetry). But two other cousins of biology also were represented, in an ethological chapter by Eckhard Hess, and a behavior genetics chapter by Gerald McClearn. These chapters were to define the major directions of biological research in the field for at least the next three decades.

As for theory, Mussen's *Handbook* was thoroughly permeated with it. Much of the theorizing was organized around the approaches that, in 1970, were known as the "three grand systems": (a) Piaget's cognitive-developmentalism, (b) psychoanalysis, and (c) learning theory. Piaget was given the most extensive treatment. He reappeared in the *Manual,* this time authoring a comprehensive (and some say, definitive) statement of his entire theory, which now bore little resemblance to his 1931/1933 sortings of children's intriguing verbal expressions. In addition, chapters by John Flavell, by David Berlyne, by Martin Hoffman, and by William Kessen, Marshall Haith, and Philip Salapatek, all gave major treatments to one or another aspect of Piaget's body of work. Other approaches were represented as well. Herbert and Ann Pick explicated Gibsonian theory in a chapter on sensation and perception, Jonas Langer wrote a chapter on Werner's organismic theory, David McNeill wrote a Chomskian account of language development, and Robert LeVine wrote an early version of what was soon to become "culture theory."

With its increased emphasis on theory, the 1970 *Manual* explored in depth a matter that had been all but neglected in the *Manual's* previous versions: the mechanisms of change that could account for, to use Murchison's old phrase, "the problem of how the infant becomes an adult psychologically." In the process, old questions such as the relative importance of nature *versus* nurture were revisited, but with far more sophisticated conceptual and methodological tools.

Beyond theory building, the 1970 *Manual* addressed an array of new topics and featured new contributors: peer interaction (Willard Hartup), attachment (Eleanor Maccoby and John Masters), aggression (Seymour Feshback),

individual differences (Jerome Kagan and Nathan Kogan), and creativity (Michael Wallach). All of these areas of interest are still very much with us at century's end.

If the 1970 *Manual* reflected a blossoming of the field's plantings, the 1983 *Handbook* reflected a field whose ground cover had spread beyond any boundaries that could have been previously anticipated. New growth had sprouted in literally dozens of separate locations. A French garden, with its overarching designs and tidy compartments, had turned into an English garden, a bit unruly but often glorious in its profusion. Mussen's two-volume *Carmichael's Manual* had now become the four-volume Mussen *Handbook,* with a page-count increase that came close to tripling the 1970 edition.

The grand old theories were breaking down. Piaget was still represented by his 1970 piece, but his influence was on the wane throughout the other chapters. Learning theory and psychoanalysis were scarcely mentioned. Yet the early theorizing had left its mark, in vestiges that were apparent in new approaches, and in the evident conceptual sophistication with which authors treated their material. No return to dust-bowl empiricism could be found anywhere in the set. Instead, a variety of classical and innovative ideas were coexisting: ethology, neurobiology, information processing, attribution theory, cultural approaches, communications theory, behavioral genetics, sensory-perception models, psycholinguistics, sociolinguistics, discontinuous stage theories, and continuous memory theories all took their places, with none quite on center stage. Research topics now ranged from children's play to brain lateralization, from children's family life to the influences of school, day care, and disadvantageous risk factors. There also was coverage of the burgeoning attempts to use developmental theory as a basis for clinical and educational interventions. The interventions usually were described at the end of chapters that had discussed the research relevant to the particular intervention efforts, rather than in whole chapters dedicated specifically to issues of practice.

This brings us to the present—the *Handbook's* fifth (but really seventh) edition. I will leave it to future reviewers to provide a summation of what we have done. The volume editors have offered introductory and/or concluding renditions of their own volumes. I will add to their efforts by stating here the overall intent of our design, and by commenting on some directions that our field has taken in the years from 1931 to 1998.

We approached this edition with the same purpose that Murchison, Carmichael, and Mussen before us had shared:

"to provide," as Mussen wrote, "a comprehensive and accurate picture of the current state of knowledge—the major systematic thinking and research—in the most important research areas of the psychology of human development."[14] We assumed that the *Handbook* should be aimed "specifically for the scholar," as Murchison declared, and that it should have the character of an "advanced text," as Carmichael defined it. We expected, though, that our audience may be more interdisciplinary than the readerships of previous editions, given the greater tendency of today's scholars to cross back and forth among fields such as psychology, cognitive science, neurobiology, history, linguistics, sociology, anthropology, education, and psychiatry. We also believed that research-oriented practitioners should be included under the rubric of the "scholars" for whom this *Handbook* was intended. To that end, we devoted, for the first time, and entire volume to "child psychology in practice."

Beyond these very general intentions, we have let chapters in the *Handbook's* fifth edition take their own shape. We solicited the chapters from authors who were widely acknowledged to be among the leading experts in their areas of the field; although we know that, given an entirely open-ended selection process and budget, we would have invited a very large number of other leading researchers whom we did not have the space—and thus the privilege—to include. With only two exceptions, every author whom we invited chose to accept the challenge.

Our directive to authors was simple: Convey your area of the field as you see it. From then on, the 112 authors took center stage—with, of course, much constructive feedback from reviewers and volume editors. But no one tried to impose a perspective, a preferred method of inquiry, or domain boundaries on any of the chapters. The authors freely expressed their views on what researchers in their areas attempt to accomplish, why they do so, how they go about it, what intellectual sources they draw on, what progress they have made, and what conclusions they have reached.

The result, in my opinion, is yet more glorious profusion, but perhaps contained a bit by some broad patterns that have emerged across our garden. Powerful theoretical models and approaches—not quite unified theories, such as the three grand systems—have begun once again to organize much of the field's research and practice. There is great variety in these models and approaches, and each is drawing together significant clusters of work. Some have been only recently formulated, and some are combinations or modifications of classic theories that still have staying power.

Among the formidable models and approaches that the reader will find in this *Handbook* are the dynamic systems theories, the life-span and life-course approaches, cognitive science and neural models, the behavior genetics approach, person–context interaction theories, action theories, cultural psychology, ecological models, neo-Piagetian and neo-Vygotskian models. Although some of these models and approaches have been in the making for some time, my impression is that they are just now coming into their own, in that researchers now are drawing on them more directly, taking their implied assumptions and hypotheses seriously, using them with specificity and with full control, and exploiting all of their implications for practice. A glance at the contents listings for the *Handbook's* four volumes will reveal the staggering breadth of concerns addressed through use of these models and approaches.

The other pattern that emerges is a self-conscious reflection about the notion of development. The reflection is an earnest one, yet it has a more affirmative tone than similar discussions in recent years. We have just passed through a time when the very credibility of a developmental approach was itself thrown into question. The whole idea of progress and advance, implicit in the notion of development, seemed out of step with ideological principles of diversity and equality.

Some genuine intellectual benefits accrued from that critique: the field has come to better appreciate diverse developmental pathways. But, like many critique positions, it led to excesses that created, for some in the field of developmental study, a kind of crisis of faith. For some, it became questionable even to explore issues that lie at the heart of human development. Learning, growth, achievement, individual continuity and change, common beliefs and standards—all became suspect as subjects of investigation.

Fortunately, as the contents of this *Handbook* attest, such doubts are waning. As was probably inevitable, the field's center of gravity has returned to the study of development. After all, the story of growth during infancy, childhood, and adolescence is a developmental story of multi-faceted learning, of acquisitions of skills and knowledge, of waxing powers of attention and memory, of formations and transformations of character and personality, of increases in understanding of self and others, of advances in emotional and behavioral regulation, of progress in communicating and collaborating with others, and of a host of other achievements that are chronicled in this *Handbook*.

Parents and teachers in every part of the world recognize and value such developmental achievements in their children, although they do not always know how to foster them. Neither do we in all cases. But the kinds of scientific understanding that the *Handbook's* authors explicate in their chapters—scientific understanding created by themselves as well as by fellow researchers in the field of developmental study—have brought us all several giant steps toward this goal.

NOTES

1. Carmichael, L. (Ed.). (1946). *Manual of child psychology.* New York: Wiley, p. viii.

2. Carmichael, L. (Ed.). (1946). *Manual of child psychology.* New York: Wiley, p. vi.

3. Carmichael, L. (Ed.). (1954). *Manual of child psychology: Second edition.* New York: Wiley, p. v.

4. Carmichael, L. (Ed.). (1946). *Manual of child psychology.* New York: Wiley, p. vi.

5. Carmichael, L. (Ed.). (1954). *Manual of child psychology: Second edition.* New York: Wiley, p. vii.

6. Murchison, C. (Ed.). (1931). *A handbook of child psychology.* Worcester, MA: Clark University Press, p. ix.

7. Murchison, C. (Ed.). (1931). *A handbook of child psychology.* Worcester, MA: Clark University Press, p. x.

8. Buhler, C. (1931). The social participation of infants and toddlers. In C. Murchison (Ed.), *A handbook of child psychology.* Worcester, MA: Clark University Press, p. 138.

9. Mead, M. (1931). The primitive child. In C. Murchison (Ed.), *A handbook of child psychology.* Worcester, MA: Clark University Press, p. 400.

10. Murchison, C. (Ed.). (1933). *A handbook of child psychology: Second edition (Revised).* Worcester, MA: Clark University Press, p. viii.

11. Murchison, C. (Ed.). (1933). *A handbook of child psychology: Second edition (Revised).* Worcester, MA: Clark University Press, p. viii.

12. Mussen, P. (Ed.). (1970). *Carmichael's manual of child psychology.* New York: Wiley, p. x.

13. Mussen, P. (Ed.). (1970). *Carmichael's manual of child psychology.* New York: Wiley, p. x.

14. Mussen, P. (Ed.). (1983). *Handbook of child psychology.* New York: Wiley, p. vii.

Acknowledgments

The fifth edition of the *Handbook* was truly a team effort. The six volume editors have my deepest gratitude for their countless hours of devoted work. No project editor has ever had a finer group of collaborators. I also thank Kelly Franklin, of John Wiley & Sons, Inc., for her inspired editorial efforts from the time of the project's inception. Without Kelly's persistence and good sense, publication in 1998 would not have been possible.

Many people contributed invaluable advice during one or another phase of the fifth edition's production. They are far too many to mention here, even if I had managed to keep systematic records of all conversations on the project's development. The final product has benefited greatly from the insights and feedback of all those who responded. In particular, I note two giants of the field whose wise counsel and generosity remain prominent in my mind: Paul Mussen and Eleanor Maccoby.

In slightly altered form, my preface was published in *Human Development* (March–April, 1997). I am grateful to Barbara Rogoff for her editorial help in this process, and to Anne Gregory for her help in obtaining background materials. Josef and Marsy Mittlemann's support has been vital in facilitating this and other scholarly activities at the Brown University Center for the Study of Human Development. My assistant, Pat Balsofiore, deserves our unending gratitude for her valiant work in helping to organize this vast endeavor.

WILLIAM DAMON

Foreword to Volume 2
Cognition, Perception, and Language

ROBERT S. SIEGLER

The goal of this volume is to depict current understanding of cognitive development. The authors of the 19 chapters form a remarkable assemblage that includes many of the deepest thinkers in the field. They have set aside large amounts of time and have dedicated the intense thought necessary to capture the progress that has been made in the field during the 15 years since publication of the previous *Handbook*. They also have sketched their visions of the issues and discoveries that lie just beyond the horizon. The result is a volume that builds on and expands the exceptional tradition of the four previous Carmichael and Mussen manuals.

Planning a volume aimed at depicting current understanding of cognitive development is quite a challenge. In approaching this task, we first independently generated possible books: sets of chapters that we thought should be included and nominees who would be good choices to write them. We were pleased to see that over half of the chapters and over half of the author choices on our lists matched. Our next task was to merge the proposals and arrive at a more manageable number than the 25 chapters that we together had suggested. Our efforts were guided by several goals. First, we wanted to represent adequately all of the main topic areas within cognitive development, broadly construed: perception, motor activity, language, learning, memory, conceptual understanding, reasoning, problem solving, social cognition, and so on. Second, we wanted to include research on all age groups from infants through adolescents. Third, we wanted to represent the most influential theoretical approaches, including neo-Piagetian, information processing, theory–theory, and cultural–contextual approaches. Fourth, we wanted authors who possessed broad understanding of their fields and whose own research was interesting and important. After a few discussions, we converged on a set of chapters and authors that met all of these goals.

We then sent letters inviting authors to contribute to the *Handbook*. The invitations asked them to emphasize four types of issues:

1. *Historical.* Who and what gave rise to the conceptual perspective and body of research covered in the chapter?
2. *Views of the current state of their research area.* Authors were asked not only to summarize the studies that had been done but also to emphasize the questions they saw as central, and the ideas and methods they saw as critical for making progress.
3. *Change mechanisms.* What were the best proposals and evidence regarding the contribution of particular change mechanisms to development in their area?
4. *Predictions and recommendations.* What were their best guesses concerning the questions that would emerge as most important in the near future, and how should those questions be approached?

Despite the challenge of these demands, and the incalculable amount of work involved in summarizing 15 years of research in a fairly broad area, in all but one case, the people we asked to write the chapters agreed to do so.

The invitations also stipulated that the chapters be no more than 35,000 words. In the context of a *Handbook* chapter, this converts to about 80 double-spaced manuscript pages plus references—not much space to cover an area as broad and popular as social cognition, semantic and conceptual development, or many of the other chapter topics. The requirement reflected the publisher's need to limit the length (and the expense) of the volume. On the plus side, this kept the chapters short enough to assign as readings in graduate courses. It also probably increased their liveliness and the number of people who will read them from beginning to end. On the minus side, a great many interesting ideas and findings could not be covered. Readers are sure to discover that some of their favorite studies are not discussed at all, or are discussed in less depth than they deserve. The fault is not the authors'; they all were forced to make impossible choices about what to put in and what to leave out. Indeed, they tried to include more; almost all of them were asked to shorten their first drafts, often by 20 or 30 pages, and occasionally by as much as 80 pages. Thus, the volume is more a survey of the most influential theories, perspectives, methods, and research findings about cognitive development than a compendium of current knowledge.

Coverage within the book overlaps that of the cognitive development volume in the 1983 edition, but it also differs in some notable ways, reflecting two types of changes. One change involves the organization of the *Handbook* as a whole. Research with infants is no longer concentrated in a separate volume; instead, it has been distributed among all of the volumes of the *Handbook*. This has resulted in the present volume's covering four topics that were in the *Infancy and Psychobiological Development* volume of the 1983 edition: (a) neural development, (b) visual perception, (c) auditory perception, and (d) infant cognition. Including these chapters in this volume creates a more consistent topical coverage. It also is congruent with the fieldwide trend toward increasing integration of research on infants with that on toddlers, preschoolers, and older children. Also reflecting this trend, many other chapters in the current volume include considerable coverage of development during infancy. Such coverage is particularly prominent in Mandler's chapter on representation, Bloom's chapter on language development in context, Woodward and Markman's chapter on semantic and conceptual development, Wellman and Gelman's chapter on knowledge acquisition, and Schneider and Bjorklund's chapter on memory development. Including this coverage of cognitive growth during infancy has allowed a more seamless depiction of development within each topical area than could otherwise have been achieved.

The second, and larger, reason for the differences between the current cognitive development volume and its predecessor is that the field has changed. A number of chapters focus on topics barely covered or not covered at all in the previous volume. These include Bertenthal and Clifton's chapter on motor skills, Rogoff's chapter on cognition as a collaborative process, Moshman's chapter on cognitive development beyond childhood, Wellman and Gelman's chapter on theory–theory approaches to conceptual understanding, and Klahr and MacWhinney's chapter on computer simulation models of development. In each instance, the new chapters describe areas in which knowledge has greatly increased since 1983.

The chapter titled "Perception and Action" is a good example. As Bertenthal and Clifton note, the last *Handbook* chapter on motor development was in the 1954 edition, more than 40 years ago. The reason for this long hiatus was that, until about 1980, relatively little research was being done in the area, and, when present, it failed to capture the imagination of the broader research community. However, increased recognition of the interdependence of perception and action, ideas from Gibsonian and dynamic systems theories, the inherent importance of motor activity for understanding development, and the advantages for the modeling of change of an area with massive amounts of observable behavior had led to a revitalization of research on perception and action. Given the area's current liveliness and inherent importance, future editions of the *Handbook* seem likely to continue to include it.

New chapters are not the only reflections of changes in the field. Topics included in previous editions of the *Handbook* often are approached quite differently in this one. For example, chapters on infant cognition, learning, semantics, representation, conceptual understanding, and social cognition appear in both the previous and the present editions. However, the chapters on these topics in the current volume focus considerably more on infants' and young children's high-level, domain-specific theories, principles, and constraints. Perhaps the most striking change is in the social cognition chapter. As Flavell and Miller note, theory of mind could not have received much coverage in the 1983 *Handbook,* because research on it was just getting started. This time, it is the dominant topic in the chapter. This status is consistent with its having become probably the single most popular research area in all of developmental psychology.

A number of other chapters also emphasize the value of viewing children's thinking in terms of domain-specific theories, constraints, and principles include those of R. Gelman and Williams on constraints on learning, Woodward and Markman on semantic and conceptual development, and Wellman and S. Gelman on children's theories of mechanics, psychology, and biology. However, the emphasis on children's theories, principles, and constraints has not met with universal approval, either in the field in general or in the chapters within the Handbook. Haith and Benson, in particular, call into question what they term "precocism," and they express skepticism about "adultocentric" cognitive interpretations of infants' looking patterns. They also discuss what has been lost by the movement toward minitheories and away from broader theories of development, such as Piaget's. Mandler and Bloom also raise important questions about the wisdom of positing such high-level understanding to account for infants' and toddlers' behavior, and they emphasize the continuing value of Piaget's legacy. The focus in so many chapters on the nature of early competence reflects the importance this issue has assumed in the field as a whole. The diverse perspectives on what infants and toddlers understand, and what types of evidence are sufficient for an inference that they possess high-level understanding, represent some of the most interesting contrasts in the volume.

At least four other major trends in the field are evident in the volume.

1. *Increased emphasis on learning.* This movement is apparent from the very first chapter, Johnson's review of neural development. Johnson describes recent research indicating that rather than neural development being largely prespecified, as has often been assumed, plasticity is a basic property of the developing brain. For example, differentiation of areas within the cortex appears in large part due to the particular input those areas receive from the thalamus. Regions of the cortex that ordinarily are involved in visual processing will instead be involved in auditory processing if the thalamus provides them with auditory rather than visual input. Aslin, Jusczyk, and Pisoni focus on the mechanisms through which people learn to segment speech into words and the mechanisms that lead to children's loss of the ability to discriminate some phonemic contrasts not present in their native language. Gelman and Williams focus on constraints that enhance the efficiency of learning. Among their insights are that all theories of learning posit constraints of some kind, and that theories differ not in whether they posit such constraints but rather in the kinds of constraints that they assume. Maratsos argues convincingly that grammars contain so many quirky and odd conventions that the mechanisms through which they are learned must be able to grind through masses of data and extract subtle regularities rather than produce sudden insights regarding appropriate transformations. Klahr and MacWhinney describe a wide range of production system and connectionist computer simulations that acquire competencies ranging from number conservation to vocabulary use. Among their most important proposals is that production system and connectionist models of learn-

ing are not as different as their proponents' depictions of them. In both types of models, learning involves considerable parallel processing; the knowledge that is acquired is distributed among many smaller entities (productions in the one case, processing units and connections in the other), and learning can occur relatively gradually as well as relatively abruptly. Rogoff depicts how participation in activity leads to learning. The learning involves not just understanding of the particular subject matter at hand, but also incorporation of values and cultural assumptions. She argues that only by analyzing the cultural traditions and historical institutions within which children develop can learning be understood.

2. *The extent and importance of variability in children's thinking and learning.* Past editions of the *Handbook,* reflecting then-contemporary understanding of cognitive development, addressed variability primarily as an issue of individual differences in cognitive styles and abilities. In the present volume, Ferrari and Sternberg ably continue this tradition. However, reflecting current understanding, a number of chapters in the present volume focus on within-child variability and its implications for development. This emphasis on within-child variability is identified by Schneider and Bjorklund as one of three major themes in current research on memory development. Such variability also is highlighted in DeLoache, Miller, and Pierroutsakos's treatment of problem solving and reasoning, in Moshman's description of research on adolescents' thinking, in Klahr and MacWhinney's descriptions of information-processing approaches, and in Bertenthal and Clifton's characterization of motor activity. Recognition of this within-child variability emerges as important not only for accurately describing development but also for predicting and understanding change.

3. *The increasing role of formal models.* This is *the* theme in Klahr and MacWhinney's chapter on information-processing approaches to development. However, it is also evident in many other contexts. Ideal observer models play a prominent role in Kellman and Banks' chapter on visual perception. Such models compare people's vision at various ages to the most acute vision possible, given anatomical and physiological constraints. They thus allow assessment of whether the immaturity of infants' brains imposes constraints on their vision beyond those imposed by their sensory systems. Aslin, Jusczyk, and Pisoni describe implications of formal analyses of auditory stimuli and performance of automatic speech recognition devices for how infants and older individuals perceive speech. In discussing conceptual development, Case presents a hierarchical learning loop model, in which associative and attentionally mediated learning exert mutually faciliative influences, and in which both are in similar bidirectional relations with the central conceptual structure in which they are embedded. These formal models are particularly helpful for specifying the mechanisms through which changes occur.

4. *The new metaphors and units of analysis that are shaping current understanding of cognitive development.* Among the most intriguing is the metaphor of the child as *bricoleur,* described by DeLoache, Miller, and Pierroutsakos. A *bricoleur* is a tinkerer, someone who makes do with whatever tools are at hand. Given children's frequent success in reaching their goals despite limited experience and lack of specialized knowledge, this seems an apt metaphor. Children usually do whatever it takes to get the job done, even though the process may not be pretty. Wellman and Gelman and Flavell and Miller depict the child as a theorist, thinking of foundational domains in terms of an organized set of basic entities, unobservable constructs, and causal relations. Case incisively contrasts four prevailing metaphors for thinking about conceptual development: (a) as a local process limited by general constraints, (b) as a sequence of theoretical revolutions, (c) as the acquisition of expertise, and (d) as a community of praxis. Each conceptualization leads to different basic questions, characteristic kinds of research, and favored forms of evidence.

Units of analysis are almost as varied as the chapters themselves: neurons, brain areas, and cortical and subcortical pathways (Johnson); perception–action links (Bertenthal and Clifton); phonemes (Aslin, Jusczyk, and Pisoni); productions, basic processing units, and connection strengths (Klahr and MacWhinney); basic memory processes, strategies, and knowledge structures (Schneider and Bjorklund); perceptual and conceptual representations (Mandler); grammatical transformations (Maratsos); constraints and principles (Woodward and Markman; Gelman and Williams); domain-specific theories (Wellman and Gelman; Flavell and Miller); central conceptual structures (Case); rules, strategies, schemas, categories, plans, analogies, and symbolic relations (DeLoache, Miller, and Pierroutsakos); activities (Rogoff); and abilities and styles (Ferrari and Sternberg). Some of these differences in basic units of analysis seem inherent to the areas; this is particularly true for neural, perceptual, and motor activity. Other differences in basic units, particularly those used to describe higher-level cognition, reflect differing theoretical approaches more than inherent differences in the content domains. It will be interesting to see whether, in the next *Handbook,* higher-level cognition continues to be depicted in these ways; whether the particular basic units of description change, but the diversity of approaches continues; or whether there will be convergence on one or a few types of basic units as the most useful for describing higher-level thought processes. For the time being, variability seems as characteristic of current approaches to children's thinking as of children's thinking itself.

A volume like this can emerge only with the help of many people. Especially important to the present effort were the many colleagues who read and commented on one or more chapters. I personally want to thank Deanna Kuhn for being a pleasure to work with and for her many excellent ideas; it was a most enjoyable collaboration. Deanna and I both want to thank Bill Damon for his help and encouragement throughout the planning and preparation of the volume. Above all, we want to thank the authors for their willingness to invest the great intellectual and personal resources needed to produce this portrayal of current knowledge of cognitive development. They have done a true service to the field.

Contents

CHAPTER 1

The Neural Basis of Cognitive Development

MARK H. JOHNSON

Development is the constructive process by which genes interact with their environment to yield complex organic structures such as the human brain and the cognitive processes it supports. The study of development is necessarily multidisciplinary since new levels of structure that emerge as a result of developmental processes often require different levels and methods of analysis from those that preceded them. For example, while embryologists usually apply molecular level analyses to unravel the first steps of brain development, and developmental neurobiologists commonly focus on the cellular level for their analyses of prenatal brain development, the functional consequences of postnatal brain development are most often studied by developmental psychologists and ethologists interested in the behavior of the whole organism. Even today these three types of scientists tend to pursue their studies relatively independently of each other. Part of the reason for this is that the methodologies and theoretical constructs of the three approaches are very different. Perhaps understandably, developmental psychologists tend to see more in common with fellow psychologists using similar methods and theories to study adult cognition, than they see in common with the test tube "bind-and-grind" studies of the molecular biologist. Over the past decade, however, the emergence of the interdisciplinary field of cognitive neuroscience has led some to the realization that the neural basis of cognitive phenomena such as perception, attention, and language can be studied. Furthermore, such investigations commonly lead to fresh insights and theories about cognitive processes. This chapter reviews current research on the neural basis of cognitive development with the view that

---

The writing of this chapter was funded by the UK Medical Research Council. I also acknowledge recent financial support from Carnegie Mellon University, the National Science Foundation, the McDonnell-Pew Foundation, and the Human Frontiers Scientific Foundation.

studies of developmental neurobiology are as relevant to cognitive developmentalists as knowledge and concepts gained from the study of adult cognitive processes.

The relative neglect of biological factors in the study of cognitive development from the 1970s to the present is somewhat surprising when viewed in the context of the history of developmental psychology. This is because, unlike the study of adult psychology which traces its roots to philosophy, the origins of developmental psychology can be traced to biologists such as Charles Darwin and Jean Piaget. Darwin (1872/1965) was one of the first to take a scientific approach to human behavioral development, and to speculate on the relations between phylogenetic and ontogenetic change. Like Darwin, Piaget viewed human behavioral development through the perspective of evolution. Piaget, who was originally trained as a biologist, also imported current theories of embryological development, mainly due to the Edinburgh biologist C. H. Waddington (1975), to generate his accounts of human cognitive development. Some of Waddington's notions have recently been resurrected by those interested in nonlinear dynamic systems approaches to cognitive development (Thelen & Smith, 1994; Elman et al., 1996). A curious aspect of Piaget's biological approach to human cognitive development was his relative neglect of the importance of brain development. Segalowitz (1994) suggests that this neglect was due to a lack of information about brain development and function resulting in Piaget being unable to articulate an integrative theory of brain and cognitive development. Another factor may have been that physiological psychologists of the day were preoccupied with associative learning, a position with which Piaget wanted to dissociate himself.

In contrast to Piaget, some early developmental psychologists in America, such as McGraw and Gesell, attempted to integrate information from brain development with what was known of behavioral ontogeny. McGraw and Gesell both focused primarily on motor development, but extended their conclusions to mental and social development (e.g., Gesell, 1929; McGraw, 1943). These scientists and their colleagues described a large number of stages in the development of motor abilities from prone positions to walking and stair climbing. McGraw proposed that the transition between these stages could be accounted in terms of the maturation of motor cortex and its inhibition of subcortical pathways. As we will see later in this chapter, the general notion that as the cerebral cortex develops postnatally it allows more intentional, purposeful, behavior (partly through the inhibition of more automatic subcortical pathways) still

provides a basis for some current research. While both McGraw and Gesell developed sophisticated informal theories that attempted to capture nonlinear and dynamic approaches to development, their efforts to relate brain development to behavioral change remained largely speculative. This failure was partly due to methodological difficulties (such as having no methods for imaging brain function) and partly due to a lack of adequate formal theoretical methods (Thelen & Smith, 1994).

In addition to Piaget and his Genevan school of developmental psychology, another (originally) European school of thought that has contributed to current thinking about biological factors in cognitive development is the discipline of Ethology, the study of the behavior of animals within their natural habitat. Two of the leading figures in ethology, Konrad Lorenz and Niko Tinbergen (contemporaries of McGraw, Gesell, and Piaget), were particularly concerned with causal factors in the development of behavior. Due to the more direct interventions possible with animals, Lorenz and his colleagues addressed issues about the relative contribution of "innate" as opposed to "experiential" contributions to behavior. The results of these experiments in which early environments were manipulated, quickly led to the realization (by Lehrmann, 1953 and others) that the dissociation of behavior into innate and acquired components was inadequate to account for the complexities of behavioral development. However, the notion that some brain and cognitive systems are more impervious to experience during development than others remains important today. Furthermore, the notion that theories of cognitive development should take into account both the whole organism and the natural environment (social and physical) within which it develops, is currently regaining popularity (e.g., Gottlieb, 1992; Hinde, 1974; Johnson & Morton, 1991; Thelen & Smith, 1994).

From the mid-1960s to the last few years, biological approaches to human cognitive development fell out of favor for a variety of reasons. Many neo-Piagetians focused their attention on the detailed stages proposed by Piaget and lost sight of the more dynamic and interactionist aspects of his theory. This was partly due to the lack of a formalism for capturing such abstract notions as "dynamic equilibrium" (Bates & Elman, 1993; Thelen & Smith, 1994; Elman et al., 1996), and partly due to his gross underestimation of the cognitive abilities of young infants (Karmiloff-Smith, 1992). In an attempt to move toward more formal computational models of cognitive development, it was not surprising that leading researchers chose to turn to models derived from consideration of digital computers. The work of McGraw, Gesell, and their contemporaries was also neglected due to a lack of direct evidence about brain-behavior relations, and the lack of formalisms for explaining the dynamic transitions they described. Additional factors no doubt included the rise of behaviorism in which reference to the brain was deemed to be largely unnecessary, and then the commonly held belief among cognitive psychologists in the 1970s and 1980s that the "software" of the mind is best studied without reference to the "hardware" of the brain. The ethological approach to human behavioral development came to be largely applied to social development and its abnormalities (Hinde, 1974) rather than to cognitive development.

THE RECENT EMERGENCE OF DEVELOPMENTAL COGNITIVE NEUROSCIENCE

In recent years, a number of factors have conspired to make an interdisciplinary approach to brain and cognitive development more feasible. This emerging interdisciplinary approach has been referred to as "Developmental Cognitive Neuroscience" (Johnson & Gilmore, 1996), and in this section I review some of the factors that have contributed to its emergence.

As stated at the beginning of this chapter, ontogenetic development involves the construction of increasingly complex structures, including the brain and the cognitive processes it supports. As more complex forms are generated, different groups of scientists use different methods and approaches appropriate for that level. Thus, as distinct from other areas of psychology, a complete account of developmental change specifically requires an interdisciplinary approach. While these considerations suggest that the study of development requires collaboration and exchange of information between scientists with different methodological expertise, the converse of this is that the study of developmental change offers an opportunity to trace the interrelationships between brain functioning and cognitive processes. Thus, as we will see later in this chapter, through development we can also shed light on the neural basis of cognition in adults.

Some have argued that many current theories of cognitive development merely give accounts of a series of static stages, rather than provide mechanisms of change (e.g., Siegler & Munakata, 1993). This may be due to the reliance on metaphors from the digital computer information processing, a type of computational machine which does

not develop in the same gradual way as organic structures, and which does not act within the context of a complex external world. Importing theories of developmental change from biological processes to cognition does not have these drawbacks. Later in this chapter we will see examples of the theories of cognitive change derived from considerations of brain development and from the functioning of the immune system.

Perhaps a more obvious reason for attempting to relate brain development to cognitive change comes from its potential value for understanding the effects of early brain injury or genetic abnormalities on subsequent cognitive development. Later in this chapter we will discuss evidence from infants with focal damage to their cerebral cortex, and children with genetic anomalies. Note that such cases can also contribute to the development of theories about the relation between the developing brain and cognition. Thus, there is a bidirectional interaction between clinical evidence and basic questions in developmental cognitive neuroscience.

Finally, the recent explosion of knowledge on brain development makes the task of relating it to cognitive changes considerably more viable than 15 years ago when the chapter on this topic was written for the previous edition of this *Handbook*. New molecular and cellular methods, along with theories of self-organizing dynamic networks, have led to great advances in our understanding of how vertebrate brains are constructed during ontogeny. There is still a very long way to go, especially for human postnatal brain development. In the next section, some of the recent methodological and theoretical developments that will facilitate the investigation of the neural basis of cognitive development are reviewed.

CONCEPTUAL APPROACHES

Conceptual Approaches to Brain Development and Cognition

For the purposes of this review, we may distinguish between two general types of conceptual approaches to understanding the relations between brain development and cognition: *causal* theories and *system* theories. Causal theories are characterized by the effort to make statements about a causal chain of events that induces or allows a cognitive change, or particular individual difference. Often correlational evidence is used to support these arguments.

The neural correlates invoked include such factors as changes in the structure of neurons and their components, electrophysiological changes, and myelinization. Commonly, some neural change is correlated in time with a cognitive change and consequently a causal relation between the two is assumed. For example, certain electrophysiological changes have been correlated in time with Piagetian stages, leading to the assumption that specific brain reorganizations cause or enable certain cognitive changes. However, evidence of temporal correlation taken in isolation is weak due to the fact that many neuroanatomical variables change gradually over the first decade of life. Also, it is nearly always possible to find some neuroanatomical variable in some brain region that shows change at a particular age. Evidence of temporal correlation can, however, be supportive when taken together with specific predictions about the nature or temporal sequence of information processing changes (e.g., Diamond, 1991; Johnson, 1990). Some causal theories propose specific pathways by which an event early in life can give rise to specific deviations from normal developmental pathways. An example of this approach is Geschwind and Galaburda's (1985) account of a causal relationship between aspects of the endocrine environment in utero, and the subsequent development of cerebral lateralization.

An alternative approach to relating brain and cognitive functioning in development is the systems approach. This approach involves applying the same *mechanism of change* to processes at the neural and cognitive level. Research within this approach usually proceeds by attempting to derive rules for changes of states at the neural level (or sometimes from other biological systems) and attempting to extend them to cognitive processes. One example of this approach is Changeux and Dehaene's (1989) and Edelman's (1987) proposals to extend the rules governing the selective loss of neural connections observed in ontogeny to processes of cognitive change. While this approach is necessarily less direct and specific than causal theories, it has the virtue that it may be applied to higher cognitive processes more readily.

Related to the relative importance of causal arguments are basic default assumptions about maturation and plasticity. Commonly (but not necessarily), the causal approach is associated with the assumption that brain development may be characterized as a maturational process. Maturational events in the brain are assumed to trigger or enable the emergence of new cognitive structures. By this view, recovery of function following early brain damage is thought to be due to specific mechanisms triggered by the injury. In contrast, those who adopt the systems approach tend, in general, to adopt the default assumption the brain is plastic, and sculpted by experience. By this view, plasticity is a fundamental and inherent property of the developing brain. As we will see, the issue then becomes how this plasticity is constrained to ensure consistent and adaptive outcomes.

A Conceptual Framework for Interpreting Issues in the Nature-Nurture Controversy

Issues of the relation between brain growth and cognitive development are inextricably entwined with the nature-nurture controversy. One misconception commonly held among developmental psychologists is that if a particular cognitive change can be demonstrated to have a neural correlate, this strengthens the evidence for it being "innate." As we will see later in this chapter, the considerable evidence for plasticity in cerebral cortex development makes such assumptions entirely fallacious.

The term *innate* has a checkered history in science in which it has been dropped from use, and even actively banned, in many areas of developmental biology. The main reason why the term has dropped from use in fields such as ethology and genetics is because it is simply no longer useful. Since it has become evident that genes interact with their environment at all levels, including the molecular, there is no aspect of development that can be said to be strictly "genetic," that is, exclusively a product of information contained within the genes. If innate refers to that which is genetic, it refers to nothing that exists in the natural world, except for genes themselves.

In the behavioral and cognitive sciences, however, use of the term has persisted despite calls for it to be dropped for the same reason as it has been dropped in other areas of development (Gottlieb, 1992; Hinde, 1974; Johnson & Morton, 1991; Oyama, 1985). Presumably this persistence is due to the usefulness of the term for analyzing development at the behavioral and cognitive level. But, as will become even clearer in the course of this chapter, the term cannot be equated with genetic. Nor is it very satisfactory to use it to refer to that which is present from birth (consider the physical changes at puberty for example).

In considering these issues, some authors have suggested that it is useful to distinguish between the various levels of interaction between genes and their environment (e.g., Greenough, Black, & Wallace, 1987; Johnson & Morton, 1991). The classification proposed by Johnson and Morton is shown in Table 1.1. By this analysis the term "innate" refers to changes that arise as a result of interactions that

TABLE 1.1   Levels of Interaction between Genes and Their Environment

Levels of Interaction	Term
Molecular	Internal environment
Cellular	Internal environment (innate)
Organism-external environment	Species typical environment (primal)
	Individual specific environment (learning)

occur within the organism. I will adopt this working definition of the term in this chapter. Interactions between the organism and aspects of the external environment that are common to all members of the species, the species-typical environment, (such as patterned light, gravity, etc.) were referred to as "primal" by Johnson and Morton. Interactions between the organism and aspects of the external environment that are specific to individual members of the species (such as exposure to a specific language) were classified as learning. Based on a series of experiments on the effects on brain structure of rearing rats in impoverished or comparatively enriched early environments, Greenough et al. (1987) proposed a similar distinction between two types of information storage induced by the environment. Changes induced by aspects of the environment that are common to all members of a species were classified as "experience-expectant" information storage, and are associated with selective synaptic loss. The second type of information incorporated by the brain through interaction with the environment was referred to as experience-dependent. This referred to interactions with the environment that are, or can be, specific to an individual and are associated with the generation of new synaptic connections.

Using the framework outlined above we can enquire into the extent to which aspects of a given neural circuit are innate (defined as the product of interactions within the organism). As we will see later in this chapter, different aspects of brain structure and function are probably differentially sensitive to the effects of postnatal experience. The analysis which follows, which for simplicity I will apply to the example of an abstract neural network, will assist in the later discussion of brain plasticity (see also a similar analysis in Elman et al., 1996). By discussing a simple abstract network, I do not mean to imply that this provides an adequate model of the complexity of real brain networks. However, by virtue of their underlying similarities to real neural networks we may be able to illustrate general principles more clearly on such simplified networks.

If we assume a simple connectionist neural network, there are a number of ways in which the structure of such a network could be plastic. First, the basic architecture of the network could alter as a result of experience—this could be a change in the number of nodes, the learning rule, the frequency with which the nodes are interconnected, and so on. Another possibility (and that most commonly observed in simple connectionist nets) is that while the basic architecture of the network is fixed, the strength of the connections between the nodes can vary according to a weight-adjustment learning rule. Since representations in connectionist nets are dependent on the particular pattern of link strengths (synaptic contacts) between nodes, allowing these to vary with the input means that different representations can be stored as a result of experience. In terms of the brain, we can think of these changes as being in the details of microcircuits, synaptic efficacy, and so on. When the basic architecture of the network is fixed but the link strengths vary as a result of input, we may say that the network imposes *architectural constraints* on the representations that emerge. If the link strengths themselves were also fixed, we could say that the network contains *innate representations*. Later in this chapter we will review evidence consistent with the view that the primate cerebral cortex has architectural constraints on the development of representations, but not innate representations. In contrast, I will suggest that some subcortical structures may contain innate representations in that the pattern and strength of synaptic contacts are specified prior to interaction with the external environment (often due to the effects of prenatal spontaneous neural activity).

EMPIRICAL METHODS

While conceptual approaches to understanding the relation between the developing brain and cognition are important, the field will also be advanced through improved empirical methods and technology. A variety of these are becoming available to developmentalists. These techniques will permit questions to be asked about the biological basis of cognitive and perceptual development more directly than in the past. One set of tools relates to brain imaging—the generation of "functional" maps of brain activity based on either changes in cerebral metabolism, blood flow, or electrical activity. Some of these imaging methods, such as positron emission tomography (PET), are of limited utility for studying transitions in cognitive development in normal infants and children due to their invasive nature (requiring the intravenous injection of radioactively labeled substances) and their relatively coarse temporal resolution (on the order of minutes). Two brain-imaging techniques currently being developed are being applied to development in normal children—high-density, event-related potentials (HD-ERP) and functional magnetic resonance imaging (F-MRI).

The electrical activity of the brain can be recorded by means of sensitive electrodes that rest on the scalp surface. These recordings can either be of the spontaneous natural rhythms of the brain (Electroencephalography-EEG), or the electrical activity induced by the presentation of a stimulus (ERP). The latter, event-related potentials, are time locked to a stimulus presentation or action. Since the ERP from many trials is averaged, the spontaneous natural rhythms of the brain that are unrelated to the stimulus presentation average to zero. With a high density of electrodes on the scalp, algorithms can be employed which infer the position and orientation of the brain sources of electrical activity (dipoles) for the particular pattern of scalp surface electrical activity. Some of the assumptions necessary for the successful use of these algorithms are actually more likely to be true of infants than adults. For example, thinner skulls and fewer cortical convolutions may improve the accuracy and interpretability of HD-ERP results in infants relative to adult subjects, but see Nelson (1994) for a comprehensive analysis of the difficulties in applying the ERP methodology to infants.

Functional-MRI allows the non-invasive measurement of cerebral blood flow (Raichle & Mallinkrodt, 1987; Kwong et al., 1992), with the prospect of millimeter spatial resolution and temporal resolution on the order of seconds, using MRI machines commonly available in modern medical facilities. This technique is beginning to be applied to children. However, the distracting noise and vibration, and the presently unknown possible effects of high magnetic fields on the developing brain, make its usefulness for subjects under 4 or 5 years of age unclear at this point.

Developmental psychobiological research on animals has contributed greatly to our understanding of the relation between developing brain and behavior. While the new functional brain imaging methods outlined above will eventually allow us to address some of the same questions in human subjects, recent techniques in molecular genetics open up new possibilities. In particular, the "lesioning" of certain genes from the genome of an animal (mainly rodents so far). A recent example of this is the deletion of the alpha-calcium calmodulin kinase II gene which results in rats being unable to perform certain learning tasks when

adults (Silva, Paylor, Wehner, & Tonegawa, 1992; Silva, Stevens, Tonegawa, & Wang, 1992). This method opens new vistas in the analysis of genetic contributions to cognitive and perceptual change in animals, and may be particularly fruitful when applied to well-studied animal models of development such as visual imprinting in chicks and song learning in passerine birds. However, it should be noted that lesioning a single gene is likely to have a cascade of effects caused by the abnormal, or absent, interactions with other genes.

Developmental cognitive neuroscience is concerned with abnormal as well as normal development. While, as discussed earlier, a better understanding of the relation between brain development and cognition will be of clinical benefit, the converse is that the study of developmental deviations, such as the effects of early focal lesions, promises to inform us about the nature and limitations of brain plasticity. Similarly, the different developmental paths presented by populations with genetic abnormalities such as Williams' and Down's syndrome, offer us a perspective in which the normal developmental path, and eventual profile of cognitive abilities, is seen as but one of a range of possibilities.

Another useful approach for linking brain development to behavior is the *marker task*. This method involves the use of a specific behavioral task that has been linked to a particular brain region or pathway in adult primates and humans by neurophysiological, neuropsychological, or brain-imaging studies, and preferably by two or three of these methods. By testing infants or children with versions of such a task at different ages, the researcher can use the success or otherwise of subjects as indicating the functional development of the relevant regions of the brain. Later in this chapter, several lines of inquiry that illustrate the marker task approach are discussed. For example, the exploration of the development of infant visual attention employs experimental methods and theoretical notions adapted from extensive studies with adults (Posner, 1980; Posner & Cohen, 1980). However, there are weaknesses to using the marker task approach. One of these is the assumption that the same brain regions or pathways necessarily are crucial for supporting similar tasks at different ages (Goldman, 1971). Consequently, the marker task approach should be viewed as an initial non-invasive approach to studying human functional brain development, which will be eventually replaced by more direct methods of analysis.

Finally, the recent emergence of connectionist neural network models offers the possibility of assessing the information-processing consequences of developmental changes in the neuroanatomy and neurochemistry of the brain. For example, O'Reilly and Johnson (1994) demonstrated how the microcircuitry of a region of vertebrate forebrain could lead to certain self-terminating, sensitive period effects, and Kertzberg, Dehaene, and Changeux (1992) have studied the emergence of clusters of Boolean functions in a simple cortical matrix model in which a selective loss of links (synapses) occurs as a result of an increasingly limited supply of growth factor. Such models promise to provide a bridge between our observations of development at the neural level and cognitive change in childhood.

CONTEMPORARY STATUS: HUMAN BRAIN DEVELOPMENT

It is not the purpose of this chapter to provide a complete review of brain development (see Purves & Lichtmann, 1985 and Brown, Hopkins, & Keynes, 1991 for more detailed reviews). Rather, I will focus on four main conclusions that I believe can be drawn about human brain development, and its comparison with that observed in other species. These four main conclusions, based on recent developmental neurobiological and neuropsychological research, are:

1. Prenatal human brain development is very similar to that of other primates, with the only major difference being in the generation of a greater quantity of cerebral cortex (and related midbrain structures), and the developmental timing of landmarks.
2. The cerebellum, hippocampus, and cerebral cortex are the structures of the brain that show the most prolonged postnatal development in humans. Immaturity of the cerebral cortex, in particular, is probably a major limiting factor on cognitive functioning in human infants and children.
3. The more extended period of postnatal brain development found in humans reveals differential timing of development both between different regions of the cerebral cortex and between different layers of the cortex. This differential development may be used to make predictions about information processing.
4. Neurobiological and brain imaging studies indicate that regions of cortex are not intrinsically prespecified to support particular classes of representations, such as those pertaining to face recognition or language

processing. Rather, the fairly consistent structure-function relations observed in the cortex of the normal human adult appear to be the consequence of multiple constraints, both intrinsic and extrinsic to the organism. Relations between brain development and experience are bidirectional.

These four conclusions will now be discussed in more detail.

Similarities between Human Brain Development and That of Other Species

The cognitive capacities thought to be unique to humans are not the result of new regions or structures in the brain. On the contrary, as far as is known, we share all of the main structures in our brain not only with other primates, but also with most other mammals. The primary difference between primates and other mammals, and between humans and primates, is in the increasing surface area of the cerebral cortex, and, relatedly, the more protracted period of postnatal development. For this reason, I will focus on the cerebral cortex in this overview (more specifically, the neocortex which is the layered part of cortex visible on the surface of the brain). Subcortical structures, such as the cerebellum and hippocampus, are very similar in structure across different mammalian species but, like cortex, may differ in their volume and developmental timetable. Postnatal development of the hippocampus and cerebellum will also be discussed where they are relevant to functional issues.

In Figure 1.1 a timetable of the main phases of development of the human brain is shown. All of the prenatal landmarks are shared in common with other primates and most mammals. As just mentioned, the main difference between humans and other mammals is in the extent of the cerebral cortex. In order to understand how this difference arises, we need to describe something of the prenatal development of cerebral cortex.

The neocortex is basically a thin, flat sheet (about 3–4 mm thick) that becomes increasingly convoluted with both phylogenetic and ontogenetic development. It has a fairly consistent internal structure throughout its extent. This does not mean, however, that this structure is simple. It is not. In fact, we still have no widely accepted computational theories of how the cortex works. Figure 1.2 shows a schematic section through an area of primate cortex, the primary visual cortex of the adult macaque monkey. This section is cut at right angles to the surface of the cortex,

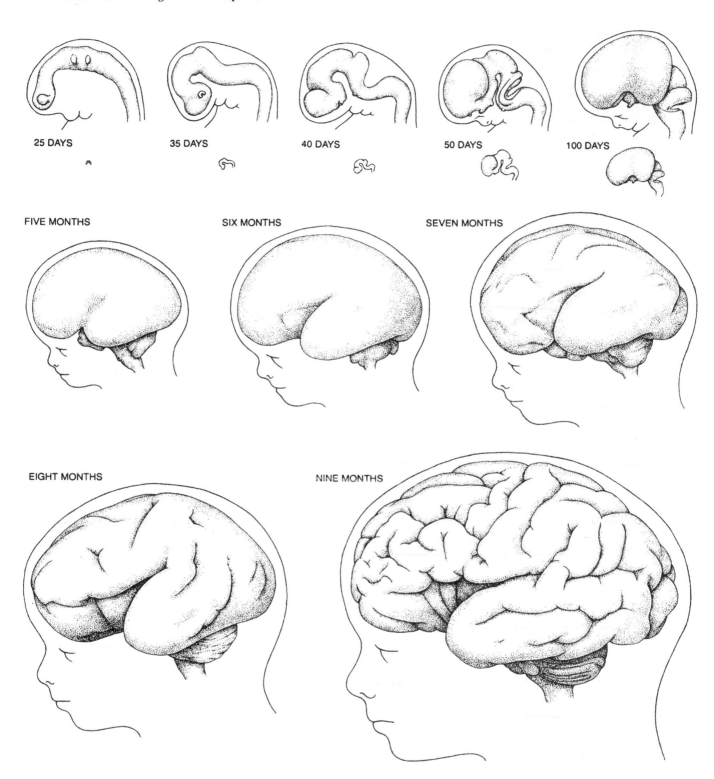

Figure 1.1 A sequence of drawings of the embryonic and fetal development of the human brain. The forebrain, midbrain, and hindbrain originate as swellings at the head end of the neural tube. In primates the convoluted cortex grows to cover the midbrain, hindbrain, and parts of the cerebellum. Prior to birth, neurons are generated in the developing brain at a rate of more than 250,000 per minute. From *The Development of the Brain,* by W. Maxwell Cowan. Copyright © 1979 by Scientific American, Inc. All rights reserved. Reprinted with permission.

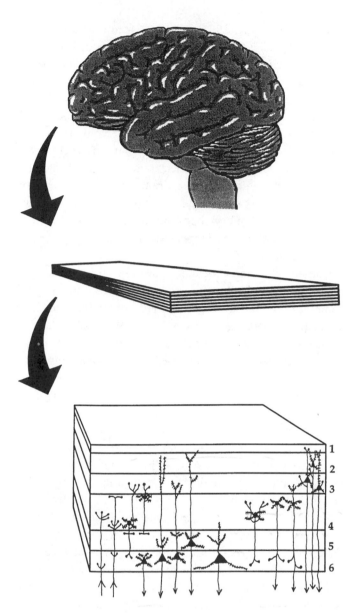

Figure 1.2 A simplified schematic diagram which illustrates that, despite its convoluted surface appearance (top), the cerebral cortex is a thin sheet (middle) composed of six layers (bottom). The convolutions in the cortex arise from a combination of growth patterns and the restricted space inside the skull. In general, differences between mammals involve the total area of the cortical sheet, and not its layered structure. Each of the layers possesses certain neuron types and characteristic input and projection patterns (see text for further details).

and reveals its laminar structure. Each of the laminae has particular cell types within it, and has particular patterns of inputs and outputs. For example, with regard to inputs and outputs, layer 4 is where inputs to the cortex from thalamic regions terminate. The deeper layers, 5 and 6, often

project back to subcortical regions that project to the corresponding layer 4, as well as other subcortical areas. More superficial layers, 2 and 3, commonly project forward to neighboring regions of cortex. Layer 1 is very diffuse and may be involved in long range cortico-cortico and cortico-limbic connections. We shall see later that the differential structure of layers in the cortex may be used to analyze developmental changes at the cognitive level.

Most cortical neurons are generated outside the cortex itself in a region just underneath what becomes the cortex, the proliferative zone. This means that these cells must migrate to take up their locations within the cortex. Rakic (1988) has proposed a "radial unit model" of neocortical development which gives an account of how the layered structure of the mammalian cerebral cortex arises. This model gives a crucial role to glial cells. According to the model, the organization of the cerebral cortex is determined by the fact that each proliferative unit gives rise to about one hundred neurones. The progeny from each proliferative unit all migrate up the same radial glial fibre, with the latest to be born travelling past their older relatives. Thus, radial glial fibers act like a climbing rope to ensure that cells produced by one proliferative unit all contribute to one radial column within the cortex. This pattern of neuronal migration stands in contrast to the more commonly observed pattern seen in most other parts of the brain in which the most recently born cells simply displace the existing ones further away from the proliferative zone.

There are some consequences of the radial unit model for the role of genetic regulation in species differences. For example, Rakic (1988) has pointed out that a single round of additional symmetric cell division at the proliferative unit formation stage would double the number of ontogenetic columns, and hence the total surface area of cortex. In contrast, an additional single round of division at a later stage, from the proliferative zone, would only increase the depth of a column by one cell (about 1%). There is very little variation between mammalian species in the layered structure of the cortex, while the total surface area of the cortex can vary by a factor of 100 or more between different species of mammal. It seems likely, therefore, that some species differences between mammals originate in the number of "rounds" of cell division that takes place within and across regions of the proliferative zone.

A related view on the evolution of mammalian brain has been put forward by Finlay and Darlington (1995). These authors compared data on the size of brain structures from 131 mammalian species and concluded that the order of neurogenesis is conserved across a wide range of species and correlates with the relative enlargement of structures as overall brain size increases. Specifically, disproportionately large growth occurs in the late-generated structures such as the neocortex. By this analysis, the structure most likely to differ in size in the relatively slowed neurogenesis of primates is the neocortex.

The Postnatal Development of the Human Brain

There are a number of ways to study the structural postnatal development of the human brain. Traditionally, investigators have used neuroanatomical analysis of postmortem tissue. Such analysis tend to be based on relatively small numbers of children due to the extensive work involved and the difficulties associated in gaining such tissue. Furthermore, those children who come to autopsy have often suffered from trauma or diseases that complicate generalizations to normal brain development. In vivo studies of adults using magnetic resonance imaging (Courchesne, Hesselink, Jernigan, & Yeung-Courchesne, 1987; Jernigan, Press, & Hesselink, 1990) and PET scanning of infants and adults (Chugani, Phelps, & Mazziotta, 1987; Petersen, Fox, Posner, Mintun, & Raichle, 1988) can inform us about the structural development of the brain. But these techniques are usually restricted to children with clinical symptoms that justify invasive neural imaging. Hence, generalizations to normal brain development must be made with caution in these cases as well. Despite these difficulties, a number of progressive and regressive neuroanatomical and neurophysiological changes have been observed during postnatal development in children. Specifically, a number of measures of brain anatomy and function show a characteristic rise-and-fall developmental pattern during this period. While the progressive and regressive processes should not be viewed as distinct stages, for the purposes of exposition I will discuss them in sequence.

A number of lines of evidence indicate substantive additive changes during postnatal development of the brain. At the most gross level of analysis, brain volume (weight) quadruples between birth and adulthood. This increase comes from a number of sources, but, in general, not from additional neurons. The formation of neurons and their migration to appropriate brain regions takes place almost entirely within the period of prenatal development in the human. Except for a few brain regions that continue to add neurons throughout life (e.g., the olfactory bulbs), the vast majority of neurons are present by around the 7th month

of gestation (Rakic, 1995). In contrast to the lack of new nerve cell bodies, there is dramatic postnatal growth of synapses, dendrites, and fiber bundles. Further, nerve fibers become covered in a fatty myelin sheath that adds further to the mass of the brain.

Perhaps the most obvious manifestation of postnatal neural development as viewed through the confocal microscope is the increase in size and complexity of the dendritic tree of most neurons. While the extent and reach of a cell's dendritic arbor may increase dramatically, it also often becomes more specific and specialized. Less apparent through standard microscopes, but more evident with electron microscopy, is a corresponding increase in measures of synaptic density.

Huttenlocher and colleagues have reported a steady increase in synaptic density in several regions of the human cerebral cortex (Huttenlocher, 1990, 1994; Huttenlocher, de Courten, Garey, & Van der Loos, 1982). While an increase in synaptogenesis begins around the time of birth for all cortical areas studied to date, the most rapid bursts of increase, and the final peak density, occur at different ages in different areas. In the visual cortex, there is a rapid burst at 3 to 4 months, and the maximum density of around 150% of adult level is reached between 4 and 12 months. A similar time course is observed in the primary auditory cortex (Heschl's gyrus). In contrast, while synaptogenesis starts at the same time in a region of the prefrontal cortex, density increases much more slowly and does not reach its peak until after the first year. There are a variety of possible measures of synaptic density—per cell, per unit dendrite, per unit brain tissue, and so forth—and careful selection is required so that factors such as increases in dendritic length do not unduly influence the results. Huttenlocher (1990) discusses some of these issues of appropriate measurement.

Another additive process is myelination. Myelination refers to an increase in the fatty sheath that surrounds neuronal pathways, a process that increases the efficiency of information transmission. In the central nervous system, sensory areas tend to myelinate earlier than motor areas. Cortical association areas are known to myelinate last, and continue the process into the second decade of life. Because myelination continues for many years after birth, there has been a great deal of speculation about its role in behavioral development (Parmelee & Sigman, 1983; Volpe, 1987; Yakovlev & Lecours, 1967). However, interest in the causal role of myelination has begun to wane in the last few years since it became clear that undermyelinated connections in the young human brain are still capable of transmitting signals.

Finally, a PET study of human infants (Chugani et al., 1987) reported a sharp rise in overall resting brain metabolism (glucose uptake) after the first year of life, with a peak approximately 150% above adult levels achieved somewhere around 4 to 5 years of age for some cortical areas. While this peak occurred somewhat later than that in synaptic density an adultlike *distribution* of resting activity within and across brain regions was observed by the end of the first year.

I now turn to regressive events during human postnatal brain development. Such events are commonly observed by those studying the development of nerve cells and their connections in the vertebrate brain (for reviews see Clarke, 1985; Cowan, Fawcett, O'Leary, & Stanfield, 1984; Hopkins & Brown, 1984; Janowsky & Findlay, 1986; Purves & Lichtman, 1985). That processes of selective loss have a significant influence on postnatal primate brain development is evident from a number of quantitative measures. For example, in the PET study alluded to above, the authors found that the absolute rates of glucose metabolism rise postnatally until they exceed adult levels, before reducing to adult levels after about 9 years of age for most cerebral cortical regions.

Consistent with these PET findings, Huttenlocher (1990, 1994) reports quantitative neuroanatomical evidence from several regions of the human cortex that following the increase in density of synapses described above there is then a period of synaptic loss. Like the timing of bursts of synaptogenesis and the subsequent peaks of density, the timing of the reduction in synaptic density varies between cortical regions. For example, synaptic density in the visual cortex returns to adult levels between 2 and 4 years, while the same point is not reached until between 10 and 20 years of age for regions of the prefrontal cortex. Huttenlocher (1990, 1994) suggests that this initial overproduction of synapses may have an important role in the apparent plasticity of the young brain, a matter which will be discussed in more detail later. There is no strong evidence for this pattern of rise and fall for either density of dendrites or for the number of neurons themselves in humans or other primates. However, in rodents and other vertebrates, cell loss may be more significant.

One explanation for the decrease in glucose uptake observed in the PET studies is that it reflects the decrease in synaptic contacts. This hypothesis was investigated in a recent developmental study conducted with cats (Chugani,

Hovda, Villablanca, Phelps, & Xu, 1991). In this study, the peak of glucose uptake in cat visual cortex was found to coincide with the peak in overproduction of synapses in this region. However, when similar data from human visual cortex is plotted (Figure 1.3), the peak of glucose uptake lags behind synaptic density. An alternative to the hypothesis that reduction of metabolic activity is the result of the elimination of neurons, axons and synaptic branches, is that the same activity may require less mental effort once a certain level of skill has been attained.

Most of the developments in the brain discussed so far concern aspects of the structure of the brain. However, there are also developmental changes in what has been known as the "soft soak" aspects of neural function, molecules involved in the transmission and modulation of neural signals. A number of neurotransmitters in rodents and humans also show the rise and fall developmental pattern (see Benes, 1994 for review). Specifically, the excitatory intrinsic transmitter glutamate, the intrinsic inhibitory transmitter GABA (gamma-aminobutyric acid), and the extrinsic transmitter serotonin all show this developmental trend.

Thus, the distinctive rise-and-fall developmental sequence is seen in a number of measures of structural and neurophysiological development in the human cortex. The number of measures and different laboratories in which this somewhat counter-intuitive developmental sequence

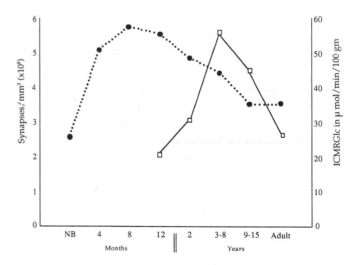

Figure 1.3 Graph showing development of density of synapses in human primary visual cortex and resting glucose uptake in the occipital cortex as measured by PET. Dotted line data taken from Huttenlocher (1990). Solid line data taken from Chugani et al. 1987. ICMRGlc is a measure of the local cerebral metabolic rates for glucose.

has been observed leads to a degree of confidence in its validity. However, it should be stressed that (a) not all measures show this pattern (e.g., myelinization), (b) measures such as synaptic density are static snapshots of a dynamic process in which both additive and regressive processes are continually in progress—in other words, there are probably not distinct and separate progressive and regressive phases, and (c) models which are exclusively dependent on regressive processes are unlikely to be adequate.

In addition to these caveats, all of the additive and subtractive events just described for normal human brain development must be weighed against a growing literature on individual differences within the normal range. As more sophisticated brain-imaging techniques are developed, it becomes increasingly evident that there is considerable variation in structure and function in normal adult subjects. For example, Gazzaniga and his colleagues (Tramo et al., 1994) reconstructed the cortical areas of two identical twins from MRI scans. Even in the case of genetically identical individuals, the variation in cortical areas was striking, with the occipital lobe occupying 13% to 17% of cortical area in one individual, and 20% in the other. These differences between individuals in brain structure may also extend to brain functioning. For example, using functional MRI, Schneider and colleagues studied the areas of activation following upper or lower visual field stimulation. While it had classically been assumed that the upper and lower visual field mapped on to the regions above and below the sulcus, there is in fact a lot of variation with some normal subjects showing an upper/lower visual field cut that straddles this structure (Schneider, Noll, & Cohen, 1993). This new evidence for variability complements an older literature on individual differences in handedness and hemispheric organization for language (e.g., Hellige, 1993; Kinsbourne & Hiscock, 1983). In view of this variability in normal adults, efforts to construct a timetable for "normal" postnatal brain development in humans must be interpreted with caution.

Dissociations between Laminar and Regional Development within Cerebral Cortex

There are at least two dimensions of specificity in the cerebral cortex: the layered structure described earlier and the orthogonal differentiation into areas or regions. Due to the very prolonged development of the human cortex that extends into postnatal life, differential development along both of these dimensions will likely influence computation.

Although most cortical neurons are in their appropriate locations by the time of birth in the primate, the "inside-out" pattern of growth observed in prenatal cortical development extends into postnatal life. Extensive descriptive neuroanatomical studies of cortical development in the human infant by Conel over a thirty-year period lead him to the conclusion that the postnatal growth of cortex proceeds in an "inside-out" pattern with regard to the extent of dendrites, dendritic trees, and myelinization (Conel, 1939/1967). The general conclusions which Conel reached have been largely substantiated with more modern neuroanatomical methods (e.g., Becker, Armstrong, Chan, & Wood, 1984; Purpura, 1975; Rabinowicz, 1979). In particular, the maturation of layer 5 (deeper) in advance of layers 2 and 3 (superficial) seems to be a very reliably observed sequence for many cortical regions in the human infant (Becker et al., 1984; Rabinowicz, 1979). For example, the dendritic trees of cells in layer 5 of primary visual cortex are already at about 60% of their maximum extent at birth. In contrast, the mean total length for dendrites in layer 3 is only at about 30% of maximum at birth. Furthermore, higher orders of branching in dendritic trees are observed in layer 5 than in layer 3 at birth (Becker et al., 1984; Huttenlocher, 1990).

The residual postnatal effects of the inside-out growth of cortex is also evident in the distribution of certain neurotransmitters (see Benes, 1994, for review). For example, acetylcholine, which originates mainly from the basal forebrain, follows the inside-out pattern of growth with the deeper cortical layers being innervated before the more superficial ones. Like acetylcholine, serotonin (which originates from the raphe nucleus) is found mainly in the deeper cortical layers at birth, consistent with the structural inside-out gradient of development. Another extrinsic cortical transmitter, dopamine (which orginates in the substantia nigra) also shows this inside-out pattern around the time of birth, at least in rats. The inside-out pattern of growth is not evident in all neuroanatomical measures, however. For example, there are no clear differences between layers in the rise and fall in synaptic density.

Turning to the orthogonal dimension of differentiation into regions and areas, as noted earlier Huttenlocher (1990, 1994) reports clear evidence of a difference in the timing of postnatal neuroanatomical events between the primary visual cortex and the frontal cortex in human infants, with the latter reaching the same developmental landmarks considerably later in postnatal life than the former. This differential development within the cerebral cortex has not been reported in other primate species (Rakic, Bourgeois, Eckenhoff, Zecevic, & Goldman-Rakic, 1986). Rakic and colleagues reported that all areas of cortex appear to hit a peak in synaptic density around the same time—around 2 to 4 months in the rhesus monkey, roughly corresponding to 7 to 12 months in the human child. Contrary to Huttenlocher's findings with human postmortem tissue, this suggests that there may be a common genetic signal to increase connectivity across all cortical regions simultaneously. While there are a number of possible explanations for this discrepancy, it is likely that the more prolonged development of the human cortex stretches out regional differences that are hard to detect within the more compressed sequence of development in the monkey.

Consistent with the reports from human postmortem tissue, a PET study also found differential development between regions of cortex (Chugani & Phelps, 1986; Chugani et al., 1987). In infants under 5 weeks of age, glucose uptake was highest in sensorimotor cortex, thalamus, brainstem, and the cerebellar vermis. By 3 months of age, there were considerable rises in the parietal, temporal, and occipital cortices, basal ganglia, and cerebellar cortex. Maturational rises were not found in the frontal and dorsolateral occipital cortex until approximately 6 to 8 months.

Cortical Plasticity

Traditionally, instances of functional recovery following damage to the cortex early in life have been attributed to a specialized adaptation response to injury. The cortex was implicitly assumed to be relatively prespecified in terms of the functional specializations of particular regions. Recently, a number of lines of research have provided evidence in support of the alternative view that plasticity is a fundamental property of the developing cortex. The new evidence comes from both developmental neuropsychology and developmental neurobiology. Some of the evidence for cortical plasticity from developmental neuropsychology will be discussed in later sections. The evidence for cortical plasticity from developmental neurobiological studies has centered around a debate about the extent to which the differentiation of the cortical surface into cytoarchitectronic and functional areas or regions is a result of factors intrinsic to the cortex itself, as opposed to being sensitive to the nature and extent of input it receives from the environment (via the thalamus). There have been two general views put forward to account for the parcellation of cortex into functional areas:

1. Rakic (1988) has proposed that the differentiation of the cortex into areas is due to a *protomap*. The protomap either involves prespecification of the proliferative zone or intrinsic molecular markers that guide the division of cortex into particular areas. One mechanism for this would be through the radial glial fiber path from the proliferative zone to the cortex. By this view, the differentiation of cortex into regions is due to factors intrinsic to the cortex.

2. The regional differentiation of cortex arises out of an undifferentiated *protocortex* that becomes divided up into specialized areas as a result of neural activity through projections from the thalamus (e.g., O'Leary, 1989). By this view, cortical differentiation is largely influenced by activity and experience-dependent factors.

While the first of these options may initially seem plausible, there is surprisingly little direct evidence for it. For example, to date there is no strong evidence for specific molecular markers or gradients that map onto the cortical areas that compose the regional divisions of cortex, something that would be expected if the regional division of cortex was prespecified (see Shatz, 1992).

In another line of evidence, Molnar and Blakemore (1991) tested the idea that molecular markers within the cortex can guide particular inputs (from the thalamus) to particular regions by seeing if sections removed from a thalamus and maintained in a petri dish innervate pieces of cortex placed close by. These petri dish experiments provided evidence for (a) laminar structure prespecification since projections from the thalamus always grew into the appropriate layer of the cortex, and (b) for thalamic afferents being attracted to innervate cortical tissue. However, further experiments of a similar kind indicated that thalamic projections do not innervate pieces of cortex from particular regions preferentially. For example, in experiments in which a piece of visual thalamus (LGN) was placed close to a variety of pieces of cortex from different areas, the visual thalamus did *not* preferentially innervate visual cortex: all cortical targets were equally acceptable to all parts of the thalamus. Molnar and Blakemore tried several different combinations of thalamic areas and cortical ones and found that regardless of the origin of the piece of thalamus or cortex, equivalent innervation of layer 4 occurs.

If these results are extended to the developing brain in situ (i.e., inside the animal, as opposed to a dish), they imply that while the cortex provides an attractive growth substrate for the thalamus, and a stop signal at the appropriate layer, there is no area-specific targeting. Thus, for example, the visual thalamus is not specifically attracted to the visual cortex by some molecular marker, and auditory thalamus is not attracted to auditory cortex.

Another alternative version of the protomap theory might be that the cortex sends connections to specific regions of thalamus that then guide the afferents from the thalamus. In other words, the developing cortex may send guidewires back down. Unfortunately for this hypothesis, however, Molnar and Blakemore found that cortical projections to thalamus lacked regional specificity in the same way as the reciprocal connections had. Any zone of embryonic cortex would innervate any zone of thalamus. These experiments indicate that there are probably no region-specific molecular signals available to guide thalamo-cortical projections.

In conclusion, therefore, there is little positive evidence for the intrinsic prespecification of cortex into areas with particular properties. However, it should be noted that there may be some exceptions to this conclusion in primate cortex. For example, in primate primary visual cortex inputs from the visual thalamus may regulate the extent of cell proliferation in the ventricular zone (Kennedy & Dehay, 1993), ensuring that this area of cortex has a rate of neuron production nearly twice that in neighboring areas.

Given that, in general, there is little evidence for a cortical protomap, how are we to account for the specificity with which particular thalamic afferents normally innervate particular regions of cortex? Molnar and Blakemore (1991) propose an account of thalamic innervation in which the regional specificity of projections between thalamus and cortex arises from a combination of timing and spatial constraints. Briefly, this account states that afferents grow from regions of the thalamus according to a particular spatio-temporal gradient. Different regions of thalamus grow projections at slightly different times, and as a new afferent grows it always grows on top of, or beside, existing afferents. By following these existing afferents, the newly grown axons terminate at an adjacent location to those that grew just before. Thus, there is a chronotopic innervation of cortex by thalamus which uses the physical presence of other afferents as a spatiotemporal constraint on the pattern of innervation.

To summarize so far, while the basic architecture of the cerebral cortex in mammals appears to be universal the overall area of cortical tissue can vary widely between species. Intrinsic cellular and molecular level interactions determine many aspects of the layered structure of cortex

and its patterns of connectivity. The differentiation of cortex into distinct areas or regions is heavily influenced by activity-dependent factors. Current evidence suggests that there are no intrinsic, predetermined functional areas in either the cortex or the thalamus; instead, both develop their area specializations as a consequence of their inputs, spontaneous activity, and the temporal (chronotopic) dynamics of neural growth. This means that normal cortical development permits a considerable degree of plasticity. That is, cortical regions could support a number of different types of representations depending on their input. A number of recent neurobiological experiments have sought to determine the extent to which cortical regions can support representations derived from different sources of input. These experiments include the following:

- When thalamic inputs are "rewired" such that they project to a different region of cortex from normal, the new recipient region develops some of the properties of the normal target tissue, for example, auditory cortex takes on visual representations (Sur, Garraghty, & Roe, 1988; Sur, Pallas, & Roe, 1990).

- When a piece of cortex is transplanted to a new location it develops projections characteristic of its new location, rather than its developmental origin, for example, transplanted visual cortex takes on the representations that are appropriate for somatosensory input (O'Leary & Stanfield, 1989).

- Reduction of the size of thalamic input to a region of cortex early in life determines the subsequent size of that region (Dehay, Horsburgh, Berland, Killackey, & Kennedy, 1989; Rakic, 1988; Schlagger & O'Leary, 1993).

- When the usual sites for higher cortical functions are bilaterally removed in infancy, that is, the temporal region with primary responsibility for visual object recognition in monkeys; regions at a considerable distance from the original site can take over the displaced function, that is, the parietal regions that are usually responsible for detection of motion and orientation in space (Webster, Bachevalier, & Ungerleider, 1995).

I will now consider the first two examples in more detail. The latter two are reviewed in Elman et al. (1996).

Cross-modal plasticity of cortical areas has now been demonstrated at the neurophysiological level in several mammalian species (for review, see Sur et al., 1990). For example, following a technique initially developed by Frost, projections from the retina can be induced to project to auditory thalamic areas, and thence to auditory cortex in the ferret by placing lesions in the normal visual cortex and in the lateral geniculate nucleus (the normal thalamic target of retinal projections). In addition, lesions are also placed such that auditory inputs do not innervate their normal thalamic target, the medial geniculate nucleus. Under these pathological conditions retinal projections will reroute to innervate the medial geniculate nucleus (MGN), which is the way station that normally handles auditory inputs. Projections from the MGN then project to the auditory cortex, in the normal fashion. The experimental question concerns whether the normally auditory cortex becomes visually responsive (i.e., in accord with its input,) or whether it retains features characteristic of auditory cortex. It turns out that auditory cortex does become visually responsive. Furthermore, cells in what would have been auditory cortex also become orientation- and direction-selective, and some become binocular.

While these observations are provocative, they do not provide evidence that the auditory cortex as a whole becomes functionally similar to the visual cortex. It is possible, for example, that the visually driven cells in the auditory cortex would fire in a random fashion unrelated to other cells. That is, there may be no organization of the representation above the level of the individual neuron. In order to address this issue, Sur and colleagues recorded from single neurons in a systematic way across the rewired cortex (Roe, Pallas, Hahm, & Sur, 1990; Sur et al., 1988). These experiments revealed that the previously auditory cortex had developed a two-dimensional retinal map. In normal ferrets, the primary auditory cortex contains a one-dimensional representation of the cochlea. Along one axis of the cortical tissue, electrode penetrations revealed a gradual shift from responses to low frequencies to responses to high frequencies. Along the orthogonal dimension of cortex, frequency remains constant (the isofrequency axis). In contrast, the visual representation developed in the rewired animals occupies both dimensions (elevation and azimuth). The authors conclude:

> Our results demonstrate that the form of the map is not an intrinsic property of the cortex and that a cortical area can come to support different types of maps. (Roe et al., 1990)

Sur and colleagues have begun a series of behavioral studies to address the further issue of whether ferrets can make use of visual input to auditory cortex. They trained adult ferrets, rewired in one hemisphere at birth, to discriminate between visual and auditory stimuli presented to the normal hemisphere. After this they probed the functioning of the rewired hemisphere by presenting visual stimuli that activated only the rewired pathway. The ferrets reliably interpreted the visual stimulus as visual rather than auditory (see Pallas & Sur, 1993). If these results continue to hold, they provide support for Sur's conclusions about the functional (as well as structural) equipotentiality of cortical mapping.

Additional evidence for cortical plasticity comes from studies in which pieces of cortex are transplanted from one region to another early in development. These experiments allow biologists to address the question of whether transplanted areas take on the structure/function of their *developmental origins,* or the structure/function of the new location in which they find themselves.

Pieces of fetal cortex have been successfully transplanted into other regions of newborn rodent cortex. For example, visual cortex neurons can be transplanted into the sensorimotor region and vice versa. Experiments such as these, conducted by O'Leary and Stanfield (1985; Stanfield & O'Leary, 1985) among others, have revealed that the projections and structure of such transplants develop according to their new spatial location rather than their developmental origins. For example, visual cortical neurons transplanted to the sensorimotor region develop projections to the spinal cord, a projection pattern characteristic of the sensorimotor cortex, but not the visual cortex. Similarly, sensorimotor cortical neurons transplanted to the visual cortical region develop projections to the superior colliculus, a subcortical target of the visual cortex, but not characteristic of the sensorimotor region. Thus, the inputs and outputs of a transplanted region take on the characteristics of their new location.

A further question concerns the detailed areal structure of the transplanted region. Will it also take on the characteristics of its new location, or will it retain the detailed areal structure of its tissue source? The somatosensory cortex of the rat (and other rodents) possesses characteristic internal structures known as *barrel fields.* Barrel fields are an aspect of the detailed areal structure of the cortex, and are clearly visible under the microscope. Each of the barrels corresponds to one whisker on the rat's face. Barrels develop during postnatal growth, and can be prevented from appearing in the normal cortex by cutting the sensory inputs to the region from the face. Furthermore, barrel structure is sensitive to the effects of early experience such as repeated whisker stimulation, or whisker removal (Killackey, Chiaia, Bennett-Clarke, Eck, & Rhoades, 1994; see also O'Leary, 1989). Hence we can ask whether transplanted slabs of visual cortex take on the barrel field structures that are typical of somatosensory cortex in the rat.

Schlaggar and O'Leary (1991) conducted a study of this kind, in which pieces of visual cortex were transplanted into the part of the somatosensory cortex that normally forms barrel fields in the rodent. When innervated by thalamic afferents, the transplanted cortex develops barrel fields very similar to those normally observed. Thus, not only can a transplanted piece of cortex develop inputs and outputs appropriate for its new location, but the inputs to that location can organize the detailed areal structure of the cortical region. However, four caveats to the conclusion that the cortex is largely equipotential should be mentioned at this stage.

First, most of the transplant and rewiring studies have involved primary sensory cortices. Some authors have argued that primary sensory cortices may share certain common developmental origins that other types of cortex do not. Specifically, since an influential paper by Sanides (1971), some neuroanatomists have argued that the detailed cytoarchitecture of the cortex is consistent with their being root, core, and belt fields of cortex (Galaburda & Pandya, 1983; Pandya & Yeterian, 1985, 1990). These lineages of cortex differ slightly in the thickness of particular layers, the shapes of certain cell types, and also in their layered projection patterns to neighboring cortical regions. While the details of this theory are complex and remain somewhat controversial, it is worth noting that each of these cortical fields is claimed to facilitate a particular type of processing. For example, the core band of cortex is associated with primary sensory cortices, the root with secondary sensory areas, and the belt field with association cortices. Assuming that the structural differences between the putative lineages is due to phylogenetic, rather than ontogenetic, factors (and this is far from clear since these hypotheses are reached following study of adult brains) it is possible that levels of stimulus processing may be attracted to certain sub-types of cerebral cortex. Thus, it is possible that certain lineages of cortex which differ in detailed ways from other areas of cortex may be more suited for dealing with certain types of information processing. With regard to the transplant experiments discussed earlier, it may be that cortex is only equipotential within a lineage (e.g., primary-to-primary or secondary-to-secondary).

The second caveat to the conclusion that cortex is equipotential is that while transplanted or rewired cortex may look very similar to the original tissue in terms of function and structure, it is rarely absolutely indistinguishable from the original. For example, in the rewired ferret cortex studied by Sur and colleagues the mapping of the azimuth (angle right or left) is at a higher resolution (more detailed) than the mapping of the elevation (angle up or down) (Roe et al., 1990). In contrast, in the normal ferret, cortex azimuth and elevation are mapped in equal detail. It should also be noted that, with the exception of the study mentioned earlier, there is still relatively little physiological or behavioral evidence indicating that the transplanted tissue behaves the way the host area normally does.

The third caveat that should be noted is that most of the experimental neurobiological studies on cortical plasticity have been performed on rodents or cats, and not primates. Indeed, at least two specific areas of the primate cortex, primary visual cortex and the entorhinal cortex, show evidence of prenatal intrinsic prespecification. In the primary visual cortex, inputs from the visual thalamus may regulate the extent of cell proliferation in the ventricular zone (Kennedy & Dehay, 1993), ensuring that this area of cortex has a rate on neuron production nearly twice that in neighboring areas. The entorhinal cortex, the region of cortex most closely associated with the hippocampus, shows some differentiation from surrounding cortex as early as 13 weeks after gestation (Kostovic, Petanjek, & Judas, 1993).

The final caveat concerns the fact that specialization resulting from activity-dependent processes need not be assumed to result from sensory or motor experience, but can be the result of intrinsic patterns of "spontaneous" firing. For example, Shatz and collaborators (see Katz & Shatz, 1996 for review) have demonstrated periodic spatially clustered waves of spontaneous firing in retinal cells during prenatal development in mammals. These waves of spontaneous firing may provide sufficiently correlated patterns of input to induce ocular dominance columns in the primary visual cortex (see next section). Other aspects of primary visual cortex structure, such as orientation tuning and columns, may be less dependent on patterned input from other regions of the brain, but may depend on waves of spontaneous activity (propagated via gap junctions, not synapses) within cortex. For example, Weliky and Katz (1997) used artificial stimulation to modify the spontaneous firing input to primary visual cortex in ferret kits before the formation of orientation selective maps. They found that although orientation selectivity in stimulated animals was significantly weaker than normal, the overall organization of orientation columns across the visual cortex was not altered. While there are a number of alternative explanations of this result, the most likely account is that the intrinsic basic architecture of cortex, or waves of gap-junction mediated firing, ensure that certain spatial clustering patterns will emerge in cortex even under a wide variety of different input pattern conditions.

In conclusion, while neither extreme view is correct, evidence tends to support the protocortex rather more than the protomap account of functional specialization within cortex, and to support the contention that there are no innate representations within cortex. That is, a variety of different representations (implemented as detailed differences in dendritic and synaptic contacts) can be supported by most regions of cortex in early development. In this sense, plasticity is a fundamental property of the developing cortex, and not just a specialized response to injury. However, this plasticity is heavily constrained by factors both intrinsic and extrinsic to the developing infant. The basic cellular and laminar architecture of the cortex puts architectural constraints on the types of representations that emerge. While the factors responsible for overall map formation may be intrinsic to the basic wiring and waves of spontaneous firing of cortex, these maps can handle a variety of different stimulus dimensions according to the structure of input generated by sensory or motor experience. In following sections we will see how other factors associated with the external environment, and other brain systems, also serve to constrain the emergence of cortical functional specificity.

CONTEMPORARY STATUS: THE NEURAL BASIS OF COGNITIVE DEVELOPMENT

The following review of the neural basis of cognitive development is necessarily selective. I have chosen to emphasize research in a number of areas in which there is (a) one or more theoretical propositions to relate to the evidence, and where (b) the neural events are related to changes in perception and cognition, as opposed to motor, emotional, or social development. There is interesting research and speculation on these excluded topics. I have clustered my review of the contemporary research under themes, some of which are domains of cognition (such as perception, attention, memory) and one which has generated a body of research, the frontal cortex. Following this

review of contemporary research, the next section focuses on some of the mechanisms of change that have been proposed by consideration of cognitive change within the context of brain development. Finally, I will outline some recommendations for future research.

Perception

Immaturities in peripheral sensory systems place limits on the perceptual capacities of young infants. For example, immaturity of the retina limits spatial acuity. The issue remains, however, whether peripheral limitations provide the major constraints on the development of perception, or whether maturation of central nervous system pathways is the primary limiting factor. While this issue remains controversial, Banks and colleagues (e.g., Banks & Shannon, 1993) have conducted an "ideal observer" analysis in which the morphology of neonatal photoreceptors and optics were compared to those of adults. From this analysis, estimates of the contribution of optical and receptor immaturity, as opposed to central immaturities, to deficits in infant spatial and chromatic vision over the first few months of life were generated. Observed differences in these aspects of vision between adults and infants turn out to be significantly greater than would be predicted on the basis of peripheral limitations only, indicating that central nervous system pathway development is an important contributing factor in the development of vision.

Given that central nervous system factors play an important role even in the development of spatial acuity, we can enquire further into the nature and source of these constraints. In one of the first attempts to relate brain development to behavioral change in the human infant in some detail, Gordon Bronson (1974, 1982) argued that the development of vision and visual orienting over the first few months of life could be attributed to a shift from subcortical visual processing, to processing in cortical visual pathways over the first six months of life. Specifically, Bronson cited evidence from electrophysiological, neuroanatomical, and behavioral studies that the primary (cortical) visual pathway is not fully functioning until around 3 months postnatal age (for more recent reviews, see Atkinson, 1984; Johnson, 1990).

A number of laboratories have followed Bronson's lead in attempting to relate aspects of cortical development to changes in visual and perceptual capacities over the first few months of life. Three of these attempts are reviewed next; (a) the development of binocular vision, (b) the development of face recognition, and (c) the development of visual recognition memory.

The Development of Binocular Vision

Ocular dominance columns are functional and anatomical structures observed in layer 4 of the primary visual cortex. These columns arise from the segregation of inputs from the two eyes. In other words, neurons in a single ocular dominance column are dominated by input from one eye in adult mammals. Ocular dominance columns are thought to be the stage of processing necessary to achieve binocular vision and, subsequently, detection of disparities between the two retinal images.

Held (1985) reviewed converging evidence that binocular vision develops at approximately the end of the fourth month of life in human infants. One of the abilities associated with binocular vision, stereoacuity, increases very rapidly from the onset of stereopsis, such that it reaches adult levels within a few weeks. This is in contrast to other measures of acuity, such as grating acuity, which are thought to increase much more gradually. Held suggested that this very rapid spurt in stereoacuity requires some equally rapid change in the neural substrate supporting it. On the basis of evidence from animal studies, he proposed that this substrate is the development of ocular dominance columns found in layer 4 of the primary visual cortex. While Held's proposal was initially based on a simple causal association between the formation of ocular dominance columns and the onset of binocularity, more recent research in his laboratory has been concerned to provide a link between the process of change at the two levels.

As discussed earlier, processes of selective loss commonly contribute to the sculpting of specific pathways in the cortex. Neurophysiological evidence indicates that the geniculocortical afferents from the two eyes are initially mixed so that they synapse on common cortical neurons in layer 4. These layer 4 cells project to disparity selective cells (possibly in cortical layers 2 and 3). During ontogeny, geniculate axons originating from one eye withdraw from the region leaving behind axons from the other eye. Held suggested that it is these events at the neural level that give rise to the sudden increase in stereoacuity observed by behavioral measures at around 4 months of age in the human infant.

This process of selective loss has the information-processing consequence that information from the two eyes which was previously combined in layer 4 of the primary visual cortex becomes segregated (Held, 1993). Specifically,

there will be a certain degree of integration between the eyes that will decline once each neuron only receives innervation from one eye. Held and colleagues elegantly demonstrated this increasing segregation of information from the two eyes by showing that younger infants (under 4 months) can perform certain types of integration between the two eyes that older infants cannot. In this experiment, Held and his colleagues presented a grating to one eye of an infant, and an orthogonal grating to the other eye. Infants under 4 months perceived a single gridlike representation instead of two sets of gratings that were orthogonal to each other. This is because, presumably, synaptic inputs from the individual eyes have not segregated into ocular dominance columns. As a result, a given cortical layer 4 neuron may have synaptic inputs from each eye and will effectively "see" the image from each eye, simultaneously. That is, information from the two eyes would be summed in layer 4, resulting in an averaging of the two signals. Since the inputs from each eye summate, in the case of the orthogonal gratings a grid was perceived. Older infants (older than 4 months of age) do not perceive this grating because neurons in cortical layer 4 of striate cortex only receive inputs from one eye. The inputs to layer 4 have been segregated from one another, and a given layer 4 neuron will receive input from one eye or the other.

The loss of these connections is probably due to the refinement of synapses by selective loss discussed earlier. The refinement of synapses most likely occurs through activity dependent neural mechanisms because the formation of ocular dominance columns can be experimentally blocked by reducing neuronal activity (Stryker & Harris, 1986). Monocular deprivation (Wiesel & Hubel, 1965) also results in abnormal ocular dominance columns; in this case, the eye that is preserved takes over more than its normal share of cortical area. Based on these experimental findings, Miller and colleagues (Miller, 1990; Miller, Keller, & Stryker, 1989) have developed a computational model of ocular dominance column development that depends on correlated neuronal firing within an eye and the comparatively uncorrelated firing between the two eyes.

The Development of Face Recognition

While there is a large literature on the development of face recognition in young infants extending back to the studies of Fantz in the early 1960s (Fantz, 1964), only recently has there been speculation about the neural basis of these abilities. Specifically, de Schonen and Mathivet (1989) and Johnson and Morton (1991; Morton & Johnson, 1991) have speculated that preferential responses to faces seen in newborn infants may be mediated by primarily subcortical visual pathways, whereas later developing abilities to recognize individual faces (on the basis of internal features) are mediated by developing cortical visual pathways.

Johnson and Morton (1991; Morton & Johnson, 1991) reviewed much of the existing literature on face recognition in infants and discussed two apparently contradictory bodies of evidence: While the prevailing view, and most of the evidence, supported the contention that it takes the infant about two or three months to learn about the arrangement of features that compose a face (for reviews, see Maurer, 1985; Nelson & Ludemann, 1989), one study (Goren, Sarty, & Wu, 1975) suggested that newborns around 10 minutes old would track, by means of head and eye movements, a facelike pattern further than various scrambled face patterns.

This newborn study was replicated by Johnson, Dziurawiec, Ellis, and Morton (1991) with minor changes to improve the methodology. As in the original study, newborn infants, around 30 minutes old, were required to track different stimuli. This procedure differs markedly from that employed by other investigators, in that the dependent measure was how far the infant would turn its head and eyes in order to keep a moving stimulus in view. The stimulus is moved slowly away from the midline and the angle at which the infant disengages its eyes from the stimulus is recorded. Three of the four stimuli used in the original Goren et al. study were used; a schematic face pattern, a symmetric scrambled face and a blank face outline stimulus. Johnson and colleagues were unable to obtain significant preferential head turning to follow the face pattern, but like Maurer and Young (1983), did successfully replicate the effect using a measure of eye movements (see Figure 1.4).

The newborn studies provided evidence in support of a nativistic account of infant face recognition, but many studies using more conventional infant testing methods, such as preferential looking, had indicated that a preference for face patterns over others was not found until 2 or 3 months after birth (for review, see Maurer, 1985; Nelson & Ludemann, 1989). For example, Maurer and Barrera (1981) used a sensitive infant control procedure, in which the infant viewed a series of singly presented static stimuli, and established that while 2-month-olds looked significantly longer at a facelike pattern than at various scrambled face patterns, 1-month-olds had no such preference. Johnson, Dziurawiec, Bartrip, and Morton (1992) replicated this result and extended the original findings by including in the

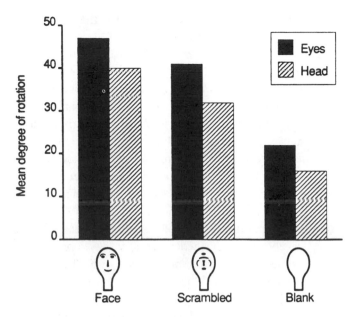

Figure 1.4 Data from Experiment 1 of Johnson et al. (1991) showing the extent of newborns' head and eye turns following a schematic face, a scrambled face, and a blank (unpatterned) stimulus. The infants tracked the face significantly further than the other stimuli by the Eyes measure.

stimulus set a "three blobs" face arrangement stimulus used in some of the newborn studies. The results replicated the previous findings: the face was looked at longer than any of the other stimuli by 10-week-olds, but a group of 5-week-olds showed no preference. The apparent contradiction between these findings and those with newborns raised a problem for existing theories of the development of face recognition that involved only one process. In order to shed some light on the issues, Johnson and Morton (1991) turned to evidence from two areas of biology: ethology and brain development.

The primary source of evidence from other species (ethology) that Johnson and Morton used to interpret the human infancy results concerned filial imprinting in the domestic chick. This topic was chosen because it is very well studied both in terms of the behavior and in terms of its neural basis. Imprinting is the process by which young precocial birds such as chicks recognize and develop an attachment for the first conspicuous object that they see after hatching (for recent reviews, see Bolhuis, 1991; Johnson & Bolhuis, 1991). While imprinting has been reported in the young of a variety of species including spiny mice, guinea pigs, chicks, and ducklings, only in precocial species (those that are mobile from birth) can we measure it using the conventional measure of preferential approach.

The domestic chick can be thought of as the "laboratory rat" of development (see Andrew, 1991), since it has proved to be an ideal species for addressing many developmental questions. The chick is also ideally placed in terms of being readily accessible to the molecular biologist and geneticist, as well as being the simplest vertebrate to show cognitive abilities of interest to the psychologist such as object recognition (Horn, 1985; Johnson, 1991; O'Reilly & Johnson, 1994). In the laboratory, chicks will imprint onto a variety of objects such as moving colored balls and cylinders. Even a few hours of exposure to such a stimulus results in strong and robust preferences for it over novel stimuli. Thus, in the absence of a mother hen, the learning is relatively unconstrained: virtually any conspicuous moving object larger than a matchbox will do. Under most circumstances this initial training object will come to be preferred over any other.

Visual imprinting involves a particular region of the chick forebrain, known as the Intermediate and Medial part of the Hyperstriatum Ventrale (IMHV) (for reviews, see Horn, 1985; Horn & Johnson, 1989). Lesions to IMHV placed before or after training on an object severely impairs preference for that object in subsequent choice tests, but does not affect several other types of visual and learning tasks (Johnson & Horn, 1986, 1987; McCabe, Cipolla-Neto, Horn, & Bateson, 1982). With a few exceptions (see Lowndes, Davies, & Johnson, 1994), similar size lesions placed in other regions of the chick forebrain do not result in significant impairments of imprinting preference (Johnson & Horn, 1987; McCabe et al., 1982).

In the laboratory, a wide range of objects such as moving red boxes and blue balls are as effective for imprinting as more naturalistic stimuli such as a moving stuffed hen. However, in the wild precocial birds such as chicks invariably imprint on their mother and not on other passing objects. These observations raise the question concerning what mechanisms ensure that this plasticity in the chick brain is constrained such that it encodes information about conspecifics, and not about the characteristics of other objects present in its early visual environment.

An answer to this issue arose from a series of experiments in which striking stimulus-dependent effects of IMHV lesions were found (Horn & McCabe, 1984). While groups of chicks trained on an artificial stimulus such as a red box were severely impaired by IMHV lesions placed either before or after training, groups of chicks trained on a stuffed hen were only mildly impaired. Other neurophysiological manipulations also turned out to show differences between the hen-trained and box-trained birds. For example, administration of the neurotoxin DSP4, which depletes forebrain levels of the neurotransmitter norepinephrine, resulted in a severe impairment of preference in birds trained on the red box, but only a mild impairment in birds trained on the stuffed hen (Davies, Horn, & McCabe, 1985). In contrast, levels of plasma testosterone correlate with preference for the stuffed hen, but not preference for the red box (Bolhuis, McCabe, & Horn 1986).

These results led Johnson and Horn (1988) to seek experimental evidence for an earlier suggestion (Hinde, 1974) that naturalistic objects such as hens may be more effective at eliciting attention in young chicks than are other objects. These authors conducted a series of experiments in which dark-reared chicks were presented with a choice between an intact stuffed hen and a variety of test stimuli created from cutting up and jumbling the pelt of a stuffed hen. Johnson and Horn (1988) concluded that chicks have a spontaneous tendency to attend toward characteristics of the head and neck region of the hen. While this untrained preference seemed to be specific to the correct arrangement of features of the face/head, it was not specific to the species. For example, the head of a duck was as attractive as that of a hen.

The results of these and other experiments led to the proposal that there are two independent neural systems that underlie filial preference in the chick (Horn, 1985; Johnson, Bolhuis, & Horn, 1985). The first is a specific predisposition for the young chick to orient toward objects resembling conspecifics. In contrast to nonspecific color and size preferences in the chick (see Johnson & Bolhuis, 1991), the predisposition system appears to be specifically tuned to the correct spatial arrangement of elements of the head and neck region. This is sufficient to pick out the mother hen from other objects the chick is likely to be exposed to in the first few days after hatching. The neural basis for this predisposition is currently unknown, but the optic tectum, the homologue of the mammalian superior colliculus, is a likely candidate. The second system acquires information about the objects to which the young chick attends and is supported by the brain region IMHV. In the natural environment, it was argued, the first system ensures that the second system acquires information about the particular individual mother hen close by. Biochemical, electrophysiological, and lesion evidence all support the conclusion that the two systems have largely independent neural substrates (for review, see Horn, 1985). For example, while selective lesions to IMHV impair preferences acquired through exposure to an object, they do not impair the predisposition (Johnson & Horn, 1986).

The other source of biological data that Johnson and Morton used to generate an account of human infant face recognition came from the postnatal development of the cerebral cortex. Both neuroanatomical and neurophysiological data indicate that visually guided behavior in the newborn infant is largely mediated by subcortical structures such as the superior colliculus and pulvinar, and that it is not until 2 or 3 months of age that cortical circuitry comes to dominate subcortical circuits. Consistent with these arguments is the position that visually guided behavior in human infants, like that in domestic chicks, is based on activity in at least two distinct brain systems. Since these systems have distinct developmental time courses, then they may differentially influence behavior in infants of different ages.

These two sources of biological evidence led Johnson and Morton (1991; Morton & Johnson, 1991) to propose a two-process theory of infant face preferences analogous to that in chicks. They argued that the first process consists of a system accessed via the subcortical visual pathway (but possibly also involving some cortical structures) and underlies the preferential tracking of faces in newborns. However, the influence of this system over behavior declines (possibly due to inhibition) during the second month of life. The second process depends upon cortical maturity, and exposure to faces over the first month or so, and begins to influence infant orienting preferences from 2 to 4 months of age.

By extension with the evidence on chicks, Johnson and Morton (1991) argued that the newborn preferential orienting system biases the input to developing cortical circuitry. This circuitry is configured in response to a certain range of input, before it itself gains control over motor output around the third month of life. Once this occurs, the cortical system has enough experience with faces to ensure that it continues to acquire further information about them. Like in the chick, the proposal is that a specific early developing brain circuit acts in concert with the species typical environment to bias the input to later developing brain circuitry.

One source of evidence that the preferential orienting toward faces found in newborn infants is primarily mediated by subcortical neural circuitry concerns its developmental time course. Although it is not feasible to test older infants with exactly the same procedure as used with newborns since they will track all patterned stimuli to the maximal extent, Johnson and colleagues (1991) devised an equivalent situation in which the infant was still required to track, by means of head and eye turning, similar stimuli. In this procedure, the infant was rotated in relation to the stimulus rather than the opposite (for details of procedure see Johnson et al., 1991 [experiment 3]). Using this procedure groups of 4-week-olds, 6-week-olds, 3-month-olds, and 5-month-olds were tested with similar stimuli to those discussed earlier. These experiments revealed that the preferential tracking of faces declines sharply between 4 and 6 weeks after birth. The time course of this response is similar to that of other newborn responses thought to be mediated by subcortical circuits such as pre-reaching (von Hofsten, 1984). It has been suggested that the disappearance of these early reflex-like behaviors in the second month of life is due to inhibition by developing cortical circuits (e.g., see Muir, Clifton, & Clarkson, 1989). This would also seem to be a plausible explanation for the decline observed in the tracking of faces. Thus, not only is it unlikely that the newborns have adequate cortical functioning to support the preferential tracking of faces, but this behavior declines at the same age as other behaviors thought to be subcortically mediated.

Why should the tracking task be so sensitive to newborns' preferences whereas standard testing procedures with static stimuli are ineffective? One reason is that the temporal visual field feeds into both the subcortical and cortical visual pathways, whereas the nasal (central) field feeds only into the cortical pathway. In a tracking task such as that described with newborns, the stimulus is continually moving out of the central visual field and toward the periphery. This movement into the temporal field may initiate a saccade to re-foveate the stimulus in newborns (for details, see Bronson, 1974; Johnson, 1990). This consistent movement toward the periphery would not necessarily arise with static presentations, and therefore preferences will rarely be elicited. Thus, the tracking task may more effectively tap into the capacities of subcortical structures such as the superior colliculus than the conventional infant testing procedures such as preferential looking at static stimuli. Preferential looking tasks in which the stimuli are far enough apart to impinge on the temporal visual field should also elicit the newborn preference, which they do (Valenza, Simion, Cassia, & Umilta, 1996).

None of the above arguments bring us any closer to specifying in detail the neural implementation of the newborn preferential tracking, and a number of different possibilities remain open, including the superior colliculus, pulvinar, deeper layers of the cortex, and any combination of these. Probably only direct methods, such as neuroimaging, will enable further progress to be made on this issue. Nevertheless, given the evidence for the preferential tracking of faces in newborns, how are we to account for the large body of evidence showing no preference for faces until 2 or 3 months of age?

Evidence from neuroimaging and brain damage in human adults, and from single unit recording in nonhuman primates, indicate that the recognition of individual faces is supported by particular regions of the cerebral cortex (for reviews, see Farah, 1990). For example, in one recent PET study on human adults a number of cortical regions were found to be activated in a face-matching task, including the anterior cingulate, frontal cortex, and anterior temporal lobe (George et al., 1993). Preliminary PET evidence indicates that 2-month-old infants show differential bilateral activation in the temporal lobes following passive exposure to faces (de Schonen, Deruelle, Mancini, & Pascalis, 1993). Indirect evidence that the later developing ability to recognize individual faces is mediated by this cortical circuitry concerns its developmental onset at 2 or 3 months of age.

A marker task for the cortical processing of faces has been devised by Vecera and Johnson (1995). This task was based upon the findings from several laboratories that cells responsive to face stimuli are found within the superior temporal sulcus (STS) of the macaque cortex (Perrett, Rolls, & Caan, 1982). Further, these cells become sensitive to faces as a result of experience (Rolls, 1989). Beyond responding to faces and particular views of faces, there is a finer level of processing within STS. Cells that are responsive to views of the head also process information concerning eye gaze direction. For example, Perrett and Mistlin (1990) report that 64% of cells in the macaque responding to the head were also responsive to eye gaze. These findings with nonhuman primates converge with findings from humans. Prosopagnosia in patients typically results from temporo-occipital lesions, although the exact neuropathology is debated. These patients are characterized by their inability to recognize or identify individual faces, and recent evidence suggests that they also have difficulty in processing the direction of another individual's eye gaze.

Campbell, Heywood, Cowey, Regard, and Landis (1990) examined the performance of both STS lesioned monkeys and two prosopagnosic patients on discriminating eye gaze direction. Following STS lesions the monkeys were impaired at this task, but not in several other face recognition tasks. Similarly, the prosopagnosic patients were unable to choose which of two faces was looking directly at them.

Vecera and Johnson (1995) tested groups of 2- and 4-month-old infants with photographs and schematic faces that differed in their direction of eye gaze. Results indicated that while 4-month-old infants can distinguish between direct and averted eye gazes, even when the difference between the two is as slight as 15°, most 2-month-olds cannot. This is consistent with the development of sensitivity to eye gaze, a "marker" for cortical face processing, developing between 2 and 4 months of age.

Biological evidence has therefore informed and constrained psychological theories of the development of face recognition in a number of ways. Evidence from the postnatal development of the brain ruled out that infants have full face recognition abilities from birth since many aspects of face recognition appear to be mediated by cortical circuits, and the cortex is relatively immature in the newborn infant. Evidence from neuroscience also generated the notion of two comparatively independent systems. Neurophysiological manipulations in the chick initially revealed the two systems, and anatomical evidence from primates (including humans) indicated the possibility of different developmental time course for cortical and subcortical systems in the human infant. Ethological considerations influenced the psychological theory by forcing a consideration of the crucial role of the external environment in supporting the development of cognitive systems. The two-process model outlined in this section holds that the species-typical environment guarantees the presence of conspecifics and their faces. The cognitive mechanisms proposed cannot be understood in isolation of the species-typical environment in which they have evolved to operate.

The Development of Visual Recognition Memory

One of the most commonly used behavioral techniques for studying the discriminative ability of young infants is habituation paradigms in which the subject is familiarized by repeated presentations of one stimulus prior to the introduction of a novel stimulus. This and related paradigms, such as the "oddball" paradigm in which an infrequent novel stimulus appears amidst repeated exposures to a familiar one, have been used with ERPs by several laboratories to study the neural correlates of visual recognition memory in infants. In a review of this literature, Nelson (1994) draws the conclusion that there are three major components of the ERP signal that emerge as important in these studies. These three components probably reflect distinct cognitive processes with different neural bases.

When infants are presented with a visual stimulus, even when it is repeated many times, a well defined negative component of the ERP is observed. This negative component occurs regardless of the whether the stimulus is familiar or novel, and Nelson (1994) suggests that it probably reflects an attentional process (and may be related to the

N400 which has been linked to attention in older subjects). One variable that influences the latency of this negative component is the age of the subjects, with it having a longer latency in younger infants (around 800 msec after stimulus onset in 4-month-olds) than in older infants (around 400 msec in 12-month-olds).

Following this component, there is often a sustained negative slow wave which Nelson suggests reflects the detection of novel stimuli. It generally occurs when an unfamiliar stimulus is detected after a sequence of familiar ones. In contrast, when a familiar stimulus is repeated the initial negative peak discussed above quickly returns to baseline. The third component is a late positive component that may be invoked by stimuli that are only partially encoded and require further processing or updating. In 6- to 8-month-olds it can be invoked by novel or rarely encountered stimuli (Nelson & Collins, 1992). This component has not been observed in infants under 6 months, and may be related in some respects to the P300 observed in adults and suggested to mark the updating of working memory.

The challenge for the future lies in identifying the brain sources of these different components of the ERP. This will allow progress in studying the multiple brain structures and pathways that underlie visual recognition memory and its development.

Visual Orienting and Attention

In the previous section, the evidence for increasing cortical involvement in perceptual processes over the first year of life was reviewed. Viewed from a broader perspective, this transition likely effects motor planning and sensory motor integration, as well as the processing of sensory input. Shifts of eye gaze and spatial attention offer the opportunity to study the effects of brain development on the integration between sensory input and motor output, while utilizing a form of action (eye gaze shifts) which infants can accomplish readily from birth. Further, over the first 6 to 8 months of life, the human infant's primary method of interacting with its environment involves shifts of eye gaze and attention. These shifts of attention allow the infant to select particular aspects of the external world for learning. For example, and as discussed in the previous section, simply by shifting the head and eyes infants can ensure that they are exposed to faces more than to other stimuli. In addition, most of what we have learned about the mental life of the infant has come from tasks in which some measure of looking behavior, such as preferential looking or habituation to a repeatedly presented stimulus, is used. Despite

the importance of shifts of attention in early infancy, however, until recently very little was known about how the development of the brain relates to changes in visual orienting and attention processes. This was despite a substantial literature on the neural basis of visual attention which comes from neuropsychological and neuroimaging studies of human adults , as well as single-cell recording and lesion studies in nonhuman primates (see Posner & Peterson, 1990 for review).

As mentioned earlier, Bronson (1974, 1982) argued that visually guided behavior in the newborn human infant is initially controlled primarily by means of the subcortical retino-collicular pathway, and that it is only by around 2 or 3 months of age that the locus of control over behavior switches to primarily cortical pathways. More recently, it has become evident that there is some, albeit limited, cortical activity in newborns, and that the onset of cortical functioning probably proceeds by a series of graded steps, rather than in an all-or-none manner. In correspondence with this, neurophysiological research on monkeys and neuropsychological research with human adults has revealed that there are multiple pathways involved in oculomotor control and attention shifts in the primate brain. A number of the structures and pathways involved are illustrated in Figure 1.5.

Most of the pathways and structures illustrated in Figure 1.5 are known to be involved in particular types of information processing related to the planning of eye movements. For brevity, only three of these pathways will be discussed here. First, the pathway from the eye to the superior colliculus. This subcortical pathway has input mainly from the temporal (peripheral) visual field, and is involved in the generation of rapid reflexive eye movements to easily discriminable stimuli. The other two pathways to be discussed here share a projection from the eye to cortical structures via the midbrain (thalamic) visual relay, the lateral geniculate nucleus (LGN), and the primary visual cortex (V1). One of these pathways goes from V1 on to a temporal area (MT) which plays an important role in the detection of motion and smooth tracking. The remaining pathway discussed here proceeds from V1 to other parts of the visual cortex and thence to the frontal eye fields (FEF). As we will see later, this FEF pathway is thought to be involved in more complex aspects of eye movement planning such as anticipatory saccades and learning sequences of scanning patterns.

The challenge has been to relate the development of these various pathways to the visuomotor competence of the infant at different ages. To date, this has involved two complementary

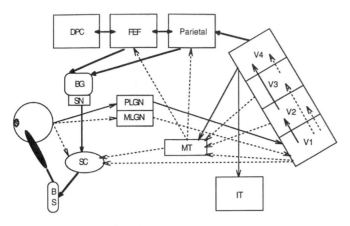

Figure 1.5 A diagram representing some of the main neural pathways and structures involved in visual orienting and attention. The solid lines indicate primarily parvocellular input, while the dashed arrows represent magnocellular. Abbreviations: V1–V4 = visual cortex, FEF = frontal eye fields, DPC = dorsolateral prefrontal cortex, BG = basal ganglia, SN = sustantia nigra, LGN = lateral geniculate (magno & parvo portions), MT = middle temporal area, IT = inferotemporal cortex, SC = superior colliculus, BS = brain stem.

approaches: predictions about the sequence of development of the pathways from developmental neuroanatomy (Atkinson, 1984; Johnson, 1990), and the administration of marker tasks to ascertain the functional development of particular structures or pathways.

An example of the first approach was an analysis by Johnson (1990) in which he proposed that first, the characteristics of visually guided behavior of the infant at particular ages is determined by which of the pathways (shown in Figure 1.5) is functional, and second the developmental state of the primary visual cortex determines which of those pathways receives structured input. The basis of this claim at the neuroanatomical level lies in three sets of observations: (a) the primary visual cortex is the major (though not exclusive) "gateway" for input to most the cortical pathways involved in oculomotor control (Schiller, 1985); (b) the primary visual cortex, like other cortical regions, shows a postnatal continuation of the prenatal "inside-out" pattern of growth with the deeper layers (5 and 6) showing greater dendritic branching, length and extent of myelinization than more superficial layers (2 and 3) around the time of birth; and (c) as discussed earlier, there are restricted inputs and outputs from different layers of the primary visual cortex (e.g., Rockland & Pandya, 1979).

By combining these observations with information about the developmental neuroanatomy of the primary

visual cortex, Johnson (1990) hypothesized a particular sequence of postnatal development of the pathways underlying oculomotor control, and then reviewed behavioral evidence consistent with this sequence. Specifically, it was hypothesized that the locus of oculomotor control in the newborn infant consisted of the subcortical pathway from the eye directly to the superior colliculus, and possibly also some cortical projections from the deeper layers of V1 to superior colliculus. This claim was argued to be consistent with following observations of newborn infants:

- Evidence from various sources, such as visually evoked potentials, indicate that visual information enters the primary visual cortex in the newborn. However, measures of the extent dendritic arborization and myelinization indicate that only the deeper layers of the primary visual cortex are capable of supporting organized information-processing activity at this age. Since the majority of feed-forward intracortical projections depart from outside these deeper layers, the cortical pathways involved in oculomotor control may only be receiving weak or disorganized input at this stage. Thus, while visual information enters the cortex in the newborn, it probably has little influence over eye movement control.

- Aslin (1981) reports that the visual tracking of a moving stimulus in the first few months of life has two characteristics. The first is that the eye movements follow the stimulus in a "saccadic" or steplike manner, as opposed to the smooth pursuit found in adults and older infants. The second characteristic is that the eye movements always lag behind the movement of the stimulus, rather than predicting its trajectory. Therefore, when a newborn infant visually tracks a moving stimulus, it could be described as performing a series of separate re-orientations as the stimulus leaves the central visual field, behavior consistent with the subcortical control of eye movements (Johnson, 1990).

- Newborns much more readily orient toward stimuli in the temporal, as opposed to the nasal, visual field (e.g., Lewis, Maurer, & Milewski, 1979). Posner and Rothbart (1980) suggest that midbrain structures such as the superior colliculus can be driven most readily by temporal field input.

- Infants in the first few months of life do not attend to stationary pattern elements within a larger frame or pattern (e.g., Maurer, 1983) unless these elements are moving (Bushnell, 1979). This is the so-called "externality effect." While a variety of explanations have been put forward to account for this phenomenon (e.g., Aslin & Smith, 1988), Johnson (1990) proposed that part of the explanation could be due to superior colliculus attempting to shift the retinal image of the most visible pattern elements into the fovea.

One important question that remained unresolved until recently was whether the subcortical pathway, in isolation of the cortical pathways, can drive saccades on its own in infants. This issue was addressed in experiments by Braddick and coworkers (1992) in which they studied two infants who had undergone complete hemispherectomy (removal of the cortex on one side) to alleviate severe epilepsy. They established that these infants were indeed able to make directed eye movements to targets that appeared in their "cortically blind" visual field, indicating that the subcortical (collicular) pathway is capable of supporting saccades in the absence of the cortex.

By 2 months of age, Johnson argued that further development of layers in V1 would allow the functioning of the pathway involving structure MT. In accordance with this prediction, at this age infants begin to show periods of smooth visual tracking, although their eye movements still lag behind the movement of the stimulus. Also at this age they first become sensitive to coherent motion in visual input (Wattam-Bell, 1991).

Due to further dendritic growth and myelinization within the upper layers of the primary visual cortex strengthening the projections to other cortical areas, around 3 months of age the pathways involving the frontal eye fields become functional. This development may greatly increase the infant's ability to make "anticipatory" eye movements and to learn sequences of looking patterns, both functions associated with the frontal eye fields. With regard to the visual tracking of a moving object, infants now not only show periods of smooth tracking, but their eye movements often predict the movement of the stimulus in an anticipatory manner.

The phases outlined above should be viewed as snapshots along a dynamic and gradually changing developmental path. Thus, the predictions from the Johnson (1990) account concern the *sequence* of development within an individual infant, rather than the exact ages of group effects.

Testing the predictions of the Johnson (1990) analysis depended on relating behavioral tasks to particular brain pathways. While there are currently studies involving more direct methods of analyzing the neural basis of sensory motor integration in infants, the majority of the recently

TABLE 1.2   Marker Tasks for the Development of Visual Orienting and Attention

Brain Region	Marker Task	Studies
Superior Colliculus	Inhibition of return;	Clohessy, Posner, Rothbart, & Vecera (1991);
	Vector summation saccades	Simion, Valenza, Umilta, & Della Barba (1995); Johnson, Gilmore, Tucker, & Minister (1995)
MT	Coherent motion detection; Structure from motion;	Wattam-Bell (1991)
	Smooth tracking	Aslin (1981)
Parietal cortex	Spatial cueing task	Hood & Atkinson (1991); Hood (1993); Johnson & Tucker (1996); Johnson (1994)
	Eye-centered saccade planning	Gilmore & Johnson (1995)
Frontal eye fields	Inhibition of automatic saccades;	Johnson (1995)
	Anticipatory saccades	Haith, Hazan, & Goodman (1988)
Dorsolateral PFC	Oculomotor delayed response task	Gilmore & Johnson (1995)

published work has involved marker tasks. Table 1.2 summarizes a number of marker tasks that have recently been developed for the functioning of structures involved in oculomotor control and visual attention shifts.

Marker tasks for the parietal cortex, frontal eye fields (FEF), and dorsolateral prefrontal cortex (DLPC) have recently been developed, and show rapid development of infant abilities between 2 and 6 months of age. One marker task for the parietal cortex is a spatial cueing task designed to measure covert shifts of spatial attention. The discussion so far has concerned overt shifts of attention due to eye and head movements. It is evident that adults are also capable of shifting their attention covertly (without moving the receptors). One way in which evidence for covert attention has been provided in adults is by studying the effect on detection of cueing saccades to a particular spatial location. A briefly presented cue serves draw covert attention to the location resulting in the subsequent facilitation of detection of targets at that location (Maylor, 1985; Posner & Cohen, 1980). While *facilitation* of detection and responses to a covertly attended location occurs if the target stimulus appears very shortly after the cue offset, with longer latencies between cue and target *inhibition* of saccades toward that location occurs. This latter phenomenon, referred to as "inhibition of return" (Posner, Rafal, Choate, & Vaughan, 1985), may reflect an evolutionarily important mechanism for preventing attention returning to a spatial location which has been very recently processed. In adults, facilitation is reliably observed when targets appeared at the cued location within about 150 msec of the cue, whereas targets that appear between 300 and 1300 msec after a peripheral (exogenous) cue result in longer detection latencies (e.g., Maylor, 1985; Posner & Cohen, 1980, 1984).

Following lesions to the posterior parietal lobe adults show severe neglect of the contralateral visual field. According to Posner and colleagues this neglect is due to damage to the "posterior attention network"—a brain circuit that includes not only the posterior parietal lobe, but also the pulvinar and superior colliculus (Posner, 1988; Posner & Peterson, 1990; see Figure 5.1 for all but the pulvinar). Damage to this circuit is postulated to impair subjects ability to shift covert attention to a cued spatial location. The involvement of these regions in shifts of visual attention has been confirmed by Positron Emission Tomography (PET) studies. Both neuroanatomical (Conel, 1939–1967) and PET (Chugani et al., 1987) evidence from the human infant indicate that the parietal lobe is undergoing substantive and rapid development between 3 and 6 months after birth in the human infant. The question arises, therefore, as to whether infants become capable of covert shifts of attention during this time.

Hood and Atkinson (1991; see Hood, 1995) reported that 6-month-old infants have faster reaction times to make a saccade to a target when it appears immediately after a brief (100 msec) cue stimulus, while a group of 3-month-olds did not. This task was regarded as "covert" since the cue stimulus was too brief to elicit a saccade on its own. Johnson (1994; Johnson & Tucker, 1996) employed a similar procedure in which a brief (100 msec) cue was presented on one of two side screens, before bilateral targets were presented either 100 msec or 600 msec later. It was hypothesized on the basis of the adult findings that the 200 msec stimulus onset asynchrony (SOA) would be short enough to produce facilitation, while the long SOA trials should result in preferential orienting toward the opposite side (inhibition of return). This result was obtained with a group of 4-month-old infants, suggesting the functioning of portions of the parietal cortex at this age. These effects were not observed in a group of 2-month-old infants. Further experiments run with older infants indicate that covert

shifts of attention may get faster between 4 and 8 months of age. At present it remains an open question whether the facilitation produced by the cue in these experiments is the result of direct priming of the eye movement system, or whether the eye movements are following an independent covert shift of attention. However, the finding that 4-month-old infants show facilitation to a cue even when it predicts the presentation of a target in the opposite direction (normally also necessitating an eye movement in the opposite direction), is more consistent with the facilitation effects being due to drawing covert attention to the location (see Johnson, Posner, & Rothbart, 1994).

Turning to marker tasks for the frontal eye fields (FEF), frontal cortex damage in humans results in an inability to suppress involuntary automatic saccades toward targets, and an apparent inability to control volitional saccades (Fischer & Breitmeyer, 1987; Guitton, Buchtel, & Douglas, 1985). For example, Guitton and coworkers (1985) studied normal subjects and patients with frontal lobe lesions or temporal lobe lesions in a so-called "anti-saccade" task. In this task subjects are instructed to *not* look at a briefly flashed cue, but to make a saccade in the opposite direction instead (Hallett, 1978). Guitton and coworkers (1985) reported that while normal subjects and patients with temporal lobe damage could do this task with relative ease, patients with frontal damage, and especially those with damage around the FEF, were severely impaired. In particular, the frontal patients had difficulty in suppressing unwanted saccades toward the cue stimulus.

Johnson (1994, 1995) developed a version of the anti-saccade task for use with infants. One cannot give verbal instruction to a young infant to look to the side opposite from where the cue stimulus appears. Instead, infants are motivated to look at the second of two opposite peripheral stimuli more than at the first stimulus. This can be done by making the second stimulus reliably more dynamic and colorful than the first. Thus, after a number of such trials infants may learn to inhibit their tendency to make a saccade to the first stimulus (the cue) when it appears, in order to respond as rapidly as possible to the more attractive second stimulus (the target). A group of 4-month-old infants showed a significant decrease in their frequency of looking to the first (cue) stimulus over a number of such trials (Johnson, 1995). A second experiment demonstrated that this decrement was not due to differential habituation to the simpler stimulus. Since 6-month-old infants are able to inhibit saccades to a peripheral stimulus, it is reasonable to infer that their frontal eye field circuit is functioning by this age.

As will be discussed in more detail in a later section, the increasing involvement of frontal lobe structures in sensory motor coordination is associated with increasingly endogenously generated (voluntary), as opposed to input-driven, action. Another manifestation of the endogenous control of attention concerns so-called "sustained" attention. Sustained attention refers to the ability of subjects to maintain the direction of their attention toward a stimulus even in the presence of distracters. Richards (1989a, 1989b) has discovered characteristic decreases in heart rate that can serve as a marker for sustained attention in infants. These heart-rate defined periods of sustained attention usually last for between 5 and 15 seconds after the onset of a complex stimulus. During these periods, it takes around twice as long for infants to shift their gaze toward a stimulus presented in the periphery as compared to when heart rate has returned to pre-stimulus presentation levels. Further, those saccades that are made to a peripheral stimulus during sustained attention are less accurate than normal, and involved multiple hypometric saccades, characteristics of superior colliculus generated saccades (Richards, 1991). Thus, the lack of distractibility during periods of sustained attention is likely to be due to cortically mediated pathways inhibiting collicular mechanisms.

To summarize, even a form of action as apparently simple as shifting the eyes involves multiple cortical and subcortical pathways. This illustrates the point that most psychological accounts of behavioral development that do not take account of brain systems are likely to grossly underestimate the complexity of the underlying computations. While the multiple pathways involved in oculomotor control are likely to have some unique functions, behavioral responses in most real world situations are likely to engage several pathways. To some extent, these pathways may have a hierarchical organization, with the latest developing pathways (commonly frontal) providing the basis of endogenous voluntary action (see also frontal cortex section). Pathways present in the newborn have less cortical involvement and tend to be more reflexive in nature. A final conclusion is that the extended laminar postnatal development of cortex can be used in certain cases to make predictions about the sequence of development of cortical pathways. These predictions can be tested with marker tasks, though in the future more direct methods will be useful.

Memory

Learning is a fundamental aspect of human cognitive development, and is represented in many of the other sections in this chapter, especially with regard to the development of face recognition, object properties, and language acquisition abilities. In these cases it is often difficult to untangle developmental processes from learning. A number of authors have, however, taken a cognitive neuroscience approach to the development of memory processes that are assumed to be independent of the acquisition of information by developing neural circuitry. In other words, they have attempted to study the development of the neurocognitive mechanisms that underlie memory processes in adults. In particular, a number of authors have speculated that deficits in memory abilities in young infants and children may be accounted for in terms of the differential development of neural systems supporting particular types of memory function. There have been a number of attempts to characterize a dissociation between two types of memory systems; one of which is variously described as "explicit," "declarative," or "cognitive," and the other of which is "procedural," "implicit," or "habit" memory. While there are some differences in the exact definitions of these terms, the same data is often used to dissociate the two systems (see Janowsky, 1993 for review).

One of the first cognitive neuroscience hypothesis about memory development was put forward by Schacter and Moscovitch (1984) who speculated that the brain mechanisms necessary for the long-term storage of information, most probably in the limbic system, are not functional for the first year or two of life. A related hypothesis was put forward by Bachevalier and Mishkin (1984), who pointed out similarities between the amnesic syndrome, in which limbic system damage in adults results in deficits in recognition memory but no deficits in learning stimulus-response "habits," and the profile of memory abilities in infants. Mishkin and colleagues had earlier demonstrated that a similar pattern of deficits to that observed in human amnesic syndrome patients could be seen in adult monkeys following surgical lesions to portions of the limbic system. These observations lead to the proposal that infant memory abilities reflected the more delayed postnatal maturation of limbic circuits.

To test the hypothesis that the putative "cognitive memory" and "habit" systems show a different ontogenetic timetable, Bachevalier and Mishkin (1984) tested infant monkeys aged 3, 6, and 12 months on two types of tasks. The first task was a visual recognition task that involved the infant monkey learning to identify the novel object of a pair following the earlier presentation of the familiar one (delayed non match to sample—DNMS). This task was thought to require a "cognitive memory" system. In the second task, a visual discrimination habit task, the infant monkey was sequentially exposed to 20 pairs of objects every day. Every day the same object of each pair was baited with a food reward, even though their relative positions were varied. The monkeys had to learn to displace the correct object in each pair.

Infant monkeys failed to learn the cognitive memory task until they were approximately 4 months old, and did not reach adult levels of proficiency even by the end of the first year. In contrast, infant monkeys of 3 or 4 months old were able to learn the visual "habit" as easily as adults. Bachevalier and Mishkin suggested that this dissociation in memory abilities in infant monkeys is due to the prolonged postnatal development of the limbic system delaying the ability of recognition and association (cognitive) memory relative to sensory-motor habit formation. This explanation could be extended to human infants since they are also unable to acquire the delayed nonmatch to sample task in early infancy (until around 15 months), and still have not reached adult levels of performance in this task at 6 years old (Overman, Bachevalier, Turner, & Peuster, 1992).

More recent evidence from both cognitive and neuroscience studies have cast some doubt on this initial two systems view of the ontogeny of memory. The cognitive evidence comes from studies indicating that human infants can recall experiences from the first year of life several years later (Rovee-Collier, 1993). These findings suggest some continuity of memory mechanisms from early infancy to later life. Further, other behavioral experiments on memory processes in infants suggest that differences between infant and adult memory processes are quantitative (retrieval time, memory span) rather than qualitative (for review, see Rovee-Collier, 1993). Thus, at least some prominent researchers believe that there is not a transition from one form of memory to another during infancy, but rather just a change in the characteristics of memory storage.

Another issue is that human infants are successful at the DNMS task at much younger ages if the response required is for the subject to merely *look* at the novel stimulus, rather than manually displacing it to obtain the reward. This suggests that the standard reaching version of DNMS requires some additional ability, such as the ability to inhibit a previously rewarded action (Diamond et al., submitted). Other tasks that tap into "cognitive" or "explicit" memory need to be studied in the future.

Perhaps even more damaging for Bachevalier and Mishkin's original hypothesis is evidence that lesions to the limbic system impair recognition memory abilities in infant monkeys in the first month of life (Bachevalier, Brickson, & Hagger, 1993), indicating that even from this early age the limbic system plays some role in memory processes. Bachevalier and colleagues measured recognition memory by a paired comparison preferential looking task similar to one used with human infants. In this task the subject is shown an object for 30 seconds. After a short delay, the subject is presented with a pair of objects, one of which is novel, and their extent of looking at each of the objects recorded. Between 15 and 30 days of age, normal infant rhesus monkeys develop a strong preference for looking toward the novel stimulus, indicating recognition of the familiar one. This preference was not found in monkeys that received medial temporal lobe lesions, including the hippocampus, in early infancy. These surprising results suggest that limbic structures make a significant contribution to visual recognition memory even at this very early age, and that other neurocognitive systems that mature more slowly may be responsible for the developments in memory ability observed in other tasks.

After reviewing much of this literature, Nelson (1995) proposes that there are more than two types of memory system that develop from infancy. Specifically, he suggests that between 8 and 18 months of age infants become able to perform DNMS and other tasks that serve as markers for explicit or cognitive memory. This form of "explicit" memory is dependent upon adequate development of the hippocampus and also related cortical areas, such as area TE. However, apparently successful performance can be elicited from infants younger than 8 months in tasks that depend solely on them showing a novelty preference, and that do not require them to dissociate how often events were presented or do not involve a delay before the response is required. Nelson (1995) hypothesizes that this "pre-explicit" memory requires only the functioning of the hippocampus, and not the related temporal cortex structures. Around 8 months of age, the development of temporal cortical areas, or their integration with the hippocampus, correlates with a transition from pre-explicit to explicit memory.

Another memory system develops around the same age but shows more protracted development, working memory. Like others, Nelson (1995) suggests that the dorsolateral prefrontal cortex is a critical component of the neural substrate for this form of memory. Nelson's suggestion corresponds with the observation (discussed in the frontal cortex section) that 6-month-olds can successfully perform a marker task for the Dorsolateral Prefrontal cortex, the oculomotor delayed response task.

The final type of memory that Nelson discusses is procedural (or implicit, or "habit") memory. This type of memory seems to be present from the first few months of life, perhaps earlier, and shows a less protracted development than the other types. It is manifest in tasks such as leg kick conditioning (Rovee-Collier, 1993), eyeblink conditioning, and the visual discrimination habit task. Some of these types of procedural learning probably involve the cerebellum.

As discussed earlier, components of recognition memory can also be studied using ERPs (Nelson, 1994). While these components of ERPs in infants have not been closely related to particular brain structures, Nelson (personal communication, 1995) speculates that a late positive component of the ERP signal may be due to medial temporal lobe activity. Possibly the emergence of this component of the ERP could be used as a marker for the development of cortical regions related to the hippocampus (such as area TE), and the transition from pre-explicit to explicit memory systems.

From the research discussed in this section, it is evident that most memory tasks likely engage multiple memory systems, in a similar way to the partially independent brain pathways that are engaged in eye movement control and attention shifts. A lack of maturity in one or more pathways may be masked in some tasks due to compensatory activity in other pathways. Possibly it is the extent of integration between different memory pathways that is the most significant change with postnatal development. If this is the case, it is not until we have a more integrative account of the relations between different brain memory pathways that we will be able to make sense of the developmental data.

In summary, some types of procedural or habit memory, probably dependent on subcortical structures such as the cerebellum and hippocampus, are present from birth or shortly thereafter. Further, some aspects of cognitive, declarative, or explicit memory develop in later life. However, a simple developmental dissociation between the two systems does not seem to account for the data. What is needed are neurocognitive models that involve the partial functioning of the latter system, and some account of the interactions between the brain structures involved.

Language Acquisition and Speech Recognition

The acquisition of language by the human child is an impressive achievement amply described elsewhere in this volume (Chapters 4, 7, 8, and 9). In recent years, a number of approaches have been taken to studying the neural correlates of language acquisition in the human infant. A general problem is that it is not possible to use animal models for studying an aspect of cognition unique to humans (although some work on speech perception has been done with other species, and work on song learning in birds may have some parallels [Marler, 1991]). However, a number of other approaches, such as ERP studies, studies of infants with focal brain damage, studies of congenital abnormalities, and correlations between phases of language acquisition and neuroanatomical developments, have been pursued. An implicit motivating question for many researchers in this field has been the extent to which language is biologically special. This issue refers to the extent to which the human infant is predisposed to process and learn about language.

In terms of research programs, two approaches have been taken. The first of these is to investigate whether there are particular parts of the cortex critical for language processing or acquisition. The second, and related, approach is to attempt to identify neural correlates of language related processing abilities present from very early in life.

Cortical Specificity and Language Acquisition

Language acquisition has become a focal point for studies designed to investigate the extent to which particular cortical areas, such as Broca's and Wernicke's areas, are prespecified to support specific functions. Two approaches to this issue have been taken, with one set of studies examining the extent to which language functions can be subserved by other regions of the cortex, and another area of research concerned with whether other functions can "occupy" regions that normally support language. The first of these approaches has been pursued through investigations of whether children suffering from perinatal lesions to "language areas" can still acquire language. The second approach has involved the testing of congenitally deaf children to see what, if any, functions are present in regions of cortex which are normally (spoken) language areas, and also by studying the effects of brain lesions on sign language.

If particular cortical regions are uniquely prespecified to support language then it is reasonable to assume that early damage to such regions will impair the acquisition of language. This implicit hypothesis has motivated a good deal of research, the conclusions of which still remain somewhat controversial. In an influential book, Lenneberg (1967) argued persuasively that if localized left hemisphere damage occurred early in life it had little effect on subsequent language acquisition. This contrasted with both the effect of similar lesions in adults or older children, and to many congenital abnormalities in which language is delayed or never emerges. Lenneberg's view lost adherents in the 1970s, as evidence accumulated from studies of children with hemispherectomies suggesting that left hemisphere removal commonly leads to selective subtle deficits in language, especially for syntactic and phonological tasks (Dennis & Whitaker, 1976). Similar results have also reported for children with early focal brain injury due to strokes (Vargha-Khadem, Isaacs, & Muter, 1994). These findings were compatible with studies of normal infants showing a left hemisphere bias at birth in processing speech and other complex sounds (Molfese, 1989), and led some researchers to the conclusion that functional asymmetries for language in the human brain are established at birth and cannot be reversed.

A number of neuroanatomical studies have shown differences between parts of left and right cerebral cortex in adults. For example, Geschwind and Levitsky (1968) reported that the left planum temporale was larger than the right in 65% of adult brains studied. A number of groups have looked for similar differences in infant brains as evidence for prespecified language abilities. Chi, Gooling, and Gilles (1977) investigated the timing of gyral and sulcal development in the fetus. In certain cases, these developed earlier on the right than on the left. In particular, a region of the temporal lobe thought to be important for language decoding and comprehension, Heschl's gyrus, was found to develop a little earlier on the right than on the left. In apparent contradiction to this finding of earlier development of the right hemisphere are several studies that report that as early as the 29th week of gestation the left planum temporale is usually larger on the left than on the right (Teszner, Tzavaras, Gruner, & Hecaen, 1972; Wada, Clarke, & Hamm, 1975; Witelson & Pallie, 1973). It is important to remember, however, that these measures refer simply to the extent of folding in the cortex. As reviewed earlier, the cerebral cortex is a thin flat sheet that becomes convoluted as it grows within the skull. Gyral and sucal measures can therefore only tell us about the quantity of cortical tissue within a region (roughly speaking, the more tissue, the more folding) and cannot be used to argue for architectural prespecification or innate representations. The latter could only be established by examining the microcircuitry of the regions concerned. Until such studies are conducted with postmortem tissue from newborn infants, no firm conclusions can be reached about different computational properties of the left and right cerebral hemispheres at birth.

In addition to these reservations about the neuroanatomical evidence, many of the secondary sources that summarized the work on hemispherectomies and/or early focal injury failed to note that the deficits shown by these children are very subtle—far more subtle than the frank aphasias displayed by adults with homologous forms of brain damage (see Bishop, 1983 for a critique of the Dennis & Whitaker study). Indeed, most of the children with left hemisphere injury that have been studied to date are within the normal range (Stiles & Thal, 1993), and those that fall outside the normal range often have complications in addition to their focal brain injury.

While most studies to date have involved assessing language competence in children that acquired perinatal lesions many years beforehand, Stiles and her colleagues have recently carried out *prospective* studies of language and spatial cognition in children who have suffered a single unilateral injury to either the right or the left hemisphere confirmed by at least one radiological technique (Stiles & Thal, 1993). Children in these studies are identified prior to the onset of measurable language skills and were examined longitudinally. This team has now studied more than twenty cases between 8 to 31 months of age, all with unilateral lesions occurred prenatally or before 6 months of age (i.e., before language development would normally begin). Regardless of the lesion site, infants with focal brain lesions were delayed suggesting, not surprisingly, that there is a general nonspecific cost to early brain injury. However, the prospective study of these infants also produced a number of rather surprising results. Based on the adult aphasia literature, we would expect delays in word comprehension to be most severe in children with damage to left posterior sites. In contrast to this, it appears that comprehension deficits are actually more common in the right hemisphere infant group—a pattern that is rarely reported in adults with right hemisphere damage. This and other findings lead Thal et al. (1991) to suggest that the regions responsible for language learning are not necessarily the regions responsible for language use and maintenance in the adult.

Another complicating factor revealed by prospective studies of focal lesion infants came from a recent study of language production (Reilly, Bates, & Marchman, in press). This study used the same population of pre- or perinatal lesions just discussed. Reilly and coworkers (in press) looked at many different aspects of lexical, grammatical, and discourse structure in a storytelling task, in focal lesion children and normal controls between 3 to 8 years of age. In this study (like many others within this age range), there were no significant differences between the left and right hemisphere groups on any of the language measures. However, the focal lesion sample as a whole performed worse than normal controls on several measures of morphology, syntax, and narrative structure. Each of these disadvantages appears to resolve over time in the focal lesion group, but each time the child moves on to the next level of development (in language acquisition), differences between the focal lesion infants and normals reappear. Thus, functional recovery does not appear to be a one-off event, but rather may reoccur at several critical points during language acquisition.

To summarize, the effects of early focal lesions on language acquisition remain complex and controversial. However, in general the evidence supports the following conclusions:

1. While regions of the left temporal lobe may be best suited to language processing, they are not critical since language can develop in a close to normal way without this region (Bates, 1994).

2. Focal pre- and perinatal lesions often cause delay in language acquisition regardless of the site of the lesion.

3. Different regions of the cortex may be involved in the acquisition of language from those which are important for language in adults.

4. Functional compensation may have to reoccur at several points in language acquisition, and is not a "one-off" event.

5. Representations related to language may initially be more widespread in the cortex, and reduce with experience.

The other approach to studying the extent to which the cortical areas supporting language are prespecified is to see whether other functions can occupy the same cortical regions. Such experiments would be analogous in logic to the neurobiological studies mentioned earlier in which input to a developing region of cortex was "rewired" such that representations generated from a new sensory modality were produced.

Neville (1991) has used ERPs to examine cortical plasticity related to intersensory competition. Evidence from visual and spatial tasks in deaf subjects suggests that cortically mediated visual processing is different among subjects reared in the absence of auditory input. Specifically,

the congenitally deaf seem more sensitive to events in the peripheral visual field than are hearing subjects. ERPs recorded over classical auditory regions, such as portions of the temporal lobe, are two or three times larger for deaf than for hearing subjects following peripheral visual field stimulation. Thus, the lack of auditory input has resulted in a normally auditory area becoming allocated to visual functions.

While cortical regions may be able to process information from different sensory modalities, particular regions (such as the left temporal lobe) may be most suited for processing the rapid temporal information that is necessary for language. Some evidence for this view comes from studies of deaf signers with acquired focal brain lesions. After reviewing evidence that sign language has many of the same formal properties as spoken languages, Bellugi, Poizner, and Klima (1989) found that deaf signers with left hemisphere lesions are aphasic for sign language, while showing intact performance on several other visuospatial tasks. Patients with right hemisphere lesions, on the other hand, showed the reciprocal pattern of performance. Commonly in this latter group signing was fluent even in areas they severely neglected outside the language domain (such as being able to converse in sign fluently about the contents of their room while showing gross spatial distortion in their description of its contents). This, and other evidence, lead Bellugi et al. to propose that it is the linguistic function, rather than its form, that determines cortical localization.

A number of developmental disorders which affect cognition such as autism (Frith, 1989) and Williams syndrome (Bellugi, Wang, & Jernigan, 1994) may also provide us with ways to examine the neural basis of language acquisition. For example, while autistic individuals commonly have severe deficits in social cognition (such as aspects of language, face recognition, and "theory of mind") (see Frith, 1989), they can be at, or above, normal levels of performance in other domains. In contrast, Williams syndrome individuals suffer from severe deficits in many aspects of cognition, but are often relatively spared in face recognition and language capabilities (Bellugi et al., 1994, Karmiloff-Smith, Klima, Bellugi, Grant, & Baron-Cohen, 1995).

Neural Correlates of Language Relevant Abilities in Infants

This general approach to investigating the extent to which language is biologically special involves attempting to identify language relevant processes in the brains of very young infants. One example of this concerns the ability to discriminate speech relevant sounds such as phonemes. Behavioral experiments have revealed that young infants show enhanced (categorical) discrimination at phonetic boundaries used in speech such as /ba/ /pa/ (see Chapter 4, this volume). These observations initially caused excitement as evidence for a language specific detection mechanism in humans. That is, a graded phonetic transition from /ba/ to /pa/ is perceived as a sudden categorical shift by infants. However, over the past decade it has become clear that other species, such as chinchillas, show similar acoustical discrimination abilities, indicating that this ability may merely reflect general characteristics of the mammalian auditory processing system, and not an initial spoken language specific mechanism (see Kuhl, 1993).

In human infants, however, Werker and Polka (1993) have reported that while young infants can discriminate a very wide range of phonetic constructs including those not found in the native language (e.g., Japanese infants, but not Japanese adults, can discriminate between "r" and "l" sounds), this ability becomes restricted to the phonetic constructs of the native language around 12 months of age. If brain correlates of this process could be identified, it may be possible to study the mechanisms underlying this language specific selective loss of sensitivity. As mentioned earlier, ERPs offer an excellent opportunity to study the neural correlates of cognition in normal infants in a relatively non-invasive manner. This excellent temporal resolution of ERPs can be complemented by some spatial resolution through the use of high-density ERPs (HD-ERP). When components of ERP differ in both latency (following the event) and spatial resolution, we may be confident that different neural circuitry is being activated. An example of this approach comes from a recent HD-ERP study of phonetic discrimination in 3-month-old infants.

Dehaene-Lambertz and Dehaene (1994) presented their infant subjects with trials in which a series of four identical syllables (the standard) was followed by a fifth that was either identical or phonetically different (deviant). The ERP was time-locked to the onset of the syllable and they observed two peaks with different scalp locations. The first peak occurred around 220 msec after stimulus onset and did not habituate to repeated presentations (except after the first presentation) or dishabituate to the novel syllable. Thus the generators of this peak, probably primary and secondary auditory areas in the temporal lobe, did not appear to be sensitive to the subtle acoustical differences that encoded phonetic information.

The second peak reached its maximum around 390 msec after stimulus onset and again did not habituate to repetitions of the same syllable, except after the first presentation. However, when the deviant syllable was introduced the peak recovered to at least its original level. Thus, the neural generators of the second peak, also in the temporal lobe but in a distinct and more posterior location, are sensitive to phonetic information. Further studies need to be done to see if the recovery of the second peak is due to the categorical perception of phonemes, or whether it would be elicited by any acoustical change. A later peak was observed over frontal regions following the deviant stimuli, a finding common to many paradigms with unexpected auditory or visual stimuli. This peak probably represents detection of novelty regardless of the input modality.

While this study must necessarily be regarded as a preliminary analysis of the neural mechanisms underlying speech discrimination and processing by young infants, it has opened up a number of intriguing avenues for further research. As mentioned earlier, infants' discrimination of phonetic constructs becomes restricted to the phonetic constructs of the native language around 12 months of age. Examining which, if any, of the three peaks observed by Dehaene-Lambertz and Dehaene (1994) declined with the loss of discrimination would be informative (Christophe & Morton, 1994).

Bates, Thal, and Janowsky (1992) have reviewed and identified a number of correlations between neuroanatomical developments in the human cerebral cortex and "landmarks" in language acquisition. As discussed earlier, it is evident that such correlations cannot be used to establish firm links between neural events and cognitive ones. However, the approach is useful for identifying specific hypotheses which can then be tested with more direct methodologies.

Bates et al. (1992) suggested that the evidence for some neuroanatomical differences between the right and left hemispheres at birth alluded to earlier may set up computational differences that "bias" language toward the left hemisphere. Similar arguments have been presented by Tallal and colleagues, who argue for the importance of rapid auditory temporal processing as a foundation for normal language acquisition (Miller & Tallal, 1995).

As discussed earlier, it is possible that these differences between the hemispheres are due to a differential developmental timetable, rather than genetic encoding of a domain specific architecture or representations. Bates et al. (1992) identify a peak transition in both behavioral and neural development at around 8 to 9 months after birth. They report the establishment of long-range connections (especially from the frontal cortex) and the onset of an adult distribution of metabolic activity (inferences derived from the PET study of Chugani (1994)) at this age, and suggest these neural developments enable the onset of a number of language related skills such as word comprehension, and the inhibition of non-native speech contrasts. Around 16 to 24 months there is a "burst" in vocabulary and grammar, and Bates et al. (1992) argue that this correlates with a steep increase in synaptic density. The increased synaptic density, they speculate, enables a larger capacity for storage and information processing. At around 4 years of age, most normal children have acquired the basic morphological and syntactic structures of their native language, and thus have reached the end of the "grammar burst." Bates et al. (1992) point out that this "stabilization" of language coincides with the decline in overall brain metabolism and synaptic density.

In conclusion, therefore, a reasonable working hypothesis is that regions of the left temporal lobe are most suitable for supporting speech and language representations. This suitability comes not from rigid genetic specification, but from a combination of spatial and temporal factors which possibly predispose this region to the processing of rapid temporal stimuli. Other regions of cortex are probably also important for the acquisition of language, and can substitute for the left temporal region if required. Language is only "biologically special" in the broadest sense in which the human species typical environment interacts with the architecture of cortex and its developmental dynamics to generate representations appropriate for the domain.

Frontal Cortex Development, Object Permanence, and Planning

The region of the frontal lobe anterior to the primary motor and premotor cortex, commonly called the prefrontal cortex, accounts for almost one-third of the total cortical surface in humans (Brodmann, 1909) and is considered by most investigators to be the locus of control for many abilities central to higher level cognition. Extensive clinical (Milner, 1982) and experimental observations of the effects of injury to this region have also supported the notion that prefrontal cortex subserves important aspects of cognition (for reviews, see Fuster, 1989; Goldman-Rakic, 1987). The particular forms of cognitive processing that have been consistently linked to frontal cortex in adults

pertain to the planning or executing of sequences of action, the maintenance of information on-line during short temporal delays, and the ability to inhibit a set of responses that are appropriate in one context but not another.

The frontal cortex shows the most prolonged period of postnatal development of any region of the human brain, with changes in synaptic density detectable into the teenage years (Huttenlocher, 1990). For this reason, it has been the cortical region most commonly associated with developments in cognitive abilities. Further, in many cases developmental abnormalities present with some "frontal" symptoms. Two alternative views of the relation between frontal cortex structural development and increases in cognitive ability in childhood have been taken. One is that structural developments in the frontal cortex occur at a particular age allowing increases in certain cognitive abilities (a recent refinement of this general view is that the frontal lobes are composed of a number of regions which subserve different functions and show differential rates of maturation, e.g., Diamond, 1991). The alternative view is that the frontal cortex is consistently involved in acquisition of new skills and knowledge from very early in life, and that it may also play a role in organizing other parts of cortex (Thatcher, 1992). By this latter view, regions of frontal cortex play a fundamental role in cognitive transitions primarily because of the region's involvement in the acquisition of any new skill or knowledge. A corollary of this is that frontal involvement in a particular task or situation may decrease with further familiarity. As we will see, there is some evidence consistent with both positions.

One of the most comprehensive attempts to relate a cognitive change to underlying brain developments has concerned the emergence of object permanence in infants. In particular, Diamond, Goldman-Rakic, and colleagues (Diamond & Goldman-Rakic, 1986, 1989; Goldman-Rakic, 1987) have argued that the maturation of prefrontal cortex during the last half of the human infant's first year of life accounts for a number of transitions observed in the behavior of infants in object permanence and object retrieval tasks.

Piaget (1954) was the first to observe that infants younger than 7½ months fail to accurately retrieve a hidden object after a short delay period if the object's location is changed from one where it was previously and successfully retrieved. Infants of this age make a particular perseverative error. They often reach to the hiding location where the object was found on the immediately preceding trial. This characteristic pattern of error, called "A not B," was cited by Piaget (1954) as evidence for the failure of infants to understand that objects retain their existence or permanence when moved from view. Between $7\frac{1}{2}$ and 9 months, infants begin to succeed in the task at successively longer delays of 1 to 5 sec. However, their performance remains unreliable up to about 12 months if the delay between hiding and retrieval is incremented as the infants age (Diamond, 1985).

Diamond and Goldman-Rakic (1989) tested monkeys in a modification of the above object permanence task. In this task, subjects are shown an object hidden at location A and are permitted to retrieve it. After a predetermined number of successful retrievals at location A (usually three), the object is then hidden at location B. Consistent with the observations on human infants, infant monkeys failed to retrieve the hidden object at location B when the delay between hiding and retrieval was 2 sec or more. Further, adult monkeys with lesions to the dorsolateral region of the prefrontal cortex (DLPC) were also impaired in this task. Lesions to other parts of the brain (parietal cortex, or the hippocampal formation) did not significantly impair performance indicating that the principal sulcus region plays a central role in delayed response tasks which require the maintenance of spatial information over temporal delays.

Thus, the infant monkeys, like young human infants, failed the object permanence tasks in ways similar to frontally lesioned monkeys. However, adult monkeys, like human infants over 9 months, succeeded in these tasks and showed an ability to withstand longer delays with age.

Further evidence linking success in the object permanence task to frontal cortex maturation in the human infant comes from two sources. The first of these is a series of EEG studies with normal human infants (Bell, 1992a, 1992b; Bell & Fox, 1992; Fox & Bell, 1990), in which increases in frontal EEG responses correlate with the ability to respond successfully over longer delays in delayed response tasks. The second source is work on cognitive deficits in children with a neurochemical deficit in the prefrontal cortex resulting from Phenylketonuria (PKU). Even when treated, this inborn error of metabolism can have the specific consequence of reducing the levels of a neurotransmitter, dopamine, in the dorsolateral prefrontal cortex. These reductions in dopamine levels in the dorsolateral prefrontal cortex result in the infants and children concerned being impaired on tasks thought to involve prefrontal cortex such as the object permanence task and an object retrieval task, and being relatively normal in tasks thought to be dependent on other regions of cortex such as delayed non-matching to sample (Diamond et al.,

submitted; Welsh, Pennington, Ozonoff, Rouse, & McCabe, 1990).

Having established a link between frontal cortex maturation and behavioral change in a number of tasks, Diamond (1991) has speculated on the computational consequence of this aspect of postnatal brain development. Specifically, she suggests that the DLPC is critical for performance when (a) information has to be retained or related over time or space, *and* (b) a prepotent response has to be inhibited. Only tasks that require both of these aspects of neural computation are likely to engage the DLPC. In the case of the object permanence task, a spatial location has to be retained over time and the prepotent previously rewarded response inhibited.

However, two recent lines of evidence suggest that the prefrontal cortex maturation hypothesis is not the whole story, and that some modification or elaboration of the original account will be required. The first of these lines of evidence concerns the fact that infants can succeed on at least one task that requires temporal spatial integration over a delay at a much younger age than is indicated by the object permanence tasks (Gilmore & Johnson, 1995). This human infant study was based on single unit recording studies in monkeys while performing a delayed response task. Funahashi, Bruce, and Goldman-Rakic (1989, 1990) have demonstrated that neurons in the DLPC have specific patterns of activity during a delayed response task. In this task, rhesus monkeys were trained to fixate a central spot while a brief cue appeared in one of eight locations in the visual periphery. The monkeys were rewarded for maintaining fixation throughout a variable delay period of 1 to 5 seconds, and for making an eye movement to the location where the cue had appeared once the central fixation stimulus had turned off. Funahashi et al. (1989, 1990) recorded neurons in the DLPC and in the frontal eye fields. They found evidence that specific neurons were maintaining a representation of the cued location during the delay period. Thirty percent of the neurons recorded in the DLPC were differentially active during the delay period, and 80% of these had receptive fields that coded the direction of the cue and subsequent eye movement. Funahashi et al. (1989, 1990) argued that these results reflect the common function of the prefrontal cortex in delayed response tasks in both the visual and motor domains: specifically the maintenance of information during short delay periods about spatial locations important for later action.

Gilmore and Johnson (1995) developed marker task versions of the oculomotor delayed response (ODR) task which involved infants either learning to delay their saccade to a spatial cue for several seconds, or to delay their saccade to a spatial location cued by an abstract central stimulus. The procedure for one version of the ODR task is shown in Figure 1.6. Infants of 6 months showed significantly greater orienting to the cued spatial location even as long as 4 seconds after the cue presentation, indicating that they were able to maintain a trial specific planned action. One mechanism for delaying the saccade to the cued location is active inhibition. However, further experiments are needed to establish whether there is inhibition during the delay phase of the marker task.

Aside from the lack of strong evidence regarding the inhibition of prepotent responses, an explanation of the discrepancy between performance in Piaget's object permanence task and the results of Gilmore and Johnson (1995) is that tasks in which the response is an eye movement (looking) are easier by virtue of the oculomotor system developing more rapidly than other forms of motor output such as reaching. This proposal is consistent with several studies showing that infants can perform successfully in analogous object permanence tasks as young as 4 or 5 months of age if looking rather than reaching performance is measured (Lecuyer, Abguegen, & Lemarie, 1992). Further, studies by Baillargeon (1987, 1993) and others entailing infants viewing "possible" and "impossible" events involving occluded objects have found that infants as young as 3.5

months look longer at the impossible events indicating that they have an internal representation of the occluded object.

To account for the apparent discrepancy between these results, and those with the reaching measures, some have provided "means-ends" explanations, arguing that infants do not know how to co-ordinate the necessary sequence of motor behaviors to retrieve a hidden object (Baillargeon, 1993; Diamond, 1991). In a series of experiments, Munakata, McClelland, Johnson, and Siegler (1994) trained 7-month-olds to retrieve objects placed at a distance from them by means of pulling on a towel or pressing a button. Infants retrieved objects when a transparent screen was interposed between them and the toy, but not if the screen was sufficiently opaque to make the object invisible. Since the same means-ends planning is required whether the screen is transparent or opaque, it was concluded that this cannot account for the discrepancy between the looking and the reaching tasks. Munakata et al. (1994) proposed an alternative "graded" view of the discrepancy implemented as a connectionist model (see later for further details).

An alternative approach to understanding the role of the prefrontal cortex in cognitive development has been espoused by several authors who have suggested that the region plays a critical role in the *acquisition* of new information and tasks. Three concomitants of this general view are that: (a) the cortical regions crucial for a particular task will change with the stage of acquisition; (b) the prefrontal cortex plays a role in organizing or allocating information to other regions of cortex; and (c) that development involves the establishment of hierarchical control structures, with frontal cortex maintaining the currently highest level of control. One example of this theoretical approach to functional prefrontal cortex development has recently been advanced by Thatcher (1992) and Case (1992) (for another related approach see Stuss, 1992).

Thatcher (1992) and colleagues have collected EEG data from a large number of subjects at various ages between 2 months and 18 years. While recording the subjects sit quietly and, as far as can be ascertained, are not responding to any stimuli. From 16 leads placed evenly across the scalp the spontaneous EEG rhythms of the brain are recorded before being subjected to a complex analysis which ascertains the extent to which the recordings from each lead "cohere" (roughly speaking, correlate) with other leads. From the large amount of raw data such an analysis generates the major factors (which leads cohere) can be adduced for each age group, and the age "peaks" of rate of increase in coherence for these leads computed. Thatcher then adds two working assumptions to this data,

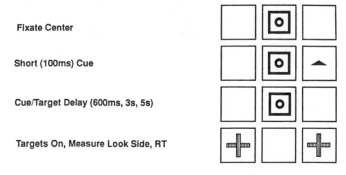

Fixate Center

Short (100ms) Cue

Cue/Target Delay (600ms, 3s, 5s)

Targets On, Measure Look Side, RT

Figure 1.6 Summary of the sequence and anatomical distribution of the coherence patterns reported by Thatcher (1992). Lines connecting electrode locations indicate a measure of strong coherence. "Microcycles" are a developmental sequence that involves a lateral-medial rotation that cycles from the left hemisphere to bilateral to right hemisphere in approximately 4 years. Note the hypothesized involvement of the frontal cortex in the "bilateral" sub-cycle. From "Working memory in infancy: Six-month-olds' performance on two versions of the oculomotor delayed response task," by R. O. Gilmore and M. H. Johnson, 1995, *Journal of Experimental Psychology, 59,* pp. 410. Copyright © 1995 by Academic Press, Inc. Reprinted with permission.

namely that scalp electrode locations provide reasonable indications of underlying cortical activity, and that the extent of correlation between the activity of regions (leads) reflects the strength of neural connections between them. The result is a hypothesis about recurring cycles of cortical reorganization orchestrated by the frontal cortex.

Figure 1.7 illustrates the hypothesis put forward by Thatcher on the basis of a complex analysis of a subset of his data. The lines in between points indicate the leads that show the greatest rate of increase in cohesion at that age. The claim made by Thatcher is that there are cycles of cortical reorganization which begin with microcycles involving reorganization of short-range connections in the left hemisphere. Following this, longer range frontal connections become important, at first only on the left side, but then bilaterally. The cycle is then completed by reorganization of short-range connections on the right-hand side. A complete cycle of this kind takes approximately four years, though subcycles and microcycles provide the basis for shorter term periods of stability and transition. By virtue of the longer range connections related to the frontal cortex, Thatcher suggests that this part of cortex plays an integral role in the reorganization of the cortex as a whole.

Case (1992) has attempted to use these EEG findings to relate brain reorganizations to cognitive change by arguing that (a) cognitive change has a similarly "recursive" character, and (b) that many limitations on cognitive performance are due to functions such as working memory commonly associated with the frontal cortex. One example used to illustrate that neural and cognitive changes may be " . . . both manifestations of a common underlying process . . . " (Case 1992, pp. 51–73) is the rate of change in EEG coherence between a particular pair of leads (frontal and parietal) and the rate of growth in working memory

span during the same ages. While the change in the rate of growth in the two variables may seem compelling at first glance, there are a number of reasons why it cannot be regarded as more than suggestive at present. One of these is that there is no clear rationale for choosing the particular pair of electrodes presented—there are, after all, 56 possible pairs to select from and there are always likely to be a few that show peaks in growth at similar ages to some developing cognitive function.

Even assuming that watertight correlations between the peaks in rates of increase in cognitive abilities and EEG coherence could be obtained, this association between brain and cognition would still be based only on temporal correlation, a form of evidence which is not very compelling. Hopefully, in the future this approach will attempt to consider the fact the EEG coherence shows phases of significant decreases of coherence as well as increases, which may be associated with "dips" in performance at the behavioral level, and more recursive, as opposed to stage-based, accounts of cognitive change.

To summarize, evidence from several sources indicate that the prefrontal cortex plays a very important role in cognitive development, possibly even a more critical role than other regions of cortex. Maturation of parts of the prefrontal cortex may underlie transitions in a variety of tasks around 9 months of age. However, it also seems likely that there is some functioning of the same regions at younger ages when looking, rather than reaching, is the required output. Moreover, the frontal cortex continues to be important in later development, possibly through a role in the cyclical reorganization of representations in other cortical regions. It seems plausible to suggest that cognitive development involves the establishment of increasing hierarchies of control, and that the prefrontal cortex maintains a position as the current top level of endogenous control.

MECHANISMS OF CHANGE

In the previous sections, a variety of approaches to understanding the relation between the postnatal development of the brain and cognitive change have been reviewed. Consideration of processes of neural change can, as mentioned earlier, inspire more biologically plausible accounts of cognitive transitions. In this section, efforts to characterize such mechanisms of change are reviewed and assessed. In particular, the following mechanisms of change will be discussed:

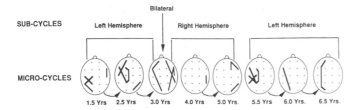

Figure 1.7 Schematic diagram showing the sequence of stimulus presentation in the spatial oculomotor delayed-response task studied by Gilmore & Johnson (1995). From "Cyclic cortical reorganization during early childhood," by R. W. Thatcher, 1992, *Brain and Cognition, 20,* pp. 24–50. Copyright © 1992 by Academic Press, Inc. Reprinted with permission.

- Graded transitions and partial representations.
- The emergence of novel representations.
- Selectionist theories of change.
- Parcellation and the emergence of modules.
- The "instinct to learn" and the role of predispositions in bootstrapping other systems.

Graded Transitions and Partial Representations

A commonly held implicit belief is that if a cognitive transition is very rapid, as opposed to gradual, it is more likely to be due to underlying brain maturation. There is no reason to believe that brain development involves rapid step-like transitions. On the contrary, most developmental transitions at both the neural and cognitive level are likely to be gradual and occur over months or years. Brain-inspired connectionist models, as well as other forms of non-linear dynamic systems (Thelen & Smith, 1994), offer the opportunity to model gradual transitions in which representations gradually increase in specificity or "strength" over a number of trials (Elman et al., in press; Munakata et al., in press).

One example of the use of connectionist modelling to investigate the graded development of partial representations concerns object permanence. Munakata and colleagues (in press) have developed simulations in which connectionist nets are trained on stimulus presentations in which objects move behind occluders. After some training the network's internal representation of the object (a particular pattern of activations across a particular set of nodes) tends to persist for some time after the occlusion of the object. With a small amount of training, the weak representation of an occluded object may be sufficient to drive a low threshold output such as looking. With further training, the representation of an occluded object gets stronger, allowing it to guide more complex forms of output such as reaching. While this simple model will require further refinement, it provides an example of how dissociations in behavior in different task contexts may be accounted for by the strength or otherwise of underlying representations.

The Emergence of Novel Representations

In the previous section a model of the strengthening of existing representations was mentioned. It is likely that cognitive development involves the emergence of new representations also. The mechanisms by which new levels or types of representations are generated at the cognitive level remain unclear (for review see Mandler, this volume). Some recent theorising inspired by brain development holds promise for the future. For example, in the frontal cortex section, the work of Thatcher and Case was discussed in which they attempt to relate putative reorganizations of cortical connectivity (as measured through EEG coherence) to reorganization of cognitive functioning. Leaving aside Case's claims about working memory, both these authors attempt to link the neural reorganizations to the cognitive ones on the basis of (a) correlations between ages of transitions, and (b) the claim that both transitions are "recursive" in nature. While this general approach is promising, a specific mechanism of change has yet to be proposed that would make this account testable.

Another brain-inspired approach to understanding the construction of new representations comes from neural network models of the formation of multiple topographic maps in the cortex. Taking the cortical visual system as an example, in many primates there are at least twenty visual areas in the cortex. Each of these areas is thought to re-map sensory space within some new dimensions. As cortical processing gets further from the primary sensory input areas, the representations map higher order dimensions of the statistical regularities present in the input. Similar multiple mappings may occur for more cognitive domains, but this is hard to ascertain without being able to guess in advance what the relevant dimensions being mapped are. A number of neuroconnectionist models of this multiple mapping process are currently under investigation.

A central question in both cognitive development, and in the formation of multiple cortical maps, is what are the factors that initiate the formation of a new mapping (representation) of information. This has sometimes been referred to as "re-representation" within the cognitive approach (Karmiloff-Smith, 1992, 1994; see Mandler, this volume). At the neural level, one contributing factor to this process may be that the input to downstream cortical areas has lower order invariances extracted (filtered) from it by the cortical regions closer to the input. If only the residual (error) information is passed on, then the system may go beyond the "success" of its initial extraction of invariances from the input, to extracting higher order components of information (see Johnson, 1997). An understanding of the neurocomputational principles that govern representation and re-representation in the cerebral cortex may provide a novel mechanism for cognitive change, and the construction of new representations.

Selectionist Theories of Change

In an earlier section, the dramatic postnatal loss of synaptic contacts within the cerebral cortex was reviewed. This ubiquitous observation has led some authors to speculate on the functional consequence of this selective loss process (Changeux, 1985; Changeux, Courrege, & Danchin, 1973; Ebbesson, 1980; Edelman, 1987). One of the broadest and most clearly explicated of "selectionist" accounts has been provided by Changeux and his collaborators. They argue that connections between classes of cells are specified genetically, but are initially labile. Synapses in their labile state may either become stabilized or regress, depending on the total activity of the post-synaptic cell. The activity of the post-synaptic cell is, in turn, dependent upon its input. Through the process of *selective stabilization,* Changeux proposes that "to learn is to eliminate," as opposed to learning taking place by instruction, or new growth.

Changeux and Dehaene (1989) extended and generalized the earlier neurocomputational account of selective loss. Specifically, they argued that there are definable biological levels in the brain (molecular, circuit level, and cognitive), and that a formalized Selectionist theory can be used to bridge these levels. They then introduced a "Darwinian version" of selectionism. By their view, a Darwinian change has two stages. The first of these is a constructive process that generates a range of possible options, while the second is a mechanism for selecting among these options. At the neural level, these two stages are implemented as an exuberance of connections specified within a particular genetic envelope, followed by the selection of particular synapses, or groups of synapses, selected as a result of either patterns of spontaneous activity within neural circuitry, and/or as a result of the information structure of sensory input.

Changeux and Dehaene (1989) then outlined how an analogous mechanism might operate at the cognitive level. The initial step, the generation of options, they suggest is achieved by the presence of "prerepresentations." Prerepresentations are described as transient, dynamic, "privileged" spontaneous activity states in neural circuits. The selection process is achieved by particular prerepresentations from the set available "resonating" with particular sensory inputs. This process probably takes place in seconds or less, whereas a more prolonged time course may be necessary for the process of attrition at the neural level.

Selectionist type theories of neurocognitive development vary along a number of dimensions. One of these

dimensions is the scale of the unit selected. For example, Edelman (1987) has proposed a similar Selectionist account to that outlined above except that particular "neuronal groups" are the unit of selection rather than single synapses (Crick [1989] suggests that such neuronal groups will be composed of around 200–1000 neurons, or a "minicolumn"). Possibly the cognitive level of selection posited by Changeux and Dehaene (1989) could be implemented as the dynamic selection of large scale neural circuits or pathways according to particular task demands. Most likely, selection occurs at multiple scales and time courses.

Another dimension along which Selectionist theories can vary is the extent to which the selective loss is responsive to sensory input, as opposed to being determined by intrinsic factors. In the model of Changeux and colleagues, sensory input or spontaneous activity determines both the pattern and the timing of the loss. Ebbesson (1988) discusses some examples in which both the pattern and timing of neural connection loss is insensitive to experience, such as when it occurs prenatally. That is, not only is the initial overwiring closely genetically specified, but so are the particular patterns and the extent of loss of connectivity. This difference between the Changeux and Ebbesson selection mechanisms is not trivial. They have distinct implications for how plasticity in a developing neural system is terminated. For Changeux the process is self-terminating, with only connections which are actively employed remaining. For Ebbesson, the end of plasticity is more rigidly determined, that is, by a given developmental stage, a certain proportion of connections *must* be lost, regardless of experience.

A "hybrid" Selectionist account of postnatal neural development which draws on aspects of both the Changeux and Ebbesson accounts has also been proposed (see Johnson & Karmiloff-Smith, 1992). The emphasis in the hybrid account is on a distinction between *timing* and *patterning* of loss. The hypothesis put forward was that while the timing and extent of loss of connections or neurones may be a product of the internal environment (possibly due to genetic modification of trophic factors), the specificity or particular pattern of that loss is determined by sensory input. By this view, there can be an intrinsically-determined termination of the phase of selective loss, while the pattern of loss within the "sensitive period" may be determined by experience-driven neural activity.

These different possibilities will require systematic investigation in real developing nervous systems, and their different effects at the computational level assessed through neural network modelling. A number of modellers have begun to investigate the functional consequences of different variations of link loss rules (Barto, Sutton, & Anderson, 1983; Kertzberg et al., 1992), including the interaction between activity-dependent link loss and overall network decreases in "trophic" factors (Shrager & Johnson, 1995).

Finally, it is important to note that selective loss is clearly only one of several aspects of postnatal neural development and that processes of directed growth may be equally important (see Purves, 1994; Quartz & Sejnowski, in press). Consequently, an exclusively selectionist account can never provide a complete account of neurocognitive development.

Parcellation and the Emergence of Modules

Some influential theorists have argued that the human infant possesses a number of specific input modules for domains such as language and visual processing. Among the various properties of these modules are that they are said to be innate and encapsulated (Fodor, 1983). Encapsulation refers to the fact that only the output, and not internal workings, of these modules are open to interaction with other brain systems. Encapsulation can be empirically demonstrated by phenomena such as visual illusions: even though a subject has the conscious knowledge that two lines are the same length, for example, he cannot help but perceive them as being of different lengths in certain contexts (Muller-Lyer illusion). Thus, the processing within a module is not affected by information in other parts of the system, only by its end product (the lines being of different length). While there is evidence that the adult mind contains such encapsulated modules, there is very little evidence that they are innate. Rather, encapsulation of particular aspects of information processing may be a consequence, rather than a generator, of postnatal development (see also Karmiloff-Smith, 1992).

How might the brain develop such encapsulated systems? Ebbesson (1984) argued that a process called *parcellation* is important in both ontogenetic and phylogenetic development. Parcellation involves the selective loss of connections between groups of neurons in an initially relatively undifferentiated brain region, resulting in the isolation of particular circuits and neuronal groups from others. This form of selectionism makes the prediction that some neural circuits will become increasingly modular with development.

Johnson and Karmiloff-Smith (1992) suggested that parcellation could be extended to the cognitive level either indirectly as a mechanism of change, or more directly by supposing that neural parcellation has cognitive consequences. Johnson and Vecera (1996) expanded on the direct approach by citing a number of examples from behavioral change where they argued that selective loss at the neuronal level gives rise to increasingly modular information processing. Specifically, some of the consequences of neural parcellation were argued to be: (a) less informational exchange between certain neurocognitive systems with development; (b) less interference between certain neurocognitive systems with increasing age/experience; and (c) increased specificity in sensory detection.

As one possible example of the information-processing consequences of neural parcellation, consider the work of Held and colleagues on the development of binocular vision discussed earlier. Held (1993) and colleagues established that prior to the segregation of inputs from the two eyes into ocular dominance columns in layer 4 of the primary visual cortex at around 4 months of age, human infants are able to integrate information between the two eyes in ways that they are not subsequently able to. Thus, after this particular parcellation event, information from the two eyes is segregated in a way that it was not previously.

Finally, it should be noted that the increasing specialization and segregation of neural circuits could also be achieved through processes of directed dendritic growth, though as yet there is relatively little information on this (Quartz & Sejnowski, in press).

Predispositions for Learning

In several of the domains reviewed above, predispositions were described as biasing or selecting the appropriate input for plastic cortical circuits. Learning in this context is usually broadly defined to include cortical plasticity. In the discussion of face recognition, evidence for a bias to orient to faces from birth was presented. Johnson and Morton (1991) argued that this bias in the newborn infants ensures that cortical circuits are exposed more to faces than to other types of visual stimuli over the first few months of life. Similiar arguments have been put forward by Kuhl (1993), Pettito (1993), Karmiloff-Smith (1992), and others for early language acquisition. While Johnson and Morton (1991) posed their argument in terms of subcortical influences on cortical plasticity, this type of argument could be extended to earlier developing cortical systems constraining the input for later developing, and still plastic, systems (Johnson, 1993).

Edelman and colleagues (e.g., Reeke, Sporns, & Edelman, 1990) have been exploring this view in the context of a self-organizing computational system, Darwin III. The behavior of this automaton emerges from representations developed during its interactions with an "environment" of simple two dimensional shapes. The automaton's interactions with the environment at any given "age" is determined by the systems which are functional earliest (sometimes corresponding to subcortical pathways). Through structured interactions with the environment, and by a process of selective loss of synapses, Darwin III comes to develop a number of sensorimotor functions such as tracking and touching objects.

The enterprise of attempting to build a neurally plausible automaton that constructs representations to "survive" in an environment promises to be very illuminating. However, it is important to bear in mind that the human infant possesses a neural network of much greater complexity which interacts with a dynamic and complex environment that includes rich interactions with conspecifics.

PREDICTIONS AND RECOMMENDATIONS FOR FUTURE RESEARCH

Recent molecular biological techniques are unquestionably going to have a major impact on our understanding of genetic contributions to cognitive change. However, it is important not to lose sight of the fact that genes code for proteins, and not functional components of cognition. Further, identifying genes involved in normal or abnormal cognitive development, does not imply determinism, or exclude a major role for the effects of experience. Rather, the interesting questions will concern how form and function emerge from the interaction between identified genes and environments at the molecular, cellular, and organismal level.

Evidence indicates that most genes involved in the formation of brain structure tend to have widespread effects throughout the brain, or gross brain regions, and are not localized to particular areas of the cortex, for example. Since brain structure is not directly "coded for" in genes, but rather is the result of complex molecular and cellular self-organizing interactive processes, any attempt to provide causal accounts of a cognitive change purely in terms of gene action are certain to be inadequate. Instead, I suggest that neural network models in which the interaction

between information processing and gene expression can be simulated, and then compared to real neurobiological systems, is likely to be a more fruitful approach. Finally, since ontogeny is the pathway from genotype to phenotype, in order to understand the proximal function and consequences of gene action in humans, I predict that molecular biologists will have to turn increasingly to developmental cognitive neuroscience over the next decade.

A common implicit assumption in cognitive development throughout the 1980s was that functional neural circuitry supporting components of cognition are either prespecified or "turned on" at specific ages due to gene expression. I caution against this rather static and deterministic view. Recent neurobiological and neuropsychological evidence indicates that plasticity is an inherent property of at least some brain structures, and we should seek to understand the mechanisms that constrain this plasticity such that particular outcomes are ensured in most individuals. This fundamental shift of underlying assumptions may take some years to filter from neurobiology to cognitive science.

There is a need for a level of computational modeling that can be related to both neural development and behavioral change. Currently, most models of cognitive development make little or no attempt to relate to brain development data. Similarly, computational models of neural development are commonly too detailed to allow any inferences about cognitive representations. In order to study the possible functional consequence of developments in neural structure, we need models at a level that make contact with both sets of data.

Many current models of cognitive development do not take the organism's interaction with the environment sufficiently into account. Taking a more ethological view of cognitive development can change our models of the types of representations that underlie behavior in at least two ways. First, the nature of the input representations, combined with the nature of the output representations, can severely restrict the possible intermediate representations. In other words, there is a need for models that, while less detailed, attempt to capture the whole pathway from input to output for a given range of tasks. Edelman's Darwin III automaton in one step in this direction.

The second, and related, point is that taking into account the structure of the external environment in which the organism develops means that the information actually represented in the brain can sometimes be relatively impoverished. The representation need be only that which is minimally sufficient for adaptive behavior in a given context. For example, Johnson and Morton (1991) argue that the face representation possessed by newborn infants may only be composed of three blobs corresponding to the locations of the eyes and mouth. This somewhat impoverished representation is sufficient for adaptive behavior, however, given that faces engage this representation, and that the species typical early environment of the infant is guaranteed to be filled with faces. A general statement is that the neural and environmental context in which a representation emerges is an important determinant of its complexity and structure.

There is a need to apply multiple methods to study the same cognitive transition. It is becoming clear that hypotheses based on a single type of behavioral task or output can be risky since other measures often lead to different conclusions. Indeed, in several domains dissociations between reaching and looking measures of performance are emerging. Applying methods such as ERP, and relating these to different behavioral measures will be important. Dissociations between different forms of behavioral output may prove to be an important phenomenon related to the gradual strengthening of representations during development.

Finally, the above points imply that collaboration between developmental neuroscience, cognitive development, and computational modelling, is essential. To facilitate these interactions we will need to train graduate students in an interdisciplinary developmental cognitive neuroscience.

ACKNOWLEDGMENTS

I thank Bob Siegler, Charles Nelson, and Paul Quinn for detailed comments on an earlier version of this chapter and my colleagues and collaborators for relevant discussion, comments, and other contributions to the chapter. In particular, I thank Liz Bates for her contribution to the sections on Brain development and on Language acquisition (which were written concurrently with, and share some text in common with, Chapter 5 of Elman et al., 1996), Rick Gilmore, Annette Karmiloff-Smith, John Morton, Charles Nelson, and Mike Posner. Sarah Hesketh, Leslie Tucker, and Sarah Minister assisted in the preparation of the chapter.

REFERENCES

Andrew, R. J. (1991). *Neural and behavioural plasticity: The use of the domestic chick as a model.* Oxford, England: Oxford University Press.

Aslin, R. N. (1981). Development of smooth pursuit in human infants. In D. F. Fisher, R. A. Monty, & J. W. Senders (Eds.), *Eye movements: Cognition and visual perception* (pp. 31–51). Hillsdale, NJ: Erlbaum.

Aslin, R. N., & Smith, L. B. (1988). Perceptual development. *Annual Review of Psychology, 39,* 435–473.

Atkinson, J. (1984). Human visual development over the first six months of life: A review and a hypothesis. *Human Neurobiology, 3,* 61–74.

Bachevalier, J., Brickson, M., & Hagger, C. (1993). Limbic-dependent recognition memory in monkeys develops early in infancy. *NeuroReport, 4,* 77–80.

Bachevalier, J., & Mishkin, M. (1984). An early and a late developing system for learning and retention in infant monkeys. *Behavioral Neuroscience, 98,* 770–778.

Baillargeon, R. (1987). Object permanence in very young infants. *Cognition, 20,* 191–208.

Baillargeon, R. (1993). The object concept revisited: New directions in the investigation of infants' physical knowledge. In C. Granrud (Ed.), *Visual perception and cognition in infancy* (pp. 265–315). Hillsdale, NJ: Erlbaum.

Banks, M. S., & Shannon, E. (1993). Spatial and chromatic visual efficiency in human neonates. In C. E. Granrud (Ed.), *Visual perception and cognition in infancy* (pp. 1–46). Hillsdale, NJ: Erlbaum.

Barto, A. G., Sutton, R. S., & Anderson, C. W. (1983). Neuron-like adaptive elements that can solve difficult learning control problems. *Institute of Electrical and Electronic Engineers Transactions on System, Man and Cybernetics, 15,* 835–846.

Bates, E. (1994). Language development in children after early focal injury [Special issue]. *Infant Behavior and Development, 17,* 426.

Bates, E., & Elman, J. L. (1993). Connectionism and the study of change. In M. H. Johnson (Ed.), *Brain development and cognition: A reader* (pp. 623–642). Oxford, England: Blackwell.

Bates, E., Thal, D., & Janowsky, J. S. (1992). Early language development and its neural correlates. In I. Rapin & S. Segalowitz (Eds.), *Handbook of neuropsychology* (pp. 69–110). Amsterdam, The Netherlands: Elsevier.

Becker, L. E., Armstrong, D. L., Chan, F., & Wood, M. M. (1984). Dendritic development on human occipital cortex neurones. *Brain Research, 315,* 117–124.

Bell, M. A. (1992a). Electrophysiological correlates of object search performance during infancy [Special issue]. *Infant Behavior and Development, 15,* 3.

Bell, M. A. (1992b). A not B task performance is related to frontal EEG asymmetry regardless of locomotor experience [Special issue]. *Infant Behavior and Development, 15,* 307.

Bell, M. A., & Fox, N. A. (1992). The relations between frontal brain electrical activity and cognitive development during infancy. *Child Development, 63,* 1142–1163.

Bellugi, U., Poizner, H., & Klima, E. S. (1989). Language, modality and the brain. *Trends in the Neurosciences, 12,* 380–388.

Bellugi, U., Wang, P. P., & Jernigan, T. L. (1994). Williams Syndrome: An unusual neuropsychological profile. In S. Broman & J. Grafman (Eds.), *Atypical cognitive deficits in developmental disorders: Implications for brain function* (pp. 23–56). Hillsdale, NJ: Erlbaum.

Benes, F. M. (1994). Development of the corticolimbic system. In G. Dawson & K. W. Fischer (Eds.), *Human behavior and the developing brain.* New York: Guilford Press.

Bishop, D. V. M. (1983). Linguistic impairment after left hemidecortication for infantile hemiplegia. A reappraisal. *Quarterly Journal of Experimental Psychology, 35A,* 199–207.

Bolhuis, J. J. (1991). Mechanisms of avian imprinting: A review. *Biological Reviews, 66,* 303–345.

Bolhuis, J. J., McCabe, B. J., & Horn, G. (1986). Androgens and imprinting. Differential effects of testosterone on filial preferences in the domestic chick. *Behavioral Neuroscience, 100,* 51–56.

Braddick, O. J., Atkinson, J., Hood, B., Harkness, W., Jackson, G., & Vargha-Khadem, F. (1992). Possible blindsight in infants lacking one cerebral hemisphere. *Nature, 360,* 461–463.

Brodmann, K. (1909). *Vergleichende Lokalisationslehre der Grosshirnrinde in ihren Prinzipien dargestellt auf Grund des Zellenbaues.* Leipzig: Barth.

Bronson, G. W. (1974). The postnatal growth of visual capacity. *Child Development, 45,* 873–890.

Bronson, G. W. (1982). The scanning patterns of human infants: Implications for visual learning. *Monographs on Infancy, 2,* 136.

Brown, M. C., Hopkins, W. G., & Keynes, R. J. (1991). *Essentials of a neural development.* Cambridge, England: Cambridge University Press.

Bushnell, I. W. R. (1979). Modification of the externality effect in young infants. *Journal of Experimental Child Psychology, 28,* 211–229.

Campbell, R., Heywood, C. A., Cowey, A., Regard, M., & Landis, T. (1990). Sensitivity to eye gaze in prosopagnosic patients and monkeys with superior temporal sulcus ablation. *Neuropsychologia, 28,* 1123–1142.

Case, R. (1992). The role of the frontal lobes in the regulation of human development. *Brain and Cognition, 20,* 51–73.

Changeux, J. -P. (1985). *Neuronal man: The biology of mind.* New York: Pantheon Books.

Changeux, J. -P., Courrege, P., & Danchin, A. (1973). A theory of the epigenesis of neuronal networks by selective stabilization of synapses. *Proceedings of the National Academy of Sciences USA, 70,* 2974–2978.

Changeux, J. -P., & Dehaene, S. (1989). Neuronal models of cognitive functions. *Cognition, 33,* 63–109.

Chi, J. G., Gooling, E., & Gilles, F. H. (1977). Gyral development of the human brain. *Annals of Neurology, 1,* 86.

Christophe, A., & Morton, J. (1994). Comprehending babythink. *Nature, 370,* 250–251.

Chugani, H. T. (1994). Development of regional brain glucose metabolism in relation to behavior and plasticity. In G. Dawson & Kurt W. Fischer (Eds.), *Human behavior and the developing brain* (pp. 153–175). New York: Guilford Press.

Chugani, H. T., Hovda, D. A., Villablanca, J. R., Phelps, M. E., & Xu, W. -F. (1991). Metabolic maturation of the brain: A study of local cerebral glucose utilization in the developing cat. *Journal of Cerebral Blood Flow and Metabolism, 11,* 35–47.

Chugani, H. T., & Phelps, M. E. (1986). Maturational changes in cerebral function determined by 18FDG positron emission tomography. *Science, 231,* 840–843.

Chugani, H. T., Phelps, M. E., & Mazziotta, J. C. (1987). Positron emission tomography study of human brain functional development. *Annals of Neurology, 22,* 487–497.

Clarke, P. G. H. (1985). Neuronal death in the development of the vertebrate nervous system. *Trends in the Neurosciences, 8,* 345–349.

Clohessy, A. B., Posner, M. I., Rothbart, M. K., & Vecera, S. P. (1991). The development of inhibition of return in early infancy. *Journal of Cognitive Neuroscience, 3,* 345–350.

Conel, J. L. (1939/1967). *The postnatal development of the human cerebral cortex* (Vols. 1–8). Cambridge, MA: Harvard University Press.

Courchesne, E., Hesselink, J. R., Jernigan, T. L., & Yeung-Courchesne, R. (1987). Abnormal neuroanatomy in a nonretarded person with autism: Unusual findings with magnetic resonance imaging. *Archives of Neurology, 44,* 335–341.

Cowan, W. M. (1979). The development of the brain. *Scientific American, 241,* 106–117.

Cowan, W. M., Fawcett, J. W., O'Leary, D. D. M., & Stanfield, B. B. (1984). Regressive events in neurogenesis. *Science, 225,* 1258–1265.

Crick, F. (1989). Neural Edelmanism. *Trends in the Neurosciences, 12,* 240–248.

Darwin, C. R. (1965). *The expression of emotions in man and animals.* Chicago: University of Chicago Press. (Original work published 1872)

Davies, D. C., Horn, G., & McCabe, B. J. (1985). Noradrenaline and learning: The effects of noradrenergic neurotoxin DSP4 on imprinting in the domestic chick. *Behavioral Neuroscience, 99,* 652–660.

Dehaene-Lambertz, G., & Dehaene, S. (1994). Speed and cerebral correlates of syllable discrimination in infants. *Nature, 370,* 292–295.

Dehay, C., Horsburgh, G., Berland, M., Killackey, H., & Kennedy, H. (1989). Maturation and connectivity of the visual cortex in monkeys is altered by prenatal removal of retinal input. *Nature, 337,* 265–267.

Dennis, M., & Whitaker, H. (1976). Language acquisition following hemidecortication: Linguistic superiority of the left over the right hemisphere. *Brain and Language, 3,* 404–433.

de Schonen, S., Deruelle, C., Mancini, J., & Pascalis, O. (1993). Hemispheric differences in face processing and brain maturation. In B. de Boysson-Bardies, S. de Schonen, P. Jusczyk, P. MacNeilage, & J. Morton (Eds.), *Developmental neurocognition: Speech and face processing in the first year of life* (pp. 149–163). Dordrecht, The Netherlands: Kluwer Academic Press.

de Schonen, S., & Mathivet, H. (1989). First come, first served: A scenario about the development of hemispheric specialization in face recognition during infancy. *European Bulletin of Cognitive Psychology, 9,* 3–44.

Diamond, A. (1985). Development of the ability to use recall to guide action, as indicated by infants' performance on AB. *Child Development, 56*(4), 868–883.

Diamond, A. (1991). Neuropsychological insights into the meaning of object concept development. In S. Carey & R. Gelman (Eds.), *The epigenesis of mind: Essays on biology and cognition* (pp. 66–110). Hillsdale, NJ: Erlbaum.

Diamond, A., & Goldman-Rakic, P. S. (1986). Comparative development in human infants and infant rhesus monkeys of cognitive functions that depend on prefrontal cortex. *Society for Neuroscience Abstracts, 12,* 742.

Diamond, A., & Goldman-Rakic, P. S. (1989). Comparison of human infants and infant rhesus monkeys on Piaget's AB task: Evidence for dependence on dorsolateral prefrontal cortex. *Experimental Brain Research, 74,* 24–40.

Diamond, A., Hurwitz, W., Lee, E. Y., Bockes, T., Grover, W., & Minarcik, C. (in press). *Cognitive deficits on frontal cortex tasks in children with early-treated PKU: Results of two years of longitudinal study.* Manuscript submitted for publication.

Ebbesson, S. O. E. (1980). The parcellation theory and its relation to interspecific variability in brain organization, evolutionary and ontogenetic development, and neuronal plasticity. *Cell and Tissue Research, 213,* 179–212.

Ebbesson, S. O. E. (1984). Evolution and ontogeny of neural circuits. *Behavioral and Brain Sciences, 7,* 321–366.

Ebbesson, S. O. E. (1988). Ontogenetic parcellation: Dual processes. *Behavioral and Brain Sciences, 11,* 548–549.

Edelman, G. M. (1987). *Neural Darwinism. The theory of neuronal group selection.* New York: Basic Books.

Elman, J., Bates, E., Johnson, M. H., Karmiloff-Smith, A., Parisi, D., & Plunkett, K. (1996). *Rethinking innateness: A connectionist perspective on development.* Cambridge, MA: MIT Press.

Fantz, R. L. (1964). Visual experience in infants: Decreased attention to familiar patterns relative to novel ones. *Science, 46,* 668–670.

Farah, M. J. (1990). *Visual agnosia.* Cambridge, MA: MIT Press.

Finlay, B. L., & Darlington, R. B. (1995). Linked regularities in the development and evolution of mammalian brains. *Science, 268,* 1578–1584.

Fischer, B., & Breitmeyer, B. (1987). Mechanisms of visual attention revealed by saccadic eye movements. *Neuropsychologia, 25,* 73–83.

Fodor, J. A. (1983). *The modularity of mind.* Cambridge, MA: Bradford Books.

Fox, N. A., & Bell, M. A. (1990). Electrophysiological indices of frontal lobe development. In A. Diamond (Ed.), *The development and neural bases of higher cognitive functions* (pp. 677–698). New York: New York Academy of Sciences.

Frith, U. (1989). *Autism: Explaining the enigma.* Oxford, England: Basil Blackwell.

Funahashi, S., Bruce, C. J., & Goldman-Rakic, P. S. (1989). Mnemonic coding of visual space in the monkey's dorsolateral prefrontal cortex. *Journal of Neurophysiology, 61*(2), 331–349.

Funahashi, S., Bruce, C. J., & Goldman-Rakic, P. S. (1990). Visuospatial coding in primate prefrontal neurons revealed by oculomotor paradigms. *Journal of Neurophysiology, 63*(4), 814–831.

Fuster, J. M. (1989). *The prefrontal cortex* (2nd ed.). New York: Raven Press.

Galaburda, A. M., & Pandya, D. N. (1983). The intrinsic architectonic and connectional organization of the superior temporal region of the rhesus monkey. *Journal of Comparative Neurology, 221,* 169–184.

George, M. S., Ketter, T. A., Gill, D. S., Haxby, J. V., Ungerleider, L. G., Herscovitch, P., & Post, R. M. (1993). Brain regions involved in recognizing emotion or identity: An oxygen-15 PET study. *The Journal of Neuropsychiatry and Clinical Neurosciences, 5,* 384–394.

Geschwind, N., & Galaburda, A. (1985). *Cerebral lateralization.* Cambridge, MA: MIT Press.

Geschwind, N., & Levitsky, W. (1968). Human brain: Left-right asymmetries in temporal speech region. *Science, 161*(837), 186–187.

Gesell, A. (1929). *Infancy and human growth.* New York: Macmillan.

Gilmore, R. O., & Johnson, M. H. (1995). Working memory in infancy: Six-month-olds' performance on two versions of the oculomotor delayed response task. *Journal of Experimental Child Psychology, 59,* 397–418.

Goldman, P. S. (1971). Functional development of the prefrontal cortex in early life and the problem of neuronal plasticity. *Experimental Neurology, 32,* 366–387.

Goldman-Rakic, P. S. (1987). Development of cortical circuitry and cognitive function. *Child Development, 58,* 601–622.

Goren, C. C., Sarty, M., & Wu, P. Y. K. (1975). Visual following and pattern discrimination of face-like stimuli by newborn infants. *Pediatrics, 56,* 544–549.

Gottlieb, G. (1992). *Individual development and evolution.* New York: Oxford University Press.

Greenough, W. T., Black, J. E., & Wallace, C. S. (1987). Experience and brain development. *Child Development, 58,* 539–559.

Guitton, H. A., Buchtel, H. A., & Douglas, R. M. (1985). Frontal lobe lesions in man cause difficulties in suppressing reflexive glances and in generating goal-directed saccades. *Experimental Brain Research, 58,* 455–472.

Haith, M. M., Hazan, C., & Goodman, G. S. (1988). Expectation and anticipation of dynamic visual events by 3.5-month-old babies. *Child Development, 59,* 467–479.

Hallett, P. E. (1978). Primary and secondary saccades to goals defined by instructions. *Vision Research, 18,* 1270–1296.

Held, R. (1985). Binocular vision: Behavioral and neuronal development. In J. Mehler & R. Fox (Eds.), *Neonate cognition: Beyond the blooming, buzzing confusion* (pp. 37–44). Hillsdale, NJ: Erlbaum.

Held, R. (1993). Development of binocular vision revisited. In M. H. Johnson (Ed.), *Brain development and cognition: A reader* (pp. 159–166). Oxford, England: Blackwell.

Hellige, J. B. (1993). *Hemispheric asymmetry: What's right and what's left.* Cambridge, MA: Harvard University Press.

Hinde, R. A. (1974). *Biological bases of human social behavior.* New York: McGraw-Hill.

Hood, B. (1993). Inhibition of return produced by covert shifts of visual attention in 6-month-old infants. *Infant Behavior and Development, 16,* 245–254.

Hood, B. (1995). Visual selective attention in the human infant: A neuroscientific approach. In C. Rovee-Collier & L. Lipsitt (Eds.), *Advances in infancy research* (pp. 10). Norwood, NJ: ABLEX.

Hood, B., & Atkinson, J. (1991). Shifting covert attention in infants. *Abstracts of the Society for Research in Child Development, 8.*

Hopkins, W. G., & Brown, M. C. (1984). *Development of nerve cells and their connections.* Cambridge, England: Cambridge University Press.

Horn, G. (1985). *Memory, imprinting, and the brain: An inquiry into mechanisms.* Oxford, England: Clarendon Press.

Horn, G., & Johnson, M. H. (1989). Memory systems in the chick: Dissociations and neuronal analysis. *Neuropsychologia, 27,* 1–22.

Horn, G., & McCabe, B. J. (1984). Predispositions and preferences. Effects on imprinting of lesions to the chick brain. *Brain Research, 168,* 361–373.

Huttenlocher, P. R. (1990). Morphometric study of human cerebral cortex development. *Neuropsychologia, 28,* 517–527.

Huttenlocher, P. R. (1994). Synaptogenesis, synapse elimination, and neural plasticity in human cerebral cortex. In C. A. Nelson (Ed.), *Threats to optimal development. The Minnesota symposia on child psychology* (Vol. 27, pp. 35–54). Hillsdale, NJ: Erlbaum.

Huttenlocher, P. R., de Courten, C., Garey, L. G., & Van der Loos, H. (1982). Synaptogenesis in human visual cortex—evidence for synapse elimination during normal development. *Neuroscience Letter, 33,* 247–252.

Janowsky, J. S. (1993). The development and neural basis of memory systems. In M. H. Johnson (Ed.), *Brain development and cognition: A reader* (pp. 665–678). Oxford, England: Blackwell.

Janowsky, J. S., & Findlay, B. L. (1986). The outcome of perinatal brain damage: The role of normal neuron loss and axon retraction. *Developmental Medicine and Child Neurology, 28,* 375–389.

Jernigan, T. L., Press, G. A., & Hesselink, J. R. (1990). Methods for measuring brain morphological features on magnetic resonance images: Validation and normal aging. *Archives of Neurology, 47,* 27–32.

Johnson, M. H. (1990). Cortical maturation and the development of visual attention in early infancy. *Journal of Cognitive Neuroscience, 2*(2), 81–95.

Johnson, M. H. (1991). Information processing and storage during filial imprinting. In P. G. Hepper (Ed.), *Kin recognition* (pp. 335–357). Cambridge, England: Cambridge University Press.

Johnson, M. H. (1993). Constraints on cortical plasticity. In M. H. Johnson (Ed.), *Brain development and cognition: A reader* (pp. 703–721). Oxford, England: Blackwell.

Johnson, M. H. (1994). Visual attention and the control of eye movements in early infancy. In C. Umilta & M. Moscovitch (Eds.), *Attention and performance: 15. Conscious and nonconscious processing* (pp. 291–310). Cambridge, MA: MIT Press.

Johnson, M. H. (1995). The inhibition of automatic saccades in early infancy. *Developmental Psychobiology, 28*(5), 281–291.

Johnson, M. H. (1997). *Developmental cognitive neuroscience: An introduction.* Oxford, England: Blackwell.

Johnson, M. H., & Bolhuis, J. J. (1991). Imprinting, predispositions and filial preference in the chick. In R. J. Andrew (Ed.), *Neural and behavioral plasticity* (pp. 133–156). Oxford, England: Oxford University Press.

Johnson, M. H., Bolhuis, J. J., & Horn, G. (1985). Interaction between acquired preferences and developing predispositions during imprinting. *Animal Behaviour, 33,* 1000–1006.

Johnson, M. H., Dziurawiec, S., Bartrip, J., & Morton, J. (1992). The effects of movement of internal features on infants' preferences for face-like stimuli. *Infant Behavior and Development, 15,* 129–136.

Johnson, M. H., Dziurawiec, S., Ellis, H. D., & Morton, J. (1991). Newborns' preferential tracking of face-like stimuli and its subsequent decline. *Cognition, 40,* 1–19.

Johnson, M. H., & Gilmore, R. O. (1996). Developmental cognitive neuroscience: A biological perspective on cognitive change. In R. Gelman & T. Au (Eds.), *Handbook of perception and cognition: Perceptual and cognitive development.* Orlando, FL: Academic Press.

Johnson, M. H., & Gilmore, R. O. (in press). *Egocentric action in early infancy: Spatial frames of reference for saccades.* Manuscript submitted for publication.

Johnson, M. H., Gilmore, R. O., Tucker, L. A., & Minister, S. L. (1996). T-18. Vector summation in young infants. *Brain and Cognition, 32*(2), 237–243.

Johnson, M. H., & Horn, G. (1986). Dissociation of recognition memory and associative learning by a restricted lesion of the chick forebrain. *Neuropsychologia, 24,* 329–340.

Johnson, M. H., & Horn, G. (1987). The role of a restricted region of the chick forebrain in the recognition of individual conspecifics. *Behavioural Brain Research, 23,* 269–275.

Johnson, M. H., & Horn, G. (1988). The development of filial preferences in the dark-reared chick. *Animal Behaviour, 36,* 675–683.

Johnson, M. H., & Karmiloff-Smith, A. (1992). Can neural selectionism be applied to cognitive development and its disorders? *New Ideas in Psychology, 10,* 35–46.

Johnson, M. H., & Morton, J. (1991). *Biology and cognitive development: The case of face recognition.* Oxford, England: Blackwell.

Johnson, M. H., Posner, M. I., & Rothbart, M. K. (1994). Facilitation of saccades toward a covertly attended location in early infancy. *Psychological Science, 5*(2), 90–93.

Johnson, M. H., & Tucker, L. A. (1993). The ontogeny of covert visual attention: Facilitatory and inhibitory effects. *Abstracts of the Society for Research in Child Development, 9,* 424.

Johnson, M. H., & Tucker, L. A. (1996). The development and temporal dynamics of spatial orienting in infants. *Journal of Experimental Child Psychology, 63,* 171–188.

Johnson, M. H., & Vecera, S. P. (1996). Cortical differentiation and neurocognitive development: The parcellation conjecture. *Behavioural Processes, 36,* 195–212.

Karmiloff-Smith, A. (1992). *Beyond modularity: A developmental perspective on cognitive science.* Cambridge, MA: MIT Press.

Karmiloff-Smith, A. (1994). Precis of beyond modularity: A developmental perspective on cognitive science. *Behavioral and Brain Sciences, 17,* 693–745.

Karmiloff-Smith, A., Klima, E., Bellugi, U., Grant, J., & Baron-Cohen, S. (1995). Is there a social module? Language, face processing and theory of mind in individuals with Williams syndrome. *Journal of Cognitive Neuroscience, 7,* 196–208.

Katz, L. C., & Shatz, C. J. (1996). Synaptic activity and the construction of cortical circuits. *Science, 274,* 1133.

Kennedy, H., & Dehay, C. (1993). The importance of developmental timing in cortical specification. *Perspectives on Developmental Neurobiology, 1*(2), 93–99.

Kertzberg, M., Dehaene, S., & Changeux, J. -P. (1992). Stabilization of complex input output functions in neural clusters formed by synapse selection. *Neural Networks, 5,* 403–413.

Killackey, H. P., Chiaia, N. L., Bennett-Clarke, C. A., Eck, M., & Rhoades, R. (1994). Peripheral influences on the size and organization of somatotopic representations in the fetal rat cortex. *Journal of Neuroscience, 14,* 1496–1506.

Kinsbourne, M., & Hiscock, M. (1983). The normal and deviant development of functional lateralization of the brain. In M. Haith & J. Campos (Eds.), *Handbook of child psychology* (pp. 157–280). New York: Wiley.

Kostovic, I., Petanjek, Z., & Judas, M. (1993). Early areal differentiation of the human cerebral cortex-entorhinal area. *Hippocampus, 3,* 447–458.

Kuhl, P. K. (1993). Innate predispositions and the effects of experience in speech perception: The native language magnet theory. In B. de Boysson-Bardies, S. de Schonen, P. Jusczyk, P. McNeilage, & J. Morton (Eds.), *Developmental neurocognition: Speech and face processing in the first year of life* (pp. 259–274). Dordrecht, The Netherlands: Kluwer Academic.

Kwong, K. E., Belliveau, J. W., Chesler, D. A., Goldberg, I. E., Weisskoff, R. M., Poncelet, B. P., Kennedy, D. N., Hoppel, B. E., Cohen, M. S., Turner, R., Cheng, H. M., Brady, T. J., & Rosen, B. R. (1992). Dynamic magnetic resonance imaging of human brain activity during primary sensory stimulation. *Proceedings of the National Academy of Sciences, 89,* 5675–5679.

Lecuyer, R., Abgueguen, I., & Lemarie, C. (1992). 9- and 5-month-olds do not make the AB error if not required to manipulate objects [Special issue]. *Infant Behavior and Development, 15,* 514.

Lehrmann, D. S. (1953). A critique of Konrad Lorenz's theory of instinctive behavior. *Quarterly Review of Biology, 28,* 337–363.

Lenneberg, E. (1967). *Biological foundations of language.* New York: Wiley.

Lewis, T. L., Maurer, D., & Milewski, A. (1979). The development of nasal detection in young infants. *Investigative Ophthalmology and Visual Science Supplement, 18,* 271.

Lowndes, M., Davies, D. C., & Johnson, M. H. (1994). Archistriatal lesions impair the acquisition of filial preferences during imprinting in the domestic chick. *European Journal of Neuroscience, 6,* 1143–1148.

Marler, P. (1991). The instinct to learn. In S. Carey & R. Gelman (Eds.), *The epigenesis of mind: Essays on biology and cognition* (pp. 37–66). Hillsdale, NJ: Erlbaum.

Maurer, D. (1983). The scanning of compound figures by young infants. *Journal of Experimental Child Psychology, 35,* 437–448.

Maurer, D. (1985). Infants' perception of facadeness. In T. M. Field & N. Fox (Eds.), *Social perception in infants* (pp. 73–100). Norwood, NJ: ABLEX.

Maurer, D., & Barrera, M. (1981). Infants' perception of natural and distorted arrangements of a schematic face. *Child Development, 47,* 523–527.

Maurer, D., & Young, R. E. (1983). Newborns' following of natural and distorted arrangements of facial features. *Infant Behavior and Development, 6,* 127–131.

Maylor, E. A. (1985). Facilitatory and inhibitory components of orienting in visual space. In M. I. Posner & O. M. Marin (Eds.), *Attention and performance* (Vol. 11, pp. 189–204). Hillsdale, NJ: Erlbaum.

McCabe, B. J., Cipolla-Neto, J., Horn, G., & Bateson, P. P. G. (1982). Amnesic effects of bilateral lesions placed in the hyperstriatum ventral of the chick after imprinting. *Experimental Brain Research, 48,* 13–21.

McGraw, M. B. (1943). *The neuromuscular maturation of the human infant.* New York: Columbia University Press.

Miller, K. D. (1990). Correlation-based models of neural development. In M. A. Gluck & D. E. Rumelhart (Eds.), *Neuroscience and connectionist theory* (pp. 267–353). Hillsdale, NJ: Erlbaum.

Miller, K. D., Keller, J. B., & Stryker, M. P. (1989). Ocular dominance column development: Analysis and simulation. *Science, 245,* 605–615.

Miller, S. L., & Tallal, P. (1995). A behavioral neuroscience approach to developmental language disorders: Evidence for a rapid temporal processing deficit. In D. Cicchetti & D. J. Cohen (Eds.), *Developmental psychopathology* (Vol. 2, pp. 274–298). New York: Wiley.

Milner, B. (1982). Some cognitive effects of frontal-lobe lesions in man. *Philosophical Transactions of the Royal Society of London, 298,* 211–226.

Molfese, D. (1989). Electrophysiological correlates of word meanings in 14-month-old human infants. *Developmental Neuropsychology, 5,* 70–103.

Molnar, Z., & Blakemore, C. (1991). Lack of regional specificity for connections formed between thalamus and cortex in coculture. *Nature, 351*(6326), 475–477.

Morton, J., & Johnson, M. H. (1991). CONSPEC and CONLERN: A two-process theory of infant face recognition. *Psychological Review, 98*(2), 164–181.

Muir, D. W., Clifton, R. K., & Clarkson, M. G. (1989). The development of a human auditory localization response: A U-shaped function. *Canadian Journal of Psychology, 43,* 199–216.

Munakata, Y., McClelland, J. L., Johnson, M. H., & Siegler, R. S. (in press). Rethinking infant knowledge: Toward an adaptive process account of successes and failures in object permanence tasks. *Psychological Review.*

Nelson, C. A. (1994). Neural correlates of recognition memory in the first potential year of life. In G. Dawson & K. Fischer (Eds.), *Human behavior and the developing brain* (pp. 269–313). New York: Guilford Press.

Nelson, C. A. (1995). The ontogeny of human memory: A cognitive neuroscience perspective. *Developmental Psychology, 31*(5), 723–738.

Nelson, C. A., & Collins, P. F. (1992). Neural and behavioral correlates of recognition memory in 4- and 8-month-old infants. *Brain and Cognition, 19,* 105–121.

Nelson, C. A., & Ludemann, P. M. (1989). Past, current and future trends in infant face perception research. *Canadian Journal of Psychology, 43,* 183–198.

Neville, H. J. (1991). Neurobiology of cognitive and language processing: Effects of early experience. In K. R. Gibson & A. C. Petersen (Eds.), *Brain maturation and cognitive development: Comparative and cross-cultural perspectives* (pp. 355–380). Hawthorne, New York: Aldine de Gruyter.

O'Leary, D. D. M. (1989). Do cortical areas emerge from a protocortex? *Trends in Neuroscience, 12,* 400–406.

O'Leary, D. D. M., & Stanfield, B. B. (1985). Occipital cortical neurons with transient pyramidal tract axons extend and maintain collaterals to subcortical but not intracortical targets. *Brain Research, 336,* 326–333.

O'Leary, D. D. M., & Stanfield, B. B. (1989). Selective elimination of axons extended by developing cortical neurons is dependent on regional locale: Experiments utilizing fetal cortical transplants. *Journal of Neuroscience, 9,* 2230–2246.

O'Reilly, R., & Johnson, M. H. (1994). Object recognition and sensitive periods: A computational analysis of visual imprinting. *Neural Computation, 6,* 357–390.

Overman, W., Bachevalier, J., Turner, M., & Peuster, A. (1992). Object recognition versus object discrimination: Comparison between human infants and infant monkeys. *Behavioral Neuroscience, 106,* 15–29.

Oyama, S. (1985). *The ontogeny of information: Developmental systems and evolution.* Cambridge, England: Cambridge University Press.

Pallas, S. L., & Sur, M. (1993). Visual projections induced into the auditory pathway of ferrets: 2. Corticocortical connections of primary auditory cortex. *Journal of Comparative Neurology, 337*(2), 317–333.

Pandya, D. N., & Yeterian, E. H. (1985). Architecture and connections of cortical association areas. In A. Peters & E. G. Jones (Eds.), *Cerebral cortex: Vol. 4. Association and auditory cortices* (pp. 3–61). New York: Plenum Press.

Pandya, D. N., & Yeterian, E. H. (1990). Architecture and connections of cerebral cortex: Implications for brain evolution and function. In A. B. Scheibel & A. F. Weschsler (Eds.), *Neurobiology of higher cognitive function* (pp. 53–84). New York: Guilford Press.

Parmelee, A. H., & Sigman, M. D. (1983). Perinatal brain development and behavior. In M. M. Haith & J. Campos (Eds.), *Infancy and the biology of development: Vol. 2. Handbook of child psychology* (pp. 95–155). New York: Wiley.

Perrett, D. I., & Mistlin, A. J. (1990). Perception of facial characteristics by monkeys. In W. C. Stebbins & M. A. Berkley (Eds.), *Comparative perception: Vol. 2. Complex signals* (pp. 187–215). New York: Wiley.

Perrett, D. I., Rolls, E. T., & Caan, W. (1982). Visual neurones responsive to faces in the monkey temporal cortex. *Experimental Brain Research, 47,* 229–238.

Petersen, S. E., Fox, P., Posner, M., Mintun, M., & Raichle, M. (1988). Positron emission tomographic studies of the cortical anatomy of single-word processing. *Nature, 331,* 585–589.

Petitto, L. A. (1993). On the ontogenetic requirements for early language acquisition. In B. de Boysson-Bardies, S. de Schonen, P. Jusczyk, P. F. MacNeilage, & J. Morton (Eds.), *Developmental neurocognition: Speech and face processing in the first year of life* (pp. 365–383). Dordrecht, The Netherlands: Kluwer Academic.

Piaget, J. (1954). *The construction of reality in the child.* New York: Basic Books.

Posner, M. I. (1980). Orienting of attention. *Quarterly Journal of Experimental Psychology, 32,* 3–25.

Posner, M. I. (1988). Structures and functions of selective attention. In T. Boll & B. Bryant (Eds.), *Clinical neuropsychology and brain function: Research, measurement and practice* (pp. 171–202). Washington, DC: American Psychological Association.

Posner, M. I., & Cohen, Y. (1980). Attention and the control of movements. In G. E. Stelmach & J. Roguiro (Eds.), *Tutorials in motor behavior* (pp. 243–258). Amsterdam, The Netherlands: North-Holland.

Posner, M. I., & Cohen, Y. (1984). Components of visual orienting. In H. Bouma & D. G. Bouwhis (Eds.), *Attention and performance* (pp. 531–556). Hillsdale, NJ: Erlbaum.

Posner, M. I., & Peterson, S. E. (1990). The attention system of the human brain. *Annual Review of Neuroscience, 13,* 25–42.

Posner, M. I., Rafal, R. D., Choate, L. S., & Vaughan, J. (1985). Inhibition of return: Neural basis and function. *Cognitive Neuropsychology, 2,* 211–228.

Posner, M. I., & Rothbart, M. K. (1980). The development of attentional mechanisms. In J. H. Flower (Ed.), *Nebraska Symposium on Motivation* (pp. 1–52). Lincoln: University of Nebraska Press.

Purpura, D. P. (1975). Normal and aberrant neuronal development in the cerebral cortex of human fetus and young infant. In N. A. Buchwald & M. A. B. Brazier (Eds.), *Brain mechanisms of mental retardation* (pp. 141–169). New York: Academic Press.

Purves, D. (1994). *Neural activity and the growth of the brain.* Accademia Nazionale Dei Lincei: Cambridge University Press.

Purves, D., & Lichtman, J. W. (1985). *Principles of neural development.* Sunderland, MA: Sinauer Associates.

Quartz, S. R., & Sejnowski, T. J. (in press). *A neural basis of cognitive development: A constructivist manifesto.* Manuscript submitted for publication.

Rabinowicz, T. (1979). The differential maturation of the human cerebral cortex. In F. Falkner & J. M. Tanner (Eds.), *Human growth: Vol. 3. Neurobiology and nutrition* (pp. 141–169). New York: Plenum Press.

Raichle, M. E., & Mallinkrodt, M. E. (1987). Circulatory and metabolic correlates of brain function in normal humans. In V. B. Mountcastle, F. Plum, & S. R. Geiger (Eds.), *Handbook of physiology—The nervous system* (pp. 643–674). Bethesda, MD: American Physiological Association.

Rakic, P. (1988). Specification of cerebral cortical areas. *Science, 241,* 170–176.

Rakic, P. (1995). Corticogenesis in human and nonhuman primates. In M. S. Gazzaniga (Ed.), *The cognitive neurosciences* (pp. 127–145). Cambridge, MA: MIT Press.

Rakic, P., Bourgeois, J. -P., Eckenhoff, M. F., Zecevic, N., & Goldman-Rakic, P. S. (1986). Concurrent overproduction of synapses in diverse regions of primate cerebral cortex. *Science, 232,* 153–157.

Reeke, G. N., Jr., Sporns, O., & Edelman, G. M. (1990). Synthetic neural modeling: The "Darwin" series of recognition automata. *Proceedings of the Institute of Electrical and Electronic Engineers, 78*(9), 1498–1530.

Reilly, J., Bates, E., & Marchman, V. (in press). Narrative discourse in children with early focal brain injury. In M. Dennis (Ed.), Discourse in children with anomalous brain development or acquired brain injury [Special issue]. *Brain and Language.*

Richards, J. E. (1989a). Sustained visual attention in 8-week-old infants. *Infant Behavior and Development, 12,* 425–436.

Richards, J. E. (1989b). Development and stability of HR-defined, visual sustained attention in 14-, 20-, and 26-week-old infants. *Psychophysiology, 26,* 422–430.

Richards, J. E. (1991). Infant eye movements during peripheral visual stimulus localization as a function of central stimulus attention status. *Psychophysiology, 28,* S4.

Rockland, K. S., & Pandya, D. N. (1979). Laminar origins and terminations of cortical connections of the occipital lobe in the rhesus monkey. *Brain Research, 179,* 3–20.

Roe, A. W., Pallas, S. L., Hahm, J. O., & Sur, M. (1990). A map of visual space induced in primary auditory cortex. *Science, 250*(4982), 818–820.

Rolls, E. (1989). Functions of neuronal networks in the hippocampus and neocortex in memory. In J. H. Byrne & W. O. Berry (Eds.), *Neural models of plasticity* (pp. 240–265). San Diego, CA: Academic Press.

Rovee-Collier, C. K. (1993). The capacity for long-term memory in infancy. *Current Directions in Psychological Science, 2*(4), 130–135.

Sanides, F. (1971). Functional architecture of motor and sensory cortices in primates in the light of a new concept of neocortex development. In C. R. Noback & W. Montana (Eds.), *Advances in primatology* (pp. 137–208). New York: Academic Press.

Schacter, D., & Moscovitch, M. (1984). Infants, amnesia and dissociable memory systems. In M. Moscovitch (Ed.), *Infant memory* (pp. 173–216). New York: Plenum Press.

Schiller, P. H. (1985). A model for the generation of visually guided saccadic eye movements. In D. Rose & V. G. Dobson (Eds.), *Models of the visual cortex* (pp. 62–70). Chichester, England: Wiley.

Schlagger, B. L., & O'Leary, D. D. M. (1991). Potential of visual cortex to develop an array of functional units unique to somatosensory cortex. *Science, 252,* 1556–1560.

Schlagger, B. L., & O'Leary, D. D. M. (1993). Patterning of the barrel field in somatosensory cortex with implications for the specification of neocortical areas. *Perspectives on Developmental Neurobiology, 1*(2), 81–91.

Schneider, W., Noll, D. C., & Cohen, J. D. (1993). Functional topographic mapping of the cortical ribbon in human vision with conventional MRI scanners. *Nature, 365,* 150–153.

Segalowitz, S. J. (1994). Developmental psychology and brain development: A historical perspective. In G. Dawson & K. W. Fischer (Eds.), *Human behavior and the developing brain* (pp. 67–92). New York: Guilford Press.

Shatz, K. (1992). Dividing up the neocortex. *Science, 258,* 237–238.

Shrager, J., & Johnson, M. H. (1995). Waves of growth in the development of cortical function: A computational model. In B. Julesz & I. Kovacs (Eds.), *Maturational windows and adult cortical plasticity* (pp. 31–44). Reading, MA: Addison-Wesley.

Siegler, R., & Munakata, Y. (1993). Beyond the immaculate transition: Advances in the understanding of change. *Society for Research into Child Development Newsletter.*

Silva, A. J., Paylor, R., Wehner, J. M., & Tonegawa, S. (1992). Impaired spatial learning in a-calcium-calmodulin kinase II mutant mice. *Science, 257,* 206–211.

Silva, A. J., Stevens, C. F., Tonegawa, S., & Wang, Y. N. (1992). Deficient hippocampal long-term potentiation in a-calcium-calmodulin kinase II mutant mice. *Science, 257*(5067), 201–206.

Simion, F., Valenza, E., Umilta, C., & Dalla Barba, B. (1995). Inhibition of return in newborns is temporo-nasal asymmetrical. *Infant Behavior and Development, 18,* 189–194.

Stanfield, B. B., & O'Leary, D. D. M. (1985). Fetal occipital cortical neurons transplanted to the rostral cortex can extend and maintain a pyramidal tract axon. *Nature, 313,* 135–137.

Stiles, J., & Thal, D. (1993). Linguistic and spatial cognitive development following early focal brain injury: Patterns of deficit and recovery. In M. H. Johnson (Ed.), *Brain development and cognition: A reader* (pp. 643–664). Oxford, England: Blackwell.

Stryker, M. P., & Harris, W. (1986). Binocular impulse blockade prevents the formation of ocular dominance columns in cat visual cortex. *Journal of Neuroscience, 6,* 2117–2133.

Stuss, D. T. (1992). Biological and psychological development of executive functions. *Brain and Cognition, 20,* 8–23.

Sur, M., Garraghty, P. E., & Roe, A. W. (1988). Experimentally induced visual projections into auditory thalamus and cortex. *Science, 242,* 1437–1441.

Sur, M., Pallas, S. L., & Roe, A. W. (1990). Cross-modal plasticity in cortical development: Differentiation and specification of sensory neocortex. *Trends in Neuroscience, 13,* 227–233.

Teszner, D., Tzavaras, A., Gruner, J., & Hecaen, H. (1972). Right-left asymmetry of the planum temporale; apropos of the anatomical study of 100 brains. *Review-Neurologique-Paris, 126*(6), 444–449.

Thal, D., Marchman, V., Stiles, J., Aram, D., Trauner, D., Nass, R., & Bates, E. (1991). Early lexical development in children with focal brain injury. *Brain and Language, 40,* 491–527.

Thatcher, R. W. (1992). Cyclic cortical reorganization during early childhood: The role of frontal lobe maturation in cognitive and social development [Special issue]. *Brain and Cognition, 20*(1), 24–50.

Thelen, E., & Smith, L. B. (1994). *A dynamic systems approach to the development of cognition and action.* Cambridge, MA: MIT Press.

Tramo, M. J., Loftus, W. C., Thomas, C. E., Green, R. L., Mott, L. A., & Gazzaniga, M. S. (1994). Surface area of human cerebral cortex and its gross morphological subdivisions. *Journal of Cognitive Neuroscience, 7*(2), 292–301.

Valenza, E., Simion, F., Cassia, V. M., & Umilta, C. (1996). Face preference at birth. *Journal of Experimental Psychology: Human Perception and Performance, 22*(4), 892–903.

Vargha-Khadem, F., Isaacs, E., & Muter, V. (1994). A review of cognitive outcome after unilateral lesions sustained during childhood. *Journal of Child Neurology, 9*(Suppl), 2S67–2S73.

Vecera, S. P., & Johnson, M. H. (1995). Eye gaze detection and the cortical processing of faces: Evidence from infants and adults. *Visual Cognition, 2,* 101–129.

Volpe, J. J. (1987). *Neurology of the newborn* (2nd ed.). Philadelphia: Saunders.

von Hofsten, C. (1984). Developmental changes in the organization of prereaching movements. *Developmental Psychology, 20,* 378–388.

Wada, J. A., Clarke, R., & Hamm, A. (1975). Cerebral hemispheric asymmetry in humans: Cortical speech zones in 100 adult and 100 infant brains. *Archives of Neurology, 32*(4), 239–246.

Waddington, C. H. (1975). *The evolution of an evolutionist.* Edinburgh, Scotland: Edinburgh University Press.

Wattam-Bell, J. (1991). Development of motion-specific cortical responses in infants. *Vision Research, 31,* 287–297.

Webster, M. J., Bachevalier, J., & Ungerleider, L. G. (1995). Development and plasticity of visual memory circuits. In B. Julesz & I. Kovacs (Eds.), *Maturational windows and adult cortical plasticity.* New York: Addison-Wesley.

Weliky, M., & Katz, L. C. (1997). Disruption of orientation tuning in visual cortex by artificially correlated neuronal activity. *Nature, 386,* 680.

Welsh, M. C., Pennington, B. F., Ozonoff, S., Rouse, B., & McCabe, E. R. B. (1990). Neuropsychology of early-treated phenylketonuria: Specific executive function deficits. *Child Development, 61,* 1697–1713.

Werker, J. F., & Polka, L. (1993). The ontogeny and developmental significance of language-specific phonetic perception. In B. de Boysson-Bardies, S. de Schonen, P. Jusczyk, P. McNeilage, & J. Morton (Eds.), *Developmental neurocognition: Speech and face processing in the first year of life* (pp. 275–288). Dordrecht, The Netherlands: Kluwer Academic.

Wiesel, T. N., & Hubel, D. H. (1965). Comparison of the effects of unilateral and bilateral eye closure on cortical unit responses in kittens. *Journal of Neurophysiology, 28,* 1029–1040.

Witelson, S. F., & Pallie, W. (1973). Left hemisphere specialization for language in the newborn. Neuroanatomical evidence of asymmetry. *Brain, 96*(3), 641–646.

Yakovlev, P. I., & Lecours, A. (1967). The myelogenetic cycles of regional maturation of the brain. In A. Minokowski (Ed.), *Regional development of the brain in early life* (pp. 3–70). Philadelphia: Davis.

CHAPTER 2

Perception and Action

BENNETT I. BERTENTHAL and RACHEL K. CLIFTON

The last chapter on motor development included in this *Handbook,* "The Ontogenesis of Infant Behavior" by Arnold Gesell, appeared over 40 years ago (Gesell, 1954). Research interests shifted following that period and it was thought unnecessary to include a chapter on motor development in subsequent volumes. This period of benign neglect is now behind us, and traditional research on motor development has given way to new conceptions and new domains of study. While Gesell was trying to show maturational changes in behavior norms, we shall highlight the complex dynamic processes that contribute to changes in motor behavior in real and developmental time. Our major focus will be on the development of three action systems: posture, reaching, and locomotion, which are the foundation of many of the later skilled behaviors of children and adults. First,

we will provide a brief historical perspective and introduce some of the new methods and analytic techniques available for studying motor performance. Then we will review the research on posture, reaching and grasping, and locomotion, and conclude by discussing some of the change mechanisms involved in the development of action systems as well as future directions for research.

It is quite remarkable to observe the dramatic turn-around that has taken place in the research on motor development in the past decade. As recently as 1980, few empirical articles or chapters were concerned with this area. Since that time, a number of special issues dedicated to perception and action have appeared in developmental journals, and numerous edited books on the development of reaching, locomotion, and other motor skills have been published (e.g., Bard, Fleury, & Hay, 1990; Bloch & Bertenthal, 1990; Clark & Humphrey, 1990; Goldfield, 1995; Hauert, 1990; Kalverboer, Hopkins, & Geuze, 1993; Kelso & Clark, 1982; Lockman & Thelen, 1993; Pick, 1989; Savelsbergh, 1993; Smith & Thelen, 1993; Thelen &

The preparation of this chapter was supported by NIH grant HD16195 to BIB, and NIH grant HD27714 and NIMH Research Scientist Award MH 00332 to RKC.

Smith, 1994; Wade & Whiting, 1986; Woollacott & Shumway-Cook, 1989). One important reason for the revitalization of this field of study is that contemporary researchers are now focusing on perceptuomotor processes and how they change over time (Bertenthal, 1996; Thelen, 1995). Unlike the study of most psychological processes, such as intelligence or attachment, motor behaviors are measured directly. Thus, it is possible to obtain a direct read-out of the behavior and to quantify how that behavior changes over different time scales. The reliable and precise quantification of behavior is a first step toward formulating more complete models of how motor behaviors change with age and experience. These new developmental models differ significantly from past models in that they emphasize not only the sequential progression of regular patterns of movement, but also the variability within and between these patterns (Bertenthal, Campos, & Kermoian, 1994; Edelman, 1992; Thelen, 1995).

Many of the new theories and approaches in the literature are inspired by a systems perspective toward motor development. This perspective underscores the limitations of viewing development as a function of a single process and emphasizes that development is necessarily a function of the confluence of many different factors that become dynamically organized (Fentress, 1989; Gottlieb, 1991; Thelen, 1989). The development of upright locomotion, for example, is not solely attributable to the development of a motor program in the brain (e.g., McGraw, 1945), but instead depends on the development of central pattern generators, balance control, muscle tone, differentiation of articulators, visual guidance, motivation, and so on (Thelen, 1986a). Although systems views were introduced long before contemporary research on motor development (Sameroff, 1983), their application to this area allows greater specification of the relevant variables and how they interact over time than heretofore discussed. It is quite understandable why many theorists in this area are attracted specifically to a dynamic systems perspective (Clark, Truly, & Phillips, 1993; Smith & Thelen, 1993; Thelen & Smith, 1994), because this view emphasizes not only the relations between different variables but also how these relations are continually changing.

It may not be apparent why "Perception and Action" is used as the title for a chapter reviewing contemporary research on the development of motor skills. Let us explain. Traditional research on motor development was rooted in the view that movements were generated solely by "motor programs" in the central nervous system. The Russian

physiologist, Nikolai Aleksandrovich Bernstein (1896–1966), was one of the first to recognize that any straightforward relation between neuromotor impulses and the coordination of movements was untenable, primarily because it ignored the many other factors, such as inertia of the limbs, reactive forces, and initial postural conditions, that always combine with active muscle forces in producing complex chains of multisegment movements. All of these factors or degrees of freedom contribute to the indeterminacy of movements and necessitate perceptual information to modulate active muscle forces to produce a functionally organized and goal-directed response.

If perceptual information were not available to detect peripheral changes and to modulate motor impulses, then, for example, even slight variations in the initial position or load of a limb, such as the arm, would preclude the repetition of the same goal-directed action, such as lifting a cup to the mouth. This inconsistency in performance is not observed because it is possible to configure different degrees of freedom (e.g., body segments and joints) to achieve the same goal by what is called *motor equivalence* (Turvey, 1990). A common example of motor equivalence is that you can write your name with pen on paper, or with chalk on a blackboard, or with a stick in the sand. Each of these actions requires a different configuration of limb movements; nevertheless, the result or the outcome is always recognizable as your signature (Lashley, 1942). The implication of this example is that coordinated actions are defined functionally and not in terms of specific body segments or movements. Sensory and motor systems contribute collectively to the outcome, which explains why they are best conceptualized as a single functional unit or action system (Reed, 1982).

A second reason for this shift in emphasis is recognition that all animals are in continual disequilibrium with their environment (Reed, 1982). Thus, it is not sufficient for them to react to intermittent stimulation; instead, it is necessary for them to act all the time and constantly evaluate their actions with respect to local conditions in the environment. As actions continue to change over time so will the modulation of the perceptual information. In essence, then, perception and action form a continuous loop in which "we must perceive in order to move, but we must also move in order to perceive" (J. Gibson, 1979, p. 223). All spatially and temporally coordinated behaviors require the coupling of perception and action. For example, reaching for an object is guided by perceptual information that changes as the reach progresses. These perceptual changes modulate the effectors to insure that the reach is successful (Jeannerod, 1994).

Similarly, perceptual information is necessary to maintain postural equilibrium, but again the information changes as the posture is adjusted in response to that information (Howard, 1986).

Although most perceptual information concerns the contemporaneous status of the environment, it is theoretically and practically significant that the perceptual information necessary to control actions is prospective. The inertia of the limbs and the time lags of neural conduction demand some anticipation of future actions (Haith, 1994; Lee, 1993; von Hofsten, 1993). Information to specify upcoming events is available directly from the spatial temporal patterning of perceptual events. For example, Lee (1974) showed that the time to contact (or tau variable) between an object and a moving observer is specified directly by the inverse of the relative expansion velocity of that object at the point of observation. This visual information has been shown to control a variety of locomotor activities, such as the stride length of long jumpers when approaching the take-off board (Lee, Lishman, & Thompson, 1982) or the wing closing of gannets when diving into the water (Lee & Reddish, 1981). Recent findings reveal some remarkable examples of prospective control by human infants, such as their ability to catch moving objects (Robin, Berthier, & Clifton, 1996; von Hofsten, 1983).

Finally, actions are systematically selected to reveal a mutuality or fit between the environment and the observer (Gibson, 1979; Warren, 1990). The observer's body size, propensities, and level of motor skill determine the functional utility of different environmental properties. It is necessary that the observer perceive both the dimensions of the environment and his or her own capabilities before determining whether or not an action should be selected (Adolph, Eppler, & Gibson, 1993b; E. Gibson, 1988). For example, bipedal locomotion is possible only when there is sufficient strength and postural control to maintain balance on two feet, and when the surface of support is relatively flat, uncluttered, rigid, and capable of supporting the weight of the moving observer. Catching a ball is possible only when the ball is restricted in size and not moving so fast as to exceed the anticipatory hand and arm responses of the person performing the action. Empirical studies inspired by these ideas suggest that at least some of the information used by adults to control their actions relative to environmental objects is specified in body-scaled units. Thus, adults determine whether or not the riser height of a staircase affords walking upright (Mark, 1987; W. Warren, 1984), or whether doorways are too narrow to pass through

without turning sideways (Warren & Whang, 1987), based on their own body proportions. Similar to other perceptual information, such as the optical variable tau, it appears that these body-scaled dimensions provide reliable perceptual information for controlling actions that does not require complex computations and comparisons.

This last argument for focusing on the unity of perception and action also highlights the dual function of perceptual information. In order to optimize the fit between the observer and the environment the observer must perceive information about the self as well as information about the spatial layout. The traditional position is that different sensory systems detect these two sources of information. One class of sensory systems (exteroceptors)—the eyes, ears, nose, mouth, and skin—is responsible for sensations of external origin; the other class (proprioceptors)—the receptors in the joints, tendons, muscles, and inner ear—is responsible for detecting self-produced stimulation. J. Gibson (1966) was one of the first theorists to criticize this classification system and asserted that most perceptual systems provide both proprioceptive and exteroceptive information. Consider, for example, a bird flying into a headwind (J. Gibson, 1958). The perspective changes in the optical flow information specify both the speed and direction of travel, whereas the invariant sources of information in the optical flow, such as an occluding edge at a precipice, specify information about spatial layout. This distinction is significant from a developmental perspective because it demands that infants and children learn to differentiate perceptual information specifying self from information specifying the external environment (Gibson & Schmuckler, 1989). It also highlights the importance of trying to understand how body-centered coordinate systems that are specified with proprioceptive information, such as an arm-centered coordinate system, are coordinated with environmental coordinate systems, such as the location of an object to be grasped, that are specified with exteroceptive information (Paillard, 1991).

In the remainder of this chapter, we will address the development of motor skills from the perspective of perception and action. Although development depends obviously on both processes, we will focus primarily on the development of actions rather than the perceptions guiding these actions. However, it is important to acknowledge from the beginning that the development of perception and action is mutual and reciprocal (Adolph et al., 1993b; Bertenthal, 1996). Thus, improvements in the scaling and coordination of actions will in turn demand greater perceptual differentiation; likewise, greater perceptual differentiation will provide children with more precise information for controlling their actions.

HISTORY

Contributions of the Early Pioneers

The study of motor behavior, like the study of child development in general, has its roots in the baby biographies of the 18th and 19th centuries. First, Tiedemann (1787, as cited by Borstelmann, 1983), then Darwin (1877) and Preyer (1882) supplied the earliest systematic accounts of a child's development, based on detailed observations of the authors' own offspring. The biological and physiological background of these early writers was reflected in what they chose to report, and continued to influence subsequent investigators. This work was the genesis of a new field of study, child development, and influenced it for decades afterward in both the questions asked and the methodology used. More than 60 years later, Preyer's work (first published in German in 1882 and in English in 1888) was cited on no fewer than 55 pages in the highly regarded standard handbook of that time (Carmichael, 1954).

Motor behavior figured prominently in all of the baby biographies, with direct observation used to generate exquisite descriptions of the infant's achievements. Out of this approach grew the longitudinal studies of the 1930s that served as the foundation of a developing field, and are still cited in textbooks and research articles today. Most notable were Myrtle McGraw's famous twin study of Johnny and Jimmy (1935), Mary Shirley's scrupulously detailed account of 25 infants during the first two years of life (1931, 1933), the Berkeley Growth Study carried out by Nancy Bayley (1933a, 1935), and the monumental work by Arnold Gesell and colleagues (Gesell, 1928; Gesell & Thompson, 1934). The work by Bayley and Gesell led to the development of infant scales of normative mental and motor development (Bayley, 1933a, 1933b, 1935, 1936; Gesell & Amatruda, 1941). The Bayley Scales were standardized and updated in 1993. The infant scales rely on motor activity to reveal mental development and consist of items such as stacking cubes, grasping a small pellet, and so on.

Although motor development occupied center stage during these early years of the field of child development, by the 1950s interest had greatly waned and by 1960 it was not viewed as a worthwhile pursuit for research. In discussing why the study of motor behavior fell out of favor, Thelen (1995) suggested that our forebears had done their work too well. Their meticulous documentations of all aspects of motor development, the determination of "motor milestones," and descriptions of stages in development left modern investigators with nowhere to go. Another factor that undoubtedly led to the fall in popularity of McGraw, Gesell, and other pioneers was their strong emphasis on maturation as an explanation for behavioral development (Clark & Whitall, 1989b; Thelen, 1987). Today maturation is rejected as an adequate explanatory process but both McGraw and Gesell were pushing against the dominant theme of behaviorism of their day (Senn, 1975). As such they represented an important countervailing influence against strict environmentalism. Nor were these pioneers so single-minded as to give maturation full control over development. Although their research was often directed at showing how ineffective training (i.e., the environment) was on acquisition of skills (Gesell & Thompson, 1929; McGraw, 1935), they never denied the interaction between heredity and environment. Gesell (1954) noted, "Growth is a unifying concept which resolves the dualism of heredity and environment. Environmental factors support, inflect, and modify; but they do not generate the progressions of development" (p. 358).

Into the theoretical vacuum following the 1950s fell J. McVicker Hunt's influential book, *Intelligence and Experience* (1961) which immediately struck a chord that resounded throughout and beyond academia into social programs such as Head Start. Piagetian theory was embraced and research turned sharply toward cognitive and perceptual development as more exciting pursuits. A final factor in the demise of interest in motor behavior may have been that it did not live up to its promise as an early index of intellectual development. The scales of infant development devised by Bayley and Gesell did not predict later intellectual development. In fact, the correlations between scores on infant scales and later IQ were so low that mid-parent IQ was a better predictor of the infant's future IQ than the infant's own score on the infant test. Many valid reasons were put forth but the failure of infant test scores to predict later mental development may have led to disenchantment not only with the usefulness of infant tests but with motor behavior in general as a theoretically worthwhile topic of study.

The resurgence of interest in motor development began in the 1970s. It was influenced by the growing interest in adult motor behavior, and spurred on a great deal by the work of Bernstein (1967). In their review of the history of motor development, Clark and Whitall (1989b) refer to the time from 1970 to the present as the "Process-Oriented Period." In the 1970s, there was increasing interest in motor development but the research remained descriptive and focused on traditional motor skills. A few psychologists, most notably Connolly (1970) and Bruner (1973), called for more interest in skill learning, approaching it as a perceptual-cognitive process. Bruner (1969) emphasized the role of exploratory behavior and intentionality in the acquisition of skills. In taking this perspective, Bruner pulled together Piaget's (1952) recognition of exploratory behavior as a motivating factor in infant development with Bernstein's (1967) characterization of movement as being neither reflexive nor random. Rather, action was seen as taking into account intentionality, or the prospective nature of the action.

Foundations of Contemporary Research

The theme of exploration was proposed as a driving force in infant behavior, beginning with Piaget (1952). The view of the infant as an active agent in the environment is an important and lasting legacy of Piagetian theory. The importance of exploratory behavior also falls directly out of the Gibsonian concept of affordance (J. Gibson, 1979) because exploratory behavior has all of the components of an affordance: perception, action, and as E. Gibson puts it, a "knowledge-gathering aspect" (E. Gibson, 1988, p. 5). E. Gibson (1988) sees the motivation for exploratory behavior as intrinsic to the infant, with external reinforcement being unimportant as a motivating agent. Cognitive development comes about as a result of the infant's spontaneous exploratory behavior and the knowledge acquired from this exploration of the environment.

Piaget and Gibson present somewhat contrasting views on the development of exploratory behaviors. They agree on its origin (it is intrinsic to the infant) and its function (to gain knowledge of the world). They differ in how they view the abilities of the newborn. E. Gibson assumes that the sensorimotor systems are somewhat coordinated from birth, whereas Piaget conceptualized visual, auditory, and haptic senses as initially uncoordinated but becoming unified through experience. E. Gibson proposes that newborn action is directed toward *external* exploration or the world, while Piaget asserted newborns did not differentiate between themselves and the world. Finally, Piaget viewed

newborn behavior as primarily reflexive, responding to external stimuli in a somewhat compulsory manner. E. Gibson sees behavior as "immature and unskilled" (E. Gibson, 1988) but nevertheless spontaneous and intrinsically driven, although affected by the environment. One example she gives is that newborn sucking can be manipulated by reinforcing high amplitude sucks to produce visual stimulation (Siqueland & DeLucia, 1969). Piaget described many variations in sucking in the first month of life but attributed the changes to accommodation of the reflex (1952, pp. 49–62). With regard to exploratory behavior, we should note that modulation of behavior in and of itself is not necessarily evidence of exploration or intentionality. Spinal animals and invertebrates will modulate their behavior (increase or decrease some response) with respect to reinforcement. Exploration should entail an active searching or variation in behavior that is not entirely due to some external change in the environment.

In comparing Piagetian and Gibsonian theories, Butterworth (1981) criticized Piagetian theory for not attributing a large enough role to perception. Butterworth described the Piagetian newborn as "locked into a role of proximal experience"; the newborn can only make reflexive responses to stimuli which come into direct contact with the body—sucking, rooting, reflexive grasping of objects placed in the hand. World knowledge must be constructed solely through experience. By contrast, the Gibsonian newborn's interaction with the environment is boosted by a more precocious sensitivity to perceptual information that does not have to be constructed by experience (J. Gibson, 1966, pp. 266–286). For example, texture gradients and occluding edges can specify depth directly; or the accretion and deletion of texture on a partially occluded, moving surface specifies the continuing existence of the unseen portion. These contrasting views of the infant from Piagetian and Gibsonian theories have led to different experimental paradigms and questions.

More recently, research on perceptuomotor development has also been conceptualized in terms of dynamic systems theory (Goldfield, 1995; Smith & Thelen, 1993; Thelen & Smith, 1994, and their chapter in Volume 1 of this *Handbook*). Much of this research as well as research inspired by Piagetian and Gibsonian views will be covered in the subsequent sections of this chapter. We will emphasize research from the beginning of the 1980s to the present, which encompasses the most productive period in the history of motor development since the golden era of the 1930s. Today's research differs from that in the former era in methods, in theory, and in the questions asked. With regard to methods, McGraw and Gesell's cinematography has given way to videotape and computer-assisted motion analysis systems. Nor do we attempt to accelerate performance by extensively training one group or one twin on motor tasks to compare with an untrained group or twin. In theory, we have moved beyond trying to pit maturation and learning against one another, and our questions couple perception and action inextricably. What today's researchers do have in common with their forebears is a dedication toward meticulous data gathering, a theoretical framework for explaining the data, and finally an interest in the whole child shown by the tying together of perception, action, and cognition.

BASIC CONCEPTS AND METHODS

The renewed interest in the study of motor development is largely attributable to the adoption of new concepts and methods by developmental researchers (Lockman & Thelen, 1993). At least some of these conceptual and methodological innovations are borrowed from allied fields such as biomechanics, neuroscience, and dynamics, and include new terms and procedures that are quite likely to be unfamiliar to the average reader. For this reason, we include this section as a reader's guide to a few of the key terms and methods that are necessary for understanding recent studies in the literature. Readers interested in more extensive discussions of these new concepts should consult one of the excellent tutorials that have been written in the past decade (e.g., Goldfield, 1995; Jeka & Kelso, 1989; Kelso, 1995; Thelen & Smith, 1994; Turvey, 1990).

Coordination and Control

In satisfying everyday demands, we engage in a multitude of coordinated actions, ranging from simple acts such as pointing or reaching to complex acts such as driving or playing the piano. The dictionary defines coordination as bringing multiple and different parts into proper relation with one another. For humans, the coordination of multiple components is a formidable task involving almost 800 muscles that act to generate and dissipate energy at approximately 100 joints (Enoka, 1988). If we make the simplifying assumption that each of these joints is a simple hinge joint, like the elbow, then coordinated actions would involve 100 mechanical degrees of freedom, each determined by two states, position and velocity (Turvey, 1990).

Reducing Mechanical Degrees of Freedom

Bernstein (1967) proposed that controlling the large number of degrees of freedom involved in a movement was accomplished by reducing the number of variables or parameters that require direct control. This reduction in degrees of freedom is accomplished by functionally linking groups of muscles often spanning several joints into a task specific unit, commonly referred to as a *synergy* or *coordinative structure* (Tuller, Turvey, & Fitch, 1982). Consider the example of aiming a gun to shoot at a target. Any change in the wrist or the shoulder will cause the bullet to deviate from the target, but skilled pistol shooters, unlike novice shooters, compensate for a change in the wrist with equal and opposite changes in the shoulder (Arutyunyan, Gurfinkel, & Mirsky, 1969). This compensation comes about with practice as the two joints become functionally related and start working as a single unit.

During coordinated movements, these muscle linkages are defined by a specific *temporal patterning* between the mechanical degrees of freedom. In other words, these linkages capture the topological rather than the metric features of movements. For example, the flexion (i.e., bending) and extension (i.e., straightening) of the knee show a stable and repetitive relation to the flexion and extension of the hip and ankle during normal walking or running (Figure 2.1). If a synergy or coordinative structure is perturbed by some

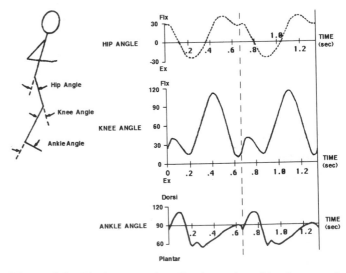

Figure 2.1 Flexion-extension (in degrees) at hip, knee, and ankle joints during treadmill running. Two complete cycles are shown. Note the consistency in the phase relations between the three joints. From "The biomechanics of lower extremity action in distance runners," by P. R. Cavanaugh, 1987, *Foot and Ankle Quarterly, 7,* pp. 197–205. Copyright © 1987 by Data Trace Medical Publishers, Inc. Reprinted with permission.

internal or external force, then all of the mechanical degrees of freedom (including those not directly involved in the action) will be adjusted quickly to preserve the goal of the task.

Constraints

If functional linkages between all degrees of freedom were equiprobable, then the development of coordinative structures would constitute an overwhelmingly complex task. Instead, there exist multiple constraints or limitations on the ways in which different limb movements are configured. Three general categories of constraints (organismic, environmental, and task) interact to determine the optimal pattern of coordination for any activity (Newell, 1986). The first category includes *neural and anatomical constraints.* It is well established that neural patterns of excitation constrain the organization of actions (Prechtl, 1984), but it is also clear that other factors relating to body composition constrain the development of new actions. For example, changes in body size and strength lead to new performatory and exploratory behaviors, such as kicking and crawling (Freedland & Bertenthal, 1994; Thelen, Fisher, & Ridley-Johnson, 1984). The second category, *environmental constraints,* includes physical as well as cultural constraints. For example, gravity will interact with the orientation of the child to differentially constrain configurations of limb movements. Likewise, locomotor and grasping patterns are constrained by the material properties of surfaces, such as hardness or smoothness. In addition, cross-cultural studies reveal that different rearing patterns lead to significant variations in the onset of early coordinated behaviors, such as sitting or reaching (Bril, Zack, & Nkounkou-Hombessa, 1989; Reed & Bril, 1995). Finally, *task constraints* relate to the goals of the action and organize the pattern of limb movements in such a way as to optimize performance. For example, the transition from walking to running is defined by the goal of minimizing energy consumption (Diedrich & Warren, 1995).

Tuning a Coordinative Structure

It is useful to distinguish between coordination and control of behaviors, especially since these two processes follow different developmental trajectories (see Locomotion section). When a coordinative structure is active, a family of functions defined by an invariant spatial-temporal organization of limb movements is established. Consider, for example, the alternating pattern of the lower limbs during walking. In order for walking to remain context specific, it is necessary that specific parameters controlling limb movements, such as displacement, amplitude, and speed, are adjusted or tuned to the exigencies of the local conditions. This tuning depends on the perception of the intrinsic (e.g., adjustable springlike muscles) and extrinsic (e.g., material properties of objects and surfaces in a gravitational force field) conditions available during the execution of the action. Much of the tuning or control of the coordinative structure is accomplished by autonomous systems, such as feedback from receptors signalling current limb positions (Turvey, 1990). Although this tuning is accomplished autonomously, the setting of the parameters for optimizing performance is learned through practice and experience (Newell, 1986). From this perspective, *skill* represents the optimal parameterization of a coordinative structure, and *control* represents the process by which the action is parameterized (Kugler, Kelso, & Turvey, 1980).

Biomechanical Analysis of Human Movements

Recent advances in understanding the organization and function of human movements have also benefitted from the application of biomechanical techniques. These techniques were developed to study the biomechanics of human movement, defined as the application of mechanical and biophysical principles to the movements of the musculoskeletal system (Bernstein, 1967). The variables included in a biomechanical analysis are derived from multiple disciplines including kinematics, kinetics, anthropometry, and electromyography (Winter, 1979). A brief discussion of these variables and their measurement is presented next.

Kinematics

By definition, *kinematics* is that part of mechanics concerned with the description of motion (Resnick & Halliday, 1977). *Kinetics,* or the dynamics of motion, is concerned with the forces that cause an object to move. As will become apparent, it is best to discuss the application of these two approaches to the study of human movements separately.

The measurement of human movements began toward the end of the last century with the development of photographic and cine techniques to capture human and animal motion. Marey (1894) used a photographic "gun" to record limb displacements in human locomotion, and at approximately the same time Muybridge (reprinted, 1955) developed a technique to sequentially trigger multiple cameras to record human and animal gait. More recently, movie film and video techniques were developed to record and measure the two- and three-dimensional displacements of the limbs during movements. The tracking of specific anatomical landmarks is accomplished by placing light reflectant material on the joints and limbs. A slightly different technique involves optoelectric markers, which require subjects to wear special lights (e.g., infrared emitting diodes) on each anatomical landmark. The lights are flashed sequentially and detected by a special camera that calculates the location (x,y) of the light. When two or more cameras are used with these techniques, it is possible to reconstruct the third dimension by calculating the disparity of the image from one camera field to the other, similar to the process by which depth is derived from binocular disparity by the human visual system. The most recent technology involves electromagnetic coils that are placed on the limbs of the subject, and provide information about the three-dimensional displacement and rotation of the limbs. Unlike camera techniques, the collection of data with coils is not interrupted by temporary occlusions of markers, and thus requires no interpolation of missing marker positions. One limitation of both coils and optoelectric techniques is that the locomotor movements of the subject are constrained because they require wire connections between the markers and the data collection equipment.

The pattern or topography of movements is reconstructed from the film or video by time sampling the three-dimensional trajectories of the markers located on anatomical landmarks, such as center of gravity of body segments, centers of rotation of joints, extremities of limb segments, and anatomical prominences, such as locations on the spine (Winter, 1979). Kinematic variables are calculated from the time-sampled data and include linear and angular displacements, velocities, and accelerations of joints and limb segments. Each of these variables can be plotted in two- or three-dimensional graphs as a time series of data to reveal how a variable, such as position or velocity, changes over time. For example, Figure 2.1 shows the joint angle displacements of the hip, knee, and ankle plotted as a function of time. A complete kinematic description of even simple movements requires an enormous volume of data and multiple graphs, which explains why most assessments focus on only a subset of the available data.

Anthropometry

This discipline is concerned with the physical measurements of the body and limbs. Biomechanical analyses require data regarding the masses of limb segments, location of mass centers, segment lengths, centers of rotation, moments of inertia (resistance to any change in angular velocity), and so on. The accuracy of any of these analyses depends critically on the anthropometric measures that are available (Winter, 1979; Zernicke & Schneider, 1993). Some of these measures for adults were determined directly from cadavers; others were determined through measurement of segment volumes in conjunction with density tables (Winter, 1979). It is also possible to approximate these body segment parameters with mathematical models. For example, Hatze (1980) models the human body with 17 segments varying in geometric shape.

Until recently, no body segment data were available for infants, and only one study reported data for children over four years of age (Jensen, 1986). To redress this situation, Schneider, Zernicke, Ulrich, Jensen, and Thelen (1990) collected anthropometric data on a group of 18 infants and developed a modified model of the adult body (Hatze, 1980). In conjunction with measurements taken on additional infants, this modified model was used to calculate the anthropometric inertia parameters (e.g., masses, center-of-mass locations, and transverse moments of inertia) for upper and lower limb segments. Regression equations that predict limb inertia parameters were developed so that estimates of these parameters can now be calculated based on an infant's age, body mass, and the length and circumference of the segment (Schneider & Zernicke, 1992).

Kinetics

This branch of biomechanics is concerned with the internal and external forces that cause a movement. Internal forces are produced by muscle activity, ligaments, friction in the muscles or joints, and motion-dependent forces that arise from the interactions among the mechanically linked segments. External forces include gravity, ground reaction forces, and active forces produced by other moving agents, such as a tackler in football. Kinetic analyses are conducted to measure a number of variables, including the moments of force produced by muscles crossing a joint, the mechanical power flowing from those same muscles, and energy changes that result from that power flow (Winter, 1979). It is also common to analyze the ground reaction forces produced by the body while locomoting or maintaining some other form of postural equilibrium with the environment (Bertenthal, 1990).

The process by which reaction forces and muscle moments are calculated requires a biomechanical link-segment model to specify how different forces are related. In this simplified model of the human body, joints are replaced by hinges, and segments are replaced by masses located at mass centers (Winter, 1979). If accurate kinematic and anthropometric measures are provided and external forces are also known, then it is possible to calculate the joint reaction forces and muscle moments using an inverse dynamics approach (Zernicke & Schneider, 1993). In essence, this approach applies Newton's Second Law (F = ma) to derive the force generated from the product of the mass and acceleration.

It is important to appreciate that the complex, multijoint organization of most actions means that multiple forces contribute to the movement of a limb. For example, the angular acceleration of the shoulder depends not only on the torques produced at the shoulder joint but also on the motion-dependent torques of mechanically linked segments, such as the angular velocity and acceleration of the forearm (Soechting & Flanders, 1991). A common method for determining the relative contribution of different forces contributing to the movement of a limb is to apply the method of inverse dynamics and then partition the torques into four factors: net joint torque, gravitational torque, motion-dependent torques, and generalized muscle torque (Schneider et al., 1990). The net joint torque is the sum of all the positive and negative torque components that act at a joint (Net joint torque = Gravitational torque + Motion-dependent torque + Generalized muscle torque). It is possible to calculate directly the net, gravitational, and motion-dependent torques; the generalized muscle torque is then derived as the residual in this analysis. The forces corresponding to generalized muscle torque include not only active muscle contractions, but also passive deformations of muscles, tendons, ligaments, and other periarticular tissues (Zernicke & Schneider, 1993). This procedure is very useful for determining whether a child or adult is successful in coordinating both the active and passive forces contributing to a limb movement (Figure 2.2).

It is also possible to measure the total force exerted by the body on the ground during sitting, standing, walking, running, and so on by calculating the ground reaction force from bi- or tridirectional force transducers that are mounted at right angles to each other on a force plate (Winter, 1979). This force is a three-dimensional vector consisting of a vertical component, and two shear components corresponding to the anterior-posterior and medial-lateral directions (Bertenthal, 1990). One standard measure derived from the force plate is the center of pressure (COP) which is measured by calculating the relative distribution of the forces on the plate and then dividing by

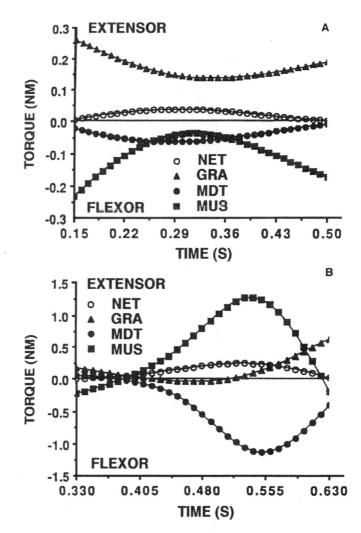

Figure 2.2 Hip joint motion during kicking by 3-month-old infants. Note how the different components (net, muscle, gravitational, and total motion-dependent torques) change for representative low-intensity (A) and high-intensity (B) kicks. From "Understanding movement control in infants through the analysis of limb intersegmental dynamics," by K. Schneider et al., 1990, *Journal of Motor Behavior, 22,* pp. 493–520. Copyright © 1990 by Heldref. Reprinted with permission.

the total vertical force. If all four forces are equal, then the COP is at the exact center of the plate.

The COP is often used for assessing postural equilibrium in standing or sitting individuals. Figure 2.3a shows how COP changes over time as a child sits on a force plate. As can be seen, the COP is not random but instead shows a periodic oscillation around the center of the plate. It is possible to partition the time-sampled COP into the different frequencies contributing to this cyclic behavior with spectral analysis (Figure 2.3b). The number and amplitude of

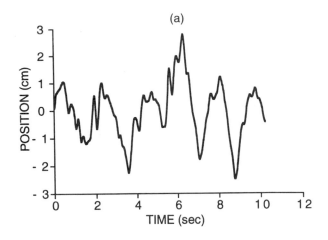

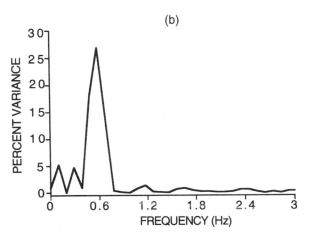

Figure 2.3 Postural sway in time and frequency domains. (a) depicts changes in center of pressure (COP) as a function of time. (b) depicts the power spectral density function for the COP data. Redrawn from "Perception-action coupling in the development of visual control of posture," by B. I. Bertenthal et al., *Journal of Experiment Psychology: Human Perception and Performance*. In Press. Copyright by the American Psychological Association. Reprinted with permission.

unique frequencies contributing to the spectrum provide an index of the stability and consistency of the postural response (Bertenthal, 1990).

Electromyography

The electrical signal associated with the contraction of a muscle is known as the *electromyogram* (EMG). Muscle tissue conducts electrical potentials similarly to the way axons transmit action potentials (Winter, 1979). Electrodes placed on the surface of a muscle or inside the muscle tissue (indwelling electrodes) will record the algebraic sum of all the electrical signals transmitted along the

muscle fibers at that point in time. Biological amplifiers are required for measuring EMGs, which introduce potential artifacts into the signal. It is important to insure that the signal is noise free and undistorted by the amplification. Winter (1979) discusses a number of important considerations when determining the level of EMG amplification. Once the EMG signal is amplified, it is often transformed by means of rectification or integration before specific analyses are conducted. Rectification of the signal involves generating the absolute value of the EMG, usually with a positive polarity. Integration involves measuring the area under the curve produced by the signal. The simplest form of integration begins measuring at some preset time and continues until muscle activation ceases.

It is important to appreciate that measures of muscle activity do not translate directly into specifying how much movement is generated at a joint. Recall that the torques generated at a joint include not only muscle activation but also motion-dependent and gravitational torques. Moreover, the muscle activation necessary to produce the same torque at a given joint changes as the joint angle changes. For example, the torque produced by the elbow flexors is greatest in midrange position (elbow angle = 1.57 rad) and least at full extension and full flexion because the length of the muscles controlling the joint changes (Enoka, 1988). Finally, the temporal patterning of the muscles is critical for determining the degree of movement. Typically, muscles will show alternating patterns of activity and quiescence when movements are produced efficiently and flexibly (see Figure 2.4a). Nevertheless, co-contraction or concurrent activity of agonist (i.e., activity causing the movement) and antagonist (i.e., activity opposing the movement) muscles is sometimes observed (see Figure 2.4b) and this activation pattern has the mechanical effect of making a joint stiffer (i.e., movement becomes more difficult). Co-contractions are produced often when learning a new task (Enoka, 1988), which suggests that this pattern of muscle activity will be especially common in infants and young children who are learning many new motor skills. For all of these reasons, it is important to exercise caution in interpreting the functional implications of EMG data.

Addendum

It is becoming increasingly common for developmental researchers to apply biomechanical techniques to the study of motor behaviors. On balance, this trend is encouraging because it provides greater opportunity for precisely exploring the processes mediating perception-action systems.

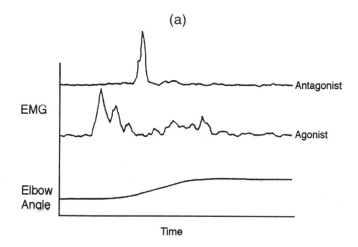

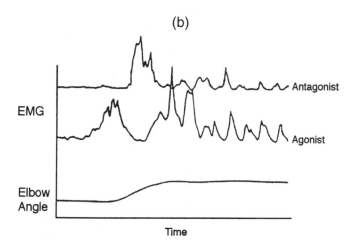

Figure 2.4 A three-burst pattern of EMG activity for an elbow-flexion movement. The EMG data are rectified and filtered. (a) A movement displaying a distinct pattern of activation. (b) A movement displaying co-contraction toward its termination. Reprinted, by permission, from R. M. Enoka, 1988, *Neuromechanical Basis of Kinesiology* (Champaign, IL: Human Kinetics Publishers), 1996.

Nevertheless, it is important to recognize that the advent of these new data collection techniques makes us increasingly vulnerable to becoming mired in data. For this reason, researchers should exercise considerable caution and forethought before investing in these techniques, and evaluate whether the added precision is truly necessary for answering the questions motivating the study. It is also important for researchers to become sufficiently knowledgable about the methods and techniques that they are employing to avoid serious confounds or misinterpretations. A number of excellent reference books are now available for researchers who are planning to conduct biomechanical analyses of

human movements (Allard, Stokes, & Blanchi, 1995; Enoka, 1988; Vaughan, Davis, & O'Connor, 1991; Winter, 1990).

POSTURE AND ORIENTATION

With this section, we begin our review of contemporary research on the development of posture, reaching, and locomotion. We have been necessarily selective, and do not provide a comprehensive summary of research on motor development. Our intended goal is to illustrate how specific actions change over time as a function of multiple neural, biomechanical, and task-related factors. We begin with the development of posture because this action system is foundational to all other movements.

In most early theories (e.g., Magnus, 1925), posture was viewed as a static state concerned with the maintenance of equilibrium by the body while sitting, standing, walking, and so on. These theories were focused on the orientation of the head relative to the trunk, because this orientation affects the inner ear and neck muscles that produce stimuli that modulate the antigravity responses of the trunk and limbs. Unlike more complex movements of the body, posture was treated as a mechanical process that was reflexively assembled from the summation of all the antigravity stretch reflexes in the body. From this perspective, it was unnecessary to consider posture when studying motor development, because posture and movement were concerned with different functions and were controlled by separate mechanisms (Reed, 1989).

Research conducted during the past two decades suggests that this traditional view is no longer tenable. Recall that human movements are the products of many different factors including neural mechanisms, environmental and task constraints, body proportions, and posture (e.g., Bertenthal, 1996; Thelen, 1995). For present purposes, we wish to emphasize the contribution of posture. Each movement is nested within a hierarchy of support structures or postures, and its organization will invariably change as a function of the specific posture selected by the individual. For example, the muscular forces necessary to reach for an object will change as a function of the passive forces (e.g., gravity, intersegmental forces) associated with whether a person is sitting or standing or lying down (Jensen, Ulrich, Thelen, Schneider, & Zernicke, 1994). The functional relation between posture and movements is nowhere better demonstrated than during early infancy when the appearance of specific responses, such as reaching or tracking a moving target, is contingent on the postural support supplied to the infant. One of the earliest and most dramatic examples of this contingency is the clinical observations of Amiel-Tison and Grenier (1986) who reported that 1- and 2-month-old infants will produce mature reaching patterns when their heads are properly supported and positioned.

It is now clear that posture should not be conceptualized as a static response to gravity, but rather as a dynamic process in which all the forces acting on the body are controlled in a flexible fashion assembled by the current task (Reed, 1989). This control demands that the body forces are perceptually modulated to local conditions. It is well-established that proprioceptive stimulation produced by the skin, joints, and muscles, and stimulation of the vestibular organs, especially the semicircular canals, contributes to postural responses (Howard, 1986). In addition, visual and auditory information provide proprioceptive sources of stimulation (J. Gibson, 1966) that contribute to the control of posture (Bertenthal & Rose, 1995). The availability of multiple sources of information to detect a change in conditions increases the likelihood of successfully controlling posture.

Systematic research on the development of posture is relatively new and fragmented. In this review we focus on developmental changes in muscle activation patterns or response synergies associated with different postures and also on the development of perceptual control of posture. A corollary focus concerns how posture interacts with the functioning of other exploratory behaviors, such as gaze stabilization.

Perceptual Control of Posture

This field is dominated by studies investigating postural compensations to optical flow; thus we begin with a brief discussion of the optical information available for specifying self-motions. When objects move in the visual field they produce local deformations in the geometric structure of the optical flow field that are congruent with their speed and direction. By contrast, movements of the eyes and head produce global changes in the structure of the optical flow field that are lawfully related to the speed and direction in which the observer is moving (J. Gibson, 1979). Stationary observers report compelling sensations of self-motion or vection when stimulated with visual fields of moving texture simulating either translation or rotation of the observer (Andersen, 1986).

Visual Control

One of the first reports of illusory self-motion dates back to an old fairground device known as the "haunted swing." People entered a chamber, and were presented with artificial scenery that moved back and forth outside the windows. The perception of the moving scenery induced a compelling illusion that the chamber was rocking, and participants experienced all the sensations of real movement, including loss of postural stability and vertigo (Wood, 1895). A similar procedure for inducing postural sway was introduced many years later by Lishman and Lee (1973). Participants stand on a stable floor surrounded by a large three-sided enclosure with a ceiling (dubbed "swinging room") that swings back and forth along a path that is parallel to the direction of gaze. They typically report that the walls are not moving, but that they themselves are swaying. The perceived direction of self-motion is opposite to the direction of the optical flow which induces participants to sway in synchrony with the flow to maintain postural equilibrium.

The first study to test infants' postural responses to optical flow was conducted by Lee and Aronson (1974) who tested infants (13- to 16-months-old) just beginning to stand in the swinging room. (A version of this apparatus used by Bertenthal and Bai (1989) is depicted in Figure 2.5. Note that it is referred to as a "moving room" since

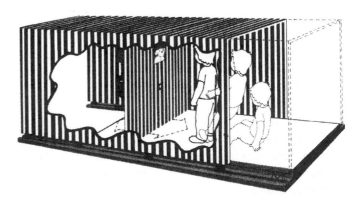

Figure 2.5 A moving room. Depicted inside the room is a child swaying backward in response to the room moving toward the child. This compensatory response would occur if the child perceived the optical flow produced by the room movement as specifying self-motion (i.e., a forward sway) rather than motion of the room. From "Infants' sensitivity to optical flow for controlling posture," by B. I. Bertenthal & D. L. Bai, 1989, *Developmental Psychology, 25*, pp. 936–945. Copyright © 1989 by the American Psychological Association. Reprinted with permission.

the walls are fastened to wheels that glide along a track.) Results from this investigation revealed that infants would compensate to the visually specified sway by responding with a sway, stagger, or fall in the appropriate direction. This finding was subsequently replicated by Butterworth and Hicks (1977) and extended by Bertenthal and Bai (1989) and Stoffregen, Schmuckler, and Gibson (1987) to show that partial flow on the sides of the visual field was sufficient to induce a postural compensation.

Since the majority of infants tested in the above studies were already walking, it remained unclear whether the visual perception of body motion necessitated experience with locomotion (cf. Butterworth & Hicks, 1977). Additional research testing younger infants disconfirms any notion that self-produced locomotor experiences are necessary for the visual perception of self-motions. Butterworth and Hicks (1977) observed that 11-month-old infants who sat in a moving room would lean in the appropriate direction when the walls moved. Bertenthal and Bai (1989) replicated this finding with a more quantitative measure of postural sway. In this study, 5-, 7-, and 9-month-old infants were passively supported in a bicycle seat, and displacements of posture were monitored by pressure transducers located under the seat. The findings revealed that 9-month-old infants showed directionally appropriate postural responses when the whole room or just the side walls moved; 7-month-old infants responded systematically when the whole room moved; and 5-month-old infants showed no evidence of systematic responding to the visual information.

One interpretation for the preceding findings is that infants are not sensitive to optical flow for specifying self-motion until 7 to 9 months of age. Yet, another possibility is that 5-month-old infants lacked the necessary muscle strength and coordination to control their own posture (mean age for sitting without support is 6.6 months, Bayley, 1969), but perceived the optical flow as specifying self-motion. This latter interpretation is apparently correct, because infants as young as 2-months-old show changes in backward head pressure when stimulated in a moving room (Butterworth & Pope, 1983).

Additional findings reveal that even neonates show directional adjustments of their head in response to peripheral stimulation from an oscillating flowfield (Jouen, 1988). This head posture is modulated by both the direction and velocity of the visual stimulation (Jouen, Lepecq, & Gapenne, in press). Mean amplitude of head responses increased linearly with the velocity of the optical flow. Interestingly, adults show a similar gain in the amplitude of

their postural sway as a function of the velocity of the optical flow (Lestienne, Soechting, & Berthoz, 1977).

These last findings with neonates are especially provocative because they reveal visual modulation of head posture long before infants control their heads without support (mean age is 2.5 months, Bayley, 1969). It thus appears that visual information combines with proprioceptive and vestibular information to control head posture even before the posture is completely functional. (A similar conclusion is true for sitting as discussed below.) Additional evidence for the intersensory control of head posture in young infants (1 to 4.5 months old) is revealed by the finding that head righting responses to vestibular stimulation vary with the orientation of the visual information (Jouen, 1984). Infants' responses to the combination of visual and vestibular information showed improvements with experience in head control. This interaction between perceptual control and experience is a theme that appears often in the contemporary literature (Bertenthal, 1996).

Multimodal Control

One puzzle presented by the above findings concerns why infants should respond primarily to visual information when somatosensory and vestibular information conflict with this information and specify either a different orientation and/or no movement. Lee and Lishman (1975) suggested that visual information dominates when learning to control a new posture, because the coupling between proprioception and muscular responses is tuned initially by visual information. If true, then postural compensations to the moving room should decrease with age, which was reported by Bertenthal and Bai (1987).

In spite of this finding, it is difficult to reconcile the visual dominance position with recent findings that young children fail to show an increase in sway amplitude when standing in the dark versus the light (Ashmead & McCarty, 1991; Hayes & Riach, 1989; Odenrick & Sandstedt, 1984). By contrast, adults show significantly more sway in the dark versus the light (Ashmead & McCarty, 1991). The improved stability shown by adults in the light is most likely attributable to their using the retinal image to stabilize posture. By minimizing the retinal slip of a fixated stationary object, observers minimize their own postural sway (Paulus, Straube, & Brandt, 1984). It is conceivable that children find it more difficult to fixate on a stationary object, which might explain why they do not show an advantage while standing in the light. Some support for this hypothesis was offered by Riach and Starkes (1987) who reported that young children show a greater number of saccades while fixating on a stationary object.

A more compelling reason for questioning the visual dominance position is that recent analyses suggest that dominance is context specific and not hard-wired into the postural control system (Bertenthal, 1996). Postural compensations are typically specified by multimodal information, but thresholds for detecting stimulation differ across sensory systems (Howard, 1986). For this reason, it would be maladaptive to seek consensus across sensory systems before responding to information specifying a change in body position. When an individual detects that support is perturbed, it is not important to determine first which sensory input channel specified a change in body position. The goal is simply to restore equilibrium, and this involves scaling the compensatory forces to the perceived displacement.

How does the infant learn that different sources of sensory input are equivalent and converge on the same motor response? If it is necessary to first coordinate sensory information across modalities before a context specific response is initiated, then it would appear necessary to learn the relations between the different inputs before appropriate compensations are produced. Indeed, this form of learning to coordinate different modalities is central to Piaget's (1952, 1954) theory of sensorimotor development. Yet, current evidence suggests that this form of associative learning is unnecessary (Bertenthal, 1996). An alternative position is that all sensory inputs related to self-motion are represented in a common amodal format that maps directly onto an appropriate pattern of muscle activations (Lee, 1993; Warren, 1990). This format insures that all sensory information is transformed into the same body-scaled information necessary for modulating the forces of the body to perform coordinated movements (Bertenthal & Rose, 1995; Savelsbergh & van der Kamp, 1993). As such, multiple sources of sensory information increase the likelihood of an adaptive response.

Development of Postural Synergies

Casual observation of young children reveals that they are posturally less stable than adults while standing. These differences are not, however, attributable to any qualitative changes in postural synergies used for controlling balance. In two studies (Forssberg & Nashner, 1982; Shumway-Cook & Woollacott, 1985), children ranging in age from 1.3 to 10 years old were tested with a movable platform and visual surround, and the measures included EMGs, reac-

tion forces, and body motions. On each trial, children's balance was disturbed as the platform moved suddenly in the anterior or posterior direction. Forssberg and Nashner (1982) reported that postural adjustments shown by the youngest children were similar to those produced by adults (using an ankle strategy in which balance adjustments are made at the ankle joint and the individual sways as an inverted pendulum) except that they were larger in amplitude and more variable. Leg muscle responses showed the same distal (lower leg) to proximal (upper leg) muscle activation pattern shown by adults. Shumway-Cook and Woollacott (1985) also observed that the youngest children in their sample showed evidence of organized leg muscle responses to postural perturbations. However, the muscle responses were again larger in amplitude and longer in latency and duration than those of adults (Figure 2.6). Curiously, 4- to 6-year-old children showed postural response synergies that were more variable and longer in latency than those observed in younger or older children. Currently, no definitive interpretation for this increased variability is available, but one possibility is that children at this age are exploring new strategies for maintaining balance (cf. Woollacott & Sveistrup, 1992).

One additional finding from these studies (Forssberg & Nashner, 1982; Shumway-Cook & Woollacott, 1985) is relevant to the previous discussion on multimodal control of posture. Both studies report that children at all ages were successful in maintaining balance when either visual or somatosensory information was absent. By contrast, children less than 7 years old were not able to balance successfully when both somatosensory and visual information were removed. Interestingly, these children did show the correct muscle activation pattern, but their latency to respond prevented them from remaining within their stability limits (Forssberg & Nashner, 1982). A possible interpretation for these findings is that young children are less sensitive to vestibular than to somatosensory or visual stimulation for detecting a postural perturbation. This interpretation should be viewed cautiously, however, because it is difficult to equate the stimulation across the different sensory conditions.

Transitions to New Postures

The preceding studies revealed only modest developmental changes in muscle response patterns once upright stance had developed. Other studies reveal more dramatic changes in the sequencing and timing of muscle responses during

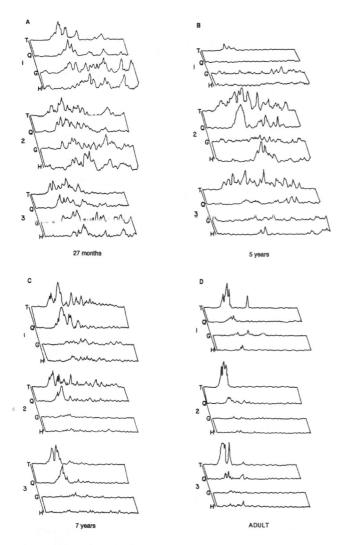

Figure 2.6 EMG patterns from three successive trials causing posterior sway. The adult (D) and the 7-year-old child (C) showed directionally specific short duration responses, with the stretched tibialis anterior (T) and quadriceps femoris (Q) muscles activated. The 27-month-old toddler (A) showed longer duration responses, with additional activation of the antagonist gastrocnemius (G) and hamstring (H) muscles. The 5-year-old child (B) showed considerable trial to trial variability. From "The growth of stability: Postural control from a developmental perspective," by A. Shumway-Cook & M. H. Woollacott, 1985, *Journal of Motor Behavior, 17*, pp. 131–147. Copyright © 1985 by Heldref. Reprinted with permission.

the development of new postures. For example, Woollacott and Sveistrup (1992) report a longitudinal study investigating infants' muscle response patterns between 7 to 15 months of age. At the onset of "pull-to-stand" behavior and then again at the onset of independent stance, response patterns showed increased variability followed by increased consistency and shorter latencies. As children gained additional experience with stance, they began to show more variability while exploring alternative response strategies, reminiscent of the behavior shown by 4- to 6-year-old children in the preceding research (Shumway-Cook & Woollacott, 1985).

Harbourne, Giuliani, and MacNeela (1993) conducted a longitudinal study on the development of sitting (mean onset age is 6.6 months, Bayley, 1969) in children between 2 and 5 months old. Children were initially supported around the trunk, and then released causing them to slump forward. Harbourne et al. reported that children younger than 4 months old showed considerable variability in the order of muscle activation, but that older infants showed a preferred pattern or synergy even though they could not yet sit without support. By contrast, Woollacott, Debu, and Mowatt (1987) report that children do not show a consistent postural response synergy while sitting until 8 months of age. Some additional support for this latter finding is provided by Hirschfeld and Forssberg (1994) who report a developmental dissociation between the activation of dorsal and ventral muscles. Children just beginning to sit independently and children not yet able to sit were tested for controlling balance while sitting on a movable platform. Following a backward sway, consistent patterns of ventral muscle activity in the hip, trunk, and neck were observed in both groups of infants. By contrast, dorsal muscles showed patterns of muscle activity following a forward sway, but only for the group capable of independent sitting. These results are difficult to reconcile with those reported by Harbourne et al. (1993), but seem more consistent with those reported by Woollacott et al. (1987). Apparently, the activation pattern of the dorsal muscles (i.e., inhibition) is fine-tuned by experience with sitting which would explain why Woollacott and Shumway-Cook did not observe a consistent postural synergy until one or more months following the onset of sitting.

A consistent theme in the preceding studies is that the development of the muscle response synergies necessary for maintaining balance do not emerge all at once and do not depend exclusively on neuromaturational development; practice and experience contribute to the spatial and temporal organization of the muscle activation patterns (Sveistrup & Woollacott, in press). A recent behavioral study on the visual control of sitting (Bertenthal, Rose, & Bai, in press) provides converging evidence for this conclusion. In this study, 5-, 7-, 9-, and 13-month-old infants were tested while seated on a force plate in a moving room that oscillated back and forth. Unlike most previous moving room studies, this task demanded that infants not only show directionally appropriate postural compensations, but also respond quickly and accurately to cyclic changes in the perceived direction of sway. By measuring the covariation (or entrainment) between the frequency of postural sway and the frequency of the wall movements, it was possible to assess the relative degree to which the visual information was scaled to the motor response. The results revealed that even 5-month-old infants showed some entrainment to the driving frequency of the walls, and this response became more consistent with age and sitting experience. It is noteworthy that posture was systematically modulated by the visual information even before infants could sit. Nevertheless, sitting experience and entrainment were highly correlated (see Rose & Bertenthal, 1995, for a replication and extension of this finding). Taken together, these findings suggest that multiple factors contribute to the control of sitting including the organization of muscle responses, practice, and sensorimotor coordination.

Nonlinear Dynamical Modeling

One limitation of the preceding research is that it rarely addresses the dynamics of postural control directly. For example, the study by Bertenthal et al. (in press) revealed a significant developmental improvement in postural control, but left unanswered whether this change reflected a quantitative improvement with practice and experience or rather a qualitative change in the underlying mechanisms. Recent analytic developments in the field of nonlinear dynamics are beginning to provide researchers with new tools for addressing these questions. It is possible to determine mathematically the number of parameters or dimensions that govern a dynamic control system by analyzing the time-sampled signal, for example, postural sway, produced by this system (see Kennel, Brown, & Abarbanel, 1992, for details). This dynamic modeling approach was followed recently to determine whether the previously collected data on postural sway revealed a different number of dimensions at different ages (Bertenthal, Boker, & Rose, 1995; Boker, Schreiber, Pompe, & Bertenthal, in press). The results revealed that the dimensionality of the postural control system did not change between 5 and 13 months of age, even though the residual noise in the data following removal of linear and nonlinear structure decreased. Taken together, these findings suggest that the structure of the control system does not change during the development of independent sitting, but it does become more stable.

It is difficult to find additional research applying nonlinear dynamical analyses to studies of motor development, but one noteworthy exception is the work of Robertson (1990) on cyclic fluctuations of spontaneous behavior in fetuses and infants. These spontaneous oscillations of motor activity occur in cycles of 1 to 4 minutes, but the period of oscillation is irregular (Robertson, 1989). In order to investigate whether this irregularity represents merely noise, or instead is attributable to the same dynamic system responsible for the observed cyclic oscillations, Robertson has pursued a program of nonlinear dynamic modeling and analysis of cyclic motility (see Robertson, Cohen, & Mayer-Kress, 1993, for details). In one recent experiment (Robertson, 1993), cyclic motor activity was studied at monthly intervals from 1 to 4 months after birth. Cyclic motility was measured with a nonlinear forecasting technique (Farmer & Sidorowich, 1987), and the results revealed that irregularity is not merely attributable to stochastic noise, but rather represents a state-specific property of the system that is developmentally stable. Before concluding this section, it is important to emphasize that these new studies emphasizing nonlinear dynamical analyses are preliminary and incomplete, but initial results are promising, especially because they offer new insights into noisy data.

Functional Significance of Posture

Early exploration of the world depends on the coordination of the head and eyes and hands (Bullinger, 1981; Trevarthen, 1984; von Hofsten, 1982). These actions require a nested hierarchy of stabilized systems in which the eyes and head are supported by the trunk in either a sitting or standing posture. It is for this reason that posture is fundamental to the functioning of these behaviors. We illustrate this relation by selectively reviewing research on posture and gaze stabilization.

Posture and Gaze Stabilization

The visual world of the infant is not stationary; some objects move frequently and so do the eyes and head. In order to process detailed information about objects, it is necessary for infants to maintain their line of gaze (i.e., imaginary line through the center of pupil and fovea) on the object (Daniel & Lee, 1990). Most studies on the development of gaze stabilization focus exclusively on the pattern of eye movements when the whole visual field moves (optokinetic response)

(Atkinson & Braddick, 1981; Kremenitzer, Vaughan, Kurtzberg, & Dowling, 1979) or when a small target moves (visual pursuit) (Aslin, 1981; Shea & Aslin, 1990). It is important to remember, however, that the eyes, head, neck, and trunk are mechanically linked and must be coordinated to achieve gaze stabilization. Studies investigating the interactions between these different reference frames (Paillard, 1991) reveal that the development of gaze stabilization depends on this coordination.

Bullinger (1983) reports that visual tracking of objects during the first month is achieved largely through rotation of the head and trunk together. As a consequence, visual tracking is spatially constrained and is often disrupted because of the poor postural stability of the trunk (Bullinger, 1981; Roucoux, Culee, & Roucoux, 1983). By 3 months, visual tracking is independent of the trunk, and the stabilized trunk serves as a base of support for visual pursuit (Bullinger, 1991). In addition, the upper limbs are no longer constrained by the movement of the head so that the hands become free to capture and manipulate objects. It is conjectured by Bullinger (1991) that these achievements are important prerequisites for the development of eye-hand coordination.

Once control of the head and trunk become individuated, infants' tracking of objects with their heads develops rapidly and is equal to the performance of adults by 25 to 28 weeks (Daniel & Lee, 1990; Owen & Lee, 1986). An important motivation for the rapid development of head movements to stabilize gaze is that reaching is developing during this same period. According to Daniel and Lee (1990) reaching for objects improves with gaze stabilization because objects are better localized with respect to the trunk (Biguer, Jeannerod, & Prablanc, 1982).

Unlike head movements, the coupling of eye movements to the target remains much less precise during this period of development (Daniel & Lee, 1990; Owen & Lee, 1986). This finding is somewhat surprising because tests of the vestibular ocular reflex (VOR), involved in stabilizing a stationary image on the retina, reveal that infants between 1 and 4 months old show perfect eye movement compensations for head movements (i.e., the gain is 1.0) at velocities between 10 and 40 deg/sec (Finocchio, Preston, & Fuchs, 1991). Although this compensatory response is opposite to that required during object tracking, it suggests that vestibular inputs are already functional and available to control eye movements. Apparently, eye-head coordination during tracking involves more than a reflexive compensation to the vestibular stimulation. One reason that

vestibular information is insufficient for controlling eye movements while tracking objects is that the gain of the eye movement depends not only on the head movement, but also on the distance of the object (Owen & Lee, 1986; Preston & Finocchio, 1993). It is also likely that eye movements will have to compensate for head movements unrelated to tracking the object (von Hofsten & Rosander, 1996). These head movements could be generated by external perturbations, such as being carried by a parent, or internal perturbations, such as yawning or loss of support. Infants begin to compensate temporally for these high-frequency and extraneous head movements by 1 month of age, but their ability to adjust their eye movements to the amplitude of the head movements develops more gradually (von Hofsten & Rosander, 1996).

In sum, the evidence reveals that postural status interacts with the accuracy of gaze stabilization. Analogous examples involving the development of posture and other actions are present in the literature and we will review some of these examples, such as the relation between posture and reaching or posture and leg movements, in subsequent sections.

REACHING AND GRASPING

Gaining control over the arms and hands is one of the major achievements of the infant. Just as greater skill in the use of the primate hand led to greater cognitive accomplishments phylogenetically (e.g., Magoun, Darling, & Prost, 1960), a similar effect occurs ontogenetically. Once infants can reach for and grasp objects, they no longer have to wait for the world to come to them; their hands now bring objects close enough for tactile, auditory, visual, and buccal exploration. The stage is set for bold advances into new cognitive problems, as the hand obtains, manipulates, and finds novel uses for objects.

The study of reaching and grasping is almost as old as the study of child development. Darwin (1877) and Preyer (1888) commented on their infants' uses of the hands in their baby diaries. Piaget (1952) was fascinated with this motor behavior, supplying detailed descriptions of reaching and object manipulation that are still useful to researchers today. The study of reaching and grasping received enormous attention during the 1930s surge in child development research, beginning with Halverson's classic work (1931, 1932) and continuing with McGraw and Gesell. Use of the hands in object manipulation became a cornerstone of the early infant development scales (Bayley, 1933a; Gesell & Amatruda, 1941), exemplified in items such as building a tower of cubes and inserting shapes correctly into a formboard. Currently, we are less interested in *when* infants achieve various "motor milestones" than in the process by which they arrive there. This requires new approaches and new thinking about the processes underlying motor achievements like reaching and grasping.

Prereaching

Successful reaching and grasping of objects appears around 4 months of age, but this achievement is preceded by a great deal of spontaneous arm movement present from birth. Trevarthen (1974) first documented the existence of these movements and termed them *prereaching;* subsequent reports have elaborated their form (e.g., Ronnqvist & von Hofsten, 1994; von Hofsten, 1982, 1984; von Hofsten & Ronnqvist, 1993). (See Figure 2.7 for an example of prereaching by a neonate.) A major issue is whether neonatal arm movements are strictly under endogenous control or whether they are responsive to visual input. Early reports by Bower and colleagues claimed that neonates reached into the near-vicinity of an object on 70% of their arm extensions (Bower, Broughton, & Moore, 1970), and that they reached more for graspable three-dimensional objects than for two-dimensional objects (Bower, 1972). Both of these claims were called into question when others attempted to replicate these findings; the 1970 result was not found by Ruff and Halton (1978) and the 1972 result was not obtained by Dodwell, Muir, and DiFranco (1976). Ruff and Halton (1978) included a "no object" control condition and found as many arm extensions in the absence of the object as in its presence. Like Ruff and Halton (1978), von Hofsten (1984) found that the presence of an object had no effect on the absolute number of forward extensions of the hand, but it did increase the relative frequency of forward extensions when the infant was fixating the object. In addition, more arm extensions and more movements were aimed close to the object during fixations on the object compared to when the infant looked elsewhere. Contrary to Bower (1972), the object was rarely touched. More recently, Ennouri and Bloch (in press) confirmed that movements initiated during fixations on the object were aimed closer to the object than were movements in a control condition with gaze on a virtual object.

These findings have been interpreted as evidence that neonates respond to objects with increased arm movements

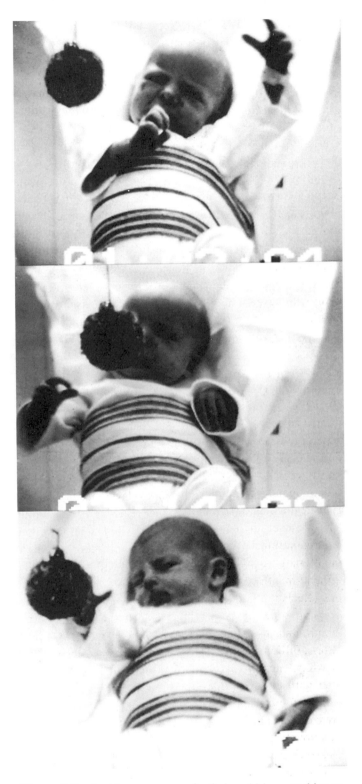

Figure 2.7   A video sequence of a 2-day-old boy reaching toward an object. From "Neonatal finger and arm movements as determined by a social and an object context," by L. Ronnqvist & C. von Hofsten, 1994, *Early Development and Parenting, 3,* pp. 81–94. Copyright © 1994 by John Wiley & Sons, Ltd. Reprinted with permission.

directed toward the general vicinity of the object if the infant is gazing in that direction. Further evidence of coordination between hand and eye at birth comes from a study by van der Meer, van der Weel, and Lee (1995) that reported newborns could direct their arm movements when given visual feedback. In this study, newborns lay supine, directly facing the ipsilateral arm or viewing the contralateral arm on a video monitor. Small weights were attached to both arms that pulled the arms toward the toes and thus out of view. Infants moved their arms against the force, keeping the position high, but only for the arm in view (Figure 2.8). This tendency of neonates to direct their arm movements toward their visual field may be related to object-directed prereaching described above. Both initial tendencies set the stage to ensure that the infant rapidly increases visual-proprioceptive coordination, and learns to bring arm movements under control in the weeks following birth.

Hand-Mouth Coordination

The earliest object-directed hand movement is undoubtedly hand-mouth contact, which has been observed even *in utero* (deVries, Visser, & Prechtl, 1985). Although long regarded as haphazard and fortuitous contact, more detailed reports indicate that hand-mouth behavior may be an early example of "intentional" or goal-directed action (Butterworth & Hopkins, 1988; Rochat, 1993). Significantly, mouth opening anticipates the movement of the hand, particularly just before a feeding (Lew & Butterworth, 1995). The presence of a sweet taste in the mouth also affects hand-mouth activity. The delivery of sucrose into the mouth with a syringe increased the frequency and duration of hand-mouth contact by 50%, compared to baseline periods (Rochat, Blass, & Hoffmeyer, 1988). The application of plain water does not increase hand transport to the mouth, and insertion of a pacifier will block the activity (Blass, Fillion, Rochat, Hoffmeyer, & Metzger, 1989), both of which suggest that hand-mouth contact may be associated with either a suckling or feeding system. This evidence of integration between different sensory systems, present from birth, has been interpreted in terms of its functional value for the newborn (Rochat, 1993). The very existence of this highly organized action pattern at birth forces a modification in Piaget's theory (1952) that newborn behaviors are primarily reflexive, uncoordinated, and functionally separate. New views of early sensorimotor behavior have been proposed by several authors that emphasize goal-directedness rather than reflexive behavior and

(a)

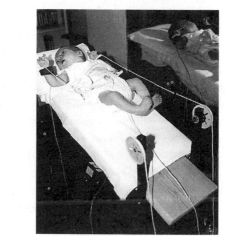

(b)

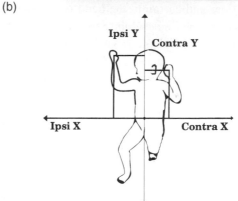

(c)

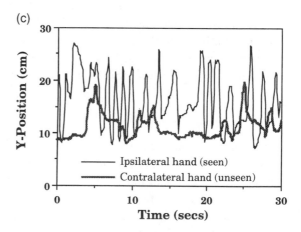

Figure 2.8 Coordination between hand and eye in neonates (van der Meer, et al.). (a) Photograph of an 18-day-old baby tested in the study. (b) Schematic representation showing how the coordinates of the hand were measured with a motion analysis system. (c) A typical plot of the movements of the two hands in the y direction. The thin line depicts the seen ipsilateral hand, the thick line depicts the unseen contralateral hand. From "The functional significance of arm movements in neonates," by A. L. H. van der Meer, F. R. van der Weel, & D. L. Lee, 1995, *Science, 267,* pp. 693–695. Copyright © 1995 by the American Academy for the Advancement of Science. Reprinted with permission.

interaction among different systems rather than separate functioning (for reviews, see Bertenthal, 1996; Bloch, 1990; Jouen, Lepecq, & Gapenne, 1993; Lockman, 1990; Thelen & Smith, 1994).

Hand-mouth coordination progresses rapidly between 1 and 6 months of age. When objects are placed in the hand, the infant begins to reliably ferry them to the mouth. Once voluntary reaching appears around 4 months, the infant will visually inspect objects before completing the journey to the mouth (Rochat & Senders, 1991). The question of how neonatal hand-mouth activity is related to the later development of reaching is still open. Piaget (1952) suggested that hand-mouth coordination is preparatory for later hand-eye coordination, and certainly the hand is transported to the mouth much earlier in development (even *in utero*) than objects are transported to the mouth. However, there are several missing links to this story. One would expect that when infants first begin to bring objects to the mouth, they would need to see the objects. Yet infants younger than 4 months (before reaching begins) can carry objects to the mouth in the dark, by-passing the visual link of hand-eye (Rochat, 1993). In addition, one would expect little hand-eye coordination before the infant becomes proficient at hand-mouth coordination; yet newborns are responsive to self-produced hand movements they can see, thus establishing a hand-eye connection long before hand-mouth contact is achieved reliably and reaching is possible (van der Meer et al., 1995). Many more aspects of these behaviors must be explored before we can fully describe the sequence of development or know the mechanisms involved in their production.

Transition to Reaching

How does the infant make the transition from prereaching arm movements to reaching and grasping objects? How is this control over the arm and hand achieved? Trevarthen (1984) suggested that the infant is endowed with innate neural structures for coordinating movement, along with a representation of the spatial field. As evidence for this claim, he noted that prereaching movements did not require a visual stimulus, but would "run off" spontaneously and ballistically. Trevarthen (1990) described how neonatal arm movements are coordinated with eye movements and contain elements of a mature reach in their form and timing. For example, opening and closing of the hand is temporally related to extension of the arm. Evidence that this coordination is present at birth, long before the infant can actually pick up or grasp an object, led Trevarthen to postulate that neural structures are responsible for this precocious motor behavior. These innate structures are modified by sensory experience, becoming refined and controlled with development.

In the past decade, alternative views on the transition to reaching have been put forward by Thelen and colleagues (1993). These authors are concerned with the intrinsic dynamics of the arm, and how the infant comes to match these dynamics to a task. Each infant has a characteristic way of moving the arms; some move slowly with highly damped movements and some more rapidly with large undamped movements. These intrinsic styles are modulated in the early weeks of the transition period to bring all infants to the point of making successful reaches. As Thelen sees it, the infant's task is to learn to adjust the intrinsic dynamics of the arm to the task through trial-and-error exploration. In contrast to traditional descriptions of the development of reaching, Thelen et al. (1993) described reaching as "*softly assembled* rather than a product of a prefigured reaching device." By softly assembled, they meant that infants organize a reach by matching the arm dynamics to the task at hand in a flexible manner, in contrast to dependence on pre-existing structures that control the reach. They concluded that there is no necessity to posit innate motor programs in the nervous system as the basis for reaching. If not some motor program, then what is the driving force behind the infant making a shift from arm movements to successful reaching? Thelen's answer (1995) is *motivation,* the desire to get something (toy, food, etc.). Once the infant has set the task, he or she explores and selects the movements that bring success. This process also implies that the infant is able to recognize success and remember what motor activity produced it. The exploration and selection process may take place over a span of days or several weeks, depending on the complexity of what is to be learned.

Within the past decade the resurgence in research on infant reaching has yielded new descriptions from kinematic and behavioral data, and new hypotheses and interpretations about those data. We are only beginning to move beyond the descriptive level in understanding this problem. Only by studying individual infants over repeated sessions will the exploration and selection process be understood. Several authors have called for intensive observation of single infants (Connolly & Dalgleish, 1989; Thelen, 1995; von Hofsten, 1989), a strategy we endorse for the study of reaching.

CONTROL AND COORDINATION OF REACHING

Posture and Reaching

The control of reaching should not be studied independent of contextual factors. In early development, posture is one of the most important influences on reaching (Savelsbergh & van der Kamp, 1993). Although there is a wealth of data on the development of reaching, most researchers have studied reaching divorced from the context of body support and posture. A welcome exception is a series of studies by Rochat and colleagues (Rochat, 1992, Rochat & Goubet, in press; Rochat & Senders, 1991) that relate the attainment of sitting alone (termed "self-sitting") to a shift from two-handed to one-handed reaching. When nonsitting infants (22–26 weeks) were placed in fully supported postures, they often chose to reach for objects with both hands. The self-sitting infants (28–38 weeks) chose to reach with one hand, regardless of the various postures in which they were placed. Rochat (1992) noted that the release from a two-handed reach gained the infants more degrees of freedom, allowing asymmetrical movements of the upper limbs. Rochat interpreted early reaching as an extension of pre-reaching and hand-mouth coordination, in which objects placed in the hands are brought to the mouth for sucking and mouthing, a behavior that occurs prior to onset of reaching (Bruner, 1969; Rochat, Blass, & Hoffmeyer, 1988).

An interesting aspect of nonsitters' behavior was their tendency to resort to one-handed reaches when put into the more precarious seated position. Reaching with two hands could easily cause a loss of balance in the unsupported infant; Rochat (1992) noted that nonsitters frequently fell forward if they attempted two-handed reaches in this posture. A similar situation prevails when infants lean forward as part of their reach. From the results of this study (Rochat, 1992), one would predict that nonsitting infants would refrain from leaning, whereas self-sitting infants would incorporate leaning into their effort to get an object. Rochat and Goubet (in press) found this to be the case, but also discovered that providing sufficient support at the hips allowed nonsitters to engage in leaning forward. Older infants (8 to 10 months) appear sensitive to whether an object placed beyond arm's length can be grasped by leaning, and at 12 months are able to use a hand-held implement to extend their lean and reach even further (McKenzie, Skouteris, Day, Hartman, & Yonas, 1993). In these situations, reaching and leaning occur together, as an integrated

act, rather than as an unsuccessful reach followed by a lean to bring the object into contact.

In summary, the research on posture and reaching has shown that from the earliest age the novice reacher is sensitive to postural support and adjusts hand involvement and extension of the body to the available support. By 8 months, infants appear to realize that leaning extends prehensile space and they smoothly incorporate it as part of the reaching act. By 12 months, they can deliberately extend their reach with a mechanical aid. The work on posture and reaching emphasizes that reaching does not occur in a vacuum, and should always be considered in the context of the entire body, including the extent of support provided by either the self or other external devices.

Changes in Reach Kinematics

As control of arm movements develops during the first year of life, infants' reaching becomes more reliable, accurate, and flexible. This developmental trend can be confirmed even by casual observation. What does a more precise kinematic analysis reveal? In 1979, von Hofsten published a very influential paper in which he provided for the first time a detailed kinematic description of infant reaching. He divided the speed plot of a reach into "movement elements" or units defined by an accelerative and decelerative phase. (Figure 2.9 displays an example of a speed plot, side view, and top view of three reaches under different lighting conditions. Movement units are designated by numbers on the speed plots.) Such units were regarded as "preprogrammed" and "ballistic" (von Hofsten, 1979), so that the movement unit had to run off without correction once it began.

The segmented reaches of infants contrast sharply with the typical adult reach consisting of a single bell-shaped curve with one accelerative phase followed by a decelerative phase as the hand approaches the object (Jeannerod, 1984). A number of developmental changes were noted in these elements of the reach when infants were tested longitudinally from 15 to 36 weeks (von Hofsten & Lindhagen, 1979). The number of movement units in a reach drops with age from about 3 to 5 units at 15 weeks to about 1 to 2 units at 36 weeks. The first unit becomes dominant, taking up the greatest proportion of the approach toward the object, and the approach path becomes straighter with age. This latter finding was interpreted by von Hofsten (1979) as the infant learning to control the arm's multiple segments.

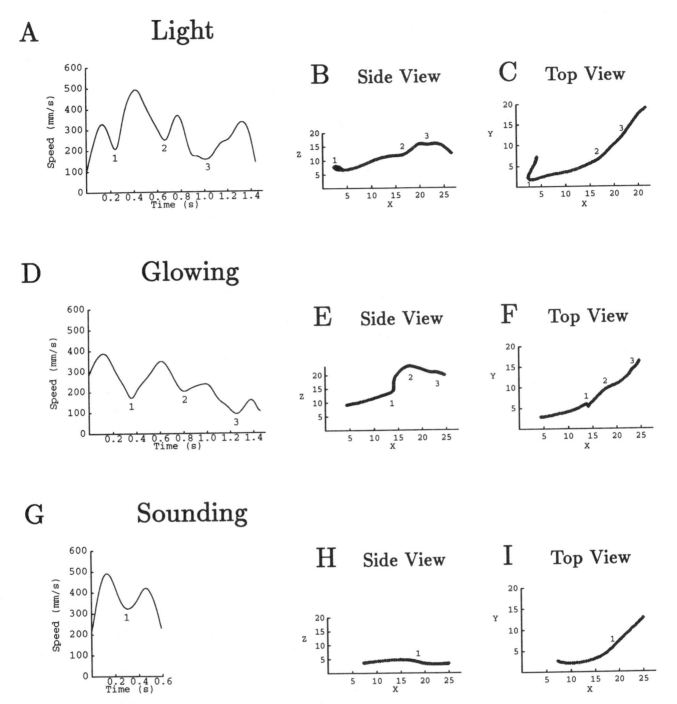

Figure 2.9. Representative reaches by a 6-month-old infant in three lighting conditions. Panels A, D, and G show the changing speed of the hand as a function of time. Movement units are separated by the numbers located at the speed minima. Panels B, E, and H show side views, and panels C, F, and I show top views of the changing position of the hand during the reach. In these position plots, the hand is moving from left to right (in cm). Movement in the x direction is toward the object in front of the infant, movement in the z direction is up, and movement in the y direction is to the sides of the infant. The numbers on the side and top view plots correspond to the hand's position at the minima in the speed plots. From "Multimodel perception in human infants," by R. K. Clifton et al., 1994, *Journal of Experimental Psychology: Human Perception and Performance, 20,* pp. 876–886. Copyright © 1994 by the American Psychological Association. Reprinted with permission.

Berthier (1996) agrees with Thelen et al. (1993) that the major task of the infant is to match the arms' intrinsic dynamics with task constraints. Like von Hofsten (1991), he was struck by the manner in which early reaching movements are composed of many submovements, but his interpretation of the function of these submovements is more developed. He noted that infants have very poor motor control when they first begin to reach. They cannot predict exactly where or how far a motor command will move the arm and hand. Given this limitation, it is better to not attempt one large continuous movement from reach onset to goal contact. By reaching with short-duration submovements that cover small distances, the infant is able to optimize accuracy. Through stochastic optimization, the infant "homes in" on the target effectively. Berthier (1996) supported the hypothesis with both computer simulations and empirical data. He reported data showing that very young infants were capable of making large continuous movements with a smooth velocity curve when they were *batting* an object, but the topology of the action changed when they were reaching in order to grasp an object. The latter movement has slower velocity, with numerous submovements, as von Hofsten and others have described. Berthier's model predicts that the number of movement segments should decrease with age. By making his hypothesis explicit in mathematical form, Berthier has pushed the search to understand infant reaching to a new level.

In spite of the success of Berthier's model in predicting changes over age in the pattern of reaching, more recent research has not consistently confirmed this developmental trend. While many of the basic observations by von Hofsten (1979) have been confirmed by Mathew and Cook (1990) and by von Hofsten himself (1991), Fetters and Todd (1987) reported no developmental change between 5 and 9 months for number of movement units, nor did temporal duration of each unit vary from an average around 200 msec. Also, reaches did not become straighter with age. Robin, Berthier, and Clifton (1996) also failed to find developmental trends in the kinematics of reaches when testing the same infants at 5 and 7 months.

Another inconsistency in the literature concerns the interpretation for movement units. Fetters and Todd (1987) concur with von Hofsten that the "speed valleys" or decelerations in hand velocity that separate movement units correspond to a change in direction. Presumably, these movement units are necessary to correct the hand path. In support of this interpretation, von Hofsten (1991) describes the hand as moving relatively straight within a unit, but

curving at the speed valleys. By contrast, Mathew and Cook (1990) found curvature *within* units, contradicting the idea that movements units were composed ballistically, that is, the movement could not be corrected once it was launched.

One explanation for these conflicting results may lie in the task because all of the studies used different objects and different modes of presentation. (This possibility is discussed in detail by von Hofsten, 1991.) It thus appears that the failure to find consistent developmental trends across labs indicates that movement units probably change from one situation to another, so broad generalizations are risky. The one consistent finding is that infant reaching does appear to be composed of multiple movement units. Even though developmental changes in the characteristics of these segments have been hard to pin down, there is general agreement that movement units are a striking fundamental property of early reaching.

Response to Object Location, Orientation, and Movement

Beginning with the onset of reaching, infants appear to take spatial relations into account. Infants as young as 15 weeks reached less often for objects placed well beyond their reach (Field, 1976), even when the objects were sized to subtend the same visual angle at each test distance. Yonas and colleagues conducted a series of studies in which a variety of visual depth cues were tested (see Yonas & Granrud, 1985, for a review of this research). They found that infants reached less often when visual information specified that the object was beyond reach, with performance improving between 5 and 7 months. Clifton and colleagues (Clifton, Perris, & Bullinger, 1991; Litovsky & Clifton, 1992) found that 6-month-old infants reached less when sounding objects in the dark were placed beyond reach, compared to placement within reach. These studies converge to show that in the early stages of reaching infants are sensitive to both visual and auditory cues specifying depth, and that they coordinate the perceptual information with their action by reaching more often when they are apt to be successful. The failure to reach for more distant objects is truly fascinating in its implication that infants are sensitive to the potential success of their action. In addition to an object's distance, infants react to the object's placement in a particular hemifield and the spatial location within that hemifield. There is a strong tendency to reach with the ipsilateral hand when the target is placed in any of several locations within a hemifield, while placement in the opposite hemifield is responded to by a switch in the reaching hand (Perris & Clifton, 1988).

In most research situations infants are presented with small graspable objects that do not require any particular hand orientation. A successful grasp will enclose the object in the hand. However, a long, thin rod can be grasped best if the hand anticipates the rod's orientation. Otherwise the outstretched fingers may jam into the rod inappropriately, as when a horizontally oriented hand grasps a vertically oriented rod, or vice versa. Infants' reaching and grasping of oriented objects may be assumed to be overt reflections of their planning and adjusting to object properties (Pieraut-Le Bonniec, 1990; von Hofsten, 1991). Infants as young as 5 months show some anticipatory hand orientation when reaching for rods (Morrongiello & Rocca, 1989; von Hofsten & Fazel-Zandy, 1984), although another study found anticipation in 9-month-olds but not 5-month-olds (Lockman, Ashmead, & Bushnell, 1984). In all of these studies, infants reached for rods in the light, and all authors discussed the role vision played in infants' anticipatory hand orientation. Although these authors stressed that increasing visuomotor control was responsible for the improvement in hand orientation across the age span tested, the process underlying this control was not examined or tested. When 7-month-olds were presented with lit rods in the dark, they preoriented their hands, suggesting that sight of the hand is not critical in making adjustments during the approach phase of the reach (McCarty, 1993).

One of the most remarkable feats of infant reaching is the ability to catch moving objects. In a series of reports von Hofsten (von Hofsten, 1980, 1983; von Hofsten & Lindhagen, 1979) described how infants intercepted objects moving at various speeds up to 120 cm/sec. Von Hofsten (1983) found evidence that infants timed their reaches to intercept the object by aiming ahead of it and decelerating the hand in its final movement before grasp. Using a paradigm similar to von Hofsten's, Robin et al. (1996) found that reaching errors were associated with faulty timing rather than failure to aim at the trajectory of the moving object. Specifically, reaches were not aimed far enough ahead to intercept it. Infants also adopted a strategy of reaching with the contralateral hand, in contrast to the ipsilateral hand used with stationary objects (Robin et al., 1996; von Hofsten, 1980). The use of the contralateral hand allows more time to prepare the reach before arrival of the object because the object moves beyond the ipsilateral hand's reaching space while still within reach of the contralateral hand.

In contrast to many behaviors (e.g., looking, sucking, heart rate change), reaching for a moving object has the great advantage of displaying the underlying plans and predictions of the infant, resulting in less need for tenuous inferences. The infant's goal is clear—to grasp the object—but movement of the object constrains success in definable ways. Variations in the movement of an object can be used to discover what strategies an infant might employ and what aspects of visual information might be critical. It is for this reason that moving object studies have such great potential to reveal the infant's ability to prepare, anticipate, and react predictively to a changing stimulus.

Changes in Visual Guidance of Reaching

In considering how the infant achieves control over the hand, vision of the surround, including sight of the hand and the object to be grasped, would seem critical. Studies of infants born blind confirm the necessity of vision in insuring anything like normal development of reaching, grasping, and coordination between the hands (Adelson & Fraiberg, 1974; Bigelow, 1986; D. Warren, 1984). However, exactly how vision contributes to the development of reaching is unclear. The classic description of "visually guided reaching" was provided by White, Castle, and Held (1964), based on their own longitudinal data and that of Piaget. They observed that infants alternated glances between hand and object when in the early stages of learning to grasp an object. Although White et al. (1964), as well as Piaget (1952), described this behavior as a transitional phase in learning to reach, the concept of early reaching as a visually guided behavior became entrenched as an explanation for how infants learn to reach. The task for the infant becomes one of matching sight of the hand with sight of the target, and as reaching becomes more practiced the infant is eventually able to forgo looking at the hand during a reach (Bushnell, 1985). This view dominated our thinking about early reaching for more than three decades and is widely cited in textbooks on infant development (Bremner, 1988, pp. 39–40; Rosenblith, 1992, pp. 321–324), in review chapters (von Hofsten, 1989), and in books on motor control (Rosenbaum, 1991). In the last decade, evidence has accumulated that this view is not correct, or at a minimum, is incomplete.

Researchers have attempted several manipulations to determine the effects of vision on reaching. McDonnell (1975) distorted vision by using prisms and Lasky (1977) occluded sight of the body and hands during the reach.

However, the McDonnell and Lasky manipulations may have been disturbing to the infant. In the case of prisms the visuo-proprioceptive map was abruptly rearranged, requiring recalibration of hand and eye. This situation is quite different from simply taking away vision and letting proprioception guide the hand. Likewise, Lasky's manipulation of occluding body parts by a strange apparatus may have been upsetting, a possibility also noted by Bushnell (1985). Presenting infants with sounding or glowing objects in pitch-black darkness gets around many of these problems. The visuo/proprioceptive map is unchanged (though inoperative) and loss of sight of the limbs may be better tolerated because nothing has been put over the body to touch or constrain it.

Bower and Wishart (1972) conducted the first study in which objects were presented to infants in the dark. Since this initial report a number of studies have indicated that infants between 4 and 8 months reach readily and accurately in the dark for sounding or luminous objects (Clifton et al., 1991; Perris & Clifton, 1988; Stack, Muir, Sherriff, & Roman, 1989; Wishart, Bower, & Dunkeld, 1978). In addition to this general finding, vision of the hand was found not necessary (1) for making anticipatory hand movements to grasp differently oriented luminous rods in the dark (McCarty, 1993), (2) for a motor action anticipating size of the object to be grasped (Clifton, Rochat, Litovsky, & Perris, 1991), and (3) for obtaining a glowing, moving object in the dark (Robin et al., 1996). A detailed comparison of the kinematics of reaching for an object in the light with reaching for a glowing object in the dark revealed no differences on any measure, including duration of reach, path length, average and peak velocity, number of peaks, and maximum or average deviation from a straight line (Clifton, Rochat, Robin, & Berthier, 1994). Finally, a longitudinal study of 7 infants tested weekly revealed that age of onset of reaching in the light was not different from onset of reaching in the dark (Clifton, Muir, Ashmead, & Clarkson, 1993).

The conclusion from these studies is that sight of the hand during reaching makes surprisingly little difference to infants when they are first learning to reach. Their skill appears to be based on proprioceptive information, which they couple with vision (sight of the target) or sound in order to direct their reach. As their reaching proficiency develops, infants begin to use sight of the hand to make fine adjustments, as adults do when threading a needle or putting a key into a lock. A few recent studies support this observation. Infants at 9 months who wore a luminescent hand marker appeared to partially adjust their reach to a suddenly displaced target (Ashmead, McCarty, Lucas, & Belvedere, 1993), indicating that visually guided reaching may begin to develop late in the first year of life. Further support for the increasing role of visual guidance during this period comes from work showing that not until around 8 to 9 months do infants preshape their thumb-finger aperture to correspond to different sized-objects (Newell, Scully, McDonald, & Baillargeon, 1989; von Hofsten & Ronnqvist, 1988). Before this age the hand conforms to an object's size and shape through haptic information after contact. In addition to these findings, more research is needed to determine at what age infants begin to make use of visual guidance of the hand.

Grasping and Manual Exploration

Detailed descriptions of infants' grasping from the 1930s remain an excellent source of information for modern researchers (Halverson, 1931, 1932). Infants between 16 and 52 weeks were cinematically recorded and scored frame-by-frame while picking up a 1-inch cube and other common objects. Halverson (1931) described three primary stages that occurred sequentially: the simple palmar grasp in which all objects are clutched in a viselike grip (20–28 weeks), a brief intermediate stage that featured some thumb opposition with palmar grasping (28–32 weeks), and finger-tip grasping in which the digits were brought fully into play with well-developed thumb opposition (32 weeks and older). This last stage is the most significant advance because it enables fine manipulation and play with objects. By contrast, infants in the earliest stage do not show thumb opposition, cannot release the cube voluntarily, and cannot transfer objects from one hand to the other—all of which would decrease visual inspection and manipulation.

Halverson's description of the progression of prehension from pawlike closure to finger-tip grip has been questioned by Newell and colleagues (1989). They claimed that the 1-inch cube offered by Halverson to all age groups did not take into account changing hand size, which molded the infants' choice of grip. Even 4-month-old infants will occasionally use the thumb and index finger when presented with the appropriate object for their hand size. While task constraints in the form of object size and shape affect grasping at every age, there is nonetheless a strong developmental progression in the frequency and skill with which infants employ various grips (Siddiqui, 1995).

Connolly and Elliott (1972) described how the object's position in the palm shifts from the ulnar or outer border of the hand at 12 weeks, over toward the thumb and index finger by 36 weeks. At the older age, finger-tip grasping is the preferred grip, shown by the common observation that around 9 months infants delight in picking up all sorts of tiny objects. What is perhaps most striking about grasping patterns is that at every age the infant shows sensitivity and adaptation to an object's properties through haptic and visual interaction. There is increasing skill in the deployment of certain grips, but from the beginning of manual interaction with the world the infant is affected by the potential match between hand and object.

This propensity to adapt the grasp to an object's size (and orientation, as noted above) extends to exploratory manipulation of objects. Palmer (1989) reported that object properties such as weight, texture, and potential for making sound, will elicit appropriate actions from 6- to 12-month-olds. By presenting objects with a broad array of characteristics, Palmer revealed a varied action repetoire that was adapted to functional possibilities. For example, sound-making toys were waved about more compared to the same toy made soundless, whereas deformable objects such as a sponge and a soft doll were squeezed more than harder objects. Gibson and Walker (1984) also had noted that infants squeezed soft objects but banged rigid objects. Ruff (1984) found that visually patterned objects were more likely to be transferred from hand to hand (which would promote visual inspection), whereas objects textured by bumps and holes were more likely to be fingered. Thus, infants appear to adapt their exploratory haptic behavior to object properties, in line with the Gibsonian concept of affordance (E. Gibson, 1988; J. Gibson, 1979), picking up information specific to their interaction with a particular object.

Bushnell and Boudreau (1993) offered a new conceptualization of how the interplay between motor control and haptic perception might work. They hypothesized that motor control of the hand both constrains and enhances haptic perception by first restricting the detection of some properties until the necessary motor abilities have been achieved, and then enabling the detection of additional properties later on. For example, the 3-month-old's tight clutch of objects placed in the hand allows perception of temperature, size, and hardness; however, haptic perception of texture and weight is delayed until the infant begins to rub and scratch the object's surface, bang it, and pass it from hand to hand between 6 and 10 months of age (Figure 2.10). Bushnell and Boudreau's (1993) position

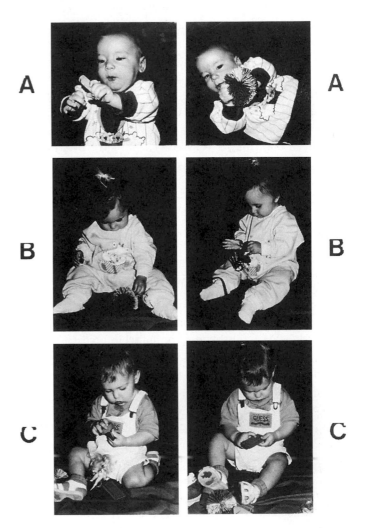

Figure 2.10 Three phases of infants' manual behavior toward objects. (A) clutching (birth through about 3 months of age), (B) rhythmical stereotypes (4 to about 10 months of age), and (C) complementary bimanual activities (10 months on). From "Motor development and the mind: The potential role of motor abilities as a determinant of aspects of perceptual development," by E. W. Bushnell & J. P. Boudreau, 1993, *Child Development, 64,* pp. 1005–1021. Copyright © 1993 by the Society for Research on Child Development. Reprinted with permission.

contrasts with more traditional views that haptic perception is constrained initially by visual perception.

Manipulation and tactual exploration can support vision, as well as being exploratory in their own right. These two aspects of hand function have been considered theoretically by Hatwell (1987) and Ruff (1989). Hatwell proposed that infants are dominated by vision after they begin to reach around 5 months of age, so the role of the hands is to support vision, with purely haptic information perhaps unattended. This subordinate role of manual exploration continues until late in the second year of life. By contrast, Ruff reviewed research, both her own and others, showing early cooperation between the two systems. She suggested that each system might benefit from the other's information and that redundant information across the two systems might facilitate perceptual learning and encoding. According to Ruff, the hand is not viewed as being in the service of vision, but rather is an equal partner in determining sequential unfolding of perceptual and cognitive abilities.

Tool Use and Social Communication

Toward the end of the first year, infants expand the use of the hand to encompass two new aspects: tool use and social communication. The earliest form of tool use might be described as using one object to get another object, as Kohler's (1925) chimpanzees did when he tested them on problem solving. This type of means-end behavior was described by Piaget (1954) and has been investigated more recently by Bates, Carlson-Luden, and Bretherton (1980), and Willatts (1984). By around 10 to 12 months of age infants will pull a string or cloth to retrieve an out-of-reach toy when it is presented singly (Bates et al., 1980) or if two cloths are presented with a toy resting on one cloth (Willatts, 1984). However, if the difficulty of a correct response is increased by covering the toy on the cloth with either a transparent or opaque cloth, performance drops to chance (Willatts, 1985). Willatts (in press) emphasized that the acquisition of the skill to use the cloth in order to get the toy is gradual, involving knowledge of action sequences and their implementation.

A skill more obvious to parents that is acquired over the same age range is learning to use a spoon. Connolly and Dalgleish (1989) observed self-feeding for 6 months in one group of infants beginning at 11 months and an older group beginning at 17 months. They found a strong hand preference had already developed in the majority of infants even at 11 months, and this increased to almost 100% of the sample by 17 months. Initially, infants tried several grasps of the spoon, some awkward, some more successful. At older ages, the more successful grip became prominent, and the contralateral hand was brought into play to hold the dish. The whole process became smoother and more economical in time and energy.

Also around 12 months infants begin to understand manual gestures as part of social communication. They follow a pointing finger to a distant object with their gaze, rather than looking at the finger itself as they did earlier (Butterworth & Grover, 1990). Around 13 to 14 months, infants use the pointing gesture themselves to attract another's attention. Franco and Butterworth (1996) stressed that pointing, unlike reaching, is a communicative gesture, and make the case that these two manual behaviors originate from different intentions and out of different contexts. The situation in their laboratory that elicited the most pointing was an interesting doll placed inaccessibly more than 2 meters away from the infant, whereas reaching was elicited by a toy placed just out of reach on a table. The authors concluded that reaching occurs when the infant wants to obtain an object, but pointing is indicative of a social connection between infant and another (usually the mother) with reference to an object. For pointing to be effective, the other person's attention must be engaged and infants appear to recognize this because they look toward the mother more often when pointing than when reaching.

Additional evidence for infants developing appreciation of the communicative function of the hands is reviewed by Petitto (1992). In one study (Petitto & Marentette, 1991) the manual activity produced by ASL deaf and hearing infants between 10 and 14 months of age was kinematically recorded and analyzed. The results revealed that those children taught sign language showed significant differences in the temporal patterning of their manual behaviors that contained linguistically-relevant units and all other manual activity. Interestingly, the linguistically-relevant manual activity was structurally similar to vocal babbling observed in hearing infants.

In summary, the infant begins life with only rudimentary control over the hand, and a minimum of hand-mouth and hand-eye coordination. Approximately one year later the infant has progressed to highly skilled reaching, haptic exploration, the beginnings of tool use, and using gestures as part of social communication. The functional significance of gaining control over the hands can hardly be overstated. The cognitive consequences of reaching, grasping, and manipulating objects are enormous, and have been widely discussed in evolutionary terms (Connolly & Elliott, 1972; Gowlett, 1984; Oakley, 1975). Along with locomotion, discussed in the next section, manual control ranks as one of the human infant's greatest achievements in the first two years of life.

LOCOMOTION

An upright mode of locomotion is one of the most distinctive features of our species. Evolutionary theorists believe that this unique form of locomotion was accompanied by a set of very successful behavioral adaptations, including the freeing of the hands to gather and carry food for long distances (Lovejoy, 1988). The functional significance of this structural change is repeated during ontogeny. It is the freeing of the hands and the affordance of greater mobility that identifies the development of upright locomotion as such a major achievement by human infants. Although most infants begin to walk by themselves at around a year of age (Bayley, 1969), the events contributing to this developmental milestone begin much earlier. Indeed, it is possible to trace the origins of locomotion from birth, which is exactly what will be done in this section.

During the early part of this century, the pioneers in this field (Burnside, 1927; Gesell & Ames, 1940; McGraw, 1935, 1940; Shirley, 1931) contributed detailed and thorough descriptions of the development of crawling and walking. Hundreds of hours were devoted to filming and describing the postures of infants at different "stages" of this developmental progression (Figure 2.11). The picture that emerged from these investigations was that the development of locomotion followed an orderly and sequential progression of changes in behavioral form. Although these investigators recognized that postural support and other environmental factors would contribute to motor performance, they advanced the position that the development of locomotion was primarily a function of the neuromaturation of the brain. For example, in explaining the development of prone progression, McGraw (1941) stated, "These successive changes in overt behavior reflect the advancing maturation of the central nervous system in a cephalocaudal direction as the controlling influence shifts from nuclear to cortical centers" (p. 110). Similar views on the role of neuromaturation are still in evidence (Forssberg, 1985; Sutherland, 1984).

Although neural development is certainly a prerequisite for the development of bipedal gait, it is misleading and overly simplistic to suggest that this one factor suffices. For an individual to move from one place to another, it is necessary not only to generate a propulsive thrust from alternating limbs, but also to maintain equilibrium and perceptually guide the direction of limb movements (Georgopoulos & Grillner, 1989). Each of these complementary processes involves multiple components that develop at different rates as a function of specific experiences (Thelen & Smith, 1994). Once these components are functional, they are flexibly organized by the task, and not by any predetermined plan (Bril & Breniere, 1991; Thelen & Smith, 1994; Whitall & Clark, 1994). It is for this reason that we emphasize research showing how

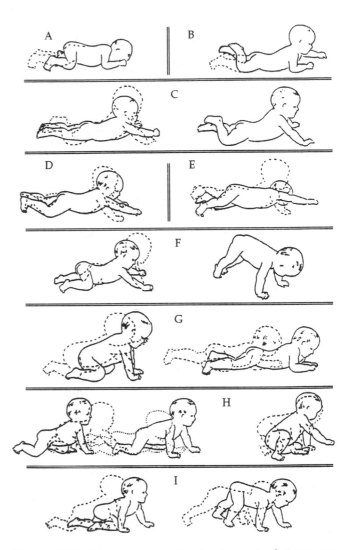

Figure 2.11 Nine phases in the development of prone progression. From "Development of neuro-muscular mechanisms as reflected in the crawling and creeping behavior of the human infant," by M. B. McGraw, 1941, *Journal of Genetic Psychology, 58*, pp. 83–111. Reprinted with permission of the Helen Dwight Reid Educational Foundation. Published by Heldref Publications, 1319 Eighteenth St., N.W., Washington, D.C. 20036-1802. Copyright © 1941.

transitions in locomotor development are a function of the interactions between neural, biomechanical, environmental, and task factors.

Developmental Transitions

Most accounts of locomotor development emphasize three dramatic transitions (e.g., Thelen & Smith, 1994). The first concerns the disappearance at around 2 months of age of the steplike patterning of the legs when infants are held upright. The second involves the reappearance of stepping movements in the second half of the first year as infants begin to bear their weight on their feet. Finally, infants begin to walk without support around one year of age. For the purposes of completeness, we add two additional transitions. One concerns the emergence of hands-and-knees crawling following a period during which infants drag their abdomens on the ground. The other concerns the development of other gait patterns besides walking.

Newborn Stepping

The stereotypical pattern for walking is an alternating and rhythmical sequence of extensions and flexions by the two legs, that is, stepping movements. Although the neonate is considered motorically immature, this same steplike pattern is produced when the infant is held upright and the feet touch the ground (McGraw, 1945). It might therefore seem that the control of this organized motor response is exclusively a function of the pattern generators in the CNS, especially since stepping and kicking patterns are also shown *in utero* (Prechtl, 1986) and by preterm infants (Heriza, 1988). Yet, a series of converging findings challenge this single mechanism explanation.

Thelen and Fisher (1982) measured the joint kinematics and EMG responses in newborns while they were stepping in a supported upright position or kicking in a supine position. Stepping was very similar to kicking when joint kinematics (i.e., timing of the phases of the cyclic extensions and flexions of the legs) and EMG responses (i.e., muscle activation patterns) were compared. This finding was surprising because infants stop stepping while held upright by 2 months of age, but continue to kick throughout the first year when sitting, supine, or prone (e.g., Thelen, Ridley-Johnson, & Fisher, 1983). If these rhythmic movements were solely attributable to a central pattern generator (CPG), then it is unlikely that they would selectively fall out at a specific age. Apparently, the production of these steplike movements involved other factors that were related to the posture of the infant.

One subtle but important factor is that more energy is needed to lift a leg to full flexion while upright than while supine. Although gravity is a constant in the environment, it only becomes a constraint after the newborn period when infants begin experiencing rapid weight gains that decrease the ratio of muscle to subcutaneous fat in the legs (Thelen & Fisher, 1982). Experimental manipulations that changed the weight of the leg or the resistance of the leg to flexion

(e.g., submerging infants in torso deep water) showed that the frequency of stepping in 4-week-old infants was systematically related to the biomechanical constraints of the situation (Thelen, Fisher, & Ridley-Johnson, 1984).

Additional evidence that newborn stepping is not entirely attributable to the presence of CPGs emerges from a comparison of EMG responses during newborn stepping and during adult walking. The defining characteristic of a CPG for walking is the precise alternation between flexor and extensor motor neurons in the limbs (Grillner, 1981). Thelen and Fisher (1983) reported that both flexors and extensors were activated by neonates at the initiation of a flexion (with somewhat stronger activation of the flexor group of muscles), but no muscles were activated at the initiation of extension. Apparently, the leg completed the cycle because potential energy was stored in the leg during flexion, and the springlike quality of the muscles and tendons combined with the force of gravity to reverse the movement of the leg at the end of the flexion phase (Thelen & Smith, 1994). Thus, the complete CPG pattern necessary for walking is not present in the neonate, even though stepping is observed.

Taken together, these results emphasize that the changing form of infants' stepping is not merely a function of neuromaturational changes, because posture and biomechanical properties of the muscles contribute as well. These and other factors will play important roles in subsequent transitions; thus it is necessary to continue to consider how these different factors interact as the component processes involved in upright locomotion develop.

Treadmill Stepping

Following the cessation of an alternating kicking mode at around 2 months of age, infants display a predominance of single-sided kicking until bilateral kicking becomes predominant again at 6 months of age (Thelen, Ridley-Johnson, & Fisher, 1983). A few months later infants begin to show coordinated stepping movements again when they are assisted in walking. It is conjectured that an important factor contributing to this transition is that stepping now involves weight bearing by the feet which produces additional information and energy to control the phasing of the legs (Thelen & Smith, 1994). As the center of gravity is shifted over the stance leg, the trailing leg is stretched backward. This stretch imparts potential energy to the leg (similar to the stretching of a spring) that is used to swing the leg forward. As the leg is maximally stretched, it provides proprioceptive stimulation that triggers the initiation of the swing (Pearson, Ramirez, & Jiang, 1992). In this way, the alternating pattern of stepping falls out of the stretching of the leg muscles.

This interpretation for the emergence of coordinated stepping during the second half of the first year is consistent with research testing infants' stepping on treadmills. When infants are supported while standing on a treadmill, their legs are stretched backward in a fashion that mimics the process that occurs when they begin to support their own weight with their feet. Thelen (1986b) supported 7-month-old infants on a small motorized treadmill and found that stepping was elicited and corresponded to a very stable alternating pattern of the legs. Without the treadmill, these same infants showed significantly less stepping. The stability of this stepping pattern was confirmed by the finding that 7-month-old infants maintain an alternating pattern of leg movements even when the two legs are driven by treadmill belts of different speeds (Thelen, Ulrich, & Niles, 1987).

In a longitudinal investigation of treadmill stepping, Thelen and Ulrich (1991) tested infants between 1 and 9 months of age. They reported that the shift between no-stepping or a multiple-step mode (combination of alternate stepping, one leg stepping, and both legs stepping together), and alternate stepping was typically quite rapid and occurred within 1 to 2 months. There were significant individual differences in the development of this behavior and multiple factors contributed to the emergence of this stepping pattern. One of the most consistent factors was a change in the flexor-extensor balance and strength of the leg muscles.

At birth, newborn infants show a flexor bias in their limbs (i.e., they are held tightly to the body) that relaxes gradually during the first few months. Also, extensor strength of the legs lags behind flexor strength for much of the first year. Thelen and Ulrich (1991) reported that postural responses of highly flexed infants and those without sufficient extensor strength showed that they rotated their foot inward and contacted the treadmill belt with their toes. As flexor and extensor tendencies of the legs became more balanced over time, infants were more likely to contact the belt with a flat foot so that their legs were stretched backward. Recall that it is the stretching of the leg muscles that swings the trailing leg forward and controls the alternating pattern of stepping. It is for this reason that improved flexor-extensor balance and strength in the legs led to significant improvements in treadmill stepping. Convergent evidence for this interpretation is provided by a test of Down syndrome infants on the treadmill (Ulrich, Ulrich, & Collier, 1992). These infants are hypotonic (low muscle tone) and showed delayed stepping on the treadmill, presumably because they lacked sufficient muscle tension to benefit from the backward stretch produced by the treadmill. It thus appears that the development of treadmill stepping offers additional evidence for the contribution of biomechanical factors in motor development.

Hands-and-Knees Crawling

One question unanswered by the preceding research is why infants selected an alternating stepping pattern instead of some other pattern, such as stepping with both legs simultaneously or taking more than one step with the same leg before stepping with the other. A plausible candidate for explaining this selection is the goal of minimizing the energy necessary to produce movements during locomotion. Many, if not most, animals use more energy for locomotion than for any other function (Alexander, 1992). As such, it is to their advantage to keep energy costs as low as possible. Research by Alexander (1984), Hildebrand (1989), and Hoyt and Taylor (1981) reveal that terrestrial animals select a gait pattern that will minimize energy expenditure at the speed that they are locomoting. Selection of the optimal gait pattern for animals is automatic and implicit as it would be for infants.

The relation between energy minimization and the emergence of new interlimb patterns of organization was addressed in a longitudinal study (Goldfield, Kay, & Warren, 1993) observing how infants through 35 weeks of age learn to optimize their bouncing while attached to a spring-mounted harness (Jolly Jumper). The results revealed that the number of bounces and their amplitude increased over sessions suggesting that foot contact information and the springlike stiffness of their leg muscles became better matched to the mechanical properties of the spring-mounted harness over sessions. This matching between the infant's behavior and the resonant frequency of the harness is not only more stable than other regimes, but it is energetically more efficient.

A consideration of the energetic costs of other interlimb patterns suggests that energy optimization contributes often to the selection of new behavioral forms. During the period of forward prone progression, the patterning of arms as well as legs contributes to the performance of the infant, especially following the onset of hands-and-knees crawling (Figure 2.11). Typically, some form of prone progression, for example, belly crawling, begins around 32 weeks of age and progresses to hands-and-knees crawling by around 42 weeks of age. Early studies on the development of hands-and-knees crawling were inconsistent regarding the interlimb pattern produced by infants. For example, Burnside (1927) reported that infants move their limbs in diagonal couplets, whereas, Hildebrand (1967) suggested that infants move one limb at a time. From a biomechanical standpoint, these different patterns of interlimb coordination are significant, because they differentially constrain the balance and mobility of the infant. A statically balanced system avoids tipping by keeping the center of mass over a polygon of support formed by three limbs (Raibert, 1986a). By contrast, a dynamically balanced system requires support by only two limbs; the smaller base of support is more flexible and more efficient than the tripod formed by three limbs (Raibert, 1986a). Logically, many different interlimb patterns conform to the requirements of a dynamically balanced system. For example, infants could support themselves with two diagonally opposite limbs, two ipsilateral limbs, or two homologous limbs.

Two recent longitudinal investigations observed developmental changes in the prone progression of infants (Adolph, Vereijken, & Denny, in press; Freedland & Bertenthal, 1994). Infants did not show any consistent interlimb pattern prior to the time that they supported their abdomens off the ground. Following the emergence of a hands-and-knees posture, infants quickly converged on an interlimb pattern involving diagonal couplets (i.e., support provided by right hand and left knee alternating with left hand and right knee). This particular interlimb pattern represents the most dynamically efficient of all two-limb patterns because it maintains a stable center of gravity (Alexander, 1992). It also shows little variability and is not perturbed by the addition of weights or the ascent up slopes (Freedland & Bertenthal, 1992). As such, this finding is consistent with other recent studies suggesting that dynamically stable coordinative structures remain invariant across a range of conditions (Clark & Phillips, 1993; Thelen & Ulrich, 1991; Whitall, 1991).

Walking without Support

The transition to independent upright locomotion is a monumental accomplishment for infants as well as parents. It is the necessity of stabilizing the mass of the body while standing on one leg and thrusting forward that makes this task so challenging. In order to propel the body forward, any terrestrial animal must apply a force against the ground in a direction opposite to the direction of forward progression. This force is produced by extending the legs that lie between the ground and the center of mass. If we stand erect and extend our legs, the ground reaction is directed vertically and we end up on tip-toes. Forward propulsion requires that we reposition our center of mass ahead of one leg, even though this posture produces a momentary imbalance. The trailing limb is lengthened to produce a ground reaction while the other leg is swung forward to keep the trunk from falling.

The cycle of limb movements produced by adults while walking is very orderly and stable. During the support or propulsive phase, which begins with footfall and ends with toe lift-off, the leg remains stationary as the body pivots over the leg; during the swing or recovery phase, which begins with toe lift-off and ends with footfall, the body remains stationary as the leg moves forward. A stride or step cycle is defined as a complete cycle of propulsion and recovery for each leg. Each step (or half-cycle) consists of a double support phase when both feet are on the ground and a swing phase for one of the two legs (Figure 2.12). For walking and slow running the gaits are usually symmetrical, that is, footfalls are evenly distributed in space and time (Forrester, Phillips, & Clark, 1993; Hildebrand, 1967; Raibert, 1986b). (See Figure 2.12.)

When infants begin walking they also show a symmetrical gait pattern, but the spatial (distance) and temporal phase relations between the two limbs are more variable (Clark, Whitall, & Phillips, 1988). This variability contributes to an unstable equilibrium, as does the small size of the child's base of support and high center of gravity. These factors are partially counterbalanced by (1) a wide spacing of the feet to increase the base of support, (2) slight flexion of the hip and knee to lower the center of gravity, and (3) raising the arms to facilitate muscular coordination (Burnside, 1927). Also the instability of the young child's walking is reduced by supporting the body with both feet firmly on the ground for 60% of the cycle (Clark & Phillips, 1993). By comparison, adults remain in a double support phase for only 20% of the cycle (Winter, 1983). One consequence of the infant's conservative strategy is that stride length is reduced and walking proceeds very slowly (Clark & Phillips, 1993). Following 2 to 3 months of walking experience, stride length and speed increases and then most gait parameters show little change through 12 months of walking experience (Bril & Breniere, 1991; Clark & Phillips, 1993). In addition, the coupling between the limbs becomes very stable following 3 to 6 months of walking experience, presumably because strength and balance are increasing as indexed by decreases in the double support phase (Bril & Breniere, 1992; Clark & Phillips, 1993; Whitall & Clark, 1994). These developmental changes parallel those seen with hands-and-knees crawling; speed increases as infants become stronger

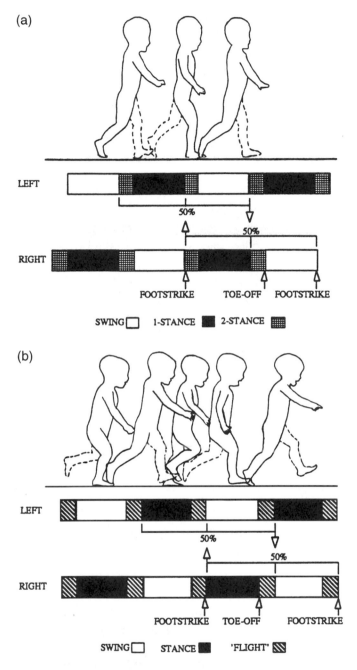

(a)

LEFT

RIGHT

50%

50%

FOOTSTRIKE   TOE-OFF   FOOTSTRIKE

SWING ☐   1-STANCE ■   2-STANCE ▦

(b)

LEFT

RIGHT

50%

50%

FOOTSTRIKE   TOE-OFF   FOOTSTRIKE

SWING ☐   STANCE ■   'FLIGHT' ▨

Figure 2.12 Walking and running cycles. (a) The walking cycle consists of each limb moving through a similar sequence of swing, double support (2-foot stance), and single support (1-foot stance) phases. The left leg begins its cycle midway through the cycle of the right leg. (b) The running cycle is also symmetric, with each limb moving through swing and stance, but a flight phase replaces double support. Reprinted from "Locomotor coordination in infancy: The transition from walking to running," by L. W. Forrester, et al., 1993. In G. J. P. Savelsbergh (Ed.), *The development of coordination in infancy* (pp. 359–393). Amsterdam, The Netherlands: Elsevier, with kind permission from Elsevier Science–NL, Sara Burgerhartstraat 25, 1055 KV Amsterdam, The Netherlands.

and show a decrease in the stance phase of their gait cycle (Adolph, Vereijken, & Denny, in press; Freedland & Bertenthal, 1994).

The control of walking involves not only interlimb coordination, but intralimb coordination as well. The leg is segmented at the knee and the movements of the thigh (upper leg) and shank (lower leg) must be coordinated to achieve a stable gait. Similar to the progress shown for interlimb coordination, intralimb coordination develops rapidly during the first 3 months following the onset of walking (Clark & Phillips, 1993). The parallel time course of intra- and interlimb coordination suggests that these two processes are complementary and are mediated by similar experiences. Other studies investigating developmental changes in stepping during the first year suggest that this synchronous development is quite common for intra- and interlimb coordination (Thelen & Fisher, 1982, 1983).

Running, Galloping, and Hopping

The emergence of upright walking marks only the beginning of the progression of new locomotor skills that will develop over the next few years. These additional skills include running, galloping, hopping, skipping, and jumping, and they will all be part of the child's locomotor repertoire by 7 years of age (Roberton & Halverson, 1984). In this section, we focus on a subset of these skills—running, galloping, and hopping—to illustrate how changes in both control and coordination contribute to the development of new modes of locomotion. Recall that coordination refers to the spatial-temporal organization of limb movements; reproducible patterns and invariance, such as the symmetrical phasing of the legs during walking, are the signatures of a stable coordination (Jensen, Phillips, & Clark, 1994). Control refers to the tuning of limb parameters, such as displacement, amplitude, and speed, necessary for adjusting performance to the context and specific task variables (Schoner & Kelso, 1988).

Running is the next locomotor skill to emerge after walking, and is distinguished from walking by a flight phase in which neither leg is in contact with the ground (Figure 2.12). Gesell and Amatruda (1941) reported that running emerges as early as 18 months in children, and is well-established by 24 months. Others report that running appears between 2.5 and 6 months after the onset of walking (Burnett & Johnson, 1971). One important reason that running emerges so soon after walking is that the two skills share the same pattern of interlimb coordination, that is, one leg is 50% out of phase with the other. Nevertheless, running does not develop simultaneously with walking, suggesting that some differences are present between the two skills (Forrester et al., 1993).

One significant difference between walking and running is that the former involves a series of controlled falls, whereas the latter involves a series of controlled leaps (Rosenbaum, 1991). In order to achieve these leaps, sufficient ground reaction forces must be generated to propel the feet off the ground (Cavanaugh & Lafortune, 1980). Running at moderate speeds creates peak vertical forces at ground contact around two times body weight (Fortney, 1983); also, running demands greater force to maintain postural equilibrium (Forrester et al., 1993). Clark and Whitall (1989a) hypothesized that the inability of newly walking infants to run is primarily attributable to their limitations in generating sufficient forces. This hypothesis was empirically confirmed in a recent study by Whitall and Getchell (in press) who used motion analysis to study four children at 5.5, 7.5, and 9.5 months after the onset of independent walking and then at 3 years of age. Kinematic analyses revealed that the children produced greater horizontal and vertical leg displacements as they acquired more experience locomoting. The improvement shown by these children to produce sufficient force to generate the greater displacements associated with running could follow from increases in muscle mass, anthropometric changes, improved motoneuron recruitment, or some combination of these factors. Although a definitive answer is not yet available, it is noteworthy that the rate limiting factor in the emergence of running is not the development of a new pattern of coordination, but rather a change in the parameterization of the variables.

Unlike running, galloping involves a new asymmetrical pattern of interlimb coordination in which the leading limb begins its cycle approximately 35% of the way through the cycle of the trailing limb (Whitall & Clark, 1994). This asymmetrical pattern corresponds to a walk with one limb and a run with the other limb (Clark & Whitall, 1989a). The gallop does not usually appear until 6 months or more following the run. In one of the few reported studies of the development of galloping, Clark, Whitall, and Phillips (cited in Clark & Whitall, 1989a) observed that the one child who they were studying showed an increase in the variability of the phasing of the limbs at around the time that galloping emerged. Although this finding is based on a single child, the increase in variability coinciding with the emergence of a new pattern of behavior is consistent with

other developmental transitions involving a change in coordinative structure.

Not surprisingly, hopping emerges later than the other locomotor skills because standing on one leg for some duration places additional demands on both balance and strength. In addition, the child must learn to differentiate the scaling of forces to the two legs since it is necessary to produce force in only one leg sufficient to lift the body off the ground. Halverson and Williams (1985) reported that only one of twenty 2-year-old children could hop, but that all the 3-year-old children could hop. In this earliest form of hopping, the swing leg is inactive and it is not until 4 or 5 years of age that the swing leg begins to move as the hop rate decreases (Halverson & Williams, 1985; Roberton & Halverson, 1988). Roberton and Halverson (1988) hypothesized that these changes could be attributed directly to the dynamics of hopping rather than to the development of a motor program. The child's hopping leg was modeled as a mass-spring system in which the speed of hopping is controlled by the stiffness of the spring. As children learn to increase their resistance to leg flexion on landing (i.e., increase stiffness), the speed of hopping will increase until some critical value is reached. Beyond that value a new interlimb pattern becomes necessary to insure that hopping remains safe and functional. It was predicted that this new pattern would involve the swinging of the nonhopping leg because oscillation of this leg produces greater flexion (reduces stiffness) in the hopping leg. Consistent with this prediction, Getchell and Roberton (1989) reported a dramatic reduction in instantaneous and estimated average whole body stiffness of 4- to 8-year-old children when their swing leg was active as opposed to inactive (Getchell & Roberton, 1989).

In sum, the development of these new locomotor skills depends heavily on improvements in controlling balance and generating the necessary forces. New patterns of interlimb coordination, such as galloping, emerge rather abruptly during periods of increased variability in the performance of other locomotor skills. Once the component variables necessary for any new locomotor skill are available to the child, the emergence of that skill in developmental time will follow the same self-organizing principles that operate during real-time behavioral transitions, such as the transition from walking to running (Diedrich & Warren, 1995). Thus, the development of these new locomotor skills does not require explicit instruction, but they do require practice and variation to become more flexible and better scaled to local conditions.

Perceptual Control of Locomotion

By now, it should be apparent that all actions are modulated and controlled by perceptual information, but locomotion places additional demands on the perceptual systems since movements are no longer limited to one location. As an observer moves through the environment, the optic flow specifies both the invariant structure of the environment as well as the changing relation between the observer and the various surfaces and objects in the environment (J. Gibson, 1979). Following Lee and Thompson (1982), we begin by distinguishing between three different sources of perceptual information. *Exteroceptive* information refers to the layout of surfaces and objects and their changes over time; *proprioceptive* information refers to the positions, orientations, and movements of body segments relative to each other; and *exproprioceptive* information refers to the position, orientation, and movement of the body as a whole, or part of the body, relative to the environment. In this section, we focus on the third source of information because most of the current research is concerned with selecting traversable surfaces and adapting locomotor strategies to the properties of those surfaces.

Traversable Surfaces

Surfaces of support available for locomotion vary along many dimensions, including slant, rigidity, smoothness, presence of obstacles, discontinuities in the path, and so on. Typically, these properties are specified by visual information before the observer chooses to move forward or avoid a surface. Other information is available through haptic exploration, but it is restricted to very proximal surfaces (cf. Gibson & Schmuckler, 1989). Although some surfaces are more easily traversed than others, for example, a roadway versus a narrow path cut in the woods, most afford some form of locomotion. One dramatic exception is a surface that ends abruptly at a precipice or cliff.

Gibson and Walk (1960) simulated the abrupt discontinuity of a cliff with their classic "visual cliff." This apparatus consists of a large sheet of plexiglass (8 ft × 4 ft) suspended 4 ft above the floor. A narrow board is placed across the middle, dividing the sheet into two sides. On one side (referred to as the shallow side), a textured checkerboard pattern is placed directly under the glass, so that it appears as a rigid and supportable surface. On the other side (referred to as the deep side), the textured pattern is placed 4 ft below the glass, so that this side simulates an apparent drop-off. In most studies, infants are placed on the centerboard and encouraged to cross to the mother who alternates standing across from the deep and shallow sides of the cliff.

Depth information at the apparent drop-off is specified by multiple sources including binocular disparity, the abrupt change in the size of the checkboard pattern, occlusion and disocclusion of texture at the edge, and motion parallax, that is, differential speed of near and far texture elements as the head and eyes move. The visual cliff was designed originally to test depth perception, but more recent research suggests that infants are sensitive to depth information prior to the age when they can be tested on the visual cliff (Yonas & Owsley, 1987). If depth perception, per se, was responsible for visual cliff performance, then infants should avoid the deep side as soon as they begin crawling. The evidence suggests, however, that avoidance represents a more complex process (Bertenthal & Campos, 1984).

Some insight into this process was first suggested by the pioneering research of Held and Hein (1963) who tested kittens on the visual cliff following selective rearing. Visuomotor experience for one group of kittens was normal and included correlated input between their active locomotion and optic flow, but visual experience for a yoked control group was restricted to passive locomotion. This latter group thus received no visual information correlated with the consequences of their own locomotion. Later, these passively reared kittens showed no avoidance of the deep side of the visual cliff, whereas the actively reared kittens avoided the deep side immediately.

Consistent with the preceding research, a number of experiments suggest that infants' avoidance of the deep side of the cliff is related to the time since crawling onset (Bertenthal & Campos, 1990; Bertenthal, Campos, & Barrett, 1984; Campos, Bertenthal, & Kermoian, 1992; Campos, Hiatt, Ramsay, Henderson, & Svejda, 1978; Richards & Rader, 1981, 1983). Many of these studies suggest that learning to avoid crossing the deep side of the cliff is directly attributable to crawling experience rather than to chronological age or some other developmental variable. Converging evidence for this conclusion is derived from studies measuring infants' heart rate as they are lowered toward the deep or shallow sides of the visual cliff (Campos, Bertenthal, & Kermoian, 1992). Prelocomotor infants show heart rate deceleration (indexing interest and attention) to the depth information as they are lowered onto the deep side of the cliff. By contrast, locomotor infants show heart rate acceleration (indexing wariness or fear). Prelocomotor infants who received 30 to 40 hours of locomotor experience in wheeled walkers also showed heart rate acceleration when tested on the visual cliff. Taken together, these findings suggest that infants learn to use the visual information specifying an apparent drop-off to control the consequences of their own locomotion (Adolph, in press; Bertenthal & Campos, 1990; Campos et al., 1992).

It is also noteworthy that haptic information specifying the continuity and rigidity of the surface on the deep side was disregarded by infants with crawling experience. These infants were resistant to crossing specifically because they come to rely on visual information to guide their locomotion. From an adaptive standpoint, this resolution to the conflicting perceptual information seems understandable because haptic information specifies the immediate conditions regarding the surface of the support, whereas visual information specifies surface conditions that will be encountered in the near future. For infants as for adults, visual information is prospective and designed to constrain actions before they become dangerous.

Locomotor Strategies

One question unanswered by the preceding research is whether the perceptual consequences of different surface properties are different for crawlers and walkers. Recall that the constraints on maintaining balance and generating sufficient force for forward progression are quite different for the two modes of locomotion. It therefore seems reasonable to expect that the capacity for traversal will depend on the fit between the mode of locomotion and the surface (Gibson & Schmuckler, 1989).

In one experiment (Gibson et al., 1987), crawling and walking infants were tested for their willingness to traverse a rigid walkway constructed of firm plywood and a nonrigid walkway constructed of a waterbed; the waterbed was gently agitated to reveal its deformability. Walking infants showed shorter latencies and less exploration of the rigid than of the nonrigid surface. Also, mode of locomotion on the rigid surface was split between walking and crawling, but all children crawled on the nonrigid surface. By contrast, crawling infants showed little differentiation in their traversing both surfaces. These results were confirmed in a second locomotor preference experiment in which both surfaces were presented simultaneously and infants chose which surface to traverse. Additional experiments compared performance on the rigid surface covered with a textured pattern or with black velvet. Both crawlers and walkers were wary of the black velvet surface because it

provided little optical information to specify its surface properties. It thus appears that the previous differences reported for crawlers and walkers are not simply attributable to greater wariness emerging in older infants. A more parsimonious interpretation is that infants perceptually explored the surfaces and then adjusted their mode of locomotion to optimize their performance relative to the different surface properties.

Similar differences between crawlers and walkers were observed when infants were tested for their willingness to ascend and descend slopes (Figure 2.13). These tasks are similar to the visual cliff in that they involve a disparity in depth between the summit and the flat surface below, but,

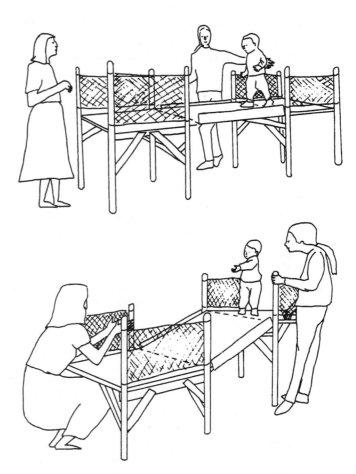

Figure 2.13 Walkway with adjustable slope. Top: Warm-up phase on flat walkway. Parent stands at one end while experimenter follows alongside the child. Bottom: Example of descending trial in which a hydraulic pump lowers the bottom platform, causing the walkway to slant at 20°. From "Crawling versus walking infants' perception of affordances for locomotion over sloping surfaces," by K. E. Adolph et al., 1993, *Child Development, 64,* pp. 1158–1174. Copyright © 1993 by the Society for Research in Child Development. Reprinted with permission.

unlike the cliff, visual and haptic information are concordant and specify a continuous slanted surface that affords support. Adults are quite good at judging the slant of a surface relative to their own action potential (Fitzpatrick, Carello, Schmidt, & Corey, 1994; Kinsella-Shaw, Shaw, & Turvey, 1992; Proffitt, Bhalla, Gossweiler, & Midgett, 1996), although they tend to overestimate slant when judgments are limited to verbal reports (Proffitt et al., 1996). From a biomechanical standpoint, ascending and descending slopes represent somewhat different tasks. Crawling or walking up a hill is energy demanding because of the greater load produced by gravity, but it is relatively easy to control and safe; crawling or walking down a hill is less energy demanding, but it is more difficult to control because body weight is supported on bent arms or legs, which makes balance more precarious (Adolph, in press).

Crawling and walking infants show differential locomotor responses on sloping walkways as a function of the angle of inclination as well as whether the task involves ascending or descending slopes (Adolph, Eppler, & Gibson, 1993a; Eppler, Adolph, & Weiner, in press). For example, Adolph et al. (1993a) tested 8.5-month-old crawling infants and 14-month-old walking toddlers on a sloping walkway (10°, 20°, 30°, and 40°). Children in both locomotor groups showed few differences in ascending slopes; they all tended to overestimate their ability and fall on the steeper slopes. By contrast, most toddlers switched from walking to sliding positions when descending slopes, but crawling infants showed little evidence of exploring alternative means for descent and were more likely to fall. Toddlers showed the greatest perceptual exploration on slopes that they could descend, whereas the opposite was true for crawling infants. A psychophysical investigation of 14-month-old walking infants' exploration and strategy choices when descending slopes suggests that the difference between toddlers and crawlers is that the older children are better at scaling their responses to the available perceptual information (Adolph, 1995). This finding is quite impressive because it suggests that young toddlers are capable of exploring surfaces and anticipating whether their repertoire of locomotor skills will allow them to descend those slopes.

A recent longitudinal study following infants from the onset of crawling through the first 10 weeks of walking reveals that crawling infants are also capable of scaling their responses to the perceptual information when provided sufficient experience (Adolph, in press). An intriguing finding from this investigation is that the scaling shown by crawling infants does not transfer when they begin walking, and it is necessary for them to learn a new scaling between the slopes and their ability to walk down these surfaces. This inability to generalize the same perceptual information across different motor skills is a recurrent theme in the literature (Bertenthal, 1996). For example, Lockman (1984) reports that crawling infants retrieve a toy that they see hidden behind a barrier one month earlier when the task involves reaching around the barrier as opposed to crawling around the barrier. From a logical standpoint, these two tasks are the same, but the actions are different and the correct reaching response develops before the correct crawling response. Apparently, perceptuomotor performance involves more than just the availability of the necessary perceptual information and motor responses. It is essential for infants to learn through active experience and exploration how perceptual information and motor responses are coupled together into an action system (Reed, 1982).

CHANGE MECHANISMS

Early research on motor development tended to oversimplify age-related changes by attributing the emergence of new behavioral patterns to a single cause, such as neuromaturation or cognitive development. From this perspective, the principal task for researchers was simply to describe sequential changes in motor skills as a proxy for the underlying mechanism. The introduction of new views concerning the indeterminacy of movement patterns by Bernstein (1967) and the direct availability of perceptual information for controlling actions by J. Gibson (1966, 1979) shifted the emphasis from descriptive to process-oriented studies. The results from these studies offer a very different perspective on the mechanisms responsible for developmental change.

In particular, recent research challenges the traditional view that infants are prescribed by some genetic plan or abstract cognitive structures to follow a fixed and sequential progression of stages in the development of new motor skills. In spite of the logical attractiveness of such a framework, the consensus conveyed by the evidence is that this position is neither valid nor informative for understanding how new movement patterns emerge or change over time. As we have increased the magnification of our observational lenses, we have begun to gain new insights into the fine structure of human actions. These insights lead to a new synthesis in which developing control of movements is seen as a dynamic and multi-determined process. Contrary to traditional views, these actions do not begin as reflexes; instead, they are spontaneous and modulated by context (Reed, 1989). Infants engage in goal-directed and exploratory behaviors from birth, and their actions become better coordinated as the perceptual information becomes more differentiated. Instead of behavioral development reflecting patterns of stability that are interrupted briefly by transitions to new behaviors, movement patterns show significant periods of variability in real and developmental time. This variability introduces new movement patterns or actions for achieving specific goals and also offers greater flexibility in adapting actions to task demands. These generalizations relating to the process of change are elaborated in the remainder of this section.

Perceptual Control of Actions

When are perception and action first coordinated? For the past few decades, the dominant view was shaped by Piaget's theory of sensorimotor development (1952, 1954). Neonatal actions are restricted to an ensemble of reflexes in which perceptions and actions are initially uncoupled and independent. Over time, these two processes become coordinated through practice and experience. A literal interpretation of this position is that the behavior of the neonate is essentially random and insensitive to any contextual information. Perhaps this position overstates the implications of Piaget's theory because it is conceivable that the theory would acknowledge that proprioception (perception of self) is available at birth to control actions, but there seems little consensus concerning this issue (Lockman, 1990). In any event, the findings reviewed in this chapter present clear and unequivocal evidence that some actions are perceptually modulated from birth.

Many of the actions showing perceptual coordination involve eye and head movements, presumably because muscle strength and other biomechanical constraints interfere less with the control of these actions. Thus, for example, newborn infants orient to sound (Clifton et al., 1981), scan differently in different stimulus conditions (Haith, 1980), visually track moving targets (Bloch & Carchon, 1992), and adjust their head posture to the direction and velocity of optic flow information (Jouen, Lepecq, & Gapenne, in press). Newborn infants also increase the frequency of hand-to-mouth contacts as a function of mouth opening or following the oral delivery of a sucrose solution (Blass

et al., 1989; Lew & Butterworth, 1995), and they show hand extensions toward objects placed in front of them (von Hofsten, 1982, 1984). All of these coordinated behaviors are fragile and inconsistent, which explains why they were missed by so many previous researchers. Nonobvious and subtle changes in stimulus factors or posture are often sufficient to disrupt the coordinated behavior. For example, neonates experience difficulty in tracking objects because of the instability of their trunks, which do not yet move independently of their heads (Bullinger, 1981; Roucoux et al., 1983).

The inconsistency of these newborn behaviors highlights a recurrent theme in this chapter. It is inaccurate and misleading to attribute an action to a single cause, such as neural development or cognitive development, and ignore all of the other variables that contribute to whether or not the action appears in a specific context (Bertenthal et al., 1994; Thelen, 1995). Muscle strength, perceptual differentiation, posture, material properties of objects and surfaces, and so on, all contribute to the successful performance of an action. Many contemporary theorists emphasize that development involves a confluence of factors that include neural, perceptual, and biomechanical changes as well as environmental and task factors (Bertenthal, 1996; Newell, 1986; Thelen, 1995). Development is a function of learning to assemble all of the contributing factors on-line to produce a task-specific response. Practice and experience with specific action systems contribute to their development (Sveistrup & Woollacott, in press; Thelen & Ulrich, 1991). As new actions are assembled and become available for learning about the world, the infant is challenged repeatedly to tune those actions to an increasingly diverse set of situations. In this way, actions become better coordinated and more flexible with experience. For example, infants and toddlers learn to traverse different surfaces more successfully by modifying their mode of locomotion as well as their speed. Infants also learn to better control the direction of their reaches and the anticipatory shaping of their hand with practice and experience. One of the most provocative findings emerging from this review is that new actions involving novel patterns of coordination, such as crawling on hands-and-knees, often appear abruptly, but the time course for tuning or scaling these actions to local conditions is much longer and depends on the experiences of the child.

The differences between the complementary processes of coordination and control are often subtle and thus demand very detailed and extensive analyses. These analyses should include repeated measurements on the same infants and children because the development of motor skills shows considerable intra- and interindividual variability (Thelen, 1989, 1995). It is for this reason that longitudinal studies are essential for studying change mechanisms in motor development (e.g., Thelen, 1995).

Dissociation between Perception and Control

New actions are assembled and controlled in response to perceptual information from the self and the spatial layout. It is important to emphasize, however, that infants' sensitivity to this perceptual information does not necessarily generalize beyond the control of a specific action. For example, 5-month-old infants are already responding to gravity and inertia when guiding their arm movements while reaching for a moving target (Robin et al., 1996; von Hofsten, 1983), yet they do not visually discriminate events that either conform to or violate these physical laws until close to the end of their first year (Spelke, 1994). One interpretation for this discrepancy is that all perception is stimulus specific, but it is more likely that this difference relates to how the perceptual information is used.

The conventional view of perception is that all sensory inputs converge on some unified representation that then guides both thought and action. Yet, recent anatomical and neurophysiological findings suggest that the perceptual control of actions and the perceptual recognition of objects and surfaces are mediated by functionally and structurally dissociable pathways (Milner & Goodale, 1995). Recently, Bertenthal (1996) summarized evidence suggesting that this functional dissociation between recognition of objects and control of actions is relevant to understanding the origins and early development of perception in human infants.

In essence, Bertenthal (1996) points out that object recognition includes processes that make contact with information perceived in the past and stored for the future. Successful recognition depends on both how the visual information is parsed and on the representational format of the stored information. As representations are expanded through new experiences, they become more abstract and differentiated and begin to guide reasoning about familiar and novel experiences. By contrast, perceptual control of actions functions in real-time with little explicit reference to past experience. These actions are modularly organized and not represented in a form that is recalled or used to guide the production of other actions. It is sufficient that infants perceive where they are and what they are doing.

All that matters is the current fit between the self and the environment. Past experience does contribute by increasing sensitivity to perceptual information and finer control of actions. However, unlike object recognition, perceptual control is implicit or procedural; it is elicited by context and not recall of explicit information about the coordination of a specific behavior.

An especially important developmental implication of this view is that perceptuomotor coordination does not readily generalize from one action to another. Perceptual control of actions is conceptualized as a nested hierarchy of modular input-output systems (Milner & Goodale, 1995). Unlike the recognition system, no representations are available for generalizing stimulus input to new motor responses. Instead, generalization depends exclusively on experience tutoring new actions. For example, infants gradually learn to scale the forces necessary to control their sitting posture in a moving room, but this learning does not readily generalize to a standing posture (Bertenthal et al., in press; Woollacott & Sveistrup, 1994). Likewise, Rochat and Senders (1991) report a progression in hand-mouth coordination from bimanual action organized in mirror image symmetry toward an asymmetrical involvement of the hands. This same progression is repeated when infants begin to visually explore objects that are grasped. Finally, recall that infants learn gradually to control their descent down a slope while crawling, but this perceptual learning does not generalize to walking down slopes (Adolph, in press). From the vantage point of a modularly organized control system, these findings are not surprising. Indeed, it seems quite reasonable for infants to require an additional apprenticeship with a task when a new response is involved because it is necessary to learn the mapping between sensory information and the response synergies necessary for controlling new limbs with different segment lengths, masses, moments of inertia, and so on.

Reciprocity between Perception and Action

Perceptual control of actions depends on both the sensitivity of the perceptual systems as well as the functionality of the motor response synergies. As simple actions, such as visual tracking and grasping, are practiced and repeated, they become better coordinated and controlled, and perceptual information necessary for this control is detected with increasing specificity. Likewise, improvements in perceptual differentiation afford infants greater control of their actions. It is for this reason that the development of perception and action is reciprocal and mutual. The two processes inform and challenge each other to become better adapted to task and environmental factors. Consider, for example, the development of infants' sensitivity to haptic properties of objects. The detection of some of these properties, such as size, demands minimal control of the hand and fingers, whereas other properties, such as weight and shape, require much greater control. As we discussed in an earlier section, infants detect some object properties, such as size and temperature, within the first few months, but texture and weight are not detected until 6 to 9 months, and shape is not detected until even later. This developmental progression corresponds closely to the developmental changes observed in the control of the hands and fingers (Bushnell & Boudreau, 1993). The close correspondence between the development of manual behaviors and haptic perception suggests that these two processes are reciprocally related. Although the evidence for this conclusion is still incomplete, it is certainly provocative and highlights the importance of considering the contribution of new motor skills for understanding perceptual development as well as the more expected contribution of perceptual skills for understanding motor development (Bertenthal & Campos, 1990; Bushnell & Boudreau, 1993).

Currently, much of the evidence consistent with the principle of reciprocity between perception and action is restricted to correlative findings, but research on the relation between self-produced locomotion and localization of hidden objects represents a noteworthy exception. Precrawling infants are expected to code the location of a hidden object with a body-centered frame of reference, presumably because this coding is initially necessary for successful orientation to the object (Bertenthal, 1996). With the emergence of crawling, infants no longer rely on this frame of reference (or at least recognize that it must be continuously updated) because their orientation relative to the spatial layout is continuously changing (Acredolo, 1985; Benson & Uzgiris, 1985; Bertenthal, Campos, & Barrett, 1984; Bertenthal et al., 1994; Bremner, 1985). Studies manipulating the availability of self-produced locomotion (e.g., independent crawling vs. passive transport) or locomotor experience (e.g., precrawling, crawling, and experience in wheeled walkers) converge to show that locomotor experience improves search performance by infants (Acredolo, Adams, & Goodwyn, 1984; Bai & Bertenthal, 1992; Benson & Uzgiris, 1985; Horobin & Acredolo, 1986; Kermoian & Campos, 1988). Apparently, the emergence

and availability of locomotion increases the sensitivity of infants to the relevant perceptual information.

Although the preceding examples emphasize perceptual information external to the infant, the information necessary for this reciprocity involves both information about the self as well as information about the environment. Perception of self-movements represents some of the most consistent and ubiquitous information available to young infants (Bertenthal & Rose, 1995). In addition, this information is almost always specified multimodally. For example, posture is specified by proprioceptive, vestibular, and visual flow information (Lishman & Lee, 1973). Recall that even neonates show some control of their head movements (Jouen, 1988; Jouen et al., in press). One likely reason that postural control develops so rapidly is that it is controlled by multiple and redundant inputs that are present virtually all the time. This consistency and redundancy increases the likelihood of detection even when stimulation of some modalities is below threshold. Also, the perception of the self, unlike the perception of objects, necessitates that the perceptual information is always correlated with the action. Every movement includes stimulation from the muscles, joints, and skin that specifies the changing position and force of the moving limbs. For this reason the development of perception and action are inextricably related when considering perception of self-movements.

Variation and Selection

One of the principal contributions of recent research on the development of perception and action is to focus attention on the variability of behavior. In contrast to conventional views of behavioral development which emphasize stable patterns of performance that are interrupted by temporary and abrupt changes, the new findings on motor development emphasize that variability is often present in the performance of an action and contributes to its further development. Thus, a complete understanding of the change mechanisms contributing to the development of motor skills requires an analysis of the variability as well as the regularity in performance (Ulrich, Jensen, & Thelen, 1991).

It is useful to begin by clarifying what is meant by variability of performance. Recall the example of expert and novice pistol shooters studied by Arutyunyan et al. (1969). Performance in this study revealed two different sources of variability. Novice pistol shooters showed high variability with regard to hitting the target, whereas expert shooters showed low variability because their shots were very accurate. By contrast, novice pistol shooters showed little variability in movement while aiming their pistols at the target, whereas expert pistol shooters showed significantly more variability in their movements because they were compensating for changes in internal and external conditions. Thus, it is important to distinguish between variability in the outcome of an action and variability in the execution of an action (Newell & Corcos, 1993). Both of these sources of variability are relevant to the development and improvement of new skills.

While learning new motor skills, it is quite common for variability in the coordination of the action to first decrease and then increase. Consider, for example, visual control of sitting in a moving room (Bertenthal et al., in press). When 5-month-old infants are tested, they show large amplitudes of postural sway and considerable variability, but this variability shows a significant decline by 7 months of age. Surprisingly, this variability increases again at 9 months of age. The reason for this flip-flop is that few 5-month-old infants control their balance while sitting, whereas most 7-month-old infants sit without support. Typically, the learning of new skills is accompanied by reducing degrees of freedom through stiffening joints to minimize unsafe and poorly controlled limb movements (Bernstein, 1967; McDonald, van Emmerick, & Newell, 1989; Rosenbaum, 1991). By 9 months of age, infants are more secure with the new skill of sitting, so they tend to reduce muscle stiffness and increase compensatory movements to maintain balance. In this example, the variability in maintaining a balanced sitting posture is first attributable to poor control of the necessary response synergy, but later variability is attributable to greater flexibility in compensating for postural perturbations. Additional examples of increased variability in movement patterns accompanying new levels of flexibility include toddlers descending slopes (Adolph, 1995, in press) and infants stepping on motorized treadmills (Thelen & Ulrich, 1991).

One question unanswered by the above examples is how infants learn new postural synergies that are more flexible. An intriguing possibility is that learning follows a stochastic process in which developmental forces induce new movement patterns (Edelman, 1987, 1992; Thelen, 1995). Some of these stochastic outcomes will be selected preferentially to other outcomes based on the complementary processes of cooperation and competition (Edelman, 1992; Kaas, 1991; Siegler, 1989). An intrinsic value (motivational) system biases selection toward those patterns that

will satisfy either implicit (e.g., minimization of energy) or explicit (e.g., intentional) goals.

In the case of motor development, variability in performance increases at certain times in response to changes in the organism or environment. For example, increases in muscle strength or the desynchronization in the movements of the hip, knee, and ankle joints, or the differentiation of head and trunk afford infants a greater repertoire of movement patterns from which they can select a subset of adaptive responses. Likewise, greater demands by the environment, such as maintaining balance against gravity in more challenging postures, or responding to new task demands presented by parents or the self, introduce more variability in performance. Note that increases in the variability of new movements are never random because they are always constrained by structural and functional demands, such as limb mass and length, gravitational and centripetal forces, or the material properties of objects. As infants explore new movement patterns that emerge with changing constraints, a distribution of intrinsic values drives the organism to store and repeat those actions that are optimally successful (Sporns & Edelman, 1993).

An exceptionally fine example of learning to store and repeat successful actions is the model developed by Berthier (1996) to explain decreases in the number of reaching submovements necessary to contact an object. As previously discussed, reaching is modeled as a stochastic optimization control problem in which infants learn by trial-and-error how to scale the force of their arm movements to achieve their goal of contacting an object. Similar to the results of the model, infants show initially considerable variability in the direction and amplitude of each submovement, but this variability decreases as infants learn to select those submovements that optimize their performance. Thus, the development of smoother and more accurate reaching is consistent with a self-organizing system in which specific visuomotor mappings are selected from a much larger distribution in order to optimize the goal of contacting the object.

One caveat before concluding. This new emphasis on variation and selection is not meant to imply that studying regularities in development is unimportant. Indeed, evidence for global or long-term stability along with local or short-term variability is the hallmark of a complex system (Goldfield, 1995; Thelen & Smith, 1994). The presence of this dualism in the behavior of the motor control system is useful for explaining why variability in the development of motor performance was overlooked for so long. Most actions typically appear stable and consistent at a global or macroscopic level, but they are revealed as variable at a more microscopic or detailed level of analysis. Readers interested in pursuing these ideas further are referred to the "Dynamic Systems Theories" chapter in Volume 1 of the *Handbook*.

FUTURE DIRECTIONS

One of our goals in writing this review was to highlight how the study of motor development has been transformed in recent years from a traditional field of inquiry to a progressive and innovative one. New technologies for analyzing behavior, innovative designs focusing on changes within and between individuals, and novel theories emphasizing the dynamic and variable nature of human performance offer new insights into the process of development. From our vantage point, it would not be surprising if many of these methodological and theoretical advances were gradually adopted by researchers in other fields (e.g., Thelen & Smith, 1994).

Before this happens, however, it will be necessary for research on perception and action to expand its focus of investigation. Our review emphasized research on the early development of posture, reaching, and locomotion partly by design, but also because there are far fewer studies conducted on older children or other behaviors. It seems that it is time to redress this imbalance by beginning to systematically investigate motor performance in older children involved in a wider range of tasks. Historically, the study of older children has focused on the development of gross motor skills, such as jumping or skipping or ball catching (e.g., Clark & Phillips, 1985; Jensen et al., 1994). This focus was almost exclusively descriptive and much too restrictive. One of the major conclusions from this review is that human movements are organized by task and not by prescription of a motor program. It thus seems reasonable to begin considering what specific tasks are relevant to the everyday life of children and how those tasks rely on specific motor skills.

Some important progress in pursuing this goal was initiated by Reed (1982) who provided a taxonomy of action systems (e.g., orienting, investigatory, appetitive) that are important to the survival of locomotor animals. Following the logic of this taxonomy, Goldfield (1995) devotes entire chapters to the development of posture and orientation, eating and drinking, locomotion, performatory actions (i.e., manual activity), and expressive actions (i.e., emotional communication). It is clear from this taxonomic

approach that motor development transcends traditional topics and is foundational to many other psychological processes, such as emotional expression or tool use or even vocal communication. Our understanding of motor responses relies on precise and quantitative measures of performance, but currently the processes controlling these less conventional motor responses are not receiving the same level of analysis.

The bulk of the research conducted in fields like emotional expression or even tool use focuses on the input and its interpretation by the child. Typically, the response is viewed as a direct index of the way the stimulus information is processed. Recent research in motor development reveals that this view of the motor response is misleading because the specific form of any movement is a function of a large number of both central and peripheral factors. It is impossible to predict that children will necessarily perform the same motor response in the same way they have done previously without full knowledge of the task. Our models of the development of many different behaviors that are measured with a motor response would be enriched if we applied the same level of precision and analysis to these responses as we do to more traditional motor responses. For example, even the interpretation for the development of object permanence measured by a search task is changed significantly when the motor response is analyzed carefully (Diamond, 1991; Thelen & Smith, 1994).

It would also be valuable to apply more detailed analyses to activities that develop first during the preschool years or later. For example, actions such as way-finding, or drawing, or writing include components that are available at fairly young ages, but are not assembled into goal-directed activities until a later age. Many of these actions involve planning and other representational components. Currently, little is known about how children assemble actions when they involve planning and other forms of higher-level control. It would be very useful to begin addressing some of these questions to learn more about how cognitive and action systems interact in the performance of different tasks. More generally, we encourage researchers to begin expanding their topics of inquiry to include how action systems constrain and promote advances in cognitive and social development.

ACKNOWLEDGMENTS

We would like to express our appreciation to the following individuals for their comments and suggestions concerning this manuscript: Karen Adolph, Neil Berthier, Roberta Collard, Jane Clark, Michael McCarty, and Claes von Hofsten.

REFERENCES

Acredolo, L. P. (1985). Coordinating perspectives on infant spatial orientation. In R. Cohen (Ed.), *The development of spatial cognition.* Hillsdale, NJ: Erlbaum.

Acredolo, L. P., Adams, A., & Goodwyn, S. W. (1984). The role of self-produced movement and visual tracking in infant spatial orientation. *Journal of Experimental Child Psychology, 38,* 312–327.

Adelson, E., & Fraiberg, S. (1974). Gross motor development in infants blind from birth. *Child Development, 45,* 114–126.

Adolph, K. E. (1995). A psychophysical assessment of toddlers' ability to cope with slopes. *Journal of Experimental Psychology: Human Perception and Performance, 21,* 734–750.

Adolph, K. E. (1997). Cognitive-motor learning in infant locomotion. *Monographs of the Society for Research in Child Development.*

Adolph, K. E., Eppler, M. A., & Gibson, E. J. (1993a). Crawling versus walking infants' perception of affordances for locomotion over sloping surfaces. *Child Development, 64,* 1158–1174.

Adolph, K. E., Eppler, M. A., & Gibson, E. J. (1993b). Development of perception of affordances. In C. Rovee-Collier & L. P. Lipsitt (Eds.), *Advances in infancy research* (Vol. 8, pp. 51–98). Norwood, NJ: ABLEX.

Adolph, K. E., Vereijken, B., & Denny, M. A. (in press). Roles of variability and experience in development of crawling. *Child Development.*

Alexander, R. M. (1984). Walking and running. *American Scientist, 72,* 348–354.

Alexander, R. M. (1992). *Exploring biomechanics.* New York: Freeman.

Allard, P., Stokes, I. A. F., & Blanchi, J. P. (Eds.). (1995). *Three-dimensional analysis of human movement.* Champaign, IL: Human Kinetics.

Amiel-Tison, C., & Grenier, A. (1986). *Neurological assessment during the first year of life.* New York: University Press.

Andersen, G. J. (1986). Perception of self-motion: Psychophysical and computational approaches. *Psychological Bulletin, 99,* 52–65.

Arutyunyan, G., Gurfinkel, V., & Mirsky, M. (1969). Investigation of aiming at a target. *Biophysics, 13,* 536–538.

Ashmead, D. H., & McCarty, M. E. (1991). Postural sway of human infants while standing in light and dark. *Child Development, 62,* 1276–1287.

Ashmead, D. H., McCarty, M. E., Lucas, L. S., & Belvedere, M. C. (1993). Visual guidance in infants' reaching toward suddenly displaced targets. *Child Development, 64,* 1111–1127.

Aslin, R. N. (1981). Development of smooth pursuit in human infants. In D. F. Fischer, R. A. Monty, & E. J. Senders (Eds.), *Eye movements: Cognition and vision perception* (pp. 31–51). Hillsdale, NJ: Erlbaum.

Atkinson, J., & Braddick, O. (1981). Development of optokinetic nystagmus in infants: An indicator of cortical binocularity? In D. F. Fisher, R. A. Monty, & J. W. Senders (Eds.), *Eye movements: Cognition and visual perception* (pp. 53–64). Hillsdale, NJ: Erlbaum.

Bai, D. L., & Bertenthal, B. I. (1992). Locomotor status and the development of spatial search skills. *Child Development, 63,* 215–226.

Bard, C., Fleury, M., & Hay, L. (Eds.). (1990). *Development of eye hand coordination across the life-span.* Columbia, SC: University of South Carolina Press.

Bates, E., Carlson-Luden, V., & Bretherton, I. (1980). Perceptual aspects of tool using in infancy. *Infant Behavior and Development, 3,* 127–140.

Bayley, N. (1933a). Mental growth during the first three years. A developmental study of sixty-one children by repeated tests. *Genetic Psychology Monographs, 14,* 1–92.

Bayley, N. (1933b). *The California First-Year Mental Scale.* Berkeley: University of California Press.

Bayley, N. (1935). The development of motor abilities during the first three years: A study of sixty-one infants tested repeatedly. *Monographs of the Society for Research in Child Development, 1,* 26–61.

Bayley, N. (1936). *The California Infant Scale of Motor Development.* Berkeley: University of California Press.

Bayley, N. (1969). *Manual for the Bayley Scales of infant development.* New York: Psychological Corp.

Bayley, N. (1993). *Bayley Scales of infant development* (2nd ed.). San Antonio: Psychological Corp.

Benson, J. B., & Uzgiris, I. C. (1985). Effect of self-initiated locomotion on infant search activity. *Developmental Psychology, 21,* 923–931.

Bernstein, N. (1967). *The coordination and regulation of movements.* Oxford, England: Pergamon Press.

Bertenthal, B. I. (1990). Application of biomechanical principles to the study of perception and action. In H. Bloch & B. I. Bertenthal (Eds.), *Sensory-motor organization and development in infancy and early childhood* (pp. 243–260). Dordrecht, The Netherlands: Kluwer.

Bertenthal, B. I. (1996). Origins and early development of perception, action, and representation. *Annual Review of Psychology, 47,* 431–459.

Bertenthal, B. I., & Bai, D. L. (1987). Visual-vestibular integration in early development. In K. Jaffe (Ed.), *Childhood powered mobility: Developmental, technical and clinical perspectives* (pp. 43–61). Washington, DC: RESNA.

Bertenthal, B. I., & Bai, D. L. (1989). Infants' sensitivity to optical flow for controlling posture. *Developmental Psychology, 25,* 936–945.

Bertenthal, B. I., Boker, S. M., & Rose, J. L. (1995). Dynamical analyses of postural development. *Journal of Sport & Exercise Psychology, 17,* 8.

Bertenthal, B. I., & Campos, J. J. (1984). A reexamination of fear and its determinants on the visual cliff. *Psychophysiology, 21,* 413–417.

Bertenthal, B. I., & Campos, J. J. (1990). A systems approach to the organizing effects of self-produced locomotion during infancy. In C. Rovee-Collier & L. P. Lipsitt (Eds.), *Advances in infancy research* (pp. 1–60). Norwood, NJ: ABLEX.

Bertenthal, B. I., Campos, J. J., & Barrett, K. C. (1984). Self-produced locomotion: An organizer of emotional, cognitive, and social development in infancy. In R. Emde & R. Harmon (Eds.), *Continuities and discontinuities in development* (pp. 175–210). New York: Plenum Press.

Bertenthal, B. I., Campos, J. J., & Kermoian, R. (1994). An epigenetic perspective on the development of self-produced locomotion and its consequences. *Current Directions in Psychological Science, 3,* 140–145.

Bertenthal, B. I., & Rose, J. L. (1995). Two modes of perceiving the self. In P. Rochat (Ed.), *The self in infancy: Theory and research* (pp. 303–324). Amsterdam, The Netherlands: Elsevier.

Bertenthal, B. I., Rose, J. L., & Bai, D. L. (in press). Perception-action coupling in the development of visual control of posture. *Journal of Experimental Psychology: Human Perception and Performance.*

Berthier, N. E. (1996). Learning to reach: A mathematical model. *Developmental Psychology, 32,* 811–823.

Bigelow, A. (1986). The development of reaching in blind children. *British Journal of Developmental Psychology, 4,* 355–366.

Biguer, B., Jeannerod, M., & Prablanc, C. (1982). The coordination of eye, head and arm movements during reaching at a single visual target. *Experimental Brain Research, 46,* 301–304.

Blass, E. M., Fillion, T. J., Rochat, P., Hoffmeyer, L. B., & Metzger, M. A. (1989). Sensorimotor and motivational determinants of hand-mouth coordination in 1–3-day-old human infants. *Developmental Psychology, 25,* 963–975.

Bloch, H. (1990). Status and function of early sensory-motor coordination. In H. Bloch & B. I. Bertenthal (Eds.), *Sensory-motor organizations and development in infancy and early childhood* (pp. 163–178). Dordrecht, The Netherlands: Kluwer.

Bloch, H., & Bertenthal, B. I. (Eds.). (1990). *Sensory-motor organization and development in infancy and early childhood.* Dordrecht, The Netherlands: Kluwer.

Bloch, H., & Carchon, I. (1992). On the onset of eye-head coordination in infants. *Behaviour Brain Research, 49,* 85–90.

Boker, S. M., Schreiber, T., Pompe, B., & Bertenthal, B. I. (in press). Nonlinear analysis of perceptual-motor coupling in the development of postural control. In H. Kanz, J. Kurths, & G. Mayer-Kress (Eds.), *Nonlinear techniques in physiological time series analysis.* Berlin: Springer-Verlag.

Borstelmann, L. J. (1983). Children before psychology: Ideas about children from antiquity to the late 1800s. In W. Kessen (Ed.), *Handbook of child psychology: History, theory, and methods* (pp. 1–40). New York: Wiley.

Bower, T. (1972). Object perception in infants. *Perception, 1,* 15–30.

Bower, T., Broughton, J. M., & Moore, M. K. (1970). Demonstration of intention in the reaching behavior of neonate humans. *Nature, 228,* 679–681.

Bower, T., & Wishart, J. (1972). The effects of motor skill on object permanence. *Cognition, 7,* 165–171.

Bremner, J. G. (1985). Object tracking and search in infancy: A review of data and a theoretical evaluation. *Developmental Review, 5,* 371–396.

Bremner, J. G. (1988). *Infancy.* Oxford, England: Basil Blackwell.

Bril, B., & Breniere, Y. (1991). Timing invariance in toddlers' gait. In J. Fagard & P. H. Wolff (Eds.), *The development of timing control and temporal organization in coordinated action* (pp. 231–244). New York: Elsevier.

Bril, B., & Breniere, Y. (1992). Postural requirements and progression velocity in young walkers. *Journal of Motor Behavior, 24,* 105–116.

Bril, B., Zack, M., & Nkounkou-Hombessa, E. (1989). Ethnotheorics of development and education: A view from different cultures. *European Journal of Psychology of Education, 4,* 307–318.

Bruner, J. S. (1969). Eye, hand, and mind. In D. Elkind & J. Flavell (Eds.), *Studies in cognitive development: Essays in honor of Jean Piaget* (pp. 223–236). New York: Oxford University Press.

Bruner, J. S. (1973). Organization of early skilled action. *Child Development, 44,* 1–11.

Bullinger, A. (1981). Cognitive elaboration of sensorimotor behavior. In G. Butterworth (Ed.), *Infancy and epistemology: An evaluation of Piaget's theory* (pp. 173–199). Brighton, Sussex: Harvester Press.

Bullinger, A. (1983). Space, the organism and objects: Their cognitive elaboration in the infant. In A. Hein & M. Jeannerod (Eds.), *Spatially oriented behaviour* (pp. 215–222). Berlin: Springer-Verlag.

Bullinger, A. (1991). Vision, posture et mouvement chez le bebe: Approche developpementale et clinique [Vision, posture and movement in infancy: A developmental and clinical approach]. In F. Jouen & A. Henocq (Eds.), *Du nouveau-ne au nourrisson: Recherche fondamentale et pediatrie* (pp. 47–63). Paris: Presses Universitaires de France.

Burnett, C. N., & Johnson, E. W. (1971). Development of gait in childhood: Part 2. *Developmental Medicine & Child Neurology, 13,* 207–215.

Burnside, L. H. (1927). Coordination in the locomotion of infants. *Genetic Psychology Monographs, 2,* 279–372.

Bushnell, E. (1985). The decline of visually guided reaching during infancy. *Infant Behavior and Development, 8,* 139–155.

Bushnell, E., & Boudreau, J. P. (1993). Motor development and the mind: The potential role of motor abilities as a determinant of aspects of perceptual development. *Child Development, 64,* 1005–1021.

Butterworth, G. (1981). Object permanence and identity in Piaget's theory of infant cognition. In G. Butterworth (Ed.), *Infancy and epistomology: An evaluation of Piaget's theory* (pp. 137–169). Brighton, Sussex: Harvester Press.

Butterworth, G., & Grover, L. (1990). Joint visual attention, manual pointing, and preverbal communication in human infancy. In M. Jeannerod (Ed.), *Attention and performance* (Vol. 13, pp. 605–624). Hillsdale, NJ: Erlbaum.

Butterworth, G., & Hicks, L. (1977). Visual proprioception and postural stability in infancy: A developmental study. *Perception, 6,* 255–262.

Butterworth, G., & Hopkins, B. (1988). Hand-mouth coordination in the new-born baby. *British Journal of Developmental Psychology, 6,* 303–314.

Butterworth, G., & Pope, M. (1983). Origine et fonction de la proprioception visuelle chez l'enfant. In S. de Schonen (Ed.), *Le developpement dans la premiere annee* (pp. 107–128). Paris: Presses Universitaires de France.

Campos, J., Bertenthal, B. I., & Kermoian, R. (1992). Early experience and emotional development: The emergence of wariness of heights. *Psychological Science, 3*(1), 61–64.

Campos, J., Hiatt, S., Ramsay, D., Henderson, C., & Svejda, M. (1978). The emergence of fear on the visual cliff. In M. Lewis & L. Rosenblum (Eds.), *The development of affect* (pp. 149–182). New York: Plenum Press.

Carmichael, L. (Ed.). (1954). *Manual of child psychology* (2nd ed.). New York: Wiley.

Cavanaugh, P. R. (1987). The biomechanics of lower extremity action in distance running. *Foot & Ankle, 7,* 197–205.

Cavanaugh, P. R., & Lafortune, M. A. (1980). Ground reaction forces in distance runners. *Journal of Biomechanics, 13,* 397–406.

Clark, J. E., & Humphrey, J. H. (Eds.). (1990). *Advances in motor development research.* New York: AMS.

Clark, J. E., & Phillips, S. J. (1985). A developmental sequence of the standing long jump. In J. E. Clark & J. H. Humphrey (Eds.), *Motor development: Current selected research* (Vol. 1). Princeton, NJ: Princeton Book.

Clark, J. E., & Phillips, S. J. (1993). A longitudinal study of interlimb coordination in the first year of independent walking: A dynamical systems analysis. *Child Development, 64,* 1143–1157.

Clark, J. E., Truly, T. L., & Phillips, S. J. (1993). On the development of walking as a limit cycle system. In E. Thelen & L. Smith (Eds.), *Dynamical systems in development: Applications.* Cambridge, MA: MIT Press.

Clark, J. E., & Whitall, J. (1989a). Changing patterns of locomotion: From walking to skipping. In M. Woollacott & A. Shumway-Cook (Eds.), *Development of posture and gait across the lifespan* (pp. 128–151). Columbia, SC: University of South Carolina Press.

Clark, J. E., & Whitall, J. (1989b). What is motor development? The lessons of history. *Quest, 41,* 183–202.

Clark, J. E., Whitall, J., & Phillips, S. J. (1988). Human interlimb coordination: The first 6 months of independent walking. *Developmental Psychobiology, 21,* 445–456.

Clifton, R. K., Morrongiello, B. A., Kulig, J. W., & Dowd, J. M. (1981). Developmental changes in auditory localization in infancy. In R. Aslin, J. Alberts, & M. Petersen (Eds.), *Development of perception: Vol. 1. Psychobiological perspectives* (pp. 141–160). New York: Academic Press.

Clifton, R. K., Muir, D., Ashmead, D. H., & Clarkson, M. G. (1993). Is visually guided reaching in early infancy a myth? *Child Development, 64,* 1099–1110.

Clifton, R. K., Perris, E. E., & Bullinger, A. (1991). Infants' perception of auditory space. *Developmental Psychology, 27,* 187–197.

Clifton, R. K., Rochat, P., Litovsky, R. Y., & Perris, E. E. (1991). Object representation guides infants' reaching in the dark. *Journal of Experimental Psychology: Human Perception and Performance, 17,* 323–329.

Clifton, R. K., Rochat, P., Robin, D. J., & Berthier, N. E. (1994). Multimodal perception in human infants. *Journal of Experimental Psychology: Human Perception and Performance, 20,* 876–886.

Connolly, K. J. (1970). *Mechanisms of motor skill development.* New York: Academic Press.

Connolly, K. J., & Dalgleish, M. (1989). The emergence of a tool-using skill in infancy. *Developmental Psychology, 25,* 894–912.

Connolly, K. J., & Elliott, J. M. (1972). The evolution and ontogeny of hand function. In N. Blurton-Jones (Ed.), *Ethological studies of child behavior* (pp. 329–383). Cambridge, England: Cambridge University Press.

Daniel, B. M., & Lee, D. (1990). Development of looking with head and eyes. *Journal of Experimental Child Psychology, 50,* 200–216.

Darwin, C. (1877). Biographical sketch of an infant. *Mind, 2,* 285–294.

deVries, J. I. P., Visser, G. H. A., & Prechtl, H. F. R. (1985). The emergence of fetal behaviour: 2. Quantitative aspects. *Early Human Development, 12,* 99–120.

Diamond, A. (1991). Neurophysiological insights into the meaning of object concept development. In S. Carey & R. Gelman (Eds.), *The epigenesis of mind: Essays on biology and cognition* (pp. 67–110). Hillsdale, NJ: Erlbaum.

Diedrich, F. J., & Warren, W. H., Jr. (1995). Why change gaits? Dynamics of the walk-run transition. *Journal of Experimental Psychology: Human Perception and Performance, 21*(1), 183–202.

Dodwell, P. C., Muir, D. W., & DiFranco, D. (1976). Responses of infants to visually presented objects. *Science, 194,* 209–211.

Edelman, G. (1987). *Neural Darwinism: The theory of neuronal group selection.* New York: Basic Books.

Edelman, G. (1992). *Bright air, brilliant fire: On the matter of mind.* New York: Basic Books.

Ennouri, K., & Bloch, H. (in press). Visual control of hand approach movements in newborns. *British Journal of Developmental Psychology.*

Enoka, R. M. (1988). *Neuromechanical basis of kinesiology.* Champaign, IL: Human Kinetics.

Eppler, M. A., Adolph, K. E., & Weiner, T. (in press). The developmental relationship between exploration and action on sloping surfaces. *Infant Behavior and Development.*

Farmer, J. D., & Sidorowich, J. J. (1987). Predicting chaotic time series. *Physical Review Letter, 59,* 845–848.

Fentress, J. C. (1989). Developmental roots of behavioral order: Systemic approaches to the examination of core developmental issues. In M. R. Gunnar & E. Thelen (Eds.), *Systems and development: The Minnesota Symposia on Child Psychology* (pp. 35–76). Hillsdale, NJ: Erlbaum.

Fetters, L., & Todd, J. (1987). Quantitative assessment of infant reaching movements. *Journal of Motor Behavior, 19,* 147–166.

Field, J. (1976). Relation of young infants' reaching behavior to stimulus distance and solidity. *Developmental Psychology, 12,* 444–448.

Finocchio, D. V., Preston, K. L., & Fuchs, A. F. (1991). Infant eye movements: Quantification of the vestibulo-ocular reflex and visual-vestibular interactions. *Vision Research, 31,* 1717–1730.

Fitzpatrick, P., Carello, C., Schmidt, R. C., & Corey, D. (1994). Haptic and visual perception of an affordance for upright posture. *Ecological Psychology, 6,* 265–287.

Forrester, L. W., Phillips, S. J., & Clark, J. E. (1993). Locomotor coordination in infancy: The transition from walking to running. In G. J. P. Savelsbergh (Ed.), *The development of coordination in infancy* (pp. 359–393). Amsterdam, The Netherlands: Elsevier.

Forssberg, H. (1985). Ontogeny of human locomotor control: 1. Infant stepping, supported locomotion and transition to independent locomotion. *Experimental Brain Research, 57,* 480–493.

Forssberg, H., & Nashner, L. (1982). Ontogenic development of postural control in man: Adaptation to altered support and visual conditions during stance. *Journal of Neuroscience, 2,* 545–552.

Fortney, V. (1983). The kinematics and kinetics of the running pattern of two-, four-, and six-year-old children. *Research Quarterly for Exercise and Sport, 54,* 126–135.

Franco, F., & Butterworth, G. (1996). Pointing and social awareness: Declaring and requesting in the second year. *Journal of Child Language, 23,* 307–336.

Freedland, R. L., & Bertenthal, B. I. (1992). Kinematic analyses of the development of creeping in human infants. *Infant Behavior and Development, 15,* 300.

Freedland, R. L., & Bertenthal, B. I. (1994). Developmental changes in interlimb coordination: Transition to hands-and-knees crawling. *Psychological Science, 5,* 26–32.

Georgopoulos, A. P., & Grillner, S. (1989). Visuomotor coordination in reaching and locomotion. *Science, 245,* 1209–1210.

Gesell, A. (1928). *Infancy and human growth.* New York: Macmillan.

Gesell, A. (1954). The ontogenesis of infant behavior. In L. Carmichael (Ed.), *Manual of child psychology* (2nd ed., pp. 335–373). New York: Wiley.

Gesell, A., & Amatruda, C. S. (1941). *Developmental diagnosis: Normal and abnormal child development.* New York: Hoeber.

Gesell, A., & Ames, L. (1940). The ontogentic organization of prone behavior in human infancy. *Journal of Genetic Psychology, 56,* 247–263.

Gesell, A., & Thompson, H. (1929). Learning and growth in identical infant twins: An experimental study by the method of co-twin control. *Genetic Psychology Monographs, 6,* 1–124.

Gesell, A., & Thompson, H. (1934). *Infant behavior: Its genesis and growth.* New York: McGraw-Hill.

Getchell, N., & Roberton, M. A. (1989). Whole body stiffness as a function of developmental level in children's hopping. *Developmental Psychology, 25,* 920–928.

Gibson, E. J. (1988). Exploratory behavior in the development of perceiving, acting, and the acquiring of knowledge. *Annual Review of Psychology, 39,* 1–41.

Gibson, E. J., Riccio, G., Schmuckler, M. A., Stoffregen, T. A., Rosenberg, D., & Taormina, J. (1987). Detection of the traversability of surfaces by crawling and walking infants. *Journal of Experimental Psychology: Human Perception and Performance, 13,* 533–544.

Gibson, E. J., & Schmuckler, M. A. (1989). Going somewhere: An ecological and experimental approach to the development of mobility. *Ecological Psychology, 1,* 3–25.

Gibson, E. J., & Walk, R. D. (1960). The "visual cliff." *Scientific American, 202,* 64–71.

Gibson, E. J., & Walker, A. S. (1984). Development of knowledge of visual-tactual affordances of substance. *Child Development, 55,* 453–460.

Gibson, J. J. (1958). Visually controlled locomotion and visual orientation in animals. *British Journal of Psychology, 49,* 182–194.

Gibson, J. J. (1966). *The senses considered as perceptual systems.* Boston: Houghton Mifflin.

Gibson, J. J. (1979). *The ecological approach to visual perception.* Boston: Houghton Mifflin.

Goldfield, E. C. (1995). *Emergent forms: Origins and early development of human action and perception.* New York: Oxford University Press.

Goldfield, E. C., Kay, B. A., & Warren, W. H. (1993). Infant bouncing: The assembly and tuning of action systems. *Child Development, 64,* 1128–1142.

Gottlieb, G. (1991). Experiential canalization of behavioral development: Theory. *Developmental Psychology, 27,* 4–13.

Gowlett, J. A. J. (1984). Mental abilities of early man: A look at some hard evidence. In R. A. Foley (Ed.), *Hominid evolution and community ecology* (pp. 167–192). London: Academic Press.

Grillner, S. (1981). Control of locomotion in bipeds, tetrapods, and fish. In V. B. Brooks (Ed.), *Handbook of physiology: Vol. 2. Motor control. Part 2* (pp. 1179–1236). Bethesda, MD: American Physiological Society.

Haith, M. M. (1980). *Rules that babies look by: The organization of newborn visual activity.* Hillsdale, NJ: Erlbaum.

Haith, M. M. (1994). Visual expectations as the first step toward the development of future-oriented processes. In M. M. Haith, J. B. Benson, R. J. Roberts, & B. F. Pennington (Eds.), *The development of future-oriented processes* (pp. 11–38). Chicago: University of Chicago Press.

Halverson, H. M. (1931). An experimental study of prehension in infants by means of systematic cinema records. *Genetic Psychology Monographs, 10,* 107–286.

Halverson, H. M. (1932). A further study of grasping. *Journal of Genetic Psychology, 7,* 34–64.

Halverson, L. E., & Williams, K. (1985). Developmental sequences for hopping over distance: A prelongitudinal screening. *Research Quarterly for Exercise and Sport, 56,* 37–44.

Harbourne, R. T., Guiliani, C., & MacNeela, J. (1993). A kinematic and electromyographic analysis of the development of sitting posture in infants. *Developmental Psychobiology, 26*(1), 51–64.

Hatwell, Y. (1987). Motor and cognitive functions of the hand in infancy and childhood. *International Journal of Behavioral Development, 10,* 509–526.

Hatze, H. (1980). A mathematical model for the computational determination of parameter values of anthropomorphic segments. *Journal of Biomechanics, 13,* 833–843.

Hauert, C. A. (Ed.). (1990). *Developmental psychology: Cognitive, perceptuo-motor, and neuropsychological perspectives.* Amsterdam, The Netherlands: Elsevier.

Hayes, K. C., & Riach, C. L. (1989). Preparatory postural adjustments and postural sway in young children. In M. Woollacott & A. Shumway-Cook (Eds.), *Development of posture and gait across the life-span* (pp. 97–127). Columbia, SC: University of South Carolina Press.

Held, R., & Hein, A. (1963). Movement-produced stimulation in the development of visually guided behavior. *Journal of Comparative and Physiological Psychology, 56,* 872–876.

Heriza, C. B. (1988). Organization of spontaneous leg movements in preterm infants. *Physical Therapy, 68,* 1340–1346.

Hildebrand, M. (1967). Symmetrical gaits of primates. *American Journal of Physical Anthropology, 26,* 119–130.

Hildebrand, M. (1989). Vertebrate locomotion: An introduction. How does an animal's body move itself along? *BioScience, 39,* 764–765.

Hirschfeld, H., & Forssberg, H. (1994). Epigenetic development of postural responses for sitting during infancy. *Experimental Brain Research, 97,* 528–540.

Horobin, K., & Acredolo, L. (1986). The role of attentiveness, mobility history and separation of hiding sites on Stage 4 behavior. *Journal of Experimental Child Psychology, 41,* 114–127.

Howard, I. P. (1986). The perception of posture, self motion, and the visual vertical. In K. R. Boff, L. Kaufman, & J. P. Thomas (Eds.), *Handbook of perception and human performance: Vol. 1. Sensory processes and perception* (pp. 18-1–18-62). New York: Wiley.

Hoyt, D., & Taylor, C. R. (1981). Gait and the energetics of locomotion in horses. *Nature, 292,* 239–240.

Hunt, J. M. (1961). *Intelligence and experience*. New York: Ronald Press.

Jeannerod, M. (1984). The timing of natural prehension movements. *Journal of Motor Behavior, 16,* 235–254.

Jeannerod, M. (1994). Object oriented action. In K. M. B. Bennett & U. Castiello (Eds.), *Insights into the reach to grasp movement* (pp. 3–15). Amsterdam, The Netherlands: Elsevier.

Jeka, J., & Kelso, J. A. S. (1989). The dynamic pattern approach to coordinated behavior: A tutorial review. In S. A. Wallace (Ed.), *Perspectives on the coordination of movement* (pp. 3–45). Amsterdam, The Netherlands: Elsevier.

Jensen, J. L., Phillips, S. J., & Clark, J. E. (1994). For young jumpers, differences are in the movement's control, not its coordination. *Research Quarterly for Exercise and Sport, 65,* 258–268.

Jensen, J. L., Ulrich, B. D., Thelen, E., Schneider, K., & Zernicke, R. R. (1994). Adaptive dynamics of the leg movement patterns of human infants: 1. The effects of posture on spontaneous kicking. *Journal of Motor Behavior, 26,* 303–312.

Jensen, R. K. (1986). Body segment mass, radius and radius of gyration proportions of children. *Journal of Biomechanics, 19,* 359–368.

Jouen, F. (1984). Visual-vestibular interactions in infancy. *Infant Behavior and Development, 7,* 135–145.

Jouen, F. (1988). Visual-proprioceptive control of posture in newborn infants. In B. Amblard, A. Berthoz, & F. Clarac (Eds.), *Posture and gait: Development, adaptation and modulation* (pp. 13–22). Amsterdam, The Netherlands: Elsevier.

Jouen, F., Lepecq, J. -C., & Gapenne, O. (1993). Frames of reference underlying early movement coordination. In G. J. P. Savelsbergh (Ed.), *The development of coordination in infancy* (pp. 237–263). Amsterdam, The Netherlands: Elsevier.

Jouen, F., Lepecq, J. -C., & Gapenne, O. (in press). Optical flow sensitivity in neonates. *Child Development*.

Kaas, J. H. (1991). Plasticity of sensory and motor maps in adult mammals. *Annual Review of Neuroscience, 14,* 137–167.

Kalverboer, A. F., Hopkins, B., & Geuze, R. (Eds.). (1993). *Motor development in early and later childhood: Longitudinal approaches*. Cambridge, England: Cambridge University Press.

Kelso, J. A. S. (1995). *Dynamic patterns: The self-organization of brain and behavior*. Cambridge, MA: MIT Press.

Kelso, J. A. S., & Clark, J. E. (Eds.). (1982). *The development of movement control and coordination*. New York: Wiley.

Kennel, M. B., Brown, R., & Abarbanel, H. D. I. (1992). Determining embedding dimension for phase-space reconstruction using a geometrical construction. *Physical Review A, 45,* 3403–3411.

Kermoian, R., & Campos, J. J. (1988). Locomotor experience: A facilitator of spatial cognitive development. *Child Development, 59,* 908–917.

Kinsella-Shaw, J. M., Shaw, B., & Turvey, M. T. (1992). Perceiving "walk-on-able" slopes. *Ecological Psychology, 4*(4), 223–239.

Kohler, W. (1925). *The mentality of apes*. London: Harcourt.

Kremenitzer, J. P., Vaughan, H. G., Kurtzberg, D., & Dowling, K. (1979). Smooth-pursuit eye movements in the newborn infant. *Child Development, 50,* 442–448.

Kugler, P. N., Kelso, J. A. S., & Turvey, M. T. (1980). On the concept of coordinative structures as dessipative structures: 1. Theoretical lines of convergence. In G. Stelmach & J. Requin (Eds.), *Tutorials in motor behavior* (pp. 1–47). Amsterdam, The Netherlands: North-Holland.

Lashley, K. S. (1942). The problem of cerebral organization in vision. *Biological Symposia, 7,* 301–322.

Lasky, R. E. (1977). The effect of visual feedback of the hand on the reaching and retrieval behavior of young infants. *Child Development, 48,* 112–117.

Lee, D. N. (1974). Visual information during locomotion. In R. B. McLeod & H. L. Pick (Eds.), *Perception: Essays in honor of James J. Gibson* (pp. 250–267). New York: Cornell University Press.

Lee, D. N. (1993). Body-environment coupling. In U. Neisser (Ed.), *Ecological and interpersonal knowledge of the self* (pp. 68–88). Cambridge, England: Cambridge University Press.

Lee, D. N., & Aronson, E. (1974). Visual proprioceptive control of standing in human infants. *Perception and Psychophysics, 15,* 529–532.

Lee, D. N., & Lishman, J. R. (1975). Visual proprioceptive control of stance. *Journal of Human Movement Studies, 1,* 87–95.

Lee, D. N., Lishman, J. R., & Thompson, J. A. (1982). Visual regulation of gait in long jumping. *Journal of Experimental Psychology: Human Perception and Performance, 8,* 448–459.

Lee, D. N., & Reddish, P. E. (1981). Plummeting gannets: A paradigm of ecological optics. *Nature, 293,* 293–294.

Lee, D. N., & Thompson, J. A. (1982). Vision in action: The control of locomotion. In D. Ingle (Ed.), *Analysis of visual behavior*. Cambridge, MA: MIT Press.

Lestienne, F., Soechting, J., & Berthoz, A. (1977). Postural readjustments induced by linear motion of visual scenes. *Experimental Brain Research, 28,* 363–384.

Lew, A. R., & Butterworth, G. (1995). The effects of hunger on hand-mouth coordination in newborn infants. *Developmental Psychology, 31,* 456–463.

Lishman, J. R., & Lee, D. N. (1973). The autonomy of visual kinaesthesis. *Perception, 2,* 287–294.

Litovsky, R. Y., & Clifton, R. K. (1992). Use of sound pressure level in auditory distance discrimination by 6-month-old infants and adults. *Journal of Acoustical Society of America, 92,* 794–802.

Lockman, J. J. (1984). The development of detour ability during infancy. *Child Development, 55,* 482–491.

Lockman, J. J. (1990). Perceptuomotor coordination in infancy. In C. A. Hauert (Ed.), *Developmental psychology: Cognitive, perceptuo-motor, and neuropsychological perspectives* (pp. 85–112). Amsterdam, The Netherlands: North-Holland.

Lockman, J. J., Ashmead, D., & Bushnell, E. (1984). The development of anticipatory hand orientation during infancy. *Journal of Experimental Child Psychology, 37,* 176–186.

Lockman, J. J., & Thelen, E. (1993). Developmental biodynamics: Brain, body, behavior connections. *Child Development, 64,* 953–959.

Lovejoy, C. O. (1988). Evolution of human walking. *Scientific American, 259*(5), 118–125.

Magnus, R. (1925). Animal posture (The Croonian Lecture). *Proceedings of the Royal Society of London, 98,* 339–352.

Magoun, H. W., Darling, L., & Prost, J. (1960). The evolution of man's brain. In M. A. B. Brazier (Ed.), *The central nervous system and behavior* (pp. 33–126). New York: Josiah Macy, Jr. Foundation.

Marey, E. J. (1894). *Movement.* Paris: Masson.

Mark, L. S. (1987). Eyeheight-scaled information about affordances: A study of sitting and stair-climbing. *Journal of Experimental Psychology: Human Perception and Performance, 13,* 360–370.

Mathew, A., & Cook, M. (1990). The control of reaching movements by young infants. *Child Development, 61,* 1238–1257.

McCarty, M. (1993) *The development of reaching in infants: Visual influences, planning and grasping, and the shoulder-elbow coupling.* Doctoral dissertation, Vanderbilt University.

McDonald, P. V., van Emmerick, R. E., & Newell, K. M. (1989). The effects of practice on limb kinematics in a throwing task. *Journal of Motor Behavior, 21,* 245–264.

McDonnell, P. M. (1975). The development of visually guided reaching. *Perception and Psychophysics, 18,* 181–185.

McGraw, M. B. (1935). *Growth: A study of Johnny and Jimmy.* New York: Appleton-Century-Crofts.

McGraw, M. B. (1940). Neuromuscular development of the human infant as exemplified in the achievement of erect locomotion. *Journal of Pediatrics, 17,* 747–771.

McGraw, M. B. (1941). Development of neuromuscular mechanisms as reflected in the crawling and creeping behavior of the human infant. *Journal of Genetic Psychology, 58,* 83–111.

McGraw, M. B. (1945). *Neuromuscular maturation of the human infant.* New York: Hafner.

McKenzie, B. E., Skouteris, H., Day, R. H., Hartman, B., & Yonas, A. (1993). Effective action by infants to contact objects by reaching and leaning. *Child Development, 64,* 415–429.

Milner, A. D., & Goodale, M. A. (1995). *The visual brain in action.* Oxford, England: Oxford University Press.

Morrongiello, B., & Rocca, P. (1989). Visual feedback and anticipatory hand orientation during infants' reaching. *Perceptual and Motor Skills, 69,* 787–802.

Muybridge, E. (1955). *The human figure in motion.* New York: Dover.

Newell, K. M. (1986). Constraints on the development of coordination. In M. G. Wade & H. T. A. Whiting (Eds.), *Motor development in children: Aspects of coordination and control* (pp. 341–360). Boston: Martinus Nijhoff.

Newell, K. M., & Corcos, D. M. (1993). Issues in variability and motor control. In K. M. Newell & D. M. Corcos (Eds.), *Variability and motor control* (pp. 1–12). Champaign, IL: Human Kinetics.

Newell, K. M., Scully, D. M., McDonald, P. V., & Baillargeon, R. (1989). Task constraints and infant grip configurations. *Developmental Psychobiology, 22,* 817–832.

Oakley, K. P. (1975). *Man the tool-maker* (6th ed.). London: British Museum.

Odenrick, P., & Sandstedt, P. (1984). Development of postural sway in the normal child. *Human Neurobiology, 3,* 241–244.

Owen, B. M., & Lee, D. N. (1986). Establishing a frame of reference for action. In M. B. Wade & H. T. A. Whiting (Eds.), *Motor development in children: Aspects of coordination and control.* Dordrecht, The Netherlands: Martinus Nijhoff.

Paillard, J. (1991). Motor and representational framing in space. In J. Paillard (Ed.), *Brain and space* (pp. 163–182). New York: Oxford University Press.

Palmer, C. F. (1989). The discriminating nature of infants' exploratory actions. *Developmental Psychology, 25,* 885–893.

Paulus, W. M., Straube, A., & Brandt, T. (1984). The visual stabilization of posture: Physiological stimulus characteristics and clinical aspects. *Brain, 107,* 1143–1163.

Pearson, K. G., Ramirez, J. M., & Jiang, W. (1992). Entrainment of the locomotor rhythm by group Ib afferents from ankle extensor muscles in spinal cats. *Experimental Brain Research, 90,* 557–566.

Perris, E. E., & Clifton, R. K. (1988). Reaching in the dark toward sound as a measure of auditory localization in infants. *Infant Behavior and Development, 11,* 473–492.

Petitto, L. (1992). Modularity and constraints in early lexical acquisition and evidence from children's first words/signs and gestures. In M. Gunnar & M. Maratsos (Eds.), *Modularity and constraints in language and cognition: The Minnesota Symposia on Child Psychology* (pp. 25–58). Hillsdale, NJ: Erlbaum.

Petitto, L., & Marentette, P. (1991). Babbling in the manual mode: Evidence for the ontogeny of language. *Science, 251,* 1483–1496.

Piaget, J. (1952). *The origins of intelligence in children.* New York: International Universities Press.

Piaget, J. (1954). *The construction of reality in the child.* New York: Basic Books.

Pick, H. L. J. (1989). Motor development: The control of action. *Developmental Psychology, 25,* 867–870.

Pieraut-Le Bonniec, G. (1990). Reaching and hand adjusting to the target properties. In H. Bloch & B. I. Bertenthal (Eds.), *Sensory-motor organization and development in infancy and early childhood* (pp. 301–314). Dordrecht, The Netherlands: Kluwer.

Prechtl, H. F. R. (Ed.). (1984). *Continuity of neural functions from prenatal to postnatal life.* Oxford, England: Blackwell.

Prechtl, H. F. R. (1986). Prenatal motor development. In M. G. Wade & H. T. A. Whiting (Eds.), *Motor development in children: Aspects of coordination and control* (pp. 53–64). Dordrecht, The Netherlands: Martinus Nijhoff.

Preston, K. L., & Finocchio, D. V. (1993). Development of the vestibulocular and optokinetic reflexes. In K. Simons (Ed.), *Early visual development: Normal and abnormal* (pp. 80–88). New York: Oxford University Press.

Preyer, W. (1882). *De seele des kindes.* Leipzig: Fernau.

Preyer, W. (1888). *The mind of the child: Pt. 1. The senses and the will* (H. W. Brown, Trans.). New York: Appleton.

Proffitt, D. R., Bhalla, M., Gossweiler, R., & Midgett, J. (1996). Perceiving geographicals land. *Psychonomic Bulletin & Review, 2,* 409–428.

Raibert, M. H. (1986a). *Legged robots that balance.* Cambridge, MA: MIT Press.

Raibert, M. H. (1986b). Symmetry in running. *Science, 231,* 1292–1294.

Reed, E. S. (1982). An outline of a theory of action systems. *Journal of Motor Behavior, 14,* 98–134.

Reed, E. S. (1989). Changing theories of postural development. In M. Woollacott & A. Shumway-Cook (Eds.), *The development of posture and gait across the life-span* (pp. 45–86). Columbia, SC: University of South Carolina Press.

Reed, E. S., & Bril, B. (1995). The primacy of action in development. In M. Latash & M. Turvey (Eds.), *Dexterity and its development.* Hillsdale, NJ: Erlbaum.

Resnick, R., & Halliday, D. (1977). *Physics.* New York: Wiley.

Riach, C. L., & Starkes, J. (1987). Visual fixation and postural sway in children. *Journal of Sport and Exercise Psychology, 9,* 56.

Richards, J. E., & Rader, N. (1981). Crawling-onset age predicts visual cliff avoidance in infants. *Journal of Experimental Psychology: Human Perception and Performance, 7*(2), 382–387.

Richards, J. E., & Rader, N. (1983). Affective, behavioral, and avoidance responses on the visual cliff: Effects of crawling onset age, crawling experience, and testing age. *Psychophysiology, 20*(6), 633–642.

Roberton, M. A., & Halverson, L. E. (1984). *Developing children—Their changing movement.* Philadelphia: Lea & Febiger.

Roberton, M. A., & Halverson, L. E. (1988). The development of locomotor coordination: Longitudinal change and invariance. *Journal of Motor Behavior, 20,* 197–241.

Robertson, S. S. (1989). Mechanism and function of cyclicity in spontaneous movement. In W. P. Smotherman & S. R. Robinson (Eds.), *Behavior of the fetus* (pp. 77–94). Caldwell, NJ: Telford.

Robertson, S. S. (1990). Temporal organization in fetal and newborn movement. In H. Bloch & B. I. Bertenthal (Eds.), *Sensory-motor organization and development in infancy and early childhood* (pp. 105–122). Dordrecht, The Netherlands: Kluwer.

Robertson, S. S. (1993). Oscillation and complexity in early infant behavior. *Child Development, 64,* 1022–1035.

Robertson, S. S., Cohen, A. H., & Mayer-Kress, G. (1993). Behavioral chaos: Beyond the metaphor. In L. Smith & E. Thelen (Eds.), *A dynamic systems approach to development* (pp. 119–150). Cambridge, MA: MIT Press.

Robin, D. J., Berthier, N. E., & Clifton, R. K. (1996). Infants' predictive reaching for moving objects in the dark. *Developmental Psychology, 32,* 824–835.

Rochat, P. (1992). Self-sitting and reaching in 5- to 8-month-old infants: The impact of posture and its development on early eye-hand coordination. *Journal of Motor Behavior, 24,* 210–220.

Rochat, P. (1993). Hand-mouth coordination in the newborn: Morphology, determinants, and early development of a basic act. In G. J. P. Savelsbergh (Ed.), *The development of coordination in infancy* (pp. 265–288). Amsterdam, The Netherlands: Elsevier.

Rochat, P., Blass, E. M., & Hoffmeyer, L. B. (1988). Oropharyngeal control of hand-mouth coordination in newborn infants. *Developmental Psychology, 24,* 459–463.

Rochat, P., & Goubet, N. (1995). Development of sitting and reaching in 5–6-month-old infants. *Infant Behavior and Development.*

Rochat, P., & Senders, S. J. (1991). Active touch in infancy: Action systems in development. In M. J. S. Weiss & P. R. Zelazo (Eds.), *Newborn attention: Biological constraints and the influence of experience* (pp. 412–442). Norwood, NJ: ABLEX.

Ronnqvist, L., & von Hofsten, C. (1994). Neonatal finger and arm movements as determined by a social and an object context. *Early Development & Parenting, 3,* 81–94.

Rose, J. L., & Bertenthal, B. I. (1995). A longitudinal study of the visual control of posture in infancy. In B. G. Bardy, R. J.

Bootsma, & Y. Guiard (Eds.), *Studies in perception and action* (pp. 251–253). Mahwah, NJ: Erlbaum.

Rosenbaum, D. (1991). *Human motor control.* New York: Academic Press.

Rosenblith, J. F. (1992). *In the beginning: Development from conception to age two* (2nd ed.). Newbury Park, CA: Sage.

Roucoux, A., Culee, C., & Roucoux, M. (1983). Development of fixation and pursuit of eye movements in human infants. *Behavioural and Brain Research, 10,* 133–139.

Ruff, H. (1984). Infants' manipulative exploration of objects: Effects of age and object characteristics. *Developmental Psychology, 20,* 9–20.

Ruff, H. (1989). The infant's use of visual and haptic information in the perception and recognition of objects. *Canadian Journal of Psychology, 43,* 302–319.

Ruff, H., & Halton, A. (1978). Is there directed reaching in the human neonate? *Developmental Psychology, 14,* 425–426.

Sameroff, A. J. (1983). Developmental systems: Contexts and evolution. In W. Kessen (Ed.), *Handbook of child psychology: Vol. 1. History, theory, and methods* (pp. 237–294). New York: Wiley.

Savelsbergh, G. J. P. (Ed.). (1993). *The development of coordination in infancy.* Amsterdam, The Netherlands: Elsevier.

Savelsbergh, G. J. P., & van der Kamp, J. (1993). The coordination of infant's reaching, grasping, catching and posture: A natural physical approach. In G. J. P. Savelsbergh (Ed.), *The development of coordination in infancy* (pp. 289–317). Amsterdam, The Netherlands: Elsevier.

Schneider, K., & Zernicke, R. F. (1992). Mass, center of mass, and moment of inertia estimates for infant limb segments. *Journal of Biomechanics, 25,* 145–148.

Schneider, K., Zernicke, R., Ulrich, B., Jensen, J., & Thelen, E. (1990). Understanding movement control in infants through the analysis of limb intersegmental dynamics. *Journal of Motor Behavior, 22,* 493–520.

Schoner, G., & Kelso, J. A. S. (1988). Dynamic pattern generation in behavioral and neural systems. *Science, 239,* 1513–1520.

Senn, M. J. E. (1975). Insights on the child development movement in the United States. *Monographs of the Society for Research in Child Development, 40*(3/4), 1–89.

Shea, S. L., & Aslin, R. N. (1990). Oculomotor responses to step-ramp targets by young human infants. *Vision Research, 30,* 1077–1092.

Shirley, M. M. (1931). *The first two years, a study of twenty-five babies: 1. Postural and locomotor development.* Minneapolis: University of Minnesota Press.

Shirley, M. M. (1933). *The first two years, a study of twenty-five babies: 2. Intellectual development.* Minneapolis: University of Minnesota Press.

Shumway-Cook, A., & Woollacott, M. H. (1985). The growth of stability: Postural control from a developmental perspective. *Journal of Motor Behavior, 17,* 131–147.

Siddiqui, A. (1995). Object size as a determinant of grasping in infancy. *Journal of Genetic Psychology, 156,* 345–358.

Siegler, R. S. (1989). Mechanisms of cognitive development. *Annual Review of Psychology, 40,* 353–379.

Siqueland, E. R., & DeLucia, C. A. (1969). Visual reinforcement of sucking in human infants. *Science, 165,* 1144–1146.

Smith, L., & Thelen, E. (Eds.). (1993). *A dynamic systems approach to development: Applications.* Cambridge, MA: MIT Press.

Soechting, J. F., & Flanders, M. (1991). Arm movements in three-dimensional space: Computation, theory, and observation. *Exercise and Sport Sciences Review, 19,* 389–418.

Spelke, E. (1994). Initial knowledge: Six suggestions. *Cognition, 50,* 431–445.

Sporns, O., & Edelman, G. M. (1993). Solving Bernstein's problem: A proposal for the development of coordinated movement by selection. *Child Development, 64,* 960–981.

Stack, D., Muir, D., Sherriff, F., & Roman, J. (1989). Development of infant reaching in the dark to luminous objects and "invisible sounds." *Perception, 18,* 69–82.

Stoffregen, T. A., Schmuckler, M. A., & Gibson, E. J. (1987). Use of central and peripheral optical flow in stance and locomotion in young walkers. *Perception, 16,* 113–119.

Sutherland, D. H. (1984). *Gait disorders in childhood and adolescence.* Baltimore: Williams & Wilkins.

Sveistrup, H., & Woollacott, M. (in press). Can practice modify the developing automatic postural response? *Experimental Brain Research.*

Thelen, E. (1986a). Development of coordinated movement: Implications for early human development. In H. T. A. Whiting & M. G. Wade (Eds.), *Motor development in children: Aspects of control and coordination* (pp. 107–124). Dordrecht, The Netherlands: Martinus Nijhoff.

Thelen, E. (1986b). Treadmill-elicited stepping in seven-month-old infants. *Child Development, 57,* 1498–1506.

Thelen, E. (1987). The role of motor development in developmental psychology: A view of the past and an agenda for the future. In N. Eisenberg (Ed.), *Contemporary topics in developmental psychology* (pp. 3–33). New York: Wiley.

Thelen, E. (1989). Self-organization in developmental processes: Can systems approaches work? In M. Gunnar & E. Thelen (Eds.), *Systems and development: The Minnesota Symposia on Child Psychology* (pp. 77–117). Hillsdale, NJ: Erlbaum.

Thelen, E. (1995). Motor development: A new synthesis. *American Psychologist, 50,* 79–95.

Thelen, E., Corbetta, D., Kamm, K., Spencer, J. P., Schneider, K., & Zernicke, R. F. (1993). The transition to reaching: Mapping intention and intrinsic dynamics. *Child Development, 64*, 1058–1098.

Thelen, E., & Fisher, D. M. (1982). Newborn stepping: An explanation for a "disappearing reflex." *Developmental Psychology, 18*, 760–775.

Thelen, E., & Fisher, D. M. (1983). The organization of spontaneous leg movements in newborn infants. *Journal of Motor Behavior, 15*, 353–377.

Thelen, E., Fisher, D. M., & Ridley-Johnson, R. (1984). The relationship between physical growth and a newborn reflex. *Infant Behavior and Development, 7*, 479–493.

Thelen, E., Ridley-Johnson, R., & Fisher, D. M. (1983). Shifting patterns of bilateral coordination and lateral dominance in the leg movements of young infants. *Developmental Psychobiology, 16*, 29–46.

Thelen, E., & Smith, L. B. (1994). *A dynamic systems approach to the development of cognition and action.* Cambridge, MA: MIT Press.

Thelen, E., & Ulrich, B. (1991). Hidden skills: A dynamic systems analysis of treadmill stepping during the first year. *Monographs of the Society for Research in Child Development, 56*(1, Serial No. 223).

Thelen, E., Ulrich, B. D., & Niles, D. (1987). Bilateral coordination in human infants: Stepping on a split-belt treadmill. *Journal of Experimental Psychology: Human Perception and Performance, 13*, 405–410.

Tiedemann, D. (1787). *Beobachtungen über die Entwickelung der Seelenfähigkeiten bei Kindern.* (New edition edited by C. Ufer, 1897.) Altenburg: Bonde.

Trevarthen, C. (1974). The psychobiology of speech development [Special issue] (E. Lenneberg, Ed.). *Neurosciences Research Program Bulletin, 12*, 570–585.

Trevarthen, C. (1984). How control of movement develops. In H. D. A. Whiting (Ed.), *Human motor actions—Bernstein reassessed* (pp. 223–261). Amsterdam, The Netherlands: North-Holland.

Trevarthen, C. (1990). Grasping from the inside. In M. Goodale (Ed.), *Vision and action: The control of grasping* (pp. 181–203). Norwood, NJ: ABLEX.

Tuller, B., Turvey, M. T., & Fitch, H. (1982). The Bernstein perspective: 2. The concept of muscle linkage or coordinative structure. In J. A. S. Kelso (Ed.), *Human motor behavior: An introduction* (pp. 253–270). Hillsdale, NJ: Erlbaum.

Turvey, M. T. (1990). Coordination. *American Psychologist, 45*, 938–953.

Ulrich, B. D., Jensen, J. L., & Thelen, E. (1991). Stability and variation in the development of infant stepping: Implications for control. In A. E. Patla (Ed.), *Adaptability of human gait* (pp. 145–164). Amsterdam, The Netherlands: Elsevier.

Ulrich, B. D., Ulrich, D. A., & Collier, D. (1992). Alternating stepping patterns: Hidden abilities in 11-month-old infants with Downs Syndrome. *Developmental Medicine in Child Neurology, 34*, 233–239.

van der Meer, A. L. H., van der Weel, F. R., & Lee, D. N. (1995). The functional significance of arm movements in neonates. *Science, 267*, 693–695.

Vaughan, C. L., Davis, B. L., & O'Connor, J. C. (1991). *Dynamics of human gait.* Champaign, IL: Human Kinetics.

von Hofsten, C. (1979). Development of visually guided reaching: The approach phase. *Journal of Human Movement Studies, 5*, 160–178.

von Hofsten, C. (1980). Predictive reaching for moving objects by human infants. *Journal of Experimental Child Psychology, 30*, 369–382.

von Hofsten, C. (1982). Eye-hand coordination in the newborn. *Developmental Psychology, 18*, 450–461.

von Hofsten, C. (1983). Catching skills in infancy. *Journal of Experimental Psychology: Human Perception and Performance, 9*, 75–85.

von Hofsten, C. (1984). Developmental changes in the organization of prereaching movements. *Developmental Psychology, 20*, 378–388.

von Hofsten, C. (1989). Mastering reaching and grasping: The development of manual skills in infancy. In S. A. Wallace (Ed.), *Perspectives on the coordination of movement* (pp. 223–258). Amsterdam, The Netherlands: North-Holland.

von Hofsten, C. (1991). Structuring of early reaching movements: A longitudinal study. *Journal of Motor Behavior, 23*, 280–292.

von Hofsten, C. (1993). Prospective control: A basic aspect of action development. *Human Development, 36*, 253–270.

von Hofsten, C., & Fazel-Zandy, S. (1984). Development of visually guided hand orientation in reaching. *Journal of Experimental Child Psychology, 38*, 208–219.

von Hofsten, C., & Lindhagen, K. (1979). Observations on the development of reaching for moving objects. *Journal of Experimental Child Psychology, 28*, 158–173.

von Hofsten, C., & Ronnqvist, L. (1988). Preparation for grasping an object: A developmental study. *Journal of Experimental Psychology: Human Perception and Performance, 14*, 610–621.

von Hofsten, C., & Ronnqvist, L. (1993). The structuring of neonatal arm movements. *Child Development, 64*, 1046–1057.

von Hofsten, C., & Rosander, K. (1996). The development of gaze control and predictive tracking in young infants. *Vision Research, 36*, 81–96.

Wade, M. G., & Whiting, H. T. A. (Eds.). (1986). *Motor development in children: Aspects of coordination and control.* Boston: Martinus Nijhoff.

Warren, D. H. (1984). *Blindness and early childhood development* (2nd ed.). New York: American Foundation for the Blind.

Warren, W. H. (1984). Perceiving affordances: Visual guidance of stair climbing. *Journal of Experimental Psychology: Human Perception and Performance, 10,* 683–703.

Warren, W. H. (1990). The perception-action coupling. In H. Bloch & B. Bertenthal (Eds.), *Sensory-motor organization and development in infancy and early childhood* (pp. 23–38). Dordrecht, The Netherlands: Kluwer.

Warren, W. H., & Whang, S. (1987). Visual guidance of walking through apertures: Body-scaled information for affordances. *Journal of Experimental Psychology: Human Perception and Performance, 13,* 371–383.

Whitall, J. (1991). The developmental effect of concurrent cognitive and locomotor skills: Time sharing from a dynamical perspective. *Journal of Experimental Child Psychology, 51,* 245–266.

Whitall, J., & Clark, J. E. (1994). The development of bipedal interlimb coordination. In S. P. Swinnen, J. Massion, & H. Heuer (Eds.), *Interlimb coordination: Neural, dynamical, and cognitive constraints* (pp. 391–411). San Diego, CA: Academic Press.

Whitall, J., & Getchell, N. (in press). From walking to running: Applying a dynamical systems approach to the development of locomotor skills. *Child Development.*

White, B., Castle, P., & Held, R. (1964). Observations on the development of visually-directed reaching. *Child Development, 35,* 349–364.

Willatts, P. (1984). The stage-4 infants' solution of problems requiring the use of supports. *Infant Behavior & Development, 7,* 125–134.

Willatts, P. (1985). Adjustment of means-end coordination and the representation of spatial relations in the production of search errors. *British Journal of Developmental Psychology, 3,* 259–272.

Willatts, P. (in press). Beyond the "couch potato" infant: How infants use their knowledge to regulate action, solve problems, and achieve goals. In J. G. Bremner, A. Slater, & G. Butterworth (Eds.), *Infant development: Recent advances.* Hove, England: Erlbaum.

Winter, D. (1979). *Biomechanics of human movement.* New York: Wiley.

Winter, D. (1983). Biomechanical motor patterns in normal walking. *Journal of Motor Behavior, 15,* 302–330.

Winter, D. (1990). *Biomechanics of motor control and human movement.* New York: Wiley.

Wishart, J., Bower, T., & Dunkeld, J. (1978). Reaching in the dark. *Perception, 7,* 507–512.

Wood, R. W. (1895). The "haunted-swing" illusion. *Psychological Review, 2,* 277–278.

Woollacott, M., Debu, M., & Mowatt, M. (1987). Neuromuscular control of posture in the infant and child: Is vision dominant? *Journal of Motor Behavior, 19,* 167–186.

Woollacott, M., & Shumway-Cook, A. (Eds.). (1989). *Development of posture and gait across the life-span.* Columbia, SC: University of South Carolina Press.

Woollacott, M., & Sveistrup, H. (1992). Changes in the sequencing and timing of muscle response coordination associated with developmental transitions in balance abilities. *Human Movement Science, 11,* 23–36.

Woollacott, M., & Sveistrup, H. (1994). The development of sensorimotor integration underlying posture control in infants during the transition to independent stance. In S. P. Swinnen, J. Massion, & H. Heuer (Eds.), *Interlimb coordination: Neural, dynamical, and cognitive constraints* (pp. 371–389). San Diego, CA: Academic Press.

Yonas, A., & Granrud, C. (1985). Reaching as a measure of visual development. In G. Gottlieb & N. Krasnegor (Eds.), *The measurement of audition and vision during the first year of postnatal life: A methodological overview* (pp. 301–322). Norwood, NJ: ABLEX.

Yonas, A., & Owsley, C. (1987). Development of visual space perception. In P. Salapatek & L. Cohen (Eds.), *Handbook of infant perception: From sensation to perception* (pp. 80–122). Orlando, FL: Academic Press.

Zernicke, R. F., & Schneider, K. (1993). Biomechanics and developmental neuromotor control. *Child Development, 64,* 982–1004.

CHAPTER 3

Infant Visual Perception

PHILIP J. KELLMAN and MARTIN S. BANKS

There has been a longstanding interest in how infants see. The great Egyptian mathematician, Alhazen, reported in the 11th century that a child who is shown two things will preferentially fixate the more attractive one (Alhazen, 1989; translated by Sabra, 1989) and deduced that some visual capability existed early in life. The evolutionary biologist, Charles Darwin, reported in the 19th century that his infant son preferred to look at some colors over others and concluded that color vision developed during early infancy (Darwin, 1877). Most of what we know about infant visual perception, however, has been learned in the past two decades, so naturally our review will focus on research during this period.

The relatively recent interest in infant visual perception arises from our natural curiosity about how sophisticated devices come to be, but there are important additional reasons. First, the experimental procedures used to study cognitive and social capabilities of infants generally involve visual stimulation, so it has become important to know what infants can and cannot see in order to ensure that immature performance in these procedures can be ascribed to cognitive or social immaturities rather than to an inability to discriminate the stimuli. Second, we learned in the 1970s that the presence of ocular abnormalities early in life (e.g., cataracts, crossed eyes, refractive errors) cause seemingly permanent deficits in a variety of visual capabilities. Early diagnosis of such abnormalities is essential to successful treatment, so there has been an increasing need to assess the vision of individual infants during their first 6 months. Third, as in many areas of science, progress in our understanding of visual development awaited the invention of techniques for measuring visual capabilities. Three important techniques were refined during the past 20 years: preferential looking (in particular, forced-choice preferential looking; Teller, 1979), visual habituation, and the visual evoked potential (Norcia & Tyler, 1985; Sokol, 1978). These techniques allowed researchers to ask more sophisticated scientific questions than were previously possible.

Understanding vision and its development requires multiple levels of analysis. In his classic work *Vision,* David Marr described three: the levels of computational theory, algorithm, and neural implementation. Computational theory involves the task to be achieved and the sources of information that make it possible. How can objects, motion, or spatial arrangements be perceived from information in reflected light? These are in general complex problems. As perception theorists have emphasized for centuries, patterns of light at the eye could imaginably arise from many causes other than the orderly arrays of objects and spatial

Supported in part by NSF Grant-9496112 to PJK and NIH Grant NIH-EY-10991 to MSB.

layouts we perceive. Thus, an important component of computational theorizing is identifying constraints—basic properties of the way the physical world works—that may simplify the mapping from optical stimulation onto physical arrangements. For example, as we walk around an object, its optical projection transforms. Using projective geometry, the visual system can recover the 3-D shape of the object from the transformations. Doing so assumes, however, that the object's 3-D shape is not changing contingent on our own motion. This constraint seems to be a reasonable one in our physical world, and it is one the visual system seems to incorporate. (This constraint is the primary source of the reality in virtual reality systems, where the optical transformations contingent on the observer's movement do not come from real world objects.)

The second level—the level of representation and algorithm—involves the ways in which information is represented and transformed. The descriptions of information processing we seek at this level, in terms of algorithms and data structures, might plausibly be similar in a human perceiver and in a computer vision system.

The third level is hardware implementation. For humans and animals, what biological mechanisms carry out the pick-up and processing of visual information? Here the human and computer visual systems diverge. Neural circuits and silicon chips may perform similar computations, but they are drastically different physical devices.

The explicit realization that all three levels must be addressed for an understanding of vision, or any complex information processing phenomenon, is a relatively recent development and one with many consequences. One is that the levels are relatively independent of each other. Finding data that disconfirm a particular neural model does not necessarily invalidate an accompanying algorithm or computational theory. At the same time, relationships among facts at the three levels are perhaps most crucial to understanding vision. One might catalog indefinitely many properties of neural structures but understand their functions only when these are tied to a particular computation and algorithm. One of Marr's (1982) favorite examples was the relation between a bird's feathers and the laws of aerodynamics. It would be rather optimistic to believe that the laws of aerodynamics could have ever been derived from intense study of feathers. The reverse is in fact true. Without knowing something about aerodynamics, we could never truly understand feathers or what they are doing on birds.

Development adds yet another dimension to our inquiry. Knowing about visual perception in the adult helps us study perceptual development. To the extent the destina-tion of development is understood, it helps us to select questions and interpret findings. On the other hand, the starting point of development may be quite remote from the destination. At every level—neural machinery, information processing, and even the computational analysis—there may be important differences between the developing perceiver and the adult. Certain classes of information may not be available to an infant before the maturation of specific neural mechanisms, for example. Even the task of perception may be different early in life (Kellman, 1993). Whereas the adult often uses vision to guide action, the young infant has little capacity to act. Early visual perception probably guides the development of action systems (von Hofsten, 1980; Bertenthal, 1996) and promotes learning about the physical and social worlds.

We will consider research relevant to visual development at all three levels of analysis and their connections. Most of this research has occurred in the last few decades, and it has replaced earlier conjecture with a reasonably detailed sketch of when various perceptual abilities emerge. More difficult has been the understanding of detailed algorithms and underlying mechanisms. Although some advances have been made, continuing to make progress from description to explanation represents a major challenge for developmental research.

Our review of infant visual perception is necessarily quite selective. The areas we have chosen to review reflect our areas of expertise and our biases concerning the most intriguing areas of research since 1983 when one of us last reviewed this field for the *Handbook of Child Psychology* (Banks & Salapatek, 1983). We begin with a discussion of object perception that includes reviews of the development of the ability to extract and partition spatial information, of the ability to detect and classify edges, of the conditions required for perceiving object unity, and of the ability to perceived three-dimensional form. We then move on to space perception including the development of the ability to use pictorial depth cues, motion-based depth cues, and binocular cues. Next is color vision and here we review recent work on infants' ability to use wavelength composition to make visual discriminations. We end with motion perception where we review the ability to make speed and direction discriminations and the ability to use motion information to perceive self- as opposed to object-motion.

OBJECT PERCEPTION

One of the most important functions of visual perception is to deliver representations of the environment in terms of discrete physical entities or *objects*. There are many imaginable ways to describe and encode the streams of light that hit the retinas of the eyes. In ordinary perceiving, however, we obtain not descriptions of light, but descriptions of the physical objects that last reflected the light. These descriptions of the locations, boundaries, shapes, sizes, and substances of objects are indispensable for action and thought. Normally, the separate objects in our perceptual world correspond to units in the physical world. Thus, perceptual knowledge allows us to predict the results of action: How the world divides, what things will detach from adjacent things, and what will remain coherent if moved, thrown or sat upon. All this we can know from a distance through vision. We perceive bounded objects as having many other attributes relevant to our actions: shapes, sizes, rigidity or flexibility, and so on. For the experienced observer, storing in memory the shapes and surface qualities of many perceived objects makes possible rapid and automatic recognition of familiar objects, even from partial information. Matched to the richness and importance of object perception is its complexity. The challenges become apparent when we see how little of human object perception can yet be emulated by artificial vision systems. For the experienced observer in a familiar environment, however, the task seems not complex, but effortless, instantaneous, almost trivial.

We begin our discussion of object perception with a review of what we know about the initial stages of visual processing; these provide the spatial information from which surface and object properties are extracted.

Extraction and Partitioning of Spatial Information

The ability to detect and encode spatial variations in the stream of light coming into the eye is fundamental to seeing surfaces and objects. For example, to identify and interact with the book in front of you, your visual system must detect and represent the variations in incoming light intensity (or wavelength) that define the boundary of the book, the letters on the page, and so forth. The study of the ability to detect and discriminate simple visual patterns has dominated research in infant visual perception, so we devote a significant proportion of this review to this topic. Most of the research has been devoted to defining the limits of detection and discrimination capacities: that is, to determining, as a function of age, what kinds of spatial variations in light intensity can be detected and discriminated and what kinds cannot. The picture that emerges from this research is that the detection and discrimination capacity of the

human infant is very limited during the first few months of life and these capacity limitations must necessarily constrain the ability to see and recognize surfaces and objects in the everyday environment.

Visual Acuity

Object recognition and identification depend on the ability to encode the spatial distribution of differences in retinal image intensity or wavelength. The study of visual acuity addresses the question of how accurate the encoding of spatial distribution is. The term *visual acuity* thus refers to the maximum resolving capacity of the visual system. The importance of this capacity is illustrated by the fact that visual acuity measurements are far and away the most common means of assessing ocular health and suitability for operating motor vehicles.

To assess acuity, high-contrast, black-and-white patterns of various sizes are presented at a fixed distance. The smallest pattern or smallest critical pattern element that can be reliably detected or identified is taken as the threshold value and is usually expressed in units of visual angle. Countless types of stimuli have been used to measure visual acuity in adults, but only two have been used in developmental studies: grating acuity and vernier acuity.

Grating acuity tasks require resolving the stripes in a repetitive pattern of stripes. The finest resolvable grating is taken as the measure of acuity and it is generally expressed in terms of spatial frequency, which is the number of stripes per degree of visual angle. Adult grating acuity under optimal conditions is 45 to 60 cycles/degree, which corresponds to a stripe width of ½ to ⅔ minutes of arc (Olzak & Thomas, 1986). By optimal conditions, we mean that the stimulus is brightly illuminated, high in contrast, presented for at least ½ second, and viewed foveally with a well-focused eye. Changes in any of these viewing parameters cause a reduction in grating acuity.

Vernier acuity tasks require the discrimination of a displacement of one small target with respect to another. For example, one task involves distinguishing whether a vertical line segment is displaced to the left or right relative to line segment just below it. In adults, the just-noticeable offset under optimal conditions is 2 to 5 seconds of arc. Because this distance is smaller than the diameter of a single photoreceptor in the human eye, this kind of performance has been called *hyperacuity* (Westheimer, 1979). As with grating acuity, the lowest vernier acuity thresholds are obtained when the stimulus is brightly illuminated, high in contrast, presented for at least ½ second, and viewed foveally with a well-focused eye.

The threshold values obtained in grating and vernier acuity tasks differ. Because the acuity limit varies from one task to another, one cannot use an acuity estimate obtained with one stimulus and task to predict the acuity for another stimulus and task. This has important implications for infant research: Specifically, one cannot use a particular acuity estimate to determine whether the pattern elements in another stimulus are visible to the infant. For example, an infant's grating acuity cannot be used in any direct fashion to determine whether the pattern elements in a schematic face are visible to the infant.

Eye movements, optics, photoreceptor properties, and postreceptoral neural mechanisms all contribute to limit acuity; one factor may dominate in a given situation, but they all contribute. Thus, a strong motivation for studying visual acuity is the expectation that it will provide insight into the oculomotor, optical, anatomical, and physiological mechanisms underlying spatial vision. Psychophysical estimates of visual acuity in adults have supported this expectation (Coletta, Williams, & Tiana, 1990; Green, 1970; Williams, 1985).

There have been numerous measurements of grating acuity (the highest detectable spatial frequency at high contrast) in human infants (Figure 3.1). The displayed results were obtained using three response measurement techniques: Forced-choice preferential looking (FPL; Teller, 1979), optokinetic nystagmus (OKN; ref), and the visual evoked potential (VEP; Norcia & Tyler, 1985).[1] Two points are illustrated by this figure. First, acuity is low at birth and develops steadily during the first year. Indeed, grating acuity during the neonatal period is so low that these children would be classified as legally blind. Second, the acuity estimates obtained with behavioral techniques such as FPL and OKN are generally lower than those obtained using electrophysiological techniques such as VEP. We will discuss the optical, receptoral, and neural factors that determine grating acuity as a function of age in the next section.

There have been fewer measurements of vernier acuity; nonetheless, some intriguing observations have been reported. Shimojo and colleagues (Shimojo, Birch, Gwiazda, & Held, 1984; Shimojo & Held, 1987) and Manny and Klein (1984, 1985) used FPL to measure the smallest offset infants could respond to at different ages. They found that vernier acuity was much poorer in 8- to 20-week-old infants than in adults. Indeed, the ratio of adult divided by 8-week vernier acuity is significantly greater than the corresponding ratio for grating acuity. A similar finding has

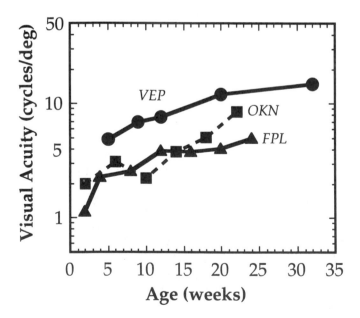

Figure 3.1 Visual acuity estimates at different ages. The highest detectable spatial frequency of a high-contrast grating stimulus is plotted as a function of age. Circles = visual evoked potential estimates from Sokol (1979); squares = optokinetic nystagmus estimates from Fantz, Ordy, & Udelf (1962); triangles = forced-choice preferential looking estimates from Allen (1978).

[1] *Forced-choice preferential looking* is a behavioral technique that relies on infants' tendency to look at the more complicated of two visual targets (e.g., Teller, 1979). The infant is shown two targets, usually side by side; one side contains the signal (for example, a grating) and the other side contains the blank (a uniform field). An adult observer, who does not know which side contains the grating, makes a forced-choice judgment indicating the side he or she believes contains the grating. It is assumed that the observer will be able to judge the correct side at a greater than chance rate when the target is visible to the child. *Visual-evoked potential* is an electrophysiological technique that relies on the fact that the components of the EEG can be driven by a time-varying visual stimulus (e.g., Norcia & Tyler, 1985). The potential is recorded at the scalp. With modern signal processing techniques, the evoked potential can be recorded quite reliably in a short period of time. It is assumed that a recordable potential will be obtained when the target is able to stimulate the visual cortex. *Optokinetic nystagmus* is a behavioral technique that relies on the a reflexive eye movement that is elicited when the infant is presented repetitive pattern that moves in one direction. The eye movement consists of a slow phase in which the eyes move at about the same rate as the pattern and a fast phase in which the eyes rotate rapidly in the opposite direction. It is assumed that the child will elicit OKN whenever the pattern is visible.

emerged from VEP measurements of vernier and grating acuity (Wesemann, Norcia, & Manny, 1996). This suggests that the visual mechanisms that limit vernier acuity undergo greater change with age than do the mechanisms limiting grating acuity. Different hypotheses have been offered concerning the differing growth rates (Banks & Bennett, 1988; Shimojo & Held, 1987), but none has been confirmed by empirical observation.

Contrast Sensitivity

The contrast sensitivity function (CSF) represents the visual system's sensitivity to repetitive striped patterns; these patterns are generally sinusoidal gratings (a series of stripes with a sinusoidal variation in luminance). Before discussing research on the development of contrast sensitivity, it is useful to describe in more detail why such measurements have played an important role in the study of infant spatial vision. More rigorous discussions of this topic can be found in Banks and Ginsburg (1985) and Wandell (1995).

The utility of contrast sensitivity measures derives from linear systems analysis, an engineering technique that has played a crucial role in the analysis of a wide range of physical and biological systems. In this approach, the system under examination is thought of as a black box with an input and output. The aim is to characterize the box so that the output can be predicted for any input. In the case of visual perception, the goal is to predict the appearance (the output) for any stimulus (the input).

Linear systems analysis is based on Fourier's theorem which states that any two-dimensional, time-invariant visual stimulus can be exactly described by combining a set of sinusoidal gratings. Such gratings are specified by four parameters: spatial frequency (which is the number of pattern repetitions, or cycles, per degree of visual angle), orientation (which refers to the grating's tilt to the left or right of vertical), phase (which is the grating's position with respect to some reference position), and contrast (which is related to the difference between maximum and minimum intensities of the grating). Fourier's theorem implies that even a complex, two-dimensional visual stimulus, such as the picture of a face, can be described exactly by the combination of a set of gratings of various frequencies, orientations, phases, and contrasts.

For linear systems (technical descriptions are given in Banks & Ginsburg, 1985; Wandell, 1995), one can characterize the system's output to any stimulus by first characterizing its output to sinusoidal gratings of various spatial frequencies. In transmission through the system, the contrast and phase of a sinusoidal grating can be altered; thus, one must estimate the input-output relationships for both contrast and phase in order to characterize the system in general. As we will see, infant work has focused to a large degree on the contrast response even though there is evidence that infants' phase response is quite immature, too.

The contrast response of the visual system is indexed by measuring the contrast sensitivity function (CSF). This function represents the minimal contrast required to detect a sinusoidal grating at different spatial frequencies. The CSF of an adult with good vision under typical indoor lighting conditions is shown in Figure 3.2. The x-axis of this plot is spatial frequency which corresponds with the number of stripes (or cycles) per degree of visual angle. (The grating pattern is becoming increasingly finer with increasing values along the x-axis.) The y-axis is contrast sensitivity which is the reciprocal of the contrast of the grating at detection threshold. (The grating pattern is becoming increasingly lower in contrast with increasing

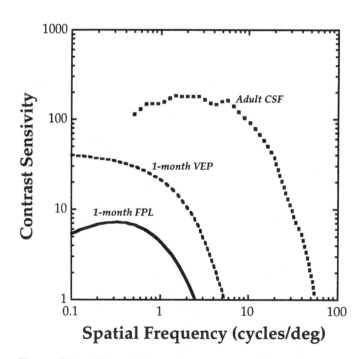

Figure 3.2 Adult and 1-month contrast sensitivity functions (CSFs). Contrast sensitivity (the reciprocal of stimulus contrast at threshold) is plotted as a function of spatial frequency (the numbers of grating cycles per degree of visual angle). The upper dotted curve is an adult CSF that was measured psychophysically. The lower solid curve is the average of 1-month CSFs, measured using forced-choice preferential looking (Banks & Salapatek, 1978). The middle dash curve is the average of 1-month CSFs, measured using the visual-evoked potential (Norcia et al., 1990).

values along the y-axis.) The curve represents the contrast sensitivities at each spatial frequency; combinations of spatial frequency and contrast that fall below the curve are visible and those that fall above are invisible. The adult CSF is bandpass with a peak sensitivity at 3 to 5 cycles/ deg, so the lowest detectable contrasts occur for gratings of medium spatial frequency. At those spatial frequencies, the just-detectable grating has light stripes that are only 1/2% brighter than the dark stripes. At progressively higher spatial frequencies, sensitivity falls monotonically to the so-called high-frequency cutoff at about 50 cycles/deg; this is the finest grating an adult can detect when the contrast is 100% and it corresponds with the person's grating acuity. At low spatial frequencies, sensitivity falls as well, although the steepness of this fall-off is quite dependent on the conditions under which the measurements are made.

In summary, gratings of medium spatial frequency pass through the visual system with minimal attenuation; gratings of low and high frequency are attenuated more. Before discussing infant contrast sensitivity, we consider the optical, receptoral, and neural factors that limit contrast sensitivity and grating acuity in adults.

The adult CSF in Figure 3.2 is typical for good lighting, foveal fixation, sufficiently long stimulus duration, and a well-focused eye. If the illumination is decreased, the function shifts downward and to the left (van Nes & Bouman, 1967); similar changes in contrast sensitivity occur when the stimulus is imaged on the peripheral retina (Banks, Sekuler, & Anderson, 1991) or the eye is not well-focused (Green & Campbell, 1965). We can understand the high-frequency falloff of the adult's CSF by examining the optical, receptoral, and retinal processes involved in spatial vision. The characteristics of these same processes also allow an understanding of how contrast sensitivity changes with illumination, the part of the retina being stimulated, and the focus of the eye. This understanding has been obtained by capitalizing on the fact that the early stages of vision can be modeled as a series of filtering stages. Visual stimuli pass sequentially through the eye's optics which are responsible for forming the retinal image, the photoreceptors which sample and transduce the image into neural signals, and two to four retinal neurons which transform and transmit those signals into the optic nerve and eventually to the central visual pathways. Considerable information is lost in these early stages of the visual process. Indeed, the high-frequency falloff observed in the adult CSF is determined, by and large, by the filtering properties

of the eye's optics and the photoreceptors (Banks, Geisler, & Bennett, 1987; Pelli, 1990; Sekiguchi, Williams, & Brainard, 1993). The loss of high-frequency sensitivity (including, of course, grating acuity) with peripheral viewing has been modeled successfully by examination of the optics, receptors, and retinal circuits of the peripheral retina (Banks et al., 1991). The sensitivity loss that accompanies a reduction in illumination has also been modeled reasonably successfully at high spatial frequencies (Banks et al., 1987; Pelli, 1990) and so has the loss that accompanies errors in the eye's focus (Green & Campbell, 1965). Given the emerging understanding of the optical, receptoral, and neural mechanisms that determine contrast sensitivity in adults, the past decade has seen a number of attempts at using similar techniques to understand the development of contrast sensitivity in human infants.

Figure 3.2 also displays infant CSFs measured using forced-choice preferential looking (Atkinson, Braddick, & Moar, 1977; Banks & Salapatek, 1978) and the visual-evoked potential (Norcia, Tyler, & Allen, 1986; Pirchio, Spinelli, Fiorentini, & Maffei, 1978). These data illustrate two common observations in this area of research. First, contrast sensitivity (and grating acuity) in young infants is substantially lower than that of adults and the disparity diminishes rapidly during the first year. Second, measurements with the visual-evoked potential typically yield higher sensitivity (and acuity) estimates than do behavioral techniques.

One way to index the development of contrast sensitivity is by the lowest detectable contrast at the peak of the CSF. Contrast sensitivity at the peak of the function develops more rapidly during the first year than does visual acuity (Norcia et al., 1990). With evoked potential measurements, peak sensitivity approaches adult values by 3 months of age. Behavioral measurements exhibit a slower developmental time course.

One would think that the anatomical and physiological causes of the striking functional deficits observed during the first few months of life would have been identified, but the specific causes are still debated. Some investigators have proposed that one can explain the low contrast sensitivity and grating acuity of neonates by an analysis of information losses caused by optical and retinal immaturities (Jacobs & Blakemore, 1988; Wilson, 1988, 1993); others have argued that those immaturities are not the whole story (Banks & Bennett, 1988; Banks & Crowell, 1993; Brown, Dobson, & Maier, 1987). Let us review briefly the development of the eye and retina because large ocular and retinal changes occur over time and they must have profound effects on the ability to see spatial patterns.

The eye grows significantly from birth to adolescence, most of the growth occurring in the first year. For instance, the distance from the cornea at the front of the eye to the retina at the back is 16 to 17 mm at birth, 20 to 21 at 1 year, and 23 to 25 mm in adolescence and adulthood (Hirano, Yamamoto, Takayama, Sugata, & Matsuo, 1979; Larsen, 1971). Shorter eyes have smaller retinal images. So, for example, a 1-deg target subtends about 200 microns on the newborn's retina and 300 microns on the adult's (Banks & Bennett, 1988; Brown et al., 1987; Wilson, 1988). Thus, if the newborn had the retina and visual brain of an adult, one would expect their visual acuity to be about 2/3 that of adults simply because they have smaller retinal images to work with.

Another ocular factor relevant to visual sensitivity is the relative transparency of the ocular media. Two aspects of ocular media transmittance are known to change with age: the optical density of the crystalline lens pigment and that of the macular pigment. In both cases, transmittance is slightly higher in the young eye, particularly at short wavelengths (Bone, Landrum, Fernandez, & Martinez, 1988; Werner, 1982). Thus, for a given amount of incident light, the newborn's eye actually transmits slightly more to the photoreceptors than does the mature eye. This developmental difference ought to favor the newborn compared to the adult, but only slightly.

The ability of the eye to form a sharp retinal image is yet another relevant ocular factor. This ability is typically quantified by the optical transfer function.[2] There have been no measurements of the human neonate's optical transfer function, but the quality of the retinal image almost certainly surpasses the resolution performance of the young visual system (Banks & Bennett, 1988). Thus, it is commonly assumed that the optical transfer function of the young eye is adult-like (Banks & Crowell, 1993; Wilson, 1988, 1993). Refractive errors or accommodation errors

diminish the sharpness of the retinal image and thereby decrease sensitivity to high spatial frequencies (Green & Campbell, 1965). For example, a person with a myopic refractive error (near-sightedness) can focus the eye to form a sharp retinal image for near targets, but cannot focus the eye for distant targets. Hyperopic (far-sighted) refractive errors are common in infants (Banks, 1980a; Howland, 1982). Astigmatic refractive errors (a condition in which the eye cannot be focused simultaneously for perpendicular stimulus orientations) are also common (Banks, 1980a). Infants also tend not to accommodate accurately until 12 weeks (Banks, 1980b; Braddick, Atkinson, French, & Howland, 1979; Haynes, White, & Held, 1965). Nonetheless, it is widely believed that infants' refractive and accommodative errors do not constrain sensitivity or visual acuity significantly (Banks, 1980a, 1980b; Braddick et al., 1979; Howland, 1982).

If optical imperfections do not contribute significantly to the visual deficits observed in young infants, receptoral and post-receptoral processes must. The retina and central visual system all exhibit immaturities at birth (Banks & Salapatek, 1983; Hendrickson, 1993; Hickey & Peduzzi, 1987; Yuodelis & Hendrickson, 1986), but there are particularly striking morphological immaturities in the fovea, particularly among the photoreceptors.

The development of the fovea is dramatic in the first year of life, but subtle morphological changes continue until at least four years of age (Yuodelis & Hendrickson, 1986). The fovea, defined as the part of the retina that contains no rods, is much larger at birth than in adulthood: Its diameter decreases from roughly 5.4 degrees at birth to 2.3 deg at maturity. Moreover, the individual cells and their arrangements are very different at birth than they will be later on. For example, the newborn's fovea possesses three discernible layers of neurons—the photoreceptors, the neurons of the outer nuclear layer, and the retinal ganglion cells—whereas the mature fovea contains only one layer that is composed of photoreceptors. The most dramatic histological differences, however, are the sizes and shapes of foveal cones. To illustrate, Figure 3.3 shows high-power micrographs of the fovea at birth, 15 months, and adulthood. In each panel, an individual cone photoreceptor is outlined for clarity. The cones' outer segments are labelled OS; the inner segments are just below the outer segments.

In mature cones, the inner segment captures light, and through waveguide properties, funnels it to the outer segment where the photopigment resides. As the light travels down the outer segment, there are several opportunities to

---

[2] The optical transfer function is the ratio of contrast in the retinal image divided by the contrast in the stimulus as a function of spatial frequency. Thus, it represents the degree to which the optics of the eye "pass" information from the stimulus to the retina. A ratio of 1 means that the retinal image contrast is the same as the stimulus contrast and therefore that the optics of the eye pass the stimulus without loss of contrast. A ratio of 0.5 means that the contrast is reduced by a factor of two in being transmitted through the eye's optics.

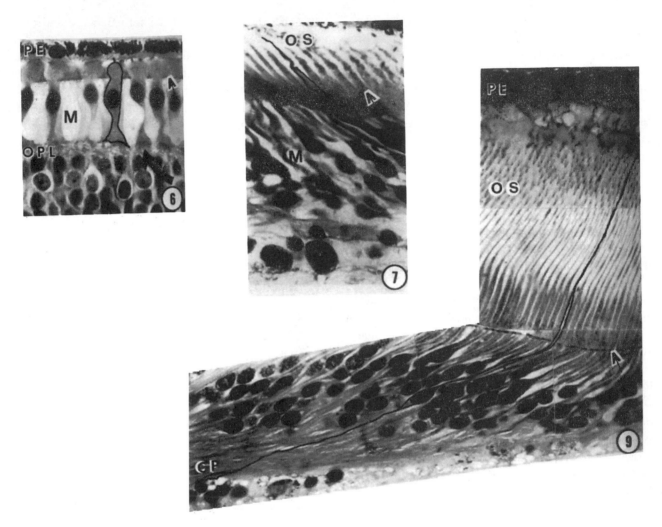

Figure 3.3   The retina near the center of the fovea at birth (#6), 15 months (#7), and adulthood (#9). The magnification is the same in each panel. An individual cone photoreceptor is outlined for clarity in each photograph. The outer segments of the photoreceptors (which contain the photopigment) are labeled OS, and the inner segments (which capture incoming photons) are just below the outer segments.

be caught by and react with photopigment molecules and thereby create visual signals that are sent through retinal circuits to the central nervous system. The micrographs reveal striking differences between neonatal and adult foveal cones. Neonatal inner segments are much broader and shorter. The outer segments are distinctly immature, too, being much shorter than their adult counterparts. All of these shape and size differences render the newborn's foveal cones less sensitive than the adult's (Banks & Bennett, 1988; Brown et al., 1987).

In order to estimate the efficiency of the neonate's lattice of foveal cones, Banks and colleagues calculated the ability of the newborn's cones to capture light in the inner segment, funnel it to the outer segment, and produce a visual signal (Banks & Bennett, 1988; Banks & Crowell, 1993). They concluded that the adult foveal cone lattice is dramatically better at absorbing photons of light and converting them into visual signals. Indeed, by their calculations, if identical patches of light were presented to newborn and adult eyes, roughly 350 photons would be effectively absorbed in adult foveal cones for each photon absorbed in newborn cones. Similar estimates were obtained by Wilson (1988, 1993). Clearly, the newborn's fovea is less able to use light entering the eye than is the mature fovea.

The cones of the immature fovea are also more widely spaced than those of the adult (Banks & Bennett, 1988; Banks & Crowell, 1993; Wilson, 1988, 1993). Cone-to-cone separation in the center of the fovea is about 2.3, 1.7, and 0.58 minutes of arc in neonates, 15-month-olds, and adults, respectively. These dimensions impose a physical limit (the so-called *Nyquist limit*) on the highest spatial frequency that can be resolved without distortion (Williams, 1985). From the current estimates of cone spacing, the foveas of newborns, 15-month-olds, and adults should theoretically be unable to resolve gratings with spatial frequencies above 15, 27, and 60 cycles/deg, respectively.

Investigators have calculated the contrast sensitivity and visual acuity losses that ought to be observed if the only difference between the spatial vision of newborns and adults were the eye's optics and the properties of the foveal cones (Banks & Bennett, 1988; Banks & Crowell, 1993; Wilson, 1988, 1993). The expected losses are substantial; contrast sensitivity to medium and high spatial frequencies is predicted to be as much as 20-fold lower in neonates than in adults. Nonetheless, the observed contrast sensitivity and grating acuity deficits in human newborns are even larger than predicted, so this analysis of information losses in the optics and receptors implies that there are other immaturities, presumably among retinal neurons and central visual circuits, that contribute to the observed loss of contrast sensitivity and grating acuity.

Another hypothesis concerning the contrast sensitivity and visual acuity of young infants has been offered. Because of the obvious immaturity of the fovea, perhaps infants use another part of the retina to process points of interest in the visual scene. Indeed, cones in the parafoveal and peripheral retina are relatively more mature at birth than their foveal counterparts, but they too undergo postnatal development (Hendrickson, 1993). Brown (1993) has speculated that neonates' contrast sensitivity and grating acuity are actually better with peripheral than with foveal viewing, but this conclusion rests on unlikely assumptions about the connections between newborn peripheral cones and retinal neurons (Banks et al., 1991; Candy, Banks, Hendrickson, & Crowell, 1993). There is also some evidence that suggests that neonates' best acuity and contrast sensitivity is obtained with foveal stimulation. Lewis, Maurer, and Kay (1978) found that newborns could detect a narrower light bar against a dark background when it was presented in central vision rather than in the periphery. Allen, Tyler, and Norcia (1989) showed that VEP acuity is higher in central than in peripheral vision in infants as young as 8 weeks. Spinelli, Pirchio, and Sandini (1983) came to a similar conclusion. These observations suggest that the newborn contrast sensitivity and acuity estimates are manifestations of foveal and parafoveal processing

rather than peripheral processing, but more direct experimental evidence, including the recording of eye position, is needed to demonstrate this conclusively.

An important question that will be pursued vigorously in the next decade is what factors not considered in the above-mentioned analyses account for the unexplained portion of the contrast sensitivity and grating acuity losses. There are numerous candidates including internal neural noise (such as random addition of action potentials at central sites), inefficient neural sampling (such as lack of appropriate cortical receptive fields for detecting sinewave gratings), poor motivation to respond, and so forth.

Pattern Discrimination

As mentioned earlier, the motivation for examining the development of contrast sensitivity comes from the fact that one can in principle use such measurements in combination with linear systems analysis to predict the visibility of a wide variety of patterns. Recall also that the basic stimuli involved in linear systems analysis can vary in spatial frequency, contrast, orientation, and phase. Research on infant vision has yielded a great deal of information on how contrast thresholds vary with spatial frequency (e.g., Atkinson et al., 1977; Banks & Salapatek, 1978; Norcia et al., 1990). There has been considerably less work on the ability of the immature system to discriminate stimuli that differ along these basic dimensions of pattern. Here we review briefly what little evidence exists concerning infants' ability to discriminate visual stimuli differing in contrast, orientation, and phase. To our knowledge, there have been no studies that bear directly on the ability to discriminate stimuli differing in spatial frequency.

The ability to discriminate on the basis of contrast differences is typically measured by presenting two sinusoidal gratings of the same spatial frequency, orientation, and phase, but differing contrasts. In adult experiments, the subject is asked to indicate the grating of higher contrast. The increment in contrast required to make the discrimination varies depending on the common contrasts of the two stimuli; as the common contrast is increased, a successively larger increment is required (Legge & Foley, 1980).

Contrast discrimination has also been measured in human infants. Six- to 12-week infants require much larger contrast increments than adults when the common contrast is near detection threshold; at high common contrasts, however, infants' discrimination thresholds approach adults' (Brown, 1993; Stephens & Banks, 1987). These findings suggest that infants' ability to distinguish spatial patterns on the basis of contrast differences is poor at low contrast and reasonably good at high contrast. Different explanations for infants' performance in this task have been offered, but none has been confirmed by empirical observation (Brown, 1993; Stephens & Banks, 1987).

The ability to discriminate patterns differing in orientation is typically measured by presenting two gratings of the same spatial frequency and contrast, but differing in orientation (e.g., vertical vs. horizontal). In adult experiments, one typically measures the smallest difference in orientation (expressed in degrees) that can be reliably discriminated. For high-contrast gratings and lines, adult observers can discriminate orientation changes of less than 1° (Thomas & Gille, 1979; Westheimer, 1981).

Sensitivity to patterns that differ in orientation has been measured in human infants using behavioral and electrophysiological techniques. Slater and Sykes (1977) reported that newborns could discriminate horizontal and vertical gratings. However, Braddick (1993) and others noted that the discrimination could have been based on differences in the perceived sharpness of the two stimuli because a significant proportion of newborns have astigmatic refractive errors (Howland & Sayles, 1985; Mohindra et al., 1978) that cause horizontal contours to be defocused relative to vertical contours (or vertical relative to horizontal). Subsequent work by Slater and colleagues (1988), however, showed more persuasively that newborns can discriminate contours differing in orientation by 90°. Other behavioral and electrophysiological work suggests that the precision of orientation discrimination improves greatly during the first few months of life (Braddick et al., 1986; Hood et al., 1992). One suspects that the immature visual system is significantly poorer at discriminating patterns differing in orientation; if so, the ability to discriminate complex visual patterns must assuredly be compromised.

Simple spatial patterns such as gratings can also differ in their spatial phase. In this context, spatial phase refers to the relative position of the spatial frequency components (the sinewave gratings) of which the pattern is composed (Piotrowski & Campbell, 1982). The importance of spatial phase is evidenced by the fact that manipulations of the phase information in a spatial pattern greatly affect its appearance and perceived identity to adults (Oppenheim & Lim, 1981). In phase discrimination tasks, the subject is asked to distinguish between two patterns—usually gratings—that differ only in the phase relationships among their spatial frequency components. Adults are able to distinguish patterns that differ only slightly in the phases of their components when the stimulus is presented to the fovea (Badcock, 1984). The ability to discriminate phase can fall dramatically, however, when the stimulus is presented in the peripheral visual field (Bennett & Banks, 1987, 1991; Rentschler & Treutwein, 1985).

To the authors' knowledge, there has only been one study of infants' ability to use phase differences to discriminate spatial patterns. Braddick, Atkinson, and Wattam-Bell (1986) presented periodic patterns composed of different spatial frequency components. When the components were added in one phase relationship, the resultant was a squarewave grating (a repeating pattern of sharp-edged light and dark stripes); when the components were added in another phase, the resultant appeared to adults to be a very different, more complex pattern. Eight-week-olds were able to discriminate these patterns. Remarkably, however, 4-week-olds seemed unable to make the discrimination.

In a similar vein, Kleiner (1987) and Kleiner and Banks (1987) examined visual preferences for patterns in which the phases of the constituent components had been altered. As has been reported many times previously, Kleiner and colleagues found that newborns and 8-week-olds exhibit reliable fixation preferences for a schematic face over a rectangle lattice (Fantz & Nevis, 1967). To examine the influence of spatial phase on fixation preference, Kleiner used an image processing technique in which the contrasts of the constituent spatial frequencies from one pattern were combined with the phases of the constituent frequencies from the other pattern. The perceptual appearance of these hybrid patterns is most closely associated with the pattern from which the phases came rather than the pattern from which the contrasts came (Oppenheim & Lim, 1981; Piotrowski & Campbell, 1982); stated another way, the hybrid pattern that appears most face-like is the one that contains the phases from the original schematic face. Not surprisingly, 8-week-olds preferred to fixate the hybrid that contained the phases of the face and the contrasts of the lattice. Newborn's preferences, however, preferred the hybrid that contained the phases of the lattice and the contrasts of the face. One possible interpretation of this finding is that newborns are relatively insensitive to spatial phase, but other interpretations are possible (Badcock, 1990; Morton, Johnson, & Maurer, 1990).

The observation that young infants seem relatively insensitive to variations in spatial phase is extremely important. If it is valid, it suggests that young infants' ability to discriminate spatial patterns has a significant deficiency that is at least qualitatively similar to the deficiency observed in the peripheral visual field of normal adults (Bennett & Banks, 1987; Rentschler & Treutwein, 1985) and in the central visual field of amblyopic adults (Levi, Klein, & Aitsebaomo, 1985).

As we have seen in the discussions of visual acuity, contrast sensitivity, and pattern discrimination, the infant visual system undergoes a dramatic change during the first few months in the ability to detect, partition, and discriminate spatial variations in light intensity coming into the eye. These abilities provide the foundations and limits for extracting information about objects. We now consider the processes by which objects and their properties are perceived.

Multiple Tasks in Object Perception

As the study of object perception has advanced, it has become clear that it is computationally complex, involving multiple tasks. The first component is *edge detection.* Edge detection involves detecting spatial variations in the optical projection. These may be intensity variations in the retinal image caused by a contour that might indicate where one object ends and another object or surface begins. They may also be discontinuities in texture, depth or motion. When we look at information for edges, we find some ambiguities in that visible contours can result from object boundaries but also from other sources, such as shadows. A second requirement, then, is *edge classification,* sorting visible contours into object boundaries as opposed to shadows, textural markings, etc. Next is *boundary assignment.* When an edge corresponding to an object boundary is located, it most commonly bounds one object, while the surface or object seen on the other side of the boundary passes behind the first object. Determining which way each boundary bounds is crucial for knowing, for example, whether we are viewing objects or object-shaped holes.

When early processes have succeeded in producing a map of visible object edges, how close are we to perceiving objects? Not very. Note that in accomplishing boundary assignment the visual system marks visible contours as bounding the surface to one side. Each time this occurs we might place a question mark on the other side. There, another surface passes behind the occlusion boundary. Where do these visible surface fragments go? How do they continue? With what other visible pieces do they link up, and what are the shapes of these linkages? These are the questions of *segmentation* and *unit formation.* A single static image raises many such complexities; more complex yet is ordinary observer motion through the environment, as well as the motions of objects. When motion occurs, the visible

fragments of objects change continuously. If the problems of unit formation can be overcome, we may be able to perceive form, that is, obtain a description of the three-dimensional arrangement of the object in space. Finally, there are perceptible properties relating to object substance: its rigidity or flexibility, surface texture, and so on.

Next we consider what is known about these components of object perception in early development.

Edge Detection and Edge Classification

What information makes edge detection possible? There are several answers, all involving discontinuities across space in some perceptible properties. First, objects tend to be homogeneous in their material composition. Parts of an homogeneous object will absorb and reflect light in similar fashion, whereas an adjacent object, made of some different material, may differ. Thus, discontinuities of luminance and spectral composition in the optic array may mark object boundaries. When average luminance and spectral characteristics are similar for adjacent objects, higher order patterns of optical variation—texture—may distinguish them. Texture may come from three-dimensional variations of orientation along the surface or from variations in the reflectance of the material. Another source of information comes from depth gradients. Depth values of visible points of a continuous object will change smoothly, but at object boundaries discontinuities will often occur. In similar fashion, optic flow provides information about edges. When the observer moves, the optical displacements for visible points will tend to vary more smoothly within objects than between objects.

None of these sources of information for detecting objects' edges is unequivocal. Discontinuities in luminance and/or spectral values may arise from reflectance differences of cast shadows along the surface of a continuous object. They may also come from surface orientation differences in a complex object, due to different geometric relations between a light source, surface patches and the observer. The same may be true for depth or motion discontinuities: they will often but not always mark object boundaries. A second requirement for object perception, then, is edge classification. Which luminance variations are probably object edges and which are illumination changes, shadows, and so on? Similar questions apply to texture, depth, and motion variations.

There is not much direct evidence about infant edge detection and edge classification abilities. It is possible to make some inferences from the literatures on visual acuity and pattern discrimination, however. Object edges are interesting in terms of their makeup from a linear systems perspective. At an abrupt edge, multiple spatial frequency components of identical orientation will be in phase (i.e., a transition from dark to light or vice versa will be at the same spatial position for the frequency components; Morrone & Burr, 1988). Eliminating the high frequency components will reduce sharpness of the edge. For this reason, studies of grating acuity place some absolute limits on edge detection from luminance variations. One implication of newborns' poor acuity relative to adults is that their ability to process object edges must be poorer.

Above acuity thresholds, edge detection may be possible but not guaranteed. The sinusoidally varying luminance patterns used to test acuity, for example, allow adults to detect pattern variation but do not specify clear edges. Positive results in infant visual acuity tests therefore do not indicate whether infants perceive any edges as opposed to gradual variations along a surface.

Early pattern perception would seem to provide a better window into elementary edge detection. If shape of a two-dimensional (2-D) pattern is detected, one might argue, then the contour comprising that edge must certainly be detected and perhaps classified as an object boundary. Since the pioneering studies of Fantz and colleagues (e.g., Fantz, Fagan, & Miranda, 1975), many studies have shown that infants discriminate patterns from the earliest weeks of life.

Discrimination, however, can be based on any registered difference between patterns; contour perception may not necessarily be implied. We noted that a visual pattern may be analyzed into sinusoidal luminance components. An object's edge may trigger responses in a population of cortical neurons sensitive to these components but not be represented as a single pattern feature. In short, different patterns might evoke different neural activity but not perception of edges or forms per se. This possibility is consistent with evidence we considered earlier that infants are somewhat insensitive to spatial phase information before about 8 weeks of age.

Other lines of research indirectly imply that edges and forms are perceived by newborns under at least some circumstances. Slater and his colleagues (Slater, Mattock, & Brown, 1990) reported evidence for some degree of size and shape constancy in the first few days of life. Size constancy is the ability to perceive the physical size of an object despite distance-dependent changes in the object's projected size. Shape constancy in this context refers to the perceiver's ability to detect a constant planar (2-D) shape despite variations in its three-dimensional (3-D) slant, for example, perceiving a rectangle despite the fact that its slant in depth produces a trapezoidal retinal projection.

Later we consider the evidence for size and planar shape constancy. Here we merely note that both would seem to require some boundary perception abilities. It is hard to imagine any way to achieve constancy if the newborn's visual representation stops at V1 with a collection of activations in independent frequency channels. More likely, higher stages of processing function to some degree to localize edges of objects. To achieve constancy, projective shape or size must be obtained. Moreover, the edge must be classified as being an object edge, not a surface marking, if its orientation in 3-D space can be detected. Even boundary assignment might be implied in this case. The objects were placed in these experiments in front of more distant, frontoparallel surfaces. Assignment of the object edges to the planar form rather than the surrounding surface seems to be implied by the detection of 3-D orientation, since the surrounding surface had a different 3-D orientation.

The earliest edge classification and boundary assignment may depend selectively on a subset of information sources available to adults. For adults, surface quality differences, for example, luminance and spectral differences alone can specify object boundaries. As noted by Rubin (1915), an area whose surround differs in luminance and/or spectral characteristics ordinarily appears as a bounded figure in front of a background surface. There is reason to believe that infants do not segregate objects using this information before about 9 months of age. Piaget (1954) noted that his son Laurent at 7 months would reach for a box of matches when it was placed on the floor but not when it was placed on a book; instead he would reach for the edges of the book. If the box slid on the book, Laurent would reach for the box. This sort of observation led to three tentative conclusions: (a) A stationary object on a large extended surface (a floor or table) may be segregated from the background; (b) a stationary object adjacent to another stationary object will not be segregated by surface quality differences; and (c) two objects can be segregated by relative motion.

Subsequent experimental work has supported Piaget's interpretations. Spelke, Breinlinger, Jacobson, and Phillips (1993) tested infants' responses to adjacent object displays. *Homogeneous* displays had parts with identical luminance, color, and texture, and the parts' boundaries were continuous at their intersection points. *Heterogenous* displays had two adjacent parts differing in luminance and color, and also had discontinuities ("T" junctions) at the intersection points. After familiarization with a display, infants viewed two test events. In one, both parts moved together whereas in the other only the top part moved, detaching from the other part. If the original display had been perceived as two separate objects, infants were expected to look longer at the event in which the whole display moved as a unit. If the two parts had been perceived as connected, infants were expected to look longer at the detachment event. Three-month-olds showed this latter result, suggesting they had perceived both the homogeneous and heterogenous displays as connected. Ambiguous results were found with 5- and 9-month-olds. In related research, von Hofsten and Spelke (1985) used infants' reaching behavior to address perceived unity. Displays were designed to approximate closely the situations considered by Piaget: Spatial and motion relationships were varied among a small, near object, a larger, further object and an extended background surface. It was assumed that reaches would be directed to perceived boundaries of graspable objects. When the whole array was stationary and the objects were adjacent, greater reaching was observed to the edges of the larger, further object. Separation of the two objects in depth led infants to reach more for the nearer, smaller object. When the larger object moved while the smaller object did not, reaching was directed more toward the smaller object. This result suggested that motion segregated the objects rather than merely attracted reaching, because infants reached more to the stationary object. From these results, it appears that discontinuities in motion or depth segregate objects, whereas luminance discontinuities and overall shape variables do not. The results make sense in that motion and depth indicate object boundaries with greater ecological validity than luminance or spectral variations alone (Kellman, 1995; von Hofsten & Spelke, 1985). That is, ambiguous or misleading cases are less likely to arise with motion or depth discontinuities.

When in development adjacent, stationary objects come to be segregated by means of surface qualities alone, and what causes this information to become effective, remain important questions for further research.

Boundary Assignment

The question of boundary assignment involves the direction in which an edge bounds an object. Most visible object boundaries mark the edge of one object. On the other side of the boundary is another surface or object that passes behind the bounded one. Many of the same considerations we raised regarding edge classification apply to boundary

assignment. Evidence that infants distinguish shapes, or figures from grounds, might indicate that boundary assignment is occurring. It is problematic, however, to prove that a shape rather than a hole is perceived. These two possibilities differ in terms of the direction of boundary assignment.

We noted above that early shape constancy seems to presuppose boundary assignment. If this inference is correct, then the relevant information probably comes from discontinuities in depth at object edges. Boundary assignment from depth discontinuities follows the straightforward rule that the nearer surface owns the boundary. Another source of boundary assignment information is accretion/deletion of texture. When one surface moves relative to a more distant surface, texture elements on the latter surface go out of sight at the leading edge of the nearer object and come into sight at the trailing edge. This information constitutes a powerful source of boundary information, depth order and shape in adult perception (Andersen & Cortese, 1989; Gibson, Kaplan, Reynolds, & Wheeler, 1969; Shipley & Kellman, 1994). Granrud et al. (1985) studied accretion-deletion of texture with infants of 5 months of age. They reported that infants reached more often to a surface specified to be nearer by accretion-deletion, a result suggesting that both depth order and boundary ownership. This interpretation incorporates previous findings that infants reaches tend to be directed toward object boundaries and to the nearest object in an array (von Hofsten & Spelke, 1985; Yonas & Granrud, 1985). Unfortunately, infants do not attain directed reaching until about 5 months of age, making it impossible to use this informative measure to assess possible earlier registration of boundary direction.

Other behavior suggests appropriate detection of object boundaries in younger infants. When an object approaches an infant, certain defensive responses often occur, including withdrawal of the head, blinking the eyes, and raising of hands (Schiff, 1965; Yonas, 1981). Although some of these behaviors may not be unique to perceived approach, evidence supports the notion that some observed responses, especially blinking, indicate defensive behavior (Yonas, Arterberry, & Granrud, 1987). The importance of boundary assignment for this ability was tested by Carroll and Gibson (1981). They presented 3-month-old infants with arrays in which all surfaces were covered with random dot texture. Using accretion-deletion of texture, an approaching object was specified in one condition and an approaching aperture (opening in the surface) was specified by the information in the other condition. Infants appeared to use the information: They responded defensively more often to approaching objects than to approaching apertures.

Perception of Object Unity

Processes of edge detection, classification and boundary assignment parse the optic array into significant pieces and reveal some of the boundaries of objects, but they do not yield representations corresponding to the physical objects in the environment. We can understand the problem in more than one way. One way is to consider the implications of boundary assignment. When we indicated that perceived boundaries bound in one direction, we implied that at each perceived boundary, some unbounded object slips behind and is partly occluded. A more general way to understand the problem is to realize that most of the processing we have so far considered could take place on a two-dimensional representation (or a 2-D representation with observer-relative depths assigned to each point, the "2.5-D sketch" hypothesized by Marr, 1982). But this kind of representation will not support our knowledge of objects and spatial layout. We need to make sense of a world layered in the third dimension, in which most objects are partly occluded by other objects, and more than one object often lies along the same line of sight from the observer.

How can the visual system move from visible pieces to complete objects when some parts of objects are partly hidden? This is the question of perceiving object unity, or unit formation. It involves problems of spatial occlusion as a 3-D world is projected onto 2-D receptive surfaces and also changes in the optic projections over time as the observer or objects move.

Early analyses of how problems of occlusion might be surmounted emphasized Gestalt principles of organization (Kanizsa, 1979; Michotte, Thines, & Crabbe, 1964; Wertheimer, 1923/1958). Common motion through space, simplicity of overall form, continuity of contours and similarity of surface qualities were all considered influences that could cause separate visible regions to be perceived as connected entities.

Separating Processes in Unity Perception. More recent analyses have separated the information for unity into two categories (Kellman & Shipley, 1991). One is the common motion process first described by Wertheimer (1923/1958): Things that move together are seen as connected. Some more rigorous definition of "move together" is needed. It turns out that the class of rigid motions as

defined in projective geometry, as well as a number of non-rigid motion correspondences, can evoke perception of unity in human adults (Johansson, 1970, 1975). The common motion process does not depend on relationships between oriented edges and for that reason has been labeled the *edge-insensitive process.*

The other process includes in refined form some of the notions embodied in Gestalt principles, especially the principle of good continuation. It has been termed the *edge-sensitive process* because it depends on relationships of oriented edges, whether in stationary or moving arrays (Kellman, 1996; Kellman & Shipley, 1991). Hidden connections between visible areas depend on edge relationships; specifically, they appear to be governed by a mathematical criterion of *relatability* that formalizes the Gestalt notion of good continuation. Informally, relatability characterizes boundary completions as smooth (diffentiable at least once) and monotonic (singly inflected). Figure 3.4 gives some examples of relatable and nonrelatable edges. These are illustrated both in occlusion cases and in illusory figure cases (in which completed surfaces appear in front of other surfaces, rather than behind). Evidence indicates that surface completion in occluded and illusory contexts depend on the same mechanisms (Kellman & Shipley, 1991; Kellman, Yin, & Shipley, 1995; Ringach & Shapley, 1996). Surface quality similarity affects unit formation within constraints established by boundary formation (Grossberg & Mingolla, 1985; Kellman & Shipley, 1991; Yin, Kellman, & Shipley,

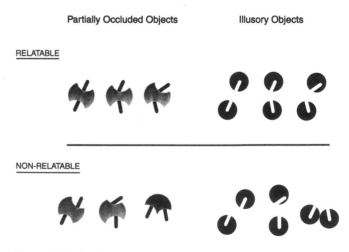

Figure 3.4   Relatable and nonrelatable edges. Connections (occluded surfaces or illusory surfaces between the two visible bars) are seen in the relatable displays, but not in the unrelatable ones.

1995). Surface quality fills in within completed boundaries, and may also spread under occlusion along the extended tangents of visible boundaries (Nakayama & Shimojo, 1992; Yin, Kellman, & Shipley, 1995).

How does unit formation get started? Understanding the processes available in early infancy and subsequent developmental changes is not only an important component of object perception but a possible window into higher visual processes, since unit formation requires contributions from the observer's system that go beyond local stimulus information.

The Edge-Insensitive Process: Common Motion.
Evidence suggests that the edge-insensitive (common motion) process appears much earlier than the edge-sensitive process. Infants' perception of partly occluded objects can be assessed using generalization of habituation (Kellman & Spelke, 1983). If two visible parts whose possible connection is occluded are perceived as connected, then after habituation of visual attention to such a display, infants should generalize habituation more to an unoccluded complete object and less to an unoccluded display containing unoccluded, separate pieces.

In a series of studies of 16-week-old infants, Kellman and Spelke (1983) found evidence that common motion of two object parts, visible above and below an occluding object, led to infants' perception of unity. After habituation to such a display, infants attend more to a moving "broken" display—two parts separated by a visible gap—than to a moving complete display. This outcome occurs whether or not the two visible parts are similar in orientation, color, and texture. Initial studies used a common lateral translation (horizontal motion, perpendicular to the line of sight), but later research indicated that vertical translation and translation in depth also specify object unity at 16 weeks (Kellman, Spelke, & Short, 1986). Translation in depth is especially informative about the underlying perceptual process, because its stimulus correlates are much different from the other translations. Whereas translation in the plane (a plane perpendicular to the line of sight) are given in terms of image displacements at the retina, or pursuit eye movements to cancel such displacements, translation in depth is specified by optical expansion or contraction in the object's project and/or by changes in convergent eye movements as the object moves. The use of a variety of stimuli that specify object translation in space suggests that infants' unity perception depends on registered object motion, not on a particular stimulus variable.

The class of motion relationships effective early in life does not appear to encompass the full range of rigid motions as defined mathematically. Rigid motions include all object displacements in 3-D space that preserve 3-D distances among object points. After habituation to a rotation display in which two visible parts rotating around the line of sight, 16-week-olds generalized habituation equally to rotating complete and broken displays (Kellman & Short, 1987a), a pattern that suggests the unity or disunity of the visible parts in the occluded display was seen as indeterminate (Kellman & Spelke, 1983). This pattern also occurred for several combinations of rotation and translation. Only when translation and rotation were combined so as to minimize any point in the motion in which the two visible parts moved in opposite directions did infants show a response pattern suggesting they perceived unity (Kellman & Short, 1987a). It appears that infants' unity perception is governed by a subset of rigid motions in which object points move in the same direction.

Motion in the Edge-Insensitive Process.   Most experiments on motion relationships in unity perception have used stationary observers and moving objects. Many theorists have observed that certain optical consequences of motion may be duplicated when a moving observer looks at a stationary object (Helmholtz, 1885/1925; James, 1890). The retinal displacement of a laterally moving object, for example, may be duplicated by an observer's head or body movement while a stationary object is in the observer's visual field. This similarity raises a crucial question about the role of motion in object unity: Does perceived unity depends on actual object motion or on certain optical events, such as image displacement, that may be caused by either observer motion or object motion?

Buried in this question is another one, at least as fundamental. Can infants tell the difference between optical changes caused by their own motion and those caused by the motions of objects? This ability is called position constancy: perceiving the unchanging positions of objects in the world despite stimulus changes due to one's own motion. If infants lack position constancy at some early stage of development, then their perceptual world might be quite bizarre. Each movement of the eyes or head might lead to impressions of objects moving as much as when objects really do move. Yet, the standard view on this question for over a hundred years has been that, given the similarities in the optical events, observers must learn to distinguish optical changes given by their own and by object motion

(Helmholtz, 1885/1925; James, 1890). A particular learning process was proposed by Helmholtz. He observed that observer-induced optical changes tend to be reversible. By moving one's head, one can make an object's image displace in one direction and then restore it to its original position by reversing the head movement. When objects move, their displacements are not in general reversible by the observer's action.

If infants cannot distinguish optical changes caused by their own and by objects' motions, then their perception of unity from motion must depend on the optical changes themselves, not uniquely on real motions of objects. The view that infant perceivers cannot distinguish real motion from observer-induced changes is not the only possible one, however. Gibson (1966, 1979) pointed out important differences between the optical consequences of observer and object motion. When an object moves, its relations to other visible objects and surfaces change. When an observer moves, certain relations among visible objects are preserved. It is possible that even young infants possess perceptual mechanisms that distinguish these cases.

Whether motion and stability can be distinguished and whether perceived unity from motion depends on one or both of them are empirical questions. Kellman, Gleitman, and Spelke (1987) took up these questions in a study of 16-week-olds. In each of two conditions, the subject's chair moved in a wide arc around a point between the observer and occlusion displays in front. In one condition (conjoint motion), the moving chair and a partly occluded object were rigidly connected underneath the display table, so that they both rotated around a point in between. In this condition, the object's motion was real; however, there was no subject-relative displacement. Thus, no eye or head movements were required to maintain fixation on the object. If perceiving the unity of this partly occluded display depends on real object motion, infants were expected to perceive unity in this condition. In the other condition (observer movement), the observer's chair moved in the same way, but the partly occluded object remained stationary. If optical displacement caused by observer motion can specify unity, infants were expected to perceive a complete object in this condition. As in earlier research, dishabituation patterns to unoccluded complete and broken displays after habituation were used to assess perception of unity. Test displays in each condition had the same motion characteristics as in habituation. Motion perception was assessed by comparing overall levels of looking in habituation and test

periods with earlier studies using similar moving or stationary displays. In those prior studies (with stationary observers), moving displays received markedly higher levels of visual attention.

Results indicated that only the infants in the conjoint motion condition perceived the unity of the partly occluded object. Analyses, based on looking time differences suggested that infants in the conjoint motion condition perceived object motion during their own motion, whereas observer movement infants responded as if they perceived the occlusion display as stationary. These results suggest that the common motion or edge-insensitive process depends on perceived object motion. The outcome makes sense ecologically, in that rigid relationships in moving visible parts are highly unlikely to occur unless the parts are actually connected. For optical displacements caused by movement of the observer, areas at similar distances from the observer will share similar displacements, yet it is hardly the case that all objects near each other are connected.

Origins of the Edge-Insensitive Process.   From findings that the motion relationships specify object unity to infants before they actively manipulate objects or crawl through the environment, Kellman and Spelke (1983) hypothesized that perceiving unity from motion is accomplished by innate mechanisms. The hypothesis also reflects the ecological importance of common motion information. Coherent motion is closely tied to the very notion of an object (Spelke, 1985), and common motion of visible areas has very high ecological validity as a signifier of object unity (Kellman, 1993).

More recent information suggests that unity may not be perceived from motion at the very beginning of life. Slater et al. (1990) replicated Kellman and Spelke's findings at 16 weeks but found different results with newborns. Newborn subjects in their experiment looked more at a complete object after habituation to an occlusion display, a pattern suggesting that the previous occluded display was perceived as containing two separate pieces. Newborns showed the same pattern of results even with larger depth separations between the occluder and the partly occluded parts (Slater, Johnson, Kellman, & Spelke, 1994).

The implications of these findings depend on what limits newborns' unity perception (Slater, Johnson, Kellman, & Spelke, 1994). One possibility is that infants begin life with an incorrect perceptual rule, assigning occlusion edges as object boundaries (Slater, Morison, et al., 1990).

This mistaken rule for parsing the world into objects might be somehow unlearned later, and rules for connecting visible parts based on common motion might be learned.

The other possibility is that newborns do not have adequate capacities to encode the crucial motion relationships. Recent evidence suggests such a limitation. Before 1 to 2 months of age, direction-selectivity of cells in visual cortex seems to be lacking, as indicated by both behavioral and electrophysiological tests (Johnson, 1990; Wattam-Bell, 1991, 1992). When a newborn views moving areas in an occlusion display, motion may be detected, but the common motion directions of the separate visible parts may not be. This might lead to the visible areas being perceived as separate, bounded fragments. The two accounts make different predictions, however, about what should be observed when directional sensitivity matures. If unity perception from common motion appears when directional sensitivity does, then it would appear that the edge-insensitive process is unlearned, awaiting only the necessary sensory inputs for its operation. Recent data suggest that the unity from motion can be found at 2 months, a finding that would tend the favor the maturational account (Johnson & Aslin, 1995).

The Edge-Sensitive Process: Unity Based on Edge Orientations and Relations.   The division of unity perception into edge-insensitive and edge-sensitive process crosscuts the earlier intuitive categorization of dynamic and static information (e.g., Kellman & Spelke, 1983; Michotte, Thines, & Crabbe, 1964). Although the common motion process is dependent only on motion relationships, the edge-sensitive process involves completion based on spatial orientations and relations of edges. These relations can be revealed in a static display or dynamically, over time, as when an observer views a scene through shrubbery. Thus, the edge-sensitive process includes object completion in stationary arrays as well as in dynamic ones where edge relationships are crucial, such as kinetic occlusion (Kellman & Shipley, 1991) and kinetic illusory contours (Kellman & Cohen, 1984). In contrast to the perception of unity from common motion, unity from relationships in static displays does not appear during the first half year of life (Kellman & Spelke, 1983; Schmidt & Spelke, 1984; Slater et al., 1990). The typical result is that after habituation to a stationary, partly occluded display, infants show equal looking to the complete and broken test displays. Based on evidence that infants do encode the visible areas and are sensitive to occlusion (Kellman & Spelke, 1983), this pattern has been interpreted as indicating the perceiver's neutrality about what happens behind the occluder.

The ineffectiveness of edge relations in specifying object unity has been found as late as 6 months of age (Bertenthal, Campos, & Haith, 1980; Schmidt & Spelke, 1984; Spelke, Breinlinger, Jacobson, & Phillips, 1993). Converging evidence comes from studies of occlusion and studies of illusory contours. For example, infants of 7 months, but not 5 months, appear to be sensitive to static and kinetic illusory contour displays (Bertenthal et al., 1980; Kaufmann-Hayoz, Kaufmann, & Walther, 1988).

Maturation, learning or some combination are the possible explanations for the later emergence of perceived unity from edge relations. Granrud and Yonas (1984) suggested that a number of pictorial depth cues appearing around 7 months of age might depend on maturation of a perceptual module, a finding bolstered by evidence from macaque monkeys (Gunderson, Yonas, Sargent, & Grant-Webster, 1993). It is possible that edge-sensitive unity perception might accompany this development. It has been noted that the depth cue of interposition is closely related to boundary completion under occlusion (Kellman & Shipley, 1991). Another argument for maturational origins comes from work on the neurophysiology of the edge-sensitive process (von der Heydt, Peterhans, & Baumgartner, 1984). It appears that boundary interpolation processes are carried out at very early stages of visual processing, certainly as early as V2 and possibly V1, the first visual cortical area (von der Heydt, Peterhans, & Baumgartner, 1984).

These observations are suggestive not conclusive. A clearer understanding of the roles of learning and maturation in the operation of the edge-sensitive process awaits further investigation.

Perception of Three-Dimensional Form

Knowing the functional possibilities of an object often depend on perceiving its form. Representations of form are also primary in object recognition. There are many levels of form—local surface topography, the two-dimensional projection of an object seen from a stationary vantage point and 3-D form, to name a few. Arguably, it is the 3-D forms of objects that are most important in human cognition and behavior. Whereas the particular 2-D projection from an object varies with the observer's position, the object's arrangement in 3-D space does not. Perceiving the unchanging object given changing optical information constitutes the important ability of *shape constancy.*

The origins of 3-D form perception have been disputed by perceptual theorists for several centuries. Adults perceive 3-D form perception in several ways, each of which suggests a different account of the development of 3-D form perception (Kellman, 1984). For example, adults can usually detect the overall form of an object from a single, stationary view. If the object is a familiar one, this ability is compatible with the idea that an object's 3-D form is a collection of 2-D views gotten from different vantage points, with any single view recalling the whole collection to mind (e.g., Mill, 1865/1965). On this account, 3-D form would develop from associating experiences of different views, perhaps guided by activity in manipulating objects (Piaget, 1954).

Another way to get whole form from a single view is to apply general rules that extrapolate 3-D form. Gestalt psychologists argued for unlearned, organizational processes in the brain that serve this purpose. An alternative account of rules of organization was suggested by Helmholtz (1885/1925) and elaborated by Brunswik (1956). Perceptual rules might be abstracted from experiences with objects. These two accounts of perceptual rules that map 2-D views into 3-D objects make opposing developmental predictions. On the Helmholtz/Brunswik account, the rules must be acquired from many experiences in seeing objects from different viewpoints and manipulating them. On the Gestalt view, organizational processes should operate as soon as the underlying brain mechanisms are mature.

Only a few decades ago, a new and different analysis of 3-D form perception emerged, based on initial discoveries such as the kinetic depth effect (Wallach & O'Connell, 1953) and later programmatic research on structure-from-motion (Ullman, 1979). The idea is that perceived 3-D form results from mechanisms specifically sensitive to optical transformations. Changes in an object's optical projection over time, given by object or observer movement, can be shown by projective geometry to be quite specific to the particular 3-D structure of an object. Several theorists have proposed that human perceivers extract this kind of information using neural mechanisms specialized for this purpose (Gibson, 1966; Johansson, 1970; Shepard, 1984). Such an arrangement would make sense for mobile organisms: The complexity and speed of human adult perception of structure from motion makes it seem unlikely that these abilities derive from general purpose mechanisms that encode motion properties and general purpose inference mechanisms that might have allowed relevant regularities to be discovered.

Optical Transformations in Infant Form Perception. Research with human infants indicates that the most basic ability to perceive 3-D form involves optical transformations. This dynamic information indicates 3-D form as early as it has been tested, whereas other sources of information about form appear unusable by infants until well past the first half year.

A method to separate responses to 3-D form from responses to particular 2-D views was developed by Kellman (1984). When an object is rotated its projection contains optical transformations over time but also might be registered as several discrete 2-D snapshots. A way to separate 3-D form from 2-D views is to habituate infants to an object rotating around one axis and test for recognition of the object (by generalization of habituation) to the same object in a new axis of rotation. For a suitably asymmetrical object, each new axis of rotation provides a different set of 2-D views, but, providing there is some rotation in depth, each conveys information about the same 3-D structure. A remaining problem is that dishabituation by infants may occur either for a novel form or a novel rotation. To combat this problem, infants were habituated to two alternating axes of rotation on habituation trials and tested afterward with familiar and a novel 3-D objects in a third, new axis of rotation. This manipulation reduced novelty responding for a changed rotation axis in the test trials. Sixteen-week-old infants tested with videotaped displays showed the effects expected if 3-D form was extracted from optical transformations. When habituated to one of two 3-D objects, they generalized habituation to the same object in a new rotation and dishabituated to a novel object in the same new rotation axis. Two control groups tested whether dynamic information was indeed the basis of response, or whether generalization patterns might have come from 3-D form perception based on single or multiple 2-D views. In the two control groups, infants were shown sequential static views of the objects taken from the rotation sequences. Two different numbers (6 and 24) of views were used along with two different durations (2 sec and 1 sec per view); in neither static view case, however, were continuous transformations available as in the dynamic condition. Results showed no hint of recognition of 3-D form based on the static views, indicating that 3-D form perception in the dynamic case was based on optical transformations.

Later research showed that this result occurs, also at 16 weeks, with wire frame objects having no surface shading information, a finding that implicates the importance of projective transformations of edges (Kellman & Short,

1987b). Yonas, Arterberry, and Granrud (1987) showed that 3-D form gotten from optical transformations could be recognized when form information was subsequently given stereoscopically. Paradoxically, transfer does not seem to go in the other direction; that is, initial representations of 3-D form do not seem to be gotten by infants from stereoscopic depth information in stationary viewing (see below).

Motion Perspective in Form Perception. The utility of 3-D form perception from dynamic information might be rather limited if infants could perceive only objects that happened to rotate while being viewed. The projective geometry of structure from motion, however, works equally well for a moving observer passing a stationary object as for the rotating object and moving observer. Kellman and Short (1987b) tested whether infants could perceive 3-D form when they were moved in an arc around a stationary object. Different axes of rotation were created by using a single vertical axis, but altering the insertion point on the object. They found the same pattern of results as in the object motion studies: Infants appeared to detect 3-D form as evidenced by their generalization of habituation to the same object in a new rotation and dishabituation to a novel object.

Static Form Perception. Form perception from optical transformations appear to be a basic foundation of human perception. It appears early and depends on complex information, suggesting the existence of dedicated neural mechanisms that map changing 2-D projections onto 3-D object representations. Another reason for looking at dynamic information as fundamental is that other sources of form information do not seem to be usable in the early months of life. This picture of early form perception turns on its head the classical empiricist notion that psychologically an object's 3-D form is a construction from stored collections of static views.

Above we described two conditions in which sequences of static views evoked no representation of 3-D form in 16-week-olds. This finding—inability to perceive 3-D form from single or multiple static views—has appeared consistently in research (Kellman, 1984; Kellman & Short, 1987b; Ruff, 1978), using real objects or photographic slides, up to an age of 9 months. The late incapacity with form from static views is perplexing given that adults easily gain 3-D form representations from single or multiple static views of objects. The one situation in which infants show some 3-D form perception from static

viewing involves recognition of 3-D forms which had previously been given kinematically (Owsley, 1983; Yonas, Arterberry, & Granrud, 1987). Perhaps this task of detecting similarity to a stored representation is simpler than developing a full 3-D object representation initially by means of static, binocular views.

Nonrigid Unity and Form. Perhaps it is obvious to say that both the concept and process of 3-D form perception are easiest to understand in the case of objects whose forms do not change, that is, rigid objects. Perception of rigid structure from motion is well understood computationally in terms of the projective geometry relating 3-D structure, relative motion of object and observer and transforming optical projections. Many objects of ordinary experience, however, do not have rigid shape. In a moving person, for example, a point on the wrist and one on the waist do not maintain a constant separation in 3-D space. Nonrigidities may be given by joints, as in animals or people, but also by flexible substances, as in a pillow that whose shape readily deforms. The possibility of perceiving or representing useful information about shape for an object whose shape varies depends on the existence of constraints on the variation. A human body can assume many, but not unlimited, variations in shape; the class of possibilities is constrained by joints and musculature, and so on. A jellyfish may be even less constrained, but even it has a shape, defined as a constrained class of possibilities, and characteristic deformations that depend on its structure and composition. Some progress has been made in the analysis of non-rigid motion, and processes that might allow us to perceive it (Bertenthal, 1993; Cutting, 1981; Hoffman & Flinchbaugh, 1982; Johansson, 1975; Webb & Aggarwal, 1982), but the problems are difficult.

Whereas scientists have not succeeded in discovering the rules for determining nonrigid unity and form, evidence suggests such rules exist in the young infant's visual processing. In work with adult perceivers, Johansson (1950, 1975) pioneered methods for testing form and event perception from motion relationships alone. His use of moving points of light in a dark surround, in the absence of any visible surfaces, has become the method of choice in structure from motion research. When such lights are attached to the major joints of a walking person, adult observers viewing the motion sequence immediately and effortlessly perceive the lights as forming a connected walking person. Turning such a display upside down eliminates recognition of a human form (Sumi, 1984).

Studies of the development of perception of non-rigid unity and form have been carried out by Bertenthal, Proffitt, and their colleagues (Bertenthal, Proffitt, & Cutting, 1984; Bertenthal, Proffitt, Kramer, & Spetner, 1987; Bertenthal, 1993). A basic finding is that when infants of 3 to 5 months are habituated to films of an upright walking person specified by light points, they subsequently dishabituate to an inverted display. This result suggests some level of perceptual organization, rather than apprehension of the displays as containing meaningless, individual points. The younger infants (at 3 months) may not perceive a person walking, however. Some later experiments used phase-shifting of the lights to disrupt the impression of a walking person. Three-month-olds discriminated phase-shifted from normal walker displays whether the displays were presented in an upright or inverted orientation (Bertenthal & Davis, 1988). Both 5- and 7-month-olds, in contrast, showed poorer discrimination with inverted than upright displays. One interpretation of these findings is that older infants, like adults, perceive only the upright, normal phase displays as a walking person so that disruption of the phase relations is salient for these displays. Because inverted displays are not perceived as people, phase disruption is not so noticeable. On this line of reasoning, 3-month-olds show perceptual organization of the displays but not classification of the upright displays as a walking person (*biomechanical motion*). The younger infants are thus sensitive to differences in upright or inverted displays.

Although a more direct measure of perception of a walking person has been difficult to devise, the findings suggest the attunement of the infant's visual system to certain nonrigid motion relationships. Detecting and encoding motion relations may begin earlier than the point at which recognition performance is measurable. Preferences for motion patterns generated by a walking person or a hand opening and closing have been demonstrated in 2-month-olds (Fox & McDaniel, 1982).

Earliest competence to perceive 3-D form depends on mechanisms that recover object structure from optical transformations. These abilities precede in development abilities to extrapolate 3-D structure from single views of objects and also precede the maturation of self-locomotion and directed reaching. Both rigid and non-rigid motion relationships provide structural information to young perceivers. What we know about early 3-D form perception fits the conjecture of ecological views that perception of structure from motion depends on dedicated perceptual machinery developed over evolutionary time (E. Gibson, 1979; Johansson, 1970; Shepard, 1984).

Perception of Size

An object of constant real size projects a larger image on the retina when it is close to the observer than when it is further away. Perception of constant physical size can be achieved by using the same geometry with a different starting point: From the projective size at the eye and information about distance, the physical size of the object can be perceived (Holway & Boring, 1941). In some situations, there may be relational variables that allow more direct perception of size, such as the amount of ground surface covered by an object in a situation where the surface has regular or stochastically regular texture (Gibson, 1950).

Among the most exciting developments in infant perception research over the last decade has been the emerging conclusion that some degree of size constancy—the ability to perceive the correct physical size of an object despite changes in viewing distance (and resulting changes in projective size)—is an innate ability of human perceivers.

Early research suggested that infants of about 5 months of age perceive an object's constant physical size at different distances and show a novelty response to a different-sized object, even when the novel object has a projective size similar to the previously seen object (Day & McKenzie, 1981). Studies of newborns have provided evidence that size constancy may be present from birth. Slater, Mattock, and Brown (1990) tested visual preferences for pairs of identically-shaped cubes of two real sizes (5.1 cm or 10.2 cm) at different distances (23–69 cm). Infants preferred the object of larger retinal (projective) size whenever it differed between the two displays. In a second experiment, infants were familiarized with either a large or small cube of constant physical size which appeared at different distances (and varying projective sizes) across trials in the familiarization period. After familiarization, infants were shown the large and small cubes successively on two test trials. Distance was adjusted so that both test stimuli had the same projective size, and this projective size was novel. (The cube that had been presented in familiarization was placed at a distance where it had not appeared earlier (61 cm away for the 10.2 cm cube and 30.5 cm away for the 5.1 cm cube). Figure 3.5 illustrates the arrangements in familiarization and test conditions. Every subject ($n = 12$) looked longer at the object of novel physical size in the test trials, and the percentage of test trial looking allocated to the novel object was about 84%. Other evidence tends to support the conclusion that size constancy is observable in neonates (Granrud, 1987; Slater & Morison, 1985). In Granrud's study, rates of habituation to sequences of

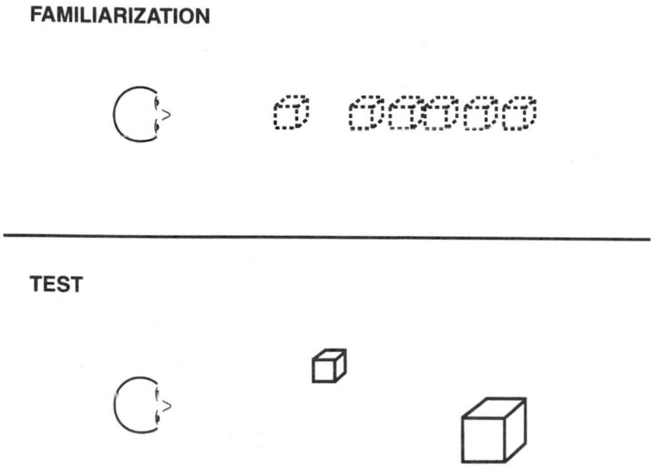

FAMILIARIZATION

TEST

Figure 3.5 The test display in the size constancy experiment (Slater, Mattock, & Brown, 1990). Each infant was familiarized with one object [either a large (10.2 cm/side) or small (5.1 cm/side) cube] at several viewing distances. The test pair consisted of the large and small cube placed at different distances (61 cm and 30.5 cm) to produce equal projective size. Object distances in the test trials were different from those used in familiarization.

objects with varying real size were slower than habituation rates to sequences with the same array of projective sizes, but unchanging physical size.

Research on newborn size perception has not addressed directly the possible information underlying constancy. This topic would seem to be an important one for future research. There are not many possibilities, however. The objects in both the Slater et al. and Granrud experiments hung in front of homogeneous backgrounds, precluding use of relational information potentially available when an object rests on a textured ground surface. In the situations used, it would appear that some information about egocentric distance, that is, distance from the observer, must be combined with projective size to allow computation of real size. Certain features of the experimental situations and newborns' abilities suggests that binocular convergence is the likely source of egocentric distance information (Kellman, 1995). Estimates of the precision of convergence vary (Aslin, 1977; Hainline, Riddell, Grose-Fifer, & Abramov, 1992; Slater & Findlay, 1975), but recent data (Hainline, Riddell, Grose-Fifer, & Abramov, 1992) and an analysis of the required precision of distance estimates needed to support size discriminations in the Slater et al. and Granrud experiments (Kellman, 1995) support this possibility.

SPACE PERCEPTION

As we have discussed, one of the more remarkable achievements of the human visual system is the ability to discern where one object ends and another begins from visual information alone. By and large, those assignments correspond with the actual boundaries of objects. However, for the perceiver to interact with objects in the visual environment, the visual system must also be able to assign them appropriate 3-D positions relative to the head and body. We now turn to this topic; that is, how does the developing visual system acquire the ability to see the spatial positions of objects in the 3-D environment?

In considering how we are able to obtain knowledge through perception, the philosopher Immanuel Kant concluded that we must bring to the task built-in (a priori) categories of space and time into which experience is organized (Kant, 1781/1902). Psychologically, understanding the origins and development of spatial perception has more nuances, as we will see. Whether we approach perception from the perspective of the philosopher, cognitive scientist, psychologist or engineer, however, we will rediscover Kant's insight that space is fundamental.

Theoretical controversy about the development of visual space perception has centered on depth perception. When we look at the human visual apparatus, it is relatively easy to see how we pick up information about two of three spatial dimensions. The optics of the eye ensure, to a high degree, that light originating from points in different directions from the observer will be mapped onto distinct points on the retina. This mapping preserves information about adjacency in two spatial dimensions (up-down and left-right). The apparent problem lies in the third (depth) dimension. Nothing in the map immediately indicates how far a ray of light has travelled to get from an object to the eye.

Traditionally, it has most often been claimed that perception of 3-D space is a product of learning (Berkeley, 1709/1963; Helmholtz, 1885/1925). Before the invention of methods to study infants' perception, arguments for this view emphasized the logical problem of recovering three dimensions of space from the two-dimensional retinal image. Learning might overcome the limitation through the storing of associations between sensations of vision and touch. It was assumed that three-dimensionality was somehow more accessible through touch; thus, the problem of seeing in 3-D could be handled by retrieval of stored tactile information when familiar visual input recurred (Berkeley, 1709/1963; Helmholtz, 1885/1925; Titchener,

1910). Piaget's view went a step further in arguing that self-initiated action and its consequences provide the necessary learning.

Modern analyses of the information available for vision have raised a radically different possibility for the origins of spatial perception. Transforming optical input given to a moving organism carries information specific to the particular 3-D layout (J. Gibson, 1966, 1979; Johansson, 1970). Humans and animals may well have evolved mechanisms to extract such information. On this *ecological* view of development (E. Gibson, 1979; Shepard, 1984), the rudiments of 3-D perception might be present even in the newborn, and their refinement might depend on sensory maturation and attentional skill, rather than on associative learning.

Research on spatial perception has gone a considerable distance toward answering this question of the constructivist versus ecological origins of the third dimension. Moreover, the emerging picture of early abilities provides important insights about functionally distinct classes of information and their neurophysiological bases. Anticipating some of these distinctions, we divide spatial perception abilities into four classes of information: Kinematic, stereoscopic, oculomotor, and pictorial. The classification reflects both differences in the nature of information and in the perceptual mechanisms at work in extracting information (Kellman, 1995; Yonas & Owsley, 1987).

Kinematic Information

For guiding action and furnishing information about the 3-D environment, kinematic or motion-carried information may be the most important class of visual information for adult humans. One reason for its centrality is that it overcomes the ambiguity in some other kinds of information, such as pictorial cues to depth. A stationary image given to one eye may be a cuddly kitten or a gigantic tiger further off, as Berkeley noted, or even a flat, 2-D cutout of a cat or tiger. To the moving observer, the transforming optic array reveals whether the object is planar or 3-D and furnishes information about relative distance and size. The mapping between the optical transformations and the 3-D scene is governed by projective geometry, and under reasonable constraints, it allows recovery of many properties of the layout (Koenderink, 1986; Lee, 1974; Ullman, 1979). Among the residual ambiguities is a problem analogous to the one Berkeley raised about a single image: If, for example, objects and surfaces in the scene *deform* (i.e., alter their shapes) contingent on the observer's motion, a unique 3-D scene is not recoverable. Now the problem is recovering

four dimensions (spatial layout plus change over time) from three (two spatial dimensions of the input plus time). In ordinary perception, simulation of the exact projective changes consistent with a particular, but not present, layout, would almost never occur by chance. It does, however, make possible the realistic depiction of 3-D space in television, motion pictures and in virtual reality set-ups. Because kinematic information about space depends on geometry, not on knowledge of what particular spatial layouts exist in the world, it is imaginable that perceptual mechanisms have evolved to make use of it. An additional reason to suspect that sensitivity to this kind of information might appear early is that early learning about the environment may be optimized by relying on sources of information that are most accurate (Kellman, 1993). On the other hand, adults acquire much kinematic information via their own movements through the environment. The human infant does not self-locomote until the second half-year of life, although kinematic information could still be made available from moving objects or when the infant is carried through the environment or from self-produced head movements.

Motion-carried information is often divided into subcategories, of which we will consider three: Relative depth surfaces can be specified by *accretion-deletion of texture*. Relative motion between an object and observer may be given by *optical expansion/contraction*. Relative depth, and under some conditions perhaps metric information about distance, can be provided by *motion parallax or motion perspective*. Another important kinematically-based spatial ability, recovery of object shape from transforming optical projections *(structure-from-motion)* was discussed earlier in the section on object perception.

Accretion/Deletion of Texture

In the late 1960s, George Kaplan, James Gibson, and their colleagues discovered a new kind of depth information, a shocking achievement given that depth perception had been systematically studied for over 200 years previously (Gibson, Kaplan, Reynolds, & Wheeler, 1969; Kaplan, 1969). Most surfaces have visible texture—variations of luminance and color across their surfaces. The new type of depth information involves what happens to visible points of texture (texture elements) when an observer or object moves. When the observer moves while viewing a nearer and further object, the elements on the nearer surface remain visible whereas those on the farther surface gradually pass out of sight along one side (deletion) of the nearer object and come into view along the other side (accretion).

The same kind of transformations occur when the motion is given by a moving object rather than a moving observer. This kind of information has been shown to be used in adult visual perception, both to establish depth order and shape, even when no other sources of information are available (Andersen & Cortese, 1989; Kaplan, 1969; Shipley & Kellman, 1994).

Shape perception from accretion-deletion of texture was studied by Kaufmann-Hayoz, Kaufman, and Stucki (1986). They habituated three-month-olds to one shape specified by accretion/deletion and tested recovery from habituation to the same and a novel shape. Infants dishabituated more to the novel shape. Although this result suggests that accretion/deletion specifies edges and shape at three months, we cannot tell much about perceived depth order from this study. That accretion-deletion does specifiy depth order at 5 to 7 months is suggested by a different study (Granrud et al., 1985). These investigators assumed that infants would reach preferentially to a surface perceived as nearer than another. Computer generated, random dot, kinematic displays were shown in which a vertical boundary was specified by only accretion-deletion information. Infants of 5 and 7 months of age were tested. Both groups showed modestly greater reaching to areas specified as nearer by accretion-deletion than to areas specified as farther.

It has been suggested (Craton & Yonas, 1990) that ordinary accretion-deletion displays actually contain two kinds of information. Besides the disappearance and appearance of texture elements, there are relationships of individual elements to the location of the boundary between surfaces. A visible element on one side of a boundary remains in a fixed relation to it, whereas an element on the other side (the more distant surface) changes its separation from the boundary over time. This separate information, termed *boundary flow*, appears to be usable by adults in the absence of element accretion-deletion (Craton & Yonas, 1990) and possibly by 5-month-old infants (Craton & Yonas, 1988).

Optical Expansion/Contraction

When an object approaches an observer on a collision course, its optical projection expands symmetrically. It can be shown mathematically that a ratio of an object point's retinal eccentricity and its retinal velocity gives its *time to contact*, that is, the time until it will hit the observer. Evidence suggests that newborns of other species show defensive responses to this kind of information (Schiff, 1965).

When presented with optical expansion patterns, human infants of 1 to 2 months of age often retract their heads, raise their arms, and blink (Ball & Tronick, 1971; Bower,

Broughton, & Moore, 1970). Not all of these responses, however, indicate perception of an approaching object (Yonas, Bechtold, Frankel, Gordon, McRoberts, Norcia, & Sternfels, 1977). Head movement may result from infants tracking visually the top contour of the pattern, and relatively undifferentiated motor behavior may cause the arms to rise in concert. Yonas et al. tested this hypothesis using a display in which only the top contour moved. This optical change is not consistent with approach of an object. Infants from 1–4 months displayed similar head and arm movements to this new display as to an optical expansion display. The result supports the hypothesis that tracking the top contour, rather than defensive responding, accounts for the behavior infants show to expansion displays.

It turns out, however, that both the tracking hypothesis and the hypothesis of defensive responding appear to be correct. When eye blinking was used as the dependent measure, reliably more responding was observed to the approach display than to the moving top contour display. It appears that blinking may best access infant perception of object approach and that it does so reliably from about one month of age (Yonas, 1981; Yonas, Pettersen, & Lockman, 1979).

Motion Perspective

Motion perspective is an important source of spatial layout information. When an observer moves and looks perpendicular to the movement direction, the visual direction of a nearer object changes at a faster velocity than that of a farther object. Comparing two such objects or points defines the classical depth cue of motion parallax. Gibson (1950, 1966) argued that perceptual systems might use relative velocities of many points, that is, that gradients of relative motion provide more information than a pair of points. To express this concept, he coined the term motion perspective. Some experimental evidence indicates that gradients are in fact used by human perceivers (Gibson, Gibson, Smith, & Flock, 1959).

Motion perspective is virtually always available to a moving observer in a lighted environment, and it ordinarily provides unambiguous indication of depth order. Given these considerations, one might expect that neural mechanisms have evolved to exploit this kind of information, and that accordingly, it might appear early in development. Several investigators have suggested that it does function quite early, but these suggestions have been based on indirect evidence (Walk & Gibson, 1961; Yonas & Owsley, 1987). Gibson and Walk (1961) studied newborns of various species on the visual cliff and noted that some species made lateral head movements before choosing the "shallow" side of the cliff over the "deep" side. It is difficult to make a similar inference about human infants, because they do not self-locomote until around 6 months of age.

Some results relevant to the development of motion perspective in 14-month-old infants were reported by von Hofsten, Kellman, and Putaansuu (1992). Subjects moved back and forth while viewing an array of three vertical bars. If motion perspective operates, the observer contingent motion should indicate that the middle rod is furthest from the subject. (See Figure 3.6.) After habituation to such an array, moving infants looked more at a stationary array consisting of three aligned, stationary rods than to another stationary array with the middle rod 15 cm further away than the others. (The latter display produced identical

motion perspective as the habituation display.) Two other experiments showed that the effect disappeared if the contingent motion was reduced from the original 0.32 to 0.16 deg/sec and that infants were sensitive to the contingency between the optical changes and their own movement. These results are consistent with infants' early use of motion perspective. They might also be explained, however, by infants responding to particular optical changes and the contingency of these optical changes on the observer's movement. In other words, the results do not show that the optical changes were taken to indicate depth. It is interesting that the experiments with these contingent optical changes found sensitivity to velocities an order of magnitude below those found in studies of motion thresholds, using noncontingent motion and stationary observers (see below). Further research is needed, however, to determine whether this enhanced sensitivity results from encoding the relative motions into depth relations via motion perspective.

Stereoscopic Information

Stereoscopic depth perception refers to the use of differences in the optical projections at the two retinas to determine depth. This ability is among the most precise available in adult visual perception. Under optimal conditions, an adult observer may detect depth when the angular difference in a viewed point's location at the two eyes (binocular disparity) is only 5 to 15 sec of arc (Westheimer & McKee, 1980). A 5 sec disparity would translate into detection of a 1.4 mm depth difference between two objects at a distance of one meter. A prerequisite for precise computation of disparity is fixation by the two eyes on a common environmental point. We can measure the disparities of other imaged points by comparison to this zero disparity fixation point. Points at roughly the same distance as the fixated point will project to corresponding retinal locations, thus, having the same angular separation and direction from the fovea on each of the two eyes.[3] Points more distant than the fixation point will have *uncrossed disparity*. The visual direction of such a point will be more to the

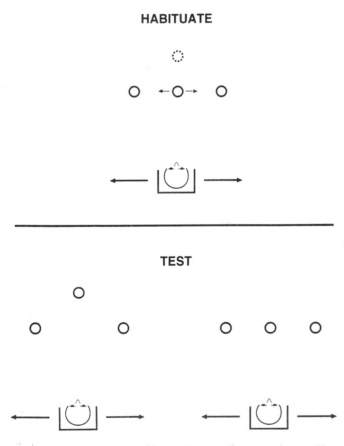

HABITUATE

TEST

Figure 3.6 Displays used in motion parallax experiment (Von Hoftsten, Kellman, & Putaansuu, 1992). *Top:* Moving observers were habituated to a linear array of rods (top view shown) in which the center rod moved in phase with the observer. The dotted line indicates the virtual object specified by motion parallax. *Bottom:* The two test arrays pictured were shown after habituation.

[3] The positions of objects that stimulate corresponding retinal locations actually lie on a circle that contains the fixation point (the place where the two foveas are directed) and the centers of the two eyes. This circle is called the Vieth-Muller Circle. Objects inside this circle create crossed disparity and those outside the circle create uncrossed disparity.

left in the visual field of the left eye than in the right eye. *Crossed disparity* characterizes points nearer than the fixated point. The visual directions of these points will be more leftward in the right eye than in the left.

Development of Stereoscopic Depth Perception

Observations from other species suggest the existence of innate brain mechanisms subserving stereoscopic depth perception, specifically, cortical cells tuned to particular disparities at birth or soon after (Hubel & Wiesel, 1970; Pettigrew, 1974; Ramachandran, Clarke, & Whitteridge, 1977).

Such single-cell recording studies are not possible in human infants; moreover, they do not directly address functional operation of stereoscopic depth perception. Evidence about human infants comes mostly from behavioral studies, and it suggests that stereoscopic depth perception arises on average around 4 months of age as a result of maturational processes.

A number of studies have used stationary displays and preferential looking as the dependent variable. One of two adjacently presented displays contains binocular disparities which might specify depth differences within the pattern. Infants are expected to look longer at a display containing detectable depth differences than at a similar one having no depth variation (Atkinson & Braddick, 1976; Held, Birch, & Gwiazda, 1980). A different method eliminates any possible monocular cues. Using random dot kinematograms, Fox, Aslin, Shea, and Dumais (1980) presented disparity information that would, if detected, specify a moving square. Using the forced-choice preferential looking method, adult observers judged the direction of motion on each trial solely by watching the infant's responses.

Estimates of the age of onset of disparity sensitivity from these methods show reasonable agreement. In longitudinal studies by Held and his colleagues (Birch, Gwiazda, & Held, 1982; Held, Birch, & Gwiazda, 1980) reliable preferences for a vertical grating pattern with disparity variation appeared at 12 weeks for crossed disparities and 17 weeks for uncrossed. Fox et al. found that 3- to 5-month-olds reliably oriented to a moving square specified by disparity, but infants younger than 3 months did not. Petrig, Julesz, Kropfl, and Baumgartner (1981) found a similar onset of sensitivity using recordings of visual evoked potentials.

A thorny issue in the interpretation of these studies is whether the observed behavioral responses index depth perception from binocular disparity or merely sensitivity to disparity itself. It is hard to settle this issue with certainty; however, some observations suggest that depth is perceived. Held, Birch, and Gwiazda (1980), for example, found that subjects who showed clear preferences for vertical line displays containing horizontal disparity showed no such preferences when the displays were rotated 90 deg to give 34 min of vertical disparity (this condition produces binocular rivalry for adults). Fox, Aslin, Shea, and Dumais (1980) observed that infants did not track a moving object specified by very large disparities which do not signal depth to adults. They found instead that infants reliably looked away from such displays. The different reactions by infants to different magnitudes of disparity might be expected if only some disparities produce perceived depth. On the other hand, the result shows that disparities per se can affect infants' fixation. Other research supports the conclusion that by 4 to 6 months, binocular information affects infants' spatial behavior (Gordon & Yonas, 1976; Granrud, 1986). Granrud's (1986) research suggests that binocular disparity (as opposed to convergence alone) is important: Disparity-sensitive infants showed substantially better reaching accuracy than disparity-insensitive infants of a similar age.

What mechanisms are responsible for the onset of stereoscopic sensitivity after several months of life? An argument for maturational causes is that sensitivity very quickly attains adultlike precision. Held, Birch, and Gwiazda (1980) reported that thresholds change over 3 to 4 weeks from greater than 60 min to less than 1 min of disparity, with the latter measured value limited by the apparatus; even so, this value is comparable to adult sensitivity under some conditions.

What mechanisms might be maturing at this time? One possibility is that disparity-sensitive cortical cells are coming on line. Another is that improvements in the mechanisms of convergence or visual acuity that are prerequisites to fine stereopsis might explain the observed onset of disparity sensitivity. Two forms of evidence suggest that the onset of stereopsis is not dependent on improvements in visual acuity (grating acuity).

First, when both acuity and disparity sensitivity are measured longitudinally in the same subjects, little or no change in grating acuity is found during the period in which stereopsis appears (Birch, 1993). Although this evidence is consistent with the hypothesis that these two aspects of vision are not causally related in development, we should point out that infant acuity and stereopsis tests generally do not have high reliability; obviously, low measurement reliability would give the appearance of a low correlation between the age-related improvement in acuity and stereopsis when there in fact might be a significant correlation.

Second, a different method pointing toward the same conclusion comes from a study by Westheimer and McKee (1980). Adult subjects were given artificially-reduced acuity and contrast sensitivity designed to approximate those present at 2 months of age. Under these conditions, stereoacuity was reduced substantially, but not sufficiently to explain infants' inability to respond to large disparities before 3 to 4 months of age. Developmental changes in convergence also appear unlikely to explain the onset of stereoacuity. Recent reassessments of the development of convergence (Hainline, Riddell, Grose-Fifer, & Abramov, 1992) indicate that it may be nearly adultlike at 1 to 2 months of age. Also, convergence changes would not explain differences in the onset of crossed and uncrossed disparity (Held, Birch, & Gwiazda, 1980).

Given the above considerations, most investigators believe the explanation for the onset of stereoscopic vision is some maturational change in cortical disparity-sensitive units. Such a mechanism underlies improvement of stereoscopic discrimination performance in kittens (Pettigrew, 1974; Timney, 1981). In humans, it has been suggested that the particular change in disparity-sensitive cells may be segregation of *ocular dominance columns* in layer 4 of the visual cortex (Held, 1985, 1988). At birth, cells in layer 4 generally receive projections from both eyes. Between birth and 6 months, inputs from the two eyes separate into alternating columns receiving input from the right and left eyes (Hickey & Peduzzi, 1987). Eye-of-origin information is needed to extract disparity information, so this neurological development is a plausible candidate for the onset of stereoscopic function.

Oculomotor Information

Oculomotor information is based on two kinds of muscular adjustments that attune the eyes to targets at different distances. The observer's eyes *accommodate* by changing the thickness of the lens (thereby changing refractive power) to attain a clearly focused image, and the two eyes converge by turning to fixate (i.e., center on the fovea) the same point in both eyes. At least since Berkeley's (1709/1910) *Essay toward a New Theory of Vision,* it has been suggested that information from receptors in the muscles that accomplish accommodation and convergence might provide information about the distance of a viewed target from the observer. This notion is plausible in that both adjustments are distance dependent. The nearer a viewed target, the greater the thickness of the lens and the turning inward of the eyes needed to achieve sharp focus and foveation respectively.

Accommodation

Research on adult perceivers has produced varied opinions about the status of accommodation as a depth cue. At best it seems to be a weak cue (Hochberg, 1971). For reasons that are somewhat complex (and not particularly relevant here), direct tests of accommodation have tended to produce negative results. Using indirect measures, however, such as the effect of accommodation on perceived size, there is reason to believe that accommodation influences perceived distance when targets are placed no more than 2 to 3 meters from the observer (e.g., Wallach & Floor, 1971).

In human infancy, accommodative responses vary somewhat with target distance but are not very accurate until about 12 weeks of age (Banks, 1980b; Braddick, Atkinson, French, & Howland, 1979; Hainline, Riddell, Grose-Fifer, & Abramov, 1992). No studies, however, have indicated whether accommodation provides depth information for infant perceivers.

Convergence

Some evidence indicates that convergence provides distance information to adult perceivers under at least some circumstances (von Hofsten, 1976; Wallach & Floor, 1971). As with accommodation, the geometry of convergence limits its effectiveness to near space, that is, within 2 to 3 meters from the observer. To equal the same convergence angle difference between two targets differing by 1 cm in depth at about 30 cm from the observer, targets at 3 meters would have to be separated by almost 1.5 meters! Thus, the precision of convergence information drops off rapidly with distance.

Early research on infant convergence suggested that achievement of appropriate convergence by young infants younger than about 5 months may occur but is quite variable (Aslin, 1977; Slater & Findlay, 1975). These assessments may have been limited by a number of methodological difficulties in precisely measuring convergence in infant subjects (Aslin, 1977). Hainline et al. (1992) reported results based on paraxial photorefraction techniques. With targets at varying distances between 25 and 200 cm, infants as young as 26 to 45 days (the youngest group tested) converged with almost adultlike accuracy. A complex question about these results is what information could produce accurate convergence in infants so young? Binocular disparities cannot be the information for convergence, given that disparity sensitivity emerges later. Convergence in adults can be triggered by accommodation, but for infants, accurate convergence seems to appear before precise accommodation. At least two possibilities remain (Hainline et al., 1992). If only a single target (or few targets) appear in each visual field, foveating the target in each eye may drive convergence. Or, convergent eye movements might occur to maximize correlated firing of separate cortical units driven by the two eyes that are sensitive to similar retinal locations. Available evidence does not permit a choice between these possibilities (Hainline et al., 1992).

Only one study (von Hofsten, 1977) has taken up directly the issue of convergence as depth information in infancy. Using convergence-altering spectacles, von Hofsten found that 5-month-olds' reaching behavior changed appropriately with convergence information. Several lines of indirect evidence suggest that convergence plays a role in early size constancy, as we considered earlier, and in perception of motion and stability (see below).

Pictorial Depth Information

The *pictorial cues* are so named because they allow depth to be portrayed in a flat, two-dimensional picture. Sometimes, these are called the classical depth cues, because they have been discussed and utilized by artists and students of perception for centuries. Theoretically, they have been central to classical arguments about the need for learning in spatial perception. The fact that the same information can be displayed in a flat picture or a real 3-D scene immediately points to their ambiguity as signifiers of reality. It is a short step to the classical perspective on the acquisition of such cues: If such cues are not unequivocally tied to particular spatial arrangements, our perception of depth from these cues must derive from learning about what tends to be the case in our particular environment. (The environment, until recently, had many more 3-D scenes offering information than 2-D representations.)

Ecologically, the pictorial cues to depth are diverse, but a number of them rest on similar foundations. The laws of projection ensure that a given physical magnitude projects an image of decreasing extent at the retina with increasing distance from the observer. Applying this geometry in reverse, it is obvious that if two physical extents are known or assumed to have the same physical (real) size, then differences in their projected size can be used to establish their depth order. This information comprises the depth cue of *relative size*. Very similar is *linear perspective*. If two lines in the world are known or assumed to be parallel, then their convergence in the optical projection may be taken to indicate their extending away from the observer in depth. Generalizing this notion to whole fields of visible elements comprises the rich source of information in natural scenes known as *texture gradients* (Gibson, 1950). If a surface is assumed to be made up of physically uniform or stochastically regular tokens (pebbles, plants, floortiles, etc.), then the decreasing projective size of texture elements indicates increasing depth. A different kind of assumed equality is illustrated by the depth cue of *shading*. If the light source comes from above, a dent in a wall will have a lower luminance at the top because the surface is oriented away from the light, whereas the bottom part, oriented toward the light, will have higher luminance. Perception of depth from these luminance variations implicitly assumes that the surface has a homogeneous reflectance; variations in luminance are then taken to indicate variations in surface orientation.

Pictorial cues are not as ecologically valid as kinematic or stereoscopic information, simply because the assumptions behind them, such as the assumption of physical equality, may be false. In a picture, it is easy to make two similar objects of different sizes or two parts of a connected surface with different reflectances, for example. Misleading cases of pictorial depth information are not too difficult to find in ordinary environments: Sometimes apparently converging lines really are converging lines, and sometimes the average size of texture elements changes with distance, as do the sizes of particles at the seashore (smaller particles get washed further up the beach).

Studies of the development of pictorial depth perception reveal a consistent pattern. Sensitivity to these cues appears to be absent until about 7 months of age. Around 7 months of age, infants seem to be sensitive to virtually all pictorial depth cues that have been tested. Much of this emerging picture of the origins of pictorial depth has come from systematic studies by Yonas and his colleagues (Yonas, Arterberry, & Granrud, 1987; Yonas & Owsley, 1987). For brevity, we consider only two examples: interposition and familiar size. The developmental course of other pictorial cues that have been studied, such as linear perspective and shading, appears to be quite similar.

Interposition

The depth cue of *interposition,* sometimes called overlap, specifies relative depth of surfaces based on contour junction information. To a first approximation, when surface edges form a T junction in the optical projection, the edge that comes to an end at the intersection point (the vertical edge in the letter T) belongs to a surface passing behind the surface bounded by the other edge (the horizontal edge in the letter T). Interposition is a powerful depth cue in human vision (Kellman & Shipley, 1991). Infant use of interposition information was tested by Granrud and Yonas (1984). They used three similar displays made of three parts each but differing in the presence of interposition information. In the interposition display, the left panel overlapped the middle which overlapped the right. In a second display, all contours changed direction at intersection points, giving indeterminate depth order. In a third display, the three surface sections were displayed slightly separated, so that there were no contour junctions relating them. Infants at 5 and 7 months of age viewed these displays monocularly (to eliminate conflicting binocular depth information), and reaching was measured. All parts of the displays were coplanar and located the same distance from the subjects. Infants' reaches to different parts of the displays were recorded. In one experiments, the interposition display was compared to the indeterminate control display and in a second experiment, the interposition display was compared to the control display having separated areas. In both experiments, 7-month-old infants reached reliably more often to the leftmost ("nearest") part of the interposition display than to the leftmost part of the control displays. Five-month-olds showed some tendency to reach more to the leftmost part of the interposition display than one of the control displays, but not the other. These results provide evidence that interposition is usable by 7 months, but they are equivocal or negative about its availability at 5 months of age.

Familiar Size

Perhaps the clearest example of learning effects in space perception is the cue of familiar size. If an object has a known physical size (and this size is represented in memory) and the object produces a particular projective size in a given viewing situation, the distance to the object can in principle be calculated (Ittleson, 1951). Using a preferential reaching method, Yonas, Pettersen, and Granrud (1982) tested infants' perception of depth from familiar size. As with perspective, 7-month-olds showed evidence of using familiar size whereas 5-month-olds did not. In a later experiment, Granrud, Haake, and Yonas (1985) tested familiar size using objects unfamiliar to the subjects before the experiment. Two pairs of objects were used. Each pair consisted of a large and small version of an object having identical shape and color. Infants were encouraged to play with the small object from one pair and the large object from the other pair for 6 to 10 minutes. After this familiarization period, infants viewed a simultaneous presentation of both large objects. It was expected that subjects would reach more often to the object whose small version had been handled during familiarization, if the cue of familiar size influenced perceived distance. (Memory for the physical sizes in the earlier exposure, combined with equal projective sizes in the test, would lead to interpretation of the previously smaller object as much closer.) Infants at 7 months of age who viewed the test displays binocularly reached equally to the two objects, but infants of the same age who viewed the test displays monocularly reached more to the previously smaller object. Five-month-olds showed no variations in reaching related to the size of objects in the familiarization period. These results suggest that by 7 but not 5 months infants may obtain depth information from familiar size, but this information is overriden when conflicting stereoscopic information is available.

A decade ago, little was known about the development of pictorial depth. Today, largely due to programmatic research by Yonas, Granrud, and their colleagues, we have a fairly clear picture about the timing of the appearance of pictorial cues. The picture is strikingly consistent across members of the category. Pictorial cues to depth arise sometime between the 5th and 7th month of age. What is not yet clear is what causes the appearance of pictorial depth perception around the midpoint of the first year. That various pictorial cues appear around the same time has been interpreted as suggesting that maturation of some higher visual processing area in the nervous system is the mechanism (Granrud & Yonas, 1984). Recent research with macaque monkeys lends additional support to a maturational explanation. Pictorial cues appear as a group around 7 to 8 weeks of life (Gunderson, Yonas, Sargent, & Grant-Webster, 1993). As they put it, this result is compatible with the idea that " . . . pictorial depth perception may have ancient phylogenetic origins, rather than being a product of enculturation." A key to this interpretation is that the timing fits the rough ratio of 1:4 in terms of time after birth in chimps and humans that fits the maturation of numerous other abilities. (In other words, a function that matures at 4 weeks in chimpanzees appears at about 16 weeks in human infants.) Alternatively, the similarity of onset of these sources of information might be explained by learning. It is suggestive that the depth cue of familiar size, which necessarily involves learning, becomes operative in the same period as other pictorial depth cues. Their appearance at this time could reflect enhanced possibilities for learning brought about by some other developmental advance, such as the appearance of crawling abilities around 6 months of age. One study that correlated individual sensitivity to linear perspective and texture gradients with crawling ability (Arterberry, Yonas, & Bensen, 1989) found no predictive relationship, however. Seven-month-olds seemed to utilize pictorial depth in their reaching regardless of whether they had learned to crawl or not.

Further research will be needed to discover the mechanisms underlying the onset of pictorial depth perception. Longitudinal studies of multiple pictorial depth cues would be helpful, as would be formulation and tests of more specific neurophysiological candidates for maturation and, alternatively, potential processes of learning.

COLOR VISION

The study of the development of color vision has been one of the most active research areas in infant perception during the past decade. Here we set the relevant background to the issues that have been examined, review recent work on the ability to discrimination on the basis of differences in wavelength composition, and review work on the development of color constancy.

Certain psychophysical observations in adults have proven to be strong indicators of the properties of the underlying physiological mechanisms and this is particularly the case in the study of color vision. Even though the experimental paradigms used in color vision may seem obscure, they are generally designed to provide significant insight into underlying mechanisms. For this reason, we devote some time in this section to describing basic features of mature color vision before we review the infant literature.

The term *color* refers to the component of visual experience characterized by the psychological attributes of *brightness, hue,* and *saturation*. Two of these—hue and saturation—are chromatic attributes and the other—brightness—is actually an achromatic attribute. Hue is primarily correlated with the dominant wavelength of the stimulus whereas brightness is primarily correlated, but not isomorphic, with stimulus intensity. Saturation is correlated with the distribution of wavelengths in a stimulus; stimuli with a broad band of wavelengths tend to be less saturated. We will refer to visual discriminations on the basis of differences in hue and/or saturation as *chromatic discriminations* and discriminations on the basis of differences in brightness as *achromatic discriminations*.

What advantage does color vision offer? There is no definitive answer, but chromatic information probably aids object segmentation and recognition in a number of everyday situations. In cases in which an object and its background are equal or nearly equal in luminance, the object's shape can be perceived from chromatic differences. Chromatic information can also help distinguish one version of an object (a red apple) from another (a green apple). Finally, it can aid the object segmentation process. For example, it can be difficult to determine whether a change in luminance in the retinal image is caused by a shadow falling across a uniform piece of material or is caused by a change in the material. A shadow generally yields a change in brightness without a change in hue whereas a change in material generally yields both. Thus, color vision may allow the perceiver to distinguish changes in the retinal image caused by shadows from other causes.

The first stage of the visual process—the photoreceptors—is the first important stage in color vision. The adult visual system, of course, has four types of photoreceptors, one type of rod and three types of cones. The cones are active under daylight viewing conditions and subserve color vision; rods are active under quite dim illumination. We will consider cones only in the remainder of our discussion of color vision.

The three cone types are sensitive to different, but overlapping, bands of wavelength. The cone types are generally called *short-wavelength-sensitive* (S), *medium-wavelength-sensitive* (M), and *long-wavelength-sensitive* (L) cones. (We prefer this terminology to the terms *blue, green,* and *red* cones because those terms imply that particular cone types are responsible for the perception of different hues and this is simply not the case.) Each type of photoreceptor responds in an untagged fashion; that is, only response quantity, and nothing else, varies with changes in the incident light. The consequences of untagged responding are profound. The output of any single photoreceptor type can be driven to a given level by virtually any wavelength of light simply by adjusting the light's intensity. Thus, information about the wavelength of a stimulus cannot be extracted from the output of a single photoreceptor type. Instead, the visual system must use the relative activities of the three photoreceptor types to infer the wavelength composition of the stimulus. Therefore, the existence of only three cone types imposes a profound limitation and leads directly to the *trichromacy* of adult color vision

Photoreceptor characteristics cannot be the whole story because the subsequent stages of the visual process must preserve wavelength information to allow the conscious experience of color. Psychophysical evidence from adult humans and physiological evidence from adult monkeys indicate that the signals of the three cone types undergo a major transformation in the retina. Signals from two or three kinds of cones are combined additively to form achromatic channels (coding brightness primarily) and are combined subtractively to form two kinds of chromatic channels (coding hue primarily). The subtractive, chromatic channels (red/green and blue/yellow) have been called *opponent processes* because different wavelength bands evoke different directions of neural response.

Many of the characteristics of photoreceptors and subsequent neural stages were originally inferred from adult behavioral studies. Part of the interest in the behavioral study of infants arises from the possibility that they will lead to similar insights concerning the development of color mechanisms. We will return to this point at the end of this section.

Development of Spectral Sensitivity and Hue Discrimination

The most basic question to ask about the development of color vision is: When can infants discriminate stimuli on the basis of hue alone? Before 1975, a large number of behavioral studies attempted to answer this question, but they all failed to eliminate the possibility that infant were basing their discriminations on brightness cues rather than hue (or saturation) cues (Kessen, Haith, & Salapatek, 1970).

To rule out brightness artifacts, one needs to know the relationship between wavelength and brightness for the individual under examination. This relationship is characterized by the *spectral sensitivity function* which plots the reciprocal of light intensity at threshold as a function of wavelength. The spectral sensitivity function manifests the sensitivities of M and L cones; S cones do not contribute to spectral sensitivity.

Infants' spectral sensitivity curve under daylight viewing conditions (favoring cones over rods) has been measured behaviorally and electrophysiologically (Dobson, 1976; Maurer, Lewis, Cavanagh, & Anstis, 1989; Moskowitz-Cook, 1979; Peeples & Teller, 1975; Teller & Lindsey, 1993). Even at 4 weeks of age, sensitivity varies with wavelength in a fashion similar to spectral sensitivity in adults. There is a tendency for infants' sensitivity to be relatively greater at short wavelengths (e.g., violet and blue), but this is probably a simple consequence of the less dense pigmentation of the lens and macula early in life (e.g., Bone, Landrum, Fernandez, & Martinez, 1988).

The general similarity of adult and infant spectral sensitivity curves suggests the presence of normal M and L cones early in life. However, the observation that M and L cones are present is not sufficient evidence that infants can distinguish lights on the basis of wavelength composition. To demonstrate this convincingly, one must show that infants can discriminate on the basis of hue alone. To do so, one must rule out brightness artifacts and two strategies have been successfully employed.

The studies have presented two stimuli differing in hue (e.g., red and green) and looked for a systematic response to one as evidence for hue discrimination. One strategy for eliminating brightness artifacts involves using the spectral sensitivity function to match the brightnesses of two stimuli to a first approximation and then by varying the luminances (a measure of stimulus intensity) of the stimuli unsystematically from trial to trial over a wide enough range to ensure that one is not always brighter than the other. Systematic responding by the infant to one of the two chromatic stimuli, across luminances, can therefore not be attributed to discrimination on the basis of brightness. Oster (1975) and Schaller (1975) used this strategy, but different response measures, to demonstrate hue discrimination in 8- and 12-week infants, respectively.

The second strategy for eliminating brightness cues was developed by Peeples and Teller (1975); subsequently, many others have used this strategy, so we will explain it in some detail. They too used spectral sensitivity data to match approximately the brightnesses of their stimuli. They then varied luminance systematically around the estimate of the brightness match. Several luminances were presented, bridging a 0.8 log unit range in small steps. Consequently, at least one of the luminance pairings must have been equivalent in brightness for each of the infants. Peeples and Teller showed that 8-week olds could discriminate red from white for all luminance pairings. They concluded that 8-week-olds can discriminate on the basis of hue alone.

Thus, three reports in 1975, using different techniques, provided the first convincing evidence that 8- to 12-week-olds can make chromatic discriminations. Young infants must have at least some rudimentary form of chromatic vision.

Infants less than eight weeks of age do not consistently demonstrate the ability to discriminate stimuli that differ in hue only, but older infants make such discriminations quite reliably (Peeples & Teller, 1975; Teller, Peeples, & Sekel, 1978; Hamer, Alexander, & Teller, 1982; Packer, Hartmann, & Teller, 1984; Varner, Cook, Schneck, McDonald, & Teller, 1985; Clavadetscher, Brown, Ankrum, & Teller, 1988; Allen, Banks, & Schefrin, 1988). Here we consider three sorts of hue discriminations—Rayleigh, tritan, and neutral-point—because they are particularly interesting theoretically.

The *neutral-point test* is based on the observation that color-normal adults are able to distinguish all spectral (single wavelength) lights from white; that is, they do not exhibit a neutral point. Peeples and Teller (1975) and Teller et al. (1978) used a neutral-point test to examine 8-week-olds' color vision. They examined both white-on-white luminance discrimination and discrimination of a variety of chromatic targets from white. The colors of the test targets and background are represented in Figure 3.7, which is a chromaticity diagram. Eight-week-olds discriminated many colors from white: red, orange, some greens, blue, and some purples; these colors are represented by the filled symbols. Eight-week-olds did not discriminate yellow, yellow-green, one green, and some purples from white; these are represented by the open symbols. Thus, 8-week-old infants seemed to exhibit a neutral zone running from short wavelengths to yellow and green. Teller et al. (1978) argued from these results that 8-week-olds may have deficient S cones (in color parlance, that they have tritanopia or tritanomalous trichromacy).

A *tritan test* is designed to assess the function of S cones. By presenting two lights that activate M and L cones equally, the test isolates the S cones. Varner et al. (1985) asked whether 4- to 8-week infants could distinguish two such lights. Specifically, they presented violet targets in a green background. Eight-week-olds distinguished the two lights at all luminances, so they do not appear to have an S-cone deficiency. Four-week-olds, on the other hand, did not discriminate the two lights reliably, suggesting that they have an S-cone defect. Allen et al.

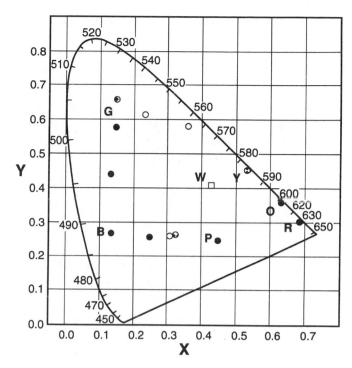

Figure 3.7 The stimuli used in neutral-point experiments (Peeples & Teller, 1975; Teller et al., 1978). Subjects in both experiments were 8-week-olds. The format of the figure is the CIE Chromaticity diagram, which allows one to plot chromatic stimuli differing in hue and saturation. Saturated colors are represented at the exterior of the diagram, and unsaturated colors toward the middle. The right corner of the diagram (labled 700) represents a hue of red, the topic of the diagram represents a hue of bluish-green (labled 520) and the lower left corner represents a hue of violet (labled 400). Each circular symbol represents a color that was presented to infants in these two experiments. Open symbols represent hues that all infants failed to discriminate from white (W). Half-filled symbols represent hues that some, but not all, infants discriminated from white. Filled symbols represent hues that all infants reliably discriminated from white.

(1988) and Clavadetscher et al. (1988) confirmed this finding: In their experiment, 3- to 4-week-olds could not distinguish a violet target on a green background, but 7- to 8-week-olds could.

Rayleigh discrimination tests involve the discrimination of brightness-matched, long-wavelength lights such as red and green. They are diagnostically important because adults with the most common color defects—deuteranopia (lacking M cones) and protanopia (lacking L cones)—are unable to make such discriminations. Hamer et al. (1982) and Packer et al. (1984) examined the ability of 4-, 8-, and 12-week-olds to make Rayleigh discriminations. Either a green or red target was presented at one of a variety of luminances on a yellow background. Most 8-week-olds and essentially all 12-week-olds made these discriminations reliably. This is clear evidence that most infants do not exhibit deutan or protan defects by 8 weeks of age. In contrast, the majority of 4-week-olds did not exhibit the ability to make either discrimination. Packer et al. also found a significant effect of target size. Twelve-week-olds were able to make Rayleigh discriminations with 4- and 8-deg targets, but not 1- and 2-deg targets. These results imply that early color vision differs from that of color-normal adults perhaps due to an absence of M and/or L cones or to an inability of post-receptoral circuits to compare M and L cone signals.

Allen et al. (1988) and Clavadetscher et al. (1988) confirmed the Rayleigh discrimination finding. They reported that 3- to 4-week-olds could not distinguish a red target on a green background; 7- to 8-week-olds could make this discrimination reliably.

Several experiments by Adams and colleagues (Adams, Maurer, & Davis, 1986; Maurer & Adams, 1987) appear to show better hue discrimination performance at comparable ages than the studies reviewed above. However, the experiments used between-subjects designs so there was no assurance that luminances were equated for each individual child. Furthermore, they used a more lenient statistical criterion than the studies reviewed above, so direct comparisons of the outcomes are difficult. More recently, however, Adams, Courage, and Mercer (1994) used a within-subjects design and an efficient behavioral procedure to assess neutral-point discriminations in newborns. They reported that the majority of newborns were able to discriminate broadband red from white and that the majority were unable to discriminate blue, green, and yellow from white. These results are quite similar to the 8-week results reported by Teller et al. (1978). They suggest that efficient procedures might reveal chromatic discrimination capabilities at younger ages.

In sum, there are no rigorous demonstrations that the majority of infants 4 weeks of age or younger make hue discriminations with the possible exception of discriminating red from white. The paucity of positive evidence is consistent with the hypothesis that human neonates are generally color deficient. Younger infants' hue discrimination failures may be due to the absence or immaturity of different cone types or because of immaturities among post-receptoral chromatic channels. Banks and Bennett (1988) have called this the *chromatic deficiency hypothesis*. There is, however, another possibility that was raised initially by Banks and Bennett (1988) and elaborated by others (Allen, Banks, & Norcia, 1993; Banks & Shannon, 1993; Brown, 1990; Teller & Lindsey, 1993). Perhaps neonates have a full complement of functional cone types and the requisite neural machinery to preserve and compare their signals, but their overall visual sensitivity is simply too poor to allow them to demonstrate their chromatic capabilities. Similarly, older infants may exhibit reliable chromatic discrimination because of increased visual sensitivity. For the purposes of this hypothesis, we define visual sensitivity as the discrimination performance of a visual system limited by optical and photoreceptor properties plus a general post-receptoral loss. This hypothesis has been called the *visual efficiency hypothesis* (Allen et al., 1993) and the *uniform loss hypothesis* (Teller & Lindsey, 1993).

The primary difference between these two explanations of the development of infant color vision can be quantified in the following way. Consider measurements of hue discrimination threshold (e.g., the chromatic contrast required to mediate the discrimination of two lights of equal brightness but different wavelength compositions) and a brightness discrimination threshold (e.g., the luminance contrast required to mediate the discrimination of two lights of the same wavelength composition but different luminances). The chromatic deficiency hypothesis predicts that the ratio of luminance discrimination threshold divided by chromatic discrimination threshold will decrease with increasing age. That is, luminance and chromatic thresholds may both become lower with age, but chromatic thresholds change more. The visual efficiency or uniform loss hypothesis predicts that the ratio of ratio of luminance threshold divided by chromatic discrimination threshold is constant with age. That is, luminance and chromatic discrimination thresholds decrease at the same rates with increasing age because they are both limited by a common factor such as overall visual sensitivity. Banks and Bennett (1988) and Banks and Shannon (1993) showed that this hypothesis can in fact predict the poor Rayleigh and neutral-point discriminations of neonates.

Recently, several investigators have tested the chromatic deficiency and visual efficiency hypotheses empirically; unfortunately, no clear consensus has yet emerged. The trick has been to develop paradigms in which infants' sensitivity can be made high enough to distinguish the predictions of the two hypotheses. In particular, recent work has focused on determining which hypothesis provides a better account of young infants' ability to use M and L cones to make Rayleigh discriminations.

Allen et al. (1993) and Morrone, Burr, and Fiorentini (1993) used VEPs and optimal spatiotemporal stimuli to examine luminance and Rayleigh discriminations at different ages. The stimuli consisted of two spatial sinewave gratings of equal contrast: one produced by modulating a saturated green stimulus (thus creating a green/black grating) and the other by modulating a saturated red (creating a red/black grating). The two sinewaves were added in counterphase (the bright red bars of one being positioned in-between the bright green bars of the other). Allen and colleagues and Morrone and colleagues then varied the ratio of red and green luminances in order to measure sensitivity for pure luminance variations and for pure chromatic variations. When the red luminance was zero (or green luminance was zero), the sinewave was an isochromatic green/black (or red/black) pattern with a variation in brightness only. When the red and green luminances were the same, the sinewave was an isoluminant pattern with a variation in hue only. The two groups of investigators measured contrast sensitivities for the various ratios in color-normal adults and in infants. The chromatic deficiency hypothesis predicted that the ratio of luminance threshold divided by chromatic threshold would increase with age and visual efficiency hypothesis predicts that the ratio would be constant with age. As expected from either hypothesis, the lowest thresholds were observed when either the red or green luminance was zero (these are luminance threshold measurements) and the highest thresholds were obtained when the red and green luminances were the same (when the grating was isoluminant). Allen et al. (1993) found that the ratio of thresholds was indeed constant from 3 weeks of age to adulthood, a finding that is consistent with the visual efficiency hypothesis. However, Morrone et al. (1993) reported that the ratio of thresholds increased with age, which is consistent with the chromatic deficiency hypothesis.

More recently, other investigators have examined the same issue using other response measures. Teller and colleagues (Teller & Lindsey, 1993; Teller & Palmer, 1996) used an ingenious OKN technique and obtained data consistent with the visual efficiency hypothesis. Brown, Lindsey, McSweeney, and Walters (1995) used a similar technique with similar results. Kelly, Borchert, and Teller (1995) used a technique similar to Allen et al. (1993) and observed a small increase with age in the luminance/chromatic threshold ratio. Thus, most of the current data is consistent with the visual efficiency hypothesis that young infants' inability to make behavioral discriminations that rely on M and L cones is due to generally poor

visual sensitivity rather than to deficits among chromatic mechanisms per se. The causes of the differences in results among some of these studies remain to be determined. Human neonates appear to have functional M and L cones and the post-receptoral neural machinery to preserve and compare their signals.

We now turn to tritan discriminations that isolate the functioning of S cones. Varner et al. (1985), Allen et al. (1988), and Clavadetscher et al. (1988) reported that few 4-week-olds and most 8-week-olds demonstrate the ability to make a tritan discrimination. Banks and Bennett (1988) and Banks and Shannon (1993) showed that the visual efficiency hypothesis cannot predict the poor tritan discrimination performance on infants less than 4 weeks of age. This theoretical finding implies that young infants may well have a tritan color defect; in particular, they may have dysfunctional or insensitive S cones or perhaps the post-receptoral blue/yellow opponent mechanisms do not develop for a couple of months. This prediction failure does not affect the interpretation of the Rayleigh discrimination experiments because they do not involve S cones.

In summary, the predictions of the visual efficiency hypothesis are consistent with the pattern of Rayleigh and neutral-point discriminations observed by Teller and colleagues. Moreover, research reports from three groups (Allen et al., 1993; Brown et al., 1995; Kelly et al., 1995; Teller & Lindsey, 1993; Teller & Palmer, 1996) have shown empirically that the chromatic information required to make a Rayleigh discrimination is transmitted to the cortex of infants as young as 3 weeks of age. Consequently, discrimination failures observed among the youngest children and for small targets among the older children do not necessarily imply deficiencies among chromatic mechanisms per se. Rather the ratio of chromatic divided by luminance sensitivity may well remain constant across age, suggesting that neonates' apparent inability to make Rayleigh and neutral-point discriminations is caused by an overall loss in visual efficiency. The predictions of the visual efficiency hypothesis are inconsistent with the tritan discriminations observed by Varner et al. (1985), Allen et al. (1988), and Clavadetscher et al. (1988). Therefore, young infants may in fact possess some form of color anomaly involving a deficiency among S cones.

Color Constancy

The wavelength composition of light reaching the eye from a reflecting surface depends not only on the properties of surfaces but also on the light illuminating the surface.

Thus, light reflected from a surface that is perceived as "white" can have a predominance of long wavelengths (e.g., yellow and red) when illuminated by sunlight at noon or can have relatively more short wavelengths (e.g., blue) when illuminated by fluorescent indoor lights. Even though the light reaching the eye can vary in this fashion, we usually do not perceive a significant change in the color appearance of the surface itself. This property of being able to perceive a surface's color despite changes in the spectrum of light illuminating the surface is called *color constancy*. The adult visual system exhibits color constancy for the relatively small variations in illumination that occur with natural lighting. There are numerous theories of color constancy (D'Zmura & Lennie, 1986; Maloney & Wandell, 1986; Marimont & Wandell, 1992), but it is as yet unclear which method or methods is employed by the mature visual system.

Dannemiller and Hanko (1987) and Dannemiller (1989) have examined the development of color constancy. In both cases, infants were presented test objects that were constructed of different sorts of reflecting material. The test objects were also illuminated by lights with different wavelength compositions. Dannemiller (1989) showed that 20-week-olds generalized habituation in a fashion consistent with the presence of color constancy. Specifically, when these infants were exposed to objects under one illuminant, they generalized habituation to the same objects viewed under a different illuminant, but did not generalize habituation to new objects viewed under the same illuminant. In other words, their behavior was consistent with discrimination based on changes in the objects themselves and not with changes in the wavelength composition of the light reaching the eye from the objects. The younger, 9-week-old infants did not exhibit this behavior. They showed a novelty preference when the objects remained the same but were viewed under a different illuminant. These findings suggest that color constancy, at least in a rudimentary form, can be demonstrated in the first half year of life. We hope that more experimental effort is devoted to this fascinating topic.

MOTION PERCEPTION

Processes of visual perception and action seem inextricably linked. To locomote safely through space and respond effectively to events require detailed information about the environment's spatial and temporal structure. Elaborate systems for acquiring such information exist only in organisms with complex action systems, and in many species, vision is the best source of this information. From these considerations alone, we may suspect that motion plays an important role in visual perception. We may intuit, for example, the relatively modern idea (Gibson, 1966; Johansson, 1970) that seeing while moving—the pickup of information over time—is basic to vision, rather than an annoying complexity added onto the decoding of static snapshots of scenes. Earlier we considered ways in which motions of objects and observers offers high-fidelity information about persisting properties of the environment such as spatial layout and object form. Here our emphasis is on the perception of change: moving objects, their trajectories, speeds, and collisions with surfaces and other objects.

Perceiving Motion and Stability

Perceiving moving objects is inextricably tied to its converse: perceiving nonmoving objects and surfaces as stationary. The latter ability is less straightforward than it might at first appear. Neural models of motion detectors suggest that these should respond to image features, such as edges, that change position on the retina over time. Yet such retinal displacement occurs in perfectly stationary environments whenever perceivers make eye, head or body movements. Perception of objects remaining at rest during observer motion, called *position constancy,* requires use of information beyond that available to individual motion-sensing units. Such information might involve comparison of retinal changes with those expected from self-produced movements (von Holst, 1954; Wallach, 1987) or more global relationships among optical changes occurring at a given time (Duncker, 1929; Gibson, 1966).

In the case of passive (i.e., nonself-produced) observer motion, relations in optic flow and/or some contribution from the vestibular system must be used in perceiving a stable world. There is some indication that young infants show position constancy under such conditions. Earlier we mentioned work in object perception (Kellman, Gleitman, & Spelke, 1987) suggesting that moving infants discriminate moving from stationary objects and perceive object unity only from real object motion. More direct studies of position constancy and motion perception by moving observers have also been carried out (Kellman & von Hofsten, 1992). In these studies, infants were moved laterally while viewing an array of objects. On each trial, one object in the array, either on the left or right, moved while others remained stationary. The object motion was parallel to the observer's motion. Whether the optical change given to the observer in this situation comes from a moving or stationary object depends on the object's distance. Thus, a stationary object placed on the opposite side of the array at a different distance matched the optical displacement of the moving object. Subjects were expected to look more at the moving object if its motion was detected. Both 8- and 16-week-olds showed this pattern when the object and observer motions were opposite in phase, but only 16-week-olds appeared to detect the motion when object and observer moved in phase (Kellman & von Hofsten, 1992). It is not clear why the younger infants showed detection of the moving object only in the opposite phase condition. Further study indicated that motion detection was eliminated in monocular viewing. It appears that some ability to distinguish moving and stationary objects during observer motion is in place as early as 8 weeks of age, and that binocular convergence may provide the distance information needed in this task (Kellman & von Hofsten, 1992).

Sensitivity to Motion

Early research on infant visual motion perception found that motion strongly attracts infant orientation and attention (Fantz & Nevis, 1967; Haith, 1983; Kremenitzer, Vaughan, Kurtzberg, & Dowling, 1979; White, Castle, & Held, 1964). In recent years, progress has been made in analyzing the limits and probable mechanisms of motion sensitivity.

Directional Selectivity

The ability to detect motion direction is one of the most basic and important perceptual capacities, but one whose development has not been much studied until recently. Using both behavioral and visual evoked potential (VEP) measures, Wattam-Bell (1991, 1992) tested directional sensitivity in longitudinal studies. In the VEP studies, it was expected that if infants detected direction reversals in an oscillating checkerboard pattern, a measurable electrical response should be found at the frequency of the stimulus reversals. Reliable VEPs were first found at a median age of 74 days for 5 deg/sec patterns and 90 days for 20 deg/sec patterns. Behavioral studies (Wattam-Bell, 1992) employed a different type of display. In one condition, an array of randomly changing dots was shown in which appeared a vertical strip of coherently (vertically) moving dots. In another condition, the vertical motion was shown against a background having opposite direction motion. A visual preference paradigm was use, in which the target display appeared adjacent to a control display having random or uniform motion. If an infant detected the vertical target strip having unique, coherent motion, he or she was expected to look longer at this display. The element displacement per frame was manipulated to find the greatest displacement that supported motion detection (d_{max}). This measure was found to increase markedly from 8 to 15 weeks of age. The younger infants (8–11 weeks) could tolerate only about a .25 deg of visual angle displacement (frame duration was 20 msec) whereas 14- to 15-week-olds showed a d_{max} of about .65. (The value for adults is about 2 deg in this task.)

Poor performance in the earliest weeks may be due to a lack of motion detectors sensitive to high velocities, that is, large displacements in short time intervals. This interpretation is supported by additional data that showed an increase in d_{max} when the temporal interval between frames was lengthened (Wattam-Bell, 1992).

Velocity Sensitivity

Human adults perceive motion over a great range of velocities. Under optimal conditions a motion as slow as 1 to 2 min of visual angle per second may be detected as motion, as may faster motions up to 15 to 30 deg/sec, at which blurring or streaking occurs (Kaufman, 1974). Estimates of the slowest velocity to which infants respond have varied. Volkmann and Dobson (1976) used checkerboard patterns (check size = 5.5 deg) and found a moving display to be clearly preferred to a stationary one by 2- and 3-month-olds for a velocity as slow as 2 deg/sec. One-month-olds showed a weaker preference. Using rotary motion displays, Kaufmann, Stucki, and Kaufmann-Hayoz (1985) estimated thresholds at about 1.4 deg/sec at one month and .93 deg/sec at 3 months, also using a visual preference technique.

More recent studies designed to distinguish various possible mechanisms by which moving patterns might be detected (see below) have yielded higher threshold estimates. Dannemiller and Freedland (1989), using unidirectional linear motion of a single bar, found no reliable motion preferences at 8 weeks. They estimated thresholds at about 5 deg/sec for 16-week-olds and about 2.3 deg/sec for 20-week-olds. For vertically moving gratings, Aslin and Shea (1990) found velocity thresholds of about 9 deg/sec at 6 weeks dropping to 4 deg/sec at 12 weeks. Thresholds for detecting a difference between two velocities were studied by Dannemiller and Freedland (1991) using paired displays with horizontal bars oscillating at different rates; their 20-month-old subjects distinguished bars moving at 3.3 deg/sec from 2.0 deg/sec, but not from 2.5 deg/sec.

Much lower thresholds for motion detection were obtained by von Hofsten, Kellman, and Putaansuu (1992). In habituation studies of observer-contingent motion with 14-week-olds, von Hofsten et al. found sensitivity to a differential velocity of 0.32 deg/sec, but not 0.16 deg/sec. Subjects were also found to be sensitive to the relation of the motion direction to their own motion. Higher sensitivity in this paradigm might have two explanations. It is possible that visual preference paradigms understate infant capacities. As is true in general with preference measures, infants might detect a difference (e.g., between moving and stationary patterns) but have no differential interest or attention to the two displays. A second possibility is that the key difference relates to observer motion contingency in the von Hofsten et al. study. It is plausible that small, observer-contingent motions are processed by the motion perspective system as specifiers of object depth, rather than as moving objects. Thus, a depth-from-motion system may have greater sensitivity than a motion detection system, and the former might be engaged only by observer movement (von Hofsten et al., 1992).

Mechanisms for Processing Moving Patterns: Velocity, Flicker, and Position

A moving stimulus may be characterized in different ways. Likewise, a response to a moving stimulus may be based on more than one kind of mechanism. Consider a vertical sine-wave grating drifting horizontally. Each edge moves at a certain velocity. At a given point, alternating dark and light areas will pass at a certain rate, presenting a modulation or flicker rate. This flicker rate depends both on the velocity of the pattern and on its spatial frequency (cycles per deg). Now consider preferential attention to such a stimulus over a non-moving grating or a blank field. The preference could be based on a direction-sensitive mechanism, a velocity-sensitive mechanism or a flicker-sensitive mechanism. Sustained flicker could be avoided by use of a single object in motion as opposed to a repetitive pattern, but then the possibility arises that the stimulus is detected by noting the change in position of some unique object feature, that is, a position-sensitive mechanism may operate. Some research on motion sensitivity has aimed to separate these possibilities experimentally.

Perhaps the first effort to disentangle velocity-sensitive, position-sensitive and flicker-sensitive mechanisms was carried out by Freedland and Dannemiller (1987). Several combinations of temporal frequency and spatial displacement were presented with random black and white checkerboard displays. Infants' preferences were affected by both of these factors and were not a simple function of velocity. The role of flicker was not directly addressed in these experiments. Sensitivity to flicker versus velocity was examined by Aslin and Shea (1990) with vertically moving, square-wave gratings. Various combinations of spatial frequency and velocity were used to vary flicker independent of velocity. For example, the flicker rate (temporal frequency) at any point in the display remains constant if spatial frequency is doubled and velocity is cut in half. Aslin and Shea (1990) found that velocity, not flicker, determines preferences in subjects 6 and 12 weeks of age. Evidence for velocity-sensitive mechanisms was also reported by Dannemiller and Freedland (1989). By using a display with motion of a single bar flanked by stationary reference bars, they excluded ongoing flicker in any spatial position. Moreover, manipulating extent of displacement allowed them to test the possibility that infants responses were determined by the extent of positional displacement. Results were consistent with velocity-sensitive mechanisms.

CONCLUSION

We close with a few general observations. Not too long ago, infant visual perception was a topic dominated mostly by speculation and inference. Over the past thirty years, laboratory research with human infants has shed much new light on the starting points of vision and its development. The developmental courses of basic visual sensitivities to pattern, motion and color are reasonably well understood. Likewise, we have gained some understanding of perception of functionally important aspects of the environment, such as objects, spatial arrangements and events. These achievements have already produced far-reaching changes in our conceptions of both perception and infant development. The idea that reality must be constructed from sensory fragments under the guidance of touch or action (Berkeley, 1709/1963; Piaget, 1954) is incorrect. Meaningful perception begins from innate foundations, and much of its improvement over the early weeks of life comes from maturation of central and peripheral mechanisms.

We have touched upon some generalizations that describe early patterns of visual development. Weakness or absence in neonates of sensitivity to basic stimulus variables, such as orientation, phase and motion direction, suggest immaturity of cortical visual mechanisms, a situation that changes markedly by 6 to 8 weeks (Johnson, 1990; Kleiner & Banks, 1987; Wattam-Bell, 1991). Many of the earliest appearing abilities to perceive objects and space involve information carried by motion, such as the use of optical transformations in perceiving object approach or 3-D form. The primacy of kinematic information may reflect the relatively early maturation of temporal processing or it may indicate the reliance of early perception on information sources of highest ecological validity (Kellman, 1993).

Yet no simple generalization encompasses the nuances of visual development. Even where visual competence begins early, infants' abilities are far worse than adults'. Refinements of various abilities follow different time courses, paced by particular courses of maturation. Some abilities, such as pictorial depth perception and 3-D form perception from static views, do not appear at all until the second half-year of life. Their origins remain unclear and may involve learning.

Further progress in understanding the characteristic pace and sequencing of visual abilities will require a deeper understanding of processes and mechanisms. One can look upon the spate of research over the past several decades as a highly successful descriptive phase in infant perception. We know when many abilities emerge, what precision they have and what information they depend on. Testing hypotheses about the use of specific perceptual computations and how these are carried out neurally stand out as challenges for future research.

ACKNOWLEDGMENTS

We thank Bob Siegler for helpful comments.

REFERENCES

Adams, R. J., Courage, M. L., & Mercer, M. E. (1994). Systematic measurement of human neonatal color vision. *Vision Research, 34*, 1691–1701.

Adams, R. J., Maurer, D., & Davis, M. (1986). Newborns' discrimination of chromatic from achromatic stimuli. *Journal of Experimental Child Psychology, 41*, 267–281.

Alhazen, I. (1989). Book of optics. In A. I. Sabra (Trans.), *The optics of Ibn al-Haytham*. Warburg Institute, University of London.

Allen, D., Banks, M. S., & Norcia, A. M. (1993). Does chromatic sensitivity develop more slowly than luminance sensitivity? *Vision Research, 33*, 2553–2562.

Allen, D., Banks, M. S., & Schefrin, B. (1988). Chromatic discrimination in human infants. *Investigative Ophthalmology and Visual Science, 29* (Suppl.), 25.

Allen, D., Tyler, C. W., & Norcia, A. M. (1989). Development of grating acuity and contrast sensitivity in the central and peripheral field of the human infant. *Investigative Ophthalmology and Visual Science, 30*(Suppl.), 311.

Allen, J. (1978). *Visual acuity development in human infants up to 6 months of age*. Ph.D. thesis, University of Washington, Seattle.

Ames, A. (1951). Visual perception and the rotating trapezoidal window. *Psychological Monographs*, (Series No. 324).

Andersen, G. J., & Cortese, J. M. (1989). 2-D contour perception resulting from kinetic occlusion. *Perception and Psychophysics, 46*, 49–55.

Arterberry, M., Yonas, A., & Bensen, A. S. (1989). Self-produced locomotion and the development of responsiveness to linear perspective and texture gradients. *Developmental Psychology, 25*, 976–982.

Aslin, R. N. (1977). Development of binocular fixation in human infants. *Journal of Experimental Child Psychology, 23*, 133–150.

Aslin, R. N., & Shea, S. L. (1990). Velocity thresholds in human infants: Implications for the perception of motion. *Developmental Psychology, 26*, 589–598.

Atkinson, J., & Braddick, O. (1976). Stereoscopic discrimination in infants. *Perception, 5*, 29–38.

Atkinson, J., Braddick, O., & Moar, K. (1977). Development of contrast sensitivity over the first three months of life in the human infant. *Vision Research, 17*, 1037–1044.

Badcock, D. R. (1984). Spatial phase or luminance profile discrimination? *Vision Research, 24*, 613–623.

Badcock, D. R. (1990). Phase- or energy-based face discrimination: Some problems. *Journal of Experimental Psychology: Human Perception and Performance, 16*, 217–220.

Ball, W., & Tronick, E. (1971). Infant responses to impending collision: Optical and real. *Science, 171*, 818–820.

Banks, M. S. (1980a). The development of visual accommodation during early infancy. *Child Development, 51*, 646–666.

Banks, M. S. (1980b). Infant refraction and accommodation: Their use in ophthalmic diagnosis. *International Ophthalmology Clinics, Electrophysiology and Psychophysics, 20*, 205–232.

Banks, M. S., & Bennett, P. J. (1988). Optical and photoreceptor immaturities limit the spatial and chromatic vision of human neonates. *Journal of the Optical Society of America, A, 5,* 2059–2079.

Banks, M. S., & Crowell, J. A. (Eds.). (1993). A re-examination of two analyses of front-end limitations to infant vision. In K. Simons (Ed.), *Early visual development: Normal and abnormal.* New York: Oxford University Press.

Banks, M. S., Geisler, W. S., & Bennett, P. J. (1987). The physical limits of grating visibility. *Vision Research, 27,* 1915–1924.

Banks, M. S., & Ginsburg, A. P. (1985). Infant visual preferences: A review and new theoretical treatment. *Advances in Child Development and Behavior, 19,* 207–246.

Banks, M. S., & Salapatek, P. (1978). Acuity and contrast sensitivity in 1-, 2-, and 3-month-old human infants. *Investigative Ophthalmology and Visual Science, 17,* 361–365.

Banks, M. S., & Salapatek, P. (1983). Infant visual perception. In M. H. & J. Campos (Eds.), *Handbook of child psychology: Biology and infancy.* New York: Wiley.

Banks, M. S., Sekuler, A. B., & Anderson, S. J. (1991). Peripheral spatial vision: Limits imposed by optics, photoreceptor properties, and receptor pooling. *Journal of the Optical Society of America, A, 8,* 1775–1787.

Banks, M. S., & Shannon, E. S. (1993). Spatial and chromatic visual efficiency in human neonates. In C. Granrud (Ed.), *Carnegie-Mellon Symposium on Cognitive Psychology.* Hillsdale, NJ: Erlbaum.

Bennett, P. J., & Banks, M. S. (1987). Sensitivity loss among odd-symmetric mechanisms underlies phase anomalies in peripheral vision. *Nature, 326,* 873–876.

Bennett, P. J., & Banks, M. S. (1991). The effects of contrast, spatial scale, and orientation on foveal and peripheral phase discrimination. *Vision Research, 31,* 1759–1786.

Berkeley, G. (Ed.). (1963). *An essay towards a new theory of vision.* Indianapolis, IN: Bobs-Merrill. (Original work published 1709)

Bertenthal, B. I. (1993). Infants' perception of biomechanical motions: Intrinsic image and knowledge-based constraints. In G. Carl (Ed.), *Visual perception and cognition in infancy. Carnegie Mellon Symposia on Cognition.* Hillsdale, NJ: Erlbaum.

Bertenthal, B. I. (1996). Origins and early development of perception, action, and representation. *Annual Review of Psychology, 47,* 431–459.

Bertenthal, B. I., Campos, J. J., & Haith, M. M. (1980). Development of visual organization: The perception of subjective contours. *Child Development, 51,* 1072–1080.

Bertenthal, B. I., & Davis, P. (1988). *Dynamic pattern analysis predicts recognition and discrimination of biomechanical motions.* Paper presented at the annual meeting of the Psychonomic Society, Chicago, IL.

Bertenthal, B. I., Proffitt, D. R., & Cutting, J. E. (1984). Infant sensitivity to figural coherence in biomechanical motions. *Journal of Experimental Child Psychology, 37,* 213–230.

Bertenthal, B. I., Proffitt, D. R., Kramer, S. J., & Spetner, N. B. (1987). Infants' encoding of kinetic displays varying in relative coherence. *Developmental Psychology, 23,* 171–178.

Birch, E. E. (1993). Stereopsis in infants and its developmental relation to visual acuity. In K. Simons (Ed.), *Early visual development: Normal and abnormal* (pp. 224–236). New York: Oxford University Press.

Birch, E. E., Gwiazda, J., & Held, R. (1982). Stereoacuity development for crossed and uncrossed disparities in human infants. *Vision Research, 22,* 507–513.

Bone, R. A., Landrum, J. T., Fernandez, L., & Martinez, S. L. (1988). Analysis of macular pigment by HPLC: Retinal distribution and age study. *Investigative Ophthalmology and Visual Science, 29,* 843–849.

Bower, T. G., Broughton, J. M., & Moore, M. K. (1970). The coordination of visual and tactual input in infants. *Perception and Psychophysics, 8,* 51–53.

Braddick, O. (1993). Orientation- and motion-selective mechanisms in infants. In K. Simons (Ed.), *Early visual development: Normal and abnormal.* New York: Oxford University Press.

Braddick, O., Atkinson, J., French, J., & Howland, H. C. (1979). A photorefractive study of infant accommodation. *Vision Research, 19,* 1319–1330.

Braddick, O., Atkinson, J., & Wattam-Bell, J. R. (1986). Development of discrimination of spatial phase in infancy. *Vision Research, 26,* 1223–1239.

Brown, A. M. (1990). Development of visual sensitivity to light and color vision in human infants: A critical review. *Vision Research, 30,* 1159–1188.

Brown, A. M. (1993). Intrinsic noise and infant visual performance. In K. Simons (Ed.), *Early visual development: Normal and abnormal.* New York: Oxford University Press.

Brown, A. M., Dobson, V., & Maier, J. (1987). Visual acuity of human infants at scotopic, mesopic, and photopic luminances. *Vision Research, 27,* 1845–1858.

Brown, A. M., Lindsey, D. T., McSweeney, E. M., & Walters, M. M. (1995). Infant luminance and chromatic contrast sensitivity: Optokinetic nystagmus data on 3-month-olds. *Vision Research, 35,* 3145–3160.

Brunswik, E. (1956). *Perception and the representative design of psychological experiments.* Berkeley: University of California Press.

Candy, T. R., Banks, M. S., Hendrickson, A. E., & Crowell, J. A. (1993). Neonatal vision and cone properties in fovea and periphery. *Investigative Ophthalmology and Visual Science, 34*(Suppl.), 1356.

Carroll, J. J., & Gibson, E. J. (1981). *Infants' differentiation of an aperture and an obstacle.* Presented at the meeting of the Society for Research in Child Development, Boston, MA.

Clavadetscher, J. E., Brown, A. M., Ankrum, C., & Teller, D. Y. (1988). Spectral sensitivity and chromatic discrimination in 3- and 7-week-old infants. *Journal of the Optical Society of America, 5,* 2093–2105.

Coletta, N. J., Williams, D. R., & Tiana, C. L. M. (1990). Consequences of spatial sampling for human motion perception. *Vision Research, 30,* 1631–1648.

Craton, L. G., & Yonas, A. (1988). Infants' sensitivity to boundary flow information for depth at an edge. *Child Development, 59,* 1522–1529.

Craton, L. G., & Yonas, A. (1990). The role of motion in infants' perception of occlusion. In T. E. James (Ed.), *Advances in psychology: 69. The development of attention: Research and theory.* Amsterdam, The Netherlands: North-Holland.

Cutting, J. E. (1981). Coding theory adapted to gait perception. *Journal of Experimental Psychology: Human Perception and Performance, 7,* 71–87.

Dannemiller, J. L. (1989). A test of color constancy in 9- and 20-week-old human infants following simulated illuminant changes. *Developmental Psychology, 25,* 171–184.

Dannemiller, J. L., & Freedland, R. L. (1989). The detection of slow stimulus movement in 2- to 5-month-olds. *Journal of Experimental Child Psychology, 47,* 337–355.

Dannemiller, J. L., & Freedland, R. L. (1991). Speed discriminations in 20-week-old infants. *Infant Behavior and Development, 14,* 163–173.

Dannemiller, J. L., & Hanko, S. A. (1987). A test of color constancy in 4-month-old human infants. *Journal of Experimental Child Psychology, 44*(22), 255–267.

Darwin, C. H. (1877). A biological sketch of a young child. *Kosmos, 1,* 367–376.

Day, R. H., & McKenzie, B. E. (1981). Infant perception of the invariant size of approaching and receding objects. *Developmental Psychology, 17,* 670–677.

Dobson, V. (1976). Spectral sensitivity of the 2-month-old infant as measured by the visual evoked cortical potential. *Vision Research, 16,* 367–374.

Duncker, K. (1929). Ueber induzierte Bewegung. *Psychologische Forschung, 22,* 180–259.

D'Zmura, M., & Lennie, P. (1986). Mechanisms of color constancy. *Journal of the Optical Society of America, 3,* 1662–1672.

Fantz, R. L., Fagan, J. F., & Miranda, S. B. (1975). Early visual selectivity. In L. B. Cohen & P. Salapatek (Eds.), *Infant perception: From sensation to cognition.* New York: Academic Press.

Fantz, R. L., & Nevis, S. (1967). Pattern preferences and perceptual-cognitive development in early infancy. *Merrill-Palmer Quarterly, 13,* 77–108.

Fox, R., Aslin, R. N., Shea, S. L., & Dumais, S. T. (1980). Stereopsis in human infants. *Science, 207,* 323–324.

Fox, R., & McDaniel, C. (1982). The perception of biological motion by human infants. *Science, 218,* 486–487

Freedland, R. L., & Dannemiller, J. L. (1987). Detection of stimulus motion in 5-month-old infants: The ontogenesis of perception [Special issue]. *Journal of Experimental Psychology: Human Perception and Performance, 13,* 566–576.

Gibson, E. J. (1979). Perceptual development from the ecological approach. In M. Lamb, A. Brown, & B. Rogoff (Eds.), *Advances in developmental psychology* (Vol. 3, pp. 243–285). Hillsdale, NJ: Erlbaum.

Gibson, E. J., Gibson, J. J., Smith, O. W., & Flock, H. R. (1959). Motion parallax as a determinant of perceived depth. *Journal of Experimental Psychology, 58,* 40–51.

Gibson, J. J. (1950). *The perception of the visual world.* New York: Appleton-Century-Crofts.

Gibson, J. J. (1966). *The senses considered as perceptual systems.* Boston: Houghton Mifflin.

Gibson, J. J. (1979). *The ecological approach to visual perception.* Boston: Houghton Mifflin.

Gibson, J. J., Kaplan, G. A., Reynolds, H. N., Jr., & Wheeler, K. (1969). The change from visible to invisible: A study of optical transitions. *Perception and Psychophysics, 5,* 113–116.

Gordon, F. R., & Yonas, A. (1976). Sensitivity to binocular depth information. *Journal of Experimental Child Psychology, 22,* 413–422.

Granrud, C. E. (1986). Binocular vision and spatial perception in 4- and 5-month-old infants. *Journal of Experimental Psychology: Human Perception and Performance, 12,* 36–49.

Granrud, C. E. (1987). Size constancy in newborn human infants. *Investigative Ophthalmology and Visual Science, 28*(Suppl.), 5.

Granrud, C. E., Haake, R. J., & Yonas, A. (1985). Infants' sensitivity to familiar size: The effect of memory on spatial perception. *Perception and Psychophysics, 37,* 459–466.

Granrud, C. E., & Yonas, A. (1984). Infants' perception of pictorially specified interposition. *Journal of Experimental Child Psychology, 37,* 500–511.

Granrud, C. E., Yonas, A., Smith, I. M., Arterberry, M. E., Glicksman, M. L., & Sorknes, A. (1985). Infants' sensitivity to accretion and deletion of texture as information for depth at an edge. *Child Development, 55,* 1630–1636.

Green, D. G. (1970). Regional variations in the visual acuity for interference fringes on the retina. *Journal of Physiology, 207,* 351–356.

Green, D. G., & Campbell, F. W. (1965). Effect of focus on the visual response to a sinusoidally modulated spatial stimulus. *Journal of the Optical Society of America, 55,* 1154–1157.

Grossberg, S., & Mingolla, E. (1985). Neural dynamics of form perception: Boundary completion, illusory figures, and neon color spreading. *Psychological Review, 92,* 173–211.

Gunderson, V. M., Yonas, A., Sargent, P. L., & Grant-Webster, K. S. (1993). Infant macaque monkeys respond to pictorial depth. *Psychological Science, 4,* 93–98.

Hainline, L., Riddell, P., Grose-Fifer, J., & Abramov, I. (1992). Development of accommodation and convergence in infancy: Normal and abnormal visual development in infants and children [Special issue]. *Behavioural Brain Research, 49,* 33–50.

Haith, M. (1983). Spatially determined visual activity in early infancy. In A. Hein & M. Jeannerod (Eds.), *Spatially oriented behavior.* New York: Springer.

Hamer, D. R., Alexander, K. R., & Teller, D. Y. (1982). Rayleigh discriminations in young infants. *Vision Research, 22,* 575–587.

Haynes, H., White, B. L., & Held, R. (1965). Visual accommodation in human infants. *Science, 148,* 528–530.

Held, R., Birch, E. E., & Gwiazda, J. (1980). Stereoacuity of human infants. *Proceedings of the National Academy of Sciences, 77.*

Helmholtz, H., von (1925). *Treatise on physiological optics.* New York: Optical Society of America. (Original work published 1885)

Hendrickson, A. E. (1993). Morphological development of the primate retina. In K. Simons (Ed.), *Early visual development: Normal and abnormal.* New York: Oxford University Press.

Hickey, T. L., & Peduzzi, J. D. (1987). Structure and development of the visual system. In P. Salapatek & L. B. Cohen (Eds.), *Handbook of infant perception: From sensation to perception.* New York: Academic Press.

Hirano, S., Yamamoto, Y., Takayama, H., Sugata, Y., & Matsuo, K. (1979). Ultrasonic observations of eyes in premature babies: Part 6. Growth curves of ocular axial length and its components. *Acta Societatis Ophthalmologicae Japonicae, 83,* 1679–1693.

Hochberg, J. (1971). Perception: Space and movement. In J. A. Kling & L. A. Riggs (Eds.), *Woodworth and Schlosberg's experimental psychology.* New York: Holt.

Hoffman, D. D., & Flinchbaugh, B. E. (1982). The interpretation of biological motion. *Biological Cybernetics, 42.*

Holway, A. H., & Boring, E. G. (1941). Determinants of apparent visual size with distance variant. *American Journal of Psychology, 54,* 21–37.

Hood, B., Atkinson, J., & Braddick, O. (1992). Orientation selectivity in infancy: Behavioral evidence for temporal sensitivity. *Perception, 21,* 351–354.

Howland, H. C. (1982). Infant eye: Optics and accommodation. *Current Eye Research, 2,* 217–224.

Howland, H. C., & Sayles, N. (1985). Photokeratometric and photorefractive measurements of astigmatism in infants and young children. *Vision Research, 25,* 73–81.

Hubel, D. H., & Wiesel, T. N. (1970). Stereoscopic vision in macaque monkey. Cells sensitive to binocular depth in area 18 of the macaque monkey cortex. *Nature, 225,* 41–42.

Ittleson, W. H. (1951). Size as a cue to distance: Static localization. *American Journal of Psychology, 64,* 54–67.

Jacobs, D. S., & Blakemore, C. (1988). Factors limiting the postnatal development of visual acuity in the monkey. *Vision Research, 28,* 947–958.

James, W. (1890). *The principles of psychology.* New York: Holt.

Johansson, G. (1950). *Configurations in event perception.* Uppsala: Almqvist & Wiksells.

Johansson, G. (1970). On theories for visual space perception: A letter to Gibson. *Scandinavian Journal of Psychology, 11,* 67–74.

Johansson, G. (1975). Visual motion perception. *Scientific American, 232,* 76–88.

Johnson, M. H. (1990). Cortical maturation and the development of visual attention in early infancy. *Journal of Cognitive Neuroscience, 2,* 81–95.

Johnson, S. P., & Aslin, R. N. (1995). Perception of object unity in 2-month-old infants. *Developmental Psychology, 31,* 739–745.

Kanizsa, G. (1979). *Organization in vision.* New York: Praeger.

Kant, I. (1902). *Critique of pure reason* (F. Max Muller, Trans.) (2nd ed.). New York: Macmillan. (Original work published 1781)

Kaplan, G. A. (1969). Kinetic disruption of optical texture: The perception of depth at an edge. *Perception and Psychophysics, 6,* 193–198.

Kaufman, L. (1974). *Sight and mind.* New York: Oxford University Press.

Kaufmann, F., Stucki, M., & Kaufmann-Hayoz, R. (1985). Development of infants' sensitivity for slow and rapid motions. *Infant Behavior and Development, 8,* 89–98.

Kaufmann-Hayoz, R., Kaufmann, F., & Stucki, M. (1986). Kinetic contours in infants' visual perception. *Child Development, 57,* 292–299.

Kaufmann-Hayoz, R., Kaufmann, F., & Walther, D. (1988). *Perception of kinetic subjective contours at 5 and 8 months* (Sixth International Conference on Infant Studies). Washington, DC.

Kellman, P. J. (1984). Perception of three-dimensional form by human infants. *Perception and Psychophysics, 36,* 353–358.

Kellman, P. J. (1993). Kinematic foundations of infant visual perception. In C. Granrud (Ed.), *Visual perception and cognition in infancy: Carnegie Mellon Symposia on Cognition.* Hillsdale, NJ: Erlbaum.

Kellman, P. J. (1995). Ontogenesis of space and motion perception. In W. Epstein & S. Rogers (Eds.), *Handbook of perception and cognition.* New York: Academic Press.

Kellman, P. J. (1996). The origins of object perception. In W. Epstein & S. Rogers (Eds.), *Handbook of perception and cognition.* New York: Academic Press.

Kellman, P. J., & Cohen, M. H. (1984). Kinetic subjective contours. *Perception and Psychophysics, 35,* 237–244.

Kellman, P. J., Gleitman, H., & Spelke, E. S. (1987). Object and observer motion in the perception of objects by infants: The ontogenesis of perception [Special issue]. *Journal of Experimental Psychology: Human Perception and Performance, 13,* 586–593.

Kellman, P. J., & Shipley, T. F. (1991). A theory of visual interpolation in object perception. *Cognitive Psychology, 23,* 141–221.

Kellman, P. J., & Short, K. R. (1987a). Infant perception of partly occluded objects: The problem of rotation. Paper presented at the Third International Conference on Event Perception and Action, Uppsala, Sweden, June.

Kellman, P. J., & Short, K. R. (1987b). Development of three-dimensional form perception. *Journal of Experimental Psychology: Human Perception and Performance, 13*(4), 545–557.

Kellman, P. J., & Spelke, E. S. (1983). Perception of partly occluded objects in infancy. *Cognitive Psychology, 15,* 483–524.

Kellman, P. J., Spelke, E. S., & Short, K. R. (1986). Infant perception of object unity from translatory motion in depth and vertical translation. *Child Development, 57,* 72–86.

Kellman, P. J., & von Hofsten, C. (1992). The world of the moving infant: Perception of motion, stability, and space. *Advances in Infancy Research, 7,* 147–184.

Kellman, P. J., Yin, C., & Shipley, T. F. (1995). A common mechanism for occluded and illusory contours: Evidence from hybrid displays. *Investigative Ophthalmology and Visual Science, 36*(Suppl.), S847.

Kelly, J. P., Borchert, K., & Teller, D. Y. (1995). Uniform vs differential sensitivity losses in infancy: Sweep VEPs to achromatic and isoluminant gratings. *Investigative Ophthalmology and Visual Science, 36*(Suppl.).

Kessen, W., Haith, M. M., & Salapatek, P. H. (1970). Human infancy: A bibliography and guide. In P. H. Mussen (Ed.), *Carmichael's manual of child psychology.* New York: Wiley.

Kleiner, K. A. (1987). Amplitude and phase spectra as indices of infants' pattern preferences. *Infant Behavior and Development, 10,* 45 55.

Kleiner, K. A., & Banks, M. S. (1987). Stimulus energy does not account for 2-month-olds' face preferences. *Journal of Experimental Psychology: Human Perception and Performance, 13,* 594–600.

Koenderink, J. J. (1986). Optic flow. *Vision Research, 26,* 161–180.

Kremenitzer, J. P., Vaughan, H. G., Kurtzberg, D., & Dowling, K. (1979). Smooth-pursuit eye movements in the newborn infant. *Child Development, 50,* 442–448.

Larsen, J. S. (1971). The sagittal growth of the eye: IV. Ultrasonic measurement of the axial length of the eye from birth to puberty. *Acta Ophthalmologica, 49,* 873–886.

Lee, D. N. (1974). Visual information during locomotion. In R. B. MacLeod & H. L. Pick (Eds.), *Perception: Essays in honor of James J. Gibson* (p. 317). Ithaca, NY: Cornell University Press.

Lee, D. N., & Aronson, E. (1974). Visual proprioceptive control of standing in human infants. *Perception and Psychophysics, 15,* 529–532.

Legge, G. E., & Foley, J. M. (1980). Contrast masking in human vision. *Journal of the Optical Society of America, 70,* 1458–1471.

Levi, D. M., Klein, S. A., & Aitsebaomo, A. P. (1985). Vernier acuity, crowding, and cortical magnification. *Vision Research, 25,* 963–977.

Lewis, T. L., Maurer, D., & Kay, D. (1978). Newborns' central vision: Whole or hole? *Journal of Experimental Child Psychology, 26,* 193–203.

Maloney, L. T., & Wandell, B. A. (1986). Color constancy: A method for recovering surface spectral reflectance. *Journal of the Optical Society of America, 3,* 29–33.

Manny, R. E., & Klein, S. A. (1984). The development of vernier acuity in infants. *Current Eye Research, 3,* 453–462.

Manny, R. E., & Klein, S. A. (1985). A three alternative tracking paradigm to measure vernier acuity of older infants. *Vision Research, 25,* 1245–1252.

Marimont, D. H., & Wandell, B. A. (1992). Linear models of surface and illuminant spectra. *Journal of the Optical Society of America, 9,* 1905–1913.

Marr, D. (1982). *Vision.* San Francisco: Freeman.

Maurer, D., & Adams, R. J. (1987). Emergence of the ability to discriminate a blue from gray at one month of age. *Journal of Experimental Child Psychology, 44*(2), 147–156.

Maurer, D., Lewis, T., Cavanagh, P., & Anstis, S. A. (1989). A new test of luminous efficiency for babies. *Investigative Ophthalmology and Visual Science, 30,* 297–303.

Michotte, A., Thines, G., & Crabbe, G. (1964). Les complements amodaux des structures perceptives. In *Studia Psycologica Louvain:* Publications Universitaires de Louvain.

Mill, J. S. (1965). Examination of Sir William Hamilton's philosophy. In R. Herrnstein & E. G. Boring (Eds.), *A source book in the history of psychology.* Cambridge, MA: Harvard University Press. (Original work published 1865)

Mohindra, I., Held, R., Gwiazda, J., & Brill, S. (1978). Astigmatism in infants. *Science, 202,* 329–330.

Morrone, M. C., & Burr, D. C. (1988). Feature detection in human vision: A phase-dependent energy model. *Proceedings of the Royal Society of London, 235,* 221–245.

Morrone, M. C., Burr, D. C., & Fiorentini, A. (1993). Development of infant contrast sensitivity to chromatic stimuli. *Vision Research, 33,* 2535–2552.

Morton, J., Johnson, M. H., & Maurer, D. (1990). On the reasons for newborns' responses to faces. *Infant Behavior and Development, 13,* 99–103.

Moskowitz-Cook, A. (1979). The development of photopic spectral sensitivity in human infants. *Vision Research, 19,* 1133–1142.

Nakayama, K., & Shimojo, S. (1992). Experiencing and perceiving visual surfaces. *Science, 257,* 1357–1363.

Norcia, A. M., & Tyler, C. W. (1985). Spatial frequency sweep VEP: Visual acuity during the first year of life. *Vision Research, 25,* 1399–1408.

Norcia, A. M., Tyler, C. W., & Allen, D. (1986). Electrophysiological assessment of contrast sensitivity in human infants. *American Journal of Optometry and Physiological Optics, 63,* 12–15.

Norcia, A. M., Tyler, C. W., & Hamer, R. D. (1990). Development of contrast sensitivity in the human infant. *Vision Research, 30,* 1475–1486.

Olzak, L. A., & Thomas, J. P. (1986). Seeing spatial patterns. In K. R. Boff, L. Kaufman, & J. P. Thomas (Eds.), *Handbook of perception and human performance.* New York: Wiley.

Oppenheim, A. V., & Lim, J. S. (1981). The importance of phase in signals. *Proceedings of the IEEE, 69,* 529–541.

Oster, H. E. (1975). *Color perception in human infants.* Ph.D. thesis, University of California, Berkeley.

Owsley, C. (1983). The role of motion in infants' perception of solid shape. *Perception, 12,* 707–717.

Packer, O., Hartmann, E. E., & Teller, D. Y. (1984). Infant colour vision, the effect of test field size on Rayleigh discriminations. *Vision Research, 24,* 1247–1260.

Peeples, D. R., & Teller, D. Y. (1975). Color vision and brightness discrimination in human infants. *Science, 189,* 1102–1103.

Pelli, D. (Ed.). (1990). *Quantum efficiency of vision.* Cambridge, England: Cambridge University Press.

Petrig, B., Julesz, B., Kropfl, W., & Baumgartner, G. (1981). Development of stereopsis and cortical binocularity in human infants: Electrophysiological evidence. *Science, 213,* 1402–1405.

Pettigrew, J. D. (1974). The effect of visual experience on the development of stimulus specificity by kitten cortical neurones. *Journal of Physiology, 237,* 49–74.

Piaget, J. (1954). *The construction of reality in the child.* New York: Basic Books.

Piotrowski, L. N., & Campbell, F. W. (1982). A demonstration of the visual importance and flexibility of spatial-frequency amplitude and phase. *Perception, 11,* 337–346.

Pirchio, M., Spinelli, D., Fiorentini, A., & Maffei, L. (1978). Infant contrast sensitivity evaluated by evoked potentials. *Brain Research, 141,* 179–184.

Ramachandran, V. S., Clarke, P. G., & Whitteridge, D. (1977). Cells selective to binocular disparity in the cortex of newborn lambs. *Nature, 268,* 333–335.

Rentschler, I., & Treutwein, B. (1985). Loss of spatial phase relationships in extrafoveal vision. *Nature, 313,* 308–310.

Ringach, D. L., & Shapley, R. (1996). Spatial and temporal properties of illusory contours and amodal boundary completion. *Vision Research, 36,* 3037–3050.

Rubin, E. (1915). Synsoplevede figurer, studier i psykologisk analyse. *Nordisk forlag.*

Ruff, H. A. (1978). Infant recognition of the invariant form of objects. *Child Development, 49,* 293–306.

Schaller, M. J. (1975). Chromatic vision in human infants: Conditioned operant fixation to "hues" of varying intensity. *Bulletin of the Psychonomic Society, 6,* 39–42.

Schiff, W. (1965). Perception of impending collision: A study of visually directed avoidant behavior. *Psychological Monographs, 79*(Whole No. 604).

Schmidt, H., & Spelke, E. S. (1984). *Gestalt relations and object perception in infancy* (International Conference on Infant Studies). New York.

Sekiguchi, N., Williams, D. R., & Brainard, D. H. (1993). Aberration-free measurements of the visibility of isoluminant gratings. *Journal of the Optical Society of America, 10,* 2105–2117.

Shepard, R. N. (1984). Ecological constraints on internal representation: Resonant kinematics of perceiving, imagining, thinking, and dreaming. *Psychological Review, 91,* 417–447.

Shimojo, S., Birch, E. E., Gwiazda, J., & Held, R. (1984). Development of vernier acuity in human infants. *Vision Research, 24,* 721–728.

Shimojo, S., & Held, R. (1987). Vernier acuity is less than grating acuity in 2- and 3-month-olds. *Vision Research, 27,* 77–86.

Shipley, T. F., & Kellman, P. J. (1994). Spatiotemporal boundary formation: Boundary, form, and motion perception from transformations of surface elements. *Journal of Experimental Psychology: General, 123,* 3–20.

Slater, A., & Findlay, J. M. (1975). Binocular fixation in the newborn baby. *Journal of Experimental Child Psychology, 20,* 248–273.

Slater, A., Johnson, S., Kellman, P. J., & Spelke, E. (1994). The role of three-dimensional depth cues in infants' perception of partly occluded objects. *Journal of Early Development and Parenting, 3*(3), 187–191.

Slater, A., & Morison, V. (1985). Shape constancy and slant perception at birth. *Perception, 14,* 337–344.

Slater, A., Morison, V., & Somers, M. (1988). Orientation discrimination and cortical function in the human newborn. *Perception, 17,* 597–602.

Slater, A., Morison, V., Somers, M., Mattock, A., Brown, E., & Taylor, D. (1990). Newborn and older infants' perception of partly occluded objects. *Infant Behavior and Development, 13,* 33–49.

Slater, A., Mattock, A., & Brown, E. (1990). Size constancy at birth: Newborn infants' responses to retinal and real size. *Journal of Experimental Child Psychology, 49,* 314–322.

Slater, A., & Sykes, M. (1977). Newborn infants' responses to square-wave gratings. *Child Development, 48,* 545–553.

Sokol, S. (1978). Measurement of visual acuity from pattern reversal evoked potentials. *Vision Research, 18,* 33–40.

Spelke, E. S. (1985). Perception of unity, persistence and identity: Thoughts on infants' conceptions of objects. In J. Mehler & R. Fox (Eds.), *Neonate cognition.* Hillsdale, NJ: Erlbaum.

Spelke, E. S., Breinlinger, K., Jacobson, K., & Phillips, A. (1993). Gestalt relations and object perception: A developmental study. *Perception, 22,* 1483–1501.

Spinelli, D., Pirchio, M., & Sandini, G. (1983). Visual acuity in the young infant is highest in a small retinal area. *Vision Research, 23,* 1133–1136.

Stephens, B. R., & Banks, M. S. (1987). Contrast discrimination in human infants. *Journal of Experimental Psychology: Human Perception and Performance, 13,* 558–565.

Sumi, S. (1984). Upside-down presentation of the Johansson moving light-spot pattern. *Perception, 13,* 283–286.

Teller, D. Y. (1979). The forced-choice preferential looking procedure: A psychophysical technique for use with human infants. *Infant Behavior and Development, 2,* 135–153.

Teller, D. Y., & Lindsey, D. T. (1993). Infant color vision: OKN techniques and null plane analysis. In K. Simons (Ed.), *Early visual development: Normal and abnormal.* New York: Oxford University Press.

Teller, D. Y., & Palmer, J. (1996). Infant color vision—motion nulls for red-green vs luminance-modulated stimuli in infants and adults. *Vision Research, 36,* 955–974.

Teller, D. Y., Peeples, D. R., & Sekel, M. (1978). Discrimination of chromatic from white light by 2-month-old human infants. *Vision Research, 18,* 41–48.

Thomas, J. P., & Gille, J. (1979). Bandwidths of orientation channels in human vision. *Journal of the Optical Society of America, 69,* 652–660.

Timney, B. (1981). Development of binocular depth perception in kittens. *Investigative Ophthalmology and Visual Science, 21,* 493–496.

Titchener, E. B. (1910). *A textbook of psychology.* New York: Macmillan.

Ullman, S. (1979). *The interpretation of visual motion.* Cambridge, MA: MIT Press.

van Nes, F. L., & Bouman, M. A. (1967). Spatial modulation transfer in the human eye. *Journal of the Optical Society of America, 57,* 401.

Varner, D., Cook, J. E., Schneck, M. E., McDonald, M. A., & Teller, D. Y. (1985). Tritan discrimination by 1- and 2-month-old human infants. *Vision Research, 25,* 821–831.

Volkmann, F. C., & Dobson, M. V. (1976). Infant responses of ocular fixation to moving visual stimuli. *Journal of Experimental Child Psychology, 22,* 86–99.

von der Heydt, R., Peterhans, E., & Baumgartner, G. (1984). Illusory contours and cortical neuron responses. *Science, 224,* 1260–1262.

von Hofsten, C. (1976). The role of convergence in visual space perception. *Vision Research, 16,* 193–198.

von Hofsten, C. (1977). Binocular convergence as a determinant of reaching behavior in infancy. *Perception, 6,* 139–144.

von Hofsten, C. (1980). Predictive reaching for moving objects by human infants. *Journal of Experimental Child Psychology, 30,* 369–382.

von Hofsten, C., Kellman, P., & Putaansuu, J. (1992). Young infants' sensitivity to motion parallax. *Infant Behavior and Development, 15,* 245–264.

von Hofsten, C., & Spelke, E. S. (1985). Object perception and object-directed reaching in infancy. *Journal of Experimental Psychology: General, 114,* 198–212.

von Holst, E. (1954). Relations between the central nervous system and the peripheral organs. *British Journal of Animal Behavior, 2,* 89–94.

Walk, R. D., & Gibson, E. J. (1961). A comparative and analytical study of visual depth perception. *Psychological Monographs, 75.*

Wallach, H. (1987). Perceiving a stable environment when one moves. In M. R. Rosenzweig & L. W. Porter (Eds.), *Annual Review of Psychology, 38,* 1–27.

Wallach, H., & Floor, L. (1971). The use of size matching to demonstrate the effectiveness of accommodation and convergence as cues for distance. *Perception and Psychophysics, 10,* 423–428.

Wallach, H., & O'Connell, D. N. (1953). The kinetic depth effect. *Journal of Experimental Psychology, 45,* 205–217.

Wallach, H., & Zuckerman, C. (1963). The constancy of stereoscopic depth. *American Journal of Psychology, 76,* 404–412.

Wandell, B. A. (1995). *Foundations of vision.* Sunderland, MA: Sinauer Associates.

Wattam-Bell, J. (1991). Development of motion-specific cortical responses in infancy. *Vision Research, 31,* 287–297.

Wattam-Bell, J. (1992). The development of maximum displacement limits for discrimination of motion direction in infancy. *Vision Research, 32,* 621–630.

Webb, J. A., & Aggarwal, J. K. (1982). Structure from motion of rigid and jointed objects. *Artificial Intelligence, 19,* 107–130.

Werner, J. S. (1982). Development of scotopic sensitivity and the absorption spectrum of the human ocular media. *Journal of the Optical Society of America, 72,* 247–258.

Wertheimer, M. (1958). Principles of perceptual organization. In D. C. Beardslee & M. Wertheimer (Eds.), *Readings in perception.* Princeton, NJ: Van Nostrand. (Original work published 1923)

Wesemann, W., Norcia, A. M., & Manny, R. E. (1996). Measurement of vernier and motion sensitivity with the rapid-sweep-VEP. *Klinische Monatsblatter fur Augenheilkunde, 208,* 11–17.

Westheimer, G. (1979). The spatial sense of the eye. *Investigative Ophthalmology and Visual Science, 18,* 893–912.

Westheimer, G. (1981). Visual hyperacuity. *Progress in Sensory Physiology, 1,* 1–30.

Westheimer, G., & McKee, S. P. (1980). Stereoscopic acuity with defocused and spatially filtered retinal images. *Journal of the Optical Society of America, 70,* 772–778.

White, B., Castle, R., & Held, R. (1964). Observations on the development of visually directed reaching. *Child Development, 35,* 349–364.

Williams, D. R. (1985). Visibility of interference fringes near the resolution limit. *Journal of the Optical Society of America, A, 2,* 1087–1093.

Wilson, H. R. (1988). Development of spatiotemporal mechanisms in infant vision. *Vision Research, 28,* 611–628.

Wilson, H. R. (1993). Theories of infant visual development. In K. Simons (Ed.), *Early visual development: Normal and abnormal.* New York: Oxford University Press.

Yin, C., Kellman, P. J., & Shipley, T. (1995). A surface spreading process complements boundary interpolation under occlusion. *Investigative Ophthalmology and Visual Science Supplements, 36,* S1068.

Yonas, A. (1981). Infants' responses to optical information for collision. In R. N. Aslin, J. Alberts, & M. Petersen (Eds.), *Development of perception: Psychobiological perspectives: The visual system.* New York: Academic Press.

Yonas, A., Arterberry, M. E., & Granrud, C. E. (1987). Space perception in infancy. *Annals of Child Development, 4,* 1–34.

Yonas, A., Bechtold, A., Frankel, D., Gordon, F., McRoberts, G., Norcia, A., & Sternfels, S. (1977). Development of sensitivity to information for impending collision. *Perception and Psychophysics, 21,* 97–104.

Yonas, A., & Granrud, C. E. (1985). Development of visual space perception in young infants. In J. Mehler & R. Fox (Eds.), *Neonate cognition: Beyond the blooming buzzing confusion.* Hillsdale, NJ: Erlbaum.

Yonas, A., & Owsley, C. (1987). Development of visual space perception. In P. Salapetek & L. B. Cohen (Eds.), *Handbook of infant perception.* New York: Academic Press.

Yonas, A., Pettersen, L., & Granrud, C. E. (1982). Infants' sensitivity to familiar size as information for distance. *Child Development, 53,* 1285–1290.

Yonas, A., Pettersen, L., & Lockman, J. J. (1979). Young infants' sensitivity to optical information for collision. *Canadian Journal of Psychology, 33,* 268–276.

Yuodelis, C., & Hendrickson, A. (1986). A qualitative and quantitative analysis of the human fovea during development. *Vision Research, 26,* 847–855.

CHAPTER 4

Speech and Auditory Processing during Infancy: Constraints on and Precursors to Language

RICHARD N. ASLIN, PETER W. JUSCZYK, and DAVID B. PISONI

HISTORY OF INFANT SPEECH PERCEPTION: THE FIRST DECADE

In the nearly 15 years since the 4th edition of this *Handbook* appeared, impressive progress has been made in our understanding of the development of the auditory system in human infants and the mechanisms used by infants to process speech sounds. Despite this progress since our earlier review (Aslin, Pisoni, & Jusczyk, 1983), several fundamental questions remain unanswered. In order to place the advances made in the past decade in perspective, we

begin this chapter with a review of several theoretical issues that were posed in the first decade of research on infant speech perception. First, however, we summarize briefly the important properties of speech sounds and their production.

Acoustic and Linguistic Structure of Speech

Two technical advances in the 1950s altered in fundamental ways the manner in which researchers viewed speech signals. The first was the sound spectrograph, which enabled for the first time the visualization of the time-varying spectral information contained in speech sounds (Koenig, Dunn, & Lacy, 1946). The second was the pattern playback, which allowed researchers to create and systematically manipulate speech synthetically (Cooper, Liberman, & Borst, 1951). Although the speech signal that impinges on the ear of the listener varies more or less

Preparation of this chapter was made possible, in part, by support to RNA from the National Science Foundation (SBR-9421064), to PWJ from the National Institutes of Health (NICHD-15795), and to DBP from the National Institutes of Health (DC-00111, DC-00012, DC-00064).

continuously over time, the adult listener perceives an utterance as consisting of a sequence of discrete units. These units—the phonemes—correspond to the basic elements that carry differences in meaning for a given natural language, such as the distinction between *bin* and *pin* in English which is carried by the different phonemes /b/ and /p/.

The situation, however, is somewhat more complicated because a given phoneme can be realized acoustically in quite different ways. For example, the phoneme /p/ in *pin* contains aspiration from the release of air as the lips are parted after complete closure, whereas the /p/ in *spin* has no aspiration. Thus, at the phonemic level both /p/s are identical (abstractly), while at the phonetic level they are quite different (though this difference carries no semantic weight in English). Phonetic differences are associated with acoustic differences, yet not all of these acoustic differences are linguistically important or discriminable by adults. For example, in English the prevoiced /b/ is not differentiated phonemically from the voiced /b/, and discrimination of these allophones of /b/ is difficult without some training (see Pisoni, Aslin, Perey, & Hennessy, 1982). For native speakers of Thai, however, where prevoiced /b/ and voiced /b/ are different phonemes, discrimination of aspiration is robust (Lisker & Abramson, 1967). Thus, subtle acoustic differences among speech sounds are preserved at a phonetic level based on their use *across* languages. In turn, some phonetic differences correspond one-to-one with phonemes, while other phonemes consist of combinations from the phonetic level depending on their use *within* a particular language.

The basic structures of the vocal tract and the manner in which these structures change to produce speech sounds are now well understood (Fant, 1960; Stevens, 1964). The vocal tract can be thought of as a tube extending from the glottis (the vocal cords) to the lips, with an ancillary tube, the nasal tract, connected in parallel by the lowering of the velum (the soft palate). Sound is generated in the vocal tract by either forcing air through the glottis to produce a quasiperiodic sound source (voicing) or by creating a noisy turbulence at some point in the vocal tract. Thus, there are two relatively independent components involved in speech production: (1) phonation, the source that generates the sound energy, and (2) articulation, the dynamic structure of the vocal tract (the filter) that modifies the sound energy. For voiced segments, such as vowels and vowel-like sounds, the source of energy consists of a glottal waveform whose spectrum contains a fundamental frequency and higher harmonics. These higher harmonics are enhanced or reduced by the properties of the vocal tract transfer function, thereby producing resonant frequencies called formants. The center frequencies of the lowest two or three formants have been shown to be sufficient to differentiate the vowels used in many languages (Hillenbrand, Getty, Clark, & Wheeler, 1995; Liljencrants & Lindblom, 1972; Peterson & Barney, 1952).

In contrast to vowels, the production of consonants involves a constricted or completely occluded vocal tract. Fricatives are produced with a noise source at the point of vocal tract constriction (either voiced: z, ð, ʒ; or unvoiced: s, θ, ʃ). The nasals are produced by a diversion of the voiced source through the nasal tract while the lips are completely (m, n) or partially (ŋ) constricted. The stop consonants (b, p, d, t, g, k), liquids (r, l), and glides (w, j) are produced by a total, or nearly total, closure of the vocal tract, followed by a more abrupt opening (or release). After the release from closure, there is a rapid spectral change characterized by transitions in the formants that occur over a very brief (for stops) or somewhat extended duration (for liquids and glides).

Fundamental Issues in Speech Perception

Linearity, Invariance, and Segmentation. In contrast to simple tones and noise bursts, speech sounds do not conform to the principles of linearity and invariance. Linearity would hold if, for each sequence of phonemes, the order of the sounds in the sequence corresponded to the order of the phonemes (Chomsky & Miller, 1963). This principle of linearity is violated in speech because of coarticulation effects. That is, the surrounding phonetic environment creates a temporal overlap of the articulatory gestures. Invariance would hold if, for each phoneme in every context, a specific set of acoustic attributes were present in the speech signal (and absent for any other phoneme). Again, coarticulation and context effects in speech violate the principle of invariance.

The failure of the principles of linearity and invariance to hold for speech signals creates a further difficulty for the processing of continuous speech. If the ordering and the specific acoustic information associated with individual phonemes are highly variable, then the segmentation of continuous speech into discrete phonemes (and their combination to form words) is made more complex. In fact, the focus on the phoneme as the basic building-block in speech recognition has been questioned, and other models based on larger units such as diphones (Fujimura & Lovins, 1978) or syllables (Massaro, 1972) have been proposed. It is interesting to note that these fundamental problems facing a human listener/perceiver are also shared by engineers who have attempted to develop machines that recognize speech (e.g., Deng & Erler, 1992; Lee, 1989). Although such speech recognition devices achieve reasonable performance for either limited vocabularies or specific (trained) talkers, a popular alternative is a "brute force" recognition based on extracting acoustic attributes from a large database of talkers without recourse to any segmentation of the speech sounds (except the sampling of the speech signal itself at regular intervals).

Mechanisms Underlying Speech Perception. The earliest experiments by Liberman and his colleagues at Haskins Laboratories (Liberman, Harris, Hoffman, & Griffith, 1957) revealed that adult listeners perceive synthetic speech sounds in a categorical manner. For some classes of speech sounds, such as stop consonants, there are discrete changes in labeling as they are varied synthetically along one or more acoustic dimensions. More importantly, for stop consonants but not vowels, the ability to discriminate two adjacent tokens from along a synthetic continuum was no better than chance if these two tokens were members of the same perceptual category. In addition, the chance discrimination performance for the within-category pair jumped to near perfection when the two tokens were drawn from different perceptual categories, even when the physical (i.e., acoustic) difference between the two tokens was the same for the within-category and the between-category pairs. This overall pattern of responding to consonants, known as categorical perception, was so different from the results typically obtained with nonspeech stimuli such as tones and noises that Liberman and his colleagues proposed categorical perception as the *sine qua non* of a specialized speech mode (Liberman, Cooper, Shankweiler, & Studdert-Kennedy, 1967). As a result, any evidence of categorical perception was taken as evidence that speech was processed by a separate perceptual module which functioned as an essential component of the larger language system unique to humans.

The pioneering study of the perception of stop consonants in human infants by Eimas, Siqueland, Jusczyk, and Vigorito (1971) confirmed that one aspect of categorical perception was present long before infants begin to produce speech. Namely, the discrimination of a synthetic /b/-/p/ continuum was shown to be discontinuous: 1- and 4-month-old infants from an English-speaking environment failed to discriminate within-category contrasts, and the region of highest discriminability straddled the voiced-voiceless

category boundary that is used by English-speaking adults. Although no labeling data were obtained from these infants, nor have labeling data been obtained from infants in any subsequent study, the conclusion that infants perceived stop consonants categorically, and that such categorical perception implied the functioning and innate determination of a specialized speech mode, was too seductive to deny.

Fueling the hypothesis that infants have such an innately specialized speech mode was a subsequent study by Eimas (1975b). Eimas reported that infants from an English speaking environment did not discriminate a prevoiced-voiced contrast that is not used phonemically in English. But, unless one believed that such infants had innate knowledge that they would be raised in an English-speaking environment where this prevoiced-voiced distinction is not used (in contrast to a Thai-speaking environment where it is used), or these infants acquired in less than one month of exposure to English knowledge that the prevoiced-voiced distinction was irrelevant, it was not clear why this non-English phonetic contrast was not discriminated.

Subsequent research raised similar questions. Streeter (1976) showed that infants from an African environment in which Kikuyu is spoken, a language like Thai that uses the prevoiced-voiced distinction phonemically, did discriminate this contrast. But Lasky, Syrdal-Lasky, and Klein (1975) reported that infants from a Spanish-speaking environment, where the prevoiced-voiced distinction is not used, and where the voiced-voiceless boundary is at a different location from the English boundary, discriminated both the Thai and the English contrasts, but not the Spanish contrast. Subsequently, Eilers, Gavin, and Wilson (1979) provided evidence that infants from a Spanish-speaking environment discriminated the Spanish contrast and the English contrast, whereas infants from an English-speaking environment discriminated only the English contrast. However, questions were raised about the methods used in the Eilers et al. (1979) study (Aslin & Pisoni, 1980a; Eilers, Gavin, & Wilson, 1980), and Aslin, Pisoni, Hennessy, and Perey (1981) reported that infants from an English-speaking environment could discriminate the non-English prevoiced-voiced distinction. In sum, it became clear across a number of studies conducted in several laboratories that *all* infants, regardless of the relevance of the "English" boundary, could discriminate it rather easily, whereas *some* infants, again regardless of the relevance of the Thai boundary, could discriminate it under some conditions. This summary suggested that the mere presence of categorical discrimination, particularly when it conformed to the English boundary, was not strong evidence for a perceptual mechanism directly relevant to the processing of one's native language.

Subsequent research added further caution to the interpretation that categorical perception, particularly as indexed solely by discrimination data, implied the operation of a specialized speech mode. Recall that the initial impetus for treating speech as a special class of auditory signals arose from the observation that stop consonants are perceived categorically, whereas simpler auditory signals are not (ignored in this view is why discrimination of vowels is *not* categorical). Perhaps the most compelling evidence of the special status of speech was a study by Mattingly, Liberman, Syrdal, and Halwes (1971) in which the formant transitions from consonant-vowel syllables were extracted and presented in isolation for labeling and discrimination. In contrast to the robust evidence for categorical perception of the formant transitions when they were presented in a "speech" context (i.e., appended to the following vowel), when these same formant transitions were presented in a "nonspeech" context (i.e., without a following vowel), categorical perception was not present. Thus, the conclusion was drawn that signals which activate the speech mode are perceived categorically, whereas those that do not activate the speech mode (presumably being limited to a lower-level auditory mode) are not perceived categorically. In essence, the presence of categorical perception became a "litmus test" for the presence of a functional speech mode of analysis. Morse (1972) and Eimas (1974) employed the logic of these tests with adults to the study of infants and reported that, while discrimination of the full speech contrasts was categorical, discrimination of the formant transitions alone was not. Thus, after five years of research on infant speech perception, the weight of the evidence continued to favor the interpretation that infants perceived speech in a special mode.

Two critical lines of evidence emerged in the mid-1970s that called into question the strong interpretation that infants perceived speech in a specialized mode. The first line of evidence came from studies of adults' perception of more complex nonspeech signals. Cutting and Rosner (1974) showed that certain classes of musical stimuli are perceived categorically. Although these stimuli were subsequently shown to be incorrectly constructed to address this question properly, two subsequent studies demonstrated that complex nonspeech signals can be perceived categorically, even when they are not heard by adults as speech. Using noise-buzz and multitone nonspeech stimuli,

Miller, Weir, Pastore, Kelly, and Dooling (1976) and Pisoni (1977) reported discrete labeling functions as well as within-category and between-category discrimination functions that matched those obtained with stop consonants. Jusczyk, Pisoni, Walley, and Murray (1980) demonstrated that the same nonspeech stimuli used by Pisoni (1977) to test adults were also discriminated categorically by infants. Thus, the mere presence of categorical discrimination performance in adults or infants does not of necessity imply the operation of a specialized speech mode.

The second critical line of evidence that called into question the strong form of a specialized speech mode came from research with nonhumans who were presented with human speech sounds. Kuhl and Miller (1975, 1978) and Kuhl (1981) demonstrated that the chinchilla, a mammal whose peripheral auditory system closely matches that of humans, displays categorical-like discrimination functions for several different synthetic speech continua, and these functions match quite closely those of human adults. Perhaps more relevant to the human, Kuhl and Padden (1982, 1983) demonstrated similar categorical perception effects in macaque monkeys. In sum, it would seem quite difficult to argue that chinchillas and macaques share a specialized speech module with human adults and infants.[1] Rather, it appears that (a) the phenomenon of categorical perception is present for a range of auditory signals not limited to human speech, (b) that whatever mechanism underlies categorical perception is not unique to humans, and (c) that the mere demonstration of categorical discrimination is not sufficient to conclude that speech signals are being processed by a mechanism specialized for natural language. It is important to note that the foregoing cautions do *not* imply that speech signals carry no special status. On the contrary, we know that in adults speech is a marvelously efficient channel for conveying complex information and we agree that speech is a special signal. The question is whether there exists a specialized mode of speech processing that is unique to humans and is present innately. By providing this historical context for models of speech perception, we hope to illustrate that a model was

---

[1] Subsequent research by Kluender (1991) and Kluender and Lotto (1994) showed that Japanese quail also exhibit context effects, similar to human adults, on their labeling boundaries for stop consonants. These context effects could not be accounted for by the effects of co-occurrence during training, suggesting that they result from a general auditory mechanism and not the activation of a specialized speech mode unique to humans.

initially proposed without the wealth of subsequent evidence required to confirm it.

A final topic relevant to the proposal of a specialized speech mode are the findings on the combination of acoustic cues that enables adults to perceive an invariant phoneme despite variations in its underlying components. This combination of acoustic cues has been termed "trading relations" because the absence or weakening of one cue can be compensated for by the presence or enhancement of a complementary cue (Repp, 1982). For example, Fitch, Halwes, Erickson, and Liberman (1980) showed that adults' perception of the [slit]-[split] contrast can be cued by differences in formant transitions in the [p] or by differences in the duration of the silence between [s] and [lit]. If one of these cues is held constant at an intermediate (ambiguous) value, then variations in the other cue will lead adults to label the continuum from good exemplars of [slit] to good exemplars of [split]. Morse, Eilers, and Gavin (1982) provided some evidence that infants respond similarly to these two cues underlying [slit] and [split]; that is, ambiguity in one cue can be offset by robustness in the other cue to yield a constant perceptual category. Similar evidence was provided by Eimas (1985) for the [say]-[stay] contrast which is signaled by the onset frequency of the first formant and by the duration of the post-frication gap.

The reason that trading relations were deemed important to the proposal of a specialized speech mode is that Best, Morrongiello, and Robson (1981) demonstrated the ineffectiveness of trading relations when adults perceived speech-like stimuli as nonspeech. That is, when degraded synthetic speech signals were presented to adults, some adults perceived the signals as speech and others perceived them as nonspeech. For those subjects who heard the signals as speech, trading relations were present, but for those who heard the signals as nonspeech, trading relations were absent. Unfortunately, because the judgment of speech or nonspeech required a subjective verbal report, an analogous experiment cannot be conducted with infants. The results of the Morse et al. (1982) and Eimas (1985) studies would suggest that trading relations are present in infancy, and, therefore, that infants have a functional speech mode. However, it is not known whether all instances of nonspeech fail to activate trading relations. Moreover, it is possible that trading relations are present in infants prior to the developmental onset of a speech mode, even if in adults it turns out that each and every instance of trading relations is associated with the activation of a speech mode. These issues continue to elude a definitive answer.

Variability and Normalization. One of the most intriguing aspects of speech perception is its robustness; that is, the ability to recognize speech in the presence of considerable variability in voice (talker), dialect, and speaking rate. These are exactly the variations that continue to plague the performance of automatic speech recognition devices. One strategy used to solve this problem is to first gather a sample of speech and then conduct a best-fit to a canonical template of phonetic segments. This fitting process could involve shifts in the spectral domain (for fundamental frequency and the formant structure of vowels) or in the temporal domain (for speaking rate). In fact, such a spectral calibration was proposed for vowel perception (Gerstman, 1968; Ladefoged & Broadbent, 1957), but Verbrugge, Strange, Shankweiler, and Edman (1976) demonstrated that adults were able to categorize vowels correctly with no preview of a particular talker's speech. More recent accounts of vowel perception propose that adults use dynamic cues embedded in formant transitions to correctly categorize vowels (Strange, 1989). Although such models have not been tested with infants, they can account for vowel perception in 4-year-olds (Murphy, Shea, & Aslin, 1989).

Several studies of infants are relevant to the issues of variability and normalization. Kuhl (1979, 1983) and Kuhl and Miller (1982) showed that infants ignored irrelevant variations in talker (fundamental frequency and pitch contour) while retaining the ability to discriminate changes in vowel category. Eimas and Miller (1980), following on work with adults by Miller and Liberman (1979), showed that infants perceive the [b]-[w] category boundary differently depending on the duration of the following vowel. This effect is analogous to the articulatory constraints present as one alters speaking rate. Unfortunately, the interpretation that infants have knowledge of the perceptual implications of speaking rate was undercut by a subsequent study by Pisoni, Carrell, and Gans (1983), which showed that similar "rate" effects are present in adults for nonspeech signals. Jusczyk, Pisoni, Reed, Fernald, and Myers (1983) subsequently showed the same "rate" effect in infants with nonspeech signals. In sum, questions of normalization and perceptual constancy in the presence of variability remain largely unexplored in infancy.

The Roles of Experience

The fact that not all phonetic differences are utilized in every natural language, combined with compelling evidence that adults often have difficulty discriminating non-native phonetic contrasts (e.g., Miyawaki, Strange, Verbrugge, Liberman, Jenkins, & Fujimura, 1975), confirmed that early language input must play a significant role in the development of speech perception. Based on the work of Gottlieb (1976), Aslin and Pisoni (1980b; see also Aslin, 1981) outlined several ways in which experience with a particular language might influence the development of speech perception (Figure 4.1). Experience with a particular language may play no role at all. But it is important to point out that this *maturational* process could still lead to significant postnatal improvement in speech perception. This developmental improvement, for example, could result from maturation of the auditory system between the inner ear and the cortex, thereby enabling finer discriminations of subtle acoustic differences. Such improvements should not depend on a specific language, but rather on exposure to any general pattern of auditory stimulation.

Language-specific effects could take one of three forms (Aslin & Pisoni, 1980b). First, exposure to a limited inventory of phonetic categories could *induce* infants to acquire the ability (via neural or attentional mechanisms) to discriminate and categorize only those phonetic categories. Second, infants could have the innate capacity to discriminate and categorize all of the phonetic contrasts used in any natural language, but based on exposure to a limited set of these phonetic categories they could *maintain* sensitivity

only to that limited set. Finally, infants may have rudimentary abilities to discriminate and categorize some of the more robust phonetic contrasts used by natural languages, and exposure to a limited set of these contrasts could *attune* them to this limited set (by enhancing sensitivity to those contrasts and attenuating sensitivity to all others).

By the end of the first decade of research on infant speech perception, it was clear that an induction model was incorrect. Several non-native speech contrasts that had never been experienced were shown to be discriminated by infants (e.g., Trehub, 1976). It was also clear, subject to concerns about false negatives resulting from insensitive methods of assessment, that infants could not discriminate all possible phonetic contrasts in early infancy, thereby ruling out the maintenance model. Thus, the attunement model appeared to offer the best overall account for the role of language-specific experience in the development of speech perception. Moreover, it was clear that *some* non-native phonetic contrasts that were not used by adults could be acquired rather easily after a period of training (Pisoni et al., 1982), whereas others could not (Miyawaki et al., 1975). This implied that the mechanism underlying language-specific experiential effects was not permanent in all cases, and probably involved attentional mechanisms rather than the atrophy of a subset of neural feature detectors.

Several limitations of the foregoing analysis were pointed out by MacKain (1982). For example, Aslin and Pisoni (1980b) and Aslin (1981) assumed that passive exposure to language input was sufficient to alter discrimination and categorization performance. They also assumed that the distribution of exemplars in the language input was sufficient to alter (by enhancement or attenuation) category boundaries. MacKain correctly noted that for many categories in which acoustic differences are not used as separate phonemes, but rather appear as allophones of a single phoneme, the infant is actually exposed to the same range of variations as an infant from a language that treats these differences as separate phonemes (although their specific distributions may differ). MacKain argued that it is only by the attachment of meaning to these differences that a phonemic rather than an allophonic use can be determined, and this attachment of meaning was not thought to occur until after the age when effects of experience were assessed.

MacKain (1982) also noted that the distribution of acoustic cues in speech production often contain significant overlap between phonetic categories. Thus, the infant would be required to analyze the distribution of the input with considerable precision to determine the precise location of a

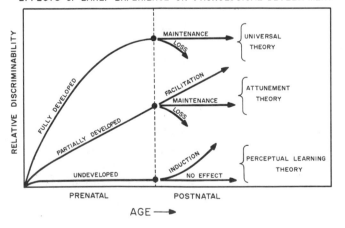

Figure 4.1 Three alternative roles that experience with early spoken language input could play in the development of speech-sound discrimination. From "Some developmental processes in speech perception and recognition," by R. N. Aslin & D. B. Pisoni, 1980, in G. H. Yeni-Komshian, J. F. Kavanagh, & C. A. Ferguson (Eds.), *Child Phonology*, Vol. 2: *Perception*. New York: Academic Press. Copyright © 1980 by Academic Press. Reprinted with permission.

category boundary. This in turn implied that infants must successfully segment the utterance into discrete phonetic units, and that they must do so reliably across utterances, which vary considerably for different talkers, speaking rates, and phonetic contexts. Clearly, this is a daunting task, and MacKain's point was that infants may be ill-equipped to perform such a complex analysis until they have been exposed to a considerable amount of language input. Although MacKain noted that speech production provides a clearer assessment of the effects of experience with a particular language, it was only two years after her article appeared that a definitive report of the effects of language experience on speech perception in infants appeared (Werker & Tees, 1984), suggesting that this complex analysis of language input was, in fact, possible in pre-productive infants.

One of the primary frustrations that faced researchers of infant speech perception during the first decade was the limited methods applicable to assessments of infants. Recall that a critical feature of categorical perception was the correspondence between category boundaries as determined by a labeling task and discrimination performance both within and between these categories. There were, and continue to be, no labeling tasks suitable for use with infants. Thus, a "category" is inferred by a *failure* to discriminate among acoustically similar tokens. This is a weak measure of "category" because such failures to discriminate can result from insensitive methods of assessment. While such failures of discrimination are typically reported in the context of positive evidence of discrimination for other contrasts, such patterns of discrimination performance obtained from adults for vowel stimuli are *not* interpreted as evidence of categorical perception. Thus, the absence of labeling data is a serious impediment to definitive interpretations of speech perception by infants.

Another limitation of methodology is the unusual context in which infants are tested. Rarely in the natural language environment are infants exposed to multiple repetitions of brief speech sounds, followed by a single change in that speech sound. Certainly, these testing paradigms are useful in mapping the discriminative capacities of infants. But it is unclear whether these perceptual capacities, sophisticated as they are, are actually used to their full extent in the processing of natural speech input, particularly since such input is presented continuously in fluent speech and not in brief phonetic or syllabic units.

Finally, infants eventually [develop, from innate biases and] from the language input, as well as from non-linguistic features of the environment, a complex system of rules for sound-combination and the attachment of meaning to these sounds. This process of extracting from the language input a system of phonological and syntactic rules, along with a lexicon that is organized according to semantic and pragmatic principles, is poorly understood. What is clear is that this transition during infancy, from a perceptual system biased by certain language-specific influences to a rule-based system that enables rudimentary speech production, is critically important (see recent reviews in Morgan & Demuth, 1996). It is this developmental transition that now occupies the attention of many researchers who are pursuing studies of infant speech perception into its third decade.

CURRENT ISSUES IN SPEECH AND AUDITORY PROCESSING BY INFANTS

As researchers entered the second decade after Eimas et al.'s (1971) report of infant speech perception capacities, two themes became apparent. One theme was the need for basic data on fundamental auditory capacities not directly related to speech signals. This also spurred researchers to seek more reliable and sensitive methods of assessment. The other theme was a search for the relation between data on the discrimination of phonetic contrasts and the acquisition of language. The first theme, whose empirical results were just emerging in the 1983 edition of this *Handbook,* has now been investigated in great detail, in part through the development of new methods of assessment. The second theme was facilitated by Werker and Tees's (1984) report on the *loss* of discrimination for nonnative phonetic contrasts in the second six postnatal months. This confirmed the longstanding belief that studies of speech perception in infancy were, in fact, relevant to language acquisition. In the following sections, we review critical findings that emerged from these two themes. But first we provide a brief summary of the methods that can be used to assess auditory processing and speech perception in human infants.

Methods of Assessment[2]

The High Amplitude Sucking (HAS) procedure was the methodological staple of the infant speech perception

---

[2] Only behavioral techniques are reviewed here. Electrophysiological techniques, such as the auditory brainstem response and otoacoustic emissions, are reviewed by Folsom and Wynne (1987) and by Bargones and Burns (1988).

literature during its first decade. In HAS, infants suck on a blind-nipple connected to a pressure transducer, with criterion-level (high-amplitude) sucks triggering the presentation of an auditory stimulus. After a predetermined decline in sucking rate, a shift and a no-shift group of infants are presented with either a novel or the familiar (unchanged) auditory stimulus, respectively. Recovery of sucking rate above the preshift level by the shift, but not the no-shift, group indicates discrimination of the novel from the familiar stimulus.

Although this technique has proven very fruitful for studies of 1- to 4-month-olds (see review by Jusczyk, 1985b), it does have several limitations. First, it provides only group data since each infant contributes only a single data point. Second, it is a sequential task that requires a stable state for 10 to 15 minutes. Subject attrition rates of 50% or higher are not uncommon. Third, HAS is used primarily as a measure of discrimination of brief stimulus materials, although variants have been used to measure a form of categorization by habituating infants to multiple exemplars (Kuhl, 1985).

A similar discrimination technique that substitutes a looking response for the sucking response in HAS was developed by Miller (1983) and used by Best and her colleagues (Best, McRoberts, LaFleur, & Silver-Isenstadt, 1995; Best, McRoberts, & Sithole, 1988). An unchanging visual stimulus elicits fixation which triggers presentation of an auditory stimulus. As duration of fixation (and listening) declines to a predetermined level, two groups of infants are presented with either a novel or the familiar auditory stimulus. As with HAS, recovery of looking in the presence of the novel auditory stimulus, compared to a no-shift control, provides evidence of auditory discrimination. Although this technique can be used with a larger age-range than HAS and has a much lower drop-out rate, it also relies on group data and is primarily used to assess discrimination rather than categorization.

A variant of the HAS technique was developed by De-Casper and Fifer (1980) to assess auditory preferences. Sucking whose interburst-intervals (IBIs) were below the median for a given infant resulted in presentation of one auditory stimulus, and IBIs above the median resulted in presentation of a different auditory stimulus. Thus, infants could control the duration of presentation of each of the two auditory stimuli, thereby expressing a preference. Because a significant preference can be exhibited only if the two auditory stimuli are discriminable, this technique also serves as a measure of discrimination. But because the absence of a preference does not imply the inability to

discriminate between the two stimuli, follow-up experiments using HAS or some other technique are usually required when no preference is obtained. As with HAS, this technique has a high attrition rate and is based on group data, but it can be used to measure categorization as well as preference/discrimination by assigning multiple tokens to each IBI-contingency.[3]

An analogous technique using visual fixation rather than a sucking response was developed by Colombo and Bundy (1981) and used by Cooper and Aslin (1990, 1994) to assess auditory preferences. Like the Miller/Best procedure, infants' fixation of an unchanging visual stimulus triggers the presentation of an auditory stimulus. One of two auditory stimuli is presented on alternate trials, thereby gathering preference data across a series of trials. This technique has proven effective with infants as young as 2 days of age and it has a lower attrition rate than the two sucking procedures (HAS and IBI). However, it too is limited to group data and, in the absence of a significant preference, must rely on another technique to verify that the two auditory stimuli are discriminable.

The conditioned headturning procedure was developed by Moore, Thompson, and Thompson (1975; see review by Kuhl, 1985) to assess auditory thresholds. An experimenter attracts the infant's gaze to a small, silent toy and an auditory stimulus is introduced from a loudspeaker located away from the infant's gaze. If the infant makes a headturn toward the loudspeaker, this criterion response is reinforced by the activation of an animated toy located adjacent to the loudspeaker (inside a smoked-plexiglas box). An experimenter, unaware of the intensity of the auditory stimulus, scores the headturn responses. No-stimulus control trials are used to establish a baseline of spontaneous headturns toward the loudspeaker/reinforcer. By systematically varying the intensity of the auditory stimulus (often using an adaptive staircase procedure), an estimate of threshold can be obtained by comparing headturns in the presence (hits) versus the absence (false alarms) of the stimulus. A variant of this technique (Schneider, Trehub, &

---

[3] Fifer (1987) has described a variant of the IBI procedure in which newborns are presented with two discriminative auditory stimuli. A sucking burst initiated during the presentation of either of two discriminative stimuli triggers the presentation of one of two auditory stimuli, such as the mother's voice or a stranger's voice. If newborns initiate sucking bursts more frequently in the presence of one discriminative stimulus than the other, then they have exhibited evidence of "preference" for the auditory stimulus paired with that discriminative stimulus.

Bull, 1979, 1980; Trehub, Schneider, & Endman, 1980) employs two loudspeakers (and reinforcers), thereby making it a two-alternative localization task rather than a yes-no detection task.

The headturning technique was first applied to the study of infant speech discrimination by Eilers, Wilson, and Moore (1977). A repeating auditory stimulus replaced the silence used to measure auditory thresholds. When the infant exhibited stable fixation of the toy being manipulated by the experimenter, the auditory stimulus was changed for several repetitions, thereby defining a temporal response window. If the infant made a headturn toward the loudspeaker/reinforcer during this response window, then the reinforcer was activated. No-change control trials assessed false alarm rates. Although this technique cannot be used with infants younger than 5 months of age (because of poor motor control and difficulty learning the stimulus-response contingency), it has a low attrition rate and can provide reliable data from individual infants, provided that a sufficient number of change and no-change trials are presented (see Aslin, Pisoni, Hennessy, & Perey, 1981).

Kuhl (1979) extended the conditioned headturning procedure to assessments of categorization by adding multiple tokens to the repeating background. In this way it was possible to measure the ease with which infants ignore these discriminable differences in the repeating background stimuli, as well as the ability to retain reliable discrimination of the auditory stimuli that define the nonbackground category. The primary limitation of this categorization technique is that it requires training on the initial discrimination task (a single repeating background and a single change-stimulus) prior to assessment of categorization, thereby typically requiring multiple test sessions.

Auditory preferences have also been measured in infants using a variant of the conditioned headturning procedure. Fernald (1985; see also Fernald and Kuhl, 1987) trained 4-month-olds to turn their head toward two interesting visual displays, with each directional headturn resulting in the presentation of a corresponding auditory stimulus. Duration of looking was used as a measure of preference for the auditory stimulus associated with each visual display.

Hirsh-Pasek et al. (1987) simplified this procedure by replacing the complex visual stimuli with two identical blinking lights. The infant's fixation was drawn to one of the blinking lights on each trial and one of two auditory stimuli was presented for the duration of the visual fixation. Initially, the side of the blinking light was associated with a particular auditory stimulus across trials, but in subsequent experiments the contingency between side and

auditory stimulus was randomized. Extensive control studies have verified that this headturn preference procedure is a reliable measure of auditory preferences in 4- to 12-month-olds (Kemler et al., 1995).

Another variant of the headturn preference procedure was developed by Jusczyk and Aslin (1995). In all previous measures of auditory preference, the preference was presumably induced by listening experience over a considerable period of time prior to the laboratory assessment. Jusczyk and Aslin were able to alter an initially neutral preference by a familiarization exposure to an auditory stimulus (or class of stimuli) immediately preceding the preference test. Thus, it was possible to determine if infants remembered auditory stimuli over brief periods, even when these stimuli were presented in different contexts (e.g., isolated words during familiarization and words embedded in sentences in the preference test).

A final method used to assess auditory thresholds as well as auditory discrimination was developed by Olsho, Koch, Halpin, and Carter (1987). Analogous to the two-alternative forced-choice looking procedure perfected by Teller (1979) for assessments of visual thresholds and discrimination, Olsho et al. reasoned that a trained observer could detect one of many possible cues from an infant who was presented with an auditory stimulus or a change in a repeating auditory stimulus. Rather than relying on a simultaneous two-choice task as used by Teller, where the infant's gaze could be directed to one of two visual stimuli, Olsho et al. (like Cooper and Aslin, 1990) used a successive trials task (called the Observer-based Psychoacoustic Procedure, or OPP) in which the observer knew that an auditory stimulus (or a change in a stimulus) was present during 50% of all observation intervals. Correct responses by the observer, like correct headturns in the conditioned headturning procedure, resulted in the presentation of a visual reinforcer. Olsho (now Werner) and her colleagues (see reviews by Werner, 1992; Werner & Bargones, 1992) have obtained reliable auditory thresholds and discrimination of auditory stimuli in infants as young as 2 weeks of age using this technique. Moreover, thresholds obtained in older infants using this technique and the conditioned headturning technique are quite similar, suggesting that the data collected from younger infants who do not perform on the conditioned headturning technique are a valid measure of threshold.

In summary, a variety of techniques have been developed or refined in the past decade to assess auditory detection, discrimination, categorization, and preference. Each technique has its advantages and limitations. In all cases, one must be careful in interpreting data collected from infants using these techniques because inattention or lack of preference may mask superior underlying capacities. As researchers begin to ask more sophisticated questions about speech perception, it is clear that developing a measure of labeling will be critical to further progress in understanding the mechanisms underlying early language acquisition.

Auditory Processing Constraints on Speech Perception

Although the infant speech perception literature highlighted the sophisticated discriminative skills of very young infants, there remained uncertainty as to whether limitations in these skills could be attributed to immaturities in the auditory system rather than to an underdeveloped speech perception mechanism per se. With the advent of the conditioned headturning procedure in the late 1970s, several researchers began to study in earnest these fundamental aspects of the auditory system using traditional psychoacoustic stimuli. Although these studies were important in their own right as descriptors of auditory development, they also held the prospect of clarifying whether limitations in intensity, frequency, and temporal processing were related to the development of speech perception capacities.

Absolute Thresholds

When the conditioned headturning procedure became well established in the late 1970s, a number of studies from several laboratories appeared which described the absolute thresholds of 6- to 18-month-olds for pure-tone and octave-band noise stimuli (Berg & Smith, 1983; Nozza & Wilson, 1984; Schneider et al., 1979, 1980; Sinnott, Pisoni, & Aslin, 1983; Trehub et al., 1980). Although there was some variability in threshold estimates across studies, it was clear that at 6 months of age infants' absolute thresholds were approximately 10 to 20 dB poorer than adults' thresholds. Moreover, the difference in thresholds between infants and adults was greater at lower frequencies than at higher frequencies.

Unfortunately, these threshold data obtained with the conditioned headturning procedure were collected from infants 6 months of age and older because of the inability of younger infants to learn the headturn contingency. To address this methodological gap, Olsho, Koch, Carter, Halpin, and Spetner (1988) obtained absolute thresholds

from 3-month-olds using OPP, as well as OPP and conditioned headturn thresholds from 6- and 12-month-olds. The thresholds from both techniques were similar at 6 and 12 months of age (10–15 dB poorer than adults), while the thresholds at 3 months of age were 15 to 30 dB poorer than adults. As shown in Figure 4.2, the greatest developmental improvement in auditory thresholds at low frequencies occurred after 12 months of age, whereas the greatest developmental improvement at high frequencies occurred between 3 and 6 months of age. This latter finding suggests that young infants may have difficulty discriminating speech contrasts, such as fricatives, that rely on high frequency information. It is also important to note that thresholds obtained free-field with loudspeakers and more recently with head or earphones have yielded very similar results.

Werner and Gillenwater (1990) have extended the use of OPP to infants as young as 2 weeks of age, but several modifications of the testing procedure were implemented. No visual reinforcer was used, and the signal/no-signal scoring interval was presented immediately after two successive stimulus intervals (signal and no-signal) so that the

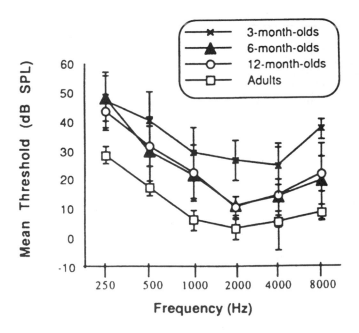

Figure 4.2 Pure-tone auditory thresholds obtained from infants using the observer-based psychoacoustic procedure and from adults. From "Pure-tone sensitivity of human infants," by L. W. Olsho et al., 1988. *Journal of the Acoustical Society of America, 84,* pp. 1316–1324. Copyright © 1988 by the American Institute of Physics. Reprinted with permission.

observer could better judge the infant's response in the context of any changes in state. Thresholds were estimated as approximately 50 dB poorer than adults. Although there remains some uncertainty about whether the absence of a visual reinforcer contributed to this infant-adult difference, it is clear that significant development in pure-tone thresholds occurs between 1 and 6 months of age (35–40 dB), and between 6 months and adulthood (10–15 dB). This threshold difference between 6-month-olds and adults is also present for speech signals (Nozza, 1987), suggesting that this difference is not the result of the reduced attentional salience of pure-tones. It is important to point out, however, that any behavioral technique for estimating thresholds is subject to criterion effects. As summarized by Bargones, Werner, and Marean (1995), infants rarely reach 100% correct on any testing procedure, and the slopes of their psychometric functions (a measure of task-sensitivity) are shallower than in adults. However, both Bargones et al. and Nozza (1995) have provided evidence that task variables do not account for the majority of the developmental differences observed between infants and adults, suggesting that these differences are primarily sensory in nature.

Frequency and Intensity Discrimination

The development of the conditioned headturning procedure as a reliable measure of absolute thresholds quickly led to its use in assessments of frequency and intensity discrimination (Olsho, 1984; Olsho, Schoon, Sakai, Sperduto, & Turpin, 1982a, 1982b; Sinnott & Aslin, 1985). For both types of discrimination, 6-month-olds could detect a change approximately twice the magnitude that adults could detect (5 dB vs. 2 dB for intensity; 2% vs. 1% for frequency).

The OPP technique developed by Olsho et al. (1987) was used to measure frequency discrimination in 3-, 6-, and 12-month-olds and to determine if the intensity of the tones affected frequency discrimination thresholds (Olsho, Koch, & Halpin, 1987). At the higher intensity, 3-month-olds' discrimination thresholds were approximately 3%, compared to 2% for 6- and 12-month-olds and slightly less than 1% for adults. This developmental difference between 3-month-olds and 6- and 12-month-olds was not present at low frequencies. Bargones and Werner (1994) have shown that at least part of this frequency-effect stems from an attentional process in which infants do not appear to selectively attend to the frequency-range within which signals are presented. This off-frequency listening effect may be relevant to any task that benefits from selective attention to one of several alternative acoustic attributes.

A final aspect of frequency discrimination relevant to speech processing was reported by Aslin (1989) who used the conditioned headturning procedure to assess 6- to 9-month-olds' discrimination of changes in pure-tones undergoing a rapid frequency sweep. These frequency sweeps were presented either in isolation or followed by a constant-frequency tone, analogous to the formant transitions of a consonant followed by a steady-state vowel. Aslin reported that infants' thresholds for discriminating a frequency sweep from a constant-frequency tone were approximately the same as for discriminating two constant-frequency tones. However, when the frequency sweep was appended to a constant-frequency tone, discrimination thresholds increased by a factor of two. Finally, when the task involved discriminating one frequency sweep from another, rather than a frequency sweep from a constant-frequency tone, infants' thresholds increased by an additional factor of 3 to 4. These results suggest that the categorical perception of consonants, which are cued in many cases by rising or falling formant transitions, may be determined, in part, by a basic limitation in the ability of the auditory system to resolve the direction and extent of frequency sweeps. While this pattern of results was also present for adults, the poorer performance of the infants may render some phonetic contrasts, such as place of articulation which relies on a subtle pattern of formant transitions, somewhat difficult to discriminate in early infancy.

Frequency Resolution and Masking

The foregoing studies of absolute thresholds and discrimination of changes in the frequency and intensity of pure-tones are perhaps less relevant for speech perception than the ability to resolve one frequency component in a broadband auditory stimulus. Several studies have used the conditioned headturning procedure to assess infants' thresholds for detecting an octave-band noise or a pure-tone in the presence of a broadband masking noise (Bull, Schneider, & Trehub, 1981; Nozza & Wilson, 1984; Schneider, Trehub, Morrongiello, & Thorpe, 1989). The masking noise elevated thresholds in infants and adults by the same relative amount, suggesting that frequency resolution is adultlike by 6 months of age. Olsho (1985), Schneider, Morrongiello, and Trehub (1990), and Spetner and Olsho (1990), using somewhat different stimulus conditions, came to a similar conclusion. The Spetner and Olsho (1990) study used OPP to test 3-month-olds as well as 6-month-olds. While the effects of masking at 500 Hz and 1000 Hz were similar at these two ages, detection at 4000 Hz was affected by a broader range of frequencies in 3-month-olds. Thus, there is evidence that at these higher frequencies young infants are less able to resolve small differences in frequency in the presence of other auditory stimuli. Werner and Bargones (1991) showed that even in 6-month-olds, who have adultlike frequency resolution, it is possible to distract them from the task (and thereby raise their thresholds) by presenting a masker whose frequency is several octaves away from the target frequency. Thus, attentional (distractor) effects can degrade infants' frequency resolution.

Temporal Resolution

The ability to detect and discriminate rapid spectral changes is essential for the categorization of phonetic segments. Moreover, durational cues are used in speech to signal segmental as well as prosodic information. Morrongiello and Trehub (1987) used the conditioned headturning procedure to assess duration discrimination and reported that 6-month-olds' thresholds were 25 msec whereas adults' were 10 msec. Werner, Marean, Halpin, Spetner, and Gillenwater (1992) used OPP to assess gap detection in 3-, 6-, and 12-month-olds. The stimulus consisted of a broadband noise that was interrupted 10 times in rapid succession. The duration of the interruption (gap) was varied across trials. By altering the low-frequency cutoff of the noise, Werner et al. were able to determine which frequencies were used by infants in this gap detection task. Although the data from 12-month-olds were inconsistent, the 3- and 6-month-olds showed gap detection thresholds 4 to 5 times longer than adults, and their thresholds (like adults') improved when high frequency information was present. However, Trehub, Schneider, and Henderson (1995), using the conditioned headturning procedure, reported that two-tone gap-detection thresholds were only approximately twice as long in 6- and 12-month-olds as in adults.

Marean and Werner (1991) used OPP to assess forward masking in 3-month-olds. A noise burst preceded a tone by a variable temporal interval. When the interval was long (200 msec), no effect of the masker was present and infant and adult thresholds were similar. But when the interval was short (5–25 msec), the noise burst elevated the threshold for detecting the tone, and this elevation in 3-month-olds was much greater than in adults. Thus, although data are limited, temporal resolution appears to be significantly poorer in 3-month-olds than in adults, and these immaturities

could have important effects on several aspects of speech processing, including the relative timing of formants that signals differences in voicing.

The foregoing summary of basic auditory development illustrates that infants undergo a substantial improvement in these capacities in the first few postnatal months. More impressively, these results indicate that by 6 months of age infants are only mildly poorer than adults on most measures of basic auditory capacities, particularly when one considers that behavioral tasks rely on the infant's natural tendency to respond in the absence of verbal instructions, and thus tend to underestimate their actual capacities. Whether infants fully utilize these sophisticated capacities in the processing of language in the natural environment is largely unknown.

Perhaps more relevant to language acquisition than speech perception itself, therefore, is the infant's ability to attend to, segment, and remember speech stimuli so that sound patterns relevant to the native language can be associated with meanings. Once these fundamental tasks have been "solved," even if only for a small set of the possible utterances to which the infant is exposed, the infant can then begin to form phonological and syntactic rules whereby novel utterances can be generated. This transition from basic speech perception capacities to rule-based systems of language structure and production is the task being addressed by many current researchers.

Speech Perception in the Context of Language Acquisition

Speech as a Biologically Significant Signal

Infants are exposed to a variety of different sounds in their native environments. Some of these are produced with great frequency by other active, nonhuman creatures, such as family pets, and others by electromechanical devices, such as alarm clocks. Yet, the sounds that infants choose to imitate, the ones which seem to attract their attention most, are the ones produced by other human beings (Colombo & Bundy, 1981; Friedlander & Wisdom, 1971; Glenn, Cunningham, & Joyce, 1981). Infants are not very remarkable in this respect. Young birds growing up in the wild learn the song patterns of their own species despite the fact that they are also exposed to the calls of many other species (Marler & Peters, 1981). Hence, of all the kinds of acoustic stimuli in the environment, there appears to be something particularly attractive about those that are produced by one's own species.

The fact that human speech sounds are salient signals for human infants is not particularly surprising. However, not all human speech sounds are equally powerful in capturing infants' attention. Rather, the speech sounds that infants appear to find most attractive are the kinds of sounds that are specifically addressed to them (Fernald, 1984, 1985). Although differences between adult- and child-directed speech had been noticed earlier (Ferguson, 1964), it was during the early 1970s that language researchers began to systematically investigate differences in the kind of speech that is typically addressed to infants, as opposed to adults (Broen, 1972; Phillips, 1973; Snow, 1972). Infant-directed (ID) speech was found to be shorter, more repetitive, and to use simpler syntactic constructions than adult-directed (AD) speech (Shatz & Gelman, 1973; Snow, 1972). Moreover, the acoustic characteristics of ID speech were noted to differ from AD speech in several important ways (Ferguson, 1977; Garnica, 1977; Grewel, 1959). For example, the average pitch of ID speech was noted to be higher, the pitch range more exaggerated, and the durations of content words longer than for AD speech (Garnica, 1977).

Subsequent investigations showed that these kinds of prosodic differences between ID and AD speech are present across a range of different languages (Fernald & Simon, 1984; Fernald, Taeschner, Dunn, Papousek, Boysson-Bardies, & Fukui, 1989; Grieser & Kuhl, 1988; Papousek, Papousek, & Haekel, 1987; Stern, Spieker, Barnett, & MacKain, 1983). More importantly, these prosodic characteristics of ID speech were shown to have an impact on infants' listening preferences. In particular, Fernald (1985) found that when given an opportunity to hear either ID or AD speech, 4-month-olds chose significantly more often to listen to ID speech. Similar preferences by English-learning infants for ID over AD speech have been reported for 7-week-olds (Pegg, Werker, & McLeod, 1992) and for 1-month-olds and newborns (Cooper & Aslin, 1990). In addition, although most studies have used stimuli based on female voices, there are indications that infants' preferences for ID over AD speech extend to male voices as well (Werker & McLeod, 1989). There is also evidence suggesting that infants' preferences for ID over AD speech hold even for non-native language materials, such as English-learning infants listening to Cantonese speech (Werker, Pegg, & McLeod, 1994).

These demonstrations that infants are attracted to ID speech raise a number of interesting questions. For instance, what role does ID speech play in development? What acoustic characteristics of ID speech do infants find

so captivating? The first of these questions generated a number of suggestions about the function of ID speech. For example, the exaggerated prosody of ID speech could serve to (a) elicit and maintain the infant's attention (Fernald & Mazzie, 1991; Kaplan, Goldstein, Huckeby, Owren, & Cooper, 1995), (b) help mark important grammatical units in fluent speech (Gleitman & Wanner, 1982; Hirsh-Pasek et al., 1987; Morgan, 1986; Peters, 1983), and (c) communicate intention and emotion to the child (Fernald, 1992). It is entirely possible that the prosodic features of ID speech may serve some or even all of these functions at various points in development.

In addition, it is possible that the prosodic characteristics of ID speech may also play some role in the precocious ability which infants show for recognizing their own mother's voice. DeCasper and Fifer (1980) demonstrated that newborn infants prefer their mother's voice over the voice of another female. That this preference for the maternal voice may be tied to prosodic characteristics is suggested by the results of several investigations. For example, Mehler, Bertoncini, Barriere, and Jassik-Gerschenfeld (1978) found that French infants between 2 and 4 weeks of age recognized their own mother's voice when she was producing ID speech, but not when she was reading words in a monotone (by reading the words of a text backwards). Spence and DeCasper (1987) presented newborns with a choice between listening to either unfiltered or low-pass filtered[4] versions of their own mother's voice. The infants did not show a significant preference for either version. One possible explanation for this result is that the low-pass versions preserved the essential information needed for infants to recognize their mother's voice. Further support for this explanation comes from a comparison of newborns' responding to unfiltered and low-pass filtered versions of unfamiliar voices. Newborns preferred listening to unfiltered versions of these voices. This suggests that the lack of a preference for the unfiltered versions of the maternal voice was not simply due to some problem in discriminating low-pass filtered and unfiltered versions of voices. Moreover, a recent study by DeCasper, Lecanuet, Busnel, Granier-Deferre, and Maugeais (1994) reported that fetal heartrate was differentially affected by a "familiar" nursery rhyme; that is, one read repeatedly by the mother for several weeks during the third trimester of pregnancy. Finally, Spence

---

[4] Low-pass filtering does not alter the intensity of sounds below a given cut-off frequency (e.g., 400 Hz) while completely attenuating all sounds above that cut-off frequency.

and Freeman (1996) have shown that newborns prefer their own mother's voice over that of another female when both voices are low-pass filtered, but not when they are whispered. These results suggest that the prosodic information carried by the fundamental frequency in low-pass but not whispered speech is important for voice-recognition. Again, this overall pattern of results suggests that prosodic information is differentially processed by the fetus.

One reason why the prosodic features of ID speech may be particularly salient for infants is the fact that this type of acoustic information is transmitted particularly well to the developing fetus. The uterine wall acts essentially as a low-pass filter, and the characteristics of speech that are best transmitted *in utero* tend to be ones associated with prosody (Armitage, Baldwin, & Vince, 1980; Griffiths, Brown, Gerhardt, Abrams, & Morris, 1994). Moreover, the speech patterns of the infant's mother are transmitted through her body to the fetus at considerably greater intensity than are sounds from the external environment (Lecanuet & Granier-Deferre, 1993; Richards, Frentzen, Gerhardt, McCann, & Abrams, 1992). Consequently, the mother's speech patterns, and particularly her prosodic characteristics, are the kinds of acoustic signals with which infants are likely to have considerable prenatal experience. These experiences could well induce infants to attend preferentially to the mother's voice and to attend to other speaking patterns which share many of the same prosodic characteristics (such as utterances in the mother's native language, as opposed to ones in a foreign language). With respect to the acquisition of a native language, a tendency to orient more toward the maternal speech patterns, particularly those in an ID speech register, could play a useful role in filtering the input. Thus, by attending most closely to ID speech patterns with similar prosodic properties to maternal speech patterns, the infant might be less likely to try to generalize across native and non-native utterances (the kind of generalization that would make the discovery of the structural features of the native language enormously complicated).

The second question regarding the acoustic characteristics of ID speech was initially addressed by Fernald and Kuhl (1987). They systematically explored the way that differences in pitch, amplitude, and rhythmic features might account for the preferences that infants display for ID over AD speech. The results of their investigation suggested that the critical differences have to do with pitch characteristics (e.g., a higher mean fundamental frequency, more exaggerated pitch changes, and an expanded fundamental frequency range) of ID speech. In particular, when amplitude and durational differences were equated, but pitch differences were present in the speech materials, 4-month-olds continued to display a preference for ID over AD speech. However, when prosodic features were equated, 4-month-olds showed no preferences for ID over AD speech, even when there were clear amplitude or durational differences between the two types of speech materials. On the basis of these results, Fernald and Kuhl (1987; see also Fernald, 1992) suggested that infants may possess an innate predisposition to orient to these salient pitch features of ID speech.

However, the results of a more recent investigation raised some questions about the origins and bases of infants' preferences for ID speech. Cooper and Aslin (1994) explored the possible bases for 1-month-olds' preferences for ID over AD speech. Although they had previously demonstrated that infants at this age prefer listening to ID speech (Cooper & Aslin, 1990), in their more recent study they found no evidence of a preference for the prosodic contours of ID speech. More specifically, 1-month-olds showed no preference for listening to low-pass filtered versions of ID as compared to AD speech samples. In another experiment, they showed that infants were able to discriminate the low-pass filtered versions of the ID samples from those of the AD samples. Hence, the lack of a preference for the prosodic contours of the ID speech samples was not simply a result of their inability to discriminate these samples from those of the AD samples. In exploring this issue further, Cooper and Aslin pitted unfiltered versions of the ID speech samples against low-pass filtered versions of these same samples. They found that 1-month-olds exhibited a significant preference for the unfiltered samples. Finally, 1-month-olds did not prefer sine wave analogues of the pitch changes present in ID speech, as had the 4-month-olds in Fernald and Kuhl (1987). On the basis of these findings, they argued that, in addition to expanded pitch contours, there are other acoustic properties, such as spectral structure, that contribute to the preference for ID speech shown by 1-month-olds. They further suggested that the preferences for the pitch contours of ID speech displayed by the 4-month-olds tested by Fernald and Kuhl (1987) may actually emerge postnatally as a result of learning to respond to such contours during the first few months of life (see also Cooper, 1993).

Learning Native Speech Sound Categories

As discussed earlier, research on infant speech perception began with investigations of the discrimination of basic phonetic contrasts. Little was known about how or when infants might have the capacity to discriminate speech sounds when Eimas, Siqueland, Jusczyk, and Vigorito (1971) first began their investigation. The discovery that infants could discriminate voicing contrasts from as early as one month of age spurred researchers to investigate a variety of different phonetic contrasts (for recent reviews of this literature see Best, 1995; Jusczyk, 1995). In general, these investigations showed that infants were capable of discriminating all possible phonetic contrasts by 6 months of age, including ones that did not appear in the infant's native language environment.

These findings contributed to the view that these perceptual capacities are either innate or determined by a maturational process independent of exposure to a specific language. Nevertheless, it is clear that during the course of development these capacities must be influenced by language experience. The sound categories and sound patterns of languages differ considerably from each other, and infants need to learn the ones appropriate to their native language. So, although young infants' perceptual capacities provide them with a preliminary analysis of the speech signal, they need to adjust or tune their capacities to optimally process native language speech patterns.

Although the relation between experience and perceptual capacities had been debated by many investigators, research on this problem began in earnest with the studies conducted by Werker and her colleagues (Werker, Gilbert, Humphrey, & Tees, 1981; Werker & Lalonde, 1988; Werker & Tees, 1984). Given that adults have difficulty discriminating phonetic contrasts that do not occur in their native language (e.g., Miyawaki et al., 1975), whereas very young infants do not (e.g., Trehub, 1976), Werker sought to determine the age at which sensitivity to non-native contrasts begins to decline. After her initial investigations indicated that the loss of sensitivity to non-native contrasts was apparent in 4-year-olds (Werker & Tees, 1983), she began to explore the possibility that these changes occur within the first year of life. Infants from English-speaking homes were tested with the conditioned head-turning procedure on English ([ba]-[da]), Hindi ([ṭa]-[t̪a]) and Nthlakapmx ([k'i]-[q'i]) contrasts at three ages: 6 to 8 months, 8 to 10 months, and 10 to 12 months. At 6 to 8 months, the infants discriminated all the contrasts. However, by 8 to 10 months, only some of the infants discriminated the non-English contrasts, and by 10 to 12 months, very few showed any evidence of discriminating the non-English contrasts. In a subsequent experiment, several Hindi- and Nthlakapmx-learning infants were tested on the contrasts appropriate to their native language. Even at 11 to 12 months, these infants

had no difficulty discriminating their native language contrasts. Thus, the failure of English-learning infants to discriminate these same contrasts is not simply attributable to a general decline in interest at this age to these particular contrasts. Rather, it is the specific language-learning background of the infants that seems to determine whether they will discriminate these contrasts. In particular, what Werker and Tees found could be described as a decline in sensitivity to certain non-native speech contrasts.

Subsequent research by Werker and Lalonde (1988) with a different, synthetically produced, Hindi contrast ([Ḍa] [da]), also indicated a similar decline in sensitivity to this contrast by English-learning infants between 6- and 12-months of age. In addition, Werker and Tees' (1984) finding of a decline in sensitivity to the Nthlakapmx contrast was later replicated by Best and McRoberts (1989) using a different testing procedure. Eimas' (1975a) demonstration that 2- to 3-month-old American infants discriminate a contrast between [ra] and [la] is an indication that Japanese infants would also be likely to do so (e.g., Gleitman, Gleitman, Landau, & Wanner, 1988). Empirical support for this speculation has recently been reported for Japanese infants by Tsushima and his colleagues (Tsushima et al., 1994).

Although initially it appeared as though the decline in sensitivity to non-native contrasts might be a case of the "use it or lose it" principle in development (i.e., capacities which do not receive sufficient environmental stimulation deteriorate), the picture has proven much more complicated. First of all, there is evidence that, with proper training, adults can regain the ability to distinguish non-native contrasts (Flege, 1989; Lively, Logan, & Pisoni, 1993; Lively, Pisoni, Yamada, Tohkura, & Yamada, 1994; Logan, Lively, & Pisoni, 1991; Pisoni et al., 1982). Consequently, the decline more likely involves attentional factors rather than the atrophy of a sensory substrate (Jusczyk, 1985a, 1992; Werker, 1991). Second, it has become apparent that the decline in sensitivity occurs for some, but not all, non-native contrasts. This fact was first demonstrated clearly in a study by Best, McRoberts, and Sithole (1988) who examined the perception of a Zulu lateral versus medial click contrast by English-learning infants. They found that at all four ages tested (6–8, 8–10, 10–12, and 12–14 months) the infants were able to discriminate this contrast. Moreover, English-speaking adults also had no difficulty in discriminating this contrast, even though it does not occur in English. Thus, unlike the contrasts that Werker and her colleagues had investigated, English-listeners show no decline in sensitivity to this non-native Zulu click contrast. In a subsequent investigation, Best (1991) reported evidence of both maintenance and loss in the discrimination of non-native contrasts. English-learning infants, between 6 and 12 months, did not show any loss of sensitivity to an Ethiopian ejective place of articulation distinction, but they did display a decline in sensitivity to a Zulu lateral fricative distinction.

How can we account for the fact that certain non-native contrasts become less discriminable during development, while others do not? An explanation, as was suggested by Werker and Lalonde (1988), that attributes the loss to a changeover from phonetic to phonemic perception (i.e., attention to only those contrasts that make meaningful distinctions between words in the native language) will not suffice. Rather, it appears that whether or not a non-native contrast undergoes a perceptual decline is related to how the non-native contrast maps onto the kinds of phonemic distinctions made in the native language (Best, 1995; Eimas, 1991; Flege, 1995; Werker, 1991). The most extensive attempt to account for developmental changes in sensitivity to non-native phonetic contrasts is the Perceptual Assimilation Model (Best, 1993, 1995). The basic premise of the model is that non-native contrasts that map onto two different native language categories or to no native language categories will be easy to discriminate, whereas those distinctions that map to a single phonemic category will be most apt to undergo a decline in discriminability (we will provide a more extensive discussion of this model in a later section).

Although much of the work on the perception of non-native speech contrasts focused on consonantal distinctions, more recent research has examined the perception of non-native vowel contrasts. Polka and Werker (1994) investigated infants' perception of certain German vowel contrasts ([U]-[Y] and [u:]-[y:]) that do not appear in English. When English-learning 10- to 12-month-olds were tested on these contrasts, they showed no evidence of discrimination. This finding is consistent with the developmental decline in the ability to discriminate non-native consonantal contrasts. However, unlike the results reported for consonantal contrasts, 6- to 8-month-olds tested on these vowel contrasts did not discriminate them, whereas a younger group of infants, 4- to 6-month-olds, were able to discriminate these same contrasts. Hence, the overall pattern of results—sensitivity to a non-native contrast, followed by a decline in sensitivity—is preserved for these vowel contrasts, but the change in sensitivity appears to occur at an earlier point in development for vowels than for consonants. One possible reason that changes in sensitivity to vowels may occur

earlier is their relative prominence in the speech stream. Vowels tend to be longer and louder than consonants, and they carry prosodic as well as phonetic information.

Consistent with this hypothesis is research on infants' perception of vowels by Kuhl and her colleagues (Grieser & Kuhl, 1989; Iverson & Kuhl, 1995; Kuhl, 1991; Kuhl, Williams, Lacerda, Stevens, & Lindblom, 1992). They have reported evidence that vowel categories may undergo some re-organization as a result of experience with native language utterances during the first 6 months of life. In particular, Kuhl and her colleagues have argued that native language vowel categories in adults are organized around prototypical instances, and that, even when they use the same vowel, different languages may vary with respect to what functions as a prototypical instance. In one study using the conditioned headturning procedure (Grieser & Kuhl, 1989), American infants were exposed to what adults judged to be either a prototypical instance or a poor instance of the English vowel [i]. The particular instance (i.e., the prototypical one or a nonprototypical one) served as a background stimulus. Novel instances from the category were used as test stimuli. Infants' discrimination of the novel instances from the familiar background stimulus was measured. Thus, the procedure assessed infants' ability to generalize from the background stimulus to novel stimuli. When a prototypical instance served as the background stimulus, infants generalized to a significantly larger number of novel instances (i.e., they were less likely to detect a change). Kuhl (1991) interpreted these findings as evidence for a "perceptual magnet effect" (but see Lively, 1993; Sussman & Lauckner-Morano, 1995). The essential idea is that the perceptual space around the prototypical instances is distorted in a way that shortens perceptual distances between the center and edges of the vowel category. New exemplars that are close to the prototype of a category are drawn to that prototype and, therefore, are perceived as belonging to that category. Kuhl et al. (1992) extended and replicated these findings by demonstrating that infants' experience with a native language is critical to the formation of vowel prototypes. American and Swedish infants were tested on two vowel prototypes: the English [i] and the Swedish [y]. Infants showed the "perceptual magnet" effect only for their own native language vowel. Swedish infants demonstrated a magnet effect for [y], but not for [i], whereas American infants showed the reverse pattern.

Kuhl's finding that infants' vowel categories may become organized around prototypical instances within the first 6 months of life is interesting in light of Polka and Werker's (1994) report that sensitivity to certain non-native vowel contrasts appears to decline at around 6 months of age. In addition, Polka and Werker also observed an asymmetry in their discrimination results that was reminiscent of the magnet effect; namely, infants found it easier to discriminate these non-native contrasts when the one that was most distant from the native language vowel served as the background stimulus. Hence, it is tempting to conclude that the same factors may be at work in organizing vowel categories around prototypical instances and in promoting the decline in sensitivity to non-native contrasts. Nevertheless, only a very limited number of vowel contrasts have been observed to date, so the generality of these effects is unclear. For example, are all native-language vowel categories organized around prototypical instances, or are only a few? In addition, the issue of talker variability has not been taken into consideration in past studies of vowel prototypes. Hence, it is not clear the extent to which these effects depend on the specific characteristics of an individual talker. These kinds of issues need to be resolved before we have a clear picture of how infants' vowel categories are organized. Nevertheless, the findings to date suggest that infants' capacities for discriminating vowel contrasts are affected by the nature of the language input to which they are exposed, even within the first 6 months of life.

The foregoing evidence suggests that experience with the native language not only affects sensitivity to contrasts outside of the native language but also sensitivity to language contrasts within the native language. There are some indications that infants may begin focusing on global, prosodic properties of the native language from a very early age. Mehler et al. (1988) found that 4-day-old French infants significantly increased their sucking rates when listening to utterances in French, as opposed to Russian. By comparison, 4-day-old infants from families whose native language was something other than French showed no tendency to suck longer in the presence of French as opposed to Russian utterances. That infants were likely responding to the prosodic qualities of the French utterances was demonstrated by the fact that the preference for French was present even when the infants were listening to low-pass filtered versions of the French and Russian utterances. Similar results for English and Spanish newborns listening to utterances in their native language have also been reported (Moon, Cooper, & Fifer, 1993; for data from 5-month-olds, see Bahrick & Pickens, 1988). More recently, Mehler and his colleagues (Bertoncini, 1993; Mehler, Dupoux, Nazzi, &

Dehaene-Lambertz, 1996) have reported evidence that French 4-day-olds are unable to distinguish changes in Japanese stimuli based on the mora—the rhythmic unit around which Japanese utterances are organized. More specifically, these 4-day-olds did not discriminate a change from 2 morae to 3 morae, even though infants at this age were able to distinguish similar changes involving syllables—the elementary rhythmic unit of French (Bijeljac-Babic, Bertoncini, & Mehler, 1993). These findings suggest that infants identify the key properties of the rhythmic organization of their native language either prenatally or during the first few days of life. Other evidence suggests that infants are able to distinguish between native and non-native patterns of word stress by at least 6 months of age. English-learning 6-month-olds listen significantly longer to words with English stress patterns than they do to words with Norwegian stress patterns, even when the words are low-pass filtered (Jusczyk, Friederici, Wessels, Svenkerud, & Jusczyk, 1993).

Beyond Segmental Contrasts: Learning about Sound Patterns in the Native Language

One of the most important changes that has occurred in infant speech research over the past decade is the shift from focusing exclusively on the discrimination of segmental contrasts to addressing wider issues in speech perception and their role in language acquisition. One of the questions that has emerged is how infants segment fluent speech and learn to recognize words in the input. Languages differ considerably in the ways words are formed (e.g., what sequences of segments are allowed), in what information is used to mark word boundaries, and in the nature of their inflectional systems (how many inflections they typically allow, what kinds, and in what orders). Thus, to be successful in recovering words from fluent speech, infants must learn something about the organization underlying sound patterns in their native language.

The organization of the sound structures of natural languages involves both segmental and suprasegmental features. For instance, languages differ in which elementary sound units—phonetic segments—they use to form words. The sound [ð], which is the first sound in the word "the," is found in English but not in French. Similarly, the sound [X], which is the last sound in the name "Bach," is found in German but not in English. As noted in the preceding section, infants seem to begin to notice the distributions of sounds in the phonetic inventories of their native language during the first postnatal year, as evidenced by their difficulty in discriminating non-native phonetic contrasts.

Beyond the inventory of the segments used in forming words, languages also differ in the constraints they impose on combinations of phonetic segments within syllables and words. For example, although English includes the sound [ʒ], as in the second consonant of the word "measure," this sound cannot appear at the beginning of words in English, although it can in Polish. Similarly, Polish permits many kinds of consonant clusters at the beginning of words (e.g., "dba," "Szczecin," "przy," "dla") that cannot occur in English words. In contrast, it is permissible for English words to end with voiced stop consonants (e.g., the last sounds in "cub," "dog," and "bird"), whereas in languages such as Polish and German all stop consonants are de-voiced in word-final position. These language-specific rules for phonetic combinations are called phonotactics.

Another key way in which the sound structures of languages differ is their suprasegmental properties (i.e., their rhythmic units, stress patterns, intonation contours, and tonal properties). As mentioned in the previous section, some languages, such as Japanese, are based on rhythmic units such as the mora, whereas others, such as French, are based on the syllable (Otake, Hatano, Cutler, & Mehler, 1993). In a language like Czech, the initial syllable is the most stressed, whereas in Russian, the syllable that receives primary stress can vary from word to word. Although many African and East Asian languages are thought to have well-developed tonal organizations, the inventory of tone levels and shapes tends to be larger and the distribution of tones within utterances is less constrained in East Asian languages (Kenstowicz, 1994).

There are many different aspects of segmental and suprasegmental organization that language-learning infants must discover about their native language. Moreover, because languages differ along so many of these dimensions, an understanding of how and when language-learners discover these properties will ultimately require cross-linguistic developmental comparisons. To the extent that speech perception capacities are optimized for dealing with the sound structures of a particular language, it is especially important to undertake such cross-linguistic investigations. At the present time, much of what we know about when the infant begins to display sensitivity to the organization of native language sound patterns comes from studies with infants from English-speaking environments.

Where might one look for evidence that infants have learned about the inventory of phonetic segments and the phonotactic organization of their native language? Certainly, the decline in sensitivity to certain non-native contrasts is suggestive that infants are learning something about the phonetic segments that typically occur in their native language. However, a more direct demonstration would be to show that infants can effectively categorize words, on the basis of their phonetic and phonotactic properties, as either belonging or not belonging to their native language. Jusczyk, Friederici, et al. (1993) used the head-turn preference procedure to explore this issue. They presented infants with lists of either native or non-native words and recorded how long infants listened to each type of list. In particular, infants were presented with different lists of either English or Dutch low-frequency words. Dutch and English are very similar with respect to their prosodic organization (Crystal & House, 1988; Reitveld & Koopmans-van Beinum, 1987), but they differ with respect to their phonetic and phonotactic properties. For example, Dutch does not have the vowel that appears in the English word "fuse," whereas English does not have the consonant that begins the Dutch word "gouda." Similarly, Dutch allows phonotactic sequences such as [kn] and [zw] to begin words, whereas English does not. English allows voiced stops to end words, whereas Dutch does not.

When tested on the English and Dutch lists of words at 6 months of age, American infants did not show any significant tendency to listen longer to either type of list. However, at 9 months, American infants listened significantly longer to the English lists. That infants were responding to the phonetic and phonotactic properties of these words, as opposed to unforeseen prosodic differences, was shown by the fact that the preference for the English words disappeared when the lists were low-pass filtered (to remove the phonetic and phonotactic cues). To determine whether 9-month-olds simply prefer listening to English or whether they had actually learned something about the properties of words in their native language, Jusczyk et al. conducted an additional experiment with both Dutch and American infants. The lists were modified so that what distinguished the words from the different languages had to do only with their phonotactic properties. Both the Dutch and American 9-month-olds listened longer to the word lists appropriate for their own native language. Thus, by 9 months of age, infants have learned something about the patterns of sound sequences which can appear in words in their native language.

There are further indications that the developing sensitivity to sound patterns of native language words goes well beyond what is required to distinguish native from foreign language words. Friederici and Wessels (1993) found that Dutch 9-month-olds are sensitive to phonotactically legal onset and offset clusters in Dutch words. Not only did the infants listen significantly longer to phonotactically legal Dutch sequences for words occurring in isolation, but they also, under some circumstances, listened longer to word sequences containing phonotactically legal clusters than to ones with phonotactically illegal clusters. The latter finding suggests that they might be able to draw on such information to help them in segmenting words from the speech stream.

Another recent investigation suggests that infants are attuned to the frequency with which certain phonotactic sequences occur in their native language (Jusczyk, Luce, & Charles-Luce, 1994). Infants were presented with different lists of monosyllables that contained phonetic sequences which were all phonotactically permissible in English words. However, half of the lists contained monosyllables with sequences for which the likelihood that one phonetic segment followed another in English words was high. The other half of the lists were composed of monosyllables with sequences that occur much less frequently within English words. Nine-month-olds, but not 6-month-olds, listened significantly longer to the lists with high frequency phonetic sequences. These results suggest that not only are infants between 6 and 9 months of age learning about the fine-grained structure of native language word patterns, but also that they are remarkably sensitive to how these patterns are distributed in the input. Sensitivity to such properties of the input could well influence the development and organization of the lexicon and word recognition processes (we will return to this point shortly when we take up the issue of word segmentation).

Some information also exists about when infants begin to respond to the suprasegmental characteristics of their native language. It has been known for some time that infants are able to discriminate speech sounds on the basis of prosodic differences such as intonation and syllable stress (Jusczyk & Thompson, 1978; Morse, 1972; Spring & Dale, 1977). Moreover, as noted earlier, French 4-day-olds appear to distinguish utterances in their native language from Russian utterances on the basis of prosodic differences (Mehler et al., 1988). Given that the kinds of utterances that Mehler and his colleagues used were long passages of connected speech, their results indicate that very young infants have some ability to recognize the global prosodic characteristics of native language utterances (such as the typical prosody of sentences, and perhaps, phrases). However, what is not addressed in these investigations is when infants begin to attend to the kinds of word-level prosodic characteristics that are potentially useful in segmenting fluent speech.

In analyzing a large corpus of spoken English utterances, Cutler and Carter (1987) found that a very high proportion of words are either stressed monosyllables or else begin with a strong syllable followed by a weak one. Thus, they identified the predominant stress pattern of English words as strong/weak (or trochaic). Jusczyk, Cutler, and Redanz (1993) investigated when English-learning infants display sensitivity to this property of their native language words. They presented American infants with lists of bisyllabic English words that either followed (i.e., strong/weak) or did not follow (i.e., weak/strong) the predominant stress pattern in the language. Half of the lists were composed of bisyllables with strong/weak patterns (e.g., "fowler," "turban") and the other half consisted of bisyllables with weak/strong patterns (e.g., "ablaze," "contrive"). Although 6-month-olds showed no difference in listening times to either type of list, 9-month-olds listened significantly longer to the lists with strong/weak stress patterns. Moreover, even when the lists were low-pass filtered, 9-month-olds listened significantly longer to the strong/weak patterns, suggesting that they were not simply responding to phonetic or phonotactic properties. Instead, it appears that American infants are also developing sensitivity to the predominant stress patterns of English words at some time between 6 and 9 months of age.

These findings from 9-month-old English-learning infants were recently replicated and extended in a study which investigated the possible bases for infants' perception of whether or not a syllable is stressed. Specifically, Turk, Jusczyk, and Gerken (1995) examined whether infants' perception of syllable stress depends on the presence of so-called "heavy" syllables. A syllable is considered to be heavy if it is closed (i.e., CVC), or if it is open (i.e., CV) but contains a tense vowel (e.g., the /i/ in beet or the /e/ in date). In some languages, only heavy syllables can receive stress. Although in most cases, stress in English is associated with heavy syllables, it can also occur on light syllables such as the first one in "beckon." Turk et al. found that when 9-month-old English-learning infants were presented with lists of items of the latter type, they still demonstrated the preference for strong/weak patterns over weak/strong ones. Hence, English-learning infants' are using more than just syllable weight to determine the predominant stress patterns of native language words.

Segmentation: A Precursor to Word-Learning

It is clear that during the first year of life infants are beginning to learn about the segmental and suprasegmental organization of their native language. Although this discovery is interesting in itself, it also may have important implications for understanding how infants learn to segment words from fluent speech. Both segmental and suprasegmental properties of speech have been hypothesized to play a role in word segmentation. Earlier we mentioned that the presence of certain types of phonotactic sequences could be a cue to word boundaries. Consider how this might work for English. If a listener is attempting to segment a sequence like redbug [rɛdbʌg], then the phonotactics of English dictate that there can be a word boundary between [d] and [b], but not between [ɛ] and [d] (because this would leave [db] as the onset of a syllable). Another potential cue to word boundaries is based on the typical contexts in which variants (or allophones) of the same phoneme appear (Bolinger & Gerstman, 1957; Lehiste, 1960). Church (1987) has pointed out that the allophonic variant of /t/ that begins words in English, such as "tap," (i.e., [tʰ]), is not found in other positions of English words, such as the /t/s in "stop" or "pat." Therefore, a listener sensitive to this property of English words could conceivably use this information in deciding whether a word boundary has occurred or not. Finally, suprasegmental properties have also been hypothesized to facilitate word segmentation in English. For example, Cutler and Carter's (1987) finding that a high proportion of words in English conversational speech begin with strong syllables led Cutler and her colleagues (Cutler, 1990, 1994; Cutler & Butterfield, 1992; Cutler & Norris, 1988) to suggest that English listeners make a first pass at segmenting fluent speech into words by assuming that each strong syllable initiates a new word onset.

What would be required for infants to use any of these potential cues to word boundaries in fluent speech? First, they must be sensitive to the distinctions that mark the presence and absence of word boundaries. Thus, in the case of the allophonic variants of /t/, they must be able to discriminate [tʰ] from [t]. Second, they must learn how these cues are distributed in the input (i.e., the contexts in which they can and cannot appear). Third, they must be able to detect and use these cues when processing fluent speech.

Several studies have been conducted to determine whether infants are sensitive to the kinds of distinctions that mark the presence or absence of word boundaries. For example, with respect to possible prosodic markers of word boundaries, Christophe, Dupoux, Bertoncini, and Mehler (1994) found that French newborns discriminate pairs of disyllabic stimuli that either contained or did not contain a word boundary. The pairs of stimuli contained the same phonetic elements (e.g., [mati] from "panorama typique" versus [mati] from "mathematician") but were

distinguished primarily in terms of prosodic differences (i.e., stress and accent). Recall, as well, that Jusczyk, Cutler, et al. (1993a) demonstrated that by 9 months of age, American infants listen longer to words with the types of stress patterns (i.e., strong/weak) that would favor a strong syllable-based segmentation strategy. Similarly, with respect to possible phonotactic cues to word boundaries, Friederici and Wessels' (1993) results show that Dutch 9-month-olds distinguish between phonotactically legal and illegal clusters at the beginnings of words. Finally, there are even some indications that infants are able to distinguish between the kinds of allophonic variants that could serve to mark word boundaries. Hohne and Jusczyk (1994) presented 2-month-olds with pairs such as "nitrate" and "night rate." The allophones of /t/ and /r/ for these items differ in ways that are consistent with the presence (for "night rate") or absence (for "nitrate") of a word boundary. Infants were able to distinguish the items on the basis of these allophonic differences, even when prosodic differences between the words were controlled via digital cross-splicing techniques.

The studies just reviewed show that infants in their first year have the prerequisite capacities to make the kinds of distinctions that could signal the presence of word boundaries. Whether they actually draw on these kinds of distinctions to segment words in the context of fluent speech is another matter. Speech researchers have only recently begun to devise procedures to investigate word segmentation abilities in infants. Still, even with the limited data that are available, it is apparent that infants begin to segment words from fluent speech at some point during the second half of their first year.

Goodsitt, Morgan, and Kuhl (1993) investigated factors that might help to separate and cluster elements within an utterance. The method they devised to examine this issue built upon previous research with the conditioned head-turning procedure which showed that 6.5-month-old infants could discriminate a phonetic contrast embedded in a string of three syllables (Goodsitt, Morse, Ver Hoove, & Cowan, 1984). In their word segmentation study, Goodsitt et al. (1993) first trained 7-month-olds to discriminate the isolated syllables [ti] and [de]. Once training was completed, the target syllables were combined with two other syllables to create a three-syllable string. These three-syllable strings were of one of three types. In invariant-order strings, the ordering of the two nontarget syllables was a fixed sequence. In variable-order stings, the two nontarget syllables could occur in either order. Finally, in redundant strings, only one of the nontarget syllables was used, but it was repeated twice in a row. The general finding was that performance was best with the invariant-order strings. This finding held regardless of whether the syllables were produced with varying intonation or as monotones. Goodsitt et al. attributed the superior performance with invariant-order strings to the fact that it was easier to group the nontarget stimuli into a single cluster and, thus, to separate them from the target syllable. This argument rests on the fact that the two nontarget syllables cohere as a unit because they always occur in the same order, whereas the ordering of the target syllable relative to them varies (sometimes before, sometimes after). Hence, the distributional properties of the input strings favor segmenting them as a two-syllable unit and a monosyllabic unit. In principle, the redundant strings should have behaved in the same fashion, but they did not. Goodsitt et al. suggested that infants were less likely to group them as a unit because the two redundant syllables were acoustically identical and lacked coarticulatory cues.

Morgan (1994) extended this line of investigation in a study that examined how rhythmic properties, in addition to distributional properties, might lead to grouping and segmenting syllables. In one experiment with 8-month-olds, he found evidence that rhythmic cues were quite effective in facilitating the grouping of the nontarget syllables into a unit. Although the most effective combination for grouping the nontarget syllables proved to be a trochaic (strong/weak) rhythmic pattern combined with an invariant syllable order, even when the syllables occurred in a variable order, the presence of a trochaic pattern appeared to induce some clustering in one of the two test sessions. Converging evidence of the effectiveness of rhythmic properties in grouping the syllables was obtained with a second measure that involved the detection of noises superimposed on the stimulus sequences. Specifically, 8-month-olds were less likely to detect the presence of the noise when it occurred between the syllables that were rhythmically clustered and invariantly ordered than when it occurred between another syllable and either of the two syllables in the cluster. In line with adult studies involving click detection (Abrams & Bever, 1969; Ladefoged & Broadbent, 1960), the interpretation of this result is that the noises are harder to perceive in syllables that are clustered together because perceptual units resist interruption. Hence, the results of this study provide some indication that rhythmic and distributional properties of the input influence how infants segment speech.

Morgan and his colleagues have conducted further investigations of how rhythmic properties affect the way that infants group syllables. In one series of studies with 9-month-olds, Morgan and Saffran (1995) extended the range of rhythmic properties by using both iambic (weak/strong) and trochaic (strong/weak) patterns. A consistent pattern of results emerged with both the conditioned headturning and click detection paradigms. Nine-month-olds appeared to integrate information about both rhythmic and distributional properties, in that performance on these tasks was best for sequences with consistent rhythmic patterns and a fixed syllable order. By comparison, 6-month-old infants appeared to respond primarily to consistent rhythmic orders, regardless of whether the syllables occurred in a fixed sequence or not. Hence, their behavior appeared to depend primarily on the presence or absence of rhythmic cues to grouping. Interestingly, there was no indication that these English-learning infants, at either age, performed differently with strong/weak versus weak/strong patterns. Morgan and Saffran suggested that the nature of their test procedure may have worked to neutralize any potential processing advantages for strong/weak patterns. Specifically, their procedures repeatedly presented the same small set of strings to infants. Any advantage for trochaic patterns might be more evident for relatively unexpected or unfamiliar strings. Morgan (1996) provided some empirical support for this view in another study with 6- and 9-month-old infants. Although familiar bisyllables were perceived similarly by both age groups, with no differences for iambic versus trochaic rhythmic patterns, 9-month-olds perceived novel bisyllables as cohesive only when they manifested a trochaic rhythmic pattern. As Morgan noted, these findings for the 9-month-olds are consistent with the use and development of a strong syllable segmentation strategy for parsing words from fluent speech.

The investigations by Morgan and his colleagues provide some indications of how rhythmic and distributional properties can lead infants to group speech input into different clusters. However, the infants in these studies did not have to deal with all the complexities that are presented by a continually changing stream of fluent speech. For instance, assuming that an infant has learned to recognize the sound patterns of some words (e.g., "cookie," "baby," "mommy") when they are presented in isolation, to what extent will they be able to recognize these words when they are embedded in a sentential context? Jusczyk and Aslin (1995) explored this issue by using the headturn preference paradigm to familiarize infants with a pair of isolated words, and then tested to see whether infants responded by listening longer to sentences containing these words, as opposed to sentences without these words. Four different monosyllabic words were used—"feet," "cup," "dog," and "bike." At the start of each experimental session, 7.5-month-olds were familiarized with two of the words on alternating trials until they accumulated 30 sec of listening time to each word. Half of the infants were familiarized with "cup" and "dog" and the other half with "feet" and "bike." During the test phase, four different passages, each consisting of six sentences, were played for the infants. For a given passage, the same test word appeared in all six sentences (although in different positions within each sentence). Two of the passages contained the words heard in the familiarization period, and the other two contained the unfamiliar (i.e., not previously heard) test words. Both the isolated words and the passages were spoken in ID speech. Infants listened significantly longer to the passages containing the familiar test words. Moreover, there was no indication that the infants' prior knowledge of the words had any important bearing on the results. Jusczyk and Aslin concluded that the exposure to the target words in isolation during the familiarization period induced a preference for infants to attend to the sentences containing these words. Interestingly, when 6-month-olds were tested in this same task, they showed no evidence of detecting the familiar words in the sentential contexts. This suggests that word segmentation skills may begin some time between 6- and 7.5-months of age.

Although it is impressive that 7.5-month-olds are able to detect a relation between a word presented in isolation and the same word in a sentential context, there is good reason to believe that language learners only acquire a relatively small proportion of words in this way. Woodward and Aslin (1990) found that even when they explicitly asked mothers to teach 12-month-olds new words, only about 20% of the new words were ever presented in isolation, and some mothers never presented the target words in isolation. Hence, many words that infants learn are likely heard only in sentential contexts. Given the tendency of fluent speakers to coarticulate words (i.e., run one word into another), learning to recognize new words from sentential contexts would appear to be more difficult than learning the same words presented in isolation. To examine the extent to which infants are able to extract new words from sentential contexts, Jusczyk and Aslin (1995) conducted another experiment in which 7.5-month-olds were first exposed to passages containing two target words, and then tested on repetitions of isolated words. The results were similar to their first experiment. Infants listened longer to isolated

words that had been embedded in the passages heard during the familiarization period. Thus, by 7.5 months of age, infants have at least some rudimentary ability to detect the appearance of a word when it occurs in different fluent speech contexts. Moreover, in a final experiment, Jusczyk and Aslin showed that, at least for monosyllabic words, alteration of a single phonetic segment was sufficient to prevent 7.5-month-olds from incorrectly matching an isolated word to a word embedded in a sentence.

Many questions remain about the precise details that infants encode about the sound properties of words in these contexts. One set of issues involves the kind of information infants use to locate the boundaries of words in fluent speech. Newsome and Jusczyk (1995) explored the possibility that English-learning 7.5-month-olds rely on prosodic cues to define word boundaries. More specifically, they investigated whether infants would find it easier to detect words in sentential contexts when the words began with a strong syllable (as is predicted by the metrical segmentation strategy proposed by Cutler and Norris, 1988). To examine this possibility, they familiarized infants with pairs of words with strong/weak stress patterns like "doctor" and "hamlet," and then measured listening times to passages that either contained or did not contain these words. As in the Jusczyk and Aslin study, the infants in Newsome and Jusczyk's study listened significantly longer to the passages containing the target words. Moreover, a preference for the familiar words was obtained even when the infants were familiarized with the words embedded in the passages first, and then tested on isolated words. By comparison, a different pattern of results occurred when Newsome and Jusczyk used words with weak/strong stress patterns like "guitar" and "surprise." Infants familiarized with these words showed no evidence of subsequently recognizing these words in sentential contexts. Instead of matching an isolated occurrence of "guitar" to "guitar" in the passages, the infants showed a significant tendency to match the strong syllable of "guitar" (i.e., "tar") to passages containing the word "guitar." That is, regardless of whether infants were familiarized to "tar" or to "guitar," they listened just as long to passages containing "guitar." In summary, differences in how infants responded to weak/strong, as opposed to strong/weak, words are consistent with a perceptual strategy based on using the occurrence of strong syllables to locate the onsets of new words in fluent speech (i.e., a metrical segmentation strategy).

Why did infants in Newsome and Jusczyk's (1995) study tend to match isolated strong syllables to ones in weak/

strong words (such as "guitar"), but not to ones in strong/weak words (such as "kingdom")? One explanation involves the distributional contexts for the strong syllables in the passages. In particular, whenever a strong/weak word (e.g., "kingdom") appeared in a sentential context in Newsome and Jusczyk's study, the strong syllable for the word (i.e., "king") was always followed by the same weak syllable (i.e., "dom"). However, this was not necessarily true for the strong syllable of the weak/strong words. Thus, the "tar" of "guitar" was followed by "is" on one occasion, by "has" on another, by a sentence boundary on another, and so on. These differences across the various contexts in which the word appears may help to signal a word boundary at the end of "guitar." Since the metrical segmentation strategy would also generate a word boundary at the beginning of the strong syllable "tar," these two factors would combine to make "tar" emerge or pop out of the context as a possible word candidate.

Houston, Jusczyk, and Newsome (1995) explored the possibility that the distributional contexts might explain why 7.5-month-olds responded to the strong syllables of the weak/strong words. They used the same set of weak/strong target words as Newsome and Jusczyk (1995), but they rewrote the sentential materials to use a constant word following a particular target word. For example, "guitar" was always followed by "is" and "surprise" was always followed by "in." In contrast to the earlier investigation, when the 7.5 month-olds were familiarized with these new passages containing "guitar is" and "surprise in," they did not listen significantly longer to the isolated syllables "tar" and "prize" during the test phase. Houston et al. suggested that this was because the distributional contexts may have led the infants to extract the pseudowords "taris" and "prizin." This interpretation was verified in another experiment in which infants who were familiarized with the same passages listened longer to the isolated pseudowords "taris" and "prizin" during the test phase. In other words, when the distributional properties are appropriate, the use of a metrical segmentation strategy may cause infants to perceive strong/weak words in places where there are not any. Therefore, although such a strategy might provide English-learning infants with a useful starting point for segmenting words from fluent speech, it will also fail in identifying some word boundaries. Consequently, English-learning infants will also need to draw on other sources of information in order to accurately locate word boundaries in the input.

There is now some evidence that, toward the end of their first year, English-learners do begin to draw on other

sources of information to locate word boundaries in fluent speech. Myers et al. (1996) examined 10.5-month-olds' capacities to detect altered word boundaries in fluent speech. In a series of experiments, they presented infants with passages that contained a number of 1 sec pauses that occurred either at boundaries between two words, or between two syllables within a word. When listening to unfiltered versions of these passages, the infants listened significantly longer to the ones in which the pauses occurred between the words. However, when listening to low-pass filtered versions of the same passages, infants displayed no significant preference for either type. This suggests that infants' preferences for the passages with the pauses between the words was based on more than how the pauses interacted with prosodic cues to word boundaries. Furthermore, in other experiments comparing performance with strong/weak words to performance with weak/strong words, Myers et al. found that infants were just as likely to perceive interruptions in weak/strong words as in strong/weak words. Myers et al. noted that the presence of robust phonotactic cues in their weak/strong words may have helped infants detect interruptions in these words. They suggest that by 10.5 months, English-learning infants may be using more than just the location of strong syllables to identify the onsets of words. Rather, at this age, they may be integrating multiple sources of information (prosodic, phonotactic, etc.) to locate the boundaries of words in fluent speech (much as Morgan & Saffran, 1995, have suggested). Additional support for the view that 10.5-month-olds are drawing on sources other than prosody to locate word boundaries comes from Houston et al. (1995). They found that 10.5-month-olds tested on their weak/strong passages were able to detect the occurrence of words such as "guitar" and "surprise" in these passages. In fact, these older infants responded to the whole weak/strong words even when their distributional contexts were not varied (e.g., when "guitar" was always followed by "is"). Moreover, unlike their 7.5-month-old counterparts, 10.5-month-olds who were familiarized with "tar" did not respond to passages containing "guitar." Hence, these older infants demonstrated considerable facility in correctly detecting weak/strong words in fluent speech.

One possible scenario, then, for the manner in which word segmentation skills develop in English-learning infants is that they begin with an approximation to locating word boundaries, such as identifying word onsets with strong syllables. This allows them to break up utterances into smaller processing units. The existence of these smaller units may, in turn, enable infants to detect the kinds of regularities (phonotactic, allophonic, etc.) within these units that may also be predictive of the presence of word boundaries. For instance, the infant may be in a better position to observe which types of sounds occur frequently at both edges of these smaller sized units (for further discussion of how working with smaller units may facilitate language acquisition, see Elman, 1993; Newport, 1990, 1991).

Relating Speech Perception Capacities to Larger Units of Linguistic Organization

The notion that the speech signal marks important aspects of the syntactic organization of utterances was proposed more than 30 years ago. McNeill (1966) considered the possibility that listeners could read the entire syntactic organization of utterances directly from the speech signal, but he dismissed this possibility on the grounds that the links between the acoustic dimensions and the syntactic organization are interpretable only if one already knows the syntax. A weaker link between prosody and syntax was put forth during the 1980s, and has come to be known as "prosodic bootstrapping" (Gleitman & Wanner, 1982; Morgan, 1986; Peters, 1983). This view holds that language learners use information in the speech signal to help them group information in utterances into units corresponding to syntactic clauses and phrases, even though the correlation between prosodic cues and syntactic categories is not perfect.

Studies of the perception of fluent speech suggest that boundaries between important units such as clauses and phrases are often marked by changes in prosody, such as increases in syllable durations, shifts in pitch contour, and pausing (Beckman & Edwards, 1990; Cooper & Paccia-Cooper, 1980; Grosjean & Gee, 1987; Klatt, 1975; Lehiste, Olive, & Streeter, 1976; Price, Ostendorf, Shattuck-Hufnagel, & Fong, 1991). In addition, the presence of such prosodic markers in the input does have an impact on adults' comprehension of utterances (Collier & t'Hart, 1975; Lehiste et al., 1976; Price et al., 1991; Scott, 1982; Scott & Cutler, 1984). Moreover, investigations of child-directed speech have shown that such prosodic markers to clausal and phrasal boundaries are present in the input that the child hears (Bernstein Ratner, 1986; Fisher & Tokura, 1996; Morgan, 1986). Of course, the presence of such markers in the input does not, in itself, prove that infants rely on such information in processing speech to identify clausal and phrasal units.

A number of studies have investigated when infants might show some indication of responding to prosodic marking of syntactic units in speech. Hirsh-Pasek et al. (1987) collected speech samples of a woman talking to an 18-month-old. They divided the samples into passages that were 15 to 20 sec long, and then modified the passages by inserting a series of 1 sec pauses in them. Two versions of each passage were produced. In one case, all the pauses were inserted at the boundaries between two clauses; in the other case, an equal number of pauses was inserted between two words in the middle of a clause. Hirsh-Pasek et al. hypothesized that if infants are sensitive to the prosodic marking of clauses in the input, they would find the versions in which the pauses coincided with the clause boundaries preferable to the versions in which the pauses did not coincide with the clause boundaries. Groups of 7- and 10-month-olds were tested using the headturn preference procedure. Both the 7- and 10-month-olds exhibited the predicted preference for the versions in which the pauses coincided with the clause boundaries. Hirsh-Pasek et al. interpreted these findings as an indication that infants as young as 7 months of age are sensitive to the presence of prosodic markers to clausal units. These findings have been replicated by Morgan, Swingley, and Miritai (1993) using a click detection procedure.

The kinds of prosodic changes observed at clause boundaries in English are also present in many other languages (Cruttenden, 1986). For this reason, American infants' responsiveness to these prosodic changes may not be a result of something they have learned about English per se, but instead may be a more general property of utterances in any natural language. Support for the latter view comes from a report that 4½-month-old American infants presented with Polish passages also listened significantly longer to the passages in which pauses coincided with clause boundaries (Jusczyk, 1989).

Although it is conceivable that infants might not need to learn about the particulars of prosodic structure in order to detect clausal units in their native language, this situation is unlikely to hold for subclausal units, such as phrases. The organization of phrasal units often differs from language to language. In languages such as English, which use word order to indicate important grammatical relations, some prosodic marking of information that occurs together within the same phrase is likely. However, case languages like Polish use affixes to mark grammatical relations and allow much freedom in ordering words within a clause. Two words within the same phrase can be separated by words from other phrases. Any prosodic marking of phrasal units in Polish is apt to be very different from that in English. Thus, infants need to discover the nature of prosodic marking of subclausal units in their native language.

Jusczyk, Hirsh-Pasek, et al. (1992) investigated when American infants might show sensitivity to prosodic marking of major phrasal units (Subject Phrase; Predicate Phrase). Again, recordings of a woman talking to a child were used to prepare the stimuli, but now pauses were inserted either between two phrasal groups (Coincident versions) or within a phrasal group (Noncoincident versions). At 6 months, the infants' listening times to the Coincident and Noncoincident versions did not differ significantly. However, by 9 months, the infants showed significantly longer listening times for the Coincident versions of the samples. Thus, in contrast to the results for clausal units, sensitivity to prosodic markers of phrasal units in English does not appear to develop until between 6 and 9 months of age.

Even when the infant can detect the prosodic organization of speech input, it is not always possible to decipher the syntactic organization from the prosody. Indeed, mismatches in the prosodic and syntactic organization may occur even in the simple sentences that are directed to infants acquiring language. Consider the following three sentences.

a. Derek drove the truck.

b. He drove the truck.

c. Did he drive the truck?

In (a), the talker is likely to produce prosodic boundary cues after the subject noun phrase (NP), "Derek." However, in (b), even two-year-old talkers (Gerken, 1991, 1994) either produce no prosodic boundary cues or produce them between the verb and the object NP, "the truck." This is because a weakly stressed pronoun subject tends to be phonologically joined (or "cliticized") to a following stressed verb, that is, the subject and verb form a prosodic unit. Hence, there is no prosodic marking of the syntactic boundary between the subject and the predicate phrases.

How do infants respond to utterances in which prosodic and syntactic boundaries are mismatched? Only a small percentage of the spontaneous speech samples (about 15%) used by Jusczyk, Hirsh-Pasek, et al. (1992) contained potential mismatches of the sort found in (b). Consequently, Gerken, Jusczyk, and Mandel (1994) created new stimulus materials to compare infants' responses to sentences with pronoun subjects, as in (b), to sentences with lexical NP subjects, as in (a). Nine-month-olds exposed to the sentences with lexical NP subjects behaved exactly like the

infants in the Jusczyk, Hirsh-Pasek, et al. study. For example, they listened significantly longer to samples in which pauses were inserted between the subject and verb phrases than to ones in which pauses were inserted between the verb and object NP phrases. In contrast, infants who heard the sentences with pronoun subjects did not show a significant preference for either type of segmentation. In an additional experiment, Gerken et al. used sentences in which there was likely to be a prosodic boundary between a pronoun subject and the verb—namely, sentences with inversions between a pronoun and an auxiliary, that is, yes-no questions as in (c). In such sentences, the pronoun and auxiliary tend to form a separate clitic group. For these sentences, 9-month-olds listened significantly longer to versions with pauses between the subject and verb phrases.

In summary, the correlation between prosodic and syntactic units in English speech is less than perfect. However, as discussed in the previous section with respect to words, the smaller subclausal sized groupings afforded by the prosody could also reduce the size of the processing window in a way that allows the language learner to detect certain distributional patterns (such as the fact that certain words like "the" may appear frequently at some points within these units—for example, at the beginning—but never at other points, for example, at the end of such a unit).

Given that infants are sensitive to prosodic markers of syntactic units, when might they actually begin using this information in segmenting speech? How can we determine if infants are truly organizing the incoming speech signal into units such as clauses or phrases? One approach is to show that such units play a role in the way infants process speech. For example, are such units used in encoding and remembering information conveyed in speech? Early studies in the field of psycholinguistics found that adults could remember information better when the materials had a linguistic, rather than an arbitrary, organization (Marks & Miller, 1964; Miller & Isard, 1963; Suci, 1967).

Analogously, prosody could provide infants with an organization for encoding and remembering speech information. Mandel, Jusczyk, and Kemler Nelson (1994) investigated whether prosodic organization enhances 2-month-olds' memory for speech. They used the HAS procedure to determine whether words that are prosodically linked within a clause are better remembered by infants than words produced as individual items from a list. If prosody helps in perceptual organization during on-line speech processing, then memory for words should be better in a sentential context than in a list. Half of the infants heard stimuli that were produced as complete sentences;

the other half heard the same sequences of words was taken from long lists of words spoken in isolation. The overall durations of both types of materials were matched. During the preshift phase, infants repeatedly heard either a single sentence or a list sequence. Following habituation to this stimulus, the preshift phase ended and was followed by a two-minute silent interval. In the postshift phase, the infants heard either the same stimulus as during the preshift phase, one that differed by one word, or one that differed by two words. The results indicated that performance was significantly better for the sentences than for the lists. A follow-up experiment replicated and extended the findings by showing that 2-month-olds' memory for information within a sentence was better than for the same information in fragments of two adjoining sentences. More recently, Mandel, Kemler Nelson, and Jusczyk (1996) examined the extent to which the presence of sentential prosody enhanced 2-month-olds' abilities to encode and remember the sequential order of information within an utterance. Once again, infants performed significantly better when the information was presented within the same sentential utterance than when it occurred as parts of two different utterances. Taken together, the results of these studies suggest that the prosodic organization afforded by sentences does facilitate infants' processing and memory for speech.

Thus, even infants as young as 2 months of age appear to benefit from the organization afforded by sentential prosody. The data available at this time indicate that not only are infants sensitive to at least some types of prosodic markers at a very early age, but these markers may play a role in what infants remember about utterances.

What Do Infants Retain about What They Hear?

Throughout the course of language development, infants must learn and retain various kinds of information about the sound patterns of their native language. For example, they must learn the different facets of the phonology of the native language, such as which sounds are included, what constraints there are on how sounds can be ordered, how sounds alternate with one another, where stresses are typically placed in words, how pronunciations change when affixes are added, etc. In addition to these general characteristics of native language sound patterns, language learners also need to retain considerable information about individual items if they are to be successful in building up a vocabulary (or lexicon) and in recognizing words. Although word recognition clearly demands that infants have sufficient discriminative capacities to distinguish the sound pattern of one word from another, it also demands that they retain sufficient information about the sound pattern of a word to recognize it when it is spoken.

In contrast to the extensive literature that exists on infants' speech discrimination capacities, considerably less is known about what information they encode and store about speech. There are some indications that information about maternal speech, particularly prosodic information, is being retained even during the prenatal period. The work of DeCasper and Fifer (1980) suggests that newborns have encoded sufficient information about their own mother's voice to prefer it over the voice of another infant's mother. Similarly, the work of Mehler et al. (1988) and Moon et al. (1993) suggests that newborn infants have extracted enough general information from their mother's speech to recognize when someone else is speaking the mother's native language or a foreign language. Moreover, there is evidence that information of an even more specific sort is retained prenatally. DeCasper and Spence (1986) had pregnant mothers read a particular story aloud during their last 6 weeks of pregnancy. Shortly after the infants were born, they were given a choice between listening to the familiar passage or a novel one. The infants exhibited a significant preference for the familiar passage. In contrast, a control group showed no significant preference for either of the two passages. Thus, the prenatal exposure to the passage subsequently affected the infants' auditory preference.

Infants are retaining some information about the speech to which they are exposed. Determining just how much detail they remember is important for understanding both the development of speech perception capacities and the development of the lexicon. With respect to speech perception capacities, there has been considerable debate about how the representations are structured. For example, do infants represent speech as strings of phonetic segments (Eimas, 1982; Werker, 1991) or as syllables (Jusczyk, 1985a; Mehler, Dupoux, & Segui, 1990)? More recently, there has been discussion as to whether infants retain abstract prototypes of speech sound categories (Kuhl, 1991) or specific exemplars of speech sounds they have heard (Jusczyk, 1992). How these issues are resolved also has implications for our understanding of the organization and development of the lexicon. For example, an indication that infants' representations of speech sounds only encode sufficient detail to distinguish an item from other items already in the lexicon, would suggest that representations become more and more refined and detailed as the size of the lexicon grows (Charles-Luce & Luce, 1990, 1995).

Investigators have used a variety of different methods to provide information about the nature of infants' representations of speech sounds. What these procedures often have in common is the presentation of a series of different stimuli rather than just a single contrastive pair. For instance, Hillenbrand (1983) used the conditioned headturning paradigm to first train 6-month-olds on a contrast between the stop [ba] and the nasal [ma]. During subsequent stages of training, he added new syllables to each category (e.g., [da] and [na]) and showed that infants could generalize to different stops and nasals. Similarly, a number of investigations with younger infants have modified the high amplitude sucking procedure to present multiple instances from a particular speech sound category (Bertoncini, Bijeljac-Babic, Jusczyk, Kennedy, & Mehler, 1988; Bijeljac-Babic et al., 1993; Jusczyk, Bertoncini, Bijeljac-Babic, Kennedy, & Mehler, 1990; Jusczyk & Derrah, 1987). For example, Jusczyk and Derrah (1987) familiarized 2-month-olds with a series of four different CV syllables beginning with an initial [b]. Then during the postshift period, a new CV syllable was added to the set of familiar ones. In one instance, the new syllable also began with [b] but contained a novel vowel. In another case, both the consonant and vowel were novel. Jusczyk and Derrah had hypothesized that if infants perceived a common [b] segment in the different syllables, then a new syllable with the familiar consonant should be less novel than a syllable that contained both a new consonant and a new vowel. In fact, infants increased their sucking significantly, and by the same amount, to both kinds of changes. A similar pattern of results with both newborns and 2-month-olds in two other investigations (Bertoncini et al., 1988; Jusczyk et al., 1990) led Jusczyk and his colleagues to claim that infants at these ages are representing speech in terms of syllabic units rather than as strings of phonetic segments.

An investigation by Bijeljac-Babic et al. (1993) arrived at the same conclusion by a slightly different means. They investigated whether infants keep track of the number of syllables in an utterance. They used the HAS procedure to present newborns with more than 70 different trisyllables (of varied phonetic composition) during the preshift period. During the postshift period, one group of infants was switched to bisyllables. The infants responded to this change in the number of syllables. In a subsequent experiment, the authors used bisyllabic utterances composed of one of two types: either four or six phonetic segments. In contrast to the earlier change involving numbers of syllables, the infants did not respond to the change in the numbers of phonetic segments. These authors interpreted this as another indication that infants at this age are representing speech in terms of syllabic units.

These kinds of methods, which employ multiple stimuli, provide information about infants' representations of speech because in order to detect a change in the stimulus set the listener must encode enough information to distinguish one element from another. In other words, because the order in which the stimuli occur is typically randomized, the infant cannot simply compare two successive stimuli and determine whether they are the same or different. Rather, detection of the new element requires that the infant compare it to some representation of the already familiar syllables. Still, these kinds of investigations only provide information about immediate memory for a train of ongoing stimuli. What is left unanswered is the extent to which infants are able to retain information over some delay period.

Several recent studies have examined infants' retention of information over brief delay periods. Jusczyk, Kennedy, and Jusczyk (1995) tested 2-month-olds with a modified version of the HAS procedure which included a delay period between the preshift and postshift phases of the experiment. During the delay, a series of slides was shown without any accompanying auditory stimulation. The infants displayed evidence of remembering considerable detail about the preshift stimuli. Even minimal changes of a single phonetic feature were detected. More recently, Jusczyk, Jusczyk, Kennedy, Schomberg, and Koenig (1995) examined the ability of infants to retain information about bisyllabic utterances. During the preshift phase, 2-month-olds were exposed to a set of bisyllabic utterances which either shared (i.e., [ba′ mIt], [ba′ zi], [ba′ lo], [ba′ dəs]) or did not share (i.e., [nɛ′ lo], [pæ′ zi], [čŭ′ dəs], [ko′ mIt]) a common syllable. The presence of a common syllable during the preshift phase did lead to a significant improvement in the infants' ability to detect the addition of a new item to the set during the postshift phase. Only infants who had heard the set with the common syllable detected the addition of a new bisyllable (e.g., [ba′ nʌl] or [na′ bʌl]) to the postshift set. Jusczyk, Jusczyk, et al. interpreted this as an indication that the presence of a common syllable enhanced the encoding of these items during the delay period, allowing them to be better remembered.

As discussed earlier, there are rather severe limitations on the methods that can be used to examine memory processes in young infants. For example, it is difficult with the HAS procedure to use a delay period longer than about two minutes because the reintroduction of any sound after this period tends to elicit spontaneous increases in sucking regardless of whether the sound is novel or not. This makes it difficult to conduct systematic investigations of the effects of different delay periods. However, the prospects of carrying out such an investigation with older infants are considerably higher because headturning techniques can be used.

There is certainly reason to believe that during the second half of the first year infants have some capacity to remember information about specific words that they have heard. Studies of the development of word comprehension suggest that infants first begin to show recognition of words around 8- to 10-months of age (Benedict, 1979; Huttenlocher, 1974). This provides some indication that infants are retaining information about the sound structures of some words to which they have been exposed. The earliest evidence that infants recognize familiar lexical items comes from a study by Mandel, Jusczyk, and Pisoni (1995) using the headturn preference procedure. Four and a half-month-olds were presented with repetitions of their own name, as well as other names that either shared the same stress pattern or had a different stress pattern (e.g., if name = "Aaron," then same-stress foil = "Corey" and different-stress foils = "Christine" and "Michelle"). Infants listened reliably longer to their name than to either the same-stress or the different-stress names. Thus, there is evidence by 4.5 months of age that infants recognize some features of their name, a highly frequent lexical item in their language environment.

Though important, the Mandel et al. (1995) study, and others documenting early word comprehension, cannot provide information about how much experience with a word is necessary for infants to recognize it on another occasion. What is required is systematic control of the amount of exposure that infants have to particular items, followed by a test of recognition of these same items. An initial step in this direction has been made by Jusczyk, Hohne, Jusczyk, and Redanz (1993; Hohne, Jusczyk, & Redanz, 1994). They arranged to visit 8-month-olds in their homes for 10 days during a two-week period. Each day the infants heard a series of tape-recorded stories produced by the same talker (half the infants heard one talker, half heard another). Approximately two weeks after the last home visit, the infants were tested in the laboratory to see what they remembered about what they had heard. One group of infants was presented with lists of words that had actually been used in the stories. The words were produced by either the familiar talker or another talker. The infants listened significantly

longer to the words produced by the familiar talker, suggesting that they had retained information about her voice quality. In another investigation (Hohne et al., 1994), infants heard a subset of the same stories for a ten-day period. However, five different talkers and two different story orders were used, so that on each day an infant heard a different talker/story order combination. Once again, after a two week delay, the infants came to the lab for testing. This time they heard lists of words that were either novel or from the stories. For a given infant, the lists were produced by a single talker. The infants who had participated in the home visits listened significantly longer to the words that came from the stories, whereas a control group (who had not heard the stories) showed no preference for either type of list. Thus, there are indications that 8-month-old infants do engage in some long-term storage of information about voices and words that they have heard. Since word comprehension skills appear to begin around this time, it is interesting that infants are storing information about the sound patterns of words, even in the absence of any clear referents for these sound patterns. Hence, word learning may occur in two directions. Sometimes infants may have a meaning in mind that they attempt to link to the right sound pattern, and sometimes they may have a sound pattern that they attempt to link to the right meaning.

Much remains to be determined about how infants' memories for speech information develop. However, the studies to date suggest that, from an early age, infants do retain some information about what they hear. Moreover, at least some of this information is retained for periods as long as two weeks.

Audio-Visual Speech Processing

One of the most intriguing aspects of speech perception was reported by McGurk and MacDonald (1976) and is referred to as the "McGurk effect." The McGurk effect occurs when a mismatch is created between the visual information for articulation and the auditory information for perception. For example, adults who view a videotape of a talker articulating the syllable [ba] while listening to an audiotape of the syllable [ga] synchronized to the videotape, typically hear the combined audio-visual stimulus as [da]. It is as if the place of articulation information (bilabial from [ba]; velar from [ga]) is blended into the intermediate alveolar [da].

Not all articulatory gestures have unique visual cues. For example, while articulation of the point vowels ([a], [i], [u]) is strongly correlated with distinct positions of the lips and jaw, several consonant distinctions ([da]-[ta], [ga]-[ka]) have articulatory gestures that are essentially invisible (see Summerfield, 1979). Nevertheless, visual cues to articulation can be useful to speech perception, particularly under degraded conditions, such as a noisy environment (Sumby & Pollack, 1954).

The enhancement of an ambiguous speech signal by visual information about articulation can only occur if the listener/observer has knowledge (by genetic or experiential factors) of the audio-visual correlations. Kuhl and Meltzoff (1982, 1984) provided the first demonstration that infants' perception of speech sounds was influenced by visual-articulatory information. They showed that 4-month-olds looked longer at a visual display of the articulation of the vowels [a] and [i] when the corresponding auditory stimulus was present. That is, infants preferred to fixate the visual and auditory events that matched articulation with perception. Interestingly, infants did not show a preference for the matching audio-visual stimuli when the sound was a pure-tone matched in duration, amplitude, and synchrony to the articulatory gesture. Thus, spectral information appeared to play some role in this preference for the audio-visual match.

Subsequent research has shown that the integration of auditory and visual information for speech perception is sometimes robust yet often subtle. For example, asynchrony of auditory and visual events can still lead to integration effects in speech perception (Massaro & Cohen, 1993), yet integration is absent for speech materials consisting of words (Easton & Basala, 1982). Moreover, integration can occur in adults for visual and auditory information that is artificially matched, such as a female face with a male voice (Green, Kuhl, Meltzoff, & Stevens, 1991), a synthetic rendering of a face with synthetic speech (Massaro & Cohen, 1990), or 3-tone nonspeech sounds with a face (Kuhl, Williams, & Meltzoff, 1991). Finally, Massaro and his colleagues (Massaro, Cohen, & Smeele, 1995; Massaro, Tsuzaki, Cohen, Gesi, & Heredia, 1993) have shown that native speakers of different languages are influenced by audio-visual speech stimuli in different ways depending on the phonetic, phonemic, and phonotactic aspects of their language.

The fact that infants did not match 3-tone nonspeech stimuli to visual displays of vowel articulation (Kuhl et al., 1991) suggests that the more subtle and language-specific influences on audio-visual matching require considerable postnatal experience. Apparently, sufficient experience has been obtained by 5 months of age because Rosenblum,

Schmuckler, and Johnson (1997) have shown that infants habituated to an audio-visual display of [va] do not dishabituate to an audio-visual display whose components are audio-[ba] and visual-[va]. However, infants did dishabituate to an audio-[da] and visual-[va] display. Because the former test display is perceived by adults as equivalent to the audio-visual [va], whereas the latter is perceived by adults as a [da], these results suggest that by 5 months of age infants are combining information from the visual and auditory modalities in a manner similar to the perceptual system of adults.

Perception of Other Complex Auditory Signals

One issue that has been frequently debated in speech research is the extent to which speech perception employs specialized neural mechanisms. For this reason, speech researchers have often carried out studies in which the perception of speech and nonspeech sounds has been compared (Best, Morrongiello, & Robson, 1981; Liberman, Harris, Kinney, & Lane, 1961; Liberman, Isenberg, & Rakerd, 1981; Miller, Weir, Pastore, Kelly, & Dooling, 1976; Pisoni, 1977). One difficulty in making such comparisons is that many nonspeech stimuli lack the complexity and systematic organization of human speech. Another difficulty is that when nonspeech stimuli are made more complex, some researchers claim that parallels between speech and nonspeech are observed because the speech processor has been tricked into processing the nonspeech signals.

Despite this interpretive difficulty associated with the use of nonspeech signals, there is another realm of human auditory perception in which listeners encounter complex and systematically organized sound patterns, namely, music. Moreover, as with spoken language, different cultures often have different systems of musical organization. Hence, there is not a single form of musical organization, but many different forms. There are also parallels between some of the structural features of language and music, such as a succession of pitch changes (melody in music; intonation in speech) and rhythmic patterns.

Research on infants' perception of musical patterns provides an interesting perspective for viewing the development of speech perception capacities. Close parallels in the way infants process speech and musical stimuli would strengthen claims that general auditory mechanisms underlie perception in both domains. Diverging patterns of results for speech and music would lend support to the view that specialized processing mechanisms handle perception of one or both types of signals.

Early studies on musical perception explored the extent to which infants could discriminate one musical pattern from another. For example, Chang and Trehub (1977) presented 5-month-olds with the same 6-tone sequence repeatedly, and then tested to see whether they could discriminate changes in the sequence. One group of infants heard a transposition that altered the absolute frequencies of the individual tones, but preserved their melodic contour. Another group heard a pattern for which the component tones were reordered. Only the latter group discriminated the change. These results have several implications. First, they indicate that 5-month-olds can discriminate one melodic pattern from another. Second, they suggest that the infants in the first group "recognized" the original melodic pattern even though it had been transposed. Note that the suggestion that infants treat transposed melodies as the same is reminiscent of what happens in speech when listeners recognize the same utterance produced by two different talkers. Although the parallel here is based on a null finding, a subsequent study (Trehub, Bull, & Thorpe, 1984) provided additional support for it. Trehub et al. tested 8- to 11-month-olds with the conditioned headturning procedure. The infants were trained to turn their heads whenever a change occurred in the contour and frequency range of a melody. The infants were able to discriminate a variety of different changes, including ones that preserved contour and interval information (i.e., transpositions), ones that preserved contour but not exact intervals, and ones that violated contour. Hence, under optimal listening conditions, the infants were able to discriminate all these types of changes. However, in a second experiment, Trehub et al. increased the task demands by inserting a distractor sequence between repetitions of the standard melody and between the standard and transformed melodies. Under these circumstances the only types of changes that infants responded to were contour-violating sequences. Trehub et al. argued that the infants treated the transpositions and contour-preserving changes as equivalent to the standard melody.

With respect to melodic contours, then, infants appeared to focus on relational as opposed to absolute pitch information. Consequently, when individual notes were changed, but the melodic contour was preserved, infants tended to treat the new pattern as equivalent to the original melody (Demany & Armand, 1984; Trehub et al., 1984; Trehub, Thorpe, & Morrongiello, 1987). By comparison, there is now evidence from several different studies that infants are very sensitive to changes in melodic contour (McCall & Melson, 1970; Melson & McCall, 1970; Trehub et al.,

1984; Trehub, Thorpe, & Morrongiello, 1985). Note that because some of these changes in melodic contour involved the re-ordering of notes from the original melody (as opposed to adding new notes), this suggests that infants are attentive to the sequential ordering of the notes. This sensitivity to sequential ordering in a well-formed musical structure parallels Mandel et al.'s (1996) finding that 2-month-olds remember the sequential order of syllables in utterances with well-formed sentential prosody.

Infants' sensitivity to the rhythmic patterning of music has also been investigated. Demany, McKenzie, and Vurpillot (1977) first reported evidence that 2- to 3-month-olds discriminate changes in rhythmic patterns. They used a series of very brief (40 ms) tone-bursts and varied the intervals between the tones. Subsequently, Trehub and Thorpe (1989) demonstrated that 6- to 8-month-olds' perception of rhythmic patterns is global (i.e., independent of the absolute durations of the individual notes). In particular, the infants were able to detect changes in the overall rhythmic pattern of a sequence, even when the tempo (i.e., whether it was played fast or slow) was varied randomly. Thus, just as infants display some capacity to normalize across different speaking rates (Eimas & Miller, 1980), so, too, do they appear to compensate for different tempos in musical sequences.

As is the case for speech, music is organized into units of varying temporal extents. A short segment may serve as a unit at one level and then join with other segments to form longer units at higher levels of organization (Deutsch & Feroe, 1981; Lehrdahl & Jackendoff, 1983). And just as speech syllables join to form words and words combine into phrases and phrases into clauses, musical tones combine to form melodic and rhythmic figures, musical phrases, and larger sections of musical pieces. As noted earlier, there is evidence that infants listening to fluent speech are sensitive to the presence of clausal and phrasal units (e.g., Hirsh-Pasek et al., 1987; Jusczyk, Hirsh-Pasek, et al., 1992). To what extent do infants display sensitivity to comparable units of musical organization? Krumhansl and Jusczyk (1990) explored this issue by presenting 4.5-month-olds with passages from Mozart minuets that were altered by inserting 1-sec pauses either at musical phrase boundaries (Coincident versions) or at other locations within a phrase (Noncoincident versions). The infants listened significantly longer to the Coincident versions of the musical pieces, suggesting that they are sensitive to phrasal units in music. Analyses of the musical passages suggested that infants were responding to markers of musical phrase boundaries such as a decline in pitch and lengthening of the final note just before the phrase boundaries. A subsequent study by Jusczyk and Krumhansl (1993) provided further evidence that the direction of pitch change (i.e., falling) and tone durations (i.e., lengthening) are the critical cues to which infants respond. It is interesting that these same cues parallel ones that are important for signaling clause boundaries in speech (i.e., declination in fundamental frequency and syllable lengthening).

There is also evidence of another kind which suggests that infants group and process patterns of tones. Thorpe and her colleagues (Thorpe & Trehub, 1989; Thorpe, Trehub, Morrongiello, & Bull, 1988) investigated the ability of 6- to 9-month-olds to detect the occurrence of a pause in musical sequences. The musical patterns consisted of three tones of one type followed by three tones of another type. The pauses were inserted either within a group of similar notes (structure-disrupting changes) or between the two different groups of notes (structure-conserving changes). The infants were better able to detect the pauses in the former condition. This finding demonstrates that the musical grouping does affect infants' abilities to react to the pauses. However, in this instance, the infants appear to behave differently with respect to speech and music. Recall that Morgan (1994) found that infants were significantly worse at detecting a noise when it occurred between two syllables within a speech unit than when it occurred between two syllables that were not part of the same perceptual unit. Whether this reflects an important difference in how infants process speech and music cannot be fully determined at this point because there were other factors that varied across the two studies (e.g., the kind of training used, the detection of a noise as opposed to silence).

An additional point of contact between research on music and speech involves how experience affects infants' perceptual capacities. Lynch, Eilers, Oller, and Urbano (1990) compared 6-month-olds' abilities to distinguish melodies based on familiar Western (major) scales or unfamiliar Javanese (pélog) scales. Unlike adult subjects who detected changes more easily for the melodies based on the Western scales, the infants performed equivalently to melodic changes based on either scale type. This suggests that in early stages of development, infants are equally adept at processing either scale type, but that culture-specific experience enhances their ability to process one type of scale over the other. A follow-up study by Lynch and Eilers (1992) compared the ability of infants at different ages to detect mistunings in Western major and augmented scales and in Javanese pélog scales. One-year-olds performed better with materials from Western major scales than they did for either the Western augmented or Javanese pélog scales. By comparison, 6-month-olds performed better with both types of Western scales than with the Javanese pélog scale. Lynch and Eilers interpret these findings as an indication that experience with musical tuning begins to affect perception in the second half of the first postnatal year. Similarly, Trehub and her colleagues have found evidence that infants from Western cultures are better able to detect changes in melodic patterns when they conform to Western scale structure than when the patterns deviate from it (Cohen, Thorpe, & Trehub, 1987; Trainor & Trehub, 1992; Trehub, Thorpe, & Trainor, 1990). Once again, these findings, which show that increasing experience with a particular musical system during the first year of life affects the perception of melodic changes, appear to parallel the kinds of changes that have been observed in the processing of native and non-native language speech contrasts. More extensive research in this area should clarify whether the parallels are simply superficial ones or indicative of some common developmental process.

A final area in which studies of speech and nonspeech have been informative of specialized versus shared underlying mechanisms is duplex perception. Duplex perception refers to the combination of two components of a speech sound, typically under dichotic listening conditions, with the resultant perception of the full speech sound *and* the "chirp" created by the rapid formant transition which serves as one of the two components. The fact that adults simultaneously perceive both a fused speech percept and a nonspeech "chirp" has been taken as strong evidence that the speech mode is separable from the remainder of the auditory system (Liberman & Mattingly, 1989). Adding fuel to this perspective was Whalen and Liberman's (1987) finding that the "chirps" presented to one ear could be below detection threshold and the integration of the components would still lead to the correct identification of the speech sound.

Eimas and Miller (1992) extended this technique to 3- and 4-month-old infants using the habituation/discrimination technique of Best et al. (1988). In one ear, infants heard all of the components of the syllable [da] or [ga] except the third formant transition which differentiated between these two stop consonants. In the other ear, infants heard the third formant transition appropriate for either [da] or [ga]. After meeting the habituation of looking criterion, each infant in the experimental group was shifted from one third-formant transition to the other, whereas the control group received the same stimulus combinations throughout the entire testing procedure. Eimas and Miller reported that infants reliably discriminated the change in the third formant, even when it was attenuated by 48 dB (which adults judged as detectable on only 4% of the trials). Thus, Eimas and Miller concluded that 3- to 4-month-olds "integrated the information from two distal sources and from different directions to form unified percepts of a presumably phonetic nature" and that "the presumed precedence of speech perception [over nonspeech perception] may be characteristic of the processing of speech by infants" (p. 344).

Unfortunately, this interpretation of duplex perception is not without controversy. Bailey and Herrmann (1993) reported that what Whalen and Liberman (1987) characterized as "below threshold chirps" were, in fact, detectable. Thus, the "precedence" of the speech over the nonspeech mode was called into question. Hall and Pastore (1992) reported that a duplex perception effect was present for nonspeech signals (musical chords), again calling into question the uniqueness of duplex perception to the speech mode. Thus, there continues to be controversy as to whether a specialized speech mode exists, particularly one that is unique to humans and that cannot be accounted for by general auditory mechanisms used to process other complex nonspeech signals.

DEVELOPMENTAL MODELS OF SPEECH PERCEPTION

Since the earliest studies of infant speech perception, a number of models have been proposed to account for the presence, onset, and developmental change in speech perception skills. These developmental models take an information processing approach similar to models proposed by cognitive psychologists rather than a computational approach, which will be discussed in a later section. In general, the models of development are of two types. The models proposed by Werker, Best, and Kuhl are primarily concerned with changes in phonetic perception. Models of the development of phonetic perception attempt to characterize the kinds of changes that occur in phonetic perception as a result of acquiring a native language. A central concern of these accounts is to explain the pattern of loss in sensitivity to certain non-native contrasts as a result of increased familiarity and experience with a native language.

In addition, these models aim to account for the native language organization of phonetic categories. In contrast, the models developed by Mehler, Dupoux, and Segui (1990), Suomi (1993), and Jusczyk (1997) attempt to relate changes in speech perception capacities to developments in word recognition. Models relating changes in speech perception to the growth of word recognition focus on how infants use their speech perception capacities to recognize words in fluent speech. These models generally take infants' early perceptual capacities for distinguishing speech contrasts as a starting point, and then consider how the task demands associated with developing efficient word recognition skills influence the organization of these capacities.

Werker's Model of the Development of Phonemic Perception

Werker (1991) described evidence suggesting that changes in sensitivity to non-native phonetic contrasts were not so much the result of a permanent sensory loss, but rather a re-organization of perceptual processes. In particular, she pointed out that adults' discrimination of non-native contrasts can be improved under different testing conditions (Werker & Tees, 1984) or with training (Logan, Lively, & Pisoni, 1991; Werker & Logan, 1985). She contrasted five possible explanations for how re-organization occurs:

1. By the manner in which experience affects auditory/perceptual development.
2. By resetting the parameters of a phonetic module.
3. By the sounds produced in cannonical babbling which mediate perceptual processes.
4. By the development of general cognitive abilities.
5. By the emergence of a phonological system in the receptive lexicon.

Werker originally favored the fifth explanation. In particular, Werker & Lalonde (1988) argued that re-organization was related to the emergence of phonemic categories toward the end of the first year. They hypothesized that infants' processing of speech shifts from a phonetic mode to a phonemic mode (i.e., one that is tied to making meaningful contrasts between different words).

Although Werker (1991) favored the fifth type of explanation, she did not rule out the fourth type of explanation, which holds that the re-organization is an instance of an initial biologically based categorization ability coming under the mediation of cognitive control. In fact, it is this type of explanation that Werker has promoted in her most recent accounts of perceptual re-organization. For example, Lalonde and Werker (1995) point to correlations between improved performance on certain cognitive and perceptual tasks and shifts in sensitivity to non-native contrasts. What these different kinds of tasks appear to have in common is that they require the ability to integrate disparate sources of information—an ability that is believed to emerge at some time during the period (8- to 10-months) when the decline in sensitivity to non-native contrasts is typically observed. The extent to which a common factor underlies the changes in performance on these different tasks remains to be determined. If Werker is correct in her hypothesis, it would be an indication that the source of the re-organization is not specific to language, but is, instead, the result of general changes in infants' information processing capacities and cognitive abilities.

Best's Perceptual Assimilation Model (PAM)

This model was an attempt to explain the pattern of results that had been reported for the perception of non-native contrasts. Best et al. (1988) were the first to observe that not all non-native contrasts undergo the same kind of decline in discriminability. Rather, some non-native contrasts such as the Zulu lateral/medial click remain easy for non-native listeners to discriminate despite their lack of experience with these contrasts. Best (1993, 1995) has proposed that whether or not the discriminability of a particular non-native contrast will show a decline depends upon the way in which the non-native phones map to existing phonemic categories in the native language. She notes that there are a number of possible relations between the phones in a particular non-native contrast and ones in the native language. All other things being equal, the better the mapping of the phones in a non-native contrast to distinct phonemic categories in the native language, the easier the discrimination. Thus, discrimination is predicted to be excellent for what Best refers to as the Two-Category case, in which each non-native phone is assimilated to a different native phoneme category. Discrimination is also predicted to be good to moderate for what Best calls the Category-Goodness case, in which both non-native phones map to the same native phoneme category but differ considerably in how close they come to a good example of the category. Similarly, good to moderate discriminability is also predicted for a Nonassimilable case (like the Zulu lateral/medial clicks) for which both non-native phones fall outside of the native language phonetic space and are heard as nonspeech sounds. Poor to moderate discriminability is predicted for the Uncategorizable case in which both non-native phones fall into regions of phonetic space that are outside of any particular native phoneme categories. Finally, the poorest discrimination is predicted for the Single-Category case, in which the non-native phones map to the same native language phoneme category but are equally distant from a good example of the category.

Best and her colleagues (Best, 1991; Best, McRoberts, Goodell, Womer, Insabella, Klatt, Luke, & Silver, 1990; Best, McRoberts, LaFleur, & Silver-Isenstadt, 1995) have selected a range of different non-native contrasts in order to test predictions of the model. Results from these investigations have generally supported the model. In addition, recent findings from other laboratories are also consistent with the predictions of PAM (Polka & Werker, 1994). One inconsistent result from Best's own investigations occurred for a Zulu lateral fricative voicing distinction (Best et al., 1990). This should have been a Two-Category case, and therefore, should not undergo a decline. However, although the 6- to 8-month-old English-learning infants did discriminate the contrast, 10- to 12-month-olds did not. Best (1995) indicates that adult non-native listeners often report hearing these sounds as impermissible phonotactic clusters in English. Thus, she speculates that the infants may not have been able to assimilate these phones to native language categories. Another problematic case involves the velar voiceless aspirated versus velar ejective contrast from Zulu. For adult listeners, this contrast is of the Category-Goodness type and is easily discriminated. However, the 10- to 12-month-olds did not discriminate this contrast. The reasons for this are not clear at present. Best has suggested that this dip in development may have to do with the discovery of higher order phonological category information at this age.

Kuhl's Native Language Magnet (NLM) Theory

Kuhl's (1993) theory is intended to cover the period during the first year prior to the time when infants acquire word meaning and contrastive phonology. The starting assumption of the theory is that infants' innate endowment provides them with the ability to categorize speech sounds into groupings that are separated by natural boundaries. The natural boundaries are not the result of any specialized phonetic processing mechanisms but, rather, stem from general auditory processing mechanisms. At some point before 6 months of age, infants develop a processing mechanism that goes beyond the auditory level. In particular, Kuhl cites investigations from her own laboratory (Kuhl, 1993) that suggest that, by this age, infants show evidence of language-specific categories for vowels. Vowel categories are hypothesized to be organized around best instances, or prototypes, which act as "perceptual magnets." The prototype for a vowel category is said to draw other stimuli toward it, effectively reducing the perceptual distance between it and other adjacent vowels. One consequence of this proposal is that stimuli that are highly similar to the prototype are assumed to be less discriminable than are stimuli near the periphery of the category. The prototype for a vowel category presumably reflects the distributional properties of different instances of the vowel that infants have heard.

The NLM explains changes in the perception of nonnative contrasts with reference to the perceptual space that represents language prototypes (note that this view of shrinking and stretching of perceptual space with the development of native language categories is very similar to one expressed by Jusczyk, 1992). In particular, perceptual magnets may cause certain boundaries to disappear as the space is reorganized to reflect the nature of the native language categories. The disappearance of certain boundaries may allow the developing magnets to pull in sounds that were discriminable by infants at an earlier point in development. Kuhl further suggests that magnet effects precede developmentally the loss of sensitivity to non-native contrasts.

The NLM offers an account for why certain changes might occur in the perception of non-native contrasts. However, at this point, the predictions of the model are much less specific than ones following from PAM. It will be interesting to see just how widespread the phenomenon of perceptual magnets is both within a particular language and across different languages. In addition, it will be useful to obtain more precise information about when perceptual magnets first appear in development.

The Syllable Acquisition, Representation, and Access Hypothesis (SARAH) Model

This model was proposed by Mehler, Dupoux, and Segui (1990) to explain the relation among speech perception capacities, word recognition processes, and the acquisition of a lexicon. The model assumes that there is a strong correspondence between the processes used by infants to acquire a lexicon and those underlying lexical access in adults. According to the model, infants initially possess three important components that make the acquisition of a lexicon possible. The first of these is a syllabic filter. In particular, SARAH postulates that this filter chops continuous speech into syllable-sized segments. Only legal syllable structures, such as CV, CVC, V, and CCVC syllables in English, for which talker-specific and speaking rate variables have been factored out, are passed by this filter. The second component is a phonetic analyzer, which provides a description of the syllable in terms of a universal set of phonetic segments. This allows the syllable to be mapped to an internal code that is related to the articulatory gestures required to produce it. The third component is a word boundary detector which uses syllabic representations and other acoustic information to compute word boundary cues.

The model posits that the change from a language general capacity to one attuned to infants' native language depends on the operation of two specialized mechanisms. The first of these is unlearning, or selective stabilization. In effect, the system becomes attuned to those phonetic contrasts, syllables, and word boundary detectors that work best for the native language. Mehler et al. are not very clear about just how this happens, but they do say that it occurs prior to the acquisition of a lexicon, and suggest that it depends on statistical extraction and parameter setting. The second specialized mechanism is compilation. This refers to the storage of syllabic templates and logogens into long term memory. These templates are extracted from the input and help to bootstrap the acquisition of lexical entries. Mehler et al. suggest that early lexical entries may differ considerably from those stored by adults. For instance, the lexical entries of language learners may include items that are not fully segmented, as in the case where a clitic or function word remains attached to a content word. Just how these entries are modified to conform to those of adults is not clear, although Mehler et al. suggest that the joint operation of bottom-up and lexical-morphological indices play some role in this process.

Suomi's Developmental Model of Adult Phonological Organization (DAPHO)

Suomi's (1993) model attempts to reconcile the view that speech consists of strings of discrete, linguistically motivated units with the observations that it is a physically continuous and unsegmented acoustic signal. In this model, phonemes are taken to be emergent units of sound structure, but speech perception and production do not actually involve the concatenation of these units. Suomi's model attempts to deal with both speech perception and production. DAPHO is a developmental model in the sense that it is derived from an earlier model (CHIPHO) that characterizes the child's early speech behavior at around the 50 word stage. Because our focus here is on how speech perception capacities develop during infancy, we will confine our discussion to the perceptual side of the DAPHO model, and deal primarily with how the model evolved from CHIPHO.

A brief overview of how DAPHO operates during word recognition in fluent speech is given here. Each word entry in the lexicon is hypothesized to consist of a motor plan and an auditory prototype. The prototypes are normalized and contain the essential auditory details that regularly occur with words across different contexts. An important assumption of the model is that these details are apprehended directly during word recognition without an intermediate stage of segmental analysis. After the incoming signal passes through a stage of auditory analysis, word boundaries are detected, and each word candidate is matched against the set of prototypes in the lexicon. Prototypes which are sufficiently similar to the word candidate are activated, and the best fitting one is selected as a match.

According to CHIPHO, during speech perception an incoming utterance undergoes a peripheral auditory analysis. Novel words are stored as holistic prototypes, whereas familiar words are matched against the existing set of prototypes in the lexicon. The meaning of the most similar prototype is activated as the result of the recognition process. One point that is not discussed is how the model determines whether an item is novel, and should be stored as a new prototype, or should be treated as a familiar item. Presumably, some criterion based on the degree of similarity to existing prototypes is required for this purpose. One other feature of the model that bears mention is that Suomi assumes that the prototypes stored in the lexicon are initially quite global and include a limited number of salient auditory features. As more items are added to the lexicon, the prototypes become increasingly more detailed to distinguish them from other lexical items. However, according to Suomi, the representations of items in the input lexicon continue to be continuous, holistic descriptions (i.e., not segmental) into adulthood. Although Suomi sees phonemes as emerging as elements in speech production,

they do not enter into the representations used in speech recognition.

The approach that CHIPHO takes to segmenting words from fluent speech is the kind of top-down approach proposed by Cole and Jakimik (1978, 1980). Words are identified in succession starting with the beginning of an utterance, with the completed recognition of one word indicating the beginning of a new word candidate. As the child acquires more and more words, more top-down information is available to facilitate word boundary detection. Unfortunately, this approach is not without its problems. In particular, an exclusively top-down approach can be expected to have difficulties with words that appear as syllables embedded within larger words, such as "can" in "candle," "toucan," "uncanny," and so on (for further discussion of this point see Jusczyk & Aslin, 1995).

Jusczyk's Word Recognition and Phonetic Structure Acquisition (WRAPSA) Model

This model is intended to account for the way in which speech perception capacities evolve to support on-line word recognition in fluent speech (Jusczyk, 1992, 1993a, 1993b, 1997). The model is an outgrowth of an earlier one proposed by Jusczyk (1985a). The model tries to account for the changeover from language-general perceptual capacities to ones optimally suited for perceiving utterances in the child's native language. A key assumption of the WRAPSA model is that the language learner develops a scheme for weighting information delivered by auditory analyzers so as to maximize the likelihood of picking up those contrasts that signify meaningful distinctions among words in the native language.

A set of auditory analyzers is assumed to provide a description of the spectral and temporal features present in the acoustic signal. The features extracted at this level are the ones provided by the inherent organization of the human auditory system. Hence, they are neutral with respect to the language that is being spoken. Jusczyk hypothesizes that it is this type of description that infants operate with during the first few months of life. As the child gains more experience with a particular native language, the output of the analyzers is weighted to highlight those features that are most critical to making meaningful distinctions in the language. The weighting scheme amounts to a way of focusing attention on certain features and de-emphasizing others. A pattern extraction process operates on the weighted output, and segments the continuous signal into word-sized units. The resulting representation of the input signal is global in the sense that it relates prominent features temporally into syllables, but does not provide an explicit breakdown into phonetic segments. However, these representations do encode information about prosodic properties, such as the relative stress, pitch, and durations of syllables within the word-sized units. The processed input representation is then matched against existing representations of known words that have been stored in the lexicon. If a close match to some item in memory is achieved, recognition occurs, and the meaning is accessed. If no close match is made, then the input is reprocessed in an attempt to find a better match, or else the item is stored as a new item in the lexicon. As was the case for Suomi's model, the criterion for determining whether an item is a familiar word or a novel one is not precisely stated.

According to the WRAPSA model, it is the development of a weighting scheme for the native language that leads to a decline in sensitivity to non-native contrasts. Originally, Jusczyk (1992) tied the development of the weighting scheme closely to the growing need of the language learner to make meaningful distinctions among words in the native language. This suggested a type of tuning of the system whereby the learner actively seeks out those properties that are most critical for making meaningful distinctions in the language. However, more recent evidence from Jusczyk (1993a, 1994) indicates that infants are sensitive to the distribution of properties in the native language input (e.g., Jusczyk, Cutler, et al., 1993; Jusczyk, Friederici, et al., 1993; Jusczyk, Luce, et al., 1994; Kuhl et al., 1992). These results suggest that the frequency with which certain sound patterns appear may also help in developing the weighting scheme.

The biggest change (and the most controversial one) between the WRAPSA model and Jusczyk's earlier model is the assumption that listeners store specific instances of words they hear rather than abstract prototypes of lexical items. Some have worried that storing individual instances might lead to an exponential explosion in the amount of material in the lexicon (Kent, 1993). However, Jusczyk (1992) has justified this move on the grounds that a growing body of evidence suggests that listeners do appear to encode and remember much detail about specific utterances that they have heard (Craik & Kirsner, 1974; Goldinger, 1992; Nygaard, Sommers, & Pisoni, 1994; Palmeri, Goldinger, & Pisoni, 1993; see section below on Talker-specific representations). Nevertheless, the final resolution of this issue depends on further empirical research to determine the

degree and extent to which infant and adult listeners store information as specific exemplars or abstract prototypes.

SUMMARY, CONCLUSIONS, AND FUTURE DIRECTIONS

Sensitivity to Speech Contrasts: Developmental Mechanisms

Understanding the basis of the decline in perceptual sensitivity to non-native contrasts is one issue that has already generated considerable interest among developmental speech researchers. As noted in the previous section, several different models have been proposed to account for changes in the perception of non-native contrasts. However, even the most elaborate of the models, Best's PAM, cannot fully account for the pattern of findings that presently exists. One current stumbling block to developing an explanatory model for changes in sensitivity to non-native contrasts is the relatively small number of phonetic contrasts that have been investigated. This is not intended as a criticism of researchers in this area. It may take a number of years to achieve a wide enough range of contrasts to reveal the factors that will determine whether a speaker of a particular language is likely to find a certain non-native contrast easy or difficult. More precise data about the organization and structure of phonetic categories in adult speakers of different languages, as well as some indication of the range of individual differences among speakers of a given language, would also be useful in understanding why certain contrasts are more likely than others to undergo a decline. A fuller explanation for the decline in sensitivity should also shed light on the underlying processes that serve speech perception. On the more practical side, it may provide new insights that will be helpful for acquiring fluency in a second language.

Interactions between Sound Patterns and Other Aspects of Language Organization

For the most part, researchers investigating language acquisition only focus on one level of organization at a time. Thus, researchers studying semantic development focus on how meanings of words are acquired, and do not typically concern themselves with the sound patterns of words. Similarly, speech researchers tend to confine their investigations to what the infant is learning about the elements of the sound structure of the native language, as opposed to the syntactic or semantic organization of the language. Such focused research strategies can provide a valuable base of information regarding language learners' capabilities within each of these areas of language organization. However, at some point, in order to fully understand and explain language acquisition, it is necessary to consider how processes at these various levels may interact during the course of development. For example, although it is reasonable to suppose that the most important factors influencing whether or not a child will learn a new word meaning have to do with semantic organization (and the child's current cognitive state), other levels of language organization may also affect the process. In particular, the demands to achieve an optimal way of processing information at some level of linguistic organization (e.g., phonological, syntactic, semantic) may well constrain the possible forms of organization at other levels. That is, the language learner has to find the best solution to satisfy task demands at all the levels of linguistic organization.

One area in which we might expect to find influences from different levels of organization is in the development of the lexicon for the native language. Current views propose that lexical entries contain information from a number of different levels of organization (e. g., see the papers in the volume by Gleitman & Landau, 1994). Thus, in addition to some description of the sound properties of a lexical item and its associated meanings, an entry may include information about the word's syntactic category and the kinds of syntactic structures that it can participate in. The assumption that lexical entries are potentially rich with information raises some interesting questions about how the lexicon, in general, and lexical entries, in particular, develop. For example, do lexical entries all begin in the same way, say as meanings that then get associated with sound patterns, and with syntactic information only added at some subsequent point? Are the only factors which limit the addition of new lexical entries ones that have to do with whether or not some particular meaning already has a sound label attached to it—along the lines of Markman's (1991) Mutual Exclusivity Principle? To what extent does the sound pattern of a particular word affect the likelihood of its being added to the lexicon?

Because this chapter is primarily concerned with the development of speech perception capacities, we will consider the problem of how the sound structure of words could impact on lexical growth. One possibility that has been suggested by child phonologists (Schwartz, 1988; Vihman, Macken, Miller, Simmons, & Miller, 1985) is that infants may avoid words that contain sounds which are difficult for them to produce. However, although this tendency would be expected to affect the nature of the lexicon underlying the child's production of words, there is no necessary reason why it should affect the words that are in the child's receptive lexicon (Schwartz, 1988). Another possibility is that the infant might at least initially avoid adding words to the lexicon that are difficult to discriminate from existing items in the lexicon. For example, models such as WRAPSA and CHIPHO assume the representations of sound patterns of early lexical items are not fully detailed descriptions. To the extent that the infant adds words with very similar sound patterns, the lack of sufficient detail in the representations might lead the infant to make recognition errors. In fact, studies based on estimates of the vocabularies of children 5 to 7 years old suggest that children's lexicons have many fewer lexical neighbors than the same words in adults' lexicons (Charles-Luce & Luce, 1990, 1995; cf. Dollaghan, 1994). Thus, this finding is consistent with the view that children may have less detailed representations of the sound structures of lexical items (see Logan, 1992). However, there is also evidence from studies of vocabulary growth that even young children do not avoid learning, and do not seem to be confused by, homonyms (Clark, 1993). Homonyms seem to lie at the most extreme end of confusability of sound patterns of words (i.e., they are identical). Nevertheless, there may be a difference between having two items with the same sound pattern, and two items that are only minimally different in their sound patterns. Ultimately, this issue will only be resolved through studies which systematically chart the growth and organization of the lexicon.

Computational Approaches

A recent trend that promises to change in substantial ways the way in which researchers conceive of the mechanisms underlying language acquisition is the use of computational models (Rumelhart & McClelland, 1986). In particular, these models have been driven by the hypothesis, rejected by most language acquisition researchers post-Chomsky, that language input is much richer than the impoverished corpus initially thought to be presented to young children. Although these computational models and their emphasis on statistical learning or distributional analyses have been applied to topics in syntax (Plunkett & Marchman, 1993) and phonology (Markey, Menn, & Mozer, 1995), they have also been applied to topics relevant to the acquisition of the lexicon (see the earlier discussions of empirical results and theories of word segmentation).

Using maternal speech transcripts, Aslin, Woodward, LaMendola, and Bever (1996) and Brent and Cartwright (1996) have shown that two classes of computational models can learn much about the location of word boundaries by the consistent ordering of sounds in fluent speech. Saffran, Newport, and Aslin (1996) have shown that these distributional analyses can actually be used by adults to segment an artificial language into "words," even when this language contains no pauses between words or between sentences and no prosodic information. Moreover, Saffran, Newport, Aslin, Tunick, and Barrueco (1997) have shown that this same artificial language can be segmented into words by 6-year-olds, even when these children are not explicitly asked to listen to the language. Finally, Saffran, Aslin, and Newport (1996) have shown that 8-month-olds can segment an artificial language composed of trisyllabic nonsense words, even when these words are solely defined by their probabilities of co-occurrence. That is, infants listened differentially to trisyllables that conformed to words of the artificial language versus trisyllables that spanned a word boundary. Because these words were defined by the sequences of sounds and not by prosodic cues or pauses between words or at the end of utterances, these results show that infants can also use statistical information from a corpus to group sounds into word-like units. Moreover, the familiarization corpus was only two minutes in length, thereby illustrating that this statistical learning of words can be accomplished very rapidly. Thus, there is strong recent evidence that many of the early stages of language acquisition may utilize general learning mechanisms based on the analysis of distributional properties of the language input. Whether these learning mechanisms are also used for subsequent analyses of language input relevant to higher levels of linguistic organization remains for further investigation.

Talker-Specific Representations

Instead of reducing or eliminating different sources of variability in speech stimuli, Pisoni and his colleagues have specifically introduced variability from different talkers and different speaking rates to study the effects of these variables on perception (Pisoni, 1990, 1992, 1996). Mullennix et al. (1989) found that the intelligibility of isolated spoken words presented in noise was affected by the number of talkers who produced the test words. Across three signal-to-noise ratios, identification performance was always better for words produced by a single talker than for words produced by multiple talkers. Mullennix et al. (1989) also measured naming latencies for the same words presented in both test conditions. Subjects were not only slower to name words from multiple-talker lists, but they were also less accurate when their performance was compared to naming words from single-talker lists. Both sets of findings were surprising because all the test words used in the experiment were highly intelligible when presented under low-noise conditions.

To assess whether attributes of a talker's voice were perceived independently of the phonetic form of the words, Mullennix and Pisoni (1990) used a speeded classification task. Subjects were required to attend selectively to one stimulus dimension (i.e., voice) while simultaneously ignoring another stimulus dimension (i.e., phoneme). Across all conditions, Mullennix and Pisoni found interference when the subjects were required to attend selectively to only one of the stimulus dimensions. This pattern of results suggested that words and voices were processed as integral dimensions; the perception of one dimension (i.e., phoneme) affects classification of the other dimension (i.e., voice) and vice versa, and subjects cannot selectively ignore irrelevant variation in the non-attended dimension. Not only was mutual interference observed, suggesting that the two sets of dimensions, voice and phoneme, are perceived in a mutually dependent manner, but Mullennix and Pisoni (1990) also found that the pattern of interference was asymmetrical. It was easier for subjects to ignore irrelevant variation in the phoneme dimension when attending to the voice dimension than it was to ignore the voice dimension when attending to the phonemes.

The results from these experiments on talker variability were surprising given the long-standing assumption in the field of speech perception that voice quality is perceived independently of the linguistic properties of these signals. These findings also suggested that the perceptual system must engage in some form of "recalibration" each time a new voice is encountered during a set of test trials. A series of followup experiments (Goldinger, 1992; Goldinger, Pisoni, & Logan, 1991; Martin, Mullennix, Pisoni, & Summers, 1989; Palmeri, Goldinger, & Pisoni, 1993) demonstrated that specific details of a talker's voice are also encoded into long-term memory, even under implicit memory conditions. Taken together, these recent findings on the effects of talker variability in perception and memory provide support for the proposal that detailed perceptual information about a talker's voice is preserved in some type of perceptual representation system (Schacter, 1990) and that these attributes are encoded into long-term memory.

Another series of experiments examined the effects of speaking rate on speech perception and memory. Sommers, Nygaard, and Pisoni (1994) found that words produced at different speaking rates (fast, medium, and slow) were identified more poorly than the same words produced at only one speaking rate. These results were compared to another condition in which differences in amplitude were varied randomly from trial to trial in the test sequences. In this condition, identification performance was not affected by variability in overall amplitude. Nygaard, Sommers, and Pisoni (1995) found that subjects recall words from lists produced at a single speaking rate better than the same words produced at several different speaking rates. Differences in speaking rate, like those observed for talker variability, suggest that perceptual encoding and rehearsal processes, which are typically thought to operate on only abstract symbolic representations, are also influenced by low-level perceptual details.

Despite the importance of stimulus variability in speech perception, very few developmental studies have been carried out with infants or young children. What is needed are studies designed to assess the extent to which infants may incur the kinds of subtle costs in processing and encoding speech that have been reported for adult listeners when dealing with variability in talker or speaking rate. One such study was conducted by Jusczyk, Pisoni, and Mullennix (1992) who examined the effects of talker variability on 2-month-old infants using the HAS technique. One experiment examined the effects of talker variability on infants' ability to detect differences between words like "bug" and "dug." Infants exposed to utterances produced by multiple talkers performed just as well as infants who heard the stimuli produced by only one talker. Another experiment examined the effects of talker variability on infants' memory for these syllables. The HAS procedure was modified by introducing a 2-minute delay period between the familiarization and test phases of the experiment. In this case, talker variability did affect infants' encoding of the test syllables. Infants who heard versions of the same syllable produced by 12 different talkers did not detect a change to a new syllable produced by the same talkers after the delay period. However, infants who heard the same syllable produced by a single talker were able to detect the change after the delay period. Other experiments carried out by Jusczyk et al. varied the range of variability and showed that although infants can detect a change in gender between voices under a 2-minute memory load, they still had difficulty detecting a phonetic change between the syllables.

The study by Jusczyk, Pisoni, et al. (1992) demonstrates that infants as young as 2 months of age have the basic capacities to cope with talker variability in speech perception. These findings replicate earlier results reported by Kuhl (1979, 1983) with 6-month-old infants. However, dealing with stimulus variability appears to carry some cost. When stimulus variability from different talkers is present, infants took longer to habituate to repetitions of a particular syllable. More importantly, the presence of variability can hamper infants' encoding of speech sounds in memory, so that they fail to detect a phonetic change after a short delay interval. Consequently, variability among different tokens of a given syllable affects primarily the way that infants remember information in the speech signal. These results are similar to those previously reported for adults. Specifically, in the absence of any noise-induced degradation of the speech signal, there is little evidence that perceptual processes related to the identification of items are significantly disrupted in adults (Mullennix et al., 1989), whereas the mere presence of talker variability is sufficient to adversely affect processes associated with the retention of speech information (Martin et al., 1989).

One of the long-term goals of research on infant speech perception as it relates to the development of the lexicon is to determine the kinds of information that infants encode about words in their language. If instance-specific information particular to the actual tokens that are heard is encoded in the representation (as the results of Hohne et al., 1994, suggest), then this has important consequences for models of word recognition. In fact, such a result would be difficult to account for in models that postulate the storage of some prototypical representation of the acoustic-phonetic characteristics of lexical items, because differences among pronunciations of the same word by different talkers are precisely the kind of information that a prototype might be expected to exclude. Instead, exemplar-based models, ones like WRAPSA postulating the storage of individual traces of particular utterances heard, would be favored by results suggesting that talker characteristics (or even characteristics of individual tokens from a particular talker) are retained in memory (Hintzman, 1986; Nosofsky, 1987, 1988).

Several other recent experiments have been carried out to study the tuning or perceptual adaptation that occurs when a listener becomes familiar with the voice of a specific talker (Nygaard et al., 1994). Subjects who had heard novel words produced by familiar voices were able to recognize words in noise more accurately than subjects who received the same novel words produced by unfamiliar voices. The findings from this perceptual learning experiment demonstrate that exposure to a talker's voice facilitates subsequent perceptual processing of novel words produced by familiar talkers. Such findings demonstrate a form of implicit memory for a talker's voice that is distinct from the retention of the individual items used and the specific task employed to familiarize the listeners with the voices (Roediger, 1990; Schacter, 1992).

These recent findings demonstrating that spoken word recognition is talker-contingent and that familiar voices are encoded differently from novel voices raise a new set of theoretical issues concerning the long-standing dissociation between the "linguistic properties" of speech—the features, phonemes and words used to convey the linguistic content of the message—and the "indexical properties" of speech—those personal or paralinguistic attributes of the speech signal that provide the listener with information about the form of the message (the speaker's gender, dialect, social class, and emotional state, among other things). The experiments on stimulus variability suggest that although the dissociation between indexical and linguistic properties of speech may be a useful dichotomy for theoretical linguists who approach language as a highly abstract formalized symbolic system, the same set of assumptions may no longer be useful for speech scientists who are interested in describing and modeling how the human nervous system encodes and stores speech signals in long-term memory or how these processes develop in infants and young children.

Longitudinal Studies

Aside from a few isolated studies (e.g., Jusczyk, Hirsh-Pasek, et al., 1992; Werker & Tees, 1984), there have been relatively few attempts to follow changes in speech perception capacities in the same infants over the course of several months. There are a number of reasons for this. First, many of the available test procedures, especially those used with younger infants, allow investigators to make comparisons among groups of infants, but not within individual infants. This is because procedures like HAS only provide one data point per infant. Moreover, young infants may undergo state changes during the course of a test session from being awake and alert to drowsy or distressed. This is especially apparent when one considers the variability of performance of infants in a no-change control condition. Some infants may show changes in sucking rates as great as infants in experimental groups. Consequently, it is not possible to say with any measure of confidence whether a particular infant detected a change or not.

Techniques such as the conditioned headturning procedure or the headturn preference procedure show more promise for use in longitudinal studies. For instance, these procedures can be used across a wider range of ages (from roughly 4.5 to 18 months of age). Thus, investigators have the possibility of testing the same infant on the same contrast at various points during this period. Moreover, since both of these types of procedures provide for a series of different change trials, they produce more reliable measures of the likelihood that a particular infant discriminated a particular stimulus pairing or displayed a preference for a particular type of stimulus. Still, some care is required to discern developmental trends with these procedures because the task demands may be different for the infants at different points in development. This is particularly true when the procedures are used with older infants who may be less interested in the experimental procedures than they were at a younger age.

Another factor that has inhibited longitudinal studies in this area has been the rather limited information concerning which abilities we might reasonably expect infants to have at various ages. It has only been during the past decade that researchers have begun to demonstrate that developmental changes in speech perception do occur during the first year of life. Furthermore, we are only just beginning to sample a wider range of speech perception abilities than just those associated with discriminating phonetic contrasts. However, as information grows about infants' abilities to segment speech, recognize and remember words, reorganize their perceptual categories, and learn about regularly occurring features of native language sound patterns, we are developing a much broader understanding of the scope of infants' capacities. This opens the door to the possibility of developing profiles of the abilities that an individual infant manifests at various points in development. It may even be possible to discern whether there are certain kinds of abilities that show a consistent pattern within a given individual. Moreover, with subsequent yearly follow-ups, it may be possible to determine whether infants, who appear to be slow in achieving speech perception landmarks during infancy, later show signs of deficits in other areas of language use. In short, longitudinal investigations could provide information of great practical, as well as theoretical, importance.

Concluding Remarks

Over the past 14 years since the publication of the previous edition of the *Handbook* our knowledge of auditory development and speech perception in infancy has expanded greatly. Many of the fundamental questions that occupied researchers in 1983, such as the role played by early language experience, still seek definitive answers. But several general aspects of early language development have been revealed quite clearly. Infants show evidence of being biased by language input as early as the third trimester of gestation, and by 6 months of age they exhibit preferences for their native language. Within the next two months, they begin to recognize familiar sequences of sounds after only a few minutes of exposure, even when those sounds are embedded in fluent speech. By the end of the first year of life, they have tuned into the speech sounds that are relevant to their native language. And, by the age at which first words are produced, infants have been exposed to a massive array of language inputs that exert powerful constraints on the course of speech perception and language acquisition. The interface between fundamental issues in speech perception and the earliest stages of language production will be a fruitful ground for studies in the next decade.

ACKNOWLEDGMENTS

We thank Robin Cooper, Jill Gallipeau, Mara Goodman, Derek Houston, Ann Marie Jusczyk, Jen Saffran, Robert Siegler, Michele Shady, and Lynne Werner for helpful comments on a preliminary version of this chapter.

REFERENCES

Abrams, K., & Bever, T. G. (1969). Syntactic structure modifies attention during speech perception and recognition. *Quarterly Journal of Experimental Psychology, 21,* 280–290.

Armitage, S. E., Baldwin, B. A., & Vince, M. A. (1980). The fetal sound environment of sheep. *Science, 208,* 1173–1174.

Aslin, R. N. (1981). Experiential influences and sensitive periods in perceptual development: A unified model. In R. N. Aslin, J. R. Alberts, & M. R. Petersen (Eds.), *Development of perception: Psychobiological perspectives: Vol. 2. The visual system.* New York: Academic Press.

Aslin, R. N. (1989). Discrimination of frequency transitions by human infants. *Journal of the Acoustical Society of America, 86,* 582–590.

Aslin, R. N., & Pisoni, D. B. (1980a). Effects of early linguistic experience on speech discrimination by infants: A critique of Eilers, Gavin, & Wilson (1979). *Child Development, 51,* 107–112.

Aslin, R. N., & Pisoni, D. B. (1980b). Some developmental processes in speech perception. In G. H. Yeni-Komshian, J. F. Kavanagh, & C. A. Ferguson (Eds.), *Child phonology: Perception* (Vol. 2). New York: Academic Press.

Aslin, R. N., Pisoni, D. B., Hennessy, B. L., & Perey, A. J. (1981). Discrimination of voice onset time by human infants: New findings and implications for the effects of early experience. *Child Development, 52,* 1135–1145.

Aslin, R. N., Pisoni, D. B., & Jusczyk, P. W. (1983). Auditory development and speech perception in infancy. In P. Mussen (Series Ed.) & M. M. Haith & J. J. Campos (Vol. Eds.), *Infancy and the biology of development: Vol. 2. Handbook of child psychology* (4th ed.). New York: Wiley.

Aslin, R. N., Woodward, J. Z., LaMendola, N. P., & Bever, T. G. (1996). Models of word segmentation in fluent maternal speech to infants. In J. L. Morgan & K. Demuth (Eds.), *Signal to syntax.* Hillsdale, NJ: Erlbaum.

Bahrick, L. E., & Pickens, J. N. (1988). Classification of bimodal English and Spanish language passages by infants. *Infant Behavior and Development, 11,* 277–296.

Bailey, P. J., & Herrmann, P. (1993). A reexamination of duplex perception evoked by intensity differences. *Perception and Psychophysics, 54,* 20–32.

Bargones, J. Y., & Burns, E. M. (1988). Suppression tuning curves for spontaneous otoacoustic emissions in infants and adults. *Journal of the Acoustical Society of America, 83,* 1809–1816.

Bargones, J. Y., & Werner, L. A. (1994). Adults listen selectively: Infants do not. *Psychological Science, 5,* 170–174.

Bargones, J. Y., Werner, L. A., & Marean, G. C. (1995). Infant psychometric functions for detection: Mechanisms of immature sensitivity. *Journal of the Acoustical Society of America, 98,* 99–111.

Beckman, M., & Edwards, J. (1990). Lengthening and shortenings and the nature of prosodic constituency. In J. Kingston & M. E. Beckman (Eds.), *Papers in laboratory phonology: 1. Between the grammar and physics of speech* (pp. 152–178). Cambridge, England: Cambridge University Press.

Benedict, H. (1979). Early lexical development: Comprehension and production. *Journal of Child Language, 6,* 183–201.

Berg, K. M., & Smith, M. C. (1983). Behavioral thresholds for tones during infancy. *Journal of Experimental Child Psychology, 35,* 409–425.

Bernstein Ratner, N. (1986). Durational cues which mark clause boundaries in mother-child speech. *Phonetics, 14,* 303–309.

Bertoncini, J. (1993). Infants' perception of speech units: Primary representational capacities. In B. B. de Boysson-Bardies, S. D. Schonen, P. Jusczyk, P. MacNeilage, & J. Morton (Eds.), *Developmental neurocognition: Speech and face processing in the first year of life.* Dordrecht, The Netherlands: Kluwer.

Bertoncini, J., Bijeljac-Babic, R., Jusczyk, P. W., Kennedy, L. J., & Mehler, J. (1988). An investigation of young infants' perceptual representations of speech sounds. *Journal of Experimental Psychology: General, 117,* 21–33.

Best, C. T. (1991, April). *Phonetic influences on the perception of non-native speech contrasts by 6–8 and 10–12 month olds.* Paper presented at the biennial meeting of the Society for Research in Child Development, Seattle, WA.

Best, C. T. (1993). Emergence of language-specific constraints in perception of native and non-native speech: A window on early phonological development. In B. de Boysson-Bardies, S. D. Schoen, P. Jusczyk, P. McNeilage, & J. Morton (Eds.), *Developmental neurocognition: Speech and face processing during the first year of life.* Dordrecht, The Netherlands: Kluwer.

Best, C. T. (1995). Learning to perceive the sound patterns of English. In C. Rovee-Collier & L. P. Lipsitt (Eds.), *Advances in infancy research.* Norwood, NJ: ABLEX.

Best, C. T., & McRoberts, G. W. (1989, April). *Phonological influences on the perception of native and non-native speech contrasts.* Paper presented at the biennial meeting of the Society for Research in Child Development, Kansas City, MO.

Best, C. T., McRoberts, G. W., Goodell, E., Womer, J., Insabella, G., Klatt, L., Luke, S., & Silver, J. (1990, April). *Infant and adult perception of nonnative speech contrasts differing in relation to the listeners' native phonology.* Paper presented at the International Conference on Infant Studies, Montreal.

Best, C. T., McRoberts, G. W., LaFleur, R., & Silver-Isenstadt, J. (1995). Divergent developmental patterns for infants' perception of two nonnative consonant contrasts. *Infant Behavior and Development, 18,* 339–350.

Best, C. T., McRoberts, G. W., & Sithole, N. M. (1988). Examination of the perceptual re-organization for speech contrasts: Zulu click discrimination by English-speaking adults and infants. *Journal of Experimental Psychology: Human Perception and Performance, 14,* 345–360.

Best, C. T., Morrongiello, B., & Robson, R. (1981). Perceptual equivalence of acoustic cues in speech and nonspeech perception. *Perception and Psychophysics, 29,* 191–211.

Bijeljac-Babic, R., Bertoncini, J., & Mehler, J. (1993). How do four-day-old infants categorize multisyllabic utterances? *Developmental Psychology, 29,* 711–721.

Bolinger, D. L., & Gerstman, L. J. (1957). Disjuncture as a cue to constraints. *Word, 13,* 246–255.

Brent, M. R., & Cartwright, T. A. (1996). Distributional regularity and phonotactic constraints are useful for segmentation. *Cognition, 61,* 93–125.

Broen, P. (1972). The verbal environment of the language learning child. *American Speech and Hearing Association Monograph, 17.*

Bull, D., Schneider, B. A., & Trehub, S. E. (1981). The masking of octave-band noise by broad-band spectrum noise: A comparison of infant and adult thresholds. *Perception and Psychophysics, 30,* 101–106.

Chang, H. W., & Trehub, S. E. (1977). Auditory processing of relational information by young infants. *Journal of Experimental Child Psychology, 24,* 324–331.

Charles-Luce, J., & Luce, P. A. (1990). Similarity neighborhoods of words in young children's lexicons. *Journal of Child Language, 17,* 205–215.

Charles-Luce, J., & Luce, P. A. (1995). An examination of similarity neighborhoods in young children's receptive vocabularies. *Journal of Child Language, 22,* 727–735.

Chomsky, N., & Miller, G. A. (1963). Introduction to the formal analysis of natural languages. In R. D. Luce, R. Bush, & E. Galanter (Eds.), *Handbook of mathematical psychology* (Vol. 2). New York: Wiley.

Christophe, A., Dupoux, E., Bertoncini, J., & Mehler, J. (1994). Do infants perceive word boundaries? An empirical approach to the bootstrapping of lexical acquisition. *Journal of the Acoustical Society of America, 95,* 1570–1580.

Church, K. (1987). Phonological parsing and lexical retrieval. *Cognition, 25,* 53–69.

Clark, E. V. (1993). *The lexicon in acquisition.* Cambridge, England: Cambridge University Press.

Cohen, A. J., Thorpe, L. A., & Trehub, S. E. (1987). Infants' perception of musical relations in short transposed tone sequences. *Canadian Journal of Psychology, 41,* 33–47.

Cole, R. A., & Jakimik, J. (1978). Understanding speech: How words are heard. In G. Underwood (Ed.), *Strategies of information processing.* New York: Academic Press.

Cole, R. A., & Jakimik, J. (1980). A model of speech perception. In R. A. Cole (Ed.), *Perception and production of fluent speech* (pp. 133–163). Hillsdale, NJ: Erlbaum.

Collier, R., & t'Hart, J. (1975). The role of intonation in speech perception. In A. Cohen & S. G. Nooteboom (Eds.), *Structure and process in speech perception* (pp. 107–121). Heidelberg: Springer-Verlag.

Colombo, J., & Bundy, R. S. (1981). A method for the measurement of infant auditory selectivity. *Infant Behavior and Development, 4,* 219–223.

Cooper, F. S., Liberman, A. M., & Borst, J. M. (1951). The interconversion of audible and visible patterns as a basis for research in the perception of speech. *Proceedings of the National Academy of Sciences, 37,* 318–325.

Cooper, R. P. (1993). The effect of prosody on young infants' speech perception. In C. Rovee-Collier & L. P. Lipsitt (Eds.), *Advances in infancy research* (Vol. 8). Norwood, NJ: ABLEX.

Cooper, R. P., & Aslin, R. N. (1990). Preference for infant-directed speech in the first month after birth. *Child Development, 61,* 1584–1595.

Cooper, R. P., & Aslin, R. N. (1994). Developmental differences in infant attention to the spectral properties of infant-directed speech. *Child Development, 65,* 1663–1677.

Cooper, W. E., & Paccia-Cooper, J. (1980). *Syntax and speech.* Cambridge, MA: Harvard University Press.

Craik, F. I. M., & Kirsner, K. (1974). The effect of speaker's voice on word recognition. *Quarterly Journal of Experimental Psychology, 26,* 274–284.

Cruttenden, A. (1986). *Intonation.* Cambridge, England: Cambridge University Press.

Crystal, T. H., & House, A. S. (1988). Segmental durations in connected speech signals: Current results. *Journal of the Acoustical Society of America, 83,* 1553–1573.

Cutler, A. (1990). Exploiting prosodic probabilities in speech segmentation. In G. T. M. Altmann (Ed.), *Cognitive models of speech processing: Psycholinguistic and computational perspectives* (pp. 105–121). Cambridge, MA: MIT Press.

Cutler, A. (1994). Segmentation problems, rhythmic solutions. *Lingua, 92,* 81–104.

Cutler, A., & Butterfield, S. (1992). Rhythmic cues to speech segmentation: Evidence from juncture misperception. *Journal of Memory and Language, 31,* 218–236.

Cutler, A., & Carter, D. M. (1987). The predominance of strong initial syllables in the English vocabulary. *Computer Speech and Language, 2,* 133–142.

Cutler, A., & Norris, D. G. (1988). The role of strong syllables in segmentation for lexical access. *Journal of Experimental Psychology: Human Perception and Performance, 14,* 113–121.

Cutting, J. E., & Rosner, B. S. (1974). Categories and boundaries in speech and music. *Perception and Psychophysics, 16,* 564–570.

DeCasper, A. J., & Fifer, W. P. (1980). Of human bonding: Newborns prefer their mothers' voices. *Science, 208,* 1174–1176.

DeCasper, A. J., Lecanuet, J.-P., Busnel, M.-C., Granier-Deferre, C., & Maugeais, R. (1994). Fetal reactions to recurrent maternal speech. *Infant Behavior and Development, 17,* .159–164.

DeCasper, A. J., & Spence, M. J. (1986). Prenatal maternal speech influences newborns' perception of speech sounds. *Infant Behavior and Development, 9,* 133–150.

Demany, L., & Armand, F. (1984). The perceptual reality of tone chroma in early infancy. *Journal of the Acoustical Society of America, 76,* 57–66.

Demany, L., McKenzie, B., & Vurpillot, E. (1977). Rhythm perception in early infancy. *Nature, 266,* 718–719.

Deng, L., & Erler, K. (1992). Structural design of hidden Markov model speech recognizer using multivalued phonetic features: Comparison with segmental speech units. *Journal of the Acoustical Society of America, 92,* 3058–3067.

Deutsch, D., & Feroe, J. (1981). The internal representation of pitch sequences in tonal music. *Psychological Review, 88,* 181–195.

Dollaghan, C. A. (1994). Children's phonological neighborhoods: Half empty or half full? *Journal of Child Language, 21,* 257–273.

Easton, R. D., & Basala, M. (1982). Perceptual dominance during lipreading. *Perception and Psychophysics, 32,* 562–570.

Eilers, R. E., Gavin, W. J., & Wilson, W. R. (1979). Linguistic experience and phonemic perception in infancy: A cross-linguistic study. *Child Development, 50,* 14–18.

Eilers, R. E., Gavin, W. J., & Wilson, W. R. (1980). Effects of early linguistic experience on speech discrimination by infants: A reply. *Child Development, 51,* 113–117.

Eilers, R. E., Wilson, W. R., & Moore, J. M. (1977). Developmental changes in speech discrimination in infants. *Journal of Speech and Hearing Research, 20,* 766–780.

Eimas, P. D. (1974). Auditory and linguistic processing of cues for place of articulation by infants. *Perception and Psychophysics, 16,* 513–521.

Eimas, P. D. (1975a). Auditory and phonetic coding of the cues for speech: Discrimination of the [r-l] distinction by young infants. *Perception and Psychophysics, 18,* 341–347.

Eimas, P. D. (1975b). Speech perception in early infancy. In L. B. Cohen & P. Salapatek (Eds.), *Infant perception: From sensation to cognition* (Vol. 2). New York: Academic Press.

Eimas, P. D. (1982). Speech perception: A view of the initial state and perceptual mechanisms. In J. Mehler, M. Garrett, & E. C. T. Walker (Eds.), *Perspectives on mental representation: Experimental and theoretical studies of cognitive processes and capacities.* Hillsdale, NJ: Erlbaum.

Eimas, P. D. (1985). The equivalence of cues in the perception of speech by infants. *Infant Behavior and Development, 8,* 125–138.

Eimas, P. D. (1991). Comment: Some effects of language acquisition on speech perception. In I. G. Mattingly & M. Studdert-Kennedy (Eds.), *Modularity and the motor theory of speech perception.* Hillsdale, NJ: Erlbaum.

Eimas, P. D., & Miller, J. L. (1980). Contextual effects in infant speech perception. *Science, 209,* 1140–1141.

Eimas, P. D., & Miller, J. L. (1992). Organization in the perception of speech by young infants. *Psychological Science, 3,* 340–345.

Eimas, P. D., Siqueland, E. R., Jusczyk, P. W., & Vigorito, J. (1971). Speech perception in infants. *Science, 171,* 303–306.

Elman, J. L. (1993). Learning and development in neural networks: The importance of starting small. *Cognition, 48,* 71–99.

Fant, C. G. M. (1960). *Acoustic theory of speech production.* The Hague: Mouton.

Ferguson, C. A. (1964). Baby talk in six languages. *American Anthropology, 66,* 103–114.

Ferguson, C. A. (1977). Baby talk as a simplified register. In C. E. Snow & C. A. Ferguson (Eds.), *Talking to children.* Cambridge, England: Cambridge University Press.

Fernald, A. (1984). The perceptual and affective salience of mothers' speech to infants. In L. Feagans, C. Garvey, & R. Golinkoff (Eds.), *The origins and growth of communication.* Norwood, NJ: ABLEX.

Fernald, A. (1985). Four-month-old infants prefer to listen to motherese. *Infant Behavior and Development, 8,* 181–195.

Fernald, A. (1992). Human maternal vocalizations to infants as biologically relevant signals: An evolutionary perspective. In J. H. Barkow, L. Cosmides, & J. Tooby (Eds.), *The adapted mind: Evolutionary psychology and the generation of culture.* New York: Oxford University Press.

Fernald, A., & Kuhl, P. K. (1987). Acoustic determinants of infant preference for motherese speech. *Infant Behavior and Development, 10,* 279–293.

Fernald, A., & Mazzie, C. (1991). Prosody and focus in speech to infants and adults. *Developmental Psychology, 27,* 209–221.

Fernald, A., & Simon, T. (1984). Expanded intonation contours in mothers' speech to newborns. *Developmental Psychology, 20,* 104–113.

Fernald, A., Taeschner, T., Dunn, J., Papousek, M., Boysson-Bardies, B. B., & Fukui, I. (1989). A cross-language study of prosodic modifications in mothers' and fathers' speech to preverbal infants. *Journal of Child Language, 16,* 477–501.

Fifer, W. P. (1987). Neonatal preference for mother's voice. In N. Krasnegor, E. Blass, & W. Smotherman (Eds.), *Perinatal development: A psychobiological perspective.* New York: Academic Press.

Fisher, C., & Tokura, H. (1996). Prosody in speech to infants: Direct and indirect acoustic cues to syntactic structure. In J. L. Morgan & K. Demuth (Eds.), *Signal to syntax.* Hillsdale, NJ: Erlbaum.

Fitch, H. L., Halwes, T., Erickson, D. M., & Liberman, A. M. (1980). Perceptual equivalence of two acoustic cues for stop-consonant manner. *Perception and Psychophysics, 27,* 343–350.

Flege, J. E. (1989). Chinese subjects' perception of the word-final English /t/-/d/ contrast: Before and after training. *Journal of the Acoustical Society of America, 86,* 1684–1697.

Flege, J. E. (1995). Second language speech learning: Theory, findings, and problems. In W. Strange (Ed.), *Speech perception and linguistic experience: Issues in cross-language research.* Timonium, MD: York Press.

Folsom, R. C., & Wynne, M. K. (1987). Auditory brain stem responses from human adults and infants: Restriction of frequency contribution by notched-noise masking. *Journal of the Acoustical Society of America, 80,* 1057–1064.

Friederici, A. D., & Wessels, J. M. I. (1993). Phonotactic knowledge and its use in infant speech perception. *Perception and Psychophysics, 54,* 287–295.

Friedlander, B. Z., & Wisdom, S. S. (1971). *Preverbal infants' selective operant responses for different levels of auditory complexity and language redundancy.* Paper presented at the annual general meeting of the Eastern Psychological Association, New York.

Fujimura, O., & Lovins, J. B. (1978). Syllables as concatenative phonetic units. In A. Bell & J. B. Hooper (Eds.), *Syllables and segments.* Amsterdam, The Netherlands: North Holland.

Garnica, O. K. (1977). Some prosodic and paralinguistic features of speech to young children. In C. Snow & C. A. Ferguson (Eds.), *Talking to children: Language input and acquisition.* Cambridge, England: Cambridge University Press.

Gerken, L. A. (1991). The metrical basis for children's subjectless sentences. *Journal of Memory and Language, 30,* 431–451.

Gerken, L. A. (1994). Young children's representation of prosodic phonology: Evidence from English-speakers' weak syllable omissions. *Journal of Memory and Language, 33,* 19–38..

Gerken, L. A., Jusczyk, P. W., & Mandel, D. R. (1994). When prosody fails to cue syntactic structure: Nine-month-olds' sensitivity to phonological vs. syntactic phrases. *Cognition, 51,* 237–265.

Gerstman, L. J. (1968). Classification of self-normalized vowels. *IEEE Transactions on Audio and Electroacoustics, 16,* 78–80.

Gleitman, L., Gleitman, H., Landau, B., & Wanner, E. (1988). Where the learning begins: Initial representations for language learning. In F. Newmeyer (Ed.), *The Cambridge Linguistic Survey.* Cambridge, MA: Harvard University Press.

Gleitman, L., & Landau, B. (Eds.). (1994). *The acquisition of the lexicon.* Cambridge, MA: MIT Press.

Gleitman, L., & Wanner, E. (1982). The state of the state of the art. In E. Wanner & L. Gleitman (Eds.), *Language acquisition: The state of the art.* Cambridge, England: Cambridge University Press.

Glenn, S. M., Cunningham, C. C., & Joyce, P. F. (1981). A study of auditory preferences in non-handicapped infants and infants with Down's Syndrome. *Child Development, 52,* 1303–1307.

Goldinger, S. D. (1992). *Words and voices: Implicit and explicit memory for spoken words* (Research on Speech Perception, Tech. Rep. No. 7). Bloomington: Indiana University.

Goldinger, S. D., Pisoni, D. B., & Logan, J. S. (1991). On the locus of talker variability effects in recall of spoken word lists. *Journal of Experimental Psychology: Learning, Memory, and Cognition, 17,* 152–162.

Goodsitt, J. V., Morgan, J. L., & Kuhl, P. K. (1993). Perceptual strategies in prelingual speech segmentation. *Journal of Child Language, 20,* 229–252.

Goodsitt, J. V., Morse, P. A., Ver Hoove, J. N., & Cowan, N. (1984). Infant speech perception in multisyllabic contexts. *Child Development, 55,* 903–910.

Gottlieb, G. (1976). Conceptions of prenatal development: Behavioral embryology. *Psychological Review, 83,* 215–234.

Green, K. P., Kuhl, P. K., Meltzoff, A. N., & Stevens, E. B. (1991). Integrating speech information across talkers, gender, and sensory modality: Female faces and male voices in the McGurk effect. *Perception and Psychophysics, 50,* 524–536.

Grewel, F. (1959). How do children acquire the use of language? *Phonetica, 3,* 193–202.

Grieser, D. L., & Kuhl, P. K. (1988). Maternal speech to infants in a tonal language: Support for universal prosodic features in motherese. *Developmental Psychology, 24,* 14–20.

Grieser, D. L., & Kuhl, P. K. (1989). The categorization of speech by infants: Support for speech-sound prototypes. *Developmental Psychology, 25,* 577 588.

Griffiths, S. K., Brown, W. S., Gerhardt, K. J., Abrams, R. M., & Morris, R. J. (1994). The perception of speech sounds recorded within the uterus of a pregnant sheep. *Journal of the Acoustical Society of America, 96,* 2055–2063.

Grosjean, F., & Gee, J. P. (1987). Prosodic structure and spoken word recognition. *Cognition, 25,* 135–155.

Hall, M. D., & Pastore, R. E. (1992). Musical duplex perception: Perception of figurally good chords with subliminal distinguishing tones. *Journal of Experimental Psychology: Human Perception and Performance, 18,* 752–762.

Hillenbrand, J. (1983). Perceptual organization of speech sounds by infants. *Journal of Speech and Hearing Research, 26,* 268–282.

Hillenbrand, J., Getty, L. A., Clark, M. J., & Wheeler, K. (1995). Acoustic characteristics of American English vowels. *Journal of the Acoustical Society of America, 97,* 3099–3111.

Hintzman, D. L. (1986). Schema abstraction in a multiple-trace memory model. *Psychological Review, 93,* 411–423.

Hirsh-Pasek, K., Kemler Nelson, D. G., Jusczyk, P. W., Wright Cassidy, K., Druss, B., & Kennedy, L. (1987). Clauses are perceptual units for young infants. *Cognition, 26,* 269–286.

Hohne, E. A., Jusczyk, A. M., & Redanz, N. J. (1994, June). *Do infants remember words from stories?* Paper presented at the 127th meeting of the Acoustical Society of America, Cambridge, MA.

Hohne, E. A., & Jusczyk, P. W. (1994). Two-month-old infants' sensitivity to allophonic differences. *Perception and Psychophysics, 56,* 613–623.

Houston, D., Jusczyk, P. W., & Newsome, M. (1995, November). *Infants' strategies of speech segmentation: Clues from weak/strong words.* Paper presented at the 20th annual Boston University Conference on Language Acquisition, Boston.

Huttenlocher, J. (1974). The origins of language comprehension. In R. L. Solso (Ed.), *Theories in cognitive psychology.* New York: Wiley.

Iverson, P., & Kuhl, P. K. (1995). Mapping the perceptual magnet effect for speech using signal detection theory and multidimensional scaling. *Journal of the Acoustical Society of America, 97,* 553–562.

Jusczyk, P. W. (1985a). On characterizing the development of speech perception. In J. Mehler & R. Fox (Eds.), *Neonate cognition: Beyond the blooming, buzzing confusion.* Hillsdale, NJ: Erlbaum.

Jusczyk, P. W. (1985b). The high amplitude sucking procedure as a methodological tool in speech perception research. In G. Gottlieb & N. A. Krasnegor (Eds.), *Measurement of audition and vision in the first year of postnatal life: A methodological overview.* Norwood, NJ: ABLEX.

Jusczyk, P. W. (1989, April). *Perception of cues to clausal units in native and non-native languages.* Paper presented at the biennial meeting of the Society for Research in Child Development, Kansas City, MO.

Jusczyk, P. W. (1992). Developing phonological categories from the speech signal. In C. A. Ferguson, L. Menn, & C. Stoel-Gammon (Eds.), *Phonological development: Models, research, implications.* Timonium, MD: York Press.

Jusczyk, P. W. (1993a). From general to language specific capacities: The WRAPSA Model of how speech perception develops. *Journal of Phonetics, 21,* 3–28.

Jusczyk, P. W. (1993b). How word recognition may evolve from infant speech perception capacities. In G. T. M. Altmann & R. Shillcock (Eds.), *Cognitive models of speech perception.* Hillsdale, NJ: Erlbaum.

Jusczyk, P. W. (1994). *The development of word recognition.* Paper presented at the International Conference on Spoken Language Processing, Acoustical Society of Japan, Yokohama, Japan.

Jusczyk, P. W. (1995). Language acquisition: Speech sounds and the beginnings of phonology. In J. L. Miller & P. D. Eimas (Eds.), *Handbook of perception and cognition: Speech, language, and communication.* Orlando, FL: Academic Press.

Jusczyk, P. W. (1997). *The discovery of spoken language.* Cambridge, MA: MIT Press/Bradford Books.

Jusczyk, P. W., & Aslin, R. N. (1995). Infants' detection of sound patterns of words in fluent speech. *Cognitive Psychology, 29,* 1–23.

Jusczyk, P. W., Bertoncini, J., Bijeljac-Babic, R., Kennedy, L. J., & Mehler, J. (1990). The role of attention in speech perception by infants. *Cognitive Development, 5,* 265–286.

Jusczyk, P. W., Cutler, A., & Redanz, N. (1993). Preference for the predominant stress patterns of English words. *Child Development, 64,* 675–687.

Jusczyk, P. W., & Derrah, C. (1987). Representation of speech sounds by young infants. *Developmental Psychology, 23,* 648–654.

Jusczyk, P. W., Friederici, A. D., Wessels, J., Svenkerud, V. Y., & Jusczyk, A. M. (1993). Infants' sensitivity to the sound patterns of native language words. *Journal of Memory and Language, 32,* 402–420.

Jusczyk, P. W., Hirsh-Pasek, K., Kemler Nelson, D. G., Kennedy, L., Woodward, A., & Piwoz, J. (1992). Perception of acoustic correlates of major phrasal units by young infants. *Cognitive Psychology, 24,* 252–293.

Jusczyk, P. W., Hohne, E. A., Jusczyk, A. M., & Redanz, N. J. (1993). Do infants remember voices? *Journal of the Acoustical Society of America, 93,* 2373.

Jusczyk, P. W., Jusczyk, A. M., Kennedy, L. J., Schomberg, T., & Koenig, N. (1995). Young infants' retention of information about bisyllabic utterances. *Journal of Experimental Psychology: Human Perception and Performance, 21,* 822–836.

Jusczyk, P. W., Kennedy, L. J., & Jusczyk, A. M. (1995). Young infants' retention of information about syllables. *Infant Behavior and Development, 18,* 27–42.

Jusczyk, P. W., & Krumhansl, C. L. (1993). Pitch and rhythmic patterns affecting infants' sensitivity to musical phrase structure. *Journal of Experimental Psychology: Human Perception and Performance, 19,* 627–640.

Jusczyk, P. W., Luce, P. A., & Charles-Luce, J. (1994). Infants' sensitivity to phonotactic patterns in the native language. *Journal of Memory and Language, 33,* 630–645.

Jusczyk, P. W., Pisoni, D. B., & Mullennix, J. (1992). Some consequences of stimulus variability on speech processing by 2-month-old infants. *Cognition, 43,* 253–291.

Jusczyk, P. W., Pisoni, D. B., Reed, M., Fernald, A., & Myers, M. (1983). Infants' discrimination of the duration of a rapid spectrum change in nonspeech signals. *Science, 222,* 175–177.

Jusczyk, P. W., Pisoni, D. B, Walley, A. C., & Murray, J. (1980). Discrimination of relative onset time of two-component tones by infants. *Journal of the Acoustical Society of America, 67,* 262–270.

Jusczyk, P. W., & Thompson, E. J. (1978). Perception of a phonetic contrast in multisyllabic utterances by two-month-old infants. *Perception and Psychophysics, 23,* 105–109.

Kaplan, P. S., Goldstein, M. H., Huckeby, E. R., Owren, M. J., & Cooper, R. P. (1995). Dishabituation of visual attention by infant- versus adult-directed speech: Effects of frequency modulation and spectral composition. *Infant Behavior and Development, 18,* 209–223.

Kemler Nelson, D. G., Jusczyk, P. W., Mandel, D. R., Myers, J., Turk, A., & Gerken, L. (1995). The head-turn preference procedure for testing auditory perception. *Infant Behavior and Development, 18,* 111–116.

Kenstowicz, M. (1994). *Phonology in generative grammar.* Cambridge, England: Blackwell.

Kent, R. D. (1993). Infants and speech: Seeking patterns. *Journal of Phonetics, 21,* 117–123.

Klatt, D. H. (1975). Vowel lengthening is syntactically determined in connected discourse. *Journal of Phonetics, 3,* 129–140.

Kluender, K. R. (1991). Effects of first formant onset frequency on VOT judgments result from processes not specific to humans. *Journal of the Acoustical Society of America, 90,* 83–96.

Kluender, K. R., & Lotto, A. J. (1994). Effects of first formant onset frequency on [-voice] judgments results from auditory processes not specific to humans. *Journal of the Acoustical Society of America, 95,* 1044–1052.

Koenig, W., Dunn, H. K., & Lacy, L. Y. (1946). The sound spectrograph. *Journal of the Acoustical Society of America, 18,* 19–49.

Krumhansl, C. L., & Jusczyk, P. W. (1990). Infants' perception of phrase structure in music. *Psychological Science, 1,* 70–73.

Kuhl, P. K. (1979). Speech perception in early infancy: Perceptual constancy for spectrally dissimilar vowel categories. *Journal of the Acoustical Society of America, 66,* 1668–1679.

Kuhl, P. K. (1981). Discrimination of speech by nonhuman animals: Basic auditory sensitivities conducive to the perception of speech-sound categories. *Journal of the Acoustical Society of America, 70,* 340–349.

Kuhl, P. K. (1983). Perception of auditory equivalence classes for speech in early infancy. *Infant Behavior and Development, 6,* 263–285.

Kuhl, P. K. (1985). Methods in the study of infant speech perception. In G. Gottlieb & N. A. Krasnegor (Eds.), *Measurement of audition and vision in the first year of postnatal life: A methodological overview.* Norwood, NJ: ABLEX.

Kuhl, P. K. (1991). Human adults and human infants show a "perceptual magnet effect" for the prototypes of speech categories, monkeys do not. *Perception and Psychophysics, 50,* 93–107.

Kuhl, P. K. (1993). Innate predispositions and the effects of experience in speech perception: The native language magnet theory. In B. D. Boysson-Bardies, S. D. Schoen, P. Jusczyk, P. McNeilage, & J. Morton (Eds.), *Developmental neurocognition: Speech and face processing in the first year of life.* Dordrecht, The Netherlands: Kluwer.

Kuhl, P. K., & Meltzoff, A. N. (1982). The bimodal perception of speech in infancy. *Science, 218,* 1138–1141.

Kuhl, P. K., & Meltzoff, A. N. (1984). The intermodal representation of speech in infants. *Infant Behavior and Development, 7,* 361–381.

Kuhl, P. K., & Miller, J. D. (1975). Speech perception by the chinchilla: Voice-voiceless distinction in alveolar plosive consonants. *Science, 190,* 69–72.

Kuhl, P. K., & Miller, J. D. (1978). Speech perception by the chinchilla: Identification functions for synthetic VOT stimuli. *Journal of the Acoustical Society of America, 63,* 905–917.

Kuhl, P. K., & Miller, J. D. (1982). Discrimination of auditory target dimensions in the presence or absence of variation in a second dimension by infants. *Perception and Psychophysics, 31,* 279–292.

Kuhl, P. K., & Padden, D. M. (1982). Enhanced discriminability at the phonetic boundaries for the voicing feature in macaques. *Perception and Psychophysics, 32,* 542–550.

Kuhl, P. K., & Padden, D. M. (1983). Enhanced discriminability at the phonetic boundaries for the place feature in macaques. *Journal of the Acoustical Society of America, 73,* 1003–1010.

Kuhl, P. K., Williams, K. A., Lacerda, F., Stevens, K. N., & Lindblom, B. (1992). Linguistic experiences alter phonetic perception in infants by 6 months of age. *Science, 255,* 606–608.

Kuhl, P. K., Williams, K. A., & Meltzoff, A. N. (1991). Cross-modal speech perception in adults and infants using non-speech auditory stimuli. *Journal of Experimental Psychology: Human Perception and Performance, 17,* 829–840.

Ladefoged, P., & Broadbent, D. E. (1957). Information conveyed by vowels. *Journal of the Acoustical Society of America, 29,* 98–104.

Ladefoged, P., & Broadbent, D. E. (1960). Perception of sequence in auditory events. *Quarterly Journal of Experimental Psychology, 12,* 162–170.

Lalonde, C. E., & Werker, J. F. (1995). Cognitive influences on cross-language speech perception in infancy. *Infant Behavior and Development, 18,* 459–475.

Lasky, R. E., Syrdal-Lasky, A., & Klein, R. E. (1975). VOT discrimination by four- to six-and-a-half-month-old infants from Spanish environments. *Journal of Experimental Child Psychology, 20,* 215–225.

Lecanuet, J. -P., & Granier-Deferre, C. (1993). Speech stimuli in the fetal environment. In B. de Boysson-Bardies, S. de Schonen, P. Jusczyk, P. MacNeilage, & J. Morton (Eds.), *Developmental neurocognition: Speech and face processing in the first year of life.* Dordrecht, The Netherlands: Kluwer Academic.

Lee, K. F. (1989). *Automatic speech recognition: The development of the SPHINX system.* Norwell, MA: Kluwer Academic.

Lehiste, I. (1960). *An acoustic-phonetic study of internal open juncture.* New York: Karger.

Lehiste, I., Olive, J. P., & Streeter, L. (1976). The role of duration in disambiguating syntactically ambiguous sentences. *Journal of the Acoustical Society of America, 60,* 1199–1202.

Lehrdahl, F., & Jackendoff, R. (1983). *A generative theory of tonal music.* Cambridge, MA: MIT Press.

Liberman, A. M., Cooper, F. S., Shankweiler, D. P., & Studdert-Kennedy, M. (1967). Perception of the speech code. *Psychological Review, 74,* 431–461.

Liberman, A. M., Harris, K. S., Hoffman, H. S., & Griffith, B. C. (1957). The discrimination of speech sounds within and across phoneme boundaries. *Journal of Experimental Psychology, 54,* 358–368.

Liberman, A. M., Harris, K. S., Kinney, J. A., & Lane, H. L. (1961). The discrimination of relative-onset time of the components of certain speech and non-speech patterns. *Journal of Experimental Psychology, 61,* 379–388.

Liberman, A. M., Isenberg, D., & Rakerd, B. (1981). Duplex perception of cues for stop consonants: Evidence for a phonetic mode. *Perception and Psychophysics, 30,* 133–143.

Liberman, A. M., & Mattingly, I. G. (1989). A specialization for speech perception. *Science, 243,* 489–494.

Liljencrants, J., & Lindblom, B. (1972). Numerical simulation of vowel quality systems: The role of perceptual contrast. *Language, 48,* 839–862.

Lisker, L., & Abramson, A. S. (1967). *The voicing dimension: Some experiments in comparative phonetics* [Proceedings of the Sixth International Congress of Phonetic Sciences]. Prague: Academia.

Lively, S. (1993). An examination of the "perceptual magnet" effect. *Journal of the Acoustical Society of America, 93,* 2423.

Lively, S., Logan, J. S., & Pisoni, D. B. (1993). Training Japanese listeners to identify English /r/ and /l/. II. The role of phonetic environment and talker variability in learning new perceptual categories. *Journal of the Acoustical Society of America, 94,* 1242–1255.

Lively, S., Pisoni, D. B., Yamada, R. A., Tohkura, Y., & Yamada, T. (1994). Training Japanese listeners to identify English /r/ and /l/. III. Long-term retention of new phonetic categories. *Journal of the Acoustical Society of America, 94,* 2076–2087.

Logan, J. S. (1992). *A computational analysis of young children's lexicons.* (Research on spoken language processing, Tech. Rep. No. 8). Bloomington: Indiana University.

Logan, J. S., Lively, S. E., & Pisoni, D. B. (1991). Training Japanese listeners to identify English /r/ and /l/: A first report. *Journal of the Acoustical Society of America, 89*, 874–886.

Lynch, M. P., & Eilers, R. E. (1992). A study of perceptual development for musical tuning. *Perception and Psychophysics, 52*, 599–608.

Lynch, M. P., Eilers, R. E., Oller, D. K., & Urbano, R. C. (1990). Innateness, experience, and music perception. *Psychological Science, 1*, 70–73.

MacKain, K. S. (1982). Assessing the role of experience on infants' speech discrimination. *Journal of Child Language, 9*, 527–542.

Mandel, D. R., Jusczyk, P. W., & Kemler Nelson, D. G. (1994). Does sentential prosody help infants to organize and remember speech information? *Cognition, 53*, 155–180.

Mandel, D. R., Jusczyk, P. W., & Pisoni, D. B. (1995). Infants' recognition of the sound patterns of their own names. *Psychological Science, 6*, 314–317.

Mandel, D. R., Kemler Nelson, D. G., & Jusczyk, P. W. (1996). Infants remember the order of words in a spoken sentence. *Cognitive Development, 11*, 181–196.

Marean, C. G., & Werner, L. A. (1991, May). *Forward masking functions of 3-month-old infants*. Paper presented at the 121st meeting of the Acoustical Society of America, Baltimore.

Markey, K. L., Menn, L., & Mozer, M. C. (1995). A developmental model of the sensorimotor foundations of phonology. In D. MacLaughlin & S. McEwen (Eds.), *Proceedings of the 19th annual Boston University Conference on Language Development*. Somerville, MA: Cascadilla Press.

Markman, E. M. (1991). The whole-object, taxonomic, and mutual exclusivity assumptions as initial constraints on word meanings. In S. A. Gelman & J. P. Byrnes (Eds.), *Perspectives on language and thought*. Cambridge, England: Cambridge University Press.

Marks, L., & Miller, G. A. (1964). The role of semantic and syntactic constraints in the memorization of English sentences. *Journal of Verbal Learning and Verbal Behavior, 3*, 1–5.

Marler, P., & Peters, S. (1981). Birdsong and speech: Evidence for special processing. In P. D. Eimas & J. L. Miller (Eds.), *Perspectives on the study of speech*. Hillsdale, NJ: Erlbaum.

Martin, C. S., Mullennix, J. W., Pisoni, D. B., & Summers, W. V. (1989). Effects of talker variability on recall of spoken word lists. *Journal of Experimental Psychology: Learning, Memory and Cognition, 15*, 676–684.

Massaro, D. W. (1972). Preperceptual images, processing time, and perceptual units in auditory perception. *Psychological Review, 79*, 124–145.

Massaro, D. W., & Cohen, M. M. (1990). Perception of synthesized audible and visible speech. *Psychological Science, 1*, 55–63.

Massaro, D. W., & Cohen, M. M. (1993). Perceiving asynchronous bimodal speech in consonant-vowel and vowel syllables. *Speech Communication, 13*, 127–134.

Massaro, D. W., Cohen, M. M., & Smeele, P. M. T. (1995). Cross-linguistic comparisons in the integration of visual and auditory speech. *Memory and Cognition, 23*, 113–131.

Massaro, D. W., Tsuzaki, M., Cohen, M. M., Gesi, A., & Heredia, R. (1993). Bimodal speech perception: An examination across languages. *Journal of Phonetics, 21*, 445–478.

Mattingly, I. G., Liberman, A. M., Syrdal, A. K., & Halwes, T. (1971). Discrimination in speech and non-speech modes. *Cognitive Psychology, 2*, 131–157.

McCall, R. B., & Melson, W. H. (1970). Amount of familiarization and the response to auditory discrepancies. *Child Development, 41*, 861–869.

McGurk, H., & MacDonald, J. (1976). Hearing lips and seeing voices. *Nature, 264*, 746–748.

McNeill, D. (1966). Developmental psycholinguistics. In F. Smith & G. A. Miller (Eds.), *The genesis of language*. Cambridge, MA: MIT Press.

Mehler, J., Bertoncini, J., Barriere, M., & Jassik-Gerschenfeld, D. (1978). Infant recognition of mother's voice. *Perception, 7*, 491–497.

Mehler, J., Dupoux, E., Nazzi, T., & Dehaene-Lambertz, G. (1996). Coping with linguistic diversity: The infant's point of view. In J. L. Morgan & K. Demuth (Eds.), *Signal to syntax*. Hillsdale, NJ: Erlbaum.

Mehler, J., Dupoux, E., & Segui, J. (1990). Constraining models of lexical access: The onset of word recognition. In G. T. M. Altmann (Ed.), *Cognitive models of speech processing*. Hillsdale, NJ: Erlbaum.

Mehler, J., Jusczyk, P. W., Lambertz, G., Halsted, N., Bertoncini, J., & Amiel-Tison, C. (1988). A precursor of language acquisition in young infants. *Cognition, 29*, 144–178.

Melson, W. H., & McCall, R. B. (1970). Attentional responses of 5-month-old girls to discrepant auditory stimuli. *Child Development, 41*, 1159–1171.

Miller, C. L. (1983). Developmental changes in male-female voice classification by infants. *Infant Behavior and Development, 6*, 313–330.

Miller, G. A., & Isard, S. (1963). Some perceptual consequences of linguistic rules. *Journal of Verbal Learning and Verbal Behavior, 2*, 217–228.

Miller, J. D., Weir, C. C., Pastore, L., Kelly, W. J., & Dooling, R. J. (1976). Discrimination and labeling of noise-buzz sequences with varying noise-lead times: An example of categorical perception. *Journal of the Acoustical Society of America, 60*, 410–417.

Miller, J. L., & Liberman, A. M. (1979). Some effects of later-occurring information on the perception of stop consonant and semivowel. *Perception and Psychophysics, 25,* 457–465.

Miyawaki, K., Strange, W., Verbrugge, R., Liberman, A. M., Jenkins, J. J., & Fujimura, O. (1975). An effect of linguistic experience: The discrimination of /r/ and /l/ by native speakers of Japanese and English. *Perception and Psychophysics, 18,* 331–340.

Moon, C., Cooper, R. P., & Fifer, W. P. (1993). Two-day-old infants prefer their native language. *Infant Behavior and Development, 16,* 495–500.

Moore, J. M., Thompson, G., & Thompson, M. (1975). Auditory localization of infants as a function of reinforcement conditions. *Journal of Speech and Hearing Disorders, 40,* 29–34.

Morgan, J. L. (1986). *From simple input to complex grammar.* Cambridge, MA: MIT Press.

Morgan, J. L. (1994). Converging measures of speech segmentation in preverbal infants. *Infant Behavior and Development, 17,* 389–403.

Morgan, J. L. (1996). A rhythmic bias in preverbal speech segmentation. *Journal of Memory and Language, 35,* 666–688.

Morgan, J. L., & Demuth, K. (Eds.). (1996). *Signal to syntax: Bootstrapping from speech to grammar in early acquisition.* Mahwah, NJ: Erlbaum.

Morgan, J. L., & Saffran, J. R. (1995). Emerging integration of sequential and suprasegmental information in preverbal speech segmentation. *Child Development, 66,* 911–936.

Morgan, J. L., Swingley, D., & Miritai, K. (1993, March). *Infants listen longer to speech with extraneous noises inserted at clause boundaries.* Paper presented at the biennial meeting of the Society for Research in Child Development, New Orleans, LA.

Morrongiello, B. A., & Trehub, S. E. (1987). Age-related changes in auditory temporal perception. *Journal of Experimental Child Psychology, 44,* 413–426.

Morse, P. A. (1972). The discrimination of speech and non-speech stimuli in early infancy. *Journal of Experimental Child Psychology, 13,* 477–492.

Morse, P. A., Eilers, R. E., & Gavin, W. J. (1982). The perception of the sound of silence in early infancy. *Child Development, 53,* 189–195.

Mullennix, J. W., & Pisoni, D. B. (1990). Stimulus variability and processing dependencies in speech perception. *Perception and Psychophysics, 47,* 379–390.

Mullennix, J. W., Pisoni, D. B., & Martin, C. S. (1989). Some effects of talker variability on spoken word recognition. *Journal of the Acoustical Society of America, 85,* 365–378.

Murphy, W. D., Shea, S. L., & Aslin, R. N. (1989). Identification of vowels in "vowelless" syllables by 3-year-olds. *Perception and Psychophysics, 46,* 375–383.

Myers, J., Jusczyk, P. W., Kemler Nelson, D. G., Charles-Luce, J., Woodward, A., & Hirsh-Pasek, K. (1996). Infants' sensitivity to word boundaries in fluent speech. *Journal of Child Language, 23,* 1–30.

Newport, E. (1990). Maturational constraints on language learning. *Cognitive Science, 14,* 11–28.

Newport, E. (1991). Contrasting conceptions of the critical period for language. In S. Carey & R. Gelman (Eds.), *The epigenesis of mind: Essays on biology and cognition.* Hillsdale, NJ: Erlbaum.

Newsome, M., & Jusczyk, P. W. (1995). Do infants use stress as a cue for segmenting fluent speech? In D. MacLaughlin & S. McEwen (Eds.), Paper presented at the 19th Boston University Conference on language development (Vol. 2, pp. 415–426). Boston, MA: Cascadilla Press.

Nosofsky, R. M. (1987). Attention and learning processes in the identification and categorization of integral stimuli. *Journal of Experimental Psychology: Learning, Memory and Cognition, 14,* 700–708.

Nosofsky, R. M. (1988). Exemplar-based accounts of relations between classification, recognition, and typicality. *Journal of Experimental Psychology: Learning, Memory and Cognition, 15,* 282–304.

Nozza, R. J. (1987). Infant speech-sound discrimination testing: Effects of stimulus intensity and procedural model on measures of performance. *Journal of the Acoustical Society of America, 81,* 1928–1939.

Nozza, R. J. (1995). Estimating the contribution of nonsensory factors to infant-adult differences in behavioral thresholds. *Hearing Research, 91,* 72–77.

Nozza, R. J., & Wilson, W. R. (1984). Masked and unmasked pure-tone thresholds of infants and adults: Development of auditory frequency selectivity and sensitivity. *Journal of Speech and Hearing Research, 27,* 613–622.

Nygaard, L. C., Sommers, M. S., & Pisoni, D. B. (1994). Speech perception as a talker contingent process. *Psychological Science, 5,* 42–46.

Nygaard, L. C., Sommers, M. S., & Pisoni, D. B. (1995). Effects of stimulus variability on perception and representation of spoken words in memory. *Perception and Psychophysics, 57,* 989–1001.

Olsho, L. W. (1984). Infant frequency discrimination as a function of frequency. *Infant Behavior and Development, 7,* 27–35.

Olsho, L. W. (1985). Infant auditory perception: Tonal masking. *Infant Behavior and Development, 8,* 371–384.

Olsho, L. W., Koch, E. G., Carter, E. A., Halpin, C. F., & Spetner, N. B. (1988). Pure-tone sensitivity of human infants. *Journal of the Acoustical Society of America, 84,* 1316–1324.

Olsho, L. W., Koch, E. G., & Halpin, C. F. (1987). Level and age effects in infant frequency discrimination. *Journal of the Acoustical Society of America, 82,* 454–464.

Olsho, L. W., Koch, E. G., Halpin, C. F., & Carter, E. A. (1987). An observer-based psychoacoustic procedure for use with young infants. *Developmental Psychology, 23,* 627–640.

Olsho, L. W., Schoon, C., Sakai, R., Sperduto, V., & Turpin, R. (1982a). Preliminary data on infant frequency discrimination. *Journal of the Acoustical Society of America, 71,* 509–511.

Olsho, L. W., Schoon, C., Sakai, R., Sperduto, V., & Turpin, R. (1982b). Auditory frequency discrimination in infancy. *Developmental Psychology, 18,* 721–726.

Otake, T., Hatano, G., Cutler, A., & Mehler, J. (1993). Mora or syllable? Speech segmentation in Japanese. *Journal of Memory and Language, 32,* 258–278.

Palmeri, T. J., Goldinger, S. D., & Pisoni, D. B. (1993). Episodic encoding of voice attributes and recognition memory for spoken words. *Journal of Experimental Psychology: Learning, Memory, and Cognition, 19,* 309–328.

Papousek, M., Papousek, H., & Haekel, M. (1987). Didactic adjustments in fathers' and mothers' speech to their three-month-old infants. *Journal of Psycholinguistic Research, 16,* 491–516.

Pegg, J. E., Werker, J. F., & McLeod, P. J. (1992). Preference for infant-directed over adult-directed speech: Evidence from 7-week-old infants. *Infant Behavior and Development, 15,* 325–345.

Peters, A. (1983). *The units of language acquisition.* Cambridge, England: Cambridge University Press.

Peterson, G. E., & Barney, H. L. (1952). Control methods used in a study of the vowels. *Journal of the Acoustical Society of America, 24,* 175–184.

Phillips, J. R. (1973). Syntax and vocabulary of mothers' speech to children: Age and sex comparisons. *Child Development, 44,* 182–185.

Pisoni, D. B. (1977). Identification and discrimination of the relative onset of two component tones: Implications for voicing perception in stops. *Journal of the Acoustical Society of America, 61,* 1352–1361.

Pisoni, D. B. (1990). *Effects of talker variability on speech perception: Implications for current research and theory.* Proceedings of the International Conference on Spoken Language Processing, Kobe, Japan.

Pisoni, D. B. (1992). Some comments on talker normalization in speech perception. In Y. Tohkura, E. Vatikiotis-Bateson, & Y. Sagisaka (Eds.), *Speech perception, production and linguistic structure.* Tokyo, Japan: IOS Press.

Pisoni, D. B. (1996). Some thoughts on "normalization" in speech perception. In K. A. Johnson & J. W. Mullennix (Eds.), *Talker variability in speech processing.* San Diego, CA: Academic Press.

Pisoni, D. B., Aslin, R. N., Perey, A. J., & Hennessy, B. L. (1982). Some effects of laboratory training on identification and discrimination of voicing contrasts in stop consonants. *Journal of Experimental Psychology: Human Perception and Performance, 8,* 297–314.

Pisoni, D. B., Carrell, T. D., & Gans, S. J. (1983). Perception of the duration of rapid spectrum changes in speech and non-speech signals. *Perception and Psychophysics, 34,* 314–322.

Plunkett, K., & Marchman, V. (1993). From rote learning to system building: Acquiring verb morphology in children and connectionist nets. *Cognition, 48,* 21–69.

Polka, L., & Werker, J. F. (1994). Developmental changes in perception of non-native vowel contrasts. *Journal of Experimental Psychology: Human Perception and Performance, 20,* 421–435.

Price, P. J., Ostendorf, M., Shattuck-Hufnagel, S., & Fong, C. (1991). The use of prosody in syntactic disambiguation. *Journal of the Acoustical Society of America, 90,* 2956–2970.

Reitveld, A. C. M., & Koopmans-van Beinum, F. J. (1987). Vowel reduction and stress. *Speech Communication, 6,* 217–229.

Repp, B. H. (1982). Phonetic trading relations and context effects: New experimental evidence for a speech mode of perception. *Psychological Bulletin, 92,* 81–110.

Richards, D. S., Frentzen, B., Gerhardt, K. J., McCann, M. E., & Abrams, R. M. (1992). Sound levels in the human uterus. *Obstetrics & Gynecology, 80,* 186–190.

Roediger, H. L. (1990). Implicit memory: Retention without remembering. *American Psychologist, 45,* 1043–1056.

Rosenblum, L. D., Schmuckler, M. A., & Johnson, J. A. (1997). The McGurk effect in infants. *Perception and Psychophysics, 59,* 347–357.

Rumelhart, D. E., & McClelland, J. L. (1986). *Parallel distributed processing: Explorations in the microstructure of cognition: Vol. 1. Foundations.* Cambridge, MA: MIT Press.

Saffran, J. R., Aslin, R. N., & Newport, E. L. (1996). Statistical learning by 8-month-old infants. *Science, 274,* 1926–1928.

Saffran, J. R., Newport, E. L., & Aslin, R. N. (1996). Word segmentation: The role of distributional cues. *Journal of Memory and Language, 35,* 606–621.

Saffran, J. R., Newport, E. L., Aslin, R. N., Tunick, R. A., & Barrueco, S. (1997). Incidental language learning: Listening (and learning) out of the corner of your ear. *Psychological Science, 8,* 101–105.

Schacter, D. L. (1990). Perceptual representation systems and implicit memory: Toward a resolution of the multiple memory systems debate. In A. Diamond (Ed.), Development and neural basis of higher cognitive function. *Annals of the New York Academy of Sciences, 608,* 543–571.

Schacter, D. L. (1992). Understanding implicit memory: A cognitive neuroscience approach. *American Psychologist, 47,* 559–569.

Schneider, B. A., Morrongiello, B. A., & Trehub, S. E. (1990). The size of the critical band in infants, children, and adults. *Journal of Experimental Psychology: Human Perception and Performance, 16,* 642–652.

Schneider, B. A., Trehub, S. E., & Bull, D. (1979). The development of basic auditory processes in infants. *Canadian Journal of Psychology, 33,* 306–319.

Schneider, B. A., Trehub, S. E., & Bull, D. (1980). High-frequency sensitivity in infants. *Science, 207,* 1003–1004.

Schneider, B. A., Trehub, S. E., Morrongiello, B. A, & Thorpe, L. A. (1989). Developmental changes in masked thresholds. *Journal of the Acoustical Society of America, 86,* 1733–1742.

Schwartz, R. G. (1988). Phonological factors in early lexical acquisition. In M. D. Smith & J. L. Locke (Eds.), *The emergent lexicon: The child's development of a linguistic vocabulary.* New York: Academic Press.

Scott, D. R. (1982). Duration as a cue to the perception of a phrase boundary. *Journal of the Acoustical Society of America, 71,* 996–1007.

Scott, D. R., & Cutler, A. (1984). Segmental phonology and the perception of syntactic structure. *Journal of Verbal Learning and Verbal Behavior, 23,* 450–466.

Shatz, M., & Gelman, R. (1973). The development of communication skills: Modifications in the speech of young children as a function of listener. *Monographs of the Society for Research on Child Development, 38*(5).

Sinnott, J. M., & Aslin, R. N. (1985). Frequency and intensity discrimination in human infants and adults. *Journal of the Acoustical Society of America, 78,* 1986–1992.

Sinnott, J. M., Pisoni, D. B., & Aslin, R. N. (1983). A comparison of pure-tone auditory thresholds in human infants and adults. *Infant Behavior and Development, 6,* 3–17.

Snow, C. E. (1972). Mothers' speech to children learning language. *Child Development, 43,* 549–565.

Sommers, M. S., Nygaard, L. C., & Pisoni, D. B. (1994). Stimulus variability and spoken word recognition: I. Effects of variability in speaking rate and overall amplitude. *Journal of the Acoustical Society of America, 96,* 1314–1324.

Spence, M. J., & DeCasper, A. D. (1987). Prenatal experience with low-frequency maternal-voice sounds influence neonatal perception of maternal voice samples. *Infant Behavior and Development, 10,* 133–142.

Spence, M. J., & Freeman, M. S. (1996). Newborn infants prefer the maternal low-pass filtered voice, but not the maternal whispered voice. *Infant Behavior and Development, 19,* 199–212.

Spetner, N. B., & Olsho, L. W. (1990). Auditory frequency resolution in human infancy. *Child Development, 61,* 632–652.

Spring, D. R., & Dale, P. S. (1977). Discrimination of linguistic stress in early infancy. *Journal of Speech and Hearing Research, 20,* 224–232.

Stern, D. N., Spieker, S., Barnett, R. K., & MacKain, K. (1983). The prosody of maternal speech: Infant age and context related changes. *Journal of Child Language, 10,* 1–15.

Stevens, K. N. (1964). Acoustical aspects of speech production. In W. O. Fenn & H. Rohn (Eds.), *Handbook of physiology—Respiration I.* Washington, DC: American Physiological Society.

Strange, W. (1989). Dynamic specification of coarticulated vowels spoken in sentence context. *Journal of the Acoustical Society of America, 85,* 2135–2153.

Streeter, L. A. (1976). Language perception of 2-month-old infants shows effects of both innate mechanisms and experience. *Nature, 259,* 39–41.

Suci, G. (1967). The validity of pause as an index of units in language. *Journal of Verbal Learning and Verbal Behavior, 6,* 26–32.

Sumby, W. H., & Pollack, I. (1954). Visual contribution to speech intelligibility in noise. *Journal of the Acoustical Society of America, 26,* 212–215.

Summerfield, A. Q. (1979). Use of visual information in phonetic perception. *Phonetica, 36,* 314–331.

Suomi, K. (1993). An outline of a model of adult phonological organization and behavior. *Journal of Phonetics, 21,* 29–60.

Sussman, J. E., & Lauckner-Morano, V. J. (1995). Further tests of the "perceptual magnet effect" in the perception of [i]: Identification and change/no change discrimination. *Journal of the Acoustical Society of America, 97,* 539–552.

Teller, D. Y. (1979). The forced-choice preferential looking procedure: A psychophysical technique for use with human infants. *Infant Behavior and Development, 2,* 135–153.

Thorpe, L. A., & Trehub, S. E. (1989). Duration illusion and auditory grouping in infancy. *Developmental Psychology, 24,* 484–491.

Thorpe, L. A., Trehub, S. E., Morrongiello, B. A., & Bull, D. (1988). Perceptual grouping by infants and preschool children. *Developmental Psychology, 24,* 484–491.

Trainor, L. J., & Trehub, S. E. (1992). A comparison of infants' and adults' sensitivity to Western musical structure. *Journal of Experimental Psychology: Human Perception and Performance, 18,* 394–402.

Trehub, S. E. (1976). The discrimination of foreign speech contrasts by infants and adults. *Child Development, 47,* 466–472.

Trehub, S. E., Bull, D., & Thorpe, L. A. (1984). Infants' perception of melodies: The role of melodic contour. *Child Development, 55,* 821–830.

Trehub, S. E., Schneider, B. A., & Endman, M. (1980). Developmental changes in infants' sensitivity to octave-band noises. *Journal of Experimental Child Psychology, 29,* 282–293.

Trehub, S. E., Schneider, B. A., & Henderson, J. L. (1995). Gap detection in infants, children, and adults. *Journal of the Acoustical Society of America, 98,* 2532–2541.

Trehub, S. E., & Thorpe, L. A. (1989). Infants' perception of rhythm: Categorization of auditory sequences by temporal structure. *Canadian Journal of Psychology, 43,* 217–229.

Trehub, S. E., Thorpe, L. A., & Morrongiello, B. (1987). Organizational processes in infants' perception of auditory patterns. *Child Development, 58,* 741–749.

Trehub, S. E., Thorpe, L. A., & Morrongiello, B. A. (1985). Infants' perception of melodies: Changes in a single tone. *Infant Behavior and Development, 8,* 213–223.

Trehub, S. E., Thorpe, L. A., & Trainor, L. J. (1990). Infants' perception of good and bad melodies. *Psychomusicology, 9,* 5–19.

Tsushima, T., Takizawa, O., Sasaki, M., Siraki, S., Nishi, K., Kohno, M., Menyuk, P., & Best, C. (1994). *Discrimination of English /r-l/ and /w-y/ by Japanese infants at 6–12 months: Language specific developmental changes in speech perception abilities.* Paper presented at the International Conference on Spoken Language Processing, 1695–1698, The Acoustical Society of Japan, Yokohama, Japan.

Turk, A. E., Jusczyk, P. W., & Gerken, L. A. (1995). Infants' sensitivity to syllable weight as a determinant of English stress. *Language and Speech, 38,* 143–158.

Verbrugge, R. R., Strange, W., Shankweiler, D. P., & Edman, T. R. (1976). What information enables a listener to map a talker's vowel space? *Journal of the Acoustical Society of America, 60,* 198–212.

Vihman, M. M., Macken, M. A., Miller, R., Simmons, H., & Miller, J. (1985). From babbling to speech: A reassessment of the continuity issue. *Language, 61,* 397–445.

Werker, J. F. (1991). The ontogeny of speech perception. In I. G. Mattingly & M. Studdert-Kennedy (Eds.), *Modularity and the motor theory of speech perception.* Hillsdale, NJ: Erlbaum.

Werker, J. F., Gilbert, J. H., Humphrey, K., & Tees, R. C. (1981). Developmental aspects of cross-language speech perception. *Child Development, 52,* 349–355.

Werker, J. F., & Lalonde, C. E. (1988). Cross-language speech perception: Initial capabilities and developmental change. *Developmental Psychology, 24,* 672–683.

Werker, J. F., & Logan, J. S. (1985). Perceptual flexibility: Maintenance or recovery of the ability to discriminate non-native speech sounds. *Perception and Psychophysics, 37,* 35–44.

Werker, J. F., & McLeod, P. J. (1989). Infant preference for both male and female infant-directed talk: A developmental study of attentional and affective responsiveness. *Canadian Journal of Psychology, 43,* 230–246.

Werker, J. F., Pegg, J. E., & McLeod, P. (1994). A cross-language investigation of infant preference for infant-directed communication. *Infant Behavior and Development, 17,* 323–333.

Werker, J. F., & Tees, R. C. (1983). Developmental changes across childhood in the perception of non-native speech sounds. *Canadian Journal of Psychology, 37,* 278–286.

Werker, J. F., & Tees, R. C. (1984). Cross-language speech perception: Evidence for perceptual re-organization during the first year of life. *Infant Behavior and Development, 7,* 49–63.

Werner, L. A. (1992). Interpreting developmental psychoacoustics. In L. A. Werner & E. W. Rubel (Eds.), *Developmental psychoacoustics.* Washington, DC: American Psychological Association.

Werner, L. A., & Bargones, J. Y. (1991). Sources of auditory masking in infants: Distraction effects. *Perception and Psychophysics, 50,* 405–412.

Werner, L. A., & Bargones, J. Y. (1992). Psychoacoustic development of human infants. In L. Lipsitt & C. Rovee-Collier (Eds.), *Advances in infancy research* (Vol. 7). Norwood, NJ: ABLEX.

Werner, L. A., & Gillenwater, J. M. (1990). Pure-tone sensitivity of 2- to 5-week-old infants. *Infant Behavior and Development, 13,* 355–375.

Werner, L. A., Marean, G. C., Halpin, C. F., Spetner, N. B., & Gillenwater, J. M. (1992). Infant auditory temporal acuity: Gap detection. *Child Development, 63,* 260–272.

Whalen, D. H., & Liberman, A. M. (1987). Speech perception takes precedence over nonspeech perception. *Science, 237,* 169–171.

Woodward, J. Z., & Aslin, R. N. (1990, April). *Segmentation cues in maternal speech to infants.* Paper presented at the 7th biennial meeting of the International Conference on Infant Studies, Montreal, Quebec, Canada.

CHAPTER 5

Infant Cognition

MARSHALL M. HAITH and JANETTE B. BENSON

Research on infant cognition has burgeoned since the last edition of the *Handbook* in 1983. While interest in early cognition has endured in some form since the rediscovery of Piaget in the 1960s, the balance of research activity in infancy has shifted noticeably from the sensory and perceptual domains toward cognitive processes over the past 15 years. This trend has created a connectedness between

infants and adults not recognized earlier. If infants can think, then perhaps their thoughts bear some resemblance to our own mental activity, in which case they should be treated as a legitimate member of the continuum of human development and not as a separate species. There is an increasing tendency for investigators to pursue concepts and lines of inquiry that were developed for older children, and theories have expanded to accommodate the infant findings (Parke, Ornstein, Rieser, & Zahn-Waxler, 1994).

However, infants are different, and that is why the inclusion of a chapter on infant cognition in this volume makes

Preparation of this manuscript was facilitated by NIMH Research Scientist Award (MH00367) to M. Haith.

sense. The dominant questions asked, the concepts used, and the methods of study in the field of early cognition are unique to infants (Horowitz, 1995). The lack of linguistic competence is key. Language is a core medium of cognitive functioning in older children and adults and an essential tool for researchers to probe cognitive activity. Yet language cannot be the vehicle for cognition in infancy, and researchers must rely on nonlinguistic indices of behavior to make inferences about cognitive abilities. They have been quite ingenious and prolific in doing so.

This struggle—between characterizing the mental processes of infants as more adultlike than previously thought, while depending on methods that are idiosyncratic to infant research—is a central theme of this chapter. Controversy rages over how data from these special methods should be interpreted, what they imply about the origins of knowledge, and how that knowledge develops. Because of the level of controversy, this will be a *critical* review of the field.

While we devote some space to topics that were reasonably well-developed by the Paul Harris chapter in the 1983 volume, such as the A, not-B search error and spatial cognition, we will devote most of our energy to newer areas.

We begin with a brief review of Piaget's legacy and a comparison of the field that Paul Harris witnessed in 1983 with what we see today. Several issues form a continuum across the areas we review; we will preview these followed by consideration of classic categories of human knowledge—object, space, time, and causality. We then move on to how infants apply these domains of knowledge when they deal with numeric information, categorize, and reason about physical phenomena.

Unfortunately, we do not have space to consider all of the topics that have a legitimate claim to inclusion in a chapter on infant cognition. Infant memory is considered in a separate chapter in this volume (Schneider & Bjorklund). We are also unable to cover research on imitation (see Meltzoff & Moore, 1992), or the prediction of later intellectual performance from early cognitive measures (see Benson, Cherny, Haith, & Fulker, 1993; Colombo, 1993; McCall & Carriger, 1993).

PIAGET'S LEGACY TO INFANT COGNITION

Piaget's theory and research still pervade the field of infant cognition. The influence of his work has been so great that it would be difficult to imagine the field in its absence. The following comments, from an anonymous review of a manuscript by Beilin (1994), makes the point for the broader field of developmental psychology:

> assessing the impact of Piaget on developmental psychology is like assessing the impact of Shakespeare on English literature or Aristotle on philosophy—impossible. The impact is too monumental to embrace and at the same time too omnipresent to detect. (p. 257)

These comments are certainly appropriate for Piaget's legacy to the study of infant cognition. Piaget focused our attention on the study of infancy as a legitimate arena from which to trace the evolution of human cognition, and he established infant cognition as a field of study in its own right. Beginning with the premise that the mental state of infants could only be inferred from direct observation of their behavior, a large part of Piaget's legacy is contained in his careful, longitudinal observations of infant behaviors. These observations formed the basis for Piaget's study of the acquisition of knowledge about fundamental dimensions of cognition, including what infants know about objects, space, time, and causality (Piaget, 1952, 1954).

Piaget's contribution was also unique in bridging the theoretical gap that spanned infancy and subsequent developmental periods. The result was an ambitious, grand theory of cognitive development that aimed to link infants' earliest attempts to make sense of the world with the higher order forms of adult logical reasoning. His developmental analysis revealed a very gradual process over the first two years of life by which infants construct knowledge about features of their world through their own actions rather than by simple observation.

Piaget was as interested in what infants could not do at each developmental stage as what they could do. The gulf between infant and adult knowledge for Piaget was a large one, and the size of the chasm has been challenged as technological advances have provided improved methodologies to assess infant abilities.

For many, Piaget's constructivism was appealing because it is developmental to the core. Development of a child's concepts was not "all or none," but rather a series of partial accomplishments or achievements that led to increasingly more comprehensive understanding. The achievement profile reflected Piaget's insistence on demanding and varied performance criteria that infants must negotiate before he was willing to endow them with mastery of a cognitive domain.

Piaget's theory has been scrutinized more than any other developmental conceptualization (Beilin, 1994), and yet hundreds of studies have verified the vast majority of the infant behaviors he described (Flavell, Miller, & Miller, 1993; Harris, 1983). Although his interpretations and the mechanisms he offered to explain development have often been attacked as too vague and abstract (i.e., assimilation, accommodation, equilibration, see Butterworth & Bryant, 1990), there is consensus that no alternative framework offers comparable scope (Flavell et al., 1993; Harris, 1983, 1989).

Some investigators have replaced Piaget's rather incompetent infant with a new and improved model that comes with an impressive list of competencies that either exist from birth (Spelke, 1991) or appear very soon thereafter (Baillargeon, 1995; Spelke, 1991). The arrival of the competent infant has diminished the value that developmentalists once placed on developmental analysis. For a prepackaged competent infant, there seems little reason to search for developmental steps toward increasing levels of mature cognitive complexity and competence. However, the behavioral criteria for assessing what infants know are much less stringent than those that Piaget required. Whether or not these altered criteria limit the conclusions that can be drawn from highly task-dependent infant behaviors is a central issue (Fischer & Bidell, 1991; Parke et al., 1994).

Despite these dismissals, Piaget's influence continues to cast a large shadow. Even so, we will not provide yet another summary of his sensorimotor stages. Several excellent overviews are available (e.g., Bremner, 1994; Harris, 1983), and the serious scholar of infant cognition will rise to the challenge to read Piaget's (1951, 1952, 1954) original infancy books.

YESTERDAY'S THEORIES AND TODAY'S MINITHEORIES

Paul Harris' (1983) infant cognition chapter, in the last edition of *The Handbook of Child Psychology*, was an exemplary critical review of theory and research. Harris systematically reviewed hundreds of empirical studies and provided a clear sense of what could be concluded and which issues remained unsettled from the products of the explosion of infant research in the 1970s.

Harris organized his chapter around three primary theoretical issues and four leading theoretical frameworks that motivated infant cognition research. The three primary theoretical concerns were the degree to which perceptual experiences required interpretation to derive meaning, the

role of experience in development, and the role of representation. The primary theoretical frameworks were those formulated by Jean Piaget, J. J. Gibson, Jerome Kagan, and Jerome Bruner.

The contrast in organization of the Harris chapter and this one reflects how the field of infant cognition has changed during the intervening years, especially with respect to the relation between theory and research. Grand developmental theories stimulated infant research in the 1960s and 1970s; not so since. These theories fell out of favor because the general principles they offered could not adequately explain the more specific features of behavior that came under the closer scrutiny of targeted research. Research today is driven more by minitheories whose behavioral sphere is much more narrowly defined (Parke, 1989; Parke et al., 1994).

Given the increasing specialization of the field, the recognition that human behavior is far too complex to be adequately explained by a small set of general principles, and the extent to which behavior can be affected by task features (Siegler, 1989; Siegler & Crowley, 1991), this trend seems reasonable. Unfortunately, there are tradeoffs. The field of infant cognition is largely composed of isolated research programs on very specific behaviors that form a series of facts that remain largely unintegrated (Horowitz, 1995). Moreover, the focus is usually so specific that age as a variable is often excluded, providing little information about age-related differences or developmental trends.

An Early Take on Our Positions

Several issues replay through the various topics we discuss, and we preview them now, while acknowledging that other authors have made several of these same points (Bogartz, Shinskey, & Speaker, in press; Butterworth, 1996; Cohen, 1995; Fischer & Bidell, 1991; Siegler, 1996).

The Rise of Precocism

Increasingly, areas of infant cognition are being incorporated into larger developmental schemes. While this trend is healthy, there are troubling byproducts. For example, an emerging trend is to document that young infants can reason about many physical concepts in ways that were once thought to be reserved for adult cognition (Baillargeon, 1993; Spelke, 1991). Some versions of this "precocism" skate on the edge of attributing full-blown, adultlike cognitive abilities to very young infants and assigning their origins to genetically determined sources, a perspective that has come to be known as neonativism (Carey & Gelman,

1991). Other versions view such early abilities more as evidence of genetic constraints that provide a starting point and direction for development (Baillargeon, 1993). Because both schemes share a tendency to attribute mature, whole-form capacities to infants with explanations that are couched in biology and evolution, conceptions of exactly what develops, the specific processes and mechanisms that guide development, and the role of additional factors, such as experience, are moot. We will challenge this shift toward a whole-process, packaged view of cognitive processes in early infancy. Our view is that infancy experiments reveal only a fragment of the large-scale concepts that experimenters address and that most cognitive concepts develop gradually over considerable time.

Perceptual and Cognitive Issues

One of the issues that Harris identified as central to infant cognitive research was the degree to which findings of infant research required attribution of meaning to perception. The distinction between perceptual and cognitive processes is clear for some phenomena, but the definitional boundaries have always caused problems for psychologists. And it is precisely at the zone of overlap where the battleground lies regarding the interpretation of many experiments in this field. There is fair agreement that infants are perceptual creatures in the first months of life. Infant cognitivists, intent on carving out a nonperceptual domain for infants, have struggled with how to eliminate perceptual interpretations so as to enhance cognitive arguments. They face several problems in doing so.

Use of Perceptual Paradigms to Address Cognitive Issues. The explosion of infant research in the late 1960s is largely attributable to the introduction of the looking-habituation paradigm, a paradigm that was designed to address sensory and perceptual issues in human infants. Several investigators have cleverly adapted this paradigm to address many other questions that fall within the cognitive domain. There are advantages to this adaptation. The habituation paradigm is well studied, and the consequences of using various procedures and measures are better known for this paradigm than for any other infancy procedure. Indexes of reliability and stability are established, and the paradigm can be executed with readily available and inexpensive equipment. Computer programs exist for administration of stimuli and for analyses of data. In brief, the habituation paradigm enjoys a level of standardization shared by no other existing infant paradigm.

There are also some drawbacks. This paradigm was originally developed to study sensory/perceptual issues, principally infant detection, discrimination, and recognition of visual patterns. Questions about detection, discrimination, and recognition have a binary quality. Can an infant detect or recognize a particular stimulus? Can one stimulus be discriminated from another? For such questions, a paradigm that depends on infant boredom and negative responding to perceptual input is suitable. However, questions about cognitive issues involve meaning and attentive processing of a more graded nature. We ask whether a paradigm that provides only binary, yes/no information can answer complex questions about infant cognition and whether the use of this paradigm encourages dichotomous rather than developmental conceptualizations.

Most importantly, differential looking in the habituation paradigm tells us only that an infant discriminates two events, not about why. The problem is that looking behavior alone is not informative about infants' *functional* knowledge about the events at issue, that is, their meaning or implications for action (Russell, 1996). When an infant reaches to a location for an object, it is not a far stretch to assume that the infant wants that object and thinks that the object is in that location; reaching is functional for that purpose. Looking behavior, while functional for getting visual information, does not tell us why the information is being gathered or what it means to infants. Any inferences about why infants look more at one thing than another go well beyond the paradigm itself.

Finally, the familiarization phase of an habituation procedure is an experience in its own right. It is often unclear whether the investigator believes that infants come to the experiment with the putative process already mastered, and the procedure is only applied to engage that process, or whether infants form the process during the familiarization sequence. Regardless, infants may use the familiarization phase as a perceptual referent so that looking may be based on the perceptual relation between the familiarization and the test events rather than on the presumptive cognitive process under study. Bogartz et al. (1997) constructed and validated a highly feasible multivariate perceptual interpretation of a well-known study by Baillargeon and her colleagues that hinged on the relation between habituation and test events, whereas the more cognitive interpretation was based on concepts infants presumably brought to the laboratory. Investigators do not typically state why they use a familiarization sequence when they believe that infants come to the laboratory with the process of interest. One might expect that infants would simply look more at an event that violates their world understanding without participating in a familiarization episode.

Favoritism for Perceptual over Cognitive Explanations. We acknowledge that we look to perceptual explanations as the first line of interpretation of studies. Perceptual interpretations are generally more parsimonious than cognitive interpretations, the processes are much better documented in the infant literature, and they require fewer inferential steps between the experimental manipulations, the presumed processes, and the observed behavior. There is a more direct tie between events and behavior for such concepts as familiarity, novelty, and salience, for example, than for beliefs, reasoning, and inference. Apparently, most investigators agree, as support for invoking cognitive processes in interpreting results usually involves a case that perceptual factors were not responsible. The need to eliminate perceptual interpretations of data that are gathered from paradigms that were designed to assess perceptual processes poses a substantial challenge to the cognitive researcher.

The Concept of "Perception" Is Limited to Features of Objects with the Assumption That Events Are Cognitive, Rather Than Perceptual. Perceptual explanations face no dispute when infants respond to an object that is (a) present, (b) static, (c) being attended, and (d) the question is about salient static physical features, such as color, size, or shape. There is also little question about response to simple motion when the question is about motion sensitivity. However, the situation gets fuzzier when the task involves complex events. What about the events in which objects participate? If parents "teach" their infants to interact with classes of objects in particular ways, for example, always hugging toy animals and always pushing toy vehicles, are we in the domain of event perception that can serve as a basis for object categorization (Gibson, 1979)? Or, does information about object function take us into the realm of meaning, a more cognitive process? Investigators often treat perceptual information as consisting only of static, physical features without much attention to the events in which objects participate or the functions that infants impose on them, arguably perceptual and sensorimotor activities in their own right.

The Issue of Representation

Related to the question of boundaries that separate perception from cognition is the issue of representation, a topic that has few rivals for center stage in discussions about cognitive development. Probably no other developmental concept attracts a wider variety of definitions and interpretations. Harris highlighted representation as one of the three major issues in his review over a decade ago, and it has not gone away. As typically discussed, representation begins when an object disappears, the baton being passed from perception to cognition; if the object is no longer present, the baby can't be operating with perception, so cognitive processes must be occurring. This version differs from Piaget's usage, which treated representation as a well-earned prize for completing the sensorimotor marathon.

The term *representation* is often used in infant work to imply that infants retain a trace of a former experience, the idea being that sensory-induced experience has been transformed in some way. Neuropsychologists use the term representation to refer to the coding of information in neural networks. For example, visual information is represented in over 30 different areas of the brain. The usage seems fair. One form of information "stands" for another, shedding some of the details in the process. The logical consequence is that even fetuses, who clearly manifest sensory sensitivity, "have" representational processes, at least for hearing and touch. Now that we recognize that even fetuses "do it," the need for a full-scale developmental model of representation that incorporates the notion of partial accomplishments is obvious. We cannot get by with a single term whose meaning spans the full distance from energy transformations in the CNS to mental manipulations of symbols. What is different about infants' representations at different moments in the performance of a task and at different stages of development? Much of the theorizing about representations in the research we review involves time intervals of less than 3 seconds; we will argue that such representations may be very closely related to the actual percepts that sensory input creates. If so, there is a question about how much we need to think about mental gyrations that the system performs on representations to account for reactions to absent objects and events. For the occlusion studies we will review, infants' responses may be to degrading perceptual information, in which case we can call on known perceptual principles, such as familiarity and response to novelty, to explain the findings.

Use of Mentalistic Terms and the Nature of Explanation

Adultocentric thinking (Fischer & Bidell, 1991) has reached a high form in some quarters of infant cognition.

We acknowledge that the role of theory is to explain phenomena to ourselves and that adultocentric accounts feel comfortable. However, words and concepts convey meaning, and how they are used guides and constrains research and explanation. While we do not adhere to stick-in-the-mud behaviorist positivism, it is fair to expect concepts to be anchored. Otherwise, there is no way to fix their meaning, and needless semantic controversies arise. Mentalistic terms such as expectations, theories, beliefs, surprise, reasoning, inference, and reflection pervade the infant cognition literature, almost as direct claims of what experiments demonstrate. While most of these terms have behavioral referents in research with older subjects, typically, the infant data only consist of infant discrimination of one stimulus or event from another.

There are at least two problems in what seems to be gratuitous and excessive usage of mentalistic terms. First, a confusion results in the infant literature because it is difficult to determine what the criteria are for evoking these processes in theoretical discussions or what the procedures are for studying them. Second, a confusion results in the developmental literature for which similar concepts may have reasonably well-established behavioral anchors. Consider surprise. Surprise has status within emotion theory, and it has been tied experimentally, on the input side, to unexpected events, and on the output side, to verbalizations, facial configurations and physiological reactions. When the concept of surprise is used in infant studies, and the only reported measure is differential looking time, potential confusion arises. Investigator X reports surprise in infants at, say 4 months, and then theorists devote energy to incorporating this "fact" into a developmental theory of emotion.[1] With respect to adultocentric thinking, an overall concept of infants emerges that grants a much more mature and adultlike mind than may be warranted; then other phenomena must be reinterpreted to accommodate this seemingly more advanced state. It is not sufficient for infancy investigators to argue that their choice of terms is only for the idiosyncratic purpose of their particular experiments. People do not choose words randomly. Science depends on conventional use of terms for clarity, effective communication, empirical extension of findings, and

theory construction. We will question the use of concepts in several areas of research.

We now consider recent research on the fundamental categories of thought that have occupied philosophers and psychologists for centuries.

THE OBJECT CONCEPT

Piaget thought that the object concept was central to an infants' understanding of all other dimensions of physical reality, and his works (Piaget, 1951, 1952, 1954) largely defined the research agenda. Research on this topic has remained lively for over 40 years since Piaget first asked, "whether the child, in its first months of life, conceives and perceives things as we do, as objects that have substance, that are permanent and of constant dimensions" (1954, p. 1). Key points to consider are:

- Piaget's theory about the object concept involved three components; investigators typically challenge Piaget's notion of the object concept on the basis of only one of these components, rarely on two, and almost never on all three. Current research typically sets performance criteria for inferences about the object concept that are much less stringent than they were for Piaget.

- Modern researchers are much less concerned about the developmental aspects of object knowledge than was Piaget, focusing instead on finding the earliest evidence for the object concept.

- While infants learn more from observation alone than Piaget believed, the challenge to his notion that sensorimotor actions were necessary for object concept development addresses only a limited aspect of his theory.

- Many puzzles remain in the object concept literature. Alternative accounts to Piaget's have difficulty in accounting for all of the behavioral phenomena, including late search, correct responding to the A location in the AB task, and incorrect responding on B trials.

Multifactor theories seem to hold the greatest promise for handling these phenomena.

The Object-Concept Complex

Our discussion focuses on recent challenges to Piaget's ideas about infant object knowledge, but first we highlight

---

[1] At least in some instances, investigators who have videotaped infants' faces during visual episodes that purportedly produce surprise have reported no facial indications of surprise in facial gestures (Bogartz, personal communication).

his main theoretical points (for detailed reviews of Piaget's sensorimotor theory, see Bremner, 1985, 1994; Gelman & Wellman, this volume; Harris, 1983, 1987; Wellman, Cross, & Bartsch, 1986).

The object concept refers to tacit knowledge about the behavior of objects that most of us take for granted and involves three core understandings that comprise the object concept complex (Piaget, 1954). First, we understand that objects maintain their permanence and substance when we no longer see them, an aspect often referred to as "object permanence." Second, we understand that we may affect objects by our actions (e.g., a pushed ball rolls off a table and falls to the floor) but that objects exist independently of our actions (e.g., gesturing from across the room will not cause a ball to move). Third, we understand that objects exist in a location in space that is independent of, but also related to, the location of other objects within a common spatial field, including the self. The object concept is thought to be so fundamental that, without it, one can barely imagine the chaotic consequences—a world in which objects rematerialize each time we make visual contact with them and that relocate arbitrarily over time. In such a world, one could not understand other dimensions of physical reality (Piaget, 1952, 1954).

Piaget's Approach: Inferences from Observations of Infant Search Behavior

Piaget created a series of clever object-hiding scenarios to assess what his own infants understood about objects. The tasks ranged from requiring only visual tracking of an object that disappeared behind a screen to manual search for an object hidden under a cover or several covers.

The hiding scenarios systematically increased in complexity with the number of possible hiding locations and whether the object was visible or invisible during displacement to its final location. Inferences about what infants understood about the hidden object were based on how they adapted their visual or manual search behaviors as task complexity increased. If infants applied a previously successful search strategy to a more difficult hiding scenario, they made search errors. For example, a young infant may succeed at finding an object hidden under one cover, but when the object is hidden under two covers in succession, she may stop after uncovering the first cover even when the object is not there. Because the hiding scenarios were graded in difficulty, Piaget could infer not only infants' current level of object concept understanding, but also how object knowledge developed.

A rather puzzling pattern of search activity, typically observed around 8 to 9 months (sensorimotor stage IV), led Piaget to the conclusion that object knowledge in infancy was incomplete at this age. Infants often searched at the location where they previously found a hidden object (location A), despite watching intently as it was hidden at a second location (location B). This striking search pattern is called the "A, not-B error."

Piaget interpreted the A, not-B error as evidence that infants viewed the object as an extension of their own actions (i.e., an action that led to the object's prior retrieval), thought the object was linked to a particular spatial location (i.e., the initial location from which it was recovered despite being moved to a new location), and believed that the object's permanence was only partial, because it was intrinsically linked to a particular spatial location and actions that were associated with it's reappearance. The object did not have an existence independent of the infant's action or a particular spatial location.

For Piaget, search errors reflect a lack of conceptual understanding, rather than a limitation in motor skill or memory capacity. That the A, not-B error occurs so late in the first year, even when infants possess requisite motor skills, is critical for Piaget's account (Harris, 1987; Wellman et al., 1986). The late appearance supports his argument that earlier behaviors, such as the visual tracking of an object as it disappears from view or the ability to manually retrieve a partially hidden object, are not evidence of complete object knowledge. Also, because infants make the A, not-B error *after* they have acquired sufficient manual skills for object search, limitations in performance can not be due to motor limitations. Alternative accounts of object concept development, especially those that claim that object knowledge occurs very early in development, must provide an explanation for the A, not-B error search pattern.

Several aspects of Piaget's empirical approach contrast with more recent approaches. Piaget set high performance criteria for infants before he was willing to infer that they had acquired all of the conceptual components of object knowledge, whereas today inferences about the object concept are often made from only discriminative looking. Piaget ruled out looking behaviors as evidence of complete object knowledge because they represent a limited behavioral repertoire. Even though there is general consensus that Piaget greatly underestimated infants' abilities, when infants were able to solve the various hiding and reaching scenarios, one could safely conclude that they possessed the three components of object knowledge that Piaget identified.

Piaget's graded hiding tasks also yielded information about the developmental sequence of acquiring object concept knowledge. Piaget viewed object knowledge as an evolving, dynamic process, rather than a static, all-or-none capacity where, for example, one day infants do not attribute objects with permanence, substance, and spatial independence and the next day they do. Although Piaget recognized that the perceptual system provides information about the world and supports sensorimotor activity, his central notion was that infants construct knowledge through sensorimotor actions on objects that transform their relations. This rendition stands in sharp contrast to alternative approaches that assume that object knowledge is innate or that observational processes alone are sufficient to account for object knowledge.

Piaget's conceptualization of object knowledge in infancy laid a logical foundation for the reasoning abilities of the adult. His attempts to bridge the developmental gaps across the periods of infancy, childhood, and adulthood remain a standard that few alternative models approach. It is unclear for alternative approaches what role the object concept plays in development of other cognitive accomplishments.

Recent Trends in Research on Object-Concept Development

Research initially attempted to replicate the sequence of object concept development that Piaget described. With almost no exceptions, these attempts supported Piaget's careful observations. In his hallmark review of the literature, Harris (1983) concluded:

> Piaget's theory of object permanence has survived very well indeed considering the fairly massive research activity that has been directed towards it. . . . We are forced then to agree with Piaget that the infant's difficulties are probably conceptual in nature. (p. 724)

Recent research has taken two general directions. One direction attempts to demonstrate that infants possess object knowledge at ages much earlier than those specified by Piaget's theory. A second focuses less on testing Piaget's theory and more on explaining the A, not-B error.

Precocist Challenges to Piaget's Theory

Object Permanence at Earlier-Than-Predicted Ages. Several challenges have arisen to Piaget's notion that objects do not exist for infants unless they can perceive them. Studies that involve occlusion of events or objects and that measure infant looking time typically provide the evidence for challenging his theory. Because these studies overlap extensively with studies of physical reasoning, we will delay extensive discussion of them for that section. However, we will make several points before we move on to studies of the A-not-B error.

Object Permanence and Substance during Occlusion. Several studies by Baillargeon and colleagues have analyzed infant looking responses to the outcome of events that seem to violate physical principles. Studies with infants as young as 3.5 months and as old as 13.5 months reported longer looking across a wide range of imaginative impossible events, including a screen that seemed to rotate through an occluded object (Baillargeon, 1987; Baillargeon, Spelke, & Wasserman, 1985), cars rolling down a ramp and through an occluded object (Baillargeon, 1986; Baillargeon & DeVos, 1991); rabbits failing to appear in a window when crossing behind a barrier (Baillargeon, 1986; Baillargeon & DeVos, 1991; Baillargeon & Graber, 1987); and objects emerging from covers with a protuberance of half their size (Baillargeon & DeVos, 1992). Baillargeon (1993) concluded that,

> contrary to what Piaget had claimed, infants as young as 3.5 months of age represent the existence of occluded objects (p. 272) . . . The infants in these experiments seemed to have no difficulty representing the existence of one, two, and even three hidden objects. (pp. 308–309)

Whether these findings pose a challenge for Piaget's account has been questioned. Fischer and Bidell (1991) argue that some researchers reject Piaget's interpretations because they either misinterpreted or misrepresented his position. For example, Fischer and Bidell (1991) cite several examples of findings from looking studies that are interpreted as a threat to Piaget's claims but are actually *consistent* with his view of object knowledge development.

Piaget argued (1969; Piaget & Inhelder, 1969; also see Fischer & Bidell, 1991, pp. 204–208) that perception was a special form of sensorimotor activity and that there is a reciprocal relation between perceptual and conceptual development. Perceptual sensitivities contribute to sensorimotor-based knowledge about objects, and similarly, sensorimotor activities influence perceptual processes. Piaget argued that neither perception nor cognition, by itself, was sufficient to explain knowledge. From this view, studies that report patterns of longer looking by infants to odd perceptual events that are occluded are consistent with claims made by Piaget about the gradual course of object knowledge development. Fischer and Bidell (1991, pp. 220–223) provide a detailed discussion of how the pattern of dishabituation of looking to an impossible event (e.g., a screen that rotates 180 degrees through the space that an object had occupied) is consistent with Piaget's description of visual search for a perceptually-absent object in sensorimotor stage 3 of object-concept knowledge. The point is that occlusion studies may capture infant perceptual sensitivities to events that violate the physical properties of objects, but this evidence does not necessarily imply that infants possess complete object knowledge.

Task Comparability and Performance Criteria

Current researchers try to investigate concepts that Piaget articulated with tasks and performance criteria that differ substantially from the ones he used. It is reasonable to ask whether these different approaches tap the same processes.

Recall that Piaget (1954) described three features of object-concept knowledge: objects are permanent and have substance; they exist independently of actions, but can be affected by them, and they occupy a spatial location that is independent from, but related to, the spatial location of other objects, including the self. Looking tasks assess whether infants look longer at displays that violate object permanence and substance (e.g., Baillargeon, 1987; Baillargeon & DeVos, 1992; Baillargeon et al., 1985; Kellman & Spelke; 1983) and whether objects maintain permanence and substance throughout changes in spatial location (e.g., Baillargeon, 1986; Baillargeon & DeVos, 1991; Baillargeon & Graber, 1987). But they do not measure the extent to which infants know anything about their own effect on objects or the spatial location of objects with respect to self. Looking tasks appear to assess information that infants have about the *physical properties of objects,* while manual search tasks measure what infants know about *what to do with objects.*

Also, there is the issue of task dependency of infant performance (Munakata, McClelland, Johnson, & Siegler, in press). If looking studies assess the same features of object concept knowledge as manual search tasks, then young infants should show the claimed high levels of object knowledge in a visual analogue of a manual search task. In a recent study, Hofstadter and Reznick (1996, experiment 2) examined the visual gaze of 5-month-old infants in a hidden object task in which infants watched as the experimenter hid an object in one of two wells that were simultaneously covered by cloths and then shielded from sight by an opaque screen. The experimenter distracted the infants during a 3 second delay, and then lowered the opaque screen, and the first gaze toward a hiding well was recorded. Infants gazed at the correct hiding location on 59% of all trials, indicating above chance correct responding ($p < .05$). However, they also made A, not-B-errors on 69% of the trials when the object shifted location after a correct response. These findings are consistent with Piaget's account that infants are prone to errors when the location of the hidden object changes, even on standard tasks that measure only looking behavior.

Finally, those who claim precocious object knowledge on the basis of looking studies must account for two findings. First, infants do not initiate manual search for hidden objects until between 7.5 and 9 months, several months after the onset of prehension, and second, infants make search errors after they do begin to search (Bremner, 1985; Harris, 1983, 1987; Piaget, 1952; Uzgiris, 1987; Wellman et al., 1986). If infants as young as 3.5 months are able to represent and reason about the location and trajectory of hidden objects in occlusion studies, why do older infants make manual search errors?

Minitheories: The AB Manual Task and the A, Not-B Error

Hundreds of studies have been conducted of manual search in the AB task, and many alternative explanations of the A, not-B search error have been offered, including those that focus on memory (e.g., Bjork & Cummings, 1984; Harris, 1986; 1989; Schacter, Moscovitch, Tulving, McLachlan, & Freedman, 1986), selective use of information (e.g., Sophian & Wellman, 1983; Sophian & Yengo, 1985); spatial coding (Bremner, 1985; Harris, 1973); object identity through space and time (Bower, 1982; Butterworth, 1975; Harris, 1983); and discrimination learning (Cornell, 1978).

How Robust Is the Late Search Phenomenon?

Infants begin to reach and grasp for objects by 4 months (e.g., Piaget, 1952, 1954; White, Castle, & Held, 1966), but not until 7.5 to 8 months do they reach for an object that is occluded by another object (e.g., Diamond, 1985; Gratch & Landers, 1971; Wishart & Bower, 1984). Moreover, 6-month-old infants interrupt an ongoing reach if the object is occluded before they contact it (e.g., Gratch, 1972; Piaget, 1954). On the basis of these and other studies (see reviews by Baillargeon, 1993; Bremner, 1985), Harris (1983,

p. 721) concluded that "it is now clear that the infant's failure to search under a cover at around 6 months cannot be attributed to a lack of manual skill." We will refer to this discrepancy as "late search," an ability to reach for an object while, at the same time, failing to reach when the object is occluded, observed between about 4 to 7.5 months of age.

How Robust Is the A, Not-B Search Error?

Numerous studies have confirmed Piaget's observation of the A, not-B search error in the AB task with some qualifications (Wellman et al., 1986), despite significant task modifications. The following examples are illustrative of the types of factors and task modifications (see reviews by Bremner, 1985; Harris, 1983, 1987; Wellman et al., 1986).

The relation between motor activity and perseverative search errors has been examined by varying the number (e.g., 1 to 5) and type (e.g., active search to simply watching) of trials at the initial A location to determine the extent to which search errors are a function of motor training (e.g., Landers, 1971). The relation between spatial cues and search has been examined by varying the distinctiveness of the covers (e.g., identical or different) that occlude the object (e.g., Bremner & Bryant, 1977), the distance between hiding locations (e.g., Horobin & Acredolo, 1986), and the movement of the infant (active or passive) or the hidden object on B trials (e.g., Benson & Uzgiris, 1985; Bremner, 1982). The role of memory and search has been examined with a wide range of task variations, including delay periods of 0 to 12 seconds between object occlusion and search (e.g., Diamond, 1985; Gratch, Appel, Evans, LeCompte, & Wright, 1974); the number of hiding locations, ranging from two to as many as five or seven (e.g., Bjork & Cummings, 1984; Cummings & Bjork, 1983; Diamond, Cruttenden, & Neiderman, 1994); and whether the object remained visible or was hidden from sight on B trials (e.g., Bremner & Knowles, 1984; Harris, 1974; Sophian & Yengo, 1985). Infants who participated typically ranged from 8 to 12 months, occasionally 16 months, and the method of hiding has varied from placing objects in cups (upright or inverted), submerged wells covered by cloths or slits through which infants reached, or behind curtains.

Wellman et al. (1986) provided a synthesis of this literature through a meta-analysis of 30 studies with 89 conditions. The meta-analysis was motivated by an attempt to determine whether search on the B trial (i.e., when the object shifts to a new location after the infant has found the object at the A location) could best be explained by one of the following models: random search, perseverative search leading to errors (one aspect of Piaget's interpretation), correct search, or a combination of both perseverative and correct search tendencies.

The meta-analysis confirmed the effect of several variables on search on the B trials. First, the likelihood of correct search on B trials increases when the hiding covers or containers differ, the number of hiding locations increases beyond two, and with age. Second, the likelihood of the A, not-B search error increases as the delay interval increases between object occlusion and search. Neither the number of search trials at the A location before the first B trial nor the distance between the hiding locations affected the error rates on B trials.

Some of the outcomes were surprising. First, the finding that the number of A trials is unrelated to correct search on B trials weakens accounts that explain the A, not-B error as the perseveration of a previous response at the A location. Second, why correct search on B trials increases when there are more than two hiding locations is puzzling, because this manipulation should increase infants' difficulty. Diamond et al. (1994) suggested that, because all locations in a multiple-location search task cannot be occluded simultaneously, the experimenter may inadvertently draw infants' attention to the target location when hiding the object. By comparison, search performance is poor in multiple-location search tasks if all locations are covered by slits, and the experimenter hides the object through a slit, rather than placing a cover over it (Diamond et al., 1994). Finally, the biggest surprise uncovered by the meta-analysis was that none of the four proposed models adequately explained the variables that affected search on B trials.

While Piaget's observation of the puzzling A, not-B search error has been confirmed, task and contextual factors do affect the tendency of 9-month olds to make the A, not-B search error. These findings do not provide support for the emphasis that Piaget placed on prior sensorimotor activity as one of the three reasons why infants return to the A location on B trials. However, these findings support Harris's (1983) conclusions that alternative accounts of the A, not-B error fare no better. Additional research has attempted to explain both late search and search errors.

Precocist Accounts of Late Search and Search Errors: Planning Means-Ends Sequences

If young infants possess object knowledge as indicated by their looking patterns to occluded and impossible events, why do they fail to apply this knowledge several months later when they show late search and manual search errors? Baillargeon (1993) attempted to explain both late search and search errors as infants' inability to perform coordinated means-ends behaviors that are involved in grasping one object (e.g., a cover) to obtain another object. This condition is not caused by a lack of object knowledge, motor-skill limitations, or a failure to visually discriminate between actions that lead to object retrieval and actions that do not (Baillargeon, 1993). Rather, infants have difficulties with generating means-ends behaviors because of an apparent conflict between the initial action required to remove the occluding object and the subsequent action required to obtain the desired object. However, no empirical evidence is presented to support this claim, nor are explanations provided for why infants would view the grasping of one object as conflicting with a subsequent grasp to obtain a second object. Even if difficulty in generating means-ends actions does hamper late search, it can not be responsible for the A, not-B search error. Remember, this error consists of making the appropriate action when the object is hidden at the A location but not when it is hidden at the B location.

Baillargeon (1993) further argues that neither short-term memory capacity nor the inability to update information held in memory are likely factors underlying search errors because 8-month-olds look longer at an impossible than possible event that involves an object disappearing in one location and a hand retrieving it at a different location, even after delays as long as 70 seconds (Baillargeon, DeVos, & Graber, 1989; Baillargeon & Graber, 1988). Infants presumably make search errors after a period of delay because they resort to "reactive" problem solving, instead of "planful" problem solving. In "reactive" problem solving, "solutions are produced immediately, without conscious reasoning," whereas the more effortful "planful" type involves problem solving in "situations in which solutions are generated through an active reasoning or computation process" (1993, p. 305). On A trials, infants presumably use "planful" problem solving to correctly retrieve the hidden object, but on B trials, they use "reactive" problem solving and "simply execute the solution they have just stored in memory, leading to perseverative errors" (1993, p. 305).

This explanation is unlikely for several reasons. No converging evidence is offered that 8-month-old infants engage in planful problem solving on the first A trial. The suggestion that "reactive" problem solving occurs after short delays while, "planful" problem solving occurs after longer delays is incomplete because the delay periods are the same

on both A and B trials (Baillargeon, 1993). Finally, this line of argument leads to a perseveration explanation of search errors which Wellman et al.'s meta-analysis revealed as inadequate (1986).

Neuropsychological Accounts of Late Search and Search Errors

Diamond offered another account of late search and search errors (Diamond, 1991a, 1991b; Diamond & Gilbert, 1989) that assumes that infants know much about the properties of objects at young ages, but the ability to demonstrate what they know about objects does not emerge until between 5 and 12 months, awaiting maturation of the frontal cortex. Like Baillargeon, Diamond (1991a; Diamond & Gilbert, 1989) explains late search not in terms of limitations in either motor skills or conceptual abilities, but rather in terms of difficulties infants have in organizing means-ends actions prior to 7 months. These claims rest on evidence that both 7- and 10-month-olds have little difficulty in reaching for visible objects if they can execute a direct reach, but only 7-month-olds have significant difficulties in obtaining a visible object if they must change the direction of their reach. Thus, young infants may not be able to link two successive actions, a skill required by most manual search tasks.

To explain why infants make the A, not-B search error, Diamond argues that two abilities are needed, memory and the inhibition of a prepotent response. In a longitudinal study, Diamond (1985) found that between 7 and 12 months the occurrence of the A, not-B error depends on the delay between hiding and search, the threshold increasing about 2 seconds per month. Thus, a delay of 2 seconds produces search errors in 7-month-olds while 12-month-olds make search errors only after a delay of 10 seconds or more. During the delay period infants must constantly update the object's new location to avoid competition between old and new information as the object shifts location.

While memory for object location is important, a memory deficit alone is not sufficient to explain the A, not-B error, because infants search at the A location even when the object is visible at the B location (Bremner & Knowles, 1984; Harris, 1974; Sophian & Yengo, 1985). Therefore, Diamond argues that infants must inhibit the tendency to reach again to the A location, which has become prepotent because that response was reinforced on prior trials. Diamond (1991a) suggests that between 5 and 9 months maturation of the supplementary motor area (SMA) of the frontal cortex serves to inhibit reflexes of the hand that appear to disrupt action sequences. Maturation of the SMA may also permit smoother coordination among sequenced actions.

Several lines of evidence support Diamond's arguments, including parallels between human and monkey infant object search performance (e.g., Diamond, 1990), lesion studies with monkeys (e.g., Diamond & Goldman-Rakic, 1989), and studies of human adults with frontal lobe lesions (Schacter et al., 1986). A recent study provides further evidence that both memory and response inhibition are important factors in explaining infant search errors. In a manual search task using 7 locations, Diamond and colleagues (1994) found that search errors were disproportionately distributed in the direction of the previously correct location (i.e., locations that were between the A and B locations) as would be expected by a memory and inhibition explanation, rather than search errors being distributed around the correct location, as would be expected by a memory only explanation.

Some concerns are raised by this account. First, Diamond's task is actually a delayed response task in which the object shifts back and forth between the A and B wells, introducing a much heavier memory demand than did Piaget's original task, in which the object usually shifts only to the B well. Second, Diamond's task further increases memory demand with a distraction during the delay between hiding and search. If Piaget included a similar distraction, it is not emphasized in his writings. Both of these procedural differences lead Diamond to focus on memory, but the error occurs even without delay and when the object is visible. Third, a recent longitudinal study (Matthews, Ellis, & Nelson, 1996) of premature and full-term infants on a modified version of AB (i.e., delayed response), recall memory, transparent barrier detour, and means-ends tasks challenges some of Diamond's proposals. Matthews et al. reported that age-corrected premature infants outperformed full-term infants on the modified and non-reaching AB tasks, calling into question Diamond's conclusion that brain maturation, rather than experience, is responsible for error-free performance. Thelen and Smith (1994) also question whether "maturity of the frontal lobes" is sufficient to explain the specific pattern of search behaviors when AB task variables, other than duration of delay, are manipulated. Their dynamic systems analysis views the task variables identified by Wellman et al. (1986) as forces that produce different searching behaviors at the A and B locations. While the dynamic systems approach provides an alternative to Diamond's account, it has yet to explain late search and occurrences of the A, not-B error when the object is visible at B.

There are several intriguing features in Diamond's account. It relies on multiple factors, including the sequence of means-ends behaviors, memory capacity, and inhibition of a prepotent response to explain late search and A, not-B search errors. It capitalizes on converging evidence from both human infants and monkeys, as well as brain-damaged adults, to bolster these claims. And, because Diamond proposes that maturation of the brain supports both memory and response control, object knowledge is not a central concern. Unlike other accounts that promote conceptual explanations of the development of object knowledge, Diamond's account focuses on search behavior and not what infants "know" about objects. While explaining more of the empirical findings than other accounts, this approach is neutral about infants' conceptualization of objects. However, research by Matthews et al. (1996) raises concerns about an emphasis on brain maturation to the exclusion of experience.

Adaptive Processes Account of Late Search and Search Errors

The presumption of many investigators about the object concept is that it is a principle that infants either understand or do not; the full object concept is in place when infants know that an object exists when it is no longer seen, felt, or heard. Munakata (in press; Munakata et al., in press) points out that the assumption that a single principle is at stake leads investigators to design tasks that reduce the performance criteria as much as possible by eliminating such factors as means-ends action sequences. Munakata proposes a process, rather than a principles, approach that assumes that infants develop an understanding of the object concept gradually and that task dependency of behavior is a tool for understanding how the object concept grows.

A series of experiments (Munakata et al., in press) examined the possibility that means-ends reaching sequences were responsible for concealing infants' knowledge of the object concept. The idea was to teach infants a simple one-step, means-ends behavior (a button press) and then see if they would use this behavior to retrieve a visible or occluded toy. For one experiment, 7-month-olds first learned to press a button to make a ledge drop that was below an opaque or transparent screen. Then the infants watched as the experimenter placed a toy on the ledge, behind the screen, and the parents demonstrated that pressing the button made the ledge drop to bring the toy within reach.

Finally, the toy was hidden behind the transparent or opaque screen on some trials, and no toy was hidden on other trials to determine under what conditions the infants would press the button. Infants were more likely to press the button when a toy was placed behind the transparent screen than when it was not. However, with the opaque screen, they were equally likely to press the button whether or not a toy was placed on the ledge. The results strongly imply that means-ends behavior was not an impediment to task performance; infants performed well when they could see the toy through the transparent screen. However, just as in the A-not B task, they seemed not to recognize that a toy existed behind the opaque screen.

To account for the discrepancy between studies that find evidence for an object concept as early as 3.5 months and those that find search errors as late as 7 months, Munakata suggests that different processes underlie performance at different ages, and these processes are integral to understanding infants' object knowledge. At the earliest age, infants do not understand that an object exists when out of sight but make predictions about events. When the predictions do not eventuate, they see the event as strange. Thus, when a screen rotates to gradually conceal an object, infants form an expectation for when the screen will stop; when the screen does not stop, there is a mismatch that produces increased looking even though infants have no representation of the hidden object. However, for reaching in the A-not B task, infants have no provision for comparing a current input with an expectation; they must generate the representation of the object internally. Munakata et al. also provide evidence from connectionist modeling to support this process-oriented approach.

Regardless of the interpretation, the findings suggest that infants do not retrieve hidden objects at 7 months even when the means-ends act is greatly simplified. Thus, they pose a serious challenge to claims that the A, not-B error occurs because infants have difficulties in linking behavioral sequences (e.g., Baillargeon, 1993; Diamond, 1991a; Spelke, 1991).

Conclusions

Evidence from looking tasks suggests that, at much earlier ages than Piaget proposed, infants are aware that objects continue to exist when they are no longer seen, at least for a few seconds. However, several findings undermine the idea that infants have a clear concept of the unseen object and that only action-sequence requirements in search tasks

impede its manifestation. When 5-month-olds are only required to look in a visual analogue of the two-location hiding task, they still make the A, not-B error (Hofstadter & Reznick, 1996), and even when 7-month-olds are only required to press a button to retrieve an object, they are no more likely to do so when an object is hidden behind an opaque screen than when no object is hidden. An all-or-none emergence of object knowledge as early as 3.5 months is not consistent with these outcomes.

While Piaget's observations of the A, not-B error and his theory have held firm, for the most part, he apparently underemphasized perceptual abilities and overemphasized the requirement for sensorimotor experience for acquisition of the object concept (Wellman et al., 1986). Diamond's multifactor account of search behavior shows considerable promise to account for performance in the two-location hiding task. The link to developing knowledge about brain circuits is also quite attractive, and we believe that the emphasis on processes rather than concepts (Munakata, in press) is wise at this stage and less likely to lead to unlikely dichotomous renditions of infant development. At the same time, it is important to note that Diamond's approach is a theory of search behavior and not of the object concept or object knowledge. Even at that, Diamond's approach will require revision to accommodate the more recent findings of Munakata et al., cited above.

It is important to restate that Piaget's theory of object concept development was broader than object permanence and search behavior in the AB task. Recent research on the object concept has been quite interesting, even fascinating, but one comes away from it with the feeling that the findings and minitheories lack the encompassing developmental and integrative character that made Piaget's account so compelling. Perhaps this trend is inevitable, but we are not yet convinced. The theory may need modification and better specification, perhaps through better identification of specific processes and neurophysiological maturation, but we are not ready to cast it aside in favor of minitheories that are far smaller in scope, some of which lack developmental analysis, and typically fare no better at providing viable alternatives.

SPACE

What infants understand about space and spatial relations naturally follows a discussion of what they know about objects because, in many ways, space is defined by relations among objects. An emphasis on the intrinsic link between space and object knowledge is not new. In their work on joint visual attention Butterworth and Jarrett (1991, p. 70) extended an argument originally made by William James. They proposed that joint visual attention permits infants and adults to view objects located in far space as mutual aspects of experience, with space serving "as a receptacle for experience." Piaget also viewed the relation between object and space knowledge as fundamental when he wrote that space "is not at all perceived as a container but rather as that which it contains, that is, objects themselves . . . the degree of objectification that the child attributes to things informs us of the degree of externality that he accords to space" (1954, pp. 109–110). Key points are:

- Piaget's theory of a developmental shift from egocentric to allocentric spatial location coding has held up well in most spatial orientation studies that involve rotation and translation of infants. However, research with newer procedures indicates that infants can employ objective spatial coding strategies at ages earlier than initially thought.
- Infants can use landmarks to maintain spatial orientation earlier when the landmark is directly associated with a target than when it only serves as a frame of reference.
- Evidence supports Piaget's claim of a developmental trend in understanding spatial referents in near space prior to far space.
- The view that the onset of locomotor skills serves to organize spatial development is an attractive idea that is widely held, but it has not yet received definitive documentation.

Piaget's Theory of Spatial Development

Piaget's account of spatial development has been the dominant theoretical framework to guide infancy researchers for many of the same reasons that his framework guided research on object knowledge. Piaget claimed that infants only gradually perceive fundamental spatial dimensions of objects, such as their shape, size, distance, and position, and they do so only as a consequence of their actions. Until 3 to 6 months, infants possess a limited awareness of the content of sensory images in terms of their figure, position, or displacements. This initial awareness takes the form of mere perceptual categories for infants that are "more or less stable, but not yet realized in objects" (1954, p. 113).

Piaget argued that objective spatial knowledge is constructed as infants gradually coordinate the effects of their actions with the resulting visual consequence, thus leading them to construct action-based spatial relations that are imposed on their perceptions. Spatial knowledge is limited by the protracted course of motor development in two ways. First, the understanding of spatial relations among objects is limited to near space before locomotion. The onset of locomotor skill provides infants with a means to experience and construct spatial relations in far space. A second prediction was that spatial knowledge would initially be egocentric, in the sense that both the self and actions form the center of the spatial nexus from which all spatial relations are constructed. A gradual decline in egocentrism would culminate in infants' ability to understand the spatial relations among many objects (including the self as one object in space) along with the ability to represent such relations.

Piaget's evidence for transitions in spatial development rested on object search behavior. Just as the onset of manual search was key to the development of the object concept, Piaget also argued that infants' attempts to uncover partially and completely hidden objects, permitted by the onset of prehension, provided evidence of the objectification of space. This evidence included the observation that young infants initially only search for a hidden object when they are already in the act of reaching and the A, not-B search error (extensively discussed in the previous section). Young infants appear to view object location and displacement as an extension of their actions.

An egocentric or self-referent spatial framework works well to encode the location of a stable hidden object, such as when reaching to the right always leads to object retrieval. However, if the location of either the infant or the hidden object changes, then egocentric spatial coding leads to localization errors. An obvious way to keep track of an object's location during self movement is to use an external frame of reference, whose spatial relation to the target remains constant. Another way is to update the object's location relative to the self as a frame of reference during movement. Piaget claimed that spatial orientation progressed from the use of an egocentric, self-referent, spatial frame of reference to an objective or allocentric spatial reference.

Finally, for Piaget, infants achieve objectification of space near the end of the sensorimotor period when they can represent the spatial relations among present and nonpresent objects by viewing themselves as one of several objects within a common space. They typically demonstrate this ability in functional detour behavior, such as when infants generate and execute an alternative spatial route when a barrier blocks a nonvisible goal.

Recent Research on Trends in Spatial Development

Piaget presumed that young infants did not attribute objects with true spatial features until such visual information could be used to guide their actions. Piaget argued that infants would understand size and shape constancy between 6 and 9 months, following the onset of prehension, and it was well into the second year, after the onset of locomotion, that he thought infants could use spatial landmarks and represent alternative routes through space. How well do Piaget's predictions stand up to empirical tests? The evidence yields a mixed picture, with some findings either refuting or supporting Piaget's view and other evidence inspiring alternative accounts. Many of Piaget's original claims about infants' early lack of spatial awareness have been challenged by research reporting that even very young infants can demonstrate visual sensitivity to size and shape constancy (e.g., Day, 1987; Kellman, Gleitman, & Spelke, 1987; Kellman, Spelke, & Short, 1986). This evidence, however, does not demonstrate that infants can use such perceptual information to guide their functional behaviors. Because other discussions are available (e.g., Bremner, 1996), we will not include classic approaches to spatial development that straddle the spatial perception-cognition boundary, including wariness of heights related to knowledge of depth as assessed in the visual cliff paradigm (see Bertenthal & Campos, 1990; Campos, Bertenthal, & Kermoian, 1992) and infants' understanding of three-dimensionality as assessed by their reactions to looming objects (e.g., Yonas et al., 1977) or attempts to reach for objects in space (McKenzie, Skouteris, Day, Hartman, & Yonas, 1993; Yonas & Granrud, 1985). We focus on research on the development of spatial orientation and joint visual attention.

Spatial Orientation

How well do infants maintain spatial orientation, or keep track of locations in space? With few exceptions, most research on this topic has used Acredolo's (1978) "training and rotation/translation-test" paradigm to confirm Piaget's predictions of a developmental trend from egocentric spatial coding to allocentric, objective spatial coding. Acredolo (1978) trained 6-, 11-, and 16-month-old infants to turn their head in one direction, to a specific spatial location, to anticipate an interesting event. After training, infants were translated and rotated 180 degrees and encouraged to look

for the event on several test trials. Six-and 11-month-olds tended to turn their heads in the same direction as during training, resulting in localization errors and suggesting that they used an egocentric spatial code that was not updated to compensate for the spatial displacement. However, 16-month-olds turned their heads in the direction opposite to training to correctly locate the target, suggesting that they updated the spatial relations during spatial displacement, since no obvious landmarks were available.

Researchers have also explored whether infants can use spatial landmarks in this situation to facilitate the maintenance of spatial orientation. Acredolo (1978) positioned a bright yellow star as a direct landmark at the target location, and observed that only 16-month-olds again turned to the correct spatial location. In a follow-up study, Acredolo and Evans (1980) provided additional landmarks at the target location (e.g., blinking lights and bright stripes) for 6-, 9-, and 11-month-old infants. The extra landmarks facilitated the spatial orientation responses of only the 9- and 11-month-olds. This series of studies and others that used a two-position manual search task (e.g., Bai & Bertenthal, 1992; Bremner, 1978a; 1978b) have generally confirmed the developmental progression of spatial orientation from the use of an egocentric (response-based) to allocentric (place-based) spatial coding strategy. Under some conditions infants as young as 9 months could maintain spatial orientation when highly salient landmarks were available. However, in the absence of landmarks, most infants under 12 months of age made localization errors.

An interesting question is why this age-related shift in spatial coding occurs. Several researchers have supported Piaget's account that the shift in spatial coding depends on the onset of locomotor skill (Acredolo, 1988; Benson, 1990; Bertenthal & Campos, 1990; Bremner, 1985, 1989). The onset of self-produced locomotion may serve as an organizing factor that prompts infants to shift spatial reference systems, because dependence on an egocentric spatial coding strategy alone, without updating, can lead to error-prone spatial orientation once infants are able to move themselves through space.

However, other researchers have challenged this proposal and raise the possibility that young infants make use of both egocentric and allocentric spatial coding strategies under certain conditions (Bremner, 1993a). For example, McKenzie and colleagues (Keating, McKenzie, & Day, 1986; McKenzie, Day, & Ihsen, 1984; Tyler & McKenzie, 1990) argued that in the usual paradigm, where infants are always trained to look in only one direction, there is no way to know whether younger infants respond on the basis of reinforcement or because they can not use spatially-relevant information (McKenzie, 1992).

To clarify this issue, McKenzie and colleagues (1984), modified the training phase of the usual paradigm so that head-eye turns in both left and right directions were required to localize a fixed target location. This was accomplished by training infants to localize a fixed location from two different orientations. With this training, 6- and 8-month-olds demonstrated above-chance responding in correctly fixating the target location after a fixed-point spatial rotation of 90 degrees. Follow-up studies (Keating et al., 1986), using a similar training procedure, found that 8-month-olds performed above chance after displacements of 45 and 90 degrees in a square room with and without landmarks, and in a circular room with landmarks. Infants responded at chance when tested in a featureless (no corners or landmarks) circular room. Tyler and McKenzie (1990) used other variations in the training procedure to demonstrate that some infants as young as 6 months, but not 4 months, are able to use visual-proprioceptive information in a landmark-free environment to update and maintain spatial orientation. They argued that their findings challenge accounts of spatial development that claim that infants' ability to maintain spatial orientation in a landmark-free environment develops only after they are able to use landmarks (e.g., Acredolo, 1985), and further suggest that such abilities are present before the onset of self-produced locomotion. However, McKenzie and colleagues did not report the level of locomotor development for infants in these studies, and it is conceivable that their older subjects had some locomotor experience. Nevertheless, these results are provocative because they suggest that when more sensitive testing procedures are employed, including extensive training, infants can demonstrate relatively sophisticated levels of spatial orientation.

These findings stand in contrast to a larger body of evidence that generally supports Piaget's account, so a few issues are worth raising. The procedures used in McKenzie's task differ from the usual paradigm in at least three important ways. First, infants are only rotated in space around a fixed spatial point compared with the more complicated spatial displacement in other studies that involves both rotation and translation. Second, the spatial rotation in McKenzie's task varied between 45 and 90 degrees compared to the more extreme spatial translations of 180 degrees in the usual paradigm. Third, infants were able to demonstrate above-chance levels of spatial orientation, but only after extensive training. Additional research is required to adequately explain why different training procedures lead to different levels of performance.

Despite these important methodological differences, it is reasonable to conclude that these findings demonstrate that the ability to keep track of relatively small rotational displacements emerges in development prior to the ability to maintain spatial orientation after larger and more complicated spatial displacements. This research also suggests the need to rethink whether egocentric and objective spatial coding strategies can be so neatly dichotomized as has been assumed. Bremner (1993a) argued that some aspects of spatial coding may involve the use of both types of spatial frameworks to maintain and update spatial orientation during either self or object displacement. Future research should address how developmental factors affect infants' choice of spatial coding strategy in conjunction with features of the spatial environment, the spatial characteristics of the displacement, the training procedure, and whether infants have control over their own spatial displacement or are passively moved.

Spatial Orientation and Landmark Use

The role of spatial landmarks in infant spatial orientation is intriguing, but there is little theoretical guidance as to the form and functions of landmarks. Most researchers have conceptualized spatial landmarks as large, immovable features in familiar environments (e.g., Acredolo, 1985) or, in the lab context, as any highly salient stimulus that becomes associated with a target location (e.g., a red ball near a visual target or a distinctive hiding cover). Most studies typically manipulate only the presence or absence of landmarks.

It is unclear exactly what constitutes a spatial landmark and how infants use landmarks to maintain spatial orientation. Once infants have constructed true objective spatial relations, they should be able to use a variety of landmarks to code a variety of spatial relations, such as landmarks that are contiguous or spatially disjoint from the target, or even coding a target by the absence of a landmark.

Research with the usual training-rotation/translation-test paradigm has yielded contradictory findings about whether infants can accurately maintain spatial orientation when landmarks are spatially separated from a target. When tested on manual search tasks, 8- to 9-month-olds can correctly code the location of a hidden object, but only when a landmark (e.g., a distinct cover) is contiguous with the target location (Bai & Bertenthal, 1992; Bremner, 1978a, 1978b). In contrast, when tested on a visual search task, 8- to 9-month-old infants can correctly code the target location when a landmark is spatially separate from the target (Keating et al., 1986). One reason for the discrepancy in performance between the visual and manual tasks is that manual tasks demand a more complex means-ends response.

Lockman and Dai (1996) asked whether infants are able to use spatially separated cues in a manual task when the usual means-ends manual response is simplified. They studied 8-month-olds in the usual training-rotation/translation-test paradigm with a manual task in which infants learned to produce a simplified motor response—a touch to one of four cylinders arranged in a row. Infants who were trained with a direct landmark that was near, but spatially separated from the target cylinder, responded allocentrically at test. Infants who learned either with no landmark or with an indirect landmark that was located near a nontarget cylinder made egocentric errors at test. The investigators concluded that these findings demonstrate that even at 8 months infants can code a target with a noncontiguous landmark. However, it is possible that what was conceived of as a landmark by the experimenters only constituted a learned association for infants.

Bushnell, McKenzie, Lawrence, and Connell (1995) addressed this issue with a new paradigm in which 12-month-olds tried to find a nonvisible target through the use of direct or indirect landmarks. In a circular enclosure, infants watched as a toy was hidden under one of 58 identical blue cushions that covered the floor. The toy was hidden 15 degrees to the right or left of center, 140 cm away, and, after a 2 second delay, infants were encouraged to locomote to the target cushion to retrieve the toy. In the first direct landmark condition (LM), a "landmark cushion" of a different color replaced a blue cushion, and the toy was hidden under it. In the direct two landmark condition (2LM), two landmark cushions, each of a different color (e.g., yellow and green), replaced two blue cushions but were separated by one blue cushion. The toy was hidden under one of the two distinctively-colored landmark cushions. In the near-landmark condition (NLM), the toy was hidden under a blue cushion placed to the left or right of a landmark cushion. Other indirect landmark conditions included hiding the toy under a blue cushion placed between (BWTN) two landmark cushions and hiding the toy under a blue cushion that was next (NEXT) to one of two landmark cushions. Infants were also tested in a no landmark condition (NoLM).

Infants showed above-chance levels of responding in most conditions, but search performance was best in the di-

rect landmark conditions (i.e., LM and 2LM), followed by lower levels of search without landmarks (i.e., NoLM). The lowest levels of performance overall were found for search in the indirect landmark conditions (i.e., NLM, BWTN, and NEXT). These findings provide additional evidence that by the end of the first year infants can associate a target location with spatial cues to maintain spatial orientation, but they are more likely to do so in the presence of direct landmarks. Distinctive cues that are not contiguous or otherwise integral to the target location were not used by infants as objective landmarks to encode spatial information about a target location. Surprisingly, infants were able to encode both the direction and distance of the target location with some degree of accuracy when landmarks were not available, suggesting that they were capable of updating an egocentric spatial code during self-movement. Finally, infants' lack of success in using indirect landmarks may have reflected confusion between an egocentric spatial code and objective spatial information from a distinctive cue.

This series of studies is important for several reasons. Bushnell et al. (1995) offer an exciting new paradigm for the study of spatial coding strategies and landmark use that does not depend on the extensive training of a limited number of behaviors, such as head turns or reaches directed to a small number of possible targets. Unlike other testing situations, this task permits researchers to observe the type of spatial coding strategies infants use when they control their own spatial displacements. Also, these findings draw attention to both advances and limitations in the spatial abilities of 12-month-old infants. While confirming that infants at this age can use direct landmarks to code a specific spatial location, these findings also provide the first demonstration that, in the absence of landmarks, infants can accurately update information about both the distance and direction of a target location when using an egocentric spatial framework. However, infants' inability to use indirect landmarks also demonstrates that they are not yet able to code basic spatial relations, such as the distance and direction between two objects, to guide successful object retrieval. This pattern of findings supports Piaget's claims that the construction of objective spatial relations between the self and objects occurs prior to the construction of objective spatial relations among many objects, including the self.

Spatial Components of Joint Visual Attention

Another prediction made by Piaget's action-based theory of spatial development is that infants understand spatial relations for objects situated in near space long before they understand such relations in far space. This question has received little direct empirical attention, but insights may be gleaned from a small body of research on the development of joint visual attention (JVA) and the comprehension of the pointing gesture.

Referential spatial communication involves the ability to follow another person's gaze or pointing gesture to an object or event located in space, presumably to achieve shared mental experience. Researchers agree that both referential and spatial components are involved in JVA (Butterworth & Jarrett, 1991; Morissette, Ricard, & Decarie, 1995) and have focused attention on determining its developmental sequence. An old French proverb illustrates the issue: "When the finger points at the moon, only the idiot looks at the finger."

Investigations of JVA (e.g., Morissette et al., 1995) involve instructing a parent to periodically break off enface interaction with an infant to direct either a visual gaze or a manual pointing gesture to a specific target, typically located within 20 to 70 degrees of the infant's visual angle at distances from the infant of .85 meters (near space) and 2.11 meters (far space). Analyses of videotape provide measures of infants' orientation and visual fixation.

In a series of systematic cross-sectional studies on JVA, Butterworth & Jarrett (1991) reported a three-stage sequence: 6-month-olds are able to look in the same general direction as their mother's gaze; 12-month-olds are able to distinguish a specific target in the direction of their mother's gaze, but only if it is the first one intercepted by their scan path; it is not until 18 months that infants can accurately locate any referenced target, including those behind them. These findings offer weak support, at best, of the near- to far-space developmental trend predicted by Piaget. It is doubtful that Piaget would predict that infants as young as 6 months would look in the same far-space direction as their mother's gaze, rather than at the more obvious near-space target—mother's face.

However, a longitudinal study conducted by Morissette et al. (1995) included both JVA and the pointing gesture and revealed different results that more strongly support a near- to far-space developmental trend. For JVA, they reported that: 6-month-olds primarily looked at their mothers face; 12-month-olds redirected their gaze in the same direction as their mother's; 15-month-olds correctly fixated only near-space targets, and it was not until 18 months that infants correctly fixated both near- and far-space targets. A slightly different age sequence was revealed for the pointing gesture that provides even stronger support for Piaget's prediction: 6- and 9-month-olds looked at the finger when it pointed to both near- and far-space targets; 12-month-olds tended to look at the near-space target, but not the far-space target, and both 15- and 18-month-olds correctly fixated both near- and far-space targets.

The Morissette et al. (1995) study describes a more protracted course of development than does the Butterworth and Jarrett (1991) study. This discrepancy probably reflects key methodological differences. These two investigations differed in many ways, including the use of different designs (e.g., cross-sectional versus longitudinal), spatial configurations of targets (e.g., 2 targets in front and behind the baby versus 2 aligned targets each to the baby's left and right), criteria for determining infant fixation (e.g., −/+ 30° around the target versus precise fixation on the target), and methods of data reduction (e.g., gaze at mother's face was considered as "no response" by Butterworth & Jarrett).

Despite these differences, both studies provide some support for Piaget's prediction about the developmental course of understanding spatial relations in near and far space. Both studies suggest the understanding of spatial relations in far space lags behind that of near space. Also, the ability to localize objects in far space does not appear until the latter part of the second year. Finally, both studies suggest developmental shifts in the ability to extrapolate a far-space location from a near-space cue at ages that correspond with the timing of motor-skill achievements that typically provide infants with a means for experiencing far space, such as crawling onset at 6 to 9 months and walking onset at 12 to 15 months. Although some evidence supports Piaget's prediction of the expansion of spatial knowledge from near to far space, additional research is needed to clarify existing discrepancies. Future research should also seek to verify this trend with convergent data generated by an alternative paradigm to determine whether this trend in spatial development is more general or specific to the social-affective nature of the JVA paradigm.

Self-Produced Locomotion as a Mechanism for Spatial Development

Almost all of the research reviewed thus far directly or indirectly implicates locomotor development as a factor in spatial development in infancy. A notable exception is the position adopted by McKenzie (1992, p. 13), who challenges the role of self-produced locomotion in the development of spatial coding strategies when she writes, " . . . correlated visual-vestibular-proprioceptive information is sufficient for target relocation and . . . active self-movement from one point in space to another is not." This view stands in sharp contrast to that of others who have argued on both theoretical and empirical grounds that the onset of self-produced locomotion is functionally related to the acquisition and performance of a wide range of cognitive and social behaviors but specifically to transitions in spatial development (for a full discussion see, Benson, 1990; Bertenthal & Campos, 1990; Bertenthal, Campos, & Kermoian, 1994; Bremner, 1993a).

A growing body of research supports a relation between locomotor experience and spatial abilities, such as spatial coding and wariness of heights on the visual cliff (Acredolo, 1985, 1989; Benson, 1990; Bertenthal & Campos, 1990; Bertenthal, Campos & Kermoian, 1994; Bremner, 1993a, 1993b). However, it has been difficult to demonstrate whether locomotor experience is a causal agent for spatial development or only a correlate.

Researchers have attempted various strategies to address this issue, including holding age constant while comparing the performance of infants with different durations of locomotor experience on tests of discriminant validity (e.g., tests of novelty-preference), for which performance should be unrelated to locomotor experience (Benson, 1990). Despite these efforts, it is not possible in any single study to control all key variables and potential confounds, including infants' age of locomotor onset, age at spatial cognitive testing, duration of locomotor experience, manipulation of type of locomotor experience, and level of locomotor skill. Researchers will need to account for these and other variables through multiple studies that converge on similar outcomes.

Conclusions

Despite the introduction of new paradigms and research questions, the study of spatial development in infancy no longer receives the attention it did in the late 1970s and early 1980s. This area is now dominated by the work of only a few researchers, who are focusing on a few key problems. Perhaps this trend reflects the decline of Piaget's theory, but it may also be a consequence of the availability of few alternative theoretical models (Bremner, 1993a) and the difficulty in neatly parsing the perceptual and conceptual processes involved in spatial understanding (Pick, 1988). Bremner (1993a, 1993b) has suggested ways in which Piagetian, Gibsonian, and Dynamic Systems Theory

constructs might be used as a general framework for spatial development. Whether such hybrid alternative approaches will be fruitful awaits future research. In the meantime, the recent progress made in better understanding how infants use landmarks in a variety of ways to code spatial location is a promising research direction.

TIME

Time is such a pervasive aspect of human life that it has been referred to as "an ever-present and inescapable part of our experience" (Lewkowicz, 1992, p. 3). Perhaps that is why it has received so little attention. Key points include:

- Time is the least-studied dimension of infant cognition.
- The evidence that does exist suggests that infants are able to sequence events in time considerably earlier than Piaget predicted.
- However, other dimensions of time knowledge remain for investigation, such as how and when infants are able to partition time into the past, present, and future.
- Evidence exists that infants begin to organize their behavior around future events early in life.

Piaget's Sensorimotor Theory of Temporal Knowledge

In the final section of *The Construction of Reality in the Child,* Piaget (1954) described how infants gradually construct an understanding of temporal relations. Initially, infants have a very primitive sense of duration and are able to anticipate simple events, but only as a product of their own actions. By 4 to 8 months, infants can sequence their own actions but not external events. They can repeat actions when they discover, by chance, that their behavior produces an interesting effect (e.g., the repeated picking up and shaking of a rattle). However, these secondary circular reactions are not evidence of intentionally ordered actions, because the relation between action and effect initially occurs by chance, and there is no systematic variation of the means that produce the effect.

A significant advance in temporal knowledge occurs at approximately 8 to 12 months. Infants begin to differentiate means from ends to create a series of actions that are coordinated in time and directed toward a goal. Now infants remove a cover to obtain a toy, pull a cloth upon which an object rests to bring it within reach, and remove an obstacle to retrieve a toy (Piaget, 1952, 1954; Willatts, 1990). But infants can not yet appreciate the temporally-ordered events that they only observe. For example, Piaget (1954, obs. 49 and 50) describes how Lucienne watches him successively hide an object in three different locations, but confines her search to the first and second hiding locations. Only at about 1 year, can infants search at the last place an object was seen when it is hidden in successive locations (Piaget, 1954).

Finally, in the last sensorimotor stage, the child can imagine the consequence of sequential actions. Piaget (1952, obs. 181, p. 339) observed his daughter, at 20 months, standing before a closed gate with objects in each hand. She placed each object on the ground, opened the gate, picked up the objects and passed through. For Piaget, this behavior demonstrated an understanding of the temporal relation of "before and after" that was used to guide a sequence of three actions. Further evidence of the representation of temporal sequence is seen now when infants use deferred imitation to represent a sequence of past events.

However, Piaget underestimated infants' perceptual sensitivities to the temporal structure of the environment (Lewkowicz, 1989, 1992). Infants can detect or discriminate particular temporal features of stimuli on the basis of duration, rate, and rhythm, the association between events on the basis of their temporal relations (e.g., the synchrony between sights and sounds), and their temporal regularities (see reviews by Lewkowicz, 1989, 1992). By at least 3 months infants can discriminate the relative temporal order of auditory elements in rhythmic sequences (Demany, McKenzie, & Vurpillot, 1977), and they can make anticipatory visual fixations to the location of a target before it becomes visible, based on prior experience with a temporal sequence (Haith, Wentworth, & Canfield, 1993).

Evidence of Temporal Knowledge in Infancy

Studies of means-ends behavior and temporally-ordered events in an elicited imitation task provide evidence of infants' understanding of temporal sequence at ages earlier than Piaget predicted.

Analyses of Means-Ends Behavior

Willatts (1984, 1990) demonstrated that 9-month-old infants can order a two-step sequence of actions to achieve a desired goal. Infants saw a toy, beyond reach, that rested on the far end of a cloth with a foam barrier between the

infant and the near end of the cloth. Infants had to remove the foam barrier (step 1) to pull the cloth (step 2) to bring the toy within reach. Nine-month-olds were significantly more likely to perform the correct sequence when the toy was on the cloth than when the toy did not touch the cloth. In a subsequent study (Willatts, 1990), 12-month-olds solved a similar 3-step task. The situation was similar to the 2-step task, except that the toy was located near the cloth, and a string that was attached to the toy lay on the far end of the cloth. Again, 12-month olds were able to remove the barrier (step 1) to pull the cloth (step 2) to retrieve the string (step 3) to obtain the toy.

Thus, several months earlier than Piaget claimed, infants can sequence their actions to create extended chains of actions, ordered in time, to obtain a desired goal. Because infants often acted appropriately in each condition on their first attempts at object retrieval, Willatts (1990; Willatts & Fabricius, submitted) argues that infants are able to represent the problem-solving sequence prior to acting. However, there is no way to determine how many steps infants represented in advance of their actions, since the execution of each step provided new information to which they could respond.

The Representation of Temporally-Ordered Events: Elicited Imitation

Additional evidence for the representation of temporally ordered information comes from infants' performance on elicited imitation tasks. In a series of experiments, Bauer and her colleagues (1995; Bauer & Hertsgaard, 1993; Bauer & Mandler, 1989, 1990, 1992) reported that children as young as 11.5 months used temporal order knowledge to recall a sequence of two-act events, and by 20 months, children recalled three-act sequences. Infants participated in an elicited imitation paradigm in which they were encouraged to imitate a sequence of actions after watching an adult use props to model either two- or three-act sequences. Analyses compared the number of all pairs of modeled acts that children produced in their correct order during baseline, immediate imitation, and deferred imitation (e.g., a delay of up to two weeks in Bauer & Hertsgaard, 1993; Bauer & Mandler, 1989). Bauer reported that very young children can accurately recall temporally organized actions based on representations of familiar and logically related events.

These two areas of research provide evidence that infants do understand aspects of temporal knowledge regarding a sequence of actions that are ordered in time. However, many questions about the development of temporal knowledge in infancy remain to be explored. We know relatively little about such basic questions as when and how infants partition time into the past, present, and future (Benson, 1994; Benson, in press).

Future-Oriented Processes

Research on infant cognition has traditionally focused on mental processes that involve current events or events that occurred in the past. For example, the AB task poses a memory problem for infants. As we will discuss, physical reasoning tasks require infants to keep track of the prior sequence of events to appreciate that a current outcome does not make sense, categorization studies depend on infants' responding to a current event based on prior experience, and studies of the perception of causality hinge on whether infants see one current event as crucial in producing another current event.

Is there evidence that infants can think ahead? Young infants can reach for their bottle as an adult brings it to them, open their mouth as a spoon approaches and, a few months later, raise arms as an adult walks near in hopes of being picked up. Infants can crawl to retrieve a toy or to enter the kitchen when they hear the sounds of meal preparation. These everyday examples seem to involve expectations for what comes next, goal setting, and future-oriented action—in short, the basis of forecasting and future thinking.

Experimental evidence for infant forecasting has the longest history in research on reaching and grasping. An elegant experiment by von Hofsten and Ronnqvist (1988) measured the timing of hand adjustment as infants reached for a target. By 5 months and still at 9 months, infants' hands began to close before contact but only near the neighborhood of the object; at 13 months hand closure occurred earlier, as part of the approach action. Other evidence is found in the work of von Hofsten and his colleagues on infants reaching for moving targets. If infants were to program a reach for a moving target at its current location, they would always miss because of the time delay required for neural transmission and because of the inertia of body mass. Yet, several studies have shown that infants can catch objects that move radially (von Hofsten, 1983; von Hofsten & Lindhagen, 1979) or in depth and, as early as 5 months, select different hands to reach, depending on whether an object is spinning clockwise or counterclockwise, a preaction choice that presumably facilitates a palm catch (Wentworth, Benson, & Haith, 1989).

A parallel exists in infant eye-movement research. In visual tracking of a moving object, infants must program eye activity ahead of the current moment for the reasons cited earlier of delays in neural conductivity and inertia of mass (although mass is not much of a problem for eye movements). If they merely respond to each current location of a moving target, successive eye movements would be jerky, and infants would always be one step behind. Visual tracking prior to 2 months often consists of a sequence of fixations and saccadic eye movements that become increasingly smooth with age (Aslin, 1981, 1987; but see Hainline & Abramov, 1992). Thus, as with reaching, evidence exists that infants can program their activity to correspond to where an object will be rather than where it is.

These studies yield evidence for "look-ahead" processes that entail performance in the presence of the event of interest. Can infants forecast nonpresent events? A favorite paradigm for asking this question involves infant eye tracking of a moving object that is occluded in its path by a tunnel or screen. One problem in interpreting eye movements that continue along the object's trajectory, when it disappears, is that infants might simply have a tendency to move their eyes in the same direction as they have been moving them, through a kind of action inertia. Muller and Aslin (1978) found evidence to support this alternative, noncognitive, interpretation by varying the occluder width and speed of object motion. The likelihood that infants would look further along the object trajectory was directly related to screen width and object motion, increasing with narrower screens and faster speeds. Wentworth and Haith (1992) also found that, even with events that appear in discrete locations, rather than along a smooth trajectory, when the event disappears, infants initially tend to move their eyes in the same direction as they moved them to foveate that event. Harris (1983) provided an extensive review of studies that fit this paradigm and concluded that solid evidence did not exist that infants engaged in predictive looking in the tracking paradigm until 9 months.

A different eye-movement paradigm utilizes discrete presentation of pictures in different locations (Haith, Hazan, & Goodman, 1988; Smith, 1984). Infants watch a series of pictures that appear in different locations that are separated by a time interval. Monitoring of infant eye movements yields evidence of forecasting, mostly by fixation of the forthcoming picture location before the picture appears. However, reaction times to picture onset also yield important information, because an expectation for a forthcoming event facilitates performance.

Infants rapidly form visual expectations and translate these expectations into action. Haith et al. (1988) found that 3.5-month-olds who watched an alternating left-right (L-R) sequence of pictures were twice as likely to shift their fixation from one side to the other during the anticipation time window and had faster RTs than infants who saw the same pictures in a random L-R sequence. Apparently, infants who simply watch a predictable sequence of events engage a *detection, expectation,* and *action* sequence in which they rapidly detect the regularity of events, form expectations for each forthcoming event, and translate those expectations into action, through anticipatory behavior or facilitated responding. Interestingly, the detection, expectation, and action sequence occurs "gratuitously" inasmuch as infants have no control over the events of interest. The events play out regardless of what infants do (Haith, 1991).

Investigators have used the Visual Expectation Paradigm (VExP), to examine the what, when, and where features of infant expectations. Evidence that infants form expectations for the "what" aspect is based on increased anticipations and faster RTs when the forthcoming picture content is predictable than when it is not (Wentworth & Haith, 1992). The presence of a time component in expectations is suggested by infants' adjustment of the timing of their anticipations depending on the duration of the interpicture interval; anticipations occur later in the interval when the duration is 1200 milliseconds than when it is 800 milliseconds (Lanthier, Arehart, & Haith, 1993). Finally, a study that used nonalternating sequences of pictures suggested a "where" component to infant expectations. Infants made appropriate anticipatory fixations for L-L-R sequences by 3 months but could not do so at 2 months (Canfield & Haith, 1991). Other studies have yielded comparable evidence of a "where" component to infant visual expectations in both 3- and 5-month-olds in a paradigm that includes as many as four potential picture locations (Arehart & Haith, 1992; Smith, 1984).

These are but the rudiments of later, more elaborated expectations that will have complex event sequences as opposed to pictures as the "what," time frames of days, months, and years as the "when," and feet and miles (rather than inches) as the "where." But expectations are surely important for a range of other future-oriented and cognitive processes (Haith, in press). In fact, investigations have shown considerable stability of individual differences in infant expectations from at least 3 months onward, within sessions (Haith & McCarty, 1990; Jacobson et al.,

1992) and between sessions, over intervals of 1 week at 3 months (Haith & McCarty, 1990) and over a month or more from 3 to 9 months (Canfield, Smith, Brezsnyak, & Snow, in press). Infants also have memory for prior expectations they have formed (Arehart, 1995; Arehart & Haith, 1990), and several studies suggest that infants' ability to form expectations and their RTs within the VExP predict to later intellectual functioning (Benson et al., 1993; DiLalla et al., 1990; Dougherty & Haith, 1997). Thus, there is evidence, as one might suspect, that expectation formation in infancy and the speed with which infants respond to events (RT) involve at least some components of stable cognitive functioning (also, see Jacobson, Jacobson, & Sokol, 1994).

There is a dearth of information on other future-oriented processes in infants. One problem is how to conceptualize what domains fit this rubric for infants. A start has been made through the creation of a Future-Oriented Processes Questionnaire (Benson, 1994; Benson & Haith, 1995; Haith, 1992) based on maternal interviews. Such approaches may provide insight into how future-oriented processes can be fruitfully conceptualized.

Conclusions

Our understanding of the development of time in general and future thought in particular is primitive at best. However, the gap has been identified. In tying together the past, present and future, future thinking is unique and deserves additional attention.

CAUSALITY

Events in the physical world do not simply occur, willy-nilly. Most happen for a reason. A rattle falls off the table of a high chair because the infant pushes it off; the baby goes hurtling through space because mom picks her up; a bottle is thrust into baby's mouth because dad put it there. Events in the world behave not in isolation but in relation to one another, often according to a causal structure. We organize many events according to this structure rather than dealing with them one by one. There is fair agreement that one of the agendas of infancy is to make sense of the flow of perceptual information, and any tools that infants can use to experience events in episodes rather than independently would be helpful. An understanding of causality could serve the function of unifying separate events and also enable infants to form expectations for what will happen next, a process that facilitates the processing of the event stream.

As for most fundamental capacities of human mind, nativists and empiricists have had their say about how an understanding of causality emerges. Kant held that the general idea of causality is given a priori, while Hume argued that causal connections only arise from repeated experience with the spatial and temporal contiguity of observed events (Oakes & Cohen, 1994). For Hume, the mind constructs the idea of causality to explain relations between events that the individual experiences. Key points include:

- Although early research suggested that infants possessed a prewired module or routine for experiencing causality that is functional at around 7 months, subsequent research has provided evidence for a more developmental course of this understanding.
- Most research that has specifically focused on infants' understanding of causality has involved their observation of physical contact between objects. This restriction in the range of causal episodes leads one to question how general the understanding of infant causality might be and whether infant responsiveness depends on the simultaneity of events as opposed to their causal relation.
- The few investigations of causality that manipulate other factors than physical contact are vulnerable to familiarity interpretations.
- Investigators have been unclear about what they mean to imply about infant cognition when they say that infants understand causality. We regard the notion of causality as a social construct, not a process that naturally accompanies one's genetic endowment.

Early Research

With few exceptions, investigators have approached the question of when and whether infants understand causality through experiments that use the billiard-ball analogy that persists as the prototypic example of physical causality. One perceives a transfer of force from one billiard ball to another as the first ball, in motion, impacts the second, stationary ball; the first ball stops moving, as the second ball suddenly begins to move along the same trajectory. One infers that the impact produces a transfer of the force of motion from the first ball to the second (Michotte, 1963).

Leslie (1984) asked whether 7-month-olds experience causality when viewing an episode that he labeled a direct-launch event. In a direct-launch film sequence, a red brick moved from one side of the screen to the middle, where it contacted a stationary green brick that then moved across the screen on the same trajectory. For this condition, there was both contact (C) and an immediate (I) reaction. After familiarization with the C-I film, infants saw a film in which the motions of the bricks were identical, but the red brick stopped 6 centimeters before contact with the green brick (NC), and about 500 milliseconds elapsed before the green brick began to move (NI). As one might expect, there was recovery of looking for the NC-NI test episode. To determine whether or not a causality shift was responsible for looking recovery, rather than simply a change in both the contact and immediacy factors, a second group also witnessed a shift in these two factors from familiarization to test, but the shift did not involve a change in causality. This second group first became familiar with a contact, nonimmediate display (C-NI) and was then tested on a noncontact, immediate display (NC-I). Thus, two features also distinguished these conditions. The logic of the experiment was that if feature changes alone determined the amount of looking recovery, then looking at the second sequence should be equivalent for the C-I → NC-NI group (causal → noncausal) and the C-NI → NC-I groups (noncausal → noncausal). However, if there were something special about causality, the first group should recover more. They did; the shift from a causal to a noncausal condition produced stronger recovery of looking. Apparently, infants did not separately analyze the filmed events into orthogonal spatial and temporal components. Rather, they saw something special about the direct-launch sequence.

Still, it is possible that infants experience causality and noncausality in terms of a global (inseparable) spatiotemporal gradient rather than dichotomously. Leslie (1984) tested this possibility with the following logic. If infants respond according to a spatiotemporal gradient, then a contrast between a causal sequence and a noncausal sequence that differs on only one factor (contact or immediacy) should produce no greater recovery than a contrast between two noncausal sequences that differ on only one factor. The results supported the spatiotemporal hypothesis. Roughly equivalent recovery occurred whether the contrast was between a causal and a noncausal sequence or between two noncausal sequences. It made little difference whether the factor that varied was contact or immediacy. Leslie concluded that infants responded in terms of a "spatiotemporal continuity gradient" with the causal sequence on one end of a pole and the noncontact/nonimmediate (NC-NI) sequence on the other, with variations in-between.

Leslie and Keeble (1987) felt, however, that they might be missing a genuinely unique response of infants to causal sequences and tried a somewhat different approach to the problem, with the following logic, again with 7-month-olds. If there is something more to the filmed causal episode than a mere spatiotemporal relation, then a reversal of events would be more noticeable for a causal than a noncausal sequence. For a causal sequence, event reversal produces a change in both the agent/recipient relation and the spatiotemporal sequence, whereas for a noncausal sequence only the spatiotemporal sequence changes. Seven-month-old infants first became familiar with either the direct-launch (C-I) or the contact nonimmediate episode (C-NI), and then saw a reversed test sequence. As predicted from the premise that infants perceive causality as special, greater recovery of looking occurred for the reversed causal episode.

The conclusion drawn from these studies was that infants do see causal sequences as special. We see a problem in assimilating this position with the findings that suggested a spatiotemporal continuum, but Leslie and colleagues seem comfortable with postulating a special status for causal sequences. Consistent with Michotte's (1963) interpretation from experiments with adults, Leslie (1988) proposed the existence of a causality module by 27 weeks that directly and automatically detects causality, bypasses thought and reasoning and, thereby, serves as a basis for infants to acquire knowledge about the covariation of events. Presumably, infants first experience causality in terms of a transfer of force between physical objects and, with development, generalize the idea of causality to a wide range of events.

Later Research

Later experiments by Oakes and Cohen present a more complex picture. First, special responding to the causal sequence seems quite fragile for 6- to 7-month-olds and depends both on what objects participate in the episodes and on the trajectory that the impacting object (A) and the impacted object (B) follow. When real toylike objects, rather than bricks, played out the direct-launch, nonimmediate, and noncontact episodes, infants in this age range did not respond differentially to the direct-launch sequence (Oakes & Cohen, 1990), but they did respond differentially when the objects were rolling balls (Oakes, 1994). Apparently,

the complexity of the objects makes a difference at this age. Further, when object B continued a trajectory identical to that of object A, 7-month-olds responded differentially to the causal sequence, but when object B took off on a trajectory that was at a 45-degree angle to the original trajectory, 7-month-olds did not respond (Oakes, 1994). Infants at 10 months responded to the causal sequence as special for both of these circumstances. If a causality module were operating at the earlier age, one would not expect such complications.

Second, even the 10-month-olds did not respond uniquely during the test phase to the direct-launch sequence when the specific objects that assumed the A and B roles varied from one familiarization trial to the next (Cohen & Oakes, 1993). That is, babies did not seem to categorize episodes as causal when the objects varied across familiarization trials, whereas they did when the same objects were used consistently. The investigators concluded that infants at this age learn about causality in a very particular way, that is, with respect to specific objects rather than as an abstract concept about how objects generally relate to one another. These results further call into question the automaticity and directness of perception of causality in infancy, expected concomitants of a causality module.

There are three components to these physical causality sequences, and it is unclear how important each is for infants. One component is the identity of object A that initially moves, a second is the action of impact, and a third is the identity of object B that continues the motion after impact. Cohen and Oakes (1993) familiarized 10-month-olds with two sequences, one direct launch (C-I) and one delayed motion (C-NI). While the A object was different for the two sequences, the B object was the same. After habituation, the specific objects that served as the causal agents reversed so that the prior A object for the C-I sequence became the agent for the C-NI sequence and vice-versa. Infant looking recovered to both test conditions, indicating that they kept track of the relation between the agent and the action in both episodes. However, when a parallel switch occurred with object B, or the recipient object, infants did not seem to notice. The authors surmised that the bond between the agent and the action is tighter than that between the recipient and the action. Given these results, the authors suggest that infants experience causality in terms of specific relations between particular agents and particular actions.

The idea of a causality module that becomes operative at around 6.5 months and that eases infants' processing task is certainly attractive in principle. However, while efficient for infants, it is not efficient in accounting for the data. Oakes and Cohen conclude that infants learn causality relations, at least initially, only for the particular objects involved, and even at that, the two participants in a causal sequence are not seen as equivalent, with the agent carrying more weight.

Comment

All of these experiments involve a particular kind of "causal" sequence, and it is worrisome when a single proto-type event serves as the platform for a construct, even more so when the concept under scrutiny is as fundamental and complex as causality. Consider the physical events of a contact, immediate reaction (C-I)—what investigators have termed a direct-launching event. Object A moves and simultaneously contacts Object B and stops. Simultaneously, Object B begins to move. Thus, three visual transitions occur: move $\rightarrow$ nonmove (object A), noncontact $\rightarrow$ contact, and nonmove $\rightarrow$ move (object B). But possibly more importantly, all three events occur *simultaneously* whereas two or fewer events occur simultaneously for control conditions. Simultaneous transitions have a special status, independent of causality, that has been ignored. For example, in musical performances, when composers call for a simultaneity in the clash of cymbals and the beat of a drum, the effect is far greater than the sum of parts. Movie directors commonly exploit the effect in surprise and terror scenes. Infants also respond to simultaneity. The synchrony between the verbal peek-a-boo, the removal of one's hands, and the appearance of an animated face is key to the peals of laughter the event produces. In brief, transitions that occur simultaneously can produce a synergistic effect. This synergy is not captured by separate conceptual analyses of the temporal and contact components of the billiard-ball analogy.

To examine the simultaneity issue, one could create episodes for which simultaneity is present but causal relations are not. Data from only one condition suggest that a simultaneity interpretation may be flawed. Oakes (1994) found that 7-month-olds discriminated between a direct-launch and nondirect condition (nonimmediate and noncontact) when the trajectory of the B object was the same as the A object, but not when the B object veered off at a 45-degree angle. Simultaneity seemed to be present for both of these conditions, so the findings could pose a problem for a simultaneity account. However, as the author

notes, Ball A obscured part of Ball B at the moment of contact only in the 45-degree condition, so 7-month-olds may not actually have perceived a contact between the two. Additionally, infants appeared to find the 45-degree condition more interesting; thus, they may have habituated less completely in this condition, masking differential recovery effects. However, the general idea of varying outcome effects while maintaining simultaneity is promising.

Several other questions concern us about the findings and interpretations of these studies. First, if the perception of causality occupies a special status for infants, why the need for a familiarization phase in each of the experiments? Why wouldn't infants be surprised by a delayed reaction, for example, after one object contacts another? Oakes and Cohen (1990) found that even 10-month-olds showed no initial looking preference for a causal versus a noncausal sequence. It is possible that infants learn something important during the familiarization sequence that they did not bring with them to the experimental setting. At least one thing they might learn is that the transitions occur synchronously or do not. Procedures should be tried to eliminate the novelty response to the objects (e.g., by repeated display of them stationary and moving) without exposing infants to the experimental sequences, so that one can examine whether they bring their dispositions to the lab or develop them during the experimental session.

A second question relates to the interplay between laboratory events and what infants experience every day. If some of the laboratory episodes look odd to babies because they are inconsistent with everyday experience, their looking activity might reflect this discrepancy. For example, infants have opportunities to witness that larger objects have more impact in collisions than smaller objects: A large dog produces a bigger effect when bounding into a chair or a ball than a cat; an adult generates a stronger outcome when pushing a chair across the room than a small child. It would be impressive if such everyday experiences can transfer to relatively abstract laboratory tasks, but such transfer would also imply that familiarity may be responsible for the reported observations rather than perception of causality or ability to calibrate the effect of causal agents.

A third question is more conceptual. We are unclear about what investigators mean when they attribute the idea of causality to infants. For us, the idea of causality implies a *must* relation between events, not just a strong correlation or even a correlation of 1.00. If A occurs, B *must* occur because of physical laws. The notion of causality implies the question of and hypothesis about why something happens.

Do infants in the first year of life ask the *why* question? We don't think so.

Conclusions

The concept of causality has occupied philosophers for centuries. Anyone who can remember back to a class on logic will recall the struggle in dealing with this deceptively transparent concept. It is unlikely that infants have a concept that is later lost and only recoverable with instruction. We believe that *causation* is a cultural construct, gradually acquired through the experiences of early childhood, and we are inclined to believe that infants have only a fuzzy idea about how one object or event makes another event happen, certainly not enough to ask for, or generate, explanations.

How then does one account for the findings that indicate that infants categorize "causal" events differently from noncausal events? First of all, they don't. Cohen and Oakes (1993) demonstrated that infants do not categorize sets of events as causal or noncausal when the events change, a standard procedure for establishing category status. For most other studies, the presence or lack of simultaneity of transitions can account for the results, with perhaps an accommodation for more attention to the initially moving object (Cohen & Oakes, 1993).

We argue that the concept of causality, per se, is socially mediated. The core of the concept is that things happen for a reason. The specific form the explanation takes depends both on the phenomena of concern and characteristics and beliefs of the culture. At least at the moment, empirical data do not convince us that infants seek explanations or understand that events have explanations. Further, we are dubious that measures of looking time alone will provide a definitive answer.

NUMBER

Research and thinking about numerical awareness in infants have been among the most focused and well-defined of the topics we discuss. The topic of number has been carefully explored by mathematicians, and the components of numeric understanding have been more explicitly articulated than for such topics as space, objects, and time. Investigators have been particularly interested in numerical awareness because it requires an abstraction that transcends immediate perceptual information, indeed, any particular set of items; theories of infant cognition that hold to a strict sensorimotor line do not permit such aperceptual abstractions. Numeric appreciation is also the foundation of mathematical and computational ability, so there is great interest in discovering its course of development. Inasmuch as genuine numeric skill requires an appreciation of relations between sets, it also bears on core issues and theories that address the development of representational thought (e.g., Fischer, 1980; Piaget, 1983). Key points include:

- Infants appear to be able to make judgments of the equivalence of sets when the quantities are small, for example, two versus three items.
- The evidence that infants can make ordinal judgments of sets is weak as is evidence that infants detect the cardinal number in a set.
- Although the evidence that infants can perform arithmetic is intriguing, the data can be accommodated by a simpler perceptual explanation that assumes that visual information persists for some period of time following its occlusion.

Evidence for Equivalence Judgments

Most research has dealt with numeric *equivalence,* whether infants can discern that two displays contain either the same or a different number of items. However, even the basic understanding of number requires more—that there also be an appreciation of the ordered relations among sets. The concept of *ordinality* refers to these relations, for example, that a set of two contains more than a set of one and less than a set of three (Klahr, 1984; Strauss & Curtis, 1984).

Early experiments on number discrimination employed displays of small numbers of dots in linear arrays. For example, infants became familiar with arrays of three dots that varied in length. Then, they saw a two-dot array of the same length as one of the three-dot arrays. Posthabituation recovery of looking provided evidence that infants discriminated the number of items in the three- and two-dot arrays independently of any particular array configuration during habituation. Discrimination of two versus three items, but not four versus six, has been reported for both 4-month-olds and newborns (Antell & Keating, 1983; Starkey & Cooper, 1980).

Further experiments addressed possible nonnumeric confounds between the larger and smaller arrays, including brightness and area of the background and dots. The items in the display sets varied over habituation trials or even moved around in the display, a manipulation that eliminated the possibility of infants discriminating spatial configurations rather the number of items. The original findings were replicated with the confounds removed, in infants ranging from 5 to 13 months (van Loosbroek & Smitsman, 1990; Starkey, Spelke, & Gelman, 1990; Strauss & Curtis, 1984). Findings are consistent for discrimination of two items from three but there is no stable evidence for discrimination of four items from five or six and only mixed evidence of discrimination between three and four items.

Can Infants Use Number Information for Action and Are Computational Processes Involved?

The studies just discussed used habituation techniques and simultaneous displays of items that raise two concerns. First, can babies only discriminate the numeric information, or can they actually use this information to guide behavior? Second, is the apprehension of item number integral to perception of small-item displays, or do infants engage more sophisticated computational processes?

"Subitizing" refers to the immediate apprehension of small numbers in displays, without counting, and investigators have tried to determine whether infants use this apparently low-level process to make equivalence discriminations. Traditionally, subitizing refers to a process that is employed with simultaneous arrays. Thus, sequential presentation of items in variously-sized arrays should bypass a subitizing process. In one study (Canfield & Haith, 1991), 2- and 3-month-old infants saw a repeating sequence of pictures in a Left$_1$-Left$_2$-Right order, separated by a 1-second interpicture interval. Three-month-olds quickly formed expectations for the spatial location of the next picture in this series, as indicated both by anticipatory visual fixations and by decreased reaction time, in comparison to a control series. Fixations were more likely to remain in the same location after the first left (Left$_1$) than right picture, and a shift in fixation location was more likely after the second left (Left$_2$) picture to anticipate the next right picture. These findings were replicated with 5-month-olds in a study that also revealed that infants could form expectations for a 3/1 series (Left$_1$-Left$_2$-Left$_3$-Right; Canfield & Smith, 1996). The appropriate eye-movement suppression and shifting could not be attributed to a timing process; the duration of the interpicture intervals varied randomly over three values in the Canfield and Smith experiment. These studies reveal that infants can both discriminate numeric displays and use numeric information to guide visual behavior. Further, numeric sensitivity is not limited to simultaneously available displays.

If numeric sensitivity is an abstraction from perceptual information, one might look for supporting evidence from intermodal studies. For example, can infants detect that a particular number of items in a visual display matches the same number in a sound display? Early findings suggested that the answer is yes. When 7-month-old infants saw two simultaneous displays, one containing two items and another containing three items, and heard either two drum beats or three drum beats, they looked longer at the visual display that corresponded to the number of drum beats (Starkey, Spelke, & Gelman, 1983, 1990). Evidence held even if the visual displays and auditory events occurred sequentially. First, infants became familiar with, say, the two-item visual display. Then, without the visual displays, drumbeats occurred, and experimenters measured the fixation time to the sound source (a black disk). Infants looked longer when the number of drum beats matched the number of items in the familiar visual display (Starkey et al., 1990). However, the differences in looking at the two sets of items were relatively small, and later studies have not replicated the results (Mix, Levine, & Huttenlocher, 1994; Moore, Benenson, Reznick, Peterson, & Kagan, 1987). Mix, Huttenlocker, and Levine (1996) found that even 3.5 to 4-year-olds were unable to make an intermodal match for set sizes of 2 versus 3 even though they could make the match if the target and comparisons were both visual. Thus, the original results should be viewed with some caution.

Regardless, the evidence pertains to small numbers of items. Infants can match sets that contain the same number of items, at least in the same sensory mode and can discriminate sets that contain different numbers of items. There is even some evidence that infants appreciate the cardinality, or largest numbered item in a small set (Canfield & Haith, 1991; Canfield & Smith, 1996). Infants appropriately shifted fixation after the third item on a side at 5 months in the latter study and, as the authors point out, one can not claim that infants were only distinguishing more from less. The second item in the 3-item series was both more than 1 and less than 3, but infants shifted side fixations less after the second than the third item. Cardinality, the assignment of the largest number to the last item in a set is a feature by which infants could understand the ordinality of numeric sets. We will return to this issue.

The Case for Infant Arithmetic

If infants understand the ordinality of sets, they have a basis for carrying out simple arithmetic operations on sets, such as addition and subtraction. Wynn (1992) presented evidence for such skills from looking-preference studies with 5-month-old infants. In a 1 + 1 condition, infants first saw a single doll on a stage, that a raised screen subsequently obscured. A hand appeared that held a second doll, moved to disappear behind the screen, and then reappeared empty. An adult would assume that the second doll was left behind the screen. When the screen dropped to reveal either one doll or two, infants looked longer when there was only one doll, presumably displaying more surprise or violated expectancy. A consistent result was obtained in a 2 − 1 condition that started with two dolls behind the screen. Here, the disembodied hand first appeared empty, moved behind the screen, and reappeared with one doll, giving the appearance of only a single doll remaining behind the screen. When the screen dropped, infants looked longer when there were two dolls than one. Did infants simply look longer when the terminal and initial displays were the same because it looked as though a change occurred when the items were hidden? Or, could infants actually keep track of the number of items in the hidden display? Another study repeated the 1 + 1 manipulation, but now the removal of the screen revealed either 2 or 3 items. If change, per se, was the operative factor, there should have been no differential looking to these displays. However, infants looked longer at the 3-item display despite their lack of a preference for this display during a pretest, suggesting they could keep track of the number of items. The capabilities demonstrated by these studies imply an understanding, not only of equivalence of numeric sets, but also of their ordinality, that is, that an operation that increases or decreases items in a set results in a specific increment or decrement in the sets.

Comment

Some fairly strong claims have been made on the basis of these data that, if true, have far-reaching implications. The data have been taken to indicate "that infants possess true numerical concepts and suggest that humans are innately endowed with arithmetical abilities . . . " (Wynn, 1992, p. 749.) Further, infants are able:

> to represent and reason about numbers of things [that are] not based on perceptual properties of displays. [They] possess procedures for operating over these representations in numerically meaningful ways, and so can appreciate the numerical relationships that hold between different numerical quantities . . . [Thus, they] possess a genuine system of numerical competence. (Wynn, in press, p. 3)

There are weighty issues that have captured several authors in this field, issues that relate to infants' ability to understand invisible manipulations, to represent events and objects, to reason about physical phenomena, and to appreciate numeric concepts innately. Before discussing the arithmetic skills of infants, we critique the numeric equivalence studies.

A critic would find it difficult to account for all of the findings of the equivalence studies by appealing to low-level perceptual factors, such as contour density or amount or brightness of the background or targets. However, it is less easy to dismiss the involvement of a perception-like process in these accomplishments as opposed to a more symbolic representational interpretation (e.g., counting).

A subitizinglike process (immediate perceptual apprehension of quantity) must be considered. Consider the numbers 0 and 1. Infants at any age can show discrimination of displays containing 0 versus 1 item, if looking time is the measure, but we would not claim that they count to 1 or require a symbolic process to do so. Now, consider 1 versus 2 items. Few would argue that a representational process is required for this discrimination; the difference between 1 versus 2 items is immediately apparent in the display, no matter what the character or size of the items involved. Is it necessary to introduce the idea of number systems or symbolic processes when we make the jump to displays that contrast 2 versus 3 items? We are dubious.

The studies do pose problems for an unqualified subitizing account. First, how can one appeal to a subitizing process when the items in displays differ in size and content as number remains constant, for example, across habituation trials (Starkey et al., 1990; Strauss & Curtis, 1981, 1984)? The answer is straightforward. If infants can subitize small quantities, and quantity remains constant over trials as everything else varies, they should habituate to that property just as they habituate to other properties, such as item or face orientation (Cohen & Strauss, 1979; McGurk, 1972) or facial expression (Ludemann, 1991). Second, subitizing is usually considered to be a simultaneous perceptual process; how can one appeal to subitizing when sequential inputs are involved, for example, in the drumbeat studies (Starkey, Spelke, & Gelman, 1983, 1990)? Perhaps we need another word for sequential input that is perceived as a pattern, but semantics is not the main issue. The issue is whether a perceptual process is involved as opposed to a more representational and conceptual, counting, process. It is worth considering that sequential stimuli can form a pattern without a symbolic overlay, for example, in bird song or the opening bars of Beethoven's *Fifth Symphony.* Few would claim that a particular species of bird counts the notes in its song or that a music appreciator needs to count the bars of the *Fifth Symphony,* for recognition. Yet, it would be no challenge to demonstrate that a bird or listener can distinguish the original from a version that has a dropped note. (In fact, one may have to reimage the opening of the *Fifth* to figure out how many bars there actually are!) A short-term, perceptual-memory process can easily account for how sequential stimuli can form the perceptual equivalent of a simultaneous array. Third, subitizing is a perceptual process that can be invoked for discrimination, but how does it account for appropriate action, as in the anticipation studies (Canfield & Haith, 1991; Canfield & Smith, 1996)? It cannot. But the problem is no different for an account that invokes representational (e.g., counting) or pattern-recognition processes. Infants "judge" whether or not there is enough input to shift fixation to another location; the question is how they make that judgment. Finally, how can a subitizing account deal with cross-modal equivalence of sets—the matching of number across visual and auditory inputs? There are two issues here, how babies detect set size in each mode and how they match across modes. By our argument, the "evaluation" of set size could be done by a subitizinglike process. How the match is done across modes is equally a problem for the subitizing or more symbolic account. In principle, this latter matching or discrimination process need be no different from that which occurs within modes, but the cross-modal aspect does imply more than low-level perceptual processing. How "representational" this process may be is another matter. Regardless, infants in these studies averaged 7 months, so the invocation of an innate process, in our view, is gratuitous.

Alternatives to Infant Arithmetic

These studies addressed the equivalence issue, whereas the Wynn studies examined the issues of ordinality and arithmetic computations. There are various issues raised by the $1 + 1$ and $2 - 1$ studies, and it helps to separate them by considering how infants might react in the following thought experiment in which there is no occluding screen. A single doll stands on a stage (the $1 + 1$ condition), and then a hand appears with a second doll, deposits it next to the first doll, and then the hand disappears. Shortly after, the second doll suddenly vanishes or nothing happens at all. It is likely that infants would look longer when the second doll vanishes

because visible vaporization is not a common occurrence. Or, two dolls stand on a stage (the $2 - 1$ condition), a hand appears and removes one doll. Shortly after, a second doll suddenly materializes on stage or nothing happens at all. Again, it is likely that infants would look longer in the materializing event, not a frequently encountered experience. For neither condition would we appeal to representational or arithmetical skills; rather, we could say that infants are unaccustomed to seeing vanishing or materializing dolls and look longer because these alterations are unfamiliar.

How must we alter our thinking when we add a screen that hides the placement ($1 + 1$ condition) or removal ($2 - 1$ condition) of the second doll? Must we appeal to arithmetic competence? Not necessarily. Imagine that infants have decaying visual information about the display after it disappears, so that after seeing one doll covered by the screen, infants still have some perceptual information about what is there.[2] When the hand appears with a second doll and then disappears behind the screen ($1 + 1$ condition), infants have some information about the motion of the doll continuing, presumably halted by the occluded stage. As the hand emerges empty, the visual information about the two dolls continue but, admittedly, in a degraded form. Then the screen disappears, to display one doll instead of two, violating the content of infants' decaying information. A similar scenario occurs for the $2 - 1$ condition. Bogartz et al. (1997) have offered a similar possibility in occlusion studies of object knowledge.

Of course, we do not believe that infants have Superman-like X-ray vision, but the thought experiment helps to clarify some issues. Infants' "representation" could be very literal and sensory-based. We need not appeal to numerical concepts, innate endowment of arithmetical abilities, numerical competence, or infants' ability to reason about numerical quantities to understand the $1 + 1$ or $2 - 1$

---

[2] We do not mean to imply by the term "decaying visual information" that infants necessarily experience a decaying visual trace. Rather, we suggest here and later that there is not a substantial change in the structure of the visual information during the few seconds of occlusion that this experiment entails. Specifically, we question whether it is necessary to assume that infants *construct* a representation and suggest, instead, that infants use gradually decaying information that was established by the display. For dynamic displays, they also use their experience of how those events continue. Unfortunately, the available vocabulary at the psychological level makes it more difficult to talk about this information psychologically than neurally.

outcomes. Viewed in this light, we can not accept these data as evidence for infants' understanding of ordinal relations of set size.

Data from a recent study seems to undermine this interpretation of the arithmetic studies, because they suggest that altering the hidden array physically without affecting the number of items produces similar results to those reported by Wynn. Simon, Hespos, and Rochat (in press) replicated the 1 + 1 and 2 − 1 conditions, but they added a manipulation that changed the identity of one of the dolls. Thus, in the 1 + 1 condition, infants might see an initial Elmo doll with a second Elmo doll added, but screen removal revealed an Elmo doll and an Ernie doll (an identity but not a number violation). By introducing identity impossibility, the authors tried to distinguish between whether the earlier results depended on the physical impossibility of objects vanishing and materializing as opposed to arithmetic impossibility. The original findings replicated. Identity impossibility did not matter, whereas existence impossibility did. However, as the authors noted, infants might have simply ignored the identity of the dolls, citing other studies for which this was the case. In the authors' own words, the results are " . . . actually consistent *both* with the interpretation that infants' surprise reactions were based on violations of physical object knowledge and with the view that the children's surprise reactions were based on arithmetical knowledge." (p. 17 of in press manuscript).

One can relax the visual information account a bit to accommodate these data. Changes in absolute identity may not be salient enough to produce differences in looking time. Although we can not argue that an absolutely isomorphic iconic image, frozen in space, underlies the results (because the results obtain over an identity change), it is possible that decaying perceptual information could preserve the existence of objects more strongly than specific features. While our account may seem stretched, the question is whether it is more plausible to grant babies many skills that seem far less likely, including understanding of ordinal numeric relations among sets, the operations of addition and subtraction, and so on. Typically, the differences in percent looking at the compatible and incompatible outcomes are quite small, so a small bias produced by even a badly degraded configuration of perceptual activation might be sufficient to produce the results.

Uller and Huntley-Fenner (1995) and Wynn (in press) obtained results that fit our interpretation. Wynn found that infants performed better in a subtraction, 3 − 1, condition than in an addition, 2 + 1, condition with the outcome being either 2 or 3. For the subtraction condition, the set to be operated on is initially seen. As Uller and Huntley-Fenner point out, it is easier for infants to actually see an array and operate on it than to construct a mental model of a larger array from a smaller array. Uller and Huntley-Fenner carried out a 1 + 1 study in which they varied infants' opportunity to see the initial object in place. In an object-first condition, they replicated the traditional procedure by showing infants a single object on stage before occluding it and then adding another object. In a screen-first condition, they started with the occluding screen in position and then added one object behind the left side of the screen and another behind the right side. The typical finding replicated only for the object-first condition; infants looked longer when the screen was removed to reveal one object than two for the object-first condition but not for the screen-first condition. Ten-month-olds performed accurately in both conditions, and even 8-month-olds could perform in the screen-first condition, but only if two screens were used rather than one. There is clearly an effect of varying infants' opportunity to build a strong image of the objects (by actually seeing one of the objects in place or by screen cues), and the ability to build such an image appears to change with age.

Conclusions

We come away from this literature convinced that infants do differentially respond to the number of items in small sets, specifically sets of 2 or 3 items, by 3 months; thus, they can detect numeric difference in small sets. However, the evidence is not compelling that they understand the ordinal numeric relations among sets before the second year of life or are able to engage in even simple arithmetic.

The number literature does provide a good object lesson, however, of the complexity we encounter in trying to determine whether infants have understandings of the grand conceptual concepts that we use, such as a "number" concept. This complexity is revealed because the components of numeric understanding are so well-articulated. We have focused here simply on the subconcepts of equivalence and ordinality. Strauss and Curtis (1984) uncovered a wonderful quote by Douglass (1925), only part of which we can include, that makes the point. After pondering what it means for a child to know the number 4, including that it is more than 3, but less than 5, that it is the square of 2 and the square root of 16, and so on. Douglass remarked:

It is clear that there is no limit which may be set to the extension or perfection of [a] concept. It is never complete, and the bounds of its development are limitless. (pp. 444–445)

We feel a need for infancy researchers to resist the temptation to dwell on grand concepts that demand a considerable developmental process and to specify carefully the details of what infants understand at each step along the way.

CATEGORIZATION

Imagine an infant who must learn anew its parent's face for each perspective rotation, each expression, and each change of hair style. Or, consider the task of an infant who must acquire a new knowledge base for each separate cat that it encounters—that each meows, drinks, eats, and so on. And, one can appreciate the utility of categorization. By incorporating individual percepts of the mom's face into a mom-face category and individual cats into a cat category, infants gain enormous leverage in accumulating knowledge. Each piece of information one acquires with an individual exemplar can generalize to the whole set, permitting appropriate expectations and behavior in encounters with completely new instances. Of course, individual exemplars may differ, so category generalization can lead one astray. A cuddly black cat and a combative tawny cat deserve different treatment. We set that issue aside. The first order of business is to determine at what age infants form categories, how inclusive these categories are, and what representational form these categories assume. Key points include:

- Infants yield evidence of the formation of categories across a broad range of materials.
- They typically respond to categories on the basis of prototypes rather than exemplars, but task parameters can determine this choice.
- The correlations among features of exemplars plays an important role in category formation.
- Whether infants form categories on a perceptual or a conceptual basis is controversial and difficult to determine; the activities in which exemplars participate may provide perceptual information that muddies the perception-conception distinction.
- More attention should be directed to the role of infants' functional activity with exemplars in the categorization process.

The Logic of Experiments and the Paradigms

Early investigations of perceptual phenomena (e.g., McGurk, 1972) demonstrated that infants were more likely to generalize behavior to a new instance if they had seen several different instances (exemplars) within the same category than if they had seen only one. McGurk showed one group of infants an arrow that appeared in a variety of rotational orientations over familiarization trials, while another group saw the arrow repeatedly in only one orientation. For the test, both groups saw a new orientation of the arrow. Whereas the single-orientation group behaved as though the test orientation was novel, the variable-orientation group responded as though it was familiar. Apparently, exposure to multiple orientations during familiarization fostered a treatment of the arrow as equivalent no matter what the orientation. This same approach to the investigation of categorization pervades virtually all studies, with one critical difference. Typically, investigators assume that infants "have" the category before the laboratory encounter. Exposure to multiple members of the category establishes a behavioral bias that should generalize to new members of the familiarized category, if it exists, but not to new members of a different category.

Paradigms in this area have been more diverse than in any other. Again, habituation-of-looking paradigms predominate; familiarization consists of presenting a variety of exemplars from, say, the category cats, with the test involving a picture of a new cat and a picture of a dog (Quinn & Eimas, in press). But concern about whether passive fixation behavior accurately taps cognitive processing, prompted the introduction of an examination paradigm. The examination paradigm permits infants to handle as well as visually explore multiple exemplars during familiarization over several trials. During the test, they receive two new exemplars on separate trials, one from the familiar category and one from a new category; more time devoted to examining the out-category exemplar constitutes evidence for categorization of the familiarized category (Mandler & McDonough, 1993; Oakes, Madole, & Cohen, 1991). Investigators have also used a combined habituation and learning paradigm, that depends on loss of interest to category exemplars. To study gender categorization of voices, for example, Miller (1983) taught infants to look at a checkerboard display to hear several different male or different female voices. When their interest in the checkerboard declined, new voices were presented, and infants recovered more when the gender changed than when it remained the same.

While these paradigms have been fruitful, they depend on a loss of interest by infants to exemplars from the familiarized category, a phenomenon that does not match the idea that categorization serves a more positive function, permitting the active formation of expectations and generalization of behavior to new instances. Several paradigms model this more active role of categorization. For example, investigators use the conjugate-learning paradigm, in which infants kick to make an attractive mobile move, to test whether the learned behavior transfers differentially to new exemplars within and outside the category (Greco, Hayne, & Rovee-Collier, 1990; Hayne, Rovee-Collier, & Perris, 1987). Investigators have also examined the generalization of imitation to in- and out-category exemplars (Mandler & McDonough, 1993).

What Types of Categories Do Infants Form?

Excellent reviews of the infant categorization literature are available in several publications (Bomba & Siqueland, 1983; Quinn & Eimas; 1986, in press; Reznick & Kagan, 1983). Investigators have explored a variety of stimulus materials to garner evidence for category formation from early infancy onward. These materials include dot and line patterns (Bomba & Siqueland, 1983; Milewski, 1979; see review in Quinn & Eimas, in press), phonemes (Meltzoff & Kuhl, 1989), gender of voices (Miller, 1983), artifacts, such as alphanumerics (Greco et al., 1990, Hayne et al., 1987), and line drawings of face-like forms (Younger, 1992) and animal-like forms (Younger, 1985). Even categorization of types of motion has been studied (Gibson, Owsley, & Johnston, 1978). However, more everyday-like stimuli have been more common, although the variety of categories has been somewhat limited. Pictures of animals or toy animals have been used most frequently (Eimas & Quinn, 1994; Eimas, Quinn, & Cowan, 1994; Mandler & McDonough, 1993; Oakes et al., 1991; Quinn, Eimas, & Rosenkrantz, 1993; Roberts & Horowitz, 1986) and pictures of vehicles and actual toy vehicles (trucks, cars, motorcycles, airplanes) have also been popular (Mandler & McDonough, 1993; Oakes et al., 1991). Pictures of real human faces and animal faces and line drawings of faces have also been studied (Cohen & Strauss, 1979; Fagan, 1976; Quinn & Eimas, in press). A recent investigation explored the category of furniture (Behl-Chadha, 1994 as cited in Quinn & Eimas, in press). Evidence for categorization exists for virtually all of these categories by around the first half-year of life or earlier. Unfortunately, with few exceptions (Madole, Oakes, & Cohen, 1993; Mandler & McDonough, 1993; Oakes, Madole, & Cohen, 1991; Younger, 1990a; Younger & Cohen, 1983, 1986; Younger & Gotlieb, 1988), laboratories have not examined multiple age groups within studies, making developmental generalizations difficult. Evidence does exist that infants become increasingly sensitive to correlations among features for exemplars within categories between 3 and 10 months (Younger & Cohen, 1983, 1986); such correlations are thought to be central to the formation of categories. Also, the ability to form categories with abstract patterns is limited to good forms at 3 months, but infants are able to categorize poorer forms at 5 and 7 months (Younger & Gotlieb, 1988).

A caveat applies to studies we discuss that do not use artificial categories. When studies use stimuli that stand for something else, that is, pictures or toy models or video displays of animals and objects, investigators' inferences about behavior almost always refer to the referenced items rather than to the stimulus materials. For example, plastic toy cars may serve as stimuli, but the inferences are about categorization of real cars or, more generally, vehicles. Unfortunately, one can not be certain to what extent infants respond to the stimulus features of the objects as opposed to the items that the experimenter intends to symbolize. Further, it is unknown whether the stimulus materials are equally effective in symbolizing items in different categories, and it is equally unknown whether age differences interact with the stimulus/real-object relations.

How Are Categories Represented?

Investigators agree that categorization in infancy, and probably, to a large extent, across the life-span, does not consist of the kind of necessary and sufficient propositional format that constitutes the basis of classical logical categories. Rather, psychological categories generally have much fuzzier boundaries. Two conceptualizations dominate thinking about how people represent categories, prototype theory and exemplar theory. Prototype theory holds that the representation of a category consists of an average of all of the features of exemplars within the category. This schema or prototype serves as a summary of all of the relevant items (Posner & Keele, 1968). Evidence for prototypic representations in infancy comes from several studies (Bomba & Siqueland, 1983; Sherman, 1985; Strauss, 1979; Younger & Gotlieb, 1988). For example, when infants see a sequence of different exemplars of faces or dot patterns and are then tested with a prototypic display that they have never seen, but that represents the average of the dimensions along which the exemplars varied, they behave as though the prototype is more familiar even than one of the exemplars that they actually saw (e.g., Younger & Gotlieb, 1988).

Medin and Schaffer (1978) presented an opposing, exemplar theory, that suggests that all of the exemplars in a category are stored, and new instances are regarded as similar or different to the category, not by virtue of their distance from an averaged prototype, but rather by the average difference between the features of the new instance and those of the exemplars in the category. While the evidence tends to favor prototype theory (Younger, 1990b, 1993), both processes may be operative either simultaneously or depending on particulars. Sherman (1985) obtained evidence that when the number of exemplars is small, the exemplars are represented individually, more in line with exemplar theory. However, when the number of exemplars is larger, infants may deal with the greater amount of information by forming an averaged representation of the whole set (Strauss, 1979). Quinn (1987) found that 3- and 4-month-olds were more likely to form prototypes if they had an opportunity to form two categories at the same time. In actuality, critical tests of exemplar versus prototype theory are quite difficult to conduct (Hayne et al., 1987; Younger, 1990b) and some feel that the exemplar theory provides the more parsimonious and less mentalistic alternative (Greco et al., 1990).

How Are Categories Formed?

Prior to the information explosion in infancy, one might have argued that the development of categories depends on adult tuition as infants gain cognitive competence. When an adult labels a bunch of different-looking dogs as "dog" and different-looking cats as "cat," infants learn markers that set the two categories of animals apart and begin to distinguish among the features that differentiate them. In fact, the provision of a common label for exemplars within superordinate categories (animals versus vehicles or tools versus animals) facilitates acquisition of the categories for 12- and 13-month-olds (Waxman, 1995). However, it is well established that infants form categories long before language input can make a difference. Waxman considers words as invitations, rather than requisites, for forming categories.

As Younger and her colleagues have noted, infants must first be able to group similar items and segregate different

items to form categories. One determinant of how easy it is to form a category is the perceptual quality of the category standard. For example, consider Figure 5.1. The cross and X at the top of the figure are bilaterally symmetrical on both the vertical and horizontal axis; they constitute good forms, whereas the forms on the bottom are not symmetrical. Three-month-olds can form prototypes from seeing exemplar variations but only of the good forms, whereas 5-month-olds form prototypes for all but the poor forms,

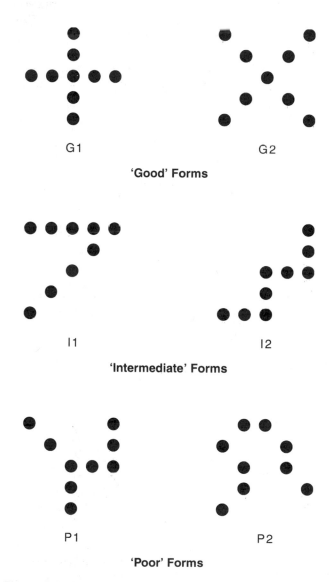

Figure 5.1 Prototypical dot patterns differing in goodness of form. From "Development of categorization skills: Changes in the nature or structure of infant form categories," by B. Younger & S. Gotlieb, 1988, *Developmental Psychology, 24*, pp. 611–619. Copyright © 1988 by the American Psychological Association. Reprinted with permission.

and 7-month-olds form prototypes for all (Younger & Gotlieb, 1988).

Another basis for segregating exemplars depends on correlations among features. One can not distinguish cats from dogs on the basis of color or size or eye distance alone, but the correlation among the features of eyes, face, tail, movement style, and sound production, makes it easy to tell a cat from a dog. Using artificial line drawings of animal-like forms, Younger demonstrated that 10-month-olds are sensitive to correlations among features such as neck length, tail width, ear separation, and leg length (Younger, 1985). A remaining problem is that real animals may have correlated features, but the features vary considerably. For example, fish differ strikingly in size and coloring from one another, but they tend to have scales (rather than fur or feathers), fins, and are limbless. When 10- and 13-month-olds see realistic pictures of animals that have features that vary, such as antlers that take different forms, or tails that vary in bushiness, they are still capable of categorizing animals on the basis of correlations of the existence or absence of those features (Younger, 1990a). The pickup of feature correlations appears to be a likely source for grouping and segregation information.

What Is the Conceptual Status of Categories?

There is a difference between infants' ability to form a category and the knowledge about what that category entails (Mandler, in press; Quinn & Eimas, 1986). Investigators generally agree that categories in early infancy consist of item grouping strictly on the basis of perceptual similarity without infants having any concept of the functional differences between members of different categories, but it is no easy task to determine when categories have meaning. As we have mentioned, habituation of looking paradigms do not provide information about the meaning that infants attach to categories, because the task does not require a functional or adaptive behavioral response.

Mandler and McDonough (Mandler, in press; Mandler & McDonough, 1983, in press) explored paradigms that engage infants in more functional activity. In one set of studies, 9- and 11-month-olds examined (including manual manipulation) different toy exemplars of one category in sequential trials and then could examine new in- and out-category exemplars. Infants performed categorically when the contrast was between the superordinate-level categories of animal and vehicle and also for the basic-level categories of car and plane, but not for the basic-level categories of dog and fish (Experiment 1). Infants also categorized at the basic level for car versus motorcycle (within-vehicle) but not for dog versus rabbit (within-animal; Experiment 2). Were infants categorizing items on the basis of perceptual features? When presented toys that had several features in common but were actually quite different—birds with their wings spread versus airplanes, infants separately categorized these two superordinate-level sets of birds and airplanes. Thus, categorization on the basis of global physical features alone seemed unlikely.

A separate set of experiments with 14-month-olds utilized a functional activity that was appropriate for one superordinate category of items but not for another (Mandler & McDonough, in press). The experimenter encouraged infants to imitate an action with toy animals and toy vehicles by modeling the action with an exemplar from one of the categories. For example, the experimenter picked up a cup and modeled giving a dog a drink, while saying "sip, sip, umm, good." Then an appropriate and inappropriate exemplar, for example, a rabbit and a motorcycle, were placed on either side of the infant. The experimenter handed the cup to the infant, the experimenter made the just-modeled sound, and infants imitated the action with one or both of the available exemplars. A putting-to-bed sequence (appropriate for animals) followed a similar routine. For the vehicles, a station wagon served as the model, with the turning of a key being the action (accompanied by "vroom, vroom") or giving a small doll a ride on the vehicle (accompanied by "go for a ride, whee"). The logic of the experiment was that if infants have formed a category, for example, of animals, they should be more likely to make an inductive generalization of the modeled action to a new in-category exemplar than to an out-category exemplar. Infants were more likely to select the in-category exemplar for imitation. This paradigm does not require training on variable exemplars before the test; thus, it depends on formation of categories prior to laboratory participation.

Similar findings were obtained when the dog and station wagon were used for the modeling sequence and testing involved atypical exemplars, an armadillo and anteater for the animal category and a forklift and shoveler for the vehicle category (Experiment 2). Even when 14-month-olds see the actions modeled for both appropriate and inappropriate exemplars, they are still more likely to select for imitation the appropriate category exemplar first. They seem to know that particular actions are more appropriate for some categories of items than others (Experiment 3).

Mandler (in press) suggests that these paradigms tap functional activity in infants that is driven more by the meaning of categories and their exemplars rather than by their physical appearance. On the other hand, infant performance in looking paradigms reflects the perceptual similarity of items. The distinction is between perceptual and conceptual categorization, the first measured by looking paradigms and the latter by paradigms that require infants' functional involvement. Conceptual categorization involves concepts, an appreciation of what things are like and a grouping on that basis rather than on the basis of how things look; noticing the physical features of a lion is very different from understanding that a lion lives in the jungle, hunts, eats other animals, and so on.

From the Mandler and McDonough view (Mandler, in press; Mandler & McDonough, in press), infants acquire conceptual knowledge about superordinate categories through perceptual analysis, a higher order abstraction of perceptual information that permits categorization on the basis of like kinds. The two examples of such information that would permit infants to distinguish animals from vehicles include the sharing, among animals, of the attributes of self-starting and of biological motion. Thus, though an anteater and rabbit cast very different perceptual images, they are conceptually alike in that they move on their own and in accord with principles of biological motion. Mandler points to a double dissociation as a key piece of evidence for her argument: infants appear to categorize at the basic level with looking paradigms but not at the superordinate level, just the opposite of what she has found with the two, more functional paradigms. Basic-level categorizing can be done on a more perceptual level, while superordinate-level categorizing depends more on an understanding of like kinds.

Comment

This analysis is intriguing and highlights the meaning component of categorization in infancy that has been alluded to by others (e.g., Quinn & Eimas, 1986) but that has not received much attention. However, we have reservations about the interpretations. A key link for the perception-conception distinction is the claim of a double dissociation, one side of which is the tendency of 9- and 11-month-olds to categorize at the superordinate level, but not at the basic level (Mandler & McDonough, 1993). (Seven-month-olds also participated in this study, but their behavior was ambiguous.) However, infants under 12-months-old did categorize at the basic level within the superordinate category of vehicles (car versus airplane and car versus motorcycle), although they did not within the superordinate category of animals. While Mandler attributes the vehicle proficiency

to unusual opportunity of Southern California infants to observe vehicles, the fact remains that the dissociation is not all that clear. (Also, see our opening comments about stimulus materials.) Additionally, others have found that infants around one year do categorize at the basic level with other paradigms (Waxman, in press), and Behl-Chadha (1994) found that even 3-month-olds can categorize at the superordinate level (furniture versus animals).

A crucial claim for the argument is that conceptual categorization is not based on salient perceptual features. However, as Quinn and Eimas (in press) point out, animals have things that vehicles do not, for example, eyes, faces, fur, and feathers. Vehicles have wheels, nontextured and shiny exteriors, and windows that animals do not share. Mandler and McDonough (1993) were sensitive to this issue when they constructed the plane exemplars for Experiment 3 in which infants categorized birds versus planes; two of the five plane exemplars contained flying tiger markings with representations of eyes. However, the data for these exemplars were not reported separately, fewer than half of the plane exemplars had such markings, and it is unclear how eyelike and facelike the markings looked to infants. We are skeptical that infants' categorization could be based on such higher-order characteristics as self-starting or biological motion. It seems unlikely that 14-month-olds would have had sufficient experience with such animals as armadillos or anteaters (not to mention musk oxes or dinosaurs that were used as distracters) to detect that they are self-starting or obey biological motion principles when they locomote; remember, infants were dealing with plastic toy figures. They might *infer* such characteristics, based on their categorization of these instances as animals, but how is the categorization accomplished in the first place? A likely possibility consists of the perceptual features proposed above.

As we noted in our opening statements, investigators often consider as "perceptual" only the static physical features of animals and objects. Why are the dynamic events that objects participate in not "perceptual"? When *events* are considered as part of perceptual experience, one realizes that there are many opportunities for infants to learn about things that go together. Parents provide furry toy animals that share the crib and teach their infants to pet them; they also model animal sounds, movements, and so on with toy animals. Siblings play with toy animals differently than with vehicles, rubbing animals against their face and sleeping with animals in their beds. Not so for vehicles. Vehicle toys are rolled and pushed, banged against one another (making noisy sounds when they crash), and flown, and may be accompanied by engine noises (such as "vroom, vroom") in sibling play or parent play-modeling. These activities could serve as a base for the superordinate categorization that investigators have observed. Moreover, they could serve as a basis for differentiation or lack of differentiation in experimental paradigms, depending on the task. For example, in an examination paradigm, in which rubbing and manipulating are key to the measure, there might be relatively little differentiation at the basic level among different animals because rubbing and manipulating are what infants see modeled in the home and have learned to do with toy animals. Such activity might not be differentiated among rabbits and dogs. But if the measure were approach versus avoidance with a dog or a rabbit in the real world, differences might emerge quite readily. To summarize, we regard the activities in which exemplars engage to be as "perceptual" as the physical features they possess and believe that such events constitute an important segue into an understanding of what objects, animals, people, and plants do. In our view, the perceptual appreciation of the function in which objects and people engage gradually encroaches into the conceptual understanding of "like-kindedness."

While disagreeing with some aspects of Mandler and McDonough's analysis, we note two important contributions of their work. The first is to balance the attention that has been given in categorization work to the static physical features of objects with consideration of the events in which entities participate. The second is to develop approaches to infant categorization that permit infants to show adaptive functional behavior with category items.

Acquiring Categories through Functional Involvement

While research on categorization with infants in the last few months of the first year and beyond has diverged from the habituation-of-looking approach with, for example, examination and imitation (Mandler & McDonough, 1993, in press), labeling (Waxman, in press), and even emotional-expression paradigms (Golinkoff & Halperin, 1983), investigators have strayed only rarely with younger infants. An exception is a research program that utilizes a learning paradigm pioneered by Watson (1966) and Rovee-Collier (Rovee & Rovee, 1969).

The paradigm permits an infant to learn that kicking activity will move an attractive crib mobile. Usually three learning sessions take place over successive days with mobiles that vary within a certain category, say color. On the fourth day, infants show categorization by kicking to a new in-category mobile (i.e., a new color) but not to an out-category mobile (e.g., a new form). Generalization fails to occur when the learning sessions do not include variable-mobile training (Hayne et al., 1987). A new in-category exemplar can also serve as a reminder of the earlier training when it occurs 13 days later, whereas an out-category exemplar is ineffective.

Infants' functional experience with the mobiles can broaden the category of mobiles considerably (Greco et al., 1990). Following normal variable training with an alphanumeric mobiles for three days, infants saw a mobile that had very different perceptual characteristics on Day 3, a mobile of a butterfly. The butterfly mobile moved and rang for only 3 minutes, either noncontingently or contingently. For only the contingent condition, the butterfly mobile served as an effective reminder of the alphanumeric mobile session 13 days later. Apparently, the Day 3 functional experience had created a broad "kickable-mobile" category for infants that merged with the alphanumeric mobiles.

The message from these experiments is that the events that exemplars participate in and the functional experience that infants have with events play a role in categorization, in agreement with a suggestion made by Nelson (1979). Even 3-month-olds are capable of establishing fairly broad categories of exemplars that are physically quite dissimilar if they have opportunities to include them in their functional activities. These are striking findings for an age group for which there has been general consensus that categories are formed only on the basis of perceptual similarity (Mandler, in press; Quinn & Eimas, 1986).

This is not to say that the role of function in categorization is complete at this early age. For example, studies of the understanding of the correlation between form and function indicate a lack of the appreciation of such relations until at least 14 months and, for some situations, not even until 18 months (Madole & Cohen, in press; Madole, Oakes, & Cohen, 1993). However, it does seem clear that the classic notion that infants process objects only in terms of their static structural features before more dynamic factors can be incorporated is as passé in considerations of infant cognition as it is for infant perception.

Conclusions

Research on categorization leaves several strong impressions. First, knowledge about the kinds of things that infants categorize can reveal a great deal about how they organize and think about events around them. Second, relatively passive looking paradigms reveal a very limited picture of what infants know about relations among classes of objects and events. Third, the functionality of events is crucial to how infants organize them, both with respect to their observation of the functions in which objects participate and with respect to their own involvement in these events. This observation is not new (e.g., Bruner, Olver, & Greenfield, 1966; Greco et al., 1990; Inhelder & Piaget, 1964; Nelson, 1973, 1974, 1979), but with few exceptions, it has been consistently ignored. Finally, comparisons of categorization skill at different ages are sorely needed. Ironically, there are few studies that examine the development of categorization, yet such studies hold the greatest potential for advances in this field.

Still unexplored are questions about infant flexibility in categorization and how flexibility develops. There are several facets to this issue. One concerns development of the ability to categorize at different levels, depending on the circumstance. Given that infants can categorize cats and dogs and can categorize animals and vehicles, what factors determine at any moment whether they choose one or another grouping alternative, that is, categorization at the basic versus superordinate level?

A second concerns shifts in categorization from one dimension to another. A dog may be a generic dog for some purposes but may be distinguished by whether it is a member of a category of familiar dogs (whose behavior is predictable) or unfamiliar dogs, for other purposes.

A third interesting issue is the question of what principles govern how far knowledge and experience generalize across various levels of category boundaries. This is an issue throughout the lifespan. Adults and even infants behave as though they distinguish among exemplars that are living and not living (animate versus inanimate). However, even though a person may know that humans and animals have genes and DNA, the typical high-school biology student is surprised to learn that bees and peas do also. And, while vehicles and rocks both fall in the category of inanimate objects, vehicles, like animals, differ from rocks in sharing the property of consuming energy. The process of categorization and the benefits it offers for generalization tap deep cognitive processes that have hardly been explored in developmental work.

Finally, the benefits of categorization have been touted broadly, but the flip side of this ability has received much less attention. How do we think about the interplay between categorization and the distinctions that infants must make among in-category members? We return to an issue that opened this section. While infants soon learn to appreciate cats as a category, they also learn differences between cats. This process is equally important to how in-category exemplars are appreciated as alike.

REASONING ABOUT PHYSICAL EVENTS

Recent research on physical reasoning has played a major role in the evolving conceptualization of infant cognition. Experiments and conceptual papers by Baillargeon and Spelke and their collaborators constitute the bulk of this effort in what we call the "precocist" perspective, a claim that complex physical reasoning occurs quite early in infancy. Piaget (1952, 1954) represented the march to cognitive maturity as more gradual. As discussed previously, the argument is that Piaget's tasks confounded complex means-ends action sequences with knowledge about events in which objects participate.

An important point of confrontation with Piagetian theory is that the precocists assert that infants can represent objects and events at an early age. Occlusion events constitute an important feature of the studies that challenge Piaget's out-of-sight, out-of-mind claim. Infants view events that are partially occluded, and their looking at compatible or incompatible outcomes provides information about whether the outcomes seem peculiar, based on the part they could see and whether they "represented" the continuation of the event during the occlusion interval.

A second claim that challenges Piaget's theory is that infants can reason about events in the absence of their acting on those events.

A third challenge to Piaget's constructionist theory is that knowledge of objects/events is either innate or depends on innately constrained, biologically-based learning mechanisms. A point of difference among these alternative perspectives is whether knowledge is innately given or whether mechanisms to acquire knowledge are given.

The rise of precocism has been accompanied by the adoption of quite sophisticated concepts to describe early cognition. In some cases, the explanatory terms include forecasting (expectations), reactions to violations of expectancy, affective consequences (surprise), and an awareness that an event is physically impossible. Very young infants are even endowed with the ability to reflect, an attribution that was unheard of a decade ago. Key points include:

- Investigators have been much too adventurous with their use of adultocentric terms.

- Infants do appear to have information that is based only on looking activity. They look at some events more than others, presumably because the events look odd to them, and this oddness must reflect information they have about normative features of their environment based on experience.
- Despite their differences with Piagetian theory, the precocists converge with that theory on a very important point. Cognition is first organized around concrete perceptual events—objects, people, and their actions. No one really disagrees on this issue, although there may be disagreement about whether cognition emerges from perception.
- While the new literature requires adjustments to Piaget's theory, a key strength of the theory endures in its developmental focus. Precocist positions are vague or noncommittal about how the infant mind becomes the mind of the older child and adolescent.

Experiments on physical reasoning can be classified on the basis of whether they use occlusion or nonocclusion events. Occlusion studies address the issue of how infants reason about events they can not see, presumably through operations on representations of those events.

Studies of Occluded Events

A description of a prototypic study will convey the major features of the paradigm and its logic. Baillargeon (1987) familiarized infants to a screen whose top rotated toward and away from them. Following the infant's familiarization with the screen rotating through its full 180-degrees extent, the experimenter laid the screen flat with the top toward the infant, and placed a box behind the pivot plane of the screen. In the "possible" condition, the top of the screen then rotated away from the infant, first obscuring the box, and then reaching a position in a few seconds where it contacted the box and stopped. In the "impossible" condition, the screen continued to rotate a full 180 degrees, as for familiarization, until it lay flat with the top facing away from the infant, invading the space that the box had occupied. Infants looked significantly longer at the impossible than the possible event. Baillargeon suggested that studies like these examine "infants' ability to represent and to reason about the *existence* of an occluded object . . . " and that the results "suggested that they (a) understood that the box continued to exist after it was occluded by the screen and (b) expected the screen to stop

and were surprised that it did not." (Baillargeon, 1991, p. 14). The assertions, therefore, implicate high-level cognitive phenomena—reasoning, representation, expectation, and surprise—upon violation of an expectation.

Issues in Occlusion Experiments

We must separate two issues in this paradigm that are easily confused, the physical events that occur and the partial occlusion of those events. When one focuses on the physical events, one set of issues arises—for example, infants' differential response to impossible and possible events may actually involve reasoning, expectation, and surprise. However, alternative interpretations must also be considered, such as whether the discrimination is based on familiarity, novelty or some other unidentified perceptual factor. The use of the possible/impossible terminology implies that, if the baby is sensitive to the contrast, she knows that the uncommon event was physically impossible. Spelke and her collaborators (Spelke, Breinlinger, Macomber, & Jacobson, 1992; Spelke, Katz, Purcell, Ehrlich, & Breinlinger, 1994) use the somewhat more neutral terms of consistent/inconsistent. We will adopt these more neutral terms, leaving for speculation what infants know about physical laws, and mean to imply that consistency or inconsistency refers to physical laws, rather than to what infants know about these laws.

An independent issue concerns whether or not events are partially occluded. One can present inconsistent events to infants that are continually visible, as will be illustrated in the next section. The point of the occlusion manipulation has been to demonstrate that infants can represent events that they can not see, and that they can logically reason about those representations. That is, infants could represent events without appreciating whether they are consistent or inconsistent, and they could appreciate consistency or inconsistency without representing events. It is easy to lose track of which studies address which issues.

Follow-Up Studies on Screen Occlusion

The studies of screen-occlusion events have followed a very systematic program and have yielded interesting results. A set of studies uncovered developmental functions that suggest growth of quantitative reasoning as well as factors that support the representation of the occluded object (Baillargeon, 1991). For example, when 4.5-month-olds saw the screen rotate only 80% of the way into the area the hidden box occupied, they failed to respond as though the event was inconsistent (Experiment 2). This finding contrasted with their response to the 100% invasion of the box area (Baillargeon, 1987). In contrast, 6.5-month-olds responded to the 80% invasion, but not an invasion of 50% (Experiment 1). Props enhanced infants' performance. When a second box stood next to the target box and remained visible throughout the screen rotation, the 6.5-month-olds now responded to the 50% rotation as though the event was inconsistent, and the 4.5-month-olds responded to both the 50% and 80% rotations (Experiments 3 and 4). Thus, the opportunity to view a second identical box that aligned perfectly with the occluded box, throughout the occlusion event, seemed to help infants secure the location of the hidden box. Alignment mattered. When the continually visible box was placed 8.5 centimeters in front of the target box, the performance of the 4.5- and 6.5-month-olds was comparable to when no comparison box was present. Other studies suggested that the physical properties of the comparison box were important also, even when the size remained identical to the target box. Baillargeon (1992, as cited in Baillargeon, 1993) found that the comparison box assisted 4.5-month-olds' performance only when its decoration was highly similar to the target box. Performance of 6.5-month-olds benefited from the presence of either a highly similar or moderately similar decoration, but not from a very dissimilar decoration. These findings imply that whether or not infants respond to inconsistency depends on the visual support available and that younger infants require a greater isomorphism between that support and the vanished object than older infants.

These data were interpreted as evidence that young infants are able to make qualitative yes/no judgments about area overlap of physical objects, but they are unable to make precise quantitative judgments (Baillargeon, 1991, 1993, 1994). With age, their ability to make quantitative judgments improves. When the comparison box is present and aligned, it serves to support the quantitative judgment, because infants can detect the exact location at which the screen intrudes upon the area of the hidden box as it moves past the front edge of the visible box. We will return to this issue after considering several experiments by Spelke and her colleagues.

The Core Principles Approach

Research by Spelke and her colleagues has also been motivated by the argument that infants know much more about their world than they can demonstrate through manual actions. In addition, these investigators believe, in contrast to Baillargeon who emphasizes innate constraints on learning, that infants have innate knowledge about how objects behave. This knowledge is based on a set of core innate principles. Three core principles are *cohesion,* the notion that objects are bounded and that their components remain connected to one another; *continuity,* the notion that an object that moves from one place to another pursues a continuous path and can not occupy the same location as another object, and *contact,* the notion that one object must contact another to make it move (Spelke, 1994; Spelke et al., 1992, 1994; Spelke, Vishton, & von Hofsten, 1995). The assertions regarding contact were based on studies by Ball (1973) and Leslie (1988), discussed earlier, and those regarding cohesion on studies by Spelke et al. (in press). A consideration of two sets of studies regarding continuity illustrates the approach.

The first set of studies involved 2.5- to 4-month-old infants who watched a ball move along a trajectory and then disappear behind a screen (Spelke et al., 1992). For example, 4-month-olds first participated in a familiarization sequence for several trials in which they saw a hand drop a ball (see Figure 5.2a); the falling ball was visible for part of its trajectory and then it disappeared behind the screen. When the experimenter removed the screen, the ball was visible on the floor of the platform. Following habituation, the test began with consistent or inconsistent events. For both conditions, the ball was dropped and disappeared, as for familiarization trials. However, when the experimenter removed the screen, now a small table stood on the platform floor. For the consistent trials, the ball lay on top of the table, and for the inconsistent trials, it lay on the floor, as though it had passed through the table top. The principle of continuity dictates that this latter condition is inconsistent; the ball could not pass through the table top. Infants looked longer on the trials that ended with the ball lying on the floor (inconsistent) than on the table, even though the table-top location was novel and that on the floor was familiar.

Infants in a control condition never saw a ball drop. During familiarization trials, they simply saw a hand place the ball on the floor, and during test trials they saw the hand place the ball on the table or floor. The screen hid the display for 2 seconds, and then the display reappeared. Unfortunately, the opportunity for controls to see the outcome display on each trial prior to screen occlusion contaminated the data for these groups, and similar contamination occurred for the other experiments in this set. Therefore, we will not consider the control data.

(a)

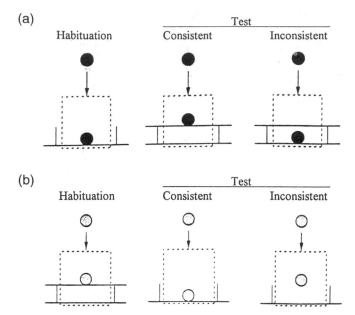

(b)

Figure 5.2 (a) Violation of continuity experiment. (b) Violation of gravity/inertia experiment. Circle indicate the initial and terminal positions of the ball. Arrows depict the path of visible motion of the ball in the experimental events. Dotted lines depict the screen when it was lowered into the display. Adapted from "Origins of knowledge," by E. S. Spelke, K. Breingler, & K. Jacobson, 1992, *Psychological Review, 99,* pp. 605–632.

Bogartz et al. (1997) and Cohen (1995) have suggested an alternative perceptual interpretation to violation-of-continuity. During familiarization, it is likely that infants tracked the visible part of the object's trajectory and continued to move their eyes along that trajectory after the ball disappeared, at least for a while. If so, the outcome revealed that the ball rested on the first surface encountered (the floor) along the infant's visual tracking path. During test trials, the ball on the table may have seemed more familiar because this condition also displayed the ball atop the first surface encountered along the infant's tracking path. However, the ball on the floor may have seemed more novel because it was the second surface encountered. Alternatively, one can completely ignore the familiarization component of the experiment and consider the two test outcomes in terms of their perceptual features. The inconsistent outcome displayed the ball enclosed by contours on all four sides, whereas the consistent outcome displayed only one contour beneath the ball. Findings from several studies have demonstrated that infants look longer at greater contour density, as long as they can resolve the contours (Haith, 1980; Haith & Campos, 1977; Karmel & Maisel,

1975). Another experiment in this series with 2.5-month-olds was virtually identical except that the ball rolled on a horizontal surface. The results were essentially the same, and so are the alternative interpretations.

Consideration of these studies illustrates the inherent ambiguity of looking measures for the purpose of inferring mental process and underlines several points we made at the outset. One difficulty is that the test-trial outcomes may be differentially attractive. The use of familiarization trials compounds the difficulty depending on the degree to which infants compare the outcome display to the familiarization display. One can ask why familiarization trials are even necessary if babies truly come to the experiment with core knowledge about what can and can not happen. Why would they not be more interested in an inconsistent outcome from the beginning? The use of a familiarization procedure leaves open the possibility that infants actually learn what is ordinary and what is not during the experiment.

The problem with the perceptual relation among test outcomes is especially apparent in Experiment 2 of this series in which 4-month-olds saw a small ball (consistent) or a large ball (inconsistent) enclosed on all sides except the top. The top had a hole in it through which the ball presumably dropped. The hole was bigger than the small ball but smaller than the large ball; thus, the larger ball could not have dropped through and, as predicted, the infants looked longer at the larger ball. However, because the chamber that contained the balls was the same size, its contours were closer to the large than small ball, and preference for greater contour density could again provide an explanation.

Finally, we should note that attempts to replicate the studies on continuity by Spelke and colleagues have not been successful with infants under 12 months (Bogartz, personal communication; Cohen, 1995; Cohen, Gilbert, & Brown, 1996).

The Principle of Continuity Compared to Gravity and Inertia

While Spelke and colleagues have taken the findings from the studies described as support for infants' sensitivity to the continuity principle, the more compelling case that the principle of continuity is privileged, that is, a part of infants' core knowledge, is based on findings that infants respond more strongly to violations of continuity than to violations of, for example, gravity and inertia (objects continue to move on a path unless impeded). During familiarization, 4-month-olds watched an experimenter drop a ball that disappeared behind a screen. Removal of the screen revealed (Spelke et al., 1992, Experiment 4) a ball lying on a table that was supported by a floor (see Figure 5.2b). Test trials were identical, except that screen removal revealed a display in which the table was removed. For consistent trials, the ball lay on the floor, in a novel location, and for inconsistent trials, the ball stood in a familiar location, now suspended in midair! Violating our intuitive expectations, infants actually looked longer at the ball on the floor, in a novel location, than at the ball suspended in midair. This finding is consistent with the idea that inertia and gravity are not principles that are members of the core knowledge family; further it is consistent with the idea that the principle of continuity may indeed be privileged.

Comment

Two caveats are important when thinking about these findings. First, Needham and Baillargeon (1993) have shown that even younger infants respond with interest when they see an object suspended if they witness the removal of support. They suggested that, because infants have ample opportunity to see objects that are apparently suspended in their everyday world, such as pictures on a wall, they may only react to midair suspension when they actually see someone remove the object's support. Because the falling ball was occluded in midtrajectory in the Spelke et al. (1992) study, there was a delay between the loss of support for the ball and the opportunity to view its suspended state. The second concern relates to the particular comparisons one makes in the habituation paradigm. The investigators chose to compare how long infants looked at the ball-on-floor versus the ball-in-air outcomes and, indeed, infants looked longer at the ball-on-floor. But this finding does not imply that infants failed to detect something odd about the ball-in-air outcome. In fact, looking time at the ball-in-air outcome was greater than for the final trials of the habituation sequence. While a statistical analysis of the recovery data was not provided, it appeared that infants were sensitive to this peculiar outcome, an apparent violation of gravity or inertia principles.

A similar concern prevails for several other experiments in the core knowledge series that use the occlusion familiarization and test paradigm to pit one outcome against another to demonstrate that responding to inertia is absent or weaker than responding to continuity (Spelke et al., 1994). Three experiments suggested that infants ranging from 4.5 to 12 months were not particularly interested in looking at an outcome in which a ball rolled on a platform, was occluded in

midtrajectory and ended up in a familiar location that it could not have reached by a linear path. At the younger ages, infants looked longer at an outcome in which the ball ended up in a novel location that could have been reached by a linear path. The authors concluded that, "None of these experiments suggest that infants expect smoothly moving objects to continue in smooth motion" (p. 153). But the analyses examined the interest of infants to violations of inertia *relative* to their interest in a novel outcome. At every single age, 4.5, 6, 8, 10, and 12 months, there was an apparent disruption of the looking-habituation trend for the nonlinear condition, produced by a recovery of looking during test trials. The recovery was just not as large for the novel-outcome condition. Other studies in this series that pitted violations of inertia against violations of continuity and found violations of continuity to produce more looking recovery are subject to the same concern. We have no way of knowing if the statistical comparisons between the last habituation trials and test trials would reveal stable recovery of looking for the inertia groups alone, either by average comparisons or by more sensitive trend tests, but some of the differences seem at least as large as those between the two test conditions.

Thus, the core knowledge argument, essentially an argument for innate knowledge of continuity but not inertia or gravity, may actually depend on a weaker, but not absent response to inertia than to continuity violations. This analysis raises a different issue. Cross-dimensional comparisons are problematic, to say the least, as one can easily illustrate by a thought experiment that asks whether infants find sounds or sights more interesting. Assuming that one could design a common measure of infant interest, how would one select the particular sounds or sights for the comparison? Based on the particular pairing, sometimes the sight would seem more interesting and sometimes the sound. Similarly, the particular instantiation of violations of inertia or continuity that one selects for study must affect the relative interest of infants in the two. We will delay until later a discussion of whether infants look longer at displays because they actually have knowledge of physical principles, like continuity or inertia, or rather, because these displays simply look odd to them. At this point, we conclude that evidence for relative responding to one violation as opposed to another can not support or weaken the claim for innate knowledge.

We turn now to two sets of studies that carried out the physical violations in full view of infants. The second set also bypassed the familiarization procedure. Consideration of these experiments will help to clarify the interpretations of the occlusion experiments.

Studies of Nonocclusion Events

Baillargeon and her colleagues carried out several experiments to examine infant's understanding of support relations between objects. In one experiment, (Baillargeon, Needham, & Devos, 1992), infants saw a person's finger push a box along the top of a platform (see Figure 5.3). In a consistent condition, the finger pushed the box until the leading edge of the box was aligned with the edge of the platform, where the box rested. In an inconsistent condition, the finger pushed the box further until its trailing edge barely maintained contact with the edge of the platform, as the rest of the box hung over the edge. This condition was inconsistent, because the box remained suspended rather than dropping to the floor. Five-month-olds did not look differentially at these two displays, whereas 6.5-month-olds looked longer at the inconsistent display. The authors' interpretation was that younger infants assumed that the platform could support the box if there was any contact at all.

Another set of experiments examined the roles of support and contact (Needham & Baillargeon, 1993). In one study, 4.5-month-olds watched a stage on which there was one box. A hand appeared from behind a curtain and placed a second box on top of the first where it remained when the hand withdrew (consistent condition). Or, the hand appeared with the second box and placed it at the height of the top of the first box, but to its side, so that when the hand withdrew, the box appeared to be suspended in midair (see Figure 5.4). Control groups saw the same events, but the hand continued to grasp the second box. Infants looked longer at the apparently suspended box than in any other condition, which the investigators interpreted to suggest that the 4-month-olds:

> (a) *believed* that the box could not remain stable without support; (b) *realized* that the box was supported when it rested on the platform or was held by the hand, but not when it was released in mid-air; and hence (c) *expected* the box to fall in the impossible event and were *surprised* that it did not. [italics added, p. 130]

A control experiment examined whether these findings reflected novelty for infants when seeing an object suspended in midair. Infants saw displays that were identical to the outcomes of the prior experiment, but no hand appeared

Familiarization Events

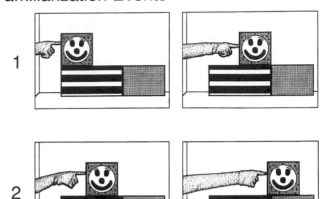

Test Events

Possible Event

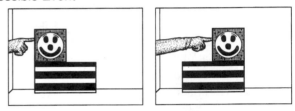

Impossible Event

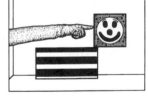

Figure 5.3 Familiarization and test events used in Baillargeon, Needham, and DeVos (1992). From "The development of young infants' intuitions about support," by R. Baillargeon, A. Needham, & J. DeVos, 1992, *Early Development and Parenting, 1,* pp. 69–78.

to introduce the second box and release it prior to the outcome. Infants looked no longer at the suspended than supported box, so it appeared that the act of hand-release and consequent suspension of the object was important in the prior study. Needham and Baillargeon (1993) suggested that there is something special about actually seeing support removed from an object which does not fall that is missing when infants only see an object suspended. As the authors note, there are many opportunities for infants to see objects that are apparently suspended in mid-air—

Possible Event

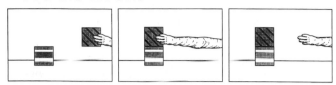

Impossible Event

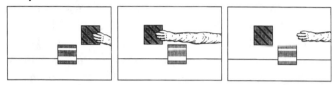

Figure 5.4 Schematic representation of the events shown to the infants in the experimental condition in Experiment 1 of Needham and Baillargeon (1993). From "Intuitions about support in 4.5-month-old infants," by A. Needham & R. Baillargeon, 1993, *Cognition, 47,* pp. 121–148. Copyright © 1993. Reprinted with kind permission of Elsevier Science-NL, Sara Burgerhartstraat 25, 1055 KV Amsterdam, The Netherlands.

model airplanes or figurines that hang from invisible nylon lines, pictures mounted on walls, mobiles, lamps, and so on. So, suspended items alone may not look odd to infants.

However the novelty factor should be considered for the combined *action* and outcome event, that is, object-release-and-consequent-suspension. Baillargeon and her colleagues have favored experiential interpretations of infants' acquisition of knowledge and have eloquently highlighted several opportunities that infants have to learn about their surroundings. For example:

> From birth, infants no doubt experience countless situations whose outcome is consistent with the notion that objects fall when they lose contact with their supports . . . infants may observe that objects typically fall when released (or swept off tables) by their parents and siblings . . . infants may also experience situations involving stable and yet apparently unsupported objects: shades on floorlamps, ceiling fans, lamps suspended in front of walls, hanging plants, or even doorknobs could all seem to be free-floating in space. (Baillargeon, Kotovsky, & Needham, in press, p. 10)

We agree with this analysis and we would go further to say that it is very infrequent that infants see a hand release an object in midair, including their own hand, and fail to see that object fall. In plain terms, this was a novel event for infants. Beliefs, reasoning, expectations, and surprise

notwithstanding, infants could simply have looked longer at an *event* (as opposed to only the outcome) because it was relatively unfamiliar.

Comment

With this foundation we now return to the question that we first asked about infant arithmetic: What is special about occlusion experiments? If violations of physical principles can be interpreted in terms of the relative peculiarity of events and/or outcomes when infants have the opportunity to see the unfolding of events, why can't the same principles be applied to occlusion manipulations? We are not convinced that occlusion experiments lead to different conclusions.

It is important to realize that occlusion experiments typically involve a period of only 2 to 3 seconds, during which the event is occluded or within which something should have happened that did not (as in the screen-rotation experiments). We must agree that these experiments do demonstrate that Piaget was wrong, literally, when he claimed that objects that were out of sight are out of mind for young infants. Whether we want to call lingering visual information that infants have a "representation" will depend on semantic proclivities; as we noted previously, Piaget reserved the term for longer-lasting cognitive episodes in which infants could transform and mentally act on symbolic information.

Now, what could be happening in a 2- to 3-second period? We use the screen-rotation experiment as an illustrative example, but the general idea relates to all brief occlusion procedures. A screen rotates toward a box and occludes it, on a course to impact the box around 2 to 3 seconds later; however, the screen keeps moving, and the infant presumably finds this event peculiar (i.e., looks relatively long). We suggest that it is gratuitous to claim that all perceptual information about the box is immediately lost. We believe that, in Baillargeon's (1991, p. 38) words, "infants keep in their mind's eye an image of the box as it stands behind the screen." That is, as for experiments that we discussed earlier on infant arithmetic, physical information about the box, its size, color, and the like, could persist for a brief period, with some features of the box fading more rapidly than others. By 3 seconds, it is unlikely that all of the perceptual information vanishes and the baby is left to deal with only a nonperceptual representation of the object. (Please see footnote 2 regarding the possibility that perceptual information need not be a fading trace in the tradition of short-term visual storage research.) In fact, evidence suggests that infants use highly concrete perceptual information during occlusion, as indicated by the importance of a continually visible comparison box whose value depended on its pattern similarity and alignment with the occluded box. Occlusion studies may only differ from nonocclusion studies in the relative *strength* of the perceptual information that is available to babies. If so, infants' response to inconsistent events may be no different for occlusion and nonocclusion studies; the inconsistent event looks peculiar because it does not fit with real-world experience.

Evidence for or against this interpretation could easily be obtained by manipulations that affect the integrity of perceptual information. For example, increasing the duration of occlusion or interpolating other perceptual information during occlusion should reduce responding to inconsistent events.

This analysis can be extended to situations in which an object moves behind an occluder in midtrajectory. Infants have plenty of opportunity to see objects move and disappear behind objects and then reappear. If there is lingering information following occlusion that includes both the event trajectory and the object, infants can still deal with degrading perceptual information, for which they have comparable experience. There is no need to suggest that infants *assume* or *reason* or *infer* that the object continues to move; the visual information is there, we suggest, for the 2- to 3-second occlusion period. If the outcome is consistent with infants' fading perceptual information and experience, the outcome will be more familiar than if it is not. There is only one finding that we have difficulty explaining with this analysis, the finding that when a person drops a ball that disappears behind a screen that is then removed, infants do not look longer at the ball suspended in midair than at the ball lying on the floor (Spelke et al., 1992). However, as we noted, the suspended outcome did produce some recovery of looking compared with preceding familiarization trials, just not as much as the ball on the floor in a novel location.

It is an error to assume that cognition necessarily begins when perceptual input ends. Perceptual processes can outlast perceptual input, certainly for several seconds, as demonstrated in adults with behavioral paradigms (Baddeley, 1990; Phillips & Baddeley, 1971).[3]

There is also substantial neurophysiological evidence that the memory for objects and events, the "representation," if you will, is distributed among many of the more than 30 visual areas of the brain and is closely tied to the sensory neurons that the object or event activates when present. For example, when macaque monkeys perform a matching-to-sample task with a delay between presentation of the sample and the match, many of the same neurons fire in the inferotemporal cortex that fired during the actual presence of the stimulus. The activity lasts, on average, approximately 16 to 18 seconds (Fuster & Jervey, 1981; Miyashita & Chang, 1988; for a review of this and related work, see Ungerleider, 1995). The delay effect is not a simple sensory afterdischarge because, among other factors, neurons in the same region may be involved during stimulus presence and not during the delay and vice-versa, and such factors as attention can affect firing during both.

In reviewing this literature, Ungerleider (1995) observed:

> Many studies have found cells whose response to the initial cue is maintained at some level throughout the delay period. Thus, the memory of the cue appears to endure by maintaining the activity of cells that represent the cue. Depending on the type of cue, cells with such properties have been found in the inferior temporal cortex (visual patterns or color cues), the posterior parietal cortex (visuospatial cues), the premotor cortex (cues for particular responses), and the prefrontal cortex (all types of cues). (p. 774)

Current thinking is that the prefrontal cortex plays a role in maintaining the delay activity in these widely distributed visual areas (Ungerleider, 1995). The point for us is that there is substantial evidence to support the idea that the kind of representational activity that investigators invoke in many infant studies, involving delays of only a few seconds, is very closely tied to sensory/perceptual activity when the object or event is present. Thus, the same factors that operate in the presence of stimuli and events—namely, familiarity, novelty, and stimulus salience, could be operative during the short delays that these experiments employ.

Conclusions

We realize that we have been highly critical of this literature. In fact, the studies that we reviewed in this section

---

[3] Cognitive processes can also proceed in the presence of perceptual input. However, given the enormous database that exists on perceptual processes and how they operate, especially data

based on looking paradigms, perceptual explanations have considerable priority when perceptual paradigms such as habituation and looking preference are employed.

have been extraordinarily ingenious in conception, design, and execution. However, we do not think that they support the heavy conceptual mantle with which they have been charged. We are concerned that the findings from these studies have frequently been cited uncritically as demonstrating the complexity of infant cognition in the early months of life, partly because there seems to be something special about infants performing in the absence of an object or event. Both the professional and lay literatures contain examples of citation of this literature as demonstrating that infants are capable of physical reasoning, inference, reflection, and many other cognitive feats, and these concepts carry a great deal of surplus meaning. We do not feel that conclusions about these abilities are warranted at this time and instead suggest the more parsimonious alternative, that straightforward perceptual analyses can accommodate the data.

SOME OBSERVATIONS

We have covered a variety of topics in this chapter beginning with the basic dimensions of object, time, space, and causality and moving on to the application of knowledge in the realms of number, categorization, and physical reasoning. One might wonder whether we have simply assembled an array of independent topics that belong to the rubric of cognitive development or whether these topics cohere in a theoretically meaningful way. The answer is mixed.

Piaget's Shadow

Piaget's gift to developmental psychology was a nice story that wove together all of the feats of early cognition. He approached his topic as a generalist. Infants' acquisition of concepts was general, transcending, for the most part, tasks, materials, and substantive content. The mechanisms by which infants acquired concepts were general, assimilation and accommodation always taking the infant to new horizons. And, the motivation for change was general—an intrinsic search for equilibrium. Importantly for Piaget, the growth of mind was not a platform for dichotomies. Biology and experience were easy partners in sculpting development, and concepts and representational abilities were dynamic and evolving. A nice story can be just a fairy tale, occupying a fond place in our hearts even though we know it to be untrue. Our impression is that many current-day theorists struggle with whether Piaget's story was simply nice because it made it so easy to comprehend the vast

complexity of early cognition or whether, in fact, it captured deep truths.

In any case, we find it much more difficult now to tell a unifying story. The battles being fought in different areas are often orthogonal to one another. In research on the object concept, there is debate over whether instrumental activity is intrinsic either to the acquisition or the execution of object knowledge or whether infants have innate knowledge about objects and/or can learn fully about them only through observation. The argument in the area of causality is over whether the concept emerges whole-spun, based on a maturational signal, or whether the concept emerges through stages, depends on experience, and reflects highly specific understandings that are dependent on particular tasks, materials, and action components. In research on categorization, disputes revolve around whether basic and superordinate categories are learned in order or in parallel, whether concepts are represented as prototypes or in terms of exemplars, the role that functionality plays, and to what extent concepts are perceptual as opposed to conceptual. These are just a few of the battlefields.

While investigators use many of the same methodologies to study infant cognition, the questions they ask, the debates they entertain, and the theoretical concepts to which they connect are quite different. We live in an era of specialization. As others have noted before us (e.g., Kessen, 1984; Parke, et al., 1994), this is a time for highly targeted minitheories, specifically tailored to the phenomena under scrutiny. Perhaps this development was inevitable. After all, we have no unifying theory of adult cognition, no theory that can contain the phenomena of social cognition, decision theory, concept formation, problem solving, memory, logical inference, and the like. Why should we have a theory of infant cognitive everything? In fact, even in the sphere of infancy, unifying theories are often not the mode. Consider infant perception. Very different questions and conceptualizations exist for visual acuity, eye movements, size and shape constancy, and color and pattern recognition. As we dig more deeply into the infant mind, less and less does the notion of undifferentiated mass seem apt, and as that notion dissolves, a generalized conceptualization to account for the growth of all mental activities seems increasingly less tenable.

However, as many of the comments we made earlier demonstrate, we are not ready to abandon Piaget, in toto. When one considers aspects of Piaget's theory on the same plane as minitheories, that is, within particular substantive areas, his notions have considerable currency, especially in his areas of focus, for example, in the object concept. He fares less well in his global generalizations about the role of instrumental activity, as seen both in the work on the object concept and in the research on physical reasoning. However we want to interpret the data, infants know more about the world than Piaget thought, and they learn much about it in the absence of instrumental activity or the coordination of action schemes. Even if we argue that infant behavior in various studies reflects common principles of familiarity and novelty rather than the understanding of general principles and concepts, there is still explaining to do. For complex events to seem familiar, especially when infants have to generalize from laboratory exposures to the real world, requires a degree of early processing that Piaget's theory does not accommodate. The unarguable contribution of the studies we have reviewed is that infants have information about physical interrelations among events that we never dreamed possible even a decade and a half ago. Although we want to make a distinction between the information infants have as opposed to their knowledge, there is no question that these studies have advanced our understanding.

As we noted in the opening of the chapter, there are some themes that do replay through even the disparate topics that currently comprise the field of infant cognition. No matter what the topic in infant cognition, investigators still struggle with the issue of nature versus nurture, representation, and the relation between perception and cognition, themes Harris identified 15 years ago. While Piaget's grand theory may not persevere, we believe that his style of explanation will enjoy a better fate, even in the realm of minitheory. We refer specifically to his deep understanding that conceptual feats are acquired gradually, rather than emerge in a dichotomous and whole-form fashion, and that a truly developmental analysis will tell how each level of understanding builds on previous ones. We value the embryological model.

The Nativist Stance

For some theorists, much of knowledge is innate. Infants are born with a portfolio of core knowledge (Spelke et al., 1994) or modules that can emerge months after birth (Leslie, 1988); elaboration proceeds from this base.

No one claims that infants and adults think alike. However, some nativist positions do hold to the view that substantive knowledge about objects is innate and forms the base for elaboration of further knowledge. Unfortunately, these positions are vague about the principles involved in the acquisition of new knowledge and how that knowledge builds on the presumed core knowledge.

A variant of the nativist approach holds that it is not knowledge, per se, that constitutes the infant's portfolio but, rather, highly constrained innate learning principles. These learning principles bias the acquisition of knowledge so that some things are acquired quite easily, others not; in brief, some things are learned more readily than others. This argument is reminiscent of Greenough, Black, and Wallace's (1987) discussion of experience-expectant phenomena. A similar argument has been made for the acquisition of visual information by newborns (Haith, 1980).

It is important to distinguish between theorists who argue that the skill itself is innate from those who suggest that the ability to *acquire* the skill is innate. Sometimes, there are shades of gray that confuse the distinction, for example, when people assert that language *ability* or numeric *ability* is innate. We see this claim to be a finesse that, to be direct, says no more than that people can learn language or numbers. In short, it is one thing to say that the content is innately given or even the strategies for learning; it is another to talk about abilities. Discussions about "innateness" of the latter amount to a tautology. If people did not inherit the potential to accomplish a skill, how could they achieve it? Discussions about innate abilities rather than content only take form when they include details about strategies or processes that generate the skill in question.

Unfortunately, there is little indication in the infant cognition literature of what these innate learning principles are and how they work. It would seem that the questions, then, concern the principles to which infants are most attuned, how these principles are acquired, and how broadly they apply (that is, only to situations that have been experienced or to all objects and events after they are acquired?). These are very interesting questions, at the crux of why infant thinking is shaped the way it is, and how it changes. We wish we knew more about the answers.

An important problem for the nativist position is that the concepts at issue often do not emerge even in partial form until many months, even into the second half of the first year of life. It is true that the emergence of these concepts, for example, the beginnings of number or category sensitivity, does not depend completely on adult language tuition, as might have been claimed a few decades ago. But it is also true that infants have more occasions for experience than we might suspect over only a few months of life. One of us estimated that infants have made 3 to 6 million eye movements by the age of 3.5 months (Haith, Hazan, &

Goodman, 1988), providing enormous opportunity for them to learn about the relation between their own action and the perceptual result. If, as so many claim, infants learn so much by simply observing, why should we fall back on nativist interpretations to account for cognitive growth? Additionally, discussions often fail to notice what portion of a complete concept does depend on adult guidance. Imagine how little children would know about numbers or taxonomic classes if they had no opportunity for schooling or adult input.

Even if one were to grant that infants come into the world with some information, the main task is to lay out the course of accomplishment and what controls that course. The focus on issues about innateness and obtaining the earliest evidence for a skill distracts us from this difficult task and, as we have written repeatedly, leads to dichotomous characterizations of cognitive growth. We are disappointed that there is a dearth of studies that include multiple age groups and a relative lack of interest in describing the course of development. More studies are needed that ask how concepts develop, with less concern about whether evidence is positive at a particular age.

The Issue of Partial Accomplishments

Nowhere is it more apparent that we need a graded approach to understanding infant cognition than in discussions of the topic of representation. We have pointed this out many times throughout this chapter. Our view, as with the case of several cognitive concepts that we have discussed, is that we have no comfortable way to think about or to model what we call partial accomplishments (Benson & Haith, 1995; Haith, 1990, 1993; but see Munakata et al., in press). The idea is that, without a model or theory of partial achievement, we are driven to think in dichotomous terms. Consider color vision in infants, for which we do not possess a model of partial skill. We ask whether an infant discriminates colors and, if so, (assuming control of a jillion confounding factors), we grant the infant color vision. But, no one really thinks that 3-month-old infants distinguish the shades of color as well as does a normal-vision adult. The problem is that we have no mental model of what some, but incomplete, color vision would be like. Now contrast this state of affairs with visual acuity. Many of us have blurred vision or have seen out of focus images, so we have a mental model of what some, but not perfect, vision is like. We even have a quantitative indicator (Snellen acuity) to reflect imperfection. Accordingly, we would never assume

that a young infant who can see can also see perfectly. Unfortunately, we do not have similar models for such topics as categorization or causality. As a result, we are led once more to dichotomous characterizations.

The problem is acute for the concept of representation. But there is a second problem with how we think about infant concepts that has received less attention. That is, even when a baby genuinely shows some evidence for acquisition of a concept at any level, let's say the concept of two items as differentiated from three, can we say that the infant is secure in that piece of knowledge? Doubtful. It seems more likely that, as with adults, when infants first begin to acquire understanding of, for example, a new basis for categorization, that the knowledge is there one moment and gone the next. Anyone who remembers the concepts acquired in trigonometry knows the feeling; only through repetition and application is the concept secured. Variability in infant performance probably reflects a genuine oscillation in understanding. Thus, our categorical representations of what goes on in the infant head is not only too categorical with respect to general concepts, it is too categorical with respect to the stability of various subconcept achievements during attainment.

We desperately need a graded model of representation. The term is often used indiscriminately to apply to any presumed process that goes on in the absence of an object and that preserves some aspect of its status. Take the idea to an absurd extreme. The eyelids briefly occlude objects during eye blinks. Must representation be involved when the baby blinks its eyes? No one we know makes that argument. If not, where is the temporal breakpoint? We suggest that many studies that occlude the object for no more than a few seconds or deal with consequences that should have occurred in only a few seconds, are addressing very different phenomena than those that involve preservation of the information for minutes, hours or days. This is not to say that the differentiation between presence and absence is meaningless for short periods. Funahashi, Bruce, and Goldman-Rakic (1990) identified areas in the prefrontal cortex that were important for maintaining location information over periods of only 1 second in macaques. Still, the evidence suggests that short-lived information in infant studies is very perceptual in nature, which makes it hard to deny perceptual interpretations of the data. Our claim is not that representational concepts should be avoided or even that this type of representation is unrelated to more advanced forms. Rather, we are arguing for differentiation among the welter of different kinds of representations and how they build on one another, something like a scheme that allows for Representation$_A$ to Representation$_Z$, so that confusion can be avoided. We could apply similar concerns to many other concepts in the area of infant cognition. Without differentiation in our concepts, there is little hope that clarity will ensue.

Where Do We Go from Here?

While we have been critical of many of the interpretations of studies in this field, we must note that research has taken the field a long way in the last 15 years or so. Previously, the manual search task dominated the study of infant cognition. There may be limitations to the newer paradigms but, at the least, they provide the investigator with a richer array of tools and an avenue for studying younger infants. Our hope is that we find a way to enrich these paradigms with other measures and techniques to bridge the gap between looking paradigms and paradigms that engage more adaptively functional behavior, like manual search. On the measures side, it would be helpful to find ways to validate the processes that are often inferred from looking alone, for example, expectations and surprise. One could imagine autonomic measures of surprise and brain measures of expectation that would help to support the claims that infants engage chains of reasoning in these paradigms.

Our understanding could be enriched by indicators other than looking of the meaning that infants take from the events they watch. Are there ways to get at infants' knowledge of the functional consequences of events that would help to validate concepts that theorists use? Obviously, we are skeptical that looking behavior alone can serve as a foundation for theorizing about infant cognition before the age that functional behaviors emerge.

Physiological research has too often been held out as the great hope for psychological constructs, and there have been more promises than products. However, progress in the last 15 years has been stunning, especially with less invasive imaging techniques and with increasingly clever methodologies for EEG research. With the early months of infancy remaining a hotbed of inquiry concerning the base for cognitive development and with the limitations that go with the territory, we must look to advances in measurement of brain activity as an important adjunct. Even now, new findings have shaped our thinking. The information from primates that areas in the prefrontal cortex are important in updating information and in coordinating action has shaped infant research and theorizing (Goldman-Rakic, 1988). Findings that suggest that

short-term memory systems are modular and closely tied to the sensory areas they serve (Ungerleider, 1995), rather than handled by a central processor, lead us to think in different ways about cognitive development. We expect mutual facilitation between neuropsychology and developmental psychology to flower in the next era.

It has become almost a catechism in both the lay and the professional literature to observe that "babies are far smarter than we think." Haith and Campos (1977) warned 20 years ago that the "gee-whiz" trend was going too far and that investigators needed to pay as much attention to infants' limitations as to their competencies. We are not about to risk heresy by saying that "infants may be dumber than many people think," but we do sound the call, once again for a more balanced view.

Elizabeth Spelke made an astute observation about the state of affairs in infant cognition that we must quote because it is consistent with our view of the field:

> There is no consensus among investigators of cognitive development about when knowledge begins, what it consists of, how it manifests itself, what causes it to emerge, how it changes with growth and experience, or what roles it plays in the development of thought and action. (1994, p. 431)

While there is little consensus on many issues, there is consensus that the issues are central to our understanding of the human mind and that they are among the most intriguing of the era. We expect that many of the issues we have reviewed will continue to excite and inspire the next generation of infancy researchers and that this field will endure through at least the next edition of the *Handbook* in the new millennium.

ACKNOWLEDGMENTS

The authors express gratitude to Leslie Cohen, Jeffrey Lockman, and Robert Siegler for their helpful comments on earlier drafts of this chapter and to Gary Haith for helpful discussions about the issues of decaying visual information.

REFERENCES

Acredolo, L. P. (1978). Development of spatial orientation in infancy. *Developmental Psychology, 14,* 224–234.

Acredolo, L. P. (1985). Coordinating perspectives on infant spatial orientation. In R. Cohen (Ed.), *The development of spatial cognition.* Hillsdale, NJ: Erlbaum.

Acredolo, L. P. (1988). Infant mobility and spatial development. In J. Stiles-Davis, M. Kritchevsky, & U. Bellugi (Eds.), *Spatial cognition: Brain bases and development* (pp. 157–166). Hillsdale, NJ: Erlbaum.

Acredolo, L. P. (1989). Coordinating perspectives on infant spatial orientation. In J. Stiles-Davis, V. Bellugi, & M. Kritchevsky (Eds.), *Spatial cognition: Brain bases and development* (pp. 115–140). Hillsdale, NJ: Erlbaum.

Acredolo, L. P., & Evans, D. (1980). Developmental changes in the effects of landmarks on infant spatial behavior. *Developmental Psychology, 16,* 312–318.

Antell, S. E., & Keating, D. P. (1983). Perception of numerical invariance in neonates. *Child Development, 54,* 695–701.

Arehart, D. M. (1995). *Young infants' formation of visual expectations: The role of memory, rule complexity, and rule change.* Doctoral dissertation, University of Denver, Denver, CO.

Arehart, D. M., & Haith, M. M. (1990, April). *Memory for space-time rules in the infant visual expectation paradigm.* Poster presented at the International Conference on Infant Studies, Montreal.

Arehart, D. M., & Haith, M. M. (1992, May). *Infants' use of visual landmarks in forming expectations for complex sequences.* Poster presented at the International Conference of Infant Studies, Miami.

Aslin, R. N. (1987). Motor aspects of visual development in infancy. In P. Salapatek & L. Cohen (Eds.), *Handbook of infant perception: Vol. 1. From sensation to perception* (pp. 43–114). New York: Academic Press.

Aslin, R. N. (1981). Development of smooth pursuit in human infants. In D. F. Fisher, R. A. Monty, & J. W. Senders (Eds.), *Eye movements: Cognition and visual perception.* Hillsdale, NJ: Erlbaum.

Baddeley, A. (1990). *Human memory.* Needham Heights, MA: Allyn & Bacon.

Bai, D., & Bertenthal, B. I. (1992). Locomotor status and the development of spatial search skills. *Child Development, 63,* 215–226.

Baillargeon, R. (1986). Representing the existence and the location of hidden objects: Object permanence in 6- and 8-month-old infants. *Cognition, 23,* 21–41.

Baillargeon, R. (1987). Object permanence in 3.5- and 4.5-month-old infants. *Developmental Psychology, 23,* 655–664.

Baillargeon, R. (1991). Reasoning about the height and location of a hidden object in 4.5- and 6.5-month-old infants. *Cognition, 38,* 13–42.

Baillargeon, R. (1992). *The role of perceptual similarity in infants' qualitative physical reasoning.* Unpublished manuscript.

Baillargeon, R. (1993). The object concept revisited: New directions in the investigation of infants' physical knowledge. In C. E. Granrud (Ed.), *Visual perception and cognition in infancy* (pp. 265–315). Hillsdale, NJ: Erlbaum.

Baillargeon, R. (1994). How do infants learn about the physical world? *Psychological Science, 3,* 133–140.

Baillargeon, R. (1995). A model of physical reasoning in infancy. In C. Rovee-Collier & L. Lipsitt (Eds.), *Advances in infancy research* (Vol. 9). Norwood, NJ: ABLEX.

Baillargeon, R., & DeVos, J. (1991). Object permanence in young infants: Further evidence. *Child Development, 62,* 1227–1246.

Baillargeon, R., & DeVos, J. (1992). *Qualitative and quantitative inferences about hidden objects in infants.* Manuscript submitted for publication.

Baillargeon, R., DeVos, J., & Graber, M. (1989). Location memory in 8-month-old infants in a nonsearch AB task: Further evidence. *Cognitive Development, 4,* 345–367.

Baillargeon, R., & Graber, M. (1987). Where is the rabbit? 5.5-month-old infants' representation of the height of a hidden object. *Cognitive Development, 2,* 375–392.

Baillargeon, R., & Graber, M. (1988). Evidence of location memory in 8-month-old infants. *Cognition, 20,* 191–208.

Baillargeon, R., Kotovsky, L., & Needham, A. (in press). The acquisition of physical knowledge in infancy. In A. J. Premack, D. Premack, & D. Sperber (Eds.), *Causal cognition: A multidisciplinary debate.* Oxford, England: Clarendon Press.

Baillargeon, R., Needham, A., & DeVos, J. (1992). The development of young infants' intuitions about support. *Early Development and Parenting, 1,* 69–78.

Baillargeon, R., Spelke, E. R., & Wasserman, S. (1985). Object permanence in 5-month-old infants. *Cognition, 20,* 191–208.

Ball, W. A. (1973, April). *The perception of causality in the infant.* Paper presented at the meeting of the Society for Research in Child Development, Philadelphia.

Bauer, P. J. (1995). Recalling past events: From infancy to early childhood. *Annals of Child Development, 11,* 25–71.

Bauer, P. J., & Hertsgaard, L. A. (1993). Increasing steps in recall of events: Factors facilitating immediate and long-term memory in 13.5- and 16.5-month-old children. *Child Development, 64,* 1204–1223.

Bauer, P. J., & Mandler, J. M. (1989). One thing follows another: Effects of temporal structure on 1- to 2-year-olds' recall of events. *Developmental Psychology, 25,* 197–206.

Bauer, P. J., & Mandler, J. M. (1990). Remembering what happened next: Very young children's recall or event sequences. In R. Fivush & J. Hudson (Eds.), *What young children remember and why—Emory Symposium in Cognition.* New York: Cambridge University Press.

Bauer, P. J., & Mandler, J. M. (1992). Putting the horse before the cart: The use of temporal order in recall of events by 1-year-old children. *Developmental Psychology, 28,* 441–452.

Behl-Chadha, G. (1994). *Perceptually driven superordinate-like categorical representations in early infancy.* Unpublished doctoral dissertation, Brown University, Providence, RI.

Beilin, H. (1994). Jean Piaget's enduring contribution to developmental psychology. In R. D. Parke, P. A. Ornstein, J. J. Rieser, & C. Zahn-Wexler (Eds.), *A century of developmental psychology.* Washington, DC: American Psychological Association. (Reprinted from *Developmental Psychology, 28,* 191–204)

Benson, J. B. (1990). The development and significance of crawling in infancy. In J. Clark & J. H. Humphrey (Eds.), *Advances in motor development research* (Vol. 2). New York: AMS Press.

Benson, J. B. (1994). The origins of future orientation in the everyday lives of 9- to 36-month-old infants. In M. M. Haith, J. B. Benson, R. J. Roberts, Jr., & B. F. Pennington (Eds.), *The development of future-oriented processes.* Chicago: University of Chicago Press.

Benson, J. B. (in press). The development of planning: It's about time. In S. Friedman & E. Scholnick (Eds.), *Why, how and when do we plan? The developmental psychology of planning.* Hillsdale, NJ: Erlbaum.

Benson, J. B., Cherny, S. S., Haith, M. M., & Fulker, D. W. (1993). Rapid assessment of infant predictors of adult IQ: Midtwin/midparent analyses. *Developmental Psychology, 29,* 434–447.

Benson, J. B., & Haith, M. M. (1995). Future-oriented processes: A foundation for planning behavior in infants and toddlers. In P. Lacasa (Ed.), *Planning, memory, and context* [Special issue]. *Infancia y Aprendizaje, 140,* 69–80.

Benson, J. B., & Uzgiris, I. C. (1985). Effects of self-produced locomotion on infant search activity. *Developmental Psychology, 21,* 923–931.

Bertenthal, B. I., & Campos, J. J. (1990). A systems approach to the organizing effects of self-produced locomotion during infancy. In C. Rovee-Collier & L. P. Lipsitt (Eds.), *Advances in infancy research* (Vol. 6). Norwood, NJ: ABLEX.

Bertenthal, B. I., Campos, J. J., & Kermoian, R. (1994). An epigenetic perspective on the development of self-produced locomotion and the consequences. *Current Directions in Psychological Science, 3,* 140–145.

Bjork, E. L., & Cummings, E. M. (1984). Infant search errors: Stage of concept development or stage of memory development? *Memory and Cognition, 12,* 1–19.

Bogartz, R. S., Shinskey, J. L., & Speaker, C. 1997). Interpreting infant looking. *Developmental Psychology, 33,* 408–422.

Bomba, P. C., & Siqueland, E. R. (1983). The nature and structure of infant form categories. *Journal of Experimental Child Psychology, 35,* 294–328.

Bower, T. G. R. (1982). *Development in infancy.* San Francisco: Freeman.

Bremner, J. G. (1978a). Spatial errors made by infants: In adequate spatial cues or evidence for egocentrism? *British Journal of Psychology, 69,* 77–84.

Bremner, J. G. (1978b). Egocentric versus allocentric coding in 9-month-old infants: Factors influencing the choice of code. *Developmental Psychology, 14,* 346–355.

Bremner, J. G. (1982). Object localization in infancy. In M. Potegal (Ed.), *Spatial abilities: Developmental and physiological foundations.* New York: Academic Press.

Bremner, J. G. (1985). Object tracking and search in infancy: A review of data and a theoretical evaluation. *Developmental Review, 5,* 371–396.

Bremner, J. G. (1989). Development of spatial awareness in infancy. In A. Slater & J. G. Bremner (Eds.), *Infant development.* Hillsdale, NJ: Erlbaum.

Bremner, J. G. (1993a). Spatial representation in infancy and early childhood. In C. Pratt & A. F. Garton (Eds.), *Systems of representation in children.* New York: Wiley.

Bremner, J. G. (1993b). Motor abilities as causal agents in infant cognitive development. In G. J. P. Savelsbergh (Ed.), *The development of coordination in infancy.* Holland: Elsevier.

Bremner, J. G. (1994). *Infancy.* Oxford, England: Blackwell.

Bremner, J. G. (1996). *Infancy.* Cambridge, MA: Blackwell.

Bremner, J. G., & Bryant, P. E. (1977). Place versus response as the basis of spatial errors made by young infants. *Journal of Experimental Child Psychology, 23,* 162–171.

Bremner, J. G., & Knowles, L. S. (1984). Piagetian stage 4 search errors with an object that is directly accessible both visually and manually. *Perception, 13,* 307–314.

Bruner, J. S., Olver, R. R., & Greenfield, P. M. (Eds.). (1966). *Studies in cognitive growth.* New York: Wiley.

Bushnell, E. W., McKenzie, B. E., Lawrence, D. A., & Connell, S. (1995). The spatial coding strategies of 1-year-old infants in a locomotor search task. *Child Development, 66,* 937–958.

Butterworth, G. (1975). Object identity in infancy: The interaction of spatial location codes in determining search errors. *Child Development, 46,* 866–870.

Butterworth, G. (1996, April). *Infant perception from a nonconceptual point of view.* Paper presented at the International Conference on Infant Studies, Providence, RI.

Butterworth, G., & Bryant, P. (1990). *Causes of development.* Hillsdale, NJ: Erlbaum.

Butterworth, G., & Jarrett, N. (1991). What minds have in common is space: Spatial mechanisms serving joint visual attention in infancy. *British Journal of Developmental Psychology, 9,* 55–72.

Campos, J. J., Bertenthal, B. I., & Kermoian, R. (1992). Early experience and emotional development: The emergence of wariness of heights. *Psychological Science, 3,* 61–64.

Canfield, R. L., & Haith, M. M. (1991). Active expectations in 2- and 3-month-old infants: Complex event sequences. *Developmental Psychology, 27,* 198–208.

Canfield, R. L. & Smith, E. G. (1996). Number-based expectations and sequential enumeration by 5-month-old infants. *Developmental Psychology, 32,* 269–279.

Canfield, R. L., Smith, E. G., Brezsnyak, M. P., & Snow, K. L. (in press). Information processing through the first year of life: A longitudinal study using the visual expectation paradigm. *Monographs of the Society for Research in Child Development.*

Carey, S., & Gelman., R. (1991). *The epigenesis of mind,* Hillsdale, NJ: Erlbaum.

Clifton, R., Rochat, P., Litovsky, R. Y., & Perris, E. E. (1991). Object representation guides infants' reaching in the dark. *Journal of Experimental Psychology: Human Perception and Performance, 17,* 323–329.

Cohen, L. B. (1995, March). *How solid is infants' understanding of solidity.* Presented at the meeting of the Society for Research in Child Development, Indianapolis.

Cohen, L. B., Gilbert, K. M., & Brown, P. S. (1996, April). *Infants' understanding of solidity: Replicating a failure to replicate.* Presented at the International Conference on Infant Studies, Providence, RI.

Cohen, L. B., & Oakes, L. M. (1993). How infants perceive a simple causal event. *Developmental Psychology, 29,* 421–433.

Cohen, L. B., & Strauss, M. S. (1979). Concept acquisition in the human infant. *Child Development, 50,* 419–424.

Colombo, J. (1993). *Infant cognition: Predicting later intellectual functioning.* London: Sage.

Cornell, E. (1978). Learning to find things: A reinterpretation of object permanence studies. In L. S. Siegel & C. J. Brainerd (Eds.), *Alternatives to Piaget: Critical essays on the theory.* New York: Academic Press.

Cummings, E. M., & Bjork, E. L. (1983). Search behavior on multi-choice hiding tasks: Evidence for an objective conception of space in infancy. *International Journal for the Study of Behavioral Development, 6,* 71–87.

Day, R. H. (1987). Visual size constancy in infancy. In B. E. McKenzie & R. H. Day (Eds.), *Perceptual development in early infancy: Problems and issues.* Hillsdale, NJ: Erlbaum.

Demany, L., McKenzie, B., & Vurpillot, E. (1977). Rhythm perception in early infancy. *Nature, 266,* 718–719.

Diamond, A. (1985). Development of the ability to use recall to guide action, as indicated by infants' performance on AB. *Child Development, 56,* 868–883.

Diamond, A. (1990). The development and neural bases of memory functions, as indexed by the AB and delayed response tasks, in human infants and infant monkeys. *Annals of the New York Academy of Sciences, 608,* 267–317.

Diamond, A. (1991a). Neuropsychological insights into the meaning of object concept development. In S. Carey & R. Gelman (Eds.), *Epigenesis of mind.* Hillsdale, NJ: Erlbaum.

Diamond, A. (1991b). Frontal lobe involvement in cognitive changes during the first year of life. In K. R. Gibson & A. C. Peterson (Eds.), *Brain maturation and cognitive development: Comparative and cross-cultural perspectives.* New York: Aldine de Gruyter.

Diamond, A., Cruttenden, L., & Neiderman, D. (1994). A, not B with multiple wells: 1. Why are multiple wells sometimes easier than two wells? 2. Memory or memory + inhibition? *Developmental Psychology, 30,* 192–205.

Diamond, A., & Gilbert, J. (1989). Development as progressive inhibitory control of action: Retrieval of a contiguous object. *Cognitive Development, 12,* 223–249.

Diamond, A., & Goldman-Rakic, P. (1989). Comparison of human infants and rhesus monkeys on Piaget's AB task: Evidence for dependence of dorsolateral prefrontal cortex. *Experimental Brain Research, 74,* 24–40.

DiLalla, L. F., Thompson, L. A., Plomin, R., Phillips, K., Fagan, J. F., Haith, M. M., Cyphers, L. H., & Fulker, D. W. (1990). Infant predictors of preschool and adult IQ: A study of infant twins and their parents. *Developmental Psychology, 26,* 759–769.

Dougherty, T. M., & Haith, M. M. (1997). Infant expectations and reaction time as predictors of childhood speed of processing and IQ. *Developmental Psychology, 33,* 146–155.

Douglass, H. R. (1925). The development of number concept in children of preschool and kindergarten ages. *Journal of Experimental Psychology, 8,* 443–470.

Eimas, P. D., & Quinn, P. C. (1994). Studies on the formation of perceptually based basic-level categories in young infants. *Child Development, 65,* 903–917.

Eimas, P. D., Quinn, P. C., & Cowan, P. (1994). Development of exclusivity in perceptually based categories of young infants. Journal of Experimental Child Psychology, 58, *418–431.*

Fagan, J. F. (1976). Infant recognition of invariant features of faces. *Child Development, 47,* 627–638.

Fischer, K. (1980). A theory of cognitive development: The control and construction of hierarchies of skills. *Psychological Review, 87,* 477–531.

Fischer, K. W., & Bidell, T. (1991). Constraining nativist inferences about cognitive capacities. In S. Carey & R. Gelman (Eds.), *The epigenesis of mind: Essays on biology and cognition.* Hillsdale, NJ: Erlbaum.

Flavell, J. H., Miller, P. H., & Miller, S. A. (1993). *Cognitive development* (3rd ed.). Englewood Cliffs, NJ: Prentice-Hall.

Funahashi, S., Bruce, C. J., & Goldman-Rakic, P. S. (1990). Visuospatial coding in primate prefrontal neurons revealed by oculomotor paradigms. *Journal of Neurophysiology, 63,* 814–831.

Fuster, J. M., & Jervey, J. P. (1981). Inferotemporal neurons distinguish and retain behaviorally relevant features of visual stimuli. *Science, 212,* 952–954.

Gibson, E., Owsley, C., & Johnston, J. (1978). Perception of invariance by 5-month-old infants: Differentiation of two types of motion. *Developmental Psychology, 14,* 407–415.

Gibson, J. J. (1979). *The ecological approach to visual perception.* Boston: Houghton Mifflin.

Goldman-Rakic, P. S. (1988). Circuitry of primate prefrontal cortex and regulation of behavior by representational memory. In V. B. Mountcastle, F. Plum, & S. R. Geiger (Eds.), *Handbook of physiology—The nervous system* (pp. 373–417). Bethesda, MD: American Physiological Association.

Golinkoff, R. M., & Halperin, M. S. (1983). The concept of animal: One infant's view. *Infant Behavior and Development, 6,* 229–233.

Gratch, G. (1972). A study of the relative dominance of vision and touch in 6-month-olds. *Child Development, 43,* 615–623.

Gratch, G., Appel, K. J., Evans, W. F., LeCompte, G. K., & Wright, N. A. (1974). Piaget's stage 4 object concept error: Evidence of forgetting or object conception. *Child Development, 45,* 71–77.

Gratch, G., & Landers, W. (1971). Stage 4 of Piaget's theory of infants' object concepts: A longitudinal study. *Child Development, 42,* 359–372.

Greco, G., Hayne, H., & Rovee-Collier, C. (1990). Roles of function, reminding, and variability in categorization by 3-month-old infants. *Journal of Experimental Psychology: Learning, Memory, and Cognition, 16,* 617–633.

Greenough, W. T., Black, J. E., & Wallace, C. S. (1987). Experience and brain development. *Child Development, 58,* 539–559.

Hainline, L., & Abramov, I. (1992). Assessing visual development: Is infant vision good enough. In C. Rovee-Collier & L. P. Lipsitt (Eds.), *Advances in infancy research* (Vol. 7). Norwood, NJ: ABLEX.

Haith, M. M. (1980). *Rules that babies look by: The organization of newborn visual activity.* Potomac, MD: Erlbaum.

Haith, M. M. (1990). Perceptual and sensory processes in early infancy. *Merrill-Palmer Quarterly, 36,* 1–26.

Haith, M. M. (1991). Gratuity, perception-action integration, and future orientation in infant vision. In F. Kessel, M. Bornstein, & A. Sameroff (Eds.), *The past as prologue in developmental psychology: Essays in honor of William Kessen.* Hillsdale, NJ: Erlbaum.

Haith, M. M. (1992, October). *From where does the future come?* Presented at the Science and Public Policy Seminar for the Federation of Behavioral, Psychological and Social Sciences, Rayburn House Office Building, Washington, DC.

Haith, M. M. (1993). Preparing for the 21st century: Some goals and challenges for studies of infant sensory and perceptual development. *Developmental Review, 13,* 354–371.

Haith, M. M. (in press). The development of future thinking as essential for the emergence of skill in planning. In S. Friedman & E. Schlonick (Eds.), *Why, how and when do we plan? The developmental psychology of planning.* Hillsdale, NJ: Erlbaum.

Haith, M. M., Benson, J. B., Roberts, R. J., Jr., & Pennington, B. F. (1994). *The development of future-oriented processes.* Chicago: University of Chicago Press.

Haith, M. M., & Campos, J. (1977). Human infancy. *Annual Review of Psychology, 28,* 251–293.

Haith, M. M., Hazan, C., & Goodman, G. S. (1988). Expectation and anticipation of dynamic visual events by 3.5-month-old babies. *Child Development, 59,* 467–479.

Haith, M. M., & McCarty, M. (1990). Stability of visual expectations at 3.0 months of age. *Developmental Psychology, 26,* 68–74.

Haith, M. M, Wentworth, N., & Canfield, R. L. (1993). The formation of expectations in early infancy. In C. Rovee-Collier & L. P. Lipsitt (Eds.), *Advances in infancy research.* Norwood, NJ: ABLEX.

Harris, P. L. (1973). Perseverative errors in search by young infant. *Journal of Experimental Child Psychology, 44,* 28–33.

Harris, P. L. (1974). Perseverative search at a visibly empty place by young infants. *Journal of Experimental Child Psychology, 18,* 535–542.

Harris, P. L. (1983). Infant cognition. In P. H. Mussen (Series Ed.) & M. M. Haith & J. J. Campos (Vol. Eds.), *Infancy and developmental psychobiology: Vol. 2. Handbook of child psychology* (4th ed., pp. 689–782). New York: Wiley.

Harris, P. L. (1986). Bringing order to the A-not-B error. *Monographs of the Society for Research in Child Development, 51,*(3, Serial No. 214).

Harris, P. L. (1987). The development of search. In P. Salapatek & L. B. Cohen (Eds.), *Handbook of infant perception* (Vol. 2). New York: Academic Press.

Harris, P. L. (1989). Object permanence in infancy. In A. Slater & G. Bremner (Eds.), *Infant development.* Hillsdale, NJ: Erlbaum.

Hayne, H., Rovee-Collier, C., & Perris, E. E. (1987). Categorization and memory retrieval by 3-month-olds. *Child Development, 58,* 750–767.

Hofstadter, M., & Reznick, J. S. (1996). Response modality affects human infant delayed-response performance. *Child Development, 67,* 646–658.

Horobin, K. M., & Acredolo, L. P. (1986). The role attentiveness, mobility history, and separation of hiding sites on stage

4 search behavior. *Journal of Child Experimental Psychology, 41,* 114–127.

Horowitz, F. D. (1995). The challenge facing infant research in the next decade. In G. J. Suci & S. S. Robertson (Eds.), *Future directions in infant development research.* New York: Springer-Verlag.

Inhelder, B., & Piaget, J. (1964). *The early growth of logic in the child.* New York: Norton.

Jacobson, S. W., Jacobson, J. L., O'Neill, J. M., Padgett, R. J., Frankowski, J. J., & Bihun, J. T. (1992). Visual expectation and dimensions of infant information processing. *Child Development, 63,* 711–724.

Jacobson, S. W., Jacobson, J. L., & Sokol, R. J. (1994). Effects of fetal alcohol exposure on infant reaction time. *Alcoholism: Clinical and Experimental Research, 18,* 1125–1132.

Karmel, B. Z., & Maisel, E. B. (1975). A neuronal activity model for infant visual attention. In L. B. Cohen & P. Salapatek (Eds.), *Infant perception: From sensation to cognition. Basic visual processes* (Vol.1, pp. 77–131). New York: Academic Press.

Keating, M. H., McKenzie, B. E., & Day, R. H. (1986). Spatial localization in infancy: Position constancy in a square and circular room with and without a landmark. *Child Development, 57,* 115–124.

Kellman, P. J., Gleitman, H., & Spelke, E. S. (1987). Object and observer motion in the perception of objects by infants. *JEP: Human Perception and Performance, 13,* 586–593.

Kellman, P. J., & Spelke, E. S. (1983). Perception of partly occluded objects. *Cognitive Psychology, 15,* 483–524.

Kellman, P. J., Spelke, E. S., & Short, K. (1986). Infant perception of object unitary from translatory motion in depth and vertical translation. *Child Development, 57,* 72–86.

Kessen, W. (1984). Introduction: The end of the age of development. In R. J. Sternberg (Ed.), *Mechanisms of cognitive development.* Prospect Heights, IL: Waveland Press.

Klahr, D. (1984). Transition processes in quantitative development. In R. Sternberg (Ed.), *Mechanisms of cognitive development.* San Francisco: Freeman.

Landers, W. F. (1971). Effects of differential experience on infants' performance in a Piagetian stage 4 object-concept task. *Child Development, 5,* 48–54.

Lanthier, E. C., Arehart, D., & Haith, M. M. (1993, March). *Infants' performance with a nonsymmetric timing sequence in the visual expectation paradigm.* Presented at the meetings of the Society for Research in Child Development, New Orleans.

Leslie, A. M. (1984). Spatiotemporal continuity and the perception of causality in infants. *Perception, 13,* 287–305.

Leslie, A. M. (1988). The necessity of illusion: Perception and thought in infancy. In L. Weiskrantz (Ed.), *Thought without language.* Oxford, England: Clarendon Press.

Leslie, A. M., & Keeble, S. (1987). Do 6 month-olds perceive causality? *Cognition, 25,* 265–288.

Lewkowicz, D. J. (1989). The role of temporal factors in infant behavior and development. In I. Levin & D. Zakay (Eds.), *Time and human cognition.* Amsterdam, The Netherlands: North-Holland.

Lewkowicz, D. J. (1992). The development of temporally-based intersensory perception in human infants. In F. Macar, V. Pouthas, & W. J. Friedman (Eds.), *Time, action, and cognition.* Dordrecht, The Netherlands: Kluwer.

Lockman, J. J., & Dai, B. (1996, April). *Landmark use by infants in a reaching task.* Poster presented at the International Conference on Infant Studies, Providence, RI.

Ludemann, P. M. (1991). Generalized discrimination of positive facial expressions by 7- and 10-month-old infants. *Child Development, 62,* 55–67.

Madole, K. L., & Cohen, L. B. (1995). The role of object parts in infants' attention to form-function correlations. *Developmental Psychology, 31,* 634–638.

Madole, K. L., Oakes, L. M., & Cohen, L. B. (1993). Developmental changes in infants' attention to function and form-function correlations. *Cognitive Development, 8,* 189–209.

Mandler, J. M. (in press). Development of categorization: Perceptual and conceptual categories. In G. Bremner, A. Slater, & G. Butterworth (Eds.), *Infant development: Recent advances.* Hillsdale, NJ: Erlbaum.

Mandler, J. M., & McDonough, L. (1993). Concept formation in infancy. *Cognitive Development, 8,* 291–318.

Mandler, J. M., & McDonough, L. (in press). Drinking and driving don't mix: Inductive generalization in infancy. *Cognition.*

Matthews, A., Ellis, A. E., & Nelson, C. A. (1996). Development of pre-term and full-term infant ability of AB, recall memory, transparent barrier detour, and means-ends tasks. *Child Development, 67,* 2658–2676.

McCall, R. B., & Carriger, M. S. (1993). A meta-analysis of infant habituation and recognition memory performance as predictors of later IQ. *Child Development, 64,* 57–79.

McGurk, H. (1972). Infant discrimination of orientation. *Journal of Experimental Child Psychology, 14,* 151–164.

McKenzie, B. E. (1992). Spatial representation in infancy. In P. C. L. Heaven (Ed.), *Life span development.* Fort Worth: Harcourt Brace Jovanovich.

McKenzie, B. E., Day, R. H., & Ihsen, E. (1984). Localization of events in space: Young infants are not always egocentric. *British Journal of Developmental Psychology, 2,* 1–9.

McKenzie, B. E., Skouteris, H., Day, R. H., Hartman, B., & Yonas, A. (1993). Effective action by infants to contact objects by reaching and leaning. *Child Development, 64,* 415–429.

Medin, D. L., & Schaffer, M. (1978). Context theory of classification learning. *Psychological Review, 85,* 207–238.

Meltzoff, A. N., & Kuhl, P. K. (1989). Infants' perception of faces and speech sounds: Challenges to developmental theory. In P. R. Zelazo & R. G. Barr (Eds.), *Challenges to developmental paradigms: Implications for theory assessment and treatment.* Hillsdale, NJ: Erlbaum.

Meltzoff, A. N., & Moore, K. M. (1992). Early imitation within a functional framework: The importance of person identity, movement, and development. *Infant Behavior and Development, 15,* 479–505.

Michotte, A. (1963). *The perception of causality.* New York: Basic Books.

Milewski, A. (1979). Visual discrimination and detection of configurational invariance in 3-month-old infants. *Developmental Psychology, 15,* 357–363.

Miller, C. L. (1983). Developmental changes in male/female voice classification by infant. *Infant Behavior and Development, 6,* 313–330.

Mix, K. S., Huttenlocher, J., & Levine, S. C. (1996). Do preschool children recognize auditory-visual numerical correspondences? *Child Development, 67,* 1592–1608.

Mix, K. S., Levine, S. C., & Huttenlocher, J. (1994, May). *Infants' detection of auditory-visual numerical correspondences: Another look.* Paper presented at the meetings of the Midwestern Psychological Association, Chicago.

Miyashita, Y., & Chang, H. S. (1988). Neuronal correlate of pictorial short-term memory in the primate temporal cortex. *Nature, 331,* 68–70.

Moore, D., Benenson, J., Reznick, J. S., Peterson, M., & Kagan, J. (1987). Effect of auditory numerical information on infants' looking behavior: Contradictory evidence. *Developmental Psychology, 23,* 665–670.

Morissette, P., Ricard, M., & Decarie, T. G. (1995). Joint visual attention and pointing in infancy: A longitudinal study of comprehension. *British Journal of Developmental Psychology, 13,* 163–175.

Muller, A. A., & Aslin, R. N. (1978). Visual tracking as an index of the object concept. *Infant Behavior and Development, 1,* 309–319.

Munakata, Y. (in press). Task-dependency in infant behavior: Toward an understanding of the processes underlying cognitive development. In F. Lacerda, C. von Hofsten, & M. Heimann (Eds.), *Emerging cognitive abilities in early infancy.* Hillsdale, NJ: Erlbaum.

Munakata, Y., McClelland, J. L., Johnson, M. J., & Siegler, R. S. (in press). Rethinking infant knowledge: Toward an adaptive process account of successes and failures in object permanence tasks. *Psychological Review.*

Needham, A., & Baillargeon, R. (1993). Intuitions about support in 4.5-month-old infants. *Cognition, 47,* 121–148.

Nelson, K. (1973). Some evidence for the cognitive primacy of categorization and its functional basis. *Merrill-Palmer Quarterly, 19,* 21–39.

Nelson, K. (1974). Concept, word and sentence: Interrelations in acquisition and development. *Psychological Review, 81,* 267–285.

Nelson, K. (1979). Explorations in the development of a functional semantic system. In W. A. Collins (Ed.), *Minnesota Symposia on child psychology: Vol. 12. Children's language and communication* (pp. 47–81). Hillsdale, NJ: Erlbaum.

Oakes, L. M. 1994). The development of infants' use of continuity cues in their perception of causality. *Developmental Psychology, 30,* 869–879.

Oakes, L. M., & Cohen, L. B. (1990). Infant perception of a causal event. *Cognitive Development, 5,* 193–207.

Oakes, L. M., & Cohen, L. B. (1994). Infant causal perception. In C. Rovee-Collier & L. Lipsitt (Eds.), *Advances in infancy research* (Vol. 9). Norwood, NJ: ABLEX.

Oakes, L. M., Madole, K. L., & Cohen, L. B. (1991). Infant's object examining: Habituation and categorization. *Cognitive Development, 6,* 377–392.

Parke, R. D. (1989). Social development in infancy: A 25-year perspective. In H. W. Reese (Ed.), *Advances in child development and behavior* (pp. 1–48). New York: Academic Press.

Parke, R. D., Ornstein, P. A., Rieser, J. J., & Zahn-Waxler, C. (1994). *A century of developmental psychology.* Washington, DC: American Psychological Association.

Phillips, W. A., & Baddeley, A. D. (1971). Reaction time and short-term visual memory. *Psychonomic Science, 22,* 73–74.

Piaget, J. (1951). *Play, dreams, and imitation in childhood.* New York: Norton.

Piaget, J. (1952). *The origins of intelligence in children.* New York: International Universities Press.

Piaget, J. (1954). *The construction of reality in the child.* New York: Basic Books.

Piaget, J. (1969). *The mechanisms of perception.* New York: Basic Books.

Piaget, J. (1983). Piaget's theory. In P. H. Mussen (Series Ed.) & W. Kessen (Vol. Ed.), *Handbook of child psychology: Vol. 1. History, theory, and methods* (4th ed., pp. 103–128). New York: Wiley.

Piaget, J., & Inhelder, B. (1969). *The psychology of the child.* New York: Basic Books.

Pick, H. L. (1988). Perceptual aspects of spatial cognitive development. In J. Stiles-Davis, M. Kritchevsky, & U. Bellugi (Eds.), *Spatial cognition: Brain bases and development* (pp. 145–156). Hillsdale, NJ: Erlbaum.

Posner, M. I., & Keele, S. W. (1968). On the genesis of abstract ideas. *Journal of Experimental Psychology, 77,* 353–363.

Quinn, P. C. (1987). The categorical representation of visual pattern information by young infants. *Cognition, 21,* 145–170.

Quinn, P. C., & Eimas, P. D. (1986). On categorization in early infancy. *Merrill-Palmer Quarterly, 32,* 331–363.

Quinn, P. C., & Eimas, P. D. (in press). Perceptual organization and categorization in young infants. In C. Rovee-Collier & L. P. Lipsitt (Eds.), *Advances in infancy research* (Vol. 11). Norwood, NJ: ABLEX.

Quinn, P. C., Eimas, P. D., & Rosenkrantz, S. L. (1993). Evidence for representations of perceptually similar natural categories by 3-month-old and 4-month-old infants. *Perception, 22,* 463–475.

Reznick, J. S., & Kagan, J. (1983). In L. P. Lipsitt (Ed.), Category detection in infancy. *Advances in Infancy, 2,* 79–111.

Roberts, K., & Horowitz, F. D. (1986). Basic level categorization in 7- and 9-month-old infants. *Journal of Child Language, 13,* 191–208.

Rovee, C. K., & Rovee, D. T. (1969). Conjugate reinforcement of infant exploratory behavior. *Journal of Experimental Child Psychology, 8,* 33–39.

Russell, J. (1996). *Agency: Its role in mental development.* Hove, East Sussex, England: Erlbaum/Taylor & Francis.

Schacter, D. L., Moscovitch, M., Tulving, E., McLachlan, D. R., & Freedman, M. (1986). Mnemonic precedence in amnesic patients: An analogue of the AB error in infants? *Child Development, 57,* 816–823.

Sherman, T. (1985). Categorization skills in infants. *Child Development, 56,* 1561–1573.

Siegler, R. S. (1989). Mechanisms of cognitive development. *Annual Review of Psychology, 40,* 353–379.

Siegler, R. S. (1996). *Emerging minds: The process of change in children's thinking.* New York: Oxford University Press.

Siegler, R. S., & Crowley, K. (1991). The microgenetic method: A direct means for studying cognitive development. *American Psychologist, 46,* 606–620.

Simon, T. J., Hespos, S. J., & Rochat, P. (in press). Do infants understand simple arithmetic? A replication of Wynn (1992). *Cognitive Development.*

Smith, P. H. (1984). Five-month-old infant recall and utilization of temporal organization. *Journal of Experimental Child Psychology, 38,* 400–414.

Sophian, C., & Wellman, H. M. (1983). Selective information use and perseveration in the search behavior of infants and young children. *Journal of Experimental Child Psychology, 35,* 369–390.

Sophian, C., & Yengo, L. (1985). Infants' search for visible objects: Implications for the interpretation of early search errors. *Journal of Experimental Child Psychology, 40,* 260–278.

Spelke, E. S. (1991). Physical knowledge in infancy: Reflections on Piaget's theory. In S. Carey & R. Gelman (Eds.), *The epigenesis of mind.* Hillsdale, NJ: Erlbaum.

Spelke, E. S. (1994). Initial knowledge: Six suggestions. *Cognition, 50,* 431–445.

Spelke, E. S., Breinlinger, K., Jacobson, K., & Phillips, A. (in press). Gestalt relations and object perception in infancy. *Perception.*

Spelke, E. S., Breinlinger, K., Macomber, J., & Jacobson, K. (1992). Origins of knowledge. *Psychological Review, 99,* 605–632.

Spelke, E. S., Katz, G., Purcell, S. E., Ehrlich, S. M., & Breinlinger, K. (1994). Early knowledge of object motion: Continuity and inertia. *Cognition, 51,* 131–176.

Spelke, E. S., Vishton, P., & von Hofsten, C. (1995). Object perception, object-directed action, and physical knowledge in infancy. In M. Gazzaniga (Ed.), *The cognitive neurosciences.* Cambridge, MA: MIT Press.

Starkey, P., & Cooper, R. S. (1980). Perception of numbers by human infants. *Science, 210,* 1033–1035.

Starkey, P., Spelke, E. S., & Gelman, R. (1983). Detection of intermodal numerical correspondences by human infants. *Science, 222,* 179–181.

Starkey, P., Spelke, E. S., & Gelman, R. (1990). Numerical abstraction by human infants. *Cognition, 36,* 97–128.

Strauss, M. S. (1979). Abstraction of prototypical information by adults and 10-month-old infants. *Journal of Experimental Psychology: Human Learning and Memory, 5,* 618–635.

Strauss, M. S., & Curtis, L. E. (1981). Infant perception of numerosity. *Child Development, 52,* 1146–1152.

Strauss, M. S., & Curtis, L. E. (1984). Development of numerical concepts in infancy. In C. Sophian (Ed.), *Origins of cognitive skills.* Hillsdale, NJ: Erlbaum.

Thelen, E., & Smith, L. B. (1994). Real time, developmental time, and knowing: Explaining the A-not-B error. In E. Thelen & L. B. Smith (Eds.), *A dynamic systems approach to the development of cognition and action.* Cambridge, MA: MIT Press.

Tyler, D., & McKenzie, B. E. (1990). Spatial updating and training effects in the first year of human infancy. *Journal of Experimental Child Psychology, 50,* 445–461.

Uller, C., & Huntley-Fenner, G. (1955, March). *On infant numerical representations.* Presented at the meeting of the Society for Research in Child Development, Indianapolis.

Ungerleider, L. F. (1995). Functional brain imaging studies of cortical mechanisms for memory. *Science, 270,* 769–775.

Uzgiris, I. C. (1987). The study of sequential order in cognitive development. In I. C. Uzgiris & J. McV. Hunt (Eds.), *Infant performance and experience.* Urbana: University of Illinois Press.

van Loosbroek, E., & Smitsman, A. D. (1990). Visual perception of numerosity in infancy. *Developmental Psychology, 26,* 916–922.

von Hofsten, C. (1983). Catching skills in infancy. *Journal of Experimental Psychology: Human Perception and Performance, 9,* 75–85.

von Hofsten, C. (1994). Planning and perceiving what is going to happen next. In M. M. Haith, J. B. Benson, R. J. Roberts, Jr., & B. F. Pennington (Eds.), *The development of future-oriented processes* (pp. 63–86). Chicago: University of Chicago Press.

von Hofsten, C., & Lindhagen, K. (1979). Observations on the development of reaching for moving objects. *Journal of Experimental Child Psychology, 28,* 158–173.

von Hofsten, C., & Ronnqvist, L. (1988). Preparation for grasping an object: A developmental study. *Journal of Experimental Psychology: Human Perception and Performance, 14,* 610–621.

Watson, J. S. (1966). The development and generalization of "contingency awareness" in infancy: Some hypotheses. *Merrill-Palmer Quarterly, 18,* 323–329.

Waxman, S. R. (1995). Words as invitations to form categories: Evidence from 12- to 13-month-old infants. *Cognitive Psychology, 29,* 254–302.

Wellman, H. M., Cross, D., & Bartsch, K. (1986). Infant search and object permanence: A meta-analysis of the A-not-B error. *Monographs of the Society for Research in Child Development, 51*(3, Serial No. 214).

Wentworth, N., Benson, J., & Haith, M. M. (1989, April). *The development of reaching for stationary and moving targets in infancy.* Poster presented at the meeting of the Society for Research in Child Development, Kansas City.

Wentworth, N., & Haith, M. M. (1987, April). *Reaction and anticipation in infant's tracking of visual movement.* Paper presented at the meetings of the Society for Research in Child Development, Baltimore, Md.

Wentworth, N., & Haith, M. M. (1992). Event-specific expectations of 2- and 3-month-old infants. *Developmental Psychology, 28,* 842–850.

White, B. L., Castle, P., & Held, R. (1966). Observations on the development of visually directed reaching. *Child Development, 35,* 349–364.

Willatts, P. (1984). The stage-4 infant's solution of problems requiring the use of supports. *Infant Behavior and Development, 7,* 125–134.

Willatts, P. (1990). Development of problem-solving strategies in infancy. In D. F. Bjorklund (Ed.), *Children's strategies: Contemporary views of cognitive development.* Hillsdale, NJ: Erlbaum.

Willatts, P., & Fabricius, W. V. (submitted). *The towels of Hanoi: The origin of forward search planning in infancy.*

Wishart, J., & Bower, T. G. R. (1984). Spatial relations and the object concept: A normative study. In C. Rovee-Collier & L. P. Lipsitt (Eds.), *Advances in infancy research* (Vol. 3). Norwood, NJ: ABLEX.

Wynn, K. (1992). Addition and subtraction by human infants. *Nature, 358,* 749–750.

Wynn, K. (in press). Origins of numerical knowledge. *Mathematical Cognition.*

Yonas, A., Bechtold, A. G., Frankel, D., Gordon, F. R., McRoberts, G., Norcia, A., & Sternfels, S. (1977). Developmental sensitivity to information for impending collision. *Perception and Psychophysics, 21,* 97–104.

Yonas, A., & Granrud, C. E. (1985). Reaching as a measure of infants' spatial perception. In G. Gottlieb & N. Krasnegor (Eds.), *Measurement of audition and vision in the first year of life: A methodological overview.* Norwood, NJ: ABLEX.

Younger, B. A. (1985). The segregation of items into categories by 10-month-old infants. *Child Development, 56,* 1574–1583.

Younger, B. A. (1990a). Infant's detection of correlations among feature categories. *Child Development, 61,* 614–620.

Younger, B. A. (1990b). Infant categorization: Memory for category-level and specific item information. *Journal of Experimental Child Psychology, 50,* 131–155.

Younger, B. A. (1992). Developmental change in infant categorization: The perception of correlations among facial features. *Child Development, 63,* 1526–1535.

Younger, B. A. (1993). Understanding category members as "the same sort of thing": Explicit categorization in 10-month-old infants. *Child Development, 64,* 309–320.

Younger, B. A., & Cohen, L. B. (1983). Infant perception of correlations among attributes. *Child Development, 54,* 858–867.

Younger, B. A., & Cohen, L. B. (1986). Developmental change in infants' perception of correlations among attributes. *Child Development, 57,* 803–815.

Younger, B. A., & Gotlieb, S. (1988). Development of categorization skills: Changes in the nature or structure of infant form categories. *Developmental Psychology, 24,* 611–619.

CHAPTER 6

Representation

JEAN M. MANDLER

In the fifteen years since the last *Handbook,* there has been a sea change in representational theories. Fifteen years ago, the most widely accepted view of the mind was that it represents information in symbolic form and carries out its processing operations by manipulating these symbols. There were a number of competing versions, of course, but symbolic forms of representation were just about the only game in town. They might be couched in the form of propositions having predicate-argument structure, or in the form of production or rule-based systems (Anderson, 1983), but all could be easily described and understood using natural language terms. Even imagery, although conceded to have analogical components, was thought to require a propositional base (Kosslyn, 1980). The hegemony of symbol systems was reinforced by the increasing prominence of computer modelling of the mind and the accompanying conception of both the mind and the computer as physical symbol systems (Newell, 1980), as well as by Chomsky's (1965) work on generative grammars, in which language was described in terms of symbols being manipulated within formal syntactic structures.[1]

In the last fifteen years, however, entirely different forms of representational systems have begun to be used; the best known of these are the subsymbolic systems of parallel distributed processing (PDP), now more commonly called *connectionism.* Although connectionist models are also representational systems, the formats are entirely different from symbolic systems and cannot be easily described or understood in natural language terms. Other nonpropositional forms of representation have appeared on the scene, along with the growth of connectionism. Analogical representation is one of these, as exemplified by the work in cognitive linguistics (e.g., Langacker, 1987). Although originally developed as an alternative to classical linguistic theory, cognitive linguistics has broadened its scope to include psychological issues such as the way we represent concepts and reason (Fauconnier, 1994; Lakoff,

---

Preparation of this chapter was supported in part by NSF grant DBS-9221867.

---

[1] A possible exception to the symbolic mainstream might be semantic network theory (e.g., Quillian, 1968), which anticipated some of the characteristics of current connectionist work in its use of spreading activation among nodes in semantic memory.

1987). This approach relies on analogical forms and spatial models to represent predicates and their arguments, rather than the traditional concatenating of atomic symbols. In this respect, it is the modern version of the imagery side of the propositional-imagery debate that was one of the major theoretical battlegrounds at the time of my last chapter in the Handbook (Mandler, 1983). Finally, a nonsymbolic development in representation, related to connectionism, is dynamic systems theory (Thelen & Smith, 1994). In this approach, representation is moved farther away from its traditionally central role. Indeed, this kind of system de-emphasizes representation to such an extent that it might be called an anti-representational theory. Because of its avoidance of representational issues, I will discuss this approach only briefly.

The diversity of approaches to representation breeds debate as to whether more than one kind of representation is necessary to describe the mind. The past decade in particular has seen heated arguments about procedural representation, associated with implicit processing, and declarative representation, associated with explicit processing. This issue is of particular interest to developmental psychologists due to Piaget's (1952) claim that there is a major transition from sensorimotor representation (which is procedural in character) to conceptual (i.e., declarative) representation between infancy and early childhood. This claim has been increasingly disputed in recent years. Thus, the larger debate about representation is reflected most obviously within developmental psychology as a debate about the foundations of mind and how to characterize the nature of knowledge in infancy. In addition, there is that other perennial troublemaker—nativism versus empiricism, a debate that also concerns representation; in this case, what needs to be built into the organism and how any built-in knowledge or bootstrapping devices should be characterized.

Because many of the most interesting disputes in cognitive development today involve infancy, I have centered this chapter on representational issues during the first two years. This focus requires careful consideration of the distinction between procedural and declarative representation, and the closely associated issue of implicit and explicit processing. Discussion of each specific topic in infancy such as categorization or memory is organized around these distinctions. In each case, I attempt to show whether the relevant information is represented procedurally or declaratively, or whether we cannot yet determine the answer. As we will see, we will have to make the dis-

tinction between the form of representation (procedural or declarative) and the type of processing being carried out (implicit or explicit). These distinctions are not identical, but because of the close association between form of representation and type of processing it is sometimes possible to collapse them and speak about implicit or explicit representation.

The plan of the chapter is as follows: In the first section (Representational Formats), I discuss several types of representation and compare different types of representational theories. We have learned a lot about possible forms of representation in recent years and now have several viable alternatives to choose from when we consider the foundations of mind. This is a confusing area, however, because as new ideas about representation came to the fore in psychology, new terminology was invented left and right. One of the main tasks of the first section of the chapter, then, is to clarify several kinds of representation, the terms that are used to refer to them, and the types of processing that are associated with them. This part of the chapter sets the background; although developmental issues arise, they do not become the main topic until later.

In the next section (Representation in Infancy), I describe the traditional theory of infant representation, namely, Piaget's (1951, 1952) theory of a sensorimotor stage. I then discuss the reasons why his view of the developmental trajectories of sensorimotor (procedural) and conceptual (declarative) representation is unlikely to be correct and consider new alternatives to his theory. It is here that I offer my own point of view on the foundations of mind and how declarative knowledge begins to be created early in infancy. I also suggest that the format of this early conceptual representation is of an analogical kind. My goal is to present the outlines of a theory of representation of knowledge in infancy that will be broad enough to account for the various empirical findings about conceptual activity that have accumulated over the past decade.

In the third section (Types of Information Infants Represent), I discuss the relevant topics in infancy that bear on these issues and that have been subjected to empirical scrutiny, namely, knowledge about objects, causality and agency, perceptual categorization, concept formation, inductive inference, language acquisition, and memory for events. One of the problems in interpreting the currently available data is that by and large, researchers do not discuss the status of the knowledge they are demonstrating. They typically show that infants have some piece of "knowledge," but it is not clear whether the information represented is sensorimotor and procedural in nature, or whether it is conceptual and therefore available for purposes of thought. For each topic, therefore, I attempt to assess the status of the knowledge involved in terms of whether it is procedurally or declaratively represented. The results of this exercise will demonstrate the many gaps in our knowledge in this regard, and how far we are from being able to support any theory of early cognitive development with definitive data.

REPRESENTATIONAL FORMATS

Nonrepresentational Theories

Representation is defined most simply as stored information. (The terms *representation* and *knowledge* can be considered synonymous, but the term *representation* emphasizes the format in which knowledge is stored.) Any organism that takes in information from the world in such a fashion that it influences its later behavior is storing information and so can be said to represent that information.[2] All learning requires storage of information and so requires representation in some form or other. However, theories vary greatly as to the relative emphases given to representation and to processing. For example, dynamic systems theory (Thelen & Smith, 1994) is explicitly antirepresentational. Thelen and Smith claim that representations are too static to account for the dynamic ever-changing character of human processing. Instead they characterize knowledge as assembled in real-time from components "that do not in and of themselves look like or contain the resultant knowledge" (p. 39). In this kind of theory, there is said to be only process, and knowledge is viewed solely "as a pattern of activity over time." Instead of representation of stable patterns of knowledge, there is a history of activity. To date, the activity investigated in this approach is largely neural activity and the self-organizing processes of sensorimotor networks. As the world is experienced, these networks gather together (into reentrant maps) correlated information from different modalities. The approach has much in common with

connectionist unsupervised learning models (discussed later in this chapter), but rejects their emphasis on uncovering stable patterns, concentrating instead on the process of change itself.

Dynamic systems theory has produced interesting theorizing about the development of motor skills. For example, Thelen and Smith (1994) provide a fascinating account of learning to walk. However, problems arise when concept formation, thought, and reasoning (what are sometimes called higher-level or symbolic functions) are to be explained. This point can be illustrated by their account of concept formation. Like many other psychologists, Thelen and Smith do not distinguish between perceptual categorization (which has to do with what something looks like) and concept formation (which has to do with the kind of thing something is), and so take learning to categorize the letter A as a representative model of learning concepts. Their account (based on work by Reeke & Edelman, 1984) emphasizes tracings of a letter's form but also uses feature lists, mapping both of these kinds of representations into a reentrant map. Thus, there is a dynamic component, but a classic type of representation, feature lists, has been slipped in as well. In this version of the theory, we are not told how such feature lists are represented, or how they are contacted by the dynamic processing mechanisms.

Differential success in accounting for different types of functioning is one theme in this chapter. Nonsymbolic approaches to representation (or, in this case, an approach that eschews representation) do best at handling nonsymbolic, sensorimotor information, that is, the kind of information that is implicit and not conceptually represented. It is not obvious, however, how to extend this kind of theory to conceptual processing. Another theme of this chapter is that to form a *concept* requires different representations and processes than to learn a motor skill or to form perceptual categories, such as the letter A. Thelen and Smith (1994) condemn what they call objective formats for representing concepts on the grounds that these formats are too static and rigid to accommodate the highly flexible and complex nature of real-world concepts. They propose a more dynamic theory; unfortunately, the example they use is not of concept formation at all, but of perceptual learning. Thus, they are in the position of rejecting a theory that accounts for one kind of knowledge while proposing a counter theory that accounts for another kind of knowledge.

Related comments can be made about Gibsonian theories. The Gibsons' own work involved perception (J. J. Gibson, 1966) and perceptual development (E. J. Gibson,

---

[2] Needless to say, information from the world is transformed by the input process. Because organisms add information of their own which is unrelated to the sensory properties of the input, the notion of representation makes no commitment to veridicality or the structure of the environment.

1969). Their approach emphasized that there is a great deal of structured information in the environment that our sensory systems either pick up from the start or else learn how to pick up. This approach fosters the view that the richness of the information available in ambient light makes representation of stored information unnecessary or of relatively minor importance. Neither theorist, however, attempted a general theory of the mind or its development that would handle issues of concept formation, reasoning, recalling the past, language acquisition, and so forth. Their views have been primarily influential in visual research, particularly in infancy (e.g., Butterworth, 1994; Spelke, 1988). In general, this kind of theory, like dynamic systems theory, seems most at home in handling responsivity to and learning about implicitly represented sensorimotor information.

Symbol Systems

Symbolic representational systems are well known to developmental psychologists, so my comments touch only on a few aspects of this kind of representation that stand in the greatest contrast to subsymbolic or analogical representational systems. Given that most of us do a lot of our thinking and all of our writing linguistically, we tend to couch our theoretical ideas, at least in a first pass, in propositional form. From there to a formal propositional or logical system is a relatively small step. Therefore, such systems seem congenial to us, even if we are not familiar with the particular notation being used. We can understand thought, problem solving, even recall of the past being couched in something like a natural language. We tend to forget that much of our recall is imaginal rather than linguistic (even though we use language to tell someone else about our recollections). And we often do not consider the difficulties that symbol systems might have with representing perceptual or motor information. As adults, we are so imbued with language that it just seems natural to us that the mind should consist of symbolic representations and their manipulation. There are symbols (roughly, words) for each of the objects we can think about. These may or may not be decomposable into parts (e.g., semantic features), but vis-á-vis thinking or reasoning, they are the basic units that are put together to form complex propositions. In this view, thinking consists of manipulating symbols in sentence-like expressions. Like language in general, this form of representation is productive; one can combine symbols in ever-longer strings and in ever-new ways. Fodor and Pylyshyn (1988) believe

that the major strength of the symbolic paradigm is that it matches language's capacity for systematicity and compositionality. The idea here is that if you can understand an expression such as "John loves the girl" you will be able to understand "The girl loves John." Any expression can be broken down into finite symbols and these same symbols can be recombined in indefinitely many ways, as long as they follow certain rules of syntax. It is this compositionality and systematicity that give symbolic systems their representational power.

In this kind of system, both programs and representations can be written in the same language. In addition, the rules to combine symbols are typically recursive so it is easy to embed statements within each other. Such recursion makes meta-statements easy since one can talk about language with language. It also makes it easy to represent beliefs and other intentional states, as in "Sam believes that John loves the girl." Reasoning is straightforward using symbolic languages; unambiguous rules of inference are easily stated as are premises and conclusions. These are some of the reasons that the higher-level cognitive processes such as logical reasoning, mathematical reasoning, planning, and so forth have tended to be modelled by symbol systems of one type or another. Typically, in such systems it is easy to learn new information, as long as the information is couched in the appropriate language. A fact can be added to the system simply by giving it the relevant sentence. This is a common way for people to learn new information. I ask you the name of the street you live on, you tell me, and (at least in the ideal case) this information is immediately added to my knowledge store. This characteristic of symbolic systems is a great boon to a programmer; it is easy to add new facts to a program just by telling it.

Given all these advantages, why might one need any other kind of representation? First of all, there is the issue of learning. Although it is easy to add new facts via language, there is no obvious way for most such systems to learn information on their own or to generalize their experiences. This may be why the topic of learning and organizing knowledge through experience is rarely considered in most symbolic treatments of representation; treating knowledge as an already acquired system that is then used for purposes of reasoning or planning in new situations is more typical. For developmental psychologists, this is a major failing. How can we take seriously any notion of representation in which the learning done by humans from birth is so difficult to specify? Second, there are other types of information that are difficult to represent in traditional symbolic formats. In particular, learning motor skills and processing perceptual information do not seem to involve mapping symbolic expressions onto each other (Dinsmore, 1992). So one of the major kinds of learning that occurs in infancy, sensorimotor learning, is not very amenable to being described in language-like form. It will not escape the reader's notice that this is the very type of learning that has tended to cause people to become interested in dynamic systems and Gibsonian theories. If one works on motor skills or basic perceptual processes, standard symbolic representation does not seem like a satisfactory notation to describe what it is that people know or how they carry out the relevant processing. Third, symbolic representational systems tend to run into trouble when faced with noise or erroneous data. For example, it is often difficult for symbolic parsers to understand ungrammatical sentences, even though people readily do so. There are ways around such difficulties, but there is something rigid and unbending about many symbolic systems that does not easily characterize the fluid and approximate thought that people often engage in.

Connectionism

Connectionism is an entirely different kind of representational system.[3] At first glance, it might not appear to be representational at all because of its strong emphasis on processing. A connectionist system consists of a large number of interconnected processing units. The connections consist of either excitatory or inhibitory weights. In a typical processing situation, signals enter the system by means of a series of input units; the activation across these input units is propagated through the system according to the strength of the weights on each connection to each unit. The end result is a series of activations across a set of output units. This may happen in a single step (i.e., the net consisting of only input and output units). However, because of limitations on what such nets can accomplish, most networks today have one or more layers of units interposed between input and output. These are called hidden units because one doesn't see their operation directly in the same way that one sees what goes into the net and what comes out.

---

[3] For an introduction to connectionist ideas, see Bechtel and Abrahamsen (1991).

A frequent method of learning in connectionist nets is to have a "teacher" examine each output to see how closely the actual output matches the desired output. A common error-correcting mechanism is back-propagation, in which the degree of error on each output unit is propagated back through the system and used to adjust the weights on each connection so as to allow a more appropriate response the next time. This process is typically slow and learning is gradual; on each trial the output activations come a tiny step closer to the teacher's view. The rate at which the system learns can be manipulated, but there is a trade-off between fast-but-poor learning and slow-but-good learning. In any case, there is no such thing as one-trial learning of the sort that is easily accomplished by symbol systems.

Connectionist systems have sometimes been criticized for requiring feedback from a teacher in order to learn, but this is a misconception, perhaps due to the popularity of back-propagation models. There are several kinds of unsupervised learning algorithms,(e.g., Hinton & Becker, 1990; Kohonen, 1984). They all have the characteristic of being self-organizing systems; they discover for themselves patterns, features, or other correlations of information that exist in the input. This is often accomplished by competitive learning, in which local groups of processing units each try to take responsibility for different parts of the input space; there are inhibitory connections among these units, so that only one unit will "win" the competition for a particular input pattern or part of a pattern. When the same or similar pattern occurs the next time, this unit is more likely to win again. In this way, the system comes to reflect the redundancy structure of the input. Unsupervised learning techniques are particularly successful in perceptual learning, that is, the kind of learning that in general goes on without instruction. (If the input is completely arbitrary, then it must be taught.) For example, in Schyns' (1991) work on perceptual category formation, categories of animals were made up from various distortions around prototypical shapes, thus creating an input space. The learning algorithm that was used (in conjunction with a Kohonen architecture which maps out spatial information; Kohonen, 1984) ordered this space on an output map that reproduced the prototypes, all without benefit of explicit feedback. Names for these categories, which are arbitrary, were taught by means of a supervised learning algorithm.

A sample of some (highly simplified) versions of connectionist networks is shown in Figure 6.1. The first panel shows a simple perceptual pattern learner. A pattern comes into the input layer and is squeezed through a relatively

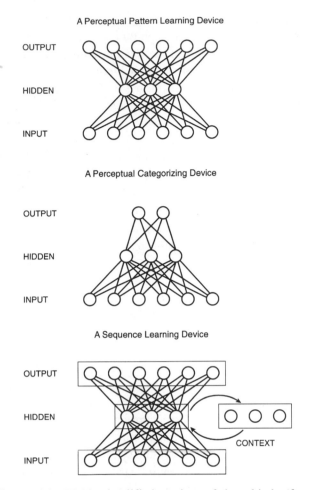

A Perceptual Pattern Learning Device

OUTPUT

HIDDEN

INPUT

A Perceptual Categorizing Device

OUTPUT

HIDDEN

INPUT

A Sequence Learning Device

OUTPUT

HIDDEN

CONTEXT

INPUT

Figure 6.1 Highly simplified versions of three kinds of connectionist systems. Typically there would be many more units in each layer.

small number of hidden units. The goal of the system is to reproduce on the output units whatever pattern is put into the input units. This turns out to be an easy job for this kind of device; it typically uncovers the highest level or most widespread features first (what would be the first principle components in a factor analysis), followed by more detailed specification as learning proceeds. The second panel shows a simple perceptual categorizer. Again, patterns of activation are fed into the input layer, but in this case the output is to say whether the pattern is an exemplar of one of four categories (which can be represented on the two output nodes as four patterns of ones and zeros). The third panel shows a slightly more complicated network, called a recurrent net (Elman, 1990), in which an additional layer of context units feeds back the activation levels of the hidden units on the previous trial

into the hidden units on the current trial (along with the current activation on the input layer). This has the effect of making the network sensitive to what has just gone before and is useful for learning sequentially ordered information, such as sentence strings. All these networks will have many more units than portrayed here, and the layering of hidden units can become quite complex.

Where is representation in these networks? There are no symbols to express the knowledge the networks are learning. Rather, knowledge is stored in patterns of activation distributed across the various units; hence, this kind of processing is called subsymbolic. Processing does not consist of manipulating symbols, but of increasing and decreasing the connection strengths among vast banks of units. Symbols can be found (at best) only in *patterns* of activation across many individual units. Although such patterns have sometimes been said to be composed of microfeatures (and thus in some sense to act like semantic features in a symbol system) this is not an apt comparison for most models. Patterns of activation across hidden units can vary from one set of trials to another, they can vary from one instantiation of a learning situation to another, and often are not interpretable by any existing set of ideas as to what microfeatures should be. Some of the difficulties involved in interpreting hidden units are shown in the following examples.

When the pattern categorizer shown in Figure 6.1b has learned to recognize instances of the four categories, examples of each of these inputs will be associated with a different pattern of activations in the hidden units. In relatively simple situations, it is sometimes possible to analyze these patterns of hidden units. For example, if one of the categories in question is zebras, one of the hidden units might become dedicated to the presence or absence of stripes. But in spite of the application of hierarchical clustering techniques and other similarity analyzers, it is often not easy to figure out how the hidden units are representing the categories in question, especially since each hidden unit typically has to handle many different pieces of information simultaneously. Although we can see that information is represented, we often cannot tell what it is. The hiddenness of hidden units is an obvious disadvantage to the theorist attempting to use these systems to characterize the nature of psychological processing. Equally distressing is the fact that interpretable patterns of activation across hidden units in early stages of learning may disappear when the task is mastered and each hidden unit is accomplishing several different functions. This kind of result is counterintuitive;

although major restructuring of knowledge sometimes happens, in general we do not expect the overall structure of a knowledge base to be lost as more details about a topic are learned.

What is represented on the hidden units is partly a function of what has been input. If stripes are to be used as a distinguishing feature, information about stripes has to be put into the input layer in some form. In some cases, it is possible to enter actual information from the world, or something near to it. For example, in NETtalk, Sejnowski and Rosenberg (1987) trained a network to recognize words and produce their sounds. Letter strings were fed into the net and the output layer was connected to a speech synthesizer so that the net could speak. On early trials, the system's pronunciation was incomprehensible, but the net gradually learned not only to pronounce words on which it had been trained, but it also generalized to new words it had never encountered before. In most cases, however, adequate sensory transducers are not available and we, as theorists, do not know what information a network needs for its job; therefore we must guess what kind of information to present to the input layer. For example, perhaps the subtle shape differences between horses and zebras is a more important clue to their differentiation than stripes. The human eye could probably tell a striped horse from a zebra without too much difficulty. But because of the complexities of the task that the hidden units are accomplishing (and because their activation also changes in unpredictable ways with experience), we cannot necessarily examine the information they are representing and learn from it. We may see that the network is doing the job but have little idea how it is doing it. That, unfortunately, is somewhat like watching people in the real world: just observing their behavior does not tell us what is going on in their heads, which is why psychology (not to mention social life) is so difficult.

So we see that one of the difficulties with this form of nonsymbolic representation is that it is not packaged in an easily interpretable form. Not only are complex packages of activation across large numbers of units difficult to interpret, but their lack of explicitness also makes it difficult for the theorist to know what to do next. The successful simulation of a task, for example, learning the past tense of verbs, does not specify just what the system knows, or, thereby, what sort of knowledge might be implicated in other aspects of language acquisition. Not only does the obscurity of the representation cause difficulty for the theorist, it also makes it difficult to transfer knowledge from one part of the system to another. To the extent that knowledge is embedded in the context of a given task, it is implicit and not available to help solve a related problem. This is very different from symbolic systems, in which knowledge representations and processing on them are distinct. The knowledge can be explicitly stored in memory so that it is available to the system when needed for quite different tasks. Although people as well cannot always find information from one task that is relevant to another, nevertheless we do have large stores of relatively context-free knowledge available for such purposes.

The fact remains that the connectionist approach has had impressive successes in handling a number of difficult tasks that characterize human cognition. Like humans, connectionist nets learn and develop, in some cases without explicit instruction. Like humans, they are skillful in learning to recognize and categorize perceptual information. Like humans, they generalize this information to new patterns. They have the eminently human characteristic of operating reasonably well with partial knowledge or in noise, and can fill in gaps with likely information. In this, they exemplify many of the characteristics of schematic processing that were prominent in the theorizing of the previous decade. Indeed, part of the motivation for developing connectionist systems was to find better ways of handling the flexible, changing characteristics of schemas than the traditional symbolic approaches could manage (Rumelhart, Smolensky, McClelland, & Hinton, 1986).

In terms of an overall evaluation of connectionist forms of representation, their successes and failures tend to be the mirror image of those of the symbolic forms. (a) Whereas symbolic representational systems have trouble learning from experience and organizing and structuring bodies of sequential experiences, connectionist representational systems do this easily and perform well. On the other hand, the rapid learning of new facts merely by being told them is easy for symbol systems and difficult, if not impossible, for connectionist systems. (b) Whereas symbolic representational systems have trouble encoding and generalizing nonpropositional information such as that involved in perceptual learning, connectionist systems do this kind of processing easily and skillfully. On the other hand, connectionist systems have not been widely applied to situations involving formal reasoning, hypothesis-testing, and planning, nor to characterizing propositional attitudes, such as belief states. (c) Both kinds of representational systems have been used successfully to characterize various aspects of language and its processing. However, the successes differ. For example, a number of recent connectionist models

have done well in modelling various aspects of language acquisition (e.g., Plunkett & Marchman, 1991, following earlier work by Rumelhart & McClelland, 1986) and language
comprehension (Bates & MacWhinney, 1989; Elman,
1990). The work that has been done, however, tends to be of
the early language-learning sort that may depend on learning distributions of sounds in one's native tongue. It is difficult to see how connectionist systems will be able to
account for the more analytic aspects of language processing, such as the explicit understanding and use of language
structure (e.g., being able to define nouns and verbs, or even
being able to count them; see Clark & Karmiloff-Smith,
1993). Part of sophisticated (but normal) language use is
metalinguistic ability, to see and comment on relationships
among words, to make judgments of the adequacy of a verbal formulation of some idea, and so forth. These are high-
level tasks that may require reasoning in symbolic form.

These differences between symbolic and connectionist
systems point to a straightforward division between them:
ease or difficulty in representing procedural versus declarative knowledge. By and large the two approaches have handled different problems. In general, the higher-cognitive
functions of reasoning, planning, hypothesis-testing, and
meta-judgments of various sorts (thinking about thinking)
appear to be aided by, and perhaps require, symbolic expressions, or at least some of the characteristics of current
symbolic systems. Sensorimotor functions, on the other
hand, such as motor skill learning, and a variety of perceptual functions such as recognition of objects, perceptual
categorization, and generalization of previously learned
responses to other members of the same category, appear to
be better characterized by nonsymbolic connectionist systems. Another way of describing the distinction is to
say that the explicit, declarative, language-saturated tasks
involved in the higher cognitive processes are different
from the implicit, procedural, prototype-forming, pattern-
learning tasks that connectionism has concentrated on.

There is by now a good deal of evidence for a division of
labor in the types of representations that will be needed to
model the various tasks that humans carry out. It is surprising, therefore, how long it has taken for hybrid systems to
be developed. That may be due to the difficulty in mastering two such different systems (consisting of different
principles, different mathematics, and requiring different
modelling skills), or it may be due to a certain proselytiz-
ing spirit that insists one's current theory can do it all.
Whatever the case, interest in hybrid systems has been slow
to take hold, although they are becoming more frequent
(see Honavar & Uhr, 1994). The gap between the symbolic

and connectionist paradigms does seem to be narrowing. In
some cases, it is the symbolic approach that incorporates
some network aspects (e.g., Pinker & Prince, 1988); in
other cases, it is the acceptance of the necessity for more
structure to be built into a connectionist architecture (e.g.,
Regier, 1992), or to incorporate some rule-based processing.[4] Even within a purely connectionist system, distributed and localist representations can be combined,
resulting in a hybrid mix of subsymbolic and symbolic processing within the same system (Lange, 1992). Recent developments suggest that some sort of hybrid system may be
the ultimate solution to the representation wars. Higher-
level structures can emerge from connectionist principles,
but these structures may need a higher level of description.
Some current work seems to ignore the hard-won insight
that the human mind is a structured processing device. But
if we forget internal structure and look only at input-output
relations, we will have returned to the poverty of radical
behaviorism.

Analogical Representation

Analogical representation as currently studied lies somewhere between the symbolic and connectionist approaches.
It has not been realized in a programming language in
the same way that symbolic systems have been translated
into BASIC or LISP, for example. Nor has it developed into
a new method of programming, such as connectionism.
Nevertheless, it is an attempt to specify the form in which
organisms represent various kinds of knowledge, from
perceptual to linguistic. The approach is not widely
known among psychologists; indeed, there is not even a
commonly agreed upon name for this school of thought that
attempts to describe cognitive activity in terms of analog
representations.

Some years ago, Ronald Langacker began work on what
has come to be known as cognitive linguistics. This work
(e.g., Langacker, 1987) is a formal linguistic theory that
eschews the standard notations used in linguistic theories,
such as that of Chomsky (1965). In their place, schematic
spatial notations, sometimes called image-schemas, are
used to represent both semantic and syntactical notions
(see also Talmy, 1988). These schemas consist of landmarks and paths through space. Hence, the grammatical

---

[4] There is one well-known hybrid system of long standing, which
makes use of both ordered symbol strings and network characteristics, namely, Anderson's (1983) ACT* system.

rules do not look like the familiar re-write rules of traditional grammars. Image-schemas are also used to represent semantics in place of the more familiar language-based symbolic representations (Johnson, 1987; Lakoff, 1987). According to these authors, image-schemas are spatial representations abstracted from perceptual processing and bodily kinesthesis. They have a dynamic character, representing movement and, in some accounts, forces acting in space. Thus, notions such as containment, part-whole, up-down, links between interacting objects, and source-path-goal relations in events have all been analyzed in terms of image-schema representations. For example, in the source-path-goal image-schema, an object is represented as going from a starting point along a path to a destination. This spatial schema is thought to underlie our understanding of what happens when one has a goal and moves toward an end point. (The use of these spatial notions in all languages is ubiquitous, as when we talk about having a long *way* to *go* before achieving a goal, or *stumbling over* an obstacle *along the way;* Lakoff, 1987). Similarly, our understanding of containment is expressed as an enclosing boundary separating an internal from an external space. Each of these image-schemas represents a primitive meaning. They are primitive, not in the sense of being unitary and indivisible symbols, but in the sense that they are the most basic meanings on which language is grounded. (To give an informal characterization of what is meant by a primitive notion, consider how you might represent the notion of self-motion if you were not allowed to speak. You might do something like put your hand at rest and then move it, thus using a simple kind of path as a representational medium. The claim is that the meaning of self-motion resides in the characteristics of such a path.) Once analogical representations of this sort are admitted as a respectable representational form, other uses of spatial forms become evident. For example, Fauconnier (1994, 1996) has developed spatial models of understanding presuppositions, counterfactual reasoning, and analogical learning of new domains.

The characteristic approach of image-schema theories is that the underlying structure of many kinds of thinking and understanding is not propositional in nature, but consists instead of manipulating spatial models. These nonlinguistic models represent the meanings onto which language is mapped. They stand in sharp contrast to the classic symbolic forms, which are associated with the idea that thought is basically linguistic in nature (Fodor, 1975). According to Fodor, the reason symbolic models are successful in describing mental representation is that they are literal reflections of the language of thought. We are born with this mental language, which is the basis on which we acquire the particular natural language of our community. The contrast between propositional and analogical models, however, does not have to do with the extent to which we think in language, but rather has to do with the nature of the underlying form of the representations we use for any kind of thinking, language-based or not. The contrast also differs from that found in the older debates between proponents of propositional and analogical forms of representation (Mandler, 1983). In that debate, the analogical view discussed imagery as the alternative representational form (e.g., Bruner, 1966; Paivio, 1971). In the current view, spatial representations are *not* images. Images have a pictorial, perceptual character that image-schemas do not. For example, an image of a container must specify a certain shape. An image-schema of containment, on the other hand, specifies only the abstract spatial relationship of inside and outside. Furthermore, images are conscious constructions based on prior meanings, whereas image-schemas represent the meanings themselves and are not available to conscious introspection (any more than other representational formats such as propositions or productions would be).

It would be possible to take image-schema representations as analog versions of symbols, and combine them according to explicit rules, thus forming a compositional system similar to other propositional forms. Indeed, people working with image-schema representations have stressed their productive and recursive character (e.g., Barsalou & Prinz, in press; Lakoff, 1987). However, there appears to be a natural affinity between image-schemas (and other analogical forms of representation) and connectionist learning systems (e.g., Regier, 1992). If you want spatial representations to be formed from perceptual input, a connectionist learning device seems a plausible route. In the particular task that Regier has been working on, the goal is to model the way that the perception of spatial relations can be mapped into any of the world's natural languages. Regier has found it necessary to build more structure into his connectionist model than is typical, but this is one of the hybrid models that I suggested earlier may be the road to the future. As another example, Barsalou (e.g., 1993) is attempting to construct a large-scale analogical representational system using what he calls perceptual symbols, that can be used in a connectionist framework.

Analogical representations are also useful for those of us interested in cognitive development in infancy. I have suggested that one of the routes threading the way between early perception and concept formation to the later learning of language is to start infants off with the capacity to turn perceptual information into simplified spatial representations (Mandler, 1992). These appear to have sufficient power to represent the kinds of global concepts that are formed in the first year of life and to enable the simple kinds of analogical and inferential reasoning that take place during this period (Mandler & McDonough, 1996a). At the same time, this form of representation provides an adequate foundation for understanding relational syntactic constructions (Mandler, 1994). In this view, there need be no propositional representation until language is learned; before that time, infants can use their ability to simplify perceptual input, including objects participating in events, to form analog sketches of what they perceive. These sketches (image-schemas) provide the first meanings that the mind forms.

To illustrate, consider very young infants observing the world around them. Given the speed with which events occur and the load that must be placed on a processing system that has not yet developed top-down expectations to guide it, they may miss most of the details of many events they see. For example, when they see an object move, they may not notice much more than that something was at rest and then began to move. Of course, they see many objects moving in many different ways, but each can be re-described in less detailed form as following a path through space. In some cases, they will notice the object begin to move and also come to rest; these aspects of an event can be represented in image-schematic form as well. Because image-schemas are analog, they have parts that can themselves be focused upon. On different occasions, the infants might focus on the path itself, its beginning or ending, and each of these analyses can lead to an image-schema in its own right. Focus on the beginnings of paths leads to differentiating objects that start motion alone versus those that do not move without being contacted by another object; I have suggested that these analyses result in image-schemas of *self-motion* and *caused motion* (Mandler, 1992). Other analyses take note of relations among objects that move contingently with respect to each other, leading to a variety of image-schemas of linked paths (Mandler, 1992). The general point here is that the most fundamental ways in which objects interact can be derived by extracting a few abstract commonalities of their motion; the image-schemas that result express the most basic meanings of *cause, self-motion, contingent motion, animate* and *inanimate motion,* and so forth. Not only are these notions basic to forming concepts such as animal, they also are basic to understanding the grammatical structuring of language itself. These

points are discussed further in the sections on *New Theories of Infant Representation* and *Prelinguistic Meanings.*

Thus, in this view, the initial conceptual representations consist of transformations of perceptual information into analogical forms, rather than the activation of a built-in propositional language of thought (Fodor, 1975). This claim that early concepts are transformations of perceptual information is partly a claim about where meaning comes from. One problem with traditional symbolic systems is what has been called the symbol grounding problem (Harnad, 1990). How do symbols in a physical symbol system get their meaning? Most simply, a symbol could be chosen arbitrarily to refer to some object in the external world. But meaning involves sense as well as reference; furthermore, it includes functional notions and abstract ideas (such as goals) that cannot be pointed to. Equally importantly, if symbols are arbitrarily assigned their meanings, they are not meaningful in themselves. They are merely pointers to concepts that are the bearers of meaning, with the origin of meaning itself left undecided. One approach to the grounding problem is to have symbols intrinsically carry meaning, as is the case in the various analog systems that have been proposed. Image-schemas by their very structure express meaningful relations.

To conclude this discussion of various representational systems, it should be noted that the viability of any one of them cannot be decided by data alone. There is no way to prove by observation that a particular form of representation is being used for any particular task. Instead, the criteria by which they will be judged are those used to decide the usefulness of any theory, namely, fruitfulness and consistency. One would like to add the criterion of completeness; however, it may be that none of these forms of representation can carry the weight of all the different kinds of processing that humans do. This is the topic of the next section.

Multiple Representational Systems: Declarative and Procedural Knowledge

The distinction between declarative and procedural knowledge is a controversial one, but it is of great importance for understanding psychological functioning. It is perhaps especially important for understanding infancy, because on one reading, it is the same as Piaget's distinction between conceptual and sensorimotor representation. Broader issues than infancy are involved, however—I have already indicated that the distinction is implicated in the dispute over symbolic and subsymbolic representational systems, because tasks involving declarative knowledge seem better handled by symbolic systems and tasks involving procedural knowledge better handled by connectionist systems. The distinction between the two kinds of knowledge appears persistently in psychology, although unfortunately in many guises. For some psychologists, the difference refers to different kinds of representation. For others, it refers to different kinds of processing. (These positions may be ultimately compatible, since different representations are apt to require different processes.) To compound the confusion, the distinction has been given many different names. A few of the most frequently used terms are shown below, listed as contrasting pairs. Although often considered to be roughly synonymous, each contrast emphasizes a different aspect. After discussing each of these dichotomies, I suggest how they dovetail with each other; in particular, how the representational and processing positions can be reconciled.

Declarative versus Procedural

Accessible versus Inaccessible

Conscious versus Nonconscious

Conceptual versus Sensorimotor

Symbolic versus Subsymbolic

Explicit versus Implicit

The terms that head the list, *declarative* and *procedural,* were borrowed from computer science, but the distinction they reflect is a much older one in the psychological literature (see Schacter, 1987, for an historical review). It is usually discussed in terms of the difference between information that can be brought to awareness and information that remains inaccessible, though it demonstrably influences behavior. Historically, memory was typically treated as conscious recall, but periodically, writers from the clinical literature (such as Freud) emphasized that information can be represented in memory in an inaccessible form. In modern times, much of the work on this kind of memory has come from the study of amnesia. One of the major aspects of this syndrome is that amnesic patients have difficulty learning or remembering new factual information, although they can learn and remember new motor and perceptual skills (Squire, 1987). The distinction between factual memory and perceptual-motor skills has traditionally been called the distinction between knowing "that" and knowing "how." We know that Christmas is celebrated on December 25 or that California borders the Pacific ocean. This is conceptual knowledge that we can think and talk about. On the other hand, we know how to ride a bike or play the piano. We can't conceptualize very well what we know in the procedural cases, but we know how to do it. This is true for perceptual recognition as much as for motor skills.

The heart of this distinction is expressed in the next two sets of terms in the list, namely, whether information can be brought to conscious awareness. Only declarative knowledge is accessible to conscious awareness. Procedural knowledge remains inaccessible (nonconscious). We can only observe the products of our procedures, not the procedures themselves. This may seem an obvious point. Everyone agrees that we have no access to the programs that control our muscles when we throw a ball. They also agree we have no access to our psychological procedures, such as retrieval or language production. On the other hand, some people believe they do have access to other motor procedures such as driving a car, typing, or tying shoelaces, as well as to perceptual procedures, such as recognition. This belief is mistaken. People can watch themselves performing certain acts and make up *theories* about how they do these things. In addition, in some instances, compiling the procedure in the first place makes use of conscious awareness and declarative knowledge, for example, in the early stages of learning to drive or type (Anderson, 1982). But using declarative knowledge to control the acquisition of procedural knowledge does not mean that the procedural knowledge itself is accessible. In most cases, we are never aware of the details of the compilation or what is happening that brings about an increase in smoothness and speed of performance. For example, most of us are unaware that as we type the first letter of a word, the fingers that will type the later letters are already beginning to raise, nor is this kind of anticipatory action what we intended to do when we learned to type in the first place.

Similarly, some people claim that they know the procedure they follow when tying their shoes. They may say, "You make a loop with the right lace, then take the left lace and wrap it around the loop, and then . . ." This is about as far as they usually get. Somehow a miracle happens and the knot is tied. Faced with the incompleteness of their description, people may say, "Well, I haven't really observed the procedure, but I could if I wanted to." This is already interesting. Why, in thousands of trials, has one not observed and learned in a declarative fashion how a knot is tied? Apparently, we can get along well without such observation, at least once the procedure is learned. When we do conceptualize a procedure, we construct a theory from observing the outcome of various steps along the way, what have been called "way stations in consciousness" (G. Mandler, 1992). Because one is not in fact observing the procedure itself, the theory that is constructed is often inaccurate (Piaget, 1976). Thus, when people say they know the procedure for tying shoes, what they mean is that they know how to do it and can offer a description of sorts, perhaps by providing labels for various parts as they watch themselves carrying it out. (This discrepancy can also work the other way, of course; people may have learned elaborate descriptions of how to put spin on a tennis ball but have no motor procedures adequate to accomplish it in action.)

Similar discrepancies exist with respect to perceptual procedures. The memory system includes huge amounts of perceptual knowledge about what things look like, most of which is not accessible to conscious awareness because it is stored in procedural form. The inaccessibility of this kind of knowledge can be illustrated by face recognition. Instead of asking someone to describe tying a knot, ask them to describe the face of their closest friend. Most people are unable to say on which side of the head the hair is parted, which side of the mouth is higher than the other (or even that the two sides are not the same), how far apart the eyes are, whether the earlobes are attached at the cheek or drop down, and so forth. We are not aware of this information, yet if it changes, we may notice the person looks different without being able to say how. In some cases, the particular bit of information has been consciously analyzed (i.e., a declarative description created). Artists, for example, are trained to do this kind of analytic work. But there are aspects of faces in general that no one knows how to describe. Fagan and Singer (1979) showed that 6-month-olds can categorize faces as male or female. But this accomplishment which we have all managed since near birth is indescribable (and without artistic training, undrawable). People make up stories about the delicacy of the female face or the strong jaw of the male face, but the actual parameters are still unknown. Some speculate that the information we use is complex proportional differences relating to the cheek bones, but I believe my point has been made. The information we have used since early infancy is not accessible to awareness.

To say that sensorimotor information is not accessible does not mean that you have no awareness of the sensations (qualia) involved in perceptual and motor learning. You see the shoe and laces and feel them in your hand; you see and may even feel the cheekbones of a face. This formulation should not be taken as indicating a zombielike lack of awareness. Rather, it means that you have not *conceptualized* the sensorimotor information and so cannot think about it. You see that a tree is green, you experience greenness, but that is not the same as thinking "This tree is green" or "Trees are green." This brings us to the next set of dichotomies in our list: *conceptual* versus *sensorimotor*. This is Piaget's version of the distinction, and it is crucial for understanding development. Piaget claimed that babies only have sensorimotor representation (Piaget, 1951, 1952). They are learning many perceptual and motor skills during the sensorimotor period, but in his theory, have not yet begun to conceptualize the information they are processing. According to Piaget, that awaits the onset of symbolic representation near the end of this period, around $1\frac{1}{2}$ to 2 years of age. Of course, he did not mean that infants are not aware of the objects in their surrounding; he meant they can't conceptualize them and so cannot call them to mind when they are absent. Notice as well that most infant procedures are not learned in the way that complex motor skills are learned in later childhood and adulthood. It takes conceptual (declarative) guidance to learn how to tie one's shoes or drive a car (even though that only means that concepts are guiding the compilation, not that one is aware of the components being compiled—these are motor movements of unknown specification). In infancy, many motor skills such as sucking or learning to reach out and grasp objects are acquired without even the step of conceptual guidance.

Factual knowledge is conceptual in nature. When we know that faces are oval, we have learned either through analyzing perceptual information or through being told; it does not come from just staring at faces. The analysis (through simplification and redescription) puts the information into conceptual form. Verbal information comes prepackaged in conceptual form. These are the kinds of knowledge that are declarative; they can be thought about and used for purposes of recall, planning, and reasoning. Sensorimotor knowledge, on the other hand, is procedural knowledge. It cannot be accessed directly; it can only be run. It can be thought about only by using the conceptual system to make up theories about its workings.

The fifth set of terms in our list is *symbolic* and *subsymbolic* knowledge. Conceptual knowledge is often referred to as symbolic knowledge. The reason for this particular terminological overlap is the equation that has often been made between symbols and words: Traditionally, symbolic representation has been treated as languagelike. The term subsymbolic, on the other hand, is used in two rather different ways. It is sometimes used to refer to procedural knowledge (knowing how), but more recently it has come to be used for the form of representation found in connectionist models (Smolensky, 1988), regardless of what is being modeled.

The final dichotomy on the list is *explicit* versus *implicit*. This set of terms has become popular in the verbal memory literature, and is favored by people who prefer to talk about a distinction in kinds of processing rather than kinds of representation (e.g., G. Mandler, 1985). One reason the distinction between explicit and implicit knowledge has become a fiercely disputed topic (e.g., Shanks & St. John, 1994) is that many current battles are taking place on the common turf of verbal processing. This is not a dispute over how to differentiate verbal or conceptual representation from motor and perceptual skills. Rather, it is how to describe different ways of processing within verbal tasks themselves. In this arena, the distinction involves the presence or absence of attention and elaboration: Verbal material that is consciously attended to and semantically analyzed, is called explicit, whereas verbal material that is unattended or at any rate, not consciously elaborated (Dorfman & Mandler, 1994; Schacter, 1992) is called implicit. Many of the disputes over the distinction stem from this verbal memory literature, in which it is sometimes difficult to know the extent to which attentive processing has taken place. The problem is that declarative knowledge, even though conceptual in nature, can on occasion be processed implicitly; it is registered but unattended or unelaborated. That is, it is not processed in terms of its semantic content, or else is processed so shallowly that it does not become integrated into the existing conceptual system. Such a situation occurs in priming experiments; subjects comprehend the information they are encoding and they show priming effects, but because of shallow processing, they have trouble with explicit tests such as recall (e.g., Graf & Mandler, 1984). The implicit priming effects stem from the procedural information being used to perceive the visual (or auditory) structure of the information in question, such as the phonological or visual shapes of words (G. Mandler, 1985; Schacter, 1992).

Thus, the procedural-declarative distinction is not identical to the implicit-explicit distinction. The procedural-declarative distinction has to do with fundamentally different kinds of information that are represented in different ways. This is a *distinction in representational format.* The implicit-explicit distinction, on the other hand, has to do with whether information can be made accessible. This

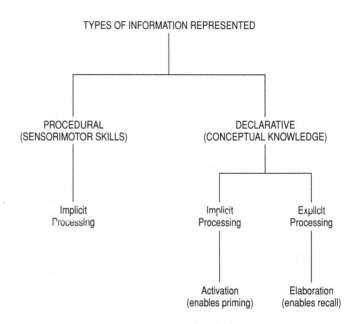

Figure 6.2 The two main classes of information the mind represents and the kinds of processes that range over them.

is a *processing distinction.* In the case of procedural knowledge, information is never accessible; we cannot process this kind of information in such a way as to bring it to awareness. In the case of declarative knowledge, the information is stored in a conceptual format and has the potential to be brought to awareness. Whether that happens on a given occasion depends on the particular kind of processing that is carried out. For example, verbal information can be either explicit or implicit depending on attention and elaboration during encoding. This family of distinctions is shown in Figure 6.2, which regroups the simple list of dichotomies I have been discussing into different types of representation and different types of processes. It can be seen that implicit processing is associated not only with procedural knowledge, but also in some circumstances with declarative knowledge. This is one of the reasons, I believe, for the confusion and proliferation of terms that have appeared in this literature.[5]

We are now in a position to summarize this family of distinctions in relation to the representational systems discussed in earlier sections. Procedural knowledge, both

---

[5] Other terms that have been proposed for similar distinctions are Shiffrin and Schneider's (1977) automatic and controlled processes, Hayes and Broadbent's (1988) selective and unselective learning, and Curran and Keele's (1993) attentional and nonattentional learning.

perceptual and motor, is inaccessible to conscious awareness and is difficult to describe in language. It is relatively slow to learn, and learning is accomplished by associative strengthening, typically over a number of trials, as in operant conditioning or perceptual schema formation. Procedural knowledge tends to be context-bound, making it difficult to get at separate parts of the information or to transfer them from one situation to another. It is sensitive to frequency, that is, how often something occurs. It does not appear to be represented in rule-like form, and is difficult to describe linguistically. For these reasons, it does not seem well suited to most symbolic forms of representation. On the other hand, these same characteristics suggest that a subsymbolic representation is an appropriate format and indeed, procedural knowledge is easy for connectionist systems to learn.

Declarative (conceptual) knowledge, in contrast, is accessible to conscious awareness and is either describable in language or (with a little training in perceptual analysis) by drawing. It requires attention to be encoded into this format; this means that it is selective (e.g., Hayes & Broadbent, 1988; Nickerson & Adams, 1979). It is potentially learnable in a single trial (in small quantities, of course) simply by being told. It seems to have a more static character than procedural knowledge, often consisting of sets of facts, but these can be reorganized and amplified through conscious thought. In some cases, the relevant knowledge can be considered knowledge of rules. It is at least potentially available for many different problem-solving and reasoning situations. It is easy to model using a variety of symbolic representations, but insofar as reasoning about new situations is involved, it is more difficult to model using connectionist architectures, or at any rate has been avoided by most connectionist modelers to date.

The human mind represents several very different kinds of information. Perceptual patterns and motor skills have a different character from symbolic reasoning. We should not be surprised if humans both learn and represent such different kinds of information in different ways. I now turn to the development of these different representational forms in infancy. Here, the distinction between procedural and declarative knowledge is crucial, primarily due to the debate as to whether the knowledge that babies have is sensorimotor or conceptual in nature. Many of the current disputes in cognitive development have this issue as their unexpressed base. When a capacity such as the object concept is stated to be present, it is not always clear whether that is considered to be a procedural or declarative

achievement. If it is procedural knowledge, then it can be made to fit traditional Piagetian theory of infants as purely sensorimotor creatures. If it is declarative knowledge, however, then Piaget's theory needs major revamping—a surefire prescription for developmental dispute.

REPRESENTATION IN INFANCY

Because Piaget's theory of representation in infancy dominated the field for so many years, it is still the standard against which new theories are evaluated. I begin this section, therefore, with a brief recap of his theory and then describe some of the criticisms—both empirical and theoretical—that have been made against it. Following this, I present some of the new theories of infant representation that challenge Piaget's view. In the last part of this section, I discuss the new debate about nativism versus empiricism that is one of the legacies of the decline in Piagetian influence.

Piaget's Theory of Representation in Infancy

Piaget was definitely not a nativist. He posited almost no inborn structures and only a single all-purpose learning mechanism. He claimed that infants are not born with any built-in cognitive structures, only sensory capacities and a small number of modifiable reflexes. In terms of inherited modes of processing, he described two domain-general principles of interacting with the environment, namely, the organization of incoming information and adaptation to it. Adaptation in turn takes place through the twin processes of assimilation and accommodation.[6] Thus, all cognitive structures (schemas) are built up through experience. In this view, essentially everything has to be learned, not just conceptual knowledge about the world, but even intersensory and sensorimotor coordination. In addition, all must be learned without any built-in structures to provide a head start, such as a face recognition device (Johnson & Morton, 1991), a causal motion detector (Leslie, 1988), or a language acquisition device (Chomsky, 1965). As a result, in

---

[6] There were some other inherited characteristics that Piaget (1952) used to account for learning, although these have not always been recognized as such. For example, the tendencies to actively seek information and to repeat or practice behavior patterns are both essential to his constructivist stance.

this theory, learning does not occur by fast mapping, but instead consists of the gradual construction of schemas, which means that change takes place only slowly.

This view of learning sets the stage for a protracted sensorimotor period. The first bit of protracted learning Piaget posited was that required for intersensory coordination. This aspect of his theory has since been shown to be incorrect. Not only are there bootstrapping devices in place from birth to speed this learning, such as the tendency to turn the eyes toward the direction of a sound (Mendelsohn & Haith, 1976), there is also evidence either for more built-in structure or more rapid learning than Piaget allowed. Thus, Meltzoff and Borton (1979) and Gibson and Walker (1984) found visual-tactual coordination at 1 month and Spelke (e.g., 1979) showed visual-auditory coordination at 4 months. Some of this intersensory coordination is quite detailed. For example, Kuhl and Meltzoff (1988) found that when 5-month-olds are presented with two films, each showing only a speaker's face, they choose the film that matches a simultaneously presented vowel sound, even when the synchrony between both films and the soundtrack is identical. Streri and Spelke (1988) showed that merely holding rings that are rigidly or loosely connected (without being able to see them) enables 4-month-olds to differentiate between visual displays representing the two situations.

The significance of this modern research is not that it disproves Piaget's theory about intersensory coordination. No one would expect his theory to be correct on the details of issues not yet subjected to experimental scrutiny at the time he wrote. Furthermore, the new results can fit easily into his theoretical framework; they merely indicate that one aspect of sensorimotor development occurs at a faster rate than was originally supposed. Instead, the significance of this work for Piaget's theory lies in the implications that derive from it. First, if infants do not have to devote so much of their learning resources to intersensory coordination, they can devote them to other kinds of learning instead. Second and more important, from a very early age there is more coherence and stability in the infant's world than Piaget suspected. One of the linchpins of Piaget's theory of infant development was the prolonged period required to achieve a stable perceptual world filled with permanent and predictable objects. Such a world is a sine qua non for conceptual development. As long as the environment presents itself as a "blooming, buzzing confusion" (James, 1890), or a succession of unrelated pictures, one could hardly expect infants to begin to form concepts about objects. If, on the other hand, infants perceive a stable world of objects and can predict their behavior from early in development, then the possibility arises that concepts about objects might develop early as well.

The second bit of protracted learning, and this Piaget (1952) documented in fine detail, was the 6-month period in which infants learn how to manipulate objects. Here, the data are not greatly in dispute, although there is evidence of more built-in structure that can be used to bootstrap the learning process than Piaget knew (von Hofsten, 1982). Nevertheless, learning to manipulate objects is slow and gradual. What has been disputed instead is the significance of this learning for cognitive development. Piaget assumed that knowledge about object properties comes from interacting with them. More controversially, his tests of what babies know about objects all involved reaching for them: in the early stages, reaching for objects in sight, in later stages, reaching for objects after they have been hidden (Piaget, 1954). There are not very many ways to test infants' knowledge, so the use of reaching tests is understandable, but it may have produced a major misunderstanding about what infants know. Baillargeon (1993), Diamond (1990), and Mandler (1988), have all noted that tests requiring infants to demonstrate their knowledge about objects by means of their immature motor system are likely to underestimate that knowledge. Nevertheless, such tests indicated to Piaget that even at the end of the first year infants could not imagine the fate of objects that move out of sight, so he assumed that they had not yet developed imagery or any other kind of conceptual system capable of representing them.

Given his view of protracted sensorimotor learning, Piaget was admirably consistent in his conception of representation in infancy. First with no intersensory coordination to provide a stable perceptual world, and then only slowly being able to build a concept of object, infants in the early months would not be in an advantageous position to acquire a declarative knowledge base. The result was Piaget's famous conclusion that the first year and a half of life consists solely of sensorimotor representation without a conceptual system. As I described in the previous Handbook (Mandler, 1983, somewhat condensed from the original):

> According to Piaget, the sensorimotor child before Stage 6 does not have a capacity for representation in the true sense, but only sensorimotor intelligence. Knowledge about the world consists only of perceptions and actions; objects are only understood through the child's own actions and perceptual

schemas. It is a most unProustian life, not thought, only lived. Sensorimotor schemas enable a child to walk a straight line but not to think about a line in its absence, to recognize his or her mother but not to think about her when she is gone. It is a world very difficult for us to conceive, accustomed as we are to spend much of our time ruminating about the past and anticipating the future. Nevertheless, this is the state that Piaget posits for the child before 1½ . . . What is missing, according to Piaget, is both a system of concepts and a mobile, flexible symbol system capable of pointing to those concepts. (pp. 424–425).

Thus, Piaget was a dual representational psychologist, but of an unusual sort: Instead of assuming that infants have both procedural (sensorimotor) and declarative (conceptual) representation from the beginning, he assumed that they start out with only one kind. They begin as strictly sensorimotor creatures, and a protracted period of learning is required before sensorimotor representation metamorphoses into a conceptual system.[7] It is also easy to see from this description why there is an affinity between connectionist learning systems and sensorimotor development. To the extent that infant development can be characterized as procedural knowledge, slow to learn, inaccessible (unrecallable), non-symbolic, then its acquisition should be amenable to connectionist modelling. The next question, however, is the extent to which Piaget's characterization of the infant as a purely procedural sensorimotor system has been challenged by recent data and theory. Is it still reasonable to assume that babies have no conceptual representation?

Criticisms of Piaget's Theory of the Sensorimotor Period

Two kinds of criticism of Piaget's view of infancy have arisen in the past decade. One is empirical; a number of techniques for exploring cognitive functioning in the laboratory have been developed and these sometimes suggest that infants know a great deal more about objects than Piaget's theory allowed. The other is theoretical; it is not easy to understand exactly how conceptual representation is created in his theory.

---

[7] Piaget restricted his use of the term *representation* to the declarative conceptual kind and did not call the procedural sensorimotor schemas representational. But that is merely a question of terminology; he was making the same distinction between the two kinds of knowledge as described in the last section.

Concerning the empirical evidence, it should be made clear at the outset that a number of the new findings that might be thought to challenge Piaget are actually compatible with the notion of infancy as a purely sensorimotor stage. Early intersensory coordination and the development of perceptual schemas that allow the recognition of familiar objects and events are sensorimotor accomplishments just as much as learning to manipulate objects. They all fall under the rubric of procedural, sensorimotor representation. Therefore, any accomplishment that can be explained in these terms poses little challenge to Piaget's theory. Some piece of learning might proceed faster than he posited or require some more innate structuring to start the learning process, but in general, these are the types of functioning that a sensorimotor theory describes well.

Here is a sampling of other abilities that have been documented in the past decade that can be incorporated into a purely sensorimotor theory of infant development. *Object perception:* By at least 2 to 3 months of age, infants parse the world into coherent, unitary, and bounded three-dimensional objects (Spelke, 1988). *Sequence learning and development of perceptual expectations:* In a few trials, 3- to 5-month-olds learn to anticipate the next event in a series of events, especially if the sequences form well-structured patterns (Haith, Hazan, & Goodman, 1988; Smith, 1984). Similarly, infants of 2½ months expect an object that is hit by another object to move (Baillargeon, 1995). *Perceptual categorization:* 3-month-olds form perceptual prototypes of geometric shapes and show standard typicality effects, such as treating the prototype as familiar even when they have not seen the prototype itself before (Bomba & Siqueland, 1983). Three-month-olds can also learn in a few trials to categorize pictures of animals, discriminating horses from zebras and dogs from cats (Eimas & Quinn, 1994; Quinn, Eimas, & Rosenkrantz, 1993). *Conditioning:* 2-month-olds learn an operant kicking response to stimuli that move contingently to the kicking (Rovee-Collier, 1989; Watson, 1972). The kicking response shows patterns of generalization, extinction, and reinstatement that are typically found in operant conditioning (e.g., Campbell, 1984). These accomplishments are all classic examples of implicit, sensorimotor learning. Conceptual representation is not necessary to describe them.

Empirical Objections

More serious in their implications for Piaget's theory are data indicating that infants develop the "object concept" in the first few months of life (Baillargeon, 1993; Spelke, Breinlinger, Macomber, & Jacobson, 1992). According to

Piaget's theory, it takes some months before infants consider objects to be 3-dimensional, solid, unitary things that are independent of themselves, and even longer to understand that objects continue to exist when out of sight. Indeed, it was the failure first to search for hidden objects, then the failure to find them, that suggested to Piaget that infants could not represent absent objects, and therefore had not yet developed a conceptual system that would enable them to do so (Piaget, 1954). However, Piaget's hiding tests were complex and call upon a number of different processes (see *Representation and Memory for Events*). There might be simpler tests that would reveal greater understanding of objects and their properties than the object-searching tasks suggest.

One of the best known techniques for studying perception in infancy is the habituation/dishabituation test (or its variant, the familiarization/preferential-looking test).[8] Baillargeon and Spelke were among the earliest to adapt this technique so that it could be used to study representation of various abstract properties of objects in addition to the kind of perceptual representation for which it had originally been devised (Baillargeon, Spelke, & Wasserman, 1985). Their work suggested that infants know a great deal more about objects than their motor behavior indicates. Whereas the previous tests of the object concept all required infants to interact with objects (find them, uncover them, pick them up, etc.), the habituation/dishabituation tests required infants to do nothing more than look at perceptual displays set before them. So not only were the object concept tests uncoupled from reliance on the still-immature motor system, they could also be conducted at a much earlier age, before infants are capable of manipulating objects at all. For the first time, a technique was available that enabled psychologists to estimate something about infants' representations of objects in the first few months of life.

This advance in technique was an important development for the field, but not surprisingly, it engendered controversy about how to interpret the data that accrued. The habituation/dishabituation technique relies upon infants' preference for novelty. The method repeatedly presents a training event until infants habituate to it, then gives them

a preference test between this event (or a closely related one) and a new event; infants will look longer at the event that seems more novel to them. The idea behind the new use of the method was to replace *perceptual* novelty with *conceptual* novelty; the latter was to be created by using impossible test events (i.e., events that could not happen in the real world) and pitting them against possible test events. For example, Baillargeon (1986) habituated 6- to 8-month-olds to a car running down an inclined track, going behind a screen, and coming out the other side. During test trials, the car was shown at the top of the track and the screen was raised to reveal a box placed either on the track (to create an impossible trial) or on one side of the track (to create a possible trial). Then the screen was lowered, the car was released as before, went behind the screen, and came out the other side. Although the sight of the car moving behind the screen and coming out the other side was the same for both kinds of test trials, the infants looked longer at the trials on which the hidden box blocked the track. This result suggested that the infants represented the box and its location even though it could not be seen behind the screen, and that they also understood that one solid object cannot move through another. Some of these representations of unseen objects are quite detailed. For example, in Baillargeon (1991), infants were sensitive not only to the fact that a box had been placed behind a screen but also roughly how far back it was placed and how high it was.

What is the status of this kind of knowledge? Is it procedural knowledge provided by the perceptual system, and thus compatible with a sensorimotor theory, or is it conceptual knowledge that implies infants have already acquired a declarative representational system? Although some of Baillargeon's and Spelke's results may be explained on the basis of looking longer at perceptually novel displays (see Bogartz, Shinskey, & Speaker, 1997), others, such as the car and track experiment just described, do seem to require the representation of absent objects. This was Piaget's sine qua non for deciding that conceptual representation was present, and so this kind of result is a serious challenge to his view of a purely sensorimotor stage. On the other hand, might it be possible for a sensorimotor system to maintain a representation of something unseen for a short space of time, without having conceptualized it? The answer to this question is not known, but must depend on the length of the delay. Sensorimotor tracking of objects behind barriers apparently requires fairly rapid trajectories, and is disrupted in infants if the object is hidden for as little as 2 seconds (Mullen & Aslin, 1978). Yet as McDonough has shown, 7-month-olds can remember the location of a hidden object

---

[8] The habituation/dishabituation technique requires the infant to reduce its amount of looking at the training stimuli to a specified low level before the test stimuli are presented. The familiarization technique is the same except that a specified number of training trials is presented, regardless of the amount of looking.

for 90 seconds (McDonough, 1997a). Moreover, tracking objects is a relatively simple perceptual function. It is more difficult to imagine a purely procedural device in which a perceptual holding function is built in that maintains a representation of an absent object but does not confuse what was seen with what is currently being seen. The most difficult aspect for such a device would presumably be to maintain details such as the height of an object and its specific location. Nevertheless, no one has seriously tackled the question of whether the perceptual system by itself, in the absence of any conceptual thought or construal of meaning, can maintain the kinds of detailed information about absent objects that Baillargeon has shown that young infants do. The customary view, of course, is that conceptual representation (an object concept) is required to do this kind of work (Piaget, 1952; see also Leslie, 1988).

Although the habituation/dishabituation data by themselves may not provide a definitive answer to the question of conceptual representation in infancy, they are supplemented by several other types of evidence. First, work on the early acquisition of signs by deaf children shows that infants begin to acquire and use communicatively ASL signs sometime between 6 and 8 months of age (Folven & Bonvillian, 1991; Meier & Newport, 1990). These gestures may have been learned originally as parts of sensorimotor routines (see Mandler, 1988), but they appear to have been extracted from the routines and then are used for referring purposes.[9] The ability to refer, of course, is one of the characteristic aspects of declarative representation. Second, as just mentioned, there is new evidence for the ability to represent absent objects or events over longer time spans than used in the habituation/dishabituation studies. At 7 months, infants are able to recall where an object has been hidden for delays of 90 seconds, which is also much longer than those used in the Piagetian object hiding tests (McDonough, 1997a). McDonough's version of Piaget's task (see *Representation and Memory for Events*) is similar to Piaget's stage III object-hiding tests, although less demanding in that the infant only has to reach in the correct direction rather than remove the object from under a cover.

---

[9] There is no indication that language in general is acquired earlier by children learning sign language than by children learning an oral language. Here we are concerned with evidence that can be used to document the onset of the conceptual function. Presumably because of earlier control over the manual system than over the vocal cords, it is easier to use sign language to express meanings.

Third, using Piaget's criterion of deferred imitation as a measure of representational ability, Meltzoff (1988a) showed that 9-month-olds can reproduce unique events seen 24 hours earlier. Indeed, deferred imitation is the best technique available to measure recall in nonverbal organisms, and provides clearcut evidence of the ability to conceptualize absent objects and events. This issue is also discussed further in *Representation and Memory for Events*.

Finally, recent experiments indicate that by 7 months, babies are beginning to form concepts of kinds of things, such as animals and vehicles (Mandler & McDonough, 1993). These concepts are closer to the usual meaning of the term concept than is the "object concept." It has not always been clear exactly what kinds of information are to be included under that rubric. But by several criteria, the concepts of animals and vehicles being formed in the middle of the first year are the sort of representations to which we usually apply the term. They are representations of kinds of things and in this sense, are different from the perceptual categories that are found in 3-month-olds. For example, they control inductive inference, which is one of the main functions of conceptual representations (Mandler & McDonough, 1996a). These data are discussed in the section on *Perceptual Categories and Concept Formation*. Bear in mind that research on this topic has only just begun; there may be more concepts of many different types and they may appear at an earlier age. Methods of studying conceptual knowledge in infants below the age of 6 months are still primitive. However, these examples, coming as they do from a range of tasks and covering a number of kinds of conceptual processing, are sufficient to call into question the notion that there is an extensive period of exclusively sensorimotor representation. If there is such a stage, present data suggest that it can last for only a few months at most.

Theoretical Objections

Piaget's theory can also be criticized for its lack of clarity about how the transformation of sensorimotor into conceptual representation takes place (Mandler, 1988, 1992). The theory states that this transformation occurs at the end of the sensorimotor period, somewhere around age 1½. Piaget actually offered two somewhat different accounts of this transition. On the one hand, he offered an associative account (Piaget, 1952): During the first year, as perceptual schemas of daily events are constructed, they come to have an anticipatory character. This is a classic view in which stimuli are assumed to acquire meaning by being associated with following events. For example, Piaget talked about conditioned signals in early infancy, in which a sight leads to the behavior associated with the next event to come, as in the case of the infant salivating at the sight of the breast. Later, he talked about prevision, in which the infant between 8 and 18 months can use one sight to predict that another sight will follow. The infant does not yet have imagery, according to Piaget, but is learning to make use of chained associations to skip ahead to the next item in the chain in a manner somewhat freer than the younger infant can manage.

But when it came to the crunch of proclaiming that the symbolic function is finally operating, Piaget switched from an associative account to one of similarity (Piaget, 1951, 1952). Imitation became the main vehicle of symbolization; by imitating the actions of others, infants gradually make a speeded-up interior copy (image) that resembles the original and so can be used to stand for or refer to it. Thus, Piaget used both of the two major views in Western thought of symbol formation (see Werner & Kaplan, 1963).[10] In this version of his theory, images are the first form of conceptual representation, but this capacity is not created until extensive practice at imitation has taken place. Piaget did not discuss exactly how imitation creates imagery, although he implied that the source lies in the analytic process infants engage in when trying to imitate complex behavior. However it happens, in this theory, imagery allows infants to re-present objects and events to themselves, and so provides the foundations for the beginning of thought. Note, however, that the claim of a purely sensorimotor form of representation during the first year and a half of life depends on the assumption that there is no imagery during this time. If younger infants can form images, then there is nothing in principle to prevent them from engaging in conceptual thought. In fact, there is no evidence that imagery is such a late-developing process. In addition, the theory leaves unsettled how images come to have more than perceptual content. How is it that forming an image of an object conceptualizes it and gives it meaning? This issue is taken up in the next section.

New Theories of Infant Representation

I have proposed that, instead of development consisting of an initial period of purely procedural representation followed by its transformation into declarative conceptual representation, conceptual representation begins early and develops in parallel with the sensorimotor system. In my view, neither system is derivative from the other (Mandler, 1988, 1992), except insofar as one must perceive stable perceptual displays in order to analyze them (and we still do not know whether a stable perceptual world exists at birth). In general, however, each kind of representation works off the same source of information, namely, perceptual displays (visual, auditory, and kinesthetic). I have also proposed that, in addition to the usual perceptual processing that humans engage in, they are also natively equipped with a mechanism of perceptual analysis that analyzes perceptual displays in a more selective way. The products of this mechanism are meanings, which in turn form the basis for conscious thought. Unless meanings are represented, one cannot think about things one has seen or heard.

Perceptual analysis uses attentive processing to analyze what is being perceived into simplified and more abstract representations, for example, the paths that objects take as they participate in the variety of spatial relations that we call events. Because the analysis is of perceptual data, an easy way to simplify would be by means of image-schema representations, as described in the earlier section on *Analogical Representation*. Consider again the example mentioned there of a young baby who has not yet developed expectations about the world, whose foveal acuity is still poor (Banks & Salapatek, 1983), but whose attention is attracted to moving objects (Arterberry, Craton, & Yonas, 1993; Kellman, 1993). What might she notice about events like the following? She sees an object nearby, she cries, the object begins to move, approaches, looms, and she is picked up. Leaving aside details such as whether she has already begun to form a perceptual schema of the "face" of the object (Johnson & Morton, 1991) she might not be able to analyze much more than that an object began to move independently of the rest of the surround, moved on a somewhat irregular path, did so contingently on her cries, and ended up by interacting with her. Even this simple description contains several problematic aspects, but I use it to illustrate the principle that perceptual analysis picks out selected aspects of a highly complex perceptual event and puts them into a simpler and more abstract form. Even if the baby only analyzes the trajectory of an object, the way the trajectory begins and ends, and the contingency between the trajectory and its own behavior, she will have gone a long way toward conceptualizing an object as animate. There is ample evidence that from an early age infants do differentiate animate from inanimate objects (e.g., Legerstee, 1992). My analysis describes a mechanism by which such differentiations can be conceptualized.

This formulation is related to that offered by Karmiloff-Smith (1992), who has proposed that humans have the capacity to redescribe established procedural information. This capacity, which she calls representational redescription, may be involved in a transition from a sensorimotor to a conceptual stage of thought, but it is more general than that. Karmiloff-Smith does not endorse a stage theory of development; rather, she claims that procedural information is continually redescribed as it becomes systematized. Initially, in learning any new domain, information is encoded procedurally; in this form, it is implicit and encapsulated. It may stay in this format for lengthy periods of time, but as experience continues with the domain, redescription begins to take place, leading to new representations that are stored independently of the procedures themselves. Since these are potentially available to the rest of the cognitive system, Karmiloff-Smith calls them explicit, but stresses that they are not yet accessible to consciousness, since further redescription is required before the information can be brought to awareness or expressed linguistically. Thus, Karmiloff-Smith equates procedural knowledge with implicit knowledge, as do I, but divides explicit knowledge into several levels, the first of which, in the terminology used in this chapter, would still be implicit since it is not yet accessible to conscious awareness. In her view, still further redescription is required for that purpose. This first "explicit" level may be roughly equivalent to a level of meanings such as image-schemas. These form the underlying structure of conceptual knowledge but are not themselves accessible to awareness. It should be noted, however, that in my view, image-schemas come from analyzing perceptual displays, not from the spontaneous redescription of previously learned perceptual procedures.

Many of the examples Karmiloff-Smith (1992) has studied involve systematic aspects of highly familiar information. Indeed, one of her claims is that extensive periods of behavioral mastery typically precede representational redescription. For instance, she has shown that French children do not become aware that the word "one" ("un") stands for both a determiner and a number until several years after they have used the single form for both

meanings without error. Similarly, children's drawing routines do not show the flexibility that allows them to be altered upon demand until several years of drawing experience have passed (Karmiloff-Smith, 1993). In this view, then, redescriptions take place on already procedurally encoded information; information is first encoded in implicit, inaccessible form, and only later is redescribed into explicit forms. Representational redescription does not take place through analysis of incoming data, but instead results from system-internal dynamics that make connections not there before.

Thus, Karmiloff-Smith's theory differs from mine in several crucial respects. I claim that all explicit knowledge is accessible, even though it may be processed implicitly under some circumstances (see Figure 6.2). I also claim that information is encoded directly into the declarative system, rather than arriving there via redescriptions of established procedural knowledge. That is, the redescription of incoming perceptual information into image-schemas takes place on-line and can take place even on new, unfamiliar sights. This issue is important for understanding concept formation in infancy. I do not believe that concepts are formed by redescribing well-established procedural information. There do not seem to be long periods of behavioral mastery in infancy before concepts about objects and events begin to be formed. If anything, Piaget's work showed us that many kinds of behavioral mastery are absent during this period. Rather than being derived from the redescription of systematized procedural knowledge, I claim that concepts are developed independently and in parallel with the sensorimotor system. They are derived in the first instance from a special kind of analysis of perceptual information, an analysis that allows them to be stored in an explicit, accessible format.

The result of the ability to conceptualize is that the post-Piagetian baby is no longer a purely sensorimotor creature who can act, but not think. The new baby seems more congenial than the old one, because it is the kind of baby we adults can understand. As I discuss in the following pages, it is a baby who has formed concepts of animate and inanimate things. It interprets other people as agents. It understands events as sequences in which agents act on objects, or in which objects cause changes in other objects. It can recall objects and events and can think about them. Finally, it is beginning to understand the world in such a way that language, which describes these kinds of understandings, can be learned. All these accomplishments are not infrequently used to describe what the 1½- to 2-year-old infant knows. They may also be what Piaget had in mind as the final accomplishments of the sensorimotor period, although he did not use this vocabulary. My point here, however, is not only that these accomplishments occur considerably earlier, but also that sensorimotor schemas are not adequate to represent them. Concepts are certainly required to think and to recall the past, but probably also even to understand sequences in terms of agents acting on objects. Piaget himself understood that at least some of these kinds of accomplishments require conceptual thought; he just didn't have the data that would have told him thought begins so early in life.

Piaget assumed that the first concepts (in his view, transformations of sensorimotor schemas into a symbolic form) constitute the basis on which language develops, but he did not specify their representational format. Indeed, until recently there has been no theory of how the first concepts are represented, perhaps because it has been easier to confine the study of early concepts to the words that newly verbal children use. But concepts and words are not the same thing, and to assess concepts only through the linguistic system, especially a system that is in the process of being formed, will surely distort our picture of what the earliest concepts are like. Concept formation is discussed in more detail in the next section *(Types of Information Infants Represent)*. Here I discuss how preverbal concepts might be represented in image-schema form. I described earlier how perceptual analysis abstracts spatial information from perceptual displays, and represents it in terms of image-schemas (Mandler, 1992). These are the same image-schemas that have been proposed by cognitive linguists as the meanings that are used to construct concepts and ultimately words. I have proposed in turn that the mechanism by which this kind of representation is formed is perceptual analysis. This mechanism can begin to operate early in life (perhaps as early as birth), and in any case must be in operation by around 7 months because concepts of animals are beginning to be formed by that age (Mandler & McDonough, 1993). I will illustrate how image-schemas can represent the core meanings involved in the notion of an animal as a particular kind of thing.

The perceptual details of animals' movement vary greatly from dogs to cats to fish to birds. But all these things move in a biological way that differs from mechanical motion. The perceptual system itself may be able to respond to the abstract parameters that characterize biological motion. Such data have not yet been collected, but Bertenthal's work (e.g., 1993) shows that as early as 3 months, babies can discriminate computer dot displays that move according to the rules of human motion from those that violate human motion. This finding suggests that babies might be able to respond similarly to the even more abstract notion of biological motion in general. Assuming that infants can categorize stimuli on the basis of biological versus mechanical motion, that is still merely a perceptual accomplishment. What perceptual analysis does is translate that perceptual feat into simpler, but potentially accessible, descriptions. These descriptions might be nothing more than representations of an irregular, rhythmic path versus a smooth and unvarying path; that is, the descriptions are considerably reduced from the much richer information used to categorize the motion in the first place. These image-schemas form a set of contrasting meanings.

Similarly, animals begin movement in perceptually very different ways. They lift limbs, flap wings, and wave fins, but in all cases, these trajectories begin by themselves without other objects coming into contact with them. Perceptual analysis can abstract this characteristic from a perceptual display, regardless of which shape is doing the moving. The resulting image-schema forms the meaning of self-motion (or self-propulsion; Premack, 1990). Similarly, other objects only move when another object comes in contact with them. Perceptual analysis of this kind of display results in an image-schema of caused-motion (Mandler, 1992; see also Leslie, 1988). Another meaning infants can create from analysis of the paths of animate and inanimate objects is that the former interact with other objects from a distance, whereas the latter do not. When these meanings are combined, they form a simple but quite effective concept of an animal as an object that moves in a certain kind of way, that starts up on its own, and that interacts with other objects from a distance, and a concept of an inanimate object as one that either doesn't move at all or if it moves, does so on a highly predictable path, does not start on its own, and never interacts with infants from a distance, no matter how hard they try to make it do so. Simple as these concepts are, they appear to be sufficient to account for the current data on conceptual categorization of animals and vehicles in the first year and for the kinds of inductive inferences that 1-year-olds make.

These meanings are derived in a straightforward fashion from perceptual information. However, their image-schematic format is a discrete, simpler, more abstract, and less context-bound form, and one that is well-suited to serve a symbolic function. In this view, meanings are not innate; there is only an innate mechanism that derives meanings from perceptual displays by abstracting some essential aspects, namely, what objects do (the roles that they take) and the relations in which they stand to other objects. Meanings, such as moves by itself, or interacts with other objects from a distance, are so basic to our ideas of animate and inanimate things, that they seem to underlie all our other notions about what things are—the core around which later knowledge about kinds of things is organized. Core conceptions of animacy and inanimacy are also the last kinds of knowledge to be lost when the conceptual system begins to break down in cases of semantic dementia (Hodges, Graham, & Patterson, 1995; Saffron & Schwartz, 1994). It seems likely that these early preverbal meanings, although greatly elaborated and perhaps even overlaid by years of linguistic representation, nevertheless remain functional throughout normal life. Are these image-schemas formed in infancy innately specified or are they merely the result of the processing of a still relatively primitive perceptual system? The latter alternative is certainly plausible. Perhaps the reason why the conceptual division of the world into animate and inanimate things occurs so early is that our perceptual systems are attuned to respond to motion; what results from perceptual analyses, then, might be predictable by the nature of our perceptual systems.

As discussed in the previous section on analogical representation, image-schematic meanings are expressed as paths through space and spatial relations among objects. These meanings are not themselves accessible. We do not have introspections about image-schemas; no representational format is directly accessible. However, these representations form the basis of the kind of information that can be made accessible. This is the heart of the proposal that procedural, sensorimotor knowledge, and declarative, conceptual knowledge are fundamentally different in kind. It says that only information that has been encoded in special ways can be explicit, that is, accessible to conscious awareness. To my knowledge, there are only two kinds of formats in which *ideas* appear in consciousness: words and images.[11] Image-schemas provide the kind of meanings that can be redescribed into words (Mandler, 1994). They may underlie image formation as well. Although image-schemas are not themselves images, imagery is constructed from what we know as well as from what we perceive. Images

are not uninterpreted copies of reality but are constructed from the underlying meanings a person has already formed (Chambers & Reisberg, 1992; Intons-Peterson & Roskos-Ewoldsen, 1989; Piaget & Inhelder, 1971). So it seems plausible that image-schemas are used to structure an image space in which specific objects and the details of their paths and relationships to each other can be filled in. In this view, image-schemas are a crucial part of our mental architecture. They are used to create meanings in the first place, then to help form the images that instantiate those meanings in consciousness, and when language is learned, to ground the words that refer to them.

Leslie (1994) offers a somewhat different, more nativist, view of the earliest meanings. Leslie suggests there is an innate, modularized, componential organization to the mind, one that shows itself not only in different sensory processors, but also in the initial conceptual system. In particular, he proposes that infants come equipped with three domain-specific modules, one that computes mechanical properties of objects (ToBy, Theory of Body Mechanism), one that computes goal-directed actions (ToMM1, first Theory of Mind Mechanism), and one that computes the states of mind of agents (ToMM2). The task of the first of these innate conceptual modules (ToBy) is to arrive at a description of the world in terms of the mechanical constitution of objects and the events they enter into. ToBy receives two main inputs from vision: an object-recognition device, similar to that posited by Spelke (1990), and a device that analyzes motion with respect to force dynamics. For this purpose, ToBy is equipped with a primitive notion of force. "Together with information on surface layout, ToBy takes, as input, descriptions that make explicit the geometry of the objects contained in a scene, their arrangement and their motions, and onto such descriptions paints the mechanical properties of the scenario" (Leslie, 1994, p. 128). This analysis of object motion also leads to causal perception in infancy (Leslie, 1988).

In part to account for his data on causality, Leslie thinks it necessary to posit an innate notion of force, which he finds incompatible with an image-schema analysis of early meaning (Leslie, 1994). He suggests that force is a necessary component of early understanding of object mechanics and is not easily represented in terms of image-schemas. Strictly speaking, Leslie's objections are relevant only to my account of the earliest image-schemas, not to the type of representation itself. It is true that I have relied as far as possible on a purely spatial analysis of early meanings, be-

---

[11] I am concerned here with thoughts and not with feelings and sensations (qualia), which may be experienced in different ways.

cause we know that infants process spatial information, and we don't yet know when they first begin to process information about force. Indeed, Proffitt and Bertenthal (1990) suggest that it is implausible that babies come into the world possessing perceptual processes that embody dynamical (forceful) constraints. They suggest that throughout the lifespan, motions are perceptually represented by kinematic parameters, and that our dynamical intuitions are formed from these parameters by development of experience-based heuristics. If this is correct, then the earliest concepts might only have spatial analyses available. In any case, I have made the simplifying assumption that the first notions of animacy, causality, agency, and so forth, are based solely on analysis of object movements and the spatial relations they enter into. As shown in Mandler (1992), these are differentiated enough to account for the asymmetry in causal roles (a doer and a done-to), and therefore may be sufficient to account for infants' responding to launching events of the sort described in Leslie and Keeble (1987).[12]

Other people, however, also relying on an image-schematic interpretation of meaning (Johnson, 1987; Talmy, 1988), have emphasized the force characteristics of image-schemas. Johnson in particular claims it is the experience of forces acting on our bodies and our forceful actions on other bodies that create many image-schemas. That is a reasonable position from the adult point of view. On the other hand, the likely limitations on infants' abilities to analyze kinesthetic information suggest that the earliest analyses might be more spatial than forceful. In general, analysis of bodily sensations seems to be a relatively late achievement. For example, it would seem easier for an infant to analyze a visual display of milk being poured into a cup in terms of containment than to analyze the experience of milk going into its body. (This point of view is supported by the widespread phenomenon in the world's languages of the vocabularies of mental states being derived from the vocabularies used to describe external

phenomena; Sweetser, 1990). Therefore, I have assumed that the notion of force is derived from experiencing force rather than being innately given. However, these are issues that are far from being resolved at this stage of theory development about the foundations of mind.

Nativism versus Empiricism

These new theories vary considerably in the extent to which they rely on inborn structures to get conceptual development started. For example, in my theory, not much more is needed than a mechanism of perceptual analysis, whereas Leslie (1994) posits several innate modules. In spite of these differences, all these views tend to get grouped together as nativist approaches. Indeed, the old debate of nativism versus empiricism, that one might have thought was well and truly buried, seems to have been given new life by the recent work in infancy. Actually, it is not clear how to label the viewpoints in the present incarnation of this debate because it is not obvious exactly what the issues are. We might call it nativism versus constructivism to imply a debate between postPiagetians (who believe that more innate structures and mechanisms are required than Piaget posited) and the Piagetian position itself (in which little needs to be built in because processing in interaction with the environment is enough to construct mental structures). Or perhaps we should call it the School of Domain-Specific Constraints, often associated with nativist views, versus the School of Domain-General Learning, more often associated with the Piagetian view. Regardless of names, at the simplest level, the argument concerns whether various capacities are innately given or whether they are learned by contact with the environment. Of course, no position is black or white. Everyone, without exception, believes there are some innate, genetically determined, species characteristics; no one thinks that children might end up behaving or thinking like camels. Also without exception, everyone believes that much of what we know is learned from interacting with the environment; no one believes that newborns think or behave like college students. So in spite of a good deal of heat, the argument in its bald form is moot; no one takes either position in the raw.

One of the sources of the upswing in dispute about nativism was Chomsky's (1965) notion of a language acquisition device, which he conceived as a special-purpose module with its own domain-specific learning mechanism, more or less unrelated to the rest of cognition. He did not specify much about this device, however, and only in recent

---

[12] Spatial information is provided most directly by the visual system. It can also be derived from touch, of course, and to a lesser extent from audition. This disparity in the usefulness of information from the various senses suggests that it is not sighted children who are held back from concept formation until they gain control over their hands, as Piaget suggested, but instead only blind infants who are at a disadvantage until their manual skills develop.

years have the developmental aspects of his program risen to the fore (Pinker, 1989). The intricate nativist claims of this position have been opposed by a number of people studying language acquisition (Bates, 1994; Braine, 1992). The main source of the dispute, however, was the new experimental research programs on conceptual development in infancy (see *Criticisms of Piaget's Theory*). Until the last decade, most of the experimental techniques for studying infant cognition were directed toward perceptual development. It was considerably easier to figure out how to study what babies see than what they think. The perceptual work was not controversial because it fit well enough with Piaget's theoretical position on infancy. However, when research began in earnest on conceptual development, as we have seen, a surprisingly wide range of knowledge about objects at an early age was uncovered. It was at this point that arguments about the new nativism began to heat up. Once Piagetian hegemony began to slip, new questions arose, not only about infant competency, but also about the extent to which there are or are not qualitative changes in cognitive development. In Piaget's theory, a kind of Copernican revolution occurs at the end of infancy, as babies come to understand objects as permanent entities independent of themselves. But if objects are understood in something like adult form early in life, what is it that makes infants different from older children or adults? Do infants operate with the same core of knowledge as adults (Spelke, 1994), or are there qualitative shifts in conceptual representation, even if different from those proposed by Piaget (Carey, 1991)? Infancy is the arena in which opposing views on these matters have clashed most strongly.

Many of the findings on infants' knowledge about objects have been demonstrated with infants as young as 2 to 4 months of age (Baillargeon, 1987; Spelke et al., 1992), suggesting that this knowledge (whether perceptual or conceptual) might be innate. However, Baillargeon, who has been responsible for much of this body of work, states that all of the knowledge she has investigated is learned (Baillargeon, 1995). Instead of a gradual unfolding of innate ideas taking place, Baillargeon claims that an innate, highly-constrained learning mechanism is applied to incoming data. This mechanism enables concepts about various physical phenomena to be learned in the first few months of life, concepts that become progressively elaborated as learning continues.

Spelke arrives at a somewhat different explanation of her data, giving a more nativist account (Spelke, 1994). First, she defines knowledge of objects, as opposed to perception of objects, as the information that allows organisms to make inferences about the properties of objects they cannot perceive (Spelke, 1994). She then suggests that some initial knowledge of objects must be innate because it conforms to environmental constraints that are not perceptually or motorically available. At $2\frac{1}{2}$ months (the age of her youngest subjects), infants have not yet begun to explore objects manually, so one of the best sources of information about their solidity and unity is still not available. She also believes that visual perceptual ability is still quite limited even at 3 months, citing Banks and Salapatek (1983), although this particular conclusion is open to question. Many of the proposed perceptual limitations come from data collected using static displays. Spelke's own work (Carey & Spelke, 1994; see also Kellman, 1993) shows that motion is crucial for many of the findings on infants' perception of the unity and coherence of objects, with various perceptual achievements being earlier when moving stimuli are used. Even with static displays, by 3 months of age, infants are learning a great deal through the perceptual system. As we have seen, they can already form perceptual categories of animals (Quinn et al., 1993). A perceptual system that can learn in a few short trials to discriminate pictures of dogs as a class from cats as a class cannot be said to be terribly limited.

In addition, Spelke questions whether one could even use the perceptual system to gain information about objects (such as that they fall when not supported, or that people move in the direction they are facing) if objects were not represented in the first place as unitary and coherent, and animate or inanimate. As she puts it: Learning systems require perceptual systems that parse the world appropriately (Spelke, 1994). In my view, this argument loses some of its force by not differentiating clearly between conceptual and perceptual representation. Spelke's own definition of innate knowledge is that which perception does not give, but she here argues for an innate basis for *perceptual* information (which few would deny). Seeing objects as unitary and coherent is an accomplishment of the perceptual system; it is procedural knowledge given by the nature of the perceptual transducers we are endowed with. It is likely to be innate, although one can imagine a dedicated learning device that could learn to parse objects in the first few weeks of life. Such knowledge can be integrated with the motor system, as is seen in the development of reaching (von Hofsten & Spelke, 1985), without having to be in explicit conceptual form. On the other hand, I see no reason why perceptual transducers should innately provide a complex distinction such as animacy and inanimacy; that can be safely left to learning. In Mandler (1992), I suggest how this distinction might be learned in the first few months of life. Parsing objects does seem essential for all further perceptual and conceptual development; parsing them as animate does not because it is easy to learn.

Even though Spelke is one of the few cognitive researchers to proclaim a sizable store of innate knowledge about the world, she also believes that a great deal of knowledge about objects is learned, much of it gradually during the first year. For example, Spelke et al. (1992) found that 2½-month-olds were sensitive to the constraints of continuity and solidity that govern object movement, but even 4-month-olds had not yet learned about various aspects of gravity or inertia. In addition, her data suggest that various Gestalt principles governing object perception are learned only gradually during the course of infancy (Spelke, 1988).

Given this emphasis on learning that is at least as strong as the emphasis on the innate component, it is surprising that Spelke and Baillargeon have been attacked as proposing an extreme and even dangerous nativist stance (Fischer & Bidell, 1991). One of Fischer and Bidell's claims is that "neo-nativists" rely on what they call the argument from precocity. This argument is that if a behavior appears early in life, it must be innate because it couldn't be learned so rapidly. However, precocity can only be defined in terms of what a given theory says *ought* to happen. It is only against the background of Piagetian theory that the many results from Spelke's and Baillargeon's laboratories suggest precocity. Without such a theory, there is nothing that specifies how much infants should know about objects or whether such learning should be slow or fast. Neither Spelke nor Baillargeon claim that the early cognitive capacities they have uncovered are mature in form, and their research shows gradual change in a number of aspects of understanding objects. Gelman (1991) emphasizes this point, noting that "it simply is not true that whenever innate factors contribute to complex behaviors, these will appear full-blown—as it were, from the head of Zeus—as soon as a 'triggering' stimulus is presented" (p. 312). What makes Fischer and Bidell's argument especially surprising is that the conclusions Fischer draws from his own work on the development of skills in this period (Fischer & Hogan, 1989) are consistent with those of Spelke and Baillargeon. For example, Fischer and Bidell (1991) say that around 3 to 4 months, infants begin to understand objects

as independently existing wholes, a conclusion that is remarkably similar to the one they attack.

One source of unhappiness with the current infancy work may be the language that has been used to describe what infants are learning. For example, both Baillargeon and Spelke say that young infants reason and make inferences about objects (e.g., Baillargeon, 1995; Spelke et al., 1992). Some psychologists disapprove of this terminology because it seems to imply explicit high-level conceptual processing of the kind we associate with much older children and adults. In my opinion, the language is not meant to imply such high-level abilities, although I understand how it might be so interpreted. Part of the problem, then, is that neither Spelke nor Baillargeon discuss the status of infants' knowledge.[13] They do not address the issue of differences between procedural, sensorimotor knowledge and declarative, conceptual knowledge; that leaves the import of the common-language terms they use uncertain and so, open to debate. Of course, these same objections could be made about Piaget, who, even as he was denying a conceptual capacity to infants, used the language of conceptual thought (curiosity, conscious awareness, contemplation, intention) quite freely even for infants as young as 2 months of age (Piaget, 1952).

It may be that if one does not actively proclaim the sensorimotor status of the knowledge in question, then usage of the common language for conceptual thought will be taken as implying that the knowledge is not only declarative, but also languagelike. Interestingly, the most elaborate nativist position (Leslie, 1994) seems to have largely escaped the criticisms that Fischer and Bidell directed toward Spelke and Baillargeon. Part of the reason for that may be that Leslie uses new terminology and also explicitly rejects the "child-as-scientist" view, in which early knowledge appears to be treated as comparable to the reflective manipulation of concepts that scientists carry out. Leslie's theory is a good example of the new nativism in that it proposes a theory of the initial state (what he calls "core architecture") and the innate endowment that is the foundation on which cognitive development rests. This endowment consists of a set of innate hierarchically arranged modules, plus some highly constrained learning mechanisms. His view is the most explicitly anti-Piagetian, because it posits innate structural modules rather than the

---

[13] Spelke (personal communication) believes there is no available evidence that bears on this issue.

domain-general learning procedures of assimilation and accommodation that Piaget used to build schemas.

The remainder of this chapter presents, in more detail, what we currently know about these issues in terms of the types of knowledge that infants represent, and in each case whether it is sensorimotor, procedural knowledge, or conceptual, declarative knowledge. The goal is for these analyses to suggest ways of resolving some of the current disputes about infant competence.

TYPES OF INFORMATION INFANTS REPRESENT

Representation of Objects

I have already discussed some of the new infancy work suggesting that infants know a good deal about objects. In particular, Baillargeon's (1993) extensive work on the topic indicates that, over the course of the first year, infants acquire many expectations about objects and the way they behave. I also discussed briefly the issue of the status of this knowledge, that is, whether it is procedural (sensorimotor) knowledge or indicative of a developing declarative (conceptual) system. In *Criticisms of Piaget's Theory,* I suggested that the ability to maintain a representation of an absent object (e.g., as found in the experiments in which a car rolls down a track hidden by a screen) implies a conceptual system, although this theoretical issue has not received much attention since Piaget first proposed using representation of absent objects as a criterion. One useful approach to the problem would be to examine carefully the different types of experimental data that are now available, scrutinizing each result with this question in mind. To that end, I will briefly discuss several other types of experiments that Baillargeon and her colleagues have conducted.

First, consider a series of studies charting the course of development of knowledge about support relations between the ages of 3 and 7 months. Needham and Baillargeon (1993) showed 4½-month-olds a possible event, in which a hand placed a box on a platform and then moved back, leaving the box supported, and an impossible event, in which the hand released the box beyond the platform, thus leaving it unsupported but still remaining in place. The infants looked longer at the impossible event. Baillargeon, Kotovsky, and Needham (1995) summarize a number of similar experiments in which the progression in responding is as follows: At 3 months of age, infants expect objects to fall if they lose contact with a supporting surface. At this

stage, any contact between an object and a surface is considered sufficient. This initial notion of support appears to be a binary distinction between contact and no contact. By 4 to 5 months of age, infants begin to distinguish between types of contact and expect that objects will be supported only if they at least partially overlap a surface, not merely abut it, although apparently any amount of overlap will do. By about 6 months, the notion has become elaborated. Babies now begin to have a more quantitative view of support, expecting objects to fall unless they substantially overlap the supporting surface.

This series of experiments is an elegant demonstration of the growing sophistication of the knowledge base being built up in infancy. But the question of interest here is what kind of knowledge is being violated by the impossible events in these experiments? In this series, infants were not required to represent something unseen; instead they only reacted to unusual sights, such as a hand letting go of an object which then remained suspended in midair. It seems possible that mere perceptual experience with the world might lead infants to find the impossible events unusual enough to produce the kind of longer looking associated with perceptual novelty. Infants are unlikely to have seen objects hovering in midair, so this impossible display should violate perceptual expectations regardless of any knowledge about the physics of support. They presumably would not have seen the other impossible displays either (such as a box supported by a small amount of overlap), but the difference between possible and impossible is less extreme in these cases. The perceptual system gains new and more detailed information with experience (E. Gibson, 1969), and the more detailed the knowledge, presumably the more detailed the expectations become. So at first, infants might not be surprised to see an object supported by a tiny amount of overlap, and only later expect it to fall without the overlap being greater. Note also that in similar experiments in which objects were shown falling, Spelke et al. (1992) found no dishabituation to displays in which an object landed in mid-air instead of on a surface. The difference between the two series of experiments may be that processing rapidly falling objects requires more experience to encode in any detail and therefore it takes longer to develop expectations about "normal" sights. Thus, more obviously than in the case of remembering the details of an object hidden behind a screen, the knowledge demonstrated in these experiments might be implicit perceptual knowledge. If the expectations are merely part of perceptual procedures, they are classic examples of sensorimotor knowledge, and as such need not consist of conceptual knowledge. If this analysis is correct, then one would not want to say that infants are reasoning about support.

On the other hand, it is possible that infants have indeed begun to conceptualize support during this period. Baillargeon's documentation of the changes in understanding, from registering contact versus no contact at 3 months, to knowing something about the amount of overlap required to provide support at 6 months, is reminiscent of the kind of perceptual analysis I have described as providing the basis for concept formation. An initial analysis of relations between objects in terms of contact versus no contact is the kind of simple transformation of perceptual information into spatial image-schemas that I have proposed is the beginning of conceptual thought (Mandler, 1992). Thus, perceptual analysis could allow a way for this kind of information to be conceptualized even at this young age. However, we don't know if this is what they are doing or not. One problem in trying to decide the nature of the processes infants are using is the lack of a detailed theory of perceptual knowledge. In spite of the great sophistication of research on perception, to my knowledge there is no theory that tells us whether binary notions such as contact versus no contact play important roles in perceptual recognition procedures.

A similar difficulty in interpretation applies to another set of experiments from Baillargeon's lab. Baillargeon and DeVos (1991) showed 3½-month-old infants either a tall carrot or a short carrot disappear behind a screen and reappear at the other side. For the test trials, a window was cut in the upper part of the screen, such that if the tall carrot now moved behind the screen it should be seen through the window, whereas if the short carrot moved behind the screen, it would still not be seen. On impossible trials, the tall carrot moved behind the screen and reappeared at the other side without being seen in the window. The infants dishabituated to this display. In a second experiment, the infants were given the same procedure, except at the beginning of the experiment they were shown two tall carrots on either side of the screen. In this experiment, the infants did *not* dishabituate on the impossible trials when the tall carrot did not appear in the window. It would seem that the pretrial procedure gave the infants a ready explanation for the impossible trials: perhaps there was a second carrot behind the screen so that the first carrot entered and stopped before reaching the window and the second carrot moved out into view from the other side. Such a conclusion seems to involve both recall and inference, since nothing in the

moving-carrot event itself suggested that there were still two carrots around. On the other hand, if the infants initially construed the situation as involving two carrots they might continue to do so during the moving-carrot event. If so, inference, in the sense of seeking an explanation for an otherwise surprising event, would not be necessary. Again, we do not know enough about the parameters involved in perceptual parsing in infancy to know whether number of objects is part of the output of perceptual recognition procedures regardless of the conceptual knowledge infants might have. There is evidence that young infants are sensitive to the number of objects in displays (Starkey, Spelke, & Gelman, 1983), but we do not know the status of this sensitivity or whether infants always parse perceptual displays in terms of the number of objects in them (Moore, Benenson, Reznick, Peterson, & Kagan, 1987).

This way of discussing these experiments is not the way that Baillargeon herself describes her work. She speaks only of what infants know about objects and how they reason about objects' movements. She has amply shown that infants know a good deal from an early age, and equally, that a great deal of what they know about objects is learned. But there is more than one way of knowing and it is this issue that I have raised here. The conclusion I come to about the studies just described is that the questions necessary to assess the status of this knowledge have not yet been asked. Therefore, at the present time, we can only speculate about how this knowledge about basic object properties is represented. At present, there is no evidence one way or the other that infants engage in explicit reasoning about objects. Such experiments have not yet been done. Nor do we know the extent to which the procedural perceptual system parses displays into number of objects, their locations, and so forth, before the organism is old enough to have an operative conceptual system. In short, we do not know how much interpretation perceptual parsing requires. The most we can say at the moment is that, either in procedural or declarative fashion, over the first few months of life, babies come to expect objects to behave in certain ways, such as moving only on continuous paths, not passing through other objects, and to fall if unsupported.

Causality and Agency

The term causality is usually used to refer to the physical effects one object has upon another, with the term agency used for the special case in which the causing object is one that moves or acts on its own. Thus, causal relations obtain between inanimate objects, and agency between an animate actor and a (typically) inanimate object. In principle, agency can be recognized without reference to intention. That is, one can observe an object move itself and act on other objects without attributing mental states to it. Poulin-Dubois and Shultz (1988) suggest that intention is an elaboration on the notion of agency, and as such is a later development than the concept of agency itself. Premack (1990), on the other hand, suggests that a notion of agency does not make any sense without some hypothesis about *why* agents act as they do; therefore, he considers intention to be part of the notion of agency itself. The same issues arise for knowledge of causality and agency in infancy as for knowledge about objects. First, what is the source of these kinds of knowledge? Are causality and agency (or intention) detectors built in, or do infants construct these notions from observing consistent differences in the relevant spatio-temporal parameters? Second, what is the status of this knowledge? Is it procedural only, or are infants able to think and make judgments about causal situations?

As in so many other areas, Piaget's (1954) account of the origins of causal understanding was the standard view for many years. In his theory, understanding of causality shows its first beginnings around 6 months of age. As infants become interested in the effects their actions have on the world and develop procedures for "making interesting sights last," they become vaguely aware that when they perform certain actions, other things happen. However, they are not yet sensitive to the spatio-temporal parameters involved, and so do not know that causes are prior to their effects or that there has to be physical contact between objects for one to move another. In addition, infants use their own feelings of force or efficacy as the basis of understanding causality, and so do not yet understand a causal relation when it is produced by forces external to themselves. Thus, a primitive sense of agency was considered the root source of causal learning. In general, the assumption underlying this view of the development of causal understanding is that observation in the world is not sufficient to produce the notion; instead our powerful belief in physical causality rests on the feelings of intention and effort that occur when we as agents move objects around.

In contrast to this view, a number of more recent investigators have suggested other origins of causal understanding. Leslie (1988) posits an innate causal-motion detector, which he considers to be part of the perceptual system. This mechanism is modular and incorrigible: It biases the system so that special attention is paid to causally connected events

and thus forms the foundation for a later-developing explicit concept of causality. Leslie based his work on that of Michotte (1963), who showed that adults are subject to a powerful illusion of causality in films in which "billiard balls" (actually circles or rectangles) appear to launch one another. He found that, contrary to Piaget's view, infants are sensitive to fine differences in spatio-temporal relations. Leslie and Keeble (1987) demonstrated the special status of causal relations by showing that 6-month-olds are more apt to dishabituate to a film of a causal launching when it is run backwards than to reversal of a film involving similar but non-launching spatio-temporal relations. In more recent writing, Leslie (1994) calls this causal detector the Michotte module, a perceptual module that is part of the larger module, ToBy, discussed earlier in *New Theories of Infant Representation*. Because the Michotte module only gives kinematic information, one of the roles of ToBy, as we saw, is to "paint" mechanical force properties onto the purely spatial motion aspects. Thus, Leslie claims that the properties of causality do not have a perceptual basis— only the *spatial* properties are given in that manner. The mechanical notion of force is innate and not learned by analyzing perceptual experience. This notion is also essential to understanding agency; therefore, both causality and agency are independently related to an innate understanding of force.

White (1988), on the other hand, attempts to show not only that causal analysis is grounded in perception, but that this kind of perception is also the root source for understanding agency. White, also basing his analyses on Michotte's work, suggests that the powerful sense of causality perceived in launching displays comes from several aspects of iconic storage, but mainly its short duration (about 250 msec). The iconic store is a large-capacity sensory store that holds visual information prior to attentive processing. The store is continuously refreshed, and this is what enables the temporal integration by which we see motion as continuous. If this temporal integration function is present in early infancy, it may be responsible for causal perception, rather than causal perception being a special innate module, as proposed by Leslie.

Michotte (1963) reported that the timing of the launching events was crucial for the causal illusion. For example, he manipulated the delay between ball A coming into contact with ball B, and B moving away (i.e., being launched). When the delay was increased from 100 to 150 msec, the causal illusion was lost, and subjects started seeing two independent movements. B also had to be present and stationary for at least 100 msec before A contacted B and B moved if a causal illusion was to occur; at shorter intervals, the impression was that there was only one object that appeared in continuous movement. Similarly, if B was not present initially and A disappeared before contacting B and then B appeared already moving, subjects had the impression of only one object. Finally, when a single ball was used and paused briefly, motion was not perceived as discontinuous until the pause was almost 100 msec. Thus, when there was one object and a pause of less than 100 msec, continuity of motion was seen. When there were two objects and the pause at contact was less than 100 msec, a causal relation was seen.

White (1988) proposes that causal processing occurs when a conflict exists between two types of continuity cues. One type (spatial discontinuity) says there are two objects, whereas the other (continuous motion) suggests a single object. The conflict is resolved by interpreting the sequence as involving two objects and the transfer of motion from one to the other (Michotte's "ampliation"). This is the launching effect. The effect disappears when the temporal parameters of the movement do not fall within the time frame of temporal integration, or if the direction of movement of A and B becomes dissimilar. White (1988) considers this phenomenon to be an implicit perceptual one, as does Leslie. However, White goes on to discuss how this procedural knowledge is used to ground later declarative beliefs about causation.[14] He points out that the main features involved in causal perception are the very factors important in the explicit causal reasoning of older children and adults. These features are: (1) temporal contiguity, (2) spatial contiguity, (3) a characteristic order, in that A first has a property and B doesn't, and then B has the property, with the transfer occurring at the moment of contact, and (4) the antecedent and consequent are similar in the sense that the property transferred is roughly the same before as after (for example, speed and direction of movement in the transfer of motion in launching). Factor 1 is important in judgments of causality at all ages (Schlottmann, 1991) and factor 2 somewhat less so (Bullock, Gelman, & Baillargeon, 1982). Factor 3 may become operative later than factors 1 and 2, but is important at least by age 5 (Shultz, Altmann, & Asselin, 1986). Finally, the belief that

results should be similar to their causes is frequently expressed at all ages (Einhorn & Hogarth, 1986).

White (1988) suggests that our understanding of agency, or intended action, stems from these same factors. The understanding of psychological causation is late compared to physical causation because the cause is an internal event (intention) and can't be apprehended by iconic processing. Instead of actual transfer of motion, it is attention that is shifted from a nonvisible internal event to the visible result. However, the same factors in continuity are operative in psychological causation, with the exception of spatial contiguity. Temporal contiguity of plan and outcome are typically involved, as well as the priority of the plan and the similarity between plan and what one does. Thus, understanding intentional action is derived by extending the processing of continuities between external events to the continuities between an internal plan and external behavior.

Premack (1990) takes a more nativist interpretation of agency and intentional action than does White. Premack assumes that just as the perception of causality is hard-wired, so is the perception of intention. In both cases, the relevant information (one object being moved by another, or an object moving itself) is fed into a higher-order device that has the interpretation of causality or intention as its output. A promising version of this kind of view is recent work by Gergely, Nadasdy, Csibra, and Biro (1995). These authors used a simplified version of the famous Heider and Simmel (1944) film showing geometrical forms moving and interacting in various ways. This film gives adults as powerful an impression of social interaction as do Michotte's films of causal interaction. Gergely et al. habituated 12-month-olds to a computer display showing two balls (circles) separated by a barrier; the balls intermittently pulsated. Then one ball approached the barrier, paused, returned to its original position, and then approached the barrier at a faster speed, jumped over it, and ended in contact with the other ball, whereupon mutual pulsing began. A control group was habituated to the same display except that the "barrier" was placed at one side of the display, rather than between the two balls, thus making the jumping action unmotivated. Test displays consisted of the same display as seen by the control group during habituation (i.e., jumping but no barrier) and also a novel action in which the first ball went in a direct line to the second one. Experimental subjects dishabituated to the old action they had seen before (the ball jumping, but now without a barrier), but not to the novel action in which, in

---

[14] White (1988) does not use the terms implicit and explicit. Instead, he uses the automatic-controlled processing distinction discussed in *Multiple Representational Systems.*

the absence of the barrier, one ball immediately moved in a direct line to the other. Gergely, Csibra, Biro, and Koos (1994) replicated this finding with 9-month-olds, but not with 6-month-olds. These data are impressive, because they imply that at a young age infants analyze agents' goals, and do not just register the characteristic ways in which agents interact with other objects. This work might be taken as support for Premack's position that the perception of intention is hard-wired, although since it does not seem to be realized until about 9 months, there is obviously time for a great deal of learning about agents to take place. Nevertheless, the young age of Gergely et al.'s subjects casts some doubt on White's thesis that the origin of understanding intentionality comes from comparing a plan with its realization.

We have seen that both Leslie and Premack assume that notions of causality and intention must be innate and perhaps independent of each other; in Leslie's view, they are parts of two specialized modular systems. White, on the other hand, has suggested that more general parameters of the perceptual system may be enough to account first for the notion of causality, and then bootstrapping from it, the notion of agency. Although Gergely et al.'s (1994) data make White's thesis seem less likely, there are other ways in which notions about causality could be acquired. I have described how both causality and agency could be acquired without innate specialized detectors (Mandler, 1992). As discussed earlier, a mechanism of perceptual analysis analyzes perceptual displays in terms of the paths that objects take. There are characteristic real-world differences between causal interactions among inanimate objects and among animate and inanimate objects. These have to do with the way that paths of motion begin and the nature of the trajectories they follow. I claim that analyses of these paths lead to image-schemas of *self-motion, caused motion,* and *animate* and *inanimate paths* (Mandler, 1992). A combination of an animate object contacting an inanimate object, which then moves, leads to an image-schema of *agency.* These analyses are quite simple and should be within the capacity of preverbal infants.

There are two advantages to this image-schema approach to causality. First, placing sensitivity to causality in perceptual analysis avoids one problem that a modular view faces, namely, that not everyone perceives the Michotte launching effect; there are also individual differences in adults' causal judgments, suggesting an interplay of conceptual and perceptual factors (Schlottmann & Anderson, 1993). Second, image-schemas provide the groundwork for

being able to make explicit judgments about causality, not just to have a set of perceptual expectations. In this view, it is the transformation of certain perceptual regularities into image-schemas that enables the formation of declarative concepts about causality. These in turn will affect the way that people *interpret* their perceptual experiences, accounting for the individual variability that is found. Whether or not the mechanism of image-schema formation is correct, both kinds of theorizing about causality are needed. First, we need a mechanism that produces the perception of causality, perhaps along the lines that White (1988) has suggested. Then we need to specify as exactly as possible the sort of mechanism that can redescribe these parameters into something more conceptual in nature, which will not only account for causal reasoning, but also the descriptions that people give about their causal perception.

Perceptual Categories and Concept Formation

As we have seen, there is considerable debate as to whether one must posit innate object, causality, or agency detectors. There is less debate about whether knowledge of specific kinds of objects (or events) is built in. Almost everyone seems to agree that humans have no innate knowledge of specific objects.[15] These, and the events they participate in, must be learned. Needless to say, this agreement does not mean that the topic is debate-free—far from it! The debate merely changes its grounds to the bases on which such learning takes place. On the one hand, the empiricist approach is that concepts are formed on the basis of categorizing objects that have common perceptual properties (Eimas, 1994; Rosch & Mervis, 1975; Smith & Heise, 1992). On the other hand, a less perceptually-based approach says that forming concepts about objects requires developing theories about "kinds" or "essences" (Gelman & Wellman, 1991; Keil, 1989).

Part of this debate is fueled by the failure to distinguish between perceptual and conceptual processes. In most of the psychological literature, categorization is treated as if it were a single process that operates in the same way for all kinds of materials, whether they be meaningless perceptual patterns (e.g., Posner & Keele, 1968), natural kinds and artifacts (Smith & Osherson, 1988), or abstract

---

[15] A possible exception to this generalization is that there may be some innate crude specification of conspecific faces, as described by Johnson and Morton (1991).

concepts, such as diseases (e.g., Nosofsky, Kruschke, & McKinley, 1992). Although the idea that all categories are formed in the same way has been around for many decades (Bruner, 1957), there have been too few tests of it (e.g., Reed & Friedman, 1973; see also Medin & Barsalou, 1987) to know whether it is correct. At the least, it is a risky assumption, and at worst it could be quite misleading. The assumption was initially based on the view that concepts are built up first out of perceptual features that later become increasingly abstract. If percepts and concepts lie on some kind of continuum, then it may not matter that the features of concepts are often functional, behavioral, or abstract properties, whereas the features of perceptual categories are typically shapes, colors, and other perceptual properties. In this view, there is essentially no difference between perceptual and conceptual categories—they shade off into each other—and so one might expect them to be learned in the same way. Indeed, Posner and Keele (1968) called their study of the formation of prototypes of random dot patterns and geometric forms *On the Genesis of Abstract Ideas,* a title suggesting that forming dot patterns is basically no different from forming superordinate concepts, such as animals and vehicles, or abstract concepts, such as justice.

If concepts could be defined in terms of perceptual properties, conflating percepts and concepts might not matter. However, most theorists today believe that concepts are not merely associative complexes of sensory or perceptual information, but have a core that specifies the sort of thing that the exemplars of a category are (Keil, 1989; Lakoff, 1987; Medin & Ortony, 1989). In the latter view, a concept is a summary representation that forms the core meaning (the intension) of a notion. It answers the question: What kind of thing is it? The concept of zebra consists of the sort of thing we think a zebra is. In this case, the minimum core meaning of zebra is that it is an animal. The concept might also specify that a zebra is an African animal and is striped. But these are details, knowledge of which depends on education and experience; they can change considerably over a lifetime and differ from person to person. One does not need to know these details to have a concept of zebra. On the other hand, if one does not know that a zebra is an animal, a concept of zebra is not present, even if the person dishabituates to a picture of a zebra after seeing a set of horses.

The term category emphasizes a concept's extension; it answers questions such as: which things are zebras? The confusion begins when no distinction is made between a conceptual category and a perceptual category. Perceptual categories are summary representations of what things look like, which is importantly not the same thing as a summary representation of what something is. Perceptual categories, such as dot patterns, do not have an intension (they have no conceptual meaning); it would probably be better to call them perceptual schemas to avoid confusion. A perceptual category or perceptual schema of zebras is a prototypical representation of what zebras look like. At least some of this knowledge is usually also part of the concept of zebra (for example, has stripes), but it doesn't work the other way around. The characterization of a zebra as an African animal, which is part of my concept, is *not* part of a perceptual prototype of what zebras look like. We also do not have access to our perceptual categories in the way that we do to our concepts. I cannot think (clearly) about the shape of zebra heads, in spite of the fact that that is probably an important part of my perceptual prototype. Indeed, aside from stripes, I can't really say how my prototype of zebras differs from my prototype of horses, yet I doubt I would be fooled by a horse with stripes painted on it. As discussed in *Multiple Representational Systems,* most of our perceptual categorical knowledge is inaccessible, whether it be what distinguishes zebras from horses or male from female faces. These perceptual categories, which are found in very young infants as well as adults, may work in a connectionist fashion (e.g., McClelland & Rumelhart, 1985); perceptual patterns get built up on top of each other, resulting in a summary representation or prototype that coexists with individual exemplar patterns. In other words, perceptual categorization is an integral part of the perceptual system itself and consists of implicit procedural knowledge. It is low-level knowledge that can be built into an industrial vision machine.

Concepts, on the other hand, are the foundation of explicit knowledge; they form the underpinnings of thought and reasoning, and let us do what the vision machine cannot. The information concepts represent is accessible to conscious thought (Mandler, 1997; Nelson, 1985). We can think about zebras, list their attributes, and argue over which of these are defining and which merely characteristic (Keil & Batterman, 1984). The upshot of these differences is that perceptual categories cannot be considered a subset of conceptual knowledge or vice versa; the two kinds of knowledge are represented in different formats with different degrees of accessibility. At least five main differences between perceptual and conceptual categories can be adduced: (a) the type of information they summarize,

(b) whether the information is accessible, (c) the amount of information they contain (with perceptual categories being richer, at least in the early stages of development), (d) the course of acquisition, and (e) the functions they serve (e.g., perceptual categories are used for recognition of objects and events; conceptual categories for the accumulation of meaning and induction). I concentrate on differences in acquisition here and discuss induction in the next section.

Infants begin to form visual perceptual categories from an early age and, in the case of auditory categorization, perhaps even prenatally (DeCasper & Spence, 1986). It is highly unlikely that these very early perceptual categories have any conceptual content (Eimas, 1994); their status appears to be implicit, procedural representation. (The perceptual information being categorized, however, can be abstract, as in the work of Bertenthal [1993] described earlier, on categorization of human motion displays.) They often require quite detailed perception. If 3-month-olds are shown a series of pictures of horses, within a few trials, they will form a perceptual category of horses that excludes cats, zebras, and giraffes (Eimas & Quinn, 1994). Similarly, if shown a series of pictures of cats, they will form a perceptual category of cats that excludes both dogs and tigers (Quinn et al., 1993). We don't know the exact basis on which this rapid categorical learning takes place, but at least for dogs and cats, it may be differences in their faces rather than overall body shape (Quinn & Eimas, 1996a). Since it seems highly likely that these pictures are merely visual patterns for 3-month-olds, it does not seem correct to talk about their having acquired concepts of dogs and cats. Later, of course, this will change; horse-patterns and cat-patterns will come to mean "animal." But perceptual categorization begins in the absence of conceptual meaning and may continue with little or no conceptual content for the first few months of life.

The arguments heat up when we ask how perceptual categories become concepts, how those horse-patterns and cat-patterns become concepts of horses and cats. One point of view is that these patterns gradually become associated with more and more information, until at some point they reach conceptual status. Eimas (1994) and Quinn and Eimas (1996b) are exponents of this position. Although previously, Quinn and Eimas (1986) claimed no one had ever successfully devised such a theory of concept formation, they now believe it can be achieved. They state that the perceptual categories of animals that 3-month-olds have are informationally rich, amodal (although since their

categorization data have to do only with visual recognition of shape, they do not provide evidence for amodality), and essentially no different from concepts. They agree with Baillargeon (1993) that even young infants engage in reasoning about objects, and since they assume that infants do so on the basis of the perceptual categories they have already formed, they assume these perceptual categories must be accessible. Thus, Quinn and Eimas claim there is no shift from perceptual representations to conceptual ones, but that with accumulated information, perceptual categories eventually come to support "what is considered conceptually-based behavior." This approach is Gibsonian in spirit: concepts are just a form of percepts. Organisms continue to gain new information perceptually throughout their lives, and concept formation and other aspects of development consist of this process of perceptual enrichment.

In contrast to the view that concepts and percepts are synonymous, Gelman and Wellman (1991), Keil (1991), Mandler (1992), and Nelson (1985) have all claimed that there is an important difference between forming perceptual categories in early infancy and forming the concepts that allow reasoning, thinking, and reflection. In this we agree with Piaget, although I do not agree with the time course his theory claims for the onset of conceptual functioning. I do not understand how concepts could arise merely by the gradual accumulation of associations to the infant's perceptual categories. Among the questions such a view raises are: When does a percept change into a concept? How does access to these categories for purposes of thought come about? What determines which aspects of perceptual categories become accessible and which do not? A separate mechanism seems to be required, one that can extract meaning from perceptual displays and put them in an accessible format. In my opinion, such a mechanism involves a different process, even though it also works on perceptual information. Rather than operating unselectively on perceptual displays to register and accumulate perceptual features and form prototypes from them, it operates selectively to abstract schematic descriptions that provide the essence of the kind of thing the object is (for example, a self-mover). Such a mechanism is unlikely to describe the world at the same level or in the same way that perceptual categorization does. Thus, we should expect to find differences in the course of acquisition of perceptual categories and conceptual descriptions of them. As I have described them, early image-schemas would not be capable of discriminating dogs and cats; they are descriptions at a higher level of generality (such as self-moving, interacting from a distance). It is worthwhile to re-emphasize the abstractness of image-schemas. The empiricist view tends to rely on language for the acquisition of abstract and functional features (i.e., features that are difficult to describe perceptually). But when abstract conceptual understanding is made a function of language, the nature of the concepts onto which the abstract language is mapped has been finessed, thus pushing the problem of the origin of abstract ideas into someone else's bailiwick.

Furthermore, the earliest concepts do not correspond well to the early perceptual categories of dogs and cats that Quinn and Eimas have been studying. At least some concept formation proceeds as a process of differentiating large, globally defined domains. Indeed, there is evidence that the earliest concept of animal is initially global in scope, although it is not yet clear whether the conceptual scope of animal consists of the entire domain or is very early divided into land-, air-, and sea-creatures (Mandler, Bauer, & McDonough, 1991; Mandler & McDonough, 1993). Between the ages of 7 and 24 months there is gradual differentiation of the animal domain into what are known (somewhat misleadingly, as I will discuss later) as basic-level categories. For example, using sequential touching of objects, we found that 18- and 24-month-olds consistently treated animals as different from vehicles, but within these domains they rarely differentiated one basic-level class from another, treating dogs and rabbits and horses as if they were all the same sort of thing, and cars and motorcycles and trucks as if they were all the same sort of thing (Mandler et al., 1991). The only within-domain distinctions made were among land-, air-, and sea-creatures and between land- and air-vehicles (boats were not tested). Similarly, 24-month-olds treated animals and plants differently, but did not make distinctions within the plant domain (trees vs. cactuses). They also differentiated kitchen items from furniture, but did not make distinctions within these domains (chairs vs. tables and spoons vs. forks). We know, of course, that they could *see* the differences between the various subclasses (and in some cases, even provide them with labels). Thus, they had formed such perceptual categories but did not treat them as if they were conceptually important, just as we often do not consider the differences between one kind of a chair and another as conceptually important.

These studies were all conducted using little objects, rather than the more commonly used pictorial stimuli. The sequential-touching task (sometimes called the object-manipulation task) was first used by Ricciutti (1965) to study infants' categorization of geometric forms. Infants below two years of age are too young to understand instructions to sort objects into piles representing categories, and relatively rarely make such separated groups spontaneously. Ricciutti put eight randomly presented objects from two categories in front of 1- to 2-year-olds. He observed how often they touched the objects from one category before touching the other, and how many objects in a category they touched in a row. These observations showed that infants systematically differentiated various kinds of forms. Later Nelson (1973) and Sugarman (1983) extended the use of this task to real-world categorical knowledge. Mandler, Fivush, and Reznick (1987) explored the statistical properties of the technique (for example, how often runs of touches to objects within a category occur by chance) so that categorization could be determined more precisely.[16] This technique works well but is too difficult for infants below about a year of age. So, a new technique to study categorization was needed. First Oakes, Madole, and Cohen (1991), then Mandler and McDonough (1993) adapted the object-examination task (Ruff, 1986), for this purpose. The task is a version of the traditional familiarization/preferential-looking task (such as used by Quinn & Eimas in their studies) but uses objects instead of pictures. Infants are given objects from one category one at a time for a given number of trials. Then two new objects are presented (usually sequentially), one of which is a new member from the same category used during familiarization and the other from a new category.

We used this technique to investigate conceptual categorization in 7- to 11-month-old infants (Mandler & McDonough, 1993). We found similar results to those we had obtained using the sequential-touching task with older infants. Infants in this age range consistently differentiated animals and vehicles, including birds and airplanes, all of whose exemplars had outstretched wings and were very similar in overall shape.[17] The infants did not differentiate dogs from fish or rabbits, however. On the other hand, there was consistent differentiation of the vehicle domain throughout this age range, with the infants treating cars,

---

[16] For the interested reader, the equation for chance run length given in the article is missing brackets around the denominator of the second term. In addition, a simpler form of the correct equation is $(2n - 1)/n$.

[17] The bird-airplane contrast was only used with 9- and 11-month-olds.

motorcycles, and airplanes as all different. McDonough and I recently extended this work to other categories. We find that by 9 months, infants differentiate furniture from both animals and vehicles, but even at 11 months, they are still not making any distinctions between chairs, tables, and beds. In addition, we tested 11-month-olds on plants and found that they differentiate plants from both animals and vehicles. Other studies that have found global categorization in infancy include Ross (1980), who showed that 12-month-olds distinguish food, animals, and furniture, even when the exemplars of these categories have little within-category perceptual similarity, and Golinkoff and Halperin (1983), who provided evidence for a global category of animals in an 8-month-old. In addition, Mandler et al. (1987), found categorization of kitchen and bathroom things in 14-month-olds (categories that have *no* perceptual similarity among the exemplars). In all of these studies, the infants examined objects instead of looking at pictures of objects. Thus, in several studies that have used objects as stimuli, infants as young as 7 months show that they have formed or are forming global domain-level categories of objects, in spite of great perceptual variability of their exemplars. When subcategories within these domains were tested in this way, less differentiation was found (except that at least in southern California, infants seem to be differentiating vehicles), suggesting that in the first year, infants are usually not conceptualizing domain subdivisions, even when they have perceptually categorized them.

In contrast, when looking at pictures is used, basic-level perceptual categories appear to precede global categorization, although this proposition has just begun to be tested. The Quinn and Eimas data discussed earlier show that 3-month-olds can form perceptual categories of several animal species. Behl-Chadha (in press) found that 3-month-olds can also discriminate chairs and tables when pictures are used, but she was unable to show that they differentiate the global categories of furniture and vehicles. The only global categorization found with young infants in picture studies has been for four-legged mammals (Behl-Chadha, in press); mammals are not a basic-level category, but the pictures she used had a good deal of perceptual similarity. In our laboratory, we have been unsuccessful in showing global categorization of animals, vehicles, furniture, or clothing when testing 11-month-olds with pictorial stimuli. Global categorization of animal pictures was also not found in 9- to 15-month-olds by Roberts and Cuff (1989).

Mandler and McDonough (1993) suggested that different processes are being measured in picture-looking and object-handling tasks. The conceptual system that guides attentive processing during object examination may not be fully engaged when young infants look at pictures. Infants certainly look at presented pictures, but they may do so shallowly, thus processing the perceptual information in the relatively unselective way characteristic of procedural processing (i.e., attention not being directed by conceptual interest). Richards and Casey (1992) point out that sustained attention occurs only some of the time when infants look at pictures, and so total fixation time is not very informative as to the types of cognitive activity taking place. In some cases, picture-looking experiments may not motivate infants greatly (although this is less likely to be true for very young infants). Manipulating objects, on the other hand, thoroughly engages infants of all ages; we never lose subjects through disinterest. Their full attention (and thus, I propose, their conceptual system) is engaged by the task. This view is supported by the analyses carried out by Ruff and her colleagues (Ruff, 1986; Ruff & Saltarelli, 1993). These investigators have shown that when objects are manipulated, examining measures a more active attentive process than does looking (see also Oakes & Tellinghuisen, 1994), and it is examining, not just looking, that is scored in the object-examination test. Thus, familiarization/preferential-looking tasks may measure different processes when pictures and objects are used, resulting in different data in the two cases. The differences illustrate the different kind of processes that are measured as a result of slight changes in method and slight differences in scoring. They also offer an object lesson in the difficulty of interpreting results from familiarization/preferential-looking tasks. The technique is one of our best tools for studying infant cognition, but the tool itself needs further analysis.

To summarize, very young infants engage in perceptual categorization, a process that relies on perceptual similarity. This means that they can categorize pictures at the basic level, and perhaps at the subordinate level as well, although the latter has not yet been tested. Superordinate (global) domains, on the other hand, typically show little within-class perceptual similarity: A lamp does not look much like a couch, or a turtle much like a bird. So unless perceptually similar members are chosen, perceptual categorization at this level is difficult. On the other hand, superordinate categorization can take place on the basis of meaning, even though exemplars do not look alike. In the early months, the meanings being associated with superordinate domains are very broad and general. Therefore, it is not surprising that global *conceptual* categories precede finer conceptual distinctions. Young infants in our culture typically have had little experience with different types of animals. At the same time, if they have observed any animals at all, they will have experienced the characteristics that differentiate animals as a global class from nonanimals, such as that they move on their own and interact with other objects from a distance (Mandler, 1992). This information characterizing the difference between animate and inanimate objects is abstract, but fundamental; as mentioned in *New Theories of Infant Representation,* the distinction between animate and inanimate is the last bit of information to disappear in cases of semantic dementia. Even for normal adults, it is easier to conceptualize how an animal differs from a piece of furniture than to conceptualize how a lion differs from a tiger. And of course, insofar as my argument is correct that to have a concept of dog *entails* the larger concept of animal, there is a logical sequence involved in the order of early concept formation as well.

These various differences between perceptual and conceptual categories illustrate the insufficiency of the widely held view that "basic-level" categories are the first to be formed (Mervis & Rosch, 1981). (I put this familiar term in quotes to indicate that we don't really know what it means.) Insofar as basic-level is understood as the categorization that occurs at a given level in a hierarchy of classes (the generic level of folk taxonomies; see Berlin, Breedlove, & Raven, 1973), the hypothesis that basic-level categories are the first to be formed has been shown by the various data discussed above to be incorrect; infants often form concepts at a more global level than the basic level. Rosch's own work (Rosch, Mervis, Gray, Johnson, & Boyes-Braem, 1976) showed that even college students do not treat the generic level as basic for the biological taxonomies from which the term was derived; instead, they tend to treat as "basic" the higher "life-form" level. Only some artifacts follow the principles Rosch described as appropriate for the basic level, and there is dispute even about some of these (e.g., Palmer, Jones, Hennessy, Unze, & Pick, 1989). Alternatively, insofar as the term is understood to mean the level of categorization in which within-category perceptual similarity is maximized and between-category similarity is minimized, no one has yet found a way to define such a level. Rosch et al. (1976) tried to use a criterion of cue validity, but cue validity has been shown to be highest at the most superordinate level rather than the basic level, and no other acceptable definition has been found (e.g., Medin, 1983; Murphy, 1982).

I have discussed the slippery status of the notion of basic-level elsewhere (Mandler, 1997). Here, I only summarize the difficulties this notion presents when characterizing early concept formation. Mervis and Rosch (1981) made it clear that the term was meant to refer to concepts and not just to perceptual categories. They claimed that basic-level categories are primary because they are more fundamental psychologically than categories at other levels, and that categorization at the level of the superordinate (global categorization) is a late development. When Rosch first proposed her theory, there was little developmental data specifically contrasting basic-level and superordinate categorization, and literally none on infants. Rosch et al. (1976) conducted two developmental experiments, but unfortunately, these did not constitute adequate tests of the hypothesis that basic-level concepts are the first to be formed, nor did they work with young enough subjects. The youngest children in their experiments were 3 years old, by which time a great deal of concept formation has already taken place.

One experiment used a sorting task in which children sorted items into either basic-level or superordinate categories of clothing, furniture, vehicles, and people. Even in the first grade, children had difficulty doing the superordinate task, which is a surprising finding. It appears that a strict criterion was used: Sorting was considered incorrect if a superordinate class was subdivided, even though the subjects were not told how many divisions to make. For example, if shoes and socks were put in one pile and shirts and pants in another pile, it would be scored as incorrect. Second, the task used a confounded design (Mandler et al., 1991). If one wishes to test whether basic-level classification is easier than superordinate classification, it is not appropriate to use sorting of, for example, dogs and cars as the basic-level classification, and contrast it with sorting of animals and vehicles. Dogs and cars are basic-level classes, but they also form a *superordinate* contrast. If children do well on this contrast, one can't tell whether they are using the basic-level or the superordinate information (or most likely both). To test ease of basic-level categorization, one must contrast dogs and rabbits, or cars and motorcycles. However, this kind of confounding of basic-level and superordinate information has characterized all the sorting tests in the literature (e.g., Saxby & Anglin, 1983), thus contributing to the belief that young children are confused about superordinate concepts. But as discussed above, young children find a true basic-level task (e.g., contrasting cars with trucks or dogs with rabbits) to be more difficult than a superordinate task contrasting animals and vehicles (Mandler et al., 1991). Using the sequential-touching measure as the precursor of sorting (Sugarman, 1983), we found a clearcut distinction being made between animals and vehicles at 1½ years, but few basic-level distinctions. Only when we used the standard confounded design, contrasting dogs with cars, did we find basic-level categorization at this age (Mandler & Bauer, 1988). For this reason, we prefer to call categories such as animals and vehicles global categories; if a superordinate such as animal is not yet divided into subcategories, it is not appropriate to speak of it as a superordinate class.

The other developmental experiment that Rosch et al. (1976) reported was a match-to-sample test with 3- and 4-year-olds, again studying superordinate versus basic-level contrasts. Children were shown a sample object and asked to choose which of two other objects was the same. Although performance was at ceiling by 4 years, the 3-year olds were roughly at chance on superordinate contrasts. This result is at variance with our data using much younger children (Bauer & Mandler, 1989a). We found a very high rate of superordinate match-to-sample in 1½- to 2½-year-olds. The poor performance of Rosch et al.'s subjects may have been due to lack of precise understanding of the instructions or to the type of pretraining procedure that was used. Match-to-sample tests have typically used pretraining that emphasizes the importance of perceptual similarity (Fenson, Cameron, & Kennedy, 1988). As Deak and Bauer (1995) have shown, this kind of instruction produces more perceptual matching than does instruction which specifies that the child is to find the same kind of thing.

Other tests of the hypothesis that basic-level concepts are primary consist of various linguistic measures, mainly dealing with the greater frequency of basic-level than superordinate terms in both children's and adults' language (Rosch et al., 1976). Indeed, the only clear evidence for a privileged level of concepts is lexical in nature. Basic-level names *are* used more frequently than superordinates in daily speech and in speech to children. This is the main reason, of course, why they are the first names children learn, since they can only learn the language they hear. As Brown (1958) noted long ago, however, the fact that basic-level names are the first to be learned does not tell us what the underlying conceptual system onto which they are mapped is like. He in fact suggested that it was likely that this underlying conceptual system was more global in nature than the vocabulary being learned to refer to it, a view

supported by the many overextensions in comprehension (Behrend, 1988; McDonough, 1977b). Interestingly, the notion that earlier formed concepts tend to be less differentiated than later ones was the dominant developmental view of that time, influenced, I believe, by Werner's (1957) orthogenetic principle that development proceeds from a state of relative globality to a state of increasing differentiation and articulation.

Rosch was sensitive to the difficulties I have outlined in giving a developmental interpretation to her data, because she later noted that the principles of categorization she espoused had to do with explaining categories coded by the language of a given culture, and did not constitute a theory of development (Rosch, 1978). Yet both Mervis and Rosch (1981) and Mervis and Mervis (1982) have also claimed that basic-level categories are the first to be acquired, and by this they do *not* mean culturally or developmentally variable concepts, but rather, a specific kind of concept, such as chair or bird (i.e., objects that have overall similar shapes, elicit similar motor patterns, and so forth, as tested in Rosch et al., 1976). This is also the interpretation that has come to be the dominant view in developmental psychology. The position is often modified by the qualification that children's basic-level categories differ from adult basic-level categories (Mervis & Mervis, 1982), but this only complicates the issue because then there are *no* criteria to delimit the term. In any case, the tension remains between Rosch's claim that the theory deals with linguistically coded categorization and the view that it speaks to the foundations of concept formation itself.

As soon as prelinguistic categorization is studied, the ambiguity about the theoretical status of basic-level categories becomes obvious. If basic-level categories are the first to be formed, does this mean they are only perceptual in nature after all? Although Rosch and her colleagues meant basic-level to refer to concepts, they did not make any distinction between conceptual and perceptual categories, so they could and did use primarily perceptual tasks to test their theory (Rosch et al., 1976). Even though most of these tests failed for the biological categories of animals and plants (see Mandler, 1997), it might be that what they were describing was some important level of perceptual categorization, for example, some level of abstraction at which it is easiest to form a perceptual prototype. However, it must be stressed that this possibility has never been addressed. To date, we simply have no information as to whether infants find subordinate perceptual categories (e.g., collies vs. dachshunds) easier or more difficult than the so-called basic-level categories (e.g., horses and zebras) that have been studied (Eimas & Quinn, 1994).

Inductive Generalization

Of the various differences between perceptual and conceptual categories, probably the most important is what they are used for. Because perceptual categories (perceptual schemas) tell us what things look like, we use them to recognize the objects and events around us. Conceptual categories, or concepts, on the other hand, represent the meaning of the objects and events that we see. One of their main functions is to enable inductive generalization, thus allowing a wide range of knowledge to be acquired from a limited set of observations. Although objects are perceptually categorized on the basis of their physical similarity, this is not the basis for generalizations about them. We generalize based on similarity of kind. As adults, we make inductive inferences about the characteristics a new object will have on the basis of our beliefs about what kind of thing it is. The role that perceptual similarity plays in this process is to help us determine if two things are of the same kind. The more two things look alike, the more likely they are to be the same kind. Even if two objects look alike, however, if for any reason we think they belong to two different kinds, no generalization from one to the other will take place.

The traditional view of inductive generalization in infancy gives a different account. The earliest inductions have been assumed to rest on perceptual similarity alone. As discussed in the previous section, infants have been said to form perceptually-based categories such as dogs and cats, and then to associate various properties with these categories. Superordinate-level inductions, such as generalizations about animals as a domain, have been considered to be more abstract and assumed to be a later achievement. Thus, the traditional doctrine is that the first inferences are *not* based on a conceptual system of kinds, but instead are generalizations based on innate responsivity to physical similarity. Physical similarity itself is described in terms of sensory qualities such as color, shape, and texture that can be directly perceived without being mediated by a conceptual system (Quine, 1977). According to this doctrine, which Keil (1991) has dubbed the doctrine of "original sim," before children develop abstract concepts or theories about the world, they are only influenced by the laws of similarity; they make associations and generalizations on the basis of what things look like. The more two things resemble each other, the more likely it is that an inductive inference from the properties of one to the other will be made. For example, an infant sees a cat eat, and from this observation (or several such observations) induces the generalization that all cats eat. Thus, in this view, induction of properties first takes place at the basic level, because of the high degree of within-category similarity at this level. With more experience, generalization gradually begins to occur at a more abstract level: Cats eat, fish eat, birds eat; perhaps, even though they have different shapes, texture, and movements, all animals eat. (Notice that there is nothing in this account to provide a stop rule at the animal boundary, since the concept of animal itself is said to arrive from these generalizations.)

Surprisingly, given a goodly amount of theoretical speculation, until recently there has been almost no research on when infants first begin to make inductive generalizations or the basis on which they do so. We have seen that before a year of age, infants have already formed concepts of animals, vehicles, and plants but we do not know exactly what these concepts consist of or whether they serve the same inductive functions that concepts do for older children and adults. They certainly do not have the advantage of high perceptual within-class similarity. They might also be too unstable or have boundaries too hazy to provide an adequate foundation for generalization. In this respect, they might be closer to what Piaget (1951) called preconcepts. Although the data base is slim, Baldwin, Markman, and Melartin (1993) showed that 9-month-olds assume that a new example of a toy (identical except for color or surface pattern) will have the same function as a previously explored toy. But these generalizations might be tied to specific objects (e.g., a comb or a pair of castanets). Presumably from an early age, babies learn to expect a comb or any other object that differs only in color to serve previously learned functions. Of greater interest for understanding induction are data by Bauer and Dow (1994) showing that 16- and 20-month-olds will generalize the props used in event sequences to different members of the same class; for example, at these ages, children will use Big Bird and a toy bed to reproduce an event sequence in which a teddy bear had been put in a toy crib. This study in particular suggests that by 16 months, infants have associated certain behaviors such as sleeping with fairly broad classes.

Aside from these few studies, research specifically designed to study how category knowledge limits induction has almost all been conducted with older children. The youngest age at which the extent of inductive generalization has been tested is 2½ years (Gelman & Coley, 1990), and most work on induction has been conducted with children 3 years or older (e.g., Gelman & Markman, 1986). Not surprisingly, these studies all involve verbal information. For example, children are told some fact about an object and are then asked to decide the categorical range over which the taught property is valid (Carey, 1985; Gelman & O'Reilley, 1988). To extend this kind of work to preverbal children, McDonough and I have been using imitation to explore the breadth of the categories that 1-year-olds use to constrain their inductions. Using little models of objects, we demonstrate a property or action characteristic of a given class (such as drinking from a cup) and then test whether the infants will generalize that action to other exemplars from the same class and/or those of a different class. For example, we model a dog drinking from a cup and then give the cup, a bird, and an airplane to the infants and see whether they will imitate and if so, which object they choose for their imitation. This technique tells us where the boundaries of various conceptual categories lie and the sorts of generalizations infants are willing to make about them. In several experiments (Mandler & McDonough, 1996a), we have shown that in their imitations, 14-month-olds generalize the properties of drinking and sleeping to all members of the animal domain and rarely to members of the vehicle domain. Similarly, they generalize the properties of being opened with a key or giving a ride to all members of the vehicle domain, but rarely to members of the animal domain. They do so for new exemplars as well as for familiar ones. Ongoing work indicates that the same results obtain for 11-month-olds and for some 9-month-olds.

In this work, we have found no effect of perceptual similarity. Only the domain boundaries of animal and vehicle constrain the inductions; infants do not restrict their inductions to the basic-level classes they have observed engage in the particular behavior, instead, they generalize across the entire domain. Interestingly, at least one of the properties we tested, using a key, is a basic-level property and not a domain-wide property, in the sense that infants would only see a key used with cars. Thus, some of the generalizations the infants make, such as that fish drink or that an airplane is opened with a key, will later have to be narrowed down to the appropriate basic-level classes. Indeed, our most recent work on this topic (McDonough & Mandler, 1997) suggests that 14-month-olds have not yet associated any specific properties with basic-level classes. For example, when we

model drinking from a teacup they generalize this to pots as well as coffee mugs, and when we model putting a baby to sleep in a crib, they generalize sleeping to bathtubs as well as beds. Not until 18 months do we find that infants begin to narrow their generalizations to basic-level classes. These findings are another indication of the broad, global nature of early conceptual understanding.

The lack of influence of similarity on infants' generalizations may seem surprising, given that research on both children and adults has generally indicated that similarity between trained and test exemplars plays at least some role in making inductions (Carey, 1985; Gelman, 1988). Similarity is usually assumed to be the reason that people make the most inductive generalizations at the subordinate level, next most at the basic-level, and the least at the superordinate level. However, similarity of exemplars is naturally confounded with height in a taxonomic tree. In general, the lower (narrower) the subclass, the more perceptually similar its members. This confounding makes it difficult to know which is the controlling factor. There is some evidence that it may not be similarity per se. Gelman (1988) examined the ratings of similarity *within* the basic-level classes she used in her study. No relationship was found between similarity of exemplars within a given basic-level class and inferences in natural kinds (although a small relationship was found for artifact categories). This finding suggests that it may be the breadth of the conceptual class that is more important in controlling induction—even for preschool children—than the similarity of the exemplars. Smaller classes may be more conducive to induction, not because their members look alike, but because there is less conceptual variation associated with them.

As we saw in the last section, infants up to the middle of the second year are not particularly sensitive to the overall perceptual similarity of one object to another when forming a concept. Since they do not rely on overall perceptual similarity for the conceptual distinctions they do make, we should not be surprised that they do not use this factor when making inductions either. Instead, the data suggest that in infancy, conceptual kind is the main factor controlling the limits on inductive generalization, with infants being, if anything, *less* influenced by similarity than are adults. The value of similarity of appearance is it indicates that two things are the same kind. The more conceptual distinctions one has made in a domain, the more useful perceptual similarity is in determining the smallest class, which in turn is useful for purposes of inductive certainty. If one has made few, if any, conceptual subdivisions in a large and variable domain such as animals, then perceptual similarity of one exemplar to another may be of little use.

Given the small amount of work carried out on preverbal induction, it is not surprising that we have no empirical information about the status of the knowledge involved. Theoretically, because the inductive inferences that have been studied involve explicit conceptual knowledge, the inferences themselves should be explicit as well. However, no direct evidence for this view is available at this time. The most we can say is that the work on induction is a powerful indication that early conceptual categories are very different in kind from the perceptual categories that traditionally have been assumed to underlie their formation.

Prelinguistic Meanings

Unfortunately, little is known about the interface between cognitive and linguistic functioning. Due in part to the Piagetian legacy, there has been a largely unremarked conflict between the age at which language begins and the view that conceptual functioning has a late onset. Most psycholinguists assume that language is mapped onto an existing conceptual system. But according to Piaget, 1-year-olds do not yet have a viable conceptual system. How is it, then, that they can learn language? This gap in Piaget's theory has been troublesome over the years. Psycholinguists who were concerned about the relation between cognition and the onset of language used such descriptions as were available to characterize the knowledge base of the young language learner. By default, these tended to be descriptions of sensorimotor schemas, not conceptual descriptions (e.g., Edwards, 1973). Uzgiris and Hunt's (1975) sensorimotor scales were often used as guides, but these are a mixture of sensorimotor and conceptual functioning, with early items tending to be sensorimotor and later items combining both sensorimotor and conceptual processes. Much of the work that went into relating language acquisition to prior cognitive development used these scales for correlational purposes, without a clear analysis of which items reflect perceptual and motor skills and which reflect a conceptual form of representation. Items were typically described as Stage 5 or Stage 6 without specifying their conceptual status more exactly. As a result, with a few exceptions (e.g., Gopnik & Meltzoff, 1987), statements about the concepts onto which language is mapped were often vague, and it was not clear exactly which linguistic function each of the separate scales was to support. Not surprisingly, then, this line of research did not turn out to be very informative (Bates, Thal, & Marchman, 1991; Bloom, Lifter, & Broughton, 1985).

In any case, this research rested on an unclear assumption. As Piaget (1951) had pointed out, language cannot be mapped onto a purely sensorimotor base, bypassing the development of a symbolic function. Sensorimotor schemas are structures controlling perception and action, not meanings to be used to interpret words. This is most obvious in the case of relational meanings and syntactical forms (the latter also being relational in character). The following example illustrates the difficulty. Two of the earliest grammatical morphemes to be learned in English are the prepositions *in* and *on*. What are the preverbal meanings the child uses to understand these prepositions during their acquisition? Assume for the sake of argument that the child has no concepts of containment, contact, or support, only sensorimotor schemas controlling actions such as pouring liquid into a container or putting an object on a surface. These schemas undoubtedly take into account information about containment and so forth, in that they monitor whether a container is filling up or an object is making contact with a surface with the right amount of force. But these are continuous and context-bound parameters and not relationships that have been isolated from the particulars of the stream of action and generalized as movable units applicable to other situations. Unless the child has analyzed these notions as units, separable from the particular context in which they are instantiated, there cannot be said to be a symbolic, or semiotic, function onto which the linguistic expressions can be mapped.

Thus, sensorimotor knowledge is not a sufficient base for much of language learning, even though the perceptual schemas built up during infancy seem to be adequate to support the ostensive learning of object names (Hall & Waxman, 1993). For language as a whole, however, an analog-digital interface is needed between sensorimotor activity, with its continuously changing dynamic parameters, and the discrete propositional system of language. There are at least two characteristics such an interface should have (Mandler, 1994): First, it should simplify and summarize the generalizable aspects of preverbal experiences, which are rich in individual detail. Not only must language squeeze meanings into small packages, but manageable preverbal meanings are also needed to carry out the kinds of concept formation and inductive generalization described in the previous sections; infants do not wait for language to begin to think. Second, the interface should be in a form onto which a discrete symbolic system can be mapped. A common assumption about this second criterion is that to meet it requires positing a propositional language of thought (Fodor, 1975), but as illustrated in the previous sections, propositional representation is not necessary to describe either concept formation or linguistic rules. Indeed, it may be that propositional representation does not exist in the human mind until language itself is learned.

One of the serendipitous aspects of an account of preverbal meanings in terms of image-schemas is that this form of representation can be used not only for concept formation, but also as the interface, or symbolic base, onto which language is mapped. For example, Brown's (1973) analyses of early language showed that children are relying on concepts of agents and patients, ongoing and completed actions, location, possession, plurality, and a variety of relations such as support and containment, and object disappearance and reappearance. Although all of these notions have often been described as sensorimotor understandings, they are more accurately described in anyone's theory as conceptual descriptions of types of action on objects and the spatial relations that obtain among objects. All of them are describable in image-schema terms (Mandler, 1992, 1994). More specific kinds of action (such as the difference between falling and climbing) are describable in image-schema terms as well (Golinkoff, Hirsh-Pasek, Mervis, Frawley, & Parillo, 1995), and Tomasello (1992) shows how such image-schemas can account for early verb acquisition.

Slobin (1985) describes a prototypical manipulative scene known to preverbal infants everywhere, in which an animate agent acts on another object. This scene is marked grammatically in various ways by the languages of the world, but all of them are learnable because each expresses the underlying meaning involved in an animate object acting causally on another object. Slobin (1985) notes that the grammatical markings that languages use to characterize this kind of transitive verb phrase are universally one of the earliest grammatical distinctions that children learn. Interestingly, transitive marking is often underextended at first, used only when the child is talking about an animate agent physically acting on an inanimate object—that is, the prototypical *agency* image-schema. As another example of a close relation between preverbal image-schemas and early grammar, I have suggested that image-schemas of *self-motion* and *caused-motion* are part of the preverbal concepts that differentiate animals from inanimate objects (Mandler, 1992). Consistent with this view, Choi and Bowerman (1991) have shown that Korean children, whose language differentially marks causative

verbs and verbs of self-motion, learn this distinction early and errorlessly.

Slobin (1985) suggests that because infants universally develop a set of preverbal conceptual notions such as the manipulative scene, they will all begin to learn language with a single set of assumptions about the structure of language. These assumptions, which he calls a universal child grammar, will match to a greater or lesser degree the particular native language to be learned. The degree of match can be used to predict the relative ease of mapping the grammatical constructions of the given language onto the underlying cognitive structures of the learner. Bowerman (1989), on the other hand, calls this view into question. Although she has been one of the major proponents of the view that underlying concepts determine language learning (Bowerman, 1987), she has suggested more recently that language itself structures the concepts that it expresses (Bowerman, 1989, 1993). In this view, learning language may not involve mapping linguistic forms onto preexisting concepts so much as it involves creating new concepts, or at least providing the major cognitive structuring for various relations.

These opposing views can be illustrated with the case of learning morphemes to express containment and support relations. As Brown (1973) and others have documented, *in* and *on* are early grammatical acquisitions in English. They are also learned virtually without error (Clark, 1977). I have suggested that one of the reasons for this errorless learning is that the meanings of these relational terms are given preverbally by image-schemas of containment and support (Mandler, 1992). Given that knowledge about these relations begins to be acquired by 3 months of age (Baillargeon et al., 1995), I would expect extensive image-schematic analyses to have been carried out in the succeeding 12 to 15 months before the first words for these relations are learned. That is, I assume that much of the work needed to map these kinds of spatial relations onto language has already been done. As mentioned earlier, in Baillargeon et al.'s (1995) analyses of support, the earliest form of knowledge about this relation seems to involve a binary distinction between contact and no contact, and somewhat later, another binary distinction between overlap or nonoverlap of surfaces. Only later in the first year do infants begin to understand something about the amount of overlap required if a support relation is to obtain. It may be that the early binary distinctions form the fundamental core of the *concept* of support. If so, then the young language learner does not have to consider countless hypotheses when attempting to understand sentences containing a preposition such as *on,* because the relevant meanings will already have been formed.

However, as Bowerman (1989) points out, languages vary as to how they express containment and support, including not only whether contact is to be specified, but also such distinctions as the horizontality or verticality of the surface involved.[18] For example, Spanish uses the single morpheme *en* to express both the *in* and *on* of English. German, on the other hand, makes the *in* versus *on* distinction, but divides *on* into two morphemes, depending on whether the supporting surface is horizontal or vertical. Dutch does something similar, except the division of *on* into two kinds (*op* and *aan*) seems to distinguish between an object being at rest when it is supported *(op)* versus requiring some kind of force or attachment for the support to be maintained *(aan)* (Bowerman, 1996). Korean uses still another three-way split (Choi & Bowerman, 1991). It uses two different morphemes (in this case, verbs rather than prepositions) for "putting in" and "putting on" when the action results in a loose, separable relation, but a single morpheme for something fitting tightly, whether that action results in "fitting tightly in" or "fitting tightly on." For example, the same verb is used to express the action of putting a glove on a hand or a hand in a glove. In this way, the language emphasizes the tightness of the fit itself rather than emphasizing one of the two parts of the enclosing/being enclosed relation. Because Korean children learn the verbs expressing loose and tight fit as early as English-speaking children learn *in* and *on,* Choi and Bowerman (1991) suggest that language is teaching (or perhaps, guiding the acquisition of) these varying concepts rather than being mapped onto a single set of underlying primitives.

Their point that the English form of these relations has no special status vis-á-vis conceptual primitives is well taken. However, the fact that there is more than one way to express various spatial relations does not mean that language itself is teaching relations previously unanalyzed by the language learner. Because English ignores the nature of the fit between the container and the contained does not mean that preverbal children have not noticed and analyzed differences between, say, a sweater fitting tightly or loosely over their heads or the difference between pop-beads that fit together tightly and ones that no longer stay together.

---

[18] The horizontal versus vertical aspect of support has not yet been studied in infancy, so we have no evidence as to whether young babies make this distinction.

(English-speaking children do not express these notions in the one-word stage, of course, because their language does not have single words for them.) Rather, it seems more likely that different languages teach children different ways to express what they have already noticed through perceptual analysis. Choi, Bowerman, McDonough, and I have recently begun to investigate this issue. We find that English- and Korean-speaking children begin to be responsive to terms for containment and support by about 18 months, and respond appropriately to the distinctions their own language makes, with English-speaking children categorizing in- and on-relations and Korean-speaking children categorizing loose- and tight-fitting relations (McDonough, Choi, Bowerman, & Mandler, in press). We have also begun to study how preverbal children respond to these same distinctions nonlinguistically. So far, we have found that between 9 and 14 months of age, infants of English-speaking parents gradually become sensitive to the distinction between loose support and tight containment, but we have yet to test the full set of distinctions the two languages make (McDonough et al., in press).

These preverbal results are preliminary, but they suggest that there may be a universal set of relational concepts that infants everywhere have analyzed before learning language. Bowerman's (1989) analyses indicate that this set is larger than that expressed in any given language. However, given the propensity for all languages to choose among a few binary or trinary distinctions for grammatical relations, the set need not be impossibly large. Fine-grained error analyses should show the extent to which a given language matches this set of preverbal conceptual distinctions, or adds new distinctions that are rarely achieved by preverbal children. For example, Bowerman (1993) reports that Dutch children have difficulty with the relatively unusual distinction that *aan* makes, and are more apt to overgeneralize *op* to cases in which adults use *aan* than the other way around. It appears that *op* expresses a more basic or earlier analyzed aspect of support. Similarly, Choi and Bowerman's (1991) analyses of overextensions in Korean children's early uses of the verb for tight-fitting suggest that the preverbal concept is broader in scope than the language will accept. The overextensions suggest that, for the preverbal child, a notion of tight-fitting includes putting clothes on tightly over the head and sticking flat magnets to a refrigerator door. Korean differentiates clothes from other objects and also reserves the verb for tight-fitting for three-dimensional objects that fit together tightly in a mutual way. These restrictions may not be part of the preverbal concept; hence, early errors occur.

I have suggested in this discussion that the concepts onto which the relational aspects of language are mapped are the result of preverbal analysis. Exactly which analyses take place before language begins to be understood and which are stimulated by language itself has yet to be determined. This is an area ripe for research. In the interim, a good guiding assumption is that the increasing sophistication in understanding object relations that occurs over the first year (Baillargeon et al., 1995) is accompanied by increasing amounts of perceptual analysis, which in turn result in a store of image-schemas representing these relations. As discussed in *New Theories of Infant Representation,* these image-schemas themselves are implicit and not accessible. However, they structure the conceptual system which *is* accessible either through imagery or language. Thus, they provide a layer of representation that acts as a kind of analog-digital transformation, mediating between sensorimotor processes and language.

Representation and Memory for Events

The accessibility of conceptual information via images and words brings us to the last topic, which is the representation of events and the extent to which memories of events are accessible in infancy. Some form of memory is operative at least from birth, since all learning requires storage of information. For example, operant conditioning is one of the most basic organismic capacities, yet it requires memory for temporal sequence. Two-month-olds can learn an operantly conditioned foot-kicking response and retain it over quite long periods of time (Rovee-Collier, 1989). Young infants also learn longer temporal sequences. For example, Smith (1984) showed 5-month-olds a picture that moved successively to each of four locations (e.g., 1 3 1 3 4 2 4 2). She tested what the infants had learned about the sequence by stopping it at various points and recording whether the infants' eyes moved to the next location. Using this technique, she was able to show that they could learn such sequential patterns in as few as 6 trials. Haith et al. (1988) also showed temporal anticipation (albeit using simpler sequences) from as early as 3 months of age.

What kind of memory is this? Smith (1984) claimed that her infants were recalling temporal order. Similarly, Rovee-Collier called the kicking her infants did to a trained stimulus after a delay, cued recall (Mandler, 1990, discussants' comments, p. 514). What Rovee-Collier (1989) actually showed was that an extinguished conditioned foot-kicking response can be reinstated by a brief re-exposure to the learning context. It is this reinstatement phenomenon

(originally studied in rats; Campbell, 1984) that Rovee-Collier calls cued recall. However, most people define recall as the bringing of past events to awareness, and neither conditioned expectations nor conditioned footkicking require such an ability. The retention of conditioned responses is among the most basic characteristics of organisms and, because it occurs even in the lowly flatworm, it cannot *require* higher-order processes such as conscious awareness. Of course, human infants are not simple organisms and they *might* be able to recall past episodes of kicking in the presence of the reinstatement cue, but it is not necessary for them to do so for a conditioned response to occur.

Similar comments can be made about recognition memory experiments in infancy. In adult recognition experiments, subjects are asked to make a conscious judgment as to whether or not they have seen a given item before. Such awareness is taken to be a different state from priming by previously presented items, which can occur in the absence of conscious awareness of their having been seen. Thus, amnesics show normal priming, even though they are not aware they have seen the material before (Warrington & Weiskrantz, 1974). Obviously babies cannot be asked questions, so habituation/dishabituation methods are used instead. However, this technique is the infant equivalent of an adult priming study, not an adult recognition memory study. The fact that babies respond differently to previously presented material than to new material shows that information has been stored, but there is no evidence for awareness of the past experiences. For this reason, I have suggested calling infant recognition memory primitive recognition, to avoid any implications of conscious, declarative memory of the past (Mandler, 1984). Again, babies *may* be consciously aware that they have seen something before or aware that it looks familiar, but since explicit remembering is not required to account for dishabituation, we should not assume that they are.

On the other hand, there is evidence for recall of events happening in the first year of life. Not surprisingly, this evidence is rarely verbal. However, Myers, Clifton, and Clarkson (1987) were able to show verbal recall in one 3-year-old child of a laboratory procedure he had participated in over a period of months from 3 to 9 months of age. The child correctly reported a picture that had been used in the procedure (a whale), even though this word had not been in his vocabulary at the time of the laboratory visits. Although this study provides a kind of existence proof for recall of events occurring at an early age, verbal recall of events taking place before a year of age is a rarity. To study the phenomenon systematically, nonverbal methods are needed. To feel confident that these methods are tapping recall, several criteria should be met (Mandler, 1990; Mandler & McDonough, 1996b). These include making sure that performance is not due to previously conditioned responses or to primitive recognition. The goal is to create a situation in which memory of the past is required, yet cannot be accounted for by sensorimotor procedures. There have been only two techniques used to study recall in preverbal infants that meet these criteria. The first of these is to have infants watch an object hidden in an unfamiliar place and find it after a delay. The second is deferred imitation, in which infants watch a new event and reproduce it after a delay. In both cases, the infant has not learned a perceptual or motor habit but instead must call upon a representation of an object or actions that can no longer be perceived.

Object-hiding tests have been used primarily to check if 6-month-olds will search for an object that has just been covered (Harris, 1987; Piaget, 1954). The technique is appropriate for studying longer-term recall, but the hiding test has mainly been used to study the development of object permanence, and its bearing on recall was a side issue; similarly for the A-not-B test, in which an object is repeatedly hidden at location A and then hidden at location B. Infants' persistent failure on this test was one of Piaget's main sources of evidence for the conclusion that up to a year of age, they have not yet formed an adequate object concept. Although recall failure was considered as one possible explanation for the errors, it gradually became obvious that the test is not a good method of studying recall. In this test, conditioned expectations are established that the object will be hidden at location A, and conditioned reaching to A is established as well. When the object is then hidden at B, if the infant reaches to A it is difficult to isolate the cause of the error. Diamond (1985, 1990) has speculated that the difficulty is due to inability to inhibit an established reaching response. Baillargeon (1993) suggests instead that once a solution has been computed to a problem, people—at all ages—tend to continue to use it whenever possible, thus leading to capture errors (Reason, 1979).[19] It could also be that the difficulty is due to the proactive inhibition that builds up in highly similar repetitive tasks. The point is, that to study whether an infant is

capable of recalling an absent object, it is advisable to use a simpler situation, not one in which so many variables come into play. Indeed, the simple object-hiding task that Piaget used with 6- to 8-month-olds would seem to be much better, but it has not yet been used systematically to study the parameters of long-term recall.

Hood and Willatts (1986) showed that 5-month-olds will reach to an object that disappears from sight, but this finding involves immediate memory. In our laboratory, we find that 7-month-olds will reach to the location where they have watched an object being hidden after delays of 90 secs (McDonough, 1997a). The memory is fragile, however; the infants begin to fail if they are removed from the room during the delay. In addition, it is not possible from this kind of design to tell exactly what has been represented; it might be the object itself or only an interesting location. It may be noted, however, that since 7-month-olds can find a hidden object after a 90 sec delay, failure on the A-not-B test, which occurs with delays as short as 2 secs, is highly unlikely to be due to inability to maintain and access a representation in memory.

The second method of studying preverbal recall is deferred imitation. The advantage of this method over hiding tasks is that when an infant reproduces the particulars of an event, we have a more detailed record of what has been recalled. When Piaget (1952) observed imitation after a delay, he considered it to be an indication that a conceptual system had been formed. For example, he described Jacqueline, at 16 months, watching a visiting child display a temper tantrum (an event that was apparently new to her) and the next day playfully reproducing the actions the child had performed. Since the event was new and she had only watched it happen, he concluded that the only way she could have reproduced it was to maintain a representation of the event that she could access. Meltzoff (1985, 1988a, 1988b) was the first to adapt this technique for laboratory use in studying the recall function. He showed that as young as 9 months of age, infants can reproduce (recall), after a 24-hr delay, novel actions they have observed only once. He also showed that 14-month-olds can reproduce novel actions after a week's delay. Using the same technique, McDonough and Mandler (1994) showed that 11-month-olds who observed a number of unusual events could reproduce one of them after a year's delay.

These experiments all involved memory for single actions. Other experiments have shown recall of multi-step event sequences, also after extensive delays. The value of using longer event sequences is not only that they seem more comparable to the kinds of recall of the past that

[19] These are the errors that occur when you try to break an established set; for example, when you plan to do something new, but find yourself executing a habitual response instead.

adults engage in, but also because the ability to reproduce a string of actions from a single observation is particularly convincing evidence that recall (as opposed to implicit processing) is taking place. Sensorimotor learning is a slow chaining process, usually requiring several trials before each action in a sequence leads to performance of the next. In the case of imitation of a sequence seen only once, there is no known process other than recall that can be used to determine the next action to perform. Bauer and Shore (1987) and Bauer and Mandler (1989b) showed that 16- and 20-month-olds could reproduce two- and three-step event sequences after delays of up to six weeks. Mandler and McDonough (1995) modelled two-step sequences for 11-month-olds, and found they could reproduce some of them after 24 hours and also three months later. Bauer, Hertsgaard, and Dow (1994) showed some recall of two-step sequences presented to 13.5-month-olds eight months later. Recently, Carver (1995) has shown that if 9-month-olds are given several presentations of two-step sequences (without being allowed to reproduce them), about half of the infants could reproduce at least one of them a month later.

One aspect of these early recall protocols is notable, and that is that at least some of the same organizational factors that affect adult recall are operative at this early age. Several studies have shown that the ease of reproducing event sequences in the first two years is governed by the structure of the event sequence itself (Bauer & Mandler, 1989b; Bauer & Travis, 1993; Mandler & McDonough, 1995). As soon as infants can reproduce a string of actions, they find it easier to do so when the actions are related causally (or by enabling relations) than when the order of the actions is arbitrary. For example, it is easier for 11-month-olds to remember how to make a rattle, in which the sequence must be performed in a given order if the goal is to be attained, than to remember an arbitrary sequence such as placing a hat on a bunny and feeding it a carrot (Mandler & McDonough, 1995). One might suspect this kind of finding to be artifactual, in the sense that infants might be able to deduce what needs to be done from memory for the goal alone, thus reducing the amount that needs to be remembered. However, Bauer (1992) has shown that this is not the case. Even 2-year-olds cannot produce these sequences when they are only shown the goal; they must be shown the steps along the way and recall them. Thus, even for preverbal infants, better recall results from better organization of the events in memory, a phenomenon long known to be true for recall of

older children (Slackman, Hudson, & Fivush, 1986) and adults (G. Mandler, 1967; Mandler, 1986).

None of the long-term recall experiments with infants provide any evidence for spatio-temporal dating of these memories. Indeed, it seems intuitively unlikely that these early episodes of recall are accompanied by awareness of when and where the events in question took place. Of course, the recall process does not require such spatio-temporal dating. It is a not uncommon occurrence even in adulthood to remember an event without being able to say when or where it happened. (It must also be said our intuitions are probably not a reliable guide in interpreting the experiences of preverbal children.) By age 2, verbal recall protocols such as those collected by Nelson and Ross (1980) suggest some possible awareness of when and where the events being recalled happened. Unfortunately, this issue has not been specifically addressed, so there is little precise information available. For example, in Fivush's studies of long-term recall during the preschool period, parents (or other interviewers) usually provide extensive information about the context and other details during the child's recall, making it difficult to know if the child independently remembers when and where the events took place (Fivush, Gray, & Fromhoff, 1987; Fivush & Hamond, 1990). A theory is needed of the cognitive abilities required to place remembered events within a spatiotemporal frame. Without such a theory, this particular aspect of recall in infancy must remain an open question.

We also do not know whether these early recall memories are autobiographical. When infants return to the laboratory after a long delay and spontaneously reproduce an event sequence they have seen, they may or may not remember that they themselves have performed these acts before. It may only be that they know what to do. This situation is comparable to that in which we as adults are asked a factual question to which we know the answer. I know that Paris is the capital of France, but I have no memory for the occasion on which I learned this fact. The information is declarative and it is explicitly brought to mind when the question is asked, but it is not an autobiographical memory. Thus, even if infants are only reminded what to do, rather than remembering they have done it themselves before, this is evidence for recall and should not be considered problematic (cf. Nelson, 1994).

Whether these early memories are autobiographical, they pass the criteria discussed earlier for assessing declarative knowledge by nonverbal means (Mandler & McDonough, 1996b). Since there can be no direct test of conscious awareness, it appears that we must rely upon theoretical and empirical consistency. For example, McDonough, Mandler, McKee, and Squire (1995) showed that amnesic patients cannot reproduce after only 24 hours the kinds of simple event sequences that infants can reproduce after a delay of several months. The logic of this approach is to assume the premise that recall requires awareness, and then to show that without such awareness, recall in the form of reproduction of observed events can no more happen than can verbal report. I take it as having been demonstrated by the amnesic and the infant data, then, that recall can occur at least by 9 months of age. This kind of memory is quintessentially declarative and is one more piece of evidence for the early development of an accessible conceptual system.

CONCLUSIONS

The preceding sections have covered an array of procedural and declarative knowledge in infancy. There are other examples, although many are less studied in this young age range, such as the representation of other minds. More generally, the issue of how infants represent human interactions (as opposed to merely engaging in them) has not figured strongly in this review, in part because of a lesser body of information on the topic in infancy, but also because I have concentrated on how infants come to represent the physical world. I should add that I found little need to mention the effects of culture on this kind of learning. Cultural influences will obviously become important in determining how children think, perhaps increasingly so as language begins to be learned. Nevertheless, the foundations of thought are built before parents or culture have much chance to play a formative role. The most fundamental issues are not what kinds of things are to be eaten but what food and eating mean; not what kinds of animals and artifacts surround one, but what animals and artifacts are; not what language is to be learned, but that language expresses meaning. Most of the functions I have discussed are the universal precursors to cultural understanding.

We have seen that conceptual representations in a number of domains begin at an early age and develop in parallel with the more familiar sensorimotor processes of infancy. The message that repeatedly comes through the types of knowledge reviewed here is that babies think. The fact that babies think raises profound issues of the form of representation that enables them to do so. I suggested that the

medium for conceptual representation, although unlikely to be subsymbolic or connectionist-like, is equally unlikely to be language-like, insofar as that implies a propositional form of representation. Perhaps I should have said instead that we have no reason to assume that early conceptual representation is language-like. Our views of representation have been strongly influenced by the philosophical community, which in turn tends to be highly linguistically oriented. Since most psychologists working on these issues study adults, they often do not notice this linguistic bias. But infants have not yet learned to speak and there is no basis for assuming that they have inherited or learned a symbol system that bears any resemblance to language during the preverbal period.

I proposed instead that infants might first develop and use an analogical form of representation for purposes of thought. Cognitive linguists have shown that in principle, an image-schema kind of representation constitutes an adequate underpinning for language, so we are not obligated to assume that preverbal infants operate with a language-like conceptual system. In addition, one of the advantages of analogical representation is that one can make a plausible account of its creation from perceptual information. A symbolic medium can thus be grounded in a sensible way without requiring a great deal of innate machinery. A mechanism of perceptual analysis allows much of this early representational system to be learned rather than built in, and the increasing sophistication and detail of the analyses that infants can perform as they develop is a natural result. These are encouraging characteristics for a developmentally relevant conceptual system, but needless to say, these arguments are not definitive. It has been amply demonstrated that one can achieve the same end through many different representational forms. In the long run, only theoretical generativity and completeness matter.

It must also be said that no one has yet proposed a plausible account of the preverbal thought that has been uncovered. The image-schemas I have suggested are still relatively unexplored. There has been a moderate amount of work on how they can be used to support chains of thought and analogical problem-solving in adults (e.g., Fauconnier, 1996; Turner & Fauconnier, 1995). But virtually nothing has been said about how children come to form the mental models that are used for these purposes. It is one thing to be able to represent a concept in image-schematic form; it is another to form the models that put these concepts in relation to each other. This, it seems to me, is one of the most important topics to be addressed before the next Handbook is written.

The fact that babies think also means that the Piagetian theory of infancy must either be abandoned or extensively revised. In spite of Piaget's fundamental insight that there is more than one kind of representation, it is no longer tenable to assume that babies operate with only one of them—a procedural sensorimotor system. This is an important advance in our thinking about infancy. Having said that, however, we have seen in a good many instances that we cannot at present determine the sensorimotor versus conceptual status of many kinds of information. Although it is clear that concepts are being formed and used, it is often difficult to say whether a particular piece of information has been encoded only as part of a sensorimotor procedure or has been conceptualized and represented in a potentially accessible form. In some cases, there has not yet been enough experimental work to provide the data base that would enable us to decide. In others, because our thinking about these issues is still primitive, we are unsure what kinds of information to seek. Sometimes we don't know how to devise a paradigm that will let us answer even a reasonably well formulated question on these issues. All of this can be expected to change in the coming decade.

The discovery that there are different forms of representation from the beginning of life leads us to ask more searching questions about how these different kinds of knowledge are organized in infancy and the kinds of processes that are available to operate on them. One of the things I have tried to do in this chapter is to explicate what some of these differences in processing might be. It appears that sensorimotor knowledge is relatively slow to learn, context-bound, and cannot be brought to conscious awareness; it is always processed implicitly. Symbolic representation is not needed for this kind of learning; instead it seems eminently suited to description by connectionist paradigms. Conceptual, declarative knowledge, on the other hand, can in principle be learned in a single episode and recalled at a later time. It can be brought to conscious awareness and manipulated there; in short, it can be made explicit. This kind of processing seems to require some form of symbolic representation, perhaps the analogical kind of representation I have described. I have also stressed that this kind of processing involves attention, and much of infants' processing (just as for adults) does not involve attentive analysis. Therefore, even when capable of encoding something declaratively, infants may not attend to and analyze the information in a conceptual way so that it becomes

part of their long-term declarative memory; it may remain implicit.

The fact that implicit processing can take place on declarative representations, which have usually been considered to be explicit (see Figure 6.2), is one of the reasons for the heated debates about these issues in psychology in the past decade. Many of these arguments took place from different vantage points. To people working in verbal learning, it seemed more plausible that different processes were involved rather than different representational systems. To others who had occasion to compare sensorimotor and verbal learning, it seemed more plausible that different representational systems were involved. As in the parable of the blind man and the elephant, it appears that both views of the elephant are correct; there is more than one kind of representation and although there is only implicit processing of procedural information, both implicit and explicit processing take place on declarative information. That the two kinds of processes influence each other is equally obvious, but here there is an almost total lack of theory to guide us.

This gap in our theoretical understanding should not be considered a failure. On the contrary, it is remarkable how much we have learned in recent years. Just two decades ago, researchers were debating whether 3- to 6-month-olds are still too young to form perceptual categories, whether young infants differentiate animate from inanimate objects, or for that matter whether they have any idea of what an object is. There was not even debate about whether they can form concepts, recall the past, or make inductive inferences, because it seemed obvious that they could not. To have learned since then that 3-month-olds are perceptual categorizers par excellence, that they understand a great deal about objects and the kinds of events they enter into, and that they are acutely sensitive to animate versus inanimate differences, is already a remarkable shift in our views of infancy. To understand further that they not only understand the world in action, but are beginning to think about it as well, is a credit to the research that has taken place in the last decade.

To close, it is possible to read this chapter as another version of the story of the super-competent infant, but such an interpretation would miss the point. Infants do not have the same skills as older children and adults. What they do have are all the elements out of which more complex processing will develop. Babies are recognizably like adults after all, in spite of the fact that they do not talk. They show sophisticated and extremely rapid pattern learning and prototyping, much of which is in an abstract form. They are very sensitive to the structure of the information that surrounds them. They are creating concepts and organizing their world into conceptual domains that will form the backbone of their thought throughout life. They are able to store episodic memories and retain them over long periods of time. Interestingly, it is motor skills at which they seem to be the most incompetent—that arena of functioning which was once considered to be one of their main accomplishments. But even with their greater knowledge in other domains, it still is true that infants are universal novices. The vast amount of learning that will accrue over the years will result in qualitative as well as quantitative changes in both behavior and thought.

ACKNOWLEDGMENTS

I am grateful to the editors of this volume and the following colleagues for their thoughtful suggestions which greatly improved this chapter: Pat Bauer, Jeff Elman, Annette Karmiloff-Smith, George Mandler, Laraine McDonough, John Morton, Kim Plunkett, Paul Quinn, Anne Schlottmann, David Shanks, and Liz Spelke.

REFERENCES

Anderson, J. R. (1982). Acquisition of cognitive skill. *Psychological Review, 82*, 369–406.

Anderson, J. R. (1983). *The architecture of cognition.* Cambridge, MA: Harvard University Press.

Arterberry, M. E., Craton, L. G., & Yonas, A. (1993). Infants' sensitivity to motion-carried information for depth and object properties. In C. E. Granrud (Ed.), *Visual perception and cognition in infancy* (pp. 215–234). Hillsdale, NJ: Erlbaum.

Baillargeon, R. (1986). Representing the existence and the location of hidden objects: Object permanence in 6- and 8-month-old infants. *Cognition, 23*, 21–41.

Baillargeon, R. (1987). Object permanence in 3½- and 4½-month-old infants. *Developmental Psychology, 23*, 655–664.

Baillargeon, R. (1991). Reasoning about the height and location of a hidden object in 4.5- and 6.5-month-old infants. *Cognition, 38*, 13–42.

Baillargeon, R. (1993). The object concept revisited: New directions in the investigation of infants' physical knowledge. In C. E. Granrud (Ed.), *Visual perception and cognition in infancy.* Hillsdale, NJ: Erlbaum.

Baillargeon, R. (1995). A model of physical reasoning in infancy. In C. R. C. Rovee-Collier & L. Lipsitt (Eds.), *Advances in infancy research* (Vol. 9). Norwood, NJ: ABLEX.

Baillargeon, R., & DeVos, J. (1991). Object permanence in young infants: Further evidence. *Child Development, 62*, 1227–1246.

Baillargeon, R., Kotovsky, L., & Needham, A. (1995). The acquisition of physical knowledge in infancy. In G. Lewis, D. Premack, & D. Sperber (Eds.), *Causal understandings in cognition and culture.* Oxford, England: Oxford University Press.

Baillargeon, R., Spelke, E. E., & Wasserman, S. (1985). Object permanence in five-month-old infants. *Cognition, 20*, 191–208.

Baldwin, D. A., Markman, E. M., & Melartin, R. L. (1993). Infants' ability to draw inferences about nonobvious object properties: Evidence from exploratory play. *Child Development, 64*, 711–728.

Banks, M. S., & Salapatek, P. (1983). Infant visual perception. In P. H. Mussen (Series Ed.) & M. M. Haith & J. J. Campos (Vol. Eds.), *Infancy and developmental psychobiology: Vol. 2. Handbook of child psychology* (pp. 435–571). New York: Wiley.

Barsalou, L. W. (1993). Flexibility, structure, and linguistic vagary in concepts: Manifestations of a compositional system of perceptual symbols. In A. C. Collins, S. E. Gathercole, M. A. Conway, & P. E. M. Morris (Eds.), *Theories of memories* (pp. 29–101). Hillsdale, NJ: Erlbaum.

Barsalou, L. W., & Prinz, J. J. (in press). Mundane creativity in perceptual symbol systems. In T. B. Ward, S. M. Smith, & J. Vaid (Eds.), *Conceptual structures and processes: Emergence, discovery, and change.* Washington, DC: American Psychological Association.

Bates, E. (1994). Modularity, domain specificity and the development of language. *Discussions in Neuroscience, 10*, 136–149.

Bates, E., & MacWhinney, B. (1989). Functionalism and the competition model. In B. MacWhinney & E. Bates (Eds.), *The crosslinguistic study of sentence processing* (pp. 3–73). New York: Cambridge University Press.

Bates, E., Thal, D., & Marchman, V. (1991). Symbols and syntax: A Darwinian approach to language development. In N. A. Krasnegor, D. M. Rumbaugh, R. L. Schiefelbusch, & M. Studdert-Kennedy (Eds.), *Biological and behavioral determinants of language development* (pp. 29–65). Hillsdale, NJ: Erlbaum.

Bauer, P. J. (1992). Holding it all together: How enabling relations facilitate young children's event recall. *Cognitive Development, 7*, 1–28.

Bauer, P. J., & Dow, G. A. (1994). Episodic memory in 16- and 20-month-old children: Specifics are generalized but not forgotten. *Developmental Psychology, 30*, 403–417.

Bauer, P. J., Hertsgaard, L. A., & Dow, G. A. (1994). After 8 months have passed: Long-term recall of events by 1- to 2-year-old children. *Memory, 2,* 353–382.

Bauer, P. J., & Mandler, J. M. (1989a). Taxonomies and triads: Conceptual organization in one- to two-year-olds. *Cognitive Psychology, 21,* 156–184.

Bauer, P. J., & Mandler, J. M. (1989b). One thing follows another: Effects of temporal structure on 1- to 2-year-olds' recall of events. *Developmental Psychology, 25,* 197–206.

Bauer, P. J., & Shore, C. M. (1987). Making a memorable event: Effects of familiarity and organization on young children's recall of action sequences. *Cognitive Development, 2,* 327–338.

Bauer, P. J., & Travis, L. L. (1993). The fabric of an event: Different sources of temporal invariance differentially affect 24-month-olds' recall. *Cognitive Development, 8,* 319–341.

Bechtel, W., & Abrahamsen, A. (1991). *Connectionism and the mind: An introduction to parallel processing networks.* Cambridge, MA: Blackwell.

Behl-Chadha, G. (in press). Superordinate-like categorical representations in early infancy. *Cognition.*

Behrend, D. A. (1988). Overextensions in early language comprehension: Evidence from a signal detection approach. *Journal of Child Language, 15,* 63–75.

Berlin, B., Breedlove, D. E., & Raven, P. H. (1973). General principles of classification and nomenclature in folk biology. *American Anthropologist, 75,* 214–242.

Bertenthal, B. (1993). Infants' perception of biomechanical motions: Intrinsic image and knowledge-based constraints. In C. Granrud (Ed.), *Visual perception and cognition in infancy* (pp. 175–214). Hillsdale, NJ: Erlbaum.

Bloom, L., Lifter, K., & Broughton, J. (1985). The convergence of early cognition and language in the second year of life: Problems in conceptualization and measurement. In M. Barrett (Ed.), *Children's single-word speech* (pp. 149–180). New York: Wiley.

Bogartz, R. S., Shinskey, J. L., & Speaker, C. (1997). *Interpreting infant looking: The event set × event set design. Developmental Psychology, 33,* 408–422.

Bomba, P. C., & Siqueland, E. R. (1983). The nature and structure of infant form categories. *Journal of Experimental Child Psychology, 35,* 294–328.

Bowerman, M. (1987). Commentary. In B. MacWhinney (Ed.), *Mechanisms of language acquisition.* Hillsdale, NJ: Erlbaum.

Bowerman, M. (1989). Learning a semantic system: What roles do cognitive predispositions play? In M. L. Rice & R. L. Schiefelbusch (Eds.), *The teachability of language* (pp. 133–169). Baltimore: Brookes.

Bowerman, M. (1993). Typological perspectives on language acquisition: Do crosslinguistic patterns predict development? In E. V. Clark (Ed.), *Proceedings of the twenty-fifth annual Child Language Research Forum* (pp. 7–15). Stanford, CA: Center for the Study of Language and Information.

Bowerman, M. (1996). The origins of children's spatial semantic categories: Cognitive versus linguistic determinants. In J. J. Gumperz & S. L. Levinson (Eds.), *Rethinking linguistic relativity.* Cambridge, England: Cambridge University Press.

Braine, M. D. S. (1992). What sort of innate structure is needed to "bootstrap" into syntax? *Cognition, 45,* 77–100.

Brown, R. (1958). How shall a thing be called? *Psychological Review, 65,* 14–21.

Brown, R. (1973). *A first language: The early stages.* Cambridge, MA: Harvard University Press.

Bruner, J. S. (1957). On perceptual readiness. *Psychological Review, 64,* 331–350.

Bruner, J. S. (1966). On cognitive growth. In J. S. Bruner, R. R. Olver, & P. M. Greenfield (Eds.), *Studies in cognitive growth.* New York: Wiley.

Bullock, M., Gelman, R., & Baillargeon, R. (1982). The development of causal reasoning. In W. Friedman (Ed.), *The developmental psychology of time* (pp. 209–254). New York: Academic Press.

Butterworth, G. (1994). Knowledge and representation: The acquisition of knowledge in infancy. In P. van Geert, L. P. Mos, & W. J. Baker (Eds.), *Annals of theoretical psychology* (Vol. 10). New York: Plenum Press.

Campbell, B. A. (1984). Reflections on the ontogeny of learning and memory. In R. Kail & N. E. Spear (Eds.), *Comparative perspectives on the development of memory.* Hillsdale, NJ: Erlbaum.

Carey, S. (1985). *Conceptual change in childhood.* Cambridge, MA: MIT Press.

Carey, S. (1991). Knowledge acquisition: Enrichment or conceptual change? In S. Carey & R. Gelman (Eds.), *Epigenesis of mind: Studies in biology and cognition.* Hillsdale, NJ: Erlbaum.

Carey, S., & Spelke, E. (1994). Domain-specific knowledge and conceptual change. In L. A. Hirschfeld & S. A. Gelman (Eds.), *Mapping the mind: Domain specificity in cognition and culture* (pp. 169–200). New York: Cambridge University Press.

Carver, L. J. (1995, March). *A mosaic of nine-month-olds' memory: ERP, looking time, and elicited imitation measures.* Poster presented at the biennial meeting of the Society for Research in Child Development, Indianapolis, IN.

Chambers, D., & Reisberg, D. (1992). What an image depicts depends on what an image means. *Cognitive Psychology, 24,* 145–174.

Choi, S., & Bowerman, M. (1991). Learning to express motion events in English and Korean: The influence of language-specific lexicalization patterns. *Cognition, 41,* 83–121.

Chomsky, N. (1965). *Aspects of the theory of syntax.* Cambridge, MA: MIT Press.

Clark, A., & Karmiloff-Smith, A. (1993). The cognizer's innards: A psychological and philosophical perspective on the development of thought. *Mind & Language, 8,* 487–519.

Clark, E. V. (1977). Strategies and the mapping problem in first language acquisition. In J. MacNamara (Ed.), *Language learning and thought.* San Diego, CA: Academic Press.

Curran, T., & Keele, S. W. (1993). Attentional and nonattentional forms of sequence learning. *Journal of Experimental Psychology: Learning, Memory, and Cognition, 19,* 189–202.

Deak, G., & Bauer, P. J. (1995). The effects of task comprehension on preschoolers' and adults' categorization choices. *Journal of Experimental Child Psychology, 60,* 393–427.

DeCasper, A. J., & Spence, M. J. (1986). Prenatal maternal speech influences newborns' perceptions of speech sounds. *Infant Behavior and Development, 9,* 133–150.

Diamond, A. (1985). The development of the ability to use recall to guide action, as indicated by infants' performance on AB. *Child Development, 56,* 868–883.

Diamond, A. (1990). Developmental time course in human infants and infant monkeys, and the neural bases of, inhibitory control in reaching. In A. Diamond (Ed.), *The development and neural bases of higher cognitive functions* (pp. 637–669). New York: New York Academy of Sciences.

Dinsmore, J. (1992). *Symbolic and connectionist paradigms.* Hillsdale, NJ: Erlbaum.

Dorfman, J., & Mandler, G. (1994). Implicit and explicit forgetting: When is gist remembered? *Quarterly Journal of Experimental Psychology, 47A,* 651–672.

Edwards, D. (1973). Sensory-motor intelligence and semantic relations in early child grammar. *Cognition, 2,* 395–434.

Eimas, P. D. (1994). Categorization in early infancy and the continuity of development. *Cognition, 50,* 83–93.

Eimas, P. D., & Quinn, P. C. (1994). Studies on the formation of perceptually based basic-level categories in young infants. *Child Development, 65,* 903–917.

Einhorn, H. J., & Hogarth, R. M. (1986). Judging probable cause. *Psychological Bulletin, 99,* 3–19.

Elman, J. L. (1990). Finding structure in time. *Cognitive Science, 14,* 179–211.

Fagan, J. F., III, & Singer, L. T. (1979). The role of simple feature differences in infant recognition of faces. *Infant Behavior and Development, 2,* 39–46.

Fauconnier, G. (1994). *Mental spaces.* Cambridge, MA: MIT Press.

Fauconnier, G. (1996). Analogical counterfactuals. In G. Fauconnier & E. Sweetser (Eds.), *Spaces, worlds, and grammar.* Chicago: University of Chicago Press.

Fenson, L., Cameron, M. S., & Kennedy, M. (1988). The role of perceptual and conceptual similarity in category matching at age two years. *Child Development, 53,* 170–179.

Fischer, K. W., & Bidell, T. (1991). Constraining nativist inferences about cognitive capacities. In S. Carey & R. Gelman (Eds.), *The epigenesis of mind: Essays on biology and cognition* (pp. 199–235). Hillsdale, NJ: Erlbaum.

Fischer, K. W., & Hogan, A. (1989). The big picture for infant development: Levels and sources of variation. In J. Lockman & N. Hazen (Eds.), *Action in social context: Perspectives on early development* (pp. 275–305). New York: Plenum Press.

Fivush, R., Gray, J. T., & Fromhoff, F. A. (1987). Two-year-olds talk about the past. *Cognitive Development, 2,* 393–410.

Fivush, R., & Hamond, N. R. (1990). Autobiographical memory across the preschool years: Toward reconceptualizing childhood amnesia. In R. Fivush & J. A. Hudson (Eds.), *Knowing and remembering in young children* (pp. 223–248). New York: Cambridge University Press.

Fodor, J. (1975). *The language of thought.* New York: Crowell.

Fodor, J., & Pylyshyn, Z. W. (1988). Connectionism and cognitive architecture: A critical analysis. *Cognition, 28,* 3–71.

Folven, R. J., & Bonvillian, J. D. (1991). The transition from nonreferential to referential language in children acquiring American Sign Language. *Developmental Psychology, 27,* 806–816.

Gelman, R. (1991). Epigenetic foundations of knowledge structures: Initial and transcendent constructions. In S. Carey & R. Gelman (Eds.), *The epigenesis of mind* (pp. 203–322). Hillsdale, NJ: Erlbaum.

Gelman, S. A. (1988). The development of induction within natural kind and artifact categories. *Cognitive Psychology, 20,* 65–95.

Gelman, S. A., & Coley, J. D. (1990). The importance of knowing a dodo is a bird: Categories and inferences in 2-year-old children. *Developmental Psychology, 26,* 796–804.

Gelman, S. A., & Markman, E. M. (1986). Categories and induction in young children. *Cognition, 23,* 183–209.

Gelman, S. A., & O'Reilley, A. W. (1988). Children's inductive inferences within superordinate categories: The role of language and category structure. *Child Development, 59,* 876–887.

Gelman, S. A., & Wellman, H. M. (1991). Insides and essences: Early understandings of the nonobvious. *Cognition, 38,* 213–244.

Gergely, G., Csibra, G., Biro, S., & Koos, O. (1994, June). *The comprehension of intentional action in infancy.* Poster presented at the 9th International Conference on Infant Studies, Paris.

Gergely, G., Nadasdy, Z., Csibra, G., & Biro, S. (1995). Taking the intentional stance at 12-months-of-age. *Cognition, 56,* 165–193.

Gibson, E. J. (1969). *Principles of perceptual learning and development.* New York: Appleton-Century-Crofts.

Gibson, E. J., & Walker, A. S. (1984). Development of knowledge of visual-tactual affordances of substance. *Child Development, 55,* 453–460.

Gibson, J. J. (1966). *The senses considered as perceptual systems.* Boston: Houghton-Mifflin.

Golinkoff, R. M., & Halperin, M. S. (1983). The concept of animal: One infant's view. *Infant Behavior and Development, 6,* 229–233.

Golinkoff, R. M., Hirsh-Pasek, K., Mervis, C. B., Frawley, W. B., & Parillo, M. (1995). Lexical principles can be extended to the acquisition of verbs. In M. Tomasello & W. Merriman (Eds.), *Beyond names for things: Young children's acquisition of verbs.* Hillsdale, NJ: Erlbaum.

Gopnik, A., & Meltzoff, A. N. (1987). The development of categorization in the second year and its relation to other cognitive and linguistic developments. *Child Development, 58,* 1523–1531.

Graf, P., & Mandler, G. (1984). Activation makes words more accessible, but not necessarily more retrievable. *Journal of Verbal Learning and Verbal Behavior, 23,* 553–568.

Haith, M. M., Hazan, C., & Goodman, G. S. (1988). Expectation and anticipation of dynamic visual events by 3.5-month-old babies. *Child Development, 59,* 467–479.

Hall, D. G., & Waxman, S. R. (1993). Assumptions about word meaning: Individuation and basic-level kinds. *Child Development, 64,* 1550–1570.

Harnad, S. (1990). The symbol grounding problem. *Physica D, 42,* 335–346.

Harris, P. L. (1987). The development of search. In P. Salapatek & L. Cohen (Eds.), *Handbook of infant perception* (Vol. 2). New York: Academic Press.

Hayes, N. A., & Broadbent, D. E. (1988). Two modes of learning for interactive tasks. *Cognition, 28,* 249–276.

Heider, F., & Simmel, M. (1944). An experimental study of apparent behavior. *American Journal of Psychology, 57,* 243–259.

Hinton, G. E., & Becker, S. (1990). An unsupervised learning procedure that discovers surfaces in random-dot stereograms. *Proceedings of the International Joint Conference on Neural Networks, 1,* 218–222.

Hodges, J. R., Graham, N., & Patterson, K. (1995). Charting the progression in semantic dementia: Implications for the organization of semantic memory. *Memory, 3,* 463–495.

Honavar, V., & Uhr, L. (1994). *Artificial intelligence and neural networks: Steps toward principled integration.* San Diego, CA: Academic Press.

Hood, B., & Willatts, P. (1986). Reaching in the dark to an objects' remembered position: Evidence for object permanence in 5-month-old infants. *British Journal of Developmental Psychology, 4,* 57–65.

Intons-Peterson, M. J., & Roskos-Ewoldsen, B. B. (1989). Sensory-perceptual qualities of images. *Journal of Experimental Psychology: Learning, Memory, and Cognition, 15,* 188–199.

James, W. (1890). *The principles of psychology.* New York: Holt.

Johnson, M. (1987). *The body in the mind: The bodily basis of meaning, imagination, and reasoning.* Chicago: University of Chicago Press.

Johnson, M. H., & Morton, J. (1991). *Biology and cognitive development: The case of face recognition.* Oxford, England: Blackwell.

Karmiloff-Smith, A. (1992). *Beyond modularity: A developmental perspective on cognitive science.* Cambridge, MA: MIT Press.

Karmiloff-Smith, A. (1993). Self-organization and cognitive change. In M. H. Johnson (Ed.), *Brain development and cognition* (pp. 592–618). Cambridge, MA: Blackwell.

Keil, F. C. (1989). *Concepts, kinds, and cognitive development.* Cambridge, MA: MIT Press.

Keil, F. C. (1991). The emergence of theoretical beliefs as constraints on concepts. In S. Carey & R. Gelman (Eds.), *The epigenesis of mind* (pp. 237–256). Hillsdale, NJ: Erlbaum.

Keil, F. C., & Batterman, N. (1984). A characteristic-to-defining shift in the development of word meaning. *Journal of Verbal Learning and Verbal Behavior, 23,* 221–236.

Kellman, P. J. (1993). Kinematic foundations of infant visual perception. In C. E. Granrud (Ed.), *Visual perception and cognition in infancy.* Hillsdale, NJ: Erlbaum.

Kohonen, T. (1984). *Self-organization and associative memory.* Berlin: Springer-Verlag.

Kosslyn, S. (1980). *Image and mind.* Cambridge, MA: Harvard University Press.

Kuhl, P. K., & Meltzoff, A. N. (1988). Speech as an intermodal object of perception. In A. Yonas (Ed.), *Perceptual development in infancy* (pp. 235–66). Hillsdale, NJ: Erlbaum.

Lakoff, G. (1987). *Women, fire, and dangerous things: What categories reveal about the mind.* Chicago: University of Chicago Press.

Langacker, R. (1987). *Foundations of cognitive grammar* (Vol. 1). Stanford, CA: Stanford University Press.

Lange, T. E. (1992). Hybrid connectionist models: Temporary bridges over the gap between the symbolic and the subsymbolic. In J. Dinsmore (Ed.), *The symbolic and connectionist paradigms* (pp. 237–289). Hillsdale, NJ: Erlbaum.

Legerstee, M. (1992). A review of the animate-inanimate distinction in infancy: Implications for models of social and cognitive knowing. *Early Development and Parenting, 1,* 59–67.

Leslie, A. M. (1988). The necessity of illusion: Perception and thought in infancy. In L. Weiskrantz (Ed.), *Thought without language* (pp. 185–210). Oxford, England: Oxford Science.

Leslie, A. M. (1994). ToMM, ToBy, and Agency: Core architecture and domain specificity. In S. A. Gelman & L. A. Hirschfeld (Eds.), *Mapping the mind: Domain specificity in cognition and culture* (pp. 119–148). New York: Cambridge University Press.

Leslie, A. M., & Keeble, S. (1987). Do six-month-old infants perceive causality? *Cognition, 25,* 265–288.

Mandler, G. (1967). The organization of memory. In K. W. Spence & J. T. Spence (Eds.), *The psychology of learning and motivation: Advances in research and theory.* New York: Academic Press.

Mandler, G. (1985). *Cognitive psychology.* Hillsdale, NJ: Erlbaum.

Mandler, G. (1992). Toward a theory of consciousness. In H. -G. Geissler, S. W. Link, & J. T. Townsend (Eds.), *Cognition, information processing, and psychophysics: Basic issues.* Hillsdale, NJ: Erlbaum.

Mandler, J. M. (1983). Representation. In P. Mussen (Series Ed.) & J. H. Flavell & E. M. Markman (Vol. Eds.), *Cognitive development: Vol. 3. Handbook of child psychology* (pp. 420–494). New York: Wiley.

Mandler, J. M. (1984). Representation and recall in infancy. In M. Moscovitch (Ed.), *Infant memory.* New York: Plenum Press.

Mandler, J. M. (1986). On the comprehension of temporal order. *Language and Cognitive Processes, 1,* 309–320.

Mandler, J. M. (1988). How to build a baby: On the development of an accessible representational system. *Cognitive Development, 3,* 113–136.

Mandler, J. M. (1990). Recall of events by preverbal children. In A. Diamond (Ed.), *The development and neural bases of higher cognitive functions* (pp. 485–503). New York: New York Academy of Science.

Mandler, J. M. (1992). How to build a baby: 2. Conceptual primitives. *Psychological Review, 99,* 587–604.

Mandler, J. M. (1994). Precursors of linguistic knowledge. *Philosophical Transactions of the Royal Society of London, Series B, 346,* 63–69.

Mandler, J. M. (1997). Development of categorization: Perceptual and conceptual categories. In G. Bremner, A. Slater, & G. Butterworth (Eds.), *Infant development: Recent advances.* Hove, England: Erlbaum.

Mandler, J. M., & Bauer, P. J. (1988). The cradle of categorization: Is the basic level basic? *Cognitive Development, 3,* 247–264.

Mandler, J. M., Bauer, P. J., & McDonough, L. (1991). Separating the sheep from the goats: Differentiating global categories. *Cognitive Psychology, 23,* 263–298.

Mandler, J. M., Fivush, R., & Reznick, J. S. (1987). The development of contextual categories. *Cognitive Development, 2,* 339–354.

Mandler, J. M., & McDonough, L. (1993). Concept formation in infancy. *Cognitive Development, 8,* 291–318.

Mandler, J. M., & McDonough, L. (1995). Long-term recall in infancy. *Journal of Experimental Child Psychology, 59,* 457–474.

Mandler, J. M., & McDonough, L. (1996a). Drinking and driving don't mix: Inductive generalization in infancy. *Cognition, 59,* 307–335.

Mandler, J. M., & McDonough, L. (1996b). Nonverbal recall. In N. L. Stein, P. O. Ornstein, B. Tversky, & C. Brainerd (Eds.), *Memory for everyday and emotional events.* Hillsdale, NJ: Erlbaum.

McClelland, J. L., & Rumelhart, D. E. (1985). Distributed memory and the representation of general and specific information. *Journal of Experimental Psychology: General, 114,* 159–188.

McDonough, L. (1997a). *Memory for location in 7-month-olds.* Manuscript submitted for publication.

McDonough, L. (1997b, April). *Overextension in the production and comprehension of basic-level nouns in two-year-olds.* Poster presented at the meeting of the Society for Research in Child Development, Washington, DC.

McDonough, L., Choi, S., Bowerman, M., & Mandler, J. M. (in press). The use of preferential looking as a measure of semantic development. In E. L. Bavin & D. Burnhope (Eds.), *Advances in infancy research.* Norwood, NJ: Ablex.

McDonough, L., & Mandler, J. M. (1997, April). *Category boundaries and inductive inference in infancy.* Poster presented at the meeting of the Society for Research in Child Development, Washington, DC.

McDonough, L., & Mandler, J. M. (1994). Very long-term memory in infancy: Infantile amnesia reconsidered. *Memory, 2,* 339–352.

McDonough, L., Mandler, J. M., McKee, R. D., & Squire, L. (1995). The deferred imitation task as a nonverbal measure of declarative memory. *Proceedings of the National Academy of Sciences, 92,* 7580–7584.

Medin, D. L. (1983). Cue validity. Structural principles of categorization. In B. Shepp & T. Tighe (Eds.), *Interaction: Perception, development, and cognition.* Hillsdale, NJ: Erlbaum.

Medin, D. L., & Barsalou, L. W. (1987). Categorization processes and categorical perception. In S. Harnad (Ed.), *Categorical perception.* New York: Cambridge University Press.

Medin, D. L., & Ortony, A. (1989). Psychological essentialism. In S. Vosniadou & A. Ortony (Eds.), *Similarity and analogical reasoning* (pp. 179–195). New York: Cambridge University Press.

Meier, R. P., & Newport, E. L. (1990). Out of the hands of babes: On a possible sign advantage in language acquisition. *Language, 66,* 1–23.

Meltzoff, A. N. (1985). Immediate and deferred imitation in fourteen- and twenty-four-month-old infants. *Child Development, 56,* 62–72.

Meltzoff, A. N. (1988a). Infant imitation and memory: Nine-month-olds in immediate and deferred tests. *Child Development, 59,* 217–225.

Meltzoff, A. N. (1988b). Infant imitation after a 1-week delay: Long-term memory for novel acts and multiple stimuli. *Developmental Psychology, 24,* 470–476.

Meltzoff, A. N., & Borton, R. W. (1979). Intermodal matching by human neonates. *Nature, 282,* 403–404.

Mendelsohn, M. J., & Haith, M. M. (1976). The relation between audition and vision in the newborn. *Monographs of the Society for Research in Child Development, 41*(Serial No. 167).

Mervis, C. B., & Mervis, C. A. (1982). Leopards are kitty-cats: Object labeling by mothers for their thirteen-month-olds. *Child Development, 53,* 267–273.

Mervis, C. B., & Rosch, E. (1981). Categorization of natural objects. *Annual Review of Psychology, 32,* 89–115.

Michotte, A. E. (1963). *The perception of causality.* London: Methuen.

Moore, D., Benenson, J., Reznick, J. S., Peterson, M., & Kagan, J. (1987). Effect of auditory numerical information on infants' looking behavior: Contradictory evidence. *Developmental Psychology, 23,* 665–670.

Mullen, A. M., & Aslin, R. N. (1978). Visual tracking as an index of the object concept. *Infant Behavior and Development, 1,* 309–319.

Murphy, G. L. (1982). Cue validity and levels of categorization. *Psychological Bulletin, 91,* 174–177.

Myers, N., Clifton, R., & Clarkson, M. (1987). When they were very young: Almost-threes remember two years ago. *Infant Behavior and Development, 10,* 123–132.

Needham, A., & Baillargeon, R. (1993). Intuitions about support in 4.5-month-old infants. *Cognition, 47,* 121–148.

Nelson, K. (1973). Some evidence for the cognitive primacy of categorization and its functional basis. *Merrill-Palmer Quarterly, 19,* 21–39.

Nelson, K. (1985). *Making sense: The acquisition of shared meaning.* San Diego, CA: Academic Press.

Nelson, K. (1994). Long-term memory for preverbal experience: Evidence and implications. *Memory, 2,* 467–475.

Nelson, K., & Ross, G. (1980). The generalities and specifics of long-term memory in infants and young children. In M. Perlmutter (Ed.), *New directions for child development—Children's memory* (pp. 87–101). San Francisco: Jossey-Bass.

Newell, A. (1980). Physical symbol systems. *Cognitive Science, 4,* 135–183.

Nickerson, R. S., & Adams, M. J. (1979). Long-term memory for a common object. *Cognitive Psychology, 11,* 287–307.

Nosofsky, R. M., Kruschke, J. K., & McKinley, S. C. (1992). Combining exemplar-based category representations and connectionist learning rules. *Journal of Experimental Psychology: Learning, Memory, and Cognition, 18,* 211–233.

Oakes, L. M., Madole, K. L., & Cohen, L. B. (1991). Infants' object examining: Habituation and categorization. *Cognitive Development, 6,* 377–392.

Oakes, L. M., & Tellinghuisen, D. J. (1994). Examining in infancy: Does it reflect active processing? *Developmental Psychology, 30,* 748–756.

Paivio, A. (1971). *Imagery and verbal processes.* New York: Holt.

Palmer, C. F., Jones, R. K., Hennessy, B. L., Unze, M. G., & Pick, A. D. (1989). How is a trumpet known? The "basic object level" concept and perception of musical instruments. *American Journal of Psychology, 102,* 17–37.

Piaget, J. (1951). *Play, dreams, and imitation in childhood.* New York: Norton.

Piaget, J. (1952). *The origins of intelligence in the child.* New York: International Universities Press.

Piaget, J. (1954). *The construction of reality in the child.* New York: Basic Books.

Piaget, J. (1976). *The grasp of consciousness: Action and concept in the young child.* Cambridge, MA: Harvard University Press.

Piaget, J., & Inhelder, B. (1971). *Mental imagery in the child.* London: Routledge & Kegan Paul.

Pinker, S. (1989). *Learnability and cognition.* Cambridge, MA: MIT Press.

Pinker, S., & Prince, A. (1988). On language and connectionism: Analysis of a processing model of language acquisition. *Cognition, 28,* 73–193.

Plunkett, K., & Marchman, V. (1991). U-shaped learning and child language acquisition. *Cognition, 38,* 43–102.

Posner, M. I., & Keele, S. W. (1968). On the genesis of abstract ideas. *Journal of Experimental Psychology, 77,* 353–363.

Poulin-Dubois, D., & Shultz, T. R. (1988). The development of the understanding of human behavior: From agency to intentionality. In J. W. Astington, P. L. Harris, & D. R. Olson

(Eds.), *Developing theories of mind* (pp. 109–125). Cambridge, England: Cambridge University Press.

Premack, D. (1990). The infant's theory of self-propelled objects. *Cognition, 36,* 1–16.

Proffitt, D. R., & Bertenthal, B. I. (1990). Converging operations revisited: Assessing what infants perceive using discrimination measures. *Perception and Psychophysics, 47,* 1–11.

Quillian, M. R. (1968). Semantic memory. In M. Minsky (Ed.), *Semantic information processing* (pp. 227–270). Cambridge, MA: MIT Press.

Quine, W. V. (1977). Natural kinds. In S. P. Schwartz (Ed.), *Naming, necessity, and natural kinds* (pp. 155–177). Ithaca, NY: Cornell University Press.

Quinn, P. C., & Eimas, P. D. (1986). On categorization in early infancy. *Merrill-Palmer Quarterly, 32,* 331–363.

Quinn, P. C., & Eimas, P. D. (1996a). Perceptual cues that permit categorical differentiation of animal species by infants. *Journal of Experimental Child Psychology, 63,* 189–211.

Quinn, P. C., & Eimas, P. D. (1996b). Perceptual organization and categorization in young infants. In C. Rovee-Collier & L. P. Lipsitt (Eds.), *Advances in infancy research* (Vol. 10). Norwood, NJ: Ablex.

Quinn, P. C., Eimas, P. D., & Rosenkrantz, S. L. (1993). Evidence for representations of perceptual similar natural categories by 3-month-old and 4-month-old infants. *Perception, 22,* 463–475.

Reason, J. T. (1979). Actions not as planned. In G. Underwood & R. Stevens (Eds.), *Aspects of consciousness*. London: Academic Press.

Reed, S. K., & Friedman, M. P. (1973). Perceptual vs. conceptual categorization. *Memory and Cognition, 1,* 157–163.

Reeke, G. N., & Edelman, G. M. (1984). Selective networks and recognition automata. *Annals of the New York Academy of Science, 426,* 181–201.

Regier, T. (1992). *The acquisition of lexical semantics for spatial terms.* Doctoral dissertation, University of California, Berkeley.

Ricciuti, H. N. (1965). Object grouping and selective ordering behavior in infants 12- to 24-months-old. *Merrill-Palmer Quarterly, 11,* 129–148.

Richards, J. E., & Casey, B. J. (1992). Development of sustained visual attention in the human infant. In B. A. Campbell, H. Hayne, & R. Richardson (Eds.), *Attention and information processing in infants and adults*. Hillsdale, NJ: Erlbaum.

Roberts, K., & Cuff, M. D. (1989). Categorization studies of 9- to 15-month-old infants: Evidence for superordinate categorization? *Infant Behavior and Development, 12,* 265–288.

Rosch, E. (1978). Principles of categorization. In E. Rosch & B. B. Lloyd (Eds.), *Cognition and categorization* (pp. 27–48). Hillsdale, NJ: Erlbaum.

Rosch, E., & Mervis, C. B. (1975). Family resemblances: Studies in the internal structure of categories. *Cognitive Psychology, 7,* 573–605.

Rosch, E., Mervis, C. B., Gray, W., Johnson, D., & Boyes-Braem, P. (1976). Basic objects in natural categories. *Cognitive Psychology, 3,* 382–439.

Ross, G. S. (1980). Categorization in 1- to 2-year-olds. *Developmental Psychology, 16,* 391–396.

Rovee-Collier, C. (1989). The joy of kicking: Memories, motives, and mobiles. In P. R. Solomon, G. R. Goethals, C. M. Kelley, & B. R. Stephens (Eds.), *Memory: Interdisciplinary approaches*. New York: Springer-Verlag.

Ruff, H. A. (1986). Components of attention during infants' manipulative exploration. *Child Development, 57,* 105–114.

Ruff, H. A., & Saltarelli, L. M. (1993). Exploratory play with objects: Basic cognitive processes and individual differences. In M. H. Bornstein & A. W. O'Reilly (Eds.), *The role of play in the development of thought* (pp. 5–16). San Francisco: Jossey-Bass.

Rumelhart, D. E., & McClelland, J. L. (1986). On learning the past tenses of English verbs. In J. L. McClelland, D. E. Rumelhart, and the PDP Research Group (Eds.), *Parallel distributed processing: Explorations in the microstructure of cognition* (Vol. 2, pp. 216–271). Cambridge, MA: MIT Press.

Rumelhart, D. E., Smolensky, P., McClelland, J. L., & Hinton, G. E. (1986). Schemata and sequential thought processes in PDP models. In J. L. McClelland, D. E. Rumelhart, and the PDP Research Group (Eds.), *Explorations in the microstructure of cognition* (Vol. 2, pp. 7–57). Cambridge, MA: MIT Press.

Saffron, E. M., & Schwartz, M. F. (1994). Of cabbages and things: Semantic memory from a neuropsychological perspective—A tutorial review. In C. Umiltá & M. Moscovitch (Eds.), *Attention and performance: 15. Conscious and unconscious information processing* (Vol. 3). Cambridge, MA: MIT Press.

Saxby, L., & Anglin, J. M. (1983). Children's sorting of objects from categories of differing levels of generality. *Journal of Genetic Psychology, 143,* 123–137.

Schacter, D. L. (1987). Implicit memory: History and current status. *Journal of Experimental Psychology: Learning, Memory, and Cognition, 13,* 501–518.

Schacter, D. L. (1992). Priming and multiple memory systems: Perceptual mechanisms of implicit memory. *Journal of Cognitive Neuroscience, 4,* 244–256.

Schlottmann, A. (1991). *Seeing it happen and knowing how it works: Temporal contiguity and causal mechanism in children's causal inferences.* Doctoral dissertation, University of California, San Diego.

Schlottmann, A., & Anderson, N. H. (1993). An information integration approach to phenomenal causality. *Memory and Cognition, 21,* 785–801.

Schyns, P. G. (1991). A modular neural network model of concept acquisition. *Cognitive Science, 15,* 461–508.

Sejnowski, T. J., & Rosenberg, C. R. (1987). Parallel networks that learn to pronounce English test. *Complex Systems, 1,* 145–168.

Shanks, D. R., & St. John, M. F. (1994). Characteristics of dissociable human learning system. *Behavioral and Brain Sciences, 17,* 367–394.

Shiffrin, R. M., & Schneider, W. (1977). Controlled and automatic human information processing: 2. Perceptual learning, automatic attending, and a general theory. *Psychological Review, 84,* 127–190.

Shultz, T. R., Altmann, E., & Asselin, J. (1986). Judging causal priority. *British Journal of Developmental Psychology, 4,* 67–74.

Slackman, E. A., Hudson, J. A., & Fivush, R. (1986). Actions, actors, links, and goals: The structure of children's event representations. In K. Nelson (Ed.), *Event knowledge: Structure and function in development.* Hillsdale, NJ: Erlbaum.

Slobin, D. I. (1985). Crosslinguistic evidence for the language-making capacity. In D. I. Slobin (Ed.), *The crosslinguistic study of language acquisition: Vol. 2. Theoretical issues* (pp. 1157–1256). Hillsdale, NJ: Erlbaum.

Smith, E. E., & Osherson, D. N. (1988). Conceptual combination with prototype concepts. In A. M. Collins & E. E. Smith (Eds.), *Readings in cognitive science.* San Mateo, CA: Morgan Kaufmann.

Smith, L. B., & Heise, D. (1992). Perceptual similarity and conceptual structure. In B. Burns (Ed.), *Percepts, concepts and categories* (pp. 233–272). Amsterdam, The Netherlands: North-Holland.

Smith, P. H. (1984). Five-month-old recall of temporal order and utilization of temporal organization. *Journal of Experimental Child Psychology, 38,* 400–414.

Smolensky, P. (1988). On the proper treatment of connectionism. *The Behavioral and Brain Sciences, 11,* 1–74.

Spelke, E. S. (1979). Perceiving bimodally specified events in infancy. *Developmental Psychology, 15,* 626–636.

Spelke, E. S. (1988). Where perceiving ends and thinking begins: The apprehension of objects in infancy. In A. Yonas (Ed.), *Perceptual development in infancy.* Hillsdale, NJ: Erlbaum.

Spelke, E. S. (1990). Principles of object perception. *Cognitive Science, 14,* 29–56.

Spelke, E. S. (1994). Initial knowledge: Six suggestions. *Cognition, 50,* 431–445.

Spelke, E. S., Breinlinger, K., Macomber, J., & Jacobson, K. (1992). Origins of knowledge. *Psychological Review, 99,* 605–632.

Squire, L. R. (1987). *Memory and brain.* New York: Oxford University Press.

Starkey, P., Spelke, E. S., & Gelman, R. (1983). Detection of intermodal numerical correspondences by human infants. *Science, 222,* 179–181.

Streri, A., & Spelke, E. S. (1988). Haptic perception of objects in infancy. *Cognitive Psychology, 20,* 1–23.

Sugarman, S. (1983). *Children's early thought.* Cambridge, England: Cambridge University Press.

Sweetser, E. (1990). *From etymology to pragmatics: Metaphorical and cultural aspects of semantic structure.* Cambridge, England: Cambridge University Press.

Talmy, L. (1988). Force dynamics in language and cognition. *Cognitive Science, 12,* 49–100.

Thelen, E., & Smith, L. B. (1994). *A dynamic systems approach to the development of cognition and action.* Cambridge, MA: MIT Press.

Tomasello, M. (1992). *First verbs: A case study of early grammatical development.* New York: Cambridge University Press.

Turner, M., & Fauconnier, G. (1995). Integration and formal expression. *Journal of Metaphor and Symbolic Activity, 10,* 183–204.

Uzgiris, I. C., & Hunt, J. (1975). *Assessment in infancy: Ordinal scales of psychological development.* Urbana: University of Illinois Press.

von Hofsten, C. (1982). Eye-hand coordination in newborns. *Developmental Psychology, 18,* 450–461.

von Hofsten, C., & Spelke, E. S. (1985). Object perception and object-directed reaching in infancy. *Journal of Experimental Psychology: General, 114,* 198–212.

Warrington, E. K., & Weiskrantz, L. (1974). The effect of prior learning on subsequent retention in amnesic patients. *Neuropsychologia, 12,* 419–428.

Watson, J. (1972). Smiling, cooing, and "the game." *Merrill-Palmer Quarterly, 18,* 323–340.

Werner, H. (1957). The concept of development from a comparative and organismic point of view. In D. B. Harris (Ed.), *The concept of development: An issue in the study of human behavior* (pp. 125–148). Minneapolis: University of Minnesota Press.

Werner, H., & Kaplan, B. (1963). *Symbol formation.* New York: Wiley.

White, P. A. (1988). Causal processing: Origins and development. *Psychological Bulletin, 104,* 36–52.

CHAPTER 7

Language Acquisition in
Its Developmental Context

LOIS BLOOM

Children acquire language in the context of their psychological development and, in particular, developments in thinking, emotionality, and social interaction. The key assumptions in this chapter, therefore, come from an explicitly psychological theory of language development rather than from specifically linguistic theories or logical arguments in the philosophy of language. Linguistic and philosophical theories are important for understanding language, to be sure. But acquiring a language is always a psychological task for the child, not a logical one, and the linguistic problems to be solved are always embedded in a personal and interpersonal context.

In order to study language acquisition, we need to look at what language does and why children acquire language. Language makes it possible for individuals to share what they have in mind at a particular moment in time through expression and interpretation, because language embodies and makes manifest the beliefs, desires, and feelings that are their intentional states (Danto, 1973; Fauconnier, 1985; Taylor, 1979). Expression and interpretation make it possible for groups of individuals to share customs, systems of

belief, and ways of living across many moments of time for the larger world view that holds a society and culture together. Thus, the motivation for learning a language, in the first place, is for expression and interpretation, so that the private and hidden contents of mind—intentional states—can be made public and shared between persons. A language will have to be learned for sustaining and promoting intersubjectivity with others beyond infancy, if child and other are to continue to "keep in touch" with what each is thinking and feeling as intentional states become increasingly elaborated with development. The multiple and detailed elements, roles, and relationships in intentional states that result from developments in cognition, emotion, and social understanding in the first few years of life can only be articulated by language.

These three concepts: (1) language as an embodiment of contents of mind; (2) the need to maintain intersubjectivity in an expanding social world; and (3) the driving force of developments in cognition, affect, and social interaction for acquiring a language provided the foundation for the model of intentionality and language development presented in om (1993). The essential thesis of the intentionality model is that development, in general, depends on a process of transaction between internal representations in intentional states and the external social and physical world. Language development, in particular, connects with all aspects of a child's physical, cognitive, emotional, social, and cultural development and is more than just acquiring words and the structures of grammar—language acquisition is not separate or special in development. The starting point of theory and research that take this explicitly psychological perspective is the mind of the young child and its development in a social world. This emphasis on mind in context has been the foundation for much of the last generation of child language research (e.g., Bates, Benigni, Bretherton, Camaioni, & Volterra, 1979; Bates & MacWhinney, 1982; Bloom, 1970, 1973, 1991, 1993; Bloom & Lahey, 1978; Budwig, 1995; Campbell, 1986; Golinkoff, 1983a, 1983b; Gopnik, 1982, 1988b; Gopnik & Meltzoff, 1985, 1987; Greenfield, 1978, 1980; Nelson, 1974, 1985; Ninio, 1995a; Ochs & Schieffelin, 1984; Schieffelin, 1990; Shatz, 1981, 1983, 1994; Snow, 1989; Tomasello, 1992a; Tomasello & Farrar, 1984; Van Valin, 1991; Zukow-Goldring, 1994, 1997). The model of intentionality and language development (Bloom, 1993) provides a unifying theory for embracing different perspectives on mind in context and encompassing the many aspects of development that determine how words and sentence structures are learned.

The intentionality model subsumes the narrower sense of "intentional communication" in instrumental definitions of language, where the assumption is that language is learned for socially and strategically influencing other persons' actions to get things done in the world, for example, "tool use" (e.g., Bates et al., 1979; Bruner, 1983a; McShane, 1980). When language is viewed primarily as an instrument, the emphasis is on the pragmatics of language use and the practical importance of language as a tool, following Vygotsky (1978). However, tool use is only one of the functions of language, and it is not basic. Expression is basic. Language influences other persons and their actions only because the words in an expression have the power to influence what others might have in mind—their beliefs, feelings, and desires—as a consequence of interpreting the expression. All the functions of language—including its personal, interpersonal, instrumental, regulatory, problem-solving, and other functions—depend on the power of language for expression and interpretation (Bloom, 1993).

Another perspective on language acquisition that is altogether different from this explicitly psychological perspective

is inherent in research and theory which has, as its starting point, the end state and one or another theory of the adult language. The question asked is how the words, structures, and procedures of the mature language system are acquired, and the evidence from children acquiring language becomes useful to the extent it can support one or another theory. In particular, acquisition research influenced by theories of syntax derived from Chomsky (1965) has typically emphasized the specifically linguistic and innate principles (or biases or constraints) that the human infant is assumed to bring to the task of language learning (e.g., Baker & McCarthy, 1981; Crain & Thornton, 1991; Deprez & Pierce, 1993; Gleitman, 1990; Hyams, 1986; Hyams & Wexler, 1993; Lust, in press; Lust, Hermon, & Kornfilt, 1994; Lust, Suner, & Whitman, 1994; Pinker, 1984; Radford, 1990; Tavakolian, 1981; Wexler & Culicover, 1980). Research concerned with how the young child acquires what the adult knows about grammar is discussed by Maratsos (Ch. 9, this Volume).

Research and theory reviewed by Woodward and Markman (Ch. 8, this Volume) also invoke the assumption that children could not otherwise acquire word meanings without explicit guidance from biases (constraints or principles) that are specific to language following, in particular, the philosophy of Quine (1960) (e.g., Golinkoff, Shuff-Bailey, Olquin, & Ruan, 1995; Landau, Smith, & Jones, 1988; Markman, 1989, 1992; Waxman, 1990; Waxman & Markow, 1995). Both Woodward and Markman (Ch. 8, this Volume) and Maratsos (Ch. 9, this Volume) make clear that such approaches to acquisition do not imply that words and grammar are learned apart from other aspects of cognition and the child's context—no one expects children to learn language in a vacuum. Nevertheless, the larger developmental contexts of language and language learning are rarely taken into account.

In contrast, the selection of theory and research topics in this chapter is concerned with the kinds of knowledge that can be attributed to children's behaviors and the factors which influence the acquisition of that knowledge. The emphasis, by and large, is on the process of change in children's knowledge in the course of development from infant abilities to adult language capacities, and the personal and interpersonal contexts in which this development is embedded. Development is not "the gradual accumulation of separate changes . . . [but] a complex dialectical process characterized by . . . qualitative transformations of one form into another [with an] intertwining of external and internal factors" (Vygotsky, 1978, p. 73). Language is just one among many aspects of human functioning, but it touches on all its aspects: "Every behavioral act, whether outward bodily movement or internalized cognitive operation, gains its significance and status in terms of its role in the overall functioning of the organism" (Werner & Kaplan, 1963, pp. 4–5). Thus, both the external linguistic behaviors that we see and hear and the hidden knowledge that gives rise to those behaviors gain their significance only in relation to other aspects of human functioning. Language, as one aspect of a child's development, depends on principles that serve development generally, rather than only principles specific to learning words and acquiring a grammar.

However, language, cognition, emotion, and socialization are ordinarily studied as categories (or domains or modules) of human functioning. The categories or domains reflected in the titles of our scholarly organizations and publications are the result of emphasizing only one or another aspect of development in efforts to explain it. Nevertheless, these categories are not discrete categories for the young child, because they represent mutual influences on development that depend on each other. Just as developments in other aspects of cognition or emotion or social interaction do not happen apart from each other or apart from language, acquiring language does not happen apart from them. But studying the convergence of multiple strands of development is a serious challenge because of the complexities involved. In experimental studies, for example, variables need to be controlled that are considered "extraneous" to a task, such as cues from the environment that can influence a child's response to the task. However, such variation, itself, often determines how language is acquired in real-life situations and contexts (e.g., Bloom, 1973, 1974; Bloom, Tinker, & Beckwith, 1995; Greenfield, 1982; Zukow-Goldring, 1994). Systematic variation is not "noise" but an essential aspect of the data of language (e.g., Labov, 1969; Sankoff, 1974), the data of language development (e.g., Bloom, 1991; Bloom, Miller, & Hood, 1975a; see Shore, 1995, for a review), and cognitive and physical competencies more generally (e.g., Thelen & Smith, 1994).

Language, itself, is typically separated into subsystems for studying acquisition of phonology, words, syntax, and discourse. Yet these subsystems are interdependent and synergistically related to each other and to the communication functions they serve (e.g., Bamberg, Budwig, & Kaplan, 1991; Bates & MacWhinney, 1982, 1987; Bloom, 1976, 1991, 1993; Bloom et al., 1975a; Budwig, 1989, 1996; Van Valin, 1991). For example, in the earliest phases of acquiring a grammar, the words in a child's sentence, the kinds of

syntactic complexity added to the basic sentence, and the conversational context in which it occurs all make variable demands on a child's cognitive resources and influence how much of the sentence the child is able to say. Two-year-olds are able to say longer sentences when they use well-known words, without added complexity in the sentence such as negation, and when they are not expected to participate in extended discourse. Conversely, sentence length is reduced when children use relatively new words, add syntactic complexity, or are pressed to respond to discourse demands (Bloom et al., 1975a). (See Langacker, 1987, for a related theoretical perspective, and Bloom et al., 1995; P. Bloom, 1990a; Boyle & Gerken,1997; and Valian, 1991, for related findings.) The child's developmental goal is the coherence of these several aspects of linguistic knowledge. The goal for those who study language development is to understand how this coherence is achieved.

In sum, one major purpose of this chapter is to emphasize that language development depends on the mutual influence among many aspects of development and is not separate and distinctive. However, this essentially integrative nature of development has not ordinarily been made explicit in theories of language development, as we shall see from the brief historical review in the next section. Following this historical review, the development of language is described in chronological order beginning with its earliest manifestations in the contexts of infancy, before the first words. In succeeding sections, three transitions provide a framework for describing language development from infancy through 3 years of age. The first of these transitions begins toward the end of the first year and continues in the second year with the emergence of words and acquisition of a basic vocabulary. The second is the transition from saying only one word at a time to combining words into phrases and simple sentences, which begins toward the end of the second year. The third transition is from simple sentences expressing a single proposition to complex sentences that express more than one proposition and the meaning relations between them. Complex sentences have their beginnings between 2 and 3 years of age but their acquisition continues well beyond the age of 3 years and into the early school years. Later developments in complex sentences are not within the scope of this chapter, but they are covered by Maratsos (Ch. 9, this Volume).

Unfortunately, space constraints on the length of this chapter have made it necessary to omit a critical factor which contributes to acquisition: the role of input from the environment. Contemporary research into the input children depend on for acquiring language originated with the classic study by Snow (1972). The role of input assumed increased importance in the ensuing years with efforts to refute or support nativist assumptions in theories of acquisition. Research is now accumulating which points to the clear correspondences between adult language input and child language output, for example, in the sentence frames and verb alternations of early syntax (Beckwith, 1988; Beckwith, Tinker, & Bloom, 1989; Naigles & Hoff-Ginsberg, 1995) and the patterning between other forms of language and their functions (e.g., Budwig, 1996). (See Gallaway & Richards, 1994.)

The description of language development that follows here is concerned with how the forms of language—words and the structures underlying simple and complex sentences—are connected to their content and use in affectively and socially driven interactions and are acquired in the context of what children know and are learning about the world of persons, objects, and events. The chapter will conclude by invoking the need for further research that embraces the child's intentionality as the driving force for language development and considers the contributions from all aspects of development to language acquisition, for a truly explanatory theory of language acquisition.

HISTORICAL PERSPECTIVES

The past two generations have seen several major shifts in child language research as one and then another theoretical perspective has gained influence and taken hold. As a consequence, the study of language development has been characterized by several theoretical tensions. These tensions have accumulated as existing theoretical perspectives have continued in the background (or foreground, depending on one's point of view), while other theories have emerged in response to new issues.

Theoretical tensions in the study of child language began as early as the late 1950s with the challenge leveled against behaviorism (notably, Skinner, 1957) from the theory of generative transformational grammar (Chomsky, 1959). Until then, few had questioned the assumption that language behaviors in the environment are sufficient for children to learn language. Chomsky's insight was that children hear sentences but they learn a grammar—the underlying rule system for generating sentences—and that grammar is not given in the environment. The assumption that children can learn language from the linguistic behaviors in the environment was strongly challenged, and the enterprise of studying language acquisition changed direction.

Chomsky proposed that acquiring a grammar must depend on what the child brings to language learning—what the child is born with that makes language learning possible. This innate endowment consists of the syntactic rules (or principles and parameters) that are universal and common to all the languages of the world (e.g., Chomsky, 1986). The question that has endured, however, concerns the relative contributions from environment and endowment to the child's becoming a competent language user. The tension between environmental and innatist explanations of language acquisition that began 40 years ago with Chomsky's critique of behaviorism continues today, and claims that human language is innately predetermined—is a gene as asserted by Pinker (1994) and others—have been vigorously contested by Elman, Bates, Johnson, and Karmiloff-Smith (1996), Tomasello (1995), and others.

Learning the forms of language depends on their function or meaning—children do not just acquire the formal syntax of the language—and they are guided in their acquisition of the semantic-syntactic structure of language by what it is they know about the world (Bloom, 1970; Brown, 1973; Schlesinger, 1971). Thus, interest in how children acquire a grammar turned, in the 1970s, to the semantics of children's language and the role of meaning for acquiring syntax. Acquiring syntax does not stand alone as a formal, linguistic construct in the scheme of a child's total development. "Rather, induction of underlying structure is intimately related to the development of cognition; accounting for the development of language competence must include an account of cognitive function" (Bloom, 1970, p. 232). The inquiry into the cognitive precursors and constraints on language learning was soon joined (e.g., Cromer, 1974; Leonard, 1976; Slobin, 1973; see Johnstone, 1985, for a review).

The initial explanatory model invoked to explain the semantic bases of early language learning was Piaget's (1954) account of cognitive development in infancy (e.g., Bates, 1976; Bloom, 1973; Brown, 1973). The result was a tension between this more general cognitive theory to explain how language as well as other aspects of symbolic behavior develop, and linguistic theory, which invoked an innate, specifically linguistic capacity for acquiring the syntax of a grammar. Inherent in this tension between specifically linguistic theories, on the one hand, and general cognitive theories, on the other, was the continuing tension between innatist and environmental emphases. Linguistic theories emphasized innate principles of universal grammar (what Chomsky called a "language acquisition device") in the child's mind. Cognitive theories emphasized how the child's mind constructs many theories about the world, including a theory of language, as a consequence of interacting with persons and acting on objects.

The attention to context required by semantically-based research was soon extended to include developments in language apart from semantics and syntax, notably the pragmatics of language use in interpersonal and instrumental contexts (Bates, 1976; Bruner, 1975a, 1975b; Dore, 1975; Ervin-Tripp, 1973; Ryan, 1974). The result was to invoke another explanatory model, one that was socially based and heavily influenced by the social context. The tension that resulted was between more general cognitive theory (e.g., Bloom, 1973, 1991, 1993; Gopnik, 1982; Greenfield, 1978; Lifter & Bloom, 1989; Shatz, 1982; Sinclair, 1989), with emphasis primarily on the individual mind of the child, and social theories, with primary emphasis on how children acquire a language in interaction with other persons (e.g., Ninio & Snow, 1988, 1996; Ninio & Wheeler, 1984; Snow, 1989; Tomasello, 1992a, 1992b; Zukow, 1990). Cognitive explanations emphasized the child's contribution to development in contrast to the emphasis on the contribution from other persons in social explanations, with the social context being, at least, a "support system" (e.g., Bruner, 1983) that is "facilitative" (Snow, 1989) or even the determiner of language learning (e.g., Dore, 1983).

The 1980s saw the introduction of yet another research paradigm—"learnability theory" (Pinker, 1984; Wexler & Culicover, 1980)—with roots in the linguistic theories of adult language, notably the theories of Chomsky and his followers. The data of child language became evidence for the correctness of one or another theory of the adult grammar, because the adequacy of any linguistic theory was judged to be how well it accounted for language acquisition. Although "analyses differ in theoretical and empirical detail, they have in common the attempt to achieve some explanatory power by predicting the simultaneous or sequential development of linguistic structures. They also share the goal of providing a principled description of the intermediate stages of development by relating them to adult grammars, and theories of Universal Grammar more generally" (Hyams & Wexler, 1993, pp. 421–422).

Research that looked to cognitive development and the social context for explanations of children's language always presumed that adult language was the goal of development— a theory of the end state is crucial to any theory. However, the difference lay in the explanatory principles that were invoked—whether they were child-centered and concerned with explaining process in development over time, or adult-centered and concerned more with the correctness of one or

another theory of adult grammar. These points of view also differed strongly in the nature of their explanatory principles (see the contributions in Piattelli-Palmerini, 1980). Cognitive and social developmental theories assumed that explanatory principles are more general, with language being only part of an individual's cognition and/or social interaction (Bates, Thal, & Marchman, 1991; Bloom, 1991, 1993; Greenfield, Nelson, & Saltzman, 1972; Shatz, 1981, 1994; Tomasello, 1992a, 1992b). Following Chomsky, learnability theory assumed that language acquisition depends on innate, specifically linguistic principles and processes (P. Bloom, Barss, Nicol, & Conway, 1994; Gleitman, 1981, 1990; Hyams, 1986; Pinker, 1984, 1994; and many others).

Most recently, a new thrust in language acquisition theory has emerged in the form of connectionist models of neurological processing for language learning (e.g., Davis, 1992; Elman et al., 1996; MacWhinney, 1989; Plunkett, 1995), following the lead of Rumelhart and McClelland (1986). Learnability theory had evolved out of the basic premise that the language input a child receives is too impoverished for learning the rules of grammar (that is, children hear only sentences but they need to acquire a grammar). In contrast, connectionist models assume that the information needed to acquire language is, indeed, available in the input, because children are not learning rules, per se. The tension that has now emerged out of these two positions is between models of the neural networks in the brain that represent information about language from the input, on the one hand, and, on the other hand, explanatory models that assume rule-based systems and invoke a strong, innately determined linguistic substructure, following Chomsky. Although the original connectionist models (Rumelhart & McClelland, 1986) and most subsequent research since used acquisition of the English past tense as the paradigm case (Davis, 1992; Marchman, 1993; Plunkett & Marchman, 1993), efforts have also been made to demonstrate connectionist models of syntactic learning (Elman, 1992; MacWhinney, 1987).

In sum, we have several theoretical tensions in language acquisition research today as a result of the last two generations of research efforts and their theoretical justifications. Even those theories of acquisition which focused more broadly on the psychology of the child beyond the child's words and sentences tended to emphasize just one or another aspect of development as central, such as cognition (e.g., Bates, Bretherton, & Snyder, 1988; Bloom, 1970, 1973; Greenfield, Nelson, & Saltzman, 1972; Nelson, 1974; Piaget, 1926, 1954); or social interaction (e.g., Bruner, 1983;

Ninio & Snow, 1988; Tomasello, 1992a; Vygotsky, 1962); or, less often, the affective life of the child (e.g., Dore, 1983). Yet, all of these things necessarily come together: If we are to achieve a truly explanatory theory of language development, our theories and research need to reach beyond language and a focus on only one or another aspect of development. Functionalist theories have begun to do this, based as they are on pragmatics and communicative uses of language (e.g., Bates & MacWhinney, 1982; Bruner, 1983; Budwig, 1995; Dore, 1975; Nelson, 1988; Ninio & Snow, 1988, 1996; Shatz & O'Reilly, 1990; Snow, Pan, Imbens-Bailey, & Herman, 1996). However, functionalist theories, by and large, emphasize the instrumental function of language and how things get done in the world. But the instrumental function is only part of what language does, and it depends on the fundamental fact that language expresses, articulates, makes manifest the contents of mind so they can be shared with other persons—the expressive power of language is basic to all its functions.

The disparate threads of explanation in language acquisition can begin to come together only when theory and research embrace the wholeness of the child in the larger context of the child's overall development. To achieve this will require setting aside the boundaries between historically separate developmental domains and embracing, instead, theories that encompass the mutual influences on development from all aspects of human thought and action (Bloom, 1993; Bloom et al., 1995; Lucariello, 1995). Although our theories, practices, and scholarly journals tend to come in categories, we cannot hope to fully understand human development unless we begin to transcend their boundaries.

The application of dynamic systems theory to understanding development (e.g., Kelso, 1995; Thelen, 1988; Thelen & Ulrich, 1991) invokes this theoretical goal. So far, however, application of systems theory has not gone beyond development within a single domain, such as in explaining early infant stepping or reaching in motor development, although efforts are being made to extend application to cognition and other aspects of development (e.g., Thelen & Smith, 1994; the papers in Smith & Thelen, 1993). Similarly, neural network or connectionist models could be applied to theories dedicated to understanding the multiple threads of influence on language development from the many personal and interpersonal contexts in which it occurs.

I have offered such an integrative model for explaining language acquisition by proposing that the core of development that brings an infant to the threshold of language at the end of the first year, and that motivates and sustains language acquisition in the succeeding years, is in the child's intentionality and the necessary convergence of developments in affect, cognition, and social connectedness to other persons (e.g., Bloom, 1993; Bloom et al., 1995). Languages are learned because children strive to maintain intersubjectivity with other persons—to share what they and others are feeling and thinking. In the first year of life, before language, this intersubjectivity depends on the affect expressions between baby and caregiver. By the end of the first year, affect expression is well developed for intersubjectivity. But 1-year-olds have also had a year of learning about the world. The result of their early cognitive development is more elaborate intentional states that require expression and need to be articulated if they are to be shared with other persons. Language expresses and also articulates the contents of intentional states in a way that the forms of affect expression cannot. Thus, if language is to keep up with developments in cognition and social connectedness taking place in the first year of life, children need to acquire words and the procedures for sentences for expression and interpretation.

The focus in the Bloom model is on the young child's intentionality—on the states of mind in consciousness that underlie all the child's actions, including acts of expression and interpretation. Development depends on a process of transaction between internal representations in intentional states and the external social and physical world. This process is governed by certain generalizations I have called the principles of relevance, discrepancy, and elaboration (Bloom, 1993). According to the principle of *relevance,* development is enhanced when events in the context bear upon and are pertinent to what the child has in mind. The principle of relevance narrows the range of possible meanings that linguistic units can have, directing a child to the formal properties to be learned. Children learn linguistic units that bear on what they have in mind. According to the principle of *discrepancy,* development is enhanced when the child acts to resolve a mismatch between contents of mind and things already evident in the context. Developments in the ability to recall past events and anticipate new events create contents of mind that cannot be known from shared perceptions and assumptions in the here-and-now. Children will have to acquire a language, because what they have in mind must be expressed if it is to be known and shared by others who cannot exploit clues from the context for understanding. And finally, the principle of elaboration presses the child to learn increasingly more of the language. According to the principle of *elaboration,* children will have to learn more words and, eventually, procedures for sentences, if they are to express and articulate the increasingly elaborated contents of mind made possible by developments in cognition and social and emotional understanding (Bloom, 1973, 1993).

A major goal in the rest of this chapter is to show how children learn the forms of language only in relation to the content and use of language forms, and how developments in language are integrated with developments in cognition, affect, and social connectedness in children's everyday actions and interactions. The origins of this integration can be found in earliest infancy.

THE ORIGINS OF LANGUAGE IN INFANCY

Infants begin to work toward acquiring language virtually from the moment of birth. The context of language development begins with certain basic capacities serving communication and language that are already in place at the start of life. In the first few hours of life, a human infant attends to sights, smells, and sounds and can make some sense of them. For instance, a newborn infant can tell the difference between its own mother's voice and a female stranger's voice (DeCasper & Fifer, 1980) and can detect the difference between two vowel sounds (Clarkson & Berg, 1983). Shortly after birth, an infant will look into another's face and, after wavering a bit, will settle on the eyes and stay there, intently gazing into another pair of eyes (Brazelton & Cramer, 1990). When only a few months old, infants can appreciate that a moving object has boundaries and obeys certain physical laws (Baillargeon, 1992; Spelke, 1988, 1991). And, from the moment of birth, infants display affect signals—frowns, whines, cries, and nascent smiles—which their caregivers interpret as meaningful. All these things contribute to the development of an intentional being in the first year of life—a person, with thoughts and feelings that include other persons and objects and events in the world. By the end of the first year, that person has begun to acquire a language for expressing this intentionality.

The behaviors in infancy that will prove to be relevant to the eventual emergence and development of language do not serve the functions of language originally. The sounds of speech are a good example. Speech sounds have their origin in the early vocalizations that accompany the infant's breathing and eating; these are gradually refined into the sounds of babbling out of which the first words

will eventually appear (Koopmans-van Beinum & van der Stelt, 1984; Oller, 1980; Ratner, 1994; Stark, 1980, 1986). The sounds of speech are an aspect of the form of language; other infant behaviors will contribute to the content or meaning of language; and the social contact and interpersonal relationships between the infant and other persons will contribute to eventual conversations and the pragmatics of language use.

Language consists of these three components: form, content, and use (Bloom & Lahey, 1978; Lahey, 1988). The shapes of words, the structures of sentences, the way the language sounds when it is spoken, or looks when it is configured by the hands in sign languages, determine the form of language. The sounds of the language make up its phonology; the words of the language make up its dictionary or lexicon; the inflectional and derivational construction of words make up its morphology; and sentence structures make up the syntax of language.

What the words and sentences mean—what they are about—is the content of language. The string of sounds /p-oh-n-i/ has meaning, is the word *pony,* only if it connects with the mental symbol of an object pony. The sentence "The pony jumped the fence" has content by virtue of the meaning of the individual words in the sentence plus the meaning relationships between the words *pony* and *jump* and *fence.* Language content depends on the semantics of language for the meaning of words and meaning relations between words. The orderly arrangement of words and their inflections in sentences according to the meaning relations they encode combines syntax, semantics, and morphology which, together, make up the grammar of the language.

The purposes of language and the different ways of saying more or less the same thing to achieve a particular purpose concern the pragmatics of language use. The use of language has to do with how we vary the forms of language in order to accomplish different purposes in different situations. How we get and give information, solve problems, organize events, get people to do things, and so forth depends on language to influence the thoughts and actions of ourselves and other persons. We need to use language differently in different sorts of circumstances in order to accomplish such purposes—taking into account where we are and to whom we are talking when we choose between, for example, "I'm thirsty," "I need a drink," "I'll have a glass of water, if you please," or "Gimme a Coke" for the same purpose.

Language is the integration of form, content, and use; the three components necessarily come together. Forms without meaning, like *dak* or *nef*, are empty; randomly connected words, like "milk chase the," are gibberish; we usually don't say words and sentences just to talk—we have some reason or purpose in mind. Unless form, content, and use come together, we cannot use language for expression and interpretation. But the behaviors in infancy that anticipate the form, content, and use of language are not integrated with each other. Neither the early behaviors that anticipate the later forms of speech and sign language nor the early turn-taking behaviors that anticipate the eventual development of conversations are endowed with the kinds of content and purpose expressed by words in later conversational exchanges (Collis, 1985; Golinkoff, 1983a). These early behaviors originally represent more or less separate threads of development. They come together only gradually during the first year of life as infant abilities and social contexts inform each other in the process of development (Bloom & Lahey, 1978).

Origins of Language Use

A key factor contributing to the social connectedness between babies and caregivers is the timing between them as they look at each other and vocalize during their interactions; these synchronous interactions have been described as a "proto-conversation" (Bateson, 1975). The timing itself cannot be separated from the entire social package in which it is embedded—the rich array of visual, auditory, and kinesthetic information in a social display (Beebe & Jaffe, 1992; Stern, 1985). Sensitivity to timing involves sensitivity to affective and cognitive information in the interaction as well. Early patterns of gazing and vocalizing between infant and caregiver, at least in Western societies, indicate that the turn-taking capacities for the give-and-take interactions of conversation are in place at least by 3 months of age, however differently caregivers in different cultures might tap into them (Bateson, 1975; K. Bloom, 1977, 1990; Stern, Jaffe, Beebe, & Bennett, 1975; Trevarthen, 1977).

Vocalization from a socially responsive adult elicits a social response from a baby, whether the adult's vocalization is contingent on the baby's own vocalization or occurs at random. However, infants who experience contingent responding are more likely to pause after the adult's response, their interactions assume the basic property of turn-taking, and they sound more speech-like than infants who experience random responding (K. Bloom, 1977, 1990; K. Bloom, Russell, & Wassenberg, 1987). Thus, the frequency and sounds of infant vocalizations in the first few months of life are responsive to social cues and other aspects of the context (Blake & de Boysson-Bardies, 1992; Delack, 1976; Delack & Fowlow, 1978; D'Odorico & Franco, 1991; Legerstee, 1991; Legerstee, Pomerleau, Malcuit, & Feider, 1987; Lewis & Freedle, 1973). Such sensitivity to context has been described by these and other investigators as the beginnings of the relationship between sound and meaning, which is critical to the eventual use of language.

An infant's vocalizations also vary according to what the infant is feeling—both physically and affectively. This is true for crying and smiling, but more fine-grained variation in expression is possible. For example, the newborn's cry begins to develop in complex ways as a function of physiological changes that take place in the vocal tract and developments in the capacity for articulatory-acoustic connections (Kent, 1981). Different patterns of cry have been identified that correspond to different internal states (Wolff, 1969). A baby's typical cry is prolonged and waxes and wanes. Discomfort cries, however, are made up of short series of cry bursts. Caregivers can attribute feelings and physiological states to a baby on the basis of the shape of the cry and other noncry vocalizations as well, at least by the last quarter of the first year. The integration of the expressive behaviors of infants—their affect expression, vocalization, gaze, and hand movements—is influenced as well by other developments, for example in their more general motor abilities (Fogel, 1992; Fogel & Thelen, 1987; van Beek, 1991; van der Stelt, & Koopmans-van Beinum, 1986).

The threads of continuity from early prelinguistic communication to later communication with language can be found in infants' affective and social connectedness to other persons, virtually from the beginning of life (Bullowa, 1979; Feagans, Garvey, & Golinkoff, 1983; Golinkoff, 1983b; Lewis & Rosenblum, 1978; Lock, 1978; Schaffer, 1977; Tronick, 1982; Ziajka, 1981). A prevailing theme is the sharing of affective meaning between baby and caregiver for the intersubjectivity that develops between them (Emde, 1984; Newson, 1977; Papousek, Papousek, & Koester, 1986; Rogoff, 1990; Stern, 1985; Trevarthen, 1977, 1979; Trevarthen & Hubley, 1978; Werner & Kaplan, 1963). The motivation for learning language is the infant's need to sustain intersubjectivity with other persons and thereby locate the self in a social world (Bloom, 1993).

Infant and caregiver indicate their mutual attention and shared understanding to an object or event through joint adjustments in posture, gaze, and head orientation toward one another. They eventually move from interactive contexts with shared affective meaning to contexts in which meaning is shared in speech (Bakeman & Adamson, 1984; Collis, 1979; Edwards, 1978; Stern, 1977), participating in what Sperber and Wilson called "ostensive-inferential communication" (1986, p. 63). Such mutual signals become particularly important in the second and third year as child and caregiver inform each other about the information in the context that might be relevant for word learning. But in the first year, shared signals sustain intersubjectivity between them and provide the foundation for the episodes of joint attention within which much of language will be learned (e.g., Akhtar & Tomasello, in press; Bruner, 1975a; 1983; Tomasello, 1988; Zukow-Goldring & Ferko, 1994).

In sum, infants can participate in organized, meaningful exchanges without words long before language begins. The early turn-taking patterns of infancy continue in the development of older 1- and 2-year-old children who are learning words and sentences for participating in conversations (Bloom, Margulis, Tinker, & Fujita, 1996; Bloom, Rocissano, & Hood, 1976; Chapman, Miller, MacKenzie, & Bedrosian, 1981; Foster, 1986; Harris, 1992; Howe, 1981; Kaye & Charney, 1980; Mannle, Barton, & Tomasello, 1992; Shatz, 1983; Snow, 1977). But developments in conversation take place because children have something to say to other persons and want to understand what others have to say to them. The mental meanings they express and interpret from the expressions of others come from what they have learned about objects, events, and relations in the world, and this knowledge gained in the first year determines the content of the language they will learn in the second and third years.

Origins of Language Content

The meanings of words make up the dictionary of a language. All who know the language share a mental dictionary of the words in the language, although individual dictionaries may differ in certain respects by virtue of differences in experience. The meanings of sentences are determined by the syntactic arrangements of words and morphological inflections on words. All who know the language share knowledge of the basic procedures for the grammar of the language. In turn, meaning in language comes from the knowledge about the world that is shared by the speakers of the language. For example, in order to know the word *more,* it is necessary to know something about the

relationship of one thing or group of things to another; one needs to know something about ponies in order to know the meaning of the word *pony*. The knowledge about the world on which the meanings of language are based begins with cognitive developments in infancy, notably the symbolic capacity and conceptual structure.

Language itself consists of symbols. Words are symbols because they stand for the elements we have in mind in acts of expression and interpretation. Mental elements are named by the forms of language in expression and are "set up mentally, pointed to, and identified" by the forms of language in interpretation (Fauconnier, 1985, p. 2). Such mental elements are, in turn, symbolic because they stand for what we know about things in the world. When a child looks at the clock on the wall and says "tick-tock," the act of reference has a mental meaning that gives rise to the behavior we observe. The mental meaning represents and refers to the object in the world; the word the child says names the representation in the mental meaning (Bloom, 1993). The symbolic capacity begins to develop in the first few months of life and makes it possible for the infant to construct mental meanings. These mental meanings are intentional states about persons, things, events, and relationships.

Constructing mental meanings or intentional states makes use of the knowledge about the world that is represented in conceptual structure in memory. Concepts and the relations between them are ultimately responsible for the content of language—both the meaning of object words like *milk,* relational words like *more,* and the relational meanings between words expressed by sentences. Concepts of objects, events, and relationships provide the bases for acquiring word meanings and the semantic structure of language. Such conceptual and eventually linguistic categories build on an infant's early experiences that result in appreciations for the consequences of movement and change. The meanings of children's words and their sentences in the second year have to do with movement and changes in location resulting from movement (Bloom, 1970, 1981, 1991; Bloom, Lightbown, & Hood, 1975b; Nelson, 1974). In turn, concepts of movement and location have been invoked for explaining the conceptual basis for adult language (e.g., Jackendoff, 1983, 1991; Langacker, 1987). The foundation for meaning and the content of language in general, then, is in the concepts of objects, movement, and location that begin to be formed in the first year of life.

The considerable literature on categorization and concept formation has been concerned, by and large, only with object concepts (see chapters by Mandler, Ch. 6, and

Woodward & Markman, Ch. 8, this Volume). However, the objective world is a world of affordances based on the relationships in which objects belong and into which they can enter (Gibson, 1979). When 1-year-olds use words like *up, more,* and *gone,* we can infer that they know something about the relational concepts for such words. But long before they use the words that express such relationships, infants show us in many ways that they already know something about the ways persons relate to objects and objects relate to each other (e.g., Bloom, 1973; Nelson, 1974; Mandler, 1992). Their earliest relational concepts are not learned through language. For example, using evidence from 1-year-old children's play, four relational concepts could be attributed to children's prelinguistic object knowledge—movement, location, containment, and support (Lifter & Bloom, 1989). Such concepts are prelinguistic because children construct relationships between objects with the general thematic relationship of containment and support long before they say the words *in* and *on*. These two words are among the earliest words children learn to say (Clark, 1973), but further research is needed for evidence of when children understand the words in relation to understanding the concepts of containment and support.

The relational concepts formed out of these kinds of appreciations of the effects of movement and change begin to develop before language and contribute to providing the content of language as it develops in the early childhood years. They include such concepts as nonexistence, disappearance, and reappearance, which contribute to learning particular words (like *gone* and *more* for instance) (Bloom, 1970, 1973; Gopnik, 1988a; Gopnik & Choi, 1990; Gopnik & Meltzoff, 1986; McCune-Nicolich, 1981). Other concepts such as containment, support, agency, effectance, and the like embrace such diverse thematic relations between objects as pouring milk into and out of cups, putting hats on heads, eating with a spoon, sitting on a chair, and so forth. These thematic relations are the everyday events with persons and objects that contribute to a child's knowledge base and, eventually, the content of language in the semantics of sentences.

Origins of Language Forms

Young infants' capacities that will eventually serve in learning the forms language can take include (a) vocalizations and speech sound perception, which anticipate learning the sound system of language; (b) hand movements, which anticipate the configurations and motions of sign language; and (c) the boundaries in sentences between words, phrases, and clauses. Although infants show us they know something rudimentary about the forms of language, these same behaviors, or behaviors derived from them, do not begin to become functional and integrated with meaning and the pragmatics of language use until the second year.

The units of mature speech are syllables, which are larger vocal-articulatory gestures than single phonemes or sounds, and they consist of consonant and vowel combinations. Their development begins in the first half year of life with maturation of the vocal-articulatory anatomy as well as the sensorimotor connections between audition and production systems (Kent, 1981; Kent & Miolo, 1995; Netsell, 1981; Oller & Eilers, 1988; Studdert-Kennedy, 1979). In addition to maturation, social factors contribute to the development of syllables. Infant vocalizing can begin to assume the contours of syllables as early as 3 months of age, when infants and caregivers engage in reciprocal and contingent vocal turn-taking. If an adult vocalizes just after the baby does, so that some representation of the infant's own vocalizing presumably remains within the infant's attention, the infant's vocalization assumes a more speechlike, syllabic quality (K. Bloom, Russell, & Wassenberg, 1987). The subcortical sensorimotor connections in such primitive articulatory matching afford a growing sensitivity to verbal input and infants' appreciation for the likenesses between the sounds they hear and the sounds they can make. These sorts of experiences lead, in the ensuing months, to the nascent cortical connections needed for the eventual approximation of speech sound categories (Kent & Miolo, 1995).

The beginning of the articulatory capabilities for actual words comes with the onset of babbling, some time between 6 and 9 months, when muscle control develops for coordinating a succession of consonant- and vowel-like sounds. In babbling, the baby's vocalizing has a clear syllabic form and consists of a series of consonant-vowel combinations. The babbling is reduplicated when each syllable in a string of babbling is the same. The consonants may be stops (like /d/), nasals (like /n/), or glides (like /y/), for example "dadadada," "nananana," "yayayaya." Adults now find it easier to imitate the baby because both the timing of syllables and the sounds themselves increasingly resemble the rhythm and sounds of adult speech. Nonreduplicated babbling, consisting of strings of syllables that combine different consonants and vowels and sound more like efforts to say words, has been reported in some studies to begin somewhat later (Elbers, 1982; Oller, 1980; Oller & Eilers, 1988; Stark, 1980, 1986). However, other studies have reported that while babbling increases over time, in general, and multisyllabic babbling becomes more frequent, in particular, both reduplicated and nonreduplicated patterns occur from the beginning of babbling at 6 to 7 months of age (Mitchell & Kent, 1990; Smith, Brown-Sweeney, & Stoel-Gammon, 1989).

Early hand positions and movements in the first few months resemble the gestures of mature language users (Fogel, 1981; Papousek & Papousek, 1977). For deaf children, these may anticipate the phonetic shapes of sign language, just as the early cry, comfort, and feeding sounds of hearing infants anticipate the eventual sounds of speech. Deaf infants, born to deaf parents who sign, babble with their hands and fingers at the same age that hearing children babble vocally, and their hand movements show the same kinds of consistency in phonetic and syllabic patterning that has been observed in hearing children's vocal babbling. These similarities in timing and structure between manual and vocal babbling suggest "a unitary language capacity that underlies human signed and spoken language acquisition" (Petitto & Marentette, 1991, p. 1495). Thus, speech is only one of the possible forms of language, and although the vocal modality is obviously favored for speech, it is not privileged for the development of language.

Early words grow out of a small number of core sounds that the infant favors in babbling, and the sounds that infants babble help to determine the words they do or do not acquire subsequently. Babbling continues after the first words begin to appear and continues to provide the phonological context out of which the young language learner will extract the sounds for words (e.g., Elbers & Ton, 1985; Georghov, 1911, cited in Ingram, 1991; Locke, 1988, 1993; Oller & Eilers, 1988; Schwartz, 1988; Smith, 1988; Stoel-Gammon, 1985; Vihman, 1992; Vihman, Macken, Miller, Simmons, & Miller, 1985; Vihman & Miller, 1988). The fact that the sounds infants babble are the same sounds they use in their first words and, indeed, in the first several years of word learning, may be due to two factors. First, frequent words in the language—the words that children also learn earliest—no doubt contain the most frequent sound patterns in the language. Second, these sound patterns may be most frequent because they are within the capacities of the infant's developing acoustic-articulatory system. Words in a language that are relatively infrequent, longer, and learned later may contain those sounds that are less likely to occur in babbling and the words of early

vocabularies (such as the fricatives, /sh/; affricates, /ch/; and liquids, /j/ and /r/). In their speech to infants, caregivers no doubt use those words that are both consistent with infants' sound-making capacities and relevant to what infants attend to and so learn about.

At the same time that very young infants' sound-making capacities are quite immature, they are able to discriminate between different computer-generated speech sounds presented to them in controlled experimental tasks. Even newborns are able to detect differences between vowel sounds when the measure of attention (orienting response) is heart rate deceleration (Clarkson & Berg, 1983). Moreover, they perceive speech sounds categorically, in the same way that adults do. This categorical perception means that they hear the differences between sounds from two different sound categories, such as /p/ and /b/, more reliably than they hear the differences between sounds from the same category, such as variants of /p/. The original findings by Eimas, Siqueland, Jusczyk, and Vigorito (1971) have since been replicated for other speech sounds and among infants learning a variety of languages (Aslin, Pisoni, & Jusczyk, 1983; Eimas & Miller, 1981; Kuhl, 1987, 1994).

Categorical perception is mediated by a general psychoacoustic processing mechanism and is not a specifically linguistic ability, even though it will serve the eventual development of speech. For example, mammals who never acquire speech are able to perceive speech sounds categorically (e.g., Aslin & Pisoni, 1980; Kuhl, 1994; Kuhl & Miller, 1975). The infant data tell us that the processing system must begin to operate virtually at birth, providing a form of perception that surely facilitates, and perhaps even makes possible, the acquisition of speech (Miller & Eimas, 1983, p. 162). Speech perception abilities are soon modified by experience in hearing speech from adults in the environment, beginning in the first few weeks of life, so that infants learn to perceive new sound contrasts and lose the ability to hear differences between other sounds that are not phonemic in the language of the adults around them (e.g., Aslin & Pisoni, 1980; Kuhl, 1994).

Early perception of syllables has also been demonstrated in the first few days of life by infants who learned to discriminate between syllables like *pat* and *tap* (Moon, Bever, & Fifer, 1992). Older infants have shown sensitivity to the boundaries between linguistic units that are larger than speech sounds and syllables—the clauses, phrases, and words in sentences—when these are cued by rhythm and pause patterns inserted at the appropriate junctures in sentences (in contrast to pauses inserted within units).

Moreover, boundaries between larger units are detected before boundaries between smaller units (Fernald & Mazzie, 1991; Hirsh-Pasek & Golinkoff, 1993). Infants as young as 6 months old prefer to listen to speech in which pauses occur between two clauses in a sentence than speech in which pauses are artificially inserted within a clause (Hirsh-Pasek et al., 1987; Jusczyk et al., 1992; Kemler-Nelson et al., 1989). By 9 months of age, infants indicate preference for sentences in which pauses separate smaller units, like noun phrase and verb phrase, over sentences with pauses inserted within a phrase (Jusczyk et al., 1992). By 11 months, they show appreciation for the perceptual boundaries that separate words in sentences.

The original interpretation from these studies of infants' perception of the boundaries between linguistic units like phrases and clauses is that infants already have an appreciation for the syntactic form of sentences, even though they are not yet able to even understand words. Another, more conservative interpretation is that infants have learned only to discriminate vocalizations in their own language that are continuous (and sound more natural) from vocalizations that are interrupted by artificially inserted pauses (Fernald & McRoberts, 1996). They are not as likely to listen to linguistic units with unusual or infrequent pause patterns, but nonetheless do appear to be sensitive to frequent patterns that are potentially important for learning syntactic structure (Gerken, 1996; Shady, Gerken, & Jusczyk, 1995). In addition, 9-month-old infants' appreciation for correspondences between prosody and linguistic boundaries is influenced by factors other than syntactic boundaries, like whether sentence subjects are nouns or pronouns and sentences are questions or statements (Gerken, Jusczyk, & Mandel, 1994).

In sum, the interplay between maturation and experience in the first year of life makes it possible for the baby to move from cries, coos, gurgles, and grunts to the tentative sounds and syllables of early words and, eventually, to the units that make up the words and sentences of the language. These productions and perceptions are never divorced from the developmental context. From the very first cries, infants are expressing something, and caregivers readily tune into their sounds and try to understand them. Many factors—cognitive, social, cultural, and linguistic—come into play as the infant moves toward learning words and acquiring the grammar of a language. Cognitively, to learn words and the syntax of sentences is to learn how to express mental meanings—intentional states that are informed by what the infant has learned about objects, events,

and relations in the world. Socially, learning words and syntax is learning how persons in a society make public what is otherwise private and internal to themselves and thereby influence each other's thoughts, feelings, and actions. Culturally, to learn words and procedures for sentences is to learn something of the values that have evolved in a society for creating and sharing a world view.

THE FIRST TRANSITION: EMERGENCE OF WORDS AND ACQUIRING A VOCABULARY

The basic contours of the emergence of language are agreed upon by most researchers; in fact, a description in an earlier edition of the *Manual of Child Psychology* more than 50 years ago remains appropriate:

> The literature is in general agreement that the first sounds of the newborn infant are the overt elements from which speech develops, that vocalizations are used as a means of communication before words proper are used; that comprehension appears before the use of words; that the normal child has a repertoire of a very few words by one year of age, that development is slow in the first months of the second year, but that toward the end of that year a great increase in the speed of progress appears; . . . that [use of words] for specific meanings is a developmental process; . . . that the first words have the force of a phrase or sentence, and combinations of words do not begin for some time. (McCarthy, 1946, p. 488, quoting Dewey, 1935, p. 251, citing a survey in French by Decroly, 1934)

We can unpack this quote from McCarthy and report that research in the succeeding years has continued to document the observation that "the first sounds of the newborn infant are the overt elements from which speech develops" (e.g., Oller, 1980; Oller, Wieman, Doyle, & Ross, 1976; Stark, 1980, 1986). Other studies have shown how vocalizations are used in the context of communication before words appear (e.g., Bateson, 1975; Bullowa, 1979; Fogel & Thelen, 1987; Harding & Golinkoff, 1979; see K. Bloom, 1990). Still other research confirmed that "development is slow in the first months of the second year," . . . that "toward the end of that year a great increase in the speed of progress appears," . . . that the use of words "for specific meanings is a developmental process," . . . that "the first words have the force of a phrase or sentence, and combinations of words do not begin for some time" (e.g., Anglin, 1977; Bates, Bretherton, &

Snyder, 1988; Bloom, 1973, 1993; Dromi, 1987; Goldfield & Reznick, 1990; Greenfield & Smith, 1976; Nelson, 1973, 1986).

First words begin at about the first birthday, give or take a few months. They are tentative, imprecise, and fragile at first, and new words are acquired slowly in the several months after words begin to appear. Some time toward the end of the second year things pick up, and children begin to learn more and more different words, begin to learn words more rapidly, and begin to use their words more easily and readily. The words infants learn in the second year are guided by the perceptual attributes of the objects they name. Words are also learned in the context of actions and the functions of the objects they name, and learning words depends on learning about objects and events in general and acquiring concepts of *particular* objects, events, and relationships (Bloom, 1973, 1993; Clark, 1973; Gopnik, 1988b; Gopnik & Meltzoff, 1986; Lifter & Bloom, 1989; McCune-Nicolich, 1981; Nelson, 1974; Nelson & Lucariello, 1985).

However, beyond these broad descriptive strokes, we have less agreement on the details of early language and even less consensus on how best to explain its development. This is so because studies of lexical development in the second year have typically looked at only one part of the "whole" child or looked only at one aspect of language development from a single theoretical perspective. Efforts to explain early word learning have invoked different theoretical models, and these have been based alternatively on either social-pragmatic factors, cognitive developments, or principles and constraints that guide word learning. The result is an essential consensus with respect to the broad outline of development, less agreement on the details, and still less agreement on theoretical explanations of how words are acquired (Bloom, Tinker, & Margulis, 1993).

First Words

Young infants who are not yet saying words often show us that they recognize the words other persons say (Hirsh-Pacek & Golinkoff, 1991; Oviatt, 1982), and they can even be taught to recognize novel labels for novel objects (e.g., Woodward, Markman, & Fitzsimmons, 1994). The average age for early word comprehension in carefully controlled experimental tests is in the range of 12 to 14 months (Golinkoff & Hirsh-Pasek, 1987; Oviatt, 1980). However, many parents report that their infants begin to understand words and even say words much earlier, sometimes as

young as 8 months of age (Bates et al., 1995; Bloom, 1993; McCarthy, 1946, 1954).

Before conventional words appear, many children use forms with some phonetic consistency that are "endowed with meaning" but are considered "nonstandard" or "unconventional," because they are not consistent in form and meaning with a conventional word in the language (Leopold, 1939, p. 164). Halliday (1975) called such words "proto-language," and Dore (1983) called them "indexical expressions." Early grunt sounds were analyzed as a particular instance of such early efforts at communicating by McCune et al. (1996). Most parents readily respond to a child's efforts to say words when the vocalizations seem relevant to the child's intent to communicate and to what is going on around them at the time.

Endowing an infant's vocalization with the status of a word is a more serious business for the researcher than it is for the parent. Parents are licensed to overattribute and, in fact, they and their infants may well enjoy and benefit from such attributions. But the researcher has the responsibility of transforming an infant's vocalizations into data for analysis in order to obtain evidence for one or another conclusion, and so the importance of the criteria used cannot be minimized (see, in particular, Dore, 1983; Dore, Franklin, Miller, & Ramer, 1976; Dromi, 1987; Halliday, 1975; Leopold, 1939; McCarthy, 1954; Plunkett, 1993; Vihman & McCune, 1994). Such criteria draw on several aspects of an infant's vocalization, including its phonetic shape, consistency, frequency, and meaningfulness in relation to something going on in the situation. The two criteria most often recruited together for crediting a child with words are aspects of phonetic shape and presumed meaning that are shared by a conventional word in the language.

Sometime toward the end of the second year, most children show a vocabulary spurt, and by the time they are 18 to 19 months old, have learned about 50 words on average (e.g., Bates et al., 1995; Bloom, 1973, 1993; Bloom et al., 1993; Dromi, 1987, 1993; Nelson, 1973). The number of new words apt to be learned on any given day during the preschool years is impressive. One estimate is that the average child who has reached the first grade is able to recognize about 10,000 words, including 6,000 main entry dictionary words in addition to derived words, and has learned an estimated 5.5 main entry words per day since the age of 18 months (Anglin, 1993). Another estimate is that children learn 13 new words a day on average before the age of 18 years—evidence of their ability to "soak up words" (Miller, 1986, p. 9; see also, Carey, 1978; Templin, 1957).

However, for statistical reasons, increase in vocabulary cannot be strictly linear because there is an inherent limitation in the number of words to be learned (Bates & Carnevale, 1993). This means that word learning probably shows several spurts in the course of development—the vocabulary spurt at around 50 words and before the transition to sentences in the second year is one; perhaps entry into school is an opportunity for another. Vocabulary spurts might be associated with other kinds of experience or cognitive development as well.

Similar developments underlie acquisition of signed words by deaf children. In some studies of the acquisition of signs, mothers of young deaf infants have reported conventional signs at a very early age—much earlier than is typically reported for words spoken by hearing children (Bonvillian, Orlansky, & Novack, 1983; Orlansky & Bonvillian, 1988; but see Newport & Meier, 1985 for discussion). Many hand movements made by both hearing and deaf infants have a counterpart in later gesture and mature sign languages—raising the question of whether deaf parents might be overinterpreting their infants' hand movements when looking for signs, just as parents of hearing children might overinterpret efforts at vocalizations as words. In studies involving more controlled observations, differences in onset of spoken and signed words have been negligible (Acredolo & Goodwyn, 1991; Petitto 1991). Nor do children learning sign language show an age advantage for later aspects of language acquisition (Newport & Meier, 1985). (See Lillo-Martin, 1996, for a full review of research in the acquisition of American Sign Language.)

Early words depend on perceptible objects and familiar actions and events for learning and subsequent retrieval and recall. Many developmental accounts of children's first words have noted the strong association between word and object, word and action, or word and event (e.g., Barrett, 1985; Barrett, Harris, & Chasin, 1991; Bates et al., 1979; Bloom, 1973; Dore, 1983; Dromi, 1987, 1993, 1996; McShane, 1980; Nelson, 1985; Nelson & Lucariello, 1985; Werner & Kaplan, 1963; Whitehurst, Kedesdy, & White, 1982). In effect, infants perform a fast mapping or association that allows them to recall a novel word when recognizing the episodic cue with which it was associated originally. Fast mapping in comprehension tasks has generally been used to explain the relative ease with which older children seem to acquire new word meanings (Carey & Bartlett, 1978; Chapman, Bird, & Schwartz, 1990; Dollaghan, 1985).

Most research accounts stress the association between words and the functions of words in the situation in which the child hears them—the circumstances perceptible to caregivers and researchers as well as to the child (see Budwig, 1996 for discussion). The internal dimension of the child's experience of a word—the feelings and desires accompanying it—contributes to the relevance of the word for learning it but is considered less often. Children exploit external resources from the social and physical context—the adults around them who talk about their objects of attention and engagement (e.g., Bruner, 1983; Nelson, 1985; Tomasello, 1988, 1992a). But they also exploit their internal cognitive and affective resources, such as their propensities to categorize objects and events (e.g., Bloom, 1973, 1993; Gopnik & Meltzoff, 1987, 1993; Lucariello, 1987a; Markman, 1984, 1989; Nelson, 1974) and their affective engagement in what is going on around them (Bloom 1993; Bloom & Beckwith, 1989; Bloom et al., 1985). These are the factors that contribute to the relevance of words for learning them.

A word the child hears is relevant when its target is part of what the child has in mind, part of the representations in consciousness that are the child's intentional states—what the child is feeling and thinking at the time. "Relevance is the single property that makes information worth processing and determines the particular assumptions an individual is most likely to construct and process" (Sperber & Wilson, 1986, p. 46). Relevance is not the same as salience. For example, the Empire State Building at 34th Street in New York City is salient to people riding the 5th Avenue bus downtown, but not necessarily relevant unless, of course, they are reminded they need to meet someone on the corner of 34th Street. In the word learning situation, something that is salient to an adult is not necessarily relevant to what the child has in mind at the time, even when the adult calls the child's attention to it. What is salient in the context becomes useful to the child only when it is pertinent and bears upon or is connected to the elements, roles, relationships in the configuration in the child's mind, that is, when it is "information worth processing" (using the felicitous phrase of Sperber & Wilson, 1986). To be sure, what the child has in mind changes on hearing words (Woodward & Markman, Ch. 8, this Volume), but that is the consequence of all acts of interpretation.

Two of a child's resources, in particular, contribute to the configurations that determine the relevance of words and hence guide the child in discovering a word's meaning. One is the child's engagement—what the child is feeling about it at the time—and engagement is an affective process. The other is the child's understanding of the objects, events, and circumstances in occasions of joint attention with caregivers, and this understanding is a function of cognitive development. Word learning is intimately related to developments in both affect and cognition.

Word Learning and Affective Development

Although affect expression and language are complementary systems of expression (Jespersen, 1922), affect has been largely left out of child language research and theory. Yet the affective life of a child has been considered crucial to other aspects of development—whether one's perspective is traditional psychodynamic theory, attachment theory, or emotions theory. For example, according to Piaget, affect is the fuel that drives the engine of cognitive development (Piaget, 1981). Theories of infant emotion and development frequently emphasize the organizing function of emotions for the motivation and organization of actions (Barrett & Campos, 1987; Izard, 1977, 1986; Izard & Malatesta, 1987; Sroufe, 1984; Stern, 1985; Thompson, 1989).

Language and affect provide two different forms of expression for expressing different aspects of mental meanings. Affect expression is already in place as the medium of sharing between infant and caregiver long before language and is the far more frequent form of expression when words begin toward the end of the first year. The onset of language in the second year does not herald a general increase in expressivity, however, because emotional expression does not also increase as speech increases between first words and a vocabulary spurt. But neither does the frequency of emotional expression decrease, and children do not express emotion less often as they learn language (Bloom, Beckwith, Capatides, & Hafitz, 1988). This finding means that children do not learn to say words instead of expressing affect. Although they learn to say more words and linguistic expression increases in the single-word period, they continue to express their feelings through displays of affect as they learn language for expressing what their feelings are about.

Words allow more explicit articulation of the elements, roles, and relations between them in intentional states than is possible with affective displays alone, and words become integrated into a child's affective life in several ways in the course of development (Bloom, 1993). Children's talk is very often about the circumstances, causes, and consequences of their emotional experiences, because these are the things that are relevant to them (Bloom & Beckwith,

1989; Bloom et al., 1988; Bloom & Capatides, 1987a; Bretherton, Fritz, Zahn-Wexler, & Ridgeway, 1986; Capatides, 1990; Capatides & Bloom, 1993; Dunn, Bretherton, & Munn, 1987; Fivush, 1993; Hood & Bloom, 1979; Miller & Sperry, 1987; Scholnick, Hall, Wallner, & Livesey, 1993). The words they learn—words like *Mama, cookie, more, cow, up*—are words that name the things their feelings are about rather than the feelings themselves. Young children do not have to tell others what it is they are feeling in those moments when they express emotion; the affect display itself is justification for attributing emotion to a child. Once they have a sizable vocabulary, by about 2 years of age, older children begin to learn emotion labels—words like *happy, mad, sad*—for naming the emotion they are feeling (e.g., Bretherton et al., 1986; Ridgeway, Waters, & Kuczaj, 1985).

When the temporal relationship between speech and affect expression was studied on-line, as they occurred in the stream of children's everyday activities and play, children were most likely to express emotion immediately after and/or at the same time they were saying words (when measured against their baseline rates of expressing emotion overall) (Bloom & Beckwith, 1989). This was interpreted to mean that the children were learning to talk about those things that were associated with their affective feeling states and, therefore, relevant to them. The two forms of expression converged and were integrated in real time because both were embodiments of aspects of the same intentional state. Similarly, gestures and spoken words have been shown to be closely integrated with each other for both expression and interpretation when children begin to say words in the second year (Morford & Goldin-Meadow, 1992). The temporal convergence of gesture and speech is attributed to children expressing the same mental "computation" (McNeill, 1987).

However, when words were said at the same time children expressed emotion, they tended to be a child's most frequent and/or earliest learned words—words that are most automatic. The emotion expressed also tended to be positive rather than negative and at low levels of intensity (Bloom & Beckwith, 1989), and most words, in fact, occurred with neutral affect. The less frequent and more recently learned words made up most of the different words the children said. The implication is that neutral affect is recruited when both expressing emotion and saying words make demands on the essentially limited cognitive resources of the young child—such as with high intensity of emotion, negative emotion, and when saying words that are less well known and automatic. Neutral affect also promotes the states of attention needed for attending to words in order to learn them, and children who spend more time in neutral affect tend to be earlier word learners (Bloom & Capatides, 1987b).

In sum, word learning is intimately connected to a child's emotional life because infants learn language to talk about and thereby to share the things their feelings are about: the persons, objects, and events that make up the goals and situations that are the causes and circumstances of emotion. But there is also a trade-off between emotional expression and learning and saying words—as indicated by the prevalence of neutral affect among earlier word learners and the tendency for children to be expressing neutral affect when using their relatively infrequent and/or more recently learned words. This collaboration between neutral affect and early word learning represents a conservation of resources for the young child and one of several developments in cognition related to language learning.

Word Learning and Cognitive Development

The relationship between language development and more general developments in cognition has been studied from different perspectives. One perspective stresses the primacy of representations in consciousness—a young child's intentional states—for all of the child's actions, including acts of expression and interpretation. In this view, intentional states—what a child's beliefs, desires, and feelings are about—direct the child to what is relevant in the environment for learning. Another focuses on the mapping relation between the conventional forms of language and a child's knowledge of objects, events, and relationships in conceptual structure in memory. In this view, it is what the child knows about the world—the knowledge base that both results from and contributes to experience—that determines language learning. Another perspective focuses on development of the processes and structures of thought needed to acquire concepts and world knowledge. And yet a fourth perspective comes from the proposal that children are endowed with a set of principles, constraints, or biases that guide their word learning. Each of these perspectives begins with a different set of theoretical assumptions and, most often, is pursued through different research paradigms.

Intentional States

The assumption of intentionality—that language expresses and articulates the representations in consciousness that are otherwise private and unobservable—is implicit in much research in language acquisition. However, it is rarely made explicit. For example, studies of communicative intent and speech acts (e.g., Bates et al., 1979; Dore, 1975; McShane, 1980; Ninio, 1995a) assume the child has a goal in mind when speaking and uses language to serve that goal. Other theorists and researchers have emphasized the importance of the representations children construct in consciousness for expression and interpretation (i.e., Campbell, 1979, 1986; Golinkoff, 1986; Greenfield, 1980). According to Gopnik (1982), the meanings of children's relational words (like *there, gone,* and *more*), in the single-word period, are directed at the plans they have in mind. They use such words to express something about their goals in relation to their actions and aspects of the context. For example, *there* expresses the success of a plan; *no* and *gone* express failure to attain a goal; *more* expresses recurrence of a goal or plan, and so forth. In a series of experiments with older, 4-year-old children that took explicit account of the computational demands attributable to underlying plans for sentence processing, certain phrases varied in difficulty for children as a function of their relative cognitive demands rather than their syntactic complexity (Hamburger & Crain, 1987).

The assumptions of intentionality provided the theoretical rationale for the principles of relevance, discrepancy, and elaboration for language development that I have proposed. The results from the study of the convergence of language and affect expression by Bloom and Beckwith (1989) and the study of early object play by Lifter and Bloom (1989) provided support for these principles (Bloom, 1993). In the study of the convergence of affect expression and language described earlier, the two forms of expression were systematically related to each other in real time because each expressed aspects of the same intentional state.

In addition, the study of object play in relation to emerging language in the second year (Lifter & Bloom, 1989, 1997) provided evidence for inferring developments in the content of the representations in consciousness that were expressed by the children's play. The children progressed from constructing general relationships of containment and support (putting one object onto or into another) to constructing thematic relations that were increasingly specific to the perceptual and culturally relevant properties of the objects (putting a child figure on a horse or feeding a doll with a spoon). The development from general to specific constructions was interpreted as evidence of the principle of elaboration—intentional states increased in number of elements and the kinds of roles and relationships between elements. Development from general to specific constructions was coextensive with the vocabulary spurt in the children's word learning. Thus, one could infer that cognitive developments taking place in this period of time made it possible for the children to have representations in mind that were increasingly discrepant from what was already available to them in the situation and also increasingly elaborated. Correspondingly, the words they were learning were not just names of things but also names for relations between things and other aspects of events, as has been reported in other studies as well (Bloom, 1973; Gopnik, 1982; Hampson & Nelson, 1993; McCune-Nicolich, 1981; Nelson, 1973; Tomasello & Farrar, 1984). Thus, the children's actions with objects and their words expressed the roles and relationships between elements in their intentional states. In turn, learning words was optimized when the words they heard other persons saying were relevant because they targeted elements, roles, and relations in these intentional state representations.

Subsequent research has now built on our earlier studies of affect and play in an investigation of how language and emotional expression are integrated with each other in relation to children's spontaneous play with objects at the time of the vocabulary spurt (Bloom, Tinker, & Beckwith, 1995). Studying language and play together with emotional expression revealed several mutual effects between them. The episodes in which the children constructed thematic relations between objects in play were treated as target events, in a form of lag sequential analysis, and the incidence of emotional expression and speech during and around the play episodes was compared to their respective base rates of occurrence. The first result was that both forms of expression were generally suppressed relative to baseline, when the children played with the objects. This was interpreted as support for the assumption that aspects of the same intentional state were expressed by the children's play, language, and emotional expression. It was necessary to conserve resources ordinarily expended in such acts of expression when they occurred within the same window of time. The children tended not to talk or express emotion when playing with objects, as has also been reported by others (Margulies & Anisfeld, 1991; Phillips & Sellito, 1990). The comparison with baseline rates of expression in the study by Bloom et al. (1995), however, gave added weight to this finding.

The second result in this study was a trade-off between the two forms of expression. Although still below baseline levels, emotional expression decreased when speech increased during the play episodes. When the children did say words, they were most likely to be saying them at the time of the actual constructing activity than in the seconds before or after. We interpreted this to mean that their earliest words were closely tied to the representations they were expressing in their actions. This assumption is consistent with the principle of relevance and many reports of young children's dependence on events in the context of their earliest word learning (Anglin, 1977; Barrett, 1986; Bates et al., 1979; Bloom 1973, 1974, 1993; Dore 1983; Greenfield, Reilly, Leaper, & Baker, 1985; Nelson, 1985; Nelson & Lucariello, 1985; Reich, 1976; Werner & Kaplan, 1963).

The children were more likely to express emotion immediately after the episode of play. Thus, as speech increased during the constructing activity, emotion changed in the opposite direction—decreasing during play and then increasing immediately after. This peak in emotional expression immediately after the offset time of a play event is consistent with the similar finding that children were most likely to be expressing emotion in the seconds immediately after saying words (reported in Bloom & Beckwith, 1989). One interpretation of these findings is that mental resources were freed for the cognitive work required for other expressive behaviors such as emotion to occur. In addition, given that most emotion expressed was positive affect, this burst of emotional expression just after a word or just after a construction in play is reminiscent of smiles of recognition (e.g., Sroufe & Waters, 1976), and smiles following mastery (Sroufe & Waters, 1976) or assimilation after "concentrated attention" (Kagan, Lapidus, & Moore, 1978).

In sum, putting two objects together in a thematic relationship was systematically related to saying words and expressing emotion. The moment-to-moment timing of object play, saying words, and expressing emotion in relation to each other showed that these different behaviors competed for a child's essentially limited cognitive and affective resources. Action of one kind might well be inhibited in order to promote action in another (Kahneman, 1973), or resources from one domain might be recruited to complement or facilitate behaviors in another (Bloom et al., 1995). Thus, collaboration between cognition and affect contributes to the developmental processes for language acquisition in the second year. The conclusion from these studies is that language development is intimately connected to other developments, and the child's intentionality provides the mediating link among them.

Concepts and Conceptual Structure

Considerable attention has been given in the child language literature to the importance of cognitive development for building the knowledge base that will inform the content of a child's language and acquisition of the meanings of words and sentence structures. Hearing words and sentences spoken in relation to an event will be helpful to a child only if at least something about the event is recognized and understood. What a child already knows about the world of persons, objects, events, and relations contributes to the relevance of the words the child hears for learning them. Linguistic and nonlinguistic data from the context become information the child can use for learning language only when they are accessible to the child's perceptual and cognitive abilities.

A major consequence of introducing meaning into the study of children's early sentences was to raise the question of where meaning comes from. It wasn't difficult to see the connection between meanings in early sentences and the cognitive developmental history of the young language-learning child (Bates, 1976; Bloom, 1973; Brown, 1973; and many others since). Many researchers have attempted to document both general and particular relationships between language development and other aspects of cognitive development in the first three years of life—in particular, how children attach the forms of language to what they know about objects, events, and relations in the world (e.g., Bloom, 1970, 1973; Gopnik & Meltzoff, 1987; Ingram, 1978; McCune-Nicolich, 1981; Mervis, 1987; Nelson, 1974, 1985; Nelson & Lucariello, 1985; and many others). The importance of conceptual development for language is, by now, noncontroversial—most simply, children learn language in relation to what they know at least something about.

Conceptual structure, however, does not lead to language in any simple way. Some aspects of language might be acquired along with their corresponding concepts, and children have many concepts without also knowing the language for them. Moreover, some aspects of the meanings of words might be acquired relatively quickly in a fast mapping, but the meanings of most words and of the syntactic structures of a language will need to be worked out tediously over months or even years—the distinction between "fast mappings and slow, extended mappings" (Carey, 1978, p. 291; see also, Anglin, 1993; Bloom & Lahey, 1978; Bowerman, 1981).

Children's earliest concepts of basic-level objects are categories such as dogs, trucks, and cookies, in which instances within a category are highly similar to each other (like oil trucks and moving vans in the category *truck*) and not at all similar to the instances in other categories (like spaniels and poodles in the category *dog*); (Anglin, 1977; Lucariello, Kyratzis, & Nelson, 1992; Mervis, 1987; Mervis & Rosch, 1981). This level is more basic than the superordinate category level (for example, animals, vehicles, or foods) because members of a superordinate category (like cars and ships in the superordinate category of *vehicles*) are more dissimilar to each other than members of the basic level (different kinds of trucks) (Rosch & Mervis, 1975; Rosch, Mervis, Gray, Johnson, & Boyes-Braem, 1976). By 16 months of age, children may begin to appreciate distinctions captured by superordinate and contextual groupings (Mandler, Ch. 6, this Volume; Mandler & Bauer, 1988; Mandler, Fivush, & Reznick, 1987; Woodward & Markman, Ch. 8, this Volume). However, the ability to fully and reliably appreciate that items belong to the same superordinate category when they are not perceptually similar (like ships and cars in the category *vehicle*) does not appear to develop until some time between 4 and 7 years of age (Golinkoff et al., 1995; Lucariello, Kyratzis, & Nelson, 1992). Learning the full extent of the meaning of words that name superordinate categories is a relatively late achievement.

Concept development is closely connected to a child's emerging theories about the world—both general theories, like theories of objects, space, time, and causality, and more circumscribed theories that depend on these general theories, like theories of biology and kinship. Concepts are embedded in networks of associations and beliefs. This fact means that there is no simple one-to-one mapping between words and corresponding items in conceptual structure (Keil, 1989, 1991). Instead, words are learned from the complicated interplay between associations with different circumstances of use and how children experience those circumstances in relation to their developing theories about the world.

The contextualization of concepts within conceptual structure and more general theories about the world highlights the importance of relationships—learning about relations between things (and between persons and things) is inherent in acquiring object concepts as well as concepts of relationships. Relational concepts like movement, location, containment, and support have importance far beyond the literal word-to-concept mappings for particular words like *in* and *on*. Rather, relational concepts provide the cognitive underpinnings for many of the grammatical properties of language (Bloom, 1973; 1981; Jackendoff, 1983, 1991; Slobin, 1985), however differently they may be realized in different languages (Bowerman, 1989). The words children learn name the objects and persons that are the participants in a relationship, words like *Mama, truck, juice, girl,* and the actions, states, or locative directions that define the relationship, words like *up, open,* and *eat.* Children eventually learn a grammar with procedures for combining relationships between more abstract linguistic categories to express increasingly abstract conceptual relationships.

Processes and Structures of Thought

Other research into cognition and early language development has centered on the development of more general theories or structures of thought. These studies were influenced originally by Piaget's description of sensorimotor cognition in the first year of life—in particular, an appreciation for relationships between means and ends and the permanence of objects in spite of their transformations in space and time (Piaget, 1954). More recent research and theory in infant cognition has challenged the notion of sensorimotor thought and sought to show infants capable of mental representation at younger ages than Piaget had suggested (e.g., Cohen, 1988; Fischer, 1980; Leslie, 1988; Mandler, 1988, Ch. 6, this Volume; Spelke, 1988, 1991). A challenge was also leveled at the idea that processes of thought are ever characterized by such notions as permanence and constancy (Thelen & Smith, 1994). However, for Piaget, "complex structures or 'configurations' in the infant's sensori-motor intelligence, [are] far from being static and non-historical, [rather] they constitute 'schemata' which grow out of one another by means of successive differentiations and integrations" (Piaget, 1960, p. 66). Piaget's theory was not the static one that has often been painted for him (Bloom, Lifter, & Broughton, 1985; Halford, 1989).

Early suggestions were that the connection between developments in infant cognition and early language was a serial one, with language depending on developments in thought, or that they developed in parallel (e.g., Bates, 1976; Bloom, 1970, 1973; Brown, 1973; Ingram, 1978, Nelson, 1974; Sinclair, 1970). Many studies have since compared developments in thought and language in the second year using ordinal scales to measure sensorimotor development, most often the instrument developed by Uzgiris and Hunt

(1975). The results of these studies have been mixed. The beginning and end of Piaget's last sensorimotor Stage 6, as measured by scale performance, coincides with the beginning and end of the single-word period in language (e.g., Bates et al., 1979; Corrigan, 1978; Lifter & Bloom, 1989, 1997). Although other global measures of language do not correlate with scale performance, more narrow and specific aspects of early language—such as the appearance of particular words—do correspond with specific object permanence tasks (e.g., Bates et al., 1979; Gopnik, 1984; Gopnik & Meltzoff, 1987; McCune-Nicolich, 1981; Menn & Hazelkorn, 1977; Smolak & Levine, 1984; Tomasello & Farrar, 1984).

The search for correspondences between developments in language and other aspects of cognition has focused on explaining the three early achievements in language: first words at the beginning of the single-word period, a vocabulary spurt toward the end of the single-word period, and the beginning of simple sentences. The evidence from a number of sources suggests that qualitative differences in an infant's capacities for thought are responsible for the quantitative change captured by an increase in vocabulary (as suggested originally by Bloom, 1973). For example, a vocabulary spurt and children's naming abilities are related to development of corresponding concepts (Lucariello, 1987a), developments in representational capacities for constructing different kinds of thematic relationships between objects in play (Lifter & Bloom, 1989, 1997), and the ability to sort objects into categories (Gopnik & Meltzoff, 1987, 1992; Poulin-Dubois & Graham, 1994; Poulin-Dubois, Graham, & Sippola, 1994–1995)—although individual differences in such sorting tasks have also been reported (Shore, Dixon, & Bauer, 1995). The vocabulary spurt is also coextensive with a sharp increase in the number of different pragmatic intentions or communicative acts that can be attributed to a child's use of single-words (Ninio, 1995a; Venezia, 1992). In turn, a vocabulary spurt is, itself, one of several developments cited as evidence of major cognitive changes at the end of the second year (e.g., Fischer, Pipp, & Bullock, 1984; Kagan, 1981; Langer, 1980).

Children's spontaneous play has often been used as a window on developments in cognition and has yielded a number of insights into the underlying cognitive changes taking place during the same time period in which children begin to learn words, acquire a working vocabulary, and approach the transition to multi-word speech and simple sentences. Piaget (1962) proposed that developments in the symbolic capacity and the ability to mentally represent a relationship between a signifier and what it signifies contributed to developments in both language and play. Many subsequent studies have provided evidence of young children's symbolic thought in the relationship between pretend play, in particular, and progress in word learning (Bates et al., 1979; Corrigan, 1978; McCune-Nicolich, 1981; Smolak & Levine, 1984); and the onset of multi-word speech (McCune, 1995; Shore, O'Connel, & Bates, 1984; see Lifter & Bloom, 1997 for reviews). The consensus has grown that developments in play and language behaviors are related to one another through the relationship of both kinds of behavior to the same underlying developments in cognition, rather than being independent and related only to general maturation (e.g., Bates et al., 1979; Bloom, 1993; Bloom et al., 1985; Lifter & Bloom, 1989, 1997; McCune, 1995; Piaget, 1954; Sinclair, 1970).

While many studies imply a causal influence of cognitive developments on language, or at least imply that they occur in parallel, language also exerts an influence on developments in cognition; the developmental influence between them is mutual. As language is acquired, it has an influence, in turn, on the content and processes of thought (e.g., Gopnik & Choi, 1990; Gopnik & Meltzoff, 1986; Hirsh-Pasek & Golinkoff, 1996; Johnstone, 1985; Lucariello, 1987a; Poulin-Dubois & Graham, 1994; Scholnick & Hall, 1991; Shatz, 1991; Sinclair, 1971; Slobin, 1973; 1985).

A number of recent psycholinguistic studies with infants and young children were brought together and synthesized in a model of developing language comprehension by Hirsh-Pasek and Golinkoff (1996). In the first phase of their model, infants hear the talk that accompanies nonlinguistic events and begin to internalize this acoustic packaging, which helps them to appreciate the boundaries of events and to begin to interpret them. Interpretation develops in the second year of life, from roughly 9 to 24 months, in a second phase of segmentation and linguistic mapping, as children analyze nonlinguistic events into the corresponding objects, actions, and relations named by the words and sentences they hear in those events (see also, Beckwith, 1988). A third phase in the Hirsh-Pasek and Golinkoff model is complex syntactic analysis between 2 and 3 years, and consists of children analyzing the relationships between clauses in the sentences they hear, in the absence of correlated events in the context for understanding.

Such developments as these in the reciprocal relationship between linguistic and nonlinguistic analysis presuppose the necessary corresponding developments in both social and conceptual knowledge.

Principles and Constraints

An altogether different cognitive perspective for explaining how children learn words is that specific constraints operate within the child to guide word learning. Citing a logical dilemma inherent in the effort to translate words from one language to another, originally posed in a philosophical argument by Quine (1960), the question is asked: How can a child ever know that a word is a word in the first place, with a meaning that has something to do with a particular object, since a new, unknown word the child hears could potentially mean many things? Hearing the word *rabbit,* for instance, how is the child to know that *rabbit* means the whole object and not some part of it (like an ear) or a quality it has (like fuzzy or white) or its action (like hopping)? How is it that the next time a rabbit hops by, and maybe even a brown one at that, the child calls it a "rabbit"? Quine's translation dilemma is a complex one, but the essential point taken from his argument was that the available data overdetermine the meaning of a word in the situation in which a child hears it. The dilemma was deemed resolved by researchers who proposed that, since so many things present themselves to a young child when someone names an object, the child must be equipped with certain a priori language-specific word learning constraints to guide them in finding the meaning of the word (e.g., Clark, 1987, 1991, 1995; Golinkoff et al., 1995; Hirsh-Pasek, Golinkoff, & Reeves, 1994; Landau, Smith, & Jones, 1988; Markman, 1989, 1992; Markman & Hutchinson, 1984; Woodward & Markman, Ch. 8, this Volume).

Different sorts of principles for word learning have been suggested. Some are quite general and described as pragmatic (e.g., Clark, 1991, 1995); others are perceptual (e.g., Landau, Smith, & Jones, 1988); still others are more linguistically driven (e.g., Landau & Gleitman, 1985; Markman, 1989, 1992). The subsequent literature contains many experimental accounts and much theorizing in efforts to prove or disprove one or another set of principles (see, in particular, reviews by Golinkoff, Mervis, & Hirsh-Pasek, 1994; Golinkoff et al., 1995; Nelson, 1988; and papers in Gelman & Byrnes, 1991). Most of the children in these studies were 3- and 4-year-olds who already knew a vocabulary of words; more recently, attention has turned to experiments in word learning by 1- and 2-year-old children (described by Woodward & Markman, Ch. 8, this Volume).

Originally, the prevailing theme was that principles for word learning took the form of biases or constraints that are biologically specified and, therefore, innate. Either the principles themselves or the ontological categories on which word meanings are based were attributed to inborn cognitive/linguistic constraints that guide language learning from the beginning (see, for example, Carey, 1982; Clark, 1987; Gathercole, 1987; Gleitman, Gleitman, Landau, & Wanner, 1988; Markman, 1989, 1992; Markman & Hutchinson, 1984; Newport, 1981; Soja, Carey, & Spelke, 1991). This view was, at least tacitly, a continuation of the innatist argument from syntactic theory. Chomsky (1959, 1965) pointed out that a child acquires the rules of a grammar despite the fact that these rules are not given in the input the child receives; he concluded that certain grammatical principles must, therefore, be a part of the child's biological endowment. However, for grammar, the argument for innateness is based on the fact that children do not experience what it is they must learn (a grammar) in their everyday interactions—this is the "poverty of the stimulus" argument. In contrast, the problem for word learning is altogether different. Here a child is supposedly presented with too much information in the situation and needs to be guided in narrowing the range of options to know what is important for the meaning of a word. Principles for word learning were invoked to provide that guidance.

More recent claims have been decidedly muted with respect to innateness, with a growing consensus that principles evolve with development at the same time they guide word learning. They appear sequentially and change as children grow older (Golinkoff et al., 1994; Golinkoff et al., 1995; Merriman, 1991; Merriman & Bowman, 1989). However, if such principles appear as children acquire a vocabulary, they more appropriately describe what it is that children are learning than explain how that learning takes place. Language learning and, in particular, principles for word learning could, therefore, be attributable to more general perceptual and learning strategies rather than being necessarily and specifically linguistic, that is, lexical principles, per se (e.g., Bloom, 1993; Braine, 1974; Dent, 1990; Falmagne, 1992; Freyd, 1983; Markman, 1992; Newport, 1981; Scholnick, 1990; Shatz, 1981; Tomasello, 1992c).

Several criticisms of the lexical principles paradigm have appeared and many of these are discussed and responded to by Woodward and Markman (Ch. 8, this Volume). One

issue that does not seem to have been raised, however, is that experiments to test the principles typically present words and objects to children in isolation—from both the nonlinguistic contexts of the events in which objects are ordinarily embedded, and the linguistic contexts of sentences and discourse in which words are ordinarily embedded.

Experimental materials in most studies of lexical constraints and principles are objects and nouns in which one or another variable is manipulated—such as shape or texture, or category versus thematic relationship—but typically in isolation from the events in which children ordinarily experience, learn, and use such words. However, children hardly ever experience objects in isolation, much less learn words for them in isolation from other words and concepts. Rather, from earliest infancy, they hear and learn words that are richly contextualized—both linguistically and nonlinguistically. Results from studies of early speech perception have shown how infants and young children learn to perceive words embedded in the envelope of syntactic, prosodic, and semantic cues to their meanings (see the papers in Morgan & Demuth, 1996).

Moreover, presenting objects and the names for them in isolation separates object names and the concepts they represent from their inherent connections to other concepts in conceptual structure (e.g., Keil, 1991; Medin & Wattenmaker, 1987) and ignores the importance of event-based learning (e.g., Lucariello & Nelson, 1987; Nelson 1986). Such experiments are reminiscent of the earlier studies of children's comprehension of the syntactic structure of sentences and early studies of memory, in which sentences or words were presented to children stripped of the relevant circumstances and contexts in which they are ordinarily experienced (see, for example, discussion by Bloom, 1973, 1974; Bloom & Lahey, 1978). However, attention to meaning and context is now virtually taken for granted in studies of memory and syntactic understanding.

The principles and constraints on word learning offered so far are typically object specific, having to do only with how children learn names for things. Important examples are the Whole Object Assumption (Markman, 1989, 1992) and the Principle of Object Scope (Golinkoff et al., 1994, 1995): On hearing a new word, a child will assume it names a whole object rather than a part of the object, one of its properties, or something related to it. Historically, most studies of word learning have focused on object names; for example, Brown (1958) and MacNamara (1982), for several reasons. For one, object names are the largest class of words in the adult language and in some early vocabularies as well. For another, they are relatively easy to study experimentally (Merriman & Tomasello, 1995).

However, we also know that children are learning different kinds of words—not just object names and, for many 1-year-olds, more than half the different words they know are not object names (e.g., Bates, Bretherton, & Snyder, 1988; Bates et al., 1994; Bates et al., 1995; Bloom, 1973; Bloom et al., 1993; Fenson et al., 1994; Gopnik, 1982, 1988a; Gopnik, Choi, & Baumberger, 1996; Hampson, 1989; Hampson & Nelson, 1993; Lieven, Pine, & Barnes, 1992; McCarthy, 1930; McCune-Nicolich, 1981; Nelson 1973; Pine, 1992; Tardiff, 1993). Even in the original study by Nelson (1973), in which more than half of some children's vocabularies were nominal forms, these were not necessarily object names but included nominals that named events like *lunch,* or nonobject things like *lap* (Nelson, Hampson, & Shaw, 1993).

When considering word tokens (all the instances of words in a child's running speech—an index of how important the word is for the child in everyday use), object names comprised only one-third of the more than 11,000 tokens said by the 1-year-olds in the study by Bloom et al. (1993). This result is consistent with the relative frequency of object names in the speech these children heard from their mothers in the same observation sessions (Beckwith, Tinker, & Bloom, 1995). In turn, the distribution of nouns in both the child and mother's speech was remarkably similar to results from analyses of a variety of written and spoken texts, from both adults and children, which show that common nouns make up about 37% of all word tokens (Hudson, 1994). It doesn't seem to matter, evidently, whether one is sampling the words used in adult or child texts, or in written or spoken texts, the relative frequency of common nouns is less than 40%. It is not at all clear why this should be. However, the message is clear enough—object names do not predominate among the everyday texts of either spoken or written discourse. Whatever differences are reported in early vocabularies, depending on different methods for obtaining the data, they can be expected to eventually disappear.

The focus on learning object names also separates the acquisition of the lexicon from acquiring all other aspects of language, particularly the grammar. Grammar is inherently *relational* in that its function is to specify the relationships within and between states and events—which include objects. Words such as *more, up, on* name relationships to things, and relational words figure prominently in

most English-speaking children's single-word vocabularies before syntax. Verbs, which are quintessentially relational, increase in frequency and number toward the end of the single-word period in anticipation of the transition to syntax (e.g., Bates, Bretherton, & Snyder, 1988; Bloom, 1973; Bloom et al., 1993; Gentner, 1982; Tomasello, 1992b). Thus, acquiring the structures of language goes hand in hand with learning the words of the language and verbs in particular (e.g., Bloom, 1981, 1991; Bloom et al., 1975a, 1975b; Pinker, 1984, 1989). Thus, both the early relational words and later verbs are central for constructing syntactic categories or "parts-of-speech."

In response to these and other criticisms, Markman (1992), Golinkoff et al. (1994), and Woodward and Markman (Ch. 8, this Volume), proposed that children would have to override the whole object assumption in order to learn the many words that do not name objects—for example, the relational words like *more, down, open* common to many young vocabularies. However, it is not at all clear what it would take to override object-specific lexical principles, and the circumstances in which they might be overridden have yet to be identified (Bloom, 1993; Bloom et al., 1993; Tomasello & Akhtar, 1995; Tomasello & Kruger, 1992). The claim is sometimes made that one or another principle could also account for learning other kinds of words (Golinkoff, Hirsh-Pasek, Mervis, Frawley, & Parillo, 1995). So far, this proposal has been empirically tested with older, 2- and 4-year-olds learning novel verbs for novel actions, with mixed results (Merriman, Marazita, & Jarvis, 1993, 1995).

One thing is clear. If many or most of the words children acquire, and most of the words they use in their running speech, are not names of objects, then object-specific lexical principles cannot be responsible for word learning. More general principles are required to explain how a child will learn any kind of word and not just object words, such as the principle of relevance (Bloom, 1993). In the intentionality model of language development that I've proposed, observations of children learning language in everyday contexts—children's actual behaviors—are taken to be more compelling for guiding both theory and research than logical arguments in philosophical theory. The principle of relevance is a generalization about the relationship between the contents of a child's mind—the here and now representations in consciousness—and the child's context. Children surely hear many words that are not relevant to what they have in mind—words in speech that they overhear as well as speech directed to them about things they neither care nor know about. But the words they will learn are those that are relevant to the things (persons, objects, events, actions, states, relationships) they do care and know about.

Words new to the child could theoretically mean many things in the situations in which they hear them—but only theoretically. How is the child to know that *rabbit* does not mean hop, ears, tail, furry, or any one of the things it could mean? When the child sees a second rabbit hop by and hears *more,* why should the word *more* mean something other than *rabbit*? The answer is that the principle of relevance narrows the range of possible meanings an utterance could have when the child hears it. Relevance in such word learning scenarios is determined by three things. One is *conceptual structure* in the knowledge base and the concepts the child is also learning—concepts of objects like rabbits and relations like recurrence. As already discussed, children more readily learn words that name something they know or are learning about (e.g., Lucariello, 1987a). The second determiner of relevance is the child's perception and *focus of attention* (e.g., Tomasello, 1988). If the focus is on the whole object, then that is what the child will take the word *rabbit* to mean. But if the focus is the rabbit's ears, then the child will assume the word *rabbit* means ears until persuaded otherwise when, in another situation, the focus is not on the ears but on the object, and the child hears *rabbit* again. The third determiner of relevance is the child's *engagement* in whatever is the focus of attention. The extent to which a child finds a task interesting will determine the level of engagement that the child brings to the task (Renninger, 1990; Renninger & Wozniak, 1985). Interest and engagement are the affective component of relevance (Bloom et al., 1995).

Similarly, hearing the word *rabbit* on several different occasions when rabbits are present, the child's focus may be on the ears, the tail, the fur, or hopping, but what all these experiences have in common each time is the whole object and the same word, *rabbit*. Frequency counts; children may well learn something about a word's meaning on a single encounter and perform a fast mapping—which is really only a first approximation of the word's meaning. Most often, however, many encounters are needed to consolidate learning—for both words (e.g., Harris, 1992; Oviatt, 1980, 1982) and syntactic frames (e.g., Beckwith, 1988).

The fact is that children do not learn words in isolation. They perform a distributional analysis in which each new experience with a word is analyzed in relation to prior experiences of the word in memory. The words stored in memory, with the circumstances in which they were experienced, are data for the child—data accumulated after hearing the same word in several or many different contexts. For example, hearing *more* in such perceptually different situations as another rabbit, another cookie, another glass of milk, the child comes to appreciate the factors—notably the fact of recurrence—which guide the distribution of *more* in these otherwise different events (see discussions of the part played by distributional learning for syntax acquisition in, for example, Beckwith, 1988; Bloom, 1991; Bloom et al., 1975a; Braine, 1963a; Maratsos & Chalkley, 1980).

An appropriate analogy is the frequent claim that adult sentences could, theoretically, have several interpretations. When hearing a sentence, however, a listener need not run through and consider all of its possible interpretations until hitting on the right one. Rather, the listener sets up an intentional state configuration for representing what the speaker might mean based on what is already available at that point in the discourse and known between them. "There will of course be choices and strategies, but the potential of a sentence, given a previous configuration, is always far less than its general potential for all possible configurations. (A brick could theoretically occupy any position in a wall, *but at any stage of the actual building process, there is only one place for it to go.*)" (Fauconnier, 1985, pp. 168–9, emphasis added). Like Fauconnier's brick, the word a child hears could *theoretically* mean any of a number of things. But, in enough situations in which the child hears it, the options are already greatly diminished by the configuration represented in the child's intentional state, and the word, like the brick, finds its target.

While not explanatory, the lexical principles or constraints on word learning that have been proposed are descriptive of children's behaviors as they learn words and acquire a vocabulary. And they are language-specific because it is language learning they describe. Two-year-old children do what the principles say they do: make reference, extend words to new exemplars, label objects that form basic level categories, and so forth. Learning a language means to acquire this sort of specific knowledge, and as such knowledge is acquired, it is used in the service of learning more about the language. Having learned a lexical principle by learning something about what words are and what they do, a child would be expected to use the principle to learn other words. Thus, if lexical principles are part of a child's cognition for word learning, they are more likely the result of learning words, rather than the starting point.

Two-year-olds perform as they do on experimental word-learning tasks because of what they already know from two years' worth of learning. Other aspects of cognitive and affective development in addition to language learning in this period of time guide a child's appreciation for the relevance of a wide variety of cues to a word's meaning (Bloom, 1993; Bloom et al., 1993; Nelson, 1988; Tomasello, 1992a; Tomasello & Akhtar, 1995). This fact is beginning to be recognized by supporters of constraints theories (e.g., Hirsh-Pasek & Golinkoff, 1996; Woodward & Markman, this volume). By now, a large number of studies have shown how children exploit a wide variety of cues for detecting what is relevant in the speech they hear. These include linguistic properties of the adult's speech such as its prosody (e.g., Echols & Newport, 1992; Fernald & Mazzie, 1991), morphology (e.g. Anglin, 1993), syntax (e.g., 1994, P. Bloom & Kelemen, 1995; Brown, 1957; Fernald & McRoberts, 1996; Gathercole, Cramer, Somerville, & op de Haar, 1995; Katz, Baker, & MacNamara, 1974), and combinations of these cues (e.g., Gerken, et al., 1994).

These kinds of linguistic cues act together with information about the function of objects (Nelson, 1974) and others), such perceptual properties of objects as their shape or substance (e.g., Baldwin, 1992; Clark, 1973; Gathercole et al., 1995; Imai, Gentner, & Uchida, 1994; Landau, Smith, & Jones, 1988; Merriman, Schuster, & Hager, 1991; Soja, Carey, & Spelke, 1991), and the presence of salient object parts (e.g., Merriman, Scott, & Marazita, 1993; Poulin-Dubois, 1995). If children are able to learn words by exploiting their own abilities to make use of a rich and wide array of cues to a word's meaning even in experimental tasks (e.g., Baldwin, 1993a, 1993b), one might well ask why lexical principles are necessary at all. Theories based on lexical principles are less than parsimonious once it is acknowledged that children do indeed make use of all such cues to learn words and that the principles can be overridden, in any event, to learn words that are not object names.

Finally, lexical principles (biases or constraints) imply an essentially passive child, one who is depending on internal mechanism rather than active process in the course of development. Research on lexical principles in the past decade has overlooked other things going on in a young child's life that contribute to the child's active engagement in word learning. Young children exploit their internal resources and take the lead in providing a rich array of cues to their intentionality—including the other words that they already know—so that other persons can make attributions of what they have in mind. Interested others are sensitive to these cues and tune into the child's focus of attention to supply information for word learning. Thus, word learning is the product of the active mind of the child, striving to find words to express the representations in intentional states, and the social and pragmatic contexts and activities of everyday living that will yield the words of the language.

Word Learning and Social Context

Language is inherently social because it has to be learned from other persons. Even learnability theory, which depends on adult linguistic theory, requires triggering encounters with appropriate language exemplars in the input children receive (e.g., Gibson & Wexler, 1994; Roeper, 1982). However, this is only the most narrow construal of the part played by contextual factors in development. In contrast, the strong version of a social theory of language acquisition assumes that the interaction between the caregiver and child is primary, with responsibility resting largely on the adult in the situation for setting up and guiding language learning. The origins of the theory are in the work of Vygotsky (1962, 1978), but its strongest contemporary proponents have been influenced by the more recent work of Bruner (1975a, 1983). Bruner suggested that a Language Acquisition Device, an innate linguistic mechanism for acquiring a grammar such as Chomsky (1965) proposed, could only operate successfully with an assist from a corresponding Language Acquisition Support System provided by caregivers. "In a word, it is the interaction between LAD and LASS that makes it possible for the infant to enter the linguistic community." The language acquisition support system is "initially under the control of the adult" who controls the transactional format within which language is learned (Bruner, 1983, p. 19).

Early formulations of the social basis for language learning emphasized the part played by adults who are in charge of their interactions with children. Support for social theories of language acquisition came from observing children and adults interacting in such scripted activities as book reading (Ninio & Bruner, 1978; Snow & Goldfield, 1983), play routines and games such as peek-a-boo (Ratner & Bruner, 1978) or a tea party (Kaye & Charney, 1980), and other routinized, repetitive, rule-governed transactions (Ninio & Wheeler, 1984) or what Bruner called *formats*.

More recent accounts broadened the base of socially mediated theories by invoking the pragmatic factors entailed when adult and child negotiate the activities of daily living (e.g., Becker, 1990, 1994; Nelson, 1985, 1988; Ninio, 1995a; Ninio & Snow, 1988,1996; Snow, 1989; Tomasello, 1992a; Tomasello & Akhtar, 1995). Developments in children's social cognition enable them to detect and pick up on a variety of pragmatic cues from the socio-cultural context for learning word meaning (e.g., Akhtar, Carpenter, & Tomasello, 1996; Greenfield, 1982; Zukow, 1990, 1991). The result is a "social-pragmatic theory of language acquisition" according to which "young children can learn new pieces of language only by entering into some type of joint attentional focus with a mature language user" (Tomasello & Akhtar, 1995, p 201). However, this assumption underestimates the opportunities children have for learning from the speech they overhear in conversations between other persons.

Optimum occasions for language learning do occur when accompanying adult speech is about the child's focus of attention, as predicted by the principle of relevance. Mothers tend to be responsive to their children's vocalizations and efforts at speech—usually responding within the first two seconds (e.g., Bloom et al., 1996; Roth, 1987; van der Stelt, 1993). Such observational data have now been complemented by a growing number of experimental studies which document the particular ostensive-inferential cues (Sperber & Wilson, 1986) children exploit for learning words in their interactions, including, for example, the direction of the adult's gaze (Baldwin, 1993a, 1993b; Tomasello & Akhtar, 1995) and the adult's affect expressions of glee or disappointment when finding or not finding an object (Tomasello & Barton, 1994). Woodward and Markman (Ch. 8, this Volume) provide a thorough review of this research and suggest that this account gives more credit to the adult rather than the child for word learning. However, their suggestion overlooks the fact that it is the child's intentional state that determines joint attention more often than not, as children invariably take the lead in their everyday conversations with adults (Bloom et al., 1996; Harris, 1992; Howe, 1981) and in their play activities as well (Bloom et al., 1995). Adults were more apt to initiate talk about distant past events in a study with 1-year-old Swiss French-speaking children, but the children initiated the majority of talk about immediate past events (Venezia & Sinclair, 1995). Mothers talk more and have longer conversations when their children talk more themselves and talk more often about the mothers' topic of conversation (Hoff-Ginsberg, 1994).

Mothers typically tune into and follow a child's lead in their typical interactions in the course of ordinary activities of daily living. The studies cited earlier in support of strong socially-based explanations of language acquisition were largely studies of picture book reading, scriptlike play such as a tea party, or direct instruction—activities in which mothers could be expected to take charge and be more directive. However, such highly formatted activities, in fact, make up only a small part of what happens between caregivers and young children in the course of a day. In addition, as the results of the study by Lucariello (1987b) would suggest, mothers might well take the lead in interacting with a child in the first five or ten minutes of a laboratory session, particularly if the situation is new for the child (as in the study by Kaye & Charney, 1980). In contrast to studies that have looked at interactions in novel or contrived contexts, studies of spontaneous everyday interactions reveal that child and mother contribute to the architecture of the early conversations between them, but, in fact, it is the child who is in charge (Bloom et al., 1995, 1996; Harris, 1992; Howe, 1981).

Mothers can differ in the timing of their response to their infants' behaviors (Roth, 1987) and also in their tendency to name what their infants are attending to. For example, among Caucasians, adolescent mothers are less responsive to their infants than adult mothers and engage in significantly less vocal turn-taking with their 12-month-old infants; their infants, in turn, engage in very little vocal responding (Barratt & Roach, 1995). But children learn more words when their mothers respond promptly to their vocalizations and also say something about the objects of their attention (Akhtar, Dunham, & Dunham, 1991; Harris, 1992; Masur, 1982; Tomasello & Farrar, 1986; see Tomasello, 1988, for review).

However important social cognition is for acquiring language, it must operate together with an understanding of the objective world and the child's affective engagement with persons and objects. Children's thinking is most likely not compartmentalized into thinking about objects and thinking about persons because persons and things typically occur in relation to each other. The same developmental principles and processes are true for knowing about both.

In sum, the social context is crucial for providing the language to be learned, to be sure, but it is no less important for providing opportunities for intersubjectivity and social connectedness to other persons. Together with cognitive developments that drive the principles of relevance, discrepancy, and elaboration, the need to maintain intersubjectivity and to function effectively with other persons determine that a language will be learned. Societies depend on children to become competent users of the language. In fact, others react less than kindly to children whose communication abilities are more limited than might otherwise be expected for a child's age (Rice, Hadley, & Alexander, 1993). However, as important as any aspect of the context for language development is, it has influence only when converging with other aspects of development. One by-product of this convergence—and one that has attracted increasing attention—is the fact that children differ in important and systematic ways in the particulars of their language acquisition.

Individual Differences in Acquiring Vocabulary

Considerable attention has been given to the ways in which children from essentially the same social and cultural backgrounds differ in their language development. The consensus now is that children vary in onset and rate of learning as well as in the different strategies they use for processing and learning language. (For reviews of individual differences in language acquisition, see Bates, Dale, & Thal, 1995; Nelson, 1981; Shore, 1995; Thal & Bates, 1990.) Children from different economic and social backgrounds also differ, particularly with respect to rate of word learning (Hart & Risley, 1995) and more socially determined, conversational aspects of language (Bloom et al., 1996).

Rate and Progress in Word Learning

Children generally differ in when they begin to say words and in their rate of progress in word learning after the first words. As an example, the wide range in the ages of 14 children when they reached three landmarks in language development: first words, a vocabulary spurt, and the beginning of sentences is shown in Figure 7.1. (See Bloom, 1993, for the individual vocabulary growth curves that contributed to these group means and ranges, and the criteria used to identify the three achievements.) The average ages of these children at the times of first words, the vocabulary spurt, and simple sentences were, respectively, about 13, 19, and 24 months. However, the individual children ranged in age from 10 to 17 months of age at first words and from 13 to 25 months at the vocabulary spurt.

The question is sometimes raised whether all children do, indeed, show a vocabulary spurt—a sharp increase in the second year in the number of new words they are learning. Observation of a vocabulary spurt could be susceptible

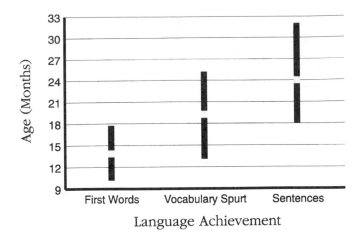

Figure 7.1 Age of language achievements (mean and range) (Bloom, 1993).

to measurement factors. One contributing factor is the comparison interval used; monthly intervals would be more likely to produce sharp increases than weekly intervals. Another factor is whether one plots a cumulative vocabulary (with all the word types—both old and new words—a child knows) or only the new words learned from one month to the next. A vocabulary spurt is more readily seen in a plot of only the new words learned from month to month and may or may not be apparent in a cumulative vocabulary count.

Smooth, continuous growth curves in vocabulary acquisition have sometimes been reported in studies that used parents' diary reports or reports in response to vocabulary items on a checklist (see, respectively, Nelson, 1973, and Goldfield & Reznick, 1990). The possibility exists that such variability reflects differences among parents in their observing and reporting skills in keeping a diary or in the accuracy in recall when responding to checklist inventories. Children's vocabularies grow slowly at first, and all children learning language normally must begin showing an increase in the number of words they learn from month to month, given the dramatic increase in word learning that takes place in the preschool years (Anglin, 1993) and the essential nonlinearity of vocabulary growth curves (Bates & Carnevale, 1993).

Children differ in the onset and development of word learning in the second year for several reasons, and both endogenous and exogenous factors have been described (Bates et al., 1988). For example, one endogenous factor is variation in infant ability to analyze the sound patterns of the speech they hear in relation to their own early sound production patterns (e.g., Goad & Ingram, 1987; Vihman,

1993). Another difference is attributed to cognitive style (e.g., Nelson, 1973, 1975; Shore, 1995) or strategy (e.g., Bates et al., 1988; Bloom, 1973; Bloom et al., 1975a). However, these endogenous factors do not operate independently of the kinds of speech the child hears, and exposure to words in the interactions around them is an important variable (Hampson & Nelson, 1993).

Another exogenous factor often suggested to explain individual differences is social and economic background; poor children are often at risk for language acquisition. Relative economic advantage—independent of gender, race, or sibling status—predicts the frequency of children's everyday experiences with language, with corresponding differences in the outcome for word learning. Children born into poverty have fewer language interactions in their homes and learn fewer words than children born into middle-class families, who, in turn, have fewer interactions and learn fewer words than children born into more affluent, professional homes (Hart & Risley, 1995). Differences in vocabulary size—object labels in particular—was the single factor that distinguished between children from working class and upper-middle-class White families in a study by Hoff-Ginsberg (1994), and economically disadvantaged White children used fewer temporal and causal connectives in their narratives than did middle-class children in a study by Peterson (1994; see also, Hall, Scholnick, & Hughes, 1987).

However, language acquisition research and theory have been biased with respect to the children typically studied. Although a great deal of attention is given to research with children learning different languages (Slobin, 1985, 1992, 1997) and learning languages in different international cultural contexts (Ochs & Schieffelin, 1984; Schieffelin & Ochs, 1986), accounts of the acquisition of English—as with studies of development generally—have not typically included children from different socio-cultural contexts (e.g., Bloom, 1975, 1992; Graham, 1992). But there are exceptions (e.g., Blake, 1993; Hall, Scholnick, & Hughes, 1987; Hart & Risley, 1995; Heath, 1982, 1983; Miller, 1982; Peterson, 1994; Stockman & Vaughn-Cook, 1982, 1989, 1992; Wells, 1981). Race and ethnicity are typically confounded with socio-economic status in those studies that have included culturally different children. One reason is that a disproportionally large number of African American children, for example, live in poverty in this country, particularly in urban communities.

Affect expression is also associated with differences in onset and rate of word learning. One-year-old children differ in the frequency with which they express emotion, and this difference is independent of the social and cultural differences among them (Bloom, 1993). More emotionally expressive infants tended to begin acquiring words somewhat later than the children who spent more time in neutral affect expression in the study by Bloom and Capatides (1987a). In this same population of children, the frequency of their emotional expressions differed longitudinally from 9 to 21 months of age. The earlier word learners, who began saying words between 10 and 13 months (children in the lower half of the range for first words in Figure 7.1), showed no change from 9 to 21 months in the frequency with which they expressed emotion. However, the later word learners increased in frequency of emotional expression from 9 to 17 months, instead of saying words early. Moreover, the frequency of their emotional expression decreased when they made their move in language toward a vocabulary spurt, between 17 and 21 months.

The direction of influence between affect expression and progress in word learning is not clear, and profiles of development in both kinds of expression could be related to a third factor, such as differences in temperament (Bates et al., 1988; Bloom, 1993). However, it may also be that the emotionality component of temperament is, itself, influenced by progress in other areas of development (Dunn, 1986), such as word learning (Bloom, 1993; Wikstrom & Bloom, 1987). That is, earlier word learning may have a damping effect on emotional expression and, therefore, may be the factor that accounts for diminished emotionality in a temperament profile. This is an area for further research.

Children do not differ only in the onset and rate of progress in word learning. They also differ in the phonological patterning of their early words (Goad & Ingram, 1987; Klein, 1981; Stoel-Gammon & Cooper, 1984; Vihman, 1993). However, this is a topic that is, unfortunately, beyond the scope permitted by the length constraints on this chapter.

The Kinds of Words 1-Year-Olds Learn

Children learn a great many different kinds of words in the single-word period in the second year. However, one thing is clear: As pointed out earlier, children's early words before syntax cannot be reliably classified, from the child's point of view, according to their parts of speech in adult language—as nouns, verbs, adjectives, prepositions, and the like. These kinds of category assignments are only valid once children begin to combine words in sentences, when linguistic categories can more appropriately be defined on the basis of their distribution in relation to each other and by their semantic and syntactic functions. (This assumption has a long history, beginning at least with McCarthy, 1946. Nevertheless, assigning words to adult parts-of-speech in single-word vocabularies has been used as an heuristic for some analyses, e.g., Bates et al., 1994.)

Other classifications of children's words have been more successful when they are based upon what a child's single words appear to be expressing. Certain words name objects, like *ball, cookie,* and *car;* other words name relationships or events, like *more, gone,* and *up.* And still other words are parts of social exchanges and routines, like *hi, bye,* and *whee* (e.g., Bloom, 1973; Gopnik, 1988a; Nelson, 1973). However, early words do not fall into neat, reliable categories according to either linguistic, conceptual, or pragmatic criteria. Even the common nouns children learn do not form a consistent class, because they name basic level objects like *shoe,* but also include words like *lap, animal,* and *lunch,* which are not names for basic objects (Nelson et al., 1993).

Again, going back to the early words of the 14 children represented in Figure 7.1, we can look at the words they learned in the period between their first words and continuing up to and including the month after their vocabulary spurt. Together, these children said a total of 11,404 words (utterance tokens) in this period in which we observed them in the playroom sessions. However, many of their words were said very frequently; in fact, only 326 different words (utterance types) were said among the more than 11,000 word tokens. The children were not learning the same words. About three fourths of the 326 different words were said by only one, two, or three of the children; only 49 different words (or 15% of all the different words learned by the group) were said by seven or more of the children. And only five words appeared in the vocabularies of all the children. These were the words *baby, ball, down, juice,* and *more* (Bloom, 1993). In sum, the diversity among young children in their vocabularies is impressive. Different kinds of words appeared among the vocabularies of seven or more of the children—words like *uhoh, hi, boom, on, this,* and *yum* occurred in the vocabularies of seven or more children, along with object names like *box, ball, girl, bottle, cookie, juice,* and *spoon.*

Descriptions of early vocabularies tend to differ, however, depending on the methods for studying them. Observational studies in which a sample of speech is used to determine the different kinds of words children use (e.g.,

Bloom, 1973; Bloom et al., 1993; Lieven, Pine, & Barnes, 1992) tend to report a lower proportion of object names than studies based on mother report measures (diaries or checklists), which report relatively more nouns. Differences between the results of mothers' reports and observational studies have been reported by, for example, Bates, Bretherton, and Snyder (1988), Gopnik (1988a), and Pine (1992).

Results from studies using either direct observation or mothers' checklist report were compared by Pine, Lieven, and Rowland (1996), and they pointed out that each method is responsive to a different research question. On the one hand, scores from a checklist, such as the MacArthur Communicative Development Inventory created by Bates and her colleagues (e.g., Bates et al., 1994; Fenson et al., 1994), are "only really meaningful in an individual differences context (i.e., as indices of [relative] differences in vocabulary size and composition across children)" (Pine et al., 1996, p. 587). On the other hand, detailed observational measures yield more reliable estimates of the absolute proportion of nouns and the distribution of kinds of words in individual vocabularies.

However, observation and mother report are both subject to bias (Pine et al., 1996). Observational data are necessarily restricted to the words used in the particular circumstances that are observed; they may, therefore, be situation-specific. Mother checklist reports are biased, in turn, because (a) nouns are overrepresented on the list relative to other words (Nelson et al., 1993), and (b) mothers are evidently biased to remember and therefore report more nouns than other sorts of words in their children's vocabularies (Pine et al., 1996). In any event, both observational data and mother report data can only provide a sample of the words a child knows, and the source of the sample varies—what mothers pay attention to and remember to report versus the contexts that can be observed by researchers. While data from observational measures are necessarily restricted to words used in the situations that are observed, data from mother report are constrained by inherent differences among mothers in the accuracy of their recall and reporting abilities. Nonetheless, as Pine et al. pointed out, both types of measures sample the words a child knows, and using both methods in the same study (e.g., Bloom et al., 1993) comes closer to the truth.

Children are learning language for interpretation and expression, and the numbers of words and the kinds of words they learn are less important than the kinds of mental meanings expressed by what they say and interpret from what others say. One-year-old children learn to talk about the objects, causes, and circumstances of their beliefs, desires, and feelings with the words that say what these are—words like *Mama, uhoh, no, cow, cookie, more, gone,* and *up*. Notably absent from early vocabularies are the words that name the different emotions like *happy, angry, sad, scared*. Rather than telling their caregivers which particular emotion they are feeling, they tell them what their feelings are about and what they might do to either maintain or change them (Bloom & Beckwith, 1989; Bretherton, Fritz, Zahn-Wexler, & Ridgeway, 1986). The words they say, and also presumably learn in the first place, are relevant to what they have in mind—the objects of their beliefs, desires, and feelings.

Children's words in the single-word period change in the kinds of mental meanings that can be attributed to them (Bloom, 1994; Bloom et al., 1988). Early words are most apt to express mental meanings about things already evident in the context, things that a child sees. However, with developments—and consistent with the principle of discrepancy—mental meanings increase that are about anticipated but imminent events. Consistent with the principle of elaboration, anticipated mental meanings about actions, particularly the child's own actions, also increase toward the end of the period. Action events entail more than one element with different roles and relations between them, such as the agent of the action, the effect that it has, the path taken by the movement of the action, and so forth. These more elaborated mental meanings will require that the child begin to learn verbs, the semantic-syntactic functions of verbs, and still other words that name persons and things and the relations between them. This development from expressing mental meanings about things that are already evident, to meanings about anticipated actions is one of the precursors to the transition from saying only one word at a time to beginning to combine words for the first phrases and simple sentences.

Once something of the language is known, it becomes a means of learning more about language itself as well as more about the world. Linguistic assumptions acquired early in language learning—assumptions the child comes to as a consequence of learning something of the language—can be expected to bootstrap subsequent language learning (Bloom, 1975, 1991). Thus, once a child begins to acquire a vocabulary, words can facilitate nonlinguistic categorization skills, concept formation, and learning other words (Brown, 1956; Lucariello, 1987a; Markman & Hutchinson, 1984; Poulin-Dubois, 1995; Waxman, 1990). The kinds of

words they know, particularly relational words, can anticipate the sorts of word combinations that are among many children's early phrases, like "more cheese," "no fit," and "this a cup." In turn, knowing something of the syntax, whether a child is yet saying combinations of words, can guide the child in discovering the meanings of new words (e.g, P. Bloom, 1994; Landau & Gleitman, 1985; Naigles, 1990). Once children know something about the syntax of sentences with different kinds of verbs, they are able to learn the meanings of the other verbs that share syntactic privileges in a category (Bloom, 1981; Bloom et al., 1975a; Fisher, Hall, Rakowitz, & Gleitman, 1994; Gleitman, 1990; Landau & Gleitman, 1985; Naigles, 1990; Tomasello, 1992b).

In sum, progress in acquiring a vocabulary and the transition to multiword speech and simple sentence grammar are not reducible in any simple way to only one or another aspect of development. Instead, all aspects of development come together by the end of the second year—cognitive, affective, social, and linguistic—in pressing a child to acquire more of the language.

THE SECOND TRANSITION: PHRASES AND SIMPLE SENTENCES

If language is to keep up with other developments in cognition, and with emotional and social understanding, the 2-year-old will need to acquire a grammar with procedures for sentences. Just as the affect displays of infancy could not express the mental meanings of the 1-year-old, the single-words that served the 1-year-old can neither express nor articulate the more elaborated and discrepant representations in the desires, beliefs, and feelings of the 2-year-old. Acquiring a grammar means learning to translate conceptual categories into linguistic categories for sentences that can express and articulate the roles and relationships in intentional states. Several theories of the adult language assume that adult linguistic categories have a conceptual basis (e.g., Bever, 1970; Jackendoff, 1983, 1990; Lebeaux, 1988), although this claim is also disputed (e.g., MacWhinney, 1987; Radford, 1990). Nevertheless, concepts that can be inferred from the semantics of children's early words and sentences—movement and location in particular—have their counterparts in adult semantic theories (Jackendoff, 1990; Lakoff, 1994). Although the details of the translation process from early child concepts to the nascent linguistic categories of early child grammars are still not agreed upon and remain to be worked out, we can point to several developments that contribute to the process.

By now, few would dispute the importance of meaning for children's early grammatical learning (e.g., Bloom, 1970, 1973, 1991; Braine, 1994; Brown, 1973; Leonard, 1976; Pinker, 1984; Schlesinger, 1971). Along with analyses of the input, what a child has learned about the world that is expressible by language determines how the child learns the semantics of the language for acquiring a grammar. Few would dispute, either, that children greatly expand the scope and frequency of the pragmatics of communication. And the words children already know or are learning, together with developments in cognition and social/pragmatic goals, contribute to acquiring the structures for the earliest phrases and simple sentences.

For many children, the beginning of phrases and the first simple sentences comes soon after a vocabulary spurt near the end of the single-word period. The increase in words expressing mental meanings with imminent actions by the child or the caregiver coincides with an increase in the number of verbs in children's single-word vocabularies (Bloom, 1994; Bloom et al., 1988; Tomasello & Kruger, 1992). Many studies have now converged on the finding that verbs naming actions and events are a relatively late development in the single-word period of English-speaking children and, even more reliably than a general vocabulary spurt, precipitate the transition to phrases and sentences (e.g., Bates, Bretherton, & Snyder, 1988; Bates et al., 1995; Bloom, 1973; Bloom et al., 1993; Gentner, 1982; Goldin-Meadow, Seligman, & Gelman, 1976; Schwartz & Leonard, 1984; Tardiff, 1993, Tomasello, 1992b; Tomasello & Kruger, 1992; but see Gopnik & Choi, 1990, 1995, and Tardiff, 1993, for exceptions to this general trend in other languages).

Children begin, tentatively at first, to put together words they had already learned to say singly, for example, "more" and "juice" become "more juice." The meaning relations between words in these early two-word sentences are determined by the meanings of their individual words, for example, "more juice" *means* recurrence because *more* means recurrence; the meanings of negation (nonexistence, rejection, denial) in little sentences like "no fit" and "no dirty soap" come from the meaning of *no*. Many observers have commented on the early acquisition of these kinds of word combinations (e.g., Bloom, 1970, 1973; Braine, 1976; Brown, 1973; Leonard, 1976; Tomasello, 1992b). The order of the words in these phrases is typically fixed and consistent with the order in which children hear the words combined with other words in adult speech. Although children are consistent in preserving the order of the words, in fact, the order relationship in such combinations is not necessarily a functional one—it does not indicate a difference in meaning or intent. This is so because the meaning of the phrase is not different from the meanings of the individual words in the phrase added together: "more juice" and "juice more" mean the same thing.

Children also might begin to repeat certain word combinations often heard in familiar routines, like "go byebye," "all gone," and "what's 'at." Again, the order of the units in these phrases is not a functional one, because the phrases are learned as single words rather than combinations of the separate words as parts. A child might even learn larger phrases as chunks and recall and say these in appropriate circumstances, for example, "I think so," before they have analyzed the phrases into their separate parts and learned how the order of the words determines the meaning relationships between them (Bloom, 1970; Gerken, 1991; Nelson, 1973; Peters, 1977, 1983).

Apart from these early formulas learned as unanalyzed phrases, and word combinations with specific words like *no* and *more* and *all gone*, children learning English need to learn the order of words for expressing meanings that are not themselves inherent in the particular words. The semantics of verbs, in particular, require that a child learn sentence frames with nouns (or pronouns) that express the arguments of the verb, for example, the relation of *girl* and *ball* to the verb *hit*. Young children on the threshold of syntax may *grope* for the right order of words to express thematic relations in English (Braine, 1976) and try out different orders of words by saying single words successively (Bloom, 1973).

Once mean length of utterance reaches 1.5 words, most of a child's phrases and simple sentences can be expected to show consistent word order in their basic constituents (Bloom, 1970; Brown, 1973). But this consistency can change dramatically as somewhat older children begin to realize that different orders are expected for different functions, and grope, once again, for the order to express more elaborate syntactic structures and the relations between them (Ervin-Tripp, 1980). An example is the following succession of utterances from a 2-year-old child, Kathryn, at mean length of utterance (MLU) = 3.3, as she looked for something to use in pretending to feed two toy lambs: "I going/ I going get some lambs for lunch/ lambs/ lambs for cereal/ I/ I want get some cereal for lambs." Kathryn evidently had a plan in mind, and knew something of the syntax for expressing what she had in mind, but struggled here for the order relations between the phrases "some cereal for lambs" and "some cereal for lunch."

Some researchers have concluded that word order is all that children learn with their first phrases, and the "earliest word combinations reflect nothing more or less than an ordering preference following adult models" (Tomasello, 1992b, p. 226), a view anticipated by Braine's (1976) "limited scope formulae," in which children learn the positions of particular words. Others have credited children with more syntactic knowledge, citing the meaning relations expressed by the order of words, to attribute nascent linguistic categories like subject and predicate. For example, the standard theory of generative transformational grammar (Chomsky, 1965) was used by Bloom (1970) as a heuristic for attributing formal relationships to the functional meaning relations expressed in sentences (whether the verb itself was actually said)—the little sentences children typically say like "Mommy pigtail," "read book," "Baby do it," "this go there." And still others assume that word order is functional from the beginning because children start out with an innate schema for the basic syntax of sentences, which guides acquisition (e.g., Gleitman, 1990; Landau & Gleitman, 1985; Pinker, 1984, 1989).

How to explain the transition to multiword speech and acquisition of linguistic categories like noun phrase and verb phrase is, perhaps, the single most disputed issue in the study of language development. Several different classes of theories have been offered, and they invoke different mechanisms. Those who have paid close attention to the social context point out that the function language serves in different settings can be the source of information about the syntax of sentences (e.g., Ervin-Tripp, 1973, 1980; Ninio, 1995a, 1995b; Ninio & Snow, 1996). Another class of theories emphasizes basic, general cognitive abilities, like being able to perceive patterns and correlations between the units of language that regularly go together, from an analysis of the ways units are distributed in the speech a child hears (e.g., Braine, 1963a, 1987, 1992; Maratsos, 1982; Maratsos & Chalkley, 1980; Olguin & Tomasello, 1993; Tomasello, 1992b). Such proposals were anticipated by Slobin's cognitive prerequisities and operating principles for grammatical development. An example is the principle "pay attention to the ends of words" in order to learn that "for any given semantic notion, grammatical realizations in the form of suffixes and postpositions will be acquired earlier than realizations in the form of prefixes or prepositions" (Slobin, 1973, p. 192).

Even more basic than such capacities for processing the distribution of linguistic units in the input is Braine's (1987, 1992) proposal that the "distinction between a predicate and its arguments [is] a primitive [logical] notion that is within the child's cognitive competence at the outset of language acquisition" and guides analysis of the input for acquiring linguistic categories (Braine, 1987, p. 85). And yet another class of theories holds that linguistic categories are, themselves, the primitives; they are innately determined and guide the acquisition of grammar from the beginning (following Chomsky, 1965, 1986), for example, P. Bloom (1990b), Gleitman (1981, 1990), Gleitman and Gillette (1995), Landau and Gleitman (1985), and Pinker (1984, 1994). Different sorts of data are cited in support of these different kinds of theories, and the issue is a long way from being resolved (see Maratsos, Ch. 9, this Volume).

One aspect of the transition to multiword speech and a grammar for simple sentences is the difference among children in the forms of their early sentences with verbs. These individual differences have been observed repeatedly and cast doubt on the notion that all children are programmed in the same way for making the transition to grammar. Such differences also point to the influence from many other factors, including the cognition of individual experience and the linguistic input children receive in their social interactions.

Individual Differences in the Transition to Syntax

Early researchers had been more or less content to describe the beginning of syntax in superficial terms, for example, the increase in length of sentences, different parts of speech, and whether sentences are complete or incomplete, simple, compound, or complex. Differences among children were described in relation to age, gender, socioeconomic status, and birth order, to name a few. These early studies were summarized by McCarthy (1954); the study by Templin (1957) represented the last and most thorough of these "count" studies.

However, the 1960s saw the introduction of generative transformational grammar to linguistic theory, with the proposal that children are learning an abstract, finite system of rules for generating the infinitely many possible sentences in a language (Chomsky, 1957, 1965). The quest was soon joined for discovering the kinds of rules that children learn and how the form of children's grammars changes over time (in particular, Braine, 1963b; Brown & Bellugi, 1964; Miller & Ervin, 1964). Implicit in Chomsky's theory and in the research it inspired was the assumption of universality, that all children are learning the same sorts of grammatical rules and in the same way. (See Bloom, 1975; Chapman, 1988; de Villiers & de Villiers, 1985; Golinkoff & Gordon, 1983; Ingram, 1989; and

Maratsos, 1983, for descriptions of this period in the history of child language research.)

The assumption of universality was challenged when the early grammars of the three children studied by Bloom (1970) were shown to differ in a more important way than simply their rate of progress. Two children combined verbs with nouns and also used nouns to indicate possession ("eat meat," "throw ball," "mommy sock"), while the third child combined verbs (or objects of possession) with pronouns (e.g., "eat it," "do this one," "my teddy"). This result "cast some doubt on the view of language development as the same innately preprogrammed behavior for all children . . . the differences among them must reflect the importance of individual differences in the interaction between cognitive function and experience, which could not be assumed to be the same for any two children" (Bloom, 1970, p. 227).

Subsequent research confirmed this basic finding of differences between pronominal and nominal (or, alternatively, holistic and analytic, or expressive and referential) strategies for early syntax. These studies documented, in particular, the developmental course of this difference after the first word combinations (Bloom et al., 1975b), its relationship to variation in children's single-word vocabularies and what has been called "cognitive style" (Nelson, 1975), the earlier developments in both language and cognition that correlate with the difference (Bates, Bretherton, & Snyder, 1988), and its relationship to differences in the input language children receive from caregivers (Goldfield, 1987; Hampson & Nelson, 1993). See the review by Shore (1995) for further documentation and discussion of these and other studies.

The basic finding is that children differ in whether they begin to combine verbs or objects of possession with nouns or pronouns in early sentences. Regardless of how they start out—whether they are more likely to combine verbs with nouns or with pronouns—the differences eventually diminish, and children become more similar to each other as they acquire more of the grammar. By the time mean sentence length exceeds 2.5 words, sentence subjects (agents, actors, experiencers) are primarily pronominal and predicate objects (the sentence theme or object affected by the action named by a verb) are primarily nominal (Bloom et al., 1975b; see also, P. Bloom, 1990a; Mazuka, Lust, Wakayama, & Snyder, 1995).

Children need to know both nominal and pronominal reference in order to learn the pragmatics of language use and conventions of everyday discourse. Nominal-pronominal variation is a motivated grammatical device for signaling shifting reference according to contingencies in the context and what is already understood between speakers (Jakobson, 1957). For example, whether one says "the bus is coming" or "it's coming" depends on whether the hearer can know what *it* refers to. At the corner bus stop, "it's coming" will make sense, but might not in another context. Although children differ in whether their early sentences are primarily nominal or primarily pronominal, they eventually learn how to use this variation between nouns and pronouns in order to shift between them to mark differences in the situation or in interpersonal factors in conversations (Garvey, 1979). As another example, by at least 29 months of age, children show sensitivity to the function of subject pronouns for marking the information in a sentence that is given or new (Levinsky & Gerken, 1995).

However, regardless of the strategy they begin with, most children make the transition to multiword speech and learning a grammar for simple sentences some time toward the end of the second year. Acquiring verbs is basic to this transition.

Verbs and Early Syntax

A key question dividing researchers bears on the extent to which children know the basic syntax of the language before they are able to learn verb meanings and the relationships between verbs and other constituents for phrases and simple sentences. At one extreme is the view from adult linguistic theory that children already know the syntax of the language, and knowing the syntax bootstraps verb learning (Gleitman, 1990; Landau & Gleitiman, 1985). At the other is the socially-based view that the structures of the language are derived from the formats for acquiring the pragmatics of language use and the conventions of discourse (Dore, 1975; Ervin-Tripp, 1973, 1980; Ninio, 1995a, 1995b; Ninio & Snow, 1996). Between these two positions is the proposal that children construct a grammar of the language in much the same way they construct their other theories about the world—that the transition to syntax and acquiring a grammar is a slow, incremental, constructive process that extends over a period of years and builds on both meaning and function (e.g., Bates & MacWhinney, 1982; Bates et al., 1988; Bloom, 1970, 1991; Bloom et al., 1975a, 1975b; Bowerman, 1976, 1981, 1987; Budwig, 1995; Sinclair, 1989, 1992; Tomasello, 1992b; Venezia, 1992).

The meanings in the majority of early sentences come from categories of verbs that name actions (for example, *do, make, push, eat*), and from the thematic roles that nouns and pronouns have as agent (the doer of the action) and theme (the object affected) in relation to those actions (e.g., Blake, 1984; Bloom et al., 1975b; Bowerman, 1973; Leonard, 1976; Miller, 1982; Stockman & Vaughn-Cook, 1989; Weist, 1982). Other kinds of verbs in early sentences name actions that involve a change of place (for example, *go, put*) with the thematic role of place or path. The importance of children's theories of objects, movement, and space—theories originating in the cognitive development of early infancy—are evident from the kinds of things expressed by early sentences.

The meanings of still other sentences come from another class of verbs children learn that name internal states, such as the verbs of volition, like *want,* and perception and epistemic verbs, like *see, know,* and *think.* The origins of such verbs as these can be traced to the early intersubjective, social connections that young infants have with their caregivers. Moreover, cultural groups may differ in the extent to which the focus in early caregiver-child interactions is on subjective or objective meanings (Blake, 1993). Young African American mothers and children from low income families tend to negotiate the more subjective aspects of relationships between people, and this interpersonal focus is reflected in relatively early and frequent use of internal state verbs in their early sentences. Mothers and children from mainstream contexts tend to focus more on objects and objective activities in their interactions. The extent to which this difference is true for children from other social-economic backgrounds remains to be determined.

Children's early verbs include a variety of descriptive verbs like *eat, ride,* and *sing,* but, in fact, most descriptive verbs occur relatively infrequently. Instead, children rely on a few all-purpose verbs or "pro-verbs" for many, if not most, early sentences (Bloom, Lifter, & Hafitz, 1980; Bloom, Merkin, & Wootten, 1982; Clark, 1978; Morehead & Ingram, 1973; Rice & Bode, 1993; Watkins, Rice, & Moltz, 1993). Pro-verbs, for example, the transitive action verb *do* and the intransitive locative verb *go,* can stand for a great many other more descriptive verbs not yet learned, like *draw* and *drive.* Having learned the syntactic frames with pro-verbs, a child can learn other verbs within a category that are more descriptive in their meanings and share the same syntactic privileges (like *chew, drink,* and *eat*).

In addition, many of the later-learned more complex structures of the language, like complementation (for example, "I want to do it" or "I see what's in there") are learned by children verb-by-verb, or one verb at a time

(e.g., Bloom et al., 1980; Bloom et al., 1989; Gordon & Chafetz, 1990; Maratsos, 1979; Tomasello, 1992b). Thus, children learn the syntax of the language first with the all-purpose pro-verbs and a few exemplars of more semantically specific, descriptive verbs. Having learned the syntactic frames in which different categories of verbs appear, a child can go on to learn new descriptive verbs that meet similar semantic and syntactic conditions (e.g., Bloom, 1981, 1991; Bloom et al., 1980).

Verb argument structures, verb inflections, *Wh*-questions (like what, who, where, and why), and many kinds of complex sentences are learned with the small number of general, all purpose pro-verbs, such as *do* and *go* and a few descriptive verb exemplars (see the papers in Bloom, 1991). Children use their knowledge of the syntax of simple sentences to learn more and different verbs, but knowledge of the constituent structure of simple sentences is learned, not innate (e.g., Bates & MacWhinney, 1982; Bloom, 1970, 1991; Bloom et al., 1975a; Budwig, 1995; Tomaselllo, 1992b). This account is consistent, in part, with the theory of "syntactic bootstrapping" (Gleitman, Gleitman, Landau, & Wanner, 1988; Landau & Gleitman, 1985) which claims that children use their syntactic knowledge to learn the syntax and semantics of other verbs that share the same syntactic functions. According to Landau and Gleitman, however, a syntactic parser is part of the linguistic endowment that the child brings to acquiring a language, and verb learning depends on this innate syntactic ability.

Initial proposals that children are learning structure and syntactic categories for expressing meaning relations were countered with assertions that the available evidence seems to support only semantic and not syntactic knowledge (Bowerman, 1973; Brown, 1973; but see Bowerman, 1987). Most recently, the transition from single words to simple sentences has been attributed to developments in the social-pragmatic uses of the single words children use before syntax by Ninio (1995a, 1995b). Ninio proposed that the increasing number and variability of children's communicative intents toward the end of the single-word period press them to learn grammatical dependency relations with rules for the permitted combinations of words. However, theories that grant knowledge of only word order, or only semantics, or only pragmatic intentions are basically discontinuous with both later learning and the adult target language in which these things are necessarily integrated. More seriously, however, they ignore the fundamentally necessary convergence of different aspects of language in the course of acquisition. Word order in sentences is never empty of either meaning or pragmatic intent; pragmatics cannot be independent of meaning. Both meaning and pragmatic intent depend on the formal properties of words, phrases, and sentences.

In sum, children tap into the verb system of the language and learn the sentence structures licensed by different categories of verbs. They may start out by analyzing the roles and relations between verbs like *put* and nouns like *truck* for phrases like "put truck," or they may begin synthetically with whole phrases or chunks, like "put it in" and "I want it" before learning the role relations between the parts. Ultimately, however, learning the argument structure of verbs and their syntactic alternations for realizing different thematic relations is the foundation for acquiring a grammar (e.g., Bates et al., 1988; Bloom, 1981, 1991; Bloom et al., 1975a, 1975b; Gropen, Pinker, Hollander, & Goldberg, 1991; MacWhinney, 1987; Pinker, 1989; Radford, 1990, 1995; Tomasello, 1992b). Many theories now assume that the different verbs children learn determine sentence structures that are continuous with later syntax and the verb system of adult English. Indeed, children learning language slowly or with difficulty have particular problems in learning verbs (e.g., Oetting, Rice, & Swank, 1995).

In contrast to this developmental, constructivist account, theories and research motivated by adult linguistic theory attribute early syntactic ability to innate knowledge of the basic grammatical principles and parameters of language (see Maratsos, Ch. 9, this Volume, for extended discussion). The realization of the innate principles and parameters in acquisition of increasingly complex structure is triggered when children hear relevant exemplars in the speech around them (e.g., Gleitman & Gillette, 1995; Hyams, 1986; Pinker, 1984; Roeper, 1982; Valian, 1991; Wexler, 1994). The difference between these two perspectives on language acquisition—one based on developmental theory and constructivism, with the assumption of more general cognitive principles, and the other based on adult linguistic theory, with the assumption of innate grammatical principles and parameters—is exemplified in two issues concerning two fundamental aspects of early child language: early sentences without subjects, and the acquisition of negation.

Subjectless Sentences

Sentence subjects are required in a grammar of English, but the early sentences of children learning English very often occur without them, for example, "read book," "ride train,"

and "no fit." Even after a child begins to say sentences with subjects, like "man making muffins" and "this go there," null-subject sentences continue to occur (Bloom, 1970; Bloom et al., 1975a; Brown, 1973). Several explanations based on adult linguistic theory have been offered (see Borer & Wexler, 1992), in particular, the theory of parameter setting (e.g., Hyams, 1986; Hyams & Wexler, 1993). Whether sentences have subjects is a parameter in universal grammar, in government and binding theory (Chomsky, 1981), but the parameter is set differently in different languages. Parameters in universal grammar have a range of values and a child depends on hearing speech in order to determine the value of a parameter in the particular language the child is learning.

Italian is a language in which sentence subjects are optional; in contrast, they are obligatory in English, which is why children's null-subject sentences attract attention. The explanation from linguistic theory is that young children learning English have not yet acquired information from the speech they hear to set the parameter for required subjects in sentences. Because they do not yet know that sentence subjects are required in English, they act as children do who are learning Italian. This explanation is a strictly linguistic one, based as it is on the assumptions in government and binding theory, and the hypothesis that subjectless sentences are the early behavioral manifestation of an innate parameter of universal grammar waiting to be set. (See Hyams, 1986, for the original statement and full logic of the theory.)

However, there are several psychologically- and developmentally-based explanations of null-subject sentences in early child speech. These accounts build on the basic observation that very young children are limited in the amount of information they are able to handle at one time. Thus, subjectless sentences occur because of limitations in their production capacities due to a variety of factors. One view is that children omit those syllables that are weakly stressed, such as pronoun sentence subjects, due to limitations in their production capacities for speech (e.g., Gerken, 1991). Others have suggested that omitting sentence subjects is pragmatically motivated: Children drop the least communicative parts of a sentence, and sentence subjects often represent information that is already given in the situation (e.g., Bates, 1976; Braine, 1974; Greenfield & Smith, 1976).

More general limitations on cognitive processing have been suggested by several researchers (e.g., Bloom, 1970; Bloom et al., 1975a; P. Bloom, 1990a; Mazuka, Lust,

Wakayama, & Snyder, 1995; Valian, 1991). In this view, what children *can say* depends on what they know about the language, but their linguistic knowledge interacts with their cognitive processing abilities to influence the variability in what they *do say*—their behaviors or performance. This account presupposes that young children have fuller knowledge of semantic-syntactic structure than is actually realized in the sentences they say, but realizing the fuller structures in complete sentences depends on development of cognitive capabilities rather than on setting innate parameters.

Saying sentences makes several demands on a young child's cognitive resources. At the least, a child needs to recall linguistic procedures, structures, and words that lexicalize linguistic categories. A child might need to add syntactic complexity, like attribution (e.g., "I wanna read *airplane* book") or negation (e.g., "Mommy *no* make pigtail"). The child might also need to respond to something someone else has said in conversation. The relative automaticity of words, added syntactic complexity, and conversational demands tap into the child's cognitive processing abilities and compete for the young child's essentially limited resources. This competition means that recalling words that are newly learned and less automatic than well-known words, or adding negation or attribution to a sentence, costs the child, and something has to give. Thus, negative sentences are shorter than affirmative sentences and lack sentence subjects initially, because negation in a sentence costs the child extra cognitive effort (Bloom, 1970; Bloom et al., 1975a; see Bates & MacWhinney, 1987; MacWhinney, 1987 for a related "competition model"). These cognitive requirements interact with what children hear of the particular language they are learning, with the result that the frequency of subjectless sentences differs between children learning English and children learning Italian (e.g., Valian, 1991) or Chinese (Wang, Lillo-Martin, Best, & Levitt, 1992). These cognitive effects are more systematic than such performance effects as fatigue, distractions, and shifts in attention and interest (described by Chomksy, 1965).

Essential to explaining the variability in early sentences is the fact that other factors can facilitate sentence subjects and increase their probability of occurrence, complementing those factors that compete for a child's limited resources (Bloom et al., 1975a). For instance, children are more likely to say longer sentences when the words they use are relatively well known and thus easily recalled. Children are less likely to include a sentence subject when

using words that were learned more recently. This "lexical familiarity effect" also influences whether children omit function morphemes, such as the object articles *a* and *the* with nouns (Boyle & Gerken, 1997). The frequency of subjectless sentences also depends on the verbs children use and is a function of syntactic role and verb category. Deaf children are more likely to drop subjects with transitive than with intransitive verbs (Feldman, Goldin-Meadow, & Gleitman, 1978; see also, P. Bloom, 1990a). In sum, the occurrence of subjects in early sentences is systematically influenced by a variety of factors that increase or decrease the probability that sentences will be complete or not. Children omit subjects when their cognitive processing abilities are exceeded—for example, when they use new verbs, nouns, or pronouns, or add negation or other kinds of complexity to a sentence, or need to respond to discourse demands that might not be relevant to what they already have in mind.

The two explanations of subjectless sentences, the cognitive load hypothesis and the parameter-setting hypothesis, independently converged on a particular component of the grammar, verb inflections (*-ing*, *-s, -ed*). While certain kinds of added complexity, like negation and two-part verbs (i.e., *take off*) reduced sentence length, adding verb inflections to modulate the meanings of verbs did not influence whether sentence subjects occur (Bloom et al., 1975a). Children were neither more nor less likely to lexicalize subjects when the verb was inflected. Thus, cognitive constraints that influence how much of a sentence a child is able to say interact selectively with aspects of the language being learned. The acquisition of inflections for marking subject-verb agreement is evidently less vulnerable to the general cognitive processing constraints that reduce the length of sentences by omitting subjects, because of the close dependency between sentence subjects and verb inflections—the bound forms that attach to verbs and nouns for modulating the meaning of simple sentences. A complementary finding was reported by Hyams (1986) in research motivated by her linguistic explanation based on principles of universal grammar. She proposed that children acquire the adult setting for the obligatory subject parameter in English at about the time they also begin to use verb inflection and auxiliaries. Others have also reported that children discover the obligatory subject requirement when they learn inflections for the distinction between tensed and untensed verbs (O'Grady, Peters, & Masterson, 1989). However, in a case study reported by Ingham (1992), the child's subjectless sentences decreased before verb inflections were reliably acquired.

Acquisition of Negation

One of the complexities that causes subject omission is negation, even though negation is one of the earliest meanings that children learn. In the first year of life, infants express negation prelinguistically—typically by shaking the head "no" (Spitz, 1957). The word *no* to express rejection/refusal is frequent in the single-word speech of many children in the second year. And negation is typically one of the earliest complexities children add to their simple sentences to express meanings such as nonexistence, rejection, refusal, and denial with words such as *no, no more, all gone,* and, eventually, *not, can't,* and *don't* (e.g., Bloom, 1970; Choi, 1988; de Villiers & de Villiers, 1979; Gopnik & Meltzoff, 1985; Klima & Bellugi, 1966; Pea, 1980, 1982). With development, the early two-word negative phrases like "no fit," "no shoe," "no more juice" (with *no more* learned as a single word) are embedded in longer sentences to express increasingly elaborated meanings, for example "I don't want more juice," "The lamb won't fit in there," and "I can't find a shoe." Negation continues to show the effects of learning and development through the preschool and school years (e.g., de Boysson-Bardies, 1977; de Villiers, Tager-Flusberg, & Silva, 1976; Hopmann & Maratsos, 1978; Klima & Bellugi, 1966).

One issue in the acquisition of negation has surfaced repeatedly since the 1960s and, as with subjectless sentences, has been a key point of debate in deciding between alternative explanations of language and its acquisition. The issue is whether early negation is external to the structure of sentences in a preliminary stage prior to the development of sentence internal negation, as the surface form of early sentences with *no* might suggest (Klima & Bellugi, 1966), or whether negation is internal to the sentence and attached to the verb in accord with the scope of negative meaning from the beginning (Bloom, 1970). Early negative sentences lack sentence subjects (as already discussed) and typically begin with *no,* for example, "no fit." The challenge comes with sentences in which *no* appears before a sentence subject, for example, "No, Mommy do it," "No, Kathryn playing self," and "No, Nathanial's a king."

The original description of sentence-external negation by Klima and Bellugi (1966) was based on the surface forms of the negative sentences of Adam, Eve, and Sara in the Roger Brown corpus (e.g., Brown, 1973; Brown & Bellugi, 1964). The challenge to external negation by Bloom (1970) was based on an interpretive analysis of sentences with *no* to determine their meaning and the child's intent (for example, "No, Kathryn playing self"). That analysis suggested that such sentences were actually affirmative, not negative. The *no* was anaphoric, meaning that it referred back to negate something either said previously or otherwise explicit in the context. For example, when Kathryn said "No, Kathryn playing self," she was asserting her intent to play with her own toys and opposing the suggestion that she play with my toys. The *no* in her sentence was a negation of my prior suggestion. Thus, when sentence subjects occurred with sentence-initial *no,* the proposition expressed in the sentence was not what was being negated (see also, Bloom, 1991).

When the early negative sentences of Adam, Eve, and Sarah were subsequently reanalyzed with the appropriate interpretive analysis by de Villiers and de Villiers (1979), "very few critical examples existed in which the negative element was nonanaphoric, and the subject was expressed . . . Clearly then, the initial-no negatives do not seem to constitute a universal first step" (de Villiers & de Villiers, 1985, p. 82). Nonetheless, they allowed that individual differences exist, citing data they collected from their son Nicholas, who said many sentences with initial *no* or *not* in front of sentence subjects between 23 and 29 months old. However, in all except one instance, the meaning of his sentences was the polite form of rejection and the *no* was an emphatic. Examples were "No Nathanial's a king" and "no Mummy do it" where the scope of negation is actually an unexpressed first person matrix verb *want* and "Mummy do it" is its complement sentence. The meaning of such sentences was glossed by de Villiers and de Villiers (1979) as "[I] no [want] Mummy do it," which anticipated the subsequent acquisition of the polite form of negation "I don't want S" or "I don't like S" (where S = sentence).

Kathryn, the child in Bloom's original study, like Nicholas, also used the complement form with first person matrix subjects (these were null initially, for example, "no want this," but, eventually, expressed, for example, "I don't want to comb hairs"). Kathryn also used anaphoric rejection or refusal frequently. The two other children in that study, in contrast, expressed *rejection* with the second person negative imperative most often ("Don't touch my block!"). However, these differences among the children probably reflected differences in the ways their caregivers talked to them. From a study of the input sentences in the Brown corpus and in their own recorded utterances to Nicholas, the de Villiers found that differences among children in the use of polite versus imperative forms of rejection corresponded to differences in the negative sentences the children heard. A complementary analysis of 10 English-speaking children has recently been reported by Drozd (1996), who looked specifically at the discourse context of sentences with *no* before the sentence-subject. He concluded that such sentences as "No Nathanial's a king" typically echo and negate a previous utterance from someone else. This interpretation is consistent with a function of exclamatory negation in adult discourse, meaning "[Don't say] 'Nathanial's a king!'"

In sum, analyses that took into account the semantic and pragmatic influences on the form of early negative sentences revealed that *no* at the beginning of an utterance is most often a negative sentence with the sentence subject omitted. When the scope of negation is indeed integral to the sentence with *no,* the inclusion of the negative marker results in shorter sentences without sentence subjects. Otherwise, when the sentence includes a subject, *no* at the beginning of the sentence is either anaphoric, an emphatic, or a form of politeness relative to the larger discourse context.

This conclusion continues to be challenged, however, most recently by Van Valin (1991) and Deprez and Pierce (1993), who used the surface forms of such examples of presentence negation to support several recent proposals in adult grammatical theory. In turn, the analysis of the three children whose speech was studied by Deprez and Pierce has now been challenged in a much more extensive study of the acquisition of negation and the status of children's early negative sentences by Stromswold (1995). She analyzed the negative utterances from 14 children in the relevant age range in the Child Language Data Exchange Systems (CHILDES) database (MacWhinney & Snow, 1985). In all, she examined over 12,000 sentences with *no* and 4,500 with *not* in relation to auxiliary and main verbs—reanalyzing, in particular, the meanings expressed in the data from the three children cited by Deprez and Pierce. She reported that children rarely used Neg-initial utterances with sentence subjects; the rate of pre-sentential negatives was not only very low, but constant throughout acquisition, indicating that it is not even an early stage. She concluded the results were more consistent with acquisition of sentence-internal negation from the beginning, rather than a switch from a Neg-initial to a Neg-internal strategy. Moreover, children distinguished between two different forms of negation, using *not* for sentential negation and *no* for anaphoric negation and quantification (Stromswold, 1995, pp. 18–19). Thus, early sentences expressing negation are immature and incomplete in critical respects, but, from the beginning, children converge on the adult structure of syntactic negation to express negative intent in their beliefs, desires, and feelings.

Subjectless sentences and the form and function of negation in early syntax are but two of the issues dividing researchers of language acquisition. They have been presented here as examples of the contrasting theoretical and empirical approaches to child language that have contributed to the theoretical tensions described in the beginning of this chapter. One class of theories begins with a child's changing behaviors in relation to the larger contexts of the child's life and invokes other aspects of the child's development for explaining language development. Other theories invoke adult linguistic theory to explain acquisition and use the data from children learning language to support that theory. Still other aspects of acquisition have been cited as a basis for deciding between competing linguistic theories, such as whether children do (e.g., Deprez & Pierce, 1993; Gerken, 1991; Peters, 1983) or do not (e.g., Radford, 1990, 1995) start out in their earliest word combinations already knowing something of inflections (see Maratsos, Ch. 9, this Volume).

In sum, once children have some understanding and facility with the syntax of simple sentences for expressing the basic semantic relationships between the agents of actions, the objects affected by an action, and the places to which and in which objects are located relative to each other, they begin to enlarge their meanings. At first, the meanings of simple sentences are modified by negation, inflections on nouns and verbs, and procedures for questions (see Bloom, 1991). With increasing sentence length, children also embed the meaning relations expressed by early two-word phrases such as "more juice" and "Mommy juice" in the verb phrase of a simple sentence, for example "get more juice" or "drink Mommy juice" (Brown, Cazden, & Bellugi, 1969).

Acquiring complex sentences, however, is an even more important development between two and three years, and provides yet another major testing ground for the exploration of competing grammatical theories. Acquiring the structures of complex sentences begins in the second year but continues well into the school years. Children need to acquire increasingly complex structures for expressing the more elaborated meanings made possible by their expanding cognitive abilities and increasing knowledge about the world, as predicted by the principle of elaboration. How children acquire the full complexity of the language has been the subject of much of the research that is driven by one or another linguistic theory to explain adult grammar—

research usually conducted with older children (see Maratsos, Ch. 9, this Volume). However, the third transition to the beginning of complex syntax depends on developments in children's thinking and occurs in the context of complementary developments in their conversational, pragmatic interactions with other persons in the activities of daily living.

THE THIRD TRANSITION: THE BEGINNINGS OF COMPLEX SENTENCES

Earlier in this chapter, considerable attention was given to developments during infancy that inform the later development of language. We saw that cognitive developments beginning in the first year result in learning about persons, objects, actions, and the relations between them. A grammar of simple sentences is acquired in the second year in order to express the thematic relations that have their origins in the knowledge about actions and the agents and recipients of action gained in the first year. Cognitive, affective, and social developments in infancy also include the earliest appreciations for relationships between events, such as one event happening before or after another, or one event being the cause of another event or its consequence. Children learn to express such increasingly elaborated relationships in intentional states—such as time and causality—when they begin to learn the increasingly complex structures of language between 2 and 3 years of age.

By the time they are 2 years old, most children have begun to realize that simple sentences can be related to each other when they are about events and states that happen together with a meaningful connection between them. Children need to acquire the syntax of complex sentences for combining the propositions underlying two simple sentences in order to express and interpret such complex meanings. They also need to learn the syntactic connectives, like *and, then, because, so, but,* and *if,* which express these meanings. However, by the time they are 3 years old, children have still only just begun to learn about syntactic connectives and meaning relations between propositions in the complex structures of conjunction, complementation, and relativization. Thus, developments in the complexity of language in the year between ages 2 and 3 can only be described in terms of emergence. Further achievement comes gradually in conjunction with other cognitive, social, and language developments in the preschool years, and development continues into the school years (e.g., Bloom, Lahey, Hood, Lifter, & Fiess, 1980; French, 1988; French & Nelson, 1985; Greenfield & Dent, 1982; Hakuta, de Villiers,

& Tager-Flusberg, 1982; Lust & Mervis, 1980; Wing & Scholnick, 1981).

The fact that children's sentences continue to increase in length is only a surface indication of the underlying developments taking place in their social and cognitive understanding. For example, the concept of causality is one of the critical aspects of both thinking and social connectedness to other persons that is expressed by a child's complex sentences. An understanding of causal connection between a person who acts and the effects of actions on objects and between objects begins in the first year of life (e.g., Leslie, 1988; Piaget, 1954, 1974). At the same time, developments are also taking place in the child's relationships with other persons and the conversational exchanges in which they participate. Giving and requesting explanations and reasons are a critical part of achieving interpersonal understanding as well as learning about the objective world. The earliest meanings of causal statements and questions between 2 and 3 have to do with the personal, emotional, or sociocultural beliefs that are the reasons for or results of actions. By the time they are 3 years old, most children have acquired the basic linguistic forms for expression of causality (e.g., Bloom & Capatides, 1987a; Donaldson, 1986; Dunn, 1988; French, 1986, 1988; Hood & Bloom, 1979; Johnson & Chapman, 1980; McCabe & Peterson, 1985).

The meanings of early complex sentences are acquired sequentially, and they are semantically cumulative, which means that they build on each other developmentally. The earliest learned meaning of conjunction is a simple additive relationship when two simple sentences are connected without another meaning relation between them. Children start out by learning the connective *and* for expressing representations in intentional states in which two events simply go together or happen together. An example is "Maybe you can carry that and I can carry this." This development has its analog in children's conceptual development: Understanding that things go together to form collections is an earlier development than learning that things can be ordered in a series or a sequence (e.g., Sinclair, 1970) or classes of things (Markman, 1984).

Complex sentences are soon learned that are additive plus something else: Two events go together but in a particular order relative to each other in time. They express temporal meanings of simultaneity or succession, for example, "I going this way, then come back." Children learn to express more semantically complex meanings when causality is added to additive and temporal meanings. The meanings of such sentences as "Maybe you can bend him so he can sit" express a causal connection (he could sit *because* you bend him) that is necessarily both additive (you bend him *and* he can sit) and temporal (you have to bend him *before* he can sit; Bloom et al., 1980; see Brown & Hanlon, 1970, for discussion of cumulative syntactic complexity and Brainerd, 1978, regarding cumulative complexity in cognitive development).

The result is a developmental sequence for acquiring conjunction with simple additive relations expressed before temporal relations, which are, in turn, expressed before causal meanings. The additive, temporal, causal sequence in acquisition of complex sentences with conjunction by 2- and 3 year-olds is echoed in 4- and 5-year-old children's understanding of the concept of a story and the developmental sequence of storytelling skills (e.g., Stein, 1988). In addition to their semantic meanings, 2-year-old children's complex sentences also express pragmatic meanings, such as expressions of causality that are requests for action or assistance, prohibitions, cautions, or reasons for a disruption in the order of things (Hood & Bloom, 1979). By the time they are 3 to 4 years old, children are able to express an adversative meaning such as a change of mind or change of focus (Peterson, 1986; see also, Wing & Scholnick, 1981).

Linguistically, children's earliest complex sentences connect the structures underlying their simple sentences (Bloom et al., 1980; Bloom, Rispoli, Gartner, & Hafitz, 1989; Bowerman, 1979; Limber, 1973). When syntactic connectives are acquired, the first connective is *and*—in English (e.g., Bloom et al., 1980; Clark, 1970; Limber, 1973) and also in other languages, for example, Swedish (e.g., Johansson & Sjolin, 1975), Japanese (Clancy, 1985), German (e.g., Werner & Kaplan, 1963). (See also, Clancy, Jacobsen, & Silva, 1976.) *And* is also the most general syntactic connective—used to express conjunction with different meaning relationships (additive, temporal, causal, and adversative) before children learn the semantically more specific connectives for expressing these meanings, such as *and then* and *when* for temporal relations, *because* and *so* for causal relations, *but* for adversatives, and *if* for conditional meaning (e.g., Bloom et al., 1980; Clark, 1970). Moreover, *and* also functions as a discourse connective, joining clauses and sentences in children's narratives and their everyday conversations. Well into the school years, *and* continues to be used ubiquitously as an all-purpose connective for cohesion in discourse—to show that successive sentences are related to each other because they share the same topic (Peterson & McCabe, 1987, 1988).

The earliest connectives learned in English—*and, then,* and *because*—are the connectives that do not also have a nonconnective function. Connectives that are homonymous—the same form having two or more meanings in the language—are learned later (Bloom, 1991; see Bever, 1970, for discussion of conceptual constraints on learning syntactically homonymous forms). For example, *what, where,* and *who* are first acquired in their non-connective contexts for asking questions (for example, "What doing?" and "Where all the people go?"), before they are learned in complex sentences with complement clauses (for example, "You know what's in this bag" and "Let's go see where Mommy is") or relativization (i.e., "the man who fixes the door"). The word *that* is learned as a connective with complement clauses (i.e., "I think that he wanna eat this") at least several months after it appears in children's speech as a demonstrative pronoun in early phrases like "that a car" (examples from Bloom, 1991). In addition, the three complex sentence structures with connectives learned in this period are learned in this sequence: conjunction before complementation before relativization. The structures of complementation with connectives and relativization are learned after conjunction in part, at least, because they require as connectives those homonymous forms *what, where,* or *that* learned earlier in other syntactic contexts.

The structures of conjunction, complementation, and relativization are also learned with different populations of verbs: Conjunction occurs overwhelmingly with action verbs like *eat* and locative verbs like *go,* relativization with the copula *to be,* and complementation primarily with state verbs, notably the perception verbs *see* and *look* and the epistemic verbs *think* and *know*. Thus, the centrality of verbs for early simple sentences continues in the acquisition of complex sentences. As was the case for verb inflections (Bloom et al., 1980) and *Wh-* questions (Bloom, Merkin, & Wootten, 1982), more complex structures tend to be learned first with only one or two individual verbs as exemplars, such as the pro-verbs *do* and *go,* before generalizing across a class or classes of more varied and descriptive verbs like *cut* and *ride* (e.g., Bloom, 1981; Maratsos, 1979; Tomasello, 1992b). Examples include the passive construction (Gordon & Chafetz, 1990) and complement clauses and connectives (Bloom et al., 1989). Only gradually do children appreciate that verbs come together to form categories as a function of the structures and aspects of grammatical meaning they share.

Does grammatical development depend on acquiring general rules first and then learning the verbs that fit the rules, or does it depend on induction as a result of learning structures one verb at a time? This question has come up in a variety of contexts (see de Villiers & de Villiers, 1985). From the perspective of linguistic theory, the basic structure of the grammar is given to begin with, and the syntax of sentences determines the verbs children learn (Gleitman, 1990; Gleitman et al., 1988). From the developmental perspective, children discover the larger grammatical structures of the language through learning how the pieces fit together. Once they've learned a basic structure with a small subset of the possible verbs that can enter into it, they can proceed to learn other verbs also permitted in that structure (Bloom, 1991). Children do not begin syntactic learning with a general category of *verb* (Tomasello, 1992b).

The different complex sentences also occur in different discourse environments. Early causal questions and statements, for example, are more likely to occur in response to what someone else says than are simple additive expressions or expressions of temporal order (Bloom, Merkin, & Wootten, 1982; Hood & Bloom, 1979). Thus, in addition to the requirements presented by the verbs in the language, requirements for conversational discourse are also a factor in learning increasingly complex structures and uses of language (e.g., Budwig, 1996). Since most research tends to be about developments in either complex sentences or discourse, more research is needed in order to understand the essential developmental relationship between them.

LEARNING LANGUAGE IN AND FOR CONVERSATIONS

Participating in conversations provides children with particularly fruitful contexts for the acquisition of complex syntax, as in the case of causality. In turn, children's use of complex sentences in conversation and narratives has provided researchers with insights into the psychological as well as logical meanings they are learning to express (e.g., Bartsch & Wellman, 1995; Falmagne, 1990; Scholnick & Wing, 1991, 1992). However, the direction of influence between syntactic learning and developments in conversation are not easy to establish, and the two kinds of development do not necessarily proceed hand-in-hand. Often, function follows form, and children may acquire the forms of the language and even use those forms in more or less relevant and appropriate contexts without learning all the details of their functions.

Acquisition of the capacity to use both nouns and pronouns for shifting reference in sentences is an early example of function following form in conversational development. Individual children start out using either nouns or pronouns primarily, but all children eventually learn to refer to a car as *it* or *car,* to a place as *there* or *floor,* and express possession with a proper noun *Kathryn's,* or a possessive pronoun, *my* (e.g., Bates, Bretherton, & Snyder, 1988; Bloom et al., 1975b; Shore, 1995). Although they acquire the capacity for shifting reference in simple sentences, they have yet to learn the social and linguistic conventions that govern use of that capacity (Bloom et al., 1975b; see also, Garvey, 1979). Among the different pronoun forms, children first learn to sort out the appropriate distinctions in reference to self before other, with first-person pronouns to mark different perspectives on agency (Budwig, 1989) and speech role (Charney, 1980).

Increasing sophistication with still other language forms often occurs with lingering naïveté about the appropriate social and personal contingencies that govern those forms. For example, a 2-year-old, Ricky, whose own TV watching was heavily monitored, responded to a 28-year-old who said he liked watching a particular TV program by exclaiming incredulously "Your mother lets you?" (Shatz, 1994, p. 326). A 2-year-old, Eric, ran after another 2-year-old who had taken off with his toy, shouting "Rob! It's not to play with!" even though it was a toy Rob was running off with (Bloom, 1970, p. 230). Thus, while children learn the pragmatics of language use and participate in conversations from the beginning of word learning, conversational skills continue to depend on development of what Shatz called "social-linguistic intelligence."

Another example of dissociation between developments in complexity and discourse was reported by Hoff-Ginsberg (1994). When equated on the basis of their average length of utterance, first-born children tended to be more proficient in syntactic ability, while second-born children showed more advanced conversational skills. This difference between children with and without siblings was attributed to differences in the kinds of interaction they each had opportunities for. First-born children typically participate in more interactions with adults, whereas second-borns also have conversations with their older siblings who provide fewer experiences with complex sentences (Hoff-Ginsberg, 1994; Toledano, 1991).

Learning language and learning to participate in conversations entails many developments in addition to developments in language. Culturally, children are not only learning the language—by learning a language, a child is learning to participate in the "give and take of everyday life" and assume a role in the cultural life of the community (Schieffelin, 1990). Social and affective developments are required because the motivation to learn a language in the first place comes from the need to sustain intersubjectivity with others and establish the self in a social world. And cognitive developments—the symbolic capacity and conceptual structure in particular—are required for constructing the increasingly discrepant and elaborate intentional states expressed by language and interpreted from the expressions of others. These are core assumptions in the intentionality model, and central to the model is the initiative and agency of the child who constructs the intentional states that determine the relevance of events for learning (Bloom, 1993).

However, much research and theory on the importance of discourse and social context for language acquisition focuses on the "very considerable role [of] the adult" (Bruner, 1983, p. 40) who interacts first with the very young infant, to provide the structure for their turn-taking and reciprocal vocal exchanges, and then with the older child to provide the "scaffolding" or "support system" for their conversation and language learning (e.g., Bruner, 1975b, 1983; Kaye & Charney, 1980). The scaffolding model assumes that adults control their interactions with young children by providing the format and structure of their exchanges, and that learning language depends on such formatted interactions. The adult's role is, therefore, primary (e.g., Bruner, 1983; Kaye & Charney, 1980; Ninio & Bruner, 1978). The essentials of the model have been endorsed by many, most notably by Dore (1983), Snow (1977), and Tomasello (1992a). (See Moerk, 1989, for a general review.) The original theoretical model for scaffolding had its roots in Vygotsky (1962)—who stressed the importance of what a child first does only with guidance from other persons. The scaffolding model was strengthened with Vygotsky's extension of his theory to learning in the "zone of proximal development" (ZPD) which is the distance between a child's actual developmental level and the level of potential development possible "under adult guidance or in collaboration with more capable peers" (Vygotsky, 1978, p. 86).

The scaffolding/ZPD account of conversational interaction and language learning has been challenged in several ways. First, such context-specific learning is culturally determined and may well be culture specific. Mothers in some non-western cultures, such as Papua New Guinea and Samoa, for example, do not engage their infants in the joint and reciprocal gazing and vocalizing described in early mother-infant interactions in western societies (Ochs,

1988; Ochs & Schieffelin, 1984; Schieffelin, 1990). Mothers and children in different cultures and even within the same culture differ also in the extent to which they participate in highly structured and conventional routines, games, and joint picture-book reading (Camaioni, 1986; Goddard, Durkin, & Rutter, 1985; Snow & Goldfield, 1983).

Second, the asymmetry inherent in traditional scaffolding/ZPD accounts was challenged by Rogoff and others in an effort to "focus on the role of children as active participants in their own development . . . [and] the complementary roles of children and caregivers in fostering children's development" (Rogoff, 1990, p. 16). Children are active participants in their interactions with others, but in Rogoff's theory, they nevertheless require guidance and direction in their shared endeavors (Rogoff, 1993). And third, the extent to which caregivers provide a structure for interaction depends on what they and their children already know about the events in which they are engaged, as well as other prior knowledge that they share (Lucariello, 1987b).

When one looks beyond the formatted routines and games such as picture-book reading, peek-a-boo, or a tea party that provided the original observations on which the scaffolding model was based, a different view of early interactions emerges—one in which the child's role is salient. It is the child who initiates conversational exchanges most often when children and caregivers are engaged in free play and other activities of daily living (Bloom et al., 1995, 1996; Harris, 1992; Howe, 1981). Mothers are more interested in maintaining a conversation by letting a child know that a message had been shared than in providing language models for the child to learn. Thus, participation in early conversations is motivated by a child's own cognitive, social, and affective agenda to express something in mind and to direct the flow of the interaction in order to share the contents of mind. Neither conversation nor language learning depend on mothers setting up formats as the occasions for scaffolded interactions (Bloom et al., 1996; Rome-Flanders, Cronk, & Gourde, 1995).

To be sure, caregivers talk to their children—some talk a great deal. Most caregiver talk is about what children are doing, thereby providing the relevant experiences with language that they need. But language learning can occur in these contexts without the child having to say something at the time. Outside of language, children take in a great deal and learn about what goes on around them all the time—without having to show the effects of that learning in their immediate nonlinguistic actions and behaviors. The language a child brings to a conversation, therefore, is language already learned from what has been heard and overheard in a multitude of actions and interactions. In fact, children can recruit cognitive resources to language more readily if their essentially limited resources are not also stretched by having to process and respond to what someone else has just said, particularly if a response is required to something that is not relevant to what the child already had in mind (Bloom, 1974, 1993; Bloom et al., 1975a, 1976; Elbers & Wijnen, 1992). Indeed, this point gains considerable support from studies of children talking in their cribs alone, before falling off to sleep. More sophisticated forms of language occur in crib speech than are observed in typical daytime interactions with other persons (Kuczaj, 1983; Nelson, 1990; Weir, 1964), because children have greater "freedom to direct their own behavior" (Kuczaj, 1983, p. 168).

The force of the child's intentionality and its centrality for language development, in general, and developments in conversation, in particular, are enhanced by the finding that the same patterns of interaction occur among different populations of children and mothers. For example, one corollary of limited economic resources is that children and caregivers in poor families engage in fewer extended conversations when compared with middle-class families (Bloom et al., 1996; Hart & Risley, 1995), and they tend to do more overlapping talking. Overlapping turns are evidently acceptable in culturally different societies and even valued by the participants in certain contexts (e.g., Cazden & Dickinson, 1981; Ervin-Tripp, 1979; Heath, 1982, 1983; Whatley, 1981). But regardless of such possible economic and/or cultural effects as these on their behaviors, children from poor homes are also the initiators and in charge of their conversations most often, and their mothers are responsive to them. As with children from less economically stressed homes, they were most likely to be talking in the moments before their mothers talked, and their mothers were most likely to be talking in the moments after they talked (Bloom et al., 1996). Thus, we have no reason to think that the role of intentionality in the developmental *process* for learning language differs for children from different cultures and societies.

CONCLUSIONS

This chapter began with an account of the theoretical tensions that have resulted from a succession of strong theories of language acquisition, each focused on a different aspect of the problem—either the child's cognition, or social interaction, or linguistic theories of the target language the child is learning. One reason these theoretical tensions endure is the strength of commitments to explanation based on such strong theories. Another reason the tensions endure, however, is that each theory is partly right—each factor invoked by these theories does, indeed, contribute to acquiring a language. The task now is to integrate the parts and embrace the whole in order to achieve a truly explanatory theory of language acquisition. This task will require constructing theories that put language development into the larger developmental context in which it occurs and that take the active mind of the child seriously in efforts to explain language acquisition.

The influences on language development originate in the child's intentionality—the contents of mind in consciousness that are determined by affective, social, cognitive, and linguistic processes. A young child's intentional states are constantly changing—as a function of development and as a function of actions and interactions in the world, including acts of expression and interpretation. Affect promotes engagement with the physical and personal world for learning and for sustaining intersubjectivity with other persons. Social developments press the child to learn a language in order to share contents of mind with other persons and thereby assume a place in culture and society. Developing cognition yields conceptual structure in the knowledge base and the symbolic capacity for the representations in consciousness that language expresses and that result from interpreting the expressions of others. Language is the goal; it influences the process as much as it is influenced by it; and all aspects of development come together in its acquisition. In contrast, when we put all the effort at explanation into only one or another of its aspects or into only the words and linguistic structures of the adult language the child needs to learn, the result is a loss of perspective on the psychology of the child. It is also a loss of perspective on language itself and the power of expression it provides.

ACKNOWLEDGMENTS

This chapter has benefited from interactions I've had with many people who generously shared their work. I thank, in particular, Nancy Budwig, LouAnn Gerken, Kathy Hirsh-Pasek, Roberta Golinkoff, Catherine Snow, Karen Stromswold, and Michael Tomasello. For their thoughtful comments on reading portions of this manuscript, I thank William Damon, Howard Gruber, Margaret Lahey, Ellen

Markman, and in particular, Joan Lucariello and Roberta Golinkoff. I am grateful to Deanna Kuhn for asking me to write the chapter in the first place and for her helpful comments and suggestions on both the form and content of the chapter as it evolved.

REFERENCES

Acredolo, L., & Goodwyn, S. (1991). *Symbolic gesture vs. word: Is there a modality advantage for onset of symbol use?* Poster presented at the meeting of the Society for Research in Child Development, Seattle, WA.

Akhtar, N., Carpenter, M., & Tomasello, M. (1996). The role of discourse novelty in children's early word learning. *Child Development, 67,* 635–645.

Akhtar, N., Dunham, F., & Dunham, P. (1991). Directive interactions and early vocabulary development: The role of joint attentional focus. *Journal of Child Language, 18,* 41–49.

Akhtar, N., & Tomasello, M. (in press). Intersubjectivity in early language learning and use. In S. Braten (Ed.), *Intersubjective communication and emotion in ontogeny.* Cambridge, England: Cambridge University Press.

Anglin, J. (1977). *Word, object, and conceptual development.* New York: Norton.

Anglin, J. (1993). Vocabulary development: A morphological analysis. *Monographs of the Society for Child Development, 58*(10, Serial No. 238).

Aslin, R., & Pisoni, D. (1980). Some developmental processes in speech perception. In G. Yeni-Komshian, J. Kavanagh, & C. Ferguson (Eds.), *Child phonology: Vol. 2. Perception and production* (pp. 67–96). New York: Academic Press.

Aslin, R., Pisoni, D., & Jusczyk, P. (1983). Auditory development and speech perception in infancy. In P. Mussen (Series Ed.) & M. Haith & J. Campos (Vol. Eds.), *Handbook of child psychology: Vol. 2. Infancy and developmental psychobiology* (pp. 573–688). New York: Wiley.

Baillargeon, R. (1992). The object concept revisited: New directions in the investigation of infants' physical knowledge. In C. Granrud (Ed.), *Visual perception and cognition in infancy* (pp. 265–315). Carnegie-Mellon Symposium on Cognition, Vol. 23. Hillsdale, NJ: Erlbaum.

Bakeman, R., & Adamson, J. (1984). Coordinating attention to people and objects in mother-infant and peer-infant interaction. *Child Development, 55,* 1278–1289.

Baker, C., & McCarthy, J. (Eds.). (1981). *The logical problem of language acquisition.* Cambridge, MA: MIT Press.

Baldwin, D. (1993a). Early referential understanding: Infants' ability to recognize referential acts for what they are. *Developmental Psychology, 29,* 832–843.

Baldwin, D. (1993b). Infants' ability to consult the speaker for clues to word meaning. *Journal of Child Language, 20,* 395–418.

Bamberg, M., Budwig, N., & Kaplan, B. (1991). A developmental approach to language acquisition: Two case studies. *First Language, 11,* 121–141.

Barrett, K., & Campos, J. (1987). Perspectives on emotional development: II. A functionalist approach to emotions. In J. Osofsky (Ed.), *Handbook of infant development* (2nd ed., pp. 555–578). New York: Wiley.

Barrett, M. (Ed.). (1985). *Children's single-word speech.* New York: Wiley.

Barrett, M. (1986). Early semantic representations and early word-usage. In S. Kuczaj & M. Barrett (Eds.), *The development of word meaning* (pp. 39–67). New York: Springer.

Barrett, M., Harris, M., & Chasin, J. (1991). Early lexical development and maternal speech: A comparison of children's initial and subsequent use of words. *Journal of Child Language, 18,* 21–40.

Barratt, M., & Roach, M. (1995). Early interactive processes: Parenting by adolescent mothers and adult single mothers. *Infant Behavior and Development, 18,* 97–109.

Bartsch, K., & Wellman, H. (1995). *Children talk about the mind.* New York: Oxford University Press.

Bates, E. (1976). *Language in context.* New York: Academic Press.

Bates, E., Benigni, L., Bretherton, I., Camaioni, L., & Volterra, V. (1979). *The emergence of symbols: Communication and cognition in infancy.* New York: Academic Press.

Bates, E., Bretherton, I., & Snyder, L. (1988). *From first words to grammar: Individual differences and dissociable mechanisms.* Cambridge, England: Cambridge University Press.

Bates, E., & Carnevale, G. (1993). New directions in research on language development. *Developmental Review, 13,* 436–470.

Bates, E., Dale, P., & Thal, D. (1995). Individual differences and their implications for theories of language development. In P. Fletcher & B. MacWhinney (Eds.), *The handbook of child language* (pp. 96–151). Oxford, England: Blackwell.

Bates, E., & MacWhinney, B. (1982). Functionalist approaches to grammar. In E. Wanner & L. Gleitman (Eds.), *Language acquisition: The state of the art* (pp. 173–218). Cambridge, England: Cambridge University Press.

Bates, E., & MacWhinney, B. (1987). Competition, variation, and language learning. In B. MacWhinney (Ed.), *Mechanisms of language acquisition* (pp. 157–193). Hillsdale, NJ: Erlbaum.

Bates, E., Marchman, V., Thal, D., Fenson, L., Dale, P., Reznick, S., Reilly, J., & Hartung, J. (1994). Developmental and stylistic variation in the composition of early vocabulary. *Journal of Child Language, 21,* 85–123.

Bates, E., Thal, D., & Marchman, B. (1991). Symbols and syntax: A Darwinian approach to language development. In

N. Krasnegor, D. Rumbaugh, R. Schiefelbusch, & M. Studdert-Kennedy (Eds.), *Biological and behavioral determinants of language development* (pp. 29–65). Hillsdale, NJ: Erlbaum.

Bateson, C. (1975). Mother-infant exchanges: The epigenesis of conversational interaction. In D. Aronson & R. Rieber (Eds.), Development psycholinguistics and communication disorders. *Annals of the New York Academy of Sciences, 263,* 101–113.

Becker, J. (1990). Processes in the acquisition of pragmatic competence. In G. Conti-Ramsden & C. Snow (Eds.), *Children's language* (Vol. 7, pp. 7–24). Hillsdale, NJ: Erlbaum.

Becker, J. (1994). Pragmatic socialization: Parental input to preschoolers. *Discourse Processes, 17,* 131–148.

Beckwith, R. (1988). *Learnability and psychologically constrained grammars.* Unpublished doctoral dissertation, Teachers College, Columbia University, New York.

Beckwith, R., Tinker, E., & Bloom, L. (1989). *The acquisition of non-basic sentences.* Paper presented at the Boston University Conference on Language Development, Boston.

Beckwith, R., Tinker, E., & Bloom, L. (1995). *Comparison of word frequencies in mother and child speech.* Unpublished data.

Beebe, B., & Jaffe, J. (1992, May). *Mother-infant vocal dialogues.* Paper presented at the International Conference on Infant Studies, Miami.

Bever, T. (1970). The cognitive basis for linguistic structures. In J. Hayes (Ed.), *Cognition and the development of language.* New York: Wiley.

Blake, I. (1984). *Language development in working class black children: An examination of form, content, and use.* Doctoral dissertation, Teachers College, Columbia University, New York.

Blake, I. (1993). The social-emotional orientation of mother-child communication in African American families. *International Journal of Behavioral Development, 16*(3), 443–463.

Blake, J., & de Boysson-Bardies, B. (1992). Patterns in babbling: A cross linguistic study. *Journal of Child Language, 19,* 51–74.

Bloom, K. (1977). Patterning of infant vocal behavior. *Journal of Experimental Child Psychology, 17,* 250–263.

Bloom, K. (1990). Selectivity and early infant vocalization. In J. Enns (Ed.), *The development of attention: Research and theory* (pp. 121–136). Amsterdam, The Netherlands: Elsevier.

Bloom, K., Russell, A., & Wassenberg, K. (1987). Turn-taking affects the quality of infant vocalization. *Journal of Child Language, 14,* 211–227.

Bloom, L. (1970). *Language development: Form and function in emerging grammars.* Cambridge, MA: MIT Press.

Bloom, L. (1973). *One word at a time: The use of single-word utterances before syntax.* The Hague: Mouton.

Bloom, L. (1974). Talking, understanding and thinking: Developmental relationship between receptive and expressive language. In R. Schiefelbusch & L. Lloyd (Eds.), *Language perspectives—Acquisition, retardation, and intervention* (pp. 285–312). Baltimore: University Park Press.

Bloom, L. (1975). Language development. In F. Horowitz (Ed.), *Review of child development research* (Vol. 4, pp. 245–303). Chicago: University of Chicago Press.

Bloom, L. (1981). The importance of language for language development: Linguistic determinism in the 1980s. In H. Winitz (Ed.), Native language and foreign language acquisition. *The New York Academy of Sciences, 379,* 160–171.

Bloom, L. (1991). *Language development from two to three.* New York: Cambridge University Press.

Bloom, L. (1992, Fall–Winter). *Racism in developmental research* (Division 7 Newsletter). Washington, DC: American Psychological Association.

Bloom, L. (1993). *The transition from infancy to language: Acquiring the power of expression.* Cambridge, England: Cambridge University Press.

Bloom, L. (1994). Meaning and expression. In W. Overton & D. Palermo (Eds.), *The ontogenesis of meaning* (pp. 215–235). Hillsdale, NJ: Erlbaum.

Bloom, L., & Beckwith, R. (1989). Talking with feeling: Integrating affective and linguistic expression. *Cognition and Emotion, 3,* 313–342.

Bloom, L., Beckwith, R., Capatides, J., & Hafitz, J. (1988). Expression through affect and words in the transition from infancy to language. In P. Baltes, D. Featherman, & R. Lerner (Eds.), *Life-span development and behavior* (Vol. 8, pp. 99–127). Hillsdale, NJ: Erlbaum.

Bloom, L., & Capatides, J. (1987a). Sources of meaning in complex syntax: The sample case of causality. *Journal of Experimental Child Psychology, 43,* 112–128.

Bloom, L., & Capatides, J. (1987b). Expression of affect and the emergence of language. *Child Development, 58,* 1513–1522.

Bloom, L., & Lahey, M. (1978). *Language development and language disorders.* New York: Wiley.

Bloom, L., Lahey, M., Hood, L., Lifter, K., & Fiess, K. (1980). Complex sentences: Acquisition of syntactic connectives and the semantic relations they encode. *Journal of Child Language, 7,* 235–261. (Reprinted in *Child language: A reader,* pp. 89–105, by M. Franklin & S. Barten, Eds., New York: Oxford University Press)

Bloom, L., Lifter, K., & Broughton, J. (1985). The convergence of early cognition and language in the second year of life: Problems in conceptualization and measurement. In M. Barrett (Ed.), *Single word speech.* London: Wiley.

Bloom, L., Lifter, K., & Hafitz, J. (1980). Semantics of verbs and the development of verb inflection in child language. *Language, 56,* 386–412.

Bloom, L., Lightbown, P., & Hood, L. (1975b). Structure and variation in child language. *Monographs of the Society for Research in Child Development, 40*(Serial No. 160).

Bloom, L., Margulis, C., Tinker, E., & Fujita, N. (1996). Early conversations and word learning: Contributions from child and adult. *Child Development, 67,* 3154–3175.

Bloom, L., Merkin, W., & Wootten, J. (1982). Wh-questions: Linguistic factors that contribute to the sequence of acquisition. *Child Development, 53,* 1084–1092.

Bloom, L., Miller, P., & Hood, L. (1975a). Variation and reduction as aspects of competence in language development. In A. Pick (Ed.), *Minnesota Symposia on Child Psychology* (Vol. 9, pp. 3–55). Minneapolis: University of Minnesota.

Bloom, L., Rispoli, M., Gartner, B., & Hafitz, J. (1989). Acquisition of complementation. *Journal of Child Language, 16,* 101–120.

Bloom, L., Rocissano, L., & Hood, L. (1976). Adult-child discourse: Developmental interaction between information processing and linguistic knowledge. *Cognitive Psychology, 8,* 521–552.

Bloom, L., Tinker, E., & Beckwith, R. (1995). *Developments in expression: Language, emotion, and object play.* Unpublished manuscript.

Bloom, L., Tinker, E., & Margulis, C. (1993). The words children learn: Evidence against a noun bias in children's vocabularies. *Cognitive Development, 8,* 431–450.

Bloom, P. (1990a). Subjectless sentences in child language. *Linguistic Inquiry, 21,* 491–504.

Bloom, P. (1990b). Syntactic distinctions in child language. *Journal of Child Language, 17,* 343–355.

Bloom, P. (1994). Possible names: The role of syntax-semantic mappings in the acquisition of nominals. *Lingua, 92,* 297–329.

Bloom, P., Barss, A., Nicol, J., & Conway, L. (1994). Children's knowledge of binding and coreference: Evidence from spontaneous speech. *Language, 70,* 53–71.

Bloom, P., & Kelemen, D. (1995). Syntactic cues in the acquisition of collective nouns. *Cognition, 56,* 1–30.

Bonvillian, J., Orlansky, M., & Novack, L. (1983). Developmental milestones: Sign language acquisition and motor development. *Child Development, 54,* 1435–1445.

Borer, H., & Wexler, K. (1992). Biunique relations and the maturation of grammatical principles. *Natural Language and Linguistic Theory, 10,* 147–190.

Bowerman, M. (1973). *Early syntactic development: A cross-linguistic study with special reference to Finnish.* London: Cambridge University Press.

Bowerman, M. (1976). Semantic factors in the acquisition of rules for word use and sentence construction. In D. Morehead & A. Ingram (Eds.), *Normal and deficient child language* (pp. 99–179). Baltimore: University Park Press.

Bowerman, M. (1979). The acquisition of complex sentences. In P. Fletcher & M. Garman (Eds.), *Language acquisition* (pp. 285–305). Cambridge, England: Cambridge University Press.

Bowerman, M. (1981). Beyond communicative adequacy: From piecemeal knowledge to an integrated system in the child's acquisition of langue. *Papers and Reports on Child Language Development, 20,* 1–24

Bowerman, M. (1987). *Mapping thematic roles onto syntactic functions: Are children helped by innate "linking rules"?* Paper presented at the Child Language Conference, Boston University.

Bowerman, M. (1989). Learning a semantic system: What role do cognitive predispositions play? In M. Rice & R. Schiefelbusch (Eds.), *The teachability of language* (pp. 133–169). Baltimore: Brookes.

Boyle, M., & Gerken, L. (1997). Effects of lexical familiarity on children's function morpheme omissions. *Journal of Memory and Language, 36,* 117–128.

Braine, M. (1963a). On learning the grammatical order of words. *Psychological Review, 70,* 323–348.

Braine, M. (1963b). The ontogeny of English phrase structure: The first phase. *Language, 39,* 1–13.

Braine, M. (1974). Length constraints, reduction rules, and holophrastic processes in children's word combinations. *Journal of Verbal Learning and Verbal Behavior, 13,* 448–456.

Braine, M. (1976). Children's first word combinations. *Monograph of the Society for Research in Child Development, 41*(Serial No. 164).

Braine, M. (1987). What is learned in acquiring word classes—A step towards an acquisition theory. In B. MacWhinney (Ed.), *Mechanisms of language acquisition* (pp. 65–87). Hillsdale, NJ: Erlbaum.

Braine, M. (1992). What sort of innate structure is needed to "bootstrap" into syntax? *Cognition, 45,* 77–100.

Braine, M. (1994). Is nativism sufficient? *Journal of Child Language, 21,* 9–31.

Brainerd, C. (1978). The stage question in cognitive-developmental theory. *The Behavioral and Brain Sciences, 2,* 173–213.

Brazelton, T., & Cramer, B. (1990). *The earliest relationship: Parents, infants, and the drama of early attachment.* New York: Addison-Wesley.

Bretherton, I., Fritz, J., Zahn-Wexler, C., & Ridgeway, C. (1986). Learning to talk about emotions: A functionalist perspective. *Child Development, 57*, 529–548.

Brown, R. (1956). Language and categories: Appendix. In J. Bruner, J. Goodnow, & G. Austin (Eds.), *A study of thinking*. New York: Wiley.

Brown, R. (1957). Linguistic determinism and the part of speech. *Journal of Abnormal and Social Psychology, 55*, 1–5.

Brown, R. (1958). How shall a thing be called? *Psychological Review, 65*, 14–21.

Brown, R. (1973). *A first language, the early stages*. Cambridge, MA: Harvard University Press.

Brown, R., & Bellugi, U. (1964). Three processes in the child's acquisition of syntax. *Harvard Educational Review, 34*, 133–151.

Brown, R., Cazden, C., & Bellugi, U. (1969). The child's grammar from I to III. In J. Hill (Ed.), *Minnesota Symposia on Child Psychology* (Vol. 2, pp. 28–73). Minneapolis: University of Minnesota Press.

Brown, R., & Hanlon, C. (1970). Derivational complexity and order of acquisition in child speech. In J. Hayes (Ed.), *Cognition and the development of language*. New York: Wiley.

Bruner, J. (1975a). From communication to language. *Cognition, 3*, 255–287.

Bruner, J. (1975b). The ontogenesis of speech acts. *Journal of Child Language, 2*, 1–19.

Bruner, J. (1983). *Child's talk: Learning to use language*. New York: Norton.

Budwig, N. (1989). The linguistic marking of agentivity and control in child language. *Journal of Child Language, 16*, 263–284.

Budwig, N. (1995). *A developmental-functionalist approach to child language*. Mahwah, NJ: Erlbaum.

Budwig, N. (1996). What influences children's patterning of forms and functions in early child language. In D. Slobin, J. Gerhardt, A. Kyratzis, & S. Jiansheng (Eds.), *Social interaction, social context, and language: Essays in honor of Susan Ervin-Tripp* (pp. 143–156). Mahwah, NJ: Erlbaum.

Bullowa, M. (Ed.). (1979). *Before speech: The beginning of interpersonal communication*. Cambridge, MA: Cambridge University Press.

Camaioni, L. (1986). From early interaction patterns to language acquisition: Which continuity? In J. Cook-Gumperz, W. Corsaro, & J. Streeck (Eds.), *Children's worlds and children's language* (pp. 69–82). Berlin: Mouton de Gruyter.

Campbell, R. (1979). Cognitive development and child language. In P. Fletcher & M. Garman (Eds.), *Language acquisition* (2nd ed., pp. 419–436). Cambridge, England: Cambridge University Press.

Campbell, R. (1986). Language acquisition and cognition. In P. Fletcher & M. Garman (Eds.), *Language acquisition: Studies in first language development* (2nd ed., pp. 30–48). Cambridge, England: Cambridge University Press.

Capatides, J. (1990). *Mothers' socialization of their children's experience and expression of emotion*. Doctoral dissertation, Columbia University, New York.

Capatides, J., & Bloom, L. (1993). Underlying process in the socialization of emotion. In C. Rovee-Collier & L. Lipsett (Eds.), *Advances in infancy research* (Vol. 8, pp. 99–135). Hillsdale, NJ: Erlbaum.

Carey, S. (1978). The child as word learner. In M. Halle, J. Bresnan, & G. Miller (Eds.), *Linguistic theory and psychological reality* (pp. 264–293). Cambridge, MA: MIT Press.

Carey, S. (1982). Semantic development: The state of the art. In E. Wanner & L. Gleitman (Eds.), *Language acquisition: The state of the art* (pp. 347–389). Cambridge, England: Cambridge University Press.

Carey, S., & Bartlett, E. (1978). *Acquiring a single new word* (Papers and Reports on Child Language Development No. 15, pp. 17–29). Department of Linguistics, Stanford University, Stanford, CA.

Cazden, C., & Dickinson, D. (1981). Language in education: Standardization versus cultural pluralism. In C. Ferguson & S. Heath (Eds.), *Language in the USA* (pp. 446–468). Cambridge, England: Cambridge University Press.

Chapman, R. (1988). Language acquisition in the child. In N. Lass, L. McReynolds, T. Northern, & D. Yoder (Eds.), *Handbook of speech-language pathology and audiology* (pp. 309–353). Toronto: Decker.

Chapman, R., Bird, E., & Schwartz, S. (1990). Fast mapping of words in event contexts by children with Down Syndrome. *Journal of Speech and Hearing Disorders, 55*, 761–770.

Chapman, R., Miller, J., MacKenzie, H., & Bedrosian, J. (1981, August). *The development of discourse skills in the second year of life*. Paper presented at the Second International Congress for the Study of Child Language, University of British Columbia, Vancouver, Canada.

Charney, R. (1980). Speech roles and the development of personal pronouns. *Journal of Child Language, 7*, 509–528.

Choi, S. (1988). The semantic development of negation: A cross-linguistic longitudinal study. *Journal of Child Language, 15*, 517–531.

Chomsky, N. (1957). *Syntactic structures*. The Hague: Mouton.

Chomsky, N. (1959). Review of B. F. Skinner: Verbal behavior. *Language, 35*, 26–58.

Chomsky, N. (1965). *Aspects of the theory of syntax*. Cambridge, MA: MIT Press.

Chomsky, N. (1981). *Lectures on government and binding*. Dordrecht, The Netherlands: Foris.

Chomsky, N. (1986). Aspects of a theory of mind. *New Ideas in Psychology, 4,* 187–202.

Clancy, P. (1985). The acquisition of Japanese. In D. Slobin (Ed.), *The crosslinguistic study of language acquisition* (Vol. 1, pp. 373–524). Hillsdale, NJ: Erlbaum.

Clancy, P., Jacobsen, T., & Silva, M. (1976). *The acquisition of conjunction: A cross-linguistic study* (Papers and Reports on Child Language Development). Department of Linguistics, Stanford University, Stanford, CA.

Clark, E. (1970). How young children describe events in time. In G. Flores d'Arcais & W. Levelt (Eds.), *Advances in psycholinguistics.* New York: Elsevier.

Clark, E. (1973). What's in a word? On the child's acquisition of semantics in his first language. In T. Moore (Ed.), *Cognitive development and the acquisition of language.* New York: Academic Press.

Clark, E. (1978). Strategies for communicating. *Child Development, 49,* 953–959.

Clark, E. (1987). The principle of contrast: A constraint on language acquisition. In B. MacWhinney (Ed.), *Mechanisms of language acquisition* (pp. 1–33). Hillsdale, NJ: Erlbaum.

Clark, E. (1991). Acquisitional principles in lexical development. In S. Gelman & J. Byrnes (Eds.), *Perspectives on language and thought* (pp. 31–71). Cambridge, England: Cambridge University Press.

Clark, E. (1995). Later lexical development and word formation. In P. Fletcher & B. MacWhinney (Eds.), *The handbook of child language* (pp. 393–412). Cambridge, MA: Blackwell.

Clarkson, M., & Berg, K. (1983). Cardiac orienting and vowel discrimination in newborns: Crucial stimulus parameters. *Child Development, 54,* 162–171.

Cohen, L. (1988). An information processing approach to infant cognitive development. In L. Weiskrantz (Ed.), *Thought without language* (pp. 211–288). Oxford, England: Oxford University Press.

Collis, G. (1979). Describing the structure of social interaction in infancy. In M. Bullowa (Ed.), *Before speech: The beginning of interpersonal communication* (pp. 111–130). Cambridge, England: Cambridge University Press.

Collis, G. (1985). On the origins of turn-taking: Alternation and meaning. In M. Barrett (Ed.), *Children's single-word speech* (pp. 217–230). New York: Wiley.

Corrigan, R. (1978). Language development as related to stage 6 object permanence development. *Journal of Child Language, 5,* 173–189.

Crain, S., & Thornton, R. (1991). Recharting the course of language acquisition: Studies in elicited production. In N. Krasnegor, D. Rumbaugh, R. Schiefelbusch, & M. Studdert-Kennedy (Eds.), *Biological and behavioral determinants of language development* (pp. 321–337). Hillsdale, NJ: Erlbaum.

Cromer, R. (1974). The development of language and cognition: The cognition hypothesis. In B. Foss (Ed.), *New perspectives in child development.* New York: Penguin.

Danto, A. (1973). *Analytical philosophy of action.* Cambridge, England: Cambridge University Press.

Davis, S. (Ed.). (1992). *Connectionism: Theory and practice.* New York: Oxford University Press.

de Boysson-Bardies, B. (1977). On children's interpretation of negation. *Journal of Experimental Child Psychology, 23,* 117–127.

de Villiers, J., & de Villiers, P. (1979, August). *Form and function in the development of sentence negation* (Papers and Reports on Child Language Development No. 17, pp. 57–64). Department of Linguistics, Stanford University, Stanford, CA.

de Villiers, J., & de Villiers, P. (1985). The acquisition of English. In D. Slobin (Ed.), *The crosslinguistic study of language acquisition* (Vol. 1, pp. 27–140). Hillsdale, NJ: Erlbaum.

de Villiers, J., Tager-Flusberg, H., & Silva, M. (1976). *The acquisition of conjunction: A cross-linguistic study.* Paper presented at the Stanford Child Language Research Forum, Stanford.

DeCasper, A., & Fifer, W. (1980). Of human bonding: Newborns prefer their mothers' voices. *Science, 208,* 1174–1176.

Delack, J. B. (1976). Aspects of infant speech development in the first year of life. *Canadian Journal of Linguistics, 21,* 17–37.

Delack, J., & Fowlow, P. (1978). The ontogenesis of differential vocalizing: Development of prosodic constrastivity during the first year of life. In N. Waterson & C. Snow (Eds.), *The development of communication* (pp. 93–110). New York: Wiley.

Dent, C. (1990). An ecological approach to language development: An alternative functionalism. *Developmental Psychobiology, 23,* 679–703.

Deprez, V., & Pierce, A. (1993). Negation and functional projections in early grammar. *Linguistic Inquiry, 24,* 25–67.

D'Odorico, L., & Franco, F. (1991). Selective production of vocalization types in different communicative contexts. *Journal of Child Language, 18,* 475–499.

Dollaghan, C. (1985). Child meets word: "Fast mapping" in preschool children. *Journal of Speech and Hearing Research, 28,* 449–454.

Donaldson, M. (1986). *Children's explanations: A psycholinguistic study.* Cambridge, England: Cambridge University Press.

Dore, J. (1975). Holophrases, speech acts, and language universals. *Journal of Child Language, 2,* 21–40.

Dore, J. (1983). Feeling, form, and intention in the baby's transition to language. In R. Golinkoff (Ed.), *The transition from prelinguistic to linguistic communication* (pp. 167–190). Hillsdale, NJ: Erlbaum.

Dore, J., Franklin, M., Miller, R., & Ramer, A. (1976). Transitional phenomena in early language acquisition. *Journal of Child Language, 3,* 13–28.

Dromi, E. (1987). *Early lexical development.* Cambridge, England: Cambridge University Press.

Dromi, E. (1993). The mysteries of early lexical development. In E. Dromi (Ed.), *Language and cognition: A developmental perspective* (pp. 32–60). Norwood, NJ: ABLEX.

Dromi, E. (1996). Early lexical development. In M. Barrett (Ed.), *The development of language.* London: UCL Press.

Drozd, K. (1996). Child English presential negation as metalinguistic exclamatory sentence negation. *Journal of Child Language, 23,* 583–609.

Dunn, J. (1986). Commentary: Issues for future research. In R. Plomin, & J. Dunn (Eds.), *The study of temperament: Changes, continuities and challenges* (pp. 163–171). Hillsdale, NJ: Erlbaum.

Dunn, J. (1988). *The beginnings of social understanding.* Cambridge, MA: Harvard University Press.

Dunn, J., Bretherton, I., & Munn, P. (1987). Conversations about feeling states between mothers and their young children. *Developmental Psychology, 23,* 132–139.

Echols, C., & Newport, E. (1992). The role of stress and position in determining first words. *Language Acquisition, 2,* 189–220.

Edwards, D. (1978). Social relations and early language. In A. Lock (Ed.), *Action, gesture, and symbol: The emergence of language* (pp. 449–469). New York: Academic Press.

Eimas, P., & Miller, J. (Eds.). (1981). *Perspectives on the study of speech.* Hillsdale, NJ: Erlbaum.

Eimas, P., Siqueland, E., Jusczyk, P., & Vigorito, J. (1971). Speech perception in infants. *Science, 171,* 303–306.

Elbers, L. (1982). Operating principles in repetitive babbling: A cognitive continuity approach. *Cognition, 12,* 45–63.

Elbers, L., & Ton, J. (1985). Play pen monologues: The interplay of words and babbles in the first words period. *Journal of Child Language, 12,* 551–565.

Elbers, L., & Wijnen, F. (1992). Effort, production skill, and language learning. In C. Ferguson, L. Menn, & C. Stoel-Gammon (Eds.), *Phonological development: Models, research, implications* (pp. 337–368). Timonium, MD: York Press.

Elman, J. (1992). Learning and development in neural networks: The importance of starting small. In C. Umilta & M. Moscovitch (Eds.), *Attention and performance: XV. Conscious and nonconscious information processing.* Hillsdale, NJ: Erlbaum.

Elman, J., Bates, E., Johnson, M., & Karmiloff-Smith, A. (1996). In J. Elman, E. Bates, M. Johnson, A. Karmiloff-Smith, D. Parisi, & K. Plunkett (Eds.), *Rethinking innateness: A connectionist perspective on development* (pp. 347–391). Cambridge, MA: MIT Press.

Emde, R. (1984). Levels of meaning for infant emotions: A biosocial view. In K. Scherer & P. Eckman (Eds.), *Approaches to emotion* (pp. 77–107). Hillsdale, NJ: Erlbaum.

Ervin-Tripp, S. (1973). *Language acquisition and communicative choice: Essays by Susan M. Ervin-Tripp.* Stanford, CA: Stanford University Press.

Ervin-Tripp, S. (1979). Children's verbal turn-taking. In E. Ochs & B. Schieffelin (Eds.), *Developmental pragmatics* (pp. 391–414). New York: Academic Press.

Ervin-Tripp, S. (1980). From conversation to syntax. Speech act theory: Ten years later. *Versus, 26/27,* 81–100.

Falmagne, R. (1990). Language and the acquisition of logical knowledge. In W. Overton (Ed.), *Reasoning, necessity and logic: Developmental perspectives* (pp. 111–134). Hillsdale, NJ: Erlbaum.

Falmagne, R. (1992). Reflection on acquisition process. In J. Alegria, D. Holender, J. Junca de Morais, & M. Radeau (Eds.), *Analytic approaches to human cognition* (pp. 395–413). Amsterdam, The Netherlands: Elsevier.

Fauconnier, G. (1985). *Mental spaces: Aspects of meaning construction in natural language.* Cambridge, MA: MIT Press.

Feagans, L., Garvey, C., & R. Golinkoff (Eds.). (1983). *The origins and growth of communication.* Norwood, NJ: ABLEX.

Feldman, H., Goldin-Meadow, S., & Gleitman, L. (1978). Beyond Herodotus: The creation of language by linguistically deprived deaf children. In A. Lock (Ed.), *Action, symbol, and gesture: The emergence of language* (pp. 351–414). London: Academic Press.

Fenson, L., Dale, P., Reznick, S., Bates, E., Thal, D., & Pethick, S. (1994). Variability in early communicative development. *Monographs of the Society for Research in Child Development, 59*(5, Serial No. 242).

Fernald, A., & Mazzie, C. (1991). Prosody and focus in speech to infants and adults. *Developmental Psychology, 27,* 209–221.

Fernald, A., & McRoberts, G. (1996). Prosodic bootstrapping: A critical analysis of the argument and the evidence. In J. Morgan & K. Demuth (Eds.), *Signal to syntax: Bootstrapping from speech to grammar in early acquisition* (pp. 365–388). Mahwah, NJ: Erlbaum.

Fischer, K. (1980). A theory of cognitive development: The control and construction of hierarchies of skills. *Psychological Review, 87,* 477–531.

Fischer, K., Pipp, S., & Bullock, D. (1984). Detecting discontinuities in development: Method and measurement. In R. Emde & R. Harmon (Eds.), *Continuities and discontinuities in development* (pp. 95–121). New York: Plenum Press.

Fisher, C., Hall, D., Rakowitz, S., & Gleitman, L. (1994). When it is better to receive than to give: Structural and conceptual cues to verb meaning. *Lingua, 92,* 333–375.

Fivush, R. (1993). Emotional content of parent-child conversations about the past. In C. A. Nelson (Ed.), *Memory and affect in development* (pp. 227–235). Hillside, NJ: Erlbaum.

Fogel, A. (1981). The ontogeny of gestural communication: The first six months. In R. Stark (Ed.), *Language behavior in infancy and early childhood* (pp. 17–44). New York: Elsevier/North-Holland.

Fogel, A. (1992). Movement and communication in infancy: The social dynamics of development. *Human Movement Science,* 387–423.

Fogel, A., & Thelen, E. (1987). Development of early expressive and communicative action: Reinterpreting the evidence from a dynamic systems perspective. *Developmental Psychology, 23,* 747–761.

Foster, S. (1986). Learning discourse topic management in the preschool years. *Journal of Child Language, 13,* 231–250.

French, L. (1986). Acquiring and using words to express logical relationships. In S. Kuczaj & M. Barrett (Eds.), *The development of word meaning* (pp. 303–338). New York: Springer-Verlag.

French, L. (1988). The development of children's understanding of "because," and "so." *Journal of Experimental Child Psychology, 45,* 262–279.

French, L., & Nelson, K. (1985). *Young children's knowledge of relational terms: Some ifs, ands, and buts.* New York: Springer-Verlag.

Freyd, J. (1983). Shareability: The social psychology of epistemology. *Cognitive Science, 7,* 191–210.

Gallaway, C., & Richards, B. (Eds.). (1994). *Input and interaction in language acquisition.* Cambridge, England: Cambridge University Press.

Garvey, C. (1979). Contingent queries and their relations in discourse. In E. Ochs & B. Schieffelin (Eds.), *Developmental pragmatics* (pp. 363–372). New York: Academic Press.

Gathercole, V. (1987). The contrastive hypothesis for the acquisition of word meaning: A reconsideration of the theory. *Journal of Child Language, 14,* 493–531.

Gathercole, V., Cramer, L., Somerville, S., & Jansen op de Haar, M. (1995). Ontological categories and function: Acquisition of new names. *Cognitive Development, 10,* 225–251.

Gelman, S., & Byrnes, J. (Eds.). (1991). *Perspectives on thought and language: Interrelations in development.* Cambridge, England: Cambridge University Press.

Gentner, D. (1982). Why nouns are learned before verbs: Linguistic relativity vs. natural partitioning. In S. Kuczaj (Ed.),

Language development: Vol. 2. Language, thought, and culture (pp. 301–333). Hillsdale, NJ: Erlbaum.

Gerken, L. (1991). The metrical basis for children's subjectless sentences. *Journal of Memory and Language, 30,* 431–451.

Gerken, L. (1996). Phonological and distributional information in syntax acquisition. In J. Morgan & K. Demuth (Eds.), *Signal to syntax: Bootstrapping from speech to grammar in early acquisition* (pp. 411–425). Hillsdale, NJ: Erlbaum.

Gerken, L., Jusczyk, P., & Mandel, D. (1994). When prosody fails to cue syntactic structure: 9-month-olds' sensitivity to phonological versus syntactic phrases. *Cognition, 51,* 237–265.

Gibson, E., & Wexler, K. (1994). Triggers. *Linguistic Inquiry, 25,* 407–454.

Gibson, J. (1979). *The ecological approach to visual perception.* Boston: Houghton Mifflin.

Gleitman, L. (1981). Maturational determinants of language growth. *Cognition, 10,* 103–114.

Gleitman, L. (1990). The structural sources of verb meaning. *Language Acquisition, 1,* 3–55.

Gleitman, L., & Gillette, J. (1995). The role of syntax in verb learning. In P. Fletcher & B. MacWhinney (Eds.), *The handbook of child language* (pp. 413–427). Cambridge, MA: Blackwell.

Gleitman, L., Gleitman, H., Landau, B., & Wanner, E. (1988). Where learning begins: Initial representations for language learning. In F. Newmeyer (Ed.), *Language: Psychological and biological aspects. Linguistics: The Cambridge Survey* (Vol. 3, pp. 150–193). Cambridge, England: Cambridge University Press.

Goad, H., & Ingram, D. (1987). Individual variation and its relevance to a theory of phonological acquisition. *Journal of Child Language, 14,* 419–432.

Goddard, M., Durkin, K., & Rutter, D. (1985). The semantic focus of maternal speech: A comment on Ninio & Bruner. *Journal of Child Language, 12,* 209–213.

Goldfield, B. (1987). The contributions of child and caregiver to referential and expressive language. *Applied Psycholinguistics, 8,* 267–280.

Goldfield, B., & Reznick, J. (1990). Early lexical acquisition: Rate, content, and the vocabulary spurt. *Journal of Child Language, 17,* 171–183.

Goldin-Meadow, S., Seligman, M., & Gelman, R. (1976). Language in the two-year old: Receptive and productive stages. *Cognition, 4,* 189–202.

Golinkoff, R. (1983a). Infant social cognition: Self, people, and objects. In L. Liben (Ed.), *Piaget and the foundations of knowledge* (pp. 179–200). Hillsdale, NJ: Erlbaum.

Golinkoff, R. (1983b). The preverbal negotiation of failed messages: Insights into the transition period. In R. Golinkoff

(Ed.), *The transition from prelinguistic to linguistic communication* (pp. 57–78). Hillsdale, NJ: Erlbaum.

Golinkoff, R. (1986). "I beg your pardon?": The preverbal negotiation of failed messages. *Journal of Child Language, 13,* 455–476.

Golinkoff, R., & Gordon, L. (1983). In the beginning was the word: A history of the study of language acquisition. In R. Golinkoff (Ed.), *The transition from prelinguistic to linguistic communication* (pp. 1–25). Hillsdale, NJ: Erlbaum.

Golinkoff, R., & Hirsh-Pasek, K. (1987, October). *A new picture of language development: Evidence from comprehension.* Paper presented at the Boston University Child Language Conference, Boston, MA.

Golinkoff, R., Hirsh-Pasek, K., Mervis, C., Frawley, W., & Parillo, M. (1995). Lexical principles can be extended to the acquisition of verbs. In M. Tomasello & W. Merriman (Eds.), *Beyond names for things: Young children's acquisition of verbs* (pp. 185–222). Hillsdale, NJ: Erlbaum.

Golinkoff, R., Mervis, C., & Hirsh-Pasek, K. (1994). Early object labels: The case for a developmental lexical principles framework. *Journal of Child Language, 21,* 125–156.

Golinkoff, R., Shuff-Bailey, M., Olquin, R., & Ruan, W. (1995). Young children extend novel words at the basic level: Evidence for the principle of categorical scope. *Developmental Psychology, 31,* 494–507.

Gopnik, A. (1982). Words and plans: Early language and the development of intelligent action. *Journal of Child Language, 9,* 303–318.

Gopnik, A. (1984). The acquisition of "gone" and the development of the object concept. *Journal of Child Language, 11,* 273–292.

Gopnik, A. (1988a). Three types of early word: The emergence of social words, names and cognitive-relational words in the one-word stage and their relation to cognitive development. *First Language, 8,* 49–70.

Gopnik, A. (1988b). Conceptual and semantic development as theory changes: The case of object permanence. *Mind and Language, 3,* 197–216.

Gopnik, A., & Choi, S. (1990). Do linguistic differences lead to cognitive differences? A cross-linguistic study of semantic and cognitive development. *First Language, 10,* 199–215.

Gopnik, A., & Choi, S. (1995). Names, relational words, and cognitive development in English- and Korean-speakers: Nouns are not always learned before verbs. In M. Tomasello & W. Merriman (Eds.), *Beyond names for things: Young children's acquisition of verbs* (pp. 63–80). Hillsdale, NJ: Erlbaum.

Gopnik, A., Choi, S., & Baumberger, T. (1996). Cross-linguistic differences in early semantic and cognitive development. *Cognitive Development, 11,* 197–227.

Gopnik, A., & Meltzoff, A. (1984). Semantic and cognitive development in 15- to 21-month-old children. *Journal of Child Language, 11,* 495–513.

Gopnik, A., & Meltzoff, A. (1985). From people, to plans, to objects—Changes in the meanings of early words and their relation to cognitive development. *Journal of Child Language, 9,* 495–512.

Gopnik, A., & Meltzoff, A. (1986). Relations between semantic and cognitive developments in the one-word stage: The specificity hypothesis. *Child Development, 57,* 1040–1053.

Gopnik, A., & Meltzoff, A. (1987). The development of categorization in the second year and its relation to other cognitive and linguistic developments. *Child Development, 58,* 1523–1531.

Gopnik, A., & Meltzoff, A. (1993). Words and thoughts in infancy: The specificity hypothesis and the development of categorization and naming. In C. Rovee-Collier & L. Lipsitt (Eds.), *Advances in infancy research.* Norwood, NJ: ABLEX.

Gordon, P., & Chafetz, J. (1990). Verb-based vs. class-based accounts of actionality effects in children's comprehension of passives. *Cognition, 36,* 227–254.

Graham, S. (1992). "Most of the subjects were white and middle-class": Trends in published research on African-Americans in selected APA journals. *American Psychologist, 47,* 629–639.

Greenfield, P. (1978). Structural parallels between language and action in development. In A. Lock (Ed.), *Action, gesture, and symbol: The emergence of language* (pp. 415–445). London: Academic Press.

Greenfield, P. (1980). Toward an operational and logical analysis of intentionality: The use of discourse in early child language. In D. Olson (Ed.), *The social foundations of language and thought* (pp. 254–279). New York: Norton.

Greenfield, P. (1982). The role of perceived variability in the transition to language. *Journal of Child Language, 9,* 1–12.

Greenfield, P., & Dent, C. (1982). Pragmatic factors in children's phrasal coordination. *Journal of Child Language, 9,* 425–443.

Greenfield, P., Nelson, K., & Saltzman, E. (1972). The development of rulebound strategies for manipulating seriated cups: A parallel between action and grammar. *Cognitive Psychology, 3,* 291–310.

Greenfield, P., Reilly, J., Leaper, C., & Baker, N. (1985). The structural and functional status of single-word utterances and their relationship to early multi-word speech. In M. Barrett (Ed.), *Children's single-word speech* (pp. 233–267). New York: Wiley.

Greenfield, P., & Smith, J. (1976). *The structure of communication in early language development.* New York: Academic Press.

Gropen, J., Pinker, S., Hollander, M., & Goldberg, R. (1991). Affectedness and direct objects: The role of lexical semantics in the acquisition of verb agreement structure. *Cognition, 41,* 153–195.

Hakuta, K., de Villiers, J., & Tager-Flusberg, H. (1982). Sentence coordination in Japanese and English. *Journal of Child Language, 9,* 193–207.

Halford, G. (1989). Reflections on 25 years of Piagetian cognitive developmental psychology. *Human Development, 32,* 325–357.

Hall, W., Scholnick, E., & Hughes, A. (1987). Contextual constraints on usage of cognitive words. *Journal of Psycholinguistic Research, 16,* 289–310.

Halliday, M. (1975). *Learning how to mean-Explorations in the development of language.* London: Edward Arnold.

Hamburger, H., & Crain, S. (1987). Plans and semantics in human processing of language. *Cognitive Science, 11,* 101–136.

Hampson, J. (1989). *Elements of style: Maternal and child contributions to the referential and expressive styles of language acquisition.* Unpublished doctoral dissertation, City University of New York.

Hampson, J., & Nelson, K. (1993). The relation of maternal language to variation in rate and style of language acquisition. *Journal of Child Language, 20,* 313–342.

Harding, C., & Golinkoff, R. (1979). The origins of intentional vocalizations in prelinguistic infants. *Child Development, 50,* 33–40.

Harris, M. (1992). *Language experience and early language development: From input to uptake.* Hove, NJ: Erlbaum.

Hart, B., & Risley, T. (1995). *Meaningful differences in the everyday experiences of young American children.* Baltimore: Brookes.

Heath, S. (1982). What no bedtime story means: Narrative skills at home and school. *Language and Society, 11,* 49–76.

Heath, S. (1983). *Ways with words.* Cambridge, England: Cambridge University Press.

Hirsh-Pasek, K., & Golinkoff, R. (1991). Language comprehension: A new look at some old themes. In N. Krasnegor, D. Rumbaugh, R. Schieffelbusch, & M. Studdert-Kennedy (Eds.), *Biological and behavioral determinants of language development* (pp. 301–320). Hillsdale, NJ: Erlbaum.

Hirsh-Pasek, K., & Golinkoff, R. (1993). Skeletal supports for grammatical learning: What infants bring to the language learning task. In C. Rovee-Collier & L. Lipsett (Eds.), *Advances in infancy research* (Vol. 8, pp. 299–338). Norwood, NJ: ABLEX.

Hirsh-Pasek, K., & Golinkoff, R. (1996). *The origins of grammar: Evidence from early language comprehension.* Cambridge, MA: MIT Press.

Hirsh-Pasek, K., Golinkoff, R., & Reeves, L. (1994). Constructivist explanations for language acquisition may be insufficient: The case for lexical principles. In W. Overton & D. Palermo (Eds.), *The ontogenesis of meaning* (pp. 237–254). Hillsdale, NJ: Erlbaum.

Hirsh-Pasek, K., Kemler-Nelson, D., Jusczyk, P., Cassidy, K., Druss, B., & Kennedy, L. (1987). Clauses are perceptual units for young infants. *Cognition, 26,* 269–286.

Hoff-Ginsberg, E. (1994). Influences of mother and child on maternal talkativeness. *Discourse Processes, 18,* 105–117.

Hood, L., & Bloom, L. (1979). What, when, and how about why: A longitudinal study of early expressions of causality. *Monographs of the Society for Research in Child Development, 44*(Serial No. 6).

Hopmann, M., & Maratsos, M. (1978). A development of factivity and negation in complex syntax. *Journal of Child Language, 5,* 295–309.

Howe, C. (1981). *Acquiring language in a conversational context.* London: Academic Press.

Hudson R. (1994). 37% of word tokens are nouns. *Language, 70,* 331–339.

Hyams, N. (1986). *Language acquisition and the theory of parameters.* Dordrecht, The Netherlands: Reidel.

Hyams, N., & Wexler, K. (1993). On the grammatical basis of null subjects in child language. *Linguistic Inquiry, 24,* 421–459.

Imai, M., Gentner, D., & Uchida, N. (1994). Children's theories of word meaning: The role of shape similarity in early acquisition. *Cognitive Development, 9,* 45–75.

Ingham, R. (1992). The optional subject phenomenon in young children's English: A case study. *Journal of Child Language, 19,* 111–131.

Ingram, D. (1978). Sensorimotor intelligence and language development. In A. Lock (Ed.), *Action, gesture and symbol: The emergence of language* (pp. 261–290). New York: Academic Press.

Ingram, D. (1989). *First language acquisition: Method, description, and explanation.* New York: Cambridge University Press.

Ingram, D. (1991). An historical observation on "Why 'Mama' and 'Papa'?" *Journal of Child Language, 18,* 711–713.

Izard, C. (1977). *Human emotions.* New York: Plenum Press.

Izard, C. (1986). Approaches to developmental research on emotion-cognition relationships. In D. Bearison & H. Zimiles (Eds.), *Thought and emotion: Developmental perspectives* (pp. 21–37). Hillsdale, NJ: Erlbaum.

Izard, C., & Malatesta, C. (1987). Perspectives on emotional development: I. Differential emotions theory of early emotional development. In J. Osofsky (Ed.), *Handbook of infant development* (2nd ed., pp. 494–554). New York: Wiley.

Jackendoff, R. (1983). *Semantics and cognition.* Cambridge, MA: MIT Press.

Jackendoff, R. (1990). *Semantic structures.* Cambridge, MA: MIT Press.

Jackendoff, R. (1991, June). *Word meanings and what it takes to learn them.* Plenary address at a meeting of the Jean Piaget Society, Philadelphia.

Jakobson, R. (1957). *Shifters, verbal categories and the Russian verb* (Department of Slavic Languages and Literatures, Russian Language Project). Cambridge, MA: Harvard University Press.

Jespersen, O. (1922). *Language: Its nature, development, and origin.* New York: Norton.

Johansson, B., & Sjolin, B. (1975). Preschool children's understanding of the coordinations "and" and "or." *Journal of Experimental Child Psychology, 19,* 233–240.

Johnson, H., & Chapman, R. (1980). Children's judgement and recall of causal connectives: A developmental study of "because," "so," and "and." *Journal of Psycholinguistic Research, 9,* 243–260.

Johnstone, J. (1985). Cognitive prerequisites: The evidence from children learning English. In D. Slobin (Ed.), *The cross-linguistic study of language acquisition* (Vol. 2, 961–1004). Hillsdale, NJ: Erlbaum.

Jusczyk, P., Hirsh-Pasek, K., Kemler, D., Nelson, K., Kennedy, K., Woodward, A., & Piwoz, J. (1992). Perception of acoustic correlates of major phrasal boundaries in young infants. *Cognitive Psychology, 24,* 252–293.

Kagan, J. (1981). *The second year.* Cambridge, MA: Harvard University Press.

Kagan, J., Lapidus, D., & Moore, M. (1978). Infant antecedents of cognitive functioning. *Child Development, 49,* 1005–1023.

Kahneman, D. (1973). *Attention and effort.* Englewood Cliffs, NJ: Prentice-Hall.

Kaplan, B. (1967). Meditations on genesis. *Human Development, 10,* 65–87.

Katz, N., Baker, E., & MacNamara, J. (1974). What's in a name? A study of how children learn common and proper names. *Child Development, 45,* 473–569.

Kaye, K. (1977). Toward the origin of dialogue. In H. Schaffer (Ed.), *Studies in mother-infant interaction* (pp. 89–117). London: Academic Press.

Kaye, K. (1979). Thickening thin data: The maternal role in developing communication and language. In M. Bullowa (Ed.), *Before speech.* Cambridge, England: Cambridge University Press.

Kaye, K., & Charney, R. (1980). How mothers maintain "dialogue" with two-year-olds. In D. Olson (Ed.), *The social foundations of language and thought* (pp. 211–230). New York: Norton.

Keenan, E., & Schieffelin, B. (1976). Topic as a discourse notion: A study of topic in the conversations of children and adults. In C. Li (Ed.), *Subject and topic* (pp. 335–384). New York: Academic Press.

Keil, F. (1989). *Concepts, kinds, and cognitive development.* Cambridge, MA: MIT Press.

Keil, F. (1991). Theories, concepts, and the acquisition of word meaning. In S. Gelman & J. Byrnes (Eds.), *Perspectives on thought and language: Interrelations in development* (pp. 197–221). Cambridge, England: Cambridge University Press.

Keller-Cohen, D., & Gracey, C. (1979). Learning to say no: Functional negation in discourse. In O. Garnica & M. King (Eds.), *Language, children, and society* (pp. 197–211). Elmsford, NY: Pergamon Press.

Kelly, C., & Dale, P. (1989). Cognitive skills associated with the onset of multiword utterances. *Journal of Speech and Hearing Research, 32,* 645–656.

Kelso, S. (1995). *Dynamic patterns: The self-organization of brain and behavior.* Cambridge, MA: MIT Press.

Kemler-Nelson, D., Hirsh-Pasek, K., Jusczyk, P., & Cassidy, K. (1989). How the prosodic cues in motherese might assist language learning. *Journal of Child Language, 16,* 55–68.

Kent, R. (1981). Articulatory-acoustic perspectives on speech development. In R. Stark (Ed.), *Language behavior in infancy and early childhood* (pp. 105–121). New York: Elsevier/ North-Holland.

Kent, R., & Miolo, G. (1995). Phonetic abilities in the first year of life. In P. Fletcher & B. MacWhinney (Eds.), *The handbook of child language* (pp. 302–334). Oxford, England: Blackwell.

Klein, H. (1981). Productive strategies for the pronunciation of early polysyllabic lexical items. *Journal of Speech and Hearing Research, 24,* 389–406.

Klima, E., & Bellugi, U. (1966). Syntactic regularities in the speech of children. In J. Lyons & R. Wales (Eds.), *Psycho linguistic papers. Proceedings of the Edinburgh Conference* (pp. 183–208). Edinburgh, England: Edinburgh University Press.

Koopmans-van Beinum, F., & van der Stelt, J. (1984). Early stages in the development of speech movements. In B. Lindblom & R. Zetterstrom (Eds.), *Precursors of early speech* (pp. 37–50). Southampton: Stockton.

Kopp, C. (1989). Regulation of distress and negative emotions: A developmental view. *Developmental Psychology, 25,* 343–354.

Kuczaj, S. (1983). *Crib speech and language play*. New York: Springer-Verlag.

Kuhl, P. (1987). Perception of speech and sound in early infancy. In P. Salapatek & L. Cohen (Eds.), *Handbook of infant perception: Vol. 2. From perception to cognition* (pp. 275–382). Orlando, Fl.: Academic Press.

Kuhl, P. (1994). Speech perception. In F. Mimifie (Ed.), *Introduction to communication sciences and disorders* (pp. 77–148). San Diego, CA: Singular.

Kuhl, P., & Miller, J. (1975). Speech perception by the chinchilla: Voiced-voiceless distinction in alveolar plosive consonants. *Science, 190*, 69–72.

Labov, W. (1969). Contraction, deletion, and inherent variability of the English copula. *Language, 45*, 715–762.

Lahey, M. (1988). *Language disorders and language development*. New York: Macmillan.

Lakoff, G. (1994). What is a conceptual system? In W. Overton & D. Palermo (Eds.), *The nature and ontogenesis of meaning* (pp. 41–90). Hillsdale, NJ: Erlbaum.

Landau, B., & Gleitman, L. (1985). *Language and experience: Evidence from the blind child*. Cambridge, MA: Harvard University Press.

Landau, B., Smith, L., & Jones, S. (1988). The importance of shape in early lexical learning. *Cognitive Development, 3*, 299–321.

Langacker R. (1987). *Foundations of cognitive grammar*. Stanford, CA: Stanford University Press.

Langer, J. (1980). *The origins of logic: Six to twelve months*. New York: Academic Press.

Lebeaux, D. (1988). *Language acquisition and the form of the grammar*. Unpublished Doctoral dissertation, University of Massachusetts.

Legerstee, M. (1991). Infant sounds. *First Language, 11*, 327–343.

Legerstee, M., Pomerleau, A., Malcuit, G., & Feider, H. (1987). The development of infants' responses to people and a doll: Implications for research in communication. *Infant Behavior and Development, 10*, 81–95.

Leonard, L. (1976). *Meaning in child language*. New York: Grune and Stratton.

Leopold, W. (1939–1949). *Speech development of a bilingual child* (Vols. 1–4). Evanston, IL: Northwestern University Press.

Leslie, A. (1988). The necessity of illusion: Perception and thought in infancy. In L. Weiskrantz (Ed.), *Thought without language* (pp. 185–210). Oxford, England: Clarendon.

Levinsky, S., & Gerken, L. (1995). Children's knowledge of pronoun usage in discourse. In E. Clark (Ed.), *The proceedings of the twenty-sixth Annual Child Language Research Forum* (pp. 189–196). Stanford, CA: Stanford University Press.

Lewis, M., & Freedle, R. (1973). Mother-infant dyad: The cradle of meaning. In P. Pliner (Ed.), *Communication and affect* (pp. 127–155). New York: Academic Press.

Lewis, M., & Rosenblum, L. (1978). Introduction: Issues in affect development. In M. Lewis & L. Rosenblum (Eds.), *The development of affect* (pp. 1–10). New York: Plenum Press.

Lieven, E., Pine, J., & Barnes, H. (1992). Individual differences in early vocabulary development: Redefining the referential-expressive distinction. *Journal of Child Language, 19*, 287–310.

Lifter, K., & Bloom, L. (1989). Object play and the emergence of language. *Infant Behavior and Development, 12*, 395–423.

Lifter, K., & Bloom, L. (1997). Assessing play skills. In M. McClean, D. Bailey, & M. Wolery (Eds.), *Assessing infants and preschoolers with special needs*. Englewood Cliffs, NJ: Prentice-Hall.

Lillo-Martin, D. (1996). Modality effects and modularity in language acquisition: The acquisition of American sign language. In T. Bhatia & W. Ritchie (Eds.), *Handbook of language acquisition*. New York: Academic Press.

Limber, J. (1973). The genesis of complex sentences. In T. Moore (Ed.), *Cognitive development and the acquisition of language*. New York: Academic Press.

Lock, A. (1978). The emergence of language. In A. Lock (Ed.), *Action, gesture and symbol: The emergence of language* (pp. 3–18). New York: Academic Press.

Locke, J. (1988). The sound shape of early lexical representation. In M. Smith & J. Locke (Eds.), *The emergent lexicon: The child's development of a linguistic vocabulary* (pp. 3–22). New York: Academic Press.

Locke, J. (1993). *The child's path to spoken language*. Cambridge, MA: Harvard University Press.

Lucariello, J. (1987a). Concept formation and its relation to word learning and use in the second year. *Journal of Child Language, 14*, 309–332.

Lucariello, J. (1987b). Spinning fantasy: Themes, structure, and the knowledge base. *Child Development, 58*, 434–442.

Lucariello, J. (1995). Understanding word learning or claiming the ethnographic child. *Cognitive Development, 10*, 299–314.

Lucariello, J., Kyratzis, A., & Nelson, K. (1992). Taxonomic knowledge: What kind and when? *Child Development, 63*, 978–998.

Lucariello, J., & Nelson, K. (1987). Remembering and planning talk between mothers and young children. *Discourse Processes, 10*, 219–235.

Lust, B. (in press). UG and first language acquisition: The continuity hypothesis. In W. Ritchie & T. Bhatia (Eds.), *Handbook of language acquisition*. New York: Academic Press.

Lust, B., Hermon, G., & Kornfilt, J. (Eds.). (1994). *Syntactic theory and first language acquisition: Cross-linguistic perspectives: Vol. 2. Binding, dependencies, and learnability.* Hillsdale, NJ: Erlbaum.

Lust, B., & Mervis, C. (1980). Development of coordination in the natural speech of young children. *Journal of Child Language, 7,* 279–304.

Lust, B., Suner, M., & Whitman, J. (Eds.). (1994). *Syntactic theory and first language acquisition: Cross-linguistic perspectives: Vol. 1. Heads, projections, and learnability.* Hillsdale, NJ: Erlbaum.

MacNamara, J. (1982). *Names for things.* Cambridge, MA: MIT Press.

MacWhinney, B. (1987). The competition model. In B. MacWhinney (Ed.), *Mechanisms of language acquisition* (pp. 249–308). Hillsdale, NJ: Erlbaum

MacWhinney, B. (1989). Competition and connectionism. In B. MacWhinney & E. Bates (Eds.), *The crosslinguistic study of sentence processing* (pp. 422–457). New York: Cambridge University Press.

MacWhinney, B., & Snow, C. (1985). The child language data exchange system. *Journal of Child Language, 12,* 271–295.

Mandler, J. (1988). How to build a baby: On the development of an accessible representational system. *Cognitive Development, 3,* 113–136.

Mandler, J. (1992). How to build a baby: II. Conceptual primitives. *Psychological Review, 99,* 587–604.

Mandler, J., & Bauer, P. (1988). The cradle of categorization: Is the basic level basic? *Cognitive Development, 3,* 237–264.

Mandler, J., Fivush, R., & Reznick, J. (1987). The development of contextual categories. *Cognitive Development, 2,* 339–354.

Mannle, S., Barton, M., & Tomasello, M. (1992). Two-year-olds' conversations with their mothers and preschool-aged siblings. *First Language, 12,* 57–71.

Maratsos, M. (1979). How to get from words to sentences. In D. Aronson & R. Reiber (Eds.), *Psycholinguistic research: Implications and applications.* Hillsdale, NJ: Erlbaum.

Maratsos, M. (1982). The child's construction of grammatical categories. In E. Wanner & L. Gleitman (Eds.), *Language acquisition: The state of the art* (pp. 240–266). Cambridge, England: Cambridge University Press.

Maratsos, M. (1983). Some current issues in the study of the acquisition of grammar. In P. Mussen (Series Ed.) & J. Flavell & E. Markman (Vol. Eds.), *Handbook of child psychology: Vol. 3. Cognitive development* (pp. 707–786). New York: Wiley.

Maratsos, M., & Chalkley, M. (1980). The internal language of children's syntax: The ontogenesis and representation of syntactic categories. In K. Nelson (Ed.), *Children's language* (Vol. 2, pp. 127–214). New York: Gardner Press.

Marchman, V. (1993). Constraints on plasticity in a connectionist model of the English past tense. *Journal of Cognitive Neuroscience, 5,* 215–234.

Margulies, M., & Anisfeld, M. (1991). *Two-year-olds reduce speech during effortful activities.* Poster presented at the biennial meeting of the Society for Research in Child Development, Seattle, WA.

Markman, E. (1984). The acquisition and hierarchical organization of categories by children. In C. Sophian (Ed.), *Origins of cognitive skills* (pp. 371–406). Hillsdale, NJ: Erlbaum.

Markman, E. (1989). *Categorization and naming in children.* Cambridge, MA: MIT Press.

Markman, E. (1992). Constraints on word learning: Speculations about their nature, origins, and domain specificity. In M. Gunnar & M. Maratsos (Eds.), *Minnesota Symposia on Child Psychology* (Vol. 25, pp. 59–101). Hillsdale, NJ: Erlbaum.

Markman, E., & Hutchinson, J. (1984). Children's sensitivity to constraints on word meaning: Taxonomic vs. thematic relations. *Cognitive Psychology, 16,* 1–27.

Masur, E. (1982). Mothers' responses to infants' object-related gestures: Influences on lexical development. *Journal of Child Language, 9,* 23–30.

Mazuka, R., Lust, B., Wakayama, T., & Snyder, W. (1995). "Null subject grammar" and phrase structure in early syntax acquisition: A cross-linguistic study of Japanese and English. *Researches Linguistiques, 24,* 55–81.

McCabe, A., & Peterson, C. (1985). A naturalistic study of the production of causal connectives by children. *Journal of Child Language, 12,* 145–159.

McCarthy, D. (1930). *The language development of the preschool child* (Institute of Child Welfare Monograph Series No.4). Minneapolis: University of Minnesota Press.

McCarthy, D. (1946). Language development in children. In L. Carmichael (Ed.), *Manual of child psychology* (1st ed., pp. 476–581). New York: Wiley.

McCarthy, D. (1954). Language development in children. In L. Carmichael (Ed.), *Manual of child psychology* (2nd ed., pp. 492–630). New York: Wiley.

McCune, L. (1995). A normative study of representational play at the transition to language. *Developmental Psychology, 31,* 198–206.

McCune, L., Vihman, M. M., Roug-Hellichius, L., Delery, D., & Gogate, L. (1996). Grunt communication in human infants (Homo sapiens). *Journal of Comparative Psychology, 110,* 27–37.

McCune-Nicolich, L. (1981). The cognitive basis of relational words in the single word period. *Journal of Child Language, 8,* 15–34.

McNeill, D. (1987). *Psycholinguistics: A new approach.* New York: Harper & Row.

McShane, J. (1980). *Learning to talk.* Cambridge, England: Cambridge University Press.

Medin, D., & Wattenmaker, W. (1987). Category cohesiveness, theories, and cognitive archaeology. In U. Neisser (Ed.), *Concepts and conceptual development: Ecological and intellectual factors in categorization* (pp. 25–62). Cambridge, England: Cambridge University Press.

Menn, L., & Hazelkorn, S. (1977). Now you see it, now you don't: Tracing the development of communicative competence. In J. Kegl (Ed.), *Proceedings of the seventh annual meeting of the Linguistic Society* (pp. 249–259). Chicago.

Merriman, W. (1991). The mutual exclusivity bias in children's word learning: A reply to Woodward and Markman. *Developmental Review, 11,* 164–191.

Merriman, W., & Bowman, L. (1989). The mutual exclusivity bias in children's word learning. *Monographs of the Society for Research in Child Development, 54*(Serial No. 220).

Merriman, W., Marazita, J., & Jarvis, L. (1993). Four-year-olds' disambiguation of action and object word reference. *Journal of Experimental Child Psychology, 56,* 412–430.

Merriman, W., Marazita, J., & Jarvis, L. (1995). Children's disposition to map new words onto new referents. In M. Tomasello & W. Merriman (Eds.), *Beyond names for things: Young children's acquisition of verbs* (pp. 147–183). Hillsdale, NJ: Erlbaum.

Merriman, W., Schuster, J., & Hager, L. (1991). *Journal of Experimental Psychology: General, 120,* 288–300.

Merriman, W., Scott, P., & Marazita, J. (1993). An appearance-function shift in children's object naming. *Journal of Child Language, 20,* 101–118.

Merriman, W., & Tomasello, M. (1995). Introduction: Verbs are words too. In M. Tomasello & W. Merriman (Eds.), *Beyond names for things: Young children's acquisition of verbs* (pp. 1–18). Hillsdale, NJ: Erlbaum.

Mervis, C. (1987). Child-basic object categories and early lexical development. In U. Neisser (Ed.), *Concepts and conceptual development: Ecological and intellectual factors in categorization* (pp. 201–233). Cambridge, England: Cambridge University Press.

Miller, G. (1986). *How school children learn words* (Cognitive Science Laboratory Report 7). Princeton, NJ: Princeton University.

Miller, J., & Eimas, P. (1983). Studies on the categorization of speech by infants. *Cognition, 13,* 135–165.

Miller, P. (1982). *Amy, Wendy, and Beth: A study of early language development in south Baltimore.* Austin: University of Texas Press.

Miller, P., & Sperry, L. (1987). The socialization of anger and aggression. *Merrill-Palmer Quarterly, 33,* 1–31.

Miller, W., & Ervin, S. (1964). The development of grammar in child language. In U. Bellugi & R. Brown (Eds.), The acquisi-

tion of language. *Monograph of the Society for Research in Child Development, 29*(Serial No. 92).

Mitchell, P., & Kent, R. (1990). Phonetic variation in multisyllabic babbling. *Journal of Child Language, 17,* 247–265.

Moerk, E. (1989). The LAD was a lady and the tasks were ill-defined. *Developmental Review, 9,* 21–57.

Moon, C., Bever, T., & Fifer, W. (1992). Canonical and non-canonical syllable discrimination by two-day-old infants. *Journal of Child Language, 19,* 1–17.

Morehead, D., & Ingram, D. (1973). The development of base syntax in normal and linguistically deviant children. *Journal of Speech and Hearing Research, 16,* 330–352.

Morford, M., & Goldin-Meadow, S. (1992). Comprehension and production of gesture in combination with speech in one-word speakers. *Journal of Child Language, 19,* 559–580.

Morgan, J., & Demuth K. (Eds.). (1996). *Signal to syntax: Bootstrapping from speech to grammar in early acquisition.* Hillsdale, NJ: Erlbaum.

Naigles, L. (1990). Children use syntax to learn verb meanings. *Journal of Child Language, 17,* 357–374.

Naigles, L., & Hoff-Ginsberg, E. (1995). Input to verb learning: Evidence for the plausibility of syntactic bootstrapping. *Developmental Psychology, 31,* 827–837.

Nelson, K. (1973). Structure and strategy in learning to talk. *Monographs of the Society for Research in Child Development, 38*(Serial No. 149).

Nelson, K. (1974). Concept, word and sentence: Interrelations in acquisition and development. *Psychological Review, 81,* 267–285.

Nelson, K. (1975). The nominal shift in semantic-syntactic development. *Cognitive Psychology, 7,* 461–479.

Nelson, K. (1981). Individual differences in language development: Implications for development and language. *Developmental Psychology, 17,* 170–187.

Nelson, K. (1985). *Making sense: The acquisition of shared meaning.* New York: Academic Press.

Nelson, K. (1986). *Event knowledge: Structure and function in development.* Hillsdale, NJ: Erlbaum.

Nelson, K. (1988). Constraints on word learning. *Cognitive Development, 3,* 221–246.

Nelson, K. (1990). *Narratives from the crib.* Cambridge, MA: Harvard University Press.

Nelson, K., Hampson, J., & Shaw, L. (1993). Nouns in early lexicons: Evidence, explanations, and implications. *Journal of Child Language, 20,* 61–84.

Nelson, K., & Lucariello, J. (1985). The development of meaning in first words. In M. Barrett (Ed.), *Single word speech* (pp. 59–86). Chichester, England: Wiley.

Netsell, R. (1981). The acquisition of speech motor control: A perspective with directions for research. In R. Stark (Ed.), *Language behavior in infancy and early childhood* (pp. 126–156). New York: Elsevier/North-Holland.

Newport, E. (1981). Constraints on structure: Evidence from American sign language and language learning. In A. Collins (Ed.), *Minnesota Symposium on Child Psychology* (Vol. 14, pp. 93–124). Hillsdale, NJ: Erlbaum.

Newport, E., & Meier, R. (1985). The acquisition of American sign language. In D. Slobin (Ed.), *The crosslinguistic study of language acquisition* (Vol. 1, pp. 881–938). Hillsdale, NJ: Erlbaum.

Newson, J. (1977). An intersubjective approach to the systematic description of mother-infant interaction. In H. Schaffer (Ed.), *Studies in mother-infant interaction* (pp. 47–61). London: Academic Press.

Ninio, A. (1995a). Expression of communicative intents in the single-word period and the vocabulary spurt. In K. Nelson & Z. Reger (Eds.), *Children's language* (Vol. 8, pp. 103–124). Hillsdale, NJ: Erlbaum.

Ninio, A. (1995b). A proposal for the adoption of dependency grammar as the framework for the study of language acquisition and language use. In G. Ben-Shakher & A. Lieblich (Eds.), *Volume in honor of Shlomo Kugelmass* (pp. 85–103). Jerusalem, Israel: Magnes Press.

Ninio, A., & Bruner, J. (1978). The achievement and antecedents of labelling. *Journal of Child Language, 5,* 1–15.

Ninio, A., & Snow, C. (1988). In Y. Lezi, I. Schlesinger, & M. Braine (Eds.), *Language acquisition through language use: The functional sources of children's early utterances* (pp. 11–30). Hillsdale, NJ: Erlbaum.

Ninio, A., & Snow, C. (1996). *Pragmatic development.* Boulder, CO: Westview Press.

Ninio, A., & Wheeler, P. (1984). Functions of speech in mother-infant interaction. In L. Feagans, C. Garvey, & R. Golinkoff (Eds.), *The origins and growth of communication* (pp. 196–223). Norwood, NJ: ABLEX.

Ochs, E. (1988). *Culture and language development: Language acquisition and language socialization in a Samoan village.* Cambridge, England: Cambridge University Press.

Ochs, E., & Schieffelin, B. (1984). Language acquisition and socialization: Three developmental stories and their implications. In R. Schweder & R. Levine (Eds.), *Culture theory: Essays in mind, self and emotion* (pp. 276–320). New York: Cambridge University Press.

Oetting, J., Rice, M., & Swank, L. (1995). Quick Incidental Learning (QUIL) of words by school-aged children with and without SLI. *Journal of Speech and Hearing Research, 38,* 434–445.

O'Grady, W., Peters, A., & Masterson, D. (1989). The transition from optional to required subjects. *Journal of Child Language, 16,* 513–529.

Olguin, R., & Tomasello, M. (1993). Twenty-five-month-old children do not have a grammatical category of verb. *Cognitive Development, 8,* 245–272.

Oller, K. (1980). The emergence of the sounds of speech in infancy. In G. Yeni-Komshian, J. Kavanagh, & C. Ferguson (Eds.), *Child phonology: Vol. I. Production* (pp. 93–112). New York: Academic Press.

Oller, K., & Eilers, R. (1988). The role of audition in infant babbling. *Child Development, 59,* 441–449.

Oller, K., Wieman, L., Doyle, W., & Ross, C. (1976). Infant babbling and speech. *Journal of Child Language, 3,* 1–11.

Orlansky, M., & Bonvillian, J. (1988). Early sign language acquisition. In M. Smith & J. Locke (Eds.), *The emergent lexicon: The child's development of a linguistic vocabulary* (pp. 263–292). New York: Academic Press.

Oviatt, S. (1980). The emerging ability to comprehend language: An experimental approach. *Child Development, 51,* 97–106.

Oviatt, S. (1982). Inferring what words mean: Early development in infants' comprehension of common object names. *Child Development, 53,* 274–277.

Papousek, H., & Papousek, M. (1977). Mothering and the cognitive head-start. In H. Schaffer (Ed.), *Studies in mother-infant interaction* (pp. 63–85). London: Academic Press.

Papousek, H., Papousek, M., & Koester, L. (1986). Sharing emotionality and sharing knowledge: A microanalytic approach to parent-infant communication. In C. Izard & P. Reed (Eds.), *Measuring emotions in infants and children* (Vol. 2, pp. 93–123). Cambridge, England: Cambridge University Press.

Pea, R. (1980). The development of negation in early child language. In D. Olson (Ed.), *The social foundations of language and thought: Essays in Honor of Jerome S. Bruner.* New York: Norton.

Pea, R. (1982). Origins of verbal logic: Spontaneous denials by 2- and 3-year-olds. *Journal of Child Language, 9,* 597–626.

Peters, A. (1977). Language learning strategies: Does the whole equal the sum of the parts? *Language, 53,* 560–573.

Peters, A. (1983). *The units of language acquisition.* Cambridge, England: Cambridge University Press.

Peterson, C. (1986). Semantic and pragmatic uses of "but." *Journal of Child Language, 13,* 583–590.

Peterson, C. (1994). Narrative skills and social class. *Canadian Journal of Education, 19,* 251–269.

Peterson, C., & McCabe, A. (1987). The connective "and": Do older children use it less as they learn other connectives? *Journal of Child Language, 14,* 375–381.

Peterson, C., & McCabe, A. (1988). The connective "and" as discourse glue. *First Language, 8,* 19–28.

Petitto, L. (1991). *Are the linguistic milestones in signed and spoken language acquisition similar or different?* Presentation at the meeting of the Society for Research in Child Development, Seattle, WA.

Petitto, L., & Marentette, P. (1991). Babbling in the manual mode: Evidence for the ontogeny of language. *Science, 251,* 1493–1496.

Phillips, R., & Sellito, V. (1990). Preliminary evidence on emotions expressed by children during solitary play. *Play and Culture, 3,* 79–90.

Piaget, J. (1926). *The language and thought of the child.* London: Kegan Paul. (Original work published 1923)

Piaget, J. (1954). *The construction of reality in the child.* New York: Basic Books. (Original work published 1937)

Piaget, J. (1960). *Psychology of intelligence.* Paterson, NJ: Littlefield, Adams.

Piaget, J. (1962). *Play, dreams and imitation in childhood.* New York: Norton. (Original work published 1945)

Piaget, J. (1974). *Understanding causality.* New York: Norton. (Original work published 1971)

Piaget, J. (1981). *Intelligence and affectivity: Their relationship during child development* (T. Brown & C. Kaegi, Trans.). Palo Alto, CA: Annual Reviews. (Original work published 1954)

Piattelli-Palmarini, M. (Ed.). (1980). *Language and learning: The debate between Jean Piaget and Noam Chomsky.* Cambridge, MA: Harvard University Press.

Pine, J. (1992). How referential are "referential" children? Relationship between maternal report and observational measures of vocal composition and usage. *Journal of Child Language, 19,* 75–86.

Pine, J., Lieven, E., & Rowland, C. (1996). Observational and checklist measures of vocabulary composition: What do they mean? *Journal of Child Language, 23,* 573–591.

Pinker, S. (1984). *Language learnability and language development.* Cambridge, MA: Harvard University Press.

Pinker, S. (1989). *Learnability and cognition: The acquisition of argument structure.* Cambridge, MA: MIT Press.

Pinker, S. (1994). *The language instinct.* New York: HarperCollins.

Plunkett, K. (1993). Lexical segmentation and vocabulary growth in early language acquisition. *Journal of Child Language, 20,* 43–60.

Plunkett, K. (1995). Connectionist approaches to language acquisition. In P. Fletcher & B. MacWhitney (Eds.), *The handbook of child language* (pp. 36–72). Oxford, England: Blackwell.

Plunkett, K., & Marchman, V. (1993). From rote learning to system building: Acquiring verb morphology in children and connectionist nets. *Cognition, 48,* 21–69.

Poulin-Dubois, D. (1995). Object parts and the acquisition of the meaning of names. In K. Nelson & Z. Reger (Eds.), *Children's language* (Vol. 8, pp. 125–143). Hillsdale, NJ: Erlbaum.

Poulin-Dubois, D., & Graham, S. (1994). Infant categorization and early object-word meaning. In A. Vyt, H. Bloch, & M. Bornstein (Eds.), *Early child development in the French tradition, contributions from current research* (pp. 207–225). Hillsdale, NJ: Erlbaum.

Poulin-Dubois, D., Graham, S., & Sippola, L. (1994–1995). *Early lexical development: The contribution of parental labelling and infants' categorization abilities* (Research Bulletin Vol. XIII). Quebec, Canada: Concordia University.

Quine, W. (1960). *Word and object.* Cambridge, MA: MIT Press.

Radford, A. (1990). *Syntactic theory and the acquisition of English syntax: The nature of early child grammars of English.* Cornwall, England: Basil Blackwood.

Radford, A. (1995). Phrase structure and functional categories. In P. Fletcher & B. MacWhinney (Eds.), *Handbook of child language* (pp. 483–507). Cambridge, England: Blackwell.

Ratner, N. B. (1994). Phonological analysis of child speech. In J. Sokolov & C. Snow (Eds.), *Handbook of research in language development using CHILDES* (pp. 324–372). Hillsdale, NJ: Erlbaum.

Ratner, N. B., & Bruner, J. (1978). Games, social exchange, and the acquisition of language. *Journal of Child Language, 5,* 391–401.

Reich, P. (1976). The early acquisition of word meaning. *Journal of Child Language, 3,* 117–123.

Renninger, A. (1990). Children's play interests, representation, and activity. In R. Fivush & J. Hudson (Eds.), *Knowing and remembering in young children. Emory Symposia in Cognition.* New York: Cambridge University Press.

Renninger, A., & Wozniak, R. (1985). Effect of interest on attentional shift, recognition, and recall in young children. *Developmental Psychology, 21,* 624–632.

Rice, M., & Bode, J. (1993). GAPS in the verb lexicons of children with specific language impairment. *First Language, 13,* 13–131.

Rice, M., Hadley, P., & Alexander, A. (1993). Social biases toward children with speech and language impairments: A correlative causal model of language limitations. *Applied Psycholinguistics, 14,* 445–471.

Ridgeway, D., Waters, E., & Kuczaj, S. (1985). Acquisition of emotion-descriptive language: Receptive and productive vocabulary norms for ages 18 months to 6 years. *Developmental Psychology, 21,* 901–908.

Roeper, T. (1982). The role of universals in the acquisition of gerunds. In E. Wanner & L. Gleitman (Eds.), *Language acquisition: The state of the art* (pp. 267–287). Cambridge, England: Cambridge University Press.

Rogoff, B. (1990). *Apprenticeship in thinking: Cognitive development in social context.* New York: Oxford University Press.

Rogoff, B. (1993). Children's guided participation and participatory appropriation in sociocultural activity. In R. Wozniak & K. Fischer (Eds.), *Development in context: Acting and thinking in specific environments* (pp. 121–153). Hillsdale, NJ: Erlbaum.

Rome-Flanders, T., Cronk, C., & Gourde, C. (1995). Maternal scaffolding in mother-infant games and its relationship to language development: A longitudinal study. *First Language, 15,* 339–355.

Rosch, E., Mervis, C., Gray, W., Johnson, D., & Boyes-Braem, P. (1976). Basic objects in natural categories. *Cognitive Psychology, 8,* 382–439.

Roth, P. (1987, April). *Longitudinal study of maternal verbal interaction styles.* Poster presented at the biennial meeting of the Society for Research in Child Development, Baltimore.

Rumelhart, D., & McClelland, J. (1986). On learning the past tense of English verbs. In J. McClellan, D. Rumelhart, & the PDP Research Group (Eds.), *Parallel distributed processing: Explorations in the microstructure of cognition: Vol. 2. Psychological and biological models* (pp. 216–271). Cambridge, MA: MIT Press.

Ryan, J. (1974). Early language development: Towards a communicational analysis. In M. Richards (Ed.), *The integration of the child into the social world* (pp. 185–213). London: Cambridge University Press.

Sankoff, G. (1974). A quantitative paradigm for the study of communicative competence. In R. Bauman & J. Sherzer (Eds.), *Explorations in the ethnography of speaking* (pp. 18–49). London: Cambridge University Press.

Schaffer, H. (Ed.). (1977). *Studies in mother-infant interaction.* London: Academic Press.

Schieffelin, B. (1990). *The give and take of everyday life: Language socialization of Kaluli Children.* New York: Cambridge University Press.

Schieffelin, B., & Ochs, E. (Eds.). (1986). *Language socialization across cultures.* Cambridge, England: Cambridge University Press.

Schlesinger, I. (1971). Production of utterances and language acquisition. In D. Slobin (Ed.), *The ontogenesis of grammar* (pp. 63–101). New York: Academic Press.

Scholnick, E. (1990). The three faces of If. In W. Overton (Ed.), *Reasoning, necessity, and logic* (pp. 159–182). Hillsdale, NJ: Erlbaum.

Scholnick, E., & Hall, W. (1991). The language of thinking: Metacognitive and conditional words. In S. Gelman & J. Byrnes (Eds.), *Perspectives in language and thought* (pp. 397–439). New York: Cambridge University Press.

Scholnick, E., Hall, W., Wallner, K., & Livesey, K. (1993). The languages of affect: Developmental and functional considerations. *Merrill-Palmer Quarterly, 39,* 311–325.

Scholnick, E., & Wing, C. (1991). Speaking deductively: Preschoolers' use of "if" in conversation and in conditional inference. *Developmental Psychology, 27,* 249–258.

Scholnick, E., & Wing, C. (1992). Speaking deductively: Using conversation to trace the origins of conditional thought in children. *Merrill-Palmer Quarterly, 38,* 1–20.

Schwartz, R. (1988). Phonological factors in early lexical acquisition. In M. Smith & J. Locke (Eds.), *The emergent lexicon: The child's development of a linguistic vocabulary* (pp. 185–222). New York: Academic Press.

Schwartz, R., & Leonard, L. (1984). Words, objects, and actions in early lexical acquisition. *Journal of Speech and Hearing Research, 27,* 119–127.

Scoville, R. (1984). Development of the intention to communicate: The eye of the beholder. In L. Feagans, C. Garvey, & R. Golinkoff (Eds.), *The origins and growth of communication* (pp. 109–122). Norwood, NJ: ABLEX.

Shady, M., Gerken, L., & Jusczyk, P. (1995). Some evidence of sensitivity to prosody and word order in ten-month-olds. In D. MacLaughlin & S. McEwen (Eds.), *Proceedings of the Boston University Conference on Language Development* (Vol. 2, pp. 553–562). Somerville, MA: Cascadilla Press.

Shatz, M. (1981). Learning the rules of the game: Four views of the relation between social interaction and syntax acquisition. In W. Deutsch (Ed.), *The child's construction of language* (pp. 17–38). London: Academic Press.

Shatz, M. (1982). On mechanisms of language acquisition: Can features of the communicative environment account for development? In E. Wanner & L. Gleitman (Eds.), *Language acquisition: The state of the art* (pp. 102–127). Cambridge, England: Cambridge University Press.

Shatz, M. (1983). Communication. In P. Mussen (Series Ed.) & J. Flavell & E. Markman (Vol. Eds.), *Handbook of child psychology: Vol. 3. Cognitive development* (pp. 841–890). New York: Wiley.

Shatz, M. (1991). Using cross-cultural research to inform us about the role of language in language development: Comparisons of Japanese, Korean, and English, and of German, American English, and British English. In M. Bornstein (Ed.), *Cultural approaches to parenting* (pp. 139–153). Hillsdale, NJ: Erlbaum.

Shatz, M. (1994a). Theory of mind and the development of social-linguistic intelligence in early childhood. In C. Lewis

& P. Mitchell (Eds.), *Children's early understanding of mind: Origins and development* (pp. 311–329). Hillsdale, NJ: Erlbaum.

Shatz, M. (1994b). Review article. *Language, 70,* 789–796.

Shatz, M., & O'Reilly, A. (1990). Conversational or communicative skill? A reassessment of two-year-olds' behavior in miscommunication episodes. *Journal of Child Language, 17,* 131–146.

Shore, C. (1995). *Individual differences in language development.* Thousand Oaks, CA: Sage.

Shore, C., Dixon, W., & Bauer, P. (1995). Measures of linguistic and non-linguistic knowledge of objects in the second year. *First Language, 15,* 189–202.

Shore, C., O'Connel, B., & Bates, E. (1984). First sentences in language and symbolic play. *Developmental Psychology, 20,* 872–880.

Sinclair, H. (1970). The transition from sensory-motor behavior to symbolic activity. *Interchange, 1,* 119–126.

Sinclair, H. (1971). Sensorimotor action patterns as a condition for the acquisition of syntax. In R. Huxley & E. Ingram (Eds.), *Language acquisition: Models and methods* (pp. 121–130). New York: Academic Press.

Sinclair, H. (1989). Language acquisition: A constructivist view. In J. Montangero & A. Tryphon (Eds.), *Language and cognition.* Geneva: Jean Piaget Archives Foundation.

Sinclair, H. (1992). Changing perspectives in child language acquisition. In H. Beilin & P. Pufall (Eds.), *Piaget's theory: Prospects and possibilities* (pp. 211–228). Hillsdale, NJ: Erlbaum.

Skinner, B. F. (1957). *Verbal behavior.* New York: Appleton-Century-Crofts.

Slobin, D. (1973). Cognitive prerequisites for the development of grammar. In C. Ferguson & D. Slobin (Eds.), *Studies of child language development.* New York: Holt, Rinehart and Winston.

Slobin, D. (1985). Crosslinguistic evidence for the language-making capacity. In D. Slobin (Ed.), *The crosslinguistic study of language acquisition* (Vol. 2, pp. 1157–1256). Hillsdale NJ: Erlbaum.

Slobin, D. (1992). *The cross-linguistic study of language acquisition* (Vol. 3). Hillsdale, NJ: Erlbaum.

Slobin, D. (1997). *The cross-linguistic study of language acquisition: Expanding the contexts* (Vol. 4). Mahwah, NJ: Erlbaum.

Smith, B. (1988). The emergent lexicon from a phonetic perspective. In M. Smith & J. Locke (Eds.), *The emergent lexicon: The child's development of a linguistic vocabulary* (pp. 75–106). New York: Academic Press.

Smith, B., Brown-Sweeney, S., & Stoel-Gammon, C. (1989). A quantitative analysis of reduplicated and variegated babbling. *First Language, 9,* 175–190.

Smith, L., & Thelen, E. (Eds.). (1993). *A dynamic systems approach to development: Applications.* Cambridge, MA: MIT Press.

Smolak, L., & Levine, M. (1984). Assessment of cognitive-linguistic relationships. *Child Development, 55,* 973–980.

Snow, C. (1972). Mothers' speech to children learning language. *Child Development, 43,* 549–565.

Snow, C. (1977). Mother's speech research: From input to interaction. In C. E. Snow & C. A. Ferguson (Eds.), *Talking to children: Language input and acquisition* (pp. 31–49). Cambridge, England: Cambridge University Press.

Snow, C. (1989). Understanding social interaction and language acquisition: Sentences are not enough. In M. Bornstein & J. Bruner (Eds.), *Interaction in human development* (pp. 83–103). Hillsdale, NJ: Erlbaum.

Snow, C., & Goldfield, B. (1983). Turn the page please: Situation-specific language acquisition, *Journal of Child Language, 10,* 551–569.

Snow, C., Pan, B., Imbens-Bailey, A., & Herman, J. (1996). Learning how to say what one means: A longitudinal study of children's speech act use. *Social Development, 5,* 56–84.

Soja, N., Carey, S., & Spelke, E. (1991). Ontological categories guide young children's inductions of word meaning: Object terms and substance terms. *Cognition. 38,* 179–211.

Spelke, E. (1988). The origins of physical knowledge. In L. Weiskrantz (Ed.), *Thought without language* (pp. 168–184). Oxford, England: Clarendon.

Spelke, E. (1991). Physical knowledge in infancy: Reflections on Piaget's theory. In S. Carey & R. Gelman (Eds.), *The epigenesis of mind: Essays on biology and cognition* (pp. 133–169). Hillsdale, NJ: Erlbaum.

Sperber, D., & Wilson, D. (1986). *Relevance: Communication and cognition.* Cambridge, MA: Harvard University Press.

Spitz, R. (1957). *No and yes.* New York: International Universities Press.

Sroufe, A. (1984). The organization of emotional development. In K. Scherer & P. Ekman (Eds.), *Approaches to emotion* (pp. 109–128). Hillsdale, NJ: Erlbaum.

Sroufe, A., & Waters, E. (1976). The ontogenesis of smiling and laughter: A perspective on the organization of development in infancy. *Psychological Review, 83,* 173–189.

Stark, R. (1980). Stages of speech development in the first year of life. In G. Yeni-Komshian, J. Kavanagh, & C. Ferguson (Eds.), *Child phonology: Vol. I. Production* (pp. 73–92). New York: Academic Press.

Stark, R. (1986). Prespeech segmental feature development. In P. Fletcher & M. Garman (Eds.), *Language acquisition: Studies in first language development* (2nd ed., pp. 149–174). Cambridge, England: Cambridge University Press.

Stein, N. (1988). The development of children's story-telling skill. In M. Franklin & S. Barten (Eds.), *Child language, a reader* (pp. 282–297). New York: Oxford University Press.

Stern, D. (1977). *The first relationship.* Cambridge, MA: Harvard University Press.

Stern, D. (1985). *The interpersonal world of the infant.* New York: Basic Books.

Stern, D., Jaffe, J., Beebe, B., & Bennett, S. (1975). Vocalizing in unison and in alternation: Two modes of communication within the mother-infant dyad. In D. Aronson & R. Rieber (Eds.), Developmental psycholinguistics and communication disorders. *Annals of the New York Academy of Sciences, 263,* 89–100.

Stockman, I., & Vaughn-Cook, F. (1982). Semantic categories in the language of working-class black children. In C. Johnson & C. Thew (Eds.), *Proceedings of the second International Child Language Conference* (pp. 312–327). Washington, DC: University Press.

Stockman, I., & Vaughn-Cook, F. (1989). Addressing new questions about black children's language. In R. Fasold & D. Schiffrin (Eds.), *Language change and variation: Current issues in linguistic theory* (Vol. 52, pp. 275–300). Philadelphia: John Benjamins.

Stockman, I., & Vaughn-Cook, F. (1992). Lexical elaboration in children's locative action expressions. *Child Development, 63,* 1104–1125.

Stoel-Gammon, C. (1985). Phonetic inventories, 15–22 months: A longitudinal study. *Journal of Speech and Hearing Research, 28,* 505–512.

Stoel-Gammon, C., & Cooper, J. (1984). Patterns of early lexical and phonological development. *Journal of Child Language, 11,* 247–271.

Stromswold, K. (1995). *The acquisition of inversion and negation in English: A reply to Deprez and Pierce.* Manuscript under revision for publication.

Stromswold, K. (1996). *Does the VP internal subject stage really exist.* Paper presented at the Boston University Conference on Language Development, Boston.

Studdert-Kennedy, M. (1979). *The beginnings of speech.* Haskins Laboratories: Status Report on Speech Research SR-58.

Tardiff, T. (1993). Nouns are not always learned before verbs: Evidence from Mandarin speakers' early vocabularies. *Developmental Psychology, 32,* 492–504.

Tavakolian, S. (Ed.). (1981), *Linguistic theory and first language acquisition.* Cambridge, MA: MIT Press.

Taylor, C. (1979). Action as expression. In C. Diamond & J. Teichman (Eds.), *Intentions and intentionality: Essays in honor of G. E. M. Anscombe* (pp. 73–89). Ithaca, NY: Cornell University Press.

Templin, M. (1957). *Certain language skills in children.* Minneapolis: University of Minnesota Press.

Thal, D., & Bates, E. (1990). Continuity and variation in early language development. In J. Colombo & J. Fagen (Eds.), *Individual differences in infancy* (pp. 359–383). Hillsdale, NJ: Erlbaum.

Thelen, E. (1988). Dynamic approaches to the development of behavior. In J. Kelso, A. Mandell, & M. Schlesinger (Eds.), *Dynamic patterns in complex systems* (pp. 348–369). Singapore: World Scientific.

Thelen, E., & Smith, L. (1994). *A dynamic systems approach to the development of cognition and action.* Cambridge, MA: MIT Press.

Thelen, E., & Ulrich, B. (1991). Hidden skills: A dynamic systems analysis of treadmill stepping during the first year. *Monographs of the Society for Research in Child Development, 56,* (Serial No. 223).

Thompson, R. (1989). Emotional self-regulation. In R. Thompson (Ed.), *Socioemotional development. Nebraska Symposium on Motivation* (Vol. 36). Lincoln: University of Nebraska Press.

Toledano, J. (1991). *Context and the language development of children with older siblings.* Unpublished Doctoral dissertation, Teachers College, Columbia University.

Tomasello, M. (1988). The role of joint attentional processes in early language development. *Language Sciences, 10,* 69–88.

Tomasello, M. (1992a). The social bases of language acquisition. *Social Development, 1,* 67–87.

Tomasello, M. (1992b). On defining language: Replies to Shatz and Ninio. *Social Development, 1,* 159–162.

Tomasello, M. (1992c). *First verbs: A case study of early grammatical development.* Cambridge, England: Cambridge University Press.

Tomasello, M. (1995). Language is not an instinct. *Cognitive Development, 10,* 131–156.

Tomasello, M., & Akhtar, N. (1995). Two-year-olds use pragmatic cues to differentiate reference to objects and actions. *Cognitive Psychology, 10,* 201–224.

Tomasello, M., & Barton, M. (1994). Learning words in nonostensive contexts. *Developmental Psychology, 30,* 639–650.

Tomasello, M., & Farrar, J. (1986). Joint attention and early language. *Child Development, 57,* 1454–1463.

Tomasello, M., & Farrar, M. (1984). Cognitive bases of lexical development: Object permanence and relational words. *Journal of Child Language, 11,* 477–493.

Tomasello, M., & Kruger, A. (1992). Joint attention on actions: Acquiring verbs in ostensive and non-ostensive contexts. *Journal of Child Language, 19,* 311–333.

Trevarthen, C. (1977). Descriptive analysis of infant communication behavior. In H. Schaffer (Ed.), *Studies in mother-infant interaction* (pp. 227–270). London: Academic Press.

Trevarthen, C. (1979). Communication and cooperation in early infancy: A description of primary intersubjectivity. In M. Bullowa (Ed.), *Before speech: The beginning of interpersonal communication* (pp. 321–347). Cambridge, England: Cambridge University Press.

Trevarthen, C., & Hubley, P. (1978). Secondary intersubjectivity: Confidence, confiding and acts of meaning in the second year. In A. Lock (Ed.), *Action, gesture and symbol: The emergence of language* (pp. 183–229). New York: Academic Press.

Tronick, E. (Ed.). (1982). *Social interchange in infancy: Affect, cognition, and communication.* Baltimore: University Park Press.

Uzgiris, I., & Hunt, J. (1975). *Assessment in infancy.* Urbana: University of Illinois Press.

Valian, V. (1991). Syntactic subjects in the early speech of American and Italian children. *Cognition, 40,* 21–81.

van Beek, Y. (1991, May). *Preterms, posture and the development of early communication.* Paper presented at a meeting of the International Society for Infant Studies, Miami.

van der Stelt, J. (1993). *Finally a word: A sensori-motor approach of the mother-infant system in its development towards speech.* Amsterdam, The Netherlands: Studies in Language and Language Use.

van der Stelt, J., & Koopmans-van Beinum, F. (1986). The onset of babbling related to gross motor movements. In B. Lindblom & R. Zetterstrom (Eds.), *Precursors of early speech* (pp. 163–173). Southampton: Stockton.

Van Valin, R. (1991). Functionalist linguistic theory and language acquisition. *First Language, 11,* 7–40.

Venezia, E. (1992). Getting expert in the old: A constructivist account of early language acquisition. *Substratum, 1,* 79–101.

Venezia, E., & Sinclair, H. (1995). Functional changes in early child language: The appearance of references to the past and of explanations. *Journal of Child Language, 22,* 557–581.

Vihman, M. (1992). Early syllables and the construction of phonology. In C. Ferguson, L. Menn, & C. Stoel-Gammon (Eds.), *Phonological development: Models, research, implications* (pp. 393–422). Timonium, MD: York Press.

Vihman, M. (1993). Variable paths to early word production. *Journal of Phonetics, 21,* 61–82.

Vihman, M., Macken, M., Miller, R., Simmons, H., & Miller, J. (1985). From babbling to speech: A reassessment of the continuity issue. *Language, 61,* 397–446.

Vihman, M., & McCune, L. (1994). When is a word a word? *Journal of Child Language, 21,* 517–542.

Vihman, M., & Miller, R. (1988). Words and babble at the threshold of language acquisition. In M. Smith & J. Locke (Eds.), *The emergent lexicon: The child's development of a linguistic vocabulary* (pp. 151–184). New York: Academic Press.

Vygotsky, L. (1962). *Thought and language.* Cambridge, MA: MIT Press.

Vygotsky, L. (1978). In M. Cole, V. John-Steiner, S. Scribner, & E. Souberman (Eds.), *Mind in society. The development of higher psychological processes.* Cambridge MA: Harvard University Press. (Original work published 1930)

Wang, Q., Lillo-Martin, D., Best, C., & Levitt, A. (1992). Null subject versus null object: Some evidence from the acquisition of Chinese and English. *Language Acquisition, 2,* 221–254.

Watkins, R., Rice, M., & Moltz, C. (1993). Verb use by language-impaired and normally developing children. *First Language, 13,* 133–143.

Waxman, S. (1990). Linguistic biases and the establishment of conceptual hierarchies: Evidence from preschool children. *Cognitive Development, 5,* 123–150.

Waxman, S., & Markow, D. (1995). Words as invitations to form categories: Evidence from 12- to 13-month-old infants. *Cognitive Psychology, 29,* 257–302.

Weir, R. (1964). *Language in the crib.* The Hague: Mouton.

Weisberg, P. (1963). Social and nonsocial conditioning of infant vocalization. *Child Development, 34,* 377–388.

Weist, R. (1982). *Verb concepts in child language—Acquiring constraints on action role and animacy.* Tubingen: Gunter Narr (Benjamins).

Wells, G. (1981). *Learning through interaction. The study of language development.* Cambridge, England: Cambridge University Press.

Werner, H., & Kaplan, B. (1963). *Symbol formation.* New York: Wiley.

Wexler, K. (1994). Optional infinitives, head movement, and the economy of derivations in child grammar. In D. Lightfoot & N. Hornstein (Eds.), *Verb movement* (pp. 305–350). Cambridge, England: Cambridge University Press.

Wexler, K., & Culicover, P. (1980). *Formal principles of language acquisition.* Cambridge, MA: MIT Press.

Whatley, E. (1981). Language among Black Americans. In C. Ferguson & S. Heath (Eds.), *Language in the USA* (pp. 92–107). Cambridge, England: Cambridge University Press.

Whitehurst, G., Kedesdy, J, & White, T. (1982). A functional analysis of word meaning. In S. Kuczaj (Ed.), *Language development: Vol. 1. Syntax and Semantics* (pp. 397–427). Hillsdale, NJ: Erlbaum.

Wikstrom, P., & Bloom, L. (1987). *The role of temperament in the emergence of language.* Paper presented at the fourth International Congress for the Study of Child Language, Lund.

Wing, E., & Scholnick, E. (1981). Children's comprehension of pragmatic concepts expressed in "because," "although," "if," and "unless." *Journal of Child Language, 8,* 347–365.

Wolff, P. (1969). The natural history of crying and other vocalizations in early infancy. In B. Foss (Ed.), *Determinants of infant behavior* (Vol. 4, pp. 81–109). London: Methuen.

Ziajka, A. (1981). *Prelinguistic communication in infancy.* New York: Praeger.

Zukow, P. (1990). Socio-perceptual bases for the emergence of language: An alternative to innatist approaches. *Developmental Psychobiology, 23,* 705–726.

Zukow, P. (1991). A socio-perceptual/ecological approach to lexical development: Affordances of the communicative context. *Anales de Psicologia, 7,* 151–163.

Zukow-Goldring, P. (1997). A social ecological realist approach to the emergence of the lexicon: Educating attention to amodal invariants in gesture and speech. In C. Dent-Read & P. Zukow-Goldring (Eds.), *Evolving explanations of development: Ecological approaches to organism-environment systems* (pp. 199–247). Washington, DC: American Psychological Association.

Zukow-Goldring, P., & Ferko, K. (1994). An ecological approach to the emergence of the lexicon: Socializing attention. In V. John-Steiner, C. Panofsky, & L. Smith (Eds.), *Sociocultural approaches to language and literacy: An interactive perspective* (pp. 170–190). New York: Cambridge University Press.

CHAPTER 8

Early Word Learning

AMANDA L. WOODWARD and ELLEN M. MARKMAN

For years investigators struggled to explain why vocabulary subscales should be the best predictors of overall intelligence. This was thought to be puzzling because vocabulary was viewed as reflecting static ("frozen"), rote memorized knowledge. But, as Sternberg and Powell (1983) pointed out, each word learned reflects the completion of an inductive inference. Word learning depends on an ability to recruit and integrate information from a range of sources to come up with the most plausible interpretation of a novel word.

Word learning, more than any other aspect of language acquisition, falls at the intersection of cognitive and linguistic development. The outstanding problem for a word learner is to figure out which of the many possible concepts a given word actually maps onto. To understand how children acquire vocabulary requires understanding how this mapping problem is solved. In other words, we need to determine what sources of information children can use to narrow down the meaning of a new term.

The kinds of input children receive influence how they acquire vocabulary. To take one example, Bowerman (1996) describes cross-linguistic differences in the ways in which languages "package" spatial relations into spatial morphemes, such as prepositions. In English, for example, the preposition *on* is used to refer to something that is on a table (a horizontal surface) and on the wall or on the door (vertical surfaces) while *in* is used for something contained in a bowl. As Bowerman points out, this implicit categorization of containment *(in)* versus contact and support with a surface *(on)* seems so basic to English speakers that we assume it reflects a natural conceptualization of space that is simply reflected in language. But, Bowerman argues, this conclusion is suspect because other languages categorize spatial relations quite differently. Finnish, for example, uses the same spatial morpheme to refer to "handle on a door" and "apple in a bowl" and a different morpheme to refer to "cup on a table." From the vantage point of Finnish speakers, attachment to an external surface is more like a kind of containment in that both reflect an intimate connection as opposed to something simply resting on a horizontal surface. As another example, Bowerman describes differences

The writing of this chapter was partially supported by a grant from the John Merck Fund to the first author.

in the way that the semantic notion of "path" is represented in representations of motion in English versus Korean. English has a general abstract representation of motion while Korean draws more specific distinctions. For example, the distinction between whether a motion is spontaneous or caused is not marked in English (e.g., "go *in* the closet" vs. "put it *in* the closet") but is distinguished in Korean. Moreover Korean, but not English, distinguishes paths depending on the shape of the objects and spaces involved. Strikingly, by 20 months of age Korean- and English-speaking children differ in the ways they express these notions, corresponding to the input language they were learning. Children learning English, for example, say "in" for spontaneous motions such as getting into a bathtub and for caused motions such as putting a toy into a small box. In contrast, children learning Korean use different morphemes in these cases. As another example, children learning Korean use different morphemes for putting something in a container depending on whether the object fits tightly or loosely, while children learning English use *in* in both cases. Bowerman argues that these differences are not readily explained by assuming a universal mode of spatial representation available to all children and invoking different mapping rules across languages. Instead, Bowerman concludes that the pattern of distribution of spatial morphemes is itself a source of information to children about how spatial relations should be represented (but see Mandler, 1996). Thus, it is an oversimplification to frame the mapping problem as only a problem of finding the right pre-existing category to go with a given term in the language. This might be a reasonable framing of the problem for object labels and property terms, but for relational terms such as spatial terms (Bowerman,1996), verbs (Gentner, 1982), and gender systems (Maratsos, 1983) the distribution of morphemes across different contexts is itself an important source of information about their meaning and use.

There are also differences within a given language in how much and in what ways parents speak to babies and young children (Nelson, 1988; Tomasello, 1992b). To take one example, Huttenlocher, Haight, Bryk, Seltzer, and Lyons (1991) have shown that which words a child acquires can be predicted by the number of repetitions of the word in parental input. But our emphasis in this chapter is on what we can conclude about the abilities of *children* that enable them to solve the mapping problem. This focus on children as learners is not meant to deny the importance of parents as tutors. In fact, we suspect that the most effective parental teaching styles will result from parents' sensitivity to ways children learn best. We conclude that there are multiple and potentially redundant sources of information in input that young children can use to infer the meanings of new words. When these sources all converge on a common hypothesis, learning will be facilitated. Parents who provide such input are likely to promote lexical acquisition in their children.

Anglin (1993) estimated that by first grade, children understand at least 10,000 words, and by fifth grade they understand approximately 40,000. This means that children acquire new words at a rate of 5.5 per day from 18 months up to the age of 6 and at an even higher rate thereafter (Anglin, 1993; see also Carey, 1978). Children produce their first words at roughly one year of age, and they understand many words before this (Benedict, 1979; Huttenlocher, 1974). Starting at about 18 months during the "naming explosion," the rate of productive vocabulary growth increases very rapidly (L. Bloom, 1973; Dromi, 1986; Goldfield & Reznick, 1990; Nelson, 1973). During the spurt, many children go from having had roughly 10 to 20 words in production for many months to having well over 100 within a couple of months (Dromi, 1986; Goldfield & Reznick, 1990), and some children at this age are reported to acquire as many as 40 new words per week (Dromi, 1986).

Many researchers have noted this salient change in language production and have hypothesized potential developmental changes as being responsible for it, including developments in categorization (Gopnik & Meltzoff, 1986), and other aspects of conceptual development (L. Bloom, 1973; L. Bloom, Lifter, & Broughton, 1985; Lifter & L. Bloom, 1989; Nelson & Lucariello, 1985), the insight that language is symbolic (Dore, 1978), and the onset of word learning constraints (Behrend, 1990a; Mervis & Bertrand, 1994). Most of the changes hypothesized as being responsible for the naming explosion would affect comprehension as profoundly as production. It is not clear, however, whether similar changes occur in comprehension at this time. On the one hand, Reznick and Goldfield (1992) found increases in receptive vocabulary size at the time of the productive spurt. On the other hand, developments in language comprehension often precede developments in production (Clark & Hecht, 1983; Goldin-Meadow, Seligman, & R. Gelman, 1976; Snyder, Bates, & Bretherton, 1981), and by some estimates, children understand many words before the spurt in production (Benedict, 1979; Hoek, Ingram, & Gibson, 1986). Moreover, even 13-month-olds can acquire a new word in comprehension based on a few minutes of training by an unfamiliar experimenter in the laboratory (Woodward, Markman, & Fitzsimmons, 1994). Thus, especially at the earliest stages of language acquisition, production alone may be an imperfect index of children's underlying abilities. Although there may well be developments in word learning ability at the time of the productive naming explosion, children have made significant progress well before it.

These achievements are all the more impressive given the inductive problem that learning a single new word could, in principle, pose. One straightforward model of word learning is that when the learner hears a new word, the first step is to generate a set of logically possible hypotheses about its meaning. Then, the learner tests each hypothesis, either by waiting for subsequent occurrences of the new word, or by explicitly asking whether new items or events can be called by that name. For example, on hearing the (new) word *abacus* in a context in which that object was in view, the learner might generate a list of possible meanings including "name for that particular object," "the name for that kind of object," "the name for the number of beads in total, on a row, and so on," "the name for the color of the beads or the frame" "the name for one of the beads," "the name for the substance of which the object or a part of it is made," "the name for the spatial relationship between the object and the table," and so forth. A learner could generate a very large number of reasonable hypotheses in this situation, even without generating all of the logically possible hypotheses, some of which might never be ruled out (cf. Goodman, 1955; Quine, 1960). If the learner considered each one in turn, it could take an extremely long time to rule out all of the incorrect hypotheses.

Does this construal of the problem fit the case of the young word learner? Perhaps infants and young children are limited in the ways they can represent the world. If this were the case, then they might be in less of a quandary than the *abacus* example implies. Limitations on information processing abilities have been theorized to play a role in young children's acquisition of syntax and morphology (Newport, 1991). According to this "less is more" hypothesis, the limitations are useful in helping to limit the hypothesis space to a manageable size. Can we make a similar case for word learning? Although there may be ways in which such limitations do help in word learning (Markman, 1989), as Clark (1983) pointed out, infancy research demonstrates that the potential hypothesis space for infants is very large. Work from this field suggests that prelinguistic infants are able to represent many different aspects of the world, including the positions and motions of objects (Baillargeon, 1993; Spelke, 1990), categorical relationships (Cohen & Younger, 1981; Mandler & McDonough, 1993; Waxman & Markow, 1995); thematic relationships (Mandler, Fivush, & Reznick, 1987), spatial relationships (Quinn, 1991), color (Bornstein, Kessen, & Weiskopf, 1976), causal relationships (Leslie & Keeble, 1987), and numerosity (Starkey, Spelke, & R. Gelman, 1990; Wynn, 1992) to name a few. Thus, although older children can consider some possible word meanings that babies cannot (e.g., integer, electricity, and ancestor), even one-year-olds have at their disposal a rich array of possible meanings for new words.

Starting with the supposition that the young child has a rich conceptual structure, which provides many possible meanings for any given new word, the child's task in word learning is to limit the range of hypotheses considered, and to zero in on the right one. A rich conceptual structure coupled with a limited ability to test hypotheses makes this problem particularly challenging. Thus, the rapidity of early word learning is especially impressive in light of limits on young children's information-processing abilities and the limits on their access to a range of linguistic and contextual sources of information that are available to older children. According to Anglin (1993), a fair amount of the vocabulary acquisition of older children reflects their knowledge of derivational morphology, a source of information not available to babies first acquiring vocabulary. Among other sources of information such as morphology, older children can use the linguistic context in which a word is presented to infer the meaning of the term (witness the cloze procedure in studies of reading comprehension). But at the initial stages of word learning, linguistic context likely contributes less and less.

Our main focus in this chapter will be on very early word learning to try to understand how babies and young children break into the semantic system in the first place, and to chart the early uses of linguistic context. This focus on babies and very young children leads us, among other reasons, to concentrate on experimental studies of children's comprehension of words, rather than production data. Children's comprehension often runs ahead of their production, so comprehension measures are likely to be more sensitive measures of young children's knowledge. And at some of the younger ages we will be exploring, children's production is very limited.

The review is organized around four main potential sources of information that could be used to infer the meaning of novel words. The first are *cues* that young children might rely on to infer what the speaker was attending to when using a novel word. We will conclude that some kind of pragmatic information is available at least in a limited way to the beginning word learner. Next, we review evidence for another means of narrowing down word meanings that is also available to the youngest word learners, namely some kinds of *biases* or *constraints* on hypotheses about what novel words are likely to mean. We then turn to evidence for somewhat older children's use of *syntactic cues* to a word's meaning. The final source of information we consider is children's use of *contrast* within a semantic domain. The evidence supports the conclusion that children draw on all of these sources of information, but in ways that change over the course of development.

SOCIAL AND PRAGMATIC CUES TO WORD MEANING

Although language learning is a remarkable intellectual achievement, it is also a form of social learning as the study of children's use of pragmatics emphasizes. Clark (1995) counts a wide range of phenomena as potential pragmatic cues, including nonlinguistic gestures, intonation, and the context, both linguistic and nonlinguistic. One question that has received a fair amount of attention is how parents adjust their communications to fit the needs, attention, and cognitive capacities of their children (L. Bloom, 1993; Fernald, 1992; Nelson, 1988; Tomasello, 1992b). Some have argued that because parents are so adept at anticipating the interests and focus of attention of their babies, constraints on learning are not necessary (e.g., Nelson, 1988). By tailoring the input to match what the baby is attending to, the argument goes, parents solve the inductive problem for their children. Although we would not want to deny the role that parental input plays in helping children acquire vocabulary, there are serious problems with the argument that input alone can account for children's achievements. Even when language learning is viewed as a form of social or cultural learning, it is critical to ask how the infant is prepared to learn in this context. As Tomasello, Kruger, and Ratner (1993) noted in their framing of the issues involved in cultural learning:

> Human beings are able to learn from one another in this way because they possess very powerful, perhaps uniquely powerful, forms of social cognition. . . . The cultural line is characterized not only by the presence of culture, . . . but also by

the uniquely human capacity to acquire cultural products. (p. 495)

Thus, as important as asking how the input is structured is asking *how* babies represent, construe, and use the information provided.

Joint Attention in Word Learning

With respect to word learning, several investigators have noticed the importance of joint attention between the baby and the adult speaker (Bruner, 1978; Masur, 1982; Messer, 1978; Murphy, 1978; Scaife & Bruner, 1975; Tomasello, Mannle, & Kruger, 1986; Tomasello & Todd, 1983). If a young child is to acquire a novel label, say, from hearing an adult label an object, then problems will arise if the baby is mistaken about which object the adult is labeling. Attentive, caring parents make an effort to talk about what their child is interested in at the time, thereby facilitating a joint focus of attention. Several studies have documented the prevalence of "follow-in" labeling, where parents label what their babies are attending to (Collis, 1977; Masur, 1982; Murphy, 1978). One interpretation of findings is that parents are taking the responsibility for ensuring that joint attention is achieved. Although this interpretation is valid to a point, parents are far from perfect at achieving joint attention (see Baldwin, 1991, for a review). The studies reveal that parents label what their babies were attending to from 50% to 70% of the time. That leaves 30% to 50% of the time when the parents have failed to establish joint attention. What happens in the not-so-rare cases when the adult is commenting on or labeling something other than what the baby is focused on? If the mechanism for ensuring joint attention were entirely dependent on adults, then we should expect errors in the cases when the adults fail. But given the high rate of failure on the part of the adults, this would be a highly risky learning mechanism. Babies would often be forming incorrect mappings between objects or events they were attending to and the language they heard their parents addressing to them at the time. Noting this problem, Baldwin (1991, 1993a, 1993b) asked what babies' contribution to achieving joint attention might be and whether it could prevent such mapping errors.

Young Children's Monitoring of Referential Cues in Word Learning

Baldwin outlined two possibilities for how joint attention is achieved during labeling. In one, the responsibility for achieving joint reference would rest solely with the parents, with babies forming mappings between words and objects through a purely associative mechanism. If babies are attending to a (novel) object at the time they hear a novel label, then they will map the label to that object. If the adult happens to be labeling an object different from the one that is the focus of the baby's attention then the baby will make a mapping error. The second possibility is that babies somehow monitor the speaker's focus of attention, maybe by checking the speaker's eyegaze or voice direction and thereby avoid errors.

To test these possibilities, Baldwin (1991) taught babies ranging in age from 16 to 19 months a novel object label under two conditions. In both conditions, babies were given a novel object to play with while a second novel object was placed in an opaque bucket. In the discrepant labeling condition, the experimenter avoided any eye contact with the baby and avoided looking at the toy the baby was playing with. Instead, the experimenter monitored the baby's eyegaze by glancing at a small side-view mirror, and when the baby was looking at and/or playing with the visible object, the experimenter looked into the bucket and said, for example, "It's a toma." Thus, as the child was looking at one object, the experimenter labeled another object that was out of sight at the time. If babies are using an associative rule that maps a novel label to a (novel) object that is currently the focus of their attention, then they should treat *toma* as the label for the object they were playing with at the time. If, on the other hand, babies check information about the speaker's focus of attention before learning a novel term, then they would avoid mapping errors in this condition. The second condition was a follow-in labeling condition where the experimenter looked at the baby's toy while saying, "It's a toma." On either account, babies were expected to learn the novel term as referring to their toy in this condition.

Babies were tested for their comprehension following the training session. To test their comprehension of the novel word, the second novel object was removed from the bucket and placed along with the baby's toy on the table. The baby was then asked to "point to the toma." To control for the relative interest of the toys, babies were asked on some trials to "point to your favorite one."

The results indicated that from 16 to 19 months of age, babies are not restricted to a simple associative mechanism to learn words. Even the younger babies were using line of regard or some other cue to the speaker's attention to determine whether a novel label referred to the object they were attending to. At both ages, babies correctly learned the labels for objects when the adult and child were attending to the same object. There was an interesting developmental difference in how babies performed in the discrepant labeling condition. At least on some measures, the older babies seemed to have inferred that the novel label referred to the toy in the bucket even though that toy was out of view at the time the label was heard. The younger babies did not correctly learn the label, but they were able to avoid mapping errors. They simply failed to learn the labels when the experimenter was not attending to their objects. Even though they heard an adult say, for example, "It's a toma" at the time they were looking at a novel toy, babies did not assume that *toma* referred to that toy. Instead they checked the experimenter's line of regard and blocked incorrect mappings.

These findings argue against a purely associative mechanism because in the discrepant condition there is greater temporal contiguity between hearing the label and viewing the baby's object than the speaker's object. Baldwin (1993a) argued that a stronger test of the associative model could be made in the discrepant labeling condition by increasing the temporal gap between hearing the label and seeing the correct object. Based on her review of the conditioning literature, Baldwin (1993a) selected 10 seconds as being well outside the usual time frame for successful conditioning. In this procedure 19- to 20-month-old babies were allowed to play with two novel objects. The objects were then taken out of view and each placed in a separate opaque container. As in the earlier study, there were two training conditions. In the discrepant training condition, the experimenter lifted the lid of one of the containers, looked inside and said, "It's a toma." She then opened the second container, removed the toy, and gave it to the baby to play with. After a minimum of 10 seconds, the experimenter then removed the toy from the first container and gave it to the baby as well. After a brief time, both toys were taken away and the test phase was begun. In the second training condition, there was only a brief temporal gap between hearing the label and seeing the correct toy. In this "coincide" condition, the experimenter lifted the lid from the first container and labeled it as before. But now the lid was removed and the object immediately given to the baby to play with. After a minimum of 10 seconds, the second container was opened and the toy removed and given to the baby to play with. Again, after a short while, both toys were removed and testing begun.

The results replicate the findings of Baldwin (1991) with this age group. Not only did the babies avoid making mapping errors in the discrepant labeling condition, but they were able to map the label onto the object that was the speaker's focus of attention. They accomplished this despite having a delay of at least 10 seconds between hearing the label and seeing the correct object and despite the presence of another novel object during this time. Akhtar and Tomasello (1996) provide strong evidence against children's reliance on temporal contiguity to learn words by constructing a situation in which the appropriate referents of a novel word are not presented at all after hearing the word. They developed scenarios in which two-year-olds expected a certain object to be involved (in the noun learning conditions) or a certain action to be performed (in the verb learning conditions). In the noun condition, for example, children played a finding game in which four toys were each found in a given location. After this routine was well established, the experimenter said "Now let's find the toma" and went to the toy barn which was one of the locations. In one condition, the expected toy was removed. In another condition, the experimenter tried to open the barn but couldn't and told the child the barn was locked. The experimenter then removed the other toys from their locations. The results indicated that children learned as well in this "referent absent" condition as in the condition when the appropriate referent was presented immediately after the novel label was introduced. Tomasello, Strosberg, and Akhtar (1996) have replicated these results with 18-month-olds. These findings provide further evidence that babies are using referential cues to guide their word-referent mappings.

Moreover, Baldwin and colleagues (1996) have evidence that babies not only monitor attentional cues of the speaker but that they appreciate that mapping words to available objects is appropriate only if signs of referential intent are apparent. Babies ranging from 15 to 20 months of age heard a novel label uttered at the time they were examining a novel object. In one condition, the speaker was seated within view of the infant and attended to the novel toy. In another condition, the speaker was out of view of the infant. As expected, when the speaker looked at the toy while labeling it, babies learned the novel label. But when the babies were unable to tell what the speaker was attending to, they did not form a stable link between the label and object even though the cooccurrence between the label and object was just as strong in this condition. Taken together these studies document that babies appreciate that a mapping between word and object is warranted only if a speaker exhibits signs of referring to that object.

Babies could be using referential cues in this way, however, without distinguishing between referential and nonreferential cues. Any action in the direction of an object might somehow increase its salience for babies. Baldwin (1993a) tested this in a condition in which the experimenter directed some nonreferential behavior towards one of the two containers. In particular, the experimenter looked at the baby while saying, for example, "I'm going to show you a toma." At the same time, the experimenter touched one of the containers and adjusted its lid, all the while looking at the baby, not the container. Then either the toy from that container or the other toy was given to the baby to play with and at least 10 seconds later the other toy was removed from its container and given to the baby. Thus conditions that parallel the discrepant and coincident training conditions of the first study were run with nonreferential cues. The results from this procedure are simply stated: Without referential cues babies do not learn mappings between novel labels and objects. Thus 19- to 20-month-olds clearly distinguish between at least some referential and nonreferential cues and will not form word-referent mapping unless they have some information about what the speaker intends to refer to.

Tomasello and Barton (1994) have shown that 2-year-olds monitor cues as to the communicative intent of speakers in learning novel verbs as well as novel nouns. They used the expression of emotion as an indication of whether an act was intentional or not. In one study, children were taught object labels by an experimenter who said, "Let's find the toma." The experimenter then picked up an object while frowning and placed it in a bucket. She then picked up a second object, frowned again, and placed it in a bucket. Finally she picked up a third object and with a gleeful expression (wide-eyed, saying "Ah!") held the object up and handed it to the child. Tomasello and Barton (1994) argue that these 2-year-olds used the emotional expression of the speaker to infer which object was the intended referent of the novel word. They might also have been using the fact that the speaker handed them one object and placed the others in buckets to infer the correct referent. In any case, 2-year-olds did not rely on temporal contiguity between hearing a label and seeing an object to form a word-referent mapping, but instead used other information to infer the communicative intent of the speaker and to map the novel label to the intended referent.

Tomasello and Barton also contrasted accidental versus intentional actions in 2-year-olds' learning of verbs. They designed toys which could support two different actions. The experimenter executed both actions on a given toy, one in an accidental manner and one in an intentional manner. Children heard the experimenter use a novel verb to announce they were going to perform an action on a well-known character, "Let's dax Mickey Mouse." In the accidental condition, the experimenter carried out one of the actions accidentally, saying "Whoops!" In the intentional condition the experimenter deliberately carried out the other action saying "There!" The results were that children could successfully map the novel verb to the intentional action, even when it was preceded by the accidental action. Here again children can overlook the temporal relationship between a novel word and potential referents in order to map the word to the intended referent, in this case an action.

The work just reviewed suggests that babies and very young children monitor and use information about a speaker's intent to communicate. This work highlights the link between children's language acquisition and emerging theory of mind (see Flavell and Miller's chapter in this volume for a review of the theory of mind literature). Very young children rely on cues to another person's attentional focus and intentional state to interpret the language they hear. Although this work establishes that children rely on information about another's mental state to interpret language, there is still the question of whether very young children try to influence the mental state of others. In particular, do very young children care whether their communicative efforts have been understood by their partner?

Young Children's Monitoring the Success of Their Communicative Efforts

When an adult fails to understand a baby's attempt to communicate, the baby will sometimes alternate eye gaze between the desired object and the adult and will modify or "repair" their communicative signals until the goal is obtained (Bates, Benigni, Bretherton, Camaioni, & Volterra, 1979; Bretherton & Beeghly, 1982; Golinkoff, 1986). Such behavior has been taken as evidence that babies understand the mental impact their signals have and are attempting to get their adult partners to understand them. None of the evidence requires such a mentalistic explanation, however. In each case, babies might simply be trying to achieve their goal and modifying their behavior to find something that works. To demonstrate that very young children care about their listener's comprehension per se, requires that the listener's comprehension not be confounded with the child's obtaining his or her goal. Shwe and Markman (in press) have developed a procedure that accomplishes this. Thirty-month-old children were shown pairs of objects—one highly attractive toy and one relatively uninteresting object. Children were asked which one they wanted to play

with and were expected to request the interesting toy. Sometimes they were given the toy they requested and sometimes the other toy. And sometimes the experimenter indicated that she had understood the child's request (by repeating the name of the requested toy) and sometimes the experimenter indicated that she had failed to understand the child's request (by mentioning the other toy). This design allows speakers' comprehension to be distinguished from the child's obtaining his or her goals. The results indicated that 2½-year-olds do care about their listener's comprehension, per se. The children clarified their signal more (e.g., by repeating the label of the requested toy) when the experimenter conveyed misunderstanding of the request, whether or not the children achieved their goal. Thus, both as speakers and as listeners, very young children make assumptions about the mental perspective of their partners.

Early Abilities to Reason about Intentions

Language learning is not the only domain in which young children would need to monitor the focus of attention or intention of their social partners. Baldwin and Moses (1994) argue that interpreting the referent of someone's emotional signals poses some of the same challenges to young children. The social referencing literature includes claims that babies as young as 10 to 12 months old are monitoring their parents' emotional reaction to strangers, novel objects, or potentially dangerous situations to decide how they should respond to the situation (Bretherton, 1992; Campos, 1983). Although babies are influenced by the emotional reactions of their parents or other adults, this could occur by some lower level mechanisms (Baldwin & Moses, 1996; Gunnar & Stone, 1984; Mumme, 1993). One possibility is that the emotional display of the adult serves as an affect induction procedure, causing babies to be happy or afraid or aroused or calm, but with no specific referent for the emotion. Mumme and Fernald (1995) provide a clear test of this hypothesis and document that for 12-month-olds the emotion picked up during social referencing is directed towards a specific object. As in the domain of language learning, one question is whether babies and young children monitor their social partner's intentional focus when attributing an emotional reaction to an object. This question was addressed by Baldwin, Moses, and Tidball (in preparation, as cited in Baldwin and Moses, 1994).

Baldwin et al. (in preparation) conducted a study in the social-emotional domain that directly parallels Baldwin's (1991, 1993a, 1993b) research on word learning where babies and adults had either a joint or a discrepant focus of attention. In the social referencing situation, 12- to 13- and 18- to 19-month-olds were shown toys, such as a furry black plastic spider, that babies should be somewhat wary of. Toys were presented in pairs with one of the toys pushed within the infant's reach. As the baby began to reach for the toy the experimenter produced either a positive emotional response (e.g., "Oh! Nice!") or a negative one (e.g., "Iiuu! Yecch!"). There were two main conditions of presentation of the emotional response. In the joint focus condition, the experimenter looked at the baby's toy while producing the emotional response. In the discrepant condition, the experimenter looked at the other toy. After producing the emotional response, the experimenter placed both toys on the table in front of the baby. The baby's reaction toward the toy and emotional expressions were recorded.

The results suggest that in the social-emotional domain as in word learning, babies monitor the focus of attention of their partners to determine the correct referent of the emotional response. Babies reacted more positively to the toy that had been the experimenter's focus of attention when the experimenter had reacted positively toward it, even in the discrepant condition where the experimenter's and the babies' focus of attention were different. There was also some generalization of affect to the toy that had not been the focus of attention of the experimenter. Nevertheless, the overall pattern provides evidence for some specificity in their reactions to the toys determined by the babies' monitoring the attentional cues of the adult. What is particularly striking about these results is that even 12- to 13-month-olds are using a social partner's discrepant focus of attention to determine the referent of her emotional reactions (see Spelke, Phillips, & Woodward, 1995, for converging evidence).

Meltzoff (1995) has explored toddlers' understanding of the kinds of behavioral cues that the two-year-olds in Tomasello and Barton's study must have drawn on in interpreting new nouns and verbs. Meltzoff asked whether 18-month-olds who saw an actor fail in the attempt to complete an action would infer what the intended action had been. Children were introduced to a series of novel toys that could be acted on in specific ways. For example, one of the toys was a box with a hole in it and a square peg that could be placed in the hole (the target action). For some of the children, an experimenter demonstrated the target action. For others, the experimenter acted out a failed intention to complete the action. For example, he picked up the peg and moved it toward the hole, but missed, hitting the

box just above the hole. A control group saw the experimenter manipulate the objects in ways that did not approximate the target action. The outcome measure was whether the babies imitated the target action. Babies in the control group seldom performed the target action, and babies who saw the target action successfully completed imitated it most of the time. Strikingly, babies who saw the failed attempt produced a correct imitation of the target action just as often as children who saw the target action completed. That is, babies did not imitate just what they saw the experimenter do (miss the hole), but instead inferred what he intended to do and imitated that action.

Woodward (1995) asked whether younger infants are able to reason about the intentions of another person in a simpler context. A very simple goal directed action is reaching for and grasping an object. Adults seeing such an action would infer that the actor had the intention of grasping the object, that is, that that object was the goal of the actor's reach. However, it is possible to construe this event only in terms of its spatiotemporal properties, for example, the path that the actor's arm moved through, the location at which her hand stopped, or how much of her arm was visible at the end of the event.

Woodward used the visual habituation paradigm to assess whether 5- and 9-month-old infants attend mainly to the goal of a reach or mainly to its spatiotemporal properties. Babies were habituated to an event in which two toys (a ball and a teddy bear) sat side by side on a stage and a person reached in from one side of the stage to grasp one of the toys. Babies saw only the actor's arm; the rest of the actor stayed hidden behind a curtain. After the infant was habituated, the positions of the two toys were switched, and infants saw two new events in alternation. In one, the actor moved her arm through the same path as in the habituation event. Since the positions of the toys had been switched, this meant that she ended up grasping a different toy than during habituation. In the other event, the actor grasped the same toy as in the habituation event, thus moving through a new path. Thus, one event presented babies with spatiotemporal properties similar to those seen during habituation, but a new goal on the part of the actor, and the other presented babies with the same goal as during habituation, but a new path of motion. Infants at both ages looked reliably longer at the event in which the goal of the reach had changed than at the event in which the spatiotemporal properties of the reach had changed. This suggests that infants were attending selectively to the goal of the actor's reach during habituation.

To test whether this effect was due to the arm simply acting as a pointer, leading the infants to attend to the toy at the end of the arm, another group of infants at each age saw similar events that did not involve a human actor. Instead, a long cylinder, which was the same approximate size and shape as the actor's arm, moved in and touched the toys. Infants in this condition showed different patterns of during the test phase in this condition than in the human actor condition. Nine-month-olds looked equally at the two test events, and 5-month-olds looked longer at the spatiotemporal change. For both groups of babies, the patterns of looking in the rod condition differed reliably from those in the human actor condition. Thus, babies attended selectively to the goal of the reach only when a person did the reaching. These findings suggest that even young infants, who are not yet able to follow line of regard, are able to reason about an actor's intentions in some situations.

In sum, well before word learning begins, babies are capable of detecting at least some kinds of information about an actor's intentions, and by the time of the naming explosion, babies can use information about intent to refer to help them solve the mapping problem.

CONSTRAINTS ON WORD LEARNING

As another early source of information about possible word meanings, a number of researchers have proposed that children's word learning is guided by a set of default assumptions or constraints on hypotheses such as, the *whole object, taxonomic* and *mutual exclusivity* assumptions (Markman, 1989; Markman & Hutchinson, 1984; Markman & Wachtel, 1988; for alternative but related formulations, see Golinkoff, Mervis, & Hirsh-Pasek, 1994; Merriman & Bowman, 1989; Mervis & Bertrand, 1993; Waxman, 1994; Waxman & Kosowski, 1990). The whole object assumption leads children to assume that new words name objects rather than parts or properties of objects, spatial relations, actions, and so on. The taxonomic assumption leads children to assume that new labels should be extended to items which are taxonomically related to the originally named item rather than to thematic associates. Mutual exclusivity leads children to assume that objects will have only one name.

These constraints should be thought of as default assumptions, akin to constraints on learning in the ethological sense, rather than absolute linguistic constraints (Behrend, 1990a; Markman, 1989; Merriman & Bowman,

1989; Woodward & Markman, 1991). If constraints on word learning are default assumptions, which can be given up in the face of counter evidence, then they can provide a useful tool for overcoming the inductive problem of word learning yet still allow for the full range of vocabulary that children must acquire. This means that these constraints alone cannot fully account for word learning.

The default nature of constraints on word learning has implications for what counts as evidence for and against the existence of these constraints. In particular, the existence of words in a child's lexicon that violate a constraint is not necessarily evidence against the constraint. The fact that children learn adjectives, action terms, prepositions, and so on, does not rule out the whole object assumption, and the fact that children can and do learn more than one word which can name the same object is not evidence against the mutual exclusivity assumption. As we will discuss in more detail below, this point addresses the criticisms of investigators who have used violations in the lexicon as evidence against these word learning constraints (L. Bloom, Tinker, & Margulis, 1993; Choi & Gopnik, 1995; Gopnik & Choi, 1990; Nelson, 1988; Nelson, Hampson, & Shaw, 1993; Tardif, 1996). This does not make constraints on word learning unfalsifiable, but it does force us to examine evidence beyond records of children's productive vocabulary. Evidence for or against constraints should be seen in the *process* of word learning as measured by children's *comprehension* of a new word. There should be evidence for a constraint in the ease with which children learn words that are consistent with the constraint versus those that violate the constraint, in children's word-learning errors, and in children's initial interpretations of new words with ambiguous reference. Conceptualizing constraints as default assumptions makes clear the need for other cues to word meaning to inform children's word learning. A number of factors, for example cues to speaker's intent to refer, syntactic cues to word meaning, and background knowledge must interact with constraints, informing and sometimes overriding them. As we review the empirical work on word learning constraints, we will discuss evidence of this sort.

The first empirical investigations of word learning constraints focused on preschool aged children (Markman, 1989; Markman & Hutchinson, 1984; Markman & Wachtel, 1988; Waxman & R. Gelman, 1986). In recent years, researchers have turned their attention to constraints in very young word learners, reasoning that these learners lack access to many sources of information that older children use to limit their hypotheses about a new word's meaning. Therefore, constraints on word learning might be most useful to very young learners, who are in need of an entering wedge into vocabulary acquisition (Echols, 1991; Golinkoff, Mervis, & Hirsh-Pasek, 1994; Liittschwager & Markman, 1994; Markman, 1994; Merriman & Bowman, 1989; Mervis & Bertrand, 1993; Waxman & Hall, 1993; Waxman & Markow, 1995; Waxman & Senghas, 1992; Woodward, 1993). As we review the empirical work on the whole object, taxonomic and mutual exclusivity assumptions, we will highlight these investigations of word learning constraints in 1- and 2-year-olds.

The Whole Object Assumption

Objects as Wholes Rather Than Their Parts or Properties

Under one formulation, the whole object assumption would lead children to assume that new words name objects as wholes rather than parts or properties of objects (Golinkoff et al., 1994; Markman, 1989; Markman & Hutchinson, 1984; Markman & Wachtel, 1988). Across many studies, learners ranging in age from two years (Soja, Carey, & Spelke, 1991) to adulthood (Imai & Gentner, 1993) have been found to treat a new label as referring to the object as a whole (or its shape) as opposed to its substance, color, or parts (Baldwin, 1989; Dickinson, 1988; Dockrell & Campbell, 1986; Golinkoff, Kenealy, & Hirsh-Pasek, 1993; Hall, Waxman, & Hurwitz, 1993; Imai & Gentner, 1993; Landau, Smith, & Jones, 1988; Markman, 1989; Markman & Wachtel, 1988; Mervis & Long, 1987; Soja, 1992; Soja et al., 1991). These results suggest that learners interpret new words as names for objects as wholes, and not their properties (but see our discussion of the shape bias below). For example, in one study, Soja, Carey, and Spelke (1991) introduced 2- year-old children to a novel object, which was made of a distinctive substance, saying, "This is my blicket." Then the children were shown an object of the same shape but different material and pieces of the material of which the original was made and asked which was "the blicket." Children chose the object of like kind, rather than pieces of the original material, even though, given the syntactic frames "my _____" and "the _____" either an object or a substance interpretation of the new word would have been valid.

In addition, children interpret new words as labeling objects as wholes rather than parts of objects (Markman & Wachtel, 1988; Mervis & Long, 1987; Poulin-Dubois,

1995). In one demonstration of this, Golinkoff, Kenealy, and Hirsh-Pasek (1993) showed adults and 5-year-olds novel objects with salient parts. When given a new label for the object, and asked whether several new items were also, for example, *daxes*, both adults and children extended the label to objects of the original kind that lacked the salient part, and to objects of the original kind that had another kind of part.

Even in the face of grammatical evidence that a new word is not an object label, young children sometimes favor object label interpretations of new words (Dickinson, 1988; Hall, Waxman, & Hurwitz, 1993; Markman & Wachtel, 1988; Soja, 1992; Waxman & Kosowski, 1990; J. Woodward & Aslin, 1991). For example, Hall, Waxman, and Hurwitz (1993) introduced 2-year-olds and 4-year-olds to new adjectives for familiar and unfamiliar objects. In one condition, the experimenter pointed to an unfamiliar object, for example, glass tongs, and said "That's a fep one." Then the experimenter showed the child two objects, one that differed in kind but shared a salient property with the original (e.g., a glass napkin ring) and one that lacked this property but was the same kind of object as the original (e.g., red plastic tongs) and asked "Can you find another one that is fep?". When the original object was unfamiliar, children at both ages chose the object of like kind. That is, children interpreted the new word as an object label rather than an adjective in spite of grammatical cues to the contrary. When the name of the original object was familiar, the older, but not the younger, children successfully interpreted the new word as an adjective. Thus, especially in very young children, the whole object assumption has a strong effect on word learning. Older children are able to use syntactic cues and other constraints (in this case, mutual exclusivity) to override the whole object assumption.

Objects versus Actions, Spatial Relations, and So On

In addition to leading children to interpret new words as labels for objects as wholes rather than their parts or properties, the whole object assumption might lead children to assume new words name objects rather than actions, spatial relations, and other non-objects (Behrend, 1990a; Echols, 1991; Golinkoff et al., 1994; Markman, 1990, 1992, 1994; Mervis & Bertrand, 1993; Woodward, 1992, 1993). This prediction stems, in part, from points originally made by Gentner (1981, 1982) who proposed that object representations form tighter perceptual and conceptual bundles than do relational representations.

(See Maratsos, 1991 for related arguments.) This has implications for word learning in that it will be easier to learn a word that names a clearly defined unit in the world.

This construal of the whole object assumption has inspired much debate. One point made by several researchers is that children learn words other than object labels from the earliest stages of language acquisition (L. Bloom et al., 1993; P. Bloom, 1994; Nelson, 1988; Nelson et al., 1993; Tomasello, 1992a; Tomasello, 1995a). Moreover, although most of children's first words tend to be nouns (Nelson, 1973), not all of these nouns are object labels. L. Bloom, Tinker, and Margulis (1993) report that object labels made up roughly 40% of children's productive vocabularies throughout the period between first words and 2 years of age. Nelson, Hampson, and Shaw (1993) report that the largest single group of words in their 18-month-old subjects' productive lexicons were names for objects, but this category accounted for only 36% of the average child's vocabulary. Nouns that were not object labels (e.g., party, day, and bath) comprised 18% of the children's productive lexicons. The rest were proper nouns (4%), mass nouns (8%), verbs (10%), dual category terms (which could be either a noun or a verb in the adult lexicon, e.g., bite, kiss) (5%), and "other" (19%). These findings show that even very young children are able to learn words that are not object labels. L. Bloom et al. (1993) and Nelson et al. (1993) argue that this fact is evidence against young children's use of the whole object assumption.

Critics of the whole object assumption are correct in noting that it cannot explain all that there is to explain about early vocabulary acquisition. From the beginnings of word learning, children must draw on other sources of information, such as pragmatic cues and an understanding of ongoing activities, in word learning. Nevertheless, based on the evidence we review next, we believe that the whole object assumption is part of the story from very early in word learning.

One source of evidence for this branch of the whole object assumption comes from anecdotal reports of children interpreting non-object labels as object labels (see Macnamara, 1982; Mervis, 1987; Mervis & Bertrand, 1993). To date, only a few studies have explored this potential effect of the whole object assumption on young children's acquisition of new words in experimental contexts. One source of evidence comes from studies in which children's ability to learn a new noun and a new verb are compared. Schwartz and Leonard (1980) provided 1- to 1½-year-olds with extensive exposure to eight new object labels and eight new action words. They found that based on their production of the new words, children learned the object labels after fewer exposures, and that they learned more of the object labels than the action words. Gentner (1982) cites a case study of one child's acquisition of a new noun and a new verb with similar results.

Given the well-documented asymmetries between young children's language comprehension and production, things might look different if the measure of acquisition were comprehension. Two studies have assessed one-year-olds' comprehension of newly taught nouns and verbs. Tomasello and Farrar (1986) found that children performed slightly better on tests of comprehension for newly taught object labels than for action words. In contrast, Oviatt (1980) found that by her measures children learned both types of word equally well. However, a problem for both of these studies is that the tasks used to assess comprehension of the new noun and verb differed from one another. For example, in Tomasello and Farrar's study, children had to choose the target object from an array with several distracters in order to show comprehension of the object label, but had to perform the target action with one of the objects in order to show comprehension of the action term. Thus, performance differences might be due to task effects rather than the ability to learn. An alternative research strategy is to present children with a new word, which might refer to either an object or a non-object, and assess which of the two the child maps the word onto.

In one study using this logic, Echols (1991) used the visual habituation paradigm to assess whether hearing a new label would enhance 13- to 15-month-old infants' attention to objects as compared to actions. Infants were shown novel objects undergoing novel motions. In one condition, infants saw a series of objects each undergoing the same motion. In another condition, infants saw the same object undergoing several different motions. Half of the infants in each condition heard a new label as they watched the displays and half did not. Echols reasoned that if infants at this age have the whole object assumption, then labeling should heighten their attention to objects. Thus, in either habituation condition, infants who had heard labels should look longer at the appearance of a new object after habituation. On the other hand, labels might draw infants' attention to the consistent elements in the display. If this were true, then infants in the consistent motion condition who had heard labels would be surprised to see a familiar object undergoing a new motion. In support of the whole object assumption, Echols found that infants in both conditions who had heard new labels looked longer at new objects than did infants who had not heard labels. Thus, regardless of which element was consistent, labeling heightened attention specifically to objects. Subsequent studies revealed that for 9-month-olds, however, labels seem to direct attention to the consistent element in the displays (Echols, 1993). This finding provides a preliminary suggestion as to the age of onset of the whole object assumption.

To test the whole object assumption, it is important to document that labeling leads babies to attend to objects per se and not just to what is salient. Woodward (1992, 1993) asked whether labeling would lead 1- and 2-year-olds to focus on objects rather than on dynamic nonsolid substances selected for their salience. Using a variant of the visual preference paradigm developed by Golinkoff, Hirsh-Pasek, Cauley, and Gordon (1987), Woodward presented children with pairs of videotaped displays. One member of each pair was a still picture of a novel object (e.g., a chinese dumpling press) and the other was a dynamic film of a nonsolid substance in motion (e.g., blue dye diffusing through green water) which violated criteria for something to be perceived as an object (Huntley-Fenner & Carey, 1995; Spelke, 1990). After children were familiarized with these items, an experimenter sitting between the two screens introduced a new label, saying, for example, "Look at the tukey." as the two images were presented side by side. On other trials, children saw similar pairs that were not accompanied by a new label. On these trials, the experimenter directed infants' attention to the video monitors with non labeling speech (saying, e.g., "Wow, look at that!"). The film pairs were constructed so that the substance displays were more interesting to watch than the object displays. This provided a stringent test of the whole object assumption, since it required labels to pull children's attention away from a highly salient display. Under these conditions, 18-month-old infants looked longer at the substance displays overall, but spent more time watching the object screen when they heard a new label than when they did not. Twenty-four-month-olds did not show these effects on looking, but their spontaneous use of the new words during the procedure suggested that they linked these selectively with the object displays. (See J. Woodward & Aslin, 1991, for similar findings.)

To summarize, there is evidence that the assumption that new words label objects rather than their parts or properties is at work in children's word learning from the age of 2 years, if not before. There is also preliminary evidence for the assumption that new words refer to objects as opposed to actions, spatial relations, and other non-object aspects of the world. However, many issues about the whole object assumption are as yet unexplored. We do not yet know whether early on, the whole object assumption is invoked for every new word the child hears. The whole object assumption might be highly context dependent—invoked only when certain cues are present, for example, when parent and child are jointly attending to some event or array, and not invoked in other situations. At the other extreme, the whole object assumption may operate any time the child hears a new word, and be given up only when information in the situation overrides it. To date, empirical investigations of the whole object assumption have introduced new words in typical labeling contexts, for example, as the experimenter and child jointly attend to some array, the experimenter uses familiar labeling frames in which the final, stressed element is a novel word. It is not clear which of these cues (if any) are crucial to invoking the whole object assumption, although Baldwin's work reviewed earlier shows that children will avoid learning a word when joint attention has not been achieved.

Origins of the Whole Object Assumption

On one account, the whole object assumption in word learning derives from nonlinguistic aspects of cognition and perception. As mentioned earlier, Gentner (1981, 1982) proposed that objects are more perceptually apparent as distinct whole units than are relations and actions, and that object concepts form more cohesive conceptual units than relational concepts do. For these reasons, objects, as compared to spatial relations, actions, and so forth may be more easily mapped onto new linguistic units. Markman (1989, 1992) has suggested several other cognitive factors that may facilitate word-object mappings. For one, young children may process stimuli holistically, and this would lead them to focus on objects as wholes rather than their component parts or properties in many situations, including word learning. In addition, Markman notes, object categories are richer than attribute categories in that they support many inferences, while attribute based categories do not. Thus, when learning a new word, children may first look for the most easily accessed, information rich unit as its referent.

Alternatively, the whole object assumption might be a strategy derived from input in which object labels are frequent and salient (Choi & Gopnik, 1995; Golinkoff et al., 1994; Gopnik & Choi, 1990; Nelson, 1988; Tardif, 1996). As is the case for many phenomena in developmental psychology, studies of the whole object assumption have mainly been conducted in children from middle class American homes. Middle-class Western parental speech has been characterized as being focused on teaching children the names for objects (Brice-Heath, 1983), and there is evidence that object labels are salient in parental speech and that many object label learning opportunities occur. Although nouns are not necessarily more frequent in parental speech than verbs or other types of words (Bridges, 1986; Goldfield, 1993), nouns are often made salient in parental speech. In American mothers' speech to 1-year-old children, names for things are the most likely word type to be loudest in an utterance (Messer, 1981), and they are the most frequent word type to come in final position in an utterance, which could make them more easy to isolate and extract (Goldfield, 1993; Messer, 1981). Bridges (1986) found that parents mention actions when they tell children what to do, but they use object labels to comment on the world and suggested that the latter, more reflective use of language is more conducive to word learning than the former. Moreover, middle-class American parents use many label teaching routines, among them picture book reading, which encourage using language to name objects (Bridges, 1986; McShane, 1979; Nelson et al., 1993; Ratner & Bruner, 1978).

Thus, based only on findings from middle-class American children, it is not possible to determine whether the whole object assumption is better characterized as a learned strategy or as a cognitively based constraint. With confounds of this sort in mind, Gentner (1982) reviewed research on early vocabulary acquisition in several different languages that varied in the extent to which nouns were emphasized in the input. She sampled languages in which object labels may be less phonologically salient (verb final languages such as Japanese and Turkish), and in which verbs may be easier to isolate because they are morphologically simple (e.g., Mandarin Chinese), in addition to a culture in which beliefs about child rearing might lead parents to focus on teaching children words other than object labels (the Kaluli people of New Guinea). Based on counts of object labels versus relational terms in children's productive lexicons gleaned from the literature, Gentner found support for the conclusion that regardless of differences in input, children initially acquired mainly object labels.

Several recent studies have looked more closely at the effects of cross-linguistic variation in input on children's early vocabulary growth. They have combined careful description of parental speech to children with assessments of the proportion of object labels in children's early speech. Two of these have compared Korean and American input and acquisition (Au, Dapretto, & Song, 1994; Choi & Gopnik, 1995; Gopnik & Choi, 1990). There are two features of Korean that could lead to a lesser emphasis on object labels in the input Korean children receive as compared to the input American children receive. For one, Korean is a verb final language, thus, verbs are more likely to occur in the salient final position of an utterance. In addition, Korean allows for nominal ellipsis: If the subject or object of a sentence is clear from context, it may be left out entirely.

Au, Dapretto, and Song (1994) recorded several Korean parents as they interacted with their one-year-old children, and compared this speech to existing records of American parents talking to children of the same age. The strongest difference in parental speech was that Korean parents were more likely to end an utterance with a verb (46% of utterances) than a noun (10% of utterances), whereas American parents were more likely to end an utterance with a noun (30% of utterances) than a verb (9% of utterances). In a similar study, Choi and Gopnik (1995) recorded the speech of Korean and American parents as they played with their children. Neither Au et al. nor Choi and Gopnik found a difference in the proportions of nouns and verbs in American versus Korean parental speech. However, Choi and Gopnik counted objects labels (as opposed to abstract nouns like *opportunity*) and action terms (as opposed to mental, attention getting, and stative verbs) and found differences between the two language groups for these word classes. Korean parents used more action terms than American parents, who used many mental verbs or attention getting verbs (e.g., look, see, think). Moreover, Korean parents produced more action terms than object labels. American parents used more object labels than Korean parents and produced more object labels than action terms.

In the face of these differences in input, do children acquiring Korean approach the task of word learning with the whole object assumption? Au et al. report that they do. They assessed vocabulary composition in Korean and American children between the ages of 15 and 24 months by means of a checklist questionnaire filled out by parents. In each of four studies, Korean and American children did not differ in the proportions of nouns and verbs in their productive lexicons and both groups had many more nouns than verbs (ranging from twice as many nouns to four times as many nouns).

In contrast to Au et al.'s findings, however, Choi and Gopnik (1995) report differences in the composition of vocabularies of the Korean- and English-speaking 12- to 26-month-olds they studied (see also Tardif, 1996, for similar findings with Mandarin-speaking children). The children learning English had many more nouns than verbs in their early vocabularies: Over several sessions, about 65% of the productive lexicon was nouns, and about 6% was verbs. The children learning Korean had closer to equal numbers of nouns and verbs: Over several sessions the proportion of nouns ranged from 38% to 47%, and the proportion of verbs ranged from 29% to 39%. Choi and Gopnik also assessed whether children had a noun spurt and a verb spurt, defined as the session in which the child had 10 new nouns or verbs in production. Of the 9 children studied, all 9 had noun spurts and 7 had verb spurts. Six children had verb spurts before they had noun spurts. This contrasted strongly with the English-speaking children: Although all of these children had noun spurts, only one had a verb spurt, and this occurred much later than the noun spurt.

Thus, although Au et al. report that children learning Korean have much higher proportions of nouns than verbs in their early productive vocabularies, Choi and Gopnik report that they have about equal proportions of each type of word. This difference in the findings of the two studies is surprising in light of the fact that for both studies, subjects were Korean parents and children living in southern California. It is not clear why the findings of the two studies differ. In any case, Choi and Gopnik did not find a reversal in the proportion of nouns and verbs in Korean children's vocabularies, even given input that stressed action terms over object labels.

Fernald and Morikawa (1993) obtained findings similar to those of Au et al. in their study of parental speech and children's vocabulary in Japanese and American parents and children. Japanese, like Korean, is verb final and allows nominal ellipsis. Based on recordings of a brief play interactions between 6-, 12-, and 19-month-old infants and their mothers, Fernald and Morikawa report that Japanese mothers, as compared to American mothers, labeled objects less often, were more likely to use several different names for the same object, and used more social routine words. To assess potential differences in children's early word acquisition, Fernald and Morikawa asked the mothers of 12- and 19-month-olds to fill out a vocabulary checklist. In spite of the differences in maternal input, American and Japanese children did not differ in the proportion of object labels in their productive lexicons: Children in both language groups produced about twice as many nouns as verbs.

The concern we outlined above, that endstate lexicons are often uninformative about the process that led to the acquisition of a word, make Choi and Gopnik's data difficult to interpret. If children are given fewer nouns in input, they will have fewer chances to learn them, and, if they are given more verbs in input, they will have more occasions to override the whole object assumption. Therefore, evidence such as that presented by Choi and Gopnik and Tardif does not necessarily rule out children's reliance on the whole object assumption. Moreover, cases such as those documented by Au and her colleagues and Fernald and Morikawa constitute one source of evidence for the whole object assumption because they demonstrate that in the face of input that stresses action terms, children may still acquire mainly object labels.

Based on the input differences just described, it could be argued that the whole object assumption would be misleading and inappropriate for children acquiring Korean, and thus that it is implausible as a mechanism to explain word learning. However, as we have begun to argue, we do not propose that the whole object assumption is the only source of information available to children. As we will describe below, mutual exclusivity offers one way for children to override the whole object assumption. Moreover, syntactic cues and pragmatic cues may also serve this function. We can imagine many ways in which input in Korean might be structured to fit a learner who had the whole object assumption as one of several sources of constraint in word learning. For example, given that mutual exclusivity can override the whole object assumption, learning would be facilitated if parents mainly introduced action terms for events involving objects with well known names. In addition, parents could provide other cues, pragmatic and syntactic, that enable children to override the whole object assumption when they need to. If it turned out that Korean parents did not provide support for overriding the whole object assumption, for example, by introducing new verbs in the context of novel objects and actions with little other information, a whole object assumption should be misleading to children. If situations like this existed and children nevertheless readily construed the novel terms as verbs, then that would be evidence against a whole object assumption.

Given the problems with using end-state lexicons as data about word learning constraints, the clearest evidence would come from experimental tests that assess children's hypotheses in word learning for groups that vary in language input. Imai and Gentner (1993) have taken a first step in this direction by using Soja, Carey, and Spelke's (1991) method to test Japanese and American children and adults. Recall that Soja et al. found that 2-year-olds who were presented with a novel object named with a novel label extended the label to other objects that had the same shape as the original but differed in substance. They did not interpret the new word as the name for the substance of which the object was made, even though the label was given in a way that allowed either interpretation.

The aspect of Japanese that interested Imai and Gentner is that, unlike English, Japanese does not differentiate syntactically between nouns that name discrete objects and nouns that name substances. Based on this difference, Imai and Gentner propose that in a task like Soja et al.'s, speakers of Japanese might be more open to the possibility that a new word names the substance of which an object was made. They found that Japanese 2- and 4-year-olds and adults responded like English speakers when the stimuli were complex objects and nonsolid substances. That is, when a new label was given to a complex solid object, Japanese speakers extended the label to objects of the same shape; when the label was given to a pile of nonsolid substance, Japanese speakers extended the new word based on substance. Japanese and English speakers differed, however, when they were given new labels for simple objects (e.g., a kidney-shaped piece of wax). On these items, English speakers extended the new word based on shape, but Japanese speakers did so based on substance. Imai and Gentner speculate that there is a psychological continuum of "objecthood" ranging from complex objects to nonsolid substances, with simple objects falling somewhere in between. Linguistic differences had an effect for items falling toward the center of the continuum, but did not have an effect for items at the endpoints. Thus, this study provides cross-linguistic evidence for the whole object assumption, but also suggests that aspects of linguistic input or cultural differences can affect the ways in which objects are conceptualized.

The Taxonomic Assumption

Another challenge facing young children is how to extend a newly learned label to the appropriate range of objects. Children are aware of many different kinds of relations between objects, including but not limited to taxonomic relations. In fact, research has long documented young

children's interest in thematic relations between objects (e.g., dogs and bones, people and cars, babies and bottles) (e.g., Inhelder & Piaget, 1964; Smiley & Brown, 1979; Vygotsky, 1962). In spite of this interest in thematic relations, young children correctly extend object labels to members of a class, not to thematically related objects, thus honoring the *taxonomic assumption* (Markman 1989, 1994; Markman & Hutchinson, 1984; for related formulations see Waxman's, 1991, 1994; Waxman & Kosowski, 1990 discussion of the *noun category bias*, and Golinkoff et al.'s, 1994, and Mervis & Bertrand's, 1993, discussion of the *principles of extendibility* and *categorical scope*).

This phenomenon has been well-documented in preschoolers as well as adults (Baldwin, 1992; D'Entrement & Dunham, 1992; Golinkoff, Hirsh-Pasek, Bailey, & Wenger, 1992; Golinkoff, Shuff-Bailey, Olguin, & Ruan, 1995; Imai, Gentner, & Uchida, 1994; Markman & Hutchinson, 1984; Mervis, 1987; Nagy & Gentner, 1990; Waxman & Kosowski, 1990). Across a number of different procedures, when given a label children extend it to the object of like kind; without a label, they are more likely to choose a thematically related object. For example, in one study, Markman and Hutchinson (1984) introduced preschoolers to new "puppet language" labels for familiar objects. On some trials, children were shown a picture of a blue jay and told that the puppet called this item a *sud*. Then, they were shown two objects, for example, a duck and a nest, and asked which was "the same as this sud." Children chose the taxonomically related item (in this case, the duck) most of the time in this condition. In contrast, when no labels were given, and children were asked "which of these is the same kind of thing as this[the original]?" they tended to choose the thematically related item (e.g., the nest). Moreover, the taxonomic assumption provides one way to highlight categorical relations for children in situations in which they might not notice them otherwise: Namely, providing novel labels (Waxman & Gelman, 1986).

There is evidence for the taxonomic assumption in children below the age of the vocabulary explosion (Markman, 1994; Waxman & Hall, 1993, but cf. Bauer & Mandler, 1989). These experimental findings concur with Huttenlocher and Smiley's (1987) analyses of 1- to 2-year-olds' spontaneous uses of nouns. Huttenlocher and Smiley found that children's uses of object labels were almost always extensions of the label to items within a basic level or superordinate category. When children used a noun in the absence of an appropriate referent (e.g., said *cookie* when there were no cookies around), there was evidence that they were using these words to request absent objects or to comment on relationships between objects, rather than extending the word thematically.

A recent series of studies by Waxman and Markow (1995) provides further evidence for the existence of the taxonomic assumption in 1-year-olds. These studies employed the logic developed by Waxman and R. Gelman (1986): If children have the taxonomic assumption, then hearing a new label should facilitate categorization. To be sensitive to the abilities of infants, Waxman and Markow used a haptic habituation paradigm to assess babies' ability to categorize a set of small toys. This method is based on the same logic as other habituation measures of categorization (e.g., Cohen & Younger, 1981; Eimas, Siqueland, Jusczyk, & Vigorito, 1971; Quinn, Eimas, & Rosenkrantz, 1993). Infants were given a series of small toys to manipulate, and the amount of time the infant attended to each toy was tallied. If infants attended less and less to each next object when given members of the same category, and if infants then attended longer to an out of category object than to an object from the familiarized category, this constituted evidence that the infants had categorized.

In their first study, Waxman and Markow introduced infants who ranged in age from 9 to 20 months to toys that were members of contrasting classes at the basic level (e.g., cars versus planes) or superordinate level (e.g., animals versus vehicles). During familiarization, the baby would first be handed a series of toys from within a category (e.g., four different cars). For one group, the experimenter labeled each of these toys as she handed it to the baby. For another group, the experimenter did not label the familiarization toys, but did draw the baby's attention to the object by talking about it (saying, for example, "Look what's here."). After familiarization, each infant was handed two objects simultaneously, a new member of the familiarized category and an object from the other category (e.g., a new car and a plane), and attention to each of these was assessed.

Infants who were shown items from different basic level categories showed evidence of having categorized whether or not they heard a new label. Infants who were shown items from different superordinate categories, in contrast, showed evidence of categorization only when the familiarization toys had been labeled. Thus, labeling facilitated categorization for sets of toys that babies would not have categorized without a label. Moreover, since the experimenter talked about the toys on unlabeled trials, the effect must be due to the introduction of a new word, not simply to speech or the presence of a sound (cf., Roberts & Jacob, 1991).

In a subsequent study, Waxman and Markow (1995) asked whether a new word that was not a noun—namely adjectives—would also facilitate categorization in 1-year-olds. Their results indicated that at least for infants with three or more words in production, new words in general, not just new nouns, promote attention to categories. Thus, the taxonomic assumption seems to be in place from very early in vocabulary growth, well before the productive vocabulary spurt.

The Role of Conceptual Categories in Children's Extensions of New Words

Children's use of the taxonomic assumption in word learning is dependent on the structure of their conceptual categories. We turn now to a brief discussion of children's conceptual categories and how they relate to the words children learn to name members of a kind. For fuller discussions of the development of conceptual categories see Markman (1989), and the chapters by S. Gelman and Wellman, and Mandler in this Volume.

Categorization and Naming at Multiple Hierarchical Levels

Children could potentially extend a new word taxonomically at several hierarchical levels, interpreting it as a basic (e.g., dog, chair), superordinate (e.g., animal, furniture) or subordinate (e.g., collie, recliner) term. By the time they are preschoolers, children can categorize many objects at multiple hierarchical levels, and even 1- and 2-year-olds may do this for some categories (Bauer & Mandler, 1989; Waxman & Markow, 1995; Waxman & Senghas, 1992). In fact, much of the evidence for this comes from word learning studies like the ones discussed earlier.

In a classic paper, Rosch and her colleagues (Rosch, Mervis, Gray, Johnson, & Boyes-Braem, 1976) proposed that the basic level of categorization reflects most clearly the correlational structure of the world, and thus, is the most accessible to both children and adults. Several properties define basic level categories: They are the most inclusive categories in which objects share the same overall shape and the highest number of common features. In addition, at the basic level both within category similarity and between category distinctiveness are high, and thus, these categories "cut the world at its joints." A number of studies have demonstrated that for adults, there is a basic level advantage across many cognitive tasks (see, e.g., Rosch et al., 1976). Similarly, findings with preschoolers suggested that children are first able to categorize at the basic level (see Markman, 1989 for a review). Based on these points, we would expect to find that children's first assumption about a new label is that it is a basic level term.

Recently, Mandler and her colleagues (Mandler & Bauer, 1988; Mandler, Bauer, & McDonough, 1991; Mandler & McDonough, 1993) have proposed that children first categorize objects into global classes, roughly equivalent in scope to superordinate classes, only later analyzing these categories further into their basic level subcategories. Mandler and Bauer (1988) noted a confound in many studies which purported to demonstrate priority of basic level sorting over superordinate sorting in preschoolers: In many of these studies basic level contrasts were also superordinate level contrasts. So for example, in the superordinate condition children might be asked to sort animals versus vehicles and in the basic level condition children might be asked to sort dogs versus boats. To eliminate this confound, Bauer and Mandler presented 16- and 20-month-olds with sets to categorize that either contrasted items from two different superordinate categories (e.g., animals versus vehicles) or items from different basic level categories from within the same superordinate category (e.g., horses versus dogs). Mandler and Bauer used the "sequential touching" measure of categorization (Ricciuti, 1965; Sugarman, 1983). Children were given sets of eight objects, four each from two contrasting sets (e.g., four dogs and four horses, or four animals and four vehicles), and allowed to play with them for two minutes. If children touched members of a kind sequentially at rates higher than expected by random responding, they were counted as having categorized. On this measure, 20-month-olds succeeded at categorizing only the superordinate sets, and 16-month-olds did not categorize either the basic level or superordinate sets.

These findings and subsequent extensions (Mandler et al., 1991; Mandler & McDonough, 1993) suggest that 1- and 2-year-old children categorize more readily at the superordinate level than at the basic level. However, as discussed in the previous section, Waxman and Markow (1995) report a failure to replicate this pattern. They found that although 12-month-olds spontaneously categorized basic level sets (e.g., cows vs. dinosaurs) they did not do so for superordinate sets (e.g., animals versus vehicles). Moreover, both Mandler et al. (1991) and Mandler and McDonough (1993) found that infants distinguished some basic level sets, and did this as young as 9 months of age

(Mandler & McDonough, 1993). Finally, researchers using different measures find that prelinguistic infants are sensitive to the similarity structure that defines basic level categories (e.g., Quinn, Eimas, & Rosenkrantz, 1993). Thus, these findings do not conclusively rule out infants' ability to categorize at the basic level, although they do provide evidence that infants can form broader categories as well.

The competing proposals put forth by Rosch et al. (1976) and Mandler and colleagues raise the question of whether children initially assume that new words label basic level classes or instead assume that new words label global classes. The first words children acquire are mainly basic level terms (Anglin, 1977; Clark, 1983; Rosch et al., 1976), but how children construe the terms is at issue. Two claims have been made about children's extensions of newly learned words: One is that new words are sometimes initially underextended or context bound, and the other is that children may also initially overextend some words to label broader classes than are labeled in the adult lexicon. As an example of the first of these, Barrett (1986) noted that his son initially produced some of his first words only in a restricted set of circumstances. For example, during the first two weeks of using the word *duck,* the child only said duck while he was in the act of pushing his rubber duck off the edge of the bathtub. This observation fits with those of other researchers for both early object labels and action terms (L. Bloom, 1973; Dromi, 1987; Harris, Barrett, Jones, & Brookes, 1988; Nelson & Lucariello, 1985; Tomasello, 1992a). These early words may initially have a status more like that of bye-bye or peekaboo in that they are part of performing a particular routine, rather than names for objects or actions.

Nevertheless, even at the earliest stages of language production children extend most of the labels they use to members of a kind (Dromi, 1987; Huttenlocher & Smiley, 1987), and some of the time they overextend terms, for example using *dog* to label all four-legged animals and *moon* to label round lamps, clocks, and fingernails as well as moons (Clark, 1983; Dromi, 1987; Mervis, 1987; Rescorla, 1980). One possible explanation for overextension is that children's conceptual categories are broader than those of adults (Barrett, 1986; Mervis, 1987). However, overextensions in production can be misleading evidence about underlying word meanings since many factors could lead children to use a word they know is not the name for an object. For example, children might be attempting communicate intentions other than labeling or might be making use of a small productive lexicon in the best way they can (see

Hoek et al., 1986; Huttenlocher & Smiley, 1987; Naigles & S. Gelman, 1995, for other possibilities). In fact, researchers who have assessed comprehension find that children do not overextend terms in comprehension to the same extent as in production (e.g., Fremgen & Fay, 1980; Huttenlocher, 1974; Naigles & S. Gelman, 1995). Even so, there are cases in which children may lack knowledge about the features that distinguish between referents of two terms in the adult lexicon (e.g., Mervis & Canada, 1983), and for some categories, determining the range of referents for a term may depend on acquiring knowledge in a domain, for example, in determining which people can be called *uncle* or *grandfather* (Benson & Anglin, 1987; Keil, 1989).

Studies of word learning in experimental contexts suggest that 2-year-olds as well as older preschoolers interpret new words as basic level terms rather than super- or subordinate terms (Callanan, 1989; Hall, 1993; Taylor & S. Gelman, 1988; Waxman, 1990; Waxman & Senghas, 1992; Waxman, Shipley, & Shepperson, 1991). Since parents tend to use basic level terms when talking to young children (Anglin, 1977; Blewitt, 1983; Callanan, 1985), children's bias to interpret words as basic level could reflect regularities in input rather than conceptual structure. On the other hand, it is possible that as Rosch et al. argued, basic level categories are privileged for both parents and children, and thus parental input and children's assumptions in word learning converge.

Hall (1993) has pointed out a different aspect of basic level kinds that is favored in children's word learning, the fact that basic level kinds share enduring properties rather than temporary or situation specific properties. Some categories, such as passenger and puppy, are organized around features that are specific to a particular time or situation, whereas others, such as person and dog, are organized around properties that are enduring. Hall (1993; Hall & Waxman, 1993) found that preschool children assume that new labels should be extended to members of enduring categories. When the experimenter explicitly told children that the new label applied to a situationally defined kind, and children already knew a basic level label for the item, children interpreted the new word as a situation specific label. Thus, preschoolers could understand situation specific terms, but assumed that new words were not terms of this sort. As is the case for basic level terms, parental labeling strategies complement children's assumptions about word meaning, in that parents tend to provide labels for enduring kinds first (Hall, 1994a).

Although preschoolers have a bias to treat new labels as referring to basic level categories, Waxman (1990) argued

that adjectives might draw children's attention to the properties that differentiated between the subordinate types, Waxman (1990) ran a sorting study in which the training instances were accompanied by novel adjectives (e.g., "sukish ones"). As predicted, hearing a novel adjective enhanced children's ability to form subordinate level categories. In another study, Waxman et al. provided children with the basic level label for the kind. When children also heard the subtypes given novel labels, they were able to sort the subordinate classes (see also Hall, 1993; Taylor & S. Gelman, 1989; Waxman & Senghas, 1992).

Thus, children apply the taxonomic assumption at multiple hierarchical levels, though their first assumption is that new labels are roughly basic level terms. To interpret a new word as a super- or subordinate class term, children may require support in the learning context. For superordinate terms, the support required seems to be minimal. Hearing a label applied to members of the same superordinate class is sufficient for children to extend the label to other members of the superordinate class (e.g., Waxman, 1990; Waxman & R. Gelman, 1986). To interpret a new label as a subordinate class term, children require more contextual support (Waxman, Shipley, & Shepperson 1991).

Nonobvious Bases of Categories

Rosch's model of categorization, like many others, focused on the perceptual bases of category structure. Recently, researchers in child development have described the ways in which children's conceptual categories go beyond the level of perceptual features (see, e.g., Carey, 1985; R. Gelman, 1990; S. Gelman, 1988; Keil, 1989; Mandler, 1992; Wellman & S. Gelman, 1987). These researchers note that for adults, natural kind categories are defined not by perceptual features, but rather by assumed deep properties, many of which may be unobservable.

Given the taxonomic assumption, it is possible that hearing two items given the same name will lead children to infer that the two objects share unobservable, category relevant features. The work of S. Gelman (1988; Gelman & Coley, 1991; Gelman & Markman, 1986) documents the ways in which even very young children make inferences of this sort for natural kinds. Gelman and Markman (1986) showed 4-year-olds triads of line drawings comprised of two standards that differed from each other in appearance and category membership (e.g., a flamingo and a bat), and a test object that looked like one of the standards but was the same kind of thing as the other (e.g., a flying bird that looked like the bat). Children were told that the standards differed in a particular property (e.g., that one fed its babies mashed up food and the other fed its babies milk) and given the category labels (*bird* and *bat*) for each. Then they were shown the test object, told it was a bird, and asked whether it fed its babies milk or mashed up food. Children inferred that items which differed perceptually but had the same name should have the same properties. That is, even though the test bird looked like the bat, children said it fed its babies mashed up food like the other bird (the flamingo). In later studies, Gelman and Coley found a similar pattern of responding in 2½-year-olds. Hearing a category label is not always necessary for children to make appropriate category-based inferences (Gelman & Coley, 1991; Gelman & Markman, 1987). Nevertheless, because children expect labels to name members of a kind, labels can provide a basis for children making inferences in the absence of other cues to category membership.

The Shape Bias

The argument we've been making is that children assume new words label members of the same taxonomic kind, thus drawing on all that they know about a category in deciding how to extend a new word. An alternative position has been put forth by Landau, Smith, and Jones (1988). They argue that given many of the findings of studies of the taxonomic assumption, another conclusion is possible, namely, that hearing a new word heightens children's attention to the single dimension shape (Jones, Smith, & Landau, 1991; Landau, Jones, & Smith, 1992; Landau et al., 1988; Landau, Smith, & Jones, 1992; Smith et al., 1992). Shape is often predictive of category membership. Thus, a taxonomic choice in these studies is often also a choice of an item of the same overall shape as the target.

Arguing along these lines, Landau, Smith, and Jones (1988) have proposed that children's word learning is governed by a shape bias, rather than the taxonomic assumption. In a series of studies, Landau, Smith, and Jones introduced preschoolers and adults to new words as names for small artifacts (e.g., wooden U-shaped blocks) (Jones et al., 1991; Landau et al., 1988; Landau, Smith, & Jones, 1992; Smith et al., 1992). Across studies, both children and adults readily extended the new labels to items with the same shape as the original, even when they differed dramatically in size, color and texture, and avoided extending labels to items that differed in shape from the original. However, since shape is diagnostic of category membership, and members of artifact kinds often do differ in color, material and size (e.g., a child's fork, a disposable plastic fork, and a large metal serving fork are all members of the fork category), subjects may have chosen the same shape

item because they believed it to be a member of the same kind as the original.

Thus, based on studies in which shape and category membership are confounded, it is impossible to tell which of the two drives children's inferences about word meaning. Recently, Baldwin (1992) and Imai, Gentner and Uchida (1994) have attempted to pull these two potential bases of word extension apart (see also Golinkoff, Shuff-Bailey, Olguin, & Ruan, 1995). In one study, Baldwin (1992) presented 4-year-olds with line drawings of known objects (e.g., a carrot), thematic associates (e.g., a rabbit) and items of the same shape but different category as the target (e.g., a rocket). As in other studies of the taxonomic assumption, one group of children was asked to "get another one" after being shown the target and children in another group heard that the target had a novel name, for example, was a *zad,* and were asked to get another *zad.* Children who did not hear a new label chose the thematic associate most of the time. Children who heard a new word chose the shape match most of the time. Thus, a shape match alone was sufficient for children to extend the new word to that item.

However, in a second study, Baldwin found that a shape match was not necessary for children to extend a new word taxonomically. In this study, children saw a target item (e.g., the carrot), a thematic associate (e.g., the rabbit), and a taxonomic match did not match the target in shape (e.g., a squash). As in the first study, half the children were asked to extend a new label while the other half were asked to chose "another one" after seeing the target. Again, children in the no label group chose the thematic associate most often. Children who were given a novel label, in contrast, were more likely to choose the taxonomically related item. Thus, although children did extend a new label based on shape when there was no category match, they also extended a new label based on category membership when there was no shape match.

In a final study, Baldwin pitted category membership against shared shape, asking which of the two 4-year-olds would base their word extensions on. In this study, children saw the target (e.g., the carrot), the shape but not category match (the rocket) and the category but not shape match (e.g., the squash) in the label and no label tasks. When they were not given a label, children chose the taxonomic match most of the time. When they were asked to extend a new label, children chose the shape and taxonomic matches equally often.

Also using line drawings as stimuli, Imai, Gentner, and Uchida (1994) replicated and extended this pattern of findings. Imai et al. report two noteworthy patterns in their data. First, there was a developmental difference in the extent to which children chose the shape match on labeled trials: 3-year-olds did this more often than 5-year-olds. Second, the more familiar children were with the category in a set of items, the more likely they were to choose the taxonomic match on labeled trials. Thus, as children learn more about categories, they are more likely to extend new words taxonomically, rather than based on shared shape. These findings, as well as Baldwin's (1992) finding that children choose taxonomically when there is no common shape between the target and test items, suggest that children do not extend new labels solely on the basis of shape, but rather that children rely heavily on shape as a cue to category membership, especially for categories that are unfamiliar.

As further evidence against the shape bias, many researchers have found that young children rely on features other than shape for extending names for items other than artifacts. For example, Ward and his colleagues (Becker & Ward, 1991; Ward, Becker, Hass, & Vela, 1991; Ward et al., 1989) introduced 3- and 4-year-olds to novel animals (depicted in line drawings) that could differ from one another on many dimensions, one of them being shape. Children were told that one item, a straight snakelike creature, was a *vibble,* and asked which of several other animals were also vibbles. Some of the test items had the straight snakelike body shape, others had snail-shaped bodies, and others had tails that were curled so that their overall shape was the same as the snaillike animals. Children at both ages were likely to extend the term vibble to animals with the same shape and to the animals with curved tails, but not to the snail-shaped animals. Thus, when the overall shape difference could be explained by a posture difference (curved versus straight tail) children extended the new word to items with a different overall shape (see also Jones, Smith, & Landau, 1991; Keil, 1989; Soja et al., 1991).

Even for artifacts, shape is an imperfect cue to category membership. Adults and older children categorize artifacts such as tools and machines based on intended function, not shape (Gentner, 1978b; Keil, 1989). However, in experiments in which shape is pitted against function, young children are more likely to extend a new name to items of the same shape as the original even though it lacks the function of the original (Gentner, 1978b; Keil, 1989; Merriman, Scott, & Marazita, 1993). To ask whether preschoolers attend to function at all in extending new labels, Kemler Nelson (1995) designed a task in which these two dimensions were not pitted against one another for all items. Children were told a name for a novel object with a distinctive shape and an interesting function. Then they were shown four test objects which varied in whether they looked similar to the first object and/or whether they could be used for the original object's function. The results were that preschoolers attended to both similarity and function.

In sum, we believe the best conclusion from the existing evidence is that young children's word learning is guided by the taxonomic assumption rather than a shape bias per se, but that children show a heavy reliance on shape as a cue to category membership.

Mutual Exclusivity

We turn now to consider another possible word learning constraint: mutual exclusivity which leads children to prefer only one label per object. Many of the same issues and debates about the other two word-learning constraints arise in the case of mutual exclusivity as well. The most extreme challenge is the claim that the mutual exclusivity constraint as such does not exist (Gathercole, 1989; Nelson, 1988). Another related claim is that to the extent that mutual exclusivity is used, it is used as a learned heuristic and therefore is: (a) not necessary for word learning and (b) used only by older children (MacWhinney, 1989). Both of these issues will be addressed throughout our discussion of the evidence. A third concern about mutual exclusivity has to do with getting the formulation of the constraint right: in particular, is mutual exclusivity best described as a lexical constraint or as a pragmatic one (Clark, 1988, 1990; Gathercole, 1989)? We concentrate here on studies that address whether mutual exclusivity is available to babies and very young children and to studies that investigate what roles mutual exclusivity plays for these young children in the acquisition of vocabulary. This section is organized by the various roles mutual exclusivity is hypothesized to play.

Avoiding Redundant Hypotheses

The simplest prediction from mutual exclusivity is probably also the most controversial, namely that children should resist learning second labels for objects. The controversy centers on the fact that second labels for objects are found in children's vocabulary. This existence of violations of mutual exclusivity has been taken as evidence that the constraint does not exist (Gathercole, 1989; Mervis, 1987; Nelson, 1988). The terminology may have been a problem here with some investigators interpreting "constraint" as implying a hard-wired, rigid mode of construal that cannot be overcome. But as we have emphasized throughout this discussion, our use of "constraint" followed that of ethologists and was not meant to imply that the belief was immutable. Instead, mutual exclusivity is thought to be a default assumption—a good first guess that can be overridden given the right circumstances. On this view, any second label that exists in children's vocabulary has a history of acquisition that needs to be known before we evaluate whether mutual exclusivity plays a role in children's word learning. Controlled experimental investigations of children's interpretation of terms at first exposure provide the best test of whether mutual exclusivity guides children's interpretation of novel terms.

In one study of second label learning, Banigan and Mervis (1988) compared the effectiveness of several different teaching methods. In each case, 2-year-old children were taught terms for objects for which they already had a label, but the objects were fairly atypical members of the object category. For example, children used the word *jacket* to refer to a vest. Each child was taught second labels for six such objects. In one training method, the objects were simply labeled. In another the critical distinguishing feature was described (e.g., for *vest* the child was told it did not have arms). In another, the critical feature was demonstrated (e.g., the experimenter put her hand through the arms) and in the final condition children both saw the demonstration and heard the description. One of the findings was that the last condition produced clear learning of the second labels. Banigan and Mervis interpret this as evidence against mutual exclusivity. But another finding was that simply labeling the objects provided no learning at all. Yet for first labels simply pointing to and labeling an object should have resulted in good learning. As Liittschwager and Markman (1994) note, the failure to learn here is a failure to learn second labels and thus may well be evidence in support of mutual exclusivity.

To test this, Liittschwager and Markman (1994) directly compared young children's learning of first versus second labels for objects. In the first study, 2-year-old children were taught a novel word, either for an object for which they had a well known name or for a novel object. Contrary to the predictions from mutual exclusivity, these 2-year-olds were equally successful at learning first and second labels. Yet these results also conflict with Banigan and Mervis' finding that labeling alone was not sufficient to teach 2-year-olds second labels since the 2-year-olds in

Liittschwager and Markman's study were learning the labels at well above chance performance. One difference between the studies is that Banigan and Mervis' children were taught six new terms while Liittschwager and Markman's were taught only one. In Liittschwager and Markman's study, the experimenter repeatedly pointed to and labeled the object. Maybe this situation was simple enough and provided enough evidence for two year olds to overcome the mutual exclusivity bias. Another related possibility that Liittschwager and Markman suggest is that mutual exclusivity may also function as a fall-back assumption—used in complex learning situations.

To test this information-processing overload hypothesis, Liittschwager and Markman (1994) again taught 2-year-olds first versus second labels for objects but now taught each child two first or two second labels rather than just one. The results of this study supported the predictions from mutual exclusivity. These 2-year-olds readily learned the first labels for objects but failed to learn the second labels.

If information processing load explains, in part, when children use mutual exclusivity, then younger children, with more limited information processing capacities, should show difficulties in learning second labels even when learning a single new word. In a third study, Liittschwager and Markman taught 16-month-olds a novel label for either an object that already had a known name or for one that did not. As predicted from mutual exclusivity, although these babies successfully learned first labels, they failed to learn the second labels for objects.

In sum, Liittschwager and Markman's (1994) findings demonstrate that mutual exclusivity is available to babies as young as 16 months of age and at least under some circumstances causes babies from 16 to 24 months of age to resist learning second labels for objects. Although this resistance to learning second labels can help children avoid redundant hypotheses, the result is mainly a failure to learn a new label. We turn now to consider some of the evidence for more positive roles that mutual exclusivity (along with other mechanisms) can play in helping children acquire vocabulary.

Providing an Indirect Means of Word-Referent Mapping

The mutual exclusivity assumption functions as a kind of indirect negative evidence leading children to reject one hypothesis about a word's meaning in favor of another. In this way, children can infer the referent of a novel term without a speaker having to explicitly point to the relevant object. If a novel label is heard in the presence of some objects with well-known names and an object without a known name, mutual exclusivity can lead children to reject a second label for the familiar objects and thereby assume that the term applies to the novel object. If a child views, for example, a car and a whisk, and is asked to "hand me the whisk," then he or she should reason that *whisk* can't refer to the car (because it is a car) and so must refer to the other thing. Note that in this situation children can fulfill both the mutual exclusivity and the whole object assumptions. It is now very well-documented that children from the age of around 2½ on will overwhelmingly map the novel label to the novel object (Au & Glusman, 1990; Golinkoff, Hirsh-Pasek, Bailey, & Wenger, 1992; Hutchinson, 1986; Markman & Wachtel, 1988; Merriman & Bowman, 1989; Merriman & Schuster, 1991). In one striking demonstration of this, Golinkoff et al. (1992) showed that in this situation, the mapping that was formed between the novel word and novel object was strong enough that, on a second trial, the newly learned word functioned as a familiar word causing children to reject another novel label for it, and leading them to map this second novel word onto a different novel object. In the example just given, having rejected *whisk* as a second label for car and assuming it must refer to the whisk instead, children would now be presented with the whisk and another novel object, say a compass. When asked to hand the experimenter the compass, children now should assume that *compass* could not be a second label for the whisk and assume that it must refer to the object that as yet has no known name. Thus, this indirect form of word learning from mutual exclusivity is robust.

Using this kind of procedure, Au and Glusman (1990) have shown children assume that mutual exclusivity holds within a language but not across languages. Both monolingual and bilingual children were placed in a word learning situation similar to the one just described. Monolingual children knew an English word for one of the objects but not the other. Bilingual children knew word for one of the objects in one language but not for the other. They then heard a novel label presented in one of two ways. They either heard the word in the same language that they already knew the relevant object label in or they heard the word in a different language. In the case of monolinguals for example, they would be led to believe they were learning another English word, or they were told it was a Spanish word. In the case where children were led to believe they were learning a second label in the same language, the results replicated the findings we have just summarized. Preschool children

overwhelmingly assume that the novel label refers to the novel object. But when they were led to think the label was from a different language, there was no tendency at all to assume that the term had to refer to the novel object. Children just as readily assume that there can be a Spanish word, say, for *car* as for *whisk*. Thus mutual exclusivity is clearly treated as language relative.

There is, then, clear evidence for preschool children preferring to map a novel label to a novel object. There are two main concerns that have been raised, however, about whether this can be taken as evidence for the existence of a mutual exclusivity assumption. The first concern is that this function of mutual exclusivity has not been demonstrated early in language acquisition, and so might be just a convenient heuristic that preschoolers have adopted rather than a necessary means to language acquisition. The second is that there is an alternative explanation for these findings. In particular, children may map a novel label to a novel object not because they are avoiding second labels for things but because they are looking for first labels (Merriman & Bowman, 1989). When children see an object for which they do not have a name, this creates a lexical gap that they want to fill, and so they are motivated to find out what the object is called. In a series of experiments, Markman and Wasow (in preparation) have addressed both these concerns. The goal of the studies was to find a situation where children would need to use mutual exclusivity to infer the referent of a novel term but where they could not be filling a lexical gap. To rule out a lexical gap explanation, children were not shown a novel object at the time they heard the novel label. Because there was no novel object around, there was no lexical gap created. Instead children saw an object with a well-known name, for example, a spoon, while the experimenter said, for example, "Can you show me the *mido?* Where's the *mido?*" In one procedure, an opaque bucket was placed on the table and the experimenter shook the bucket to indicate that something was inside. The babies were 16- and 19-month-olds and at both ages there was clear evidence for babies relying on mutual exclusivity to locate a potential referent for the novel term. Babies were significantly less likely to indicate the known object when they heard a novel word compared to both when they heard the object's appropriate name and when they were simply asked to "find one." And babies were significantly more likely to search either by reaching for the bucket or by looking around the room when they heard a novel term than in the other comparison conditions. In a variant of this procedure, the study was run without the bucket. A single object with a well-known label was placed on the table and again the experimenter said, "Can you show me the *mido?*" The question here was whether babies would search the room by looking around the perimeter or on the floor. Again, 15- and 18-month-olds who viewed a familiar object and heard a novel label searched the room as if looking for an appropriate referent for the object.

Thus, mutual exclusivity can serve as an indirect means of word learning for babies as young as 15 months of age. Markman and Wasow (in preparation) found no evidence, however, that this function is available to 13- to 14-month-olds. It could be that mutual exclusivity is not yet available to babies this young. Even if it were, however, babies as young as 13 months might not be able to use it in this context. This indirect word-learning situation requires a kind of syllogistic reasoning: The novel word could refer to either object A or B. It does not refer to object B, by reason of mutual exclusivity, therefore it must refer to object A. It is all the more impressive then that 15-month-olds can use mutual exclusivity in this way.

Overcoming the Whole-Object Assumption

One of the main functions of the mutual exclusivity assumption is to help override the whole object assumption. Although the whole object assumption plays a critical role in helping early language learners break into the language system and begin to acquire vocabulary, by itself it would severely limit children's vocabulary. Object labels are fundamental building blocks for a vocabulary but children must also learn words that refer to parts, substances, sizes, texture, colors, and other properties as well as terms that refer to actions and relations between objects. When mutual exclusivity comes into conflict with the whole-object assumption, it serves as a means of motivating children to acquire much needed vocabulary for properties, actions, relations, and so on. Moreover, mutual exclusivity or lexical contrast works within a semantic domain to help children acquire more a more differentiated lexicon. There is now evidence that mutual exclusivity serves to overcome the whole-object assumption and thereby motivate children to learn terms for adjectives, mass nouns, and parts. The logic of the studies is to compare children's interpretation of a novel term depending on whether it is applied to an object for which the child knows a name to one for which the child has no known name. The prediction is that children will be better able to acquire terms for parts, properties, and so on when they are attributed to objects with known names because children will not be so ready to treat the

terms as labels for the object itself. We have already mentioned some of this evidence in the discussion of the whole object assumption, namely that children are better able to learn terms for properties and substances when they already have a label for the object (Hall, Waxman, & Hurwitz, 1993; Markman & Wachtel, 1988). Most of this work involves preschool children. We will summarize in more detail some recent work on children's use of mutual exclusivity to use part terms because it focuses on younger children.

As we discussed earlier, Markman and Wachtel (1988) demonstrated that preschool children were more likely to treat a term as referring to an object's part if the object had a known label than if it were familiar. Recently Mervis, Golinkoff, and Bertrand (1994) have concluded that 2½-year-olds have no reluctance to learn second labels for objects and do not opt to treat a potential second label as a part term. Deciding whether children have interpreted a label as a referring to the part or the whole poses some tricky methodological problems however. A design that comes first to mind would be to have children choose between the object minus the part in question versus the part alone. This is likely to be problematic, however. First, removing a salient part of an object might change the object so that it is no longer recognizable or no longer viewed as the same kind of thing. But if the part remained on the object, then there is the problem that children could point to the object but be referring to the part. Selecting the whole object including the part could be ambiguous as to which was being selected. Another related problem is the question of whether the disembodied parts would still be recognizable to children. Mervis et al.'s (1994) study had children choose between whole objects including the parts and the disembodied parts. The design Markman and Wachtel used was to ask children whether the novel term referred to the whole object (while the experimenter circled the object) or just the part (while the experimenter circled the part). But this method is not appropriate for younger children.

To get around these problems, Markman and Wasow (in preparation) designed a procedure where they could get reliable measures of whether very young children were indicating the whole object or its part. To do this, they placed objects with salient parts on the table in front of the children but the parts were always oriented away from the child. This way in order to indicate a part, the child would have to make a deliberate slightly awkward reach around the object instead of just pointing or reaching straight ahead. Following the logic of the Markman and Wachtel

(1988) procedure, children were taught potential part terms for objects either with or without known names. The results were exactly as predicted on the whole-object and mutual exclusivity assumptions for children as young as 24 months old; that is, these children interpreted a novel term as a part term significantly more often if they already knew a label for the object.

Overcoming the Taxonomic Assumption

Mutual exclusivity might also play a role in helping children to learn proper names by overriding the taxonomic assumption. According to the taxonomic assumption, children will assume that an object label should extend to things of like kind. But proper names refer to specific individuals and should not be generalized. Hall (1991) argued that mutual exclusivity could play a role in the acquisition of proper names and predicted that children should be better able to learn a proper name for an object whose category label is already known than for an object without a known label. This study will be described in more detail in the section on proper names, however, as predicted, 2½-year-olds were better able to learn proper names for objects with well-known labels.

Functions of Mutual Exclusivity

Mutual exclusivity thus serves a range of functions—some of which are available very early in word learning and some of which may appear somewhat later. Some investigators have questioned why children might rely on a principle which, because it is not true of languages in general, will have to frequently be violated (Clark, 1987, 1988; Nelson, 1988). Mutual exclusivity would rule out hierarchically organized terms, for example, yet hierarchies are common in natural language. The answer to this that Markman (1992) posed is that some kinds of simplification may be essential for learning and organizing information in complex domains. Mutual exclusivity may be in language the instantiation of a more general tendency to exaggerate regularities, ignore counterexamples, and stick with one reasonable hypothesis even when presented with others.

Markman (1992) suggested that phenomenon across a wide range of domains serve this kind of simplifying function, including blocking and overshadowing in classical conditioning, illusory correlations, overjustification, and other examples of the discounting principle in social psychology. In each of these cases, the principles that help the organism learn associations or that help people understand their own and others' behavior also generate systematic

errors. A guiding learning principle does not have to be perfect to be useful. Mutual exclusivity can generate errors that need to be corrected but it can also help young children avoid redundant hypotheses, provide an indirect source of negative evidence about word-referent mapping, and help override the whole object and taxonomic assumptions.

Mutual Exclusivity—A Lexical or Pragmatic Assumption?

There are two proposals suggesting that mutual exclusivity is a pragmatic rather than a lexical constraint. First, as discussed earlier, Markman and Wasow's (in preparation) studies were designed to distinguish between children's use of mutual exclusivity and the pragmatic tendency to fill lexical gaps proposed by Merriman and Bowman (1989). Second, Clark (1987, 1988, 1990, 1993) has proposed that language acquisition is facilitated by a pragmatic constraint, the principle of contrast (see also Gathercole, 1987, 1989). Under this proposal, language users assume that any difference in form implies a difference in meaning. This pragmatic constraint could play a role in children's learning of many aspects of language, including word learning. On hearing a new word, given this constraint, children would reason that if the speaker had meant to refer to a familiar object, they would have use the conventionally agreed on name for it. Therefore, by using a new word, the speaker must mean to refer to something else. Thus, this pragmatic constraint can predict some of the same findings as mutual exclusivity (Clark, 1987, 1988, 1990; Gathercole, 1987, 1989). There are not many empirical tests designed to distinguish between the two, but the one study that has been done supports the existence of mutual exclusivity per se (Nowinski & Markman, in preparation).

Nowinski and Markman (in preparation) examined the task where children are presented with two objects, one with a well-known name and another with no known name, say a shoe and a whisk. An adult then requests one of the objects using a novel label and avoiding giving any cues such as eyegaze as to which object he or she is referring to. In this case, the experimenter might say "Please hand me the item." Young children overwhelmingly interpret *item* as referring to the object that they do not yet know a name for. Here are the two explanations for this result. According to the lexical constraint version of mutual exclusivity, children prefer not to have two labels for the same object. According to the pragmatic version, children reason that if the speaker meant to refer to the shoe he or she would have said *shoe*. Both of these hypotheses may be true, and it was not the intent of the study to argue against the existence of such a (reasonable) pragmatic constraint. The goal was, however, to construct a situation where the pragmatic version could be ruled out in order to determine whether a lexical version of mutual exclusivity was operating. The critical manipulation was to introduce a brief period prior to the request for the, say *item* where the experimenter made it clear that she in fact meant to refer to the familiar object as an *item*. So, for example, the experimenter looked at and pointed to the shoe and said "Look at the item." The shoe and whisk would then be placed on the table and the experimenter would then say "Can you hand me the item?" On the pragmatic account, given that the pragmatic or referential intent of the speaker had been clarified by explicit pointing and labeling of the shoe as the item, the child should now be free to treat *item* as applying to shoe. According to the lexical version of mutual exclusivity, in contrast, children should be reluctant to learn second labels and might still treat *item* as referring to the novel whisk rather than the familiar shoe. This is what Nowinski and Markman have found. Moreover, it is consistent with Liittschwager and Markman's (1994) finding that second labels are harder for young children to learn even when adults are looking at, pointing at, and touching the familiar objects as they label them. The findings are also consistent with anecdotal evidence that children will "correct" an adult who has provided a second label for an object and refuse to accept the label (Macnamara, 1982). This resistance occurs in the face of an adult who is making their intent to refer to a given object with a given label quite clear.

We take this work as evidence that mutual exclusivity does not reduce to a pragmatic constraint. This is not to refute the existence of the pragmatic principle of contrast, but to support the existence of the mutual exclusivity constraint. There may well be both a lexical constraint that biases children against accepting two labels for the same object and a pragmatic constraint that if the speaker had meant to refer to a given object he or she would have used the best known label.

GRAMMATICAL CUES TO WORD MEANING

As children learn about the syntax and morphology of their language, they acquire new ways of narrowing down the range of possible meanings for a new word. In this section, we describe children's use of form class cues in learning new words, focusing on the ways in which form class and other information interact in children's learning of proper and common nouns. Then, we turn to two other ways in which children's knowledge of linguistic structure can aid word learning: the use of argument structure as a cue to verb meaning and the use of compounding and derivational morphology to coin and interpret new terms.

The Role of Form Class in Learning Proper versus Common Names

The grammatical frame that surrounds a word carries information about a word's potential meaning that can be used to narrow down the likely meaning of a novel term. As one example of this, a child who can use grammatical form class cues to determine whether a novel word is a noun, adjective, or verb, for example, could hypothesize that the term refers to an object, property, or action, respectively. The correlation between grammatical form class and type of meaning is far from perfect. *Activity* and *enthusiasm* are nouns, for example, while *own* and *believe* are verbs. Moreover, as Pinker (1994) points out, several different grammatical devices may be used to express a single concept. As an example, Pinker gives *being interested* which can be expressed as a noun (Her interest in . . .), a verb (It is starting to interest her . . .), an adjective (She appears interested in . . .) or an adverb (Interestingly, . . .). Although grammatical categories are not rigidly assigned a fixed kind of meaning, the correlation between a form class and its typical meaning is robust enough to be worth using as a source of information about a term's meaning. It may be especially useful in speech to children where presumably the correlation is stronger and so nouns might be more likely to refer to objects and verbs to actions than in the language as a whole.

In a classic demonstration of preschool children's use of grammatical cues to a word's meaning, Brown (1957) found that they interpreted *a wug* as referring to an object, *some wug* as referring to a mass and *wugging* as referring to a novel activity. Recent studies have shown that children as young as 2 years of age attend to form class cues at least some of the time in distinguishing between count versus mass nouns, nouns versus verbs, and nouns versus adjectives (Soja, 1992; Waxman & Kosowski, 1990; J. Woodward & Aslin, 1991). However, a finding that consistently emerges in these studies is that when form class cues conflict with word learning constraints even preschoolers may ignore them in service of maintaining the constraint (Au & Markman, 1987; Dickinson, 1988; Hall et al., 1993;

Heibeck & Markman, 1987; Landau, Smith, & Jones, 1992; Markman & Wachtel, 1988; Smith, Jones, & Landau, 1992; Soja, 1992; J. Woodward & Aslin, 1991).

We turn now to examine in detail young children's use of form class cues in learning proper versus common nouns and some of the more subtle ways in which this cue may interact with other sources of information, such as conceptual knowledge and word learning constraints. The contrast between proper and common names is between whether an individual is named as an individual per se (e.g., *Fido*) or as a member of a class (e.g., *dog*). Katz, Baker, and Macnamara (1974) hypothesized that young children would recruit two sources of information in deciding whether a novel term was a common noun or a proper name (see also Macnamara, 1982). The first is the grammatical form class cues which in this case is the presence or absence of an article. The second is the conceptual domain, the argument being that only some kinds of objects are candidates for taking proper names. People, for example, are categories of objects where individuals may well be singled out and given proper names, while spoons or blocks are categories of objects where this is unlikely. Katz et al. (1974) predicted that young children will treat a novel term as a proper name only when both the syntactic cues and the conceptual domain are appropriate. In their first study, 2-year-olds were taught either a proper name ("This is Zav.") or a common name ("This is a zav.") for either a doll or a plastic block with a ribbon around it. After hearing the object labeled, children were then shown two objects—the originally labeled object and another similar one. The two dolls were identical except for hair color and the two blocks were identical except for color. Each child was then asked to find *a zav* or *Zav* depending on the condition. The measure of whether children treated the terms as a proper name was whether they selected the named object at above chance (50%) levels. The prediction was that children who heard the doll called by a proper name should treat the term as a proper name but that children in the other three conditions should treat the term as a common name and thus be willing to pick the similar object just as often as the originally named object. In sum, children should treat a common name given to a doll and either a common or a proper name to a block as common names. The 2-year-old girls showed the predicted pattern: above chance selection of the named doll when it was given a proper name and chance performance in the other conditions. Boys, however, failed to show this pattern and were at chance in every condition. Two-year-old girls, at least, seem capable of integrating the syntactic and conceptual information needed to make the proper/common noun distinction.

In a second study, Katz et al. asked whether girls younger than 2 had already mastered this distinction. Pilot work suggested that younger girls would not be above chance in selecting the named doll so to make the dolls more distinctive they were given different clothing as well as different hair color. In the study proper there were two conditions: 17-month-olds were taught either a common name or proper name for a doll (the blocks were eliminated from this study). There were five girls in each condition. When asked to find *Zav,* the children selected the named object at above chance levels. When asked to find *a zav* they selected the named object around 50% of the time. The results suggest that girls as young as 17 months old can distinguish between proper and common names.

S. Gelman and Taylor (1984) were troubled by the fact that in the Katz et al. procedure, the evidence for a common noun interpretation was chance performance. This could be because of a common noun interpretation but it could also have indicated confusion and random guessing. Guessing has some plausibility because Katz et al. (1974) used familiar objects for which children already had labels so, in the common noun condition, children were presented with second labels which violates mutual exclusivity. To avoid these problems, Gelman and Taylor used novel objects, rather than familiar ones, and, during testing, had children select from four objects, two similar objects and two distracters, rather than just the two similar objects. Gelman and Taylor tested 2- to 3-year-old children and found that both boys and girls used both the conceptual and linguistic cues to infer a proper name versus a count noun.

Hall (1991) pointed out that two word-learning biases could affect how likely it is that children would construe a novel term as a common noun versus a proper name. The taxonomic assumption should lead children to assume that a novel label is a label for an object kind, rather an individual. Children hearing a proper name attributed to a novel object have two conflicting sources of information then. The syntax which should lead them to treat the term as a proper name and their implicit knowledge of the taxonomic assumption which should lead them to treat the term as a kind term. This conflict would be reduced in cases where children were learning proper names for objects whose kind terms were already known. The mutual exclusivity assumption should lead children to reject a second kind term for a given object thus enabling them to weigh the syntactic cues more heavily. Thus children should be better able to learn proper names for objects whose labels are known than for novel objects.

Hall (1991) tested this prediction by teaching 2-year-olds novel proper names for toy animals. In one condition, the toy animals were cats and the 2 year-olds knew the label *cats* while in the other condition the animals were monsterlike animals unknown to the children. Using Gelman and Taylor's (1984) method Hall then tested whether children treated the novel term as a proper name more often when taught on a familiar than a novel animate object. The results of this study and a second replication revealed that 2-year-olds are better able to learn a proper name for objects with known labels than for novel objects. When the object was unfamiliar children would reasonably often treat a proper name (e.g., "This is Dax.") as if it were a common name. Thus, proper name syntax alone or rather the syntax supported by the conceptual domain of animate objects was not always sufficient to get children to treat the term as referring to the specific individual named. Children's tendency to treat novel terms as category terms (the taxonomic assumption) still exerted some influence on their interpretation of these novel terms. But when the objects had known labels and the taxonomic assumption could be overridden by mutual exclusivity, children more readily interpreted the novel terms as proper names.

There are now several studies indicating that from about 24 months children integrate information from the conceptual domain and syntax (S. Gelman & Taylor, 1984; Katz et al., 1974) and the mutual exclusivity assumption (Hall, 1991) to decide whether a new term should be treated as a proper or common name. The evidence for younger children is somewhat tenuous. Katz et al. (1974) found evidence for the distinction in 17-month-old girls but not boys and there were only five girls in this age group who were taught a proper name, and there have been no other studies we are aware of with children this young.

Even the results with the older children are not as straightforward as they might first appear. Selecting the named toy at above chance performance does not necessarily imply that children interpreted the term as a proper name. As S. Gelman and Taylor (1984) and Hall (1994b) have pointed out, children might be treating these terms as adjectives or mass nouns. The English syntax that was used to teach proper names in these studies is ambiguous. In a sentence such as "This is dax," *dax* could be a proper name, a predicate adjective, or a mass noun. Children seeing a blond doll as in Katz et al. (1974) and hearing "This is dax" might interpret *dax* as meaning blond. If so, when

presented with a blond and brunette doll and asked to indicate *dax,* the children would consistently select the blond doll. Hall (1994b) dealt with this problem by adding distracters to test for property interpretations but it is hard using this kind of a design to rule out the possibility of some subset interpretation.

Liittschwager and Markman (1993) devised a task that can unambiguously establish whether children are treating a term as referring to a specific individual rather than a subtype. The main idea is to require that children track an individual without being able to rely on distinguishing characteristics to tell it apart from other members of the same category. In this study, 3-year-olds were taught either a proper name or a common name for two familiar objects—one inanimate object (e.g., a shoe) or one animate object (e.g., a stuffed bear). At the beginning of each trial, the child was shown an object with a distinctive feature, for example, a bear wearing a bib, and placed in a fixed location on the table. The experimenter then labeled the object using either a common label ("This is a mido.") or a proper name ("This is Mido.") depending on the condition. The experimenter then moved the object to a new location on the table and removed the distinguishing property (e.g., took off the bear's bib). A second object that was identical to the first was then placed on the table in the original location on the table (i.e., the place where the first object had been labeled). The child now would see two identical objects that differ only in location with the new object in the original location. At this point, children are asked either to "Find a mido." or to "Find Mido." depending on the condition. Note that at this point, there is no subset information that children could use to identify the originally labeled object. The two objects are identical except for location. If children had thought that the original label referred to a given object in a given location then they would consistently be wrong in selecting the second object that is now in the original location. Thus, neither the appearance nor the location of the object could be used to identify the original object because both were changed from the time of initial labeling. If children consistently choose the original object it is because they have tracked that object per se.

The results establish that 3-year-olds are treating proper names as names for individuals and not for properties or subtypes. Children were above chance in selecting the target object in the proper name but not the common name condition. Overall, there was not, however, a significant difference between the animate and inanimate objects, which is a failure to replicate both Katz et al. (1974) and

S. Gelman and Taylor (1984). In Liittschwager and Markman's (1993) study children were taught labels for both an inanimate and an animate object and it turned out there were large order effects. When the data were analyzed with only the first item taught, thus treating animate versus inanimate as a between-subjects comparison, then the typical effect of animacy was found: Children interpreted the proper name as referring to the originally labeled object 81% of the time for animate objects and only 38% of the time for inanimate objects. A second study provided further support for children's tendency to assume a proper name refers to an animate object. In this study, Liittschwager and Markman showed children two unfamiliar objects, one animate and one inanimate. The children were then asked to find the referent of a novel proper or common name (e.g., "Where is the mido?" versus "Where is Mido?"). Children selected the animate object at above chance levels (78% of the time) when they heard a proper name compared to chance levels (59% of the time) when they heard a common name, the difference between the two conditions being marginally significant. These two studies, then, confirm that three-year-olds combine information from syntax and animacy to decide whether a term is a proper or common name and that their proper name responses can be validly interpreted as tracking a specific individual and not just a subtype. Whether younger children are tracking individuals per se has not yet been so clearly documented.

The Liittschwager and Markman (1993) procedure capitalized on people's belief that the identity of an individual does not change in the face of some kinds of transformations. Removing an article of clothing from a person, for example, does not change the person's identity. This is a clear case, but to fully characterize what kinds of transformations preserve identity is a deep and challenging philosophical problem. It is a problem that one must face in any complete analysis of proper names. Proper names refer to the same individual over time so we need some notion of what constitutes the same individual. Several philosophers have argued that we cannot judge the identity of an individual without reference to some substance sortal or classification of its kind (Geach, 1968; Macnamara, 1986; Moravcsik, 1990). The idea here is that it makes no sense to ask whether an individual is the same without knowing the same what? Liittschwager (1994) quotes a passage from Moravcsik (1990) that illustrates this point well:

> When we ask whether Socrates is the same in two distinct projections, we assume that we are asking this question about a human. . . . If Socrates can be a human here, a mountain there, and the number 13 elsewhere, then there is no fact in virtue of which he could be the same or different across projections. (p. 150)

Similarly, Macnamara (1986) argues that identity must be traced relative to something approximating a basic-level sortal. A very general sortal such as "thing" or "physical object" will not suffice according to this argument. Liittschwager (1994) translated this claim into a testable hypothesis: The identity of an individual should be readily maintained in transformations that preserve the basic-level kind but not in transformations that change the basic-level kind.

In a series of studies designed to test this hypothesis, Liittschwager told children and adults stories in which a person was transformed into something else. When the character was first introduced it was given a proper name, say George. After the transformation the subjects had to judge whether the transformed object was still George. In the first study, the transformations included a state change (from wet to dry), a change in physical appearance (long hair to short hair), a change in role (painter to ice skater), a change in age (child to old man), a change in sex (girl to boy) an change in basic-level kind (boy to rabbit), a change in superordinate kind (woman to flower), a change in living kind (girl to chair), and a change in ontological kind (man to smoke). In each case, the original object and transformed object were represented by drawings. In two preliminary studies, adults ranked the transformations either according to how dramatic the transformations were or according to how similar the pre- and post-transformation objects were. These ratings provided an a priori ordering of the transformations against which the children's judgments could be compared.

One possible outcome is that our (and children's) conceptual system is flexible enough that we can preserve identity across virtually any change in an object's category. At least at some level we can comprehend statements that a witch, say, turned George into a frog or even into smoke, and at least some adults can retain the belief that the frog or smoke is still George. So with a compelling enough scenario, identity of an individual might be readily retained across even changes in ontological kinds. Alternatively, it could be that the more dramatic the transformation, the less likely people are to believe the identity of the individual has been preserved. This predicts there should be a linear decline in the degree to which identity is preserved and the prior ratings of similarity of the pairs. The third possibility Liittschwager considered is the one predicted by Macnamara (1986) that there should be a discontinuity at the level of basic-level kind.

The results of the study gave very little support to the notion that the basic-level was somehow fundamental to the tracking of identity. There was no evidence of an abrupt drop in identity judgments after changes at the basic level. Instead, in this and the other studies in Liittschwager (1994), there was a relatively smooth drop in identity judgments according how dramatic the transformation was.

In addition to the magnitude of the transformation, the degree of continuity by which an object is transformed plays a critical role in our conception of identity. The parable of Theseus' ship has been used for generations to make this point with a thought experiment. Imagine a ship that undergoes a series of repairs. As each plank is worn out it is replaced by a new one. Over time every plank might be replaced yet we would still judge it to be the same ship. In contrast, if the ship were torn down, the old planks thrown out, and a new ship built from new wood, we would not consider it the same ship. The continuity of most of the parts in the face of some transformations allows us to preserve the identity of an individual. Liittschwager (1994) examined what role the continuity of the transformations might play across a wide range of transformations. In this study (Study 4b), 4-year-olds were told stories that depicted either gradual or abrupt transformations of a person into another object and pictures were drawn to indicate the intermediate stages. Not surprisingly continuity had the predicted effect of increasing the number of identity judgments children made (though the manipulation was not so influential for adults). Of particular interest, however, is that the effect of continuity did not interact with the degree of transformation. Instead from minor changes in state all the way to changes in ontological kind, a scenario that described the continuous intermediate stages better enabled children to preserve the identity of the individual.

General Syntax-Semantics Links

P. Bloom (1994) has proposed that children are endowed with a large set of innate semantic-syntactic linkages that guide word learning. Children are proposed to have grammatical categories such as count noun, mass noun, proper noun, transitive verb, intransitive verb, and so on, and a set of mapping rules linking these syntactic classes to semantics. In particular, Bloom proposes the following three

mappings, which offer an alternative account for many of the findings taken as evidence for the whole object and taxonomic assumptions.

Mapping 1. Noun phrases refer to individuals.

Mapping 2. Count nouns refer to kinds of individuals.

Mapping 3. Mass nouns refer to kinds of portions.

The proposal is that when children hear a count noun, their first step is to look for an individual that could be named by the word and then extend the new name to all members of that kind. The notion of individual is broader than the class of concrete objects. It includes anything that "can play an independent causal role in a conceptual domain" (p. 319), and thus includes, objects, organized groups (e.g., forest, army), sounds, ideas, and units of time, among other entities. Bloom points out that this account has the power to explain how children acquire nouns other than object labels, as well as words other than nouns, since there are rules of this sort for all syntactic classes.

Even if they have these innate semantic-syntactic mappings, early in language development, children will not yet know how or if their language marks distinctions between count nouns and mass nouns, and so on. Bloom argues that the inductive problem posed by word learning is still limited for these very young learners since a new word must map onto one of the innate syntactic categories. Once children acquire an understanding of how their language marks syntactic classes such as count noun and mass noun, they can begin to draw on the mapping rules in interpreting new words.

A problem for this account is posed by the fact that even children who have productive use of a grammatical distinction may ignore it when interpreting a new word. As we discussed earlier, children ranging in age from toddlerhood to five years often ignore form class cues that a new word is a mass noun or adjective, interpreting it instead as an object label (e.g., Dickinson, 1988; Hall, Waxman, & Hurwitz, 1993; Markman & Wachtel, 1988; Soja, 1992; Waxman & Kosowski, 1990; J. Woodward & Aslin, 1991). Bloom notes these findings and proposes that they are due to a cognitive bias to see discrete physical objects as individuals extraordinaire. This would explain why a child might be biased to interpret count nouns as one sort of an individual rather than another (e.g., *tree* rather than *forest*). However, if children have knowledge of a grammatical distinction, under Bloom's account, they should draw on this knowledge in word learning. That is, on hearing mass noun syntax, they should invoke Mapping 3, not Mapping 2. In order to account for children's interpretations of mass nouns and adjectives as object labels, it is necessary to propose that in addition to the syntax-semantics mappings described above, children also are biased to interpret new words as object labels, that is, that children have the whole object assumption.

Markman (1994) has suggested that Bloom's syntax-semantics mappings are a developmental achievement rather than a starting point. That is, after a while babies will begin to detect the fairly consistent way in which count nouns refer to objects. Then upon hearing count nouns applied to things such as "a crowd" or "a movie" children might somewhat metaphorically give objectlike status to such nonobjects.

The Use of Grammatical Information in Verb Learning

Children learn words to describe events from the earliest stages of language acquisition (L. Bloom, 1973; Bowerman, 1974; Gopnik & Meltzoff, 1986; Huttenlocher, Smiley, & Charney, 1983; Nelson, 1973; Tomasello, 1992a), although for children acquiring English, these are often not verbs, but rather words like *up, down, more, allgone, hi,* and *bye* (Choi & Bowerman, 1991; Clark, 1983; Tomasello, 1992a). Even so, Tomasello (1992a) noted words that would be classified as verbs from an adult standpoint in his daughter's vocabulary as young as 16 months of age.

Even if the child has the understanding that new verbs refer to actions and could use form class to determine that a new word is a verb, there are still many possible interpretations of any new verb given in reference to an event. Gleitman (1990) has outlined the ways in which this is the case. For one, a verb might refer to the manner of an action (e.g., *roll*), the path of an action (e.g., *enter*), or the outcome of an action (e.g., *paint*), or some combination of these. A verb that describes a transitive action could describe what the actor is doing (e.g., *pushing*) or what the item that is being acted upon is doing (e.g., *moving*). Repeated exposure to a verb in different contexts could, in principle, help the learner to narrow the range of options of which aspects of an event a verb referred to. However, a problem remains for verbs such as *flee* and *chase,* or *buy* and *sell,* that describe different perspectives on the same event which always cooccur (e.g., every act of chasing, by definition, is accompanied by an act of fleeing, and vice versa). Similarly, verbs that are subsets of others (e.g., see, look, and orient) can be used to describe the same event.

Finally, mental verbs refer to aspects of an event that can only be inferred. Thus, for verbs, Gleitman argues, information in the context alone is insufficient to narrow the range of hypotheses about the word's meaning.

Perhaps there are biases in event perception that make some interpretations of new verbs more salient than others. This proposal has been considered by a number of researchers, who have had little success at locating strong biases of this sort. For example, some researchers have found that given a choice between interpreting a new verb as encoding the outcome of an action (e.g., fill, break) and the manner of the action (e.g., pour, run), children prefer the outcome interpretation (Behrend, 1990b; Behrend, Harris, & Cartwright, 1995), but other findings suggest just the opposite (Gentner, 1978a; Gropen, Pinker, Hollander, & Goldberg, 1991; Huttenlocher et al., 1983). Moreover, Behrend (1990b, 1995) reports that these effects depend upon whether the verb is given in the present or past tense and whether the bias is assessed for familiar actions or newly taught verbs, as well as on the aspects of the event that are varied in training. In addition, some researchers report that children are conservative verb learners in the lab in that they are apt to accept as other referents of a newly taught verb only those actions that are the same as the original on almost all dimensions (Behrend, 1995; Forbes & Farrar, 1993; Forbes, Poulin-Dubois, & Shulman, 1995). Moreover, given the variability in the elements that may be lexicalized in the verb (Gentner, 1982; Talmy, 1974), a bias to link verb meaning to one particular feature of an event would not serve the learner very well.

Syntactic Bootstrapping

For verbs, a crucial cue to meaning is provided by the grammatical structure of the sentences in which it can be used. This is because verbs are relational terms—they specify relations between objects. Thus, information about the subject and objects of a verb, the number of arguments it can take, and the relation these arguments bear to one another can be useful in determining the meaning of the verb. Use of this information in word learning has been termed "syntactic bootstrapping" by Gleitman and her colleagues. Gleitman (1990) provides one illustration of this notion,

> Verbs that describe externally caused transfer or change of possessor of an object from place to place . . . fit naturally into sentences with three noun phrases, for example, *John put the ball on the table* . . . That is, "putting" logically implies one who puts, a thing put, and a place into which it is put; a

noun phrase is assigned to each of the participants in such an event. In contrast, because one can't move objects from place to place by the perceptual act of looking at them, the occasion for using *look* in such a structure hardly, if ever, arises. (p. 30)

To further illustrate the ways in which grammatical structure could provide a source of information about verb meaning, we take examples discussed by Fisher, Hall, Rakowitz, and Gleitman (1994). Fisher et al. focused on the problems presented by verbs like *flee* and *chase* and *give* and *take,* that describe different perspectives on the same event. For example, suppose a young child sees an episode in which a rabbit gives a ball to an elephant, who takes the ball, and hears an adult say "look, giving." Based on just this information, how is the child to know whether the verb names the giving or the taking? Fisher et al. point out that the sentential frames that generally surround new verbs can provide several sources of evidence about the meaning of words like give and take. For example, take these four sentences:

1. The rabbit is giving the ball to the elephant.
2. The elephant is taking the ball from the rabbit.
3. The rabbit is pushing the elephant.
4. The elephant is falling.

If a child did not understand the verbs *give, take, push,* and *fall,* he or she would be able to make a good first guess at these words' meanings given sentential cues. For one, so long as the child could identify the subject of the sentence, he or she could infer that (1) is about what the rabbit is doing and (2) is about what the elephant is doing. The number of arguments in (3) versus (4) suggests that the verb in (3) names a transitive action and the verb in (4) names an intransitive one. In addition, the prepositions *to* and *from* in (1) and (2) specify relations between the elephant, rabbit and ball that would allow the child to differentiate between *give* and *take.*

One critique of syntactic bootstrapping is that it does not provide sufficient information to narrow the range of hypotheses to a usefully small number (Maratsos & Deak, 1995; Pinker, 1994). For example, Pinker (1994) notes that verbs with different meanings often appear in the same syntactic frames—syntactic cues do not differentiate between *slide, roll, bounce, skip, slip, skid, tumble, wiggle,* and *shake,* or between *hope, think, pray, decide, say,* and *claim,* to name just a few. Gleitman, Fisher, and colleagues (Fisher, Gleitman, & Gleitman, 1991; Fisher et al., 1994; Gleitman, 1990)

allow that much information about a verb's meaning will not be signaled by the syntactic frames in which it occurs, but argue that nevertheless, these frames provide critically important information about meaning.

Given that these grammatical cues to meaning are present, can preschoolers use them to interpret new verbs given in reference to events they observe? To ask this, Fisher et al. (1994) presented 3- and 4-year-olds with videotaped scenes in which puppets acted out fleeing/chasing, giving/taking, eating/feeding, and other events of this type. Children were introduced to a puppet, whose "puppet talk" they were asked to translate. The puppet provided invented words as labels for the videotaped events. On some trials, the invented word was presented with no informative sentential frame ("Look, ziking."). On other trials, the new word was presented in a frame that provided the kinds of information described above. Thus one child who saw the push/fall vignette might hear "The rabbit is ziking the elephant" and another child might hear "The elephant is ziking" while seeing the same vignette.

The grammatical context had a strong effect on children's interpretations of the new verbs. Both 3- and 4-year-olds almost always interpreted the puppet talk verbs in accord with the sentence frames when such frames were given. For example, they said that "The rabbit is ziking the elephant" meant that the rabbit was pushing the elephant, but that "The elephant is ziking" meant that the elephant was falling.

When children heard verbs without sentential cues to meaning that would discriminate between the two possible interpretations ("look, ziking"), they did not chose randomly between the two possible interpretations. Rather, they tended to chose the causal action (e.g., feeding rather than eating, pushing rather than falling). Fisher et al. suggest that children have a general "agency bias"—that is, that they interpret new words as the name for the most causal action in sight, in the absence of other cues to meaning. Thus, syntax had the effect of overriding the most salient interpretation of the new verb when it worked against this bias, that is, when the new verb was non-agentive.

These findings do not specify which of several potential grammatical cues to word meaning children were relying on. For one, if children were able to identify the subject of the sentence, then this information would enable them to interpret the new verbs correctly. In addition, in some of the items, prepositions like *to* and *from* provided another cue to verb meaning, and in others, number of nouns in the sentence provided one cue to whether the verb was transitive or intransitive. Fisher (1996) has begun to pull the various cues apart, exploring children's use of the number of arguments in a sentence and their use of prepositions such as *to* and *from* in interpreting novel verbs. Three- and 5-year-olds were shown videotaped novel events involving two female actors. In one set of events, one of the actors moved the other in a novel way. As they saw these, children heard sentences such as these:

5. She's blicking her around.

6. She's mooping around.

Since both actors were female, the use of the pronouns *she* and *her* made it impossible for children to map the participants onto the subject and object of the sentence. Here, the only cue to meaning was that *blick* takes two arguments, whereas *moop* takes one. After seeing the events, children were asked to point to the person who was blicking or mooping. Both 3- and 5-year-olds pointed to the actor who was moving the other one when they heard sentences like (5). That is, hearing a new verb in a sentence with a subject and an object led children to interpret it as a transitive verb. When they heard sentences like (6), children chose each actor equally often. Fisher points out that either a transitive or intransitive interpretation is possible given (6), since many transitive verbs can occur with no direct object (e.g., eat). Once again, children who heard the new verb in the absence of sentential cues ("Look, mooping.") were likely to chose the more causal of the two actors (the pusher rather than the pushee) as the one who was mooping.

In another set of events, children saw one actor pass an object to the other, who accepted it, again in novel ways. For this set, children heard sentences like (7) and (8), and were asked to point to the actor who was *fliffing* or *korping*.

7. She's fliffing the ball to her.

8. She's korping the ball from her.

For these sentences as well, children made use of the isolated grammatical cue, in this case the prepositions *to* and *from*, in interpreting the verbs. That is, they pointed to the giver when they heard sentences like (7), but were more likely to point to the givee when they heard sentences like (8).

These studies demonstrate that preschoolers use aspects of the syntax of a sentence surrounding a new verb to make an educated guess about the verb's meaning when given a single sentence. Gleitman and her colleagues

(Fisher et al., 1991; Gleitman, 1990; Lederer, Gleitman, & Gleitman, 1995) have proposed that in addition to this, the range of sentence frames in which a new verb appears provides the learner with a method of greatly narrowing the range of hypotheses about a new verb's meaning. To illustrate how multiple sentence frames might inform a learner, we take another example from Fisher et al. (1994), contrasting the verbs *give, explain, go,* and *think.* Both *give* and *explain,* but not *go* and *think,* can occur in sentences with three noun phrases, which are associated with verbs of transfer. For example,

9. Ed gave the horse to Sally.

10. Ed explained the facts to Sally.

In addition to this, *explain* and *think,* but not *give* and *go,* can occur with sentence complements, a feature associated with mental verbs. For example,

11. Jane thinks/explains that there is a mongoose in the parlor.

*12. Jane gives/goes that there is a mongoose in the parlor.

Thus, *explain,* both a mental verb and a verb of transfer, occurs in frames that are associated with these elements of meaning, whereas *think* does not occur in frames associated with transfer, and *give* and *go* do not occur in frames associated with mental verbs.

At least some of the time, then, multiple sentence frames are a potentially useful source of information about a new verb's meaning. One question that arises is how general these cues to word meaning are. Do verbs that appear in the same sets of subcategorization frames generally have similar meanings? To address this question, Fisher, Gleitman, and Gleitman (1991) asked one group of adult subjects to judge the pairwise similarity of each of 24 commonly used verbs, and another group of adult subjects to judge the range of syntactic frames that each of the verbs could enter into. They found that verbs that were rated as being similar in meaning were rated as occurring grammatically in the same subcategorization frames. As expected, mental verbs occurred with sentential complements, verbs of motion occurred with prepositional phrases, and verbs of transfer occurred in sentences with three noun phrases. Moreover, verbs that involve the transfer of information or an idea from one person to another were associated with both sentential complements and three noun phrase sentences. This study provides preliminary evidence for linkages between argument structure and verb meaning for several classes of verbs. (See Fisher, 1994, for other such linkages, and Maratsos & Deak, 1995, Pinker, 1994, and Rispoli, 1995, for arguments against the generality of these correspondences.)

Lederer et al. (1995) and Naigles and Hoff-Ginsburg (1995) have found similar correspondences between subcategorization frames and meaning for verbs used in parental speech to small children. Although, at this point, we do not know whether children make use of this evidence when learning a new verb, two pieces of evidence suggest that they may. For one, work by Pinker and Gropen (Gropen, Pinker, Hollander, & Goldberg, 1991; Pinker, 1989) suggests that children exploit the linkages between semantics and argument structure in the other direction, namely to determine the allowable range of argument frames for a new verb based on its meaning.

In addition, Naigles (Naigles, Fowler, & Helm, 1992; Naigles, Gleitman, & Gleitman, 1992) has found that presenting known verbs in a new sentence frames can affect young children's interpretations of these verbs. Naigles and her colleagues asked children ranging in age from 2 to 12 years and adults to act out sentences in which known verbs occurred in ungrammatical as well as grammatical sentence frames. In the context of playing with a Noah's Ark set of toys, subjects were asked to enact intransitive verbs used in transitive frames, for example "The zebra goes the lion," and transitive verbs in intransitive frames, for example "The zebra brings." Adults and older children given sentences such as these tended to ignore the conflicting sentence frame in service of acting out the verb appropriately. Thus, they might move only the zebra, ignoring the lion, given the first mismatch sentence, and add an object for the zebra to bring given the second. Preschoolers, in contrast, tended to follow the frame rather than the verb. Thus, they were likely to respond to "The zebra goes the lion" as if it meant "The zebra moves the lion," and to "The zebra brings" as if it meant "The zebra comes."

One possible explanation for these findings is that young children may be more compliant in the face of seeming pragmatic demands to reinterpret familiar verbs. However, Naigles, Fowler, and Helm (1992) found that the shift from reliance on the frame to reliance on the verb occurred at different ages for different frames and that subjects across ages were reliant on the same frames to different extents for different verbs. Thus, it seemed unlikely to them that developmental differences in response

to pragmatic demands could account for their findings. Rather, they concluded children who are in the early stages of learning verbs will be more open-minded about the possible range of meanings and uses of a new verb, and will thus respond to the appearance of a familiar verb in a novel frame. As children gain more experience with a verb and the range of sentence frames in which it can appear, they become resistant to reinterpreting the verb based on hearing it in a new syntactic frame.

Although Naigles et al. chose verbs that were limited to occurring in either transitive or intransitive sentences, many verbs in English can occur in both kinds of frames; that is, the same verb can be used to describe caused motion and experienced motion, for example, "The door opens"/"Sal opens the door," "The ship sinks"/"Lou sinks the ship," and "The ball drops"/"The crew drops the ball." Therefore, another reason for the young verb learners in Naigles et al.'s studies to remain open-minded is that, given this pattern in English, a verb they had encountered only in a transitive frame, could, potentially also be used intransitively. Bowerman's (1977, 1978, 1985) work illustrates that young children understand this pattern, in that they sometimes overgeneralize it. Bowerman noted that beginning at about 3 years of age her daughters produced errors such as "I come it closer so it won't fall" (meaning bring) and "I'm singing him" (meaning making a toy sing). Since these verbs were used correctly prior to this time, Bowerman concluded that these errors were evidence that her daughters had re-analyzed familiar verbs, noting the correspondence between meaning and form.

As noted earlier, Choi and Bowerman (1991) noted similar patterns in younger children's use of path markers such as *up* and *off* to describe motion events in English. By the age of 20 months, the English-acquiring children they studied readily used the same term to describe caused and experienced motion. This contrasted with the early verb use of a group of Korean children. Korean differs from English in that it requires that different verbs be used to describe caused and experienced motion. The Korean children studied by Choi and Bowerman never used the same verb to describe both caused and uncaused motion. Thus, the patterns seen for both groups suggest that children pick up on language specific patterns from an early age.

The Age of Availability of Syntactic Cues to Verb Meaning

The age at which children are first able to use argument structure in verb learning is an open question. In the first study that explored very young children's use of grammatical information in verb learning, Naigles (1990) found that even 2-year-olds can use some of these cues. Since her subjects were 25 months of age on average, Naigles used a visual preference task to assess their reasoning about new verbs. In the first phase of the study, children saw a single event, involving a duck and bunny, that included a causal action (the duck pushed down on the bunny's head, causing the bunny to squat) and a non-causal action (both the duck and the bunny waved their arms in large circles). As children watched this event, they heard a new verb. For some children, the verb was embedded in transitive sentence ("The duck is gorping the bunny."), and for others the verb was embedded in an intransitive sentence ("The duck and the bunny are gorping.").

After the introduction of the new verb, children were shown two video scenes simultaneously, each of which contained only one of the actions seen in the first video. That is, one screen showed the two characters waving their arms in circles, and the other showed one character pushing the other into a squat. As these two events were presented, children were asked "Where's gorping?" and the amount of time they looked at each of the two screens was coded. Children who had heard the verb in transitive frame looked longer at the causal action (pushing down) and children who had heard the verb in an intransitive frame looked longer at the non-causal action (arm circling). Thus, this provides evidence that 2-year-olds can use some aspects of the grammar of a sentence surrounding a new verb to decide which of two potential actions the verb names (see also Hirsh-Pasek & Golinkoff, 1993, 1996; Naigles & Kako, 1993).

However, Tomasello (1995a; Olguin & Tomasello, 1993; Tomasello & Kruger, 1992) has recently argued that for 1- and 2-year-olds, verb meanings are not linked to general syntactic representations of verbs. In a diary study of his daughter's early verb acquisition, Tomasello (1992a) noted that at this age, his daughter was conservative in her use of verbs, confining a given verb to a narrow range of the allowable argument structures. When she had mastered a construction for a particular verb, she did not generalize this construction to other verbs. Tomasello concluded that this was because his daughter lacked the grammatical category *verb* at this age. Instead, she organized her sentences around particular verbs, applying what she had learned about the allowable sentences for each verb individually.

To test this proposal with a larger sample of children, Olguin and Tomasello (1993) taught a group of 25-month-olds a series of novel verbs, each of which was introduced in a limited set of sentence frames. For example, one verb might be introduced in sentences with agents, but no patients ("Ernie's gaffing."), another might be introduced in sentences with patients but no agents ("Look, gaffing cookie monster."), and another might be introduced with no surrounding argument structure ("Look, gaffing."). Then, children's spontaneous uses of each new word were recorded and analyzed. Children rarely used a verb in a sentence frame they had not heard it in. When they did produce a verb with an argument position not previously modeled, it always took the form of putting a noun in front of the verb, and in several cases the noun put in first position was not the agent of the action. Moreover, even though they were given an elicitation task for the past tense, none of the children added the past tense marker -ed to any of the new verbs. Based on these findings, Olguin and Tomasello concluded that 25-month-olds do not have a general category of transitive verbs to which new verbs are added. Rather, they argued that children at this age learn the range of sentences frames a verb can enter on a verb by verb basis, only later abstracting cross-verb grammatical patterns.

In light of these findings, Tomasello (1992a, 1995a) has argued that the first verbs are learned without the aid of grammatical constraints. Instead, children set up their first verb meanings based on contextual information and by assessing the intentions of their interlocutors (see also Tomasello, 1995a). This is clearly an issue that requires more study. There may well be a point at which children's ability to draw on grammatical information in verb learning is extremely limited or nonexistent. Other sources of information about a new verb's meaning would be critical at this stage. Moreover, as we noted earlier, even preschoolers may need to draw on other sources of information to distinguish between verbs that can occur in the same syntactic frames. We turn now to a brief discussion of some of the other sources of information children may draw on in verb learning.

Other Sources of Information about Verb Meaning

One source of information in verb learning is provided by the words the child already knows. These could help to narrow the range of possible verb meanings in at least two ways. For one, knowledge of some nouns and likely relations between them may help narrow the range of hypotheses. Even if children did not have access to syntactic cues, if they heard a sentence with *baby* and *cookie* in it, they might assume that the new verb meant *eat* (Pinker, 1994;

Tomasello, 1995a; but see Fisher et al., 1994, and Gleitman, 1990, for a discussion of the limits of this cue to meaning).

In addition, children may follow mutual exclusivity or the principle of contrast in verb learning (Clark, 1983, 1987, 1993; Pinker, 1994). If children hear a new verb in reference to an event for which they already have a verb, they may reject that verb's meaning as a possible interpretation of the new verb. For example, suppose a child who already knew the verbs *drop* and *fall* heard "Look, it's drifting" while seeing a person drop a feather, which then falls to the ground. On the basis of contrast or mutual exclusivity, the child could correctly decide that *drift* referred to some other aspect of the event. Clark (1993), Golinkoff et al. (1995), and Merriman, Marazita, and Jarvis (1995) review evidence that preschoolers do this sort of reasoning when introduced to new verbs for partially familiar events.

Tomasello and his colleagues have documented some of the ways in which very young children draw on their understanding of the situation in which a new verb is introduced, and the intentions of the persons involved. As we described earlier, Tomasello and Barton (1994) found that 2-year-olds are adept at deciding, based on behavioral cues, whether an action is accidental or intended, and use this information in interpreting a new verb. Tomasello and Akhtar (1995) found that in addition to this, 2-year-olds can use pragmatic cues to decide whether a new word is the name for an action as opposed to an object. When a novel action, as opposed to an object, was the new element in the communicative context, or when the experimenter made obvious preparations related to the novel action prior to introducing the new word, children interpreted the word as the name for the new action rather than an object label.

Moreover, 2-year-olds are able to make inferences about an actor's unrealized intentions in verb learning. Akhtar and Tomasello (1996) introduced children to several activities (e.g., a curved platform that catapulted another toy into the air). After the child had been shown how each of these activities worked, the experimenter took one of them out and said "Let's meek Big Bird now." Then, for some children, the experimenter pulled out Big Bird and proceeded to (for example) catapult him. For other children, the experimenter pretended not to be able to find Big Bird, and then put the catapult away. Both groups of children were then shown the other activities again. Then children were given elicited production and comprehension tasks for the verb *meek*. Children in both groups did well on comprehension trials, even those children who did not see the action after hearing the verb. Thus, children must have inferred the experimenter's intended action and, even though the intention was not fulfilled, mapped it onto the new verb.

When learning an object label, as we discussed earlier, children rely on attaining joint visual attention on an object with the adult in order to determine which object the adult is labeling. Verb learning presents a problem for this kind of joint attention, since actions are typically fleeting and attempting to attend to both the action and the new label at once may make either or both difficult to process. Moreover, the pragmatic contexts in which verbs are introduced may differ from those in which nouns are introduced. Specifically, verbs may occur frequently as requests for action, thus occurring before the referent action takes place. With this in mind, Tomasello and Kruger (1992) asked whether children typically hear verbs as they watch an ongoing action, or instead just before or just after the action. Overwhelmingly, the parents of 1-year-olds they studied labeled actions just prior to the actions occurring, and most often they labeled actions that the child was about to produce, either by requesting an action or by anticipating one.

In a subsequent study, Tomasello and Kruger asked whether this behavior on parents' part had any implications for toddler's ability to learn new verbs. They brought a group of 2-year-olds into the lab and introduced them to a novel action and a novel verb. For some of the children, the experimenter only labeled the action when it was ongoing, that is, when either the experimenter or the child was in the midst of producing the action. For other children, the new verb was introduced either just after or just before the child or experimenter produced the action. After training, children's spontaneous and elicited production and their comprehension of the new verb was assessed. Children were most likely to produce the new verb after training when it had been introduced prior to the action, and were least likely to perform correctly on the comprehension test when they had heard the verb at the same time as the action occurred. Thus, parents' labeling strategies seem to fit well with children's learning abilities.

As a final source of evidence in verb learning, we point briefly to the role of conceptual structure. In order to learn a relational term, the child must understand the relation it encodes. Thus, one source of information critical to verb learning will be the child's developing understanding of the kinds of relations that exist. Gopnik and Meltzoff (1986) have argued that some early relational terms may be learned as the child is coming to understand the relations involved. For example, they noted a strong correlation between the onset of the ability to solve means-ends tasks and the acquisition of terms to describe success and failure (e.g., *there* and *uh-oh*). Some examples of this in older children that have received attention from researchers are verbs that relate to a person's intentions or other mental states (e.g., Huttenlocher et al., 1983; Johnson & Wellman, 1980; Shatz, Wellman, & Silber, 1983), cooking terms, legal terms, and other cultural creations (Keil, 1989), and verbs that describe biological processes (Carey, 1985).

To summarize, 2-year-olds draw on pragmatic information, as well as their developing understanding of situations and relations to help them interpret new verbs. At this age, there is also evidence that children use grammatical information in learning verbs: By the age of 2, there is evidence that children can use the presence of verb morphology, for example, the -ing suffix, to determine that a new word is a verb (J. Woodward & Aslin, 1991), and by the time they are 25 to 27 months there is evidence to suggest that children can use the number and position of arguments in a sentence to interpret a new verb (Hirsh-Pasek & Golinkoff, 1996; Naigles, 1990; Naigles & Kako, 1993). As Tomasello (1992a) and others have noted, children can acquire some verbs before the age of two. We do not yet know the extent to which children use grammatical cues in this very early verb learning.

Children's Use of Knowledge about Compounds and Derivational Morphology in Word Learning

Another kind of information about word meaning can come from the form of the new word itself. Clues to meaning are given by the subcomponents of compounds such as *butter knife* and derived forms such as *agreeable*. If a child understood the rules for compound formation in English and knew the functions of affixes such as *un-, -er, -ish,* and *-able,* he or she could make intelligent guesses about the meaning of derived words such as *untie, adapter, boyish,* and *agreeable* and compounds such as *lawn mower* and *pain killer.* Evidence from children's coinages of new terms suggests that even preschoolers are able to make use of this kind of information in word learning.

Clark and her colleagues (Clark, 1993; Clark & Berman, 1987; Clark, S. Gelman, & Lane, 1985) have found that a very early strategy for coining new terms is to create compounds. Children as young as 2 will do this, for example using *fixman* to describe a person who fixes things. Children's use of coined noun-noun compounds in

English honors the rule that the second word is the head noun, that is, the name for the kind of object being described, and the first, stressed word is the modifier (Clark, 1993; Clark, S. Gelman, & Lane, 1985). Clark and colleagues (1985) found that 3-year-olds also show their understanding of this rule in interpreting unfamiliar compounds. When children were asked to interpret a new compound, such as *apple knife,* they correctly indicated that it referred to a kind of knife rather than a kind of apple, and that it referred, in particular, to a kind of knife that would be used to cut apples.

After they have begun to produce and comprehend compounds, preschoolers begin to show an understanding of some aspects of derivational morphology. At around 3 or 4 years of age, children begin to use the suffix -er productively, using the term *fixer* instead of *fixman* (Clark, 1993; Clark & Cohen, 1984; Clark & Hecht, 1982). Children seem to understand the agentive -er suffix as young as 3 years of age, in that they correctly interpret unfamiliar terms such as *holder* and *puller* (used to describe both people and tools) (Clark & Hecht, 1982). Bowerman (1985) reports that at about three years of age, her daughters began using the prefix *un-* productively with verbs to talk about reversals of actions, such as *unshorten* (for lengthen), *unhang* (for taking a stocking down from the fireplace), and *unhate* (see also Clark, 1993). Many aspects of derivational morphology are acquired later in childhood (see Anglin, 1993, for a review); nonetheless, these findings suggest that even preschoolers can draw on some aspects of this cue to word meaning.

The findings of Anglin's (1993) study of vocabulary growth during grade school suggest that derivational morphology becomes an increasingly useful source of information in word learning for children in the middle to late grade school years. By testing children on a randomly selected sample of words drawn from an unabridged dictionary of English, Anglin was able to estimate the size and composition of first, third and fifth grade children's vocabularies. He found that vocabulary grew at an ever increasing rate during this period: Estimated vocabulary size increased from about 10,000 words in first grade to 19,000 in third grade, and nearly 40,000 in fifth grade. Anglin also found that between third and fifth grades, derived words (e.g., unbribable, semiliquid, foundationless) were by far the largest class of words acquired, accounting for 40% of total vocabulary by fifth grade.

For this class of words, it is possible that a child who had not yet learned the meaning of a derived word, but knew the root word, could figure out the meaning of the derived word during the comprehension test. Anglin searched the transcripts of the test sessions for signs of this "morphological problem solving," and found evidence that fifth graders used this technique for about half of the words tested. For example, one fifth grader asked to define *semi-liquid,* said the following,

> . . . like liquid is a wet substance like, but semi- could mean half, like half liquid or something. Like something could be half liquid, half solid, like maybe ice cream . . . on top of pop or something. (p. 99)

Anglin concludes that by fifth grade, and perhaps before, children have not only a vocabulary of known words, but also a set of "potentially knowable" words that they could decode based on their existing vocabulary and knowledge of derivational morphology.

CONTRAST WITHIN SEMANTIC DOMAINS

As children acquire more and more language, the linguistic context becomes a crucial source of information for acquiring new words. As we have just seen, grammatical form class can be used to limit the hypotheses children need to consider about a new word's meaning. Even so, the class of potential word meanings remains very large if grammatical form class alone were the only information. Knowing that a given word is likely to refer to a property in the case of an adjective, or an action or even a transitive action in the case of a verb, still leaves open many alternative construals of the word. But coupled with a compelling situational context, grammatical form class can lead children to effectively focus on a reasonable approximation to the meaning of a new word. We turn now to consider contrast within a semantic domain—a kind of linguistic information that has the potential to much more fully specify a word's meaning. While an adjective, for example, might specify some property or other, knowing that the adjective is a color word narrows the possibilities to a much greater extent. Often, however, it is not possible to simply state the semantic domain: In some cases, the child may not know the supernym for the domain (e.g., texture) and in some cases the domain has no readily available nontechnical supernym. In these cases an effective way to indicate the domain might be to simply contrast the new word with a familiar word from the domain. Saying that something is beige, not red could be sufficient to indicate that *beige* is a color word. This was the strategy used by Carey and Bartlett (1978) in their

seminal study of young children's learning from lexical contrast.

Carey and Bartlett (1978) were interested in establishing the limits of young children's word learning ability. In their studies, 3- and 4-year-old children were given a single exposure to a novel word. They were tested for their knowledge of the word only after a delay of one week. Lexical contrast was used to teach the novel term *chromium* for the color olive. In a naturalistic context children were asked to bring an adult the "chromium tray, not the red one," in the presence of an olive tray and a red tray. After this single exposure, about half of the children showed some learning of the term *chromium* even after a week's delay. At first sight, Carey and Bartlett's finding would seem to document the power of lexical contrast as a means of teaching young children novel words. Hearing *chromium* contrasted with *red* presumably leads children to learn, at a minimum, that *chromium* is a color word. At the same time, viewing the olive-colored tray could enable children to determine the precise color *chromium* refers to. Despite the compelling rationale and impressive findings, the conclusions about how children learn from lexical contrast are not so simple. We will now review some of the subsequent findings.

Heibeck and Markman (1987) conducted a modified replication of Carey and Bartlett with several goals in mind. First, they wanted to test the generality of children's use of lexical contrast in acquiring word meanings. The only domain Carey and Bartlett (1978) tested was color and within that domain, only a single color, olive, was taught. To begin to test how generally children can use lexical contrast, Heibeck and Markman (1987) examined three lexical domains: color, texture, and shape. Another problem in assessing the generality of Carey and Bartlett's findings is that it turned out the color olive was a reasonably salient choice for the meaning of *chromium* even for control children who had not been taught the novel word. To avoid this problem and further test the generality of the effect, Heibeck and Markman used a pool of colors, shapes, and textures, and randomly selected items from the pool as training items. Thus different children were taught different color, shape, and texture terms. Examples of novel terms taught are *beige, chartreuse, maroon,* for color; *hexagon, oval, trapezoid,* for shape; and *fleecy, granular, woven,* for texture.

The second goal of Heibeck and Markman's (1987) first study was to develop more sensitive measures of what children have learned about the novel word. One of the important goals of Carey and Bartlett's work was to track the partial or incomplete lexical entries of children. A child might learn that, say, *chromium* is a color word without knowing what color it is. To test for this partial knowledge, Carey and Bartlett (1978) used a hyponym task where they asked children straightforward questions about the domain such as "Is red a color?" catch questions such as "Is noisy a color?" and the target question, "Is chromium a color?" As it turned out, these questions were too hard for the children and provided very little information. Heibeck and Markman (1987) introduced a simpler hyponym task that proved much more successful in detecting partial knowledge. Children did not need to understand or use the supernyms for the domain such as *color, texture,* or *shape,* to show that they thought the novel word was part of that domain, but instead had to contrast the novel word with a well-known example from the semantic domain. To take texture as an example, children who learned the new texture term *granular* would be shown a smooth box and be told: "See this box? It is not granular because it is _____" with the children expected to fill in the blank. Children who knew that *granular* was a texture term would be expected to supply the known term *smooth* or *soft* as the contrast as opposed to a term from some other domain such as color, shape, size, and so forth.

Heibeck and Markman (1987) extended the age range down to include 2-year-olds as well as 3- and 4-year-olds. They also tested children's learning of the novel words about 10 minutes after the introducing event rather than using the one week delay of Carey and Bartlett (1978). The main findings of this first study are simply stated: The effectiveness of lexical contrast is not limited to the color domain. Even 2-year-olds are capable of learning the lexical domain of a new word on the basis of hearing it contrasted with a known word from a given domain. Some of the details of the study are worth considering in light of other findings. First, of the three measures of learning used—a production task, a comprehension task, and a hyponym task, by far the least sensitive was production. Production was a particularly weak measure of learning in the texture and color domains. In color for example, only 4% of the children could produce the new word compared to 64% who could successfully identify the correct color upon hearing the novel word and 89% who knew it was a color term and provided a color contrast in the hyponym task. This reinforces the concern we've expressed throughout this chapter about relying too much on children's production to infer the process of lexical acquisition. Second, there were significant differences between the domains.

Children were better able to learn a novel shape term than a novel color term, and better able to learn a novel color term than a texture term. The superiority of shape echoes the earlier discussion of the whole objects and taxonomic assumptions. Shape may be a particularly good predictor an object's category.

Although children's success in this and in Carey and Bartlett's study suggests that young children can use linguistic contrast to narrow a word's meaning, there is an alternative explanation for these results. In both studies, children saw two objects, for example two cups, that were identical except for one attribute, say color. This nonlinguistic context may have highlighted the appropriate domain sufficiently. (Note that the fact that the two cups are identical except for color does not logically limit the contrast to color. A novel term could mean something like *expensive, ugly, near,* or perhaps refer to some unseen properties such as *fragile* or *contains lead*). In this kind of a situation, the linguistic contrast could have served to simply rule out one of the objects and not necessarily to specify the dimension. But since the objects differ on one salient dimension, children may have used the situational contrast to infer that the new word referred to that dimension. In a second study, Heibeck and Markman (1987) tested this hypothesis by adding a condition where children were introduced to novel words without any lexical contrast. They would hear, for example, "Bring me the maroon one, not the other one." The results indicated that children were just as able to infer the meaning of the new word with this implicit contrast as with the explicit lexical contrast. Thus, from this work we are not justified in concluding that children are using the linguistic contrast per se to achieve the fast mapping of novel words.

To determine whether linguistic contrast is of benefit requires using a situation that does not highlight the relevant semantic domain to such a great extent as in these earlier studies. To this end, Au and Markman (1987) showed children only a single object when they introduced the novel term so there was no nonlinguistic contrast available. Moreover, each training item was a small square of a given material and color. Children could then be tested to see if they interpreted the novel term as a name for the color or the material. The two experimental conditions were

1. A Material name contrast where the novel word was contrasted with known material term (e.g., "Can you bring me the rattan square? See, this is not wood, and this is not cloth. This is rattan.").

2. A Color Name contrast where the novel word was contrasted with known color words (e.g., "Can you bring me the mauve square. See, this is not red and this is not green. This is mauve.").

As in Heibeck and Markman (1987), children were tested with comprehension and hyponym tasks. To take a concrete example of the comprehension task, a child might see a mauve rattan square as a training item. For comprehension (of *mauve* or *rattan* depending on the condition) children would see a chartreuse rattan triangle (same material) and a mauve paper triangle (same color) as choices. The results revealed that 3- and 4-year-olds could in fact make use of linguistic contrast to narrow the meaning of a novel term, but only under some favorable circumstances. In this case, children used linguistic contrast successfully to acquire a novel material term but not a color term. Hearing that a given square was chartreuse, "not red" and "not green" did nothing at all to elevate children's baseline level of treating the term as a color term. There are hints in the data that children were more likely to treat the term as material term having heard it contrasted with known color words. This surprising result is consistent with findings of Dockrell (1981) and Au (1985). Although lexical contrast was not used successfully by children to learn color words, it was used to learn material words.

In a series of papers Au (1985, 1990; Au & Laframboise, 1990; Au & Markman, 1987) has considered a number of possible explanations for why children did not benefit from lexical contrast in the domain of color. In Au and Markman (1987) we know that material was favored over color from children's baseline preference assessed in a Label Only condition. Perhaps lexical contrast works only to heighten an already favored interpretation. But Au (1990) ruled this out by using items that varied in shape as well as material. Although shape was the preferred dimension in this task, children continued to learn well from lexical contrast with known material terms. The best explanation rests on an interaction between children's use of lexical contrast and the reliance on word-learning constraints. In this case, mutual exclusivity may be preventing children from learning the color words. Most children will readily extend a known color word to cover atypical colors. When children look at the yellowish-green of chartreuse, for example, they will readily call it yellow or green. Given that they believe they already have a term to cover that color, they may resist learning another color word. Au provides two sources of evidence to support this

interpretation. In Au and Laframboise (1990), children were taught color words using lexical contrast as in the earlier studies, but in one condition the known color word was the child's term for that color rather than the unrelated color words used in the earlier work. A child who called maroon *purple,* for example, would be told that the square was maroon, not purple. If preemption by a known word was blocking children's learning of color terms, then this condition should result in improved learning. This is exactly what was found. Children as young as three could successfully learn a new color term through lexical contrast if the contrast was with the word they would have extended to the novel color.

The second source of evidence that preemption by a known term was competing with children's ability to use lexical contrast came from Au's (1990) study where children were taught novel shape and material terms. Au was able to predict how successfully children would learn the novel word from how willing children were to extend a known term to the novel shape or material. Children readily labeled a crescent shape as *moon,* for example, but had a hard time coming up with a term for a trapezoid. As predicted, lexical contrast was more effective in helping children learn *trapezoid,* than *crescent.* The correlation between the difficulty in naming the particular shape or material and children's success in learning a new name through lexical contrast was .86. Thus children's preference for keeping terms mutually exclusive effects their ability to learn from lexical contrast.

Taken together these studies of lexical contrast demonstrate that young preschoolers are capable of using lexical contrast to fast map a novel word but only under some circumstances. In particular information from lexical contrast may be suppressed when it conflicts with word-learning constraints, such as the whole object assumption (Au, 1990; Dockrell, 1981) and mutual exclusivity (Au, 1990; Au & Laframboise, 1990). Although lexical contrast might become more decisive with age and more readily override the word-learning constraints (Au & Markman, 1987), Au's (1985) work with adults reveals that the problem of coordinating information from semantic contrast and word learning constraints persists into adulthood.

CONCLUSIONS

We began by considering the remarkable success of very young word learners given the inductive problems posed by needing to determine the meaning of a new word. The research of the past decade has shed light on many of the sources of information that young children bring to bear on this problem. The evidence suggests that even before the productive naming explosion children have at least two sources of information to use in word learning: their incipient understanding of the communicative intentions of other people and a set of default assumptions about what words are likely to mean. By 16 to 18 months, there is evidence that babies check for and use cues to a speaker's intentions in learning a new word (Baldwin, 1991; Tomasello et al., 1996), as well as evidence that they honor the whole object, taxonomic and mutual exclusivity assumptions (e.g., Echols, 1991; Liittschwager & Markman, 1994; Waxman & Markow, 1995; Woodward, 1992).

By the age of 2 years, children are able to draw on some aspects of grammatical structure to inform word learning. We do not yet know precisely how much children are able to use this cue to word meaning before the age of 2, but by this age there is evidence that children can use form class cues in some contexts to identify new words, for example, as proper versus common nouns, and aspects of argument structure to distinguish between transitive and intransitive verbs. The ability to use linguistic structure in word learning is elaborated over the preschool and school aged years, as children become able to use a range of argument structures to inform verb learning, aspects of derivational morphology to guess at the meanings of new words, and lexical contrast to determine whether a new term is, for example, a color term or a shape term.

Thus, over the course of development, the range of information available to the child in word learning changes. In addition, the child's weighting of different sources of information changes with development. For example, 1-year-olds, who likely lack an understanding of form class cues, do not differentiate between adjectives and nouns on tasks which assess the taxonomic assumption (Waxman & Markow, 1995). In contrast, 2-year-olds override the taxonomic assumption in some cases when they hear a new adjective rather than a new noun (Waxman & Kosowski, 1990). However, even 4-year-olds may ignore form class information specifying that a new word is an adjective, interpreting it instead as a count noun (Hall et al., 1993). Children are most apt to follow form class to override the taxonomic assumption when they already know a category term for the object (Hall et al., 1993) or when a property is made especially salient (Smith et al., 1992). Later in development, form class alone may be sufficient to override

some of the word learning constraints (see, e.g., Landau, Smith, & Jones, 1992).

The conclusion that we draw from our review of the research is that no single source of information can account for the ways in which children learn new words. Instead, multiple cues to meaning work together, at times converging, at times conflicting. Increasingly, however, arguments are being proposed that children's knowledge of pragmatics might be able to account for their success in word learning (Baldwin, 1991, 1993a, 1993b, 1995; Baldwin et al., 1996; Baldwin & Moses, 1994; Clark, 1987, 1990, 1995; Tomasello, 1992b, 1995a, 1995b; Tomasello & Akhtar, 1995; Tomasello et al., 1993; Tomasello et al., 1996). In their strongest form, these arguments hold that constraints of any kind are not necessary given both adults' care at using language in ways that children cannot misinterpret and young children's facility at deciphering adults' communicative intent. L. Bloom (1993) argues that studies of lexical development have routinely neglected the importance of the social context in which language is learned and the role adults play in providing utterances they know their children can understand. Bloom cites Nelson (1988) who argues:

> The typical way children acquire words in their first language is almost completely the reverse of the Quinean paradigm . . . Children do not try to guess what it is that the adult intends to refer to; rather they have certain conceptions of those aspects of the world they find interesting and, in successful cases of word acquisition it is the adult [at least in western middle-class societies] who guesses what the child is focused on and supplies an appropriate word. (p. 240)

Bloom's (1993) Principle of Relevance assumes a similar position though one that places greater emphasis on the role of the child:

> In the typical word-leaning situation, infant and adult exploit their mutual signals of ostensive-inferential communication to share a focus of attention and the most likely candidate for what a word means . . . But the chances are that the intentional states of both child and adult will have been expressed ostensively, so that the target of translation is conspicuous. Words are learned when they are relevant to what the child has in mind. (pp. 86–87)

Although to some extent both of these positions may be true, they are overstating the case and basing much of the explanatory work of their theories on unspecified mechanisms that somehow ensure both the adult and child are attending to the same thing. The claims are overstated because we have already shown in the work on word learning constraints that children will learn words to refer to aspects of a situation that are *not* the most salient to them. Take the early work of Markman and Hutchinson (1984) which showed that in the absence of a label children sort pictures according to thematic relations but hearing a novel label causes them to sort taxonomically. The point of that demonstration and the work that followed from it is that children will extend words taxonomically even under conditions where the children would otherwise focus more on the thematic relations. As another example, take Woodward's (1992) test of the whole object assumption where babies viewed a static object and a dynamic display. If children operated according to some principle that assumed that adults will label what children are most likely to find salient, then they should have assumed the label would refer to the dynamic display. Contrary to this and in support of the whole object assumption, children looked more at the object, not the dynamic display, when they heard a novel word. As another example, take the Markman and Wasow (in preparation) study of the learning of part terms. Despite adult gestures outlining the parts of objects, 2-year-olds often treated the novel term as referring to the whole object. When these gestures were boosted by the mutual exclusivity assumption, however, these young children did override the whole object assumption and learn part terms. In these studies and many others designed to document the role of word learning constraints, there was always an empirical demonstration that one aspect of the situation was more salient to children, but upon hearing a novel word children would map that word onto a different less salient or interesting aspect of the situation. This is not explained by invoking adults tailoring their labels to fit what the children are focused on nor to claims that "words are learned when they are relevant to what the child has in mind." Hearing the words *changes* what the child attends to as predicted by the word learning constraints.

Adults often succeed in anticipating the focus of attention of children and in adjusting their input accordingly. And, the studies of Baldwin and Tomasello and their colleagues document that babies and young children monitor and use cues to the referential intent of their speakers to acquire words. But neither of these facts can be taken as proof that lexical constraints are not necessary nor do they explain the large amount of experimental evidence that early word learning is a constrained form of learning.

A second line of argument has been to acknowledge that early word learning is constrained by biases that more or less conform to the whole object and mutual exclusivity assumptions or something similar, but that these are pragmatic, not lexical, constraints. This is an interesting and certainly logically coherent position. For example, as we discussed earlier, the principle of contrast, a pragmatic constraint (Clark, 1987, 1988, 1990; Gathercole, 1987, 1989) can account for some of the findings explained by mutual exclusivity. To date, very few empirical tests exist that could distinguish the hypotheses. Moreover, as the scope of what counts as pragmatic expands, as in Clark (1995), it becomes harder to distinguish the two accounts. Based on the evidence we have so far, our best guess is that there are often pragmatic biases that parallel lexical ones. In the case just described, there may be both a lexical constraint that biases children against accepting two labels for the same object and a pragmatic constraint that if the speaker had meant to refer to a given object he or she would have used the best known label. Take reference as another example. Proponents of the pragmatic view claim that words don't refer, people do. But surely both do. On the one hand, it is by assuming the conventional referents of words that listeners are able to infer a speaker's intent in using a given word on a given occasion. And conversely, it is by inferring a speaker's intent that listeners may be able to infer the intended meaning and referent of a novel word. Following Markman (1992) we are arguing that pragmatic and lexical constraints will often provide redundant sources of information thereby helping a child converge on a given hypothesis about the meaning of a novel term.

One benefit of having multiple cues to meaning is that it allows the learner to be flexible. We have highlighted many examples of this throughout the chapter, for example, cases in which pragmatic or grammatical cues override the interpretation provided by a default assumption such as the whole object constraint or mutual exclusivity. In earlier work (Woodward & Markman, 1991), we likened these findings to findings from ethologists that document the benefit of default cues in animals' learning to solve problems such as navigation between home and a food source.

Ethologists have also documented many cases where multiple mechanisms converge helping animals solve important problems. In word learning as well, multiple cues will often converge, providing redundant, rather than conflicting interpretations. For example, pragmatic factors as well as mutual exclusivity may support a child's interpretation of a new label as the name for an unfamiliar object rather than a familiar one. Or a child might be introduced to the verb *dance* in a context in which grammatical cues, knowledge of the situation, and pragmatic cues all point to the correct interpretation. Studies of word learning in the lab are valuable in that they can help us isolate the sources of information that children draw on in learning new words. However, they do not allow us to see the ways in which these cues converge in natural word learning contexts.

Domains that involve social learning require not only redundancy but some degree of coordination among the mechanisms used by the partners in the social exchange (Fernald, 1992). Threat or courtship displays by one member of a species can be effective only if they have the desired effect on the partners in the interaction. Coordination of mechanisms is needed between males and females during courtship, between caregivers and offspring, and between adults as providers and children as recipients of information.

Word learning, then, requires some coordination between adults as sources of information and children as learners. Coordination between parental input such as labeling strategies and children's word-learning biases should be expected. Finding that adults often label objects, for example, should not be taken as evidence against the existence of a whole object assumption. When parents aim to teach words other than object labels, we predict that the most effective input will provide support for overriding the whole object assumption, using some of the other cues that children have access to. Thinking of word learning from the perspective of the ethology of learning would lead us to expect both redundancy and coordination of word learning biases and other sources of information such as parental input and pragmatics.

ACKNOWLEDGMENTS

We thank Robert Siegler, Deanna Kuhn, and Lois Bloom for their helpful comments on an earlier draft of this chapter.

REFERENCES

Akhtar, N., & Tomasello, M. (1996). Two-year-olds learn words for absent objects and actions. *British Journal of Developmental Psychology, 14,* 79–93.

Anglin, J. M. (1977). *Word, object and conceptual development.* New York: Norton.

Anglin, J. M. (1993). Vocabulary development: A morphological analysis. *Monographs of the Society for Research in Child Development, 58*(10, Serial No. 238).

Au, T. K. (1985). Children's word learning strategies. *Papers and Reports on Child Language Development, 24,* 22–29.

Au, T. K. (1990). Children's use of information in word learning. *Journal of Child Language, 17,* 393–416.

Au, T. K., Dapretto, M., & Song, Y. (1994). Input vs. constraints: Early word acquisition in Korean and English. *Journal of Memory and Language, 33,* 567–582.

Au, T. K., & Glusman, M. (1990). The principle of mutual exclusivity in word learning: To honor or not to honor? *Child Development, 61,* 1474–1490.

Au, T. K., & Laframboise, D. E. (1990). Acquiring color names via linguistic contrast: The influence of contrasting terms. *Child Development, 61,* 1808–1823.

Au, T. K., & Markman, E. M. (1987). Acquiring word meanings via linguistic contrast. *Cognitive Development, 2,* 217–236.

Baillargeon, R. (1993). The object concept revisited: New directions in the investigation of infants' physical knowledge. In C. E. Granrud (Ed.), *Visual perception and cognition in infancy: Carnegie Mellon Symposia on Cognition* (pp. 265–316). Hillsdale, NJ: Erlbaum.

Baldwin, D. A. (1989). Priorities in children's expectations about label reference: Form over color. *Child Development, 60,* 1291–1306.

Baldwin, D. A. (1991). Infants' contribution to the achievement of joint reference. *Child Development, 62,* 875–890.

Baldwin, D. A. (1992). Clarifying the role of shape in children's taxonomic assumption. *Journal of Experimental Child Psychology, 54,* 392–416.

Baldwin, D. A. (1993a). Early referential understanding: Infants' ability to recognize referential acts for what they are. *Developmental Psychology, 29,* 832–843.

Baldwin, D. A. (1993b). Infants' ability to consult the speaker for clues to word meaning. *Journal of Child Language, 20,* 395–418.

Baldwin, D. A. (1995). Understanding the link between joint attention and language. In C. Moore & P. Dunham (Eds.), *Joint attention: It's origins and role in development* (pp. 131–158). Hillsdale, NJ: Erlbaum.

Baldwin, D. A., Markman, E. M., Bill, B., Desjardins, R. N., Irwin, R. N., & Tidball, G. (1996). Infants' reliance on a social criterion for establishing word-object relations. *Child Development, 67,* 3135–3153.

Baldwin, D. A., & Moses, L. M. (1994). Early understanding of referential intent and attentional focus: Evidence from language and emotion. In C. Lewis & P. Mitchell (Eds.), *Origins of an understanding of mind* (pp. 133–156). Hillsdale, NJ: Erlbaum.

Baldwin, D. A., & Moses, L. M. (1996). The ontogeny of social information gathering. *Child Development, 67,* 1915–1934.

Baldwin, D. A., Moses, L. M., & Tidball, G. (in preparation). *Social referencing versus social receptiveness: Evidence for referential understanding in the emotions domain at 12 and 18 months.* Manuscript in preparation.

Banigan, R. L., & Mervis, C. B. (1988). Role of adult input in young children's category evolution: 2. An experimental study. *Journal of Child Language, 15,* 493–504.

Barrett, M. D. (1986). Early semantic representations and early word usage. In S. A. Kuczaj & M. D. Barrett (Eds.), *The development of word meaning* (pp. 39–68). New York: Springer-Verlag.

Bates, E., Benigni, L., Bretherton, I., Camaioni, L., & Volterra, V. (1979). *The emergence of symbols: Cognition and communication in infancy.* New York: Academic Press.

Bauer, P. J., & Mandler, J. M. (1989). Taxonomies and triads: Conceptual organization in one- and two-year-olds. *Cognitive Psychology, 21,* 156–184.

Becker, A. H., & Ward, T. B. (1991). Children's use of shape in extending novel labels to animate objects: Identity versus postural change. *Cognitive Development, 6,* 3–16.

Behrend, D. A. (1990a). Constraints and development: A reply to Nelson, 1988. *Cognitive Development, 5,* 313–330.

Behrend, D. A. (1990b). The development of verb concepts: Children's use of verbs to label familiar and novel events. *Child Development, 61,* 681–696.

Behrend, D. A. (1995). Processes involved in the initial mapping of verb meanings. In M. Tomasello & W. E. Merriman (Eds.), *Beyond names for things: Young children's acquisition of verbs* (pp. 251–273). Hillsdale, NJ: Erlbaum.

Behrend, D. A., Harris, L. L., & Cartwright, K. (1995). Morphological cues to verb meaning: Verb inflections and the initial mapping of verb meanings. *Journal of Child Language, 22,* 89–106.

Benedict, H. (1979). Early lexical development: Comprehension and production. *Journal of Child Language, 6,* 183–200.

Benson, N. J., & Anglin, J. M. (1987). The child's knowledge of English kin terms. *First Language, 7,* 41–66.

Blewitt, P. (1983). Dog versus collie: Vocabulary in speech to young children. *Developmental Psychology, 19,* 602–609.

Bloom, L. (1973). *One word at a time: The use of single word utterances before syntax.* The Hague: Mouton.

Bloom, L. (1993). *The transition from infancy to language: Acquiring the power of expression.* Cambridge, England: Cambridge University Press.

Bloom, L., Lifter, K., & Broughton, J. (1985). The convergence of early cognition and language in the second year of life: Problems in conceptualization and measurement. In M. Barrett (Ed.), *Children's one-word speech* (pp. 149–180). New York: Wiley.

Bloom, L., Tinker, E., & Margulis, C. (1993). The words children learn: Evidence against a noun bias in early vocabularies. *Cognitive Development, 8,* 431–450.

Bloom, P. (1994). Possible names: The role of syntax-semantics mappings in the acquisition of nominals. *Lingua, 92,* 297–329.

Bornstein, M. H., Kessen, W., & Weiskopf, S. (1976). The categories of hue in infancy. *Science, 191,* 201–207.

Bowerman, M. (1974). Learning the structure of causative verbs: A study in the relationship of cognitive, semantic and syntactic development. *Papers and Reports on Child Language Development, 8,* 142–178.

Bowerman, M. (1977). The acquisition of rules governing "possible lexical items": Evidence from spontaneous speech errors. *Papers and Reports on Child Language Development, 13,* 148–158.

Bowerman, M. (1978). Systematizing semantic knowledge: Changes over time in the child's organization of meaning. *Child Development, 49,* 977–987.

Bowerman, M. (1985). Reorganizational processes in lexical and syntactic development. In E. Wanner & L. R. Gleitman (Eds.), *Language acquisition: The state of the art* (pp. 319–346). Cambridge, England: Cambridge University Press.

Bowerman, M. (1996). Learning how to structure space for language: A crosslinguistic perspective. In P. Bloom, M. A. Peterson, L. Nadel, & M. F. Garrett (Eds.), *Language and space* (pp. 385–436). Cambridge, MA: MIT Press.

Bretherton, I. (1992). The origins of attachment theory: John Bowlby to Mary Ainsworth. *Development Psychology, 28,* 759–775.

Bretherton, I., & Beeghly, M. (1982). Talking about internal states: The acquisition of an explicit theory of mind. *Developmental Psychology, 18,* 906–921.

Brice-Heath, S. (1983). *Ways with words: Language, life and work in communities and classrooms.* Cambridge, England: Cambridge University Press.

Bridges, A. (1986). Actions and things: What adults talk about to 1-year-olds. In S. Kuczaj & M. Barrett (Eds.), *The development of word meaning* (pp. 225–255). Berlin: Springer-Verlag.

Brown, R. W. (1957). Linguistic determinism and the parts of speech. *Journal of Abnormal and Social Psychology, 55,* 1–5.

Bruner, J. (1978). From communication to language: A psychological perspective. In I. Markova (Ed.), *The social context of language.* New York: Wiley.

Callanan, M. A. (1985). How parents label objects for young children. *Child Development, 56,* 508–523.

Callanan, M. A. (1989). Development of object categories and inclusion relations: Preschoolers' hypotheses about word meanings. *Developmental Psychology, 25,* 207–216.

Campos, J. J. (1983). The importance of affective communication in social referencing: A commentary on Feinman. *Merrill-Palmer Quarterly, 29,* 83–87.

Carey, S. (1978). The child as word learner. In M. Halle, J. Bresnan, & G. A. Miller (Eds.), *Linguistic theory and psychological reality.* Cambridge, MA: MIT Press.

Carey, S. (1985). *Conceptual change in childhood.* Cambridge, MA: MIT Press.

Carey, S., & Bartlett, E. (1978). Acquiring a single new word. *Papers and Reports on Child Language Development, 15,* 17–29.

Choi, S., & Bowerman, M. (1991). Learning to express motion events in English and Korean: The influence of language specific lexicalization patterns. *Cognition, 41,* 83–121.

Choi, S., & Gopnik, A. (1995). Early acquisition of verbs in Korean: A crosslinguistic study. *Journal of Child Language, 22,* 497–529.

Clark, E. V. (1983). Meanings and concepts. In J. H. Flavell & E. M. Markman (Eds.), *Handbook of child psychology: Vol. 3. Cognitive development* (pp. 787–840). New York: Wiley.

Clark, E. V. (1987). The principle of contrast: A constraint on acquisition. In B. MacWhinney (Ed.), *Mechanisms of language acquisition: The 20th annual Carnegie Symposium on Cognition* (pp. 1–34). Hillsdale, NJ: Erlbaum.

Clark, E. V. (1988). On the logic of contrast. *Journal of Child Language, 15,* 317–335.

Clark, E. V. (1990). On the pragmatics of contrast. *Journal of Child Language, 17,* 417–431.

Clark, E. V. (1993). *The lexicon in acquisition.* Cambridge, England: Cambridge University Press.

Clark, E. V. (1995). *Pragmatics and lexical acquisition: Discussant, Symposium on "Constructing meanings in context: Constraints and pragmatics in semantic development.* Symposium at the biennial meetings of the Society for Research in Child Development, Indianapolis, IN.

Clark, E. V., & Berman, R. A. (1987). Types of linguistic knowledge: Interpreting and producing compound nouns. *Journal of Child Language, 14,* 547–567.

Clark, E. V., & Cohen, S. R. (1984). Productivity and memory for newly formed words. *Journal of Child Language, 11,* 611–625.

Clark, E. V., Gelman, S. A., & Lane, N. M. (1985). Compound nouns and category structure in young children. *Child Development, 56,* 84–94.

Clark, E. V., & Hecht, B. F. (1982). Learning to coin agent and instrument nouns. *Cognition, 12,* 1–24.

Clark, E. V., & Hecht, B. F. (1983). Comprehension, production, and language acquisition. *Annual Review of Psychology, 34,* 325–349.

Cohen, L., & Younger, B. (1981). *Perceptual categorization in the infant.* Paper presented at the eleventh annual Jean Piaget Symposium, Philadelphia.

Collis, G. M. (1977). Visual co-orientation and maternal speech. In H. R. Schaffer (Ed.), *Studies in mother-infant interaction.* London: Academic Press.

D'Entremont, B., & Dunham, P. J. (1992). The noun-category bias phenomenon in 3-year-olds: Taxonomic constraint or translation? *Cognitive Development, 7,* 47–62.

Dickinson, D. K. (1988). Learning names for materials: Factors limiting and constraining hypotheses about word meaning. *Cognitive Development, 3,* 15–35.

Dockrell, J. (1981). *The child's acquisition of unfamiliar words: An experimental study.* Doctoral dissertation, University of Stirling, Scotland.

Dockrell, J., & Campbell, R. (1986). Lexical acquisition strategies in the preschool child. In S. Kuczaj & M. Barrett (Eds.), *The development of word meaning* (pp. 121–154). Berlin: Springer-Verlag.

Dore, J. (1978). Conditions for the acquisition of speech acts. In I. Markova (Ed.), *The social context of language* (pp. 87–111). New York: Wiley.

Dromi, E. (1986). The one-word period as a stage in language development: Quantitative and qualitative accounts. In I. Levin (Ed.), *Stage and structure: Reopening the debate* (pp. 220–245). Norwood, NJ: ABLEX.

Dromi, E. (1987). *Early lexical development.* Cambridge, England: Cambridge University Press.

Echols, C. (1991). *Infants' attention to objects and consistency in linguistic and non-linguistic contexts.* Paper presented at the biennial meetings of the Society for Research in Child Development, Seattle, WA.

Echols, C. (1993). *Attentional predispositions and linguistic sensitivity in the acquisition of object words.* Paper presented at the biennial meetings of the Society for Research in Child Development, New Orleans, LA.

Eimas, P., Siqueland, S., Jusczyk, P., & Vigorito, J. (1971). Speech perception in infants. *Science, 171,* 303–306.

Fernald, A. (1992). Human maternal vocalizations to infants as biologically relevant signals: An evolutionary perspective. In J. H. Barkow, L. Cosmides, & J. Tooby (Eds.), *The adapted mind: Evolutionary psychology and the generation of culture* (pp. 391–428). Oxford, England: Oxford University Press.

Fernald, A., & Morikawa, H. (1993). Common themes and cultural variation in Japanese and American mothers' speech to infants. *Child Development, 64,* 637–656.

Fisher, C. (1994). Structure and meaning in the verb lexicon: Input for a syntax-aided verb learning procedure. *Language and Cognitive Processes, 9,* 473–917.

Fisher, C. (1996). Structural limits on verb mapping: The role of analogy in children's interpretation of sentences. *Cognitive Psychology, 31,* 41–81.

Fisher, C., Gleitman, H., & Gleitman, L. (1991). On the semantic content of subcategorization frames. *Cognitive Psychology, 23,* 331–392.

Fisher, C., Hall, D. G., Rakowitz, S., & Gleitman, L. (1994). When it is better to receive than to give: Syntactic and conceptual constraints on vocabulary growth. *Lingua, 92,* 333–375.

Forbes, J. N., & Farrar, M. J. (1993). Children's initial assumptions about the meaning of novel motion verbs: Biased and conservative? *Cognitive Development, 8,* 273–290.

Forbes, J. N., Poulin-Dubois, D., & Shulman, J. (1995). *Event specificity in 20-month-olds' extensions of familiar action verbs.* Paper presented at the biennial meetings of the Society for Research in Child Development, Indianapolis, IN.

Fremgen, A., & Fay, D. (1980). Overextensions in production and comprehension: A methodological clarification. *Journal of Child Language, 7,* 205–211.

Gathercole, V. C. (1987). The contrastive hypothesis for the acquisition of word meaning: A reconsideration of the theory. *Journal of Child Language, 14,* 493–532.

Gathercole, V. C. (1989). Contrast: A semantic constraint? *Journal of Child Language, 16,* 685–702.

Geach, P. (1968). Subject and predicate. In A. P. Martinich (Ed.), *The philosophy of language* (pp. 189–199). New York: Oxford University Press.

Gelman, R. (1990). First principles organize attention to and learning about relevant data: Number and the animate/inanimate distinction as examples. *Cognitive Science, 14,* 79–106.

Gelman, S. A. (1988). The development of induction within natural kind and artifact categories. *Cognitive Psychology, 20,* 65–95.

Gelman, S. A., & Coley, J. D. (1991). The importance of knowing a dodo is a bird: Categories and inferences in 2-year-old children. *Developmental Psychology, 26,* 796–804.

Gelman, S. A., & Markman, E. M. (1986). Categories and induction in young children. *Cognition, 23,* 183–209.

Gelman, S. A., & Markman, E. M. (1987). Young children's inductions from natural kinds: The role of categories and appearances. *Child Development, 58,* 1532–1541.

Gelman, S. A., & Taylor, M. (1984). How two-year-old children interpret proper and common names for unfamiliar objects. *Child Development, 55,* 1535–1540.

Gentner, D. (1978a). On relational meaning: The acquisition of verb meaning. *Child Development, 49,* 988–998.

Gentner, D. (1978b). What looks like a jiggy but acts like a zimbo? A study of early word meaning using artificial objects. *Papers and Reports on Child Language Development, 15,* 1–6.

Gentner, D. (1981). Some interesting differences between verbs and nouns. *Cognition and Brain Theory, 4,* 161–178.

Gentner, D. (1982). Why nouns are learned before verbs: Linguistic relativity versus natural partitioning. In S. Kuczaj (Ed.), *Language development: Language, cognition and culture.* Hillsdale, NJ: Erlbaum.

Gleitman, L. (1990). The structural sources of verb meanings. *Language Acquisition, 1,* 3–55.

Goldfield, B. A. (1993). Noun bias in maternal speech to one-year-olds. *Journal of Child Language, 20,* 85–99.

Goldfield, B. A., & Reznick, J. S. (1990). Early lexical acquisition: Rate, content and the vocabulary spurt. *Journal of Child Language, 17,* 171–183.

Goldin-Meadow, S., Seligman, M., & Gelman, R. (1976). Language in the two-year-old. *Cognition, 4,* 189–202.

Golinkoff, R. M. (1986). I beg your pardon? The preverbal negotiation of failed messages. *Journal of Child Language, 13,* 455–476.

Golinkoff, R. M., Hirsh-Pasek, K., Bailey, L. M., & Wenger, N. R. (1992). Young children and adults use lexical principles to learn new nouns. *Developmental Psychology, 28,* 99–108.

Golinkoff, R. M., Hirsh-Pasek, K., Cauley, K. M., & Gordon, L. (1987). The eyes have it: Lexical and syntactic comprehension in a new paradigm. *Journal of Child Language, 14,* 23–45.

Golinkoff, R. M., Hirsh-Pasek, K., Mervis, C. B., Frawley, W. B., & Parillo, M. (1995). Lexical principles can be extended to the acquisition of verbs. In M. Tomasello & W. E. Merriman (Eds.), *Beyond names for things: Young children's acquisition of verbs* (pp. 185–222). Hillsdale, NJ: Erlbaum.

Golinkoff, R. M., Kenealy, L., & Hirsh-Pasek, K. (1993). *Object scope: Labels promote attention to whole objects.* Unpublished manuscript.

Golinkoff, R. M., Mervis, C. B., & Hirsh-Pasek, K. (1994). Early object labels: The case for a developmental lexical principles framework. *Journal of Child Language, 21,* 125–155.

Golinkoff, R. M., Shuff-Bailey, M., Olguin, R., & Ruan, W. (1995). Young children extend novel words at the basic level: Evidence for the principle of categorical scope. *Developmental Psychology, 31,* 494–507.

Goodman, N. (1955). *Fact, fiction and forecast.* Cambridge, MA: Harvard University Press.

Gopnik, A., & Choi, S. (1990). Do linguistic differences lead to cognitive differences? A cross-linguistic study of semantic and cognitive development. *First Language, 10,* 199–215.

Gopnik, A., & Meltzoff, A. N. (1986). Words, plans, things and locations: Interactions between semantic and cognitive development in the one-word stage. In S. Kuczaj & M. Barrett (Eds.), *The development of word meaning* (pp. 199–223). New York: Springer-Verlag.

Gropen, J., Pinker, S., Hollander, M., & Goldberg, R. (1991). Syntax and semantics in the acquisition of locative verbs. *Journal of Child Language, 18,* 115–151.

Gunnar, M. R., & Stone, C. (1984). The effects of positive maternal affect on infant responses to pleasant, ambiguous and fear-provoking toys. *Child Development, 55,* 1231–1236.

Hall, D. G. (1991). Acquiring proper names for familiar and unfamiliar objects: Two-year-olds' word learning biases. *Child Development, 62,* 1142–1154.

Hall, D. G. (1993). Basic-level individuals. *Cognition, 48,* 199–221.

Hall, D. G. (1994a). How mothers teach basic level and situation specific count nouns. *Journal of Child Language, 21,* 391–414.

Hall, D. G. (1994b). Semantic constraints on word learning: Proper names and adjectives. *Child Development, 65,* 1299–1317.

Hall, D. G., & Waxman, S. R. (1993). Assumptions about word meaning: Individuation and basic-level kinds. *Child Development, 64,* 1550–1570.

Hall, D. G., Waxman, S. R., & Hurwitz, W. M. (1993). How two- and four-year-old children interpret adjectives and count nouns. *Child Development, 64,* 1651–1664.

Harris, M., Barrett, M., Jones, D., & Brookes, S. (1988). Linguistic input and early word meaning. *Journal of Child Language, 15,* 77–94.

Heibeck, T. H., & Markman, E. M. (1987). Word learning in children: An examination of fast mapping. *Child Development, 58,* 1021–1034.

Hirsh-Pasek, K., & Golinkoff, R. M. (1993). Skeletal supports for grammatical learning: What infants bring to the language learning task. In C. K. R. Collier & L. P. Lipsitt (Eds.), *Advances in infancy research* (Vol. 8, pp. 299–338). Norwood, NJ: ABLEX.

Hirsh-Pasek, K., & Golinkoff, R. M. (1996). *The origins of grammar: Evidence from early language comprehension.* Cambridge, MA: MIT Press.

Hoek, D., Ingram, D., & Gibson, D. (1986). Some possible causes of children's early word overextensions. *Journal of Child Language, 13,* 477–494.

Huntley-Fenner, G., & Carey, S. (1995). *Individuation of objects and portions of nonsolid substances: A pattern of success (objects) and failure (substances).* Paper presented at the biennial meetings of the Society for Research in Child Development, Indianapolis, IN.

Hutchinson, J. E. (1986). *Children's sensitivity to the contrastive use of object category terms.* Paper presented at the Stanford Child Language Research Forum, Stanford, CA.

Huttenlocher, J. (1974). The origins of language comprehension. In R. Solso (Ed.), *Theories in cognitive psychology* (pp. 331–368). Hillsdale, NJ: Erlbaum.

Huttenlocher, J., Haight, W., Bryk, A., Seltzer, M., & Lyons, T. (1991). Early vocabulary growth: Relation to language input and gender. *Development Psychology, 27,* 236–248.

Huttenlocher, J., & Smiley, P. (1987). Early word meanings: The case of object names. *Cognitive Psychology, 19,* 63–89.

Huttenlocher, J., Smiley, P., & Charney, R. (1983). Emergence of action categories in the child: Evidence from verb meanings. *Psychological Review, 90,* 72–93.

Imai, M., & Gentner, D. (1993). *Linguistic relativity vs. universal ontology: Cross-linguistic studies of the object/substance distinction.* Paper presented at the Chicago Linguistic Society, Chicago.

Imai, M., Gentner, D., & Uchida, N. (1994). Children's theories of word meaning: The role of shape similarity in early acquisition. *Cognitive Development, 9,* 45–75.

Inhelder, B., & Piaget, J. (1964). *The early growth of logic in the child.* New York: Norton.

Johnson, C. N., & Wellman, H. M. (1980). Children's developing understanding of mental verbs: Remember, know and guess. *Child Development, 51,* 1095–1102.

Jones, S. S., Smith, L. B., & Landau, B. (1991). Object properties and knowledge in early lexical learning. *Child Development, 62,* 499–516.

Katz, N., Baker, E., & Macnamara, J. (1974). What's in a name? A study of how children learn common and proper names. *Child Development, 45,* 469–473.

Keil, F. C. (1989). *Concepts, kinds and cognitive development.* Cambridge, MA: MIT Press.

Kemler Nelson, D. G. (1995). Principle-based inferences in young children's categorization: Revisiting the impact of function on the naming of artifacts. *Cognitive Development, 10,* 347–380.

Landau, B., Jones, S., & Smith, L. (1992). Perception, ontology and naming in young children: Commentary on Soja, Carey & Spelke. *Cognition, 43,* 85–91.

Landau, B., Smith, L. B., & Jones, S. S. (1988). The importance of shape in early lexical learning. *Cognitive Development, 3,* 299–321.

Landau, B., Smith, L. B., & Jones, S. (1992). Syntactic context and the shape bias in children's and adults' lexical learning. *Journal of Memory and Language, 31,* 807–825.

Lederer, A., Gleitman, H., & Gleitman, L. (1995). Verbs of a feather flock together: Semantic information in the structure of maternal speech. In M. Tomasello & W. E. Merriman (Eds.), *Beyond names for things: Young children's acquisition of verbs* (pp. 277–297). Hillsdale, NJ: Erlbaum.

Leslie, A. M., & Keeble, S. (1987). Do six-month-olds perceive causality? *Cognition, 25,* 265–288.

Lifter, K., & Bloom, L. (1989). Object knowledge and the emergence of language. *Infant Behavior and Development, 12,* 395–423.

Liittschwager, J. C. (1994). *Children's reasoning about identity across transformations.* Doctoral dissertation, Stanford University, Stanford, CA.

Liittschwager, J. C., & Markman, E. M. (1993). *Young children's acquisition of proper versus common nouns.* Paper presented at the biennial meetings of the Society for Research in Child Development, New Orleans, LA.

Liittschwager, J. C., & Markman, E. M. (1994). Sixteen and 24-month-olds' use of mutual exclusivity as a default assumption in second label learning. *Developmental Psychology, 30,* 955–968.

Macnamara, J. (1982). *Names for things.* Cambridge, MA: MIT Press.

Macnamara, J. (1986). *A border dispute: The place of logic in psychology.* Cambridge, MA: MIT Press.

MacWhinney, B. (1989). Competition and lexical categorization. In R. Corrigan, F. Eckman, & M. Noonan (Eds.), *Linguistic categorization* (pp. 195–241). Amsterdam, The Netherlands: John Benjamin.

Mandler, J. M. (1992). How to build a baby: 2. Conceptual primitives. *Psychological Review, 99,* 587–604.

Mandler, J. M. (1996). Preverbal representation and language. In P. Bloom, M. A. Peterson, L. Nadel, & M. F. Garrett (Eds.), *Language and space* (pp. 365–384). Cambridge, MA: MIT Press.

Mandler, J. M., & Bauer, P. J. (1988). The cradle of categorization: Is the basic-level basic? *Cognitive Development, 3,* 247–264.

Mandler, J. M., Bauer, P. J., & McDonough, L. (1991). Separating the sheep from the goats: Differentiating global categories. *Cognitive Psychology, 23,* 263–298.

Mandler, J. M., Fivush, R., & Reznick, J. (1987). The development of contextual categories. *Cognitive Development, 2,* 339–354.

Mandler, J. M., & McDonough, L. (1993). Concept formation in infancy. *Cognitive Development, 8,* 291–318.

Maratsos, M. P. (1983). Some current issues in the study of the acquisition of grammar. In J. H. Flavell & E. M. Markman (Eds.), *Handbook of child psychology: Vol. 3. Cognitive development* (pp. 707–786). New York: Wiley.

Maratsos, M. P. (1991). How the acquisition of nouns may be different from that of verbs. In N. A. Krasnegor, D. M. Rumbaugh, R. L. Schiefelbusch, & M. Studdert-Kennedy (Eds.), *Biological and behavioral determinants of language acquisition* (pp. 67–88). Hillsdale, NJ: Erlbaum.

Maratsos, M. P., & Deak, G. (1995). Hedgehogs, foxes, and the acquisition of verb meaning. In M. Tomasello & W. E. Merriman (Eds.), *Beyond names for things: Young children's acquisition of verbs* (pp. 377–404). Hillsdale, NJ: Erlbaum.

Markman, E. M. (1989). *Categorization and naming in children: Problems of induction.* Cambridge, MA: MIT Press.

Markman, E. M. (1990). Constraints children place on word meanings. *Cognitive Science, 14,* 57–78.

Markman, E. M. (1992). Constraints on word learning: Speculations about their nature, origins and domain specificity. In M. R. Gunnar & M. P. Maratsos (Eds.), *Modularity and constraints in language and cognition: The Minnesota Symposium on Child Psychology* (pp. 59–101). Hillsdale, NJ: Erlbaum.

Markman, E. M. (1994). Constraints on word meaning in early language acquisition. *Lingua, 92,* 199–227.

Markman, E. M., & Hutchinson, J. (1984). Children's sensitivity to constraints on word meaning: Taxonomic versus thematic relations. *Cognitive Psychology, 16,* 1–27.

Markman, E. M., & Wachtel, G. F. (1988). Children's use of mutual exclusivity to constrain the meanings of words. *Cognitive Psychology, 20,* 121–157.

Markman, E. M., & Wasow, J. (in preparation). *Evidence for very young children's use of mutual exclusivity to guide their interpretations of novel terms.* Manuscript in preparation.

Masur, E. (1982). Mothers' responses to infants' object-related gestures: Influences on lexical development. *Journal of Child Language, 9,* 23–30.

McShane, J. (1979). The development of naming. *Linguistics, 17,* 79–95.

Meltzoff, A. M. (1995). Understanding the intentions of others: Re-enactments of intended acts by 18-month-old children. *Developmental Psychology, 31,* 838–850.

Merriman, W. E., & Bowman, L. L. (1989). The mutual exclusivity bias in children's word learning. *Monographs of the Society for Research in Child Development, 54* (Serial No. 220).

Merriman, W. E., Marazita, J., & Jarvis, L. (1995). Children's disposition to map new words onto new referents. In M. Tomasello & W. E. Merriman (Eds.), *Beyond names for things: Young children's acquisition of verbs* (pp. 147–184). Hillsdale, NJ: Erlbaum.

Merriman, W. E., & Schuster, J. M. (1991). Young children's disambiguation of object name reference. *Child Development, 62,* 1288–1301.

Merriman, W. E., Scott, P. D., & Marazita, J. (1993). An appearance-function shift in children's object naming. *Journal of Child Language, 20,* 101–118.

Mervis, C. B. (1987). Child-basic object categories and early lexical development. In U. Neisser (Ed.), *Concepts and conceptual development: Ecological and intellectual factors in categorization* (pp. 201–233). Cambridge, MA: Cambridge University Press.

Mervis, C. B., & Bertrand, J. (1993). Acquisition of early object labels. In A. P. Kaiser & D. B. Gray (Eds.), *Enhancing children's communication: Research foundations for intervention* (pp. 287–316). Baltimore: Brooks.

Mervis, C. B., & Bertrand, J. (1994). Acquisition of the novel name nameless category (N3C) principle. *Child Development, 65,* 1646–1663.

Mervis, C. B., & Canada, K. (1983). On the existence of competence errors in early comprehension: A reply to Fremgen & Fray and Chapman & Thompson. *Journal of Child Language, 17,* 357–374.

Mervis, C. B., Golinkoff, R. M., & Bertrand, J. (1994). Two-year-olds readily learn multiple labels for the same basic-level kind. *Child Development, 65,* 1163–1177.

Mervis, C. B., & Long, L. (1987). *Words refer to whole objects: Young children's interpretation of the referent of a novel word.* Paper presented at the biennial meetings of the Society for Research in Child Development, Baltimore.

Messer, D. J. (1978). The integration of mothers' referential speech with joint play. *Child Development, 49,* 781–787.

Messer, D. J. (1981). The identification of names in maternal speech to infants. *Journal of Psycholinguistic Research, 10,* 69–77.

Moravcsik, J. M. (1990). *Thought and language.* London: Routledge & Kegan Paul.

Mumme, D. L. (1993). *Rethinking social referencing: The influence of facial and vocal affect on infant behavior.* Doctoral dissertation, Stanford University, Stanford, CA.

Mumme, D. L., & Fernald, A. (1995). Infants' use of gaze in interpreting emotional signals. Manuscript under review.

Murphy, C. M. (1978). Pointing in the context of shared activity. *Child Development, 49,* 371–380.

Nagy, W., & Gentner, D. (1990). Semantic constraints on lexical categories. *Language and Cognitive Processes, 5,* 169–201.

Naigles, L. G. (1990). Children use syntax to learn verb meanings. *Journal of Child Language, 17,* 357–374.

Naigles, L. G., Fowler, A., & Helm, A. (1992). Developmental shifts in the construction of verb meanings. *Cognitive Development, 7,* 403–427.

Naigles, L. G., & Gelman, S. A. (1995). Overextensions in comprehension and production revisited: Preferential looking in a study of dog, cat and cow. *Journal of Child Language, 22,* 19–46.

Naigles, L. G., Gleitman, H., & Gleitman, L. R. (1992). Children acquire word meaning components from syntactic evidence. In E. Dromi (Ed.), *Language and cognition: A developmental perspective* (pp. 104–140). Norwood, NJ: ABLEX.

Naigles, L. G., & Hoff-Ginsburg, E. (1995). Input to verb learning: Evidence for the plausibility of syntactic bootstrapping. *Developmental Psychology, 31,* 827–837.

Naigles, L. G., & Kako, E. T. (1993). First contact in verb acquisition: Defining a role for syntax. *Child Development, 64,* 1665–1687.

Nelson, K. (1973). Structure and strategy in learning to talk. *Monographs of the Society for Research in Child Development, 38*(Serial No. 149).

Nelson, K. (1988). Constraints on word learning? *Cognitive Development, 3,* 221–246.

Nelson, K., Hampson, J., & Shaw, L. K. (1993). Nouns in early lexicons: Evidence, explanations and implications. *Journal of Child Language, 20,* 61–84.

Nelson, K., & Lucariello, J. (1985). The development of meaning in first words. In M. Barrett (Ed.), *Children's single word speech* (pp. 59–83). New York: Wiley.

Newport, E. L. (1991). Contrasting concepts of the critical period for language. In S. Carey & R. Gelman (Eds.), *The epigenesis of mind: Essays on biology and cognition* (pp. 111–130). Hillsdale, NJ: Erlbaum.

Nowinski, V., & Markman, E. M. (in preparation). *Construing young children's word mappings in indirect label learning: A lexical or pragmatic choice?* Manuscript in preparation.

Olguin, R., & Tomasello, M. (1993). Twenty-five-month-old children do not have a grammatical category of verb. *Cognitive Development, 8,* 245–272.

Oviatt, S. L. (1980). The emerging ability to comprehend language: An experimental approach. *Child Development, 51,* 97–106.

Pinker, S. (1989). *Learnability and cognition: The acquisition of argument structure.* Cambridge, MA: MIT Press.

Pinker, S. (1994). How could a child use verb syntax to learn verb semantics? *Lingua, 92,* 377–410.

Poulin-Dubois, D. (1995). Object parts and the acquisition of the meaning of names. In K. E. Nelson & A. Reger (Eds.), *Children's language* (Vol. 8, pp. 125–143). Hillsdale, NJ: Erlbaum.

Quine, W. V. O. (1960). *Word and object.* Cambridge, MA: MIT Press.

Quinn, P. C. (1991). *Categorization of spatial relationships by young infants.* Paper presented at the biennial meetings of the Society for Research in Child Development, Seattle, WA.

Quinn, P. C., Eimas, P. D., & Rosenkrantz, S. L. (1993). Evidence for representations of perceptually similar natural categories by 3-month-old and 4-month-old infants. *Perception, 22,* 463–475.

Ratner, N., & Bruner, J. (1978). Games, social exchange and the acquisition of language. *Journal of Child Language, 5,* 391–401.

Rescorla, L. A. (1980). Overextension in early language development. *Journal of Child Language, 7,* 321–335.

Reznick, J. S., & Goldfield, B. A. (1992). Rapid change in lexical development in comprehension and production. *Developmental Psychology, 28,* 406–413.

Ricciuti, H. (1965). Object grouping and selective ordering behavior in infants 12- to 24-months-old. *Merrill-Palmer Quarterly, 11,* 129–148.

Rispoli, M. (1995). Missing arguments and the acquisition of predicate meanings. In M. Tomasello & W. E. Merriman (Eds.), *Beyond names for things: Young children's acquisition of verbs* (pp. 331–352). Hillsdale, NJ: Erlbaum.

Roberts, K., & Jacob, M. (1991). Linguistic vs. attentional influences on nonlinguistic categorization in 15-month-old infants. *Cognitive Development, 6,* 355–375.

Rosch, E., Mervis, C. B., Gray, W. D., Johnson, M. D., & Boyes-Braem, P. (1976). Basic objects in natural categories. *Cognitive Psychology, 7,* 573–605.

Scaife, M., & Bruner, J. S. (1975). The capacity for joint visual attention in the infant. *Nature, 253,* 265–266.

Schwartz, R. G., & Leonard, L. B. (1980). Words, objects, and actions in early lexical acquisition. *Papers and Reports in Child Language Development, 19,* 29–36.

Shatz, M., Wellman, H. M., & Silber, S. (1983). The acquisition of mental verbs: A systematic investigation of the first reference to mental states. *Cognition, 14,* 301–321.

Shwe, H., & Markman, E. M. (in press). Young children's appreciation of the mental impact of their communication signals. *Developmental Psychology.*

Smiley, S. S., & Brown, A. L. (1979). Conceptual preference for thematic or taxonomic relations: A nonmonotonic age trend from preschool to old age. *Journal of Experimental Child Psychology, 28,* 249–257.

Smith, L. B., Jones, S. S., & Landau, B. (1992). Count nouns, adjectives, and perceptual properties in children's novel word interpretations. *Developmental Psychology, 28,* 273–286.

Snyder, L., Bates, E., & Bretherton, I. (1981). Content and context in early lexical development. *Journal of Child Language, 8,* 565–582.

Soja, N. N. (1992). Inferences about the meanings of nouns: The relationship between perception and syntax. *Cognitive Development, 7,* 29–45.

Soja, N. N., Carey, S., & Spelke, E. S. (1991). Ontological categories guide young children's inductions of word meaning: Object terms and substance terms. *Cognition, 38,* 179–211.

Spelke, E. S. (1990). Principles of object perception. *Cognitive Science, 14,* 29–56.

Spelke, E. S., Phillips, A. T., & Woodward, A. L. (1995). Infants' knowledge of object motion and human action. In A. J. Premack, D. Premack, & D. Sperber (Eds.), *Causal cognition: A multidisciplinary debate* (pp. 44–77). Oxford, England: Clarendon Press.

Starkey, P., Spelke, E. S., & Gelman, R. (1990). Numerical abstraction by human infants. *Cognition, 36,* 97–127.

Sternberg, R., & Powell, J. S. (1983). Comprehending verbal comprehension. *American Psychologist, 38,* 878–893.

Sugarman, S. (1983). *Children's early thought: Developments in classification.* Cambridge, England: Cambridge University Press.

Talmy, L. (1974). Semantics and syntax of motion. In J. Kimball (Ed.), *Syntax and semantics* (Vol. 4, pp. 181–238). Academic Press.

Tardif, T. (1996). Nouns are not always learned before verbs: Evidence from Mandarin speakers' early vocabularies. *Developmental Psychology, 32,* 492–504.

Taylor, M., & Gelman, S. A. (1988). Adjectives and nouns: Children's strategies for learning new words. *Child Development, 59,* 411–419.

Taylor, M., & Gelman, S. A. (1989). Incorporating new word into the lexicon: Preliminary evidence for language hierarchies in two-year-old children. *Child Development, 60,* 625–636.

Tomasello, M. (1992a). *First verbs: A case study of early grammatical development.* Cambridge, England: Cambridge University Press.

Tomasello, M. (1992b). The social bases of language acquisition. *Social Development, 1,* 67–87.

Tomasello, M. (1995a). Pragmatic contexts for early verb learning. In M. Tomasello & W. E. Merriman (Eds.), *Beyond names for things: Young children's acquisition of verbs* (pp. 115–146). Hillsdale, NJ: Erlbaum.

Tomasello, M. (1995b). Thinking in niches: Sociocultural influences on cognitive development: Comment. *Human Development, 38,* 46–52.

Tomasello, M., & Akhtar, N. (1995). Two-year-olds use pragmatic cues to differentiate reference to objects and actions. *Cognitive Development, 10,* 201–224.

Tomasello, M., & Barton, M. (1994). Learning words in nonostensive contexts. *Developmental Psychology, 30,* 639–650.

Tomasello, M., & Farrar, J. (1986). Object permanence and relational words: A lexical training study. *Journal of Child Language, 13*, 495–505.

Tomasello, M., & Kruger, A. C. (1992). Joint attention on actions: Acquiring verbs in ostensive and non-ostensive contexts. *Journal of Child Language, 19*, 311–333.

Tomasello, M., Kruger, A. C., & Ratner, H. H. (1993). Cultural learning. *Behavioral and Brain Sciences, 16*, 495–552.

Tomasello, M., Mannle, S., & Kruger, A. C. (1986). Linguistic environment of 1- to 2-year-old twins. *Developmental Psychology, 22*, 169–176.

Tomasello, M., Strosberg, R., & Akhtar, N. (1996). Eighteen-month-olds learn words in non-ostensive contexts. *Journal of Child Language, 23*, 157–176.

Tomasello, M., & Todd, J. (1983). Joint attention and lexical acquisition style. *First Language, 4*, 197–212.

Vygotsky, L. S. (1962). *Thought and language.* Cambridge, MA: MIT Press.

Ward, T. B., Becker, A. H., Hass, S. D., & Vela, E. (1991). Attribute availability and the shape bias in children's category generalization. *Cognitive Development, 6*, 143–167.

Ward, T. B., Vela, E., Peery, M. L., Lewis, S. N., Bauer, N. K., & Klint, K. A. (1989). What makes a vibble a vibble? A developmental study of category generalization. *Child Development, 60*, 214–224.

Waxman, S. R. (1990). Linguistic biases and the establishment of conceptual hierarchies: Evidence from preschool children. *Cognitive Development, 5*, 123–150.

Waxman, S. R. (1991). Convergences between semantic and conceptual organization in the preschool years. In J. P. Byrnes & S. A. Gelman (Eds.), *Perspectives on language and cognition: Interrelations in development.* Cambridge, England: Cambridge University Press.

Waxman, S. R. (1994). The development of an appreciation of specific linkages between linguistic and conceptual organization. *Lingua, 92*, 229–257.

Waxman, S. R., & Gelman, R. (1986). Preschoolers' use of superordinate relations in classification and language. *Cognitive Development, 1*, 139–156.

Waxman, S. R., & Hall, D. G. (1993). The development of a linkage between count nouns and object categories: Evidence

from fifteen- to twenty-one-month-old infants. *Child Development, 64*, 1224–1241.

Waxman, S. R., & Kosowski, T. D. (1990). Nouns mark category relations: Toddlers and preschoolers word learning biases. *Child Development, 61*, 1461–1473.

Waxman, S. R., & Markow, D. B. (1995). Words as invitations to form categories: Evidence from 12- to 13-month-old infants. *Cognitive Psychology, 29*, 257–302.

Waxman, S. R., & Senghas, A. (1992). Relations among word meanings in early lexical development. *Developmental Psychology, 28*, 862–873.

Waxman, S. R., Shipley, E. F., & Shepperson, B. (1991). Establishing new subcategories: The role of category labels and existing knowledge. *Child Development, 62*, 127–138.

Wellman, H., & Gelman, S. A. (1987). Children's understanding of the nonobvious. In R. J. Sternberg (Ed.), *Advances in the psychology of human intelligence.* Hillsdale, NJ: Erlbaum.

Woodward, A. L. (1992). *The role of the whole object assumption in early word learning.* Doctoral dissertation, Stanford University, Stanford, CA.

Woodward, A. L. (1993). The effect of labeling on children's attention to objects. In E. V. Clark (Ed.), *Proceedings of the 24th annual child language research forum* (pp. 35–47). Stanford, CA: CSLI.

Woodward, A. L. (1995). *Infants' reasoning about the goals of a human actor.* Paper presented at the biennial meetings of the Society for Research in Child Development, Indianapolis, IN.

Woodward, A. L., & Markman, E. M. (1991). Constraints on learning as default assumptions: Comments on Merriman and Bowman's "The mutual exclusivity bias in children's word learning." *Developmental Review, 11*, 137–163.

Woodward, A. L., Markman, E. M., & Fitzsimmons, C. M. (1994). Rapid word learning in 13- and 18-month-olds. *Developmental Psychology, 30*, 553–566.

Woodward, J. Z., & Aslin, R. N. (1991). *Two-year-olds' object and action biases in lexical development.* Paper presented at the biennial meetings of the Society for Research in Child Development, Seattle, WA.

Wynn, K. (1992). Addition and subtraction by human infants. *Nature, 358*, 749–750.

CHAPTER 9

The Acquisition of Grammar

MICHAEL MARATSOS

Grammar, and thus its acquisition, comprises a complex and heterogeneous system. This fact makes it impossible to give a simple answer to the question "What is grammar acquisition like?" Imagine someone asking "What is the human body like?" and expecting a one-sentence reply. Such a question requires a textbook for an answer.

Furthermore, it can be misleading to infer too much even from a valid general characteristic of such systems.

To the question "What is the human body like?" a possible answer is, "The human body is 86% water." But from this general characteristic, it is a mistake to draw inferences like "The human body is 86% water; water is chemically simple; so the body is mostly chemically simple."

For the study of grammatical acquisition, the problem is happily exacerbated by the generous outpouring of results on acquisition in many languages (e.g., Slobin, 1985b, 1992a). These results show that there is not even a "general course of acquisition." For example, most textbooks state that children's first grammatical combinations are combinations of simple, uninflected stems, e.g., "mommy sock" or "no cereal." Morphological inflections such as noun plurals ("dog + s") or verb tensing and aspect ("fall + s," "go + ing") come later. But in many languages with rich morphological systems, the first grammatical combinations include inflected stems (Slobin, 1992b). It is probably safe to say that in general, children's early sentences are missing parts that later development supplies. But this is hardly surprising.

Because there is no general acquisitional path to describe, any chapter on grammatical acquisition must be selective. This chapter will focus on those related aspects of grammatical acquisition that probably provide its central characteristic interest: complexity and innateness. It is the complexity of much of grammar, combined with children's surprising ability to cope with this complexity, that suggests that species-specific innate mechanisms buffer and guide the process. Simultaneously, these very concepts—innateness and complexity—themselves comprise heterogeneous domains. Public discussions often seem to oversimplify the term *innateness* in misleading ways. Accordingly, the initial section of this chapter attempts to articulate the conceptual structure of innateness, illustrating its variety of meanings, to provide a ground for the subsequent discussion, which addresses sequentially three kinds of complexity in grammatical processes: massive, configurational, and abstruse. The sections that illustrate these qualities provide a necessarily selective analysis of a few grammatical acquisitional problems beginning with the massive information-processing complexity involved in the acquisition of individual morphological markers. The surprising acquisitional results found here support several central conclusions about grammatical development.

The discussion continues by considering how such individual grammatical markers are systematically organized acquisitionally to make up the formal grammatical categories of grammar, such as subject and verb. This problem illustrates *configurational* complexity. Finally, the last section presents some general characteristics of current Chomskyan nativist approaches. Here *abstruse* complexity—the complexity of odd, idiosyncratic primitive analytic properties—becomes a paramount problem. As the chapter proceeds, domain-characteristic, potentially idiosyncratic aspects of grammatical competence will be explored.

My goal in using this progression is not simply to follow a conceptual-logical format. Although not all grammar is complex, a great deal of it is. The presentation of this chapter is designed to help readers appreciate just how remarkable these acquisitional phenomena are.

CONCEPTS OF INNATENESS AND MODULARITY: WHAT DOES INNATENESS MEAN?

Innateness, a key concept in language acquisition, has many meanings. Presumably, innateness refers to the biological specification of how variably the organism can respond to variability in environmental inputs. Theoretically, the organism's response potential ranges from rather high variability (e.g., Skinnerian psychology) to relatively low (e.g., ethological analyses of some behavioral systems).

But a general scaling of this sort is still quite inadequate. The extant animal literature shows that innateness means many things across different species behaviors (Gallistel, Brown, Carey, Gelman, & Keil, 1991).

Fixed Reaction Patterns and Targeted Innateness

Some cases of innateness do in fact correspond to most people's prototypical idea of this quality: The organism innately emits certain fixed behaviors in response to certain fixed stimuli. Male stickleback fish attack any object with a red dot that approaches their nest during mating season (Tinbergen, 1951). Male sticklebacks grow such a dot during this season, and thus the fish defend their nests. They do not learn this behavior from observing other sticklebacks when they are young; it is a fixed reaction pattern, with red dot as the trigger stimulus of the innate attack behavior. In this chapter, such prespecified innate knowledge of the eliciting stimulus or elicited response will be called *targeted innateness.*

Special Learning Systems in Animals: Innate Specifications about Learning

Studies of animal behavior show, however, that many animal behaviors are partly learned and thus do not correspond to simple target nativism. Such behaviors, however, often also have crucial innate components. Sometimes, the organism begins with a partly specified innate target. For example, mature vervet monkeys make three warning cries, to air, land, and crawling predators (some snakes). Initially, however, infant vervet monkeys make the "snake" call to any long thin object on the ground. Experience with other monkeys tunes this to the particular dangerous snakes in the vicinity (some snakes are harmless). So there is a partially innate stimulus target, followed by further learning.

In still other partly innate systems, there is virtually no innate specification of the stimulus target. Geese and many other birds form most of their idea of their social targets for the rest of their lives from exposure during a brief period after birth to (preferably moving) objects. But the bird can learn to attach to anything, including a human, or even a boulder moving around a track. So the period of learning is what is innately specified; this gives the familiar name *critical period* to such stages of learning.

Many partly innately governed learning patterns, however, do not involve critical periods. For example, organisms most typically form conditioning patterns to stimuli that are very close to each other in time. If Pavlov had rung his bell 20 minutes before presenting food, no dog would have learned to salivate to the bell by itself. But suppose one makes a rat sick 20 minutes (or more) after it encounters a novel taste. The rat will now avoid that food. This learning pattern is specific to novel taste and illness. Electric shock 20 minutes after a novel taste does not work, nor does illness 20 minutes after a new food shape (Garcia & Koeling, 1966). There is no critical period for this kind of special interval learning; it applies any time in the rat's life.

Finally, such specialized learning systems may involve surprisingly complex tabulation and inference systems. In many ant species, the ants, having wandered complexly away from their nest, go back to it in a straight line. How can they do this? Apparently, some internal mechanism keeps track of how long and how fast the ant went in each direction, and adds up the direction-velocity-duration vectors. (Part of the evidence for this is that if one picks up the ant and moves it 30 feet away, it goes in a straight line to a point 30 feet from its nest; the ant has to tabulate its own body movements.)

Such data indicate that even in presumably relatively simple animal systems, there is no uniform "signature" or structural nature for innateness, or for learning either. Nor do researchers have even a Guttman scale (if A is not innate, B will not be; if B is innate, A will be). The expression of innateness in animal behavioral systems is enormously heterogeneous. Evolution is apparently both too haphazard and too opportunist to provide neatly organized, homogeneously organized systems. The assumption in this chapter is that grammar acquisition, itself a highly complex system, also comprises a heterogeneously organized system: This assumption reduces the possibility of drawing broad generalizations about the whole, from the study of some of its parts.

Is Grammar Encapsulated?

Chomsky's Supposed Views on Encapsulation

It is also necessary in the study of grammar to dispense with the homogeneous view: that grammar must be either completely "encapsulated," or completely interactive with other mental systems. Chomsky's own nativist theory, in particular, is commonly believed to imply that grammar is completely separate from other functions. For example, Fowler (1990) writes, "One cannot conduct language development research without at least acknowledging the hypothesis that language is acquired, processed, and represented independently of other cognitive domains" (p. 303), clearly meant to be a statement of the Chomskyan "modularity" position on language. This understanding is reflected commonly in my own conversations with graduate and undergraduate students; it is also evidenced in texts like Cole and Cole (1992), in public discussions (e.g., Churchland, 1992), and in private ones. Arguments about whether cognitive and social development might affect grammatical development often take much of their force only in reference to the presupposed Chomskyan argument that grammatical abilities are completely isolated from other abilities. Because otherwise, one might ask, who could doubt that aspects of cognitive development would affect grammatical development?

In fact, it seems impossible that grammar acquisition would have nothing to do with cognition and perception in general. Grammar is part of the mechanism by which language maps meaning onto a publicly perceived medium (usually sound). To learn that mapping system, one must relate meaning (from concepts) to the public perceptual medium. For example, if someone believed that one can say either "Mary kissed John" or "John kissed Mary" to mean that Mary initiated the act of kissing, it would be obvious that the person lacked knowledge of English grammar. Some mapping of event structure onto grammatical sequences is necessary to learn grammar.

Chomsky's Actual Position

Chomskyan linguistic theory has in fact always had a role for semantics and speech situational factors, even if such aspects of the whole system are typically rather briefly discussed, or sometimes serve as depositories for unwanted aspects of structural analyses (see Harris, 1992). Space does not permit much further explication of this problem, however, so I will simply quote the generally agreed on chief protagonist in the matter:

> The idea that language is completely isolated from other cognitive and perceptual functions cannot have been proposed by anyone. What could that possibly mean? that language is not perceived? that it doesn't enter into thought? I've come across arguments of that sort, but rarely comment on them. Life's too short. . . . As far as is known, there are properties of language that are specific to it, and indeed, rare-to-unknown in the organic world. . . . But from that fact, it plainly does not follow that every aspect of language is language-specific, or that language is completely isolated from other functions. The inference is utterly irrational. (N. Chomsky, 1994, p. 1)

Similarly, it is commonly believed that according to Chomskyan theory, all grammatical universals or near-universals arise from qualitatively unique language-specific factors. Yet Chomsky (1994) cites iconicity and smaller-elements-first (Bever, 1970) as general perceptual and cognitive processing factors that partially determine cross-linguistic trends in grammatical structures.

Without seeking to sort out the rhetorical history of how this highly polarized view of language specificity has come about, I will assume that in Chomskyan theory, grammar is not completely encapsulated from nonlinguistic functions, but it does have some faculty-unique elements. As a corollary, showing that some aspect of grammatical acquisition rests on cognitive or social development thus does not disprove the Chomskyan hypothesis of considerable faculty specificity. Nor, for that matter,

would evidence that some things about grammar look fairly unique show that grammatical acquisition as a whole has nothing to do with more general cognition or perception. Assuming that a domain problem is characterologically homogeneous, certainly makes the drawing of domain-general inferences from specific findings much easier. But again, there is no reason to expect evolution has made matters so straightforward.

Modularity and Grammar Revisited

The notion of complete encapsulation or isolation of a faculty or domain is often associated with *modularity* (Fodor, 1983). So does Chomsky's acceptance that nonlanguage elements interact with language imply that grammar could not be in any respect modular? Actually, *modularity* does not definitionally entail complete encapsulation; modularity properly understood just means a coherent system of operations that *restricts* the information it can receive from other systems, as well as the information it sends on to them (Maratsos, 1992). A Chomskyan nativist like Pinker (1984) can posit that grammar acquisitional systems receive information from social and cognitive systems; this corresponds to a modular system as long as the information flow is restricted rather than totally open.

General Degrees of Nativism

It is a goal here to eliminate any simple choice between innate versus not innate; it is also a goal to point out that general "more-or-less innate" scalings also do not mean much, because of the qualitative heterogeneity of innate-environmental interactions in the animal literature. Nevertheless, one general scaling is probably conceptually useful: widespread versus species-specific versus faculty-specific innateness:

1. *Fairly widespread innate perceptual, social, or cognitive factors.* Some innate cognitive and perceptual processes are common to many species. For example, human infants innately categorically perceive voiced-unvoiced boundaries between language sounds such as /b/ versus /p/ or /d/ versus /t/ (Eimas, Siqueland, & Vigorito, 1971); these boundaries sometimes play a role in various grammatical operations. But rhesus monkeys, minks, and chinchillas innately categorically perceive the same auditory boundaries (Kuhl & Miller, 1975). So these auditory boundaries are indeed innate, but not even particular to humans.

2. *Species-specific innate properties.* There are also, without doubt, human-specific cognitive and perceptual processes that contribute to many behavioral domains at once, grammar among them. For example, humans are particularly good at analyzing sequences, an ability relevant to grammar. Humans have a highly developed frontal cortex, which allows them relatively great inhibition of habitual and competing responses, a probable prerequisite for the functioning of complex mental-behavioral systems. Very young humans show uniquely flexible joint attention to both social interactants and objects in play situations, which probably is prerequisite for figuring out speech-encoded meanings in speech situations. Such species-specific innate abilities are accepted by many non-Chomskyans who reject Chomskyan faculty-specificity (e.g., Bates & MacWhinney, 1989; O'Grady, 1987).

3. *Chomskyan faculty-specificity.* Chomsky, of course, believes that at least some elements of grammar are unique to grammar. He believes, for example, that children innately know abstract grammar-particular primitives (such as noun, verb, or hierarchical subjacency). Chomskyan nativism thus includes strong belief in much faculty-specific target nativism. Chomskyan nativist accounts also often specify modular routings of perceptual and cognitive properties from nonlinguistic systems to specific grammatical systems (e.g., Pinker & Bloom, 1990).

4. *Non-Chomskyan faculty specificity.* Faculty specificity in general is typically identified with Chomskyan views. But it seems plausible to hypothesize faculty-specific aspects of grammatical acquisition that are weaker forms of nativism than Chomskyan proposals. Bates (1979) proposes that grammar is a "new machine made of old parts." Perhaps much of grammatical acquisition involves faculty-specific routing of elements and operations from such old parts to one another. For example, suppose sequence analysis, perception of meaning in social exchange, and category building to be "old parts." Suppose further that aspects of these systems are specifically routed to each other in ways that naturally give language-particular grammatical categories as a result, without the child's system knowing in advance what the particular outcomes will be. This would comprise a form of faculty specificity, but it would be a weaker form than the highly targeted innate knowledge of grammatical categories that Chomskyans typically hypothesize. Belief in a considerable amount of non-Chomskyan faculty specificity is suggested in Slobin (1985a) or Maratsos (1989).

Possibilities 1 through 4 all seem worth distinguishing theoretically. Simultaneously, it is important to see that they are not mutually exclusive. One could easily be a Chomskyan nativist, for example, but also believe that other innate properties generally widespread among higher animals, or specific to humans but not to grammar, all contribute to grammatical acquisition. For terminological convenience, the words "innateness" or "innate" in this chapter will always mean "species-specific" or "faculty-specific" innateness. If Chomskyan faculty specificity is specifically meant, I will say "Chomskyan innateness" or "Chomskyan nativism."

Chomsky and Skinner

The preceding discussion should make it obvious that Chomsky's principal opponents no longer come from Skinnerian ranks. Most developmental psychologists are, in one way or another, no longer Skinnerians: They typically believe children go beyond forming simple uniform flat stimulus-association chains strengthened by reinforcing stimuli, and this is what Skinnerianism means. (Even believing in rewards and punishments does not make one a Skinnerian; e.g., if one believes an organism actively and complexly plots to get rewards and avoid punishments—as I think most parents rightly believe their children do—one is not a Skinnerian.) Chomsky's opponents now include many who believe with him that human behavior is complexly and "deeply" structured, even partly by species-specific innate functions. Identifying the Chomskyan/non-Chomskyan debate with Chomsky versus Skinner is historically outmoded and plays no significant role in the present chapter.

With this conceptual background in mind, it is possible to proceed with the "journey into grammatical complexity" promised earlier. We begin with a set of problems where in fact, basic English grammar does not seem particularly complicated. But as will become apparent, familiarity with the analogous competences in other languages gives a very different and informative perspective on children's grammar acquisition.

ENGLISH AND NON-ENGLISH ENCODINGS OF THEMATIC ROLE RELATIONS

Textbooks typically remark that children's acquisition of grammar is quite an achievement because grammar is highly complex, yet children learn it without the overt instruction they receive for other complicated subjects such as algebra or physics. Unfortunately, from this appropriate beginning, the discussion often moves on to a discussion of early English grammar where the reader encounters not particularly impressive examples of grammar such as "mommy walk" or "more popsicle." Such utterances seem unlikely to convince anyone about the complexity of children's grammatical achievements. This is especially unfortunate, because a developmentalist is likely to believe that early beginnings are characteristic of later development, which can be thought of as "more of the same."

There is nothing wrong with early English as an example of aspects of grammar. But the normal range of languages also includes many languages in which basic sentence structure presents quite different grammatical problems. Again unfortunately, most speakers of a given language tend to see their own language as "normal," and therefore representative of other languages. All this follows from natural tendencies of human thought: Belief in one's own central normality, belief that a given domain (e.g., grammar) is essentially homogeneous, all lead naturally to the belief that early acquisition is much the same throughout languages.

Luckily, recent years have brought an outpouring of early acquisitional data from many non-English languages (Slobin, 1985b, 1992a). Although basic propositional structures in many of these languages are quite "English-like," in others the basic processes are different in ways that illustrate how grammar can be very complex. So I shall first briefly describe some relevant foundational ideas illustrated in some of the early English data (see Bloom, Ch. 7, this Volume, for much fuller discussion). From there, the discussion will move to the surprising complexity of non-English systems in dealing with analogous aspects of basic propositional structure.

Mapping Meanings onto Morpheme Sequences: The Basic Problem

The basic linguistic unit of meaning is generally said to be the *morpheme*. This is usually defined as the smallest sound sequence that has a distinct assigned meaning. It is not the same as a word. For example, the word *dogs* has two morphemes, the stem "dog" and the noun plural "-s," each of which carries a meaning.

Sentences combine morphemes to give meanings not already explicit in the individual morphemes. For example, consider the morphemes "John," "Sarah," "scratch," and verb past tense "-ed." These refer individually to a male and female individual, a particular action, and a past tense. When the words are said as a randomly ordered list, the hearer might guess that there was an act of scratching between John and Sarah in the past. But only when someone says "Sarah scratched John" in that order does the listener know it was Sarah who initiated the scratching. The grammatical arrangement *adds* the meaning that Sarah was the agent of the scratching, and John was the patient (recipient of force of the action). (Interestingly, we must typically observe such grammatical arrangements even when the meaning would be clear without them (e.g., "Sarah scratched the post," where it is hardly likely the post could have scratched Sarah).

Grammaticization, Agent-Patient Relations, and Definiteness

Aspects of sentence meaning control how morphemes are ordered in sentences. But not all aspects of the conceptual world play major roles in controlling grammar. Across the world's languages, there is a relatively small set of characteristically "grammar-important" concepts. Such meanings are said to be *grammaticized* by the relevant language. Initially, I will concentrate on just two of these:

1. *Agent-patient relations.* All languages allow speakers to talk about events in which one object, typically an animate being, initiates an action, the force of which falls on a second object. The first class of event-roles for objects is called *agent,* and the second class is often called *patient.* Typically the action-encoder is a *verb,* and the words central for encoding the agent and patient sentence constituents are *nouns.* (I call these role-encoders *constituents* because sometimes they are multiword phrases; e.g., "the little boy" denotes the agent in "the little boy ate the carrot"; the noun "boy" is taken to be the central word in the agent-constituent.)

In English, basic active sentences have a simple pattern: agent-action-patient. This pattern holds true for literally thousands of verbs. Basic English distinguishes agents from patients by constituent order: agents before actions; actions before patients.

2. *Definiteness-indefiniteness.* Definiteness seems semantically more subtle than agent-patient relations; but it plays a surprisingly major role in the basic sentence-grammar of many languages. Definiteness means a reference to a specific member or subset of a category, which is furthermore referentially specific for both speaker and listener in the speech situation (Brown, 1973).

Specificity-nonspecificity can be illustrated in this way: Suppose someone says, "I don't have a cat." This utterance is probably not about a specific cat; it means, "I don't have any member of the class 'cat.'" Nonspecific references are typically indefinite, encoded by indefinite articles like "a" or pronouns like "something" (exceptions: generic statements such as "the early bird gets the worm," which have no particular referents).

But conceptual specificity is not enough to account for the definite indefinite distinction. For example, suppose someone was scratched by some particular cat. It would still be odd for him to walk into a room full of people who had no knowledge of this particular cat, and say "*the cat* scratched me." This is because "the cat" is not just a specific reference, it is also a *definite* reference. Definite references are typically reserved for specific referents that are known to speaker and listener alike as a specific member of the class of objects. The reference could first be established for speaker and listener(s) alike by saying something like "*a cat* (indefinite specific reference) scratched me." After this introduction, definite specific references to "the cat" or "he" would be appropriate.

Both agent-patient relations and definite-indefinite relations are *grammaticized* in English. Agent-patient relations are grammaticized by constituent order. Definite-indefinite status is grammaticized by obligatory marking before common nouns in noun constituents (e.g., one must say "I saw *a* cat," not just "I saw cat"). These relations can be used *productively* to encode or comprehend new agent-action-patient or new definiteness-marking sequences the speaker has never heard before. For example, if you were told some new animal was *a gimel,* you could make up new sentences such as "the gimel scratched the post," or "I wonder if gimels eat vegetables or meat"; these are novel because "gimel" would not have been heard in particular sequences with "scratch" or "eat" or "the" before.

English Acquisition of Agent-Patient Marking

In discussing English, the important early acquisitional results concern children's use of agent-patient grammar; definite-indefinite encoding will become important in the discussion of non-English languages. English-speaking children typically encode agent-action-patient orders appropriately from an early period on. At first, it is true, they do so in incomplete sentences, making statements such as "eat cereal" or "mommy eat." But typically by 24 months, complete agent-action-patient sequences are present; research suggests children probably know much of the relevant grammar earlier than their overt speech indicates (Hirsh-Pasek & Golinkoff, 1991; Ingram, 1989). There is much subtle argument over the details of this process (see Bloom, Ch. 9, this Volume), but virtually all investigators have agreed on the centrality of agent-action-patient structure in early English acquisition (e.g., Bloom, 1970; Bowerman, 1973; Braine, 1976; Brown, 1973; Radford, 1990; Schlesinger, 1971).

Significance of Early Use of Agent-Patient Relations

These findings have greatly influenced people's thinking about grammar. When Schlesinger (1971) and Bloom (1970) proposed these analyses, Chomskyan rhetoric had typically claimed that meaning would play little role in the children's acquisition of grammar (Chomsky, 1965; McNeill, 1970). Children's early use of meaning-based grammar implied a refutation of Chomskyan ideas about grammar acquisition that remained a setback until Grimshaw (1981), Pinker (1984), and other Chomskyans showed how semantic-conceptual notions such as agent could also be profitably employed in Chomskyan theorizing (discussed later in this chapter).

Agent-Action-Patient and the Naturalness of Grammar

The discovery of children's early use of agent-action-patient grammar had another important effect—and not a good one: It led people to overestimate the "naturalness" of grammar in general. To most English speakers, the agent-action-patient order indeed seemed to be the conceptually natural one. Agents begin actions, which proceed on to the patient. So agent-action-patient appears to be a natural mapping from content to form (Bruner, 1975). In fact, in nearly all languages that use grammatical order to encode agent-patient relations, agents do typically precede patients (Greenberg, 1966). In addition to political and economic causes, the naturalness and simplicity of English basic propositional structure has probably aided its adoption as a near-universal language.

If early English acquisition is representative, children's earliest grammatical agent-patient codes may transparently mirror conceptual-perceptual representations. Acquisition of the grammatical code might be correspondingly straightforward. Perhaps a child could hear just one or two such sequences (e.g., "Mommy ate the cereal," or "I'll kiss you") and record the natural agent-action-patient sequence. The child might indeed virtually notice agent-action-patient order from a few input examples.

A Mistaken Significance

But looking only at early English agent-action-patient acquisition as an "exemplar" of grammatical acquisition is misleading in at least three ways. First, it can give the impression that if the beginning foundations of grammar are so straightforward, then perhaps later grammatical acquisition is also not so very complex. This conclusion follows from the notion that a complex domain is essentially homogeneous: Later acquisition will just be "more of the same" as early grammar, except perhaps a little more complicated. Even constrained to English acquisition, this conclusion is simply wrong (see later discussion).

Second, not all languages use fixed constituent order to encode agent-patient relations even in basic sentences. I will point out far different acquisitional implications in the basic-clause structure when I describe the acquisition of agent-patient encoding in non-English languages.

Third, when adults consider acquisition in their own language, they are naturally egocentric. Adults already tacitly know the solution to the relevant acquisitional problem in their own language. So unconsciously, when they think of a child trying to "break the code" in language-learning situations, what "sticks out" to an adult are just those aspects of the situation that the child should attend to get the right answer. This makes it hard to see that there is an acquisitional problem. Looking at languages where this egocentric projection does not work highlights the complexity of the acquisitional problem.

Marking of Agent-Patient and Definiteness Relations in Other Languages

Fixed constituent order is not the universal way of conveying agent-patient relations. In many languages, such relations are conveyed by morphological inflections on nouns (e.g., Turkish), on associated determiners (e.g., Greek, German), or even mostly on the main verb (e.g., Tagalog).

Turkish: A Nonconstituent-Order Agent-Patient Language

Bowerman (1973) and Slobin (1982) first studied the acquisition of morphologically inflected agent-patient relations. The structure and acquisitional data from Turkish are especially useful for understanding certain basic, complicated-looking analytic problems; they also show children being surprisingly good in solving them.

Turkish Use of Major Constituent Order for Focus

To begin with, major constituent order in Turkish is not used to convey agent-patient relations. Instead, it is used to convey what is called *Focus*. An element is in focus if it is new information, or makes a claim contrasted with someone else's. Suppose someone says, "John ate something last night," and a second person asks, "What did he eat?" The answer might be in English, "He ate some curried chicken." "He" encodes old information, because we already know who "he" is, and know he was an eater. The new information is 'some curried chicken.' Thus this information is in Focus. In Turkish (and many other languages), Focus is expressed by major constituent order. In Turkish, focused elements have to be placed before the main verb. One could say 'Some curried chicken ate John' or 'John some curried chicken ate,' but not 'John ate some curried chicken' or 'Ate John some curried chicken.' Thus, agent-patient have no fixed-order encoding. Young Turkish children hear all possible orders of agents, patients, and actions in early input (Slobin, 1982).

Morphological Marking of Agent-Patient Relations

So how does Turkish convey agent-patient relations? It uses inflectional morphology on nouns. Agents are distinctive in *not* being inflected. Patients, however, are inflected. For example, any combination of 'John-u,' 'kissed,' and 'Ann' would mean 'Ann kissed John,' because -/u/ (sounds like 'oo') marks patients.

Obviously children cannot just notice a natural order to figure out Turkish agent-patient relations. They must instead analyze the role of morphological inflections. How can they do so?

It is very difficult to cope with how potentially difficult this problem is. For a first pass at the problem, let us falsely assume that in Turkish, patients are always consistently marked by a single inflection, /-u/; the purpose is to demonstrate why the induction problem might be difficult even for this relatively simple situation.

The essence of the problem is this: It is easy enough to learn all patients are marked by "-u" *if someone tells you*. But a language-learning child is not told; the child simply hears sound-sequences in situations and is supposed to analyze out sequences of meaningful morphemes, and then analyze what those morphemes mean. For example, to start with, the child must analyze that 'Ann' and 'Annu' both refer to someone named Ann, and analyze 'Annu' into 'stem + /u/,' part of the *segmentation problem* for grammar (Peters, 1983).

Assume the child has completed this preliminary analysis of 'Ann-u' into two morphemes, 'Ann' + /-u/ (see Braine, 1987; Peters, 1983; Pinker, 1984). How will the child figure out what meaning '-u' conveys? Knowing the answer, one assumes that the child will hear '-u' in a situation in which '-u' is attached to a patient of an action, and so will naturally "notice" that '-u' encodes patienthood.

A Problem: Many Meanings Are Present at Once

But in any situation, the referent of the word to which /-u/ is attached has many *other* properties to which /-u/ might be referring. For example, suppose in an appropriate situation, the child hears 'Ann-u kissed daddy,' (meaning 'daddy kissed Ann'). In this situation, 'Ann' does refer to a patient. But 'Ann' also refers to a feminine being; to a human being; to someone who also comprises the goal-endpoint in space of an action; to a relatively long-thin object (vs. flat-round objects); to an alive being; perhaps to someone who has relatively high status, compared with the speaker or listener; perhaps to someone who is affectionately regarded; probably to something that is socially deemed inedible; perhaps to a family member, rather than a stranger; perhaps to someone the speaker or listener regards as morally good; perhaps to someone who is a good cook (maybe daddy kissed Ann because he was happy about a well-cooked meal); perhaps to someone who is wearing bright clothes; and so on.

All of these might supply candidate meanings for '-u.' Again, no one is telling the child the right one. Furthermore, many of these possible meanings actually *do* control the meanings for inflectional morphemes in *some* language. In Tagalog, someone who is kissed is grammatically treated as the goal-endpoint of a movement-transfer action rather than as a patient; many languages mark for relative social status of objects; or for animacy; or for humanness; or for whether the object is affectionately regarded; or for long-thin general shape (humans are long-thin in such languages). So the child had *better* be able to guess these meanings as prospective meanings for morphological inflections on nouns. Furthermore, some of the possible meanings do not happen to be encoded morphologically in languages, but otherwise seem important enough to be candidates on general conceptual grounds. These include 'thought to be a morally good individual' or 'thought to be a good cook' or 'wearing bright clothes' (children are supposed to be perceptually oriented). So perhaps they are also prospective meanings for '-u.' In fact, for any referent in a situation, many things are true of it at once, and most of them *are* encoded in some language or another. So the child cannot plausibly be expected to look at the situation and luckily notice just the right answer required by her own language.

Property Registers: Storing Possible Properties

Consequently, to sort out what their own language is doing with a particular inflection, children must at least be capable of guessing any of the meanings languages actually assign. This task, in turn, requires that minimally, children have what can be called a *property register*. This property register must minimally include all the meanings that languages could encode with inflections; perhaps it includes more. As situations are encountered, children can register whether or not individual register properties are present when some morphological inflection is used.

Sifting: Getting the Right Property out of Many Possible Ones

The morphological inflection property register is obviously not likely to supply the right answer in a single situation-registration. In any single situation, as in the previously described example, many properties that must be in the register will be present in the input and thus are potential candidates for the meaning of the inflection.

How could the child proceed? First, assume there really is an initially limited property register—that not all the possible conceptual-perceptual properties in the world are part of the register. This still leaves a fairly extensive set to be sifted through. How can the child test properties against input for '-u?' There are two basic poles for induction sifters: serial and parallel. In the serial model (Pinker, 1984), the child selects one property, perhaps randomly, and tests this against further input. Suppose, for example, the child selected 'human' as the potential meaning for '-u.' Now the child could see whether, in future input, 'human' was consistently true of the stems to which '-u' markers are added. Of course, it would not be—the child would hear sentences like 'chicken-u ate John,' in which '-u' marks a nonhuman. Over time, 'human' would be disconfirmed. Then another property could be tried. Eventually 'patient' would be tried, and prove to match the input consistently.

The other analytic pole consists of multiple-property (parallel) induction, in which all (or many) properties are tested simultaneously against the input data (e.g., MacWhinney & Chang, 1992; Rispoli, 1991). Over time, the property that consistently predicts the new stem marker will emerge as the correct predictor.

Neither model, obviously, would be expected to converge on the right answer in just one lucky guess; in fact, criteria would probably be built in to require stable convergence over a period of time, to avoid misidentification resulting from a few inputs in a row matching a wrong initial guess.

Inflections That Mark More than One Thing: Exacerbating the Induction Problem

Thus, even when a morphological inflection is controlled by just one meaningful property, it is unlikely the child can just "notice" the right answer in a single instance. There are too many possible "right answers" across languages, or viewed another way, too many plausible wrong ones.

In fact, typical induction situations are much worse, because languages rarely use just one meaningful property to control morphological choice. Let us now look at how the Turkish accusative-marking actually works. In reality, Turkish has four accusative markers—rounded /i/ (pronounced 'ee') and /u/, and unrounded /i/ and /u/. (Rounding refers to whether the lips are rounded when pronouncing the vowel.) English has only rounded /u/ and unrounded /i/, but Turkish has all four possibilities, and each one is a meaningfully separate phoneme, as meaningfully separate as rounded /u/ versus unrounded /i/ in English. So the Turkish child will hear the equivalent of 'Bob-u kissed Sarah' to mean 'Sarah kissed Bob,' but would hear 'Ted-i kissed Sarah' to mean 'Sarah kissed Ted.'

Definiteness and Patient Marking. Moreover, some patients are not inflectionally marked at all. 'John pushed the bed' might be realized as 'bed-i pushed John,' but the equivalent to 'John pushed a bed' would come out 'bed pushed John,' with 'bed' unmarked.

What could explain this? Turkish *fuses* two meanings into patient marking, *and* also uses stem vowel phonological properties to choose markers. First, the semantic fusion: In Turkish, only semantically definite patients are inflectionally marked; indefinite ones are not. That is why accusative 'bed' is unmarked in the equivalent to 'John pushed a bed.'

Vowel Harmony and Definite-Patient Marking. Second, the phonology of the noun stem dictates the choice of definite-patient marker. Vowels differ in lip roundedness, as already noted. Vowels also vary in where in the mouth the tongue is highest. Pronounce 'ee' versus 'oo' to yourself. The tongue is higher toward the front for /i/

("ee"); it is higher towards the back for /u/. So /i/ is a front vowel, as is /e/ ("eh"); /u/ is a back vowel, as are /a/ ("ah") or /o/ ("oh"). The patient marker must harmonize with the stem vowel in both roundedness and front-backness. So for "bed," which has an unrounded front vowel, the definite-patient marker will be unrounded front /i/; for "pan," it is unrounded /u/.

At this point, I hope the reader begins to see this as a complicated-looking problem because patients are not consistently marked by any single marker. Again, the child does not know any of this in advance, and no one is telling her.

Multiply-Determined Case Markers Complicate the Induction-Sifting Task. Earlier it was assumed that the child could test to see whether, whenever a hypothesized meaning occurred, the hypothesized inflection marker was used. This assumption allows just one negative instance to falsify a marker-meaning guess. Now the same induction process will not work. For example, suppose the child heard "Ann-u kissed daddy" and guessed (appropriately) that /-u/ marks patienthood, as a lucky chance choice from the properties in the general property register. Will the child now find in future input, that patients are consistently marked by unrounded /u/? Of course not. In fact, most patients will *not* be marked by unrounded /u/. They will sometimes be marked by rounded /u/, or rounded and unrounded /i/, and sometimes not be marked at all. So the child, by this previous simple input-property induction criterion, will throw out 'patient' as a candidate. This is too bad, because it is part of the right answer.

How can the child proceed? In a serial procedure, suppose the child (tacitly) entertains the possibility that /u/ marks patients. If the induction criterion requires a complete match, this correct possibility will have to be thrown out. But suppose the child has a much lower provisional criterion: If a marker is associated with a meaning some "significant portion" of the time (probably around 5–10%), it might be kept as a "provisional candidate," to see if it works better in conjunction with other properties. Other properties then have to be tested serially, to see how they work out. Then a final procedure is needed to see how the provisional properties work in combination.

The second approach is some kind of parallel processing. *All* the properties in the "property register" are tested in parallel against the input, to see which combinations of possible register properties consistently co-occur with a particular marker in speech situations. The child might have heard "Ann-u kissed daddy" and recorded that for this situation, /-u/ went with an animate, human, feminine, long-thin, goal-endpoint, socially high status, affectionately regarded, definite, particular individual, patient. The various phonological properties naturally also have to be part of the register: The child might record that /-u/ went with a stem that has a nasal consonant at the end (stem-ending consonants often affect inflectional choice), a mid-back, unrounded, unnasalized vowel, and so on. Over time, the child could keep retesting the whole property battery against uses of /-u/; only some will consistently tend to occur, these being 'patient,' 'definite,' and 'back stem vowel,' and unrounded 'stem vowel.' This particular parallel process will also turn out to be defective for certain inflection-learning problems, but is still an improvement over the single inflection-single meaning match procedure.

Turkish Is Not Atypically Complex

These approaches are examples of minimally adequate approaches to the problem; no doubt there are others. But all of them must cope with the same basic acquisitional problems. Furthermore, there is nothing wildly complicated about the Turkish case-marking system; other case-marking systems typically have other complexities. It is remarkable, in its way, that virtually no human language seems to just pick out a single inflectional marker for patients and stick to it. Other properties are almost always implicated.

Acquisition of Turkish Case-Marking: Early and Error-Free

Most English speakers see Turkish case-marking as tremendously complex, and guess it would take a young child many error-filled years to figure it out. According to Aksoy and Slobin (1985), Turkish children typically use the accusative (patient-centered) case and other noun markers appropriately and productively by or before the age of 2 years. In fact, the child's first grammatical combinations typically include stem+definite-patient combinations. No "positive errors of commission" (using one accusative marker in place of another, or on indefinite nouns) are recorded, though markers are sometimes omitted ("errors of omission"). In experimental tests, Turkish children comprehend morphologically marked agent-patient sentences (using all possible orders) perhaps a little earlier than English-speaking children comprehend fixed-order agent-action-patient sequences. This role system is "complicated" to the conscious mind; but not to a young child learning grammar.

Polish Noun Subclass Case Marking

In the past decades, research efforts have brought forth a plethora of acquisitional data on different case-marking systems (e.g., Imedadze & Tuite, 1992; Katis, 1984; Pye, 1992; Smoczynska, 1985; Stephany, 1995; Walter, 1975; Weist, 1990). All these systems combine other properties with agent-patient marking. Polish (Smoczsynska, 1985; Weist, 1990) illustrates case marking crossed with arbitrary noun-class-set (formal gender), a system type that will also prove useful for discussion later in this chapter.

Case and Formal Noun Gender in Polish

Polish distinguishes six main cases, in the traditional grammatical sense: nominative, accusative, genitive, dative, locative, and instrumental. Accusative marks most patients; but if the action is performed incompletely ('John ate [some of] the carrot') or negated ('John didn't eat a carrot'), the case marking is genitive instead. Genitive also marks simple possessors (like the "-s" of "John's dog" in English). Dative marks recipients of objects (e.g., "Mary" in "Sarah gave a cat to Mary"). Nominative marks agents of actions, but also experiencers of emotions and things that are described (e.g., "ball" in "the ball is big"). Locative marks a location for an action, or the nonrecipient endpoint of a movement action. Instrumental marks some object used to carry out an action.

As in Turkish, these relations are not expressed by fixed constituent order. Morphological inflections on the nouns give the main information. Again, these inflections are multiply determined; one event-role (like agent) is not consistently marked by just one inflection. Table 9.1 gives the overall marking paradigm.

TABLE 9.1   Polish Case Marking

	Noun Class I	Noun Class II	Noun Class III
Nominative	-a	-	-o/-e
Accusative	-e	ANIMATE: -a/(-u) INANIMATE: -	-o/-e
Genitive	-y/-i*	-a/(-u)	-a
Dative	-e/-i*	-owi/(-u)	-a
Locative	-e/-i	-e/-u	-e/-u*
Instrumental	-a	-em	-em

* means "used after a palatalized stem consonant."
(-) means "use controlled by some noun stem phonological characteristic not outlined here."
From Smoczynska 1985, *The Acquisition of Polish* (pp. 595–686).

Arbitrariness and Productivity of Case-Marking System

Again, there is no standard agent marker, no standard patient marker, and so on. There are instead three major *sets* of markers, for three different noun-sets. Such case-marking noun-sets in Indo-European languages are usually called "noun gender" sets, because sometimes masculine nouns tend to fall into one, and feminine into another. But in reality, true gender is a very unreliable indicator. For example, 'boy' and 'girl' and 'child' are all neuter gender in Greek; 'girl' and 'child' are neuter in German. 'Back' is feminine in Greek and 'chest' is neuter. Other semantic correspondences that have been found are highly conditional and generally riddled with exceptions. Currently, there is no evidence that children attempt to break into these noun-sets by concentrating on some particular organizing meaning first (Bohm & Levelt, 1979; Maratsos & Chalkley, 1980). They are called "formal gender" sets for convenience, but natural gender probably plays no role in their acquisition. Thus no key semantic property predicts set membership.

Deducing Polish Word-Sets

Assume that a child has analyzed the meanings that go with the individual markers. In addition, however, the child must record *which individual nouns* the case markers appear on. Some nouns take /-a/ to mark agents (or described objects), some nouns take /-o/ to describe agents, and some add no marker. Some nouns take /-e/ to mark (completed action) patients, some nouns take /o/, some take nothing or /u/, and so on.

But a person who has (unconsciously) learned the system can do better than this. For example, hearing a new noun used in a nominative use, the person can predict other case uses. Hearing "gimel-a" as a nominative use, a knowledgeable speaker knows to say "gimel-e" for accusative uses, "gimel-y" for genitive uses, and so on. This is because in the previous input, the different noun-operation uses are *correlated:* over and over again, individual nouns that take marker /-a/ in nominative contexts, take marker /-e/ in accusative contexts, marker /-y/ in genitive contexts, and so on: This is what the category "Noun Class I" (see Table 9.1) encodes. Thus children can form grammatical categories by this initial item-operation analysis, followed by an internal analysis of how many individual nouns share the same case-marker *set.* Once formed, this set analysis itself comprises part of what determines new uses of individual case markers, in conjunction with the case-relevant meanings. Thus the child's analysis of internal noun-to-marker patterns, itself comes to determine part of how individual case markers are to be applied.

Acquisitional Data: Efficient Learning

Again, one might expect a long, drawn-out acquisitional period, with many errors of commission. Smoczynska (1985), however, reports that Polish children productively use the greater part of the formal case-gender system by age 2, with few such errors reported (also Weist, 1990).

It is striking how rare "positive errors" (using morphological inflections on the wrong noun, or wrong case) are in both Turkish and Polish. It is tempting to attribute this success to simple memorization: The child initially memorizes word-inflection combinations as single units, without respect to what the inflections actually mean, so the word-forms are always "accurate" word forms.

But such rote word-form memorization, if it literally means "word" memorization would actually produce many positive errors. Think of a Class I noun, the hypothetical word "gimel." Suppose the child memorizes "gimel-a" as a unit, when it is heard in a nominative-case context. But now suppose the child wants to talk about "gimel" in an accusative or genitive context. If the child has simply memorized "gimel-a" as a word unit, without analyzing any of the general properties that control when /-a/ can be used, the child will wrongly say "gimel-a," instead of the appropriate "gimel-e" or "gimel-y." So extensive positive errors of commission would result. Thus simple word-inflection memorization will *not* produce accuracy; it will produce large numbers of positive errors. Thus unanalyzed memorization of simple stem inflection is *not* a viable explanation for general early lack of error.

Another Morphological Acquisition Problem: Nonlocal Dependences

In Turkish and Polish, at least, the meanings that case markings encode are associated with the referent of the noun: its situational role, its definiteness, and so on. The semantic control is thus in some sense "local." Remarkably enough, languages commonly include systems where noun marking is dependent on qualities of some *other* constituent of the sentence, and hence is nonlocal. Thus the property register must include properties of other constituents of the sentence besides the inflected stem. Georgian case marking is an example of such a system.

Georgian Noun Case Marking: Partly Controlled by Verb Aspect

In Georgian (Imedadze & Tuite, 1992), agent-patient noun case marking is partly controlled by the aspect of the *verb* of the sentence. What does this mean?

Aspect Marking on Verbs.   Verb aspect refers to several characteristics; chiefly it refers to whether the action is complete or incomplete at the time of reference. Consider "John was eating" and "John will be eating." One is past, one is future, but both refer to an action of eating that is not completed at the respective past or future time. This is *incomplete* aspect. On the other hand, "John ate the banana, and then left," or "John will eat the banana, and then leave," both refer to *completed* eating actions, whether past or future. Languages commonly encode event-aspect on verbs. In Georgian, however, verb-aspect also partly controls *noun* case marking.

How Verb Aspect Controls Noun Case Marking. Georgian has three relevant verb classes, but this discussion will be limited to agents and transitive patient marking for Class I verbs, which include most of the simple action verbs of Georgian. The basic system is as follows:

	Agents	Patients
Incomplete Aspect	SWITCH	INCOMPL-PAT
Complete Aspect	COMPL-AG	SWITCH

There are three main sets of case markers which I will call SWITCH, INCOMPL-PAT (incomplete-patient) and COMPL-AG (complete-agent). Each of these actually refers to a small set of inflectional markers (e.g., SWITCH can be /-i/ or nothing, depending on noun stem phonology) but, for convenience, they will be treated here as single case markers.

The SWITCH marker is used to mark agents if the action is incomplete, but used to mark patients if the action is completed. INCOMPL-PAT is used for incomplete-action patients, and COMPL-AG is used for agents of completed actions. For example, imagine an act of kissing in which a girl is agent, and a boy is patient. Suppose one is referring to the action at a time when it is not yet complete. Then agent 'girl' is marked with SWITCH, and patient 'boy' with INCPAT. Suppose one is referring to a time at which the action is completed. Then agent 'girl' is marked with COMPL-AG, and SWITCH now marks the patient 'boy.'

Extending the Properties of the Property Register

What is new here? Before, the property register for noun inflection had to consider semantic properties of the noun and its referent. Now, the property register for noun case must also refer to possible properties of other constituents of the sentence and their referents, such as the verb. This expands greatly the necessary set of register properties to be analyzed in the input.

This looks very complicated indeed, but again, the developmental data are remarkably bland. Imedadze and Tuite (1992) report on three children for whom detailed diaries were kept. These children started marking aspect on verbs around 3 years of age. At this time, noun-case-markings appeared. When the case marking system came in, it entered without positive error.

Is Morphological Acquisition Always Errorless?

Some scholars familiar with the case-marking literature or morphological literature may protest that the data covered here are overconsistent. Children in some languages are sometimes recorded as making gender-case errors, such as those reported for Russian by Slobin (1973). In Serbo-Croatian, an especially complicated and confusing system, various problems seem to persist until age 5 (Slobin, 1982).

This is certainly true. But often the errors seem to result from particular subsystem problems. For example, the Russian system resembles the Polish system in the singular (Smoczynska, 1985). But the Russian system includes a small subgroup of nouns for which even the nominative case use is not a consistent indicator of uses in other cases; this seems to be where persistent errors are concentrated (Maratsos & Chalkley, 1980).

The relatively few selected positive errors in some languages do not furthermore, negate the fact that acquisition is generally surprisingly fast and free of positive error throughout the bulk of nearly all such systems. This has to be a "natural fact" for acquisition models. Developmentalists, like people in general, tend to notice and treasure the salient, interesting fact or occurrence. It is not easy to notice or get interested in "the dog that did not bark in the night." Children in some languages do make some errors; but over and over, the dominant acquisitional fact is how few errors of commission occur amidst the many opportunities for misanalysis (see also data in the following section). The core acquisitional problem, in my view, is not why occasional salient errors occur. The central phenomenon is that these systems are so obviously complex, and yet children are so stably skilful in acquiring them.

SOME CONCLUSIONS ABOUT ASPECTS OF GRAMMATICAL ACQUISITION RELATED TO COMPLEX CASE MARKING

Some implications about aspects of grammatical development follow especially sharply from these examinations of case-marking acquisition—much more sharply, in fact, than from problems to be considered in later sections. So we pause, so to speak, to make these implications clear. I have arranged these conclusions in a kind of "spreading wave." I will first discuss conclusions, or implications, that center on the focal problems of this chapter: complexity and innateness in acquisition. This is followed by consideration of other general developmental problems. In these latter general discussions, case-marking data in conjunction with a wider range of developmental data are used to discuss the role of social and linguistic input and methodological problems in interpreting developmental errors and sequences.

Complexity of Acquisition: A Lot of Basic Grammar Acquisition Really Is Complicated

Earlier it was claimed that the acquisition of fixed-order agent-action-patient grammar could be misleading, because it seems so transparent and basically straightforward. From this conclusion, in conjunction with the assumption that grammar acquisition is basically homogeneous, one might infer that perhaps grammar acquisition is not so complicated after all.

To the adult conscious mind, however, grammatical operations such as Turkish or Polish or Georgian basic agent-patient marking typically *do* seem complex. Yet, as has been seen, young children really are quite good at acquiring them. The basic conclusion to draw is that young children are indeed, as claimed, often very good at acquiring complex grammatical systems. English agent-patient grammar just does not happen to provide a very clear illustration of this conclusion.

A corollary conclusion is that such acquisitional problems we call complex because they are complex for adults to think about consciously. But children can acquire these complex-looking (to adult thought) case-marking systems surprisingly early, with little or no recorded overt error. It is essential to dissociate "adult conscious complexity"

from "child acquisitional complexity," and give up the assumption that what is complicated for adults to think about is necessarily complicated for children to acquire. Henceforth in this chapter, "complex" will just mean "hard for adults to think about"; it has no implications for the course of development whatsoever.

"Noticing Things" versus "Sifting" Data

There is a central point to the *kind* of complexity these case-marking systems exemplify. In years of teaching, I have found that when students are asked how a child might acquire some morphological marker, or constituent order, they say something like "the child notices that . . ." (e.g., "the child notices that '-ed' is used to mark a past tense,"). They seem consistently to believe (or hope) that the child could "notice" or "intuit" the right grammatical rule, from maybe just one fortunate analysis in one speech situation.

For all we know, maybe children *do* notice content-form schemas such as 'agent-action-patient' from one or two fortunate examples. But I hope it is obvious to any reader that no child would just notice one day from a single happy guess that unrounded /-u/ marks definite-patient meaning if the noun-stem has a back unrounded vowel. And no child would intuit from a particularly fortunate instance that in Georgian, SWITCH markers mark agents of incompleted actions, but patients of completed actions. In all these and other cases, it is simply inconceivable that the child could just notice the right properties, and only the right properties, from a single instance. Instead, apparently, the child's acquisitional system has long-term "sifting" procedures that induce the right combinations of properties by analyzing fruitful correlations of many different properties, from many different situation- and sentence-sources; these correlations must be analyzed over a large number of separate sentence+situation inputs to give the right result.

Massive Complexity

The complexity here has a particular, distinctive aspect: I call it *massive* complexity because of the masses of different kinds of data that have to be dealt with and sorted over many data inputs. Furthermore, such massive systems are necessary for the analysis of most morphological inflections, not just case marking.

Case Marking and Different Kinds of Innateness

As noted earlier, to most developmentalists, *innateness* in grammatical acquisition tends to mean highly targeted

Chomskyan innateness: extensive, detailed knowledge of possible target outcomes, quickly triggered by only one or two key pieces of prespecified inputs. But this is clearly not possible for the analyses of complex case markers. Who could preknow Georgian or Turkish case marking as a well-detailed innate option? The appropriate analyses could never be "triggered" by just one or two fortunate inputs.

Furthermore, the relevant input properties to case marking (and much else in morphology) obviously draw heavily off the cognitive-social-perceptual domains of thought; they include properties such as definiteness, ongoing versus completed aspect, or agent-patient relations. Case-marking analysis is hardly autonomous or encapsulated vis-à-vis other domains of thought. This seems to contradict common ideas of Chomskyan modularity.

Actually, Chomskyan nativism, properly understood, is not disconfirmed by these findings. First, Chomsky has not claimed that all grammar is autonomous, as discussed earlier, just that aspects of it are; *modularity* means only that inputs to a system from other systems are restricted, not cut off. Second, as will be seen, he also does not believe that all grammar is learned the same way; highly targeted, quickly triggered processes might only apply to certain aspects of grammar (see later discussion).

Disentangling Innateness from Chomskyan Innateness

More important, one of the purposes of this chapter is partly to disentangle "innateness" from "Chomskyan innateness." Again, the former does not perfectly coincide with the latter. As will be recalled, faculty-specific innateness could be realized in many different ways: highly innate, targeted faculty-specific knowledge is only one of these. Others include faculty-specific highly restricted access to material in other systems; another might even be simple access to enormous amounts of neural-computational space (massive morphological analysis problems look as though they would require such computational space). So let us look at the problem keeping in mind the perspective that faculty-specific or species-specific innateness does not necessarily mean Chomskyan innateness.

Stability and Efficiency of Acquisition.   First, it is certainly impressive that these complicated problems are solved so reliably by children in a wide range of intellectual abilities and inclinations, across a wide range of both favorable and relatively unfavorable-looking social situations. Children essentially have to have certain acute forms of organic damage not to learn such systems. As far

as social environments are concerned, most adults in many cultures are *not* interested in having conversations with young children (Heath, 1983), unlike the prototypical Western middle-class mother. Adults and older children in Walbiri culture actually tease younger children about their linguistic incompetence (Bavin, 1992). So it seems fair to say that the acquisition of these complex systems shows robustness across many circumstances; such robustness is often a developmental indicator of species-specific or faculty-specific systems (or both).

The Necessity of Limiting the Property Register. Second, there is an important problem that many Chomskyans and non-Chomskyans alike have discussed (see, e.g., Pinker, 1984; Slobin, 1985a; Talmy, 1985). As has been seen, languages display impressively diverse factors that can control morphological marking; these include wide-ranging semantic and phonological properties, potentially from a number of different local and nonlocal sentence sources.

But the property register cannot include as potential properties every possible aspect of sentences and the speech situations in which they are used; there are simply too many possible properties. In fact, Talmy (1985) argues that across languages, the number of meaningful properties that can control morphological inflection is relatively small (compared with all the possible conceptual properties in the child's world). Properties that are commonly grammaticized in morphology include certain aspects of event roles (e.g., agent or patient), tense, aspect, number, person, agency, definiteness, tense, locative path, gender, status, and a few others. Perhaps an innately selected set of semantic and phonological properties has specified access to grammatical systems like those that analyze small morphological segments (Pinker, 1984). This restriction might arise from species-specific aspects of the general conceptual-perceptual system. But then again, perhaps the restriction arises from specifically language-related evolutionary adaptations. In that case, it would constitute a faculty-specific modular property of grammatical systems, even if the induction process that uses the properties is somewhat open as to how they can be fused into individual inflections.

Connectionism and Restricted Property Registers

One might object that in fact, these massive induction-sifting systems look a great deal like connectionist pattern-analyzing systems (e.g., MacWhinney & Chang, 1995; Rumelhardt & McClelland, 1986), which are generally said to be nonnativist induction systems. But as analysts (e.g., Karmiloff-Smith, 1992) have noted, these neural network systems are always *implicitly* limited as to what input features can enter into the induction process. They *have* to be limited; no computer-simulation system can include all possible features as input. Furthermore, careful inspection of actual simulations shows careful choice of the right input features to give the right result (explicitly analyzed in Lachter & Bever, 1989; implicitly exemplified in MacWhinney & Chang, 1995). Indeed, Smolensky (1992) has proposed a "connectionist" system in which many of the input features are faculty-specific features drawn from current linguistic theory; the inductive system then compares these register properties against the input to give the appropriate language-particular feature weightings. So although an induction system may have a massive sifting quality, faculty-specific innateness may enter into the initial choice of features.

Thus even if complex case markers cannot be completely targeted, this does not mean other forms of species and faculty specificity do not enter the analysis. The robustness and efficiency of children's acquisitional systems and the need to restrict the property register provide general diagnostics that something faculty-specific may be at work, in conjunction with highly efficient species-specific mechanisms, though researchers cannot presently determine their relative proportion.

Grammar and the Social Environment

Are Social Knowledge and Social Interaction "Central"?

Grammatical acquisition takes place in a social interactional environment. To many developmentalists (e.g., Cole & Cole, 1992; Shaffer, 1996), acquisitional theories like Chomsky's seem to emphasize a rather asocial picture of grammatical development, in which the role of the child's social interactants is minor at best. Perhaps most developmentalists would hope to find instead central roles for adult input to children, and the social context, in grammatical acquisition. Chomskyan developmentalists (and some non-Chomskyans) seem conversely to argue that such interaction has little role in grammatical acquisition. I will argue here for more temperate conclusions at both ends.

Positive Roles for Social Knowledge and Interaction. Positive roles for social interaction, and the child's social knowledge, stem from a basic fact: Many basic grammaticized meanings are highly social in nature. Focus, as discussed earlier, controls basic constituent order in Turkish and other languages. Focus refers to whether information is new to the listener or makes claims that contrast with previous claims in the conversation; such meanings have a clear social aspect. Definiteness partly means conceptual specificity, but it also partly means that a reference is specific for speaker and listener alike (Brown, 1973; Maratsos, 1976)—again an obviously partly social meaning.

If interlocutors speak to a child in a manner that is insensitive to whether the information they impart is established, new, or old, the child will receive confusing or noninformative input. In addition, a child who does not have the social knowledge to analyze such social-grammatical properties will not make the right meaning-form mappings. Tager-Flusberg (1988) indeed finds grammatically advanced autistic children to be deficient in just those aspects of grammar that require such social mapping of shared information.

Asocial Sifting-Induction Processes. But what about the other side? Showing that social knowledge and interaction are necessary does not show they are by themselves sufficient. Nor does it show that all grammatical acquisition is guided by shared knowledge, or is molded by the usage of insightful older language users. First, the child has to *see* the shared information; autistic persons prove this is not the automatic response of any intelligent organism to generally species-appropriate input. Second, and more central, all these arguments only apply to the child's analysis of individual social situations. As noted earlier, however, part of the massive complexity of morphological analysis lies in how the inductive system has to operate internally over data inputs from many speech situations, using extensive long-term storage and sifting processes, to converge on just the right property combinations to analyze morphological markers. This convergence-over-many-uses analysis has to be done by systems internal to the child; no one can point out the right property correlations to the child. Nor can any single situation, no matter how well structured, "give" them to the child. So this long-term sifting-induction aspect of the acquisitional processes is indeed relatively asocial and autonomous. Although case marking certainly does not fit the targeted-triggered Chomskyan acquisitional mold, it demonstrates a partly asocial character to grammatical acquisition that cannot be eliminated. Attempts to show either that "social input is central" or "social input is irrelevant" show the usual problems of trying to impose homogeneous solutions on a heterogeneous problem.

Feedback on Grammaticality: A More Specific Social Input Problem

For more than 40 years, a second social-interactional issue has also figured heavily in arguments about acquisition. This issue can be divided into two questions: Do the child's conversants provide feedback on whether the child's utterances are relatively grammatical? and, If such feedback is potentially available, would it critically help children learn grammar? (e.g., Bohannon, MacWhinney, & Snow, 1990; Gordon, 1990; Morgan & Travis, 1989).

Is There Consistent Feedback?

Let us start with the first question. Brown and Hanlon (1970) found that children are *not* more likely to hear positive feedback such as "that's right" or "yes" after grammatically correct utterances, nor are they more likely to hear negative feedback such as "that's wrong" or "no" after grammatically incorrect utterances. They found that such clear parental feedback is contingent on whether the child's utterance was factually *true*, not whether it was grammatical. They also investigated whether relatively grammatical utterances were more likely to be followed by reasonable conversations on the part of parents and found no differences between more or less grammatical child utterances.

Bohannon et al. (1990) note, however, that among middle-class English-speaking children, parents sometimes repeat most or all of what a child says, typically as a way to carry on the conversation (Brown & Hanlon, 1970, noted this). If the child says something ungrammatically, or leaves something out, the parent's repetition quite naturally is likely to correct it or fill in the missing part, because parents generally speak grammatically (e.g., if a child says "he melt it" [for a past act], the parent's counterpart is likely to be "he melted it," filling in the missing "-ed" form). Bohannon et al. believe such implicit feedback could supply specific useful information to the child on the relative adequacy of the child's forms, and help shape the child's grammatical analysis.

Unclarity in the Feedback. The feedback, however, is not really very good statistically. It has been found that about 10% of the time, parents actually imitate ungram-matical utterances. More important, about 30% of the time, they *change* something in repeating a child's grammatical utterance. This is not so surprising. A child might say "the boy's eating," to which a parent might naturally say "yes, he's eating" ("he's" instead of "the boy's"). Or the parent might also *expand* the child's utterance by saying something like "yes, he's eating, *isn't he?*"

These changes mean that some parental responses are implicit corrections, but about 30% are merely optional expansions or other noncorrecting changes. The question is, How is the child supposed to know which changes are implicit corrections and which are just remarks for continuing the conversation? To distinguish among these possibilities, the child probably must know most of the relevant grammar already.

Low Utility of Properly Understood Feedback: Multiplicity of Possible Wrong Properties in Case Marking. Second, how useful is such feedback when it is understood to be feedback? In acquiring case markers in Turkish, Polish, or Georgian, typically the child's errors are errors of omission, not commission—the child leaves out a marker. So the corrections could only be the older speaker filling in something that was missing. How much of the relevant required information can such feedback supply to the child? Suppose the child is working on analyzing Polish case marking, and leaves a case marker off a Class I noun accusative (e.g., says 'eat pear' instead of 'eat pear-e'). So the adult says 'eat pear-e.' What should the child conclude? The child might somehow conclude that *something* in the speech-meaning-grammatical system required /-e/ to be used here. But what? Was it the animacy of the noun? The fact that it is edible? The fact that it is roundish? The fact that its stem vowel is /e/? The child still has all the same problems of analyzing *which properties* are the reason the adult's usage disagreed with hers; this just replicates the original sifting-through-properties inductive problem.

Or suppose the child did occasionally produce a wrong marker (e.g., says 'I eat pear-u' in Turkish), and even is told it is wrong (which in reality seems virtually never to happen). What information does this give the child? It does not tell the child *what* is wrong. When we look at such "feedback-exchanges" in our own language, we tacitly know the right determining properties, so we "see" them as obvious in the situation. If they were so obvious, the child probably would not have made the error in the first place. Most grammatical constructions are like case marking in that many properties codetermine correct usage. For all such constructions, the same arguments apply.

Frequency of Input

This discussion of input would be incomplete without consideration of a last environmental factor: simple frequency of input. The sifting-induction processes discussed for case marking apparently require a good deal of input to work properly. But other well-known findings for morphological acquisition indicate that input frequency is not very important.

Brown (1973) studied the acquisitional sequence of 14 English small-word functors (e.g., articles, prepositions "in" and "on" and forms of "be"), and morphological inflections (e.g., verb present and past tense, progressive aspect, irregular past, noun plural and possessive inflections). Using an acquisition criterion of 90% use in obligatory contexts, he found that children acquire the morphemes in a highly stable overall order. Relative input frequency turned out not to be a predictor of acquisition order. For example, the articles "a" and "the" were the most frequent morphemes in parental input, but were acquired relatively later than most of the other morphemes.

Brown's findings imply relative frequency is unimportant, whereas the previous discussion implies that a good deal of input is required for acquisition. Yet in fact, there is no contradiction. For methodological reasons, all of Brown's 14 morphemes (see Brown, 1973) were highly frequent in the input. He showed that when various morphemes are all high in frequency, *further* relative differences in frequency do not affect acquisitional order. He did not claim that extremely infrequent input would provide sufficient data for acquisition, or make no difference for time of acquisition.

In fact, major frequency-differences probably do matter. Passives, for example, are extremely infrequent in English input to young children (Pinker, 1984), and are acquired relatively late (Bever, 1970). But passives are relatively common in the input to Sesotho children, who appear accordingly to have significantly earlier knowledge of them (Demuth, 1990). More generally, in various Third World rural areas in which people talk to children relatively rarely, reports show markedly slower acquisition trends (Bavin, 1992; Tolbert, 1979). If this is a low-baseline-frequency problem, the result would only be surprising if one expected children to be able to notice the right answer from one or two data inputs. It is not at all surprising for the kinds of morphological analysis processes considered here.

Errors, Sequences, and the Study of Development

We now deal with methodological questions to which case-marking results are sharply pertinent: To what degree can developmentalists count on phenomena such as grammatical errors or sequences of development, to provide direct information about basic underlying processes of development? My own conclusions are, unfortunately, basically pessimistic; in fact, I would happily see strong counter-arguments to the conclusions I present here. A key point is the overwhelming absence of expectable errors during case-marking development, so the discussion begins with some implications of these "nonfindings."

The Underground Nature of Morphological Acquisition

As noted earlier, in acquiring complex case markers, children surprisingly often fail to make any positive errors of commission (e.g., using one morphological inflection where another is required). The basic pattern is an absence of use, followed by instances that appear completely correct. This result is not particular to case marking; it is also obtained in many other morphological acquisitions, such as verb-agreement marking (e.g., Aksoy & Slobin, 1985; Gonzalez, 1984).

What can this lack of observed positive error of commission mean? One possibility is that children do not use the morphemes for some time because they have *no idea* of what they mean. Then suddenly, one day, they "catch on," and produce them correctly. They thus proceed from "no use" to correct use, with no intermediate stages of knowledge.

But as discussed earlier, this sudden noticing hypothesis seems inconceivable. How could a child go instantly from no knowledge to highly accurate knowledge of any particular Polish or Georgian case marker? As far as we can tell, for even a single case marker, there must be long drawn-out induction processes; these processes must have intermediate states during which the child's knowledge of appropriate properties is partly but not wholly developed. But if children produced morphemes using this incomplete knowledge, they would show positive errors of commission. The inevitable conclusion is that somehow, children generally do not produce the relevant inflectional markers during these intermediate periods; production only occurs when the underlying development is largely complete. But if this is true, then development during this intermediate period is "underground," uninstantiated in overt behavior.

Implications of Underground Development

Underground development has two sharp ramifications, one substantive and one methodological. Substantively, there is the interesting problem of why these underground systems do not "report out" responses in intermediate states. But although these substantive issues may be interesting, the methodological ramifications appear uniformly unfortunate. Developmentalists quite reasonably would like to see the intermediate states of developing knowledge systems mapped directly onto overt behavior, so they can see how the system progresses to mature competence. This could tell us much about the basic mechanisms. But underground development, when it occurs, largely defeats this hope; intermediate states of knowledge do not show up in overt behavior.

Errors of Commission versus Errors of Omission. At this point, it might be objected that analysts (e.g., Brown, 1973) have shown that overtly evidenced morphological development is indeed "gradual." But what Brown showed was that children sometimes omit required morphemes, and gradually supply them more and more reliably in obligatory contexts. When uses are supplied, however, they are generally accurate. The observed errors are thus errors of *omission*. As Brown noted, errors of omission in themselves are not very informative. The literature is full of good arguments that many errors of omission in fact show little about the state of underlying knowledge, but may instead reflect "adjunct" problems such as short-term memory processing constraints, as will be discussed. It is errors of *commission*, the use of one morpheme where another is required, or where none should be used, that potentially provide the most information about intermediate internal analyses. But as a result of underground acquisition, the rates of errors of commission in morphological and small-word functors are commonly low or nonexistent.

Other Empirical Support for Underground Acquisition. Other findings support the claim that much grammatical acquisition proceeds underground. Hirsch-Pasek and Golinkoff (1991) find that children understand agent-action-patient sequences well before they produce any. Gerken (1987) produces impressive experimental evidence that even before children produce morphological inflections and various small words, they comprehend sentences that contain them better than sentences that lack them although the latter sentences more closely resemble the child's own productions. Gerken's findings do not tell us what the children know about the use of the markers when they are not being produced, but they show that the children know *something*. My guess is that they know a good deal.

Grammatical Acquisition and the Sequences of Acquisition: The Problem of Adjunct Competence

If acquisition errors are not necessarily going to be very informative, one might hope that observation of the *sequences* in overt behavior would provide information about underlying processes. If B follows A in overt behavior, one might reason, B probably follows A in underground analysis; this fact might, when carefully analyzed, give important clues about basic language-analyzing mechanisms.

There is good reason to doubt this somewhat optimistic conclusion. To see why this is so, it is necessary to define *core* and *adjunct* competences.

Core Competence and Adjunct Competence

Any underlying competence in which a researcher is interested can be called a "core competence" for that researcher. Some other knowledge or processing mechanism can be called an "adjunct competence" if it is necessary to realize the "core competence." For example, suppose an investigator is focusing on children's knowledge of some sequential schema. Even if children have a mental representation of the relevant schema (the core competence), they will not be able to "program" this underlying knowledge reliably in overt behavior unless they have adequate short-term sequential memory capacity. For in "reading out" any sequential schema, the child has to keep in mind what has been produced and what needs to be produced, and compare these against the underlying schema.

(In making this core-adjunct distinction, keep in mind that one investigator's "core competence" is another investigator's "adjunct competence." An investigator whose central interest was short-term sequential memory capacity *would* see sequential memory capacity as core competence.)

Core versus Adjunct Competences in Cognitive Development

From the viewpoint of core versus adjunct competence, much of the recent history of cognitive development has consisted of demonstrations that children often have some core Piagetian competence much earlier than previous experiments had indicated (Gelman & Baillargeon, 1983). This was typically shown by reducing the adjunct competences required by the tasks (e.g., attention, memory-processing demands, unfamiliar stimuli materials), and this task simplification resulted in earlier demonstrated behavioral competence. In other words, it was adjunct competences that had controlled age of passing the tasks, not core competence.

Why Sequences Are "Noisy" Developmental Information Requirements

There is no reason to think grammatical development would be immune to these problems. For example, many investigators believe that English-speaking children omit sentence subjects not because of lack of underlying knowledge, but because of problems in short-term memory processing during production (see Bloom, Ch. 9, this Volume, for extensive discussion).

But if overt behavior is a poor indicator of when a single core competence is observed, then observed behavioral *sequences* must also be poor indicators of underlying *sequences* of core competences. This argument is implicit in some current analyses of the well-known "14-morpheme" acquisitional sequence that Brown (1973) discovered. Brown's criterion for judging a morpheme to be "acquired" was a stable high production rate: a morpheme had to be produced 90% of the time in contexts where it was obligatory (e.g., saying "I see a dog" instead of "I see dog"—an article is obligatory and missing in "I see dog"). But when such a stable production rate is required, then adjunct mechanisms relevant to programming individual productions of morphemes could constitute the major source of acquisitional order. Two such nonmutually exclusive adjunct competence explanations are provided by Tolbert (1981) and Pye (1992).

Tolbert (1981) points out that the individual morphemes differ considerably in how much nonlocal control there is of their appropriate use. For example, "-s" on verbs (e.g., "eat-s") is controlled by properties of the verb (present tense) and the sentence subject (third-person singular). Noun plural "-s" is largely controlled by the number properties of the noun itself. So verb "-s" has much more nonlocal control.

But more nonlocal control naturally entails more demands on short-term memory during morpheme production; there is more information from more parts of the sentence to keep track of. For such morphemes, the relevant information may be lost more often, and the production, essentially, canceled. Tolbert (1981) shows that the number of nonlocal controllers of a morpheme exactly predicts

much of the "stable production" acquisitional order that Brown obtained.

Along another track, Pye (1992) shows that simple phonological salience of individual markers also predicts order of acquisition of frequent morphemes in both Mayan Quiché and English. He argues forcefully that this phonological salience affects which morphemes are easier to "lose" while programming productions. Gerken (1991) produces experimental evidence that the weak rhythmic stress of English definite articles in certain sentence locations contributes greatly to their tendency to be omitted in overt production; this finding supports Pye's conclusions.

Thus, at a general level, developmental sequences of observed behavior might commonly be caused by sequences of adjunct competence acquisition, rather than by underlying sequences of core competence acquisition. This greatly reduces the value of observed behavior sequences as tools for analyzing underlying core competence acquisitional mechanisms.

Conclusions about Methodological Problems

The ramifications of these combined arguments—underground acquisition, low rates of errors of commission, the interpretive ambiguity of behavioral sequences—seem by and large unfortunate. Many facts about acquisition certainly retain their importance; it is a basic empirical fact that parents do not overtly instruct children, and that children yet efficiently analyze tremendously complex case markers like those of Georgian, Polish, and Turkish. But overt behavior does not transparently map out the underlying mechanisms by which children do this. Nor can experiments readily substitute for behavioral observation in solving these problems. For young children's limited attention spans restrict how much data one can obtain from each child; thus experiments must be narrowly focused, and they lack the richness of knowledge sampling that naturalistic observations can provide.

General Summary and Conclusions

To summarize, children are astonishingly efficient in carrying out the massive sifting-induction analyses required to analyze individual case markers in languages such as Turkish, Polish, and Georgian. Though the relevant mechanisms could not be innately targeted, there must be restrictions on the cognitive-perceptual-social properties that can be part of the property register for the basic system.

Both social-interactive and asocial processes play a role, but the asocial ones dominate in the long-term sifting-induction operations. Finally, the phenomenon of underground acquisition, and the interpretive difficulties posed by the strong behavioral influence of adjunct competence, show that developmental data are often missing when needed, or irrelevant when present; the basic mechanisms involved in these complex analyses not only run smoothly but quietly. Investigators cannot expect overt behavioral data to map out the underlying course of development in any transparent way.

FORMAL GRAMMATICAL CATEGORIES: SYSTEMS OF GRAMMATICAL OPERATIONS

The preceding section has shown how easily children can handle grammar systems of surprising complexity. But the focus has mostly been at a relatively low level—the analysis of individual grammatical markers. The acquisition of formal grammatical categories is a higher level problem: How are such individual grammatical analyses organized into higher order "formal category" systems? Historically, this problem has provided a central focus in work on grammar development (Ingram, 1989).

Formal Categories and the Partial Autonomy of Grammar

Formal grammatical categories include the familiar repertory of grade school: subject, direct object, noun, verb, adjective, and preposition (or, in some languages, postpositions). Formal categories are not isomorphic with semantic categories such as agent, or action, though the memberships of formal and semantic categories often overlap greatly. Formal categories are partly created by the very pattern of grammatical structure itself; they thus account for much of what is often called the *autonomy* of grammar.

Interestingly, the strong differences among theories actually preclude finding a neutral description of acquisitional questions. Chomskyans believe, for example, that children innately know what the major formal categories are before they acquire any grammar at all (Grimshaw, 1981; Pinker, 1984). So in Chomskyan views, children do not really *acquire* the categories at all; rather they must somehow come to *recognize* examples of them in the input, on the way to figuring out how the categories specifically work in their own language. In contrast, non-Chomskyans believe children *construct* these categories.

Before we look at these different theories of formal category development, however, we should try to gain some understanding of what constitutes a "formal" rather than a "semantic" category in the first place. Greek provides a helpful example from a non-English language.

Modern Greek Verbs: Distinguishing Semantic from Formal Categories

I will start with a specific question: Why do we not just say that "verb" means "action word" while "adjective" means "state word"? Or that "subject" means "agent" and "direct object" means "patient"? Certainly these correspondences express probabilistically valid *tendencies*. But most linguists would agree that formal categories are in fact defined by the sets of grammatical operations in which their members participate, not by their meanings.

Modern Greek provides an example of this operation-determining principle in its number-person forms for the present tense of the concepts 'run' (a prototypical action-concept) and '(to be) sleepy' (a clear state concept). To say the equivalent of 'I run,' one says 'treh-o.' To say '(s)he runs,' one would say 'treh-i.' 'You (sing.) run' would be expressed by 'treh-is.' There is a specific number-person-present affix for every number-person-present-tense combination.

How would a Greek express the equivalent present-number-person meanings for 'sleepy'? 'I am sleepy' would be 'nistaz-o.' 'He is sleepy' would be 'nistaz-i.' 'You are sleepy' would be 'nistaz-is.' In Greek, in fact, the predicate that means 'sleepy' acts grammatically in just the same way as the word for 'run' in *all* 20 aspect-tense-person-number combinations, even though 'sleepy' expresses a state concept, while 'run' expresses an action concept.

Linguists classify both words as *verbs,* despite their semantic differences. They do this because the two predicates are treated identically for the roughly 20 different tense-number-person combinations that can be marked on intransitive verbs. Each of these grammatical markers constitutes a *grammatical operation.* "Verb" then means a set of predicates that take a common set of grammatical operations, regardless of whether the predicate semantically denotes an action or a state.

English State versus Action Verbs

English has comparable examples. For example, consider the concepts expressed by "fond," "like," and "kill." Surely of this concept triad, "like" and "fond" are the semantically similar duo, and "kill" is the odd one. Yet grammatically, "like" shares verb-grammatical operations with "kill," not "fond." One says in the simple past either "he killed it" or "he-liked it," but not "he fonded (of) it." Or to express first-person-present-tense negation (first-person subject), one says "I *don't kill* those" or "I *don't like* those," but not "I *don't fond* (of) those." Use of "-ed" past, or preceding "*do*-forms" for negation + tense + person are characteristic English verb-set operations. Thus although the state meaning of "like" is so similar to the state meaning of "fond," "like" is grammatically a verb. English has many transitive state predicates, such as "feel," "consist," "belong," "resemble," "know," "believe," "have," "own," all of which are main verbs.

Most linguists furthermore agree that many adjectives (e.g., "quick," "brave," "nasty," "loud," "noisy") are actually highly *actional* predicates (Fillmore, 1968; Lakoff, 1971). They are nevertheless adjectives because they take the same grammatical operations as words such as "warm" or "sad" or "smart."

Some Developmental Data

Acquisitionally, children do quite well at analyzing verb-adjective operation-sets. Two- or three-year-old English-speaking children, for example, generalize '-ed' past to nonactional irregular verbs (e.g., "feeled," "heared," "seed") about as readily as to action verbs (e.g., "runned," "goed") (Maratsos, Kuczaj, Fox, & Chalkley, 1979). Presumably, they do so because these nonaction predicates share in other verb operations (e.g., "I *don't feel* good" or "he *feels* bad"). Furthermore, they do not generalize verb operations to more actional adjectives—they do not say things like "he noisied" or "he louded" (Maratsos, 1982). So it appears that they have appropriately analyzed the grammatical operation-sets that comprise verb versus adjective distinctions, and that cut across action-state boundaries.

Verb-Adjective Variation across Languages

Cross-linguistic patterns buttress the conclusion that the verb-action, adjective-state correspondence is unreliable. Across languages, verbs tend statistically to include the primary action predicates of languages, whereas adjectives tend to include more state concepts. But this distinction is highly labile. Many concepts that are expressed as adjectives in one language are expressed by verbs in another. In modern Greek, 'sad,' 'warm,' 'cold,' 'unpopular,' 'hungry,' 'thirsty,' 'responsible,' or 'in danger,' when said of animate beings, are all main verbs, not adjectives. In fact, many African and American Indian languages have no grammatical adjective-verb distinction at all; all major predicate concepts are treated grammatically in verblike fashion (e.g., morphological inflection on the stem for aspect-tense-person qualities). One says 'he bigs' just as one says 'he runs' (Comrie, 1988).

Grammatical Subjects and Agents

The case of agent and subject seems potentially more promising for a semantic account. In the basic clause structure of probably 95% of the world's languages, transitive agents consistently differ from transitive patients in grammatical treatment. These agent-distinctive grammatical properties undergo a set of distinctive grammatical operations shared by many nonagent predicate roles. This agent-distinctive set thus comprises the grammatical subject properties for the language.

For example, in English basic tensed clauses, the following grammatical operations are distinctive to transitive agents as opposed to transitive patients:

- The transitive agent occurs before the main verb, while patients appear after the main verb (e.g., "Mary/killed/John"; "the dog/is eating/the bone").
- Agents control number-person agreement on the main verb or the verb "to be." For example, the use of singular "he" versus plural "they" controls the difference between "he *eats* carrots" versus "they *eat* carrots," or between "he *is* eating carrots" versus "they *are* eating carrots."
- Agents are encoded by certain pronouns that do not encode transitive patients, these being "I," "we," "they," "she," "he" (e.g., "*she* cured *her*"; "*they* cured *them*"). These agent-characteristic pronouns are called *nominative* pronouns.

Subject is called a *formal* category, however, because nonagent noun arguments also undergo this set of operations. For example, in "he resembles John" or "he is smaller than John," the pronoun "he" does not express the agent of an action when it denotes someone who is small, or someone who resembles someone. But "he" is encoded initially, it controls number-person agreement, and it is expressed by a nominative pronoun. So the noun phrase roles 'small one' or 'resembler' share in the same set of grammatical operations as do agentive roles such as pushers, crushers, cookers, or eaters. The agent-patient distinctions seem to set up a distinctive operational framework that can be applied to nonagents and nonpatients.

Agent Subjects in Other Languages

Subjects and direct objects have partly different grammatical properties in different languages. Turkish agent subjects have no fixed constituent order; what they share is the same case inflection marking (no inflection, which is distinctive in Turkish), and control of agreement properties on verbs. But at a deep level of analysis, English and Turkish subjects are highly similar: In both languages, the basic-clause properties that distinguish agents from patients seem to form the grammatical "matrix" for the subject category. In both languages, the agent-distinctive grammatical operations, generalized to nonagents, define the subject set.

The tendency of languages to have similar semantic formal relations naturally suggests some developmental relation between the semantic categories and the formal ones. Probably most developmentalists have felt that somehow, the core semantic categories like agent, patient, action, object, and state, provide the initial framework for organizing grammatical operation-sets in languages (e.g., Bates & MacWhinney, 1982; Braine, 1994; Grimshaw, 1981; MacNamara, 1982; Pinker, 1984; Schlesinger, 1982). There are, however, formal category structures that do not fit this semantic framework view, and I have been a proponent of formal category acquisition theories that do not rely on such frameworks. But the greater intuitive naturalness of what are usually called "semantic bootstrapping" views makes them a good place to begin a discussion of category formation.

Semantic Bootstrapping (or Assimilation) Theories of Formal Category Formation: General Format

Semantic bootstrapping theorists hypothesize that the child uses central semantic categories such as agent and action to provide an initial framework for the analysis of formal operation-sets. Semantic bootstrapping theories exist in diverse forms, including Chomskyan (Grimshaw, 1981; Pinker, 1984, 1987) and non-Chomskyan forms (Bates & MacWhinney, 1982; Braine, 1994; perhaps MacNamara, 1982; Schlesinger, 1982). Most of these approaches, however, propose roughly the following general developmental progression:

1. The child uses the canonical semantic cue properties (e.g., agent, patient, action, object, physical state) to form initial "protocategories." These will be the ancestors of the adult formal categories. Semantically noncanonical words or constituents such as "need" or "have" are not initially incorporated into these categories.

2. The child's acquisitional system analyzes the language-particular individual grammatical operations in which members of these semantically organized protocategories participate. This gives the grammatical operation-set for the protocategory.

3. The child subsequently incorporates semantically noncanonical words and constituents into the protocategories; thus the protocategory gradually loses its semantic homogeneity, and becomes defined instead by category-distinctive grammatical operation-sets.

Noncanonical Words and Constituents

What is meant by a "noncanonical" word or constituent? It is a word or constituent with some major semantic properties that do not fit any of the canonical meanings: It is not an agent, or an action, or a patient, and so on. For example, the predicate "need" denotes an emotional state; it is thus a predicate, but not an action predicate or a physical-state predicate. Nor are its argument roles (needer and needed) identifiable as agents or patients. So initially, when the child hears a sentence such as "mommy needs a glass," "mommy" will not be analyzed as referring to a proto-subject, "need" will not be analyzed as a proto-verb, and "a glass" will not be analyzed as a proto-direct-object ("mommy" and "glass" however, are analyzable as proto-nouns, because they denote concrete objects).

Later in development, however, the child will have analyzed grammatical operations characteristic of the protocategories; at this point, the noncanonical constituents of "mommy needs a glass" can be absorbed into the protocategories. Thus "needs" will be analyzed as an English main verb, because it is marked with third-person singular present tense "-s," which comprises a distinctive English verb grammatical operation. "Mommy" will be analyzed as a subject, because it is the initial noun argument of a verb, and controls the number-person agreement on the verb in a manner characteristic of proto-subjects.

Canonical Violators: Stipulated Absent in Early Input

"Need" and its argument roles are thus initially ignored by the early protocategory identification mechanisms. Some grammatical items (by *item* I mean "word" or "constituent") in languages, however, constitute what can be called "canonical violators": their semantic properties do give them a canonical protocategory classification, but it is the wrong one. For example, *physical action* provides the cue for "protoverb." But words such as "bath" and "trip" are physical-action words, and yet they are nouns, not verbs. In actional passives such as "he was helped by some friends," "he" is the transitive patient, which would require its absorption into the proto-direct-object category. The agent is 'some friends,' which would cue its absorption into the protosubject category. If such canonical violators appear in early input, they *will* be classified in a protocategory, because they fit the appropriate semantic canonical property. Thus they would carry their grammatical properties into the inappropriate protocategory. As a result, the sentences the child hears in early input must be stipulated not to have such canonical violators (Grimshaw, 1981; Pinker, 1984).

Centrality of Grammatical Cues: A Basic Developmental Property

Eventually, children must encounter violators such as action nouns or passives. A child who was still using the canonical semantic cues as category identifiers would misclassify them. So somehow, between the early protocategory period and this later point, the child must "turn off" or deemphasize the use of canonical semantic-cue properties, and use only the category-distinctive grammatical cues. Thus, any semantic bootstrapping theory requires a provision for this "deactivation." Non-Chomskyans typically seem to assume this deemphasis will occur naturally as a result of general cognitive properties of human category-forming systems. Pinker (1984) addresses this problem in a Chomskyan framework by directly stipulating an innate maturational deactivation of the early canonical semantic cues as category identifiers, and a clear switchover to the use of grammatical operation cues. Whatever one's theory, this eventual dominance of grammatical cues in formal-category formation appears to be a central fact, one to be discussed again later.

Non-Chomskyan versus Chomskyan Semantic Bootstrapping Accounts

Non-Chomskyans (e.g., Bates & MacWhinney, 1989; Braine, 1994; Schlesinger, 1982) believe that semantic bootstrapping does *not* reflect any faculty-specific mechanisms. In their view, the child's general cognitive systems naturally pick out the canonical semantic properties as initial category organizers simply because such properties are central event-concept properties. As language-particular

grammatical operations become distinctively characteristic of these categories, the child's category-assimilation system naturally begins to use them as new category identifiers (Braine, 1994).

Chomskyan Semantic Bootstrapping Theories

Chomskyans, in contrast, believe that children innately know the repertory of the major formal categories, and furthermore know in advance that they are formally defined by grammatical operation-sets, not semantically defined. Why, then, should the child go through the intermediate stage of having semantically defined protocategories?

As Grimshaw (1981) points out, even if the child knows in advance that there are formal categories like subject and noun, the child does not know ahead of time how they act grammatically *in the child's own language*. Indeed, across languages, categories we identify as the "same" category, can act quite differently in their grammar. As noted earlier, Turkish subjects have no fixed order, unlike English subjects. A single regular verb may have up to 3,000 different inflectional forms in some languages (e.g., Turkish), and only one form (the stem) in others (e.g., Chinese). So even the knowledge that there are subjects and verbs, in itself, will not allow the child to *recognize* any instances of them by their grammatical behavior in sentences. But the child needs to recognize *some* valid instances of the targeted categories to proceed with analyzing their language-particular grammatical properties. Grimshaw proposed that the canonical semantic properties would provide good heuristic cues for identifying clear individual instances of subjects, verbs, nouns, and so on. Having done so, the child could go on to analyze their category-distinctive grammatical properties.

It is important to note that in this account, the canonical semantic properties do not initially *define* the protocategories: They are only useful symptoms of category membership. In general, *identifying* properties are distinguishable from *defining* properties. For example, in wartime, wearing a French soldier's uniform *identifies* someone as a Frenchman, even though wearing a French uniform is not a *defining* property of being a French national. Similarly, Grimshaw and Pinker looked at the canonical semantic properties as useful *identification* properties for formal categories, not as defining properties.

This semantic bootstrapping identification procedure thus solves the problem of cross-language variation in grammatical behavior, by using central conceptual-semantic cues to recognize instances in the input. Hence, as Grimshaw

(1981) and Pinker (1984) showed, a Chomsky targeted system might advantageously be programmed to use nonlanguage properties evolved previously in evolution (Bickerton, 1981; Pinker & Bloom, 1990). This does not explain, however, why the languages do not just all treat the same formal categories in the same grammatical manner (Maratsos, 1989); no adequate Chomskyan answer has been given to this question, to my knowledge.

Difficulties for Semantic Bootstrapping Theories

Semantic bootstrapping theories, whether Chomskyan or non-Chomskyan, are intuitively appealing because they allow the child to use intuitively salient conceptual-semantic properties to lay down quickly the grammatical framework for the adult system (Grimshaw, 1981; Pinker, 1984). But they have that one very clear theoretical condition: Canonical violators cannot appear in the early input. Sometimes this condition is fully met. Object words are nouns in all early input, because they are nouns in all adult grammars. English early input contains no passives (Pinker, 1984) and so contains no agents that are not subjects. Yet the condition is also violated surprisingly often; for some languages, in fact, this violation is a regular state of affairs. I will begin with English violations, before discussing non-English cases.

Problems in English: Early Nonverb Action Words

As just noted, early English input meets the no-violators condition for object words and agents. But Pinker (1984) found that although 85% of the action words in early input were adult verbs, 15% were adult nouns, and thus had grammatical properties of nouns. According to the theory, this means that 15% of the input for protoverbs would be misleading, and carry nonverb grammatical properties into the protoverb category. Nelson (1994) provides evidence that young children comprehend and sometimes use nonverb action words such as "bath." Furthermore, in children's early English combinations, nonverb action words such as "up," "down," and "away" are often used as the major action predicate of sentences like "car away" (Maratsos & Chalkley, 1980) and thus constitute probable spontaneous "mis-classifications" on children's part.

Other generally canonical languages also have some frequent input violations. In Sesotho, for example, passives are common in input to young children; Sesotho-speaking children use passives earlier than English-speakers, so they probably attend to this counter-canonical input (Demuth, 1990).

Agent-Patient "Switch" Languages

More generally, and more devastating, in 95% of the world's languages, it is true that agents are indeed consistently adult subjects in basic sentences. But what about the other 5%? In these languages, agents and patients often "switch off" on which argument role is the subject even in "basic clauses" of the language; neither one stably commands the role. For example, one such language is Tagalog, a characteristic language among the 120 languages and dialects spoken in the Philippines (Schachter & Otanes, 1976).

Does Tagalog have a grammatical subject? Though languages differ in subject properties, there is a prototypical list of about 35 grammatical and semantic properties that grammatical subjects across the world's languages seem to draw from (Keenan, 1976). Convergence on a number of these identifies the Tagalog "subject." For example, there is a standard set of nominative noun markers for intransitive subjects and the subject of multiargument sentences. This same noun-argument controls aspect-marking forms on the verb. Finally, in most languages, grammatical subjects strongly tend to be semantically definite; in some, like Tagalog, the subject is required to be definite (one cannot say the equivalent of 'a dog was barking' or 'a girl laughed').

One might expect that in Tagalog basic clauses, the agent role would consistently be chosen to govern these subject properties. But instead, for agent-patient verbs (e.g., 'throw,' 'give,' or 'read'), the system works as follows: (a) If the patient is semantically definite, it governs the subject properties; (b) if the patient is semantically indefinite, *any other* major noun role can govern the subject properties. For example, in the Tagalog equivalent of 'the boy gave *the book* to the girl,' the definite patient *book* would control grammatical subject properties. But in 'the boy gave *a book* to the girl,' the patient constituent 'a book' is indefinite; thus either the agent 'the boy' or the recipient-goal 'the girl' could control subject-properties (the choice seems to be highly optional).

So the child could *not* properly analyze the Tagalog grammatical subject by initially placing all agents into the protosubject category, and analyzing the grammatical properties of this category. Many agents are nonsubjects; so the protosubject category would contain both subject and nonsubject grammatical properties.

One might think the complex and odd grammar of this language would cause many false starts, errors, and other developmental disruptions. In fact, Gonzalez (1984), who kept a diary on his nephew and niece on weekends, reports acquisition of the main properties of the system by about age 3, with no errors of case marking or verb-agreement marking (the verb aspect marking agrees with the subject in semantic-grammatical case).

In other languages, agents and patients may switch off being subject depending on other contingencies such as the relative humanness of the nouns, or their relative focus, or which is closer to first person (Rispoli, 1991). Developmental reports (Rispoli, 1991; Slobin, 1992b) again fail to indicate that children learning these languages find them in any way "odd" or "deviant" (see Rispoli, 1991, for a property register matrix-grid account of how children could analyze such systems).

Such agent-patient switch languages are relatively uncommon, and so statistically "deviant." But as Slobin (1992b) notes, nothing about children's acquisition of them indicates that children find them in any way odd or deviant. Their acquisition appears to be a *natural* acquisitional fact, not a deviant one. Such languages provide extremely serious problems for semantic bootstrapping theories.

Formal Categories That Have No Semantic Cores

Furthermore, many Indo-European languages have minor formal categories that are defined by distinctive grammatical operation-sets, but that have no consistent semantic "core" properties to provide developmental frameworks for these operation-sets. One example of such formal category systems is Polish case-marking noun-subsets. A subfragment of the system follows, for convenient reference:

	Set I	Set III
Nominative	stem + a	stem + o
Accusative	stem + e	stem + o
Genitive	stem + y	stem + a

As discussed earlier, in these systems, a child cannot predict on semantic grounds which noun-set a particular noun will fall into. But once analyzed, the system is productive and systematic: Knowing a noun takes /-a/ nominative marking, one can predict it will take /-y/ genitive marking; knowing a noun takes /-o/ nominative marking, one can predict it will take /-a/ genitive marking, and so on.

What makes a noun a member of Set I, is that it takes a distinctive set of grammatical case-marking operations; what makes a noun a member of Set III, is that it takes a different distinctive set of case-marking operations. These formal gender categories are indeed *formal categories,* but they are ones that have no semantic core tendency.

Other Indo-European languages also have minor categories consisting of different operation-sets for marking noun case. In Russian and Greek, noun stem marks form different case-marker sets. In German and Greek, the noun-set markings are carried by the definiteness-marking determiners for the nouns (the equivalents of 'a,' 'the,' 'this,' 'that') and the pronouns that refer to the nouns. In these latter languages, different sets of case markers go with semantically nondistinctive sets of nouns; the determiners fuse definiteness marking with case marking.

Acquisitional Data

As described earlier, Polish-speaking children, by age 2, master their own complex noun gender systems with little acquisitional error. What about other languages? Katis (1984) and Stephany (1995) report largely error-free learning of the Greek noun and determiner markers by 3 years. Naturalistic observations of German-speaking children show no errors of wrong gender-class marking (Walter, 1975). Greek also has a formal *verb conjugation* system (different sets of verb markers to mark aspect-number-person-tense); this system also shows little developmental error (Katis, 1984; Stephany, 1995) and is learned by 3 years.

Slobin (1973) did report persistent gender-class marking errors for Russian-speaking children until the age of 7, which he attributed to the lack of semantic differentiation of the noun classes. But it turns out that the most persistent of these errors occur in a small formally eccentric part of the Russian system, in which even knowledge of the nominative form of a noun cannot predict other case uses reliably (Maratsos & Chalkley, 1980). Smoczynska (1985) notes that in the singular, the Polish case-marking system is very similar to the Russian system, but it lacks the "eccentric" subpart; this may partly account for the precociously early and error-free Polish acquisitional data.

Distributional Analysis and Minor Categories

As discussed earlier, in systems like Polish noun gender, acquisitional systems would have to keep track of how individual nouns had individual case markers applied to them; over time, various subsets of these nouns would turn out to have similar grammatical properties (i.e., similar operation-sets that apply to them) and would take the same distinctive set of case markers. Nouns of each subset would be grouped together on the basis of sharing distinctive operation-sets, with an internal category designated for each subgroup. (Verb conjugation analysis would work similarly, for sets of tense-aspect-number-person markers.)

This process is, basically, an example of a general form of pre-Chomskyan linguistic analysis called *distributional analysis* (Maratsos, 1979), though there are some differences at a finer level. Distributional analysis constitutes a second major approach to formal category formation to which we now turn our attention.

Distributional Analysis of Formal Categories

Distributional mechanisms work generally as follows:

- For each word or constituent (or, for each "grammatical item"), grammatical operations that apply to them are recorded.

- Over time in long-term storage, semantically heterogeneous grammatical items turn out to take highly overlapping operation-sets.

- Such overlap in operation-sets causes the items to be classified together, and a novel category designated to refer to items of that class.

Judging from their skill in constructing minor formal categories, children's acquisitional systems employ such distributional mechanisms quite efficiently.

Generalizing Distributional Mechanisms to Major Formal Categories

Though distributional mechanisms apply especially clearly to minor formal categories, the mechanisms can be generalized to explain the construction of major formal categories such as subject and verb. For as discussed earlier, major formal categories are also defined as semantically heterogeneous words or constituents to which a distinctive common set of grammatical operations can be applied. The formal verb-adjective distinction, for example, largely corresponds to different grammatical operation-sets for encoding the tense, aspect, and number-person information relevant to different sets of predicates.

In Maratsos and Chalkley (1980), we accordingly argued that item-by-item distributional analysis comprises the basic acquisitional mechanism that constructs both minor and major formal categories. Appropriately applied, this mechanism would not only capture more familiar major formal category systems such as English verb or subject, but

also the "deviant" agent-patient switch systems such as Tagalog, which cause fatal difficulties to semantic bootstrapping systems. For children would not have to find some nonexistent "core" semantic property with which to bootstrap such formal categories. They would move directly from the analysis of how individual items take common grammatical properties, to the analysis of the relevant formal category structure.

We also believed that these arguments point to another conclusion: Formation of major formal categories is *not* innately targeted (children do not know the major formal categories in advance). We reasoned as follows:

1. Many minor formal categories would not be on any nativist's targeted list.

2. Nontargeted distributional mechanisms are necessary to capture these minor formal categories.

3. The same nontargeted distributional mechanisms can construct major formal category systems.

4. Therefore, it is unnecessary to hypothesize innate knowledge of major categories; in fact, it is theoretically unparsimonious to do so.

Criticisms of Unrestricted Distributional Analysis

Our original analysis, however, had its own difficulties. One of these, that there are too many possible "grammatical operations" for the system to register, is highly correctable; the other problem, the question of *why* semantic core properties tend to predict major formal category membership, is more serious.

Too Many Grammatical Properties.   As part of our antinativist stance, we (Maratsos & Chalkley, 1980) assumed that the child is a kind of "inductive vacuum cleaner" that tabulates all the grammatical properties of all words and constituents in sentences, so that the distributional systems can flexibly find the "best" distributional systems for any language system.

But there are too many possible grammatical properties in the input for any analytic system to tabulate (Keil, 1981). Pinker (1984) shows that even using an impoverished criterion "grammatical property," a seven-word sentence has 9 billion possible such properties. Both Keil and Pinker thus argued that a distributional analyzer would have to be selective about which properties to record at all. This argument seems irrefutably correct. (I considered some additional distributional problems in Maratsos, 1991.)

Privileged Grammatical Operation Types. The cross-linguistic literature provides some clues about the possible nature of these "privileged" grammatical property types. Although the grammatical properties of major formal categories vary across languages, certain grammatical property types strongly *tend* to recur as central for defining major formal categories. For example, operation-sets for marking tense, aspect, and person agreement consistently prove central in defining verb categories. Operation-sets for marking definiteness and quantity typically define formal noun categories. Some of these "privileged properties" even play roles in defining more than one formal category. Definiteness, for example, often also constitutes a grammatical subject property (Keenan, 1976); it often fuses with thematic role (e.g., agent, patient) as part of the case-marking system (e.g., Turkish, German, Tagalog, Greek).

Restricting Input Properties and Innateness. Thus, let us accept that distributional systems are innately specified only to accept certain grammatical property types as input. Does this entail that formal categories are "completely innate" after all? Pinker (1984) argued that accepting such restrictions was already contrary to the antinativist spirit of our original arguments, which had assumed the child unbiasedly analyzes all possible grammatical properties. So, he argued, one might as well accept a Chomskyan targeted account like his own (Pinker, 1984).

But this argument is incorrect. If the conditions of argument were "either something is not at all innate, or it is all innate," Pinker's argument would have been decisive in favor of targeted innateness. But as outlined early in the chapter, there is no reason to hold to an "all-or-none" homogeneous view of innateness. A distributional account that accepts species-specific or faculty-specific restrictions on which grammatical properties can be tabulated, still comprises a much weaker form of faculty-specific innateness than a Chomskyan innately targeted account, in which all the major formal categories are known in advance.

Any formal category-analysis system moreover, has to specify which grammatical property-types it can tabulate as input. For example, a semantic bootstrapping mechanism that arrived at 'subject' by analyzing all the conceivable grammatical properties of agents, would have far too many agent-grammatical properties to tabulate (Pinker, 1987, implicitly makes this argument). Thus, a restricted property register for formal category analysis must be part of any formal category acquisitional system.

Why Are There Any Cross-language Semantic-Formal Tendencies?

So distributional mechanisms, appropriately restricted, are highly flexible in their ability to analyze a wide variety of formal category systems. But oddly enough, as Braine (1994) points out, such purely distributional approaches are a little *too* flexible. If category systems are so flexible, why do 95% of the world's languages have such strong agent-patient → subject-direct object correspondences in basic clauses? Why is it that in all (or nearly all) languages, object words are consistently clustered together in the noun category (Maratsos, 1991)? Even when languages reverse the typical semantic-formal correspondences, the usual canonical semantic properties generally retain some important partial predictive role. For example, although Tagalog may not give agent the usual priority for being the subject in basic clauses, like many agent-patient switch languages, it gives priority instead to (definite) patients—but patienthood is another core semantic property. These cross-linguistic semantic-formal trends persuade me that semantic properties must also have some partial weight as potential category-unifying properties in early formal category formation, operating in conjunction (not prior to) with distributional processes.

Other Changes of Mind

The years of theoretical and empirical dispute have, as they should, partly affected most of the participants. For example, Pinker (1987, 1990) currently agrees that the straightforward semantic bootstrapping approaches he had earlier advocated will not work (see Pinker, 1987, for extensive sets of reasons); Pinker (1990) furthermore agrees that the highly general applicability of distributional analysis to many different kinds of formal category systems cannot be a coincidence; thus in his current views, distributional analyses of item-grammatical properties must constitute part of formal category analysis from the start, in conjunction with weighted semantic category cues. Nor does he continue to hypothesize instantly triggered category identifications; he agrees that language variation makes such instant identifications vulnerable to serious classification errors.

Summary and Conclusions. When originally clear theoretical oppositions partly dissolve into agreement, onlookers may have the feeling that not much has been accomplished. To the contrary, however, I think a great deal that is surprising and interesting has been learned, even if no "pure" acquisitional theories remain plausible, and central questions remain open. I will try to list here what seem to me some major resulting conclusions and persistent open issues.

Children's Acquisitional Facility with "Odd" Language Systems.   In this formal category section, I have again emphasized children's skill in acquiring grammatical systems that contradict "natural intuitions" of English speakers. These especially include the distributionally organized minor formal noun- and verb-subset category systems of many Indo-European languages, and the agent-patient subject-switch systems of languages like Tagalog and other non-Indo-European languages. Many English speakers, I think, tend to hope that acquisitional theory could be based on a firm English-like foundation, with unusual category systems treated as odd footnotes (or nonexistent). But the acquisitional evidence once again shows that for children, "unusual" systems are ordinary acquisitional problems (just as Turkish or Georgian case markers are). Such language systems must comprise "natural facts" for grammatical acquisitional theory, not annoying footnotes.

Distributional Systems and the Dominance of Operation-Sets.   Semantic properties such as agent-patient and action-state distinctions play central roles in aspects of both children's and adults' grammar. Yet in formal category formation, grammatical operation-sets end up with strongly dominant defining weight over such canonical semantic properties. Because semantic-conceptual properties are so cognitively central, it does not seem intuitively obvious on general grounds that such grammatical operation-set properties would have such dominant category-defining weight; this feature of formal category acquisition increasingly seems to me to indicate faculty-specific features of acquisition.

Similarly, distributional analysis—the *process* of analyzing individual grammatical properties of items, and analyzing similarities among items in their operation-sets plays a pervasive role even in early acquisition. One would hardly expect 1-year old Polish children or 2-year old Greek children to be carrying out such complex analyses, on the basis of what is known about their general cognitive abilities; yet the developmental data show it must be so. Furthermore, these organized detailed analyses are somehow configured in a systematic way with partial weightings for relevant semantic properties. I find it increasingly difficult not to perceive at least some faculty-specificity in these precocious distributional processes and their smooth co-working with semantic properties.

Unsettled Questions of Target Innateness.   In a way, knowing that so much in formal-acquisition systems must be arranged properly to work so well, makes it less urgent to answer the specific question of whether children actually know in advance the major formal category repertory. In fact, they cannot preknow everything: Some languages have no adjective-verb distinction; some languages do not have agent-centered subject-systems; many languages have minor formal systems. Yet evolutionary systems often have partly targeted initial knowledge that can be partly tuned or modified by associated learning systems; the vervet monkey, for example, initially makes its "snake" warning cry to any long thin object on the ground, before monkey-culture environment tunes this innate response to apply to the local set of dangerous snakes. Pinker and Bloom (1990) imply that acquisition of major formal category variations might correspond to a similarly partly targeted, partly tuned innate system.

On the other hand, it is plausible that sufficiently restricted semantic + distributional analyses may operate naturally to *construct* the right major and minor category outcomes, without knowing which particular categories it is moving toward (Ingram, 1989; Maratsos, 1989; Slobin, 1985a). The great naturalness of acquisition of minor or noncanonical major formal category systems gives such constructional accounts a great deal of appeal, in my view.

The truth is, the years of theoretical dispute have caused many major opposing targeted and constructional positions to converge enough in subpropositions that clear evidential distinctions among them are not easy to find. Again, this may seem unfortunate; in reality, however, the partial convergences probably represent considerable progress in understanding. I do not believe we would have been able to understand how interesting some of our acquisitional results really are, without having had the theoretical disagreements that brought out their significance.

CURRENT CHOMSKYAN APPROACHES TO SOME ABSTRUSE PROBLEMS

The previous section included a good example of Chomskyan targeted innateness: the nativist semantic bootstrapping theory proposed by Grimshaw (1981) and Pinker (1984; revised in Pinker, 1987). Yet in reality, we have not really centered on the most characteristic kinds of Chomskyan arguments except in passing; nor have we looked at phenomena that in many ways comprise the stronghold of Chomskyan confidence in highly targeted faculty-specific innateness.

The goal of this section is to discuss such ideas and problems directly. It is important to note that we cannot claim a thorough explication here, for two reasons. First, a thorough explication would presuppose a year or two of linguistic background. Second, Chomskyan linguistics itself is going through one of its periodic episodes of rapid change (e.g., "deep structure" and "surface structure," concepts familiar to most psychologists in some form or another, have been abolished in Chomsky, 1992). Chomskyan acquisitional theories can be expected to change as the linguistic theories do. Yet at a basic level, certain aspects of Chomskyan acquisitional logic are likely to remain constant throughout these changes, and I will try to concentrate on such aspects.

Basic Chomskyan Ideas

Nonunique Chomskyan Beliefs

In fact, some foundational Chomskyan stipulations accord quite well with some of the conclusions already reached in dealing with other acquisitional problems. Let us make these shared stipulations explicit.

1. *Languages differ from each other in various respects.* For any basic dimensional value on which languages differ (e.g., properties involved in marking patients in one language vs. another), there must be a corresponding property in a property register that can register the presence or absence of the relevant property in the respective languages.

2. *The property register cannot include every theoretically imaginable property value or property combination* (because there are too many of these). Moreover, the property variation range that languages display seems to show some highly specific restrictions, whether these are due to faculty-specific restriction, more general species-specific restriction, or both.

3. *There must be specific inductive processes that go from initial register property-input correlations, to grammatical form;* again, these may be faculty-specific, species-specific (or mammal-specific) in nature.

More Characteristically Chomskyan Ideas

To these basic foundational ideas, Chomskyans typically add the following hypotheses:

4. *Language-particular, innate, often "abstruse" register properties.* In Chomskyan theory, some central initial register properties are viewed to be faculty-specific; many of these look highly abstruse to conscious thought. Thus abstruse complexity can be added to massive and configurational complexity as a complexity type. These abstruse register properties include grammar-particular categories such as "Comp(lementizer)"; they also include subtle formal differences in sentence boundaries within sentences, or of formal hierarchical relations among sentence constituents; these are hypothesized *not* to be eventually reducible to properties borrowed from other domains, though they must eventually connect with such other-domain properties somehow.

5. *Limited variation in acquisitional choices and inferences.* Furthermore, for a core set of property dimensions, acquisitional analysis need choose only among a highly limited, preknown set of possible values. This variation-range can be called the parametric range for a property continuum; analyzing the right property value or setting for a particular language generally can be called "setting the parameter" for that language. This resembles the "restricted property register" discussed earlier, but is believed to be both much more highly configured and much more restricted in Chomskyan theory.

6. *Relatively instant "triggering" of parametric choices.* For the core parameters of variation, the range of possibilities is hoped to be highly restricted, and well specified. Acquisitionally, if these conditions are met, it becomes possible to posit that a single, appropriate input datum could immediately trigger the right parametric choice for a child learning a particular language. This contrasts with the slow, grinding inductive processes frequently outlined in previous sections.

7. *Multiple parameter-setting.* Furthermore, it is hoped, parameter settings for many different parametric dimensions might be exactly correlated across the world's languages. Abstractly speaking, any language that has some value *x* for Dimension 1, is guaranteed to have some value *y* for Dimension 2, and so on. If this is so, and the child innately knows these correlations, then setting one parameter appropriately would immediately set one or more of the others.

The Chomsky theorist thus hopes that for certain key processes, grammar acquisition resembles ethological fixed reaction patterns as much as possible, except that complex internal knowledge states, rather than overt behavioral responses, are what is triggered by preselected input stimuli.

Parameter Setting: Some Perspectival Amendments

In considering Chomskyan ideas, it is important to keep track of some important perspective amendments. The following seem central:

- *Limits of core grammar.* Chomsky himself (1992) pointedly notes that core grammar does not include all grammatical processes. Thus, no single validation or disproof of a particular grammatical process could prove or disprove whether core grammar as a whole is a viable hypothesis.

- *Nonfaculty specific sources of some basic register properties.* Even for the core grammar, many of the proposed innate register properties are not grammar-specific in likely origin. Aspects of agency, noun definiteness, and verb tense, for example, play central roles in many core acquisitional processes. These properties are probably recruited from more general conceptual and social systems, even if their routing to core grammar is faculty-specific.

- *Logical independence of some of the propositions.* It is commonly assumed that all the preceding acquisitional hypotheses *must* go together, because they are commonly asserted together by Chomskyans. This implies that attacking one of them, for example, constitutes an attack on all; conversely, supporting one constitutes support for all.

  In fact, like most theories in psychology, the constituent propositions are mostly logically independent. For example, as noted earlier, non-Chomskyans may hold that analyses such as agent-action-patient are instantly obtainable from one or two inputs because of their general cognitive naturalness. So "instant acquisition" is not logically equivalent to "innately known grammar-specific properties." Conversely, one could easily hypothesize that the child often uses grammar-particular, highly abstruse-looking register properties, but feeds these property registrations into a "slow, grinding" induction-over-many-occurrences inducer (Smolensky, 1992, proposes such a system in a connectionist implementation). Thus, the different claims do not necessarily rise and fall together; validation or falsification of one does not necessarily falsify or validate others.

A Preliminary Evaluation

My own belief is that among the claims, the most theoretically central, and most plausible one, is that some grammatical register properties may be both faculty-specific and abstruse in nature. First, this claim has remained most constant over the years; the proposed induction processes (and indeed, particular basic register properties themselves) have often changed radically. Second, I would judge on various grounds that the other claims do not seem to be doing very well.

The full range of evidence relevant to these evaluations is too extensive, and too technical, for clear explication here. But it is possible to indicate briefly some reasons for these overall evaluations. I will begin by giving reasons for the negative evaluation of multiple parameter setting and instant triggering.

Against Multiple Parameter-Setting

The idea that setting the value for one parameter might automatically set the value for one or more others was first suggested in comparisons of Italian versus English (Hyams, 1986; Rizzi, 1982). Italian allows Pro(noun)-drop; that is, tensed clauses do not have to have overt grammatical subjects (see later discussion). It also has a much richer subject-verb agreement morphology, and allows a specific range of *wh-questions* not allowable in English (e.g., it allows questions equivalent to "which tornado does John believe that destroyed the village?"). Such parameter values, it was proposed, all strictly predict each other across languages; thus the child, analyzing one, would automatically know the others.

Soon, in linguistics itself, much cross-linguistic research was devoted to searches for mutually restricted parameter settings. In fact, however, it is impossible to say any convincing candidates for mutually restricting settings have been found yet. For example, not only morphologically rich languages like Italian and Spanish allow Pro(noun)-drop. So do morphologically bare languages like Chinese. To try to save the parameter-setting account of Pro(noun)-drop, it has been proposed that "morphologically uniform" languages allow it: that is, languages with rich agreement morphology, or none at all (and thus are "uniform") (Hyams, 1989). But this proposal is both unconvincingly ad hoc, and empirically probably unsound (Chomsky, 1989; Comrie, 1990). Papers in Webelhuth (1995a), such as Webelhuth (1995b), Harbert (1995), and Hendrick (1995) comment that in general, clear corestrictions among parameters have turned out to be much less common than had been hoped. Promising proposals that emerge from the study of a few languages typically fail when more languages are investigated. The relative failure of the program has probably partly contributed to recent basic changes in linguistic theory such as those in Chomsky (1992).

Obviously, past failure does not guarantee future failure; but it is impressive that no consistent examples have emerged yet after years of concentrated search. Before acquisitional studies are pursued to empirically support multiply-correlated parameter settings (or other cross-language equivalence patterns), psycholinguists might well wait for linguists to come up with multiple correlations that actually survive after 10 or 15 years of linguistic studies.

Instant Triggering of Single Grammatical Analyses: Vulnerability to Erroneous Input

Suppose no convincing proposals for highly correlated parameters (or other pattern correlations) emerged from cross-linguistic studies. It remains theoretically possible that individual input data could trigger the right parameter setting for each single grammatical parameter decision, which is still an impressive induction savings. Braine (1971), however, long ago noticed an important vulnerability in all single-input hypothesis-testing theories: They require the input to be absolutely error-free. If a system is so keenly tuned that a single input can "set" a parameter, it is also so keenly tuned that a single erroneous input can *mis*-set a parameter (Meisl, 1995; Valian, 1990). Adult speech to children is certainly, on the whole, high in accuracy (Newport, Gleitman, & Gleitman, 1977; Snow, 1972); but "high in accuracy" is not the same as "without error." Adult speech does contain occasional errors for various grammatical processes, and a single-input system is automatically susceptible to them.

Valian (1990), who certainly believes in central aspects of the Chomskyan program, discusses this problem extensively for Pro(noun)-drop, and concludes, using empirical data from English-speaking and other samples, that potential adult error in the input does indeed occur. Even standard English speakers occasionally omit pronominal subjects from sentences (around 5 to 10% of the time), as part of a general "editing" procedure that allows many initial elements of sentences to be dropped in colloquial speech (e.g., "probably won't come, if it's raining"; "doesn't like that, does he?"). In theory, there are ways for the child to ferret out when such input is incorrect. But these error-ferreting procedures require the child to use probabilistic evidence gathered across sentences, in ways

that single-instance parameter setting was supposed to make unnecessary.

As a concrete example of the problem in a more abstruse grammatical domain, we can consider the following instance, recorded by the author when Jessica Maratsos was 5 years old. In one exchange between Jessica and her mother, the latter said, quite interpretably in context, "That's a program that I know some (people) that got a degree in." This sentence is ungrammatical in English, but is of a general type that is grammatical in Swedish (Engdahl & Ejerhed, 1982). Thus it constitutes a legitimate input for the parameter-setting processes for relative clause analysis. Again, the sentence was highly interpretable in context. No adult corrected the use immediately, and the conversation continued in a natural way after its utterance. At the age of 5, Jessica had sufficient control of complex embedded-sentence relativization grammar to make it likely she could analyze the grammatical form of the input. For example, she had previously uttered the sentence "They're mad at him for getting mad at who they thought was a god," an accurate description of an incident she was watching in *Star Wars*.

So suppose she analyzed the input sentence appropriately. In single-input theory, such an analysis of this one sentence would have been sufficient for Jessica to set the relevant relative-clause parameter incorrectly for a Swedish value. None of her subsequent productions indicate she did so. Suppose one posits she did misset the relevant parameter, but somehow "undid" this initial setting. But a mechanism to undo incorrect settings of this kind would probably have to include in the acquisitional equipment the kinds of sifting probabilistic mechanisms that were supposed to be eliminated. A single-input induction theory of this kind thus appears too vulnerable to occasional input error, or it appears to require probabilistic adjustment mechanisms that oppose the original spirit of the proposal.

Abstruse Variables Illustrated for Wh-Question Processes

So far it has been (rather quickly) concluded here both that "multiple-setting" and "single input-trigger" acquisitional theories have serious current problems. I would give their prospects of future success a very low Bayesian estimate, myself. But as discussed earlier, such negative conclusions, even if correct, would not bear very heavily on the proposal that "abstruse grammar-specific" properties play a role in core grammar acquisition. Although there is no conclusive evidence regarding this latter proposal, there are certainly some abstruse-looking basic processes to look at; one fragment of a relevant grammatical process will be discussed, that of wh-processes.

Nonabstruseness of Some Core Grammar Problems

Before discussing wh-processes, I want to stress that not *all* proposed core grammar processes appear to be equally abstruse. For example, as discussed above, it has been proposed there is a basic parametric variation among languages in whether pronominal subjects can be dropped (Italian, Greek, Spanish) for tensed clauses or not (English, German). But this does not seem (to me, anyway) to be an overwhelmingly difficult inductive problem; in fact, it does not really seem particularly worse than other problems that apparently have to be solved anyway with a less initially restricted and targeted set of acquisitional mechanisms (e.g., correlations among case marking, definiteness, and vowel harmony for Turkish). The wh-processes about to be illustrated are thus not claimed to be representative of all core grammar processes in potential abstruseness; support for abstruseness here, does not constitute support for abstruseness everywhere in core grammar.

Restrictions on Wh-Processes: an Exemplary Abstruse Problem

As stated earlier, a few cross-linguistic variation problems and their relevant "boundary-properties" (as these language-differentiating properties will now be called), probably supply the central confidence of Chomskyans that some acquisitions in grammar require grammar-specific innate knowledge, because the relevant boundary properties seem highly abstruse and, for that matter, highly focused in their application to a limited range of grammatical problems. Noncoincidentally, the relevant abstruse properties require probably a year or two of linguistic background for full explication; this is obviously impossible to supply here. So I hope to be able to illustrate the problems, without saying exactly what they are claimed to be. In particular, I will describe restrictions on what are called wh-gaps in sentences, a grammatical problem that has remained theoretically central since the ground-breaking linguistic analyses in Ross (1967).

Wh-questions: Neither All "Form," Nor All "Content." "Wh-processes" refers to a broad-range of grammatical processes which seem to play a role in many grammatical constructions. They are called "wh-processes"

after the wh-question, a key exemplar of them. Wh-questions are questions which question particular sentence-constituents; English examples include sentences like "*What did you see?*" or "*For which reasons* will John go?" Again, we want to emphasize that such grammatical processes are not utterly isolated from nonlinguistic social and cognitive analysis. Indeed, asking such questions appropriately requires detailed appropriate social-informational analysis. For example, consider "What will John eat?" This corresponds to roughly the following, using "X" to mean the to-be-questioned part: Both listener and speaker share knowledge that "John will eat X." The speaker does not know the nature of "X," and thinks the other conversant can supply this knowledge. The wh-question requests this additional, new information. Thus acquiring the form of wh-questions requires the child to be able to analyze what is shared and unshared knowledge in speech events, to be able to analyze the nature of social requests for information, and so on.

But cross-linguistic variation proves that the information content of such questions does not automatically dictate their form. The following sentences compare Chinese, Welsh, and English versions of 'What will John eat?' (I have put the auxiliary verb 'will' in English-like position in all three translations, just to avoid distraction from the main concern, the different treatment of the central wh-constituents in the three languages):

1. John will eat what? (Chinese)
2. What-i will John eat it-i? (Welsh, Arabic)
3. What-i will John eat _____ -i?

(Reasons for the "-i" indices will be explained.)

Intuitively, one can see that Chinese simply leaves the wh-constituent in its "normal" position, the same that would be used for nonquestions such as 'John will eat—something' or 'John will eat—this radish.' In Welsh and Arabic, the wh-constituent is placed at the front of the clause, as in English. But a pronoun 'it' is also left in the normal position for the questioned constituent. This 'it' is understood to refer to the same referent as the 'what' at the front. 'What-i will John eat it-i?' means 'what is it such that John will eat it?' The use of the index "-i" on both 'what-i' and 'it-i' signals that they refer to the same thing, or are *coreferential*.

Finally, English simply places the wh-constituent in front, and leaves behind a "gap" where the normal placement of the relevant constituent would have occurred. This gap almost certainly corresponds to something psychologically real that English speakers process in both production and comprehension. One must remember, in producing a wh-question, not to put anything in the "normal" position. In comprehension, one must analyze where the gap occurs, to obtain the appropriate semantic-grammatical interpretation of the initial wh-constituent. The different position of the gap supplies the interpretive difference between, for example, 'Who(m)-i did Mary talk to _____-i about the boss?' versus 'Who(m)-i did Mary talk to the boss about _____-i?'

More Abstruse Cross-Linguistic Differences in Wh-Questions. Capturing the right language-particular wh-question structure for these languages, however, might so far be considered within the acquisitional abilities of a generally good analyzer of symbolic sequences, as human children must be conceded to be. Currently of greater interest are the subtle cross-linguistic differences in where wh-gaps can occur, in different languages. A set of wh-gap sentences follows, with the relevant "grammatical context" of the wh-gap marked by [   ]. In this set, only questions 1 and 2 exemplify types acceptable to most English speakers. (Asterisks signal that the sentence is unacceptable to most English speakers.)

1. What-i does John think [(that) Mary will eat _____-i?]

2. What-i does John think [_____-i will eat Mary?]

3. *What-i does John think [that _____-i will eat Mary?] (This has the same meaning as (2), related to 'John thinks that X will eat Mary.')

4. *What-i does John wonder [who ate _____-i?]

5. *What diseases-i does John deny [the claim that doctors can cure _____-i?]

6. *What diseases-i does John admire [doctors who can cure _____-i?]

7. *What diseases-i does John admire [the doctors who can cure _____-i?]

Of the preceding, Italian allows questions 1 through 4, but not 5 through 7. Norwegian allows questions 1 through 5; Danish, 1 through 6 (probably); and Swedish, 1 through 7. So there is a fairly regular continuum ranging from more restricted (here, English) to less restricted, with boundary points consisting of wh-gap context properties that children must analyze as allowed, or not allowed, in their own language. The ability to make this analysis without overt instruction seems to decline gradually into puberty (Johnson & Newport, 1989), but is robust in childhood.

No simple general hypotheses explain the cross-linguistic differences. For example, acceptability is not determined by whether a speaker has heard the *specific* wh-sentences before; all these sentences are presumably novel as specific sequences of words. Nor is it that the unacceptable sentences are just "very generally novel." For example, one can introduce a wholly new word, such as 'symdex,' and adults will accept as grammatical a novel wh-question that contains 'symdex' in it, such as "Which symdex-i do you think Mary will buy _____-i for John?" In some ways, such a sentence is more generally "novel" than the less acceptable sequence *"What kind of car does John admire anybody who owns -i?" in which every word and concept is familiar.

Only certain specific grammatical properties seem to act as cross-linguistic differentiators. Making the right language-particular analysis of the wh-question input, apparently means analyzing for the presence or absence of a rather particular set of properties of wh-gap contexts in one's own language. This set of potential wh-gap delineators can be called *wh-gap properties.*

Some Important Acquisitional Considerations. Furthermore, some general acquisitional facts are important to keep in mind. First, there is no evidence adults teach children the general restrictions overtly; adults do not know them consciously themselves. Nor is there evidence children make errors of exceeding their own language's boundaries and thus no evidence they get adult feedback for ungrammatical utterances. Besides, even if error-feedback events occurred, the child would have to figure out what property of the many properties of the speech situation and sentence was actually causing the difficulty. So the child would still have to carry out the same property-space search.

What Are the Wh-Gap Properties Like? If the wh-gap properties that differentiate languages, or differentiate usages within languages, turned out to be obvious general cognitive or perceptual properties, then there would be nothing very surprising or interesting here. The properties, however, do not seem to be obvious ones. Most English speakers will not find themselves having any obvious ideas of what is wrong with questions 3 through 7 (furthermore, when people try to guess, they are typically wrong). The relevant properties are not obvious at all. In fact, linguists are still arguing over what the right within-language and cross-language boundary properties are; if those properties were obvious, such arguments would have been settled years ago.

Not All the Boundary Properties are Faculty-Specific. Some of the relevant boundary properties, though, do turn out to be ones that are probably recruited from more general cognition and social understanding. For example, consider the difference between "What-i does John like [pictures of _____-i]?" versus *"What-i does John like [those pictures of _____-i]?" (unacceptable for most speakers). The main difference is that 'pictures of X' is semantically indefinite, whereas 'those pictures of X' is definite. Wh-gaps in semantically definite expressions are typically more problematic, both within and across languages (Chomsky, 1986; Engdahl & Ejerhed, 1982).

Abstruse Boundary Properties. On the other hand, many of the other boundary properties look more abstruse and faculty-specific. They include various subtle distinctions among formal types of embedded sentence boundaries that languages may allow to intervene between wh-constituents and later gaps; language differences may be determined by how many of these selected structural boundaries may occur directly next to each other, in the path between the front of the clause and the wh-gap. Just because of their "abstruse" grammar-particular quality, these boundary properties cannot be briefly explained here.

Unused Potential Boundary Properties. Furthermore, the choice of wh-gap boundaries appears to be highly restricted. Many other possible properties do not seem to determine acceptability or nonacceptability in any known language: Is the question about an action versus a state? about an animate or inanimate? does the speaker approve of the questioned event? None of these important-looking properties ever seem to matter. Perhaps children could learn languages in which such properties partly control wh-gaps. Most linguists would guess they could not, though we have no way of knowing. But again, it is certainly impossible that *all* such potential properties and property combinations should play roles.

A Brief Statement of the Argument. This, then, is the heart of the Chomskyan case: Children must record the presence or absence of certain key grammatical properties, in order to analyze the right "restriction profile" for wh-gaps (and many other related grammatical processes) in their own language. The relevant properties seem to be highly selective, and often quite linguistically abstruse. Chomskyans feel confident that it is unlikely these analyses follow solely from generally natural cognitive-perceptual properties of sentences.

Non-Chomskyan Alternative Formulations for Wh-Processes: "Natural Processing Arguments"

If the automatically registered boundary properties are indeed in part so idiosyncratically grammar-particular, the Chomskyan case here is very strong. Are there any alternatives? Some analysts have tried to show instead that within a particular language, some, most, or even all such "odd-looking" restrictions follow from the social-communicative naturalness of the construction, once the social-informational purpose of the relevant construction is fully understood (e.g., Bever, 1970; Eretschik-Shir, 1982; Kuno, 1988; Van Hoek, 1995; these references include discussions of both wh-processes and other abstruse processes). At least some of these arguments are highly plausible. For example, as noted earlier, within and across languages, whether or not a noun constituent is semantically definite influences the acceptability of wh-gaps inside the constituent. Wh-gaps that occur inside definite noun expressions are on the whole less acceptable (e.g., compare "Which dogs-i does John like [pictures of _____-i]?" with "Which dogs-i does John like [those pictures of _____-i]?"). As was discussed earlier, definite expressions are supposed to be ones for which speaker and listener can already uniquely identify the referent. Thus questioning some part of them runs counter to their "presupposed, old-information" discourse referent status (Eretchik-Shir, 1982, has excellent discussions of such arguments, applied within Swedish).

It remains controversial whether all proposed restrictions can somehow be recast this way. Probably a majority of linguists would guess they cannot, though the scope and influence of such "speech-event-information" analyses seems to be growing. Even if such explanations are widely applicable, however, they encounter a puzzling situation in the context of cross-linguistic differences. If the relevant restrictions are indeed wholly natural products of the social-cognitive processing of grammar, presumably they would apply universally across different languages because speakers across languages use the same basic social-informational and cognitive processes. Instead, different language communities observe different boundary properties. Aside from the puzzling fact that such major cross-linguistic variation occurs at all, there is the acquisitional problem as well: There must still be a language-acquisition inductive process that automatically registers different property values in different languages. Without specification how a "natural" analyzer would carry out this task across languages, it is difficult to say the Chomskyan problem has been solved.

A General Evaluation of Wh-Processes

Space limitations preclude further examination of these complex questions. But it is surely evident that whatever they are, the relevant cross-language boundary properties here are not typically obvious to the conscious mind. Yet young children efficiently and unconsciously register the appropriate relevant wh-gap property profile that characterizes their own language as opposed to others. This developmental robustness and efficiency is quite striking, no matter what one's general theory of the analytic primitives. Nor does further study of the problems in these domains typically make them more straightforwardly transparent. The odd and abstruse complexity of these and related problems gives many Chomskyans their core confidence that at least some of grammar acquisition must involve highly grammar-specific, innate mechanisms. Certainly it is reasonable for them conditionally to draw confidence in this way, even if the relevant linguistic issues are still without final resolution.

Acquisitional Studies and Complex Restriction Issues

One might naturally hope that acquisitional studies would add important, even decisive information here. I believe that when the issues are understood adequately, developmental data, currently unfortunately do not play this decisive role, for a number of reasons.

Why Quickness of Acquisition Is Not Decisive

I think most acquisitional investigators are convinced, for example, that the quickness of acquisition is itself a key issue for Chomskyan nativism in general. Quick acquisition of complicated-looking systems is stereotypically associated with highly targeted Chomskyan innateness (e.g., Crain, 1992; Maratsos, 1979). Slower acquisition might then be reactively associated with non-Chomskyan acquisition (if children know everything in advance, why is acquisition taking so long?).

Why Fast Acquisition Is Not Decisive

But these associations are not logically necessary. Suppose, for example, acquisition of some relevant systems is quick (e.g., Crain, 1992; DeVilliers, 1995; Roeper & DeVilliers, 1992). Chomskyans would (and do) find such findings rewarding. As mentioned earlier, however, some anti-Chomskyans also believe some acquisitions may be quick (e.g., agent-action-patient schemas). A non-Chomskyan can believe in quick acquisition when analysis of the property space is believed to be highly natural. Thus, suppose a cognitive-processing non-Chomskyan natural set of basic analytic properties can be found for wh-processes; then the basic property-register mechanisms might yet again work very efficiently. The point is, analyses can be natural for varied reasons: because they fit a faculty-specific analytic process (Chomskyans), or because they fit a species-specific set of natural processes.

Why Slow Acquisition Is Not Decisive

On the other hand, suppose acquisition for some abstruse grammatical processes turns out to be relatively slow (e.g., Wexler & Mancini (1987), for various pronominal and reflexive restrictions in English and other languages). Either side could claim that the basic register properties are indeed "natural," but development is held up by the delayed development of various adjunct systems. For example, some grammatical processes involve dependencies between widely separated parts of sentences (Elman, 1992; Johnson & Newport, 1989). The resulting adjunct sequence-memory problems could slow down acquisition in any kind of account.

Or suppose acquisition was relatively slow because it requires a highly extended sifting-grinding process. This only addresses the quick-triggering aspect of Chomskyan hypotheses. If no one can think of non-faculty-specific properties that can analytically take the place of Chomskyan proposed abstruse properties in the relevant property register, then it does not really matter whether acquisition comes from "triggering" or "grinding through."

Why Developmental Errors or Nonerrors Are Not Decisive

Finally, whether or not there is a great deal of developmental error might seem to be decisive. Lack of errors of commission seems intuitively to support highly targeted Chomskyan accounts. But as shown earlier, in many systems that cannot be highly targeted in advance, such as gender-case-marking systems (e.g., Polish), low error rates are also common. High error rates, if ever observed, could be written off to adjunct causes by either side.

The view taken here is that the complexity of the problems and the noise in our developmental data currently ensure no simple decisive acquisitional predictions. If qualitatively different acquisitional behavioral outcomes could be shown to follow clearly from opposing analyses of the basic boundary properties, and if the noise in acquisitional studies could be filtered out, perhaps decisive acquisitional evidence on these problems could be gathered. Presently, it is difficult to see that opposing views allowing such discrete differentiation exist; in effect, the main problem lies with what analyses of basic properties can be gotten in the first place. In fact, analyses of these matters are still fluctuating strongly among linguists themselves, so no stable boundary-property analysis is currently available, much less clear and complete opposing analyses.

SUMMARY AND CONCLUSIONS

I have argued above that we should not currently expect any "smoking gun" decisive evidence on questions like these. This does not mean individuals cannot draw, and argue for, Bayesian evaluations of the whole set of phenomena. For example, whatever the actual nature of the relevant boundary properties for wh-processes, the language-particular inductions required for them are probably not something the conscious mind would have intuitively predicted young children would automatically be doing. Any reasonably objective observer should be impressed by the robustness and efficiency of the acquisitional systems that deal with these complex grammatical problems. It seems likely that some rather idiosyncratic species-specific and probably some faculty-specific human characteristics are at work here.

INVESTIGATIONS OF CLINICAL SYNDROMES

By this point, many readers have wearied of the theoretical and barely empirically based nature of much of the discussion. It can only be pointed out that this high degree of theoretical complexity is ultimately related to the reasons that grammatical acquisition is such a remarkable phenomenon.

But who would deny a desire for more straightforward empirical evidence about the faculty specificity of grammar? In recent years, studies of clinical conditions, such as retardation syndromes, or results of brain lesions, have seemed to produce compelling relevant findings. Indeed, the writer of this chapter was himself at one time highly compelled by such findings (Maratsos, 1989). But a closer look at the phenomena, accompanied by more recent findings, often shows less relevance to high-level core grammatical processes, and more relevance to adjunct competences, than one would have hoped. The literature is extensive, and so only two research domains are discussed here (see Maratsos & Matheny, 1994, for wider review).

Brain Localization

Why Brain Localization Is Not Equivalent to Organizational Modularity

It is a natural hypothesis that if grammar is organizationally modular, the physical organization of the brain would reflect this (Fodor, 1983). That is, there would be physically separate "language" or "grammar" areas in the brain. In considering this hypothesis, however, it is important to note that grammatical *organizational* modularity does not logically require corresponding physical localization. Many corporations, for example, comprise organizational modules. But the physical input-output extensions of a large corporation are found in widespread, noncontiguous areas of the world, where they can take advantage of convenient labor sources, physical resources, consumer markets, and so on. Likewise, grammatical abilities utilize widespread cognitive, perceptual, and social abilities. Even if there were a "grammatical module," its physical extensions in the brain might be widepsread for analogous reasons.

Brain Localization Evidence

Still, if grammatical competence were to be physically localized in the brain, this would intuitively comprise powerful evidence for organizational modularity (Fodor, 1983). In the nineteenth century, Broca noted the evidence that traumas or disease lesions in a certain part of the left hemisphere seem specifically to damage sentence production (Broca's area). Wernicke later found that lesions in certain posterior left hemisphere areas produced fluent speakers who made little sense, and comprehended poorly. In contrast, right-hemisphere lesions do not seem to affect language ability very much. Rather, they affect most (not all) spatial-analytic abilities (Kosslyn & Koenig, 1992).

In the 1970s, Zurif and Caramazza (1976) furthermore theorized that Broca's area corresponds to the control of sentence grammar, especially morphology, and Wernicke's area is the home for sentence semantics. Poizner, Bellugi, and Klima (1987) found that native sign language users showed quite analogous grammar-related difficulties for left-hemispheric damage, even though sign language is heavily spatial-analytic in many respects; this strengthened the language-localization hypothesis.

Difficulties for Grammar Localization Hypotheses

But in fact, there have always also been difficulties for the straightforward versions of localization hypotheses. Left-handed persons also usually have left hemispheric localization for language, but about 15% seem to have right hemispheric or bihemispheric localization. More striking are various acquisitional phenomena. For example, gradual rather than fast lesion of Broca's area often results in no loss of language function (Broca, 1965), which is rather surprising.

Even complete loss of the left hemisphere can be overcome. The left hemispheres of a very few infants are surgically removed because of extremely severe epileptic seizure. Such infants grow up to speak quite normally. Their overall cognitive ability is lower than average, not surprisingly (Huttenlocher, 1993); but qualitatively, their speech is normal, even for complex morphological systems such as German noun-gender case-marking.

Some investigators have found that children without a left hemisphere show somewhat lower-than-average language syntactic processing in experimental studies of complex constructions (Dennis & Whittaker, 1976). This is not very impressive for several reasons. First, the relevant children speak normally. To say they are simply "passing"—acting as though they have acquired normal language when they have not—reminds one of claiming that a tone-deaf person could manage successfully in a professional string quartet. Second, such children have lost a hemisphere; they have fewer general adjunct resources to draw on in complex tasks. Third, we have no idea of how much damage to the remaining hemisphere might have been caused while the eventually removed hemisphere was causing seizures; seizures are not confined to one hemisphere. (This fact makes it less impressive that children who lose their left hemispheres later in life show a wider range of language outcomes; it is not known how much the remaining right hemisphere was damaged by the seizures.)

Broca's Aphasics and the End of Grammar Localization

For most investigators, current hopes for strict localization of grammatical ability fell apart after the remarkable results reported by Schwartz, Linebarger, and Saffran (1985). They investigated very severely impaired Broca's aphasics, who could barely put together two words to make utterances and could not reliably understand differences between sentences such as "the boy kissed the girl" versus "the girl kissed the boy." Smith and Schwarz thought of having these subjects judge fairly subtle grammaticality differences among sentences. For example, there is only a small morphological-control difference between 'did he going?' and 'is he going?' Or what is the difference between 'we ate the cake that she made' versus 'we ate the cake after she made.' It has to do

with the ways in which relative pronouns like 'that' license later gaps in English clauses, whereas conjunctions like 'after' do not. The severely impaired Broca's aphasics were able to judge grammatical versus ungrammatical sentences with surprisingly good ability, despite their devastated productive and comprehensional abilities. Their behavioral deficits must arise from problems in adjunct competences, not in basic grammatical knowledge. As a result of these and many fascinating related results (see, e.g., Bates, Wulfeck, & MacWhinney, 1991; Heechen, 1985), most aphasia researchers no longer believe that Broca's versus Wernicke's area corresponds to qualitatively different deficits in grammatical core competence. Rather, workers in the field speak in terms of adjunct competence "excitation versus inhibition functions" or "temporal integration" functions. In fact, no one has any clear idea of what might be going on (Bates, 1994), but clear localization of modularly separated grammatical abilities is not a current candidate.

Odder Results about Brain Localization

Actually, I have not yet even mentioned the oddest set of brain-grammar results. Newborns occasionally suffer from hydrocephaly (liquid in the brain), and some decades ago, current shunting techniques were not available. The typical result was extensive or virtually complete loss of the upper brain cortex. Surprisingly, while averaging lower than normal cognitive and language function, a substantial proportion of these children nevertheless ended up functioning in the normal range. One well-certified case who has pretty much no upper cortex (Lewin, 1980) has a tested adult IQ of 126 and has received a degree in mathematics from Sheffield University. He seems completely normal to those around him. These results seem currently unassimilable by any neurological developmental theory.

Conclusions about Localization

The truth is, we do not know where in the brain grammar might be. We probably do not even know what this question means. But whatever the eventual answer, current localization studies offer no straightforward support for grammatical faculty specificity.

Retardation Syndromes: Down versus Williams Syndrome

Different clinical retardation syndromes, like different brain lesions, also often show distinctive patterns of mental deficits: One syndrome may affect one set of abilities relatively sharply, whereas another syndrome more sharply affects a different set. Turner's syndrome in girls, for example, typically affects spatial-analytic ability more than verbal intelligence. Behavior-genetic and psychometric studies also support some general "verbal" abilities (including tests of reasoning about similarities and differences, vocabulary) versus spatial-analytic abilities (Plomin, 1990).

Even within spatial-analytic measures, in fact, different syndromes have different impacts. Williams syndrome children, for example, have good facial recognition, but draw relatively badly when young, relative to their overall IQ. Down syndrome children's drawings are at least recognizable, but facial recognition is relatively impaired (Bellugi, Bihrle, & Corina, 1991).

For the claims about grammatical faculty specificity, however, a general "verbal" ability (which includes many general cognitive abilities) versus "spatial" ability difference is not decisive. It would be more interesting to find that, for example, grammatical core competence abilities showed some clear dissociation from other verbal-higher cognition measures. Some recent studies have been taken to show just such fractionation or separation (Bellugi et al., 1991). In particular, investigators have compared the ability profiles of two syndromes, Down syndrome and Williams syndrome, to show that grammatical and other cognitive abilities can "dissociate." That is, it is claimed that Williams syndrome children do well at acquiring grammar, even though their other cognitive abilities are very poor. Down syndrome children contrastively appear to do much worse at grammar, relative to other cognitive abilities. If grammar and other verbal cognition shared in a fully "general" cognitive capacity, both should rise and fall together. So perhaps these results do show faculty specificity for grammar. But again, further analysis is required to come to conclusions.

Let us first discuss the two syndromes separately. Down syndrome children are moderately retarded, with general IQs averaging around 50, which constitutes roughly the first percentile for IQ. Their grammatical progress, however, as measured by speech samples, is relatively even slower. Many Down syndrome adolescents speak and comprehend at the level of normal 2- to 3-year-old children. Their vocabulary acquisition rate is very slow; and furthermore, when it reaches a point where grammatical acquisition normally "takes off," it does not (Chapman, 1995). It is important to note, however, their grammatical progress does not *qualitatively* differ from that of normal children; it is only extremely slow (Chapman, 1995; Fowler, 1990). If

their central conceptual-analytic core for analyzing input relevant to grammar were qualitatively deviant, qualitative differences would show up. The fact that the main problem is very slow progress, suggests that the main problem may be a low-level one, such as difficulties in getting input into the analytic system. I shall return to this hypothesis soon.

Williams syndrome children also test low in IQ, with an average around 55. Their vocabulary acquisition is also slow. But when it reaches the normal "critical mass," grammatical acquisition progresses fairly normally.

On other cognitive abilities, they seem relatively impaired, compared with their overall IQ. For example, some Williams syndrome adolescents can pass Piagetian conservation tests, but others cannot, though they are relatively fluent in language (Bellugi et al., 1991). This finding of relatively fluent final grammatical knowledge, compared with very poor abilities in other cognitive areas, has led commentators like Damasio and Damasio (1992) to write:

> The maturation of language processes may not be dependent on the maturation of conceptual processes, since some children with defective conceptual systems have nevertheless acquired grammar. The neural machinery for some syntactic operations does seem capable of developing autonomously. (p. 89)

Flavell, Miller, and Miller (1993) write of "language independent of cognition," and Maratsos (1989) cites the Williams results as supporting faculty specificity.

Questioning "Independence from Cognition"

But in fact, even the original observations on Williams syndrome children do not support such strong conclusions. For example, consider the claim of "language independent of cognition." What would this mean, taken literally? Williams syndrome children speak semantically sensible sentences. They describe ordinary events and objects in normal ways. Sensible sentences are sensible because they make conceptual sense. It is not easy to say what "grammar without concepts" would look like: Perhaps the product would be sentences like Chomsky's famous "green ideas sleep furiously," in which grammatical structure is correct but there is no sensible content. No one claims Williams syndrome children speak this way.

Besides, as discussed earlier in the chapter, aspects of grammatical acquisition heavily recruit from general cognition or social analysis (e.g., agency, definiteness, tense, and aspect distinctions). Any adequately speaking child must have access to all the required cognitive-grammatical primitives. Furthermore, at a more microcognition level, the basic vocabulary of Williams syndrome children means just what normal people's vocabulary means for the same words; recent claims of exceptional associative responses in certain laboratory tasks (Bellugi et al., 1991) have been countered by results from a more representative Williams sample (Mervis, Morris, & Bertrand, in press). It also has been reported that Williams syndrome children do relatively well in narrating stories, given a picture-story like the "frog" story (Rossem, 1993). If they are good at narrations, they must have memories adequate for tying together past, present, and future events (as they apparently do when telling stories), abilities to estimate what other people can understand, and the like.

Nor does the other evidence prove that their grammatical and language abilities develop without "adequate" conceptual support. For example, many Williams syndrome children become fluent speakers without passing Piagetian conservation tasks. The same thing can be said of most normal 4- and 5-year olds. In fact, no one currently knows why children fail conservation tasks in the first place; many researchers believe the task problems lie in adjunct rather than core competences (Gelman & Baillargeon, 1983).

Low-Level Explanations of Syndrome Differences

Recently, in fact, Mervis and her colleagues (in press) have found surprisingly straightforward low-level adjunct cognitive abilities may explain much of the within- and between-syndrome variance in grammatical progress. Within Williams subjects, for example, there is a normal distribution of grammatical abilities, and 70% of the variance can be explained by the additive effect of just two measures: Peabody Vocabulary Test, and backward digit span, a low-level test of short-term memory for sequences. To take in the basic input for grammar, one of course must have short-term memory for sequences; individual differences in this adjunct ability appear to explain a good deal of within-syndrome variance. What about the difference between Williams and Down syndrome children? Much of this difference is again explicable in terms of low-level ability differences. Down syndrome children, in particular, score at the bottom of the first percentile on the backward digit span, indicating their short-term memory for sequences is weaker than their overall IQ. Again, to take in grammatical input in the first place requires short-term sequence memory. Down syndrome children's extremely poor specific short-term memory capacity thus can explain much of their relatively very slow grammatical progress. Mervis (personal communication, 1996) is currently studying a 7-year-old Down syndrome child who has backward digit span ability in the low-normal range, and indeed has syntactic ability in the low-normal range as well.

Conclusions: Clinical Syndromes and Low-Level Adjunct Abilities

The results from Broca's versus Wernicke's aphasias, and Down versus Williams syndromes, thus currently come to remarkably similar general conclusions: What seem to be profound core competence-behavioral deficits may mostly result from impairment of adjunct abilities, such as "excitation versus inhibition" functions, or short-term sequence memory.

These results might tempt one to wonder if in reality, grammar itself is nothing but a coordinated collection of low-level abilities. If one defines *low-level* and *coordinated collection* carefully, this could be theoretically feasible. But there is another possibility, one which seems more likely. To use an analogy, suppose investigators were studying various syndromes that attack gifted painters and affect their painting ability. These investigators might assume initially that the syndromes were attacking the painters' high-level artistic talents, since that is what we are chiefly interested in. But instead, it turns out that the syndromes act largely through attacking low-level processes (e.g., most of them are painless arthritic processes that attack the hands and thus affect the artistic output). The researchers would be unlikely to conclude that in reality, there are no high-level abilities involved in being a gifted artist. Similarly, the failure of clinical syndromes to affect core grammatical ability does not show there are no "core grammatical abilities." This failure may simply show that clinical syndromes typically attack adjunct competences, not that adjunct competences are all that exist.

The data from normal and non-normal acquisitional and language use thus agree completely in one respect. Differences in adjunct functions control much of observable overt behavior. Nature has not arranged for deep underlying acquisitional and knowledge to be transparently observable by a careful, informed observer using common sense.

GENERAL CONCLUSIONS

Grammar and the Mind

What conclusions can be reached about grammatical development from the incomplete evidence and discussions here? First, it should be obvious that *no* claim is being made that grammar as a whole is isolated from other aspects of cognitive or social life. Grammatical acquisition, it has been stressed, draws from a wide variety of social, perceptual, and cognitive sources. Nor is it claimed that *all* of grammar is surprisingly complex. Some parts of it, like English fixed order agent action-patient schemas, really may be transparently related to "natural" cognitive-perceptual schemas.

But since grammatical acquisition is not homogeneous, these conclusions can only characterize aspects of it. Other aspects of grammar and its acquisition seem tremendously complex. This complexity itself lacks homogeneity. "Massive" complexity may consist of the child sifting through many possible property correlations to analyze case marker or agreement marker properly, or the massive complexity of forming related-operation formal category systems. Or the complexity of grammar may lie in the configurational complexity of property relations in formal categories, or the abstruse complexity of some properties that restrict wh-processes, and other, undiscussed, abstruse coreferential processes. In all these cases, innate restrictions on the mass of possible influencing input properties seemed required, whatever their source, in the service of dealing coherently with cross-linguistic variability.

Such complexities, and the child's ability to configure them correctly without overt instruction, points to a partly innately buffered set of acquisitional processes. But as was stressed initially, *innate* can mean many things: innate processes characteristic of many species, innate processes characteristic of only one species, or innate processes characteristic of a particular faculty. Even among faculty-specific innate processes, there is a difference between highly targeted, faculty-specific innate knowledge, or more weakly, a highly structured interaction of non-faculty-specific processes. Nor are any of these processes mutually incompatible, on the whole.

This is a natural point in the chapter for readers to expect the author to "resolve" many of the questions, or at least express a general opinion. Personally, like Slobin (1985a), I would guess that a mixture of all the above causes, in some right proportion not easily guessed, is likely to be right. But to me, at least, there seem to be no available "smoking gun" arguments that settle the interesting particulars of many current hypotheses.

Another Interpretation of the Basic Issues

Throughout all this, I have accepted the general view that faculty specificity in particular is the central problem of the field. But now I would like to propose there has always been a more general issue, which seems to me furthermore to have a reasonable current answer. This issue is whether, according to the standards of the conscious mind, the mind itself is a rational, accurate, comprehensible cognitive system; or whether the mind is, in fact, shot through with qualities of idiosyncracy and oddness. The latter, at a general level, is taken here to be partly implicit in what Chomsky is arguing.

Let us go back in history a little. When Chomsky emerged as one of the foremost opponents to Skinnerian views, it was natural to assume that Chomsky supported opposite views. Skinner claimed there is no such thing as a rational, comprehensible, accurate mind; this is definitional to behaviorism. The obvious opposite is that the mind is in fact rational, adaptive, and accurate. Certainly Piaget was a distinguished representative of this "rational mind" approach, with his belief in the "child as young scientist," and probably most information-processing researchers would support the same view, in some form or another. It was natural to assume that Chomsky also supported such a view.

But as it turns out, Chomsky was not on the side of general rationality and logic after all. He called his views "rationalism," but this just borrows Descartes' name for nativism. Certainly to most outsiders, Chomsky's view of the mind entails that at least the grammatical part of it is "quirky" and "idiosyncratic" rather than generally "rational." He also believes, simultaneously, that grammar, though connected to other mind processes, does represent a partly separate faculty.

Because the "quirkiness" of grammar and its faculty specificity go together in Chomsky's own views, they are typically taken to be logically equivalent. Thus, much of the opposition to Chomsky holds that if grammar is not acquired through the use of a separate faculty, it is acquired by a generally rational, comprehensible, adaptive, accurate cognitive faculty, as Piaget or many information-processing researchers would claim.

But logically, the questions of quirkiness and faculty specificity can be separated. If grammar is partly quirky, then the mind that acquires it is likely to be odd in part as well, whether this "odd quality" is hypothesized to be localized in one component or spread out through the workings of the mind in less localized fashion.

In the writer's view, aspects of the complexity of grammar really are odd. Many aspects of grammar are often more complex, often oddly so, than they need to be for straightforward communicative purposes. Those aspects of grammar where Chomskyans find their greatest confidence, such as the varied restrictions on wh-processes, furthermore, often seem qualitatively odd. They are not something one would have predicted beforehand. Intelligent and well-educated persons who just lack specific linguistic training, in fact, usually find full explications of these processes to be unintelligible. Yet normal children unconsciously deal quite equally with all these peculiar-seeming grammatical problems, with little noticeable behavioral perturbation. This seems to demonstrate that at least some aspects of grammar do not overlap very well with the presumably more general rational processes available to the conscious mind.

Therefore my personal conclusion is that the mind, like many evolutionary systems (Lewin, 1984), does indeed have many quirks and odd-looking (to the conscious mind) idiosyncracies running through it, even as it also contains straightforward and expectable aspects as well (e.g., Pinker & Bloom, 1990, emphasize some evolutionarily straightforward parts of grammar, and are correct in doing so). From this perspective, arguments over faculty specificity are interesting, but only concern how localized the odd-looking mind properties are. My view is that Chomsky has been claiming, at least implicitly, that much of the mind's working is indeed quite "odd" from the perspective of conscious, rational, logical thought; at this general level, the hypothesis looks strong. Grammatical acquisition currently provides the strongest support for this general hypothesis; this may in turn provide its most important current contribution to our understanding of the mind.

ACKNOWLEDGMENTS

I would like to acknowledge the exceptionally helpful advice of the volume editors and chapter reviewer in greatly improving the expositional form of this chapter.

REFERENCES

Aksoy, S., & Slobin, D. I. (1985). The acquisition of Turkish. In D. I. Slobin (Ed.), *The crosslinguistic study of language acquisition* (Vol. 1, pp. 15–68). Hillsdale, NJ: Erlbaum.

Bates, E. (1979). *The emergence of symbols: Cognition and communication in infancy.* New York: Academic Press.

Bates, E. (1994). Colloquium held at University of Minnesota, Minneapolis.

Bates, E., & MacWhinney, B. (1982). Functionalist approaches to grammar. In E. Wanner & L. Gleitman (Eds.), *Language acquisition: The state of the art* (pp. 173–218). Cambridge, England: Cambridge University Press.

Bates, E., & MacWhinney, B. (1989). Functionalism and the competition model. In B. MacWhinney & E. Bates (Eds.), *The cross-linguistic study of sentence processing.* New York: Cambridge University Press.

Bates, E., Wulfeck, B., & MacWhinney, B. (1991). Cross-linguistic research in aphasia: An overview. *Brain Language, 41,* 123–148.

Bavin, E. (1992). The acquisition of Warlbiri. In D. I. Slobin (Ed.), *The crosslinguistic study* (Vol. 2, pp. 310–372). Hillsdale, NJ: Erlbaum.

Bellugi, U., Bihrle, A., & Corina, D. (1991). Linguistic and spatial development: Dissociations between cognitive domains. In N. A. Krasnegor, D. Rumbaugh, R. Schiefelbusch, & M. Studdert-Kennedy (Eds.), *Biological and behavioral determinants of language development* (pp. 363–398). Hillsdale, NJ: Erlbaum.

Bever, T. (1970). The cognitive basis for linguistic structures. In J. R. Hayes (Ed.), *Cognition amd the development of language* (pp. 279–352). New York: Wiley.

Bickerton, D. (1981). *The roots of language.* Ann Arbor, MI: Karoma.

Bloom, L. (1970). *Language development: Form and function in emerging grammar.* Cambridge, MA: MIT Press.

Bohannon, J. N., III, MacWhinney, B., & Snow, C. (1990). No negative evidence revisited: Beyond learnability, or who has to prove what to whom. *Developmental Psychology, 26,* 221–226.

Bohm, K., & Levelt, W. J. M. (1979). *Children's use and awareness of natural and syntactic gender.* Paper presented at the conference on linguistic awareness and learning to read, Victoria, British Columbia.

Bowerman, M. (1973). *Early syntactic development: A cross-linguistic study with special reference to Finnish.* Cambridge, England: Cambridge University Press.

Braine, M. D. S. (1971). On two models of the internalization of grammar. In D. I. Slobin (Ed.), *The ontogenesis of grammar: A theoretical symposium* (pp. 153–188). New York: Academic Press.

Braine, M. D. S. (1976). Children's first word combinations. *Monographs of the Society for Research in Child Development, 41.*

Braine, M. D. S. (1987). What is learned in acquiring word classes: A step towards an acquisition theory. In B. MacWhinney (Ed.), *Mechanisms of language acquisition* (pp. 65–88). Hillsdale, NJ: Erlbaum.

Braine, M. D. S. (1994). Is nativism sufficient? *Journal of Child Language, 21,* 1–23.

Broca, P. (1965). Sur la siege de la faculte du language articule. *Bulletin Societe Anatomique Paris, 6,* 336–357.

Brown, R. (1973). *A first language: The early stages.* Cambridge, MA: Harvard University Press.

Brown, R., & Hanlon, C. (1970). Derivational complexity and order of acquisition in child speech. In J. Hayes (Ed.), *Cognition and the development of language* (pp. 11–54). New York: Wiley.

Bruner, J. (1974–1975). From communication to language: A psychological perspective. *Cognition, 3,* 255–287.

Cazden, C. B. (1968). The acquisition of noun and verb inflections. *Child Development, 39,* 433–448.

Chapman, R. (1995). Language development in children and adolescents with down syndrome. In P. Fletcher & B. MacWhinney (Eds.), *The handbook of child language* (pp. 641–663). Oxford, England: Basil Blackwell.

Chomsky, A. N. (1965). *Aspects of the theory of syntax.* Cambridge, MA: MIT Press.

Chomsky, A. N. (1986). *Barriers.* Cambridge, MA: MIT Press.

Chomsky, A. N. (1989). Colloquium held at University of Minnesota, Minneapolis.

Chomsky, A. N. (1992). A minimalist program for linguistic theory. In K. Hale & S. Keyser (Eds.), *The view from building 20: Essays in linguistics in honor of Sylvain Bromberger.* Cambridge, MA: MIT Press.

Churchland, P. (1992, April). Colloquium held at University of Minnesota, Minneapolis.

Cole, M., & Cole, S. (1992). *The development of children* (2nd ed.). San Francisco: Freeman.

Comrie, B. (1988). Linguistic typology. In J. Newmeyer (Ed.), *Linguistics: The Cambridge Survey* (Vol. 1, pp. 447–461). Cambridge: Cambridge University Press.

Crain, S. (1992). Language acquisition in the absence of experience. *Brain Behavioral Science, 14,* 597–611.

Damasio, A. R., & Damasio, H. (1992). Brain and language. *Scientific American., 117,* 89–95.

Demuth, K. (1990). Subject, topic, and Sesotho passive. *Journal of Child Language, 17,* 67–84.

Dennis, M., & Whitaker, H. (1976). Language acquisition following hemidecortication. *Brain Language, 10,* 287–317.

DeVilliers, J. (1985). Learning how to use verbs: Lexical coding and the influence of the input. *Journal of Child Language, 12,* 587–595.

DeVilliers, J. (1995). Empty categories and complex sentences: The case of wh-questions. In P. Fletcher & B. MacWhinney (Eds.), *The handbook of child language* (pp. 508–540). Oxford, England: Basil Blackwell.

Eimas, P., Siqueland, E. R., & Vigorito, J. (1971). Speech perception in infants. *Science, 171,* 303–306.

Elman, J. (1992). Learning and development in neural networks: The importance of starting small. In C. Umilta & M. Moscovitch (Eds.), *Attention and performance: XV. Conscious and unconscious information processing* (pp. 13–26). Hillsdale, NJ: Erlbaum.

Engdahl, E., & Ejerhed, E. (1982). *Readings on unbounded dependencies in Scandinavian languages.* Stockholm: Almqvist & Wiksell.

Eretschik-Shir, E. (1982). Extractability in Danish and the pragmatic principle of dominance. In E. Engdahl & E. Ejerhed (Eds.), *Readings on unbounded dependencies in Scandinavian languages* (pp. 175–192). Stockholm: Almqvist & Wiksell.

Fernald, A., & Roberts, G. (in press). Prosodic bootstrapping: A critical analysis of the argument and the evidence. In J. Morgan & K. Demuth (Eds.), *Signal to syntax: Bootstrapping from speech to grammar in early acquisition.* Hillsdale, NJ: Erlbaum.

Fillmore, C. J. (1968). The case for case. In E. Bach & R. T. Harms (Eds.), *Universals in linguistic theory* (pp. 1–90). New York: Holt, Rinehart and Winston.

Flavell, J. H., Miller, P. H., & Miller, S. A. (1993). *Cognitive development.* Englewood Cliffs, NJ: Prentice-Hall.

Fletcher, P., & MacWhinney, B. (1995). *The handbook of child language.* Oxford, England: Basil Blackwell.

Fodor, J. (1983). *Modularity of mind* (2nd ed.). Cambridge, MA: MIT Press.

Fowler, A. E. (1990). Language abilities in children with down syndrome. In D. Ciccheti & M. Beeghly (Eds.), *Child with down syndrome: A developmental perspective* (pp. 302–328). New York: Cambridge University Press.

Gallistel, C. R., Brown, A. L., Carey, S., Gelman, R., & Keil, F. (1991). Lessons from animal learning for the study of cognitive development. In S. Carey & R. Gelman (Eds.), *The epigenesis of mind: Essays on biology and cognition* (pp. 1–36). Hillsdale, NJ: Erlbaum.

Garcia, J., & Koelling, R. A. (1966). The relation of cue to consequence in avoidance learning. *Psychonomic Science, 4,* 123–124.

Gelman, R., & Baillargeon, R. (1983). A review of Piagetian concepts. In J. H. Flavell & E. Markman (Eds.), *Handbook of child development* (Vol. 3, pp. 167–230). New York: Wiley.

Gerken, L. A. (1987). Telegraphic speaking does not imply telegraphic listening. *Papers and Reports on Child Language Development, 26,* 48–55.

Gerken, L. A. (1991). The metrical basis for children's subjectless sentences. *Journal of Memory and Language, 30,* 431–451.

Gonzalez, A. (1984). *Acquiring Pilipino as a first language: Two case studies.* Manila: Linguistic Society of the Philippines.

Gordon, P. (1990). Learnability and feedback. *Developmental Psychology, 26,* 217–220.

Greenberg, J. (1966). Some universals of language with particular reference to the order of meaningful elements. In J. Greenberg (Ed.), *Universals of language* (2nd ed., pp. 73–113). Cambridge, England: Cambridge University Press.

Grimshaw, J. (1981). Form, function, and the language acquisition device. In C. L. Baker & J. McCarthy (Eds.), *The logical problem of language acquisition.* Cambridge, MA: MIT Press.

Harbert, W. (1995). Binding theory, control, and *pro.* In G. Webelhuth (Ed.), *Government and binding theory and the minimalist program* (pp. 177–240). Oxford, England: Blackwell.

Harris. R. L. (1992). *The linguistic wars.* Oxford, England: Oxford University Press.

Heath, S. B. (1983). *Ways with words: Language, life, and work in communities and classrooms.* Cambridge, England: Cambridge University Press.

Heeschen, C. (1985). Agrammatism versus paragrammatism: A fictitious opposition. In M. Kean (Ed.), *Agrammatism* (pp. 207–248). New York: Academic Press.

Hendrick, R. (1995). Morphosyntax. In G. Webelhuth (Ed.), *Government and binding theory and the minimalist program* (pp. 297–348). Oxford, England: Blackwell.

Hirsch-Pasek, K., & Golinkoff, R. M. (1991). A new look at some old themes. In N. Krasnegor, D. Rumbaugh, R. Schiefelbusch, & M. Studdert-Kennedy (Eds.), *Biological and behavioral determinants of language development* (pp. 301–320). Hillsdale, NJ: Erlbaum.

Hyams, N. (1986). *Language acquisition and theory of parameters.* Dordrecht, The Netherlands: D. Reidel.

Hyams, N. (1989). The null subject parameter in language acquisition. In O. Jaeggli & K. J. Saffir (Eds.), *The null subject parameter* (pp. 215–238). Dordrecht, The Netherlands: Kluwer.

Imedadze, N., & Tuite, K. (1992). The acquisition of Georgian. In D. I. Slobin (Ed.), *The crosslinguistic study of language acquisition* (Vol. 2, pp. 39–110). Hillsdale, NJ: Erlbaum.

Ingram, D. (1989). *First language acquisition: Method, description and explanation.* Cambridge, England: Cambridge University Press.

Jackendoff, R. (1972). *Semantic interpretation in generative grammar.* Cambridge, MA: MIT Press.

Johnson, J. S., & Newport, E. L. (1989). Critical period effects in second language learning. *Cognitive Psychology, 21,* 60–99.

Karmiloff-Smith, A. (1979). *A functional approach to child language: A study of determiners and reference.* Cambridge, MA: MIT Press.

Karmiloff-Smith, A. (1992). *Beyond modularity: A developmental perspective on cognitive science.* Cambridge, MA: MIT Press.

Katis, D. (1984). *The acquisition of the modern Greek verb.* Doctoral dissertation, University of Reading, Reading, England.

Kean, M. (Ed.). (1985). *Agrammatism.* New York: Academic Press.

Keenan, E. O. (1976). Toward a universal definition of "subject." In C. Li (Ed.), *Subject and topic* (pp. 206–257). New York: Academic Press.

Keil, F. (1981). Constraints on knowledge and cognitive development. *Psychiatric Review, 88,* 197–227.

Kosslyn, S., & Koenig, K. (1992). *Wet brain.* Cambridge, MA: Harvard University Press.

Krasnegor, N. A., Rumbaugh, D., Schiefelbusch, R., & Studdert-Kennedy, M. (Eds.). (1991). *Biological and behavioral determinants of language development.* Hillsdale, NJ: Erlbaum.

Kuhl, P., & Miller, J. D. (1975). Speech perception by the chinchilla: Voice-voiceless distinction in alvealar plosive consonants. *Science, 190,* 69–72.

Kuno, S. (1988). *Functional syntax.* Chicago: University of Chicago Press.

Lachter, J., & Bever, T. G. (1989). The relation between linguistic structure and associative theories of language learning: A constructive critique of some connectionist learning models. In S. Pinker & J. Mehler (Eds.), *Connections and symbols* (pp. 195–248). Cambridge, MA: MIT Press.

Lewin, R. (1980). Is your brain really necessary? *Science, 210,* 1323–1334.

Lewin, R. (1984). Why is development so illogical? *Science, 224,* 1327–1329.

MacNamara, J. (1982). *Words for things: A study of language development.* Cambridge, MA: Harvard/Bradford Books.

MacWhinney, B. (1978). The acquisition of morphophonology. *Monographs of the Society for Research in Child Development, 43*(1/2).

MacWhinney, B., & Chang, D. (1995). Connectionism and language learning. In C. Nelson (Ed.), Basic and applied perspectives on learning, cognition, and development. *The Minnesota Symposia on Child Psychology, 28,* 33–59.

MacWhinney, B., Leimbach, J., Taraban, R., & McDonald, J. (1989). Language learning: Cues or rules? *Journal of Memory and Cognition, 28,* 255–277.

Maratsos, M. (1976). *The use of definite and indefinite reference in young children: An experimental study of semantic acquisition.* Cambridge, England: Cambridge University Press.

Maratsos, M. (1979). How to get from words to sentences. In D. Aaronson & R. Reiber (Eds.), *Perspectives in psycholinguistics.* Hillsdale, NJ: Erlbaum.

Maratsos, M. (1982). The child's construction of grammatical categories. In E. Wanner & L. Gleitman (Eds.), *Language acquisition: The state of the art* (pp. 240–266). Cambridge, England: Cambridge University Press.

Maratsos, M. (1989). Innateness and plasticity in language development. In M. Rice & R. Schiefelbusch (Eds.), *The teachability of language* (pp. 109–125). Baltimore: Brookes.

Maratsos, M. (1991). How the acquisition of nouns may be different from that of verbs. In N. A. Krasnegor, D. Rumbaugh, R. Schiefelbusch, & M. Studdert-Kennedy (Eds.), *Biological and behavioral determinants of language development* (pp. 67–88). Hillsdale, NJ: Erlbaum.

Maratsos, M., & Chalkley, M. A. (1980). The internal language of children's syntax. In K. Nelson (Ed.), *Children's language* (Vol. 2, pp. 127–213). New York: Gardner Press.

Maratsos, M., Kuczaj, S., Fox, D., & Chalkley, M. A. (1979). Some empirical studies in the acquisition of transformational relations: Passives, negatives, and the past tense. In W. A. Collins (Ed.), *Minnesota Symposium on Child Psychology* (Vol. 12, pp. 1–28). Hillsdale, NJ: Erlbaum.

Maratsos, M., & Matheny, L. (1994). Language specificity and elasticity: Brain and clinical syndrome studies. In M. Rosenzweig & L. Porter (Eds.), *Annual Review of Psychology, 45,* 487–516.

McNeill, D. (1970). *The acquisition of language: The study of developmental psycholinguistics.* New York: Harper & Row.

Meisl, J. M. (1995). Parameters in acquisition. In P. Fletcher & B. MacWhinney (Eds.), *The handbook of child language* (pp. 10–35). Oxford, England: Basil Blackwell.

Mervis, C., Morris, C. A., Bertrand, J., & Robinson, B. F. (in press). Williams syndrome: Findings from an integrated program of research. In H. Tager-Flusberg (Ed.), *Neurodevelopmental disorders: Contributions to a new framework from the cognitive neurosciences.* Cambridge, MA: MIT Press.

Morgan, J., & Demuth, K. (Eds.). (in press). *Signal to syntax: Boostrapping from speech to grammar in early acquisition.* Hillsdale, NJ: Erlbaum.

Morgan, J., & Travis, L. (1989). Limits on negative information in language acquisition. *Journal of Child Language, 16,* 531–551.

Nelson, K. (1994). The dual category problem in the acquisition of action words. In M. Tomasello & B. Merriman (Eds.), *Beyond words for things: Young children's acquisition of verb meanings* (pp. 57–76). Hillsdale, NJ: Erlbaum.

Newport E., Gleitman L., & Gleitman, H. (1977). Mother I'd rather do it myself: Some effects and non-effects of maternal speech style. In C. E. Snow & C. A. Ferguson (Eds.), *Talking to children: Language input and acquisition* (pp. 126–165). Cambridge, England: Cambridge University Press.

O'Grady, W. (1987). *Principles of grammar and learning.* Chicago: University of Chicago Press.

Peters, A. (1983). *The units of language acquisition.* Cambridge, England: Cambridge University Press.

Pinker, S. (1984). *Language learnability and language development.* Cambridge, MA: Harvard University Press.

Pinker, S. (1987). The bootstrapping problem in language acquisition. In B. MacWhinney (Ed.), *Mechanisms of language acquisition* (pp. 399–441). Hillsdale, NJ: Erlbaum.

Pinker, S. (1990). In D. Osherson & H. Lasnik (Eds.), *An invitation to cognitive science* (Vol. 1, pp. 199–243). Cambridge, MA: MIT Press.

Pinker, S., & Bloom, P. (1990). Natural language and natural selection. *Behavioral Brain Science, 13,* 723–824.

Plomin, R. (1990). *Nature and nurture: An introduction to human behavioral genetics.* Pacific Grove, CA: Brooks/Cole.

Plunkett, K. (1995). Connectionists approaches to language acquisition. In P. Fletcher & B. MacWhinney (Eds.), *The handbook of child language* (pp. 36–72). Oxford, England: Basil Blackwell.

Poizner, H., Klima, E. S., & Bellugi, U. (1987). *What the hands reveal about the brain.* Cambridge, MA: MIT Press.

Pye, C. (1992). The acquisition of Quiche' Mayan. In D. I. Slobin (Ed.), *The crosslinguistic study of language acquisition* (Vol. 2, pp. 221–309). Hillsdale, NJ: Erlbaum.

Radford, A. (1990). *Syntactic theory and the acquisition of English syntax: The nature of early child grammars of English.* Oxford, England: Blackwell.

Rispoli, M. (1991). Mosaic theory of grammatical acquisition. *Journal of Child Language, 18,* 517–551.

Rizzi, L. (1982). *Issues in Italian syntax.* Dordrecht, The Netherlands: Foris.

Roeper, T., & Devilliers, J. (1991). Ordered decisions in the acquisition of wh-questions. In J. Wessenborn, H. Goodluck, & T. Roeper (Eds.), *Theoretical issues in language acquisition* (pp. 191–236). Hillsdale, NJ: Erlbaum.

Ross, J. R. (1967). *Constraints on variables in syntax.* Doctoral dissertation, Massachusetts Institute of Technology, Cambridge.

Rossem, R. (1993, May). *The fractionation of language and cognition in Williams' syndrome.* Colloquium presented at University of Minnesota.

Rumelhardt, D. E., & McClelland, J. L. (1986). On learning the past tense of English verbs. In J. L. McClelland, D. E. Rumelhardt, & the PDP Research Group (Eds.), *Parallel distributed processing: Explorations in the microstructure of cognition: Vol. 2. Psychological and biological models.* Cambridge, MA: Bradford Books/MIT Press.

Schachter, P., & Otanes, R., (1976). *A Tagalog grammar.* Berkeley: University of California Press.

Schwartz, M. G., Linebarger, M. C., & Saffran, E. M. (1985). The status of the syntactic deficit theory of agrammatism. In M. Kean (Ed.), *Agrammatism* (pp. 83–124). New York: Academic Press.

Schlesinger, I. M. (1971). The production of utterances and language acquisition. In D. I. Slobin (Ed.), *The ontogenesis of grammar: A theoretical symposium* (pp. 63–102). New York: Academic Press.

Schlesinger, I. M. (1982). *Steps to language.* Hillsdale, NJ: Erlbaum.

Shaffer, D. (1996). *Developmental psychology: Childhood and adolescence.* Pacific Grove, CA: Brooks/Cole.

Slobin, D. I. (Ed.). (1971). *The ontogenesis of grammar: A theoretical symposium.* New York: Academic Press.

Slobin, D. I. (1973). Cognitive prerequisites for the development of grammar. In C. A. Ferguson & D. I. Slobin (Eds.), *Studies of child language development.* New York: Holt, Rinehart and Winston.

Slobin, D. I. (1982). Universal and particular in the acquisition of language. In E. Wanner & L. Gleitman (Eds.), *Language acquisition: The state of the art* (pp. 128–172). Cambridge, England: Cambridge University Press.

Slobin, D. I. (1985a). Crosslinguistic evidence for the language-making capacity. In D. I. Slobin (Ed.), *The crosslinguistic study of language acquisition* (Vol. 1, pp. 1157–1256). Hillsdale, NJ: Erlbaum.

Slobin, D. I. (Ed). (1985b). *The crosslinguistic study of language acquisition* (Vol. 1). Hillsdale, NJ: Erlbaum.

Slobin, D. I. (Ed.). (1992a). *The crosslinguistic study of language acquisition* (Vol. 2). Hillsdale, NJ: Erlbaum.

Slobin, D. I. (1992b). Introduction. In D. I. Slobin (Ed.), *The crosslinguistic study of language acquisition* (Vol. 2, pp. 1–14). Hillsdale, NJ: Erlbaum.

Smoczynska, R. (1985). The acquisition of Polish. In D. I. Slobin (Ed.), *The crosslinguistic study of language acquisition* (Vol. 1, pp. 595–686). Hillsdale, NJ: Erlbaum.

Smolensky, P. (1992). *An optimality model of connectionist models.* Colloquium presented at University of Minnesota, Minneapolis.

Smiley, P., & Huttenlocher, J. (1994). In M. Tomasello & B. Merriman (Eds.), *Beyond words for things: Young children's acquisition of verb meanings* (pp. 124–146). Hillsdale, NJ: Erlbaum.

Snow, C. (1972). Mother's speech to children learning language. *Child Development, 43,* 549–565.

Stephany, U. (1995). *The acquisition of Greek.* Institut fur Sprachwissenschaft, Univeritat zu Koln. Arbeitspapier nr. 22.

Tager-Flusberg, H. (1988). On the nature of a language acquisition disorder: The example of autism. In F. Kessel (Ed.), *The development of language and language researchers: Essays in honor of Roger Brown* (pp. 249–268). Hillsdale, NJ: Erlbaum.

Talmy, L. (1985). Lexicalization patterns: Semantic structure in lexical forms. In T. Shopen (Ed.), *Language typology and syntactic description: Vol. 3. Grammatical categories and the lexicon.* Cambridge, England: Cambridge University Press.

Thelen, E. (1989). Self-organization in development processes: Can systems approaches work? In M. R. Gunnar & E. Thelen (Eds.), *Systems and developmental psychology: The Minnesota Symposium on Child Psychology* (22, pp. 77–118). Hillsdale, NJ: Erlbaum.

Tinbergen, N. (1951). *The study of instinct.* Oxford, England: Clarendon Press.

Tolbert, M. C. (1979). *Morphological acquisition in Spanish.* Doctoral dissertation, Harvard University, Cambridge.

Tolbert, M. C. (1981). A new look at acquisitional sequences in grammar. *New Directions for Child Development, 12,* 1–46.

Tomasello, M. (1992). *First verbs: A case study of early language development.* Cambridge, England: Cambridge University Press.

Tomasello, M., & Merriman, B. (Eds.). (1994). *Beyond words for things: Young children's acquisition of verb meanings.* Hillsdale, NJ: Erlbaum.

Valian, V. (1990). Null subjects: A problem for parameter-setting models of language acquisition. *Cognition, 35,* 105–122.

Van Hoek, K. (1995). Conceptual reference points: A cognitive grammar account of pronominal anaphora constraints. *Language, 71,* 310–340.

Van Valin, R. (1992). An overview of ergative phenomena and their implications for language acquisition. In D. I. Slobin (Ed.), *The crosslinguistic study of language acquisition* (Vol. 2, pp. 15–38). Hillsdale, NJ: Erlbaum.

Walter, S. (1975). *Zur Entwicklung morphologischer Strukturen bei Kinder.* Heidelberg: Diplomarbeit.

Wanner, E., & Gleitman, L. (Eds.). (1982). *Language acquisition: The state of the art.* Cambridge, England: Cambridge University Press.

Webelhuth, G. (Ed). (1995a). *Government and binding theory and the minimalist program.* Oxford, England: Blackwell.

Webelhuth, G. (1995b). X-bar theory and case theory. In G. Webelhuth (Ed.), *Government and binding theory and the minimalist program* (pp. 17–96). Oxford, England: Blackwell.

Weist, R. M. (1990). Neutralization and the concept of subject in Polish. *Linguistics, 28,* 1331–1351.

Wexler, K., & Mancini, M. (1987). Parameters and learnability in binding theory. In T. Roeper & E. Williams (Eds.), *Parameter-setting* (pp. 41–89). Dordrecht, The Netherlands: D. Reidel.

Zurif, E. G., & Caramazza, A. (1976). Psycholinguistic structures in aphasia: Studies in syntax and semantics. In H. Whitaker & H. A. Whitaker (Ed.), *Studies in neurolinguistics* (Vol. 1, pp. 147–174). New York: Academic Press.

CHAPTER 10

Memory

WOLFGANG SCHNEIDER and DAVID F. BJORKLUND

Memory development has been one of the most-studied topics in all of cognitive development, and deservedly so. Memory is at the center stage of cognition, varying as a function of both basic-level and higher-order processes and being involved in almost every act of complex cognition. The importance of memory development is not new. Although it is widely known that the scientific study of memory began with the classic work of Ebbinghaus (1885), it is not equally well-known that research on memory *development* also started at that date. Around the turn of the cen-

tury, numerous experiments were carried out in Europe to investigate developmental and individual differences in immediate memory and long-term retention. (See Schneider & Pressley, 1997, for a more detailed review.) These studies helped to overcome common misconceptions held at that time, for example, that children, because they practice their memory skills in school almost every day, are better at remembering verbal material than adults. These early developmental studies also contradicted the popular assumption that boys have a better memory than girls. These findings helped bring about coeducation in German classrooms at the beginning of this century.

Although early research on memory development was strongly influenced by practical considerations, basic research was not neglected. Numerous experimental studies

This chapter was completed while the second author was supported by National Science Foundation research award SBR-9422177.

explored theoretically interesting issues such as the impact of type of learning material (e.g., verbal vs. nonverbal) and the retention interval on memory performance. In one of the most impressive early studies on memory development, Brunswik, Goldscheider, and Pilek (1932) provided a general description of memory between the ages of 6 and 18 years of age. The subjects were tested with a large battery of predominantly verbal memory tasks that tapped both immediate and long-term retention. The authors tried to assess children's "memory strength" by aggregating scores across all memory measures. The resulting curve of "general memory development," based on scores of about 700 students, indicated linear and steep rises in performance from 6 to 11 years of age, followed by a flatter slope and a plateau in performance during early and late adolescence. Notwithstanding several methodological shortcomings of this study, the findings obtained by Brunswik et al. (1932) correlate well with results of contemporary studies exploring the course of memory development in children (e.g., Weinert & Schneider, 1995).

How does modern research on memory development differ from the historical approaches? One of the crucial differences concerns a shift from an emphasis on describing developmental differences in memory performance to an emphasis on identifying the underlying mechanisms of change. Another difference concerns the theoretical frameworks used. Since the mid-1960s, research on memory development has been influenced strongly by theoretical models derived from information-processing and neuroscience approaches.

In writing this chapter, three themes became apparent. First is the theme that memory is multifaceted. There is no one thing that can be appropriately called "memory." Rather, different types of memory have different underlying neurological systems (e.g., Squire, 1992). Therefore, we should not expect that the various memory skills for any given child will be homogeneous. Just as there is great unevenness in general cognitive abilities (e.g., Fischer, 1980), so too is there much heterogeneity of memory abilities. Similarly, we should expect that different types of memory abilities will have different developmental functions. Some memory abilities may develop slowly over childhood and be greatly influenced by environmental factors; others may be developmentally invariant, showing near-adult levels early in life and be relatively impervious to instruction.

Second, and related to the first, is the theme of variability. Children's performance will vary not only as a function of *type* of memory systems that is being tapped (e.g., implicit vs. explicit), but there is also substantial intrasubject variability on highly similar tasks. There are many factors that influence children's memory performance and these factors can vary over brief intervals and affect children's memory behavior. Variability can no longer be viewed as error variance in cognitive development but may be the stuff upon which developmental change is based (Bjorklund, 1997; Siegler, 1996, 1997).

This brings us to our third and perhaps most important theme: the development of memory can be understood only by examining behavior at a variety of levels. Research looking at basic-level processes tells us much about the developing child and his or her memory abilities. So, too, does research taking a more "macro" perspective, examining, for example, the role of metacognition or the social construction of memory. Either perspective alone, however, misses the larger point that memory abilities are part of the basic biology of the developing child, which have evolved to function in a complex social community. Although it may be necessary to study only small parts of the developing memory system at any one time, we should not lose track of the fact that memory development occurs in a dynamic system of interacting factors, ranging from the genetic to the cultural (Lerner, 1991). This recognition of the importance of considering multiple levels of memory development has become increasingly obvious in the past decade or so as research in nondeliberate memory, often involving basic-level and nonstrategic processes, has exploded. Research on deliberate and strategic memory remains important and active, but there has been a noticeable shift away from such "potentially conscious," macroprocesses to unconscious and microprocesses.

In our review of the literature, we begin with a discussion of the memory system, focusing on developmental differences in the capacity of working memory. This is followed by a look at memory in infancy. We next examine the development of strategic memory, an area that dominated memory development research for most of the last 30 years, followed by an examination of factors that influence declarative memory development. We then review developmental research on nonstrategic memory, including unintentional and implicit memory, fuzzy-trace theory, long-term retention and forgetting, and event memory, including children's eyewitness testimony and infantile amnesia. This is followed by a section examining the consistency and stability of memory.

THE MEMORY SYSTEM

Basic Models and Theoretical Concepts

The first information-processing model to influence research on memory development was Atkinson and Shiffrin's (1968) multistore model, which emphasized the fact that memory processes are time dependent. A distinction was made between a sensory register (SR), a short-term store (STS), and a long-term store (LTS). New information first enters the SR, where it forms memories of very short duration (less than a second). It then moves on to the STS, a system of limited capacity. The activities of the STS are represented as various control processes (e.g., rehearsal), which keep alive selected information and transfer it to permanent storage in the LTS. Atkinson and Shiffrin distinguished between encoding/storage and retrieval activities. Whereas *learning* may be a good synonym for storage, the term *remembering* describes what is meant by various retrieval activities such as recognizing, recalling, and reconstructing. Although the basic logic of the multistore model has been challenged (e.g., by process-oriented approaches such as the levels-of-processing model of Craik & Lockhart, 1972), the STS-LTS structural distinction has been supported by research carried out in biology, neuroscience, and psychopharmacology (see Parkin, 1993; Squire, Knowlton, & Musen, 1993, for reviews).

Regarding the permanent LTS, various content-specific taxonomies have been offered to describe its organization (e.g., Tulving, 1985). In most taxonomies, a distinction is made between declarative and nondeclarative memory. Whereas the former has been defined as the conscious remembering of facts and events, the latter refers to unconscious memory for skills (i.e., procedural memory), priming, and operant as well as classical conditioning. Declarative memory is composed of two different but interacting components, episodic and semantic memory. Whereas episodic memory can be defined as an individual's autobiographical record of past experiences, semantic memory refers to our "world knowledge," that is, knowledge of language, rules, and concepts (Tulving, 1985). Although the contents of semantic and episodic memory are ordered and organized differently (i.e., conceptually vs. temporally), both systems are similar in that they can be accessed consciously.

In the last few years, an alternative distinction concerning the nature of LTS has been put forward. This approach attempts to explain LTS by examining how it responds to explicit and implicit memory tests (Parkin, 1993). Explicit memory involves conscious recollection of previous experiences and can be tested directly using free recall, cued recall, and recognition. Implicit memory is an unconscious form of retention, or "memory without awareness," that is assessed with tasks testing memory indirectly. The distinction between these two LTS components is supported by numerous experiments with brain-damaged patients, showing severe impairment in explicit (declarative) memory but preserved functioning in implicit (nondeclarative) memory (Schacter, 1992). Apparently, processes of declarative and nondeclarative memory can be located in neurologically and anatomically distinct brain areas: whereas the various subcomponents of nondeclarative memory seem to function separately from neocortical structures, processes related to declarative memory are linked to structures in the medial temporal lobe as well as the hippocampus (Squire, 1992).

Most of the research reviewed in this chapter is related to children's explicit, declarative memory, but not all. It has become increasingly obvious in recent years that regardless how important intentional and explicit memory are to everyday functioning, much of what children remember is acquired without intention and retrieved without awareness. There are different memory systems with different underlying neurological organizations, and because of this, we should anticipate different patterns of developmental function.

Developmental Differences in Capacity

The idea of limited capacity is central to all information-processing accounts of development and is an implicit or explicit assumption in nearly all contemporary theories of cognitive development in general (Case, 1985; Fischer, 1980) and memory development in particular (Bjorklund, Muir-Broaddus, & Schneider, 1990; Kee, 1994). With respect to memory, capacity usually refers to the amount of information that can be held in the various memory stores or the length of time that information will persist in those stores. For all practical purposes, the long-term store can be considered to have infinite storage. In contrast, the capacities of the sensory register and short-term store are finite. Recently, psychologists have come to realize that "how much" one can hold in mind is related to how quickly one can process information, and age differences in speed of processing play a central role in our discussion of developmental changes in capacity.

The Sensory Register

The most studied sensory register is the *iconic store*. When visual information is flashed (e.g., 100 msec) to adults and they are asked to recall what they saw, most people report only a few items but have the feeling that they saw more. For example, Sperling (1960) developed the partial-report technique, in which subjects were shown briefly a series of nine letters in a 3×3 array. Immediately following the visual display, a marker pointed to one row, and subjects were asked to recall the three items in that particular row. Under these conditions, recall was nearly perfect, suggesting that all the visual information had entered the iconic store but that it deteriorated so rapidly that by the time subjects recalled three or four items the sensory memory for the remainder of the display had decayed, leaving them with the impression that they had seen more than they could recall.

Variants of the partial-report technique have been used with children, and results suggest minimal age differences in the actual capacity of the iconic store, although there are substantial age differences in the transfer of information to the STS (Hoving, Spencer, Robb, & Schulte, 1978; LeBlanc, Muise, & Blanchard, 1992; Sheingold, 1973). This is reflected by comparable recall of items for people of all ages when brief delays between the presentations of the stimulus and the cue are involved (e.g., 50 msec), but significant age differences with longer delays (e.g., 100 msec and longer). One explanation for these findings is that children are less able than adults to use strategies such as visual rehearsal, verbal encoding, or more focused attention to specific parts of the visual icon in transferring information between the iconic and short-term stores (e.g., Hoving et al., 1978). An alternative explanation is that the information deteriorates at a faster rate for children than adults, due to age differences in the speed with which information is processed, and there is strong empirical support for this latter interpretation (LeBlanc et al., 1992). Because the processing of younger children is slower than that of older children, they "lose" more information before it can be encoded in the STS, accounting for the developmental differences observed at longer delays.

The Short-Term Store

Developmental differences in the capacity of the STS have been studied extensively, with these differences, in one form or another, being associated with global cognitive changes, effective use of strategies, and individual differences on a host of cognitive and educational tasks (Case, 1985; Kee, 1994; Siegel, 1993). The task most often associated with the capacity of the STS is *memory span*. Memory span is defined as the number of rapidly presented items that a person can recall in exact order. Digits are the most frequently used stimuli for memory-span tests, and regular age differences are found in digit span between the ages of 2 years and young adulthood (Dempster, 1981). Tests of *working memory* are similar to memory-span tasks in that subjects must remember a series of items in exact order, but they are embedded in an additional task in which subjects must transform information held in the STS (Case, 1985; de Ribaupierre & Bailleux, 1995; Siegel & Ryan, 1989). For instance, children may be given a set of sentences for which they must add the final word (e.g., "In the summer it is very_____."). After completing a number of these sentences, they are asked to recall the final word from each sentence in the order they were presented (Siegel & Ryan, 1989). In general, working-memory tasks show the same developmental pattern as memory-span tasks, although the absolute level of performance on the working-memory tasks is usually about two items less than for memory-span tasks (Case, 1985).

The Role of Knowledge Base on Memory Span

The robustness of these differences makes very attractive the interpretation that the actual capacity of the STS is increasing with age. As appealing as this is, however, it is too simple. Research over the past two decades has made it clear that memory (and working-memory) span is *not* a domain-general phenomenon that is essentially identical regardless of what type of information is being remembered. Rather, how much a person knows about the class of stimuli he or she is remembering affects memory span, with knowledge presumably having its effect by influencing speed of processing.

Evidence for this position comes from experiments assessing the memory span of chess-expert versus chess-novice children for chess positions on a chess board and for other types of items, such as digits (Chi, 1978; Roth, 1983; Schneider, Gruber, Gold, & Opwis, 1993). The general findings are that chess-expert children and adults have higher spans for the chess positions than for digits. This suggests that memory span is *domain specific,* varying with a person's background knowledge for the to-be-remembered material. One reason for the regular age-related improvements observed on most memory-span tasks is that older children typically know more about the background knowledge than younger children. When this relation is modified, so is memory span (see Dempster, 1985 and discussion of role of knowledge base below).

Speed of Processing

Knowledge seems to have its greatest effect on memory span by increasing the rate with which children process information. For example, chess-expert children and adults have been shown to process chess information faster than chess-novice agemates, with speed of processing predicting memory span (Roth, 1983). It has been well established that speed of information processing increases with age across a wide range of tasks (Case, 1985; Kail, 1991; Kail & Salthouse, 1994). As such, developmental differences in this presumably domain-general mechanism would account for the regular age-related changes in memory span that are observed for most domains. In fact, in an extensive review, Dempster (1981) concluded that the only factor to account for developmental differences in memory-span performance was ease, or speed, of item identification.

A model of working memory that accounts for age differences in memory span primarily in terms of speed of processing has been developed by Baddeley and Hitch (Baddeley, 1986; Baddeley & Hitch, 1974; Hitch & Towse, 1995). They propose that phonological information is stored in the *articulatory loop,* with these verbal memory traces decaying rapidly. However, the phonological information can be maintained in memory via verbal rehearsal. Research has suggested that there are few, if any, developmental differences in the rate with which information decays in working memory (Engle, Fidler, & Reynolds, 1981), making rehearsal rate the primary reason for age differences in memory span. Faster rehearsal results in maintaining more information active in working memory for longer periods of time, resulting in enhanced levels of memory span.

Research has provided support for Baddeley and Hitch's position. For example, there is a strong, positive relation between age, the rate at which children are able to identify words, and memory span (Hitch & Halliday, 1983; Hulme, Thompson, Muir, & Lawrence, 1984). Figure 10.1 presents the relation among these three factors and illustrates the strength of these relations. In other research, when adults' speed of item identification is slowed down to be comparable to that of 6-year-olds, their levels of memory and working-memory span are correspondingly reduced (Case, Kurland, & Goldberg, 1982).

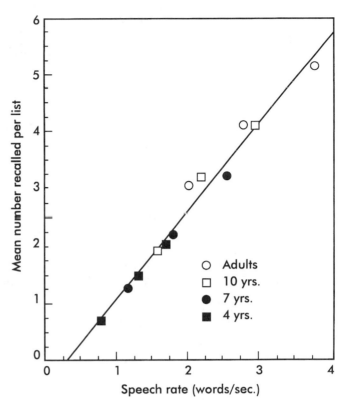

Figure 10.1 The relationship between word length, speech rate, and memory span as a function of age. As speech rate increases, more words are recalled, with both speech rate and words recalled increasing with age. From "Speech rate and the development of spoken words: The role of rehearsal and item identification processes," by C. Hulme et al., 1984, *Journal of Experimental Child Psychology, 38,* pp. 241–253. Copyright © 1984 by Academic Press, Inc. Reprinted with permission.

Differences in articulation rate are related to language differences in memory span. For example, Chinese speakers have significantly longer digit spans than English speakers, with this difference being apparent as early as age 4 (Chen & Stevenson, 1988; Geary, Bow-Thomas, Fan, & Siegler, 1993). The Chinese advantage is due to differences in how rapidly number words (e.g., "one," "two") can be articulated in the two languages. Chinese number words are relatively short and articulated more quickly compared to the corresponding English words. As a result, verbal rehearsal is more efficient for Chinese than English speakers, resulting in enhanced digit span.

The impact of language differences on memory span was also demonstrated for a group of bilingual children (Ellis & Hennelley, 1980). Ellis and Hennelley recruited a sample of children whose first language was Welsh and whose second language was English and assessed their digit spans in both languages. Intraindividual comparison revealed that significantly higher digit spans were obtained in English, the children's *second* language, than in Welsh. Although this finding may be surprising at first glance, it is in accord with the results of the Chinese–English comparisons, in that larger digit spans were found for the language with number words that are more quickly articulated (i.e., English).

Speed of processing, whether it be in terms of rate of item identification (Dempster, 1981) or articulation rate (Hitch & Towse, 1995), seems to be the primary influence on memory span, with knowledge base having its effect on span by increasing processing rate for domain-specific material. Age differences in speed of processing are clearly influenced by maturational factors, such as mylination of neurons in the associative cortex (Lecours, 1975), but also by experiential factors, such as expertise in a particular domain or the language one happens to speak.

MEMORY DEVELOPMENT IN INFANCY

Memory must begin early in development, at birth or even before. However, unlike other aspects of children's memory, the questions of what preverbal infants remember, and when and how they remember it, were not believed amenable to empirical science during the early decades of this century. New technologies beginning with the work of Fantz (1958) on infant perception, changed this, and now investigations of infant memory are very much a part of mainstream cognitive developmental psychology.

In this section, we divide research in infant memory into two broad categories: memory in early infancy, examining the memory abilities of infants over the first year, and memory in later infancy, investigating memory in preverbal toddlers, from about 12 to 20 months of age. Age is not the only distinction in this dichotomy; the methods of studying memory also differ between these two age groups, with young infants' memory being assessed primarily by means of recognition or operant-conditioning techniques, and memory in older infants being assessed primarily by means of cued-recall techniques, specifically via deferred imitation.

Memory in Early Infancy

Habituation/Dishabituation Procedures

When can infants form memories? The first technique widely used to assess infant memory involved variants of the habituation/dishabituation procedure, in which infants are presented repeatedly with a stimulus (visual, auditory, tactile) until their attention to the stimulus decreases (habituates) from its initial level (usually by 50%). Immediately following the final habituation trial, a novel stimulus is presented. Increased attention to the novel stimulus (dishabituation) is used as an indication that the infant can discriminate the novel stimulus from the earlier, habituated stimulus, with this discrimination being made between one stimulus that is physically present (the novel stimulus) and one that is present only memorially (the habituated stimulus). Using this technique, several researchers have demonstrated habituation and dishabituation for newborns (Friedman, 1972; Slater, Mattock, Brown, & Bremner, 1991), suggesting that neonates can form at least a brief memory of a perceptual experience.

A variant of the habituation/dishabituation paradigm is the preference for novelty procedure. In this technique, infants are habituated to a stimulus. Then, some time later, ranging from seconds to weeks, they are presented with two different stimuli, one being the "old," habituated stimulus and the other being a "new," or novel stimulus. The extent to which infants prefer (i.e., attend to) the novel stimulus relative to the old stimulus is used as a measure of their memory for the original stimulus. Joseph Fagan (1973, 1974) pioneered this technique and demonstrated that infants can retain briefly experienced visual information over substantial delays. In one study, 5- and 6-month-old infants formed visual memories that lasted up to two weeks (Fagan, 1974). More recent research using the preference-for-novelty technique has shown that infants as young as 3 months can retain a memory for object motion across intervals of 1 and 3 months (Bahrick & Pickens, 1995).

Research has indicated that infants' rates of habituation and preferences for novelty are related to later measures of childhood IQ. Infants who habituate faster or show a stronger preference for novelty have higher childhood IQs than infants who are slower to habituate or show less of a novelty preference (Fagan, 1984; Rose, Feldman, & Wallace, 1992; Thompson, Fagan, & Fulker, 1991). Two reviews of the literature have demonstrated the reliability of these findings, reporting median correlations between infant measures of habituation and/or preference for novelty and later IQ ranging between .37 and .49 (Bornstein, 1989; McCall & Carriger, 1993). Not only does infant preference for novelty predict childhood IQ, but one study has found that it correlates significantly with a measure of recognition memory at 36 months of age (Thompson et al., 1991), arguing for a continuity of the cognitive mechanisms underlying memory functioning between infancy and early childhood. Candidates for these underlying mechanisms include the encoding, storing, and categorization of stimuli, the comparison and discrimination of a present stimulus with a memory representation, the ability to process novelty, and the ability to inhibit responding to a familiar stimulus, among others (Bornstein, 1989; Fagan, 1992; McCall & Carriger, 1993). Each of these processes is critical to memory in later childhood, and also to most other aspects of intellectual functioning.

Mobile Conjugate Reinforcement

The preference-for-novelty procedure is limited to assessing memories of things perceived and cannot be used effectively for memories of actions performed. Adapting techniques from operant-conditioning paradigms, Carolyn Rovee-Collier and her colleagues have developed procedures that assess the memories of young infants for their own actions (specifically, foot kicks) over delays of up to six weeks (Rovee-Collier & Fagen, 1981; Rovee-Collier & Shyi, 1992). In their procedure, a ribbon, connected to a mobile suspended over a crib, is tied to an infant's ankle so that when the infant moves its leg the mobile moves. The typical experiment begins with a 3-minute baseline period, when the ribbon is not connected to the mobile. Next comes a 9-minute reinforcement phase (acquisition), with the ribbon being connected to the mobile. Most infants quickly learn that when they kick their feet, the mobile moves. Some time later (ranging from a few minutes to weeks), the infant is again hooked up to the ribbon with a mobile overhead. If he or she resumes kicking at rates greater than baseline when the ribbon and mobile are *not* connected, it implies memory of the earlier reinforcement phase. If the kicking rate is low and comparable to baseline, the implication is that the infant has forgotten the earlier contingency.

Using variants of this procedure, Rovee-Collier and her colleagues have demonstrated long-term memories in very young infants. For example, retention of conditioned responses was found over a 2-week period for infants as young as 8 weeks of age, although evidence of memory was obtained only under optimal conditions (distributing training over several sessions) (Vander Linde, Morrongiello, & Rovee-Collier, 1985). Slightly older infants (e.g., 6-month-olds) show retention for periods up to 6 weeks, especially when "reminders" (e.g., aspects of the acquisition environment, such as a noncontingent mobile or the distinctive crib in which training occurred) are given sometime between

acquisition and testing (Rovee-Collier & Shyi, 1992; Rovee-Collier, Sullivan, Enright, Lucas, & Fagen, 1980). These results indicate that young infants can remember events over long intervals, although these skills do improve over the first several months of life.

One focus of Rovee-Collier's recent work has been the contribution of *context* to long-term retention. In these experiments, Rovee-Collier and her colleagues vary aspects of the acquisition and testing environments, such as the cribs in which infants are tested or the color or pattern of the crib liners. In one study, 6-month-old infants were tested following standard procedures, although the testing situation was made highly distinctive (Rovee-Collier, Schechter, Shyi, & Shields, 1992). The infant sat in an infant seat placed in a playpen, which was draped with a distinctive cloth (for example, a yellow liner with green squares). Some infants were tested 24 hours later with the same cloth ("No Change" condition), whereas others were placed in the playpen that was draped with a blue liner and vertical red felt strips ("Context Change" condition). Infants in the "No Change" condition remembered the contingencies significantly better than infants in the "Context Change" condition, illustrating the important role of context in infant memory.

Based on this and other experiments, Rovee-Collier et al. (1992) concluded that infants do not respond to the context "as a whole," but rather process individual components of the context. For instance, reversal of the foreground and background (e.g., yellow liner with green squares versus green liner with yellow squares) or changes in visual patterns (e.g., stripes versus squares) disrupted memory, but changes in color did not. Rovee-Collier and Shyi (1992) speculated that the infants' reliance on specific aspects of a context may be adaptive, preventing them from retrieving memories in "inappropriate" situations. This may be especially important given infants' poor inhibitory abilities (Diamond, 1991), which may lead them to retrieve previously acquired actions (memories) in a wide range of often inappropriate situations unless there were some potent constraints on the memory system, such as context specificity.

Search Tasks

A less frequently used technique to assess memory in early infancy involves search tasks, which are variants of Piaget's object-permanence problems (Diamond, 1985, 1995; Horobin & Acredolo, 1986). In research by Diamond (1985), infants were followed longitudinally between the ages of 7.5 and 12 months of age on an adaptation of

Piaget's A-not-B task. Infants watched as the experimenter hid objects several times at one location (A) in front of them, retrieving the object each time after it was hidden. On the critical B trial, the object was hidden in a different location (B), as the infants watched. Diamond varied the length of time between hiding the object and allowing the infant to search for it during the B trial. She reported that the delay between hiding and searching that was necessary to produce the A-not-B error (i.e., searching at the previously correct A location even though seeing it hidden at B) increased with age at a rate of about 2 seconds per month. That is, 7.5-month-old infants erred with only a 2-second delay, whereas, by 12 months of age, infants made the error only if approximately 10 seconds transpired between the hiding of the object and the beginning of the search. These data indicate that infants' memories for their actions are improving steadily between the ages of 7.5 and 12 months. However, in addition to indicating memory as a critical factor, Diamond proposed that infants' abilities to inhibit prepotent responses (i.e., reaching to the previously correct A location) also played an important role in infants' performance (Diamond, 1985, 1991). This is consistent with a recent claim by Rovee-Collier that infants have poor inhibitory abilities and that their long-term memories are highly susceptible to the effects of interference (Rovee-Collier & Boller, 1995; Rovee-Collier & Shyi, 1992).

Memory in Later Infancy

The infant-memory system, illustrated by the preference-for-novelty, conjugate reinforcement procedures, and search tasks, is generally consistent with traditional conceptions of sensorimotor intelligence as described by Piaget (1952) and others. Rovee-Collier's research suggests that secondary circular reactions may be within the capability of infants several months younger than proposed by Piaget, but hers are not the first data to suggest this (Willatts, 1990), and the findings do not call for a radical change in how memory or infant cognition is viewed. The memory demonstrated by these experiments is all implicit. No conscious awareness is necessary, and there is no need to postulate advanced cognitive representations (i.e., symbols). The same cannot be said for recent research examining memory in older infants. The canonical perspective, following Piaget (1952, 1962) and neo-Piagetians (Case, 1985, 1992; Fischer, 1980), holds that it is not until late in the second year that infants possess symbolic abilities. However, a new variant on an old technique, that of *deferred imitation,* seriously questions this

assumption, and results from this work are causing developmental psychologists to rethink not only the nature of infant memory development, but also of infant cognition in general.

Deferred, or delayed, imitation was listed by Piaget (1962) as one of several demonstrations of the symbolic (or semiotic) function, appearing usually between the ages of 18 and 24 months. In deferred imitation, children observe a model and imitate the modeled behavior some appreciable time thereafter, retrieving from memory some representation of the observed behavior. It is thus an example of recall, presumably requiring the retrieval of a mental (symbolic) representation.

In 1985, evidence first appeared that deferred imitation might be within the capability of much younger infants (Abravanel & Gingold, 1985; Meltzoff, 1985). Most experiments follow a procedure in which infants are shown a series of novel actions performed by a model, often involving a new toy. For example, an infant may be shown a toy shaped like a dumbbell. The model picks it up and removes one end in a particular way (Meltzoff, 1988a). Infants do not play with the toy at this time, but only observe the model. At some later time, infants are again shown the toy and encouraged to interact with it. The extent to which they reproduce the behavior they had earlier observed is contrasted with the behavior of children of the same age, who are given the toy for the first time. If experimental infants display the novel behavior to a greater extent than the control infants, it is indication of deferred imitation and thus memory.

This research has shown that the memories of preverbal toddlers can be long lasting indeed, with deferred imitation being reported for 11- to 20-month olds for novel behaviors over delays of one (Abravanel, 1991; Abravanel & Gingold, 1985; Meltzoff, 1985) and two days (Hanna & Meltzoff, 1993), one week (Bauer & Dow, 1994; Bauer & Hertsgaard, 1993; Meltzoff, 1988a), one to 12 months (Bauer & Wewerka, 1995; Mandler & McDonough, 1995; McDonough & Mandler, 1994; Meltzoff, 1995), and over a 24-hour period for samples of 9-month-olds (Meltzoff, 1988b). Although levels of deferred imitation are typically greater for older than younger infants (e.g., Abravanel & Gingold, 1985; Meltzoff, 1985), the findings indicate that the neurological systems underlying long-term recall are present, in at least a rudimentary form, by the beginning of the second year of life. These findings also have important implications for theories of infantile amnesia, and will be discussed later in this chapter.

Is deferred imitation a type of explicit memory? The claim by most researchers using deferred imitation is that the procedure taps a nonverbal, declarative (i.e., explicit) memory system, different from the implicit memory assessed by preference-for-novelty and operant conditioning techniques (Bauer, 1995; McDonough & Mandler, 1995; Meltzoff, 1995). As such, the type of memory observed for toddlers with deferred-imitation tasks is conceptually similar to the verbal recall observed in older children. Support for this contention comes from experiments that report that adult amnesiacs, who fail to perform "normally" on declarative memory tasks, also fail on deferred imitation tasks (McDonough, Mandler, McKee, & Squire, 1994). This finding suggests, counter to earlier claims (e.g., Bachevalier & Mishkin, 1984), that infants' brains are sufficiently mature to form declarative memories. This claim is not without its critics, however (e.g., Nelson, 1994), and it may be impossible to obtain from preverbal infants the type of information needed (e.g., evidence of conscious awareness) to unambiguously classify deferred imitation as a form of explicit memory. Despite the lack of consensus, the evidence of infants' retention of observed acts over long delays clearly suggests that the cognitive and memory systems of infants in their second year are more like those of older children than had been previously believed.

THE DEVELOPMENT OF MEMORY STRATEGIES

The modern era of memory development began with the study of strategies (Flavell, Beach, & Chinsky, 1966) and dominated the field well into the 1980s. Historically, examinations of children's memory strategies can be traced to mediation theories developed by neobehaviorists. (See Harnishfeger & Bjorklund, 1990a; Howe & O'Sullivan, 1990, for a historical sketch.) Mediation theorists assumed that young children's problems in discrimination-learning tasks were due to a failure to construct verbal mediators of their perceptual experiences in such tasks. Neobehaviorists did not refer to verbal mediators as "strategies," although their descriptions of "intervening mediators" come close to current conceptualizations of memory strategies.

Most researchers accept a characterization of strategies as potentially conscious, deliberate, and controllable cognitive plans adopted to enhance performance in memory tasks (Pressley, Forrest-Pressley, Elliot-Faust, & Miller, 1985; Pressley & Van Meter, 1993). The majority of developmental studies have dealt with encoding strategies, such as rehearsal, organization, and elaboration strategies carried out during study. Other investigations focused on retrieval strategies, that is, processes of accessing information in the LTS. Before giving a brief overview of the development of these strategies, we first discuss briefly a few concepts developed to describe and explain young children's strategies. We then discuss the distinction between recognition and recall memory.

Mediation, Production, and Utilization Deficiencies

Working in the tradition of the mediation theorists, Reese (1962) first described young children as being mediationally deficient, or unable to use a verbal mediator. A *mediational deficiency* refers to children being unable to benefit from the use of a strategy even if one is imposed on them. Flavell (1970) coined the term *production deficiency* to describe children who can be instructed to use a strategy effectively but do not use it spontaneously. In contrast to the long history of research investigating mediational and production deficiencies, the third type of deficiency, *utilization deficiency* (Miller, 1990), has only recently been identified. According to Miller, a utilization deficiency occurs during the early phases of strategy acquisition when a child spontaneously produces an appropriate strategy but does not benefit from it in terms of task performance, or experiences less benefit from it than an older child using the same strategy. Although utilization deficiencies have only recently been identified, evidence of their existence can be found in memory development research from its inception. In their review of developmental memory research between the years 1974 and 1992, Miller and Seier (1994) found 59 studies that could be evaluated for utilization deficiencies. Of these, 56 (95%) found partial or clear evidence of utilization deficiencies, although, until recently, few researchers discussed this unanticipated aspect of their results (see also Bjorklund & Coyle, 1995). More recently, a review of memory *training* studies reported evidence of utilization deficiencies in over 50% of experiments reviewed (Bjorklund, Miller, Coyle, & Slawinski, 1997).

Because children become strategic on some tasks before others, the three deficiencies described above occur at different ages on different tasks. For a given strategy, however, it is assumed that these deficiencies occur in a fixed sequence, with mediation deficiencies occurring first, followed by production deficiencies, and utilization deficiencies showing up last before children eventually benefit from the strategy at hand.

Recall versus Recognition

Most studies of strategic memory involve recall, with substantial developmental differences typically being found, particularly when free recall (i.e., without specific prompts) is used. However, smaller developmental differences are usually found for nonstrategic recognition memory (Perlmutter, 1984). That young children can recognize stimuli suggests that they are able to encode the learning materials; that they cannot freely recall them suggests that they are not very good at searching their memories and that they may need more specific prompts to get information "out" of memory (e.g., category cues for recall of categorizable lists) (Ackerman, 1987; Ceci, Lea, & Howe, 1980; Emmerich & Ackerman, 1978).

Recognition memory is particularly good for spatial location, even for very young children. Research using hide-and-seek tasks, reconstruction tasks (Ellis, Katz, & Williams, 1987), and the game "Concentration," or "Memory" (Baker-Ward & Ornstein, 1988; Schumann-Hengsteler, 1996) has shown that this type of memory develops early, reducing or even eliminating age differences in performance. Two factors may contribute to young children's remarkable performance on such tasks: (1) visuospatial memory skills are well-developed at an early age and are much better than verbal memory skills; although pronounced age effects can be found for the latter, only weak developmental trends are reported for the former kind of memory (Schumann-Hengsteler, 1992); and (2) substantial deficits in strategic memory skills. Young children's performance on recognition tasks illustrates that they are able to encode and retain information well; they show particular problems, however, when other cognitive operations (i.e., strategies) must be used in the service of remembering.

Evidence of Strategic Behavior in Preschool Children

Although there is considerable evidence that preschoolers have problems with free-recall tasks, more recent evidence suggests that preschoolers have more strategic competence than was initially supposed. Brown, Bransford, Ferrara, and Campione (1983) noted that two major techniques have been used to demonstrate early competence: (1) simplifying the tasks as much as possible in order to reveal their cognitive requirements in the easiest way, and (2) situating the experiment in a familiar context. Somerville, Wellman, and Cultice (1983) explored young children's prospective memory for everyday activities, that is, the ability to plan ahead and keep in mind a particular event. Two- to 4-year-old children were instructed to carry out a particular activity at a specified future time. The to-be-remembered event was either one that was highly appealing to the child (e.g., getting candy) or one that would be of little interest (e.g., getting the wash out of the washer). There was better memory at all ages for the interesting event, suggesting that even 2-year-olds are capable of intentional memory.

Young children were found to be similarly strategic when memory for spatial locations was assessed. Using an overlearned hide-and-seek game, DeLoache, Cassidy, and Brown (1985) let children aged 18 to 24 months watch an experimenter hide a toy (Big Bird) under a pillow. The children were told that they should remember Big Bird's location so that they could find him later. Although children were then distracted with attractive toys for several minutes, they frequently interrupted their activities to check Big Bird's hiding place (e.g., looking at the pillow, or pointing at it). These activities seemed to be attempts to remember the locations, since they did not occur in a control condition when Big Bird was put on top of the pillow.

Other research on intentional memory for location has produced mixed results. For example, although some studies found almost no evidence that children under 3 years of age benefit from retrieval cues (Loughlin & Daehler, 1973; Ratner & Myers, 1980), others demonstrated that 2- to 3-year-olds can make use of retrieval cues under certain conditions (Blair, Perlmutter, & Myers, 1978; Sophian & Wellman, 1983). Preschoolers seem to benefit from retrieval cues when the task is very simple and retrieval cues are visible to them (Geis & Lange, 1976; Ritter, Kaprove, Fitch, & Flavell, 1973; Schneider & Sodian, 1988). On the other hand, preschoolers and kindergarten children require prompting when the task is more difficult and requires children to prepare for retrieval themselves (Beal & Fleisig, 1987; Ritter, 1978; Whittaker, McShane, & Dunn, 1985). There is evidence of effective strategies, no strategies, and "faulty strategies" (i.e., strategic behaviors that do not help remembering; see Wellman, 1988) in young children.

Although studies on preschoolers' memory have shown surprising competence in 2- to 4-year-olds (Baker-Ward, Ornstein, & Holden, 1984), we should not over interpret these findings. As noted by Brown et al. (1983), young children's memory activities tend to be fragile and are restricted to limited domains. In the current trend to demonstrate the early emergence of mnemonic strategies, we should not overlook the obvious fact that older schoolage children are able to show their memory skills in a wider range of situations, including laboratory tasks. In the following section, we will examine these skills carefully.

Development of Encoding and Retrieval Strategies

Rehearsal

Research interest in rehearsal was partially motivated by the crucial role of rehearsal in both multistore and "levels-of-processing" memory models, and by John Flavell's early work establishing rehearsal as a strategy that developed between 5 and 10 years of age. In a now-classic study, Flavell, Beach, and Chinsky (1966) developed a unique method for studying list learning by 5-, 7-, and 10-year-olds. The children wore space helmets while preparing for serial recall of picture lists. The helmets covered the children's eyes but exposed their lips, allowing the experimenter to determine if the children were verbally rehearsing the materials. Flavell et al. demonstrated that production of the rehearsal strategy increased with age and was positively correlated with level of performance. In particular, it was assumed that frequency of rehearsal determines memory performance.

Later research by Ornstein, Naus, and Liberty (1975) questioned Flavell's frequency interpretation. Ornstein and colleagues used an overt-rehearsal procedure that required children to repeat the items of a word list aloud, permitting the experimenter to determine exactly what the children were doing. Ornstein and his colleagues found that children in the early elementary-school years tended to rehearse each item singularly as it was presented (passive rehearsal style), whereas older children rehearsed each item with several previously presented ones (active, or cumulative rehearsal style). Based on these and other data, the researchers asserted that the important developmental changes are in terms of *style* rather than *frequency* of rehearsal. (See also Guttentag, Ornstein, & Siemens, 1987; Ornstein & Naus, 1985.)

Naus, Ornstein, and Aivano (1977) provided evidence that the differences in rehearsal between younger and older elementary-school children reflected a production deficiency by the younger children. Third graders who did not use the cumulative rehearsal strategy spontaneously could be easily trained to use three-item rehearsal sets and their recall increased accordingly, thus demonstrating a causal relationship between the quality of the rehearsal strategy

and memory performance. What differs in development, then, is children's inclination to implement an active rehearsal strategy and not so much their ability to use it.

Organization

One of the most frequently studied encoding strategies involves organizing pictures or words into semantic categories. In sort-recall tasks, children are typically given a randomly ordered list of categorizable pictures or words, such as animals, furniture, and the like. Children are then told that their task is to remember the items later on, and that they are free to do anything with the materials that may help their recall. Following a short study period, children are asked to recall as many stimuli as they can. Children's organization of items during study (sorting) and recall (clustering) has been measured using the adjusted ratio of clustering (ARC) (Roenker, Thompson, & Brown, 1969) or the ratio-of-repetition (RR) (Bousfield & Bousfield, 1966). For both of these measures, values close to 1 represent almost perfect organization of stimuli, whereas values close to 0 indicate random responding.

As noted by Flavell, Miller, and Miller (1993), the developmental story for organizational strategies is much the same as for rehearsal. In most cases, preschoolers, kindergartners, and young elementary-school children show a production deficiency. That is, they fail to use organizational strategies when given "neutral" instructions (Carr, Kurtz, Schneider, Turner, & Borkowski, 1989; Moely, Olson, Halwes, & Flavell, 1969). Older children are more likely to group the items on the basis of meaning and to study same-category items together, with higher levels of sorting and clustering yielding higher levels of recall (Hasselhorn, 1992; Schneider, 1986). However, even young children can use organizational strategies and display elevated levels of memory performance when instructed to group items on the basis of meaning (Black & Rollins, 1982; Lange & Pierce, 1992). Furthermore, small changes in stimulus presentation procedures considerably influence sorting behavior in preschool children (Guttentag & Lange, 1994). These findings demonstrate the fragility of memory strategies in this age group. Yet, such interventions rarely eliminate age differences, and young children will only generalize a trained organizational strategy if training is extensive (Carr & Schneider, 1991; Cox & Waters, 1986; Waters, & Andreassen, 1983).

Higher levels of organization are not always accompanied by higher levels of recall. Such utilization deficiencies have been shown in several studies with both preschoolers and elementary-school children (Bjorklund, Coyle, & Gaultney, 1992; Lange, Guttentag, & Nida, 1990; Lange & Pierce, 1992; Miller, Haynes, DeMarie-Dreblow, & Woody-Ramsey, 1986). It appears that using an organizational strategy is only a first step. Once the mechanics of the strategy are learned, children need some time before they can execute it proficiently. Typically, spontaneous and effective use of organizational strategies cannot be observed before the end of elementary school (Hasselhorn, 1992; Schneider, 1986). From Grade 4 on, most children spontaneously and successfully employ organizational strategies across a wide variety of materials and instructions, as indicated by substantial intercorrelations among sorting, clustering, and recall.

Elaboration

Elaboration involves the generation of relations between pairs of items, and deals with possibilities to improve paired-associate learning. (See Kee, 1994; Pressley, 1982; Rohwer, 1973; Schneider & Pressley, 1989, for reviews.) According to Rohwer (1973), elaboration in noun-pair learning refers to the process of generating an event that can serve as the common referent for the members of each pair. More specifically, elaboration involves associating two or more items by creating a visual or verbal representation of them. Most research exploring the effects of imagery and verbal elaboration has used variants of the method of paired-associates, in which children are presented pairs of unrelated nouns (e.g., cat–apple, arrow–glasses) to memorize on a study trial. At testing, only the stimulus is presented, with the child being required to recall the associated response. A verbal elaboration for the pair cat–apple could involve generating a sentence that describes an event involving the two, for example, "The cat rolled the apple around." A visual elaboration concerning this noun pair could involve creating an image of a cat rolling an apple around.

Early research concerning the use of elaboration strategies revealed production deficiencies during the preschool and childhood years (Flavell, 1970; Rohwer, 1973). Unlike rehearsal and organizational strategies, elaboration strategies are rarely observed before adolescence (Beuhring & Kee, 1987; Pressley & Levin, 1977). Moreover, even many adults need to be prompted to use elaboration on paired-associate tasks (Rohwer, 1980). However, as with the other two mnemonics, young children can be trained to use elaboration strategies with corresponding increases in memory performance (Pressley, 1982; Siaw & Kee, 1987). When younger children do generate elaborations, they typically are not as effective as those produced by older children (Reese, 1977), reflecting a utilization deficiency.

Strategies for Remembering Complex Materials

Most studies of strategy development have focused on processes that improve rote recall of words or pictures. As already noted by Brown et al. (1983), this is not the only form of learning. Deliberate strategies can also be applied to understand, store, and retrieve complex, meaningful information such as texts. Learning to read and write requires strategic activities rarely observed in elementary-school children. In particular, early research carried out by Brown and her colleagues has shown that processes such as identifying, underlining, and summarizing the main ideas of text passages develop during the high school years (Brown et al., 1983; Pressley, Forrest-Pressley et al., 1985).

Although these strategies develop rather late, the developmental pattern found between Grades 6 and 12 resembles that found for rote-recall memory strategies between Grades 1 and 6. That is, these activities are only sporadically observed, followed by more frequent, robust application in a broader variety of learning situations. As is true for simpler strategies, such as rehearsal and organization, initial use of strategies for understanding and remembering texts is often accompanied by production deficiencies and poor performance. It is only after prolonged periods of practice that mature, successful strategy application can be observed.

Complicated text-processing strategies can be effectively taught to normal, elementary-school children (Gaultney, 1995; Paris & Oka, 1986; Pressley, 1995a) and to poor readers (Palincsar & Brown, 1984; Short & Ryan, 1984). However, spontaneous production of strategies for learning and remembering complex text material is the exception rather than the rule, and even adults may fail to use such strategies routinely. It appears that traditional summaries of the development of memory strategies focusing on rote-recall memory tasks frequently underestimate the variation of age-related development in natural strategic competence. Whereas simple strategies can already be detected in early childhood, more sophisticated and complex procedures are not commonly observed even in bright and mature subjects, such as university students (Pressley & Afflerbach, 1995; Pressley & Van Meter, 1993).

Retrieval Strategies

Once information has entered the LTS, something has to be done to get it out. Retrieval strategies refer to planful operations individuals undertake in order to access stored information. Like encoding strategies, retrieval strategies vary considerably in complexity and sophistication. Age differences in the effective use of retrieval strategies have been frequently observed (Kobasigawa, 1977; Pressley & MacFadyen, 1983). Kobasigawa listed several potential deficiencies in children's retrieval: (1) Children often fail to perceive that internal or external memory cues are potential memory aids; (2) they may lack strategies for locating target information in memory, and (3) they may not have enough experience with the problem to evaluate when the search process should be considered finished.

Regarding the first potential deficiency cited by Kobasigawa, several studies have demonstrated young children's problems with using external memory cues. For example, Kobasigawa (1974) presented lists of categorizable items to children in Grades 1, 3, and 6 to learn for subsequent recall. He also presented cue cards that served to classify the objects (e.g., pictures of animals went with a cue card of a zoo). The younger children did not spontaneously use these retrieval cues at testing to guide their recall, and they also displayed no benefits when told that the retrieval cues could be used (available-cue condition). However, their recall was much improved and comparable to that of the older children when they were explicitly told to use the cues at recall (directive-cue condition). These findings suggest that the younger children had stored as much information about the target stimuli as the older children. Their major problem was getting it out (Howe, Brainerd, & Kingma, 1985).

A study by Keniston and Flavell (1979) illustrates another retrieval problem of younger children referred to by Kobasigawa (1977), namely, lack of adequate search strategies. First-, third-, seventh-graders, and college students were read a list of 20 different letters of the alphabet, which they wrote down. Unexpectedly, subjects were asked to recall these letters. An effective retrieval strategy is to go through the entire alphabet and identify the letters that have been recently seen, thus transforming the difficult free-recall task into a much easier recognition task. If items are recalled in alphabetical order, one can infer that such a retrieval strategy was used. Results showed that the younger children in the study could use the recognition strategy effectively and skillfully when told to do so, although they did not use the strategy spontaneously. In contrast, no specific feedback was required for the older subjects to use the alphabetic retrieval strategy.

These and other related findings suggest that young children benefit more from the imposition of retrieval cues than older children, presumably because the older children spontaneously generate appropriate retrieval plans. As noted by Flavell et al. (1993), much of what develops in the area of memory retrieval consists of the ability to search the LTS system intelligently, that is, systematically, flexibly, exhaustively, and selectively—whatever the retrieval problem at hand demands. In general, this ability develops rather late in childhood, particularly when the use of internal memory cues is required. On the other hand, we have already shown that even preschool children demonstrate the ability to effectively use retrieval cues when searching the external world (Wellman, 1985).

How Important Are Strategies? The Case of Utilization Deficiencies

The study of strategies dominated the field of memory development throughout most of the 1970s and 1980s. This dominance was due in large part to the belief that using strategies yielded enhanced memory performance, with strategic children performing better than nonstrategic children. This canonical perspective began to be questioned in the late 1980s as evidence accumulated that children's memory performance often was *not* enhanced by using strategies or was enhanced less for younger than for comparably strategic older children (Bjorklund & Bjorklund, 1985; Bjorklund & Harnishfeger, 1987; Miller et al., 1986), a phenomenon Miller (1990, 1994) labeled as a utilization deficiency.

The finding that strategies often fail to improve young children's performance, and sometimes actually hinder it, is counterintuitive given the perspective that the purpose of strategies is to increase memory. The explanation for this discrepancy favored by most researchers is that executing strategies consumes too much of children's limited mental capacity. As a result, they do not have sufficient resources remaining to devote to the actual retrieval of items from memory (Bjorklund & Coyle, 1995; Miller, 1994; Miller & Seier, 1994). Several experiments have manipulated the mental effort requirements of memory tasks and have found empirical evidence for this position (Bjorklund & Harnishfeger, 1987; Miller, Seier, Probert, & Aloise, 1991). Several other factors have been hypothesized to influence utilization deficiencies. For example, young children may not be able to inhibit the execution of inefficient strategies (Miller, 1994). Utilization deficiencies may also be related to metacognition, with young children failing to monitor their task performance and thus failing to realize that a strategy is not enhancing their performance (Bjork-lund & Coyle, 1995). Another possibility is that children use a strategy, even if it doesn't help their performance, simply for the novelty of using it. Children may enjoy exercising a new strategy for its own sake (similar to Piaget's idea of functional assimilation), without consideration for its consequences (Siegler, 1996). The end result may be adaptive. As the novelty wears off, the strategy becomes less effortful to execute (as a result of repeated use), resulting in eventual memory benefits (Bjorklund et al., 1992). Whatever the reasons, utilization deficiencies are real and are at odds with the idea that children use increasingly sophisticated strategies with age and show corresponding improvements in memory performance.

Multiple- and Variable-Strategy Use

From this discussion of strategy development, one could get the impression that children use one strategy at a time, progressing stagelike from less to more effective strategies. Research has made it clear, however, that this is not the case. Rather, there is substantial inter- and intrasubject variability in strategy use, with children using different strategies and combinations of strategies on any given problem. This position has been championed by Robert Siegler (Siegler, 1995, 1996), who views cognitive development not as a series of stagelike steps, but rather as changes in the frequency with which children use different strategies. Rather than using a staircase metaphor of development (Case, 1992), Siegler views developmental change as a series of overlapping waves; strategies occur with different frequencies over time and compete with one another for use. With time, the modal strategy children use to solve a problem will typically increase in efficiency, replacing less effective strategies; but simple and complicated strategies co-exist in a child's cognitive repertoire and compete for use. Depending on aspects of the task, the learning context, and the child, different strategies will be used on different trials.

Although most of Siegler's empirical work on strategy variability, competition, and selection has been done with arithmetic (Siegler, 1987; Siegler & Jenkins, 1989), some research based on this framework also has been done with memory strategies. For example, McGilly and Siegler (1989, 1990) assessed the different strategies 5- to 9-year-old children used on a serial-recall task. Although task performance increased with age and older children typically used more sophisticated strategies than younger children,

children of all ages used multiple strategies on the task, with even the youngest children sometimes using the most sophisticated strategy (repeated rehearsal). In other research, Coyle and Bjorklund (1997) reported multiple- and variable-strategy use for children in Grades 2, 3, and 4 on a multitrial sort-recall task with categorized sets of items. Strategies children used included sorting items into groups, category naming, rehearsal, and clustering. Although the average number of strategies children used increased over the five trials and increased with age, there was substantial variability in the number of strategies children used per trial at all grades, with greater than one-third of the second-grade children using two or more strategies on a majority of the trials. Children of all ages also varied the strategies they used. No age differences were found in the incidence of switching strategies (i.e., using one combination of strategies on one trial and a different combination on the next trial), with children at all grades showing a switch on about half of the trials. Strategy effectiveness was also related to age, with older children typically improving their memory performance when they increased the number of strategies they used on adjacent trials, whereas younger children actually showed a decrement in recall when they increased the number of strategies they used. This pattern reflects a utilization deficiency (Miller, 1994), with young children failing to benefit from the spontaneous use of a strategy.

Siegler (1996) proposes that variability enhances learning, and that this is especially advantageous for infants and young children. By generating a variety of alternative strategies, children can experiment with different approaches to a problem, discovering what works well, when, and where. Strategies are not always selected because they worked in the past or because they are apt to produce the best performance. Sometimes strategies are selected because they are novel. Task outcome may not be enhanced (as in a utilization deficiency), but with practice, a strategy initially selected for its novelty may come to be effective and eventually used to enhance task performance.

FACTORS THAT INFLUENCE (VERBAL) MEMORY DEVELOPMENT

Although charting age-related differences in memory behavior is an important task, equally important is finding the factors that underlie these differences. Researchers have identified a variety of factors that, in combination, have been shown to have a significant impact on memory development, particularly (though not exclusively) the development of strategic memory, and we examine some of these factors in the following section.

The Role of Metamemory

More than 25 years ago, John Flavell (1971) introduced the term *metamemory* to refer to knowledge about memory processes and contents. From a developmental perspective, this concept seemed well-suited to explain young children's production deficiencies on a broad variety of tasks. Because young children only occasionally get into situations that require intentional memorizing, they do not learn much about the advantages of strategies. This changes as children enter school. From that point on, they are regularly confronted with various memory tasks that help them discover the advantages of strategies and improve their metamemory.

In their taxonomy of metamemory, Flavell and Wellman (1977) distinguished between two main categories, "sensitivity" and "variables." The sensitivity category included knowledge of when memory activity is necessary (e.g., awareness that a particular task in a particular setting requires the use of memory strategies). This component has also been called "procedural metacognitive knowledge," indicating implicit, unconscious behavioral knowledge (Brown et al., 1983; Paris & Lindauer, 1982). The variables category was divided into three subcategories: (a) person characteristics, (b) task characteristics, and (c) knowledge about potentially applicable memory strategies. This component refers to explicit, conscious, factual knowledge also called "declarative metacognitive knowledge." An example of a person variable is the child's mnemonic self-concept, including ideas about his or her memory strengths and weaknesses. Task variables denote factors that influence task difficulty, such as item familiarity, list length, or study time. The strategy variable includes all changes in knowledge about advantages and problems of memory strategies.

Other theorists have contributed to the development of metamemory theory. (For useful reviews and critiques, see Borkowski, Milstead, & Hale, 1988; Nelson, 1992; Schneider, 1985; Wellman, 1985.) For instance, Paris and colleagues (Paris & Lindauer, 1982; Paris & Oka, 1986) introduced a component called "conditional metacognitive knowledge" that focused on children's ability to justify or explain their decisions concerning memory

actions. Whereas declarative metamemory assessed by Flavell and colleagues focuses on "knowing that," the component added by Paris and coworkers particularly deals with "knowing why" information. Although the "knowing what" and "knowing why" components should be closely related from a theoretical point of view, this is not necessarily the case. For example, young school children may know that organizational strategies are better than naming or rehearsal in sort-recall tasks but are unable to give appropriate reasons. On the other hand, both knowledge components are highly interrelated in older school children (Hasselhorn, 1992; Schneider, 1986).

Whereas Flavell and colleagues focused on declarative metamemory, Brown's research group explored the procedural metamemory component, that is, children's ability to monitor and regulate their memory behavior ("knowing how"). Here, the frame of reference was the competent information processor, one possessing an efficient "executive" that regulated cognitive behaviors. Brown and colleagues took the perspective that memory monitoring and regulation processes play a large role in executive actions and that considerable developmental differences can be observed for these variables. In particular, monitoring and regulating behaviors seem to be crucial in more complex cognitive tasks such as comprehending and memorizing text materials (Baker & Brown, 1984; Brown et al., 1983; Garner, 1987).

Declarative Metacognitive Knowledge

How do we know what children know about their memory? One straightforward way of finding out is to ask them. Kreutzer, Leonard, and Flavell (1975) conducted a comprehensive interview study of kindergarten, first-, third-, and fifth-grade children's metamemory concerning person, task, and strategy variables. Children were asked if they ever forget things, if it would be easier to remember the gist of a story than to recall it verbatim, and if learning pairs of opposites (e.g., boy–girl) would be easier or harder than learning pairs of unrelated words (e.g., Mary–walk). Other questions were more demanding. Children's knowledge of retrieval strategies was tested by asking them to think of all the things they could do to try to find a jacket they had lost while at school.

Overall, the results of the Kreutzer et al. study indicated that, although young children display metamnemonic competence in some situations, they experience many problems in evaluating the impact of person, task, and strategy variables on memory performance. Even 3- and 4-year-olds realize that remembering many items is more difficult than remembering just a few, and a majority of the kindergarten children knew that using external devices (e.g., writing phone numbers down) help in remembering information. However, large age effects were found for most interview items. Regarding person variables, only the 9- and 11-year-olds realized that memorization skills vary from person to person and from situation to situation. In contrast, the kindergarten and first-grade children were convinced that they always remember well and that they are better at remembering than their friends. This finding is consistent with other demonstrations that the memory-related self-concept of young children is overly optimistic (Flavell, Friedrichs, & Hoyt, 1970; Yussen & Levy, 1975).

Several studies evaluating children's knowledge of task and strategy factors yielded similar developmental trends. (For a review, see Schneider & Pressley, 1997.) Factual knowledge about these aspects of memory develops greatly once children enter school. Preschoolers and kindergartners have only rudimentary knowledge regarding task and strategy factors (Yussen & Bird, 1979). It is not before the middle of elementary school that the importance of task variables is well understood (Borkowski, Peck, Reid, & Kurtz, 1983; Cavanaugh & Borkowski, 1980; Kurtz & Borkowski, 1984; Schneider, Borkowski, Kurtz, & Kerwin, 1986; Weinert, 1986). For example, only 55% of the kindergartners, but 100% of Grade 5 subjects in the Kreutzer et al. (1975) study knew that gist recall is easier than verbatim recall. Similarly, only the 9- and 10-year-olds but not the 7-year-olds in Moynahan's (1978) study knew that taxonomically organized items are easier to recall than conceptually unrelated words. Finally, although the majority of preschool and kindergarten children know that memory tasks are easier when retrieval cues are available (Schneider & Sodian, 1988), sophisticated understanding of retrieval cues and how they work develops later during the grade-school years (Beal, 1985).

One problem with evaluating findings concerning declarative metacognitive knowledge is that verbal interviews and questionnaires were used in most studies addressing this issue. Young children's verbal skills are often inadequate for them to articulate their knowledge about memory, making nonverbal assessments desirable. For example, Justice (1985, 1986) developed a procedure that involves presenting various memory strategies (e.g., looking, naming, rehearsing, and grouping) on a videotape. After watching the videotape, children made paired comparisons of the four strategies. For each pair, they were asked to state which strategy was better suited for free recall. The studies based on this paradigm produced consistent data (Justice, 1985, 1986; Schneider, 1986; Schneider, Körkel, & Vogel, 1987), and demonstrated that kindergarten and young elementary-school children recognized differential effectiveness only when strategies produced dramatic differences in performance. Older children, however, detected more subtle differences in strategy effectiveness. By and large, then, these findings corroborate those obtained with verbal assessment procedures.

Taken together, the empirical evidence illustrates that some knowledge of facts about memory is available in preschool children and develops quickly over the elementary-school years. Although some studies suggest that declarative metamemory may be complete by 11 or 12 years of age, research dealing with rather complex materials such as texts shows that this is not the case. There is increasing evidence that even adolescents and young adults have problems understanding the advantages of some advanced memory strategies and also with understanding complex task- and person-variable interactions (Schneider & Pressley, 1997).

Procedural Metamemory: Self-Monitoring and Self-Regulation

One possibility for exploring the role of metamemory in actual behavior is to look at how children use their knowledge to monitor their own memory status and regulate their memory activities. According to Nelson and Narens (1994), self-monitoring and self-regulation correspond to two different levels of metacognitive processing. Self-monitoring refers to keeping track of where you are with regard to your goal of understanding and remembering, (bottom-up process). On the other hand, self-regulation refers to central executive activities and includes planning, directing, and evaluating your behavior (top-down process).

Self-Monitoring. A variety of developmental studies on memory monitoring have addressed children's ability to predict future memory performances from previous performances (*performance-prediction accuracy*). As noted earlier, these studies have consistently found that preschool and kindergarten children overpredict their memory performance, whereas elementary-school children are much more accurate (Schneider et al., 1986; Worden & Sladewski-Awig, 1982). Several studies have tried to identify young children's difficulties in making accurate performance predictions. It was found that predictions tended to be more accurate in familiar than in unfamiliar, laboratory-type situations (Justice & Bray, 1979; Wippich, 1980). Moreover, nonverbal assessments of memory span yielded more accurate judgments than the traditional verbal procedure (Cunningham & Weaver, 1989). Also, young children can be rather accurate when asked to predict the performance of other children, as compared to their own performance (Stipek, 1984). Thus, young children's poor performance predictions seems not to be primarily due to metacognitive deficiencies, but they may be strongly affected by motivational factors such as wishful thinking or beliefs in the power of effort (Stipek, 1984; Wellman, 1985). Because such motivational processes are not similarly influential in school children, performance on the performance-prediction task indeed reflects memory monitoring in this population. Although performance prediction can be already accurate in young elementary-school children, there are subtle improvements during the elementary-school years (Pressley & Ghatala, 1990; Schneider, 1986; Schneider & Uhl, 1990).

Similar trends were observed when children's "postdictions" (i.e., their judgments of performance accuracy after the fact) were evaluated (Bisanz, Vesonder, & Voss, 1978; Pressley, Levin, Ghatala, & Ahmad, 1987). For instance, Pressley, Levin, et al. (1987) compared 7- and 10-year-olds' postdictions for word lists and individual items. There were two interesting findings: (a) although rather accurate postdictions were found even for the younger age group, the older children were significantly better; and (b) those children who were most accurate with regard to estimating performance on individual items were not similarly accurate when asked to postdict performance on the entire list, and vice versa. It appears, then, that these two tasks tap different aspects of the estimation process (see also Nelson & Narens, 1994).

A number of developmental studies have explored children's *feeling-of-knowing (FOK) accuracy* (Cultice, Somerville, & Wellman, 1983; DeLoache & Brown, 1984; Posnansky, 1978; Wellman, 1977). Children were shown a series of items and then asked to name them. When children could not recall the name of an object given its picture, they were asked to indicate whether the name would be recognized if the experimenter provided it. These FOK ratings were then related to subsequent performance on the recognition test. Taken together, the findings demonstrated that even preschoolers can be fairly accurate when the task is simply structured and involves highly meaningful test materials such as faces. Most studies indicate that FOK accuracy improves continuously across childhood and adolescence

(e.g., Zabrucky & Ratner, 1986; but see Butterfield, Nelson, & Peck, 1988, for discrepant findings).

Control and Self-Regulation.   Several studies examined whether school children and adults were more likely to spend more time on less well-learned material *(allocation of study time)*. Masur, McIntyre, and Flavell (1973) asked first graders, third graders, and college students to learn a list of pictures for free recall. After the first trial, subjects were instructed to select half the pictures for additional study. Masur et al. found that, although all of the subjects could distinguish between recalled and unrecalled items, the older children and adults were more likely to select previously unrecalled items for further study. Similar findings were reported by Bisanz et al. (1978) and Dufresne and Kobasigawa (1989) for a paired-associate task. The results indicate that even young grade-school children can discriminate between recalled and unrecalled items as well as between easy and difficult items. However, it is unlikely that they use this information for subsequent learning.

Another example of self-regulation concerns knowledge of *recall readiness*. One variation involves asking subjects to continue studying until their memory of the to-be-learned materials is perfect. For instance, Flavell et al. (1970) found that 5- to 6-year-old children are often too optimistic about their readiness for a test and have low levels of recall after they say they are ready for a test. Recall readiness estimates of the second- and fourth-grade children were considerably more accurate. Flavell et al. (1970) concluded that older children's more accurate assessments were due to their greater use of self-testing during study.

One problem with this interpretation is that relatively short lists corresponding to each child's memory span were used in this study. Recall readiness assessment skills are typically overestimated when children learn materials that are not particularly difficult (Markman, 1973). Later studies including memory tasks other than serial recall (e.g., free recall, memory for text) showed that older elementary-school children are not particularly proficient at determining when they have studied items long enough to master the material (Dufresne & Kobasigawa, 1989; Gettinger, 1985; Leal, Crays, & Moely, 1985). Self-testing strategies were rarely observed in these studies. Apparently, most grade-school children do not spontaneously use task-relevant regulation strategies, a finding that may explain their difficulties with allocating study time well. However, there is no doubt that they can be successfully trained to do so. Several studies have shown that training in memory monitoring and self-regulation is responsible for the effectiveness and maintenance of strategy training (Ghatala, Levin, Pressley, & Goodwin, 1986; Paris, Newman, & McVey, 1982).

Metamemory-Memory Relations

One of the main motivations to study metamemory has been the assumption that there are important relationships between knowing about memory and memory behaviors (Brown, 1978; Flavell & Wellman, 1977; Weinert, 1986). However, early investigations did not find substantial relations between the two (Cavanaugh & Borkowski, 1980), and it was concluded, counter to initial expectations, that the links between memory knowledge and memory behavior are rather weak (Cavanaugh & Perlmutter, 1982).

More recent research has shown that the relation one finds between metamemory and memory is much stronger than previously assumed (Cantor, Andreassen, & Waters, 1985; Schneider, 1985; Wellman, 1983). In a first statistical meta-analysis of empirical studies addressing this issue, Schneider (1985) reported an overall correlation of .41, which was based on 27 studies and a total of 2231 subjects. A second meta-analysis carried out a few years later and based on a considerably larger sample (i.e., 60 publications and 7079 subjects) replicated the .41 correlation (Schneider & Pressley, 1989). Thus, children's metamemory makes a reliable and moderately strong contribution to their memory behavior and performance. Schneider and Pressley (1989) concluded that the metamemory-memory relation depends on several factors, such as the type of task (e.g., organizational strategies or memory monitoring), age of the child, task difficulty, and presentation of the metamemory assessment (before or after the memory task). The relation appears to be stronger (a) for older than for younger children, and (b) after experience with a memory task rather than before. However, the type of task turns out to be an important moderator variable. For example, studies looking at metamemory-memory relations in categorization and elaboration tasks do not yield strong connections between the two factors until the elementary-school years (Lange et al., 1990), and not consistently until age 10 (Hasselhorn, 1992). Yet, when the task is simple and familiar and the metamemory questions are highly related to successful task performance, substantial metamemory-memory relations are found even for preschool children (e.g., Schneider & Sodian, 1988).

In general, the research evidence points to a bidirectional relationship between metamemory knowledge and memory behavior (Brown, 1978; Schneider, 1985). Metamemory can influence memory behavior, which in turn leads to enhanced metamemory. Several studies (Fabricius & Hagen, 1984; Hasselhorn, 1986; Kurtz & Weinert, 1989; Schneider, Körkel, & Weinert, 1987) have used multivariate causal modeling procedures to examine the causal interrelationships among metamemory, memory behavior, and memory performance. These analyses permit the conclusion that even relatively young elementary-school children possess strategy knowledge that has direct influence on strategic behaviors, which in turn adds to their task-specific metamemory.

Strategy-Capacity Relations

One reason for young children's production deficiencies may be that the deployment of strategies is too demanding given their limited attentional resources. To test this hypothesis, a dual-task procedure can be used. In these procedures, children execute two tasks, a primary memory activity, and a secondary, irrelevant activity (e.g., finger tapping), both separately and together. The crucial outcome variable is the degree of interference between the two tasks, with higher levels of interference indicating that the aggregate demand for attentional resources exceeds the capacity limitations.

Guttentag (1984) used the dual-task procedure to explore the capacity requirements of a cumulative rehearsal strategy. While second-, third-, and sixth-grade children rehearsed a list of unrelated words, they were required to perform the finger tapping task as quickly as possible. This tapping rate during rehearsal was compared to a baseline rate of tapping only. Guttentag found that children of all grades were able to execute the cumulative rehearsal task and that dual-task deficits decreased with age. Guttentag interpreted this finding as showing that younger children allocated more mental effort to execute a cumulative rehearsal strategy than older children. In accord with this interpretation, Guttentag et al. (1987) found that some children who used a passive rehearsal strategy under normal presentation conditions switched to an active, cumulative rehearsal strategy under conditions in which the resource demands of the active strategy were reduced (e.g., when the items remained visible during study). Similar developmental differences in dual-task performance were obtained for other strategies, including organization (Bjorklund & Harnishfeger, 1987), elaboration (Kee & Davis, 1988, 1990), and selective attention (Miller, Seier, Probert, & Aloise, 1991). It appears, then, that age differences in the resource demands of strategy use may be at least partially responsible for age differences in strategy selection and efficiency (but see Brainerd & Reyna, 1989).

The Impact of the Knowledge Base

Since the late 1970s, there has been increasing evidence for the impressive effects of knowledge on performance in various memory tasks (cf. Bjorklund, 1987; Chi & Ceci, 1987; Ornstein, Baker-Ward, & Naus, 1988; Schneider, 1993a). In most domains, older children know more than younger ones. The more people know about a topic, the easier it is for them to learn and remember new information about it. Most researchers investigating the acquisition of content knowledge assume that it is a sort of mental dictionary of objects and their relationships (Bjorklund, 1987; Chi, 1985; Chi & Rees, 1983). They posit modified network models of semantic memory, assuming that every item or concept in semantic memory is represented by nodes that are connected to each other. Developmental changes in the network affect the number of available items and their accessibility. New features are added with experience, with additional features permitting more elaborate codings when items are presented as stimuli in a memory task.

In our view, the primary effect that an elaborated knowledge base has on memory is to increase the speed of processing for domain-specific information. Research using dual-task paradigms has shown that younger children require greater mental effort to use memory strategies than older children. Mental effort is reduced when highly familiar stimuli are used, leaving more of one's limited capacity to search for individual items or to execute a complex strategy (Guttentag, 1989; Kee, 1994). If that faster processing can be equated with more efficient processing, the result is greater availability of mental resources.

According to Bjorklund (1987), age differences in content knowledge can affect memory in three general ways: (a) by increasing the accessibility of specific items (item-specific effects); (b) by the relatively effortless activation of relations among sets of items; and (c) by facilitating the use of deliberate strategies.

Item-Specific Effects

These effects are most easily observed when children are asked to recall sets of unrelated items (e.g., tree, clock, dress, nail, rain). Whereas recall of such lists typically improves with age, no corresponding improvements in subjective organization are found (Knopf, Körkel, Schneider, & Weinert, 1988; Ornstein, Hale, & Morgan, 1977). One

interpretation of these findings is that individual items are more richly represented (i.e., have more features) in the semantic memories of older than younger children, resulting in greater ease of retrieval. This conclusion has been supported by experiments using lists of unrelated items that were equally meaningful for children of different ages, effectively eliminating age differences in knowledge for the to-be-remembered information. Under these conditions, no age differences in recall were obtained (Chechile & Richman, 1982; Ghatala, 1984). In a similar vein, Lindberg (1980) demonstrated that children can actually outperform adults when the task material refers to content that they know better, such as titles of children's television programs and books.

Nonstrategic Organization

One way in which having an elaborated knowledge base facilitates recall is through the relatively automatic activation of relations between items in long-term memory. The result is highly organized retrieval without the need of deliberate, effortful strategies. These effects increase with age, as knowledge becomes better established and integrated in semantic memory. For example, Bjorklund and Zeman (1982) asked children in Grades 1, 3, and 5 to recall the names of their current classmates. Age differences in recall were small and were significantly less than age differences found for lists of categorically related words. Furthermore, children's recall of classmates' names typically was highly organized in terms of seating assignments, reading groups, or sex. Yet, when asked how they went about remembering the names, most of the children in all grades were unaware of using any specific strategy. In a follow-up study, Bjorklund and Bjorklund (1985) induced children to use a specific retrieval strategy (e.g., recall names by seating arrangement). Although children followed these organizational schemes almost perfectly, there was no improvement in recall as a function of strategy use. Bjorklund and Bjorklund (1985) argued that although the outcome of the children's recall looked to be strategic, the processes underlying their performance were not. Rather, the results were consistent with the position that performance was mediated by the relatively automatic activation and retrieval of relations among items in memory, and that the use of intentional memory strategies has only a minimal effect on performance in this type of task.

Facilitating Strategies

Several developmental studies have shown substantial relationships between conceptual knowledge and strategy use.

Experimental manipulations have often concerned children's knowledge of categorical relations among items, such as, *category typicality* (Bjorklund, 1988; Rabinowitz, 1984; Rabinowitz & Kee, 1994), or have explored *interitem associativity* (Bjorklund & Jacobs, 1985; Frankel & Rollins, 1985; Schneider, 1986). Frankel and Rollins (1985) assessed the impact of associative versus categorical relations by manipulating high and low category relatedness and high and low interitem associativity. They found that fourth- and tenth-grade children showed high levels of organization in recall whenever category typicality and/or associative strength were high. In contrast, kindergartners displayed greater category clustering only when associations among items were high. Schneider (1986) used a similar experimental design with second and fourth graders. In general, more clustering was found for the highly associated lists. The fourth graders had higher levels of sorting, clustering, and recall than the younger children. More importantly, there was a striking age-by-list associativity interaction in the clustering data, such that low associativity particularly penalized the younger children. Using the relation between clustering and recall as an indicator of strategic processing (as suggested by Lange, 1973), only the oldest children could be considered strategic.

Taken together, this research clearly demonstrates that differences in the meaningfulness of words considerably influences the processing of verbal information. One reason proposed for the conceptual knowledge effect is that semantic relations between high associates are activated with relatively little mental effort, resulting in retrieval that appears organized and strategic even in young children, but does not require the use of a deliberate strategy. Whereas young children's strategic competencies may be underestimated in situations where complex, effort-consuming strategies such as cumulative rehearsal are required (see above), they actually may be overrated in situations where high associativity among items automatically guides the structure of recall (see Bjorklund, 1987).

Strategic effects of the knowledge base are not restricted to categorization tasks but have been similarly observed for other memory paradigms (Chi & Ceci, 1987; Hasselhorn, 1995; Rabinowitz & Chi, 1987). Thus, the general proposition is that an elaborated knowledge base allows for the effective use of memory strategies. Later in development, when children have a more sophisticated knowledge base and more experience, even complex strategies may become automated. In support of this, a number of studies have shown that children (and adults) more readily acquire and generalize strategies to new sets of material when more familiar (as opposed to less familiar) stimuli are used (Best, 1993; Rabinowitz, Freeman, & Cohen, 1992).

The Role of Expertise

If knowledge does play a central role in memory functioning, particularly strong effects of content knowledge on memory are to be expected for people possessing high levels of expertise in the domain under investigation (Chi & Ceci, 1987; Rabinowitz & Chi, 1987; Schneider, 1993b). From a developmental perspective, the major advantage of the expert-novice paradigm is that knowledge and chronological age are not necessarily confounded, a problem inherent in most studies addressing knowledge-base effects.

We discussed earlier some of the findings concerning memory spans for chess-expert children (Chi, 1978; Roth, 1983; Schneider, Gruber, Gold, & Opwis, 1993). In the study by Schneider and his colleagues (1993), groups of child and adult experts and novices were compared on various chess board and control board reconstruction tasks. No performance differences between adult and child experts were found. The effects of expertise on performance decreased with decreasing meaning of chess piece constellations (i.e., in the random board reconstruction task), and were almost completely eliminated in a control task that required the reconstruction of wooden pieces on a board that had little in common with a chess board. It appears that context factors such as the familiarity with the constellation of chess pieces and the familiarity with the characteristics of the chess board (e.g., geometrical pattern, form and color of chess pieces) significantly contributed to the experts' superior performances. Taken together, the chess studies provided evidence that content knowledge enables a child expert to perform like an adult expert and better than an adult novice, showing the disappearance or even reversal of usual developmental trends.

Superior recall of child experts has not only been demonstrated in the domain of chess, but also of dinosaurs (Chi & Koeske, 1983), soccer (Schneider, Körkel, & Weinert, 1989), baseball (Recht & Leslie, 1988), and "Star Wars" (Means & Voss, 1985), among others. Perhaps the most robust finding in the literature on knowledge effects is that experts in an area learn more when studying "new" information in their domain of expertise than do novices (but see DeMarie-Dreblow, 1991 and Muir-Broaddus, Rorer, Braden, & George, 1995).

Undoubtedly, experts and novices in a domain differ considerably in terms of *quantity* of knowledge. However, there is also evidence that experts and novices differ *qualitatively* in the way their knowledge is represented. For example, Means and Voss (1985) found that their "Star Wars" experts differed from novices in that they constructed a more complete hierarchical structure of "Star Wars" that contained high-level goals, subgoals, and basic actions. Even more interestingly, there were age-related representational differences within the sample of "Star Wars" experts. Whereas the older experts seemed to interpret "Star Wars" in relation to an "international conflict" schema involving interrelated political-moral-military components, the younger experts tended to interpret "Star Wars" in reference to a military-oriented "good guy–bad guy" schema. Similarly, qualitative differences between experts and novices were also observed in the chess studies. For instance, Schneider et al. (1993) found that most experts in their sample not only tended to pick up chess pieces in a similar order when reconstructing the meaningful chess positions, but also created similar patterns. Most of these patterns were "collectively reconstructed" by more than 50% of the experts. There were no similar effects for the novices, indicating that the novices did not represent common features of the chess positions in the same way as experts did. (See Körkel & Schneider, 1992 for an illustration of qualitative differences in text recall of soccer experts and novices.)

How is such a rich knowledge base acquired? The few available longitudinal studies indicate that expertise is based on a very long-lasting process of motivated learning. Building up a rich knowledge base not only requires cognitive abilities but also high levels of interest and motivation. In several domains, it is the amount of practice and not so much the level of general aptitude that determines exceptional performance (Schneider, 1993b). The importance of practice was illustrated in a follow-up study of the Schneider et al. (1993) chess experiment (Gruber, Renkl, & Schneider, 1994). In that study, children were presented with the same chess board reconstruction tasks they had worked on three years earlier. The most interesting outcome was that those children who had lost their expert status because of lack of interest and motivation reconstructed fewer chess positions from memory than those children who had shifted from novice to expert status. Whereas the latter group had improved considerably over the years, only small gains in memory for chess positions were observed for the former

group. Similarly, in a longitudinal study of young tennis talents, Schneider, Bös, and Rieder (1993) found that the amount and intensity of practice as well as the level of achievement motivation significantly predicted the tennis rankings obtained five years later. Together, these findings indicate that cognitive ability seems less important than noncognitive factors such as interest, endurance, dedication, and concentration when the major goal is to build a rich knowledge base (Renninger, Hidi, & Krapp, 1992).

There is one peculiar finding concerning the effects of expertise and knowledge on strategic memory performance that deserves attention here, and that is that the greater recall typically found for experts on many strategic memory tasks is only partially mediated through greater strategy use. For example, several expert/novice studies using either free- or sort-recall procedures reported substantially greater recall performance for expert children, but only marginally greater evidence of strategy use (Gaultney, Bjorklund, & Schneider, 1992; Schneider & Bjorklund, 1992; Schneider, Bjorklund, & Maier-Brückner, 1996). These findings suggest that the enhanced performance on strategic tasks for expert children are primarily mediated by item-specific effects associated with their more elaborated knowledge base rather than through more effective use of strategies (Bjorklund & Schneider, 1996).

The Impact of Environmental/Contextual Factors

Evidence has accumulated from cross-cultural studies that strategy acquisition does not occur naturally, but is broadly situated in the cultural context and cultural institutions in which memory skills are practiced (Rogoff, 1990; Rogoff & Mistry, 1990; Wagner, 1981). Results have shown a powerful effect of schooling on strategy use and memory performance (Rogoff, 1981, 1990). Since differences between schooled and nonschooled children do not generally appear until the schooled children have received several years of formal instruction, it appears that experience at school influences the acquisition of memory strategies (Rogoff & Mistry, 1990).

Although nonschooled children and adults are unlikely to engage spontaneously in memory strategies such as organization, they are able to make use of them when interitem associations are made explicit (Sharp, Cole, & Lave, 1979). Moreover, cross-cultural differences in memory performance disappear when information can be integrated in a meaningful context and is linked to everyday experiences (and not the amount of schooling), as demonstrated for the recall of stories and spatial memory (e.g., Kearins, 1981; Mandler, Scribner, Cole, & De Forest, 1980; Rogoff & Waddell, 1982). These findings clearly illustrate that individual differences in strategy use and memory performance are not determined solely by maturational factors but depend greatly on prior familiarity with to-be-remembered stimulus materials.

Educational effects on strategy use can also be observed in cross-national studies where the amount of formal schooling is comparable for subjects under study. The available evidence suggests that individual differences in task demands placed in different school systems play an important role (Carr, Kurtz, Schneider, Turner, & Borkowski, 1989; Kurtz, Schneider, Carr, Borkowski, & Rellinger, 1990; Schneider, Borkowski, Kurtz, & Kerwin, 1986). These training studies revealed systematic and reliable differences in American and German school children's use of organizational strategies. German second and third graders showed higher levels of sorting and clustering than their American peers before training. However, levels of sorting, clustering, and recall were equally high for both groups after training, indicating that the pretraining difference was mainly due to a production deficiency on the part of the American children. Results from parent and teacher questionnaires showed that differences in reported strategy instruction of parents and teachers paralleled strategic differences of American and German children. Furthermore, parents' strategy instruction was also associated with children's metamemory. Accordingly, differences in educational practices and instructional systems do have an impact on strategy acquisition.

Recent studies by Moely and her colleagues (Moely, Hart, Leal, et al., 1992; Moely, Hart, Santulli, et al., 1986; Moely, Santulli, & Obach, 1995) conducted within different schools in the United States indicate that teachers vary enormously in their amount of strategy instruction. Classroom observations revealed that generally low strategy instruction was found for a broad range of activities. The amount of strategy instruction provided varied as a function of subject matter, with suggestions for strategy use most likely offered during the teaching of math problem solving. Furthermore, it was shown that children from high-strategy instruction classrooms benefited more from subsequent strategy instruction on an experimental memory task than did children from low-strategy instruction classrooms (Moely et al., 1995). These and other findings (see Folds, Foote, Guttentag, & Ornstein, 1990; Kurtz, 1990) illustrate that individual differences in school experiences not only influence the acquisition of memory strategies but also affect the development of children's metacognitive knowledge base.

Strategy Use and Motivation

Most research investigating motivational influences on children's memory strategies can be summarized as reflecting three motivational dimensions: extrinsic motivation effects, attributional (metacognitive) determinants of motivation, and effects of mastery motivation (Guttentag & Lange, 1994). Early studies focusing on extrinsic motivation effects assumed that external incentives such as monetary reward would increase strategy use and subsequent recall among school children. For example, Kunzinger and Witryol (1984) manipulated extrinsic motivation by assigning a monetary value to items on a serial recall list, with the recall of some words worth 1 cent and the recall of others worth 10 cents. In the control group, children were given 5 cents for the recall of each item. As predicted, children in the experimental condition rehearsed more actively than the control children, with 10-cent items for children in the experimental condition being rehearsed more than twice as much as 1-cent items. These findings support the view that extrinsic motivation incentives can influence strategy use even in young elementary school children (see also Gelabert, Torgesen, Dice, & Murphy, 1980).

Studies focusing on the impact of *intrinsic* motivation on children's memory strategies have yielded mixed results. Theoretically, metacognitive knowledge should lead to attributional beliefs about the reasons underlying academic success. For instance, children attributing performance gains to effortful strategy use should be more motivated to work hard in contrast to peers who attribute academic outcomes to uncontrollable factors such as luck or task difficulty (Kurtz, 1990; Paris, 1988). Overall, the evidence seems to support such a view. Children's attributional beliefs about effort were found to be related to their performance on memory tasks (Fabricius & Hagen, 1984; Kurtz & Borkowski, 1984). However, in most cases the relation was only moderate in size. For example, Schneider et al. (1986) found that correlations between measures of attribution and intrinsic motivation on the one hand and strategy use in a sort-recall task on the other hand were mostly significant but did not exceed .30. In another study (Kurtz & Weinert, 1989), the evidence was even less favorable in that no significant relations between effort attributions and strategy use were found.

The third line of studies related young children's mastery motivation to their strategic memory (Lange, MacKinnon, & Nida, 1989; Lange, Guttentag, & Nida, 1990). Again, this research added little support for the hypothesis that academic mastery motivation is linked to strategy use, at least not for preschool children. The correlations between preschoolers' mastery orientation and strategy use were generally low (Lange et al., 1989), and mastery orientation did not predict strategy use once other potential predictors such as metacognitive knowledge about strategies had been taken into account (Lange et al., 1990).

Although the evidence is rather mixed, there is little doubt that individual differences in intrinsic motivation can influence memory behavior and performance. As noted by Pressley, Borkowski, and O'Sullivan (1985), a crucial part of instruction is getting students to attribute their improvements in academic performance to the use of strategies. Rather than encouraging students to attribute improved performance to effort alone, they should be encouraged to attribute success to effort expended through strategies well-matched to task requirements. Training studies focusing on this goal have yielded support for the assumption that durable use of strategies is secured by encouraging children to attribute their successes to the use of strategies matched to task requirements (Borkowski & Turner, 1990; Borkowski, Weyhing, & Carr, 1988; Pressley & Van Meter, 1993).

The Influence of Intelligence/Aptitude on Strategic Memory

The effects of intelligence and academic aptitude (e.g., reading ability, learning disabilities) on children's strategic memory have been extensively studied, often in interaction with other factors (Bjorklund & Schneider, 1996; Borkowski & Turner, 1990; Schneider & Weinert, 1990). In general, children with higher IQs remember more than children with lower IQs (Borkowski & Peck, 1986; Bray & Turner, 1986), and children with academic disabilities, such a poor readers, remember less than children without disabilities (Bauer, 1979; Worden, 1983). There have been many reasons hypothesized for these differences, most prominent among them being that more intellectually advantaged children have better metacognition, have greater knowledge bases, use strategies more efficiently, and/or have better developed basic-level information processing abilities than less intellectually advantaged children.

Not surprisingly, differences in metacognition have been found consistently between mentally retarded and nonretarded children (Borkowski, Reid, & Kurtz, 1984). More controversial are differences in metacognition between children within the normal-to-above-normal IQ range (see Alexander, Carr, & Schwanenflugel, 1995). Many studies have demonstrated superior metamemory for high-IQ relative to lower-IQ children (Borkowski & Peck, 1986; Carr, Borkowski, & Maxwell, 1991; Schneider, Körkel, & Weinert, 1987). For example, gifted children have been shown to generalize the benefits of a trained strategy (Borkowski & Peck, 1986) and to be more likely to recognize the benefits of strategy use for memory performance (Gaultney, Bjorklund, & Goldstein, 1996) than nongifted children. However, many other studies find only small or no differences in metacognition between high- and low-IQ children (Alexander & Schwanenflugel, 1994; Kurtz & Weinert, 1989; Scruggs & Mastropieri, 1988). One factor that seems important in whether IQ differences are found is the type of metamemory skill assessed. In a review examining metacognitive differences between gifted and nongifted children, Alexander et al. (1995) concluded that gifted children have an advantage at all ages when declarative metacognition is assessed, whereas differences are less apt to be found for cognitive monitoring. Alexander et al. concluded that the metacognitive advantage for gifted children is most robust when looking at transfer of training effects, with high-IQ children being more aware of the benefits of strategy training and being better able to use those strategies in new contexts than children of less intellectual aptitude.

Differences in memory performance between children of different aptitudes has been shown to be greatly influenced by differences in background knowledge (Bjorklund & Schneider, 1996). For example, Bjorklund and Bernholtz (1986) asked 13-year-old good and poor readers to rate items from 12 natural-language categories in terms of typicality. The category ratings of the good readers were more similar to those of adults for each of the 12 categories than those of the poor readers, whose rating were similar to those of children five years their junior. These findings indicated a developmental delay in the category knowledge of the poor readers. Recall lists of categorizable words were then generated based on each child's self-generated ratings. This insured that the lists would be comparably familiar for all children, essentially equating knowledge for the stimulus items between the good and poor readers. Under these conditions, no significant differences in recall or strategy use were found between the good and poor readers. This was contrasted with the significant difference in recall found when lists consisting of adult-defined sets of categorized items were used as stimuli. These findings suggest that the memory differences typically found between good and poor readers are due to the greater knowledge base of the good readers for the things they are asked to remember, not to differences in underlying memory abilities, per se.

Children's memory performance can be influenced more by their expertise in a specific domain than by their general intellectual ability. This was shown by Schneider and colleagues (1989, 1990), who read soccer-expert and soccer-novice children in Grades 3, 5, and 7 a story about a soccer game. The children were further classified with regard to general ability, as good or poor learners. Not surprisingly, the experts recalled the story better than the novices and made more text-consistent inferences. The findings also confirmed the results of the chess studies described earlier in that a reversal of developmental trends was observed: Grade-3 experts recalled more text information than Grade-7 novices. Even more striking, expertise was much more predictive of performance than was general ability, regardless of age. (See Recht & Leslie, 1988; Walker, 1987, for similar findings.) The same pattern of results was found when children were retested one year later (Schneider & Körkel, 1989). Subsequent studies by Schneider and Bjorklund (1992; Schneider et al., 1996) attempted to generalize the main finding concerning the role of general ability to a strategic memory task (i.e., sort-recall). Expert-novice differences on these tasks were found, although high-IQ children remembered more than low-IQ children in both the expert and novice groups. Thus, knowledge seems to fully compensate for the effect of low IQ for some tasks (e.g., text recall), but not for others (e.g., sort-recall).

Although most studies looking at strategic memory between high- and low-IQ children report greater strategy use for the higher-IQ children (Borkowski & Peck, 1986), others fail to find differences (Harnishfeger & Bjorklund, 1990b; Scruggs & Mastropieri, 1988). Moreover, there is evidence that on some tasks, strategy use is more important for performance for nongifted than for gifted children. In one study, for example, the advantage to recall for strategic relative to nonstrategic children was greater for nongifted than for gifted seventh-grade children (Gaultney et al., 1996). Gifted children in this study had relatively high levels of recall regardless of whether they used memory strategies or not, whereas high levels of recall for nongifted children were limited to those children classified as strategic.

Patterns such as those reported by Gaultney et al. (1996) suggest that some of the benefit high-IQ children experience on memory tasks is due to nonstrategic factors, such as faster or more efficient information processing. Evidence for this comes from studies demonstrating that gifted children show faster processing on a variety of elementary cognitive tasks than nongifted children (Cohn, Carlson, & Jensen, 1985; Jensen, Cohn, & Cohn, 1989). These differences are found even when differences in knowledge base are eliminated (Kranzler, Whang, & Jensen, 1994). Differences in basic-level processes can translate into substantial differences in memory performance by making overall processing more efficient and strategy implementation easier. In fact, resource-consuming strategies can actually be detrimental if information can be retrieved without them.

The effect of intelligence/aptitude on children's memory performance is complex. In some situations, higher-IQ children appear to be more strategic, to have better metacognition, and to have greater knowledge for the to-be-remembered materials than lower-IQ children; however, in other situations, IQ effects are still observed but in the absence of strategic, metacognitive, and knowledge differences. We believe that intelligence is a multifaceted thing, and that no single factor can account for the superior performance typically found for high-IQ children. Among these factors, we believe, is an ability to process novel stimuli (Sternberg, 1985) and to process information quickly and efficiently (Kranzler et al., 1994). We believe that much of the benefit that high-IQ children have over low-IQ children in memory performance is not strategic (or metastrategic) in nature, but due instead to more efficient basic-level processing of information (Bjorklund & Schneider, 1996). Children's level of memory performance can only be understood by considering a multitude of interacting factors, some strategic and some not.

Models of Good Strategy Use and Good Information Processing

Michael Pressley, John Borkowski, Wolfgang Schneider, and their colleagues have developed a model based on the assumption that good memory is the product of a number of interacting factors such as strategies, knowledge base, metamemory, capacity, and motivation (Borkowski, Carr, Rellinger, & Pressley, 1990; Borkowski & Turner, 1990; Pressley, 1994, 1995b; Pressley, Borkowski, & Schneider, 1987, 1989; Schneider & Pressley, 1997). Whereas their earlier model ("The Good Strategy User") particularly focused on the importance of sophisticated strategy use for good and efficient thinking, their more recent model ("Good Information Processing") emphasizes the fact that strategies never operate in isolation but must be considered in light of other factors.

One of the merits of the Good Information Processing model is that it provides a detailed account of interactional processes in the acquisition of strategies and metacognitive knowledge. These authors conceive of metamemory as a number of interacting, mutually dependent components. The process of knowledge acquisition is characterized by the following steps:

1. Children are taught by parents or teachers to use a strategy, and with repetition, come to learn about the attributes and advantages of the strategy *(specific strategy knowledge)*. If children's environments at home and in the school are stimulating, more strategies will be encountered, leading to expanded specific strategy knowledge.

2. Teachers may demonstrate similarities and differences of multiple strategies in a domain, allowing children to structure strategies based on their shared features *(relational knowledge)*.

3. At this point, children recognize the general utility of being strategic, leading to *general strategy knowledge*. Children then learn to attribute successful learning outcomes to effort expended in strategy deployment and also acquire higher-order skills such as selecting and monitoring strategies appropriate for the task *(metacognitive acquisition procedures)*.

The core assumption of the model is that such higher-order skills and also attributional beliefs about the utility of strategies are highly important for producing generalized thinking and problem solving.

The Good Information Processing model seems well-suited to integrate research findings concerning interactions among sources of memory development. It highlights the impact of educational experiences on the development of memory skills, and thus emphasizes the role of parents and teachers in the acquisition of strategies and knowledge. One of the obvious implications of this work is to transfer strategy instruction from the lab to real-world educational settings. Recent research by Pressley and colleagues illustrates how this can be accomplished (Pressley, 1994, 1995b).

NONSTRATEGIC FACTORS IN MEMORY DEVELOPMENT

Through most of the 1980s, research into deliberate, usually strategic, memory, dominated the field of memory development. This concentration on strategy development, however, grossly misrepresented age changes in how and what children remember. Despite the importance of deliberate, strategic memory, perhaps especially for those of us living in information-age societies, much of what children and adults remember is acquired without intention and often retrieved without awareness. Routine events surely have profound impact on the developing child, yet children rarely intentionally commit to memory the mundane experiences of everyday life.

In the sections that follow, we review a variety of contemporary topics in memory development that focus on nonstrategic processing. Topics include research on unintentional and implicit memory; fuzzy-trace theory, which looks at developmental differences in storage and retrieval of memory traces; long-term retention and forgetting; and event and autobiographical memory, including the role parents play in "teaching" their children to remember, children as eyewitnesses, and new ideas about the nature of infantile amnesia.

Unintentional and Implicit Memory

Unintentional Memory

By definition, unintentional, or incidental, memory is not influenced by the use of deliberate encoding strategies, which contribute substantially to development differences on intentional memory tasks. Instead, memory representations are formed as part of ongoing, often naturalistic, activity. (Note that although there may be no intention to *acquire* information in incidental memory, people may use strategies when they later try to *retrieve* information.)

Several researchers have speculated that, in some cases, unintentional, involuntary, "naturalistic" learning may actually yield higher levels of performance than more deliberate memorization attempts, particularly for young children (Istomina, 1975; Piaget & Inhelder, 1973). The now classic study by Istomina has been frequently cited as evidence supporting this. Preschool children in that study were instructed to learn a list of items either in a real-world situation (a shopping game) or in an artificial context (laboratory-type list-learning condition). Istomina reported higher levels of recall for the shopping task than for the list-learning task for children of all ages and interpreted the better performance in the game context as being due to motivational factors. Although serious methodological problems were identified in the original study (Schneider & Hasselhorn, 1994) and later replication attempts led to mixed findings (Rogoff & Mistry, 1990; Schneider & Brun, 1987; Weissberg & Paris, 1986), there is more recent evidence suggesting that naturalistic contexts may sometimes produce higher levels of recall. For example, Newman (1990) found that 4- and 5-year-olds remembered more toys when instructed to play with the toys than to remember the toys, consistent with Istomina's position that unintentional memory can be better than intentional memory in young children.

Although these studies demonstrate the potential advantages of unintentional memory for young children, they make no claims about developmental differences. Other researchers have examined developmental differences in unintentional memory by asking children to make judgments of a series of words (e.g., DOG: "Is it written in capital letters?" or "Is it an animal?") then later, unexpectedly, asking them for recall of the words. This is a manipulation of depth of processing, with semantic orientation resulting in "deeper" processing than the nonsemantic orientation. Age differences in these tasks, in which children were not attempting to remember the stimulus items for later on, are usually limited to situations in which children are asked to make some meaning-based judgments about words during the orienting task (e.g., "Is it an animal?"). This effect is usually attributed to older children's and adults' richer, more detailed knowledge bases. Age differences are smaller and often nonexistent when the orienting task requires subjects to make some assessment of the physical characteristic of the words (e.g., "Is it written in capital letters?") (e.g., Lindberg, 1980; Naito, 1990). The fact that recall varies minimally with age when nonsemantic-orienting tasks are used suggests that when "pure" unintentional memory can be assessed, independent of the effects of background knowledge, few developmental differences are found. This implies that there is little development in the processes influencing unintentional memory, and that young children have the cognitive and neurological capacity to acquire much information "in context," counter to the findings for intentional memory. Nevertheless, unintentional memory is still influenced by some of the same, nonstrategic factors that affect intentional memory (specifically, knowledge base), reminding us of the impossibility of studying any type of memory processing in isolation from other aspects of the developing cognitive system.

Implicit Memory

Implicit, or indirect, memory is "memory without awareness," or demonstrating memory for some information without being consciously aware that one is remembering (Jacoby, 1991; Schacter, 1992). One task that has been frequently used to assess implicit memory is the word-stem completion task, in which subjects are shown a series of words in an initial cognitive task (e.g., an explicit recognition task), and later given word fragments and asked to complete the words (e.g., cab _____ for cable). Some of the word stems can be completed with words that were seen on the initial task ("old" words), whereas others are "new" words. Implicit memory is indicated when subjects complete more stems for "old" than for "new" words, despite having no recollection of experiencing the "old" words previously.

Although there has been relatively little developmental research on implicit memory, the extant findings are consistent. In contrast to explicit memory tasks, few developmental differences are observed for implicit memory (Ausley & Guttentag, 1993; Drummey & Newcombe, 1995; Greenbaum & Graf, 1989; Naito, 1990; Parkin & Streete, 1988; Perrig & Perrig, 1993; Russo, Nichelli, Gibertoni, & Cornia, 1995; Wippich, Mecklenbräuker, & Brausch, 1989). In a study by Newcombe and Fox (1994), 9- and 10-year-old children were shown photographs of 4- and 5-year-old children and asked to identify those who had been classmates of theirs in preschool. This is an explicit memory task. While children were viewing the pictures, changes in Galvanic Skin Response (GSR) were being recorded. Greater changes in GSR when viewing former classmates' pictures as opposed to the pictures of unfamiliar children reflect implicit recognition (i.e., recognition without the need of conscious awareness). Newcombe and Fox (1994) reported that GSR readings were the same for children who had performed well and those who had performed poorly on the explicit memory task, suggesting that even children whose conscious recognition was no greater than chance still recognized, implicitly, many of their former classmates.

Well-developed unintentional and implicit memory systems would seem to be of critical importance in situations in which cultural learning occurs through observations of adults and involvement in daily activities, as was the case for our pre-industrial ancestors and is found in contemporary traditional societies (Rogoff, Mistry, Göncü, & Mosier, 1993). Well-developed unintentional and implicit memory systems are important in every human culture, whereas more sophisticated intentional and explicit memory abilities become increasingly important as the complexity of a culture's technology increases.

Fuzzy-Trace Theory and Memory Development

Aspects of both unintentional and implicit memory are performed without awareness or the need of conscious, strategic intervention. An increasingly popular theory that attempts to explain memory and cognitive development without invoking conscious awareness is fuzzy-trace theory developed by Charles Brainerd, Valerie Reyna and their colleagues (e.g., Brainerd & Kingma, 1985; Brainerd & Reyna, 1990, 1993; Reyna, 1995; Reyna & Brainerd, 1991, 1995). Fuzzy-trace theory provides a developmental description of the nature of memory traces and the processes that act on those traces when people perform cognitive tasks. It is a basic-process theory, eschewing concepts such as strategies or metacognition to account for developmental patterns of thinking. In this section, we provide a brief description of the developmental aspects of fuzzy-trace theory, followed by a section describing *cognitive triage,* a model that accounts for patterns of free recall by applying tenets of fuzzy-trace theory.

Assumptions of Fuzzy-Trace Theory

Brainerd and Reyna propose that memory representations exist on a continuum from literal, verbatim representations to fuzzy, skeletal, gistlike traces and that multiple-memory traces exist for any event one experiences. Memory representations of an event are not either verbatim or fuzzy, but may exist in a variety of forms simultaneously, each of which is independent from the others (Reyna & Kiernan, 1994). The type of trace people use will depend on the nature of the task, the durability of the trace, and the processing preferences of an individual. People of all ages extract the gist from a message. This is what Brainerd and Reyna refer to as the *reduction to essence rule.* They propose that "it is a natural habit of mind to process traces that are as near to the fuzzy ends of fuzzy-to-verbatim continua as possible" (1990, p. 9). According to Brainerd and Reyna, fuzzy traces are more easily accessed and used and are less susceptible to interference and forgetting than verbatim traces.

Although the reduction to essence rule may apply universally, there are developmental differences in gist extraction. Children of all ages extract gist, but young children are biased toward storing and retrieving verbatim traces, resulting in a verbatim→gist shift, occurring sometime during the early elementary school years, although the timing of this shift may vary with the nature of the task. This means that the memory system for processing verbatim information develops earlier than the system for processing gist. Brainerd and Reyna further propose that the processing efficiency of verbatim information declines in adolescence.

Evidence for this verbatim→gist shift has been inferred from the results of several experiments (Brainerd & Gordon, 1994; Reyna & Kiernan, 1994). In one study, Brainerd and Gordon (1994) gave simple numerical problems to preschool and second-grade children. Children were told that "Farmer Brown owns many animals. He owns 3 dogs, 5 sheep, 7 chickens, 9 horses, and 11 cows." They were then asked a series of questions, some requiring verbatim knowledge for their correct answer, such as: "How many chickens does Farmer Brown own, 7 or 5?" and others requiring only gist information, such as: "Which of Farmer Brown's animals are the most, cows or horses?" or "Does Farmer Brown have more cows or more horses?" They reported that preschool children performed their best on the verbatim questions, whereas second graders performed better on questions involving gist information. Moreover, whereas performance on the verbatim questions was comparable between the two groups of children, the second graders outperformed the preschool children for questions requiring gist information.

An important set of processing assumptions in fuzzy-trace theory concerns the role of *output interference* on task performance, with the act of making responses serving to hinder subsequent performance (cf., Dempster, 1992). Two forms of output interference are proposed: *scheduling effects* and *feedback effects.* Scheduling effects are due to the serial nature of response systems. Although different cognitive operations may be executed in parallel, responses are made serially, with the various possible responses competing for priority of execution. This produces feedback of irrelevant information "that reverberates through the system, degrading performance as it goes. . . . introducing noise into working memory" (Brainerd & Reyna, 1990, p. 29). Similar to the theorizing of inhibition theorists (Bjorklund & Harnishfeger, 1990; Hasher & Zacks, 1988), the "noise" in working memory competes with task-relevant information, reducing performance. Also consistent with inhibition and resistance-to-interference theorists (Dempster 1992; Harnishfeger & Bjorklund, 1994), children become increasingly able to resist the adverse effects of interference with age. This age difference is related to young children's greater reliance on verbatim traces, which are more susceptible to interference than are fuzzy traces.

Cognitive Triage

Cognitive triage conceptualizes free recall as a process in which the most difficult items are recalled first, analogous to the battlefield surgical practice of treating the most difficult cases first. Brainerd, Reyna, and colleagues developed the *optimization model* to account for this phenomenon (Brainerd, 1995; Brainerd, Reyna, Harnishfeger, & Howe, 1993; Brainerd, Reyna, Howe, & Kevershan, 1991; Reyna & Brainerd, 1995).

The basic prediction of the optimization model is that recall should begin by recalling items with relatively weak memory strength *(weak priority)*. On multitrial tasks, weak items are defined as those that have not been recalled (or have been recalled infrequently) on earlier trials. Brainerd and Reyna point out that most theories of free recall make exactly the opposite prediction, with strong items (i.e., those that have been remembered frequently on earlier trials) being the first to be recalled, primarily because these items would be those most easily activated in long-term memory (Reyna & Brainerd, 1995). Despite the counterintuitive nature of their claim, research findings support Brainerd and Reyna's contention. In fact, the predominant pattern of recall, also predicted by the theory, is weaker→stronger→weaker, with the recall of the most salient, or strongest, items being sandwiched between weaker items. This *nonmonotonic emergence* effect is depicted in Figure 10.2, demonstrating that items of low memory strength are recalled earlier in the recall stream than items of high memory strength, which in turn are recalled before items of medium strength (based on data from Brainerd et al., 1991). The theory also predicts that the weak priority and nonmonotonic emergence effects become more pronounced with age, a finding that is also reflected in Figure 10.2. The principal reason for this is that younger children are more susceptible to the effects of interference than older children, and these interference effects adversely influence retrieval of even the stronger memory traces.

Brainerd and Reyna state that two general factors must be taken into consideration when predicting order of recall: episodic activation, which facilitates the recall of

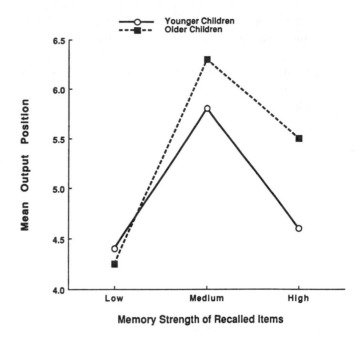

Figure 10.2 Relation between output positions in free-recall queues and trichotomous memory strength measure for younger children and older children. These plots are based on data reported in "Fuzzy-trace theory and cognitive triage in memory development" by C. J. Breinerd et al., 1991, *Developmental Psychology, 27*, pp. 315–369.

additional words, and output interference, which inhibits the recall of additional words. The recall of the most strongly activated memory traces activates other traces in the episodic memory network, facilitating the retrieval of other items. If this were all there was to free recall, one would expect that strong items would be retrieved before weak items. However, output interference also plays a critical role. Irrelevant feedback is generated when a trace is retrieved, hindering subsequent performance. According to the model, output interference is especially detrimental to the recall of weaker memory traces. Thus, weak traces are more likely to be retrieved when interference is low. The model also predicts that output interference subsides as episodic activation increases. This means that interference will be greater following the recall of weaker traces than the recall of stronger traces.

Taken together, the model predicts that weak traces are most apt to be recalled when interference is at its lowest, which would be during the beginning of a trial. As weak traces are retrieved, interference will mount, making the further recall of weak traces difficult. However, the high activation of the stronger traces means that they can still be retrieved during levels of high interference. The recall of several strong traces results in a reduction of interference, making the retrieval of weaker traces possible again. This yields the weaker→stronger→weaker pattern observed in experimental data.

Several experiments have directly contrasted strategic versus triage models of free recall, with results yielding a closer fit with the triage than with the strategic model (Brainerd, Reyna et al., 1993; Harnishfeger & Brainerd, 1994). Cognitive triage also seems to be good for recall performance, in that there is a positive relation between a subject's "goodness of triage" ratings and levels of recall (Brainerd, Reyna, et al., 1993; Harnishfeger & Brainerd, 1994).

Cognitive triage is real. Application of the optimization model, an extension of fuzzy-trace theory, resulted in the discovery and explanation of counterintuitive patterns of order of output in free recall. Its avoidance of strategic and other types of executive processes is consistent with the explanatory style currently popular in cognitive science, and its application of output interference to explain patterns of performance is in line with other recent accounts of cognitive development (Dempster, 1992; Diamond, 1991; Harnishfeger, 1995). Cognitive triage, and other basic-level cognitive theories, should be taken seriously in any account of memory development. We are not yet ready to eliminate concepts such as strategies and metacognition from the developmental study of memory; but neither do we believe that these "higher-level" processes can be fruitfully studied without also investigating the basic-level mechanisms that underlie them.

Long-Term Retention and Forgetting

Since the beginning of scientific research on memory development at the turn of the century, studies on relatively short-term memory have dominated the field. The paucity of research on long-term retention and forgetting may be due to a failure to find age differences in forgetting rates (Brainerd, Reyna, Howe, & Kingma, 1990; Howe & Brainerd, 1989; Reyna & Brainerd, 1995). For instance, most research through the 1980s failed to find any substantial age differences in forgetting (Fainsztejn-Pollack, 1973; Lehman, Mikesell, & Doherty, 1985; Merriman, Azmita, & Perlmutter, 1988; Morrison, Haith, & Kagan, 1980; Vertes, 1913), suggesting that forgetting rates for both semantic and nonsemantic information are age invariant, at

least from preschool to late adolescence. Given the "no development" outcome in most of these studies, it is not surprising that developmental memory researchers have not shown much interest in the issue of long-term forgetting.

On the other side of the coin of forgetting is *reminiscence*, the remembering of something at time B that could not be remembered at some earlier time A. Although early research on this phenomenon revealed developmental patterns, the findings were not consistent (Ballard, 1913; Piaget & Inhelder, 1973; Vertes, 1913). Whereas several studies investigating children's memory for prose found that younger children exhibited greater reminiscence than older ones (Ballard, 1913) the reverse finding was reported by Vertes (1913) who used a paired-associate learning procedure. Vertes found that recall improvements assessed after one week were restricted to children 10 years of age and older. Younger children's recall declined during this retention interval. As noted by Howe and Brainerd (1989), problems with the consistency of the Age × Reminiscence interaction and the appropriate interpretation of the effects led to disinterest in research on reminiscence.

The empirical evidence described above is in conflict with popular assumptions about developmental trends in forgetting and reminiscence. Several theorists (e.g., Underwood, 1964) claimed that retention is positively related to how well or how rapidly information is acquired: because older children learn almost anything faster than younger ones, they should forget more slowly. Given this discrepancy between belief and data, Brainerd, Howe, Reyna, and colleagues implemented a research program designed to examine the development of long-term retention and reminiscence (Brainerd, Reyna, Harnishfeger, & Howe, 1993; Brainerd, Reyna, Howe, & Kingma, 1990; Howe, 1991; Howe & Brainerd, 1989; Howe, Kelland, Bryant-Brown, & Clark, 1992; Reyna & Brainerd, 1995). Before describing the theoretical framework and the research outcomes of these studies in more detail, we first discuss design problems of the earlier research that made the "no development" findings described above hard to interpret. In particular, Brainerd et al. identified three problem variables that they labeled *recognition insensitivity, floor effects,* and *levels-of-learning confounds.*

Recognition insensitivity refers to the problem that recognition tests used in most studies of long-term retention and forgetting were not sensitive to age change. There have been a number of studies showing that null age effects are the most common results because even young children display high levels of recognition accuracy, making it unlikely that reliable age differences in forgetting can be obtained using recognition measures.

Floor effects in forgetting rates indicate that no significant declines in performance between the immediate and delayed memory tests are found. In fact, most studies exploring developmental differences in forgetting were not only based on recognition measures but also short delay intervals (e.g., 1 day) and used very memorable items (e.g., pictures). Because the average performance decline was typically found to be small (about 5%), there was little room for age variability.

The third problem, *stage-of-learning confound*, seems more complicated. As noted by Underwood (1964), the absence of controls for level of learning poses serious difficulties for the interpretation of retention data. Because older children will learn almost everything faster than younger ones, age differences in long-term retention might be due to processes operating during the retention interval, but could also be due to age differences in learning. Accordingly, differences in immediate levels of learning can mask age differences in the subsequent amounts of forgetting.

How did Brainerd and colleagues deal with these problems in their own research? They avoided recognition insensitivity by switching to cued or free recall tasks. Floor effects were eliminated by using less memorable materials, and longer forgetting intervals (e.g., 2 weeks rather than 1 day). Finally, the levels-of-learning problem was dealt with by requiring subjects of all age levels to learn the material to a perfect-recall criterion. Although age differences in the rate at which the criterion is reached may determine individual differences in forgetting and thus introduce a potential confound of its own (Guttentag, 1990; Wang, 1991), subsequent tests of this hypothesis found no support for it: when age and learning rate were entered as predictors in a path analysis to explain developmental differences in forgetting rates, it could be shown that age influenced both forgetting and the rate of learning, but that rate of learning had no direct effects on forgetting rates (Brainerd & Reyna, 1990). In a first series of experiments controlling for the design problems described above, Brainerd, Howe, and colleagues found substantial developmental differences in long-term retention in that older children retained more (and thus forgot less) than younger ones (Brainerd, Kingma, & Howe, 1985; Howe, 1987). Consistent improvements in retention were documented from the early elementary school years to adolescence.

Why does forgetting develop? Mainstream theories of forgetting distinguished between forgetting in the sense

of progressive loss of memory traces (storage failure) and forgetting in the sense of progressive loss of the ability to access intact traces (retrieval failures), and have varied as to the relative contribution of these two processes (see Loftus & Loftus, 1980). Overall, however, the retrieval hypothesis has remained the predominant explanation (Brainerd et al., 1990). Based on earlier work on acquisition processes in long-term memory and also on aspects of fuzzy-trace theory, Brainerd, Howe, Reyna, and colleagues (Brainerd et al., 1990; Howe & Brainerd, 1989; Reyna & Brainerd, 1995) developed a theoretical framework (disintegration/redintegration theory) and a mathematical model (trace-integrity model) that seemed suited to explore the relative contributions of storage and forgetting failures to forgetting within and between age levels.

The disintegration/redintegration theory assumes that, during acquisition, an item's core semantic representation is enriched with sufficient episodic information to produce reliable retrieval. Episodic features encoded during study serve as retrieval cues activating the item's core representation. The quality of feature integration not only depends on the age of a person but also on the nature of the features, with some features (e.g., taxonomic, visual) providing better integration than others. Featural integration is regarded as a key determinant of trace discriminability: the more clearly a trace stands out against the background of competing memory "noises," the higher the probability it will be retrieved later. Following the acquisition period, traces may consolidate for a short time, depending on the stringency of the learning criterion and the completeness of initial learning. Next, the complementary process, featural disintegration, begins. It is hypothesized that featural bonds loosen and traces fade as disintegration progresses. Thus it becomes harder to retrieve and locate traces that match the episodic information encoded on memory tests. The last process in the theory, featural redintegration, refers to attempts to recover previously stored information, such as retention tests, and aims at explaining the "spontaneous" recovery of items (reminiscence). It is postulated that test-induced recovery arises from featural redintegration of traces. The simple activity of attempting to recall previously learned material initiates a process that reverses some of the disintegration that has accumulated during the forgetting interval.

Brainerd, Howe, Reyna, and colleagues subsequently translated this theoretical approach into mathematical models designed to provide precise measurements of age changes in storage failure, retrieval failure, and redintegration.

These Markov models contain some parameters that measure the rate at which traces disintegrate over forgetting intervals and some other parameters that assess the rate at which the still-intact items are unavailable for retrieval. (See Brainerd et al., 1990; Howe & Brainerd, 1989, for a detailed description.) These models have been applied in several recent forgetting experiments covering a broad age range (preschoolers, elementary school children, adults, and the elderly), and have yielded similar results (Brainerd et al., 1990; Howe, 1991, 1995; Howe, Courage, & Bryant-Brown, 1993; Howe et al., 1992).

As a major finding, these experiments revealed that the storage-failure rate (i.e., rate of losing memory traces) clearly exceeded the retrieval-failure rate (i.e., rate of ability to access intact traces), regardless of age. Substantial amounts of storage failure were measured in all of these experiments. Storage failure often contributed more to age variability in forgetting rates than retrieval failure did. Thus, the findings did not support the retrieval-failure hypothesis still prominent in contemporary theories of forgetting. In accord with assumptions derived from fuzzy-trace theory, it was found that forgetting was more a matter of verbatim failure than of gist failure at all age levels.

The most consistent and important conclusions from this research are that storage failures are a more frequent cause of forgetting than retrieval failures, and that age differences in long-term retention and forgetting are the rule rather than the exception. It should be noted, however, that these interpretations are restricted to the particular methodology used in the research and to the authors' definitions of what constitutes forgetting in their model (Guttentag, 1990). For example, it may be difficult to generalize findings from a paradigm that requires perfect learning to the world outside the laboratory where perfect learning of a set of items is rare (Bjorklund, 1995). Nonetheless, the theoretical approach chosen by Brainerd, Howe, Reyna, and colleagues seems important in that it has great explanatory power for certain phenomena not easily accounted for by more traditional views.

The Development of Event and Autobiographical Memory

Most of what people remember during their everyday lives is about things that have happened to them, or about *events*. When such *event memory* is about personal experiences, it has been described as *autobiographical memory*. Autobiographical memory is based heavily on language skills, with children using the structure of language to recall what happened to whom, when, and where. Several researchers have proposed that it is children's increasing sophistication with language between their second and fourth years of life that is primarily responsible for the development of autobiographical memory (Fivush & Hamond, 1990; Leichtman & Ceci, 1993; Nelson, 1993). Four aspects of event memory development will be discussed here. The first section examines the constructive nature of event memory, focusing particularly on the role of scripts in encoding and recalling events. The second section concerns the role of parents and other social agents in "teaching" children how to use language to remember. The third section looks at children's eyewitness memory and the possibility that children are more susceptible to suggestion than adults. The final section examines when autobiographical memory begins and looks for explanations of infantile amnesia.

The Constructive Nature of Event Memory

One's memory for an event is based not only on the actual experience, but also on what one already knows about the event in question. Children, and adults, do not encode or recall events verbatim but *construct* a memory. According to a constructivist perspective, the act of encoding into memory is a Piagetian assimilation-type process of constructing an internal representation affected by personal interpretations. Similarly, retrieval is conceived as an active and assimilatory process of reconstruction rather than a passive copying out of what is stored in the LTS. The constructivists assume that we are constantly making spontaneous inferences and interpretations when processing, storing, and retrieving information.

Important developmental changes in constructive memory are changes in the knowledge structures guiding recall. It has been shown that young children acquire *scripts,* that is, knowledge structures referring to real-life routines such as baking cookies or going to a restaurant. A script is characterized by a causal-temporal sequence of events that is constant across its occurrences, thus facilitating the storage and retrieval of material that can be easily assimilated into it. Children learn what "usually happens" in a situation and remember novel information in the context of these familiar events (Farrar & Goodman, 1992; Mistry & Lange, 1985; Nelson, 1986).

There has been substantial research over the past decade demonstrating that even very young children organize information temporally in a scriptlike fashion (Bauer & Fivush, 1992; Fivush, Kuebli, & Clubb, 1992). Moreover, such schematic organization for events does not seem to change much into adulthood (Fivush & Hudson, 1990). Young children's tendencies to organize information in a scriptlike fashion seems to make it difficult for them to remember more specific (that is, nonscript) information. For example, Fivush and Hamond (1990) found that the 2.5-year-old children in their study were not very specific when asked questions about recent special events (e.g., a trip to the beach, a ride in an airplane, a camping trip). Rather than recalling the novel aspects of these events, the children tended to focus on more routine information such as waking up, eating, and going to bed. Apparently, the younger the children, the more they may need to embed novel events into familiar routines.

In a similar vein, the organization of stories (scripted vs. nonscripted) may influence young children's recall more than that of older children. For example, the 3- to 4-year-olds of the Munich Longitudinal Study (LOGIC; see Weinert & Schneider, 1986; Weinert & Schneider, 1995) recalled a scripted story (Birthday party) significantly better than a similarly familiar, nonscripted story (Playing in the afternoon). The difference in recall of these two stories disappeared in later assessments (cf. Knopf & Waldmann, 1991). Furthermore, when presented with stories about scripted events such as birthday parties that deviate from the canonical order, even preschool children tend to repair these temporal violations in several ways, primarily omitting acts that are presented out of sequence, or reordering and transforming acts (Nelson & Hudson, 1988). For example, preschoolers may state that the "children took presents (i.e., favors) home" in place of the misordered act "children brought presents" which was placed toward the end of a birthday party story (Hudson & Nelson, 1983). Taken together, the numerous studies on young children's constructive memory provide evidence that scripts yield an automatic organizational structure for children's recall of stories and real-world events. While using scripts does not necessarily increase the amount of information recalled, they certainly do guide output.

On the other hand, possessing familiar scripts can cause memory problems. For example, Nelson and Hudson (1988) reported no structural differences between 3- to 5-year-olds' *general* scripts about birthday parties and their reports about *specific* birthday parties. Nelson and Hudson argued that this represented a blending of the specific episode with the general script. According to Farrar and Goodman (1990), schema- or script-based processing involves two phases, a schema-confirmation phase and a schema-deployment phase. In the schema-confirmation phase, children try to use a schema (e.g., going-to-a-restaurant script) in order to understand an event. Next, in the schema-deployment phase, children process script-deviant information (e.g., a puppet show at the restaurant). Young children may remember only the script-consistent information or confuse the script and episodic memories because processing is too difficult for them to start with the second phase. On the other hand, older children are able to process schema-consistent information quickly and then concentrate on processing inconsistent information mainly because of their large repertoire of well-developed scripts. This may explain why younger children have more difficulty than older children with keeping script-consistent and script-deviant events separate in memory.

The Social Construction of Memory

Remembering events requires the ability to identify the critical aspects of an experience and organize it in a temporally appropriate way so that causal links are maintained. In other words, remembering events requires telling stories. This is something that is done universally, although different cultures may have somewhat different ways in which stories are told (Nelson, 1993). Several researchers have proposed that children learn to tell stories by interacting with their parents—that autobiographical memory is socially constructed, with parents teaching children how to create narratives so they can store and later remember their experiences (Fivush & Hamond, 1990; Fivush & Reese, 1992; Nelson, 1993). For example, Hudson (1990) has suggested that young children initially view remembering as "an activity that is at first jointly carried out by parent and child and then later performed by the child alone" (p. 172). Hudson suggests that in most families parents' early requests for recall involves talking about past events. They ask children series of questions about recent events (e.g., "Where did we go yesterday? What did we see? Who was there with us?"). Interchanges such as these serve as lessons in how to organize narratives. Children are learning what aspects of events are important (e.g., the location, the interactants) and the importance of sequencing events in temporal and causal order. Hudson also notes that parents not only ask questions, but also supply some of the answers, further demonstrating how narratives and conversations are organized. Children also are learning that they may remember more than they think they know, as parents' specific cues yield elevated levels of memory (Price & Goodman, 1990). In fact, Fivush and Hudson (1990) have claimed that young children merely require more memory questions (cues) to remember as much event information as older children.

Support for the contention that how parents interact with their young children influences how they remember comes from studies that examine differences in parent-child conversations and relate these differences to children's later memory performance. For example, Ratner (1984) found a relation between the number of questions mothers of 2- and 3-year-olds asked their children and subsequent memory performance of the children. Mothers who asked more questions had children with better memories. Other research has shown that mothers who provide their preschool children with more evaluations of their memory performance and use more elaborative language when talking about memory with their children, have children who remember past events better than children with less elaborative mothers (Reese, Haden, & Fivush, 1993). In general, girls are more likely to receive the type of experiences conducive to good memory performance than boys and as a result show superior memory abilities (Cowan & Davidson, 1984; Reese, Haden, & Fivush, 1996). The role of the children in influencing this dyadic interaction should not be overlooked, however. It is possible that girls' greater verbal skills and social orientation may play a role in eliciting memory-enhancing behavior from their parents.

The research suggests that children's early autobiographical memory is guided by interactions with adults who help them identify the important aspects of an experience so that it can later be remembered. Nelson (1993) has emphasized the social significance for the development of autobiographical memory, stating that language makes possible the sharing of memories with other people, which becomes the primary goal of remembering:

> Memories become valued in their own right—not because they predict the future and guide present action, but because they are shareable with others and thus serve a social solidarity function. I suggest that this is a universal human function, although one with variable, culturally specific rules. In this respect, it is analogous to human language itself, uniquely and universally human but culturally—and individually—variable. (p. 12)

Children as Eyewitnesses

One form of children's autobiographical memory that has received substantial attention in the last decade has been eyewitness memory (Ceci & Bruck, 1993; Doris, 1991). With children being increasingly called upon to provide testimony in legal cases, issues about how much and how accurately children remember, and the degree to which they are influenced by suggestion, has become a high-priority research interest.

Age Differences in Children's Eyewitness Memories. In most respects, eyewitness memory is no different than any other type of event memory. Children may witness events staged at their schools, videotaped events, or recollections of some potentially traumatic experiences, such as visits to the dentist, emergency room, or doctor. Children are typically first questioned using general prompts (e.g., "Tell me what happened in your classroom yesterday morning"), usually followed by more specific questions (e.g., "What did the man who came into your class yesterday morning do?"). (Children's eyewitness memory is covered in greater detail in Chapter 11 by Ceci & Bruck on "The Child Witness" in Volume IV.)

Consistent with other research on children's event memory, levels of recall to general questions is typically low in preschool and early schoolage children and increases with age (e.g., Cassel & Bjorklund, 1995; Ornstein, Gordon, & Larus, 1992; Poole & Lindsay, 1995). Despite low levels of free recall, what preschoolers do recall is usually accurate. When examining the ratio of incorrect to correct information remembered, most studies report no age differences (Fivush & Hamond, 1989; Howe, Courage, & Peterson, 1994; Rudy & Goodman, 1991), although others report somewhat higher accuracy for young children than for adults (Cassel & Bjorklund, 1995; Poole & White, 1991). Also, what little young children do recall spontaneously tends to be central to the witnessed event (Goodman, Aman, & Hirschman, 1987; Howe et al., 1994; Poole & White, 1991).

As is the case for memory in general, levels of correct recall for an eyewitnessed event increase for people of all ages when more specific cues are provided (Ornstein et al., 1992; Poole & Lindsay, 1995). However, unbiased cues also produce increased levels of inaccurate recall (Goodman, Quas, Batterman-Faunce, Riddlesberger, & Kuhn, 1994; Poole & Lindsay, 1995), although not always (Howe, Courage, & Peterson, 1994). Increased error rates to unbiased-cued questions is illustrated in research by Cassel, Roebers, and Bjorklund (1996), who showed kindergarten, second-grade, and fourth-grade children and adults a video, followed by free recall and then a set of unbiased questions, merely requesting more information about an aspect of the event, not suggesting any particular interpretation. They reported that the unbiased cues yielded age-related increases in levels of correct recall for all subjects, but also produced substantial levels of inaccurate recall, especially for the kindergarten children (43% of responses; inaccurate recall = 36%, 26%, and 16% for second graders, fourth graders, and adults, respectively).

There has been some debate concerning the stability of children's false memories. When relatively brief delays are involved, there is evidence that children who recall something incorrectly at one point in time are *not* likely to recall the same false memory at a later time (Cassel & Bjorklund, 1995). However, when longer delays are involved (Poole, 1995) or when recognition procedures are used (Brainerd, Reyna, & Brandse, 1995; Reyna & Brainerd, 1995), there is evidence that false memories are as persistent (or slightly more persistent) over lengthy delays as true memories. This counterintuitive finding has been interpreted in terms of fuzzy-trace theory. Correct recognition is based on verbatim traces, which are more susceptible to forgetting than gist traces. False recognition, on the other hand, must be based on gist traces (there are no verbatim traces for false memories), which are more resistant to forgetting. As a result, gist-based false memories are more likely to be remembered after long delays than are the verbatim-based true memories.

There are many factors that can influence children's eyewitness memory, one of which is knowledge (Ornstein, Shapiro, Clubb, Follmer, & Baker-Ward, 1996; Stein, Wade, & Liwag, 1996). Knowledge has been found to affect young children's recollections of stressful medical procedures (Clubb, Nida, Merritt, & Ornstein, 1993; Goodman et al., 1994; Ornstein et al., 1996). Research has shown that children's recall of an invasive medical procedure is related to their knowledge of the procedure; children who knew more about the procedure remembered more accurate information (Clubb et al., 1993) and recalled less inaccurate information and were less susceptible to suggestion (Goodman et al., 1994) than less knowledgeable children.

Another factor related to children's memory for traumatic events is style of parent-child interaction. In the study by Goodman and her colleagues (1994), mothers who were emotionally supportive of their children and who discussed the medical procedure with them, had children who recalled less inaccurate information and were less suggestible than children with less sympathetic or talkative

mothers. One possible reason for this effect may be related to knowledge base; mothers who talk more to their children may have children with a better understanding of the procedure than other children. These results are consistent with the findings that mothers who use a more elaborative style in talking with their children about past events have children with better memories (Reese et al., 1993).

Another possible reason for young children's false memories is related to their ability to monitor the source of their memories. Research has shown that preschool and early schoolage children sometimes have difficulty discerning whether they actually performed an act or just imagined it (Foley & Johnson, 1985; Foley, Santini, & Sopasakis, 1989). Similarly, preschool children often incorrectly recall that an action carried out by another person during a joint activity was actually performed by them (Ackil & Zaragoza, 1995; Foley, Ratner, & Passalacqua, 1993). These findings have led some researchers to speculate that young children's difficulties in monitoring the source of their knowledge may contribute to the accuracy of their memories for witnessed events (Ceci & Bruck, 1993).

Age Differences in Suggestibility. An important topic in children's eyewitness memory concerns age differences in susceptibility to suggestion. In most suggestibility paradigms, participants witness or experience an event and are later either presented with some post-event information that contradicts events observed earlier (misinformation) or are asked sets of misleading questions, suggesting an inaccurate "fact" (Ceci, Ross, & Toglia, 1987; Dale, Loftus, & Rathburn, 1978; Goodman et al., 1994). People of all ages are susceptible to both misinformation and misleading questions. The primary concern of developmental researchers has been whether or not there are age differences in suggestibility.

This has been a controversial area of research, with findings varying as a function of how and when questions are posed. However, most studies that have looked for developmental differences in suggestibility have found them, although often only in certain conditions, with preschool children being particularly susceptible to suggestion (Ceci et al., 1987; Goodman & Clarke-Stewart, 1991, Experiment 6; Goodman & Reed, 1986). For example, when 3- and 6-year-old children were asked to remember a visit to the doctor's office one and three weeks after its occurrence, levels of correct recall were relatively high. When these children were asked misleading questions, 3-year-olds were much more likely to be swayed by the misleading questions than the 6-year-olds (Ornstein et al., 1992).

Young children's erroneous answers do not necessarily reflect an actual change in memory representation. It is likely that some of the young children's compliance with misleading questions is related to the social demand characteristics of the situation, and some research has shown that children who were deliberately misled to give an incorrect answer later remembered the correct "fact" when given a multiple-choice test (Cassel et al., 1996). However, other research suggests that misinformation and misleading questions actually result in changes in the underlying memory representations, with young children being more likely to make such changes than older children (Leichtman & Ceci, 1993; Reyna, 1995).

Long-Term Retention of Autobiographical Memories and Infantile Amnesia

One important question for researchers of autobiographical memory concerns the duration of those memories. Most of the research discussed earlier assessed memory for events over relatively brief intervals, usually minutes or, at the most, days. How accurate are autobiographical memories over lengthy delays, and does accuracy vary with age? A related issue concerns the earliest age that autobiographical memories can be formed and later retrieved.

Long-Term Retention of Autobiographical Memories.   Some memories may last a lifetime, but others are quickly forgotten, and the memories we do have from earlier years may be reconstructions rather than accurate recollections of actual experiences. Research has shown, however, that even preschool children are able to form stable autobiographical memories and retain them for lengthy periods (Nelson & Ross, 1980). Hamond and Fivush (1991) interviewed 3- and 4-year-old children about their trip 6 or 18 months after they had visited Disney World. Although 3-year-olds required more prompts to remember aspects of the trip than the 4-year-olds, both groups of children recalled a substantial amount of information about the event, even 18 months after the trip. These and other similar findings (e.g., Baker-Ward, Gordon, Ornstein, Larus, & Clubb, 1993; Howe & Courage, 1993) suggest that even 3-year-olds can retain a specific, novel experience for periods of greater than one year.

A number of studies have examined the effects of delay on children's autobiographical memory, with delays ranging from several weeks to over a year. Most research assessing the effects of delays of one month or less report that the total amount of information recalled and the overall accuracy of recall (that is, the ratio of inaccurate to accurate information) is comparable to what it was when recall was tested immediately after witnessing the event, regardless of age (Baker-Ward et al., 1993; Cassel & Bjorklund, 1995). Age differences are observed, however, for longer delays. Poole and White (1993) reported that, although 6-, 8-, and 10-year-olds recalled about as much accurate information as adults following a 2-year delay, they recalled significantly more *inaccurate* information (20%) than the adults (7%), with no differences being observed among the three groups of children. Flin, Boon, Knox, and Bull (1992) similarly reported that the ratio of incorrect to correct recall was higher for a group of 6-year-olds than for adults after a 5-month delay, although, in this case, levels of incorrect recall were comparable between the two age groups, with adults remembering more accurate information than the children (see also Howe et al., in press). Thus, age differences in the long-term retention of autobiographical memory are found, although they are greatest when delays are longest.

Infantile Amnesia.   Related to age differences in the long-term retention of autobiographical memories is the question of "When does autobiographical memory begin?" Based on reports from adults and older children about their earliest recollections, it would seem that few stable memories are formed much before the age of 3.5 or 4 years, with memories much before the age of 6 or 7 being rare (Cowan & Davidson, 1984; Sheingold & Tenney, 1982). There have been many explanations proposed for infantile amnesia, including Freud's (1963) idea that this represents an active process of repression of the traumatic events of infancy and early childhood. Alternatives to Freud's repression hypothesis include the possibility that infants and young children cannot store autobiographical information for long-term retention and that information is represented differently by infants and toddlers than by older children and adults (see Spear, 1984; White & Pillemer, 1979).

Research findings have been accumulating over the past 15 years suggesting that the first alternative is not likely. For example, research using deferred-imitation techniques discussed earlier in this chapter (Bauer, 1995; Meltzoff, 1995) indicates that infants between 9 and 16 months of age can encode and retain an experience for periods of up to one year. These researchers argue that such deferred imitation reflects explicit memory, although there is still debate whether such memories should be classified as autobiographical (Nelson, 1994). Nevertheless, these, and other research findings (Myers, Clifton, & Clarkson, 1987; Nelson & Ross, 1980; Perris, Myers, & Clifton, 1990) make it unlikely that infants and toddlers are *incapable* of forming long-term memory representations.

The second alternative, that infants and young children encode information differently than older children and adults, is consistent with stage theories of cognitive development (Bruner, 1966; Case, 1985; Piaget, 1983). When adults attempt to retrieve memories, they do so by reconstructing the events in terms of their current cognitive structures, which are not suitable for interpreting events encoded in infancy and early childhood (Neisser, 1962). However, 3- and 4-year-old children are clearly using language and other symbolic forms of representation to encode their experiences, making the "different representation" argument not wholly satisfying (Fivush & Hamond, 1990).

Nevertheless, updated variants of the "different representation" hypothesis have been generated that can better account for the data. One alternative explains infantile amnesia in terms of fuzzy-trace theory. For example, Leichtman and Ceci (1993) proposed young children's bias toward encoding events with the less stable, verbatim traces increases the likelihood that they will be unavailable after significant time delays. Leichtman and Ceci (1993) also suggest that the encoding shift from verbatim toward fuzzy traces is accompanied by an increasing facility with language, which is used to represent experiences (Bruner, 1966; Vygotsky, 1962) as well as to communicate. With language, children are better able to represent information in a form that will be accessible later on. This proposal, that it is children's developing language abilities that is the basis for autobiographical memory, has been championed by several theorists (Fivush & Hamond, 1990; Nelson, 1993). As we discussed in an earlier section, parents play a significant role in "teaching" their children how to form narratives so that they can represent events in ways that can be recounted to others. From this perspective, the commencement of autobiographical memories (and the cessation of infantile amnesia) represents a transition in cognitive development based on everyday adult-child interaction and the developing language system. Support for this comes from a study by Fivush, Haden, and Adam (1995), who reported that children's narratives about a novel event became increasingly complex, coherent, and more richly elaborated over the preschool years. They suggested that children's "very early memories might not be organized as

coherent narratives and would therefore become more difficult to access as individuals grow older and begin to form a narratively organized life story" (p. 49).

One other hypothesis relies less on differences in how children represent experiences and more on how they represent themselves (Fivush, 1988; Howe & Courage, 1993; Howe et al., 1994). A child's *self-concept* develops gradually over the preschool years (e.g., Brooks-Gunn & Lewis, 1984; Howe & Courage, 1993). This means that children's early memories were formed when their sense of self was poorly developed, providing them with an unstable and unreliable anchor for retrieving such memories later in life. Howe and Courage (1993) state explicitly that unless events can be related to the self they cannot be retrieved at a later time.

The various factors that have been suggested as causes of infantile amnesia share a common bond—a reliance on a developing underlying representational system (see Mandler, Ch. 6, this Volume). Even theorists who believe that infants possess symbolic abilities acknowledge that the nature of representation changes over the first two years of life (Meltzoff, 1995). The nature of this underlying system may be debated, but it appears to us that differences in how information is represented early versus later in life is at the core of why memories from infancy and early childhood are so elusive.

Despite the preponderance of evidence for people's general inability to retrieve detailed memories from their early childhood, American psychotherapists have reported a startling number of reports of repressed memories of sexual and satanic ritualistic abuse. These events supposedly occurred in childhood but were remembered only in adulthood, usually discovered in the process of psychotherapy (see Loftus & Ketchum, 1994). If these memories are "real," it suggests that stressful and repetitive experiences in infancy and early childhood can indeed be coded in memory and then completely forgotten (repressed) until years later. This has caused a great debate between clinical psychologists and memory researchers over the validity of these memories. Given the lack of physical and corroborating evidence for the abuse, most memory researchers suggest that the ideas of abuse are unintentionally planted in the process of psychotherapy, with the client coming to believe in their veracity.

Recent research has demonstrated that false memories from childhood can be easily planted in the mind of an adult, making this interpretation plausible. For example, Loftus and Pickrell (1995) presented four scenarios of specific childhood events to people, three of which had actually happened to the participants (based on reports of parents or older siblings) and one of which, being lost in a mall at age 5, was fabricated. The participants were asked to write about each of the four events in detail and were later interviewed about these events. Participants accurately remembered 68% of the true events; they also recalled 25% of the false events, sometimes vividly. Other research has found similar results of successfully implanted memories for less mundane activities, such as an overnight hospital stay for an ear infection and attending a wedding and accidentally spilling a punch bowl (Hyman, Husband, & Billings, 1995). False-memory creation using similar procedures has also been demonstrated in preschool children (Ceci, Loftus, Leichtman, & Bruck, 1994). Although these findings do not prove that the memories of satanic ritual abuse were similarly implanted, they do indicate that such false memories *can* be implanted. People apparently use their general knowledge of the world and integrate the suggested information with it to create a memory. They use schematic information to support the false event, making the false memory as real to them as a true memory.

MEMORY: DOMAIN-GENERAL FACULTY OR SET OF DOMAIN-SPECIFIC ABILITIES?

How can we test the assumption that memory may not be a domain-general skill but rather may be composed of different domain-specific abilities? One suitable way to explore this issue is to administer different memory tasks to children and assess the intertask correlations. A few developmental studies conducted in the late 60s and 70s reported moderate intraindividual consistency in performance across several memory tasks (Cavanaugh & Borkowski, 1980; Kail, 1979; Stevenson, Hale, Klein, & Miller, 1968). In particular, the relatively high intercorrelations found by Cavanaugh and Borkowski (1980) gave rise to the assumption that there is not only a general memory ability but also a general strategy ability, at least for children 8 years of age and older. However, one obvious problem with the generalization of these findings was that the laboratory tasks used in this study were very similar in structure.

Later research used a wider variety of tasks, including laboratory tasks such as sort-recall and memory-span tasks as well as everyday memory tasks such as story recall

(Knopf et al., 1988; Weinert, Schneider, & Knopf, 1988). On average, these studies reported lower intertask correlations. For example, Knopf et al. (1988) computed correlations among sort-recall, text-recall, and memory-span measures obtained for a total of 578 third-, fifth-, and seventh-graders. Although the correlations between recall for clusterable and nonclusterable word lists were moderately high for all age groups (about .50 on average), comparisons among text-recall and sort-recall variables yielded only low correlations. Kurtz-Costes, Schneider, and Rupp (1995) administered kindergarten, second-, and fourth-grade children a set of 12 memory tasks including laboratory tasks (sort-recall and paired-associate measures), school-related tasks (e.g., recalling a story, remembering a geography lesson), and everyday memory tasks (e.g., "shopping" for items at a store). In general, little intertask consistency was found among the 12 memory tasks. Although the average correlations among tasks increased with age (average correlations = .07, .08, .13 for kindergartners, second-, and fourth-grade children, respectively), only a few developmental differences were found.

Schneider and Weinert (1995) replicated the Kurtz-Costes et al. findings using data from the Munich Longitudinal Study on the Genesis of Individual Differences (LOGIC; Weinert & Schneider, 1986, 1992). In this study, the same group of children was administered a broad variety of memory tasks at 4, 6, 8, 10, and 12 years of age. Schneider and Weinert reported relatively high intercorrelations among structurally similar tasks (e.g., parallel measures of story recall, or word span and listening span). However, similar to the cross-sectional studies described above, the longitudinal analyses yielded only low intertask correlations for structurally dissimilar memory tasks (e.g., recall for word lists and stories) and few significant development changes.

Taken together, these findings suggest that deliberate memory may be better thought of as a set of specific abilities rather than a domain-general construct. Given the lack of change in the relations among memory tasks with development, the findings indicate that this position may hold across the life-span.

STABILITY OF MEMORY PERFORMANCE OVER TIME

A related issue is that of intraindividual stability over time. Here, the question is whether children who remember well, for example, at one age also remember well on the same or a similar task some time later. Longitudinal data are necessary to answer this question. In the LOGIC study mentioned above, *group stabilities* (test-retest correlations) were calculated for various memory measures (Schneider & Sodian, 1991; Schneider & Weinert, 1995). Overall, group stabilities were only moderate in size for most memory measures, indicating that many children did not maintain their position in rank order over time.

The most detailed analyses are available for a traditional sort-recall task that was presented five times within a period of ten years (Schneider & Weinert, 1995; Sodian & Schneider, in press). Group stabilities for recall were generally low, ranging from .16 over a six-year period to .39 over a two-year period (see Schneider & Weinert, 1995). Stabilities for sorting and clustering were even lower, indicating long-term instability over time. To decide whether the amount of instability found for the sort-recall data was due to unreliability of measures or to true fluctuation/change in the variables, their stability over short time intervals (2 weeks) was also assessed. The generally high short-term stabilities suggest that most memory variables could be reliably assessed even at the earliest measurement point (at the age of 4). Consequently, low long-term stabilities must be attributed to individual differences in the rate of memory development over the course of elementary school.

Schneider and Weinert (1995) noted comparably higher long-term stabilities for other memory measures such as memory span and text recall. For these variables, test-retest correlations were mostly in the .40 to .70 range. These authors concluded that the considerably lower long-term stability for the sort-recall variables, as compared to the text-recall and memory-span measures, may be related to the substantially greater strategic component required for the sort-recall task. According to this view, the degree of long-term stability varies as a function of the strategic component inherent in the memory task.

Sodian and Schneider (in press) provided a detailed longitudinal analysis of the sorting and clustering strategies variables used in the sort-recall task. One of the major goals of the study concerned whether typical cross-sectional findings could be replicated by the longitudinal data. In particular, the question was whether the impression of gradual developmental increases in strategy use and recall derived from cross-sectional studies could be confirmed by the longitudinal findings. The answer was positive: overall, the longitudinal analyses on the group level indicated that the findings were comparable to what was known about memory development from previous cross-sectional studies in the sort-recall paradigm.

A second goal of the longitudinal analysis conducted by Sodian and Schneider was to follow up the low stabilities for the strategy and recall variables described above. If individual children change their relative positions in the sample considerably between measurement points (as indicated by the low stabilities), the model of gradual improvement that fits the group data well does not seem to hold for strategy acquisition in individual children. A closer inspection of children's sorting quickly showed that a pattern of gradual, steady increases over time was rarely found. About 81% of the children "jumped" from chance level (sorting scores < .30) to near perfection (sorting scores > .80) between subsequent measurement points. The remaining children fell into three groups: about 3% never discovered the strategy, 8% were nearly perfect from the start, and another 8% showed a pattern of gradual increase as suggested by the group data. There was also considerable variation in the age at which children first used the strategy, and many children who used it at early measurement points lost it subsequently and "rediscovered" it at some later point. Thus some of the instability of strategic behavior over time can be explained by individual variation in the time of strategy "discovery": Children go from chance levels of sorting to perfection, but they do it at different points in time. Furthermore, their patterns of strategy development show "leaps" and U-shaped curves. These findings are consistent with new evidence of multiple- and variable-strategy use in children discussed earlier in this chapter (Siegler, 1996).

Taken together, these findings indicate that the group data on strategy acquisition that have been reported in cross-sectional studies (and replicated in the longitudinal group analysis) obscure individual developmental paths. The analyses of individual developmental patterns conducted by Sodian and Schneider (in press) helped solve the puzzle of low individual stabilities in highly regular group data. They also showed that longitudinal analyses of memory development can go far beyond the possibilities of (cheaper) cross-sectional studies.

CONCLUDING REMARKS

Our overview of the literature has shown that the area of memory development is still a very active field three decades after John Flavell and his colleagues began with their classic studies. Due to space restrictions, it was not possible to provide a representative picture of all relevant research activities. For instance, although the study of visuospatial memory and memory for actions has attracted many researchers during the last decade (cf. Ratner & Foley, 1994; Schumann-Hengsteler, 1992), we decided to focus on the development of verbal memory because this research area has clearly dominated the field. Furthermore, we had to restrict ourselves to the description of developmental processes during childhood and adolescence, despite the fact that assessments of memory development in adults and the elderly have received much attention (Weinert et al., 1988). Nonetheless, we believe that the present review of the literature provides an idea about how fast the field is growing. This is particularly true for the area of infant memory, but also holds for both classic lines (e.g., strategy development) as well as recent research trends such as the study of autobiographical memory.

How does the field cope with previous criticisms that bemoaned its focus on artificial memory situations, its neglect of social context and everyday-life activities, and its dependence on theories and methods derived from nondevelopmental research (Perlmutter, 1988; Schneider & Pressley, 1989)? Weinert (1988) summarized the problems of the state-of-the-art in the late 1980s as follows:

1. The use of memory strategies and the availability of domain-specific knowledge are often studied in isolation, thereby neglecting motivational and social factors;

2. Intentional learning dominates over incidental learning, and verbal memory gets much more attention than nonverbal memory;

3. Whereas the emphasis of most studies is on short-term recognition and recall, long-term retention and forgetting processes are rarely investigated;

4. Research has been primarily conducted under laboratory-type experimental conditions, with systematic observations of memory processes in natural, real-life situations being the exceptions; and

5. Memory research has focused on universal changes in memory processes, thereby neglecting intra- and interindividual differences.

A closer look at current research activities reveals that most of the shortcomings noted by Weinert have been overcome. We do know a lot more about the complex interplay among memory capacity, strategy development, and various forms of knowledge than we did ten years ago. Recent attempts to describe these relations led to models that explicitly included motivational and context factors (e.g., the Good Information Processing model). Although studies of deliberate memory processing still dominate the field, the number of investigations exploring developmental differences in implicit learning and memory have increased considerably during the 1990s. In a similar vein, developmental models and empirical studies of long-term memory and forgetting have complemented classic research lines that emphasized short-term memory functioning. Moreover, a large number of studies primarily dealing with aspects of autobiographic memory have used real-life scenarios to assess episodic memory in children. Finally, recent research on the role of aptitude and other personality variables as well as longitudinal research dealing with intraindividual consistency of memory behavior and performance over time have emphasized the importance of these variables for a proper understanding of individual memory development.

Although we believe that the research conducted during the last decade has helped in eliminating numerous problems of earlier studies, this does not imply that it managed to solve all puzzles of memory development in children. On the contrary, the evidence from large scale longitudinal studies indicates that the diversity of ontogenetic changes in memory has been clearly underestimated in traditional cross-sectional approaches that focused on prototypical developmental sequences and tacitly assumed intraindividual homogeneity and interindividual consistency in developmental changes. In our view, one major challenge for the next generation of studies will be to identify sources of inter- and intraindividual variation in patterns of memory development. This may require a multimethod approach, including fine-grained microgenetic studies as well as large-scale real-life assessments. Given the complexity of the phenomenon under study, future research should also emphasize interdisciplinary approaches (e.g., the cooperation with neurosciences) in order to get closer to the ambitious goal of understanding memory development.

ACKNOWLEDGMENTS

We would like to thank Barbara Bjorklund, Charles Brainerd, Marcus Hasselhorn, Elizabeth Kennedy, Michael Pressley, Kristina Rosenblum, Robert Siegler, and Harriet Waters for comments on earlier drafts of this manuscript. We would like to thank Claudia Roebers and Ralph Carpenter for technical support in facilitating transatlantic communication.

REFERENCES

Abravanel, E. (1991). Does immediate imitation influence long-term memory for observed events? *Journal of Experimental Child Psychology, 51,* 235–244.

Abravanel, E., & Gingold, H. (1985). Learning via observation during the second year of life. *Developmental Psychology, 21,* 614–623.

Ackerman, B. P. (1987). Descriptions: A model of nonstrategic memory development. In H. W. Reese (Ed.), *Advances in child development and behavior* (Vol. 20). Orlando, FL: Academic Press.

Ackil, J. K., & Zaragoza, M. S. (1995). Developmental differences in eyewitness suggestibility and memory source monitoring. *Journal of Experimental Child Psychology, 60,* 57–83.

Alexander, J. M., Carr, M., & Schwanenflugel, P. J. (1995). Development of metacognition in gifted children: Directions for future research. *Developmental Review, 15,* 1–37.

Alexander, J. M., & Schwanenflugel, P. J. (1994). Strategy regulation: The role of intelligence, metacognitive attributes, and knowledge base. *Developmental Psychology, 30,* 709–723.

Atkinson, R. C., & Shiffrin, R. M. (1968). Human memory: A proposed system and its control processes. In K. W. Spence & J. T. Spence (Eds.), *The psychology of learning and motivation* (Vol. 2). New York: Academic Press.

Ausley, J. A., & Guttentag, R. E. (1993). Direct and indirect assessments of memory: Implications for the study of memory development. In M. L. Howe & R. Pasnak (Eds.), *Emerging themes in cognitive development: Vol. 1. Foundations.* New York: Springer-Verlag.

Bachevalier, J., & Mishkin, M. (1984). An early and late developing system for learning and retention in infant monkeys. *Behavioral Neuroscience, 98,* 770–778.

Baddeley, A. D. (1986). *Working memory.* Oxford, MA: Clarendon Press.

Baddeley, A. D., & Hitch, G. J. (1974). Working memory. In G. Bower (Ed.), *The psychology of learning and motivation: Advances in research and theory* (Vol. 8). New York: Academic Press.

Bahrick, L. E., & Pickens, J. N. (1995). Infant memory for object motion across a period of three months: Implications for a four-phase attention function. *Journal of Experimental Child Psychology, 59,* 343–371.

Baker, L., & Brown, A. L. (1984). Metacognitive skills and reading. In P. D. Pearson, M. Kamil, R. Barr, & P. Mosenthal (Eds.), *Handbook of reading research.* New York: Longman.

Baker-Ward, L., Gordon, B. N., Ornstein, P. A., Larus, D. M., & Clubb, P. A. (1993). Young children's long-term retention of a pediatric visit. *Child Development, 64,* 1519–1533.

Baker-Ward, L., & Ornstein, P. A. (1988). Age differences in visual-spatial memory performance: Do children really outperform adults when playing concentration? *Bulletin of the Psychonomic Society, 26,* 331–332.

Baker-Ward, L., Ornstein, P. A., & Holden, D. J. (1984). The expression of memorization in early childhood. *Journal of Experimental Child Psychology, 37,* 555–575.

Ballard, J. (1913). Obliviscence and reminiscence. *British Journal of Psychology Monograph Supplements, 1,* 1–82.

Bauer, P. J. (1995). Recalling past events: From infancy to early childhood. *Annals of Child Development, 11,* 25–71.

Bauer, P. J., & Dow, G. A. (1994). Episodic memory in 16- and 20-month-old children: Specifics are generalized but not forgotten. *Developmental Psychology, 30,* 403–417.

Bauer, P. J., & Fivush, R. (1992). Constructing event representations: Building on a foundation of variation and enabling relations. *Cognitive Development, 7,* 381–401.

Bauer, P. J., & Hertsgaard, L. A. (1993). Increasing steps in recall of events: Factors facilitating immediate and long-term memory in 13.5- and 16.5-month-old children. *Child Development, 64,* 1204–1223.

Bauer, P. J., & Wewerka, S. S. (1995). One- and two-year-olds recall of events: The more expressed, the more impressed. *Journal of Experimental Child Psychology, 59,* 475–496.

Bauer, R. H. (1979). Memory, acquisition, and category clustering in learning-disabled children. *Journal of Experimental Child Psychology, 27,* 365–383.

Beal, C. R. (1985). Development of knowledge about the use of cues to aid prospective retrieval. *Child Development, 56,* 631–642.

Beal, C. R., & Fleisig, W. E. (1987, April). *Preschooler's preparation for retrieval in object relocation tasks.* Paper presented at the biennial meeting of the Society for Research in Child Development, Baltimore.

Best, D. L. (1993). Inducing children to generate mnemonic organizational strategies: An examination of long-term retention and materials. *Developmental Psychology, 29,* 324–336.

Beuhring, T., & Kee, D. W. (1987). The relationships between memory knowledge, elaborative strategy use and associative memory performance. *Journal of Experimental Child Psychology, 44,* 377–400.

Bisanz, G. L., Vesonder, G. T., & Voss, J. F. (1978). Knowledge of one's own responding and the relation of such knowledge to learning. *Journal of Experimental Child Psychology, 25,* 116–128.

Bjorklund, D. F. (1987). How age changes in knowledge base contribute to the development of children's memory: An interpretive review. *Developmental Review, 7,* 93–130.

Bjorklund, D. F. (1988). Acquiring a mnemonic: Age and category knowledge effects. *Journal of Experimental Child Psychology, 45,* 71–87.

Bjorklund, D. F. (1995). An interim evaluation of fuzzy-trace theory: Cautiousness, confirmation, and consciousness. *Learning and Individual Differences, 7,* 105–115.

Bjorklund, D. F. (1997). In search of a metatheory for cognitive development (or, Piaget's dead and I don't feel so good myself). *Child Development, 68,* 142–146.

Bjorklund, D. F., & Bernholtz, J. E. (1986). The role of knowledge base in the memory performance of good and poor readers. *Journal of Experimental Child Psychology, 41,* 367–393.

Bjorklund, D. F., & Bjorklund, B. R. (1985). Organization versus item effects of an elaborated knowledge base on children's memory. *Developmental Psychology, 21,* 1120–1131.

Bjorklund, D. F., & Coyle, T. R. (1995). Utilization deficiencies in the development of memory strategies. In F. E. Weinert & W. Schneider (Eds.), *Memory performance and competencies: Issues in growth and development.* Hillsdale, NJ: Erlbaum.

Bjorklund, D. F., Coyle, T. R., & Gaultney, J. F. (1992). Developmental differences in the acquisition and maintenance of an organizational strategy: Evidence for the utilization deficiency hypothesis. *Journal of Experimental Child Psychology, 54,* 434–448

Bjorklund, D. F., & Harnishfeger, K. K. (1987). Developmental differences in the mental effort requirements for the use of an organizational strategy in free recall. *Journal of Experimental Child Psychology, 44,* 109–125.

Bjorklund, D. F., & Harnishfeger, K. K. (1990). Children's strategies: Their definition and origins. In D. F. Bjorklund (Ed.), *Children's strategies: Contemporary views of cognitive development.* Hillsdale, NJ: Erlbaum.

Bjorklund, D. F., & Jacobs, J. W. (1985). Associative and categorical processes in children's memory: The role of automaticity in the development of organization in free recall. *Journal of Experimental Child Psychology, 39,* 599–617.

Bjorklund, D. F., Miller, P. H., Coyle, T. R., & Slawinski, J. L. (1997). Instructing children to use memory strategies: Evidence of utilization deficiencies in memory training studies. In D. F. Bjorklund & P. H. Miller (Eds.), New themes in strategy development [Special issue]. *Developmental Review.*

Bjorklund, D. F., Muir-Broaddus, J. E., & Schneider, W. (1990). The role of knowledge in the development of strategies. In D. F. Bjorklund (Ed.), *Children's strategies: Contemporary views of cognitive development.* Hillsdale, NJ: Erlbaum.

Bjorklund, D. F., & Schneider, W. (1996). The interaction of knowledge, aptitudes, and strategies in children's memory performance. In H. W. Reese (Ed.), *Advances in child development and behavior* (Vol. 25). San Diego, CA: Academic Press.

Bjorklund, D. F., & Zeman, B. R. (1982). Children's organization and metamemory awareness in the recall of familiar information. *Child Development, 53,* 799–810.

Black, M. M., & Rollins, H. A. (1982). The effects of instructional variables on young children's organization and free recall. *Journal of Experimental Child Psychology, 33,* 1–19.

Blair, R., Perlmutter, M., & Myers, N. A. (1978). Effects of unlabeled and labeled picture cues on very young children's memory for location. *Bulletin of Psychonomic Society, 11,* 46–48.

Borkowski, J. G., Carr, M., Rellinger, E. A., & Pressley, M. (1990). Self-regulated strategy use: Interdependence of metacognition, attributions, and self-esteem. In B. F. Jones (Ed.), *Dimensions of thinking: Review of research* (pp. 53–92). Hillsdale, NJ: Erlbaum.

Borkowski, J. G., Milstead, M., & Hale, C. (1988). Components of children's metamemory: Implications for strategy generalization. In F. E. Weinert & M. Perlmutter (Eds.), *Memory development: Universal changes and individual differences.* Hillsdale, NJ: Erlbaum.

Borkowski, J. G., & Peck, V. A. (1986). Causes and consequences of metamemory in gifted children. In R. J. Sternberg & J. C. Davidson (Eds.) *Conceptions of giftedness.* Cambridge, England: Cambridge University Press.

Borkowski, J. G., Peck, V. A., Reid, M. K., & Kurtz, B. E. (1983). Impulsivity and strategy transfer: Metamemory as mediator. *Child Development, 54,* 459–473.

Borkowski, J. G., Reid, M. K., & Kurtz, B. E. (1984). Metacognition and retardation: Pragmatic, theoretical and applied perspectives. In P. H. Brooks, R. Sperber, & C. McCauley (Eds.), *Learning and cognition in the mentally retarded.* Hillsdale, NJ: Erlbaum.

Borkowski, J. G., & Turner, L. A. (1990). Transsituational characteristics of metacognition. In W. Schneider & F. E. Weinert (Eds.), *Interactions among aptitudes, strategies, and knowledge in cognitive performance.* New York: Springer-Verlag.

Borkowski, J. G., Weyhing, R. S., & Carr, M. (1988). Effects of attributional retraining on strategy based reading comprehension in LD children. *Journal of Educational Psychology, 80,* 46–53.

Bornstein, M. H. (1989). Stability in early mental development: From attention and information processing in infancy to language and cognition in childhood. In M. H. Bornstein & N. A. Krasnegor (Eds.), *Stability and continuity in mental development: Behavioral and biological perspectives.* Hillsdale, NJ: Erlbaum.

Bousfield, A. K., & Bousfield, W. A. (1966). Measurement of clustering and of sequential constancies in repeated free recall. *Psychological Reports, 4,* 39–44.

Brainerd, C. J. (1995). Interference processes in memory development: The case of cognitive triage. In F. N. Dempster & C. J. Brainerd (Eds.), *New perspectives on interference and inhibition in cognition*. New York: Academic Press.

Brainerd, C. J., & Gordon, L. L. (1994). Development of verbatim and gist memory for numbers. *Developmental Psychology, 30,* 163–177.

Brainerd, C. J., & Kingma, J. (1985). On the independence of short-term memory and working memory in cognitive development. *Cognitive Psychology, 17,* 210–247.

Brainerd, C. J., Kingma, J., & Howe, M. L. (1985). On the development of forgetting. *Child Development, 56,* 1103–1119.

Brainerd, C. J., & Reyna, V. F. (1989). Output-interference theory of dual-task deficits in memory development. *Journal of Experimental Child Psychology, 47,* 1–18.

Brainerd, C. J., & Reyna, V. F. (1990). Gist is the grist: Fuzzy-trace theory and the new intuitionism. *Developmental Review, 10,* 3–47.

Brainerd, C. J., & Reyna, V. F. (1993). Domains of fuzzy trace theory. In M. L. Howe & R. Pasnak (Eds.), *Emerging themes in cognitive development: Vol. 1. Foundations.* New York: Springer-Verlag.

Brainerd, C. J., Reyna, V. F., & Brandse, E. (1995). Are children's false memories more persistent than their true memories? *Psychological Science, 6,* 359–364.

Brainerd, C. J., Reyna, V. F., Harnishfeger, K. K., & Howe, M. L. (1993). Is retrievability grouping good for recall? *Journal of Experimental Psychology: General, 122,* 249–268.

Brainerd, C. J., Reyna, V. F., Howe, M. L., & Kevershan, J. (1991). Fuzzy-trace theory and cognitive triage in memory development. *Developmental Psychology, 27,* 315–369.

Brainerd, C. J., Reyna, V. F., Howe, M. L., & Kingma, J. (1990). The development of forgetting and reminiscence. *Monographs of the Society for Research in Child Development, 55*(Serial No. 222).

Bray, N. W., & Turner, L. A. (1986). The rehearsal deficit hypothesis. In N. R. Ellis & N. W. Bray (Eds.), *International review of research in mental retardation* (Vol. 14). New York: Academic Press.

Brooks-Gunn, J., & Lewis, M. (1984). The development of early self-recognition. *Developmental Review, 4,* 215–239.

Brown, A. L. (1978). Knowing when, where, and how to remember: A problem of metacognition. In R. Glaser (Ed.), *Advances in instructional psychology*. Hillsdale, NJ: Erlbaum.

Brown, A. L., Bransford, J. D., Ferrara, R. A., & Campione, J. C. (1983). Learning, remembering, and understanding. In J. H. Flavell & E. M. Markman (Eds.), *Handbook of child psychology* (Vol. 3). New York: Wiley.

Bruner, J. S. (1966). On cognitive growth. In J. S. Bruner, R. R. Olver, & P. M. Greenfield (Eds.), *Studies in cognitive growth*. New York: Wiley.

Brunswik, E., Goldscheider, L., & Pilek, E. (1932). Zur Systematik des Gedächtnisses [A systems view of memory]. In E. Brunswik (Ed.), *Beihefte zur Zeitschrift für angewandte Psychologie, 64*(Suppl.), 1–158.

Butterfield, E., Nelson, T., & Peck, G. (1988). Developmental aspects of the feeling of knowing. *Developmental Psychology, 24,* 654–663.

Cantor, D. S., Andreassen, C., & Waters, H. S. (1985). Organization in visual episodic memory: Relationships between verbalized knowledge, strategy use, and performance. *Journal of Experimental Child Psychology, 40,* 218–232.

Carr, M., Borkowski, J. G., & Maxwell, S. E. (1991). Motivational components of underachievement. *Developmental Psychology, 27,* 108–118.

Carr, M., Kurtz, B. E., Schneider, W., Turner, L. A., & Borkowski, J. G. (1989). Strategy acquisition and transfer among American and German children: Environmental influences on metacognitive development. *Developmental Psychology, 25,* 765–771.

Carr, M., & Schneider, W. (1991). Long-term maintenance of organizational strategies in kindergarten children. *Contemporary Educational Psychology, 16,* 61–72.

Case, R. (1985). *Intellectual development: Birth to adulthood.* New York: Academic Press.

Case, R. (1992). *The mind's staircase: Exploring the conceptual underpinnings of children's thought and knowledge.* Hillsdale, NJ: Erlbaum.

Case, R., Kurland, M., & Goldberg, J. (1982). Operational efficiency and the growth of short-term memory span. *Journal of Experimental Child Psychology, 33,* 386–404.

Cassel, W. S., & Bjorklund, D. F. (1995). Developmental patterns of eyewitness memory and suggestibility: An ecologically based short-term longitudinal study. *Law & Human Behavior, 19,* 507–532.

Cassel, W. S., Roebers, C. E. M., & Bjorklund, D. F. (1996). Developmental patterns of eyewitness responses to increasingly suggestive questions. *Journal of Experimental Child Psychology, 61,* 116–133.

Cavanaugh, J. C., & Borkowski, J. G. (1980). Searching for metamemory-memory connections: A developmental study. *Developmental Psychology, 16,* 441–453.

Cavanaugh, J. C., & Perlmutter, M. (1982). Metamemory: A critical examination. *Child Development, 53,* 11–28.

Ceci, S. J., & Bruck, M. (1993). Suggestibility of the child witness: A historical review and synthesis. *Psychological Bulletin, 113,* 403–439.

Ceci, S. J., Lea, S. E. G., & Howe, M. J. A. (1980). Structural analysis of memory traces in children from 4- to 10-years-of-age. *Developmental Psychology, 16,* 203–212.

Ceci, S. J., Loftus, E. F., Leichtman, M., & Bruck, M. (1994). The role of source misattributions in the creation of false beliefs among preschoolers. *International Journal of Clinical Experimental Hypnosis, 62,* 304–320.

Ceci, S. J., Ross, D. F., & Toglia, M. P. (1987). Suggestibility of children's memory: Psycholegal implications. *Journal of Experimental Psychology: General, 116,* 38–49.

Chechile, R. A., & Richman, C. L. (1982). The interaction of semantic memory with storage and retrieval processes. *Developmental Review, 2,* 237–250.

Chen, C., & Stevenson, H. W. (1988). Cross-linguistic differences in digit span of preschool children. *Journal of Experimental Child Psychology, 46,* 150–158.

Chi, M. T. H. (1978). Knowledge structure and memory development. In R. Siegler (Ed.), *Children's thinking: What develops?* Hillsdale, NJ: Erlbaum.

Chi, M. T. H. (1985). Interactive roles of knowledge and strategies in the development of organized sorting and recall. In S. F. Chipman, J. W. Segal, & R. Glaser (Eds.), *Thinking and learning skills: Vol. 2. Research and open questions.* Hillsdale, NJ: Erlbaum.

Chi, M. T. H., & Ceci, S. J. (1987). Content knowledge: Its role, representation, and restructuring in memory development. In H. W. Reese (Ed.), *Advances in child development and behavior* (Vol. 20). Orlando, FL: Academic Press.

Chi, M. T. H., & Koeske, R. D. (1983). Network representation of a child's dinosaur knowledge. *Developmental Psychology, 19,* 29–39.

Chi, M. T. H., & Rees, E. T. (1983). A learning framework for development. In M. T. H. Chi (Ed.), *Trends in memory development research.* Basel/München: Karger.

Clubb, P. A., Nida, R. E., Merrit, K., & Ornstein, P. A. (1993). Visiting the doctor: Children's knowledge and memory. *Cognitive Development, 8,* 361–172.

Cohn, S. J., Carlson, J. S., & Jensen, A. R. (1985). Speed of information processing in academically gifted youths. *Personality and Individual Differences, 6,* 621–629.

Cowan, N., & Davidson, G. (1984). Salient childhood memories. *The Journal of Genetic Psychology, 145,* 101–107.

Cox, D., & Waters, H. S. (1986). Sex differences in the use of organization strategies: A developmental analysis. *Journal of Experimental Child Psychology, 41,* 18–37.

Coyle, T. R., & Bjorklund, D. F. (1997). Age differences in, and consequences of, multiple- and variable-strategy use on a multitrial sort-recall task. *Developmental Psychology, 33,* 372–380.

Craik, F. I. M., & Lockhart, R. S. (1972). Levels of processing: A framework for memory research. *Journal of Verbal Learning and Verbal Behavior, 11,* 671–684.

Cultice, J. C., Somerville, S. C., & Wellman, H. M. (1983). Preschooler's memory monitoring: Feeling-of-knowing judgments. *Child Development, 54,* 1480–1486.

Cunningham, J. G., & Weaver, S. L. (1989). Young children's knowledge of their memory span: Effects of task and experience. *Journal of Experimental Child Psychology, 48,* 32–44.

Dale, P. S., Loftus, E. F., & Rathburn, L. (1978). The influence of the form of the question on eyewitness testimony of pre-school children. *Journal of Psycholinguistic Research, 7,* 269–277.

DeLoache, J. S., & Brown, A. L. (1984). Where do I go next? Intelligent searching by very young children. *Developmental Psychology, 20,* 37–44.

DeLoache, J. S., Cassidy, D. J., & Brown, A. L. (1985). Precursors of mnemonic strategies in very young children's memory. *Child Development, 56,* 125–137.

DeMarie-Dreblow, D. (1991). Relation between knowledge and memory: A reminder that correlation does not imply causality. *Child Development, 62,* 484–498.

Dempster, F. N. (1981). Memory span: Sources of individual and developmental differences. *Psychological Bulletin, 89,* 63–100.

Dempster, F. N. (1985). Short-term memory development in childhood and adolescence. In C. J. Brainerd & M. Pressley (Eds.), *Basic processes in memory development: Progress in cognitive development research.* New York: Springer.

Dempster, F. N. (1992). The rise and fall of the inhibitory mechanism: Toward a unified theory of cognitive development and aging. *Developmental Review, 12,* 45–75.

de Ribaupierre, A., & Bailleux, C. (1995). Development of attentional capacity in childhood: A longitudinal study. In F. E. Weinert & W. Schneider (Eds.), *Research on memory development: State-of-the-art and future directions.* Hillsdale, NJ: Erlbaum.

Diamond, A. (1985). Development of the ability to use recall to guide action as indicated by infants' performance on AB. *Child Development, 56,* 868–883.

Diamond, A. (1991). Frontal lobe involvement in cognitive changes during the first year of life. In K. R. Gibson & A. C. Petersen (Eds.), *Brain maturation and cognitive development: Comparative and cross-cultural perspectives.* New York: Aldine de Gruyter.

Diamond, A. (1995). Evidence of robust recognition memory in early life even when assessed by reaching behavior. *Journal of Experimental Child Behavior, 59,* 419–456.

Doris, J. (Ed.). (1991). *The suggestibility of children's recollections: Implications for eyewitness testimony.* Washington, DC: American Psychological Association.

Drummey, A. B., & Newcombe, N. (1995). Remembering versus knowing the past: Children's explicit and implicit memories for pictures. *Journal of Experimental Child Psychology, 59,* 549–565.

Dufresne, A., & Kobasigawa, A. (1989). Children's spontaneous allocation of study time: Differential and sufficient aspects. *Journal of Experimental Child Psychology, 47,* 274–296.

Ebbinghaus, H. (1885). *Über das Gedächtnis* [About memory]. Leipzig: Duncker.

Ellis, N. C., & Hennelley, R. A. (1980). A bilingual word-length effect: Implications for intelligence testing and the relative ease of mental calculation in Welsh and English. *British Journal of Psychology, 71,* 43–52.

Ellis, N. R., Katz, E., & Williams, J. E. (1987). Developmental aspects of memory for spatial location. *Journal of Experimental Child Psychology, 44,* 401–412.

Emmerich, H. J., & Ackerman, B. P. (1978). Developmental differences in recall: Encoding or retrieval? *Journal of Experimental Child Psychology, 25,* 514–525.

Engle, R. W., Fidler, D. S., & Reynolds, L. M. (1981). Does echoic memory develop? *Journal of Experimental Child Psychology, 32,* 459–473.

Fabricius, W. V., & Hagen, J. W. (1984). The use of causal attributions about recall performance to assess metamemory and predict strategies memory behavior in young children. *Developmental Psychology, 20,* 975–987.

Fagan, J. F., III. (1973). Infants' delayed recognition memory and forgetting. *Journal of Experimental Child Psychology, 16,* 424–450.

Fagan, J. F., III. (1974). Infant recognition memory: The effects of length of familiarization and type of discrimination task. *Child Development, 45,* 351–356.

Fagan, J. F., III (1984). The relationship of novelty preferences during infancy to later intelligence and recognition memory. *Intelligence, 8,* 339–346.

Fagan, J. F., III (1992). Intelligence: A theoretical viewpoint. *Current Directions in Psychological Science, 1,* 82–86.

Fainsztein-Pollack, G. (1973). A developmental study of decay rate in long-term memory. *Journal of Experimental Child Psychology, 16,* 225–235.

Fantz, R. L. (1958). Pattern vision in young infants. *Psychological Record, 8,* 43–47.

Farrar, M. J., & Goodman, G. S. (1990). Developmental differences in the relation between script and episodic memory: Do they exist? In R. Fivush & J. Hudson (Eds.), *Knowing and remembering in young children.* Cambridge, England: Cambridge University Press.

Farrar, M. J., & Goodman, G. S. (1992). Developmental changes in event memory. *Child Development, 63,* 173–187.

Fischer, K. W. (1980). A theory of cognitive development: The control and construction of hierarchies of skills. *Psychological Review, 87,* 477–531.

Fivush, R. (1988). The functions of event memory: Some comments on Nelson and Barsalou. In U. Neisser & E. Winograd (Eds.), *Remembering reconsidered: Ecological and traditional approaches to the study of memory.* New York: Cambridge University Press.

Fivush, R., Haden, C., & Adam, S. (1995). Structure and coherence of preschoolers' personal narratives over time: Implications for childhood amnesia. *Journal of Experimental Child Psychology, 60,* 32–56.

Fivush, R., & Hamond, N. R. (1989). Time and again: Effects of repetition and retention interval on 2-year-olds' event recall. *Journal of Experimental Child Psychology, 47,* 259–273.

Fivush, R., & Hamond, N. R. (1990). Autobiographical memory across the preschool years: Toward reconceptualizing childhood amnesia. In R. Fivush & J. A. Hudson (Eds.), *Knowing and remembering in young children.* Cambridge, England: Cambridge University Press.

Fivush, R., & Hudson, J. A. (1990). *Knowing and remembering in young children.* Cambridge, England: Cambridge University Press.

Fivush, R., Kuebli, J., & Clubb, P. A. (1992). The structure of event representations: A developmental analysis. *Child Development, 63,* 188–201.

Fivush, R., & Reese, E. (1992). The social construction of autobiographical memory. In A. Conway, D. C. Rubin, H. Spinnler, & W. A. Wagenaar (Eds.), *Theoretical perspectives on autobiographical memory.* Amsterdam, The Netherlands: Kluwer.

Flavell, J. H. (1970). Developmental studies of mediated memory. In H. W. Reese & L. P. Lipsitt (Eds.), *Advances in child development and behavior.* New York: Academic Press.

Flavell, J. H. (1971). First discussant's comments: What is memory development the development of? *Human Development, 14,* 272–278.

Flavell, J. H., Beach, D. R., & Chinsky, J. H. (1966). Spontaneous verbal rehearsal in a memory task as a function of age. *Child Development, 37,* 283–299.

Flavell, J. H., Friedrichs, A. G., & Hoyt, J. D. (1970). Developmental changes in memorization processes. *Cognitive Psychology, 1,* 324–340.

Flavell, J. H., Miller, P. H., & Miller, S. A. (1993). *Cognitive development* (3rd ed.). Englewood Cliffs, NJ: Prentice-Hall.

Flavell, J. H., & Wellman, H. M. (1977). Metamemory. In R. V. Kail & J. W. Hagen (Eds.), *Perspectives on the development of memory and cognition.* Hillsdale, NJ: Erlbaum.

Flin, R., Boon, J., Knox, A., & Bull, R. (1992). The effect of a five-month delay on children's and adult's eyewitness memory. *British Journal of Psychology, 83,* 323–336.

Folds, T. H., Foote, M., Guttentag, R. E., & Ornstein, P. A. (1990). When children mean to remember: Issues of context specificity, strategy effectiveness, and intentionality in the development of memory. In D. F. Bjorklund (Ed.), *Children's strategies: Contemporary views of cognitive development.* Hillsdale, NJ: Erlbaum.

Foley, M. A., & Johnson, M. K. (1985). Confusions between memories for performed and imagined actions: A developmental comparison. *Child Development, 56,* 1145–1155.

Foley, M. A., Ratner, H. H., & Passalacqua, C. (1993). Appropriating the actions of another: Implications for children's memory and learning. *Cognitive Development, 8,* 373–401.

Foley, M. A., Santini, C., & Sopaskis, M. (1989). Discriminating between memories: Evidence for children's spontaneous elaborations. *Journal of Experimental Child Psychology, 48,* 146–169.

Frankel, M. T., & Rollins, H. A. (1985). Associative and categorical hypotheses of organization in the free recall of adults and children. *Journal of Experimental Child Psychology, 40,* 304–318.

Freud, S. (1963). Three essays on the theory of sexuality. In J. Strachey (Ed. & Trans.), *The standard edition of the complete psychological works of Sigmund Freud* (Vol. 7). London: Hogarth Press.

Friedman, S. (1972). Habituation and recovery of visual response in the alert human newborn. *Journal of Experimental Child Psychology, 13,* 339–349.

Garner, R. (1987). *Metacognition and reading comprehension.* Norwood, NJ: ABLEX.

Gaultney, J. F. (1995). The effect of prior knowledge and metacognition on the acquisition of a reading comprehension strategy. *Journal of Experimental Child Psychology, 59,* 142–163.

Gaultney, J. F., Bjorklund, D. F., & Goldstein, D. (1996). To be young, gifted, and strategic: Advantages for memory performance. *Journal of Experimental Child Psychology, 61,* 43–66.

Gaultney, J. F., Bjorklund, D. F., & Schneider, W. (1992). The role of children's expertise in a strategic memory task. *Contemporary Educational Psychology, 17,* 244–257.

Geary, D. C., Bow-Thomas, C. C., Fan, L., & Siegler, R. S. (1993). Even before formal instruction, Chinese children outperform American children in mental arithmetic. *Cognitive Development, 8,* 517–529.

Geis, M. F., & Lange, G. (1976). Children's cue utilization in a memory-for-location task. *Child Development, 47,* 759–766.

Gelabert, T., Torgesen, J., Dice, C., & Murphy, H. (1980). The effects of situational variables on the use of rehearsal by first-grade children. *Child Development, 51,* 902–905.

Gettinger, M. (1985). Time allocated and time spent relative to time needed for learning as determinants of achievement. *Journal of Educational Psychology, 77,* 3–11.

Ghatala, E. S. (1984). Developmental changes in incidental memory as a function of meaningfulness and encoding condition. *Developmental Psychology, 20,* 208–211.

Ghatala, E. S., Levin, J. R., Pressley, M., & Goodwin, D. (1986). A componential analysis of the effects of derived and supplied strategy-utility information on children's strategy selection. *Journal of Experimental Child Psychology, 41,* 76–92.

Goodman, G. S., Aman, C. J., & Hirschman, J. (1987). Child sexual and physical abuse: Children's testimony. In C. J. Ceci, M. P. Toglia, & D. F. Ross (Eds.), *Children's eyewitness memory.* New York: Springer-Verlag.

Goodman, G. S., & Clarke-Stewart, A. (1991). Suggestibility in children's testimony: Implications for sexual abuse investigations. In J. Doris (Ed.), *The suggestibility of children's recollections: Implications for eyewitness testimony.* Washington, DC: American Psychological Association.

Goodman, G. S., Quas, J. A., Batterman-Faunce, J. M., Riddlesberger, & Kuhn, J. (1994). Predictors of accurate and inaccurate memories of traumatic events experienced in childhood. *Consciousness and Cognition, 3,* 269–294.

Goodman, G. S., & Reed, R. S. (1986). Age differences in eyewitness testimony. *Law and Human Behavior, 10,* 317–332.

Greenbaum, J. L., & Graf, P. (1989). Preschool period development of implicit and explicit remembering. *Bulletin of the Psychonomic Society, 27,* 417–420.

Gruber, H., Renkl, A., & Schneider, W. (1994). Expertise und Gedächtnisentwicklung. Längsschnittliche Befunde aus der Domäne Schach [Expertise and memory development: Longitudinal findings from the chess domain]. *Zeitschrift für Entwicklungspsychologie und Pädagogische Psychologie, 26,* 53–70.

Guttentag, R. E. (1984). The mental effort requirement of cumulative rehearsal: A developmental study. *Journal of Experimental Child Psychology, 37,* 92–106.

Guttentag, R. E. (1989). Age differences in dual-task performance: Procedures, assumptions, and results. *Developmental Reviews, 9,* 146–170.

Guttentag, R. E. (1990). Issues in the study of age differences in forgetting. Commentary to Brainerd, Reyna, Howe, & Kingma, The development of forgetting and reminiscence. *Monographs of the Society for Research in Child Development, 55*(Serial No. 222).

Guttentag, R. E., & Lange, G. (1994). Motivational influences on children's strategic remembering. *Learning and Individual Differences, 6,* 309–330.

Guttentag, R. E., Ornstein, P. A., & Siemens, L. (1987). Children's spontaneous rehearsal: Transitions in strategy acquisition. *Cognitive Development, 2,* 307–326.

Hamond, N. R., & Fivush, R. (1991). Memories of Mickey Mouse: Young children recount their trip to Disneyworld. *Cognitive Development, 6,* 433–448.

Hanna, E., & Meltzoff, A. N. (1993). Peer imitation by toddlers in laboratory, home, and day care contexts: Implications for social learning and memory. *Developmental Psychology, 29,* 701–710.

Harnishfeger, K. K. (1995). The development of cognitive inhibition: Theories, definitions, and research evidence. In F. Dempster & C. Brainerd (Eds.), *New perspectives on interference and inhibition in cognition.* New York: Academic Press.

Harnishfeger, K. K., & Bjorklund, D. F. (1990a). Children's strategies: A brief history. In D. F. Bjorklund (Ed.), *Children's strategies: Contemporary views of cognitive development.* Hillsdale, NJ: Erlbaum.

Harnishfeger, K. K., & Bjorklund, D. F. (1990b). Memory functioning of gifted and nongifted middle school children. *Contemporary Educational Psychology, 15,* 346–363.

Harnishfeger, K. K., & Bjorklund, D. F. (1994). Individual differences in inhibition: Implications for children's cognitive development. *Learning and Individual Differences, 6,* 331–355.

Harnishfeger, K. K., & Brainerd, C. J. (1994). Nonstrategic facilitation of children's recall: Evidence of triage with semantically related information. *Journal of Experimental Child Psychology, 57,* 259–280.

Hasher, L., & Zacks, R. T. (1988). Working memory, comprehension, and aging: A review and a new view. In G. H. Bower (Ed.), *The psychology of learning and motivation: Advances in research and theory* (Vol. 22). San Diego, CA:

Hasselhorn, M. (1986). *Differentielle Bedingungsanalyse verbaler Gedächtnisleistungen bei Schulkindern* [Assessing the determinants of verbal memory performance in school children]. Frankfurt/Main: Lang.

Hasselhorn, M. (1992). Task dependency and the role of category typicality and metamemory in the development of an organizational strategy. *Child Development, 63,* 202–214.

Hasselhorn, M. (1995). Beyond production deficiency and utilization inefficiency: Mechanisms of the emergence of strategic categorization in episodic memory tasks. In F. E. Weinert & W. Schneider (Eds.), *Memory performance and competencies: Issues in growth and development.* Hillsdale, NJ: Erlbaum.

Hitch, G. J., & Halliday, M. S. (1983). Working memory in children. *Philosophical Transactions of the Royal Society, B302,* 324–340.

Hitch, G. J., & Towse, J. (1995). Working memory: What develops? In F. E. Weinert & W. Schneider (Eds.), *Research on memory development: State-of-the-art and future directions.* Hillsdale, NJ: Erlbaum.

Horobin, K., & Acredolo, L. (1986). The role of attentiveness, mobility history, and separation of hiding sites on Stage IV search behavior. *Journal of Experimental Child Psychology, 41,* 114–127.

Hoving, K. L., Spencer, T., Robb, K. Y., & Schulte, D. (1978). Developmental changes in visual information processing. In P. A. Ornstein (Ed.), *Memory development in children.* Hillsdale, NJ: Erlbaum.

Howe, M. L. (1987). *The development of forgetting in childhood.* Paper presented at the biennial meeting of the Society for Research in Child Development, Baltimore.

Howe, M. L. (1991). Misleading children's story recall: Forgetting and reminiscence of the facts. *Developmental Psychology, 27,* 746–762.

Howe, M. L. (1995). Interference effects in young children's long-term retention. *Developmental Psychology, 31,* 579–596.

Howe, M. L., & Brainerd, C. J. (1989). Development of long-term retention. *Developmental Review, 9,* 302–340.

Howe, M. L., Brainerd, C. J., & Kingma, J. (1985). Development of organization in recall: A stages-of-learning analysis. *Journal of Experimental Child Psychology, 39,* 230–251.

Howe, M. L., & Courage, M. L. (1993). On resolving the enigma of infantile amnesia. *Psychological Bulletin, 113,* 305–326.

Howe, M. L., Courage, M. L., & Bryant-Brown, L. (1993). Reinstating preschoolers' memories. *Developmental Psychology, 29,* 854–869.

Howe, M. L., Courage, M. L., & Peterson, C. (1994). How can I remember when "I" wasn't there: Long-term retention of traumatic experiences and emergence of the cognitive self. *Consciousness and Cognition, 3,* 327–355.

Howe, M. L., Courage, M. L., & Peterson, C. (1995). Intrusions in preschoolers' recall of traumatic childhood events. *Psychonomic Bulletin and Review, 2,* 130–134.

Howe, M. L., Kelland, A., Bryant-Brown, L., & Clark, S. L. (1992). Measuring the development of children's amnesia and hypermnesia. In M. L. Howe, C. J. Brainerd, & V. L. Reyna (Eds.), *Development of long-term retention.* New York: Springer.

Howe, M. L., & O'Sullivan, J. T. (1990). The development of strategic memory: Coordinating knowledge, metamemory, and resources. In D. F. Bjorklund (Ed.), *Children's strategies: Contemporary views of cognitive development.* Hillsdale, NJ: Erlbaum.

Hudson, J. A. (1990). The emergence of autobiographical memory in mother-child conversation. In R. Fivush & J. A. Hudson (Eds.), *Knowing and remembering in young children.* Cambridge, England: Cambridge University Press.

Hudson, J. A., & Nelson, K. (1983). Effects of script structure on children's story recall. *Developmental Psychology, 19,* 625–635.

Hulme, C., Thompson, N., Muir, C., & Lawrence, A. (1984). Speech rate and the development of spoken words: The role of rehearsal and item identification processes. *Journal of Experimental Child Psychology, 38,* 241–253.

Hyman, I. E., Husband, T. H., & Billings, F. J. (1995). False memories of childhood experiences. *Applied Cognitive Psychology, 9,* 181–197.

Istomina, Z. M. (1975). The development of voluntary memory in preschool-age children. *Soviet Psychology, 13,* 5–64.

Jacoby, L. L. (1991). A process dissociation framework: Separating automatic from intentional uses of memory. *Journal of Memory and Language, 30,* 513–541.

Jensen, A. R., Cohn, S. J., & Cohn, C. M. G. (1989). Speed of information processing in academically gifted youths and their siblings. *Personality and Individual Differences, 10,* 29–33.

Justice, E. M. (1985). Categorization as a preferred memory strategy: Developmental changes during elementary school. *Developmental Psychology, 21,* 1105–1110.

Justice, E. M. (1986). Developmental changes in judgments of relative strategy effectiveness. *British Journal of Developmental Psychology, 4,* 75–81.

Justice, E. M., & Bray, N. W. (1979). *The effects of context and feedback on metamemory in young children.* Paper presented at the biennial meeting of the Society for Research in Child Development, San Francisco.

Kail, R. V. (1979). Use of strategies and individual differences in children's memory. *Developmental Psychology, 15,* 251–255.

Kail, R. V. (1991). Development of processing speed in childhood and adolescence. In H. W. Reese (Ed.), *Advances in child development and behavior* (Vol. 23). San Diego, CA: Academic Press.

Kail, R. V., & Salthouse, T. A. (1994). Processing speed as a mental capacity. *Acta Psychologica, 86,* 199–225.

Kearins, J. M. (1981). Visual spatial memory in Australian aboriginal children of desert regions. *Cognitive Psychology, 13,* 434–460.

Kee, D. W. (1994). Developmental differences in associative memory: Strategy use, mental effort, and knowledge-access interaction. In H. W. Reese (Ed.), *Advances in child development and behavior* (Vol. 25). New York: Academic Press.

Kee, D. W., & Davis, L. (1988). Mental effort and elaboration: A developmental analysis. *Contemporary Educational Psychology, 13,* 221–228.

Kee, D. W., & Davis, L. (1990). Mental effort and elaboration: Effects of accessibility and instruction. *Journal of Experimental Child Psychology, 49,* 264–274.

Keniston, A. H., & Flavell, J. H. (1979). A developmental study of intelligent retrieval. *Child Development, 50,* 1144–1152.

Knopf, M., Körkel, J., Schneider, W., & Weinert, F. E. (1988). Human memory as a faculty versus human memory as a set of specific abilities: Evidence from a life-span approach. In F. E. Weinert & M. Perlmutter (Eds.), *Memory development: Universal changes and individual differences.* Hillsdale, NJ: Erlbaum.

Knopf, M., & Waldmann, M. R. (1991). Die Rolle von Ereignisschemata beim Lernen im Vorschulalter [The impact of event schemata on learning in preschoolers]. *Zeitschrift für Entwicklungspsychologie und Pädagogische Psychologie, 23,* 181–196.

Kobasigawa, A. (1974). Utilization of retrieval cues by children in recall. *Child Development, 45,* 127–134.

Kobasigawa, A. (1977). Retrieval strategies in the development of memory. In R. V. Kail & J. W. Hagen (Eds.), *Perspective on the development of memory and cognition.* Hillsdale, NJ: Erlbaum.

Körkel, J., & Schneider, W. (1992). Domain-specific versus metacognitive knowledge effects on text recall and comprehension. In M. Carretero, M. Pope, R. J. Simons, & J. I. Pozo (Eds.), *Learning and instruction—European research in an international context* (Vol. 3). New York: Pergamon Press.

Kranzler, J. H., Whang, P. A., & Jensen, A. R. (1994). Task complexity and the speed and efficiency of elemental information processing: Another look at the nature of intellectual giftedness. *Contemporary Educational Psychology, 19,* 447–459.

Kreutzer, M. A., Leonard, C., & Flavell, J. H. (1975). An interview study of children's knowledge about memory. *Monographs of the Society for Research in Child Development, 40*(Serial No. 159).

Kunzinger, E. L., & Witryol, S. L. (1984). The effects of differential incentives on second-grade rehearsal and free recall. *The Journal of Genetic Psychology, 144,* 19–30.

Kurtz, B. E. (1990). Cultural influences on children's cognitive and metacognitive development. In W. Schneider & F. E. Weinert (Eds.), *Interactions among aptitudes, strategies, and knowledge in cognitive performance.* New York: Springer-Verlag.

Kurtz, B. E., & Borkowski, J. G. (1984). Children's metacognition: Exploring relations among knowledge, process, and motivational variables. *Journal of Experimental Child Psychology, 37,* 335–354.

Kurtz, B. E., Schneider, W., Carr, M., Borkowski, J. G., & Rellinger, E. (1990). Strategy instruction and attributional beliefs in West Germany and the United States: Do teachers foster metacognitive development? *Contemporary Educational Psychology, 15,* 268–283.

Kurtz, B. E., & Weinert, F. E. (1989). Metamemory, memory performance, and causal attributions in gifted and average children. *Journal of Experimental Child Psychology, 48,* 45–61.

Kurtz-Costes, B. E., Schneider, W., & Rupp, S. (1995). Is there evidence for intraindividual consistency in performance across memory tasks? New evidence on an old question. In F. E. Weinert & W. Schneider (Eds.), *Research on memory development: State of the art and future directions.* Hillsdale, NJ: Erlbaum.

Lange, G. (1973). The development of conceptual and rote recall skills among school age children. *Journal of Experimental Child Psychology, 15,* 394–406.

Lange, G., Guttentag, R. E., & Nida, R. E. (1990). Relationships between study organization, retrieval organization, and general strategy-specific memory knowledge in young children. *Journal of Experimental Child Psychology, 49,* 126–146.

Lange, G., MacKinnon, C. E., & Nida, R. E. (1989). Knowledge, strategy, and motivational contributions to preschool children's object recall. *Developmental Psychology, 25,* 772–779.

Lange, G., & Pierce, S. H. (1992). Memory-strategy learning and maintenance in preschool children. *Developmental Psychology, 28,* 453–462.

Leal, L., Crays, N., & Moely, B. E. (1985). Training children to use a self-monitoring study strategy in preparation for recall: Maintenance and generalization effects. *Child Development, 56,* 643–653.

LeBlanc, R. S., Muise, J. G., & Blanchard, L. (1992). Backward masking in children and adolescents: Sensory transmission, accrual rate and asymptotic performance. *Journal of Experimental Child Psychology, 53,* 105–114.

Lecours, A. R. (1975). Myelogenetic correlates of the development of speech and language. In E. H. Lenneberg & E. Lenneberg (Eds.), *Foundations of language development: A multidisciplinary approach.* New York: Academic Press.

Leichtman, M. D., & Ceci, S. J. (1993). The problem of infantile amnesia: Lessons from fuzzy-trace theory. In M. L. Howe & R. Pasnak (Eds.), *Emerging themes in cognitive development: Vol. 1. Foundations.* New York: Springer-Verlag.

Lehman, E. B., Mikesell, J. W., & Doherty, S. C. (1985). Long-term retention of information about presentation modality by children and adults. *Memory and Cognition, 13,* 21–28.

Lerner. R. M. (1991). Changing organism-context relations as the basic process of development: A developmental contextual perspective. *Developmental Psychology, 27,* 27–32.

Lindberg, M. (1980). The role of knowledge structures in the ontogeny of learning. *Journal of Experimental Child Psychology, 30,* 401–410.

Loftus, E. F., & Ketcham, K. (1994). *The myth of repressed memory.* New York: St. Martin's Press.

Loftus, E. F., & Loftus, G. R. (1980). On the permanence of stored information in the human brain. *American Psychologist, 35,* 409–420.

Loftus, E. F., & Pickrell, J. E. (1995). The formation of false memories. *Psychiatric Annals, 25,* 720–725.

Loughlin, K. A., & Daehler, M. A. (1973). The effects of distraction and added perceptual cues on the delayed reaction of very young children. *Child Development, 44,* 384–388.

Mandler, J. M., & McDonough, L. (1995). Long-term recall of event sequences in infancy. *Journal of Experimental Child Psychology, 59,* 457–474.

Mandler, J. M., Scribner, S., Cole, M., & De Forest, M. (1980). Cross-cultural invariance in story recall. *Child Development, 51,* 19–26.

Markman, E. M. (1973). *Factors affecting the young child's ability to monitor his memory.* Unpublished doctoral dissertation, University of Pennsylvania, Philadelphia.

Masur, E. F., McIntyre, C. W., & Flavell, J. H. (1973). Developmental changes in apportionment of study time among items in a multitrial free recall task. *Journal of Experimental Child Psychology, 15,* 237–246.

McCall, R. B., & Carriger, M. S. (1993). A meta-analysis of infant habituation and recognition memory performance as predictors of later IQ. *Child Development, 64,* 57–79.

McDonough, L., & Mandler, J. M. (1994). Very long-term recall in infants: Infantile amnesia reconsidered. *Memory, 2,* 339–352.

McDonough, L., Mandler, J. M., McKee, R. D., & Squire, L. R. (1995). The deferred imitation task as a nonverbal measure of declarative memory. *Proceedings of the National Academy of Sciences, 92,* 7580–7584.

McGilly, K., & Siegler, R. S. (1989). How children choose among serial recall strategies. *Child Development, 60,* 172–182.

McGilly, K., & Siegler, R. S. (1990). The influence of encoding strategic knowledge on children's choices among serial recall strategies. *Developmental Psychology, 26,* 931–941.

Means, M., & Voss, J. (1985). Star wars: A developmental study of expert and novice knowledge structures. *Memory and Language, 24,* 746–757.

Meltzoff, A. N. (1985). Immediate and deferred imitation in fourteen- and twenty-four-month-old infants. *Child Development, 56,* 62–72.

Meltzoff, A. N. (1988a). Infant imitation after a 1-week delay: Long-term memory for novel acts and multiple stimuli. *Developmental Psychology, 24,* 470–476.

Meltzoff, A. N. (1988b). Infant imitation and memory: Nine-month-olds in immediate and deferred tests. *Child Development, 59,* 217–225.

Meltzoff, A. N. (1995). What infant memory tells us about infantile amnesia: Long-term recall and deferred imitation. *Journal of Experimental Child Psychology, 59*, 497–515.

Merriman, W. E., Azmita, M., & Perlmutter, M. (1988). Rate of forgetting in early childhood. *International Journal of Behavioral Development, 11*, 467–474.

Miller, P. H. (1990). The development of strategies of selective attention. In D. F. Bjorklund (Ed.), *Children's strategies: Contemporary views of cognitive development.* Hillsdale, NJ: Erlbaum.

Miller, P. H. (1994). Individual differences in children's strategic behavior: Utilization deficiencies. *Learning and Individual Differences, 6*, 285–307

Miller, P. H., Haynes, V. F., DeMarie-Dreblow, D., & Woody-Ramsey, J. (1986). Children's strategies for gathering information in three tasks. *Child Development, 57*, 1429–1439.

Miller, P. H., & Seier, W. L. (1994). Strategy utilization deficiencies in children: When, where, and why. In H. W. Reese (Ed.), *Advances in child development and behavior* (Vol. 25). New York: Academic Press.

Miller, P. H., Seier, W. L., Probert, J. S., & Aloise, P. A. (1991). Age differences in the capacity demands of a strategy among spontaneously strategic children. *Journal of Experimental Child Psychology, 52*, 149–165.

Mistry, J. J., & Lange, G. W. (1985). Children's organization and recall of information in scripted narratives. *Child Development, 56*, 953–961.

Moely, B. E., Hart, S. S., Leal, L., Santulli, K. A., Rao, N., Johnson, T., & Hamilton, L. B. (1992). The teacher's role in facilitating memory and study strategy development in the elementary school classroom. *Child Development, 63*, 653–672.

Moely, B. E., Hart, S. S., Santulli, K., Leal, L., Johnson, T., Rao, N., & Burney, L. (1986). How do teachers teach memory skills? *Educational Psychologist, 21*, 55–71.

Moely, B. E., Olson, F. A., Halwes, T. G., & Flavell, J. H. (1969). Production deficiency in young children's clustered recall. *Developmental Psychology, 1*, 26–34.

Moely, B. E., Santulli, K. A., & Obach, M. S. (1995). Strategy instruction, metacognition, and motivation in the elementary school classroom. In F. E. Weinert & W. Schneider (Eds.), *Memory performance and competencies: Issues in growth and development.* Hillsdale, NJ: Erlbaum.

Morrison, F. J., Haith, M., & Kagan, J. (1980). Age trends in recognition memory for pictures: The effects of delay and testing procedures. *Bulletin of the Psychonomic Society, 16*, 480–483.

Moynahan, E. D. (1978). Assessment and selection of paired associate strategies: A developmental study. *Journal of Experimental Child Psychology, 26*, 257–266.

Muir-Broaddus, J., Rorer, R., Braden, T., & George, C. (1995). The effects of a knowledge base manipulation on individual differences in processing speed and recall. *Contemporary Educational Psychology, 20*, 403–409.

Myers, N. A., Clifton, R. K., & Clarkson, M. G. (1987). When they were very young: Almost threes remember two years ago. *Infant Behavior and Development, 10*, 123–132.

Naito, M. (1990). Repetition priming in children and adults: Age-related dissociation between implicit and explicit memory. *Journal of Experimental Child Psychology, 50*, 462–484.

Naus, M. J., Ornstein, P. A., & Aivano, S. (1977). Developmental changes in memory: The effects of processing time and rehearsal instructions. *Journal of Experimental Child Psychology, 23*, 237–251.

Neisser, U. (1962). Cultural and cognitive discontinuity. In T. E. Gladwin & W. Sturtevant (Eds.), *Anthropology and human behavior.* Washington, DC: Anthropological Society of Washington.

Nelson, K. (1986). Event knowledge and cognitive development. In K. Nelson (Ed.), *Event knowledge: Structure and function in development.* Hillsdale, NJ: Erlbaum.

Nelson, K. (1993). The psychological and social origins of autobiographical memory. *Psychological Science, 4*, 7–14.

Nelson, K. (1994). Long-term retention of memory for preverbal experience: Evidence and implications. *Memory, 2*, 467–475.

Nelson, K., & Hudson, J. (1988). Scripts and memory: Functional relationship in development. In F. E. Weinert & M. Perlmutter (Eds.), *Memory development: Universal changes and individual differences.* Hillsdale, NJ: Erlbaum.

Nelson, K., & Ross, G. (1980). The generalities and specifics of long-term memory in infants and young children. In M. Perlmutter (Ed.), *New directions for child development: Children's memory.* San Francisco: Jossey-Bass.

Nelson, T. O. (Ed.). (1992). *Metacognition: Core readings.* Boston: Allyn & Bacon.

Nelson, T. O., & Narens, L. (1994). Why investigate metacognition? In J. Metcalfe & A. P. Shimamura (Eds.), *Metacognition—Knowing about knowing.* Cambridge: MIT Press.

Newcombe, N., & Fox, N. A. (1994). Infantile amnesia: Through a glass darkly. *Child Development, 65*, 31–40.

Newman, L. S. (1990). Intentional and unintentional memory in young children: Remembering vs. playing. *Journal of Experimental Child Psychology, 50*, 243–258.

Ornstein, P. A., Baker-Ward, L., & Naus, M. J. (1988). The development of mnemonic skill. In F. E. Weinert & M. Perlmutter (Eds.), *Memory development: Universal changes and individual differences.* Hillsdale, NJ: Erlbaum.

Ornstein, P. A., Gordon, B. N., & Larus, D. M. (1992). Children's memory for a personally experienced event:

Implications for testimony. *Applied Developmental Psychology, 6,* 49–60.

Ornstein, P. A., Hale, G. A., & Morgan, J. S. (1977). Developmental differences in recall and output organization. *Bulletin of the Psychonomic Society, 9,* 29–32.

Ornstein, P. A., & Naus, M. J. (1985). Effects of the knowledge base on children's memory strategies. In H. W. Reese (Ed.), *Advances in child development and behavior* (Vol. 19). New York: Academic Press.

Ornstein, P. A., Naus, M. J., & Liberty, C. (1975). Rehearsal and organizational processes in children's memory. *Child Development, 46,* 818–830.

Ornstein, P. A., Shapiro, L. R., Clubb, P. A., Follmer, A., & Baker-Ward, L. (1996). The influence of prior knowledge on children's memory for salient medical experiences. In N. Stein, P. A. Ornstein, C. J. Brainerd, & B. Tversky (Eds.), *Memory for everyday and emotional events.* Hillsdale, NJ: Erlbaum.

Palincsar, A. S., & Brown, A. L. (1984). Reciprocal teaching of comprehension-fostering and comprehension-monitoring activities. *Cognition and Instruction, 1,* 117–175.

Paris, S. G. (1988). Motivated remembering. In F. E. Weinert & M. Perlmutter (Eds.), *Memory development: Universal changes and individual differences.* Hillsdale, NJ: Erlbaum.

Paris, S. G., & Lindauer, B. K. (1982). The development of cognitive skills during childhood. In B. Wolman (Ed.), *Handbook of developmental psychology.* Englewood Cliffs, NJ: Prentice-Hall.

Paris, S. G., Newman, R. S., & McVey, K. A. (1982). Learning the functional significance of mnemonic actions: A microgenetic study of strategy acquisition. *Journal of Experimental Child Psychology, 34,* 490–509.

Paris, S. G., & Oka, E. R. (1986). Children's reading strategies, metacognition, and motivation. *Developmental Review, 6,* 25–56.

Parkin, A. J. (1993). *Memory: Phenomena, experiment and theory.* Oxford, England: Blackwell.

Parkin, A. J., & Streete, S. (1988). Implicit and explicit memory in young children and adults. *British Journal of Psychology, 79,* 361–369.

Perlmutter, M. (1984). Continuities and discontinuities in early human memory paradigms, processes, and performance. In R. V. Kail & N. E. Spear (Eds.), *Comparative perspectives on the development of memory.* Hillsdale, NJ: Erlbaum.

Perlmutter, M. (1988). Research on memory and its development: Past, present, and future. In F. E. Weinert & M. Perlmutter (Eds.), *Memory development: Universal changes and individual differences.* Hillsdale, NJ: Erlbaum.

Perrig, W. J., & Perrig, P. (1993). Implizites Gedächtnis: Unwillkürlich, entwicklungsresistent und altersunabhängig? [Implicit memory: Unconscious, developmentally invariant, and age-independent?] *Zeitschrift für Entwicklungspsychologie und Pädagogische Psychologie, 25,* 29–47.

Perris, E. E., Myers, N. A., & Clifton, R. K. (1990). Long-term memory for a single infancy experience. *Child Development, 61,* 1796–1807.

Piaget, J. (1952). *The origins of intelligence in children.* New York: Norton.

Piaget, J. (1962). *Play, dreams, and imitation in childhood.* New York: Norton.

Piaget, J. (1983). Piaget's theory. In P. H. Mussen (Gen. Ed.) & J. H. Flavell & E. M. Markman (Eds.), *Cognitive development: Vol. 3. Handbook of child psychology* (4th ed.). New York: Wiley.

Piaget, J., & Inhelder, B. (1973). *Memory and intelligence.* New York: Basic Books.

Poole, D. A. (1995). Strolling fuzzy-trace theory through eyewitness testimony (or vice versa). *Learning and Individual Differences, 7,* 87–93.

Poole, D. A., & Lindsay, D. S. (1995). Interviewing preschoolers: Effects of nonsuggestive techniques, parental coaching and leading questions on reports of nonexperienced events. *Journal of Experimental Child Psychology, 60,* 129–154.

Poole, D. A., & White, L. T. (1991). Effects of question repetition on the eyewitness testimony of children and adults. *Developmental Psychology, 27,* 975–986.

Poole, D. A., & White, L. T. (1993). Two-years later: Effects of question repetition and retention interval on the eyewitness testimony of children and adults. *Developmental Psychology, 29,* 844–853.

Posnansky, C. J. (1978). Age- and task-related differences in the use of category-size information for the retrieval of categorized items. *Journal of Experimental Child Psychology, 26,* 373–382.

Pressley, M. (1982). Elaboration and memory development. *Child Development, 53,* 296–309.

Pressley, M. (1994). Embracing the complexity of individual differences in cognition: Studying good information processing and how it might develop. *Learning and Individual Differences, 6,* 259–284.

Pressley, M. (with McCormick, C.). (1995a). *Advanced educational psychology.* New York: HarperCollins.

Pressley, M. (1995b). What is intellectual development about in the 1990s? Not strategies!: Good information processing, not strategies instruction!: Instruction cultivating good information processing. In F. E. Weinert & W. Schneider (Eds.),

Memory performance and competencies: Issues in growth and development. Hillsdale, NJ: Erlbaum.

Pressley, M., & Afflerbach, P. (1995). *Verbal protocols of reading: The nature of constructively responsive reading.* Hillsdale, NJ: Erlbaum.

Pressley, M., Borkowski, J. G., & O'Sullivan, J. T. (1985). Children's metamemory and the teaching of memory strategies. In D. L. Forrest-Pressley, G. E. MacKinnon, & T. G. Waller (Eds.), *Metacognition, cognition, and human performance* (Vol. 1). Orlando, FL: Academic Press.

Pressley, M., Borkowski, J. G., & Schneider, W. (1987). Cognitive strategies: Good strategy users coordinate metacognition and knowledge. In R. Vasta & G. Whitehurst (Eds.), *Annals of child development* (Vol. 5). New York: JAI Press.

Pressley, M., Borkowski, J. G., & Schneider, W. (1989). Good information processing: What is it and what education can do to promote it. *International Journal of Educational Research, 13,* 857–867.

Pressley, M., Forrest-Pressley, D. J., Elliott-Faust, D. J., & Miller, G. E. (1985). Children's use of cognitive strategies, how to teach strategies, and what to do if they can't be taught. In M. Pressley & C. J. Brainerd (Eds.), *Cognitive learning and memory in children.* New York: Springer.

Pressley, M., & Ghatala, E. S. (1990). Self-regulated learning: Monitoring learning from text. *Educational Psychologist, 25,* 19–34.

Pressley, M., & Levin, J. R. (1977). Task parameters affecting the efficacy of a visual imagery learning strategy in younger and older children. *Journal of Experimental Child Psychology, 24,* 53–59.

Pressley, M., Levin, J. R., Ghatala, E. S., & Ahmad, M. (1987). Test monitoring in young grade school children. *Journal of Experimental Child Psychology, 43,* 96–111.

Pressley, M., & MacFadyen, J. (1983). Mnemonic mediator retrieval at testing by preschool and kindergarten children. *Child Development, 54,* 474–479.

Pressley, M., & Van Meter, P. (1993). Memory strategies: Natural development and use following instruction. In R. Pasnak & M. L. Howe (Eds.), *Emerging themes in cognitive development: Vol. 2. Competencies.* New York: Springer.

Price, D. W. W., & Goodman, G. S. (1990). Visiting the wizard: Children's memory for a recurring event. *Child Development, 61,* 664–680.

Rabinowitz, M. (1984). The use of categorical organization: Not an all-or-none situation. *Journal of Experimental Child Psychology, 38,* 338–351.

Rabinowitz, M., & Chi, M. T. H. (1987). An interactive model of strategic processing. In S. J. Ceci (Ed.), *Handbook of the cognitive, social, and physiological characteristics of learning disabilities* (Vol. 2). Hillsdale, NJ: Erlbaum.

Rabinowitz, M., Freeman, K., & Cohen, S. (1992). Use and maintenance of strategies. The influence of accessibility to knowledge. *Journal of Educational Psychology, 84,* 211–218.

Rabinowitz, M., & Kee, D. (1994). A framework for understanding individual differences in memory: Strategy-knowledge interactions. In P. A. Vernon (Ed.), *Handbook of neuropsychology of individual differences.* New York: Academic Press.

Ratner, H. H. (1984). Memory demands and the development of young children's memory. *Child Development, 55,* 2173–2191.

Ratner, H. H., & Foley, M. A. (1994). A unifying framework for the development of children's activity memory. In H. W. Reese (Ed.), *Advances in child development and behavior* (Vol. 25). New York: Academic Press.

Ratner, H. H., & Myers, N. A. (1980). Related picture cues and memory for hidden-object location at age two. *Child Development, 51,* 561–564.

Recht, D. R., & Leslie, L. (1988). Effect of prior knowledge on good and poor readers' memory of text. *Journal of Educational Psychology, 80,* 16–20.

Reese, E., Haden, C. A., & Fivush, R. (1993). Mother-child conversations about the past: Relationships of style and memory over time. *Cognitive Development, 8,* 403–430.

Reese, E., Haden, C. A., & Fivush, R. (1996). Mothers, fathers, daughters, sons: Gender differences in autobiographical reminiscing. *Research on Language and Social Interaction, 29,* 27–56.

Reese, H. W. (1962). Verbal mediation as a function of age level. *Psychological Bulletin, 59,* 502–509.

Reese, H. W. (1977). Imagery and associative memory. In R. V. Kail & J. W. Hagen (Eds.), *Perspectives on the development of memory and cognition.* Hillsdale, NJ: Erlbaum.

Renninger, A., Hidi, S., & Krapp, A. (Eds.). (1992). *The role of interest in learning and development.* Hillsdale, NJ: Erlbaum.

Reyna, V. F. (1995). Interference effects in memory and reasoning: A fuzzy-trace theory analysis. In F. N. Dempster & C. J. Brainerd (Eds.), *New perspectives on interference and inhibition processes in cognition.* San Diego, CA: Academic Press.

Reyna, V. F., & Brainerd, C. J. (1991). Fuzzy-trace theory and children's acquisition of mathematical and scientific concepts. *Learning and Individual Differences, 3,* 27–59.

Reyna, V. F., & Brainerd, C. J. (1995). Fuzzy-trace theory: An interim synthesis. *Learning and Individual Differences, 7,* 1–75.

Reyna, V. F., & Kiernan, B. (1994). Development of gist versus verbatim memory in sentence recognition: Effects of lexical familiarity, semantic content, encoding instructions, and retention interval. *Developmental Psychology, 30,* 178–191.

Ritter, K. (1978). The development of knowledge of an external retrieval cue strategy. *Child Development, 49,* 1227–1230.

Ritter, K., Kaprove, B. H., Fitch, J. P., & Flavell, J. H. (1973). The development of retrieval strategies in young children. *Cognitive Psychology, 5,* 310–321.

Roenker, D. L., Thompson, C. P., & Brown, S. C. (1969). Comparison of measures for the estimation of clustering in free recall. *Psychological Bulletin, 76,* 45–48.

Rogoff, B. (1981). Schooling and development of cognitive skills. In H. C. Triandis & A. Heron (Eds.), *Handbook of cross-cultural psychology* (Vol. 4). Boston: Allyn & Bacon.

Rogoff, B, (1990). *Apprenticeship in thinking: Cognitive development in social context.* New York: Oxford University Press.

Rogoff, B., & Mistry, J. J. (1990). The social and functional context of children's remembering. In R. Fivush & J. A. Hudson (Eds.), *Knowing and remembering in young children.* Cambridge, England: Cambridge University Press.

Rogoff, B., Mistry, J., Göncü, A., & Mosier, C. (1993). Guided participation in cultural activity by toddlers and caregivers. *Monographs of the Society for Research in Child Development, 58*(Serial No. 236).

Rogoff, B., & Waddell, K. J. (1982). Memory of information organized in a scene by children from two cultures. *Child Development, 53,* 1224–1228.

Rohwer, W. D., Jr. (1973). Elaboration and learning in childhood and adolescence. In H. W. Reese (Ed.), *Advances in child development and behavior* (Vol. 8). New York: Academic Press.

Rohwer, W. D., Jr. (1980). An elaborative conception of learner differences. In R. E. Snow, P. A. Federico, & W. E. Montague (Eds.), *Aptitude, learning, and instruction: Vol. 2. Cognitive process analyses of learning and problem.* Hillsdale, NJ: Erlbaum.

Rose, S. A., Feldman, J. F., & Wallace, I. F. (1992). Infant information processing in relation to six-year cognitive outcomes. *Child Development, 63,* 1126–1141.

Roth, C. (1983). Factors affecting developmental changes in the speed of processing. *Journal of Experimental Child Psychology, 35,* 509–528.

Rovee-Collier, C., & Boller, K. (1995). Interference or facilitation in infant memory? In C. J. Brainerd & F. N. Dempster (Eds.), *Interference and inhibition in cognition.* San Diego, CA: Academic Press.

Rovee-Collier, C., & Fagen, J. W. (1981). The retrieval of memory in early infancy. In L. P. Lipsitt & C. K. Rovee-Collier (Eds.), *Advances in infancy research* (Vol. 1). Norwood, NJ: ABLEX.

Rovee-Collier, C., Schechter, A., Shyi, C.-W. G., & Shields, P. (1992). Perceptual identification of contextual attributed and infant memory retrieval. *Developmental Psychology, 28,* 307–318.

Rovee-Collier, C., & Shyi, C.-W. G. (1992). A functional and cognitive analysis of infant long-term retention. In M. L. Howe, C. J. Brainerd, & V. F. Reyna (Eds.), *Development of long-term retention.* New York: Springer-Verlag.

Rovee-Collier, C., Sullivan, M. W., Enright, M., Lucas, D., & Fagen, J. W. (1980). Reactivation of infant memory. *Science, 208,* 1159–1161.

Rudy, L., & Goodman, G. S. (1991). Effects of participation on children's reports: Implications for children's testimony. *Developmental Psychology, 27,* 527–538.

Russo, R., Nichelli, P., Gibertoni, M., & Cornia, C. (1995). Developmental trends in implicit and explicit memory: A picture completion study. *Journal of Experimental Child Psychology, 60,* 566–578.

Schacter, D. L. (1992). Understanding implicit memory. *American Psychologist, 47,* 559–569.

Schneider, W. (1985). Developmental trends in the metamemory-memory behavior relationship: An integrative review. In D. L. Forrest-Pressley, G. E. MacKinnon, & T. G. Waller (Eds.), *Cognition, metacognition, and human performance* (Vol. 1). Orlando, FL: Academic Press.

Schneider, W. (1986). The role of conceptual knowledge and metamemory in the development of organizational processes in memory. *Journal of Experimental Child Psychology, 42,* 218–236.

Schneider, W. (1993a). Acquiring expertise: Determinants of exceptional performance. In K. A. Heller, F. J. Mönks, & A. H. Passow (Eds.), *International handbook of research and development of giftedness and talent.* Oxford, England: Pergamon Press.

Schneider, W. (1993b). Domain-specific knowledge and memory performance in children. *Educational Psychology Review, 5,* 257–273.

Schneider, W., & Bjorklund, D. F. (1992). Expertise, aptitude, and strategic remembering. *Child Development, 63,* 461–473.

Schneider, W., Bjorklund, D. F., & Maier-Brückner, W. (1996). The effects of expertise and IQ on children's memory: When knowledge is, and when it is not enough. *International Journal of Behavioral Development, 19,* 773–796.

Schneider, W., Borkowski, J. G., Kurtz, B. E., & Kerwin, K. (1986). Metamemory and motivation: A comparison of strategy use and performance in German and American children. *Journal of Cross-Cultural Psychology, 17,* 315–336.

Schneider, W., Bös, K., & Rieder, H. (1993). Leistungsprognose bei jugendlichen Spitzensportlern [Performance prediction in adolescent top tennis players]. In J. Beckmann, H. Strang, & E. Hahn (Eds.), *Aufmerksamkeit und Energetisierung.* Göttingen: Hogrefe.

Schneider, W., & Brun, H. (1987). The role of context in young children's memory performance: Istomina revisited. *British Journal of Developmental Psychology, 5,* 333–341.

Schneider, W., Gruber, H., Gold, A., & Opwis, K. (1993). Chess expertise and memory for chess positions in children and adults. *Journal of Experimental Child Psychology, 56,* 328–349.

Schneider, W., & Hasselhorn, M. (1994). Situational context features and early memory development: Insights from replications of Istomina's experiment. In R. van der Veer, M. Van IJzendoorn, & J. Valsiner (Eds.), *Reconstructing the mind: Replications in research on human development.* Norwood, NJ: ABLEX.

Schneider, W., & Körkel, J. (1989). The knowledge base and text recall: Evidence from a short-term longitudinal study. *Contemporary Educational Psychology, 14,* 382–393.

Schneider, W., Körkel, J., & Vogel, K. (1987). Zusammenhänge zwischen Metagedächtnis, strategischem Verhalten und Gedächtnisleistungen im Grundschulalter: Eine entwicklungspsychologische Studie [Relationships among metamemory, strategic behavior, and memory performance in school children: A developmental study]. *Zeitschrift für Entwicklungspsychologie und Pädagogische Psychologie, 19,* 99–115.

Schneider, W., Körkel, J., & Weinert, F. E. (1987). The effects of intelligence, self-concept, and attributional style on metamemory and memory behavior. *International Journal of Behavioral Development, 10,* 281–299.

Schneider, W., Körkel, J., & Weinert, F. E. (1989). Domain-specific knowledge and memory performance: A comparison of high- and low-aptitude children. *Journal of Educational Psychology, 81,* 306–312.

Schneider, W., & Pressley, M. (1989). *Memory development between 2 and 20.* (1st ed.) New York: Springer.

Schneider, W., & Pressley, M. (1997). *Memory development between 2 and 20* (2nd ed). Mahwah, NJ: Erlbaum.

Schneider, W., & Sodian, B. (1988). Metamemory-memory behavior relationships in young children: Evidence from a memory-for-location task. *Journal of Experimental Child Psychology, 45,* 209–233.

Schneider, W., & Sodian, B. (1991). A longitudinal study of young children's memory behavior and performance in a sort-recall task. *Journal of Experimental Child Psychology, 51,* 14–29.

Schneider, W., & Uhl, C. (1990). Metagedächtnis, Strategienutzung und Gedächtnisleistung: Vergleichende Analysen bei Kinder, Jüngeren Erwachsenen und altern Mecnschen [Metamemory, strategy use, and memory performance: A comparison among children, young adults, and the elderly.] *Zeitschrift für Entwicklungspsychologie und Pädagogische Psychologie, 22,* 22–41.

Schneider, W., & Weinert, F. E. (1990). The role of knowledge, strategies, and aptitudes in cognitive performance. In W. Schneider & F. E. Weinert (Eds.), *Interactions among aptitudes, strategies, and knowledge in cognitive performance.* New York: Springer-Verlag.

Schneider, W., & Weinert, F. E. (1995). Memory development during early and middle childhood: Findings from the Munich longitudinal study (LOGIC). In F. E. Weinert & W. Schneider (Eds.), *Memory performance and competencies: Issues in growth and development.* Hillsdale, NJ: Erlbaum.

Schumann-Hengsteler, R. (1992). The development of visuospatial memory: How to remember location. *International Journal of Behavioral Development, 15,* 455–471.

Schumann-Hengsteler, R. (1996). Children's and adults' visuospatial memory: The game Concentration. *Journal of Genetic Psychology, 157,* 77–92.

Scruggs, T. E., & Mastropieri, M. (1988). Acquisition and transfer of learning strategies by gifted and nongifted learners. *Journal of the Education of the Gifted, 9,* 105–121.

Sharp, D., Cole, M., & Lave, C. (1979). Education and cognitive development: The evidence from experimental research. *Monographs of the Society for Research in Child Development, 44*(Serial No. 178).

Sheingold, K. (1973). Developmental differences in intake and storage of visual information. *Journal of Experimental Child Psychology, 16,* 1–11.

Sheingold, K., & Tenney, Y. (1982). Memory for a salient childhood event. In U. Neisser (Ed.), *Memory observed: Remembering in natural contexts.* San Francisco: Freeman.

Short, E. J., & Ryan, E. B. (1984). Metacognitive differences between skilled and less skilled readers: Remediating deficits through story grammar and attribution training. *Journal of Educational Psychology, 76,* 225–235.

Siaw, S. N., & Kee, D. W. (1987). Development of elaboration and organization in different socioeconomic-status and ethnic populations. In M. A. McDaniel & M. Pressley (Eds.), *Imagery and related mnemonic processes: Theories, individual differences, and applications.* New York: Springer-Verlag.

Siegel, L. S. (1993). The cognitive basis of dyslexia. In R. Pasnak & M. L. Howe (Eds.), *Emerging themes in cognitive development: Vol. 2. Competencies.* New York: Springer-Verlag.

Siegel, L. S., & Ryan, E. B. (1989). The development of working memory in normally achieving and subtypes of learning disabled children. *Child Development, 60,* 973–980.

Siegler, R. S. (1987). The perils of averaging data over strategies: An example from children's addition. *Journal of Experimental Psychology: General, 116,* 250–264.

Siegler, R. S. (1995). Children's thinking: How does change occur. In W. Schneider & F. E. Weinert (Eds.), *Memory performance and competencies: Issues in growth and development.* Hillsdale, NJ: Erlbaum.

Siegler, R. S. (1996). *Emerging minds: The process of change in children's thinking.* New York: Oxford University Press.

Siegler, R. S., & Jenkins, E. (1989). *How children discover strategies.* Hillsdale, NJ: Erlbaum.

Slater, A., Mattock, A., Brown, E., & Bremner, G. J. (1991). Form perception at birth: Cohen and Younger revisited. *Journal of Experimental Child Psychology, 51,* 395–406.

Sodian, B., & Schneider, W. (in press). Memory strategy development—Gradual increase, sudden insight or roller coaster? In F. E. Weinert & W. Schneider (Eds.), *Individual development from 3 to 12: Findings from the Munich Longitudinal Study.* Cambridge, England: Cambridge University Press.

Somerville, S. C., Wellman, H. M., & Cultice, J. C. (1983). Young children's deliberate reminding. *The Journal of Genetic Psychology, 143,* 87–96.

Sophian, C., & Wellman, H. M. (1983). Selective information use and preservation in the search behavior of infants and young children. *Journal of Experimental Child Psychology, 35,* 369–390.

Spear, N. E. (1984). Ecologically determined dispositions control the ontogeny of learning and memory. In R. V. Kail, Jr., & N. E. Spear (Eds.), *Comparative perspectives on the development of memory.* Hillsdale, NJ: Erlbaum.

Sperling, G. (1960). The information available in brief visual presentations. *Psychological Monographs, 74*(No. 11).

Squire, L. R. (1992). Memory and the hippocampus: A synthesis from findings with rats, monkeys, and humans. *Psychological Review, 99,* 195–231.

Squire, L. R., Knowlton, B., & Musen, G. (1993). The structure and organization of memory. *Annual Review of Psychology, 44,* 453–495.

Stein, N. L., Wade, E., & Liwag, M. D. (1996). A theoretical approach to understanding and remembering emotional events. In N. L. Stein, P. A. Ornstein, B. Tversky, & C. J. Brainerd (Eds.), *Memory for everyday and emotional events.* Hillsdale, NJ: Erlbaum.

Sternberg, R. J. (1985). *Beyond IQ: A triarchic theory of human intelligence.* Cambridge, England: Cambridge University Press.

Stevenson, H. W., Hale, G. A., Klein, R. E., & Miller, L. K. (1968). Interrelations and correlates in children's learning and problem solving. *Monographs of the Society for Research in Child Development, 33*(Serial No. 123).

Stipek, D. (1984). Young children's performance expectations: Logical analysis or wishful thinking? In J. G. Nicholls (Ed.), *Advances in motivation and achievement: Vol. 3. The development of achievement motivation.* Greenwich, CT: JAI Press.

Thompson, L. A., Fagan, J. F., & Fulker, D. W. (1991). Longitudinal prediction of specific cognitive abilities from infant novelty preference. *Child Development, 62,* 530–538.

Tulving, E. (1985). Memory and consciousness. *Canadian Psychology, 26,* 1–12.

Underwood, B. J. (1964). Degree of learning and the measurement of forgetting. *Journal of Verbal Learning and Verbal Behavior, 3,* 112–129.

Vander Linde, E., Morrongiello, B. A., & Rovee-Collier, C. (1985). Determinants of retention in 8-week-old infants. *Developmental Psychology, 21,* 601–613.

Vertes, J. O. (1913). Das Wortgedächtnis im Schulkindesalter [Memory for words in school children]. *Zeitschrift für Psychologie, 63,* 19–128.

Vygotsky, L. S. (1962). *Thought and language.* Cambridge, MA: MIT Press.

Vygotsky, L. S. (1978). *The mind in society: The development of higher psychological processes.* Cambridge, MA: Harvard University Press.

Wagner, D. A. (1981). Culture and memory development. In H. C. Triandis & A. Heron (Eds.), *Handbook of cross-cultural psychology* (Vol. 4). Boston: Allyn & Bacon.

Walker, C. H. (1987). Relative importance of domain knowledge and overall aptitude on acquisition of domain-related information. *Cognition and Instruction, 4,* 25–42.

Wang, A. Y. (1991). Assessing developmental differences in retention. *Journal of Experimental Child Psychology, 51,* 348–363.

Waters, H. S., & Andreassen, C. (1983). Children's use of memory strategies under instruction. In J. R. Levin & M. Pressley (Eds.), *Cognitive strategy research: Psychological foundations.* New York: Springer-Verlag.

Weinert, F. E. (1986). Developmental variations of memory performance and memory-related knowledge across the life-span. In A. Sörensen, F. E. Weinert, & L. R. Sherrod (Eds.), *Human development: Multidisciplinary perspectives.* Hillsdale, NJ: Erlbaum.

Weinert, F. E. (1988). Epilogue. In F. E. Weinert & M. Perlmutter (Eds.), *Memory development: Universal changes and individual differences.* Hillsdale, NJ: Erlbaum.

Weinert, F. E., & Schneider, W. (Eds.). (1986). *First report on the Munich Longitudinal Study on the Genesis of Individual Competencies (LOGIC).* Munich: Max Planck Institute for Psychological Research.

Weinert, F. E., & Schneider, W. (Eds.). (1992). *The Munich Longitudinal Study on the Genesis of Individual Development (LOGIC), Report No. 8: Results of wave 6* (Tech. Rep.). Munich: Max Planck Institute for Psychological Research.

Weinert, F. E., & Schneider, W. (Eds.). (1995). *Memory performance and competencies: Issues on growth and development.* Hillsdale, NJ: Erlbaum.

Weinert, F. E., Schneider, W., & Knopf, M. (1988). Individual differences in memory development across the life-span. In P. B. Baltes, D. L. Featherman, & R. M. Lerner (Eds.), *Life-span development and behavior* (Vol. 9). Hillsdale, NJ: Erlbaum.

Weissberg, J. A., & Paris, S. G. (1986). Young children's remembering in different contexts: A reinterpretation of Istomina's study. *Child Development, 57,* 1123–1129.

Wellman, H. M. (1977). Preschoolers' understanding of memory-relevant variables. *Child Development, 48,* 1720–1723

Wellman, H. M. (1983). Metamemory revisited. In M. T. H. Chi (Ed.), *Trends in memory development research.* Basel: Karger.

Wellman, H. M. (1985). A child's theory of mind: The development of conceptions of cognition. In S. R. Yussen (Ed.), *The growth of reflection in children.* New York: Academic Press.

Wellman, H. M. (1988). The early development of memory strategies. In F. E. Weinert & M. Perlmutter (Eds.), *Memory development: Universal changes and individual differences.* Hillsdale, NJ: Erlbaum.

White, S. H., & Pillemer, D. B. (1979). Childhood amnesia and the development of a socially accessible memory system. In J. F. Kihlstrom & F. J. Evans (Eds.), *Functional disorders of memory.* Hillsdale, NJ: Erlbaum.

Whittaker, S., McShane, J., & Dunn, D. (1985). The development of cueing strategies in young children. *British Journal of Developmental Psychology, 3,* 153–161.

Willatts, P. (1990). Development of problem-solving strategies in infancy. In D. F. Bjorklund (Ed.), *Children's strategies:*

Contemporary views of cognitive development. Hillsdale, NJ: Erlbaum.

Wippich, W. (1980). Meta-Gedächtnis und Gedächtnis-Erfahrung [Metamemory and memory experience]. *Zeitschrift für Entwicklungspsychologie und Pädagogische Psychologie, 12,* 40–43.

Wippich, W., Mecklenbräuker, S., & Brausch, A. (1989). Implizites und explizites Gedächtnis bei Kindern: Bleiben bei indirekten Behaltensprüfungen Altersunterschiede aus? [Implicit and explicit memory in children: Do developmental differences disappear in indirect memory tests?] *Zeitschrift für Entwicklungspsychologie und Pädagogische Psychologie, 21,* 294–306.

Worden, P. E. (1983). Memory strategy instruction with the learning disabled. In M. Pressley & J. R. Levin (Eds.), *Cognitive strategy research: Psychological foundations.* New York: Springer-Verlag.

Worden, P. E., & Sladewski-Awig, L. J. (1982). Children's awareness of memorability. *Journal of Educational Psychology, 74,* 341–350.

Yussen, S. R., & Bird, J. E. (1979). The development of metacognitive awareness in memory, communication, and attention. *Journal of Experimental Child Psychology, 28,* 300–313.

Yussen, S. R., & Levy, V. M. (1975). Developmental changes in predicting one's own span of short-term memory. *Journal of Experimental Child Psychology, 19,* 502–508.

Zabrucky, K., & Ratner, H. H. (1986). Children's comprehension monitoring and recall of inconsistent stories. *Child Development, 57,* 1401–1418.

CHAPTER 11

Knowledge Acquisition in Foundational Domains

HENRY M. WELLMAN and SUSAN A. GELMAN

In this chapter, we examine the emergence and development of children's foundational knowledge. By foundational knowledge we mean those concepts or bodies of knowledge that engender, shape, and constrain other conceptual understandings. To illustrate, according to Piaget (1954), late in infancy children begin to understand that physical objects co-exist with the self and that objects continue to exist whether or not the child perceives them. He claims that this fundamental insight frames the child's subsequent understanding of mechanical causation, human instrumental actions, space, time, and natural physical phenomena such as astronomy and geography. Arguably any piece of knowledge, no matter how obscure, could affect at least some other conceptions. However, certain understandings are also much more influential than others (e.g., the object concept vs. knowledge that cars are more often black than pink). The point here is not to draw a sharp dividing-line between foundational and nonfoundational knowledge, but rather to direct attention to knowledge that has a potentially powerful impact, during and throughout childhood.

Thought has structure, function, and content (Piaget, 1953). Knowledge is the content on which the mind works. Without knowledge, there would be no thought. Thus, it is not surprising that scholars have been interested in children's knowledge for decades. The array of content areas that have been explored is vast; including the shape of the earth, distinctions between dreams and waking reality, whether plants are alive, illness, numerosity, print, magnetism, and more. Until recently, however, the focus has rarely been on children's knowledge itself. Rather, theorists proposed that examining knowledge would provide a window onto more fundamental, domain-general structures and processes that children were using, such as categorization, memory, or logic. Piaget's research epitomizes this approach. He provided some of the most intriguing accounts of early knowledge, yet disavowed any interest in the "surface" level—that is, the knowledge itself.

Support for the preparation of this chapter was provided by NICHD grant HD-22149 to Wellman and NSF grant 91–00348 to Gelman.

Currently, however, there is a renewed interest in knowledge, how it is organized, and how it changes over time. One reason for this interest is the recognition that specialized knowledge can exert powerful effects on cognition. In a variety of domains, experts—both children and adults—make use of concepts, principles, and procedures not available to novices (Chase & Simon, 1973; Chi, 1978).

Renewed interest in knowledge also derives from studies of naive, folk, or common sense theories. Common sense theories are people's ordinary understandings of certain bounded bodies of information, such as the set of ideas that nonscientists hold about celestial phenomena (folk astronomy). Various claims have been advanced by anthropologists, cognitive developmentalists, educators, and other cognitive scientists: that human concepts, for adults and children, are entrenched in naive theories (e.g., Murphy & Medin, 1985); that cultural worldviews are instantiated in folk theories that shape ways of thinking within particular societies (e.g., Holland & Quinn, 1987); that young children rapidly acquire certain basic theories that shape further cognitive acquisitions (e.g., Carey, 1985); and that naive theories deeply constrain learning via instruction (e.g., Vosniadou & Brewer, 1987).

A third source of increased interest in knowledge is the contemporary concern with domain-specific "modules" of thought. The general claim here is that the mind is heterogeneous—not general—different cognitive systems are designed to process and represent some sorts of information, not others (e.g., words vs. numbers). Several writers have strongly argued that domain-specific cognition has an evolutionary-neurological basis (e.g., Pinker, 1994; Sperber, 1994). Animals evolve special physical and sensory adaptations designed to solve certain problems or to take advantage of certain environmental affordances (e.g., eyes and ears, sight vs. echolocation, wings vs. fins). The same pressures could yield special conceptual adaptations as well—systems that process only specific sorts of information to arrive at specific sorts of representations. In humans, language is arguably a prime example (but see Bates, Bretherton, & Snyder, 1988; Tomasello, 1995). Developmentally, the representations generated by specific modules may provide a basic infrastructure for knowledge and its acquisition.

From several directions, therefore, foundational knowledge has become central to our efforts to understand cognitive development. The relevant research does not form a unitary literature; it abounds with competing assumptions, explanations, kinds of evidence, and conclusions.

Nonetheless, a set of common questions guides these efforts: Are there core domains of human cognition? If so, how are these best characterized—as pockets of expertise, naive theories, or mental modules? When do these first appear in development—as early infrastructure or the later culmination of conceptual achievement? What accounts for their emergence? How much and in what ways do they change? Current research that tackles these questions sheds light on some of the most basic issues in the field.

Any approach to addressing these issues necessarily embodies certain assumptions. We outline some of the features and limits of our approach in the following three sections.

Target Domains

A claim of those interested in foundational knowledge is that certain systems of knowledge are especially important to human understanding. We focus on three that are arguably central to survival and everyday interactions: the domains of physics, psychology, and biology. Knowledge about other humans enables negotiating social interactions and managing important tasks of mating and childrearing; knowledge about plants and animals fosters food-gathering, avoiding predators, and maintaining health; knowledge about physical objects allows prediction of the effects of one's own and others' physical actions, the creation and use of tools, and so on. Moreover, these domains represent three areas in which considerable exciting research is being conducted. Other content areas, too, clearly have broad significance for children's reasoning but will not be covered here. These include language, number, space, time, morality, and social kinds (including gender and race). Most are covered elsewhere in this *Handbook*.

The three domains we review have roots in Piaget's work (Piaget, 1929, 1930). He argued that psychological, physical, and biological reasoning were fundamental systems of adult thinking and knowing. Thus, he conducted investigations of children's understanding of physical, psychological, and biological phenomena, prefiguring current work in these areas. Importantly, Piaget concluded that children's thinking does *not* honor fundamental adult distinctions among these domains; basic knowledge of these phenomena was said to develop relatively late in childhood. Young children, Piaget claimed, are animists, construing various physical phenomena (clouds moving, rivers flowing) as alive; they are realists, construing mental phenomena as concrete and physical (e.g., ideas are visible and tangible objects); and they are artificialists, construing natural phenomena as the products of human invention and intention (e.g., clouds come from the chimneys of houses). Piaget's arguments underscore a key question: Do children distinguish these three possible domains, and if so, when? Our review is shaped by two orienting perspectives for addressing this question. One concerns the nature of the evidence researchers might use to address the question. The other concerns possible explanatory accounts theorists have proposed for domain differences.

Evidence: Ontologies, Causes, and Unobservables

In order to infer that children's thought reflects distinct domains of understanding, it is not sufficient to demonstrate that children know about different sorts of things—that they have some information about people, some about physical objects, and some about plants and animals. Instead, we need evidence that children view these as distinctively different phenomena that require different sorts of reasoning. Although one could adopt a neurological approach (do different brain systems serve these different understandings?), instead we adopt a cognitive approach, and draw from philosophy of science for more conceptual criteria. Scientific bodies of knowledge certainly carve the world into distinctive domains. Consider the differences between physics and psychology. What features distinguish such profoundly different domains? Philosophers of science wrestle with this issue when they discuss paradigms or research traditions as opposed to specific scientific theories. Specific theories are detailed formulations about a delimited set of phenomena. Beyond specific theories, scientific endeavors also reflect more global paradigms (Kuhn, 1962), research programs (Lakatos, 1970), research traditions (Laudan, 1977), or what we have called framework theories (Wellman, 1990; Wellman & Gelman, 1992). Most important for the current discussion, framework theories carve out basic domains for scientific reasoning. They do so by outlining the ontology, basic causal devices, and underlying constructs pertinent to a domain.

> A research tradition provides a set of guidelines for the development of specific theories. Part of those guidelines constitute an ontology which specifies, in a general way, the types of fundamental entities which exist in the domain or domains within which the research tradition is embedded. The function of specific theories within the research tradition is to explain all the empirical problems in the domain by "reducing" them to the ontology of the research tradition. . . . Moreover, the research tradition outlines the different modes by which

these entities can interact. Thus, Cartesian particles can only interact by contact, not by action-at-a-distance. Entities within a Marxist research tradition can only interact by virtue of the economic forces influencing them. (Laudan, 1977, p. 79)

Whether or not there are *everyday* framework theories (Brewer & Samarapungavan, 1991; Wellman, 1990), a consideration of these scientific frameworks highlights several features that we take to be critical to a consideration of core domains of thought: ontological distinctions, domain-specific causal modes of reasoning, underlying "theoretical" or nonobvious constructs, and coherent, interrelated systems of concepts. We aim to address when and in what ways children: (a) divide the world into fundamentally different kinds of "things"—for example, thoughts versus solid physical objects, (b) appreciate fundamentally different sorts of causes—for example, processes activated by collisions with solid objects versus processes activated by desires and intentions, (c) appeal to distinctive underlying constructs in their understandings—for example, the states that underpin human behavior versus the atoms and substances out of which solid objects are composed, and (d) create larger systems within which these concepts, causes, and constructs cohere.

In contrast to this sort of domain-specific reasoning, children's thinking could be based exclusively on more domain-general principles (Keil, 1989). For example, children might classify all sorts of objects—physical devices, persons, plants, and animals—using general principles of similarity (classifying entities by overall color, shape, movement). Children might reason causally about all phenomena in similar ways—identifying as causally important those events that reliably precede and covary with various outcomes, whatever their nature may be. We also want to consider, therefore, whether children at first understand phenomena in terms of domain-general, manifest features rather than domain-specific underlying constructs.

In sum, in what follows we consider whether and when children's thinking is shaped into three core domains of knowledge—naive physics, psychology, and biology—by considering whether children honor ontological distinctions among these domains, whether children use distinctive causal principles in reasoning about these domains, and whether children's beliefs within a domain appeal to unobservable, underlying constructs and cohere into interconnected networks of reasoning. These are empirical questions. Without examining children's language and behavior, one cannot know if children's thinking ever assembles itself in this fashion, or if so, at what point developmentally. Moreover, although framework scientific theories arguably demonstrate these qualities, children's thinking could be characterized by one, several, or none of these features. Similarly, we need not require that all these different qualities be evident in order to conclude that there are core domains of everyday cognition. Core domains could be defined in ways that privilege one or two rather than all these features. Consideration of ontological categories, coherence, causal beliefs, and understandings of the nonobvious, however, provides relevant distinctions to evaluate these and other claims.

Explanatory Accounts: Modules, Expertise, and Theories

Suppose children's thinking, early or late, demonstrates distinctive physical, biological, and psychological modes of reasoning. How might we account for these developments? Our second orienting perspective is to consider three classes of theoretical accounts that correspond, roughly, to three different metaphors of children's thought: child-as-adult, child-as-novice, and child-as-alien. These accounts differ with regard to several questions: How similar are the knowledge systems of children and adults? How can one characterize these knowledge systems? How similar are the mechanisms by which children and adults revise their knowledge (the process of conceptual change)? We focus primarily on the first two questions, though the third is also quite important (e.g., Kuhn, 1995).

On the child-as-adult metaphor, children are cognitively just like adults in having the same core conceptions and organizing knowledge in essentially the same ways. On this account, apparent differences between children's and adults' thought are essentially superficial. This view fits well with a common intuition that wholly new fundamental understandings may be impossible. If you don't already view the world as consisting of individual objects (as opposed to ever changing flashes of light and form), how could you ever discover this and how could you communicate with others who do? Even the simple conversational exchanges of parents and 2-year-olds would be impossible to achieve without a common set of concepts (e.g., "want" or "cookie") on which to draw. True, children often appear to lack fundamental adult knowledge or even to misconstrue simple phenomena. On this view, children's behavioral limitations—their limited memory,

language, processing speed—obstruct our view of their knowledge. This competence-performance distinction intuitively fits with our common experience of knowing something but not being able to access or articulate it.

In contrast, the child-as-novice metaphor assumes that children start out knowing little or nothing of the world around them. Beginning with ignorance, children develop by gaining experience and so incrementally adding to their knowledge base. The power of expertise is seen with something so ordinary as the act of reading. We start out, as children, painstakingly deciphering words letter-by-letter, not even understanding what we read, but after many hours, then months, then years, of experience, we can perform the task so rapidly, so automatically, that the thoughts evoked by the writer seem to leap into our minds without effort.

Finally, the child-as-alien metaphor assumes that children's view of the world is potentially quite different from that of adults. (Note that the presumption of this metaphor is that children's knowledge is alien from adults; not that their brains are alien.) Basic conceptions that we cannot imagine someone without (such as expecting objects to continue to exist when out of sight) may not be shared by children. The point is that, rather than ignorance, children are thought to have their *own* ways of understanding the world. Intuitive insight into this view can be garnered from considering the qualitative changes that have occurred in the history of science (e.g., from a Newtonian to an Einsteinian physics). Moreover, something like cognitive revolutions occur within the minds of individuals (e.g., grasping algebra in high school, learning a new language, religious conversion).

These three metaphors correspond roughly to three distinctive theoretical approaches to knowledge acquisition, domain-specificity, and foundational knowledge. The counterparts to child-as-adult views are innatist, modular theories, the counterparts to child-as-novice views are expertise theories, and the counterparts to child-as-alien views are theory theories. Table 11.1 presents a summary of some of the distinctive characteristics of these three approaches.

Modular Theories

Chomsky argued that the mind is modular—"consisting of separate systems with their own properties" (Chomsky, 1988, p. 161). Claims of other theorists regarding modularity have varied in at least two respects: whether modularity is restricted to perceptual processes or affects central cognitive processes as well, and whether modularity is innate

TABLE 11.1   A Schematic Comparison among Modular, Theory Theory, and Expertise Approaches

	Dominant Metaphor	Mechanism	Role of Input	What Is Innate	Variability in Outcome	Sample Domains
Modules	child as adult	biological constraints	input as "trigger"	mandatory input-output systems	highly fixed and constrained	language, vision, theory of mind
Theories	child as alien	causal-explanatory understandings	input as source of data	skeletal principles and ontologies	variable within broad constraints	psychology, physics, biology
Expertise	child as novice	information-processing skills	input/experience foundational	information-processing strategies	highly variable	reading, dinosaurs, physics

or constructed. Modularity need not imply evolved innate modules (Karmiloff-Smith, 1992) but for most modular proponents it does, and that is the sort of modularity we address here. Nonetheless, all modularity views assume domain-specificity. Chomsky's focus was on language, and more specifically syntax or universal grammar. Evidence for the status of syntax as a module was its innate, biologically driven character—evident in all and only humans; its neurological localization and breakdown—the selective impairment of syntactic competence in some forms of brain damage; its rapid acquisition in the face of meager environmental data—syntactic categories of great abstraction, such as verb or subject, are easily acquired by small children faced with impoverished input; and the presence of critical periods and maturational timetables (Pinker, 1994). Fodor (1983) extended the logic of modules to cognitive abilities more broadly. He distinguished between central logical processes and perceptual systems, arguing for modularity of the latter. In Fodor's analysis, modules are innately specified systems that take in sensory inputs and yield necessary representations of them. The visual system as characterized by Marr (1982) provides a prototypic example—a system that takes visual inputs and generates $2\frac{1}{2}$ dimensional representations of objects and space. Like the visual system, by Fodor's analysis, modules are not only innately specified, their processing is mandatory and encapsulated, and (unlike central knowledge and beliefs) their representational outputs are insensitive to revision via experience. Experience provides specific inputs to modules which yield mandatory representations of inputs. Certain experiential inputs may be necessary to trigger the module's working in the first place, but the processes by which the module arrives at its representations are mandatory rather than revisable.

Extending Fodor, several writers have argued that certain conceptual processes, not just perceptual ones, are modular (Karmiloff-Smith, 1992; Sperber, 1994) or supported by systems of cognitive modules (e.g. Atran, 1995; Baron-Cohen, 1995; Leslie, 1994). In these claims each module works independently, achieving its own special representations. Thus, for the most part, cognitive modules are like Fodor's perceptual ones, except that "perceptual processes have, as input, information provided by sensory receptors, and as output, a conceptual representation categorizing the object perceived . . . [whereas] conceptual processes have conceptual representations both as input and as output" (Sperber, 1994, p. 40).

It is important to distinguish the general claim that there is innate knowledge from the stronger claim that there are innate modules (e.g., Gopnik, 1993). It is conceivable that certain representations may be innately specified, yet fail to be modular, either because the knowledge is domain-general or because it is readily revisable on the basis of new experience. All sorts of knowledge, including expertise or naive theories, may include or begin from a base of innately specified representations. A crucial difference between nativist modular accounts and the others, therefore, concerns the nature of the interplay between experience and conceptual structure. Modular processes are mandatory in the sense that, assuming they come on line (and are not impaired), they result in conceptions that are necessary conversions of the relevant inputs into special representations, specified by that module.

Developmentally, this distinction between innate knowledge and innate modules concerns how open in principle development is considered to be: Are there a limited number of predetermined developmental endpoints or an essentially open-ended array of endpoints depending only on the information given and amount of time development takes? Modular accounts specify a limited number of endpoints in each domain; theories and expertise accounts encompass considerably more variable developmental possibilities.

Some modular accounts allow several alternative developmental endpoints arrived at by several branching routes. In these parameter-setting accounts, the modular representation can take one form or another depending on which value of a key parameter is available in that organism's developmental environment (e.g., Hyams, 1986). However, the relation between input and system here is still one of triggering; hence, the developmental options are fixed, and once set, the parameter cannot be readjusted. Modularity accounts may invoke external information processing limitations or performance constraints to explain certain sorts of developments. Still, on this view, early conceptual structures are like later ones; only various performance limitations prevent children from demonstrating their knowledge.

Expertise

The claim that expertise carves out domains begins with the following observation. With enough practice at a task, whether that task is the game of chess or the gathering of factual knowledge about dinosaurs, an ordinary person begins to look extraordinary. With sufficient experience, a person attains amazing feats of memory (Chase & Ericsson, 1981), reorganizes knowledge into complex hierarchical systems, and develops rich networks of causally related information (Chi, Hutchinson, & Robin, 1989). These abilities are so striking that they can even erase the usual developmental finding that adults outperform children (e.g., Chi, 1978).

Just as important, these abilities cannot be explained as individual differences in the general processing talents of experts. The same individual who is remarkable on the chessboard shows mundane performance on tasks outside the skill domain. For example, the chess expert's memory for a string of digits is quite ordinary. It seems, then, that these abilities are domain-specific, at least in some sense of domain. Furthermore they are foundational in that expertise influences further learning, attention to, and understanding of new domain-related information.

The notion of skill domains molded by expertise is distinct from modularity. With the former, there is no appeal to innate modules, innate constraints, or evolutionary forces. Consideration of expertise-driven skill domains poses an interesting challenge to other notions of domain specificity and foundational knowledge. First, the effects of expertise demonstrate the far-reaching influences of intensive experience. They remind us to take seriously the capacity of human cognition to shape itself to the world it finds as opposed to a world it may evolutionarily expect.

Early humans could not have evolved special cognitive capacities to read; there was no world of print until humans invented it millennia later. Yet even relatively young children become expert readers evidencing a complex network of knowledge and processes of domain-like scope. A second point is that studies of expertise challenge us to consider what can count as a domain. From the perspective of Chomsky, Fodor, and their followers, it has been assumed that domains constitute large and natural chunks of cognition—language, perception, mathematics, and music. Yet from the expertise literature, it seems that domains might include invented and smaller corners of experience.

Theory Theory

The view that children possess strikingly different thoughts and knowledge from adults is argued most comprehensively by Piaget (e.g., 1953). As is well known to students of cognitive development, Piaget uncovered many surprising childhood errors: Infants seem to believe objects go out of existence when they go out of sight, preschoolers can't conserve and hence apparently believe that amount and weight change when an object's shape changes, and pre-adolescents seemingly can't engage in propositional reasoning. Moreover, as it is generally understood (but see Chapman, 1988), Piaget claimed that certain general cognitive structures (sensorimotor, preoperational, concrete operational, and formal operational stages of thought) underlie children's knowledge and reasoning across a wide variety of content areas. Thus concrete operational thinking uniformly structures such disparate conceptions as number, time, weight, morality, classification, and causal reasoning. Considerable research suggests that Piaget's domain-general stage theory is incorrect, and that cognition seems domain-specific in ways that pose considerable challenges to domain-general theories more broadly (see Gelman & Baillargeon, 1983, for one review).

However, the proposal of qualitative ontogenetic changes in conceptual knowledge has re-emerged in the theory theory—the proposal that children's knowledge is organized into coherent, causal-explanatory systems (e.g., Brewer & Samarapungavan, 1991; Carey, 1985; Wellman, 1990). According to this view, like Piaget's, children have early understandings, but ones that nonetheless differ importantly from adults'. Unlike general stage theories, however, theory theories postulate that these understandings and the changes they undergo are inherently dependent on specific contents and not others. Compare scientific fields such as psychology versus geophysics. Their theories differ fundamentally because their contents differ—the first dealing with behavior, emotion, representation, and learning, the second with planetary forces, plate tectonics, and volcanic activity. Additionally, theories characterize knowledge in ways that go beyond collections of facts. The content of knowledge changes with place and time, so that uncovering what a child in 1994 in Ann Arbor, Michigan, knows about X cannot generalize to a child of 1934 or a child of 2054, or even to a child in 1994 Bombay. As Piaget convincingly argued, the ever-changing details of an inventory of the child's knowledge base may say little about cognitive development more broadly (although they may have important instructional or other applied implications). A focus on everyday theories is an attempt to focus on more enduring and informative knowledge. The aim is a level of analysis that captures structured knowledge systems, as do scientific theories rather than scientific observations.

Beyond a loose use of theories to refer to children's developing knowledge—a usage often adopted even by advocates of expertise and modular accounts—theory theories draw stronger parallels between cognitive development and certain aspects of the development of scientific theories. "Two of the clearest and most impressive instances we have of . . . learning [about the nature of the world] are the acquisitions of children and the achievements of science. . . . The hypothesis of the theory theory is that there are deep similarities between the underlying cognitive mechanisms involved in the epistemological endeavors of childhood and of science" (Gopnik & Wellman, 1994, p. 259). To be clear, the theory theory claim is not that everyday folk, especially children, are doing science. Everyday knowledge is not formalized in explicit canons that are grounded in empirical research; children do not engage in scholarly, scientific reasoning. Instead, the claim is that there are two sorts of theories: everyday and scientific. Everyday theories are coherent systems of knowledge that organize and structure everyday thinking, akin to how theories organize and constrain scientists' thinking. Everyday theories are resistant to change, yet at the same time they are partly grounded in evidence and thus subject to change. Indeed, initial conceptions can give way to radically reorganized conceptions, as is evident in scientific revolutions across history. The essential idea is that initial theory-based conceptions are used by the child to explain, interpret, and make predictions about the world. In this process, initial conceptions encounter theoretical anomalies—facts that don't fit, predictions that consistently fail. At first these anomalies can be ignored, but if they persist, they cause conceptual reorganization and accommodation that lead to revised theories, or in the extreme, to new qualitatively different theories. Just how theory change differs among children versus adults is a matter of some debate. Some suggest that the processes by which children and adults revise their theories are primarily the same (Brewer & Samarapungavan, 1991; Gopnik & Wellman, 1994), whereas others argue that there are important age-related differences (Kuhn, 1989; Klahr, Fay, & Dunbar, 1993).

In contrast to expertise accounts, theory-theory accounts contend that development rarely begins with ignorance; rather, prior systems of concepts constrain and shape learning, beginning with innately evolved strategies or representations for parsing or understanding the world. In contrast to modular accounts, however, theory-theory accounts emphasize initial conceptions that are revisable—via experience and processes of theory change rather than brain maturation alone. Thus, later theories, concepts, and even domains can potentially differ radically from earlier ones.

Summary

In this chapter, we consider children's early understanding of physical, biological, and psychological phenomena. We ask whether—and if so, when and in what fashion—these early understandings form three distinctive domains. In the process, we consider modular, expertise, and theory-theory accounts of the development of foundational knowledge. Currently available research and theory require us to consider some topics in greater or lesser depth, depending on the domain. We begin by considering children's conceptions of physical phenomena, which provide the most comprehensive data concerning infancy. Within this area, we can consider whether foundational, content-full knowledge systems are possible early on, even before the child has language to describe these understandings. We next take up children's understanding of psychological phenomena. By contrasting physical and psychological conceptions, we can consider when in development these represent distinctively different domains—different ontological and causal-explanatory understandings. Moreover, discussion of children's naive psychology has generated the clearest contrasts between theory theory and innate modular accounts of cognitive development. We then turn to biological understandings. Debates concerning understanding of biology again address issues regarding what constitutes a domain, and how one domain might break off from another parent domain developmentally. Moreover, in the case of biological knowledge especially, researchers have raised the question of whether domain-general processes, such as categorization and similarity-based abstraction, might more simply account for children's knowledge acquisition.

NAIVE PHYSICS

Ordinary thought often concerns itself with solid objects and their interactions—rocks falling, balls bouncing, cans stacking, sides containing, and floors supporting. That physical objects exist and have certain predictable properties thus seems foundational to many other conceptions. But this knowledge could be acquired early or later in development. Moreover, the two core framework notions here—physical objects and physical-mechanical causes— are potentially vast in scope. Physical entities include not only solid objects, but unbounded masses (sand and water), gases (air), and the insides and substances of objects; physical causes include not only the dynamics of object contact but also processes like flight, dissolving, combustion, and melting. We focus this section on two primary issues: (a) Descriptively, what kinds of physical knowledge are present in infants and children? Here we start with early infancy, then proceed to later infancy and childhood. (b) Theoretically, how can we best characterize such knowledge, in particular, in modular, expertise, or theory-theory terms?

Early Infancy

Objects

Piaget (1954) concluded that younger infants did not see the world as composed of solid object-like entities. An understanding of the independent existence of objects was instead acquired late in infancy, an insight based on the infant's interactions with objects, especially searching for visible, then invisible, then invisibly moved objects. In the past 10 years, this conclusion has been systematically overturned, both with alternative interpretations of findings using Piagetian tasks (e.g., Bertenthal, 1996; Wellman et al., 1986) and with altogether different methods, such as preferential looking paradigms. For example, Baillargeon et al. (1985) demonstrated that infants as young as 3 and 4 months expect objects to continue to exist when they are out of view. Infants looked longer at a physically anomalous display where a rectangular panel apparently moved right through a solid box than they did at a physically possible

event where the panel stopped on contact with the box. This finding suggests that such young infants were puzzled when the screen did not stop on expected contact with the box and thus believed the box continued to exist even when hidden from view behind the panel.

Based on extended findings of this sort (e.g., Baillargeon, 1986; Baillargeon & DeVos, 1991; Spelke et al., 1992), Spelke (1988, 1994) has proposed that very young infants have certain core concepts that constrain their conception and perception of physical objects. For example, physical objects move on paths that are connected (according to the continuity constraint) and cannot move through physical obstructions (solidity constraint). To illustrate, 4-month-old infants were habituated to a display in which a ball was dropped behind a screen, depicted in Figure 11.1 (Spelke et al., 1992). First infants saw the background wall and floor, then a screen covered the display, and a hand holding a ball appeared and dropped it behind the screen. The screen was then removed, revealing the ball at the bottom of the display. After habituation to multiple trials of this event, infants saw a shelf placed in the display in the path of the falling ball. They then saw two contrasting test items where again the ball fell out of sight behind the screen. For the consistent test event, the display was uncovered to reveal the ball on the shelf, consistent with the principles of continuity and solidity. For the inconsistent test event, the ball was revealed in the old position on the floor at the bottom of the display. Four-month-olds looked longer at the inconsistent than the consistent test event, registering enhanced attention if the ball failed to behave in accord with solidity and continuity.

Note that the inconsistent test event is actually most perceptually similar to the habituation presentation—in this case, the outcome is identical, as the ball is shown on the

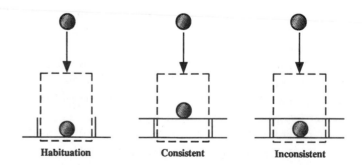

Figure 11.1 Schematic depiction of the habituation and test events used in one of Spelke's studies of infants' knowledge of solidity and continuity. (After "Origins of knowledge," by E. S. Spelke, K. Breingler, & K. Jacobson, 1992, *Psychological Review, 99*, pp. 605–632.

floor at the bottom of the display. In contrast, the consistent test event shows the ball in a novel position on the shelf. If infants are responding on the basis of perceptual similarity or novelty alone, they should look longer at the consistent event because of its greater dissimilarity to the habituation event. However, they look longer at the inconsistent event, suggesting that infants interpret the movements in terms of solidity and continuity, not just perceptual similarity. In addition, note how the study is designed to tap conceptions about objects, not just object perception, in that it assesses infants' expectations about unseen events—the object's unwitnessed path of movement behind the screen. The relation between infant object perception and object conception is theoretically intriguing and also contested—perhaps early object conceptions are induced from earlier perceptual experiences or perhaps they correspond to innate representations of the physical world (Baillargeon, Kotovsky, & Needham, 1995; Bertenthal, 1996; Karmiloff-Smith, 1992; Mandler, 1988, 1992; Spelke, 1994). But studies such as these with hidden objects demonstrate that, at the least, conceptual representations are evident by 3 to 4 months of age.

Physical Causality

Understanding of physical causal forces also seems evident early in infancy. For example, Leslie (Leslie, 1982; Leslie & Keeble, 1987) showed 6-month-olds a film of either one object colliding with and launching a second object, or control events such as a first object making contact with a second one that began to move only after a considerable delay (violating temporal aspects of the causal dynamics). Leslie reasoned that since the control events do not specify causal connections, an infant habituated to one of those events should be unsurprised if the event was reversed (since the reversal, too, provides no causal regularity). For the target event, however, reversal of the sequence specifies a real reversal of causal roles: The cause is now the effect. In several converging studies, Leslie found dishabituation only upon reversing the properly causal sequence, suggesting an early appreciation of at least some aspects of mechanical causation.

Cohen and Oakes (Cohen & Oakes, 1993; Oakes & Cohen, 1990) dispute the age at which infants perceive causality in these displays. In a habituation-dishabituation paradigm, they found that 10-month-olds distinguished between causal and non-causal events, but 6-month-olds did not. Further, when causal agent and recipient varied from trial to trial, even 10-month-olds did not process events as causal in a general way. Also, it is not clear whether infants

demonstrate conceptual (vs. perceptual) understanding (Mandler, 1988), since the events are visible in their entirety in these displays. Again, this issue can be addressed in part by assessing infants' understanding of hidden object movements. For example, Spelke (1991, 1994) argues that young infants understand several principles that define the nature of simple mechanical causation, especially contact and no-action-at-a-distance: "objects act on each other if and only if they touch" (Spelke et al., 1995, p. 49). To test these understandings, infants were first habituated to one object moving behind a screen and another object emerging from behind the same screen at the other side. After habituation, the infants were shown two test sequences with no screen. In the consistent event, children saw the first object move up to and contact the second object, thereby launching its movement, consistent with the principle of contact. In the inconsistent event, they saw the first object go toward but not touch the second object, which then moved off on its own. Even 6-month-olds looked longer at the inconsistent event (Spelke & Van de Walle, 1993; Van de Walle et al., 1994), evidently inferring that the two objects met behind the screen during habituation and thus being surprised to see the no-contact test event. Kotovsky and Baillargeon (reviewed in Baillargeon et al., 1995) provide additional demonstrations of infants' appreciation of the role of contact in causing physical movements.

Developments Later in Infancy

Suppose we grant that young infants represent objects as continuing to exist, as moving due to contact collisions, and as moving along continuous paths even when out of view. What other basic object understandings might there be, and when do they appear? Spelke argues that, although an understanding of solidity and contact appears early in infancy, an understanding of such physical notions as gravity and support appear only later in the first year. Thus, in an experiment analogous to the one depicted in Figure 11.1 (Spelke et al., 1992), 4-month-olds were habituated to a hand releasing a ball behind a screen, which was then removed to show the ball at rest on a shelf suspended above the floor of the apparatus. For the test events, the shelf was removed. In the consistent test event, infants saw the hand release the ball behind the screen, then when the screen was removed, subjects saw the ball at rest on the floor of the apparatus. In the inconsistent test event, when the screen was removed, the ball was revealed in the same position it had occupied during habituation—but, with the shelf now absent, the object appeared to float in midair. Four-month-olds looked equally at these two test events; only older infants looked longer at the inconsistent event. Thus, 4-month-olds in the original experiment seemed surprised if the ball appeared to pass through a solid shelf, but in a parallel situation, were not surprised if it appeared to be suspended without support against gravity.

Another later development seems to be the capacity to reason quantitatively about events which previously were understood only qualitatively (Baillargeon, 1994). For example, 4-month-olds represent an occluded object as continuing to exist when out of sight, but it is not until several months later that they represent just how big that occluded object is (e.g., its height).

In the sorts of studies reviewed thus far, infants individuate different objects in terms of spatio-temporal cues (these two things are spatially separate, so they must be two objects) and movement cues (object X moving on path A cannot be object Y that is moving on path B). Indeed, infants can keep track of whether there are 1, 2, or 3 different objects in a display, apparently forming some kind of numerical count (e.g., Antell & Keating, 1983; Starkey, 1992; Wynn, 1992). But how do infants individuate and represent objects more precisely? Adults understand not only that each object is spatially distinct from other objects and that objects move through space on distinctive paths, but also that identity and property information individuate objects. If I see a car at one time and place, A, and then later see the identical car, down to its distinguishing dents and marks, at another time and place, B, I assume I have encountered the same car even though the two instances are separate in space and even without knowledge of the spatial movements that would bring it from A to B. In contrast, if I see a green car go into a short tunnel and a red one emerge on the exact spatio-temporal trajectory as the first, I would probably assume there are two cars in spite of the continuous path of movement from one to the next. It is possible, however, that young infants ignore property information.

Recent research by Xu and Carey (1996) illustrates this point. Suppose adults are shown a display with an occluding screen and see one object (a toy rabbit) emerge from one side of the screen and then return, alternating with a different object (a cup) emerging and returning from the other side. Adults infer there must be two objects behind the screen. Note that, in terms of spatio-temporal movements alone, it is equally possible that: (a) there are two objects, or (b) a single object unspecified as to property features of any sort is emerging first from one side then

from the other. Property/identity features (cup vs. rabbit) automatically specify to adults that there are two objects, sharing in some way common spatial trajectories, but do young infants have the same conception? Indeed, if infants look to movement rather than properties to individuate objects, they should not know if there are one or two objects behind the screen; the movements alone do not specify one or two objects, only the properties do. In a set of experiments, Xu and Carey (1996) presented infants with variations on this demonstration, showing them a series of screened emergences, then testing the infants' conceptions by raising the screen and showing them displays of one or two objects. Ten-month-olds were able to use spatiotemporal information but failed to used property/identity information to represent distinct individual objects. However, 12-month-olds, like adults, individuated objects in terms of property/kind information. In essence, the younger infants were unsurprised to find either one or two objects when the screen was raised, though perfectly able to keep track of one versus two objects in analogous hidden displays using movements to individuate the objects.

Relatedly, as Gopnik and Meltzoff (1997) point out, 5- and 6-month-olds will track the trajectory of an object that disappears behind one side of a narrow screen, then emerges at the other side (e.g., Bower et al., 1971; Meltzoff & Moore, 1995; but see Gratch, 1982, or Muller & Aslin, 1978, for failures to replicate). These younger infants will not show disrupted tracking if one object disappears and a completely different one emerges, as long as the spatio-temporal path is continuous (Bower, 1982; Meltzoff & Moore, 1995; Moore et al., 1978). In short, these data suggest that late in the first year of life, infants' object concepts may undergo a change, with infants first coming to distinguish objects, as adults do, on the basis of property/kind information. It is not that before this time infants fail to discriminate between objects that look different; they do (e.g., Cohen & Younger, 1983). However, such property features do not mark identity for younger infants, in the sense of specifying distinctive individual objects that continue in time and space.

Older Children

Objects

Toddlers and preschoolers, like infants, expect objects to continue to exist and to move on continuous paths. Toddlers regularly solve search problems requiring them to understand that objects continue to reside in a location even when nonvisible (see e.g. Sophian, 1984). For example, if an object is hidden under a cover, 18-month-olds will search for it there and be surprised if they find not the original object, but a different one (LeCompte & Gratch, 1972); indeed, they will continue to search for the original object. In invisible displacement tasks (in which an object is first hidden in a container which is moved to several locations, then shown to be empty), toddlers logically work out where the object must be, given the movement of the container and the object sightings (e.g., Haake & Somerville, 1985). Toddlers will display an object at the bottom of a cup-like cylinder to someone else by holding it so that the other can see the object—thereby making it invisible to themselves (Lempers, Flavell, & Flavell, 1977). They regularly use words to comment on the existence of out-of-sight objects, their comings and goings ("all gone"), their locations and identities (e.g., Gopnik, 1984).

Not all understandings of objects, however, concern existence, solidity, paths, and appearances. Indeed, it could be argued that such aspects concern the outer, phenomenal, apparent aspects of objects. Adults appeal as well to a variety of less obvious features and underlying constructs to explain and make sense of the physical world—for example, an object's center of balance, its molecular composition, or its inner working parts. Recent evidence suggests that quite young children begin reasoning about such unobservable physical constructs. Consider children's understanding of the insides of objects, such as the gears of a watch or the bones of an animal. Insides are often unobserved (though in principle observable), but they are often particularly important for understanding what items are and how they function (e.g., the gears of a watch vs. its glass crystal). Children know a significant amount about the insides of familiar objects by age 3 years. If asked to report the contents of various objects, 3-year-olds offer different answers for animate and inanimate things, typically reporting that animates have blood, bones, and internal organs (such as hearts or muscles), whereas inanimates have either nothing or have material such as cotton, paper, hair, or "hard stuff" (R. Gelman, 1990; Simons & Keil, 1995). By age 4 years, children seem ready to assume that members of a particular category are likely to have the same internal parts and substance as one another, claiming, for example, that all dogs have "the same kinds of stuff inside" (S. Gelman & O'Reilly, 1988).

These kinds of responses may represent nothing more than reports of common associates—responding "skin" or "shell" to questions about outsides and "stuffing" or "blood" to questions about insides. Similarly, children may report that since all watches are similar, their insides are similar. However, in a different sort of task, S. Gelman and Wellman (1991) asked children to reason about triads in which internal similarity did not correspond to external similarity, for example, triads such as an almond, a very similar-looking rock, and a dissimilar-looking peanut. Children were asked which two items looked most alike and which had the same kinds of insides. To answer correctly about insides, children had to select two items that looked different on the outside. Even 3-year-olds were significantly correct at distinguishing insides and outsides. In a second study, 4- and 5-year-olds judged that nonobvious insides were often essential to an object's identity or function. If asked, for example, whether an egg would still be an egg, or a watch still a watch, if its outside (shell or glass) versus insides (white and yolk, or gears and other parts) were removed, 4- and 5-year-olds affirmed that insides were more essential than outsides. Other demonstrations suggest that young children's understanding of objects depends on conceptions of kinds, not just on perceptual similarities.

Objects like watches not only have distinct insides and distinct structural identities, they are also composed of material substances such as metal and glass. Smith et al. (1985) showed that 4-year-olds understand that various kinds of objects are composed of material substances and that such material kinds are different from object kinds. For example, they showed several items (e.g., a paper cup) to 4-, 5-, 7-, and 9-year-olds who judged what they were and what they were made of. Then the items were cut into small pieces as the children watched, and children were asked whether each item was still the same kind of object and whether it was still the same kind of stuff. At all ages children knew that the cut-up bits were no longer the same kinds of objects but that they were the same material kinds (e.g., still paper but not still a cup). Thus, at this age children appear to have a conception of structured objects, but also a conception of the substances out of which physical objects are composed. Moreover, Kalish and Gelman (1992) found that children appropriately draw different kinds of inferences based on material substance versus object kind. They report, for example, that wooden pillows are hard and glass frying-pans break—even though they had never before encountered a hard pillow or a breakable frying pan.

Unlike watches and eggs, objects such as a wooden pillow or a sugar cube are homogeneous substances throughout, all of one physical kind, such as wood or sugar. Au (1994) studied children's conception of such substances. Children between the ages of 3 and 8 years were shown chunks of a variety of natural and artificial substances (e.g., wood vs. playdough) with familiar and novel names (e.g., wood vs. carbonate). Children were then shown these substances transformed in three ways: (a) large chunks broken into smaller chunks, (b) chunks turned into powder, and (c) powders dissolved in water. Note that transformations of type (a) change size but not appearance. Type (b) transformations change size *and* appearance in the sense of texture and feel. Type (c) transformations change appearance in the extreme sense of making the substance invisible. Children correctly asserted that the items still had the same names and were still of the same stuff under these transformations. Transformations of type (c) were most difficult, but even 3-year-olds were 65% to 70% correct on these questions. In another study, children were asked questions about the properties of the substances. Some properties were material-relevant, such as what the substance would taste like, or how it would react to heat (e.g., melt vs. turn black in a hot oven); some properties were object-relevant but material-irrelevant, such as size (fit into a matchbox) and weight. Young children were again largely correct, appropriately distinguishing between material-relevant and irrelevant properties for most items and transformations.

These data show that even quite young children know that larger objects are composed of smaller pieces and these pieces, even if invisible, have enduring physical existence and properties. Au et al. (1993) and Smith et al. (1985; Carey, 1991) suggest that these insights constitute the basis of a naive atomic theory of matter, wherein everyday objects are, in the final analysis, composed of tiny bits of matter.

Consider further the distinction between chunks and powders presented above. Ontologically, physical entities are divided into solid bounded objects that have form and individuation versus aggregates or unbounded masses (water, piles of sand) that do not (Keil, 1979; Sommers, 1963). Young children know that both are physical entities—4-year-olds judge it is impossible for water to fill a box that is already filled by a steel block (Carey, 1991). At the same time, Soja et al. (1991) demonstrated that 2-year-old English-speaking children appreciate that solid physical objects differ from massed aggregates in terms of their distinctive properties and ontological status. This conceptual distinction is in place prior to children's linguistic mastery of mass versus count nouns in language.

Physical Causality

The above studies demonstrate that quite young children understand much about physical objects and reason about them in terms of underlying constructs and properties, beyond just their surface features. Equally important are children's conceptions of and inferences about the causal interactions that determine object movements and transformations. Following Hume, causal inferences might be construed solely in terms of content-independent logical principles. Causes might be induced whenever events (of whatever sort) exhibit requisite patterns of temporal and spatial contiguity and covariation. Developmental research on children's understanding of causality, following Piaget, began by documenting children's developing ability to make logical causal inferences on the basis of covariation. One conclusion of such research concerned preschoolers' consistent failures to reason causally in these logical ways (Shultz & Kestenbaum, 1985). In the 1980s, however, researchers questioned this conclusion, sensing that a Humean analysis missed an essential content-dependent aspect of human thinking about causal events. Specifically, a Humean analysis fails to consider the attribution of causal powers, that is, the force or source that actually generates its effect. In physical systems in particular, we reason about specific mechanisms whereby some cause produces some effect by transmitting a force or blocking such a force (Bullock et al., 1982; Cheng, 1993; Shultz, 1982). If knowledge about physical objects and physical causal mechanisms constitutes a domain of understanding, and if children early on acquire a rich understanding of that domain, then they should make appropriate causal inferences in that domain, even if their logical reasoning in other domains is limited.

Bullock et al. (1982) addressed this issue by demonstrating that preschool children consider intermediate mechanisms—not just input-output correlations—to make predictions about causal events. For example, in one study, children were presented with a domino-like array consisting of a series of blocks, each of which caused the next to topple. A device with a rod through a hole preceded the first block; when the rod was pushed through the hole it toppled the first block. Even 3-year-olds accurately predicted which modifications to the device would be relevant to how it worked (e.g., removing intermediate blocks) and which would be irrelevant (e.g., using a glass vs. wooden rod).

Similarly, Shultz (1982) found that preschool-age children reason sensibly about several sorts of causal transmissions.

In several ingeniously controlled situations, preschoolers appropriately attributed the snuffing out of a candle to a blower that was on rather than to one that was off, or the appearance of a spot of light to a lamp that was on as opposed to one that was off—despite competing Humean cues. The spotlight effect, for example, was instantaneous, rather than obviously prior in time, and involved no mechanical-spatial contiguity. Shultz thus claimed that young children figure out specific causal mechanisms and often reason properly about them, rather than deduce causes from raw patterns of temporal sequence and covariation. (See Cheng, 1993, for a related analysis but a revised account of these experiments.)

Goswami and Brown (1989) considered the possibility that, with respect to physical causality, young children (3–6 years) might be able to engage in sophisticated, analogical reasoning. Piagetian theory suggests that analogical reasoning of the classical a:b::c:d form is very difficult for children before the age of formal operations, and considerable research supports the claim that such reasoning appears only late in middle childhood (Goswami, 1991). However, the analogies used in these studies rely on relations such as semantic opposites (black:white::hard:?) or isolated facts (bird:air::fish:?)—not physical causal mechanisms that children may understand well. Goswami and Brown (1989) first tested 3- to 6-year-olds' understanding of such familiar causal acts or transformations as cutting or melting. Causal reasoning about such transformations was typically very good, even for 3-year-olds; they knew, for example, that a knife cutting through a whole loaf of bread yields cut-up bread. Then Goswami and Brown tested children's ability to reason analogically about such relations such as, Playdoh:cut-up Playdoh::apple:?. After being presented with the first three terms in this problem, children had to choose the correct answer for the missing last term of the analogy from several carefully composed alternatives:

1. A correct choice (cut-up apple);
2. A correct object but wrong physical change (bruised apple);
3. A wrong object but correct physical change (cut-up bread);
4. A mere appearance match for the third term (red ball);
5. A semantic associate of the third term (banana).

Even 3-year-olds were significantly correct on these sorts of problems. Goswami and Brown conclude that "as long as the child understands the causal relation, he or she can solve an analogy based on that relation" (1989, p. 79). Goswami (in press) further articulates and reviews recent empirical evidence for this claim.

Although these studies emphasize early developmental achievements, we do not wish to imply that children's causal understandings are wholly accurate. Indeed, even adults hold some persistent misconceptions. Consider the literature on understanding of object dynamics in children and adults (Proffitt et al., 1990). In these studies, people must predict, for example, the trajectories of balls rolling out of curved tubes or the weight or direction of the movement of colliding balls. These studies show that adults' naive understanding of such motions is coherent (McCloskey, 1983), although often in error. Proffitt and Kaiser conclude that even children are relatively competent with simple problems in which motion and force transmission involve essentially simple symmetrical objects whose action can be adequately seen in terms of a single particle of mass (Proffit et al., 1990). However, what Proffitt et al. (1990) call extended body problems—problems that require an understanding of more than point masses—are typically poorly understood even by adults. By studying people's understanding of the dynamics of wheels, where, for example, both a center of gravity and a distribution of mass or a set of rotational forces are involved, they find that even very familiar events may be completely misunderstood.

How to Characterize the Physical Domain

What might account for these early achievements and developments in physical understanding? On an expertise account, even infants may rapidly learn about physical phenomena because the world is full of objects that all obey core principles; hence even 4- and 5-month-olds could have received massive amounts of experience sufficient to develop early expertise in these matters. Spelke argues, however, that this early knowledge is innate (e.g., Spelke, 1994). In part, her argument is logical—how could infants learn about object movements at such an early age if they do not single out objects for consideration to begin with? But there are also empirical arguments. For example, since all objects cast shadows, infants have been exposed to massive amounts of experience with shadows as well. If experience leading to expertise determines infants' understanding of objects, one might expect infants to be similarly expert at the nature and behavior of shadows. Note, however, that shadows do not conform to the core principles used to understand objects. Shadows are not solid and they embody action at a distance—if the light source at a distance moves, so does the shadow; thus, it is not launched by contacting objects. Spelke and her colleagues (Spelke et al., 1995) have shown that 5- and 8-month-old infants misconstrue shadows. It is not just that infants are ignorant about them; instead, apparently, they expect them to act like objects. Infants' early, correct construal of objects, but not shadows, poses a challenge for an expertise approach.

One possible account of such findings is to posit the existence of an early developing module dedicated to understanding solid objects and at first misapplied to related entities (such as shadows). Leslie (1987, 1994) proposes the existence of such a module, and Spelke (1994; Carey & Spelke, 1994) argues for something like this in characterizing initial knowledge of objects as innate and domain-specific. In principle, there are strict limitations on the modifiability of innate modules over development. Therefore, Spelke distinguishes between core physical concepts (such as solidity and contact) that appear early and with minimal input, and noncore physical concepts (such as gravity) that appear later and require more extensive experience. Spelke suggests that infants' core principles persist into and throughout adulthood. These early beliefs are foundational in that they define an immutable core of physical knowledge, always constraining what will be selected as entities for further consideration.

Other researchers, however, advance different accounts, ones that provide a bigger role for learning and development in a basic understanding of objects themselves. For example, Cohen (1988) outlines an information-processing account of infant cognition, and Baillargeon et al. (1995) contends that infants begin not with innate knowledge, but with a domain-specific learning mechanism. Differential experiences result in different kinds of learning; this process, rather than core versus noncore knowledge, shapes development.

Baillargeon has examined infants' understanding of various physical phenomena: collisions, containment, occlusion, and so on. At a broad level, her empirical results are in accord with those summarized thus far (e.g., Baillargeon et al., 1995). However, Baillargeon argues that infants' understandings emerge in a precise sequence that does not fit Spelke's account. Consider Spelke's claim that infants are born with the core belief that objects are solid, but that infants must acquire noncore beliefs, such as those about support, via observation and learning. "One prediction suggested by this distinction is that core principles would be demonstrated earlier than non-core beliefs, and would be revealed uniformly in all situations in which they are

implicated" (Baillargeon, 1994, p. 112). According to Baillargeon's recent research, however, even 3-month-olds understand certain aspects of support, hypothesized by Spelke to be a later-developing, noncore belief. Perhaps more telling, Baillargeon argues that such things as barrier phenomena (that solid barriers are obstacles to objects and mechanical forces), passing-through phenomena (that in the absence of a barrier, object and forces can pass through space), and containment and veiling phenomena (that one object can be concealed by another object in the same space by being contained or covered by it) should all reveal a general understanding of object solidity, *if* infants possess such a core concept. But, she contends, infants learn about some of these phenomena long before others. Thus, according to Baillargeon et al. (1995), the pattern of infants' successes and failures at a young age does not suggest the presence of a general core principle such as that objects are solid. Instead, infants "go about the world identifying basic ways in which objects behave or interact. These types of interaction are akin to conceptual roles, i.e., infants reason about objects and occluders, objects and gaps, objects and supports, objects and barriers . . ." (p. 113). These concepts are initially quite separate. They speculate:

> Three-month-old infants have already learned that objects fall when released in mid-air . . . because this expectation is consistent with countless observations (e.g., watching their carers drop peas in pots, toys in baskets, clothes in hampers) . . . Infants do not begin to recognize what type of contact is needed between objects and their supports until 4.5 months . . . because unilateral visually guided reaching emerges at about 4 months. . . . With this new-found ability, infants may have the opportunity deliberately to place objects against other objects, and to observe the consequences of these actions . . . It is not until 6.5 months that infants begin to appreciate how much contact is needed between objects and their supports because . . . the ability to sit without support emerges at about 6 months of age; infants then become able to sit in front of tables . . . relieved from the encumbrance of postural maintenance and thus free to manipulate objects. (pp. 110–111)

In short, as the infants' motoric abilities emerge, their experience of the world changes and their object understandings follow suit.

This sort of developmental scenario is similar in form to one advanced by Campos and Bertenthal with regard to infants' understanding of space and distances, especially as indexed by their fear of heights (e.g., Bertenthal & Campos,

1990; Campos et al., 1978). They claim that self-produced locomotion—rather than age—critically advances the infant's understanding and induces a wariness of heights. This hypothesis is supported by systematic studies in which infants are given early locomotor experiences via wheeled walkers (Campos et al., 1992). Similarly, Bushnell and Boudreau (1993) argue that infants' understanding of objects from haptic exploration develops in a sequence that is best explained by developmental changes in abilities to control the hands and fingers.

Do infants' early conceptions of objects undergo radical changes when developing into adults' and older children's conceptions, or—as Spelke maintains—does infants' initial knowledge remain intact as the unchanging core of adult knowledge? On this difficult question, Carey (e.g., 1991) and Gopnik and Meltzoff (1997) propose that there are radical conceptual changes in the child's basic understanding of objects, and they interpret these changes in theory-theory terms. Consider the change, noted earlier, from individuating objects in terms of spatial coordinates and movement alone to using property features to do so. It could be argued that, for adults, identity or property information is more important than spatial information for tracking and identifying individual objects. In contrast, Gopnik and Meltzoff (1997), following Bower (1974), suggest that babies reidentify objects by their movements *rather than* their properties. If children undergo this developmental shift, it would surely qualify as a radical conceptual reorganization, one that directly affects conceptions of identity, individuation, and sameness. Adults who tracked objects by path of motion rather than featural cues—believing that an object could enter a tunnel as a duck and come out of it as a ball, for example—would be so unlike normal adult humans that they might indeed constitute examples of the metaphorical alien considered at the beginning of this chapter.

Likewise, consider again children's conception of material substance. Carey (1991) and her colleagues suggest that preschoolers have a conception of material substances (as reviewed earlier), but that in addition, children's understanding of matter and substance changes profoundly beyond the preschool years. Like adults, young children judge that large chunks of styrofoam are made of small bits of styrofoam. But unlike adults and older children, preschool children judge that visible pieces of styrofoam weigh nothing at all. Thus having weight, having matter, and occupying space may not be coextensive aspects of objects for young children as they are for adults—implying

that children's conception of objects undergoes an important conceptual revolution.

The theory-theory position is supported not only by evidence of radical changes with age, but also evidence of coherence among children's beliefs—especially when such coherence demonstrates a mismatch with the input children are receiving. Thus, note that young children's reasoning about physical objects and physical-mechanical systems of the sorts reviewed above coheres in several important ways. Coherence is evident when children make novel inductive inferences (Au, 1994), when they reason analogically (Goswami, in press), and when they maintain sensible yet incorrect beliefs—at times even in the face of instruction. For example, according to Au's research, children believe that substances are homogeneous throughout—sugar in cubes is composed of sugar particles, which are composed of still smaller particles, and so on. Every bit of sugar is composed of still smaller bits of sugar. At the extreme, however, this homogeneous conception of matter becomes incorrect. At some point when sugar is broken down into smaller and smaller bits, the smaller pieces would be hydrogen, carbon, and oxygen pieces, not sugar. A scientific understanding of matter is particulate—in terms of fundamental particles of matter—not homogeneous in terms of substances. Of course, a homogeneous conception is adequate for and consistent with everyday observations. When children are taught the scientific particulate theory, however, they have difficulty mastering it, and maintain instead an everyday homogeneity view; some students insist on the homogeneity view even when they take chemistry courses in college (Gabel & Samuel, 1987; Novick & Nussbaum, 1981).

In a similar vein, Vosniadou and Brewer have studied children's understanding of everyday astronomy (Vosniadou, 1989, 1994; Vosniadou & Brewer, 1992, 1994): conceptions of the earth's shape (flat or round), the movement of the planets, and so forth. Conceivably, children could just learn from their elders the relevant facts. However, children's understanding reveals the imprint of their larger coherent theories of physical objects. In spite of being told that the earth is round, most young children at first believe the earth is flat, consistent with their everyday observation of the physical earth stretching before them as a relatively flat plane and their everyday notions of support (if the earth were spherical, people on the bottom would fall off). These coherent notions are specially visible in the numbers of children who assert that the earth is round, consistent with received instruction, but then go on to explain that it is round like a pizza, or that it is round like a large shallow bowl, with all the people safely on the inside and the sky above. Vosniadou and Brewer's studies demonstrate the coherence of children's physical beliefs by showing their conceptual systematicity even in cases where children's conclusions are wrong, at odds with, or only partly adjusted to adult beliefs and input.

Conclusions

Certain core beliefs about the nature and causal interactions of physical objects appear to constitute early foundational human knowledge, emerging in infancy and rapidly becoming enriched to include a deeper understanding of objects (for example, support and gravity), as well as later understanding of insides, of substances, of planetary systems, and more. Conceptions of physical objects also appear to change more profoundly, for example, by undergoing revisions to include property/kind object identification. In the extreme, in some persons at least (e.g., expert physicists), conceptions become reorganized into systems involving such sophisticated concepts as fundamental particles (quarks), space-time continua, and matter-energy interchangeability. Before drawing conclusions regarding the modular, expertise, and theory-theory positions as explanations for such changes, we examine the domains of psychology and biology.

NAIVE PSYCHOLOGY

Naive psychology focuses on our everyday understanding of psychological states and experience. It is thus one aspect of social cognition (Flavell & Miller, this Volume), a topic that includes understanding of social relationships such as kinship, social groups such as families, social institutions such as schools and governments, and social conventions such as manners and morals. Philosophers, ethologists, and psychologists have increasingly argued that naive psychology is a specially evolved human competence, a distinctive everyday theory, a foundational system of human thought (Cheney & Seyfarth, 1990; Churchland, 1981; Dennett, 1987; Humphrey, 1993; Povinelli, 1993; Wellman, 1990). Moreover, for adults, psychological reasoning seems to contrast quite starkly with physical reasoning. Rocks, centers of gravity, and melting are all quite different from emotions, minds, and dreaming.

Research on children's developing psychological understanding has mushroomed in the last 10 to 15 years under the rubric of the child's theory of mind, a phrase first introduced by Premack and Woodruff (1978) to question whether chimpanzees share with us a mentalistic understanding of purposeful actions. We divide our discussion of naive psychology into two parts, first by considering the understanding of verbal children age 3 years and older, and second by taking up similar questions regarding infancy. In each of these parts, we consider (a) what kinds of psychological knowledge are present in children, and (b) how to characterize that knowledge. A further question of special import concerns whether psychological understandings form a distinctive conceptual domain for young children, separable from other potential domains. This question—and the parallel question for children's understanding of physical phenomena—can be addressed by comparing physical and psychological conceptions with one another. For example, do children make a fundamental ontological distinction between physical objects (e.g., a rock) and psychological entities (e.g., a thought about a rock)? Do children distinguish and reason differently about mechanical and psychological causation?

Preschoolers

Mental Entities

When Piaget argued that preschoolers were realists, he was claiming, in part, that they do not honor a distinction between mental and physical phenomena and hence think of mental entities as tangible, physical ones: "The child cannot distinguish a real house, for example, from the concept or mental image or name of the house" (Piaget, 1929, p. 55). In contrast, current research demonstrates that children as young as 3 years firmly distinguish the mental and physical worlds. These studies use more precisely constructed judgment tasks, rather than relying on interpreting young children's often cryptic responses to open-ended interview questions. For example, if told about one boy who has a dog and another one who is thinking about a dog, young children correctly judge which dog can be seen, touched, and petted (Harris et al., 1991; Wellman & Estes, 1986). Moreover, if told about someone who has a dog that ran away and about someone who is thinking of a dog, they know that although neither dog can be seen or petted, one is mental ("just in his mind," "only imagination") whereas the other is physically real but unavailable (Estes et al., 1989). Even if asked to consider certain specially vivid mental entities, such as a mental image of an object depicted by a thought bubble, 3-, 4-, and 5-year-olds still distinguish mental phenomena appropriately from comparable physical objects, such as a picture of an object hidden in a box (Estes et al., 1989; Wellman et al., 1996). By 3 years of age, young children also understand something of the subjectivity of thoughts. In appropriately simple tasks, they are able to state, for example, that while they think a particular cookie tastes yummy, someone else could think it's yucky, or that while Mary thinks a particular box has a doll in it, Bill thinks it contains a teddy bear (e.g., Flavell et al., 1990).

Psychological Causes and Explanation

Adults' psychological understandings arguably constitute a specific system of causal-explanatory reasoning. A useful shorthand description of this system is to characterize it as a belief-desire reasoning framework (D'Andrade, 1987; Fodor, 1987; Wellman, 1990). According to this analysis, at the center of our everyday psychology is a basic triad: beliefs, desires, and actions. Why did Jill go to the swimming pool? She *wanted* to swim and *thought* the pool was open. The fundamental, albeit common idea is that people engage in actions because they believe those actions will satisfy certain desires. Everyday psychology builds on this basic infrastructure in a variety of ways. For example, it encompasses reasoning such as: Why did John go to the candy machine? He was hungry and wanted a candy bar, and thought he'd seen the kind he liked in that machine; boy, will he be surprised. That is, naive psychology incorporates beliefs, desires, and actions centrally, but also a network of related constructs such as physiological states (e.g., "he was hungry") that ground one's desires, and perceptual experiences (e.g., "he'd seen that kind") that ground one's beliefs. Furthermore, actions lead to outcomes in the world, and these outcomes lead to emotional reactions, such as surprise, happiness, sadness, anger.

Note that under this characterization, psychological reasoning involves a coherent system of constructs, and depends on appeals to unobservable mental states. Individual phenomenal experiences are arguably directly experienceable in ourselves (e.g., my longing for that chocolate bar), but we attribute unobserved mental states to others as well as to self. Moreover, beliefs, desires, actions, emotions, and so on are intertwined. Because an actor has certain beliefs and desires, he or she engages in certain intentional acts, the success and failure of which lead to emotions, revised beliefs, renewed desires, and so on. Such a system of reasoning seems notably different from the one used for

physical reasoning, which relies on mechanical causes, physical forces, contact, and solidity.

If preschool children are asked to explain simple human actions (e.g., Jane is looking for her kitty), they, like adults, predominantly advance belief-desire explanations (she wants her kitty, she thinks the kitty is missing). They do so in laboratory situations (Bartsch & Wellman, 1989; Wellman & Banerjee, 1991) and in everyday conversations (Bartsch & Wellman, 1995; Dunn & Brown, 1993). Stein and Trabasso, among others, have systematically shown that 3-, 4-, and 5-year-olds are quite good at understanding the psychological causality depicted in simple stories about human characters who want certain goals, possess certain beliefs, use the information in their beliefs to execute certain plans to overcome obstacles to their goals, and are appropriately happy or sad or angry when they have attained or failed to attain these goals (Stein, 1988; Stein & Trabasso, 1982; Trabasso & Nickels, 1992; Trabasso, Stein, & Johnson, 1981).

By 3 or 4 years, children's psychological understandings also form a coherent system of interrelated constructs. In their explanations, young children reason backwards from actions to beliefs and desires, and can do so in prediction tasks as well (Robinson & Mitchell, 1995). They can also reason forward from characters' beliefs and desires to predict their actions, emotions, or statements (e.g., Hadwin & Perner, 1991; Harris et al., 1989; Wellman & Bartsch, 1988; Wimmer & Perner, 1983). At this age, children also know that perception informs beliefs (Pillow, 1989; Pratt & Bryant, 1990; Wimmer et al., 1988) and something of how various sources of information shape distinctive mental states (O'Neil & Gopnik, 1991; Woolley & Bruell, 1996). Moreover, they conceive of emotions as subjective states (Wellman et al., 1995), understand that emotional reactions are dependent on other mental states such as goals and intentions (e.g., Stein & Levine, 1989; Yuill, 1984), and even understand that some emotions (e.g., happiness) are more dependent on desires whereas others (e.g., surprise), are more dependent on beliefs (Hadwin & Perner, 1991; Wellman & Banerjee, 1991). Again, some of the most telling demonstrations of children's ability to follow and to construct coherent psychological accounts come from their abilities to comprehend and create narratives (e.g., Stein & Albro, in press). Moreover, young children's use of mental terms demonstrates an interlocking network of related constructs. When asked to explain the nature of mental entities, children—like adults—do so in terms of other mental constructs: about a dream, "it's only pretend"; about a false memory, "he's imagining it"; about a mental image, "I could only touch it with my dream hands" (Wellman, 1988). By age 3 or 4 at least, it can be argued that children's naive psychology, like adults', reveals much of the character of a naive framework theory.

Consequently, as early as 3 years, children appropriately distinguish psychological from physical causes and explanations. By 3 years, many children report that physical force is necessary to manipulate physical objects (e.g., to open and close a real pair of scissors) but that "just thinking" is sufficient to affect mental changes (e.g., to open and close the image of a pair of scissors in your mind; Estes et al., 1989). Children 3 and 4 years old precisely distinguish thinking from doing, one as internal, private, and "just" mental, the other as overt, public, and physically consequential (e.g., Flavell et al., 1995; Wellman et al., 1996). Even in their understanding of human action and movement, 3- and 4-year-olds can distinguish sharply between psychological versus physical causes. Human movements can be object-like (e.g., being blown by the wind) and hence explainable in physical causal terms, or they can be voluntary (e.g., desiring and deciding to go outdoors and doing so) and hence explainable in belief-desire terms. Early in the preschool years, children make such explanatory distinctions (Schult & Wellman, in press).

Much of the above analysis depends in part on granting young children an understanding of a variety of mental states, such as beliefs and desires. Developmentally, however, several researchers claim that children understand some of these states—in particular desires, emotions, and perceptions—before others—notably beliefs. For these and other reasons, children's understanding of beliefs has received special research attention. False beliefs have been investigated especially intensively because false beliefs neatly contrast with reality itself (e.g., Jane believes it is raining, but it is not).

Many studies now show that by 4 and 5 years, children reason competently about false beliefs at least in clear, simplified situations. For example, if children of this age are shown a distinctive candy box that actually contains pencils, they can correctly predict that a naive viewer of the box will falsely believe it contains candy, not pencils (Gopnik & Astington, 1988; Perner et al., 1987). Or, if 4- and 5-year-olds see a person notice where an object is placed, and then see that the person is absent and thus cannot observe when the object is moved to a new location, they can accurately predict that the person will mistakenly look for, and falsely think that, the object is in the original location

(Avis & Harris, 1991; Moses & Flavell, 1990; Wimmer & Perner, 1983). Intriguingly, although 4-year-olds often pass these sorts of false belief tasks, in many studies, younger children, typically 3-year-olds, fail them. In this, 3-year-olds do not just answer randomly or confusedly, they make a specific error. For example, they say that the other person will think that the box contains pencils, or that the person will look for the object in the new, correct location. That is, they predict the other's action and they attribute to the other thoughts based on objective reality rather than the person's subjective beliefs. This developmental difference from 2 or 3 to 4 or 5 years has been found with a variety of tasks and methods—when the questions are about mental states directly or when they are about behavior (where the person will search or look), when the target person is a story character, a videotaped character, a puppet, a child, or an adult, and even in tasks that focus on the child's own beliefs.

These findings, among others, lead to the developmental hypothesis of a major reorganization in children's naive psychologies in the ages from 2 to 5. According to this hypothesis, younger children construe persons as relating to the world directly as it is (or at least as the child himself believes it to be), whereas older preschoolers construe people as relating to the world through their representations of it. To be clear, it is *not* that children below age 4 lack a naive psychology; several lines of research suggest that very young children have a clear understanding of some mental states. The claim is that this early understanding is different from the representational understanding of older children and adults.

How to Characterize Preschoolers' Psychological Understandings

Theory-theory, modular, and expertise accounts provide alternative characterizations of these psychological conceptions and developments. Theory-theory accounts characterize preschool children as proceeding from an earlier simple desire (Wellman, 1990), situational (Perner, 1991), or "connections" (Flavell, 1988) theory of mind to a later representational theory. Gopnik and Wellman (1994) claim that young children's psychological understandings are demonstrably theory-like in that unobservable theoretical constructs—such as beliefs and desires—are evident in how children explain and predict human behavior and states, and in their theory-based interpretation of evidence. For example, 3-year-olds not only fail to attribute false beliefs to others, they similarly fail to understand their own false beliefs and misinterpret their own psychological states (Gopnik, 1993). Moreover, the process of developmental change—from understanding of desires and emotions but not beliefs, to understanding of beliefs but still explaining behavior only in terms of other states, to only later incorporating an understanding of beliefs into psychological explanations—closely mimics a process of theory change. According to this account, a conception of belief is first absent, and then developed only as a marginal auxiliary hypothesis, before becoming theoretically central to children's understanding.

In contrast, a nativist, modular account of the same data is advanced by theorists such as Fodor (1983, 1992) and Leslie (1987, 1994). Fodor's claim is that naive psychological understanding is designed into the human conceptual apparatus by evolution, that it necessarily encompasses an understanding of both beliefs and desires, that such an understanding is present extremely early in life, and that it requires little, if any, learning. Such a position leads to questions regarding the data purporting to show that understanding of beliefs is absent in 3-year-olds and emerges only in 4- and 5-year-olds. Several studies now show that at least in some situations 3-year-olds, too, perform correctly on false belief tasks. In several studies, downplaying the salience of the real state of affairs (e.g., that the candy box contains real pencils, not candy) or making salient the prior mental state (e.g., that the child first thinks it is a candy box) helps young children correctly identify the character's false belief (Mitchell & Lacohee, 1991; Woolley, 1995; Zaitchik, 1991). In addition, 3-year-olds at times perform well if they are more actively engaged in deceiving the target person (Chandler et al., 1989; Sullivan & Winner, 1993; but see Sodian, 1994), if the key features of the false belief narrative are overlearned (Lewis et al., 1994), or if certain ways of phrasing the false belief question are used rather than others (e.g., Lewis & Osborne, 1990; Siegal & Beattie, 1991).

The data have also fueled proposals that understanding belief specifically, and developing belief-desire reasoning more generally, are due to increasing expertise (e.g., Dunn, Brown, & Beardsall, 1991; Siegal, 1991; Stein & Trabasso, 1982). One of these expertise accounts—simulation theory—deserves special mention because it is uniquely domain-specific. As described thus far, children possess mental state representations that function like theoretical constructs, allowing children to interpret behavior in intentional terms by attributing to themselves and others mental states such as beliefs and desires, and thereby to predict and explain actions, understand others' minds, and so on. Even modular theorists such as Fodor (1992) adopt this sort of basic characterization. In contrast, simulation theory contends that ordinary reasoning about persons and minds is instead based on our own first-hand experience of mental life (Goldman, 1992; Gordon, 1986; Harris, 1991). Since we are creatures possessing mental state experiences, we certainly come to refer to states such as beliefs and desires, but our capacity to do so does not depend on developing concepts and theories of such states. Rather, we simply experience and report our own mental experiences. Attributing such experiences to others, relatedly, proceeds not via a series of conceptual inferences but instead via a process of simulation. To think about others' minds, we project ourselves into the other person's situation, imaginatively consider what we would experience in that situation ourselves, and then attribute that (simulated) experience to the other.

Expertise is needed in this process because children must learn not to attribute their own states to others, but to simulate others' states from information about their situation. According to Harris (1992), who has articulated a simulation account in most detail, children's simulations operate against a backdrop of two default settings, namely the mental states of the self and the real state of the world. Simulations are more or less difficult depending on how many defaults the child must override. To simulate someone else's desire or belief, for instance, one must ignore one's own state and imagine the state of the other. Suppose a child does not know what is in a box, but thinks it holds a doll. To simulate the belief of someone who thinks it holds a toy truck, the child must override his own belief and simulate the other's contrasting belief. An understanding of false beliefs, however, requires the child to override not only her own mental stance, but reality as well. Thus, if the child knows the box holds a doll and must simulate the thought of someone else who mistakenly believes it holds a truck, then the child must set aside known reality and imagine someone else as having a different intentional stance toward that reality.

Empirically testing theory-theory, modularity, and simulation accounts presents several difficulties. For example, each account acknowledges that children's performance on false belief tasks may change with age, while offering different explanations of that change—e.g., that such tasks reveal only performance, not competence limitations, or that they reflect genuine conceptual change.

The different accounts tend to generate and privilege different sorts of data as well. In particular, modular theorists early considered and generated theory-of-mind research with individuals with autism. In this line of research, the theory-of-mind hypothesis for autism proposes that the social and communicative deficits of autism reflect neurological impairment to a theory-of-mind module leading to deficits in the normally developing ability to construe persons in terms of mental states (Baron-Cohen et al., 1993). This hypothesis has proven both productive and controversial—sparking considerable research on the understanding that people with autism have mental states and sparking alternative proposals as to the central impairments of autism. For example, several studies show impairment in reasoning about mental states in high-functioning people with autism who, at the same time, show very good reasoning about physical phenomena (e.g., Baron-Cohen, 1995). A precise comparison has targeted the understanding that people with autism have false beliefs versus false photographs. Parallel tasks requiring recognition of a false mental representation—an individual's outdated and hence false belief—versus recognition of a false physical representation—an outdated and hence incorrect photograph—yield similar results for normal 4-year-olds but very different results for children with autism (Leekam & Perner, 1991; Leslie & Thaiss, 1992). High-functioning individuals with autism show very good performance on false photos, yet poor performance on false beliefs. Thus, their false belief errors are not due to an inability to reason logically or to follow the target tasks, but instead strongly imply a specific deficit in mental state understanding. These sorts of deficits in psychological reasoning are not apparent in control groups of subjects with Downs Syndrome, general retardation, or specific language delays (Baron-Cohen, 1995).

At the least, these data provide further support for domain-specific differences in reasoning about persons versus physical objects. In addition, they provide initial support for the notion of a theory of mind mental module. One implication of positing a theory of mind module, however, is that individuals who are *not* impaired in that module—that is, do not have autism—should achieve landmark mental state understandings on a roughly standard maturational timetable. In contrast, if expertise or theory-theory accounts more adequately capture these developing abilities, individuals who are exposed to very different amounts of mental state data should acquire mental state understandings on different timetables. In this regard, consider deaf individuals raised by hearing parents. Many hearing parents cannot sign, and even hearing parents who learn signing in order to communicate with their deaf children are generally poor signers, typically using short phrases about here-and-now referents and avoiding talk about complex, unobservable phenomena such as mental states (Marschak, 1993; Peterson & Siegal, 1995). Thus, most deaf children of hearing parents have relatively little access to mental state conversation until they join a community of fluent signers (often not until primary school). Two recent studies of such deaf preschool children's performance on theory-of-mind tasks show delays and deficiencies comparable to those of children with autism (Gale et al., 1996; Peterson & Siegal, 1995). These preliminary data thus challenge neurological maturational accounts such as the modular ones of Baron-Cohen and Leslie.

Data from 2-year-olds also help contrast different explanatory accounts. Consider young children's use of mental-psychological language. Children begin referring to people's emotions, desires, perceptions, and even thoughts and knowledge at an early age via such words as *happy, sad, want, think,* and *know* (Bretherton & Beeghley, 1982; Furrow et al., 1992; Ridgeway et al., 1985). Moreover, children use these terms to refer to people's internal mental states distinct from their external behaviors, physical features, and facial expressions (Shatz et al., 1983; Wellman et al., 1995). In everyday discourse, young children refer to the mental states of self and others (Bartsch & Wellman, 1995; Dunn, Brown, Slomkowski, Tesla, & Youngblade, 1991; but see Smiley & Huttenlocher, 1989), and while they refer to desires and emotions by 2 years or younger, they do not refer to thoughts and beliefs until about 3 years (Bartsch & Wellman, 1995; Brown & Dunn, 1991). Such very young children refer to desires and emotions, but not beliefs and thoughts, even though parents talk to them about beliefs and thoughts, as well as desires and emotions (Bartsch & Wellman, 1995).

These data pose challenges to an innatist account such as Fodor's. If children are born knowing about both beliefs and desires, if they eagerly communicate about mental states generally, why talk about desires but not beliefs? The data also provide some evidence relevant to theory theory versus simulation accounts. On Harris's simulation account, for example, talk about one's own desires and one's own beliefs should develop before talk about others' desires and beliefs. Talk about false beliefs, however, should be notably later because here reality is known and needs to be overridden as well. On a theory-theory account, however, talk about desires should include attributions to self and other—desires are generic constructs used to explain states or acts of both self and other—and talk about desires should precede talk about beliefs because these two are quite different theoretical constructs. The data from everyday conversations conform closely to theory-theory expectations: children talk about desires for self and others early on; they fail to talk about beliefs, even their own beliefs or theoretically easy-to-simulate beliefs, and when talk about beliefs first appears, it includes reference to false beliefs as well as beliefs of self and others (Bartsch & Wellman, 1995).

Infants

Even quite young infants demonstrate certain distinctive social behaviors. They cry, smile, and begin to become emotionally attached to others; they preferentially attend to faces—or, at first, the sorts of complex, detailed, high-contrast stimuli that faces represent (Banks & Salapatek, 1983; Johnson & Morton, 1991; Nelson, 1987); they imitate certain human actions, especially facial movements (Meltzoff & Moore, 1983). In short, infants attend to people as a special sort of object. Consequently, in infancy, children appear to develop certain expectations about persons that contrast with their expectations about physical objects. Within the first year of life, infants will imitate the actions of persons (Meltzoff & Moore, 1983), but not similar activities of mechanical objects (e.g., Legerstee, 1991), and they are upset in still-face research when people do not behave actively and expressively (see review by Muir & Haines, 1993). From about 3 months on, infants discriminate animate-biological motions versus random or artificial ones (e.g., Bertenthal, 1993), and toward the middle of the first year, may distinguish persons as self-propelled movers in contrast to physical objects that must be launched by external forces. For example, at 7 months (and perhaps earlier), infants appear surprised if objects begin moving without some external force causing them to do so as described in our section on naive physics, but not if people do so (Spelke, Phillips, & Woodward, 1995). At 10 months (and perhaps earlier), infants easily learn to push a lever in order to set an inanimate object (a picture) in motion but are unable to learn to push the lever in order to make a person wave and smile (Golinkoff et al., 1984).

Understanding that certain objects move on their own whereas others do not helps infants separate animate from inanimate things and helps infants recognize "that they are like other human beings as opposed to inanimate stimuli" (Legerstee, 1992, p. 65). But conceiving of persons as animate in the sense of self-moving requires no distinctive psychological conception of them; fleas are animate entities and cars are self moving, but neither requires a theory of mind to be understood. A psychological conception of persons and states requires more than a conception of self-propulsion or animacy. A common claim is that it requires something like an understanding of intentionality, as philosophers use that term (Baldwin & Moses, 1994; Brentano, 1874; Dennett, 1987; Perner, 1991; Wellman, 1993). Both beliefs and desires are intentional states in that they are internal experiences about or toward some object—a belief about an apple. Note that, in this sort of analysis, an ordinary intentional act—deliberately reaching for an apple—manifests intentionality in two related senses. In the narrower everyday sense, it is intentional because it is purposeful. In the broader philosophical sense, it reflects an intentional state, such as a goal (to get the apple), a desire (for the apple), or a belief (that's an apple). Intentional acts and states in this sense are very different from merely self-propelled motion.

Researchers describe a transition in social interaction, evident in the period from 8 to 14 months, in which the infant comes to see self and others in notably different terms. Infants at this age are said to show a sense of subjectivity (Stern, 1985), secondary intersubjectivity (Trevarthen & Hubley, 1978), intentional communication (Bates et al., 1979), triadic awareness (Adamson & Bakeman, 1985), or even an implicit theory of mind (Bretherton et al., 1981). The common claim here, we believe, is that infants come to view persons in intentional terms. These descriptions rest on findings that older infants (10 to 14 months or so) show emerging understanding of others' visual gaze (Butterworth, 1991; Scaife & Bruner, 1975) and pointing gestures to nearby objects (Murphy & Messer, 1977), they begin to comprehend words and engage in simple communicative interchanges with words and gestures (Bates et al., 1979), and they engage in social referencing (Feinman, 1982; Sorce et al., 1985). These descriptions of the development of intentional understanding at around 12 months are intriguing, insightful, and may eventually prove correct. At present, however, it is unclear whether behaviors that begin to appear at the end of the first year do or do not demonstrate an intentional understanding of persons, as we illustrate with three examples: infants' interpretation of gaze, social referencing, and word learning.

Older infants achieve considerable skill at following others' direction of gaze, thereby focusing on the other person's object of attention (e.g., Butterworth, 1991), and often achieving joint reference (e.g., Adamson & Bakeman, 1985). From roughly 12 to 18 months, infants achieve the ability to locate objects looked at by others even if those objects are behind the infant (outside his/her immediate visual space), if two or more targets lie in the same general direction (e.g., Butterworth & Grover, 1988; Butterworth & Jarrett, 1991). Butterworth argues, however, that at these ages, infants solve these problems geometrically, following lines of sight and probably using the nose as an important cue. If solving these problems geometrically, the infant need not construe the looker as actually seeing the object—as having perceptual experiences about the target referent. Infants, even at ages 14 to 18 months, might simply be monitoring others' gaze as a reliable cue for producing an interesting perceptual experience.

The classic social referencing phenomenon is that in certain situations, infants as young as 10 months glance to the parent and then subsequently behave toward the object or situation in accord with the affect shown by the parent. For example, when a baby is placed across a visual cliff from its mother, if the mother smiles, the baby is likely to cross, but if she appears fearful, the baby is likely to stay where she is (Sorce et al., 1985). These results are not simply due to mood contagion (e.g., seeing a negative expression causes the infant to become fearful or anxious), because infants' social referencing reactions are object specific (Hornick et al., 1987; Walden & Ogan, 1988). A rich interpretation of these demonstrations is that infants seek emotional information from parents and interpret emotional displays as providing evidence as to the parent's internal feeling about the object or situation. However, even establishing that infants' reactions are object specific does not establish that infants understand that parents' emotions are *about* objects. In Hornick et al.'s study, for example, the infants themselves were already focused on the target object (because of its novelty and salience in the experimental situation) at the time the mothers expressed their affect facially and verbally. In this situation children did not necessarily need to read the parental emotion as being about an object. Infants might simply associate parental affect to the object with which they (the infants) were presently engaged.

Even children's early comprehension of words is not clear evidence of intentional understanding of communication (Baldwin, 1991). When parents name objects for infants, their labels help pick out objects, but infant word learning could take place in either of two ways. Associatively, infants might pair adults' labels with the objects of their own (the infant's) attention. Or, intentionally, infants could understand that speakers use words to pick out specific objects

and thus attempt to pair labels with the object of the speaker's intent or attention. In several studies, Baldwin has compared infants in two word-learning conditions: follow-in labeling and discrepant labeling (Baldwin, 1991, 1993). In each condition, infants were shown two novel objects. In follow-in labeling, the speaker waited until the infant first looked at one toy and then the speaker also looked at and labeled that toy. In discrepant labeling, the speaker waited for the infant to focus on one toy and then looked at and labeled the other toy. Later, infants' word learning was assessed; infants were again shown the two toys and asked comprehension questions (essentially, "Which is the [new label]?"). Baldwin found that 14-month-old infants fail to learn in either situation, 16-month- and 18-month-old infants learn in follow-in conditions, but only 18-month-olds learn correctly in the discrepant conditions. These older infants noted the attentional discrepancy, checked the speaker's attentional focus, and understood the new label as concerning the speaker's object of attention. We believe that Baldwin's data thus show intentional understanding of speakers' communicative intents by about 18 months, but not necessarily earlier. Other recent research also suggests that 18-month-olds understand human acts in intentional, goal-directed terms (e.g., Repacholi & Gopnik, 1997). For example, Meltzoff (1995) demonstrated that when imitating human actions, such as an adult who tried, but failed at some act, 18-month-olds inferred the intention and thus re-enacted successful, completed acts. This behavior was appropriately distinguished from that of children who saw the full target act, appropriate other comparison acts, or who saw an inanimate object execute the same movements that the person had.

The importance, yet ambiguity, of naive psychological understandings in infants younger than 18 months, however, has created fertile ground for competing accounts of infants' psychological understanding—modular, theory-theory, and expertise accounts. We believe that data testing these alternative accounts of infant development are as yet unavailable. Nonetheless, it is useful to contrast them briefly.

Modular accounts that propose some single theory of mind module available early in life, such as Fodor's, have trouble accommodating data that reveal developmental changes in infants' or young children's conceptions. But more generally, mental modules are part of a larger view of the mind as having a componential architecture, that is, as being composed of specialized subsystems. Theory of mind capacities themselves need not be subserved by a single module; that system might be composed of separate subsystems or modules. A series of modules triggered or maturing at separate points in development could then underlie the developmental data.

Leslie (1987) initially offered an analysis of the special sort of cognitive representations needed by a computational device in order to understand mental states—representations not just of objects or states of the world, but representations of representational states themselves, that is, metarepresentations (or lately, m-representations). He argued that mental state understanding depends on a specialized module for representing these m-representations—ToMM, or the theory of-mind mechanism. More recently, both Leslie (1994) and Baron-Cohen (1995) have proposed a developmental sequence of mental modules culminating in ToMM. To illustrate, we consider Baron-Cohen's proposal.

According to Baron-Cohen, infants start with two modules—an Eye-Direction Detector (EDD) and an Intentionality Detector (ID)—which are followed at about 10 to 12 months of age by a Shared Attention Mechanism (SAM), and then ToMM still later. Based on research with human infants and with non-human primates, Baron-Cohen argues that attending to others' eyes is evolutionarily and developmentally important, and that an early developing module (EDD) takes in information about eyes and represents others as looking at objects in the intentional sense. Beyond representing the other as directed toward particular objects, eventually infants need to represent self and other as directed simultaneously toward the same objects. Such a shared attention representation underlies older infants' understandings of gesture and gaze according to Baron-Cohen, hence the need for SAM. Still later ToMM comes on line, which can then yield representations of persons in terms of a variety of deeper psychological-mentalistic construals—desiring, knowing, and believing things.

In arguing for the plausibility of this modular account, Baron-Cohen marshalls both developmental and clinical-neurological data. Developmentally, behaviors demonstrating shared attention (e.g., social referencing) appear late in the first year, after earlier attention to faces and eyes. Such shared attention capacities in turn precede the later onset of pretense, mental state language, and success on various theory of mind tasks. Baron-Cohen argues that there are probably two subgroups of autism: an early onset group—resulting from an impairment of SAM (Mundy & Sigman, 1989)—and a later onset group of individuals who show normal development until about 18 to 24 months (Volkmar & Klin, 1993)—resulting from an impairment to ToMM alone. Both rich and intriguing, this account is still very promissory: No evidence exists that attention to eyes in early infancy yields a representation in terms of intentional states, and the best interpretation of data from children with autism is still in dispute (see the chapters in Baron-Cohen et al., 1993), leaving ample room for alternative accounts.

Moore (Barresi & Moore, 1996; Moore, 1996; Moore & Corkum, 1994), for example, advances an expertise account—claiming that general learning mechanisms produce infants' psychological understandings and their development. Moore stresses that infants must come to understand persons in intentional terms, and stresses that this understanding must be applicable to others as well as the self. That is, in some way, the child must overcome the problem of other minds (see also Hobson, 1993; Smiley & Huttenlocher, 1989). Developmentally, according to Moore, the child arrives at a representation of psychological relations that fuses a first person and a third person perspective. The infant must come to understand the other's behavior from the inside and understand his own internal experiences from the outside, so as to see both self and other as similar, psychologically related objects.

In Moore's account, infants slowly learn a variety of interpersonal behaviors and routines over the first year of life because of certain attentional dispositions—such as preference for faces—and certain general learning mechanisms—such as imitation and contingency learning. One outcome of these factors is that by the end of the first year, the infant increasingly shares attention with others, that is, the infant and adult attend to and behave similarly with the same objects. Importantly, at this point, the infant does not yet appreciate that both persons are psychologically relating to (looking at, thinking about) objects. Nonetheless, the infant tends to be engaged with adult partners in such special matching situations. Similarly, adults' tendency to imitate infants means that adults are often behaviorally providing visual displays coincidentally matched to infants' inner experiences. These situations provide the infant with matched first person and third person information about the same person-object relation. In these special situations, according to Moore and colleagues, the infant first achieves a rudimentary representation of intentional relations, a representation that literally fuses first and third person views and is not attributable independently to either self or other. Only at the end of infancy, late in the second year, based on experience in such matched situations and on increasing cognitive ability to hold multiple sources of information in mind in a common representation, does the infant become able to represent a generic psychological relation attributable to either self or other.

Gopnik and Meltzoff (1997) provide a detailed theory-theory account of developments from infancy on. They argue that infants begin life with an initial theory of action, but then accumulate transitional auxiliary hypotheses leading to several intermediate theories that result in a first theory of mind. The infant's first theory of mind is nonrepresentational and so must develop further into a representational theory of mind. Like Moore, Gopnik and Meltzoff assume that it is crucial for the infant to be able to represent self and other similarly in a common format. However, they assume that such a representation is the starting state for infant understanding of persons rather than the culmination of two years of developing expertise and experience. For Gopnik and Meltzoff, evidence for this claim comes from demonstrations of infants', even neonates' (Meltzoff & Moore, 1983), imitation of facial gestures. Since the infant cannot see his or her own face, imitating facial gestures requires mapping visual perceptions of others' movements along with internally felt experiences of self's unseen movements in the same representation.

This initial "like me" representation is strictly tied to bodily movements and is the basis for an initial understanding of bodily movement, an initial theory of action. Importantly, the initial theory provides the starting state for several expansions to the infant's understanding. Specifically, Gopnik and Meltzoff (1997) spell out a series of transitional states leading from early infancy to the 9-month-old theory. This later theory includes a distinction between persons and objects, and between the sorts of physical actions needed to act on objects versus the different sorts of actions needed to interact with persons. Experience, including various forms of imitation, provides the data that transform the intial theory into the later one. By the end of the first year, the infant achieves an understanding of persons as special psychological actors acting on a world of objects and interacting with other people.

Conclusions

Whether modular, expertise, or theory-theory accounts of crucial developments during infancy turn out to be most useful, the clear fact remains that children by preschool age in a variety of countries—North America, England, Europe, Australia, Turkey, Japan, and the Cameroons—

construe people in terms of mental states that determine how they act and interact. This naive psychological understanding contrasts quite clearly with an understanding of physical objects and forces. Even young children believe that contents and states of mind are mental, subjective, and immaterial, whereas contents and states of the physical world are substantial, objective, and material. This distinction is evident in basic form in toddlers, arguably based on a still earlier distinction in infants between inanimate object properties and motions and animate self-propelled entities and motions. One question we address in the next section is: Do young children understand that people and animals are also biological creatures, and thus, do they distinguish a domain of biological phenomena from psychological ones?

NAIVE BIOLOGY

Biological understandings concern the distinction between living and nonliving things, the relation of humans to other species, and natural processes such as illness, digestion, and birth. At minimum, thinking biologically requires the realization that certain entities operate outside the forces of mechanical or belief-desire causation. Moreover, thinking biologically requires an understanding of specifically biological causal forces such as growth, reproduction, and inheritance. Biological conceptions have recently received considerable attention for at least two reasons. Like physics and psychology, biological understandings are important and far-reaching, encompassing the living world at large, ourselves, plants, and other animals. Moreover, biological phenomena are linked to issues of categorization. Plants and animals are richly-structured, inference-promoting entities (Gelman & Markman, 1986; Keil, 1989) and are universally organized into hierarchically structured taxonomic systems (Atran, 1990; Berlin, 1992; Malt, 1995). Although biological categories may or may not be privileged in this respect (as discussed later), classification systems of biological kinds provide a paradigm case for considering issues of categorization.

As in the previous sections, our discussion focuses on two issues of central importance: When in development is there a separate biological domain, and how can that domain best be characterized? Most of the relevant evidence comes from studies of children preschool age and older, though we also refer to research with infants.

When Is There a Separate Biological Domain?

Biology constitutes a domain separate from physics or psychology for adults in our culture. Adults recognize a variety of specifically biological processes (e.g., inheritance, photosynthesis). They attribute being alive to a set of entities that share few outwardly perceivable similarities, but many important structures and functions (animals and plants are alive, but not dolls or fake plants). They report that all and only living things can reproduce, or need to eat or breathe, and recognize the existence of biological processes even in atypical organisms (e.g., germs). Furthermore, adults treat the living-nonliving distinction as ontological, for example, reporting that it is not simply false but rather makes no sense to say things such as "the chair is alive."

It is clear that at least the more sophisticated versions of these beliefs develop. Newborns do not conceive of germs, and 3-year-olds do not understand how the circulatory system works. At what point can children be said to distinguish a separate domain of biology? There are at least two plausible ways in which young children may fail to do so. First, biology could be confused in children's minds with psychology—children may think that all animate phenomena are governed by an organism's motivations, feelings, or beliefs, or social forces such as convention and morality (Carey, 1985). Second, biology could also fail to function as a distinct domain if domain-general principles govern children's understandings. For example, children may classify animals and plants using domain-general principles of similarity, failing to give special weight to specifically biological features (Gelman & Coley, 1991; Keil, 1989).

Biological Entities

As noted earlier, even infants readily distinguish animals (especially people) from inanimate objects. For example, older infants distinguish animals from vehicles based on properties such as the capacity to drink or sleep (Mandler & McDonough, in press). However, grasping a distinction between animate and inanimate things, albeit basic to a mature grasp of biology, is insufficient evidence for a specifically biological understanding. To provide evidence for a biological distinction, it is crucial to ask children about items that unconfound animacy and life—items such as plants, which are living but inanimate, or robots, which are animate-like but not alive. In fact, when asked if plants are alive, elementary school children often say "no" (Carey, 1985; Hatano et al., 1993; Richards & Siegler,

1986). However, there are two different interpretations consistent with this error. On the one hand, children may use psychological criteria (e.g., desires and goals) rather than biological criteria to respond, categorizing plants as non-living because plants cannot think, want, or plan. This would imply failure to appreciate a biological domain. On the other hand, perhaps young children recognize a distinct biological domain, but one that excludes plants. According to this view, children could recognize the appropriate ontological domain (biology), but err in its scope of application (i.e., determining precisely which things are biological). This second account would also imply that under certain circumstances, young children might readily learn to treat plants as biological entities.

In support of the second account, more recent studies suggest that 3- and 4-year-olds distinguish living things (including plants) from human artifacts in several respects. These studies differ from past work in precisely focusing children on specific biological properties rather than generally asking them to classify items as alive or not alive. Thus, preschool children recognize that plants, like animals, can grow (Hickling & Gelman, 1995; Inagaki & Hatano, 1996), heal without human intervention (Backscheider, Shatz, & Gelman, 1993), or decompose and become noxious (Springer, Ngyuen, & Samaniego, 1996). Preschoolers may also distinguish biological from non-biological natural things in terms of whether their parts or properties have a predetermined function or purpose (also known as a teleological construal). For example, the green color of a plant helps it to acquire energy, whereas the green color of an emerald has no function for that emerald (Keil, 1992, 1994). There is currently debate as to whether children's teleological explanations (e.g., "the heart works because it wants to move the blood around the body") stem from a distinctive vitalistic biology (Inagaki & Hatano, 1993) or a psychological understanding of biological phenomena (Carey, 1995).

Biological Causal Mechanisms

Recent studies demonstrate that preschool children view at least some biological processes as *outside* the domains of psychology or physics. For example, 4- and 5-year-olds judge that processes such as breathing, getting tired or sleepy, and gaining weight cannot be controlled or modified by merely psychological interventions (Inagaki & Hatano, 1993; Schult & Wellman, in press). Similarly, they say that people cannot prevent an animal from growing (Inagaki & Hatano, 1987). At the same time, young children hold many misconceptions regarding certain biological processes, particularly internal bodily processes that involve specialized structures, such as respiration, digestion, or circulation of the blood (Carey, 1985).

Demonstrating that children understand that some phenomena fall outside of the scope of psychological and mechanical forces does not necessarily demonstrate a specifically biological causal understanding. What might be distinctive biological processes and mechanisms (in the way that mechanical-dynamic collisions are distinctively physical, say) that children could plausibly grasp early in life? We suspect, as have other researchers, that likely candidates include the processes of biological movement, growth, inheritance, and illness. There may be a basic level of phenomena that children focus on in their early conceptualizations—topics that are neither too broad (such as evolution), nor too narrow (such as cellular mitosis). Movement, growth, inheritance, and illness are notable in this regard because they involve the entire visible animal or plant, rather than the workings of parts (e.g., lungs, heart) or obscure processes (e.g., digestion). Perhaps more importantly, movement, growth, inheritance, and illness/injury have broad implications for interpreting an animal's behavior and judging its identity. For example, adults rely on movement to make decisions regarding agency; they rely on growth to track identity of an animal over time; and they use biological inheritance when predicting or explaining the characteristics of offspring. Furthermore, parents may be more likely to talk about movement, growth, kinship, and illness than internal bodily processes.

It is plausible to suspect that children's earliest understandings of biological processes concern movement, given the primacy of movement in infancy (e.g., Bertenthal et al., 1985). Moreover, children's causal explanations differ for animal versus artifact movement (Gelman, Durgin, & Kaufman, 1995; Massey & Gelman, 1988). Children aged 3 and 4 years realize that animals, but not simple artifacts, move as the result of self-generated powers (R. Gelman, 1990; S. Gelman & Gottfried, 1996). Children as young as 3 years of age honor domain differences even with item movements that appear to be self-generated (e.g., a hopping chinchilla is said to move by itself; a toy that seemingly propels itself across a table is said to move not by itself but rather as a result of human intervention).

Children also understand several aspects of growth by preschool age. They understand that growth and development are constrained: animals get bigger with age, not smaller; animals can take on a more complex form (e.g.,

caterpillar to butterfly), but not a simpler form (e.g., butterfly to caterpillar; Rosengren, Gelman, Kalish, & McCormick, 1991). Only animals and plants undergo the distinctive process of growth; human artifacts such as toys or machines cannot (Carey, 1985; Rosengren et al., 1991). Similarly, Backscheider et al. (1993) found that 3- and 4-year-old children report that living things are capable of self-healing; artifacts are not. For example, if the fur is removed from a dog, children report that it can grow back by itself. But if the hair is cut off a doll, children report that it requires human intervention to be restored.

Preschool children appear to understand the constraints on growth much earlier than they understand the constraints on nonbiological processes of change involving animals. With nonbiological processes such as surgical operations, children below age 7 accept as wide a range of transformations as possible, including those adults deem impossible (e.g., a cat becoming a dog; DeVries, 1969; Keil, 1989). But for natural transformations, children realize that the changes that can occur are bounded and that identity remains constant across those changes (Gelman, 1993; Rosengren et al., 1994). In this way, young children give evidence that they are sensitive to whether the mechanism inducing change is a natural, biological one or an artificial one.

Inheritance is a specifically biological process; all and only living things have offspring to which they are capable of passing along inherited characteristics. Although learning the details of the process certainly requires instruction, young children have an early grasp of some of the basic aspects. Springer (1992; Springer & Keil, 1989) asked preschool children to predict which features of parents would be inherited by their offspring. For example, they were told that "Mr. and Mrs. Bull . . . were both born with pink hearts inside their chests instead of normal-colored hearts," and were asked to predict whether their children would be born with a normal-colored heart or a pink heart. Subjects more often treated a feature as inherited when it led to biological outcomes (e.g., the capacity to eat more) than when it led to psychological outcomes (e.g., anger), thus suggesting that preschool children believe that the process of inheritance operates over specifically biological properties. Preschool children also have reasonable expectations about the means by which biological properties are transmitted from parent to offspring, for example, appealing to internal causal mechanisms rather than psychological or artificialistic explanations to explain why a biological entity is a certain color (Springer & Keil, 1991). Importantly, Springer

(1992) found that preschool children are aware of the biological implications of kinship. They expect animals of the same family to share physical features (e.g., tiny bones inside), even in the strong case when perceptual similarity is placed in conflict with kinship.

Related to the notion of inheritance is the understanding that individuals have a certain innate potential that is determined at or before birth and emerges in a broad array of environmental contexts. For example, a mouse may be genetically programmed to have black-and-white fur, even though it is hairless at birth. By age 4 years, children appreciate that animals have innate potential of this sort, and they quickly apply this understanding to plant seeds as well. When children are told about infant animals and seeds that are raised in an environment more suited to another species (e.g., a calf raised among pigs; a seed that came from an apple and was planted in a pot full of flowers), they report that the animals and plants will have species-appropriate characteristics (e.g., the adult cow will moo and have a straight tail; Gelman & Wellman, 1991). Children believe that this sort of innate potential exists for humans as well as other animals. Taylor (1993) found that young children expect that gender-linked characteristics (e.g., play preferences and aptitudes) are innately determined and unaffected by environmental opportunities. Children do not start to acknowledge the importance of environmental influence until middle childhood (roughly age 9 or 10 years; Taylor, 1993).

These data are consistent with the interpretation that children expect each category member to possess an underlying essential nature that persists even in the absence of a normal environment. It is possible, however, that children make these judgments without having a specifically biological understanding. Carey (1995) rightly warns of the danger of overattributing understandings to children based on similarities between children's and adults' knowledge. Specifically, Solomon et al. (1996) argue that in Gelman and Wellman's study, children could still apply a psychological rather than biological construal. Solomon et al. conducted a set of studies that highlighted the nurturing, family-like aspects of the adoptive family, and tested both biological and psychological properties. Using this task, it was not until 7 years of age that children relied on biological parents for drawing inferences about the adopted child. Similarly, children did not distinguish biological from psychological properties until age 7. However, Solomon et al.'s task was considerably more complex than that of Gelman and Wellman, and other evidence suggests that preschool

children do grasp that crucial properties are determined by the birth parents, when the experimental task is presented in a clear and simple manner (Hirschfeld, 1996; Springer, 1995). We suggest, therefore, that preschoolers grasp the general principle that birth parents are more predictive of certain properties than are adoptive parents, but that children still must sort out which particular properties are heritable (the latter being an issue that scientists continue to debate).

In sum, we believe that children show an early grasp of biological processes, at least when focusing primarily on animals and on aspects that (a) involve the whole organism at a basic level of consideration, (b) have implications for important, everyday behaviors and identities, and (c) are likely to be topics of discussion with others. Data regarding early understanding of movement, growth, and inheritance suggest—with some controversy—a generally sensible grasp of several biological processes in preschool-age children.

Unobservables

Unobservable constructs can lead to classifications in which category instances differ from one another in salient ways, yet share underlying properties relevant to the domain. For example, adults generally classify plants and animals together into a category of living things, largely because of beliefs regarding their biological commonalities (e.g., both plants and animals grow, reproduce, take in nutrients, and can heal themselves). Without such knowledge, there may be no reason for grouping plants and animals together; as noted earlier, young children often fail to treat them as a single category of living things.

How might children demonstrate an appreciation of unobservables in the biological realm? Consider contamination and illness, both of which can (for adults) make reference to germs. On the one hand, children might have considerable difficulty understanding contamination and illness, because both phenomena would seem to arise out of nowhere—for example, a person may go to bed feeling fine but wake up in the morning with a nasty rash and high fever. The causal underpinnings of particular cases of illness and contamination are not visible, the effects or visible symptoms are often delayed (by hours, days, even weeks or years), and nonbiological accounts are plausible (e.g., immanent justice, wrath of God, bad luck).

On the other hand, the very fact that contamination and illness can become evident without apparent cause may facilitate children's understanding. The existence of seemingly inexplicable, yet highly salient events may pique children's interest and lead them to search for identifiable, albeit non-apparent, causal agents (such as germs). Recent evidence suggests that preschool children appreciate that, with both illness and contamination, an entity can induce illness or be contaminated despite lack of visible evidence (Au et al., 1993; Rosen & Rozin, 1993; Siegal, 1988). For example, Kalish (1996) finds that 4- and 5-year-olds make predictions about who will get sick (in cases of contamination and contagion) based on the presence or absence of invisible germs: Children judge that Bobby will get sick if he eats an apple that falls in the garbage—unless they learn that there were no germs in the garbage.

In biology, another important example of unobservables is a category essence—an underlying nature hypothesized to determine identity and the observable qualities that category members have in common (Gelman, Coley, & Gottfried, 1994; Medin, 1989). For example, the essence of the tiger category may be a distinctive DNA profile; the essence of the water category may be H_2O (Putnam, 1973; Schwartz, 1979; but see Malt, 1994). Even without knowing precisely what it is that holds category members together, children and adults may assume that some fundamental, common feature(s) exist, thus leaving a placeholder for an essence that will eventually be discovered (Atran, 1990; Gelman & Medin, 1993). The claim that children treat categories as having essences does not imply a particular set of beliefs concerning what that essence is. It does, however, imply some general properties: that the essence resides within the organism, is fixed and relatively unmalleable, and is responsible for numerous other features including those not yet known or discovered.

Children's biological categorizations demonstrate two sorts of evidence that are consistent with essentialist reasoning: Children treat internal parts as privileged, and they regularly draw inductive inferences on the basis of category membership rather than surface appearances. Regarding internal parts, children are highly sensible if not specifically accurate about the possible internal parts of animals by 3 or 4 years of age (R. Gelman, 1990; S. Gelman & O'Reilly, 1988; Simons & Keil, 1995). Moreover, as noted earlier, children draw inferences about identity and capacity to function based on internal parts (S. Gelman & Wellman, 1991). Relatedly, children draw a rich array of inferences from one category member to another very dissimilar category member or even to the entire category. For example, S. Gelman and Markman (1986) presented preschool children with items in which category membership was put into conflict with superficial appearances, such as a brontosaurus, a rhinoceros, and a triceratops, which were labeled as *dinosaur, rhinoceros,* and *dinosaur,* respectively. Category labels and outward appearances conflicted: The brontosaurus and triceratops are members of the same category, whereas the rhinoceros and triceratops looked more alike. Then children learned a new property of the brontosaurus and the rhinoceros (that they had cold blood and warm blood, respectively), and were asked which property was true of the triceratops. The results of this and other related experiments showed that by 2½ years of age, children base inferences on category membership, despite conflicting surface appearances (S. Gelman & Coley, 1990; Shipley, 1993).

The claim that young children think of biological entities in terms of underlying essences has been called into question by the suggestion that children have a general shape bias in their interpretations of novel count nouns. According to this proposal, new words (e.g., a "dax") are assumed to refer to a set of objects that share a common shape, even objects that are taxonomically unrelated for adults (Imai, Gentner, & Uchida, 1994; Landau, Smith, & Jones, 1988). A shape bias would thus mean that underlying, essential status is irrelevant when extending words (e.g., toy bears and real bears are both bears because they have a common shape, despite the fact that children understand that toys are not real). In favor of this position, many studies indicate that shape is salient for children, particularly in word-learning contexts (Baldwin, 1992; Smith, Jones, & Landau, 1992). However, children may attend to shape not because it is the basis on which words are extended, but rather because it correlates with and thus provides good information about what kind of thing an object is (Soja, Carey, & Spelke, 1992). Indeed, children override similarity (including shape) when extending novel words at the basic level (Golinkoff, Shuff-Bailey, Olguin, & Ruan, 1995), and children make use of information other than shape, such as object function and syntax, to extend new words (Gathercole, Cramer, Somerville, & Op de Haar, 1995).

In any case, the shape-bias hypothesis seems incomplete, given that features are either highlighted or downplayed, depending on how the child conceptualizes the larger category to which the object belongs. For example, Jones, Smith, and Landau (1991) found that when 2- and 3-year-olds were asked to classify simple novel objects (e.g., geometric shapes made of wood, wire, or sponge), children attended primarily to shape, yet when the same items had plastic eyes attached, subjects attended to both shape and texture. Apparently, the addition of eyes changed the child's conception of the object's ontological status (from object to animal), which in turn influenced categorization judgments. Similarly, Ward, Becker, Hass, and Vela (1991) found that although children generally rely on shape for classifying and extending novel words, they do not do so when the shape is a temporary one (e.g., a snake curled into a circle). Moreover, Soja, Carey, and Spelke (1991) demonstrated that although children use shape when learning words for objects, they do not do so when learning words for substances.

Coherence

To what extent do young children's biological beliefs cohere into a biological system? Although the issue has rarely been examined, evidence suggests that there is some interrelatedness of children's biological knowledge by late preschool. Backscheider (1993) told 4-year-olds about items that possessed either a biological or a non-biological property, then asked children to infer the presence or absence of other biological and non-biological properties. Children were not permitted to see the item during questioning. For example, they were told for one item, "This is something that grows" and were asked whether it was held together with nails and screws, whether if it got a scratch it would get better all by itself, and so forth. When told that an item had one biological property, subjects inferred that it had other biological (but not nonbiological) properties; when told that an item had one nonbiological property, they inferred that it had other nonbiological (but not biological) properties.

Intriguingly, children's assumption that biological properties intercorrelate may at times be stronger than that of adults. Kalish (1996) found that, for preschool children, the concept of illness may be "more coherent and inferentially rich" than for adults. Specifically, whereas adults saw no strong links among illness and other features (e.g., fevers), children viewed illnesses as strongly predictive of fevers and consistently requiring medicine, and they viewed contagion as based on a single underlying cause (i.e., infection). Thus, children may search for and expect causal interconnections among biological phenomena even when they don't exist.

Finally, an issue central to addressing children's coherent biological reasoning concerns the inductive function of categories, that is, their potential to generate novel inferences. For adults, categories function to extend knowledge beyond what is obvious or already known. For example, after learning that one dog has leukocytes inside it, subjects are likely to infer that other dogs also have leukocytes inside them (Gelman & Markman, 1986). Categories that are tied to theories or larger framework understandings promote especially many inferences concerning novel features (Markman, 1989; Quine, 1977). As reviewed above, even very young children use biological categories (e.g., "dinosaur") to generate novel inferences about unfamiliar organisms.

How to Characterize the Biological Domain

In the biological domain, as in naive physics and psychology, modularity, theory-theory, and expertise approaches have offered different characterizations of the relatively rich knowledge base young children have acquired.

Modularity Position

One proposal is that children have an innate biological module. For example, Pinker (1994) proposes four "distinctive properties of living things" that humans are predisposed to notice: (a) Organisms fall into species in which members share tight clusters of similar features, (b) There is a distinctive logical (non-overlapping, hierarchical) structure that we use to classify biological species, (c) Biological organisms, being self-preserving systems, are "governed by dynamic physiological processes that are lawful even when hidden," and (d) Members of a biological kind have a hidden essence that remains unchanged across outward changes, such as growth or reproduction.

Although Pinker cites some evidence for these properties, he does not demonstrate that they are either innate or domain-specific. For example, appreciation of physiological processes could require formal schooling, or essentialism may be a more general feature of concepts, and not specifically biological.

Perhaps the most sustained argument for the notion of biology as a distinct innate module comes from Atran (1990, 1994), who studies classification systems cross-culturally. Building on Berlin's (Berlin et al., 1973) seminal work, he finds striking cross-cultural similarities in how people organize categories of plants and animals: the existence of taxonomies, the lack of overlap among categories within a given level, the number of levels in the taxonomies, the level that is most accessible and most powerful for induction (e.g., Lopez, Atran, Coley, Medin, & Smith, 1997). He also argues that each category at the basic level of a hierarchy (the species/genus level, such as rat) is assumed by language-users to capture an underlying essence. Thus, Atran claims that biological reasoning—especially taxonomic, essentialist reasoning—is separate, special, and the result of an innate module. Three components of Atran's claims are crucial here: that taxonomic and essentializing principles are innate, that they are specific to the domain of living kinds (see also Wierzbicka, 1984), and that they are atheoretical.

In contrast to Atran's claim that taxonomizing and essentializing grow out of innate biological understandings, others suggest that taxonomizing and essentializing arise from domain-general properties of language (Carey, 1995). Some researchers (e.g., Rosch, 1978; Rosch et al., 1976) claim to find parallel hierarchical classification systems in biological and nonbiological domains, at least for adults. Shipley (1993) also advances an alternative domain-general account of how categories become organized into hierarchies. And several developmental studies find no obvious domain differences in hierarchical reasoning in young children (Anglin, 1977; Blewitt, 1989; S. Gelman et al., 1989; Waxman, 1990). Similarly, there is evidence suggesting that young children may apply essentialistic reasoning more broadly than just to biological categories (e.g., applying it to substances such as gold; S. Gelman & Markman, 1986). However, because the developmental study of class inclusion hierarchies has been dominated by the Piagetian domain-general perspective, researchers have rarely examined whether domain differences exist. These issues are in need of sustained research.

Theory View

Whereas modularity theorists focus on biological categories and their organization into hierarchies, theory theorists focus on the content of beliefs: the ontological distinction between living and nonliving things, and the distinctive biological processes of growth, reproduction, and so forth. The view that children's biological knowledge inheres in early theories has at least two distinct forms: (a) Children hold a distinctly biological theory from the start (S. Gelman & Coley, 1991; Hatano & Inagaki, 1994; Keil, 1992), and (b) children have a theoretical understanding of living things, but one that at first is psychological and only gradually emerges as a separate biological domain (Carey, 1985).

Because both these positions hold that children have specifically biological theories by age 10 (or perhaps

earlier), we focus on Carey's (1985) claim that children's biological theories emerge out of their psychological theories. Carey's evidence includes children's difficulty with the concepts of life and death; their socio-psychological interpretations of biological concepts such as growth, reproduction, gender; their difficulty merging animals and plants into a concept of living things; and so forth. In all of these studies, children appeared to be ignorant about biological processes—often re-interpreting them within a psychological framework.

In contrast, the studies reviewed in the previous section indicate that children do recognize a distinctively biological domain by 4 to 6 years of age. For example, studies of gender or species constancy have found dramatically improved performance in even younger children by switching the order of items to reduce pragmatic biases (Siegal & Robinson, 1987), presenting children with potential cross-ontological changes rather than within-ontological changes (e.g., a porcupine that appears to be a cactus; Keil, 1989), or presenting children with transformations in which they need reason about only one identity at a time instead of two (S. Gelman & Wellman, 1991).

Early competence is found even in children's reasoning about humans, where psychological construals might be expected to be particularly strong. For example, Schult and Wellman (in press) specifically asked 4-year-olds about human behaviors that were either psychologically or biologically caused (e.g., hanging from a tree branch, then letting go—either because of a desire to let go or because of muscle fatigue despite a desire to hang on), and subjects provided appropriately distinct explanations for these behaviors. Similarly, Inagaki and Hatano (1993) posed direct contrasts to children—for example, a child who wanted to be fat but ate very little versus a child who wanted to be thin but ate large quantities—and found that even preschoolers could accurately report the biological consequences (e.g., which character would gain weight). It appears, then, that although the psychological may at times inappropriately intrude upon the biological, children can perform quite well when directed to think about the relevant conceptual distinctions between these two domains. At the very least, distinctively biological reasoning seems evident at 4 or 5 years rather than 9 or 10.

However, this conclusion leaves open the same two alternatives mentioned earlier. On the one hand, children's understanding of biological phenomena may be distinctly biological at all prior points in development. The recent history of studies of cognitive development suggests healthy skepticism regarding claims of developmental incompetence. Furthermore, at present there is no principled reason to expect that biological understandings clearly revealed at age 5 could not also be uncovered at ages 4, 3, or even earlier. On the other hand, however, children's biology may split off from psychology (as Carey suggested), but at an earlier point than initially proposed. At this point, there is no evidence for a specifically biological theory in infants or toddlers, but this seems to be due to a lack of appropriate methods to test the hypothesis rather than the presence of evidence contradicting the view that the domains are distinct early in development.

Expertise

Modular and theory views of children's developing understanding of biological phenomena predominate in current theorizing. However, perhaps the most intuitive, common sense view of how children's biological knowledge grows is an expertise view: that children learn these things because people teach them. Certainly expertise influences knowledge acquisition in the biological domain (Chi, Hutchinson, & Robin, 1989; Inagaki, 1990; Tanaka & Taylor, 1991). For example, Springer (1995) found that learning that babies grow inside their mothers prior to birth may be a pivotal piece of knowledge leading to children's understanding of kinship as biological. A greater amount of specific knowledge about biological phenomena, typically acquired from more knowledgeable adults, plays a powerful role in children's developing biologies.

Expertise rests on acquiring increasing information about a domain and thus implies close linkages between sources of informational input and knowledge. One way to evaluate the expertise approach, therefore, is to ask how close a link can be found between sources of expertise (specifically, information in the environment available to the child) and children's knowledge. One set of issues involves timing, specifically whether there is a critical period for input, suggesting that other developmental factors—not input alone—influence rates and patterns of learning. Another set of issues concerns untaught beliefs (beliefs that emerge either without input or on the basis of only slight, indirect, or subtle input), or self-constructed errors (those that are not merely incomplete versions of the input or confusions of the input). If there are variations in learning due to timing or content, or mismatches between the input and the conceptual understanding, then factors other than expertise may be responsible.

At the very least, what is needed is a more detailed description of the kinds of input available to children concerning biological categories and processes. Moreover, this same prescription applies for the domains of physical and psychological reasoning. The few studies that exist suggest that although parents provide a richly informative database concerning category labels, taxonomic relatedness, and even some of the apparent properties that are characteristic of categories at different taxonomic levels (e.g., Callanan, 1985, 1990), their discussion of biological essences and causal processes is at best incomplete (S. Gelman, Coley, Rosengren, Hartman, & Pappas, 1995). The data suggest that parental input may provide useful information for children, yet is unlikely to be the sole or primary source of children's biological beliefs.

Furthermore, biological knowledge seems to entail untaught or self-constructed errors. We illustrate with two examples: evolutionary accounts of speciation, and understanding of the relation between humans and non-human animals. Evolutionary theory has been widely accepted in the scientific community for many years, yet nonscientists (children and adults alike) are remarkably resistant to it, either by rejecting it outright or by misinterpreting its claims (e.g., Almquist & Cronin, 1988; Engel, Clough, & Wood-Robinson, 1985). Evans (1994) suggests that this resistance to evolutionary theory arises in part because of pre-existing psychological and biological beliefs. In her own work, Evans examined beliefs about species origins ("How do you think the first X [e.g., human] got here on earth?") in children from 5 to 13 years of age. In addition to open-ended questions, children heard possible explanations that they could accept or reject, including spontaneous generationist ("it came out of the ground"), evolutionist ("it changed from a different kind of animal"), creationist ("God made it"), and artificialist ("humans made it") choices. Half the subjects were from fundamentalist Christian backgrounds, and the remainder were from non-fundamentalist backgrounds, but otherwise the groups did not differ in parent educational levels. As predicted, the older subjects in the two groups differed markedly in their explanations of species origins: Those from a fundamentalist background tended to endorse creationist accounts, whereas those from a non-fundamentalist background tended toward some form of evolutionary/adaptationist account. In contrast, the younger subjects from the two backgrounds gave remarkably similar answers, both favoring creationist accounts overall. Group differences in beliefs did not appear until middle childhood. At the earlier ages, children from distinctly different ideological backgrounds seem to have constructed remarkably similar explanations for these biological phenomena.

Relatedly, children also misconstrue the place of humans within the animal kingdom. Specifically, children appear to have great difficulty thinking of humans as one kind of animal among many—instead, they tend not to think of humans as animals at all (Carey, 1985). This tendency can be seen in Johnson, Mervis, and Boster's (1992) study of animal classifications. Children and adults were presented with triads (e.g., chimpanzee, human, dog) and asked to pair together the two instances that were the same sort of thing. Subjects—especially children—often isolated the human by grouping together the chimpanzee and the dog. Coley (1993) presented subjects with even more extreme examples (e.g., chimpanzee, human, caterpillar), and found that children again tended to isolate the human, in this case grouping together the highly dissimilar chimpanzee and caterpillar. This example again argues for powerful beliefs in childhood that do not just evidence ignorance of adult understandings, but rather conflict with them.

Conclusions

Children seem to appreciate a distinct biological domain by 4 or 5 years of age. They honor an ontological distinction between living things (including plants and animals) and non-living things; they understand something of the biological importance of self-generated movement, growth and healing, inheritance, and germs; they appeal to nonobvious biological properties; and they recognize the interrelatedness among biological properties. Below preschool age, infants and toddlers are certainly attentive to animals and animal properties (e.g., distinguishing animals from artifacts with respect to properties such as the need for water), yet there is little research with young children to demonstrate convincingly that these seemingly biological understandings are distinct from either psychological or domain-general ones.

Several theoretical positions compete to account for the developmental changes and constancies found in children's biological reasoning. There may be an innate module dedicated to the biological domain, most forcefully argued to be manifest in children's biological categories—both their internal structure (shown in an essentializing tendency) and their external structure (shown in hierarchical taxonomies). Another possibility is that children's beliefs cohere into an early-emerging (possibly innate) biological theory, in which simple heuristics such as essentialism and teleology pave the way for an increasingly sophisticated grasp of biological processes and functions. Note that, as Inagaki and Hatano remind us, it is possible that children honor a domain of biology but one that differs in fundamental ways from that of adults (scientists or lay people). A third possibility is that children may develop a biological theory itself out of a more primary psychological theory. We are skeptical of a fourth option, associated with an expertise perspective, that children develop biological knowledge primarily out of piecemeal, extensive exposure to biological information from parents, siblings, other caregivers, and the media; our skepticism reflects the powerful presuppositions children hold that endure in the face of disconfirming evidence.

CONCLUSIONS AND CHALLENGES

There are two classic questions concerning conceptual development: the descriptive question of what sorts of knowledge children have when, and the explanatory question of what sorts of mechanisms account for this knowledge. Our focus on children's ontological knowledge, understanding of unobservable entities, and causal-explanatory notions addresses the descriptive question; modular, expertise, and theory-theory accounts propose explanations for development.

Descriptions of Children's Knowledge

Within and across the three domains we have reviewed, young children reveal a core of systematic beliefs and distinctions. Even toddlers search for causes, maintain firm ontological boundaries, acknowledge unobservable entities. Most of the research on understanding of biology focuses on somewhat older children than do studies of physics and psychology, yet preschool children demonstrate insightful understanding of biological phenomena as well. These findings support a strong claim: At a young age, children distinguish at least three foundational domains of thinking. It is not yet clear how many domains children distinguish in all, nor which analytic criteria identify foundational domains of thought. Some consensus has emerged in the research, but how to identify domains remains problematic and deserves more attention.

The findings we have reviewed could conceivably be viewed as consistent with traditional characterizations of knowledge development, except for demonstrating competence at earlier ages than expected. Even this modest interpretation has broad-ranging implications, as it necessitates explaining how the knowledge is acquired so rapidly. However, we prefer a more radical interpretation, one that up-ends several assumptions about cognitive development. Specifically, it is often assumed that young children begin by attending to the perceptual, overt, surface features of phenomena and only slowly come to penetrate to more underlying, nonobvious understandings. Relatedly, children are assumed to confuse certain distinctions basic to adult thought—such as mind/body, animate/inanimate, and subjective/objective—the sorting out of which requires considerable developmental construction. Similarly, children's reasoning is often depicted as first focusing on acausal correlations between salient occurrences and only later reflecting a genuine appreciation of causal regularities and causal explanations. However, we believe that rather than being later developmental *outcomes,* concepts of causes, ontologies, and unobservables are more properly early *contributors* to knowledge development, at least in the domains of reasoning we have reviewed. If this portrait is correct, it requires a revolution in how we think about knowledge— what is most basic, what is derived, and how knowledge develops.

Causal Explanations

By preschool age at least, causal understandings are central in children's reasoning about physics, psychology, and biology. We propose that in these cases, causality is a developmental primitive, emerging early in development and influencing categorization and knowledge acquisition. In natural conversation, young children readily invoke causal reasoning, and in comparison to older persons, young children may *overattribute* causality to events. For example, randomness is quite difficult for preschoolers to comprehend; young children tend to assume that random events are causally determined (Green, 1978; Kuzmak & Gelman, 1986; Piaget, 1930). Thus, children may be causal determinists, actively expecting events to have causes (S. Gelman & Kalish, 1993).

Children's reasoning about magic further suggests that children search for causes (Harris, 1994). If children readily accepted uncaused events, they would have no need to appeal to magic. What is baffling and amusing about so-called magical events is that they have apparently either no antecedent causes or extraordinary causes. Magical events thus differ from events with merely unknown causes. Consider the rabbit-hat trick versus an electric garage-door opener. The latter is assumed to have a causal physical mechanism, so that even though the mechanism is unknown to the child, it is presumed to result somehow physically from the remote-control device. The appearance of the rabbit in the hat, in contrast, seems outside the realm of possible physical causes. It is interesting that this contrast between the magical and the merely inexplicable is available to the young child (Rosengren & Hickling, 1994).

A possible objection to this interpretation is that very young children (those below 3½, say) are notoriously poor audiences for magic. Conceivably, these very young children have yet to care about causes. Our counterinterpretation is that young children may hold so strongly to a causal view of the world that they simply don't conceive of extraordinary events and causes. This general expectation is coupled, often, with a lack of knowledge as to specific causal mechanisms: "This is another one of those events I can't yet explain; of course it has a cause—I just don't know yet what it is." Baillargeon (1994) reports that in certain cases, babies fail to be surprised by events that are impossible and should be surprising (e.g., one solid object passing through another), but that in these cases one can show that infants make auxiliary assumptions in order to resolve the apparent puzzle. In other words, even babies may at times work to avoid concluding that an event is impossible.

We assume, in fact, that in the three domains we have targeted, causal determinism works in a framework fashion: Children may be ignorant about specific causal factors but still expect that events have relevant domain-specific causes of some sort. This seems particularly likely for younger children, who are continually surrounded by inexplicable events. Why does a balloon float up to the sky instead of fall to the ground? What makes a garage door opener work? In short, an expectation that events generally have sensible causes is not the result of painstakingly observing many particular causal sequences and inferring from them the generalization that there are always causes at work. Instead, a disposition to expect causal regularity seems well in place even when children have scant knowledge of particular causes. This faith of the young child that the world is a predictable, orderly, *knowable* place enables children to proceed to understand the world in increasingly more sophisticated ways.

Ontological Knowledge

By referring to a distinction as ontological, we mean that it captures basic conceptions of what sorts of entities there are in the world. Ontological kinds are distinguishable in principle because they engender category mistakes rather than simple falsehoods (Keil, 1979; Sommers, 1963). The statement "cork is heavier than gold" is false, but the statement "ideas are heavier than gold" is neither true nor false; it is a category mistake. Ideas are not the kind of thing that can be light or heavy (except metaphorically). Similarly, the only way to understand a category mistake such as "My TV died" is by imposing a metaphorical interpretation (it broke).

Keil (1979) studied children's ontological understandings by asking children to judge category mistakes versus simple falsehoods. This method, however, requires metalinguistic judgments that are beyond the capacity of children much younger than kindergarten age. Thus, the research we have reviewed has relied on other measures. The thrust of the findings are clear: Children distinguish three very distinct kinds of entities quite early in development: bounded physical objects, mental entities, and living kinds. They judge that thoughts cannot be touched—not because thoughts are far away or behind barriers, but because they are distinctly different kinds of things from physical objects. They judge that damaged artifacts cannot heal by themselves but damaged animals can—again, not because of contextual limitations (e.g., shortage of bandages or doctors), but because only animals are capable of this. In fact, one of the more intriguing findings of the research we have reviewed is the existence of adult-like ontological distinctions at very early ages. Preschoolers, toddlers, and even babies distinguish animate from inanimate, solid object from unbounded mass, object from event, mental from physical.

The ontological distinctions demonstrated early in life are not the only ones we make as adults. That is, we are not necessarily restricted to a small, innate, or early-developing set. For example, as Carey (1991) argues, the development and emergence of new scientific theories yields the emergence of new ontologies (e.g., the distinction between heat and temperature) even for adults. What seems less clear, however, is whether the ontological distinctions we are born with can ever be erased. We suspect not—which could account in part for the enduring errors and folk beliefs that continue to undermine scientific training. For example, the (folk) ontological distinction between space and time renders the Einsteinian view of the universe (with its space-time continuum) nearly incomprehensible to most adults. Similarly, although certain folk-biological categories (e.g., tree) have no scientific counterpart, it appears that even expert botanists can't help but think in terms of them (Atran, 1990).

Children's distinctions among physical, psychological, and biological phenomena are interesting not only for how they carve up the world, but also for how children try to reason across these ontological divides. Children's attempts to understand how different domains intersect provide fruitful sources of fiction, imagination, and analogy. For example, magic typically entails human actions overriding physical laws; astrology entails physical (celestial) objects influencing the thoughts, desires, or behaviors of humans; parapsychology entails humans effecting physical consequences via mental means. These might all be considered ontological suspensions, even confusions—but of a relatively advanced sort. Ontological confusions of the less advanced sort would include a complete failure to distinguish ontological types, and (interestingly) seem not to exist even in very young children in these domains. Ontological confusions of the more advanced sort involve stretching the scope of application of one domain onto an inappropriate realm; these exist in childhood, though possibly only after the stable domain distinctions are worked out to begin with. That is, this second-level ontological confusion may represent a conceptual advance over an initially clean set of ontological distinctions. Support for this notion is the finding that magical explanations appear only at about 4 or 5 years of age (not 3)—after the infrastructure of the core domains is already in place.

Unobservables

In the domains we have reviewed, in their search for understanding and explanations, children do not simply explain overt events in terms of overt factors; they appeal instead to unobservable constructs and forces. Unobservables sometimes refer to literally invisible entities: essences, nonvisible particles, mental states. More broadly, children distinguish between at least two levels of analysis: evidential phenomena themselves (such as a parent's offspring or a person's behavior) versus explanatory, abstract concepts used to account for the evidence (such as innate potentials or beliefs). For example, consider the goal of attempting to explain why a person jumps into a swimming pool while clothed (Murphy & Medin, 1985). One could describe the covariation of related factors, all at the same behavioral level (e.g., whether others are doing the same thing, or whether the target person tends to do this on other days). In contrast, one could explain the behavior in terms of a mechanism that is phrased at a different level of analysis (e.g., the person's physiological state—inebriated—or psychological state—giddy). Adults and even young children appeal to the latter sort of explanation (Ahn et al., 1995; White, 1995).

One implication of this early appeal to unobservables is that, as Simons and Keil (1995) recently argued, children's reasoning may in places proceed not from concrete to abstract, as is commonly assumed, but rather from abstract to concrete (or global to specific; Mandler et al., 1991). Indeed, in the domains we have reviewed, our argument is precisely of this sort. Children understand and appeal to certain framework notions in a very general way, prior to knowledge of the concrete details. Importantly, however, in other areas the concrete-to-abstract view is probably correct; for certain phenomena, children undoubtedly build more abstract understandings off a database of particulars. Thus, an interesting question becomes *when* development shifts from abstract to concrete, and *when* the reverse. We suggest that the abstract-to-concrete direction of change will be found for domains in which core understandings are in place early (e.g., theory of mind), whereas concrete-to-abstract change will result in other areas (e.g., chess). Indeed, such shifts might serve as a method for uncovering children's foundational knowledge domains.

Commonalities across These Early Domains of Understanding

The full story of foundational knowledge acquisition requires the consideration of multiple domains. To examine children's understanding of physics, it is necessary to consider an alternative domain such as psychology; to examine biology, it must be contrasted with physics and psychology. Comparisons across these domains of thought also raise intriguing questions. Consider the claim that in these three domains, children easily appeal to unobservable entities. Does this represent the workings of a domain-general learning assumption—a general essentialist assumption, say, that all phenomena have underlying essences? Or do we have three different domain-specific assumptions, one tied to the essences underlying biological categories, one to the mental states underlying behavior, and one to the forces

and entities (centers of gravity, insides, and atoms) underlying physical matter and events?

In part, we argue that apparent uniformity across domains, when it occurs, is more apparent than real; children are developing distinctive domain-specific notions that are similar only by adopting a quite general level of analysis. But in part, language as a system of understanding may also be influential. Language is a domain in its own right—a system of regularities, meaning-form matches and mismatches that children work on and restructure. That is, regardless of the specific characterization of the language domain—for example, in terms of innate modules (Pinker, 1994) or in terms of a functional expertise (Tomasello, 1995)—it certainly seems plausible to argue that language and communication constitute a domain of knowledge separable from naive physics, psychology, and biology. Although it is separate, language understanding can nonetheless contribute to knowledge acquisition in other domains, just as an understanding of naive psychology can be employed by analogy to understand other complex devices—computers, thermostats (Carey & Spelke, 1994). Indeed, one of the most fruitful domains for this sort of influence, at least early in development, may well be language. At the age that children are acquiring naive physics, psychology, and biology, they are rapidly acquiring language as well. Even minimal communicative competence permits social transmission of information about the physical, psychological, and biological worlds. Moreover, languages universally have certain conceptual presuppositions: They parse up the world into objects, events, and properties (roughly, nouns, verbs, and adjectives); nouns label kinds that may be presumed to share common features; categories are organized into class-inclusion hierarchies; animacy is highly predictive of which kinds of things are most likely to be the subjects of verbs or to take certain kinds of markers (such as gender); languages agree more or less as to which sorts of things are more or less animate (Silverstein, 1976); and there is a conceptually basic sentence structure common among children across the world—an animate agent is performing an action on an inanimate object. (See Comrie, 1981; Croft, 1990; Greenberg, 1966; Slobin, 1985 for a rich set of conceptual properties embedded in language.)

Thus, to illustrate, a search for unobservable essences may be a consequence of the logic of nouns (Carey, 1995; Mayr, 1991): Nouns impose categorical structure on the world. Our strong intuition that all dogs are in some deep sense the same may derive unconsciously from the forms of language: We say that a chihuahua is a dog, an Irish Setter is a dog, and a poodle is a dog. The implication is that these outwardly distinct entities are the same in some important sense. Languages encourage this assumption, not only in the sense of informing children which specific instances fall within a particular category, but perhaps also more generally by employing nouns. In the future, it will be necessary to consider more comprehensively how children's acquisition of language influences their knowledge acquisition in the domains we have reviewed.

Mechanisms in Children's Acquisition of Foundational Knowledge

Expertise

To a degree, the picture that emerges from the research we have considered is one of several domains of early expertise. In these areas, children seem like experts in that they possess considerable knowledge, they recognize underlying nonobvious constructs, they are able to reason logically, and their special attention to phenomena within these domains facilitates the practice and experience that underwrite additional learning and an enriched knowledge base.

However, traditional expertise accounts fall short in several ways. Somewhat ironically, expertise accounts seem intrinsically domain general. Practice and experience as applied to any area of knowledge yield expertise; witness experts of such contrived subjects as baseball, chess, and the Beatles. General processes of memory, information acquisition, information organization, and inference are often posited to produce experts. The picture is one of a level conceptual playing field that only differentiates according to the dictates of experience and practice. However, children appear to be more easily expert in some domains than others—such as naive physics versus reading. A challenge to expertise accounts, therefore, is to explain why some kinds of expertise are easy for even young humans to acquire. One possibility consistent with an expertise account is that the domains we have reviewed may include the kinds of things parents most often talk about, the sorts of objects children most often encounter, the modes of explanation a culture finds most useful, and the experiences children (and adults) find most interesting. However, this argument becomes circular without a means of explaining why children and adults have these preferences and interests to begin with.

A deeper challenge is that expertise accounts are typically bottom-up in character. Experts must build up, then work from, a large store of specific facts and observations.

Experts do not merely reason well—they know a lot. As just noted, however, at least in the three domains we have reviewed, development seems to proceed as much from abstractions to specifics as the reverse. As we would put it, children seem to have something like framework theories before they hold specific theories. Thus, from an expertise account alone, young children seem like strange mixtures—grasping certain basic frameworks but often without knowledge of the facts and particulars that seem so implicated to adults. It may even be that parents' and researchers' common experience of seeing children as precocious yet ignorant, both wise and witless, stems from this mismatch between children's knowledge and our common sense expectations of expertise.

Modules

Characterizing these three domains of knowledge in terms of innate conceptual modules can answer the question of why expertise arises so early and rapidly: Evolution has shaped the human mind to attend to and represent these domains in special ways. Modular accounts also provide an obvious explanation for why knowledge in these domains might be resistant to change and to instruction: The way that modules mandatorily convert certain inputs into particular representations precludes serious revision. Two strengths, therefore, of nativist modular accounts are their ability to account for very early knowledge and their ability to account for developmental continuities. An additional strength of modular approaches is that they exploit and develop links between cognitive development, cognitive neuroscience, and evolutionary psychology (see e.g., Baron-Cohen, 1995).

In terms of mechanisms, modular accounts are notably parsimonious. The initial emergence of representations and subsequent conceptual change have the same explanation—the relevant module comes on line. Note, however, that on this explanation the sources of change are all exogenous, outside the conceptual system itself. Conceptual change is due to brain maturation rather than either the accumulating effects of information or reorganizations in the content and structure of concepts themselves. Cognitive development reduces to neurological development. It seems undeniable, however, that other factors account for conceptual revisions; at the very least, they do so in the course of intellectual history. Einstein's theory of physics represents a radical departure from Newton's, yet we do not account for this change by neurological mechanisms—an Einsteinian mental module coming on line historically. Rather the explanation for these conceptual changes, whatever their specifics might be, is couched in part in terms of developments within the system of relevant concepts themselves; the later theory builds off of but revises the earlier one. It is an empirical question whether the changes that characterize ontogenetic development include the sorts of endogenous conceptual transformations that can be seen in historical development; but many scholars argue that they do (e.g., Carey, 1985; Gopnik & Wellman, 1994; Karmiloff-Smith, 1992; Munakata, McClelland, Johnson, & Siegler, in press; Piaget, 1954; Plunkett, 1995).

Relatedly, a major question continues to be how much and what sorts of conceptual restructuring are apparent in children's understanding of the world. To reiterate, modules once on-line automatically convert their proprietary inputs into mandatory representations, hence, those representations are essentially unrevisable. Modular accounts of this sort thus allow no fundamental changes in the child's basic concepts themselves, only enrichment or extension of the existing mandatory notions and removal of performance obstacles to the demonstration of innate conceptions. A challenge to such accounts, therefore, is the demonstration that fundamentally new or revised conceptual systems can develop. Take Spelke's (1994) core notions of physical objects as solid and moving on continuous paths. She posits that these early notions fundamentally constrain the cognizable entities in the domain of physics and thus that these notions not only capture infant conceptions of objects but also "constitute the core of mature knowledge." Yet expert physicists' core notions are radically different—space and time merge, objects act on objects at a distance, and so on. Of course, such conceptions were difficult to come up with historically, are difficult to convey to students and novices even in the present day, and likely co-exist with, rather than displace, more everyday conceptions of the physical world in the mind of any individual. But, if Spelke were literally correct, such conceptions would be impossible—never even conceived because they fall outside the confines of our innate conceptual endowment, much as humans can never grow wings, because to do so would fall outside our innate physiological endowment. If any of the claims reviewed in this chapter of developmental conceptual revolutions regarding objects, minds, and biology are even approximately correct, they pose major challenges to an innatist modular approach.

A final related challenge to innatist modular theories comes from an expansion of evolutionary arguments themselves. Some writers argue that an evolutionary account of cognition requires a modular view of the mind (Cosmides & Tooby, 1994). Other evolutionary accounts focus on the evolution of cognitive complexity and flexibility (e.g., Bennett & Harvey, 1985; Gould, 1977). Organisms have evolved not only definite structures to cope with particular tasks—for example, wings to exploit aerial ecological niches, imprinting to attach offspring to parent—but they have evolved ways for their offspring to put off adapting until born into the specific environment they find. Learning in its myriad forms is the prime example. Humans in particular are characterized by a long period of childhood that allows for learning and ontogenetic rather than phylogenetic adaptations. Relatedly, Tomasello, Kruger, and Ratner (1993) have recently argued that humans have evolved several special social-cognitive abilities that allow for and account for cultural learning. These abilities lead to the creation and use of cultural tools such as language, mathematics, and science, and also to specific cultural systems of meaning and interpretation. Tomasello et al.'s is only one proposal among many (e.g., Bruner, 1990; Cole, 1988; Rogoff, 1990; Vygotsky, 1978). Our point here is that human children have evolved to be able to change conceptually and thus are able to adapt and contribute to changing knowledge. Indeed, Gopnik and Wellman (1994) go so far as to suggest that our adult capacity for scientific discovery, as well as for lifelong education, may well be a holdover of our capacities as children to engage in fundamental conceptual construction and learning—a sort of cognitive neotony. At the very least, modular proposals need to specify more clearly how to account for such varied and flexible innovation and learning, given only an architecture of nonrevisable innate conceptual modules (e.g., Sperber, 1994).

Theories

In some senses, theory-theory accounts stand between modules and expertise. Like modular accounts, they posit early conceptual structures that determine representation and understanding. Like expertise accounts, they emphasize change and the fit between resulting conceptual structures (theories) and evidence or experience (data). The theory theory is not simply a compromise position between modular and expertise views, however; it is a specific proposal with its own detailed positions. For example, in their construal of cognitive structures as theory and their acceptance of early innate concepts, theory-theory proposals are quite unlike Piaget's: There is no denial of rich innate structure and thus no recourse to action as the necessary well-spring of conception. There is no insistence on domain-general logical stages that are independent of specific contents. Rather, theories are domain-specific, content-full structures that are shaped by the acquisition of knowledge in the domain itself.

In their construal of cognitive change as like theory change, however, theory theorists reaffirm some of Piaget's proposals. Specifically, Piaget insisted on and attempted to characterize the relation between abstract cognitive structures, input from the experiential world, and newly revised structures. Assimilation and accommodation were, in part, his mechanisms for this process. Characterizing cognitive change in terms of theory change confronts this same problem. Theories are structures based on interpreting evidence; evidence speaks to old theories and can transform them into new ones. But how, more precisely? One challenge for theory theories is to articulate and model how such a process of conceptual revision works. How do structure and experience interpenetrate; how do theories and data influence each other in the unfolding of individual cognitive development? These are difficult questions. It is noteworthy, however, that the question of how to characterize conceptual acquisition and change is reasonably simple for either modular or expertise perspectives. Those accounts have straightforward, albeit sometimes complex, answers—new concepts either emerge innately or are governed by domain-general learning processes. In contrast, the theory theory must confront more directly the problem of specifying the mechanisms for conceptual change. Assimilation and accommodation proved too vague; theory theories may flounder on the same issue.

One attraction of the theory theory, as we see it, is the distinction between *specific* versus *framework* theories. Framework theories are neither domain general, as are Piaget's logico-mathematical structures, nor are they small corners of experience such as skill domains (e.g., chess). Despite its considerable scope, for example, a theory of mind explains only mental things, not physical things. In one way or another, scholars of cognitive development are finding the need to characterize such framework understandings. Related proposals include R. Gelman's skeletal principles that define domains (1990), Mandler's global rather than specific categories (e.g., Mandler, Bauer, & McDonough, 1991), Simons and Keil's (1995) abstract concepts that precede rather than result from concrete understandings, and Case's (1992) central conceptual structures. A consideration of framework theories, we believe, helps pose and address questions about such structures.

As just one example, a large problem for discussions of domain-specificity continues to be, what domains are there? There is no tidy answer here as yet, but theory theory offers a process for addressing the question. Each framework theory defines its own domain. Identifying the domains of human cognition thus is an empirical question, answered by identifying the framework theories. Moreover, such theories evolve and one can differentiate out of another, so there is nothing to say that human domains need to carve up the world in some tidy, comprehensive, developmentally stable, or philosophically elegant, fashion.

If the early developments we have reviewed are framework theories, however, it seems curious that children seem to be acquiring at least two and perhaps all three of these theories on such an apparently similar timetable. Certainly the history of science gives no reason to expect the development of physics, psychology, and biology to proceed along similar timetables. Empirical studies of naive psychology, biology, and physics have almost never attempted detailed comparisons of understandings across these domains; the findings only suggest a rough parallelism in that knowledge in all three domains emerges rapidly in the early years. Gopnik and Meltzoff (1997), however, describe a theory-theory account of young children's understanding of objects, of human actions, and of classes during the time period of birth to about 2 years. They argue that sizable conceptual revolutions in each of these domains takes place at about 9 to 12 months. If this developmental description is correct, it underscores the challenge we are raising here: Nothing in theories and theory development per se suggests that three such different strands of conception should develop on similar timetables. To the contrary, if theories are separate, content-dependent structures, and theory developments require separate content-dependent experiences, it would be a striking coincidence to find such similar developmental milestones.

Other Proposals and Processes

Theories, modules, and expertise certainly do not exhaust ideas about mechanisms of cognitive change. In recent years, we have witnessed a renewed interest in the mechanisms of cognitive development, along with a number of substantive and methodological proposals (e.g., Karmiloff-Smith,1992; Mandler, 1988; Ribaupierre, 1989; Rogoff, 1990; Siegler, 1989; Sternberg, 1984). At a more general level, several writers have argued for a general reorientation in our thinking about mechanisms (Bertenthal, 1996; Plunkett, 1995; Siegler, 1989, 1995). These writers, among others, note that cognitive-developmental research has yielded a wealth of descriptive information about children's thoughts at different ages, yet much less information about how cognition changes. Part of the problem, they suggest, is an emphasis on consistency rather than variability. There are at least two problems with insisting that "children of a given age think about a task in a given way" (Siegler, 1995, p. 406). First, it makes the conceptualization of change hard—if children's thinking is all of one sort at one age and then becomes different, "why would they suddenly form a different understanding?" (p. 407). Second, empirically, such descriptions seem wrong: Findings concerning children's strategies, concepts, and problem solutions suggest that performance is quite variable. Not only do individuals differ, but more importantly, each individual shows a mix of alternative, even contradictory procedures at any one time. Using microgenetic methods (cf. Kuhn & Phelps, 1982), Siegler has studied computational strategies—how children solve arithmetic problems—and documents that children exhibit multiple strategies which advance and recede over time. More generally, cognitive change exhibits processes of competition between ongoing alternatives (see also MacWhinney, 1987). Successful procedures compete with and overtake less successful ones, new strategies emerge as variants of old ones, conceptual construals conflict with one another. Microgenetic methods often focus on these variations as well as allow researchers to examine the process of change in more detail from repeated measurements within a relatively brief period of time (Kuhn, Garcia-Mila, Zohar, & Andersen, 1995; Siegler & Crowley, 1991).

The research we have reviewed could both fit with and amplify this sort of thinking about cognitive change. First, children are developing several alternative conceptual frameworks—not just a monolithic understanding of the world, but rather distinctly physical, psychological, and biological construals. Even to young children, animals are both animate *and* physical objects; persons are not only psychological entities, but biological and physical entities as well. These alternative systems provide children with the sorts of conceptual multiplicity required to afford processes of cognitive competition; knowledge from multiple domains multiplies children's approaches, strategies, and conceptual resources.

Moreover, it is important to reiterate that by our analysis, children's reasoning within these domains systematically incorporates at least two levels of analysis—one that captures more surface phenomena versus another that penetrates to deeper theoretical levels. Young children see that blackbirds and bats look alike in terms of appearance, yet also realize they are structured differently inside, perhaps that they manifest different essences. Young children distinguish between a person's mistaken belief and the actual state of the world. Young children distinguish between appearances and realities in the realms of objects, animals, representations, and mental states (e.g., Flavell et al., 1986). Essences, underlying mental states, and invisible particles of material substances all reflect children's appreciation of at least two contrasting representations of a situation. Thus, children entertain not only alternative problem-solving procedures, they regularly entertain alternative conceptual perspectives on the world, and such alternatives fuel attempts to compare, share, merge, and create new conceptions. The general point is that if cognitive development requires alternative construals—as highlighted in models of strategy choice, cognitive conflict, disequilibrium, theory change, and analogical reasoning—then these three domains of thought, and children's early framework understandings of these domains, provide several of the needed alternatives.

Culture and Variation

Foundational knowledge might appear early and be formative for later conceptual development, yet still be specific in place and time and dependent on specialized socialization practices. To what extent are the domains of knowledge we have sketched specific to the children of only one culture? This is a question that as yet has no clear answer. However, it is important to point out that a number of the findings we review seem to be common in a variety of English-speaking countries—the United States, Canada, England, Scotland, Australia—and non-English-speaking European countries as well—Austria, the Netherlands, Germany, Turkey. The relatively scarce data available from nonwestern children, such as those from Japan (e.g., Inagaki & Hatano, 1993), and from nonliterate cultures, such as the Baka from the Cameroons (Avis & Harris, 1991), or the Yoruba from Nigeria (Jeyifous, 1986), are typically in accord with the English-speaking data in demonstrating early expertise for these domains of knowledge. Nonetheless, rarely has research precisely targeted nonliterate cultures or cultures hypothesized to contrast in interesting ways with the naive theories evident in western English-speaking countries.

The possibility that cultures vary substantially, even in their basic understandings, is important to consider in all three domains we have reviewed, but it is especially easy to illustrate in the domain of naive psychological reasoning (e.g., Lillard, 1995). In this case, anthropologists have made explicit ethnographic claims that adults in some cultures understand persons in decidedly different ways from a Western belief-desire construal.

> The most challenging and interesting thing about the Baining from the point of view of ethnopsychological studies is that they appear not to have a folk psychology. The Baining exhibit a pervasive avoidance of modes of discourse about psychology. If we understand the latter to be a domain of culture which includes a concern with affect and emotions, concepts of person and self . . . interpretations of behavior, and ideas about cognition and personality development, the Baining manifest very little interest in these areas. (Fajans, 1985, p. 367)

At the moment, it is possible either that basic mental state reasoning (of some characterizable sort) is a human universal (although unremarked in certain ethnographic reports designed to probe cultural differences), or that there are no universal, foundational, folk psychological conceptions of the mind; instead, each culture socializes its children into quite different understandings.

We believe that demonstrations of early understandings of the sort we have reviewed, are particularly relevant to these unfolding discussions. Consider again naive psychology. If a mentalistic belief-desire understanding in our culture is the endproduct of extensive enculturation and socialization, it is easy to imagine alternative cultures with a very different sort of end product. On the other hand, if very young English-speaking children begin the process of person understanding with the assumption that persons have internal mental lives, it is easier to imagine that social understanding in all cultures might honor this assumption in one form or another. Very young English-speaking children, we argue, approach the task of learning about persons, and acquiring the vocabulary for actions, emotions, reactions, and mental states, with certain framework assumptions. In particular, they begin by interpreting persons in internal, mentalistic fashions and assuming that certain terms refer to those nonobvious states and experiences rather than or in addition to bodily movements or facial displays. Similarly, they quickly adopt initial framework understandings for physical objects and for certain biological phenomena. Certainly, as we have outlined in this chapter, it is impressive how rapidly young English-speaking children can understand and talk about such phenomena so appropriately—including nonobvious aspects and underlying constructs.

Again this hypothesis—that young children have impressive foundational knowledge—argues only for the existence of very general frameworks within which children still must engage in much culture-specific learning. On the one hand, the hypothesis predicts certain constraints on folk theories across cultures, deriving from framework assumptions present in children and continuing in adults. On the other hand, such constraints may be enabling as much as constraining, because they operate developmentally. As *framework* understandings, young children's early physical, psychological, and biological notions must necessarily be fleshed out, and these early notions may develop in a variety of fashions to constitute quite different specific theories. In the extreme, cultural communities have centuries in which to develop their own specific theories. And such communities have many years—at the least, from infancy to adulthood—in which to train and enculturate each member into an ethnotheory. The result may well be a host of ethnotheories quite different from one another and from the initial assumptions of 2- and 3-year-olds.

This sort of analysis suggests that young children's understanding in core domains may be more similar across a variety of cultures and languages than is adults' understanding. This is not a new idea. Mead (1932), in her study of children's understanding of causality in Manus, argued that these children had a straightforward physicalistic understanding of events, such as a canoe going adrift. Just like adults (and, we contend, children) in Western English-speaking societies, children in Manus explained such events in terms of commonplace physical events, such as ropes unfastening, or the water's currents. But adults in Manus explained such events in terms of ghosts, evil intents, and animistic forces. Similarly, Kohlberg (1969) argued that the dream concepts of American and Atayal children were quite similar until age 6 or 7. Only after that point did American and Atayal judgments differentiate, with older children and adults in each community holding to two dramatically different conceptions—in the one case, that dream events are internal, mental phenomena and in the other, that they are real, visible, external phenomena. Harris (1990) has argued that young children's understanding of persons and minds may show basic commonalities across cultures that become submerged in or replaced by very different elaborated adult ethnotheories.

Alternatively, young children in different cultures may acquire very different frameworks rapidly, as the result of early and rich enculturation (see e.g., Lillard, in press). In any event, the existence of early foundational knowledge in some children argues for the need for research across a wider array of cultures and experiences.

Final Remarks

Research on foundational knowledge systems has exploded in the last several years, with studies of infants' and children's understanding of physical, psychological, and biological phenomena leading the way. The intensified interest in knowledge systems has several sources: a rediscovery of the importance of domains of thought in everyday life; conceptual analyses of the domains themselves—their core principles, naive theories, coherent knowledge systems; and, empirical studies that cleverly tackle these topics, revealing sense, structure, and development in these areas, and thus inspiring further research. These areas of knowledge acquisition, individually and together, have proven fertile ground for advancing and testing basic accounts of cognitive development, including modular, expertise, and theory-theory positions. The work brings into focus our ignorance as well as our knowledge. This is a sign of scientific good health: A mix of agreement and disagreement, known and unknown, knowledge gained and knowledge sought, seems especially fitting for a field whose substantive topic is knowledge acquisition itself.

ACKNOWLEDGMENTS

We gratefully thank John Flavell, Chuck Kalish, Catherine Sophian, Marjorie Taylor, and Jacqui Woolley for their helpful comments on an initial draft. In addition we wish to thank our editors Deanna Kuhn and Bob Siegler for their help and patience.

REFERENCES

Adamson, L. B., & Bakeman, R. (1985). Affect and attention: Infants observed with mothers and peers. *Child Development, 5*, 582–593.

Ahn, W., Kalish, C. W., Medin, D. L., & Gelman, S. A. (1995). The role of covariation versus mechanism information in causal attribution. *Cognition, 54*, 299–352.

Almquist, A. J., & Cronin, J. E. (1988). Fact, fancy, and myth on human evolution. *Current Anthropology, 29*, 520–522.

Anglin, J. M. (1977). *Word, object, and conceptual development.* New York: Norton.

Antell, S. E., & Keating, D. P. (1983). Perception of numerical invariance in neonates. *Child Development, 54*, 695–701.

Atran, S. (1990). *Cognitive foundations of natural history.* Cambridge, England: Cambridge University Press.

Atran, S. (1994). Core domains versus scientific theories. In L. A. Hirschfeld & S. A. Gelman (Eds.), *Mapping the mind* (pp. 316–340). New York: Cambridge.

Atran, S. (1995). Causal constraints on categories and categorical constraints on biological reasoning across cultures. In D. Sperber, D. Premack, & A. J. Premack (Eds.), *Causal cognition: A multidisciplinary debate* (pp. 205–233). New York: Oxford University Press.

Au, T. K. (1994). Developing an intuitive understanding of substance kinds. *Cognitive Psychology, 27*, 71–111.

Au, T. K., Sidle, A. L., & Rollins, K. B. (1993). Developing an intuitive understanding of conservation and contamination: Invisible particles as a plausible mechanism. *Developmental Psychology, 29*, 286–299.

Avis, J., & Harris, P. L. (1991). Belief-desire reasoning among Baka children. *Child Development, 62*, 460–467.

Backscheider, A. G. (1993). *Preschoolers' understanding of living kinds.* Doctoral dissertation, University of Michigan, Ann Arbor.

Backscheider, A. G., Shatz, M., & Gelman, S. A. (1993). Preschoolers' ability to distinguish living kinds as a function of regrowth. *Child Development, 64*, 1242–1257.

Baillargeon, R. (1986). Representing the existence and the location of hidden objects: Object permanence in 6- and 8-month-old infants. *Cognition, 23*, 21–41.

Baillargeon, R. (1994). Physical reasoning in young infants: Seeking explanations for impossible events. *British Journal of Developmental Psychology, 12*, 9–33.

Baillargeon, R., & DeVos, J. (1991). Object permanence in young infants: Further evidence. *Child Development, 62*, 1227–1246.

Baillargeon, R., Kotovsky, L., & Needham, A. (1995). The acquisition of physical knowledge in infancy. In D. Sperber, D. Premack, & A. Premack (Eds.), *Causal cognition: A multidisciplinary debate* (pp. 79–116). New York: Oxford University Press.

Baillargeon, R., Spelke, E. S., & Wasserman, S. (1985). Object permanence in 5-month-olds. *Cognition, 20*, 191–208.

Baldwin, D. A. (1991). Infants' contribution to the achievement of joint reference. *Child Development, 63*, 875–890.

Baldwin, D. A. (1992). Clarifying the role of shape in children's taxonomic assumption. *Journal of Experimental Child Psychology, 54*, 392–416.

Baldwin, D. A. (1993). Early referential understanding: Infants' ability to recognize referential acts for what they are. *Developmental Psychology, 29*, 832–843.

Baldwin, D. A., & Moses, L. J. (1994). Early understanding of referential intent and attentional focus: Evidence from language and emotion. In C. Lewis & P. Mitchell (Eds.),

Children's early understanding of mind. Hove, England: Erlbaum.

Banks, M. S., & Salapatek, P. (1983). Infant visual perception. In M. Haith & J. Campos (Eds.), *Handbook of child psychology: Vol. 2. Infancy and developmental psychology.* New York: Wiley.

Baron-Cohen, S. (1995). *Mindblindness: An essay on autism and theory of mind.* Cambridge, MA: MIT Press.

Baron-Cohen, S., Tager-Flusberg, H., & Cohen, D. J. (1993). *Understanding other minds: Perspectives from autism.* Oxford, England: Oxford University Press.

Barresi, J., & Moore, C. (1996). Intentional relations and social understanding. *Behavioral and Brain Sciences, 19,* 107–154.

Bartsch, K., & Wellman, H. M. (1989). Young children's attribution of action to beliefs and desires. *Child Development, 60,* 946–964.

Bartsch, K., & Wellman, H. M. (1995). *Children talk about the mind.* New York: Oxford University Press.

Bates, E., Benigni, L., Bretherton, I., Camaioni, L., & Volterra, V. (1979). *The emergence of symbols: Cognition and communication in infancy.* New York: Academic Press.

Bates, E., Bretherton, I., & Snyder, L. (1988). *From first words to grammar.* New York: Cambridge.

Bennett, K., & Harvey, P. (1985). Brain size, development and metabolism in birds and mammals. *Journal of Zoology, 207,* 491–509.

Berlin, B. (1992). *Ethnobiological classification: Principles of categorization of plants and animals in traditional societies.* Princeton, NJ: Princeton University Press.

Berlin, B., Breedlove, D., & Raven, P. (1973). General principles of classification and nomenclature in folk biology. *American Anthropologist, 75,* 212–242.

Bertenthal, B. I. (1993). Perception of biomechanical motions by infants. In C. Granrud (Ed.), *Visual perception and cognition in infancy* (pp. 175–214). Hillsdale, NJ: Erlbaum.

Bertenthal, B. I. (1996). Origins and early development of perception, action, and representation. *Annual Review of Psychology, 47,* 431–459.

Bertenthal, B. I., & Campos, J. J. (1990). A systems approach to the organizing effects of self-produced locomotion during infancy. *Advances in Infancy Research, 6,* 51–98.

Bertenthal, B. I., Proffit, H. D. R., Spetner, N. B., & Thomas, M. A. (1985). The development of infant sensitivity to biomechanical motions. *Child Development, 56,* 531–543.

Blewitt, P. (1983). "Dog" versus "collie": Vocabulary in speech to young children. *Developmental Psychology, 19,* 602–609.

Blewitt, P. (1989). Category hierarchies: Levels of knowledge and skill. *Genetic Epistemologist, 17,* 21–30.

Bower, T. G. R. (1974). *Development in infancy.* San Francisco: Freeman.

Bower, T. G. R. (1982). *Development in infancy* (2nd ed.). San Francisco: Freeman.

Bower, T. G. R., Broughton, J. M., & Moore, M. K. (1971). Development of the object concept as manifest in changes in the tracking behavior of infants between 7- and 20-weeks-of-age. *Journal of Experimental Child Psychology, 11,* 182–193.

Brentano, F. (1973). *Psychology from an empirical standpoint* (A. C Rancurello, D. B. Terrell, & L. L. McAlister, Trans.). London: Routledge & Kegan Paul. (Original work published 1874)

Bretherton, I., & Beeghly, M. (1982). Talking about internal states: The acquisition of an explicit theory of mind. *Developmental Psychology, 18,* 906–921.

Bretherton, I., McNew, S., & Beeghly-Smith, M. (1981). Early person knowledge as expressed in gestural and verbal communication: When do infants acquire a "theory of mind?" In M. Lamb & L. Sherrod (Eds.), *Social cognition in infancy* (pp. 333–373). Hillsdale, NJ: Erlbaum.

Brewer, W., & Samarapungavan, A. (1991). Children's theories vs. scientific theories: Differences in reasoning or differences in knowledge? In R. Hoffman & D. Palermo (Eds.), *Cognition and the symbolic processes* (pp. 209–232). Hillsdale, NJ: Erlbaum.

Brown, J. R., & Dunn, J. (1991). "You can cry, mum": The social and developmental implications of talk about internal states. *British Journal of Developmental Psychology, 9,* 237–256.

Bruner, J. S. (1990). *Acts of meaning.* Cambridge, MA: Harvard University Press.

Bullock, M., Gelman, R., & Baillargeon, R. (1982). The development of causal reasoning. In W. J. Friedman (Ed.), *The developmental psychology of time* (pp. 209–254). New York: Academic Press.

Bushnell, E. W., & Boudreau, J. P. (1993). Motor development and the mind: The potential role of motor abilities as a determinant of aspects of perceptual development. *Child Development, 64,* 1005–1021.

Butterworth, G. E. (1991). The ontogeny and phylogeny of joint visual attention. In A. Whiten (Ed.), *Natural theories of mind.* Oxford, England: Blackwell.

Butterworth, G. E., & Grover, L. (1988). The origins of referential communication in human infancy. In L. Weiskrantz (Ed.), *Thought without language.* Oxford, England: Clarendon Press.

Butterworth, G. E., Harris, P. L., Leslie, A. M., & Wellman, H. M. (Eds.). (1991). *Perspectives on the child's theory of mind.* Oxford, England: Oxford University Press.

Butterworth, G. E., & Jarret, N. L. M. (1991). What minds have in common is space. *British Journal of Developmental Psychology, 9,* 55–72.

Callanan, M. A. (1985). How parents label objects for young children: The role of input in the acquisition of category hierarchies. *Child Development, 56,* 508–523.

Callanan, M. A. (1990). Parents' descriptions of objects: Potential data for children's inferences about category principles. *Cognitive Development, 5,* 101–122.

Campos, J. J., Bertenthal, B. I., & Kermoian, R. (1992). Early experience and emotional development: The emergence of wariness of heights. *Psychological Science, 3,* 61–64.

Campos, J. J., Hiatt, S., Ramsay, D., Henderson, C., & Svejda, M. (1978). The emergence of fear of heights. In M. Lewis & L. Rosenblum (Eds.), *The development of affect* (pp. 149–182). New York: Plenum Press.

Carey, S. (1985). *Conceptual change in childhood.* Cambridge, MA: MIT Press.

Carey, S. (1991). Knowledge acquisition: Enrichment or conceptual change? In S. Carey & R. Gelman (Eds.), *The epigenesis of mind: Essays on biology and cognition* (pp. 257–291). Hillsdale, NJ: Erlbaum.

Carey, S. (1995). On the origin of causal understanding. In D. Sperber, D. Premack, & A. Premack (Eds.), *Causal cognition: A multidisciplinary debate* (pp. 268–302). New York: Oxford University Press.

Carey, S., & Gelman, R. (1991). *The epigenesis of mind: Essays on biology and cognition.* Hillsdale, NJ: Erlbaum.

Carey, S., & Spelke, E. (1994). Domain-specific knowledge and conceptual change. In L. A. Hirschfeld & S. A. Gelman (Eds.), *Mapping the mind: Domain specificity in cognition and culture* (pp. 169–200). Cambridge, England: Cambridge University Press.

Case, R. (1992). *The mind's staircase.* Hillsdale, NJ: Erlbaum.

Chandler, M., Fritz, A. S., & Hala, S. (1989). Small-scale deceit: Deception as a marker of 2-, 3-, and 4-year-olds' early theories of mind. *Child Development, 60,* 1263–1277.

Chapman, M. (1988). *Constructive evolution: Origins and development of Piaget's thought.* New York: Cambridge University Press.

Chase, W. G., & Ericsson, K. A. (1981). Skilled memory. In J. R. Anderson (Ed.), *Cognitive skills and their acquisition.* Hillsdale, NJ: Erlbaum.

Chase, W. G., & Simon, H. A. (1973). Perception in chess. *Cognitive Psychology, 4,* 55–81.

Cheney, D. L., & Seyfarth, R. M. (1990). *How monkeys see the world.* Chicago: University of Chicago Press.

Cheng, P. W. (1993). Separating causal laws from casual facts: Pressing the limits of statistical relevance. In D. L. Medin (Ed.), *The psychology of learning and motivation* (Vol. 30, pp. 215–264). San Diego, CA: Academic Press.

Chi, M., Hutchinson, J., & Robin, A. (1989). How inferences about novel domain-related concepts can be constrained by structured knowledge. *Merrill-Palmer Quarterly, 35,* 27–62.

Chi, M. T. H. (1978). Knowledge structure and memory development. In R. Siegler (Ed.), *Children's thinking: What develops?* (pp. 73–96). Hillsdale, NJ: Erlbaum.

Chomsky, N. (1988). *Language and problems of knowledge.* Cambridge, MA: MIT Press.

Churchland, P. M. (1981). Eliminative materialism and propositional attitudes. *Journal of Philosophy, 78,* 67–90.

Clough, E. E., & Wood-Robinson, C. (1985). Children's understanding of inheritance. *Journal of Biological Education, 19,* 304–310.

Cohen, L. B. (1988). An information processing approach to infants cognitive development. In L. Weiskrantz (Ed.), *Thought without language* (pp. 211–228). Oxford, England: Oxford University Press.

Cohen, L. B., & Oakes, L. M. (1993). How infants perceive a simple causal event. *Developmental Psychology, 29,* 421–433.

Cohen, L. B., & Younger, B. A. (1983). Perceptual categorization in the infant. In E. Scholnick (Ed.), *New trends in conceptual representation.* Hillsdale, NJ: Erlbaum.

Cole, M. (1988). Cultural psychology: A once and future discipline. *Nebraska Symposium on Motivation,* 279–335. Lincoln: University of Nebraska Press.

Coley, J. D. (1993). *Emerging differentiation of folkbiology and folkpsychology: Similarity judgments and property attributions.* Doctoral dissertation, Department of Psychology, University of Michigan, Ann Arbor.

Comrie, B. (1981). *Language universals and linguistic typology.* Chicago: University of Chicago Press.

Cosmides, L., & Tooby, J. (1994). Origins of domain specificity: The evolution of functional organization. In L. A. Hirschfeld & S. A. Gelman (Eds.), *Mapping the mind.* New York: Cambridge.

Croft, W. (1990). *Typology and universals.* Cambridge, England: Cambridge University Press.

D'Andrade, R. (1987). A folk model of the mind. In D. Holland & N. Quinn (Eds.), *Cultural models in language and thought.* Cambridge, England: Cambridge University Press.

Dennett, D. C. (1987). *The intentional stance.* Cambridge, MA: MIT Press.

DeVries, R. (1969). Constancy of generic identity in the years 3 to 6. *Monographs of the Society for Research in Child Development, 34*(3, Serial No. 127).

Dunn, J., & Brown, J. (1993). Early conversations about causality: Content, pragmatics and developmental change. *British Journal of Developmental Psychology, 11,* 107–123.

Dunn, J., Brown, J., & Beardsall, L. (1991). Family talk about feeling states and children's later understanding of others' emotions. *Child Development, 27,* 448–455.

Dunn, J., Brown, J., Slomkowski, C., Tesla, C., & Youngblade, L. (1991). Young children's understanding of other people's feelings and beliefs: Individual differences and their antecedents. *Child Development, 62,* 1352–1366.

Engel Clough, E., & Wood-Robinson, C. (1985). How secondary students interpret instances of biological adaptation. *Journal of Biological Education, 19,* 125–130.

Estes, D., Wellman, H. M., & Woolley, J. D. (1989). Children's understanding of mental phenomena. In H. Reese (Ed.), *Advances in child development and behavior* (pp. 41–87). New York: Academic Press.

Evans, M. (1994). *God or Darwin? The development of beliefs about the origin of species.* Unpublished doctoral dissertation, University of Michigan, Ann Arbor.

Fajans, J. (1985). The person in social context: The social character of Baining "Psychology." In G. White & J. Kirkpatrick (Eds.), *Person, self, and experience: Exploring pacific ethnopsychologies* (pp. 367–397). Los Angeles: University of California Press.

Feinman, S. (1982). Social referencing in infancy. *Merrill-Palmer Quarterly, 28,* 445–470.

Flavell, J. H. (1988). The development of children's knowledge about the mind: From cognitive connections to mental representations. In J. Astington, P. Harris, & D. Olson (Eds.), *Developing theories of mind* (pp. 244–267). New York: Cambridge University Press.

Flavell, J. H., Flavell, E. R., Green, F. L., & Moses, L. J. (1990). Young children's understanding of fact beliefs versus value beliefs. *Child Development, 61,* 915–928.

Flavell, J. H., Green, F. L., & Flavell, E. R. (1986). Development of knowledge about the appearance-reality distinction. *Monographs of the Society for Research in Child Development, 51*(Serial No. 212).

Flavell, J. H., Green, F. L., & Flavell, E. R. (1995). Young children's knowledge of thinking. *Monographs of the Society for Research in Child Development,* (Serial No. 243).

Fodor, J. A. (1983). *Modularity of mind.* Cambridge, MA: MIT Press.

Fodor, J. A. (1987). *Psychosemantics: The problem of meaning in the philosophy of mind.* Cambridge, MA: MIT Press.

Fodor, J. A. (1992). A theory of the child's theory of mind. *Cognition, 44,* 283–296.

Furrow, D., Moore, C., Davidge, J., & Chiasson. (1992). Mental terms in mothers' and children's speech: Similarities and relationships. *Journal of Child Language, 19,* 617–631.

Gabel, D. L., & Samuel, K. V. (1987). Understanding of the particulate nature of matter. *Journal of Chemical Education, 64,* 695–697.

Gale, E., de Villiers, P., de Villiers, J., & Pyers, J. (1996). Language and theory of mind in oral deaf children. In A. Stringfellow, D. Cahana-Amitay, E. Hughes, & A. Zukowski (Eds.), *Proceedings of the 20th Annual Boston University Conference on Language Development, Vol. 1.* Cascadilla Press.

Gathercole, V. C. M., Cramer, L. J., Somerville, S. C., & op de Haar, J. (1995). Ontological categories and function: Acquisition of new names. *Cognitive Development, 10,* 225–251.

Gelman, R. (1990). First principles organize attention to and learning about relevant data: Number and the animate-inanimate distinction as examples. *Cognitive Science, 14,* 79–106.

Gelman, R., & Baillargeon, R. (1983). A review of some Piagetian concepts. In J. H. Flavell & E. M. Markman (Eds.), *Handbook of child psychology: Vol. 3. Cognitive development* (pp. 167–230). New York: Wiley.

Gelman, R., Durgin, F., & Kaufman, L. (1995). Distinguishing between animates and inanimates: Not by motion alone. In D. Sperber, D. Premack, & A. J. Premack (Eds.), *Causal cognition* (pp. 150–184). Oxford, England: Clarendon Press.

Gelman, S. A. (1988). The development of induction within natural kind and artifact categories. *Cognitive Psychology, 20,* 65–95.

Gelman, S. A. (1993). Early conceptions of biological growth. In J. Montangero et al. (Eds.), *Conceptions of change over time* (pp. 197–208). Foundation Archives Jean Piaget, No. 13.

Gelman, S. A. (1994). Competence versus performance. In R. J. Sternberg (Ed.), *Encyclopedia of human intelligence* (Vol. 1, pp. 283–286). New York: Macmillan.

Gelman, S. A., & Coley, J. D. (1990). The importance of knowing a dodo is a bird: Categories and inferences in 2-year-old children. *Developmental Psychology, 26,* 796–804.

Gelman, S. A., & Coley, J. D. (1991). Language and categorization: The acquisition of natural kind terms. In S. A. Gelman & J. P. Byrnes (Eds.), *Perspectives on language and thought: Interrelations in development* (pp. 146–196). New York: Cambridge University Press.

Gelman, S. A., Coley, J. D., & Gottfried, G. M. (1994). Essentialist beliefs in children: The acquisition of concepts and theories. In L. A. Hirschfeld & S. A. Gelman (Eds.), *Mapping the mind: Domain specificity in cognition and culture* (pp. 341–365). New York: Cambridge University Press.

Gelman, S. A., Coley, J. D., Rosengren, K. S., Hartman, E., & Pappas, A. (1995). *Parent-child conversations about categories during picturebook reading.* Paper presented at the biennial meeting of the Society for Research in Child Development.

Gelman, S. A., & Gottfried, G. M. (1996). Children's causal explanations of animate and inanimate motion. *Child Development, 67,* 1970–1987.

Gelman, S. A., & Kalish, C. W. (1993). Categories and causality. In R. Pasnak & M. L. Howe (Eds.), *Emerging themes in cognitive development* (Vol. 2, pp. 3–32). New York: Springer-Verlag.

Gelman, S. A., & Kremer, K. E. (1991). Understanding natural cause: Children's explanations of how objects and their properties originate. *Child Development, 62*, 396–414.

Gelman, S. A., & Markman, E. M. (1986). Categories and induction in young children. *Cognition, 23*, 183–209.

Gelman, S. A., & Medin, D. L. (1993). What's so essential about essentialism? A different perspective on the interaction of perception, language, and conceptual knowledge. *Cognitive Development, 8*, 157–167.

Gelman, S. A., & O'Reilly, A. W. (1988). Children's inductive inferences within superordinate categories. *Child Development, 59*, 876–887.

Gelman, S. A., & Wellman, H. M. (1991). Insides and essences: Early understandings of the non-obvious. *Cognition, 38*, 213–244.

Gelman, S. A., Wilcox, S. A., & Clark, E. V. (1989). Conceptual and lexical hierarchies in young children. *Cognitive Development, 4*, 309–326.

Goldman, A. I. (1992). In defense of simulation theory. *Mind and Language, 1*, 104–119.

Golinkoff, R. M., Harding, C. G., Carlson, V., & Sexton, M. E. (1984). The infant's perception of causal events: The distinction between animate and inanimate objects. In L. L. Lipsitt & C. Rovee-Collier (Eds.), *Advances in infancy research* (Vol. 3, pp. 145–165). Norwood, NJ: ABLEX.

Golinkoff, R. M., Shuff-Bailey, M., Olguin, R., & Ruan, W. (1995). Young children extend novel words at the basic level: Evidence for the principle of categorical scope. *Developmental Psychology, 31*, 494–507.

Gopnik, A. (1984). The acquisition of *gone* and the development of the object concept. *Journal of Child Language, 11*, 273–292.

Gopnik, A. (1993). How we know our minds: The illusions of first person knowledge of intentionality. *Behavioral and Brain Sciences, 16*, 1–14.

Gopnik, A., & Astington, J. W. (1988). Children's understanding of representational change and its relation to the understanding of false belief and the appearance-reality distinction. *Child Development, 59*, 26–37.

Gopnik, A., & Graf, P. (1988). Knowing how you know: Young children's ability to identify and remember the sources of their beliefs. *Child Development, 59*, 1366–1371.

Gopnik, A., & Meltzoff, A. (1993). Minds, bodies, and persons. In S. Parker, M. Boccia, & R. Mitchell (Eds.), *Self-awareness in animals and humans*. New York: Cambridge University Press.

Gopnik, A., & Meltzoff, A. (1997). *Words, thoughts and theories*. Cambridge, MA: MIT Press.

Gopnik, A., & Wellman, H. M. (1994). The theory theory. In L. A. Hirschfeld & S. A. Gelman (Eds.), *Domain specificity in cognition and culture*. New York: Cambridge University Press.

Gordon, R. M. (1986). Folk psychology as simulation. *Mind and Language, 1*, 158–171.

Goswami, U. (1991). Analogical reasoning: What develops? A review of research and theory. *Child Development, 62*, 1–22.

Goswami, U. (in press). Analogical reasoning and cognitive development. In H. Reese (Ed.), *Advances in child development and behavior* (Vol. 26).

Goswami, U., & Brown, A. L. (1989). Melting chocolate and melting snowmen: Analogical reasoning and causal relations. *Cognition, 35*, 69–95.

Gould, S. J. (1977). *Ontogeny and phylogeny*. Cambridge, MA: Harvard University Press.

Gratch, G. (1982). Responses to hidden persons and things by 5-, 9-, and 16-month-old infants. *Developmental Psychology, 18*, 232–237.

Green, M. (1978). Structure and sequence in children's concepts of chance and probability. *Child Development, 49*, 1045–1053.

Greenberg, J. H. (1966). *Language universals*. The Hague: Mouton.

Haake, R. J., & Somerville, S. C. (1985). The development of logical search skills in infancy. *Developmental Psychology, 21*, 176–186.

Hadwin, J., & Perner, J. (1991). Pleased and surprised: Children's cognitive theory of emotion. *British Journal of Developmental Psychology, 9*, 215–234.

Harris, P. L. (1990). The child's theory of mind and its cultural context. In G. Butterworth & P. Bryant (Eds.), *The causes of development* (pp. 215–237). Hemel Hempstead, England: Harvester Wheatsheaf.

Harris, P. L. (1991). The work of the imagination. In A. Whiten (Ed.), *Natural theories of mind* (pp. 283–304). Oxford, England: Basil Blackwell.

Harris, P. L. (1992). From simulation to folk psychology: The case for development. *Mind and Language, 7*, 120–144.

Harris, P. L. (1994). Magic [Special issue]. *British Journal of Developmental Psychology, 12*, 1–108.

Harris P. L., Brown, E., Marriot, C., Whithall, S., & Harmer, S. (1991). Monsters, ghosts and witches: Testing the limits of the fantasy-reality distinction in young children. *British Journal of Developmental Psychology, 9*, 105–123.

Harris, P. L., Johnson, C. N., Hutton, D., Andrews, G., & Cooke, T. (1989). Young children's theory of mind and emotion. *Cognition and Emotion, 3*, 379–400.

Hatano, G., & Inagaki, K. (1994). Young children's naive theory of biology. *Cognition, 50*, 171–188.

Hatano, G., Siegler, R. S., Richards, D. D., & Inagaki, K. (1993). The development of biological knowledge: A multi-national study. *Cognitive Development, 8*, 47–62.

Hickling, A. K., & Gelman, S. A. (1995). How does your garden grow? Early conceptualization of seeds and their place in the plant growth cycle. *Child Development, 66,* 856–876.

Hirschfeld, L. A. (1996). *Race in the making.* Cambridge, MA: MIT Press.

Hirschfeld, L. A., & Gelman, S. A. (1994). *Mapping the mind: Domain specificity in cognition and culture.* New York: Cambridge University Press.

Hobson, R. P. (1993). *Autism and the development of mind.* Hillsdale, NJ: Erlbaum.

Holland, D., & Quinn, N. (1987). *Cultural models in language and thought.* Cambridge, England: Cambridge University Press.

Hornick, R., Risenhoover, N., & Gunnar, M. (1987). The effects of maternal positive, neutral, and negative affective communications and infant responses to new toys. *Child Development, 58,* 937–944.

Humphrey, N. (1993). *A history of the mind.* London: Vintage Books.

Hyams, N. M. (1986). *Language acquisition and the theory of parameters.* Dordrecht, The Netherlands: Reidel.

Imai, M., Gentner, D., & Uchida, N. (1994). Children's theories of word meaning: The role of shape similarity in early acquisition. *Cognitive Development, 9,* 45–75.

Inagaki, K. (1990). The effects of raising animals on children's biological knowledge. *British Journal of Developmental Psychology, 8,* 119–129.

Inagaki, K., & Hatano, G. (1987). Young children's spontaneous personification as analogy. *Child Development, 58,* 1013–1020.

Inagaki, K., & Hatano, G. (1993). Young children's understanding of the mind-body distinction. *Child Development, 64,* 1534–1549.

Inagaki, K., & Hatano, G. (1996). Young children's recognition of commonalities between animals and plants. *Child Development, 67,* 2823–2840.

Jeyifous, S. (1986). *Atimodemo: Semantic and conceptual development among the Yoruba.* Unpublished doctoral dissertation, Cornell University.

Johnson, K. E., Mervis, C. B., & Boster, J. S. (1992). Developmental changes within the structure of the mammal domain. *Developmental Psychology, 28,* 74–83.

Johnson, M. H., & Morton, J. (1991). *Biology and cognitive development: The case of face recognition.* Oxford, England: Basil Blackwell.

Jones, S. S., Smith, L. B., & Landau, B. (1991). Object properties and knowledge in early lexical learning. *Child Development, 62,* 499–516.

Kalish, C. W. (1996). Preschoolers' understanding of germs as invisible mechanisms. *Cognitive Development, 11,* 83–106.

Kalish, C. W. (1996). Causes and symptoms in children's understanding of illness. *Child Development, 67,* 1647–1670.

Kalish, C. W., & Gelman, S. A. (1992). On wooden pillows: Young children's understanding of category implications. *Child Development, 63,* 1536–1557.

Karmiloff-Smith, A. (1992). *Beyond modularity.* Cambridge, MA: MIT Press.

Keil, F. C. (1979). *Semantic and conceptual development.* Cambridge, MA: Harvard University Press.

Keil, F. C. (1989). *Concepts, kinds, and cognitive development.* Cambridge, MA: MIT Press.

Keil, F. C. (1992). The origins of an autonomous biology. In M. A. Gunnar & M. Maratsos (Eds.), *Minnesota Symposium on Child Psychology* (Vol. 25, pp. 103–138). Hillsdale, NJ: Erlbaum.

Keil, F. C. (1994). The birth and nurturance of concepts by domains: The origins of concepts of living things. In L. A. Hirschfeld & S. A. Gelman (Eds.), *Mapping the mind: Domain specificity in cognition and culture* (pp. 234–254). New York: Cambridge University Press.

Klahr, D., Fay, A., & Dunbar, K. (1993). Heuristics for scientific experimentation: A developmental study. *Cognitive Psychology, 25,* 111–146.

Kohlberg, S. (1969). Stage and sequence: The cognitive-developmental approach to socialization. In D. A. Goslin (Ed.), *Handbook of socialization theory and research* (pp. 347–480). New York: Rand McNally.

Kuhn, D. (1989). Children and adults as intuitive scientists. *Psychological Review, 96,* 674–689.

Kuhn, D. (1995). Microgenetic study of change: What has it told us? *Psychological Science, 6,* 133–139.

Kuhn, D., Garcia-Mila, M., Zohar, A., & Andersen, C. (1995). Strategies of knowledge acquisition. *Monographs of the Society for Research in Child Development, 60*(4), vol. 128.

Kuhn, D., & Phelps, E. (1982). The development of problem-solving strategies. In H. Reese (Ed.), *Advances in child development and behavior* (Vol. 17). New York: Academic Press.

Kuhn, T. (1962). *The structure of scientific revolutions.* Chicago: University of Chicago Press.

Kuzmack, S. D., & Gelman, R. (1986). Young children's understanding of random phenomena. *Child Development, 57,* 559–566.

Lakatos, I. (1970). Falsification and the methodology of scientific research programmes. In I. Lakatos & A. Musgrave (Eds.), *Criticism and the growth of knowledge* (pp. 91–196). Cambridge, England: Cambridge University Press.

Landau, B., Jones, S. S., & Smith, L. (1992). Perception, ontology, and naming in young children: Commentary on Soja, Carey, and Spelke. *Cognition, 43,* 85–91.

Landau, B., Smith, L. B., & Jones, S. S. (1988). The importance of shape in early lexical learning. *Cognitive Development, 3,* 299–321.

Laudan, L. (1977). *Progress and its problems: Towards a theory of scientific growth.* Berkeley: University of California Press.

LeCompte, G., & Gratch, G. (1972). Violation of a rule as a method of diagnosing infants' level of object concept. *Child Development, 43,* 385–396.

Leekam, S., & Perner, J. (1991). Does the autistic child have a "metarepresentational" deficit? *Cognition, 40,* 203–218.

Legerstee, M. (1991). The role of person and object in eliciting early imitation. *Journal of Experimental Child Psychology, 51,* 423–433.

Legerstee, M. (1992). A review of the animate-inanimate distinction in infancy. *Early Development and Parenting, 1,* 59–67.

Lempers, J. D., Flavell, E. R., & Flavell, J. H. (1977). The development in very young children of tacit knowledge concerning visual perception. *Genetic Psychology Monographs, 95,* 3–53.

Leslie, A. M. (1982). The perception of causality in infants. *Perception, 11,* 173–186.

Leslie, A. M. (1987). Pretense and representation: The origins of "theory of mind." *Psychological Review, 94,* 412–426.

Leslie, A. M. (1994). ToMM, ToBy, and agency: Core architecture and domain specificity in cognition and culture. In L. A. Hirschfeld & S. A. Gelman (Eds.), *Mapping the mind: Domain specificity in cognition and culture* (pp. 119–148). New York: Cambridge University Press.

Leslie, A. M., & Keeble, S. (1987). Do 6-month-old infants perceive causality? *Cognition, 25,* 265–288.

Leslie, A. M., & Thaiss, L. (1992). Domain specificity in conceptual development: Neuropsychological evidence from autism. *Cognition, 43,* 225–251.

Lewis, C., Freeman, N. H., Hagestadt, E., & Douglas, H. (1994). Narrative access and production in preschoolers' false belief reasoning. *Cognitive Development, 9,* 397–424.

Lewis, C., & Osborne, A. (1994). Three-year-olds' problems with false belief: Conceptual deficit or linguistic artifact? *Child Development, 61,* 1514–1519.

Lillard, A. (in press). Ethnopsychologies and the origins of a theory of mind. *Psychological Bulletin.*

Lindberg, M. A. (1980). Is knowledge base development a necessary and sufficient condition for memory development? *Journal of Experimental Child Psychology, 30,* 401–410.

Lopez, A., Atran, S., Coley, J. D., Medin, D., & Smith, E. E. (1997). The tree of life: Universals and cultural features of folk biological taxonomies and inductions. *Cognitive Psychology, 32,* 251–295.

MacWhinney, B. (1987). The competition model. In B. MacWhinney (Ed.), *Mechanisms of language acquisition.* Hillsdale, NJ: Erlbaum.

Malt, B. C. (1994). Water is not H_2O. *Cognitive Psychology, 27,* 41–70.

Malt, B. C. (1995). Category coherence in cross-cultural perspective. *Cognitive Psychology, 29,* 85–148.

Mandler, J. M. (1988). How to build a baby: On the development of an accessible representational system. *Cognitive Development, 3,* 113–136.

Mandler, J. M. (1992). How to build a baby: II. Conceptual primitives. *Psychological Review, 99,* 587–604.

Mandler, J. M., Bauer, P. J., & McDonough, L. (1991). Separating the sheep from the goats: Differentiating global categories. *Cognitive Psychology, 23,* 263–298.

Mandler, J. M., & McDonough, L. (in press). Drinking and driving don't mix: Inductive generalization in infancy. *Cognition.*

Markman, E. M. (1989). *Categorization and naming in children.* Cambridge, MA: MIT Press.

Marr, D. (1982). *Vision.* New York: Freeman.

Marschark, M. (1993). *Psychological development in deaf children.* New York: Oxford University Press.

Massey, C. M., & Gelman, R. (1988). Preschooler's ability to decide whether a photographed unfamiliar object can move itself. *Developmental Psychology, 24,* 307–317.

Mayr, E. (1991). *One long argument: Charles Darwin and the genesis of modern evolutionary thought.* Cambridge, MA: Harvard University Press.

McCloskey, M. (1983). Naive theories of motion. In D. Gentner & A. Stevens (Eds.), *Mental models* (pp. 299–324). Hillsdale, NJ: Erlbaum.

Mead, M. (1932). An investigation of the thought of primitive children with special reference to animism. *Journal of the Royal Anthropological Institute, 62,* 173–190.

Medin, D. (1989). Concepts and conceptual structure. *American Psychologist, 44,* 1469–1481.

Meltzoff, A. N. (1995). Understanding the intentions of others: Re-enactment of intended acts by 18-month-old children. *Developmental Psychology, 31,* 838–850.

Meltzoff, A. N., & Gopnik, A. (1993). The role of imitation in understanding persons and developing theories of mind. In S. Baron-Cohen, H. Tager-Flusberg, & D. J. Cohen (Eds.), *Understanding other minds.* New York: Cambridge University Press.

Meltzoff, A. N., & Moore, M. K. (1983). Newborn infants imitate adult facial gestures. *Child Development, 54,* 702–719.

Meltzoff, A. N., & Moore, M. K. (1995). Infants' understanding of people and things. In J. Bermudez, A. J. Marcel, & N. Eilan

(Eds.), *The body and the self* (pp. 43–69). Cambridge, MA: MIT Press.

Mitchell, P., & Lacohee, H. (1991). Children's early understanding of false belief. *Cognition, 39,* 107–127.

Moore, C. (1996). Theories of mind in infancy. *British Journal of Developmental Psychology, 14,* 19–40.

Moore, C., & Corkum, V. (1994). Social understanding at the end of the first year of life. *Developmental Review, 14,* 349–372.

Moore, M. K., Borton, R., & Darby, B. L. (1978). Visual tracking in young infants. *Journal of Experimental Child Psychology, 25,* 183–198.

Moses, L. J., & Flavell, J. H. (1990). Inferring false beliefs from actions and reactions. *Child Development, 61,* 929–945.

Muir, D. W., & Hains, S. M. J. (1993). Infant sensitivity to perturbations in adult facial, vocal, tactile, and contingent stimulation during face to face interactions. In B. de Boysson-Bardies, S. de Schonen, P. Jusczyk, P. McNeilage, & J. Morton (Eds.), *Developmental neurocognition: Speech and face processing in the first year.* Dordrecht, The Netherlands: Kluwer.

Muller, A., & Aslin, R. (1978). Visual tracking as an index of the object concept. *Infant Behavior and Development, 1,* 309–319.

Munakata, Y., McClelland, J. L., Johnson, M. H., & Siegler, R. S. (in press). Rethinking infant knowledge: Toward an adaptive process account of successes and failures in object permanence tasks. *Psychological Review.*

Mundy, P., & Sigman, M. (1989). The theoretical implications of joint-attention deficits in autism. *Development and Psychopathology, 1,* 173–184.

Murphy, C. M., & Messer, D. J. (1977). Mothers, infants and pointing: A study of a gesture. In H. R. Schaffer (Ed.), *Studies in mother-infant interaction.* London: Academic Press.

Murphy, G. L., & Medin, D. L. (1985). The role of theories in conceptual coherence. *Psychological Review, 92,* 284–316.

Nelson, C. A. (1987). The recognition of facial expressions in the first two years of life: Mechanisms of development. *Child Development, 58,* 889–909.

Novick, S., & Nussbaum, J. (1981). Pupils' understanding of the particulate nature of matter. *Science Education, 65,* 187–196.

Oakes, L. M., & Cohen, L. B. (1990). Infant perception of a causal event. *Cognitive Development, 5,* 193–207.

O'Neill, D. K., & Gopnik, A. (1991). Young children's ability to identify the sources of their beliefs. *Developmental Psychology, 27,* 390–397.

Perner, J. (1991). *Understanding the representational mind.* Cambridge, MA: MIT Press.

Perner, J., Leekam, S. R., & Wimmer, H. (1987). Three-year-olds' difficulty with false belief. *British Journal of Developmental Psychology, 5,* 125–137.

Peterson, C. C., & Siegal, M. (1995). Deafness, conversation and theory of mind. *Journal of Child Psychology and Psychiatry, 36,* 459–474.

Piaget, J. (1929). *The child's conception of the world.* London: Routledge & Kegan Paul.

Piaget, J. (1930). *The child's conception of physical causality.* London: Routledge & Kegan Paul.

Piaget, J. (1953). *The origins of intelligence in the child.* London: Routledge & Kegan Paul.

Piaget, J. (1954). *The construction of reality in the child.* New York: Basic Books.

Pillow, B. H. (1989). Early understanding of perception as a source of knowledge. *Journal of Experimental Child Psychology, 47,* 116–129.

Pinker, S. (1994). *The language instinct.* New York: Penguin Books.

Plunkett, K. (1995). Connectionist approaches to language acquisition. In P. Fletcher & B. MacWhinney (Eds.), *Handbook of child language* (pp. 36–72). Oxford, England: Blackwell.

Povinelli, D. J. (1993). Reconstructing the evolution of mind. *American Psychologist, 48,* 493–509.

Pratt, C., & Bryant, P. E. (1990). Young children understand that looking leads to knowing (so long as they are looking into a single barrel). *Child Development, 61,* 973–982.

Premack, D., & Woodruff, G. (1978). Does the chimpanzee have a theory of mind. *Behavioral and Brain Sciences, 4,* 515–526.

Proffitt, D. R., Kaiser, M. K., & Whelan, S. M. (1990). Understanding wheel dynamics. *Cognitive Psychology, 22,* 342–373.

Putnam, H. (1973). Meaning and reference. *Journal of Philosophy, 70,* 699–711.

Quine, W. V. (1977). Natural kinds. In S. P. Schwartz (Ed.), *Naming, necessity, and natural kinds* (pp. 155–175). Ithaca, NY: Cornell University Press.

Repacholi, B. M., & Gopnik, A. (1997). Early reasoning about desires: Evidence from 14- and 18-month-olds. *Developmental Psychology, 33,* 12–21.

Ribaupierre, A. (1989). *Transition mechanisms in child development.* Cambridge, England: Cambridge University Press.

Richards, D. D., & Siegler, R. S. (1984). The effects of task requirements on children's abilities to make life judgments. *Child Development, 55,* 1687–1696.

Richards, D. D., & Siegler, R. S. (1986). Children's understandings of the attributes of life. *Journal of Experimental Child Psychology, 42,* 1–22.

Ridgeway, D., Waters, E., & Kuczaj, S. (1985). Acquisition of emotion-descriptive language: Receptive and productive vocabulary norms for ages 18 months to 6 years. *Developmental Psychology, 21,* 901–908.

Robinson, E. J., & Mitchell, P. (1995). Making children's early understanding of the representational mind: Backwards explanation versus prediction. *Child Development, 66,* 1022–1039.

Rogoff, B. (1990). *Apprenticeship in thinking: Cognitive development in social context.* New York: Oxford University Press.

Rosch, E. H. (1978). Principles of categorization. In E. H. Rosch & B. B. Lloyd (Eds.), *Cognition and categorization* (pp. 27–48). Hillsdale, NJ: Erlbaum.

Rosch, E. H., Mervis, C. B., Gray, W., Johnson, D., & Boyes-Braem, P. (1976). Basic objects in natural categories. *Cognitive Psychology, 3,* 382–439.

Rosen, A. B., & Rozin, P. (1993). Now you see it, now you don't: The preschool child's conception of invisible particles in the context of dissolving. *Developmental Psychology, 29,* 300–311.

Rosengren, K. S., Gelman, S. A., Kalish, C. W., & McCormick, M. (1991). As time goes by: Children's early understanding of growth in animals. *Child Development, 62,* 1032–1320.

Rosengren, K. S., & Hickling, A. K. (1994). Seeing is believing: Children's explanations of commonplace, magical and extraordinary transformation. *Child Development, 65,* 1605–1626.

Rosengren, K. S., Kalish, E. W., Hickling, A. K., & Gelman, S. A. (1994). Explaining the relations between preschool children's magical beliefs and causal thinking. *British Journal of Developmental Psychology, 12,* 69–82.

Scaife, M., & Bruner, J. S. (1975). The capacity for joint visual attention in the infant. *Nature, 253,* 265.

Schult, C. A., & Wellman, H. M. (in press). Explaining human movements and actions. *Cognition.*

Schwartz, S. P. (1979). Natural kind terms. *Cognition, 7,* 301–315.

Shatz, M., Wellman, H. M., & Silber, S. (1983). The acquisition of mental verbs: A systematic investigation of first references to mental state. *Cognition, 14,* 301–321.

Shipley, E. T. (1993). Categories, hierarchies, and induction. In D. Medin (Ed.), *The psychology of learning and motivation* (Vol. 30, pp. 265–301). New York: Academic Press.

Shultz, T. R. (1982). Rules of causal attribution. *Monographs of the Society for Research in Child Development, 194.*

Shultz, T. R., & Kestenbaum, N. R. (1985). Causal reasoning in children. In G. Whitehurst (Ed.), *Annals of child development* (Vol. 2, pp. 195–244). Greenwich, CT: JAI Press.

Siegal, M. (1988). Children's knowledge of contagion and contamination as causes of illness. *Child Development, 59,* 1353–1359.

Siegal, M. (1991). *Knowing children: Experiments in conversation and cognition.* Hove, England: Erlbaum.

Siegal, M., & Beattie, K. (1991). Where to look first for children's understanding of false beliefs. *Cognition, 38,* 1–12.

Siegal, M., & Robinson, J. (1987). Order effects in children's gender constancy responses. *Developmental Psychology, 23,* 283–286.

Siegler, R. S. (1989). *Mechanisms of cognitive development: Annual review of psychology* (Vol. 40, pp. 353–379). Palo Alto, CA: Annual Reviews.

Siegler, R. S. (1995). Children's thinking: How does change occur? In F. E. Weinert & W. Schneider (Eds.), *Memory performance and competencies: Issues in growth and development* (pp. 405–430). Mahwah, NJ: Erlbaum.

Siegler, R. S., & Crowley, K. (1991). The microgenetic method: A direct means for studying cognitive development. *American Psychologist, 46,* 606–620.

Silverstein, M. (1976). Hierarchy of features and ergativity. In R. M. W. Dixon (Ed.), *Grammatical categories in Australian languages* (pp. 112–171). Canberra: Australian Institute for Aboriginal Studies.

Simons, D. J., & Keil, F. C. (1995). An abstract to concrete shift in the development of biological thought. *Cognition, 56,* 129–163.

Slobin, D. I. (1985). Crosslinguistic evidence for the language-making capacity. In D. I. Slobin (Ed.), *The crosslinguistic study of language acquisition: Vol. 2. Theoretical issues* (pp. 1157–1256). Hillsdale, NJ: Erlbaum.

Smiley, P., & Huttenlocher, J. (1989). Young children's acquisition of emotion concepts. In C. Saarni & P. Harris (Eds.), *Children's understanding of emotion.* New York: Cambridge University Press.

Smith, C., Carey, S., & Wiser, M. (1985). On differentiation: A case study of the development of the concepts of size, weight, and density. *Cognition, 21,* 177–237.

Smith, L. B., Jones, S. S., & Landau, B. (1992). Count nouns, adjectives, and perceptual properties in children's novel word interpretations. *Developmental Psychology, 28,* 273–286.

Sodian, B. (1994). Early deception and the conceptual continuity claim. In C. Lewis & P. Mitchell (Eds.), *Children's early understanding of mind.* Hove, England: Erlbaum.

Soja, N. N., Carey, S., & Spelke, E. S. (1991). Ontological categories guide young children's inductions of word meaning: Object terms and substance terms. *Cognition, 38,* 179–211.

Soja, N. N., Carey, S., & Spelke, E. S. (1992). Discussion: Perception, ontology, and meaning. *Cognition, 45,* 101–107.

Solomon, G. E. A., Johnson, S. C., Zaitchik, D., & Carey, S. (1996). The young child's conception of inheritance. *Child Development, 67,* 151–171.

Sommers, F. (1963). Types and ontology. *Philosophical Review, 72,* 327–363.

Sophian, C. (1984). Developing search skills in infancy and early childhood. In C. Sophian (Ed.), *Origins of cognitive skills.* Hillsdale, NJ: Erlbaum.

Sorce, J. F., Emde, R. N., Campos, J. J., & Klinert, N. D. (1985). Maternal emotional signaling: Its effect on the visual cliff behavior of 1-year-olds. *Developmental Psychology, 20,* 195–200.

Spelke, E. S. (1988). Where perceiving ends and thinking begins: The apprehension of objects in infancy. In A. Yonas (Ed.), *Perceptual development in infancy* (Vol. 20, pp. 197–234). Hillsdale, NJ: Erlbaum.

Spelke, E. S. (1991). Physical knowledge in infancy. In S. Carey & R. Gelman (Eds.), *The epigenesis of mind: Essays on biology and cognition* (pp. 133–169). Hillsdale, NJ: Erlbaum.

Spelke, E. S. (1994). Initial knowledge: Six suggestions. *Cognition, 50.*

Spelke, E. S., Breinlinger, K., Macomber, J., & Jacobson, K. (1992). Origins of knowledge. *Psychological Review, 99,* 605–632.

Spelke, E. S., & Van de Walle, G. (1993). Perceiving and reasoning about objects. In N. Eilan, W. Brewer, & R. McCarthy (Eds.), *Spatial representation.* New York: Blackwell.

Spelke, S. S., Phillips, A. T., & Woodward, A. L. (1995). Infants' knowledge of object motion and human action. In A. Premack (Ed.), *Causal understanding in cognition and culture.*

Sperber, D. (1994). The modularity of thought and the epidemiology of representations. In L. A. Hirschfeld & S. A. Gelman (Eds.), *Mapping the mind.* New York: Cambridge University Press.

Springer, K. (1992). Children's awareness of the biological implications of kinship. *Child Development, 63,* 950–959.

Springer, K. (1995). Acquiring a naive theory of kinship through inference. *Child Development, 66,* 547–558.

Springer, K., & Keil, F. C. (1989). On the development of biologically specific beliefs: The case of inheritance. *Child Development, 60,* 637–648.

Springer, K., & Keil, F. C. (1991). Early differentiation of causal mechanisms appropriate to biological and nonbiological kinds. *Child Development, 62,* 767–781.

Springer, K., Ngyuen, T., & Samaniego, R. (1996). Early understanding of age- and environment-related noxiousness in biological kinds: Evidence for a naive theory. *Cognitive Development, 11,* 65–82.

Starkey, P. (1992). The early development of numerical reasoning. *Cognition, 43,* 93–126.

Stein, N. L. (1988). The development of children's storytelling skill. In M. B. Franklin & S. Barten (Eds.), *Child language* (pp. 279–282). New York: Oxford University Press.

Stein, N. L., & Albro, E. R. (in press). Building complexity and coherence: Children's use of goal-structured knowledge in telling good stories. In M. Bamberg (Ed.), *Learning how to narrate: New directions in child development.* San Francisco: Jossey-Bass.

Stein, N. L., & Levine, L. J. (1989). The causal organization of emotional knowledge: A developmental study. *Cognition and Emotion, 3,* 343–378.

Stein, N. L., & Trabasso, T. (1982). Children's understanding of stories. In C. Brainerd & M. Pressley (Eds.), *Verbal processes in children* (Vol. 2, pp. 161–188). New York: Springer-Verlag.

Stern, D. N. (1985). *The interpersonal world of the infant.* New York: Basic Books.

Sternberg, R. J. (1984). *Mechanisms of cognitive development.* New York: Freeman.

Sullivan, K., & Winner, E. (1993). Three-year-olds' understanding of mental states: The influence of trickery. *Journal of Experimental Child Psychology, 56,* 135–148.

Tanaka, J. W., & Taylor, M. (1991). Object categories and expertise: Is the basic level in the eye of the beholder? *Cognitive Psychology, 23,* 457–482.

Taylor, M. G. (1993). *Children's beliefs about the biological and social origins of gender differences.* Unpublished doctoral dissertation, University of Michigan, Ann Arbor.

Tomasello, M. (1995). Language: Not an instinct. *Cognitive Development, 10,* 131–156.

Tomasello, M., Kruger, A. C., & Ratner, H. H. (1993). Cultural learning. *Behavioral and Brain Sciences.*

Trabasso, T., & Nickels, M. (1992). The development of goal plans of action in the narration of picture stories. *Discourse Processes, 15,* 249–275.

Trabasso, T., Stein, N. L., & Johnson, L. R. (1981). Children's knowledge of events: A causal analysis of story structure. In G. H. Bower (Ed.), *Learning and Motivation* (Vol. 15). New York: Academic Press.

Trevarthen, C., & Hubley, P. (1978). Secondary intersubjectivity: Confidence, confiding and acts of meaning in the first year. In A. Lock (Ed.), *Action, gesture and symbol: The emergence of language* (pp. 183–229). New York: Academic Press.

Van de Walle, G., Woodward, A. L., & Phillips, A. (1994). *Infants' inferences about contact relations in a causal event.* Paper presented at the meetings of the International Society for Infants Studies, Paris.

Volkmar, F. R., & Klin, A. (1993). Social development in autism: Historical and clinical perspectives. In S. Baron-Cohen, H. Tager-Flusberg, & D. J. Cohen (Eds.), *Understanding other minds* (pp. 40–57). New York: Oxford University Press.

Vosniadou, S. (1987). Children and metaphors. *Child Development, 58,* 870–885.

Vosniadou, S. (1989). On the nature of children's naive knowledge. *Proceeding of the 11th Annual Conference of the Cognitive Science Society* (pp. 404–411). Hillsdale, NJ: Erlbaum.

Vosniadou, S. (1994). Universal and culture-specific properties of children's mental models of the earth. In L. A. Hirschfeld & S. A. Gelman (Eds.), *Mapping the mind.* New York: Cambridge University Press.

Vosniadou, S., & Brewer, W. F. (1987). Theories of knowledge restructuring in development. *Review of Educational Research, 57,* 51–67.

Vosniadou, S., & Brewer, W F (1992). Mental models of the earth: A study of conceptual change in childhood. *Cognitive Psychology, 24,* 535–585.

Vosniadou, S., & Brewer, W. F. (1994). Mental models of the day/night cycle. *Cognitive Science, 18,* 123–183.

Vygotsky, L. S. (1978). *Mind in society: The development of higher psychological processes.* Cambridge, MA: Harvard University Press.

Walden, T. A., & Ogan, T. A. (1988). The development of social referencing. *Child Development, 59,* 1230–1240.

Ward, T. B., Becker, A. H., Haas, S. D., & Vela, E. (1991). Attribute availability and the shape bias in children's category generalization. *Cognitive Development, 6,* 143–167.

Waxman, S. R. (1990). Linguistic biases and the establishment of conceptual hierarchies: Evidence from preschool children. *Cognitive Development, 5,* 123–150.

Wellman, H. M. (1988). First steps in the child's theorizing about the mind. In J. Astington, P. Harris, & D. Olson (Eds.), *Developing theories of mind.* New York: Cambridge University Press.

Wellman, H. M. (1990). *The child's theory of mind.* Cambridge: MIT Press.

Wellman, H. M. (1993). Early understanding of mind: The normal case. In S. Baron-Cohen, H. Tager-Flusberg, & D. J. Cohen (Eds.), *Understanding other minds: Perspectives from autism* (pp. 10–39). Oxford, England: Oxford University Press.

Wellman, H. M., & Banerjee, M. (1991). Mind and emotion: Children's understanding of the emotional consequences of beliefs and desires. *British Journal of Developmental Psychology, 9,* 191–124.

Wellman, H. M., & Bartsch, K. (1988). Young children's reasoning about beliefs. *Cognition, 30,* 239–277.

Wellman, H. M., Cross, D., & Bartsch, K. (1986). Infant search and object permanence: A meta-analysis of the A-not-B error.

Monographs of the Society for Research in Child Development, 51(Serial No. 214).

Wellman, H. M., & Estes, D. (1986). Early understanding of mental entities: A reexamination of childhood realism. *Child Development, 57,* 910–923.

Wellman, H. M., & Gelman, S. A. (1992). Cognitive development: Foundational theories of core domains. *Annual Review of Psychology, 43,* 337–375.

Wellman, II. M., Harris, P. L., Banerjee, M., & Sinclair, A. (1995). Early understanding of emotion: Evidence from natural language. *Cognition and Emotion, 9,* 117–149.

Wellman, H. M., Hollander, M., & Schult, C A (1996). Young children's understanding of thought-bubbles and of thoughts. *Child Development, 67,* 768–788.

White, P. A. (1995). *The understanding of causation and the production of action: From infancy to adulthood.* Hove, England: Erlbaum.

Wierzbicka, A. (1984). Apples are not a 'kind of fruit': The semantics of human categorization. *American Ethnologist, 11,* 313–328.

Wimmer, H., Hogrefe, J., & Perner, J. (1988). Children's understanding of informational access as source of knowledge. *Child Development, 59,* 386–396.

Wimmer, H., & Perner, J. (1983). Beliefs about beliefs: Representation and constraining function of wrong beliefs in young children's understanding of deception. *Cognition, 13,* 103–128.

Woodward, A. (1995). *Infants' reasoning about the goals of a human actor.* Paper presented at the meetings of Society for Research in Child Development, Indianapolis, IN.

Woolley, J. D. (1995). The fictional mind: Young children's understanding of pretense, imagination, and dreams. *Developmental Review, 15,* 172–211.

Woolley, J. D., & Bruell, M. J. (1996). Young children's awareness of the origins of their mental representations. *Developmental Psychology, 32,* 335–346.

Wynn, K. (1992). Addition and subtraction by human infants. *Nature, 358,* 749–750.

Xu, F., & Carey, S. (1996). Infants' metaphysics: The case of numerical identity. *Cognitive Psychology, 30,* 111–153.

Yuill, N. (1984). Young children's coordination of motive and outcome in judgments of satisfaction and morality. *British Journal of Developmental Psychology, 2,* 73–81.

Zaitchik, D. (1991). Is only seeing really believing? Sources of true belief in the false belief task. *Cognitive Development, 6,* 91–103.

CHAPTER 12

Enabling Constraints for Cognitive Development and Learning: Domain Specificity and Epigenesis

ROCHEL GELMAN and EARL M. WILLIAMS

All theories of cognitive development make assumptions about constraints on learning, even those which commonly are seen as nonconstraint theories. We do not ask whether a constraint theory or a nonconstraint theory is better. Instead, we ask what kind of theory best accommodates key facts about cognitive development and concept learning. Our answer follows in three sections. We begin by reviewing what we consider these relevant facts to be, in the form of seven postulates about cognitive development and learning.

In the second section, we turn to a review of theories and the notions of constraint embedded within them. This allows us to bring out key sources of misunderstanding and confusion about what constraints are and how they function. We emphasize the fact that the meaning of theoretical terms including *constraint* and *learning* can differ considerably across theories. For example, some treat constraints as *learning enablers,* while others consider them to be limiting mechanisms that make learning unnecessary. We also point out instances in which seemingly different theories share overlapping assumptions about the nature of constraints.

In the third section, we move to a combined consideration of evidence and theory, and develop our reasons for

Partial support for the work came from NSF Grant No. DBS-92009741 to R.G.

favoring a rational-constructivist theory of cognitive development. The rationalist side of the theory is motivated in part by the many findings of conceptual competence in infants and animals, competencies that extend well past the simple perceptual abilities to which they were once thought to be limited. The constructivist side is motivated by the evidence that learning at all ages involves an active interchange between structures in the mind and "structure-able" information from the environment. We share with Piaget the hypothesis that our young join their mental structures with processes, such as assimilation and accommodation, to actively contribute to their own cognitive development and epigenesis.

Rather than pairing these self-modifying mental processes with Piaget's set of innate reflexes, however, we prefer to pair them with domain-specific skeletal structures. We do so for two reasons. First, there are now simply too many demonstrations of infant conceptual competence to accept Piaget's nonconceptual account of infancy. Second, reflexes do not provide an adequate foundation for learning: they cannot self-modify, but depend instead for their modification on other neural processes. For example, the vestibulo-ocular reflex (which keeps our eyes stable as our heads move) depends on separate neural machinery for calibration. When that separate machinery is removed, the reflex can no longer calibrate itself. By contrast, skeletal structures *do* provide an adequate foundation for subsequent learning because they can and do self-modify. If we accept the idea that from the start, our young apply their constructivist tendencies to the skeletal structures they are endowed with, then we have a way to account for how beginning learners come to share knowledge structures with their elders. Existing structures of mind help novices move onto learning paths that are domain-relevant rather than domain-irrelevant. Domain-relevant paths lead learners to inputs that are consistent with the structure of the domain to be learned; domain-irrelevant ones do not. More generally, the idea is that constraints function to enable and facilitate the acquisition and use of domain-relevant knowledge. Like other experientially modifiable biological structures (e.g., muscles), mental structures both require and contribute to epigenetic interactions with their environment (Dickinson & Dyer, 1996; Gottlieb, 1983; Lehrman, 1970).

Considerations of evolutionary, comparative, cultural, and Piagetian perspectives inform our assumptions that the mind has certain skeletal, innate domains of knowledge which actively contribute to its epigenesis of knowledge. Humans' ability to acquire novel knowledge in areas that are not grounded on innate skeletal principles leads us to distinguish between *core* and *noncore* kinds of domains. We do not appeal to different learning mechanisms to explain the acquisition of each kind, however. For us, the key learning tool in both cases is structure-mapping, in which information from the environment is mapped with existing information in the mind. The mind's ever-present proclivity to find and map relevant data is enabled whenever there are already-present structures, no matter how skeletal they might be. Even skeletal structures can provide novices the wherewithal to find and map inputs that share their structure. Similarly, these structures can call on other mental learning tools, especially a frequency-computing tool, to collect information about the relative predictive validity of different cues as indicators of the appropriate interpretation or role assignment for an object/event. Skeletal structures give young minds a mental running start and serve as the engines of learning.

Where mental structures have to be acquired de novo—as is surely the case for topics such as chess, Newtonian mechanics, the theory of evolution, the stock market—learners have to acquire domain-relevant structure in addition to the content of the domain (Brown, 1990). Acquisition of noncore domains should therefore be difficult, since it is not easy to assemble truly new conceptual structures (e.g., Carey, 1991; Chi, 1992; Chi, Glaser, & Farr, 1988; Kuhn, 1970), and lengthy formal instruction is often required. Efforts to provide such instruction must recognize and overcome a crucial challenge: learners may assimilate inputs to existing conceptual structures even when those inputs are intended to force accommodation and conceptual change (Gelman, 1993, 1994; Slotta, Chi, & Joram, 1995).

To summarize, given that all theories of cognitive development and concept learning contain some notion of constraint, the preference for one class of theories over another should be guided by the degree to which facts about the mind in general and about cognitive development in particular are accommodated. We turn to marshaling the kinds of evidence that led us to a theory which embeds a learning-enabling notion of constraints.

KEY POSTULATES ABOUT LEARNING AND COGNITION

The last 25 years or so have provided a wealth of important data about cognition and cognitive development. Here we highlight seven postulates which attempt to capture theoretical advances and certain classes of findings that are especially relevant to the consideration of different accounts of learning and concept acquisition. In the past, when appreciated at all, these postulates have commonly been considered individually or in small groups, rather than as a coherent and interconnected package. By bringing them all together here, we hope to build a solid theoretical and empirical standard against which subsequent discussions of constraints and their influence on learning can be measured. Where possible, we refer the reader to relevant chapters elsewhere in this *Handbook* for a greater degree of empirical detail. To anticipate the argument which we will develop later in this chapter, we believe that these postulates implicate a learning-enabling view of constraints within a rationalist-constructivist theory of mind.

Postulate 1: Inputs Can Be Divergently and Convergently Ambiguous, Requiring Interpretation

The would-be learner must cope with two fundamental challenges: perceptual and conceptual inputs are often either *divergently* or *convergently* ambiguous. Inputs that can be interpreted in more than one way are *divergently ambiguous* (the familiar sense of ambiguity). For example, many sentences are syntactically ambiguous, such as "They are baking apples," or "Jane likes Bill better than Will," or "Does he write on time?" Homophonic words are ambiguous by definition: the word "bat" can refer to an animate object, an inanimate object, or a verb. Notation systems provide other examples of divergent ambiguity. The notation F(2,4) can stand for a fraction, a musical time signature, or even a statistical analysis-of-variance result. When used as a fraction, one can say that ¾ is equal to $^{100}/_{200}$ but not ⅝. In contrast, the time signature ¾ can be rendered meaningfully into a ⅝ rhythm, but there is no such thing as the time signature $^{100}/_{200}$. For a child learning both Spanish and English, the sound *si* can mean "yes" or "see" depending on whether it is meant to be interpreted as a word in Spanish or English.

Inputs can also be *convergently ambiguous* in their mapping to mental representations: that is, multiple perceptual inputs can converge on a common meaning. A single mental representation can have multiple perceptual instantiations. Bilingual language learners confront especially compelling examples of items which differ in their surface appearance but nevertheless have the same meaning. The French-English bilingual child has to master the fact that *un, deux, trois* and *one, two, three* share the same meaning, even though they are perceptually different. Turning to the mathematics of rational numbers again, the fractional

expressions ½, $^{33}/_{66}$, $^{4.5}/_{9.0}$, and .50 are all equivalent and therefore share the same meaning, even though they look very different from one another. Similarly, the printed and written versions of individual letters vary extensively by case, font, and handwriting, even though they all share the same phonemic interpretation. When an adult and a child utter the same sentence, the much higher pitch range used by the child does not change the sentence's meaning. In general, much of the surface variability in what we perceive is discarded as irrelevant when we interpret its meaning.

Convergent and divergent ambiguities present a deep challenge to any learner, because they eliminate the possibility of a guaranteed, invariant, one-to-one mapping between a particular environmental input and a particular "correct" mental representation of that input that is to be learned. How do we learn what entities constitute the possible extensions and meaning of a concept? How do we learn particular mappings which are consistent from one occasion to the next, let alone consistently shared with other people with whom we might wish to communicate? These questions pose deep difficulties for any theory of conceptual development that seeks to build knowledge entirely from sensory and perceptual inputs.

Some readers might dispute our postulation of divergent and convergent ambiguity, denying the existence of these problems by arguing that the real world in which people live and act is contextually rich and full of structured information. There is no problem of stimulus impoverishment, so the argument continues, since people are able to use context to pick up and disambiguate relevant inputs (e.g., E. J. Gibson, 1984; J. J. Gibson, 1983; Greeno, Smith, & Moore, 1992; Lave & Wenger, 1991; Nelson, 1987, 1988; Rogoff & Chavayah, 1995; Rogoff & Lave, 1984). We believe that this response begs the question of how learners could accomplish this disambiguation. As can be seen in Figure 12.1, environments can present ambiguities about edges of objects, what is a "real" object as opposed to its reflection, and which occluded bits go together to form a whole object. The more novel and complex the physical environment, the more likely it is that objects and events will overlap. The environment by itself does not specify an interpretation, nor does it tell the mind what goes with what. We agree that there surely are cases where the structure of the environment affords or dictates particular solutions (picking up, pushing) and not others (twigs on trees do not afford standing-on). We particularly agree that relevant environmental inputs are often structured, a point to which we return below. However, we disagree that the world itself suffices to define what is relevant.

Figure 12.1 Where does what start (end) and what goes with what? Photograph by Adam H. Gallistel. Reproduced with permission.

If left to their own devices, novices are at risk for mixing together inputs that do not lead to a coherent perception or cognition, and for achieving perceptual organizations of the environment that differ radically from ones reached by others (Neisser, 1966). This is true even when the information source is social. For instance, contrary to our intuitions, the sound stream of spoken speech does not have gaps of silence in between words. Linguists have shown that this "segmentation problem" is a real challenge to language learners, because it is not obvious how to divide up the continuous speech stream into discrete words (let alone phonemes). Misinterpretations of well-known lyrics provide clear evidence of segmentation errors. Examples from both children and adults abound, including, "Gladly the

cross-eyed bear" (Gladly the cross I bear), "Our father Wishart in heaven" (Our Father, which art in heaven), and "One nation, underground, invisible" (One nation, under God, indivisible). In addition to demonstrating the problem of divergent ambiguity, these errors often reveal the action of top-down processes in children's active attempts to construct a coherent interpretation of what they hear. In the third example above, being underground and being invisible fit together well, giving the entire phrase a certain (unfortunately incorrect) coherence.

More generally, the notion of "context" as an ambiguous input's general surrounding is itself ambiguous. What counts as context for an ambiguous input can be adjacent inputs, or concepts, or points of view, or instructions, or knowledge of a language, or who else is present, or what one saw on the news, and so on indefinitely. Whether one "sees" a fossil or a stone depends on the prior knowledge and expertise one brings to the setting. What we "see" when faced with ambiguous inputs often depends on our mindset, on how our minds interpret a given surface input: we can "see" five individual animals or a cooperating group, an inclined plane or the affordance of something to slide on, a space between words or a fill-in-the-blank test item, a poor child or a dirty child, and so on.

The prevalence of divergent and convergent ambiguity points to an additional corollary: inputs which are incomplete can often still be constructed by the learner. What a child learns need not be fully grounded on what we as adults think are the relevant data "out there" in the world. Relevance is defined by the learner, not the teacher or the outside observer. For example, despite the seeming lack of "relevant" input, blind children learn that barriers interfere with visual perspective-taking in sighted individuals (Landau & Gleitman, 1985). Deaf children learn about complex aspects of the structure of American Sign Language (ASL) morphology which are not part of the input offered them by their signing parents (Johnson & Newport, 1991; Newport, 1990). Children create their own non-standard words that are nevertheless consistent with linguistic principles and rules (Clark, 1993; Marcus et al., 1992), as for example "mouses" (mice), "gursh" (ice cream, for one of our children), "furniture-animal" (statue), "undisappear" (to make appear again), "breaked" (broke), and "twenty-nine-ten" (thirty). Likewise, some children use idiosyncratic count lists that honor counting principles even though they differ from the conventional list of their language, for example, "1, 2, 3, 4, 5, 6, 7, H, I, J" (Gelman & Gallistel, 1978; Hartnett, 1991). A specific or complete set of inputs to be matched is not required for learning to proceed. Learners can construct inputs that on their own are ambiguous or incomplete.

Postulate 2: The Mind Is an Active Learner, Not a Passive Receptacle

From the beginning, learners actively apply their motoric, sensory, perceptual, conceptual, and social-emotional capacities to their environments, immature as such capacities may be. Even babies have a ubiquitous tendency to use their limited repertoire of responses to explore and seek information from their world, including sucking, head-turning, eye-tracking, kicking, touching, crawling, standing, looking over or around barriers, etc. (e.g., Gibson, 1988; Haith, this volume; Piaget, 1952). Five- to 12-month-old infants not only like to look at pictures, they are willing to suck a pacifier at a particular rate in order to bring them into focus (Kalnins & Bruner, 1973). One-month-old infants will suck or turn their heads in order to hear speech sounds (Eimas, 1974; Mehler & Christophe, 1995), and will move their eyes around to explore objects (Banks & Salapatek, 1983; Haith, 1980). Infants also engage in actions which can have causal effects: they repeat an action to make interesting things last or reappear (Piaget, 1952). They kick in order to move a mobile attached to their foot by a string (e.g., Watson, 1987; Rovee-Collier & Bhatt, 1993), and they both start and stop attending to their caregivers who respond in kind (Stern, 1977; Tronick, 1989).

Toddlers manually explore the edges of an undulating surface such as a waterbed, and then get down and crawl on it (Gibson, Riccio, Stoffregen, Rosenberg, & Taormina, 1987). They spontaneously touch objects within one category in sequence before doing the same for those in another category, even when the categories are abstract ones like animate and inanimate (see Mandler, this volume). They point to things in their environment and ask "What's that?" sometimes so relentlessly as to tax the patience of their caretakers! As preschoolers, they persist at balancing blocks while exploring their physical characteristics (Karmiloff-Smith & Inhelder, 1974/1975). They spontaneously count things, including steps, cracks in sidewalks, puzzle pieces, raisins, train cars, and cows in the fields they pass on a trip (Gelman & Gallistel, 1978). They ask causal questions such as "why" and "how" (Koslowski & Winsor, 1981). It is hard to overemphasize the significance of these child-initiated perceptual and cognitive engagements of their environments. The following is an especially articulate defense by Eleanor Gibson of the active perceiver

(Gibson, 1988, p. 5), although see above for our differences with her views on the necessity of interpretation:

> The old view of perception was that "input" from stimuli fell upon the retina, creating a meaningless image composed of unrelated elements. Static and momentary, this image had to be added to, interpreted in the light of past experiences, associated with other images, etc. Such a view of perception dies hard, but die it must. There is no shutter on the retina, no such thing as a static image. Furthermore, perceiving is active, a process of obtaining information about the world (J. J. Gibson, 1966). We don't simply see, we look.

Readers familiar with Piaget's writings can surely generate their own parallel passages to support the conclusion that neither child nor adult are passive receivers of conceptual inputs. We seek out and even create environments that nurture our active construction of knowledge (e.g., Piaget, 1971). As next illustrated, we also are very selective about what counts as relevant data for learning.

Postulate 3: Cognition and Learning Are Always Selective

The inbound flow of information-bearing signals from learners' sensory systems far exceeds their information processing capacities. We cannot perceive or learn about everything at once; by necessity, only a particular subset of the information with which we are continually bombarded can be perceived, learned, or thought about. Extensive research has been devoted to selectivity in vision, audition, attention, learning, and recall (e.g., Bregman, 1990; Broadbent, 1958; Garcia & Koelling, 1966; Trabasso & Bower, 1968; Treisman, 1982). We call attention here to just a few examples of this selectivity.

Selective Visual Attention

Neisser and his colleagues provide particularly compelling demonstrations of selective visual attention abilities in adults as well as 4-month-old infants (Bahrick, Walker, & Neisser, 1981; Neisser & Becklen, 1975). Subjects were shown two film events superimposed on each other, for example a handball game and a hand-clapping sequence. Care was taken to select movies that elicited comparable levels of attention when shown individually. Subjects were cued to attend to only one of the two events on the film: adults were told which one to attend to, and infants were played only one event's soundtrack (e.g., bouncing or clapping sounds).

Both studies demonstrated selective attention abilities. Adults readily followed instructions to monitor one of the superimposed events, and when asked to monitor both events at once, declared the task difficult or impossible. Selective attention in the infants was demonstrated by the method of habituation, which takes advantage of infants' preference for novelty. Having repeatedly seen the superimposed films while hearing only one of the two soundtracks, infants were tested by being shown the two movies silently and separated side-by-side. In this test situation, the infants looked reliably more at the movie that was silent during the initial phase, presumably because they had not been attending to it previously and it was therefore novel to them.

These selection effects were among the results used to support Neisser's (1966) view of perception in both infants and adults, in which schemata are formed and actively tuned based on initial uptakes of relevant, attended-to information. Information about irrelevant events is not noticed, for the simple reason that no schemata for processing such events are generated.

Selective Learning in Spatial Localization

Studies of how rats (Cheng, 1986) and toddlers (Hermer & Spelke, 1994; Spelke & Hermer, 1995) learn object locations in space add strength to the proposal that schemata and conceptual models are responsible for selective "screening-out" effects in learning. Both rats and toddlers use certain types of information to locate themselves in space, but not others. For example, Cheng made concerted efforts to encourage rats to use various types of landmark information when orienting themselves in space: odor, texture, and surface information presented at the same place as food. None of these three types of information were learned, despite their high salience to humans; rats preferred instead to use the overall shape of the experimental environment. This reliance on overall shape was demonstrated even in situations where shape was a particularly uninformative cue, for instance in a rectangular four-arm radial maze. In one such study, after learning a particular food location (e.g., a well-marked corner) and then being disoriented and placed at the center of the rectangular box, the animals chose randomly between the correct corner and the one 180° opposite. They did this despite the perfect association between the food and nearby background cues. Had they used these cues, they should have made few errors.

Spelke and Hermer (1995) report the same response pattern in studies with toddlers. Toddlers first watched as a toy was hidden in one corner of a rectangular room. They were then blindfolded and turned several times before being allowed to search for the hidden toy. As with Cheng's rats, seemingly salient landmark information (a blue cloth covering one end of the room) was ignored in favor of ambiguous geometric information about the overall shape of the environment (e.g., "it's in the corner"). "Obvious" pairings were not learned (or at least, not sufficiently to guide successful searching behavior). The children looked for the toys equally often at geometrically equivalent places (diagonally opposite corners of the rectangular room).

Selective Learning and Domain-Specific Cue Salience

Studies of the learning conditions under which young children do or do not use color information provide another major example of selectivity. We know that infants perceive colors categorically, that is, like adults they divide the continuous color spectrum into discrete categories such as red and blue (Bornstein, 1985). Further, there are ample opportunities for young children to encounter differently colored blocks, letters, toys, stacking cups, pieces of paper, stickers, and so on. Thus, it would seem that the conditions for acquiring color-relevant concepts and knowledge are met at an early age. Nevertheless, preschoolers have substantial difficulty learning the names for different colors, and they do not use salient color differences in many concept learning tasks (for reviews, see Bornstein, 1985; Landau & Gleitman, 1985; Macario, 1991). By contrast, at the same age, these children do learn quite a few number names (Shatz & Backscheider, 1991).

Hirschfeld's (1996) studies of how preschoolers assign individuals to different categories provide another example in which color is not a significant variable. Children did not base their classifications on skin color: again, the suggestion is that this inattention follows from the children's own ideas about what is relevant and irrelevant. Macario's (1991) studies of 2- to 5-year-olds' use of color are especially interesting in this regard. When children were presented with novel objects and thought they were learning about new foods, they used the color information provided with ease. When the same novel objects were thought to be exemplars of new toys, however, color was treated as irrelevant.

These demonstrations of the variable salience of color information share a common theme. The fact that a perceptual attribute is ubiquitously present in the environment does not guarantee its psychological relevance, nor its ready uptake for perceptual processing and concept learning. Relevance at the psychological level is very much a matter of structure, a point to which we will return below in Postulate 7. Selectivity in learning and cognition is a necessary byproduct of sensory overload. How do we define what is relevant, and choose the particular information subset we do? Selectivity can be accomplished either randomly or nonrandomly, and random selectivity is inconsistent with what we know about commonalities in learning paths and outcomes across individuals and cultures. The remaining alternative is nonrandom selectivity, and our preferred explanation emphasizes the role of enabling constraints in defining relevance within core domains.

Postulate 4: Animals, Infants, and Young Children Are Not Perception-Bound Learners

We draw attention to an important feature of our discussions of selective attention and structured inputs. Many of our examples show infants and very young children selectively attending to and using inputs that are more abstract than concrete (see also Postulate 7). We surely have not exhausted the list of such examples. For example, it is now known that young children appeal to invisible entities in explaining their belief that something is contaminated (Au, Sidle, & Rollins, 1993); they invoke internal or invisible causal forces to explain why objects move and stop (S. Gelman & Gottfried, 1996; Massey & Gelman, 1988; Williams & Gelman, 1995); they reason about internal body parts and their functions (Carey, 1985) or the contrast between the insides and outsides of unfamiliar animals (Gelman, 1990; Massey, 1989); and they can readily pretend that the same empty cup is first a full cup and then an empty cup (Leslie, 1994a). In this section we extend our review of conceptual abilities to encompass animal cognition. More and more students of animal behavior are demonstrating that animals have nonverbal conceptual abilities and are not limited to instinctual sensing, perceiving, and reacting. As a result of ethological and experimental research with animals over the past fifty years, we now have solid evidence that many animal species have evolved complex representational abilities related to solving particular adaptive problems (see reviews in Gallistel, 1990, 1995; Gallistel et al., 1991).

The demonstrated abilities of animals and infants to use abstract information and acquire abstract concepts are inconsistent with the long-standing view that they are preconceptual, "perception-bound," and limited to concrete reasoning or stimulus-response pairings. Gallistel (1990) provides a review of the findings showing that all kinds of animals orient themselves in space with reference to a cognitive map, that is, a representation of the relative positions of points, lines, and surfaces in their surroundings. He also reviews the extensive studies demonstrating the surprising abilities of rats and pigeons to represent numerosity and temporal intervals, as well as to perform common arithmetic operations upon these quantities such as computing sums and ratios. Below, we introduce two highlights from these remarkable findings: evidence for numerical abilities (see also Postulate 7 for a discussion of numerical abilities in infants), and evidence for cognitive-mapping abilities.

Since several chapters in this Volume provide extensive coverage of the young child's considerable reasoning and representational abilities (DeLoache, Miller, & Pierroutsakos, Ch. 16; Mandler, Ch. 6; Wellman & S. Gelman, Ch. 11, this Volume), we will not dwell on them further (see also Gelman & Baillargeon, 1983). Instead, we describe a compelling example of abstract reasoning and concept acquisition by infants: mechanical/biomechanical reasoning about inanimate and animate objects.

Numerical Abilities in Animals

Platt and Johnson (1971) provide an excellent demonstration of rats' numerical abilities. The animals in their experiment were required to press a lever a certain number of times ($N = 4$–24) to arm a feeder that operated silently. After the N presses on the lever, the rat could poke its head into a feeding alcove and obtain food. If the rat failed to press the lever the requisite number of times before poking his head into the alcove, the counter was reset to zero. The observed median number of presses corresponding to the required value of N, showing that rats can count up to at least 24 (nonverbally, of course). Platt and Johnson's study is but one of many examples of animals counting beyond very small numbers (e.g., Capaldi & Miller, 1988; Meck & Church, 1984), indeed for N as large as 50 (Rilling, 1967). These data, together with demonstrations of the chimpanzee's and parrot's abilities to use numerical symbols in arithmetically correct ways (Boysen & Bernston, 1989; Pepperberg, 1987), have encouraged the view that animals can and do have abstract cognitions, despite the fact that they do not possess a rich linguistic capacity.

Cognitive Maps in Animals: More on Spatial Abilities

In our discussion of selectivity under Postulate 3 above, we introduced evidence that rats can form cognitive maps of their environment. A compelling earlier demonstration of this ability comes from Morris (1981). Rats were dropped into a pool of opaque water, in which they had to swim until they found a barely submerged brick on which to perch. On subsequent trials, they were able to swim directly to the perch, whether or not it had a flag placed on it to identify its location. This kind of orientation would not be possible if the rat could not place the position of its goal within the framework of a cognitive map of the macroscopic shape of its environment.

An additional example of cognitive mapping abilities in the absence of immediate perceptual information comes from research with gobie fish (Aronson, 1951). These fish live in tide pools, and can become stranded by receding tides. In order to escape to the open sea, they accurately leap out of the water from pool to pool, despite being unable to see the destination of their jumps in advance. Through experimental manipulations with artificial tide pools, Aronson demonstrated that jumping accuracy depended on experience during a rising tide which allowed the fish to learn a cognitive map of the spatial arrangement of the pools.

Conceptual Abilities in Infants: "Baby Object Mechanics and Biomechanics"

Work on infants' knowledge of objects and how they move adds strength to the idea that concept learning can go from the abstract to the particular. Very young infants have been shown to respond in ways which are consistent with highly abstract principles about the nature of moveable physical objects, distinguishing between those that are animate and those that are inanimate (Mandler & Wellman, Ch. 6, this Volume; Sperber, Premack, & Premack, 1996). In general, these demonstrations have found that infants look longer at "impossible events" (in which objects appear to violate physical laws) than they do at "possible events." For example, 5-month-old infants respond in ways consistent with the beliefs that one solid object, a rotating screen, cannot pass through another solid object, a block hidden behind the screen (Baillargeon, Spelke, & Wasserman, 1985) and that an inanimate object cannot propel itself (Leslie, 1995).

Spelke (1991) provides similar evidence with 3- and 4-month-old infants, in a habituation study for which both the possible and impossible events were novel. To start each habituation trial, a ball was held above a screen and then dropped behind it, after which the screen was removed to reveal the ball resting on the surface of the table. This event sequence was repeated until infants habituated, that is until they looked less than half as long during a trial than they once did. During the posthabituation trials, the ball was again dropped, but this time the screen was removed after the drop to reveal the object resting either on top of or underneath a novel shelf that had been placed surreptitiously into the display. For the latter case, the ball ended up in a familiar position, on top of the table. But to get there, it would have had to pass through the shelf that sat between the dropping point and the table. Therefore, although both of the posthabituation events were novel, only the latter event (ball-on-table) was impossible. Once again, infants looked longer at the impossible event. In a control set of conditions, infants saw the same final displays in the posthabituation phase but the balls were not dropped. Therefore, neither outcome was impossible. Now infants preferred to look at the ball that was resting in a novel place, that is, on the shelf as opposed to the table. A series of follow-up studies by Baillargeon and colleagues have confirmed this finding, extended it to still younger infants (Needham & Baillargeon, 1993), and also investigated infants' understanding of physical phenomena including support, collision, and unveiling (Baillargeon, 1995; Baillargeon, Kotovsky, & Needham, 1995).

These findings are joined by a series of studies demonstrating infants' ability to distinguish between novel examples of mechanical and biomechanical motion (Bertenthal, 1993). Infants distinguish between objects and events which are animate or inanimate on the basis of differences in the conditions that cause movement. Spelke, Phillips, and Woodward (1995) provide especially compelling evidence here since they controlled for differences in size and surface characteristics between animates and inanimates. The authors contrasted infants' reactions to both animate and inanimate pairs of videotaped displays. Inanimate pairs of stimuli were two 5- and 6-foot-tall objects that had distinctive novel shapes and contrasting bright colors and patterns. The animate pairs were two people. With each pair of objects, infants watched two events: (a) the objects moved toward each other, touched each other, and then changed direction; and (b) the objects moved toward each other, stopped briefly before touching each other, and then changed direction. During test trials, infants looked reliably longer at the no-contact inanimate event; they showed no such preference in the animate event trials. This higher looking time is usually an indication of either surprise or a violated expectation: The authors' conclusion is that 7-month-olds know that a causal event between two inanimate objects requires contact, but the same is not true of two animate objects. In other words, animates are capable of action at a distance, but inanimates are not. This pattern of results is exactly what one should observe if the innards and external-agent causal principles proposed by Gelman (1990) aid infants in interpreting the motion paths of animate and inanimate objects.

Converging evidence that infants interpret the same motion path differently, depending on whether the moving object is animate in kind or not, can be found in Golinkoff and Harding (1980), Poulin-Dubois and Shultz (1989), and Premack and Premack (1995). This line of work is joined by studies showing an early ability to distinguish animate from inanimate objects and to distinguish the causal conditions for their differing kinds of motion and transformations. For instance, Mandler and McDonough (1996; this volume) have demonstrated that 7-month-old infants can categorize replicas of animals and nonanimals, as revealed by their reliable tendency to touch items within one abstract category before switching to explore those in another.

There are several reports of young children applying a "no action at a distance" principle of physical causality for inanimate objects but not animate ones (e.g., Bullock & Gelman, 1979; Bullock, Gelman, & Baillargeon, 1982; Koslowski, Spilton, & Snipper, 1981). When the 3- and 4-year-old children in the Bullock and Gelman studies were shown an event that had a gap between the cause and outcome (cf., Leslie & Keeble, 1987), they either inferred a mechanism ("When I wasn't looking, the ball slided over"), talked about magic, or made it clear that something was not quite right ("What? How did that happen? It's a trick, right?"). Similarly, we find that young children produce predominantly external causal attributions for the motion of familiar inanimate objects but not the motion of familiar animate objects (S. Gelman & Gottfried, 1996; Massey & Gelman, 1988; Williams & Gelman, 1995). For animate objects, children offered attributions that were related to the object class itself: these included the object's capacity for various self-propelling actions, its limbs, and some combination of blood, bones, and food. When this pattern is compared with their answers to questions about the insides of animates (Gelman, 1990), we are reminded of René Descartes' suggestion that animate action resembles the motions created by the hydraulic system controlling the statues in the Gardens of Versailles, and of Claude Bernard's description of people as nothing but a bag of bones filled with and surrounded by liquids and foods. Hence, we are much inclined to limit ourselves to an account of the early conceptual understanding of animates in terms of a theory of internal mechanistic action (Williams & Gelman, 1995), rather than an early theory of biology (cf., Au & Romo, 1996; Carey, 1995).

In sum, how can we account for young novices' selective and successful use of abstract data before they have induced the necessary abstractions in the first place? How do 5- to 7-month-old infants know to perceive simple collision events in terms of the causal roles played by the striking

object (agent) and the struck object (recipient), rather than solely in terms of the spatiotemporal relations between the objects (Leslie & Keeble, 1987; Leslie, 1995)? The existence of so many abstract cognitive abilities in infants, young children, and animals requires us to answer this fundamentally important question. One way to do this for the findings on number, causality, and the animate-inanimate distinction is to propose that domain-specific skeletal principles enable construction of a model of the world. If these model-building principles define the structure of a domain, and if the mind actively uses whatever structure it has as a basis of induction, then inputs that are related in complex ways to the inductions drawn from them will be favored.

Postulate 5: Learning Is Not a Single "Process" Since There Are Different Domain-Specific Kinds of Learning

We now know of an ever-increasing number of cases in which the rate of learning varies as a function of what is being learned and when. Some learning proceeds smoothly and at a relatively rapid pace. The course and conditions of such early learning in core domains can contrast strongly with the slow and uncertain learning in noncore domains of knowledge—even when we think a core and noncore domain are closely related. Studies of complex learnings in animals have been central in the development of domain-specific accounts of animal learning (e.g., Gould & Marler, 1987; Shettleworth, 1993) that were fueled by demonstrations of species-specific learnings about illness (Garcia & Koelling, 1966; Rozin, 1976) and danger signals (Bolles, 1970). These types of learning include bird song, categories of predators, the time of day at which events occur, the rates of event occurrence, and navigational information such as the solar ephemeris and the center of rotation of the night sky. Many of the abilities and behaviors exhibited by animals cannot be explained by traditional behaviorist or associationist learning models (Gallistel, 1990, 1995; Gallistel et al., 1991; Rozin & Schull, 1988).

Theoretical developments within evolutionary and animal learning theory have encouraged us and other students of conceptual development to adopt a key idea from evolutionary theory: learning is the product of behavioral mechanisms with elaborated internal structures that have evolved to guide domain- and species-relevant learning (see Carey & Gelman, 1991; Hirschfeld & Gelman, 1994). Additional examples of such learning in humans (see also above) include foods which are safe to eat (Siegal, 1995), the faces of others in a newborn infant's world (Johnson &

Morton, 1991), the syntax of language (Pinker, 1991), and probably implicit rules of conversation (Grice, 1975).

Within this theoretical frame of reference, concept learning is not a homogeneous or content-neutral process. Rather, it benefits from multiple mental structures that support attention to and learning about domain-relevant, structured data sets (Cosmides & Tooby, 1994a; Fodor, 1972, 1975; Gallistel, 1995; Gardner, 1992; S. Gelman, 1991, 1993; Hirschfeld & S. Gelman, 1994; Leslie, 1995; Medin, Goldstone, & Gentner, 1993). This view of learning differs in fundamental ways from theories grounded on general processes, for example, Skinner (1938, 1950), Hull (1952), Thorndike (1913), Watson (1913), Rumelhart and McClelland (1986), Simon (1972), and Siegler (1991). Information processes embodied in abstract domain-specific structures privilege attention to domain-relevant, structured data, an especially important idea which we develop at length below. This means a critical condition is met for learning; the learner's active structure-mapping tendencies (see below) can be put to work in the service of early concept development and learning, no matter what specific learning theory we embrace.

To say that knowledge acquisition in core domains benefits from innate skeletal structures is not to say that there is no need for learning. The knowledge in question will not appear full-blown immediately when the individual encounters an example of relevant data. We do not hold such a position, nor do most other theorists working within a domain-specific framework. Our goal is to achieve an account of learning that better handles the evidence. Ours is not a theory that falls within the empiricist class of theories about cognitive development and concept acquisition; nevertheless, it is a theory of learning. Variability is a fundamental fact about cognitive development.

Postulate 6: Epigenesis Leads to Variability and Requires Supporting Environments

With rare exception, any genetic developmental program carries with it extensive requirements for interactions with environments that can nurture, support, and channel the differentiation of adult structure. In the absence of those environments, the program will almost certainly fail. The same is surely true for skeletal mental structures; the existence of a primordial input-structuring mechanism does not guarantee that related knowledge will spring forth full blown the moment the individual encounters a single example of the requisite environment. Without opportunities to interact with, learn about, and construct domain-relevant inputs, as well as to practice components of relevant action plans, the contributions of skeletal structures will remain unrealized, or will lead to atypical developments. It follows that learners must encounter opportunities to interact with and assimilate relevant supporting environments (cf., Scarr, 1993). It also follows that variability is a characteristic of any learning, whether about core domains that benefit from skeletal structures or noncore domains that do not.

Marler's work on birdsong learning provides an especially compelling example of epigenetic variability from the animal literature. His work on the course of songbird learning in the male white-crowned sparrow provides us with an important case of animal learning in which skeletal structures guide learning but also lead to variability. These findings in combination with ones from several developmental laboratories illustrate the point of this postulate: be the learning in a core or noncore domain, variability is to be expected, and is entirely consistent with a theory that invokes *enabling* constraints on learning.

Songbird learning mechanisms are specific adaptations, designed to operate in environmentally specific contexts to ensure the uptake of adaptive information. Innately-determined representations guide selection of what is to be learned, and how that subset is both extracted from diverse input and selectively remembered in constructing a song. Of major interest here is the fact that song sparrows who grow up in different places end up singing different songs, namely, songs with the characteristics of the dialect they are exposed to plus individual signature elements. White-crowned sparrows, like many songbirds, have a sensitive period somewhere during the first year of their life. If they do not get to hear the song of an adult sparrow during this time, the song they sing will be decidedly odd when they grow up. The sensitive period has the effect of "tuning" the bird's template for a particular class of song. But exposure during an early period of life does not suffice to guarantee that the young bird will grow up to sing the represented song, or that his adult song will be normal. He has to go through periods of subsong learning and crystallization, again during the first year of life.

The subsong learning period is especially interesting for us, because only at this time does the young bird start to sing (after the sensitive period for exposure). The initial efforts look very much like trial-and-error, and in some ways are like a human infant's babbling; the song sounds not at all like the adult target model. The data gathered by Marler and colleagues compel the conclusion that the bird is working at converging on a particular output plan, one that generates a song that is consistent with the mentally represented song template. Without any more input than what the young bird creates himself at this point, the bird gradually moves toward singing a song that contains more and more notes and phrasal units of the adult song (Marler, 1991; Nelson & Marler, 1993). Yet because of the idiosyncratic nature of this learning process, no two adult songs are identical: there is variability in the outcome.

It is hard to resist comparing the young white-crowned sparrow's learning path with examples of children's learning. One case that seems especially pertinent comes from beginning language learners' efforts to master the count list of their language. The evidence is that children detect the relevant list of count words at a very young age (Gelman, 1990; Shatz & Backscheider, 1991; Wynn, 1992). Yet only much later will they reliably produce even the first ten words in the list and use this verbal knowledge without error (Fuson, 1988; Hartnett, 1991; Miller, Smith, Zhu, & Zhang, 1995; Wynn, 1992). Karmiloff-Smith and Inhelder's (1974–1975) microgenetic analyses of children's block-balancing show similar developmental patterns, from seeming trial-and-error-like efforts to systematic, rule-governed actions. We are cautious about labeling these early counting and block-balancing efforts as examples of trial and error, however, for even this variable performance is domain-relevant and far from random. Siegler and Crowley's (1994) experiments on how 5-year-olds achieve arithmetic solutions by converging on the use of a novel strategy, and how 10-year-olds learn to succeed at tic-tac-toe, are particularly relevant in this regard. They provide elegant demonstrations of the importance of paying special attention to learners' goals and abilities to attempt nonrandom solutions en route to a successful solution.

Like Siegler and colleagues (Siegler, 1991; Siegler & Crowley, 1991), Kuhn's (1995) review of a variety of microgenetic studies examining change processes in learning concludes that variability is a fact about learning, no matter what one's theory of learning might be. Systematic within- and across-condition variability in the extent to which performance conforms to abstract principles is consistent with traditional learning and developmental theories in which unprincipled "habits" are acquired prior to the induction of principles. But contrary to widespread assumption, such variability is equally consistent with and predicted by rationalist accounts of cognitive development. It therefore behooves us to consider potential sources of variability more carefully, and examine how different theories account for these. Variability could conceivably result from random noise in learning mechanisms, different learning solutions for the same underlying structure, different task demands, cultural differences in the interpretation of test settings, differences in the development of planning abilities, or a lack of achieved competence. We will return to the issue of variability below and the possibility that there may be different but systematic sources of variability that are due to conceptual learning goals, cultures, physical environments, settings, tasks, etc. (Cole, 1995; Donaldson, 1978; Gelman & Greeno, 1989; Gelman, 1993; Rogoff & Chavayah, 1995; Siegal, 1991).

Postulate 7: Environments and Minds Share Universal Structures, Not Universal Surface Characteristics

In our final postulate, we bring together elements from several of the foregoing postulates. In core domains, learners apply enabling structures in order to map structured information from the environment onto skeletal mental structures. We emphasize two aspects of the phrase "structured information from the environment." The first is that such information can be abstract rather than directly perceivable or concrete; nevertheless, the active mind is capable of selectively seeking out and learning the relevant abstract information. The second is that skeletal mental structures are attuned to information in the environment at the level of structural universals, not the level of surface characteristics. This means that enabling mental structures can be universal and yet still produce variability across individuals and cultures. We will develop these arguments by going into deeper empirical detail than in our discussion of the previous postulates. Our focus will be on research in a highly abstract area which we believe to be a core domain: numerical reasoning.

More and more we are gaining evidence that children all over the world acquire knowledge in core domains without explicit instruction, just as they do with their native language. This learning takes place automatically, given of course that they have access to the everyday cultural, social, and physical environments of their community (Carey & Gelman, 1991; Hirschfeld & S. Gelman, 1994; Hirschfeld, 1996; Keil, 1981; Mandler, this volume; Leslie, 1994b, 1995; Premack, 1990; Sperber, Premack, & Premack, 1996). In the core domain of numerical reasoning, all children develop a principled understanding of verbal counting and use it to add and subtract, whether or not they receive formal schooling (for reviews, see Gelman & Meck, 1992; Miller et al., 1995; Resnick, 1989; Sophian 1994). Children all over the world also quickly learn about the differences between animate and inanimate objects (Atran, 1994; Carey, 1995; Inagaki & Hatano, 1987; Jeyifous, 1986; Simons & Keil, 1995; Wellman & S. Gelman, Ch. 11, this Volume).

In both of these cases there are differences about the details learned, for instance in the particular count list and the particular kinds of animals and nonanimals. It could not be otherwise, given that different cultures use different languages and live in different parts of the world. These kinds of findings challenge any account of development that builds knowledge from bits of sensory inputs, but they fit well with an account that sees young learners as using abstract domain-specific structures. As long as the encountered exemplars are consistent with the structure that outlines the domain, they can serve as domain-relevant food for thought. Number-specific principles can identify and assimilate the examples of count lists in one's native language. Similarly, causal principles that distinguish between animates and inanimates can encourage attention to the kinds of information that will support learning about which particular moveable objects are self-moveable and which need an agent to move them (Gelman, Durgin, & Kaufman, 1995; Premack & Premack, 1995).

From this perspective we should and do find that young children are able to use information about objects other than simply their surface perceptual features (see Postulate 4). For example, Massey and Gelman (1988) found that 3- and 4-year-old children do not always use overall surface similarities when judging which of a series of novel items can move both up and down a hill. Moreover, when justifying their yes-no answers, they often either denied visible information when it conflicted with their conceptually-based classifications, or invented information that was not perceptually available. Two examples were the following: "it does not have feet" (for a statue whose "feet" were clearly visible), and "it uses the feet" (for an animal whose feet were not visible). Children ignored obvious but superficial similarities between a statue and the living thing whose form it reproduced, treating the statue more like the wheeled objects in the study than the animate objects. Simons and Keil (1995), S. Gelman and Gottfried (1996), and Kremer and S. Gelman (1991) all report a similar preference among young children for abstract as opposed to surface information when sorting or reasoning about novel examples of animate and inanimate objects.

The conclusion that early learners use structured data is reinforced by the generality of the demonstrations of infants' conceptual abilities. These results have been obtained across a wide range of samples, including infants from the culturally diverse and low-income areas of downtown New York City, Philadelphia, Washington, and London, as well as more homogeneous areas such as Champaign and Ithaca (in the United States), Geneva, and Japan (see chapters in this volume by Banks & Kellman, and Haith). An especially interesting set of studies are those on number.

Young Children's Alleged Numerical Incompetence

Not so long ago, most developmental psychologists and educators concurred that children's ability to achieve numerical concepts was relatively late to develop. Preverbal infants and nonverbal animals certainly lacked numerical abilities, given that they were restricted to processing data at a sensorimotor or perceptual level. Young children lacking concrete operational structures were therefore also limited to the perceptual level. For example, they failed in Piaget's (1952) conservation of number experiment because they could not help but focus on perceptual attributes as opposed to the shared one-to-one correspondence of the two arrays. Although the claim that "primitive" people and young children lack abstract numerical abilities is less prevalent than it once was (see Crump, 1990), the theme continues (see, e.g., Andrews, 1977; Bidell & Fischer, 1992; Hallpike, 1979; Hurford, 1987; Ifrah, 1985; McCleish, 1992, for a discussion of this theme within fields of education). The following excerpt is but one of many examples that could be cited:

> Even human beings, for whom the abstract activity of counting seems the most natural thing in the world, find it incredibly difficult to learn. One of the discoveries of the 20th-century scientists (made independently by Montessori, Piaget, and Vygotsky) was that adults forget how gradual and time-consuming the process of learning to think in the abstract is. (McCleish, 1992, p. 8)

Subitizing versus Counting: A Perception-Only Account of Number After All?

Several studies of infants' use of numerical information have revealed a set size limitation, in which infants reason accurately with displays of no more than 3 or 4 items. These results encourage many to continue to argue that infants use non-numerical representations rather than abstract numerical representations. The favored mechanism is called "perceptual subitizing," a process that is assumed to allow subjects to make discriminations between small set sizes without any implicit or explicit understanding of numerical principles (e.g., Cooper, 1984; Cooper, Campbell, & Blevins, 1983).

It is true that ultimate mastery of the count list can take a very long time (Hartnett, 1991; Miller et al., 1995), However, this alone is insufficient reason to reject the proposal that the learning process is guided by implicit counting and arithmetic reasoning principles. It is important to distinguish between the ease of finding a learning path at all and the final mastery of the knowledge on that path (see Postulate 6 for a discussion of factors contributing to variability in count list learning). Similarly, although it is true that infants' ability to discriminate numerosities appears limited to small set sizes, it is far from clear that a perception-only model can accommodate the data.

The problem for perception-only models is that infants can process numerical displays with an extremely diverse range of object and event types, enough so as to constitute an abstract category. Starkey, Spelke, and Gelman (1990) showed photographs of common household items to 6- to 8-month-old infants, including a comb, pipe, lemon, scissors, and corkscrew. These items varied in color, shape, size, and texture. Each photograph showed two or three different items, and the spatial arrangement of the items was unique from trial to trial. Thus, the only common characteristic of the 3-item and 2-item displays was their numerical value. To start, half the infants were habituated to 3-item displays, half to 2-item displays. Despite all the variations in the objects' surface characteristics, infants were able to attend to number (set size): recovery from habituation occurred when infants saw a display with the other set size (e.g., when seeing a 3-item display after having been habituated to a series of 2-item displays). Wynn (1995) has demonstrated that infants can attend to numerical information not only with concrete objects but with dynamic events. Events are particularly difficult to attend to within an associationist learning theory because they occur across time, rather than consisting of co-occurring sensations that can be associated. In Wynn's studies, infants were able to keep track of the number of times a puppet jumped up and down, for instance dishabituating to a two-jump event after having been habituated to a series of three-jump events. Finally, an especially interesting demonstration of infants' ability to notice abstract number information in the environment is presented by Canfield and Smith (1996). These authors report that 5-month-old infants' anticipatory eye-movements reflect an ability to keep track of the number of pictures presented in one location and use this running count to predict whether the next picture will be at that same location or another one.

Infants in these various studies could have focused on perceptual attributes of the items such as shape, motion, textural complexity, and so on, but they did not. To date, there is no known simple perceptual mechanism that can do this, that is, attend to number across an ever-increasing set size while ignoring item kind, color, size, shape, location, event type, degree of stimulus overlap, a wide range of visual angles, modality, the difference between simultaneous and sequential presentations, and so on. More and more it becomes difficult to continue to maintain that infants are restricted to some simple, low-level sensory or perceptual mechanism.

Because infants can process numerical information across sensory modalities (Starkey et al., 1990) and across time (Wynn, 1995), a mechanism that selectively attends to number must deal with the things being counted at a level far removed from their basic sensory or configurational properties. Two kinds of current explanations meet this requirement. One is that the infants use something akin to a set theoretic definition of "thing," where "thing" is a member of the class of all classes of objects and events. Numerical abilities are then attributed to the use of a one-to-one correspondence rule (see also Starkey & Cooper, 1995). The other is that infants use a less rarefied notion of "thing," the one embedded in the nonverbal counting principles of one-to-one, stable-ordering, and cardinality in the counting plus arithmetic reasoning model proposed by Gelman and Gallistel (1978) and Gallistel and Gelman (1992). If counts are governed by an implicit understanding of the how-to-count principles, then it follows that counting will be indifferent to item type (Gelman & Greeno, 1989). All that matters is that the collection of items in a to-be-counted set are perceptually or conceptually separable from one another. From this point of view, a "thing" is as basic a concept as one can specify (Gallistel & Gelman, 1990), reflecting the differentiation of figure/event from background, which is widely recognized to be one of the most fundamental operations in perception and cognition (Kellman & Banks, Ch. 3, this Volume; Spelke, 1990). In this account, infants need not even notice the color or kind of things they encounter when they are engaged in numerical processing (Xu & Carey, 1996). The numerical abilities follow from application of a structure that relates the counting principles to the effects of addition and subtraction.

One further line of argument is in order before leaving the issue of subitizing versus counting. Conclusions that infants use a perception-only "subitizing" mechanism are based in large part on a methodological decision to score infants' numerical discriminations as correct (exact) or not, rather than looking at the variance in errors that are produced for larger set sizes. This method is unable to determine whether errors are due to an inability to use a preverbal counting process, or instead to increases in inherent variability. Thus, the claim that infants cannot deal at all with larger numbers is problematic. To distinguish between these alternatives, it will be necessary to find ways to obtain infants' estimates of variability as a function of set size. This has not yet been done, but corresponding studies have already been done with animals that reveal an ability to use set sizes much greater than 3 or 4 (see Postulate 4 for more on animals' numerical abilities). Since the infant data that do exist in other areas of numerical reasoning map well onto the animal data, Gallistel and Gelman (1992) have proposed that infants use a mechanism like the Meck and Church (1984) animal counting model.

In the Platt and Johnson (1971) studies of rat counting described above, the greater the particular numerosity to be represented, the more likely it was that the animals confused it with adjacent or nearby values of N. The fact that the variance of the distribution for each N increases with N in all of the animal counting experiments has implications for how studies with infants are interpreted. We attribute this increase in variance to two systematic sources (Gelman, 1993). The first is generated by the counting process itself; increasing set sizes involve greater information processing demands and therefore an increasing chance of errors (Gelman & Gallistel, 1978; Gelman & Tucker, 1975). The second source is the scalar variability in the mental magnitudes with which animal and human brains represent scalar variables like number and the duration of temporal intervals (Gallistel, 1992; Gibbon, Church, & Meck, 1984). The coefficient of variation in these quantity-symbolizing magnitudes is constant, that is, the standard deviation of the accuracy with which a mental magnitude may be read increases in proportion to the magnitude. This coefficient of variation may be greater in young children than in adults. Thus, the variability in the representation of a given numerosity increases with increasing numerosity, both because longer counts have more counting errors and because the mental magnitudes by which numerosities are represented have intrinsic scalar variability. This increase in the variability or uncertainty means that something like Weber's law applies to the discrimination of remembered numerosities: for a fixed difference between two numerosities, the bigger they are, the proportionally more difficult they are to discriminate.

In sum, infants' errors at set sizes where $N \leq 3$ may not implicate subitizing or a lack of numerical reasoning ability, but instead may indicate the presence of one common preverbal counting mechanism similar to the one used by animals. Indeed, Balakrishnan and Ashby's (1992) analyses of a huge number of trials generated by adult subjects over a two-week period show that there is good reason to assume that the same holds for adults. These authors conclude that there is but one underlying process controlling adult judgments of set sizes that are both smaller and greater than three or four.

Numerical Reasoning Beyond Counting

A key to the question of whether infants possess nonverbal numerical principles is whether they can reason about number with set sizes, even if no greater than three or four (Gelman, 1972). More and more it appears that infants are capable of reasoning about the effects of the arithmetic operations of addition and subtraction. For example, Wynn's (1992) 5-month-old infants responded appropriately when they saw addition and subtraction. The infants first had repeated experience with two objects; then a screen covered the objects and the infants watched as an object was added to or removed from the hidden display. The screen was then removed, revealing one or two items; in each case, infants looked longer at the numerically incorrect display. Data like these implicate a process that relates the effect of adding or removing items to a numerical representation of the initial display (Wynn, 1992, 1995).

Evidence of infants' ability to use the numerical ordering relations ($<$, $>$) strengthens the conclusion that they can reason numerically (for more on this point, see Gelman & Gallistel, 1978, Chapter 11). Although we know of no such data for infants as young as Wynn's, they do exist for older infants. Cooper (1984) showed that 12-month-olds can learn to compare successive visual displays on the basis of whether they have an equal or unequal number of items. Sophian and Adams (1987) took advantage of 14-month-old infants' preference for the larger of two sets. To start, they showed infants two displays with the same number of items in each. Then the displays were both screened and infants watched as an item was either added to, or subtracted from, one of the displays. When allowed to reach out, they had a reliable preference for the screen hiding the effect of subtraction, demonstrating their ability to relate the equivalent of an arithmetic operation to ordering.

Proposals about innate, universal skeletal domains of knowledge need not, and cannot, rest on our ability to show that infants are extremely competent in these domains. The human ability to walk upright is largely dependent on innate contributions, but nobody expects 3- or 4-month-old infants to walk. Alternative accounts of the "baby arithmetic" results (e.g., Simon & Klahr, 1995) are better countered by a cumulative body of converging evidence generated with many different methods. We do not rest our case on the infant results described here.

The Effects of Novelty on Numerical Reasoning

Just such a converging body of evidence is provided by comparisons between how normal and retarded children generate novel solutions to counting problems, together with evidence of cross-cultural structural commonalities in numerical reasoning. The successful ability to invent novel counting strategies implicates at least implicit conceptual understanding of the counting principles, just as the ability to generate novel sentences or make up words implicates implicit understanding of relevant language rules. On the assumption that existing structures encourage children to find successful solutions, indirect hints should suffice to encourage movement toward the generation of a correct solution. But if children lack the requisite conceptual structure, even explicit hints should do little to improve performance (Campione, Brown, Ferrara, & Bryant, 1984).

Gelman and Cohen's (1988) study of normal and Down Syndrome children's solutions to a novel counting problem illustrates this point. It is well known that retarded persons can have problems with numerical tasks, this being especially so for Down Syndrome individuals (Edgerton, 1967; Thurlow & Turner, 1977). The retarded children's school where Gelman and Cohen's study was conducted took this into account, and incorporated counting opportunities into almost all activities of the school day. Frequency of exposure therefore favored this sample of children over the normal preschool sample in the study. Indeed, nothing in our own observations of preschoolers in a variety of settings suggests that the exposure of normal preschoolers to explicit instruction in counting is as intense and pervasive as it is in the curriculum at the retarded children's school. Still, significant differences favoring the preschoolers were found in the two groups' abilities to count (Gelman, 1982). These differences are consistent with the view that some retarded children do not count with understanding because they lack the core skeletal structure that normal children have. Eight of the Down Syndrome students in the Gelman and Cohen study were poor counters; two were excellent

counters. These differences were perfectly related to the students' ability to invent successful counting solution for Gelman and Gallistel's (1978) novel "doesn't matter" counting task.

Children start the "doesn't matter" counting task by counting a row of heterogeneous items. This done, an experimenter uses a puppet to ask the child to do a counting trick, which is to count all the items but in a way that involves tagging the second item as "the one," or "the three," or "the four," and so on. *Skip-around* and *correspondence-create* are two kinds of solutions children come up with to solve the problem. For example, given a 5-item display, one child pointed to the second item in the row while saying "one," then backed up to point to the first item and say "two," and then skipped over the second item to say "three" while pointing to the third item, and so forth. Another child switched the positions of the first and second item and then simply counted from one end of the row to the other as usual.

The preschool children were more likely to find an acceptable solution as soon as they were given a target problem than were the group of school-aged retarded children who were of comparable mental age but had been scored as poor counters. The preschoolers also benefited extensively from indirect hints, whereas the retarded children failed to benefit at all from either indirect or direct hints. Even when the retarded children were shown an example of a successful trial, they did not transfer on a subsequent trial. Finally, the two groups of children produced different error patterns. The preschool children sometimes rearranged words in the count list instead of objects in the display, for example, "one, three, two, four, five." Although they violated the stable-ordering principle, they at least met the task constraint and ended their count with the correct cardinal value of the display. Down Syndrome children altered their count lists in a different way. When asked, for example, to make the second item "three," they started with that item and said "three" and then continued on in the count list until they tagged all items ("three, four, five, six, seven, eight"). This violated the cardinal principle, an error that is taken by many as evidence for a lack of understanding of the counting principles (e.g., Fuson, 1988).

In short, the various analyses of the different solution efforts of the retarded children who could not count converge on one conclusion. Even though these children received a great deal of counting input, they did not assimilate it with understanding. All indications are that they lacked the implicit counting principles and related arithmetic structures under discussion. In contrast, the data from the preschool children buttress the hypothesis that they have the implicit principles that outline the relevant domain, even though the relevant inputs they receive are less frequent and picked up on the fly (Gelman, Massey, & McManus, 1991).

Young children's ability to deal with novel number conditions come to the fore again when they are given addition and subtraction problems. In these tasks, they sometimes invent solutions which use counting (e.g., Groen & Resnick, 1977; Siegler & Robinson, 1982; Sophian, 1994; Starkey & Gelman, 1982). This is illustrated in the following protocol from an experiment where children encountered the unexpected effects of the experimenter surreptitiously removing two items from a display of five items (Gelman & Gallistel, 1978, p. 172). It also is an example of the kind of evidence that led Gelman and Gallistel to conclude that young children know that addition increases numerosity and subtraction decreases it, but that they do not know the inverse rule, that is, that the addition of X can be canceled by the subtraction of exactly X.

Child: Must have disappeared.

Experimenter: What?

Child: The other mouses?

. . .

Experimenter: How many now?

Child: One, two, three.

Experimenter: How many at the beginning of the game?

Child: There was one there, one there, one there, one there, one there.

Experimenter: How many?

Child: Five—this one is three now but before it was five.

Experimenter: What would you need to fix the game?

Child: I'm not really sure because my brother is real big and he could tell.

Experimenter: What do you think he would need?

Child: Well I don't know . . . Some things have to come back.

Experimenter: [Hands the child some objects including four mice.]

Child: [Puts all four mice on the plate.] There. Now there's one, two, three, four, five, six, seven! No . . . I'll take these [points to two] off and we'll see how many.

Child: [Removes one and counts.] One, two, three, four, five, no—one, two, three, four. Uh . . . there were five, right?

Experimenter: Right.

Child: I'll take out this one here [on the table] and then we'll see how many there is now.

Child: [Takes one off and counts.] One, two, three, four, five. Five! Five.

Structural Universality and Cross-Cultural Surface Variability

The structure of such invented solutions is common across tasks (Starkey & Gelman, 1982) and in people from all over the world, be they in schooled environments or not. Although different cultures use different lists and although older individuals might work with numbers in their head and use larger values, the underlying structure of the reasoning is the same. Different count lists all honor the same counting principles (Gelman & Gallistel, 1978) and different numbers are made by adding, subtracting, composing, and decomposing natural numbers that are thought of in terms of counting sets. The mathematical operations involved are always addition and subtraction, even if the task is stated as a multiplication or division one. In the latter case, people use repeated addition and subtraction to achieve an answer. Those who have learned to count by multiples of one, for example, by fives, tens, fifties, hundreds, are at an advantage since they can count and add faster than if they had to count by one (Nunes, Schliemann, & Carraher, 1993; Resnick, 1989; Vergnaud, 1983). This commonality of structure across tasks and settings is an important additional line of evidence for the idea that counting principles and some simple arithmetic principles are universal. So, too, are the cross-cultural studies of "street" arithmetic.

Further evidence for the worldwide use of counting and the arithmetic principles of addition and subtraction comes from studies of "Street Arithmetic." Reed and Lave (1977) found that Liberian tailors who had not been to school solved arithmetic problems by laying out a set of familiar objects (e.g., buttons, pebbles), or drawing lines on paper, and then counting them. Nunes, Schliemann, and Carraher (1993) found that 9- to 15-year-old street vendors were able to indicate what a number of coconuts would cost by performing a chain of additions on known numbers. For example, a 9-year-old said "Forty, eighty, one twenty" when asked the cost for 3 coconuts at a price of 40 cruzeiros each. When another child was asked to determine how much a customer would have to pay for 15 of an item costing 50 cruzeiros each, he answered, "Fifty, one hundred, one fifty, two hundred, two fifty. (Pause). Two fifty, five hundred, five fifty, six hundred, six fifty, seven hundred, seven fifty" (p. 43).

Variations in performance levels and time to learn the count list are systematically related to schooling, the transparency of a given language's system for generating count words above ten, the degree to which numbers are used in the everyday activities of a culture, and what functions the count list serves (e.g., Gelman & Gallistel, 1978; Miller, 1996; Zaslavsky, 1973; Saxe, 1979). In the past, some conclusions about non-Western inabilities to count have been due to investigators not knowing to avoid cultural taboos against counting certain classes of things. Others probably followed from their failure to recognize the arithmetization of count-2 systems and/or a failure to recognize that some cultures use hand configurations and body positions as the tagging entries in their count list (Zaslavsky, 1973). It is true that some languages only have two or three count words. It does not follow, however, that the people who use these languages cannot count in a principled way. The Bushmen of South Africa are a case in point. They indeed have but two separate count words. However, this does not keep them from counting at least to 10. They manage the latter by using the operation of addition to generate terms that represent successive larger cardinal values. For example the word for eight translates as "two+two+two+two." This is the very same addition solution that plays so significant a role in "street mathematics." Thus, despite notable differences in the particular verbal counting solutions that different cultures endorse, at the structural level there appears to be a critical overlap.

The Oksapmin of New Guinea use a count list that has 29 unique entries. It starts with the right thumb, which corresponds to "1," the right index finger to "2," and so on (Saxe, 1979). Tagging continues to the right, up through points on the right arm and shoulder, around the outside of the head, down the left shoulder and arm, and ending with the left thumb which corresponds to "29." Should these count lists be rejected as not being "real" count lists because they are "concrete?" No; Saxe (1981) reported that the Oksapmin use their lists in a principled way. Participants in his study were told a story in which people in a far away village count starting on the left side of their bodies instead of the right side. They were then told that men from both villages counted sweet potatoes, ending their counts at

the same body part (e.g., left shoulder). Finally, they were asked who had counted more potatoes. If participants had said that both men counted the same number, we could conclude that they were not using body parts as arbitrary symbols in an ordered list. However, since the participants did answer appropriately, depending on which villager's system was used, we can conclude that they were able to use both counting and reasoning principles.

When the focus is on the abstract level of structure, multiple lines of evidence fit together to support the conclusion that skeletal principles of counting and arithmetic reasoning form a core domain. Similar conclusions are reached by others in their studies of biological classifications (Atran, 1994; Simons & Keil, 1995; Wellman & S. Gelman, Ch. 16, this Volume) and the animate-inanimate distinction (Gelman et al., 1995; Premack & Premack, 1995). This makes it possible for cognitive universals to live alongside culturally-specific interpretations (Boyer, 1995; Gelman & Brenneman, 1994; Sperber, 1994).

The seven postulates described in this section form an interconnected theoretical and empirical framework which any theory of learning and constraints must accommodate. It rests firmly on converging lines of evidence, and does not rely on any one particular study or interpretation. In the next section, we will review different theories of learning and attempt to measure them against this framework.

DIFFERING THEORETICAL PERSPECTIVES ON CONSTRAINTS AND LEARNING

Different theoretical approaches to cognitive development embody different views about the way constraints function in the service of knowledge acquisition and problem solving. Those based on empiricist assumptions about concept acquisition are grounded on the idea that to start, we are limited to processing bits of sensations. This constraint on the nature of first inputs means that inductions about abstract or relational concepts can follow only as a function of the build-up of associative strength. For domain-specific theorists, on the other hand, the principles that organize a domain draw attention to abstract or relationally structured inputs from the outset. Both domain-specific and stage theories share this learning-enabling point of view, whether or not they posit innate skeletal mental structure. These two kinds of theories differ however in that the latter typically focus on broad-based structures of mind. Information processing theorists draw attention to the existence of limits on our real-time cognitive processes (Shatz, 1978, 1983; Simon, 1972). This, too, is a view of constraints that places limits on the learner. But in contrast with the associationist view, here the limits are about considerations of what learners can do in a given amount of time, not about the learning mechanism itself.

It is not always easy to uniquely identify particular authors as Associationist, Information Processing, Stage, or Domain-Specific theorists. Some assumptions about the role of constraints can be shared across different theories of cognitive development, and some theories contain multiple assumptions about constraints (for a related discussion, see Keil, 1990). The same points apply to domain-general stage theories, as well as approaches including Situated Learning, Cultural Psychology, and Evolutionary Psychology. Many theorists combine two or more approaches. For example, researchers including Case (1992), Halford (1993), and Kuhn, Garcia-Mila, Zohar, and Anderson (1995) combine key Piagetian and information processing notions. Resnick (1994) works with a combination of information processing, situated learning, and domain-specific notions. Parisi (1996) has explicitly set out to develop connectionist models that are consistent with evolutionary and Piagetian approaches. Domain-specific accounts of early cognitive development often do consider maturational constraints (e.g., Johnson & Morton, 1991). Nevertheless, their emphasis is on considerations pertaining to a domain as opposed to general structures of mind or limits on a general processor.

The different usages of the notion of constraint are often joined with qualitatively different usages of other shared terms, especially *learning*. This is because qualitatively different ideas about learning mechanisms are embedded in the foundational principles of the theory. We expand on this point before continuing with a discussion of how different classes of theories deploy the concept of constraint.

About Terms and Their Role in Scientific Theories

Scientific and technical terms are defined separately from nontechnical words in dictionaries, and for good reason: they derive their meaning from the theories within which they are embedded. Technical definitions for terms are often inconsistent with their everyday usage. For example, *multiply* always means *to increase* in everyday use. This is not true in mathematics wherein two fractions multiplied by each other render a smaller number. In the same way, there can be different intended meanings when different scientific theories of learning use the same word. We already have seen that the notion of *constraint* changes in significant ways

as a function of the theoretical context in which it is embedded. So, too, do its semantic brethren *boundary, innate, biological,* and *instinct.* The everyday meanings of such terms are commonly paraphrased as *restricted, required, not voluntary, not spontaneous, hemmed in,* and *forced.* They are pitted against words like *acquired, learned, educated, experienced,* and so on.

This why we expect some readers to be puzzled by our use of the term "learning" in the context of discussions of innate contributions, since for many, "that is not what learning is really about." The long-standing tendency to paraphrase *innate* as *not-learned* persists in much of psychology. It fits well with the nontechnical definition of *innate* in the *American Heritage Dictionary:* "Of or produced by the mind rather than learned through experience." The same dictionary includes amongst its definitions of *constraint* and *constrain,* "The state of being restricted or confined within prescribed bounds," and "To compel by physical, moral, or circumstantial force; oblige." The broad intuitive appeal of these definitions is as it should be, capturing the terms' everyday meaning-in-use.

It is noteworthy that Hinde and Stevenson-Hinde (1973, p. 470) considered as "unfortunate" the choice of the term "constraint" for the title of the conference that led to their book *Constraints on Learning.* They worried that researchers rooted in the traditions of associationism and learning theory would move to talk about "too-powerful general laws [of association] hedged by constraints," as opposed to "some quite new formulation [that] would seem more profitable." Unfortunately, in many cases, their worry proved prophetic. The alternative they had in mind was a theory of learning founded on the assumption of different domain-specific learning mechanisms, one where the very notion of learning was qualitatively different than one based on associationist assumptions.

It is well to recall that there are many examples in the history of science (e.g., Kitcher, 1982; Kuhn, 1970; Lakatos, 1970) where the meanings of terms differ as a function of the theory about the phenomena to which they refer. Indeed, differences in the intended meaning of terms can be a clue that there either is an ongoing theory change among scientists about the domain in question, or a situation in which qualitatively different scientific theories coexist. Such co-existence characterizes the current state of affairs with respect to the nature of concept learning and development in animals and man (Gelman, 1993; Gallistel, 1995). The same can be said of fields including linguistics (e.g., Chomsky, 1972; Pinker, 1991), comparative cognition and ethology (e.g., Gould & Marler, 1987), and cognitive science (Gold,

1967; Osherson, Stob, & Weinstein, 1986). Given that current assumptions about the "laws of learning" and related mechanisms can vary in fundamental ways, we should be on the lookout for differences in the intended meanings of phrases like *learning theory,* as well as differences in assumptions about the different theoretical premises they entail. A key case in point is how different kinds of learning theorists view the role of innate knowledge.

Anti-nativists who reject the idea that there is anything like innate knowledge typically use what is now an outmoded biological version of the notion, namely some form of genetic determinism. This usage is exacerbated by discussion in the popular and sometimes even scientific press of genes "for" particular traits. In this view, innate contributions are always in a mature steady-state, waiting to generate perfect and therefore nonvariable performance at all times. This perspective is readily recognizable in writings that reject the idea that there are constraints on cognitive and language development. To illustrate, Nelson (1988) wrote, "A true constraint would be manifested in all or none type responses; . . . . If the constraint is universal (cognitive or linguistic), all children should follow the pattern. . . . If they are innate, they should apply from the beginning of the language learning process" (pp. 227–228).

Ideas like these about the way our biology makes complex contributions to our cognitive development do not take into account the explosion of work and theory in developmental biology, ethology, animal cognition, behavioral genetics, and evolutionary psychology. Such efforts have led a number of researchers across these and other fields to use the terms *innate* and *learned* in ways that are complementary. Gould and Marler (1987; Marler, 1991) write about the "instinct to learn." Fodor (1983) writes about domain-specific learning modules. Gallistel et al. (1991, p. 30) writes about domain-specific learning engines whose computational processes are suited to the many specific problems the animal confronts:

> Within each functionally defined domain of animal endeavor, there can be dramatic differences in the need for flexibility, and thus in the need for learning. There must always be a strong learning component in any mobile organism's ability to develop a representation of the spatial location of objects in the world, as it is extremely implausible that such information is prewired. But in other domains, such as the identification of food or the recognition of conspecifics, species differ as to how much demand on learning their solution to the problem requires. These differences are reflected in the existence and the complexity of specific learning mechanisms.

In each of these latter lines of research, the idea is to work on a kind of learning theory that differs from those in the empiricist tradition. Within this framework, the notion of constraint shifts from one about limits on domain-general learning processes, to one about the enabling effects of domain-specific learning systems and their particular structures. This difference in theoretical perspective has important consequences for how one interprets common terms in the two classes of theories. Some terms can have notably different meanings, just as do the common terms used by children, college students, and physics experts to talk and reason about the nature of heat, light, and electrical current (Gentner & Stevens, 1983; Slotta, Chi, & Joram, 1995; Wiser, 1987). Put differently, the current theoretical environment for discussions about cognitive development and the mechanisms of change is itself dealing with something akin to a theory change. Readers would do well to keep this in mind, especially when the discourse is about learning and constraints.

Constraints in Associationist Theories

Associationist theories of animal learning and human concept formation remain popular (e.g., for treatments of modern versions, see Gluck & Bower, 1988; Kehoe, 1988; McClelland & Rumelhart, 1986; Pearce, 1994; Schwartz & Reisberg, 1991). Modern associationist theories carry forward the key assumptions of Empiricism, including the one that acquisition of knowledge about the world and how to respond to it is derived from the capacity to form associations about sensory data in a lawful way. Initially, the British Empiricists formulated two laws of association: (a) the law of frequency (the more exposures there are to a particular association, the stronger the association); and (b) the law of contiguity (the closer together that the occurrence of an association's components are in time and space, the more likely it is that an association will be formed). Modern versions of the theory add several laws to these original ones. These include: (c) the law of similarity (the more similar the stimuli, responses, and/or existing associations are to each other, the greater the chance that an association will be formed); (d) the law of effect (reinforced pairings and behaviors are more likely to be learned than nonreinforced ones); and (e) the law of contingency (to be learned, the components of an association must be contingently related and not simply contiguous in time and/or space: the first component must predict the second in some sense).

The original theory of association emphasized the principle of equipotentiality: all effective sensory inputs and all observable responses were treated as equally potential contributors to the associative process. In other words, learning was thought to be a singular, content-independent process. Learning about language, causality, space, time, biology, physics, fishing, number, and other people's minds should therefore be traceable to the same fundamental laws of association that explain a rat's learning to avoid poisonous food, or a pigeon's ability to learn the temporal parameters of a reinforcement schedule. Nothing in classical association theory limits the nature of stimuli or responses that can be associated with each other. Similarly, it provides no principled reason to expect learning to vary as a function of development.

It is probably considerations like these that lead some to think that traditional "learning theory" makes no assumptions about constraints on the learner; that the mind is a completely flexible learning machine. However, association theory does embed one key constraint on the infant learner: young infants are constrained to process and form associations between bits of sensations, or between sensations and reflexes. If their sensory systems are not yet functioning, or their capacity to form associations is weak, then little or no learning can occur. It follows that blind individuals should not be able to learn about the visual world.

These constraints on inputs and associative processing are consistent with classical empiricist dogma: the assumption of an initially blank mind (tabula rasa), and the related idea that "there is nothing in the mind that was not first in the senses" (Locke, 1690). However, their implications are strikingly inconsistent with the postulates and supporting evidence reviewed above. Some alternative is needed to encompass the reviewed facts, including ones which show that the mind is actively engaged in its own knowledge acquisition; that some data for learning are supplied by the learners themselves and not from sensory input; that even infants can prefer structured inputs to unstructured bits of sensory experiences; and that cognitive development is nonrandomly selective from the start.

There are different kinds of theoretical responses to these findings of conceptually-driven selectivity, domain-specificity, and non-equipotentiality in early learning. One involves efforts to accommodate such results within the general process theory of association (Schwartz & Reisberg, 1991, Ch. 1). Within modern associationist accounts, constraints act to limit a too-general or too-powerful learning process. A parallel notion of constraint is used in Connectionist theories that assume an associative theory of mind (for a discussion, see Davis & Pérusse, 1988). Most

connectionist accounts limit the construction of knowledge to the build-up of nonsymbolic association networks of knowledge (Bates & Elman, 1993; Elman, 1990; McClelland & Rumelhart, 1986). Here, constraints are added to the model to take into account real-time limits, the nature of human perceptual systems, and so on. However, there are also symbolic connectionist models of learning and cognitive development that build in structural constraints (Parisi, 1996).

The class of accounts of cognitive development which we favor treat the mind as a structure-using and structure-creating device (see below and Karmiloff-Smith, 1992). But even here there are fundamental differences between theorists, especially with regard to the nature and origin of mental structures, and how the notion of learning is construed. Some accounts remain within the associationist tradition, attributing the acquisition of mental structures to the build-up of associative networks (for examples, see T. Simon & Klahr, 1995). Other accounts forge a new path outside the associationist tradition, attributing the acquisition of mental structures to domain-specific information processes that possess specialized functions.

Constraints and Mental Structure I: Information Processing Theories

Among theorists who emphasize the role of mental structures, there are various proposals about how mental structures function as constraints on learning. One class of proposals is information processing theories of cognitive development. Although some information processing theorists include domain-specific knowledge structures in their hypotheses about the architecture of cognition (e.g., McShane, 1991; Mandler, Ch. 6, this Volume), most do not. Still, as McShane points out, there is a shared frame of reference for information processing theorists, this being that the mental architecture is divided into processing components like attention, short-term memory, working memory, and long-term memory. Research topics, not to mention textbook chapter headings, are organized around the idea that there are real-time processing constraints on these cognitive components (Anderson, 1995; Cosmides & Tooby, 1994b).

Information processing accounts of development focus on some limiting effects of an immature brain on the capacities to sense, act, remember, and plan (e.g., Anderson, 1995; Kail & Bisanz, 1992; Newport, 1990; Siegler, 1983, 1991; Simon, 1972). There are straightforward reasons for the existence of constraints on what infants can process: their sensory system, motoric abilities, and brain functions are all immature. Compared to other primate species, human infants appear to be born early, with brains that continue to develop for months at a rate comparable to that before birth. The cortex in particular develops substantially during the first year of life, particularly in differentiation, myelination, and connectivity (Rabinowicz, 1979).

The upshot of this ongoing development is that immature brain mechanisms may mistakenly give us the impression that infants lack conceptual knowledge. For example, infants 4 months of age and younger are guaranteed to fail any task that requires them to accurately perceive the details of an object across the room. Since their visual system is too immature to process such information (Held, 1993; Johnson & Gilmore, 1996; Kellman, 1996), it is hardly fair to conclude that they lack the conceptual ability required for the task. Likewise, when the stimulus conditions of a task unwittingly elicit a reflexive response that interferes with an infant's overall plan of action, it is inappropriate to reach conclusions about competence (Diamond, 1991). If there are developmental functions on processing capacities, then there will be changes in children's ability to deal with the real-time demands of understanding and performance.

Information processing theorists often pair assumptions of constraints on real-time processing and the knowledge base with hypotheses about how the mind attempts to circumvent these limits. In this vein, development is characterized as involving the increasing release from processing limits, either as a function of maturation, an increasing knowledge base, and/or improved abilities to use organizational strategies (Siegler, 1991; Simon 1981). Information processing approaches to the role of constraints have generated a wealth of interesting research programs, including ones about developments in attentional capacity or strategies (Simon, 1972; Kemler, 1983), processing space (Case, 1992; Halford & Wilson, 1980), expertise (Chi, 1992), processing speed (Kail & Bisanz, 1992), and strategies for circumventing information processing limits (Bjorklund, this volume; Brown, Bransford, Ferrara, & Campione, 1983; Ornstein & Naus, 1978).

Newport (1990) and her colleagues take a very different tack when they argue that maturational constraints facilitate early learning about the structure of language. They have been working on the intriguing idea that limits young children's information processing capacities actually assist their language learning rather than hindering it. These limits lead children to miss much of the linguistic data in their

environment, and instead to attend to bits and pieces of it. Since such language-relevant data can be characterized as features (for example, the markers "-ed" and "-s" indicating past tense or plurals), the resulting focus on bits and pieces is well suited to the task of inducing the morphemic and syntactic structure of the input language. From this perspective, one might even expect young learners to do better at learning the structure of a language than older ones.

Newport and her colleagues have provided support for this hypothesis (e.g., Johnson & Newport, 1991; Newport, 1990; Newport & Supalla, 1990). They were able to conduct a natural experiment about the effect of starting to learn American Sign Language (ASL) as either a Native learner (born to deaf parents and exposed to ASL from birth), an Early learner (a 4- to 6-year-old whose first encounter with ASL occurred when they started a school for the deaf), or a Late learner (not exposed to ASL until at least the age of 12 and eventually attending a school for the deaf, meeting ASL-speaking deaf friends or a spouse). All participants in the Newport project had at least 30 years of daily exposure to ASL, and all did well on word-order and syntactic phrase parsing tests. Nevertheless, differences favoring the Native learners emerged, having to do with knowledge and ability of how to use the component structure of the morphology and syntax. For example, Late learners had a far larger number of "frozen" signs in their vocabulary, signs that they could not decompose into morphological units. Early learners shared these vocabulary items but could also use them in nonfrozen ways, making up novel words with their components.

Siegler and his collaborators (e.g., Siegler & Crowley, 1994), working within the information-processing frame of reference, have developed an important version of the constraint-as-enabler view, encompassing the conditions that a general purpose central action-assembler has to take into account in order to generate a successful plan of action. Their focus is on the development of competent plans of action, for example, for solving novel arithmetic and tic-tac-toe problems. Siegler and Crowley (1994) propose that 5- and 10-year-olds generate a *goal sketch* that functions to help them generate potentially goal-relevant candidate strategies. Children's ability to judge which of several strategies would be better for a given problem is but one line of evidence presented in support of the proposal. As Siegler and Crowley point out, to accomplish these tasks successfully, it is necessary to select goal-relevant strategies and have some way to evaluate whether they work.

Closely related arguments are found in Gallistel (1985) and Gelman and Greeno (1989), even though both are domain-specific theorists. Gallistel's emphasis is on the way domain-specific goals potentiate and depotentiate relevant action components to assemble functionally coherent behavioral sequences. Gelman and Greeno's effort is focused on how numerical *conceptual competence* in conjunction with *interpretative competence* relates to the ability to generate competent plans of action for a given task and setting.

All of these lines of research highlight the fact that the ability to create a competent plan of action requires much more than a general problem-solving facility: it requires a solution to what has been called the "frame problem." For instance, Newell, Simon, and Shaw's (1958) General Problem Solver model does not on its own have the capacity to assemble task-relevant and content-relevant solutions. As such, it could go on forever making up solutions that have nothing to do with a non-assigned problem. Siegler and Crowley's goal sketch helps solve the frame problem by virtue of its ability to search existing knowledge bases that might be relevant to the task at hand, and also to use the search results to put together a plausible strategy (at least some of the time). The result is a planning process that benefits from enabling constraints.

Constraints and Mental Structure II: Stage Theories of Cognitive Development

Within stage theories, structures of mind are typically described with reference to single structures or formats that are domain-general and content-independent. For example, the Piagetian stage of Concrete Operations encompasses the ability to identify, learn, and reason about well-classified data, various kinds of orderings, and number. Domain-specific theories instead postulate multiple structures with domain-specific organizing principles, for instance about number, animate natural kinds, and so forth. The learner's ability or inability to find relevant inputs is due to the availability or non-availability of mental structures that can be mapped to domain-relevant data.

Piaget's Concrete Operations are well-known for their role as mental structures that enable the ability to organize data into hierarchical classification schemes and reach inductions about the inclusion relationships between superordinate and subordinate levels of a given classification (Piaget & Inhelder, 1956). Within the theory, preoperational children have yet to achieve operational structures

and therefore are constrained to make classifications on the basis of surface, perceptual similarities. This leads them to solutions that count as failures on a wide range of classification tasks. For example, they respond to class-inclusion questions on the basis of the perceptual data given. When shown a display of ten roses and two tulips, and asked, "Which is more, the flowers or the roses," they chose the roses, as if they interpreted the question as, "Which has more, the bunch of roses or the bunch of tulips?" (Piaget & Inhelder, 1956).

There are many challenges to Piaget's theory and findings about classification. Some of these are taken up below in our discussion of the nature of concepts. At the moment however, we focus on a key feature of stage theories. Stages are structures of mind that not only limit but also enable cognition and learning. For example, sensorimotor schemes constrain infants to learn about sensory and motoric representations, pre-operational thought constrains children to learn about the perceptual aspects of their world, and so on. But stages also have a facilitating function, especially when they achieve the status of a logical structure. For Piaget, concrete operations underlie several abilities: to think about sets of objects in terms of the dimensions that characterize them, to find the intersecting values of two dimensions, and to reach inferences about members of a class-inclusion hierarchy. Similarly, logical structures enable the use and understanding of classifications, seriations, and numerical concepts (Inhelder & Piaget, 1956; Piaget, 1971). When children have developed Concrete Operations, they can use them to organize a seemingly disparate set of objects into systematic subclasses.

Constraints and Mental Structure III: Domain-Specific Theories of Concept Learning

A shared assumption across stage- and domain-specific theories of mind is that mental structures find, interpret, and assimilate data whose structure they overlap with. For this reason, domain-specific knowledge structures, even when they are skeletal, can enable learning by helping individuals find inputs that have the potential to nurture further learning about a domain. Because domain-specific structures lead learners to select one class of inputs over others, one might say they also have a limiting role. But in this case, the limiting role is due to their ability to select from the vast flow of possible data those inputs that are relevant for learning about a domain. It is not that learners cannot learn about other things, but rather that different mental structures support different kinds of learning. In all cases, the mental structures actively seek out data that are structurally consistent with the principles that organize them. The result is that learners are more likely to encounter domain-relevant learning paths and the consequent benefits that we discuss below.

Among domain-specific theorists, some assume that there are innate skeletal learning systems for core domains. Domain-specific theorists also differ on whether infants' core domains are already content-rich enough to be called theories. Whereas Spelke (Carey & Spelke, 1994) is willing to grant infants an implicit theory of physical objects, we prefer to limit the attribution to the different skeletal principles organizing the causes of movement and change of animate and inanimate objects (Gelman et al., 1995). Although we prefer the view that core domains start as different sets of skeletal principles, there are others who refer to such domains as being organized by core theories (e.g., Carey & Spelke, 1994; Gopnik & Wellman, 1994; Wellman & S. Gelman, Ch. 11, this Volume). To the extent that theories are organized by a set of domain-specific principles, they certainly meet our definition of a domain (Gelman, 1993; and below).

The open question is how much infants already know about the content of a domain and therefore whether it is best to assume their knowledge is skeletal in form. In either case, the move to postulate core domains paired with an assumption of domain-specific learning systems was much influenced by students of animal learning who work within an evolutionary perspective. These lines of influence are illustrated below in our development of the idea that constraints often serve as enablers of learning, that the mind will use existing knowledge structures to actively learn more about a particular conceptual domain.

Our preference for a domain-specific structural theory of concept learning is reinforced by the need to deal with the well-known empirical and theoretical difficulties with stage theories of classification abilities (Gelman & Baillargeon, 1983). Since stage theories of classification are grounded in the classical theory of concepts, these difficulties are shared with the classical (Empiricist) account of concepts. This account assumes concepts are built up from a primitive set of features available to the mind. Like other cognitive developmentalists and cognitive scientists, we believe that the difficulties faced by the classical theory warrant adopting the position that the meaning of a concept is embedded within the structure of the domain to which it belongs. This is one of the main reasons for our view that

enabling constraints privilege some learning over others and are structural and conceptual in kind. Examples of conceptual constraints include Markman's (1989) mutual-exclusivity constraint on the labels for items in a common classification structure (for considerations pro and con of word-learning constraints, see Markman, Ch. 8, this Volume; Keil's [1989] M-constraint on the members of ontological categories; or Gelman & Gallistel's [1978] constraint on double-counting embedded in the one-to-one counting principle).

Summary

To recapitulate our review of differing perspectives on constraints, the term *constraint* does not stand alone. As shown in Table 12.1, its meaning varies as a function of the theory in which it functions, as well as each theory's foundational assumptions about mental architecture and knowledge acquisition mechanisms. Given a domain-specific epigenetic theory of concept acquisition, enabling constraints serve the learner in significant ways. However, this claim is not tied to the assumption that a particular domain of knowledge is a core domain which develops from innate skeletal principles. In the remainder of the chapter, we further develop the idea of enabling constraints. It is not the presence of domain-relevant conceptual constraints that stands in the way of learning and problem solving; rather it is their absence. Readers should notice the overlap between this conclusion and the one above about Siegler and Crowley's (1994) concept of a goal sketch. The account of cognitive development that we will articulate in the remainder of the chapter introduces the idea that mental learning tools are recruited along with domain-specific knowledge as facilitators of learning and problem solving.

ENABLING CONSTRAINTS, EPIGENESIS, AND DOMAIN SPECIFICITY IN LEARNING

A successful theory of concept acquisition and cognitive development must address and accommodate all of the following issues: (a) the sources of both initial and subsequent knowledge structures; (b) the ways those structures foster learning; (c) the characterization of relevant inputs for both early and subsequent learning; (d) the characterization of the sources of those structured inputs, including the physical and sociocultural environment; (e) the nature of the individual's active participation in the elaboration of

TABLE 12.1   Summary of the Relationship between Theories of Concept Acquisition and Their Notions of Constraint

Framework	Kinds of Constraints	Examples/Implications
I. Traditional Associationism	1. Learning is governed by the laws of association: frequency and spatial/temporal contiguity.	• Only stimuli that fall within the associative window (closely paired in time and space) can be associated.
	2. Nothing is in the mind that is not first in the senses. (John Locke)	• Blind children should not be able to learn the meaning of "see," because they have no experience of seeing.
	3. Concepts are built from sensory primitives.	• Young infants do not have concepts.
II. Biological Boundaries on Associationism	1. Same implications as above, except the parameters of the associative mechanism may differ from domain to domain. Some knowledge is *implicit* in these parameter settings.	• Taste is more readily associated with illness than is visual appearance. • Taste-illness associations can develop even when illness occurs hours after the taste. • *Implicit* knowledge in the above two parameter settings: the fact that poisons act by virtue of their chemical composition (which is better indicated by taste than vision), and that poisons may act slowly.
III. Connectionism* (Nonsymbolic)	1. Much the same as traditional Associationism, plus the Delta Rule (the Rescorla-Wagner law).	• Acquisition of the past tense "rule" is due to amount of training, not a language-specific domain.
IV. Information Processing	1. Domain-general information processing mechanisms make it possible to extract structure from input.	• Chunking makes it possible to organize information into learnable chunks.
	2. Real-time constraints on domain-general information processing mechanisms limit what can be learned.	• Short term memory limits what can be learned without considerable effort, e.g., complex syntactic constructions, or long non-rule-governed count lists.
	3. In some cases, these limits may simplify the learning task.	• Newport's (1990) "less is more" account of language acquisition.
	4. However, nothing in these general-purpose mechanisms endows the learned representation with any explicit structure that was not in the sensory input to begin with.	• Rules and principles must be induced, e.g., the counting principles.
V. Stage Theories	1. The structure of one's stage limits what can be attended to and learned in that stage.	• A child can assimilate only those inputs that fit their level of mental structure.
	2. The assimilation of experience can, however, lead to a metamorphosis, a change to a new structure that enables successful solutions to a broad set of problems.	• The cumulative impact of inputs that don't fit causes accommodation of the child's mental structure. Format change during Concrete Operations supports ability to form abstract concepts.
VI. Domain Specific Learning Mechanisms	1. Skeletal learning mechanisms enable active attention to and processing of domain-relevant data. Different core domains benefit from different learning mechanisms.	• Mechanisms for song learning make it possible for birds to learn their species' song but do not contribute to the learning of counting, a map of the environment, or other domains. • Language learning mechanisms make language learning possible. • First principles of counting and arithmetic support acquisition of natural number concepts.
	2. Some of what is *explicitly* represented may derive from the domain-specific information processing mechanism.	• Space (spatial relations) is explicitly represented as three-dimensional even though all visual input is two-dimensional and all auditory input lacks a spatial dimension entirely.
	3. Existing structures may interfere with learning of expert knowledge if they do not map to the structure of the expert knowledge.	• Newtonian mechanics, calculus, chess, etc., are noncore domains and require learning new principles. Mastery is hard, requiring time and considerable practice.

TABLE 12.1   *(Continued)*

Framework	Kinds of Constraints	Examples/Implications
VII. Ecological Constraints	1. The acquisition mechanism itself is not specified, because the environment has such a rich structure that it dictates the structure of what will be learned.	• Affordances of the kind addressed in the Gibsons' theory (e.g., J. Gibson, 1983), such as learning about the difference between icy and smooth surfaces.
VIII. Situated Cognition	1. Version of VII in which it is argued that what is learned is specific to the situation or context in which it is learned; hence, there is no cross-situational transfer.	• Street Math does not transfer to School Math.

*The last few years have witnessed rapid changes in the nature of Connectionist models, including examples of domain-specific structural models (e.g., Marcus, 1995), or even a combination of associationism and structuralism.

their knowledge structures; (f) the mechanisms of change which relate initial learning to later learning; (g) the variability in performance levels during learning, across tasks and cultures; and (h) the existence of cross-cultural universals of cognition. A tall order, to be sure.

Most children in nondeprived learning environments acquire core knowledge bases and a conceptual worldview which is shared with the rest of their community if not beyond. They do this despite facing a great deal of ambiguity during their formative early learning years. We do not deny that this commonality of outcome surely must be nurtured by relevant commonalities in learning environments. Again, however, environments alone are insufficient. How do novice learners of any age find these relevant commonalities, given that environments are variously ambiguous and undetermined? How do learners know what is relevant, given that there is an unending flow of possible inputs? How does the mind select what subset of the world to attend to, interpret, and learn about?

In the foregoing sections, we have begun to lay out our reasons for favoring a rationalist-constructivist theory of learning and cognitive development. We believe such a theory to have the best hope for answering these questions, and also for meeting the desiderata listed above. Our view emphasizes the role that domain-specific constraints play in enabling early learning and cognitive development within core domains. The mind starts out with certain core skeletal domains of knowledge that include the ability to actively engage with and benefit from potential relevant environments. Enabling constraints guide learning by allowing the mind to actively and selectively seek out domain-relevant information, and by privileging particular interpretations of that often ambiguous information. They capture universal structural principles about core domains, yet they also lead to variability in learning outcomes due to

epigenetic interaction with particular local environments. Many of these structural principles are abstract, encoding notions such as number, causality, force, and mental states which are not directly perceivable by the senses.

Knowledge growth in core domains comes about as a function of an epigenetic, reciprocal interaction between multiple sources of structured information. Key players in the epigenesis of knowledge include the following: (a) existing domain-specific knowledge structures, be they skeletal or not; (b) the surrounding and internal physical and biological environments; (c) the social and cultural milieus; and (d) the domain-relevant data that the mind itself generates and sets up as it acquires a knowledge base.

We turn now to expand on our view of enabling constraints and epigenesis, and we begin by discussing an evolutionary perspective on learning. This perspective provides a line of converging theory and evidence that meshes well with our view and with the postulates described at the beginning of the chapter. In addition, it fits poorly with traditional associationist views of learning. We then attempt a more detailed development of what enabling constraints are and how they function, followed by a discussion of difficulties faced by the alternative views of constraints reviewed in the previous section. Because of our commitment to learning as an epigenetic mind-environment interaction, we turn next to a characterization of the structured environments in which learning takes place. Last, we address the important issue of conceptual learning in noncore domains. We introduce the idea of mental learning tools, including structure mapping and frequency computing, as mechanisms which operate both in core and noncore domains. They, too, "enable" learning, but in a different way from enabling constraints: they provide bridges between early and late learning, and between domain specificity and domain generality.

Constraints as Learning Enablers:
An Evolutionary Perspective

The brain is no less a product of natural selection than the rest of our body's structures and functions. The mind, like all other biological organs, puts its structures to work to accomplish their functions once prerequisite sensory, motoric, and brain maturation levels are reached. Some of these mental structures serve regulatory purposes, such as temperature maintenance, while others involve learning. The function of this latter type of structure is to find, assimilate, and use relevant structured information in order to learn about particular domains and solve domain-related problems. Complex adaptive functional organization is the hallmark of natural selection (Dawkins, 1995), and is a feature of mental processes such as learning just as it is of nonmental processes such as respiration. Complex structures evolve to fulfill a function, to enable the implementation of an adaptive process. Hearts evolved to pump blood, livers evolved to extract toxins, and some mental structures evolved to enable the learning of certain types of information that are necessary for adaptive behavior.

As was the case with sociobiology in the 1970s, current efforts to frame psychology within evolutionary theory (sometimes referred to as "evolutionary psychology") have been criticized for "just-so" storytelling. Debate over the merits of the "adaptationist program" has pointed out the difficulties of identifying adaptations (e.g., Daly & Wilson, 1995; Gould, 1991; Gould & Lewontin, 1979; Mayr, 1983; Piattelli-Palmarini, 1989; Symons, 1990, 1992). These difficulties particularly beset the search for mental adaptations, whose functional structure cannot be directly perceived under the microscope. In addition, evolutionary psychology as a "grand theory" (e.g., Tooby & Cosmides, 1992) must beware of overreaching its applicability throughout the cognitive sciences, and also of underemphasizing converging theoretical and empirical contributions from sources which do not draw on evolutionary theory. Premack (1996) summarizes many of these cautions in his review of the research programs described in Barkow, Cosmides, and Tooby's (1992) book *The adapted mind*. Notwithstanding these potential pitfalls, the adaptive-evolutionary approach provides important insights into the role of constraints in enabling learning (see also Rozin, 1976; Rozin & Schull, 1988). These insights converge with formal theoretical work on learnability (e.g., Chomsky, 1965), as well as empirical findings from learning and cognition in young children, infants, and animals (see Postulates 4 and 7 above).

From an evolutionary perspective, learning cannot be a process of arbitrary and completely flexible knowledge acquisition. In core domains, learning processes are the means to functionally defined ends: acquiring and storing the particular sorts of relevant information which are necessary for solving particular problems. An important class of these problems involves making predictions. These predictions can be about matters such as the future actions of friends and foes; the prospects of other people as mates, allies, or prey; or the likelihood of finding food at a particular location. Predictive strength is much more important than simple associative strength: compared to a vast number of arbitrary correlations, there are relatively few predictive/causal links in the world. As described above, behavior theory has moved in this direction, emphasizing contingency over simple contiguity, partly in response to empirical evidence of selectivity in associations (e.g., Garcia & Koelling, 1966).

The associationist proposal that all types of information are equally learnable (equipotentiality) is inconsistent with the evolutionary view of learning as a set of complex functional solutions to individual adaptive problems (Rozin & Schull, 1988). The mind does not learn all different sorts of information with equal facility, because different sorts of problem solving require different sorts of information about the world to be learned (Gallistel, 1990). More significantly, we should no longer think of information as entirely "out there in the environment," isolated from the information-processing problem(s) whose solution requires that it be learned. There are many types of adaptive information-processing problems: object perception, object classification, navigation, and mate selection to name but a few. Accordingly, there are many different types of learning. Core domains encompass those adaptive problem-solving behaviors which are universal, in which learning proceeds rapidly and without formal instruction.

Enabling constraints embodied in mental structures that support core domains solve the two deep obstacles to learning discussed above: convergent/divergent ambiguity, and the need for guided (nonrandom) selectivity. They selectively guide the learner's attention to relevant inputs, and they selectively guide the learner's interpretations of those inputs toward accurate and adaptively useful ends. These twin functions enable the learner to travel a successful learning path. We wish to emphasize here our use of "a" successful learning path rather than "the" successful learning path: enabling constraints do not inflexibly require an exact set of inputs to be matched, and neither do they force all learners to learn exactly the same thing.

The evolutionary history of our species has made us good learners in certain problem-relevant areas and poor learners in other areas. Other species of animals may be good or poor learners in a different set of areas, owing to differences in their problem-solving needs (Gallistel, 1990). Human specialties include visual pattern recognition, navigation, and language, while humans are completely outclassed by the location memory of certain nut-hiding birds (Vander Wall, 1982) and the taste-learning abilities of the white rat (Rozin & Kalat, 1971). The fields of cognitive psychology and artificial intelligence have traditionally focused on the flexibility and generality of human learning abilities, usually in the "higher learning" sense that (for instance) a college student can choose to study any academic field. Yet this apparent flexibility should not obscure underlying species-specific conceptual learning mechanisms which are specifically tuned to certain types of information.

All adaptations, both mental and non-mental, have an informational component: they embody information about the environment in which they evolved. Information is at the heart of the well-accepted biological concept of adaptedness in an ecological niche:

> As Young (1957), Lorenz (1966), and others have emphasized, we recognize adaptedness as an informational match between organism and environment. An animal that is well adapted to its environment can be regarded as embodying information about its environment, in the way that a key embodies information about the lock that it is built to undo. A camouflaged animal has been said to carry a picture of its environment on its back. (Dawkins, 1982, p. 173)

If core domain structures of mind were not related to data structures in the world, infants would be at risk for missing evolutionarily important inputs (the selectivity problem) or making up representations of non-existent worlds (the ambiguity problem). In core domains, structural regularities which carve the physical learning environment into different domains have been internalized into the cognitive architecture of the mind (cf., Shepard, 1994). This allows children to focus on domain-relevant aspects of data, and to recognize the often abstract relationships between entities in a domain.

Having evolved to function successfully in a certain environment, like a key, adaptations may or may not perform as successfully in a different environment. Sperber's discussion of relevance (Sperber, 1994; Wilson & Sperber, 1986) is especially helpful here. He distinguishes between the "proper" and "actual" domains of a cognitive module. Learning mechanisms evolved to serve specific functions: to attend to and store particular sorts of information. The proper domain of a learning mechanism consists of the information that it is functionally designed to learn, that it is in some sense "expecting." The actual domain is whatever structured information in the modern world and in a particular cultural setting is able to engage the learning mechanism; a new lock for an old key. This distinction between old solutions and new problems undercuts a common misconceived criticism of the application of evolutionary theory to psychology. It is often claimed that evolutionary theory expects all modern behavior to be adaptive or even "optimal" since it has survived the process of natural selection. Of the many reasons why this is not so, the most striking is that modern environments can differ dramatically from the environments in which human beings evolved as hunter-gatherers. Adaptations well-suited to the "environment of evolutionary adaptedness," be they mental or non-mental, sometimes fit less well in modern environments. For example, our lungs perform their function poorly in the oxygen-poor environments found at extreme altitudes or in polluted cities.

Returning to enabling constraints as information-processing adaptations, maladaptive learning and performance can occur when there are mismatches between the expected and actual information coming from the environment. Cognitive mechanisms may produce incorrect solutions when provided with inputs whose structure is unexpected. For example, shape detectors in the human visual system appear to "assume" an overhead direction of illumination, and can be fooled in indoor settings where artificial lighting comes from below (Ramachandran, 1988). In general, learning in a noncore domain can be either facilitated or hindered by the degree to which it is consistent or inconsistent with a core learning mechanism that has evolved to selectively "expect" particular types of structured information (Slotta & Chi, 1996). Relatedly, mental structures which evolved to serve one function may take on additional functions when presented with modern inputs whose structure overlaps with that of the inputs they are expecting; Piattelli-Palmarini (1989) and Gould (1991) describe these modern functions as "exaptations." We take up these issues of transfer in more detail below.

What Enabling Constraints Are and Are Not

Constraints in Core Domains: Defining Relevance and Structuring Early Representations

Stage theories and the classical theory of concepts both run into the same problem: neither has an a priori rule of salience (see Postulate 3 above). What leads us to think that color is usually a relevant feature of a tomato but not a car? The oft-favored rule of salience, that surface features are most relevant to our concepts about objects, turns out to fail under a variety of conditions. If 3- and 4-year-old children are asked to name red foods to take on a picnic, they will include watermelon alongside tomato, ketchup, and plums, even though the outside of a watermelon is green (Macario, 1991). Although color has some predictive value for our ability to identify foods, color does not have good predictive value for identifying cars (save perhaps for some subordinate-level cars with special functions). Similarly, if adults or 3- and 4-year-old children are asked to select or group pictures of items that can go up and down a hill by themselves, their choices do not appear to follow simple similarity. They pick out an echidna, a tarantula, a child, a sloth, and even a lobster, but they do not select statues or dolls—even though these share human parts such as faces, legs, and arms (Massey, 1989).

The difference in the predictive value of color for identifying instances of the categories of cars versus foods has led some to adopt a theory of concepts that assigns different weights to the same perceptual features for different concepts. We could say that the weight for color approaches 0 given the concept of car, and approaches 1 given the concept of food. But this approach will not do either. As soon as we start to assign different weights to the exact same attributes as a function of concept type, we slip in a circular decision rule that embeds in it an understanding of the very thing that is to be understood. In other words, the weighting method assumes that we use our different concepts to decide what weights to assign to the seemingly "same" features. If so, then they cannot be independent, content-free, decomposable intensional features as required by classical learning theory. We therefore are back to square one with regard to the question of what leads us to decide that a perceptual attribute is more or less important, or more or less similar to ones already learned about.

To restate the problem, we cannot avoid a basic question when asking how children learn a concept (or anyone does for that matter): how should we define relevance or salience? Some argue that the problem is solved for us by others, because we attend to what others bring to our atten-

tion (Tomasello, 1992). There is no question that if we did not use such information, matters would be even worse (Leslie, 1995). Nevertheless, how do different individuals converge on a common interpretation of what to both look at? Quine's (1960) "gavagai" problem still remains: each individual could be attending to any of a very large number of aspects of that part of the world within view. For example, an adult might be looking at the fur of a cat while a child is looking at its moving tail. What makes it more likely that a novice will attend to what another person has in mind? How do blind children develop visual concepts as they do (Landau & Gleitman, 1985), including the idea that sighted people cannot see through barriers?

Given the facts of selective attention and ambiguity (Postulates 1 and 3), we can assume that initial choices of inputs and interpretation are made either randomly or in a principled manner. For us, the existence of shared, early, on-the-fly, universal learnings argue against the random selection alternative. So, too, does the fact that infants and animals actively attend to domain-relevant structured inputs, rather than focusing on bits of light, sound, pressure, smells, and so on.

These observations fit with the evolutionary perspective discussed above, that treats core domain learning mechanisms as functional information-processing adaptations that evolved to use particular classes of data to solve particular problems. The determination of what is perceptually relevant is a function of the learner's current domain-specific goals. If she is concerned about classifying different birds, then she is more likely to attend to color. If she wants to figure out how to move a given object, she had better attend to its size and weight. But if the aim is to count the number of objects in a room, she can ignore attributes such as size, weight, and color. This is why we conclude that domain-specific knowledge structures help us determine what kinds of inputs are relevant to their use. Whether perceptual data are relevant or not depends on the conceptual goal we set.

If we grant infants skeletal domain-specific structures of mind, we can develop an account of which concepts might and might not be universally shared. These structures encourage learners to move onto learning paths that will lead them to the kinds of domain-relevant structured environments that can nurture the build up of shared knowledge structures. Assuming that the learning path is strewn with cases of potential inputs that share the structure of the core domain—be these inputs offered by knowledgeable members of the community, developed by the child, or part of the artifact environment—progress is highly likely given the learner's inclinations to use existing mental structures when interacting with the environment. We emphasize that there must be such domain-relevant learning paths: otherwise, domain-specific, innate contributors to knowledge acquisition will remain skeletal or even wither. On the one hand, were there no skeletons to dictate the shape and contents of the bodies of pertinent knowledge, then the acquired representations would not cohere. On the other hand, were there no supporting environments for learning to interact with, influence, and be influenced by, then epigenesis could not take place.

More on the Notions of Domain and Principle[1]

We define a domain of knowledge in much the same way that formalists do, by appealing to the notion of a set of interrelated principles. A domain's principles and the rules of their application serve to identify the entities belonging to that domain, and exclude those entities which do not. Since different structures are defined by different sets of principles, we can say that a body of knowledge constitutes a domain of knowledge to the extent that we can show that a set of interrelated principles organize the entities and related knowledge as well as the rules of operation on these. Principles "carve the psychological world at its joints," producing distinctions which guide our differential reasoning about entities in one domain versus another. In this way, domain-specific structures encourage attention to inputs that have a privileged status because they have the potential to nurture learning about a domain; they help learners find inputs that are relevant for knowledge acquisition and problem solving within the domain.

General processes like discrimination, or general processing mechanisms like short-term memory, do not constitute domains. Nor does a script structure constitute a domain. Scripts are analogous to the heuristic prescriptions for solving mathematical problems, which should not be confused with the mathematical domains themselves (algebra, calculus, theory of functions, and so on). Still, information processing limits on short-term memory can influence whether a given domain-specific problem is solved correctly or not. For example, although there is nothing in Gelman and Gallistel's (1978) counting principles that requires children to place items in a row and count from one end to the other, efforts to honor the one-to-one principle favor this kind of a solution. In order to count without error, they should not double-count or leave any items out. If they

---

[1] This section was based on Gelman 1991, 1993.

generate an orderly plan of action, we can say that they have a well-formed plan for solving the task.

There is nothing about our definition of a domain that limits domains to those that have an innate basis, or that requires all principle-based, domain-specific knowledge be built on an innate foundation. For instance, dog show judges' knowledge of various species of dogs constitutes a noncore domain of knowledge, rather than an innate core domain (Carey, 1996). In this regard, our insistence on the distinction between core and non-core domains helps deal with a key worry about domain-specific accounts of the mind. As Leslie (1994b) put it: "The trouble with the notion of domain specificity is that there could turn out to be too many domains" (p. 120). We concur with the suggestion that the number of innate domains is likely to be limited to ones that are universally shared, and not dependent on access to formal schooling (a very recent invention). There are few Leonardo DaVincis who acquire a remarkable number of noncore domains of knowledge, but there are some. More typically, different people acquire expertise in different noncore domains as a function of their interests and their commitment to the extended learning effort required for achieving principled understanding.

Only core domains benefit from what we call skeletal knowledge structures. Leslie's (1994b, 1995) idea of "core cognitive architecture" refers to "those human information-processing systems that form the *basis* for cognitive development *rather than its outcome*" (emphasis added). If children are able to interact within the bounds of the everyday environments of their communities, they will acquire knowledge about core domains early on, and with relative ease. Not only do the principles of a domain help children find relevant inputs, they also collect and keep together assimilated pieces of relevant information. In a sense, they are like memory files for storing pieces of domain-relevant knowledge together. This allows for the collection of a database, one that eventually can become large enough to warrant review, support inductive reasoning, and perhaps be reorganized (cf., Karmiloff-Smith, 1992).

Noncore, nonprivileged domains of knowledge are typically acquired later—from middle childhood on into adulthood—and usually are dependent on structured lesson plans and/or focused study. Although not impossible, it is difficult to acquire these new conceptual structures. As discussed above, their acquisition requires the concurrent acquisition of both new organizing principles and a coherent body of relevant knowledge governed by them. It is not surprising that learning about noncore domains generally is effortful and time-consuming (e.g., Anderson, 1995). Core domains of knowledge can sometimes be barriers to the later acquisition of noncore domain-specific learning (Hartnett & Gelman, in press; Slotta, Chi, & Joram, 1995; see also our discussion of structure mapping at the end of the chapter).

In sum, when we suspect something is a conceptual domain, we can test whether it is by seeing whether it is possible to characterize it in terms of a coherent set of operating principles and their related entities. This definition of a knowledge domain is neutral about the origin of the domain; it can start as an innate skeletal set of principles or be learned from scratch. There is no necessary link between knowledge's domain specificity and its time of acquisition; we should not conclude that early learning is domain-specific and later learning is not.

Constraints, Epigenesis, Universals, and Variability

The classes of relevant inputs for a domain are defined in terms of the structures of that domain, not particular surface features. The actual examples of inputs to learners can differ from one time to another and from one culture to another. This means that although different cultures can offer their young different subsets of domain-relevant inputs, the children will develop concepts that share common structural cores across cultures. Universal innate concept learning mechanisms do not rule out culture-specific knowledge for a given domain, however. Surface differences, for instance in languages or local wildlife, need not alter structural regularities that can still be learned with different exemplars. Just as children in different language environments share knowledge about linguistic universals, so, too, children who encounter different kinds of toys, artifacts, food, physical environments, and so on, will share knowledge about counting principles, the key differences between animate and inanimate objects, and so on. All will encounter animate and inanimate objects, separably moveable objects, collections of things, and so on. The upshot in many cases is that children in different cultures assimilate different domain-relevant knowledge to their shared skeletal principles.

The above examples demonstrate one source of variability that is consistent with a domain-specific account of core domains of knowledge. Another is variability due to limits or differences in knowledge of conversational rules and task requirements, opportunities to practice, planning abilities, and levels of knowledge. Siegal (1991, 1996) presents a wealth of evidence on the way children's limited knowledge of conversational rules can mask their ability to display conceptual competence. Some might conclude that these sources of variation implicate a situation-specific model of cognition (e.g., Lave & Wenger, 1991). However, there is an alternative to the situated cognition approach, and this is to take on the task of uncovering and describing the sources of systematic variation and how they interact with a model that assumes conceptual competence (Gelman, 1978).

Gelman and Greeno (1989) offer one example of this approach. They identify the understanding of conversational and task variables with the development of interpretive competence, and detail how the acquisition of levels of knowledge is related to the growth of conceptual competence. Recent studies by Kuhn (e.g., Kuhn et al., 1995) and Siegler (e.g., Siegler & Shipley, 1995) provide additional examples of how to seek careful accounts of the kinds of sources that make systematic contributions to variable performance. Researchers can and should return to the problems presented by competence-performance distinctions across development (see Gelman, 1993, for further discussion).

Problems with Alternative Views of Constraints

Associationist Constraints and Theory: Empirical Difficulties

The Postulates section at the start of this chapter reviews some remarkable results which fit very poorly with traditional theories of learning and constraints. "Screening-out" effects, in which young children and animals prefer geometrically ambiguous information over seemingly salient contingent information, are hardly what one might expect if committed to an associationist theory of mind. Relatedly, the many demonstrations of infants' active use of organized perceptual and conceptual inputs mean that we can no longer assume that infants wait passively for bits of sensory data to impinge on their sensoria. They seek out and structure the material that they learn.

How therefore should we characterize the raw data that a learner can learn about (more on this topic below)? This question helps make explicit a theme that is woven throughout this chapter. When the learner was thought to be passive, the "objective" structure of data "in the environment" might be imagined to determine the structure of what was learned. But when the learner helps structure the data, it is much more difficult to know how best to characterize it from a psychological point of view. We continue our discussion of this theme by focusing on the fact that the great stage theories of cognitive development carry with them a commitment to the classical theory of concepts, a theory that is grounded in the Associationist account of mind.

Domain-General Stage Theories and the Classical Theory of Concepts: Empirical Difficulties

Whatever the differences between Bruner's, Piaget's, or Vygotsky's theories of cognitive development, they all converge on the conclusion that there is an ordered shift from a stage where children use non-hierarchical rules to one where they have the capacity to represent hierarchical classification systems. Therefore, the form of young children's concepts differs qualitatively from those of older children and their elders. They can think about complexes (Bruner, Greenfield, Olver, et al., 1966), pseudoconcepts (Vygotsky, 1962), or preconcepts (Inhelder & Piaget, 1956), but not about "true" concepts. Two kinds of evidence challenge this stage view of classification and cognitive development. These include demonstrations of young children's success on classification tasks, and penetrating challenges to the classical theory of concepts with its reliance on the mental ability to operate logically with classes. Fodor (1972) points out that traditional stage theories of concept development are grounded on the classical theory of concepts. His argument continues that since the classical theory is deeply flawed, so, too, are traditional stage characterizations of cognitive development.

Domain-Specific Classification Effects.   Young children's failure on a variety of classification tasks is well-documented (Inhelder & Piaget, 1964). They concluded that there are three stages in the development of classification abilities. Initially (around 2 to 5½ years) children produce "graphic" solutions, in which items are grouped for no apparent reason or on the basis of a shifting classification criterion. Examples include a train and a cake, or a sequence of objects which taken pairwise have overlapping properties, such as red square, red circle, yellow circle, yellow triangle, and so forth. In the second stage (5 to 8 years), "nongraphic" solutions dominate that are more mature. At the end of this stage, children can consistently use a single criterion for classifying a set of objects, and can then reclassify the objects using a different criteria. Despite this advance, children who generate such solutions are still considered pre-operational when they fail on class-inclusion tasks. In an example of these tasks, children are shown a set of flowers, most of which are roses and the rest of which are another type of flower, and are then asked, "Which is more,

the flowers or the roses?" Young children typically respond that there are more roses, mistakenly comparing subset to subset rather than set to subset as asked. When children answer the question correctly, Inhelder and Piaget (1956) consider them able to use a class-inclusion structure inferentially, reasoning on the basis of the logical relationship that holds between classes and their subclasses. This achievement is considered indicative of concrete operational thought.

Different classification tasks were used by Bruner and his collaborators (e.g., Bruner et al., 1966), as well as by Vygotsky (1962). Nevertheless, their findings parallel Inhelder and Piaget's. For example, in one study Bruner et al. presented 6- to 19-year-old subjects a series of concrete nouns and asked them to tell how each new item in the list was like or different from all the ones they had already heard. Subjects who previously had heard the words *banana* and *peach* next heard *potato,* and were asked how a potato was like a banana and peach and how it was different. Younger subjects favored perceptual solutions, for instance, based on the color of the items. With development, solutions based on function and nominal criteria increasingly predominated. Vygotsky's data on children's ability to classify blocks on the basis of whether they have a common nonsense word on their underside converge on those of Piaget's and Bruner's. Like Inhelder and Piaget, he found that 5- to 8-year-old children reach a point where they can use a consistent criterion. Still, not until they are about 10 years old could they use a classification criterion based on the intersection of two dimensions (e.g., red and square).

We do not dispute that young children's failures on these traditional classification tasks are reliable and well documented. However, by now the same can be said about children's ability to succeed on different classification tasks (for reviews, see Gelman & Baillargeon, 1983; Mandler, Ch. 6, this Volume; Markman, 1989, Ch. 8, this Volume; Rosser, 1991; Wellman & S. Gelman, 1992). Especially pertinent to this chapter are those studies that reveal the potent effect of a knowledge base. When children know a great deal about something, so much so that we can say they have achieved a principled organization of it, there is no question that they can deploy hierarchical classification structures. Our favorite case comes from Gobbo and Chi's (1986) studies of preschool dinosaur experts. These children can sort dinosaurs on the basis of whether they are land-living or not, meat-eating or not, and so on. Since children who know much less about dinosaurs generate data that resembles the results from the traditional classification tasks, it is hard to escape the conclusion that the key variable here is knowledge, not the presence or absence of classification abilities per se (cf., Carey, 1985). These knowledge effects buttress domain-specific theories of cognitive development.

Problems with the Classical Theory of Concepts. Logical and empirical challenges to the classical theory of concepts reinforce efforts to find alternative models for our ability to form and use concepts (e.g., Armstrong, Gleitman, & Gleitman, 1983; Carey, 1985; Fodor et al., 1980; Goodman, 1972; Keil, 1989; Markman, 1989; Medin, 1989). The many demonstrations that young children put together items that older children and adults never would, while excluding from their groupings exemplars that are obvious to their elders, can be summarized as follows. Young child cannot correctly "use" concepts when our model of competence derives from the classical definition of what a concept is. According to the classical view of concepts, concepts are defined by their *intension* and their *extension*. The *intension* of a concept is its set of necessary and sufficient fundamental features, none of which can be broken down into smaller sub-features. The *extension* consists of the set of instances that are consistent with the intensional definition, and excludes all instances that are not. Boolean rules of logic organize and generate concepts.

The problems with the classical theory of concepts are well-known. Most importantly, it turns out to be very hard to find examples of everyday concepts that actually have intensional definitions, for example, for which we can articulate the required list of necessary and sufficient nondecomposable features (Armstrong, Gleitman, & Gleitman, 1983; Fodor, 1972). Even baby birds, who cannot fly and have no feathers, are still birds. Second, different people assign the same exemplar to different categories: is a whale a fish or a mammal, and is a tomato a fruit or a vegetable? Third, people treat some exemplars as better examples of a concept than others, as for example rating a robin as a "better" bird than a penguin. Finally, as discussed above, what counts as a relevant feature is concept dependent, and concept salience can vary as a function of context. For example, a snow shovel is more typical in the contexts of Minneapolis and Montreal than it is in the contexts of Los Angeles and Tel Aviv.

The recognition of these problems led to the development of the prototype and family resemblance theories of concepts (Rosch, Mervis, Gray, Boyes-Braem, & Johnson, 1976). The central idea for both is that given a set of exemplars, we form an abstraction that summarizes them. Novel instances are accepted as further exemplars on the basis of a similarity match to the summary; the more similar an exemplar is to the prototype, the more likely it will be accepted as an instance of the concept. Our ability to categorize faces as familiar is often cited in favor of a prototype or family resemblance theory. Ponder the ability to meet someone you do not know and say, "You must be so-and-so's sister. You sure look at lot like her," despite the fact that the stranger and her sister do not share all of the same features. Consider also our ability to form a concept like *game,* even though we cannot give a classical definition of it that encompasses all cases of games and no cases of nongames (Wittgenstein, 1953).

Despite their improvements over the classical theory of concepts, the similarity-based prototype and family resemblance theories have serious problems as well (see reviews in Armstong et al., 1983; Fodor & Lepore, 1996; Medin, 1989; Wellman & S. Gelman, Ch. 11, this Volume). For example, the prototype theory fails the test of concept combination. The combination of the representations of a prototypical pet (dog or cat) and a prototypical fish (salmon or trout) does not generate the common belief that the prototypical pet fish is a goldfish. Additionally, there is no a priori definition of similarity and relevance for attributes. The assumption that similarity translates to "close to" fails more often than not. We might say that 3 is more like 4 than 5 because it is closer to 4. But is it still, if we are concerned about the concepts of odd or prime numbers (Armstrong et al., 1983)? Likewise, we might say that a doll is more like a person than is a lobster, because it shares more relevant perceptual features. But this would not be so if we were concerned about the concept of animacy and the capacity for self-generated motion (Massey & Gelman, 1988).

Again, we need an account of why some attributes are treated as relevant for a concept and why others are not. Why do we think that some things are similar to each other even if they are not perceptually alike on their surfaces? What leads us to select a given input as relevant on one occasion but not on another? With core concepts, our answer is: our domain-specific knowledge structures, for both cognitive development and adult concept learning. Indeed, we think some of the best evidence for this position comes from demonstrations of early conceptual competence (see Postulate 4). Our discussion of how domains enter into the definition of similarity begins with a consideration of what count as primary input data for learning.

Characterizing the Learning Environment

Primary Data: Structured, Relational, and Abstract

Within the associationist framework, sensory data are the primary data for concept learning. Sensations that contribute to the build-up of association strength occur frequently, and in proximity to each other in time and space. In turn, associations between existing sensory-based associations are formed; this makes it possible for learners to move on to use perceptual information. Eventually enough examples of perceptual inputs are encountered and learned about to supposedly allow the induction of an abstract concept.

In contrast, our theory views the ability to organize data according to abstract criteria as foundational, not derived. We define primary data in structural terms: a domain's organizing principles lead learners to attend to relations and abstract principles when interacting with the environment, not bits of sensations. This is not to say that sensory data are totally irrelevant and never noticed. It is just that they do not form the foundation for getting concept learning off the ground. Babies use abstract principles about the nature of concepts to find exemplars in the world. Once they have identified exemplars, they can go on to learn whether objects are red, shiny, and so forth (Gelman & Brown, 1986).

Our characterization of primary data for learning in terms of relationships and structures, as opposed to bits of sensations, reverses the traditional developmental rank ordering assigned by associationist theories. That is, the different theories have opposite rankings regarding what kinds of inputs are initially salient and pertinent to both perceptual and cognitive development. Being able to attend to color makes it possible for infants to learn the color of a moving object, but only after the object has been identified as an object at all, distinct from its background (Spelke, 1990). Having nonverbal number-relevant principles makes it possible to attend to the numerosity of a display, no matter what color, shape, size, and so on, the items are.

To review so far: first principles help focus attention on inputs that are relevant for the acquisition of concepts in their domain. It matters not that these first principles are implicit, preverbal, and sketchy in form. What matters is that they are structured. Their active application leads infants and young children to find and store structurally related examples of domain-relevant inputs. Of course, the more examples of data that are present in the child's everyday environments, the greater the opportunity for this kind of learning device to do its work. There is a need for inputs

that share the same expected structure with one another (structural repetition), but there is no requirement for frequent exposure to the exact same inputs (literal repetition). If learners had no mental clues about the surface features of relevant environments, they would have no reason to put together bits of inputs that cohere as objects, that provide clues about causal agents, and so on. Bits of sense experiences do not make an object "out there," let alone an "agent." Selection at this level requires some conceptual organizer. If this is an appropriate way to characterize the nature of relevant data, then we should find that young children and infants are able to respond at abstract levels, and we do (see Postulate 4). Toward the end of the chapter we return to reconcile the conclusion that concepts derive their meaning from a set of related principles with the kinds of facts that lead some to still favor prototype models.

The current literature on mathematics learning adds weight to the theme that learning benefits when the abstract is introduced—alongside the usual concrete examples. A judicious mix of the concrete and the abstract can enhance the development of understanding (Silver, Mamona-Downs, Leung, & Kenney, 1996). Lampert's (1986) successful efforts to bring her 10-year-old students to a principled understanding of multi-digit multiplication algorithms illustrates this point. In one series of lessons she first had fourth grade students (average age = 8.5 years) learn to tell "math" stories, for example, about the total number of children attending parties when 43 children go to 26 parties, versus when 26 children go to 43 parties. Next they were asked to make up stories for multiplication problems. For example:

Teacher: Can anyone give me a story that could go with this multiplication: 12×4?

Jessica: There were 12 jars and each had 4 butterflies in it.

Teacher: And if I did this multiplication and found the answer, what would I know about the jars and the butterflies?

Jessica: You'd know that you had that many butterflies altogether.

The class then proceeded to concretely represent Jessica's story. They also took groups apart and made new groups of different sizes, which demonstrated the numerical principles of decomposition and recomposition as well as the distributive and associative laws of multiplication. Eventually, students could make up multiplication algorithms, a clear index of their principled understanding of multiplication. The children themselves never talked about the distributive law or any other mathematical laws, but they were encouraged to talk in ways that are consistent with the language and structure of mathematics, something that many researchers now consider to be especially important (Brown, Collins, & Duguid, 1989; Gelman, 1991; Silver, Mamona-Downs, Leung, & Kenney, 1996; Stigler & Fernandez, 1995).

Other recent success stories about teaching mathematics share a commitment to introducing the abstract (structural) level of mathematics from the start, mixing it with "concrete" examples (Anderson, Corbett, Koedinger, & Pelletier, 1995). Again, the idea is not to replace experience with doing problems or applications. Rather it is to render these examples mathematically coherent by providing domain-relevant data, including its specialized language. No one thinks that doing this will produce one-trial learning, nor would that be desirable given what we know about learning and retention. But there is good reason to propose that the chances for learning with understanding are increased. The next sections expand on this conclusion.

Learning Structured Information: The Constructivist Learning Laws of Redundancy and Ubiquity

Amongst those theorists in developmental and cognitive psychology who have moved to embrace a structural constructivist theory of mind are those who emphasize the social-cultural aspects of supporting environments, especially the fact that these are organized by members of the community (for recent reviews, see Rogoff, Ch. 14, this Volume, and Rogoff & Chavayah, 1995). Such community and cultural organizations often are cited as reason enough to reject theories such as ours, which give all learners a shared set of innate, skeletal knowledge structures with which to find, interpret, and learn about environments. The thrust of this argument should be familiar by now: there is said to be no need for nativist assumptions because all learners will encounter comparable environments. Again, there are two problems with this counter to the idea that we all share a set of core skeletal domains. We have already discussed one in Postulate 1: the problem of environmental ambiguity and incompleteness. The second problem follows from the fact that individuals interpret environments with reference to what they already know.

Since learners actively participate in their own knowledge acquisition, we have to give up the idea that the frequent presentation of data will suffice for learning to take place. We repeatedly have said that a constructivist theory of knowledge acquisition is inconsistent with the idea that learning occurs simply because a given set of inputs are frequently present in the real world. This is because we cannot assume that the learner shares with us the same definition of data, let alone whether some datum has been presented X number of times.

In fact, the entire notion of frequency (counts per unit time) is problematic, because it is not clear what counts as a single learning trial. Once we allow learners to contribute to their own cognitive development, we lose the control we may have once thought we had over what counts as relevant. Learners may or may not attend at a given time. A novice's interpretation of the environment "out there" need not overlap with ours. Naive learners might even treat inputs as relevant that we, the "experts," do not think of as relevant. It is possible that even the same input is treated as different on each occasion it is noticed, with different aspects being attended to each time. Most importantly, constructivist learners can themselves make up data that will feed the growth of existing structures. Compelling examples of self-generated data have been provided by those who study the problems of confabulation in eyewitness testimony (Loftus, 1991).

None of these facts fit with an associationist theory of learning that requires frequent exposure to the exact same input. No matter how conceptually competent a child's parents, teachers, and other socializing agents might be, we cannot have a theory of environment that fails to recognize and accommodate the learner's active role in determining what is relevant. To achieve this, we need to develop further the implications of assuming a rational-constructivist theory of mind, one that is founded on the assumption that structures of mind can both define and seek out structured inputs. The structured nature of environments has to be placed alongside the given of a similarly structured mind. The latter is what makes it possible for learners to benefit from the richly structured environments in which they develop.

Given a structural definition of relevance, particular examples can vary in their surface details as long as their structure maps to that of the mental conceptual domain being learned about. For example, $(1 + 1)$ is equivalent to $(0 + 2)$, $(90 - 88)$, and so on. Since we can say that examples within an equivalence class are redundant, we now have a straightforward way to state the laws of input for a constructivist theory of learning: learning is favored under conditions of structural *redundancy* and structural *ubiquity*. The more structurally redundant and ubiquitous examples of domain-relevant information the learner gets, the more likely it is that the learner's existing mental structures, related attentional inclinations, and potential supporting environment will be mutually compatible.

The principle of ubiquity is *not* the associationist principle of frequency in disguise. The idea is that learners will ordinarily encounter many different exemplars of structurally equivalent inputs. This maximizes the probability that they will recognize enough of them as relevant. The surface details of particular examples typically *differ* from one another, possibly occurring no more than once each. A straightforward count of these details would yield experienced frequency counts of $N = 1$, which is hardly enough to meet the requirement of the associationist law of frequency.

The functions of the ubiquity principle and redundancy principle cannot be separated: they work together as follows. The ubiquitous presence of structurally equivalent (redundant) examples of domain-relevant data is likely to move individuals further along a domain-relevant domain's learning path. This is well illustrated by children's language learning accomplishments. Within a given language environment, children seldom hear the exact same utterance twice. Further, speakers from different cultures vary in the extent to which they simplify their talk to beginning language learners (Schieffelin & Ochs, 1986). Indeed, congenitally deaf children hear neither motherese nor any other variant of spoken language, and whether they see exemplars of sign language varies both within and across countries (Alibali & Goldin-Meadow, 1993; Newport, 1990). Still, both hearing and deaf children all over the world master the syntax of their language group at about the same age, presumably because they encounter many different examples of the surface structure of the syntax that underlies these outputs, and because deaf children somehow find the relevant inputs (Johnson & Newport, 1991).

Language comprehension in general articulates the principles of ubiquity and redundancy. People seldom generate the exact same utterance. Nevertheless, they do produce many acceptable sentences that reflect the operation of their implicit knowledge of syntactic principles. Put differently, sentences are patterns of sound that are isomorphic exemplars of the structure in question. It does not matter whether two examples of relevant data are identical in surface detail, or produced by the same source. They can be offered by peers, adults, television, and so on. What matters is that utterances produced at two different times, by either the same or a different person, reflect a shared structure. When this happens, a child who shares with others the same core domain structure (at least to a considerable

extent) will find the relevant data. To learn their language, children need not hear these data at a given time or from a particular teacher. We hold that the same considerations apply for privileged domains of concept learning, which is why we choose to characterize relevant data in terms of the constraints on the structure of a domain and the principles of ubiquity and redundancy.

The ubiquity and redundancy principles have important practical consequences. They mitigate against the fact that experts' guesses about relevant data sometimes will be wrong, and can even lead to our withholding what young learners would consider to be possible inputs. A theory that allows novices more than one information source in more than one setting makes evolutionary sense, for it acknowledges the possibility of multiple learning routes which are structurally related. This fits well with the important fact that there can be both universals of cognitive development and also culture-specific variability.

Sources of Structured Information in the Learning Environment

We emphasize again that since what novice learners know can differ from what is known by their siblings, parents, tutors, extended family members, and friends, we cannot assume that there are standard countable trials of learning as required by the associationist law of frequency. This shows why it is not a trivial task to develop a theory of the environment for conceptual development that is consistent with any version of a constructivist theory of mind, be it ours, Piaget's, Rogoff's, Vygotsky's, or anyone else's. There are many sources of potentially relevant inputs. Some kinds of learning may lean heavily on one particular source; other kinds will benefit from the potential for redundancy across multiple sources. For example, the idea that one's elders should be respected is surely dependent on inputs from the social-cultural milieu, but probably owes little to the structure of the physical environment. However, the world of physical objects is likely to be the key source for the belief that solid objects cannot pass through one another, even though our perceptions appear to allow this possibility (Leslie, 1988). Individuals might also provide themselves with novel cases of concept data, such as when they contemplate the effect of adding one to a very large number (Hartnett & Gelman, in press). Still, from our point of view, any effort to assign more significance to one kind of environmental source than another in the epigenesis of knowledge is akin to asking whether height or width contributes more to a rectangle. With this caveat in mind, we turn to considering some of the kinds of relevant input that can support cognitive development.

Structure in the Sociocultural Environment

Human beings largely create their own environment. They also tend to structure the learning environment that their children encounter (Rogoff, Ch. 14, this Volume). Sperber (1994) calls this source of experience the "cultural" domain that the learner lives in and interacts with, an extension of his idea of an "actual" domain (see p. 601). The cultural domain consists of the sorts of information that learners experience due to the particular emphases and representational tools of their peers, teachers, and general culture. Sociocultural influences on learning play an important role in the transmission of knowledge, not only in formal educational settings but in informal settings such as parent-child interactions. From our point of view, they are one of the sources of data that children encounter on a given learning path. Greenfield's studies (1993) of how daughters of the Zinacenteco (a Mayan people of Southern Mexico) learn to weave provide a particularly compelling example of this conclusion, in one of the best examples we know of learning that is scaffolded, informal, and relatively error-free.

When Greenfield first visited the Zinacenteco, the mothers were ever-present teachers who continually guided their daughters' efforts to learn to weave. Indeed, they were model scaffolders in the Vygotskian sense, ready to provide explanations and demonstrations that were especially well tuned for their daughters' skill level, so much so as to create the conditions for errorless learning. Some twenty years later, after trucking and tourism became part of the community's ongoing activities, this teaching style has all but disappeared. Mothers are no longer at home—they make fabrics and sell them to tourists—and girls have joined their brothers at the local school. Girls still learn to weave, but not in the same way; much of their learning is self-initiated and self-monitored. Older sisters frequently serve as teachers, but they do not use the scaffolding teaching style. The learner now has to ask explicitly for help from her sister, who often is more interested in other ongoing events. The upshot is that trial-and-error learning has become the rule, not the exception.

Greenfield (1993) expected these changes in teaching style and mode, as well as a change in kinds of fabrics that were made. In order to keep up with tourist demands, women shifted from producing expensive, time-consuming traditional patterns to cheaper and novel patterns. Under these circumstances, the premium is on novelty and speed. A trial-and-error method of learning is more likely to generate variable outputs, some of which are correct and some of which are not. Since cheaper materials are used, the cost to the group of errors drops considerably. At the same time, girls can be encouraged when they produce interesting variations that appeal to tourists, or when they show a particular talent for weaving.

Lest one treat Greenfield's follow-up study as evidence for the idea that culture is a source of infinite variability, it is important to point out that the girls were still learning to weave, and still producing recognizable patterns. That is, despite cultural changes, there was a shared commitment to the same class of activities and products and this guaranteed that exemplars of the target class of artifacts were available to the learners when they sought them out. Despite dramatic changes in the culture's teaching style, there still were plenty of examples of the structure of the skill to be learned. The cultural unconscious of the Zinacenteco still includes ubiquitous and redundant examples of its commitment to weaving, and the assumption that the skill will be passed from female to female (see also Gelman et al., 1991, on the role of museums as institutions of informal learning).

Thus, when it comes to the arena of cognitive development, it is important to keep in mind the structural universality of some ontological worldviews and social premises (cf., Boyer, 1995; Brown, 1990; Hirschfeld, 1996; Sperber, 1994). For instance, consider that the physical environments in which children are raised vary widely in exposure to animals, for example, a house in the country versus a high-rise apartment in the city. These differences are likely to influence how much children come to know about the core differences between animate and inanimate objects, but nevertheless all children will acquire organized knowledge about these differences. Carey (1995) and Keil (1995) develop a related argument about the cross-cultural evidence for a naive theory of biology.

Structure in the Physical World

Several recent movements in psychology and cognitive science have also called attention to an analysis of the structure of the learning environment. Ecological psychology, founded by J. J. and E. R. Gibson, describes the learning environment as providing an information flow that constantly bombards the perceiving mind with an enormous amount of information, an amount which greatly exceeds the mind's ability to attend to and store all of it. It argues against associationist theory by showing that the learning environment is structured, and therefore that the senses pick up structured as opposed to punctate bits of information. Three types of structure in the learning environment are particularly important here. First, there are structural regularities in the physical nature of the environment which remain constant over time (Shepard, 1987). Examples include the direction of gravity, the rising and setting of the sun, the fact that solid objects do not pass through one another, and the fact that different surfaces offer different degrees of support. Structural regularities do not mean surface constancies or invariances: for example, the particular time and position of the sunrise is not constant. Nevertheless, there are regularities about the sunrise that can be learned: the fact that the sun does rise every day, and the annual cycle to its north-south variability.

A second type of structure in the environment comes from the division of types of objects into natural kinds. In the case of animate objects, this structure is taxonomic and hierarchical, and has arisen through the multiplication of species during the course of evolution. Animate objects tend to share properties such has having eyes, limbs, and so on. In the case of inanimate objects, diversity has arisen because of differences in raw materials (e.g., granite versus clay) as well as differences in the physical forces that have shaped them (e.g., wind versus water). In both cases, objects belong to structured classes which have many predictable properties and can often be arranged hierarchically (Atran, 1995; Keil, 1995).

A third type of structure in the environment exists at the personal level of the learner: objects in the world interact differently with the learner and offer differing functional possibilities. Animate objects tend to move and interact with their environment, raising the possibility of threat or benefit to the learner. Inanimate objects can also move, but their motions result only from external forces rather than from internal motives. The Gibsons' concept of affordance is closely related to the functional aspect of this type of structure: only certain objects in the environment can be walked on, picked up, or thrown. Children quickly catch on to the relevance of these kinds of affordances. For example, 3- and 4-year-old children say they cannot touch the sun because it is too far away, and if it were not, it would be too hot anyway (Gelman, Spelke, & Meck, 1983).

Again, we must emphasize that the types of structure in the learning environment just described need not be concrete and directly perceivable in the empiricist sense.

Some regularities are temporal, such as the seasons of the year. Other regularities are internal, such as concepts of causation and mechanism which underlie reasoning about animate versus inanimate motion. Still other aspects of structure are abstract, as in the case of numerical regularities. None of these examples of structure could be learned by traditional empiricist means, in which punctate sensations have to be proximate to each other in time and space in order to be associated.

Structure in the Mind

There are a variety of ways in which the mind is capable of generating data for its own benefit, a capacity mentioned several times above and which Piaget referred to as "logical experience." Self-generated data certainly play an important role in language learning: throughout infancy, babies babble to themselves as they try out and refine new speech sounds. A similar role is played by early stages of birdsong learning (see discussion in Postulate 6 above of Marler's work in this area). Gelman and Hartnett (in press) provide a variety of examples of how young children use thought experiments to generate counting-relevant data: counting to some large number, or continually adding one to a number they already think is rather big. Indeed, it was parents' reports of their preschoolers wondering about whether the numbers ended that led Gelman and her students to study children's learning about the successor principle for natural numbers.

We are only beginning to learn about this self-generated source of cognitive development, especially the conditions that engender the spontaneous generation of questions and inferences that can attract appropriate inputs from those who are more knowledgeable. Brown and Campione's (1996) "communities of learners" in elementary schools, like microgenetic studies of a focused learning problem (e.g., Karmiloff-Smith & Inhelder, 1974–1975; Kuhn et al., 1995; Siegler & Crowley, 1991) are extremely promising on this front. They provide detailed accounts of acquisition curves as well as the kinds of input learners both generate and use.

Mental Learning Tools: Beyond Initial Enabling Constraints and Core Domains

Up to this point our focus has been on the role of enabling constraints and the nature of conceptual domains. In the remainder of the chapter we turn to what we call "mental learning tools." By mental learning tools, we mean an armament of learning mechanisms such as structure mapping, the computation of frequencies and contingencies, imitation, template tuning, parameter setting, pattern seeking, action-planning, and so on.[2] For us, mental learning tools contribute to the active construction of knowledge, and are neither domain-specific nor domain-general in the usual sense. They are more specific than truly domain-general processes such as formal logic, and yet more general than the enabling constraints in core domains.

Mental learning tools are more "central" than enabling constraints in Fodor's (1983) sense of peripheral versus central modularity. This is because they often take as inputs the data which has already been selected as relevant by domain-specific enabling constraints. A learning tool is applied whenever the learner is faced with data having the particular structure with which that learning tool "resonates" (Shepard, 1994), in something like what Keil (1994) refers to as a "mode of construal" and Dennett (1987) refers to as a "stance." For instance, if a task requires mastering the frequency with which particular exemplars of a concept appear in the learner's environment, then the frequency computation device will be engaged (see below).

Mental learning tools are therefore not strictly domain-specific, in that they can operate on structured information from more than one domain, but neither are they completely domain-general, since they resonate only with a specific type of informational structure. They provide a way to construct higher-order combinations from the outputs of different domain-specific learning mechanisms, in order to produce more flexible and general learning. It is combinations of this sort which we believe create the *appearance* of domain-generality. Higher-order combinations of information by learning tools also address the issue of evolvability raised by Tooby and Cosmides (1992) in their sweeping rejection of domain-general processes. They argue that truly domain-general solutions to adaptive problems are always weaker than problem-specific solutions, and therefore could not have evolved. Tooby and Cosmides' objection does not apply to learning tools, however, since

they are not truly domain general. Learning tools create potentially useful extensions of domain-specific processes. This potential usefulness creates a gradient which satisfies the conditions of evolvability: some benefit is better than none, and therefore gradual improvements in learning tools could evolve (see Dawkins, 1995, Ch. 3).

Our list of mental learning tools above might strike some as unusual, even perverse. It brings together processes that are sometimes pitted against each other, for example, imitation and parameter setting. Discussions of imitative learning as a domain-general process have often been embedded in noncognitive social learning theories (e.g., Bandura & Walters, 1965; Miller & Dollard, 1941). This fact surely contributed to treatments of imitation in parameter-setting theories as a poor stepsister of general associative learning mechanisms (Chomsky, 1959, 1965; Piattelli-Palmarini, 1989). Even so, what might be true about syntax acquisition need not apply for all domains of learning. We agree with Premack and Premack's (1995) thesis that imitation serves young human learners' efforts to accomplish many knowledge acquisition tasks, including norms of human interaction. In doing so, we reject the idea that imitation is best accounted for within a content-neutral S-R social learning theory like Bandura and Walters'. We share with Piaget (1929) and other cognitive developmentalists the position that imitation serves learning. We consider it an extremely potent example of structure-mapping, the first of two mental learning tools described in the next section. Frequency computing is the second learning tool featured.

Structure Mapping

The ability to map from existing mental structures to new structures during knowledge acquisition is among the most important of the mental learning tools. This follows from our assumption that principles of a domain make possible the assimilation of domain-relevant data, that is, data that share a common structure with the domain's principles. In core domains, the skeletal principles themselves define initial representations which become the repository of all data whose structure can be mapped to them. Structure mapping serves learners' abilities to identify relevant inputs when going beyond old learnings, given the ever-present tendency to apply existing mental structures to new learnings. A similar mechanism can be invoked to address Wilson and Sperber's (1986) account of relevance.

Our claim that structure mapping is a key learning tool has an important implication: learning will be a function of

---

[2] We are much aware of the ability of humans to develop and use a host of metacognitive learning skills and artifacts with varying degrees of facility, including physical, symbolic, computational, and communication tools. Our focus here is not on these metacognitive tools that learners can deploy to their benefit once they are mastered, but rather on online mental learning tools whose use does not depend on their intentional deployment.

the degree to which existing mental structures (be they in core or noncore domains) overlap with the structure of the input. Environments that share relevant structural relations with existing domains of knowledge are ones that are conducive to rapid knowledge acquisition. Our premise is that learners have a better chance of assimilating an input if there is potential for a structural map between what is to be learned and what is already known. The fit can also be dependent on whether there is a match between the number of common *structural units* a student can process and the number embodied in the data (cf., Case, 1992; Halford, 1993). In the absence of such potential structural maps and fits, there is a risk that the input will be ignored or mistakenly assimilated into the existing (inconsistent) structure and knowledge base (Gelman, 1991).

Work on analogical reasoning provides especially compelling examples of the foregoing ideas about structure mapping. There is an emerging consensus that successful analogical transfer depends on the extent to which structure mapping is possible. The probability that transfer will occur is very high if learners achieve representations that are structural isomorphs but very low if learners have to rely on surface cues of perceptual similarity (Brown, 1990; Gentner, Rattermann, & Forbus, 1993; Holyoak & Thagard, 1995). For instance, by taking advantage of very young children's principled knowledge about causality, Goswami and Brown (1990) were able to illustrate that children solve analogies of the a : b : : c : d form when a common causal transformation forms the basis of the analogy. In another example of analogical reasoning and transfer, Catrambone and Holyoak (1989) presented subjects with multiple analogous word problems and measured transfer to the solution of a superficially different word problem; transfer was facilitated when the problems were worded so as to emphasize their structural similarities.

The potential role of a structure-mapping learning tool is also featured in the literatures on mathematics and science learning. There are a number of differences between mathematics classes in Japan and the United States for 6- and 7-year-olds, including how children are taught number facts such as multiplication tables (Stevenson & Stigler, 1992). In the United States, children often are introduced to their number facts with manipulable objects so as to render the symbolic level "concrete." The roots of this practice lie in the mistaken belief that young children are limited to concrete (non-abstract) reasoning. Although the same manipulable materials can be found in Japanese classrooms, they are used in a very different way; Japanese

teachers relate them to abstract mathematical representations in their discussions about the many possible ways to state particular number facts. Both errors and correct answers are included in the discussion, in an effort to encourage all children to think of different but structurally equivalent ways to state a single mathematical problem, for example, $2 + 5 = 7$ and $1 + 1 + 1 + 1 + 1 + 1 + 1 = 7$. Although the left-hand sides of these two equations are perceptually very different, they are structurally equivalent within the domain of natural number arithmetic, making structure mapping to the principles of the domain possible, and thereby facilitating a deeper understanding of number facts beyond mere rote memorization. Efforts to promote structure mapping and overall coherence are also characteristic of Japanese lesson plans, and are a leading hypothesis proposed by Stigler and his colleagues (e.g., Stevenson, Lee, & Stigler, 1986; Stigler & Fernandez, 1995) for why Japanese elementary school math lessons lead children to better understandings than American lessons.

Gallistel and Gelman's (1992) conclusion that preverbal counting processes are isomorphic to verbal counting processes serves as another example of how the domain of number can take advantage of structure mapping. Preverbal principles provide a framework that makes the verbal counting process intelligible to the young learner; a structure mapping learning tool makes possible the assimilation of the count list encountered in the child's environment (Gelman, 1993). Gelman and Gattis' (1995) review of mathematics learning contains other examples of structure mapping as a learning tool. These include Lampert's (1986) successful efforts to bring her elementary-school students to a principled understanding of multidigit multiplication algorithms (see p. 607), and Nesher and Sukenik's (1991) successful program for teaching high school students about ratios and proportions.

Further examples of the workings of structure mapping as a learning and problem-solving tool are found in the literature on science learning. White's (1993) ThinkerTools program for teaching Newtonian mechanics to sixth graders takes as given the assumption that science learning should be built around causal principles and relations. Studies from the literature on expertise and novice-expert differences also illustrate how a domain can take advantage of a structure-mapping tool. Chi, Feltovich, and Glaser (1981) asked novices and experts to sort physics textbook problems in any way they wished. Novices did so on the basis of the perceptual aspects of the diagrams or the apparatus, for example, inclined plane, balance beam, and so on.

Experts instead classified the problems on the basis of the underlying physics principles needed to solve the problem, for example, Newton's second law. Put differently, experts were able to map the organizing principles of their (non-core) domain of knowledge to the different problems. Since the novices did not share such principled knowledge, they could not achieve a structural map based on the laws of physics. This being so, they could either use a perceptual default strategy to classify problems on the basis of common surface information, or map the input to whatever existing mental structures they had available. Both kinds of solutions occurred: the former were classified as examples of perceptual solutions, the latter as examples of misconceptions.

Young children have a ubiquitous tendency to persist until they get something right (Brown et al., 1983; Gelman & Brown, 1986). This means that in addition to their tendencies to apply their existing mental structures, they have a way to monitor the relationship between their outputs and the target they aim for. Our designation of structure mapping as a learning tool provides an important piece of the solution to the problem of accounting for self-initiated and self-guided learning within a domain. A structure-mapping device can provide at least a *match/no-match* test of whether a solution is correct. Repeated efforts can be scrutinized in the same way, and accepted or rejected to the degree that they map structurally to the principles of the domain governing the learning or problem solving. Learnings that can take advantage of existing structures are at an advantage in this account, a prediction that is supported by the wealth of data showing that learning is always better when there is an existing mental structure.

The foregoing leads to a principled statement about structure mapping: Learning is a function of the degree to which existing knowledge structures can be mapped to—in Piagetian terms, projected onto—the to-be-learned materials. Theory and ongoing research on the relation between early domain knowledge and later learning lends strong support to this conclusion (Hartnett & Gelman, in press).

Learners' proclivities to map available structures to environments helps explain some rather precocious abilities in young children. Before they are taught to write, they can generate different plans of action in response to a request to either write a word or draw a picture for a given line drawing (Brenneman, Massey, Machado, & Gelman, 1996). They can also develop writing systems (Tolchinsky-Landsmann, 1990), and they can distinguish between a string of marks on paper that are "good for writing" as opposed to "good for numbers" (e.g., Lee & Karmiloff-Smith, 1996).

How do the young even begin to sort out the fact that there are different kinds of marks on paper? We suggest that young children's structure mapping tendencies serve them well in this case. The idea is that each of the symbol systems has its own structure and related constraints. For example, we know that young children have implicit knowledge about the structure of inanimate objects and language. The former have bounded surfaces and are solid. Drawings of objects map these characteristics, at least often enough. An orange is drawn as a continuous circle and filled in with the color orange. Language is represented as a sequence of sound units; print (at least in the cultures studied) consists of a sequence of marks with spaces between them, and so on. Such differences in structural relations do not begin to define the full range of our implicit knowledge about objects and speech, on the one hand, and drawing and writing conventions on the other hand. Still, they might suffice from the viewpoint of young learners whose goal is likely to be limited to an attempt to distinguish between the kinds of marks on paper that they encounter. This goal can be served by their omnipresent tendency to engage in structural mapping. Young children's beginning representations of the difference between drawing and writing are hardly complete. What matters is that they exist at all. Once they do, a learning path opens up—and in this case there will be many eager to encourage and support movement along it (Cole, 1996).

Frequency Computing

As indicated, skeletal principles in core domains draw attention to the class of relevant inputs, and organize the assimilation and early representation of noticed cases. Skeletal structures start to accumulate flesh as structured examples are assimilated. In addition, they take advantage of an automatic (nonconscious) ability to keep a running frequency count of encountered exemplars and their relevant aspects. Such a learning tool contributes to the build up of knowledge of the predictive validity of the different attributes of encountered exemplars. For example, certain surface properties and form attributes characterize animate objects, as opposed to different properties and attributes which characterize inanimate objects.

The registration of attribute frequencies and the computation of their predictiveness, that is, of the contingency between a given concept and the possession of a given surface attribute, is carried out by what we call a frequency/contingency learning tool. This learning tool is a good example of the middle ground described above between domain generality and domain specificity; it operates specifically on frequency data, but it also performs the same frequency-computing function in many different domains.

There is good evidence that animals and humans of all ages keep track *automatically* of the frequency of relevant events and objects (Gallistel, 1990; Hasher & Zacks, 1979; Marcus et al., 1992). For example, Hasher and Zacks (1979) showed children ages 5 to 8 years a series of pictures, in which each picture appeared 0 to 4 times. Afterward, children in all age groups were highly and equally successful at reporting how many times a picture had been shown, despite not receiving any instructions to keep track of this information. Similarly robust abilities to pick up frequency information about objects or events abound. Hasher and Zacks (1984) have documented frequency learning across populations (college students, learning-disabled children, and depressed and elderly persons), as well as across a wide range of variable-frequency materials (letters of the alphabet, familiar words, surnames, and professions). Marcus et al. document people's ability to keep track of the different frequencies of irregular past tense and plural words. Infants' abilities to adjust the frequency with which they suck or turn their heads in order to achieve presentations of sounds, well-focused photographs, mobiles they control, and so on, add to the list of cases where we find the mind keeping track of frequencies of items or events of interest (Watson, 1987).

Saffran, Aslin, and Newport (1996) provide another impressive demonstration of frequency detection and learning. They presented 8-month-old infants with just two minutes of synthesized speech in a monotone female voice. The speech stream contained four three-syllable "words," repeated in random order with no pauses. Despite the lack of pauses, the infants were able to detect the boundaries between words in the continuous speech stream. The only information available to them for this task was frequency information: the transitional probabilities between particular pairs of syllables (higher within words than across word boundaries). In one experiment, infants reliably distinguished words from nonwords where the nonwords consisted of familiar syllables in an unfamiliar order. In a second experiment, they successfully made an even more difficult distinction, in which the nonwords consisted of the final syllable from one word and the first two syllables from another word. The syllable order of each nonword was therefore familiar, but statistically its syllables did not correspond to a word. Saffran et al. concluded that these results were attributable to an innately biased statistical learning mechanism. This mechanism could be language-specific, or (as we believe) more generally applicable to distributional analyses of environmental stimuli.

We are sure that readers know which is more frequent, white or green cars and are very impressed with Macario's (1991) preschool children who could play his "what will we take on a picnic" game—they were able to generate possible foods on the basis of a color cue. We endorse the thesis put forth by Hasher and Zacks (1979, 1984), that learning about the frequency of *noticed* objects and events occurs automatically and without awareness. So apparently do Tversky and Kahneman (1973) who simply assume that we can use base rate information. In fact, we believe that humans share this extremely potent learning tool with other animal species. Gallistel (1990) reviews evidence that animals in classical and instrumental conditioning paradigms are learning the rate/frequency of reinforcement and its contingency on available cues, rather than the associative pairings predicted by associationist theory. From raw frequencies the animals are computing contingencies, that is, the extent to which the frequency of reinforcement in the presence of a conditioned stimulus is different from the frequency observed in its absence. As with humans, these computations are automatic and continuous.

Once again our use of a term, in this case, frequency, admits possible misinterpretations. In our view, the foundational structure in core domains always comes from the skeletal principles embodied in enabling constraints; frequency data about relevant encounters are *subsequently* recorded and attached to that existing framework. Frequency information does not help the learner to recognize encounters in the first place. Thus, our idea that a frequency counting computational device is a mental learning tool is not a variant of the associationist law of frequency governing the learning of associations. Within association theory, frequency serves to build associative strength; it is not specifically encoded and represented, nor does it feed a device that keeps a running total of frequency per se. Certain associations are stronger than others because they have had the benefit of more frequent encounters with particular pairings of stimuli, longer rewards, and/or rewards at shorter delays. That is, many different factors combine to determine associative strength, but the factors contributing to that strength, for example, frequency, are not represented by associative strength and therefore are not recoverable as inputs for learning.

Thus, to say a cue has predictive validity is not to say that it is defining; lettuce does not have to be green, and a green leaf does not guarantee the presence of lettuce. Similarly, the distinction between a malleable versus a rigid form is strongly correlated with the animate-inanimate distinction. To be sure, the rigidity cue has considerable predictive validity for animacy/inanimacy, as do attributes such as uniform versus variable surface textures, and the presence or absence of limbs, eyes, ears, and so on. Although none of these are defining it still helps to learn their relative frequencies and related contingencies. Such computations allow us to make an informed guess about the animacy status of a novel or unidentified item, and then to check if the guess is consistent with the requirements of the domain. Informed guesses can be disconfirmed by subsequent information which violates core principles about a domain; no matter how much something looks like a rock, we will no longer believe it to be a rock if it gets up and walks away. And no matter how unlikely a particular example of a category might be, we can accept it if it can be assimilated to the domain's principles. Thus, a green lemon is still a lemon, and a three-legged dog is still a dog.

Parenthetically, the above makes it possible to make sense of the data that are used to favor a prototype theory of concepts. These are the data that show learners have knowledge of particular relevant features as well as their centrality (see Schwartz & Reisberg, 1991, for an excellent review). For example, wings are particularly relevant features of birds, and robins are more "central" exemplars of birds than are ostriches. From our point of view, these studies provide evidence that we do have a frequency-counting mental learning tool. This is why high-frequency features are more memorable, and why exemplars with many high-frequency features are judged better examples of a category. How such frequency information is used depends on the domain in question. Individuals will not say that a high-frequency irregular verb is a better example of verb than a relatively novel verb with a regular past tense (Marcus, 1996).

The proposal that a mental learning tool computes the frequency of relevant encounters converges with conclusions drawn by other authors. Schwartz and Reisberg (1991) suggest that we may need a three-part theory of concepts, in which "concepts are represented by a prototype, some set of specifically remembered cases, and some further abstract information" (p. 391), where the parts all interact to accomplish correct similarity judgments and inferences. In our account, the recorded knowledge of frequencies and contingencies underlies subjects' abilities to answer questions in ways that make them look like they learn prototypes and some salient domain-relevant exemplars. Keil (1995) has proposed that "concepts in theories"

structures are supplemented by domain-general feature tabulation processes. Armstrong, Gleitman, and Gleitman (1983) concluded that we know the difference between saying an object is an instance of a concept, versus characterizing it as a good or bad instance. More generally, our account provides a way to reconcile these response patterns with the compelling arguments against the idea that concepts are based on prototypes (Fodor & Lepore, 1996).

Further converging lines of thought exist with respect to children's understanding of causality. Bullock, Gelman, and Baillargeon (1982) argue that causal principles lead children to search for causal mechanisms and assimilate causally relevant information about events, including the cue value of spatial and temporal cues. Ahn, Kalish, Medin, and S. Gelman (1995) conclude that information about covariation and about causal mechanisms play complementary roles in our decisions about causes. Cheng (in press) shows that people relate their computations of contingency to their beliefs in causal principles. Finally, several authors have offered accounts of how children learn to classify moving objects as animate or inanimate based on the causal conditions of animate versus inanimate motion (Gelman, 1990; Gelman, Durgin, & Kaufman, 1995; S. Gelman, & Gottfried, 1996; Williams & Gelman, 1995).

Mental Learning Tools and Later Learning: Structure Mapping Can Help or Hinder

A central tenet of a structural constructivist theory of mind is that existing mental structures influence later learning, whether they be the result of prior learning or of enabling constraints in core domains. Learning is fastest in core domains, when enabling constraints are engaged by the types of inputs they are functionally designed to "expect," allowing the rapid uptake and interpretation of information. Learning is slowest when no existing structures are close enough to the structure of the new information to be useful (e.g., tax law, calculus). In such cases, the learner has the double burden of learning both the information and the structure with which to interpret and store it. As the literature on expertise acquisition in noncore domains has shown, novice learners often settle into nonprincipled organizing structures which appear to reflect fall-back strategies such as perceptual similarity (e.g., Gibson & Gibson, 1955); with enough experience and concentrated study, learners are able to reorganize their structures in a principle-based manner which reflects the underlying regularities in the knowledge domain. For instance, as noted earlier, novice physics students appear to structure their knowledge of physics around formulas and perceptual similarities, such as the presence of pendulums or inclined planes. In contrast, expert physicists structure their knowledge around underlying physical principles (Hardiman, Dufresne, & Mestre, 1989; Larkin, McDermott, Simon, & Simon, 1980).

Between these two extremes of particularly fast and particularly slow learning lie instances in which some partial mapping is possible between existing knowledge structures and the structure of the information being learned. When this mapping is particularly accurate and consistent, analogical reasoning provides an important mental tool for rapid uptake of the new structure (Gentner, 1989; Holyoak & Thagard, 1995; Vosniadou & Ortony, 1989). There are cases however where existing knowledge structures actually hinder the acquisition of new knowledge. This can occur when entities and concepts which have previously been learned about within one structure, particularly as part of a core domain, are being learned about within a new structure (e.g., Slotta & Chi, 1996). When entities and concepts are shared in the new structure, the learner is likely to assume that the old structural relations between them are still valid. If the new structure turns out to be inconsistent with the old structure, the learner is in for a hard time. We illustrate these implications with an example of our effort to document the contrast between easy and difficult mappings.

An Example: Why Learning about Fractions Is Difficult and Infinity Is Not

Existing knowledge structures may or may not facilitate the learning of new knowledge structures. When the structure of the to-be-learned data does not map to the structure of what is known, existing knowledge can become a barrier or obstacle to new learning. That is, when there is inconsistency between the intended interpretations of inputs for new learning and the actual way a learner is likely to interpret the data, new learnings may not occur. For better or for worse, our constructivist minds sometimes can put new learning at risk, not because we intentionally go astray or intentionally misinterpret inputs, but rather because we cannot help but interpret inputs in terms of what we know and/or believe—just as in the Müller-Lyer illusion, when we see one stick as longer than the other when in fact they are equal. We find consistency even in the face of inconsistency. We do not do this to be ornery, any more than we intentionally err in length judgments when shown the Müller-Lyer display. In both cases, the interpretation of

data follows from structures of the mind which continually attempt to make sense of the world. As we have seen in various sections of this chapter, such structures usually serve us well, helping us select and organize relevant inputs, making sense of the novel, and so on. That they can also lead us astray when we encounter certain input conditions is to be expected. This is one of the pitfalls of the fact that our minds do have knowledge structures.

The idea that there will be some structure-environment pairings that lead to "trouble" is not unique to constructivist theories of mind. Armies have learned to have soldiers break stride when crossing bridges in order to minimize the likelihood that the bridge will collapse. Bridges collapse when they resonate at their natural frequency and it is possible to generate this frequency with certain marching paces. The point for developmental psychologists—indeed all psychologists who care about knowledge acquisition—is this: Even when we lack the structures needed for the correct interpretation of given inputs, we interpret them nevertheless. At such times, the fundamental tendency of our constructivist minds is to apply existing structures, be these about knowledge domains, beliefs, social schemes, etc. Under such conditions, our minds can therefore lead us astray.

There is abundant evidence that schooled and non-schooled individuals all over the world share a common theory about numbers, given that there are some number-relevant activities within a culture. These can include tailoring, cab driving, selling, shopping in supermarkets, or going to Weight Watchers, to name a few. The crux of this theory is that "numbers are what you get when you count."[3] Children in the United States start to receive formal instruction about fractions in kindergarten or Grade 1. Number lines are a ubiquitous feature of kindergarten classes. Blackboards prominently display fraction numergraphs and numerlogs, for example, ½ and "one half." Textbooks include illustrated lessons on the labels of *X* equal parts of shapes, where *X* is at least 2, 3, and 4 and the related fractions are ½, ⅓, and ¼. They also offer instruction on how to label the *X* equal parts, for example, "this circle has 2 equal parts, each is one half of a circle," "We can write *one-half* as ½," and so on. Finally, children have some opportunities to mix fractions with whole numbers, in either fractional

---

[3] There are disagreements about the developmental origins of this theory, but not whether it is shared by the time children start school.

notation or natural language (e.g., 1½ and "one and one half").

In contrast, young children are almost never taught about the successor principle for natural numbers, that is, that every natural number has a successor and therefore that there is no last number. However, the mathematical structure of the natural number successor principle is consistent with what children already know about numbers, whereas the mathematical structure for the notion of a fraction is not. For these reasons, we (Gelman, Cohen, & Hartnett 1989; Hartnett & Gelman, in press) reasoned that despite these different schooling opportunities, young children would (a) come to understand the successor principle with relative ease; and (b) make systematic interpretative errors about fractions.

Mathematically, a fraction is defined as one cardinal number divided by another. Since division is an operation that is outside the knowledge of the young child, the idea of a fraction as a number is not conceptually consistent with the counting principles. The definition maps to a tripartite symbol, for example, ½ is made up of symbols for 1, 2, and division. Although the rule of one-to-one correspondence of the counting principles readily maps to single entities like digits, nothing in the counting principles can be mapped to the symbol for a fraction, be it in fraction or decimal format. To make matters even worse, there is no successor principle for fractions; that is, there is no "next" fraction. This follows from the fact that there are infinitely many numbers between any two rational numbers.

The expected differential successes with successor and fraction tasks have indeed been found (e.g., Gelman, 1991; Gelman, Cohen, & Hartnett, 1989; Hartnett & Gelman, in press). As expected, children between 5 and 8 years of age quickly catch onto the fact that they can keep adding 1 to whatever number they are thinking about. In contrast, children within the same age range consistently misinterpreted inputs meant to represent fractions. For example, when Gelman, Cohen, and Hartnett (1989) asked kindergarten, first-, and second-grade children to place circle representations of fractions on a special number line that represented whole numbers with sets of N circles, the majority of the children used whole number count strategies to solve the task. When asked to put a card with 1½ circles on the number line, most children placed it at the position for 2 since the card had two objects on it. Similarly, many children placed all of the representations of unit fractions (one-fourth, one-third, one-half) at the position for 1 on the number line, often telling us that each was "one thing."

Further, although these same children pointed correctly to the card that "showed one half," when their choice was between ½ and ¼, they systematically misordered these same two fraction symbols, choosing ¼ as larger. Similarly, they seldom read ½ correctly as "one half." Instead they came up with a variety of alternatives, including "one and two," "one and a half," "one plus two," "twelve," and "three." The most frequent misreading was "one and a half." These are but some examples of early conceptual difficulties with fractions and concepts that are related to the underlying mathematical structure.

There is an ever-growing literature that adds weight to our proposal that children's knowledge of natural numbers (a core domain) serves as a conceptual barrier to later learning about other numbers and their mathematical structures, for example, fractions, ratios, proportions, multiplication, and division (see, for example, Leinhardt, Putnam, & Harttrup, 1992; Nunes & Bryant, 1996; Sophian, 1994). Many children eventually do achieve a mathematical understanding of fractions despite the difficulty. Gelman (1991) suggests that they accomplish this by finding a series of local structural commensurates between their knowledge of the counting numbers and bits of knowledge about fractions. In the absence of an existing relevant conceptual structure, these local mappings serve as mental stepping stones which can begin to assimilate relevant data, and thus for some learners to begin to fashion a skeletal structure for learning. But since the learning task requires the simultaneous acquisition of both the relevant structure and the entities that give the structure its content, it should be no surprise that it takes a long time.

CONCLUSION

We have argued for a theory of concept learning and cognitive development that combines converging lines of theoretical and empirical work from across the cognitive sciences. These influences include deep empirical and theoretical challenges to previous theories of learning and cognition; the recognition of domain-specific and modular learning mechanisms in humans and animals; and an appreciation of evolutionary perspectives on learning. Because so many terms are shared across very different theories of learning, we have emphasized the theory-dependent nature of terms, particularly "constraint." Constraints of one form or another are embedded in all learning theories, not just those which endow learners with innate mental structures. We believe that among the alternatives, a view of constraints as learning enablers is best suited to charting the complex interaction between biological and environmental influences on development. Distinguishing between core and noncore domains facilitates a more productive approach to a variety of long-standing controversies: the degree of innateness in mental architecture, the existence of cognitive universals, and the helping/hindering relationship between early and later learning.

In his review of evolutionary psychology's attempts to serve as a new grand theory for the social sciences, Premack (1996) expressed the opinion that "the cutting edge of [developmental psychology] is entirely modular . . . the villains have already been met and, as much as villains can ever be, were slain." While this may be true of traditional but now empirically untenable learning theories, our impression is that many underlying tenets of Empiricism and associationist theory have survived the demise of behaviorism. Domain-general, equipotential, anti-abstract, and extreme anti-nativist sentiments are alive and well in cognitive science, particularly within many information-processing and connectionist accounts of learning. For those within these camps, therefore, our theory of concept learning still represents a difficult theory change, containing many counterintuitive aspects; all we can propose is that intuition is often a poor guide when it comes to understanding both adaptations (Dawkins, 1987) and psychological theories (Cosmides & Tooby, 1994b). This is particularly true of theories whose support derives even in part from evolutionary arguments, and which therefore commonly face what Dawkins (1987, p. 38) describes as the "Argument from Personal Incredulity." Yet unless we wish to return to Descartes' dualism, we must avoid the inconsistency of accepting adaptive evolutionary arguments for anatomical structures but rejecting them for mental structures. The brain with all its functional complexity and differentiation is a product of natural selection just like the rest of us.

So does our rational-constructivist account constitute a new grand theory of learning? We do not think so. Our attention to terminological definitions and criticisms of traditional views should not be taken as a shield which allows any criticism to be deflected as "misunderstandings." We are just beginning to draw many complementary threads together, to recognize their implications, and to attempt to weave a consistent theory of learning which fits the available evidence better than its predecessors. Our contribution is not limited to the proposal that innate

skeletal constraints enable learning in core domains; the theory itself can be seen as a skeletal structure to which we hope future accounts of learning will cohere. Much work remains to be done in order to develop the idea of mental learning tools, and our hope is that such work will prove fruitful in exploring the interactions between domain-specific and domain-general learning mechanisms. Further development of the theory must continue to rely on converging lines of evidence, based on data from infants, different cultures, animals, atypical development functions, systematic cross-task manipulations, microgenetic analyses, and theoretical predictions about the nature of variability and the role of learning environments. It also remains to be seen to what extent explanations of additional types of learning beyond concept acquisition can be accommodated by the framework: declarative fact learning, event memory, perceptual learning, implicit learning, motor skill learning, and so on.

In closing, we call attention to the scientific goal of parsimony. Learning theorists' traditional interpretation of parsimony, borrowed from physics, has always been to postulate a small set of simple and domain-general learning mechanisms which are minimally constrained by a few domain-specific preferences. We believe that the theoretical and empirical considerations which motivate our effort call for this definition of parsimony to be turned upside down. We view the mind as a collection of complex, functional, domain-specific adaptations tied together by higher-level adaptations including partially domain-general learning tools. Constraints enable learning, rather than limiting a supposedly general-purpose learning mind. Conceptual learning in core domains would be impossible were it not for the presence of domain-specific enabling constraints which solve the deep problems of selectivity and ambiguity. This view may be counterintuitive for some, but it fits well with the available evidence and with an evolutionary perspective on the origins of the mind. In this new view of parsimony, domain-general learning processes should be seen as the exception rather than the rule.

ACKNOWLEDGMENTS

The final draft of this chapter was written at New York University where Rochel Gelman was a Visiting Scholar in the Psychology Department. We thank Stephanie Reich, Randy Gallistel, and our editors, Deanna Kuhn and Robert Siegler, for their insightful comments on earlier drafts.

REFERENCES

Ahn, W., Kalish, C. W., Medin, D. L., & Gelman, S. A. (1995). The role of covariation versus mechanism information in causal attribution. *Cognition, 54,* 299–352.

Alibali, M. W., & Goldin-Meadow, S. (1993). Gesture speech mismatch and mechanisms of learning: What the hands reveal about a child's state of mind. *Cognitive Psychology, 25,* 468–523.

Anderson, J. R. (1995). *Learning and memory: An integrated approach.* New York: Wiley.

Anderson, J. R., Corbett, A. T., Koedinger, K. R., & Pelletier, R. (1995). Cognitive tutors: Lessons learned. *The Journal of the Learning Sciences, 4,* 167–207.

Andrews, F. E. (1977). *Numbers, please.* New York: Teacher's College Press, Columbia University.

Armstrong, S. L., Gleitman, L. R., & Gleitman, H. (1983). What some concepts might not be. *Cognition, 13,* 263–308.

Aronson, L. R. (1951). Further studies on orientation and jumping behavior in the gobiid fish, *Bathygobiis soporator. Annals of the New York Academy of Sciences, 188,* 378–392.

Atran, S. (1994). Core domains versus scientific theories: Evidence from systematics and Itza-Maya folkbiology. In L. A. Hirschfeld & S. A. Gelman (Eds.), *Mapping the mind: Domain specificity in cognition and culture* (pp. 316–340). New York: Cambridge University Press.

Atran, S. (1995). Causal constraints on categories and categorical constraints on biological reasoning across cultures. In D. Sperber, D. Premack, & A. J. Premack (Eds.), *Causal cognition: A multidisciplinary debate* (pp. 205–233). New York: Clarendon Press/Oxford University Press.

Au, T. Kit-Fong, & Romo, L. R. (1996). Building a coherent conception of HIV transmission: A new approach to AIDS education. In D. L. Medin (Ed.), *The psychology of learning: Advances in research and theory* (pp. 193–241). New York: Academic Press.

Au, T. Kit-Fong, Sidle, A. L., & Rollins, K. B. (1993). Developing an intuitive understanding of conservation and contamination: Invisible particles as a plausible mechanism. *Developmental Psychology, 29,* 286–299.

Bahrick, L. E., Walker, S., & Neisser, U. (1981). Selective looking by infants. *Cognitive Psychology, 13,* 377–390.

Baillargeon, R. (1986). Representing the existence and the location of hidden objects: Object permanence in 6- and 8-month-old infants. *Cognition, 23,* 21–41.

Baillargeon, R. (1995). Physical reasoning in infancy. In M. S. Gazzaniga (Ed.), *The cognitive neurosciences* (pp. 181–204). Cambridge, MA: MIT Press.

Baillargeon, R., Kotovsky, L., & Needham, A. (1995). The acquisition of physical knowledge in infancy. In D. Sperber, D. Premack, & A. J. Premack (Eds.), *Causal cognition: A multidisciplinary approach* (pp. 79–116). Oxford, England: Oxford/Clarendon Press.

Baillargeon, R., Spelke, E. S., & Wasserman, S. (1985). Object permanence in five-month-old infants. *Cognition, 20,* 191–208.

Balakrishnan, J. D., & Ashby, F. (1992). Subitizing: Magical numbers or mere superstition? *Psychological Research/Psychologische Forschung, 54,* 80–90.

Bandura, A., & Walters, R. H. (1965). *Social learning and personality development.* New York, Chicago, San Francisco, Toronto, London: Holt, Rinehart and Winston.

Banks, M. S., & Salapatek, P. (1983). Infant visual perception. In M. M. Haith & J. Campos (Eds.), *Infancy and biological development* (pp. 453–572). New York: Wiley.

Barkow, J. H., Cosmides, L., & Tooby, J. (Eds.). (1992). *The adapted mind: Evolutionary psychology and the generation of culture.* New York: Oxford University Press.

Bates, E., & Elman, J. L. (1993). Connectionism and the study of change. In M. H. Johnson (Ed.), *Brain development and cognition.* Cambridge, MA: Blackwell.

Behr, M. J., Lesh, R., Post, T. R., & Silver, E. A. (1983). Rational-number concepts. In R. Lesh & M. Landua (Eds.), *Acquisition of mathematics concepts and processes* (pp. 91–126). New York: Academic Press.

Berthental, B. I. (1993). Infants' perception of biomechanical motions: Intrinsic image and knowledge-based constraints. In C. Granrud (Ed.), *Visual perception and cognition in infancy: Carnegie Mellon symposia on cognition* (pp. 175–214). Hillsdale, NJ: Erlbaum.

Biddell, T. R., & Fischer, K. W. (1992). Cognitive development in educational contexts: Implications for skill learning. In A. Demetriou, M. Shayer, & A. Efklides (Eds.), *Neo-Piagetian theories of cognitive development* (pp. 11–31). London and New York: Routledge & Kegan Paul.

Bolles, R. C. (1970). Species-specific defense reactions and avoidance learning. *Psychological Review, 77,* 32–48.

Bolles, R. C. (1988). Nativism, naturalism, and niches. In R. C. Bolles & M. D. Beecher (Eds.), *Evolution and learning* (pp. 1–15). Hillsdale, NJ: Erlbaum.

Bornstein, M. H. (1985). Color naming versus shape naming. *Journal of Child Language, 12,* 387–393.

Boyer, P. (1995). Causal understandings in cultural representations: Cognitive constraints on inferences from cultural input. In D. Sperber, D. Premack, & A. J. Premack (Eds.), *Causal cognition: A multidisciplinary approach* (pp. 615–644). Oxford, England: Oxford/Clarendon Press.

Boysen, S. T., & Berntson, G. G. (1989). Numerical competence in a chimpanzee *(Pan troglodytes). Journal of Comparative Psychology, 103,* 23–31.

Bregman, A. S. (1990). *Auditory scene analysis: The perceptual organization of sound.* Cambridge, MA: MIT Press.

Brenneman, K., Massey, C. M., Machado, S., & Gelman, R. (1996). Notating knowledge about words and objects: Preschoolers' plans differ for "writing" and drawing. *Cognitive Development, 11,* 397–419.

Broadbent, D. A. (1958). *Perception and communication.* London: Pergamon Press.

Brown, A. L. (1990). Domain-specific principles affect learning and transfer in children. *Cognitive Science, 14,* 107–133.

Brown, A. L., Bransford, J. D., Ferrara, R. A., & Campione, J. C. (1983). Learning, remembering, and understanding. In J. H. Flavell & E. M. Markman (Eds.), *Cognitive development.* New York: Wiley.

Brown, A. L., & Campione, C. (1996). Psychological theory and the design of innovative learning environments: On procedures, principles and systems. In L. Schauble & R. Glaser (Eds.), *Contributions of instructional innovation to understanding theory* (pp. 229–270). Hillsdale, NJ: Erlbaum.

Brown, D. E. (1991). *Human universals.* Philadelphia: Temple University Press.

Brown, J. S., Collins, A., & Duguid, P. (1989). Situated cognition and the culture of learning. *Educational Researcher, 18,* 32–44.

Bruner, J. S. (1964). The course of cognitive growth. *American Psychologist, 19,* 1–15.

Bruner, J. S., Greenfield, P. M., Olver, et al. (1966). *Studies in cognitive development.* Cambridge, MA: Harvard University Press.

Bullock, M., & Gelman, R. (1979). Preschool children's assumptions about cause and effect: Temporal ordering. *Child Development, 50,* 89–96.

Bullock, M., Gelman, R., & Baillargeon, R. (1982). The development of causal reasoning. In W. J. Friedman (Ed.), *The developmental psychology of time* (pp. 209–253). New York: Academic Press.

Campione, J. C., Brown, A. L., Ferrara, R., & Bryant, N. R. (1984). The zone of proximal development: Implications for individual differences and learning. *New Directions for Child Development, 23,* 77–91.

Canfield, R. L., & Smith, E. G. (1996). Number-based expectations and sequential enumeration by 5-month-old infants. *Developmental Psychology, 32,* 269–279.

Capaldi, E. J., & Miller, D. J. (1988). Counting in rats: Its functional significance and the independent cognitive processes which comprise it. *Journal of Experimental Psychology: Animal Behavior Processes, 14,* 3–17.

Carey, S. (1985). Are children fundamentally different kinds of thinkers and learners than adults? In S. Chipman, J. Segal, & R. Glaser (Eds.), *Thinking and learning skills: Research and open questions.* Hillsdale, NJ: Erlbaum.

Carey, S. (1991). Knowledge acquisition: Enrichment or conceptual change? In S. Carey & R. Gelman (Eds.), *Epigenesis of mind: Studies in biology and cognition.* Hillsdale, NJ: Erlbaum.

Carey, S. (1995). On the origin of causal understanding. In D. Sperber, D. Premack, & A. J. Premack (Eds.), *Causal cognition: A multidisciplinary approach* (pp. 268–308). Oxford, England: Oxford/Clarendon Press.

Carey, S. (1996). Perceptual classification and expertise. In R. Gelman & T. Kit-Fong Au (Eds.), *Perceptual and cognitive development* (pp. 49–69). San Diego, CA: Academic Press.

Carey, S., & Gelman, R. (Eds.). (1991). *The epigenesis of mind: Essays on biology and cognition.* Hillsdale, NJ: Erlbaum.

Carey, S., & Spelke, E. (1994). Domain-specific knowledge and conceptual change. In L. A. Hirschfeld & S. A. Gelman (Eds.), *Mapping the mind: Domain specificity in cognition and culture* (pp. 169–200). New York: Cambridge University Press.

Case, R. (1992). Neo-Piagetian theories of intellectual development. In H. Beilin & P. B. Pufall (Eds.), *Piaget's theory: Prospects and possibilities* (pp. 21–38). Hillsdale, NJ: Erlbaum.

Catrambone, R., & Holyoak, K. (1989). Overcoming contextual limitations on problem solving transfer. *Journal of Experimental Psychology: Learning, Memory, and Cognition, 15,* 1147–1156.

Cheng, K. (1986). A purely geometric module in the rat's spatial representation. *Cognition, 23,* 149–178.

Cheng, P. W. (in press). From covariation to causation: A causal power theory. *Psychological Review, 103.*

Chi, M. T. H. (1992). Conceptual change within and across ontological categories: Examples from learning and discovery in science. In R. Giere (Ed.), *Cognitive models of science: Minnesota studies in the philosophy of science* (pp. 129–186). Minneapolis: University of Minnesota Press.

Chi, M. T. H., Feltovich, P. J., & Glaser, R. (1981). Categorization and representation of physics problems by experts and novices. *Cognitive Science, 5,* 121–152.

Chi, M. T. H., Glaser, R., & Farr, M. J. (Eds.). (1988). *The nature of expertise.* Hillsdale, NJ: Erlbaum.

Chomsky, N. (1959). Review of the book *Verbal behavior. Language, 35,* 26–58.

Chomsky, N. (1965). *Aspects of the theory of syntax.* Cambridge, MA: MIT Press.

Chomsky, N. (1972). Psychology and ideology. *Cognition, 1,* 11–46.

Clark, E. V. (1993). *The lexicon in acquisition.* Cambridge, England: Cambridge University Press.

Cole, M. (1995). Culture and cognitive development: From cross-cultural research to creating systems of cultural mediation. *Culture and Psychology, 1,* 25–54.

Cooper, R. G., Jr. (1984). Early number development: Discovering number space with addition and subtraction. In C. Sophian (Ed.), *Origins of cognitive skill* (pp. 147–192). Hillsdale, NJ: Erlbaum.

Cooper, R. G., Jr., Campbell, R. L., & Blevins, B. (1983). Numerical representation from infancy to middle childhood: What develops? In D. L. Rogers & J. A. Sloboda (Eds.), *The acquisition of symbolic skills* (pp. 523–533). New York: Plenum Press.

Cosmides, L., & Tooby, J. (1994a). Origins of domain specificity: The evolution of functional organization. In L. A. Hirschfeld & S. Gelman (Eds.), *Mapping the mind: Domain specificity in cognition and culture* (pp. 85–116). New York: Cambridge University Press.

Cosmides, L., & Tooby, J. (1994b). Beyond intuition and instinct blindness: Toward an evolutionarily rigorous cognitive science. *Cognition, 50,* 41–77.

Crump, T. (1990). *The anthropology of numbers.* Cambridge, England: Cambridge University Press.

Daly, M., & Wilson, M. (1995). Evolutionary psychology: Adaptationist, selectionist, and comparative. *Psychological Inquiry, 6,* 34–38.

Davis, H., & Pérusse, R. (1988). Numerical competence in animals: Definitional issues, current evidence, and a new research agenda. *Behavioral and Brain Sciences, 11,* 561–615.

Dawkins, R. (1982). *The extended phenotype: The long reach of the gene.* Oxford, England: Oxford University Press.

Dawkins, R. (1987). *The blind watchmaker: Why the evidence of evolution reveals a universe without design.* New York: Norton.

Dawkins, R. (1995). *River out of Eden: A Darwinian view of life.* New York: Basic Books.

Dennett, D. C. (1987). *The intentional stance.* Cambridge, MA: MIT Press.

Diamond, A. (1991). Neuropsychological insights into the meaning of object concept development. In S. Carey & R. Gelman (Eds.), *The epigenesis of mind: Essays on biology and cognition* (pp. 67–110). Hillsdale, NJ: Erlbaum.

Dickinson, J., & Dyer, F. (1996). How insects learn about the sun's course: Alternative modeling approaches. In S. Wilson & et al. (Eds.), *From animals to animats* (Vol. 4). Cambridge, MA: MIT Press.

Donaldson, M. (1978). *Children's minds.* New York: Norton.

Edgerton, R. B. (1967). *The cloak of competence: Stigma in the lives of the mentally retarded.* Berkeley: University of California Press.

Eimas, P. D. (1974). Linguistic processing of speech by young infants. In R. L. Shiefelbusch & L. L. Lloyd (Eds.), *Language perspectives: Acquisition, retardation, and intervention.* Baltimore: University Park Press.

Elman, J. (1990). Finding structure in time. *Cognitive Science, 14,* 179–211.

Flegg, G. (Ed.). (1989). *Number through the ages: Reader in the history of mathematics.* London, England: Macmillin/The Open University.

Fodor, J. A. (1972). Some reflections on L. S. Vygotsky's *Thought and language. Cognition, 1,* 83–95.

Fodor, J. A. (1975). *The language of thought.* New York: Thomas.

Fodor, J. A. (1983). *The modularity of mind.* Cambridge, MA: MIT Press.

Fodor, J. A., Garrett, M. F., Walker, E. C. T., & Parkes, C. H. (1980). Against definitions. *Cognition, 8,* 263–367.

Fodor, J. A., & Lepore, E. (1996). The red herring and the pet fish: Why concepts still can't be prototypes. *Cognition, 58,* 253–270.

Fuson, K. C. (1988). *Children's counting and concepts of number.* New York: Springer-Verlag.

Gallistel, C. R. (1985). Motivation, intention and emotion: Goal-directed behavior from a cognitive-neuroethological perspective. In M. Frese & J. Sabini (Eds.), *Goal-directed behavior: The concept of action in psychology.* Hillsdale, NJ: Erlbaum.

Gallistel, C. R. (1990). *The organization of learning.* Cambridge, MA: MIT Press.

Gallistel, C. R. (1992). Classical conditioning as an adaptive specialization: A computational model. In D. L. Medin (Ed.), *The psychology of learning and motivation: Advances in research and theory* (pp. 35–67). New York: Academic Press.

Gallistel, C. R. (1995). The replacement of general purpose theories with adaptive specializations. In M. S. Gazzaniga (Ed.), *The cognitive neurosciences* (pp. 1255–1267). Cambridge, MA: MIT Press.

Gallistel, C. R., Brown, A. L., Carey, S., Gelman, R., & Keil, F. C. (1991). Lessons from animal learning for the study of cognitive development. In S. Carey & R. Gelman (Eds.), *The epigenesis of mind: Essays on biology and cognition* (pp. 3–36). Hillsdale, NJ: Erlbaum.

Gallistel, C. R., & Gelman, R. (1990). The what and how of counting. *Cognition, 34,* 197–199.

Gallistel, C. R., & Gelman, R. (1992). Preverbal and verbal counting and computation: Numerical cognition [Special issue]. *Cognition, 44,* 43–74.

Garcia, J., & Koelling, R. (1966). Relation of cue to consequence in avoidance learning. *Psychonomic Science, 5,* 123–124.

Gardner, H. (1992). *Frames of mind*. New York: Basic Books.

Gelman, R. (1972). The nature and development of early number concepts. In H. W. Reese (Ed.), *Advances in child development* (Vol. 3.). New York: Academic Press.

Gelman, R. (1978). Cognitive development. *Annual Review of Psychology, 29,* 297–332.

Gelman, R. (1982). Basic numerical abilities. In R. J. Stemberg (Ed.), *Advances in the psychology of intelligence* (pp. 181–205). Hillsdale, NJ: Erlbaum.

Gelman, R. (1990). First principles organize attention to and learning about relevant data: Number and the animate-inanimate distinction as examples. *Cognitive Science, 14,* 79–106.

Gelman, R. (1991). Epigenetic foundations of knowledge structures: Inititial and transcendent constructions. In S. Carey & R. Gelman (Eds.), *The epigenesis of mind: Essays on biology and cognition* (pp. 293–322). Hillsdale, NJ: Erlbaum.

Gelman, R. (1993). A rational-constructivist account of early learning about numbers and objects. In D. Medin (Ed.), *Learning and motivation* (pp. 61–96). New York: Academic Press.

Gelman, R. (1994). Constructivism and supporting environments. In D. Tirosh (Ed.), *Implicit and explicit knowledge: An educational approach* (pp. 55–82). Norword, NJ: ABLEX.

Gelman, R., & Baillargeon, R. (1983). A review of some Piagetian concepts. In J. H. Flavell & E. M. Markman (Eds.), *Cognitive development* (pp. 167–230). New York: Wiley.

Gelman, R., & Brenneman, K. (1994). First principles can support both universal and culture-specific learning about number and music. In L. A. Hirschfeld & S. Gelman (Eds.), *Mapping the mind: Culture and domain-specificity* (pp. 369–390). Cambridge, England: Cambridge University Press.

Gelman R., & Brown. (1986). Changing views of cognitive competence in the young. In N. Smelser & D. Gerstein (Eds.), *Discoveries and trends in behavioral and social sciences* (pp. 175–207). Commission on Behavioral and Social Sciences and Education, Washington, DC: National Research Council Press.

Gelman, R., & Cohen, M. (1988). Qualitative differences in the way Down's Syndrome and normal children solve a novel counting problem. In L. Nadel (Ed.), *The psychobiology of Down's Syndrome* (pp. 51–99). Cambridge, MA: MIT Press.

Gelman, R., Cohen, M., & Hartnett, P. (1989). To know mathematics is to go beyond thinking that "Fractions aren't numbers." In *Psychology of mathematics education. Volume 11 of the North American Chapter of the International Group for Psychology.* Rutgers, NJ.

Gelman, R., Durgin, F., & Kaufman, L. (1995). Distinguishing between animates and inanimates: Not by motion alone. In D. Sperber, D. Premack, & A. J. Premack (Eds.), *Causal cognition: A multidisciplinary approach* (pp. 150–184). Oxford, England: Oxford/Clarendon Press.

Gelman, R., & Gallistel, C. R. (1978). *The child's understanding of number.* Cambridge, MA: Harvard University Press.

Gelman, R., & Greeno, J. G. (1989). On the nature of competence: Principles for understanding in a domain. In L. B. Resnick (Ed.), *Knowing and learning: Essays in honor of Robert Glaser* (pp. 125–186). Hillsdale, NJ: Erlbaum.

Gelman, R., & Hartnett, P. M. (in press). Early understandings of number: Paths or barriers to the construction of new understandings? *The Journal of the European Association for Learning and Instruction, 4.*

Gelman, R., & Lee Gattis, M. (1995). Trends in educational psychology in the United States. In *Recent trends and developments in educational psychology: Chinese and American perspectives.* Paris, France: UNESCO.

Gelman, R., & Massey, C. (1987). The cultural unconscious as contributor to the supporting environments for cognitive development. Commentary on Saxe, Guberman & Gearhart. *Society for Research in Child Development Monographs, 52*(2, Serial No. 216), 138–151.

Gelman, R., Massey, C., & McManus, M. (1991). Characterizing supporting environments for cognitive development: Lessons from children in a museum. In J. M. Levine & L. B. Resnick (Eds.), *Socially shared cognition* (pp. 226–256). Washington, DC: American Psychological Association.

Gelman, R., & Meck, B. (1992). Early principles aid initial but not later conceptions of number. In J. Bideaud, C. Meljac, & J. Fischer (Eds.), *Pathways to number* (pp. 171–189). Hillsdale, NJ: Erlbaum.

Gelman, R., Spelke, E. S., & Meck, B. (1983). What preschoolers know about animate and inanimate objects: Implications for research on social cognition. In D. Rogers & J. A. Sloboda (Eds.), *The acquisition of symbolic skills* (pp. 297–326). New York: Plenum Press.

Gelman, R., & Tucker, M. F. (1975). Further investigations of the young child's conception of number. *Child Development, 46,* 167–175.

Gelman, S. A., & Gottfried, A. (1996). Children's causal explanations of animate and inanimate motion. *Child Development, 67,* 1970–1987.

Gelman, S. A., & Kremer, K. E. (1991). Understanding natural cause: Children's explanations of how objects and their properties originate. *Child Development, 62,* 396–414.

Gentner, D. (1989a). Structure mapping: A theoretical framework for analogy. *Cognitive Science, 7,* 155–170.

Gentner, D. (1989b). The mechanisms of analogical learning. In S. Vosniadou & A. Ortony (Eds.), *Similarity and analogical reasoning* (pp. 199–241). New York: Cambridge University Press.

Gentner, D., Rattermann, M. J., & Forbus, K. (1993). The roles of similarity in transfer: Separating retrievability from inferential soundness. *Cognitive Science, 25,* 524–575.

Gentner, D., & Stevens, A. L. (1983). Flowing waters or teeming crowds: Mental models of electricity. In D. Gentner & A. Stevens (Eds.), *Mental models.* Hillsdale, NJ: Erlbaum.

Gibbon, J., Church, R. M., & Meck, W. H. (1984). Scalar timing in memory. In J. Gibbon & L. Allan (Eds.), *Timing and time perception* (pp. 52–77). New York: New York Academy of Sciences.

Gibson, E. J. (1984). Perceptual development from the ecological approach. In M. C. Lamb, A. L. Brown, & B. Rogoff (Eds.), *Advances in development* (pp. 243–286). Hillsdale, NJ: Erlbaum.

Gibson, E. J. (1988). Exploratory behavior in the development of perceiving, acting, and the acquiring of knowledge. In M. R. Rosenzweig & L. W. Porter (Eds.), *Annual review of psychology* (pp. 1–41). Palo Alto, CA: Annual Reviews.

Gibson, E. J., Riccio, G., Stoffregen, T. A., Rosenberg, D., & Taormina, J. (1987). Detection of the transversability of surfaces by crawling and walking infants. *Journal of Experimental Psychology: Human Perception and Performance, 13,* 533–544.

Gibson, J. J. (1966). *The senses considered as perceptual systems.* Boston, MA: Houghton Mifflin.

Gibson, J. J. (1983). Notes on affordances. In E. Reed & R. Jones (Eds.), *Reasons for realism* (pp. 401–418). Hillsdale, NJ: Erlbaum.

Gibson, J. J., & Gibson, E. J. (1955). Perceptual learning: Differentiation or enrichment? *Psychological Review, 62,* 32–41.

Gluck, M., & Bower, G. (1988). Evaluating an adaptive network model of human learning. *Journal of Memory and Language, 27,* 166–95.

Gobbo, C., & Chi, M. (1986). How knowledge is structured and used by expert and novice children. *Cognitive Development, 1,* 221–237.

Gold, E. M. (1967). Language identification in the limit. *Information and Control, 16,* 447–474.

Golinkoff, R. M., & Harding, C. G. (1980). Infants' expectations of the movement potential of inanimate objects. In *International Conference on Infant Studies.* New Haven, CT.

Goodman, N. (1972). *Fact, fiction, and forecast* (3rd ed.). Indianapolis, IN: Bobbs-Merrill.

Gopnik, A., & Wellman, H. M. (1994). The theory theory. In L. A. Hirschfeld & S. Gelman (Eds.), *Mapping the mind: Domain specificity in cognition and culture* (pp. 257–293). New York: Cambridge University Press.

Goswami, U., & Brown, A. (1990). Melting chocolate and melting snowmen: Analogical reasoning and causal relations. *Cognition, 35,* 69–95.

Gottlieb, G. I. E. (1983). The psychobiological approach to developmental issues. In M. M. Haith & J. J. Campos (Eds.), *Infancy and developmental psychobiology* (pp. 1–26). New York: Wiley.

Gould, J. L., & Marler, P. (1987). Learning by instinct. *Scientific American, 256,* 74–85.

Gould, S. J. (1991). Exaptation: A crucial tool for an evolutionary psychology. *Journal of Social Issues, 47*(3), 43–65.

Gould, S. J., & Lewontin, R. (1979). The spandrels of San Marco and the Panglossian program: A critique of the adaptationist programme. *Proceedings of the Royal Society of London, 250,* 281–288.

Greenfield, P. M. (1993). International roots of minority child development: Introduction to the special issue. *International Journal of Behavioral Development, 16*(3), 385–394.

Greeno, J. G., Smith, D. R., & Moore, J. L. (1992). Transfer of situated learning. In D. Detterman & R. J. Sternberg (Eds.), *Transfer on trial: Intelligence, cognition, and instruction.* Norwood, NJ: ABLEX.

Grice, H. P. (1975). Logic and conversation. In P. Cole & J. Morgan (Eds.), *Syntax and semantics: 3. Speech acts.* New York: Academic Press.

Groen, G. J., & Resnick, L. B. (1977). Can preschool children invent addition algorithms? *Journal of Educational Psychology, 69,* 645–652.

Haith, M. (1980). *Rules that babies look by.* Hillsdale, NJ: Erlbaum.

Halford, G. S. (1987). A structure-mapping approach to cognitive development: The neo-piagetian theories of cognitive development; toward and integration [Special issue]. *International Journal of Psychology, 22,* 609–642.

Halford, G. S. (1990). Is children's reasoning logical or analogical? Further comments on Piagetian cognitive developmental psychology. *Human Development, 33*(6), 356–361.

Halford, G. S. (1993). *Children's understanding: The development of mental models.* Hillsdale, NJ: Erlbaum.

Halford, G. S., & Wilson, W. H. (1980). A category theory approach to cognitive development. *Cognitive Psychology, 12,* 356–411.

Hallpike, C. R. (1979). *The foundations of primitive thought.* Oxford, England: Clarendon Press.

Hardiman, P. T., Dufresne, R., & Mestre, J. P. (1989). The relation between problem categorization and problem solving among experts and novices. *Memory and Cognition, 17,* 627–638.

Hartnett, P. M. (1991) *The development of mathematical insight: From one, two, three to infinity.* Doctoral dissertation, University of Pennsylvania.

Hartnett, P. M., & Gelman, R. (in press). Early understandings of number: Paths or barriers to the construction of new understandings? *The Journal of the European Association for Learning and Instruction, 4.*

Hasher, L., & Zacks, R. T. (1979). Automatic and effortful processes in memory. *Journal of Experimental Psychology, 108,* 356–388.

Hasher, L., & Zacks, R. T. (1984). Automatic processing of fundamental information: The case of frequency of occurrence. *American Psychologist, 39,* 1372–1388.

Held, R. (1993). What can rates of development tell us about underlying mechanisms? In C. Granrud (Ed.), *Visual perception and cognition in infancy: Carnegie Mellon symposia on cognition* (pp. 75–89). Hillsdale, NJ: Erlbaum.

Hermer, L., & Spelke, E. S. (1994). A geometric process for spatial reorientation in young children. *Nature, 370,* 57–59.

Hinde, R. A., & Stevenson-Hinde, J. S. (Eds.). (1973). *Constraints on learning.* New York: Academic Press.

Hirschfeld, L. A. (1996). *Race in the making.* Cambridge, MA: MIT Press.

Hirschfeld, L. A., & Gelman, S. A. (Eds.). (1994). *Mapping the mind: Domain specificity in cognition and culture.* New York: Cambridge University Press.

Holyoak, K., & Thagard, P. (1995). *Mental leaps: Analogy in creative thought.* Cambridge, MA: MIT Press.

Hull, C. L. (1952). *A behavior system.* New Haven, CT: Yale University Press.

Hurford, J. R. (1987). *Language and number.* Cambridge, England: Cambridge University Press.

Ifrah, G. (1985). *From one to zero.* New York: Viking.

Inagaki, K., & Hatano, G. (1987). Young children's spontaneous personification as analogy. *Child Development, 58,* 1013–1020.

Inhelder, B., & Piaget, J. (1956). *The growth of logical thinking from childhood to adolescence.* New York: Basic Books.

Inhelder, B., & Piaget, J. (1964). *The early growth of logic in the child.* New York: Harper & Row.

Jeyifous, S. W. (1986). *Altimodemo: Semantic conceptual development among the Yoruba.* Doctoral dissertation, Cornell University, Ithaca, NY.

Johnson, M. H., & Gilmore, R. O. (1996). Developmental cognitive science: A biological perspective on cognitive change. In R. Gelman & T. Kit-Fong Au (Eds.), *Perceptual and cognitive development: Handbook of perception and cognition* (pp. 333–372). San Diego, CA: Academic Press.

Johnson, M. H., & Morton, J. (1991). *Biology and cognitive development: The case of face recognition.* Cambridge, England: Blackwell.

Johnson, J. S., & Newport, E. L. (1991). Critical period effects on universal properties of language: The status of subjacency in the acquisition of a second language. *Cognition, 39,* 215–258.

Kail, R., & Bisanz, J. (1992). The information-processing perspective on cognitive development. In R. J. Sternberg & C. A. Berg (Eds.), *Intellectual development.* New York: Cambridge University Press.

Kalnins, I. V., & Bruner, J. S. (1973). The coordination of visual observation and instrumental behavior in early infancy. *Perception, 2,* 307–314.

Karmiloff-Smith, A. (1992). *Beyond modularity: A developmental perspective on cognitive science.* Cambridge, MA: MIT Press.

Karmiloff-Smith, A., & Inhelder, B. (1974–1975). If you want to get ahead, get a theory. *Cognition, 3,* 195–212.

Kehoe, E. J. (1988). A layered network model of associative learning: Learning to learn and configuration. *Psychological Review, 95,* 411–433.

Keil, F. C. (1981). Constraints on knowledge and cognitive development. *Psychological Review, 88,* 197–227.

Keil, F. C. (1989). *Concepts, kinds, and cognitive development.* Cambridge, MA: MIT.

Keil, F. C. (1990). Constraints on constraints. Surveying the epigenetic landscape. *Cognitive Science, 14,* 135–168.

Keil, F. C. (1994). The birth and nurturance of concepts by domains: The origins of concepts of living things. In L. A. Hirschfeld & S. Gelman (Eds.), *Mapping the mind: Domain specificity in cognition and culture* (pp. 234–254). Cambridge, England: Cambridge University Press.

Keil, F. C. (1995). The growth of causal understandings of natural kinds. In D. Sperber, D. P. Premack, & A. J. Premack (Eds.), *Causal cognition: A multidisciplinary approach* (pp. 234–267). Oxford, England: Oxford/Clarendon Press.

Kellman, P. (1996). The origins of object perception. In R. Gelman & T. Kit-Fong Au (Eds.), *Perceptual and cognitive development* (pp. 3–48). New York: Academic Press.

Kemler, D. (1983). Holistic and analytic modes in perceptual and cognitive development. In T. Tighe & B. E. Shepp (Eds.), *Perception, cognition, and development: Interactional analyses.* Hillsdale, NJ: Erlbaum.

Kitcher, P. (1982). *The nature of mathematical knowledge.* New York: Oxford University Press.

Klahr, D., & Wallace, J. G. (1973). The role of quantification operators in the development of conservation of quantity. *Cognitive Psychology, 4,* 301–327.

Koslowski, B. (1996). *The development of scientific reasoning.* Cambridge, MA: MIT Press.

Koslowski, B., Spilton, D., & Snipper, A. (1981). Children's beliefs about instances of mechanical and electrical causation. *Journal of Applied Developmental Psychology, 2,* 189–210.

Koslowski, B., & Winsor, A. P. (1981). *Preschool children's spontaneous explanations and requests for explanations: A non-human application of the child-as-scientist metaphor.* Unpublished manuscript, Department of Human Development, Cornell University, Ithaca, NY.

Kuhn, D. (1996). *Microgenetic study of change. What has it told us?* Unpublished manuscript, Psychology, Teacher's College, Columbia University, New York.

Kuhn, D., Garcia-Mila, M., Zohar, A., & Andersen, C. (1995). Strategies of knowledge acquisition. *Monographs of the Society for Research in Child Development, 60*(4, Serial No. 241), 1–158.

Kuhn, T. S. (1970). *The structure of scientific resolutions* (2nd ed.). Chicago: University of Chicago Press.

Lakatos, I. (1970). Falsification and the methodology of scientific research programmes. In I. Lakatos & A. Musgrave (Eds.), *Criticism and the growth of knowledge* (pp. 91–196). Cambridge, England: Cambridge University Press.

Lampert, M. (1986). Knowing, doing, and teaching multiplication. *Cognition and Instruction, 3,* 305–342.

Landau, B., & Gleitman, L. (1985). *Language and experience: Evidence from the blind child.* Cambridge, MA: Harvard University Press.

Larkin, J. H., McDermott, J., Simon, D., & Simon, H. A. (1980). Models of competence in solving physics problems. *Cognitive Science, 4,* 317–345.

Lave, J., & Wenger, E. (1991). *Situated learning: Legitimate peripheral participation.* Cambridge, MA: Cambridge University Press.

Lee, K., & Karmiloff-Smith, A. (1996). The development of external symbol systems: The child as a notator. In R. Gelman & T. Kit-Fong Au (Eds.), *Perceptual and cognitive development* (pp. 185–211). San Diego, CA: Academic Press.

Lehrman, D. S. (1970). Semantic and conceptual issues in the nature–nurture problem. In L. Aaronson, E. Tobach, D. S. Lehrman, & J. S. Rosenblatt (Eds.), *Development and evolution of behavior: Essays in memory of T. C. Schneirla* (pp. 17–24). San Francisco: Freeman.

Leinhardt, G., Putnam, R., & Harttrup, R. A. (Eds.). (1992). *Analysis of arithmetic for mathematics teaching.* Hillsdale, NJ: Erlbaum.

Leslie, A. M. (1988). Some implications of pretense for mechanisms underlying the child's theory of mind. In J. W. Astington, P. L. Harris, & D. R. Olson (Eds.), *Developing theories of mind* (pp. 19–46). Cambridge, England: Cambridge University Press.

Leslie, A. M. (1994a). Pretending and believing: Issues in the theory of ToMM. *Cognition, 50,* 211–238.

Leslie, A. M. (1994b). ToMM, ToBy, and Agency: Core architecture and domain specificity. In L. A. Hirschfeld & S. Gelman (Eds.), *Mapping the mind: Domain specificity in cognition and culture* (pp. 119–148). New York: Cambridge University Press.

Leslie, A. M. (1995). A theory of agency. In D. Sperber, D. Premack, & A. J. Premack (Eds.), *Causal cognition: A multidisciplinary approach* (pp. 121–141). Oxford, England: Oxford/Clarendon Press.

Leslie, M., & Keeble, S. (1987). Do six-month-old infants perceive causality? *Cognition, 25,* 265–288.

Locke, J. (1690). *An essay concerning human understanding.*

Loftus, E. F. (1991). Made in memory: Distortions in recollection after misleading information. In G. H. Bower (Ed.), *The psychology of learning and motivation: Advances in research and theory* (Vol. 27, pp. 187–215). San Diego, CA: Academic Press.

Lorenz, K. (1966). *Evolution and modification of behavior.* London: Methuen.

Macario, J. F. (1991). Young children's use of color and classification: Foods and canonically colored objects. *Cognitive Development, 6,* 17–46.

Mandler, J. M. (1996). Development of categorization: Perceptual and conceptual categories. In G. Bremner, A. Slater, & G. Butterworth (Eds.), *Infant development: Recent advances.* Hove, England: Erlbaum.

Mandler, J. M., & McDonough, L. (1993). Concept formation in infancy. *Cognitive Development, 8,* 291–318.

Mandler, J. M., & McDonough, L. (1996). Drinking and driving don't mix: Inductive generalization in infancy. *Cognition, 59,* 307–335.

Mandler, J. M., & Orlich, F. (1993). Analogical transfer: The roles of schema abstraction and awareness. *Bulletin of the Psychonomic Society, 31,* 485–487.

Marcus, G. F. (1996). Why do children say "breaked"? *Current Directions in Psychological Science, 5*(3), 81–85.

Marcus, G. F., Pinker, S., Ullman, M., Hollander, M., Rosen, T. J., & Xu, F. (1992). Over regularization in language acquisition. *Monographs of the Society for Research in Child Development, 57*(4, Serial No. 228), 1–182.

Markman, E. M. (1989). *Categorization and naming in children.* Cambridge, MA: MIT Press.

Marler, P. (1991). The instinct to learn. In S. Carey & R. Gelman (Eds.), *The epigenesis of mind* (pp. 37–66). Hillsdale, NJ: Erlbaum.

Massey, C. M. (1989). The development of the animate-inanimate distinction in preschoolers. *Dissertation Abstracts International, 50*(n2-B), 766.

Massey, C. M., & Gelman, R. (1988). Preschoolers decide whether pictured unfamiliar objects can move themselves. *Developmental Psychology, 24,* 307–317.

Mayr, E. (1983). How to carry out the adaptationist program. *The American Naturalist, 121,* 324–334.

McCleish, J. (1992). *The history of numbers and how they shape our lives.* New York: Fawcette Columbine.

McClelland, J., & Rumelhart, D. (1986). *Parallel distributed processing* (Vol. 2). Cambridge, MA: MIT Press.

McCloskey, M., & Cohen, N. J. (1989). Catastrophic interference in connectionist networks: The sequential learning problem. In G. H. Bower (Ed.), *The psychology of learning and motivation* (pp. 109–165). New York: Academic Press.

McShane, J. (1991). *Cognitive development: An information process approach.* Cambridge, MA: Basil Blackwell.

Meck, W. H., & Church, R. M. (1984). The numerical attribute of stimuli. In H. L. Roitblatt, T. G. Bever, & H. S. Terrace (Eds.), *Animal cognition* (pp. 445–464). Hillsdale, NJ: Erlbaum.

Medin, D. L. (1989). Concepts and conceptual structure. *American Psychologist, 44,* 1469–1489.

Medin, D. L., Goldstone, R. L., & Gentner, D. (1993). Respects for similarity. *Psychological Review, 100,* 254–278.

Mehler, J., & Christophe, A. (1995). Maturation and learning of language in the first year of life. In M. S. Gazzaniga (Ed.), *The cognitive neurosciences* (pp. 943–954). Cambridge, MA: MIT Press.

Miller, K. F. (1996). Origins of quantitative competence. In R. Gelman & T. Kit-Fong Au (Eds.), *Perceptual and cognitive development* (pp. 213–241). San Diego, CA: Academic Press.

Miller, K. F., Smith, C. M., Zhu, J., & Zhang, H. (1995). Preschool origins of cross-national differences in mathematical competence: The role of number-naming systems. *Psychological Science, 6,* 56–60.

Miller, N. E., & Dollard, J. (1941). *Social learning and imitation.* New Haven, CT: Yale University Press.

Morris, R. G. M. (1981). Spatial localization does not require the presence of local cues. *Learning and Motivation, 12,* 239–260.

Needham, A., & Baillargeon, R. (1993). Intuitions about support in 4.5-month-old infants. *Cognition, 47,* 121–148.

Neisser, U. (1966). *Cognitive psychology.* New York: Appleton-Century-Crofts.

Neisser, U., & Becklen, R. (1975). Selective looking: Attending to visually specified events. *Cognitive Psychology, 7,* 480–494.

Nelson, D. A., & Marler, P. (1993). Innate recognition of song in white-crowned sparrows: A role in selective vocal learning? *Animal Behaviour, 46,* 806–808.

Nelson, K. (1978). How children represent knowledge of their world in and out of language: A preliminary report. In R. S. Siegler (Ed.), *Children's thinking: What develops?* Hillsdale, NJ: Erlbaum.

Nelson, K. (1987). Nativist and functionalist views of cognitive development: Reflections on Keil's review of "Making sense: The acquisition of shared meaning." *Cognitive Development, 2,* 237–247.

Nelson, K. (1988). Constraints on word learning? *Cognitive Development, 3,* 221–246.

Nesher, P., & Sukenik, M. (1991). The effects of formal representation on the learning of rational concepts. *Learning and Instruction, 1,* 161–175.

Newell, A., Simon, H. A., & Shaw, (1958). Elements of a theory of human problem solving. *Psychological Review, 65,* 151–166.

Newport, E. L. (1990). Maturational constraints on language learning. *Cognitive Science, 14,* 11–28.

Newport, E. L., & Supalla, T. (1990). *A critical period effect in the acquisition of a primary language.* Unpublished manuscript, University of Rochester, Rochester, NY.

Nunes, T., & Bryant, P. (1996). *Children doing mathematics.* Cambridge, MA: Blackwell.

Nunes, T., Schliemann, A. D., & Carraher, D. W. (1993). *Street mathematics and school mathematics.* Cambridge, England: Cambridge University Press.

Ornstein, P. A., & Naus, M. J. (1978). Rehearsal processes in children's memory. In P. A. Ornstein (Ed.), *Memory development in children.* Hillsdale, NJ: Erlbaum.

Osherson, D. N., Stob, M., & Weinstein, S. (1986). *Systems that learn: An introduction to learning theory for cognitive and computer scientists.* Cambridge, MA: MIT Press.

Parisi, D. (1996). Computational models of developmental mechanisms. In R. Gelman & T. Kit-Fong Au (Eds.), *Perceptual and cognitive development* (pp. 373–412). San Diego, CA: Academic Press.

Pearce, J. M. (1994). Discrimination and categorization. In N. J. Mackintosh (Ed.), *Animal learning and cognition: Handbook of perception and cognition* (2nd ed., pp. 109–134). San Diego, CA: Academic Press.

Pepperberg, I. M. (1987). Evidence for conceptual quantitative abilities in the African grey parrot: Labeling of cardinal sets. *Ethology, 75,* 37–61.

Piaget, J. (1929). *The child's conception of the world.* London, England: Routledge & Kegan Paul.

Piaget, J. (1952). *The child's conception of number.* London, England: Routledge & Kegan Paul.

Piaget, J. (1970). Piaget's theory. In P. H. Mussen (Ed.), *Carmichael's manual of child psychology*. New York: Wiley.

Piaget, J. (1971). *Biology and knowledge*. Chicago: University of Chicago Press.

Piaget, J., & Inhelder, B. (1956). *The growth of logical thought*. London, England: Routledge & Kegan Paul.

Piattelli-Palmarini, M. (1989). Evolution, selection, and cognition: From "learning" to parameter setting in biology and in the study of language. *Cognition, 31*, 1–44.

Pinker, S. (1991). Rules of language. *Science, 253*, 530–544.

Platt, J. R., & Johnson, D. M. (1971). Localization of position within a homogeneous behavior chain: Effects of error contingencies. *Learning and Motivation, 2*, 386–414.

Poulin-Dubois, D., & Shultz, T. (1989). The infant's concept of agency: The distinction between social and nonsocial objects. *Journal of Genetic Psychology, 151*(1), 77–90.

Premack, D. (1990). The infant's theory of self-propelled objects. *Cognition, 36*, 1–16.

Premack, D. (1996). Piggyback with Darwin. *Contemporary Psychology, 41*, 207–212.

Premack, D., & Premack, A. J. (1995). Intention as psychological cause. In D. Sperber, D. Premack, & A. J. Premack (Eds.), *Causal cognition: A multidisciplinary debate* (pp. 185–199). New York: Clarendon Press/Oxford University Press.

Quine, Q. V. (1960). *Word and object*. Cambridge, MA: MIT Press.

Rabinowicz, T. (1979). The differentiate maturation of the human cerebral cortex. In F. Falkner & J. M. Tanner (Eds.), *Human growth: Vol. 3. Neurobiology and nutrition*. New York: Plenum Press.

Ramachandran, V. S. (1988). Perception of shape from shading. *Nature, 331*, 163–166.

Reed, H. J., & Lave, J. (1979). Arithmetic as a tool for investigating relations between culture and cognition. *American Ethnologist, 6*, 568–582.

Resnick, L. B. (1989). Developing mathematical knowledge. *American Psychologist, 44*, 162–169.

Resnick, L. B. (1994). Performance puzzles: Educational reform through national standards and assessment [Special issue]. *American Journal of Education, 102*, 511–526.

Rilling, M. (1967). Number of responses as a stimulus in fixed interval and fixed ratio schedules. *Journal of Comparative and Physiological Psychology, 63*, 60–65.

Rogoff, B., & Chavayah, P. (1995). What's become of research on the cultural basis of cognitive development? *American Psychologist, 50*, 859–877.

Rogoff, B., & Lave, J. (1984). *Everyday cognition: Its development in social context*. Cambridge, MA: Harvard University Press.

Rosch, E. H., Mervis, C. B., Gray, W. D., Boyes-Braem, P., & Johnson, D. N. (1976). Basic objects in natural categories. *Cognitive Psychology, 8*, 382–439.

Rosser, R. (1991). *Cognitive development: Psychological and biological perspectives*. Boston: Allyn & Bacon.

Rovee-Collier, C., & Bhatt, R. S. (1993). Evidence of long-term memory in infancy. In R. Vasta (Ed.), *Annals of child development* (pp. 1–45). London, England: Jessica Kingsley.

Rozin, P. (1976). The evolution of intelligence and access to the cognitive unconscious. In J. A. Sprague & A. N. Epstein (Eds.), *Progress in psychobiology and physiological psychology* (pp. 245–280). New York: Academic Press.

Rozin, P., & Kalat, J. W. (1971). Specific hungers and poison avoidance as adaptive specializations of learning. *Psychological Review, 78*, 459–486.

Rozin, P., & Schull, J. (1988). The adaptive-evolutionary point of view in experimental psychology. In R. C. Atkinson, R. J. Herrnstein, G. Lindzey, & R. D. Luce (Eds.), *Learning and cognition* (pp. 503–546). New York: Wiley.

Rumelhart, D. E., & McClelland, J. L. (Eds.). (1986). *Parallel distributed processing*. Cambridge, MA: MIT Press.

Saffran, J. R., Aslin, R. N., & Newport, E. L. (1996). Statistical learning by 8-month-old infants. *Science, 274*, 1926–1928.

Saxe, G. B. (1979). Developmental relations between notational counting and number conservation. *Child Development, 50*, 180–187.

Saxe, G. B. (1981). Body parts as numerals: A developmental analysis of numeration among the Oksapmin in Papua, New Guinea. *Child Development, 52*, 306–316.

Saxe, G. B. (1990). *Culture and cognitive development: Studies in mathematical understanding*. Hillsdale, NJ: Erlbaum.

Scarr, S. (1993). Genes, experience, and development. In D. Magnusson, P. Jules, & M. Casaer (Eds.), *Longitudinal research on individual development: Present status and future perspectives. European network on longitudinal studies on individual development* (pp. 26–50). Cambridge, England: Cambridge University Press.

Schieffelin, B. B., & Ochs, E. (1986). Language socialization. *Annual Review of Anthropology, 15*.

Schwartz, B., & Reisberg, D. (1991). *Learning and memory*. New York: Norton.

Shatz, M. (1978). The relationship between cognitive processes and the development of communication skills. In C. B. Keasey (Ed.), *Nebraska Symposium on Motivation* (pp. 1–42). Lincoln: University of Nebraska Press.

Shatz, M., & Backscheider, A. (1991, November). *Acquiring the normative concepts of color and number*. Presented at the meeting of the Psychonomic Society, Seattle, WA.

Shepard, R. N. (1987). Evolution of a mesh between principles of the mind and regularities of the world. In J. Dupré (Ed.), *The latest on the best: Essays on evolution and optimality.* Cambridge, MA: MIT Press.

Shepard, R. N. (1994). Perceptual-cognitive universals as reflections of the world. *Psychonomic Bulletin and Review, 1,* 2–28.

Shettleworth, S. J. (1993). Varieties of learning and memory in animals. *Journal of Experimental Psychology: Animal Behavior Processes, 19,* 5–14.

Siegal, M. (1991). *Knowing children: Experiments in conversations and cognition.* Hove and London, England: Erlbaum.

Siegal, M. (1995). Becoming mindful of food and conservation. *Current Directions, 4,* 177–181.

Siegal, M. (1996). Conversation and cognition. In R. Gelman & T. Kit-Fong Au (Eds.), *Perceptual and cognitive development* (pp. 185–211). San Diego, CA: Academic Press.

Siegler, R. S. (1983). Information processing approaches to cognitive development. In W. Kessen (Ed.), *History, theory and methods.* New York: Wiley.

Siegler, R. S. (1991). *Children's thinking* (2nd ed.). Englewood Cliffs, NJ: Prentice-Hall.

Siegler, R. S. (1995). How does change occur: A microgenetic study of number conservation. *Cognitive Science, 28,* 225–273.

Siegler, R. S., & Crowley, K. (1991). The microgenetic method: A direct means for studying cognitive development. *American Psychologist, 46,* 606–620.

Siegler, R. S., & Crowley, K. (1994). Constraints on learning in nonprivileged domains. *Cognitive Psychology, 27,* 194–226.

Siegler, R. S., & Robinson, M. (1982). The development of numerical understanding. In H. W. Reese & L. P. Lipsitt (Eds.), *Advances in child development and behavior.* New York: Academic Press.

Siegler, R. S., & Shipley, C. (1995). Variation, selection, and cognitive change. In T. Simon & G. Halford (Eds.), *Developing cognitive competence: New approaches to process modeling* (pp. 31–76). Hillsdale, NJ: Erlbaum.

Silver, E. A., Mamona-Downs, J., Leung, S. S., & Kenny, P. A. (1996). Posing mathematical problems: An exploratory study. *Journal for Research in Mathematics Education, 27,* 293–309.

Simon, D. P., & Simon, H. A. (1978). Individual differences in solving physics problems. In R. S. Siegler (Ed.), *Children's thinking: What develops?* Hillsdale, NJ: Erlbaum.

Simon, H. A. (1972). On the development of the processor. In S. Farnham-Diggory (Ed.), *Information processing in children.* New York: Academic Press.

Simon, H. A. (1981). *The sciences of the artificial.* Cambridge, MA: MIT Press.

Simon, T. J., & Klahr, D. (1995). A computational theory of children's learning about conservation. In T. J. Simon & G. S. Halford (Eds.), *Developing cognitive competence: New approaches to process modeling* (pp. 315–354). Hillsdale, NJ: Erlbaum.

Simons, D. J., & Keil, F. C. (1995). An abstract to concrete shift in the development of biological thought: The insides story. *Cognition, 56,* 129–163.

Skinner, B. F. (1938). *The behavior of organisms.* New York: Appleton-Century-Crofts.

Skinner, B. F. (1950). Are theories of learning necessary? *Psychological Review, 57,* 193–216.

Slotta, J. D., & Chi, M. T. H. (1996). *Understanding constraint-based processes: A precursor to conceptual change in physics.* Cognitive Science Society. La Jolla, CA: Erlbaum.

Slotta, J. D., Chi, M. T. H., & Joram, E. (1995). Assessing students' misclassifications of physics concepts: An ontological basis for conceptual change. *Cognition and Instruction, 1*(3), 373–400.

Sophian, C. (1994). *Children's numbers.* Madison, WI: WCB Brown & Benchmark.

Sophian, C., & Adams, N. (1987). Infants' understanding of numerical transformations. *British Journal of Developmental Psychology, 5,* 257–264.

Spelke, E. S. (1990). Principles of object perception. *Cognitive Science, 14,* 29–56.

Spelke, E. S. (1991). Physical knowledge in infancy: Reflections on Piaget's theory. In S. Carey & R. Gelman (Eds.), *The epigenesis of mind: Essays on biology and cognition. The Jean Piaget Symposium series* (pp. 133–169). Hillsdale, NJ: Erlbaum.

Spelke, E. S., & Hermer, L. (1995). Early cognitive development: Objects and space. In R. Gelman & T. Kit-Fong Au (Eds.), *Perceptual and cognitive development* (pp. 72–114). San Diego, CA: Academic Press.

Spelke, E. S., Phillips, A., & Woodward, A. L. (1995). Infants' knowledge of object motion and human action. In D. Sperber, D. P. Premack, & A. J. Premack (Eds.), *Causal cognition: A multidisciplinary debate* (pp. 44–78). Oxford, England: Clarendon Press/Oxford University Press.

Sperber, D. (1994). The modularity of thought and the epidemiology of representations. In L. A. Hirschfeld & S. A. Gelman (Eds.), *Mapping the mind: Domain specificity in cognition and culture* (pp. 39–67). New York: Cambridge University Press.

Sperber, D., Premack, D., & A. J. Premack (Eds.). (1995). *Causal cognition: A multidisciplinary approach.* Oxford, England: Clarendon Press/Oxford University Press.

Starkey, P., & Cooper, R. G. (1995). The development of subitizing in young children. *British Journal of Developmental Psychology, 13,* 399–420.

Starkey, P., & Gelman, R. (1982). The development of addition and subtraction abilities prior to formal schooling. In T. P.

Carpenter, J. M. Moser, & T. A. Romberg (Eds.), *Addition and subtraction: A developmental perspective.* Hillsdale, NJ: Erlbaum.

Starkey, P., Spelke, E. S., & Gelman, R. (1990). Numerical abstraction by human infants. *Cognition, 36,* 97–127.

Stern, D. (1977). *The first relationship: Infant and mother.* Cambridge, MA: Harvard University Press.

Stevenson, H. W., Lee, S. L., & Stigler, J. W. (1986). Mathematics achievement of Chinese, Japanese, and American children. *Science, 231,* 693–699.

Stevenson, H. W., & Stigler, J. W. (1992). *The learning gap.* New York: Summit Books.

Stigler, J. W., & Fernandez, C. (1995). Learning mathematics from classroom instruction: Cross-cultural and experimental perspectives. In C. A. Nelson (Ed.), *Basic and applied perspectives on learning, cognition, and development. The Minnesota Symposia on Child Psychology* (Vol. 28, pp. 103–130). Mahwah, NJ: Erlbaum.

Symons, D. (1990). Adaptiveness and adaptation. *Ethology & Sociobiology, 11,* 427–444.

Thorndike, E. L. (1913). *Educational psychology.* New York: Teacher's College, Columbia University.

Thurlow, M. L., & Turner, J. E. (1977). Children's knowledge of money and time: Effective instruction for the mentally retarded. *Education and Training of the Mentally Retarded,* 203–212.

Tolchinsky-Landsmann, L. (1990). Early writing development: Evidence from different orthographic systems. In M. Spoolers (Ed.), *Literacy acquisition.* Norwood, NJ: ABLEX.

Tomasello, M. (1992). *First verbs: A case study of early grammatical development.* Cambridge, England: Cambridge University Press.

Tooby, J., & Cosmides, L. (1992). The psychological foundations of culture. In J. Barkow, L. Cosmides, & J. Tooby (Eds.), *The adapted mind: Evolutionary psychology and the generation of culture.* New York: Oxford University Press.

Trabasso, T., & Bower, G. H. (with Gelman, R.). (1968). *Attention in learning.* New York: Wiley.

Treisman, A. (1982). Perceptual grouping and attention in visual search for features and for objects. *Journal of Experimental Psychology: Human Perception and Performance, 8,* 194–214.

Tronick, E. Z. (1989). Emotions and emotional communication in infants. *American Psychologist, 44,* 112–119.

Tversky, A., & Kahneman, D. (1973). Availability: A heuristic for judging frequency and probability. *Cognitive Psychology, 5,* 207–232.

VanderWall, S. B. (1982). An experimental analysis of seed recovery in Clark's nutcracker. *Animal Behavior, 30,* 84–94.

Vergnaud, G. (1983). Multiplicative structures. In R. Lesh & M. Landau (Eds.), *Acquisition of mathematics concepts and processes.* New York: Academic Press.

Vosniadou, S., & Ortony, A. (1989). *Similarity and analogical reasoning.* New York: Cambridge University Press.

Vygotsky, L. S. (1962). *Thought and language.* Cambridge, MA: MIT Press.

Watson, J. B. (1913). Psychology as the behaviorist views it. *Psychological Review, 20,* 158–177.

Watson, J. S. (1987). Reactions to response-contingent stimulation in early infancy. In J. Oates & S. Sheldon (Eds.), *Cognitive development in infancy.* Hove, England: Erlbaum.

Waxman, S. (1990). Convergences between lexical and conceptual organization. In J. P. Byrnes & S. A. Gelman (Eds.), *Perspectives on language and cognition: Interrelations in development.* Cambridge, England: Cambridge University Press.

Wellman, H. M., & Gelman, S. A. (1992). Cognitive development: Foundational theories of core domains. *Annual Review of Psychology, 43,* 337–375.

White, B. Y. (1993). ThinkerTools: Causal models, conceptual change, and science education. *Cognition and Instruction, 10,* 1–100.

Williams, E. M., & Gelman, R. (1995, April). *Preschoolers' theory of action: Causal accounts of why familiar animate and inanimate objects move and stop.* Poster presented at the biennial meeting of the Society for Research in Child Development, Indianapolis, IN.

Wilson, D., & Sperber, D. (1986). *Relevance.* Oxford, England: Blackwell.

Wiser, M. (1987). Novice and historical thermal theories. In S. Strauss (Ed.), *Ontogeny, phylogeny, and the history of science.* Norwood, NJ: ABLEX.

Wittgenstein, L. (1953). *Philosophical investigations.* New York: Macmillan.

Wynn, K. (1990). Children's understanding of counting. *Cognition, 36,* 155–193.

Wynn, K. (1992). Addition and subtraction by human infants. *Nature, 358,* 749–750.

Wynn, K. (1995). Infants possess a system of numerical knowledge. *Current Directions in Psychological Science, 4,* 172–177.

Wynn, K. (1996). Infants' individuation and enumeration of actions. *Psychological Science, 7,* 164–169.

Xu, F., & Carey, S. (1996). Infants' metaphysics: The case of numerical identity. *Cognitive Psychology, 30,* 111–153.

Young, J. Z. (1957). *The life of mammals.* Oxford, England: Oxford University Press.

Zaslavsky, C. (1973). *Africa counts.* Boston: Prindle, Wever & Schmidt.

CHAPTER 13

Information Processing

DAVID KLAHR and BRIAN MACWHINNEY

SEARCHING FOR MECHANISMS OF TRANSITION AND CHANGE

In every field of science, questions about transition and change have challenged generations of researchers. In physics, the goal is to understand the processes involved in the origin of the universe. In biology, researchers attempt to discover the processes underlying cell differentiation, growth, and death. In the field of cognitive development, the fundamental questions are about the structure and content of children's knowledge, and the nature of the transition mechanisms that allow the child to move between progressive knowledge states.

Developmentalists have long sought an adequate language for formulating these questions and for proposing

answers to them. Vygotsky (1962) viewed inner speech as a way of building temporary mental representations, but he never specified how these temporary representations could lead to long-term developmental changes. Piaget sought to explain knowledge structures and transition processes by adapting the formalisms available at the time. Using logic and mathematics, he constructed a representational system (Piaget, 1953) and from biology he borrowed the notion of assimilation and accommodation (Piaget, 1975). However, subsequent researchers have found these constructs to be exasperatingly ambiguous (Brainerd, 1978; Cohen, 1983; Klahr, 1982; Miller, 1983).

About 30 years ago, with the emergence of what came to be known as "the information processing approach" (see McCorduck, 1979; Palmer & Kimchi, 1986 for a succinct history), a new set of conceptualizations and methodologies were proposed as a means of addressing questions about cognitive development. In the past three decades, most of what has been discovered about children's thinking deals, in one way or another, with how they process information. Today, few psychologists would disagree with the

Preparation of this chapter was supported in part by a grant from the National Institute of Child Health and Human Development (R01-HD25211) to the first author and by a grant from the National Institute for Deafness and Communicative Disorders (R01-DC01903) to the second author.

claim that cognitive development involves changes in the content, structure, and processing of information.

However, beyond this diffuse consensus, there is substantial diversity in the kinds of answers that different information-processing researchers would give to more focused questions, such as: What do we mean by information and by processing? What is the stuff that gets processed? What are the characteristics of the processor? With what information and what processes is the neonate endowed? Which of these change with development? In this chapter, we focus on the way in which one particular subgroup of researchers—sometimes characterized as members of the "hard core" information-processing camp (see Klahr, 1992 for an overview)—has used computational models to suggest answers to such questions. Thus, from the very broad topic of information processing, we limit our discussion to developmentally relevant computational models of cognition and language.

First, we provide a short historical account of the emergence of computational approaches to studying cognitive development. Then we discuss three broad classes of computational models and provide a brief overview of each. Following that, we describe in depth the two most widely used types of computational models: production systems and connectionist systems. Finally, we close with a comparison of the two approaches and with some speculations about the future of computational modeling.

PRECURSORS OF COMPUTATIONAL MODELS OF DEVELOPMENT

More than 30 years ago, Herbert Simon—one of the founders of the cognitive revolution, but not a cognitive developmentalist—sketched the path that a computational approach to cognitive development might take:

> If we can construct an information-processing system with rules of behavior that lead it to behave like the dynamic system we are trying to describe, then this system is a theory of the child at one stage of the development. Having described a particular stage by a program, we would then face the task of discovering what additional information-processing mechanisms are needed to simulate developmental change—the transition from one stage to the next. That is, we would need to discover how the system could modify its own structure. Thus, the theory would have two parts—a program to describe performance at a particular stage and a learning program governing the transitions from stage to stage. (Simon, 1962, pp. 154–155)

Simon's suggestion contained two ideas that departed radically from the then-prevailing views in developmental psychology. The first idea was that cognitive theories could be stated as computer programs. These "computational models of thought," as they have come to be known, have one important property that distinguishes them from all other types of theoretical statements: They independently execute the mental processes they represent. That is, rather than leaving it to the reader to interpret a verbal description of such processes as encoding an external stimulus or searching a problem space, computational models actually do the encoding or searching. Consequently, the complex implications of multiple processes can be unambiguously derived.

The second idea in Simon's suggestion followed from the first: If different states of cognitive development could be described as programs, then the developmental process itself could also be described as a program that took the earlier program and transformed it into the later one. Such a program would have the capacity to alter and extend its own processes and structures. That is, it would be a computational model possessing some of the same self-modification capacities as the child's developing mind.

This two-step view—proposing a performance model and then seeking an independent set of "transition mechanisms" that operate on that performance model—was influential in the early years of computational modeling of cognitive development (Baylor & Gascon, 1974; Klahr & Wallace, 1976; Young, 1976) and we have included several examples of it in this chapter. However, over the years, the sharp distinction between performance models and learning models has become blurred. Today the most promising approaches are those that formulate computational models that are always undergoing self-modification, even as they perform at a given "level" or "stage."

Classes of Computational Models

It is not easy to construct computational models that achieve an appropriate balance between performance and adaptation. Consequently, two relatively distinct—and at times adversarial—approaches to computational modeling of developmental phenomena have emerged. We will describe these two broad classes of systems: production systems and connectionist systems.[1] They approach issues of performance and adaptation from different points of departure. In

---

[1] This dichotomy has also been characterized as between symbolic models (production systems) and subsymbolic (connectionist

general, production systems emphasize performance over adaptation, while connectionist systems emphasize adaptation over performance. However, as we will explain later in the chapter, the distinctions between the two approaches are diminishing as both fields devote more effort to addressing developmental issues. Most of the rest of this chapter will be aimed at clarifying and defending this assertion. In addition, we will briefly describe some computational efforts that are neither production systems nor connectionist systems.

Production Systems

One of the paradoxes of cognition is that it is simultaneously serial and parallel. Massive amounts of parallelism are manifest both deep within the system at the neural level as well as at the surface where the organism's perceptual and motor systems interact with the environment. Paradoxically, rational thought, attention, and motor acts, from speech to locomotion, require a nontrivial degree of seriality. For example, if your phone rang while you were reading this chapter, you would immediately consider what to do about it: Pick up the receiver? Let your answering machine screen the call? Ask someone else to answer the phone? Your mind must contain some rules that can respond to this kind of unexpected input, while at the same time containing other rules that enable you to systematically and sequentially scan the page from left to right and top to bottom (with necessary regressions) while reading. What kind of processing system can account for these phenomena? Production-systems models of cognition were invented as a response to this challenge (Newell & Simon, 1972).

Production systems are a class of computational models consisting of two interacting data structures:

1. A *working memory* consisting of a collection of symbol structures called working memory *elements*.
2. A *production memory* consisting of condition-action rules called *productions,* whose conditions describe configurations of working memory elements and whose actions specify modifications to the contents of working memory.

Production memory and working memory are related through the *recognize-act* cycle, which consists of three distinct processes:

1. The *recognition* (or matching) process finds productions whose conditions match against the current state of working memory. Because the components of a production's conditions are usually stated as variables, a given production may match against working memory in different ways, and each such mapping is called an instantiation. Moreover, several different productions may be instantiated (or satisfied) at once.
2. The *conflict resolution* process determines which instantiated productions will be applied (or fired).
3. The *act* process applies the instantiated actions of the selected productions. Actions can include the modification of the contents of working memory, as well as external perceptual-motor acts.

The recognize-act process operates iteratively. As productions fire, the contents of working memory change. This leads to another recognition cycle, which leads to a different set of productions being satisfied.[2]

Production systems can be thought of as collections of complex, dynamic systems of stimulus-response (S-R) pairs. The S corresponds to the condition sides of the productions that search, in parallel, structures in working memory. The relation between the working memory of production systems and the working memory construct in experimental psychology has always been somewhat vague. Production-system working memory has been variously conceptualized as short-term memory (Waugh & Norman, 1965), M-space (Pascual-Leone, 1970), short-term plus intermediate-term memory (Bower, 1975; Hunt, 1971), the currently activated portion of long-term memory, or simply as the current state of awareness of the system. More recent models of working memory (Baddeley, 1986, 1990) are more complex than the initial "box of slots" conceptualizations. However, regardless of the mapping between these theoretical constructs and the working memory of production-system architectures, the effect of this architectural feature is clear. The immediacy and recency of information that can satisfy productions serves to maintain context, while still admitting of abrupt shifts in attention, if either internal processing or perceptual input effects relevant changes in that context. Thus, production systems

systems). The subsymbolic characterization was introduced by connectionists who view their models as explanations of the "micro-structure of cognition" (Rumelhart & McClelland, 1986).

[2] Many of the constraints implicit in this simple description have been relaxed and modified during the 20 years or so that production-system architectures have been under development. We will describe these developments in the main section on production systems.

resolve the parallel-serial paradox by providing a parallel associative recognition memory on the condition side and a serial response on the action side.

Connectionist Systems

Connectionist models share a set of assumptions about the nature of neural computation: its connectivity, its representation of knowledge, and the rules that govern learning. Connectionist systems use neither symbols nor rules to manipulate those symbols. The basic premises in these systems are inspired by our knowledge of how the brain is "wired." Connectionist systems consist of elementary nodes or units, each of which has some degree of activation. Nodes are connected to each other in such a way that active units can either excite or inhibit other units. Connectionist networks are dynamic systems that propagate activation among units until a stable state is reached. Information or knowledge is represented in the system not by any particular unit, but rather by the pattern of activation over a large set of units, any one of which may participate to some degree in representing any particular piece of knowledge. McClelland (1995, p. 158) succinctly characterizes the essence of these models:

> On this approach—also sometimes called the parallel-distributed processing or PDP approach—information processing takes place through the interactions of large numbers of simple, neuron-like processing units, arranged into modules. An active representation—such as the representation one may have of a current perceptual situation, for example, or of an appropriate overt response—is a distributed pattern of activation, over several modules, representing different aspects of the event or experience, perhaps at many levels of description. Processing in such systems occurs through the propagation of activation among the units, through weighted excitatory and inhibitory connections.

As already suggested, the knowledge in a connectionist system is stored in the connection weights: it is they that determine what representations we form when we perceive the world and what responses these representations will lead us to execute. Such knowledge has several essential characteristics: First, it is inchoate, implicit, completely opaque to verbal description. Second, even in its implicit form it is not necessarily accessible to all tasks; rather it can be used only when the units it connects are actively involved in performing the task. Third, it can approximate symbolic knowledge arbitrarily closely, but it may not; it admits of states that are cumbersome at best to describe by rules; and fourth, its acquisition can proceed gradually, through a simple, experience-driven process.

Because connectionist systems are inherently learning systems, the two-step approach (first performance models, then transition models) has not been used. Instead, designers of connectionist models have focused on models that learn continuously, and they have attempted to illustrate how different distributions of connectivity among the nodes of their networks correspond to different knowledge levels in children. The earliest applications were in the area of language acquisition, but more recent models have begun to examine conceptual development and problem solving.

Ad Hoc Models

In many cases, a researcher may have a theory about some phenomenon that is sufficiently complex that only a computational model will enable one to derive predictions from it. However, the modeler may not be prepared to make a commitment to the theoretical claims of either connectionist or production-system approaches. In such cases, one simply chooses to focus on the knowledge structures and computational processes, and employs an ad hoc computational architecture in which to formulate and run the model. This approach enables the model builder to focus on the complexities of the domain under consideration without being constrained by global architectures or particular learning algorithms. One advantage of ad hoc systems is that, because they are not constrained by global theoretical concerns, they often achieve extremely precise and fine-grained fits to empirical measures of children's performance. The disadvantages are that their range of application is relatively narrow, and their relation to the total cognitive system is not specified.

Example: A Computational Model for Children's Strategy Choice in Arithmetic. The focus of this chapter is on production systems and connectionist systems. However, in order to demonstrate the way in which computational models can enhance our understanding of developmental phenomena even when there is no strong commitment to a particular cognitive architecture, we will describe one such model.

Siegler and his colleagues have developed a series of computational models to account for children's performance on simple addition problems (Siegler & Shipley, 1995; Siegler & Shrager, 1984). The basic phenomenon is that children use a variety of strategies to solve problems such as $3 + 4$. One strategy is to simply retrieve the answer from memory. Another is to start a count at 4, and then count up 3 steps to 7. Yet another is to count on their fingers: first three fingers, then four fingers, and then to count all the extended fingers. The relation between the use of these strategies and their speed and accuracy is highly systematic. Siegler's models address two basic questions. How do each of the distinct strategies work? How do children choose among them?

The key feature in the first computational model (Siegler & Shrager, 1984) was a data structure in which, for every pair of integers, there was a distribution of associations to possible answers (both correct and incorrect). For example, the problem 3 + 5 has associated with it not only 8, but also other possible responses that might have been given in the past, just as 6, 7, and 9. The distribution of response strengths to possible answers gives each problem a characteristic shape, and these distributions can be classified along a dimension of *peakedness*. In a problem with a peaked distribution, most of the associative strength is concentrated in a single answer, ordinarily the correct answer. At the other extreme, in a *flat distribution,* associative strength is dispersed among several answers, with none of them forming a strong peak.

This data structure is then used by the model to decide whether to produce an answer through direct retrieval—with the response determined by the probability distribution associated with that problem, or via some other, more deliberate counting-based strategy. When run on a variety of data sets, the model provided an excellent fit to both speed and accuracy data from children's performance on the same type of problems that were presented to the model. In fact, it facilitated the derivation of some nonintuitive predictions about the correlation between error rates and strategy selection that were supported by the empirical results. Moreover, the model challenges the notion that metacognitive processes play a role in children's choice of addition strategies. Instead, intelligent strategy choices emerge from the application of simpler, more basic processes. This kind of "emergent property" is a particularly important feature of computational models, and we will discuss it further at the end of this introductory section.

But the model had its shortcomings. Siegler and Shipley (1995) were able to analyze its behavior with extreme precision and conclude that "it was too inflexible, too limited in its explicitness, and too dumb." Harsh words, but true. (But could one ever assess a verbally based theory with such exactness?)

In order to remedy this problem, Siegler and Shipley formulated a second computational model—the Adaptive Strategy Choice Model (ASCM). Their goal was to create a more flexible, more precise, and more intelligent model of strategy choice. In ASCM, each strategy has associated with it a database containing information about its accuracy, speed, and novelty, as well as its *projected* accuracy, speed and special features. The improved model was designed to account for variability in strategies, answers, and individual performance patterns, as well as the order in which strategies were considered. ASCM was able to make adaptive choices on novel as well as familiar problems and to make good choices among its alternative strategies.

Thus, ad hoc computational models offer theoretical advances, even though they do not entail the more global systemic assumptions of either production-system or connectionist frameworks. Indeed, in a review of over a score of computational models relevant to cognitive development, Rabinowitz, Grant, and Dingley (1987) indicate the influential role of ad hoc models. A more recent example of ad hoc computational modeling is the work on analogical reasoning described by Gentner and her colleagues (Gentner, Rattermann, Markman, & Kotovsky, 1995). However, because such models are quite diverse in the assumptions that they make, for the remainder of this chapter we will focus only on production systems and connectionist systems.

Psychological Theory and Computer Simulation

Before leaving this preliminary section, we will make a few general comments about computational modeling as a form of theory building in psychology. In particular, we want to address a common misconception about the role of the computer in psychological theory.

Critics of the hard-core information-processing approach often attribute to computational modelers the belief that the digital computer is an appropriate model for the mind. For example, Ann Brown (1982) correctly points out that "A system that cannot grow, or show adaptive modification to a changing environment, is a strange metaphor for human thought processes which are constantly changing over the life span of an individual." Although the statement clearly applies to computers, it equally clearly does *not* apply to computational models—even though they are implemented on computers. For example, we have just described how the ASCM model demonstrates adaptive change, and we will describe several other adaptive models later in this chapter.

The misattribution derives from a failure to distinguish between the theoretical content of a program that runs on a computer and the psychological relevance of the computer itself. Hard-core information-processing theories are sufficiently complex that it is necessary to run them on computers in order to explore their implications. But this does not imply that a theory bears any necessary resemblance to the computer on which it runs. Meteorologists who run computer simulations of hurricanes do not believe that the atmosphere works like a computer. Furthermore, the same theory could be implemented on computers having radically different underlying architectures and mechanisms.

Note that this distinction between computational models and computers holds not only for symbolically based simulations but also for connectionist simulations. Even such inherently parallel, highly interconnected systems sit atop computing hardware that is statically organized in a fashion bearing no relation at all to the living neural tissue that the human brain comprises.

The goal of computational approaches to cognitive development is to determine the extent to which the emergence of intelligent behavior can be accounted for by a computational system that is manifested in the physical world. Consequently, because both computers and brains are computational systems, some of the theoretical constructs and insights that have come out of computer science may be relevant for cognitive developmental theory.

One such insight is what Palmer and Kimchi (1986) call the *recursive decomposition* assumption: Any nonprimitive process can be specified more fully at a lower level by decomposing it into a set of subcomponents and specifying the temporal and informational flows among the subcomponents. This is a good example of how abstract ideas from computer science have contributed to computational models of psychological processes: "it is one of the foundation stones of computer science that a relatively small set of elementary processes suffices to produce the full generality of information processing" (Newell & Simon, 1972, p. 29). An important consequence of decomposition is that

> ... the resulting component operations are not only quantitatively simpler than the initial one, but *qualitatively different* from it.... Thus we see that higher level information-processing descriptions sometimes contain *emergent properties* that lower level descriptions do not. It is the *organization* of the system specified by the flow relations among the lower level components that gives rise to these properties. (Palmer & Kimchi, 1986, p. 52)

The importance of emergent properties cannot be overemphasized, for it provides a route to explaining how intelligence—be it in humans or machines—can be exhibited by systems comprised of unintelligent underlying components—be they synapses or silicon. Even if one defines "underlying components" at a much higher level—such as production systems or networks of activated nodes, emergent properties still emerge, for that is the nature of complex systems.

The emergent property notion provides the key to our belief that computational approaches provide a general framework, particular concepts, and formal languages that make possible the formulation of powerful theories of cognitive development. The fundamental challenge is to account for the emergence of intelligence. Intelligence must develop from the innate kernel. The intelligence in the kernel, and in its self-modification processes, will be an emergent property of the *organization* of elementary (unintelligent) mechanisms for performance, learning, and development.

In the rest of this chapter, we will first describe production systems, and their use in cognitive developmental theory. Next we will give a similar treatment to connectionist systems. Finally, we will discuss the similarities and differences between these two approaches to computational modeling, with special emphasis on issues of direct relevance to cognitive development.

PRODUCTION-SYSTEM ARCHITECTURES

"What is happening in the human head to produce human cognition?" asks John Anderson in the opening chapter of his most recent book on the ACT-R theory of human thought (Anderson, 1993). The question is as fundamental to developmentalists as it is to those who focus on adult cognition. Anderson's answer is unequivocal:

> Cognitive skills are realized by production rules. This is one of the most astounding and important discoveries in psychology and may provide a base around which to come to a general understanding of human cognition. (p. 1)

Anderson goes on to point out that

> production systems are particularly grand theories of human cognition because they are cognitive architectures ... relatively complete proposals about the structure of human cognition.... Just as an architect tries to provide a complete specification of a house (for a builder), so a ... cognitive architecture tries to provide a complete specification of a system. There is a certain abstractness in the architect's specification, however, which leaves the concrete realization to the builder. So too, there is an abstraction in a cognitive or

computer architecture. One does not specify the exact neurons in a cognitive architecture, and one does not specify the exact computing elements in a computer architecture.[3] (pp. 3–4)

In this section we describe production systems and their relevance and potential for advancing our understanding of cognitive development. Before we get to production systems, as such, a bit of preliminary work is necessary. First we discuss a few issues surrounding the notion of "symbol systems." Then we describe a cognitive architecture that represents the standard view of adult cognition that gained widespread acceptance in the 1970s and 1980s. With those preliminaries out of the way, we describe production systems proper.

Symbol Systems

Production systems represent the most elaborated and extensive examples of what has come to be called (more by its critics than its advocates) the "symbolic approach" to computational modeling of cognition and cognitive development. It is important to provide a brief introduction to the theoretical assumptions inherent in this approach. The role of symbols, symbol structures, and symbol manipulation in computational models is best described by Newell (1980). He defines a physical symbol system as one that

> Is capable of having and manipulating symbols, yet is also realizable within our physical universe . . . [This concept] has emerged from our growing experience and analysis of the computer and how to program it to perform intellectual and perceptual tasks. The notion of symbol that it defines is internal to this concept of a system. Thus, it is a hypothesis that these symbols are in fact the same symbols that we humans have and use everyday of our lives. Stated another way, the hypothesis is that humans are instances of physical symbol systems, and by virtue of this, mind enters into the physical universe. (p. 136)

Perhaps the most remarkable aspect of Newell's characterization of physical symbol systems is that it solves the venerable "mind-body problem." The essential property of

a symbol (physically represented in silicon or neurons) is that it can designate something else (represented as a symbol structure). Such symbols comprise the elementary units in *any* representation of knowledge including sensory-motor knowledge or linguistic structures. Moreover, because these representations encode information about the external physical and social world, they have a semantics as well as a syntax.

Philosophical distinctions between dense and articulated symbols (Goodman, 1968) or personal and consensual symbols (Kolers & Smythe, 1984) emphasize the likelihood of idiosyncratic symbol structures for specific individuals, and the difference between internal symbol structures and their external referents. However, they are entirely consistent with Newell's physical symbol system hypothesis.

A First-Order Cognitive Architecture

Most of the work on both symbolic and connectionist cognitive architectures has focused on adult cognition, rather than on cognitive development. Nevertheless, developmentalists interested in a variety of cognitive processes have adopted—either implicitly or explicitly—the general view of the adult information-processing system that emerged in the late 1960s and early 1970s (Atkinson & Shiffrin, 1968; Craik & Lockhart, 1972; Norman, Rumelhart, & Group, 1975). In this section, we describe a system intended to depict the essential cognitive architecture of a normal adult. This standard description includes three major architectural components:

1. Several buffers in which information from various sensory modalities remains briefly active and available for further processing—such as a visual "iconic" memory and an "acoustic buffer";

2. A limited-capacity memory (of from two to seven "chunks" of information) that can retain material for a few seconds if unrehearsed but for much longer if continually rehearsed. As noted earlier, this memory has been variously conceptualized as short-term memory, working memory, and immediate memory. In some models, these distinctions are specific and theoretically important, while in others they are indistinguishable.

3. An (effectively) unlimited, content-addressable long-term memory.

Although this characterization was inspired by, and is analogous to, the gross functional features of computer

---

[3] Anderson continues: "This abstractness even holds for connectionist models that claim to be 'neurally inspired.' Their elements are in no way to be confused with real neurons. . . . " In the final section of this chapter we will discuss this claim and others related to the neural realism of connectionist models of cognition.

architectures, it also represents an attempt to account for the plethora of empirical findings that have emerged from experimental studies of human information processing. As we have already explained, the analogy to computer architectures in no way rests on the assumption that, at more microscopic levels of underlying hardware, computers bear any resemblance to neural circuitry.

The notion of a cognitive architecture was originated by Newell (1973, 1981) and has since gone through several successive refinements. One of the most detailed is Card, Moran, and Newell's (1983) model of the human information-processing system that includes not only the gross organization of the different information stores and their connections, but also estimates of processing rates and capacities. This Model Human Processor (MHP) was designed to facilitate predictions about human behavior in a variety of situations involving interactions between humans and computers. It was based on a vast amount of empirical data on human performance in perceptual, auditory, motor, and simple cognitive tasks.

The MHP is illustrated in Figure 13.1 and its principles of operation are listed in Table 13.1. It includes a long-term memory; a working memory; two perceptual stores for visual and auditory information; and three subsystems for cognitive, motor, and perceptual processing. For each of these stores, there are associated estimates of storage capacity, decay times, cycle times, and the type of code as well as connectivity to the rest of the system.

The perceptual system consists of sensors and associated buffer memories, the most important buffer memories being a Visual Image Store and an Auditory Image Store to hold the output of the sensory system while it is being symbolically coded. The cognitive system receives symbolically coded information from the sensory image stores in its Working Memory and uses previously stored information in Long-Term Memory to make decisions about how to respond. The motor system carries out the response.

For some tasks (pressing a key in response to a light), the human must behave as a serial processor. For other tasks (typing, reading, simultaneous translation), integrated, parallel operation of the three subsystems is possible, in the manner of three pipe-lined processors: information flows continuously from input to output with a characteristically short time lag showing that all three processors are working simultaneously. The memories and processors are described by a few parameters. The most important parameters of a memory are: μ, the storage capacity in items; d, the decay time of an item; and k, the main code type (physical, acoustic, visual, semantic). The most important parameter

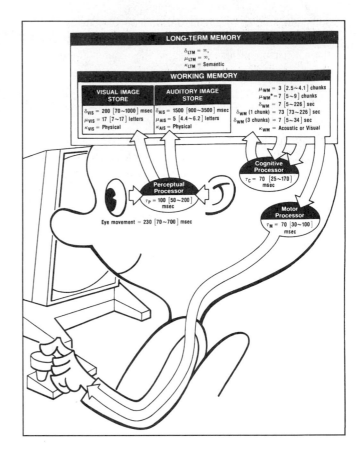

Figure 13.1 The model human processor—memories and processors. Sensory information flows into Working Memory through the Perceptual Processor. Working Memory consists of activated chunks in Long-Term Memory. From *The Psychology of Human-Computer Interaction* by S. Card, T. P. Moran, & A. Newell, 1983. Hillsdale, NJ: Erlbaum. Copyright © 1983 by Lawrence Erlbaum Associates. Reprinted with permission.

of a processor is t, the cycle time (Card et al., 1983, pp. 24–25).

The MHP was formulated to account for the perceptual and motor behavior of adults interacting with computers, and it has been used successfully to help design and evaluate human-computer interfaces (Gray, John, & Atwood, 1993). It was definitely *not* designed to advance developmental theory. Nevertheless, we include it here because we believe that it exemplifies the more general attempt to formulate a cognitive architecture that is consistent with the massive amount of empirical data on human performance. As such, it presents an obvious challenge to developmentalists: What would an MHP look like for an infant, for a preschooler, or for an adolescent? Which of the architectural features, processing rates, and information capacities

TABLE 13.1   Principles of Operation for the Model Human Processor (From Card et al., 1983)

P0.   *Recognize-Act Cycle of the Cognitive Processor.* On each cycle of the Cognitive Processor, the contents of Working Memory initiate actions associatively linked to them in Long-Term Memory; these actions in turn modify the contents of Working Memory

P1.   *Variable Perceptual Processor Rate Principle.* The Perceptual Processor cycle time t_r varies inversely with stimulus intensity

P2.   *Encoding Specificity Principle.* Specific encoding operations performed on what is perceived determine what is stored, and what is stored determines what retrieval cues are effective in providing access to what is stored.

P3.   *Discrimination Principle.* The difficulty of memory retrieval is determined by the candidates that exist in the memory, relative to the retrieval clues.

P4.   *Variable Cognitive Processor Rate Principle.* The Cognitive Processor cycle time t_c is shorter when greater effort is induced by increased task demands or information loads; it also diminishes with practice.

P5.   *Fitt's Law.* The time T_{pos} to move the hand to a target of size S which lies a distance D away is given by:

$$T_{pos} = I_M \log_2(D/S + .5),$$

where $I_M = 100 [70 \sim 120]$ msec/bit.

P6.   *Power Law of Practice.* The time T_n to perform a task on the nth trial follows a power law:

$$T_n = T_1 n^{-a},$$

where a = .4 [.2 ~ .6].

P7.   *Uncertainty Principle.* Decision time T increases with uncertainty about the judgment or decision to be made:

$$T = I_C H$$

where H is the information-theoretic entropy of the decision and $I_C = 150(0 \sim 157)$ msec/bit. For n equally probable alternatives (called Hick's Law),

$$H = \log_2 (n + 1)$$

For n alternatives with different probabilities, p_i, of occurrence,

$$H = \Sigma_i \, p_i \log_2 (1/p_i + 1)$$

P8.   *Rationality Principle.* A person acts so as to attain his goals through rational action, given the structure of the task and his inputs of information and bounded by limitations on his knowledge and processing ability:

Goals + Task + Operators + Inputs + Knowledge
+ Process-limits Æ Behavior

P9.   *Problem Space Principle.* The rational activity in which people engage to solve a problem can be described in terms of (1) a set of states of knowledge, (2) operators for changing one state into another, (3) constraints on applying operators, and (4) control knowledge for deciding which operator to apply next.

that so effectively characterize a normal adult would have to change in these "kiddy" versions of the MHP? Finally, what additional features would an MHP need to have in order to develop from the neonate processor to the adult version?

The answers to such questions will occur at two levels. At the level of rates and parameters, the kind of results emerging from Kail's (1988, 1991) extensive chronometric studies may ultimately inform theories about the developmental course of the basic cognitive processes that support the system architecture. At present, however, the developmental range of variation from childhood to adulthood in things such as visual scanning rates, STM scanning rates, and so on, is of the same order of magnitude as the MHP estimates for adults, so the experimental results do not constrain the computational models. For example, Card and colleagues estimate a basic cycle time for the MHP between 25 and 170 msec, while Kail's results show a STM scanning rate that varies from about 125 msec per item for eight-year-olds to 50 msec per item for adults. In order for the chronometric results to constrain the broader architectural theories, it will be necessary to combine such "hardware" estimates with more detailed task analyses of the "software" that utilizes the hardware.

At the architectural level, it is necessary to go beyond the global characterizations provided by the MHP and create computational models that utilize that architecture. The creation of production-system models of children's cognitive processes represents a path toward that goal. In the next section we describe this kind of work.

Production Systems for Different Knowledge States

Production systems were first used in computer science without any particular reference to human cognition.[4] With respect to cognitive modeling, the most important early developments include Newell's first computer implementation of a production-system language called PSG (1973) and Anderson's production systems for adult cognitive tasks (Anderson, 1983; Anderson, Kline, & Beasley, 1978) which combined production systems with semantic nets. These systems took the standard model—described in the previous section—and transformed it into specific proposals about the dynamics of the human cognitive architecture.

At their inception, production systems were used to account for adult problem-solving performance in situations requiring a systematic accumulation of knowledge about a problem space as well as an ability to opportunistically change the focus of the problem (Newell & Simon, 1972).

---

[4] A brief history of production systems—both in computer science and in psychology—is presented in Neches, Langley, and Klahr (1987).

Although the models cast in this form were able to dynamically accumulate knowledge, revise it, and eventually construct a solution to a problem, these initial models did not themselves change. However, issues of change, learning, adaptation—more generally termed "self-modification"—quickly became an issue, and the early literature on production systems includes work on "adaptive production systems" (Waterman, 1975).

The initial use of production systems by developmentalists was the "sequence of models" approach. As noted earlier, the approach seeks to produce a sequence of production-system models for a specific task such that each model represents a different level of performance. The premise was that once such a sequence of models had been created and validated, it would be possible to examine the differences between successive models in order to infer what a transition mechanism would have to accomplish. Although it is now clear that the clean distinction between performance models and transition models was an oversimplification, such models constituted most of the early work in this area, so we will describe a few of them here.

An Example from Conservation

Consider the moment, repeated tens of thousands of times by developmental investigators, when a child is asked the "crucial" conservation question: "Are there more objects in this row, or in this row, or do the two rows have the same number of objects?" How can we represent the mental computations that the child performs in attempting to reply?

Klahr and Wallace (1976) approached this question by formulating a series of increasingly complex production-system models to account for children's understanding of quantitative concepts, starting with models for encoding discrete quantities via subitizing and counting, and ending with children's ability to understand questions about class inclusion, transitivity, and conservation. Their most "mature" model contains productions dealing with several different levels of knowledge. At the highest level are productions that represent general conservation rules, such as "If you know about an initial quantitative relation, and a transformation, then you know something about the resultant quantitative relation." At the next level are productions representing pragmatic rules, such as "If you want to compare two quantities, and you don't know about any prior comparisons, then quantify each of them." At an even lower level are rules that determine which of several quantification processes will actually be used to encode the external display (e.g., subitizing, counting, or estimation).

Finally, at the lowest level, are productions for carrying out the quantification process.

Later in this chapter, we will describe the most recent version of a production-system model of conservation knowledge (Simon & Klahr, 1995). In this section, we use the earlier work to illustrate some important aspects of production-system models. Table 13.2 lists a few of the key productions from the Klahr and Wallace (1976) model.

At first glance, and when read in the pseudo-formalism used in Table 13.2, the first three productions appear to be nearly identical. But there are important differences between them. P1 corresponds to a situation in which the system has no goals with respect to quantitative comparison, but has just received some external query (from the ubiquitous conservation investigator). P2 corresponds to a situation in which there *is* a goal of determining a relationship, so it establishes the first subgoal along the path to such a determination, which is to compare the quantity of the two collections. Eventually, the system will determine that relationship, and when it does, P3 will notice that it has both a goal to determine a relationship and the requisite information to satisfy that goal.

Now let us consider in more detail just what each of these productions does. P1 detects an element in working memory that results from the encoding of a verbal query. The linguistic processing is not modeled here, but the

TABLE 13.2   Some Productions for Quantity Conservation. Italicized terms represent variables whose values will be determined by the working memory elements that they happen to match. (Adapted from Klahr & Wallace, 1976, Chapter 5)

P1:   If you have been asked about a *quantitative relationship* between *collection X* and *collection Y*
then set a goal to determine the relationship between *collection X* and *collection Y.*

P2:   If the goal is to determine a *quantitative relationship* between *collection X* and *collection Y*
then set the goal of comparing *collection X* and *collection Y.*

P3:   If the goal is to determine a *quantitative relationship* between *collection X* and *collection Y*
and you know a *relationship* between *collection X* and *collection Y*
then respond by saying the *relationship.*

P4:   If your goal is to apply knowledge about quantity conservation
and you know that *collection X* and *collection Y* were quantitatively equivalent
and that *collection Y* underwent a quantity-preserving transformation, changing *Y* into *Y'*
then you know that *collection X* and *collection Y'* are quantitatively equivalent.

assumption is that a variety of questions would produce the three pieces of information: one about the relationship, and the other two about the identity of the focal collections. This production illustrates what is meant by "multiple instantiations" of the same production. This production could be satisfied by several different combinations of matching elements, depending on the precise form of the question (e.g., Which is longer the top row or the bottom row? or Which is less, the red ones or the blue ones?) and on whether or not there exists in working memory more than one active element that is a member of the *relationship* concept, or the *collection* concept. For example, the second of the two questions above would form the following matches or bindings: *relationship*–less, *collection X*–red ones, *collection Y*–blue ones. But if another referent to a collection—such as "round things" was still active in working memory, another instantiation of the same production might be: less, red, round.

In addition to multiple instantiations of the same production, it is possible (and common) for several different productions to match the contents of working memory at the same time. For example, because the conditions of P2 are a proper subset of the conditions for P3, whenever P3 is satisfied, so is P2. It is up to the conflict resolution process (described below) to decide how to handle such multiple instantiations of the same production, as well the instantiation of more than one production.

P4 is one of several productions in the original model that represent cross products of the three possible relationships between initial quantities (>, =, <) and three classes of transformations (those that effect increases, decreases, or no change). One of the surprising discoveries that came out of the formulation of production-system models of the conservation task was that there were many different kinds of knowledge required before a child could really be said to "have" quantity conservation. Another was that, in addition to productions about conservation as such, the system needs a large number of quantity-specific problem-solving productions, of the sort represented in Table 13.2, that establish the requisite information and the appropriate goal structure for correctly responding to a conservation query.

Knowledge States for Balance Scale Predictions

Klahr and Siegler (1978) used production systems in a different way: to take a noncomputational information-processing model that had already shown an excellent fit to children's performance and recast it as a production-system in order to get a better idea of its dynamic properties.

The production-system models were based on earlier investigations of children's performance on Piaget's balance scale prediction task. Siegler (1978, 1976) proposed an elegant analysis of rule sequences characterizing how children (from 3 years to 17 years old) make predictions on this task (as well as in several other domains having a similar formal structure). This work has provided the basis for many subsequent empirical and theoretical analyses, including computational theories cast as both production systems and connectionist networks. Because we will be discussing these models in some detail, we next describe the balance scale task on which they are based.

The type of balance scale used consisted of a two-arm balance, with several pegs located at equal intervals along each arm. Small circular disks, all of equal weight, were placed on the pegs in various configurations, while the balance was prevented from tipping. The child's task was to predict the direction in which the balance scale would move if it were allowed to.

The basic physical concept that underlies the operation of the balance scale is torque: The scale will rotate in the direction of the greater of the two torques acting on its arms. The total torque on each arm is determined by summing the individual torques produced by the weights on the pegs, and individual torques are in turn computed by multiplying each weight by its distance from the fulcrum. Since the pegs are at equal intervals from the fulcrum, and the weights are all equal, a simpler calculation is possible. It consists of computing the sum of the products of number of weights on a peg times the ordinal position of the peg from the fulcrum. This is done for each side, and the side with the greater sum of products is the side that will go down. (If they are equal, the scale will balance.)

Siegler (1976) demonstrated that the different levels of knowledge that children have about this task could be represented in the form of a sequence of four increasingly "mature" binary decision trees, depicted in Figure 13.2. A child using Model I considers only the number of weights on each side: If they are the same, the child predicts balance, otherwise he predicts that the side with the greater weight will go down. For a Model II child, a difference in weight still dominates, but if weight is equal, then a difference in distance is sought. If it exists, the greater distance determines which side will go down, otherwise the prediction is balance. A child using Model III tests both weight and distance in all cases. If both are equal, the child predicts balance; if only one is equal, then the other one determines the outcome; if they are both unequal, but on the

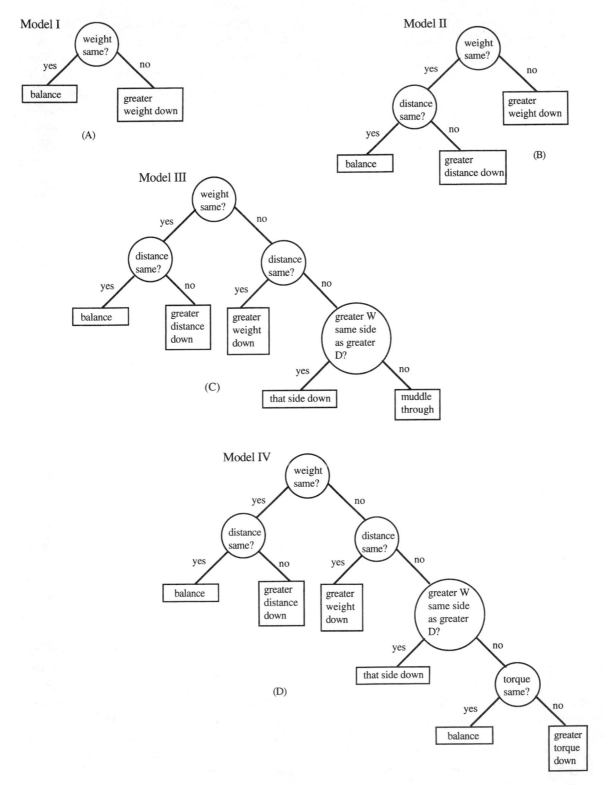

Figure 13.2 Decision tree representation for models I–IV of balance scale predictions. From "The representation of children's knowledge," by D. Klahr & R. S. Siegler, 1978, in H. W. Reese & L. P. Lipsitt (Eds.), *Advances in Child Development and Behavior* (Vol. 12, pp. 61–116). New York: Academic Press. Copyright © 1978 by Academic Press. Reprinted with permission.

same side with respect to their inequality, then that side is predicted to go down. However, in a situation in which one side has the greater weight, while the other has greater distance, a Model III child, although recognizing the conflict, does not have a consistent way to resolve it. This child simply "muddles through" by making a random prediction. Model IV represents "mature" knowledge of the task: Since it includes the sum-of-products calculation, children using it will always make the correct prediction, but if they can base their prediction on simpler tests, they will do so. The components of this knowledge are acquired over a remarkably long span of experience and education. Although children as young as 5 years old usually know that balances such as teeter-totters tend to fall toward the side with more weight, most college students are unable to consistently solve balance scale problems.

Production Systems for Balance Scale Rules. The binary decision trees make clear predictions about the responses that would be made by a child using one of these rules for any specific configuration of weights. However, they are silent on the dynamics of the decision process, and they do not make a clear distinction between encoding processes and decision processes. By recasting the rules as production systems, Klahr and Siegler were able to make a more precise characterization of what develops than was afforded by the decision-tree representation.

The production system is listed in Table 13.3. Consider, for example, Model II in Table 13.3. It is a production system consisting of three productions. The condition elements in this system are all tests for sameness or difference in weight or distance. The actions all refer to behavioral responses. None of the models in Table 13.3 contain a representation for any more detailed knowledge, such as the actual amount of weight or distance, or the means used to encode that information. Nor is there any explicit representation of how the system produces the final verbal output. It is simply assumed that the system has processes—or "operators" that produce encoded representations of the relational information stated in the conditions.

On any recognize-act cycle, only one of these productions will fire, depending on the type of knowledge that the encoding processes have placed in working memory. If the weights are unequal, then P2 will fire; if the weights are equal and the distances are not, then both P1 and P3 will be satisfied, and this "conflict" has to be resolved by the production system architecture. For the production system that Klahr and Siegler proposed, the conflict is resolved by a

TABLE 13.3 Production System (P) Representations for Models I-IV. D = distance; W = weight. See text for further explanation. (From Klahr & Siegler, 1978)

Model I

P1: ((Same W) → (Say "balance"))
P2: ((Side X more W) → (Say "X down"))

Model II

P1: ((Same W) → (Say "balance"))
P2: ((Side X more W) → (Say "X down"))
P3: ((Same W) (Side X more D) → (Say "X down"))

Model III

P1: ((Same W) → (Say "balance"))
P2: ((Side X more W) → (Say "X down"))
P3: ((Same W) (Side X more D) → (Say "X down"))
P4: ((Side X more W) (Side X less D) → muddle through)
P5: ((Side X more W) (Side X more D) → (Say "X down"))

Model IV

P1: ((Same W) → (Say "balance"))
P2: ((Side X more W) → (Say "X down"))
P3: ((Same W) (Side X more D) → (Say "X down"))
P4: ((Side X more W) (Side X less D) → (get Torque))
P5: ((Side X more W) (Side X more D) → (Say "X down"))
P6: ((Same Torque) → (Say "balance"))
P7: ((Side X more Torque) → (Say "X down"))

Transitional requirements

	Productions	Operators
I → II	add P3	add distance encoding and comparison
II → III	add P4, P5	
III → IV	modify P4; add P6, P7	add torque computation and comparison

specificity principle that always selects the more specific of two productions when one is a special case of the other.[5] Finally, if both weights and distances are equal, then only P1 will be satisfied and it will fire. (Note that a production maintains its label across the four models.)

We can compare the four models to determine the task facing a transition model. At the level of productions, the requisite modifications are straightforward: transition from Model I to Model II requires the addition of P3; from Model II to III, the addition of P4 and P5; and from Model III to IV, the addition of P6 and P7 and the modification of P4 to P4′.

Thus far we have compared the models at the level of productions. But productions need information provided by the operators that encode the external configuration.

---

[5] More recent production-system architectures have dropped the "specificity principle." Conflict resolution will be discussed later in the chapter.

Consequently, it is informative to compare the four models at a finer level of analysis by looking at the implicit requirements for encoding and comparing the important qualities in the environment. The production system for Model I tests for sameness or difference in weight. Thus, it requires an encoding process that either directly encodes relative weight or encodes an absolute amount of each and then inputs those representations into a comparison process. Whatever the form of the comparison process, it must be able to produce not only a same-or-different symbol, but if there is a difference, it must be able to keep track of which side is greater. The production system for Model II requires the additional capacity to make these decisions about distance as well as weight. This might constitute a completely separate encoding and comparison system for distance representations, or it might be the same system except for the interface with the environment.

Model III's production system needs no additional operators at this level. Thus, it differs from Model II only in the way it utilizes information that is already accessible to Model II. The Model IV production system requires a much more powerful set of quantitative operators than any of the preceding models. In order to determine relative torque, it must first determine the absolute torque on each side of the scale, and this in turn requires exact numerical representation of weight and distance. In addition, the torque computation would require access to the necessary arithmetic production systems to actually do the sum of products calculations.

Although we have compared the four models at two distinct levels—productions and operators—the levels are not really that easily separated. Missing from these models is a set of productions that would indicate the interdependence: productions that explicitly determine which encoding the system will make. That is, in these models, there are almost no productions of the form: (want to compare weights) → (attend to stimulus and notice weight). The sole exception to this occurs in P4′ in Model IV. When this model is confronted with a nonconflict problem, either P1, P2, P3, or P5 will fire on the first recognize cycle. For a conflict problem, P4′ fires, and the system attempts to "get torques." The result of this unmodeled action, as described above, would be to produce a knowledge element that could satisfy either P6 or P7 on the next cycle.

Representing the Immediate Task Context. One advantage of a production-system formulation is that it facilitates the extension of a basic model of the *logical* properties of a task to include the processing of verbal instructions, encoding of the stimulus, keeping track of where the child is in the overall task, and so on. For example, in their analysis of *individual* subject protocols on the balance scale, Klahr and Siegler proposed several distinct models to account for some children's idiosyncratic—but consistent—response patterns. Some of these models included not only the basic productions for a variant of one of Siegler's four models for balance scale predictions, but also knowledge about the instantaneous task context.

These models are too detailed to present here. However, it is instructive to consider the way in which such detailed models are able to characterize how much more than balance scale knowledge, as such, is required by a child performing this task. For example, one of the Klahr and Siegler models for an individual subject dealt with the way in which the child maintained, in working memory, the following pieces of information: which side has *more* weight or distance, which side has a *big* weight or distance, what the current criterion value is, what the scale is expected to do, what the scale actually did, whether the prediction is yet to be made or has been made, and whether it is correct or incorrect.

Thus, their model makes a strong claim about how much of the encoded knowledge (i.e., the contents of working memory) must be available at any one moment. Although production-system models do not generally impose any clear constraints on the size of working memory they provide the potential for such an analysis. One of the relatively unexplored areas for future computational modelers is to attempt to integrate the theoretical constructs and empirical results described by working memory capacity theorists, such as Case (1986) and Bidell and Fischer (1994) with the added formalisms and precision of production-system models. Promising steps in this direction are represented by recent work by Halford and his colleagues (Halford, 1993; Halford et al., 1995).

The two examples in this section—conservation and balance scale knowledge—represent the nontransition phase of production system modeling. The primary goal was to explore the nature of the system that could display the different levels of performance observed in the children's responses to these tasks. Thus they exemplify the two-step approach that characterized such early models, even though they did not address the transition process itself. The next step in the progression came in the form of self-modifying production systems.

Production-Systems Approaches to Self-Modification

Many general principles for change have been proposed in the developmental literature. These include equilibration, encoding, efficiency, redundancy elimination, search reduction, self-regulation, consistency detection, and representational redescription. However, such principles are not computational mechanisms. That is, they do not include a specification of how information is encoded, stored, accessed, and modified. It is one thing to assert that the cognitive system seeks equilibration or that a representation is redescribed; it is quite another to formulate a computational model that actually does so.

Adoption of a production-system architecture allows one to pose focused questions about how broad principles might be implemented as specific mechanisms. One way to do this is to assume the role of a designer of a self-modifying production system, and consider the issues that must be resolved in order to produce a theory of self-modification based on the production-system architecture. The two primary questions are:

1. *What* are the basic change mechanisms that lead to new productions? Examples are generalization, discrimination, composition, proceduralization, strengthening, and chunking.
2. *When* are these change mechanisms evoked: when an error is noted, when a production fires, when a goal is achieved, or when a pattern is detected?

Possible Loci of Development in Production-System Architectures

There are two primary classes of changes that can affect the behavior of a production system and each provides a potential site for a partial account of cognitive development. One class of changes is at the level of productions, and involves creating new productions or modifying existing ones. The other class of changes involves the rules of execution of the production system itself. These include changes in the conflict resolution rules and changes in the size or complexity of working memory elements.

Production Changes.   One way to generate new productions is to modify the conditions of existing productions. Anderson, Kline, and Beasley (1978) were the first to create production-system models that learned via *generalization* and *discrimination*. The first mechanism creates a new production that is *more* general than an existing

production, while retaining the same actions. The second mechanism—discrimination—creates a new production that is *less* general than an existing production, while still retaining the same actions. The two mechanisms lead to opposite results, though in most models they are not inverses in terms of the conditions under which they are evoked.

Various change mechanisms have been proposed that lead to productions with new conditions *and* actions. *Composition* was originally proposed by Lewis (1978) to account for speedup as the result of practice. This method combines two or more productions into a new production with the conditions and actions of the component productions. But conditions that are guaranteed to be met by one of the actions are not included. For instance, composition of the two productions AB→CD and DE→F would produce the production ABE→CDF. The most advanced form of this type of self-modification—chunking—is embodied in the Soar model to be described in the next section.

Another mechanism for creating new productions is *proceduralization* (Anderson, Greeno, Kline, & Neves, 1981). This involves constructing a highly specific version of some general production, based on some instantiation of the production that has been applied. This method can be viewed as a form of discrimination learning because it generates more specific variants of an existing production.

Production System Architecture Changes.   As noted earlier, it is often the case that more than a single production is satisfied during the recognition phase of the recognize-act cycle. Thus, conflict resolution offers another decision point at which the behavior of the system can be affected. Production system designers have employed a number of schemes for performing conflict resolution, ranging from simple fixed orderings on the productions, to various forms of weights or strengths (usually based on feedback about the effectiveness of prior production firings), to complex schemes that are not uniform across the entire set of productions, to no resolution at all. Some important aspects of cognitive development, such as attentional increases and the ability to suppress prepotent responses, might be accounted for by developmental changes in these conflict resolution processes.

Another type of architectural change that might be used to explain some aspects of developmental change would be changes in the size and complexity of the working memory elements that can be matched against productions. At present, there are no detailed proposals along these lines, but such an account might provide an integration between existing capacity theories of cognitive development, such as Case (1985), Halford et al. (1995), and computational models of the type described in this chapter.

Chunking and Its Use in a Model of Conservation Acquisition

A basic mechanism for change via chunking was initially proposed by Rosenbloom and Newell (1982, 1987) and first used to explain the power law of practice (the time to perform a task decreases as a power function of the number of times the task has been performed). The learning curves produced by their model are quite similar to those observed in a broad range of learning tasks. The chunking mechanism and the production-system architecture to support it has evolved into a major theoretical statement about the nature of the human cognitive system. The system (called Soar) is one of the most fully-elaborated examples of a complete cognitive theory—a "unified theory of cognition" as Newell (1990) calls it. It would require a substantial extension of the present chapter to give a comprehensive overview of Soar. However, because the Soar architecture has been used in a recently developed theory of conservation acquisition to be described below, we will briefly summarize its main features here.

The Soar architecture is based on formulating all goal-oriented behavior as search in problem spaces. A problem space consists of a set of states and a set of operators that move between states. A goal is formulated as the task of reaching one of a desired set of states from a specified initial state. Under conditions of perfect knowledge, satisfying a goal involves starting at the initial state, and applying a sequence of operators that result in a desired state being generated. Knowledge is represented as productions. When knowledge is not perfect, the system may not know how to proceed. For example, it may not know which of a set of operators should be applied to the current state. When such an impasse occurs, Soar automatically generates a subgoal to resolve the impasse. These subgoals are themselves processed in additional problem spaces, possibly leading to further impasses. The overall structure is one of a hierarchy of goals, with an associated hierarchy of problem spaces. When a goal is terminated, the problem solving that occurred within the goal is summarized in new productions called chunks. If a situation similar to the one that created the chunk ever occurs again, the chunk fires to prevent any impasse, leading to more efficient problem solving.

Soar contains one assumption that is both parsimonious and radical. It is that all change is produced by a single mechanism: chunking. The chunking mechanism forms productions out of the elements that led to the most recent goal achievement. What was at first a search through a hierarchy of subgoals becomes, after chunking, a single production that eliminates any future search under the same conditions. Chunking is built into the Soar architecture as an integral part of the production cycle. It is in continual operation during performance—there is no place at which the performance productions are suspended so that a set of chunking productions can fire. Chunking occurs at all levels of subgoaling, and in all problem spaces. Chunking reduces processing by extending the knowledge base of the system.

Simon and Klahr (1995) used Soar as the theoretical context in which to formulate a computation model of how children acquire number conservation. Their model, called Q-Soar, simulates a training study (Gelman, 1982) in which 3- and 4-year-old children were given a brief training session that was sufficient to move them from the classical nonconserving behavior to the ability to conserve small and large numbers. Q-Soar is designed to satisfy several desirable features of computational models of cognitive development:

1. It is based on a principled cognitive architecture (in this case Newell's Soar theory of cognition).
2. It is constrained by general regularities in the large empirical literature on number conservation.
3. It generates the same behavior as do the children in the specific training study being modeled. That is, it starts out by being unable to pass number conservation tasks, and then, based on the chunks that it forms during the training study, it is able to pass post tests that include both small and large number conservation tests.

Q-Soar asserts that young children acquire number conservation knowledge by measurement and comparison of values to determine the effects of transformation on small collections of discrete objects. Having been shown a transformation on a set of objects, the model first categorizes the transformation. This processing creates new knowledge about this kind of transformation, which becomes available on future occurrences in similar contexts. Eventually, the transformation's effects can be stated without the need for any empirical processing.

Processing Capacity in a Production-System Model

Halford et al. (1995) describe a model of strategy development in transitive inference tasks called the Transitive

Inference Mapping Model (TRIMM). The model—written as a self-modifying production system—is similar to Siegler and Shipley's (1995) ASCM model for strategy choice in arithmetic, in the way it chooses strategies on the basis of their strength (here represented as the strength of productions). In addition, where no strategy is available, TRIMM develops a new strategy by making analogical mappings from earlier representations of situations similar to the current context. One of the novel features of TRIMM is that these mappings are subject to a processing load factor that operates only when new strategies are being developed, but not when existing strategies are adequate. Thus, the model implements and combines both associative and metacognitive mechanisms for strategy development. Once new productions have been formed, they are strengthened or weakened according to their success on the transitive inference tasks presented to the system.

Halford and colleagues make an important observation about the implications of this kind of model for the learning-maturation dichotomy that is so pervasive in discussions about cognitive development.

> It is obvious enough that the question of cognitive development cannot be a matter of learning *or* maturation. However, it is equally inappropriate to propose the question in any other form. For example, it makes no sense to ask whether cognitive development is a matter of capacity *or* knowledge acquisition, capacity *or* expertise, capacity *or* relational encoding, and so on. All of these are really alternate forms of the learning or maturation question. We take it as self-evident that experience-driven processes such as accumulation and organization of a knowledge base, skill acquisition, and efficient encoding, are all important in cognitive development. Modeling some of those processes in detail is what . . . [computational modeling] is about. The question of capacity is not whether it is an alternative to any of these processes, but whether, and how, it interacts with them. (p. 124, emphasis added)

Necessary and Sufficient Mechanisms

Thus far, we have described two classes of potential changes in production systems that can be used to account for developmental phenomena: changes at the level of productions and changes at the level of the production-system architecture. We have illustrated a handful of examples of production systems that use such processes on familiar tasks from the cognitive development literature. But production system modelers have a much more ambitious goal: to explain cognitive development "in the large," rather than

on a task by task basis. Indeed, this is one of the reasons why more recent work tends to use production-system architectures that derive from overarching cognitive theories such as Newell's SOAR or Anderson's ACT-R.

One of the fundamental research questions in this area is the extent to which the self-modification processes included in such theories are necessary and/or sufficient to explain cognitive development. For example, it is not yet clear whether the "basic" production modification processes described earlier—such as generalization, discrimination, composition, proceduralization, and chunking—can account for the apparent reorganization necessary to get from novice to expert level (Hunter, 1968; Larkin, 1981; Lewis, 1981; Simon & Simon, 1978). Such reorganization may involve much more than refinements in the productions governing *when* sub-operations are performed. These refinements could be produced by generalization and discrimination mechanisms. However, producing a new procedure requires the introduction of new operators that, in turn, may require the introduction of novel elements or goals—something that generalization, discrimination, composition, and chunking are not clearly able to do.

Some additional mechanisms and processes have been proposed, but they remain to be implemented in computational models. For example, Wallace, Klahr, and Bluff (1987) proposed a novel production-system architecture that included a hierarchically-organized set of nodes, each of which is a semi-autonomous production system, communicating via a shared working memory. Each of these nodes can be simultaneously activated. The basic developmental process involved the construction of new nodes by processing a representation of episodic sequences for the systems' previous behavior (the time line). Another example of a plausible concept that remains to be computationally implemented is Karmiloff-Smith's (1992) "representational redescription"—a process in which the underlying engine of cognitive development involves increasingly efficient reorganizations of knowledge structures and the processes that operate upon them.

Such "soft-core" notions presents challenges to the "hard-core" approach: either implement these ideas, or show that they are theoretically unnecessary, or create a computational alternative that accomplishes the same thing.

Summary: Production Systems as Frameworks for Cognitive Developmental Theory

The production-system approach to theory building in cognitive development rests on three fundamental premises:

1. The human information-processing system architecture is isomorphic to a production-system architecture. This premise derives from observations about similarities in terms of both structural organization and behavioral properties. Structurally, production systems provide a plausible characterization of the relations between long-term memory and working memory, and about the interaction between procedural and declarative knowledge. Behaviorally, strong analogies can be seen between humans and production systems with respect to their abilities to mix goal-driven and event-driven processes, and with their tendency to process information in parallel at the recognition level and serially at higher cognitive levels.

2. Change is a fundamental aspect of intelligence; we cannot say that we fully understand cognition until we have a model that accounts for its development. The first 20 years of information-processing psychology devoted scant attention to the problems of how to represent change processes, other than to place them on an agenda for future work. Indeed, almost all of the information-processing approaches to developmental issues followed the two-step strategy outlined in the Simon quotation that opened this chapter: First construct the performance model, and then follow it with a change model that operates on the performance model. In recent years, as researchers have begun to work seriously on the change process, they have begun to formulate models that inextricably link performance and change. Self-modifying production systems are one such example of this linkage.

3. All information-processing-system architectures, whether human or artificial, must obey certain constraints in order to facilitate change. It is these constraints that give rise to the seemingly complex particulars of individual production-system architectures. Thus, an understanding of production-system models of change is a step toward understanding the nature of human development and learning.

CONNECTIONIST SYSTEMS

In this section we examine work conducted from the connectionist perspective. Because both production system modelers and connectionists are pursuing common goals, there are many points where their pathways converge. Both approaches rely heavily on computational modeling. Both approaches understand the importance of matching theory to data. Both perspectives have come to understand the importance of emergent properties in understanding transition mechanisms. Since the final understanding of transition mechanisms may well require insights from both perspectives, it makes little sense to advance strong claims for superiority of one approach over the other. Rather, we need to understand why researchers are currently exploring different paths, invoking different incantations, and wielding different computational weapons. To do this, we need to better understand the differences in the goals and constraints assumed by the two approaches.

We start with a brief description of the basic features of connectionist models. Then we address a few important aspects of connectionism that distinguish it from production system approaches. One basic distinction comes from the fact, noted earlier, that production systems take the symbol as their basic building block, while connectionist systems take a "sub-symbolic" perspective. Although we have reserved most of the "compare and contrast" discussion in this chapter for the final section, it is important to treat this distinction at the outset of our presentation of connectionist models. Following that discussion we turn to a review of actual work conducted in the connectionist framework.

Basic Principles of Neural Networks

Connectionist models are implemented in terms of artificial neural networks. Neural networks that are able to learn from input are known as "adaptive neural networks." In practice, all current neural network frameworks are based on adaptive neural networks. The architecture of an adaptive neural network can be specified in terms of eight design features:

1. *Units.* The basic components of the network are a number of simple elements called variously neurons, units, cells, or nodes. In Figure 13.3, the units are labeled with letters such as "x_1."

2. *Connections.* Neurons or pools of neurons are connected by a set of pathways which are variously called connections, links, pathways, or arcs. In most models, these connections are unidirectional, going from a "sending" unit to a "receiving" unit. This unidirectionality assumption corresponds to the fact that neural connections also operate in only one direction. The only information conveyed across connections is activation information. No signals or codes are passed. In Figure 13.3, the connection between units x_1 and y_1 is marked with a thick line.

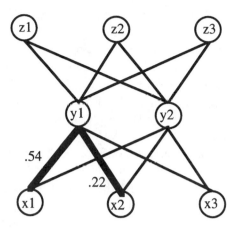

Figure 13.3   The general shape of a neural network.

3. *Patterns of connectivity.* Neurons are typically grouped into pools or layers. Connections can operate within or between layers. In some models, there are no within-layer connections; in others all units in a given layer are interconnected. Units or layers can be further divided into three classes:

   (a) *Input units* which represent signals from earlier networks. These are marked as x units in Figure 13.3.

   (b) *Output units* which represent the choices or decisions made by the network. These are marked as z units in Figure 13.3.

   (c) *Hidden units* which represent additional units juxtaposed between input and output for the purposes

of computing more complex, nonlinear relations. These are marked as y units in Figure 13.3.

4. *Weights.* Each connection has numerical weight that is designed to represent the degree to which it can convey activation from the sending unit to the receiving unit. Learning is achieved by changing the weights on connections. For example, the weight on the connection between x_1 and y_1 is given as .54 in Figure 13.3.

5. *Net inputs.* The total amount of input from a sending neuron to a receiving neuron is determined by multiplying the weights on each connection to the receiving unit times the activation of the sending neuron. This net input to the receiving unit is the sum of all such inputs from sending neurons. In Figure 13.3, the net input to y_1 is .76, if we assume that the activation of x_1 and x_2 are both at 1 and the x_1y_1 weight is .54 and the x_2y_1 weight is .22.

6. *Activation functions.* Each unit has a level of activation. These activation levels can vary continuously between 0 and 1. In order to determine a new activation level, activation functions are applied to the net input. Functions that "squash" high values can be used to make sure that all new activations stay in the range of 0 to 1.

7. *Thresholds and biases.* Although activations can take on any value between 0 and 1, often thresholds and bias functions are used to force units to be either fully on or fully off.

8. *A learning rule.* The basic goal of training is to bring the neural net into a state where it can take a given input and produce the correct output. To do this, a learning rule is used to change the weights on the connections. *Supervised* learning rules need to rely on the presence of a target output as the model for this changing of weights. *Unsupervised* learning rules do not rely on targets and correction, but use the structure of the input as their guide to learning.

All connectionist networks share this common language of units, connections, weights, and learning rules. However, architectures differ markedly both in their detailed patterns of connectivity and in the specific rules used for activation and learning. For excellent, readable introductions to the theory and practice of neural network modeling, the reader may wish to consult Bechtel and Abrahamsen (1991) or Fausett (1994). For a mathematically more advanced treatment, see Hertz, Krogh, and Palmer (1991).

To illustrate how connectionist networks can be used to study cognitive development, let us take as an example the

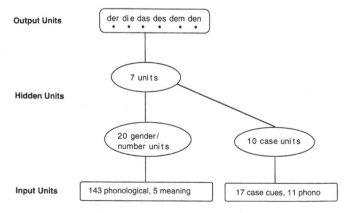

Figure 13.4   A network for learning the use of the German definite article. Based on "Language learning: Cues or rules?" by B. J. MacWhinney, J. Leinbach, R. Taraban,& J. L. McDonald, 1989, *Journal of Memory and Language, 28,* pp. 255–277. Copyright © 1989 by Academic Press, Inc. Reprinted with permission.

model of German gender learning developed by MacWhinney, Leinbach, Taraban, and McDonald (1989). This model was designed to explain how German children learn how to select one of the six different forms of the German definite article. In English we have a single word "the" to express definiteness. In German, the same idea can be expressed by *der, die, das, des, dem,* or *den.* Which of the six forms of the article should be used to modify a given noun in German depends on three additional features of the noun: its gender (masculine, feminine, or neuter), its number (singular or plural), and its role within the sentence (subject, possessor, direct object, prepositional object, or indirect object). To make matters worse, assignment of nouns to gender categories is often quite nonintuitive. For example, the word for fork is feminine, the word for spoon is masculine, and the word for knife is neuter. Acquiring this system of arbitrary gender assignments is particularly difficult for adult second language learners. Mark Twain expressed his own consternation at this aspect of German in a treatise entitled "The aweful German language" (Twain, 1935) in which he accuses the language of unfairness in assigning pretty young girls to the neuter gender, while allowing the sun to be feminine and the moon masculine. Along a similar vein, Maratsos and Chalkley (1980) argued that, since neither semantic nor phonological cues can predict which article accompanies a given noun in German, children could not learn the language by relying on simple surface cues.

Although these relations are indeed complex, MacWhinney et al. show that it is possible to construct a connectionist network that learns the German system from the available cues. This model, like most current connectionist models, involves a level of input units, a level of hidden units, and a level of output units (Figure 13.4). Each of these levels or layers contains a number of discrete units or nodes. For example, in the MacWhinney et al. model, the 35 units within the input level represent features of the noun that is to be modified by the article. Each of the two hidden unit levels includes multiple units that represent combinations of these input-level features. The six output units represent the six articles in the German language that correspond to the word the in English.

As noted, a central feature of such connectionist models is the very large number of connections among processing units. As shown in Figure 13.4, each input-level unit is connected to first-level hidden units; each first-level hidden unit is connected to second-level hidden units; and each second-level hidden unit is connected to each of the six output units. None of these hundreds of individual node-to-node connections are illustrated in Figure 13.4, since graphing each individual connection would lead to a blurred pattern of connecting lines. Instead a single line is used to stand in place of a fully interconnected pattern between levels. Learning is achieved by repetitive cycling through three steps. First, the system is presented with an input pattern that turns on some, but not all of the input units. In this case, the pattern is a set of sound features for the noun being used. Second, the activations of these units send activations through the hidden units and on to the output units. Third, the state of the output units is compared to the correct target and, if it does not match the target, the weights in the network are adjusted so that connections that suggested the correct answer are strengthened and connections that suggested the wrong answer are weakened.

MacWhinney et al. tested this system's ability to master the German article system by repeatedly presenting 102 common German nouns to the system. Frequency of presentation of each noun was proportional to the frequency with which the nouns are used in German. The job of the network was to choose which article to use with each noun in each particular context. After it did this, the correct answer was presented, and the simulation adjusted connection strengths so as to optimize its accuracy in the future.

After training was finished, the network was able to chose the correct article for 98% of the nouns in the original set. The ability to learn the input set is not a demonstration of true learning, since the network may have simply memorized each presented form by rote. However, when the simulation was presented with a previously encountered noun in a novel context, it chose the correct article on 92% of trials, despite the noun's often taking a different article in the new context than it had in the previously encountered ones. This type of cross-paradigm generalization is clear evidence that the network went far beyond rote memorization during the training phase. In addition, the simulation was able to generalize its internalized knowledge to entirely novel nouns. The 48 most frequent nouns in German that had not been included in the original input set were presented in a variety of sentence contexts. On this completely novel set, the simulation chose the correct article from the six possibilities on 61% of trials, versus 17% expected by chance. Thus, the system's learning mechanism, together with its representation of the noun's phonological and semantic properties and the context, produced a good guess about what article would accompany a given noun, even when the noun was entirely unfamiliar.

The network's learning paralleled children's learning in a number of ways. Like real German-speaking children, the network tended to overuse the articles that accompany feminine nouns. The reason for this is that the feminine forms of the article have a high frequency because they are used both for feminines and for plurals of all genders. The simulation also showed the same type of overgeneralization patterns that are often interpreted as reflecting rule use when they occur in children's language. For example, although the noun *Kleid* (which means clothing) is neuter, the simulation used the initial "kl" sound of the noun to conclude that it was masculine. Because of this, it invariably chose the article that would accompany the noun if it were masculine. Further, the same article-noun combinations that are the most difficult for children proved to be the most difficult for the simulation to learn and to generalize to on the basis of previously learned examples.

How was the simulation able to produce such generalization and rule-like behavior without any specific rules? The basic mechanism involved adjusting connection strengths between input, hidden, and output units to reflect the frequency with which combinations of features of nouns were associated with each article. Although no single feature can predict which article would be used, various complex combinations of phonological, semantic, and contextual cues allow quite accurate prediction of which articles should be chosen. This ability to extract complex, interacting patterns of cues is a particular characteristic of the type of connectionist algorithm, known as back-propagation, that was used in the MacWhinney et al. simulations. What makes the connectionist account for problems of this type particularly appealing is the fact that an equally powerful set of production system rules for German article selection would be quite complex (Mugdan, 1977) and learning of this complex set of rules would be a challenge in itself.

Connectionist Constraints on Computational Models

As we pointed out earlier, theoretical claims regarding production-system models do not extend to the underlying architecture of the computer on which they run. However, production systems have the potential to embody the same computational power as the von Neumann serial computer. Such models only become plausible as theories of human cognition when additional constraints are added, such as the size of working memory, the total amount of activation, and so on. However, some connectionists have not been satisfied with this analysis of the relation between von Neumann

machines and human cognition. Instead, they have argued that the very nature of the underlying neural system yields emergent properties that are quite different from those implicit in production-system architectures. In particular, adaptive neural network models (Grossberg, 1987; Hopfield, 1982; Kohonen, 1982) deliberately limit this descriptive power of their models by imposing two stringent limitations on their computational models: a prohibition against symbol passing and an insistence on self-organization rather than hand wiring. We will describe each of these constraints below.

Thou Shalt Not Pass Symbols

The brain is not constructed like a standard digital computer. The crucial difference between the two machines lies in the structure of memory storage and access (Kanerva, 1993). In the random-access memory of a standard digital computer (von Neumann, 1956), there are a series of hard locations, each of which can store a single "word" of data. The size of the memory depends on the length of the word of data. Because the computer is built out of highly reliable electrical components, the integrity of each memory location can be guaranteed. Neural hardware is made out of noisy, unstable components and no such guarantees can be issued. To compensate for the lower reliability of individual components, the brain relies on massive parallelism and distributed memory encodings. In the type of neural memory that appears to be implemented in the cerebellum (Albus, 1981; Marr, 1969), the address space is huge and sparse. Because the system cannot rely on locating individual hard addresses at the site of individual neurons (Kanerva, 1993), it must perform retrieval by locating addresses in the general vicinity of the stored memory. These addresses are called "soft" memory addresses, since they refer not to a single location, but to a general position in address space. The address space has a huge number of dimensions; but, because it is so sparsely populated, retrieval of memories does not require the exact determination of hard addresses.

An alternative method for passing symbols between neurons would view individual neurons as separate processing units capable of sending and receiving signals. But we know that the signals sent and received by neurons are entirely limited in shape. Neurons do not send Morse code down axons, symbols do not run across synapses, and brain waves do not pass phrase structures. In general, the brain provides no obvious support for the symbol passing architecture that provides the power underlying the von Neumann machine.

Instead, computation in the brain appears to rely ultimately on the formation of redundant connections between individual neurons.

The ways in which the brain has adapted to these limitations are not yet fully understood. The cerebellar addressing system is probably only one of several neural memory systems that use soft addresses and other storage techniques. We know that the hippocampus is also involved in aspects of memory storage (Schmajuk & DiCarlo, 1992) and it appears that its role may involve techniques involving data compression. There are also various rehearsal pathways designed to implement the learning of verbal material (Gathercole & Baddeley, 1993; Gupta & MacWhinney, 1994, 1996). Our emerging understanding of the various memory systems of the brain points to a complex interaction between cortex, thalamus, hippocampus, cerebellum, and other brain structures that work both on line and during sleep to facilitate storage, learning, and retrieval of memories. All of this work is done in ways that circumvent the limitations on symbol passing imposed by the biological structure of neurons.

Thou Shalt Not Hand-Wire

By itself, the requirement that computation be performed locally without symbol passing or homunculi is not enough to fully constrain the descriptive power of our models. One could still hand-wire a neural network to perform a specific function or to model a particular behavior. In neural networks, hand-wiring can be accomplished by creating a little program or homunculus that gets inside the network and sets weights on individual links between nodes. For example, we could hand-wire an animal category by linking nodes labeled "cat," "dog," and "tiger" to a hand-coded node labeled "animal." By detailed weight setting and the use of gating and polling neurons, virtually any function can be wired into a neural network (Hertz et al., 1991). An early example of a fully hand-wired neural network was Lamb's (1966) stratificational grammar. More recently, we have seen hand-wired neural networks in areas such as interactive activation models of reading (McClelland & Rumelhart, 1981), speech errors (Dell, 1986; MacWhinney & Anderson, 1986; Stemberger, 1985), ambiguity resolution (Cottrell, 1985), and lexical activation (Marslen-Wilson, 1987). Although these networks fit within the general framework of connectionist models, the fact that they are constructed through hand-wiring makes them less interesting as developmental models.

Certain "hybrid" models move the process of hand-wiring away from the network level onto an alternative

symbolic level. This "implementational" approach to hand-wiring spares the modeler the tedium of hand-wiring by running the wiring procedure off symbolic templates. For example, Touretzky (1990) has shown that there are techniques for bottling the full power of a LISP-based production-system architecture into a neural net. These demonstrations are important because they show how difficult it is to control excessive modeling power.

Ideally, we want to match the constraint against symbol passing with the requirement that networks be *self-organizing*. We want to make sure that specific representations are not hand-wired and that the connections between units are developed on the basis of automatic learning procedures. Although we will always be forced to "label" our input nodes and output nodes, we want our labelling systems to be general across problems and not hand-crafted anew for each particular problem. Rather, we want to use general forms of representation that lead to robust and emergent learning without recourse to hand-wiring. It is the emergent, self-organizing properties of neural networks that make them particularly interesting to the developmental psychologist. Such models can display further interesting and important properties, such as stage transitions (Shultz, Schmidt, Buckingham, & Mareschal, 1995), category leakage (McClelland & Kawamoto, 1986), graceful degradation (Harley & MacAndrew, 1992; Hinton & Shallice, 1991; Marchman, 1992), and property emergence (MacWhinney et al., 1989).

Alternative Network Architectures

One of the principal goals of connectionist theory over the last thirty years has been the exploration of the properties of competing network architectures. In this section we will review the most important network architectures with an eye toward understanding the types of developmental processes for which each might be most relevant. There is a great deal of evidence to suggest that no single architecture is ideal for all purposes and that the human brain probably uses different patterns of neural connectivity to solve different cognitive problems.

Perceptrons

In the late 1950s, researchers (e.g., Rosenblatt, 1959; Block, 1962; Widrow & Hoff, 1960) explored the properties of a simple connectionist model called a perceptron. This model connected a series of input units to one or more output units using simple unidirectional connections. The weights in the network were trained using an algorithm called the perceptron learning rule. The perceptron learning rule comes along with the rather attractive guarantee that, if a perceptron can be configured to solve a problem, the algorithm will succeed in finding the solution. The rub is that it often turns out that perceptrons cannot solve even very simple problems. For example, Minsky and Papert (1969) showed that perceptrons can encode a relation such as "black and tall," but not a relation such as "black but not tall." The problem with perceptrons is not with the learning rule, but with the strength of the basic computational mechanism. Today, perceptrons are only of historical interest.

Pattern Associators and Backpropagation

The successors to the perceptron are the pattern associators, and there are dozens of pattern associator architectures. Typically, these devices are designed as models of retrieval in human memory. They rely for their power on the holographic quality of neural networks which are able to retrieve stored patterns through vector manipulations. For example, a pattern associator should be able to take the sound /bal/ and retrieve the spelling B-A-L-L or it can take the smell of a rose and retrieve the vision of the thorns of the rose. Networks of this type are often trained using the delta rule or the extended delta rule. These rules compare the network's output patterns against some target signal and make weight adjustments to bring the network into line with the target.

The backpropagation architecture (Werbos, 1974) achieves additional computational power by adding an additional level of units between the input and output layers. These additional units are called "hidden units" because they have no direct connection to either the input or the output. Networks using backpropagation with hidden units and the delta rule can solve many types of problems that are difficult for simpler machines such as the perceptron. In fact, most current work in computational modeling of developmental phenomena makes use of the backpropagation framework. This single, simply characterized algorithm has demonstrated an ability to learn a wide variety of subtle patterns in the data.

Despite the proven success of backpropagation, there are several crucial problems that arise when we try to use this single architecture as an account for all aspects of cognitive and linguistic development. Each of the problems encountered by backpropagation has served as a stimulus to the development of interesting alternative frameworks. One basic problem that arises immediately as we try to match the backpropagation algorithm up to the brain is the fact that backpropagation assumes that connections which fire in a feed-forward fashion can also be trained in a feed-backward direction. However, we know that real neurons fire in only one direction and that this type of backwards training is not neurologically plausible. However, as Fausett (1990) shows, one can devise backpropagation networks that can be trained in a unidirectional and local manner by adding additional arrays of controlling units.

The study of the actual mechanics of weight changing in neural networks is very much the province of the cellular neurophysiologist. In this area, there is increasing evidence emphasizing the extent to which the neuron can compute complex functions. Hebb (1949) suggested that learning occurs when two cells fire simultaneously and the output of the postsynaptic cell functions to strengthen the firing of the synapse connecting the two cells. Although work by Kandel and Hawkins (1992) with the sea slug supports aspects of the Hebbian model of learning, Alkon and colleagues (1993) have found computationally more complex learning in higher organisms such as rabbits and rats. This non-Hebbian learning takes place locally on small areas of the dendritic cell membrane. Alkon has implemented a network model called Dystal that faithfully mimics these aspects of membrane activity and also works well as a connectionist pattern associator.

Networks That Deal with Time

In the standard backpropagation framework, processing is idealized as occurring at a single moment in time. This idealization may make sense for processes that are extremely brief or for decisions in which many factors are being weighed without time constraints. However, for problems such as word recognition, sentence production, seriation, and speeded chess playing, temporal components are crucial components of the task. One network architecture that deals with this problem is a variation on back propagation developed by Jordan (1986) and Elman (1990). This variation takes the standard three-layer architecture of pools A, B, and C shown in Figure 13.5 and adds a fourth input pool D of context units which has recurrent connections to pool B. Because of the recurrent or bidirectional connections between B and D, this architecture is known as *recurrent backpropagation.*

A recurrent backpropagation network encodes changes over time by storing information regarding previous states in the pool of units labeled as D. Consider how the network deals with the processing of a sentence such as "Mommy loves Daddy." When the first word comes in, pool C is activated and this activation is passed on to pool B and then

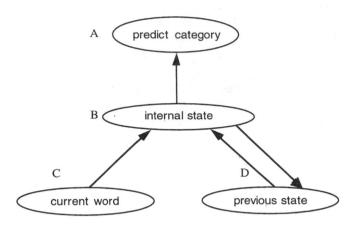

Figure 13.5 A recurrent backpropagation network.

pools A and D. The complete state of pool B at Time 1 is stored in pool D. The activation levels in pool D are preserved, while pools A, B, and C are set back to zero. At time 2 the networks hears the word "love" and a new pattern of activations is established on pool C. These activations are passed on to pools B, C, and D. However, because pool D has stored activations from the previous word, the new state is blended with the old state and pool C comes to represent aspects of both "Mommy" and "love."

Processing in a network of this type involves more than just storage of a superficial sequence of words or sounds. For example, in the simulations of sentence processing developed by Elman (1993), the output units are trained to predict the identity of the next word. In order to perform in this task, the network needs to implicitly extract part-of-speech information from syntactic co-occurrence patterns. Alternatively, the output units can be used to represent comprehension decisions, as in the model of MacWhinney (1996). In that model, part-of-speech information is assumed and the goal of the model is to select the agent and the patient using a variety of grammatical and pragmatic cues.

Another method for dealing with temporal ordering was developed by Grossberg (1978). In this system, linear ordering of elements such as the phonemes in a word is controlled by cluster units which sit above the component phoneme units and control their ordering as what Grossberg calls an "avalanche." The Elman and Grossberg systems are designed for markedly different problems. Grossberg's system works well for the learning of invariant serial orderings such as those found in lexical phonology and Elman's system is more appropriate for the learning of flexible, variant patterns of serial ordering, such as those found in syntax. It

would not be surprising to find that other problems in serial ordering required still other network architectures.

Avoiding Catastrophes. A serious limitation of the backpropagation algorithm is its tendency toward developmental instability. A backpropagation network trained on one set of inputs can undergo a process of "catastrophic interference" (McCloskey & Cohen, 1989) when the input corpus is shifted to a markedly different structure. The problem of catastrophic interference shows up clearly when a network is trained with one language (L1) and then suddenly switched to dealing with input from a second language (L2). What happens is that learning of L2 wipes out knowledge of L1 (MacWhinney, 1996). Of course, no such catastrophic interference occurs in real life. When we learn a second language in real life, our knowledge of our first language remains firm.

Catastrophic interference occurs in backpropagation networks because new memories tend to overwrite old memories. One class of solutions tries to address this problem by making minor changes to backpropagation. This can be done by making weight changes only for novel aspects of the input (Kortge, 1990), hand-tuning the input corpus to avoid sudden changes (Hetherington & Seidenberg, 1989), localizing the receptive fields for units (Kruschke, 1992), or adding units with different learning rates (Hinton & Plaut, 1987). Although these solutions solve the problem of catastrophic interference, they often force us to make overly restrictive assumptions about the possible distributions of cues in the environment.

Localized Memories. A more general approach to the problem of catastrophic interference and other forms of crosstalk focuses on the role of neuronal topology in controlling neuronal recruitment and memory development. In topological models, units are more specifically devoted to specific memories, interactions between memories tend to be confined to local areas, and major shifts in the character of the input do not overwrite these localized memories.

Kanerva's Sparse Distributed Memory (SDM) is one such topological approach. The SDM model allows for one-shot storage of new memories without crosstalk. However, memories must be stored at several neighboring locations to guarantee consistent retrieval. A similar framework has been proposed by Read, Nenov, and Halgren (1995) on the basis of Gardner-Meadwin's (1976) model of hippocampal functioning.

The idea of encoding memories through topological organization in the brain is further elaborated in the self-organizing feature map (SOFM) approach developed by Kohonen (1982) and Miikkulainen (1990). Self-organizing feature maps use an unsupervised, competitive learning algorithm. All input units are connected to cluster units which are organized in a two-dimensional topological grid (see Figure 13.6), which is actually a compressed representation of a multidimensional space. When an input is presented, the cluster unit that responds most strongly becomes the winner. The winning unit then decrements the units that are just outside its immediate neighborhood so that they are less likely to respond to a similar input when it is next presented. The pattern of inhibition follows the "Mexican hat" format found in cells of the visual cortex. In this way, two units that initially respond to the same set of inputs start to pull away from each other. As this process continues, the radius for each unit decreases and its specificity increases. MacWhinney (1996) found that a self-organizing feature map of 10,000 units was able to learn an array of 6,000 words with 99% accuracy. Thus, it seems that the SOFM architecture is well-suited for the learning of arbitrary associations such as words.

The success of feature maps in the learning of arbitrary associations, such as the sound-meaning associations involved in words, stands in marked contrast to the problems that backpropagation networks have with the same task. The backpropagation architecture is designed to detect patterns, rather than to encode arbitrary associations. When a backpropagation network is trained with a long list of English words, it will lose its ability to acquire new words after learning the first 700 words or so. Adding more hidden units to the network does not help at this point, since the limitation seems to be in the basic resolution of the weight space. The reason that backpropagation reaches saturation for learning new words is not because of the shortage of nodes, but because of problems with the basic algorithm. Backpropagation uses hidden units not as individual address spaces for individual lexical items, but as pattern detectors that search for commonalities between words. However, because words are really arbitrary associations between sounds and meanings, backpropagation is frustrated in its attempt to pick up meaningful or useful patterns. The SOFM architecture, on the other hand, can be used to simply throw a large number of only weakly associated memories onto a large feature map. As MacWhinney (1996) has found, feature maps and sparse distributed maps can learn items up to the size of the feature map. In this regard, they seem better suited to the task of lexical learning than does an architecture such as backpropagation.

Networks That Grow. In addition to the crosstalk problem that lies at the root of catastrophic interference, backpropagation networks also suffer from a problem with commitments to local minima during early phases of training. These networks tend to isolate the major patterns in the input early on and are often incapable of picking up secondary strategies that conflict with the basic patterns in the input. One way of solving this problem is to force the network to "start small." By giving the network only minimal resources at first and allowing it to recruit new resources when the problem becomes more difficult, it is possible to force the network to treat basic statistical regularities as fundamental, while still learning higher-order regularities later.

Within the backpropagation framework, there have been quite a few recent proposals about how to add new units during learning (Azimi-Sadjadi, Sheedvash, & Trujillo, 1993; Fahlman & Lebiére, 1990; Frean, 1990; Hirose, Yamashita, & Hijiya, 1991; Kadirkamanathan & Niranjan, 1993; Platt, 1991; Wynne-Jones, 1993). One of

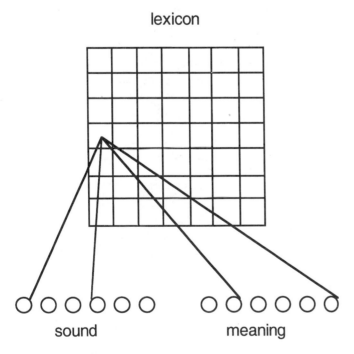

Figure 13.6 A self-organizing feature map illustrating connections for one lexical item.

these models is the "cascade correlation" approach of Fahlman and Lebiére (1990) which adds units when error reduction is not otherwise possible. The network begins its existence with only input and output units and no hidden units. In this form, it is equivalent to a perceptron. During training, new hidden units are added to the net in an effort to continually reduce the error in the output. As we will see below, this expansion of computational space through recruitment allows cascade-correlation networks to solve developmental problems that stymie standard backpropagation networks.

The idea of adding new units to networks to increase their computational capacity can be found in many frameworks. Within the framework of Adaptive Resonance Theory or ART (Carpenter, Grossberg, Markuzon, Reynolds, & Rosen, 1992; Carpenter, Grossberg, & Reynolds, 1991; Grossberg, 1987), recruitment is a basic part of network functioning. For example, Grossberg (1987) adds new units to a network when no current unit matches a new input within a certain level of tolerance. Blackmore and Miikkulainen (1993) present a self-organizing feature map (SOFM) approach to incremental grid growing that allows for the expansion of a feature map to correct for errors in the compression of high dimensional feature space onto the two-dimensional topological grid.

A crucial insight incorporated in the various recruitment models is the idea that, by starting off with minimal computational resources, the learning system is forced to deal first with the most general patterns in the data. In effect, the system can only deal with the first of the various factors that can be extracted by principal components analysis (PCA). Once this first factor is learned, the network finds that there is still some residual error and it recruits new units to extract additional regularities. However, these new units are then largely dedicated to a second aspect of the problem. In this way, the network comes closer to modeling the type of stage-like learning we see in the child.

Recruitment versus Deletion

Models that rely on the recruitment of new neurons have been criticized on the grounds that they go against facts of developmental neurobiology. We know that new neurons are not added after birth. In fact, development is more characterized by neuronal loss than by neuronal addition. Some theorists have seized on this fact to argue that, like the immune system, neural development works by generating a vast array of potential cognitive structures which are then weeded out during development (Changeux & Danchin, 1976; Edelman, 1987; Jerne, 1967). Extending

the analysis to issues in human development, Siegler (1989), Piatelli-Palmarini (1989), and Campbell (1960) have argued for the importance of "blind variation and selective retention" in creative thought and cognitive development.

Recent work calls into question some of the assumptions of this selectionist approach. Although it is true that there is a rapid loss of both cells and dendritic branches during the first months of life, the period of loss does not continue through development. Reassessing earlier claims about ongoing losses in synaptic density, Bourgeois, Goldman-Rakic, and Rakic (1994) have found ongoing synaptogenesis in prefrontal cortex during development. These findings match up with reports of increased volume of frontal cortex during development (Dekaban & Sadowsky, 1978; Jernigan et al., 1991) which indicate that brain development is not fundamentally selectionist and that additional resources may well be recruited during learning. This is not to say that the actual mechanisms supporting recruitment have yet been identified, only that models that use recruitment cannot be excluded on neurological grounds.

CONNECTIONISM AND DEVELOPMENT

We now turn to an examination of connectionist models of specific developmental processes. We will first look at models of the various component processes in language development. Second, we will examine general issues in cognitive development and their realization in connectionist models of specific cognitive tasks. Third, we will look at models of additional issues in development, including motor development and early brain maturation.

Connectionism and Language Development

The learning of language is a complex process that extends over the course of many years and which relies on interplay between several complex cognitive processes. Some recent accounts of language learning (Lightfoot, 1989; Pinker, 1994) tend to focus rather exclusively on the learning of grammatical markings and syntax, but language learning is more than just the learning of a few rules of grammar. In fact, the child devotes far more attention to tasks such as word learning, concept acquisition, articulatory control, discourse structuring, and conversational maintenance. No symbolic or connectionist model has been formulated that can handle all levels of language learning, although MacWhinney (1978, 1982, 1987a, 1988) and Pinker (1984) offered initial sketches in the symbolic framework. In the next sections, we will look at current work in connectionist models with an eye to discerning the shape of a new, more detailed, synthetic approach.

Word Learning

Current research in sentence processing (Juliano & Tanenhaus, 1993; Trueswell & Tanenhaus, 1991, 1992) has stressed the importance of individual words as determiners of sentence-level processing. The central role of words in phonological development and auditory learning has been recognized for nearly two decades (Ferguson & Farwell, 1975). Even discourse processes and narrative structures are grounded on specific lexical constructions (Goldberg, 1995).

For symbolic models, lexical learning is a computationally trivial problem, since symbolic models have no trouble picking up arbitrary numbers of arbitrary associations. However, the symbolic view of word learning as mere association does not match up well with developmental data. We know that children can learn new words quickly on the basis of a single encounter (Carey, 1978; Dollaghan, Biber, & Campbell, 1995), but only a few new words can be picked up at the same time. If we present a child with dozens of new words at once, learning starts to fall apart. Moreover, the exact nature of the representation constructed by the child learner or the adult second language learner (Atkinson, 1975) is often heavily dependent on the context of presentation (Kay & Anglin, 1982).

Networks that use backpropagation and hidden units have exactly the opposite problem with modeling lexical learning. These networks typically cannot learn more than about 700 lexical forms. After this level, the hidden units are so fully invested in distinguishing phonological and semantic subtypes and their associations that there is simply no room for new words. Adding more hidden units doesn't solve this problem, since all the interconnections must be computed and eventually the learning algorithm bogs down.

The problems faced by backpropagation are not general to all network models. Building on earlier models from Grossberg (1978, 1987), Houghton (1990), and Burgess and Hitch (1992), Gupta and MacWhinney (1996) have constructed a lexical learning model that uses three hierarchically-ordered layers, as illustrated in Figure 13.7. The lowest layer is a set of phonological units for the sounds of a word. Above this layer, is a set of phonological chunks representing the various syllable patterns of the language. On the top is a programmable level that controls

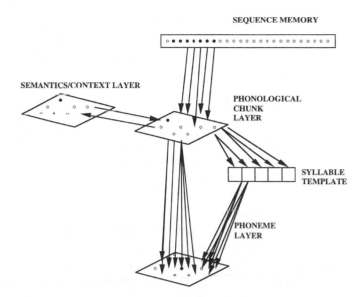

Figure 13.7   A lexical learning model using three hierarchically-ordered layers. From "Vocabulary acquisition and verbal short-term memory: Computation and neural bases," by P. Gupta & B. MacWhinney, 1996, *Brain and Language*. In Press. Copyright © 1996 by Academic Press, Inc. Reprinted with permission.

the order of syllables within the word. Each new word is learned as a new node on the top layer and a series of weights on the connections from this layer to lower layers. Gupta and MacWhinney show that this model does a good job of accounting for a wide variety of well-researched phenomena in the literature on word learning, immediate serial recall, interference effects, and rehearsal in both adults and children (Gathercole & Baddeley, 1993).

A major limitation of the Gupta and MacWhinney model is its reliance on a rigid fixed level of items for the top-level word nodes. Once the initial number of nodes has been used up, the system would need to recruit a new node for each new word. However, simply inserting a fresh node into the model for each new word requires us to make excessively strong assumptions about neuronal plasticity, while also failing to capture the ways in which new words interact with old lexical structures. As we noted earlier in our discussion of the model of MacWhinney (1996), by relying on a fuller address space of the type proposed by Kanerva or Miikkulainen, problems with the learning of new lexical items can be minimized.

Word Meaning

The task of simulating the semantic aspects of word learning is extremely challenging, because of the open-ended nature of meaning. Connectionist models have found two ways of dealing with this problem. One approach structures the world as a miniature perceptual system. This mini-world approach was developed first by Chauvin (1989) and echoed in a replication by Plunkett and Sinha (1992). The goal of the Chauvin model is to associate dot patterns with arbitrary labels. Learning is done using *autoassociation.* First the net is given an image and asked to activate a label, next it is given a label and asked to activate an image, and then it is given a trial with both image and label presented together. Plunkett and Sinha note that the cue validity of the label in their input corpus is higher than that of the image, since the label predicts a unique image, but an image does not predict a unique label. Unfortunately, it is difficult to see how a relation of this type can map onto the facts involved in real lexical structures where the opposite is usually the case.

Because the Chauvin/Plunkett-Sinha model uses back-propagation, it does not perform well in the basic lexical acquisition task. However, it does succeed in capturing some of the other phenomena associated with lexical learning. In particular, Plunkett and Sinha claim that their model captures these three phenomena:

1. *The prototype effect.* This effect replicates the original findings of Posner and Keele (1968; 1970) and has been observed in other connectionist models (McClelland & Rumelhart, 1985; Schyns, 1991), as well.

2. *The word learning spurt.* The model only starts producing labels after the first 20 epochs. At this point, Plunkett and Sinha view the onset of learning as similar to the "word spurt" that occurs in children. However, the cause of the delay in the model is the low validity of the image as a cue to the label and it is difficult to see how this structuring of lexical validities maps onto the real facts of lexical structures. Thus, it appears that the model is demonstrating the word learning spurt for the wrong reason.

3. *The superiority of comprehension over production.* Here, again, the reason for the superiority of comprehension is the higher cue validity of the label and it appears that the model is displaying the correct behavior for the wrong reasons.

Despite these limitations, the Chauvin/Plunkett and Sinha model serves as a useful starting point for thinking about comprehension-production relations in development (Mac-Whinney, 1990).

In another exploration within the mini-world framework, Schyns (1991) applied a Kohonen network to the task of learning three competing categories with prototype structures. The three categories were geometric patterns that were blurred by noise in order to create a prototype structure, although the actual prototypes were never displayed. The simulations showed that the network could acquire the patterns and demonstrate human-like categorization and naming behavior. When presented with a fourth new word that overlapped with one of the first three words, the system broke off some of the territory of the old referent to match up with the new name. Schyns interpreted this as evidence that the network was obeying the mutual exclusivity constraint of Markman (1989). However, the operation of his network can be understood even more clearly in terms of the forces of contrast and competition described by Clark (1987) and MacWhinney (1989).

An alternative approach to the development of word meaning focuses on the learning of small fields of real words. Three studies have been conducted to date. Shultz, Buckingham, and Oshima-Takane (1994) use the cascade-correlation algorithm to acquire the use of "you" and "me" from two types of input: child-directed speech and speech directed to a third party. The problem with learning the meaning of words like "you" and "me" is that the actual reference of the word is constantly changing. The best way to figure out the meanings of these words is to observe two other people using them. In this way, the child is able to see that "you" is used for the addressee and "me" for the speaker and that these words only have meaning in the context of the speaker-listener relation. Research by Oshima-Takane, Goodz, and Derevensky (in press) has shown that learning is faster when children are exposed to relatively more speech addressed to a third party, typically an older sibling, since this input makes the use of "you" clearer. By comparing input corpora with varying amounts of speech directed to a third party, Shultz et al. were able to model this effect.

Another study of meaning development by Li and Mac-Whinney (1996) used a standard backpropagation architecture to model the learning of reversive verbs that used the prefix "un-" as in untie or "dis-" as in disavow. The model succeeded in capturing the basic developmental stages reported by Bowerman (1982) and Clark, Carpenter, and Deutsch (1995) involving the production of errors such as unbreak or disbend. The network's performance was based on its internalization of what Whorf (1938; 1941) called the "cryptotype" for the reversive which involved a "covering, enclosing, and surface-attaching meaning" that is present in a word like untangle, but absent in a form such as un-break. Whorf viewed this category as a prime example of the ways in which language reflects and possibly shapes thought.

The various models of learning word meaning we have discussed so far all treat meaning as if it were a fixed set of elements for any given word. However, nothing could be farther from the truth. Virtually every common word in our vocabulary has many alternative meanings and shades of meanings. In extreme cases, such as the verbs "put" and "run," the dictionary may list up to 70 alternative meanings. Typically, the choice of one meaning over another is determined by the other words in the sentence. For example, when we say that "the ball rolled over the table," we are thinking of the word over as meaning across. However, when we say that "Jim placed the snuffer over the candle," we are thinking of over as meaning covering. These competitions between the various alternative readings of words like "over" were discussed from a general connectionist perspective by MacWhinney (1989). Subsequently, an implemented connectionist model of the learning of the meanings of "over" by a network was developed by Harris (1990; 1994b). The Harris model is capable of taking new input test sentences of the type "the pin rolled over the table" and deciding on the basis of past learning that the meaning involved is across, rather than covering or above. It does this only on the basis of the co-occurrence patterns of the words involved, rather than on information from their individual semantics. Thus, it learns that combinations like ball, roll, and table tend to activate across without regard to facts such as knowing that balls are round and can roll or knowing that tables are flat and that rolling involves movement.

Inflectional Morphology

One of the most active areas of connectionist modeling has been the study of the child's learning of the ways in which words change when they are combined with grammatical markings such as suffixes or prefixes. These markings are called *inflections* and the system that governs the use of these inflections is called *inflectional morphology*. A simple case of inflectional learning is the system of patterns that help us choose to say "bent" instead of "bended" as the past tense of the verb bend. Inflectional learning is also involved in the learning of the correct form of the German definite article that we examined earlier. There are now well over thirty empirical studies and simulations investigating this topic from a connectionist perspective. The majority of work on this topic has examined the learning of English verb morphology with a particular focus on the English past tense. The goal of these models is the learning of irregular forms such as went or fell, along with regular past tense forms such as wanted and jumped. Other areas of interest include German noun declension, Dutch stress placement, and German participle formation. This work has examined six core issues:

1. *Cues versus rules.* The most central issue addressed in this research is whether or not one can model the learning of inflectional morphology without using formal rules. Pinker (1991) has argued that irregular forms are indeed produced by connectionist networks, but that regular forms are produced by a regular rule. However, Pinker's attempts to preserve a role for rules in human cognition runs into problems with the fact that even the most regular patterns or "rules" display phonological conditioning and patterns of gradience (Bybee, 1993) of the type that are easily captured in a connectionist network.

2. *Phonological representation.* Most current models of inflectional learning use a system for phonological representation like the one introduced by MacWhinney, Leinbach, Taraban, and MacDonald (1989). This system assigns each node a status on each of three coding systems. The first coding system indicates the position of the node in the syllable, the second indicates the position of the syllable in the word, and the third represents the presence or absence of a phonetic distinctive feature. Because this representational system relies on standard linguistic concepts, it addresses most of the concerns expressed by Pinker and Prince (1988) with earlier connectionist models of inflectional learning. An elaborated version of this same representational system can be found in Gasser (1991, 1992). Gasser's models emphasize the serial quality of morphological formations by relying on predictive recurrent networks. The system Gasser proposes uses three separate recurrent subnetworks for phonemic structure, syllabic structure, and metrical structure. On the top level, the three levels would be integrated in terms of lexical items. However, exactly how this integration of separate recurrent subnetworks should occur remains unclear, since Gasser never fully implemented his model.

3. *U-shaped learning.* A major shortcoming of nearly all connectionist models has been their inability to capture

the patterns of overgeneralization and recovery from overgeneralization known as u-shaped learning. Empirical work by Marcus et al. (1992) has shown that strong u-shaped learning patterns occur only for some verbs and only for some children. The models of MacWhinney and Leinbach (1991) and Plunkett and Marchman (1991) showed levels of u-shaped learning in rough conformity with the patterns observed by Marcus et al. Moreover, Plunkett and Marchman showed that u-shaped learning levels could be affected by changes in the type and token frequencies of irregular verbs in the input.

4. *Rote learning of irregulars.* Although models like MacWhinney and Leinbach or Plunkett and Marchman succeed in demonstrating some u-shaped learning, this success is at least in part misleading. In order to correctly model the child's learning of inflectional morphology, models must go through a period of virtually error free learning of irregulars, followed by a period of learning of the first irregulars accompanied by the first overregularizations (Marcus et al., 1992). No current model consistently displays all of these features in exactly the right combination. MacWhinney (1996) has argued that models that rely exclusively on backpropagation will never be able to display the correct combination of developmental patterns and that a two-process connectionist approach will be needed. The basic process is one that learns new inflectional formations, both regular and irregular, by rote as items in self-organizing feature maps. The secondary process is a backpropagation network that uses the information inherent in feature maps to extract secondary productive generalizations.

5. *The role of semantic factors.* The first attempts to model morphological learning focused exclusively on the use of phonological features as both input and output. However, it is clear that the formation of past tense forms must also involve semantic factors. In English, the use of semantic information is associated with the irregular patterns of inflection. The idea is that, since we cannot access "went" by combining "go" and "-ed," it might be that we can access it directly by a semantic route. Of course, this idea is much like that underlying the dual-route theory. In German gender, the role of semantic information is much clearer. Köpcke and Zubin (Köpcke, 1994; Köpcke & Zubin, 1983, 1984; Zubin & Köpcke, 1981, 1986) have shown that a wide variety of both phonological and semantic factors are used in predicting the gender of German nouns and their plural.

Some of the features involved include: alcoholic beverages, superordinates, inherent biological gender, gem stones, body parts, rivers inside Germany, and light versus heavy breezes. Simulations (Cottrell & Plunkett, 1991; Gupta & MacWhinney, 1992; MacWhinney, 1996) have integrated semantic and phonological information in various ways. However, a better understanding of the ways in which semantic factors interact during word formation will require a more extensive modeling of lexical items and semantic features.

6. *Extensions of irregular patterns to new words.* Extending earlier work by Bybee and Slobin (1982), Prasada and Pinker (1993) examined the abilities of native English speakers to form the past tense for nonsense words like plink, plup, or ploth. They found that, the further the word diverged from the standard phonotactic rules for English verbs, the more likely the subjects were to form the past tense by just attaching the regular "-ed" suffix. Ling and Marinov (1993) noted that the original verb-learning model developed by Rumelhart and McClelland (1987) failed to match these new empirical data, largely because of its tendency to overapply irregular patterns. To correct this problem, Ling and Marinov created a nonconnectionist symbolic pattern associator which did a better job modeling the Prasada and Pinker data. However, MacWhinney (1993) found that the network model of MacWhinney and Leinbach (1991) worked as well as Ling and Marinov's symbolic model in terms of matching up to the Prasada and Pinker generalization data.

Phonology

In the area of speech processing, connectionist models have been developed primarily as ways of simulating aspects of adult word recognition. The recurrent backpropagation architecture has been used in word recognition models developed by Norris (1994), Waibel, Hanazawa, Hinton, Shikano, and Lang (1988), and Watrous, Shastri, and Waibel (1987). Recently, Markey (1994) has developed a realistic physical representation of the young child's vocal apparatus and used it to model the development of phonetic and phonological skills. Markey's model is able to capture some of the basic aspects of early phonological development. Hopefully, we will soon see additional models that will allow us to better understand how much of early phonological development is determined by the articulatory apparatus and how much by the structure of the words being learned.

Reading

Sejnowski and Rosenberg (1988) presented an entertaining demonstration of a system called NETtalk that learned to read aloud. The system took as its input the orthographic representation of English words and was trained to produce computerized speech as its output. At first the network made only crude approximations to the sounds of the words and then moved phonologically closer and closer through training. In this regard, the network fails to actually capture the nature of early reading in the child where words are fully formed phonologically and the task is to extract enough cues to effect retrieval of the full word form (Simon, 1976; Simon & Simon, 1973). However, a positive aspect of the NETtalk model is its ability to extract local graphemic linear dependencies that a beginning reader might use to derive the sound of a word.

A more complete picture of the development of early reading skills was provided in a backpropagation model developed by Seidenberg and McClelland (1989). An important quality of this model is that it emphasizes the ways in which both regular spellings such as hint or mint can be controlled by the same computational mechanism that also controls irregular spellings such as pint. In the traditional symbolic approach (Marshall & Newcombe, 1973), a distinction is made between rote storage for irregular forms and pattern-based storage for regular forms. This distinction motivates a dual-process or dual-route approach to reading. Seidenberg and McClelland show that one can model the learning and usage of both regulars and irregulars in a single model with a single set of processes.

The Seidenberg-McClelland model has been challenged on empirical grounds (Behrman & Bub, 1992; Besner, Twilley, McCann, & Seergobin, 1990; Coltheart, Curtis, Atkins, & Haller, 1993). One problem with the model was its inability to acquire its own training set. However, by using a phonological input representation much like that developed by MacWhinney et al. (1989), Plaut, McClelland, Seidenberg, and Patterson (1995) were able to improve on the performance of the original model. A second problem with the model arose in connection with the modeling of data from neurological patients with deep dyslexia. For these patients, the model underestimated the sparing of high-frequency regular and irregular forms, as predicted by the dual-route model. Here, again, the revised coding system of Plaut et al. was able to improve on the performance of the original model.

In evaluating the status of the debate between single-route and dual-route accounts of reading and lexical processing, it is important to recognize that connectionist theory makes no specific commitment to the single-route concept. Moreover, it may be impossible to avoid some aspects of duality, even in the most homogeneous model. For example, Kawamoto (1993; Kawamoto & Zemblidge, 1992) has shown that subjects tend to produce incorrect pronunciations of irregulars more quickly than correct pronunciations. Thus, the pronunciation of pint to rhyme with hint is faster than the correct pronunciation of pint. Kawamoto models this effect using a ART-type model. At first, the large number of words with the regular "-int" shape activate a common pattern. If the subject produces a reading of the word at this time, it will be an error. A few milliseconds later, the slower connections to the irregular pronunciation start to dominate and the correct pronunciation will be produced. This is still a single mechanism, but the presence of two routes is simulated by contrasting pattern activations at different time points during the settling of the network.

Syntactic Classes

Psycholinguists working in the standard symbolic tradition (Chomsky, 1965; Fodor & Pylyshyn, 1988; Lachter & Bever, 1988) have pointed to the learning of syntax as a quintessential problem for connectionist approaches. One of the key abilities involved in the learning of syntax is the abstraction of syntactic classes or "parts of speech," such as nouns, verbs, or prepositions. In the theory of universal grammar, these categories are innately given. However, their actual realization differs so much from language to language that it makes sense to explore accounts that induce these categories from the input data. Elman (1993) has presented a connectionist model that does just this. The model relies on a recurrent architecture of the type presented in Figure 13.7 above. The training set for the model consists of dozens of simple English sentences such as "The big dog chased the girl." By examining the weight patterns on the hidden units in the fully trained model, Elman showed that the model was conducting implicit learning of the parts of speech. For example, after the word big in our example sentence, the model would be expecting to activate a noun. The model was also able to distinguish between subject and object relative structures, as in "the dog the cat chased ran" and "the dog that chased the cat ran."

Even more interestingly, Elman found that the network only learned to pick up these positional expectations when it began with a narrow perceptual window of two or three words. If the network started with too large a window, it could not focus on detection of the most basic determinants of syntactic positioning. Elman interpreted this contrast as underscoring the "importance of starting small." In many ways, this analysis is much like the one offered by Schultz for the importance of a learning algorithm that starts off with limited resources and only recruits new resources when it is unable to further reduce error.

Lexical Segmentation and Masking

In order to process sentences effectively, we need to be able to segment out words from the ongoing speech stream. Norris (1994) proposes a system called ShortList which uses a recurrent net of the type given in Figure 13.5 to process incoming phonemes left-to-right. A network of this type does fine with many words. However, it has trouble with words like catalog which have what Norris calls a "right context" problem. When processing the word catalog, a simple recurrent net would recognize the word cat and decide that this word had actually occurred, if it were not somehow forced to hold off and process further right context. In order to prevent this from happening, Norris suggests that there must be a short list of competitors that include words like cat, cattle, catalog, and others like them that will compete for full recognition of the input material. The ShortList implementation of this process uses a hand-wired word list. However, Miikkulainen (1993) has suggested that it would be possible to model this same process using self-organizing feature maps.

Once a word has been successfully detected, the sounds that activated it need to be masked out, in order to block multiple recognition of the same input by alternative competitors. Take a sentence like "I gave my cat a Miranda doll." Once the word cat has been selected, its component phonemes are "masked" in order to avoid the additional activation of the form "catamaran" on the basis of the string "cat a Miran." Once a word is fully recognized and its component sounds are masked, it must then begin to participate in higher level syntactic and semantic patterns. The exact nature of this conversion is not yet clear. There have been several suggestions regarding the nature of this short-term verbal memory:

1. As soon as words are linked together into conceptual clusters, they can be used to activate a unique underlying meaning that no longer requires verbal storage.
2. Before this linkage occurs, words may be retained in a phonological loop (Baddeley, 1986). This immediate

rehearsal requires that words be present in a primarily articulatory form (Gupta & MacWhinney, 1994).

3. It is also possible that some additional mechanism operates on lexical items to encode their serial occurrence without reference to either meaning or sound. This could be done in terms of some additional episodic, possibly hippocampal, mechanism that stores activation levels of words prior to masking. A system of this type is close to the Competitive Queuing mechanism proposed first by Grossberg and then again by Houghton.

Further experimental work will be needed to decide which of these three mechanisms is involved at which points in the storage of short term verbal memories. However, there is already good (Gupta & MacWhinney, 1996) evidence that various neural mechanisms are available to support masking in the lexicon.

Bilingualism

The study of bilingualism and adult second language learning is a particularly promising and challenging area for connectionist research. Recent research in second language acquisition (Dechert & Raupach, 1989; Flege & Davidian, 1984; Hancin-Bhatt, 1994; Harrington, 1987; Johnson, 1989; MacWhinney, 1992; Odlin, 1989; Sasaki, 1994) has underscored the importance of transfer of first language skills to the learning of the second language. Because of its emphasis on pattern generalization, the backpropagation algorithm is well-suited to modeling transfer effects. In one of the first simulations designed to examine these issues, Gasser (1990) constructed an auto-associative network that used backpropagation training for the learning of basic word orders in second language learning. In one simulation, the network was first trained with a first language order of Subject-Verb (SV) and then exposed to a set of second language sentences with Verb-Subject (VS) order. In the other "mirror-image" simulation, the network began with VS in the first language and then shifted to SV in the second language. The network demonstrated a strong tendency to transfer the first language word order to the second language, particularly for words that were similar semantically. This type of lexically-based transfer for word order is exactly what one would expect for a strong pattern generalizing network. However, there is not yet any actual empirical data that would support the importance of this effect in real second language learning.

MacWhinney (1996) reports on unpublished work by Janice Johnson that adapts the architecture of the recurrent network shown in Figure 13.5 to the problem of second

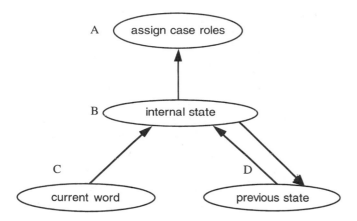

Figure 13.8 Architecture for the Johnson-MacWhinney model for second language learning.

language learning. The exact shape of the model is given again as Figure 13.8.

In these simulations, the input in pool C is a pattern that represents the status of the "current word" along the dimensions of animacy, number, case, agreement-marking, part-of-speech, and language. We assume that this information is available through the individual lexical item. Note that this highly structured form of the input differs radically from the raw word level input used by Elman (1993). Because of the highly structured shape of the input, this network performs much better than the Elman net as a sentence processor and interpreter. The task of the network is to assign the agent, object, and perspective roles to the correct words. In order to get these assignments right, the network must activate the correct output units in pool A. For example, the network can choose between activating a node that assigns the first noun as agent and a competing node that assigns the second noun as agent. Training involves the presentation to the network of sentences, one word at a time. For example, the input could be "the dog is chased by the cat." In this case, the network might begin by thinking that "the dog" is the agent. However, once the passive form of the verb is detected, the weight on this role assignment is decreased and the second noun is selected as agent instead. When the network is processing passive sentences, we find that it goes through an on-line reversal or "garden-path," first activating a choice of the first noun as agent and then reversing this activation to choose the second noun as the agent.

The network was trained initially with a wide variety of English sentence patterns. At the end of this initial training, it was performing well in the role assignment task for English. Then, the input was extended to include a full

corpus of parallel sentences for Dutch. After a period of mixed training, the network then continued with Dutch-only training for a further period. The first basic finding of this research was that the exact weights of the various cues in the model matched up well with a large body of empirical research summarized in MacWhinney and Bates (1989). In particular, the model learned the basic English SVO pattern quickly and then continued to learn the VOS and OSV patterns found in adult speakers. The second finding was that, when learning Dutch, the model showed exactly the type of word order transfer effects reported by McDonald (1987, 1989) for the learning of Dutch by English speakers and the learning of English by Dutch speakers. Finally, the model also showed a clear tendency toward "catastrophic interference" if the period of mixed-language training was omitted. A more robust, general approach to the catastrophic interference problem in this network and others like it could be developed if the network were given a firmer grounding on the learning of syntactic patterns on the basis of generalization from particular lexical items, as we noted earlier.

Connectionism and Developmental Theory

Connectionism offers a fresh perspective on a variety of issues of ongoing concern to developmentalists, including the emergence of symbols and representations, the movement between developmental stages, and the role of nonlinearities in development.

Stages and Transitions

The simplest developing system is one that shows only one type of uniform change over time. For example, a falling ball undergoes only one type of transition during its downward movement. We can use Galileo's equation for acceleration to compute the distance traveled as a function of acceleration a and time t. For this simple, uniform system, we have a clear rule that allows us to predict the state of the system at each time t.

More complex systems can go through a series of stages during state transitions. For example, a drop of rain can begin as cloud vapor, form into a droplet, freeze into hail, fall to the ground, and then melt into slush. Each of these state transitions delimit specific stages in the life of the droplet. In the human child, stages of this sort abound. For example, after learning the first word, children spend several months slowly picking up a few additional words. Then, suddenly, we see a rapid growth in vocabulary that has been called the vocabulary "burst." The vocabulary burst does not emerge overnight, but builds over the course of several weeks. However, if we plot the size of the vocabulary on the y-axis and the child's age on the x-axis we will note a marked upward acceleration at the beginning of this period. Such changes indicate a stage-like quality in development.

Piaget has characterized the intellectual growth of the child in terms of four major epochs, each composed of several periods with some further divisions of the periods into subperiods. However, Piaget's characterization of these stages as invariant properties of human development is no longer widely accepted and few researchers are interested in developing simulations to account for the child's movement through the classical set of Piagetian stages. This is not to deny the reality of major qualitative changes in cognition as the child moves from infancy to adolescence. However, attempts to capture these changes across skill domains have not been successful. Because of this, connectionist models of stagelike transitions have tended to focus not on broad changes in cognition, but on local discontinuities within the development of specific skills. The areas that have been most closely investigated are the balance beam, velocity computation, and seriation.

Balance Beam

One of the clearest analyses of stage transitions in cognitive development is the case of the balance beam problem studied first by Piaget. Earlier we examined the production-system accounts for learning of the balance beam problem by Klahr and Siegler (1978). McClelland (1989, 1995) has noted that, although these production-system models provide a good description of the four balance beam rules discussed earlier, they tell us little about the forces that drive the child from one rule system to the next.

McClelland was able to construct a backpropagation model of the balance beam problem that used 20 input units. There were 10 positional units devoted to the 5 positions to the left of the fulcrum and the 5 positions to the right of the fulcrum. The 10 weight units were dedicated to represent the numbers of weights stacked up at a position with 5 units for the possible number of weights on the left and 5 units for the possible weights on the right. A given problem could be encoded with a total of 4 units turned on. For example, take a problem with 4 weights at a distance of 3 right and 5 weights at a distance of 2 left. The units turned on would then be 4-right-weight, 5-left-weight, 3-right-distance, and 2-left-distance. In order to bias the network toward reliance on the weight cue over the distance cue, McClelland included a large number of cases in which

the distance cue was neutralized, thereby focusing the network's attention to the weight cue.

Using this type of representation, McClelland was able to model many aspects of the learning of this task. The network began with performance that relied on Rule 1 and moved on to learn Rule 2 and then Rule 3. It never acquired full use of Rule 4, but, McClelland argues, this is because some aspects of the use of Rule 4 in adults involve the application of full mathematical analysis. However, the network was able to capture aspects of the rather subtle "torque distance effect" detected in studies by Ferretti and Butterfield (1986) and Wilkening and Anderson (1982). These studies have shown that subjects perform best and most consistently on balance beam problems when it is clear perceptually that one side has an overwhelming combination of weight and distance in its favor. When the balance between the two sides is closer numerically, decisions are less consistent. Torque distance effects indicate that subjects are not simply applying an all-or-none rule, but are performing a type of cue-weighting that is much like that conducted inside a neural network.

Shultz, Schmidt, Buckingham, and Mareschal (1995) extended McClelland's model by using the cascade correlation variation of the backpropagation algorithm. Shultz et al. argue that static backpropagation networks with only a few hidden units can succeed at modeling the first stages of development, but are unable to reach higher levels of performance, because their weights become too closely tuned to solving the basic levels of the problem. This was true for McClelland's balance beam model, which learned Rules 1, 2, and aspects of 3, but was unable to learn Rule 4. However, using the cascade correlation framework, Shultz et al. were able to model successful learning of all four rules.

These models make two important points. First, both the McClelland and the Shultz et al. models show that connectionist models can provide good accounts of perceptual aspects of learning such as the torque distance effect. Second, Shultz's model shows that static networks that begin life with abundant numbers of extra hidden units may fail to perform the type of architectural decomposition of a problem space that is required for successful mastery. Models that start out small and are forced to recruit new units when they run out of steam are more likely to be able to focus first on the core of a problem and then add the details as elaborations of this core.

Other Physical Coordinations

In addition to their work on the balance beam problem, Shultz and his colleagues have developed connectionist models for three other types of physical coordinations. These include the learning of seriation, potency-resistance, and velocity-distance-time relations. Mareschal and Shultz (1993) developed a model of seriation that attempts to simulate the developmental progression reported by Piaget (1965). The model's task is to order a series of six sticks, each with a different length, so that the shortest is on the left and the longest is on the right. This is done by placing one stick in position at a time. The network is composed of two independent modules—a "which" module and a "where" module (Jacobs, Jordan & Barto, 1991). The "which" module is given the task of deciding which stick to move at a given point in the problem. The "where" module is given the task of deciding where to position each stick in terms of one of six possible spatial positions.

The results for these simulations of seriation learning match up closely with the empirical findings reported by Piaget. In stage 1, performance is close to chance. In stage 2, the network forms pairs and triplets that are correctly ordered, but the whole array is not correct. In stage 3, the whole array is ordered, but through largely trial-and-error repetition of subgroup ordering. In stage 4, seriation is performed correctly with previous analysis.

Buckingham and Shultz (1994) developed a model of the learning of the relations inherent in the physical relations expressed by these equations: $d = vt$, $v = d/t$, and $t = d/v$. These equations relate distance, velocity, and time through multiplicative relations. Wilkening (1981) found that children tend to progress through three levels of information integration in learning these relations. First, they relate each quantity only to itself. Second, they take into account the effect of the other two determining variables, but employ subtraction or addition instead of the correct division or multiplication rules. Third, they acquire the correct division or multiplication rules. Buckingham and Shultz (1994) were able to capture this three-stage developmental sequence in a neural network model. As in the other simulations reported by Shultz et al. (1995), the movement through these stages was facilitated by use of the cascade-correlation algorithm which tends to force simple solutions at early periods, but allows for the recruitment of additional resources to solve problems in more complex ways later on. In order to reach the more extreme values required by the multiplicative rule, weights have to first move through a set of values that match the additive rule. As additional units are recruited, these weights move closer to approximating a multiplicative relation.

Finally, Shultz and his colleagues have also studied the learning of resistance-potency relations. When a force with a given potency goes directly against a force with a certain resistance, the resultant force is computed by subtracting the two vectors. However, when a ramp is included in the physical system, the sum of the two vectors is computed by division, rather than subtraction. Shultz et al. (1995) were able to simulate the learning of both types of computations and showed that the subtractive relations were learned earlier than the division relations. Again, these effects seem to emerge from basic facts about the process of weight changes in neural networks.

Attachment

Van Geert (1991) developed a dynamic systems model designed to model growth curve developments in both vocabulary acquisition and the formation of attachment relations. One particularly interesting aspect of his model is the analysis he provides for the interaction between two competing developmental strategies. Van Geert shows how a variety of growth curves can arise from the competition and that the shapes of these curves depend on the internal stability of the two separate processes. In a system with optimally sensitive parenting, attachment grows steadily over time to reach a ceiling level. In a system with insensitive parenting, attachment grows weakly to reach a lower, but steady state. In a system with inconsistently sensitive parenting, the resulting attachment behavior of the child is extremely variable and unstable. These patterns of growth match up well with empirical data on the development of attachment under conditions of consistent and inconsistent parenting (Ainsworth, Blehar, Waters, & Wall, 1978; Belsky, Rovine, & Taylor, 1984).

Connectionism and Brain Development

Connectionist theory is extremely rich in terms of its implications for brain development. The first major area for which connectionism is relevant is brain development during embryogenesis. Here, connectionist models suggest that the commitment and inductance of particular neural areas to particular functions is driven by connections between areas and sensorimotor functions. The idea is that the shape of the brain emerges under the real physical constraints of the sensory and motor systems to which it is linked, rather than out of response to some abstract genetic blueprint for a set of disembodied innate ideas. To consider an example of how this works, consider the development of columns in the visual cortex (Hubel & Weisel, 1963). Miller, Keller, and Stryker (1989) have formulated network models that show how this columnar organization can arise from competitive interactions between signals from the two eyes. In general, it may be true that patterns of connectivity in the brain arise from the competition between signals arriving from different sensory systems and signals being sent to motor processes (Walsh & Cepko, 1992, 1993).

Connectionism may also help us to understand some of the mysteries of brain development during infancy and early childhood. Work on children with perinatal brain lesions (Aram & Eisele, 1992; Dennis, 1980; Feldman, 1993; Feldman, Janosky, Scher, & Wareham, 1994; Thal et al., 1991) has demonstrated the remarkable ability of the young brain to acquire normal language functioning after even the most severe early lesions. How the brain reorganizes to achieve this dynamic response is one of the great challenges facing developmental psychology and it is one in which connectionist modeling can play an important role. Recent constructivist accounts of brain development (Montague & Sejnowski, 1994; Quartz & Sejnowski, 1995) point out some possible mechanisms for changes in brain function, even after major damage. These models note that the continual refinement of patterns of connectivity is driven by local mechanisms, including dendritic growth, synaptogenesis, myelinization, and changes in membrane potential. In a constructivist model of the brain new synaptic connections are viewed as emerging through the action of nitrous oxide. When a cell fires, it broadcasts nitrous oxide to nearby cells and encourages the development of projections in the direction of the gradient of diffusion. A mechanism of this type fits in well with ideas about topological organization which we discussed earlier such as the self-organizing feature map models of Kohonen and Miikkulainen or the sparse distributed memory of Kanerva. However, a full account of reorganization after early brain damage may require more than just the local reorganization offered by these models.

The various connectionist models described in this section represent only a first step toward resolving some of the enduring issues in cognitive development. Bechtel and Abrahamsen (1991) outline the further potential of such models, including: (a) a new interpretation of the distinction between maturation and learning; (b) a computational instantiation of the distinction between accommodation and assimilation; (c) an account of context effects (in which minor task variations have large effects on preschooler's performance [Gelman, 1978]); and (d) explanations of many of the phenomena and anomalies associated with stages and transitions.

FUTURE DIRECTIONS

Having presented a description of the two principal approaches to computational modeling of cognitive development, we close with a discussion of their similarities, differences, and current inadequacies. Three themes run through this final discussion. One is that the two approaches are not as distinct as their practitioners often claim. The second is that—for all of their accomplishments—both approaches must solve some very difficult remaining problems. The third theme is that such challenges can only be met by infusing computational techniques into the training of the next generation of cognitive developmentalists.

Comparing Connectionist and Production-System Models

Although connectionist forays into cognitive development are often accompanied by the dismissal of "symbolic" approaches as unsuited to the task, we wonder whether the differences are as substantial as are sometimes claimed. Connectionist models are usually proposed as radically different from production-system architectures, and more neuronally plausible. However, one can ask where the fundamental differences lie: in the parallelism of the processing, in the distributed knowledge, or in the connectivity of that knowledge?

1. Parallelism can not be the source of the difference, because during the "match" or "recognize" phase of a production system's recognize-act cycle, the condition side of all productions are matched in parallel with all the elements in working memory.[6] In some systems, working memory is defined as the set of elements in a vast semantic memory that are above some threshold, so the match process is massively parallel and the connectivity between working memory elements and the productions is dynamic and potentially unbounded.

2. What about distributed knowledge? The extent to which knowledge is distributed or modularized in a production system depends entirely upon the grain size that elements or productions are supposed to capture. Thus, a

---

[6] The actual implementation of this parallel match occurs in a serial Von Neumann machine. But so too do the implementations of the learning algorithms in PDP models. This microlevel of implementation is not regarded as part of either theoretical stance.

single production might represent a very explicit and verbalizable rule; it might represent a small piece of processing for a complex, implicit piece of knowledge; or it might represent a complex pattern of cue associations much like those found in connectionist models (Ling & Marinov, 1993). Similarly, in PDP models, the individual element can represent knowledge at any grain size: from an individual neuron, to an assembly of neurons, to the word "neuron." There is nothing inherent in either formulation that specifies what this grain should be, until additional constraints are imposed on the model. Such constraints might include attempting to match production-system cycles to human reaction times, or the connectivity of connectionist models to neural connectivity.

3. Another purported difference between PDP models and production-system models is the gradualism of the former and the abruptness of the latter. But as evidenced by some of the models described earlier, one can create a production-system architecture with continuously varying strengths of productions—hence production systems can exhibit gradualism. Conversely, the higher order derivatives of different learning functions in connectionist systems can assume large values. Given the appropriate grain size on a performance window, such models would appear to be undergoing discontinuous changes (cf. Newell's 1973 classic analysis of process-structure distinctions in developmental psychology).

These many points of similarity have also been noted by advocates of the connectionist approach. Bechtel and Abrahamsen summarize some of these areas of potential overlap and rapprochement:

> Most of the modifications incorporated in the most recent symbolic models have narrowed the gap between symbolic and network models. . . . First, a large number of rules at a fine grain of analysis (microrules) can capture more of the subtleties of behavior than a smaller number of rules at a larger grain of analysis. Second, rule selection, and perhaps rule application as well, can be made to operate in parallel. Third, the ability to satisfy soft constraints can be gained by adding a strength parameter to each rule and incorporating procedures that use those values in selecting rules. Fourth, resilience to damage can be gained by building redundancy into the rule system (e.g., making multiple copies of each rule). Fifth, increased attention can be given to learning algorithms, such as the genetic algorithm (Holland, 1975; Koza, 1992), knowledge compilation and "chunking" of rules into

larger units (Anderson, 1983; Newell, 1990), and ways of applying old knowledge to new problems, such as (Falkenheiner, Forbus, & Gentner, 1989).

> . . . There presently is no adequate research base for determining what differences in empirical adequacy might result from these differences, but the differences are likely to be small enough that empirical adequacy will not be the primary determinant of the fate of symbolic versus connectionist models. Within either tradition, if a particular inadequacy is found, design innovations that find some way around the failure are likely to be forthcoming. Personal taste, general assumptions about cognition, the sociology of science, and a variety of other factors can be expected to govern the individual choices that together will determine what approaches to cognitive modeling will gain dominance. (Bechtel & Abrahamsen, 1991, pp. 18–19)

Problems Facing Computational Models

Scalability

To date, both symbolic and subsymbolic models of cognitive development have focused on highly circumscribed domains, and within those domains, on small scale exemplars of the domain. For all of the work on connectionist models of language, no one has yet been able to construct a complete connectionist model of language acquisition. For example, developmental neural networks are often constrained to well-defined topics such as the acquisition of the English past tense (Cottrell & Plunkett, 1991), or learning German gender (MacWhinney et al., 1989). The toy model approach often reduces large problems such as question answering (St. John, 1992) or word sense disambiguation (Harris, 1994a) to small problems by using only a few dozen sentences or words in the input corpus. In fact, there is not even a reasonably complete account for smaller skill domains such as word learning or syntactic development. For all of the work on Piagetian and other types of problem solving, no one has constructed a production system or a neural net that performs the full range of tasks encountered by a normal 5-year-old child. In essence, all of the work so far has been on toy versions of larger domains.

Computational modelers argue, either explicitly or implicitly, that in principle, such models could be expanded substantially with no major theoretical modifications. But could they? Here, the plausibility of the claim varies according to the approach, with the symbolic models having the better track record. Although there are no large scale developmental production systems, there do exist several very large production systems that start with a few hundred initial "hand-coded" productions and go on to learn over 100,000 productions. Domains include both AI-type tasks and cognitive models. (See Doorenbos, 1995 for a review and evaluation of several such large-scale production systems.)

With respect to scaling up connectionist systems, there are grounds for skepticism. For example, in the language learning domain, when one attempts to add additional words or sentences to many of the connectionist language models, their performance begins to degenerate. One of the major challenges for computational models then, is a direct attack on this scalability problem.

Ad Hoc Assumptions about the Environment

Another problem facing both connectionist and production-system models is the lack of a principled, data-constrained theory of the *effective* environment in which such models operate. For many models, the "training" to which they are exposed is based on arbitrary, unprincipled, ecologically ungrounded assumptions about the environmental inputs that the child receives. Until we have better ways of measuring the actual properties of patterns in the effective environment, we cannot really claim that our models are being properly constrained by real empirical data.

Fortunately, there are two promising research avenues that may soon begin to alleviate this problem. The first avenue is the development of rich computerized databases. In the area of language development the Child Language Data Exchange System (CHILDES) database (MacWhinney, 1995) has collected transcript data from dozens of major empirical projects. These transcripts contain both the language input to the child and the child's developing conversational competence. More recently, these data are being supplemented by digitized audio and video records that give researchers access to the full richness of the original interactions. Because this database is computerized according to a standardized format, it is possible to use a wide variety of computer programs for search and analysis of patterns in both the input and the child's productions. Increasingly, simulations of language learning are being based on properties of the input as computed from the CHILDES database and similar computerized sources.

A second promising development is the growth of microgenetic studies. This research is designed to capture developmental processes as they occur by looking at fine-grained moment-to-moment changes in cognition and behavior. Kuhn (1995) has applied microgenetic techniques to the study of scientific reasoning, and Siegler and Crowley (1991) and Alibali (1993) have applied this methodology to the study of strategy development in mathematics. However, the technique can be used equally well with basic behaviors such as walking (Adolph, 1995) or reaching (Thelen & Smith, 1994). Because microgenetic methods have such a fine-grained level of analysis, they collect quantities of data that are rich enough to support interesting tests of connectionist (MacWhinney & Leinbach, 1991), symbolic (Marcus et al., 1992), and dynamic systems (van der Maas & Molenaar, 1992) approaches to cognitive development.

Hybrid Models

By now the reader has come to appreciate the degree to which connectionist models focus on low-level cognition, leaving the more complex aspects of cognitive performance to full symbolic models. There are not yet connectionist models of processes such as the learning of double-digit addition, gaining expertise in solving the Tower of Hanoi, or solving cryptarithmetic problems. Is it possible that neural networks are only appropriate as models of perception and low-level aspects of language and cognition? If so, it would make sense to graft together models that use neural networks for low-level tasks and production systems for high-level tasks.

There are reasons to believe that it would be premature to explore the construction of hybrid models of this type. Before we start building Centaurs and mermaids, we should complete our exploration of more complex, multicomponential neural network models. By linking up systems for arbitrary pattern association such as SOFM or SDM with other modules that use backpropagation or ART to extract regularities and patterns, we can increase the power of our models, while retaining the connectionist framework. When we look at the complex architecture of processing types implemented in brain structures such as the hippocampus, thalamus, and cerebellum, we realize that neuronally plausible connectionist models of tomorrow will make the simple backpropagation models of today seem primitive indeed.

Once this basic exploration of complex connectionist architectures has been completed, it may be propitious to examine the ways in which connectionist models implement algorithms developed in symbolic models such as SOAR, IBL, or ACT-R. A detailed example of close computational equivalence between a low-level symbolic model and a structured connectionist model can be found in the dialog between Ling and Marinov (1993) and MacWhinney (1993).

Why Compute?

Why should someone interested in cognitive development be concerned about computational models of the sort described in this chapter? The primary justification for focusing on such systems is the claim that self-modification is *the* central question for cognitive developmental theory. We are convinced that in order to make major theoretical advances, it will be necessary to formulate computational models at least as complex as the systems described here.

As we noted previously, early commentators on computational models often faulted them for being insufficiently attentive to the issue of self-modification. Such criticism strikes us as misplaced and ironic. While it is easy to find developmentalists who fault computational models, it is even easier to find criticisms of the entire field of developmental psychology for its inability to deal adequately with transition and change:

> I have asked some of my developmental friends where the issue stands on transitional mechanisms. Mostly, they say that developmental psychologists don't have good answers. Moreover, they haven't had the answer for so long now that they don't very often ask the question anymore—not daily, in terms of their research. (Newell, 1990, p. 462)

Is this too harsh a judgment? Perhaps we can dismiss it as based on hearsay, for Newell himself was not a developmental psychologist. But Newell's comments simply echoed an earlier assessment from one of the central figures in the field:

> ... serious theorizing about basic mechanisms of cognitive growth has actually never been a popular pastime, ... It is rare indeed to encounter a substantive treatment of the problem in the annual flood of articles, chapters, and books on cognitive development. The reason is not hard to find: Good theorizing about mechanisms is very, very hard to do. (Flavell, 1984, p. 189)

Even more critical is the following observation on the state of theory in perceptual development from one of the area's major contributors in recent years:

> Put simply, our models of developmental mechanisms are disappointingly vague. This observation is rather embarrassing because the aspect of perceptual developmental psychology that should set it apart from the rest of perceptual psychology is the explanation of how development occurs, and such an explanation is precisely what is lacking. (Banks, 1987, p. 342)

It is difficult to deny either Newell's or Bank's assertions that we don't have good answers, or Flavell's assessment of the difficulty of the question. However, the good news is that the question is no longer being avoided: many developmentalists have been at least asking the right questions recently. In the past decade or so, we have seen Sternberg's (1984) edited volume *Mechanisms of Cognitive Development,* MacWhinney's (1987b) edited volume *Mechanisms of Language Acquisition,* and Siegler's (1989) *Annual Review* chapter devoted to transition *mechanisms.* So the question *is* being asked.

And the answers are, increasingly, coming in the form of computational models. Only a few of the chapters in the 1984 Sternberg volume specify mechanisms any more precisely than at the flow-chart level, and most of the proposed "mechanisms" are at the soft end of the information-processing spectrum. However, only five years later, Siegler (1989) in characterizing several general categories for transition mechanisms (neural mechanisms, associative competition, encoding, analogy, and strategy choice) was able to point to computationally-based exemplars for all but the neural mechanisms (Bakker & Halford, 1988; Falkenheiner et al., 1989; Holland, 1986; MacWhinney, 1987a; Rumelhart & McClelland, 1986; Siegler, 1988). The recent Simon and Halford (1995) book, consisting entirely of computational models of developmental processes, provides a clear indication of this trend toward "hardening the core" (Klahr, 1992).

The advantage of such computational models is that they force difficult questions into the foreground, where they can be neither sidetracked by the wealth of experimental results nor obscured by vague characterizations of the various "essences" of cognitive development. The relative lack of progress in theory development—noted by Banks, Flavell, and Newell—is a consequence of the fact that, until recently, most developmental psychologists have avoided moving to computationally-based theories, attempting instead to attack the profoundly difficult question of self-modification with inadequate tools. In contrast, computational models render these issues into a form sufficiently specific that it is possible to assess theoretical progress (see Mareschal & Shultz, 1996, for a cogent example).

The Future of Computational Models of Cognitive Development

That brings us to our final topic: The education of future cognitive developmentalists. As this book goes to press, the conceptual and technical skills necessary for computational modeling of developmental phenomena are taught in only a handful of graduate programs. However, we see the current situation as analogous to earlier challenges to the technical content of graduate training. When other kinds of computational technology that are now in common use—such as statistical packages—were first being applied to psychological topics, journal articles invariably included several pages of description about the technique itself. Writers of those early articles correctly assumed that their readers needed such background information before the psychological issue of interest could be addressed. Today, writers of papers using analysis of variance, or path analysis, or logistic regression simply assume that their readers have had several courses in graduate school learning the fundamentals.

Similarly, in the early years of computer simulation, the necessary resources of large "main frame" computers were limited to very few research centers, and exposure to computational modeling was inaccessible to most developmentalists. Even today, very few developmental psychologists have had any training with computational models, and only a handful of computational modelers have a primary interest in cognitive development. Nevertheless, as evidenced by the work described in this chapter, the intersection of these two areas of research is growing. Moreover, with the increasing availability of powerful workstations, the proliferation of computer networks for dissemination of computational models, the increasing number of published reports on various kinds of computationally-based cognitive architectures, the appropriate technology and support structures—such as summer workshops—are becoming widely accessible. All of these activities will increase the pool of appropriately trained developmentalists.

Even then, mastery of these new tools for computational modeling will not be easy. Nevertheless it appears to be a necessary condition for advancing our understanding of cognitive development. As Flavell and Wohlwill (1969) noted nearly thirty years ago: "Simple models will just not do for developmental psychology."

ACKNOWLEDGMENTS

We thank Robert Siegler and Chris Schunn for comments on earlier versions.

REFERENCES

Adolph, K. (1995). Psychophysical assessment of toddlers' ability to cope with slopes. *Journal of Experimental Psychology, 21,* 734–750.

Ainsworth, M. D. S., Blehar, M. C., Waters, E., & Wall, S. (1978). *Patterns of attachment: A psychological study of the Strange Situation.* Hillsdale, NJ: Erlbaum.

Albus, J. S. (1981). *Method and apparatus for implementation of the CMAC mapping algorithm.* Peterborough, NJ: McGraw-Hill.

Alibali, M. (1993). Gesture-speech mismatch and mechanisms of learning: What the hands reveal about a child's state of mind. *Cognitive Psychology, 25,* 468–523.

Alkon, D. L., Blackwell, K. T., Vogl, T. P., & Werness, S. A. (1993). Biological plausibility of artificial neural networks: Learning by non-Hebbian synapses. In M. Hassoun (Ed.), *Associative neural memories: Theory and implementation.* New York: Oxford University Press.

Anderson, J. (1983). *The architecture of cognition.* Cambridge, MA: Harvard University Press.

Anderson, J. (1993). *Rules of the mind.* Hillsdale, NJ: Erlbaum.

Anderson, J., Greeno, J., Kline, P., & Neves, D. (1981). Acquisition of problem-solving skill. In J. Anderson (Ed.), *Cognitive skills and their acquisition.* Hillsdale, NJ: Erlbaum.

Anderson, J. R., Kline, P. J., & Beasley, C. M. (1978). *A general learning theory and its application to schema abstraction* (Tech Report 78-2). Pittsburgh: Carnegie Mellon University.

Aram, D. M., & Eisele, J. (1992). Plasticity and recovery of higher cortical functions following early brain injury. In F. B. J. Grafman (Ed.), *Handbook of neuropsychology: Child neuropsychology.* Amsterdam, The Netherlands: Elsevier.

Atkinson, R. D. (1975). Mnemotechnics in second-language learning. *American Psychologist, 30,* 821–828.

Atkinson, R. D., & Shiffrin, R. (1968). Human memory: A proposed system and its control processes. In K. Spence & J. Spence (Eds.), *The psychology of learning and motivation* (Vol. 2). New York: Academic Press.

Azimi-Sadjadi, M. R., Sheedvash, S., & Trujillo, F. O. (1993). Recursive dynamic node creation in multilayer neural networks. *IEEE Transactions on Neural Networks, 4,* 242–256.

Baddeley, A. D. (1986). *Working memory.* Oxford, England: Oxford University Press.

Baddeley, A. D. (1990). *Human memory: Theory and practice.* Needham Heights, MA: Allyn & Bacon.

Bakker, P. E., & Halford, G. S. (1988). *A basic computational theory of structure-mapping in analogy and transitive inference.* (Tech. Report No. 88-1): Brisbane: University of Queensland.

Banks, M. (1987). Mechanisms of visual development: An example of computational models. In J. Bisanz, C. J. Brainerd, & R. Kail (Eds.), *Formal methods in developmental psychology: Progress in cognitive development research.* New York: Springer-Verlag.

Baylor, G. W., & Gascon, J. (1974). An information processing theory of aspects of the development of weight seriation in children. *Cognitive Psychology, 6,* 1–40.

Bechtel, W., & Abrahamsen, A. (1991). *Connectionism and the mind: An introduction to parallel processing in networks.* Cambridge, MA: Basil Blackwell.

Behrman, M., & Bub, D. (1992). Surface dyslexia and dysgraphia: Dual routes, a single lexicon. *Cognitive Neuropsychology, 9,* 209–258.

Belsky, J., Rovine, M., & Taylor, P. (1984). The Pennsylvania Infant and Family Development Project: 3. The origins of individual differences in infant-mother attachment: Maternal and infant contributions. *Child Development, 55,* 718–728.

Besner, D., Twilley, L., McCann, R., & Seergobin, K. (1990). On the association between connectionism and data: Are a few words necessary? *Psychological Review, 97,* 432–446.

Bidell, T. R., & Fischer, K. (1994). Developmental transitions in children's early on-line planning. In M. Haith, J. Benson, R. Roberts, & B. Pennington (Eds.), *The development of future-oriented processes.* Chicago: University of Chicago Press.

Blackmore, J., & Miikkulainen, R. (1993). *Incremental grid growing: Encoding high-dimensional structure into a two-dimensional feature map.* Proceedings of the IEEE International Conference on Neural Networks, San Francisco.

Block, H. D. (1962). The perception: A model for brain functioning: 1. *Review of Modern Physics, 34,* 123–135.

Bourgeois, J. P., Goldman-Rakic, P. S., & Rakic, P. (1994). Synaptogenesis in the prefrontal cortex of rhesus monkeys. *Cerebral Cortex, 4,* 78–96.

Bower, G. H. (1975). Cognitive psychology: An introduction. In E. R. Hilgard & G. H. Bower (Eds.), *Theories of learning* (pp. 25–80). Englewood Cliffs, NJ: Prentice-Hall.

Bowerman, M. (1982). Reorganizational processes in lexical and syntactic development. In E. Wanner & L. Gleitman (Eds.), *Language acquisition: The state of the art.* New York: Cambridge University Press.

Brainerd, C. (1978). The stage question in cognitive-developmental theory. *The Behavioral and Brain Sciences, 2,* 173–213.

Brown, A. L. (1982). Learning and development: The problem of compatibility, access and induction. *Human Development, 25,* 89–115.

Buckingham, D., & Shultz, T. (1994). *A connectionist model of the development of velocity, time, and distance concepts* (Proceedings of the sixteenth annual conference of the Cognitive Science Society). Hillsdale, NJ: Erlbaum.

Burgess, N., & Hitch, G. (1992). Toward a network model of the articulatory loop. *Journal of Memory and Language, 31,* 429–460.

Bybee, J. L. (1993). *Regular morphology and the lexicon.* Unpublished manuscript.

Bybee, J. L., & Slobin, D. I. (1982). Rules and schemas in the development and use of the English past. *Language, 58,* 265–289.

Campbell, D. T. (1960). Blind variation and selective retention in creative thought as in other knowledge processes. *Psychological Review, 67*(6), 380–400.

Card, S., Moran, T. P., & Newell, A. (1983). *The psychology of human-computer interaction.* Hillsdale, NJ: Erlbaum.

Carey, S. (1978). The child as word learner. In J. B. G. M. M. Halle (Ed.), *Linguistic theory and psychological reality.* Cambridge, MA: MIT Press.

Carpenter, G., Grossberg, S., Markuzon, N., Reynolds, J., & Rosen, D. (1992). Fuzzy ARTMAP: A neural network architecture for incremental supervised learning of analog multidimensional maps. *IEEE Transactions on Neural Networks, 3.*

Carpenter, G., Grossberg, S., & Reynolds, J. (1991). ARTMAP: Supervised real-time learning and classification of nonstationary data by a self-organizing neural network. *Neural Networks, 4,* 565–588.

Case, R. (1985). *Intellectual development: A systematic reinterpretation.* New York: Academic Press.

Case, R. (1986). The new stage theories in intellectual development: Why we need them; what they assert. In M. Perlmutter (Ed.), *Perspectives for intellectual development* (pp. 57–91). Hillsdale, NJ: Erlbaum.

Changeux, J., & Danchin, A. (1976). Selective stabilization of developing synapses as a mechanism for the specification of neuronal networks. *Nature, 264,* 705–712.

Chauvin, Y. (1989). *Toward a connectionist model of symbolic emergence* (Proceedings of the eleventh annual conference of the Cognitive Science Society). Hillsdale, NJ: Erlbaum.

Chomsky, N. (1965). *Aspects of the theory of syntax.* Cambridge, MA: MIT Press.

Clark, E. (1987). The principle of contrast: A constraint on language acquisition. In B. MacWhinney (Ed.), *Mechanisms of language acquisition.* Hillsdale, NJ: Erlbaum.

Clark, E., Carpenter, K., & Deutsch, W. (1995). Reference states and reversals: Undoing actions with verbs. *Journal of Child Language, 22,* 633–652.

Cohen, D. (1983). *Piaget: Critique and assessment.* London: Croom Helm.

Coltheart, M., Curtis, B., Atkins, P., & Haller, M. (1993). Models of reading aloud: Dual-route and parallel distributed processing approaches. *Psychological Review, 100,* 589–608.

Cottrell, G. (1985). *A connectionist approach to word sense disambiguation.* Rochester, NY: University of Rochester.

Cottrell, G., & Plunkett, K. (1991). *Learning the past tense in a recurrent network: Acquiring the mapping from meaning to sounds. Proceedings of the thirteenth annual conference of the Cognitive Science Society.* Hillsdale, NJ: Erlbaum.

Craik, F. I. M., & Lockhart, R. S. (1972). Levels of processing: A framework for memory research. *Journal of Verbal Learning and Verbal Behavior, 11,* 671–684.

Dechert, H., & Raupach, M. (Eds.). (1989). *Transfer in language production.* Norwood, NJ: ABLEX.

Dekaban, A. S., & Sadowsky, D. (1978). Changes in brain weights during the span of human life: Relation of brain weights to body heights and body weights. *Annals of Neurology, 4,* 345–356.

Dell, G. (1986). A spreading-activation theory of retrieval in sentence production. *Psychological Review, 93,* 283–321.

Dennis, M. (1980). Strokes in childhood: 1. Communication intent, expression, and comprehension after left hemisphere arteriopathy in a right-handed nine-year-old. In R. W. Reiber (Ed.), *Language development and aphasia in children.* New York: Academic Press.

Dollaghan, C., Biber, M., & Campbell, T. (1995). Lexical influences on nonword repetition. *Applied Psycholinguistics, 16,* 211–222.

Doorenbos, R. B. (1995). *Production matching for large learning systems.* Unpublished doctoral thesis, Carnegie Mellon University, Pittsburgh.

Edelman, G. (1987). *Neural Darwinism: The theory of neuronal group selection.* New York: Basic Books.

Elman, J. (1990). Finding structure in time. *Cognitive Science, 14,* 179–212.

Elman, J. (1993). Incremental learning, or the importance of starting small. *Cognition, 49,* 71–99.

Fahlman, S. E., & Lebiére, C. (1990). The cascade-correlation learning architecture. In D. Touretzky (Ed.), *Advances in neural information processing systems* (Vol. 2). Los Altos, CA: Morgan Kaufmann.

Falkenheiner, B., Forbus, K. D., & Gentner, D. (1989). The structure-mapping engine: Algorithm and examples. *Artificial Intelligence, 41,* 1–63.

Fausett, D. W. (1990). Strictly local back propagation. *International Joint Conference on Neural Networks, 3,* 125–130.

Fausett, L. (1994). *Fundamentals of neural networks.* Englewood Cliffs, NJ: Prentice-Hall.

Feldman, H. M. (1993). The course of language development after early brain damage. In H. Tager-Flusberg (Ed.), *Constraints on language acquisition: Studies of atypical children.* Hillsdale, NJ: Erlbaum.

Feldman, H. M., Janosky, J. E., Scher, M. S., & Wareham, N. L. (1994). Language abilities following prematurity, periventricular brain injury, and cerebral palsy. *Journal of Communicative Disorders, 27,* 71–90.

Ferguson, C., & Farwell, C. B. (1975). Words and sounds in early language acquisition. *Language, 51,* 419–439.

Ferretti, R. P., & Butterfield, E. C. (1986). Are children's rule assessment classifications invariant across instances of problem types? *Child Development, 57,* 1419–1428.

Flavell, J. H., & Wohlwill, J. F. (1969). Formal and functional aspects of cognitive development. In D. Elkind & J. H. Flavell (Eds.), *Studies in cognitive development* (pp. 67–120). New York: Oxford University Press.

Flavell, J. J. (1984). Discussion. In R. J. Sternberg (Ed.), *Mechanisms of cognitive development* (pp. 187–210). New York: Freeman.

Flege, J., & Davidian, R. (1984). Transfer and developmental processes in adult foreign language speech production. *Applied Psycholinguistics, 5,* 323–347.

Fodor, J., & Pylyshyn, Z. (1988). Connectionism and cognitive architecture: A critical analysis. *Cognition, 28,* 3–71.

Frean, M. (1990). The upstart algorithm: A method for constructing and training feedforward neural networks. *Neural Computation, 2,* 198–209.

Gardner-Medwin, A. R. (1976). The recall of event through the learning of associations between their parts. *Proceedings of the Yoyal Society of London B, 194,* 375–402.

Gasser, M. (1990). Connectionism and universals of second language acquisition. *Second Language Acquisition, 12,* 179–199.

Gasser, M. (1991). *Learning to recognize and produce words: Towards a connectionist model* (Proceedings of the thirteenth annual conference of the Cognitive Science Society). Hillsdale, NJ: Erlbaum.

Gasser, M. (1992). *Learning distributed representations for syllables* (Proceedings of the fourteenth annual conference of the Cognitive Science Society). Hillsdale, NJ: Erlbaum.

Gathercole, V., & Baddeley, A. (1993). *Working memory and language.* Hillsdale, NJ: Erlbaum.

Gelman, R. (1978). Cognitive development. *Annual Review of Psychology, 29,* 297–332.

Gelman, R. (1982). Accessing one-to-one correspondence: Still another paper about conservation. *British Journal of Psychology, 73,* 209–220.

Gentner, D., Rattermann, M. J., Markman, A., & Kotovsky, L. (1995). Two forces in the development of relational similarity. In T. J. Simon & G. S. Halford (Eds.), *Developing cognitive competence* (pp. 263–314). Hillsdale, NJ: Erlbaum.

Goldberg, A. (1995). *Constructions.* Chicago: University of Chicago Press.

Goodman, N. (1968). *Languages of art.* Indianapolis, IN: Bobbs-Merrill.

Gray, W. D., John, B. E., & Atwood, M. E. (1993). Project Ernestine: Validating a GOMS analysis for predicting and explaining real-world task performance. *Human-Computer Interaction, 8,* 237–309.

Grossberg, S. (1978). A theory of human memory: Self-organization and performance of sensory-motor codes, maps, and plans. *Progress in Theoretical Biology, 5,* 233–374.

Grossberg, S. (1987). Competitive learning: From interactive activation to adaptive resonance. *Cognitive Science, 11,* 23–63.

Gupta, P., & MacWhinney, B. (1992). *Integrating category acquisition with inflectional marking: A model of the German nominal system* (Proceedings of the fourteenth annual conference of the Cognitive Science Society). Hillsdale, NJ: Erlbaum.

Gupta, P., & MacWhinney, B. (1994). Is the articulatory loop articulatory or auditory? Re-examining the effects of concurrent articulation on immediate serial recall. *Journal of Memory and Language, 33,* 63–88.

Gupta, P., & MacWhinney, B. (in press). Vocabulary acquisition and verbal short-term memory: Computational and neural bases. *Brain and Language.*

Halford, G. S. (1993). *Children's understanding: The development of mental models.* Hillsdale, NJ: Erlbaum.

Halford, G. S., Smith, S. B., Dickson, J. C., Mayberry, M. T., Kelly, M. E., Bain, J. D., & Stewart, J. E. M. (1995). Modeling the development of reasoning strategies: The roles of analogy, knowledge, and capacity. In T. Simon & G. Halford (Eds.), *Developing cognitive competence: New approaches to process modeling.* Hillsdale, NJ: Erlbaum.

Hancin-Bhatt, B. (1994). Segment transfer: A consequence of a dynamic system. *Second Language Research, 10,* 241–269.

Harley, T., & MacAndrew, S. (1992). *Modelling paraphasias in normal and aphasic speech* (Proceedings of the fourteenth annual conference of the Cognitive Science Society). Hillsdale, NJ: Erlbaum.

Harrington, M. (1987). Processing transfer: Language-specific strategies as a source of interlanguage variation. *Applied Psycholinguistics, 8,* 351–378.

Harris, C. (1990). Connectionism and cognitive linguistics. *Connection Science, 2,* 7–33.

Harris, C. (1994a). Coarse coding and the lexicon. In C. Fuchs & B. Victorri (Eds.), *Continuity in linguistic semantics* (pp. 205–229). Amsterdam, The Netherlands: John Benjamins.

Harris, C. (1994b). Back-propagation representations for the rule-analogy continuum. In J. Barnden & K. Holyoak (Eds.), *Analogical connections* (pp. 282–326). Norwood, NJ: ABLEX.

Hebb, D. (1949). *The organization of behavior.* New York: Wiley.

Hertz, J., Krogh, A., & Palmer, R. (1991). *Introduction to the theory of neural computation.* New York: Addison-Wesley.

Hetherington, P. A., & Seidenberg, M. S. (1989). *Is there "catastrophic interference" in connectionist networks?* (Proceedings of the eleventh annual conference of the Cognitive Science Society) (pp. 26–33). Hillsdale, NJ: Erlbaum.

Hinton, G., & Shallice, T. (1991). Lesioning an attractor network: Investigations of acquired dyslexia. *Psychological Review, 98*(1), 74–95.

Hinton, G. E., & Plaut, D. C. (1987). *Using fast weights to deblur old memories* (Proceedings of the ninth annual conference of the Cognitive Science Society) (pp. 177–186). Hillsdale, NJ: Erlbaum.

Hirose, Y., Yamashita, K., & Hijiya, S. (1991). Back-propagation algorithm which varies the number of hidden units. *Neural Networks, 4,* 61–66.

Holland, J. H. (1975). *Adaptation in natural and artificial systems.* Ann Arbor: University of Michigan Press.

Holland, J. H. (1986). Escaping brittleness: The possibilities of general purpose machine learning algorithms applied to parallel rule-based systems. In R. S. Michalski, J. G. Carbonell, & T. M. Mitchell (Eds.), *Machine learning: An artificial intelligence approach* (pp. 593–624). Los Altos, CA: Morgan-Kaufmann.

Hopfield, J. J. (1982). Neural networks and physical systems with emergent collective computational abilities. *Proceedings of the National Academy of Sciences, 79,* 2554–2558.

Houghton, G. (1990). The problem of serial order: A neural network model of sequence learning and recall. In R. Dale, C. Mellish, & M. Zock (Eds.), *Current research in natural language generation.* London: Academic Press.

Hubel, D., & Weisel, T. (1963). Receptive fields of cells in striate cortex of very young, visually inexperienced kittens. *Journal of Neurophysiology, 26,* 994–1002.

Hunt, E. (1971). What kind of computer is man? *Cognitive Psychology, 2,* 57–98.

Hunter, I. M. L. (1968). Mental calculation. In P. C. Wason & P. N. Johnson-Laird (Eds.), *Thinking and reasoning* (pp. 341–351). Baltimore: Penguin Books.

Jacobs, R., Jordan, M., & Barto, A. (1991). Task decomposition through competition in a modular connectionist architecture: The what and where vision tasks. *Cognitive Science, 15,* 219–250.

Jerne, N. (1967). Antibodies and learning: Selection versus instruction. In G. C. Quarton, T. Melnechuk, & F. O. Schmitt (Eds.), *The neurosciences: A study program.* New York: Rockefeller University Press.

Jernigan, T. L., Archibald, S. L., Berhow, M. T., Sowell, E. R., Foster, D. S., & Hesselink, J. R. (1991). Cerebral structure on MRI: Part 1. Localization of age-related changes. *Biological Psychiatry, 29,* 55–67.

Johnson, J. (1989). Factors related to cross-language transfer and metaphor interpretation in bilingual children. *Applied Psycholinguistics, 10,* 157–177.

Jordan, M. (1986). *Serial ordering: A parallel distributed processing approach* (ICS Report 8604). La Jolla: University of California.

Juliano, C., & Tanenhaus, M. (1993). *Contingent frequency effects in syntactic ambiguity resolution* (Proceedings of the fifteenth annual conference of the Cognitive Science Society). Hillsdale, NJ: Erlbaum.

Kadirkamanathan, V., & Niranjan, M. (1993). A function estimation approach to sequential learning with neural networks. *Neural Computation, 5,* 954–975.

Kail, R. (1988). Developmental functions for speeds of cognitive processes. *Journal of Experimental Child Psychology, 45,* 339–364.

Kail, R. (1991). Processing time declines exponentially during childhood and adolescence. *Developmental Psychology, 27,* 259–268.

Kandel, E. R., & Hawkins, R. D. (1992). The biological basis of learning and individuality. *Scientific American, 266,* 40–53.

Kanerva, P. (1993). Sparse distributed memory and related models. In M. Hassoun (Ed.), *Associative neural memories: Theory and implementation.* New York: Oxford University Press.

Karmiloff-Smith, A. (1992). *Beyond modularity: A developmental perspective on cognitive science.* Cambridge, MA: MIT Press.

Kawamoto, A. (1993). Non-linear dynamics in the resolution of lexical ambiguity: A parallel distributed processing account. *Journal of Memory and Language, 32,* 474–516.

Kawamoto, A., & Zemblidge, J. (1992). Pronunciation of homographs. *Journal of Memory and Language, 31,* 349–374.

Kay, D. A., & Anglin, J. M. (1982). Overextension and underextension in the child's expressive and receptive speech. *Journal of Child Language, 9,* 83–98.

Klahr, D. (1982). Non-monotone assessment of monotone development: An information processing analysis. In S. Strauss & R. Stavy (Eds.), *U-shaped behavioral growth.* New York: Academic Press.

Klahr, D. (1992). Information processing approaches to cognitive development. In M. H. Bornstein & M. E. Lamb (Eds.), *Developmental psychology: An advanced textbook* (3rd ed.). Hillsdale, NJ: Erlbaum.

Klahr, D., & Siegler, R. S. (1978). The representation of children's knowledge. In H. W. Reese & L. P. Lipsitt (Eds.), *Advances in child development and behavior* (Vol. 12, pp. 61–116). New York: Academic Press.

Klahr, D., & Wallace, J. G. (1976). *Cognitive development: An information-processing view.* Hillsdale, NJ: Erlbaum.

Kohonen, T. (1982). Self-organized formation of topologically correct feature maps. *Biological Cybernetics, 43,* 59–69.

Kolers, P. A., & Smythe, W. E. (1984). Symbol manipulation: Alternatives to the computational view of mind. *Journal of Verbal Learning and Verbal Behavior, 23,* 289–314.

Köpcke, K. -M. (1994). Zur rolle von schemata bei der Pluralbildung monosyllabischer Maskulina. *Linguistische Arbeit, 319,* 81–93.

Köpcke, K. -M., & Zubin, D. (1983). Die kognitive Organisation der Genuszuweisung zu den einsilbigen Nomen der deutschen Gegenwartssprache. *Zeitschrift fur germanistische Linguistik, 11,* 166–182.

Köpcke, K. -M., & Zubin, D. (1984). Sechs Prinzipien fur die Genuszuweisung im Deutschen: Ein Beitrag zur natürlichen Klassifikation. *Linguistische Berichte, 93,* 26–50.

Kortge, C. A. (1990). *Episodic memory in connectionist networks* (Proceedings of the thirteenth annual conference of the Cognitive Science Society) (pp. 764–771). Hillsdale, NJ: Erlbaum.

Koza, J. R. (1992). *Genetic programming: On the programming of computers by means of natural selection and genetics.* Cambridge, MA: Bradford Books.

Kruschke, J. (1992). ALCOVE: An exemplar-based connectionist model of category learning. *Psychological Review, 99,* 22–44.

Kuhn, D. (1995). Microgenetic study of change: What has it told us? *Psychological Science, 6,* 133–139.

Lachter, J., & Bever, T. (1988). The relation between linguistic structure and associative theories of language learning: A constructive critique of some connectionist learning models. *Cognition, 28,* 195–247.

Lamb, S. (1966). *Outline of stratificational grammar.* Washington, DC: Georgetown University Press.

Larkin, J. H. (1981). Enriching formal knowledge: A model for learning to solve textbook physics problems. In J. R. Anderson (Ed.), *Cognitive skills and their acquisition* (pp. 311–334). Hillsdale, NJ: Erlbaum.

Lewis, C. (1978). *Production system models of practice effects.* University of Michigan.

Lewis, C. (1981). Skill in algebra. In J. R. Anderson (Ed.), *Cognitive skills and their acquisition* (pp. 85–110). Hillsdale, NJ: Erlbaum.

Li, P., & MacWhinney, B. (1996). Cryptotype, overgeneralization, and competition: A connectionist model of the learning of English reversive prefixes. *Connection Science, 8,* 3–30.

Lightfoot, D. (1989). The child's trigger experience: Degree-0 learnability. *Behavioral and Brain Sciences, 12,* 321–275.

Ling, C., & Marinov, M. (1993). Answering the connectionist challenge. *Cognition, 49,* 267–290.

MacWhinney, B. (1978). The acquisition of morphophonology. *Monographs of the Society for Research in Child Development, 43*(Whole no. 1).

MacWhinney, B. (1982). Basic syntactic processes. In S. Kuczaj (Ed.), *Language acquisition: Vol. 1. Syntax and semantics.* Hillsdale, NJ: Erlbaum.

MacWhinney, B. (1987a). The Competition Model. In B. MacWhinney (Ed.), *Mechanisms of language acquisition.* Hillsdale, NJ: Erlbaum.

MacWhinney, B. (Ed.). (1987b). *Mechanisms of language acquisition.* Hillsdale, NJ: Erlbaum.

MacWhinney, B. (1988). Competition and teachability. In R. Schiefelbusch & M. Rice (Eds.), *The teachability of language.* New York: Cambridge University Press.

MacWhinney, B. (1989). Competition and lexical categorization. In R. Corrigan, F. Eckman, & M. Noonan (Eds.), *Linguistic categorization.* New York: Benjamins.

MacWhinney, B. (1990). Connectionism as a framework for language acquisition theory. In J. Miller (Ed.), *Progress in research on child language disorders.* Austin, TX: Pro-Ed.

MacWhinney, B. (1992). Transfer and competition in second language learning. In R. Harris (Ed.), *Cognitive processing in bilinguals.* Amsterdam, The Netherlands: Elsevier.

MacWhinney, B. (1993). Connections and symbols: Closing the gap. *Cognition, 49,* 291–296.

MacWhinney, B. (1995). *The CHILDES Project: Tools for analyzing talk* (2nd ed.). Hillsdale, NJ: Erlbaum.

MacWhinney, B. (1996). Lexical connectionism. In P. Broeder & J. M. J. Murre (Eds.), *Models of language acquisition: Inductive and deductive approaches.* Cambridge, MA: MIT Press.

MacWhinney, B., & Anderson, J. (1986). The acquisition of grammar. In I. Gopnik & M. Gopnik (Eds.), *From models to modules.* Norwood, NJ: ABLEX.

MacWhinney, B., & Bates, E. (Eds.). (1989). *The crosslinguistic study of sentence processing.* New York: Cambridge University Press.

MacWhinney, B., & Leinbach, J. (1991). Implementations are not conceptualizations: Revising the verb learning model. *Cognition, 29,* 121–157.

MacWhinney, B., Leinbach, J., Taraban, R., & McDonald, J. L. (1989). Language learning: Cues or rules? *Journal of Memory and Language, 28,* 255–277.

Maratsos, M., & Chalkley, M. (1980). The internal language of children's syntax: The ontogenesis and representation of syntactic categories. In K. Nelson (Ed.), *Children's language* (Vol. 2). New York: Gardner Press.

Marchman, V. (1992). Constraint on plasticity in a connectionist model of the English past tense. *Journal of Cognitive Neuroscience, 5,* 215–234.

Marcus, G., Ullman, M., Pinker, S., Hollander, M., Rosen, T., & Xu, F. (1992). Over regularization in language acquisition. *Monographs of the Society for Research in Child Development, 57*(4).

Mareschal, D., & Shultz, T. R. (1993). *A connectionist model of the development of seriation* (Proceedings of the fifteenth annual conference of the Cognitive Science Society). Hillsdale, NJ: Erlbaum.

Mareschal, D., & Shultz, T. R. (1996). Generative connectionist networks and constructivist cognitive development. *Cognitive Development, 11,* 571–603.

Markey, K. (1994). *The sensorimotor foundations of phonology.* Boulder, CO: University of Colorado.

Markman, E. (1989). *Categorization and naming in children: Problems of induction.* Cambridge, MA: MIT Press.

Marr, D. (1969). A theory of cerebellar cortex. *Journal of Physiology, 202,* 437–470.

Marshall, J. C., & Newcombe, F. (1973). Patterns of paralexia: A psycholinguistic approach. *Journal of Psycholinguistic Research, 2,* 175–199.

Marslen-Wilson, W. D. (1987). Functional parallelism in spoken word-recognition. *Cognition, 25,* 71–102.

McClelland, J. L. (1989). Parallel distributed processing: Implications for cognition and development. In R. G. M. Morris (Ed.), *Parallel distributed processing: Implications for psychology and neurobiology.* Oxford, England: Oxford University Press.

McClelland, J. L. (1995). A connectionist perspective on knowledge and development. In T. J. Simon & G. S. Halford (Eds.), *Developing cognitive competence: New approaches to process modeling.* Hillsdale, NJ: Erlbaum.

McClelland, J. L., & Kawamoto, A. (1986). Mechanisms of sentence processing: Assigning roles to constituents. In J. L. McClelland & D. E. Rumelhart (Eds.), *Parallel distributed processing.* Cambridge, MA: MIT Press.

McClelland, J. L., & Rumelhart, D. E. (1981). An interactive activation model of context effects in letter perception: Part 1. An account of the basic findings. *Psychological Review, 88,* 375–402.

McClelland, J. L., & Rumelhart, D. E. (1985). Distributed memory and the representation of general and specific information. *Journal of Experimental Psychology: General, 114,* 159–188.

McCloskey, M., & Cohen, N. (1989). Catastrophic interference in connectionist networks: The sequential learning problem. In G. Bower (Ed.), *The psychology of learning and motivation* (Vol. 23). New York: Academic Press.

McCorduck, P. (1979). *Machines who think.* San Francisco: Freeman.

McDonald, J. L. (1987). Assigning linguistic roles: The influence of conflicting cues. *Journal of Memory and Language, 26,* 100–107.

McDonald, J. L. (1989). The acquisition of cue-category mappings. In B. MacWhinney & E. Bates (Eds.), *The crosslinguistic study of language processing.* New York: Cambridge University Press.

Miikkulainen, R. (1990). *A distributed feature map model of the lexicon* (Proceedings of the twelfth annual conference of the Cognitive Science Society). Hillsdale, NJ: Erlbaum.

Miikkulainen, R. (1993). *Subsymbolic natural language processing.* Cambridge, MA: MIT Press.

Miller, K., Keller, J., & Stryker, M. (1989). Ocular dominance column development: Analysis and simulation. *Science, 245,* 605–615.

Miller, P. H. (1983). *Theories of developmental psychology.* San Francisco: Freeman.

Minsky, M., & Papert, S. (1969). *Perceptions.* Cambridge, MA: MIT Press.

Montague, P., & Sejnowski, T. (1994). The predictive brain: Temporal coincidence and temporal order in synaptic learning mechanisms. *Learning and Memory, 1,* 1–33.

Mugdan, J. (1977). *Flexionsmorphologie und Psycholinguistik.* Tübingen: Gunter Narr.

Neches, R., Langley, P., & Klahr, D. (1987). Learning, development, and production systems. In D. Klahr, P. Langley, & R. Neches (Eds.), *Production system models of learning and development.* Cambridge, MA: MIT Press.

Newell, A. (1973). Production systems: Models of control structures. In W. G. Chase (Ed.), *Visual information processing* (pp. 463–526). New York: Academic Press.

Newell, A. (1980). Physical symbol systems. *Cognitive Science, 4,* 135–183.

Newell, A. (1981). Reasoning problem solving and decision processes: The problem space as a fundamental category. In R. Nickerson (Ed.), *Attention and performance* (Vol. 8, pp. 693–718). Hillsdale, NJ: Erlbaum.

Newell, A. (1990). *A unified theory of cognition.* Cambridge, MA: Harvard University Press.

Newell, A., & Simon, H. (1972). *Human problem solving.* Englewood Cliffs, NJ: Prentice-Hall.

Norman, D. A., Rumelhart, D. E., & Group, L. R. (1975). *Explorations in cognition.* San Francisco: Freeman.

Norris, D. (1994). Shortlist: A connectionist model of continuous speech recognition. *Cognition, 52,* 189–234.

Odlin, T. (1989). *Language transfer: Cross-linguistic influence in language learning.* New York: Cambridge University Press.

Oshima-Takane, Y., Goodz, E., & Derevensky, J. L. (in press). Birth order effects on early language development: Do second children learn from overheard speech? *Child Development.*

Palmer, S. E., & Kimchi, R. (1986). The information processing approach to cognition. In T. J. Knapp & L. C. Robertson (Eds.), *Approaches to cognition: Contrasts and controversies* (pp. 37–77). Hillsdale, NJ: Erlbaum.

Pascual-Leone, J. (1970). A mathematical model for the transition rule in Piaget's developmental stages. *Acta Psychologica, 32,* 301–345.

Piaget, J. (1953). *Logic and psychology.* Manchester, England: Manchester University Press.

Piaget, J. (1965). *The child's conception of number.* New York: Norton.

Piaget, J. (1975). *L'equilibration des structures cognitives* [The equilibration of cognitive structures]. Paris: Presses Universitaires de France.

Piatelli-Palmarini, M. (1989). Evolution, selection, and cognition: From "learning" to parameter setting in biology and in the study of language. *Cognition, 31,* 1–44.

Pinker, S. (1984). *Language learnability and language development.* Cambridge, MA: Harvard University Press.

Pinker, S. (1991). Rules of language. *Science, 253,* 530–535.

Pinker, S. (1994). *The language instinct.* New York: Morrow.

Pinker, S., & Prince, A. (1988). On language and connectionism: Analysis of a Parallel Distributed Processing Model of language acquisition. *Cognition, 29,* 73–193.

Platt, J. C. (1991). A resource-allocating network for function interpolation. *Neural Computation, 3,* 213–225.

Plaut, D. C., McClelland, J. L., Seidenberg, M. S., & Patterson, K. (1995). Understanding normal and impaired word reading: Computational principles in quasi-regular domains. *Psychological Review, 103,* 56–115.

Plunkett, K., & Marchman, V. (1991). U-shaped learning and frequency effects in a multi-layered perceptron: Implications for child language acquisition. *Cognition, 38,* 43–102.

Plunkett, K., & Sinha, C. (1992). Connectionism and developmental theory. *British Journal of Development Psychology, 10,* 209–254.

Posner, M., & Keele, S. (1968). On the genesis of abstract ideas. *Journal of Experimental Psychology, 77,* 353–363.

Posner, M., & Keele, S. (1970). Retention of abstract ideas. *Journal of Experimental Psychology, 83,* 304–308.

Prasada, S., & Pinker, S. (1993). Generalization of regular and irregular morphological patterns. *Language and Cognitive Processes, 8,* 1–56.

Quartz, S. R., & Scjnowski, T. J. (in press). The neural basis of cognitive development: A constructivist manifesto. *Behavioral and Brain Sciences.*

Rabinowitz, R. M., Grant, M. J., & Dingley, H. L. (1987). Computer simulation, cognition, and development: An introduction. In J. Bisanz, C. J. Brainerd, & R. Kail (Eds.), *Formal methods in developmental psychology: Progress in cognitive development research* (pp. 263–301) New York: Springer-Verlag.

Read, W., Nenov, V. I., & Halgren, E. (1995). Inhibition-controlled retrieval by an autoassociative model of hippocampal area CA3. *Hippocampus, 5,* 79–91.

Rosenblatt, F. (1959). Two theorems of statistical separability in the perception. In M. Selfridge (Ed.), *Mechanisation of thought processes: Proceedings of a symposium held at the National Physical Laboratory.* London: HM Stationery Office.

Rosenbloom, P. S., & Newell, A. (1982). *Learning by chunking: Summary of a task and a model.* Paper presented at the second national conference on Artificial Intelligence, Los Altos, CA.

Rosenbloom, P. S., & Newell, A. (1987). Learning by chunking: A production system model of practice. In D. Klahr, P. Langley, & R. Neches (Eds.), *Production system models of learning and development* (pp. 221–286). Cambridge, MA: MIT Press.

Rumelhart, D. E., & McClelland, J. L. (1986). On learning the past tense of English verbs. In J. L. McClelland & D. E. Rumelhart (Eds.), *Parallel distributed processing: Explorations in the microstructure of cognition.* Cambridge, MA: MIT Press.

Rumelhart, D. E., & McClelland, J. L. (1987). Learning the past tenses of English verbs: Implicit rules or parallel distributed processes? In B. MacWhinney (Ed.), *Mechanisms of language acquisition.* Hillsdale, NJ: Erlbaum.

St. John, M. (1992). The story gestalt: A model of knowledge-intensive processes in text comprehension. *Cognitive Science, 16,* 271–306.

Sasaki, Y. (1994). Paths of processing strategy transfers in learning Japanese and English as foreign languages. *Studies in Second Language Acquisition, 16,* 43–72.

Schmajuk, N., & DiCarlo, J. (1992). Stimulus configuration, classical conditioning, and hippocampal function. *Psychological Review, 99,* 268–305.

Schyns, P. (1991). A modular neural network model of concept acquisition. *Cognitive Science, 15,* 461–508.

Seidenberg, M., & McClelland, J. (1989). A distributed, developmental model of word recognition and naming. *Psychological Review, 96,* 523–568.

Sejnowski, T. J., & Rosenberg, C. R. (1988). NETtalk: A parallel network that learns to read aloud. In J. A. Anderson & E. Rosenfeld (Eds.), *Neurocomputing: Foundations of research.* Cambridge, MA: MIT Press.

Shultz, T., Buckingham, D., & Oshima-Takane, Y. (1994). A connectionist model of the learning of personal pronouns in English. In S. J. Hanson, T. Petsche, M. Kearns, & R. L. Rivest (Eds.), *Computational learning theory and natural learning systems: Vol. 2. Intersection between theory and experiment.* Cambridge, MA: MIT Press.

Shultz, T., Schmidt, W. C., Buckingham, D., & Mareschal, D. (1995). Modeling cognitive development with a generative connectionist algorithm. In T. J. Simon & G. S. Halford (Eds.), *Developing cognitive competence: New approaches to process modeling.* Hillsdale, NJ: Erlbaum.

Siegler, R. (Ed.). (1978). *Children's thinking: What develops?* Hillsdale, NJ: Erlbaum.

Siegler, R. (1988). Strategy choice procedures and the development of multiplication skill. *Journal of Experiment Psychology: General, 117,* 258–275.

Siegler, R. (1989). Mechanisms of cognitive development. *Annual Review of Psychology, 40,* 353–379.

Siegler, R., & Crowley, K. (1991). The microgenetic method: A direct means for studying cognitive development. *American Psychologist, 46,* 606–620.

Siegler, R., & Shrager, J. (1984). Strategy choices in addition and subtraction: How do children know what to do? In C. Sophian (Ed.), *Origins of cognitive skills.* Hillsdale, NJ: Erlbaum.

Siegler, R. S. (1976). Three aspects of cognitive development. *Cognitive Psychology, 8,* 481–520.

Siegler, R. S., & Shipley, C. (1995). Variation, selection, and cognitive change. In G. Halford & T. Simon (Eds.), *Developing cognitive competence: New approaches to process modeling* (pp. 31–76). Hillsdale, NJ: Erlbaum.

Simon, D. (1976). Spelling, a task analysis. *Instructional Science, 5,* 277–302.

Simon, D., & Simon, H. (1973). Alternative uses of phonemic information in spelling. *Review of Educational Research, 43,* 115–137.

Simon, D., & Simon, H. (1978). Individual differences in solving physics problems. In R. Siegler (Ed.), *Children's thinking: What develops?* (pp. 325–348). Hillsdale, NJ: Erlbaum.

Simon, H. A. (1962). An information processing theory of intellectual development. *Monographs of the Society for Research in Child Development, 27.*

Simon, T., & Klahr, D. (1995). A theory of children's learning about number conservation. In T. Simon & G. Halford (Eds.), *Developing cognitive competence: New approaches to process modeling.* Hillsdale, NJ: Erlbaum.

Simon, T., & Halford, G. (Eds.). (1995). *Developing cognitive competence: New approaches to process modeling.* Hillsdale, NJ: Erlbaum.

Stemberger, J. (1985). *The lexicon in a model of language production.* New York: Garland.

Sternberg, R. J. (Ed.). (1984). *Mechanisms of cognitive development.* New York: Freeman.

Thal, D. J., Marchman, V. A., Stiles, J., Aram, D., Trauner, D., Nass, R., & Bates, E. (1991). Early lexical development in children with focal brain injury. *Brain and Language, 40*(4), 491–527.

Thelen, E., & Smith, L. (1994). *A dynamic systems approach to the development of cognition and action.* Cambridge, MA: MIT Press.

Touretzky, D. (1990). BoltzCONS: Dynamic symbol structures in a connectionist network. *Artificial Intelligence, 46,* 5–46.

Trueswell, J. C., & Tanenhaus, M. K. (1991). Tense, temporal context, and syntactic ambiguity resolution. *Language and Cognitive Processes, 6,* 303–338.

Trueswell, J. C., & Tanenhaus, M. K. (1992). *Consulting temporal context during sentence comprehension: Evidence from the monitoring of eye movements in reading* (Proceedings of the fourteenth annual conference of the Cognitive Science Society). Hillsdale, NJ: Erlbaum.

Twain, M. (1935). *The awful German language. The family Mark Twain.* New York: Harper & Brothers.

van der Maas, H., & Molenaar, P. (1992). Stagewise cognitive development: An application of catastrophe theory. *Psychological Review, 99,* 395–417.

van Geert, P. (1991). A dynamic systems model of cognitive and language growth. *Psychological Review, 98,* 3–53.

von Neumann, J. (1956). Probabilistic logics and the synthesis of reliable organisms from unreliable components. In C. Shannon & J. McCarthy (Eds.), *Automata studies.* Princeton, NJ: Princeton University Press.

Vygotsky, L. (1962). *Thought and language.* Cambridge, MA: MIT Press.

Waibel, A., Hanazawa, T., Hinton, G., Shikano, K., & Lang, K. (1988). Phoneme recognition using time-delay neural networks. *IEE Transactions on Acoustics, Speech and Signal Processing, 37.*

Wallace, J. G., Klahr, D., & Bluff, K. (1987). A self-modifying production system for conservation acquisition. In D. Klahr, P. Langley, & R. Neches (Eds.), *Production system models of learning and development.* Cambridge, MA: MIT Press.

Walsh, C., & Cepko, C. L. (1992). Clonally related cortical cells show several migration patterns. *Science, 255,* 434–440.

Walsh, C., & Cepko, C. L. (1993). Widespread dispersion of neuronal clones across functional regions of the cerebral cortex. *Science, 362,* 632–635.

Waterman, D. (1975). *Adaptive production systems.* Proceedings of the Fourth International Joint Conference on Artificial Intelligence, 296–303. Tbilisi, USSR.

Watrous, R. L., Shastri, L., & Waibel, A. H. (1987). Learned phonetic discrimination using connectionist networks. In J. Laver & M. A. Jack (Eds.), *Proceedings of the European conference on Speech Technology.* Edinburgh: CEP Consultants.

Waugh, E., & Norman, D. (1965). Primary memory. *Psychological Review, 72,* 89–104.

Werbos, P. (1974). *Beyond regression: New tools for prediction and analysis in the behavioral sciences.* Unpublished Ph.D. thesis, Harvard University, Cambridge, MA.

Whorf, B. (1938). Some verbal categories of Hopi. *Language, 14,* 275–286.

Whorf, B. (1941). The relation of habitual thought and behavior to language. In L. Spier (Ed.), *Language, culture, and personality: Essays in memory of Edward Sapir.* Ogden: University of Utah Press.

Widrow, B., & Hoff, M. E. (1960). Adaptive switching circuits. *IRE WESCON Convention Record* (part 4), 96–104.

Wilkening, F. (1981). Integrating velocity, time, and distance information: A developmental study. *Cognitive Psychology, 13,* 231–247.

Wilkening, F., & Anderson, N. H. (1982). Representation and diagnosis of knowledge structures in developmental psychology. In N. H. Anderson (Ed.), *Contributions to integration theory: Vol. 3. Developmental.* Hillsdale, NJ: Erlbaum.

Wynne-Jones, M. (1993). Node splitting: A constructive algorithm for feed-forward neural networks. *Neural Computing and Applications, 1,* 17–22.

Young, R. M. (1976). *Seriation by children: An artificial intelligence analysis of a Piagetian task.* Basel, Switzerland: Birkhauser.

Zubin, D. A., & Köpcke, K. M. (1981). Gender: A less than arbitrary grammatical category. In C. M. R. Hendrick & M. Miller (Eds.), *Papers from the seventeenth regional meeting.* Chicago: Chicago Linguistic Society.

Zubin, D. A., & Köpcke, K. M. (1986). Gender and folk taxonomy: The indexical relation between grammatical and lexical categorization. In C. Craig (Ed.), *Noun classes and categorization.* Amsterdam, The Netherlands: John Benjamins.

CHAPTER 14

Cognition as a Collaborative Process

BARBARA ROGOFF

As civilized human beings, we are the inheritors, neither of an inquiry about ourselves and the world, nor of an accumulating body of information, but of a conversation, begun in the primeval forests and extended and made more articulate in the course of centuries. It is a conversation which goes on both in public and within each of ourselves. . . . [Each new generation enters] an initiation into the skill and partnership of this conversation. And it is this conversation which, in the end, gives place and character to every human activity and utterance. (Oakeshott, 1962, p. 199)

This chapter asks how cognitive development occurs in and is promoted by individuals' collaboration with others. I examine theory and research on processes of collaboration and their implications for cognitive development, as well as on how collaborative processes develop as people participate in the activities of their communities.

My definition of collaboration is broad—including face-to-face mutual involvements such as routine conversation, teaching, tutoring, and cooperative learning; side-by-side engagements; and participation in shared endeavors without physical copresence (such as occurs between correspondents, between authors and readers of articles, or in remembered conversations). These engagements may or may not strive to promote cognitive development (or learning—a term that I use interchangeably with development in this chapter).

Cognitive development occurs as new generations collaborate with older generations in varying forms of interpersonal engagement and institutional practices. For example, in some communities, conversation between adults and young children is common, but children seldom have the opportunity to observe and participate in adult activities; in other communities, engagement between adults and young children occurs in the context of children's involvement in the mature activities of the community, but not in peerlike conversation (Rogoff, 1990). The topic of cognition as a collaborative process necessarily includes all such forms of collaboration.

The idea that cognition is a process involving more than the solo individual is still new to many cognitive developmentalists. For some, it is a foreign concept to think of cognition as something other than an individual activity. For others, the idea of cognition involving social processes is comfortable, but somewhat inchoate. As I will argue, a great deal of research simply adds social factors to the default unit of analysis of the field—the individual—thereby assimilating but not accommodating sociocultural ideas that shift from the individual to sociocultural activity as the basic unit of analysis.

This chapter attempts to elucidate the conceptual shift from individual to sociocultural activity as unit of analysis, as well as key themes in research on cognition as a collaborative process. The paradigm shift required to move from thinking of cognition as a property of individuals to thinking of cognition as an aspect of human sociocultural activity (without attempting to locate the process only in individuals) is at the edge of the "zone of proximal development" of the field at this point. This chapter is primarily addressed to those who are interested in exploring this edge.

Sociocultural scholars are currently struggling with issues of how concepts of cognition and of individual development need to be reformulated to be consistent with assumptions of a sociocultural approach and appropriate empirical methods. Sociocultural research involves integration across topics that have traditionally been segregated

in different disciplines, such as psychology, anthropology, sociology, sociolingistics, and history (see Rogoff & Chavajay, 1995). It also integrates topics traditionally treated as distinct phenomena—such as cognitive, social, emotional, motivational, and personal identity processes. Although research may focus on one of these, it is recognized that they are not independent phenomena.

The study of cognition as a collaborative process is still emerging, and researchers are not of one mind regarding how to proceed. I hope that my review of key research done from differing perspectives (with their internal tensions) will help the field to further articulate central sociocultural concepts and their use in research. This chapter includes my view of how a sociocultural approach leads to reformulations in concepts of cognition and of the individual's relation with the community, and to a recasting of research questions and methods. I anticipate that the next edition of this *Handbook* will contain extensive reviews of sociocultural processes spread through chapters on the development of literacy, planning, remembering, learning, interpersonal problem solving, and so on, incorporating the new lines of empirical work that are based on the assumption that cognition occurs in shared involvement in community/institutional endeavors.

The chapter begins with consideration of two historically central theoretical approaches to the study of cognition as a collaborative process that emerged in the early decades of the 20th century. These are (a) the cultural/historical theorizing of Vygotsky, Leont'ev, and their colleagues, who argued that individual development was an aspect of cultural/historical activity and (b) Piagetian theorizing about cognitive development occurring through co-operation as individuals attempt to resolve conflicts between their perspectives.

The next section examines the conceptual frameworks of two more recent approaches to understanding the collaborative nature of cognition. These are a family of sociocultural approaches that, for about two decades, have been building on the classic theoretical work of the early decades of the century, especially the cultural/historical theory of Vygotsky and Leont'ev. The other is less explicitly theoretical, but its underlying assumptions constitute a position that has formed the basis of a great deal of the research in this area for decades. I call this the "social influence" approach, because it uses the generic individual as the basic unit of analysis and adds social factors as external influences.

The next section of the chapter discusses the differences in research and methodologies for the observation or evaluation of individuals' development from sociocultural and social influence approaches. In social influence approaches, researchers struggle to standardize the social context and isolate the individual to assess learning; in sociocultural approaches, researchers attempt to study individuals' learning as they participate in ongoing and varied sociocultural activities.

The central section of the chapter addresses key concepts and research on cognition as a collaborative process, beginning with a brief overview of the nature and limitations of the available research. I first focus on how experts aid novices in learning and then go on to discuss how peers assist each other in learning.

The section on experts' support of novices' learning begins with a discussion of how sociocultural approaches to this question differ from closely related work on scaffolding. Then it examines findings from research on techniques that experts use to support novices' learning (scaffolding, tutoring, and so on). This section includes conceptualization and research on the ways that experts adjust their support to novices' needs for assistance, the mutual roles of children and adults in structuring adult-child interaction, and the role of the expert's expertise.

The section on how peers assist each other in learning addresses concepts and research on collaboration in peer play and child caregiving, the role of similarity of status in collaborative argumentation, and peers' facilitation of each other's learning in classrooms. It also includes consideration of how children and the adults and institutions that work with them learn to collaborate, emphasizing a central theme of this chapter—that individual learning occurs through participation in sociocultural activities that include individuals' own contributions as well as the developing contributions of other people and cultural institutions.

The concluding section focuses on collaboration in sociocultural activities beyond the didactic and dyadic interactions between children and adults or peers that have provided most of the research to date. I argue that collaboration involves groups larger than dyads and includes specialized asymmetrical as well as symmetrical roles between participants, discord as well as harmony, and collaboration among people of different eras and locations.

I begin by considering two central schools of thought of our predecessors, with whom we collaborate in advancing our understanding of cognition as a collaborative process.

CLASSIC THEORETICAL APPROACHES TO COGNITION AS A COLLABORATIVE PROCESS

This section focuses on the cultural/historical theoretical approach inspired by Vygotsky, Leont'ev, and their colleagues, and on the social interactional aspects of Piaget's work. It is a curious coincidence that these classic theoretical works were developed by scholars born in the same year—Vygotsky and Piaget were both born in 1896. Vygotsky's immediate personal involvement ended with his death in 1934, was carried on by his students and colleagues in the USSR for some years, and is now being transformed by a renaissance of international interest. Piaget's own oeuvre continued until his death about four decades after Vygotsky's, but most of his work on the social context of cognition occurred early in the century; his legacy in this area continues with his students and colleagues.

Although these two theories are often placed in opposition, they are compatible in many ways (see Tudge & Rogoff, 1989) and built on many of the same scholarly insights of previous generations. Their influence is pervasive in current sociocultural efforts that form the theoretical basis for much of the ongoing interest in cognition as a collaborative process.

One of the key commonalities between the cultural/historical and Piagetian approaches to cognition as a collaborative process is an emphasis on achievement of shared thinking. In the process of everyday communication, people share their focus of attention, building on a common ground that is not entirely shared (for each person works with a somewhat unique perspective). To engage in shared endeavors, there must be some common ground, even to be able to carry out disputes. Lomov (1978) argued that the first stage in communication is:

> the *determination of common "coordinates"* of joint activity (reference points, reference models). These serve as a basis that, in a certain sense, guides the construction of the entire process of communication and the distribution and coordination of the operations carried out by each member of the communicating group. (p. 20)

Mutual understanding between people in communication has been termed *intersubjectivity,* a process that occurs *between* people; it cannot be attributed to one person or the other in communication (Berger & Luckmann, 1966; Newson & Newson, 1975; Riegel, 1979; Rommetveit, 1985;

Trevarthen, 1980; Wertsch, 1979b). Some modifications in the perspectives of each participant are necessary to understand the other person's perspective. The modifications can be seen as the basis for development—as the participants adjust to understand and communicate, their new perspectives involve greater understanding and are the basis for further growth (Wertsch, 1984). Newson and Newson (1975) argued that from infancy, children are guided by intersubjectivity in social interaction:

> Knowledge itself originates within an interaction process (highly active on the part of the infant) between the infant himself and other, more mature, human individuals who already possess shared understandings with other communicating beings. . . . In short, the child only achieves a fully articulated knowledge of his world, in a cognitive sense, as he becomes involved in social transactions with other communicating human beings. (p. 438)

Although cultural/historical and Piagetian theories differ in their conceptions of shared thinking (discussed later), both emphasize its role in cognitive development (Forman & Kraker, 1985; Perret-Clermont & Schubauer-Leoni, 1981; Rogoff, 1986, 1990; Tudge & Rogoff, 1989; Wertsch, 1984; Youniss, 1987).

Cultural/Historical Theory of Vygotsky, Leont'ev, and Their Colleagues

In contrast with much of the tradition of research in child development, which has focused on the individual as the unit of analysis, cultural/historical theory posits that individual development is a function of participation in and extension of cultural/historical as well as phylogenetic processes. Vygotsky (1978) argued that rather than deriving explanations of psychological processes from the individual's characteristics plus secondary social influences, analysis should focus on the social, cultural, and historical processes in which individual functioning develops (Wertsch, 1985; Wertsch, Tulviste, & Hagstrom, 1993).

Vygotsky proposed the integrated study of four interrelated, dynamic levels of development involving the individual and the social world in their different time frames—microgenetic, ontogenetic, phylogenetic, and sociohistorical development (Scribner, 1985; Wertsch, 1985; Zinchenko, 1985). Developmental psychologists traditionally deal with ontogenetic development—changes in thinking and behavior arising in the history of individuals, such

as across childhood. This is merely a different grain of analysis from the other three developmental levels: Phylogenetic development is the slowly changing species history that leaves a legacy for the individual in the form of genes. Cultural/historical development is the changing cultural history that leaves a legacy for the individual in the form of technologies such as literacy, number systems, and computers, as well as value systems and scripts and norms for the handling of situations met by the individual. Microgenetic development is the moment-to-moment learning of individuals in particular problem contexts, built on the individual's genetic and cultural/historical background.

From this perspective, since human development necessarily builds upon both the historical endowment with which humans are born as members of their species and their communities, it is a false dichotomy to focus on "nature" and "nurture" as separable influences on development. Babies enter the world equipped with patterns of action from their genes and prenatal experience, as well as with caregivers who structure their biological and social worlds in ways deriving from their own and their ancestors' phylogenetic and cultural history (Rogoff, 1990). As Als (1979) stated, the human newborn is biologically a social organism. At the same time, new generations transform cultural institutions and practices, and contribute to biological evolution.

Central to Vygotsky's theory is the idea that children's participation in cultural activities with the guidance of others allows children to "internalize" their community's tools for thinking. Thus, efforts to understand individual cognitive development must consider the social roots of both the tools for thinking that children are learning to use and the social interactions that guide children in their use. Vygotsky's concept of the zone of proximal development posits that development proceeds through children's participation in activities slightly beyond their competence with the assistance of adults or more skilled children (Laboratory of Comparative Human Cognition, 1983; Valsiner & van der Veer, 1993; Vygotsky, 1978; Wertsch, 1979a).

Interactions in the zone of proximal development are the crucible of development *and* of culture (Cole, 1985) in that they allow children to participate in activities that would be impossible for them alone, using cultural tools that must be adapted to the specific practical activities at hand, and thus passed on to as well as transformed by new members of the community. People working together use and adapt tools provided by predecessors and, in the process, create new tools and new uses for old ones.

Vygotsky proposed that the most basic unit of analysis of human development and learning should be not the individual, but one that preserves the inner workings of larger events of interest. He argued that using the individual as the unit of analysis separates human functioning into elements that no longer function in the ways that the larger living unit does. He sought a unit that

> designates a product of analysis that possesses *all the basic characteristics of the whole.* The unit is a vital and irreducible part of the whole. The key to the explanation of the characteristics of water lies not in the investigation of its chemical formula but in the investigation of its molecule and its molecular movements. In precisely the same sense, the living cell is the real unit of biological analysis because it preserves the basic characteristics of life that are inherent in the living organism. (Vygotsky, 1987, p. 46)

Vygotsky attempted to determine the psychological analogue of the living cell, and focused on the unit of word meaning. Although other scholars following Vygotsky have questioned this particular unit of analysis or emphasized others—such as practical activity, use of intellectual tools, propositions, or dialogue—the basic concept of using a unit of activity that maintains the functions of the larger system is one of Vygotsky's important contributions (Bakhtin, 1981; Cole, 1985; Leont'ev, 1981; Wertsch, 1985; Zinchenko, 1985). Bakhtin's approach has been used to extend the unit of analysis from Vygotsky's focus on the *word* to a more satisfying focus on *dialogue,* in which people engage with each other (even in monologue), building on cultural genres (Wertsch, 1991; Wertsch et al., 1993). Leont'ev (1981) extended Vygotsky's search for a unit of analysis by elaborating the concept of *activity.* He stated that an activity is:

> a system with its own structure, its own internal transformations, and its own development. . . . If we removed human activity from the system of social relationships and social life, it would not exist and would have no structure. With all its varied forms, the human individual's activity is a system in the system of social relations. (pp. 46–47)

Similarly, inspired by the work of Vygotsky, Leont'ev, and Luria, the Laboratory of Comparative Human Cognition (1983) focused on cultural practices as a unit of analysis. Cultural practices were defined as learned systems of activity in which knowledge consists of standing rules for behavior appropriate to a particular socially assembled situation, embodied in the cooperation of individual members of a culture.

The history of sociocultural theory itself provides an interesting example of intellectual development through collaboration in ways that illustrate the theory. The cultural/historical theory initiated by Vygotsky in the 1920s and 1930s was elaborated as well as criticized by his students and colleagues. An outgrowth of the associated scholarly tensions (as well as the political realities of the Soviet Communist state) was the development of the psychological theory of activity, especially by Leont'ev (Vygotsky's student, follower, and critic). Leont'ev and Vygotsky themselves built on philosophical notions of activity available several decades before Vygotsky's work. The roots of Soviet cultural/historical theory included wide interdisciplinary reading and discussion of European and American authors in the arts, literature, philosophy, and the infant social sciences of the early 1900s. Further developments of the theory in the Soviet Union were influenced by national and worldwide political events, especially during Stalin's time. For a fascinating account of the development of these Soviet strands of cultural/historical and sociocultural theorizing through the twentieth century, see Zinchenko (1995; also John-Steiner, 1992; Kozulin, 1990; van der Veer & Valsiner, 1991; Wertsch, 1985).

The uptake of Soviet cultural/historical theory in the United States involved some contact in earlier eras of the twentieth century, with publications in English of Vygotsky's work in 1929 and 1962. However, deeper international interest awaited the translation of Vygotsky's work by Cole, Scribner, John-Steiner, and Souberman. Their 1978 volume, *Mind in Society,* marks the beginning of widespread use of Vygotskian ideas in the United States and Western Europe. Deep interest in the theory in the United States midway through the 20th century may have been prevented by incompatibility with the zeitgeist of psychology of the times (including behaviorism and information processing approaches). The change in receptivity may have been encouraged by the impact of efforts to examine cognition in widely varying cultural communities, which resulted in awareness of the limitations in then-contemporary theories to account for contextual variations in performance and the social nature of cognition (see Rogoff & Chavajay, 1995).

Contemporary approaches that have built on Soviet cultural/historical theory, in conjunction with other compatible theoretical views (especially from cultural theory and sociolinguistic approaches), are building a family of sociocultural approaches (key among them are Cole, 1990; Heath, 1983; John-Steiner, 1985; Laboratory of Comparative Human Cognition, 1983; Lave & Wenger, 1991; Ochs, 1988; Rogoff, 1990, in press; Schieffelin, 1991; Valsiner, 1987; Wertsch, 1991, 1995). Valsiner and van der Veer (1993) provided an excellent account of how the concept of the zone of proximal development emerged in Vygotsky's own work and its further development in contemporary sociocultural theory.

Dewey's (1916) theory of development through experience developed concurrently with Vygotsky's (and was inspired by some of the same prior scholarship). Dewey's theory is quite compatible with cultural/historical theory and is providing further inspiration to current work in sociocultural theory development and research. Dewey emphasized a shift in focus from the individual to the event as the basic unit of analysis (Dewey & Bentley, 1949)—a very similar proposal to cultural/historical theory's emphasis on the activity as the unit of analysis. Both perspectives emphasized the importance of studying thinking in process, and both placed children and other people as active participants in shared endeavors of their communities and insisted that individual cognition depends upon engagement in such activities.

> The social environment . . . is truly educative in its effects in the degree in which an individual shares or participates in some conjoint activity. By doing his share in the associated activity, the individual appropriates the purpose which actuates it, becomes familiar with its methods and subject matters, acquires needed skill, and is saturated with its emotional spirit. (Dewey, 1916, p. 26)

Bandura's social learning theory is sometimes erroneously considered part of the same family. It shares an interest in studying how children learn from the social world, but separates the person from the social world and maintains the individual as the basic unit of analysis. Although Bandura's concept of reciprocal determinism states that it is shortsighted to focus only on the individual or only on the environment, as each determines the other, the theory seems still to treat them as independently defined entities (see Tudge & Winterhoff, 1993a). The emphasis is on how other people influence the individual, and how the individual in *turn* learns from others. This is a marked difference from Vygotskian and Deweyan approaches, which view the individual as well as cultural tools and institutions as mutually constituting contributors to activities or events.

Piaget's classical developmental theory has also contributed to understanding cognition as a collaborative process. Although Piaget's theorizing on the role of collaboration in cognitive development was not central to his theory, it offered some important complementary ideas, discussed in the next section.

Piaget's Foray into Development through Co-Operation

In some of his early writing, Piaget focused directly on cognitive development through co-operation with peers. In the late 1920s, his writings examined the relation between the individual and the social. Piaget provided cogent speculation that individual development is facilitated by cooperation between peers in resolving cognitive conflicts provided by their differing perspectives.

> When I discuss and I sincerely seek to understand someone else, I become engaged, not just in avoiding contradicting myself, in avoiding playing on words, etc., but also in entering into an indefinite series of viewpoints other than my own. . . . It is a moving equilibrium. . . . The engagements . . . that I make by nature of cooperation lead me I don't know where. (Piaget, 1977 [1928], p. 237)

Piaget's statements that reflection is internalized dialogue resemble Vygotsky's principle that higher mental functions are internalized from social interaction: "Reflection is an internal discussion. . . . In social conflict is born discussion, first simple dispute, then discussion terminating in a conclusion. It is this last action which, internalized and applied to oneself, becomes reflection" (Piaget, 1977 [1928], p. 219).

Despite the lucidity of Piaget's comments on collective activity, it did not become a major focus of his theory or research. In addition, there are key differences from cultural/historical theory in Piaget's conception of social processes. A major difference is that Piaget's speculations on the social world were largely limited to the interpersonal context, without substantial or sustained consideration of the cultural or historical context of the intellectual problems and solutions of cognitive development.

Piaget also differed from Vygotsky in his approach to treating the individual as the locus of change. According to Vygotsky's perspective, joint problem solving occurs *between* partners, whereas in Piaget's view, individuals work with independence and equality on each other's ideas. In reference to Piagetian theory, Vygotsky (1987) stated: "The child is not seen as a part of the social whole, as a subject of social relationships. He is not seen as a being who participates in the societal life of the social whole to which he belongs from the outset. The social is viewed as something standing outside the child" (p. 83).

According to Piaget (1926), social influence fosters change through the induction of cognitive conflict and the logical operations carried out by children attempting to reconcile their differing views to achieve cognitive equilibrium. The Piagetian model of effective social interaction is thus cooperation between equals who attempt to understand each other through reciprocal consideration of their alternative views. Piaget considered cooperation to be a form of logic in which children discuss propositions that provoke cognitive conflict and its logical resolution, yielding equilibrium with a system of propositions that are free from contradiction and are reversible:

Cooperation itself constitutes a system of co-operations: putting in correspondence (which is an operation) the operations of one partner with those of the others, uniting (which is another operation) the acquisition of one partner with that of others, etc.; and in case of conflicts, raising the contradictions (which presupposes an operational process) or above all differentiating the different points of view and introducing between them a reciprocity (which is an operational transformation). (Piaget, 1977 [1963], p. 347)

Piaget laid out three conditions under which equilibrium is achieved in intellectual exchange (Piaget, 1977). First, the partners need a common language and system of ideas, providing a key that allows each to translate into common terms the differing views. Second, they need to recognize a conservation of their propositions in which one does not contradict oneself, and in which the partners search for agreement on propositions or find facts justifying their difference in points of view. The third condition for equilibrium is that there is a reciprocity between partners such that the propositions of each are treated interchangeably. Thus, for Piaget, cognitive development through collaboration occurs if the partners have a common language and system of ideas and use reciprocity in examining and adjusting for differences in their opinions.

According to Piaget, the very young child is largely impervious to social influence because egocentricity blocks the establishment of reciprocity and cooperation in considering differing points of view. Thus, according to Piaget

(1977), it is not until middle childhood that children routinely benefit from social interaction, when logical argument between children with varying points of view becomes more possible (see also Azmitia & Perlmutter, 1989).[1] Piaget thought that young children would usually either continue to see things from their own perspective or switch to the other person's perspective without understanding the rationale and, hence, without actually advancing developmentally (though occasionally entering into genuine exchange of ideas; see Tudge & Winterhoff, 1993a).

For Piaget, the meeting of minds involves two separate individuals, each operating on the other's ideas, using the back-and-forth of discussion for each to advance his or her own development. The discussion is the product of two individuals considering alternatives provided socially, rather than the construction of a joint understanding between partners. Forman (1987) contrasted Vygotskian intersubjectivity—a process that takes place between people—with Piagetian perspective-taking or decentering, which are individual processes working on socially provided information.

Several other authors have argued that individuals' use of other people's ideas to advance their own is not the same as collaboratively developed ideas that extend beyond the understanding of the individuals. For example, Crook

---

[1] For the kind of argumentation on which Piaget focused, clarity of communication and taking others' perspective may be necessary in a way that differs from what is needed for the collaboration involved in young children's understanding of the language, concepts, and routines of their community from the first year of life. Although French and U.S. toddlers have been observed to collaborate in play through coordination of actions, elaboration of each other's ideas, co-construction, and guidance (Brownell & Carriger, 1991; Verba, 1994), studies of collaboration of 3- to 5-year-old children in cognitive tasks have been quite variable in their results (Cooper, 1980; Freund, 1990; Gauvain & Rogoff, 1989; Göncü & Rogoff, submitted; Mistry & Rogoff, submitted; Pacifici & Bearison, 1991; Perlmutter, Behrend, Kuo, & Muller, 1989; Rogoff et al., 1995; Wood et al., 1978; Wood, Wood, Ainsworth, & O'Malley, 1995). The age at which children learn from their interactions with other people may be a function of the nature of the activity as well as of the collaborative processes involved in communicating about the decisions and information at hand (Rogoff, 1990). The argumentation emphasized by Piaget may characterize a specific kind of discourse in a particular type of activity.

(1994) argued that turn-taking exchanges in which individuals try to compare the quality of their ideas fall short of collaboration, in which individuals seek a fusion of reference that creates a platform for subsequent joint action (see also Lomov, 1978). Matusov (1995) argued that intersubjectivity is a process of coordinating individual participation in joint sociocultural activity, not a relationship of correspondence of individuals' ideas or actions to each other. Similarly,

> Each participant's thinking becomes more and more an integrative part of what everyone else thinks in the group, and therefore neither the meaning nor the mode of construction of each participant's cognition can be explained as isolated, individual mental entities. (Miller, 1987, p. 235)

In work groups or family discussions in which individuals participate in a joint construction, the participants change their understanding and may have difficulty determining "whose" idea an insight was (Rogoff, 1990).

For Piaget, the social process provides individuals the opportunity to see alternatives and explore the logical consequences of their own positions in a meeting of individual minds, as opposed to a shared thinking process. To understand how individuals learn and develop through participation in the sociocultural world, it is necessary to grant that meaning is more than a construction by individuals. Piaget's use of the isolated individual as the unit of analysis, in my view, makes it impossible to develop a sociocultural approach to cognition using his theory as the basis; sociocultural aspects of cognition are not merely the addition of individual changes in thinking resulting from social interaction.

Nonetheless, Piagetian theory has added important ideas to the sociocultural theoretical endeavor. Most notably, Piaget's (1926) emphasis on peer interaction has drawn attention to the exploration of cognitive conflict between companions of equal status. Piaget asserted that only when children are able to discuss problems as equals are they likely to take into account new ways of thinking. Other scholars have extended Piaget's discussion to include the effects of peer interaction on the development of Piagetian concepts. Some of this work considers the sociocultural context in addition to the interpersonal context, developing the seed of Piaget's ideas about the social world beyond his own work. A later section of this chapter examines peers' similar status in collective argumentation and presents research and conceptual points of scholars closely influenced by Piaget.

Thus, it seems fair to say that the conceptual perspective offered by Vygotsky and his colleagues forms the theoretical inspiration of sociocultural work on cognition as a collaborative process, with the emphasis of Piaget on peer interaction adding substantively to the endeavor.

The next section presents the central concepts of contemporary sociocultural theories. It also contrasts them with another perspective—the social influence approach—whose implicit set of assumptions provides a widespread, though little-articulated, conceptual system for much recent research which is at odds in many ways with the tenets of sociocultural theories.

SOCIOCULTURAL AND SOCIAL "INFLUENCE" CONCEPTUALIZATIONS

In this section, I summarize the theoretical position of a family of sociocultural theories regarding cognition as a collaborative process, and attempt to distinguish it from the assumptions of the social influence approach. In sociocultural theories, individuals' cognitive development is regarded as inherently involved with the sociocultural activities in which they engage with others in cultural practices and institutions, in a mutually constituting relationship. The sociocultural activity is the unit of analysis (see also Rogoff & Chavajay, 1995).

The social influence approach uses the individual as the unit of analysis, and adds social interaction as an "influence" on individual development, treating the partner or their "input" as an independent variable, and the later performance of the target individual as a dependent variable (see also Wertsch & Toma, 1995). Researchers using social influence conceptualizations do not identify their approach as a theory. However, the implicit assumptions and questions within this approach are often treated as the default theory in empirical work. This often occurs even if the study's rationale refers to Vygotsky's or Piaget's theories. Nicolopoulou and Cole (1993) pointed out that in research referring to Vygotsky, the social context of development has often been reduced to face-to-face interaction in dyadic pairs, "a truncated and inadequate conception of the sociocultural dimension of Vygotsky's theory" (p. 283).

I have the impression that a unifying metaphor underlying social influence approaches is a tool of widespread use in U.S. psychological research: the Analysis of Variance (ANOVA). The ANOVA provides pervasive guidance for the research that has appeared in developmental journals, and it seems, by extension, to provide a way of looking at the phenomena researched. One of the key tenets in the use of ANOVA is that human phenomena are to be divided into separate factors, defined independently of each other, and varied without respect to each other. The assumption is that by examining the effects of these independent factors one at a time or with a few others in (statistical) interaction, the nature of human phenomena can be determined.

My remarks here are not meant to criticize statistics, metaphors, or other tools of thought and communication, but to articulate the assumptions of a particular metaphor that is widely used but usually unexamined. We make use of tools such as ANOVA, graphs, two-dimensional diagrams, or analysis of transcripts to organize our ideas about the human phenomena we seek to understand. The tools (and metaphors of communication as well) are essential for our work, but the limitations of the tools should not become limitations in our understanding. I am simply suggesting that we reflect on the assumptions necessary to use metaphors and tools of analysis, rather than assume that the phenomena are structured in the same way as the metaphors and tools (see also Gellatly, 1989).

Sociocultural theory is still emerging and is not a single consolidated view. In this overview, I present my own views and those of others that are closely related. I have argued that development and learning entail individuals' *transformation of participation* in sociocultural activity; their roles are not separate entities from the activities in which they participate, although their contributions can become the focus of attention for particular analyses (Rogoff, 1990, 1995). Similar emphasis on transformation of participation has been made by Lave, Ochs, Shieffelin, Heath, and Dewey. For example, Dewey (1916) argued:

> The living creature is a part of the world, sharing its vicissitudes and fortunes, and making itself secure in its precarious dependence only as it intellectually identifies itself with the changes about it, and, forecasting the future consequences of what is going on, shapes its own activities accordingly. If the living, experiencing being is an intimate participant in the activities of the world to which it belongs, then knowledge is a mode of participation, valuable in the degree in which it is effective. It cannot be the idle view of an unconcerned spectator. (p. 393)

Some sociocultural scholars may disagree with my points here—especially those who work within a social influence approach or something in between (as I myself have done in my earlier work). So, this section should not be taken as representing the thinking of all members of the "sociocultural family," but as my efforts, along with those of some other scholars, to explicate how learning and development occur as a process of transformation of participation in sociocultural activity.

The remainder of this section examines conceptual issues that distinguish transformation of participation and social influence views:

- Nonindependence versus independence of individual, interpersonal, and community processes.
- Learning conceived as changing participation in activities versus internalization across boundaries.
- Observing dynamic processes of understanding versus locating stored knowledge.
- Changing participation versus competence in reaching a developmental goal.
- Relation of participation across activities versus transfer of knowledge.

Nonindependence versus Independence of Individual, Interpersonal, and Community Processes

Sociocultural theories, such as the transformation of participation approach, have in common a premise that individual, interpersonal, and cultural processes are not independent entities (Lave, 1988b; Packer & Scott, 1992; Rogoff, 1982, 1992; Valsiner, in press; Wertsch & Toma, 1995). Analysis may focus primarily on one of them, but not without reference to the others as if they could exist in isolation from each other (Rogoff, 1995). As Bakhurst put it, "the study of mind, of culture, and of language (in all its diversity) are internally related: that is, it will be *impossible* to render any one of these domains intelligible without essential reference to the others" (1988, p. 39).

With the view that individual, social, and cultural processes constitute each other, it is essential to note that individuals transform culture as they participate in its practices, altering the practices with their generation to fit their circumstances. Individuals develop as they participate with others in shared endeavors that both constitute and are derived from community traditions (Rogoff, 1990). For example, children's play occurs in organized social institutions that predate the children's involvement, but the children also elaborate the possibilities available to them (Packer & Scott, 1992).

Rogoff (1995) suggested that the examination of individual, interpersonal, and community/institutional developmental processes involves differing planes of observation and analysis, with any one plane being the focus, but with the others necessarily observed in the background (see Figures 14.1 and 14.2). In an analysis focusing on individual contributions to sociocultural activities, the individual's

Figure 14.2   Analyzing the personal, interpersonal, and community/institutional planes in this activity could entail a focus on one child as she writes (personal plane), the engagement of that child with her classmates and teacher (interpersonal plane), or the classroom arrangements—such as seating arrangements and literacy and numeracy tools on the wall and desks—as well as the recent adoption of this European-derived institution in this Mayan community (community/institutional plane). (© Barbara Rogoff)

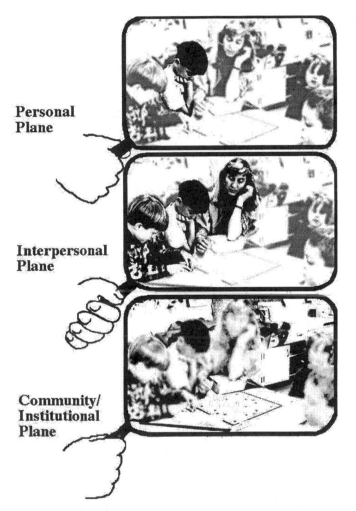

Personal Plane

Interpersonal Plane

Community/ Institutional Plane

contributions are in focus while those of the other people are blurred, but one cannot interpret what the individual is doing without understanding how it fits with ongoing events. It is not as if the individual could be taken outside of the activity to have their development analyzed. They are involved—part of the activity. Individual, interpersonal, and community processes on which researchers focus do not entail "boundaries" between separate entities.[2] This is my reason for stressing the term *planes* of analysis, which contrasts with prevailing notions of *levels* of analysis that treat personal, interpersonal, and community processes as separate entities rather than simply analytic distinctions.

Figure 14.1   Using personal, interpersonal, and community/institutional planes of analysis involves focusing on one plane, but still using background information from the other planes, as if with different lenses. In this image, the viewer can focus on the boy planning a word to spell (a personal plane of analysis), the interaction between the boy and the woman helping him and his competitors (an interpersonal plane of analysis), or the scrabble game, dictionary, classroom arrangement, and middle-class U.S. version of a European-derived institution (a community/institutional plane of analysis). Analysis focusing on each of these planes requires some attention to background information regarding the others. (© Barbara Rogoff)

[2] Compatible units of analysis seem to be employed by some researchers studying events in the brain (such as the functioning of neurons or the development of brain matter) and perception-and-action (such as coordination of limbs in the context of action in real circumstances). For example, Pribram (1990) discussed the hologram metaphor, which he attributed to the parallel distributed processing approach: "The properties of holograms are expressed by the principle that 'the whole is contained or enfolded in its parts,' and the very notion of 'parts' is altered, because parts of a hologram do not have what we think of as boundaries" (pp. 92–93; see also Gibson, 1982; Winograd & Flores, 1987).

An example of how individual cognitive processes constitute and are constituted by interpersonal and community processes was provided by a study of planning Girl Scouts' cookie sales (Rogoff, Baker-Sennett, Lacasa, & Goldsmith, 1995). The individual Scouts' cognitive activity in planning and keeping track of orders, money, and routes occurred in close collaboration with other Scouts, family members, customers, and adult troop leaders, and involved cognitive tools provided by the institution (such as memory and calculation aids on the order form). At the same time that the girls' work fit existing practices, it contributed to transforming them with use of new technologies (such as using post-it notes to organize orders). Attention to the individual, interpersonal, and community/institutional planes of analysis was necessary to understand the complex problem solving of this activity, each becoming the focus of different analyses; treating them as independent entities would not have resulted in a coherent understanding of the roles of individuals, other people, and the community.

Learning as Changing Participation IN Activities versus Internalization ACROSS Boundaries

The concept of internalization has been used in a variety of theoretical approaches to account for how shared thinking results in changes in an individual (Aronfreed, 1968; Bandura, 1986; Zinchenko, 1985). However, the concept of internalization often involves a strict boundary between the individual mind and the external world. Individuals are considered to possess preexisting knowledge, then have a social experience, and then internalize it so that it becomes a part of their own bag of tricks. The internalization process is necessary in social influence approaches to account for the movement of information from outside the boundary to inside it.

From the transformation of participation perspective, learning from shared thinking does not involve *taking* or *being given* something from an external model. Instead, by participating in shared endeavors in sociocultural activity, the individual is continually in the process of developing and using their understanding. In the process of participation, individuals *change,* and their later involvement in similar events may reflect these changes.

Participation in sociocultural activities does not involve copying what is already invented or available in the thinking of the participating individuals; it is a creative process. Leont'ev (1981) stressed the creative process when he claimed that the very form of mental reflection of reality

changes in the course of each person's development in each new generation, as he or she participates in practical activity developed in human society. The social influence view is not usually a copy theory either—"incoming" information is often treated as being transformed by the individual, but this occurs within the individual's acquisition of the external information. This is a different process than in sociocultural theories, where individuals are regarded as transforming their understanding and roles, becoming people that play varying roles in the community with changing understanding and interpersonal relations, as an inherent aspect of their participation in sociocultural activity (Forman & McPhail, 1993; Lave & Wenger, 1991; Litowitz, 1993; Rogoff et al., 1995).

Observing Dynamic Processes of Understanding versus Locating Stored Knowledge

The central research questions raised in the social influence model deal with attempting to locate where knowledge resides and how it moves from one location to another through the impact of social interaction—from external events to the brain, from the brain to executed action, and from one situation to another (Rogoff, in press).

These questions are premised on a storage metaphor, in which learning and development are conceived as the accumulation of mental objects such as plans, memories, or reading skills (Kvale, 1977; Rogoff, Baker-Sennett, & Matusov, 1994; Wertsch & Toma, 1995). The storage metaphor seems to be necessitated by the assumptions of a boundary between the person and the rest of the world, accompanied by assumptions that the present is bounded off from the past and future. Gauvain (1993) discusses the storage model in her account of spatial thinking from a sociocultural perspective:

> Spatial knowledge is not a general, underlying "piece" of knowledge that exists inside the head, to be externalized for use when needed. Spatial understanding may not be separate from the activity in which the knowledge is used and, thus, may be less like a representation, such as a route or a map, and more like a problem-solving process. (p. 70)

The storage metaphor rests on an assumption that time is segmented into past, present, and future, with boundaries between them. Relations across time periods are handled by assuming that the individual stores memories of the past that are somehow retrieved and used in the present, and that the individual makes plans in the present and (if they are stored effectively) executes them in the future. This involves crossing boundaries between time periods, like the boundary between the person and the rest of the world in social influence approaches (Rogoff, Baker-Sennett, & Matusov, 1994).

From a transformation of participation perspective, change and development in the process of participation are assumed to be inherent, with prior and upcoming events involved in (not independent of) the ongoing present event. Any event in the present is an extension of previous events and is directed toward goals that have not yet been accomplished. As such, the present extends through the past and future and is not independent of them (see Ochs, 1994; Pepper, 1942; Rogoff, in press). When a person acts on the basis of previous experience, their past is present. It is not merely a stored memory called up in the present; the person's previous participation contributes to the event at hand by having prepared it. The present event is different than it would have been if previous events had been different; the explanation does not require a storage model of past events. Thinking and acting in the present involves reference to prior events and activities, as well as others that are anticipated in the future.

The contrast between treating interacting people as separate individuals versus contributors to a dynamic, integrating event is illuminated by Felton (personal communication, October 1993), who suggested that it is necessary to think of cognitive development as a process, as people move *through* understanding rather than *to* understanding (seen as a platform, or level of achievement). In discussing the concept of intersubjectivity, she argued that "the difficulty in working with intersubjectivity as a concept is that it isn't located in space; it may be inferred through activity, or seen in the products of creative endeavour" (p. 2). She illustrated her points with observations of dance:

> Contact improvisation [is] a dance form founded on and directed towards an articulation of the intersubjective process. (A way I'd never describe it in other circles, but this is essentially what it is.) The locus of attention and activity resides between two partners moving in unrehearsed concert with each other. This improvisational form is based on moving without resistance and working with the impulses that are constructed between partners. We work with blending our movements, giving and taking weight, and falling with gravity. This intersubjective focus allows us to effortlessly lift partners much heavier than ourselves because we work with momentum generated through our interactions. Dancing with one partner (or more) our attention is focused on what

is occurring between us from moment to moment. These moments aren't fixed places that we move from and to. The dance is not an exchange from one person to another, or from one pose or posture to another. If we had to wait for our partner to arrive at the destination of each movement, the momentum for the dance would be gone. If we take a slow motion look at this, we see that the dance isn't a series of static postures strung together, but is a constantly unfolding, emerging activity. The dancer never gets to or departs from any specific place. . . . The dance can't rely on the skill of one partner or of the other; if the intersubjective realm is not attended to, no amount of expertise will save the dance from being static. (1993, pp. 2–3)

The view that development is a transformation of participation of people engaged in shared endeavors avoids the idea that the social world is external to the individual and that development consists of *acquiring* knowledge and skills. Rather, a person develops through participation in an activity, *changing* to be involved in the situation at hand in ways that contribute both to the ongoing event and to the person's preparation for involvement in similar events. Instead of studying a person's possession or acquisition of a capacity or a bit of knowledge, the focus is on people's active changes of understanding and involvement in dynamic activities in which they participate (Arievitch & van der Veer, 1995; Gibson, 1979; Leont'ev, 1981; Pepper, 1942; Rogoff, 1990; Rogoff et al., 1994). Communication and coordination during participation in shared endeavors involve adjustments between participants (with varying, complementary, or even incompatible roles) to stretch their common understanding to fit with new perspectives in the shared endeavor. Such stretching to accomplish something together is development. As Wertsch and Stone (1979, p. 21) put it, "the process is the product." The central questions raised in the transformation of participation view deal with how people's roles and understanding change as an activity develops, how different activities relate to each other, and how people prepare now for what they expect later on the basis of their prior participation (Rogoff, in press).

Changing Participation versus Competence in Reaching a Developmental Goal

The effort to chart internal competence often appears in social influence views, conceived as acquisition of mental objects underlying actual but impure performance. The distinction between competence and performance is not relevant to studying the structure of people's developing involvement in sociocultural activities. From a transformation of participation perspective, we examine how children actually participate in sociocultural activities to characterize how they contribute to those activities. The emphasis changes from trying to infer what children *can* think to interpreting what and how they *do* think (see also Packer & Scott, 1992; Rogoff et al., 1994).[3]

If we do not search for the acquisition of mental objects or competence, this move also recasts the question of the onset of new competences (Rogoff, 1996). The question of when a person *begins* to have plans, perspective-taking skills, or language treats transitions as if they were contained in the child, who either does or does not have the knowledge or skill. The onset question in developmental psychology generally searches for the earliest time one can find evidence of the skill or knowledge in question, yielding continual efforts to demonstrate that the child "has it" at an earlier age than asserted by Piaget or some other scholar, by changing the nature of the task situation (see Bruner, 1978; Elbers, 1991). From the transformation of participation perspective, developmental transitions are to be studied in people's roles in sociocultural activities rather than through assuming that developmental change involves the acquisition of a competence solely within the individual.

In addition, the definition of development changes from one in which people ascend levels toward a given (often uniform) developmental endpoint, to a sociocultural definition in which transformations are qualitative developmental changes in particular directions. The direction of development varies locally in accord with cultural values, interpersonal needs, and specific circumstances, but it does not require specification of universal or ideal endpoints of development. Further, the applicability of sociocultural ideas about learning and development is not restricted to directions that are considered desirable by

experts or other segments of the community. They apply also to explaining how people develop through participation in community activities that many would criticize. What is key is transformation in the process of participation in community activities, not acquisition of competences defined independently of the sociocultural activities in which people participate.

Relating Participation across Activities versus Transferring Knowledge across Situations

In a transformation of participation view, the relation between processes in different activities is a central matter for investigation. Processes are not automatically assumed to be general, nor are they assumed to be so particular that we cannot extend from any particular observation to others. Rather, researchers can observe how processes observed in one situation relate to those in others.

The question of relating activities to each other differs from questions of transfer or generalization using a storage metaphor. The focus is on determining how activities relate to each other and how people's participation in one activity relates to their participation in another, rather than on how mental objects are transferred (as if they existed in isolation in the head) or how physical similarities in the materials elicit transfer (as if the materials carry meaning outside of their use). Rather, the idea is that individuals change and handle later situations in ways prepared by their own participation and changing responsibility in previous activities (Rogoff, 1994, 1995, in press).

In the social influence perspective, since individual competence is traditionally seen as separate from environmental circumstances, researchers examine relations across situations by means of statistical interactions between person and situation (Rogoff, 1982). Social influence approaches conceptualize the complex whole as an enormous collection of variables that are defined independently of each other. The search for interactions between separately defined person and situation factors yields infinite interactions, leading to "a hall of mirrors that extends to infinity" (Cronbach, 1975, p. 119).

Those who become concerned that the study of contextual issues leads towards chaos are likely to be considering those infinite interactions from a social influence perspective rather than seeking the regularities and simplifications of patterns available when individuals are conceived as participants in—rather than separate from—sociocultural activity. Greater parsimony is to be found, I have argued

---

[3] This contrast does not imply a recommendation to attend only to behavior. Determining what and how people think is still inferential and is not simply a matter of recording simple aspects of behavior or of peoples' responses to questions or cognitive tasks. Neither the view of observers nor of people themselves is a "true" window on cognitive processes. Researchers should take advantage of whatever evidence is available from their own observations as well as from the reports of other observers and the people involved to create a plausible account that advances understanding (see Edwards, 1993; Kvale, 1977).

(Rogoff, 1996), in recognizing and studying regularities and coherence in the existing richness of structure of human activities.

The question from a participation view is to understand the transformations that occur in children's participation in particular kinds of activities, which themselves transform—how do children change from this kind of participation to that kind of participation, and how do the activities in which they participate change with the children's and others' involvement? For example, to examine children's progress in learning to read, researchers would examine transformations in how children make sense of letters in particular kinds of texts with specific kinds of social and cultural organization of the reading activity, such as the kind of social support provided for the child's participation in reading and the purpose of the reading effort. These are inherently part of the process of reading, not potential confounds or features that need to be controlled in order to identify the child's "level" of reading competence. The activity in which children's reading is observed would be part of the evaluation of the children's progress, since no setting provides a context-free window on hard-to-see competence that the individual "has" (Rogoff, in press).

In sum, the basic contrast is that in sociocultural views, individual development is seen as contributing to as well as constituted by the sociocultural activities in which people participate, whereas social influence approaches maintain a focus on the individual as the basic unit of analysis and examine the influence of "outside" social forces.

The next section considers ramifications for the central research questions and methods regarding the study of individuals' development that stem from the conceptual differences between sociocultural and social influence perspectives. The sociocultural approach does not just add new variables (e.g., whether or not people have a partner), but is developing a worldview that differs in some fundamental ways from the assumptions on which much developmental research has been based.

RESEARCH QUESTIONS AND ASSOCIATED WAYS OF OBSERVING DEVELOPMENT

Sociocultural and social influence approaches both address classical cognitive developmental questions such as how people learn to plan, remember, solve problems, classify information, perceive, communicate and understand each other, read and write, understand mathematical and

linguistic systems, and extend their understanding to new situations. However, in sociocultural approaches, such cognitive processes are regarded as an aspect of how people act intelligently within specific types of sociocultural activity, whereas they are seen as residing within individuals in the social influence approach (with domain specificity of skills used to account for differences in how people think in different activities).

This section outlines some of the key differences in research questions and methodological approaches for observing individuals' development from sociocultural and social influence perspectives. Sociocultural researchers are still in the process of developing research methods consistent with the assumption system of the sociocultural perspective. As Vygotsky (1978) argued, "any fundamentally new approach to a scientific problem inevitably leads to new methods of investigation and analysis. The invention of new methods that are adequate to the new ways in which problems are posed requires far more than a simple modification of previously accepted methods" (p. 58).

It is challenging for researchers to attend both to the learning of the children whose development is of interest and to the contributions of their partners and communities. The challenges to researchers working with the sociocultural perspective are to develop methods to examine individual contributions in relation to the course of their participation in sociocultural activity (not to treat the individual's contribution as existing separately from the dynamic interpersonal and sociocultural aspects of the activity). Researchers working from the social influence perspective attempt to standardize or separately define the social influences "impacting" the individual and isolate the individual for the sake of examining their learning.

These differences between the two approaches involve both conceptual and methodological issues, with quite different units of analysis: the individual (as an independent entity) versus the activity (with contributions by varying people whose roles are mutually defining). The different units of analysis are reflected in the central research questions regarding cognition as a collaborative process in the two approaches. With the social influence approach, researchers ask what external influences affect the individual's development and how individuals generalize what they have acquired to new tasks; with the sociocultural approach, researchers ask how individuals' understanding and roles transform in their participation in sociocultural activities and how people relate participation in one activity to another.

Examining Development in Social Influence Approaches

In social influence approaches, the assumption is that in order to evaluate learning, the individual must be isolated from other influences and a standard procedure applied to "measure" competence as pieces of knowledge that have been obtained. Methodological manipulations are used to clear away situational artifacts that "get in the way" of evaluating children's possessions of skills or concepts. This often involves using standardized tests or pretest-treatment-posttest designs to isolate the individual's competence. However, this approach is plagued by difficulties in applying equivalent procedures as well as in truly isolating the individual (Rogoff, in press).

Standardization of Procedures as an Attempt to Hold Constant the Situation

Standardization requires that situations have the same meaning for different individuals or groups; it is not necessarily achieved by applying the same procedures. The same procedures often carry very different meanings to differing people.

For example, U.S. middle-class children with different schooling backgrounds differed in treating an experimenter as a tester or a collaborator, making the children's "independent" performance noncomparable even though the experimenter acted the same way with both groups (Matusov, Bell, & Rogoff, unpublished data). Children whose schooling emphasized collaboration with adults (see Figure 14.1) treated the experimenter as a collaborator, attempting to converse with him about the problems and trying to involve him in the activities, though he sat reading a book to indicate that he was not supposed to be interacting. Children from a school that employed little collaboration seldom tried to involve the experimenter; they were more used to having adults withdraw as they worked or displayed their knowledge. For the experimenter to refuse to be involved with the children from the collaborative school was a violation of their expectations of the social situation, though it was consistent with the expectations of the children from the less collaborative school. Thus, it was not possible to compare the "independent" performance of the two groups of children, because the experimenter was treated by the children as playing different roles.

The expected relationships between child and examiner in a test or experiment are familiar to some research participants, but not to others of differing cultural or social backgrounds. Relations with a tester entail a particular form of display of knowledge and of social interaction that is valued in many schools and experiments (Rogoff, 1982; Rogoff, Radziszewska, & Masiello, 1995; Schubauer-Leoni, Bell, Grossen, & Perret-Clermont, 1989). For example, in many communities, the role of children may be to observe and to carry out directives, but not to initiate conversation or talk back to a person of higher status (Blount, 1972; Harkness & Super, 1977; Ward, 1971). In tests, reliance on a companion for help may be considered cheating, whereas in everyday situations in many communities, not to employ a companion's assistance may be regarded as folly or egoism.

Schooled people are familiar with an interview or a testing situation in which a person who already knows the answer asks the question anyway (Mehan, 1979). In some cultural settings, however, the appropriate behavior may be to show respect to the questioner or avoid being made a fool of by giving the obvious answer to what must be a trick question (otherwise why would a knowledgeable person be asking it?). Irvine (1978) suggested that Wolof subjects' interpretation of an experimenter's purpose in a conservation procedure may conflict with their giving straightforward answers to questions. She reported that it is uncommon, except in schoolroom interrogation, for Wolof people to ask one another questions to which they already know the answers: "Where this kind of questioning does occur it suggests an aggressive challenge, or a riddle with a trick answer" (p. 549).

The particular forms of cognitive activity that are considered central to intellectual life in research are closely tied to the definitions of thinking employed in academic settings. Schubauer-Leoni et al. argued that schooled children often assume that relations with a researcher follow the "didactic contract" that they are familiar with from their relations with their teachers, entering a research setting with the tendency to function as a pupil with the associated "systems of rights, obligations, rules, and tacit agreements embedded within the institutional framework" (1989, p. 681).

Like other societal institutions, schooling provides practice in the use of specific tools and technologies for solving particular problems (Scribner & Cole, 1981). Such tools include mnemonic devices; language genres such as essayist prose and story problems; and formats for calculation and record keeping, such as arithmetic and writing. Societal institutions and tools of thought carry with them values that define important goals to reach, significant problems to solve, and sophisticated approaches to use in addressing the problems and reaching the goals. The values differ in their emphasis on independent versus interdependent performance, social responsibility versus technological advance, analysis of freestanding puzzles versus synthesis of patterns in practical contexts, speed of action versus considered deliberateness, and many other contrasts (Goodnow, 1976; Lutz & LeVine, 1982; Rogoff, 1981; Rogoff & Chavajay, 1995; Scribner, 1976; Serpell, 1982).

Skills for mastering specific forms of assessment—such as the "objective" tests in schools and national standardized assessments—themselves become a central part of many institutions designed to foster learning, with instruction focusing on success in these specific activities (Frederiksen & Collins, 1989). Such differences in values and practices make it unlikely that standardized procedures will have the same meaning to different people, especially as their backgrounds differ (Cole & Means, 1981; Frederiksen & Collins, 1989).

Attempting to Isolate the "Individual" from Social Situations

Most information on children's cognitive development has been obtained in situations in which children are treated as if they were revealing their thinking in a situation free of social and cultural constraints. According to Brown (1994), in the 1960s, children were often tested in "cages" (the Wisconsin General Test Apparatus, designed by Harlow for use with monkeys that bite) in order to minimize interaction of the experimenter and the child. The procedure kept the child from seeing the experimenter's facial expressions behind a one-way mirror, in order to "control" for social influences.

A common method for attempting to isolate the individual from social influence in order to assess learning is the treatment-posttest design, in which researchers arrange for exposure to external knowledge or skill, and then examine evidence of acquisition as the person retrieves the acquired knowledge or skill "independently." However, there *is* no pure observation of what the individual does independent of their prior and concurrent participation in sociocultural activity (Schubauer-Leoni et al., 1989; Wertsch et al., 1993). For example, posttests do not reveal purely individual performance. The subject in a posttest is working within the constraints and supports provided by the experimenter and the research tradition and scholarly institutions that encompass the procedures and interpretation of posttests. The posttest proceeds

according to a communicative contract that delineates the appropriate form of communication and resources available in responding to the problems posed by the experimenter (Crook, 1994; Forman & McPhail, 1993; Perret-Clermont, 1993; Perret-Clermont, Perret, & Bell, 1991; Rogoff et al., 1995).

Experimenters or testers are collaborators in children's production of test performance (Newman, Griffin, & Cole, 1984; Scribner, 1976). Young children attempt to use researchers as collaborators, making use of the examiner's nonverbal cues, such as direction of gaze and hesitations to answer standardized questions (Mehan, 1976). Tudge (1992) suggested that, in a situation in which the experimenter provided no feedback on children's solutions to balance beam problems, the experimenter's silence is nonetheless social information. "Silence on the part of an adult typically implies consent—or surely an incorrect answer would be challenged" (p. 1377). Tudge suggested that the stability of incorrect and correct responses in his study might have been due to an inadvertent strengthening by the adult of the views expressed by the children.

Even when experimenters and subjects are not directly engaged, they are indirectly engaged together. For example, researchers attempt to tailor the problems on which children work to their age level or abilities (Tudge & Winterhoff, 1993b), and the materials, instructions, and experimental script are used to communicate to children what they are to do, and to support their playing their role in the study. Cognitive researchers easily note that preschool children have difficulty following the experimenter's plans or focusing on the experimental goals unless their role is carefully supported by the researcher and the experimental procedures.

Researchers seldom analyze how they themselves are involved in the cognitive activities of their subjects when the contact is indirect, such as through instructions in advance of a task, provision of materials or of constraints on available methods, or written or electronic communication with research participants. An example of how individuals relied on indirect collaboration with researchers occurred in a study noting that white upper-middle-class U.S. fourth-graders who worked solo on a computer-based tutorial accessed a computer helpscreen summarizing the meaning of symbols to be learned (a form of contact with the experimenters) more often than did students working in groups (Hooper, Temiyakarn, & Williams, 1993).

For researchers to examine our own assumptions and personal and institutional engagements in cognitive tests is a challenging endeavor, because people are notably unaware of the institutions in which they themselves act. Berger and Luckmann (1966) speculated that habitual relations between people become institutionalized as expected and accepted rules and approaches that humans come to regard as external to their functioning. Shotter (1978) explained:

> For the structure of human exchanges, there are precise foundations to be discovered in the *institutions* we establish between ourselves and others; institutions which implicate us in one another's activity in such a way that, what we have done together in the past, *commits us* to going on in a certain way in the future, ... The members of an institution need not necessarily have been its originators; they may be second, third, fourth,[and so forth] generation members, having "inherited" the institution from their forebears. And this is a most important point, for although there may be an intentional structure to institutional activities, practitioners of institutional forms need have no awareness at all of the reason for its structure—for them, it is just "the-way-things-are-done." The reasons for the institution having one form rather than another are buried in its *history*. (p. 70)

Efforts by scholars to understand the cultural-historical nature of academic institutions and activities are aided by the discourse across disciplines, nations, and historical time periods that are inherent to the sociocultural approach, and by the aims of this line of work to understand the mutually constituting nature of individual functioning and interpersonal and community/institutional processes (Rogoff, 1995; Rogoff & Chavajay, 1995). In sociocultural approaches, the idea of separating the individual from social influences is seen as an analytic device that has been used by researchers using a particular assumption system that fits with prevalent academic institutions.

Observing Development as Transformation of Participation

From the perspective that development occurs as individuals transform their participation in sociocultural activities, the point is not to try to dissect individuals apart from sociocultural activity, but to try to understand their roles in, contributions to, and changes through the sociocultural activities in which they participate. Moving from the individual to the activity as the unit of analysis has been informed by methodological approaches prevalent in disciplines other than psychology, notably ethnographic analyses and graphical analyses.

Sociocultural approaches do not limit analyses to particular methods, but rather inspire broadening of methodological tools through using methods of examining evidence used in other disciplines. Depending on the question, researchers from a sociocultural approach choose among or combine methodological tools that have previously been regarded as belonging within the domain of particular disciplines. Sociocultural research emphasizes both qualitative approaches to understanding the meaning of events from a perspective that fits the practices of the community being studied, and quantitative approaches that can be useful in understanding patterns that appear across cases or settings. It is beyond the scope of this chapter to go into detail on methodological innovations; I refer the reader to Chapter 3 of Rogoff, Mistry, Göncü, and Mosier (1993) for discussion and examples of integrating qualitative and quantitative approaches that can support sociocultural analyses.

An important aspect of the sociocultural approach to understanding scholarly inquiry itself is an examination of the methods that are used in analyzing phenomena (see Kindermann & Valsiner, 1989; Valsiner, 1986). This involves putting the question first, and then looking for ways to study it, rather than limiting what is studied to the phenomena that can be analyzed exclusively with the methodological tools of a particular discipline. I suspect that the default assumptions employed in the social influence approach are maintained with tenacity due in part to the firm placement of ANOVA (and related statistical tools) as a rite of passage for researchers becoming psychologists.

From the perspective that development is a process of transformation of participation, evaluation of development focuses on how individuals participate in and contribute to ongoing activity rather than on "outcome" and individuals' possessions of concepts and skills. Evaluation of development examines the ways people transform their participation, analyzing how they coordinate with others in shared endeavors, with attention to the purposes and dynamic nature of the activity itself and its meaning in the community. The investigation of people's actual involvement and changing goals in activities becomes the basis of understanding development rather than simply the surface to try to get past. (See also Packer & Scott, 1992.)

The central question becomes: How do people participate in sociocultural activity and how does their participation change from being relatively peripheral participants (cf. Lave & Wenger, 1991), observing and carrying out secondary roles, to assuming various responsible roles in the management or transformation of such activities? Rogoff (in press) suggested that these features of an individual's participation in shared endeavors can be used to evaluate their learning:

- The roles people play (including leadership and support of others), with what fidelity and responsibility;
- Their changing purposes for being involved, commitment to the endeavor, and trust of unknown aspects of it (including its future);
- Their flexibility and attitude toward change in involvement (interest in learning rather than rejection of new roles or protection of the status quo);
- Their understanding of the interrelations of different contributions to the endeavor and readiness to switch to complementary roles (e.g., to fill in for others);
- The relation of the participants' roles in this activity to those in other activities, with individuals extending to other activities or switching to different modes of involvement as appropriate (such as skillfully generalizing or switching approaches to participation in certain roles at school and at home, or to involvement in different ethnic communities); and
- Their flexibility and vision in contributing to revision of ongoing community practices.

For example, graduate students' progress in learning how to do research is commonly evaluated according to these features of their involvement with their advisor's research team.

A participation perspective is routinely used in the classroom evaluation of children's learning in an innovative public elementary school in which tests are rarely given, but teachers have rich information on children's development and learning (Rogoff, Matusov, & White, in preparation; see also Clay & Cazden, 1990). Evaluation derives from collaboration with the children and observation of the roles that the children begin to carry out in the learning activities. Teachers evaluate learning to write, for example, in terms of whether children are at the point of needing assistance in becoming involved at all in writing, or write with interest of their own. Do they write only in response to requests to do so or to initiate communication through writing? Is their writing embedded in a very limited range of activities or is it broadly used? As they write, do they consider whether a reader will understand their written communication, or are they tied to writing for themselves alone? Do they take responsibility for editing for meaning

and legibility or is this a role that needs close support from another person? Do they assist others with writing activities? Do they effectively adjust their writing to differing circumstances, such as writing collaboratively when this is called for and writing solo when required? Does their writing achieve its purpose?

These kinds of observations provide teachers with detailed understanding of the children's development as writers, and simultaneously with information about how the teachers could support further development. The evaluation necessarily includes examination of the teachers' own involvement, the writing situation and supports, as well as the child's role in the writing activity. It is a formative evaluation that assesses learning within ongoing activity and simultaneously informs practice. It resembles Frederiksen and Collins' (1989) recommendation that test makers, teachers, and assessors make clear guidelines regarding the central skills and understanding of a particular kind of learning (e.g., developing geometric proofs or technical and creative skill in ice skating) and focus assessment as well as instruction on directly and explicitly involving students in these activities.

Experimental situations can similarly be analyzed in terms of how people (including the researchers) arrange their relative contributions, such as in children's learning how to plan maze routes with the involvement of their mothers and the experimenter in both practice and posttest events (Rogoff et al., 1995). Evaluation would include examination of how the children, mothers, and experimenter collaborated and avoided collaborating in the practice and posttest sessions (according to the rules of the experiment, which would also be an object of study), and how each person's role in planning the maze routes transformed and was transformed by those of others. The maze planning itself would be viewed as a function of the contributions of the participants in the sociocultural activity, and the similarities across the training and posttest events would reveal the nature of responsibility taken by the different contributors.

The theoretical systems involved in social influence and sociocultural perspectives fit with very different questions and ways of observing the learning and development of individuals. The sections of this chapter that focus on research findings are inclusive of differing conceptions and methods of studying cognition as a collaborative process. I provide some overview of limitations of the body of research to date, but I do not focus on the assumptions or the methods used in each study. Rather, I include studies employing a wide range of approaches and attempt to convey the extent to which the findings are convincing or simply suggestive.

A great proportion of the work appears to be based primarily on social influence assumptions, perhaps because these assumptions require only the addition of social factors to the traditional psychological focus on the individual as the basic unit of analysis. However, a great deal of the research reveals efforts to break out of that assumption system toward the sociocultural perspective. The research corpus reflects the field's efforts to move beyond the individual as unit of analysis. The inconsistencies in assumption systems across (and often within) studies may reflect a developmental transition in the field.

THE STATUS OF RESEARCH TO DATE

The next sections summarize research on cognition as a collaborative process, with the aim of examining regularities that are appearing in our empirical understanding. Some of the work is based on the cultural/historical theory of Vygotsky and Leont'ev or on sociocultural theory, some is based on Piagetian theory, and a great deal fits largely within the social influence model. In beginning to extend the study of cognition beyond the isolated individual to include another person, research often still analyzes the contributions of the individual and a partner separately, rather than as collaborating participants in an integrated activity (see Rogoff, 1986, for my own shift between these two stances).

Although my preference for sociocultural theory necessarily guides my interpretation and organization of this account of research questions and findings, much (but not all) of the work done from other perspectives can be interpreted from a sociocultural perspective. The diversity of approaches to the study of cognition is a resource, not a shortcoming to be avoided—diverse questions, goals, and methods provide us with a more flexible and insightful complex of understanding of our subject matter.

The research literature on cognition as a collaborative process has grown dramatically in the last two decades. Some efforts have examined *whether* interaction with others fosters cognitive development, with varying correlations between adult "input" and children's skills. Because it seems clear that the role of social interaction in cognitive development varies with the circumstances rather than yielding a yes-or-no answer to the question of whether social interaction makes a difference, it is of

greater interest to determine *how* individuals engage with others and how such participation relates to their later involvement in related activities. For this reason, the focus of this review is on the processes of individuals' participation in shared endeavors with others, and the relation of their engagement in one activity with their later engagement in related activities.

The available research on cognition as a collaborative process has several systematic shortcomings, which are not surprising given the field's focus on use of the individual as the unit of analysis and the relative paucity of information about development in situations other than the laboratory and in cultural groups other than those of the researchers. There is still insufficient study and analysis of the following aspects of collaboration:

- There has been little study of the social and cultural aspects of how people determine the problems, goals, and means of their collaborative efforts, perhaps because research has focused largely on activities devised by researchers. Even outside of laboratory settings, researchers are often a part of the activities without examining their own roles (e.g., when they ask mothers to play with their children naturally); the researchers' roles in phenomena are seldom studied.

- We know little about collaboration when children and adults are in each other's presence without interaction as their agenda; when interaction is initiated and controlled by children seeking assistance, entertainment, or companionship; or when groups of children are not in the presence of adults.

- The dynamics of groups larger than a dyad have received little attention. Even when larger groups have been studied, they are often treated simply as collections of more individuals, interacting with each other as successive dyads rather than as integrated groups.

- There is insufficient information regarding populations other than middle-class European American groups, or in situations other than those devised or managed by middle-class European American researchers. Existing research examines the types of interactional settings (dyadic, often face-to-face) and institutions (e.g., schooling) that are of importance in that setting. Some studies cautiously limit generalization to the populations, institutions, and situations observed, but still, many slip to inferences that the research generalizes to "the child" or "the mother" or "the teacher."

- Insufficient research attention has been paid to the role of cultural tools, such as language for categorization and analysis of events, taxonomies for organizing lists of information to be remembered, and conventions such as genres of communication and maps for planning efficient routes in advance of navigation. There has also been little attention to the functioning of the institutions in which children's collaborations are observed—the ways that thinking and collaborating are aspects of cultural practices in laboratories, schools, and families.

The most interesting research on cognition as a collaborative process has moved beyond these limitations. However, even the research within these limitations provides useful information. Rather than repeating my concerns with these limitations with each research topic, I ask readers to interpret the findings of research that focuses exclusively on dyads (usually from European American middle-class populations) as representing a particular sociocultural setting organized by researchers within the cultural traditions of research (and often, of schooling). Although the sociocultural aspects of these particular activities may not have been analyzed by the researchers, results should not be automatically generalized beyond the populations and situations observed.

The major sections that follow review conceptual and empirical work on how adults as experts support novices' learning and how peers assist each other in learning. In the concluding section, I give greater emphasis to how collaboration includes cultural and institutional processes among people in different eras and locations, with collaboration involving asymmetries and disagreements as well as equal or harmonious agreement.

ADULTS AS EXPERTS SUPPORTING NOVICES' LEARNING

Research from various traditions has addressed the question of how experts structure novices' engagement in activities. Much of the work has focused exclusively on the means of support and stimulation that experts provide to novices, using methods such as scaffolding, Socratic dialogue, and tutoring. The earliest work in this tradition was very important in expanding the field's perspective on cognitive development beyond the solo individual. It yielded important findings regarding the importance of contingency between a tutor's assistance and a novice's

performance in the task, which might be regarded as a rudimentary form of mutuality, although it treats the tutor's and novice's acts separately.

Nonetheless, from a sociocultural perspective, much of the early and current work is incomplete because it often pays relatively little attention to the ongoing mutual process of understanding (focusing often on the expert's treatment of the novice, with the novice contributing correct or incorrect behavior). More importantly, this literature often overlooks the institutional and cultural aspects of the joint problem-solving activities that are observed. In many cases, the unit of analysis is separate individuals influencing each other, rather than sociocultural activity in which mutually engaged individuals collaborate in reaching goals.

Most of the research that I report focuses on adult-child interaction, but I also include some work done with college-age novices that helps to document the specific processes employed in such interactions. I do not focus on the question of age differences in forms of support for children's learning. This is due in part to insufficient information thus far to systematically examine this question. However, my impression is that a more fruitful question is more socioculturally cast: How does experts' support of novices' learning vary with the novices' extent of experience and interest in the activity in question and the experts' and the community's goals for the novices to move beyond the particular interaction to become participants in broader frames of activities? Answers to this question would include attention to the maturity of children as it relates to their involvement with immediate and broader sociocultural activities.

In the section that follows, I examine the distinction between sociocultural approaches to studying experts' support of novices' learning and approaches that focus on particular techniques of providing support, such as scaffolding. Then I review research and conceptual work that focuses on the techniques through which experts support novices' learning (much of it fitting the concept of scaffolding, but also tutoring and Socratic dialogue). I then turn to consideration of ways in which experts change their supports for novices becoming more skilled in the activities in which they participate, mutuality in communication between adults and children, and the role of expertise itself.

Sociocultural and Scaffolding Approaches to Experts' Support of Novices' Learning

The notion of scaffolding is often mentioned in the same breath as working in the zone of proximal development.

However, the two concepts are distinct in several ways. One of them, which I do not detail here, is that interactions in the zone of proximal development occur in pretend play among peers in addition to interactions between children and more expert partners (Vygotsky, 1967), whereas scaffolding is not regarded as inherent to pretend play among peers. (The collaborative aspects of play are discussed in a later section. Here I focus on interactions between people who vary in expertise, treating expert and novice as relative terms pertaining to the activity in question, not absolute designations—though we all vary in expertise, we all also have more to learn.)

Scaffolding is a specific technique focusing on what experts provide for novices, with individuals as the basic units of analysis and attention to particular instructional moves that can be operationally defined as epitomizing scaffolding (Greenfield, 1984). The originators of the concept of scaffolding, Wood, Bruner, and Ross (1976), described the functions of the tutor in scaffolding a child's performance as involving the following functions:

- Recruiting the child's interest in the task as it is defined by the tutor.
- Reducing the number of steps required to solve a problem by simplifying the task, so that the learner can manage components of the process and recognize when a fit with task requirements is achieved.
- Maintaining the pursuit of the goal, through motivation of the child and direction of the activity.
- Marking critical features of discrepancies between what a child has produced and the ideal solution.
- Controlling frustration and risk in problem solving.
- Demonstrating an idealized version of the act to be performed.

As a metaphor, scaffolding has been criticized as being too mechanical (Griffin & Cole, 1984; Valsiner & van der Veer, 1993). For example, Packer (1993) pointed out that in construction work, scaffolding is meant to hold up a passive structure (the building = the child?) until external efforts to construct it are completed, but children, as well as adults, are active and can manage the interaction.

Scaffolding focuses on the tutor's efforts as they relate contingently to the novice's successes and failures. It makes a very important advance over efforts that considered adult instruction in a way that was not linked with children's roles at all. Such unlinked ways of studying instruction examined only what the expert did (e.g., by counting frequency of questions, directives, or praise) without examining the instructional context involving the novice's current state of understanding or reaction to the expert's instruction. The scaffolding notion explicitly includes the novice's progress in the concept, recognizing that a tutor's moves mean quite different things if they follow upon an error or successful attempt by a novice.

Equating scaffolding and working in the zone of proximal development is a frequent occurrence in the literature, which seems to be an assimilation of Vygotsky's complex ideas to a more familiar approach. The concepts of scaffolding and working in the zone of proximal development serve quite different functions and involve different units of analysis (Griffin & Cole, 1984). Nicolopoulou and Cole (1993) criticized the "interactional reductionism" implicit in much Vygotskian-inspired research, which too seldom goes beyond studying specific interactions to place them in the context of a cultural and institutional framework.

The concept of the zone of proximal development is not a characterization of what the more expert partner does to the other. It is a way of describing an activity in which someone with greater expertise assists someone else (or participants in play stretch) to participate in sociocultural activities in a way that exceeds what they could do otherwise. Sociocultural approaches to the study of experts assisting novices focus on examining how participants mutually contribute to learning, with attention to institutional, historical aspects of how the activity functions in the communities in question.

Research on the zone of proximal development involves a more broadly dialogic analysis of the novices' contributions to the shared endeavor than does research on the original concept of scaffolding (Stone, 1993). Investigation of the zone of proximal development focuses on the process of communication that builds "a continually evolving mutual perspective on how to conceive the situation at hand (Stone, 1993, p. 180)" rather than limiting analysis of novices' roles simply to their success or their errors in the task. For example, observations of some adults' assistance to young children's narrative productions examine the collaborative process by which the adults and children together provide the structure for the children's accounts, together creating support for children's development in their community's narrative script (Eisenberg, 1985; McNamee, 1980; Reese, Haden, & Fivush, 1993).

Analysis of interactions in the zone of proximal development also involves attention to how participants and institutions determine the goals, means, and situation definition of the activities observed (Forman & McPhail, 1993). Wertsch and Hickmann (1987) suggested that "the child becomes 'aware' of the *functional significance* of the behaviors he has been performing under the guidance of an adult, in the sense of grasping how these behaviors constitute appropriate means to reach a particular goal" (p. 262).

The concept of scaffolding does not refer to the institutional and cultural context in which it occurs, whereas the concept of zone of proximal development requires attention to processes of communication and the relation of the interaction at hand to institutional, cultural, and historical processes. The shared endeavors of novices and experts are regarded as aspects of cultural activities with intellectual tools elaborated by society, which participants contribute to developing as they interact (Forman & McPhail, 1993; Moll & Whitmore, 1993; Rogoff, 1990; Wertsch et al., 1993). For example, strategic assistance of children's problem solving varies depending on the instructional goals and institutional practices of teachers and parents—especially whether the goal is error-free performance or exploration with errors, and whether the adults consider the task as school-related or home-related (Rogoff, Ellis, & Gardner, 1984; Wertsch, Minick, & Arns, 1984).

However, the Vygotskian concept of the zone of proximal development has tended to focus on face-to-face dyadic and didactic instruction, due to Vygotsky's emphasis on schooled interactions supporting the learning of academic concepts. It has missed the routine and tacit engagements and arrangements involving children and their caregivers and companions in varying cultural communities.

Cultural research has found important variations in adult ways of interacting with children—such as in face-to-face dyadic interactions or in multiparty engagements, and in treating children as conversational peers or not—that connect with children's roles in their community, ideal social relations toward which they are developing, and opportunities to observe mature members of the community (Heath, 1983; Martini & Kirkpatrick, 1981; Ochs, 1988; Rogoff et al., 1993; Schieffelin, 1991; Ward, 1971). For example, middle-class teachers' and mothers' collaborative assistance of students' narrative accounts focus on literate scripts for discourse (Reese et al., 1993), which differ from conventions of skilled discourse in some other communities (Michaels & Cazden, 1986; Mistry, 1993). Collaboration in language socialization has been observed to relate to the preparation of preschool-age children to the literate discourse of schooling for middle-class white and black children, but not for working-class white and black children (Heath, 1983).

In order to call attention to learners' roles and to the tacit as well as explicit arrangements involved in children's learning through their everyday engagement with others in their community, I introduced the concept of guided participation (see Rogoff, 1990). The concept of guided participation has sometimes been assimilated to the more familiar didactic instructional concepts prevalent in middle-class researchers' concepts of what teaching and learning involve (see Rogoff, 1994). It has been interpreted as embodying a particular form of instructional communication, however, it is not intended to portray a particular model (as I think the concept of scaffolding is). Rather than being a particular technique, guided participation is a perspective for examining people's opportunities to learn through diverse processes of participation in the valued activities of their various communities.

In later sections of this chapter, I focus on cultural and institutional aspects of collaboration, collaboration among people in different eras and locations, and asymmetries and disagreements as well as equal or harmonious agreement in collaboration, which are essential aspects of cognition as a collaborative process. These are aspects of collaboration that are not captured simply by attention to scaffolding of novices' roles by experts in sensitive face-to-face contexts, but they are essential aspects of collaboration from a sociocultural perspective.

Techniques through Which Experts Structure Novices' Problem Solving: Scaffolding, Tutoring, and Socratic Dialogue

A variety of techniques for supporting or stimulating novices' learning in tutorial situations have been studied, led by work on scaffolding that examines the contingency between experts' assistance and novices' performance. Some techniques, unlike scaffolding, appear to focus exclusively on the expert's efforts in social interaction, unrelated to the children's contributions to the ongoing social interaction. For example, providing challenging questions that encourage children to distance themselves from the immediate task has been proposed to stimulate skill in representation (Sigel, 1982; Sigel & Cocking, 1977).

In an influential series of studies with preschool children constructing complex block pyramids, Wood and his colleagues found that middle-class adults tailored their support of children's efforts according to the children's skill and that such contingency may have helped children to advance their skills (Wood, Bruner, & Ross, 1976). When mothers helped their 3- to 4-year-olds, most of them tailored their instruction to their children's needs, guiding at a level that was near the limits of the children's performance, taking into account the children's responses to the most recent instruction, and adjusting the specificity of instruction according to whether the child had been successful on that step (Wood & Middleton, 1975). Children performed best on a posttest of independent construction if their mothers had intervened in their region of sensitivity to instruction and had adjusted to their success; the *number* of interventions did not relate to the children's performance. Wood and Middleton suggested that the region of sensitivity to instruction ideally involves one extra operation or decision beyond the level at which the child is currently performing.

When a tutor followed the mothers' patterns in systematically accommodating her instruction to children's needs, the 3- to 4-year-old children's performance with the puzzle improved (Wood, Wood, & Middleton, 1978). Children who were taught contingently—with the tutor moving to less intervention after success and to more intervention after failure—were more capable of carrying out the task in the posttest than were children who were taught according to scripts that focused on either modeling the whole task, describing the task, or arbitrarily switching between these levels of intervention.

Other studies have also noted the role of contingency of scaffolding, finding that the middle-class European American mothers studied adjusted their help to the children's success or errors in the task, and that sometimes this related to children's later performance in the task. Mothers' attempts to teach 7-month-olds to reach around a barrier to grasp an object were tailored to the infants' motivation, attention, and success—they assisted when the infants looked back at the toy after having just looked away or when infants had been close to success but were becoming fretful, but not when the infants were reaching for the toy (Kaye, 1977). Mothers working with preschoolers in a counting task adjusted the level of their assistance to children's correctness, giving children more responsibility for managing the task when they made accurate counts and giving more specific directives when children counted inaccurately (Saxe, Gearhart, & Guberman, 1984). Mothers who assisted 4-year-olds in solving mazes often provided strategic assistance when children got stuck and refrained from directing or taking over when children were not having difficulty; such contingency correlated with the extent of advance planning later used by the children solving mazes without their mothers' assistance (Rogoff et al., 1995). Toddlers whose parents more frequently asked for

context information in the toddlers' narratives more often provided a listener with when-and-where information in their stand-alone narratives 18 months later (Peterson & McCabe, 1994).

Some studies of tutoring or cognitive apprenticeship (Brown, Collins, & Duguid, 1989; Hennessy, 1993) employ a more sophisticated analysis of what is effective for the tutee than simply providing contingent assistance at one step beyond the level at which the tutee is currently performing. A tutor may consider what kinds of errors are instructive (and therefore worth focusing on) and what kind need simply to be corrected to maintain focus on key ideas.

In a study of college-age computer novices learning basic programming concepts, Merrill, Reiser, Merrill, and Landes (1995) found that two U.S. university student tutors corrected almost all errors that had to do with arbitrary details, but if an error concerned a conceptual aspect of programming or problems with keeping track of the goals, the tutors pointed out the general location of the error to the student (and if relevant, reminded them of the current goal). They allowed the student to participate in recovery from the error—recognizing what was incorrect, inferring the nature of the error, setting a goal to repair it, and implementing a repair—with support from the tutor to keep the student from floundering. Merrill et al. suggested that the tutors' responses to errors involved comparing the relative benefits of the learning opportunity with its costs. When learners' involvement provided the possibility of important learning, the tutors allowed them to do as much of the error recovery as possible, but if involving the student in the repair would yield little learning, tutors simply told the student how to repair the error, thereby keeping the student on track of the larger issues and protecting the student from floundering in arbitrary details. Similar tailoring occurred in tutors' interventions in remedial algebra tutoring by U.S. high school teachers (McArthur, Stasz, & Zmuidzinas, 1990).

Socratic dialogue also involves complex prioritizing of instructional moves based on students' growing understanding. Socratic dialogue techniques include encouraging students to specify their working hypotheses and to evaluate them, suggesting systematically varying cases to develop a hypothesis and counterexamples to test students' conclusions, and trapping students in incorrect statements to reveal faulty reasoning (Collins & Stevens, 1982). When adult experimenters engaged children in challenging and exploratory discussion regarding the causes of a physical event, Spanish 5- to 8-year-olds showed greater reflectiveness regarding the causes of a physical event than did children interacting with an experimenter who merely asked for description or explanations of what had happened (Lacasa & Villuendas, 1990).

Brown and Palincsar (1989) characterized Socratic dialogues as involving discussions guided by teachers' instructional priorities:

> They tend to take up errors before omissions, easy misconceptions before fundamentally wrong thinking, prior steps in theory before later steps, important factors before less important ones, and so on. . . . There is also order in the teachers' method for selecting teaching examples and analogies—ones that exemplify important factors and cases are stressed and grouped together so that significant generalizations can be reached. Finally the teacher fields questions based on his or her model of the students' knowledge, skipping topics assumed to be known (too simple) or beyond their existing competence (too advanced), and concentrating on what students can assimilate now. Given the continual growth in knowledge, such models of student understanding must be constantly adjusted. (p. 412)

A number of approaches focus explicitly on the changing nature of experts' assistance as novices develop in their understanding of the activity at hand—the topic of the next section.

Adult Experts Adjusting Support of Novices' Development

As children gain skill in handling a process, they and their more expert partners in informal family interactions and in deliberate instruction can encourage or even demand them to take greater responsibility (Greenfield, 1984; Rogoff & Gardner, 1984). For example, middle-class U.S. mothers helping their children plan imaginary routes or sorting miniature objects differed in the nature of their assistance depending on the children's ages (Freund, 1990; Gauvain, 1992); Mayan mothers' assistance in weaving was much greater for girls who were relatively inexperienced in weaving than for those who had already completed several pieces of cloth (Greenfield, 1984); middle-class European American parents gave more explicit prompts for clarification of statements regarding the location of objects to 3-year-olds than to 4-year-old children (Plumert & Nichols-Whitehead, 1996); and one-on-one tutoring by New Zealand teachers in the Reading Recovery program involves beginning with familiar work, gradually introducing unfamiliar aspects of reading strategies, and passing increasing control of the

activity to the child (Clay & Cazden, 1990). (As mentioned later, novices can also resist a shift in responsibility.)

Researchers in prelinguistic development have noted that middle-class European American adults carry on conversations with infants in which the adult's role as conversational partner is adjusted to the baby's repertoire, with adults stepping up their expectations as the baby's skills increase:

> Mothers work to maintain a conversation despite the inadequacies of their conversational partners. At first they accept burps, yawns, and coughs as well as laughs and coos—but not arm-waving or head movements—as the baby's turn. They fill in for the babies by asking and answering their own questions, and by phrasing questions so that a minimal response can be treated as a reply. Then by seven months the babies become considerably more active partners, and the mothers no longer accept all the baby's vocalizations, only vocalic or consonantal babbles. As the mother raises the ante, the child's development proceeds. (Cazden, 1979, p. 11)

In communicating with young children, middle-class caregivers often support verbal messages with enough redundant verbal and nonverbal information to ensure understanding. As their infants become able to comprehend verbal messages, these adults decrease the redundant information and explicitness of statements (Bellinger, 1979; Bernstein, 1981; Greenfield, 1984; Messer, 1980; Ochs, 1979; Schneiderman, 1983; Snow, 1977; Zukow, Reilly, & Greenfield, 1982).

Some caregivers also seem to adjust their labeling of objects to children's growing conceptual understanding. For example, mothers observed by Adams and Bullock (1986) labeled penguins "penguins" rather than "birds" until children had established the bird prototype, at which time they began remarking that "penguins are birds." At 38 months of age, children provided most of the basic level names (e.g., bird), and their labels conformed to adult usage, but naming of atypical exemplars (e.g., penguin) showed roughly equal contributions of adult and child.

In early picture-book reading, European American middle-class mothers have been observed to adjust their demands according to their child's development, and reported that their adjustments were deliberate (DeLoache, 1984). Mothers of 12-month-olds carried the whole conversation, primarily labeling the pictures. With 15-month-olds, they named the objects and asked children simply to confirm the label ("Is that an elephant?") or they answered their own "What's this?" questions. When children began labeling objects, mothers skipped pictures with which they thought their children were unfamiliar. With older children, mothers began requesting information that was not directly visible in the picture ("What do bees make?")—if children did not reply, some mothers gave clues, apparently avoiding responding to their own question (though mothers of younger children routinely answered their own questions) but aiding children in getting the right answer.

European American middle-class mothers' assistance in a memory task also often involved support to prevent noticeable errors, such as redundant verbal and nonverbal information to ensure correct performance (Rogoff & Gardner, 1984). For example, a mother developing an idea for associating category labels with their locations increasingly involved her child in its development. The mother devised a story incorporating the first three out of six category boxes, explaining, "We'll remember those things go there . . . we'll make a little story," as she invented mnemonics involving a daily routine. The child contributed slightly to the story for the fourth category, and invented part of the story for the last two category boxes. The mother attempted to involve the child in developing the story by pausing and looking at the child at junctures and pointing to the next box without filling in that part of the story. The partners seemed to seek a level of responsibility in which the children could extend their role without making errors of a magnitude that would require notice.

The same sort of subtle evaluation of learner's readiness, with attendant support from an expert for taking the next step, was evidenced in tutoring university-level science and math students (Fox, 1988, 1993). Tutors made use of the timing of the students' participation in discourse to infer understanding of the points, providing pauses to allow students to take the responsibility for an idea by anticipating or completing the tutor's idea. Tutors made use of information regarding the number and length of each response opportunity that students passed up, taking into account whether the information being discussed was new, the effectiveness of the tutor's invitation to the student to respond, and what the student was doing during the passed-up opportunity (e.g., looking blank versus calculating). If students passed up two or three opportunities, tutors were likely to continue with an explanation, and if no evidence of understanding occurred during the explanation, the tutor was likely to repeat or reformulate it. Both partners showed a preference for having the student handle the problem before the tutor intervened, and for the tutor's intervention to

involve a collaborative redirection of the student's efforts. Tutors used collaborative completion of statements as a way to find out what the student understood, with a rising intonation to cue the student to complete the statement. If the student provided an inappropriate completion, the tutor could provide the correct answer simply by completing her own sentence without appearing to correct the student. A common form of tutorial assistance that avoided direct correction was to ask a "hint" question whose answer helps the student get unstuck if the student can determine how the answer is a resource.

Although classroom situations involving many students seldom allow this sensitivity of exchange, teachers may nonetheless attempt to discern students' level of understanding by the looks on their faces and their uptake of questions. Pettito (1983) observed a fourth-grade teacher structuring a long-division lesson into stages involving decreasing explicitness of formal steps, with adjustment according to the skills of individual students. Brown and Campione (1984) observed that in initial sessions of reading instruction, a teacher primarily modeled strategies for comprehension, but gradually the teacher's demands for student involvement increased as students began to perform parts of the task until finally the students independently produced strategic behavior that resembled that modeled by the teacher. The students improved in both reading comprehension and guidance skills as they took on the roles practiced with the teacher; they gradually served as experts to each other (Brown & Reeve, 1987). Reviewing studies successful in training reading comprehension, Pearson and Gallagher (1983) stressed the importance of careful release of responsibility for applying the skills from teacher to students.

The flexibility of support and shared understanding characteristic of tutoring has proven difficult to model with technological attempts to create teaching tools (Crook, 1994; McArthur et al., 1990). Fox argued that computer systems lack the necessary cognitive flexibility and multiple interpretations of ongoing interaction in context used by human tutors, which involve interpretation of the ongoing interaction in the context of the history of the preceding discourse (1988). Merrill et al. (1995) found that tutors instructing computer programming did not follow a path through a curriculum script or simply correct students and review curriculum material; instead, they carefully tracked student reasoning and modulated the timing and nature of their assistance depending on the type of difficulty encountered and the current problem-solving context.

Similarly, Schallert and Kleiman (1979) suggested that elementary students understand teachers better than they understand textbooks because teachers tailor their presentations to children's level of understanding and monitor students' comprehension to adjust messages. Schallert and Kleiman quoted Socrates from the dialogue *Phaedrus:* "Written words seem to talk to you as though they were intelligent, but if you ask them anything about what they say . . . they go on telling you the same thing forever."

In summary, the subtle and tacit skills of determining a learner's current understanding and designing a supportive situation for advancement have been observed in parent-infant interaction, both verbal and nonverbal, and in interaction in tutoring situations by adults working with children or other adults. In all these situations, mutual interactional cues—the timing of turns, nonverbal cues, and what each partner says or does not say—are central to the partners' achievement of a challenging and supportive structure for learning that adjusts to the partners' changes in understanding. Research on techniques of supporting novices' learning have moved far beyond examining the aid provided by expert partners independent of the contributions of learners, or simple contingencies between adult aid and learners' success in the task (with each partner's moves defined independently of the other). The next section considers the mutual role of adults and children, emphasizing the leadership of both children and adults in shared thinking. Later sections address the roles of adult expertise and of peer guidance.

The Mutual Roles of Children and Adults in Structuring Adult-Child Interaction

The research reviewed in the preceding sections indicated the importance of considering the mutual roles of expert and novice. In this section, I review work that emphasizes the mutual roles of adults and children in collaboration, and the leadership of both adults and children in initiating and managing their shared endeavors. (I am not implying that adults and children are always eager and conscientious in their relations; as I discuss in a later section, collaboration involves both discord and harmonious relations.)

Mutual involvement in routine shared activities provides children and adults with many learning opportunities. For example, Ferrier (1978) and Newson and Newson (1975) argued that language development occurs in routine participation in shared experience and efforts to communicate as caregivers and infants carry out the thousands of diaperings, feedings, baths, and other recurring activities of daily life.

Around the world, children and their caregivers engage with each other in shared activities (Rogoff et al., 1993). At the same time, the particular norms for adult and child responsibility for organizing learning vary. In some communities, children have great responsibility to learn, with extensive opportunities for observation and engagement in community activities along with the support of caregivers; in other communities, adults take major responsibility for structuring lessons and motivating children to learn (Lamphere, 1977; Ochs, 1988; Ochs & Schieffelin, 1994; Rogoff, 1990; Rogoff et al., 1993; Schieffelin, 1991). In some communities where children are usually segregated from observing and participating in community events, their learning takes place in specialized adult-run settings such as lessons created by adults for children to learn adult-promoted skills (Morelli, Rogoff, & Angelillo, submitted; Rogoff, 1990; Scribner & Cole, 1973).

In the specialized adult-child collaboration of schools, the responsibilities of children and adults vary with the structure of the school. In U.S. schools, the structure often involves an adult attempting to control the behavior and stimuli in the classroom, with students simply supposed to receive the information presented to them (Cuban, 1984). The teacher does most of the talking and students are allowed to talk only when called upon to respond to a question or directive from the teacher, often following a format where the teacher tests a student with a question, the student responds briefly, and the teacher evaluates the correctness of the response (Mehan, 1979). In other school structures of growing interest in U.S. schools, teachers arrange for students to work with each other in structured collaborative learning sessions directed by the teacher (more about this in a later section). The organization occasionally involves adult leadership of a community of learners in which children and adults engage in multi-way collaboration with each other on topics of mutual interest, with adults learning as well as facilitating the students' learning (see Figure 14.1; Brown et al., 1993; Rogoff, 1994; Tharp & Gallimore, 1988; Wells, Chang, & Maher, 1990).

Throughout these cultural and institutional variations in relative responsibility of adults and children, it is nonetheless the case that both adults and children collaborate in the arrangements of children's time, resources, and companionship. The following subsections focus in turn on how adults make arrangements for and with children and how children themselves manage their activities with adults.

Adults' Arrangements for and with Children

Adults around the world frequently select activities they consider appropriate for children of a particular developmental status or interest level (Laboratory of Comparative Human Cognition, 1983; Valsiner, 1984). Whiting (1980) cogently pointed out the importance of parents and other adults in arranging children's learning environments:

> The power of parents and other agents of socialization is in their assignment of children to specific settings. Whether it is caring for an infant sibling, working around the house in the company of adult females, working on the farm with adults and siblings, playing outside with neighborhood children, hunting with adult males, or attending school with age mates, the daily assignment of a child to one or another of these settings has important consequences on the development of habits of interpersonal behavior, consequences that may not be recognized by the socializers who make the assignments. (p. 111)

Adults' choices also include arrangements of children's material environment that may or may not be deliberately planned for children's instruction. For example, adults provide specialized objects to assist children in achieving developmental milestones, such as the varying forms of baby walkers used around the world to help infants practice walking—ranging from wheeled vehicles to bamboo railings to siblings assigned to "walk" the baby. Their arrangement of objects in the home make certain activities available or unavailable to children.

From early in infants' first year of life, caregivers and infants participate in exchanges that involve infants in the practices and systems of meaning of their families and communities. A compelling example was provided in observations of a musically inclined family in which the adults assisted a child in musical engagement in her first two years by providing constant musical interaction and instruction.

> [By 24 months, the toddler's] singing was characterized by accurate pitch and rhythm, distinct diction, basically correct lyrics, vocal technique, and musical expression. These songs primarily developed from the mother reading and singing nursery rhymes and stories at bedtime using a "scaffolding" procedure mentioned by Ninio and Bruner (1976), where the child filled in words. On morning waking and at play, the child would sing or pretend-read songs to herself. The mother corrected songs and sang along on difficult passages. At times the father accompanied the songs at the piano. Of interest here is the development of vocal technique. On one occasion the child was having difficulty with an octave interval jump. Noticing this problem while riding in the car, the grandmother told her she could sing that note if she "breathed in a great big breath with lots of air, opened her throat as if she yawned a great big yawn, and then sang the note." The child followed these instructions and the note was easily sung. (Kelley & Sutton-Smith, 1987, pp. 38–39)

Mothers from some communities regulate joint attention during the first year, often by following infants' direction of gaze, by touching or shaking an indicated object, or introducing it between themselves and the infant (Bruner, 1983; Kaye, 1982; Lempers, 1979; Schaffer, 1984; Schaffer, Hepburn, & Collis, 1983). They often provide verbal and nonverbal interpretation for babies' actions, their own actions, and events in the environment (Harding, 1982; Kruper & Uzgiris, 1985; Packer, 1983; Shotter, 1978; Shotter & Newson, 1982; Snow, 1984). For example, for babies learning to eat from a spoon, middle-class U.S. adults frequently provided cues regarding the appropriate action for the child—opening their own mouths wide at the time the baby was to do the same (Valsiner, 1984).

Studies of early language development include emphasis on adults' roles with mutuality in communication. For example, some infants in the one-word period build discussions with others through successive turns that layer comments on topics of joint attention, as in "Shoe" . . . "Is that your shoe?" . . . "On" . . . "Oh, shall I put on your shoe?" (Greenfield & Smith, 1976; Ochs, Schieffelin, & Platt, 1979; Scollon, 1976; Zukow et al., 1982). By filling in slots in social routines managed by their elders, such as saying hello or naming family members and in social games such as Peek-a-boo and All Gone, infants may learn the structure of such events as well as memorized phrases to apply in conversation (Snow, 1984). The dinnertime conversations of European American families provide routine and extensive opportunities to collaboratively build and test theories to account for everyday events, as family members narrate and contest the meaning of events and their telling (Ochs, Taylor, Rudolph, & Smith, 1992).

Language development occurs within a system in which the primary goal is achieving understanding between child and companions (Camaioni, de Castro Campos, & de-Lemos, 1984; John-Steiner & Tatter, 1983; Tomasello, in press, 1992). In introducing labels, mothers have been observed to focus on immediate communicative concerns rather than on technical accuracy such as whether whales are fish (Adams & Bullock, 1986; Mervis, 1984), a practice that may assist children in some communities in understanding category hierarchies and learning labels (Adams, 1987; Callanan, 1985, 1991). In working with young children on puzzles, mothers often began by ensuring that their children perceived the overall puzzle in the same way the mothers did (as a truck), by asking the children to identify the overall array and its pieces (Wertsch, 1979b). This establishment of a common ground enabled the mothers' later references to pieces by terms that both partners understood (e.g., "wheels," "headlights").

According to Ochs and Schieffelin (1994), in all societies, members attempt to "get their intentions across to children" (p. 76) and modify their language to do so. (However, in diverse communities, prevalence and situations in which adults modify their speech vary—in particular, the age at which children begin to be treated as conversational partners varies widely.)

Consistent with the perspective that language development occurs in the context of mutual and functional communication, research shows a relationship between the responsivity of adult-child interaction and children's language development, largely in middle-class European American samples (Adamson, Bakeman, & Smith, 1990; Hoff-Ginsberg & Shatz, 1982; Masur, 1982; Nelson, Denninger, Bonvillian, Kaplan, & Baker, 1984; Olson, Bates, & Bayles, 1984; Tomasello & Farrar, 1986). Several studies have demonstrated that labels for objects were learned better if young children's attention was already focused on the objects of reference (Dunham, Dunham, & Curwin, 1993; Tomasello & Farrar, 1986; Valdez-Menchaca, 1987).

Thus, a great deal of research has focused on adult leadership in children's learning, while underlining the mutual involvement of children in the process. Another research line supporting this view focuses on the role of children's narration with adults for their memory development (McNamee, 1980; Nelson, 1995). For example, joint discussions between mothers and young children in a museum led to greater memory of the information discussed, no matter which member of the pair initially focused attention on that detail (Tessler, cited by Fivush, 1988); details that the children pointed out but did not become a focus of joint discussion were not remembered as well by the children. In the next subsection, the focus shifts to children's leadership in learning with the mutual involvement of adults in the process.

Children's Management of Activities with Adults

In many circumstances, children initiate their involvement with adults, who may support children's learning by fitting their assistance into children's already occurring interests and efforts (Wood, 1986). Carew (1980) reported that 82% of middle-class European American toddlers' interactions in their natural activities at home were initiated by the toddlers.

Children are very active in choosing their own activities and companions, directing adults toward desirable and away from undesirable activities. Rheingold (1969) argued that even the youngest babies direct adults to fulfill their goals, socializing their caregivers, teaching them what the infants need to have them do through the power of the cry and the rewards of smiles and vocalization. "From his behavior they learn what he wants and what he will accept, what produces in him a state of well-being and good nature, and what will keep him from whining" (p. 786).

During the first year, infants have been observed to deliberately seek information and direct activities (Trevarthen & Hubley, 1978). During the first half of the first year, European American middle-class babies have been observed to maintain eye contact, smile, and cooperate with adults trying to get them to play as long as the adults meshed their agenda with the baby's interests and were sensitive to the baby's cues, and by the last half of the first year, they use adults instrumentally to reach their own goals (Bretherton, McNew, & Beeghly-Smith, 1981; Kaye, 1977; Mosier & Rogoff, 1994; Rogoff, Malkin, & Gilbride, 1984; Rogoff et al., 1992; Sugarman-Bell, 1978).

Infants in a number of communities look to the interpretation of companions to determine how to proceed in ambiguous circumstances (Feinman, 1982; Gunnar & Stone, 1984; Rogoff et al., 1993; Sorce, Emde, Campos, & Klinnert, 1985). Such social referencing is facilitated by infants' efforts during the first year to obtain information from the direction in which caregivers point and gaze (Bruner, 1983, 1987; Butterworth, 1987; Butterworth & Cochran, 1980; Churcher & Scaife, 1982; Scaife & Bruner, 1975; Tomasello, 1995). Young infants also seem to interpret intonation contours, timing, and emotional tone of adult commentary to understand the gist of messages (Fernald, 1988; Papousek, Papousek, & Bornstein, 1985).

A key debate regarding infants' responsibility for managing learning has involved the question of the origins of intersubjectivity (Rogoff, 1990; Schaffer, 1977). Some have suggested that adults act as if infants achieve communication (e.g., Kaye, 1982), arguing that adults lend meaning to infants' facial expressions, hand movements, and gaze patterns and insert social meaning into the autonomous patterning of infant behavior, assisting babies in adding meaning to their initially random or nonsocial actions. Other scholars have argued that infants engage their social partners with mutual contingency and contribute to the structure formed by both partners, even in the first months of life (Beebe, Jaffe, Feldstein, Mays, & Alson, 1985; Brazelton, 1983; Luria, 1987; Murray & Trevarthen, 1985; Newson, 1977; Trevarthen, Hubley, & Sheeran, 1975; Tronick, 1982).

From a sociocultural perspective, the question is not when intersubjectivity is acquired, but rather how it transforms as children and their social partners change (see Rogoff, 1996). The form of intersubjectivity between infants and their caregivers differs from the kind of communication possible in early linguistic communication a few years later. Consistent with this view, Vygotsky (1987) argued that from the beginning of life, children are involved in social exchanges that guide cognitive development, but with an enormous transition occurring "when speech becomes intellectual and thinking verbal" (p. 111).

Facility with verbal and gestural means of communication allows for greater clarification of purpose by both children and adults, as can be seen in an interaction between an adult and a 14½-month-old European American middle-class baby as the adult tried to determine which toy the baby (restrained in a high chair) wanted to handle.

> The adult began looking for a toy in the toy box. When he touched the tower of rings, the baby exclaimed, "Aa!" The adult asked, "Aa?," picking up the tower. The baby continued looking at the toy box, ignoring the tower, so the adult showed the baby the tower and again asked, "Aa?" The baby pointed at something in the toy box, grunting, "Aa . . . aa. . . . " The adult reached toward the toy box again, and the baby exclaimed, "Tue!" The adult exclaimed "Aa!" as he picked up the peekaboo cloth and showed it to the baby. But the baby ignored the cloth and pointed again at something in the toy box, then impatiently waved his arm. The adult exclaimed, "Aa!" and picked up the box of blocks. Offering it to the baby, the adult asked, "Aa?" But the baby pointed down to the side of the toy box. The adult discarded the blocks in the indicated spot. Then they repeated the cycle with another toy. . . . When the adult picked up the jack-in-the-box, asking "This?" the baby opened his hand toward the toy, and they began to play. (Rogoff, Malkin, & Gilbride, 1984, pp. 42–43)

Shatz (1987) argued that young children are equipped with procedures for structuring and making use of language input—eliciting talk in relevant situations, and maintaining discourse and using overheard linguistic information even with only partial understanding. Of course, this process could not occur without social interaction, and

may be assisted by other people's efforts to simplify language and support children's growing understanding (Waxman & Gelman, 1986).

Young children often attend to adults' activities and how adults use objects. Rheingold (1982) found that toddlers spontaneously and energetically helped their parents or a stranger in the majority of the household chores that the adults performed in a laboratory or home setting (although many of these middle-class parents reported that they commonly circumvented their child's efforts to participate at home by trying to do chores while the child was napping). Several studies indicate that infant attentiveness, skill, and learning new uses for objects was enhanced by adult object demonstration, focusing of attention, and collaborative engagement with objects, with markedly similar actions performed on the objects by the children (Bornstein, 1988; Eckerman, Whatley, & McGhee, 1979; Hay, Murray, Cecire, & Nash, 1985; Henderson, 1984; Hodapp, Goldfield, & Boyatzis, 1984; Parrinello & Ruff, 1988; Rogoff, Malkin, & Gilbride, 1984).

Children are also active in recruiting adults' help as early as the second half of the second year (Heckhausen, 1984). In explicit teaching situations, older children may direct adults' assistance through seeking help (Nelson-Le Gall, 1985, 1992). At times, they lead in structuring a learning situation (Rogoff, 1990; Toma, 1992). In a classification task carried out by middle-class European American 9-year-olds and their mothers (Ellis & Rogoff, 1986; Rogoff & Gardner, 1984), a few children took over management of instruction, despite their mothers' assigned responsibility to prepare them for an upcoming test and the fact that only the mothers had access to a cue sheet indicating the correct placement of items. One 9-year-old took control when his mother indicated that she was totally confused and the items were in disarray. The child told her, politely but insistently, to look at the cue sheet, and led her through the process of checking the correct placement of items, picking up one item at a time and asking, "Is this one right? . . . Look at the sheet." The child elicited the information about correct placement from his mother to independently infer the category organization (Rogoff & Gardner, 1984).

Children, as well as adults, manage their shared endeavors in ways that involve them in shared thinking. Even very young children are expert beyond any of their companions in some aspects of their lives. Children and adults can be simultaneously regarded as providing leadership in some areas while continuing to learn (though often about different things). The next section examines the role of expertise as an aspect of adult structuring of children's learning; subsequent sections focus on the roles of children in collaboration with each other.

The Role of Adult Expertise

Observations in infancy suggest that interactions with mothers are more sensitive and contingent than are interactions with other children.[4] Working-class Mexican American toddlers were less likely to respond to and expand on each others' comments than their mothers' comments, and their mothers in turn were more responsive partners than were peers (Martinez, 1987). Similarly, middle-class European American mothers were more likely to support infants' conversational skills through responding contingently and constructing exchanges around the infants' actions than were preschool siblings, who were less contingent and less likely to involve the infants' interests (Vandell & Wilson, 1987).

The importance of the roles of expertise and status of partners have been addressed in several studies by comparing the processes of interaction and the later performance of children who work on a task with adults versus with peers. The adults have been used to represent skilled partners and the peers as less skilled partners, in tasks such as remembering and planning in laboratory situations. In these situations, which are also designed and managed by adults (the researchers), adult partners seem to provide children with advantages in learning, compared with peer partners. Thus, adults seem to have a special role in guiding children's learning in the constrained cognitive tasks of the laboratory.

---

[4] Less sensitive partners, however, offer other opportunities for learning. For example, with fathers who are less involved with their young children, the limited shared understanding may stimulate children to stretch to explain themselves and to understand their partner (Barton & Tomasello, 1994; Mannle & Tomasello, 1989). Familiar partners may give children the experience of complex sharing of ideas with people who do not require much background in order to proceed with a new thought, and seem to be more likely to engage in productive discussions of differences of perspective that foster learning (Azmitia, 1996; Azmitia & Hesser, 1993; Azmitia & Montgomery, 1993). However, less familiar or less sensitive partners may provide the challenge to develop new ways of expressing notions that could otherwise be taken for granted in interactions with a very familiar and skilled partner.

In learning a classification system to organize sets of common objects, 6-year-old European American middle-class children performed better after having the assistance of their mothers than of 8-year-old acquaintances (Ellis & Rogoff, 1982, 1986). The mothers almost always explained the tasks before beginning to place items, referred to the need to categorize, and provided category rationales for the groups of items; less than half of the child teachers did so. Most of the mothers prepared their learners for the memory test through rehearsal and mnemonics for the classification system, whereas very few of the child teachers provided explicit preparation for the test beyond admonishing their partners to study. The children whose mothers provided guidance and who participated in working out the organization of items and in preparing for the test remembered the items and the conceptual organization better in a posttest (Rogoff & Gauvain, 1986).

The child teachers often appeared not to consider their partners' need to learn in this task; they appeared to focus on the immediate task of sorting items (Ellis & Rogoff, 1986). The peer dyads did not evidence the shared decision making observed with the mother-child dyads—more than half of them did not include the learners in the task, placing the items themselves without explanation and often without even looking to see if the learners were watching; others required the learners to perform the task with minimal guidance, having them guess the location of items without explanation. (On occasion, it appeared that this was the child teachers' idea of the role of a teacher, as they used school-teacher intonations to praise the learners' correct guesses.) Similar contrasts between the teaching interactions of adults and children teaching younger children have been found by McLane (1987), Foot, Shute, Morgan, and Barron (1990), and Koester and Bueche (1980). The child teachers seemed to focus on accomplishing the concrete task rather than ensuring that their partners understood the rationale, and they usually did too much (taking over the performance of the task) or too little (insisting that their young partners "figure it out" without giving them guidance in doing so).

In two studies of 10-year-old children's planning of imaginary errands, similar contrasts were observed between children's collaboration with adults and with peers, even when peers were trained in the task. Compared with adult-child dyads, peer dyads planned less efficient routes, with destinations scattered around and decisions involving one item at a time rather than coordinating several destinations into one efficient route (Radziszewska & Rogoff,

1988, 1991). In addition, peers were less likely to explain their strategies or talk-aloud their decisions than were adults, and they were less likely to share in joint decision making in skilled planning. During collaboration with adults, children usually participated in managing the sophisticated strategies organized by the adults.

There has been little research examining the roles of peers in activities in which children may be equally or more expert than adults. However, there are a few indications that such situations warrant study. For example, U.S. suburban third and sixth graders were more accurate than adults (most of whom were experienced teachers) in interpreting filmed children's understanding and nonunderstanding of a lesson on the basis of slight nonverbal cues (Allen & Feldman, 1976). In collaborative learning of computer games in which all participants were novices (but 9-year-olds were more comfortable than adults), peer and adult-child dyads did not differ substantially in collaborative processes (Tudge, Fordham, Lawrence, & Rogoff, 1995).

Even in the tasks in which interaction with adults appeared to foster children's learning more than interaction with peers, peer involvement may nonetheless have also been helpful to the children. (The studies did not provide comparisons of children working without a partner at all.) In other activities, peers play many roles that adults do not, and adult and peer partners appear to complement each others' roles in shared endeavors—which often involve both adult and peer partners, not one to the exclusion of the other. The next section considers the roles of peers assisting each other in learning; it and subsequent sections also consider the integrated involvement of adult and child collaborators in varying roles.

PEERS ASSISTING EACH OTHER IN LEARNING

Children's engagement with their peers and with adults can be regarded as involving complementary, multifaceted roles in shared sociocultural activity, rather than considering peers and adults as contrasting influences. Research on how peers may assist each other in learning focuses on how children contribute to each other's learning in peer play and in child caregiving activities, the role of peers' similar status in collaborative argumentation, and how peers facilitate each other's learning in classrooms.

I use the term *peer* broadly to refer to companions of roughly equal status, to include sibling and neighbor groups of generally similar age and status, not just the unrelated same-age classmates that have been a primary focus of peer research. The roles of unrelated and related similar-age children vary extensively around the world, requiring greater research than is presently available to systematically distinguish the contributions of siblings and unrelated peers to children's cognitive development.

Children Learning with Each Other in Peer Play and Child Caregiving

In some communities, play is considered as children's domain (Rogoff et al., 1993), but even in middle-class communities where adults often act as playmates with young children, adults are likely to take differing roles than child companions in play. Dunn and Dale (1984) found that the play of 2-year-olds with their older siblings commonly involved close meshing of the partners' actions in complementary pretend roles, whereas mothers generally observed and supported the play without entering it by performing pretend roles or actions.

Vygotsky suggested that play "creates its own zone of proximal development of the child. In play a child is always above his average age, above his daily behavior; in play it is as though he were a head taller than himself." (1967, p. 552; see also Göncü, 1987; Nicolopoulou, 1993). Vygotsky regarded play as the "leading activity" (the central goal) of development during early childhood. In play, children experiment with the meanings and rules of serious life, but place these meanings and rules in the center of attention—for example, two sisters focus on the rules of sisterhood as they "play sisters." In such play, children free themselves from the situational constraints of everyday time and space and the ordinary meaning of objects or actions, to develop greater control of actions and rules and understanding.

Role play and dramatic play among peers may be arenas for children to work out the "scripts" of everyday life—adult skills and roles, values and beliefs (see Figure 14.3; Hartup, 1977; Hollos, 1980). In addition, the freedom to play with the rules of activities and to creatively recast goals from moment to moment may be unique and valuable in peer interaction (John-Steiner, 1985; Sylva, Bruner, & Genova, 1976). In addition to learning about the given structure of social life, middle-class European American children in their play adapt and restructure the social order (Packer, 1994). Forbes, Katz, and Paul (1986) stated that "through active manipulation of representations in the

Figure 14.3 These Mayan children engage in pretend play, preparing and serving a meal of leaf tortillas and dirt meat. The older children, at other times, help their mothers with actual meal production (note the skilled slapping of 'tortillas' by the girl on the right). Child caregiving that is occuring simultaneously in the play provides younger children with the opportunity to observe and to participate in the enactment (with modifications) of a mature activity of their community. (© Barbara Rogoff)

course of original fantasy creation, the child comes to know the nature of the socially accepted world in a much fuller way than might be possible if play were to consist of simply recreations or recapitulations of observed social phenomena" (p. 262).

Play appears to be important in the development of novel, adaptive behavior as well as in the socialization and practice of established skills (Lancy, 1980; Vandenberg, 1980). For example, a study with third-graders of a variety of ethnic backgrounds noted that children benefitted most from collaborative writing who balanced their planning and revising activities with playful approaches to language, academic concepts, reality, and each other (Daiute & Dalton, 1993).

Children's collaborative play also often requires efforts to take the perspectives of others and to clarify communication as play partners negotiate scripts and rules of play (Bretherton, 1984; Corsaro & Rizzo, 1988; Göncü, 1987). Children may force each other to work to be understood and to understand (Barton & Tomasello, 1994; Cicirelli, 1976; French, 1987; Garvey, 1986; Rogoff, 1990). Coordination between young children in pretend play involves co-elaboration and clarification of meaning in ways that build beyond each person's contribution (Verba, 1993). An example of the coordination of ideas in very young children's play was given by Verba (1994), who observed two French

toddlers aged 1 year 4 months and 1 year 2 months as they developed a common play idea:

> As the children sat next to each other on the floor, Child A tapped two beads against each other and repeated the action several times. Child B manipulated a rubber band while glancing at A's action. A took two cubes and tapped several times. B looked at A and stopped manipulating the rubber band, then took a bead, explored, and glanced at A. A looked at B, and took an identical bead and gave it to B. B took the bead and tapped the two beads twice.

Peers' efforts to achieve shared understanding and action involve cognitive stretches that contribute to their development, as Gearhart (1979) observed with 3-year-olds who were planning episodes of playing store and learned that their partner had a separate plan for playing and that coordination of plans is necessary for play to run smoothly. The children developed more explicit and sophisticated plans over the course of repeated play episodes, addressing directly the shortcomings in their plan and its communication that had impeded joint action in earlier episodes. Similarly, Baker-Sennett, Matusov, and Rogoff (1992) noted that a group of middle-class European American children's planning of a classroom play required flexibility in coordinating their often discrepant ideas, which resulted in ideas that were more than the sum of the individual contributions.

In many communities children play a more central role with each other than in the European American middle class, serving from the age of 4 or 5 as caregivers of younger siblings and working and playing in mixed age groups responsible for their own functioning (see Figure 14.3; Rogoff, Sellers, Pirrotta, Fox, & White, 1975; Watson-Gegeo & Gegeo, 1989; Weisner & Gallimore, 1977; Whiting & Edwards, 1988; Whiting & Whiting, 1975). Under such circumstances, children have opportunities to develop skills in guiding other children which are less available to children with little responsibility for other children and more limited contact with children of ages different from their own. For example, Heath (1983) noted that the play-songs invented by working-class Black girls are tailored to language teaching for young children, with nonsense wordplay, number counting, and naming body parts—topics handled in middle-class adult-child interaction through nursery rhymes and routines.

In West Africa, peer and sibling caregiving usually involves multi-age teams of children ranging from about 20 months to 6 or 7 years of age, under the guidance and mentorship of one or two older siblings aged 8 to 10 years

(Nsamenang, 1992). In these teams, children learn collective roles, responsibility, and peer mentoring, and how to handle conflicts and compromises. Previously, such teams were used as a training ground for leadership roles and (when members became old) as part of the government and law enforcement system.

Once Marquesan (Polynesian) babies can walk, they enter the care of 3- to 4-year-old siblings (Martini & Kirkpatrick, 1992). According to mothers, toddlers want to be with and be like their older siblings, so they learn to run, feed and dress themselves, and help with household chores by imitating preschool children. The preschoolers (who enjoy the company of the toddlers and the mature status among peers that comes from being a caregiver) teach the toddlers that they can stay with the children's group only if they keep themselves safe and stay out of the way of the group activity. The toddlers learn to be self-reliant and nondisruptive, and play on the edge of the group and watch the group intently until they can keep up with the play. Martini (1994) observed 13 members of a stable play group of 2- to 5-year-olds daily for 4 months as they played several hours a day without supervision while older siblings attended school. The children organized activities, settled disputes, avoided dangers such as strong surf and dangerous objects that were often left around, and dealt with injuries without adult intervention. Tasks are also often assigned to the children as a unit, leaving them to decide who does what, with all held responsible for task completion.

Thus peers may fill important roles seldom taken by adults. Peer interaction may foster exploration without immediate goals, which in the long run may lead to insightful solutions to unforeseen problems. Peers may also provide each other with engagement in building their own social structure and opportunities to learn to take others' perspectives. For children with extensive opportunities to fill responsible roles with other children, there seem to be rich opportunities to learn how to take the perspective of others and to collaborate in groups, skills that have become of widespread interest in schooling and in research on peers' collaborative argumentation.

Peers' Similar Status in Collaborative Argumentation

Peer interaction has been suggested as offering children the opportunity to explore ideas in a more equal relationship than is possible with adults. Piaget (1926, 1977) argued that similarity of status is essential for social interaction that supports a change of perspective. He also stated that interaction with an adult is essentially unequal due to the adult's power, which disrupts the condition of reciprocity for achieving equilibrium in thinking through discussion and cooperation. According to Piaget (1977/1928), the effect of lessons from adults is for young children to abandon their own ideas for those presented, since their ideas are poorly formulated and exist only as an "orientation of the spirit" that cannot compete with the views of adults, so children agree without examining the idea.

In this section, I examine the importance of shared thinking in problem solving among peers, as well as suggestions that differences in expertise or perspective are important for learning among peers. I conclude the section with a discussion of whether adults are necessarily in positions of authority and peers are necessarily in positions of equal status, and argue that the roles of peers and adults (or equal and different status and expertise) can be seen as complementary resources in cognitive development through collaboration.

The importance of intersubjective reasoning and problem solving has been increasingly noted by scholars studying peer interaction (Berkowitz & Gibbs, 1985; Forman & Cazden, 1985; Mercer, 1995; Mugny, Perret-Clermont & Doise, 1981; Rubtsov & Guzman, 1984–1985). Miller (1987) claimed that a collective process in children's argumentation with adults and peers functions as a basic developmental mechanism where the coordination of arguments leads participants toward a set of collectively valid statements. He gave the example of one 5-year-old centering on weight as the principle for explaining what will balance on a scale, and another focusing on distance from the fulcrum. When contradictions are detected, the participants seek a change in their understanding to resolve the contradiction:

> Even if these children do not yet have any idea of what these changes will eventually look like, i.e., even if the structurally higher level knowledge remains undefined (transcendent) relative to their already attained knowledge, they nevertheless know where it has to be found. It must be a structural solution of the contradiction between their mutually exclusive points of view—a contradiction they have created themselves and which now begins to determine their ascension to a higher level of knowledge. (p. 237)

Several studies report that decision making that occurs jointly with a balanced exploration of differences of perspective among peers is most likely to contribute to children's progress in understanding (Glachan & Light, 1982; Kobayashi, 1994; Kruger, 1993; Light, Foot, Colbourn, &

McClelland, 1987). Peers who engaged with each other's ideas were more likely to gain in skill and understanding of a logical game and math and science tasks than peers who did not discuss the ideas or whose discussions focused on their roles or behavior (Damon & Phelps, 1987; Light & Glachan, 1985). Middle-class European American preschool children who worked together on an imaginary errand planning task performed better in subsequent solo planning than children who worked alone only if they shared in decision making (Gauvain & Rogoff, 1989). British 11-year-olds who worked in pairs on a computer errand planning game with discussion of planning, co-construction of knowledge, and negotiation performed better on the task by themselves later than did children who less often engaged in such discussion (Light, Littleton, Messer, & Joiner, 1994).

Collective accomplishment of 11- to 13-year-olds judging whether pictures were by the same artist was usually substantially higher than the best individual performance of either partner, with solutions not originally proposed by either of the partners (Bos, 1937).

> Both came to a new way of thinking, arrived at fresh viewpoints, so that in this case it would be impossible to establish the individual share of each partner. The same things happen in cases where, in lively exchange of thoughts, adults discuss a problem. Through the interpretation of the other, which is rejected by us, we arrive at ideas, which in their turn are taken over, eventually are further elaborated, and thereby lead to a result. Whom shall we give credit for the solution? It was fortunate, that our young candidates did not bother about the authorship and after intensive collaboration, simply declared, that they had worked out the problems *together*. (pp. 363–364)

The children who managed such cooperative activity (half of the dyads) achieved 76% of the maximum score possible. The others who took one another's opinions into account only in rejecting them, without discussion or justification, achieved 56% of the maximum, and those who worked individually in alternating participation in the execution of the task, *being* together but not *working* together, reached only 42%.

Piaget's idea that children may be freer to examine the logic of arguments when interacting with peers than with adults is supported by several studies of moral reasoning. Middle-class children of 7 and 11 years expressed logical arguments more with their peers than with their mothers (Kruger & Tomasello, 1986). Although mothers requested idea clarification more than did peers, children produced more self-generated clarifications of logic and were more likely to make comments operating on their partner's logic when interacting with peers. Kruger (1992) found that 8-year-olds who had discussed moral dilemmas with peers progressed more in their moral reasoning than did children who had discussed the dilemmas with their mothers. The more interactive logical discussion of partners' ideas that characterized peer discussions were positively correlated with progress in moral reasoning.

However, several studies investigating Piagetian physical and mathematical concepts have not found the same pattern. With conservation tasks, lower-to-middle-class European American children made more progress working with adults than with nonconserving peers (and working with conserving peers yielded intermediate results); interactions with adults involved a slightly greater extent of partners discussing each others' ideas (Radziszewska, 1993). Heber (1981) found improvement in seriation skills in a condition in which an adult engaged each child in dialogue about the child's seriation decisions, especially when the dialogue encouraged the child to specify the rationale for decisions (to an "ignorant" puppet) or guided the child in discussing relations of "more" and "less." In contrast, there was no improvement for children who received a didactic explanation of the rationale, worked with peers of equal skill, or worked independently, compared with children who received no opportunity to work on the problem. It appears that both expertise and shared thinking may be important for learning from social interaction.

In Piagetian theory, differences in children's views of appropriate ways to solve a problem is presumed to induce "cognitive conflict" among the partners which impels them to seek equilibrium at a higher level (Bearison, 1991; Sigel & Cocking, 1977). Cognitive conflict in conservation tasks is often operationalized by pairing children with a partner with greater or different expertise; progress in conservation seems often to relate to the partner's expertise (Azmitia & Perlmutter, 1989; Ellis, Klahr, & Siegler, 1993; Lacasa & Villuendas, 1990). Several authors suggest that children are most likely to advance in their thinking when faced with a perspective that fits reality better than their own, especially if it involves problem solving at a level *just* beyond that of the child (see Azmitia, 1988; Kuhn, 1972; Mugny & Doise, 1978; Tudge, 1992; Tudge & Rogoff, 1989).

In a meta-analysis involving studies with children of varying racial and economic status, Johnson and Johnson (1987) reported that peer cooperation tended to promote transitions to higher levels of reasoning in about half of the studies, to show no difference in half, and not to favor individual arrangements in any studies. Nonconservers often learned how to conserve when engaged cooperatively with conservers, and when group members expressed differences of opinion, thinking was enhanced—findings consistent with the idea that cognitive conflict involves differences of expertise as well as with the idea that shared engagement with ideas matters.

There are substantial inconsistencies in the results of research pairing children with partners similar or different in conservation. Although working with a partner who is slightly more skilled may be most effective, working with a partner equal in skill, or even one less advanced, has sometimes yielded progress (Forman & Kraker, 1985; Glachan & Light, 1982; Howe, Tolmie, & Rodgers, 1990; Light & Glachan, 1985; Light et al., 1994; Rubtsov, 1981; Rubtsov & Guzman, 1984–85). Occasionally, however, there is no such progress, as when partners are equal in understanding of seriation problems (Heber, 1981), or there may even be "regression," as when children interact with less advanced partners on balance beam problems (Tudge, 1992) or simply trade strategies in classifying objects (Fonzi & Smorti, 1994). In scientific reasoning on a problem that often evokes misconceptions among adults, transactive discussions among middle-class Israeli youth led some to progress in their thinking, but others to regress in a way that could be considered compatible with adult views in their community; similar transactions on a Piagetian task not subject to misconceptions among adults yielded progress in the participants' understanding (Levin & Druyan, 1993). Thus, the role of cognitive conflict and transactive discussion may well fit together with the role of expertise, with understanding moving toward group or community consensus rather than necessarily toward an outside definition of correctness.

The literature on peer argumentation is not yet coherent enough to allow conclusions about what aspects of peer engagement are most important. However, the occurrence of actual engagement of partners with each other's thinking seems to be crucial, and this may at least sometimes be facilitated by differences of perspective or expertise.

Some of the differences that have been observed in peer learning under varying circumstances may be explained by Damon's (1984) conjecture that interaction with more expert partners (e.g., in peer tutoring) may be especially helpful when children are learning information or skills that do not require conceptual change, whereas the free exchange of ideas and feedback among equals may be ideal for wrestling with difficult new principles to stretch the boundaries of understanding. Damon's suggestion is especially useful in its focus on differences and similarities of status among children. To finish this section, I suggest that adults are not necessarily in positions of authority and peers not necessarily in positions of equality, and I argue for the importance of considering the patterns of interaction that involve peers and adults as joint contributors to children's learning.

Questioning the Notions That Adult = Authority and Peer = Equal Status

In many accounts, it is assumed that adults are more likely to play an authority role with children, and peers are more likely to play an equal status role that allows true collaboration. Although Piaget argued that children's interaction with adults does not promote their cognitive development, his focus was on the use of adult authority. He allowed for the possibility that adults may be able to interact with children in a cooperative fashion that permits the sort of reciprocity required for children to advance to a new level of equilibrium: "It is despite adult authority, and not because of it, that the child learns. And also it is to the extent that the intelligent teacher has known to efface him or herself, to become an equal and not a superior, to discuss and to examine, rather than to agree and constrain morally, that the traditional school has been able to render service" (Piaget, 1977/1928, p. 231).

Adult-child interaction does not necessarily involve invoking authority (Radziszewska, 1993). Changes in the use of adult authority have occurred across the decades of the twentieth century in many nations, including Piaget's Switzerland. Toma (1992) provided an example of historically changing adult-child roles in examining a case in which a Japanese boy challenged his father's perspective on a problem and advised his father on how he could have handled the problem better; such discourse would have been improbable in pre-World War II Japan, but was not surprising in Japan of the early 1990s. Further study of cultural changes and differences in conceptions of adult-child relations (in families and schools) would enhance understanding of the roles of expertise and status as adults direct or assist children in learning.

There are also important issues of what being peers involves—a question that is often focused on age similarity, but even this definition is problematic. One study noted advantages from working with an agemate but not from working with a slightly older child, indicating that being close in age does not necessarily lead to balanced involvement in problem solving. In planning routes, middle-class

U.S. 5-year-olds were more involved in decision-making and strategy formulation with 5-year-old expert partners than with 7-year-old expert partners; over time, their involvement increased with the same-age partners, but decreased with the slightly older partners (Duran & Gauvain, 1993). Later solo performance was better for the children who had worked with a same-age expert than for children who had had no partner but not for those who had worked with slightly older experts.

Even with people who are of the same age, equality of status may be rare, due to other differences such as their varying social status in the group, differing expertise, or differing interest in controlling the activity (Verba & Winnykamen, 1992). Observations of U.S. elementary school students' collaboration at computers noted wide spontaneous variations in how the pairs worked—in some, one member tutored a less-skilled partner; in others the partners explicitly divided jobs such as the "thinkist" and the "typist" (Hawkins, 1987, p. 11); others worked simultaneously together at a detailed level of action; a few employed more extended joint work with partners proposing and critiquing each other's ideas. With college student peers, Gillam, Callaway, and Wikoff (1994) noted struggles with issues of authority among peers when one was designated as a writing tutor—with tutors pondering whether their relationship was one of equals or of authority based on expertise and on institutional role-designation. The quandary was especially complicated when the writing tutor was younger than the student to receive their assistance.

Research on peer relations thus indicates the importance of considering not only the age of the partners but their roles in the social group, their personal relationships, and their relative expertise. The previous section also pointed to cultural differences in children's opportunities to learn how to collaborate with siblings and other peers through their involvement with each other in responsible family and play roles. A later section focuses on how children learn how to collaborate and the roles of adults and of the structure of institutions (such as schooling) in which children habitually interact, in children's patterns of collaboration with each other.

Adults and Peers: Joint Contributors to Children's Learning in the Activities of Their Community

There are other possibilities of relationship in addition to adults-as-authority figures and children-as-equal-partners. A variety of educational prescriptions urge teachers to depart from their traditional authority roles to engage more in dialogue with students (Sutter & Grensjo, 1988; Tharp & Gallimore, 1988). In classrooms in which teachers exert control through commands and questions, children respond tersely, whereas when teachers substitute noncontrolling talk (such as commentary on their own ideas and demonstration of their own uncertainty) and increase the amount of time allowed for children to respond, children are more active and equal participants (Subbotskii, 1987; Wood, 1986).

The literature on adult-child relations (in both parenting and classroom teaching) often casts two models in opposition, one with adults as authorities transmitting information to children and controlling children's behavior ("adult-run") and the other with children "free" from adult authority ("children-run"; Rogoff, 1994). These are often regarded as opposite extremes of a pendulum swing in discussions among researchers focusing on freedom and control in classrooms and families as well as on issues of restructuring schools and evaluating child-centered versus didactic approaches (see Eccles et al., 1991; Giaconia & Hedges, 1982; Greene, 1986; Stipek, in press). However, both adult-run and children-run models are alike in relegating control and activity to one side of adult versus child relations. The controversy over whether learning is best structured with adults (or experts) in charge or with the learner or equal peers in charge simply switches which side of an assumed dichotomy is active and in control.

A distinct model is that adults and children are not necessarily on different sides; they can collaborate with varying roles and responsibilities of different members of the group (Dewey, 1938; Engeström, 1993; Kohn, 1993; Rogoff, 1994). This view is reflected in discussions of community of learners models of classroom and family relations, based on theoretical notions of learning as a process of transformation of participation in which people engage with each other in shared activities, in varying leadership and responsibility roles (Bartlett, Goodman Turkanis, & Rogoff, in press; Brown & Campione, 1990; Newman, Griffin, & Cole, 1989; Rogoff, 1994; Tharp & Gallimore, 1988; Wells, Chang, & Maher, 1990). It is also reflected in the Japanese Hypothesis-Experiment-Instruction method of science education, which is based on the idea that conceptual change occurs through discussion of ideas among peers, with "scaffolding" of the peers' discussion by a teacher who defines the target issue, reviews possible alternatives, encourages participants to use informal knowledge, and proposes ways to get further information (Kobayashi, 1994).

In a community of learners model, adults and children make varying contributions to each others' learning, with all active and involved (see Figure 14.4). This often fits with the model of apprenticeship learning in trades, where learning involves a system of relations of an apprentice and other apprentices as well as a master, rather than the tutorial expert-novice dyadic relation to which the apprenticeship metaphor seems often to be assimilated. It is also consistent with the kind of social interaction that has been observed to foster discoveries in microbiology laboratories, in which differences of perspective and expertise among professors, postdoctoral fellows, and graduate students provide productive grounds for reconceptualizing problems and promoting conceptual change by all members of the research team (Dunbar, 1995).

The community of learners model of instruction fits well with the theoretical perspective that learning is a process of transformation of participation in community activities, where individual learning is seen as a function of individuals' active, ongoing involvement in sociocultural activities rather than the passive result of transmission from others or the active but solo (or at most peer-based) result of acquisition of outside information (Rogoff, 1994; Rogoff, Matusov, & White, 1996). In both the community of learners instructional model and the transformation of participation theory, the dichotomy that is often drawn between adult and peer contributions to children's learning is superseded. Both the instructional model and the theory

Figure 14.4 This activity illustrates the involvement of children in both symmetrical and asymmetrical collaboration, as they engage with each other and with an adult in a multiplication lesson laying out tiles to represent the numerical concept. (© Barbara Rogoff)

emphasize that children's participation in sociocultural activities is complexly and multidimensionally structured, with important contributions from individuals, their social partners of varying status and expertise, and the structure of the cultural/historical activities in which they participate and which they contribute to shaping further.

Peers Facilitating Each Other's Learning in the Classroom

Although much of U.S. schooling occurs according to a model that places the responsibility for teaching exclusively on adult teachers, increasing efforts make use of peers as tutors or as collaborators in each others' learning in the classroom (see Figures 14.1 and 14.4). Both peer tutoring and peer collaboration appear to be effective learning formats for the students who are regarded as needing the greatest help as well as for those who serve as tutors or are very well prepared academically (Allen, 1976; Allen & Feldman, 1973; Bruffee, 1993; Daiute & Dalton, 1993; Palincsar, Brown, & Martin, 1987; Phelps & Damon, 1989).

This section first examines the role of cooperative learning in the development of children's academic skills, a topic that has received a great deal of investigation. Then it turns to issues of how children learn to collaborate, as collaboration itself involves complex problem solving. Finally, this section addresses the role of adult collaboration in children's cooperative learning, a topic that has often been overlooked when the role of peers is examined. This section also emphasizes the role of the institution of schooling in children's opportunities to collaborate and the form of their collaboration.

The Value of Cooperative Learning for the Development of Academic Skills

Numerous studies support the idea that cooperative learning enhances individual academic achievement (Brandt, 1991; Slavin, 1990). For example, cooperative organization of classrooms was associated with greater learning in Israeli and German classrooms, compared with traditional classroom instruction where an adult addresses the class as a whole and children do not work together (Huber & Eppler, 1990; Lazarowitz & Karsenty, 1990; Sharan & Shaulov, 1990). U.S. college students and third graders of a variety of ethnic backgrounds wrote and studied essays and stories more effectively when working in pairs than alone, and this cooperative advantage carried over to individual writing and comprehension tasks (Daiute & Dalton, 1993; O'Donnell & Dansereau, 1992; O'Donnell et al., 1985).

A meta-analysis carried out by Johnson and Johnson (1987) on 378 studies compared the achievement of people working individually versus in cooperative groups or in competitive arrangements. More than half of the studies favored cooperation; less than 10% favored individualistic efforts. These results were similar regardless of the age of participants (ranging from elementary school through college), the duration of the study (from 1 to more than 30 sessions), whether the studies employed research laboratories or field settings, or involved published or unpublished studies.

Participating in cooperative groups often facilitates (and does not hurt) the achievement of individuals who are already proficient, and clearly benefits the achievement of individuals who are achieving at medium or low levels before the study (Johnson & Johnson, 1989). Other studies comparing cooperative and individual arrangements for "high ability" elementary age European American middle-class students have found that cooperative arrangements promoted greater learning and high-level reasoning (Hooper et al., 1993; Johnson, Johnson, & Taylor, 1993).

Almost all the studies analyzed by Johnson and Johnson (1989) were conducted in North America; no differences were found according to the socioeconomic class or ethnic background of participants. Sharan (1990) reviewed studies employing different ethnic and socioeconomic groups and similarly found cooperative learning arrangements to be beneficial to all groups. Some authors suggest that cooperative learning structures are especially appropriate for Latino, African American, Native American, and Native Hawaiian students, and for other groups whose community values are more in line with cooperative than individualistic arrangements (Duran, 1994; Haynes & Gebreyseus, 1992; Little Soldier, 1989; Manning & Lucking, 1993; Tharp & Gallimore, 1988).

In addition to the goals of academic and cognitive development, cooperative learning in the classroom often has other goals that are extremely important, but beyond the scope of this chapter: promoting children's learning how to get along with others, intergroup relations among varying ethnic groups or children with differing skills, and respect and responsibility in social relations.

A limitation of much of this research is how it usually evaluates learning, which (with important exceptions) seems to involve no change from traditional school practices treating knowledge as an individual possession (Packer, 1993). Collaboration between peers is generally handled as a "treatment" intended to produce an "outcome" that is conceived as individual "in-the-head" learning. Some inspiring but rare exceptions consider alternatives to the traditional definition of learning, sometimes approaching learning as a change in peoples' ways of participating in sociocultural activities (including literate and numerate activities that are basic to schooling).

There have been some efforts to delineate what aspects of cooperative learning are involved in successful arrangements for children to learn from each other in groups in the classroom. In the next subsections, I examine motivating structures of group activities, the importance of intersubjectivity, and the group's engagement with "big" ideas. Then later sections address the related questions of how children learn how to collaborate and assist each other in learning and the roles of adults and institutions in children's collaboration.

Motivational Processes in Cooperative Learning. Motivation to engage in learning activities is one of the key aspects proposed to account for the enhancement of achievement through cooperative classroom arrangements (Knight & Bohlmeyer, 1990). Johnson and Johnson's (1989) meta-analysis supports the idea that motivation to learn is enhanced by cooperative learning arrangements— in 51% of the studies, cooperation promoted greater task involvement than did individualistic efforts; only 4% of the studies favored individualistic efforts. Sharan and Shaulov (1990) found that cooperative learning increased fifth- and sixth-grade Israeli students' likelihood of choosing to forego the chance to go out to play in favor of continuing their schoolwork; such motivation was a very strong predictor of the children's achievement. Sharan and Shaulov suggested that the explanation for their finding was positive peer social relations and enhanced involvement of students in decision making regarding their own work in the cooperative learning situation. Similarly, European American middle-class high school students made greater gains and expressed greater intrinsic motivation to learn the concepts of algebra in a peer cooperative than in an individualistic arrangement (Nichols & Miller, 1994).

The motivating and supporting context that students can provide each other also includes reciprocal assistance and encouragement to take intellectual risks (Knight & Bohlmeyer, 1990). An example is provided in a study that compared middle-class multi-ethnic U.S. children aged 8 to 11 working either alone or in pairs on an unsolvable spatial logic problem (Gauvain, 1994). The pairs generated more attempts to solve the problem, less often erroneously believed that they had solved it, and more frequently attributed their lack of success to the unsolvability of the problem than to the problem being too hard for them. The pairs that collaborated (rather than taking turns) made suggestions regarding each others' ideas and remembered and kept track of prior moves and attempts to a greater extent, monitoring and editing plans together, thereby supporting each other in developing novel solutions.

Researchers disagree on the role of extrinsic rewards in cooperative learning. Some have argued that group rewards along with individual accountability are essential (e.g., Slavin, 1990). Others have argued that it is more effective for group work to build on student-student interdependence in projects and on interest in working together on projects of inherent interest, or to focus on the relation of the activity to what is to be learned from it (Johnson & Johnson, 1987; Kohn, 1992; Meloth & Deering, 1994; Sharan & Sharan, 1992; see also Forman & McPhail, 1993). Phelps and Damon (1989) suggested that different notions of the aims of education underlie this debate, and argued that the conceptual changes that education should promote are jeopardized by extrinsic motivation. They argued for collaboration based on intrinsic incentives such as the children's natural search for knowledge, competence, and stimulating communication.

Intersubjectivity in Cooperative Learning. Discussions of the process by which classroom cooperative learning aids cognitive development are consistent with the earlier discussion of intersubjectivity based on other literatures. Johnson and Johnson (1989) argued on the basis of their meta-analysis that positive interdependence among students' goals is important for individuals to learn from their engagement in a group—students' parallel work had no advantage over individual work for their transfer to later individual work. Roschelle (1992) and Pontecorvo and Girardet (1993) emphasized the importance of the development of a common understanding ("convergence") between partners. Ellis, Klahr, and Siegler (1994) noted that fifth graders from a multiethnic middle-income population were more likely to move to a correct strategy for solving decimal problems if partners clearly explained their ideas and considered each others' proposals; correct strategies that were proposed but were not met with interest were likely to be abandoned.

An important aspect of cognition as a collaborative process seems to be the learning that derives from explaining ideas and resolving controversies through attempts to understand and persuade (Webb, 1982). College students learned more from a history passage if they taught it to someone else than if they just prepared to teach it or if they read it without the aim of teaching it (Annis, 1983). Johnson and Johnson (1989) summarized a number of studies indicating that understanding and reasoning were enhanced by the combination of explaining one's knowledge and summarizing another person's perspective. They argued that people learn something more deeply if they learn it in order to teach someone else: "A person actively teaching someone else may reorganize or clarify material on the spot, both of which allow the teacher to see the issue from new perspectives, enabling him or her to see previously unthought of new relationships" (p. 67).

Brown and Palincsar (1989) noted that although conflict has been repeatedly pointed to as an impetus for cognitive change, it may not be the conflict but the processes of co-elaboration which support cognitive progress, as several points of view are examined and modified to produce a new idea that takes into account the differing standpoints:

> Change is not the automatic outcome of group problem solving. . . . It is the result of certain social settings that force the elaboration and justification of various positions. Groups, peers, and adults can cause change, if they set into motion the appropriate processes. By extension, experienced learners can cause change on their own by adopting these process roles in thought experiments, or by "internalizing" role models from their experiences of group discussion in later intrapersonal dialogues. (p. 408)

Conceptual Change through Cooperative Learning. In general, researchers suggest that cooperative learning is most useful for learning that involves conceptual change (Kobayashi, 1994). Johnson and Johnson (1987) stated that cooperative learning is effective for any instructional task but note that "the more conceptual and complex the task, the greater the superiority of cooperative learning over competitive or individualistic learning" (p. 44).

Based on their meta-analysis, Johnson and Johnson (1989) argued that cooperative arrangements promote the use of higher quality cognitive reasoning strategies and metacognitive approaches than in individual arrangements. They reported that when cooperative situations were structured appropriately, groups of children working together induced new ideas or general principles that none of the group members could induce alone. Their 1989 meta-analysis found no difference among studies according to academic subject area, but reported that on lower-level learning tasks, individuals' achievement is the same whether they have worked cooperatively or by themselves, while on higher-level learning tasks having worked with a group benefits individuals' later solo achievements. Phelps and Damon (1989) noted that peer collaboration promoted deep conceptual development (such as understanding the notion of proportionality) but was not the best medium for fostering rote learning (such as multiplication tables and copying skills). Kruger (1994) found more shared thinking in spontaneous collaboration on discovery tasks than on skill tasks.

The conceptual advances that are possible in groups are not an automatic outcome of putting peers together. As the research of the previous sections revealed, cognitive development in peer collaboration is likely to require engagement between members of the group, with collective and individual understanding developing from such engagement. For such understanding to fit with adult definitions of cognitive development may require some members or facilitators of the group (whether children or adults) to induce the group to consider alternative concepts and information that fits with what is regarded as more sophisticated concepts or approaches. For example, with preliminary instruction by a teacher, ethnically mixed U.S. community college students who discussed chemistry concepts in cooperative group tasks structured to elicit misconceptions showed far fewer misconceptions as well as greater understanding of concepts such as the conservation of matter and energy than did students who received the preliminary instruction but not the cooperative tasks (Basili & Sanford, 1991).

An impressive example of peer collaboration with expert help is reciprocal teaching, in which peers aid each other with facilitation by an expert who helps the group in the subject matter as well as in group thinking processes (Brown & Palincsar, 1989). The group is responsible together for understanding and evaluating the meaning of a text; each member serves (in different turns, following a teacher's model) as a learning leader responsible for orchestrating the dialogue and as a listener or critic in the joint construction of meaning. Studies of reciprocal teaching indicate that in this system, U.S. students from first through eighth grades learned how to look for and comprehend the meaning of information presented, and performed better on tests. Brown and Palincsar argued that working in groups provides learners of varying levels of understanding with the opportunity to engage with deeply meaningful concepts for fundamental restructuring of knowledge, supported by the understanding and diversity of skills in the group. "Change is more likely when one is required to explain, elaborate, or defend one's position to others, as well as to oneself; striving for an explanation often makes a learner integrate and elaborate knowledge in new ways" (p. 395).

Brown and Palincsar emphasized that reciprocal teaching is a system that simultaneously involves cooperative learning among peers and direct instruction by an adult who models strategies and provides temporary scaffolding to bolster the group's process (a combination that they pointed out resembles apprenticeship). Students witness others' enactment of differentiated spontaneous roles such as the executive who designs plans, the skeptic who questions premises and plans, the instructor who explains and summarizes for the less involved members of the group, the recordkeeper, and the conciliator who strives to minimize interpersonal stress. This provides learners with support for their own development of corresponding thinking strategies that they are learning to manage for themselves, such as defining the problem, isolating important features of it, referring to information and general principles, and evaluating progress. The next section considers how children learn to participate skillfully in shared thinking.

Children Learning How to Collaborate and Assist Each Other in Learning

Developmental research suggests that children's shared decision making is not easy for many European American children (Patterson & Roberts, 1982; Peterson, Wilkinson, Spinelli, & Swing, 1982). There is evidence that they develop greater skills in collaboration as they develop, such as increasing use of attention-focusing statements, responsiveness to a partner, and explicitness of reference to objects from age 3 to 5 years (Cooper, 1980).

However, collaboration among European American middle-class elementary and secondary school students is often still a challenge (Socha & Socha, 1994). For example, pairs of 9-year-old European American "teachers" who were asked to teach 7-year-olds to play a game often offered two parallel, unrelated lines of instruction, whereas pairs of Navajo 9-year-olds were more likely to build on each other's comments in teaching a 7-year-old (Ellis & Gauvain, 1992). The Navajo children provided a higher proportion of useful task information and remained engaged in the task, observing their partners even when they were not controlling the game moves; European American children were distracted when they were not controlling the game, sometimes to the point of leaving the task.

Extent of experience collaborating may play a role in children's learning to coordinate ideas. Rodrigo and Batista (1995) found that three 11-year-old middle-class Spanish children who had worked together on reasoning tasks for 9 sessions advanced in their collaboration skills, and these skills seemed to carry over to a later errand-planning task; three other girls who had done the reasoning tasks solo for 9 sessions evidenced less skill in managing the coordination of ideas on the shared errand-planning task. Through experience with solving the problems of collaboration, and perhaps also with development of relationships among people engaging in shared thinking, children may develop skill in coordinating their ideas with each other.

An example of progress in children's collaboration with experience is available in Socha and Socha's (1994) study in which two groups of U.S. 6-year-olds progressed in their problem-solving discussions over 5 sessions. The difficulties of coordinating ideas in the first session are evident in the interactions of a group of nine children, upon being asked to decide how they would spend the day together if given an imaginary day off from school (with specific questions such as what they would all eat):

> The children began their discussion by whispering to the person seated next to them. The teacher had to re-explain the concept of "group" decision making to them. The children subsequently talked louder and also talked with the child across from them, but still did not talk to the entire group. Small coalitions formed as a result of this, characterized by such statements as, "Me and R. are going to J's house" [in response to the question of whose house the whole group would go to]. Once these subgroups decided their response to a question, they proceeded to the next question without the rest of the group. . . . They reached agreement by shouting their responses in unison. It seemed that whoever yelled the loudest, first, "won." For example, one child yelled "Cheese pizza" (in response to what to eat), and the others yelled, "Yeah, cheese pizza." The group also had difficulty handling disagreements. One girl pouted and cried when she did not get things her way. The teacher had to intervene and teach the group about ways to compromise (e.g., "Next time we could do things your way"). The other decision-making strategy they chose was [using the counting-out rhyme] "e-nee, me-nee, mi-nee, mo." (p. 237)

These children's (and teacher's) reliance on ways of dividing up the task fits with their difficulties in coordinating their efforts to think together. By the fifth discussion (on another topic), this group engaged in a more orderly discussion, having been supported over the five sessions by the teacher's occasional suggestions and rules.

The pervasiveness of the lack of cooperative opportunities and of support in learning how to cooperate in traditionally organized schools makes it easy for researchers as well as students to assume that European and European American children's usual lack of skill in collaborating is simply "natural" (Forman & McPhail, 1993; Sharan & Sharan, 1992). Johnson and Johnson (1987) pointed out that students who are used to working in competitively structured individualistic classrooms assume that this is the natural structure unless assisted in learning about the nature of interdependence in goal structures and the skills necessary to work in groups. In British primary schools, Bennett and Dunne (1991) pointed out, students often work *in* groups (as a collection of children who sit together) but seldom work *as* groups. In German classrooms, cooperative learning organization was observed to be rare; without support in learning to cooperate (such as by prioritizing group reflection on the process of working together), students often simply divided the task, preventing their enlarging their individual resources by learning in collaboration (Huber & Eppler, 1990). A sociocultural approach urges attention to the role of institutional arrangements in children's development.

A growing literature supports the idea that peers solve problems cooperatively and tutor collaboratively when the social structure of the classroom supports such interactive patterns (Aronson, Blaney, Stephan, Sikes, & Snapp, 1978; Cazden, Cox, Dickinson, Steinberg, & Stone, 1979; Cooper, Marquis, & Edward, 1986; Damon, 1984). Pairs of middle-class European American children from a school structured collaboratively were more likely to work together with consensus, building on each other's ideas collaboratively, and to assist each other collaboratively in out-of-class math and categorization tasks than were children from a neighboring traditional school that had less emphasis on collaboration (Matusov, Bell, & Rogoff, submitted).

Middle-class U.S. third-graders learned more if their studying was done in cooperative groups that included discussion of how well their group was functioning and how they could improve its effectiveness than if they were in cooperative groups without group processing (Yager, Johnson, Johnson, & Snider, 1986). (However, students in cooperative groups without group processing nonetheless learned more than students in an individualistic condition.) A follow-up study with African American high school seniors and college freshmen (Johnson, Johnson, Stanne, & Garibaldi, 1989) replicated these findings with the added result that a combination of teacher and student processing was even more effective:

> The results of hundreds of studies on group dynamics indicate that communication, leadership, trust, decision-making, and conflict management skills are required for effective cooperative action. Individuals must be taught the interpersonal and small group skills needed for high quality cooperation, and be motivated to use them. . . . It is a truism in group dynamics that to be productive groups have to "process" how well they are working and take action to resolve any difficulties members have in collaborating together productively. (Johnson & Johnson, 1989, pp. 74–75)

The emphasis on learning to think and develop ideas together goes beyond individuals developing skill in interpersonal understanding. Crook (1994) warned against looking for successful collaboration solely in terms of individual characteristics such as age, stage, or "skill" in comprehending the intentions of another or in communicating. Crook contrasted an emphasis on individual social-cognitive skills with development of an "intersubjective attitude" that transcends the characteristics of individuals, as collaborators work toward constructing joint understanding. "If intersubjectivity does become a resource to support collaboration, it is because the conventions, rituals, institutions and goals of organized social life arrange that it should do so. This is the phenomenon we need to understand. Teachers and others need to understand how best to mobilize an intersubjective attitude towards the particular purposes of joint problem-solving" (p. 145).

In some communities, assisting children in learning to coordinate with others is central to the social structure of classroom and/or family life (Martini & Kirkpatrick, 1992; Rogoff et al., 1993; Toma, 1991a). Hatano (1994) contrasted the Western ideal of individualized instruction with Japanese educators' unanimous recommendation that instruction be organized to maximize multiway interaction and group norms emphasizing understanding. In Japanese elementary school classrooms, it is very common for teachers to explicitly teach children discourse forms for building on each other's ideas (Toma, 1991b). A Japanese teacher explained:

> As a first step before addressing the teacher, children discuss among themselves. For example, "I think such and such but what do you think, B-kun?" Then in return, "I think in such and such a way but what do you think?" Just like that. Children question and respond among themselves and by doing this, they deepen their understanding of the content (which they are supposed to be learning in the class session). The teacher comes into the picture at the very end when it is time to make sure that the main points are learned. As a first step before all of this, we need to teach speech forms, otherwise the discussion goes in chaotic ways. (p. 5)

This instruction often uses lists on classroom walls suggesting phrasings to begin a statement, including the following phrasings quoted by Toma (1991b, pp. 3–4): for agreeing with someone else ("I agree with [name]'s opinion. This is because . . ."), for disagreeing ("I disagree with [name]'s opinion. This is because . . ."), for requesting clarification ("I would like to ask [name]. Did you mean to say. . . ?"), and for extending an argument ("Does anyone have another idea [opinion]?" or "I would like to add . . . to [name's] idea").

In a Mayan community in Guatemala, children of 3 to 5 years collaborate with and support their younger siblings, voluntarily allowing the younger one leeway in access to resources with allowance for a toddler's lack of social understanding (Mosier & Rogoff, submitted). The 3- to 5-year-olds may act in a socially responsible way with regard to the toddlers in part because that is the way they themselves have been treated. They are no longer the one that is given the leeway but are already part of the system in which responsibility to other people is an inherent part of human relations. Learning to collaborate may be easiest if one has been treated in a collaborative fashion by adults and others in positions of responsibility. The next section focuses further on the roles of adults and of cultural institutions in collaboration with and among children.

Adult and Institutional Roles in Children's Collaborative Learning

Previous sections have touched on the important roles that adults play in children's collaborations with each other, for example, in the work of Brown and Palincsar (1989), Kobayashi (1994), and studies of communities of learners. Groups of Spanish 13- to 14-year-old students planned writing assignments in a more sophisticated fashion when working on a common group outline than on individual outlines; the difference was even stronger if the teacher assisted the children in developing a common outline (Lacasa, Herranz-Ybarra, Martín-del-Campo, & Pardo-de-León, 1994).

There is a great need for more focused attention on how children's collaboration with each other is integrated with adult roles. In most work on peer collaboration, adults are practically hidden collaborators, as teachers or researchers who structure or even script the tasks and attempt to facilitate the ongoing process and the participants' reflections on it. The adults' roles are usually referred to only in the background of the situation. In collaborative learning research, often the comparison serving as the "individual" condition is actually children's learning in whole-class instruction where the teacher addresses the children as a class. This is a form of interaction between the children and the adult; it is individual only in the sense that collaboration among peers is discouraged.

It is also common for researchers to treat experimenters as a neutral background feature of the experiment rather than to consider their role as collaboration. In one example, the researchers treated the learning through problem solving with a peer partner as "social interaction" and noted that receiving feedback regarding correctness of answers either while working "alone" or with a peer was also effective for the children's learning. The children receiving the adult researchers' feedback were regarded as working "alone," although the adults communicated correctness (with an arrow under a sticker indicating the correct answer) and presumably gave the children instructions and interacted with them during the experimental session.

Beyond the roles of adults, the institutional or cultural processes involved in experiments or in cooperative learning sessions are rarely examined directly. For example, usually it is assumed that cooperative activities occur as separate sessions within otherwise "traditional" academic settings in which most of the day involves teachers instructing the whole class at once (or individuals) and students are not allowed to help each other and are judged in comparison with each other. Exceptions are research in schools or communities where the everyday structure of communication is collaborative and the cooperative learning events are studied in relation to everyday classroom or family communication (e.g., Graves, 1992; Haynes & Gebreyseus, 1992; Johnson & Johnson, 1987; Kohn, 1992; Little Soldier, 1989; Matusov, Bell, & Rogoff, submitted).

Attempts to understand or to promote cooperative learning in the classroom require consideration of the roles of adults in children's cooperative learning and the overall structure of the classroom, and the roles of adults outside the classroom in supporting adults' collaboration with children within the classroom (Tharp & Gallimore, 1988).

Nicolopoulou and Cole's (1993) research on creating collaborative learning after-school activities noted the essential role played by the "common culture" (collaborative or not) of the institutions in which their activities were initiated.

Literature on school restructuring suggests that for children to learn through collaboration (or to sustain it once encouraged and helped to do it) requires rethinking adults' roles in children's learning and in relation to each other. Teachers have difficulty learning to guide rather than to control children's behavior when attempting to change from traditional teacher-controlled whole-class activities to cooperative learning activities (Solomon, Watson, Schaps, Battistich, & Solomon, 1990). For teachers to learn to use cooperative learning approaches, it appears that they themselves need to have participated in such learning activities rather than to have been lectured regarding the importance of cooperative learning (Johnson & Johnson, 1987; Sharan & Sharan, 1992; Sharan & Shaulov, 1990). Solomon et al. (1990) and Sharan and Sharan (1992) have described programs helping teachers learn how to help children learn how to support each other's work in the classroom through collaboration.

The same processes of learning through collaboration through shared purposes are important for adults as for children's learning of the school curriculum (Bruffee, 1993; Clokey, Cryns, & Johnston, in press; Lubomudrov, in press; Rogoff, Matusov, & White, 1996). Thus the structure of the school as a whole appears to relate to the success of efforts for children and teachers to learn to collaborate—principals' and district administrators' collaboration with teachers supports teachers' collaboration with each other as they learn to collaborate with the children, rather than each "level" of responsibility seeing itself as the repository of knowledge or authority for those "lower" (Shedd & Weaver, 1995; Tharp, 1993; Tharp & Gallimore, 1988). Cooperative learning in elementary and secondary school classrooms also requires university researchers and educators to learn to collaborate with educators of younger students, in order to promote the cognitive development we all seek for the children. Thus, the cooperative learning of children involves the collaboration of adults who carry out institutional roles ranging from the setting in which the children sit to distant universities.

My point in this section on the role of peer interaction in children's cognitive development has been to underline the roles of shared thinking between the peers and to expand the field of vision beyond the specific interactions of the children themselves to include the roles of others who are involved in the interaction or arrangements for its structure, as well as the roles of institutional and cultural traditions in the structure of children's collaborative thinking with each other and with adults.

This is a sociocultural view of cognitive development through collaboration that extends far beyond the simple examination of the "social influence" of putting another person together with the individual child being studied. Although research has begun to effectively include more than one person in studies of cognitive development, our scope has been largely limited to observations of interacting individuals (especially those who are deliberately engaged in teaching and learning situations). Most of the work to date thus fits the social influence perspective more than the sociocultural perspective.

To conclude this chapter, I suggest that we need to devote greater attention to the processes of collaboration in other sociocultural activities beyond social interaction with experts or with peers in situations that are largely intended as instructional. A broader view of collaboration as a sociocultural process includes other forms of collaboration between people than those that are usually the focus of research on social impacts on cognitive development. In particular, a sociocultural view emphasizes examining how the relations between partners and the contributions of individuals may vary as they participate in different activities of their community, and how individual and interpersonal aspects of activities are constituted by and themselves constitute cultural practices and institutions.

INTERPERSONAL AND COMMUNITY ASPECTS OF COLLABORATION IN SOCIOCULTURAL ACTIVITIES

The work on how adults as experts support novices' learning and how peers assist each other in learning has extended our purview of cognitive development beyond the role of the individual to include the involvement of other people, largely in instructional situations. The work includes some research that moves beyond dyadic and didactic settings, such as research on play among peers, integration of adult roles in peer interactions, and cultural variation in the structure of adult-child or peer interaction. The need to conceptualize the roles of individuals in sociocultural activities is clear in an observation by Schrage (1990):

An ethnographer studying a group of machine technicians came to a blunt rethinking of what expertise means in the context of the workplace. His analysis was that expert knowledge among technicians is less a matter of what each individual knows than of their joint ability to produce the right information when and where it's needed. . . . In other words, expertise is a social affair. (p. 49)

This concluding section extends the effort to understand how the thinking and interactions of individuals and their social partners fit with group, institutional, and cultural processes.

Moving beyond the notion that cognition is the property of isolated individuals opens important research questions regarding how individuals' participation in sociocultural activities proceeds and how it prepares those individuals for participation in other activities. It focuses cognitive developmental researchers' attention to a greater extent on the proximal and distal relations of individuals with other individuals, the roles of individuals in groups, and the structural arrangements of people's roles in institutions that extend beyond the lifespan and lifespace of individuals.

The shortcomings in the available research that I mentioned prior to reviewing the research on adult and peer roles in cognition as a collaborative process are important directions for future research. We need greater attention to the social and cultural aspects of how people determine the problems, goals, and means of their collaborative efforts, and to researchers' roles in phenomena under study. We also need to study collaboration in circumstances in which partners are mutually engaged but without interaction or instruction as their goal. We need to attend to the role of cultural tools—such as tools of language, genres of communication, and material technologies involved in problem solving—as well as to the functioning of the institutions in which collaboration occurs—the ways that thinking and collaborating are aspects of cultural practices in laboratories, schools, and families.

We need far greater understanding of collaboration and cognition in populations other than middle-class European American groups, or in situations other than those devised or managed by middle-class European American researchers. The available research is very limited as to the cultural communities represented. I have attempted to avoid overgeneralizing findings beyond the populations studied in three ways:

1. Frequently mentioning the communities in which the research has taken place,

2. Discussing cultural similarities and differences where research provides sufficient evidence, and

3. Referring to findings as observations that have occurred with particular participants in research ("these children did such-and-such") rather than in a general form ("children do such-and-such").

Related to some of the suggestions of cultural variation in collaboration is the need to study the dynamics of groups larger than dyads, without reducing them to collections of individuals or dyads. Evidence suggests that the dynamics are often quite different in larger groups than in dyads (examine the relations in Figures 14.1 to 14.4). For example, the presence of a second child can change mother-child conversations (Feinman & Lewis, 1983; Snow, 1982; Tomasello, Mannle, & Kruger, 1986; Wells, 1975).

Dyads may be the prototypical social relationship in some but not all communities. In Martini's (1994) observations of 3- to 5-year-olds, U.S. children played alone in 36% of observations and with just one partner in 35% of observations, whereas Marquesan (Polynesian) children almost never played alone (0%) or with just one other child (7%)—they played in groups of 3 to 6 children in 75% and in groups of 7 to 10 children in another 18% of the observations. Toddlers in a Mayan community in Guatemala and in a tribal community in India interacted in multiway engagement in groups about half of the time, whereas middle-class Turkish and European American toddlers engaged as members of a group during only about a tenth of the occasions—they more commonly acted alone or in successive dyadic relations with one person at a time, even though a group was always present during the observations (Rogoff et al., 1993). Even in large groups such as classrooms, middle-class European American interaction is usually structured dyadically—the students are to speak only to the teacher, who takes a speaking turn between each child turn (Lerner, 1993; Mehan, 1979). This contrasts with the structure in Japanese elementary school classrooms in which children build on each other's ideas as a group in exploring a problem (Toma, 1991b) and researchers argue that the involvement of more than two people is important for cognitive development (Hatano & Inagaki, 1991).

Although research on collaboration has focused on symmetrical conversations between two partners as a prototype for investigation, collaboration involves varied arrangements that warrant much more study. In the remaining sections, I focus on cognitive development through collaboration that involves specialized as well as symmetrical roles of participants, the role of conflictual as

well as harmonious relations in collaboration, and the roles of distant collaborators, such as those who are not physically or temporally present.

Specialized as Well as Symmetrical Roles in Collaboration

The literature often applies the term collaboration to instances in which partners engage with equal or symmetrical contributions. However, interactions involving symmetrical exchanges—in which each partner accords the other equal latitude and in which exchanges resemble smooth and fair turn taking between partners of equal status engaged on the same topic—are simply one form of collaboration.

Collaboration also includes interactions in which participants' roles are complementary or with some leading and others following, supporting, or actively observing (see Figures 14.1 to 14.5). Under varying circumstances, different partners may be more responsible for initiating and managing shared endeavors. For example, middle-class European American toddlers' attention to their mothers' activity increased during times that the mothers had not been asked to interact with their toddlers compared with times that the mothers had been directed to either encourage the toddlers to play with them or to play separately (Goldsmith & Rogoff, unpublished data).

As long as an endeavor and its thought process occurs at least partially in common, I regard the activity as involving collaboration. A person who is actively observing and following the thinking or decisions made by another is

Figure 14.5 Two young Mayan girls observe the skilled practice of backstrap weaving by the older girls and women in their family. (© Barbara Rogoff)

participating whether or not he or she contributes directly to decisions as they are made. A lecture can involve collaboration if either the lecturer or the audience (or both) manage to engage in thinking together. Collaboration can even occur without people being in each other's presence (discussed in a later section). The particular balance of responsibility is extremely interesting to examine (Rogoff et al., 1993).

Observation is an important collaborative process in child development, one that is often mistakenly regarded as passive. Children's active monitoring of events happening around them provides them with important information, even when the events are not staged for the children's benefit or adjusted to their viewing (see Figure 14.5). Children often pick up information from observing the actions of other people (Bandura, 1986; Hay et al., 1985; Lewis & Feiring, 1981; Verba, 1994; Zimmerman & Rosenthal, 1974). For example, toddlers have been observed to evaluate the character of a stranger by observing the reactions of others (Feiring, Lewis, & Starr, 1983). Likewise, 5-year-old children whose performance in Lego construction improved spent three times longer observing their expert partners, and their partners spent five times longer monitoring and observing them, than members of dyads in which novices' performance did not improve (Azmitia, 1988). In a group setting, some Japanese students, even when they did not speak, evaluated and incorporated other students' ideas to achieve deeper and more accurate understanding (Hatano, 1994).

In informal learning in many communities, children learn through participation with adults in community activities, and in some apprenticeships novices learn through the opportunity to observe and work with others varying in skills and roles in learning a craft as they contribute to the work of the shop (Goody, 1989; Lave & Wenger, 1991; Rogoff, 1990; Rogoff et al., 1993). Learners may play very central roles in managing their own learning and involvement, with adults or experts potentially (but not necessarily) facilitating their observation and growing participation.

Lave and Wenger (1991) pointed out that learners are often involved in *legitimate peripheral participation,* in which they have access to observe and begin to participate in the activities of a community of practice. The novices carry great responsibility for their involvement, and more competent practitioners may support their learning by structuring the activities in which they are allowed to engage directly. The "curriculum" of apprenticeship for Vai (Liberian) tailors involves novices observing masters and advanced apprentices, and participating in successive steps for approaching the overall body of tailoring skill and knowledge. The structuring of tasks in the relationship between master and apprentices provides the opportunity for an alert apprentice to observe the next step while participating in production of steps already under control, involved in a way that allows understanding of the overall process while contributing to a small section of it.

As legitimate peripheral participants, children often observe in contexts in which they are preparing to or already participate on other occasions. Their observations build upon their current understanding based on participation in social activities with caregivers and peers in previous situations and on their projected roles in managing cultural activities using cultural tools of understanding and action.

Although observation has been noted as an important means for children to come to an understanding with others in their community, there has been little research on how children go about observing, how participants in a situation in which children are observing communicate and foster or structure children's attention, or how children's observation of incidental activities may differ from their observation of purposefully modeled activities. A study focused on this issue indicated that in a Mayan community emphasizing learning by observation, toddlers and their caregivers frequently focused simultaneously on several competing ongoing events, without attention to one event disrupting attention to others (Rogoff et al., 1993). Such attentional management may facilitate being alert to important surrounding events. In contrast, in a middle-class European American community with less emphasis on learning by observation, toddlers and their caregivers more frequently attended to one event at a time, switching between competing events or appearing to ignore important surrounding events.

I have referred to "shared" thinking in this section as a key aspect of collaboration. Since many people seem to regard any form of "sharing" as the sort of rosy engagement desired between children in many preschools, I should clarify that I regard both harmonious and discordant interactions as involving shared thinking, as long as there are some premises in common. Collaboration and shared thinking does not require agreement on all points—just some common topic or starting point. The important role of disagreement is worth expanding, in the following section.

Discord as Well as Harmony in Collaboration

Collaboration does not imply smooth relationships or that everyone is happily supporting each other all the time.

Collaboration may involve disagreements about who is responsible for what aspect of the endeavor, or about the direction of the effort itself. Collaborative engagement in shared endeavors includes contested roles and disagreements, as well as moments of smoothly coordinated ongoing activity (Baker-Sennett, Matusov, & Rogoff, 1992; Gutierrez, Kreuter, & Larson, 1995; Matusov, 1995).

The notion that collaboration includes conflict appears to be a difficult idea, as the terms cooperation and collaboration to some people imply a lack of disagreement. In the United States, children and adults often use the term "cooperation" to mean "behaving" or avoiding conflict with an authority, as when parents and teachers tell children they "need their cooperation" or children report that they cooperate with others by withdrawing or avoiding disagreement (Holloway, 1992).

During collaboration, disagreements are an important tool for learning. Indeed, much research based on Piaget's theory and on collaboration in classrooms posits a central role for conflict in sparking advances in understanding (see Bruffee, 1993; Kruger, 1993; Nelson & Aboud, 1985). For example, discussions in which fifth-grade friends (from mostly Caucasian, low-to-middle income families) engaged in exploring their disagreements were associated with advances in scientific reasoning (Azmitia & Montgomery, 1993).

Several scholars have underlined the productive role of discord in learning through collaboration (Kohn, 1992). Hawkins (1987) noted that episodes of U.S. elementary students' collaboration at computer work that involved reorienting a problem-solving episode generally involved dissent between partners. Francis Crick, who discovered the double helix with James Watson, observed a similar phenomenon:

> "Our . . . advantage was that we had evolved unstated but fruitful methods of collaboration. . . . If either of us suggested a new idea, the other, while taking it seriously, would attempt to demolish it in a candid but nonhostile manner." (In fact, Crick once told a BBC interviewer at the time he got the Nobel that "Politeness is the poison of all good collaboration in science." Candor—if not rudeness—is at the heart of most successful collaborative relationships.) (Schrage, 1990, p. 42)

In accord with this notion is Zinchenko's (1995) moving account of the productive tension between the theoretical strands of cultural-historical psychology and the psychological theory of activity of Vygotsky and Leont'ev and their colleagues and students in the former USSR: "There

are *vital* (i.e., *life-giving*) *contradictions* between cultural-historical psychology and the psychological theory of activity and . . . these are a point of growth for both directions" (p. 51).

Beyond the role of disagreement in friendly collaborations, even participants in an unfriendly argument can be considered collaborators. Participants in an argument share some rules about the proceedings and are contesting for some common goal; through their argument they may assist in sharpening their own and the other combatants' ideas (even if this is contrary to their intent). Schoenfeld pointed to the importance of collaboration with unsympathetic partners in his description of his approach to math instruction at U.C. Berkeley:

> The general tenor of these discussions followed the line of argumentation outlined in Mason, Burton, and Stacey's (1982) *Thinking mathematically:* First, convince yourself. Then, convince a friend. Finally, convince an enemy. (That is, first make a plausible case, and then buttress it against all possible counter-arguments.) In short, we focused on what it means to truly understand, justify, and communicate mathematical ideas. (1993, p. 14)

Of course, the consequences of conflict (and of social interaction) are not necessarily beneficial, or intended to foster learning.

Even children's closest relationships often involve disagreement or efforts by partners or by children themselves to avoid some kinds of learning opportunities. Children often resist attempts to direct their learning (Litowitz, 1993). And as Goodnow (1987) pointed out, there are many topics that adults protect or divert children from learning (e.g., sexuality, family income), and adults are not always eager to participate in instructional situations. Parents are often busy with their own activities and sometimes stressed; they are not constantly focused on preparing each of their children for their future occupations or ensuring that their child is learning at each moment of the day (Goldsmith & Rogoff, 1995, 1997). Middle-class mothers interacting with their children when they think they are not being observed are much less involved and less instructive than when they are aware of being observed (Graves & Glick, 1978). Often parents' goal of the moment is to get a job done, not to instruct. When lower- to middle-income U.S. mothers worked with their 4-year-olds in planning routes through a model grocery store, they shared more responsibility with their children if they had been told that the children would later carry out the task on their own;

otherwise they somewhat more frequently carried out key aspects of the task without involving the child (Gauvain, 1995).

Adults often constrain children's opportunities to explore, as for example in refusing to let a one-year-old near a fire (Valsiner, 1984, 1987). Carew's (1980) observations of toddlers at home revealed that their activities were restricted during 8% of the observations, compared with being facilitated during 12% and engaged in mutually with another person during 21% of the observations. Such constraints are a part of the arrangements for children's learning that I believe are essential for understanding the collaborative nature of cognitive development—they are key to understanding both children's opportunities for learning and community or more local values and practices that inherently contribute to children's development in shared endeavors of their community.

Collaboration does not imply harmonious relations, but rather some degree of shared thinking and effort, which can be the sort that is necessary for an argument to proceed, or for a child to observe their family's and other companions' values and solutions to everyday problems. Indeed, shared thinking and effort can occur without people being in each other's presence or even without each knowing about the other.

Collaboration among People of Different Eras and Locations

Although collaboration and intersubjectivity are prototypically treated as processes occurring among people who are in each other's presence, they also characterize the shared thinking of people involved in shared endeavors at a distance or in different time periods. This point is central to sociocultural approaches to development.

Individual cognitive development occurs in collaboration with a community of thinkers in which more than one person is working on a particular problem, with historical and material aspects of other people's solutions available to each thinker in their extended conversation (Bruffee, 1993; Hutchins, 1995; John-Steiner, 1985, 1992; Schrage, 1990). Patricia MacLachlan described how she relied on both an anticipated reader and an absent editor to solve problems in writing:

> I try to anticipate the experience of the reader. I myself, of course, am the first reader, and I try to envision a small, objective, heartless Patty MacLachlan looking over my shoulder

saying, "Aw, come on!" when I am clumsy or self-indulgent. But the small Patty MacLachlan somehow turns into a Charlotte Zolotow [MacLachlan's editor]. Her voice has become ingrained in my consciousness; I can hear her.

> I've passed this on. My daughter Emily is becoming a wonderful, imaginative writer herself, and we spend a good deal of time discussing her work. "When I write a theme in class," she told me the other day, "I hear your voice in my ear." (1989, pp. 740–741)

In Schoenfeld's (1989) tracing of the development of the ideas of a research project, he noted the importance of the discussions among group members as well as of conversations with other colleagues, on other topics, in apparently extraneous events. These conversations at the time did not seem significant to the research problem, but analysis in retrospect revealed their centrality to the research endeavor, across time and contexts. Schoenfeld noted that "ideas in the air" in the local research culture (at U.C. Berkeley's School of Education) led to synergistic ideas that could not have derived from the work of any one individual working alone, or in another local research culture.

Such communities of thinkers may not be particularly organized, they may be competitive or supportive, and they may not coexist in time. Striking examples of collaboration across time are provided by Michaelangelo's study of ancient sculpture and by the creative grounding of cello virtuosity of Pablo Casals in his daily morning exercise of playing from Bach (John-Steiner, 1985). Exceptionally creative writers, painters, and physicists discover their own teachers from the past, engaging with "an intense and personal kinship that results when the work of another evokes a special resonance in them. . . . In this way, they stretch, deepen, and refresh their craft and nourish their intelligence" (p. 54). Collaborators may also be individuals in the future, such as a writer must consider in order to write in a way that will make sense to a future generation.

Collaboration and intersubjectivity between people participating in shared activity at a distance are often mediated by technologies for indirect involvement, such as computers, fax machines, telephones, television, and literacy (see Figure 14.6; Bruffee, 1993; Crook, 1994; Pea & Gomez, 1992; Schrage, 1990). For example, in classrooms, some forms of guidance can be provided by either a computer or a human partner (Zellermayer, Salomon, Globerson, & Givon, 1991); either option involves collaboration with human partners acting either indirectly through a device or directly in face-to-face interaction. Or a published

Figure 14.6 A boy, apparently alone on the lakeshore, is engaged socially with the ideas of a distant author of a book and with a nearby researcher taking a photograph. (© Barbara Rogoff)

artifact may be used for extending a topic beyond the prior contributions of an absent author, as with the use of a phase-transition diagram to re-represent ideas in ongoing discussion in a physics research group (Ochs, Jacoby, & Gonzales, 1994).

Tools for thinking provide a form of collaboration that may be easily overlooked. Kobayashi (1994) pointed out that in the Japanese science education method of Hypothesis-Experiment-Instruction, in which students are presented with a question along with three or four possible answers to choose among and to discuss, the problem setup itself serves as guidance in the learning process. The question and the alternatives guide how students verify their predictions, simply in the way the questions are asked and the alternatives worded. The alternatives provide a range of possibilities that encompass the common misconceptions in the domain of the question. This aids students in discerning both which opinions are plausible and which predictions are accurate when feedback is sought, providing students with clues as to how to restructure their naive understanding into scientific concepts. Without considering the collaborative role of those who devise such cognitive tools and the structure of the tools themselves, the students' learning process would be incompletely understood.

It is fascinating that one tool, the computer, is coming to be regarded by many as an "interactive" partner itself. Hawkins (1987) suggested that computers as partners have special value in being able to quickly and efficiently

display the results of substeps in problem solving and thus invite reconsideration and revision. Schrage (1990) argued that use of computers as a collaborative tool in scientific and business work can enhance creative problem solving by externalizing the discussion in print or graphic symbols. Of course, thinking with the aid of a computer also involves remote collaboration with the people who designed the hardware, the software, and the computer setting in use (see Figure 14.7). Pea (1993) provided an apt illustration of reconceptualizing intelligence and its development to include computer use, in describing a presentation by Papert at a 1987 National Science Foundation meeting:

> Papert described what marvelous [LEGO-Logo] machines the students had built, with very little "interference" from teachers. . . . On reflection, I felt this argument missed the key point about the "invisible" human intervention in this example—what the designers of LEGO and Logo crafted in creating just the interlockable component parts of LEGO machines or just the Logo primitive commands for controlling these machines. For there are only so many ways in which these components can be combined. Considerable intelligence has been *built into* these interpart relations as a means of constraining what actions are possible with the parts in combination. What I realized was that, although Papert could "see"

Figure 14.7 These U.S. students working at computers are at least as engaged with distant people's ideas through the use of the programs and the information on the screen as they are with the people next to them. Notice also the asymmetrical collaboration of the standing girl observing the problem-solving of a classmate and of the adult in the foreground who is observing and available to help. At least one of the children is also clearly engaged with the researcher documenting the activity. (© Barbara Rogoff)

teachers' interventions (a kind of social distribution of intelligence contributing to the child's achievement of activity), the designers' interventions (a kind of artifact-based intelligence contributing to the child's achievement of activity) were not seen. . . . [The child] could be scaffolded in the achievement of activity either explicitly by the intelligence of the teacher, or *implicitly* by that of the designers, now embedded in the constraints of the artifacts with which the child was playing. (pp. 64–65)

Material artifacts such as books, orthographies, computers, buildings, and hammers are essentially social, historical objects, transforming with the ideas of both their designers and their later users, forming and being formed by the practices of their use and by related practices, in historical and projected communities (Brown & Duguid, 1994; Gauvain, 1993; Rogoff et al., 1994). Artifacts serve to amplify as well as to constrain the possibilities of human activity as the artifacts participate in the practices in which they are employed (Cole & Griffin, 1980; Wertsch, 1991). They are representatives of earlier solutions to similar problems by other people, which later generations modify and apply to new problems, extending and transforming their use.

Consider the example of the development of current practices in drafting a written composition, which in recent years have been transformed by the advent of word processing on computers, replacing drafts on tablets of lined paper and supporting revision of text in new ways. Before the Middle Ages in Europe, all elaboration of the ideas and expression of text occurred before the material was set to written form (Alcorta, 1994). The person who composed the text was not the one who wrote it—the text's author merely dictated it to a scribe who wrote it exactly on the parchment. In the Middle Ages, it became possible to work with an intermediate draft—with the innovation of using a wax tablet—and some authors began to fill all three roles: the composer of the text, the writer on the wax tablet, and the transcriber to parchment for the final, neat document. It was not until the 1880s in France that schoolchildren were expected to express themselves in writing, rather than simply write to put lectures to paper. Literate people may now take for granted the tool for thinking that written composition provides, but this cognitive practice has evolved through the centuries from earlier roots in oral traditions, along with material inventions, in a collaboration of people extending over great periods of time.

Children's cognitive development is inherently related to their community's historical traditions, such as whether formal schooling or literacy are prevalent or observation of parents' work is easily accessible. Each new generation builds on and modifies the inventions and arrangements of prior generations, in a process of continuing involvement with people no longer present (who may or may not be of the same ancestry).

Thus collaboration is a process that can take many forms, whether intended or accidental, mutual or one-sided, face-to-face, shoulder-to-shoulder, or distant, congenial or contested; the key feature is that in collaboration, people are involved in others' thinking processes through shared endeavors. Many of these forms of collaboration have not yet received much research attention. It will be important to investigate the ways that individual, interpersonal, and community aspects of shared thinking function in the rich variety of sociocultural activities in which children participate.

CONCLUSION

Research on collaboration has derived largely from the perspective of the social influence approach, in which individuals serve as the unit of analysis and the impact of external influences is studied. Such research examines the roles of characteristics of the separate individuals who are interacting—such as age, expertise, or status of the developing learner or of the partner, or the kind of technique used by the partner in influencing the learner.

Much of this research can be interpreted from a sociocultural perspective (though sometimes requiring great effort in avoiding overgeneralization to other populations or situations). The largest shortcomings of the literature at present are that most of the research leaves unanalyzed the cultural/historical aspects that are important in all the situations observed (whether in laboratories, schools, homes, Girl Scout troops, or other organized settings in any community) and devotes insufficient attention to what is meant by learning or development (relying on unquestioned habits of thinking of learning/development as acquisition of mental objects).

In this chapter, I have provided an overview of the research as well as commentary suggesting that sociocultural approaches can lead us further in understanding cognition as a collaborative process. Sociocultural approaches broaden the focus to include cultural/historical aspects of the phenomena and, at least from the perspective that I take in thinking of learning as transformation of participation, to rethink what is meant by learning and development.

Theoretical, research, and methodological issues in the sociocultural study of cognition as a collaborative process center on the following themes: A sociocultural approach goes beyond regarding the individual as a separate entity that is the base unit of analysis to examine sociocultural activity as the unit of analysis, with examination of the contributions of individual, interpersonal, and community processes. Thus, analysis goes beyond the individual and the dyad to examine the structured relations among people in groups and in communities, across time.

With sociocultural activities as the units, analysis emphasizes the purposes and dynamically changing nature of events. Analysis examines the changing and meaningful constellations of aspects of events, not variables that attempt to be independent of the purpose of the activity. Central to analysis of cognition as a collaborative process is a focus on the shared meaning in endeavors in which people engage in common. Cognition is not conceptualized as separate from social, motivational, emotional, and identity processes—people's thinking and development is conceived as involved in social relations, with purpose and feeling central to their involvement in activities, and transformation of their roles as a function of participation.

Developmental transitions are of great interest; they are conceived as properties of people's participation in sociocultural activities, not as properties of people independent of their involvements. Development and learning are evaluated in terms of the transformation of people's participation in sociocultural activities. The extent to which individuals' changing roles and understandings are used in other activities is a matter for empirical investigation; generality is not assumed and is not attributed to either the individual's or to the situation's characteristics, but to the processes of participation of the individual and others (present and historical) in the activity. Generalization focuses on processes rather than personal or situational attributes. Analysis of cognition as a collaborative process includes consideration of how the researcher and the research tradition itself plays a role in the activities under consideration. Cognition is a widely collaborative process.

I hope that my comments in this chapter help support development of the field in these areas, and that when the next volume of the *Handbook* appears in a dozen years or so, some of the issues reported here can be seen as transitional to a more adequate understanding of cognitive development as a collaborative process involving individuals engaged with others in sociocultural activities. Understanding how people develop, that is, how they change in their participation in sociocultural activities, requires attention to the changing activities themselves, to people's changing responsibilities and roles, and to how their participation relates to their becoming a member of a community with specific but changing institutions, technologies, and definitions of intelligent involvement. The field has made considerable progress in moving beyond considering cognitive development as a property exclusively of solitary individuals; we have much left to do to incorporate the insights of sociocultural theory into our research and practices. The learning and development that we seek as a field is itself a collaborative process, like the phenomena we study.

ACKNOWLEDGMENTS

I am grateful to the Spencer Foundation for their support for my writing of this chapter, to Margarita Azmitia, Maureen Callanan, Michael Cole, Bill Damon, Deanna Kuhn, Eugene Matusov, Bob Siegler, and Chikako Toma for their suggestions on earlier drafts, and to Cindy White for her help in preparing the manuscript.

REFERENCES

Adams, A. K. (1987, January). *"A penguin belongs to the bird family": Language games and the social transfer of categorical knowledge.* Paper presented at the third International Conference on Thinking, Honolulu.

Adams, A. K., & Bullock, D. (1986). Apprenticeship in word use: Social convergence processes in learning categorically related nouns. In S. A. Kuczaj & M. D. Barrett (Eds.), *The development of word meaning: Progress in cognitive development research* (pp. 155–197). New York: Springer-Verlag.

Adamson, L. B., Bakeman, R., & Smith, C. B. (1990). Gestures, words, and early object sharing. In V. Volterra & C. Erting (Eds.), *From gesture to language in hearing and deaf children* (pp. 31–41). New York: Springer-Verlag.

Alcorta, M. (1994). Text writing from a Vygotskyan perspective: A sign-mediated operation. *European Journal of Psychology of Education, 9,* 331–341.

Allen, V. L. (Ed.). (1976). *Children as teachers: Theory and research on tutoring.* New York: Academic Press.

Allen, V. L., & Feldman, R. S. (1973). Learning through tutoring: Low-achieving children as tutors. *Journal of Experimental Education, 42,* 1–5.

Allen, V. L., & Feldman, R. S. (1976). Studies on the role of tutor. In V. Allen (Ed.), *Children as teachers: Theory and research on tutoring* (pp. 113–129). New York: Academic Press.

Als, H. (1979). Social interaction: Dynamic matrix for developing behavioral organization. In I. C. Uzgiris (Ed.), *Social interaction and communication during infancy* (pp. 21–39). San Francisco: Jossey-Bass.

Annis, L. F. (1983). The processes and effects of peer tutoring. *Human Learning, 2,* 39–47.

Arievitch, I., & van der Veer, R. (1995). Furthering the internalization debate: Gal'perin's contribution. *Human Development, 38,* 113–126.

Aronfreed, J. (1968). *Conduct and conscience: The socialization of internalized control over behavior.* New York: Academic Press.

Aronson, E., Blaney, N., Stephan, C., Sikes, J., & Snapp, M. (1978). *The jigsaw classroom.* Beverly Hills: Sage.

Azmitia, M. (1988). Peer interaction and problem solving: When are two heads better than one? *Child Development, 59,* 87–96.

Azmitia, M. (1996). Peer interactive minds. In P. B. Baltes & U. M. Staudinger (Eds.), *Interactive minds.* Cambridge, England: Cambridge University Press.

Azmitia, M., & Hesser, J. (1993). Why siblings are important agents of cognitive development: A comparison of siblings and peers. *Child Development, 64,* 430–444.

Azmitia, M., & Montgomery, R. (1993). Friendship, transactive dialogues, and the development of scientific reasoning. *Social Development, 2,* 202–221.

Azmitia, M., & Perlmutter, M. (1989). Social influences on children's cognition: State of the art and future directions. In H. Reese (Ed.), *Advances in child development and behavior* (Vol. 22, pp. 89–144). Orlando, FL: Academic Press.

Baker-Sennett, J., Matusov, E., & Rogoff, B. (1992). Sociocultural processes of creative planning in children's playcrafting. In P. Light & G. Butterworth (Eds.), *Context and cognition: Ways of learning and knowing* (pp. 93–114). New York: Harvester Wheatsheaf.

Bakhtin, M. M. (1981). In M. Holquist (Ed.), *The dialogical imagination.* Austin: University of Texas Press.

Bakhurst, D. (1988). Activity, consciousness and communication. *Newsletter of the Laboratory for Comparative Human Cognition, 10,* 31–39.

Bandura, A. (1986). *Social foundations of thought and action: A social cognitive theory.* Englewood Cliffs, NJ: Prentice-Hall.

Bartlett, L., Goodman Turkanis, C., & Rogoff, B. (in press). *Learning as a community.* New York: Oxford University Press.

Barton, M. E., & Tomasello, M. (1994). The rest of the family: The role of fathers and siblings in early language development. In C. Gallway & B. J. Richards (Eds.), *Input and interaction in language acquisition* (pp. 109–134). New York: Cambridge University Press.

Basili, P. A., & Sanford, J. P. (1991). Conceptual change strategies and cooperative group work in chemistry. *Journal of Research in Science Teaching, 28,* 293–304.

Bearison, D. J. (1991). Interactional contexts of cognitive development: Piagetian approaches to sociogenesis. In L. T. Landesman (Ed.), *Culture, schooling, and psychological development* (pp. 56–70). Norwood, NJ: ABLEX.

Beebe, B., Jaffe, J., Feldstein, S., Mays, K., & Alson, D. (1985). Interpersonal timing: The application of an adult dialogue model to mother-infant vocal and kinesic interactions. In T. M. Field & N. Fox (Eds.), *Social perception in infants* (pp. 217–247). Norwood, NJ: ABLEX.

Bellinger, D. (1979). Changes in the explicitness of mothers' directives as children age. *Journal of Child Language, 6,* 443–458.

Bennett, N., & Dunne, E. (1991). The nature and quality of talk in co-operative classroom groups. *Learning and Instruction, 11,* 103–118.

Berger, P. L., & Luckmann, T. (1966). *The social construction of reality.* New York: Doubleday.

Berkowitz, M. W., & Gibbs, J. C. (1985). The process of moral conflict resolution and moral development. In M. W. Berkowitz (Ed.), *Peer conflict and psychological growth* (pp. 71–84). San Francisco: Jossey-Bass.

Bernstein, L. E. (1981). Language as a product of dialogue. *Discourse Processes, 4,* 117–147.

Blount, B. G. (1972). Parental speech and language acquisition: Some Luo and Samoan examples. *Anthropological Linguistics, 14,* 119–130.

Bornstein, M. H. (1988). Mothers, infants, and the development of cognitive competence. In H. E. Fitzgerald, B. M. Lester, & M. W. Yogman (Eds.), *Theory and research in behavioral pediatrics* (Vol. 4, pp. 67–99). New York: Plenum Press.

Bos, M. C. (1937). Experimental study of productive collaboration. *Acta Psychologica, 3,* 315–426.

Brandt, R. S. (Ed.). (1991). *Cooperative learning and the collaborative school.* Alexandria, VA: Association for Supervision and Curriculum Development.

Brazelton, T. B. (1983). Precursors for the development of emotions in early infancy. In R. Plutchik & H. Kellerman (Eds.), *Emotion: Theory, research, and experience* (Vol. 2, pp. 35–55). New York: Academic Press.

Bretherton, I. (Ed.). (1984). *Symbolic play: The development of social understanding.* Orlando, FL: Academic Press.

Bretherton, I., McNew, S., & Beeghly-Smith, M. (1981). Early person knowledge as expressed in gestural and verbal communication: When do infants acquire a "theory of mind"? In M. E. Lamb & L. R. Sherrod (Eds.), *Infant social cognition* (pp. 333–373). Hillsdale, NJ: Erlbaum.

Brown, A. L. (1994). The advancement of learning. *Educational Researcher, 23,* 4–12.

Brown, A. L., Ash, D., Rutherford, M., Nakagawa, K., Gordon, A., & Campione, J. C. (1993). Distributed expertise in the classroom. In G. Salomon (Ed.), *Distributed cognitions: Psychological and educational considerations* (pp. 188–228). New York: Cambridge University Press.

Brown, A. L., & Campione, J. C. (1984). Three faces of transfer: Implications for early competence, individual differences, and instruction. In M. E. Lamb, A. L. Brown, & B. Rogoff (Eds.), *Advances in developmental psychology* (Vol. 3, pp. 143–192). Hillsdale, NJ: Erlbaum.

Brown, A. L., & Campione, J. C. (1990). Communities of learning and thinking, or a context by any other name. In D. Kuhn (Ed.), *Developmental perspectives on teaching and learning thinking skills: Contributions in human development* (Vol. 21, pp. 108–126). Basel: Karger.

Brown, A. L., & Palincsar, A. S. (1989). Guided, cooperative learning and individual knowledge acquisition. In L. B. Resnick (Ed.), *Knowing, learning, and instruction.* Hillsdale, NJ: Erlbaum.

Brown, A. L., & Reeve, R. A. (1987). Bandwidths of competence: The role of supportive contexts in learning and development. In L. S. Liben (Ed.), *Development and learning: Conflict or congruence?* (pp. 173–223). Hillsdale, NJ: Erlbaum.

Brown, J. S., Collins, A., & Duguid, P. (1989). Situated cognition and the culture of learning. *Educational Researcher, 18,* 32–42.

Brown, J. S., & Duguid, P. (1994). Borderline issues: Social and material aspects of design. *Human-Computer Interaction, 9,* 3–36.

Brownell, C. A., & Carriger, M. S. (1991). Collaborations among toddler peers. In L. B. Resnick, J. M. Levine, & S. D. Teasley (Eds.), *Perspectives on socially shared cognition* (pp. 365–383). Washington, DC: American Psychological Association.

Bruffee, K. A. (1993). *Collaborative learning. Higher education, interdependence, and the authority of knowledge.* Baltimore, MD: Johns Hopkins University Press.

Bruner, J. S. (1978). The child's conception of language. In A. Sinclair, R. J. Jarvella, & W. J. M. Levelt (Eds.), *The child's conception of language* (pp. 241–256). Berlin: Springer-Verlag.

Bruner, J. S. (1983). *Child's talk: Learning to use language.* New York: Norton.

Bruner, J. S. (1987). The transactional self. In J. Bruner & H. Haste (Eds.), *Making sense: The child's construction of the world* (pp. 81–96). London: Methuen.

Butterworth, G. (1987). Some benefits of egocentrism. In J. Bruner & H. Haste (Eds.), *Making sense: The child's construction of the world* (pp. 62–80). London: Methuen.

Butterworth, G., & Cochran, G. (1980). Towards a mechanism of joint visual attention in human infancy. *International Journal of Behavioral Development, 3,* 253–272.

Callanan, M. A. (1985). How parents label objects for young children: The role of input in the acquisition of category hierarchies. *Child Development, 56,* 508–523.

Callanan, M. A. (1991). Parent-child collaboration in young children's understanding of category hierarchies. In S. A. Gelman & J. P. Byrnes (Eds.), *Perspectives on language and thought: Interrelations in development* (pp. 440–484). Cambridge, England: Cambridge University Press.

Camaioni, L., de Castro Campos, M. F. P., & deLemos, C. (1984). On the failure of the interactionist paradigm in language acquisition: A re-evaluation. In W. Doise & A. Palmonari (Eds.), *Social interaction in individual development* (pp. 93–106). Cambridge, England: Cambridge University Press.

Carew, J. V. (1980). Experience and the development of intelligence in young children at home and in day care. *Monographs of the Society for Research in Child Development, 45*(6/7, Serial No. 187).

Cazden, C. B. (1979). Peek-a-boo as an instructional model: Discourse development at home and at school. In *Papers and reports on child language development* (No. 17). Department of Linguistics, Stanford University, Standford, CA.

Cazden, C. B., Cox, M., Dickinson, D., Steinberg, Z., & Stone, C. (1979). You all gonna hafta listen: Peer teaching in a primary classroom. In W. Collins (Ed.), *Children's language and communication: The Minnesota Symposium on Child Psychology* (Vol. 12, pp. 183–231). Hillsdale, NJ: Erlbaum.

Churcher, J., & Scaife, M. (1982). How infants see the point. In G. Butterworth & P. Light (Eds.), *Social cognition: Studies of the development of understanding* (pp. 110–136). Chicago: University of Chicago Press.

Cicirelli, V. G. (1976). Siblings teaching siblings. In V. Allen (Ed.), *Children as teachers: Theory and research on tutoring* (pp. 99–111). New York: Academic Press.

Clark, H. H., & Wilkes-Gibbs, D. (1986). Referring as a collaborative process. *Cognition, 22,* 1–39.

Clay, M. M., & Cazden, C. B. (1990). A Vygotskian interpretation of Reading Recovery. In L. Moll (Ed.), *Vygotsky and education* (pp. 206–222). Cambridge, England: Cambridge University Press.

Clokey, M., Cryns, T., & Johnston, M. (in press). Teachers learning together. In L. Bartlett, C. Goodman Turkanis, & B. Rogoff (Eds.), *Learning as a community.* New York: Oxford University Press.

Cole, M. (1985). The zone of proximal development: Where culture and cognition create each other. In J. V. Wertsch (Ed.), *Culture, communication, and cognition: Vygotskian perspectives* (pp. 146–161). Cambridge, England: Cambridge University Press.

Cole, M. (1990). Cognitive development and formal schooling: The evidence from cross-cultural research. In L. C. Moll (Ed.), *Vygotsky and education* (pp. 89–110). Cambridge, England: Cambridge University Press.

Cole, M., & Griffin, P. (1980). Cultural amplifiers reconsidered. In D. R. Olson (Ed.), *The social foundations of language and thought* (pp. 343–364). New York: Norton.

Cole, M., & Means, B. (1981). *Comparative studies of how people think: An introduction.* Cambridge, MA: Harvard University Press.

Collins, A., & Stevens, A. L. (1982). Goals and strategies of inquiry teachers. In R. Glaser (Ed.), *Advances in instructional psychology* (Vol. 2, pp. 65–119). Hillsdale, NJ: Erlbaum.

Cooper, C. R. (1980). Development of collaborative problem solving among preschool children. *Developmental Psychology, 16,* 433–440.

Cooper, C. R., Marquis, A., & Edward, D. (1986). Four perspectives on peer learning among elementary school children. In E. C. Mueller & C. R. Cooper (Eds.), *Process and outcome in peer relationships* (pp. 269–300). Orlando, FL: Academic Press.

Corsaro, W. A., & Rizzo, T. A. (1988). *Discussione* and friendship: Socialization processes in the peer culture of Italian nursery school children. *American Sociological Review, 53,* 879–894.

Cronbach, L. J. (1975). Beyond the two disciplines of scientific psychology. *American Psychologist, 30,* 116–127.

Crook, C. (1994). *Computers and the collaborative experience of learning.* London: Routledge & Kegan Paul.

Cuban, L. (1984). *How teachers taught: Constancy and change in American classrooms, 1890–1980.* New York: Longman.

Daiute, C., & Dalton, B. (1993). Collaboration between children learning to write: Can novices be masters? *Cognition and Instruction, 10,* 281–333.

Damon, W. (1984). Peer education: The untapped potential. *Journal of Applied Developmental Psychology, 5,* 331–343.

Damon, W., & Phelps, E. (1987, June). *Peer collaboration as a context for cognitive growth.* Paper presented at Tel Aviv University School of Education, Tel Aviv.

DeLoache, J. S. (1984). What's this? Maternal questions in joint picturebook reading with toddlers. *Quarterly Newsletter of the Laboratory for Comparative Human Cognition, 6,* 87–95.

Dewey, J. (1916). *Democracy and education.* New York: Macmillan.

Dewey, J. (1938). *Experience and education.* New York: Macmillan.

Dewey, J., & Bentley, A. F. (1949). *Knowing and the known.* Boston: Beacon Press.

Dunbar, K. (1995). How scientists really reason: Scientific reasoning in real-world laboratories. In R. J. Sternberg & J. E. Davidson (Eds.), *The nature of insight* (pp. 365–395). Cambridge, MA: MIT Press.

Dunham, P. J., Dunham, F., & Curwin, A. (1993). Joint-attentional states and lexical acquisition at 18 months. *Developmental Psychology, 29,* 827–831.

Dunn, J., & Dale, N. (1984). I a daddy: Two-year-olds' collaboration in joint pretend with sibling and with mother. In I. Bretherton (Ed.), *Symbolic play: The development of social understanding* (pp. 131–158). Orlando, FL: Academic.

Duran, R. P. (1994). Cooperative learning for language minority students. In R. A. DeVillar, C. J. Faltis, & J. Cummins (Eds.), *Cultural diversity in schools: From rhetoric to practice* (pp. 145–159). Buffalo, NY: SUNY Press.

Duran, R. T., & Gauvain, M. (1993). The role of age versus expertise in peer collaboration during joint planning. *Journal of Experimental Child Psychology, 55,* 227–242.

Eccles, J. S., Buchanan, C. M., Flanagan, C., Fuligni, A., Midgley, C., & Yee, D. (1991). Control versus autonomy during early adolescence. *Journal of Social Issues, 47,* 53–68.

Eckerman, C. O., Whatley, J. L., & McGhee, L. J. (1979). Approaching and contacting the object another manipulates: A social skill of the 1-year-old. *Developmental Psychology, 15,* 585–593.

Edwards, D. (1993). But what do children really think?: Discourse analysis and conceptual content in children's talk. *Cognition and Instruction, 11,* 207–225.

Eisenberg, A. R. (1985). Learning to describe past experiences in conversation. *Discourse Processes, 8,* 177–204.

Elbers, E. (1991). The development of competence and its social context. *Educational Psychology Review, 3,* 73–94.

Ellis, S., & Gauvain, M. (1992). Social and cultural influences on children's collaborative interactions. In L. T. Winegar & J. Valsiner (Eds.), *Children's development within social context* (Vol. 2, pp. 155–180). Hillsdale, NJ: Erlbaum.

Ellis, S., Klahr, D., & Siegler, R. S. (1993, March). *Effects of feedback and collaboration on changes in children's use of mathematical rules.* Paper presented at the meetings of the Society for Research in Child Development, New Orleans.

Ellis, S., Klahr, D., & Siegler, R. S. (1994, April). *The birth, life, and sometimes death of good ideas in collaborative problem-solving.* Paper presented at the meetings of the American Educational Research Association, New Orleans.

Ellis, S., & Rogoff, B. (1982). The strategies and efficacy of child versus adult teachers. *Child Development, 53,* 730–735.

Ellis, S., & Rogoff, B. (1986). Problem solving in children's management of instruction. In E. Mueller & C. Cooper (Eds.), *Process and outcome in peer relationships* (pp. 301–325). Orlando, FL: Academic.

Engeström, Y. (1993). Developmental studies of work as a test-bench of activity theory: The case of primary care medical practice. In S. Chaiklin & J. Lave (Eds.), *Understanding practice: Perspectives on activity and context* (pp. 64–103). Cambridge, England: Cambridge University Press.

Feinman, S. (1982). Social referencing in infancy. *Merrill-Palmer Quarterly, 28,* 445–470.

Feinman, S., & Lewis, M. (1983). Is there social life beyond the dyad? A social psychological view of social connections in infancy. In M. Lewis (Ed.), *Beyond the dyad* (pp. 13–41). New York: Plenum Press.

Feiring, C., Lewis, M., & Starr, M. D. (1983, April). *Indirect effects and infants' reaction to strangers.* Paper presented at the meetings of the Society for Research in Child Development, Detroit.

Fernald, A. (1988, November). *The universal language: Infants' responsiveness to emotion in the voice.* Paper presented at the Developmental Psychology Program, Stanford University, Stanford, CA.

Ferrier, L. (1978). Word, context and imitation. In A. Lock (Ed.), *Action, gesture and symbol: The emergence of language* (pp. 471–483). New York: Academic.

Fisher, R. (1969). An each one teach one approach to music notation. *Grade Teacher, 86,* 120.

Fivush, R. (1988). *Form and function in early autobiographical memory.* Unpublished manuscript, Emory University, Atlanta.

Fonzi, A., & Smorti, A. (1994). Narrative and logical strategies in socio-cognitive interaction between children. *International Journal of Behavioral Development, 17,* 383–395.

Foot, H. C., Shute, R. H., Morgan, M. J., & Barron, A. -M. (1990). Theoretical issues in peer tutoring. In H. C. Foot, M. J. Morgan, & R. H. Shute (Eds.), *Children helping children.* New York: Wiley.

Forbes, D., Katz, M. M., & Paul, B. (1986). "Frame talk": A dramatistic analysis of children's fantasy play. In E. C. Mueller & C. R. Cooper (Eds.), *Process and outcome in peer relationships* (pp. 249–265). Orlando, FL: Academic Press.

Forman, E. A. (1987). Learning through peer interaction: A Vygotskian perspective. *Genetic Epistemologist, 15,* 6–15.

Forman, E. A., & Cazden, C. B. (1985). Exploring Vygotskian perspectives in education: The cognitive value of peer interaction. In J. V. Wertsch (Ed.), *Culture, communication, and cognition: Vygotskian perspectives* (pp. 323–347). Cambridge, England: Cambridge University Press.

Forman, E. A., & Kraker, M. J. (1985). The social origins of logic: The contributions of Piaget and Vygotsky. In M. W. Berkowitz (Ed.), *Peer conflict and psychological growth* (pp. 23–39). San Francisco: Jossey-Bass.

Forman, E. A., & McPhail, J. (1993). A Vygotskian perspective on children's collaborative problem-solving activities. In E. A. Forman, N. Minick, & C. A. Stone (Eds.), *Contexts for learning: Sociocultural dynamics in children's development* (pp. 213–229). New York: Oxford University Press.

Fox, B. A. (1988). *Cognitive and interactional aspects of correction in tutoring* (Tech. Rep. No. 88-2). Institute of Cognitive Science, University of Colorado, Boulder.

Fox, B. A. (1993). *The Human Tutorial Dialogue Project: Issues in the design of instructional systems.* Hillsdale, NJ: Erlbaum.

Frederiksen, J. R., & Collins, A. (1989). A systems approach to educational testing. *Educational Researcher, 18,* 27–32.

French, L. (1987). *Effects of partner and setting on young children's discourse: A case study.* Unpublished manuscript, University of Rochester, New York.

Freund, L. S. (1990). Maternal regulation of children's problem-solving behavior and its impact on children's performance. *Child Development, 61,* 113–126.

Garvey, C. (1986). Peer relations and the growth of communication. In E. C. Mueller & C. R. Cooper (Eds.), *Process and outcome in peer relationships* (pp. 329–345). Orlando, FL: Academic Press.

Gauvain, M. (1992). Social influences on the development of planning in advance and during action. *International Journal of Behavioral Development, 15,* 377–398.

Gauvain, M. (1993). Spatial thinking and its development in sociocultural context. *Annals of Child Development, 9,* 67–102.

Gauvain, M. (1994, August). *Spatial planning, peer collaboration, and the problem of the Konigsberg bridges.* Paper presented at the meetings of the American Psychological Association, Los Angeles.

Gauvain, M. (1995). Influence of the purpose of an interaction on adult-child planning. *Infancia y Aprendizaje, 69–70,* 141–155.

Gauvain, M., & Rogoff, B. (1989). Collaborative problem solving and children's planning skills. *Developmental Psychology, 25,* 139–151.

Gearhart, M. (1979, March). *Social planning: Role play in a novel situation.* Paper presented at the meetings of the Society for Research in Child Development, San Francisco.

Gellatly, A. (1989). The myth of cognitive diagnostics. In A. Gellatly, D. Rogers, & J. A. Sloboda (Eds.), *Cognition and social worlds* (pp. 113–131). Oxford, England: Clarendon Press.

Giaconia, R. M., & Hedges, L. V. (1982). Identifying features of effective open education. *Review of Educational Research, 52,* 579–602.

Gibson, E. J. (1982). The concept of affordances in development: The renascence of functionalism. In W. A. Collins (Ed.), *Minnesota Symposium of Child Psychology* (Vol. 1, pp. 55–81). Hillsdale, NJ: Erlbaum.

Gibson, J. J. (1979). *The ecological approach to visual perception.* Boston: Houghton Mifflin.

Gillam, A., Callaway, S., & Wikoff, K. H. (1994). The role of authority and the authority of roles in peer writing tutorials. *Journal of Teaching Writing, 12,* 161–198.

Glachan, M., & Light, P. (1982). Peer interaction and learning: Can two wrongs make a right? In G. Butterworth & P. Light (Eds.), *Social cognition: Studies of the development of understanding* (pp. 238–262). Brighton, England: Harvester Press.

Goldsmith, D., & Rogoff, B. (1995). Sensitivity and teaching by dysphoric and nondysphoric women in structured versus unstructured situations. *Developmental Psychology, 31,* 388–394.

Goldsmith, D., & Rogoff, B. (1997). Mothers' and toddlers' coordinated joint focus of attention: Variations with maternal dysphoric symptoms. *Developmental Psychology, 33,* 113–119.

Göncü, A. (1987). Toward an interactional model of developmental changes in social pretend play. In L. G. Katz & K. Steiner (Eds.), *Current topics in early childhood education* (Vol. 7, pp. 126–149). Norwood, NJ: ABLEX.

Göncü, A., & Rogoff, B. (submitted). *Children's categorization with varying adult support.* Manuscript submitted for publication.

Goodnow, J. J. (1976). The nature of intelligent behavior: Questions raised by cross-cultural studies. In L. B. Resnick (Ed.), *The nature of intelligence.* (pp. 169–188). Hillsdale, NJ: Erlbaum.

Goodnow, J. J. (1987, November). *The socialization of cognition: What's involved?* Paper presented at the conference on Culture and Human Development, Chicago.

Goody, E. N. (1989). Learning, apprenticeship and the division of labor. In M. W. Coy (Ed.), *Apprenticeship: From theory to method and back again* (pp. 233–256). Albany: State University of New York Press.

Graves, L. N. (1992). Cooperative learning communities: Context for a new vision of education and society. *Journal of Education, 174,* 57–79.

Graves, Z. R., & Glick, J. (1978). The effect of context on mother-child interaction. *Quarterly Newsletter of the Institute for Comparative Human Development, 2,* 41–46.

Greene, M. (1986). Philosophy and teaching. In M. C. Wittrock (Ed.), *Handbook of research on teaching* (3rd ed., pp. 479–501). New York: Macmillan.

Greenfield, P. M. (1984). A theory of the teacher in the learning activities of everyday life. In B. Rogoff & J. Lave (Eds.), *Everyday cognition: Its development in social context* (pp. 117–138). Cambridge, MA: Harvard University Press.

Greenfield, P. M., & Smith, J. (1976). *The structure of communication in early language development.* New York: Academic Press.

Griffin, P., & Cole, M. (1984). Current activity for the future: The zo-ped. In B. Rogoff & J. V. Wertsch (Eds.), *Children's*

learning in the *"zone of proximal development"* (pp. 45–64). San Francisco: Jossey-Bass.

Gunnar, M. R., & Stone, C. (1984). The effects of positive maternal affect on infant responses to pleasant, ambiguous, and fear-provoking toys. *Child Development, 55,* 1231–1236.

Gutierrez, K., Kreuter, B., & Larson, J. (1995). Script, counterscript and underlife in the classroom: James Brown vs. *Brown vs. the Board of Education. Harvard Education Review, 65,* 445–471.

Harding, C. G. (1982). *Prelanguage vocalizations and words.* Paper presented at the International Conference on Infant Studies, Austin, TX.

Harkness, S., & Super, C. M. (1977). Why African children are so hard to test. In L. L. Adler (Ed.), *Issues in cross-cultural research. Annals of the New York Academy of Sciences, 285,* 326–331.

Hartup, W. W. (1977, Fall). Peers, play, and pathology: A new look at the social behavior of children. *Newsletter of the Society for Research in Child Development.*

Hatano, G. (1994). Introduction: Conceptual change—Japanese perspectives. *Human Development, 37,* 189–197.

Hatano, G., & Inagaki, K. (1991). Sharing cognition through collective comprehension activity. In L. B. Resnick, J. M. Levine, & S. D. Teasley (Eds.), *Perspectives on socially shared cognition* (pp. 331–348). Washington, DC: American Psychological Association.

Hawkins, J. (1987, April). *Collaboration and dissent.* Paper presented at the meetings of the Society for Research in Child Development, Baltimore.

Hay, D. F. (1980). Multiple functions of proximity seeking in infancy. *Child Development, 51,* 636–645.

Hay, D. F., Murray, P., Cecire, S., & Nash, A. (1985). Social learning of social behavior in early life. *Child Development, 56,* 43–57.

Haynes, N. M., & Gebreyseus, S. (1992). Cooperative learning: A case for African American students. *School Psychology Review, 21,* 577–585.

Heath, S. B. (1983). *Ways with words: Language, life, and work in communities and classrooms.* Cambridge, England: Cambridge University Press.

Heber, M. (1981). Instruction *versus* conversation as opportunities for learning. In W. P. Robinson (Ed.), *Communication in development* (pp. 183–202). London: Academic Press.

Heckhausen, J. (1984). *Mother-infant dyads in joint object-centered action.* Unpublished doctoral dissertation, University of Strathclyde, Glasgow.

Henderson, B. B. (1984). Parents and exploration: The effect of context on individual differences in exploratory behavior. *Child Development, 55,* 1237–1245.

Hennessy, S. (1993). Situated cognition and cognitive apprenticeship: Implications for classroom learning. *Studies in Science and Education, 22,* 1–41.

Hodapp, R. M., Goldfield, E. C., & Boyatzis, C. J. (1984). The use and effectiveness of maternal scaffolding in mother-infant games. *Child Development, 55,* 772–781.

Hoff-Ginsberg, E., & Shatz, M. (1982). Linguistic input and the child's acquisition of language. *Psychological Bulletin, 92,* 3–26.

Hollos, M. (1980). Collective education in Hungary: The development of competitive, cooperative and role-taking behaviors. *Ethos, 8,* 3–23.

Holloway, S. (1992). A potential wolf in sheep's clothing: The ambiguity of "cooperation." *Journal of Education, 174,* 80–99.

Hooper, S., Temiyakarn, C., & Williams, M. D. (1993). The effects of cooperative learning and learner control on high- and average-ability students. *Educational Technology Research and Development, 41,* 5–18.

Howe, C., Tolmie, A., & Rodgers, C. (1990). Physics in the primary school: Peer interaction and the understanding of floating and sinking. *European Journal of Psychology of Education, 5,* 459–475.

Huber, G. L., & Eppler, R. (1990). Team learning in German classrooms: Processes and outcomes. In S. Sharan (Ed.), *Cooperative learning: Theory and research* (pp. 151–171). New York: Praeger.

Hutchins, E. (1995). *Cognition in the wild.* Cambridge, MA: MIT Press.

Irvine, J. T. (1978). Wolof "magical thinking": Culture and conservation revisited. *Journal of Cross-Cultural Psychology, 9,* 300–310.

Johnson, D. W., & Johnson, R. T. (1987). *Learning together and alone: Cooperative, competitive, and individualistic learning* (2nd ed.). Englewood Cliffs, NJ: Prentice-Hall.

Johnson, D. W., & Johnson, R. T. (1989). *Cooperation and competition: Theory and research.* Edina, MN: Interaction.

Johnson, D. W., & Johnson, R. T. (1990). Cooperative learning and achievement. In S. Sharan (Ed.), *Cooperative learning: Theory and research* (pp. 23–37). New York: Praeger.

Johnson, D. W., Johnson, R. T., Stanne, M. B., & Garibaldi, A. (1989). Impact of goal and resource interdependence on problem-solving success. *Journal of Social Psychology, 129,* 621–629.

Johnson, D. W., Johnson, R. T., & Taylor, B. (1993). Impact of cooperative and individualistic learning on high-ability students' achievement, self-esteem, and social acceptance. *Journal of Social Psychology, 133,* 839–844.

John-Steiner, V. (1985). *Notebooks of the mind: Explorations of thinking.* Albuquerque: University of New Mexico Press.

John-Steiner, V. (1992). Creative lives, creative tensions. *Creativity Research Journal, 5,* 99–108.

John-Steiner, V., & Tatter, P. (1983). An interactionist model of language development. In B. Bain (Ed.), *The sociogenesis of language and human conduct* (pp. 79–97). New York: Plenum Press.

Kaye, K. (1977). Infants' effects upon their mothers' teaching strategies. In J. D. Glidewell (Ed.), *The social context of learning and development* (pp. 173–206). New York: Gardner Press.

Kaye, K. (1982). Organism, apprentice, and person. In E. Z. Tronick (Ed.), *Social interchange in infancy* (pp. 183–196). Baltimore: University Park Press.

Kelley, L., & Sutton-Smith, B. (1987). A study of infant musical productivity. In J. C. Peery, I. W. Peery, & W. Thomas (Eds.), *Music and child development* (pp. 35–53). New York: Springer-Verlag.

Kindermann, T., & Valsiner, J. (1989). Strategies for empirical research in context-inclusive developmental psychology. In J. Valsiner (Ed.), *Child development in cultural context* (pp. 13–50). Toronto: Hogrefe & Huber.

Knight, G. P., & Bohlmeyer, E. M. (1990). Cooperative learning and achievement: Methods for assessing causal mechanisms. In S. Sharan (Ed.), *Cooperative learning.* New York: Praeger.

Kobayashi, Y. (1994). Conceptual acquisition and change through social interaction. *Human Development, 37,* 233–241.

Koester, L. S., & Bueche, N. A. (1980). Preschoolers as teachers: When children are seen but not heard. *Child Study Journal, 10,* 107–118.

Kohn, A. (1992). Resistance to cooperative learning: Making sense of its deletion and dilution. *Journal of Education, 174,* 38–56.

Kohn, A. (1993, September). Choices for children: Why and how to let students decide. *Phi Delta Kappan,* 8–20.

Kozulin, A. (1990). *Vygotsky's psychology: A biography of ideas.* New York: Harvester Wheatsheaf.

Kruger, A. C. (1992). The effect of peer and adult-child transactive discussions on moral reasoning. *Merrill-Palmer Quarterly, 38,* 191–211.

Kruger, A. C. (1993). Peer collaboration: Conflict, collaboration, or both? *Social Development, 2,* 165–182.

Kruger, A. C. (1994). Task influences on spontaneous peer learning in the classroom. In H. C. Foot, C. J. Howe, A. Anderson, A. K. Tolmie, & D. A. Warden (Eds.), *Group and interactive learning* (pp. 459–464). Southampton, England: Computational Mechanics.

Kruger, A. C., & Tomasello, M. (1986). Transactive discussions with peers and adults. *Developmental Psychology, 22,* 681–685.

Kruper, J. C., & Uzgiris, I. C. (1985, April). *Fathers' and mothers' speech to infants*. Paper presented at the meetings of the Society for Research in Child Development, Toronto.

Kuhn, D. (1972). Mechanisms of change in the development of cognitive structures. *Child Development, 43,* 833–842.

Kuhn, D. (1995). Microgenetic study of change: What has it told us? *Psychological Science, 6,* 133–139.

Kvale, S. (1977). Dialectics and research on remembering. In N. Datan & H. W. Reese (Eds.), *Life-span developmental psychology: Dialectical perspectives on experimental research* (pp. 165–189). New York: Academic Press.

Laboratory of Comparative Human Cognition. (1983). Culture and cognitive development. In P. H. Mussen (Series Ed.) & W. Kessen (Vol. Ed.), *Handbook of child psychology: Vol. 1, History, theory, and methods* (pp. 294–356). New York: Wiley.

Lacasa, P., Herranz-Ybarra, P., Martín-del-Campo, B., & Pardo-de-León, P. (1994, July). *The role of children's goals when they plan texts together in the classroom*. Paper presented at the International Congress of Applied Psychology, Madrid.

Lacasa, P., & Villuendas, D. (1990). Adult-child and peer relationship: Action, representation, and learning process. *Learning and Instruction, 2,* 75–93.

Lamphere, L. (1977). *To run after them: Cultural and social bases of cooperation in a Navajo community*. Tucson: University of Arizona Press.

Lancy, D. F. (1980). Play in species adaptation. *Annual Review of Anthropology, 9,* 471–495.

Lave, J. (1988a, May). *The culture of acquisition and the practice of understanding* (Rep. No. IRL 88-0007). Palo Alto, CA: Institute for Research on Learning.

Lave, J. (1988b). *Cognition in practice*. Cambridge, England: Cambridge University Press.

Lave, J., & Wenger, E. (1991). *Situated learning: Legitimate peripheral participation*. Cambridge, England: Cambridge University Press.

Lazarowitz, R., & Karsenty, G. (1990). Cooperative learning and students' academic achievement, process skills, learning environment, and self-esteem in tenth-grade biology classrooms. In S. Sharan (Ed.), *Cooperative learning: Theory and research* (pp. 123–149). New York: Praeger.

Lempers, J. D. (1979). Young children's production and comprehension of nonverbal deictic behaviors. *Journal of Genetic Psychology, 135,* 93–102.

Leont'ev, A. N. (1981). The problem of activity in psychology. In J. V. Wertsch (Ed.), *The concept of activity in Soviet psychology* (pp. 37–71). Armonk, NY: Sharpe.

Lerner, G. H. (1993). Collectivities in action: Establishing the relevance of conjoined participation in conversation. *Text, 13,* 213–245.

Levin, I., & Druyan, S. (1993). When sociocognitive transaction among peers fails: The case of misconceptions in science. *Child Development, 64,* 1571–1591.

Lewis, M., & Feiring, C. (1981). Direct and indirect interactions in social relationships. In L. P. Lipsett (Ed.), *Advances in infancy research* (Vol. 1, pp. 129–161). Norwood, NJ: ABLEX.

Light, P., Foot, T., Colbourn, C., & McClelland, I. (1987). Collaborative interactions at the microcomputer keyboard. *Educational Psychology, 7,* 13–21.

Light, P., & Glachan, M. (1985). Facilitation of individual problem solving through peer interaction. *Educational Psychology, 5,* 217–225.

Light, P., Littleton, K., Messer, D., & Joiner, R. (1994). Social and communicative processes in computer-based problem solving. *European Journal of Psychology of Education, 9,* 93–109.

Litowitz, B. E. (1993). Deconstruction in the zone of proximal development. In E. A. Forman, N. Minick, & C. A. Stone (Eds.), *Contexts for learning* (pp. 184–196). New York: Oxford University Press.

Little Soldier, L. (1989). Cooperative learning and the Native American student. *Phi Delta Kappan, 71,* 161–163.

Lock, A. (1978). The emergence of language. In A. Lock (Ed.), *Action, gesture and symbol: The emergence of language* (pp. 3–18). London: Academic Press.

Lomov, B. F. (1978). Psychological processes and communication. *Soviet Psychology, 17,* 3–22.

Lubomudrov, C. (in press). Decision making in a learning community. In L. Bartlett, C. Goodman Turkanis, & B. Rogoff (Eds.), *Learning as a community*. New York: Oxford University Press.

Luria, A. R. (1987). Afterword to the Russian edition. In R. W. Rieber & A. S. Carton (Eds.), *The collected works of L. S. Vygotsky: Vol. 1, Problems of general psychology* (pp. 359–373). New York: Plenum Press.

Lutz, C., & LeVine, R. A. (1982). Culture and intelligence in infancy: An ethnopsychological view. In M. Lewis (Ed.), *Origins of intelligence: Infancy and early childhood* (pp. 1–28). New York: Plenum Press.

MacLachlan, P. (1989). Dialogue between Charlotte Zolotow and Patricia MacLachlan. *Horn Book, 65,* 740–741.

Magkaev, V. K. (1977). An experimental study of the planning function of thinking in young schoolchildren. In M. Cole (Ed.), *Soviet developmental psychology: An anthology* (pp. 606–620). White Plains, NY: Sharpe.

Manning, M. L., & Lucking, R. (1993). Cooperative learning and multicultural classrooms. *Clearing House, 67,* 12–16.

Mannle, S., & Tomasello, M. (1989). Fathers, siblings, and the Bridge Hypothesis. In K. Nelson & A. van Kleeck (Eds.),

Children's language (Vol. 6, pp. 23–42). Hillsdale, NJ: Erlbaum.

Martinez, M. A. (1987). Dialogues among children and between children and their mothers. *Child Development, 58,* 1035–1043.

Martini, M. (1994). Peer interactions in Polynesia: A view from the Marquesas. In J. L. Roopnarine, J. E. Johnson, & F. H. Hooper (Eds.), *Children's play in diverse cultures.* Albany, NY: SUNY Press.

Martini, M., & Kirkpatrick, J. (1981). Early interactions in the Marquesas Islands. In T. M. Fields, A. M. Sostek, P. Vietze, & P. H. Leiderman (Eds.), *Culture and early interactions* (pp. 189–213). Hillsdale, NJ: Erlbaum.

Martini, M., & Kirkpatrick, J. (1992). Parenting in Polynesia: A view from the Marquesas. In J. L. Roopnarine & D. B. Carter (Eds.), *Parent-child socialization in diverse cultures: Vol. 5. Annual advances in applied developmental psychology* (pp. 199–222). Norwood, NJ: ABLEX.

Masur, E. F. (1982). Mothers' responses to infants' object-related gestures: Influences on lexical development. *Journal of Child Language, 9,* 23–30.

Matusov, E. L. (1995, April). *Intersubjectivity without agreement.* Paper presented at the American Educational Research Association, San Francisco.

Matusov, E. L., Bell, N., & Rogoff, B. (submitted). *Collaboration and assistance in problem solving by children differing in cooperative schooling backgrounds.* Manuscript submitted for publication.

McArthur, D., Stasz, C., & Zmuidzinas, M. (1990). Tutoring techniques in algebra. *Cognition and Instruction, 7,* 197–244.

McLane, J. B. (1987). Interaction, context, and the zone of proximal development. In M. Hickmann (Ed.), *Social and functional approaches to language and thought* (pp. 267–285). Orlando, FL: Academic Press.

McNamee, G. D. (1980). *The social origins of narrative skills.* Unpublished doctoral dissertation, Northwestern University, Evanston, IL.

Mehan, H. (1976). Assessing children's school performance. In J. Beck, C. Jenks, N. Keddie, & M. F. D. Young (Eds.), *Worlds apart* (pp. 161–180). London: Collier Macmillan.

Mehan, H. (1979). *Learning lessons: Social organization in the classroom.* Cambridge, MA: Harvard University Press.

Meloth, M. S., & Deering, P. D. (1994). Task talk and task awareness under different cooperative learning conditions. *American Educational Research Journal, 31,* 138–165.

Mercer, N. (1995). *The guided construction of knowledge: Talk amongst teachers and learners.* Clevedon, England: Multilingual Matters.

Merrill, D. C., Reiser, B. J., Merrill, S. K., & Landes, S. (1995). Tutoring: Guided learning by doing. *Cognition and Instruction, 13,* 315–372.

Mervis, C. B. (1984). Early lexical development: The contributions of mother and child. In C. Sophian (Ed.), *Origins of cognitive skills* (pp. 339–370). Hillsdale, NJ: Erlbaum.

Messer, D. J. (1980). The episodic structure of maternal speech to young children. *Journal of Child Language, 7,* 29–40.

Messer, D. J., Joiner, R., Loveridge, N., Light, P., & Littleton, K. (1993). Influences on the effectiveness of peer interaction: Children's level of cognitive development and the relative ability of partners. *Social Development, 2,* 279–294

Michaels, S., & Cazden, C. B. (1986). Teacher/child collaboration as oral preparation for literacy. In B. B. Schieffelin & P. Gilmore (Eds.), *The acquisition of literacy.* Norwood, NJ: Erlbaum.

Miller, M. (1987). Argumentation and cognition. In M. Hickmann (Ed.), *Social and functional approaches to language and thought* (pp. 225–249). Orlando, FL: Academic Press.

Mistry, J. (1993). Cultural context in the development of children's narratives. In J. Altarriba (Ed.), *Cognition and culture: A cross-cultural approach to psychology* (pp. 207–228). New York: Elsevier.

Mistry, J., & Rogoff, B. (in press). *Meaningful purpose in children's remembering.* Manuscript submitted for publication.

Moll, L. C., & Whitmore, K. F. (1993). Vygotsky in classroom practice: Moving from individual transmission to social transaction. In E. A. Forman, N. Minick, & C. A. Stone (Eds.), *Contexts for learning* (pp. 19–42) New York: Oxford University Press.

Morelli, G. A., Rogoff, B., & Angelillo, C. (submitted). *Cultural variation in children's involvement in mature activities or in specialized child activities.* Manuscript submitted for publication.

Mosier, C. E., & Rogoff, B. (1994). Infants' instrumental use of their mothers to achieve their goals. *Child Development, 65,* 70–79.

Mosier, C. E., & Rogoff, B. (submitted). *Cultural variation in young siblings' roles: Autonomy and responsibility.* Manuscript submitted for publication.

Mugny, G., & Doise, W. (1978). Socio-cognitive conflict and structure of individual and collective performances. *European Journal of Social Psychology, 8,* 181–192.

Mugny, G., Perret-Clermont, A. -N., & Doise, W. (1981). Interpersonal coordinations and social differences in the construction of the intellect. In G. M. Stephenson & J. M. Davis (Eds.), *Progress in applied psychology* (Vol. 1, pp. 315–343). New York: Wiley.

Murray, L., & Trevarthen, C. (1985). Emotional regulation of interactions between 2-month-olds and their mothers. In

T. M. Field & N. Fox (Eds.), *Social perception in infants* (pp. 177–197). Norwood, NJ: ABLEX.

Nelson, J., & Aboud, F. E. (1985). The resolution of social conflict between friends. *Child Development, 56,* 1009–1017.

Nelson, K. E. (1995, April). *Social narrative as a "cure" for childhood amnesia.* Paper presented at the meetings of the Society for Research in Child Development, Indianapolis.

Nelson, K. E., Denninger, M. S., Bonvillian, J. D., Kaplan, B. J., & Baker, N. D. (1984). Maternal input adjustments and nonadjustments as related to children's linguistic advances and to language acquisition theories. In A. D. Pellegrini & T. D. Yawkey (Eds.), *The development of oral and written language in social contexts* (pp. 31–56). Norwood, NJ: ABLEX.

Nelson-Le Gall, S. (1985). Help-seeking behavior in learning. In E. W. Gordon (Ed.), *Review of research in education* (Vol. 12, pp. 55–90). Washington, DC: American Educational Research Association.

Nelson-Le Gall, S. (1992). Children's instrumental help-seeking: Its role in the social acquisition and construction of knowledge. In R. Hertz-Lazarowitz & N. Miller (Eds.), *Interaction in cooperative groups.* Cambridge, England: Cambridge University Press.

Newman, D., Griffin, P., & Cole, M. (1984). Social constraints in laboratory and classroom tasks. In B. Rogoff & J. Lave (Eds.), *Everyday cognition: Its development in social context* (pp. 172–193). Cambridge, MA: Harvard University Press.

Newman, D., Griffin, P., & Cole, M. (1989). *The construction zone: Working for cognitive change in school.* Cambridge, England: Cambridge University Press.

Newson, J. (1977). An intersubjective approach to the systematic description of mother-infant interaction. In H. R. Schaffer (Ed.), *Studies in mother-infant interaction* (pp. 47–61). New York: Academic Press.

Newson, J., & Newson, E. (1975). Intersubjectivity and the transmission of culture: On the social origins of symbolic functioning. *Bulletin of the British Psychological Society, 28,* 437–446.

Nichols, J. D., & Miller, R. B. (1994). Cooperative learning and student motivation. *Contemporary Educational Psychology, 19,* 167–178.

Nicolopoulou, A. (1993). Play, cognitive development, and the social world: Piaget, Vygotsky, and beyond. *Human Development, 36,* 1–23.

Nicolopoulou, A., & Cole, M. (1993). Generation and transmission of shared knowledge in the culture of collaborative learning. In E. A. Forman, N. Minick, & C. A. Stone (Eds.), *Contexts for learning* (pp. 283–314). New York: Oxford University Press.

Nsamenang, A. B. (1992). *Human development in cultural context: A third-world perspective.* Newbury Park, CA: Sage.

Oakeshott, M. J. (1962). *Rationalism in politics, and other essays.* New York: Basic Books.

Ochs, E. (1979). Introduction: What child language can contribute to pragmatics. In E. Ochs & B. Schieffelin (Eds.), *Developmental pragmatics* (pp. 1–17). New York: Academic Press.

Ochs, E. (1988). *Culture and language development: Language acquisition and language socialization in a Samoan village.* Cambridge, England: Cambridge University Press.

Ochs, E. (1994). Stories that step into the future. In D. Biber & E. Finegan (Eds.), *Sociolinguistic perspectives on register* (pp. 106–135). New York: Oxford University Press.

Ochs, E., Jacoby, S., & Gonzales, P. (1994). Interpretive journeys: How physicists talk and travel through graphic space. *Configurations, 1,* 151–171.

Ochs, E., & Schieffelin, B. B. (1994). The impact of language socialization on grammatical development. In P. Fletcher & B. MacWhinney (Eds.), *Handbook of child language.* Oxford, England: Blackwell.

Ochs, E., Schieffelin, B. B., & Platt, M. (1979). Propositions across utterances and speakers. In E. Ochs & B. B. Schieffelin (Eds.), *Developmental pragmatics.* New York: Academic Press.

Ochs, E., Taylor, C., Rudolph, D., & Smith, R. (1992). Storytelling as a theory-building activity. *Discourse Processes, 15,* 37–72.

O'Donnell, A. M., & Dansereau, D. F. (1992). Scripted cooperation in student dyads: A method for analyzing and enhancing academic learning and performance. In R. Hertz-Lazarowitz & N. Miller (Eds.), *Interaction in cooperative groups: The theoretical anatomy of group learning* (pp. 120–141). Cambridge, England: Cambridge University Press.

O'Donnell, A. M., Dansereau, D. F., Rocklin, T., Lambiotte, J. G., Hythecker, V. I., & Larson, C. O. (1985). Cooperative writing: Direct effects and transfer. *Written Communication, 2,* 307–315.

Olson, S. L., Bates, J. E., & Bayles, K. (1984). Mother-infant interaction and the development of individual differences in children's cognitive competence. *Developmental Psychology, 20,* 166–179.

Pacifici, C., & Bearison, D. J. (1991). Development of children's self-regulations in idealized and mother-child interactions. *Cognitive Development, 6,* 261–277.

Packer, M. J. (1983). Communication in early infancy: Three common assumptions examined and found inadequate. *Human Development, 26,* 233–248.

Packer, M. J. (1993). Away from internalization. In E. A. Forman, N. Minick, & C. A. Stone (Eds.), *Contexts for learning* (pp. 254–265). New York: Oxford University Press.

Packer, M. J. (1994). Cultural work on the kindergarten playground: Articulating the ground of play. *Human Development, 37*, 259–276.

Packer, M. J., & Scott, B. (1992). The hermeneutic investigation of peer relations. In T. Winegar & J. Valsiner (Eds.), *Children's development within social context: Vol. 2. Research and methodology* (pp. 75–111). Hillsdale, NJ: Erlbaum.

Papousek, M., Papousek, H., & Bornstein, M. H. (1985). The naturalistic vocal environment of young infants. In T. M. Field & N. Fox (Eds.), *Social perception in infants* (pp. 269–298). Norwood, NJ: ABLEX.

Palincsar, A. S., Brown, A. L., & Martin, S. M. (1987). Peer interaction in reading comprehension instruction. *Educational Psychologist, 22*, 231–253.

Parrinello, R. M., & Ruff, H. A. (1988). The influence of adult intervention on infants' level of attention. *Child Development, 59*, 1125–1135.

Patterson, C., & Roberts, R. (1982). Planning and the development of communication skills. In D. Forbes & M. Greenberg (Eds.), *Children's planning strategies: New directions for child development* (pp. 29–46). San Francisco: Jossey-Bass.

Pea, R. D. (1993). Practices of distributed intelligence and designs for education. In G. Salomon (Ed.), *Distributed cognitions* (pp. 47–87). Cambridge, England: Cambridge University Press.

Pea, R. D., & Gomez, L. M. (1992). Distributed multimedia learning environments: Why and how? *Interactive Learning Environments, 2*, 73–109.

Pearson, P. D., & Gallagher, M. C. (1983). The instruction of reading comprehension. *Contemporary Educational Psychology, 8*, 317–344.

Pepper, S. C. (1942). *World hypotheses: A study in evidence.* Berkeley: University of California Press.

Perlmutter, M., Behrend, S. D., Kuo, F., & Muller, A. (1989). Social influences on children's problem solving. *Developmental Psychology, 25*, 744–754.

Perret-Clermont, A. -N. (1993). What is it that develops? *Cognition and Instruction, 11*, 197–205.

Perret-Clermont, A. -N., Perret, J. F., & Bell, N. (1991). The social construction of meaning and cognitive activity in elementary school children. In J. M. Levine, L. B. Resnick, & S. Behrend (Eds.), *Socially shared cognition* (pp. 41–62). New York: APA Press.

Perret-Clermont, A. -N., & Schubauer-Leoni, M. -L. (1981). Conflict and cooperation as opportunities for learning. In P. Robinson (Ed.), *Communication in development* (pp. 203–233). London: Academic Press.

Peterson, C., & McCabe, A. (1994). A social interactionist account of developing decontextualized narrative skill. *Developmental Psychology, 30*, 937–948.

Peterson, P., Wilkinson, L., Spinelli, F., & Swing, S. (1982). *Merging the progress-product and the sociolinguistic paradigms: Research on small-group processes.* Paper presented at the conference on "Student Diversity and the Organization, Processes and Use of Instructional Groups in the Classroom," Wisconsin Center for Educational Research, Madison.

Petitto, A. L. (1983). *Long division of labor: In support of an interactive learning theory.* Unpublished manuscript, University of Rochester, New York.

Phelps, E., & Damon, W. (1989). Problem solving with equals: Peer collaboration as a context for learning mathematics and spatial concepts. *Journal of Educational Psychology, 81*, 639–646.

Piaget, J. (1926). *The language and thought of the child.* New York: Harcourt, Brace.

Piaget, J. (1977/1928). Logique génétique et sociologie. In *Etudes sociologiques* (pp. 203–239). Geneva, Switzerland: Librairie Droz. (Reprinted from *"Revue Philosophique de la France et de l'Etranger,"* 53, nos. 3 and 4, pp. 161–205, 1928)

Piaget, J. (1977). Les operations logiques et la vie sociale. In *Etudes sociologiques* (pp. 143–171). Geneva, Switzerland: Librairie Droz.

Piaget, J. (1977/1963). Problèmes de la psycho-sociologie de l'enfance. In *Etudes sociologiques* (pp. 320–356). Geneva, Switzerland: Librairie Droz. (Reprinted from *Traité de sociologie*, pp. 229–254, by G. Gurvitch, 1963, Paris: PUF)

Plumert, J. M., & Nichols-Whitehead, P. (1996). Parental scaffolding of young children's spatial communication. *Developmental Psychology, 32*, 523–532.

Pontecorvo, L., & Girardet, H. (1993). Arguing and reasoning in understanding historical topics. *Cognition and Instruction, 11*, 365–395.

Pribram, K. H. (1990). From metaphors to models: The use of analogy in neuropsychology. In D. E. Leary (Ed.), *Metaphors in the history of psychology* (pp. 79–103). Cambridge, England: Cambridge University Press.

Radziszewska, B. (1993, April). *Sociocognitive processes in adult-child and peer collaboration on conservation of area and volume tasks.* Unpublished manuscript, California State University, Long Beach.

Radziszewska, B., & Rogoff, B. (1988). Influence of adult and peer collaborators on children's planning skills. *Developmental Psychology, 24*, 840–848.

Radziszewska, B., & Rogoff, B. (1991). Children's guided participation in planning imaginary errands with skilled adult or peer partners. *Developmental Psychology, 27*, 381–389.

Reese, E., Haden, C. A., & Fivush, R. (1993). Mother-child conversations about the past: Relationships of style and memory over time. *Cognitive Development, 8*, 403–430.

Rheingold, H. L. (1969). The social and socializing infant. In D. A. Goslin (Ed.), *Handbook of socialization theory and research* (pp. 779–790). Chicago: Rand McNally.

Rheingold, H. L. (1982). Little children's participation in the work of adults, a nascent prosocial behavior. *Child Development, 53,* 114–125.

Riegel, K. F. (1979). *Foundations of dialectical psychology.* New York: Academic Press.

Rodrigo, M. J., & Batista, M. L. (1995). Planificar para razonar y planificar para trazar rutas: Aprendizaje y transferencia de la planificación en colaboración y por adelantado. *Infancia y Aprendizaje, 69–70,* 183–202.

Rogoff, B. (1981). Schooling and the development of cognitive skills. In H. C. Triandis & A. Heron (Eds.), *Handbook of cross-cultural psychology* (Vol. 4, pp. 233–294). Rockleigh, NJ: Allyn & Bacon.

Rogoff, B. (1982). Integrating context and cognitive development. In M. E. Lamb & A. L. Brown (Eds.), *Advances in developmental psychology* (Vol. 2, pp. 125–170). Hillsdale, NJ: Erlbaum.

Rogoff, B. (1986). Adult assistance of children's learning. In T. E. Raphael (Ed.), *The contexts of school-based literacy* (pp. 27–40). New York: Random House.

Rogoff, B. (1990). *Apprenticeship in thinking: Cognitive development in social context.* New York: Oxford University Press.

Rogoff, B. (1992). Three ways to relate person and culture. *Human Development, 35,* 316–320.

Rogoff, B. (1994). Developing understanding of the idea of community of learners. *Mind, Culture, and Activity, 1,* 209–229.

Rogoff, B. (1995). Observing sociocultural activity on three planes: Participatory appropriation, guided participation, and apprenticeship. In J. V. Wertsch, P. del Rio, & A. Alvarez (Eds.), *Sociocultural studies of mind* (pp. 139–164). Cambridge, England: Cambridge University Press.

Rogoff, B. (1996). Developmental transitions in children's participation in sociocultural activities. In A. Sameroff & M. Haith (Eds.), *The five to seven year shift: The age of reason and responsibility* (pp. 273–294). Chicago: University of Chicago Press.

Rogoff, B. (in press). Evaluating development in the process of participation: Theory, methods, and practice building on each other. In E. Amsel & A. Renninger (Eds.), *Change and development: Issues of theory, application, and method.* Hillsdale, NJ: Erlbaum.

Rogoff, B., Baker-Sennett, J., Lacasa, P., & Goldsmith, D. (1995). Development through participation in sociocultural activity. In J. J. Goodnow, P. J. Miller, & F. Kessel (Eds.), *Cultural practices as contexts for development* (pp. 45–65). San Francisco: Jossey-Bass.

Rogoff, B., Baker-Sennett, J., & Matusov, E. (1994). Considering the concept of planning. In M. M. Haith, J. B. Benson, R. J. Roberts, Jr., & B. F. Pennington (Eds.), *The development of future-oriented processes* (pp. 353–373). Chicago: University of Chicago Press.

Rogoff, B., & Chavajay, P. (1995). What's become of research on the cultural basis of cognitive development? *American Psychologist, 50,* 859–877.

Rogoff, B., Ellis, S., & Gardner, W. (1984). The adjustment of adult-child instruction according to child's age and task. *Developmental Psychology, 20,* 193–199.

Rogoff, B., & Gardner, W. P. (1984). Adult guidance of cognitive development. In B. Rogoff & J. Lave (Eds.), *Everyday cognition: Its development in social context* (pp. 95–116). Cambridge, MA: Harvard University Press.

Rogoff, B., & Gauvain, M. (1986). A method for the analysis of patterns, illustrated with data on mother-child instructional interaction. In J. Valsiner (Ed.), *The individual subject and scientific psychology* (pp. 261–290). New York: Plenum Press.

Rogoff, B., Gauvain, M., & Ellis, S. (1984). Development viewed in its cultural context. In M. H. Bornstein & M. E. Lamb (Eds.), *Developmental psychology* (pp. 533–571). Hillsdale, NJ: Erlbaum.

Rogoff, B., Malkin, C., & Gilbride, K. (1984). Interaction with babies as guidance in development. In B. Rogoff & J. V. Wertsch (Eds.), *Children's learning in the "zone of proximal development"* (pp. 31–44). San Francisco: Jossey-Bass.

Rogoff, B., Matusov, E., & White, C. (1996). Models of teaching and learning: Participation in a community of learners. In D. Olson & N. Torrance (Eds.), *Handbook of education and human development: New models of learning, teaching, and schooling.* London: Basil Blackwell.

Rogoff, B., Mistry, J., Göncü, A., & Mosier, C. (1993). Guided participation in cultural activity by toddlers and caregivers. *Monographs of the Society for Research in Child Development, 58*(7, Serial No. 236).

Rogoff, B., Mistry, J., Radziszewska, B., & Germond, J. (1992). Infants' instrumental social interaction with adults. In S. Feinman (Ed.), *Social referencing and the social construction of reality in infancy* (pp. 323–348). New York: Plenum Press.

Rogoff, B., Radziszewska, B., & Masiello, T. (1995). Analysis of developmental processes in sociocultural activity. In L. Martin, K. Nelson, & E. Tobach (Eds.), *Sociocultural psychology: Theory and practice of doing and knowing* (pp. 125–149). Cambridge, England: Cambridge University Press.

Rogoff, B., Sellers, M. J., Pirrotta, S., Fox, N., & White, S. H. (1975). Age of assignment of roles and responsibilities to children: A cross-cultural survey. *Human Development, 18,* 353–369.

Rommetveit, R. (1985). Language acquisition as increasing linguistic structuring of experience and symbolic behavior control. In J. V. Wertsch (Ed.), *Culture, communication, and cognition: Vygotskian perspectives* (pp. 183–204). Cambridge, England: Cambridge University Press.

Roschelle, J. (1992). Learning by collaborating: Converging conceptual change. *Journal of the Learning Sciences, 2,* 235–276.

Rubtsov, V. V. (1981). The role of cooperation in the development of intelligence. *Soviet Psychology, 19,* 41–62.

Rubtsov, V. V., & Guzman, R. Y. (1984–1985). Psychological characteristics of the methods pupils use to organize joint activity in dealing with a school task. *Soviet Psychology, 23,* 65–84.

Sarbin, T. (1976). Cross-age tutoring and social identity. In V. Allen (Ed.), *Children as teachers: Theory and research on tutoring* (pp. 27–40). New York: Academic Press.

Saxe, G. B., Gearhart, M., & Guberman, S. B. (1984). The social organization of early number development. In B. Rogoff & J. V. Wertsch (Eds.), *Children's learning in the "zone of proximal development"* (pp. 19–30). San Francisco: Jossey-Bass.

Scaife, M., & Bruner, J. (1975). The capacity for joint visual attention in the infant. *Nature, 253,* 265–266.

Schaffer, H. R. (Ed.). (1977). *Studies in mother-infant interaction.* New York: Academic Press.

Schaffer, H. R. (1984). *The child's entry into a social world.* London: Academic Press.

Schaffer, H. R., Hepburn, A., & Collis, G. M. (1983). Verbal and nonverbal aspects of mothers' directives. *Journal of Child Language, 10,* 337–355.

Schallert, D. L., & Kleiman, G. M. (1979, June). *Some reasons why teachers are easier to understand than textbooks* (Reading Ed. Rep. No. 9). Urbana-Champaign: University of Illinois, Center for the Study of Reading. (ERIC Report No. ED 172 189)

Schieffelin, B. B. (1991). *The give and take of everyday life: Language socialization of Kaluli children.* Cambridge, England: Cambridge University Press.

Schneiderman, M. H. (1983). "Do what I mean, not what I say!" Changes in mothers' action directives to young children. *Journal of Child Language, 10,* 357–367.

Schoenfeld, A. H. (1989). Ideas in the air: Speculations on small group learning, environmental and cultural influences on cognition, and epistemology. *International Journal of Educational Research, 13,* 71–88.

Schoenfeld, A. H. (1993, February). *Reflections on doing and teaching mathematics.* Unpublished manuscript, University of California, Berkeley.

Schrage, M. (1990). *Shared minds.* New York: Random House.

Schubauer-Leoni, M.-L., Bell, N., Grossen, M., & Perret-Clermont, A.-N. (1989). Problems in assessment of learning: The social construction of questions and answers in the scholastic context. *International Journal of Educational Research, 13,* 671–684.

Scollon, R. (1976). *Conversations with a 1-year-old.* Honolulu: University of Hawaii Press.

Scribner, S. (1976). Situating the experiment in cross-cultural research. In K. F. Riegel & J. A. Meacham (Eds.), *The developing individual in a changing world* (Vol. 1, pp. 310–321). Chicago: Aldine.

Scribner, S. (1985). Vygotsky's uses of history. In J. V. Wertsch (Ed.), *Culture, communication, and cognition: Vygotskian perspectives* (pp. 119–145). Cambridge, England: Cambridge University Press.

Scribner, S., & Cole, M. (1973). Cognitive consequences of formal and informal education. *Science, 182,* 553–559.

Scribner, S., & Cole, M. (1981). *The psychology of literacy.* Cambridge, MA: Harvard University Press.

Serpell, R. (1982). Measures of perception, skills and intelligence. In W. W. Hartup (Ed.), *Review of child development research* (Vol. 6, pp. 392–440). Chicago: University of Chicago Press.

Sharan, S. (1990). Cooperative learning and helping behaviour in the multi-ethnic classroom. In H. C. Foot, M. J. Morgan, & R. H. Shute (Eds.), *Children helping children* (pp. 151–176). New York: Wiley.

Sharan, S., & Shaulov, A. (1990). Cooperative learning, motivation to learn, and academic achievement. In S. Sharan (Ed.), *Cooperative learning: Theory and research* (pp. 173–202). New York: Praeger.

Sharan, Y., & Sharan, S. (1992). *Expanding cooperative learning through Group Investigation.* New York: Teachers College Press.

Shatz, M. (1987). Bootstrapping operations in child language. In K. E. Nelson & A. van Kleeck (Eds.), *Children's language* (Vol. 6, pp. 1–22). Hillsdale, NJ: Erlbaum.

Shedd, J. B., & Weaver, B. M. (1995, April). *Reconstructing processes inside and outside the classroom: Curriculum emphasis and adult collaboration in elementary schools.* Paper presented at the meeting of the American Educational Research Association, San Francisco.

Shotter, J. (1978). The cultural context of communication studies: Theoretical and methodological issues. In A. Lock (Ed.), *Action, gesture, and symbol: The emergence of language* (pp. 43–78). London: Academic Press.

Shotter, J., & Newson, J. (1982). An ecological approach to cognitive development: Implicate orders, joint action, and intentionality. In G. Butterworth & P. Light (Eds.), *Social cognition studies in the development of understanding* (pp. 32–52). Brighton, England: Harvester Press.

Sigel, I. E. (1982). The relationship between parental distancing strategies and the child's cognitive behavior. In L. M. Laosa & I. E. Sigel (Eds.), *Families as learning environments for children* (pp. 47–86). New York: Plenum Press.

Sigel, I. E., & Cocking, R. R. (1977). Cognition and communication: A dialectic paradigm for development. In M. Lewis & L. A. Rosenblum (Eds.), *Interaction, conversation, and the development of language: The origins of behavior* (Vol. 5, pp. 207–226). New York: Wiley.

Slavin, R. E. (1987). Developmental and motivational perspectives on cooperative learning: A reconciliation. *Child Development, 58,* 1161–1167.

Slavin, R. E. (1990). *Cooperative learning: Theory, research, and practice.* Boston: Allyn & Bacon.

Snow, C. E. (1977). Mother's speech research: From input to interaction. In C. Snow & C. Ferguson, (Eds.), *Talking to children* (pp. 31–49). Cambridge, England: Cambridge University Press.

Snow, C. E. (1982). Are parents language teachers? In K. Borman (Ed.), *Social life of children in a changing society* (pp. 81–95). Hillsdale, NJ: Erlbaum.

Snow, C. E. (1984). Parent-child interaction and the development of communicative ability. In R. Schiefelbusch & J. Pickar (Eds.), *The acquisition of communicative competence* (pp. 69–107). Baltimore: University Park Press.

Socha, T. J., & Socha, D. M. (1994). Children's task-group communication. In L. R. Frey (Ed.), *Group communication in context: Studies of natural groups* (pp. 227–246). Hillsdale, NJ: Erlbaum.

Solomon, D., Watson, M., Schaps, E., Battistich, V., & Solomon, J. (1990). Cooperative learning as part of a comprehensive classroom program designed to promote prosocial development. In S. Sharan (Ed.), *Cooperative learning: Theory and research* (pp. 231–260). New York: Praeger.

Sorce, J. F., Emde, R. N., Campos, J., & Klinnert, M. D. (1985). Maternal emotional signaling: Its effect on the visual cliff behavior of 1-year-olds. *Developmental Psychology, 21,* 195–200.

Stipek, D. J. (in press). Is child-centered early childhood education really better? In S. Reifel (Ed.), *Advances in early education and day care.* Greenwich, CT: JAI Press.

Stone, C. A. (1993). What is missing in the metaphor of scaffolding? In E. A. Forman, N. Minick, & C. A. Stone (Eds.), *Contexts for learning* (pp. 169–183). New York: Oxford University Press.

Subbotskii, E. V. (1987). Communicative style and the genesis of personality in preschoolers. *Soviet Psychology, 25,* 38–58.

Sugarman-Bell, S. (1978). Some organizational aspects of preverbal communication. In I. Markova (Ed.), *The social context of language* (pp. 49–66). New York: Wiley.

Sutter, B., & Grensjo, B. (1988). Explorative learning in the school? Experiences of local historical research by pupils. *Quarterly Newsletter of the Laboratory of Comparative Human Cognition, 10,* 39–54.

Sylva, K., Bruner, J. S., & Genova, P. (1976). The role of play in the problem-solving of children 3–5 years old. In J. S. Bruner, A. Jolly, & K. Sylva (Eds.), *Play: Its role in development and evolution* (pp. 244–257). New York: Basic Books.

Tharp, R. G. (1993). Institutional and social context of educational practice and reform. In E. A. Forman, N. Minick, & C. A. Stone (Eds.), *Contexts for learning* (pp. 269–282). New York: Oxford.

Tharp, R. G., & Gallimore, R. (1988). *Rousing minds to life: Teaching, learning, and schooling in social context.* Cambridge, England: Cambridge University Press.

Toma, C. (1991a, April). *Speech genre of school in U.S. and Japan.* Paper presented at the meeting of the American Educational Research Association, Chicago.

Toma, C. (1991b, October). *Explicit use of others' voices for constructing arguments in Japanese classroom discourse: An analysis of the use of reported speech.* Paper presented at the Boston University Conference on Language Development, Boston.

Toma, C. (1992, September). *Who is in control? An analysis of the discourse space among a child and parents.* Paper presented at The First Conference for Socio-Cultural Research, Madrid.

Tomasello, M. (1992). The social bases of language acquisition. *Social Development, 1,* 67–87.

Tomasello, M. (1995). Joint attention as social cognition. In C. Moore & P. Dunham (Eds.), *Joint attention: Its origins and role in development* (pp. 103–129). Hillsdale, NJ: Erlbaum.

Tomasello, M. (in press). The cultural roots of language. In B. Velichkovsky & D. Rumbaugh (Eds.), *Naturally human: Origins and destiny of language.* Princeton, NJ: Princeton University Press.

Tomasello, M., & Farrar, M. J. (1986). Joint attention and early language. *Child Development, 57,* 1454–1463.

Tomasello, M., Mannle, S., & Kruger, A. C. (1986). Linguistic environment of 1- to 2-year-old twins. *Developmental Psychology, 22,* 169–176.

Trevarthen, C. (1980). Instincts for human understanding and for cultural cooperation: Their development in infancy. In M. von Cranach, K. Foppa, W. Lepenies, & D. Ploog (Eds.), *Human ethology: Claims and limits of a new discipline* (pp. 530–594). Cambridge, England: Cambridge University Press.

Trevarthen, C., & Hubley, P. (1978). Secondary intersubjectivity: Confidence, confiding and acts of meaning in the first year. In A. Lock (Ed.), *Action, gesture and symbol: The emergence of language* (pp. 183–229). London: Academic Press.

Trevarthen, C., Hubley, P., & Sheeran, L. (1975). Les activites innees du nourrisson. *La Recherche, 6,* 447–458.

Tronick, E. Z. (1982). *Social interchange in infancy: Affect, cognition, and communication.* Baltimore: University Park Press.

Tudge, J. R. H. (1992). Processes and consequences of peer collaboration: A Vygotskian analysis. *Child Development, 63,* 1364–1379.

Tudge, J. R. H., Fordham, J., Lawrence, C., & Rogoff, B. (1995, March). *When adult-child and peer dyads collaborate: Learning how to use educational and recreational computer games.* Paper presented at the meetings of the Society for Research in Child Development, Indianapolis.

Tudge, J. R. H., & Rogoff, B. (1989). Peer influences on cognitive development: Piagetian and Vygotskian perspectives. In M. Bornstein & J. Bruner (Eds.), *Interaction in human development* (pp. 17–40). Hillsdale, NJ: Erlbaum.

Tudge, J. R. H., & Winterhoff, P. (1993a). Vygotsky, Piaget, and Bandura: Perspectives on the relations between the social world and cognitive development. *Human Development, 36,* 61–81.

Tudge, J. R. H., & Winterhoff, P. (1993b). Can young children benefit from collaborative problem-solving? Tracing the effects of partner competence and feedback. *Social Development, 2,* 242–259.

Valdez-Menchaca, M. C. (1987, April). *The effects of incidental teaching on vocabulary acquisition by young children.* Paper presented at the meetings of The Society for Research in Child Development, Baltimore.

Valsiner, J. (1984). Construction of the zone of proximal development in adult-child joint action: The socialization of meals. In B. Rogoff & J. V. Wertsch (Eds.), *Children's learning in the "zone of proximal development"* (pp. 65–76). San Francisco: Jossey-Bass.

Valsiner, J. (Ed.). (1986). *The individual subject and scientific psychology.* New York: Plenum Press.

Valsiner, J. (1987). *Culture and the development of children's action.* New York: Wiley.

Valsiner, J. (in press). Bounded indeterminacy in discourse processes. *Infancia y Aprendizaje.*

Valsiner, J., & van der Veer, R. (1993). The encoding of distance: The concept of the zone of proximal development and its interpretations. In R. R. Cocking & K. A. Renninger (Eds.), *The development and meaning of psychological distance* (pp. 35–62). Hillsdale, NJ: Erlbaum.

Vandell, D. L., & Wilson, K. S. (1987). Infants' interactions with mother, sibling, and peer: Contrasts and relations between interaction systems. *Child Development, 58,* 176–186.

Vandenberg, B. (1980). Play, problem-solving, and creativity. In K. H. Rubin (Ed.), *Children's play* (pp. 49–68). San Francisco: Jossey-Bass.

van der Veer, R., & Valsiner, J. (1991). *Understanding Vygotsky.* Oxford, England: Blackwell.

Verba, M. (1993). Cooperative formats in pretend play among young children. *Cognition and Instruction, 11,* 265–280.

Verba, M. (1994). The beginnings of collaboration in peer interaction. *Human Development, 37,* 125–139.

Verba, M., & Winnykamen, F. (1992). Expert-novice interactions: Influence of partner status. *European Journal of Psychology of Education, 7,* 61–71.

Vygotsky, L. S. (1967). Play and its role in the mental development of the child. *Soviet Psychology, 5,* 6–18.

Vygotsky, L. S. (1978). *Mind in society: The development of higher psychological processes.* Cambridge, MA: Harvard University Press.

Vygotsky, L. S. (1987). *Thinking and speech.* In R. W. Rieber & A. S. Carton (Eds.), *The collected works of L. S. Vygotsky* (N. Minick, Trans.) (pp. 37–285). New York: Plenum Press.

Ward, M. C. (1971). *Them children: A study in language learning.* New York: Holt, Rinehart and Winston.

Watson-Gegeo, K. A., & Gegeo, D. W. (1989). The role of sibling interaction in child socialization. In P. G. Zukow (Ed.), *Sibling interaction across cultures: Theoretical and methodological issues* (pp. 54–76). New York: Springer-Verlag.

Waxman, S., & Gelman, R. (1986). Preschoolers' use of superordinate relations in classification and language. *Cognitive Development, 1,* 139–156.

Webb, N. M. (1982). Peer interaction and learning in cooperative small groups. *Journal of Educational Psychology, 74,* 642–655.

Weisner, T. S., & Gallimore, R. (1977). My brother's keeper: Child and sibling caretaking. *Current Anthropology, 18,* 169–190.

Wells, G. (1975). The contexts of children's early language experience. *Educational Review, 27,* 114–125.

Wells, G., Chang, G. L. M., & Maher, A. (1990). Creating classroom communities of literate thinkers. In S. Sharan (Ed.), *Cooperative learning: Theory and research* (pp. 95–121). New York: Praeger.

Wertsch, J. V. (1979a). From social interaction to higher psychological processes. *Human Development, 22,* 1–22.

Wertsch, J. V. (1979b, March). *The social interactional origins of metacognition.* Paper presented at the meetings of the Society for Research in Child Development, San Francisco.

Wertsch, J. V. (1984). The zone of proximal development: Some conceptual issues. In B. Rogoff & J. V. Wertsch (Eds.), *Children's learning in the "zone of proximal development"* (pp. 7–18). San Francisco: Jossey-Bass.

Wertsch, J. V. (1985). *Vygotsky and the social formation of mind.* Cambridge, MA: Harvard University Press.

Wertsch, J. V. (1991). *Voices of the mind.* Cambridge, MA: Harvard University Press.

Wertsch, J. V. (1995). The need for action in sociocultural research. In J. V. Wertsch, P. del Río, & A. Alvarez (Eds.), *Sociocultural studies of mind* (pp. 56–74). New York: Cambridge University Press.

Wertsch, J. V., & Hickmann, M. (1987). Problem solving in social interaction: A microgenetic analysis. In M. Hickmann (Ed.), *Social and functional approaches to language and thought* (pp. 251–266). Orlando, FL: Academic Press.

Wertsch, J. V., Minick, N., & Arns, F. J. (1984). The creation of context in joint problem-solving. In B. Rogoff & J. Lave (Eds.), *Everyday cognition* (pp. 151–171). Cambridge, MA: Harvard University Press.

Wertsch, J. V., & Stone, C. A. (1979, February). *A social interactional analysis of learning disabilities remediation.* Paper presented at the International Conference of the Association for Children with Learning Disabilities, San Francisco.

Wertsch, J. V., & Toma, C. (1995). Discourse and learning in the classroom: A sociocultural approach. In L. P. Steffe & J. Gale (Eds.), *Constructivism in education.* Hillsdale, NJ: Erlbaum.

Wertsch, J. V., Tulviste, P., & Hagstrom, F. (1993). A sociocultural approach to agency. In E. A. Forman, N. Minick, & C. A. Stone (Eds.), *Contexts for learning* (pp. 336–356). New York: Oxford University Press.

Whiting, B. B. (1979). *Maternal behavior in cross-cultural perspective.* Paper presented at the meeting of the Society for Cross-Cultural Research, Charlottesville, VA.

Whiting, B. B. (1980). Culture and social behavior: A model for the development of social behavior. *Ethos, 8,* 95–116.

Whiting, B. B., & Edwards, C. P. (1988). *Children of different worlds: The formation of social behavior.* Cambridge, MA: Harvard University Press.

Whiting, B. B., & Whiting, J. W. M. (1975). *Children of six cultures: A psycho-cultural analysis.* Cambridge, MA: Harvard University Press.

Winograd, T., & Flores, F. (1987). *Understanding computers and cognition.* Reading, MA: Addison-Wesley.

Wood, D. (1986). Aspects of teaching and learning. In M. Richards & P. Light (Eds.), *Children of social worlds* (pp. 191–212). Cambridge, MA: Polity Press.

Wood, D., Bruner, J. S., & Ross, G. (1976). The role of tutoring in problem-solving. *Journal of Child Psychology and Psychiatry, 17,* 89–100.

Wood, D., & Middleton, D. (1975). A study of assisted problem-solving. *British Journal of Psychology, 66,* 181–191.

Wood, D., Wood, H., Ainsworth, S., & O'Malley, C. (1995). On becoming a tutor: Toward an ontogenetic model. *Cognition and Instruction, 13,* 565–581.

Wood, D., Wood, H., & Middleton, D. (1978). An experimental evaluation of four face-to-face teaching strategies. *International Journal of Behavioral Development, 2,* 131–147.

Yager, S., Johnson, R. T., Johnson, D. W., & Snider, B. (1986). The impact of group processing on achievement in cooperative learning groups. *Journal of Social Psychology, 126,* 389–397.

Youniss, J. (1987). Social construction and moral development: Update and expansion of an idea. In W. M. Kurtines & J. L. Gewirtz (Eds.), *Moral development through social interaction* (pp. 131–148). New York: Wiley.

Zellermayer, M., Salomon, G., Globerson, T., & Givon, H. (1991). Enhancing writing-related metacognitions through a computerized writing partner. *American Educational Research Journal, 28,* 373–391.

Zimmerman, B. J., & Rosenthal, T. L. (1974). Observational learning of rule-governed behavior by children. *Psychological Bulletin, 81,* 29–42.

Zinchenko, V. P. (1985). Vygotsky's ideas about units for the analysis of mind. In J. V. Wertsch (Ed.), *Culture, communication and cognition: Vygotskian perspectives* (pp. 94–118). Cambridge, England: Cambridge University Press.

Zinchenko, V. P. (1995). Cultural-historical psychology and the psychological theory of activity: Retrospect and prospect. In J. V. Wertsch, P. del Río, & A. Alvarez (Eds.), *Sociocultural studies of mind* (pp. 37–55). New York: Cambridge University Press.

Zukow, P. G., Reilly, J., & Greenfield, P. M. (1982). Making the absent present: Facilitating the transition from sensorimotor to linguistic communication. In K. E. Nelson (Ed.), *Children's language* (Vol. 3, pp. 1–90). New York: Gardner Press.

CHAPTER 15

The Development of Conceptual Structures

ROBBIE CASE

Children's early concepts differ in interesting ways from those of adults; even when they use the same word to describe a particular object (e.g., dog) the conceptual meaning that they attach to this word often differs substantially from the adult one (Anglin, 1993; Clark, 1983). It has also been claimed that the entire structure of children's conceptual understanding is different from that of adults. When unpacked, this claim may normally be seen to involve one or more of the following propositions: (a) distinctive general patterns may be discerned in children's conceptual understanding, ones which are present across a wide variety of local exemplars (e.g., mother, father, brother); (b) these

patterns reflect a fundamental difference—not just in the content of children's conceptual knowledge—but in the way that knowledge is organized; and (c) the reason children's knowledge is organized differently from that of adults is not just because children have had less experience, but because the architecture of their cognitive systems is different in some fundamental way. The foregoing claims, or ones much like them, show up in the earliest writings on children's cognitive development, and have inspired some of the most controversial work that has been done in the field throughout this century. In the present chapter I review this work, with special attention to the age range for which the largest body of empirical data has been gathered: namely, 4 to 10 years.

Most previous treatments of this topic have been organized in one of four ways: chronological, substantive, thematic, or theoretical. When adopting the chronological approach, the standard procedure is to review the conceptual structures that have been hypothesized for children at different ages, beginning in infancy and passing on to higher stages; then to evaluate the evidence that has been gathered and the conclusions that have been drawn for each. When adopting the substantive approach, the standard procedure is to lay out the major domains or types of concepts for which structural claims have been made (for example, those having to do with causality, time, and space); then to summarize the structural progression that has been hypothesized within each domain, the studies have been conducted, and the conclusions that have been drawn. The thematic approach is compatible with either of the foregoing forms of organization and is sometimes combined with them. Its distinctive feature is that a general set of issues or questions are presented at the outset: Do general conceptual structures exist at all? What sort of data would we need to gather to support or refute this claim? Are the conceptual structures at different stages of development qualitatively different? Is the transition from one form of structure to the next a gradual or a rapid one? Each of these questions has a long history in the field; accordingly, each can be treated in a separate section. Alternatively, the questions as a group can be used as a leitmotif to provide unity and coherence to the material that is reviewed throughout. The final form of organization is theoretical. Here the strategy is to devote a different section to each of the major theories that has been proposed in the field of cognitive development and to outline the position that each has taken on the structural question; then to attempt some sort of systematic comparison and/or integration of these positions at the chapter's end.

A modified form of this latter organization will be used in the present chapter. The basic thesis that underlies the present review, and that distinguishes it from other reviews on the same topic, is that many of the most enduring issues and controversies in this field are actually epistemological in nature; that is to say, they have to do with background assumptions that their authors make about the fundamental nature of human knowledge, and the process by which that knowledge is acquired. Although investigators have not always stated their background assumptions explicitly, these assumptions have nevertheless had a profound effect, both on the nature of the theories to which they have been attracted, and on the methodologies that they have regarded as most appropriate for investigating these theories. In order to highlight the role that background assumptions of this sort have played in the history of the field, the theories that are covered in the present chapter are organized into three broad epistemological categories. The history of the field is then described as a dialectic one, in which a succession of new and/or improved theories is seen as emerging within each of the three categories, in response to criticisms that were levelled at the previous theory by those subscribing to a rival epistemological position.

This chapter is organized in six sections. In the first, I provide a brief description of the major epistemological positions that have influenced the field, and the background assumptions that they entail about human knowledge. In subsequent sections, I describe (a) the view of children's conceptual structures that has been proposed in each tradition; (b) the dialogue that has taken place among the traditions, as the relative merits of the different positions have been debated and their points of disagreement clarified; (c) the work that has been done in each of the traditions in the last decade in response to the most recent round in this debate; and (d) several new lines of investigation: ones that suggest a way in which work in the three traditions may possibly be integrated. Finally, in the last two sections, I consider the question of how to conceptualize the process of structural change. After a brief review of the mechanisms that have been proposed in each of the three traditions, I conclude by suggesting a way in which these different proposals may be integrated.

For readers who are new to the topic of conceptual structures, my hope is that the present chapter will constitute a good introduction. All the classic positions on the topic are covered, as are the different substantive domains for which these positions have been developed, the data that have been gathered and the issues that have emerged. For readers who are already sophisticated students in this field, or active contributors to it, my hope is that my treatment of the history of the field will be of some interest as well. The assignment of theories to groups is somewhat different from the one that we have become accustomed to, as is the treatment of certain of the classic controversies. My hope is that the reader will find these differences to be productive, both in terms of the light that they cast on past work in the field, and the promise that they offer for the future.

THREE THEORETICAL TRADITIONS IN THE STUDY OF CONCEPTUAL GROWTH

Research on children's conceptual structures has been conducted within several different epistemological frameworks. Although a number of schemes have been proposed for classifying these frameworks (Beilin, 1983; Overton, 1984, 1990, 1996), the scheme that will be used in this chapter is one that distinguishes three traditions: each with its own pioneers, its own methods, and its own tradition of progressive inquiry.

The Empiricist Tradition

The epistemological roots of the first tradition lie in British empiricism, as articulated by Locke and Hume (1955/1748). According to the empiricist position, knowledge of the world is acquired by a process in which the sensory organs first detect stimuli in the external world, and the mind then detects the customary patterns or "conjunctions" in these stimuli. Developmental psychologists who accept this view have tended to view the goals of psychology as being to describe (a) the process by which new stimuli are discriminated and encoded (perceptual learning); (b) the way in which correlations or associations among these stimuli are detected (cognitive learning); and (c) the process by which new knowledge is accessed, tested, and/or used in other contexts (transfer). The general method that has been favored includes the following three steps:

1. Make detailed empirical observations of children's learning, in a fashion that can be replicated with reliability.
2. Generate explanations for these observations that are clear and testable.
3. Conduct carefully controlled experiments to test these hypotheses: ones that rule out any rival hypotheses.

In the field of child development, early attempts to apply this perspective led to two main kinds of investigation. The first was directed toward clarifying the nature of the perceptual stimuli that infants could detect at birth, and documenting the forms of learning that were possible (Lipsitt, 1967). The second was directed to clarifying the sort of higher order learning that children could engage in at older ages, once they could make the required perceptual discriminations. Of particular interest was the learning of verbal concepts. To study this latter type of learning, children were presented with pairs of sensory stimuli that varied along a number of dimensions (e.g., form, color, pattern), and then asked to play a game where they had to figure out which stimulus feature was associated with receipt of a small reward (e.g., square stimulus on top of container = raisin inside container; circular stimulus on top = nothing inside). On each trial children were allowed one guess as to which stimulus would be rewarded. When they had succeeded in picking the correct stimulus on some predetermined number of trials (typically 9 out of 10), they were said to have acquired the concept. At that point, a different attribute was selected, and a fresh sequence of experimental trials was initiated.

The results that were obtained from these studies were as follows. Although preschool children could learn to select a stimulus on the basis of its shape, color, or pattern by the age of 3 to 4 years, and could also learn to change the basis for their selection when the criterion was changed, they did so in a rather slow and laborious manner, with the result that their learning curves looked much like those exhibited by lower primates (Kendler, Kendler, & Wells, 1960). By the age of 5 to 6 years, children's original learning became much more rapid. They also became capable of relearning much more rapidly, typically within one or two trials (Kendler & Kendler, 1962). However, this was true only if the new criterion was one that required attention to the same general stimulus dimension (e.g., shape). If they were required to shift to a different dimension, particularly one that was perceptually less salient than the first dimension, the capability for rapid relearning did not emerge until the age of 7 to 10 years of age (Mumbauer & Odom, 1967; Osler & Kofsky, 1966).

When these phenomena were first observed, the change in children's learning on such tasks was hypothesized to be part of a larger pattern, which White (1967) referred to as the "5 to 7 shift." In keeping with the learning theories of the time, Kendler and Kendler (1962) proposed that the pattern was caused by a shift from unmediated to verbally mediated learning. The notion was that children under the age of 5, like lower primates, can learn to differentiate objects that are associated with reward from other objects. However, since they do not covertly label each object using dimensional terms (e.g., square), they have to learn about each object in a rather local fashion. By contrast, since older children and adults do engage in this sort of covert verbal labelling, they are capable of much more rapid initial learning; they are also capable of much more rapid re-learning, since all they have to do is substitute one dimensional term for another, not learn a whole new set of associations. This same change, that is, the change from unmediated to verbally mediated learning, was believed to have a wide variety of other consequences for children's cognition, especially the sort that is required in school (Kendler & Kendler, 1967; Rohwer, 1970).

In interpreting the data in this fashion, investigators in this tradition were subscribing to the first two classical hypotheses that were stated at the outset, namely (a) that a distinctive *pattern* may be discerned in young children's conceptual understanding, which is present across a wide variety of different local exemplars and (b) that this pattern reflects a fundamental difference, not just in the content of children's conceptual knowledge, but in the way that knowledge is organized. The third hypothesis that was mentioned—namely, that this difference does not derive from experience, but from a fundamental difference in the architecture of children's cognitive systems—was not necessarily subscribed to. Indeed, a good deal of work was devoted to showing that children *could* encode the relationship to be learned in the required fashion with a little instruction, but did not do so spontaneously (Kendler & Kendler, 1967). This latter datum was interpreted as indicating a "performance" rather than a "structural" deficiency in children's verbal mediation.

In retrospect, what can be said about the early work on children's concept formation in this tradition? From a theoretical point of view, the harvest was relatively meager. Although the notion of verbal mediation continued to play some role in other epistemological traditions (see below), it was by and large abandoned in the empiricist tradition, because it did not fit the overall pattern that emerged, as further training and transfer studies were conducted. (See Stevenson, 1972; Ch. 9 for a review.) From a methodological point of view, the harvest was not as rich as it might have been, either. For a variety of reasons that will be described below, subsequent investigators decided that this sort of perceptually-based learning paradigm was not the best one to use during this age range, in order to reveal the full conceptual understanding of which children are capable.

To say that the harvest from these early studies was relatively meager is not to say that there was no harvest at all, however. First, the data that were gathered were extremely reliable and formed a lasting part of the general corpus that subsequent investigators felt obliged to explain, in building a model of the change that takes place in children's cognition in this age range (Case, 1985; Gholson, 1985). Second,

the general paradigm embodied a number of methodological canons that proved enduring. Of particular importance were:

1. There is much to be learned, in studying any complex conceptual structure, by examining the manner in which children encode its constituent elements.
2. There is also much to be gained by selecting a carefully circumscribed task, and varying its parameters.
3. Finally, there is much to be learned by examining the performance of different age groups, in a multiple-trial task where learning can be observed directly.

All three of these features have been preserved (or rather reintroduced) by subsequent investigators in this tradition (Siegler, 1978, 1996).

The Rationalist Tradition

The second theoretical tradition in which children's conceptual structures have been studied drew its inspiration from Continental rationalism rather than British Empiricism. In reaction to British empiricists, philosophers such as Kant (1961/1796) suggested that knowledge is acquired by a process in which order is imposed by the human mind on the data that the senses provide, not merely detected in these data. Examples of concepts that played this foundational role in Kant's system were space, time, causality, and number. Without some pre-existing concept in each of these categories, Kant argued that it would be impossible to make any sense of the data of sensory experience: to see events as taking place in space, for example, as unfolding through time, or as exerting a causal influence on each other. For this reason he believed that these categories must exist in some a priori form rather than being induced from experience.

Developmental psychologists who were influenced by Kant's view tended to see the study of children's cognitive development in a different fashion from those who were influenced by empiricists. They thought that one should begin by exploring the foundational concepts with which children come equipped at birth; then go on to document any change that may take place in these concepts with age. The first developmental theorist to apply this approach was Baldwin (1968/1894). According to Baldwin, children's conceptual schemata progress through a sequence of four universal stages, which he termed the stages of "sensorimotor," "quasilogical," "logical," and "hyper-logical" thought, respectively. In any given stage, Baldwin believed that new experience is "assimilated" to the existing set of schemata, much in the manner that the body assimilates food. He saw transition from one form of thought to the next as driven by "accommodation," a process by which existing schemata are broken down and then reorganized into new and more adaptive patterns. Finally—and in this he was attempting to go beyond Kant—he saw children's conceptual understanding in each of Kant's categories as something that they construct, not something that is inborn. The only primitive elements with which he saw children being endowed at birth were entities that he called "circular reactions." He called for subsequent generations to explore these reactions, and to chart the process by which they are assembled into higher order schemata.

Although Baldwin was the first to articulate a general theory of conceptual development, it was Piaget's (1960, 1970) acceptance of Baldwin's challenge, and his reworking of Baldwin's theory, that had the greatest impact on the field. The most important feature that Piaget added to Baldwin's theory was the notion of a "logical structure," that is, a coherent set of logical operations that can be applied to any domain of human activity, and to which any cognitive task in the domain must ultimately be assimilated. Piaget hypothesized that the form of children's structures is different at different stages of their development, and that it is this difference that gives the thought of young children its unique character. To highlight the importance of these structures, he relabelled Baldwin's second and third stages of development, calling them the stages of "pre-operational" and "operational" thought, respectively. He also divided the stage of operational thought into the "concrete" and "formal" periods.

Together with his collaborators at the University of Geneva, Piaget conducted a vast number of studies that were designed to reveal the details of children's conceptual understanding in each of Kant's categories, and the process by which this understanding is arrived at. The basic procedure was to present children with a wide variety of simple problems or tasks, in order to see how they would respond to them; then to interview them in order to determine the reasoning on which these responses were based. A final step was to look for a common pattern in children's reasoning at different ages, and to treat this pattern as a clue regarding the underlying logical structure that was present.

The conservation task is perhaps the most famous of Piaget's problems (Piaget, 1952). A precursor to this task had actually been studied by Binet (1900), who asked children to judge which of two objects was bigger under a variety of illusory conditions. Binet and his colleagues had shown that preschool children could not perform successfully on such tasks, that is to say, they could not overcome the perceptual illusion that the stimulus situation presents. By contrast, school-aged children were able to overcome the illusion, and to make an accurate judgment of quantity (Binet & Simon, 1905). Piaget modified this task so that children of all ages would have a more certain, logical basis for making a judgment about relative quantity. First, he presented children with a pair of objects whose quantity was equal, under perceptual conditions that were not illusory, and asked them if they thought the two objects were equal in quantity (typically children decided that they were). Next, he transformed one of the two objects, in full view, so that it looked bigger or smaller than the other object. If dealing with two lumps of plasticene, for example, he might pull one of the two lumps into a long, loglike shape. After the transformation was complete, Piaget's final step was to ask the children if they still thought the quantities were equal, or if one was now bigger (or contained more) than the other. Once they had answered, he asked them to explain why they thought this was the case.

The results are by now well-known. Notwithstanding the fact that "logic" argued that the two quantities must still be equal, preschool children were misled by the evidence of their senses into concluding that one of the two arrays contained more than the other. By contrast, older children concluded that the amount in each array must still be the same. At the age of 7 to 8, the most frequent explanation was that nothing had been added to, or taken away from, the original array. Justifications that were sometimes added at a later age included the argument that—while one array does look bigger now along one dimension (e.g., length)—it looks smaller along another (e.g., width).

Piaget's explanation for the change in children's justifications was that they had acquired a new logical structure: one in which the illusions of the sensory world can be compensated for by a set of internal, logico-mathematical operations. He further asserted that these operations were systemwide in their applicability, and signalled a major change in the architecture of their cognitive systems. Note that—while Piaget's interpretation included all three of the components that were mentioned at the outset of the chapter—it was quite different from the interpretation that had been advanced by empiricists, in order to explain the change that they had observed during the same time period. Rather than seeing children as learning to recognize and label the basic dimensions of the empirical world, as a result of experience with it, Piaget saw them as constructing a powerful new form of logic, one which enabled them to overcome the illusions to which empirical experience would otherwise subject them.

In this particular case, the logical structure that Piaget presumed children had to assemble was one in which compensation plays a vital role, and that can be symbolized by the following formula:

$$A_1 \times B_1 = A_2 \times B_2$$

where A_1 stands for the value of the first dimension at time 1, B_1 stands for the value of the second dimension at time 1, A_2 stands for the value of the first dimension at time 2, and B_2 stands for the value of the second dimension at time 2.

As Piaget became interested in logical structures of this sort, he devised a number of tasks that he hoped would document their existence more directly (Inhelder & Piaget, 1958, 1964). Included among these was another task that became a classic: namely, the task of class inclusion. In this problem, children are shown an array of shapes (say, a set of square and round shapes). They are then asked to compare the set comprised of all the shapes with the larger of the two subordinate sets, and say which set is bigger. Once again, the result is by now well known. Prior to the age of 7, most children assert that the subordinate set (e.g., square shapes) is larger than the superordinate set (all shapes). They then justify their response by comparing the two subordinate sets. By the age of 7 to 10, most children reverse their earlier decision and conclude that the superordinate set is larger. Moreover, they appear to experience this fact as a "logical necessity." For Piaget, the switch to the correct response, coupled with the feeling of logical necessity, provided further evidence that children were acquiring a new set of logico-mathematical structures.

As it happens, the class inclusion task is rather similar to the concept learning task in certain respects. Both tasks present children with a simple set of shapes that can be classified in a number of different ways (by shape, color, etc.). Both tasks require children to overcome their "natural" or "habitual" way of classifying a set of stimuli. Both tasks require children to sustain a focus on subordinate stimulus values, without losing sight of a superordinate classification. Finally, both tasks are passed for the first time during the same general age range: 7 to 10 years. The form of interpretation that the two groups of theorists developed to explain the developmental change, however, was

quite different. For learning theorists, the switch to a new form of response was seen as the result of applying a learned set of labels to stimuli, and forming associations among them; in short, it was seen as the result of a verbally mediated learning process. For Piaget and those who followed him, the switch was seen as the result of acquiring a new logical structure: one in which superordinate and subordinate categories were differentiated and integrated. This structure, in turn, was seen as emerging from an internal process of reflection, not from a process in which exposure to empirical experience played the major role.

The difference between the two groups in their view of children's developing cognitive competencies was paralleled by a difference in their view of the methods that were most appropriate for studying these processes. The approach favored by empiricists was to focus on a single task that involved some form of empirical learning, then to systematically vary its parameters. By contrast, the approach favored by Piaget and his colleagues was to focus on children's understanding across a broad range of tasks, in which the results of empirical learning had to be overcome in some fashion. The form of response that the two groups analyzed was also different. Empiricists offered children a choice between two clear cut alternatives, then examined their success rate and the strategies that led to it. By contrast, Piaget and his colleagues gave a much higher weight to children's explanations, probing the reasoning that lay behind these explanations in a clinical manner. Like the differences in their theories, these differences in methodology were a function of differences in epistemology.

The Sociohistoric Tradition

A third epistemological tradition within which children's conceptual understanding has been studied has its roots in the sociohistoric epistemology of Hegel, Marx, and the modern continental philosophers (Kaufmann, 1980). According to the sociohistoric view, conceptual knowledge does not have its primary origin in the structure of the objective world (as empiricist philosophers suggested). Nor does it have its origin in the structure of the subject and his spontaneous cogitation (as rationalist philosophers suggested). It does not even have its primary origin in the interaction of between the structure of the subject and the structure of the objective world (as Baldwin and Piaget maintained). Rather, it has its primary origin in the social and material history of the culture of which the subject is a member, and the tools, concepts, and symbol systems that the culture has developed for interacting with its environment.

Developmental psychologists who adopted the sociohistoric perspective viewed the study of children's conceptual understanding in a different fashion from empiricists or rationalists. They believed that one should begin one's study of children's thought by analyzing the social, cultural, and physical contexts in which human cultures find themselves, and the social, linguistic, and material tools that they have developed over the years for coping with these contexts. One should then proceed to examine the way in which these intellectual and physical tools are passed on from one generation to the next, in different cultures and at different time periods.

The best known of the early sociohistoric theories was Vygotsky's (1962). According to Vygotsky, children's thought must be seen in a context that includes both its biological and its cultural evolution. Three of the most important features of human beings as a species are: (a) that they have developed language; (b) that they fashion their own tools; and (c) that they transmit the discoveries and inventions of one generation to the next. From the perspective of Vygotsky's theory, the most important milestone in children's early development is the acquisition of language, not the construction of some logical structure, or exposure to a set of universal stimuli and labels. Children first master language for social (interpersonal) purposes. Next, they internalize this language and use it for intra-personal (self-regulatory) purposes. Finally, as this change takes place, their culture recognizes their new capabilities, and begins an initiation process that includes an introduction to the forms of social practice in which they will have to engage as adults. In modern literate societies this initiation process normally includes the teaching of skills such as reading, writing, and enumeration in primary school, followed by such subjects as science and formal mathematics in secondary school. Followers of Vygotsky often saw the acquisition of the first set of skills as being causally related to the appearance of the concrete logical competencies that children develop in middle childhood, and the second set as being causally linked to the emergence of the more formal competencies that appear in adolescence.

Early research in the sociohistoric tradition led to a number of interesting new findings. One of the most provocative was that adults in a traditional agricultural culture, especially ones who have not attended school, tend to score at a much lower level than adults who *have* attended school, on tests of mnemonic and formal logical capabilities such

as syllogisms (Luria, 1976; Vygotsky, 1962). To Vygotsky, this finding indicated that modern schooling, not some universal process of reflexive abstraction, is the major instrument of cognitive growth. This inference has not gone unchallenged in recent years. Nevertheless, the datum was an important one, and one that has led to many further studies. In most of the early studies, strong schooling effects were found, not just on the sort of tasks that Luria and Vygotsky had used, but on tasks that had been used in the other two traditions as well. (Cole, Gay, Glick, & Sharp, 1971; Goodnow, 1962; Greenfield, Reich, & Oliver, 1966). Although the results differed somewhat from study to study, the general pattern was that children moved through the 5 to 7 shift at a considerably later age if they did not attend school; very often, too, they failed to show the teenage shift to a more abstract or "formal" type of response. Instead, the shift that they showed was one that could only be understood by studying their culture, its beliefs, and its socialization practices (Bruner, 1964; Greenfield, 1966). As this tradition developed, ethnographic and historical methods were utilized with increasing frequency in order to place children's reasoning in context. Use of these methods further differentiated the sociohistoric tradition from the empiricist and rationalist traditions.

Comparing the Three Traditions and Clarifying Their Differences

Before proceeding, it is worthwhile to review the differences among the three traditions, and the challenge that these differences posed to subsequent investigators. The first difference was in the data that were collected on children's conceptual growth. Studies in the empiricist tradition demonstrated that, during the early years of schooling, children show a change in the strategies that they employ on tests where some novel association must be learned (e.g., square = correct; circle = wrong). They also showed that these strategies can be manipulated by instruction, at least to some extent. Studies in the rationalist tradition demonstrated that, during the same age range, a change takes place children's understanding of fundamental properties of the world: properties such as quantity, time, and space. They also showed that a change was present in children's tendency to base their response on the structure of the perceptual world, rather than the structure suggested by reasoning or "logic." Finally, studies in the sociohistoric tradition demonstrated that the emergence of a "logical" (and supposedly universal) pattern of responding during this age range is affected by variables such as culture and schooling. Indeed, for certain formal tasks (e.g., syllogistic reasoning) the pattern that emerges does not appear to be a universal one at all.

The first challenge that these three groups of data posed to subsequent investigators was to fashion a theory that provides a unified account of all three sets of findings. A second challenge had to do with the most appropriate methods to use in exploring such accounts, or trying to decide among them. As indicated above, each group had a natural affinity with a particular set of methods, because it was motivated by a distinctive set of epistemological questions. For this reason, it was not clear how to combine the results of the different methods, or how to weigh the different evidence that each one generated. This task was further complicated by the fact that the different traditions did not just hold different views of children's conceptual development. As indicated in Table 15.1, they also held different views

about such basic constructs as learning, intelligence, and experience. Finally, and perhaps most problematically, the three groups held different views about what constituted "good science."

Although the activities of scientists are different in a great many respects from those of children, they are similar in that they often share a common goal: namely, the acquisition of knowledge. Because knowledge and its acquisition were viewed so differently in the three traditions, subtle disagreements arose on what constituted good science. From the empiricist perspective, good science was science that focused on a clearly identified empirical phenomenon, that developed explicit and testable causal hypotheses regarding this phenomenon, and that tested these hypotheses in a rigorous fashion. General theories were valued, but the best method for arriving at them was presumed to be a bottom-up one, in which theoretical constructs were induced from specific phenomena,

TABLE 15.1   Comparison of the Three Views of Knowledge and Their Embodiment in Philosophy, Psychology and Education

Psychological Constructs	Empiricist	Rationalist	Sociohistorical
Knowledge	Repertoire of patterns or problems that one has learned to detect and operations that one can execute on them.	Structure created by human mind and evaluated according to rational criteria such as coherence, consistency and parsimony.	Creation of a social group, as it engages in its daily interaction and praxis, and both adapts to and transforms the environment around it.
Learning	Process that generates knowledge; begins when one is exposed to a new problem, continues as one learns to respond to that problem and generalize one's response to other contexts.	Process that takes place when the mind applies an existing structure to new experience, in order to understand it.	Process of being initiated into the life of a group, so that one can assume a role in its daily praxis.
Development	Cumulative learning.	Long-term, transformational change that takes place in the structures to which new experience is assimilated.	The emergence and training of the symbolic and tool-using capacities that make social initiation possible.
Intelligence	Individual trait that sets limit on the maximum rate at which cumulative learning takes place.	Adaptive capability that all children possess, to apply and modify their existing cognitive structures; this capability grows with age (and is transformed).	Distributed across a group, and intimately tied to the tools, artifacts and symbolic systems that the group develops.
Motivation	Internal state that is subject to external influence, and that affects the deployment of attention.	Set of natural tendencies that draw human beings of all ages toward epistemic activity.	Identification: i.e., the natural tendency of the young to see themselves as being like their elders and to look forward to the day when they will assume their elders' role.
Education	Process by which the external conditions that affect children's learning and motivation are carefully arranged and sequenced so that socially desirable goals may be achieved.	Child-centered process: one that involves the provision of an environment that will stimulate children's natural curiosity and constructive activity, and promote active reflection on the results of that activity.	Process by which a community takes charge of its young, and moves them from a peripheral to a central role in its daily practices.

and retained a close linkage to them. This meant that the general structure of empiricist theories often resembled a list of "factors," together with a set of operational procedures for measuring the factors in a particular situation, and predicting their combined effect.

From the rationalist perspective, such theories often appeared to be oversimplified, pedestrian, and/or trivial. In the rationalist tradition, good science was seen as involving the articulation of a sophisticated intellectual system, and the exploration of its implications across a wide range of circumstances. Although a theory's power to accommodate new data was acknowledged to be important, theoretical change was seen as equally likely to result from the discussion, clarification, and rationalization of the elements of the system itself. Thus, the theories that emerged in this tradition were more likely to resemble a complex system of interwoven arguments, assertions, and constructs than they were a list of factors, principles, or even general laws. By the same token, the development of new methods of observation, the gathering of more detailed data, and the use of new statistical techniques was not seen as having much scientific import in and of itself. What was seen as being of importance was the extent to which any given method flowed from, or could contribute to, an advance in general theoretical understanding.

Finally, from the third perspective, science was seen first and foremost as a social activity. Like any other social activity, it was viewed as having evolved in a particular cultural and historical context, and as depending on a particular set of intellectual tools and representations. It was also viewed as being practiced by individuals who acquired a particular status because of their practice, and who shared a particular set of biases and beliefs. From this perspective, cross cultural investigation was seen as a vital tool in building up a general model of any social phenomenon, not just something one could conduct after the fact, in order to explore the possibility of "social influences." At the same time, scientific results of this sort were also seen as being open to distortion, due to the tendency of the members of any one cultural group to take their own views and practices as the standard, against which the practices of all other cultural groups should be measured. In this tradition, then, good science was seen as science that was critically aware of its own social origins, modest in the generality of its claims, and neutral in its evaluation of ultimate developmental outcomes.

This third perspective is worthwhile to keep in mind, in evaluating the strengths and weaknesses of the three traditions. The empiricist tradition was born in England, and had its greatest impact on the conduct of social science in that country, and its former colonies. The rationalist position was born in continental Europe, and had its greatest impact in this sphere of influence. Finally, the sociohistoric tradition was born in postrevolutionary Russia, and had its main impact, at least in its early years, in the countries of the Soviet bloc. Thus, it should be realized that—to some extent, at least—the early discussion and debate that took place among the three traditions involved a confrontation between different cultures and world views, not just different views of knowledge, of children, or of social science.

DIALOGUE BETWEEN THE EMPIRICIST AND RATIONALIST TRADITIONS

Early Empiricist Critiques of Piaget's Theory

Up until the late 1950s, North American psychology was dominated by empiricism of a rather extreme form: namely, the school of "logical positivism." Although the influence of this school was rather short lived in philosophy, its hold on North American psychology lasted much longer, and served to justify the radical Behaviorism that developed on that continent. During the late 1950s and early 1960s, however, North American behaviorism began to come under fire from within North America as well as outside it. The most common criticism was that behaviorism failed to do justice to the organization of human behavior, and the complex inner processes that are responsible for generating it (Bruner, Goodnow, & Austin, 1956; Chomsky, 1957; Miller, Gallenter, & Pribram, 1960; Newell, Shaw, & Simon, 1958). At the same time as this criticism was being voiced, computers were emerging as a new economic force, and a new discipline was being created whose province was the design of software for them. Eventually, investigators from the newly formed discipline of computer science joined hands with psychologists, linguists, and other social scientists, in an effort to describe the cognitive processes that are necessary to generate and control complex human behavior. This event became known as the "cognitive revolution" and the new discipline became known as "cognitive science" (Gardner, 1985).

Although theories of learning underwent a profound transformation during this time period, the underlying epistemology on which they were based changed relatively little. By and large, North American investigators still presumed that the ultimate locus of knowledge was the empirical world, and that the acquisition of knowledge by psychologists should follow the traditional canons of empiricist methodology. In the field of cognitive development, the result was an interesting ambivalence. On the one hand, there was a great surge of interest in the sort of work that Piaget had pioneered: When Flavell's (1963) English language summary of Piaget's work became available, it was widely read and discussed. Although reactions were varied, by and large Piaget's theory was seen as offering a far deeper understanding of children's conceptual understanding than had been possible from the perspective of learning theory, and a wealth of new data. On the other hand, Piaget's theory was often read with empiricist glasses. Thus, many investigators found the manner in which his theory was formulated to be excessively abstract, vague, and difficult to operationalize. They also found it too impregnated with general philosophical arguments and hence difficult to verify or falsify. They had problems with the substance of the theory, as well: in particular, they thought that the general logical structures Piaget hypothesized probably did not exist, and that such cognitive structures as did exist were more likely to be the result of empirical learning than "reflexive abstraction." Finally, they viewed Piaget's method of interviewing children as too clinical and subjective, and his methods of sampling and data-analysis as too unsystematic.

The continuing split between the two epistemological traditions, and the ambivalent way in which Piaget's theory was received in North America as a result, was well reflected in the way in which children's conceptual development was characterized in the 1970 edition of the present handbook. Four chapters were devoted to this topic. The first was Stevenson's (1970) description of research on children's learning, which covered work that had been done in the empiricist tradition. The second was Piaget's chapter, which described his own theory and research (Piaget, 1970). The third was White's (1970) look at research in both traditions, and its dependence on epistemological priors. Finally, the fourth was a chapter by Flavell (1970), which was devoted almost exclusively to an evaluation of Piaget's work, from a perspective that Piaget classified as friendly but foreign, due to its strong empiricist emphasis (Piaget, in Flavell, 1963, p. vii).

For the purpose of the present review, the most interesting of these four chapters is the one written by Flavell, since it provides such a clear view of the different perspectives that the two traditions bring to bear on the task of studying children's conceptual development, and the difficulties

confronting any attempt to build a bridge between them. The first task that Flavell undertook was simply to describe Piaget's theory in terms that would render it more comprehensible to an audience grounded in detailed empirical research and precise, operational definitions. The second task was to describe, in simple terms, the more specific conceptual changes that Piaget hypothesized in each of Kant's major conceptual categories. The third task was to describe the measurement instruments that Piaget had devised, and the data he had gathered, to support his model of children's conceptual growth in each of these areas. The fourth task was to review the empirical data that had been gathered using these instruments. Included in this category were: (a) original data gathered by Piaget; (b) new data gathered by investigators elsewhere, to see if Piaget's findings could be replicated (by and large the answer to this question was affirmative); (c) data gathered on instruments that had been modified in various ways (here the general pattern was that modifications produced differences in the passing age of tasks, but not the general sequence); and (d) instructional studies that had been done, in an attempt to determine whether the overall sequence could be accelerated (here the answer appeared to be that the effects of the interventions were positive but modest).

The mere fact of undertaking these four tasks already represented a major effort at bridging the gap between the two traditions. The final task that Flavell set himself, however, was perhaps the most challenging. This was to tackle the question of how Piaget's most general theoretical claims could be tested empirically. In particular, how could one test the claims having to do with the existence of general logical structures, the process by which they are formed, and their supposedly stage-like development? One view at the time was that—if Piaget's stage theory was valid—children should be found to acquire a wide range of logical competencies relatively rapidly, that is, within a relatively tight age range (Brainerd, 1976). Flavell spent a good deal of effort documenting the difficulties that were involved in testing this assertion. Since it is difficult to establish an indisputable operational criterion for determining when, exactly, any logical competence is fully in place to begin with, it is doubly difficult to determine whether two or more such competencies emerge in the same age range, in a synchronous fashion.

In retrospect, Flavell's most prescient comment was perhaps the one in which he raised the question of whether these were the most appropriate criteria to be using in the first place, in order to document the existence of general conceptual structures. As he put the matter:

I assume that my knowledge of developmental psychology is in some sense a cognitive structure rather than a collection of independent pieces of information. However, it would be factually wrong to argue that this structure emerged at a given point in my adult development—elements, relations, and all— and logically absurd to claim that, since it did not, it could not now be a genuine structure. (Flavell, 1970, p. 1039)

Note that, in making this comment, Flavell was separating the question of whether or not conceptual structures exist from several other questions, including (a) whether or not these structures emerge in a saltatory as opposed to continuous fashion, (b) whether or not they are age- or stage-specific, and (c) whether or not they depend on the presence of an underlying logico-mathematical competence. In subsequent years, these distinctions turned out to be crucial.

Subsequent Developments of the Empiricist Critique

During the decade that followed Flavell's chapter, work on Piaget's theory in the empiricist tradition continued, and dissatisfaction mounted concerning the theory's assumptions about the role of logico-mathematical structures in children's thought. Thus, when Gelman and Baillargeon (1983) reviewed the theory 13 years later, they were able to cite at least five different strands of empirical research—all of which were by now well developed—which called Piaget's general view of these structures into question. The relevant data were: (a) data on intertask correlations, which were often substantial but which did not assume a pattern that bore any obvious relation to the structures Piaget had hypothesized; (b) data on the sequence of cognitive development, which rarely showed logicomathematical structures emerging before the conceptual competencies they were supposed to generate; (c) data on preschool cognition, which often demonstrated the presence of logical competencies years before many Piagetians would have predicted; (d) data on the training of concrete operational concepts, which likewise indicated that they could often be acquired during the pre-operational period; and (e) data on logical competencies in adolescence and adulthood, which often demonstrated the *absence* of logical competencies at an age when they would have been long since been expected.

In suggesting which aspects of Piaget's theory were likely to prove lasting, Gelman and Baillargeon cited his emphasis on the active nature of children's cognitive processes, his suggestion that these processes were organized into coherent (though not necessarily logical) structures, and his elucidation of concepts such as assimilation and accommodation. Elsewhere, Gelman (1979) also mentioned the many tasks that Piaget's group had created, and the provocative data that they had generated, as significant and enduring contributions. The aspects of Piaget's theory that were seen as having received *no* support, however, and being unlikely to last, were (a) his view of the role played by children's logicomathematical structures in their cognitive development; and (b) his view of the stagelike nature of children's cognitive growth.

This general evaluation was a pervasive one among empiricists in the late 1970s and early 1980s. (For a dissenting view, see Chapman, 1988.) The dilemma with which it left investigators, however, was a perplexing one. How could one create an account of children's development that would eliminate the weaknesses of Piaget's theory, without also eliminating its strengths? How could one characterize the development of children's conceptual understanding in a fashion that captured its specificity, without also eliminating any ability to capture its overall shape? How could one create a weaker and less logic-bound characterization of children's conceptual structures, which would not also weaken the powerful heuristic utility that Piaget's account had shown?

NEW MODELS OF CHILDREN'S CONCEPTUAL UNDERSTANDING

Several different lines of inquiry have been pursued since the publication of the last *Handbook,* in response to this dilemma. In the present section I consider four of these. The first (often referred to as neo-Piagetian theory) had its origins in an attempt to integrate the core assumptions of the empiricist and rationalist traditions. The other three had their origins in attempts to re-think the core assumptions of one of the three classic traditions, in the light of the criticisms that had been levelled at it from other quarters, or new developments that had taken place within the tradition itself.

Conceptual Development as a Local Process, Limited by General Constraints

The first line of theoretical inquiry to emerge was one that became known as "neo-Piagetian" theory. This theoretical enterprise involved a direct attempt to build a bridge between the assumptions and methods that had underpinned

Piaget's research program and the assumptions and methods of empiricism. Neo-Piagetians accepted Piaget's position that children construct their own understanding of the world, and that reflexive abstraction plays an important role in this process. They also accepted Piaget's contention that development is a very general process, in which changes that cannot be tied to any form of specific external stimulation play an important role. Finally, they accepted the implicit methodological canons underlying Piaget's research: including (a) the notion that misleading tasks provide a particularly important window on children's conceptual understanding, and (b) the notion that the best way to develop a balanced view of children's intellectual capabilities is to examine their cognition on a broad spectrum of tasks, which span all the major categories of human understanding.

At the same time, however, neo-Piagetians also agreed with empiricists that much of children's knowledge of the world is acquired in a more piecemeal fashion than Piaget had indicated, and that local task factors, specific experience, and associative processes play a crucial role in this process. They also accepted the notion that one must examine and explain children's performance in specific contexts in great detail, and model the process of learning. Finally, they accepted the necessity of defining their constructs and task situations in operational terms. The notion of a scheme, for example, was defined in the first neo-Piagetian system as an ordered pair of responses, s-r (Pascual-Leone, 1970).

Different neo-Piagetian theorists proposed somewhat different views of the general architecture of the cognitive system, and the way in which that system develops. Nevertheless, there was a core set of propositions to which they all subscribed which included the following: Children's cognitive development does show a general pattern of growth across many different domains. However, this is not because of the existence of systemwide logicomathematical structures. Rather, it is because the local structures that children construct are all subject to a common, systemwide constraint in information processing capacity, and this constraint gradually lifts with age. Different theorists focused on different aspects of children's information processing capacity, such as their short-term memory, their working memory, and/or their information processing speed (Biggs & Collis, 1982; Case, 1985; Fischer, 1980; Halford, 1982; Pascual-Leone, 1970). They also used different metrics for calibrating the load that any given task places on children's information processing capacity. Regardless of the specifics, however, there was general agreement that a far more detailed analysis of specific task requirements was necessary than Piaget had attempted, and that these specific requirements had to be related to children's more general information-processing capacities—not just to their logical competencies.

In order to get a sense of the changed view of children's conceptual structures that neo-Piagetian analyses generated, it is worthwhile to consider a specific example. Consider, therefore, an early analysis of conservation. According to Piaget's analysis, it will be remembered, what children need in order to pass this task is a general logico-mathematical structure. By contrast, what neo-Piagetians claimed was necessary was a set of specific schemes of the following sort (Case, 1972a; Pascual-Leone, 1969):

E   An executive scheme representing the task instructions ("Do the two arrays still contain the same amount?") and directing an appropriate scan of the stimulus array.

F_1 A figurative scheme representing the fact that the two arrays originally had the same quantity.

F_2 A figurative scheme representing the rule (constructed from prior experience) that—if nothing is added or taken away—then the quantity should remain the same. (Note: If 4-year-olds do not actually witness the result of the transformation, this is their prediction.)

The thing that made the conservation task so problematic, according to this analysis, was that 4-year-old children also have another scheme, constructed on the basis of previous experience, namely:

F_m A misleading figurative scheme representing the rule that arrays of objects which look larger normally contain more substance.

Since the conservation task was deliberately designed in order to insure that F_m would be activated, children were believed to need three general things in order to pass it. First, they need a learned repertoire of schemes such as those indicated. Such a repertoire, it was hypothesized, can only be acquired through experience. Second, they need an information processing capacity of at least $e + 2$ units, in order to activate E, F_1, and F_2. According to the theory (see Table 15.2), an information processing capacity of $e + 2$ units is not available until the age of about 5 to 6 years. Even with appropriate experience, therefore, it is unlikely

TABLE 15.2 Hypothesized Mental Capacity Values (M) at Different Piagetian Stages and Substages

Piagetian Stage and Substage	Age	Modal Value of Mental Power or Capacity (M)
Early Preoperational	3–4 yrs.	$e + 1$*
Late Preoperational/ Early Concrete	5–6 yrs.	$e + 2$
Early/Middle Concrete	7–8 yrs.	$e + 3$
Late Concrete	9–10 yrs.	$e + 4$
Early Formal	11–12 yrs.	$e + 5$
Middle Formal	13–14 yrs.	$e + 6$
Late Formal	15–16 yrs.	$e + 7$

*In this notation, e stands for the capacity required to activate an executive schema representing the general task goal, and directing a scan of the perseptual situation

that children will pass the task before this age, and for variants of the problem where a second dimension needs to be focused on in order to arrive at a judgment, they will be unlikely to pass it before 7 to 8 years (Case, 1977). Third, children need a cognitive style of field independence: that is, a style that will allow them to integrate the first three schemes, (E, F_1, and F_2) and reach a logical conclusion, even in the face of the misleading schema F_m. If they do not have such a style, their acquisition of conservation will be considerably delayed.

In support of this analysis and others like it, neo-Piagetian theorists gathered several new kinds of data. Among the most important were the following:

1. Tests of children's information processing capacity do reveal an increase with age which follows the scale in Table 15.2 (Case, 1972b, 1995a; Pascual-Leone, 1970).

2. Subjects whose information processing capacity develops in an unusually rapid or slow manner show a corresponding acceleration or delay in acquiring new conceptual understandings of the sort studied by Piaget (Case, 1985; Crammond, 1992).

3. Subjects whose information processing capacity is normal, but who have a field dependent cognitive style, do not pass the most misleading of Piaget's tasks until 1 to 2 years after other children (Globerson, 1985; Pascual-Leone, 1969, 1974, 1989).

Finally, the age at which conceptual tasks are passed can be reduced by two years, by training studies that chunk two schemes together (Case, 1972a). Conversely, it can be increased by two years by task modifications that increase

the number of schemes that must be coordinated, in order to arrive at a successful task solution (Case, 1972b; Pascual-Leone & Smith, 1969).

In keeping with the general rationalist tradition, such demonstrations were not just attempted for logical tests such as conservation or classification. They were also attempted for high level logical tasks (DeRibaupierre & Pascual-Leone, 1979) and for a very broad range of other tasks, including those involving language (Johnson, Fabian, & Pascual-Leone, 1989; Johnson & Pascual-Leone, 1994), art (Bleiker, 1995; Dennis, 1992; Morra, Moizo, & Scopesi, 1988), classical learning tasks (Halford, 1982), social interaction (Fischer, Hand, Watson, Van Parys, & Tucker, 1984), motor skill (Todor, 1979) and even attachment (Case, 1995b). Finally, an attempt was also made to analyze the data from the concept learning studies cited earlier in order to show that they, too, showed a similar pattern. In this case, the suggestion was that in order to focus on a single dimension, children had to abstract its relevance by focusing on at least two lower order schemes. For this reason, it was argued, initial learning does not become rapid until children have an information processing capacity of $e + 2$ units. By the same token, if children are to decenter from this dimension, and focus on some other, less salient dimension, then they need an information processing capacity of $e + 3$ units (Case, 1985, p. 200). For this reason it was argued, relearning does not become rapid until 7 to 8 years of age, unless the second dimension happens to be more salient than the first one.

As work in this tradition progressed, neo-Piagetian analyses of individual tasks became much more detailed. They also became a good deal broader, and expanded to include an analysis of skills, (Fischer, 1980) executive control structures (Case, 1985), and mental models (Case, 1992a; Halford, 1993). Finally, an attempt was made to account for the growth of information processing capacity itself, on the basis of neurological change on the one hand (Case, 1985, 1995a; Pascual-Leone et al., 1990), and automaticity and improved speed of processing on the other (Case, 1985). The basic postulates described above, however, remained at the core of the endeavor.

Conceptual Development as a Sequence of Theoretical Revolutions

In contrast to the first line of work, which attempted to integrate the assumptions of the empiricist and rationalist traditions, the second line of work stayed more squarely within the rationalist tradition itself. Rather than turning to information processing theory for inspiration, theorists who took this second direction turned to two other sources: Chomsky's work on the acquisition of the structures of natural language, and T. Kuhn's (1962) work on theory change in science. According to Chomsky (1957), the reason that children come to understand and speak language as rapidly as they do is that they have an innate language acquisition device: one that is modular in nature, and that sensitizes them to the features in their environment that are relevant. According to T. Kuhn (1962), progress in science does not take place evenly. Rather it takes place in spurts: ones in which relatively short periods of revolutionary change are punctuated by long periods of problem solving within the general paradigm that any new theory affords.

Putting these two notions together, investigators in this second group suggested that the mind is best conceived as a loosely connected set of modules, each of which is specialized for executing its own particular function in the same way as is the system for natural language (Carey, 1985; Fodor, 1982; Gardner, 1983). Certain theorists in this school believed that children possess "naive theories" of the world at birth, one whose properties are universal (Spelke, 1988). Other theorists in this school emphasized the innate property of theories less strongly (see Gelman & Wellman, this volume). Regardless of the degree to which they took an innatist stance, however, theorists in this school were agreed that, by the preschool years, children possess a coherent, albeit a naive theory of the world, which they then rework as they enter their years of formal schooling (Carey, 1985, 1988). Such reworkings were seen as taking place in one of two fashions: Existing concepts can be related in new ways, as children encounter more experience with the world, or more experience in trying to understand adult explanations. (This sort of change is analogous to the sort that occurs during stable periods in science, when new data are being gathered, and the problems with the existing theoretical structure are being worked out.) Alternatively, existing conceptual structures can be radically restructured. This corresponds to the change that takes place during scientific revolutions. When this second, more revolutionary form of transformation takes place, three cognitive changes were hypothesized to take place in close synchrony:

1. The first involves a change in the phenomena that children see as needing explanation in the domain in question.

2. The second involves a change in the nature of what counts as an explanation in their eyes.

3. The third involves a change in the concepts that form the core of such explanations (Carey, 1985).

Once again, a specific example may help to clarify the theory-theory position. According to Carey and her colleagues, preschoolers have one naive theory that they apply to human beings and animals, in which action is explained in terms of social and motivational factors. They have a second naive theory that they apply to objects such as rocks, bicycles, or trees, in which action is explained in terms of mechanical causation. However, they do not yet have a uniquely biological theory: one that applies equally to humans, animals, or plants, and that explains surface phenomena in terms of underlying biological processes. Between the ages of 4 and 10 they acquire such a theory, or at least its rudiments. The result is that a major change takes place in their conceptual understanding.

This change has many of the revolutionary properties described above, and provides children with a radically different framework for responding to a wide variety of tasks, situations, and questions. To understand this transformation, theorists in this school developed a number of interesting new tasks. In one, children were told about an imaginary new human organ (e.g., an omenta) and how it works. They were then asked what other things they think might possess an omenta (a sheep? a worm? a cloud? a rock?). In another task, they were told about a biological process with which they have some first-hand knowledge (e.g., breathing), and asked about the range of objects to which this process applies. (Does a worm breathe? Does a rock breathe? Do clouds breathe?) In still another task, children were shown a situation in which one animal was made to look like another by the application of paint, and asked whether they thought it was still "really" the same kind of animal, or whether it had been changed into an animal that fit more with its appearance (Keil, 1986). These questions were interspersed with questions of the sort posed by Piaget in his work on children's naive concepts, namely, questions concerning what sorts of objects are and are not alive.

The general results across all these tasks were quite similar. At the age of 4, children presume that animals whose faces look like human faces will tend to have the same organs and processes as humans, but that animals which do not look like humans (e.g., snakes) will not. They also assume that, when the appearance of an animal is changed in some way, its behavior will tend to change also. By the age of 8 to 10 years, children's view of the natural world is quite different. Now they presume that most of the organs found in humans will be found in all other animals, and will not be found in inanimate objects, regardless of their visual similarity to humans. They also presume that plants will share certain underlying processes with humans, (e.g., the need for air), and that changes in the appearance of any living thing will not impact its behavior, unless they impact these underlying biological processes.

The foregoing changes fit well with one set of changes documented by Piaget: namely, the change from an "animistic" to a more "scientific" way of explaining natural phenomena, which normally occurs somewhere between the age of 5 and 7 years. And indeed, theorists in this school sided with Piaget, not with empiricists, in asserting that animistic responses are ones involving a genuine *mis*understanding on the part of the child, not simply the absence of empirical experience with the object being talked about, or a lack of familiarity with the type of question being posed (Carey, 1985, 1988). It is important to realize, however, that the theory-theory explanation for these changes was also *different* from Piaget's in two important respects. It was different, first, in the locus of conceptual change that it proposed. Change was not held to occur as a function of some system-wide transformation, such as the development of "concrete logical operations," or an increase in information processing capacity. Rather, it was held to occur as a result of a change that was modular, that is, domain-specific. Second, the particular *kind* of domain-specific change proposed by theory-theorists was different from the one proposed by Piaget. The change was not one in which an animistic response was replaced with a more "logical" one. Rather, the change was one in which a social/psychological theory was replaced by a biological one.

Children's theories of biological life are not the only ones that were studied from the theory-theory perspective. A second line of work examined children's theories of human intentionality (Astington, Harris, & Olson, 1989; Wellman, 1990). This work will be described in a later section. For the moment, the general point is simply this. The theory-theory view of conceptual development remained more squarely in the rationalist tradition than did neo-Piagetian theory, by characterizing children's conceptual development as a series of qualitative transformations in internal structures, whose field of application was quite broad, and which were relatively impervious to experience of a task-specific sort. As a consequence, this view also

remained united with classical Piagetian theory in adopting a research strategy that examined children's reasoning across a broad range of situations, on tasks where some sort of misleading feature had to be overcome, rather than examining one task in detail in a multi-trial learning context.

Conceptual Development as the Acquisition of Expertise

A third view of conceptual structures that has been proposed since the last *Handbook* has its origins in the empiricist tradition, in work on expert systems. Early studies of chess experts revealed—somewhat to everyone's surprise—that these individuals do not appear to have a set of general problem-solving heuristics that are more powerful than those of novices. Nor do they have more powerful spatial memories. To be sure, they can perform powerful feats of memory. For example, if presented with a chess board for only a few seconds, they can reproduce the entire configuration of pieces without error. However, this is true only if the pieces are placed in the sort of configuration that they might typically assume in a real chess game. If the pieces are placed on the board randomly, the ability of experts to remember their position is no better than that of novices (DeGroot, 1966). This study, and others like it, convinced many investigators that the main thing which distinguishes chess experts from others—other than some innate love of, or talent for, the game—is that they possess a huge repertoire of chess patterns that they can recognize (e.g., presence of an open file), and good moves that they can make in response to these patterns (e.g., move a rook to this file). This notion of expertise fit well with attempts to simulate the performance of chess experts on a computer. With about 10,000 patterns of the above sort, computer programs were created that did a very good job of simulating expert performance: beating human novices in the same general fashion, and in the same number of moves, as would a real expert, and losing to world champions or grand masters.

This early work on expertise was soon extended to domains of knowledge that were less perceptually based, such as Medicine and Physics. Studies in these domains also found that the distinguishing feature of experts was the vast network of specific knowledge that they possessed—not a more powerful set of general heuristics or strategies. Equipped with this specific knowledge, experts would classify new problems in a different fashion from novices, typically according to the deep "principles" that they embodied, rather than with regard to their superficial features (Chi & Rees, 1983). Once the problems were classified in this fashion, experts were able to solve them with *less* effort, and *less* elaborate problem solving processes than were novices. Once again, attempts to create expert systems on a computer were more successful when they built a huge repertoire of specific knowledge, and a powerful way of representing that knowledge, than when they tried endowing the system with more powerful problem solving strategies.

As Hayes (1985) pointed out, a repertoire of the magnitude required by these simulations takes many years for humans to acquire. Indeed, his review of the literature suggested that—even in the extreme case of "child prodigies"—one never finds a lasting contribution to a field being made until at least ten years of study have been logged, with a daily investment on the order of 8 to 10 hours. Needless to say, one of the obvious things that distinguishes 10-year-olds from newborns is that they have had ten additional years of experience. It was not long, therefore, before developmentalists in the empiricist tradition began to view the work on expert systems as providing a model for children's intellectual development. According to their view, extremely young children are best viewed as "universal novices," while adults are best viewed as individuals who have become expert in the wide range of problems that daily life (and/or school) presents.

In an early series of studies designed to demonstrate this point, Chi and her colleagues modeled children's knowledge about a particular class of objects (dinosaurs), in terms of the features of each dinosaur that they were aware of, and could talk about (has sharp teeth, eats meat, is large, etc.). She then showed that, as children's knowledge of dinosaurs increases, the knowledge network that they possess becomes increasingly coherent, in the sense that local groups of dinosaurs acquire more and more internal connecting links, which serve to distinguish them from other groups (Chi & Koeske, 1983). Finally, she showed that 6-year-olds with a lot of dinosaur experience (and coherent knowledge networks) tend to sort dinosaurs in the classic hierarchical fashion that is normally not seen until the age of 7 years (after the 5 to 7 shift), while 7-year-old children with the same I.Q. who have had little experience (and whose knowledge networks are not well differentiated) tend to sort dinosaurs in the syncretic and error prone fashion that is normally typical of children who are 5 years of age or younger (Chi, Hutchinson, & Robin, 1989). Chi's interpretation of Piaget's findings on classification and class-inclusion, therefore, was that the

performance typically displayed by young children often results from an immature knowledge network, not from the absence of some powerful general logic that specifies how classes and subclasses are related, or some powerful general "processing capacity." Indeed, Chi, (1976) suggested that the age-related growth of processing capacity itself might just be an epiphenomenon. The real source of growth, she proposed, might be the acquisition of a huge knowledge-network, one which is in turn acquired through the accumulation of a vast amount of specific experience.

Chi's interpretation of the data that had been gathered by theory-theorists was more subtle. While she agreed with them that the fundamental source of children's cognitive growth was knowledge, she preferred to see the underlying process as one in which different knowledge networks gradually become more elaborate and coherent, rather than as one in which one type of theory is replaced with another as a result of some sort of "cognitive revolution." In accord with this interpretation, she pointed out that Carey's own (1985) data on children's acquisition of biological knowledge betokens a rather gradual (6 year) rather than a revolutionary change. Extending this point of view downwards, one could argue that infants are not born with—nor do they construct—naive "theories" about the world around them. Rather, they are born with a biological pre-disposition to pay attention to certain broad classes of features in the world, which disposition leads them to create certain general types of knowledge network. To begin with, different knowledge networks may be rather restricted in their domain of application. However, as children acquire more experience, their networks gradually become more tightly linked with each other, and hence more general.

This view of conceptual development, based as it is on the gradual accumulation of elements via experience, is consistent with the classical empiricist view of cognitive development. As will be shown later, it is also consistent with contemporary attempts to model cognitive development via "neural nets." One problem that this account raises, however, is how to account for the sort of revolutionary changes that occur in the history of science. For certain developmental theories, this might not be a problem: One could simply argue that the two sets of phenomena are only superficially similar, and thus require no deep or integrating explanation. Since the "expertise" view of children's development holds that the underlying mechanisms of knowledge acquisition are identical in the two cases (or at least very similar), however, the problem of explaining revolutionary theory change in science is a serious one. If scientific knowledge networks are also acquired gradually, and more powerful ones emerge by the linking of specific networks, how is one to explain those dramatic watersheds in the history of science—the ones that theory-theorists take as models for the watershed in children's cognition between 4 and 10 years of age?

In response to this problem, Chi (1994) pointed out that many major theoretical changes in the history of science have lacked the revolutionary character that T. Kuhn's theory postulates. The historical discovery of the principles governing blood and its circulation, for example, was quite slow, and took place over a long time period. What about the sort of change that took place when Einstein's theory was adopted? This change did have a revolutionary character, Chi acknowledges. However, her claim is that the revolutionary character of this change did not stem from the fact that it conflicted with an existing theory (which, of course, any new theory must do) but from the fact that it conflicted with a fundamental and universal way of categorizing reality. Things that are normally placed into one primitive and universal ontological category (the category of objects) had now to be placed into a different but equally primitive ontological category (the category of a process). Whenever this requirement for radical re-parsing is present, Chi argued, a new theory will be difficult to understand. By the same token, however, when it *is* understood, it will have the potential to produce changes that are sweeping and revolutionary in their nature.

Conceptual Development as Initiation into a Community of Praxis

The fourth line of inquiry in the post-Piagetian era had its roots in the sociohistoric tradition. The general starting point from which this work took off was Vygotsky and Luria's demonstration that the performance of adults in a traditional agricultural setting, on a set of high level mnemonic and logical tasks, is a function of their degree of exposure to modern schooling. Several important questions were raised by this finding. First, how general is this effect? Is it one that applies across-the-board, and produces a change in the full range of intellectual competencies that individuals in the culture display, or is it restricted to school-type tasks? Second, what aspect of schooling is responsible for producing this effect? Is it the acquisition of a new symbol system, such as that involved in literacy and numeracy (Olson, 1977)? Is it exposure to a new form of instruction, one that originally evolved to teach these systems, and that did so in a "decontextualized" context (Greenfield & Bruner, 1966)? Is it the mastery of the formal systems of

Western thought: ones which the new symbolic systems were designed to represent, and that evolved with them?

A good deal of work has been devoted to pursuing these questions since the publication of the last *Handbook*. Although many questions remain to be answered, the pattern of the findings that has emerged is remarkably coherent. Consider first the work that has been devoted to analyzing the acquisition of literacy, and its cognitive consequences. Early studies suggested that the acquisition of literacy—both within a culture and within an individual child—produces a transformation in cognitive structures that is revolutionary in its consequences, and that applies to the full range of activities in which a literate individual engages (Olson, 1977). More recent work, while continuing to reinforce the notion that literacy is important, has suggested that its effects are a good deal more differentiated, as a function of the local social, economic, and institutional context (Olson, 1994).

The classic study that led to this conclusion was one conducted by Cole and his colleagues in Liberia, with the Vye. What made the Vye so interesting for Cole's purpose was that, some time during the late eighteenth century, they developed a script of their own. Of even greater interest, this script is still taught today, in several different institutional contexts. In one context (secular schools), it is taught via a form of schooling that resembles the one that is used in the West; once acquired in this context, the script is then used for Western purposes. In another context (religious schools), it is taught via chant and recitation, so that it can be used for further reading, memorization, and recitation of the Koran. In a third (family) context, it is taught more informally, so that it can be used by relatives who are separated but want to stay in touch with each other by writing letters. Cole and his collaborators demonstrated that each of these contexts leads to a unique pattern of cognitive consequences. There is no universal transformation that takes place, which differentiates the thinking of those who are literate from those who are not. Rather, the particular transformation that takes place is a function of the context in which literacy is acquired, and the use to which it is put (Scribner & Cole, 1981).

In the face of this evidence, and other evidence implicating such factors as economic exchange and authority (Street, 1984), even those who still view literacy as the gateway to higher cognitive functioning now take a much more differentiated view of the process by which this transformation takes place, and the aspects of literate practice that are crucial for it (Olson, 1994). The same applies to the acquisition of other paper-based cultural systems, such as those involved in the use of arithmetic (Damerow, in press; Hoyrup, 1994), money (McDermott, 1994) or cartography (Olson, 1994, Ch. 10). Although interesting cognitive consequences often do appear to be associated with the acquisition of these systems, the nature of the effects that they produce appears to be a function of the context and purpose of their use. Literacy, by itself, does not appear to be sufficient to produce a conceptual transformation.

Nor does literacy appear to be necessary for the acquisition of sophisticated conceptual structures. Neisser (1976) was one of the first to make this point. Drawing on the work of Gladwyn (1970) with the Pulawatt, Neisser pointed out that the navigational competence of this group is remarkable. With the knowledge acquired from their elders, young Pulawatt men can travel thousands of miles across uncharted stretches of ocean in small outrigger canoes, arriving precisely at their intended destination. This remarkable achievement does not appear to depend on any formal logical system of the sort that Piaget postulated. Nor does it depend on literacy or the use of modern Western artifacts such as a compass or a map. On the other hand, it *does* depend on the acquisition of a complex knowledge structure: one that entails principled and sophisticated understanding of celestial movements in the region, and that utilizes this understanding for navigational purposes (Oatley, 1977).

In a related study, this line of reasoning was taken further. Frake (1985) studied the system that was used by medieval sea-farers for the reckoning of tides. The conceptual framework that was used for this purpose in Northern Europe during the middle ages was a highly sophisticated one, which related solar and lunar time via the device of the compass rose. With an understanding of this system, mariners could calculate the time at which high and low tide would occur at any harbor they might visit—provided only that they had knowledge of the height the tide had reached there on one prior date and time. In analyzing this capability, Frake made a number of interesting points. One is that this capability did not require any formal ability to read and write. Like the Pulawatt, seafarers in the middle ages were often illiterate. Another is that the acquisition of the relevant structure did not produce a general change in the mental capabilities of those who understood it. Rather, it produced a change that was domain-specific. A third point is that—with the transition to literacy and modern technology—this remarkable capability has been lost. Modern tide tables give the tidal heights at all harbors in an area, for any given date and time of the day. Deprived of

this table, most modern seafarers cannot begin to use their general understanding of tides, lunar movement, and local conditions to calculate the height of the tide in a particular location. Not only can non-Western cultures develop structures that are as powerful as ours, then, it would appear that our own culture has had structures in the past which were more powerful than those we use now—at least in certain respects. Frake's conclusion is that one should not see conceptual development as proceeding in a unique or privileged direction, even within the West, as we move from the pre-industrial to the post-industrial period.

If the conceptual capabilities of adults are particular to their geographic locale and historical period, it follows that social transmission must play a vital role in the developmental process. In our own culture, much of this transmission takes place via schooling. As mentioned above, one early hypothesis about modern schools had to do with their "decontextualized" nature. The notion was that protracted formal schooling—which originally emerged as a vehicle for teaching children to read and write—also exposes children to a form of learning that is unique and extremely powerful: namely, one where the conceptual content that must be mastered is learned in a context remote from that in which it must ultimately be applied. In an early essay on this topic, Greenfield and Bruner (1966) suggested that this decontextualized form of learning might produce a corresponding decontextualization of children's thought, that is, the ability to apply that thought, in a more logical, principled fashion, across a wide variety of contexts.

Just as the presumed superiority of Piaget's formal structures was challenged by cross cultural investigations, however, so was the presumed superiority of formal schooling. The most widely cited studies were those that looked at the development of children's conceptual understanding of the whole numbers, and the base system that underlies their use. These understandings show a typical pattern of development during the early school years which progresses from an understanding of how small whole numbers work, through to an understanding of groupings and exchanges, to an understanding of the principles underlying such operations such as multiplication and division (Resnick, 1989).

One might think that, if formal schooling had any advantage, it would manifest itself in this precise and well articulated domain. In fact, however, this does not appear to be the case. Studies with unschooled children who work as street vendors in Brazil have shown that these children's understanding of the number system proceeds quite normally in such unschooled contexts (Carraher, Carraher, & Schliemann, 1985). Indeed, children who grow up in this environment often display an understanding of numerical principles and operations that is *superior* to that displayed by children who learn their mathematics in school. These latter children sometimes apply the algorithms that they learn in a rote or unprincipled fashion, whereas children who grow up as street vendors rarely if ever make mistakes of this sort. If the problem that is presented is *unique* to a schooled setting (as is the case for certain kinds of ratio problems), schooled children do show occasional competencies that are superior to those of street vendors (Saxe, 1988). By and large, however, what is more salient is that the informal learning in the market is every bit as powerful as, and perhaps more powerful than, the decontextualized learning provided by the academy. These results, and others like them have been used by Lave (1988) to argue for the superiority of contextually based "apprenticeship" over more formal learning. Intellectual competencies can then be seen as being acquired through a sort of "apprenticeship" in thought (Rogoff, 1990).

Summary

Early work in the sociohistoric tradition accepted Vygotsky's notion that children's conceptual development depends on the acquisition of an intellectual and physical technology: one that is normally acquired in school and that depends on the acquisition of literacy and numeracy. Recent work in this tradition has continued the emphasis on the importance of mastering the intellectual technology that one's culture provides. However, it has painted a picture that is a good deal more complex and context-specific. Not only is there no formal structure that applies across all contexts, but literate structures are not necessarily superior to other structures, and may in fact lead to practices that are less rather than more sophisticated. The same holds for the institutions with which literacy has been associated, and the historical practices that have developed within them. Although they may offer certain advantages, they may also offer certain disadvantages that are equally important to understand.

Comparing the New Models and Abstracting Common Principles

As will no doubt be apparent, the epistemological differences that divide different schools of thought in the post-Piagetian era are still considerable, as is the view which the

different schools offer of the process of conceptual growth. For expertise-theorists, the growth of knowledge is still by and large seen as being under the control of local learning factors, and the relationship between learning and development is still seen as the one indicated under the empiricist rubric in Table 15.1. What has changed, largely as a result of developments in cognitive science, is the sophistication of the models of knowledge that can be proposed and the ease with which they can be simulated on a computer. A similar point may be made for theory-theorists. By and large theorists in this school still view children's knowledge as qualitatively different from that of adults, and still subscribe to most of the general propositions that are listed under the rationalist rubric in Table 15.1. However, their attempt to model the structure of children's conceptual understanding has been enriched by contemporary analyses of theory-change in science. Contemporary sociohistoric theorists, too, still by and large see conceptual change in the fashion described in the original sociohistoric position. However, as a result of developments in Cognitive Anthropology, their models have become less Euro-centric, and more contextualized in their analysis of cognitive benefits and debits. Of the four groups reviewed, neo-Piagetian theorists have made the most explicit attempt to cross the epistemological boundaries that are indicated in the table. Even in this group, however, most theorists still lean quite strongly in either the empiricist or rationalist direction in their foundational assumptions; the principle new postulates which they hold in common are: (a) conceptual growth is neither a monolithic process, nor a process that is driven by a universal logic; (b) notwithstanding its specificity, there are still general maturational constraints to which the process is subject; (c) using the best analytic tools available, detailed models must be created which specify how general-maturational and more specific domain- and task- and cultural factors interact, to influence children's conceptual growth on particular tasks and in particular contexts.

Given the continuing commitment to different epistemologies, it is perhaps not surprising that the methods that have been employed to explore the different positions continue to be quite distinctive, and that each group occasionally fires methodological broadsides across the bows of another. The primary methodological innovation that expertise theorists have introduced has been the coupling of detailed studies on children's learning with studies designed to diagnose the semantic organization of children's knowledge (Chi, Hutchinson, & Robin, 1989). The primary methodological innovation in the rationalist tradition has been the introduction of new tasks for probing children's semantic (as opposed to logical) structures—especially tasks relating to their theory of life (Carey, 1985) their theory of mind (Astington, Harris, & Olson, 1989) and their theory of the physical world (McCloskey, 1983). The primary methodological innovation in the sociohistoric tradition has been the examination of different forms of cultural praxis and learning, and the tighter linkage of these to cognitive performance. Finally, the primary innovation in the neo-Piagetian tradition has been the combination of studies of conceptual development with assessment of change in more basic cognitive capacities such as speed of processing or working memory. Since the methods of the various traditions have continued to vary so greatly, so, too, has the new database that has been built up, and the interpretative stances that have been taken toward it.

To say that large differences still separate the different traditions is not to say that the process of dialogue has had no effect. To the contrary, if one looks at the general structure of the new theories in each tradition, and compares them to their predecessors, one sees a number of important points of convergence that were not present in previous years. In contrast to the state of affairs that obtained 20 years ago, for example, contemporary theorists in each school are now agreed (a) that the notion of a systemwide cognitive structure should be replaced by a notion of structures that are more specific; (b) that children's cognitive structures should not be modeled as systems of logical operations, but as systems for making meaning, each with its own distinctive conceptual and/or symbolic content (this is a move that Piaget also made in his later years; Piaget & Garcia, 1991); and (c) that children's physical and/or social experience should be assigned a much more central role in explaining the process of structural change than early theories gave it.

For theorists in the empiricist tradition, the move to this middle ground meant a move away from a view of knowledge that focuses exclusively on isolated elements and their associations, and toward a view where broad structural and/or disciplinary coherencies are considered as well. For theorists in the rationalist tradition, the move to this middle ground has meant a move away from analyses that are systemwide, and toward a detailed consideration of factors that are domain specific. For theorists in the sociohistoric tradition, the new position has entailed a similar movement away from a general and unilinear model of social and intellectual change, and toward a model in which culture

practices and patterns of reasoning are viewed in terms that are more specific.

Given the trend toward greater convergence, it seems possible that we may see a greater convergence still in the years to come. In the extreme, it seems possible that the different perspectives may ultimately be seen as more complementary than incompatible, and that it may be possible to contemplate the possibility of a more general and unified theoretical framework. With this possibility in mind, I turn now to a description of several recent lines of inquiry: ones which give some hint of the outline that such a framework might ultimately assume.

TOWARD AN INTEGRATED VIEW OF CHILDREN'S CONCEPTUAL STRUCTURES

Considerable progress has been made in the last few years in clarifying children's understanding of a number of foundational domains of knowledge (see Wellman & Gelman, Ch. 11, this Volume). Three lines of work that are of particular relevance in the present context are those dealing with children's understanding of number, space, and narrative.

Young Children's Understanding of Number

Throughout the 1980s and 1990s, increasingly strong empirical evidence was obtained that children are born with a natural sensitivity to number (Starkey, 1992; Wynn, 1992) and that—by the time they enter school (if not earlier)—their intuitions with regard to small numbers are well developed. By the preschool years, children possess a good deal of intuitive knowledge that permits them to answer questions about the effects of addition, subtraction, and spatial transformation when these operations are applied to small quantities. The top panel of Figure 15.1 lays out the major semantic nodes and relations that appear to underlie these competencies.

As Gelman (1978) has shown, preschoolers also possess a good deal of knowledge about counting. They can reliably count a set of objects by the age of 4 years. They can also understand that the answer to the question "How many objects are there in this group?" is the final number tag assigned to a set. Finally, they can respond with insight to a variety of novel counting requests: such as the request to begin counting in the middle of a line of objects rather than at the end. Although there is some disagreement as to whether this capacity stems from a conceptual or a procedural knowledge base (Gelman, 1978; Siegler, 1992), there

(A) Global Quantity Schema

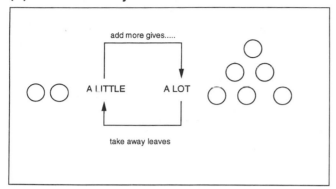

(B) Counting Schema

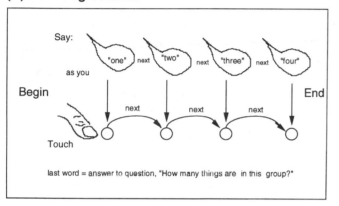

Figure 15.1   Central numerical structures hypothesized in preschool children, circa 4 years of age. Panel A illustrates the global quantity schema that permits children to answer questions about "more" and "less." Panel B illustrates the counting schema that permits children to state how many objects are in a set.

is no disagreement that it implies the existence of a complex knowledge network. One possible way of representing this network is illustrated in the bottom panel of Figure 15.1.

Although children assemble knowledge structures for generating number tags and for making non-numerical judgments of quantity during the preschool period, they appear to be incapable of integrating these two competencies (Resnick, 1989). Thus, when asked "Which is more (or which is bigger), 4 or 5?" they respond at chance level, even though they can successfully count to 5 and make relative quantity judgments about arrays containing 5 versus 4 objects (Siegler & Robinson, 1982). On magnitude comparisons which involve a big difference in quantity (e.g., 6 versus 3) they do a good deal better. However, the point is that they do not appear to use a number's position in a

counting string, in and of itself, as an indicator of its quantity relative to other numbers. Using Chi's metaphor, one could say that children's numerical knowledge and their quantity knowledge are stored in different "files" which are as yet not fully "merged."

As children move from age 4 to age 6 they gradually become capable of answering such questions. It seems reasonable to hypothesize, therefore, that these two earlier structures have become merged and that a new conceptual structure, one which integrates the two previous structures, is now available. In our own work, Sandieson, Griffin, and I have provided a detailed model of this structure (Case & Griffin, 1990; Case & Sandieson, 1988). The most recent version of this model is reproduced in Figure 15.2.

Since the structure that is illustrated in Figure 15.2 will be treated as a prototype for the rest of the present chapter, it is worthwhile to explicate the notation that it employs. The top row of entries in the figure (row a) indicates that children can recognize the written numerals from 1 to 5, and that these written symbols are "grafted on," as it were, to a structure that is more fundamental and that appears below the dotted lines. This more fundamental structure has four basic components, which appear as interconnected

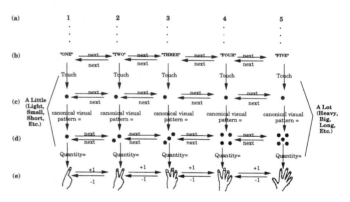

Figure 15.2   Central numerical structure (the "mental number line") hypothesized to emerge circa 6 years, as a result of the elaboration and merging of the two earlier schemas shown in Figure 15.1. The five rows indicate, respectively, (a) knowledge of written numerals, (b) knowledge of number words, (c) knowledge of how to assign numbers to objects when counting, (d) knowledge of the visual patterns formed by sets of different sizes, and (e) knowledge that one can move from one of these patterns to the next by an addition or subtraction of one unit. Vertical arrows indicate knowledge that each row maps conceptually on to the next; horizontal arrows indicate knowledge that entire structure can be used as a vehicle for determining relative amount (weight, height, length, etc.) of quantities composed of identical units.

rows below the dotted lines. The first of these rows, (row b) is the "verbal labeling" line. What the notation is intended to indicate is that children can recognize and generate the number words "one," "two," "three," and so on. The row immediately below this (row c) is intended to indicate that children have a routine for pointing at or "tagging" a set of objects as they say the number words, in such a fashion that each object is tagged once and only once in the process. The next row in the figure (row d) is the "perceptual configuration" line. What the entries in this row are intended to indicate is that children understand that each act of tagging an object is equivalent to forming a set that has a certain number of objects in it, and that also has a certain characteristic perceptual form (e.g., as displayed on dice). What the bottom row (e) indicates is that children can form an internal representation of these patterns (initially with their fingers) and move from one pattern to the next by the addition or subtraction of one unit.

Consider next the arrows in the figure. In each case, the horizontal arrows indicate the "transformations" or "rules for movement" that allow children to move from one item to the next in any row, and back. The vertical arrows signify children's understanding that there is a one-to-one mapping between each row and the next. Thus, movement from one item to the next in any row must necessarily be accompanied by a similar movement from one item to the next in all other rows as well. The wide brackets at the edge of the figure indicate children's understanding that movement forward or backward along the four rows is simultaneously a movement toward "more" or "less" of some quantity. Thus, counting can be used for making predictions or assessments of quantity along a wide variety of dimensions. In our own work we have shown that the dimensions to which children can apply the structure in the figure include time, distance, musical tonality, and monetary value (Capodilupo, 1992; Griffin, Case, & Sandieson, 1992; Marini, 1992; Okamoto & Case, 1996).

For each of the forgoing dimensions, children appear to progress through three recognizable phases: In the first (5–6 years), they build a "mental model" of the dimension that is numerical in nature. In the second (7–8 years), they begin to differentiate two sub-dimensions or "scales" for each of these dimensions (e.g., hours and minutes for time; feet and inches for distance; black notes and white notes for musical tonality; ounces and pounds or grams and kilograms for weight). Finally, in the third (9–10 years), they can not only differentiate these scales; they can formulate and apply an explicit rule for modeling the relationship between them.

Children might progress through a common sequence such as this across a broad variety of dimensions for any number of reasons. The particular hypothesis that we have investigated is that they progress through this common sequence because the conceptual understanding of number which the figure reflects is a general one, which impacts their understanding across a broad range of specific tasks and procedures. In order to validate this claim, we have conducted three sorts of study. In the first, we have shown that children's progress through the common developmental sequence occurs at a common rate: namely, that hypothesized by the model (Case & Sowder, 1990; Griffin, Case, & Siegler, 1994; Okamoto & Case, 1996). In the second, we have shown that correlational analyses of children's performance reveal a consistency across these various tasks: one that permits the presence of an underlying latent structure to be induced (Okamoto & Case, 1996). Finally, in the third we have shown that, when the hypothesized structure is trained, children show transfer to the full range of dimensions and tasks cited above (Griffin & Case, 1996) but not to others (Case, Okamoto, Henderson, & McKeough, 1993).

Young Children's Social Understanding and their Construction of a "Theory of Mind"

A great deal of research has also been conducted in recent years on children's early social understanding. This work has shown that preschoolers possess some rudimentary understanding that people have mental representations by the age of about 3 years, and that they understand the way in which mental states can be modified by external events by the age of 4 to 5 years (Astington, 1994; Astington et al., 1989; Wellman, 1990). Another general understanding that is in place by this age is that of "scripts": 4- to 5-year-old children understand how familiar sequences of events unfold, and the way in which one event can follow another, or prepare the way for still another event that follows it. They can also describe these familiar "scripts" in language (Nelson, 1978; Nelson & Gruendel, 1978). The content that is represented in each of these two knowledge structures is depicted in Figure 15.3.

Although 4-year-olds are quite skilled at operating within each of these domains of social knowledge, they are much less skilled at moving across the two. For example, if asked why a mother responds in some fashion in a familiar action sequence, they have no trouble referring to the previous action or event that triggers this response. Nor do they have any trouble extrapolating forward, and predicting

(A) Inner State Schema

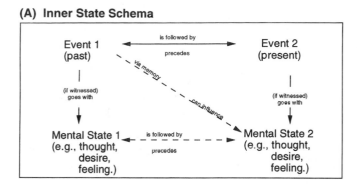

(B) External Action Schema

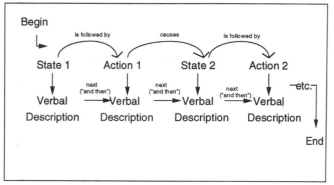

Figure 15.3   Central narrative structures hypothesized in preschool children, circa 4 years of age. Panel A illustrates the inner state schema that permits children to infer the thoughts or feelings of others, and to solve the classic "false belief" task. Panel B illustrates the schema that permits children to verbalize the social scripts with which they are familiar and make causal statements and/or predictions about what will happen next (see Nelson, 1978).

what action or response will come next. But even if probed with further questions, they do not spontaneously shift their focus, and refer to the role of the mother's internal state in motivating her action (Goldberg-Reitman, 1992). As was the case with numerical understanding, one could say that children of this age have their knowledge of familiar scripts and their knowledge of familiar mental states stored in separate "files," which they have great difficulty in "merging." Between the ages of 5 and 6 years, children become capable of answering such questions. One can therefore suggest that they have now merged the two original files, and have formed a superordinate structure such as that illustrated in Figure 15.4. As the figure suggests, children can now think of any familiar human activity as a coordinated sequence of events involving two components: a "landscape of action," which is the behavioral component of any event sequence (row c), and a "landscape of

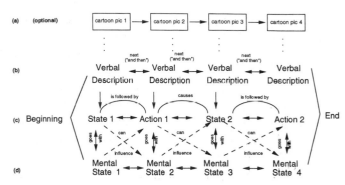

Figure 15.4   Central narrative structure (the "mental story line") hypothesized to emerge during the school years, circa 6 years of age, as a result of the elaboration and merging of the two earlier schemas shown in Figure 15.3. The four rows indicate, respectively, (a) (optional) knowledge that states and actions can be represented with visual symbols or "icons," (b) knowledge of sentence forms for describing familiar events and actions, (c) knowledge of familiar states and actions, together with the causal or "enabling" relations that they bear to each other, and (d) knowledge of the role that those events play in influencing mental states and vice-versa. External brackets indicate that entire structure is understood to have a characteristic beginning, middle, and end.

consciousness," which is the internal or "intentional" component (row d) (Bruner, 1986).

As a comparison of Figures 15.2 and 15.4 will reveal, there is a similarity in the general form of children's narrative and numerical thought at the age of 6, notwithstanding the many differences. In effect, the structure depicted in Figure 15.4 may be viewed as a mental "story line" that corresponds in its general form to the mental "number line" with which children of this age approach quantitative tasks. This parallel between 6-year-olds' social and numerical understanding applies at older ages as well. Between the ages of 6 and 10 there is a progression from uni-intentional to bi-intentional and then to integrated bi-intentional thought, which directly parallels the corresponding progression in the domain of number: that is, the progression from uni-dimensional to bidimensional to integrated bidimensional thought (Bruchkowsky, 1992; Goldberg-Reitman, 1992; Griffin, 1992; McKeough, 1992a).

Young Children's Understanding of Space

A similar progression also appears to take place in the domain of space. By the age of 4 years, most children (or at least most Western, middle-class children) have developed a general schema for representing familiar three-dimensional objects on a two-dimensional surface. This representation correctly captures the shape of the objects to be depicted, as well as the shape of their most salient component parts, and the adjacency and inclusion relations that obtain among them. Thus, a tree is typically represented as a circle (for the branches and the leaves) with a line extending downwards from the bottom (for the trunk). Similarly, the human figure is typically represented as a circle for the body, with two dots and a semi-circle inside for the eyes and mouth, and two straight lines extending downwards from the circle for the legs (Kellogg, 1969; Luquet, 1927). The implicit knowledge that underlies these representational capabilities is illustrated in the top panel of Figure 15.5.

At the same age, children also learn to represent the location of any familiar three-dimensional object on a

two-dimensional surface by noting its position vis à vis the scene of which it is a part. As this knowledge develops, children become capable of reproducing the position of a single dot that is placed on a 3 × 3 grid (Crammond, 1992), or a line of dots that goes along some particular edge (Halford & McDonald, 1977). They also become capable of placing pre-drawn "stick figures" in the correct position in a scene. A related task that has been studied by DeLoache (1989) is that of locating a hidden object in a three-dimensional room by noting its position in a photograph or model. Children can find an object using this sort of representation in relatively easy conditions by the age of 3, and under conditions that include some sort of misleading property by the age of 4 or 5. The emergence of these competencies suggests that children acquire some sort of "object-location" schema during the preschool years. One way of representing the core elements of this schema is indicated in the bottom panel of Figure 15.5.

Once again, although preschool children possess both these sorts of knowledge, they have great difficulty in integrating the two in any systematic fashion. Thus, if asked to draw a picture of two people standing side by side on the grass, they tend to reproduce the internal relations of each person correctly, but ignore the relations that obtain between the people and their general environment (Dennis, 1992). By the age of 6 years, this task poses little problem. One may therefore infer that they have merged the two lower-order structures into a superordinate structure in which each individual object can simultaneously be seen as a configuration of two-dimensional shapes with its own internal structure, and as one component in a broader spatial field. During this age range children's drawing shows quite a dramatic re-organization, as each object is now carefully positioned with respect to a common ground line or "reference axis." The knowledge that permits children to draw figures that are arranged in this fashion is illustrated in Figure 15.6.

Between the ages of 6 and 10, children's ability to represent the location of a group of objects in relation to a "mental reference line" increases in a systematic fashion. By the age of 8, they appear capable of mentally dividing any group of objects into two subgroups, each positioned with respect to a different mental reference line. Finally, by the age of 10, they appear capable of examining any set of objects in a spatial array and noting their position with regard to two orthogonal reference lines simultaneously. This "conjoint referencing capability" can be used for understanding the system of Cartesian coordinates that is used

(A) Object Shape Schema

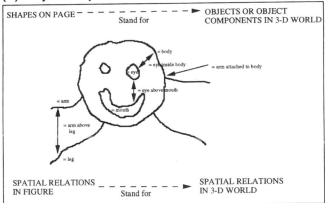

(B) Object Location Schema

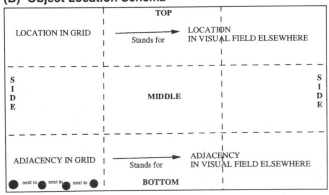

Figure 15.5 Central spatial structures hypothesized in preschool children, circa 4 years of age. Panel A illustrates the shape schema that permits children to symbolize the consitutent two-dimensional shapes of which a three-dimensional object is comprised, and the relations among them. Panel B illustrates the location schema that permits children to represent the general shape of a rectangular field, and the location of objects within it.

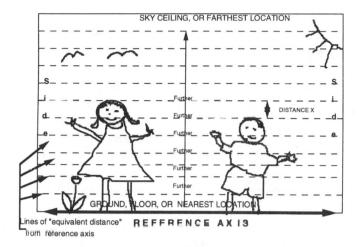

Figure 15.6 Central spatial structure hypothesized to emerge during the school years, circa 6 years of age, as a result of the elaboration and merging of two earlier schemas shown in Figure 15.5. Note that structure permits children to represent relationship of object components to each other (head is above body, body is above legs, etc.) as well as relationship of objects to each other. (Girl's skirt is higher than flower, girl is taller than boy, etc.). Note that these latter judgments can only be made with reference to the ground line. It is the construction of this line, and the referencing of all objects in the window to it, that gives the schema its name (the Mental Reference Axis).

in graphs, or the system of projective representation that is used to render perspective in Western art (Case et al., 1996; Piaget & Inhelder, 1956). The overall progression is illustrated in Figure 15.7.

Abstracting a Common Pattern of Development across Different Domains

There is a similarity in the general form of children's numerical, narrative, and spatial development—or at least in the graphic representations of this development that I have presented—between the ages of 4 and 10 years. In each domain, 4-year-olds appear to posses two separate structures, each of which represents a fairly elaborate set of first-order symbolic relations. In each domain, an integration or "merging" of these structures takes place between the ages of 4 and 6 years, with the result that children begin to construct a system of second-order symbolic relations. Finally, in each domain, there is a parallel progression between the ages of 6 and 10, as children move from partial to complete mastery of the second order system. The structures that are constructed at 6 years all appear to be linelike ones, which integrate knowledge regarding the internal components of

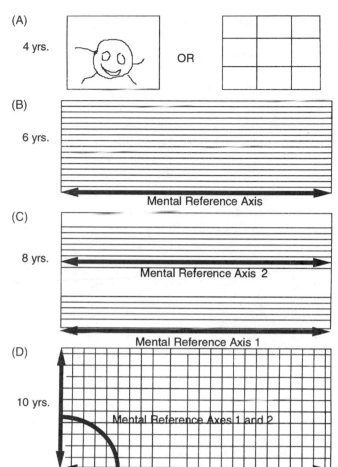

Figure 15.7 Hypothesized progression in children's central spatial structures between 4 and 10 years of age. Panel A indicates the pre-axial schemas possessed by 4-year-olds for representing the component shapes of an object, and the location of an object in a rectangular field (see Figure 15.5). Panel B indicates the uniaxial schema possessed by 6-year-olds, which can conjointly specify an object's internal shapes and their relations and its location relative to the edge of a field (Figure 15.6). Panel C indicates the new "biaxial" capability acquired by 8-year-olds; that is, the capability of setting up two discrete representations in different locations, each referenced to a different axis. Panel D indicates that 10-year-olds can now conjointly reference a whole field of objects to two discrete mental reference axes that are orthogonal to each other.

an individual object or event with knowledge about its position in an overall sequence or field. The structures that are assembled between 7 and 8 years of age all appear to be ones in which two line- or fieldlike structures are integrated in a tentative fashion. Finally, the structures that are assembled at 9 to 10 years appear to be ones in which multiple linelike or fieldlike structures of this sort are integrated, with more explicit rules that can be generalized to an entire system.

On the basis of this analysis, the general claim that we have made in our own work is this: in each of these three domains, children's understanding is underpinned by a set of central conceptual structures (CCSs) such as those illustrated in the figures. These structures are central in several different senses. They are central in that they form the conceptual core or "center" of children's understanding of a broad array of situations, both within and across culturally-defined disciplines or content areas. They are central in that they form the foundational elements out of which more elaborate structures will be constructed in the future; in effect, they constitute the central conceptual kernels on which children's future conceptual growth will depend. Finally, they are central in that they are the product of children's central processing: Although the content that they serve to organize is modular, the structures themselves reflect a set of principles and constraints that are systemwide in their nature, and that change with age in a predictable fashion.

The foregoing hypothesis draws on elements from all three of the classic research traditions. As suggested by classical Piagetian theory, CCS's undergo a clear differentiation and integration between the ages of 4 and 6. This in turn leads to a qualitative shift, and an emergent ability for children to understand or "enter in" to a new conceptual system. In keeping with theory-theory, children's internal representations of these systems (their CCSs) exert a strong influence on the questions that they see as significant, and the methods they see as appropriate for investigating these questions, in the relevant content domains. In keeping with expertise theory, CCSs are better represented as "knowledge networks" than as formal conceptual systems. When they are represented in this fashion, it becomes apparent that they contain associative as well as conceptual links, and that both sorts of links are vital to their functioning. In keeping with neo-Piagetian theory, the structures are seen as being subject to a general set of influences and constraints, which produce a parallel pattern of development in the different content domains. Finally, in keeping with sociohistoric theory—and in contrast to Piaget's theory—the systems that children begin to understand are cultural creations; they therefore show a good deal of variation in their content, both from one cultural group to another in our current era and from one historical era to the next, within our own culture.

There is a certain intuitive appeal to the notion that the parallel form and rate of development displayed by

children's CCSs comes from a set of constraints that are internal and systemwide in their nature, whereas the differences in content come from differences in the domains themselves, coupled with differences in the systems that our culture has evolved for representing these domains. On the other hand, it is not always easy to spot the presence of culturally-specific content in something that is as seemingly universal and logical as a mental number line. Surely, one might think, this mental representation must also be a universal, which stems from the sort of universal logical operations that Piaget described. In actual fact, the cultural component of the mental number line is quite pronounced. Not all cultural groups use their fingers in learning to count; some use other body parts (Saxe, 1981). Yet digital representations are an essential part of the structure as portrayed in the figure (see Row e, Figure 15.2). Not all cultures have counting words for numbers higher than 3 or 4, yet these numbers, and the words that we use for representing them, are also essential parts of the structure as it is portrayed in the figure (see Row b). Not all cultures give the numbers from 1 to 6 the canonical visual representations that ours does, yet these, too, form a critical part of the structure (Row d). Not all cultures use the sorts of linguistic terms that we do for labeling the numbers from 1 to 10, or label the relations between the numbers in the explicit manner that we do ("next," "up," "down," etc.). Finally, and perhaps most importantly, not all cultures link the movement of one unit forward or backward in the counting string with the addition or subtraction of one unit of quantity (Damerow, Englund, & Nissen, 1995). With all these elements that are unique to the modern representation of number, the overall mental number line that children construct must clearly be classified as a creation of our culture, not just our nervous systems. A similar analysis may be advanced for the other two structures that children construct during this same age range: that is, the mental story line and the mental reference line (Case, 1996b).

Since the CCSs that have been described are all social constructions, it follows that they must be transmitted from one generation to the next by a social process. And this in turn means that the parallels that they exhibit across domains, both in form and in rate of development, may lie in the social institutions that transmit them, not just in the minds to which they are transmitted. In the present case, the most obvious candidate to focus on is the school, since children enter school for the first time during the age range when the structures first emerge and are exposed to a number of different activities there which could facilitate the process of structural assembly. The lessons that children encounter in early arithmetic are directly relevant to children's progress in understanding the CCS for number, and have been shown to be capable of facilitating the acquisition of this structure (Griffin & Case, 1996). Instruction in handwriting (keeping letters on schoolbook lines, etc.) are directly relevant to children's structures for organizing two dimensional space, and can impact the acquisition of this structure (Case, Marra, Bleiker, & Okamoto, 1996). Finally, instruction in reading—because it normally includes exposure to a large number of stories—is relevant to children's structures for interpreting narrative, and under appropriate conditions can exert an impact on the acquisition of this structure (McKeough, 1992b). Of course, there is a chicken and egg problem here, since the decision to begin formal schooling during the age from 5 to 7, and to teach these three subjects at this time, has evolved at least in part in response to the fact that the majority of children appear to be responsive to such instruction at this time, but not before (Mounoud, 1986). Still, even if biological maturation plays a big role, it seems unlikely that the time period in which the structures are acquired would be as narrowly constrained as it is *without* the influence of social-institutional factors such as schooling.

What sort of biological factors might enable children to profit from schooling during this age range, and to begin constructing mental number, story, and reference lines? Important neurological changes take place in the human cortex between the ages of 4 and 7. The tracts connecting to the two hemispheres become increasingly myelinated, for example (Yakovelev & Lecours, 1967), and the activity in the two hemispheres becomes better differentiated and integrated (Witelson, 1983). Since the mental processing lines of this sort involve the integration of sequential and parallel components, and since the two hemispheres are generally regarded as playing a differential role in these two types of activity, this sort of change might be one general potentiator of, or constraint on, the changes that take place in children's central conceptual structures during this age range.

Another important biological change is in the fibres connecting the frontal with the posterior lobes. These fibers show a strong pattern of dendritic growth during this age range. Moreover, as this growth takes place, there is a gradual synchronization of electrical activity across the frontal and posterior regions (Thatcher, 1992). As the reader may be aware, the size of the frontal cortex is one of the features that most strongly distinguishes the human brain from the brains of other primates. The frontal lobes are

also generally regarded as the seat of the executive control function, and the function that is responsible for generating novel mappings between existing knowledge networks (Stuss & Benson, 1986). Since all the mental structures that are constructed at the age of 5 or 6 require this sort of mapping and control (Halford, 1982, 1993), the change in the "connectedness" of frontal and posterior regions might constitute a second change that would potentiate or constrain the construction of the different CCS's, in a common manner.

The frontal lobes are not just the seat of the executive and mapping functions. They are also the seat of "working memory" (Goldman-Rakic, 1989b). During the years between 4 and 6, children's working memory for the sort of content that these structures entail increases from 1 to 2 units (Crammond, 1992). A working memory of 2 would be an advantage if one wanted to make new mappings between two existing knowledge networks or "files," since it would enable one to keep both files "open" while one did so (Case, 1995a; Case & Okamoto, 1996, Ch. 8). The increase in working memory during this age range, and the frontal factors that contribute to this increase, might therefore constitute a third potentiator and/or constraint that would tend to standardize the rate of progress that took place across different domains, during this age range (for a more extended presentation of this latter argument, and an analysis of the evidence on working memory growth, see Case, 1995a).

Broadening the Search for Commonalities to Other Domains

If the cultural and biological factors listed above are, in fact, the most powerful ones that are responsible for producing the common pattern of conceptual development that is observed in children's CCSs during this age range, a further question that arises is whether a similar pattern may also be present in *other* specific domains of functioning, especially ones that are subject to the same broad set of cultural and biological influences. What might these domains be?

One theorist who has tackled this question in a systematic fashion is Gardner (1983). Drawing on Fodor's (1982) notion of mental modularity, and Goodman's (1976) notion of culturally created symbol-systems, Gardner has proposed that there are a number of core intellectual capacities, or "intelligences" which are fundamental to all human activity. The criteria that he has proposed for identifying these intelligences are as follows:

1. *Universality.* Any intellectual capacity that is proposed as fundamental should be evident and assigned at least some value in all known cultures.

2. *Psychological Distinctiveness.* Any such capacity should draw on a distinct set of psychological operations, and be capable of being studied in relative isolation from other capacities.

3. *Neurological Modularity.* Any primary capacity should be capable of suffering severe damage, or of developing to prodigious levels, without any major impact on any of the other capacities.

4. *Developmental Distinctiveness.* Any primary capacity should have a distinctive developmental history, both phylogenetically and ontegentically.

5. *Cultural Distinctiveness.* Any primary capacity should be capable of being encoded by a distinctive symbolic system, and developed to exceptionally high levels by a dedicated group of practitioners.

Using these general criteria, the core list of intelligences that Gardner has proposed are as follows:

1. *Logicomathematical.*
2. *Spatial.*
3. *Social.*
4. *Linguistic.*
5. *Musical.*
6. *Bodily/kinesthetic.*

Since each of the first three intelligences is associated with a different CCS, it follows that the others on the list may also be associated with CCSs of equal distinctiveness and psychological importance.

Gardner's parsing of the mind into core modules is of course not the only one that is possible. In recent years, a different and more empirical approach to the parsing problem has been taken by a team of investigators at the University of Thessalonika led by Andreas Demetriou. In their early work, Demetriou and his colleagues converted a broad range of Piagetian measures into psychometric format, and administered them to children from several different cultures and social classes (Demetriou & Efklides, 1987). They then analyzed the pattern of individual differences, using Gustafsson's (1988) variant of structural modeling. This analytic technique avoids most of the problems pointed out by Flavell (1970) in the critique that

was mentioned earlier. It does not presume that all components of a structure must emerge synchronously, or in a saltatory fashion. Rather, what it presumes is that—if a structure exists—then (a) its components should tend to show the same correlational pattern in a cross-sectional study, and (b) they should also tend to change together in a longitudinal study. These criteria seem well suited for revealing the sort of coherence that theorists in the rationalist tradition have always cited as a defining feature of cognitive structures, but which they have not always been able to define in an operational manner. The criteria also seem appropriate for isolating the sort of domain-based cognitive structures that Flavell referred to, when he cited his own understanding of developmental psychology as an example.

Using his battery of Piagetian-style tasks, Demetriou and his colleagues have demonstrated the presence of five factors, across many different ages, cultures, and social classes (Shayer, Demetriou, & Pervez, 1988). In their early work, they suggested that these factors indicated the existence of a core set of underlying "capacity-spheres." In their more recent work, they have taken the factors as also suggesting the presence of "specific structural systems" of which the CCS's described above may be representative exemplars (Demetriou, Efklides, & Platsidou, 1993). The names they has have given to these specific systems are (a) *the quantitative/relational,* (b) *the imaginal/spatial,* (c) *the verbal/propositional,* (d) *the qualitative/analytic,* and (e) *the causal/experimental* systems. They have also postulated a sixth structural system, which their original measures were not designed to assess, but which their more recent measures have focussed on, namely (f) *the social/affective system.*

For each of these domains, Demetriou and his colleagues propose that there exists a unique set of cognitive operations, a unique domain of application in the empirical world, a unique form of symbolization that is most appropriate, and perhaps even a unique kind of "logic" (Demetriou, Efklides, & Platsidou, 1993). At the same time, across the six domains, they postulate a common pattern of four-stage growth : one which is compatible with the characterization that has been proposed in the Piagetian and neo-Piagetian traditions. Finally, they postulate two further systems that are distinct from, and bear a hierarchical relationship to, those mentioned above. These are, (a) the *hypercognitive system,* whose goal is to build models of, and/or to direct, the activity that goes on the other systems (Demetriou, Kazi, Platsidou, Sirmali, Efklides, & Kiosseoglou, 1996), and (b) the *processing system,* in which this sort of activity actually takes place, and for which differences exist in speed, span, and executive control. The importance of the first system in development has been stressed by Flavell (1979), Kuhn (1983), and Campbell and Bickhart (1986). The importance of the second system has been stressed by neo-Piagetian and information-processing theorists (Kail, 1995). The overall structure that emerges when all these systems are combined is illustrated in Figure 15.8.

There is considerable overlap between the core capacities proposed on theoretical grounds by Gardner, and those identified empirically by Demetriou. If Gardner's first candidate (logical mathematical intelligence) is divided into its two primary components, then one finds a core set of five entries on each list, namely: *numerical, spatial, social, verbal, and qualitative analytic (i.e., logical).* With these core capacity spheres specified, there is only one entry on Demetriou's list that does not appear on Gardner's, namely, the *causal/experimental* capacity.

An extensive body of evidence supports the importance of causal/experimental knowledge, and the foundational role that it plays in human cognition. (See Wellman &

Gelman, Ch. 11, this Volume.) Thus, there is good evidence from other sources that this item should feature prominently in any attempt to specify the core domains in which CCSs are likely to play a prominent role. It is also important to point out that there is nothing in Demetriou's data that rules out the two additional entries that appear on Gardner's list, namely *musical* and *bodily* intelligence. Had measures for assessing this sort of performance appeared in Demetriou's original test battery, they might well have emerged as distinctive factors in his structural analysis also.

Elsewhere, I have attempted to specify what the content of children's CCSs in this full set of domains might look like (Case, 1996a). To conclude the present section, however, I would like to say a word about the general endeavor: that is, the attempt to map out the core set of domains of human functioning in a fashion that takes account of both biology and culture. Diagrams of the sort presented in Figure 15.8 have a long history in the psychometric tradition: one which goes back through Guilford's cube (Guilford, 1967) to the branching models of earlier theorists (e.g., Spearman, 1922). Such diagrams have been criticized as being descriptive rather than explanatory, and as oversimplifying the fundamental nature, structure and functioning of human intelligence. These criticisms are not without merit and can be applied in the present case as well. For example, the diagram in Figure 15.8 does not, in and of itself, explain the architecture of the developing cognitive system. What it does do, however, is provide a way of describing that architecture that is economical, and that makes the hypothesized relationship among its components apparent. Moreover—and this is in contrast to earlier psychometric models—the diagram (or more properly, the model on which it is based) offers a potential bridge between several different subfields in psychology whose data have rarely been integrated: namely cognitive psychology, the psychology of individual differences, and developmental psychology. (For the importance of this effort, see DeRibaupierre, Rieben, & Lautrey, 1991; Keating & Bobbitt, 1978; Snow, Kyllonen, & Marshalek, 1984). Finally, the model may also be useful in building a bridge to contemporary neuroscience: for example, one could look at the systems that are specified around the periphery of the cylinder as being localized in the posterior cortex, and one could look at the systems at the center of the cylinder as being localized in the frontal lobes, and as playing an important role in orchestrating the performance of all the peripheral systems. Any representation which has the potential to bridge

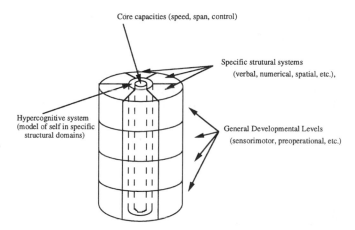

Figure 15.8 Basic architecture of the cognitive system according to Demetriou's model. The top surface of the cylinder shows the different systems that are hypothesized, with those that are presumed to be central (the processing system and the hypercognitive system) at the center, and those that are presumed to be more modular (the specific capacity systems) around the periphery. The vertical dimension represents development. Thus, the four sections of the cylinder along the vertical axis indicate the levels of structure that are built up in each specific system, during the four classic stages of development (i.e., the sensorimotor stage, the pre-operational [relational] stage, the concrete operational [or dimensional] stage, and the abstract or formal stage).

several different ways of looking at the human mind, it seems to me, should as a minimum be treated as having heuristic value, for the enterprise of creating a mere unified view of conceptual development.

Summary

In the first half of the century, each of the major epistemological traditions developed its own unique analysis of children's conceptual structures, and the way in which these structures change with age. Empiricists saw developmental changes in children's concepts as stemming from a general change in their capacity for learning, one which resulted from the replacement of a perceptually based, associative system by a system that permitted verbal mediation. Rationalists saw the same developmental changes as stemming from the construction of a powerful logicomathematical structure: ones that emerged as lower order structures were gradually differentiated and coordinated via reflexive abstraction. Sociohistoric theorists saw the underlying structures as resulting from the gradual re-construction by the child of representational systems that themselves were the result of a long developmental process: not just across species, but across long periods of cultural history. In their view, it was these systems, and the social institutions that had evolved for transmitting them, that were the most interesting subjects for developmental investigation.

In the last third of the century, there has been a general recognition that the overall pattern of conceptual development is a good deal less monolithic than was originally believed. Depending on the particular tradition, however, the underlying reason that development has the (more specific) pattern that it does has been conceived in a quite different manner. Empiricists have seen the pattern as resulting from the gradual development of domain-specific knowledge networks, which become increasingly linked to each other as children moved through middle childhood. Rationalists have seen the pattern as the result of a sequence of domain-specific theoretical revolutions, each following its own time course, and each being followed by long periods of consolidation and extension. Sociohistoric theorists have seen the pattern as resulting from the construction and utilization of new forms of representation: cultural creations that are designed to solve particular problems, and that must be used for particular purposes in particular contexts. Finally, Neo-Piagetian theorists have suggested that children's acquisition and deployment of any cognitive structure—no matter how cultural its elements—is still subject to certain very general constraining influences of a biological nature:

particularly those involving the speed and span of information processing. While there is much more specificity in development than originally believed, therefore, one should not ignore the fact that there is also a good deal of generality.

As we reach the end of the 20th century, it is possible to discern the outline of a more integrated framework: one that acknowledges the contribution of all three of the major epistemological traditions, and the theories to which they have given rise. Within such a framework, the existence of distinctive conceptual structures can be acknowledged within domains, while the existence of general biocultural constraints can be acknowledged across domains as well as within them. In modeling the development of these structures, an attempt can be made to highlight both their general structural characteristics and the unique sociocultural content that they entail. Finally, it can be acknowledged that such structures contain associative as well semantically based and logical linkages.

As we move toward characterizing children's conceptual structures in this more integrated fashion, and make an attempt to understand the full range of domains in which such structures are important, it seems possible that a second form of integration may also be possible: one that not only spans the classical traditions of inquiry within the field of cognitive development, but also spans other related fields in which advances have been made in recent years such as cognitive psychology, differential psychology, and neuropsychology. As we create such integrated frameworks, debate on the best way of understanding children's conceptual progress will not cease. However, the new issues that emerge and the new debates that take place will be played out on a broader stage, and will be constrained by a broader set of data.

THE PROCESS OF CONCEPTUAL CHANGE

Historically, students of children's conceptual structures have been concerned with two questions:

1. How to characterize the general properties of children's conceptual understanding at different points in time, and

2. How to characterize the process by which they move from one of these points to the next.

The proposal that was advanced in the previous section provides one possible way of answering the first question: one that takes account of the work that has been done in the three classical developmental traditions, as well as related work that has been done in other disciplines. However, the proposal offers relatively little guidance with regard to the second question, other than to suggest that several different classes of transition mechanism must be considered. In the present section, I review the transition models that have been proposed in recent years in each of the classic and neo-classical traditions. I then consider the question of whether it is possible to integrate these models in a fashion that does justice to their underlying concepts on the one hand, and to the proposal that was advanced in the previous section on the other.

Models of Conceptual Change in the Empiricist Tradition

In the classical empiricist tradition, high-level cognitive structures were presumed to be acquired by a continuous process, in which new associations were formed between existing cognitive units and/or new cognitive units were added to the existing repertoire. In her expertise-based model of children's cognitive structures, Chi distinguished two different types of associative process: the sort that links elements within an existing file, and the sort that links elements across files. As yet, she has not constructed a model of how either process might proceed. One obvious possibility, however, is the one that has been developed by contemporary connectionists.

Models of Conceptual Change Based on (Unidirectional) Associative Learning

Arguably the most influential body of work that has accumulated since the writing of the last *Handbook* is the work on parallel distributed processing, which is also known as "neo-connectionism" (McClelland, Rumelhart, & Hinton, 1987). The general architecture that most such models presume is illustrated in Figure 15.9. As may be seen, there is a layer of units that is stimulated directly by input from the external world, which appears at the bottom of the figure. There is layer of units that is responsible for producing some sort of output, which appears at the top of the figure. In between, there is a layer of "hidden" units, which are connected to the layers above and below them with facilitatory and inhibitory links of various strengths. In order to get such a network to respond in a structured or rulelike fashion one presents the system with a series of stimuli exemplifying some sort of concept, and forces it to make a

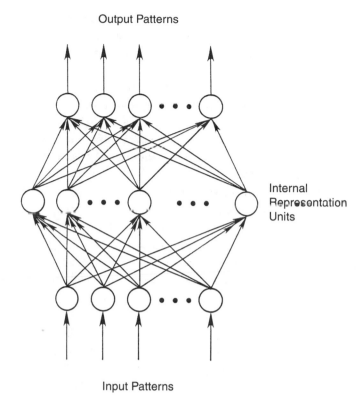

Output Patterns

Internal Representation Units

Input Patterns

Figure 15.9 Pattern of nodes and connections used in simulating learning in a connectionist system. The nodes at the bottom are turned on by specific inputs. Those at the top are turned on by the weighted sum of inputs from below them. Any given connection may be either positive or negative. The values of the weights are adjusted in the course of learning, in order to maximize the probability that a particular value of the input (say input detectors ABC on, DEF off, and G on) will generate a pattern of output that is considered "appropriate."

choice. One then presents feedback on the adequacy of this choice, followed by another example. In short, one exposes the system to much the same situation that children were confronted with in the classic concept learning experiments that were described at the beginning of the chapter.

The remarkable thing is that such systems respond in much the same fashion as do young children: that is to say, they gradually acquire the ability to correctly identify all exemplars of the concept in question. The learning algorithm with which such systems are most frequently programmed—and that enables them to accomplish this feat—is called the "Backward Propagation Rule." This algorithm begins at the top level in the hierarchy (i.e., the level closest to the output) and adjusts the weights of the hidden units in such a fashion as to increase the likelihood that, if a new set of trials is produced which is the same as the set of trials to date, then the correct answer will be given on as many trials as possible. From a mathematical point of view, what the algorithm does is to conduct a sort of nonlinear regression analysis, using the response to be predicted as the dependent variable.

This general sort of model has proved remarkably successful in simulating certain types of perceptual and motor learning. It has also been applied to the simulation of more complex cognitive behaviors, including those that have been studied in the developmental literature. Three cognitive developmental tasks that have been modeled are: (a) the learning of the past tense in linguistics (Rumelhart & McClelland, 1987); (b) the concept learning task described at the beginning of the chapter (Kruske, 1992); and (c) the balance beam task (McClelland, 1995). In the first task, the system goes through the same "over-regularizing" phase as children. In the second task, the system acquires the same concepts, and learns to deal with intra-dimensional shifts in the same fashion as 6-year-olds (though not adults). In the final task, the system goes through the same general sequence of rules as do children in the range from 4 to 10 years, providing it is fed example problems in a sensible order, and with a reasonable set of relative frequencies.

As might be expected, given the historic rivalry between empiricism and rationalism, such demonstrations have been criticized on a number of grounds. One of the most telling of these criticisms is simply that connectionist learning takes too long: that is to say, it takes more trials than does children's learning (typically thousands more). One possible response to this criticism has been proposed by Shultz (1991, 1997), who has suggested modifying the standard learning algorithm. Shultz's algorithm uses a procedure that is referred to as "Cascade Correlation." Basically, the algorithm has two components, one that adjusts weights via backward propagation, and one that keeps track of its own "hit rate" in correctly identifying new exemplars of the concept. When the second system detects the fact that the first system is reaching an asymptote in its learning, it sets up a new layer of hidden nodes, thus increasing the potential complexity of its response. As a test of the adequacy of the revised algorithm, Shultz and Schmidt (1991) have shown that a system that uses it can learn the balance beam problem much more rapidly than other systems, and in a series of spurts of the sort that classical Piagetian theory postulates.

The modification that permits the system to exhibit these spurts is not a trivial one since it implies (a) that some sort of "hypercognitive," or "metacognitive" system exists (Demetriou et al., 1993; Kuhn, 1983), and (b) that this system constitutes the real source of children's conceptual development. Still, it is of interest to note that, with this one modification, connectionist systems can be made to exhibit the sort of stepwise progression that classical developmental theory postulates.

A Model of Change Combining Associative and Rule-Based Learning

Whether or not real children actually exhibit such spurts in performance, however, has been questioned by Siegler (1996). Siegler began his research on children's conceptual development by modeling children's understanding of balance beam principles via a set of rules, each of which required some sort of more advanced encoding and/or computation than the previous one. In his recent work, he has turned his attention to the acquisition of strategies in elementary arithmetic: for example, strategies for deciding whether to retrieve the answer to a problem such as $2 + 5$ from long-term memory, or to answer the problem by modeling the transformation it describes with a set of tokens (e.g., the fingers). The strategy he has modeled in greatest detail is one referred to as the "min strategy" (Groen & Parkman, 1972). This is a strategy where the subject solves the problems by counting tokens, but minimizes the work that is involved by counting forward from the highest digit. By tracking children's learning across multiple trials, Siegler has shown that the sequence of strategy shifts that moves from simple counting through the min strategy to retrieval from long-term memory is better modeled as a sequence of "overlapping waves" than a sequence of steps or spurts. These waves are illustrated in the top panel of Figure 15.10. In the bottom panel of the same figure, data are presented on children's first major cognitive developmental transition: namely, from reflexive to cortically-based motor movement (McGraw, 1943).

Given that the overlapping wave pattern is observed across such a wide range of ages and types of response as those illustrated in the figure, it seems likely that it may emerge in a good many other situations as well. In fact, this appears to be the case. (See Kuhn, in press, for a review.) Thus, Siegler (1997) has proposed that it is this pattern of overlapping waves, and not the classical staircase pattern, that developmentalists should take as normative and attempt to model. In his own simulations, he has continued to use rule-based approaches; however, he has combined them with a variant of associative learning in an attempt to capture the most important features of each. In the above case, for example, it is the association strength of the correct answer to any particular addition problem, vis à vis its possible competitors, that his system uses as a cue as to whether

(a) Siegler's model

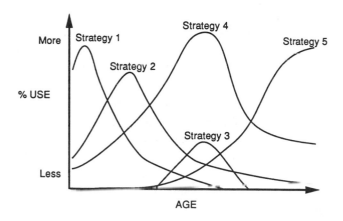

(b) McGraw's data

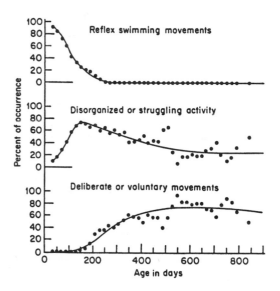

Figure 15.10 Probability of observing different strategies in the course of development. In (a), Siegler's model is shown. This model asserts that—at any age—one sees a variety of strategies, and that, with increasing age, increasingly sophisticated strategies become more probable, and less sophisticated strategies become less probable. In (b), data from the classic study of motor development by McGraw (1943) are shown, as tabulated by Lipsitt. Whether the intermediate behavior should be considered a strategy in its own right is perhaps moot, but the general sequence appears to follow the general pattern suggested by Siegler quite nicely.

to work out the answer from scratch, or retrieve the answer from long-term memory. However, the strategy itself is generated in a rule-based fashion.

As is the case with McClelland's balance beam model—or any model in which a new way of looking at or approaching a

problem is consolidated by associationist means—such models run the risk of getting "stuck" on an existing approach, even if it is not the most adequate one, simply because the existing approach is frequently reinforced and thus becomes so habitual. In the classic developmental terms proposed by Baldwin (1894), one could say that these systems need some process to "break down" an old habit, and open up the possibility of accommodation. In more modern connectionist terms, one could say that such systems need something to move them out of "local optima." In the sort of model designed by McClelland, this problem is addressed by making sure that the feature on which higher order success is dependent is encoded by the system from the start, but has a very low association strength. In Siegler's simulations, the same function is achieved by introducing an inherent response variability in the system from the outset, together with an attraction to novelty. In effect, then, his system engages in a sort of operant learning, which is based on Darwinian principles of variability and selection. Whenever a new possibility emerges, the system tries it out. If the new response meets with some success, then its strength gradually increases, and it eventually overcomes the dominating approach (Siegler, 1997). More recent simulations involve a conceptual evaluation of the new approach as well (Siegler & Shraeger, 1997).

In testing the validity of this model, Siegler has introduced a methodological innovation to parallel the conceptual one. Recall that, in the classic empiricist tradition, the paradigm that investigators used was to sample children's learning at two points in development: one where it operated according to one set of principles or strategies (typically rather inefficient ones) and a second where it operated according to a different set of principles or strategies (typically more efficient ones). The innovation Siegler introduces is a variant of the "epigenetic method" (Kuhn & Phelps, 1982; Werner, 1948). First, he selects children at an intermediate age range. Next he presents a large number of trials, and charts the gradual transition from one strategy to the next, videotaping each trial en route. Finally, he reviews the entire videotaped sequence in order to learn more about the circumstances that surrounded each strategy's first emergence. Interestingly, he finds that more efficient strategies normally emerge at a very low level of probability, and well before children appear to have much conscious awareness of their utility.

Children may be presented with problems that are designed to dramatize the need for the new strategy at any point in the learning sequence. The problem 2 + 21, for example, is one that dramatizes the need for the min strategy, since the amount of counting that is required if this strategy is not used is rather tedious. One might think that problems of such sort are the ones that motivate children to discover the min strategy in the first place. This does not appear to be the case, however: such problems have little effect if the child has not already used the min strategy on his or her own, on at least one prior occasion. Once the strategy is in the child's repertoire, the results are quite different. At that point such problems have a major impact: children adapt the min strategy rapidly, and are articulate about the advantages that it offers. Not only does Siegler's model generate the classic ogival shape of learning curves, then, and not only does it map on to the sort of response data that empiricists have classically been most attracted to, but it also maps on well to children's conscious experience and to their verbal explanations. Not all investigators in the empiricist tradition agree with Siegler that conceptual development follows the wavelike pattern that his model generates (Brainerd, 1993). However, for cases where it does follow this pattern, it is a clear contender.

A Model of Change Based on Two-Way Associative Learning

One final model is important to mention (Hinton, Dayan, Frey, & Neal, 1995). This model uses the same general connectionist architecture as shown in Figure 15.9. However, it uses a learning algorithm that is quite different from either Backward Propagation or Cascade Correlation. In fact, it uses two algorithms. In the first (upstream) algorithm, each successive hidden layer attempts to reconstruct the pattern of stimulation in the previous layer, in a fashion that is as economical as possible. The second (downstream) algorithm operates in the opposite direction. Beginning with the pattern of activation that emerged in the highest hidden level on the upstream sweep, each hidden layer attempts to reconstruct the pattern of stimulation in the layer above it as economically as possible. An iterative feedback loop is thus set up, in which economy of representation takes the place of external input as the criterion for correctness. The net result that the system conducts a sort of nonlinear factor analysis on the input rather than a nonlinear regression analysis.

Hinton and his colleagues refer to their pair of algorithms as the "wake-sleep" algorithm, because the "upstream" weights are turned off before the downstream weights are computed and harmonized with them. They also point out: (a) that their model produces much more rapid learning than conventional connectionist simulations

(thus solving the problem noted by Shultz); (b) that it does so in a fashion that better fits the functioning of real neurological systems (where all major pathways have efferent as well as afferent projections); and (c) that it permits learning to take place without any form of didactic instruction (thus solving the problem of how children learn in situations where they are not coached).

Although Hinton's model has not yet been applied to the acquisition of complex developmental competencies, it seems ideally positioned to do so. It could also be combined with a feature analogous to the one suggested by Shultz: one where a new level of analysis is introduced from time to time. As Klahr and Wallace (1976) pointed out, one of the best ways to get a system to engage in "self-modification" is to build an additional (hypercognitive) tier, which reads the productions of the existing tier, and extracts patterns from them. The techniques that Klahr and Wallace used for this purpose are such things as "searching for similarity" and the "elimination of redundancy," since their model is based on production system rather than connectionist modeling. If such a tier were added to the Hinton model, however, and if this tier took the output from several existing wake-sleep algorithms as its input, it could perform this same sort of pattern extraction by connectionist means. Neurologically, such an addition might be equivalent to adding an extra layer to the frontal lobes of the association cortex. Mathematically, such an addition might be like performing nonlinear factor analysis in a recursive or hierarchical fashion.

Neurological Models of Associative Learning

The foregoing comment about the associative cortex, like Hinton's comments about the function of two-way projection in the nervous system, illustrates an interesting fact about modern connectionist theory, which is that the theory explicitly asserts that our models of human perception and cognition should—wherever possible—operate in a fashion that is similar to the human nervous system. In this regard, it is perhaps worthwhile to note that most contemporary neurological models of learning have their roots in the pioneering theoretical work of two theorists, Hebb (1949) and Luria (1973). Hebb argued that the external objects that we see in the world are represented cortically by groups of cells, which "feed back" on themselves, and reverberate for a short period of time. According to Hebb's model, this reverberation leads to the formation of new connections among existing neurons, because it produces chemical changes in the dendrites that make them more likely to activate the axons of the next cell in the loop on a repeated excitation.

One way to look at Hinton's wake-sleep algorithm is that it constitutes a procedure for producing a learning cycle of this reverberatory sort: one directed toward representing the pattern in any given input as economically as possible, rather than just producing a correct response. For this reason it is worthwhile to note that modern neuro-biology has by and large confirmed Hebb's original model. Chemical changes do take place in dendritic terminals during repeated activation of a group of cells, and these changes do alter the probability that each element in the circuit will re-activate the next one in a subsequent trial. Interestingly, developmental research has also shown: (a) that "waves of dendritification" take place in the visual cortex in the course of early development; (b) that these waves produce immense opportunities for the formation of such experientially based circuits; and (c) that neurons that do not come to participate in such circuits in the course of development tend to lead rather short lives. The process has thus been referred to as "branching and pruning" (Greenough, Black, & Wallace, 1987) and it has been proposed as basis for a neurological model of development that has been referred to as "neural Darwinism" (Edelman, 1987).

What about higher order processing? Here what Hebb argued is that existing cell assemblies are assembled into units of a higher order still, which he called "phase sequences." He also asserted that the formation of such "phase sequences" is the primary function of the association cortex. The foregoing suggestion with regard to hierarchical processing, then, may be regarded as a sort of Hebbian extension of Hinton's model: one intended to let it engage in higher level associative learning, with the results of lower level learning as its input. Such higher order circuits would appear to be well suited to the task of detecting structure across existing networks, and building higher order ones. In short, they would appear to be well suited to modeling the second sort of association that Chi describes in her developmental models.

Models of Conceptual Change in the Rationalist Tradition

In the context of classical Piagetian theory, the major factor that was believed to produce conceptual change was the child's own cognitive activity: particularly the activity of differentiating and coordinating lower order structures and then abstracting a higher order structure from

them. This process was presumed to lead to a series of qualitative shifts, at each of which children's capability for learning underwent a significant (indeed, revolutionary) transformation (Piaget, 1964, 1985). In the present section, I describe several recent models in the rationalist tradition that have tried to explicate these classic notions, and expand on them.

A Model of Change Combining Associative and Attentionally-Mediated Learning

In the context of Pascual-Leone's system, the notion of attentionally mediated change is used to distinguish two different kinds of learning. The first is Conditioning, or C-learning. This sort of learning is hypothesized to occur very gradually and in a Hebbian manner. Whenever two previously unconnected schemes are repeatedly co-activated in a particular context, and one of these is strongly activated (say, by a salient feature in the environment) while the other is more weakly activated (say, by a less salient feature), what happens is that the weakly activated scheme gradually becomes incorporated into the strongly activated structure and eventually serves as an additional "releaser" or "cue" for it. As Fischer (1980) suggested, the process that results can often mimic development by chaining together a set of related schemes, rather than re-assembling them into a higher order structure. In my own work, I have attempted to show that—by making the sequential activation of existing structures more automatic—this sort of process can play a vital role in higher order development, too, freeing up additional attentional capacity for new learning (Case, 1985, Ch. 16).

As has already been noted, a system that is only endowed with an associative process such as C-learning is unlikely to learn things at the rate that humans do. It is also likely to get stuck in a "local optimum," and to have trouble generating novel behavior. To account for behavior that avoids these traps, Pascual-Leone postulated a second form of learning: one that takes existing schemes as input and mobilizes some subset of these schemes—independent of their original degree of activation. Whenever two or more schemes are co-activated in this fashion, while other schemes are actively inhibited, Pascual-Leone proposed that a different, and much more rapid form of learning occurs: one which leads to connections that are more flexible, reciprocal, and open to conscious inspection. Since this form of learning was the process that he believed was responsible for producing Piaget's logical structures, he referred to it as L (for logical) learning.

In addition to C- and L-learning, Pascual-Leone proposed a third mechanism of conceptual change: the one for which neo-Piagetian theory became best known. In order to construct genuinely novel conceptual products under conditions where existing products serve as misleading cues, Pascual-Leone proposed that a change also needs to take place in the *number* of schemes to which children can attend simultaneously. The particular number of schemes that he hypothesized as being necessary at different ages was mentioned earlier (see Table 15.2), and the process that he hypothesized as producing the change in this Mental power was maturation. In the present context, what is important is that each increase in M-power was presumed to induce a new wave of L-learning, in much the same way as does the addition of a new layer of hidden units in Shultz's model. The prime difference is that Shultz's new waves of learning are always task-specific, whereas Pascual-Leone's waves of M-induced L-learning are system-general.

To test the notion that new waves of L-learning can be facilitated by increases in Mental power, early studies provided various forms of perceptual and/or conceptual training, and followed the progress of children with attentional capacities of different magnitudes. In the typical study, the high capacity children showed rapid acquisition of the concept being studied whereas low capacity children showed a gradual mastery of its components, but no integration. If the complexity of the task was decreased, this pattern changed, and both groups showed rapid learning. If the complexity of the task was increased beyond its original level, then the pattern changed again and neither group showed rapid learning. (See Case, 1985, Ch. 15 for a review.) In other studies, the same basic idea has been tested, using a longitudinal rather than a cross-sectional design (Lewis & Ash, 1992).

A Catastrophe Model of Attentionally Mediated Learning

For Pascual-Leone, growth in M-power was presumed to be continuous, but its application to specific tasks—especially misleading ones—was presumed to yield changes that could be quite abrupt. This notion has recently been given an elegant formulation in the context of dynamic systems theory, by van der Maas and Molenaar (1992). As the reader may be aware, dynamic systems theory has dealt quite extensively with the general problem of how new forms emerge from a set of previously independent elements. The particular version of dynamic systems theory that van der Maas and Molenaar have used is catastrophe

theory. As it happens, catastrophe theory is well suited for modeling sort of dynamic re-configuring of elements that Pascual-Leone postulated. What it proposes is that—when two conflicting external responses are possible, and each of these is mobilized by a different factor—a number of outcomes are possible which can best be modeled via a "catastrophe surface." In the classic illustration used by Zeeman (1976) the two competing response tendencies were fight and flight, and the two competing control factors were fear and anger. In the illustration that van der Maas and Molenaar present, the two incompatible responses are conservation and nonconservation, and the two competing control variables are those specified by Pascual-Leone's theory, namely, (a) the misleading appearance of the perceptual array, and (b) the mobilizing power of the child's attention. What happens with development is that the size of children's attentional capacity grows in a continuous fashion, until it eventually reaches the critical point where all the relevant schemes can be activated at once, and the misleading scheme can be inhibited. At that point, the system spontaneously reorganizes itself, and a change takes place in reasoning. This outcome is illustrated graphically in Figure 15.11.

Note that two different developmental pathways are possible within the context of this model, which both lead to the same ultimate outcome. At certain (rather low) values in the misleading vector (shown on the X axis), the transition to a new form of response can be rather gradual. The transition that children make under these conditions is indicated by the arrow at the back of the figure. Under other (rather high) values in the misleading vector, development proceeds along a different pathway, namely the one indicated at the front of the figure. Here subjects reach a point where they make a sudden "leap" from the bottom to the top of the catastrophe surface: that is to say, their responses suddenly go from nonconservation to conservation, without passing through any intermediate zone. The notion that two different pathways to the same outcome are possible is an interesting one, which seems to offer a potential resolution to the problem of whether development is steplike or wavelike. The answer would be that it can be either, depending on whether the general situation (and the particular problem) is facilitating or misleading, and on the pattern of change that the subject's mental capacity is undergoing. In short, the pattern observed should depend on both the specific problem and the individual child.

Tracking individual developmental pathways in misleading and facilitating situations, deciding what does and does

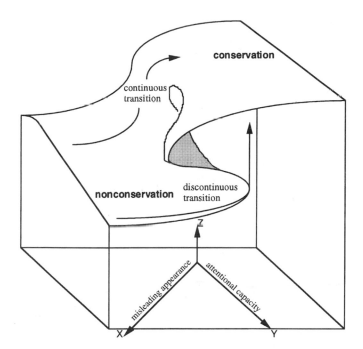

Figure 15.11 Catastrophe surface, after Zeeman (1967) and van Der Maas (1996). The top surface indicates the various positions a child can occupy, along the road from non-conservation to conservation. The two axes in the bottom of the diagram indicate the two independent variables that control the subject's position on the surface. These are perceptual misleadingness (on the X axis) and attentional capacity (on the Y axis). The Z axis indicates the probability of conservation. It is 1 at the top right, and 0 at the bottom left. The folding of the surface is pronounced at the front of the diagram, and vanishes at the back. Transition from one state to the other is thus discontinuous at the front of the figure and continuous at the back, as the arrows indicate.

not count as a genuine strategy change, and sorting out what sort of change is observed under what conditions is a process that may take some time. However, the process has already begun, and there is reason to be optimistic about the outcome (Case, 1997; Siegler, 1996; van der Maas, 1996). In the meantime, it is of interest to note that the catastrophe model also allows one to consider the conditions under which a new structure will be *dis*organized, with a resulting regression in development. The key notion here can be seen by inspecting the figure again, beginning at the front left, and letting one's eyes ascend slowly to the right until they encounter the cusp and have to jump to the top surface. Once one has moved one's eyes along this track, one should move them back to the left along the top surface, until they reach the cliff of the cusp and "drop back" to the lower surface. What one will note, if one traces out these

two journeys, is that the two transitions do not take place at exactly the same point on the X axis.

This sort of asymmetry in transition points has interesting analogies in nature, to situations where new structures are formed and un-formed. When water freezes, for example, a structural reorganization takes place, with the water molecules assuming a rigid, lattice structure. The parameter that controls this qualitative shift is temperature: at 0 degrees Celsius (32 degrees Fahrenheit) water molecules spontaneously self-organize themselves into the lattice pattern, and the water freezes. If one warms the ice back up again, however, one discovers that the lattice bonds do not break up at the same temperature. One must heat ice significantly above 0 degrees Celsius in order to melt the ice and return it to its original, fluid state.

Van der Maas and Molenaar propose that this property, which is known as hysteresis, may also be observed in cognitive development. Children who have just understood conservation in all its ramifications, and committed themselves to it, should still be able to be convinced by a nonconservation argument. However, this should only be possible under perceptual conditions that are a good deal more illusory than they originally encountered. To test this prediction, van der Maas (1996) first decreases the strength of the misleading vector in a computer-controlled conservation task, until children appear to catch on to conservation, and start giving convincing, correct answers. Then he gradually increases the strength of the illusory vector again, and shows that, as the vector becomes stronger, children eventually abandon their conservation response and begin to reason like nonconservers again. Finally, he shows that the two transitions do not occur at the same absolute levels. In the same way that it requires extra heat to melt ice, it appears to require an extra degree of illusion to cause a regression from conservation to nonconservation. This phenomenon is an exciting one, and it will be interesting to see what happens, as it is investigated further.

Models Distinguishing Major from Minor Conceptual Change

Neither Pascual-Leone nor van der Maas and Molenaar make a distinction that featured rather prominently in Piaget's theory: namely the distinction between the major conceptual transitions that occur *across* stages and the more minor ones that occur *within* stages. In the context of theory-theory, conceptual development is presumed to be domain-specific rather than general. However, the general

Piagetian distinction is preserved, with revolutionary conceptual changes corresponding to *across*-stage transitions, and progressive elaborations corresponding to *within*-stage transitions (Carey, 1985). In my own theory, the claim is much like Carey's but for a system in which conceptual structures are subject to general systemic constraints. *Within*-stage change is presumed to involve a progressive elaboration of existing structures with a concomitant increase in complexity, while *across*-stage change is presumed to involve a more radical restructuring: one which requires a move to a new level of processing, and the hierarchical integration of structures that were formerly quite discrete (Case, 1985).

In Fischer's (1980) skill theory, a tripartite distinction is made. Certain *across*-stage transitions (e.g., the change from sensorimotor to symbolic thought) are presumed to involve a major change in the "tier" of cognition. Within each broad tier, four qualitative shifts are presumed to take place in the "level" of children's thought (the 5 to 7 shift being one such example). Finally, within each of these levels, a series of more minor steps takes place which are more continuous in nature and which can vary in number from one task to the next. In a recent series of papers, Fischer and Van Geert have developed a dynamic model which simulates both the major, qualitative change that takes place across levels, and the more minor and continuous change that takes place in small steps. (See Van Geert, 1994, Ch. 8 for a summary.) In this model, incremental changes take place in each skill in the child's repertoire as a function of two classes of factor: (a) factors that are unique to this skill, and that give it a characteristic growth rate, and (b) the facilitation or interference that the skill receives from other related skills within the same level. By contrast, major qualitative change (i.e., change from one level to another) takes place by the periodic introduction of a new skill: one which is connected to many of the existing skills in a hierarchical fashion and has the potential to transform them, but which cannot become active until these other skills reach some critical level in their own growth.

As is the case for the catastrophe model, Van Geert and Fischer's model makes a number of interesting and novel predictions. One is that—depending on the particular parameters that are involved—major qualitative change can assume a form that is linear, wavelike, or saltatory; it can also assume two other forms, namely, (a) a small developmental regression prior to a major spurt, or (b) a chaotic or oscillatory transition period. By examining time series data in

detail, they have found examples that illustrate all five sorts of change and are in the process of developing more rigorous analytic techniques for fitting these patterns of data to their model (Fischer & Granott, 1995; Fischer & Kennedy, in press; Ruland & Van Geert, 1996).

Neurological Models

Before concluding, it is worthwhile to mention that theorists in the rationalist tradition have also begun to take an interest in neurological models. While connectionists have drawn primarily on the work of Hebb (1949), however, researchers in the rationalist tradition have drawn more heavily on the work of Luria (1966). In contrast to Hebb, who focused primarily on the neuronal structure of the association cortex, Luria focused primarily on the more molar, modular structure of the brain, and the circuits that appeared to be hard wired into it. Drawing on the large population of patients with neurological injuries to which he had access (by one account all Soviet soldiers with gunshot wounds in World War II!) he created a functional map of the brain that was divided into three broad systems: (a) a motivational and arousal system, located in the limbic region; (b) a cognitive or information-representing system, located in the posterior lobes (and divided into subsystems such "visual pattern recognition," etc.); and (c) an attentional or "executive" system located in the frontal lobes. As was the case with Hebb's model, Luria's model has stood up rather well to more modern neurological investigations. Using various forms of imaging techniques, investigators have, by and large, confirmed the existence of the general systems that Luria postulated.

Not surprisingly, given their interest in attentionally mediated and executive processes, neo-Piagetians have become particularly interested in Luria's third system, the one that is localized in the frontal lobes. Pascual-Leone has suggested that frontal lobe maturation may play a major role in mediating the sort of attentionally mediated conceptual change that takes place on tasks like conservation, by exerting a "priming" effect on the rest of the cortex. According to his model, this priming takes place via downstream projection to the limbic system, and re-afferent energization of the cortex. As a result of this energization, a change takes place in the number of cell assemblies that can be kept in a state of full activation, on the one hand, and the number of assemblies that can be actively inhibited on the other. As a preliminary test of this hypothesis, he has shown that children who show evidence of strong frontal activity tend to be more advanced than other children on cognitive tasks which require activating a large number of novel psychological units, while inhibiting the activation of units stimulated by a perceptual array (Pascual-Leone, Hamstra, Benson, Khan, & Englund, 1990).

A related model has been proposed by Thatcher (1992, 1993), although the postulated mechanism is somewhat different. According to Thatcher, waves of branching and pruning take place in the long-distance axons connecting the frontal and posterior system in the course of development, and these waves give the frontal lobes the chance to play an increasingly powerful role in integrating and orchestrating the activity in the posterior systems. In his empirical work, Thatcher has shown that the EEG patterns in the posterior and frontal lobes become increasingly more "coherent," that is to say "in phase." He has also shown that these increases take place in waves. In my own work (Case, 1992b), I have drawn on Thatcher's notions and shown that the rate and shape of the developmental change in EEG patterns follows quite closely the wave-like change in attentional capacity that takes place, during the same time periods (Figure 15.12). I have also suggested that—accompanying the change in attentional capacity—there are several other changes as well. One of these is the ability to construct a new executive structure; another is the ability to reflect on one's own performance, and abstract a higher order pattern in it. Still another is the ability to inhibit the activation of lower order structures in the limbic system. Since these three functions are also known to be localized in the frontal system, the suggestion is that their growth may be related to waves of frontal growth and/or connectivity, too (Case, 1992b).

As yet, only one study has examined the connection between increases in coherence and cognitive performance directly. In a study by Bell and Fox (1992), it was shown that subjects for whom frontal-posterior coherence was most prominent were also the ones that showed the most advanced performance on Piagetian tests of object permanence. Related work by Diamond (1991) with primates had implicated the dorso-lateral prefrontal cortex in this cognitive transition, and this work dovetails with that work quite nicely. Other, more specific, changes in coherence have been found between certain particular frontal and posterior sites, which appear to map onto other, more specific patterns of cognitive change. As Fischer and Rose (1993) caution, however, the overall pattern is still far from clear.

The foregoing proposals regarding the functioning of the frontal lobes and the role that they may play in cognitive development are still in an early stage of development.

(A)

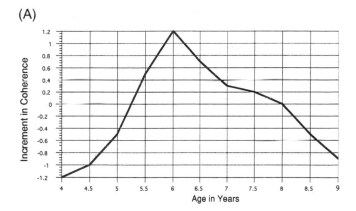

(B)

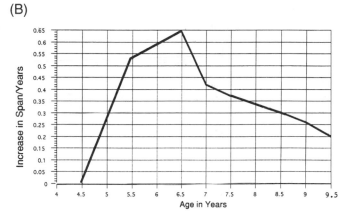

Figure 15.12 Working memory EEG correspondence. Panel A shows the rate of growth of EEG coherence between frontal and posterior lobes during middle childhood ($F_7 - P_3$) (Thatcher, 1992). Panel B shows the rate of growth of working memory during the same age range, aggregated over all existing studies using two measures: the counting span and the spatial span.

Still, it is worthwhile reiterating that they fit rather well with existing phylogenetic and ontogenetic data. Cross-species comparisons have made it clear that no other primate species ever attains the conceptual capabilities of the human 5-year-old. Indeed, the *strongest* claims that have been advanced on behalf of other primates are only for competencies that can be found in the human child at the age of 3 to 4 (Savage-Rumbaugh et al., 1993), and these are often disputed. Anatomical comparisons across species have also made it clear that a critical feature that distinguishes humans from other primates (including Neanderthal man) is the increased size of the frontal lobes. The emerging data from neurological investigations complement these findings very nicely, then, inasmuch as that they show (a) that a primary function of the frontal lobes is regulating precisely those functions that most clearly distinguish humans from other primates (Stuss & Benson, 1986), and (b) that a major "wave of coherence" in the EEG patterns between frontal and posterior sites takes place during the same time period in human ontogenesis, during which these functions begin to outstrip those found in the adults of other species.

Models of Conceptual Change in the Sociohistoric Perspective

The issues that have emerged from recent work on conceptual change in the sociohistoric tradition are different from those in the empiricist and rationalist traditions, but equally important. Recall that, in the classic sociohistoric tradition, intellectual development was seen as resulting from the development of language and the subsequent utilization of language for mastering the intellectual systems and technology of the culture. Particular attention was devoted to the conceptual and notational systems that the culture had acquired (e.g., those involved in reading, mathematics, and science) because these systems were presumed to be associated with the highest levels of thought. Given the nature of this position, two sorts of change process are of interest. The first is the sort of change that takes place in an entire culture, as it undergoes some form of technological or social transformation, and evolves a new form of intellectual or notational system. The second is the sort of change that takes place in individual children, as they begin to assume a more adult-like role in the life of the culture, and are initiated into its various systems of thought and practice.

Processes of Change in Developing Cultures

Consider first the change that takes place in an entire culture. Such change takes place across a very long time scale: one that normally spans many generations, and sometimes many centuries. Thus, the problems that are involved in its study are extremely challenging. Still, in recent years, considerable advances have been made, particularly in regard to the study of conceptual structures for representing number. As the reader may be aware, the ancient Babylonians were pioneers in the development of mathematics (Neugebauer, 1969). The conceptual and notational system that they developed was a very sophisticated one, which involved higher order units of 10, 60, and 360. The influence of this system is still reflected in our own system for representing time, where 60 seconds equals 1 minute and 60 minutes equals 1 hour. It is also evident in our system for calculating angular distance, where 1 degree equals 60 minutes and 360 degrees equals one full revolution.

The way in which this system appears to have evolved is this. When the only settlements in Mesopotamia were small villages (from about 10,000 to 4000 BC), villagers kept track of their livestock and grain using small tokens (Schmandt-Besserat, 1978, 1986). As technological and social development took place, the small villages in the region gradually grew into larger units. Eventually (circa 4000 BC), a form of city state emerged in which agricultural surpluses were brought from the countryside to the city, where they were stored and distributed by the city's ruling priests. As this form of civilization took root, the need arose for keeping records regarding the transport, storage, and allocation of agricultural goods. It was at that point that the first written symbols arose, and the first computations that resemble modern arithmetic. At first, the new symbols were merely impressions made in clay by pushing the tokens into it (Schmandt-Besserat, 1978, 1986). Gradually stylized pictures of these impressions began to dominate, and a system emerged in which symbols representing higher order groupings were written with a stylus on the left of clay tablets and single units on the right.

In one fascinating study of these written symbols, Damerow, Englund, and Nissen (1995) used computer analysis of all existing clay tablets and shards in the region, to determine the grouping system that such records utilized. Their analysis revealed that the first symbols which referred to multiple objects did not have a meaning that was context or content independent. For example, a symbol which looks much like a triangle (and which was represented earlier by a token with a conical shape) was always used to indicate higher order groupings, but the size of those groupings varied from one context to the next. When used to tally animals, the mark represented a group of 60. When used to tally grain, it referred to 3 rather than 60 units. It was not until the end of the fourth millennium (circa 3200 BC) as the first regional empires began to emerge, that evidence is found of a higher order grouping system, one that is context independent. At that point, the base 60 system became standard in one empire (the Sumerian) and the base 10 system in another (the Elamite). It is these two systems that were drawn on by the Babylonians, who then went on to develop the sophisticated system of arithmetic that is in evidence in the archaeological records by the year 2000 BC, and that involves addition, subtraction, multiplication, and division of whole numbers and their reciprocals.

Damerow (1995, in press) draws several conclusions from this developmental progression:

1. The first is that the early symbols should not be misinterpreted as representing numbers. A better interpretation for a symbol like the triangle would be something like "measure," since one would not expect the standard measure for any two commodities to be the same.

2. A second conclusion follows directly from the first, which is that the emergence of a system of representation, in and of itself, does not automatically precipitate any reorganization in the existing conceptual structures. To the contrary, the existing structures for representing quantity stayed in place for hundreds if not thousands of years after the invention of a writing system.

3. A third conclusion is that Piaget's high level operative structures for representing number (i.e., those beyond the simple conservation of number), were very probably not available to the early Mesopotamians, precisely because they did not have any higher order system for representing numbers. Although this latter point is perhaps moot for the sort of understanding that Piaget was interested in studying, it is true by definition for the sort of understanding that many contemporary developmentalists have studied, such as the understanding of the base ten system.

4. Damerow's final conclusion follows directly from his third. This is that many of the logical insights that Piaget took to be universal, and which he presumed were abstracted from individual patterns of activity and reflection, are neither individual nor universal. Rather, they are cultural creations, which are originally abstracted from advanced economic and social activity and only then become an object of individual reflection.

Although this last point may appear to be counterintuitive, it is supported by contemporary studies of traditional cultures. A good example comes from a recent study by Saxe (1995), who examined the counting system of the Oksapmin. The Oksapmin are a hunter-gatherer people in the interior of Papua New Guinea, who have a counting system in which different body parts rather than fingers are used for making tallies (for example, the number for 7 might be represented as "left elbow"). Saxe found that number conservation in these children emerged in a normal fashion, somewhere during middle childhood. Even adults, however, showed no understanding of an insight which in our culture

emerges in the early primary school, with the construction of the mental number line. This is the understanding that the addition of 4 physical units to a group of X units is calculable simply by counting forward 4 units from X. Saxe attributes the absence of this insight to the absence of any commercial activity in Oksapmin culture for which this sort of computation would be useful. In support of this interpretation, he notes what happened when a trading store came into one Okaspmin valley, and commercial problems of this sort began to take on considerable significance. Although they kept their indigenous counting system, the Oksapmin introduced innovations in its use which precisely parallel those that modern children use, when they adopt the min strategy. This finding is clearly in line with Damerow's final conclusion, as are several others (e.g., Fiati, 1992).

Not all modern conceptual innovations, of course, can be traced directly to the new needs that are encountered, and the new problems that must be solved, in the course of social and economic development. Still, many modern conceptual developments have taken place in the context of our universities, which serve a clear economic purpose of their own. It is therefore of interest to note (a) that the school first came into existence in the Babylonian era, for the training of skill in the use of the new symbols, and (b) that it did not immediately assume its current form. This latter point has been made with some force by Hoyrup (1994), who has studied the gradual evolution of mathematics in the various empires that succeeded the Babylonian one, as well as the changes that took place in pre-Babylonian and Babylonian times. One of the interesting points he makes is that certain mathematical problems, analogous to modern puzzles or brain-teasers may be found in the records of the early schools, and appear to have been used both a means of training novices and as a sign of insider knowledge and power. This sort of educational experience, in which special problems are invented for training and presented in an organized "curriculum," is quite un-characteristic of learning that takes place by apprenticeship, as Lave and her colleagues have convincingly shown (Lave & Wenger, 1991). That this activity is characteristic of the earliest symbol-learning environments is therefore of some interest.

Of even greater interest is the fact that the sort of reasoned conceptual process that we take as protypical of mathematical activity, involving inquiry and proof, does not appear to have emerged in the history of mathematics until well after such schools were in existence. Hoyrup (1994) has shown that it is not until the evolution of the

Greek city state, in which rhetoric and argumentation become a normal part of political life, that one sees the importation of this sort of activity into academic life. This turned out to be a watershed in the development of mathematics, which produced a major shift in both the nature and the rate at which new mathematical discoveries were made.

Processes of Change in Developing Children

With the focus on school as an agent of conceptual transmission, work in the sociohistoric tradition comes full circle. Recall that early studies in the sociohistoric tradition found that certain high level structures did not appear to develop in traditional cultures, and that strong schooling effects were found in cultures that were in a process of cultural transition. Both these findings are clarified by the studies of historical and cultural change reported above. This work also clarifies the findings on social class, which indicate that children from higher SES groups perform at a higher level on Piagetian tasks than do children from lower SES groups (Gaudia, 1972; Shayer et al., 1988). In a recent longitudinal study, Edelstein, Keller, and Schroeder (1990) found that these differences are rather small in the early years, but widen as children progress through the school system, as a result of factors that are clearly identifiable in the early years (Edelstein, 1996).

Drawing on studies such as these, as well as the literature on educational reform, there have been several recent attempts by developmentalists in the United States to improve the process of schooling for low SES children (Brown & Campione, 1994; Confrey, 1996; Griffin & Case, 1996). Most of these attempts share three features in common: first they make an attempt to focus on the deep principles and structures that underlie the discipline, not merely surface procedures or computational tricks. Second, they all encourage more genuine intellectual autonomy and more discussion, than does traditional instruction for such groups. Finally, they all encourage children to identify with their school achievement in some fashion, and to see it as centrally related to their developing sense of power and self. One could therefore say that they are re-instituting, in a more modern cultural context, three of the main features that appear to have been critical in the original development of these academic disciplines in the first place.

Unfortunately for the present review, few of these intervention studies have attempted to assess children's conceptual structures using standard cognitive-developmental tasks. In the one that did, however, a gradual change was shown over time, with the low SES children who received the special schooling eventually reaching and surpassing the level of their middle class peers (Griffin, in press). Although we do not have a full sense of the way in which socioeconomic circumstances and schooling contribute to children's conceptual growth, then, a picture is certainly emerging that is consistent across widely different forms of methodology, and that is consistent with the general tenets of sociohistoric thought.

Correlating Change in a Culture and Its Socialization Practices

One final study is worth mentioning, because it examined the effects of cultural change on the way in which children are initiated into cultural practices, as well as the practices themselves (Greenfield, 1989, 1995). The group Greenfield studied are the Zinacantel, a Mexican agricultural group who weave their own clothing. Prior to a period of close contact with representatives of modern urban life, Greenfield noted that young girls were taught how to weave the 4 classic patterns of clothing in a manner that was strongly adult-scripted, and that resulted in a rather rigid pattern of classification and symbolization. Over a 20-year period, as the Zinacantel came into increasing contact with the broader culture of Mexico, the economic basis of their life underwent a considerable transformation and this pattern changed. The Zinacantel now began to weave products for trade rather than just their own usage. They were also exposed to a broader range of fabrics and patterns by their new trading partners. Among the changes that Greenfield documents during this time period, and which she attributes to this change, were: (a) a change in the range of patterns that began to emerge in adult weaving patterns; (b) an increased interest in representation and representational diversity more broadly; and (c) a change in the method of initiating young people into the weaving process: one that was much less highly adult-scripted, and more oriented toward individual discovery. Once again, then, we see that changes in economic activity and social organization, changes in representational forms, and changes in the form of teaching and learning are closely linked. Similar though less pronounced effects may be taking place in our own culture, as it goes through its current process of social, economic, and technological growth (Greenfield, 1994).

Trends and Convergences among the Three Traditions

As will no doubt be apparent, the differences that separate the three traditions on the topic of conceptual change are every bit as large as the differences that separate them on the question of how to characterize children's conceptual structures to begin with. Investigators in the empiricist tradition remain as committed as they were thirty years ago to viewing the change process as incremental, and closely tied to the tasks to which children are exposed on a daily basis (compare Siegler, 1996, Ch. 8, with Gagné, 1968). Investigators in the rationalist tradition remain committed to the view that developmental change has a strong endogenous component, which from time to time permits a major restructuring of children's existing conceptual understanding to take place (compare van der Maas, 1996, with Piaget, 1970). Finally, sociohistoric theorists remain committed to the proposition that economic, social, and technological changes are the major factors that have produced conceptual revolutions in the past and that it is the initiation into these practices that plays the major role in children's intellectual development in the present (compare Damerow, 1995, with Vygotsky, 1962).

Notwithstanding their continued commitment to different views of change, however, there has been gradual convergence of the three traditions on a number of points. This convergence is perhaps most obvious in the case of the empiricist and the rationalist traditions. Although the new connectionism has produced a revival of the view that was temporarily discredited during the cognitive revolution—namely, that a core set of associational processes can lead to the acquisition of very complex cognitive structures—several notions have also crept into empiricist thought, in the process of actually building systems that can achieve this feat, which are strongly reminiscent of work in the rationalist tradition. These include the following: (a) it is important to distinguish between change within and across existing structures (Chi, 1988); (b) new "levels" of cognition may be necessary to model higher order growth (Shultz, 1991); (c) curiosity (i.e., a bias toward novelty) may also be required (Siegler, 1996); and finally (d) some sort of top-down "abstraction" process may be necessary, in addition to a bottom-up one (Hinton et al., 1995; Klahr & Wallace, 1976; Shultz, 1991; Siegler & Shraeger, 1997).

By the same token, while rationalists continue to focus on transformational change with an endogenous component, a number of notions have been introduced which have been of long standing interest in the empiricist tradition. These include the suggestions: (a) that associative learning plays a vital part in preparing a system for transformational change (Case, 1985; Fischer, 1980; Pascual-Leone, 1970); (b) that new waves of development depend on the attainment of critical levels of specific learning (Case, 1992a;

Van Geert, 1991); and (c) that endogenous change involves a quantitative as well as a qualitative component. The way in which endogenous change has been conceptualized has also developed in a fashion that makes it much more compatible with empiricist thinking. Suggestions which move the theory in this direction are: (a) that periodic reorganizations follow the general laws of dynamic systems (Pascual-Leone, 1970; van der Maas & Molenaar, 1992; Van Geert, 1991); and (b) that the quantitative parameters which control such re-organizations have objective, neurological underpinnings (Case, 1992b; Fischer & Rose, 1993; Pascual-Leone et al., 1990; Thatcher, 1992). Finally, there has been a clear convergence in the methods used in the two traditions, which have come to rely increasingly on dense time-series sampling, and computer simulation.

On the surface, the sociohistoric tradition has proceeded entirely in its own direction, with little accommodation to the other two. In fact, however, there are several substantive trends in common which include the de-emphasis on logic as the underlying mechanism of growth, and the increased emphasis on conceptual and notational systems. There are also several common methodological trends, which include the increased emphasis on modeling change, and on sampling the variable being modeled more densely, as it actually occurs, in a specific context.

To the foregoing sets of convergences may be added one final one, which is the most concealed but perhaps the most important of all. This is the increased (albeit implicit) acceptance that the form of explanation being developed in any one tradition has its limits—and that any complete account of conceptual change must ultimately take account of the data and ideas in the other traditions as well. In short, there is an increased acceptance that the sort of major conceptual changes that we see in children's thinking in middle childhood would not assume the form that they do: (a) without a long period of initiation into a culture, and the forms of interaction and thought that it has developed; (b) without an equally long period of learning, both associative and purposeful, in which the cultural systems that are inherited are applied to solving a set of specific tasks and problems; and (c) without a change in the level of reflexive analysis that children become capable of, at the approximate age when formal schooling is initiated. Acceptance of the above three propositions is by no means universal. Given that it is present at all, however, it seems worthwhile to conclude by addressing the question of how we might take account of all three sorts of change-factor at once, within the context of a single theoretical system.

TOWARD AN INTEGRATED VIEW OF CONCEPTUAL CHANGE

In thinking about how to combine the models and concepts in the previous section, it is worthwhile to focus on a specific example. Consider, therefore, the requirements that would have to be met for the 6-year-old mental number line (Figure 15.2) to be constructed from the two lower order schemas that are its precursors: namely, the schemas for global quantification and enumeration (Figure 15.1). From a purely formal point of view, it is clear that at least five requirements would have to be met:

1. The content of the existing schemas would have be differentiated and elaborated.
2. The content of the existing schemas would have to be linked.
3. The new (linked) schema would have to be re-organized.
4. A new (2nd order) symbol system would have be mastered, to represent the elements of the new schema.
5. The new structure would have to be put to work for mastering a new set of tasks, both social and intellectual.

Some progress toward an integrated account of conceptual change may be made by considering each one of these requirements separately.

Differentiating and Elaborating the Content of Existing Schemas

Consider first the requirement for adding new content to existing schemas. What sort of process would one need to postulate, in order to produce the sort of additions that are observed during this age range? This content could not be added without exposure to the forms that already exist in the culture. Equally clearly, the process must be subject to some form of general constraint, since children who receive daily exposure do not show much learning of this content until the age of 3 to 4 years. Elsewhere (Case, 1985, Ch. 10) I have provided detailed analyses of how new content can be acquired by independent exploration, modeling, and/or direct instruction. Regardless of the global process, the underlying mechanism appears to be the same. A situation must be set up where children activate the existing elements of a schema (e.g., they mentally count from 1 to 4) in a context where there is at least some peripheral activation of an additional element (e.g., 5).

The process that connectionists have modeled in such detail, and that Pascual-Leone has termed C-learning would be one possible way of insuring that such a process got started: Indeed, it might be the preferred way, since it would not require the child to play too active a role in the process until a general spatio-temporal frame had been established. Since the number 5 occurs right after 4 in many contexts where counting takes place one would expect that, as a result of C-learning, a positive association would naturally build up between the sub-schemas for 4 and 5, while a negative association built up between the sub-schema for 4 and other possible content (e.g., 6, 10). This sort of associative learning would clearly be facilitated by exposure to a cultural model, provided that the neurological prerequisites were in place. At the neurological level, the process would be facilitated by any change that increased the availability of facilitory and inhibitory connections in the cortical system that is responsible for representing the type of content in question. As Thatcher (1992) has pointed out, there is evidence from EEG studies that such a process of branching takes place within each of the posterior lobes during this time period.

Although C-learning would be an excellent way to begin a learning process of this sort, one would ideally want a more active process as well, one that would—at some point—involve the subject's conscious attention, and would produce more rapid learning. The process that Pascual-Leone has labeled *L-learning* would appear to be ideal in this regard. Moreover, if L-learning gradually took over after a preparatory phase of C-learning, the overall growth curve would assume the wavelike form that Siegler has documented.

The likelihood that L-learning would be involved would also increase as a function of both experiential and neurological factors, although they might be somewhat different ones. Among the prime experiential factors would be: (a) increased exposure to counting as a task as a result of entry into a new social institution such as a nursery school or kindergarten; (b) a change in the degree to which the missing element in the child's existing routine was rendered salient, by peers or older role models; and (c) increased availability of existing attentional resources, due to the automization of existing counting routines. The relevant neurological factors would be ones that involve the frontal lobes, since they appear to control executive processes and working memory. As mentioned above, Thatcher's (1992) data suggest that a developmental process takes place during this time period, in the long distance fibers connecting the frontal and posterior lobes. A good deal of development may also take place within the frontal lobes themselves.

Linking Existing Schemas from Different Modules

What about the second requirement: the requirement for linking two previously discrete schemas? As a brief glance at television aimed at preschoolers will confirm, the tasks of learning to count and learning to make quantity (more/less) judgments are recognized as important ones in our culture and are given considerable attention in instructional efforts aimed at preschool children. By and large, however, these two tasks appear to take place in separate contexts. There may also be executed by different neurological modules (see Dehaene & Changeux, 1993; Dehaene & Cohen, 1995). Finally, there is empirical evidence that children who have well elaborated schemas for each do not necessarily find it easy to link them. Being able to count to 5 flawlessly, and being able to judge that 5 physical objects is more than 4 objects is no guarantee that one will know that the number 5 automatically entails more quantity than the number 4 (Okamoto & Case, 1996; Siegler & Robinson, 1982).

In principle, it seems to me that the same basic learning processes would be likely to be involved in making linkages across schemas as within schemas (i.e., C- and L-learning). The only difference would be that there would be likely to be more resistance in the system, and thus a greater necessity for some increase in attentional capacity (M) before the process of cross-schema linkage could really get started. As has already been mentioned, an important neurological requirement for this latter growth may be improved frontal functioning, and/or improved connections between the frontal and posterior cortex. Additional changes that would facilitate the linkage of previously discrete schemas would be those involving improved connectivity among the various posterior centers on which the particular structures in question depend, and/or their increased lateralization. The posterior centers and connections that are involved in the particular case under consideration are shown in Figure 15.13 (based on work which shows by Dehaene & Changeux, 1993; Dehaene & Cohen, 1995), the circuitry that is involved in making magnitude judgments in response to auditorily present numbers. Although the subjects were adults, the task they were asked to perform (number comparison) is one that has been taken as criterial for the acquisition of a mental number line in the developmental literature. Thus, one can presume that anything which improved the functioning and/or communication

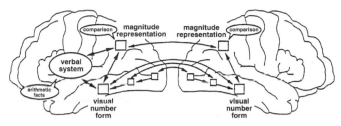

Figure 15.13 Dehaene's diagram of the neural centers and pathways that are involved in making comparisons of magnitude. The model assumes that numerals (Row a, Figure 15.1) are stored in the ventral occipital lobes, which are labelled *visual number form* in the diagram. Number words (Row b, Figure 15.1) are stored in the left temporal lobe, which is labeled *verbal system* in the diagram. The magnitude of each number is presumed to be represented analogically, and these representations are stored in the parieto-occipital-temporal junctions, which are indicated as *magnitude representations* in the diagram. Analogical representation is presumed to be bilateral, although it may be superior in the right hemisphere. Verbal representation is lateralized in the left hemisphere. For any more complex use of number representations, the frontal lobes are intimately involved. The hypothesized circuitry for these latter connections is shown in Dehaene and Cohen (1995).

between the centers indicated in the diagram would also help to facilitate the assembly of the mental number line in younger children.

As with any set of neurological developments, the caveat is that the structure in question (in this case, the mental number line) must be a significant one in the culture, and that social mechanisms must be in place for making this importance manifest to children, in order for these developments to take place. School constitutes a major mechanism of this sort.

Reorganizing the Existing Schematic Repertoire

In order to generate the 6-year-old conceptual structures from those that are present at the age of 4, it is not sufficient simply to elaborate the existing structures and link them together. In addition, one needs to re-organize the resulting network. First of all, one needs to *interleave* the content of the two schemas (Case, 1985, 1992a; Demetriou, 1996; Neches & Hayes, 1978). In the case of children's numerical development, the analogic representation for three must be linked with the counting word "three," the analogic representation for four must be linked with the counting word "four" and so on. Second, one needs to *map* the content of one on to the other, in such a fashion that a new principle can be abstracted (Demetriou, 1996; Halford, 1982). In the case of children's numerical development, the new principle is the idea that the addition or subtraction of a unit to any canonical set always yields a number that is adjacent in the counting string: a principle that only gradually emerges in children's strategies for adding and subtracting during the age range from 5 to 7 years (Davydov, 1982; Fuson, 1982).

The psychological mechanism that I would propose for achieving this reorganization is the one that I hinted at in the discussion of Hinton's work: namely, the addition of a new level of hidden unit—a new level of processing, if you will—to the higher order system that receives input from the first order processing system, and is responsible for abstracting the patterns of covariance in it. In terms of Demetriou's model (Figure 15.8) this suggestion corresponds to the suggestion that a new a new level of processing is added to the hypercognitive system. This of course implies an acceptance of Piaget's proposal that "reflexive abstraction," or "hierarchical integration" plays a major role in the developmental process, a claim that Kuhn (Kuhn, 1983; Kuhn, Garcia-Mila, Zohar, & Anderson, 1995) has championed, and Campbell and Bickart (1986), have made central to their "levels of knowing" model.

Modern "dynamic system" theorists in the empiricist tradition have resisted this suggestion quite strongly; they have seen it as building in an internal "homunculus" to read abstract patterns from existing processes, rather than allowing existing processes to "self-organize," in response to a change in a control parameter (Smith & Thelan, 1993). Dynamic systems theorists in the rationalist tradition have seen this criticism as unnecessarily restrictive, however (van der Maas, 1996). Moreover, anyone who has tried to simulate this sort of high-level change on a computer—whether using rule-based methods (Klahr & Wallace, 1976; Siegler & Shraeger, 1997) or connectionist methods (Halford, 1993; Shultz, 1991)—has found it necessary to include some sort of change of a hypercognitive nature. Once one accepts the presence of such a system, one can see how it would also facilitate both prior forms of learning just mentioned: namely, the initial formation of connections within and across existing schemes.

In neurological terms, the proposal that improved hypercognitive learning plays an important role in conceptual development corresponds to the suggestion that a new layer of processing is added to the frontal lobes—or a new level of connectedness between the frontal and the posterior regions (Case, 1992b). The relevant social factors have also been considered, at least in general terms.

One particular social activity that is relevant to the reorganization of children's mathematical understanding in the early years is worthy of mention, namely, the playing of board games in which the addition of one unit to a total is always accompanied by one move forward along a line of numerals, and the subtraction of one unit is always accompanied by one move backward. The presence of board games in the home correlates strongly with success in early school mathematics. Moreover the programs that have been most successful in stimulating early mathematical growth have used board games as a strong component (Griffin, in press). Similar games may facilitate the re-organization of other emerging structures.

Mastering a New (Second-Order) Symbol System

First-order symbol systems normally involve verbal or gestural language. Second-order symbol systems often (though not necessarily) involve some form of written notation. The use of such written notation carries many advantages, since it in effect creates second-order visual "objects" which can be thought about and talked about in the same fashion as first-order objects, with little or no interference (Brooke, 1968; Olson, 1994). These advantages are clearly apparent in children's acquisition of the central conceptual structure for numbers. Not only does the existence of a visually mediated place value system make it easier to acquire the base ten system, it also gives one a set of objects that one can talk about as entities, thus facilitating the acquisition of the notion that a number can be treated as an object in its own right, rather than just as a counting tag.

For children to acquire such systems, it is necessary that they be exposed to some form of culturally mediated, symbolic learning, which may well require a certain set of unique and biologically specific mechanisms. School is one place where children learn about written numerals in our culture. Through number books and games, a good deal of learning also goes on in the home. Neurological factors that are relevant would include those mentioned above, as well as any additional factors that were unique to left temporal lobe development, and the linkage of left temporal with other circuits in the cortex.

Putting the New System to Work

At the same time as children are abstracting a new set of principles and learning a new set of symbols, they are of course also encountering a new set of social and cognitive tasks, and developing a new set of executive strategies for dealing with these tasks. In the empiricist tradition, new executive structures are normally seen as being "learned" in one context, and "transferred" to another. In the rationalist tradition, new structures are normally seen as being "abstracted" from the processing that takes place across a variety of contexts and then gradually consolidated in a fashion that also transcends any specific context. On this point it may be unnecessary to chose between the two traditions. In my own recent work, for example, I have proposed a model in which both sorts of change take place in concert. On the one hand, specific changes are gradually "fed-up" to a more general level; on the other hand, general changes are "fed down" to more specific contexts, thus changing increasing the likelihood of local learning. In effect, I have proposed a *hierarchical learning loop,* in which conceptual changes of a general nature and changes of a more specific nature are reciprocally coupled, and constrained by general efficiency of the overall system (Case, 1996).

The operation of such a loop is illustrated in Figure 15.14. As may be seen, specific learning is seen as involving an iterative process, in which associative (C) and attentionally mediated (M) learning facilitate each other. The operation of this sort of loop is in turn embedded within the broader loop provided by the central conceptual and more specific structures. Although the model is only a preliminary one, it has been mathematized and tested against several different kinds of data, and shown to provide a reasonable fit to them. These data include: (a) growth curves from tasks to which children receive different degrees of specific exposure; (b) growth curves from children in widely differing cultures; (c) growth curves from children from different social classes; and (d) growth curves for misleading as well as facilitating tasks (Case, 1997). Like the notion of a central conceptual structure, then, it would appear that the notion of a hierarchical learning loop offers the potential for mediation across different traditions of inquiry.

Once the operation of such a loop is understood, one can see how it would not only facilitate the gradual expansion of tasks to which a new structure is relevant, but the original assembly and consolidation of the structure in the first place. Depending on the external conditions (facilitory versus inhibitory) and the internal conditions (multiplicative versus additive interaction among levels), such a system could contribute to slow, wave-like acquisition, or acquisition that was quite abrupt (Case, 1997). In and of itself, the model cannot explain the full range of acquisition phenomena that have been reported in the developmental literature, and which include such behaviors as temporary regression,

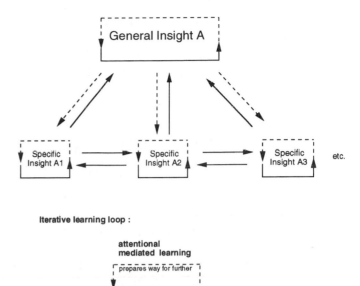

Figure 15.14 Hierarchical learning loop. Children's associative learning and their attentional learning in specific situations "feed" on each other, in an iterative feedback loop. A similar feedback loop connects children's learning in specific situations with their more general (structural) understanding. One result of this hierarchical feedback process is that the rate of learning in low-exposure situations is faster than one might otherwise expect, since it is mediated by general understanding (which is "fed" by insights acquired in high exposure situations).

oscillation, and asymmetrical gestalt-shifts or "hysteresis" (Fischer & Kennedy, in press; van der Maas & Molinaar, 1996; Van Geert, 1994). However, if inhibitory as well as facilitory links among units were included (as is the case in most dynamic approaches that focus on these phenomena) then the present model might help to move this enterprise forward as well. What one would end up with would be a model that captured the complex interactions—both positive and negative—among cognitive units at multiple levels, in a system whose basic capacities and capability for reflexive abstraction were gradually expanding, and which was highly sensitive to the facilitating or misleading patterns in its environment.

SUMMARY AND CONCLUSION

Throughout this century, research on children's conceptual structures has been conducted in three epistemological traditions: the empiricist tradition, the rationalist tradition, and the sociohistoric tradition. Each tradition has brought its own preconceptions about the origins of human knowledge to the enterprise, and each has produced its own pioneers, its own theories, and its own tradition of progressive empirical inquiry. In the first half of the century, each tradition labored in relative isolation from the others. Events during the second half of the century did much to break down these original barriers, however, and to open up new lines of communication.

In the first round of dialogue, there was a fair amount of misunderstanding and criticism across the three traditions. With time, though, the grounds of disagreement gradually became clarified, and a new set of models emerged. Expertise theory and neo-connectionism emerged in the empiricist tradition, from the ashes of earlier s-r theory. Theory-theory emerged in the rationalist tradition, from the merger of classical Piagetian theory with Chomsky's notion of a module-specific structure, and Kuhn's model of theory-change in science. New theories emerged in the sociohistoric tradition from the merger of Vygotsky's theory with notions of cognitive representation and cultural practice that had been developed in cognitive and cultural anthropology. Finally, neo-Piagetian theory emerged from an attempt to combine the core assumptions of rationalism and empiricism, using the tools provided by the newly emerging discipline of cognitive science.

As these new theoretical positions were developed, an improved set of empirical techniques emerged in each tradition, and a process began in which the new models were honed in the light of the new methods and data. Further refinement also took place as a result of continued dialogue across the traditions. This process continues to this day, as investigators begin to build models that focus on the process of conceptual change, and to study this process more directly.

Notwithstanding the continued differences among the various traditions, it seems clear that one result of the dialogue has been a move toward a "middle ground" by proponents of all three general positions. Rationalists and sociohistoric theorists have begun to define conceptual structures in such a fashion that they are confined to particular domains, rather than being systemwide in their scope and implications. By the same token, empiricists have begun to define conceptual structures in a fashion that is considerably broader than their original, rather atomistic models. They have also begun to examine such general properties as conceptual coherence and organization, and to

postulate the existence of top-down processing and/or some form or reflexive abstraction.

In my own work, I have attempted to extend this trend toward convergence, by building a theory that draws on concepts from all three classic traditions. Two constructs are central to this theory (a) the notion of a *central conceptual structure:* that, is a powerful schema which captures the core ideas of a domain, and which children reconstruct, via a series of differentiations and integrations, in the course of their social and cognitive growth, and (b) the notion of a *hierarchical learning loop:* that is, a two-level structure in which the emerging top level reads patterns that are present within or across lower levels, and then feeds back the results to the lower levels themselves, thus facilitating the ongoing dynamic that is present at that level between and associative and attentional learning. As the power of the higher level system expands, such loops acquire the ability to produce a new wave of learning, of just the sort that is observed in the critical years of middle childhood. Although this model has so far been tested only on data for the 4- to 10-year age period, it seems at least possible that it may provide an equally good fit to the waves of structural learning that take place later (during the teenage years) or earlier (during the preschool years) in the overall sequence of children's conceptual development.

Given the history of the field to date, what predictions can one hazard about the future? The safest prediction, it seems to me, is that continued progress in the field will result from the same three sources as it has in the past, namely: (a) the natural tension and dialogue *among* the three traditions, and the refinement, clarification, and occasional attempts at integration that this dialogue provokes; (b) the natural tension between theory and data *within* each of the three traditions, coupled with the search for improved concepts and methods; and (c) the impact of intellectual events taking place *outside* the three traditions: both in the general zeitgeist, and in other disciplines. Two related disciplines in which great strides are currently being made are dynamic systems theory, and neuroscience. In the fifth section, I reviewed several models of structural change that have already been influenced by work in these areas, and speculated on further connections that might be made as this work continues to develop. As we look toward the future, it seems likely that developments in these other fields will continue to influence the study of conceptual structures. It also seems likely that new intellectual forces will arise whose shape we cannot discern at the moment, and whose roots will be much clearer in retrospect than they were in prospect. One would of course not wish things to be otherwise, especially in a field devoted to the study of complex conceptual structures, and their development over long periods of time.

REFERENCES

Anglin, J. M. (1993). Vocabulary development: A morphological analysis. *Monographs of the Society for Research in Child Development, 58*(10, Serial No. 238).

Astington, J. W (1994). *The child's discovery of mind.* New York: Cambridge University Press.

Astington, J. W., Harris, P. L., & Olson, D. R. (1989). *Developing theories of mind.* New York: Cambridge University Press.

Baldwin, J. M. (1968). *The development of the child and of the race.* New York: Augustus M. Kelly. (Original work published 1894)

Beilin, H. (1983). The new functionalism and Piaget's program. In E. K. Scholnick (Ed.), *New trends in conceptual representation* (pp. 3–40). Hillsdale, NJ: LEA.

Bell, M. A., & Fox, N. A. (1992). The relation between frontal brain electrical activity and cognitive development during infancy. *Child Development, 63,*1142–1163.

Biggs, J., & Collis, K. (1982). *Evaluating the quality of learning: The SOLO taxonomy.* New York: Academic Press.

Binet, A. (1900). *La suggestibilite.* Paris: Schleicher et Frères.

Binet, A., & Simon, T. (1916/1905). *The development of intelligence in children.* Baltimore: Williams & Wilkens.

Bleiker, C. (1995). *The role of central conceptual structures in children's drawing.* Unpublished doctoral dissertation, Stanford University, Stanford, CA.

Brainerd, C. J. (1976). Stage, structure, and developmental theory. In G. Steiner (Ed.), *The psychology of the twentieth century.* Munich: Kindler.

Brainerd, C. J. (1993). Cognitive development is abrupt (but not stage-like). *Monographs of the Society for Research in Child Development, 58*(9), 170–190.

Brooke, L. R. (1968). Spatial and verbal components of the act of recall. *Canadian Journal of Psychology, 22,* 349–369.

Brown, A. L., & Campione, J. C. (1994). Guided discovery in a community of learners. In K. McGilly (Ed.), *Classroom lessons* (pp. 229–272). Cambridge, MA: MIT Books.

Bruchkowsky, M. (1992). The development of empathic cognition in middle and early childhood. In R. Case (Ed.), *The Mind's Staircase: Exploring the conceptual underpinnings of children's thought and knowledge* (pp. 153–170). Hillsdale, NJ: Erlbaum.

Bruner, J. S. (1964). The course of cognitive growth. *American Psychologist, 19,* 1–15.

Bruner, J. S. (1986). *Actual minds, possible worlds.* Cambridge, MA: Harvard University Press.

Bruner, J. S., Goodnow, J. J., & Austin, G. A. (1956). *A study in thinking.* New York: Wiley.

Campbell, R. L., & Bickart, M. H. (1986). *Knowing levels and developmental stages.* Basel: Karger.

Capodilupo, A. M. (1992). A neo-structural analysis of children's response to instruction in the sight-reading of musical notation. In R. Case (Ed.), *The Mind's Staircase: Exploring the conceptual underpinnings of children's thought and knowledge* (pp. 99–115). Hillsdale, NJ: Erlbaum.

Carey, S. (1985). *Conceptual change in childhood.* Cambridge, MA: MIT Press.

Carey, S. (1988). Reorganization of knowledge in the course of acquisition. In S. Strauss (Ed.), *Ontogeny, phylogeny, and historical development* (pp. 1–27). New York: ABLEX.

Carraher, T. N., Carraher, D. W., & Schliemann, A. D. (1985). Mathematics in the streets and schools. *British Journal of Developmental Psychology, 3,* 21–29.

Case, R. (1972a). Learning and development: A neo-Piagetian interpretation. *Human Development, 15,* 339–358.

Case, R. (1972b). Validation of a neo-Piagetian capacity construct. *Journal of Experimental Child Psychology, 14,* 287–302.

Case, R. (1977). Responsiveness to conservation training as a function of induced subjective uncertainty, M-space, and cognitive style. *Canadian Journal of Behavioral Science, 9,* 12–25.

Case, R. (1985). *Intellectual development: Birth to adulthood.* New York: Academic Press.

Case, R. (1992a). *The Mind's Staircase: Exploring the conceptual underpinnings of children's thought and knowledge.* Hillsdale, NJ: Erlbaum.

Case, R. (1992b). The role of the frontal lobes in the regulation of cognitive development. *Brain and Cognition, 20,* 51–73.

Case, R. (1995a). Capacity based explanations of working memory growth: A brief history and a reevaluation. In F. M. Weinert & W. Schneider (Eds.), *Research in memory development and competencies* (pp. 23–44). Hillsdale, NJ: Erlbaum.

Case, R. (1995b). The role of psychological defenses in the representation and regulation of close personal relationships across the lifespan. In G. Noam & K. Fischer (Eds.), *Development and vulnerability in close relations.* Hillsdale, NJ: Erlbaum.

Case, R. (1996a). Modeling the dynamic interplay between general and specific change in children's conceptual understanding. In R. Case & Y. Okamoto (Eds.), The role of central conceptual structures in the development of children's thought. *Monographs of the Society for Research in Child Development, 60*(5/6), 156–188.

Case, R. (1996b). Summary and conclusions. In R. Case & Y. Okamoto (Eds.), The role of central conceptual structures in the development of children's thought. *Monographs of the Society for Research in Child Development, 60*(5/6).

Case, R. (1997, April). *A dynamic model of general numerical understanding, and its development in specific contexts.* Paper presented at the biennial meetings of the Society for Research in Child Development. Washington.

Case, R., & Griffin, S. (1990). Child cognitive development: The role of central conceptual structures in the development of scientific and social thought. In C. A. Hauert (Ed.), *Advances in psychology, developmental psychology* (pp. 193–230). Amsterdam, The Netherlands: Elsevier.

Case, R., Marra, K., Bleiker, C., & Okamoto, Y. (1996). Central spatial structures and their development. In R. Case & Y. Okamoto (Eds.), The role of central conceptual structures in the development of children's thought. *Monographs of the Society for Research in Child Development, 60*(5/6).

Case, R., & Okamoto, Y. (1996). The role of central conceptual structures in the development of children's thought. *Monographs of the Society for Research in Child Development, 60*(5/6).

Case, R., Okamoto, Y., Henderson, B., & McKeough, A. (1993). Individual variability and consistency in cognitive development: New evidence of the existence of central conceptual structures. In R. Case & W. Edelstein (Eds.), *The new structuralism in developmental theory and research: Analysis of individual developmental pathways.* Basel: Karger.

Case, R., & Sandieson, R. (1988). A developmental approach to the identification and teaching of central conceptual structures in middle school science and mathematics. In M. Behr & J. Hiebert (Eds.), *Research agenda in mathematics education: Number concepts and operations in the middle grades* (pp. 236–270). Hillsdale, NJ: LEA.

Case, R., & Sowder, J. (1990). The development of computational estimation: A neo-Piagetian analysis. *Cognition and Instruction, 7,* 79–104.

Chapman, M. (1988). *Constructive evolution: Origins and development of Piaget's thought.* New York: Cambridge University Press.

Chi, M. T. H. (1976). Short term memory limitations in children: Capacity or processing deficits? *Memory and Cognition, 23,* 266–281.

Chi, M. T. H. (1988). Children's lack of access and knowledge reorganization: An example from the concept of animism. In M. Perlmutter & F. E. Weinert (Eds.), *Memory development: Universal changes and individual differences* (pp. 169–194). Hillsdale, NJ: Erlbaum.

Chi, M. T. H. (1994). Conceptual change within and across ontological categories: Examples from learning and discovery in science. In R. Giere (Ed.), *Cognitive models of science: Minnesota studies in the philosophy of science.* Minneapolis: University of Minnesota Press.

Chi, M. T. H., Hutchinson, J. E., & Robin, A. F. (1989). How inferences about novel domain-related concepts can be constrained by structured knowledge. *Merrill-Palmer Quarterly, 35,* 27–61.

Chi, M. T. H., & Koeske, R. D. (1983). Network representation of a child's dinosaur knowledge. *Developmental Psychology, 12,* 29–39.

Chi, M. T. H., & Rees, E. (1983). A learning framework for development. *Contributions to Human Development, 9,* 71–107.

Chomsky, N. (1957). *Syntactic structures.* The Hague: Mouton.

Clark, E. V. (1983). Concepts and meanings. In J. H. Flavell & E. D. Markman (Eds.), *Carmichael's handbook of child development* (4th ed.) (Vol. 3, pp. 787–840). New York: Wiley.

Cole, M. (1991). Cognitive development and formal schooling: The evidence from cross cultural research. In L. C. Moll (Ed.), *Vygotsky and education: Instructional implications and applications of sociohistorical psychology* (pp. 89–110). New York: Cambridge University Press.

Cole, M., Gay, J., Glick, J. A., & Sharp, D. D. (1971). *The cultural context of learning and thinking.* New York: Basic Books.

Confrey, J. (1996, April). *Methodological considerations of a 3-year longitudinal teaching experiment designed to investigate splitting ratio, and proportion.* Paper presented at the annual meeting of the American Educational Research Association, New York.

Crammond, J. (1992). Analyzing the basic developmental processes of children with different types of learning disability. In R. Case (Ed.), *The Mind's Staircase: Exploring the conceptual underpinnings of children's thought and knowledge* (pp. 285–302). Hillsdale, NJ: Erlbaum.

Damerow, P. (in press). Prehistory and cognitive development. In J. Langer & M. Killen (Eds.), *Piaget, evolution and development.* Hillsdale, NJ: Erlbaum.

Damerow, P., Englund, R. K., & Nissen, H. J. (1995). The first representations of number and the development of the number concept. In R. Damerow (Ed.), *Abstraction and representation: Essays on the cultural evolution of thinking. Boston studies in the philosophy of science* (Vol. 175, pp. 275–297). Dordrecht, The Netherlands: Kluwer Academic.

Davydov, V. V. (1982). The psychological characteristics of the formation of elementary mathematical operations in children. In T. P. Carpenter, J. M. Moser, & T. A. Romberg (Eds.), *Addition and subtraction: A cognitive perspective* (pp. 67–82). Hillsdale, NJ: Erlbaum.

DeGroot, A. (1966). Perception and memory versus thought: Some old ideas and recent findings. In B. Kleinmuntz (Ed.), *Problem solving.* New York: Wiley.

Dehaene, S., & Changeux, J.-P. (1993). Development of elementary numerical abilities: A neuronal model. *Journal of Cognitive Neuroscience, 5,* 390–407.

Dehaene, S., & Cohen, L. (1995). Towards an anatomical and functional model of number processing. *Mathematical Cognition, 1,* 83–120.

DeLoache, J. S. (1989). The development of representation in young children. In H. W. Reese (Ed.), *Advances in child development and behavior* (Vol. 22). New York: Academic Press.

Demetriou, A. (1996). *Modelling change in the development of mind.* Unpublished manuscript, University of Thessalonika, Greece.

Demetriou, A., & Efklides, A. (1987). Towards a determination of the dimensions and domains of individual differences in cognitive development. In E. DeCorte, H. Lodewijks, R. Parmentier, & P. Span (Eds.), *Learning and instruction: European research in an international context.* Oxford, England: Pergamon Press.

Demetriou, A., Efklides, A., & Platsidou, M. (1993). The architecture and dynamics of developing mind. *Monographs of the Society for Research in Child Development, 58*(5/6, Serial No. 234).

Demetriou, A., Kazi, S., Platsidou, M., Sirmali, K., Efklides, A., & Kiosseoglou, G. (1996). *Self-image and cognitive development: Structure, development, and functions of self-evaluation and self-representation in adolescence.* Unpublished monograph, University of Thessalonika.

Dennis, S. (1992). Stage and structure in the development of children's spatial representations. In R. Case (Ed.), *The Mind's Staircase: Exploring the conceptual underpinnings of children's thought and knowledge* (pp. 229–245). Hillsdale, NJ: Erlbaum.

DeRibaupierre, A. (1993). Structural invariants and individual differences: On the difficulty of dissociating developmental and differential processes. In R. Case & W. Edelstein (Eds.), *The new structuralism in cognitive development: Theory and research on individual pathways* (pp. 11–33). Basel: Karger.

DeRibaupierre, A., & Pascual-Leone, J. (1979). Formal operations and M-power: A neo-Piagetian investigation. In D. Kuhn (Ed.), *Intellectual development beyond childhood: New directions in child development* (pp. 1–43). San Francisco: Jossey-Bass.

DeRibaupierre, A., Rieben, L., & Lautrey, J. (1991). Developmental change and individual differences: A longitudinal study using Piagetian tasks. *Genetic, Social and General Psychology Monographs, 117,* 285–311.

Diamond, A. (1991). Frontal lobe involvement in cognitive changes during the first year of life. In K. Gibson, M. Konner, & A. Peterson (Eds.), *Brain and behavioral development.* New York: Aldine Press.

Edelman, G. M. (1987). *Neural Darwinism: The theory of neuronal group selection.* New York: Basic Books.

Edelstein, W. (1996). The social construction of cognitive development. In G. Noam & K. W. Fischer (Eds.), *Development and vulnerability in close relationships.* Hillsdale, NJ: Erlbaum.

Edelstein, W., Keller, M., & Schroeder, E. (1990). Child development and social structure: A longitudinal investigation of individual differences. In P. B. Baltes, D. L. Fotherman, & R. M. Lerner (Eds.), *Life span development and behavior* (Vol. 10, pp. 152–185). Hillsdale, NJ: Erlbaum.

Eimas, P. D. (1966). Effects of overtraining and age on the intradimensional and extradimensional shifts in children. *Journal of Experimental Child Psychology, 3,* 348–355.

Fiati, T. A. (1992). Cross cultural variation in the structure of children's thought. In R. Case (Ed.), *The Mind's Staircase* (pp. 189–206). Hillsdale, NJ: Erlbaum.

Fischer, K. W. (1980). A theory of cognitive development: The control and construction of hierarchies of skills. *Psychological Review, 87,* 477–531.

Fischer, K. W., & Granott, N. (1995). Beyond one-dimensional change: Parallel, concurrent, socially distributed processes in learning and development. *Human Development, 38,* 302–314.

Fischer, K. W., Hand, H. H., Watson, M. W., Van Parys, M. M., & Tucker, J. L. (1984). Putting the child into socialization: The development of social categories in preschool children. In L. Katz (Ed.), *Current topics in early childhood education* (Vol. 5, pp. 27–72). Norwood, NJ: ABLEX.

Fischer, K. W., & Kennedy, B. (in press). Tools for analyzing the many shapes of development: The case of self-in-inrelationships in Korea. In K. A. Renninger & E. Amsel (Eds.), *Processes of development.* Hillsdale, NJ: Erlbaum.

Fischer, K. W., Knight, C. C., & Van Parys, M. M. (1993). Analyzing diversity in developmental pathways. In R. Case & W. Edelstein (Eds.), *The new structuralism in cognitive development: Theory and research on individual pathways* (pp. 33–56). Basel: Karger.

Fischer, K. W., & Rose, S. P. (1993). Development of coordination of components in brain and behavior: A framework for theory and research. In G. Dawson & K. W. Fischer (Eds.), *Human behavior and the developing brain.* New York: Guilford Press.

Flavell, J. H. (1963). *The developmental psychology of Jean Piaget.* Princeton, NJ: Van Nostrand.

Flavell, J. H. (1970). Concept development. In P. H. Mussen (Ed.), *Carmichael's handbook of child development* (pp. 983–1060). New York: Wiley.

Flavell, J. H. (1979). Metacognition and cognitive monitoring: A new area of cognitive developmental inquiry. *American Psychologist, 34,* 906–911.

Fodor, J. (1982). *The modularity of mind.* Cambridge, MA: MIT Press.

Frake, C. O. (1985). Cognitive maps of time and tide among medieval seafarers. *Man, 20,* 254–270.

Fuson, K. C. (1982). An analysis of the counting-on solution procedure in addition. In T. P. Carpenter, J. M. Moser, & T. A. Romberg (Eds.), *Addition and subtraction: A cognitive perspective* (pp. 67–82). Hillsdale, NJ: Erlbaum.

Gagné, R. M. (1968). Contributions of learning to human development. *Psychological Review, 75,* 177–191.

Gardner, H. (1983). *Frames of mind.* New York: Basic Books.

Gardner, H. (1985). *The mind's new science: A history of the cognitive revolution.* New York: Basic Books.

Gaudia, G. (1972). Race, social class, and age of achievement of conservation of Piaget's tasks. *Developmental Psychology, 6,* 158–165.

Gelman, R. (1978). Counting in the preschooler: What does and what does not develop? In R. Siegler (Ed.), *Children's thinking: What develops?* (pp. 213–242). Hillsdale, NJ: Erlbaum.

Gelman, R. (1979). Why we will continue to read Piaget. *Genetic Epistemologist, 8*(4), 1–3.

Gelman, R., & Baillargeon, R. (1983). A review of some Piagetian concepts. In P. H. Mussen (Ed.), *Carmichael's handbook of child development* (4th ed.) (Vol. 3, pp. 167–230). New York: Wiley.

Gholson, B. (1985). *The cognitive developmental basis of human learning: Studies in hypothesis testing.* New York: Academic Press.

Gladwyn, T. (1970). *East is a big bird: Navigation and logic on a Pulawatt Atoll.* Cambridge, MA: Harvard University Press.

Globerson, T. (1985). Field dependence/independence and mental capacity: A developmental approach. *Developmental Review, 5,* 261–273.

Goldberg-Reitman, J. R. (1992). Children's conception of their mother's role: A neo-structural analysis. In R. Case (Ed.), *The Mind's Staircase: Exploring the conceptual underpinnings of children's thought and knowledge* (pp. 135–152). Hillsdale, NJ: Erlbaum.

Goldman-Rakic, P. (1989a, June). *Working memory and the frontal lobes.* Paper presented at the Toronto General Hospital, Toronto, Canada.

Goldman-Rakic, P. (1989b). *Cellular and circuit basis of working memory in prefrontal cortex of nonhuman primates.* Paper prepared for *The prefrontal cortex.* Amsterdam, The Netherlands: Netherlands Institute for Brain Research.

Goodman, N. (1976). *Languages of art: An approach to a theory of symbols.* Indianapolis, IN: Hackett.

Goodnow, J. J. (1962). A test of milieu differences with some of Piaget's tasks. *Psychological Monographs, 36*(Whole No. 555).

Greenfield, P. M. (1966). On culture and conservation. In J. S. Bruner, R. R. Oliver, & P. M. Greenfield (Eds.), *Studies in cognitive growth* (pp. 225–256). New York: Wiley.

Greenfield, P. M. (1989). From birth to maturity in Zinacantan: Ontogenesis in cultural context. In V. Brinker & G. Gossen (Eds.), *Ethnographic encounters in southern Mesoamerica: Celebratory essays in honor of Evon Z. Vogt.* Albany, NY: SUNY Press.

Greenfield, P. M. (Ed.). (1994). Effects of interactive entertainment technologies on development. *Journal of Applied Developmental Psychology, 15,* 1–139.

Greenfield, P. M. (1995, June). *Development evolution and culture.* Paper presented at the annual meeting of the Jean Piaget Society, Berkeley, CA.

Greenfield, P. M., & Bruner, J. S. (1966). Culture and cognitive growth. *International Journal of Psychology, 1,* 89.

Greenfield, P. M., Reich, L. M., & Oliver, R. R. (1966). On culture and equivalence: II. In J. S. Bruner, R. R. Oliver, & P. M. Greenfield (Eds.), *Studies in cognitive growth* (pp. 270–319). New York: Wiley.

Greenough, W. T., Black, J. E., & Wallace, C. S. (1987). Experience and brain development. *Child Development, 58,* 539–559.

Griffin, S. A. (1992). Young children's understanding of their inner world: A neo-Piagetian analysis of the development of intrapersonal intelligence. In R. Case (Ed.), *The Mind's Staircase: Exploring the conceptual underpinnings of children's thought and knowledge* (pp. 189–206). Hillsdale, NJ: Erlbaum.

Griffin, S. A. (in press). Evaluation of a program designed to teach number sense to children at risk for school failure. *Journal of Research in Mathematics Education.*

Griffin, S. A., & Case, R. (1996). Evaluating the breadth and depth of training effects, when central conceptual structures are taught. In R. Case & Y. Okamoto (Eds.), The role of central conceptual structures in the development of children's thought. *Monographs of the Society for Research in Child Development, 60*(5/6).

Griffin, S. A., Case. R., & Sandieson, R. (1992). Synchrony and asynchrony in the acquisition of children's everyday mathematical knowledge. In R. Case (Ed.), *The Mind's Staircase: Exploring the conceptual underpinnings of children's thought and knowledge* (pp. 75–98). Hillsdale, NJ: Erlbaum.

Griffin. S. A, Case, R., & Siegler, R. S. (1994). Rightstart: Providing the central conceptual prerequisites for first formal learning of arithmetic to students at risk for school failure. In

K. McGilly (Ed.), *Classroom lessons: Integrating cognitive theory and classroom practice* (pp. 1–50). Cambridge, MA: MIT Press.

Groen, G. G., & Parkman, J. M. (1972). A chronometric analysis of simple addition. *Psychological Review, 79,* 329–343.

Guilford, J. P. (1967). *The nature of human intelligence.* New York: McGraw-Hill.

Gustafsson, J. E. (1988). Broad and narrow abilities in research on learning and instruction. In R. J. Sternberg (Ed.), *Advances in the psychology of intelligence* (Vol. 4). Hillsdale, NJ: Erlbaum.

Halford, G. S. (1982). *The development of thought.* Hillsdale, NJ: Erlbaum.

Halford, G. S. (1993). *Children's understanding: The development of mental models.* Hillsdale, NJ: Erlbaum.

Halford, G. S., & McDonald, C. (1977). Children's pattern construction as a function of age and complexity. *Child Development, 48,* 1096–1100.

Hayes, J. R. (1985). Three problems in teaching general skills in S. Chipman, J. Segal, & R. Glaser (Eds.), *Thinking and learning skills* (Vol. 2, pp. 391–407). Hillsdale, NJ: Erlbaum.

Hebb, D. O. (1949). *The organization of behavior.* New York: Wiley.

Hinton, G. E., Dayan, P., Frey, B. J., & Neal, R. M. (1995). The "wake-sleep" algorithm for unsupervised neural networks. *Science, 268,* 1158–1161.

Hoyrup, H. (1994). Varieties of mathematical discourse in premodern socio-cultural contexts: Mesopotamia, Greece, and the Latin middle ages. In J. Hoyrup (Ed.), *In measure, number and weight: Studies in mathematics and culture* (pp. 1–22). Albany, NY: SUNY Press.

Hume, D. (1955). *An inquiry concerning human understanding.* New York: Bobbs-Merrill. (Original work published 1748)

Inhelder, B., & Piaget, J. (1958). *The growth of logical thinking from childhood to adolescence.* New York: Basic Books.

Inhelder, B., & Piaget, J. (1964). *The early growth of logic in the child.* London: Routledge & Kegan Paul.

Johnson, J., Fabian, V., & Pascual-Leone, J. (1989). Quantitative hardware stages that constrain language development. *Human Development, 32,* 245–271.

Johnson, J., & Pascual-Leone, J. (1994). Developmental levels of processing in metaphor interpretation. *Journal of Experimental Child Psychology, 48,* 1–31.

Kail, R. (1995). Processing speed, memory, and cognition. In F. E. Weinert & W. Schneider (Eds.), *Memory performance and competencies: Issues in growth and development* (pp. 71–88). Hillsdale, NJ: Erlbaum.

Kant, I. (1961). *Critique of pure reason.* New York: Doubleday Anchor. (Original work published 1796)

Kaufmann, W. (1980). *Discovering the mind: Goethe, Kant and Hegel.* New York: McGraw-Hill.

Keating, D. P., & Bobbitt, B. L. (1978). Individual and developmental differences in cognitive processing components of mental ability. *Child Development, 49,* 155–167.

Keil, F. C. (1986). On the structure-dependent nature of stages of cognitive development. In I. Levin (Ed.), *Stage and structure: Reopening the debate* (pp. 144–163). Norwood, NJ: ABLEX.

Keil, F. C. (1994). The birth and nurturance of concepts by domains: The origins of concepts of living things. In L. A. Hirschfeld & S. A. Gelman (Eds.), *Mapping the mind: Do main specificity in cognition and culture* (pp. 234–254). New York: Cambridge University Press.

Kellogg, R. (1969). *Analyzing children's art.* Palo Alto, CA: National Press.

Kendler, H. H., & Kendler, T. S. (1962). Vertical and horizontal processes in problem solving. *Psychological Review, 69,* 1–16.

Kendler, T. S., & Kendler, H. H. (1967). Experimental analysis of inferential behavior in children. In L. P. Lipsitt & C. C. Spiker (Eds.), *Advances in children's development and behavior.* New York: Academic Press.

Kendler, T. S., Kendler, H. H., & Wells, D. (1960). Reversal and nonreversal shifts in nursery school children. *Journal of Comparative and Physiological Psychology, 53,* 83–88.

Klahr, D., & Wallace, J. G. (1976). *Cognitive development: An information-processing view.* Hillsdale, NJ: Erlbaum.

Kruske, J. K. (1992). ALCOVE: An exemplar-based connectionist model of category learning. *Psychological Review, 99,* 22–44.

Kuhn, D. (1983). On the dual executive and its role in the development of developmental psychology. In D. Kuhn & J. Meachum (Eds.), *On the development of developmental psychology: Contributions to human development* (Vol. 8). Basel: Karger.

Kuhn, D. (in press). Microgenetic study of change. What has it told us? *Psychological Science.*

Kuhn, D., Garcia-Mila, M., Zohar, A., & Anderson, C. (1995). Strategies of knowledge acquisition. *Monographs of the Society for Research in Child Development, 60*(245).

Kuhn, D., & Phelps, E. (1982). The development of problem solving strategies. In H. Reese (Ed.), *Advances in child development and behavior* (Vol. 17). New York: Academic Press.

Kuhn, T. S. (1962). *The structure of scientific revolutions.* Chicago: University of Chicago Press.

Lave, J. (1988). *Cognition in practice.* New York: Cambridge University Press.

Lave, J., & Wenger, E. (1991). *Situated learning: Legitimate peripheral participation.* Cambridge, England; Cambridge University Press.

Lewis, M. D., & Ash, A. J. (1992). Evidence for a neo-Piagetian stage transition in early cognitive development. *International Journal of Behavioral Development, 15,* 337–358.

Lipsitt, L. P. (1967). Learning in the human infant. In H. W. Stevenson, E. Hess, & H. L. Rheingold (Eds.), *Early behavior: Comparative and developmental approaches* (pp. 147–196). New York: Wiley.

Luquet, G. H. (1927). *Le dessin enfantin* [Children's drawing]. Paris: Alcan.

Luria, A. R. (1966). *Higher cortical functions in man.* New York: Basic Books.

Luria, A. R. (1973). *The working brain.* London: Penguin Books.

Luria, A. R. (1976). *Cognitive development: Its cultural and social foundations.* Cambridge, MA: Cambridge University Press.

Marini, Z. A. (1992). Synchrony and asynchrony in the development of children's scientific reasoning. In R. Case (Ed.), *The Mind's Staircase: Exploring the conceptual underpinnings of children's thought and knowledge* (pp. 55–74). Hillsdale, NJ: Erlbaum.

McClelland, J. L. (1995). A connectionist perspective on knowledge and development. In T. J. Simon & G. S. Halford (Eds.), *Developing cognitive competence: New approaches to process modeling* (pp. 157–204). Hillsdale, NJ: Erlbaum.

McClelland, J. L., Rumelhart, D. E., & Hinton, G. E. (1987). *The appeal of parallel distributed processing: Explorations in the microstructure of cognition* (Vol. 1, pp. 3–44). Cambridge, MA: MIT Press.

McCloskey, M. (1983). Naive theories of motion. In D. Gentner & A. Stevens (Eds.), *Mental models* (pp. 229–324). Hillsdale, NJ: Erlbaum.

McDermott, R. (1994). *Money as technology of the mind.* Unpublished manuscript, School of Education, Stanford University, Stanford, CA.

McGraw, M. (1943). *The neuromuscular maturation of the human infant.* New York: Columbia University Press.

McKeough, A. (1992a). A neo-Piagetian analysis of narrative and its development. In R. Case (Ed.), *The Mind's Staircase: Exploring the conceptual underpinnings of children's thought and knowledge* (pp. 207–228). Hillsdale, NJ: Erlbaum.

McKeough, A. (1992b). Testing for the presence of a central conceptual structure: Use of the transfer paradigm. In R. Case (Ed.), *The Mind's Staircase: Exploring the conceptual underpinnings of children's thought and knowledge* (pp. 189–206). Hillsdale, NJ: Erlbaum.

Miller, G. A., Galanter, E., & Pribram, K. H. (1960). *Plans and the structure of behavior.* New York: Holt, Rinehart and Winston.

Morra, S., Moizo, C., & Scopesi, A. M. (1988). Working memory (or the M-operator) and the planning of children's drawing. *Journal of Experimental Child Psychology, 46,* 41–73.

Mounoud, P. (1986). Similarities between developmental sequences at different age periods. In I. Levin (Ed.), *Stage and structure: Reopening the debate.* Norwood, NJ: ABLEX.

Mumbauer, C. C., & Odom, R. D. (1967). Variables affecting the performance of preschool children in intradimensional, reversal and extradimensional shifts. *Journal of Experimental Psychology, 75,* 180–187.

Neches, R., & Hayes, J. R. (1978). Progress toward a taxonomy of strategy transformations. In A. Lesgold, J. Pellegrino, S. Fokkema, & R. Glaser (Eds.), *Cognitive psychology and instruction* (pp. 253–269). New York: Plenum Press.

Neisser, U. (1976). *Cognition and reality: Principles and implications of cognitive psychology.* San Francisco: Freeman.

Nelson, K. (1978). How children represent their knowledge of the world in and out of language: A preliminary report. In R. S. Siegler (Ed.), *Children's thinking: What develops?* (pp. 255–274). Hillsdale, NJ: Erlbaum.

Nelson, K., & Greundel, J. (1978). Generalized event representations: Basic building blocks of cognitive development. In M. E. Lamb & A. L. Brown (Eds.), *Advances in developmental psychology* (Vol. 1). Hillsdale, NJ: Erlbaum.

Neugebauer, O. (1969). *The exact sciences in antiquity* (2nd ed.). New York: Dover.

Newell, A., Shaw, J. C., & Simon, H. A. (1958). Elements of a theory of human problem solving. *Psychological Review, 65,* 151–166.

Oatley, K. (1977). Inference, navigation and cognitive maps. In P. N. Johnson-Laird & P. Waron (Eds.), *Thinking: Readings in cognitive science.* Cambridge, MA: Cambridge University Press.

Okamoto, Y., & Case, R. (1996). Exploring the microstructure of children's central conceptual structures in the domain of number. In R. Case & Y. Okamoto (Eds.), The role of central conceptual structures in the development of children's thought. *Monographs of the Society for Research in Child Development, 60*(5/6).

Olson, D. R. (1977). From utterance to text. *Harvard Educational Review, 47,* 257–281.

Olson, D. R. (1994). *The world on paper: The conceptual and cognitive implications of writing and reading.* New York: Cambridge University Press.

Osler, S. F., & Kofsky, E. (1966). Structure and strategy in concept attainment. *Journal of Experimental Child Psychology, 4,* 198–209.

Overton, W. F. (1984). World views and their influence on psychological theory and research: Kuhn-Lakatos-Laudon. In H. W. Reese (Ed.), *Advances in child development and behavior.* New York: Academic Press.

Overton, W. F. (1990). The structure of developmental theory. In P. van Geer & L. P. Mos (Eds.), *Annals of theoretical psychology.* New York: Plenum Press.

Overton, W. F. (1997). Developmental psychology, philosophy, concepts and methods. In R. M. Lerner (Ed.), *Handbook of child psychology: Vol. 1. Theoretical models of human development*. New York: Blackwell.

Pascual-Leone, J. (1969). *Cognitive development and cognitive style*. Unpublished doctoral dissertation, University of Geneva, Geneva.

Pascual-Leone, J. (1970). A mathematical model for the transition rule in Piaget's development stages. *Acta Psychologica, 32*, 301–345.

Pascual-Leone, J. (1974, July). *A neo-Piagetian process-structural model of Witkin's psychological differentiation*. Paper presented at the Symposium on Cross Cultural Studies of Psychological Differentiation in the meetings of the Internal Association for Cross Cultural Psychology, Kingston, Ontario, Canada.

Pascual-Leone, J. (1989). An organismic process model of Witkin's field-dependence-independence. In T. Globerson & T. Zelniker (Eds.), *Cognitive style and cognitive development*. Norwood, NJ: ABLEX.

Pascual-Leone, J., Hamstra, N., Benson, N., Khan, I., & Englund, R. (1990). *The P300 event-related potential and mental capacity*. Paper presented at the 4th International Evoked Potentials Symposium, Toronto, Canada.

Pascual-Leone, J., & Smith, J. (1969). The encoding and decoding of symbols by children: A new experimental paradigm and a neo-Piagetian theory. *Journal of Experimental Child Psychology, 8*, 328–355.

Piaget, J. (1952). *The child's conception of number*. London: Routledge & Kegan Paul. (Original work published in French 1941)

Piaget, J. (1960). *The psychology of intelligence*. Totowa, NJ: Littlefield, Adams.

Piaget, J. (1964). Development and learning. In R. E. Ripple & V. N. Rockcastle (Eds.), *Piaget rediscovered* (pp. 7–20). Ithaca, NY: Cornell University School of Education Press.

Piaget, J. (1970). Piaget's theory. In P. H. Mussen (Ed.), *Carmichael's handbook of child development* (pp. 703–732). New York: Wiley.

Piaget, J. (1985). *The equilibration of cognitive structures: The central problem of intellectual development*. Chicago: University of Chicago Press.

Piaget, J., & Garcia, R. (1991). *Toward a logic of meanings*. Hillsdale, NJ: Erlbaum.

Piaget, J., & Inhelder, R. (1956). *The child's conception of space*. London: Routledge & Kegan Paul. (Original work published in French 1948)

Resnick, L. B. (1989). Developing mathematical knowledge. *American Psychologist, 44*, 162–169.

Rogoff, B. (1990). *Apprenticeship in thinking: Cognitive development in social context*. New York: Oxford University Press.

Rohwer, W. D. (1970). Implications of cognitive development for education. In P. H. Mussen (Ed.), *Carmichael's handbook of child development* (pp. 1379–1454). New York: Wiley.

Ruland, R., & van Geert, P. (1996). *Jumping into syntax: Transitions in the development of closed class words*. Unpublished manuscript, University of Groningen, the Netherlands.

Rumelhart, D. E., & McLelland, J. C. (1987). Learning the past tenses of English verbs: Implicit rules or parallel distributed processing? In B. MacWhinney (Ed.), *Mechanisms of language acquisition*. Hillsdale, NJ: LEA.

Savage-Rumbagh, E. S., Murphy, J., Sevick, R. A., Brakke, K. E., Williams, S. L., & Rumbagh, D. (1993). Language comprehension in ape and child. *Monographs of the Society for Research in Child Development*, (Serial No. 233).

Saxe, G. B. (1981). Body parts as numerals. A developmental analysis of numeration among the Oksapmin of New Guinea. *Child Development, 52*, 306–316.

Saxe, G. B. (1988). The mathematics of street vendors. *Child Development, 59*, 1415–1425.

Saxe, G. B. (1995, June). *Culture, changes in social practices, and cognitive development*. Paper presented to the annual meeting of the Jean Piaget Society, Berkeley, CA.

Schmandt-Besserat, D. (1978, June). The earliest precursor of writing. *Scientific American, 238*, 40–49.

Schmandt-Besserat, D. (1986). Tokens: Facts and interpretations. *Visible Language, 20*, 259–272.

Scribner, S., & Cole, M. (1981). *The psychology of literacy*. Cambridge, MA: Harvard University Press.

Shayer, M., Demetriou, A., & Pervez, M. (1988). The structure and scaling of concrete operational thought: Three studies in four countries. *Genetic, Social, and General Psychology Monographs, 114*, 307–376.

Shultz, T. Z. (1991). Simulating stages of human cognitive development with connectionist models. In L. Biumbaum & G. Collins (Eds.), *Machine learning: Proceedings of the eighth international workshop* (pp. 105–109). San Mateo, CA: Kauffman.

Shultz, T. Z., & Schmidt, W. C. (1991). A cascade-correlation model of balance scale phenomena. In *Proceedings of the thirteenth annual conference of the cognitive science society* (pp. 635–640). Hillsdale, NJ: Erlbaum.

Siegler, R. S. (1978). The origins of scientific reasoning. In R. S. Siegler (Ed.), *Children's thinking: What develops?* Hillsdale, NJ: Erlbaum.

Siegler, R. S. (1992). In counting, young children's procedures precede principles. *Educational Psychology Review, 32*, 127–135.

Siegler, R. S. (1997). *Emerging minds*. New York: Oxford University Press.

Siegler, R. S., & Robinson, M. (1982). The development of numerical understanding. In H. W. Reese & L. P. Lipsitt (Eds.), *Advances in child development and behavior* (Vol. 16, pp. 241–312). New York: Academic Press.

Siegler, R. S., & Shrager, J. (1997, April). *A model of strategy discovery*. Paper presented at the biennial meeting of the Society for Research in Child Development, Washington, DC.

Smith, L. B., & Thelan, E. (1993). *A dynamic systems approach to development: Applications*. Cambridge, MA: MIT Press.

Snow, R. E., Kyllonen, P. C., & Marshalek, B. (1984). The topography of ability and learning correlations. In R. Sternberg (Ed.), *Advances in the psychology of intelligence* (pp. 47–103). Hillsdale, NJ: Erlbaum.

Spearman, C. (1922). *The abilities of man: Their nature and measurement*. New York: Macmillan.

Spelke, E. S. (1988). Where perceiving ends and thinking begins: The apprehension of objects in infancy. In A. Yonas (Ed.), *Perceptual development in infancy: Minnesota Symposia in Child Psychology* (pp. 197–234). Hillsdale, NJ: Erlbaum.

Starkey, P. (1992). The early development of numerical reasoning. *Cognition, 43*, 93–126.

Stevenson, H. W. (1970). Learning in children. In P. H. Mussen (Ed.), *Carmichael's handbook of child development* (pp. 849–938). New York: Wiley.

Stevenson, H. W. (1972). *Children's learning*. New York: Appleton-Century-Crofts.

Street, B. (1984). *Literacy in theory and practice*. New York: Cambridge University Press.

Stuss, D. T., & Benson, D. F. (1986). *The frontal lobes*. New York: Oxford University Press.

Thatcher, R. W. (1992). Cyclical cortical reorganization during early childhood. *Brain and Cognition, 20*, 24–50.

Thatcher, R. W. (1993). Maturation of the human frontal lobes: Physiological evidence for staging. *Developmental Neuropsychology*.

Thelan, E., Fogel, A., & Kelso, J. A. S. (1987). Self organizing systems and infant motor development. *Developmental Review, 7*, 39–65.

Thelan, E., & Smith, L. B. (1994). *A dynamic systems approach to the development of cognition and action*. Cambridge, MA: MIT Press.

Todor, J. I. (1979). Developmental differences in motor task integration: A test of Pascual-Leone's theory of constructive operations. *Journal of Experimental Child Psychology, 28*, 314–322.

Tuddenham, R. D. (1969). A 'Piagetian' test of cognitive development. In W. B. Dockerell (Ed.), *On intelligence*. Toronto: The Ontario Institute for Studies in Education.

Turiel, E. (1983). *The development of social knowledge: Morality and convention*. Cambridge, MA: Cambridge University Press.

van der Maas, H. L. J. (1996). Beyond the metaphor? *Cognitive Development, 10*, 621–642.

van der Maas, H. L. J., & Molenaar, P. C. M. (1992). Stagewise cognitive development: An application of catastrophe theory. *Psychological Review, 99*, 395–417.

van der Maas, H. L. J., & Molenaar, P. C. M. (1996). Catastrophe analysis of discontinuous development. In *Categorical variables in developmental research: Methods of analysis* (pp. 77–105). New York: Academic Press.

Van Geert, P. (1991). A dynamic systems model of cognitive and language growth. *Psychological Review, 98*, 3–53.

Van Geert, P. (1994). *Dynamic systems of development: Change between complexity and chaos*. Hemel Hempstead, Herefordshire: Harvester Wheatsheaf.

Vygotsky, L. S. (1962). *Thought and language* (E. Hanfmann & G. Vaker, Trans.). Cambridge, MA: MIT Press. (Original work published 1934)

Wellman, H. (1990). *The child's theory of mind*. Cambridge, MA: MIT Press.

Werner, H. (1948). *Comparative psychology of mental development*. New York: International Universities Press.

White, S. H. (1967). Some general outlines of the matrix of developmental changes between five and seven years. *Bulletin of the Orton Society, 20*, 41–57.

White, S. H. (1970). The learning theory tradition and child psychology. In P. H. Mussen (Ed.), *Carmichael's handbook of child development* (pp. 657–702). New York: Wiley.

Wiser, M. (1988). The differentiation of heat and temperature: History of science and novice-expert shift. In S. Strauss (Ed.), *Ontogeny, phylogeny, and historical development* (pp. 28–48). New York: ABLEX.

Wiser, M., & Carey, S. (1982). When heat and temperature were one. In D. Gentner & A. Stevens (Eds.), *Mental models* (pp. 267–297). Hillsdale, NJ: Erlbaum.

Witelson, S. (1983). Bumps on the brain: Right-left anatomic asymmetry as a key to functional laterization. In S. J. Segalowitz (Ed.), *Language functions and brain organization*. London: Academic Press.

Wynn, K. (1992). Addition and subtraction by human infants. *Nature, 358*, 709–750.

Yakovlev, P. I., & Lecours, A. R. (1967). The myelogenetic cycles of regional maturation of the brain. In *Regional development of the brain in early life* (pp. 1–70). Oxford, England: Blackwell.

Zeeman, E. C. (1976). Catastrophe theory. *Scientific American, 234*(4), 65–83.

CHAPTER 16

Reasoning and Problem Solving

JUDY S. DELOACHE, KEVIN F. MILLER, and SOPHIA L. PIERROUTSAKOS

1. Abe (4 years): "If it doesn't break when I drop it, it's a rock. . . . It didn't break. It must be a rock." (Scholnick & Wing, 1995, p. 342)

2. Laura (3 years), removing opened can of soda from refrigerator, to mother: "Whose is this? It's not yours 'cause it doesn't have lipstick."

3. Colette (3 years): "Mommy, I have special powers. If I concentrate really hard, I can know everybody's private parts."

4. Ross (5½ years): Looking at the tombstones while driving past a cemetery, "Mom, are the ones with the biggest rocks kings?"

5. Jessie (4 years): After relating to her mom that she had been in trouble for talking at preschool, she explained that she "had to tell the new girl how to sit on the line—she wasn't sitting the right way."

6. Tristan (3 years): "Why doesn't my blood come out when I open my mouth?"

7. Michael (4 years): Explaining to his mother why the moon changes shape. "Because there's a piece of blue, a piece of sky over it."

8. Nathan (5 years): In response to a friend's claim that the tooth fairy is really one's mother, Nathan scornfully retorted: "Benjamin, that's stupid. The tooth fairy comes into your room in the middle of the night. How could your mom come into your room in the middle of the night!"

9. Matt (11 years) wanted to go to a hobby store on Memorial Day. Mother, doubting it was open, told him to call. Matt went off to the phone, returned, and said, "Let's go." They arrived to find the store closed. The frustrated mother inquired: "I thought you called." Matt: "I did, but they didn't answer, so I figured they were too busy to come to the phone."

10. Adolescent John was informed that he would have to rake the leaves. John: "How long do I have to rake?" Father, seeing that it was 10:30 in the morning, replied, "Until lunchtime." John agreed and went to get a rake. Ten minutes later his father discovered him in the kitchen, eating a peanut butter sandwich. Father: "What are you doing?" John: "Having lunch." (Dumas, 1995)

Preparation of this chapter was supported in part by NICHD grant HD-25271 to the first author and NIMH grants MH-50222 and MH-01190 to the second author.

11. Antoine (3 years): Watching his mother futilely trying to retrieve a helium-filled balloon that had lodged underneath a high-ceilinged stairwell, "Mommy, just make it go over to the side and then you can walk upstairs and get it."

The preceding examples of everyday thinking fall into many of the standard categories studied by psychologists. Abe's inference (1) that some nonbreakable entity must be a rock constitutes a case of that staple of deductive reasoning, *modus ponens—if p, then q; p; therefore, q.* Three-year-old Laura's deduction (2) that the can of soda, sans lipstick, could not belong to her mother is an example of *modus tollens—if p, then q; not q; therefore, not p.* ("If an open can of soda belongs to my mother, then it will have lipstick. This can has no lipstick; therefore, this is not my mom's soda.") Three-year-old Colette (3) is engaged in *induction*—proceeding from the anatomical characteristics of a few cases she knows to offer a broad generalization. Ross (4) reasoned by *analogy* when he equated size of tombstone with degree of earthly power. Jessie (5) has induced a *rule* governing appropriate preschool behavior.

The reasoning embodied in these examples is all the more impressive when one recognizes that some of the quotations actually involve a relatively long chain of reasoning with several steps or premises. Three-year-old Tristan's query (6), for example, is based on his understanding that liquid can escape containers with holes in them, his knowledge that his body contains blood that sometimes escapes through holes (cuts) in its "container" (skin), and his conception of the mouth as a hole. This knowledge is combined to prompt his naive question.

Some of our examples involve the kind of charming errors that constitute the basis for many favorite family stories. However, such cases are typically not errors of logic; Ross's (4) and Tristan's (6) amusing questions follow quite sensibly from the state of their knowledge, that is, from their premises. Michael's conclusion (7) about the phases of the moon is based on what he has observed. Indeed, some investigators argue that children rarely if ever actually violate the basic rules of inference (e.g., Braine & O'Brien, 1991). They may reach conclusions that are untrue, but not that are illogical (given their premises). Their errors stem from several other sources. A frequent one is reasoning from a *false* premise, for example, Nathan's assumption (8) that his mother must be asleep the same time he is. An *incomplete* set of true premises can be equally

problematic, as illustrated by Matt's inference (9) from the unanswered hobby shop telephone. The leaf-raking example (10) is a form of what Kunda (1990) refers to as *motivated reasoning,* a common "error" familiar to every parent. Antoine's strategy (11) for retrieving the balloon is a classic example of problem solving using means-end analysis. His suggestion does not lead directly to his mother being able to reach the balloon, but is instead a strategy for moving the balloon to a new location where she can reach it.

REASONING AS BRICOLAGE

The quotes with which we opened this chapter testify to the rich, heterogeneous nature of children's reasoning, as well as its dependence on context and knowledge. In traditional views of the development of reasoning, such as that of Piaget, children's thinking is typically compared with normative models of Aristotelian logic or hypothetico-deductive reasoning, which adults are assumed to exemplify. Children are seen as illogical and seriously deficient at problem solving, whereas adults are viewed as highly skilled, logical reasoners. Both sides of this inequality have fallen under attack. Research has revealed that adults are substantially less logical and rational than was previously believed: Logical fallacies are the rule rather than the exception, and adult reasoners are prey to many biases and heuristic shortcuts that lead them to err in systematic ways (Kahneman & Tversky, 1982; Klayman & Ha, 1987). At the same time, recent research has shown children to be more rational and capable reasoners than previously believed.

Furthermore, a good case can be made that they are more active thinkers than adults. Young children have less experience and world knowledge so they more often encounter novel situations. Their cognition is less automatized; hence, more problem solving is required for the negotiation of everyday life (e.g., Siegler, 1991). Gaps in their knowledge often force them to attempt to resolve inconsistencies. In E. Langer's terms (1992), children can be said to be generally "mindful," whereas adults often behave in a "mindless" fashion, avoiding thinking or reasoning whenever possible (Campbell & Olson, 1990).

In post-Piagetian views of children's thought, domain knowledge has been accorded a central role. A familiar pattern has emerged: Repeatedly, what had been taken as evidence of structural deficits has turned out to stem instead from knowledge deficits. When care is taken to ensure that children have the background knowledge relevant to a particular task or problem, they often display competent performance. In the most extreme cases, some abilities that Piaget believed did not develop until adolescence have been demonstrated (in simple forms) by preschool children, toddlers, and sometimes even infants.

Many examples of this pattern appear in this chapter because the crucial role of domain knowledge in reasoning and problem solving is a recurrent theme. However, our review also underscores that although knowledge is necessary, it is not always sufficient for particular abilities to be manifest. Other factors are also important.

We think that either extreme view—the child as insufficiently logical or as knowledge-challenged—fails to capture important aspects of the development of reasoning. We seek an alternative to monolithic views of children as having some particular abilities and lacking others. Instead, we wish to emphasize the heterogeneous nature and context dependence of children's reasoning. To this end, we have adopted a metaphor from Levi-Strauss (1962/1967), who described "primitive" thought with the term *bricolage,* a French word whose closest English translation is "tinkerer." Levi-Strauss (1962/1967) argued that neither science nor engineering provides a satisfactory model for thinking:

> The *bricoleur* is adept at performing a large number of diverse tasks; but, unlike the engineer, he does not subordinate each of them to the availability of raw materials and tools conceived and procured for the purpose of the project . . . the rules of his game are always to make do with "whatever is at hand." (p. 17)

Children reason about wide-ranging situations and problems for which they have no special-purpose tools. From an early age, their reasoning shows opportunism and heterogeneity; they bring to bear varied processes and strategies, gradually coming through experience to select those that are most effective. As the bricolage metaphor implies, children's ability to solve problems depends on many factors in addition to the mastery of abstract reasoning principles including domain knowledge, motivation, their own problem-solving goals, the social context, and so forth. Young bricoleurs, like the adults described by Levi-Strauss, make do with whatever cognitive tools are at hand.

The focus in this chapter is compatible with our metaphor of reasoning and problem solving that is not constrained to a single correct model such as propositional logic. Before reviewing relevant research, however, we should briefly define what the term reasoning means in general and then distinguish between forms of reasoning that are more and less relevant to our purposes.

DEFINING THE DOMAIN

Although *reasoning* is an everyday term that everyone feels confident he or she understands, there is no consensus regarding its precise meaning. In the psychological literature, as Galotti (1989) has noted, "Boundaries for the usage of the term *reasoning* are unclear, leaving it very difficult for a reader to know if two investigators, each purporting to study a kind of reasoning, are really studying a common entity" (p. 331). Many developmentalists, including Moshman (1995) and Overton (1990), have made explicit distinctions between reasoning and other varieties of cognition. Wason and Johnson-Laird's (1972) generous view provides a useful definition:

> It is obvious . . . that when an individual draws a conclusion from premises according to traditional Aristotelian laws of logic, he is engaged in reasoning. It is also feasible to assert that an individual solving a crossword puzzle, planning to buy a new house, or determining the best route from one town to another, is also engaged in reasoning. (p. 1)

A defining feature of reasoning and problem solving is that it is *goal-directed cognitive activity* (thus ruling out reminiscing, daydreaming, etc.). The goal can be *general,* involving efforts simply to understand something, to resolve uncertainty, to draw conclusions. Young children's incomplete knowledge often leaves them struggling to make sense of their experiences, actively seeking information to fill in their cognitive blanks and to resolve contradictions. Reasoning goals can also be highly *specific* and explicit, such as those involved in problem solving.

Reasoning and problem solving typically involve *inference,* that is, going beyond the information given to reach a new conclusion, form a generalization, find a solution. New knowledge is usually the result: "Once we know at least one fact about something we may be able to reason from that fact, and add other facts to our knowledge" (Garnham & Oakhill, 1994, p. 58). In the example at the beginning of this chapter, Collette's generalization gave her new knowledge about human anatomy.

FORMAL VERSUS INFORMAL, EVERYDAY REASONING

Many psychologists have contrasted formal, decontextualized reasoning with reasoning immersed in the everyday context. A similar distinction appears in other genres, including detective novels. A "rationalist" or deductive approach is embodied by Hercule Poirot, Agatha Christie's fussy Belgian detective, and Nero Wolfe, the corpulent and indolent creation of Rex Stout. These detectives prefer to solve crimes from the comfort (and safety) of their armchairs, with the use of the "leetle grey cells" in Poirot's case. They rely on logic more than observation, with the conclusion of their cerebration announced at a climactic scene with all the characters gathered to hear the brilliant detective detail the process of deduction through which he solved the crime. Other popular mystery writers take what might be called an "empiricist" or inductive approach. V. I. Warshawski, Sara Paretsky's heroine, and all the protagonists in Dick Francis novels solve crimes by ferreting out the facts themselves. They visit the scene of the crime, actively interview witnesses, and gradually fit the pieces together to solve the mystery. (They typically make several miscalculations and get beaten up at least once in the inductive process.)

Similar, albeit less colorful, distinctions have been made in the psychological literature on reasoning: closed system versus adventuresome (Bartlett, 1958); laboratory versus everyday (Perkins, 1986); theoretical versus practical (Scribner, 1986); pure versus practical (Wason & Johnson-Laird, 1972). We generally follow Galotti's (1989) distinction between formal and informal or everyday reasoning, recognizing that there is substantial variation within and overlap between them.

Formal Reasoning

In *formal* reasoning, the *form* of an argument, not its semantic content, is crucial. *Logical,* not empirical, truth matters: The internal logical consistency of a set of premises and the conclusion drawn from them is all that counts, not whether or how they map onto the real world. World knowledge is irrelevant; indeed, it should be quarantined to avoid infecting the pure reasoning process. In research on formal reasoning, all the information about which individuals are to reason is contained in a set of premises provided to them; they are simply asked to draw a conclusion, and the correct answer is clear and certain.

People are notoriously bad at pure reasoning. Even when one makes active conscious efforts to adopt a purely formal, analytic stance, knowledge tends to seep into the process, for better and for worse. When general knowledge is compatible with the premises of a formal argument, people are more successful than when they have no relevant knowledge or knowledge that conflicts with the premises (e.g., Kahneman & Tversky, 1982; Wason & Johnson-Laird, 1972). Part of the difficulty that children have in formal reasoning situations stems from their lack of understanding of the "rules of the game." They do not realize that they should eschew content, attend only to the precise wording of problems, and ignore violations of conversational principles. The development of formal reasoning is, to a large extent, the development of metareasoning.

Furthermore, in everyday life, it is sometimes appropriate to violate logical principles when pure logic and pragmatics conflict. Consider, for example, a young child who is told, "If it rains this afternoon, you must stay indoors." If the child then sees rain, she is likely, however reluctantly, to reach the correct conclusion that she must remain in the house. This would be good deductive reasoning, an example of modus ponens: *If p then q; p; therefore, q* (if it's raining, stay in; it's raining; therefore, stay in). If the skies clear and the sun comes out, however, any child we know will immediately infer that she can go outside to play. Such a perfectly reasonable inference does not necessarily follow in formal logic, in which *not p* (no rain) does *not* imply *not q* (don't stay in). The relation is indeterminate; *not q* is a permissible inference from *not p,* but not a certain one. Drawing the inference *not q* is known as the classic error of *denying the consequent.* In such a case, pragmatics, past experience with parental strictures, and motivation conspire to lead the child to a firm and probably appropriate conclusion not dictated by logic.

Informal Reasoning

In contrast to decontextualized formal reasoning, *informal reasoning* (everyday, practical) is *contentful: Informal reasoning is about something. Empirical truth* is of primary concern; the individual is reasoning about the world, typically attempting to achieve a functional, veridical representation of reality. Premises are derived from experience and world knowledge, and a successful outcome depends on correct and truthful premises. Often, the individual does not start with all the necessary information; like the bricoleur, he or she must search for and decide what information is relevant and useful. Informal reasoning is characterized by uncertainty; although the individual's goal may be clear, how to reach it may not be. There may be no obvious answer, or there may be several acceptable answers. The ultimate conclusion may be uncertain; it may simply be judged "more likely" than other possibilities.

FOCUS AND PLAN OF THE CHAPTER

The topic of reasoning and problem solving is so broad and encompasses such a vast literature that it would be impossible to cover all the research that fits under this commodious umbrella in any one chapter. Hence, we have limited our scope and focus in several ways, governed both by conceptual and practical considerations. The major narrowing of focus is to *informal or everyday reasoning,* the kind encompassed by our bricolage metaphor. Formal reasoning is addressed in Chapter 19, by Moshman, in this Volume. Because informal reasoning is still a huge topic, we will restrict our coverage to research published since the preceding edition of the *Handbook* and emphasize areas of intense activity in the past few years.

The rest of the chapter is organized into three major sections. In the first, we focus on different kinds of relations that serve as the basis for reasoning. This section covers five disparate literatures—perceptual similarity, concepts and theories, analogical reasoning, symbol-based reasoning, and rule induction and use. These topics are not usually reviewed together under the rubric of reasoning, but they illustrate the heterogeneity of children's reasoning processes. In the second section, we summarize research specifically investigating problem solving, and the selection is more traditional. Although we see no principled difference between reasoning and problem solving, the two literatures are for the most part quite distinct; their separation here is primarily for convenience. The third major section focuses on scientific reasoning. This topic blends the issues emphasized in both the reasoning and problem-solving sections, particularly the complex relation between normative models of reasoning and the more heterogenous thought processes that children use.

REPRESENTATIONAL BASES FOR REASONING

Reasoning is based on mental representations of relations between entities. Using one's representation of the relation between x and y, an inference can be drawn from what one knows about x to y; something known about x and the relation between x and y leads one to conclude something about y. The person now knows something new about y. The following kinds of represented relations can be used as a basis for reasoning and drawing inferences.

Perceptual Similarity. Because x and y are perceptually similar in some respect(s), we assume they are probably alike in other ways as well.

Conceptual. If we believe that x and y are the same kind of thing, that is, belong to the same category, we can reason that x and y will share various characteristics. Hence, if we know that x has a particular feature, we can infer that y will probably possess that same feature.

Analogical. If we know that a and b are related in some way, and if we further know that x has the same relation to a that y has to b, we may assume that x and y are related in the same way that a and b are.

Symbolic If we know that x is a symbol for y, then we may be able to conclude that a feature or relation we identify in x will also be present in y.

Rule. If we learn a rule that specifies that some relation holds between any two variables of particular sorts, and if we know that x and y are relevant entities, then we know what relation will exist between x and y.

In the following sections, we review recent research on children's reasoning based on each of these five kinds of relations. There are core differences between the relations, but there is also a great deal of overlap: Perceptual and conceptual similarity are often tightly linked, and the relation between a given pair of entities can sometimes be characterized as analogical, symbolic, or rule-based. Nevertheless, even though their boundaries can be quite fuzzy, the important core differences between these relational bases make it useful to examine them separately.

Similarity Relations

One general kind of relation that supports reasoning is similarity, limited in this discussion here to perceptual similarity: If one judges that two (or more) entities are similar in some respect, then one is likely to infer that they may be similar in other respects as well. A world without similarity is unimaginable; if nothing resembled anything else, or if people were insensitive to similarity, then generalization, induction, and categorization would all be impossible. "Similarity is one of the most central theoretical constructs in psychology" (Medin, Goldstone, & Gentner, 1993, p. 254).

The power of similarity comes from its usefulness and informativeness: "One function of similarity is to allow people to make educated guesses in the face of limited knowledge" (Medin et al., 1993, p. 258). Because perceptual features do not vary independently, perceptual appearance gives a good clue as to the identity of most entities in the world (Medin & Ortony, 1989). Members of one natural or basic level category usually look (sound, taste, smell, or feel) more like one another than like members of any different category (Rosch & Mervis, 1975). Most dogs look and sound more like other dogs than they look and sound like cows, cats, or clarinets. A similarity heuristic thus gets one into the conceptual ballpark and usually to first base as well.

Similarity is not simple; making a similarity judgment is not just a matter of calculating the number of features two or more entities share. There is, in fact, no unique answer to the question of how similar any two entities are (Murphy & Medin, 1985); instead, there are various answers, depending on what the domain is and which particular attributes or features are used for the comparison. As Smith and Heise (1992) have emphasized, similarity is not "given in the stimulus"; rather, the perception of similarity is a dynamic process.

Similarity is thus variable and flexible and depends on selective attention. A factor that governs attention to one set of features versus another is the perceiver's *goal:* Whether a child momentarily thinks of a ballpoint pen as more similar to a crayon or to an airplane depends on whether the child wants to draw a picture or pretend to be flying a plane. Attention is also governed by *context,* even for infants. Infants who see a series of stimuli that vary on everything but color of objects, gender of faces, or number of elements eventually habituate and then recover to a change in color, gender, or numerosity, but not to a change in another dimension (Bornstein, 1985; Fagen, 1979; and Strauss & Curtis, 1981, respectively). Thus, exposing infants to multiple stimuli that remain the same in one respect while varying in others directs their attention selectively to the constant element.

This flexibility in the perception of similarity must also be true of similarity-based reasoning. The inferences that reasoners draw from the relation between two entities will necessarily be determined by the features they have identified as relevant. In this section, we make two main points:

(a) Perceptual similarity is highly serviceable as a basis for reasoning; and (b) children's similarity judgments and the inferences drawn depend on context.

Inductive Inferences Based on Perceptual Similarity

Even infants are sensitive to perceptual information and use it to make judgments. To cite just one example, 4½-month-old infants who saw a screen rotate toward and occlude a solid object could calibrate where the screen should stop when a second object, identical or highly similar to the first, was visible to the side of the screen (Baillargeon, 1993). If the reference object was less similar, the infants did not use it to figure out how far the screen should rotate. Thus, the similarity between the two objects led the infants to use one to reason about the other.

To examine young children's similarity-based inductive inferences, we resorted to gleaning information from the control conditions of several studies in which the investigators were more interested in children's ability to ignore perceptual information in favor of something else. Davidson and S. Gelman (1990) presented 4- to 5-year-old children with pictures of novel animals, plants, and artifacts. (Note: We use "novel" or "imaginary" to refer to made-up stimuli and "unfamiliar" for real entities or words that a young child is unlikely to know.) On each trial, the child saw a target picture (e.g., a gnu-like animal with an elephant-like trunk) and was told some property possessed by the target, such as, "This has four stomachs." The child was then shown four test pictures, one at a time, and asked whether each pictured object shared the property of the target: "Do you think this has four stomachs like this [target]?"

Perceptual similarity strongly influenced the children's inferences: They drew significantly more inferences to the test items that were perceptually similar to the target than to those that were dissimilar. In other words, they thought that a test picture that differed from the gnu-cum-trunk target only in color and tail was more likely to have four stomachs than was a giraffe-shaped creature with a trunk, fuzzy-looking coat, and large and peculiar ears (or possibly antlers). Similar results have been reported for 3- to 6-year-old children for both novel and familiar stimuli (Florian, 1994; Lopez, S. Gelman, Gutheil, & Smith, 1992). Thus, young children expect entities that look alike to share other nonobvious characteristics as well.

Children as young as 2½ years have this expectation. S. Gelman and Coley (1990) found that children of this age readily inferred that the test item most similar in appearance to a target shared one of its properties, and they reliably declined to attribute the property to the test item most dissimilar to the target. Thus, for a target bird that "lives in a nest," the children inferred that another bird virtually identical to the target would also live in a nest, were unsure or inconsistent about the domicile of a dodo or a pterodactyl, and inferred that a stegosaurus did not live in a nest. Like older children, these 2½-year-old children used perceptual similarity as the basis for drawing inductive inferences.

Context Effects in Similarity Judgments

Given that young children use similarity relations as a basis for drawing inductive inferences from one entity to another, we can ask whether their judgments, like those of adults, are context dependent. Relevant evidence has come from a number of studies examining the basis on which young children extend word meaning. (This research is reviewed by Woodward & Markman, Ch. 8, this Volume, with respect to word learning.)

Words provide a context that differentially directs young children's attention (Waxman & Braig, 1996). In the first of an elegant series of studies, Landau, Smith, and Jones (1988) investigated the effect of naming something on young children's selective attention. They presented 24- and 36-month-old children with novel objects that varied in shape, size, and surface texture (see Figure 16.1). In the No Label condition, the children were simply asked to choose which test item was like the target. No dimension was given precedence. In the Label condition, the experimenter introduced the target object with a novel count noun, saying, for example, "This is a dax." For each of the test objects, the experimenter asked if it was "also a dax." Highly systematic responses occurred: The children generalized the name to objects of the same shape, even if they were different in size or texture. Thus, labeling induced a *shape bias.* Hearing a name applied to a novel object led the children to think that the objects most similar to it were those of the same shape.

The shape bias presumably indicates that young children assume that objects with the same name typically belong to the same category (Waxman & Hall, 1993). Hearing an object named suggests to the children that the task is to find another of the same kind of thing. In general, overall shape is highly diagnostic of category membership, especially for natural categories, so such a bias would usually be helpful for inferring which of the large number of possible alternatives a heard word denotes.

The dynamic nature of young children's similarity-based reasoning is illustrated by other context effects.

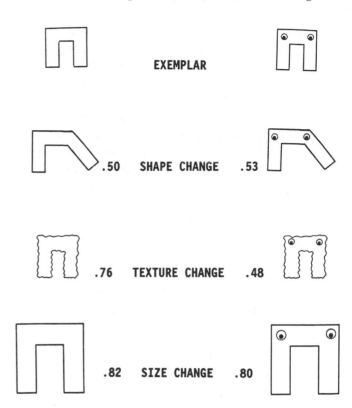

Figure 16.1 On the left are examples of the objects used by Landau, Smith, and Jones (1988) to study the effect of naming on children's inferences for word meaning. The proportions come from the Label condition and show that children extended the label to objects of similar shape. Adding eyes to the stimuli, as Jones, Smith, and Landau (1991) did, led children to generalize on the basis of texture.

Becker and Ward (1991b) presented 3½- to 4½-year-old children with pictures of a flat, snake-like creature that was referred to as a "diffle." The children judged other flat, snake-like creatures to be diffles and, to a lesser extent, they also accepted curled-up versions of the same creatures. They rejected snail-like creatures, even though their outline shape was identical to that of the curled ones. Thus, these children tended to ignore overall shape when it appeared to reflect a temporary postural change. Similarly, when an animal target was described as "wide awake" and children were told that it "lives in a nest," they did not infer that a "wide awake" test item would also live in a nest (Gelman & Coley, 1990). Thus, a temporary state attribution did not serve as the basis for an inference.

Jones, Smith, and Landau (1991) induced a *texture* bias when they added eyes to nonsense objects like those used by Landau et al. (1988). In one condition, 36-month-olds were presented with stimuli that had eyes attached to them; in the other condition, the same objects were eyeless (see

Figure 16.1). When the target object was not named and the children were simply asked if the test objects were like it, they responded indiscriminately in both conditions. When a label was provided in the No Eyes condition, a shape bias emerged, just as reported by Landau et al. (1988). The most interesting result came when labels were applied in the Eyes condition. The children were even more selective in their judgments; they generalized only when *both* shape and texture were the same. In other words, they thought that a test object was similar to a target with eyes only when the two objects shared both shape and texture. The presence of eyes—a "conceptually-laden perceptual property" (Jones & Smith, 1993)—presumably activated particular category knowledge (either of real or toy animals, or both), thus suggesting to the children that surface texture was relevant.

Hall, Waxman, and Hurwitz (1993) elicited a texture bias with an even simpler intervention. When an emphatic adjective phrase was applied to a familiar object ("This is a very zavish one"), 4-year-olds tended to generalize to another object of the same material kind. Thus, in a match-to-target task, when a metal cup was labeled as being "very zavish," children preferred a metal spoon to a plastic cup.

Attention to texture rather than shape can also result from the nature of the stimuli themselves. When the referent of a novel word is a non-solid substance (e.g., piles or blobs of instant coffee, sawdust, Play-Doh®), 2- and 2½-year-olds (Soja, Carey, & Spelke, 1991) and 3- to 5-year-olds (Dickinson, 1988) ignore the overall shape of the stimuli. Instead, they generalize the label to stimuli of the same substance (i.e., texture and probably color).

This substance/texture bias turns out, as was true for shape, to be further sensitive to context, specifically, to category knowledge. Becker and Ward (1991a) presented 4- to 6-year-old children with a three-dimensional substance. In one condition, it was labeled as "a pile of daf" and the children were told that daf is a kind of food. In the second condition, the same stimulus was called "a daf," and the children were told that a daf is an animal that lives in the zoo. The children who thought the target was a kind of food selected test items that matched it in texture (spongy or granular), ignoring overall shape. Children who thought the target was some kind of zoo animal relied on shape.

It is interesting—and instructive—to note that Becker and Ward (1991a) did not find a texture bias when they showed children *pictures* of piles of material similar to those used in their study. Thus, representational medium is another contextual factor that can affect children's attention to

one feature or another. It does not, however, always do so. Baldwin (1989), reported the same results for real objects and pictures of them. Presumably, three-dimensional materials are more important for judgments based on texture, where the relevant information may be less salient in a picture; indeed, all three studies described here that reported a texture bias used three-dimensional objects or substances.

Context can also direct young children's attention to *color,* even though they generally tend not to use color as a basis for extending a novel label, either to familiar (e.g., Baldwin, 1989) or novel objects (e.g., Landau et al., 1988). Macario (1991) elicited attention to color by invoking a familiar category for which color is relevant—food. On each trial, 3- and 4-year-old children were presented with colored shapes made of paraffin—a target and two test objects that matched the target either in shape or color. Children who were asked to select which of the probes would *taste the same* as the target object chose on the basis of color. Thus, these children apparently inferred that two items of food that were similar in color were more likely to taste similarly than two items of different colors. However, children who were asked which of the test objects was the *same kind of thing* to play with made their selection on the basis of shape. Thus, as Becker and Ward (1991a) reported, different features of the same objects were used to draw inferences, depending on what category was involved.

Smith, Jones, and Landau (1992) also succeeded in directing children's attention to color in a study in which the target was a salient glittery gold color, and the test items matched on either shape or color. Although the 36-month-old children initially showed inconsistent responses to color, a simple manipulation induced a strong color bias. The children looked through the opening of a "cave" to view the objects illuminated by a spotlight, a procedure that rendered their glittery color extremely salient. The children now generally accepted a test object as a "dax one" only if it was of the same color as the exemplar.

Similarity and Development

The flexibility that children show in selecting which aspect of similarity to attend to has consequences for earlier claims of a global *perception-to-conception shift* with development (e.g., Piaget, 1929; Vygotsky, 1978a). This view assumes that young children are more susceptible to and more influenced by perceptual factors than older children are; that is, different processes govern their behavior.

An alternative view attributes differences in children's reliance on perceptual variables to differences in the extent of their knowledge of which attributes are relevant in a domain or task (S. Gelman & Medin, 1993; Jones & Smith, 1993). By this account, child bricoleurs (and adults as well) will use any relevant information they have to reason and solve problems. Infants and young children have perceptual information from the beginning, but relatively little knowledge. With development, they have increasing amounts of conceptual information to draw on; as a result, their conceptual knowledge increasingly often overrides their perceptual knowledge on those occasions (probably relatively rare outside the psychology laboratory) in which the two conflict. Several theorists, including Gentner and Rattermann (1991) and Keil (1989), have emphasized the impact of increasing knowledge on similarity judgments.

As illustrated in this section, perception and conception do not play distinct roles in the reasoning of young children, and we see no reason to think they become divorced with development. People never escape or become insensitive to perceptual similarity, and it interacts with knowledge throughout life (Medin & Ross, 1989). An excellent demonstration of the conception/perception interaction was described by Mervis, Johnson, and Scott (1993), who studied the similarity judgments of individuals of differing levels of expertise in two content domains—shorebirds and dinosaurs. Novices generally based their judgments on global perceptual features such as shape, size, and color. Experts relied on more subtle perceptual features such as tooth structure. The authors argue that with increased knowledge, more weight is placed on those features that are diagnostic of category membership. They note, "Expert knowledge remains rooted in perception throughout the continuum of knowledge acquisition" (p. 154).

Conceptual Relations

Conceptual structures—including what have been varyingly described as categories, concepts, theories, and scripts—support inferences among entities. Knowing that some entities are conceptually related leads one to infer that they will have many features in common. The crucial role of knowledge in cognition has for some time been a dominant theme and an active realm of inquiry in many areas, including cognitive development. Investigators have become increasingly aware that myriad changes accompany the shift from novice to expert in a given domain.

An inevitable concomitant of the knowledge revolution has been increasing disenchantment with Piagetian theory. The current emphasis on knowledge is at best orthogonal, and in many ways antithetical, to the Piagetian approach, a major feature of which has been the attempt to exclude

knowledge as a contaminant in research on "pure" logical reasoning, the topic deemed to be of real interest. A shift has occurred from domain-general accounts of development, as exemplified by Piaget's theory, to domain-specific ones. A cardinal assumption of most current investigators is that we should not expect to see monolithic developmental changes in cognition; rather, children will exhibit different levels of cognitive skills and abilities as a function of their level of knowledge in different domains.

With the recognition of the importance of knowledge development, research on concepts and categories has changed. Rather than investigating the process by which highly artificial categories are learned, a substantial portion of current research focuses on the natural concepts that children acquire from their everyday experience, how those concepts become theories, and how children's existing knowledge supports reasoning.

Category-Based Inductions

The area of research most relevant here is work on inductive inferences based on children's conceptual knowledge and their theories of particular domains. As mentioned before, much of this work overlaps with research reviewed in the preceding section, since some of the most dramatic effects of knowledge on young children's judgments have come from experiments that pitted category knowledge against perceptual information. As much of this research is reviewed in detail in other chapters of this Volume (see Wellman & S. Gelman, Ch. 11, and Woodward & Markman, Ch. 8), we only briefly describe some of the basic phenomena relevant to conceptual relations as an important basis for reasoning.

In a study of category-based inference, 10½-month-old infants, saw a series of demonstration events in which salt was poured into a cylindrical container and then dumped out (Kolstad & Baillargeon, 1997). Then the infants' reactions were assessed to two new containers: One was perceptually similar to the familiar one but was bottomless and hence should not be able to function as a container. The other test object had a bottom, and hence could function as a container, but differed markedly in its perceptual appearance. In the test events, the infants were surprised (looked longer) when the perceptually similar bottomless object appeared to hold salt poured into it than when the perceptually different object with a bottom did so. Thus, the infants gave precedence to a functional property rather than perceptual similarity as the basis for generalization.

Kemler-Nelson (1995) recently reported interesting knowledge effects of a similar sort with 3- to 5-year-olds. Using the familiar extension of a novel word paradigm, she provided children with relevant knowledge about a complex, novel object (see Figure 16.2) by demonstrating its function. The object was named "stennet," and the children were asked whether various test objects were also stennets. The unique feature of this study was that the real target object afforded two very different functions. Half the children saw a demonstration of painting with the target object: The four paintbrushes at the top were dipped into paints and used to paint four parallel lines on paper. The other half of the children saw the target object used as a musical instrument: The three strings were plucked to play a simple tune. There were no demonstrations with the test objects, and the children were not allowed to manipulate them. Hence, they had to infer the objects' functional

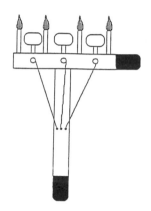

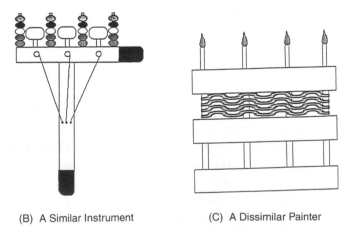

(A) The Original Stennet

(B) A Similar Instrument   **(C) A Dissimilar Painter**

Figure 16.2 One of the objects used by Kemler-Nelson (1995). Children generalized a novel label from the target object (A) to the dissimilar object that afforded the same function as the target. They generalized to (B) when the target was used for making music and (C) when the function demonstrated was painting.

possibilities from the presence and arrangement of critical elements.

Although perceptual similarity affected the children's judgments to some extent, the functional affordances of the objects had a much larger effect. A given test object was preferred or rejected depending on whether it afforded the same function as the target. This judgment was based on whether certain critical features were present and functional: In the context of painting, test objects with no brushes or inaccessible brushes were not considered to be stennets. In the context of music, the children focused on the presence and arrangement of the strings. Although the objects used in this study were both novel and complex, the critical features embedded in them were familiar, and the causal structure of the objects was simple. Thus, the children's general knowledge about painting and music making could direct their attention to the relevant features.

S. Gelman and her colleagues have conducted a highly influential series of studies of preschool children's inductive inferences on the basis of category membership. In the original research by S. Gelman and Markman (1986, 1987), 3- and 4-year-old children were presented with a trio of pictures and asked to attribute an unknown property based either on shared category membership or on perceptual similarity. The children were taught novel facts about two of the depicted entities. For example, pointing to a picture of a flamingo, the experimenter told the child, "This bird gives its babies mashed-up food." Pointing to the picture of a bat in flight, the experimenter said, "This bat gives its babies milk." The child was then asked about the picture of a blackbird in flight, "Does this bird give its babies mashed-up food like this bird [the flamingo] or milk like this bat?" The 4-year-olds consistently relied on category membership rather than perceptual similarity as the inferential basis for their judgments. They believed that the blackbird would feed its offspring in the same way as the other member of the same category rather than as the perceptually similar but conceptually dissimilar creature.

In a large number of studies using this basic format, S. Gelman and her colleagues have demonstrated reliance on category knowledge for drawing inferences across a wide spectrum of subjects (2½-year-olds to adults), stimuli (artifacts as well as natural kinds, including plants and animals, both real and imaginary), labels (familiar and novel), and attributes (diet, domicile, insides, behavior, growth patterns, etc.). (For a review of this program of research, see Wellman & S. Gelman, Ch. 11, this Volume.) This research testifies to the faith that children have in categories as a basis for making inferences. Very young bricoleurs, like adults, bring whatever knowledge they have to bear when reasoning.

Concepts in Theories

Although much of the work on conceptually based inferences focuses on particular categories (e.g., birds), it is generally assumed that children do not rely solely on their knowledge of the categories when making their judgments. Rather, the assumption is that many categories, especially natural kinds, are embedded in more extensive, elaborate conceptual frameworks, and that children operate on the basis of these concepts-in-theories (Murphy & Medin, 1985). Carey (1985) first proposed that children's conceptual knowledge in many domains is organized into theories in the sense that it is coherent and structured around a set of core beliefs linked by causal principles. Inferences are drawn from the constellations of concepts and beliefs that constitute a theory, and some inferences have priority over others.

Children's reasoning has been examined from this perspective in several domains, including biology (Carey, 1985), astronomy (Brewer & Samarapungavan, 1991), and animacy (R. Gelman, 1995). Massey and R. Gelman (1988) presented 3- and 4-year-olds with photographs of unfamiliar animate and inanimate objects and asked about each object's capacity for self-propelled locomotion, specifically, whether the entity could go both up and down a hill on its own. The children were very consistent and very accurate in their judgments, even though the objects were unfamiliar and presented in static pictures. The children answered that the depicted animals could move themselves up and down a hill. They judged that objects with wheels might be able to come down but could not go up a hill by themselves. Statues and nonwheeled objects were deemed incapable of either type of self-movement.

In making these inferences, the children actively searched for and used perceptual data in the pictures to make a determination of animacy. In many cases, however, their conceptual knowledge overrode perception:

> Some children even claimed that an unknown animate object could move itself because it had legs, a rather startling claim for objects like the echidna whose limbs were not visible in the photograph. However, "limbs" *per se* did not suffice for a child: Statues with limbs were not able to move themselves because they lacked "real" feet, they were "furniture animals," "pretend," or . . . they were made of the "wrong stuff." (R. Gelman, 1995, p. 180)

Having identified the echidna (a spiny anteater) as an animal, the children inferred from that categorization that it possessed legs, driving the further inference that it was capable of self-produced locomotion. Thus, their reasoning was based on their beliefs about animate creatures in general, specific anatomical features related to animacy, and the relation of those features to behavior. Keil's research program has focused on children's theories about natural kinds. He has also taken the familiar tack of forcing children to make and rationalize judgments based on perceptual appearance *versus* conceptual knowledge. One series of studies (described in Keil, 1989) compared the judgments of 6-, 8-, and 10-year-old children about the identity of different kinds of entities—natural kinds or artifacts—following a transformation that altered their appearance. In one example, children were shown pictures of a horse and a zebra and told the following story:

> A scientist took this horse and did an operation on it. He put black and white stripes all over its body. He cut off its mane and braided its tail like this. He taught it to run away from people. No one could ride it anymore. He taught it to eat grass instead of oats and hay. He also taught it to live out in the wild part of Africa instead of in a stable. Did he change it into a zebra, or is it still a horse? (p. 200)

In some cases, as in this example, the change was from one natural kind to another similar one (tiger/lion) or from one artifact to another (nail/needle); in other cases, a natural kind was changed into a very different kind (porcupine/cactus).

All three age groups accepted that an artifact could be transformed into a different artifact, and they all generally resisted the idea that a different-kind transformation could occur. However, large developmental differences occurred for the similar-kind changes. The 10-year-old children denied that the changed perceptual appearance of the natural kinds altered their identity. Their explanations made it clear that they accorded absolute priority to the insides of the natural-kind stimuli: As long as the internal elements were unchanged, identity was retained. The 6-year-olds typically relied on perceptual appearance in making their judgments; for the preceding example, they thought the horse had become a zebra. Their explanations were less coherent than those of the older children, but they were sometimes quite committed to their judgments. One child, obviously frustrated with the experimenter's persistent questioning about a raccoon painted to look like a skunk, said emphatically: "A skunk. Because it looks like a skunk, it smells like a skunk, it acts like a skunk, and it sounds like a skunk."

Keil attributes these developmental differences to increased domain knowledge and specifically to the existence of increasingly more coherently organized theories. Theories specify that some factors are more causally central than others and hence must be accorded precedence in making judgments. The importance of internal composition becomes a central tenet of children's theories about biological organisms and hence comes to override perceptual appearance as a basis for their judgments.

Concepts and Development

As this review shows, the development of knowledge profoundly influences children's reasoning, not because the inferential process changes, but because the conceptual basis for those inferences changes. From infancy and early childhood on, the bricoleur uses whatever relevant knowledge he or she possesses to reason. Apparent differences in the processes involved in reasoning have often turned out to be differences in the extent of knowledge.

As described in the preceding section, perceptual similarity and conceptual knowledge are intricately intertwined. Perceptual information is vital in the formation of many early concepts, and it is used in identifying the relevant categories in a given situation, but it is sometimes deemed less informative when it conflicts with conceptual knowledge. Such situations may be relatively rare in everyday experience; most of the time we, like Keil's young subject, get by quite well following the old saw, "If it looks like a duck, walks like a duck, and quacks like a duck, it probably *is* a duck." In analogical reasoning discussed in the following section, knowledge continues to play a crucial role.

Analogical Relations

A third kind of relation that supports reasoning is analogy. Analogical reasoning is based on relational similarity. It involves *relational mapping*—applying what one knows about the relations among some set of elements to the relations among a different set. An analogy asserts that the relations that hold between *a* and *b* (and *c* and *d* and . . . *n*) are the same as the relations between *a'* and *b'* (and *c'* and *d'* and . . . *n'*). There need be no perceptual similarity between *a* and *a'* or *b* and *b'*. In using an analogy, mapping is selective: Only those objects and relations that are part of

the higher-order relational structure common to both domains are mapped, a process Gentner (1983) and Halford (1993) describe as "structure mapping."

Consider, for example, *horse is to race as Miss Texas is to the Miss America pageant.* The common relation is contestants vying to win a competition. Note the near absence of attributes common to the corresponding objects; to the extent that Miss Texas resembles a horse, she would be less likely to win a beauty contest. In our initial example in which 5½-year-old Ross (4) asked, "Are the ones with the biggest rocks kings?" he was saying, in essence, "a monarch is to a commoner as a large tombstone is to a small tombstone."

Analogies can serve many different functions, from simply drawing attention to already known relations to providing a basis for genuine insight, the acquisition of new knowledge, and the reorganization and deepening of existing knowledge. From Spearman (1923) on, many cognitive theorists have regarded analogical reasoning as a central component of cognition (e.g., Gentner, 1983; Holyoak, 1984; Sternberg, 1986; Vosniadou & Ortony, 1989). Developmental theorists have proposed it as a powerful developmental mechanism (Brown, 1989; Gentner, 1989; Gentner & Rattermann, 1991; Goswami, 1991, 1992) and even as the origin of many logical rules (Halford, 1992, 1993).

The early developmental literature on analogical reasoning was dominated by the Piagetian tradition, and it supported Piaget's claim that analogical reasoning does not develop before formal operations. Piaget and his colleagues (Inhelder & Piaget, 1958; Piaget, Montangero, & Billeter, 1977) and many other investigators used classical analogies of the format *a: b:: c: d* (read as "*a* is to *b* as *c* is to *d*"). An example of a problem used by Piaget is *bicycle: handlebars:: ship: ?* Children were typically given pictures of the first three items and asked either to generate the answer "rudder" or to select the correct picture from a set of alternatives. Not until adolescence did children successfully meet the threefold criterion for analogical ability—giving the correct answer, explaining the basis for the answer, and resisting countersuggestions.

The analogy problems presented to the children in this research were typically fairly complex and often quite abstract, and little attention was paid to whether the children knew the relations on which the analogies were based (e.g., whether the children tested knew that the steering mechanism of a ship is its rudder). Thus, as has often been the case in cognitive development research, knowledge deficits and structural deficits were confounded. To illustrate, it can be assumed that everyone reading this chapter is capable of reasoning by analogy, but many might nevertheless fail to solve some of the following:

beat: 45 degrees :: reach : ?
. : i :: - : ?
runaway baby carriage: Eisenstein :: sinking piano: ?
Jack Snipe : King Alfred :: Kaufmann : ?

(The answers and relevant domains are *90 degrees*—sailing; *t*—Morse code; *Campion*—films; *Darwin*—flowering bulbs.)

As these examples show, failure to solve an analogy when one's knowledge is deficient is not evidence of a lack of analogical ability. The research reviewed in this section reveals that when children are asked to reason about familiar relations (that is, when they have the knowledge on which the analogy is based), analogical reasoning is present very early in life.

The first highly influential demonstration that young children are capable of analogical reasoning was a study by Holyoak, Junn, and Billman (1984). They examined the use of analogies by 4- to 6- and 11- to 12-year-old children in a problem-solving context that involved a meaningful situation and familiar relations among real objects. The children had to figure out how to transfer some balls from one bowl on a table to a second, out-of-reach bowl. The table held a variety of objects, including an aluminum cane, a long hollow tube, a large sheet of heavy paper, scissors, string, and so forth.

The children were presented with stories designed to serve as analogies to help them solve the problem. The stories involved a genie who wished to move his precious jewels from a nearby bottle to one further away. In one story, the genie achieved his goal by using a "magic staff" to pull the far bottle close to the other. The preschool children profited from the magic staff story; half of them spontaneously used the aluminum cane to pull the out-of-reach bowl to the other one, and the rest did so after receiving a hint that the story could help them. Thus, these young children transferred the approach used by a fantasy character in a story to their own solution of a problem with real objects. What was transferred from the base to target problem was the higher-order relation common to both—employing a long rigid object to pull a goal object within reach.

Many successful demonstrations of analogical transfer by young children followed. For example, in a charming series of studies, Brown and her colleagues (Brown & Kane, 1988; Brown, Kane, & Long, 1989) taught 3- and 4-year-old children novel biological facts, such as various animal defense mechanisms. In a series of problems on visual mimicry, the children heard stories about creatures such as the hawkmouth caterpillar, which looks like a poisonous snake when it rolls over; the crested rat, which can part its fur to reveal skunk-like markings; and the capricorn beetle, which looks like a wasp when it opens its wings.

The young children readily abstracted and transferred the general idea that some animals look like other animals as a means of protecting themselves from predators. One 3-year-old noted that a hawkmouth caterpillar and porcupine fish are the same because "they both have the same kind of problem. . . . Both of them have a mean guy that wants to eat them all up. . . . They both get mean and scary so they [predators] run away" (Brown, 1989, p. 393).

In certain circumstances, even toddlers solve problems by analogy. In a study described by Brown (1989), children between 20 and 30 months were presented with an attractive but out-of-reach toy, along with an array of potential tools, including long and short sticks, a cone, and a hooked cane, all gaily decorated with red and white stripes. After using the cane to pull the toy within reach, the children were presented with a new set of tools. They preferred a solid-color long rake that could effect the pulling strategy over tools that looked more similar to the training tool but were ineffective for the task (candy-striped sticks, a too-short cane). Knowledge of functional affordances, rather than perceptual similarity, was the basis for transfer.

Even earlier analogy use was reported by Chen, Sanchez, and Campbell (in press). One-year-old infants were presented with an attractive but out-of-reach toy (a red car) with a black string attached. The string was also out of reach, but it was lying curled up on a blue cloth that was within reach but that was behind a barrier (a white box). The infants effected the three-step solution to this problem, either spontaneously or with parental modeling, by removing the barrier (box), pulling the cloth, and then pulling the string to get the toy. On subsequent test trials, the infants successfully applied this solution to problems with dissimilar materials (e.g., a multi-colored rocking horse as the goal, a brown string, an orange-and-white striped cloth, and a blue box). To succeed, they had to resist another cloth with a string that was not attached to the target object.

Classical analogies—the type originally studied by Piaget—have turned out to also be solvable by very young children, provided they have the requisite knowledge.

Goswami and Brown (1989, 1990) used classical analogies (*a : b :: c : ?*) that were based on simple relations understood by preschool children. In one study (Goswami & Brown, 1989), children saw picture analogies of familiar objects that had undergone a familiar physical transformation (for example, *chocolate : melted chocolate :: snowman : ?* ; *Play-Doh : cut Play-Doh :: apple : ?*). Pictures for the *a : b :: c* terms were laid out, along with five additional pictures from which the child was to choose the correct *d* term. They included the correct picture (e.g., cut apple) and four distractors—a different object that had undergone the same transformation (cut bread), the correct object with a different transformation (a bruised apple), an object of similar appearance to the correct term (a ball), and a semantic associate of the correct item (a banana). Performance increased with age, but even the 3-year-old children were above chance (3-year-olds—52% correct, 4-year-olds—89%, and 6-year-olds—99%).

A particularly important result of this study was a significant conditional relation between the children's knowledge and their analogy performance. In a test of their knowledge of the specific causal relations on which the analogies were based, the children had to choose the appropriate causal agent for a particular transformation. For the cutting analogy, they saw pictures of a cut apple, cut bread, and cut-up Play-Doh, and they had to choose the picture of the common agent (a knife). Children who selected the correct answer in the knowledge test were also likely to select the correct picture in the analogy task. This result directly links knowledge and analogizing and hence provides strong support for the claim that young children's poor performance in earlier research on analogical reasoning had more to do with deficient knowledge than with deficient ability to use analogies per se.

In a study by Goswami (1996), 4- and 5-year-old children successfully mapped abstract relations (such as "decrease") *across* perceptual dimensions: for example, *fat toadstool : thin toadstool :: tall girl : short girl*. This age group was also successful on cross-dimensional mappings of ordered *triplets* (monotonic increase or decrease) such as the following: *thin toadstool: medium-size toadstool : fat toadstool :: short girl : medium-height girl : tall girl*. An additional result of this series of studies was successful mapping of relations even with no perceptual similarity between the *c* and *d* terms. For example, the 4- and 5-year-old children in one study were above chance when asked to complete analogies such as *acorn : oak tree :: bud : flower*.

Bauer and her colleagues (Freeman, McKie, & Bauer, 1994) have demonstrated successful solution of classical analogies by 24-month-olds. In each of a series of problems, the children were shown a real object, were told, "This is going to change," and then were asked to choose which of three objects represented the correct transformation. One set of problems involved a "broken-to-fixed" transformation. The experimenter first showed the children that the correct choice to go with a broken umbrella was an intact umbrella and that the correct choice for a broken piece of wood was a whole piece. On the test trial, the children saw a broken eggshell and chose from an array consisting of the correct object (whole eggshell), the correct transformation but wrong object (whole umbrella), or the correct object but wrong transformation (broken eggshell strung on a string). Thus, the children had to resist an alternative object that presumably looked as much like the exemplar as the correct object did. Their performance was above chance, indicating that even 2-year-old children can use higher-order relations in a classical analogy format.

Clues to Relational Structure

To reason by analogy, children must not only *have* the relevant knowledge; they must detect the relational similarity between what they know and the problem to be solved. As bricoleurs, young children generally benefit from a variety of different kinds of clues—virtually anything that highlights the relational structure of their existing knowledge or the relational similarity of two analogs.

One kind of clue to common underlying relational structure is surface similarity, both for adults (Holyoak & Koh, 1987) and children. In the study by Holyoak et al. (1984), the younger (4-year-old) children solved the genie jewel-transport problem much better when there was a high level of perceptual similarity between the analogous tools than when there was less perceptual support. Several other studies have reported positive effects of object similarity, with greater benefit typically occurring for younger children (e.g., Chen et al., in press; Chen, Yanowitz, & Daehler, 1995).

Differential effects of similarity as a function of age are consistent with Gentner's (1989; Gentner & Rattermann, 1991) *relational shift* account of the development of analogical reasoning. She claims that younger (less knowledgeable) children are generally more affected by surface similarity than older (more knowledgeable) individuals and that with age (and increased knowledge), children become more sensitive to underlying relational structure. This position is supported by results such as those reported by Gentner and Toupin (1986): Although both age groups in their study benefited from surface similarity, it had a larger effect for the younger children; and only the older children used the higher-order relational structure of the story analogs to map between them.

Familiarity is another factor that can influence analogical success. Practice with the original story problem improved analogical transfer by 4- and 5-year-olds of quite complex solutions to problems of the missionaries-and-cannibals genre (Gholson, Dattel, Morgan, & Eymard, 1989). In addition, *familiar schemas* already firmly represented in children's semantic memory can facilitate relational mapping. Halford (1992) argues that many kinds of reasoning problems, such as transitive inference, are initially solved through analogy by mapping a novel problem onto a familiar ordered structure already in memory. For example, the ordering structure *top-middle-bottom* can be used for this problem: *Ben is taller than Jerry. Larry is taller than Ben. Who is the tallest?* Children map the three terms of the premises onto the schema (Ben—middle, Jerry—bottom, Larry—top.) The correct answer emerges from the mapping of the novel elements into the familiar structure.

Goswami (1995) reported a facilitative effect of a familiar schema on young children's analogical reasoning. Three- and 4-year-old children exploited the relational structure of the highly familiar "Goldilocks and the Three Bears" story to solve a series of transitive inference problems involving ordered dimensions. For example, the children mapped three bowls of porridge described as "boiling hot," "hot," or "warm" onto Daddy Bear > Mummy Bear > Baby Bear.

Clues to common relational structure can also be provided directly. Hints that two analogs are related have been shown to help both adults and children gain access to an analogy (e.g., Gick & Holyoak, 1983; Holyoak et al., 1984). Drawing children's attention to the underlying goal structure of a story (Brown & Kane, 1988; Brown et al., 1989; Chen & Daehler, 1989) or inducing them to reflect in some way on their knowledge (Brown & Kane, 1988; Crisafi & Brown, 1986) facilitates analogical transfer. Similarly, communicating the underlying moral of a story can help older children map it onto another story with a similar structure (Gentner & Toupin, 1986).

Metacognitive Knowledge

Metacognition plays an important role in young children's analogical reasoning and suggests how analogy could be an important developmental mechanism. The existence of early explicit metacognitive understanding is nicely illustrated by 4-year-old Lucas in Goswami (1996):

Lucas was trying to solve the analogy *bird:nest::dog:?* We had asked him to predict the correct solution to the analogy before looking at the distractors, and Lucas first told us that the correct solution was *puppy*. He argued, quite logically, "Bird lays eggs in her nest [some eggs appeared in the nest in the b-term picture] . . . dog . . . dogs lay babies, and the babies are . . . umm . . . and the name of the babies is puppy!" Lucas had used the relation *type of offspring* to solve the analogy, and was quite certain that he was correct. "I don't have to look [at the distractor pictures]—the name of the baby is puppy!" Once he did agree to look at the different solution options, however, he decided that the *dog house* was the correct response. (p. 102)

Lucas understood that he was supposed to be looking for relations, but he did not yet realize that there can be multiple relations between two entities and that more information is needed to be certain of the correct answer.

Brown and her colleagues (Brown & Kane, 1988; Brown et al., 1989) report increases in metacognitive understanding in the form of *learning to learn*. In several experiments, young children received a series of six story problems—three sets of two problems each. The children were first given two problems with a common solution (e.g., stacking something to reach something or visual mimicry as an animal defense mechanism). If they failed to solve the first problem of the pair, the experimenter demonstrated the solution. The children typically did not transfer the solution from the first to the second problem in this initial set.

The children then received the two additional sets of problem pairs. There was more transfer on the second pair than on the first; by the third pair, nearly 90% of the children transferred the novel solution from the first to the second problem in the pair. The extent to which some children were aware of problem similarity is illustrated in the following examples. The first is an exchange between the experimenter and a 3-year-old subject (Brown & Kane, 1988, p. 503):

E: You said my games are the same. How are they the same?

C: They both have to put things on top.

E: Could you tell me a little more?

C: In the farmer game we put these green things [yellow bales of hay] on top.

E: Umm.

C: In the game we pile up wheels like before. Both games are for you to pile up things to reach.

In another example, 4-year-old Billy, after having just received two problems involving a rolling solution, commented at the beginning of a third story problem: "And all you need to do is get this thing rolled up? I betcha!" (Brown & Kane, 1988, p. 517).

Brown and Kane (1988) concluded that their subjects had formed a "mind-set to look for analogies." The children's repeated experience with analogy problems induced them to look for structural similarity between new problems. They *"expect to extract a general rule,* they *look for the rules of the game. . . .* [They] come to expect what they learn to be relevant elsewhere" (pp. 519–520). This demonstration of the formation of a set to transfer per se lends plausibility to the idea that analogical reasoning could constitute a powerful developmental mechanism.

Analogy and Development

According to Goswami's (1995) analogical primacy view, the capacity to reason by analogy is present in infancy. Age differences in performance are primarily attributable to differences in knowledge. Halford (1992, 1993) proposes a developmental progression that is closely linked to age and that corresponds generally to the major Piagetian stages. Children's ability to reason by analogy develops as increased processing capacity makes possible the representation of increasing relational complexity. According to Gentner's (1989) relational shift account, briefly described earlier, the ability to reason about object similarity developmentally precedes the ability to reason about relational similarity, and reasoning about simple, "first-order" relations is possible earlier than reasoning about "higher-order" relations: "Young children focus on common object descriptions, whereas older children and adults focus on common relations" (Gentner & Rattermann, 1991, p. 227). Although this quote seems to imply a maturational, domain-general relational shift, Gentner differs from Halford by emphasizing that the relational shift is primarily a function of increasing knowledge within domains.

Most of the researchers that have been discussed emphasize the potential power of analogical reasoning as a developmental mechanism: A presumed function is acquisition of new knowledge and the reorganization of existing knowledge. Since knowledge has been shown to play a vital role in many aspects of cognition, this is an important contribution. Changes in the level at which knowledge is represented have also been proposed to result from repeated analogizing. According to Gentner and her colleagues (Gentner, Rattermann, Markman, & Kotovsky, 1995), more abstract and general—and hence more powerful—knowledge representations result from the process of repeated "structural alignment." Halford (1992, 1993) similarly proposes that many abstract (logical) rules grow out of the repeated use of familiar schemas as analogies.

Symbolic Relations

Symbols constitute a fourth kind of relational support for reasoning. There are many kinds of symbols, some of which carry information and hence can serve as a basis for making predictions and drawing inferences. Thus, for some symbols, if we know that x is a symbol for y, then we assume that some of what we know about x will also be true of y. As a consequence, we can learn about y by learning about x. In this discussion, we restrict ourselves to external (i.e., not purely internal or mental symbols) and nonlinguistic symbols. Failure to distinguish between mental and other kinds of representations has probably hampered the understanding of any of them (DeLoache, 1995).

Symbolic relations are distinguished from the other kinds of relations considered here in two main ways. One is intentionality; for something to be a symbol, someone must intend that it be interpreted primarily in terms of something other than itself (DeLoache, 1995). Also, in symbolic relations there is always a qualitative difference between symbol and referent; they are different kinds of things. This is obvious when the symbol is a different medium—a picture, film, or map—from its referent—a sweetheart, birthday party, or landscape. Symbols that do not differ in medium from their referents have different functional affordances. For example, a real room affords movement and other activities not possible in a small scale model of the room.

Symbols expand the realm of reasoning by enabling us to represent, draw inferences from, and make predictions about objects and events we have never directly experienced. No one alive personally experienced Napoleon's ill-fated campaign into Russia, but it is possible to learn a great deal about it from Minard's famous map (Tufte, 1983). This remarkably informative document depicts a map of Europe and western Russia with a band representing the path of Napoleon's march into and out of Russia. The dates and sites of all major battles are marked. The width of the band represents the number of soldiers, and one can easily infer the disastrous course of the campaign from the progressive narrowing of the band. One can infer which battles were the most devastating, and one can also tell how the number of troops declined precipitously during the Russian winter even without any major battles being fought. A poignantly slim line leads back to Paris.

Understanding the Representational Nature of Symbols

The components of symbol-referent relations are not transparent, even though they often seem so to adults who have a lifetime of experience with a vast array of symbols. Very young children may fail to appreciate any and all of them. That young children might initially be unaware of the representational nature of totally arbitrary symbols like printed words is not surprising. Nothing about a printed word gives a clue as to its function and significance, and many young children are read to for months or years before realizing that the squiggly marks on a page mean something.

The representational nature of iconic symbols—those that closely resemble their referents—is not necessarily clear either, at least not to individuals with limited symbolic experience. Pierroutsakos (1995) and her colleagues (DeLoache, Pierroutsakos, Uttal, Rosengren, & Gottlieb, 1997; Pierroutsakos & DeLoache, 1996) have established that 9-month-old infants are confused about what *pictures* are. When presented with realistic color photographs of a single object, infants manually explore the depicted objects and even try to grasp and pick them up. They apparently assume that a picture and its referent share more properties than is in fact the case. By 20 months of age, this kind of manual exploration rarely occurs. Experience with pictures has presumably led infants to learn that pictures contain only a few of the properties of their referents.

Nevertheless, children continue to evidence picture-referent confusions. Beilin and Pearlman (1991) reported that preschool children occasionally believe that a picture shares the properties of its referent; for example, they might claim that a picture of an ice cream cone would be cold to the touch or that a photograph of a rose would smell sweet. In a similar vein, Flavell, Flavell, Green, and Korfmacher (1990) reported that young children predicted that turning a video monitor upside-down would cause a filmed tower of blocks to tumble down.

Symbol-referent confusions occur with noniconic symbols as well. The first step in *reading* is "print awareness" (Teale & Sulzby, 1986): "The child must induce *that print symbolizes language*" (Adams, 1990, p. 335). Children then have to work out how letters and sounds and printed and spoken words are related. They start with various guesses and misconceptions about these symbol-referent relations.

Beginning readers often apply the similarity heuristic that has been so useful to them and assume that there should be some physical resemblance between printed words and their referents. For example, they expect the size of an object to be reflected in the size of the word that represents it. Given the words "banana" and "car," they assume that the longer word denotes the larger entity (Bialystok, 1991; Lundberg & Torneus, 1978). These children thus confuse the properties of the symbol and its referent. Young children are also uncertain about what invests a printed word with meaning. Bialystok (1991) showed prereaders, who could identify printed letters, a card with a word printed on it that was sitting next to a picture of its referent. The word was read aloud to the children. When the card was moved next to a different picture, they now thought that the word on the card was the name for the second picture because they had a flawed understanding of the representational relation between letters and sounds.

Similar symbol-referent confusions occur with respect to *writing*. Levin and Tolchinsky Landsmann (1989) reported that 5-year-old children imported features of the referent into their pretend "writing" of the names of objects. Their written expression for "rope" was elongated compared with that for "ball," "elephant" was written in larger letters than was "ant," and "tomato" and "cucumber" were written in red and green ink, respectively. Again, this suggests a misguided assumption that perceptual similarity matters in symbol-referent relations.

Research on children's interpretation and use of *maps* provides another example. Liben and Downs (1986, 1991) have reported that even when children can identify that something is a map or other kind of place representation, they may still have problems like those evidenced by beginning readers—they try to use an inappropriate perceptual similarity heuristic, and they often confuse properties of the symbol and its referent.

Liben and Downs (1986, 1991) presented children ranging in age from 3½ to 6½ years with various place representations, such as a standard road map of Pennsylvania and an aerial photograph of downtown Chicago. The children rejected many of the experimenter's suggestions about the identity of particular features on the representations because they were not sufficiently similar to their referents. One area on the photograph could not be grass "because grass is green"; the red lines on the road map could not be roads because real roads are not red. Other features could not be cars "because they're too tiny" or buildings "because buildings are bigger." Interpretive errors went the other direction as well: Some children expected that the real road represented by a red line would itself be red. These children evidenced a "fusion between the properties of the referent and of the representation" (Liben & Downs, 1991, p. 163). They believed that characteristics of the referent should necessarily appear in its representation, and they also attributed characteristics of the representation to its referent. Only with experience do children come to understand how symbols and referents are related and hence what inferences are permissible.

Using Symbols as Information

DeLoache and her colleagues have examined symbol understanding and use by very young children. Because the goal of this research was to investigate the origins of symbolic understanding, all the symbols studied have been iconic representations (what Vygotsky, 1978b, referred to as first-order symbols). For the same reason, search tasks have been employed, because the goal can be conveyed with a minimum of verbal instructions, the children's response is nonverbal and unambiguous, and even toddlers enjoy and are highly motivated by object-retrieval games.

One set of studies (DeLoache, 1987, 1991; DeLoache & Burns, 1994) examined very young children's ability to draw an inference from pictures, the first external symbol to which most children and even infants are exposed (at least in middle-class Western homes). The results indicate that by 2½ years of age, children readily use pictures as a source of information about something of which they have no direct knowledge. In each study, the experimenter presented children with a picture, explaining that it showed where a toy had been hidden in a room. The pictures that were used varied across studies and included a wide-angle photograph of the room, a line drawing of the same, and a series of photos depicting individual pieces of furniture in the room. In some studies, the hidden toy appeared in the pictures; in others, it did not. A group of 2½-year-olds averaged over 80% errorless retrievals, regardless of the pictures used. A group of 2-year-olds presented a stark contrast; they rarely succeeded in retrieving the hidden toy, indicating that they failed to use the pictures as information. Several concerted efforts to improve the performance of 2-year-olds in these tasks failed (DeLoache & Burns, 1994).

The results of this research indicate that by 2½ years of age, children are capable of using a symbol-referent relation as the basis for making an inference about an unseen event. They understand that the picture tells them where to find the hidden toy; in other words, they understand the relation between the picture and its referent. Although pictures are a familiar medium, this research asked children to use them in an unfamiliar way: as a source of information about a specific, existing state of affairs and as a means to solve a problem. Children rarely if ever experience pictures in such a context. Nevertheless, 2½-year-olds, like good bricoleurs, flexibly adopted pictures as a new problem-solving tool.

This pattern of performance has recently been replicated with another highly familiar visual medium—television. Troseth and DeLoache (1996) explained and demonstrated for 2- and 2½-year-old children that a video camera was filming "live." Children then observed televised hiding events in which an experimenter hid a toy in the room next door. They were then asked to retrieve the toy. The results were the same as for still pictures: The 2½-year-olds inferred from the video events where to find the toy, but the 2-year-olds failed to do so.

The younger children's failure was not due to memory or motivational problems; when a different group of 2-year-olds directly watched the same hiding event through a window, rather than on a monitor, they were 100% correct in their searching. This indicates that seeing the hiding event on a television screen prevented these children from connecting it with the real toy and the real room. They did not comprehend the symbol-referent relation.

Another series of studies has examined young children's understanding of scale models, using a similar retrieval task. A realistic scale model is used to stand for a room (either a full-sized real room or a tentlike portable room). There is a high degree of physical similarity between the miniature items of furniture in the model and their full-sized counterparts. On each trial, children watch as a miniature toy is hidden behind or under a piece of furniture in the model. They are told that a similar but larger toy is hidden in the corresponding place in the room. If the children appreciate the symbol-referent relation, then they can infer from their knowledge of where the miniature toy is hidden in the model where to search for the larger toy in the room.

In numerous studies using this task (DeLoache, 1987, 1991, 1995; DeLoache, Kolstad, & Anderson, 1991; Marzolf & DeLoache, 1994; Uttal, Schreiber, & DeLoache, 1996), 3-year-old children have typically succeeded (>75% errorless retrievals); based on their knowledge of the location of one toy, they readily infer where the other must be. In contrast, 2½-year-olds have usually performed very poorly (<20%). As was true for the 2-year-olds in the picture studies, the younger children's failure in the model task is not due to a lack of knowledge or motivation: When brought back to the model, they reliably retrieve the toy they originally observed being hidden. Their problem seems to be in understanding the relation between the model and room and in realizing that their knowledge of the first is relevant to figuring out the second.

Reasoning from model to room is not simply a matter of detecting similarity relations. It is not the case, as has sometimes been suggested (e.g., Lillard, 1993; Perner, 1991), that children can succeed simply by noticing the correspondence between individual items in the two spaces. The claim is that on each trial, they independently map single similarity relations (miniature couch to large couch, then small pillow to large pillow, etc.), without ever recognizing the presence of any higher-order relation between the spaces. One piece of evidence against this claim is a study (Troseth & DeLoache, 1995) in which 2½-year-old children were simply asked to pick out the larger objects in the room that were "like" (i.e., that corresponded to) the smaller ones in the model. The children easily constructed the individual correspondences between the objects in the two spaces. Nevertheless, when they were then given the standard model task involving a representational relation, they failed, just like other 2½-year-olds. Thus, representing a set of lower-order, similarity relations is not a sufficient basis for using a model as a source of information.

Similarity is, however, helpful in young children's understanding of the model-room relation (DeLoache et al., 1991). Three-year-olds are successful in the task only if there is a high level of similarity between the furniture in the two spaces. Furthermore, even 2½-year-olds can succeed if the model and room are made quite similar in size (i.e., if the "room" is only twice as big as the model). High levels of physical similarity may help children both with noticing the model-room relation and mapping between the two spaces (just as it assists with gaining access to and mapping an analogy).

Several other factors also affect performance in the model task. One is a long delay between when children see the toy being hidden in the model and when they are allowed to search in the room. When 3-year-olds have to wait 5 minutes, they fail to use their memory for the hiding event to infer where to search in the room (Uttal, Schreiber, & DeLoache, 1995). Three-year-olds also perform poorly when multiple relations must be mapped from model to room. Marzolf (1996) hid a miniature toy in one of four

tiny boxes in a scale model. To know which of the identical boxes held the toy, the children had to encode the relation between the box and a landmark—one of the pieces of miniature furniture in the model. To find the larger toy that had been hidden in the corresponding larger box in the room, the children had to map two relations—the toy-box relation and the box-landmark relation from the model to the room. The 3-year-olds in this series of studies always searched in a box, indicating they had represented the toy-box relation. However, they were barely above chance in their choice of the correct box, indicating that they did not consistently map the second, box-landmark relation. They had, however, represented that relation: When asked to retrieve the miniature toy from the model, they readily did so. A group of 4-year-olds was very successful: They clearly represented and mapped both relations.

DeLoache (1987, 1991, 1995) has proposed that the developmental differences observed in the model task stem in part from the need for *dual representation:* To use a model as a symbol for something else, the child has to simultaneously represent both its concrete and abstract nature. All external symbols have a "double reality" (Gibson, 1979; Gregory, 1970; Potter, 1979; Sigel, 1978), in that they have both a concrete existence and an abstract function. To the extent that one's attention is drawn to the physical properties of a symbol, it will be more difficult to interpret it abstractly, to represent it as a term in a "stands for" relation.

By this analysis, some of the very characteristics of the model that make it appealing to young children may pose a representational challenge. The younger children are, the more likely they are to have difficulty disengaging or distancing themselves from the model as an interesting object in its own right and hence the less likely they are to use it as a symbol for something other than itself. As S. Langer (1942) pointed out, a peach would not be a good symbol, because we are too interested in the peach itself.

The dual representation hypothesis has received very strong support, beginning with the fact that 2½-year-old children successfully exploit pictures as a source of information at the same time that they fail to use a model (DeLoache, 1987, 1991). Unlike models, pictures are relatively nonsalient and uninteresting as objects, so there is nothing about them to distract children from their primary, representational role.

In a direct test of dual representation (described in DeLoache, 1995), the salience of the model itself was *decreased* by placing it behind a window, thus preventing children from interacting directly with it. As predicted, a group of 2½-year-olds was more successful than this age group typically is in the standard model task. In a second test, the opposite approach was taken: The salience of the model as an object was *increased* for a group of 3-year-olds by allowing them to play with it for several minutes before participating in the standard task. Again as predicted, their performance was worse than the usual level for that age group. The support for the dual representation hypothesis provided by these three findings is especially strong, given that each of them is counterintuitive and not predicted on any other grounds.

The most stringent—and counterintuitive—test of dual representation involved an effort to *eliminate* the need for dual representation altogether from a version of the model task (DeLoache, Miller, & Rosengren, 1996). A group of 2½-year-olds was convinced that a "shrinking machine" could shrink a room (the tentlike portable room used in many model studies). The reasoning was that if the children believe that the machine has shrunk the room (into the scale model of that room), then there is no representational relation between model and room. There is instead an identity relation: The model is not a symbol for the room; it *is* the room. As a consequence, children who fail to reason from one space to the other based on the symbolic model-room relation should be more successful with an identity relation between the same two entities.

A group of 2½-year-olds was introduced to "Terry the Troll" and his room (the portable room). Then the powers of the shrinking machine (an oscilloscope with flashing green lights) were demonstrated. The troll was placed in front of the machine, the machine was "turned on," and the child and experimenter waited in the adjoining area, listening to computer-generated tones described as the "sounds the shrinking machine makes while it's working." The child then returned to discover a miniature troll in place of the original one. Three more demonstrations established that the machine could also make the troll "get big again," that it could shrink the room, and that it could return the room to its original size.

On the first test trial, the child watched as the experimenter hid the larger doll in the portable room. After waiting while the machine shrank the room (and toy), the child was asked to find the toy. The miniature troll was hidden in the model in the place corresponding to where the child had seen the larger troll being hidden in the room. The subsequent trials alternated between hiding events in the model and room. Just as in the symbolic model task, the child in the shrinking room task had to use his or her knowledge of

where the toy was hidden in one space to draw an inference about where to search in the other. The only difference was the nature of the child's mental representation of the relation between the two spaces.

As predicted, performance was significantly better in the nonsymbolic shrinking room task (76%) than in a control task involving the usual symbolic relation between model and room (19%). The superior performance occurred even though the delay between the hiding event and the child's retrieval was longer than in the standard model task, a factor known to adversely affect children's performance (Uttal et al., 1996). This study thus provides very strong support for the dual representation hypothesis.

More generally, these results mean that any explanation of children's performance in both the shrinking room and standard model tasks must invoke the children's mental representation of the relation between the model and room. What, if any, inferences are drawn from one to the other depends crucially on what, if any, relation is represented.

One other important result of the series of scale model studies is that experience with one symbol transfers to others. More precisely, experience with a symbol-referent relation that they understand facilitates children's subsequent detection of other relations. Several transfer studies employing a basic easy-to-hard format have found significant transfer, both for 2½- and 3-year-old children, including transfer from pictures to model, from an easy model task to a more difficult one, and from a simple map to the model task (DeLoache, 1991; Marzolf & DeLoache, 1994).

In the most impressive test to date (Marzolf, Pacha, & DeLoache, 1996), transfer occurred in the absence of any supportive context. A group of 2½-year-olds was given the relatively easy similar-scale model task on the first day, using two toy dogs. On the second day, they went to a different building on the other side of campus where they were tested in the more difficult standard model task by a different experimenter using two trolls as hidden objects. The children were successful (63%) in the more difficult task and significantly better than a control group who experienced it twice. The same level of transfer occurred even after a one-week delay. The only basis for transfer was the similar structure of the two tasks. There were no common objects, people, or settings. Transfer had to be based on some fairly abstract understanding, such as the fact that in both cases a scale model served as a source of information about another space.

Simple *maps* can also serve as a source of information and inferences for preschool children, as shown in the classic work of Bluestein and Acredolo (1979) and Presson (1982, 1987). More recently, Uttal and Wellman (1989) investigated the effect of exposure to a simple map on young children's mental representation of a space. Children between the ages of 4 and 7 had to learn a route through a playhouse. The house comprised six contiguous rooms (two rows of three rooms), each distinguished by a particular stuffed animal (bunny, cat, pig, etc.) sitting in the room. A map was used to teach half of the children the animal locations before they ever entered the space. All the children then repeatedly traveled through the playhouse. Comparing the performance of the symbol-assisted group with the group given direct experience only, Uttal and Wellman found that exposure to the map was helpful in two ways. First, the children who had experience with the map subsequently learned a particular route through the playhouse faster, that is, they more quickly learned the correct sequence of animals. Second, these children also performed better when asked to identify rooms out of the learned sequence. Thus, having a map of a space helped these young children achieve a more coherent, complete mental representation of the space.

Uttal, Lio, and Taxy (1995) have evidence that the characteristics of a map affect its usefulness to young children. When identifiable structure is apparent in a map, young children are more successful at mapping information to the represented space. Children aged 3 and 5 were presented with an array of 27 cups on the floor of a room. Although the cups were arranged in the shape of a dog, this was not readily apparent. All the children were given a map with dots representing the array of cups. Half the children received a map with lines connecting the dots, which made the dog structure readily apparent; the other children received a map on which the dots were unconnected and the structure less obvious. In the test, the experimenter pointed to one of the dots on the map, asking the child to retrieve a sticker hidden under the corresponding cup in the room. In the no lines condition, this was a very difficult task: The 3-year-olds searched the correct cup less than 20% of the time, and the 5-year-olds succeeded only about 50% of the time. However, in the lines condition in which the dog-shape was evident, the performance of the older children was enhanced. The 5-year-olds in the lines condition were successful 72% of the time. Thus, the structure that was apparent in the map with lines made the 5-year-olds more successful at mapping information from it to the represented array. The map-provided structure presumably facilitated performance by revealing the structure in the real

array and by making it easier to match the elements on the map with the corresponding cups.

Young children can also reason in the opposite direction; they can use their knowledge about a space to interpret a map of it. Liben and Yckel (1996) presented 4½- to 5½-year-old children with the two maps of their preschool classroom (shown in Figure 16.3). The "plan" map showed an overhead view of the room and objects in it, and the "oblique" map depicted a partial side view as well. The children received the maps in counterbalanced order, and their task was to place a sticker on the map to indicate the location of a target object (toy bear, lunch box) in the room itself. To succeed, children had to understand the overall map-room relation, and they also had to be able to match the locations (objects and places) in the room with their symbols on the map.

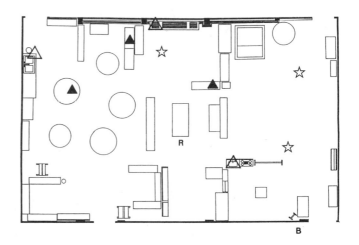

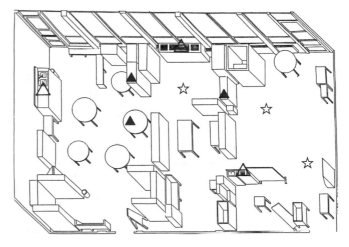

Figure 16.3   Maps of a preschool classroom used by Liben and Yekel (in press). Children were more successful using the *oblique* map (bottom) than the *plan* map.

Although virtually all the children knew that the maps represented the room, many had difficulty carrying out the task. Their performance differed as a function of the two maps and the order in which they received them. Children who received the plan map first rarely identified the correct locations on it, but they did significantly better when they were subsequently given the oblique map. Children who received the oblique map first performed very well, both with it and later with the plan map.

There were thus two main results. One was a relatively straightforward similarity effect like those found with scale models (DeLoache et al., 1991). The additional features in the oblique map made the depicted objects resemble their referents in the room and thereby helped the children match them, that is, helped the children carry out the requisite mapping. The second result was transfer: As in Marzolf and DeLoache's (1994) model studies, prior experience with a symbol (map) they could interpret helped the children use a more difficult one.

Symbols and Development

Unlike the relations reviewed in the preceding sections, symbolic relations are not available as tools for reasoning in infancy. Many steps are required to become a proficient symbolizer, starting with learning that some entities are to be responded to primarily in terms of what they represent. Once children are able to detect symbolic relations and map between symbols and referents, their intellectual horizons transcend both time and space. The product of development becomes a major source of further development. Symbols become one of the most powerful tools in the bricoleur's box.

Rule-Based Relations

Rules constitute an economical and powerful basis for reasoning. A rule specifies a relation across two or more variables, where the variables can take any of some range of values. Not only is the content of the variables open, but the nature of the relation itself varies greatly. Much of our cognition and action is governed by mentally represented rules. We are fully aware of some of the rules that we follow, but we are totally unaware of the rulelike basis for many of our other behavioral regularities.

There are two distinct traditions of theory and research on rule-based reasoning, both with long histories in psychology. The first focuses on the development of purely formal, logical rules. Piaget, like Aristotle and many other philosophers and psychologists, believed that the rules of logic reflect the rules of thought: "Reasoning is nothing more than the propositional calculus itself" (Inhelder & Piaget, 1958, p. 305). Piaget's theory was geared toward explaining how cognitive development culminates in formal propositional logic, the ability to reason on the basis of the pure form of an argument, irrespective of its content. A number of developmentalists share Piaget's belief that human reasoning is based on logical principles (Overton, 1990); however, some emphasize the logical inferences that people routinely make in everyday, practical reasoning and conversation (Braine & O'Brien, 1991; Scholnick & Wing, 1995) and how logical rules could develop out of one's everyday experience of environmental contingencies (Falmagne, 1990). (The development of formal logical reasoning is addressed in Chapter 19, by Moshman in this Volume.)

The idea that logic describes thinking processes has been forcefully challenged by many theorists who are skeptical that the mind operates with formal, content-free rules. Johnson-Laird (1983) has proposed mental models as an alternative representational basis for reasoning. Although mental models are more abstract than is often assumed, they represent particular situations and hence are contentful. Another alternative representational format is pragmatic inference schemas, clusters of generalized rules defined in relation to particular classes of goals. An example is the "permission" schema, a set of rules about situations in which a given action can be taken only if some precondition is satisfied (Cheng & Holyoak, 1985). Social exchange theorists (Barkow, Cosmides, & Tooby, 1992) propose even more context-specific mental representations underlying reasoning. They argue that humans have evolved various special-purpose reasoning schemas applicable to particular goals of universal importance, such as the detection of cheating in social contexts. Some research has examined mental models in children's reasoning (Halford, 1992; Johnson-Laird, Oakhill, & Bull, 1986), but there has been little developmental work on either pragmatic inference schemas or social exchange theory.

The second traditional line of inquiry in rule-based reasoning focuses on the processes involved in learning or *inducing* a rule from experience and in *following* a rule that one has represented. These rules are by nature contentful; they are distillations of environmental regularities that enable one to predict and draw inferences, as well as to regulate behavior.

Young children represent and sometimes follow large numbers of behavior-control rules, some of which are explicitly taught by others and some that they induce from experience. Parents diligently teach, "Look both ways before crossing the street," "Don't ever hit anyone," "Eat your vegetables before your dessert." Preschools are a source of numerous additional rules: "Raise your hand before talking in group-time," "Stay on your cot during nap-time," "Paint on the paper, not the table." In the example that opened this chapter, Jessie (5) had not only learned her preschool's rule about sitting quietly on a line on the floor, she saw herself as an appropriate enforcer of the rule. Children are also taught more abstract rules, such as those described in the previous section for mapping alphabet letters onto sounds. They induce from experience with parental behavior, "Only 47 drinks of water after the absolute, final, last goodnight."

Rule Induction

Children's ability to induce a rule from experience has been examined in two very different programs of research. Both series of studies have revealed that young children can learn general rules and that the underlying complexity of a rule affects how readily they do so.

Smith, DeLoache, and Schreiber (1995) examined very young children's ability to induce abstract rules. One set of studies examined 24- and 30-month-old children's learning of a "sameness" rule; specifically, the rule was that for *any* hidden object, the object could be found in a box with a matching picture on its lid. (A second box had a nonmatching picture on it.) Knowing the sameness rule could enable the child to retrieve any target object.

In the training phase, each child received several trials designed to teach two *specific* rules from which the general rule could be induced. For example, the children were taught that a toy frog was always found in the box with a picture of a frog on top of it; and then they were taught a second specific rule, for example, that a hammer could be found in the box with the hammer picture. In the test phase, the children were asked to search for a series of novel objects that were always hidden with the matching picture. As a new toy was used on each trial and the children never observed the hiding event, the only way to succeed was by using a general, abstract rule that transcended their previous experiences. To formulate this general rule, the children had to relate the two specific rules formed in the first two phases to one another. Only by doing so could the common relational core—the general rule—be discovered.

The 30-month-old children were very successful (93% correct) on the test trials with the novel objects, and nearly all the children met the success criterion of 5 out of 6 correct searches. The 24-month-olds were significantly less successful, although their performance (68%) was above chance and some of them did reach criterion. Thus, 30-month-olds readily induced the abstract rule in this situation, and some of the 24-month-olds also learned it.

Two subsequent studies demonstrated that similarity was not relevant to inducing the rule. In the most extreme test of similarity, each target object was hidden, not in a box with a picture, but in a larger version of the object itself. For example, a small doll's boot was hidden in a real boot. The performance of a group of 24-month-olds was just the same as in the original experiment. It is possible that the interest value of the object hiding places may have been counterproductive; reminiscent of the scale model research reviewed in the previous section, the children in this experiment may have focused on the specific objects themselves, to the detriment of the abstract relation.

Something that did help 24-month-olds induce the general rule was having the relation labeled. In one study, the experimenter repeatedly labeled the specific relations in the two training series, for example, "You found the frog in the frog box," and "You found the hammer in the hammer box." Over half the 24-month-olds now reached criterion in the test trials. Thus, drawing the children's attention to the relation between the toys and the pictures helped them abstract the general rule.

Similar results were obtained in other studies that employed a different training procedure, different stimuli, and a different rule—a *same-color* rule. From a series of demonstration trials, children had to figure out that a brightly colored jelly bean could always be found under the one of two small cups that was the same color as the candy. Just as was true for the same-object rule, 30-month-olds readily induced the general rule, but 24-month-olds did not. Labeling the relevant dimension and relation increased the performance of the 24-month-olds just as it did in the same-object studies.

Another set of studies probed limitations in the rule learning of 30-month-olds by examining their induction of more complex rules. A procedure reminiscent of that employed by Marzolf (1996) was incorporated into the same-object task: As the child watched, the target toy was inserted into a small box. Then, without the child observing, that box was placed inside the larger one with the picture cue on its lid. Thus, everything was exactly the same as in the original study, except that an additional relation intervened between the matching object and picture. This more complex rule was more difficult for the 30-month-old subjects, who were less successful (72%) than those in the original study. Although the addition of the extra box seems like an inconsequential change to an adult, the extra relation obviously added representational complexity for the children.

Remarkably convergent results for young children's rule learning have emerged in work by Overman and his colleagues (Overman, Bachevalier, Miller, & Moore, 1996), taking an approach unlike that employed by Smith et al. They have examined different kinds of rules and have used procedures that include two classic psychological paradigms—oddity learning and delayed nonmatch to sample (DNMS). Whereas the subjects in the Smith et al. research received a few trials in a single session, Overman's heroic subjects often experienced hundreds of learning trials over many days.

In DNMS, a sample object is presented, and the child finds a reward (e.g., a Cheerio® or raisin) under it. Next, two alternative objects are presented, one identical to the sample, one different. The child is rewarded for picking the different—the nonmatching—object. The rule that is involved here is straightforward: "Choose the target that is different from the sample." Its execution is also straightforward, in that only a single comparison is required—a comparison of one alternative versus the target. If x is different from the target, choose x. (There is no need to inspect y.) If x is the same as the target, choose y. (Again, there is no need to examine the second object.) This problem is readily solved by children as young as 27 to 32 months, and even by younger subjects (Overman, 1990; Overman et al., 1996).

Overman et al. (1996) found that young children had more trouble with a rule that was representationally more complex. Oddity problems, in which children must select whichever of three alternative objects is the "odd one" (different from the other two), require making multiple comparisons (rather than the single comparison necessary for success on DNMS problems). For children below the age of 6, oddity problems were much more difficult than DNMS problems. Verbally telling the children the oddity rule led to immediate success. Thus, these young children had no problem following a rule, even though they had extreme difficulty inducing that same rule.

The results of the Smith et al. (1995) and Overman et al. (1996) research are remarkably congruent, given the extremely different situations and rules involved. In both cases, (a) 2½-year-old children induced a simple abstract rule, (b) more complex rules were more difficult, and (c) giving children clues to or teaching them a rule enabled them to represent and follow it.

Rule Following

Zelazo and his colleagues have examined children's ability to follow rules. This research reveals both that the ability to follow rules develops early and that young children become increasingly flexible in their rule-based reasoning.

Zelazo and Reznick (1991) told young children two simple rules for sorting pictures, explicitly stating them in several different ways. For example, the children were told, "All the bugs go in this box and all the animals go in that box. We don't put any bugs in that box. No way. If it's a bug it goes here. If it's an animal it goes there." The children were then asked to place individual pictures in the appropriate boxes. Categories included both natural ones (e.g., bugs vs. animals, clothes vs. tools), and ad hoc categories, (e.g., things that make noise vs. things that are quiet, things that go inside the house vs. things that go outside). A relatively dramatic age difference occurred: Children 36 months of age were very successful at following the sorting rule regardless of category type. However, children a few months younger were markedly less successful, particularly with the ad hoc categories. Only half of the 31- and 33½-month-old children performed above chance.

The younger children's difficulty following the sorting rule was not due to a knowledge deficit, as revealed by probes of their knowledge of each object's category membership. For example, children were shown a bicycle and asked "Is this something you can ride or make music with?" Children in all three age groups were very successful at this task. Thus, having the relevant knowledge is not tantamount to being able to execute a rule based on that knowledge. Many 2½-year-old children who know a rule and have all the requisite conceptual knowledge for applying the rule nevertheless fail to use it to regulate their behavior. Furthermore, they are remarkably impervious to efforts to improve their rule use. Zelazo, Reznick, and Piñon (1995) gave 32-month-old children extra help in the sorting task, including feedback and reinforcement, labeling pictures in terms of the appropriate categories, and regular reminders of the rule. Even with all this assistance, the 32-month-olds did not perform above chance. Thus, rapid development occurs in the ability to execute simple if-then rules, independent of children's knowledge of those rules.

After children become capable of rule following, the ability remains fragile and context bound. Three-year-olds who can execute an if-then sorting rule have great difficulty switching to a different rule. Zelazo, Frye, and Rapus (1995) asked children to sort a set of pictures either by color or by shape (category). The children were very successful at this part of the task. However, after five trials they were told to use a new rule. Thus, children who had been sorting pictures into green versus yellow ones were now supposed to put the green and yellow objects of the same type together.

Three-year-olds failed this sorting task, while 4- and 5-year-olds were successful. The younger subjects' failure to switch to the new rule was not due to any inability to understand or remember it; they were able to answer knowledge questions such as, "Where do the cars go in the shape game?" They knew the rule but did not use it to guide their sorting. The 3-year-olds failed to switch to a new rule even when they had experienced only a single trial with the original rule and they did not actually have to sort the cards but merely had to verbally respond to "where does this go?" Thus, 3-year-olds are extremely inflexible in their rule use, despite an understanding of the rule that is on a par with that of older children.

Rules and Development

Comparing across the three separate programs of research reviewed in this section, it is clear that by 2½ years of age, children can induce a simple (one-relation) rule from their experience, especially when the relevant dimension is made salient to them. They are not, however, successful at following a pair of simple rules that have been explicitly taught to them.

The reason for this large difference is not immediately clear. Zelazo and his colleagues attribute it to changes in the ability to exercise conscious control over behavior. It may also have to do with complexity: Perhaps the difficulty young children have following explicitly taught rules has to do with there being two rules that involve two relations. Performance in the Zelazo rule-following studies is, in fact, quite similar to that in the embedded rule (extra box) tasks used by Smith et al.

Summary

Our review of the representational bases for reasoning reveals no compelling evidence of global shifts in inferential processes. Rather, consistent with our bricolage metaphor, we see a cascade of local increments. Changes in the five kinds of relations we have identified are inextricably linked.

Perceptual similarity among particular entities is the initial relation from which inferences are drawn, and it remains a vital basis of reasoning throughout life. With the development of conceptual knowledge, the kinds of similarity relations that afford reasoning expand. As knowledge broadens and deepens, more complex conceptual structures make it possible to detect structural similarity among perceptually dissimilar entities, thus permitting the use of analogy. Analogizing further enhances knowledge acquisition, as more knowledge is acquired and existing knowledge is reorganized. Increased knowledge is also responsible, at least in part, for the expansion of children's information processing capacity, which in turn makes possible more complex analogies. As the number of relations that can be represented and used together expands, symbolic relations become an increasingly potent basis for reasoning. The advent of symbol use liberates children's reasoning from direct experience, and the mastery of symbolic tools vastly expands the possible realms of reasoning. Similarly, regularities can be summarized together into rules that serve as the basis for further inferences. Rules provide mental economy, by encompassing in a single representation the relation between any number of variables. Through repeated use and reflection, these relational bases can become explicitly represented and even more powerful as a consequence.

Two points implicit in this summary should be made explicit. First, the same factors often constitute both the source and outcome of development. All the relations reviewed are simultaneously developmental products and processes.

There are core differences among these relations, but also a great deal of overlap at their boundaries. An example of overlap among all five relations is provided by De-Loache's (1995) research on young children's understanding of scale models. Perceptual similarity and conceptual knowledge both support children's reasoning from model to room. A symbolic relation is the basis for reasoning in this task, in that the scale model was designed and is used to stand for the room. However, inferring where the larger toy is hidden based on knowledge of the location of the miniature one could also be characterized as analogical reasoning: Mapping the relation between two elements in one space onto the relation between two elements in another space permits the crucial inference to be drawn. In addition, one could think of what the child represents in this task as a rule: "If the small toy is hidden in location x in the model, then the larger toy will be hidden in location x in the room."

This example illustrates that many of the distinctions we make about reasoning may be more in the mind of the researcher than in the mind of the child. It seems unlikely that some children in the scale model task are manipulating symbols, while others are doing analogies and still others are following rules. Thus, the inferential process itself may be the same once a relation between mental entities has been represented.

The young bricoleurs featured in this section use a variety of tools for reasoning, including analogies, symbols, and rules. We turn now to the area of research traditionally referred to as problem solving, in which heterogeneity is again a cardinal characteristic.

PROBLEM SOLVING

A problem-solving situation consists of a goal, one or more obstacles that make achieving the goal not immediately possible, one or (typically) more strategies that can be used to solve the problem, other resources (knowledge, other people, etc.) that can affect which strategies are used, and evaluation of the outcome of the problem-solving process. This chapter has emphasized the adaptive and goal-oriented nature of children's reasoning, so the distinction between reasoning and problem solving is neither clear nor principled. The research reviewed in this section emphasizes children's developing ability to adaptively marshal resources in pursuit of a goal and to monitor and evaluate their efforts toward achieving that goal. The bricolage metaphor provides a good characterization of problem solving throughout development. Children's problem solving is marked by flexibility and opportunism from an early age, but their performances are limited by the strategies they have access to, the resources available for problem solving, their ability to manage the process of solving problems, and the social contexts in which problems are presented and vanquished.

The adolescent's ingenious solution to the problem of leaf raking until lunchtime (Dumas, 1995) cited at the beginning of this chapter highlights several key aspects of problem solving. The father had a goal (getting the leaves raked without too much effort on his part) that he presented to his son. The son apparently had his own, different goals. Through the son's question, a small but critical change in the shared goal was negotiated, so that it became raking leaves until lunchtime. The goals of the father (getting the leaves raked) and the son (doing as little leaf raking as possible) differed significantly. From the strategies available, the son chose a solution (eating lunch at 10:40 A.M.) that accomplished his goal at the expense of

his father's. As this anecdote reminds us, problem solving often occurs in a social context in which the goals of various participants may differ, there typically are several strategies for achieving one's goals, and successful attainment of a goal requires management of the problem-solving process. In this case, the father failed to adequately monitor the process to ensure his goals were met; in other cases problem solvers may fail to solve problems either because they fail to plan their actions in advance or they fail to evaluate the outcome of those solution attempts.

The basic requirements of problem solving—goals, obstacles, strategies for overcoming obstacles, and evaluation of the results—appear very early in life. Evidence of goal-directed behavior appears within the first 6 months of life. Lewis, Alessandri, and Sullivan (1990) presented infants from 2 to 8 months of age with a task in which pulling a lever produced an interesting event (presentation of a color slide of a baby's face accompanied by a song). Even 2-month-olds quickly learned to pull the lever at twice the rate of nonreinforced infants. When lever-pulling no longer produced the interesting event, infants of all ages responded by decreasing the frequency of pulls and showing observable signs of anger.

The necessity of choosing among alternative problem-solving strategies also emerges early in life. Willats and Fabricius (1993) presented 18-month-olds with a task in which they had to choose which cloth to pull in order to obtain a desired toy. Three identical toys were aligned in a row out of direct reach, but only one toy was actually sitting on a cloth (and thus could be retrieved by pulling it). Infants showed a variety of scanning and reaching strategies, including pulling two cloths at the same time, and they shifted strategies often after both successful and unsuccessful trials. There was some evidence of adaptive choice among these strategies, although the strategy of pulling two cloths randomly was the only one for which infants were significantly more likely to switch after failure than after success. The variability of strategy use in this task illustrates two points about early problem solving: first, apparently simple problems such as identifying which cloth to pull to retrieve a doll can be quite complex; second, even young infants show some indication of opportunism in seizing on strategies that increase the likelihood they will achieve their goals.

While problem solving in its most basic form exists from very early in life, there are enormous changes with development in the scope and complexity of the problems children can solve. The development of problem solving can be characterized as the process of overcoming cognitive limitations to make problem solving more reliable, systematic, and efficient. Development of problem solving can be described in terms of changes in (a) the solution strategies children bring to bear, (b) the resources (knowledge, representational tools, etc.) children have available to them, (c) children's ability to plan and manage the solution process, and (d) the social contexts in which problem solving occurs. The following sections review each of these components of problem solving in turn.

Development of Problem-Solving Strategies

Knowledge-Lean Problem-Solving Strategies: Trial and Error, Means-End Analysis, and Hill-Climbing

Problem-solving strategies can be classified into those that are general across domains (termed *knowledge-lean* methods by Newell, 1990) and those tailored to the characteristics of particular domains (*knowledge-intensive* methods). Three examples of knowledge-lean problem solving—trial and error, means-end analysis, and hill-climbing—vary in the amount of cognitive overhead they impose (Wickelgren, 1974). Trial-and-error problem solving involves trying all possible strategies until one works. Trial-and-error problem solving requires only that one notice when the goal has been achieved. It is more efficient if one keeps track of which strategies have already been tried, but it does not require any analysis of which strategy would be most appropriate to solving a problem. The behavior of 2-month-olds in the contingent lever-pulling paradigm used by Lewis et al. (1990) is an example of basic trial-and-error learning. Infants presumably pulled the lever as part of their exploration of the environment, then noticed that pulling the level produced an interesting event. When the strategy no longer worked, infants changed their rate of pulling and showed signs of anger.

From early in life, children show evidence of knowledge-lean strategies that are more sophisticated than trial and error. Perhaps the prototype of a knowledge-lean method is means-end analysis (Newell & Simon, 1972). Means-end analysis requires that the problem solver evaluate the difference between the current situation and the goal, and then take action that reduces the difference between them. When, as is usually the case, the goal cannot be achieved directly, the problem solver can reason backward from the goal to set subgoals that will reduce the difference between the current state of affairs and the goal.

The example of 3-year-old Antoine (11) cited at the start of this chapter demonstrates means-end analysis resulting in the establishment of a new subgoal for problem solving. In that case, his mother was not tall enough to reach the balloon directly where it was stuck. Antoine therefore suggested a new subgoal, moving the balloon laterally far enough that it would float up to the top of the stairwell, where the primary goal—retrieving the balloon—could be achieved. Successful means-end problem solving requires knowledge about the problem domain and the kinds of actions that will achieve goals and subgoals, but the basic strategy of means-end analysis is one that is general across domains.

The basic ability to perform means-end action sequences appears some time after the middle of the first year of life. Nine-month-olds, but not 6-month-olds, pull on a cloth to retrieve an object placed out of reach on the end of the cloth (Willats, 1990). Failure to do so might reflect absence of means-end problem-solving ability, or as with adult problem solving, failure may reflect an inability to think of the relevant solution procedure. If accessing the solution is the problem, a hint concerning the proper procedure should be effective in improving performance (Ross, 1989). Following this logic, Kolstad and Aguiar (1995) have shown that hints dramatically improve infants' performance on this task. The hints did not have to demonstrate pulling the toy with the cloth; instead demonstration of a similar action sufficed. At age 6½ months, infants who watched an adult cover the toy with the cloth, then pull it away to reveal the toy, subsequently succeeded 58% of the time (compared with 8% for infants who did not see the hint), even though removing a cover is a different means-end sequence from pulling a cloth to bring the object within reach. Infants' ability to perform even the most basic means-end sequences is quite limited, but as with adults and older children, hints concerning useful means to a desired end can improve that performance substantially.

Means-end problem solving is difficult because of the cognitive load imposed by generating, ordering, and remembering subgoals, and then using these goals to regulate problem solving. The complexity of these processes is illustrated well in a study by Bullock and Lütkenhaus (1988) of the development of volitional behavior in children from 15 to 35 months of age. They looked at children's ability to perform the following tasks (chosen to be within their manual capacity) at an adult's request: stacking blocks to copy a house built by an adult, cleaning a blackboard, and placing blocks to cover a toy figure. Substantial developmental change was found across this period in children's ability to focus on the specific outcomes requested, organize a series of actions in the correct order, and to monitor their problem solving and make corrections where necessary. The youngest group, averaging 17 months old, engaged in relevant activities such as building something with the blocks, but attempts to achieve the specific goal (copying the model house) were not evident in most children until 26 months. Monitoring of performance also showed substantial development. At 17 months of age, 45% of children corrected the position of one block on at least one trial, but only 9% showed evidence of monitoring the overall outcome. By 26 months of age, 95% of children corrected the position of a single block, and 85% carefully stacked all the blocks on at least one tower building trial. Bullock and Lütkenhaus also measured an aspect of problem solving that is often overlooked, the affective reaction children showed on completing the tasks. There was a reliable increase with age in observable responses such as smiling or frowning after building the tower, from 36% in the 17-month-olds to 90% in the 32-month-olds. Although basic means-end problem solving can be found during infancy, this research shows that there is substantial development in the generality and flexibility of children's problem solving during the toddler years.

Means-end problem solving in adults is often studied with reference to puzzles that are unfamiliar and can vary in terms of the number and complexity of the subgoals that must be generated. One of the most commonly used tasks is the Tower of Hanoi puzzle, which consists of an apparatus with a row of three vertical pegs on which a series of disks varying in size may be placed. Solvers are required to move disks from an initial configuration to a final configuration, subject to the constraints that only one disk may be moved at a time and a larger disk may never be placed on top of a smaller disk. These constraints generally make it impossible to move directly to the goal state. Solving this puzzle efficiently thus requires means-end problem solving, because solvers must identify and achieve subgoals that will eventually put them in position to move directly to the goal. Piaget (1976) reported that younger subjects (5- and 6-year-olds in the examples cited) could not solve problems that required moving a three-disk tower to a different peg. He reported that they could successfully move two-disk towers "... but only after all sorts of attempts to get around the instructions and without being conscious of the logical links" (p. 288).

A more encouraging picture of children's ability to engage in means-end problem solving emerged from research by Klahr and Robinson (1981), who developed an engaging analog of the Tower of Hanoi problem shown in Figure 16.4. In their version, the major task constraint, that disks must be placed in order of size, was instantiated as a physical constraint by using cans of increasing diameter in place of disks. A smaller can cannot be placed on a larger can without falling off, simplifying the problem of discriminating legal from illegal moves. Klahr and Robinson looked at children's planning ability by asking participants to describe the entire sequence of moves they would make before beginning to move the cans.

Configurations differ in the complexity of solution sequences that must be considered. Tower-ending problems, in which the blocks end up stacked in a tower, are generally easier than Flat-ending problems, in which the blocks end up spread across the pegs, because in Tower-ending problems the rules of the game dictate that the largest disk must be put in place first. In Flat-ending problems it is unclear which disk must be positioned first, so there are additional potential moves making the problem more difficult. Klahr and Robinson found that configuration had a large effect on children's performance. For Tower-ending problems, most 5-year-olds and nearly all 6-year-olds could produce perfect four-move solutions, and most 6-year-olds could produce perfect six-move solutions; performance was noticeably worse on the Flat-ending

Figure 16.4 "Monkey cans" version of the Tower of Hanoi problem (Klahr & Robinson, 1982). Child is required to tell the experimenter how to move cans from the initial state (on the experimenter's side) to the goal state (on the child's side).

problems. Welsh (1991) administered a variant of the Tower of Hanoi task in which children did not have to describe their plans beforehand; she obtained somewhat better performance by younger subjects, but observed a similar pattern of deterioration in planfulness and in the adaptiveness of self-corrections as the number of moves increased, as well as a tendency of children at all ages to resort to simpler fall-back strategies for more complex problems. Across this age range, children show evidence of means-end problem solving, but there are important increases in the complexity of problems to which they are able to apply this approach.

Despite its generality, means-end problem solving can impose a daunting cognitive load, requiring children to reason backward from the goal to identify obstacles that stand in the way of achieving it, and then generate subgoals of removing those obstacles, repeating as necessary. Hill-climbing is a simpler knowledge-lean problem solving strategy that only requires the solver to reason forward from the current state in the direction of the desired goal. Hill-climbing requires choosing strategies that will move the solver closer to the goal, as in climbing a hill by continually taking the path that appears to lead upward fastest. Hill-climbing can result in the problem solver reaching a local maximum, that is, a state that does not reach the goal but is closer to it than all surrounding states, but it has the advantage of not requiring the solver to envision the entire path from the current state to the goal. Perhaps because of the cognitive overhead imposed by means-end analysis, hill-climbing appears to be a good characterization of the problem-solving behavior of preschoolers on unfamiliar problems. Klahr (1985) presented 4- to 6-year-old children with a puzzle in which they had to move a set of animals (dog, cat, and mouse) to their favorite foods (bone, fish, and cheese, respectively). Consistent with a hill-climbing strategy, the children preferred to (a) make moves that took them toward the goal, (b) avoid backing up (moving away from the goal state), and (c) look no more than two moves ahead.

The tendency to prefer hill-climbing strategies to the complexity of means-end analysis is not limited to children. Adults also resist making moves that appear to lead away from their ultimate goal (Mayer, 1992). Hill-climbing represents one way around the complexity of means-end analysis. Another way around the cognitive load imposed by means-end analysis and other knowledge-lean problem-solving procedures is to use domain-specific, knowledge-intensive strategies that take advantage of the specific content of problems to be solved to organize the problem-solving process. Because knowledge-intensive strategies

exploit the structure of specific domains, they do not generalize across domains. The repeated finding that both children and adults show substantial variability across different conceptual domains in the ability to solve formally identical problems (Bjorklund, Muir-Broaddus, & Schneider, 1990) indicates the importance of knowledge-intensive strategies in problem solving throughout development. A great deal of current research on children's problem solving reflects the importance of knowledge-intensive strategies by focusing on how children solve problems in particular content domains.

Strategies and Strategy Choice

Recent research on children's problem solving has demonstrated that children use a variety of strategies in solving problems, making adaptive choices among them. This new picture of children's strategy selection emerges largely from research that employs a microgenetic approach to understanding development (e.g., Kuhn, Schauble, & Garcia-Milas, 1992; Siegler & Crowley, 1991). Although the microgenetic methodology (Werner, 1948) is not new, there has been a resurgence in studies using this approach, characterized by (a) observations of individual children throughout a period of change, (b) a high density of observations relative to the rate of change in the process being studied, and (c) analyses of changes across these short intervals intended to reveal the process by which change is effected (Siegler & Crowley, 1991).

An example of this approach is Siegler's (1995) description of 5-year-old children's acquisition of number conservation. Piaget (1952) argued that the foundation for mathematical development is the realization that numerical relations are conserved across changes in the physical alignment of sets. Later studies have shown that preschool children possess a well-organized understanding of basic numerical relations well before they pass conservation tasks (R. Gelman, 1990). Number conservation would seem an unpromising setting in which to look at strategy diversity, because following a simple logical rule (only addition and subtraction of material affects amount) leads to correct performance.

Siegler (1995) gave nonconserving children training on number conservation tasks under three training conditions. One group received feedback concerning whether responses were correct or not without further elaboration. A second group of children received feedback and were also asked to explain their reasoning. A third group received feedback and then were asked to explain the experimenter's reasoning. The final condition was adapted from research by Chi and her colleagues, who have shown that effective college students are more active than other students in generating explanations for textbook examples of physics problems (Chi, Bassok, Lewis, Reimann, & Glaser, 1989), and that prompting eighth graders to generate such explanations while reading texts leads to improvements in understanding (Chi, de Leeuw, Chiu, & LaVancher, 1994).

As predicted, children who were asked to explain the experimenter's reasons for the correct judgments showed considerably more progress than did those in other conditions. One striking result of this study was the variability of explanations that children gave throughout the study (in the two conditions where explanations were solicited). Children used multiple types of explanation throughout the experiment, and those children who were required to explain the experimenter's reasons showed a greater variety than did those asked to explain their own reasons. Even when children began to give explanations based on the transformation involved (adding vs. rearranging), they tended not to immediately extend that justification to all kinds of problems.

This diversity of strategy use both between and within individuals is apparent in many domains. Siegler (1988) described individual differences in strategy choices among first graders performing simple arithmetic, including "perfectionist" children who tended to use backup strategies even on problems for which they could correctly retrieve the answer. Diversity of strategy use across different levels of expertise characterizes a number of other domains, from time-telling (Siegler & McGilly, 1989) to causal reasoning (Schultz, Fisher, Pratt, & Rulf, 1986). Diversity of strategies is also evident in cases where children represent contradictory information in their spoken and gestural communication, a phenomenon that characterizes children's behavior during a transitional state of knowledge acquisition (Goldin-Meadow, Alibali, & Church, 1993). Perry, Church, and Goldin-Meadow (1988) looked separately at the gestures and spoken statements of 9- to 10-year-old children solving problems that involve mathematical equivalence. Children showing mismatches between their gestures and speech were more likely to benefit from instruction than did those who did not.

One of the more intriguing findings from research on changes in children's strategy use is that success rather than failure often leads to strategy or representational change, arguing that necessity is not necessarily the mother of invention. Siegler and Jenkins (1989) reported this result in a microgenetic study of the discovery and generalization of the *min* strategy for adding two numbers. This strategy involves counting up from the larger of two addends to reach the sum, rather than starting from the number one and counting up both addends. They presented 4½- and 5-year-old children with concentrated experience in solving addition problems over a practice phase consisting of three sessions a week for 11 weeks. Children showed varied strategies for adding numbers, but there was no evidence that impasses led them to discover new strategies. Once the min strategy was discovered, however, it was particularly likely to be used on problems (such as 2 + 21) where it saved the most work.

Karmiloff-Smith (1984, 1992) reported a similar finding in studies of children's representational abilities in domains as diverse as balancing objects and making drawings. Karmiloff-Smith (1984, 1992) described a three-phase model of children's problem solving. The first step consists of a "procedural phase" in which children emphasize getting the correct outcome without concern for understanding. This is followed by a second "metaprocedural phase" in which the procedural representations learned in the first phase themselves become the object of interest as children become interested in understanding why a procedure works. This can cause temporary decreases in performance, as children emphasize consistency over correctness of judgments. The final step is a "conceptual phase," in which children combine the correct performances of the procedural phase with the organized understanding of the metaprocedural phase.

The persistence of strategy diversity is consistent with the *bricolage* metaphor in emphasizing the heterogenous nature of children's problem solving. This diversity makes it more difficult to characterize the development of problem solving. To a large extent, developmental change in strategy use is less a matter of global shifts from one strategy to another than it is a change in an overall ecology of strategies, with some approaches becoming more prevalent and others falling out of favor. Siegler (1996) has argued that variability in processing is adaptive in itself, and provides an important mechanism for developmental change. Diversity of strategies often predicts progress in later instruction (Alibali & Goldin-Meadow, 1993; Graham & Perry, 1993; Siegler, 1996). Variability in strategies may encourage children to explore why some approaches work and others do not, to learn the circumstances under which some approaches are useful, and to provide a repertoire of alternative strategies to respond to new problems.

With development, children show increased facility with both general problem-solving strategies and knowledge-intensive strategies that take advantage of the causal structure of particular domains. Even when children are familiar with strategies, they often fail to take advantage of them, in part because executing new strategies takes a great deal of effort (Flavell, Beach, & Chinsky, 1966; P. Miller, 1990). Another important source of developmental change in problem solving is changes in the resources children can bring to bear which will be considered next. These include factors such as expertise in particular domains and representational tools that can organize and simplify problem solving.

Developing Resources for Problem Solving

Expertise: Changes in the Knowledge Base

Familiar problem contexts and content facilitate problem solving from infancy. Acredolo (1979) demonstrated this with 9-month-old infants, who watched while an object was hidden under a cloth to their left or a cloth to their right. They were then moved to the opposite side of the table and allowed to search. If an object is hidden on their right, after infants are moved to the other side of the table, they will typically search in the location on their right, even though the correct location is now to their left. Infants tested in a landmark-free laboratory and an unfamiliar landmark-filled office demonstrated this pattern, but infants tested in their own homes did not. Seeing this task in a rich, familiar environment helped infants respond in terms of a nonegocentric spatial reference system.

Similar familiarity or knowledge effects have been found in many domains. Preschoolers' memory performance on list-learning tasks improves when these tasks are embedded in the context of a game that requires them to remember items on a grocery list in order to retrieve them from a "store" (Istomina, 1975; Schneider & Brun, 1987). For both adults and children, the problem-solving performance of those with experience in particular domains of knowledge can differ dramatically from that of novices. Furthermore, a large body of research indicates that the distinctive feature of expertise is the acquisition of a large and well-organized body of domain-specific knowledge (Bedard & Chi, 1992).

Developmentally, expertise-related differences have been advanced to account for some or all of the differences in problem solving and memory performance between children and adults. Chi (1978) demonstrated that child chess experts outperformed psychology graduate students in a chess recall task, but showed the expected poorer performance on a digit span task. Roth (1983) compared child and adult experts and novices on a chess board comparison task, finding that differences in expertise accounted for most of the time differences observed in performance. Schneider, Gruber, Gold, and Opwis (1993) replicated this finding that child chess experts outperform adult novices in recall of meaningful configurations. Schneider et al. also included adult experts, and found no age-related differences between the child and adult experts.

The phenomenon of expert knowledge being better organized than the knowledge of novices has been found in preschoolers as well. Chi and Koeske (1983) described the knowledge structure of one 4½-year-old dinosaur expert, showing that his knowledge was much more integrated and cohesive for familiar than for unfamiliar dinosaurs. Gobbo and Chi (1986) explored the dinosaur representations of a group of 7-year-olds classified as either dinosaur novices or experts. Supporting the view that knowledge is better organized in familiar domains, expert children used more connective information and used relevant features such as type of teeth and defensive armament to judge whether an unfamiliar dinosaur was a meat eater. McPherson and Thomas (1989) showed that tennis skill is associated with a similar change in representation of the variables relevant to tennis game decision making. Thus in many domains, experts can be identified by the amount and organization of their domain-relevant knowledge.

The basic finding that expertise in specific domains helps problem solvers overcome limitations in reasoning and problem solving holds up well for children as well as for adults. However, research on adult experts has revealed some important limitations in expert processing. In some domains, including clinical decision making, expert knowledge appears to have remarkably little impact on performance (Camerer & Johnson, 1991). Actuarial models based on expert evaluations of different symptoms consistently outperform the diagnoses of those same experts, in part because human beings are overly prone to make exceptions (Meehl, 1954). The claim that expert knowledge is limited to particular content domains is also coming under reevaluation. In one of the more dramatic examples, Lehman, Lempert, and Nisbett (1988) found that graduate training in different disciplines was associated with differential improvement on reasoning tasks. Graduate training in psychology, and to a lesser extent in medicine, resulted in improvement on statistical and methodological reasoning problems, such as understanding the effects of base rates and sample size on everyday phenomena. Graduate study in chemistry and law, however, produced no discernible improvement on these kinds of problems. Training in psychology, medicine, and law all produced improvement on conditional reasoning problems that tested participants' understanding of deductive reasoning.

Most developmental research on expertise has focused on demonstrations that expert knowledge can enable children to overcome processing limitations. With notable exceptions, there has been relatively little research on understanding the causes and consequences of expertise in childhood. An important exception is research by Ericsson and his colleagues (Ericsson, Krampe, & Tesch-Römer, 1993), whose studies of the development of elite performers in several domains have provided new descriptions of the processes and conditions under which expertise develops. In most domains of expertise, elite performers began during childhood a regimen of deliberate practice extending for a minimum of 10 years, with amount of practice the best and sometimes the only predictor of level of skill attained (Stigler, Chalip, & K. Miller, 1986). Incorporating research on expertise into an overall understanding of the role of domain-specific knowledge in reasoning and problem solving awaits further research on the cognitive, social, and motivational conditions that lead to the development of expert abilities, and an understanding of the impact of such knowledge on problem solving within and beyond the domain of expert knowledge (see Holyoak, 1991).

Cognitive Tools for Problem Solving

Problem solving occurs within a cultural context that includes cognitive tools that structure how problems are represented and solved (Vygotsky, 1978b). A child who wants to determine whether she will have to go to school on her birthday next year can consult a calendar, turning a formidable computational problem into a simple matter of looking up information. K. Miller and Paredes (1996) argue that there are three ways in which the structure of symbol systems such as numbers, calendars, and writing systems can affect the development of problem solving. First, mastering a symbol system is a prerequisite to using it in problem solving, and the structure of the system can have a major impact on the difficulty children have in acquiring it. Second, even after children have acquired a symbol system, its structure can continue to affect the process of solving problems. Finally, the organization of symbols can clarify or obscure the underlying conceptual structure of problems.

As an example of how symbol structure can affect its acquisition, K. Miller, Smith, Zhu, and Zhang (1995) showed that differences in consistency between English

and Chinese number names are reflected in differences in acquisition by children of the two number naming sequences. Both systems consist of an unpredictable sequence of names in the range 1–10 (i.e., having learned to count to four, there's no way to predict that the next number is five), and children show equivalent difficulty in acquiring number names in this range. After 10, Chinese follows a strict base-10 system of names (e.g., the name for 12 can be translated as "10–2," and the name for 24 as "2-10-4"). English, on the other hand has a complex system of names in the teens with unpredictable names for 11 and 12, and names in the range 13–19 that follow a different rule (smaller value named first, then larger one) than is used for larger two-digit numbers. This complexity in names is reflected in both overall difficulty in learning to count and in the kinds of errors children make in learning to count. These differences are quite large; at age 5 years, the median level of abstract counting (reciting the list of number names) was 100 for Chinese children compared with only 49 for U.S. children.

Once children have mastered a symbol system, its properties can continue to affect how it is used in problem solving. Kelly, Feng, and Fang (1995) looked at how differences in the formation of calendar names in Chinese and English would affect performance on a simple calendar calculation task. Chinese uses a numerical system for names for days of the week and months of the year; that is, the name for January can be translated as "1-month," and the name for Monday as "Weekday 1" (the only exception to this rule is the name for Sunday, which is nonnumerical). The numerical structure of the Chinese calendar could facilitate some kinds of calendar tasks, such as figuring out what month is 5 months from now. In order to see whether children take advantage of this numerical system in making time calculations, Kelly et al. asked children in Grades 2 and 4, as well as adults, to do calendar calculation tasks. Participants were asked to figure out the day that a plant would sprout (if it took 4 days to sprout) and the month when a plant would blossom (if it took 7 months to grow). These tasks were presented in both forward (e.g., If the plant is planted in March, when will it blossom?) and backward conditions (e.g., If the plant blossoms in March, when was it planted?). Results showed a dramatic difference in calculation speed across countries for all calculation tasks, with particularly big differences on the backward conditions. For the months backward task, Chinese fourth graders were faster than American college students. Chinese subjects reported using the numerical structure of the lists and U.S. subjects reported a variety of algorithms, with counting through the list the most common one. Thus, even after children master a symbol system its organization can continue to affect their use of these symbols in problem solving.

Symbolic tools can also affect problem solving by clarifying the relevant variables and relations that must be considered. Venn diagrams produce a physical representation of the logical relation of class-inclusion, potentially making it more accessible to reasoners. Agnoli (1991) demonstrated the efficacy of Venn diagrams for alerting children to the logical relations involved in class inclusion problems. Most of her Italian seventh graders initially judged that there would be more tanned women than women at the beach in the summertime. A training session in the use of Venn diagrams to represent inclusion and disjunction relationships led to a substantial drop in such errors for both sixth and eighth graders that was maintained in a later follow-up session. Symbolic tools for problem solving can have a significant developmental impact; because acquiring such symbolic tools is itself difficult, this effect will usually be to magnify differences between younger and older children, but teaching younger children symbolic problem-solving tools can be an effective way of increasing their competence.

Child as Manager: Developmental Changes in the Planning and Regulation of Problem Solving

Planning how to solve a problem and monitoring and correcting the solution process can themselves be difficult problems. By at least 5 years of age, children report planning in the context of recurrent daily actions, such as laying out clothes to put on in the morning (Kreitler & Kreitler, 1987). When confronted with more difficult problems, children often fail to show evidence of planning (Friedman, Scholnick, & Cocking, 1987). Failure to plan is not limited to children. In a difficult combination-of-liquids task, Pitt (1983) found that chemistry professors were much less likely to succeed in identifying the unknown liquid when allowed to conduct tests without planning than when forced to describe how they were going to test the liquids.

Ellis and Siegler (1997) summarized the reasons that children fail to plan a course of action before beginning problem solving: Planning entails delay and requires suppression of more activated procedures, it can be difficult and time-consuming, and there is no guarantee that it will be successful. Furthermore, there are social and pragmatic barriers to planning; children may assume that others will take care of planning and/or monitoring for them in a given situation (Goodnow, 1987).

In general, planning and regulation appear to constitute a late-emerging aspect of problem solving. In a survey of parents, Benson (1994) found that reports of planning lagged behind other future-oriented abilities such as anticipating events, with few reports of planning before 24 months of age. In some contexts, however, infants show evidence of monitoring problem solving. Fabricius and Schick (1995) reported that 18-month-olds self-corrected their errors in a task that required them to choose among routes around a barrier. DeLoache, Sugarman, and Brown (1985) found that children of the same age would attempt to correct their mistakes in a task requiring them to stack a set of nesting cups.

The extent to which young children plan and monitor their problem solving is greatly affected by factors such as the familiarity and complexity of the problem-solving task, the nature of children's participation in it, and the goals children bring to the problem-solving situation. Gauvain and Rogoff (1989) looked at organization and planning in a familiar setting using a problem-solving task that required children to retrieve a series of items from the shelves of a model grocery store. Most 5-year-olds engaged in an inefficient item-by-item search. By 9 years of age, however, children were more likely to scan through the entire store and then use their knowledge of object locations to organize a much more efficient search. In a variation of this task, Hudson and Fivush (1991) showed that 3-year-olds were able to show organized "shopping" under supportive conditions, where items were spatially organized and children only had to select items of a single type (e.g., breakfast items) at a time. Where children had to select items that met multiple criteria (e.g., breakfast and birthday party items), 3-year-olds often forgot their goals and failed to monitor their performance.

Although preschoolers can show rudimentary evidence of planning, they show little evidence of planning and monitoring of performance before age 5 years in more complex situations, such as the route-planning tasks of Fabricius (1988) in which children had to devise a route that would allow them to retrieve a series of objects without backtracking. In more complex tasks, such as planning a large party, substantial developmental change occurs even between adolescence and adulthood (Chalmers & Lawrence, 1993).

Variations in planning and regulation of problem solving across different contexts also emerge as a function of children's participation in the tasks. Hudson, Shapiro, and Sosa (1995) studied children's generalized event representations of familiar activities such as going to the beach or going grocery shopping, and also asked them how one might remedy various mishaps that might occur in these contexts, such as forgetting the grocery list. Although both situations are familiar to most children, most 3-year-olds were able to generate a plan to remedy the two beach mishaps (forgetting lunch or having your castle knocked down by a wave), but it was not until age 4 that most children could describe a plan to remedy two grocery shopping mishaps (forgetting the shopping list or not having enough money). Hudson et al. suggested that one factor accounting for the differences between the two events may be that children actively participate in more activities related to a trip to the beach than they do in the context of grocery shopping.

Another important reason for developmental differences in planning may be differences in the goals that subjects of different ages set. In deciding how much effort to expend on planning, children are quite sensitive to task demands. Gardner and Rogoff (1990) required 4- to 9-year-old children to solve mazes varying in difficulty, with instructions emphasizing either accuracy alone or both speed and accuracy. When presented with difficult mazes and instructions emphasizing accuracy alone, both younger and older children generated complete route plans before beginning to draw on the mazes. Given simple mazes, or instructions emphasizing speed as well as accuracy, children generally generated partial plans, executed them, and then corrected their mistakes. Planning and regulating problem solving is one of the more complex aspects of the problem-solving process, and often decreases as the complexity and unfamiliarity of tasks increase. Planning is also particularly likely to be embedded in social contexts, in part because complex problems of the sort that require explicit organization may also require group activity for solution. Furthermore, the necessity of organizing and coordinating group activity is likely to demand explicit planning. As with other aspects of reasoning, problem solving is greatly affected by the social contexts in which it occurs.

The Social Contexts of Problem Solving

In its most basic form, the ability to enlist others to help accomplish one's ends emerges very early in life. Mosier and Rogoff (1994), found that 6-month-olds attempted to use their mothers as means to desired ends, including using conventionalized gestures to request objects, often accompanied by attention-getting grunts. As children grow older, the complexity of the social regulation of problem solving increases apace.

The importance of social regulation of problem solving has been stressed in several models of cognitive development. Vygotsky (1978a) argued that cognitive change primarily occurs in the "zone of proximal development," defined as the distance between the child's capabilities as measured by independent problem solving and the level of performance possible with the guidance of an adult or an expert peer. This concept that a supportive environment promotes both cognitive functioning and cognitive development was also captured in Wood, Bruner, and Ross's (1976) description of scaffolding.

Group Problem Solving

Research on scaffolding indicates that in regulating children's problem solving (a) parents are quite sensitive to children's abilities and limitations, and (b) there are important differences between adults and children as promoters of cognitive change. From at least 2½ years of age, regulation of young children's problem-solving strategies by parents is contingent on the difficulties children face and is associated with both increased success and greater transfer to new problems (Pacifici & Bearison, 1991). A similar pattern was found for more complex planning tasks with older children. Mothers of 4-year-olds focused on clarifying task procedures and rules, whereas mothers of 8-year-olds stressed more general strategies (Gauvain, 1992).

Research on peers as tutors yields a more complex picture, with children generally being less effective tutors than adults. An important variable that seems to account for variation in results is the degree to which all members of the group actively participate in planning or problem solving. It is common for children to adopt a directive teaching style when tutoring younger peers, which may deny them the opportunity to plan independently (Ellis & Rogoff, 1986). In a cross-age design in which children were tutored either by their older siblings or by peers of the older children, Azmitia and Hesser (1993) found that siblings were more effective tutors than peers, because older siblings provided more explanations and positive feedback and gave learners more control of the task than did older peers. Also, the younger children were more active when paired with siblings than with older peers, asking more questions and asserting greater task involvement.

Active involvement can also be affected by the age of the tutor. Duran and Gauvain (1993) compared 7-year-old and 5-year-old experts as tutors of 5-year-old novices on a planning task. Children tutored by younger experts showed more involvement during the training task than did those tutored by older experts, and they were more successful in a posttest.

Teasley (1995) studied the role of talking in problem solving, asking dyads and individual fourth-graders to solve problems, with half of the children in each condition specifically required to work together and half requested not to talk as they worked on the problems. Children in the dyadic talk conditions generated better hypotheses than did those requested not to talk, although there was no difference between the talking and no-talking conditions for those who solved the problems individually. Radziszewska and Rogoff (1991) looked at dyadic problem solving by 9-year-olds in an errand planning task with three kinds of collaborators—novice peers, peers trained in errand planning, or untrained adults. The route planning by groups that contained either expert peers or adults was equally sophisticated, but groups including adults had more discussion of planning strategies and more involvement of the target child in the planning task, as well as better performance by the target child in an individual posttest. The critical variable across these studies appears to be the extent to which the tutored child takes an active role in the process of learning; this can be mediated by factors such as status and expertise differences between participants, the teaching style adopted by the tutor, and the tutor's skill in adjusting to the needs of the tutee.

Another important difference between peers and adults as tutors may be a consequence of the general tendency not to provide feedback in collaborative problem-solving studies. The tutored child may be unwilling to accept a peer's claims concerning the correct solution, but this problem is less likely to arise when the tutor is an adult. If this is the case, then combining peer tutoring with feedback concerning the correct answer should increase the effectiveness of peer tutoring. Ellis and Klahr (1993) conducted a collaborative problem-solving study looking at fifth graders' understanding of decimal fractions. Dyads who received feedback were more successful than either dyads who received no feedback or children who worked alone (whether or not they were given feedback). Working with a partner and receiving feedback was more likely to lead to generation of rules that were consistent with the feedback.

Cultural Differences in Problem Solving

Cultures may differ in extent to which they value planned versus spontaneous problem solving. Ellis and Schneiders (1989) argue that Navajo culture emphasizes planned and deliberative decision making, and this was echoed in their finding that Navajo third graders showed substantially more planning than their Anglo peers on novel segments of route-finding problems in both solitary and group conditions. Cultures also differ in the kinds of problem-solving responsibilities children are expected to take on at a given age. Studies of Japanese preschools (Peak, 1991; Tobin, Wu, & Davidson, 1989) emphasize the extent to which preschoolers are expected to resolve interpersonal problems, such as fights, on their own without adult intervention. More generally, Rogoff, Mistry, Göncü, and Mosier (1993) describe two main patterns of adult-child teaching, distinguishing the teaching model in which children are segregated in special learning environments from an apprenticeship model in communities where children are integrated into adult activities and can learn adult roles through active observation and guided participation in those activities. Rogoff et al. (1993) conducted a cross-cultural study of toddler-caregiver interaction in a Mayan Indian village in Guatemala, a tribal village in India, and middle-class urban neighborhoods in Turkey and the United States. They reported that the problems children confronted and the management of teaching by adults varied as a function of type of community organization. Parents in the middle-class neighborhoods tended only to provide instruction and assistance in special teaching situations, whereas parents in the other communities were more consistent in providing support across all the problem situations that were presented.

Cultures also differ in the kinds of problems that are presented to children at different ages. In a large-scale study of the contexts of academic achievement in Taiwan, Japan, and the United States, Stevenson et al. (1990) found that mothers reported children in Chinese elementary school spent about four times as much time on homework as their U.S. peers, and more than twice as much as Japanese children of the same age. American parents were much more likely to report that their children had assigned chores to do at home than were parents in either of the Asian countries. Hatano (1990) argued that, in the same way that countries can have national sports that are valued above other athletic activities, countries can also vary in those national intellectual pursuits in which success is particularly valued. Cross-cultural variation in the value placed on the ability to solve different kinds of problems, and beliefs in the appropriateness of particular problem-solving situations for children of a given age results in variation in children's opportunities to learn to solve particular kinds of problems, which is in turn an important variable in the development of problem-solving abilities.

From early in infancy, children's problem solving is marked by efforts to adapt available resources to achieve their ends. Like Lévi-Strauss's bricoleur, the young problem solver faces important limitations in experience, knowledge, and the cognitive tools available for solving problems. The general processes of using these resources to overcome problems appears to be constant across development, but changes in the resources available for problem solving and in the child's ability to use and manage these resources can lead to enormous developmental differences in problem-solving competence.

SCIENTIFIC REASONING

Scientific reasoning is an appropriate final topic in this chapter, because the development of scientific reasoning incorporates all the major themes previously considered, particularly the tension between normative models of reasoning and the more complex, heterogenous thinking processes characterized as bricolage. The term *scientific reasoning* is used in two different ways. Scientific reasoning can refer to an idealized model of thinking, typically the hypothetico-deductive method described by Popper (1962). In this model, scientists generate rival hypotheses that are evaluated by critical experiments, the results of which lead directly to the rejection of some hypotheses and the formation and modification of theories. In addition to this normative sense of the term scientific reasoning, it can also refer to the larger set of processes by which human beings (from children to scientists) reason about the regularities and causal structure of the natural world.

An apt historical example of the differences between the two senses of "scientific reasoning" comes from Bradshaw's (1992) analysis of the invention of the airplane. Bradshaw argues that the process of invention engaged in by the Wright brothers differed in a fundamental way from that of their many competitors. The Wright brothers' competitors took a classic *bricolage* approach, in which they constructed many models that varied along many dimensions; after testing a plane they typically made multiple changes along many dimensions in producing their next model. In so doing, they adopted what Bradshaw termed a *design-space* search, in which there were nearly 13 million possible combinations of design options to be considered.

The Wright brothers, on the other hand, adopted a *function-space search,* which is similar to what a classical model of scientific reasoning would recommend. They analyzed the problems that a plane must solve, such as lift, lateral control, and propulsion. Each of these problems could then be attacked in isolation. In contrast to the multiple models their rivals built (e.g., Langley tested over 30 different models), the Wright brothers built only three models before making their successful airplane. Function-space searches can still be laborious, and, indeed, the Wright brothers tested over 80 different wing shapes in their wind tunnel. This approach is still vastly more efficient than the alternative, because it avoids the need to test each wing shape in combination with each propulsion option.

Two lessons can be drawn from Bradshaw's description of the different thought processes used by the Wright brothers and their competitors. The first is that the classical hypothesis testing model is very powerful: The Wright brothers' method of invention closely resembles an ideal model of scientific reasoning and their success demonstrates the power of that approach. The second lesson, though, concerns the rarity of this approach. The fact that the Wright brothers' achievement was so exceptional cautions against using their methods as a basis for describing ordinary reasoning about scientific problems. Scientific reasoning in this sense can be viewed as something of an unnatural act that requires considerable cognitive sophistication to accomplish (Kuhn, Amsel, & O'Loughlin, 1988).

Scientific reasoning as practiced by the Wright brothers' rivals fits the bricolage metaphor quite well. Reasoning about the natural world by both children and working scientists involves a complex *mélange* of goals for understanding, analogies from other domains of experience, theories that differ in their scope and sophistication, procedural tools for exploring a domain and generating evidence that can be used to evaluate theories, and processes for defending and revising theories in the face of conflicting evidence. Development can occur in all these aspects of scientific reasoning, which furthermore can differ across different conceptual domains. Research on the development of scientific reasoning processes and on changes in children's understanding of the natural world will be reviewed in turn.

Developing Processes of Scientific Reasoning: The Child as Experimenter

Distinguishing between Theory and Evidence

At the heart of scientific reasoning lies a set of processes for forming a harmonious relationship between evidence and theories (Kuhn, 1989). They include processes involved in generating experiments to discriminate between different theoretical beliefs and in modifying theories when they do not conform to data.

Kuhn and her colleagues (Kuhn et al., 1988) have studied the development of understanding the relation between theory and evidence in tasks involving the covariation of multiple variables in determining some outcome. For example, they presented a hypothetical experiment involving the relation between eating different foods and catching colds to sixth graders, ninth graders, philosophy graduate students, and a group of adults of varying ages and educational experiences. Participants were initially interviewed to determine which foods they thought were associated with getting colds. Based on this interview, pairings between foods (e.g., baked potato vs. French fries) and outcomes (healthy vs. sick) were constructed for individual participants. The pairings included two foods that covaried perfectly with outcome (one that was consistent with the participant's initial belief, and one that conflicted with it), as well as two that were independent of outcome (one that the participant believed was related to colds, and one that he or she believed was not). Data concerning effects of food on health were presented in a series of pictures. Each contained a group of either sick or healthy children surrounded by a set of four food choices depicting their diet. After each card was presented, the participants were asked to judge whether each food item was associated with getting colds. This was followed by a probe question asking how the participant knew that a food did or did not have an effect (or why he or she couldn't tell), and, if needed, a probe in which participants were explicitly asked how the evidence presented indicated that a food did or did not cause colds.

Of particular interest was the extent to which the participants produced explanations that explicitly took the evidence into account (e.g., "Tomato soup doesn't matter because it's with healthy children here and sick children here"), as opposed to simply drawing on their personal experience (e.g., "The liver makes you healthier, because when I eat pork I get sick"), or other extra-experimental beliefs ("The juice makes a difference because my mother says orange juice is better for you"). As more evidence was presented, all adults made at least some spontaneous evidence-based responses, but 30% of the sixth graders never produced spontaneous evidence based responses.

Children were less likely than adults to spontaneously refer to the experimental evidence, but the probe questions were sufficient to eliminate differences in overall frequency of evidence-based responses (but not to eliminate all differences; the children still made more inappropriate inferences from the evidence). Thus, children could evaluate the evidence when it was called to their attention. This study also suggested important differences related to expertise. Although data from the philosophy graduate students were not included in the statistical analyses, the difference between them and other adult subjects on many of the measures was nearly as great as that between the sixth graders and the nonphilosopher adults.

Kuhn et al. (1988) argue that systematic scientific reasoning emerges so late in life because it requires metareasoning, in which children must think *about* theories rather than only thinking *with* them, to represent evidence as an entity separate from a theory, and to reason hypothetically about the implications of particular pieces of evidence for that theory. When children fail to integrate theory and evidence, they often fall back on one of two simpler approaches. Kuhn (1989) characterized some children as "theory-bound investigators," who were so bound to their original theories that they failed to attend to evidence or generate useful evidence. Given conflicts between theory and evidence, theory-bound children frequently adjusted the evidence to maintain a fit between theory and evidence. Other children take a "data-bound" approach, failing to organize evidence into an integrated theory, focusing instead on explaining local patterns of isolated results.

The idea that difficulty in integrating evidence and theory is the stumbling block in scientific reason lies at the heart of a model of scientific reasoning developed by Klahr and Dunbar (1988). In this model, integrating theory and evidence is described in terms of coordinating a dual search in two cognitive spaces, hypothesis space and experiment space. In the hypothesis space, reasoners must explore potential explanatory hypotheses that vary in their plausibility and consistency. In the experiment space, reasoners must design experiments that will be informative in ruling out potential hypotheses. Klahr, Fay, and Dunbar (1993) described developmental changes in children's exploration of a computerized microworld, in which participants had to determine the effect of programming commands on a tank that could move, turn, and fire. In one task, participants had to develop experiments to figure out what a command ("RPT N") might mean, and they were asked to test hypotheses that previous research had shown were viewed as either plausible ("Repeat the last command N times") or implausible ("Repeat the Nth step once"). In contrast to adults, third and sixth graders conducted a limited set of experiments and designed experiments that were often difficult to interpret. When presented with the implausible hypotheses, younger children tended to ignore them and instead generate a more plausible one, then concentrate on collecting evidence to confirm this new hypothesis. Adults were much better than children at organizing their search through these dual cognitive spaces of experiments and hypotheses, systematically pruning the range of possibilities to be explored.

The extent of consistency across domains in children's developing scientific reasoning ability was assessed in a microgenetic study by Kuhn, Garcia-Mila, Zohar, and Andersen (1995), in which adults and preadolescent children were presented with scientific reasoning problems in a context designed to assess transfer of knowledge to a new domain. Two problems involving relations among variables were designed for both a physical domain (determining what factors affect the speed of a car and of a boat moving through water) and a social domain (determining what factors affect student achievement in school and what determines children's ratings of television shows). Participants explored one problem from each domain for 10 sessions, then switched to a new problem in each domain. The view that participants were learning general processes of scientific reasoning was supported by the finding of substantial transfer to new problems, particularly among the adults.

Although feedback in experiments is typically perfect, learning in the context of noisy feedback was described in a microgenetic study by Schauble (1996). In this study, fifth through sixth graders and noncollege adults conducted experiments over 6 half-hour sessions to explore the causal structure of two physical science domains. The first task required participants to determine the factors that affect the movement of immersed objects through fluids. The second task involved objects suspended from springs and lowered into fluids; participants were required to determine the factors that affect spring extension. Both children and adults improved, but the adults substantially outperformed the child participants.

Across all these studies, a number of important similarities in children's design and interpretation of experiments emerged. First, children had a great deal of difficulty designing informative experiments, often varying every factor between consecutive trials in a manner that made it impossible to draw conclusions. Second, children focused on cases where a factor was associated with a positive outcome (a fast boat or a good serve), neglecting cases where it was associated with a negative result. Klayman and Ha (1987) have argued that even adults show a general positive test strategy, tending to focus on instances expected to have the property of interest at the expense of those expected to lack it. The results of the studies reviewed suggested that some fundamental aspects of scientific reasoning are common across content domains, and that the ability to correctly design and properly interpret a scientific experiment is a very late-developing cognitive skill.

Contexts in Which Children Distinguish between Theory and Evidence

Although children (and often adults) have great difficulty testing relations between theory and evidence, there are some contexts in which much younger children properly distinguish theory and evidence. Sodian, Zaitchik, and Carey (1991) demonstrated that at least by the second grade, children can coordinate simple beliefs and the evidence required to test those beliefs. They asked children how they could determine the size of a mouse based on the size of box it could enter. Children were shown two food-containing mouse boxes with large and small openings, respectively, and asked a series of questions about which box to use if they wanted to find out the size of the mouse as opposed to just feeding it, as well as about what could be concluded from evidence that the mouse had visited one or the other of the boxes. Fifty-five percent of first graders and 86% of second graders both selected the appropriate box and gave logical justifications for their choice. A later study by Ruffman, Perner, Olson, and Doherty (1993) also demonstrated impressive understanding of the process of evidence interpretation in preschoolers. They found that 81% of 5-year-olds could correctly determine a simple correlation (eating red food and tooth decay); the children also understood that someone who saw a different relation (eating green food causing tooth decay) would draw a different conclusion.

There are at least two critical differences between contexts in which young children demonstrate successful scientific reasoning and those in which they do not. Preadolescent children do particularly badly when they are required to act as principal investigators, generating their own experiments and producing their own hypotheses. They also have a very hard time accepting or even exploring hypotheses that seem implausible. These findings suggest specific limitations in children's experimental abilities and the relatively late development of the ability to generate informative experiments. The second difficulty, which has to do with testing implausible hypotheses, may result from a heuristic response to the difficulty of generating experiments. A simple way of pruning down the hypothesis space is to rule out implausible hypotheses a priori. This may represent a rational strategy of maximizing the use of limited cognitive resources, but it results in very poor performance in situations where initially implausible hypotheses turn out to be correct.

The Content of Children's Scientific Beliefs: The Child as Theorist

Children's Theories and Scientists' Theories

Looking at the content of children's beliefs about the natural world, rather than their ability to design experiments and to reason scientifically, reveals a mixed developmental picture. Children possess beliefs that are often substantially at variance with adult theories, although the processes they use in forming and revising these beliefs resemble those of adults in important ways. Carey (1992) has argued that children's and adults' theories are often incommensurable, with different understandings of basic scientific terms. An important example is the distinction between material and immaterial entities. Although both adults and school-age children understand that objects such as wood and water are material things that take up space, a majority of first graders include air as an immaterial substance that takes up no space at all. Given such differences, part of developmental change in scientific understanding consists of redefining and differentiating the terms of scientific discourse, a process that occurred in the history of science as well as in individual development (Wiser & Carey, 1983).

In reviewing children's scientific theories, we will generally focus on their developing understanding of biology. To have a scientific theory, one must define the domain over which that theory applies (e.g., Wellman & S. Gelman, 1992). Hatano and Inagaki (1994) argued that there are three components to naive biological knowledge. First, it must specify the domain of biology, which requires a distinction between living and nonliving things, as well as a mind-body distinction. Second, there must be some way to infer the attributes and behaviors of biological entities. Third, children must develop a nonintentional causal framework to understand the mechanisms of biological change. They argue that children develop this model from many sources, including personal experience and models provided by their culture.

Carey (1985) suggested that children's biological models develop out of an earlier, psychologically based framework. In her view, 4- and 5-year-olds have a theory of biology that is based largely on psychological characteristics, in which similarity between a particular animal and human beings is an important criterion for deciding whether or not some property applies to a particular animal. By 10 years of age, children have developed distinct theories of biology and psychology.

More recent research, however, has indicated that even young children are not limited to similarity-based judgments of biological concepts. Rosengren, Gelman, Kalish, and McCormick (1991) showed that even 3-year-olds expect animals but not objects to change in size over time. Keil (1992) has shown that providing 4-year-olds additional context about why humans do certain things (e.g., we eat in order to live and grow) can lead them to make biologically based judgments.

Cultural factors appear to play some role in children's initial biological beliefs. Hatano et al. (1993) explored the relation between culture and early biological concepts. They studied understanding of the characteristics of humans, other animals, plants, and inanimate objects among kindergarten, 2nd-, and 4th-grade children in Israel, Japan, and the United States, asking questions such as whether a tulip could feel sad. They noted that a combination of attitudinal and linguistic factors might lead Japanese children to be more accepting of the attribution of animate characteristics to plants and even to inanimate objects than their U.S. peers, and Israeli children to draw a stricter distinction between animals and other entities (i.e., both plants and nonliving objects). Consistent with these cultural/linguistic patterns, they found that Japanese children were most likely to attribute properties possessed by living things to inanimates, and Israeli children were the most likely to fail to attribute to plants qualities shared by all living things. Thus, in forming initial biological concepts children appear to be sensitive to classifications that are implicit in their culture and language.

Where valid biological inferences cannot be drawn from cultural models or direct experience, development involves moving away from early inferences based on these sources. An interesting example is children's developing differentiation between real and impossible transformations. Rosengren, Kalish, Hickling, and Gelman (1994) reported that parents encourage children to believe in the reality of magical figures. Four- and 5-year-olds draw a clear distinction between possible and impossible biological changes.

They do not invoke magic as an explanation for biological changes; they tend to reject as impossible changes such as metamorphosis that lead to enormous changes in appearance. Nonetheless, most children believe that a magician can accomplish even impossible biological changes.

Taken together, these studies suggest that very young children do possess non-similarity-based biological concepts, but these concepts must compete with an alternative similarity-based system. Hatano and Inagaki (1994) concluded that children possess the framework for a domain of biology by the time of school entry. These early frameworks set the stage for later development, which largely consists of fleshing out these models by learning the specific mechanisms that account for biological change.

Theory Change in Children and Adults

Continuity between scientific reasoning by children and adults has been emphasized by Brewer and his colleagues in a different domain (Brewer & Samarapungavan, 1991; Vosniadou & Brewer, 1992). They have shown remarkable misconceptions on the part of children at the same time that both children and adult scientists respond in similar ways to anomalies between their beliefs and experience. In their research on children's cosmological beliefs, Vosniadou and Brewer (1992) found that a large number of elementary school-age children have models of the earth's shape and motion that are strikingly deviant from normative descriptions. Many of these deviant models originate in children's attempt to reconcile their daily experience of living on an apparently flat world with the information provided by adults that the earth is a round planet. Among children's cosmological theories are beliefs that the earth is shaped like a hollow hemisphere, a rectangle, a flattened sphere or a disk or, most strikingly, a "dual earth" position which distinguishes between a flat surface ("the world") and a spherical planetary body ("the earth") floating somewhere above us in space. This view can be diagnosed by asking children to point to the earth; children who hold this view are likely to point upward!

Vosniadou and Brewer note that children's naive cosmological beliefs resemble models developed by adult thinkers of earlier eras, and argue that they represent resolutions, termed "synthetic models," between apparently contradictory assertions about the astronomical world. The dual earth model, for example, preserves the proposition that the earth is a round planet against the experience that the world is a roughly flat place by distinguishing the entities to which these contradictory propositions apply.

Chinn and Brewer (1993) have argued that the processes by which children respond to anomalies between theory and data are quite similar to responses to anomalous data found in the history of science. They identified seven responses to anomalous data: ignoring, active rejection, exclusion, holding it in abeyance, reinterpreting the data, making a peripheral change to the theory, or making a major theory change. They argue that both children and adult scientists engage in the same processes of trying to defend their beliefs against apparently contradictory data and show the same reluctance to make major theoretical changes. A classic example of holding data in abeyance comes from Karmiloff-Smith and Inhelder's (1975) study of children's attempts to balance blocks on their center of gravity. Some blocks had a hidden weight implanted so their center of gravity did not correspond to their geometric center. Many 6- and 7-year-old children, who believed that things balance in the center, simply rejected the weighted blocks as being impossible to balance, without modifying their belief that objects balance in the center.

The general processes of theory change, and the general tendency to resist change, appear to be part of development from early childhood. Whether there are essential changes in children's ability to relate theory and evidence is a matter of continuing controversy. Those who have studied children's ability to generate and interpret experiments have emphasized the dramatic changes between middle childhood and adulthood in the ability to organize and manage the process of scientific reasoning. Those who have studied children's preexisting scientific concepts have tended to emphasize the continuity of processes by which children and adults develop theories based on observations and reluctantly change them in response to contradictory experience.

Summary

Drawing evidence-based conclusions about causal relationships is the essence of scientific reasoning. For both children and adults, Popperian hypothetico-deductive scientific reasoning is a difficult activity, often simplified through heuristic processes (such as focusing on positive evidence) that can lead to erroneous conclusions. From an early age, children show at least a rudimentary ability to distinguish between theory and evidence and they organize their understanding of the world into models that bear important resemblances to scientific theories. Children respond to evidence that contradicts their beliefs in ways similar to adults. Their ability to systematically organize experiments that will verify their beliefs is quite limited, however, and children are more likely than adults to improperly interpret the results of such experiments.

The analogy between child and scientist can be overdrawn (Harris, 1994; Kuhn, 1989). Adult scientists are capable of reflection on their theories in ways that children are not. Scientific reasoning by children and adults may be well characterized as bricolage, but the example of the Wright brothers and their competitors points out the limitations of that mode of thinking. As Harris (1994) summarized this point, ". . . the theoretical consistency, parsimony, and progress that we take to be the hallmark of a mature scientific discipline is achieved despite and not because of any similarities between the cognitive processes of children and scientists" (p. 313).

CONCLUSION

To conclude this chapter, we return to the metaphor of reasoning as bricolage, or cognitive tinkering. The bricoleur adaptively employs a diverse set of procedures, processes, and strategies as tools in the pursuit of reasoning and problem-solving goals. Different tools are available at different ages, but at every age people use a variety of cognitive tools to cope with limited resources. One will always encounter problems that exceed memory capacity, domain knowledge, relevant strategies, and so forth. Extremely young reasoners have extremely limited resources compared with older reasoners, but they are often trying to solve different—usually easier—problems with more social support while doing so.

Inherent in the bricolage metaphor is an emphasis on the diversity and continuity of development. It is antithetical to any monolithic, normative view of reasoning, that is, the idea that the forces of development march single file toward one most mature, eventually dominant mode of thought. Instead, reasoning is at every age including adulthood characterized by heterogeneity, even within individuals. Thus, across domains, children will sometimes make judgments based primarily on perceptual similarity and sometimes not, and they will sometimes reason by analogy and sometimes not, depending on their knowledge in the different areas. Within a domain, and even on a given problem, a child is likely to employ a diverse set of more and less sophisticated strategies.

The bricolage metaphor is incompatible with a position that posits discontinuity or stages in development. In the literature reviewed here, we see little evidence of omnibus qualitative changes in reasoning and problem solving. There are certainly large, important changes in the resources available at different ages, and hence in the way individuals perform. However, we see more heterogeneity, from the individual to the cultural level, than can be comfortably accommodated by universal stages.

With respect to domain-general versus domain-specific aspects of development, the bricolage metaphor encompasses both. Some of the tools in the bricoleur's box are widely applicable. Reasoning by analogy is helpful in any domain, and literacy probably affects the course of development in most. Other tools, processes, and procedures are specific to particular domains. The min strategy is important in early arithmetic, but nothing else, and map-reading skills are applicable only to spatial problems.

Reasoning becomes more powerful as the bricoleur develops new and improved resources, many of which are both the product and the source of development. Increments in domain knowledge produce a cascade of effects. With increasing knowledge, conceptual relations among entities provide a supplement or an alternative to perceptual similarity. More comprehensive and coherent theories support children's scientific reasoning (although preconceptions can also have negative effects on hypothesis testing and evaluation). More knowledge begets even more knowledge, as adequate knowledge in a domain enables children to reason by analogy, thus discovering new relations both within the domain and between it and other ones. Repeated analogizing leads to more abstract and hence more powerful representations (Gentner & Rattermann, 1991; Halford, 1992).

Increasing knowledge about the process of reasoning and problem solving—metareasoning—is a particularly powerful source of further development. Older children and adolescents can reflect on their own reasoning processes and consciously select more efficient and more powerful ones (Kuhn et al., 1992). Similar effects occur for young children, who learn from experience a mind-set to look for analogies (Brown & Kane, 1988) or who become increasingly sensitive to potential symbolic relations (Marzolf & DeLoache, 1994). Metareasoning is especially important in formal logical reasoning (Moshman, Ch. 19, this Volume) in which the reasoner must understand the need to ignore problem content and put aside prior world knowledge and preconceptions.

The generation of new strategies and the selection of more effective and efficient ones is a crucial developmental phenomenon. The strategy selection process is twofold, involving both increased reliance on successful strategies and also the ability to inhibit others. Throughout development, new more powerful approaches can become dominant only to the extent that old, less powerful ones are relinquished. Giving up an old strategy is often the most difficult part of developmental progress (Kuhn & Phelps, 1982). As Siegler (1988) has emphasized, we rarely abandon earlier strategies completely; problem solvers typically bring to bear a mix of strategies of varying efficacy and appropriateness.

The diversity of available tools expands as the bricoleur masters the various symbol systems of his or her culture, opening up whole new arenas of reasoning and problem solving. Calculus affords generating and solving problems not amenable to finger counting. Understanding the representational nature and informational capacity of visual media liberates the child from reliance on direct experience for learning.

An additional resource exploited by bricoleurs is the social context. We have repeatedly emphasized how input, support, and guidance from other people is a major factor in reasoning and problem solving at every stage of development, from the effect of saying a word on infants' assumptions about word meaning to the role of cultural factors in early concepts. What we wish to emphasize here is that the social context "develops" along with the child. The increasing importance of peers in the child's life creates new problems to be solved, new strategies for solving them, and a dramatically altered social context for cognition. As children become more competent, adults place increasing demands on them, hold them to higher standards, and give them more difficult problems. The degree and kind of scaffolding and social support change as well, as parents and teachers implicitly target their interventions to the child's current zone of proximal development. In addition, different tools and resources are supplied as the child develops: Bedtime storybook reading is replaced by help with homework; nesting cups are supplanted by computers.

ACKNOWLEDGMENTS

We thank Renée Baillargeon, Shari Ellis, Cynthia Fisher, David Klahr, Karl Rosengren, Brian Ross, Linda Smith, and Sandra Waxman for providing helpful comments on earlier versions of the manuscript. We also thank Deanna Kuhn and Robert Siegler for their great patience and many helpful suggestions.

REFERENCES

Acredolo, L. P. (1979). Laboratory versus home: The effect of environment on the 9-month-old infant's choice of spatial reference system. *Developmental Psychology, 15,* 666–667.

Adams, M. J. (1990). *Beginning to read: Thinking and learning about print.* Cambridge, MA: MIT Press.

Agnoli, F. (1991). Development of judgmental heuristics: Training counteracts the representativeness heuristic. *Cognitive Development, 6,* 195–217.

Alibali, M. W., & Goldin-Meadow, S. (1993). Gesture-speech mismatched mechanisms of learning: What the hands reveal about a child's state of mind. *Cognitive Psychology, 25*(4), 468–523.

Azmitia, M., & Hesser, J. (1993). Why siblings are important agents of cognitive development: A comparison of siblings and peers. *Child Development, 64,* 430–444.

Baillargeon, R. (1993). The object concept revisited: New directions in the investigation of infants' physical knowledge. In C. E. Granrud (Ed.), *Visual perception and cognition in infancy: Carnegie Mellon Symposia on Cognition.* Hillsdale, NJ: Erlbaum.

Baldwin, D. A. (1989). Priorities in children's expectations about object label reference: Form over color. *Child Development, 60,* 1291–1306.

Barkow, J. H., Cosmides, L., & Tooby, J. (Eds.), (1992). *The adapted mind.* New York: Oxford University Press.

Bartlett, F. (1958). *Thinking.* New York: Basic Books.

Becker, A. H., & Ward, T. B. (1991a, April). *Children's use of shape and texture with objects and substances.* Paper presented at the 1991 biennial convention of the Society for Research in Child Development, Seattle, WA.

Becker, A. H., & Ward, T. B. (1991b). Children's use of shape in extending novel labels to animate objects: Identity versus postural change. *Cognitive Development, 6,* 3–16.

Bedard, J., & Chi, M. T. H. (1992). Expertise. *Current Directions in Psychological Science, 1,* 135–139.

Beilin, H., & Pearlman, E. G. (1991). Children's iconic realism: Object vs. property realism. In H. W. Reese (Ed.), *Advances in child development and behavior* (Vol. 23). New York: Academic Press.

Benson, J. B. (1994). The origins of future orientation in the everyday lives of 9- to 36-month-old infants. In M. Haith, J. B. Benson, R. J. Roberts, Jr., & B. F. Penington (Eds.), *The development of future-oriented process.* Chicago: University of Chicago Press.

Bialystok, E. (1991). Letters, sounds, and symbols: Changes in children's understanding of written language. *Applied Psycholinguistics, 12,* 75–89.

Bjorklund, D. F., Muir-Broaddus, J. E., & Schneider, W. (1990). The role of knowledge in the development of strategies. In D. F. Bjorklund (Ed.), *Children's strategies.* Hillsdale, NJ: Erlbaum.

Bluestein, N., & Acredolo, L. P. (1979). Developmental changes in map-reading skills. *Child Development, 50,* 691–697.

Bornstein, M. H. (1985). Human infant color vision and color perception. *Infant Behavior & Development, 8,* 109–113.

Bradshaw, G. (1992). The airplane and the logic of invention. In R. N. Giere (Ed.), *Cognitive models of science: Vol. 15. Minnesota studies in the philosophy of science.* Minneapolis: University of Minnesota.

Braine, M. D. S., & O'Brien, D. P. (1991). A theory of *If:* A lexical entry, reasoning program, and pragmatic principles. *Psychological Review, 98,* 182–203.

Brewer, W. F., & Samarapungavan, A. (1991). Children's theories vs. scientific theories: Differences in reasoning or differences in knowledge? In E. R. Hoffman & D. S. Palermo (Eds.), *Cognition and the symbolic processes: Applied and ecological perspectives.* Hillsdale, NJ: Erlbaum.

Brown, A. L. (1989). Analogical learning and transfer: What develops? In S. Vosniadou & A. Ortony (Eds.), *Similarity and analogical reasoning.* Cambridge, England: Cambridge University Press.

Brown, A. L., & Kane, M. J. (1988). Preschool children can learn to transfer: Learning to learn and learning from example. *Cognitive Psychology, 20,* 493–523.

Brown, A. L., Kane, M. J., & Long, C. (1989). Analogical transfer in young children: Analogies as tools for communication and exposition. *Applied Cognitive Psychology, 3,* 275–293.

Bullock, M., & Lütkenhaus, P. (1988). The development of volitional behavior in the toddler years. *Child Development, 59,* 664–674.

Camerer, C. F., & Johnson, E. J. (1991). The process-performance paradox in expert judgment: How can experts know so much and predict so badly? In K. A. Ericsson & J. Smith (Eds.), *Toward a general theory of expertise: Prospects and limits.* New York: Cambridge University Press.

Campbell, R., & Olson, D. (1990). Children's thinking. In R. Grieve & M. Hughes (Eds.), *Understanding children.* Oxford, England: Blackwell.

Carey, S. (1985). *Conceptual change in childhood.* Cambridge, MA: MIT Press.

Carey, S. (1992). The origin and evolution of everyday concepts. In R. N. Giere (Ed.), *Cognitive models of science: Vol. 15. Minnesota studies in the philosophy of science* (pp. 89–128). Minneapolis: University of Minnesota.

Chalmers, D., & Lawrence, J. A. (1993). Investigating the effects of planning aids on adults' and adolescents' organization of a complex task. *International Journal of Behavioral Development, 16,* 191–214.

Chen, Z., & Daehler, M. W. (1989). Positive and negative transfer in analogical problem solving by 6-year-old children. *Cognitive Development, 4,* 327–344.

Chen, Z., Sanchez, R. P., & Campbell, T. (in press). From beyond to within their grasp: The rudiments of analogical problem solving in 10- and 13-month-olds. *Developmental Psychology.*

Chen, Z., Yanowitz, K. L., & Daehler, M. W. (1995). Constraints on accessing abstract source information: Instantiation of principles facilitates children's analogical transfer. *Journal of Educational Psychology, 87,* 445–454.

Cheng, P. W., & Holyoak, K. J. (1985). Pragmatic reasoning schemas. *Cognitive Psychology, 17,* 391–416.

Chi, M. T. H. (1978). Knowledge structures and memory development. In R. S. Siegler (Ed.), *Children's thinking: What develops?* Hillsdale, NJ: Erlbaum.

Chi, M. T. H., Bassok, M., Lewis, M. W., Reimann, P., & Glaser, R. (1989). Self explanations: How students study and use examples in learning to solve problems. *Cognitive Science, 13,* 145–182.

Chi, M. T. H., de Leeuw, N., Chiu, M. H., & LaVancher, C. (1994). Eliciting self explanations improves understanding. *Cognitive Science, 18,* 439–477.

Chi, M. T. H., & Koeske, R. (1983). Network representation of a child's dinosaur knowledge. *Developmental Psychology, 19,* 29–39.

Chinn, C. A., & Brewer, W. F. (1993). The role of anomalous data in knowledge acquisition: A theoretical framework and implications for science instruction. *Review of Educational Research, 63,* 1–49.

Crisafi, M. A., & Brown, A. L. (1986). Analogical transfer in very young children: Combining two separately learned solutions to reach a goal. *Child Development, 57,* 953–968.

Davidson, N. S., & Gelman, S. A. (1990). Inductions from novel categories: The role of language and conceptual structure. *Cognitive Development, 5,* 151–176.

DeLoache, J. S. (1987). Rapid change in the symbolic functioning of very young children. *Science, 238,* 1556–1557.

DeLoache, J. S. (1991). Symbolic functioning in very young children: Understanding of pictures and models. *Child Development, 62,* 736–752.

DeLoache, J. S. (1995). Early symbol understanding and use. *The Psychology of Learning and Motivation.* New York: Academic Press.

DeLoache, J. S., & Burns, N. M. (1994). Early understanding of the representational function of pictures. *Cognition, 52,* 83–110.

DeLoache, J. S., Kolstad, V., & Anderson, K. N. (1991). Physical similarity and young children's understanding of scale models. *Child Development, 62,* 111–126.

DeLoache, J. S., Miller, K., & Rosengren, K. (1997). The credible shrinking room: Very young children's performance in symbolic and non-symbolic tasks. *Psychological Science.*

DeLoache, J. S., Pierroutsakos, S. L., Uttal, D. H., Rosengren, K., & Gottlieb, A. (1997). *Grasping the nature of pictures.* Manuscript submitted for publication.

DeLoache, J. S., Sugarman, S., & Brown, A. L. (1985). The development of error correction strategies in young children's manipulative play. *Child Development, 56,* 928–939.

Dickinson, D. K. (1988). Learning names for materials: Factors constraining and limiting hypotheses about word meaning. *Cognitive Development, 3,* 15–35.

Dumas, G. (1995, May). When youngsters say things that crack you up, write them down. *Smithsonian,* 140.

Duran, R. T., & Gauvain, M. (1993). The role of age versus expertise in peer collaboration during joint planning. *Journal of Experimental Child Psychology, 55,* 227–242.

Ellis, S., & Klahr, D. (1993, March). *Effects of feedback and collaboration on changes in children's use of mathematical rules.* Paper presented at the biennial meeting of the Society for Research in Child Development, New Orleans, LA.

Ellis, S., & Rogoff, B. (1986). Problem solving in children's management of instruction. In E. C. Mueller & C. R. Cooper (Eds.), *Processes and outcomes in peer relationships* (pp. 301–325). Orlando, FL: Academic Press.

Ellis, S., & Schneiders, B. (1989, April). *Collaboration on children's instruction: A Navajo versus Anglo comparison.* Paper presented at the biennial meeting of the Society for Research in Child Development, Kansas City, MO.

Ellis, S., & Siegler, R. S. (1997). Planning and strategy choice, or why don't children plan when they should? In S. L. Friedman & E. K. Scholnick (Eds.), *Why, how, and when do we plan: The developmental psychology of planning.* Hillsdale, NJ: Erlbaum.

Ericsson, K. A., Krampe, R., & Tesch-Römer, C. (1993). The role of deliberate practice in the acquisition of expert performance. *Psychological Review, 100,* 363–406.

Fabricius, W. (1988). The development of forward search planning in preschoolers. *Child Development, 59,* 1473–1488.

Fabricius, W., & Schick, K. (1995, April). *Strategy construction and choice in 18- to 36-month-olds: Flexibility in early spatial problem solving.* Paper presented at the biennial meeting of the Society for Research in Child Development, Indianapolis, IN.

Fagen, J. W. (1979). Behavioral contrast in infants. *Infant Behavior & Development, 2,* 101–112.

Falmagne, R. J. (1990). Language and the acquisition of logical knowledge. In W. Overton (Ed.), *Reasoning, necessity and logic: Developmental perspectives.* Hillsdale, NJ: Erlbaum.

Flavell, J. H., Beach, D. H., & Chinsky, J. M. (1966). Spontaneous verbal rehearsal in a memory task as a function of age. *Child Development, 37,* 283–299.

Flavell, J. H., Flavell, E. R., Green, F. L., & Korfmacher, J. E. (1990). Do young children think of television images as pictures or real objects? *Journal of Broadcasting and Electronic Media, 34,* 399–419.

Florian, J. E. (1994). Stripes do not a zebra make, or do they? Conceptual and perceptual information in inductive inference. *Developmental Psychology, 30,* 88–101.

Freeman, K., McKie, S., & Bauer, P. (1994, March). *Analogical reasoning in 2-year-olds.* Paper presented at the biennial conference on Human Development, Pittsburgh, PA.

Friedman, S. L., Scholnick, E. K., & Cocking, R. R. (1987). Reflections on reflections: What planning is and how it develops. In S. L. Friedman, E. K. Scholnick, & R. R. Cocking (Eds.), *Blueprints for thinking: The role of planning in cognitive development.* New York: Cambridge University Press.

Galotti, K. M. (1989). Approaches to studying formal and everyday reasoning. *Psychological Bulletin, 105,* 331–351.

Gardner, W., & Rogoff, B. (1990). Children's deliberateness of planning according to task circumstances. *Developmental Psychology, 26,* 480–487.

Garnham, A., & Oakhill, J. (1994). *Thinking and reasoning.* Oxford, England: Blackwell.

Gauvain, M. (1992). Social influences on the development of planning in advance and during action. *International Journal of Behavioral Development, 15,* 377–398.

Gauvain, M., & Rogoff, B. (1989). Collaborative problem solving and children's planning skills. *Developmental Psychology, 25,* 139–151.

Gelman, R. (1990). First principles organize attention to and learning about relevant data: Number and the animate-inanimate distinction as examples. *Cognitive Science, 14,* 79–106.

Gelman, R. (1995). Epigenetic foundations of knowledge structures: Initial and transcendent constructions. In S. Carey & R. Gelman (Eds.), *The epigenesis of the mind: Essays on biology and cognition.* Hillsdale, NJ: Erlbaum.

Gelman, S. A., & Coley, J. D. (1990). The importance of knowing a dodo is a bird: Categories and inferences in 2-year-old children. *Developmental Psychology, 26,* 796–804.

Gelman, S. A., & Markman, E. M. (1986). Categories and induction in young children. *Cognition, 23,* 183–209.

Gelman, S. A., & Markman, E. M. (1987). Young children's inductions from natural kinds: The role of categories and appearances. *Child Development, 58,* 1532–1541.

Gelman, S. A., & Medin, D. L. (1993). What's so essential about essentialism? A different perspective on the interaction of perception, language, and conceptual knowledge. *Cognitive Development, 8,* 157–167.

Gentner, D. (1983). Structure-mapping: A theoretical framework for analogy. *Cognitive Science, 7,* 155–170.

Gentner, D. (1989). The mechanisms of analogical learning. In S. Vosniadou & A. Ortony (Eds.), *Similarity and analogical reasoning.* London: Cambridge University Press.

Gentner, D., & Rattermann, M. J. (1991). Language and the career of similarity. In S. A. Gelman & J. P. Byrnes (Eds.), *Perspectives on language and thought: Interrelations in development.* Cambridge, England: Cambridge University Press.

Gentner, D., Rattermann, M. J., Markman, A., & Kotovsky, L. (1995). Two forces in the development of relational similarity. In. T. J. Simon & G. S. Halford (Eds.), *Developing cognitive competence: New approaches to process modeling.* Hillsdale, NJ: Erlbaum.

Gentner, D., & Toupin, C. (1986). Systematicity and surface similarity in the development of analogy. *Cognitive Science, 10,* 277–300.

Gholson, B., Dattel, A. R., Morgan, D., & Eymard, L. A. (1989). Problem solving, recall, and mapping relations in isomorphic transfer and nonisomorphic transfer among preschoolers and elementary school children. *Child Development, 60,* 1172–1187.

Gibson, J. J. (1979). *The ecological approach to visual perception.* Boston: Houghton Mifflin.

Gick, M. L., & Holyoak, K. J. (1983). Schema induction and analytical transfer. *Cognitive Psychology, 15,* 1–38.

Gobbo, C., & Chi, M. (1986). How knowledge is structured and used by expert and novice children. *Cognitive Development, 1,* 221–237.

Goldin-Meadow, S., Alibali, M. W., & Church, R. B. (1993). Transitions in concept acquisition: Using the hand to read the mind. *Psychological Review, 100,* 279–297.

Goodnow, J. J. (1987). Social aspects of planning. In S. L. Friedman, E. K. Scholnick, & R. R. Cocking (Eds.), *Blueprints for thinking: The role of planning in cognitive development.* New York: Cambridge University Press.

Goswami, U. (1991). Analogical reasoning: What develops? A review of research and theory. *Child Development, 62,* 1–22.

Goswami, U. (1992). *Analogical reasoning in children.* Hillsdale, NJ: Erlbaum.

Goswami, U. (1995). Transitive relational mappings in 3- and 4-year-olds: The analogy of Goldilocks and the Three Bears. *Child Development, 66,* 877–892.

Goswami, U. (1996). Analogical reasoning and cognitive development. In H. Reese (Ed.), *Advances in child development and behavior* (Vol. 26). New York: Academic Press.

Goswami, U., & Brown, A. (1989). Melting chocolate and melting snowmen: Analogical reasoning and causal relations. *Cognition, 35,* 69–95.

Goswami, U., & Brown, A. (1990). Higher-order structure and relational reasoning: Contrasting analogical and thematic relations. *Cognition, 36,* 207–226.

Graham, T., & Perry, M. (1993). Indexing transitional knowledge. *Developmental Psychology, 29,* 779–788.

Gregory, R. I. (1970). *The intelligent eye.* New York: McGraw-Hill.

Halford, G. S. (1992). Analogical reasoning and conceptual complexity in cognitive development. *Human Development, 35,* 193–217.

Halford, G. S. (1993). *Children's understanding: The development of mental models.* Hillsdale, NJ: Erlbaum.

Hall, D. G., Waxman, S. R., & Hurwitz, W. M. (1993). How two- and four-year-old children interpret adjectives and count nouns. *Child Development, 64,* 1651–1664.

Harris, P. L. (1994). Thinking by children and scientists: False analogies and neglected similarities. In L. A. Hirschfeld & S. A. Gelman (Eds.), *Mapping the mind: Domain specificity in cognition and culture.* New York: Cambridge University Press.

Hatano, G. (1990). Toward the cultural psychology of mathematical cognition. In H. W. Stevenson & S. Lee (Eds.), *Contexts of achievement. Monographs of the Society for Research in Child Development, 55*(1/2, Serial No. 221).

Hatano, G., & Inagaki, K. (1994). Young children's naive theory of biology. *Cognition, 50,* 171–188.

Hatano, G., Siegler, R. S., Richards, D. D., Inagaki, K., Stavy, R., & Wax, N. (1993). The development of biological knowledge: A multi-national study. *Cognitive Development, 8,* 47–62.

Holyoak, K. J. (1984). Analogical thinking and human intelligence. In R. J. Sternberg (Ed.), *Advances in the psychology of human intelligence* (Vol. 2). Hillsdale, NJ: Erlbaum.

Holyoak, K. J. (1991). Symbolic connectionism: Toward third-generation theories of expertise. In K. A. Ericsson & J. Smith (Eds.). *Toward a general theory of expertise: Prospects and limits.* New York: Cambridge University Press.

Holyoak, K. J., Junn, E. N., & Billman, D. O. (1984). Development of analogical problem-solving skill. *Child Development, 55,* 2042–2055.

Holyoak, K. J., & Koh, K. (1987). Surface and structural similarity in analogical transfer. *Memory and Cognition, 15,* 332–340.

Hudson, J. A., & Fivush, R. (1991). Planning in the preschool years: The emergence of plans from general event knowledge. *Cognitive Development, 6*(4), 393–415.

Hudson, J. A., Shapiro, L. R., & Sosa, B. B. (1995). Planning in the real world: Preschool children's scripts and plans for familiar events. *Child Development, 66,* 984–998.

Inhelder, B., & Piaget, J. (1958). *The growth of logical thinking from childhood to adolescence.* New York: Basic Books.

Istomina, M. (1975). The development of voluntary memory in preschool-age children. *Soviet Psychology, 13,* 5–64.

Johnson-Laird, P. N. (1983). *Mental models.* Cambridge, England: Cambridge University Press.

Johnson-Laird, P. N., Oakhill, J., & Bull, D. (1986). Children's syllogistic reasoning. *Quarterly Journal of Experimental Psychology: Human Experimental Psychology, 38,* 35–58.

Jones, S. S., & Smith, L. B. (1993). The place of perception in children's concepts. *Cognitive Development, 8,* 113–139.

Jones, S. S., Smith, L. B., & Landau, B. (1991). Object properties and knowledge in early lexical learning. *Child Development, 62,* 499–516.

Kahneman, D., & Tversky, A. (1982). Judgement under uncertainty: Heuristics and biases. In D. Kahneman, P. Slovic, & A. Tversky (Eds.), *Judgement under uncertainty: Heuristics and biases.* Cambridge, England: Cambridge University Press.

Karmiloff-Smith, A. (1984). Children's problem solving. In M. E. Lamb, A. L. Brown, & B. Rogoff (Eds.), *Advances in developmental psychology* (Vol. 3). Hillsdale, NJ: Erlbaum.

Karmiloff-Smith, A. (1992). *Beyond modularity: A developmental perspective on cognitive science.* Cambridge, MA: MIT Press.

Karmiloff-Smith, A., & Inhelder, B. (1974). If you want to get ahead, get a theory. *Cognition, 3,* 195–212.

Keil, F. C. (1989). *Concepts, kinds and development.* Cambridge, MA: MIT Press.

Keil, F. C. (1992). The origins of an autonomous biology. In M. R. Gunnar & M. Maratsos (Eds.), *Modularity and constraints in language and cognition: Minnesota Symposium on Child Psychology.* Hillsdale, NJ: Erlbaum.

Kelly, M., Feng, G., & Fang, G. (1995, April). *Counting the days: Language effects on calendar processing by Chinese and U.S. children.* Paper presented to the biennial meeting of the Society for Research in Child Development, Indianapolis, IN.

Kemler-Nelson, D. G. (1995). Principle-based inferences in young children's categorization: Revisiting the impact of function on the naming of artifacts. *Cognitive Development, 10,* 347–380.

Klahr, D. (1985). Solving problems with ambiguous subgoal ordering: Preschoolers' performance. *Child Development, 56,* 940–952.

Klahr, D., & Dunbar, K. (1988). Dual space search during scientific reasoning. *Cognitive Science, 12,* 1–48.

Klahr, D., Fay, A. L., & Dunbar, K. (1993). Heuristics for scientific experimentation: A developmental study. *Cognitive Psychology, 25,* 111–146.

Klahr, D., & Robinson, M. (1981). Formal assessment of problem solving and planning problems in children. *Cognitive Psychology, 13,* 113–148.

Klayman, J., & Ha, Y. (1987). Confirmation, disconfirmation, and information in hypothesis testing. *Psychological Review, 94,* 211–228.

Kolstad, V., & Aguiar, A. (1995, March). *Means-end sequences in young infants.* Paper presented at the biennial meeting of the Society for Research in Child Development, Indianapolis, IN.

Kolstad, V., & Baillargeon, R. (1997). *Appearance- and knowledge-based responses of 10.5-month-old infants to containers.* Manuscript in preparation.

Kreitler, S., & Kreitler, H. (1987). Conceptions and processes of planning: The developmental perspective. In S. L. Friedman, E. K. Scholnick, & R. R. Cocking (Eds.), *Blueprints for thinking: The role of planning in cognitive development.* New York: Cambridge University Press.

Kuhn, D. (1989). Children and adults as intuitive scientists. *Psychological Review, 96*(4), 674–689.

Kuhn, D., Amsel, E., & O'Loughlin, M. (1988). *The development of scientific thinking skills.* New York: Academic Press.

Kuhn, D., Garcia-Mila, M., Zohar, A., & Andersen, C. (1995). Strategies of knowledge acquisition. *Monographs of the Society for Research in Child Development, 60*(4, Serial No. 245).

Kuhn, D., & Phelps, E. (1982). The development of problem-solving strategies. In H. Reese (Ed.), *Advances in child development and behavior* (Vol. 17). New York: Academic Press.

Kuhn, D., Schauble, L., & Garcia-Milas, M. (1992). Cross-domain development of scientific reasoning. *Cognition and Instruction, 9,* 285–327.

Kunda, Z. (1990). The case for motivated reasoning. *Psychological Bulletin, 108,* 480–498.

Landau, B., Smith, L. B., & Jones, S. S. (1988). The importance of shape in early lexical learning. *Cognitive Development, 3,* 299–321.

Langer, E. J. (1992). Matters of mind: Mindfullness/mindlessness in perspective. *Consciousness and Cognition: An International Journal, 1*(4), 289–305.

Langer, S. K. (1942). *Philosophy in a new key.* Cambridge, MA: Harvard University Press.

Lehman, D. R., Lempert, R. O., & Nisbett, R. E. (1988). The effects of graduate training on reasoning. *American Psychologist, 43,* 431–442.

Lévi-Strauss (1967). *Savage thought. [La Pensée sauvage].* Chicago: Chicago. [Original work published 1962]

Levin, I., & Tolchinsky Landsmann, L. (1989). Becoming literate: Referential and phonetic strategies in early reading and writing. *International Journal of Behavioral Development, 12,* 369–384.

Lewis, M., Alessandri, S. M., & Sullivan, M. W. (1990). Violation of expectancy, loss of control, and anger expressions in young infants. *Developmental Psychology, 26,* 745–751.

Liben, L. S., & Downs, R. M. (1986). *Children's production and comprehension of maps: Increasing graphic literacy* (Report No. G-83-0025). National Institute of Education. Washington, DC.

Liben, L. S., & Downs, R. M. (1991). The role of graphic representations in understanding the world. In R. M. Downs, L. S. Liben, & D. S. Palermo (Eds.), *Visions of aesthetics, the environment, and development: The legacy of Joachim Wohlwill.* Hillsdale: NJ: Erlbaum.

Liben, L. S., & Yekel, C. A. (1996). Preschoolers' understanding of plan and oblique maps: The role of geometric and representational correspondence. *Child Development, 67,* 2780–2796.

Lillard, A. S. (1993). Pretend play skills and the child's theory of mind. *Child Development, 64,* 348–371.

Lopez, A., Gelman, S. A., Gutheil, G., & Smith, E. E. (1992). The development of category-based induction. *Child Development, 63,* 1070–1090.

Lundberg, I., & Torneus, M. (1978). Nonreaders' awareness of the basic relationship between spoken and written words. *Journal of Experimental Child Psychology, 25,* 404–412.

Macario, J. F. (1991). Young children's use of color in classification: Foods and canonically colored objects. *Cognitive Development, 6,* 17–46.

Marzolf, D. P. (1996, April). *Representing and coordinating multiple relations in symbolic tasks.* Poster presented at the biennial meeting of the International Conference on Infant Studies, Providence, RI.

Marzolf, D. P., & DeLoache, J. S. (1994). Transfer in young children's understanding of spatial representations. *Child Development, 65,* 1–15.

Marzolf, D. P., Pacha, P., & DeLoache, J. S. (1996, April). *Transfer of a symbolic relation by young children.* Poster presented at the biennial meeting of the International Conference on Infant Studies, Providence, RI.

Massey, C. M., & Gelman, R. (1988). Preschooler's ability to decide whether a photographed unfamiliar object can move itself. *Developmental Psychology, 24,* 307–317.

Mayer, R. E. (1992). *Thinking, problem solving, cognition* (2nd ed.). New York: Freeman.

McPherson, S. L., & Thomas, J. R. (1989). Relation of knowledge and performance in boys' tennis: Age and expertise. *Journal of Experimental Child Psychology, 48,* 190–211.

Medin, D. L., Goldstone, R. L., & Gentner, D. (1993). Respects for similarity. *Psychological Review, 100*(2), 254–278.

Medin, D. L., & Ortony, A. (1989). Psychological essentialism. In S. Vosniadou & A. Ortony (Eds.), *Similarity and analogical reasoning.* Cambridge, England: Cambridge University Press.

Medin, D. L., & Ross, B. H. (1989). The specific character of abstract thought: Categorization, problem solving, and induction. In R. J. Sternberg (Ed.), *Advances in the psychology of human intelligence* (Vol. 5). Hillsdale, NJ: Erlbaum.

Meehl, P. E. (1954). *Clinical versus statistical prediction: A theoretical analysis and review.* Minneapolis: University of Minnesota.

Mervis, C. B., Johnson, K. E., & Scott, P. (1993). Perceptual knowledge, conceptual knowledge, and expertise: Comment on Jones and Smith. *Cognitive Development, 8,* 149–155.

Miller, K. F., & Paredes, D. R. (1996). On the shoulders of giants: Cultural tools and mathematical development. In R. Sternberg & T. Ben-Zeev (Eds.), *The nature of mathematical thinking.* Hillsdale, NJ: Erlbaum.

Miller, K. F., Smith, C. M., Zhu, J., & Zhang, H. (1995). Preschool origins of cross-national differences in mathematical competence: The role of number naming systems. *Psychological Science, 6,* 56–60.

Miller, P. (1990). Strategies of selective attention. In D. F. Bjorklund (Ed.), *Children's strategies.* Hillsdale, NJ: Erlbaum.

Moshman, D. (1995). Reasoning as self-constrained thinking. *Human Development, 38,* 53–64.

Mosier, C. E., & Rogoff, B. (1994). Infants' instrumental use of their mothers to achieve their goals. *Child Development, 65,* 70–79.

Murphy, G. L., & Medin, D. L. (1985). The role of theories in conceptual coherence. *Psychological Review, 92,* 289–316.

Newell, A. (1990). *Unified theories of cognition.* Cambridge, MA: Harvard University Press.

Newell, A., & Simon, H. A. (1972). *Human problem solving.* Englewood Cliffs, NJ: Prentice-Hall.

Overman, W. H. (1990). Performance on traditional match-to-sample, non-match to sample, and object discrimination tasks by 12–32 month-old children: A developmental progression. In A. Diamond (Ed.), *The development and neural basis of higher cognitive functions* (Vol. 608). New York: New York Academy of Sciences Press.

Overman, W. H., Bachevalier, J., Miller, M., & Moore, K. (1996). Children's performance on "animal tests" of oddity: Implications for cognitive processes required for tests of oddity and delayed non-match to sample. *Journal of Experimental Child Psychology, 62,* 223–242.

Overton, W. F. (Ed.). (1990). *Reasoning, necessity, and logic: Developmental perspectives.* Hillsdale, NJ: Erlbaum.

Pacifici, C., & Bearison, C. (1991). Development of children's self-regulations in idealized and mother-child interactions. *Cognitive Development, 6,* 261–277.

Peak, L. (1991). *Learning to go to school in Japan: The transition from home to preschool life.* Berkeley: University of California.

Perkins, D. N. (1986, April). *Reasoning as it is and could be: An empirical perspective.* Paper presented at the AREA Conference, San Francisco, CA.

Perner, J. (1991). *Understanding the representational mind.* Cambridge, MA: MIT Press.

Perry, M., Church, R. B., & Goldin-Meadow, S. (1988). Transitional knowledge in the acquisition of concepts. *Cognitive Development, 3,* 359–400.

Piaget, J. (1929). *The child's conception of the world.* New York: Harcourt, Brace and Company.

Piaget, J. (1952). *The child's conception of number.* New York: Norton.

Piaget, J. (1976). *The grasp of consciousness.* Cambridge, MA: Harvard University Press.

Piaget, J., Montangero, J., & Billeter, J. (1977). Les correlats. In J. Piaget (Ed.), *L'abstraction reflechissante.* Paris: Presses Universitaires de France.

Pierroutsakos, S. L. (1995, April). *When do infants grasp the nature of pictures?* Poster presented at the biennial meeting of the Society for Research in Child Development, Indianapolis, IN.

Pierroutsakos, S. L., & DeLoache, J. S. (1996, April). *Understanding the object of a picture.* Poster presented at the biennial meeting of the International Conference on Infant Studies, Providence, RI.

Pitt, R. (1983). Development of a general problem-solving schema in adolescence and early adulthood. *Journal of Experimental Psychology: General, 112,* 547–584.

Popper, K. R. (1962). *Conjectures and refutations: The growth of scientific knowledge.* New York: Basic Books.

Potter, M. C. (1979). Mundane symbolism: The relations among objects, names, and ideas. In N. R. Smith & M. B. Franklin (Eds.), *Symbolic functioning in childhood.* Hillsdale, NJ: Erlbaum.

Presson, C. C. (1982). The development of map-reading skills. *Child Development, 53,* 196–199.

Presson, C. C. (1987). The development of spatial cognition: Secondary uses of spatial information. In N. Eisenberg (Ed.), *Contemporary topics in developmental psychology.* New York: Wiley.

Radziszewska, B., & Rogoff, B. (1991). Children's guided participation in planning imaginary errands with skilled adult or peer partners. *Developmental Psychology, 27,* 381–389.

Rogoff, B., Mistry, J., Göncü, A., & Mosier, C. (1993). Guided participation in cultural activity by toddlers and caregivers. *Monographs of the Society for Research in Child Development, 58*(179).

Rosch, E., & Mervis, C. B. (1975). Family resemblances: Studies in the internal structure of categories. *Cognitive Psychology, 7,* 573–605.

Rosengren, K. S., Gelman, S. A., Kalish, C. W., & McCormick, M. (1991). As time goes by: Children's early understanding of growth. *Child Development, 62,* 1302–1320.

Rosengren, K. S., Kalish, C. W., Hickling, A. K., & Gelman, S. A. (1994). Exploring the relation between preschool children's magical beliefs and causal thinking: Magic [Special issue]. *British Journal of Developmental Psychology, 12,* 69–82.

Ross, B. H. (1989). Distinguishing types of superficial similarities: Different effects on the access and use of earlier problems. *Journal of Experimental Psychology: Learning, Memory, & Cognition, 15,* 456–468.

Roth, C. (1983). Factors affecting developmental change in the speed of processing. *Journal of Experimental Child Psychology, 35,* 509–528.

Ruffman, T., Perner, J., Olson, D. R., & Doherty, M. (1993). Reflecting on scientific thinking: Children's understanding of the hypothesis-evidence relation. *Child Development, 64,* 1617–1636.

Schauble, L. (1996). The development of scientific reasoning in knowledge-rich contexts. *Developmental Psychology, 32,* 102–119.

Schneider, W., & Brun, H. (1987). The role of context in young children's memory performance: Istomina revisited. *British Journal of Developmental Psychology, 5,* 333–341.

Schneider, W., Gruber, H., Gold, A., & Opwis, K. (1993). Chess expertise and memory for chess positions in children and adults. *Journal of Experimental Child Psychology, 56,* 328–349.

Scholnick, E. K., & Wing, C. S. (1995). Logic in conversation: Comparative studies of deduction in children and adults. *Cognitive Development, 10,* 319–346.

Scribner, S. (1986). Thinking in action: Some characteristics of practical thought. In R. J. Sternberg & R. Wagner (Eds.), *Practical intelligence.* Cambridge, England: Cambridge University Press.

Shultz, T. R., Fisher, G. W., Pratt, C. C., & Rulf, S. (1986). Selection of causal rules. *Child Development, 57,* 143–152.

Siegler, R. S. (1988). Individual differences in strategy choices: Good students, not-so-good students, and perfectionists. *Child Development, 59,* 833–851.

Siegler, R. S. (1991). *Children's thinking* (2nd ed.). Englewood Cliffs, NJ: Prentice-Hall.

Siegler, R. S. (1995). How does change occur: A microgenetic study of number conservation. *Cognitive Psychology, 28,* 225–273.

Siegler, R. S. (1996). *Emerging minds: The process of change in children's thinking.* Oxford, England: Oxford University Press.

Siegler, R. S., & Crowley, K. (1991). The microgenetic method: A direct means for studying cognitive development. *American Psychologist, 46,* 606–620.

Siegler, R. S., & Jenkins, E. (1989). *How children discover new strategies.* Hillsdale, NJ: Erlbaum.

Siegler, R. S., & McGilly, K. (1989). Strategy choices in children's time-telling. In I. Levin & D. Zakay (Eds.), *Time and human cognition: A life span perspective.* Amsterdam, The Netherlands: Elsevier.

Sigel, I. E. (1978). The development of pictorial comprehension. In B. S. Randhawa & W. E. Coffman (Eds.), *Visual learning, thinking, and communication.* New York: Academic Press.

Smith, L. B., DeLoache, J. S., & Schreiber, J. C. (1995). *Induction of a sameness rule by young children.* Unpublished raw data.

Smith, L. B., & Heise, D. (1992). Perceptual similarity and conceptual structure. In B. Burns (Ed.), *Percepts, concepts and categories.* Amsterdam, The Netherlands: Elsevier.

Smith, L. B., Jones, S. S., & Landau, B. (1992). Count nouns, adjectives, and perceptual properties in children's novel word interpretations. *Developmental Psychology, 28,* 273–286.

Sodian, B., Zaitchik, D., & Carey, S. (1991). Young children's differentiation of hypothetical belief from evidence. *Child Development, 62,* 753–766.

Soja, N. N., Carey, S., & Spelke, E. S. (1991). Ontological categories guide young children's inductions of word meaning: Object terms and substance terms. *Cognition, 38,* 179–211.

Spearman, C. E. (1923). *The nature of "intelligence" and the principles of cognition.* London: Macmillan.

Sternberg, R. J. (1986). Toward a unified theory of human reasoning. *Intelligence, 10,* 281–314.

Stevenson, H. W., Lee, S. Y., Chen, C., Stigler, J. W., Hsu, C.-C., & Kitamura, S. (1990). Contexts of achievement: A study of American, Chinese, and Japanese children. *Monographs of the Society for Research in Child Development, 55*(1/2, Serial No. 221).

Stigler, J. W., Chalip, L., & Miller, K. F. (1986). Consequences of skill: The case of abacus training in Taiwan. *American Journal of Education, 94,* 447–479.

Strauss, M. S., & Curtis, L. E. (1981). Infant perception of numerosity. *Child Development, 52,* 1146–1152.

Teale, W. H., & Sulzby, E. (1986). Emergent literacy: A perspective for examining how young children become writers and readers. In W. H. Teale & E. Sulzby (Eds.), *Emergent literacy: Writing and reading.* Norwood, NJ: ABLEX.

Teasley, S. D. (1995). The role of talk in children's peer collaborations. *Developmental Psychology, 31,* 207–220.

Tobin, J. J., Wu, D. Y. H., & Davidson, D. H. (1989). *Preschool in three cultures: Japan, China, and the United States.* New Haven, CT: Yale University Press.

Troseth, G. L., & DeLoache, J. S. (1995). *Young children's detection of correspondence.* Unpublished raw data.

Troseth, G. L., & DeLoache, J. S. (1996, April). *The medium can obscure the message: Understanding the relation between video and reality.* Poster presented at the biennial meeting of the International Conference on Infant Studies, Providence, RI.

Tufte, E. R. (1983). *The visual display of quantitative information.* Cheshire, CT: Graphics Press.

Uttal, D. H., Lio, P. A., & Taxy, B. E. (1995, April). Seeing the big picture: Children's mental representation of maps. In J. Plumert (Chair), *Developmental change in the coding of spatial location.* Presented at the biennial meeting of the Society for Research in Child Development, Indianapolis, IN.

Uttal, D. H., Schreiber, J. C., & DeLoache, J. S. (1995). Waiting to use a symbol: The effects of delay on children's use of models. *Child Development, 66,* 1875–1891.

Uttal, D. H., & Wellman, H. M. (1989). Young children's representation of spatial information acquired from maps. *Developmental Psychology, 25,* 128–138.

Vosniadou, S., & Brewer, W. F. (1992). Mental models of the earth: A study of conceptual change in childhood. *Cognitive Psychology, 24,* 535–585.

Vosniadou, S., & Ortony, A. (1989). Similarity and analogical reasoning: A synthesis. In S. Vosniadou & A. Ortony (Eds.), *Similarity and analogical reasoning.* Cambridge, England: Cambridge University Press.

Vygotsky, L. S. (1978a). *Mind and society.* Cambridge, MA: MIT Press.

Vygotsky, L. S. (1978b). In M. Cole, V. John-Steiner, S. Scribner, & E. Souberman (Eds.), *Mind in society.* Cambridge, MA: Harvard University Press.

Wason, P. C., & Johnson-Laird, P. N. (1972). *Psychology of reasoning: Structure and content.* London: Batsford.

Waxman, S. R., & Braig, B. (1996, April). *Stars and starfish: How far can shape take us?* Poster presented at the biennial meeting of the International Conference for Infant Studies, Providence, RI.

Waxman, S. R., & Hall, D. G. (1993). The development of a linkage between count nouns and object categories: Evidence from fifteen- to twenty-one-month-old infants. *Child Development, 64,* 1224–1241.

Wellman, H. M., & Gelman, S. A. (1992). Cognitive development: Foundational theories of core domains. *Annual Review of Psychology, 43,* 337–375.

Welsh, M. C. (1991). Rule-guided behavior and self-monitoring on the Tower of Hanoi disk-transfer task. *Cognitive Development, 6,* 59–76.

Werner, H. (1948). *Comparative psychology of mental development.* New York: International Universities Press.

Wickelgren, W. A. (1974). *How to solve problems.* San Francisco, CA: Freeman.

Willats, P. (1990). Development of problem solving strategies in infancy. In D. F. Bjorklund (Ed.), *Children's strategies.* Hillsdale, NJ: Erlbaum.

Willats, P., & Fabricius, W. (1993, March). *The origin of forward search planning in infancy.* Paper presented to the biennial meeting of the Society for Research in Child Development, New Orleans, LA.

Wiser, M., & Carey, S. (1983). When heat and temperature were one. In D. Gentner & A. Stevens (Eds.), *Mental models.* Hillsdale, NJ: Erlbaum.

Wood, D., Bruner, J. S., & Ross, G. (1976). The role of tutoring in problem solving. *Journal of Child Psychology and Psychiatry, 17,* 89–100.

Zelazo, P. D., Frye, D., & Rapus, T. (1996). An age-related dissociation between knowing rules and using them. *Cognitive Development, 11,* 37–63.

Zelazo, P. D., & Reznick, J. S. (1991). Age-related asynchrony of knowledge and action. *Child Development, 62,* 719–735.

Zelazo, P. D., Reznick, J. S., & Piñon, D. E. (1995). Response control and the execution of verbal rules. *Developmental Psychology, 31,* 508–517.

CHAPTER 17

Social Cognition

JOHN H. FLAVELL and PATRICIA H. MILLER

An experimenter shows a 5-year-old a candy box with pictures of candy on it and asks her what she thinks is in it. "Candy," she replies. She then gets to look inside and discovers to her surprise that it actually contains pencils. What would another child who had not yet looked inside think was in it, the experimenter next asks. "Candy," says the child, amused at the deception. The experimenter then tries the same procedure with a 3-year-old. The response to the first question is the expected "candy," but the response to the second is an astonishing and unamused "pencils." More surprising yet, the younger child also claims, in response to further questioning, that he himself had initially thought that pencils would be in the box—and had even *said* there were (e.g., Gopnik & Astington, 1988; Perner, Leekam, & Wimmer, 1987; Wimmer & Hartl, 1991). The two children's identical response to the initial question attests to an unremarkable bit of physical knowledge that both have acquired: Boxes usually contain what is shown on their outside covers. Their different responses to the

other questions suggest a remarkable developmental difference in their social-cognitive knowledge: The older child seems to know what a false belief is whereas the younger one seemingly does not.

Social cognition has as its objects humans and human affairs; it means cognition and knowledge about people and their doings. Machines, mathematics, and mental states are all objects of cognition, for example, but only people's knowledge about mental states would be regarded as a topic within *social* cognition. Social cognition bears on the strictly social and psychological world, not the physical and logical-mathematical ones, even though all three worlds obviously have people's fingerprints all over them. Social cognition is currently of great interest to psychologists, nondevelopmental (e.g., Fiske, 1993) as well as developmental. However, its actual practice has undoubtedly been of even greater importance in people's everyday lives since the dawn of the species. Numerous motives, ranging from self-preservation to simple curiosity, must continually impel people the world over to try to make sense of themselves, other people, interpersonal relations, and other interesting phenomena within the social world (Wegner & Vallacher, 1977). It is not surprising that psychologists

---

Author Flavell's contribution to the chapter was supported in part by National Institutes of Mental Health Grant MH40687.

would want to learn about the nature and development of processes that are that significant in everyday mental life.

We begin with a brief history of the field that includes a characterization of current emphases. Two long sections on infancy and developments after infancy make up the bulk of the chapter. We then address intracultural, intercultural, and interspecies differences in development. Finally, looking to the future, we propose fruitful points of contact between recent work on children's understanding of the mind and other topics in social cognition with a long history of research.

History of Research on Social-Cognitive Development

In her chapter on social-cognitive development in the previous edition of this *Handbook,* Shantz (1983) reviewed the history of work in this area up to about 1980; for a more recent history, see Bennett (1993a). Shantz identified three streams of theory and research that had helped to shape the field as it was then. First and by far the most important was work stemming directly or indirectly from Piaget's theory. Werner's (1948) theory was also influential, but to a lesser degree. A central Piagetian claim was that children begin development by being cognitively *egocentric* (Flavell, 1992). By this, Piaget meant that they initially do not know that there exist such things as conceptual, perceptual, and affective perspectives or points of view. As a consequence, they naturally cannot know that they themselves have such perspectives vis-à-vis external objects and events, or that others do, or that their own perspective may differ from those of others, or that they may be unwittingly reporting their own perspectives when asked to report another person's. Piaget also considered as egocentric children who have some awareness that perspectives exist but who are not skilled at discriminating their own from another person's. Piaget and his colleagues used egocentrism and other concepts to interpret their developmental studies of a wide range of social-cognitive topics: perceptual perspective-taking; egocentric communication; the misattribution of mental characteristics to physical objects (animism) and physical characteristics to mental events (realism); and understanding of thoughts, dreams, intentions, and morality. Research on these and related topics continues to the present day, although usually not from a Piagetian theoretical perspective (e.g., Flavell, 1992; Flavell, Green, & Flavell, 1995b; Woolley & Wellman, 1992). Shantz (1983) also describes more recent stage theories of various aspects of social-cognitive development in the Piagetian tradition (Damon, 1977; Selman, 1980; Turiel, 1975) as well as re-

porting numerous studies of perspective-taking and related Piagetian topics by Borke, Chandler, Feffer, Flavell, Selman, and many other investigators.

The second stream cited by Shantz (1983) is attribution theory, as developed by social psychologists Heider, Kelley, and others. Attribution theory mainly investigates what inferences adults make about the causes of their own and other people's behavior. Do they think the cause of a particular behavior lies mainly in the person (e.g., the person's traits, abilities, attitudes, effort) or in the situation in which the behavior occurred? Similarly, is this particular performance mainly explainable by the performer's ability or by his or her effort? Shantz (1983) reviews a number of developmental studies testing, for example, whether or when children use various attribution principles (covariation principle, discounting) that have been identified in adults. (See also Miller & Aloise, 1989 and Flavell, Miller, & Miller, 1993, pp. 208–216 for reviews of more recent developmental work in the general area of causal attribution.) Children's understanding of the causes of behavior continues to be an active area of research (see *Intentions* and *Other Psychological Causes* sections) but, as with research on topics that Piaget first studied, most current work on this topic does not appear to be explicitly guided by attribution theory.

Shantz' (1983) third stream is not identified with any single theory, but is rather a perspective on what social knowledge is and how it should be studied. In Shantz' words: "It takes the position that the way to reveal explicit and tacit knowledge and reasoning is to observe social interaction, that is, the child not as a knower *about* the social world but as an actor *in* it" (Shantz, 1983, p. 497). Advocates of this position argue that the way to find out what social-cognitive knowledge children possess is to observe them in natural social settings rather than test them in experimental situations such as the false-belief one previously described. Observational methods continue to be used extensively in this area today (e.g., Bartsch & Wellman, 1995; Dunn, Brown, & Beardsall, 1991) and, here as in other areas of developmental psychology, there is continued debate about the merits of observational versus experimental methods (Astington & Olson, 1995; Lewis, 1993; Raver & Leadbeater, 1993).

Two other areas of research have made important contributions to our understanding of social-cognitive development: metacognitive development and theory-of-mind development. For reviews of work on metacognitive development and citations of other reviews, see Brown, Bransford, Ferrara, and Campione (1983), Flavell, Miller, and

Miller (1993), and the chapters by Moshman and by Schneider and Bjorklund in this Volume. Metacognition (cognition about cognition—hence the "meta") has been defined as any knowledge or cognitive activity that takes as its cognitive object, or that regulates, any aspect of any cognitive activity (Flavell, Miller, & Miller, 1993, p. 150). Metacognition can encompass people's knowledge about the nature of people as cognizers, about the nature of different cognitive tasks, and about possible strategies for coping with different tasks. It can also include executive skills for monitoring and regulating one's cognitive activities. The majority of developmental studies classified as metacognitive have investigated children's metamemory, that is, their knowledge about variables affecting memory performance and, especially, their knowledge and use of memory strategies. The rubric has also been applied to numerous studies of children's cognition concerning comprehension, communication, language, perception and attention, and problem solving.

Research on metacognitive development is not usually included in reviews of social-cognitive development (e.g., Shantz, 1983). The probable reason is that it seems less "social" than other types of social cognition. Take the case of the development of knowledge and use of memory strategies, for instance—a paradigmatic instance of metacognition. What is known about and used here are one's own memory strategies rather than another person's, and this knowledge and use serves a basically nonsocial goal (i.e., remembering something) rather than a social one. Metacognitive processes identified by Piaget (formal operations, reflective abstraction) are not usually regarded as social-cognitive processes either, and probably for much the same reason. Nevertheless, metacognition qualifies as a genuine instance of social cognition because it is clearly cognition about things that people rather than objects do— that is, people's cognitive acts of remembering, communicating, and so forth. To put it another way, our knowledge of what people know about people would surely be incomplete if it did not include their intuitions about human memory, comprehension, and the like.

The Theory-of-Mind Approach

The final research trend could not have been included in Shantz' (1983) history because it was just getting underway at about the time her review was published. We refer to the very exciting new line commonly referred to as theory-of-mind research. Prior to about 1983, most investigators of children's knowledge about people would probably classify their work as either metacognitive, attribution-theoretical,

or in the general Piagetian tradition. Today the great majority would say they are doing one or another kind of theory-of-mind research. In fact, they would likely use that label as a shorthand, easily recognizable characterization of the general line of work they are in, even if they were not convinced, as some are not, that children actually acquire bona fide theories of mind rather than just knowledge and skills concerning it. At this writing, theory-of-mind research is one of the hottest, most active research areas in all of developmental psychology. Indeed, the flood of papers and posters on this topic at recent Society for Research in Child Development conventions reminds us of the way Piagetian research used to dominate the program. How did all this come to pass, and what is theory-of-mind research all about?

In a 1978 issue of *Behavioral and Brain Sciences,* Premack and Woodruff reported some research in which they attempted to test whether chimpanzees have a theory of mind, which they defined as follows:

> An individual has a theory of mind if he imputes mental states to himself and others. A system of inferences of this kind is properly viewed as a theory because such states are not directly observable, and the system can be used to make predictions about the behavior of others. As to the mental states the chimpanzees may infer, consider those inferred by our own species, for example, *purpose* or *intention,* as well as *knowledge, belief, thinking, doubt, guessing, pretending, liking,* and so forth. (Premack & Woodruff, 1978, p. 515)

In their commentaries on this article, three philosophers independently suggested that one might be able to find out whether an animal possessed the concept of belief in something in the following fashion (Bennett, 1978; Dennett, 1978; Harman, 1978). The subject animal sees another individual put object X in container A and then leave the scene. The subject then sees someone else move X from A into container B while the individual is still absent. The subject animal should then be credited with some understanding of belief if it acts as if it expects that the returning individual will search for X in A rather than B: "If the subject chimpanzee expects the second chimpanzee to reach into the pot which originally contained the banana, that would seem to show that it has a conception of mere belief" (Dennett, 1978, p. 557). Philosophers and researchers consider false-belief tasks to be better tests of the concept of belief than are true-belief tasks because children could be correct on true-belief tasks by egocentrically assuming that others know what they themselves know.

These ideas were taken up in the early 1980s by two Austrian psychologists, Josef Perner and Heinz Wimmer. In a famous and highly influential series of studies, they used the "unexpected transfer" method proposed by the philosophers to test young children's understanding of false belief (Wimmer & Perner, 1983). Similarly, Bretherton and her colleagues examined infants' gestural and verbal communication for evidence that they have "what Premack and Woodruff (1978) have called a 'theory of mind'" (Bretherton, McNew, & Beeghly-Smith, 1981, p. 339). Around the same time, Wellman and his co-workers had independently begun to conceptualize children's developing metacognitive knowledge and understanding of mental terms as the development of a theory of mind (e.g., Johnson & Wellman, 1980; Shatz, Wellman, & Silber, 1983; Wellman, 1983, 1985). In addition, a number of other researchers who had not yet begun to conceptualize children's social-cognitive development in quite this way had been doing research that subsequently became part of the theory-of-mind movement. An example would be the work on children's knowledge about perception and about the appearance-reality distinction by Flavell and colleagues (e.g., Flavell, Flavell, Green, & Wilcox, 1980; Flavell, Flavell, & Green, 1983; see Astington, Harris, & Olson, 1988, for other such projects).

The movement was given added identity and coherence by two conferences that were held in the spring of 1986: the International Conference on Developing Theories of Mind, organized by Janet Astington, Lynd Forguson, Alison Gopnik, and David Olson at the University of Toronto, and the Workshop on Children's Early Concept of Mind, organized by Paul Harris at the University of Oxford. The papers presented at these two meetings were subsequently published in a book entitled *Developing Theories of Mind* (Astington, Harris, & Olson, 1988), and the movement was officially launched. A look through this milestone publication provides an immediate sense of the broad and diverse array of acquisitions judged to be instances of theory-of-mind development, and more have been added since. What it does not convey is the high excitement felt by the conference participants at the birth of a new approach to social-cognitive development.

The rest, as they say, is history. Publications concerned with theory-of-mind development must number in the hundreds by now and the flow continues. Good reviews of work in this large and still-burgeoning area can be found (Astington, 1993—a particularly good, easy-to-read summary of the whole area; Astington & Gopnik, 1991a; Astington, Harris,

& Olson, 1988; Baron-Cohen, Tager-Flusberg, & Cohen, 1993; Bartsch & Wellman, 1995; Bennett, 1993b; Butterworth, Harris, Leslie, & Wellman, 1991; Flavell, Miller, & Miller, 1993; Forguson, 1989; Frye & Moore, 1991; Harris, 1989; Hirschfeld & Gelman, 1994; Karmiloff-Smith, 1992; Lewis & Mitchell, 1994; Moses & Chandler, 1992; Perner, 1991; Taylor, 1996; Wellman, 1990; Wellman & Gelman, 1992; Whiten, 1991).

It is not surprising that philosophers were invited to comment on the Premack and Woodruff (1978) article. For many years, philosophers of mind have been interested in the lay person's theory of mind, which they commonly refer to as "folk psychology." (See, for example, Christensen & Turner, 1993; Churchland, 1984.) Two of them have recently described it as follows:

> Folk psychology is a network of principles which characterizes a sort of common-sense theory about how to explain human behavior. These principles provide a central role to certain propositional attitudes, particularly beliefs and desires. The theory asserts, for example, that if someone desires that *p*, and this desire is not overridden by other desires, and he believes that an action of kind *k* will bring it about that *p*, and he believes that such action is within his power . . . then *ceteris paribus,* the desire and the beliefs will cause him to perform an action of the kind *k*. The theory is largely functional, in that the states it postulates are characterized primarily in terms of their causal relations to each other, to perception and other environmental stimuli, and to behavior. (Horgan & Woodward, 1993, p. 144)

For philosophers of mind, there are a number of unresolved questions concerning folk psychology (Christensen & Turner, 1993): Should it be regarded as a theory? If so, what type of theory is it? Is it a good theory? That is, does it adequately characterize, predict, and explain our thoughts and actions? Will it eventually be reducible to a lower level neurobiological theory (the view of identity theorists) or will it not be reducible, either because it is false and will eventually have to be abandoned (the position of eliminative materialists), or because it constitutes a valid but autonomous and irreducible level of explanation (the functionalists' view)?

Developmental psychologists who work in this area have been mainly concerned with the first two of these questions (whether a theory, and if so, what kind) plus three others: What is the structure and content of the lay adult theory of mind? What are the developmental steps in its acquisition during childhood? How should this acquisition be explained? The work of Henry Wellman (1990) provides a good initial illustration of how such questions are addressed by developmentalists. (See also Gopnik & Wellman, 1994; Perner, 1991; Wellman & Gelman, 1992.)

Wellman and colleagues argue that our knowledge about the mind does comprise a theory—not an actual scientific theory, but an everyday "framework" or "foundational" theory. To constitute such an informal theory, they claim, a body of knowledge must have three properties. First, it must specify a set of entities or processes (an ontology, philosophers call it) that are found in its domain of application and in no other domain. Second, it must use causal principles that are likewise unique to the theory's domain. Finally, the body of knowledge must comprise a system of interrelated concepts and beliefs rather than just a collection of unrelated contents.

Wellman and others believe that our informal theory of mind satisfies all three of these conditions. First, entities or processes such as beliefs, desires, thinking, and so forth,

are found only in the domain of the mental, and thus satisfy the ontological criterion. Second, psychological causality (she tried to get it because she wanted it and thought she could get it, etc.) is also found only in the domain of the psychological; physical objects are not caused to move by such mental states. Finally, our knowledge about the mind is organized and richly interconnected, with different mental states conceptualized as being causally linked to one another, to environmental input, and to behavioral output.

Figure 17.1 illustrates these three criteria and also shows part of Wellman's proposed structure and content of the adult theory of mind; for other parts, see p. 115 of his book. This diagram suggests, among other things, that adults believe that what we perceive influences what we think about and believe; that what we believe may bias what we perceive; that various mental and physiological states engender our desires; that beliefs and desires may lead to behavioral intentions which in turn may lead to goal-directed actions; and that the success or failure of these

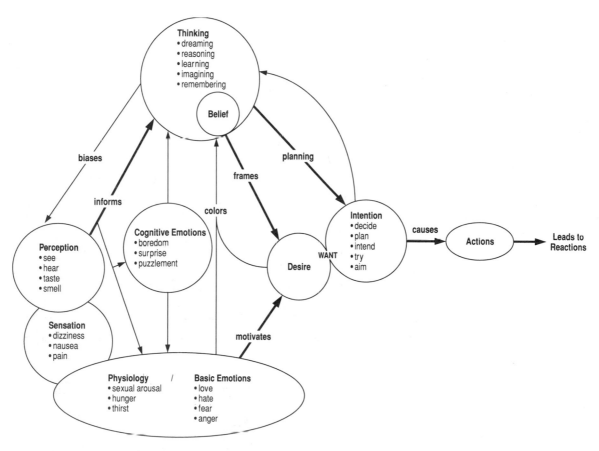

Figure 17.1   Belief-desire reasoning. From *The Child's Theory of Mind,* by H. M. Wellman (1990), p. 109, Cambridge, MA: MIT Press. Copyright © 1990 by MIT Press. Reproduced with permission.

actions will cause emotional reactions which will in their turn engender additional mental and behavioral activity.

As we will discuss in subsequent chapter sections, researchers have identified a number of steps or milestones in children's developmental itinerary toward the adult theory of mind. For example, Wellman (1990, 1993) has suggested that by the age of 2, children understand that people have the inner experiences of perceiving, feeling, and desiring, but do not yet understand believing. Later they change from having just a "desire psychology" to having a "belief-desire psychology," according to Wellman.

We will also discuss various mechanisms or processes that have been proposed to explain this developmental itinerary. For instance, researchers such as Wellman and Gopnik, who think of the acquisitional process in this area as one of theory construction, stress the role of experienced failures of the child's early theory (e.g., desire psychology) in engendering the subsequent construction of a more adequate one (e.g., belief-desire psychology; Gopnik & Wellman, 1994).

There are several features of the theory-of-mind approach to the study of social-cognitive development that tend to distinguish it from its predecessors. First, it tends to focus more on very basic knowledge about the mind, that is, the child's knowledge that there are such things in the inner world as desires, beliefs, and other mental states. To illustrate, a study of memory development in the metacognitive tradition would be likely to inquire as to the child's knowledge about the effects of various task variables and memorization strategies on memory performance. In contrast, a study done from a theory-of-mind perspective would be likelier to test for more fundamental knowledge: For example, does the child even know what it means to remember or forget something, let alone know how to help the former and hinder the latter (Lyon & Flavell, 1994)? This focus has led researchers to identify previously unstudied or little-studied acquisitions, for example, a basic understanding of what a belief is and how it affects the believer's behavior, and to invent ingenious new tasks to assess them, for example, the false-belief tasks previously described. Another outcome is the focus on very young children rather than older ones. Here, as in other areas of developmental psychology, the discovery of new and important-seeming developables coupled with fruitful methods for studying them has resulted in a rush of productive scientific activity.

The approach is also distinctive in that it advocates a focus on the child's theorylike conception of the whole mental system, rather than just random bits of isolated metacognitive knowledge. This feature is important for at least three reasons. First, it helps to integrate the study of social-cognitive development with that of other developments. For example, the child's acquisition of knowledge in the physical and biological domains is also currently being conceptualized as instances of naive theory development (Wellman & Gelman, 1992; Wellman & Gelman, this Volume). Likewise, theory-of-mind acquisition is increasingly being seen as highly relevant to lexical, emotional, and other developments (e.g., Baldwin & Moses, 1994). Second, it links social-cognitive growth to various nondevelopmental areas, including philosophy, cognitive psychology, and even cognitive anthropology (D'Andrade, 1987). For example, the nature of mental representations is a topic of vital concern in all areas of cognitive science, and is also relevant to theory-of-mind development (e.g., Perner, 1991); the interest of philosophers of mind in folk psychology has already been mentioned. Finally, a focus on the child's developing knowledge of the entire structure and content of the mind has allowed us to ask new versions of the traditional developmental questions. We refer here to the questions mentioned in previous paragraphs: When and in what order does the child gain some understanding of all the major mental entities (beliefs, desires, etc.) and their causal interrelationships with one another, with the perceived environment, and with behavior? What causes the child to achieve all this understanding?

We will particularly emphasize theory-of-mind research in this chapter because of its current preeminence in the field of social-cognitive development. It is simply the case that theory-of-mind research is where most of the scientific action is at present in this field. For more thorough coverage of research in the Piagetian, attribution-theoretical, and metacognitive traditions, see reviews by Bennett (1993b), Flavell, Miller, and Miller (1993), Moshman (this Volume), Schneider and Bjorklund (this Volume), and Shantz (1983). We will also say little about other topics that could properly be classified as social-cognitive, such as representation and the development of self, personality, and morality, because these topics have their own chapters in this *Handbook*.

DEVELOPMENTS DURING INFANCY

There recently has been a quickening of research interest in social-cognitive development during infancy. Useful reviews of work in this area include Astington (1993), Baldwin and Moses (1994), Bretherton, McNew, and Beeghly-Smith (1981), Butterworth (1994), Flavell, Miller, and Miller (1993), Golinkoff (1983), Harris (1989), Hobson (1994), Legerstee (1992), Moore (1996), Moore and Corkum (1994), Moore and Dunham (1995), Mumme, Fernald, and Herrera (1996), Schaffer (1984), Tomasello (1995), and Wellman (1993). The principal questions of interest here are the following: What behaviors do infants of different ages show that seem relevant to the development of knowledge about people? How should these behaviors be interpreted? That is, exactly how much and what kind of social-cognitive knowledge (if any) should we attribute to infants who exhibit them? Researchers differ widely in the generosity of their interpretations here (Baldwin & Moses, 1994). Where some see evidence of genuine knowledge about people's minds, others see evidence only of knowledge about people's behavior—knowledge that at most may provide a developmental foundation for later-developing knowledge about the mind. Finally, how can we explain the infant's knowledge and ability to acquire new knowledge? For example, have human beings evolved innate or early-maturing mechanisms specialized for understanding persons? If so, what might such mechanisms be like? We address the first two questions here, and the third, briefly, in a later section entitled "Principal Views Concerning the What, When, and How of Development."

Infant Behaviors and Abilities

Infants are born with or quickly acquire a number of abilities and dispositions that will help them learn about people. They find human faces, voices, and movements particularly interesting stimuli to attend and respond to. They also possess and further develop impressive abilities to perceptually analyze and discriminate human stimuli.

Basic Discrimination Abilities

In the case of faces, infants develop considerable skill in discriminating different facial expressions over the first two years of life, and there is reason to suspect that a component of the ability to recognize facial expressions is unlearned (Nelson, 1987). By the end of the first half year of life, they can abstract the invariant features of, say, a happy facial expression, and can therefore detect a similarity among happy expressions even when they appear on different people's faces (Nelson, 1987). Young babies have also been found to respond differently and appropriately to facial and vocal expressions of different emotions; for example, they tend to look happier and be more responsive when their mother looks and sounds happy than when she looks and sounds sad (Harris, 1989). Infants are also very at-

tracted to people's eyes and develop the ability to follow another person's eye gaze (Butterworth & Jarrett, 1991). This ability to use gazing to detect what another person is looking at makes it possible for the infant to initiate acts of joint visual attention with an adult, acts that will serve to improve the infant's communicative and other social-cognitive abilities.

In the case of voices, infants are highly attentive to them from the beginning and can distinguish one voice from another. Incredibly, young infants have even been shown capable of distinguishing their mother's voice from another woman's based upon prenatal, intrauterine auditory experience with her voice (Cooper & Aslin, 1989). Young babies also have an unlearned ability to hear fine differences between consonant sounds and to perceive them categorically (Kuhl, 1987).

In the case of motor movements, young infants can discriminate biological motion from other kinds of motion. Thus, by 3 months of age, babies show more interest in and dishabituate more to patterns of moving lights that specify human motion (e.g., the pattern of movement of lights attached to the limbs of a walking person) than to random arrays of moving lights (Bertenthal, Proffitt, & Cutting, 1984). Studies by Meltzoff and others (e.g., Meltzoff & Moore, 1994) have demonstrated that, remarkably, even newborns are able to perceptually represent and imitate movements of another person that they cannot see themselves make (though more conservative interpretations of the results are possible, e.g., Anisfeld, 1991). For example, the neonate will imitatively stick out its tongue after it has seen an adult do this; although the adult's action is visible to the infant, the infant's imitative copy of that action is not visible to it, only felt. Older infants apparently know when they are being imitated and they prefer to attend to adults who imitate them (Meltzoff, 1990). Infants are also capable of other feats of intermodal perceptual representation involving people. For instance, by the middle of the first year of life, they can apparently match a happy voice with a happy face, a parent's voice with that same parent's face, the voice of one sex with a face of that same sex, and a spoken monologue with the person delivering it, achieved by detecting the temporal synchrony between the pattern of speech sounds heard and the pattern of lip movements seen.

All this intense and differentiated responsiveness to people must serve the infant's social-cognitive development. If one wanted to design an infant that would learn a lot about people, one would obviously want to start by making it deeply interested in and attentive to them. One would also want to design it so that its appearance and behavior would cause adults to interact with it, and by doing so, provide additional evidence as to what people—both the adults and the infant—are like. Human infants do indeed seem to be built with these two developmentally useful properties: They are impelled to attend to and interact with other people and they impel other people to attend to and interact with them.

There is evidence that infants respond differently to people than they do to objects and seem to expect people to behave differently than objects do (Golinkoff, 1983; Legerstee, 1992; Spelke, Phillips, & Woodward, 1995). Legerstee (1992) reports a longitudinal study in which babies were presented with familiar objects, novel objects, and people. The objects or people either responded contingently to the baby's response or remained passive and unresponsive, depending on the trial. The infants produced significantly more social responses (smiles, vocalizations) toward people than toward objects even when they were only 2 months old. Legerstee (1991) also found that 5- to 8-week-old babies would imitate mouth openings and tongue protrusions produced by an adult, but would not imitate similar-looking behaviors produced by an object.

In their reviews, Golinkoff (1983), Legerstee (1992), and Spelke et al. (1995) report other interesting differentiations between objects and persons that infants of one age or another seem capable of making. Infants try to retrieve a just-disappeared object by reaching toward its place of disappearance, but try to retrieve a just-disappeared person merely by vocalizing to the person (Legerstee, 1992). Similarly, they find it easy to learn to push a knob to produce an inanimate event (the appearance of a picture) but not to produce an animate one (a person waving and saying "Hi!"), as if they realize that people's behavior, unlike that of objects, is not ordinarily influenced by such actions (Golinkoff, 1983). They also tend to act more surprised when an inanimate object seems to move entirely on its own, with nothing pushing it, than when a person does (Golinkoff, 1983; Poulin-Dubois & Shultz, 1988; Spelke et al., 1995). In summary, infants come to construe people as what we have called "compliant agents" (Flavell, Miller, et al., 1993, p. 184): that is, entities that are self-propelled and capable of independent movement (agents), but also influenceable at a distance by communicative signals (compliant). People may come to be seen, from the child's point of view, as both more and less controllable than objects are: More, because unlike most objects, they can be influenced from a distance; less, because unlike most objects, they are sometimes unresponsive even to proximal, physical-force efforts at influence (e.g., unlike the child's doll, they won't always come when you tug at them).

Understanding "Aboutness"

As just described, early in the first year, infants begin to learn how people differ from objects. Late in the first year, they begin to learn how people relate to objects psychologically. Philosophers have noted that people and other animates are related to objects in ways that other objects are not. This special relation is called "aboutness" or "intentionality" (intentionality in a broad sense—not just in the narrow sense of "on purpose"). A person's behavior is "about" an object in this sense if he or she perceptually attends to it, labels it, thinks about it, wants it, fears it, intends or tries to get it, or relates to it in any other psychological way (e.g., Astington, 1993; Wellman, 1993). Wellman (1993) summarizes this development nicely:

> The young infant attends to and interacts with people and a bit later, attends to and manipulates objects. At about nine to twelve months the older infant begins to attend to both simultaneously. This is evident in studies of gaze, where older infants attend back and forth between an object and another person (see, for example, Bakeman and Adamson, 1984). Beyond evidencing a more sophisticated ability to juggle attention between two foci, these interactions begin to reveal a conception of people and objects as connected together—the person directed toward the object. Conceiving of people as connected to objects in this directional fashion is, at the least, a step toward an understanding of intentionality. Beyond that, in the second year, I believe that infants come to recognize persons in intentional terms: the person as experiencing something *about* an object, that object as an object *of* attention or intention. (Wellman, 1993, p. 21)

Infants do a variety of things that reflect a dawning awareness of intentionality or some precursor thereof. They attempt to engender new "aboutnesses" in others through various communicative gestures, and they also check to see if their attempts have succeeded. For example, they may look at, point to, hold up, or vocalize about an object or event and check to see if the other person looks at, comments on, or otherwise responds to it (Bates, 1976; Flavell, Miller, et al., 1993). They also develop skill at reading the aboutnesses the other person already has going. As one example, we have already noted that babies become able to follow another person's direction of gaze and thereby succeed in looking at what the person is looking at. This state of joint attention, in which baby and adult achieve a common cognitive focus, is of course requisite for all communication and communication development (Moore & Dunham, 1995). Recent studies by Meltzoff (1995) have also shown that 18-month-olds can infer what action another person is trying to perform (e.g., detaching one object from another object), even though the person is unsuccessful in the attempt and therefore never actually demonstrates the intended action.

Research reported by Spelke et al. (1995) further suggests that 12-month-olds expect a person to reach for an object that she is looking at with positive affect, rather than another one to which she is not attending. Infants also learn the names for things by noting what object the adult appears to be attending to when he or she says the label. Some clever studies of this kind of aboutness-reading have been done recently (see Baldwin & Moses, 1994; Markman & Woodward, this Volume; Tomasello, 1995). Baldwin (1991, 1993; Baldwin & Moses, 1994) showed that infants of 19 to 20 months of age sense that the verbal label an adult utters refers to the object the adult shows clear signs of attending to at that moment. They recognize that it does not refer to other perceptually salient objects she is not focused on: for example, an object that they rather than she is currently attending to, or an object that she calls to their attention but in such a way as to not appear to be labeling it. In short, infants of this age seem to recognize that it is the adult's attentional focus rather than their own that gives clues as to the adult's referential intent. Tomasello and Barton (1994; Tomasello, 1995) found that children of about 24 months could even distinguish accidental verb-action pairings from intentional ones. An adult picked up a doll and said "Let's dax Mickey Mouse." She then subjected Mickey to two novel actions, one done as if accidentally (saying "Woops!") and the other done intentionally (saying "There!"). Almost none of the subjects took *dax* to mean the accidental-seeming action, suggesting that they could accurately read the experimenter's referential intent from the accidental versus intentional look of her actions.

Social Referencing

As we have just seen, infants develop the ability to learn what an object is called by reading the adult's attentional focus when the adult labels it. They also develop the ability to learn what an object is like by reading the adult's attentional focus when the adult is expressing a positive or negative emotional reaction to it. That is, they can recognize that the adult's emotional display refers to or is about a particular object, just as they can recognize that the adult's

spoken label refers to or is about a particular object. Seeking or using information about objects' positive or negative qualities conveyed by adults' emotional reactions to these objects has been called *social referencing;* the developmental literature on social referencing has recently been ably reviewed by Mumme (1993), Mumme, Fernald, and Herrera (1996), and Robinson (1993). Parents often present young children with this kind of evaluative information, as when they try to interest them in a new toy by acting as if it were the greatest thing ever ("Wow, look at *this!* See what *this* does!" etc.).

One question in the social referencing literature is whether the baby actually realizes that the adult's expressions of affect are about the object. An alternative possibility is that these expressions just alter the baby's mood, which in turn alters the baby's reactions to all objects, for example, dampening them when the mood thus induced is negative. However, recent studies strongly suggest that, although such mood modification effects also can occur, by 12 months or so, infants do have some understanding that the adult's behavior is about the object the adult is attending to when expressing the positive or negative affect (Baldwin & Moses, 1994; Hornik, Risenhoover, & Gunnar, 1987; Mumme, Won, & Fernald, 1994). For example, in a study by Mumme, Won, and Fernald (1994), 12-month-olds watched video displays of an actress directing neutral, happy, or fearful emotional signals at one of two novel objects in front of her. The infants then had the opportunity to play with the actual objects that had just been shown in the video. There was clear evidence of referent specificity: Infants tended to prefer the object that the actress was attending to except when she acted as if she were afraid of it; when she acted that way they avoided it.

Other Social-Cognitive Skills

Older infants also do other things suggestive of a beginning understanding of human psychology. They sometimes appear to be trying to manipulate other people's emotional responses rather than, as in social referencing, just reading these responses for the information about reacted-to objects that they may provide. Even toddlers occasionally seem to try to change other people's feelings, or at least change their affective behavior. In the second year of life they begin to comfort younger siblings in distress by patting, hugging, or kissing them, and may even bring a security blanket to an adult in pain (Wolf, 1982; Zahn-Waxler, Radke-Yarrow, Wagner, & Chapman, 1992). Less positively, young children sometimes tease or otherwise annoy siblings, as if hoping to frustrate or anger them (Dunn, 1988; see also Reddy, 1991). They often do this by destroying a favorite possession or taunting, but occasionally their attempts are more subtle, as when one 24-month-old child teased her sister by pretending to be her imaginary friend (Dunn & Munn, 1985). Such behaviors, positive or negative, are revealing, for they suggest that young children are beginning to identify the conditions that elicit or change emotions or behaviors.

As we will describe in subsequent chapter sections, around 1½ to 2 years of age, children may also begin to evince a more explicit understanding of certain mental states by using words that refer to them (Bartsch & Wellman, 1995; Bretherton & Beeghly, 1982; Huttenlocher & Smiley, 1990; Wellman, 1993). The states most commonly talked about at this early age are seeing ("I see a car"), wanting ("Want juice"), and reacting emotionally ("Those ladies scare me") (Wellman, 1993). Older infants likewise show signs of having acquired at least the beginnings of a self concept (see the chapter on self development by Harter, Volume 3).

Problems of Interpretation

It is apparent from the foregoing review that infants show a number of behaviors that seem relevant to the development of knowledge about people. As Baldwin and Moses (1994), Moore and Corkum (1994), and others have pointed out, however, there is considerable disagreement in the field as to how richly these behaviors should be interpreted. Do the available findings indicate that infants actually represent people as having inner mental states or do they merely show that infants represent various regularities in people's overt behaviors? A number of investigators are relatively generous in their interpretations here, crediting infants with at least some genuine understanding of some mental states (e.g., Baldwin & Moses, 1994; Baron-Cohen, 1993, 1994; Bretherton et al., 1981; Dunn, 1988; Leslie, 1994; Premack, 1990; Tomasello, 1995; Trevarthen & Hubley, 1978; Wellman, 1993). Others are more cautious, preferring leaner, less mentalistic explanations of infants' actions (e.g., Butterworth, 1994; Moore & Corkum, 1994; Perner, 1991). To illustrate the latter stance, Moore and Corkum (1994) present a thoughtful and well-reasoned argument for the position that social behaviors such as joint visual attention, social referencing, and various communicative acts should not be taken as evidence that 1-year-olds have any sort of theory of mind. For example, they argue that

behaviors such as showing objects to people and checking to see if the people's eyes orient towards those objects do not warrant the inference that infants are actually aware that people have seeing experiences and mentally attend to objects (see also Perner, 1991). Although such behaviors may constitute developmental stepping stones to an eventual awareness of mental states, according to these authors they do not attest to the present existence of any such awareness in the 1-year-old.

It is easy to be sympathetic with such lean interpretations. They seem scientifically parsimonious, and they appeal to familiar, general-purpose learning mechanisms rather than to mysterious inborn sensitivities to mental states or the like. Moreover, a convincing case can be made that infants would not necessarily need to be aware of people's mental states to do many of the social-cognitive things that they do (Perner, 1991). For example, they would not actually have to realize that their mother felt afraid of an object in order for them to learn to avoid it in cases of social referencing. They would only have to read her visible expressions of fear as meaning "this object is dangerous," something they could have learned through some conditioning process. That is, the received message could be all about the object rather than about both the object and her inner feelings regarding it. Similarly, infants could respond appropriately in many situations if they could just predict people's overt behavior from their gaze direction. They would not actually have to be aware that the people are also having perceptual and cognitive experiences as their eyes move about (Moore & Corkum, 1994).

On the other hand, a case could be made that we ought not to be overly conservative in our interpretation of infants' behavior in this domain, even when—usually the case—a knock-down argument for a rich interpretation cannot be made. If our pet puppy looks like it is attributing seeing and other mental states to us, we are right to interpret that look conservatively, because it is not clear that even adult dogs make such attributions. In contrast, older human infants who show a similar look are undeniably going to be making genuine mental state attributions in a few short months. Given that fact, it is not unreasonable to suppose that they might be doing some precursor to or early version of the same thing now. There is also the argument that it would be hard to imagine how they could learn to make mental state attributions later if *wholly* incapable of it earlier. In the case of older children, developmentalists often argue that subjects who look as if they lack a certain understanding in task situations (e.g., of false belief, of conservation of quantity) may nevertheless "really" possess that understanding. Real competence often lurks beneath apparent lack of competence, they say. In the present case, in contrast, the parsimoniously-inclined are wont to deny social-cognitive understanding to infants who look as if they *possess* it rather than lack it. Our argument, then, is that if infant members of a mindreading species give us the strong feeling that they are doing some kind of mindreading, they probably are.

Sometimes a longer look on our part reinforces the mentalistic look of their behavior. For example, we have observed that infants usually show their caretakers an interesting new object only once, even though their indulgent caretakers would probably also socially reinforce additional showings with appropriate expressions of interest and approval. They may repeat other interchanges endlessly, to the point of adult tedium, but usually seem to feel the need to show things just once. Why? Our guess is that they somehow sense that the adult has received the new information on the first showing, and thereafter continues to—what?—"know it," one wants to say. They seem not merely to want the other person to look at or see the object—that would be as effectively accomplished on the nth showing as on the first—but in some sense to "know" what it is and that it is there. Such observations lead us to think that infants may at times be attributing to other people *something* inner and unobservable, even though we are at a loss to imagine what that attribution experience might be like for creatures so unknowledgeable and nonverbal.

A final argument for some charity in interpretation here is that older infants do not do just one or two things suggestive of a mentalistic conception of others. Rather, they do a variety of things, all of which point to the dawning of some such conception (Baldwin & Moses, 1994; Tomasello, 1995; Wellman, 1993):

> For example, around this age, important developments take place in areas as diverse as pretense . . . , self-recognition . . . , imitation . . . , empathy . . . , and internal state language . . . , suggesting that infants may have already achieved some general conceptual insight into the minds of others. (Baldwin & Moses, 1994, p. 150)

LATER DEVELOPMENTS

The beginning social-cognitive knowledge described thus far shows dramatic development after infancy. We will discuss several areas that have emerged as important: perception and attention, desires and emotions, intentions, other psychological causes, beliefs and related mental representations, knowledge, pretense, and thinking.

Perception and Attention

What do children know about perception and attention, and when do they acquire this knowledge? Useful reviews of work on these questions can be found in Cox (1980), Flavell (1992), Flavell, Miller, and Miller (1993), Gopnik, Slaughter, and Meltzoff (1994), Miller (1985a), Newcomb (1989), Perner (1991), Pillow (1988, 1989a), Shantz (1983), and Winer (1991). Most of the research in this area has dealt with knowledge about visual perception, the topic to which we turn first.

Visual Perception

We have already cited evidence suggesting that older infants, at least, have some understanding that people see things. They follow the direction of other people's gaze. They try to get others to direct their gaze toward the things they are trying to show them, and may check to make sure they do: "In compelling cases, the infant will begin to point only when the other is attending to him or her, execute the point, check the other's visage, keep pointing or augment the behavior if the other is not correctly directed, and only stop when the other orients or comments on the object" (Wellman, 1993, p. 22). They also start using vision-related words like *see* correctly as early as 1½ to 2 years of age. In fact, all of the evidence on infant joint attention, communication, lexical acquisition, and social referencing reported in the previous section can also be interpreted as plausible evidence for some early intuitions about visual perception.

There is other evidence as well. If asked to show a picture to a person who has covered her eyes with her hands, the 18-month-olds will move the hands or try to put the picture between the hands and the eyes (Lempers, Flavell, & Flavell, 1977). They tend to show pictures to another person in such a way that they can also continue to see them while the other person does, rather than turning them away from the self and facing them toward the other, as 24-month-olds tend to do (Lempers et al., 1977). Consequently, when asked to show a small picture glued to the inside bottom of an opaque cup, 1½-year-olds tend to hold the cup low and tilt its opening back and forth so that both they and the other person can get alternating glimpses of it.

Infants have many opportunities to learn that closing and opening their eyes, looking in this direction versus that, seeing objects appear and disappear from view, and the like, changes their own visual experiences. It may not be too difficult for them to infer that similar behaviors have similar effects on other people, and especially that other people do indeed have visual experiences (Gopnik, Slaughter, & Meltzoff, 1994; Novey, 1975).

Assuming that at some quite early age children do begin to realize that people have inner visual experience or percepts, what do they know about these percepts? There is evidence for at least two roughly distinguishable developmental levels or stages of knowledge about visual percepts (Flavell, 1978, 1992; Hughes & Donaldson, 1979; Masangkay et al., 1974). At the higher one, called Level 2, children clearly understand the idea of people having different perspectives or views of the same visual display. Level 2 children can represent the fact that although both they and another person see the very same thing from different station points, the other person nonetheless sees it a bit differently, or has a somewhat different visual experience of it, than they do. For example, they realize that a dog that they see right side up in a picture book will look upside down to someone who views the book wrong side up. At earlier-developing Level 1, children understand that the other person need not presently see something just because they do and vice-versa. For example, they realize that whereas they see what is on their side of a vertically-held card, another person, seated opposite, does not. Thus, they are clearly not profoundly and pervasively egocentric in the Piagetian sense; they definitely do have some knowledge about visual perception. Unlike Level 2 children, however, they do not yet conceptualize and consciously represent the fact of perspective-derived differences between their and the other person's visual experience of something that *both* people currently see. They know whether the other person sees X, but cannot yet calculate exactly how X looks.

Flavell and colleagues have made direct tests of this hypothesized developmental sequence by comparing the same children's performance on Level 1 and Level 2 tasks (Flavell, Everett, Croft, & Flavell, 1981; Masangkay et al. (1974). The results of their studies suggest that there is a real and robust difference between Level 1 and Level 2 knowledge, with the former regularly developing earlier than the latter. Furthermore, relevant experience appears not to readily induce Level 2 thinking in Level 1 children, even when that experience consists of literally supplying them with the correct answer to the question. For a summary of these and other studies of Level 1 and 2 knowledge, see Flavell (1992). For the few studies dealing with the development of knowledge about perception in other modalities, see Flavell, Green, and Flavell (1989), Winer (1989), and Yaniv and Shatz (1988).

Attention

As already described, infants come to understand that people show, by their gaze direction and other actions, that they are psychologically "about" various objects and events in the world. In this sense, infants clearly could be said to possess at least a rudimentary understanding of attention. Indeed, some developmentalists are inclined to credit the infant with a quite rich understanding of attention (e.g., Baron-Cohen, 1995). The evidence suggests that children also go on to acquire other important insights about attention (Fabricius & Schwanenflugel, 1994; Flavell, Green, & Flavell, 1995a; Miller, 1985a; Pillow, 1988, 1989a, 1995). First, attention is selective. We do not see or hear everything that is in our field of vision or in earshot; perceptibility does not automatically imply perceived. We may even not devote much attention to the things we perceive, and therefore may not comprehend, reflect on, or remember them. Second, as implied in this last, attention entails constructive processing of what has been attended to. It involves a Level 2-like interpretation and elaboration of the sensory input, rather than just a Level 1-like internal registering or copying of it; as a consequence, one person's cognitive representation of what has been perceived may differ from another person's. Third, attentional capacity is limited. If we try to pay full attention to one thing, we will not normally be very aware of other things in the perceptual field—unless the other things are very attention-capturing (e.g., visually salient or loud), in which case, attention to the first thing will suffer correspondingly.

The following are sample studies illustrating these developmental acquisitions. Young children's view of attention is that unless the situation is noisy, a person will hear and comprehend what someone says to him (Miller & Bigi, 1979). By about age 8, children begin to realize that the mind has some control over the attentional process. They know that people shut out something boring (usually a teacher!) even if the room is quiet, and successfully attend to something interesting, even in a noisy room. In less demanding testing situations, older preschoolers sometimes demonstrate this awareness of the contribution of psychological states to the attention process. (Miller & Bigi, 1979; Miller & Shannon, 1984; Miller & Zalenski, 1982; Pillow, 1988, 1989a).

Pillow (1989a) tested preschoolers' and elementary-school children's understanding that trying to comprehend verbal input in one ear (a story, or block-building instructions) would result in failure to comprehend an incidental story presented to the other ear. He found that "whereas most 4 year-olds demonstrated little understanding of selective listening, some 5-year-olds, most 6-year-olds, and nearly all 8-year-olds understood that attending selectively to one event may diminish the information one obtains about other events" (Pillow, 1989a, p. 441).

Flavell, Green, and Flavell (1995a) tested children of 4, 6, and 8 years of age for their understanding that a person who is mentally focused on one thing will be devoting little or no simultaneous attention or thought to another, totally irrelevant thing. For instance, while one is busy trying to recognize the people in a group photograph, one will not be simultaneously paying any significant amount of attention to the photograph's visible but unremarkable picture frame. Likewise, when trying to recall the movies one has seen recently, one will not also be thinking about something totally unrelated, such as one's piano. Whereas most of the 6- and 8-year-olds demonstrated an understanding that task-oriented thought and attention are selectively focused in this way, most of the 4-year-olds showed no such understanding. These results are consistent with those obtained by Miller and Pillow, just cited. Flavell et al. (1995a) speculated that 4-year-olds may implicitly conceive of the mind as more like a lamp than like a flashlight, that is, as a device that can radiate attention and thought in all directions at once, rather than in only one direction at a time.

Finally, a program of studies by Fabricius and Schwanenflugel (1994) is showing some intriguing further developments in children's understanding of attention and other mental phenomena after the age of 8. As examples, older children seem to acquire a clearer distinction between attention and comprehension, a more abstract, supramodal conception of selective attention, and more generally, a more process-oriented, constructivist conception of the mind (cf., Pillow, 1995). We will return to issues of constructivism and perception-cognition relations in later sections.

Desires and Emotions

There are important commonalities between desires and emotions. Together with perception, desires and emotions tend to be the first mental states that young children talk about (Bartsch & Wellman, 1995; Wellman, 1993). Moreover, some mental states, such as that of liking or disliking something, seem to be mixtures of desires and emotions. Desires and emotions are also causally linked within our naive theory of mind. For example, we believe that people will normally tend to feel good if they get what they desire and feel bad if they do not. Likewise, we think that people will usually come to like previously neutral things with which they have had positive emotional experiences and dislike those associated with negative experiences. As we will show, young children also represent these causal links.

Desires

There are a number of good reviews of research on children's developing knowledge about desires: Astington (1993), Astington and Gopnik (1991b), Bretherton and Beeghly (1982), Perner (1991), Wellman (1990, 1991), Wellman and Woolley (1990), and especially, Bartsch and Wellman (1995). Much of the evidence concerning young children's understanding of desires comes from research by Wellman and his colleagues. Particularly important is an ambitious recent study by Bartsch and Wellman (1995) which made use of the Child Language Data Exchange System (CHILDES), a growing collection of child language corpora contributed by different researchers (MacWhinney & Snow, 1990). Bartsch and Wellman examined samples of the everyday speech of ten children in the CHILDES database from before they were 2 years old until they were 5 years old. Of the approximately 200,000 utterances searched, about 12,000 included thought and belief terms such as *think, know,* and *wonder,* and desire terms such as *want, hope,* and *wish.*

Bartsch and Wellman (1995) found that the children in their sample began using desire terms very early—by 1½ to 2 years of age. More important, by the time the children were 2 to 2½, they were using these terms in ways that strongly suggested some genuine understanding of desire as a mental state. They would contrast what they wanted with what they actually had or were about to have, suggesting that they did not equate desires with existing objects, actions, or states of affairs. For example, one 2-year-old said, after his mother promised to turn the TV on later, "I don't want it on later . . . I want it on now" (said while TV is clearly off and remains off; Bartsch & Wellman, 1995, p. 90). Around this same age, the children also appeared to sense that desires are subjective, and that different people might differ in what they want or like. The authors concluded that their 2-year-olds' use of desire terms "revealed an understanding that different people have different desires; identical objects may differ in desirability among different people; and desires are essentially experiential states that motivate action but that are also separate from the external world of overt acts and outcomes" (Bartsch & Wellman, 1995, p. 93).

Bartsch and Wellman (1995) found that their subjects used and seemed to understand desire terms much earlier than thought and belief terms. Other observational or diary studies have also shown the same thing (Bretherton, McNew, & Beeghly-Smith, 1981; Brown & Dunn, 1991; Shatz, Wellman, & Silber, 1983). Bartsch and Wellman (1995) conclude that their data support the following three-step developmental sequence. First, around the age of 2, children acquire a *desire psychology*. This includes an elementary conception, not only of simple desires, but also of simple emotions and simple perceptual experience or attention. The conception is elementary in that, although mentalistic, it is nonrepresentational rather than representational. That is, the child understands that people are subjectively related to things in the sense of having the inner experience of wanting them, fearing them, seeing them, and so forth, but does not yet understand that people mentally represent these things, accurately or inaccurately, as being a certain way. Second, around the age of 3, children begin to talk about beliefs and thoughts as well as desires, and seem to understand that beliefs are mental representations that can be false as well as true and can differ from person to person. However, at this age, they continue to explain their own and other people's actions by appeal to desires rather than beliefs. The authors refer to this second level of understanding as a *desire-belief psychology*. Finally, at about age 4, children begin to understand that what people think and believe, as well as what they desire, crucially affects how they behave. That is, they acquire our adult *belief-desire psychology*, in which beliefs and desires are thought to determine actions jointly.

Experimental studies also confirm the observational, language-diary evidence that children have some genuine understanding of desires by the age of 2½ to 3 years. They show that children of this age tend to grasp simple causal relations between desires, outcomes, and emotions; that is, they believe that people will feel happy if they get what they want, and sad or mad if they do not (Hadwin & Perner, 1991; Stein & Levine, 1989; Wellman, 1990; Wellman & Banerjee, 1991; Yuill, 1984). In addition to predicting the emotion from the desire-outcome relation, they are also able to explain the emotion by referring back to the initial desire (Stein & Levine, 1989; Wellman, 1990; Wellman & Banerjee, 1991). Wellman and Woolley (1990; Wellman, 1990) further showed that 2½-year-olds can not only infer

feelings of happiness and sadness from desire-outcome matches and mismatches, they can also predict some subsequent behavior—specifically, that a person who found the desired object he or she had been searching for would quit searching, whereas a person who found nothing, or even another attractive object, would continue searching (but see Perner, 1991, Note 9.1, p. 312, for less impressive performance by 3-year-olds on this task).

A study by King (1994) tested 3-year-olds' understanding of simple attitudes (likes-dislikes). All of her subjects gave evidence of believing that positive and negative experiences with an object would lead, respectively, to liking and disliking that object. Thus, they evinced some knowledge about how attitudes can get formed through experience. Most of her 3-year-olds also understood that two story characters who had opposite emotional and behavioral reactions to the very same sleeping, unresponsive animal would form different attitudes toward it; that is, the one who thought the animal would bite and withdrew from it would not like it, whereas the one who thought it would play and approached it would like it. Similarly, Flavell, Mumme, Green, and Flavell (1992) found that 3-year-olds had no trouble grasping the possibility that even though they themselves do not like coffee, an adult might. Recall that Bartsch and Wellman (1995) likewise found that children of this age understand that different people can have different desires and attitudes regarding the very same things. Contrary to a conjecture by Perner (1991), young preschoolers seem to construe desire more as a personal, subjective relation to things rather than viewing desirability and undesirability as inherent, objective properties of things.

Emotions

Emotions are objects of people's thinking as well as felt experiences. It is difficult to imagine a socially competent human who lacked an understanding of emotions and their relation to cognition and behavior. This understanding helps children identify the feelings of other people toward them, anticipate whether their parents will be angry or pleased about their behavior, and hide their socially inappropriate feelings. Moreover, such knowledge can promote positive relationships with others, effective self-presentation, and the attainment of rewards or interpersonal advantage. Perhaps reflecting the importance of this topic, research in the area has boomed in the last several years.

Useful sources include Astington (1993); Bretherton, Fritz, Zahn-Waxler, and Ridgeway (1986); Flavell, Miller, and Miller (1993); Gross and Ballif (1991); Lewis and Saarni (1985); Perner (1991); Saarni and Harris (1989); and especially, Harris (1989) and Meerum Terwogt and Harris (1993). In addition, research relevant to this sprawling topic is also reviewed in several chapters of Volume 3 of this *Handbook*. Likewise, there is important recent work on the family antecedents of individual differences in children's emotion knowledge and social behavior (Dunn & Brown, 1994) that we unfortunately do not have space to discuss.

Studies have shown that children tend to begin producing some emotion words late in their second year and that the use of emotion-descriptive language increases rapidly during the third year (Bretherton & Beeghly, 1982; Bretherton, McNew, & Beeghly-Smith, 1981; Brown & Dunn, 1991; Dunn, Bretherton, & Munn, 1987; Ridgeway, Waters, & Kuczaj, 1985; Smiley & Huttenlocher, 1989; Wellman, Harris, Banerjee, & Sinclair, 1995). Words such as *happy, sad, mad,* and *scared* are among the earliest to appear. Examples of 2-year-old emotion talk are: "Santa will be happy if I pee in the potty"; "You sad, Daddy?"; "I feel bad"; "Bees everywhere. Scared me!"; "Don't be mad, Mommy!" (Bretherton & Beeghly, 1982, p. 913).

What do young children think such words refer to? What is their conception of emotions? As Wellman et al. (1995) point out, they might conceive of emotions merely as scriptlike situation-action regularities. For example, *scared* might be thought to refer, not to an internal, subjective-experiential state, but to a fear-inducing stimulus or situation, or to the expressive and instrumental behaviors (a fear face, running away) that such situations elicit in people, or to some combination of these. Alternatively, they might conceive of them as internal feeling states, as Bretherton, Dunn, and other less conservative theorists have believed all along.

Wellman et al. (1995) tried to find out by carefully analyzing the emotion- and pain-related utterances from the CHILDES study previously discussed in the *Desires* subsection (Bartsch & Wellman, 1995). These utterances proved to be very revealing. They frequently specified the target of the emotion, that is, the person, object, or event that the self or some other individual was afraid of, mad at, happy or sad about, and so forth. In contrast, although children cited the causes of pains, they did not seem to conceptualize pains as having intended targets—that is, things that they were about. Children also seemed able to distinguish feeling states from the actions they commonly engender. Although some of their cited evidence might be given a

leaner, nonmentalistic interpretation, we tend to believe their conclusion that young children "evidence an understanding of emotions as experiential states of persons, as distinguished from the actions (e.g., hitting) and expressions (e.g., smiling) that emotions cause, and they distinguish between the subjective emotional experiences of different individuals" (Wellman et al., 1995, p. 118).

There is obviously much more for children to learn about emotions than that they are mental states that have causes and consequences—facts they seem to have some grasp of even during the preschool years. During the preschool and elementary school years, children's knowledge about emotions becomes more complex. For example, concepts of emotion evolve from a global *feels good* and *feels bad* to a range of differentiated emotions, for instance, *mean* and *excited* by age 3 (Ridgeway, Waters, & Kuczaj, 1985), *proud, jealous,* and *worried* by age 7, and *relieved* and *disappointed* by preadolescence (Harris, Olthof, Meerum Terwogt, & Hardman, 1987).

Moreover, young children extend their ability to infer emotions from facial expressions to making this inference when they cannot see the face, when the real emotion is masked by a different facial expression, or when the emotion is one that is not easily detected in the face. Children are increasingly likely to use some organizing principle to unite diverse events—breaking a favorite toy, having to eat spinach, being hurt by a friend—into a single category of sadness. How might children detect emotion in these cases? One possibility (Harris, 1989) is that children could draw on their own experiences to cognitively simulate the underlying emotion that someone else would have in the situation (see also Smiley & Huttenlocher, 1989). Another possibility (Stein & Levine, 1989) is that children may label an emotion according to whether a goal is satisfied, rather than according to the overt situation (e.g., a smile, a birthday party). This account is plausible because preschoolers have some grasp of the causal relations among desires, outcomes, and emotions.

Another major change is that children become aware of multiple sources of information for inferring emotions. Suppose that a child is trying to decide whether to ask another child, who has a toy she desires, to share that toy, and is trying to assess his emotional state. She might look at his face, consider the context (e.g., Is he playing a game he likes? Has he had a frustrating day?), recall that he generally is a happy child, and ponder that boys at that school tend to become angry when asked to share. She may be cognitively limited in several ways when making these judgments. First, preschoolers are often cognitively overwhelmed by multiple sources of information, probably due to capacity limitations. Second, young children have difficulty inferring emotions from information about a person's group membership (e.g., gender, age, race) and specific personal experiences such as prior negative interactions with the person. Third, young children have trouble sorting out conflicting cues, for instance, when a person feels sad but tries to look happy.

Regarding this third point, preschoolers rarely show an understanding of such facial display rules, though one study showed that they can produce misleading facial displays under some circumstances (Cole, 1986). Most of the change comes later. In one study (Gnepp & Hess, 1986), children had to decide which facial expression a child in a story would display and what the child would say. For example, in one story, a child failed to win a talent contest and watched everyone applaud the winner. From ages 6 to 10, children showed increased levels of understanding that the child would smile to hide his disappointment (see also Harris & Gross, 1988; and Saarni, 1984). School-age children also know the value of hiding one's feelings in certain situations, but recognize that it is maladaptive to carry this to the extreme of rarely expressing one's real feelings. Among 6- to 13-year olds, the majority assert that such a child would be maladjusted, disliked, and difficult to get to know (Saarni, 1988). As one psychodynamically-oriented 13-year-old remarked, "if she kept everything inside her all the time, she'd consume all her anger, jealousy, whatever, and then one day she'd explode, commit suicide, and get emotionally disturbed" (p. 289).

Interestingly, when children acquire an understanding of facial displays, they in a sense unlearn a rule they had learned earlier—that physical evidence such as behavior, facial expressions, and speech provide clues to emotions and other mental states. They learn that such evidence is unreliable, inaccurate, and sometimes even a deliberate attempt by others to deceive. More generally, the notion that social appearances may not correspond to social realities strikes us as a major developmental step in social cognition (Flavell, Green, & Flavell, 1986; Flavell, Lindberg, Green, & Flavell, 1992; Harris & Gross, 1988). Understanding facial displays also is important because it is "an important element in children's understanding of the potential privacy of their mental world" (Meerum Terwogt & Harris, 1993, p. 76).

Thus far we have discussed conflicting information sources regarding emotion when facial and situational cues conflict. But another kind of conflicting information involves the experience of two or more conflicting emotions, for example, feeling happy about going to a birthday party but feeling sad that a friend was not invited. Although even toddlers experience ambivalence, as when they both approach and avoid an interesting but strange phenomenon such as a department store Santa, they apparently cannot conceptualize their emotional state until many years later (Harter & Buddin, 1987; Harter & Whitesell, 1989). Until 6 or 7 years of age, children generally can conceive of two successive conflicting emotions, at best. Later, they have the concept of concurrent emotions, but only if they have the same valence, such as mad and sad, and refer to a single target. Only by age 10 or so do children understand that people can simultaneously experience two opposite-valenced emotions, such as sad and happy: "I was happy that I got a present but mad that it wasn't what I wanted" (Harter & Buddin, 1987, p. 393). Without this understanding, children may not try to take another emotional perspective, for example, look on the bright side of a disappointing event. For reports of earlier competencies in this area, see Kestenbaum and Gelman (1995) and Stein and Trabasso (1989).

Other major developments in concepts of emotions include the following (e.g., Flapan, 1968; Harris, 1989; Rothenberg, 1970; Savitsky & Izard, 1970): Children learn that emotions typically wane with time, and that waiting a while before acting when in the grip of a strong emotion is often a wise thing to do (Meerum Terwogt & Harris, 1993). In addition, children become increasingly likely to try to infer feelings spontaneously and to try to explain them. They also become more accurate at diagnosing emotional states, and need fewer obvious clues. Moreover, children learn that a person's emotional reaction to an event may be influenced by an earlier emotional experience or by the person's current mood. For example, they realize that a person's brooding about an earlier bad experience could dampen his feelings about a current pleasant event. In contrast, a younger child is likely to predict the person's feelings only on the basis of the present event. In addition, older children can draw on a broader perspective to make more complex and abstract inferences about emotions. As an example, an adolescent might be aware of, and sympathize with, the suffering of a group in another country as well as the more obvious and salient distress of someone they know well (Hoffman, 1978). Children's increasingly abstract and mentalistic conception of emotions paves the way for profound and pervasive changes in their social cognition and social behavior.

Children also apply their knowledge of emotions to the control of their own mental state to some extent. In one study, younger boys at an English boarding school tended to distract themselves from feelings of homesickness by using situational strategies such as getting absorbed in games or other activities (Harris, 1989, chapter 7). Later, by age 10 or so, they also could provide psychological explanations about how this strategy helped. Similarly, children help delay gratification by changing their cognitive state, for example, by mentally transforming a marshmallow into a puffy cloud or a yucky-tasting object (Mischel & Mischel, 1983). Additional evidence concerning the development of strategies for coping with stress is described in other *Handbook* chapters.

Intentions

Developing the concept of intentionality is highly significant for at least two reasons. First, it clarifies how people differ from other objects; humans, unlike other objects, are driven by intentions, motives, goals, and plans. Second, children must draw on intentions in order to understand responsibility and morality (Shantz, 1983). In fact, most early research on understanding intentions (Shultz, 1980; see chapter on morality in Volume 3) focused on whether children use intentions when making moral judgments rather than examine knowledge about intentions per se. Subsequently, researchers more directly studied children's understanding of intentionality. Useful sources include Astington (1991, 1993), Bloom (this Volume), Flavell, Miller, and Miller (1993), Karniol (1978), Moses (1990, 1993), Shantz (1983), Shultz (1980), and Shultz and Wells (1985).

As we noted earlier, there is evidence that infants come to construe people as agents, that is, as animate beings that, unlike inanimate objects, can move and behave on their own steam. Shultz (1991) argues that children elaborate their early, possibly innate (Premack, 1990), concept of agent into the concept of intentions. The latter goes beyond notions of agency and animacy by positing an internal mental state that guides behavior. People not only *can* act; they *want* and *try* to act. By age 3, children may have some ability to distinguish intended actions from nonintentional behaviors such as reflexes and mistakes (Shultz, 1980). When children tried to repeat a tongue twister (e.g., "She sells sea shells by the sea shore"), but made errors, they reported that they did not mean to say the sentence wrong. This also was found with peer bystanders, regardless of whether they

had previously experienced the task themselves. Thus, even a child who had not yet tried to repeat the tongue twister knew that another child who said it incorrectly did not "mean to say it like that." It was less clear whether the 3-year-olds understood that a knee-jerk reflex was not done "on purpose."

These appropriate uses of *mean to* and *on purpose* by 3-year-olds may reflect a genuine understanding of the intentional-unintentional distinction. However, children may simply have formed an association between the phrase *not on purpose* and errors. Or, children may infer that a behavior is intended only if a desire is fulfilled as suggested in research by Astington (1991, 1993). Children heard two stories. In one, a girl takes some bread outside, throws crumbs to the birds, and the birds eat them. In a second story, another girl's mother gives her some bread, which she takes outside to eat. Some crumbs accidentally drop behind her and the birds eat them. The two stories had the same outcome, in both cases caused by the child's behavior, but only in the first is the action intended. When 4- and 5-year-olds were asked which girl meant for the birds to eat the crumbs, they correctly chose the first girl, but the 3-year-olds were equally likely to choose either girl. Astington suggested that Shultz's 3-year-olds inferred intentionality only when a person's desire is fulfilled. When there was not a match between a desire and the outcome, as when wanting to repeat a tongue twister correctly but making an error, children believed that the behavior was not intended. Thus, when outcomes are identical and desires are not stated explicitly, as in the bread crumbs study, 3-year-olds are unable to detect that the two girls differed in their intent to achieve the outcome. They do not fully understand intentionality because they do not understand that an intention could be unfulfilled, and that a desired outcome could happen fortuitously, rather than by the child's intention. Possibly their "desire theory of mind" (Bartsch & Wellman, 1995) causes them to confuse intent and desire, perhaps because each is either fulfilled or not fulfilled by the outcome. Recent studies by Abbot, Lee, and Flavell (1996) support Astington's interpretation.

In summary, infants seem to have some notion of people as agents. By age 3, children often can distinguish between intentional behavior and mistakes or accidents, but children probably fail to understand intent as a prior causal mental state independent of the outcome of actions until at least age 4. It appears that an adequate understanding of intent involves at least two components: (a) a nonaccidental behavior that is related to desires but differentiated from outcomes; and (b) a prior mental state of planning an action and believing that one will carry it out (Moses, 1993). What causes the development of this knowledge? Certain experiences may facilitate the understanding of intentionality. Adults may respond to unintended and intended actions differently—for example, telling the child that her harmful action was done on purpose, and punishing her for it. Children might work out various rules of thumb for making the distinction. For example, they might come to assume that an outcome is likely to be intended if it matches the agent's stated intention, if the agent looked as though he was trying to achieve it, and if he does not look disappointed, surprised, or puzzled when it occurs. Also, in the case of one's own behavior, intended and unintended actions and outcomes engender very different thoughts and feelings in oneself—very different metacognitive experiences (Flavell, Miller, & Miller, 1993).

Other Psychological Causes

As described earlier, even toddlers sometimes talk about such psychological causes as emotions, intentions, and desires. Interestingly, young children tend to talk about social rather than physical causes (Bloom & Capatides, 1987; Hood & Bloom, 1979). It may be that 2-year-olds have more need to communicate their needs and desires, rather than physical causes, to other people. Moreover, young children may understand more about possible psychological mechanisms, such as desires, than they do about physical causal mechanisms (Miller & Aloise, 1989), which is not surprising if they do in fact already have a desire theory of mind (Bartsch & Wellman, 1995).

Over the next few years, children become able to predict how a variety of emotions, abilities, perceptual perspectives, beliefs, and motives affect behavior. At the same time, they are acquiring event or script knowledge that allows them to fit psychological states into event sequences involving causes. For example, they know that someone will go to a birthday party because she wants to have fun and takes a piece of cake because she believes she will want to eat it. Not until middle or late childhood, however, do children fully differentiate certain closely related causes such as ability and effort (e.g., Skinner, 1990; Stipek, 1992; Stipek & MacIver, 1989). Children also become aware of more subtle psychological causes, for example, the unconscious motivation underlying displaced aggression (Miller & DeMarie-Dreblow, 1990; Weiss & Miller, 1983).

One type of psychological causal explanation is a trait that causes the person to behave in a consistent way over time and situations. Although preschoolers occasionally use trait words when describing a person, they may be referring to specific behaviors rather than general dispositions (Rholes, Newman, & Ruble, 1990). And they rarely use traits to explain behavior. It appears that age 5 to 7 is a transitional period, with some studies (e.g., Gnepp & Chilamkurti, 1988; Ruble, Newman, Rholes, & Altshuler, 1988) reporting children's appropriate predictions of behaviors based on traits, and other studies (e.g., Rholes & Ruble, 1984; Stipek & Daniels, 1990) reporting less competence. As an example of the latter, children may overpredict and say that a person with a positive trait would do well in unrelated domains, for instance, predicting that a nice classmate would jump over higher hurdles than not-so-nice classmates (Stipek & Daniels, 1990). On the other hand, they may underpredict due to their shaky understanding that a person can express a trait in different, but related, behaviors (Rholes & Ruble, 1984). Thus, young children may detect regularities in a person's behavior, apply a trait label, and perhaps treat it as a cause, but may not see the trait as a stable, abiding, differentiated psychological cause until age 8 to 10. For useful reviews, see Rholes, Newman, and Ruble (1990), Yuill (1992, 1993), and Ruble and Dweck (1995).

A main question about causal attributions of behavior concerns young children's preference for using external versus internal-psychological causes. Children may know about mental states, but how salient are these states? Suppose a child observes another child grasping his mother's hand tightly as a large, unfamiliar dog approaches. She could encode this event as "He's holding his mommy's hand" or "He's scared of the dog." Note that, like psychologists, young children could be considered either "behaviorists" or "mentalists" in their description of this behavior. Traditionally, young children have been considered behaviorists, tending to describe events in observable, physical terms and to explain behavior in terms of physical causes. One reason for this view is that young children are known to describe others mainly in terms of their appearance, behavior, and possessions. Moreover, they use facial expressions to infer emotions, desirable outcomes to infer intentionality, and the amount of damage done rather than intentions to make moral judgments (Miller & Aloise, 1989).

In recent years, researchers have challenged this apparent developmental change from external to internal attributions (e.g., Lillard & Flavell, 1990; Miller & Aloise, 1989). As described earlier, young children in fact do have some knowledge about mental states and may even have a coherent theory of mind. Moreover, when researchers make their assessments less verbally demanding or make internal states more salient, young children can use psychological states to describe or explain behavior, and often even prefer to do so. To illustrate, Lillard and Flavell (1990) examined 3-year-olds' preferred way of describing events. Children saw three differently colored copies of the same picture. The experimenter described the first picture in terms of the mental state of the person in the picture, and the second picture in terms of the person's behavior, or vice versa. Then the child was asked to tell a puppet about the third picture. In this way, the child could choose between the mental and behavioral description. The pictures had no cues to either the behavior or the mental state. For example, in one picture, a child was sitting on the floor leaning over a glass of spilled milk; neither his face nor his behavior (wiping up the milk) was visible. Thus, the two possible available descriptions ("He's feeling sad about his spilled milk" and "He's wiping up his spilled milk") were equally plausible. The children tended to choose mentalistic descriptions, both in this study and in a second study with pictures biased toward behavioristic descriptions, for example, with the behavior fully visible. Thus, young children may prefer to use mentalistic accounts of behavior, if available, even when a behavioristic description is more salient. Similarly, Miller (1985b) showed that 4-year-olds preferred internal psychological causes to external ones when both were made salient and were pitted against each other on a task requiring children to choose one cause.

Young children do not, however, always prefer psychological causes. Several studies (e.g., Higgins & Bryant, 1982) report preschoolers have a preference for nonpsychological causes—causes outside of the person. In fact, adults often prefer to attribute behavior to external causes, especially when explaining their own behavior rather than that of others (e.g., Nisbett, Caputo, Legant & Marcek, 1973). In general, though, it appears that preschoolers tend to prefer psychological causes unless the relevant information for making this inference is too complex or subtle (Miller & Aloise, 1989).

Beliefs and Related Mental Representations

There have been a great many investigations of children's developing understanding of "serious" mental representations, that is, nonpretense mental states meant by their owners to portray reality accurately. The majority of these have dealt with children's comprehension of representations that differ from person to person or differ from reality. Principal examples are studies dealing with the appearance-reality distinction (perceptual appearance versus reality), Level 2 perspective taking (perceptual appearance from one position versus another vis-à-vis some visual display), interpretation and constructive processing, deception, and most studied of all, false belief. Reviews of work in these areas can be found in many books and articles, including Astington (1993), Astington and Gopnik (1991a), Bartsch and Wellman (1995), Flavell (1992), Flavell, Miller, and Miller (1993), Lewis and Mitchell (1994), Perner (1991), Pillow (1995), and Wellman (1990).

Introduction

A brief sampling of some of the more common research methods and developmental findings will serve to introduce this area. Experimenters usually test children's understanding of beliefs by using one or another variation of the two false-belief tasks described previously: the unexpected-transfer task (p. 853) and the deceptive-box task (p. 851). The usual finding has been that 3-year-olds tend to fail these tasks. In the unexpected-transfer task they tend to say, incorrectly, that the returning individual will think the object is where it really is and will look there, and in the deceptive-box task that the naive observer will think the box contains what it really contains. In both cases, they err by reporting what is really the case rather than what the misled individual would falsely believe to be the case. In contrast, 4- and 5-year-olds usually pass such tests.

Similarly, 3-year-olds often seem not to understand that one can induce false beliefs in people by providing them with misleading information. As a case in point, Russell, Mauthner, Sharpe, and Tidswell (1991) tried to teach 3- and 4-year-old subjects a competitive game in which they were supposed to point deceptively to a box that does not contain candy rather than one that does, so as to keep the candy for themselves rather than let their opponent get it. Unlike the 4-year-olds, who quickly caught on, the 3-year-olds continued for trial after trial to point to the box containing the candy rather than the empty one. They did this despite their obvious desire to win the candy for themselves and their obvious frustration as they inexplicably kept losing it to their opponent.

Similar developmental trends are usually seen when children's grasp of the appearance-reality distinction is assessed—another case in which an erroneous mental impression is pitted against a known reality. For example, after pretraining on the appearance-reality distinction and associated terminology, subjects may be presented with a sponge made to look like a rock or a little object that looks big when viewed through a magnifying glass (Flavell, 1992; Flavell, Green, & Flavell, 1986). After discovering each object's true identity or property, subjects are asked how the object currently appears to their eyes (rock; big) and how or what it really and truly is (sponge; little). The common result has been that 3-year-olds tend to give the same answer to both questions, reporting either the appearance twice or the reality twice, as if they did not distinguish conceptually between the misleading perceptual appearance and the underlying reality. On the other hand, children of age 4 and older typically show some command of the distinction. The distinction between perceptual appearance and reality is conceptually very similar both to the distinction between false belief and reality and to the previously described Level 2 distinction between two different perceptual appearances resulting from different observer perspectives. Consistent with this fact, there is some correlational evidence that these distinctions develop together: Young children who perform well (or poorly) on appearance-reality tasks also tend to perform well (or poorly) on false belief tasks, Level 2 visual perspective-taking tasks, and other conceptually related measures (Flavell, Green, & Flavell, 1986; Friend & Davis, 1993; Gopnik & Astington, 1988; Moore, Pure, & Furrow, 1990; Taylor, Gerow, & Carlson, 1993; but see also Slaughter & Gopnik, 1996).

Finally, it is clear that children's knowledge about mental representations continues to increase after the age of 4. In particular, it is not until middle childhood and later that children appear to gain any appreciable understanding of the mind as an interpretive, constructive processor (Chandler, 1988; Fabricius & Schwanenflugel, 1994; Flavell, 1988; Lalonde, Chandler, & Moses, 1993; Pillow, 1995; Pillow & Henrichon, 1996; Taylor, 1988; Wellman, 1990; Wellman & Hickling, 1994). For example, recognizing that the way people interpret an ambiguous event may be influenced by their preexisting biases or expectations seems to be a middle-childhood rather than an early-childhood insight (Pillow, 1993a; Pillow & Henrichon, 1996).

Many investigators believe that the core knowledge that is developing in this area can be characterized roughly as follows: People mentally represent (construe, interpret, perceive, etc.) the world as being a certain way. However, their mental representations are not always accurate, and can also vary from person to person and within the same person over time. As now-familiar examples: Their present belief about something may be false, or it may differ from someone else's belief or from their own at a previous time; how things appear perceptually may differ from how they really are or from how they appear from a different viewing position. Finally, in the case of beliefs, it is recognized that people really believe their beliefs, their false ones as well as their true ones. That is, people think and act in accordance with their false beliefs rather than in accordance with the true state of affairs that these beliefs refer to and incorrectly represent. False-belief tasks are intended to assess this knowledge, especially the last part. For example, in the unexpected-transfer task, subjects are supposedly tested for their understanding that the protagonist has a false representation, believes it to be true, and therefore searches where it says to search rather than where the hidden object actually resides.

This knowledge, usually referred to as a *representational theory of mind,* is obviously of supreme importance for the child's social-cognitive development. It is hard to imagine a human society in which the adult members did not realize that they and their fellow members could harbor false as well as true beliefs and would behave as if these false beliefs were true. It is not surprising, therefore, that developmental studies of false-belief, deception, appearance-reality, and related phenomena have mushroomed since Wimmer and Perner's (1983) pioneering investigations. In fact, children's understanding of false belief has been the most-studied topic in the whole field of social-cognitive development in recent years.

There are many tangled issues concerning exactly *what* develops in this area, *when* and *how* it develops, and there are many different positions taken on these issues—so many, in fact, that a book rather than a chapter section would really be needed to treat them adequately. Inasmuch as only the latter is available to us here, we attempt only two things in this section. First, we summarize briefly the principal positions taken on the what, when, and how issues. Then we present our own best guess as to what the right developmental story might be, particularly concerning the what and when issues. The reader should bear in mind, however, that an adequate picture of what is currently going on in this large and complex area simply cannot be gotten from our brief review alone. One final caution: The differing theoretical positions we will describe also concern the development of knowledge about mental states other than just beliefs and their kin. They are presented in this section partly for expository convenience.

Principal Views Concerning the What, When, and How of Development

A number of investigators believe that *what* gets acquired here is some version of the representational theory of mind just described. This group includes, among others, Astington, Flavell, Gopnik, Olson, Perner, Wellman, and their coworkers (see, e.g., Astington & Gopnik, 1991a; Bartsch & Wellman, 1995; Flavell, 1988; Forguson, 1989; Gopnik & Wellman, 1994; Perner, 1991, 1995; Ruffman, Olson, & Astington, 1991; Wellman, 1990). Perner's (1991) theory is a prototypical example of this view. According to Perner, children are initially able to form only single mental models of the world—single models that they continually update. Then, during late infancy and the early preschool years, they become able to model more than one situation at a time. For example, they can model both a past and a present situation, or both a real and a pretend situation. Perner argues that this multiple-models capability enables the young child to become what he calls a *situation theorist,* with a *mentalistic theory of behavior.* With this theory, the child can understand that a person can be mentally related to real or imaginary states of affairs in various ways. As examples, the young situation theorist understands that another person can want A, think about B, pretend C, and imagine D. This conception of the young preschooler's understanding is somewhat similar to Wellman's desire psychology (Bartsch & Wellman, 1995, p. 195) and Flavell's Level 1 knowledge about the mind (Perner, 1991, p. 277). Finally, around age 4, children develop a *metarepresentational* ability and understanding, that is, an ability to represent that one thing (or one person) is representing something else as being a certain way. This new ability enables children to understand the representational nature and function of pictures and other external symbols. More importantly in the present context, it also enables them to understand that the mind is a representational device, and that people act on the basis of their mental representations of reality rather than the reality itself. In short, they develop an understanding of representations in general, and a representational theory of mind in particular. It is the emergence of this new theory that allows children to really understand false belief, deception, appearance-reality contrasts, and the like.

Other theorists have different views about what gets acquired here. For a variety of alternative positions, see the Open Peer Commentaries on Gopnik (1993). Leslie (1994; Leslie & Roth, 1993) believes that young children are not

acquiring a theory about mental and other representations at all. Rather, he postulates the acquisition through neurological maturation of a succession of three domain-specific and modular mechanisms for dealing with agents versus nonagent objects. The first, called Theory of Body mechanism (ToBy), develops early in the first year. It allows the baby to recognize, among other things, that agents have an internal source of energy that permits them to move on their own. The next two, called Theory of Mind mechanisms (ToMM), deal with the intentionality or aboutness of agents rather than with their mechanical properties. $ToMM_1$, which comes into play later in the first year, will allow the infant to construe people and other agents as perceiving the environment and as pursuing goals. Finally, $ToMM_2$ begins to develop during the second year of life. This important mechanism allows children to represent agents as holding attitudes toward the truth of propositions—what philosophers refer to as *propositional attitudes.* Propositional attitudes are mental states such as *pretending that, believing that, imagining that, desiring that,* and the like. Equipped with $ToMM_2$, children are able to compute that Mary is pretending that this empty cup is filled with tea, that John thinks that this candy box contains candy, and other propositional attitudes. Other theorists proposing innate or early-maturing modular mechanisms dedicated to mental state computations are Fodor (1992), Mitchell (1994), and especially, Baron-Cohen (1993, 1994, 1995).

Johnson (1988) and Harris (1991, 1992) propose a different alternative to the representational theory of mind view. According to these investigators, children are introspectively aware of their own mental states and can use this awareness to infer the mental states of other people through a kind of role-taking or simulation process. For example, children could predict where the protagonist would look for the hidden object in the unexpected-transfer false-belief task by imagining or mentally simulating what they would believe and where they would look if they were in his shoes and had only his information to go on. What develops is the ability to make increasingly accurate simulations of this kind. Although not denying that people also resort to theories in predicting and explaining behavior, Harris (1992) stresses the importance of such mental-simulation processes in the development of social-cognitive knowledge and skills.

There are still other alternatives to the theory view. Hobson (1991) argues that, although children acquire considerable understanding of persons as they develop, they do not acquire anything that could properly be termed a *theory* of mind. Although generally friendly to the theory view, Wimmer has argued that children's mastery of false belief and related tasks is mediated principally by a growing understanding of how thoughts are caused by informational inputs rather than by a growing understanding of the representational nature of belief (Wimmer & Weichbold, 1994).

There is considerable controversy at present concerning the *when* of development as well as the *what*. The traditional view has been that the standard false-belief, deception, appearance-reality, and Level 2 perspective-taking tasks are reasonably valid measures of children's understanding of mental representations, and that since these tasks are not usually passed until about age 4, this understanding is also not present prior to about that age. In fact, as already noted, some have stressed that a clearly constructivist, representational conception of the mind does not fully develop until well after that age (e.g., Chandler & Hala, 1994). However, there has recently been a number of studies purporting to show that the standard tasks underestimate younger children's understanding in this area, with the attendant claim that 3-year-olds do in fact possess this understanding. Chandler, Fritz, and Hala (1989) have colorfully dubbed those holding the traditional, more skeptical view of 3-year-olds' abilities as "scoffers," and those holding the more liberal, 3-year-olds-do-understand-beliefs view as "boosters."

Why might the standard tasks be thought to underestimate 3-year-olds' understanding? One line of argument in the case of false-belief tasks has to do with the relative cognitive salience, for the young child, of the true reality versus the false belief. The following is a composite or blend of a number of arguments of this kind; for the details of the different variants of this line of thinking see, for example, Fodor (1992), Leslie (1994), Leslie and Roth (1993), Mitchell (1994), Mitchell and Lacohee (1991), Moses (1993), Robinson and Mitchell (1994, 1995), Russell, Mauthner, Sharpe, and Tidswell (1991), Wellman (1990), and Zaitchik (1991). In false-belief task situations, the reality is more cognitively salient for 3-year-olds than the false belief is. It is more salient for one or more of the following reasons: First, the reality is objectively more salient because the subject has perceived it directly; it is one of the givens in the task situation. In contrast, the false belief has to be inferred from consideration of the information that is and is not available to the protagonist, for example, from the fact that she did not see that the object was moved to a new place in the unexpected-transfer task. Second, they have learned that beliefs are supposed to match or copy reality, and usually do. Consequently, they find it

natural to think immediately of the reality when asked about the belief. Third, they also know that people try to do whatever satisfies their desires. On unexpected-transfer false-belief tasks, searching where the transferred object presently is (the reality) will satisfy the protagonist's desire to obtain it. Therefore, young children find it natural to say, incorrectly, that the protagonist will search there. Finally, young children are generally more oriented to what actually is the case than to what someone might think is the case; in Mitchell's words, they have an "excessive reality orientation" (Mitchell, 1994, p. 25). Some of these same arguments have been used to account for 3-year-olds' failures on deception and appearance-reality tasks.

Other investigators attribute 3-year-olds' failures on false-belief and related tasks to more domain-general information-processing or "performance" (as contrasted with "competence") problems, such as limited executive or memory abilities (Case, 1989; Frye, Zelazo, & Palfai, 1992; Halford, 1992; Lewis, 1994; Olson, 1993; Russell, Jarrold, & Potel, 1994). Fodor (1992), Leslie (1994), and other "salience" theorists would also construe their position as one of performance limitations. For example, Russell, Jarrold, and Potel (1994) suggest that 3-year-olds' difficulty on the Russell et al.(1991) deceptions task, described in the introduction to this section, may be caused by a limitation in their executive functioning—specifically, a limitation on their ability to inhibit a dominant response. Recall that in order to succeed on this task, children have to inhibit their natural, dominant tendency to point to the box that contains the candy and instead point to the empty box. Russell, Jarrold, and Potel (1994) argue that 3-year-olds may be just too neurologically immature to inhibit this overlearned tendency to point to where things are rather than to where they aren't. The other authors just cited argue that young children have general, nondomain-specific difficulties in holding in mind, coordinating, or reasoning about several pieces of information at a time, and that the structure of the standard tasks requires these abilities; for a critique of this cognitive-complexity line of argument, see Bartsch and Wellman (1995, pp. 191–194).

As Russell, Jarrold, and Potel (1994) rightly point out, performance-limitations arguments here could take one of two forms. One form holds that 3-year-olds do already have the representational understanding in question, but cannot show this understanding on the standard tasks because of information-processing limitations of the sorts just described. The other argues that 3-year-olds have not yet acquired this understanding and that an improvement with age in these information-processing capacities will make its acquisition possible. Some theorists favor the first of these two possibilities (e.g., Fodor, 1992; Leslie, 1994; Mitchell, 1994), whereas Russell et al. (1994) and most of the other investigators previously cited favor the second.

Other researchers have faulted the standard tasks as being insensitive measures of young children's understanding in still other ways; for reviews of this work, see Chandler and Hala (1994), Mitchell (1994), and Siegal and Peterson (1994). Some argue that young children may fail these tasks because they fail to understand precisely what is being asked of them (Lewis & Osborne, 1990; Siegal & Beattie, 1991; Siegal & Peterson, 1994). For example, they may interpret the experimenter's "Where will he look?" question in an unexpected-transfer false-belief task as "Where *should* he look?" rather than, as intended, "Where will he look *first*?" (Siegal & Peterson, 1994). Others worry that the standard tasks do not sufficiently engage the interests of young subjects, or involve them actively and personally enough in the task events (Chandler & Hala, 1994; Dunn, 1994; Freeman, Lewis, & Doherty, 1991). In Chandler and Hala's words, "these procedures have typically turned on matters that are often static, hypothetical, third-party, and of no immediate relevance or personal interest to the young subjects in question" (1994, p. 412). Finally, Bartsch and Wellman (1995) believe that 3-year-olds' frequent difficulties with the standard tasks do reflect a genuine conceptual limitation (namely, possession of a desire-belief theory of mind rather than a belief-desire one), but not the total absence of a representational conception of the mind.

Not surprisingly, theorists' views about the *how* of development in this area are often predictable from their views about the what and the when. Although all theorists recognize that, here as elsewhere, both nature and nurture play a role in development, they differ in the relative weight they give to each factor. On the nature side, Baron-Cohen (1995), Fodor (1992), and Leslie (1994) posit innate or early-maturing modular mechanisms that directly enable the child to compute mental states. Others also emphasize the role of maturation but see it as making a more indirect contribution to development. That is, they argue that the development through maturation of various domain-general information-processing skills makes it computationally possible for children to infer false beliefs and the like (e.g., Case, 1989; Frye, Zelazo, & Palfai, 1992; Halford, 1992; Olson, 1993). However, they would presumably agree that, once these skills had matured sufficiently, the child would still have to learn from experience that such mental states exist and how to infer them.

Similarly, among those who put more emphasis on nurture or experience, some assign it a direct formative role and others an indirect one. Gopnik, Perner, Wellman, and other "theory theorists" (e.g., Astington & Gopnik, 1991a; Bartsch & Wellman, 1995; Gopnik & Wellman 1994; Sodian, 1994) clearly envision a direct role. They believe that experience provides young children with information that cannot be accounted for by their present theory of mind, information that will eventually cause them to revise and improve that theory. For example, desire psychologists will gradually become belief-desire psychologists by repeatedly seeing people behave in ways that require for their explanation a concept of belief as well as a concept of desire. Thus, the role of experience is viewed as similar to that in Piaget's equilibration theory: That is, experience engenders disequilibrium and, eventually, a new, higher state of equilibrium (a new theory). Simulation theorists (e.g., Harris, 1991) also assume that experience makes a direct contribution, in that it is through practice in role taking that children improve their simulation skills. Likewise, those who stress the developmental importance of interactions with parents and siblings (e.g., Dunn, 1994) assume that children learn about mental states more or less directly through these experiences. Finally, theorists such as Siegal (e.g., Siegal & Peterson, 1994) appear to envisage a more indirect developmental role for experience. That is, they argue that experience improves children's conversational and other communicative skills and these skills help them interpret correctly the experimenter's questions in false-belief and other tasks. However, acquiring these communicative skills, like acquiring general information-processing skills, would presumably only remove a barrier to the child's knowledge acquisition rather than supply that knowledge directly.

A Possible Developmental Sequence

What can one conclude about the *what* and *when* of development in this area from the mountains of data now available? Unfortunately, it is hard to draw firm and confident conclusions because there is so much disagreement in results and interpretations at present. However, the tentative picture that we have formed is the following: The proposed ages are approximate, and would be expected to vary somewhat from sample to sample. In any case, it is the sequence rather than the exact ages that matters most.

Until about their third birthday, most children probably have no understanding at all of beliefs and other serious mental representations. Although 2-year-olds sometimes talk about desires, emotions, and perceptions, they virtually never talk about beliefs or perceptual appearances. They also show no convincing evidence of trying to create false beliefs in other people by deceptive ploys. Finally, they rarely exhibit any clear signs of understanding even when given very easy, child-friendly false-belief, appearance-reality, or Level 2 percept knowledge tasks. Although a case might be made that something akin to Leslie's (1994) ToMM$_2$ is mediating some understanding of pretense representations at this age (although, as we will see, even this is debatable), it is hard to argue convincingly that it is subserving any understanding of belief as yet.

However, there are suggestions from recent research that, unlike 2-year-olds, young 3-year-olds may possess at least some minimal understanding. In everyday conversations at home, some children of this age may on rare occasions say, for example, that someone thinks this or that is the case when it is not. They may also sometimes show apparent signs of understanding in false-belief, deception, appearance-reality, and Level 2 percept knowledge tasks, particularly in special, nonstandard tasks designed to be as easy as possible for young children and, occasionally, in naturalistic, nonlaboratory conditions. We say "sometimes" and "apparent" because there is much disagreement in the area as to how robust these findings are and how convincing they are as indicative of early competence. For examples of difference in results or interpretation of results, see Chandler and Hala (1994) versus Sodian (1994) and Speer, Sullivan, and Smith (1992); Leslie and Thaiss (1992) versus Riggs and Robinson (1995); Fodor (1992) versus Wimmer and Weichbold (1994); and Siegal and Beattie (1991) versus Clements and Perner (1994).

Our own present guess is that many young 3-year-olds probably do have some beginning understanding, but this understanding is severely limited in several respects: It is fragile, with its expression easily impeded by information-processing and other limitations. Even systematic efforts at training may not always reveal evidence of understanding (Taylor & Hort, 1990; but compare Slaughter & Gopnik, 1996). It is probably rarely accessed spontaneously in the child's everyday, extralaboratory life in addition to being hard to access in the laboratory. Although it may be there in some form in the child's cognitive system, we suspect that the child of this age is seldom able to use it to predict or explain people's actions. Finally, the understanding itself may be different from what the older child possesses—more implicit, more procedural, less accessible to reflection and verbal expression.

A very interesting recent study by Clements and Perner (1994) provides evidence of its implicit nature. In an unexpected-transfer false-belief task, preschoolers of different ages were asked two questions about a cardboard mouse whose cheese had been surreptitiously moved from one box to another: "I wonder where he is going to look?" followed by "Which box will he open?" As would be expected, there was the usual steady improvement with age from 2½ to 4½ years in correct responding for the second question, a traditional verbal test of false-belief understanding. Much more interesting was the developmental pattern of nonverbal responding to the first question. Not surprisingly, the older 3-year-olds and the 4-year-olds responded to it by looking immediately at the original, now-empty box, whereas the 2½-year-olds responded by looking at the box that now contained the cheese. Very surprisingly, however, an intermediate group of young 3-year-olds (2:11–3:2 years) spontaneously looked at the empty box just as the older subjects did, even though they then indicated the other box immediately afterwards when asked which box the mouse would open. The authors conclude that in the case of the young 3-year-olds:

> . . . we are dealing with a different type of knowledge: implicit as opposed to explicit knowledge. This demonstration is particularly impressive since the very same paradigm is used as in the traditional false belief task. (Clements & Perner, 1994, p. 394)

How to model precisely the young 3-year-old's competence in this area remains one of the most intractable problems in social-cognitive development (cf. Chandler & Chapman, 1991; Clements & Perner, 1994; Falmagne, 1993, pp. 176–177; Siegler, 1994, pp. 195–196).

Beginning at the age of 4 or late 3, children show clearer and more consistent evidence of understanding. They show it in their spontaneous mental state talk and occasional deceptive behavior, and also in their generally good performance on the standard tasks. Although it is hard to characterize precisely the 4- and 5-year-old's understanding just as it is the 3-year-old's, virtually everyone believes that the older child's knowledge is decidedly more robust, more accessible, more clearly "there." Nevertheless, as indicated previously, there is considerable evidence that the older preschooler still has a great deal to learn about beliefs, appearances, and the interpretive, constructive nature of the mind in general. We do not have space here to describe this evidence, but invite the interested reader to consult, for example, Chandler (1988), Chandler and Lalonde (1996), Fabricius and Schwanenflugel (1994), Flavell (1988), Flavell, Flavell, and Green (1989), Flavell, Green, and Flavell (1986), Lalonde, Chandler, and Moses

(1993), Perner and Howes (1992), Pillow (1995), Pillow and Henrichon (1996), Taylor (1988), Wellman (1990), and Wellman and Hickling (1994). It is not clear when or where this later development stops. For example, there is evidence that even adults often forget that it is people's mental representations of events rather than the events themselves that dictate their thoughts and actions regarding them (Griffin & Ross, 1991).

Knowledge

A good deal of research has been directed at the child's developing understanding of knowledge. For reviews of this work, see Astington (1993), Bartsch and Wellman (1995), Lyon (1993), Moore and Furrow (1991), O'Neill (1996), and especially Montgomery (1992), Perner (1991), and Taylor (1996). Much of the literature on belief is also pertinent to knowledge because the two concepts are closely related (see previous section).

The following appear to be the major facts about knowledge that most people probably learn (cf. Montgomery, 1992; Perner, 1991). Knowledge is a mental state. More specifically, it is a belief that is true rather than false: Although one can *believe* things that are not true, one can only be said to *know* true things. Because knowing is an internal, mental state rather than an external, physical one, it should not be confused with successful behaviors or outcomes. A person might have been correct in some decision or successful in some action because of a lucky guess or other chance factors rather than because of the knowledge the person possessed. The external validity of the knowledge is also usually mirrored by an inner sense of relative certainty. One usually feels quite certain that one knows when one actually does know, but not when one is merely speculating or guessing (unfortunately, one also usually feels quite certain of one's false beliefs).

Adults likewise understand that acquisition of new knowledge requires access to an information source. In fact, the sense of certainty that one knows something comes in part from remembering the information source of the knowledge. Although one can also increase one's knowledge by reflecting on what one already knows, the information source is commonly a perceptual one. For instance, adults realize that of two people who are initially ignorant of some fact, only the person who sees, hears, or otherwise receives adequate information concerning that fact will likely know it. The words "adequate" and "likely" indicate that exposure to relevant information may be a necessary condition, but is not a sufficient one. On the one hand, the information presented has to be adequate enough to engender a true and certain belief, that is, genuine knowledge. If the information is meager or ambiguous, the individual may not be able to achieve a correct mental representation of the situation. On the other hand, a correct representation is also unlikely to be achieved if the individual is inattentive, or lacks the cognitive maturity or background knowledge to construct it from the information presented. One implication of these last two facts is that knowledge acquisition is an interpretive process, requiring inferences from what is perceived, as well as simple apprehension of the perceptual givens. Another implication is that different people can end up knowing or believing different things despite being exposed to identical information, due to differences in their cognitive skills and biases, in their background knowledge, and so on.

When do children acquire these facts? It is clear that by the age of 4 or 5, children possess at least some of them (Montgomery, 1992). They seem to have some sense that knowing is a mental state that is experienced as certain and refers to a true state of affairs. Although they are prone to confuse the internal state of knowledge with behavioral success or other external indicators, they have some ability to distinguish them. To illustrate, in a study by Johnson and Wellman (1980), preschoolers initially saw where an object was hidden but later, because of an experimenter trick, failed to find it there. Despite their lack of behavioral success, a majority of 4-year-old subjects claimed that they had known where it was (see also Perner, 1991, pp. 156–158). Likewise, Moore and Furrow (1991) and Montgomery (1992) cite evidence that by 4 or 5 years of age, children realize that the word *know* expresses more speaker certainty than the words *think* or *guess* and is a surer guide to the true state of affairs. There is correlational evidence suggesting that an understanding of knowledge, certainty, false belief, and appearance-reality all develop together, perhaps as different manifestations of a developing representational theory of mind (Moore & Furrow, 1991).

There is also considerable development during the preschool period in children's understanding of the conditions that provide a person with knowledge. In a study by Gopnik and Graf (1988), 3-, 4-, and 5-year-olds learned about the contents of a drawer in three different ways: by seeing them, by being told about them, or by inferring them from a clue. They were later asked how they knew about the drawer's contents. The oldest subjects had little difficulty identifying the specific source of their knowledge, but the youngest were quite poor at this task (see also O'Neill &

Gopnik, 1991). Consistent with this evidence, Aksu-Koc (1988, Ch. 8) found that, among Turkish children, 4-year-olds are more aware than 3-year-olds of verb endings in that language that tell the listener how the speaker knows about an event, namely, by actually witnessing it (one verb ending) versus being told about it or inferring it (a different verb ending). This also suggests a developing sensitivity during the preschool period to sources of knowledge. Research by Taylor, Esbenson, and Bennett (1994) has shown that young preschoolers are also often unclear about when they acquired a piece of knowledge. For instance, they tend to say that they have known for a long time both familiar, long-known information and new information that the experimenter has just taught them.

Several studies have tested young children's understanding of the importance of perceptual access in acquiring knowledge. Some have found that even 3-year-olds will tend to attribute knowledge of a box's contents to a person who looks inside the box rather than to one who just touches the box (Pillow, 1989b; Pratt & Bryant, 1990). Other investigations have shown that they have considerable difficulty in isolating perceptual access as a critical condition for knowledge (Perner & Ogden, 1988; Ruffman & Olson, 1989; Wimmer, Hogrefe, & Perner, 1988). For example, Lyon (1993) found that 3-year-old subjects tended to attribute knowledge of a box's contents to a doll that did not look inside the box but moved toward it, in preference to one that did look inside but moved away from it. In both this and another study by Lyon (1993), 3-year-olds tended to attribute knowledge on the basis of something like desire or engagement rather than perceptual access, whereas 4-year-olds did so on the basis of perceptual access alone (see also Montgomery & Miller, 1992, in press). It seems, then, that children of this age will sometimes wrongly deny knowledge to a person with perceptual access as well as wrongly attribute knowledge to a person without access, suggesting that they are often unclear about the perceptual conditions that lead to knowledge (Taylor, 1996; see also Montgomery, 1992, p. 423). Their uncertain understanding of the nature of knowledge and the role of perceptual access in knowledge formation would not help them on false-belief tasks: It is hard to infer that a person who does not have perceptual access to some state of affairs may have a false belief about it if one does not even understand that the person lacks knowledge of it because of the lack of perceptual access.

In the late preschool and middle childhood periods, children discover that perceptual information needs to be adequate as well as merely present. For example, whereas 3-year-olds are apt to believe that a person could learn the color of an object by just feeling it, 5-year-olds realize that the perceptual access must be modality-appropriate—in this case, visual (O'Neill, Astington, & Flavell, 1992; Pillow, 1993b). Children also learn that even when it is modality-appropriate, perceptual information may be inadequate because it is too scanty or ambiguous to ensure the target knowledge. For example, preschoolers tend to believe that a naive other person can tell that a picture contains a giraffe even if only a small, nondescript part of the giraffe is visible to the person. In contrast, older children realize that, although the person does indeed see the giraffe (there is visual access), he or she does not see enough of it to be able to identify it as a giraffe (Chandler & Helm, 1984; Taylor, 1988; for information about related studies by others, see Montgomery, 1992, p. 421, and Taylor, 1996). There is a similar age trend with respect to understanding something like the opposite: A person may sometimes be able to infer information to which the person does not have direct visual access (Sodian & Wimmer, 1987). Older children also discover that what gets known or believed depends upon the perceiver as well as the quality of the available information (see the references cited in last paragraph of the preceding section). For example, they come to realize that people's preexisting biases or expectations may influence their interpretation of the perceptual evidence (Pillow & Henrichon, 1996). Finally, there is substantial improvement with age in children's metacomprehension and comprehension-monitoring skills—their ability to determine what they themselves do and do not know (Flavell, 1981). The chapter by Moshman in this Volume describes additional knowledge about the nature and limits of knowledge (called *epistemic cognition*) that some adolescents and adults acquire.

O'Neill (1996) has recently uncovered what might be some sort of developmental precursor to the preschooler's fledgling knowledge about knowledge. She found that 2-year-olds, no less, will sometimes communicate about a situation more fully to a parent who had not shared that situation with them just previously (and therefore needed more information about it), than to a parent who had. This behavior superficially resembles the shape-what-you-say-to-fit-what-the-listener-needs-to-know communication strategy extensively studied by developmental and social psychologists such as Flavell, Glucksberg, and Krauss in previous decades (Flavell, Miller, & Miller, 1993, pp. 296–298). O'Neill (1996) argues that 2-year-olds probably do not yet have a mentalistic conception of knowledge, but do have a nonmentalistic version that takes the form "Tell others about experiences not shared with me." Whether this nonmentalistic conception helps children acquire their later mentalistic one is not yet known.

Children also acquire some understanding of the closely related mental state or process of memory during the preschool and later periods (Lyon & Flavell, 1993, 1994; Schneider & Bjorklund, Ch. 10, this Volume). Finally, older preschoolers are sometimes able to distinguish between knowing something and actively thinking about it (Flavell, Green, & Flavell, 1995b), and older elementary school children show some sensitivity to the distinction between remembering something and comprehending it (Lovett & Flavell, 1990; Lovett & Pillow, 1995, 1996; cf., Fabricius & Schwanenflugel, 1994).

Pretense

The development of pretend-play skills during early childhood has been studied for many years (Rubin, Fein, & Vandenburg, 1983). Only recently, however, has it been viewed as part of the development of children's knowledge about the mind, thanks largely to an important analysis by Leslie (1987). For useful reviews of this more recent, theory-of-mind-related work on pretense, see Astington (1993), Harris (1994a), Harris and Kavanaugh (1993), Harris, Lillard, and Perner (1994), Leslie (1987), Lillard (1993a, 1993b, 1994), Perner (1991), Perner, Baker, and Hutton (1994), and Taylor (1996). According to Leslie (1987, 1994), the maturation of a modular theory-of-mind mechanism, ToMM$_2$ (see the "Beliefs and Related Mental Representations" section), permits the 18- to 24-month-old to engage in pretend play and to understand as pretense the pretend actions of others. This *metarepresentational* capacity, as Leslie calls it, prevents the child from being confused when, for example, someone pretends that a banana is a telephone. It does so by *decoupling,* or quarantining off cognitively, the temporary pretend identity of the banana (i.e., telephone) from its permanent real identity (banana). The child can then compute the relation: "this person is pretending that this banana is a telephone" (for further details, see Leslie, 1987).

Leslie's idea that the ability to understand pretense and the ability to understand false belief and other mental states are mediated by a common, early-maturing metarepresentational or theory-of-mind mechanism is certainly plausible on its face. "Pretending that" and "believing that" are both propositional attitudes. Moreover, both are understood by adults as being mental representations or construals of something as being a certain way—either for real (belief) or just temporarily, for play purposes (pretense). Nevertheless, Leslie's claim is currently very controversial, and there are arguments and evidence both for it and against it.

One argument against it is the marked age gap between children's comprehension of pretense and their comprehension of false-belief, deception, appearance-reality, and Level 2 perceptual perspectives. Harris and Kavanaugh (1993) have convincingly demonstrated that even young 2-year-olds read other people's pretend actions correctly. They readily infer that the other person is pretending the banana is a telephone and they will draw all the needed pretend-world inferences, for example, that they should talk into the banana when it is their turn. In contrast, we have seen that children seldom evince any clear understanding of false belief and the like until age 3 or 4. Similarly, Flavell, Flavell, and Green (1987) showed that 3-year-olds find it significantly easier to make a pretend-real distinction than an apparent-real one, even using the same false objects as stimuli. If understanding of pretense and understanding of false belief are both mediated by Leslie's ToMM$_2$, then why does the former appear so much earlier in childhood than the latter? Although Leslie, Fodor, and others have argued that performance obstacles explain the late display of false-belief understanding on standard tests, as noted in the "Beliefs and Related Mental Representations" section, it is hard for most of us to credit that 2-year-olds really do understand false belief.

We have described two possibilities so far. One, advocated by Leslie and company, is that children correctly construe both pretense and beliefs as mental states by the age of 2. The other is that they interpret pretense mentalistically by age 2, but do not interpret beliefs this way until they are about 4 years of age. However, Harris, Lillard, and Perner have recently proposed a third possibility: 2-year-olds lack a fully mentalistic conception of pretense as well as of belief (Harris, 1994a; Harris & Kavanaugh, 1993; Harris, Lillard, & Perner, 1994; Lillard, 1993a, 1993b, 1994, 1996; Perner, 1991; Perner, Baker, & Hutton, 1994). Lillard (1993b, 1996) has provided some striking experimental support for this third possibility. One of her methods was to present children with, for example, a doll named Moe who knows nothing at all about rabbits but chances to be hopping like one. The children were then asked if Moe was or was not pretending to be a rabbit. The majority of the 4-year-olds and even many 5-year-olds claimed that Moe was indeed pretending to be a rabbit, despite their having agreed that he did not know how rabbits hop. Other studies by Lillard indicate that preschoolers think dolls who are not trying to be like rabbits are nevertheless pretending to be rabbits if they hop like them (personal communication). Lillard (1996) has further demonstrated that many children of this age classify pretense with physical activities, such as clapping one's hands, rather than with mental activities, such as thinking. By the age of 7 or 8, most children responded like adult subjects to such tasks, insisting that pretense actions were necessarily generated by pretense mentation.

As Lillard (1996, personal communication) has pointed out, however, there is also evidence consistent with Leslie's position. The fact that autistics both tend not to pretend and also tend to perform poorly on theory-of-mind tasks (Baron-Cohen et al., 1993) is consistent with the possibility that understanding pretense and understanding other mental states do have a common mediator and develop together. In addition, studies by Hickling, Wellman, and Gottfried (1994) and Custer (1996) suggest that preschoolers might have a more mentalistic conception of pretense than Lillard's tasks give them credit for. Perhaps these studies are assessing a more rudimentary understanding of pretense than Lillard has been tapping.

There is also some interesting recent research on children's understanding of the distinction between the real and the mental or imaginary; for reviews of this work, see Lillard (1994) and Woolley (1995). In several important studies, Wellman and colleagues (Estes, Wellman, & Woolley, 1989; Wellman & Estes, 1986) have found that even 3-year-olds can distinguish between real objects and imaged or imagined ones. Like adults, they recognize that whereas a real dog is externally visible, tangible, public, and enduring, the internal image of a dog they form at the experimenter's request is none of these things. Woolley and Wellman (1992) have shown that most preschoolers also recognize that dreams are internal, private mental states, different from external, "real" events. However, research by Harris, Brown, Marriott, Whittall, and Harmer (1991) suggests that the imagined-real distinction may be less clear for young children when the imagined object is scary. When their 4- and 6-year-old subjects pretended that an empty box contained a monster, they claimed that the monster was not real, just as adults would. So far, so good. However, they subsequently avoided that box in favor of a box containing an imaginary puppy and they also preferred

to poke a finger into the puppy box and a stick into the monster box, rather than the reverse (see also Woolley & Wellman, 1993). The authors conclude that "children systematically distinguish fantasy from reality, but are tempted to believe in the existence of what they have merely imagined" (Harris et al., 1991, p. 105). Research by Rozin, Millman, and Nemeroff (1986) shows that adults may not be all that different from children in this regard. Their subjects saw sugar poured into two bottles and then put a "sodium cyanide" label on one bottle and a "sugar" label on the other. Despite their certain knowledge that the first bottle did not really contain poison, they were reluctant to eat from it. Finally, Taylor and her colleagues (Taylor, Cartwright, & Carlson, 1993; Taylor, Gerow, et al., 1993) have begun an ambitious study of children who have imaginary companions. One of their intriguing findings is that, contrary to what one might expect, these children are not inferior to their peers in their ability to distinguish between fantasy and reality.

Thinking

Most theory-of-mind research has focused on children's understanding of mental states, such as beliefs, knowledge, intentions, desires, and emotions. In contrast, until recently there has been little investigation of children's knowledge about mental activities such as thinking, that is, the mental things people could be said to *do* rather than just *have* (D'Andrade, 1987). During the past several years, however, Flavell and colleagues and other investigators have begun to explore this and related topics (Flavell, 1993; Flavell, Green, & Flavell, 1993, 1995a, 1995b; plus unpublished work); see also, for example, studies by Estes (in press) and Wellman, Hollander, and Schult (1996).

The evidence indicates that children acquire some important elementary knowledge and skills concerning thinking during the early preschool years (see Flavell et al., 1995b for a summary). First, preschoolers seem to know that thinking is an activity that only people and perhaps some other animates engage in (Dolgin & Behrend, 1984). Second, as mentioned in the "Pretense" section, work by Wellman and colleagues (e.g., Estes et al., 1989) has shown that preschoolers also realize that mental entities like thoughts and images are internal, in-the-head affairs, not to be confused with physical actions or other external objects and events. Similarly, they regard the mind and the brain as necessary for mental actions (Johnson & Wellman, 1982). Third, they realize that, like desires and other mental entities, thinking has content and makes reference, and that thoughts can take as their objects nonpresent and even nonreal things (Estes et al., 1989; Flavell et al., 1995b). Thus, preschoolers have been shown to understand some of the most basic and important facts about thinking: Namely, that it is an internal human activity that refers to or represents real or imaginary things. Recent studies of 3- and 4-year-olds' understanding of thoughts and "thought bubbles" (the bubbles above comic-strip characters' heads that depict their thoughts) by Wellman et al. (1996) reinforce this picture of preschoolers' knowledge. Finally, preschoolers have some ability to infer the presence of thinking in another person, provided that the cues are very strong and clear, and also can differentiate thinking from other activities in such situations (Flavell et al., 1995b).

However, there are also important knowledge and skills concerning thinking that preschoolers clearly lack. Many of their difficulties can be summarized by saying that they tend to be poor at determining both *when* a person (self or other) is thinking and *what* the person is and is not thinking about. As to the *when,* they greatly underestimate the amount of mental activity that goes on in people. They do not realize that people are continually experiencing mental content of one kind or other spontaneously—the ever-flowing "stream of consciousness" described by William James (1890). Flavell et al. (1993, 1995b) have shown in several studies that, unlike older subjects, preschoolers do not consistently attribute any mental activity at all to a person who just sits quietly, waiting. Even more surprising, they do not automatically assume that something must be going on in a person's mind, or that the person's mind must be doing something, even when they know that the person is looking at or listening to something, reading, or talking to another person—activities that adults would regard as necessarily involving some cognition. As to the *what,* on those occasions when they do assert that a person is thinking, they are often surprisingly poor at inferring what the person is and is not thinking about, even when the evidence is very clear.

These same difficulties are equally evident when preschoolers are asked to report their own mental activity rather than another person's. That is, they tend to be very poor at recalling or reconstructing both the fact and the content of their own recent or present thinking, even in situations especially designed to make such introspection extremely easy (Flavell et al., 1995b; but see Estes, in press). As one of many examples, 5-year-olds who at the experimenter's instigation had clearly just been thinking silently about which room in their house they keep their toothbrush

in, often denied that they had just been thinking; moreover, in those instances when they did say they had been thinking, they often did not mention either a toothbrush or a bathroom when asked what they had been thinking about. In sharp contrast, subjects of 7 or 8 years of age proved to be much more skilled than 5-year-olds at this and other introspection tasks. Consistent with these results, research by Flavell, Green, Flavell, and Grossman (1997) has shown that preschoolers are largely unaware of their own ongoing inner speech and may not even know that speech *can* be covert.

Recent research has also demonstrated that preschoolers have less understanding than school-aged children of what Gordon and Flavell (1977) called *cognitive cueing,* that is, the tendency of one mental content to trigger the occurrence of another mental content that is related to it in some way in the thinker's experience (Cohen, 1993; Gordon & Flavell, 1977; Schneider & Sodian, 1988; Sodian & Schneider, 1990); they do have some understanding of it, however (Lagattuta, Wellman, & Flavell, in press). Flavell et al. (1995b) have hypothesized that this and the other preschooler shortcomings described in this chapter section may stem in part from the absence of a causal theory of thinking: Unlike adults, preschoolers may regard thoughts as isolated, mysterious mental events, not linked to preceding causes or subsequent effects. Finally, unpublished research by Flavell, Green, and Flavell indicates that younger children are more inclined than older children and adults to attribute self-awareness and decision-making abilities to an unconscious person ("sound asleep and not dreaming"). In one study, for instance, the percentage of 5-year-olds, 7-year-olds, 8-year-olds, and adults claiming that people know they are asleep while deeply asleep and not dreaming were 61%, 39%, 28%, and 11%, respectively. Taken together with the other results reported in this chapter section, these findings suggest that young children do not have a very clear idea of what it is like, experientially, to be conscious as opposed to unconscious. In particular, they tend to attribute too little ongoing ideation to a conscious person (e.g., the stream of consciousness) and too much to an unconscious one.

DIFFERENCES IN DEVELOPMENT

Thus far, we have presented the typical course of development of social cognition, but now will turn to the important issue of variations in development. From a developmental perspective, individual differences in social-cognitive competencies can be of one of two types—*rate* and *product*. On the one hand, two individuals may end up with the same social-cognitive knowledge or skills, but may acquire them at different ages or rates (rate differences). On the other hand, they may not possess the same knowledge or skills when development is completed (product differences). In this section, we briefly review research on intracultural, intercultural, and interspecies differences in rate and product of social-cognitive development.

Intracultural Differences

There have been several recent investigations of individual differences in rate of acquisition among normal children within the same culture; for reviews, see Astington (1993) and Harris (1994b). Their principal objective has been to identify social experiences that foster social-cognitive development. For example, in a longitudinal study of American children, Dunn, Brown, Slomkowski, Tesla, and Youngblade (1991) found significant correlations between parent and child talk about feelings when the children were 33 months of age and the same children's performance on affect-labeling, affective-perspective-taking, and false-belief tasks at 40 months. Similarly, in another longitudinal study with British children, Dunn, Brown, and Beardsall (1991) found that individual differences in frequency of conversations about feeling states with parents and siblings at 3 years of age predicted affective-perspective-taking skill at 6 years. Importantly, the correlations obtained in both of these investigations continued to be significant even when subjects' verbal ability and other potentially confounding variables were controlled. For related studies, see Brown, Donelan-McCall, and Dunn (1996), Howe (1991), and Tesla (1991). Other research suggests that interactions with siblings may facilitate social-cognitive development. Jenkins and Astington (1996) and Perner, Ruffman, and Leekam (1994) have both shown that preschoolers who have more siblings to interact with perform better on false-belief tasks than preschoolers who have fewer or none. Perner, Ruffman, and Leekam (1994) argue that these results favor a social-experiential explanation of theory-of-mind development more than a maturationist one.

There are also individual differences in developmental product as well as in developmental rate to be found within a single culture. The most striking example is the almost total lack of knowledge about mental states shown by most children and adults with autism. Research by Baron-Cohen,

Leslie, and many others has shown that subjects with autism perform far worse than both unimpaired subjects and subjects with mental retardation of the same mental age on false-belief, appearance-reality, Level 2 perspective-taking, and other theory-of-mind tasks. Although not all experts agree on this point, there is reason to believe that people with autism have a marked cognitive impairment that is specific to social cognition. One of the many interesting features of this research is its vivid demonstration of what our lives would be like if we lacked knowledge of mental states. For details of this very lively research area, see, for example, Baron-Cohen, Tager-Flusberg, and Cohen (1993) and relevant chapters in Volume 4 of this *Handbook*. Also consult other *Handbook* chapters for accounts of significant, if less extreme, differences in social cognition obtaining between normal individuals and those with other types of psychopathology, such as psychosis, sociopathy, and extreme aggressiveness.

What about intracultural product differences among unimpaired individuals? Dweck and her coworkers have identified some intriguing ones (e.g., Dweck & Leggett, 1988). They do not find some unimpaired adults who have a concept of false belief and others who lack it—nothing akin to normal-autistic differences. However, they do find important individual differences in people's implicit theories of intelligence. Some people think of it as a fixed, uncontrollable trait or entity *(entity theory),* others as a malleable, controllable quality that can be improved with effort and training *(incremental theory).* Moreover, these differences in people's naive theory of intelligence have important consequences for their achievement motivation and intellectual performance. A perusal of textbooks in the fields of personality, social psychology, and social cognition would reveal many other ways that normal adults have been shown to differ from one another in their naive theories and knowledge regarding themselves and other people, and of course psychologists and other scientists have espoused widely different conceptions of human cognition and personality over the years.

Intercultural Differences

The question of intercultural similarities and differences in this area is a fascinating one. How universal are the developments we have described in this chapter? Several studies have shown striking similarities across cultures not only in developmental product but, more surprisingly, in developmental rate as well. Flavell, Zhang, Zou, Dong, and

Qi (1983) found that Beijing preschoolers mastered physical appearance-reality tests (e.g., involving a sponge that looks like a rock) at the same age as California preschoolers, and also showed very similar error patterns prior to that age. Similarly, Japanese, American, and British children all develop the ability to solve emotional appearance-reality tasks (in which, for example, a person really feels sad but looks happy by putting on a happy face) at about the same age (Harris & Gross, 1988). Although the children in these groups were clearly of different cultural and linguistic backgrounds, they were all from literate, industrialized societies. Not so the pygmy children from a preliterate hunter-gatherer group (the Baka) in an African rain forest tested by Avis and Harris (1991). Nevertheless, these children also showed belief-desire reasoning at about the same age as do children from literate, industrialized nations. More specifically, after Baka 3- to 5-year-olds had surreptitiously moved an adult's food from its original container to a different one, many of them correctly predicted that the unsuspecting adult would approach the original container rather than the new one, would feel happy before lifting its cover, and would feel sad after lifting it. Sound familiar?

On the other hand, a number of anthropologists have reported intercultural product differences in social cognition, for example, differences in how adults from different cultures structure the domain of emotions (e.g., Heelas & Lock, 1981; Lutz, 1983). Vinden (1996) also obtained experimental evidence for such differences. An important review of the literature on this question by Lillard (in press) allows for some intercultural similarities, but also mostly weighs in on the side of intercultural differences.

Interspecies Differences

Recall that the theory-of-mind movement essentially began with Premack and Woodruff's (1978) attempts to find out whether chimpanzees have any understanding of mental states ("History of Research on Social-Cognitive Development"). Since that time, the question of interspecies similarities and differences in theory of mind has continued to be addressed in both observational and experimental studies. For accounts of this work, see Cheney and Seyfarth (1990), Gómez, Sarriá, and Tamarit (1993), Povinelli (1993), Povinelli and Eddy (1996), and Whiten (1991, 1993). Comparative-psychological research in this area is important for at least two reasons. First, it may help us understand how various social-cognitive competencies

evolved—indeed, how the mind evolved (Povinelli, 1993; Povinelli & Eddy, 1996). Second, it may lead to the invention of new nonverbal methods that can be used to test for these competencies in preverbal human subjects, much as nonverbal methods originally devised to test perceptual abilities in animals were successfully appropriated for the study of human infant perception.

Do chimps have any knowledge of mental states? One would certainly think so, based on observations such as the following (Byrne & Whiten, 1988, 1991): Chimp A observed Chimp B acting as though no food were available at a feeding hopper, although there really was food there. Then Chimp A appeared to depart, but actually hid behind a nearby tree and watched until Chimp B took the food, whereupon Chimp A emerged from hiding and snatched it from him! A series of experimental studies by Povinelli and his co-workers also suggested that chimps may have some of this kind of knowledge (Povinelli & deBlois, 1992; Povinelli, Nelson, & Boysen, 1990; Povinelli, Parks, & Novak, 1991; see also Premack, 1988). On each of a series of trials, subjects in their experiments saw one experimenter (the knower) hide a desirable object in one of four containers after another experimenter (the guesser) had left the room; the hiding was done in such a way that the subjects could not see in which specific container the object was hidden. Following this, each experimenter pointed to a different container, the knower always to the correct one and the guesser always to an incorrect one. Subjects then had only one try to identify the correct container and obtain the object; if they failed, they went unrewarded on that trial. Some subjects never learned to always follow the knower's advice rather than the guesser's, even after many trials. These subjects were adult monkeys and human 3-year-olds. Others did, either immediately or after just a few trials, or only following many trials. The immediate-or-few-trials subjects were human 4-year-olds and the many-trials subjects were adolescent (7- to 9-year-old) chimps. The 4-year-olds also could say that the guesser didn't know where the object was.

However, Povinelli and Eddy (1996) give three reasons why we should hesitate to conclude that chimps, like 4-year-olds, understand the seeing-knowing relation. First, the fact that the chimp subjects required so many trials could mean that they had simply learned a mindless (theory-of-mindless?) discrimination. Second, in an attempted replication of these experiments, younger chimps (3- to 4-year-olds) never learned to consistently choose the container that the knower pointed to, responding instead like the monkeys and the 3-year-old children (Povinelli, Rulf, & Bierschwale, 1994).

Finally, a subsequent series of 15 very careful studies by Povinelli and Eddy (1996) raise serious doubts as to whether chimps even have a mentalistic versus behavioristic conception of seeing. The subjects were six 4- to 5-year-old chimps who had previously learned to beg for food by extending their hand(s) toward a person who had some to give rather than to an adjacent person who had none. In front of them on each test trial were two experimenters standing or sitting side by side. One of them obviously could see the subject and the other obviously could not—"obviously" to any human observer, at least. The latter was unable to see the subject for different reasons in different experiments: back turned, blindfolded, hands covering eyes, bucket covering head, opaque screen held in front of face, eyes closed, or eyes directed upwards and away from the subject. What Povinelli and Eddy (1996) wanted to know was whether the subjects would systematically address their food-begging gesture to the experimenter who could see them rather than to the one who could not. The answer was very surprising: The chimps systematically gestured to the experimenter who could see them only when the one who could not had his or her back turned to them, not in any other condition. Although here, as elsewhere, they looked at the experimenters' eyes and followed their eye gazes (e.g., they looked up and away when the experimenter looked up and away), they did not seem to comprehend the psychological significance of the gazes. In contrast, a group of young 3-year-old human subjects had little difficulty with these tasks, quite consistently gesturing only to the adult who could see them. It is of course possible that older chimps would perform better on these tasks, as they did on the knower-guesser task, but Povinelli and Eddy (1996) doubt it. In research with nonhuman primates, as in research with human infants, it can be maddeningly difficult to know what one's nonverbal subjects really know about the mind.

IS THERE A NEW DEVELOPMENTAL SOCIAL COGNITION?

Rarely does an area of study change as rapidly as has the field of social-cognitive development during the years since the last edition of the *Handbook*. The focus on theory of mind in this chapter reflects the domination of this new area. Now that we have an impressive corpus of information about children's theory of mind, it is time to pause and contemplate where we have come and where we should go from here. Although in this chapter, we have attempted to integrate theory-of-mind and other social-cognitive research, we now will more explicitly propose ways in which they could enrich each other. In the present section, we will take a new look at the broader field of social cognition through the lenses of the theory-of-mind approach and, in the opposite direction, identify some limitations, and thus needed future directions, of theory-of-mind research from the perspective of the broader field of social cognition. We present our vision of an emerging new field of social cognition that incorporates the best of the past and present. Based on such an integration, we sketch out a possible research agenda, including hypotheses that seem plausible, based on past research.

Implications of Theory of Mind for Social Cognition More Broadly

In the previous *Handbook* chapter on social cognition, Shantz (1983) organized this domain into the developing conceptions of

1. Other people's behavior and psychological nature, including their causes,
2. Relations between two individuals, including authority, friendship, and conflict relations, and
3. Intragroup relations, including social structure and social roles.

Developmentalists have continued to address these important topics (e.g., Bennett, 1993a; Eisenberg, 1994; Erwin, 1993; Forrester, 1992), especially the cognitive basis of friendship, conflict, moral judgments, gender roles, and attachment (see other chapters in this *Handbook*). However, due to changes in the field, the topics in the current chapter seem somewhat different: developing conceptions of mental states such as perception, attention, desires, emotions, intentions, dispositions, beliefs, pretense, thinking, and knowledge. Let us now explore how this recent focus on mental states might give a new spin to the still-important areas more traditionally considered as social cognition. We believe that the focus on children's coherent, causal-explanatory theories of mind provides a fruitful new way to organize and invigorate the potpourri of social-cognitive research (for other ideas in this regard, see Lyon, 1993, and Taylor, 1996). Theory-of-mind research suggests that the understanding of mental states is central to social cognition, and that a theory of mind provides a causal explanatory system involving interconnections among events, mind, and behavior.

Understanding Mental States

The understanding of mental states, especially the representational nature of mind, is central to the development of social cognition. A theory-of-mind perspective recasts earlier models of social cognition about the self, others, and social relations. In a recast, young children use mental states to predict and explain behavior, and there is much social-cognitive activity even during infancy. From a theory-of-mind perspective, previous social-cognitive research has focused on children's understanding of a subset of mental states such as intentions and emotions, while slighting certain important mental states, particularly desires, beliefs, thought, and knowledge.

The focus on a variety of mental states would generate certain hypotheses about children's developing perceptions of other people: Children become increasingly proficient at accessing and using information about mental states for person perception and the understanding of social relationships. Moreover, the relative salience of various mental states used for social understanding changes as children move from a desire to a desire-belief, to a belief-desire, to an active-interpretive theory of mind (Bartsch & Wellman, 1995). Young children's desire psychology may make desires salient and lead them to use people's desires to infer their knowledge or behavior (Lyon, 1993; Montgomery & Miller, 1995). Relatedly, young children's tendency to be overoptimistic about their abilities and achievements (e.g., Bjorklund & Green, 1992) may reflect their belief in the power of desire or effort to help them perform well. Beginning around age 4, a child may start to perceive other people's beliefs as an important part of who they are and what they do. The understanding that people can differ in their representations of reality surely impacts peer collaboration, friendship, and other social relationships. For example, knowing that two people's conflicting representations of the same event caused them to behave differently surely encourages children to try to resolve social conflicts. Still later, a theory of mind as interpretive may affect attributions. As an example, Pillow (1991) found that between 5 and 8 years of age, children come to understand that Child A's belief (based on prior experience) that Child B, who damaged his model airplane,

is mean rather than nice, biases Child A to infer that Child B's behavior was intentional.

Importantly, children's theory of mind informs them that the world is not always as it seems. Studies of pretense, deception, false belief, the appearance-reality distinction, and facial displays that hide one's emotions could provide a fresh and promising perspective on more traditional areas of social-cognitive research. Examples are causal attributions (choosing between overt physical and covert psychological information), concepts of friendship (a false friend), person perception (distrust of apparently benign strangers), and self presentation (deceptively positive image).

The focus of theory-of-mind research on children's understanding of the sources of information leading to particular beliefs or knowledge raises new questions about person perception. Can children identify the sources of their knowledge and beliefs about another person, such as facial expressions, behavior, utterances, inferences from prior experience with the person, or information from other people? How do they view the reliability of these various sources? For example, in the social-cognitive paradigm of discounting, children use their beliefs about the certainty of information. Older children discount uncertain information about internal motivation (i.e., intrinsic interest) if there is more certain information about an external cause, such as a promised reward for engaging in the behavior (see Miller & Aloise, 1990, for a review). Children's concepts of authority may also influence the relative attention to different people who serve as sources of information; people endowed with authority may have more credibility. In addition, as older children develop an understanding of the mind as an interpretive device and become aware of informational ambiguity, they realize that events per se are sometimes ambiguous sources of information. An example of individual differences in this knowledge is that highly aggressive boys interpret an ambiguous event, such as being hit by a ball thrown by a peer, as intentional rather than as possibly accidental, whereas normal boys do not (Dodge & Frame, 1982).

Understanding Links and Interconnections

As a causal-explanatory system, a theory of mind helps children understand not only simple links between a psychological cause and a behavior, but also a larger system of interconnections among events, mind, and behavior. If children's theory of mind is in fact an informal theory of the whole mental system, it not only refers to X, Y, and Z (what the other perceives, feels, knows, etc.) in isolation, but also gives them a larger picture of how various mental states or dispositions relate to each other and to the observable world. For example, children may not simply hold a specific rule concerning the relations among effort, ability, and outcome, but instead possess a general belief system concerning desires to achieve, methods for achieving, achievement-related dispositions, and external support or barriers to achievement. As another example, in children's conceptions of people, how are others' perceptions, desires, intentions, emotions, beliefs, and knowledge related? When do children understand that external events and internal mental events interact to determine behavior? How many behavioral instances do children of various ages think are needed to infer a particular mental state or psychological trait (Aloise, 1993)? How does a theory of mind contribute to older children's theories about complex social phenomena such as social roles, kinship systems, political systems, systems of justice, and the distribution of wealth? A focus on the causal-system nature of theory of mind leads researchers to ask new questions about social cognition.

To illustrate more fully how a theory-of-mind perspective can invigorate the field of social cognition by providing an alternative explanation for certain findings, we examine children's increasing awareness of traits (see also Yuill, 1993). Previous social-cognitive research views this primarily as a developmental shift from focusing on observable physical characteristics, regularities in observable behaviors, or global (and perhaps temporary) internal tendencies, to inferring specific permanent traits (Shantz, 1983). From a theory-of-mind perspective, children may conceive of a trait as an organized, enduring tendency to have certain mental states, for example, intent to harm, optimistic beliefs, or desires for particular outcomes. Children may construct another person's traits from that person's history of desires, beliefs, thoughts, intentions, and emotions. If a child has repeated experiences with a person who helps others, and the child repeatedly infers the person's mental states of desiring to help others, believing that others deserve help, thinking about helping others, intending to help others, and feeling happy after helping others, then she may construct a permanent mental state tendency, or trait, for that person—a "helpful" person. The trait of helpfulness would be seen as a stable, generalized disposition to generate certain mental states. Thus, a child could use traits to both predict (working forward) or explain (working backward) a particular mental

state. An extension of theory-of-mind work on tastes or preferences (e.g., Flavell, Mumme, Green, & Flavell, 1992) may be a good starting point for this research.

Several new questions, then, would arise:

1. What do children of various ages understand about the relations between temporary mental states and enduring traits? This understanding that mental states contribute to traits and that traits influence current mental states is an essential part of a mature theory of mind.

2. When does the understanding of traits actually become theorylike? A systematic causal-explanatory "theory of traits" or "theory of personality" would include an understanding of the connections (a) among traits, (b) among an event, a trait, and a behavior, and (c) among traits, desires, beliefs, emotions, and knowledge. Even 3-year-olds have some nascent sense of an organized personality rather than of unrelated behaviors (Eder, 1990). For example, children who choose, as being like them, the high end of the bipolar dimension for one aggression item tend to do the same for other aggression items and also choose the low end of the self-control factor.

3. Does the understanding that people can change their representations of people, objects, and events contribute to the understanding of personality change in others and the self?

4. Do developmental changes in understanding sources of information affect what information is used to attribute traits? For example, knowing that other people's prior experiences affect their knowledge, beliefs, emotions, and expectations may help children use others' backgrounds and experiences to infer personality differences or cognitive styles.

Implications of Social Cognition More Broadly for Theory-of-Mind Research

Now turning our gaze in the other direction, the social-cognitive perspective identifies certain limitations of theory-of-mind research and, more positively, suggests important future directions for research. These directions include: (a) a theory of mind-in-relationships; (b) the roles of social knowledge and social biases; (c) the on-line cognitive activities involved while using a theory of mind; and (d) the developments in theory of mind in older children and adolescents.

A Theory of Mind as a Theory of "Mind-in-Relationships"

Given that this is a chapter on social cognition, readers might expect to encounter work on the developing understanding of social relationships. Instead, theory-of-mind research focuses on understanding the mental states of individuals. Many social-cognitive perspectives would question this individualistic cast and argue for an interpersonal account (e.g., Forrester, 1992; Selman, 1980). At some point, a theory of mind surely includes an understanding that people form mental representations about people and relationships between people, in addition to representations about objects and events. Children learn to take into account how other people's relationships and past interactions affect their representations of each other's mental states and behaviors. In other words, children learn that there is a community of mental states—a network of psychological connections among people. Mental states exist in a social context; minds interact and influence each other, for example, in recursive thinking—"He's thinking that she's thinking that I'm thinking . . . " (Miller, Kessel, & Flavell, 1970).

Combining theory-of-mind research and other social-cognitive research suggests the following developmental progression of representations of mental states involved in friendship, agonistic, and nurturing relationships: Just as desires and emotions are valenced mental states, so are the positive and negative mental leanings toward, or away from, other people in positive and negative relationships. Liking, caring, hating, and rejecting all involve states of mind that must be understood in order to make sense of the social world. Children may have an early understanding of mind-in-relation-to-others based on one-way, and later two-way, mental leanings between people, for example, "she likes him" and "he likes her." This may lead to more understanding of social-cognitive reciprocity. Children may perceive a thinking-acting person who at the same time is the object of thoughts and actions from others. In addition, children's understanding of the appearance-reality distinction may be applied to relationships, as in the inference that "they act like they like each other, but they really don't." Later may come a view of minds as actively influencing minds: Minds can persuade, agree, disagree, empathize, collaborate, co-construct, and share knowledge. Also, children surely become aware of the dynamic, changing quality of interpersonal mental states, as, for example, when friendships develop and dissolve.

During late childhood and adolescence, children come to understand recursive thinking, which involves a highly sophisticated understanding of representation, namely, that several people simultaneously possess belief states about each other; mental representations can recursively include other mental representations. This increasing abstractness and complexity of representations can also be seen in the relatively late grasp of concepts such as intimacy and trust. Adolescents may also acquire an awareness of a broad range of possible social influences on beliefs, such as people's stereotypes, gender, culture, social class, and ethnicity. Like "standpoint" epistemologists (e.g., Hartsock, 1983), adolescents become increasingly aware that knowledge is situated in a personal and social-historical context (see also Moshman, this Volume). More generally, the broader field of social cognition would posit important advances in theory of mind beyond the preschool years—the focus of most theory-of-mind research.

Effects of Social Knowledge on Detection and Use of Mental State Information

Social knowledge and biases in social reasoning may affect children's detection of mental states and their use of this information. Social-cognitive research has documented the influence of general knowledge about the social world and differential knowledge about specific other people on children's attributions about people's behavior (e.g., Miller & Aloise, 1990). Regarding the former, theory-of-mind research has given little attention to how general social knowledge might underlie individual or developmental differences in theories of mind (but see our earlier sections on intracultural and intercultural differences in development). Researchers have given even less attention to the latter—the influences of different knowledge about different types of people on assessing others' mental states. For example, preschoolers are more likely to detect the manipulative intent behind a bribe from a "big mean brother" than from their mother (Aloise & Miller, 1991). The acquisition of such social knowledge and other social knowledge about categories based on gender, race, age, and relationship to oneself is likely to lead to inferences of different mental states in different people. In general, knowledge about the mental states of specific, significant other people, such as family members and close friends, may be more advanced because of a shared history (Dunn, 1994). Familiar regularities in the behavior of others may help children access their knowledge about others' likely mental representations. Thus, a child's differential knowledge about specific other people may cause unequal application of her theory of mind across people and situations.

Several social-cognitive biases (e.g., Miller & Aloise, 1990) suggest other influences on the particular mental state inferred. An optimism bias (e.g., Peterson & Gelfand, 1984) refers to young children's tendency to believe that people are inherently good, even in the face of information to the contrary. An application to theory-of-mind research, then, might be that children tend to infer positive desires, beliefs, intentions, and thoughts, rather than negative ones. This tendency to be positive about other people may also account for young children's overattribution of knowledge to people (see our "Knowledge" section). A second bias, that good things go together (Kun, 1977), could contribute to young children's understanding that a positive desire (wanting a toy) leads to a positive outcome (obtaining that toy) and a positive emotion (happiness). Third, the belief that people have personal control over their behavior (e.g., Smith, 1978) may lead young children to look for the causes of behavior in mental states, particularly intentions, rather than external forces. Thus, social-reasoning biases suggest fruitful new directions for theory-of-mind research.

Theory-of-Mind Thinking as Thinking "On-Line"

Much social-cognitive research, especially that conducted from an information-processing perspective (e.g., Crick & Dodge, 1994), addresses the actual functioning of social-cognitive thought. Social cognition is an activity as well as a set of knowledge, dynamic as well as static. From this perspective, theory-of-mind research focuses too much on what a child understands at age X or Y rather than how this understanding is actually applied at any one point in time. After we know what children know, and consequently what inferences they can make, we need a detailed account of how this knowledge is expressed, moment by moment. This expression may include detecting the need to attempt an act of social cognition, encoding and interpreting social information, accessing prior social knowledge, detecting one or more mental states, combining external and internal causes over time, and selecting a behavior. In other words, children at some point understand that others can have thoughts that differ from their own, but we know little about the process by which they actually infer what those desires, beliefs, and intentions are. For example, a theory of mind may guide the search for information about mental states. Children may gather this information by looking at a person's face (e.g., a smile or pensive expression), observing her behavior (e.g., aggression, helping behavior), asking questions, looking at her line of sight, checking for visual barriers, retrieving and integrating information about the person's behavior in similar situations, and so on.

CONCLUSIONS

In this chapter, we have tried both to capture the exciting findings of the thriving new area of children's theory of mind and to show their importance by placing them into a broader context of social-cognitive development. Our sense is that researchers now understand the general landscape of theory-of-mind development in young children. However, we see the need to explore both the "vertical" and "horizontal" ties between the heavily studied theories of mind of 3- to 5-year-olds and other phenomena. Regarding vertical ties, we see the origins of children's theories in remarkably early rudimentary knowledge seemingly possessed by infants and preschoolers, and the later transformations of this knowledge during middle childhood and adolescence. Future research should give close attention to the mechanisms of development underlying these vertical linkages. We know little regarding the construction and revision of children's theories. Some mechanisms are general, such as the interactive contributions of biological and experiential factors. Examples of more specific possible mechanisms are bootstrapping from self-understanding to understanding others (e.g., Harris, 1989), theory change through gradual accommodation to evidence inconsistent with the child's initial theory (Gopnik & Wellman, 1994), and social experiences such as parent language focused on emotions and other mental states (e.g., Fivush, 1994). Other specific mechanisms may include increasingly powerful information-processing capabilities (e.g., Case, 1989) and brain development (Baron-Cohen & Ring, 1994), and imitative, instructed, and collaborative learning (Tomasello, Kruger, & Ratner, 1993).

We are struck not only by these vertical ties, but also by probable, though scarcely studied, horizontal ties to other important developments. Work on theory of mind has remained somewhat isolated from work on other areas of development. Children's theory of mind surely affects, and is affected by, social behaviors such as peer interaction, social play, friendship, attachment, verbal persuasion, social referencing, aggression, and self-regulation. What does each new theory-of-mind acquisition permit children to do in the social world that they could not do before? Developmentalists are beginning to trace ties between young children's theory of mind and their socialization (e.g. Dunn, 1994), particularly the process by which parent-child conversations about past and present events and emotions contribute to the construction of the self, autobiographical memories, personal narratives, and the meaning of emotions and other mental phenomena (e.g., Fivush, 1994; Miller, 1994; Nelson, 1993; Welch-Ross, 1995).

Accounts of vertical and horizontal links are likely to form some of the major empirical and theoretical contributions in future theory-of-mind research. A main challenge is to understand the developmental processes involved in these links.

ACKNOWLEDGMENTS

The authors wish to thank Shari Ellis, Frances Green, Deanna Kuhn, Scott Miller, Derek Montgomery, Robert Siegler, and Marjorie Taylor for their valuable advice and help in the writing of this chapter.

REFERENCES

Abbott, K., Lee, P. P., & Flavell, J. H. (1996). *Children's understanding of intention.* Unpublished research, Stanford University, Stanford, CA.

Aksu-Koc, A. A. (1988). *The acquisition of aspects and modality.* Cambridge, England: Cambridge University Press.

Aloise, P. A. (1993). Trait confirmation and disconfirmation: The development of attribution biases. *Journal of Experimental Child Psychology, 55,* 177–193.

Aloise, P. A., & Miller, P. H. (1991). Discounting in preschoolers: Effects of type of reward agent. *Journal of Experimental Child Psychology, 57,* 70–86.

Anisfeld, M. (1991). Neonatal imitation. *Developmental Review, 11,* 60–97.

Astington, J. W. (1991). Intention in the child's theory of mind. In D. Frye & C. Moore (Eds.), *Children's theories of mind.* Hillsdale, NJ: Erlbaum.

Astington, J. W. (1993). *The child's discovery of the mind.* Cambridge, MA: Harvard University Press.

Astington, J. W., & Gopnik, A. (1991a). Theoretical explanations of children's understanding of the mind. *British Journal of Developmental Psychology, 9,* 7–32.

Astington, J. W., & Gopnik, A. (1991b). Developing understanding of desire and intention. In A. Whiten (Ed.), *Natural theories of mind: Evolution, development and simulation of everyday mindreading.* Oxford, England: Basil Blackwell.

Astington, J. W., Harris, P. L., & Olson, D. (Eds.). (1988). *Developing theories of mind.* Cambridge, England: Cambridge University Press.

Astington, J. W., & Olson, D. R. (1995). The cognitive revolution in children's understanding of mind. *Human Development, 38,* 179–189.

Avis, J., & Harris, P. L. (1991). Belief-desire reasoning among Baka children: Evidence for a universal conception of mind. *Child Development, 62,* 460–467.

Bakeman, R., & Adamson, L. B. (1984). Coordinating attention to people and objects in mother-infant and peer-infant interaction. *Child Development, 55,* 1278–1289.

Baldwin, D. A. (1991). Infants' contribution to the achievement of joint reference. *Child Development, 62,* 875–890.

Baldwin, D. A. (1993). Early referential understanding: Infants' ability to recognize referential acts for what they are. *Developmental Psychology, 29,* 832–843.

Baldwin, D. A., & Moses, L. J. (1994). Early understanding of referential intent and attentional focus: Evidence from language and emotion. In C. Lewis & P. Mitchell (Eds.), *Children's early understanding of mind: Origins and development.* Hillsdale, NJ: Erlbaum.

Baron-Cohen, S. (1993). From attention-goal psychology to belief-desire psychology: The development of a theory of mind, and it's dysfunction. In S. Baron-Cohen, H. Tager-Flusberg, & D. J. Cohen (Eds.), *Understanding other minds: Perspectives from autism.* Oxford, England: Oxford University Press.

Baron-Cohen, S. (1994). How to build a baby that can read minds: Cognitive mechanisms in mindreading. *Cahiers de Psychologie Cognitive, 13*(5), 513–552.

Baron-Cohen, S. (1995). *Mindblindness: An essay on autism and theory of mind.* Cambridge, MA: MIT Press.

Baron-Cohen, S., & Ring, H. (1994). A model of the mind reading system: Neuropsychological and neurobiological perspectives. In C. Lewis & P. Mitchell (Eds.), *Children's early understanding of mind: Origins and development.* Hillsdale, NJ: Erlbaum.

Baron-Cohen, S., Tager-Flusberg, H., & Cohen, D. J. (1993). *Understanding other minds: Perspectives from autism.* Oxford, England: Oxford University Press.

Bartsch, K., & Wellman, H. M. (1995). *Children talk about the mind.* New York: Oxford University Press.

Bates, E. (1976). *Language and context: The acquisition of pragmatics.* New York: Academic Press.

Bennett, J. (1978). Some remarks about concepts. *Behavioral and Brain Sciences, 1,* 557–560.

Bennett, M. (1993a). Introduction. In M. Bennett (Ed.), *The development of social cognition: The child as psychologist.* New York: Guilford Press.

Bennett, M. (Ed.). (1993b). *The development of social cognition: The child as psychologist.* New York: Guilford Press.

Bertenthal, B. I., Proffitt, D. R., & Cutting, J. E. (1984). Infant sensitivity to figural coherence in biomechanical motions. *Journal of Experimental Child Psychology, 37,* 213–220.

Bjorklund, D. F., & Green, B. L. (1992). The adaptive nature of cognitive immaturity. *American Psychologist, 47,* 46–54.

Bloom, L., & Capatides, J. B. (1987). Sources of meaning in the acquisition of complex syntax: The sample case of causality. *Journal of Experimental Child Psychology, 43,* 112–128.

Bretherton, I., & Beeghly, M. (1982). Talking about internal states: The acquisition of an explicit theory of mind. *Developmental Psychology, 18,* 906–921.

Bretherton, I., Fritz, J., Zahn-Waxler, C., & Ridgeway, D. (1986). Learning to talk about emotions: A functionalist perspective. *Child Development, 57,* 529–548.

Bretherton, I., McNew, S., & Beeghly-Smith, M. (1981). Early person knowledge as expressed in gestural and verbal communication: When do infants acquire a "theory of mind"? In M. Lamb & L. Sherrod (Eds.), *Social cognition in infancy.* Hillsdale, NJ: Erlbaum.

Brown, A. L., Bransford, J. D., Ferrara, R. A., & Campione, J. C. (1983). Learning, remembering, and understanding. In P. H. Mussen (Series Ed.) & J. H. Flavell & E. M. Markman (Eds.), *Handbook of child psychology: Vol. 3. Cognitive development.* New York: Wiley.

Brown, J. R., Donelan-McCall, N., & Dunn, J. (1996). Why talk about mental states? The significance of children's conversations with friends, siblings and mothers. *Child Development, 67,* 836–849.

Brown, J. R., & Dunn, J. (1991). 'You can cry, mum': The social and developmental implications of talk about internal states. *British Journal of Developmental Psychology, 9,* 237–256.

Butterworth, G. (1994). Theory of mind and the facts of embodiment. In C. Lewis & P. Mitchell (Eds.), *Children's early understanding of mind: Origins and development.* Hillsdale, NJ: Erlbaum.

Butterworth, G., Harris, P., Leslie, A., & Wellman, H. W. (Eds.). (1991). Perspectives on the child's theory of mind [Special issues]. *British Journal of Developmental Psychology, 9,* (1, 2).

Butterworth, G., & Jarrett, N. (1991). What minds have in common in space: Spatial mechanisms serving joint visual attention in infancy. *British Journal of Developmental Psychology, 9,* 55–72.

Byrne, R. W., & Whiten, A. (1988). Toward the next generation in data quality: A new survey of primate tactical deception. *Behavioral and Brain Science, 11,* 267–283.

Byrne, R. W., & Whiten, A. (1991). Computation and mindreading in primate tactical deception. In A. Whiten (Ed.), *Natural theories of mind: Evolution, development and simulation of everyday mindreading.* Oxford, England: Basil Blackwell.

Case, R. (1989, April). *A neo-Piagetian analysis of the child's understanding of other people, and the internal conditions which motivate their behavior.* Paper presented at the biennial meeting of the Society for Research in Child Development, Kansas City, MO.

Chandler, M. (1988). Doubt and developing theories of the mind. In J. W. Astington, P. L. Harris, & D. R. Olson (Eds.), *Developing theories of mind.* Cambridge, England: Cambridge University Press.

Chandler, M., & Chapman, M. (1991). *Criteria for competence: Controversies in the conceptualization and assessment of children's abilities.* Hillsdale, NJ: Erlbaum.

Chandler, M., Fritz, A. S., & Hala, S. M. (1989). Small scale deceit: Deception as a marker of 2-, 3-, and 4-year-olds' early theories of mind. *Child Development, 60,* 1263–1277.

Chandler, M., & Hala, S. (1994). The role of personal involvement in the assessment of early false belief skills. In C. Lewis & P. Mitchell (Eds.), *Children's early understanding of mind: Origins and development.* Hillsdale, NJ: Erlbaum.

Chandler, M., & Helm, D. (1984). Developmental changes in the contributions of shared experience to social role-taking competence. *International Journal of Behavioral Development, 7,* 145–156.

Chandler, M., & Lalonde, C. E. (1996). Shifting to an interpretive theory of mind: 5- to 7-year-olds' changing conceptions of mental life. In A. Sameroff & M. Haith (Eds.), *The 5 to 7 year shift: The age of reason and responsibility.* Chicago: University of Chicago Press.

Cheney, D. L., & Seyfarth, R. M. (1990). *How monkeys see the world.* Chicago: University of Chicago Press.

Christensen, S. M., & Turner, D. R. (Eds.). (1993). *Folk psychology and the philosophy of mind.* Hillsdale, NJ: Erlbaum.

Churchland, P. M. (1984). *Matter and consciousness.* Cambridge, MA: Bradford/MIT Press.

Clements, W. A., & Perner, J. (1994). Implicit understanding of belief. *Cognitive Development, 9,* 377–395.

Cohen, J. (1993). *Children's understanding of spontaneous cognitive cueing.* Unpublished honor's thesis, Department of Psychology, Stanford University.

Cole, P. M. (1986). Children's spontaneous control of facial expression. *Child Development, 57,* 1309–1321.

Cooper, R. P., & Aslin, R. N. (1989). The language environment of the young infant: Implications for early perceptual development. *Canadian Journal of Psychology, 43,* 247–265.

Cox, M. V. (1980). Visual perspective-taking in children. In M. V. Cox (Ed.), *Are young children egocentric?* New York: St. Martin's Press.

Crick, N. R., & Dodge, K. A. (1994). A review and reformulation of social information-processing mechanisms in children's social adjustment. *Psychological Bulletin, 115,* 74–101.

Custer, W. L. (1996). A comparison of young children's understanding of contradictory references in pretense, memory, and belief. *Child Development, 67,* 678–688.

Damon, W. (1977). *The social world of the child.* San Francisco: Jossey-Bass.

D'Andrade, R. (1987). A folk model of the mind. In D. Holland & N. Quinn (Eds.), *Cultural models in language and thought.* Cambridge, England: Cambridge University Press.

Dennett, D. C. (1978). Beliefs about beliefs. *Behavioral and Brain Sciences, 1,* 568–570.

Dodge, K. A., & Frame, C. L. (1982). Social cognitive biases and deficits in aggressive boys. *Child Development, 53,* 620–635.

Dolgin, K. G., & Behrend, D. A. (1984). Children's knowledge about animates and inanimates. *Child Development, 55,* 1646–1650.

Dunn, J. (1988). *The beginnings of social understanding.* Oxford, England: Basil Blackwell.

Dunn, J. (1994). Changing minds and changing relationships. In C. Lewis & P. Mitchell (Eds.), *Children's early understanding of mind: Origins and development.* Hillsdale, NJ: Erlbaum.

Dunn, J., Bretherton, I., & Munn, P. (1987). Conversations about feeling states between mothers and their young children. *Developmental Psychology, 23,* 132–139.

Dunn, J., & Brown, J. (1994). Affect expression in the family, children's understanding of emotions, and their interactions with others. *Merrill-Palmer Quarterly, 40,* 120–137.

Dunn, J., Brown, J., & Beardsall, L. (1991). Family talk about feeling states and children's later understanding of others' emotions. *Developmental Psychology, 27,* 448–455.

Dunn, J., Brown, J., Slomkowski, C., Tesla, C., & Youngblade, L. (1991). Young children's understanding of other people's feelings and beliefs: Individual differences and their antecedents. *Child Development, 62,* 1352–1366.

Dunn, J., & Munn, P. (1985). Becoming a family member: Family conflict and the development of social understanding in the second year. *Child Development, 56,* 480–492.

Dweck, C. S., & Leggett, E. L. (1988). A social-cognitive approach to motivation and personality. *Psychological Review, 95,* 256–273.

Eder, R. A. (1990). Uncovering young children's psychological selves: Individual and developmental differences. *Child Development, 61,* 849–863.

Eisenberg, N. (1994). *Social development.* Thousand Oaks, CA: Sage.

Erwin, P. (1993). *Friendship and peer relations in children.* New York: Wiley.

Estes, D. (in press). Young children's understanding of the mind: Imagery, introspection, and some implications. *Journal of Applied Developmental Psychology.*

Estes, D., Wellman, H. M., & Woolley, J. D. (1989). Children's understanding of mental phenomena. In H. W. Reese (Ed.), *Advances in child development and behavior.* San Diego, CA: Academic Press.

Fabricius, W. V., & Schwanenflugel, P. J. (1994). The older child's theory of mind. In A. Demetriou & A. Efklides (Eds.), *Intelligence, mind, and reasoning: Structure and development.* Amsterdam, The Netherlands: Elsevier.

Falmagne, R. J. (1993). Review of M. Siegal, Knowing children: Experiments in conversation and cognition. *Human Development, 36,* 174–177.

Fiske, S. (1993). Social cognition and social perception. *Annual Review of Psychology, 44,* 155–194.

Fivush, R. (1994). Constructing narrative, emotion, and self in parent-child conversations about the past. In U. Neisser & R. Fivush (Eds.), *The remembering self: Construction and accuracy in the life narrative.* New York: Cambridge University Press.

Flapan, D. (1968). *Children's understanding of social interaction.* New York: Teachers College Press.

Flavell, J. H. (1978). The development of knowledge about visual perception. In C. B. Keasey (Ed.), *Nebraska Symposium on Motivation* (Vol. 25). Lincoln: University of Nebraska Press.

Flavell, J. H. (1981). Cognitive monitoring. In W. P. Dickson (Ed.), *Children's oral communication skills.* New York: Academic Press.

Flavell, J. H. (1988). The development of children's knowledge about the mind: From cognitive connections to mental representations. In J. W. Astington, P. L. Harris, & D. R. Olson (Eds.), *Developing theories of mind.* Cambridge, England: Cambridge University Press.

Flavell, J. H. (1992). Perspectives on perspective taking. In H. Beilin & P. Pufall (Eds.), *Piaget's theory: Prospects and possibilities.* Hillsdale, NJ: Erlbaum.

Flavell, J. H. (1993). Young children's understanding of thinking and consciousness. *Current Directions in Psychological Science, 2,* 40–43.

Flavell, J. H., Everett, B. A., Croft, K., & Flavell, E. R. (1981). Young children's knowledge about visual perception: Further evidence for the Level 1–Level 2 distinction. *Developmental Psychology, 17,* 99–103.

Flavell, J. H., Flavell, E. R., & Green, F. L. (1983). Development of the appearance-reality distinction. *Cognitive Psychology, 15,* 95–120.

Flavell, J. H., Flavell, E. R., & Green, F. L. (1987). Young children's knowledge about the apparent-real and pretend-real distinctions. *Developmental Psychology, 23,* 816–822.

Flavell, J. H., Flavell, E. R., & Green, F. L. (1989). A transitional period in the development of the appearance-reality distinction. *International Journal of Behavioral Development, 12,* 509–526.

Flavell, J. H., Flavell, E. R., Green, F. L., & Wilcox, S. A. (1980). Young children's knowledge about visual perception. Effect of observer's distance from target on perceptual clarity of target. *Developmental Psychology, 16,* 10–12.

Flavell, J. H., Green, F. L., & Flavell, E. R. (1986). Development of knowledge about the appearance-reality distinction. *Monographs of the Society for Research in Child Development, 51*(1, Serial No. 212).

Flavell, J. H., Green, F. L., & Flavell, E. R. (1989). Young children's ability to differentiate appearance-reality and level 2 perspectives in the tactile modality. *Child Development, 60,* 201–213.

Flavell, J. H., Green, F. L., & Flavell, E. R. (1993). Children's understanding of the stream of consciousness. *Child Development, 64,* 387–398.

Flavell, J. H., Green, F. L., & Flavell, E. R. (1995a). The development of children's knowledge about attentional focus. *Developmental Psychology, 31,* 706–712.

Flavell, J. H., Green, F. L., & Flavell, E. R. (1995b). Young children's knowledge about thinking. *Monographs of the Society for Research in Child Development, 60*(1, Serial No. 243).

Flavell, J. H., Green, F. L., Flavell, E. R., & Grossman, J. B. (1997). The development of children's knowledge about inner speech. *Child Development, 68,* 39–47.

Flavell, J. H., Lindberg, N. A., Green, F. L., & Flavell, E. R. (1992). The development of children's understanding of the appearance-reality distinction between how people look and what they are really like. *Merrill-Palmer Quarterly, 4,* 513–524.

Flavell, J. H., Miller, P. H., & Miller, S. A. (1993). *Cognitive development* (3rd ed.). Englewood Cliffs, NJ: Prentice-Hall.

Flavell, J. H., Mumme, D. L., Green, F. L., & Flavell, E. R. (1992). Young children's understanding of different types of beliefs. *Child Development, 63,* 960–977.

Flavell, J. H., Zhang, X.-D., Zou, H., Dong, Q., & Qi, S. (1983). A comparison between the development of the appearance-reality distinction in the People's Republic of China and the United States. *Cognitive Psychology, 15,* 459–466.

Fodor, J. (1992). A theory of the child's theory of mind. *Cognition, 44,* 283–296.

Forguson, L. (1989). *Common sense.* London: Routledge & Kegan Paul.

Forrester, M. A. (1992). *The development of young children's social cognitive skills.* Hillsdale, NJ: Erlbaum.

Freeman, N. H., Lewis, C., & Doherty, M. J. (1991). Preschoolers' grasp of a desire for knowledge in false-belief prediction. *British Journal of Developmental Psychology, 9,* 139–158.

Friend, M., & Davis, T. L. (1993). Appearance-reality distinction: Children's understanding of the physical and affective domains. *Developmental Psychology, 29,* 907–914.

Frye, D., & Moore, C. (Eds.). (1991). *Children's theories of mind: Mental states and social understanding.* Hillsdale, NJ: Erlbaum.

Frye, D., Zelazo, P. D., & Palfai, T. (1992). *The cognitive basis for theory of mind.* Unpublished manuscript, New York: New York University.

Gnepp, J., & Chilamkurti, C. (1988). Children's use of personality attributions to predict other people's emotional and behavioral reactions. *Child Development, 59,* 743–754.

Gnepp, J., & Hess, D. L. R. (1986). Children's understanding of verbal and facial display rules. *Developmental Psychology, 22,* 103–108.

Golinkoff, R. M. (1983). Infant social cognition: Self, people, and objects. In L. S. Liben (Ed.), *Piaget and the foundations of knowledge.* Hillsdale, NJ: Erlbaum.

Gómez, J. C., Sarriá, E., & Tamarit, J. (1993). The comparative study of early communication and theories of mind: Ontogeny, phylogeny, and pathology. In S. Baron-Cohen, H. Tager-Flusberg, & D. J. Cohen (Eds.), *Understanding other minds: Perspectives from autism.* Oxford, England: Oxford University Press.

Gopnik, A. (1993). How we know our minds: The illusion of first-person knowledge of intentionality. *Behavioral and Brain Sciences, 16,* 1–14.

Gopnik, A., & Astington, J. W. (1988). Children's understanding of representational change and its relation to the understanding of false belief and the appearance-reality distinction. *Child Development, 59,* 26–37.

Gopnik, A., & Graf, P. (1988). Knowing how you know: Young children's ability to identify and remember the sources of their beliefs. *Child Development, 59,* 1366–1371.

Gopnik, A., Slaughter, V., & Meltzoff, A. (1994). Changing your views: How understanding visual perception can lead to a new theory of mind. In C. Lewis & P. Mitchell (Eds.), *Children's early understanding of mind: Origins and development.* Hillsdale, NJ: Erlbaum.

Gopnik, A., & Wellman, H. M. (1994). The 'theory' theory. In L. A. Hirschfeld & S. A. Gelman (Eds.), *Mapping the mind: Domain specificity in cognition and culture.* Cambridge, England: Cambridge University Press.

Gordon, F. R., & Flavell, J. H. (1977). The development of intuitions about cognitive cueing. *Child Development, 48,* 1027–1033.

Griffin, D., & Ross, L. (1991). Subjective construal, social inference, and human misunderstanding. *Advances in Experimental Social Psychology, 24,* 319–359.

Gross, A. L., & Ballif, B. (1991). Children's understanding of emotion from facial expressions and situations: A review. *Developmental Review, 11,* 368–398.

Hadwin, J., & Perner, J. (1991). Pleased and surprised: Children's cognitive theory of emotion. *British Journal of Developmental Psychology, 9,* 215–234.

Halford, G. S. (1992). *Children's understanding: The development of mental models.* Hillsdale, NJ: Erlbaum.

Harman, G. (1978). Studying the chimpanzee's theory of mind. *Behavioral and Brain Sciences, 1,* 576–577.

Harris, P. L. (1989). *Children and emotion.* Oxford, England: Basil Blackwell.

Harris, P. L. (1991). The work of the imagination. In A. Whiten (Ed.), *Natural theories of mind: Evolution, development and simulation of everyday mindreading.* Oxford, England: Basil Blackwell.

Harris, P. L. (1992). From simulation to folk psychology: The case for development. *Mind and Language, 7,* 120–144.

Harris, P. L. (1994a). Understanding pretense. In C. Lewis & P. Mitchell (Eds.), *Children's early understanding of mind: Origins and development.* Hillsdale, NJ: Erlbaum.

Harris, P. L. (1994b). The child's understanding of emotion: Developmental change and the family environment. *Journal of Child Psychology and Psychiatry, 35,* 3–28.

Harris, P. L., Brown, E., Marriott, C., Whittall, S., & Harmer, S. (1991). Monsters, ghosts and witches: Testing the limits of the fantasy-reality distinction in young children. *British Journal of Developmental Psychology, 9,* 105–123.

Harris, P. L., & Gross, D. (1988). Children's understanding of real and apparent emotions. In J. W. Astington, P. L. Harris, & D. R. Olson (Eds.), *Developing theories of mind.* Cambridge, England: Cambridge University Press.

Harris, P. L., & Kavanaugh, R. D. (1993). Young children's understanding of pretense. *Monographs of the Society for Research in Child Development, 58*(1, Serial No. 231).

Harris, P. L., Lillard, A., & Perner, J. (1994). Commentary: Triangulating pretense and belief. In C. Lewis & P. Mitchell (Eds.), *Children's early understanding of mind: Origins and development.* Hillsdale, NJ: Erlbaum.

Harris, P. L., Olthof, T., Meerum Terwogt, M., & Hardman, C. E. (1987). Children's knowledge of the situations that provoke emotion. *International Journal of Behavioral Development, 10,* 319–344.

Harter, S., & Buddin, B. (1987). Children's understanding of the simultaneity of two emotions: A five-stage developmental acquisition sequence. *Developmental Psychology, 23,* 388–399.

Harter, S., & Whitesell, N. R. (1989). Developmental changes in children's understanding of single, multiple, and blended emotion concepts. In C. Saarni & P. L. Harris (Eds.), *Chil-dren's understanding of emotion.* Cambridge, England: Cambridge University Press.

Hartsock, N. (1983). The feminist standpoint: Developing the ground for a specifically feminist historical materialism. In S. Harding & M. Hintikka (Eds.), *Discovering reality: Feminist perspectives on metaphysics, epistemology, methodology, and philosophy of science.* Dordrecht, The Netherlands: Reidel.

Hcelas, P., & Lock, A. (1981). *Indigenous psychologies.* London: Academic Press.

Hickling, A. K., Wellman, H. M., & Gottfried, G. M. (in press). Preschoolers' understanding of others' mental attitudes toward pretense. *British Journal of Developmental Psychology.*

Higgins, E. T., & Bryant, S. L. (1982). Consensus information and the fundamental attribution error: The role of development and in-group versus out-group knowledge. *Journal of Personality and Social Psychology, 43,* 889–900.

Hirschfeld, L. A., & Gelman, S. A. (Eds.). (1994). *Mapping the mind: Domain specificity in cognition and culture.* Cambridge, England: Cambridge University Press.

Hobson, R. P. (1991). Against the theory of "theory of mind." *British Journal of Developmental Psychology, 9,* 33–51.

Hobson, R. P. (1994). Perceiving attitudes, conceiving minds. In C. Lewis & P. Mitchell (Eds.), *Children's early understanding of mind: Origins and development.* Hillsdale, NJ: Erlbaum.

Hoffman, M. L. (1978). Empathy: Its developmental and prosocial implications. In C. B. Keasey (Ed.), *Nebraska Symposium on Motivation* (Vol. 25). Lincoln: University of Nebraska Press.

Hood, L., & Bloom, L. (1979). What, when, and how about why: A longitudinal study of early expressions of causality. *Monographs of the Society for Research in Child Development, 44*(6, Serial No. 181).

Horgan, T., & Woodward, J. (1993). Folk psychology is here to stay. In S. M. Christensen & D. R. Turner (Eds.), *Folk psychology and the philosophy of mind.* Hillsdale, NJ: Erlbaum.

Hornik, R., Risenhoover, N., & Gunnar, M. (1987). The effects of maternal positive, neutral, and negative affective communications on infant responses to new toys. *Child Development, 58,* 937–944.

Howe, N. (1991). Sibling-directed internal state language, perspective-taking, and affective behavior. *Child Development, 62,* 1503–1512.

Hughes, M., & Donaldson, M. (1979). The use of hiding games for studying the coordination of viewpoints. *Educational Review, 31,* 133–140.

Huttenlocher, J., & Smiley, P. (1990). Emerging notions of persons. In N. L. Stein, B. Leventhal, & T. Trabasso (Eds.), *Psychological and biological approaches to emotions.* Hillsdale, NJ: Erlbaum.

James, W. (1890). *The principles of psychology* (Vol. 1). New York: Henry Holt.

Jenkins, J. M., & Astington, J. W. (1996). Cognitive factors and family structure associated with theory of mind development in young children. *Developmental Psychology, 32,* 70–78.

Johnson, C. N. (1988). Theory of mind and the structure of conscious experience. In J. W. Astington, P. L. Harris, & D. R. Olson (Eds.), *Developing theories of mind.* Cambridge, England: Cambridge University Press.

Johnson, C. N., & Wellman, H. M. (1980). Children's developing understanding of mental verbs: Remember, know, and guess. *Child Development, 51,* 1095–1102.

Johnson, C. N., & Wellman, H. M. (1982). Children's developing conceptions of the mind and brain. *Child Development, 53,* 222–234.

Karmiloff-Smith, A. (1992). *Beyond modularity.* London: Bradford/MIT Press.

Karniol, R. (1978). Children's use of intention cues in evaluating behavior. *Psychological Bulletin, 85,* 76–85.

Kestenbaum, R., & Gelman, S. A. (1995). Preschool children's identification and understanding of mixed emotions. *Cognitive Development, 10,* 443–458.

King, J. E. (1994). *Young children's understanding of attitudes.* Unpublished honor's thesis, Department of Psychology, Stanford University, Stanford, CA.

Kuhl, P. K. (1987). Perception of speech and sound in early infancy. In P. Salapatek & L. Cohen (Eds.), *Handbook of infant perception: Vol. 2. From perception to cognition.* Orlando, FL: Academic Press.

Kun, A. (1977). Development of the magnitude-covariation and compensation schemata in ability and effort attributions of performance. *Child Development, 48,* 862–873.

Lagattuta, K. H., Wellman, H. M., & Flavell, J. H. (in press). Preschoolers' understanding of the link between thinking and feeling: Cognitive cueing and emotional change. *Child Development.*

Lalonde, C. E., Chandler, M. J., & Moses, L. (1993, March). *Children's early understanding of the interpretive nature of knowing.* Paper presented at the biennial meeting of the Society for Research in Child Development, New Orleans, LA.

Legerstee, M. (1991). The role of person and object in eliciting early imitation. *Journal of Experimental Child Psychology, 51,* 423–433.

Legerstee, M. (1992). A review of the animate-inanimate distinction in infancy: Implications for models of social and cognitive knowing. *Early Development and Parenting, 1,* 59–67.

Lempers, J. D., Flavell, E. R., & Flavell, J. H. (1977). The development in very young children of tacit knowledge concerning visual perception. *Genetic Psychology Monographs, 95,* 3–53.

Leslie, A. M. (1987). Pretense and representation: The origins of "theory of mind." *Psychological Review, 94,* 412–426.

Leslie, A. M. (1994). ToMM, ToBy, and agency: Core architecture and domain specificity. In L. A. Hirschfeld & S. A. Gelman (Eds.), *Mapping the mind: Domain specificity in cognition and culture.* Cambridge, England: Cambridge University Press.

Leslie, A. M., & Roth, D. (1993). What autism teaches us about metarepresentation. In S. Baron-Cohen, H. Tager-Flusberg, & D. J. Cohen (Eds.), *Understanding other minds: Perspectives from autism.* Oxford, England: Oxford University Press.

Leslie, A. M., & Thaiss, L. (1992). Domain specificity in conceptual development: Neuropsychological evidence from autism. *Cognition, 43,* 225–251.

Lewis, C. (1994). Episodes, events, and narratives in the child's understanding of mind. In C. Lewis & P. Mitchell (Eds.), *Children's early understanding of mind: Origins and development.* Hillsdale, NJ: Erlbaum.

Lewis, C., & Mitchell, P. (Eds.). (1994). *Children's early understanding of mind: Origins and development.* Hillsdale, NJ: Erlbaum.

Lewis, C., & Osborne, A. (1990). Three-year olds' problems with false belief: Conceptual deficit or linguistic artifact? *Child Development, 61,* 1514–1519.

Lewis, M. (1993). Commentary. *Human Development, 36,* 363–367.

Lewis, M., & Saarni, C. (Eds.). (1985). *The socialization of emotions.* New York: Plenum Press.

Lillard, A. S. (1993a). Pretend play skills and the child's theory of mind. *Child Development, 64,* 348–371.

Lillard, A. S. (1993b). Young children's conceptualization of pretense: Action or mental representational state? *Child Development, 64,* 372–386.

Lillard, A. S. (1994). Making sense of pretense. In C. Lewis & P. Mitchell (Eds.), *Children's early understanding of mind: Origins and development.* Hillsdale, NJ: Erlbaum.

Lillard, A. S. (1996). Body or mind: Children's categorization of pretense. *Child Development, 67,* 1717–1734.

Lillard, A. S. (in press). Ethnopsychologies and the origins of a theory of mind. *Psychological Bulletin.*

Lillard, A. S., & Flavell, J. H. (1990). Young children's preference for mental state versus behavioral descriptions of human action. *Child Development, 61,* 731–741.

Lovett, S. B., & Flavell, J. H. (1990). Understanding and remembering: Children's knowledge about the differences between comprehension and memory. *Child Development, 61,* 1842–1858.

Lovett, S. B., & Pillow, B. H. (1995). The development of the ability to make distinctions between comprehension and memory: Evidence from strategy-selection tasks. *Journal of Educational Psychology, 87,* 523–536.

Lovett, S. B., & Pillow, B. H. (1996). The development of the ability to make distinctions between comprehension and memory: Evidence from goal-state evaluation tasks. *Journal of Educational Psychology, 88,* 546–562.

Lutz, C. (1983). Parental goals, ethnopsychology, and the development of emotional meaning. *Ethos, 11,* 246–262.

Lyon, T. D. (1993). *Young children's understanding of desire and knowledge.* Unpublished doctoral dissertation, Stanford University, Stanford, CA.

Lyon, T. D., & Flavell, J. H. (1993). Young children's understanding of forgetting over time. *Child Development, 64,* 789–800.

Lyon, T. D., & Flavell, J. H. (1994). Young children's understanding of "remember" and "forget." *Child Development, 65,* 1357–1371.

MacWhinney, B., & Snow, C. (1990). The child language data exchange system: An update. *Journal of Child Language, 17,* 457–472.

Masangkay, Z. S., McCluskey, K. A., McIntyre, C. W., Sims-Knight, J., Vaughn, B. E., & Flavell, J. H. (1974). The early development of inferences about the visual percepts of others. *Child Development, 45,* 237–246.

Meerum Terwogt, M., & Harris, P. L. (1993). Understanding of emotion. In M. Bennett (Ed.), *The development of social cognition: The child as psychologist.* New York: Guilford Press.

Meltzoff, A. N. (1990). Foundations for developing a concept of self: The role of imitation in relating self to other and the value of social mirroring, social modeling, and self-practice in infancy. In D. Cicchetti & M. Beeghly (Eds.), *The self in transition: Infancy to childhood.* Chicago: University of Chicago Press.

Meltzoff, A. N. (1995). Understanding the intentions of others: Re-enactment of intended acts by 18-month-old children. *Developmental Psychology, 31,* 838–850.

Meltzoff, A. N., & Moore, M. K. (1994). Imitation, memory, and the representation of persons. *Infant Behavior and Development, 17,* 83–89.

Miller, P. H. (1985a). Metacognition and attention. In D. Forrest-Pressley, G. E. MacKinnon, & T. G. Waller (Eds.), *Metacognition, cognition, and human performance: Vol. 2. Instructional practices.* New York: Academic Press.

Miller, P. H. (1985b). Children's reasoning about the causes of human behavior. *Journal of Experimental Child Psychology, 39,* 343–362.

Miller, P. H., & Aloise, P. A. (1989). Young children's understanding of the psychological causes of behavior: A review. *Child Development, 60,* 257–285.

Miller, P. H., & Aloise, P. A. (1990). Discounting in children: The role of social knowledge. *Developmental Review, 10,* 266–298.

Miller, P. H., & Bigi, L. (1979). The development of children's understanding of attention. *Merrill Palmer Quarterly, 25,* 235–250.

Miller, P. H., & DeMarie-Dreblow, D. (1990). Social-cognitive correlates of children's understanding of displaced aggression. *Journal of Experimental Child Psychology, 49,* 488–504.

Miller, P. H., Kessel, F. S., & Flavell, J. H. (1970). Thinking about people thinking about people thinking about. . . . A study of social cognitive development. *Child Development, 41,* 613–623.

Miller, P. H., & Shannon, K. (1984). Young children's understanding of the effect of noise and interest level on learning. *Genetic Psychology Monographs, 110,* 71–90.

Miller, P. H., & Zalenski, R. (1982). Preschoolers' knowledge about attention. *Developmental Psychology, 18,* 871–875.

Miller, P. J. (1994). Narrative practices: Their role in socialization and self construction. In U. Neisser & R. Fivush (Eds.), *The remembering self: Construction and accuracy in the self narrative.* New York: Cambridge University Press.

Mischel, H. N., & Mischel, W. (1983). The development of children's knowledge of self-control strategies. *Child Development, 54,* 603–619.

Mitchell, P. (1994). Realism and early conception of mind: A synthesis of phylogenetic and ontogenetic issues. In C. Lewis & P. Mitchell (Eds.), *Children's early understanding of mind: Origins and development.* Hillsdale, NJ: Erlbaum.

Mitchell, P., & Lacohee, H. (1991). Children's early understanding of false belief. *Cognition, 39,* 107–127.

Montgomery, D. E. (1992). Young children's theory of knowing: The development of a folk epistemology. *Developmental Review, 12,* 410–430.

Montgomery, D. E., & Miller, S. A. (1992). *Young children's judgments of an unintended listener's knowledge.* Unpublished manuscript, University of Florida, Gainesville, FL.

Montgomery, D. E., & Miller, S. A. (in press). Young children's attributions of knowledge when speaker-intent and listener-access conflict. *British Journal of Developmental Psychology.*

Moore, C. (1996). Theories of mind in infancy. *British Journal of Developmental Psychology, 14,* 19–40.

Moore, C., & Corkum, V. (1994). Social understanding at the end of the first year of life. *Developmental Review, 14,* 349–372.

Moore, C., & Dunham, P. J. (Eds.). (1995). *Joint attention: Its origins and role in development.* Hillsdale, NJ: Erlbaum.

Moore, C., & Furrow, D. (1991). The development of the language of belief: The expression of relative certainty. In

D. Frye & C. Moore (Eds.), *Children's theories of mind: Mental states and social understanding.* Hillsdale, NJ: Erlbaum.

Moore, C., Pure, K., & Furrow, D. (1990). Children's understanding of the modal expression of speaker certainty and uncertainty and its relation to the development of a representational theory of mind. *Child Development, 61,* 722–730.

Moses, L. J. (1990). *Young children's understanding of intention and belief.* Unpublished doctoral dissertation, Stanford University, Stanford, CA.

Moses, L. J. (1993). Young children's understanding of belief constraints on intention. *Cognitive Development, 8,* 1–25.

Moses, L. J., & Chandler, M. J. (1992). Traveller's guide to children's theories of mind. *Psychological Inquiry, 3,* 286–301.

Mumme, D. (1993). *Rethinking social referencing: The influence of facial and vocal affect on infant behavior.* Unpublished doctoral dissertation, Stanford University, Stanford, CA.

Mumme, D. L., Fernald, A., & Herrera, C. (1996). Infants' responses to facial and vocal emotional signals in a social referencing paradigm. *Child Development, 67,* 3219–3237.

Mumme, D. L., Won, D., & Fernald, A. (1994, June). *Do 1-year-old infants show referent specific responding to emotional signals?* Poster presented at the meeting of the International Conference on Infant Studies, Paris, France.

Nelson, C. A. (1987). The recognition of facial expressions in the first two years of life: Mechanisms of development. *Child Development, 58,* 889–909.

Nelson, K. (1993). The psychological and social origins of autobiographical memory. *Psychological Science, 4,* 7–14.

Newcomb, N. (1989). The development of spatial perspective taking. In H. W. Reese (Ed.), *Advances in child development and behavior* (Vol. 22). San Diego: Academic Press.

Nisbett, R. E., Caputo, C., Legant, P., & Marcek, J. (1973). Behavior as seen by the actor and as seen by the observer. *Journal of Personality and Social Psychology, 27,* 154–165.

Novey, M. S. (1975). *The development of knowledge of others' ability to see.* Unpublished doctoral dissertation, Harvard University, Cambridge, MA.

Olson, D. R. (1993, March). *What are beliefs and why can a 4-year-old child but not a 3-year-old child understand them?* Paper presented at the biennial meeting of the Society for Research in Child Development, New Orleans, LA.

O'Neill, D. K. (1996). Two-year-olds' sensitivity to a parent's knowledge state when making requests. *Child Development, 67,* 659–677.

O'Neill, D. K., Astington, J., & Flavell, J. H. (1992). Young children's understanding of the role that sensory experiences play in knowledge acquisition. *Child Development, 63,* 474–490.

O'Neill, D. K., & Gopnik, A. (1991). Young children's ability to identify the sources of their beliefs. *Developmental Psychology, 27,* 390–397.

Perner, J. (1991). *Understanding the representational mind.* Cambridge, MA: MIT Press.

Perner, J. (1995). The many faces of belief: Reflections on Fodor's and the child's theory of mind. *Cognition, 57,* 241–269.

Perner, J., Baker, S., & Hutton, D. (1994). Prelief: The conceptual origins of belief and pretense. In C. Lewis & P. Mitchell (Eds.), *Children's early understanding of mind: Origins and development.* Hillsdale, NJ: Erlbaum.

Perner, J., & Howes, D. (1992). 'He thinks he knows': And more developmental evidence against the simulation (role taking) theory. *Mind and Language, 7,* 72–86.

Perner, J., Leekam, S. R., & Wimmer, H. (1987). Three-year-olds' difficulty with false belief: The case for a conceptual deficit. *British Journal of Developmental Psychology, 5,* 125–137.

Perner, J., & Ogden, J. (1988). Knowledge for hunger: Children's problem of representation in imputing mental states. *Cognition, 29,* 47–61.

Perner, J., Ruffman, T., & Leekam, S. R. (1994). Theory of mind is contagious: You catch it from your sibs. *Child Development, 65,* 1228–1238.

Peterson, L., & Gelfand, D. M. (1984). Causal attributions of helping as a function of age and incentive. *Child Development, 55,* 504–511.

Pillow, B. H. (1988). Young children's understanding of attentional limits. *Child Development, 59,* 38–46.

Pillow, B. H. (1989a). The development of beliefs about selective attention. *Merrill-Palmer Quarterly, 35,* 421–443.

Pillow, B. H. (1989b). Early understanding of perception as a source of knowledge. *Journal of Experimental Child Psychology, 47,* 116–129.

Pillow, B. H. (1991). Children's understanding of biased social cognition. *Developmental Psychology, 27,* 539–551.

Pillow, B. H. (1993a, March). *Children's understanding of biased interpretation.* Poster presented at the biennial meeting of the Society for Research in Child Development, New Orleans, LA.

Pillow, B. H. (1993b). Preschool children's understanding of the relationship between modality of perceptual access and knowledge of perceptual properties. *British Journal of Developmental Psychology, 11,* 371–389.

Pillow, B. H. (1995). Two trends in the development of conceptual perspective-taking: An elaboration of the passive-active hypothesis. *International Journal of Behavioral Development, 18,* 649–676.

Pillow, B. H., & Henrichon, A. J. (1996). There's more to the picture than meets the eye: Young children's difficulty understanding biased interpretation. *Child Development, 67,* 802–819.

Poulin-Dubois, D., & Shultz, T. R. (1988). The development of the understanding of human behavior: From agency to intentionality. In J. W. Astington, P. L. Harris, & D. R. Olson (Eds.), *Developing theories of mind.* Cambridge, England: Cambridge University Press.

Povinelli, D. J. (1993). Reconstructing the evolution of mind. *American Psychologist, 48,* 493–509.

Povinelli, D. J., & deBlois, S. (1992). Young children's (Homo Sapiens) understanding of knowledge formation in themselves and others. *Journal of Comparative Psychology, 106,* 228–238.

Povinelli, D. J., & Eddy, T. J. (1996). What young chimpanzees know about seeing. *Monographs of the Society for Research in Child Development, 61* (3, Serial No. 247).

Povinelli, D. J., Nelson, K. E., & Boysen, S. T. (1990). Inferences about guessing and knowing by chimpanzees (Pan troglodytes). *Journal of Comparative Psychology, 104,* 203–210.

Povinelli, D. J., Parks, K. A., & Novak, M. A. (1991). Do rhesus monkeys (Macaca mulatta) attribute knowledge and ignorance to others? *Journal of Comparative Psychology, 105,* 318–325.

Povinelli, D. J., Rulf, A. B., & Bierschwale, D. (1994). Absence of knowledge attribution and self-recognition in young chimpanzees (Pan troglodytes). *Journal of Comparative Psychology, 108,* 74–80.

Pratt, C., & Bryant, P. E. (1990). Young children understand that looking leads to knowing (so long as they are looking through a single barrel). *Child Development, 61,* 973–982.

Premack, D. (1988). 'Does the chimpanzee have a theory of mind?' revisited. In R. W. Byrne & A. Whiten (Eds.), *Machiavellian intelligence.* Oxford, England: Oxford University Press.

Premack, D. (1990). The infant's theory of self-propelled objects. *Cognition, 36,* 1–16.

Premack, D., & Woodruff, G. (1978). Does the chimpanzee have a theory of mind? *Behavioral and Brain Sciences, 1,* 515–526.

Raver, C. C., & Leadbeater, B. J. (1993). The problem of the other in research on theory of mind and social development. *Human Development, 36,* 350–362.

Reddy, V. (1991). Playing with others' expectations: Teasing and mucking about in the first year. In A. Whiten (Ed.), *Natural theories of mind: Evolution, development and simulation of everyday mindreading.* Oxford, England: Basil Blackwell.

Rholes, W. S., Newman, L. S., & Ruble, D. N. (1990). Understanding self and others: Developmental and motivational aspects of perceiving persons in terms of invariant dispositions.

In E. Higgins & R. Sorrentino (Eds.), *Handbook of motivation and cognition: Foundations of social behavior* (Vol. 2). New York: Guilford Press.

Rholes, W. S., & Ruble, D. N. (1984). Children's understanding of dispositional characteristics of others. *Child Development, 33,* 550–560.

Ridgeway, D., Waters, E., & Kuczaj, S. A. (1985). The acquisition of emotion descriptive language: Receptive and productive vocabulary norms for 18 months to six years. *Developmental Psychology, 21,* 901–908.

Riggs, K. J., & Robinson, E. J. (1995). Children's memory for actions based on a false belief. *Journal of Experimental Child Psychology, 60,* 229–244.

Robinson, E. J., & Mitchell, P. (1994). Young children's false-belief reasoning: Interpretation of messages is no easier than the classic task. *Developmental Psychology, 30,* 67–72.

Robinson, E. J., & Mitchell, P. (1995). Masking of children's early understanding of the representational mind: Backwards explanation versus prediction. *Child Development, 66,* 1022–1039.

Robinson, K. (1993). *Social referencing in infants and toddlers: The understanding of specific referents of emotions.* Unpublished paper, Stanford University, Stanford, CA.

Rothenberg, B. B. (1970). Children's social sensitivity and the relationship to interpersonal competence, intrapersonal comfort, and intellectual level. *Developmental Psychology, 3,* 335–350.

Rozin, P., Millman, L., & Nemeroff, C. (1986). Operation of the laws of sympathetic magic in disgust and other domains. *Journal of Personality and Social Psychology, 50,* 703–712.

Rubin, K. H., Fein, G. G., & Vandenburg, B. (1983). Play. In P. H. Mussen (Series Ed.) & E. M. Hetherington (Ed.), *Handbook of child psychology: Vol. 4. Socialization, personality, and social development.* New York: Wiley.

Ruble, D. N., & Dweck, C. S. (1995). Self-conceptions, person conceptions, and their development. In N. Eisenberg (Ed.), *Social development.* Thousand Oaks, CA: Sage.

Ruble, D. N., Newman, L. S., Rholes, W. S., & Altshuler, J. (1988). Children's "naive psychology": The use of behavioral and situational information for the prediction of behavior. *Cognitive Development, 3,* 89–112.

Ruffman, T. K., & Olson, D. R. (1989). Children's ascription of knowledge to others. *Developmental Psychology, 25,* 601–606.

Ruffman, T. K., Olson, D. R., & Astington, J. W. (1991). Children's understanding of visual ambiguity. *British Journal of Developmental Psychology, 9,* 89–103.

Russell, J., Jarrold, C., & Potel, D. (1994). What makes strategic deception difficult for children—the deception or the strategy? *British Journal of Developmental Psychology, 12,* 301–314.

Russell, J., Mauthner, N., Sharpe, S., & Tidswell, T. (1991). The "windows task" as a measure of strategic deception in preschoolers and autistic subjects. *British Journal of Developmental Psychology, 90,* 331–350.

Saarni, C. (1984). An observational study of children's attempts to monitor their expressive behavior. *Child Development, 55,* 1504–1513.

Saarni, C. (1988). Children's understanding of the interpersonal consequences of dissemblances of nonverbal emotional-expressive behavior. *Journal of Nonverbal Behavior, 12,* 275–294.

Saarni, C., & Harris, P. L. (Eds.). (1989). *Children's understanding of emotion.* Cambridge, England: Cambridge University Press.

Savitsky, J. C., & Izard, C. E. (1970). Developmental changes in the use of emotion cues in a concept-formation task. *Developmental Psychology, 3,* 350–357.

Schaffer, H. R. (1984). *The child's entry into a social world.* London: Academic Press.

Schneider, W., & Sodian, B. (1988). Metamemory-memory relationships in preschool children: Evidence from a memory-for-location task. *Journal of Experimental Child Psychology, 45,* 209–233.

Selman, R. L. (1980). *The growth of interpersonal understanding.* New York: Academic Press.

Shantz, C. U. (1983). Social cognition. In P. H. Mussen (Series Ed.) & J. H. Flavell & E. M. Markman (Eds.), *Handbook of child psychology: Vol. 3. Cognitive development.* New York: Wiley.

Shatz, M., Wellman, H. M., & Silber, S. (1983). The acquisition of mental verbs: A systematic investigation of the first reference to mental state. *Cognition, 14,* 301–321.

Shultz, T. R. (1980). Development of the concept of intention. In W. A. Collins (Ed.), *Minnesota symposia on child psychology: Vol. 13. Development of cognition, affect, and social relations.* Hillsdale, NJ: Erlbaum.

Shultz, T. R. (1991). From agency to intention: A rule-based, computational approach. In A. Whiten (Ed.), *Natural theories of mind: Evolution, development and simulation of everyday mindreading.* Oxford, England: Basil Blackwell.

Shultz, T. R., & Wells, D. (1985). Judging the intentionality of action-outcomes. *Developmental Psychology, 21,* 83–89.

Siegal, M., & Beattie, K. (1991). Where to look first for children's knowledge of false beliefs? *Cognition, 38,* 1–12.

Siegal, M., & Peterson, C. C. (1994). Children's theory of mind and the conversational territory of cognitive development. In C. Lewis & P. Mitchell (Eds.), *Children's early understanding of mind: Origins and development.* Hillsdale, NJ: Erlbaum.

Siegler, R. S. (1994). The other Alfred Binet. In R. D. Parke, P. A. Ornstein, J. Rieser, & C. Zahn-Waxler (Eds.), *A century of developmental psychology.* Washington, DC: American Psychological Association.

Skinner, E. A. (1990). Age differences in the dimensions of perceived control during middle childhood: Implications for developmental conceptualizations and research. *Child Development, 61,* 1882–1890.

Slaughter, V., & Gopnik, A. (1996). Conceptual coherence in the child's theory of mind: Training children to understand belief. *Child Development, 67,* 2967–2988.

Smiley, P., & Huttenlocher, J. (1989). Young children's acquisition of emotion concepts. In C. Saarni & P. L. Harris (Eds.), *Children's understanding of emotion.* Cambridge, England: Cambridge University Press.

Smith, M. C. (1978). Cognizing the behavior stream. *Child Development, 48,* 736–743.

Sodian, B. (1994). Early deception and the conceptual continuity claim. In C. Lewis & P. Mitchell (Eds.), *Children's early understanding of mind: Origins and development.* Hillsdale, NJ: Erlbaum.

Sodian, B., & Schneider, W. (1990). Children's understanding of cognitive cueing: How to manipulate cues to fool a competitor. *Child Development, 61,* 697–704.

Sodian, B., & Wimmer, H. (1987). Children's understanding of inference as a source of knowledge. *Child Development, 58,* 424–433.

Speer, J. R., Sullivan, G. M., & Smith, N. (1992, June). *Hiding paradigm affords no evidence of deceptive intent in 2.5-year-olds.* Paper presented at the meeting of the American Psychological Society, San Diego, CA.

Spelke, E. S., Phillips, A., & Woodward, A. L. (1995). Infant's knowledge of object motion and human action. In D. Sperber, D. Premack, & A. J. Premack (Eds.), *Causal cognition: A multidisciplinary debate.* Oxford, England: Clarendon Press.

Stein, N. L., & Levine, L. J. (1989). The causal organization of emotional knowledge: A developmental study. *Cognition and Emotion, 3,* 343–378.

Stein, N. L., & Trabasso, T. (1989). Children's understanding of changing emotional states. In C. Saarni & P. L. Harris (Eds.), *Children's understanding of emotion.* Cambridge, England: Cambridge University Press.

Stipek, D. J. (1992). The child at school. In M. H. Bornstein & M. E. Lamb (Eds.), *Developmental psychology: An advanced textbook* (3rd ed.). Hillsdale, NJ: Erlbaum.

Stipek, D. J., & Daniels, D. H. (1990). Children's use of dispositional attributions in predicting the performance and behavior of classmates. *Journal of Applied Developmental Psychology, 11,* 13–18.

Stipek, D. J., & MacIver, D. (1989). Developmental change in children's assessment of intellectual competence. *Child Development, 60,* 521–538.

Taylor, M. (1988). The development of children's ability to distinguish what they know from what they see. *Child Development, 59,* 703–718.

Taylor, M. (1996). A theory of mind perspective on social cognitive development. In R. Gelman, & T. Au (Eds.) & E. C. Cartcrette & M. P. Friedman (Gen. Eds.), *Handbook of perception and cognition: Vol. 13. Perceptual and cognitive development.* New York: Academic Press.

Taylor, M., Cartwright, B. S., & Carlson, S. M. (1993). A developmental investigation of children's imaginary companions. *Developmental Psychology, 29,* 276–285.

Taylor, M., Esbensen, B. M., & Bennett, R. T. (1994). Children's understanding of knowledge acquisition: The tendency for children to report they have always known what they have just learned. *Child Development, 65,* 1581–1604.

Taylor, M., Gerow, L. E., & Carlson, S. M. (1993, March). The relation between individual differences in fantasy and theory of mind. In J. Woolley (Chair), *Pretense, imagination, and the child's theory of mind.* Symposium presented at the biennial meeting of the Society for Research in Child Development, New Orleans, LA.

Taylor, M., & Hort, B. (1990). Can children be trained in making the distinction between appearance and reality? *Cognitive Development, 5,* 89–99.

Tesla, C. (1991, March). *Early correlates of young children's ability to understand other people's feelings and beliefs.* Paper presented at the biennial meeting of the Society for Research in Child Development, Seattle, WA.

Tomasello, M. (1995). Joint attention as social cognition. In C. Moore & P. Dunham (Eds.), *Joint attention: Its origins and role in development.* Hillsdale, NJ: Erlbaum.

Tomasello, M., & Barton, M. (1994). Learning words in non-ostensive contexts. *Developmental Psychology, 30,* 639–650.

Tomasello, M., Kruger, A. C., & Ratner, H. H. (1993). Cultural learning. *Behavioral and Brain Sciences, 16,* 495–552.

Trevarthen, C., & Hubley, P. (1978). Secondary intersubjectivity: Confidence, confiding, and acts of meaning in the first year. In A. Lock (Ed.), *Action, gesture, and symbol: The emergence of language.* New York: Cambridge University Press.

Turiel, E. (1975). The development of social concepts: Mores, customs, and conventions. In D. J. DePalma & J. M. Foley (Eds.), *Moral development: Current theory and research.* Hillsdale, NJ: Erlbaum.

Vinden, P. G. (1996). Junín Quechua children's understanding of mind. *Child Development, 67,* 1707–1716.

Wegner, D. M., & Vallacher, R. R. (1977). *Implicit psychology: An introduction to social cognition.* New York: Oxford University Press.

Weiss, M. G., & Miller, P. H. (1983). Young children's understanding of displaced aggression. *Journal of Experimental Child Psychology, 35,* 529–539.

Welch-Ross, M. K. (1995). An integrative model of the development of autobiographical memory. *Developmental Review, 15,* 338–365.

Wellman, H. M. (1983). Metamemory revisited. In M. T. H. Chi (Ed.), *Trends in memory development research.* Basel: Karger.

Wellman, H. M. (1985). The child's theory of mind: The development of conceptions of cognition. In S. R. Yussen (Ed.), *The growth of reflection in children.* San Diego, CA: Academic Press.

Wellman, H. M. (1990). *The child's theory of mind.* Cambridge, MA: MIT Press.

Wellman, H. M. (1991). From desires to beliefs: Acquisition of a theory of mind. In A. Whiten (Ed.), *Natural theories of mind: Evolution, development and simulation of everyday mindreading.* Oxford, England: Basil Blackwell.

Wellman, H. M. (1993). Early understanding of mind: The normal case. In S. Baron-Cohen, H. Tager-Flusberg, & D. Cohen (Eds.), *Understanding other minds: Perspectives from autism.* Oxford, England: Oxford University Press.

Wellman, H. M., & Banerjee, M. (1991). Mind and emotion: Children's understanding of the emotional consequences of beliefs and desires. *British Journal of Developmental Psychology, 9,* 191–214.

Wellman, H. M., & Estes, D. (1986). Early understanding of mental entities: A reexamination of childhood realism. *Child Development, 57,* 910–923.

Wellman, H. M., & Gelman, S. A. (1992). Cognitive development: Foundational theories of core domains. In M. R. Rosenzweig & L. W. Porter (Eds.), *Annual review of psychology* (Vol. 43). Palo Alto, CA: Annual Reviews.

Wellman, H. M., Harris, P. L., Banerjee, M., & Sinclair, A. (1995). Early understandings of emotion: Evidence from natural language. *Cognition and Emotion, 9,* 117–149.

Wellman, H. M., & Hickling, A. K. (1994). The mind's "I": Children's conception of the mind as an active agent. *Child Development, 65,* 1564–1580.

Wellman, H. M., Hollander, M., & Schult, C. A. (1996). Young children's understanding of thought bubbles and of thoughts. *Child Development, 67,* 768–788.

Wellman, H. M., & Woolley, J. D. (1990). From simple desires to ordinary beliefs: The early development of everyday psychology. *Cognition, 35,* 245–275.

Werner, H. (1948). *Comparative psychology of mental development.* Chicago: Follett.

Whiten, A. (Ed.). (1991). *Natural theories of mind: Evolution, development and simulation in everyday mindreading.* Oxford, England: Basil Blackwell.

Whiten, A. (1993). Evolving theories of mind: The nature of non-verbal mentalism in other primates. In S. Baron-Cohen, H. Tager-Flusberg, & D. J. Cohen (Eds.), *Understanding other minds: Perspectives from autism.* Oxford, England: Oxford University Press.

Wimmer, H., & Hartl, M. (1991). Against the Cartesian view on mind: Young children's difficulty with own false beliefs. *British Journal of Developmental Psychology, 9,* 125–138.

Wimmer, H., Hogrefe, A., & Perner, J. (1988). Children's understanding of informational access as source of knowledge. *Child Development, 59,* 386–396.

Wimmer, H., & Perner, J. (1983). Beliefs about beliefs: Representation and constraining function of wrong beliefs in young children's understanding of deception. *Cognition, 13,* 103–128.

Wimmer, H., & Weichbold, V. (1994). Children's theory of mind: Fodor's heuristics or understanding informational causation. *Cognition, 53,* 45–57.

Winer, G. A. (1989). Developmental trends in the understanding of perceptual adaptation. *Journal of Experimental Child Psychology, 48,* 293–314.

Winer, G. A. (1991). Children's understanding of perception and perceptual processes. In R. Vasta (Ed.), *Annals of child development* (Vol. 8). London: Jessica Kingsley.

Wolf, D. (1982). Understanding others: A longitudinal case study of the concept of independent agency. In G. E. Forman (Ed.), *Action and thought.* New York: Academic Press.

Woolley, J. D. (1995). The fictional mind: Young children's understanding of imagination, pretense, and dreams. *Developmental Review, 15,* 172–211.

Woolley, J. D., & Wellman, H. M. (1992). Children's conceptions of dreams. *Cognitive Development, 7,* 365–380.

Woolley, J. D., & Wellman, H. M. (1993). Origin and truth: Young children's understanding of imaginary mental representations. *Child Development, 64,* 1–17.

Yaniv, I., & Shatz, M. (1988). Children's understanding of perceptibility. In J. W. Astington, P. L. Harris, & D. R. Olson (Eds.), *Developing theories of mind.* New York: Cambridge University Press.

Yuill, N. (1984). Young children's coordination of motive and outcome in judgments of satisfaction and morality. *British Journal of Developmental Psychology, 2,* 73–81.

Yuill, N. (1992). Children's conception of personality traits. *Human Development, 35,* 265–279.

Yuill, N. (1993). Understanding of personality and dispositions. In M. Bennett (Ed.), *The development of social cognition: The child as psychologist.* New York: Guilford Press.

Zahn-Waxler, C., Radke-Yarrow, M., Wagner, E., & Chapman, M. (1992). Development of concern for others. *Developmental Psychology, 28,* 126–136.

Zaitchik, D. (1991). Is only seeing really believing? Sources of the true belief in the false belief task. *Cognitive Development, 6,* 91–103.

CHAPTER 18

The Development of Mental Abilities and Styles

MICHEL FERRARI and ROBERT J. STERNBERG

One of the most striking things about any group of children is how much they differ from one another in both their mental abilities and in their styles of using those abilities. Yet part of the difficulty in exploring children's mental abilities and styles can be attributed to the many varied traditions in psychology that have addressed these topics.

The psychometric approach identifies human mental abilities through correlations among test performances (e.g., among verbal or mathematical test performance). The information-processing approach identifies abilities by comparing children's efficiency in manipulating symbolic information (e.g., how rapidly children can recognize English versus non-English words). The contextualist approach explores the importance of context to performance (e.g., children's vocabulary when talking with their parents as opposed to their skill as shown in a typical psychometric vocabulary test). Finally, the developmental approach postulates additional developmental mechanisms that regulate entire classes of performance in children of different ages. Thus, virtually no children speak in well-formed sentences before 18 months of age, whereas by three years of age virtually all children have begun to do so.

Similarly, the concept of cognitive style has theoretical roots in many different literatures. The psychodynamic, or

Research for this article was supported under the Javits Act Program (Grant # R206R50001) as administered by the Office of Educational Research and Improvement of the U.S. Department of Education. Grantees undertaking such projects are encouraged to express freely their professional judgments. This article, therefore, does not necessarily represent positions or policies of the Government and no official endorsement should be inferred.

ego psychology approach to styles explores how cognitive styles relate to other ego structures such as motivation. The Gestalt psychology approach examines stylistic consistency across perceptual or categorization tasks. Finally, educational psychology approaches to styles focus on how different types of learners, learning activities, and learning contexts influence learning.

The goal of this chapter is to present a broad sweep of recent theories and research on mental abilities and styles as they relate to child psychology and to each other. We begin by defining ability and style and explaining why these concepts are important.

Abilities refer to the quality or state of being able to perform some physical or mental action (Carroll, 1993, 1996). As such, abilities are hypothetical constructs used to explain how an individual adapts effectively and often flexibly to different environments. This chapter focuses on the concept of *mental ability*. Mental abilities are those abilities that require cognitive representation and processing, and for which individual differences in sensory acuity and in physical strength or agility generally constitute a small part of the total variance in performance (Jensen & Weng, 1994).

The concept of ability is important because it provides a way of classifying the almost infinite variety of human actions as emanating from a relatively small set of dimensions along which individuals vary (for example, variations in verbal, numerical, and spatial abilities, to name three widely cited dimensions). In child psychology, individual differences in performance on these different dimensions have important implications for selection of remedial or gifted learners for special education, for training children in special skills such as music or dance, and for the design of performance assessments, among other things. By testing or training children on a few relatively broad dimensions, one can thus assess or promote their potential future performance on a wide variety of tasks. Importantly, the term ability is entirely neutral with regard to whether an individual's ability results from inherited characteristics, learning, or some combination of the two (Carroll, 1996; Sternberg, 1996).

Four major approaches to the study of mental abilities in children are examined in this chapter: psychometric, information-processing, contextualist, and developmental. The psychometric approach has helped illuminate the structure of the human mind, that is, the dimensions of ability along which individuals differ. The information-processing approach has focused on the functional and procedural aspects of intellectual ability. The contextualist

approach emphasizes how different abilities such as mathematical or verbal abilities are used in different contexts. Finally, the developmental approach seeks to explain differences among mental structures at different ages, as well as the dynamic processes and mechanisms underlying the transformation from one structure to another throughout development. However, actual performances on any given task are not solely an expression of one's mental abilities; task performance also depends on stylistic differences in how individuals typically express their mental abilities.

Cognitive styles refer to the dominant or typical ways that children use their cognitive abilities in situations complex enough to allow a choice among equally valid responses, or even among different situations (Messick, 1994; Royce & Powell, 1983). For example, children can use either broad or narrow categories when making perceptual judgments, so consistent use of either sort of categorization is viewed as a difference in style. Styles are also measured in terms of contrasts between performances along a particular stylistic dimension (e.g., breadth of categorization). In this case, children are tested on both extremes of a particular dimension (broad and narrow categorization), and their style reflects the type of categorization that they perform most effectively (Messick, 1994). Thus, contrasted measures of performance can also demonstrate a child's stylistic mobility or flexibility (Witkin & Goodenough, 1981).

Despite several excellent comprehensive reviews of the enormous literature on styles (Grigorenko & Sternberg, 1995; Kagan & Kogan, 1970; Kogan, 1983), the theoretical and empirical bases of the styles construct remain problematic. Indeed, different theorists seem to use the term *style* to mean different things. Three main literatures dealing with the styles construct are examined in this chapter: the psychodynamic ego-psychology perspective, exemplified by the original study of cognitive "attitudes" or "controls"; the Gestalt-psychology perspective, exemplified in the study of field articulation; and the educational perspective, exemplified by attempts to study types of thinkers and types of learning situations.

Styles and abilities mutually influence each other. Styles influence not only the use of cognitive structures but also their development. Styles of functioning shape the information that is attended to and, hence, the very material upon which abilities operate (Messick, 1994). For example, if a child enjoys discussing the global themes of a novel, then he or she may pay less attention to the specific details of the plot. When asked to reason about the motivations of the characters in the novel, these details will not be available to inform his or her judgments. In this way, styles help shape the nature of ability and the organization of knowledge, making styles important predictors of achievement in different ability domains. By the same token, innate predispositions to acquire specific abilities may predispose one to adopt styles congruent with those abilities.

Children may find tasks that match their cognitive style to be more intrinsically motivating and interesting than are tasks that do not. Thus, given the same basic level of ability, children whose styles are mismatched to the task may perform less effectively than matched children, depending on their stylistic flexibility and on how strongly motivated they are by contextual demands (Royce & Powell, 1983; Witkin & Goodenough, 1981). Consider the child studying a novel, mentioned earlier. She would be more likely to excel, and to learn more, when asked to write an essay about the important message of the novel, and to do poorly on multiple choice questions about the details of the plot. Over many months or years, this child would develop her knowledge on matched tasks by meeting the challenges of her assignments, whereas on mismatched tasks she would probably become increasingly discouraged by failure.

Certain styles of information processing appear to be favored by particular cultures, and socialization practices work to develop these styles in members of these societies (Berry et al., 1986; Witkin & Goodenough, 1981). Years of training or schooling in tasks requiring high levels of abstraction may also shape one's predisposition toward performance of a wide range of tasks and effectively shape one's habitual cognitive style (Ericsson & Lehmann, 1996).

In the next section, after briefly examining some historical ideas about abilities, we explore various models of individual differences in mental ability. We then go on to show how differences in cognitive style influence the ways in which children acquire and express abilities in everyday, real-world performances.

DIMENSIONS OF INDIVIDUAL DIFFERENCES IN MENTAL ABILITY

This section is organized into four main parts. In the first part we look briefly at historical views of individual differences in mental abilities. In the second part we examine several factor-analytic models of the structure of mental abilities and the dimensions along which abilities may differ. In the third section we consider the theory of multiple intelligences. In the fourth and final part, factor-analytic models of mental abilities and the theory of multiple intelligences are compared.

Historical Roots of the Modern Concept of Abilities

The notion of individual differences in abilities is as old as recorded history. All cultures appear to have mythical stories of heroes who obtained exceptional levels of physical prowess or spiritual insight (Campbell, 1988; Ericsson & Charness, 1994). However, such ideas seem very far from modern notions of individual differences in mental abilities. Precursors of modern concepts of individual differences in abilities can be found among the ancient Greeks. Plato, in his famous discussion of knowledge, compared the minds of different individuals to blocks of wax of different sizes and consistencies—some blocks too soft to retain any impression of ideas, others too hard to permit any impression to be formed in them (Plato, ~300/1961). Aristotle argued that one's intellectual powers correspond both to one's age and to individual differences in mental potential (Aristotle, ~300/1984). During the medieval period, the scholastics, most eminently Thomas Aquinas and Duns Scotus, advanced a two-process theory of mental abilities in which a passive intellect (phantasmata) is acted upon by sensory data, and an active intellect (intellectus agens) allows stimulation to engage the passive intellect, permitting abstractions (universals) to be discerned in the particulars. These ideas about mental abilities remained essentially unchanged until the 20th century, although rationalist, empiricist, and biological perspectives on mental abilities were drawn into sharper contrast (Robinson, 1994).

Modern scientific advances in conceptions of mental abilities are intricately connected to ways of measuring individual differences in abilities. In fact, one might argue that advances in the power to measure mathematical relations between cognitive performances ushered in the modern era in mental-ability assessment (Boring, 1950; Cattell, 1971/1987). Galton (1869) explored individual differences in intelligence as reflected in differences in the achievements of geniuses and those with lesser talent. Indeed, Galton (1883) laid the groundwork for contemporary theories of cognitive abilities by proposing a series of tests to measure individual differences in mental abilities. Galton measured four components: body length, body breadth, visual acuity, and reaction time (note that only the last is still considered a measure of cognitive ability). Disappointingly, Galton found no significant relations between reaction time and any societal correlates of intelligence, such as occupational and educational categories (but see Deary,

1994; Johnson et al., 1985, for recent re-analyses of these data). The results of these early perceived failures to measure intelligence produced two relatively separate currents of research: research into tests predictive of success in real-world settings (e.g., academic or professional excellence) and research into the basic mental abilities (e.g., verbal, mathematical, etc.) common to performances on all cognitive tasks.

Binet and Simon (1905, 1908) attempted to design tests that were adapted to real-world settings—especially academic settings—and that could serve to predict how well children would perform in school. They developed a scale to distinguish normal children from children deficient in mental abilities. The scale consisted of a series of 30 verbal and nonverbal reasoning tasks of increasing difficulty. Terman (1916) adapted this scale for use in the United States. After the moderate success of these individually-administered tests at predicting academic performance, group tests of cognitive ability were developed by Burt (1911) and by Otis (1918), the latter for use in testing recruits during World War I. More recently, computer-generated tests have been developed that adjust the difficulty of the questions given to the examinee as a function of the success rate for previously generated questions (Mead & Drasgow, 1993). Although originally Binet did have a theory of intelligence (Binet & Simon, 1905, 1908; Sternberg, 1990a), the essentially atheoretical nature of many subsequent cognitive ability tests led some researchers to seek out dimensions that might underlie success or failure on any given set of psychological test items.

A second current of research, established by Spearman and Thurstone, set out to determine the underlying structure of mental abilities and the number of dimensions or factors necessary to account for performance across the full range of human tasks. The first of the major factor-analytic theories was that of the British psychologist C. E. Spearman and was inspired by Galton's writings. In a seminal work, Spearman (1904a, 1904b) presented a study of school children in which he explained correlations among complex mental tests in terms of individual differences in intelligence. Spearman's analyses of these and later test data suggested to him that just two kinds of factors underlie all individual differences in test scores. The first and more important kind of factor Spearman labeled the "general factor," or g, which is said to pervade performance on all tasks requiring intelligence. The second kind of factor is specifically related to performance on each particular test. However, as evidence mounted for the existence of classes of tests that are intercorrelated, Spearman acknowledged that some tests measure additional group factors (such as verbal ability and spatial ability) beyond the general factor (Carroll, 1993; Spearman, 1927/1981).

The American psychologist L. L. Thurstone argued that the appearance of just a single factor was an artifact of Spearman's use of an unrotated factorial solution to determine his factors. In the first of two major studies, 56 tests were given to 240 subjects, resulting in the clear identification of seven primary factors or mental abilities (verbal comprehension, verbal fluency, number, spatial visualization, inductive reasoning, memory, and perceptual speed) (Thurstone, 1938). However, the results of a later study examining the primary-ability scores of school children (Thurstone & Thurstone, 1941) obliged Thurstone to grant that his seven primary factors were intercorrelated.

As we shall see, in the light of contemporary hierarchical factor-analytic models, the main disagreement between Spearman and Thurstone concerns the relative importance each wished to attribute to general and specialized abilities. Spearman and his school placed greater emphasis on the general factor; Thurstone and his school emphasized factors representing narrower and more specialized abilities. In the next section, we consider current hierarchical models of the structure of mental abilities that have sought to reconcile these two views.[1]

Hierarchical Factor-Analytic Models of Mental Abilities

The hierarchical approach originated in the British research tradition (Burt, 1949; Vernon, 1971). Several hierarchical models of abilities have been proposed, but the

---

[1] Many other historically important figures are necessarily absent from such a cursory treatment of the history of models of individual differences. For example, Guilford (1967) tried to arrange the many primary factors he and others had discovered into what he called the Structure-of-Intellect model. These primary factors were achieved by crossing different mental processes, contents, and products. Guilford's model initially generated enthusiasm, but was later criticized on logical grounds for proposing a taxonomic system in which universal parameters interact in all possible ways and for his use of factor-analytic methods—especially overfactorization, complete reliance on orthogonal factors, and statistically compromised forms of rotation (see Carroll, 1993; Cattell, 1971/1987; Undheim & Horn, 1977).

basic idea in all of these models is that abilities are hierarchically structured groups of correlated traits that reflect increasingly complex or general levels of behavior (Cardon & Fulker, 1994; Carroll, 1993; Gustafsson, 1994). These factors are presumed to account for almost all of the abilities measured by IQ tests and by neuropsychological test batteries (Horn, 1994).

One of the most popular hierarchical models is that of Cattell and Horn (Cattell, 1943; Horn, 1968; Horn & Cattell, 1966), which proposes two general subfactors of general mental ability *(g)*: fluid and crystallized intelligence.[2] *Fluid intelligence* is purported to reflect biological and neurological capacity, and is best measured in unfamiliar tasks, that is in tasks involving adaptation to novel conditions that require a minimum of prior knowledge. Manipulations of geometrical and other relations are often used to measure fluid intelligence (Cattell, 1971/1987). *Crystallized intelligence* reflects complex knowledge or expertise acquired throughout life and is central in verbal-conceptual tasks. It is best measured in familiar tasks in which performance is influenced by education, acculturation, or both.

Horn (1994; Horn & Hofer, 1992) has recently proposed a *broadened theory of fluid and crystallized intelligence,* which sets the number of primary abilities at about 40. According to Horn, the pattern of intercorrelation among these 40 primary abilities shows that they represent about 10 second-strata abilities. In turn, an analysis of the correlations between these 10 factors produced two more general factors, crystallized and fluid ability, which themselves are positively correlated (see also Carroll, 1993; Gustafsson, 1984, 1994, for similar models).[3]

Typically, hierarchical models focus their attention on the second stratum of ability, a pragmatic solution given that conclusions about the interrelations among about 10 constructs are more easily intelligible than would be conclusions about 40-odd primary abilities. Rather than enter into the fine distinctions among these different hierarchical models, we center on Horn's (1994; Horn & Hofer, 1992) model as an illustrative example of this sort of hierarchical factor analysis of human mental abilities.

The 10 dimensions of ability constituting the primary mental abilities (PMA) system identified by Horn are the following: (1) *fluid reasoning,* involved in tasks that require inductive, deductive, conjunctive, or disjunctive reasoning to understand relations among stimuli, to grasp implications, or to draw conclusions (e.g., concept formation, logical analysis); (2) *crystallized or acculturated knowledge,* measured in tasks requiring breadth and depth of concepts and forms of reasoning that have been developed by an entire culture over centuries, and that are interiorized through acculturation (e.g., vocabulary, riddles); (3) *short-term memory* (apprehension-retention), measured by tests indicating awareness of, and ability to recall the elements of immediate stimulation, or those occurring within approximately the past minute (e.g., memory for digits, words); (4) fluency of retrieval from *long-term memory,* measured by tasks that require associations to previously stored information (e.g., delayed recall, memory for names); (5) *visual processing,* measured by tasks involving visual constancy and closure, and mental manipulation of objects (e.g., pattern analysis, object recognition, mental imagery); (6) *auditory processing,* measured by tasks involving perception of distorted sound patterns, awareness of order or rhythm among sounds, or the elements of groups of sounds (e.g., sound blending, chord recognition); (7) *rapid visual sensory detection* of curvature, symmetry, wedges, etc.; (8) *rapid auditory sensory detection* (i.e., echoic memory); (9) *processing speed,* measured most purely in rapid scanning (e.g., visual symbol matching, digit symbol coding); and finally, (10) *correct decision speed* for questions that require deliberate reflection. Note that *quantitative knowledge,* measured by tasks that require understanding and skill in mathematics (e.g., calculation and solving equations), is logically a form of crystallized intelligence, but factor analyses consistently find that patterns of individual differences in quantitative knowledge are distinct from those found for other forms of crystallized knowledge, suggesting that quantitative knowledge constitutes a separate eleventh factor of ability (Horn, 1994).

Evidence for these ability factors comes from five main sources: (1) structural evidence of individual differences in scores on psychometric tests; (2) developmental evidence of changes across the life span; (3) neurocognitive

---

[2] A recent task force on intelligence (Neisser et al., 1996) concludes that there is still no full agreement on what *g* means: *g* has been considered a statistical regularity (Ceci, 1994); a kind of mental energy (Spearman, 1981); a generalized abstract reasoning ability (Gustafsson, 1984); and an index of neural processing speed (Reed & Jensen, 1992; Vernon, 1993). All of these conceptions of *g* are still being explored in contemporary research on intelligence and mental abilities.

[3] Gustafsson (1984, 1994) has consistently found the loading of fluid intelligence on *g* to be unity, implying that both of these factors are equivalent.

evidence of patterns of neurological and physiological functioning and breakdown; (4) achievement evidence, based on predicted academic and occupational levels of performance, including effects of transfer and training; and (5) behavioral-genetic evidence, based on relationships among biologically-related individuals (Horn, 1994; Horn & Hofer, 1992).

Horn prefers to consider each of the second-order abilities as distinct but not unrelated intelligences (Horn & Hofer, 1992). Structural evidence argues for the distinctiveness of these different abilities due to their construct independence. In other words, each ability relates differently to the physiological structure of the brain and to genetic and environmental determinants of mental abilities. Horn (1994) remarked that a complete theory of crystallized and fluid intelligence should logically also contain concepts to represent organization among other sensory functions, such as those of kinesthesis or olfaction. Just as one can think in terms of sights and sounds, one can also think in terms of smells and physical sensations, but little is known scientifically about these other sorts of mental abilities.

Relevant to child psychology, Horn (1994) suggests that this hierarchy reflects both increasingly abstract functions of information processing and increasingly more sophisticated developmental levels. In terms of information processing, visual and auditory sensory detection capabilities feed into and support visual and auditory associative processing. Associative processing in turn feeds into and supports organizational functions such as broad visual, auditory, and spatial abilities. These functions, in turn, are needed to exercise relational thinking functions which involve the eduction of relations and correlates in fluid intelligence needed to develop crystallized intelligence. Furthermore, the development of these capabilities is purported to parallel their functional organization, with higher levels of abstraction in function emerging through restructuring of more concrete information. Horn (1994) even ventures to draw a parallel between crystallized and fluid intelligence and the Piagetian notions of accommodation and assimilation (p. 448).[4]

---

[4] Space does not permit a discussion of Cattell's (1971/1987) own variant on the original theory of crystallized and fluid intelligence. The interested reader might wish to consider how Cattell's innovative theory suggests ways of reconciling psychometric, contextualist, information-processing, and developmental theories of mental abilities.

The Theory of Multiple Intelligences

Cattell (1971/1987) makes the important point that although at least 40 primary abilities have now been identified, without a principled approach to determining the range of mental abilities, it is impossible to know whether one has achieved a comprehensive picture of all possible primary mental abilities. Such a principled approach to identifying the range of human abilities has been developed by Gardner (1993a, 1993b, 1995, 1997; Granott & Gardner, 1994; Torff & Gardner, in press) in his theory of multiple intelligences (MI theory).

Although an ardent critic of psychometric theories, Gardner (1993a, 1995) has used a different rationale and set of methods (a critical review of the literature, or what he calls a "subjective factor analysis") to produce a taxonomy of mental abilities that has the same form as a psychometric theory, namely, a listing of abilities. The factors generated by the psychometric theories mentioned earlier were based on the mathematical properties of correlations among subtests. Gardner's method of analysis, however, is a more wide-ranging, but perhaps looser inductive attempt to organize existing data on the range of human abilities, using criteria never before considered conjointly. These criteria reflect three main concerns or aspects of mental abilities, all three of which are required to isolate particular mental abilities: (1) *definition*, including identifiable core operations capable of being encoded in a symbol system, for example, sensitivity to pitch relations and rhythm in music; (2) *measurement*, including experimental psychological support (such as selective priming or interference), psychometric support, potential isolation by brain damage, and the existence of exceptional individuals (such as prodigies, idiots savants, etc.); and (3) *development*, as reflected by tracing the evolutionary, ontogenetic, and adult course of skill acquisition.

In considering a wide range of culturally-valued human activities, Gardner (1993a) originally isolated seven factors or dimensions of mental abilities (or "intelligences") along which individuals differ: linguistic, logical-mathematical, spatial, musical, bodily-kinesthetic, interpersonal, and intra-personal. More recently, Gardner (1997) has added another "1½ intelligences" to his taxonomy, to which we will return shortly.

MI theory is framed in light of the presumed biological origins of universal human problem-solving skills. Gardner's theory of multiple intelligences states, in general, that individuals are born with biological proclivities for interpreting patterns of information available to several distinct and modular information-processing systems. Such proclivities can range from extreme giftedness to extreme retardation in any given intelligence. Mental abilities (intelligences), in this view, are manifested in solving problems or fashioning products that are valued (i.e., are of consequence) for a given culture or community. Intelligences are seen as raw biological potentials, visible in their pure form only in abnormal individuals. Normally, intelligences work together to solve problems and to yield certain cultural end-states (vocations, avocations, etc.). Part of the appeal of this model is that it provides a framework for using different domains of cultural activity to identify different sorts of human abilities.

In this view, the modules underlying performance are not merely learned abilities that are aspects of a single intelligence but, rather, truly distinct intelligences. Combinations of intelligences develop into talents in particular domains (e.g., as musical and bodily-kinesthetic intelligence are combined in a figure skater, ballet dancer, or orchestra conductor). Skill at specific occupations develops through children's interactions with culturally sanctioned experts in different domains. Each domain is codified through second-order cultural symbol systems that experts in the field use to transmit knowledge to novices about each intelligence. For example, linguistic intelligence is codified through storytelling or writing; music is codified in musical forms or notations. However, the relations between successful use of different intelligences and an understanding of the second-order symbol systems created to teach them remain unclear (but see Piaget, 1974a, 1974b).

Like Horn, Gardner grants that his list of seven intelligences may need to be divided or rearranged on the basis of future evidence. For example, consider taste and olfaction, proposed as intellectual abilities by both Horn (1994) and Cattell (1971/1987), especially as these relate to food. While more evidence may be needed to establish this point firmly, understanding of food is certainly encoded into cultural activities as far ranging as gastronomy or wine tasting, each with its acknowledged symbol systems, experts, and evolutionary history (Rozin, 1996). Thus, intelligence concerning food might be a candidate for inclusion in a future reworking of Gardner's taxonomy.

Indeed, Gardner himself has recently proposed a similar eighth intelligence in his taxonomy, called naturalistic intelligence. Naturalistic intelligence allows one to make consequential distinctions in the natural world (e.g., among flora and fauna), and to use this ability productively in

activities like fishing or biological science (Gardner, 1995, 1997; Torff & Gardner, in press). He is also ambivalent about another possible candidate intelligence, one relating to the human ability to pose foundational questions (e.g., "What is the meaning of life?" or "Where did the universe come from?"), hence his playful suggestion (Gardner, 1997) that his system now includes "8½ intelligences." Gardner does not elaborate on why these particular additions are the most fitting extensions of his original taxonomy.

Multiple Intelligences and Hierarchical Factor-Analytic Models of Mental Ability Compared

Several different factorial models of abilities have been proposed in the literature, only some of which have been described here. It is often hard to distinguish among these models because the results of the factor analyses used to support them depend on so many different things, including the type of information included in the factor analysis (or in one's assessment of the existing literature, in the case of Gardner). Sternberg (1990a) has suggested that these various models are basically not so different from each other. Although they differ in the particular abilities proposed, all the theories have in common their claim that (objectively or subjectively determined) structural factors are the basic units of human abilities.

Furthermore, close examination shows that common threads run through all of these various models. True, many of the hierarchical factor-analytic models discussed earlier hold that a general factor (characterized by fluid-reasoning ability) permeates all intellectual tasks. However, these models also hypothesize that there exist some relatively independent "modules" in the form of independent factors for attributes such as quantitative ability, visuo-spatial abilities and auditory abilities (Carroll, 1993; Horn, 1994). Some of these second-order abilities are similar to Gardner's intelligences. In fact, Carroll (1993, p. 641) draws a close analogy between Gardner's *linguistic intelligence* and his own proposed *crystallized intelligence,* between Gardner's *musical intelligence* and his proposed *auditory ability,* and between Gardner's *spatial intelligence* and his proposed *spatial ability.* At least as far as more abstract problems are concerned, Horn and his associates (Horn, 1994; Horn & Stankov, 1982) have found significant overlap between Gardner's characterization of *linguistic* and *musical intelligence* and their own second-order factors of *verbal* and *auditory ability,* respectively.

Thus, each of Gardner's intelligences is analogous to a "higher-order factor structure"—with many parallels to the second-order factors proposed by these models. One possible advantage of MI theory, however, is that it provides additional criteria by which to specify the range of primary mental abilities, by observing how patterns of human abilities are used in different ways by different cultures.

THE HERITABILITY OF MENTAL ABILITIES

As mentioned earlier, Galton (1869) was interested in individual differences in intelligence as reflected in differences in achievement of geniuses and those with lesser talent. Galton believed observed differences to be largely hereditary, a belief that is only partially supported by more sophisticated work in behavior genetics. Family, twin, and adoption studies consistently show that general cognitive ability, *(g)* as measured by psychometric tests of intelligence, is one of the more highly heritable of personal traits (Plomin & McClearn, 1993; Plomin & Neiderhiser, 1991).

Estimating Genetic and Environmental Contributions to IQ

Bouchard, McGue, and their colleagues (Bouchard & McGue, 1981; McGue, Bouchard, Iacono, & Lykken, 1993), in their thorough and systematic review of the world's literature on behavior-genetic research on IQ, clearly demonstrated the existence of genetic influences on general cognitive ability, as indexed by IQ. Recently, Chipuer, Rovine, and Plomin (1990) subjected these data to a LISREL analysis. Their model included additive and nonadditive genetic parameters (i.e., linear versus interaction effects), and shared and unshared environmental parameters (i.e., common culture and family experience versus unique personal experiences). The authors found that when assortative mating (or the tendency for individuals to marry someone around their own level of intelligence) was taken into account when estimating the parameters of the model, both additive and nonadditive genetic variance contributed to general cognitive ability, as indexed by IQ.

The estimate of heritability (.51) produced by this model resembles that of most experts, who suggest that about half (+/− .2) of the current variation in IQ currently observed in U.S. and European Caucasian populations is a result of genetic differences (Jensen, 1997; McGue et al.,

1993; Scarr, 1992). This means that approximately half of the population variation in general mental ability is due to hereditary factors, but that the rest is not. It is important to remember that this statistic does not mean that half of an individual's general mental ability is due to heredity. Heritability is defined as a characteristic of a population, not as an individual trait or indicator that could be used to compare populations (Carroll, 1993; Plomin, 1988). Indeed, heritability may vary as a function of the population being studied. For example, greater heritability of intelligence has been found among Norwegians, perhaps due to the more egalitarian nature of this society, which reduces environmental variation and thus allows genetic factors to vary proportionally more (Tambs, Sundet, & Magnus, 1984).

Environmental influences are as important as genetic influences to heritability estimates. The correlation between parental socioeconomic status and a child's cognitive ability is about .30 (White, 1982)—socioeconomic status and its correlates are purported indicators of the "richness" of the child's intellectual environment. However, an association between any characteristic of the parent and that of the child may indicate the influence of genetic mechanisms and/or that of environment, since both mutually influence each other (Scarr, 1997; Wachs, 1993).

An elegant way out of this dilemma is to study families with adopted children. Several large-scale studies of adopted children—the Texas (Loehlin, Horn, & Willerman, 1989), Colorado (DeFries, Plomin, & Fulker, 1994; Plomin, DeFries, & Fulker, 1988), and Minnesota studies (Bouchard, Lykken, McGue, Segal, & Tellegen, 1990), in particular—have produced surprising results. Such studies have shown that environmental differences between families (such as socioeconomic status, cultural background, parent's occupation and background, childrearing practices, physical environment, and so on) account for little or none of the variance in the IQs of adolescents and adults—although between-families sources of environmental variance account for about half the total environmental variance in the IQs of preadolescent children (McGue et al., 1993). Thus, these studies suggest that the heritability of intelligence increases with age, meaning that people's IQs as adults are more predictable from the IQs of their parents than are people's IQs as children. In children, the proportion of shared environmental variance among relatives increases with degree of relatedness (i.e., twins > siblings > parents > cousins) (Chipuer et al., 1990). The effect of this variance on IQ are small but notable. By contrast, for adolescents and adults, the effects of shared environment (between-families) dwindles to almost zero; the effect of nonshared environmental variance remains unchanged; and the effect of genetic variance increases.

Thus, surprisingly, most of the strictly environmental (i.e., nongenetic) variance exists within families, that is, in the parental and social influences unique to each sibling of a given family. This observation remains true despite the fact that adoptive families differ widely on measures of socioeconomic status and childrearing practices. This fact, which contradicts popular belief, is one of the major findings of behavior genetics in the last decade (Chipuer et al., 1990; Jensen, 1997; Plomin, 1988).

However, this finding is not without its critics. Some researchers point out that the population-genetics approach as a whole does not address the issue of individual development, resulting in a nondevelopmental understanding of developmental outcomes (Gottlieb, 1995; Horowitz, 1993). More specifically, behavior-genetics research has been criticized for its analysis of environmental influences. Indeed, environmental influences are often measured differently from one study to the next, and sometimes simply refer to the variance that remains after genetic effects on performance have been partialed out (Goldsmith, 1993; Horowitz, 1993; Wachs, 1993). These limitations should be borne in mind when considering findings from behavior-genetic research. Let us now look at the possible relations between genetic and environmental influences proposed by behavior-genetic research in more detail.

Genotype-Environment Correlation and Interaction

Genotype-environment correlation is the result of the nonrandom occurrence of different genotypes in different environments. For example, persons with genotypes favorable to the development of a certain trait (e.g., musical talent) are likely to grow up in an environment that favors the development of this trait—that is, to have parents with musical interests—thereby increasing the phenotypic variance for this trait through increased exposure to the domain in question. Interactions between genotypes and diverse environments affect the development of intelligence in domains related to those interactions (e.g., the development of perfect pitch). This sort of interaction is known as passive genotype-environment correlation. Reactive genotype-environment correlation refers to the special treatment that a child receives as a result of his or her gene-influenced activities. In this case, genotype-environment correlations include the effect of differential treatment by parents,

teachers, and peers, whose responses are largely evoked by the person's distinctive genotypic characteristics. For example, a child who understands ideas quickly may be provided with more complex and detailed explanations by teachers and parents. Finally, active genotype-environment correlation refers to the fact that children with given genetic attributes may actively seek out and create environments that let them develop their particular genetic potentials; for example, they may actively question elders, or they may join groups that allow them to develop their intellectual abilities (Scarr, 1992; Scarr & McCartney, 1983). A review of the existing adoption studies suggests a passive genotype-environment correlation of about .20 to .30 exists for IQ (Loehlin & DeFries, 1987). Active and reactive genotype-environment correlations have been less studied.

There is little direct evidence of a genetic-environmental interaction component for IQ, in a statistical sense, based on existing studies of monozygotic adopted twins (Jensen, 1997; Loehlin, 1994). However, some theorists argue that even if particular combinations of genotypes do produce different results in different environments over and above the combined average effects of both, current research methods work against discovering these sorts of interactions (Goldsmith, 1993; Horowitz, 1993; Rowe & Waldman, 1993; Wachs, 1993).

Even so, the term emergenesis has been coined to account for unexpected extremes in ability that may result from interactions between systems involving many genes (i.e., polygenic systems) and environmental context (Lykken, McGue, Tellegen, & Bouchard, 1992). In emergenesis, the unusual development of certain abilities and talents may depend on a rare combination of genes that simultaneously influence several different abilities and other traits. Because both parents provide each child with a unique combination of their genes, a given child may sometimes have proclivities that are not present in either parent, and that are possible due only to a rare match of a particularly favorable combination of parental genes. Only if this critical combination is present does the talent appear, given the appropriate environment. Emergenesis is essential for understanding conspicuous phenotypic differences in certain traits between close relatives (e.g., geniuses in music or mathematics who come from relatively undistinguished parents). Such differences seem too exceptional to result from the additive effect of polygenes or differences in upbringing—although some theorists argue that such exceptional abilities may be largely developed through deliberate practice (Ericsson & Lehmann, 1996).

Heritability of Specific Cognitive Abilities

Behavioral-genetic evidence seems fairly conclusive in indicating that a single genetic factor does not account for all genetic influences on cognitive ability (Cardon & Fulker, 1993, 1994; Pedersen, Plomin, & McClearn, 1994); thus, some researchers have examined to what extent specific abilities are subject to genetic influences over and above genetic influences on general cognitive ability. Many childhood-twin and family studies have suggested that verbal ability is influenced in some degree by genetic factors, and that perceptual speed and memory show little genetic influence. Spatial tests show conflicting results regarding heritability (Segal, 1986; Vandenberg, 1968; Wilson, 1983). However, these early studies typically aimed to determine whether general or specific mental abilities are influenced by genetic factors (i.e., they compared the theories of Spearman and Thurstone). However, lack of congruence (i.e., different measures of performance, size and composition of samples, and statistical analyses) in these early studies led to disagreements regarding the magnitude and generality of genetic influences on different specific mental abilities (Cardon & Fulker, 1993).

More recent research on specific cognitive abilities has aimed to incorporate more contemporary hierarchical theories of intelligence, such as were presented earlier in this chapter. For example, Pedersen, Plomin, and McClearn (1994) found that data for 12 of 13 tests used in the Swedish Adoption/Twin Study of Aging (SATSA)—measuring both fluid and crystallized intelligence, and specific abilities such as verbal ability, spatial ability, memory, and perceptual speed—showed significant genetic influence on tests of specific cognitive ability, even after g was partialed out. Nevertheless, tests with the highest genetic overlap with g also tend to show the highest phenotypic loading on g (e.g., synonyms and block design tests). Indeed, a correlation of .77 was found between the heritabilities on these tests and their phenotypic (i.e., psychometric test) g-loadings after controlling for test reliabilities.

Cardon and Fulker (1993, 1994) developed a hierarchical longitudinal path model to analyze the genetic influence on specific cognitive abilities in twin and sibling data from the Colorado Adoption Project at four different ages. Specifically, children were administered tests of four primary abilities (verbal, spatial, perceptual speed, and visual memory) at ages 3, 4, 7, and 9. Results showed genetic and environmental origins of both general and specific cognitive abilities. At the early ages (3 and 4), specific abilities, with the possible exception of spatial ability, are substantially influenced by both genes and environment. Surprisingly, genetic influence on specific abilities increases at age 7. By age 9, shared environment effects emerge for spatial ability and perceptual speed, and (with the exception of verbal ability) the genetic components of these abilities appear to generalize into a common genetic factor (Cardon & Fulker, 1993). Cardon and Fulker (1993) admit that these results may partly reflect incongruities in how abilities are measured at different ages. However, these data also raise the intriguing possibility that genetic and environmental influences may exert fleeting or lasting effects on different mental abilities over time.

Unfortunately, the problem with all of these behavior-genetic studies is that they are limited to measures of *how much* variance is attributed to genetic and environmental influences on specific mental abilities in a given population. It is very difficult, if not impossible, for these models to address the question of *how* different genetic and environmental influences promote or hinder individual cognitive development. Indeed, addressing this question may require innovative research designs that assess genetic and environmental influences on specific types of individuals (Bronfenbrenner & Ceci, 1993; Rowe & Waldman, 1993). These efforts may hinge on advances in molecular genetic techniques for measuring cognitive abilities, the topic we turn to now.

Molecular Genetics and Mental Abilities

The data reported so far have all dealt with genetic and environmental influences on test performances. An exciting new direction in genetic research on cognitive abilities is the possibility of using new molecular-genetic techniques to identify some of the genes responsible for the heritability of cognitive abilities found in correlational studies of mental ability (Aldhous, 1992; Plomin & McClearn, 1993). For example, Plomin and his associates (Plomin et al., 1994, 1995) have attempted to distinguish between children from 6 to 12 years of age at the high and low ends of the IQ dimension by using DNA markers on or near genes likely to be relevant for neural functioning, that is, using an allelic association strategy. (See Plomin, 1993, for a brief yet comprehensive introduction to these new molecular-genetic techniques.) However, these initial studies remain exploratory and the influence of specific DNA markers on behavioral traits (such as reflect differences in mental abilities) has so far proved difficult to replicate (Plomin et al., 1994, 1995).

The major implications of identifying quantitative trait loci will be for basic research. Even if markers can be identified that clearly differentiate high and low mental-ability groups, these markers will probably not be useful for identifying high- and low-ability children in the general population (Plomin et al., 1994). But such markers will make it possible to measure genotypes for individuals without relying on indirect inferences about family resemblances, as is currently the case. Given such markers, it will become possible to study the effects of different environments on individuals with comparable genetic potentials. Such knowledge is bound to raise important ethical issues, but Plomin and his associates remain optimistic that the increased potential for understanding normal and abnormal phenotypic variation in mental abilities will far outweigh the potential abuses of this technique.

The theories presented so far in this chapter have focused on individual differences in scores on mental tests, and on the relationships of these differences to neurological, genetic, and environmental influences—all of which are essentially static snapshots of the range and source of existing human abilities. In the next two sections we examine how individuals use and develop their mental abilities. We begin by examining information-processing theories of abilities.

INFORMATION-PROCESSING THEORIES OF ABILITIES

Information-processing theories of ability seek to explain how information is coded, stored, and applied in specific tasks. Thus these theories examine how individuals (or machines) translate sensory input into conceptual representations, translate one representation into another, or translate conceptual representations into actions. In this section, we begin by discussing metacognitive ability, which many consider essential to optimal information processing. We then examine information processing in two major types of abilities typically identified through psychometric test batteries—reasoning abilities and mathematical abilities.

Metacognitive Abilities

Many cognitive researchers believe that the overall efficiency of the intellectual system depends upon metacognitive abilities, or "knowing about knowing" (Flavell, Green, & Flavell, 1995; Kuhn, Garcia-Mila, Zohar, &

Andersen, 1995; Sternberg, 1985, 1988a). This meta-level is in some sense separable from that of the object of cognition, as Nelson (1996) shows in the following example. Clearly the phrase, "Thiss sentence contains threee errors" contains two-object level errors—the spelling of *this* and of *three*—, but it also contains a meta-level error, namely, that there are only two errors in the sentence, not three. In this sense, metacognitive abilities stand over and above the abilities required to be successful at cognitive tasks, yet are key to monitoring or controlling the overall efficiency of performances.

Most theories of metacognitive ability have been inspired by the seminal work of Flavell on metacognitive knowledge (Flavell, 1976; Flavell et al., 1995), and of Brown (1978; 1987) on metacognitive or self-regulatory control during problem solving. Many recent models represent some synthesis of these two original research strands (e.g., Nelson, 1996; Nelson & Narens, 1994; Paris & Winograd, 1990; Pinard, 1992). Perhaps the most interesting feature of these recent synthetic models of metacognition is their attempt to coordinate metacognitive knowledge and metacognitive activity.

Metacognitive knowledge involves monitoring and reflecting on one's current or recent thoughts (Flavell et al., 1995). Such reflection will necessarily concern both *factual knowledge*—about the task, one's goals, or one's self—and *strategic knowledge* about how and when to use specific procedures to solve the problem at hand (Pinard, 1992). *Metacognitive activity* involves using self-awareness (Ferrari & Sternberg, in press) to adapt and manage the strategies applied during thinking and problem solving (Kuhn et al., 1995; Schraw, Dunkle, Bendixon, & DeBacker Roedel, 1995).

The quality of this metacognitive activity varies under certain conditions. That is, some independent variables show no effect on learning but do affect how accurately one can metacognitively monitor that learning (Mazzoni & Nelson, 1995). For example, research has shown that active reflection on one's performance, and especially delayed judgments of learning enhance one's metacognitive abilities, whereas negative emotional reaction and debilitating internal dialogue tend to inhibit it (Dunlosky & Nelson, 1994; Nelson & Dunlosky, 1991; Pinard, 1992). Note that metacognitive knowledge and metacognitive activity do not have to be perfectly accurate to be useful, or to influence behavior; rather, individuals' monitoring of their cognitive activity must simply be shown to influence the control they exert over their own behavior (Nelson, 1996; Paris & Winograd, 1990; Pinard, 1992).

Some of the most exciting research on metacognitive abilities in children has examined what young children understand about their own minds and those of other individuals. Children as young as two-and-a-half years old appreciate that to hide an object from another person they must use deceptive tactics such as laying false trails or erasing their own tracks (Hala, Chandler, & Fritz, 1991). Three-year-olds already understand that thinking is an internal mental event that has content, is referential (i.e., refers to real or imaginary events), and is unique to human beings (and perhaps other animate objects). They can also distinguish thinking from knowing (Flavell et al., 1995).

However, preschoolers greatly underestimate the amount of mental activity people engage in; they do not necessarily attribute any mental activity or consciousness to someone who is merely "waiting" (Flavell, Green, & Flavell, 1993), or even to someone who is reading or listening. They have a poor understanding of attentional focus and attentional limits (Flavell et al., 1995; Pillow, 1989). Preschoolers also have limited awareness of the source of their beliefs, even when these beliefs were acquired only minutes before (e.g., they have difficulty recalling whether they learned the contents of a drawer because they saw the objects themselves or because someone told them what was in it) (Gopnik & Graf, 1988). Even by age five, they have difficulty in determining what someone is thinking about, given the available evidence, or in remembering or reconstructing what they themselves were thinking earlier (Flavell et al., 1995). Preschoolers also have little appreciation of the importance of "cognitive cueing" for memory. Cognitive cueing involves situations in which one is reminded of something by some external cue or phrase such as, "Don't you remember, we were at the beach?" (Sodian & Schneider, 1990).

By age 7 or 8, however, children improve markedly at appreciating the value of cognitive cueing, perhaps because they become increasingly aware of the "stream of consciousness" of their own thoughts and those of others (Flavell et al., 1993, 1995). Many theorists currently believe that children develop increasingly constructivist, process-oriented conceptions of mind during middle childhood and adolescence (Chandler & Carpendale, in press; Pillow, in press); however, this area of research is still in its early stages (Flavell et al., 1995).

Children's understanding of mind necessarily affects their metacognitive awareness of factors influencing achievement when performing specific tasks (e.g., the value of task specific strategies) (Bouffard & Vezeau, in press). Research on memory shows that the value of metacognitive awareness is especially apparent when children are asked about their metacognitive activity during or immediately following memory-task performance (Best & Ornstein, 1986; Schneider & Sodian, 1991); links between decontextualized declarative metacognitive knowledge about memory and memory performance have typically not been found (Best & Ornstein, 1986). Furthermore, the effectiveness of metacognitive abilities is greatly tied to general knowledge about the task, with metacognition being especially important when children have low knowledge of the domain (Alexander & Schwanenflugel, 1994; Schneider & Korkel, 1989). Metacognitive abilities may also be linked to general reasoning abilities, although this link remains controversial (Alexander, Carr, & Schwanenflugel, 1995).

In the next section we will examine information-processing accounts of inductive and deductive reasoning abilities, and how these interact with metacognitive monitoring and control.

Reasoning Abilities

Information-processing models have been developed to explain both inductive and deductive reasoning abilities. We begin with *inductive reasoning*, which refers to the ability to induce a general rule, pattern, or schema from a series of instances, examples, or events, and sometimes then to apply that schema to predicting a new event (Holland, Holyoak, Nisbett, & Thagard, 1986; Holyoak & Thagard, 1997; Johnson-Laird, 1993). Most inductive reasoning problems involve classifications, series completions, or analogies. In classification problems, children must find the common rule or characteristic that unites two or more items and, often, what item does not fit the rule (e.g., Montréal, New Orleans, San Francisco, Texas). In series-completion problems, children must select or generate an item that continues a series of given items (e.g., abc, aabbcc, _____). Analogies require children to map the relations between a new problem and similar successfully-solved problems to arrive at a solution (Anderson & Thompson, 1989). Analogies typically have the form A:B::C: _____, in which children must generate or select D, whose relation to C is analogous to that of B to A. The terms of the analogy may be verbal, pictorial, or mathematical. These types of inductive reasoning problems show high loadings on the so-called general intelligence, or *g*, factor mentioned earlier (Sternberg & Gardner, 1982).

Some fairly general information-processing components involved in inductive reasoning are encoding, inference, mapping, application, comparison, justification, and response (Sternberg, 1985, 1988a). Consider the following analogy: LAWYER : CLIENT :: DOCTOR : (a) PATIENT, (b) MEDICINE. In encoding, one retrieves the semantic attributes that are potentially relevant for solving the analogy from semantic memory. In inference, one determines the relation between the first two terms of the analogy (here, LAWYER and CLIENT). In mapping, one determines the higher order relation that links the first half of the analogy, headed by LAWYER, to the second half of the analogy, headed by DOCTOR. In application, one carries over to the second half of the analogy the relation inferred in the first half, generating a possible completion for the analogy. In comparison, one compares each of the answer options to the mentally-generated completion, deciding which, if any, is correct. In justification—used optionally if none of the answer options matches the mentally-generated solution—one decides which, if any, of the options is close enough to constitute an acceptable solution to the question. In response, one indicates an option by, for example, pressing a button, making a mark on a piece of paper, etc. (Sternberg, 1985).

Generating a relevant analogy requires that one determine the "deep" structure of the problem at hand and not be distracted by surface similarities to irrelevant problems. Similarly, spurious correlations between examples can lead children to make false inductions (Lewis & Anderson, 1985). The ability to see the deeper structure or pattern of an analogy often depends on one's level of expertise in the particular domain from which the analogy is drawn (Chi, Hutchinson, & Robin, 1989).

Let us now consider *deductive reasoning*. Deductive reasoning refers to the process of reaching a necessary and valid conclusion, given a particular set of premises. One theory of deductive reasoning postulates that the mind contains inference rules that are part of a mental logic (Braine, 1990; Rips, 1994). These rules are general and, in principle, content free. For example, given the rule, "If dogs are amphibious (p), then they can live on Mars (q)," and the statement, "Dogs are amphibious (p)," one can logically deduce that "Dogs can live on Mars (q)." According to this theory, the preceding deduction is made in three steps. First, one removes the specific content of the inference to get at the underlying skeleton of the argument (i.e., if p then q; p; therefore q). Second, the skeleton is matched to arguments with a similar structure in one's repertoire of

possible arguments, and a series of logical steps required by that form is implicitly carried out to reach a conclusion (as a logician would do explicitly). Third, the specific content (e.g., dogs, Mars) is overlaid on this structure and a specific conclusion is reached. Arguments that have an atypical form—for example, if p then q; not q; therefore not p—are more difficult because they have no direct match in one's repertoire, so one cannot apply an inference rule directly.

The major problem with this mental logic theory is that it cannot account for the impact of different types of content on reasoning using the same basic skeletal argument. Many demonstrations of the importance of content have centered around variants of the classic Wason selection task (Wason, 1968), in which subjects are given four cards—A, 4, B, 7—and the following rule: If there is a vowel on one side of the card, then there is an even number on the other side. The task is to choose which of the four cards one should turn over in order to determine whether the rule is true. Most people correctly choose card A but fail to choose card 7, although if the 7 card has a vowel on the other side, the rule is false. This relation becomes much clearer when one uses realistic content. For example: to drink beer, a customer must be over 18. Given four cards— beer, over 18, coke, under 18—most people correctly choose the first and last cards, and can justify why their choices are necessary. On the other hand, content can also draw people into making invalid inferences, a problematic finding for a theory based on mental logic (Johnson-Laird & Byrne, 1991; Markovits & Nantel, 1989).

A second theory of deductive reasoning ability (Cheng & Holyoak, 1985; Holland et al., 1986) proposes that children's use of inference rules is sensitive to context. These authors argue that reasoning ability relies on domain-specific *pragmatic reasoning schemas* that reflect one's knowledge of events and relations in the real world, such as are involved in determining permission or obligation. Because inferences that are pragmatic in one situation may not be in another, reasoning depends on the type of schema evoked. For example, the *obligation schema* provides a set of rules for situations in which a given condition necessitates an action (e.g., if you are caught stealing, you will be punished). The *permission schema* is similar, but concerns situations in which a precondition must be met before a desired action is taken (e.g., if you want to buy this toy, you must first find or earn $20). These two types of schema have been the most researched. However, Cheng and Holyoak (1985) also proposed two additional schemas, *causal schemas* concerning rules for dealing with cause and effect relations (e.g., if you drop the camera, it will break) and *contingency schemas* dealing with correlated events (e.g., if a man is an American citizen, he speaks English). Recently, Thompson (1995) suggested adding another type of schema, the *definitional schema,* concerning categorical relations between objects (e.g., if it is a bird, it has two legs).

According to this pragmatic theory of deductive reasoning, realistic versions of a task are easier because they cue the relevant pragmatic schema, whereas an abstract version of the task does not. However, this theory fails to explain how individuals do manage to make valid deductions with abstract or unfamiliar problems (Byrne, 1994). Furthermore, Markovits and Savary (1992) found that the effects of schema category varied across task domain. Subjects were given problems using the Wason selection task (Wason, 1968), and problems in the form of logical arguments that needed to be evaluated. In the latter form of the problems, subjects were given a logical statement such as: "If this is a tree, then it has roots." They were then asked to evaluate the following four situations: (1) "This is not a tree: Does it have roots?" (2) "This plant has roots: Is it a tree?" (3) "This plant has no roots: Is it a tree?" and (4) "This plant is a tree: Does it have roots?" Surprisingly, while individuals were more likely to give conditional responses on a conditional reasoning problem than on a causal reasoning problem when performing the Wason selection task, the reverse was true when the same problems were framed as logical arguments evaluated as valid or invalid. This inconsistency in subjects' answers challenges the notion of an all-purpose rule structure applicable to all contexts requiring similar deductive inferences.

Efklides, Demetriou, and Metallidou (1994), based on a model of mental development which they call *experiential structuralism,* tested 261 adolescents aged 12 through 16 (approximately 50 per age group) and 26 college students (a total of six groups) on a battery of 58 logical arguments. Subjects were also asked to rate the perceived difficulty and similarity of each of these arguments; their explanations of why arguments were similar were also rated. These ratings were used to measure metacognitive awareness and metacognitive knowledge of performance. A series of confirmatory factor analyses showed that logical relations function as powerful organizing principles for propositional reasoning. A further series of cross-sectional analyses showed that difficulty ratings decreased up to age 16, and increased thereafter. College students' ratings of increased difficulty were associated with improved performance, especially on invalid arguments, suggesting that older students had superior metacognitive abilities to monitor their problem solving.

In contrast to the theories of reasoning discussed so far, which are based on syntactic structure, two other theories (Johnson-Laird, 1983, 1993; Piaget & Garcia, 1991) base their explanations of reasoning on the semantic implications between premises. According to the theory of *mental models* (Johnson-Laird, 1983, 1993) individuals construct mental models of events, and use these models to make logical inferences. In this theory, deduction involves three steps. (1) Build an initial mental model of the situation based on one's perceptions, imaginations, or verbal descriptions that make explicit the objects, properties, and relations relevant to potential actions. Many models contain elements that cannot be directly visualized (e.g., negation). What is important is not subjective experience of the model but its structure. A model makes explicit those objects, properties, and relations that are relevant to potential actions without the need for further processing. (2) Generate a novel, parsimonious conclusion not explicit in the premises. (3) Evaluate the validity of the conclusion by establishing that no alternative model exists that will invalidate the current model.

Because people have only a limited amount of working memory, alternative models are typically considered implicitly (Johnson-Laird, Byrne, & Schaeken, 1992). Limits on human working-memory capacity lead to two principal predictions: (a) deductions requiring a greater number of explicit models should be harder to make; and (b) because individuals do not necessarily exhaust all possible models before drawing a conclusion, errors should reflect conclusions that are true in a subset of possible models of the situation. Content helps when making inferences because familiar content makes alternative models easier to imagine (Johnson-Laird & Byrne, 1991). Likewise, children presumably reason less well than do adults because they have less experience with which to generate initial and alternative models.

One objection to the mental-model approach is that it relies on a covert use of mental logic to choose one model as necessarily superior to another, or to decide that no further models are possible (Leslie, 1994; see also Braine, 1990). However, this criticism may over-emphasize the structure of logical reasoning in mental-model building, and under-emphasize the semantic meaning of the elements represented in the model. This point is made even more explicit in the next model of reasoning to be presented.

In one of his last published works, Piaget and his associates (Piaget & Garcia, 1991) explored children's understanding of the role played by *meaning relations,* such as relevance and necessity, in the development of reasoning. Piaget's studies were based on an intensional logic not easily accessible upon first reading. However, Piaget and Johnson-Laird seem to agree that the key to understanding logic lies in the semantic implications between propositions. Consistent with his theory of development, Piaget further argued that logic is rooted in the implications between sensorimotor actions. From a particular subject's point of view, all actions have meaning, as does every abstract operation later developed on the basis of these actions. Furthermore, these meanings are not isolated, but rather are organized in a system of implications in which some meanings are relevant or necessary to other meanings. To take a very simple example, the meaning of *rain* necessarily includes the meaning of *wet.* Rain is wet, so that what one knows about wetness is relevant to what one knows about rain. Note that certain objective facts, such as the fact that snow will turn to rain at a certain temperature, may not be subjectively known, or may not be viewed as relevant to a particular problem and therefore will not be included in one's reasoning about an issue.

In an ingenious series of studies, Piaget and his associates traced the development of the logic of meanings, from instrumental behavior in infants to more abstract tasks such as the consideration of arithmetic implications and meanings. For example, in one study children are asked to determine cardinal and ordinal numbers in a collection of buttons arranged in a circle. Younger children are able correctly to count the number of buttons, but cardinal and ordinal numbers remain undifferentiated. By around age 8, however, children begin to differentiate cardinal and ordinal numbers and come to realize that the (ordinal) number of second elements is twice the (cardinal) number of buttons. In other words, any button can be deemed the "first button," and one can then proceed to count in either direction. This possibility results in twice as many "second (or third or fourth, etc.) buttons" as there are "first buttons" (Piaget & Garcia, 1991).

These studies are important because they respond to many of the criticisms leveled against Piaget's earlier texts on reasoning. Furthermore, these studies of the "logic of meanings," as well as the studies by Johnson-Laird, also help to explain how expertise aids in problem solving (Chi, Glaser, & Farr, 1988; Ericsson & Lehmann, 1996), why expertise relies on case-based reasoning (Riesbeck &

Schank, 1989), and why mistaken beliefs (false knowledge) can interfere with the use and acquisition of correct knowledge, even if one engages in systematic reasoning (Ben-Zeev, 1995). In all of these cases, reasoning and understanding depend upon the subjective meaning and relevance of specific knowledge to the task at hand.

Finally, *connectionist* information-processing models of reasoning, based on similarity-based retrieval and on the generalization of knowledge elements, have been gaining increasing attention as an alternative to rule-based models of reasoning (Sloman, 1996). In connectionist models, reasoning is faster and simpler than in rule-based models and is actually considered to reflect how representations are encoded. For example, these models permit analogies to be drawn automatically, based on the extent to which features of the new problem overlap with those of a previously solved problem. Thus, analogies are not between problems or concepts, but between subcomponents of concepts (Smolensky, 1988). The preferred metaphor for reasoning among connectionists is that of settling into a stable state. In other words, an inference is the result of a constraint satisfaction process which, in principle, eventually settles upon the relevant representation (Sloman, 1996). A major problem for these models is that of tracing a conceptual hierarchy of representations (for example, from mammal to bird to robin) that requires multiple representations of the same object, one at each level of the hierarchy.

Sloman (1996) argues that both associative and rule-based reasoning systems are used when individuals reason in everyday contexts. He presents examples in which individuals hold simultaneous yet contradictory solutions to a given problem that reflect the workings of these two systems. For example, Osherson, Smith, Wilkie, Lopez, and Shafir (1990) asked people which of two arguments seemed stronger: (1) Robins have an ulnar artery. Therefore, birds have an ulnar artery. Or (2) Robins have an ulnar artery. Therefore, ostriches have an ulnar artery. Most people chose the first argument, because robins are more similar to most other birds than to ostriches. Subjects conceded, however, that logically the second argument is just as strong as the first because ostriches are birds, too. This and similar examples suggest that feature overlap plays an important role in reasoning, and competes with rule-based reasoning when reaching a conclusion.

Sloman (1996) argues that associative and rule-based reasoning are interwoven in development, just as they are in task performance. People use associative processes when they do not have access to knowledge or rules. However, individuals use and invent rules when trying to structure their conceptual understanding, creating lay theories of a domain to test against new evidence. Thus, associative and rule-based reasoning may also be important to developing tacit and analytic knowledge, respectively, although this connection has yet to be studied empirically (Sternberg, Wagner, Williams, & Horvath, 1995).

Theories of inductive and deductive reasoning serve as the basis for research on other major abilities. In light of the findings from the psychometric literature, this fact should not be surprising: Reasoning ability appears to be more general than these other abilities and contributes to individual differences in performance of them. We now briefly look at information processing in a specific domain, that of mathematical reasoning and problem solving.

Mathematical Abilities

Models of mathematical ability have generally been framed in terms of more limited subdomains of information processing. In this section we deal with two such subdomains, basic computational abilities and complex mathematical problem solving.

Some researchers consider basic computational abilities, such as numerosity (i.e., determining the number of objects without any need for counting), ordinality (i.e., relative quantities indicated as "more or less," "larger or smaller," etc.), counting, conservation of number, and simple arithmetic (e.g., addition or subtraction) to be governed by biological influences, since they emerge spontaneously in all cultures and in virtually all children who develop in typical environments (Bisanz, Morrison, & Dunn, 1995; Gallistel & Gelman, 1992; Geary, 1993, 1996; Wynn, 1992). According to Gelman and Gallistel (1978; Gallistel & Gelman, 1992), counting by preschoolers is governed by five implicit principles: one-to-one correspondence, stable order, cardinality, abstraction, and order irrelevance. In this view, implicit knowledge of these principles precedes and thus governs the acquisition of counting procedures. An alternative view is that children first use these basic abilities (e.g., counting) by rote, and only later develop a conceptual representation of their activity (Briars & Siegler, 1984; Siegler & Jenkins, 1989; Siegler & Shrager, 1984). Regardless of which of these two views is correct, counting knowledge is related to skill in using computational strategies to solve arithmetic problems (Geary, Bow-Thomas, & Yao, 1992).

From an early age, children rely on a variety of strategies to solve simple arithmetic problems. For example, if the answer cannot be recalled or if the problem is novel, kindergarten and first-grade children in the United States tend to count on their fingers or out loud (Geary, 1996). By the end of the first grade, children typically use the min (or count-on) procedure. In other words, more able first-grade children asked to add 5 + 2 will start from five and count to seven (they will count on from the largest number). Less skilled children use the sum (or count-all) procedure (Groen & Parkman, 1972), in which they count the first number from the beginning and then keep counting with the second one. Some problems, such as those in which both elements of the addition are identical (e.g., 3 + 3), are recalled faster than would be predicted by using either of these methods, suggesting that these sums are stored in memory (Groen & Parkman, 1972). Thus, mathematical problem solving involves both deliberate strategies and habitualized or implicit knowledge.

These findings reflect what are probably the two main approaches to understanding basic computational skill. The first is to use information-processing modeling to estimate reaction times in solving computational problems. The second approach is to predict errors in order to understand student misconceptions about mathematical operations. However, in both approaches, mastering basic skills is seen as a necessary prerequisite for more complex mathematical problem solving (Sternberg, 1988b).

A second important aspect of mathematical ability is complex problem-solving. Mayer (Hegarty, Mayer, & Monk, 1995; Mayer & Hegarty, 1996) and Schoenfeld (1992) have proposed overlapping models that isolate five component processes of mathematical problem solving: (1) mathematical knowledge; (2) translating and integrating problem elements; (3) execution of mathematical operations; (4) supervising mathematical problem solving performance (i.e., planning, monitoring, and evaluating); and (5) student beliefs and affect. Let us consider each of these components in light of a simple mathematical problem: Three marbles represent what proportion of a dozen marbles?

First, solving such a math problem requires both declarative and procedural *mathematical knowledge*. For complex problems, mathematical reasoning often relies on increasingly complex chunks of declarative mathematical knowledge (Fayol, Abdi, & Gombert, 1987). Chunking occurs when isolated knowledge elements of mathematical knowledge are integrated (chunked) into a single unit, freeing attention for higher level processes (e.g., one can realize that multiplication is a special case of addition and that division is its necessary complement). Procedural knowledge refers to one's knowledge (sometimes implicit knowledge) of legal mathematical operations within a given mathematical system (e.g., knowing that dividing by zero is an illegal procedure). As individuals address more and more complex mathematical problems, their abilities rely increasingly on knowledge and procedures that are part of a specific cultural heritage, acquired through sustained instruction by experts (teachers and mathematicians) (Geary, 1996; Parker & Leinhardt, 1995).

Translating and integrating involve using mathematical knowledge to create a mental representation of a given problem. Children often have trouble translating between symbol systems (e.g., translating verbal propositions into numerical propositions), sometimes due to a lack of knowledge. For example, one must know that the word "dozen" refers to the number 12. Integrating involves building a coherent mental representation (i.e., a mental model) of the problem situation. Thus, one must see the marble problem as one of determining a fraction or proportion of a larger quantity, and such integration often requires schematic knowledge of problem types (e.g., proportions, ratios, etc.). Less successful children tend to directly translate key words and numbers into mathematical statements (e.g., they will immediately translate one dozen into the number 12), whereas more successful children construct a mental model of the problem situation (e.g., they will picture 3 marbles as a subset of a large quantity of 12 marbles) (Hegarty, Mayer, & Monk, 1995; Mayer & Hegarty, 1996). However, the ability to generate mental models of mathematical problems improves with training (Lewis & Mayer, 1987; Robins & Mayer, 1993) and appears to be key in developing the most sophisticated forms of mathematical reasoning (Dreyfus & Eisenberg, 1996).

Executing involves performing some mathematical operation. Using operations requires procedural knowledge of the correct algorithm to apply, and their effective utilization is limited by short-term memory capacity (Sweller, 1989). Perhaps not surprisingly, when students do not know the correct algorithm they often create their own reasonable algorithm to solve a problem, one that is sometimes incorrect because it is based on an overspecialized or overgeneralized use of familiar examples (Ben-Zeev, 1995; VanLehn, 1990).

Supervision (planning/monitoring/evaluating) involves devising and revising the problem-solving procedure. Note that this component of mathematical problem solving involves children's metacognitive abilities, mentioned earlier. Understanding of mathematics can be greatly enhanced by encouraging students at all levels to monitor their progress during problem solving and to ask questions when important

information seems to be missing (Delclos & Harrington, 1991; Graesser & McMahen, 1993). For example, problem solving can be assessed and taught by having subjects reflect on the problem, or by providing worked-out examples (Chi et al., 1989; Schoenfeld, 1992).

Finally, sometimes student *beliefs and affect* influence student goals and motivation and may undermine sophisticated mathematical problem solving (Pajares & Miller, 1994; Schoenfeld, 1992). For example, one such belief is that there is only one right answer to any given mathematical problem, which limits any motivation to attempt a creative solution or to develop an alternative solution to a given math problem (Schoenfeld, 1992). Indeed, different beliefs about the value of mathematics, and how much mathematical achievement depends on personal effort, may be one of the reasons why Asian and Asian-American students outperform other ethnic groups in mathematics from elementary school on (Chen & Stevenson, 1995). The importance of such beliefs in orienting performance will be discussed further when we examine their impact on cognitive styles.

In conclusion, mathematical abilities involve a number of information-processing skills, many of which are hierarchically related. For example, problem-solving skills presuppose some computational skills, and computational skills in turn presuppose counting skills. However, information-processing analyses of mathematical ability often tend to obscure the overall picture of how these various skills combine to produce the correlation patterns found on psychometric tests of this ability (Sternberg, 1988b). Finally, mathematicians such as Dreyfus and Eisenberg (1996) insist that mathematical thought involves more than simply the ability to develop some mathematical knowledge or to solve some mathematical problem. Rather, it is closely tied to the elegance of one's solution (that is, its explanatory coherence and parsimony); such elegance typically reflects an expert understanding of the mathematical problem.

The information-processing account of mathematical ability briefly outlined here illustrates how this approach to the study of mental ability focuses on the processes and representations that underlie competent functioning in the mathematical domain. However, as with other abilities, mathematical ability does not exist in a vacuum; it is always embedded in a context (Sternberg, 1988b). Contextual theories have emphasized the importance of the meaning and relevance of different tasks (as specifically reflected by subjects' familiarity and interest in a given context) to individual performances involving particular abilities. We next briefly examine how context influences both the expression and the acquisition of different mental abilities.

ABILITIES IN CONTEXT

The cognitive theories mentioned so far emphasize the importance of process and knowledge over context (Ceci & Roazzi, 1994). But many researchers have argued that knowledge is inseparable from the activities and environments that generate it and in which it is applied (Rogoff, this volume; Rogoff, Mistry, Göncü, & Mosier, 1993; Sternberg & Wagner, 1994; Williams, in press; Wozniak & Fischer, 1993). Rather than attempt to cover all of the research that has been done in this area, we focus on the bioecological theory of intellectual development (Bronfenbrenner & Ceci, 1993; Ceci, 1990; Ceci & Roazzi, 1994), which is typical of this entire class of theories. The bioecological theory of intellectual development seeks to explain the unevenness of intellectual performance in different contexts (e.g., the street vendor who can give change in half a dozen currencies, but cannot solve simple academic math problems). The theory includes three main tenets: (1) multiple innate abilities exist, not a single ability; (2) innate biological potentialities provide a range of possibilities that develop, fail to develop, or atrophy in interaction and synergy with environmental potentials; and (3) motivation is important to the acquisition of different mental abilities.

Like recent psychometric theories (Carroll, 1993; Cattell, 1971/1987; Horn & Hofer, 1992) and the theory of multiple intelligences (Gardner, 1993a) mentioned earlier, the biological part of the theory holds that human intellectual potential comprises a system of biological resources, each responsible for a different aspect of information processing (e.g., visual processing, auditory discrimination, etc.). Like the multiple-intelligences theory, the bioecological theory also denies the existence of a general factor (g) permeating all intellectual performances. Correlations permitting the emergence of g are seen as arising from overlap between tasks, not from a single common ability factor that permeates all performances.

According to the bioecological theory, these abilities are developed and maintained through interaction with various aspects of the environment and will atrophy otherwise. At each point in development, the interplay between biology and ecology produces changes that permit or inhibit the possibility of further changes, in what might be called a domino or cascade effect (Bronfenbrenner & Ceci, 1993; see also Gottlieb, 1995). Hence, intellectual change is nonlinear, with small changes to the environment sometimes producing dramatic long-term effects. Furthermore, some periods in development may be sensitive ones in which prerequisite skills must be promoted by the environment for later use. For example, exposure to language at an early age, certainly before puberty, appears to be essential to a native full mastery of that language (Ceci, 1994; Ericsson & Charness, 1994).

The bioecological theory further holds that the efficient use of cognitive processes (self-regulation) depends on three principal types of environmental context: (a) the physical context; (b) the social context; and (c) the mental context. The *physical context* is especially important to the extent that one has not explicitly conceptualized his or her understanding of a given phenomenon (Piaget, 1974a, 1974b). For example, young children may be able to predict the effect of cutting an orange in half, but not that of cutting a watermelon (Ceci & Roazzi, 1994), and even adults require repeated exposure to novel objects before achieving an abstract understanding of them (Granott & Gardner, 1994; Piaget, 1974a).

The *social context* refers to the fact that how well a child performs is intimately bound to the social context in which learning and performance occur. For example, during a concept-formation task requiring prediction of how geometric shapes will migrate across a computer screen based on their size, form, and color, children were unable to determine the rules governing the movement of these shapes, even after 750 trials. However, when the task was modified into a video game in which the objects became birds, bees, and butterflies, and children had to place a butterfly net where the new objects would migrate, they were able to achieve near-perfect performance after only about 300 trials (Ceci & Bronfenbrenner, 1985). In a follow-up study, children were able to implicitly transfer the rule from the contextualized task to the more abstract geometric-shape task, but only if the laboratory context immediately followed the video-game context and the room itself remained unchanged (Ceci & Roazzi, 1994).

Finally, the *mental context* refers to the way in which individuals represent the problem at hand. A more elaborate knowledge base leads to a more elaborate conception of how problems are classified and of what possible strategies can be deployed (Ceci, 1994; Ericsson & Lehmann, 1996). Level of expertise and motivation in a particular context and knowledge domain both help to determine how actively and strategically individuals will approach a given problem, and how perseverant they will be in the face of obstacles or difficulties (Bandura, 1986, in press; Pinard, 1992). Individuals must be motivated to profit from their experiences and thus acquire expertise in a given environment. Given the analogous sort of complex reasoning needed to excel at scientific reasoning and at racetrack betting, for example, it is reasonable to assume that individuals who excel at betting (Ceci & Liker, 1986) would be able to excel at similar sorts of scientific reasoning, given exposure to, and motivation to profit from, environments that encourage them to do so.

For this reason, the bioecological theory views multiple human cognitive abilities as only imperfectly measured by conventional intelligence tests, and perhaps by all psychometric tests. IQ tests, for example, are viewed simply as achievement tests that closely resemble other tests in academic settings, and are thus susceptible to the same sorts of influences on performance (prior knowledge, motivation, and aptitude for these types of tasks). Hence it not surprising that IQ reflects number of years of schooling (as well as math and reading achievement scores), and may help explain the fact that IQ test scores have been rising around the world for the last 60 years. In fact, in what has come to be known as the "Flynn effect," average test takers today score an entire standard deviation higher than did average test takers in 1932 (Flynn, 1987; Williams, in press). Furthermore, once individuals leave school, their IQs begin to decline, suggesting that IQ is not simply a reflection of innate capacity, but is influenced by learning (Cattell, 1971/1987; Ceci, 1990).

The bioecological theory is not alone in considering both contextual and biological influences on development. However, other theories of mental abilities have proposed that the influence of context is bounded by maturational influences on how mental abilities develop. Let us turn to these theories of development next.

LEVEL OF COGNITIVE DEVELOPMENT AND MENTAL ABILITIES

The question of whether the human mind develops in a general or a specific way has been controversial throughout the history of psychology (Case, 1992; Feldman, 1993). As mentioned earlier, some theories propose that ability is context-bound, that is, limited to culturally-defined "knowledge domains" (Carey, 1985), or to neurologically-defined "mental modules" (Fodor, 1983; Gardner, 1993a; Horn, 1994). New paradigms in infancy research, for example, suggest that the human mind has evolved such that it is sensitive to specific classes of knowledge (e.g., language and spatial relationships) from the outset (Geary, 1996; Spelke, Breinlinger, Macomber, & Jacobsen, 1992). Without these initial constraints on processing, it is hard to see how a child could even begin to learn a language or appreciate music, for example (Karmiloff-Smith, 1992). Yet a look at other cultures shows that human beings are able to develop many different symbol systems from the input supporting different cognitive modules (Gardner, 1993a, Karmiloff-Smith, 1992; Miller & Parades, 1996). So, while all children learn a language, specific children learn very different languages, or even several languages, depending upon the culture in which they are raised. While some forms of cognitive ability (e.g., reading) emerge only in some cultures, cross-cultural comparisons in constellations of cognitive abilities suggest that the emergence of some abilities (e.g., counting and spatial abilities) are driven by biological influences. According to Geary (1996), biologically primary abilities like counting should thus manifest themselves in activities such as play that appear pan-culturally; by contrast, biologically secondary abilities unique to specific cultures, like reading, are acquired more slowly and effortfully and must be specifically trained through guided participation (Rogoff et al., 1993) and deliberate practice (Ericsson & Charness, 1994) of activities that promote their acquisition.

Several theories, while acknowledging the importance of specific bodies of knowledge to ability, have proposed that the development of ability is regulated by system-wide changes in information-processing capacity (Fischer, 1980; Halford, 1982; Pascual-Leone, 1988; Piaget, 1970/1983). These theories have particular trouble with situations in which child prodigies appear to perform at adult levels on a single class of tasks (e.g., tasks involving musical ability), or specific skills (e.g., chess). Prodigious performances such as these seem to require: (a) the opportunity to acquire a rich and extensive knowledge base associated with the task, that is, to become an expert (Chi & Koeske, 1983); or (b) high motivation and a particular talent for specific domains or skills from an early age (Feldman, 1991).

Recently, neo-Piagetian theories of mental development have attempted to reconcile prodigious performance with the notion of universal stages that are presumed to limit domain-general processes (Case, 1992; Karmiloff-Smith, 1992). Although each of these theories has certain unique features, the model proposed by Case provides a good example of this class of theories. Case and his associates (Case, 1992, Ch. 15, this Volume; Case & Okamoto, 1996) administered both general measures of ability (e.g., measures of working memory and processing speed) and measures of cognitive competence in specific domains (e.g., mathematical, social, and physical domains). Based on findings from a number of studies involving analogous cognitive structures in a variety of different content domains (e.g., everyday mathematics, sight reading in music, understanding of social roles, etc.), Case argues that children assemble a *central conceptual structure* (i.e., knowledge representation) applicable across a range of tasks and use this knowledge structure to construct specific strategies required for particular tasks within a content domain.

As the theory predicts, children given analogous tasks in two content areas tend to perform at about the same developmental level. Children who do not perform at the expected level tend to perform below the level predicted by the theory in one of several content areas, often due to lack of task-specific knowledge in that domain (Case, 1992). Even gifted children and prodigies performed at a level of representational complexity only slightly ahead of their peers. However, exceptional children were extremely prolific in their domain of expertise relative to their performance in other content domains, sometimes approaching or even exceeding adult levels of productivity (Poarth, 1992).

Based on these and similar data, Case (1992) proposed a reconciliation between modular and system-wide developmental approaches. He classifies children's cognitive processes into basic "domains of functioning." As in the theory of multiple intelligences and in the hierarchical theories of mental abilities mentioned previously (Gardner, 1993a; Horn, 1994), these domains are presumed to originate in the modular structure of the human nervous system, with each module processing information of relevance to its particular specialization. Children's most important conceptual structures build directly on these early modular systems, resulting in children having a theory of social knowledge very different from, say, numeric knowledge (see also Carey, 1985). The root of such conceptual systems is a set of core conceptual elements organized into what Case (1992) calls central conceptual structures, which are semantic networks constructed through domain-specific experiences and which remain largely specific to the domain studied (Case & Okamoto, 1996).

Recent research suggests that young children's knowledge of different conceptual domains has a theory-like

organization that exhibits properties such as consistency, comprehensiveness, and explanatory power (Brewer & Samarapungavan, 1991; Case & Okamoto, 1996; Gelman & Wellman, this volume; Kuhn et al., 1995). For example, in Keil's (1989) studies of categorization, children and adults were asked to classify ambiguous biological entities and cultural artifacts that had the surface appearance of one object (e.g., a horse) but the insides of another (e.g., a cow). Kindergartners classified both artifacts and biological objects based on their external perceptual appearance, whereas older children and adults classified biological objects based on their internal constitution. However, even the youngest children would not accept cross-ontological transformations (e.g., a biological horse given mechanical insides was always considered a mechanical object). The key point is that children (and adults) develop theories of biological entities from which they abstract critical features by which to classify new instances. These theories should be intimately connected to children's conceptual structures in any given domain.

However, Case (1992, this Volume) maintains that children's central conceptual structures are nevertheless limited by common developmental constraints on the executive and/or working-memory systems that apply across domains, and that these constraints have some sort of biological basis. Qualitative shifts in understanding are brought about by structural reorganization of children's central conceptual structures. These qualitative shifts proceed from contextually specific action-based knowledge (i.e., sensorimotor knowledge) to increasingly abstract, general, and complex knowledge systems. Major reworkings of children's conceptual structures are likely to occur across domains, whereas minor restructuring is likely to occur within domains (Case, 1992; Fischer, 1980). Relatively little research has been done on the mechanisms that govern these changes, although some studies indicate that change will be more difficult to achieve under certain conditions, for example if it crosses ontological categories (Chi, 1992, 1997), or involves replacement of a causal belief by a non-causal one (Kuhn et al., 1995).

The cognitive strategies that individuals employ on any particular task are greatly influenced by the nature of their central conceptual structure in a given domain (Case & Okamoto, 1996; Inhelder & Cellérier, in press). However, the content of children's central conceptual structures is increasingly shaped by exposure to culturally specific experiences (Okamoto, Miura, & Tajika, 1995). Social interactions, including schooling and direct apprenticeship, play an ever more important role in providing such experiences by familiarizing children with a culture's symbol systems and the concepts and conventions that underlie their use (Bisanz et al., 1995; Granott & Gardner, 1994; Rogoff, this volume; Vygotsky, 1934/1986). Thus, an individual's central conceptual structures develop both in content and in level of complexity as a culture's symbol system itself continues to evolve (Case, 1992; Piaget & Garcia, 1987). This means that as music as a discipline evolves, so an individual's understanding of music will also evolve, given the appropriate training and biological potential (Feldman, 1993).

Indeed, different domains may require deliberate practice at culturally prescribed activities to develop the very specific cognitive control structures required to become an expert in them (Ericsson & Lehmann, 1996). Also it is sometimes easy to underestimate the extent to which difficulty in mastering a particular topic may depend on the specific organization of the symbol system itself, which has its own historical development. Thus, different difficulties that Chinese and American children encounter when learning to count depend on how the spoken number systems are organized in these two cultures. American children are obliged to decipher a strange set of terms between numbers 10 and 20 and find these numbers difficult to learn, whereas Chinese children are obliged to tackle a new term that appears between the numbers 100 and 110, and have great difficulty with these numbers (Miller, Smith, Zhu, & Zhang, 1995). Different written number systems also present their own difficulties for doing mathematical calculations, and their historical development is independent of spoken representations for mathematical concepts. However, the influence of these differences between symbol systems on performance may decrease as expertise in a domain increases (Miller & Parades, 1996).

Finally, according to Karmiloff-Smith (1992; see also Inhelder & Cellérier, 1992/in press; Piaget, 1974a, 1974b), development and learning involve both a gradual process of *proceduralization* (making behavior less consciously accessible) and a process of *representational redescription* (abstracting knowledge from successful performance of specific tasks, and thus more consciously accessible). Children's explicit conceptualizations build upon innately specified predispositions to attend to certain classes of information in the physical and cultural environment that are triggered and subsequently shaped by actual encounters with these classes of information. For example, all children are sensitive to the ways in which language parses and structures sequences of sound, but the specific "language module" that children develop will depend upon the structure of the language to which they become acculturated. Individuals become increasingly able to exploit the information implicitly stored in these modules by redescribing their own representations in ways that make it accessible to other parts of the system. Such explicit conceptual knowledge is essential to the effective functioning of the metacomponents postulated by many cognitive models. Although there is insufficient space to explore this important distinction, this difference between implicit and explicit knowledge seems to parallel similar distinctions in abilities such as learning and memory (Kihlstrom, 1987), and in the field of intelligence more generally (Sternberg et al., 1995).

As is obvious from our discussion so far, mental abilities have been studied in a variety of ways in different areas of psychology. For example, individual differences in ability have been studied through performance on a wide variety of tests that reflect both biological and genetic influences on mental ability. Type of information processing, context, and level of cognitive development also affect one's actual performance on any given task. However, actual task performance does not depend on ability alone. Performance on a given task also reflects consistent cognitive styles in one's disposition to use one's abilities. These stylistic concerns are the focus of the remainder of the chapter.

COGNITIVE STYLES

Cognitive styles refer to the dominant or typical ways children use their cognitive abilities across a wide range of situations, when the situation is complex enough to allow a variety of responses (Grigorenko & Sternberg, 1995; Messick, 1987, 1994; Royce & Powell, 1983). For example, a child may excel at tasks that require using broad perceptual categories, but may find it very difficult to perform tasks that require using narrow perceptual categories. This advantage for broad categorization should hold for all performances involving that child's mental abilities. From the standpoint of theory, there are at least three major literatures that address styles: psychodynamic ego psychology, Gestalt psychology, and educational psychology. As was the case with abilities, we begin our discussion of styles by first examining some historical views on determinants of cognitive processing. We then provide a brief survey of three of the main literatures that address cognitive style, with a special emphasis on cognitive styles in children and how they develop.

Historical Views on Determinants of Cognitive Processing

Early historical writings clearly show an appreciation of how people's use of their cognitive capabilities reflects their personality and motives. For example, the classic story of the Iliad (Homer, c. ~800/1990) alludes to the modern idea of cognitive styles in its portrayal of the consistent ways in which the personalities of Odysseus and Achilles influence their use of their cognitive abilities. Achilles is forthright and honest and uses his intellectual abilities in ways that reflect his personality. Odysseus makes a very different use of his intellectual abilities than does Achilles. Odysseus is crafty and it is by using his intellect in crafty ways, including his idea of building the Trojan horse, that Troy is conquered and that (after another entire epic) he eventually finds his way home. Similar examples of cognitive styles shaping a character's use of mental abilities appear in the literature of many cultures throughout history.

In the history of psychology, precursors to contemporary ideas of cognitive styles can be found in fields as varied as act-psychology, behaviorism, social psychology, and the psychology of personality. According to Boring (1950; see also Mischel & Shoda, 1995), psychology has always been preoccupied with factors that determine human actions, although the notion of the "dynamic principle" or the specific determinant of a psychological event has assumed a number of different aliases. In fact, Boring (1950) lists many terms that all address the distinction between more or less general and more or less implicit influences on performance. The notions of goal-directed behavior and of unconscious influences on consistent choices has also been a part of psychology from its inception. Lewin (1935), in particular, by considering people within the context of their total lifespace (or their environment as they conceive of it), and of their desires within that lifespace, paved the way for the notion of styles as dispositions to use cognitive abilities that are expressions of personality. Allport (1937) may have been the first explicitly to link personality and intellectual style when he referred to "styles of life" as means of identifying distinctive types of behavior. Thurstone (1944), already mentioned as a key figure in early research on abilities, clearly stated that an individual's spontaneous attitude toward perceptual judgments in some way reflected parameters that characterize him or her as a person. Thurstone identified two such "perceptual attitudes": (a) speed and strength of closure (how quickly one restructures incomplete or unorganized stimulus arrays into meaningful patterns); and (b) flexibility of closure (how readily one can break one meaningful pattern to form another). Similarly to Witkin and his associates (Witkin & Goodenough, 1981; Witkin, Lewis, Hertzman, Machover, Meissner, & Wapner, 1954), Pemberton (1952) found subjects high in flexibility to be more analytical and socially retiring, whereas those high in speed of closure were more sociable and nontheoretical.

Despite these precursors, interest in cognitive styles originated in part because traditional psychometric research on abilities and IQ had failed to address the manner or form of specific performances in any given ability domain (Grigorenko & Sternberg, 1995; Kogan, 1983). As a result, psychologists started looking for new ways to describe cognitive functioning that incorporated deeper, more enduring adaptive mechanisms centered in personality. We begin our discussion of styles by examining stylistic constructs developed by two main groups who began the study of cognitive styles: (a) the Menninger Foundation group (Gardner, Holzman, Klein, Linton, & Spence, 1959; Klein, 1954; Klein & Schlesinger, 1949), who studied the notion of cognitive controls, and later cognitive styles, within the context of ego psychology; and (b) Witkin and his associates (Witkin & Goodenough, 1981; Witkin et al., 1954), who studied the specific style construct of field dependence-independence. These sections will be followed by a review of work on styles originating in educational psychology.

The Concept of Styles as It Originated in Ego Psychology

Cognitive Controls

The Menninger Foundation group was one of the original research groups to examine cognitive styles. This group viewed consistencies in performance on a variety of experimental tasks in light of key concepts in psychoanalytic ego psychology, which presumably reflected the deepest levels of personality (Gardner et al., 1959; Klein, 1954; Klein, & Schlesinger, 1949). In this tradition, Thurstone's notion of perceptual attitudes (Thurstone, 1944) was first generalized to cognitive attitudes (Klein & Schlesinger, 1949).

Cognitive attitudes were later called cognitive controls, viewed as adaptive regulatory mechanisms for balancing internal strivings and environmental demands. Cognitive controls governed a range of situations requiring similar adaptive requirements, and not simply responses to similar physical stimuli or identical behaviors (Gardner et al., 1959; Klein, 1954).

A major line of research in the study of cognitive controls involved individual differences in categorizing style, also known as cognitive differentiation. The major findings of studies of categorizing styles indicate that individual consistencies in categorization are demonstrable across a wide range of activities, such as learning and teaching, as well as in experimental tests (Gardner & Schoen, 1962). Other cognitive-control distinctions within this tradition include tolerance for unrealistic experience, leveling versus sharpening (the tendency to exaggerate or minimize remembered differences), conceptual differentiation (the number of distinctions an individual makes among concepts), and scanning versus focusing (Gardner et al., 1959; Gardner & Schoen, 1962).

Although research in this tradition mainly examined adults and is more or less exhausted, certain recent theories of styles with important implications for child psychology have evolved out of it. For example, cognitive complexity is a logical outgrowth of Gardner's notion of conceptual differentiation. *Cognitive complexity,* as opposed to simplicity, refers to a bias toward viewing the world (especially the social world) in multidimensional ways. A complex individual's conceptual system is highly *differentiated* (including many distinct dimensions or concepts), finely *articulated* (with the strength and magnitude of stimuli discriminated within each dimension), and flexibly *integrated* (with multiple interrelations of dimensions allowing one to adopt alternative perspectives) (Harvey, Hunt, & Schroeder, 1961; Messick, 1994). An undifferentiated cognitive structure might apply a single metric (such as, "How is this good for me?") to any situation or action; a more differentiated cognitive structure would consider information from additional perspectives (such as, "What are the long-term versus short-term benefits, and at what cost to others?"). Integration is used to coordinate the information from different dimensions or perspectives (for example, although cheating a business associate may be of short term-benefit, it is unfair and will ultimately undermine cooperation and trust between both parties).

In one of its most recent variants, the *integrative complexity* approach (Suedfeld, Tetlock, & Streufert, 1992)

considers complexity to be a situation-specific state variable, as opposed to a dispositional trait. This contextualization of a cognitive style has an obvious link to the views of Ceci (1990), mentioned earlier, according to which context largely determines the form and level of one's mental abilities. However, complexity is not necessarily beneficial (Goldstein & Blackman, 1978), especially when unaccompanied by higher-order integration of information (Sheldon & Emmons, 1995), as high levels of cognitive complexity may lead individuals to become confused by irrelevant information and to appear more indecisive (Messick, 1994)

Cognitive complexity has been measured in two main ways. Some researchers use an early test by Kelly (1955) called the Construct Repertory Test. This test asks subjects to think of ways in which two people resemble each other, but not a third person, along several construct dimensions specified by the test. A matrix is then constructed of how different people relate to different constructs. A simple cognitive structure is shown by highly similar ratings across constructs. Factor analysis and individual ratings of preselected constructs have also been used, as have other sophisticated forms of computer analyses (Gaines & Shaw, 1980, 1992); again, the more factors one obtains, or the more the ratings differ, the higher an individual's level of cognitive complexity. Kelly's test and its variants have typically shown low correlations with IQ (around .20) and with academic achievement. The major alternative to this method of measuring cognitive complexity is the Paragraph Completion Test (Schroeder, Driver, & Streufert, 1967), which involves having subjects write a short text on a preset theme. Specially-trained judges then analyze these texts in terms of their level of differentiation and integration of ideas. More recently, this method has been generalized to any connected verbal material, including verbal interviews and narrative text (Suedfeld et al., 1992).

A direct test of the association between the Paragraph Completion Test and four common measures of mental ability (verbal ability, crystallized intelligence, fluid ability, and divergent thinking) revealed modest correlations—from .14 to .28—between the PCT and verbal ability, crystallized intelligence, and especially divergent thinking. Although the Paragraph Completion Test shows low correlations for adults, it has shown consistently higher positive correlations with IQ among subjects of high-school age or younger, suggesting that a certain threshold of verbal skill is needed to express highly differentiated and complex concepts (Suedfeld, 1994; Suedfeld & Coren, 1992).

Other recently proposed stylistic dimensions are also closely tied to the original conceptions of cognitive controls. For example, uncertainty orientation (Sorrentino & Short, 1986), that is, an individual's willingness to incorporate new information when there is uncertainty about the self and the environment, bears a strong resemblance to an earlier dimension of cognitive control called "tolerance for unrealistic experience" (Gardner et al., 1959). Sorrentino and his associates have found that uncertainty-oriented individuals seek to confront situations that involve uncertainty, whereas certainty-oriented individuals will seek to avoid such situations—whether the uncertainty concerns one's self (i.e., one's skill) or the situation (i.e., whether the outcome is due to chance) (Sorrentino, Hewitt, & Rasco-Knott, 1992).

Cognitive Controls and Self-Regulation

The original notion of cognitive controls developed by the Menninger group closely resembles recent views of self-regulation, especially theories that incorporate situation-specific personality constructs, such as motivation (Deci & Ryan, 1991), self-concept (Cross & Markus, 1994; Marsh, 1992), control beliefs (Skinner, Chapman, & Baltes, 1988), attributions about success (Borkowski, Carr, Rellinger, & Pressley, 1990; Paris & Winograd, 1990; Weiner, 1994), and perceived self-efficacy (Bandura, 1986, in press; Schunk & Zimmerman, 1994) into explanations of consistent patterns of self-regulation. Recent research has found that students' self-systems (an integral part of many contemporary theories of personality) consistently influence how they regulate their performance across a range of contexts that have similar adaptive requirements (Mischel & Shoda, 1995).

For example, Dweck and her associates (Chiu, Hong, & Dweck, 1994; Dweck, 1991; Dweck & Leggett, 1988) propose that children develop one of two general theories about their own mental abilities: (a) an entity theory, which views mental ability as a fixed and stable trait, or entity, which people possess in varying amounts, or (b) an incremental theory, which views mental abilities as a set of skills developed through experience. These two theories have different motivational impacts on performance.

Dweck argues that an entity theory is associated with extrinsic motivation and is oriented toward maximizing positive social evaluations of competence (usually associated with good grades). Entity theorists, believing that ability is fixed, make little effort to improve and are likely to be discouraged by failure. By contrast, an incremental theory is associated with intrinsic motivation and is oriented toward increasing mastery. Incremental theorists believe that ability can improve through effort and continually strive to develop and expand their repertoire of skills, leading to increased persistence and challenge seeking.

In conditions of success, there is little noticeable difference between children who hold these two theories, but under conditions of failure, Dweck has shown that the two orientations result in stable differences between children on measures of test anxiety and task persistence. As a result, the two orientations are significant predictors of short-term academic success. For example, girls have been found initially to perform at a superior level to boys in mathematics, but eventually to fall behind them. Dweck (1986) found that able girls attributed failure to lack of ability more than able boys; boys attributed failure to low effort, high task difficulty, or bad luck. Attributing failure to low ability probably decreased girls' motivation to pursue advanced mathematics in high school when difficulty increased and new types of skills were required.

A recent study (Bouffard, Boisvert, Vezeau, & Larouche, 1995) suggests, however, that performance and mastery goals may have different impacts on academic self-regulation and achievement for boys and girls, at least during late adolescence, with successful boys placing greater emphasis on performance goals than do successful girls. This study also shows that the most successful students are those who coordinate both sorts of goals during learning, and that this more integrated goal orientation improves the efficiency with which these students use cognitive and metacognitive strategies to self-regulate their own learning.

These self-system influences on how individuals evaluate their own mental abilities and regulate their performance on cognitive tasks resemble the cognitive controls mentioned earlier. At the very least, research on how personality influences self-regulation forces one to consider how dispositional moderators of competence relate to situation-specific moderators of specific performances, for example, children's achievement in mathematics or reading, or in other settings that share prototypical features (Mischel & Shoda, 1995; Schunk & Zimmerman, 1994). Motivational influences on children's performance are further explored when we examine style constructs in the educational psychology literature.

Cognitive Controls versus Cognitive Styles

Klein (1958) originally distinguished cognitive controls from cognitive styles. Cognitive controls refer to the specific independent dimensions of cognitive regulation (e.g., leveling-sharpening, conceptual differentiation, etc.), whereas cognitive style refers to an individual's patterning or profile of such control principles, and was viewed as a "superordinate level of control within the personality system." Although this distinction has not always been acknowledged, some recent treatments of styles have revived the notion of stylistic profiles that incorporate a number of control dimensions. For example, Miller (1988) has developed a model in which three dimensions (analytic-holistic, emotionally stable-unstable, and subjective-objective) are presumed to be superordinate to individual differences on many of the original cognitive control dimensions and their more recent variants.

Royce (1983; Royce & Powell, 1983) proposed an ambitious theory of individuality that addresses the question of cognitive styles at two levels of integration. Royce argued that human individuality (or personality) involves the individual's total psychological system comprising six main subsystems, organized in four levels. Level I is the level of *information transmission,* and is composed of (1) *sensations,* and (2) *motor behavior,* both of which involve spatiality and temporality. Level II is the level of *information transformation,* and is composed of (3) *affect* (i.e., emotional stability, emotional independence, introversion/extroversion) and (4) *cognitions* (i.e., perceiving, conceptualizing, symbolizing). Level III is the level of *information transduction,* and is composed of (5) *values* (intrinsic, self, social) and (6) *styles* (rational, empirical, metaphoric). Level IV is the level of *personal integration* (world view, self image, lifestyle).

Royce also defined two main personality types (or styles) at the highest level of integration in his model: *Assimilators* adapt to new situations by assimilating as much new information as possible into already existing personality structures, and should show low mobility on various cognitive style/control dimensions; *accommodators* adapt by accommodating to new information by changing their world view, and thus should show greater mobility in their use of various cognitive styles. As we shall see, some theories in educational psychology define learning style as one's general assimilative and accommodative stance toward learning and experience (e.g., Kirton, 1976, 1977; Kolb, 1977). Thus, individuality theory provides a rare link between theories of cognitive controls, cognitive styles, and learning styles.

Although Carroll (1993) was unable to detect the three broad dimensions of cognitive styles proposed by individuality theory, Royce's (1983) main point may be that empirical research is needed to determine the latent structure of these different stylistic dimensions—a point emphasized by a number of other researchers (Goldstein & Blackman, 1978; Grigorenko & Sternberg, 1995). Furthermore, innovative confirmatory factor-analytic techniques using criterion-based measures (cf., Efklides et al., 1994) may provide a better test of this complex and interesting theory. Likewise, new methods of measuring the impact of general disposition on situation-specific cognitions and affect (Mischel & Shoda, 1995) may help to show how the components of individuality theory might generate consistent styles of behavior.

In the next section we examine the stylistic construct of field dependence-independence, before going on to discuss styles in the educational psychology literature.

The Concept of Styles as It Originated in Gestalt Psychology: Field Dependence-Independence

Field dependence-independence, or field articulation, is certainly one of the most extensively studied cognitive styles. The Menninger Foundation group viewed field articulation as simply one of many cognitive controls; however, given the relatively independent and ongoing research tradition associated with this construct, we discuss it in a separate section.

The principal work on field dependence-independence was directed by Witkin, a student of both Köhler and Wertheimer. Thus, and perhaps not surprisingly, the Gestalt movement's focus on issues of form was particularly influential in this work. The construct of field articulation evolved from research on basic perceptual processes. Individuals who were unable to ignore misleading perceptual cues were labeled field-dependent, whereas those who were able to isolate themselves (Body Adjustment Task) or a rod (Rod and Frame Task) from the surrounding perceptual field were labeled field-independent (Witkin et al., 1954). The *Embedded Figures Test* (EFT) was later found to correlate with both the Rod and Frame Task and the Body Adjustment task, and the theory increasingly emphasized the ability to overcome an embedding context (Witkin, Oltman, Raskin, & Karp, 1971). The Weschler block design, picture completion, and object-assembly subtests were later included in the measurement model, and the field dependence-independence dimension came to be described in terms of global and articulated field effects. More recently, self-concept, defense mechanisms, and pathological

symptoms have been included in the concept of field articulation, which is now seen as explaining individual differences in degree of psychological differentiation (Messick,
1994).

However, many researchers (especially those engaged in
the psychometric study of mental abilities) claim that differences in field articulation simply reflect individual differences in spatial or fluid ability (Cronbach & Snow,
1977; MacLeod, Jackson, & Palmer, 1986). Indeed, Goldstein and Blackman (1978), in their review of twenty studies, found generally consistent indications that various
measures of field independence are related to both verbal
and performance aspects of intelligence. The correlations
between field independence and intelligence were mostly
in the .40–.60 range. Furthermore, MacLeod, Jackson, and
Palmer (1986), in their LISREL analysis of field independence and spatial ability, found no evidence to support the
claim that the two are distinct constructs. These results
called into question the usefulness of the field dependence-
independence construct.[5]

In order to clearly specify the style-like quality of field
articulation, Witkin and Goodenough (1981) presented a
new version of the theory that considered autonomy and reliance on external referents as two poles of a single dimension. Both poles of field articulation now had adaptive
advantages, with field independence leading to greater autonomy and field dependence leading to greater interpersonal competency. Thus, for example, field-independent
children (indexed by the Embedded Figures Task) should
excel on cognitive tasks that involve restructuring, whereas
field-dependent children (indexed by the Rod and Frame
Task) should excel at various interpersonal skills. In addition, individuals were believed to be more or less mobile,
that is, more or less able to adjust their degree of autonomy
depending upon the demands of different tasks and situations (Witkin & Goodenough, 1981). Despite the theoretical appeal of this reformulation, results have so far shown
that although field-dependent individuals are oriented

toward, and attentive to, the social world, they do not show
increased social skill (Davis, 1991; Kogan & Block, 1991).
These findings cast doubt on the validity of Witkin's final
attempt at reformulation of the field-articulation construct.

Some recent studies have treated degree of field articulation as a performance variable, focusing on how field-
dependent and field-independent children differ in their
information-processing strategies (cf. Davis & Cochran,
1989). For example, Pascual-Leone (1989) has proposed a
theory in which both attentional energy (M-processes) and
inhibitory processes (I-processes) influence sensitivity to
gestalt field effects (the F-factor). He argues that children's sensitivity to field effects should be measured by
contrasting their performance on the Rod and Frame Task
and the Embedded Figures Task. Other microanalyses of
task performance have shown clear differences between
the performances of individuals who excel on the *Rod and
Frame* task and those who excel on the *Embedded Figures*
task (Goodenough, Oltman, Snow, Cox, & Markowits,
1991). These and other recent studies described by Globerson and Zelniker (1989), Wapner and Demick (1991), and
Messick (1994) show that interest in the field-articulation
construct continues to flourish.

The Concept of Styles as It Is Addressed in Educational Psychology

In educational settings, styles have been framed in terms of
types of learners and types of learning activity (learning
styles). More recently, studies have also examined how
types of learning contexts interact with student personality
to produce consistent dispositions toward learning (Ramsden, 1992). We begin by looking at types of learners and
then examine learning styles and learning contexts.

Types of Learners

Several theories of styles in educational psychology can be
traced back to Jung's (1923) theory of personality types,
which characterized individual differences by crossing two
attitudes (extraversion and introversion), two perceptual
functions (intuition and sensing), and two judgment functions (thinking and feeling). The contemporary Myers-
Briggs theory of styles, for example, is closely based on
Jung's theory of types. According to Myers (1981; Myers
& McCaulley, 1985), there are 16 types of personality
styles, resulting from all possible combinations of four different functions, each containing two categories: (1) *perceiving*—sensing versus intuition; (2) *judging*—thinking

---

[5] However, an individual's underlying personality may serve as
an organizing tendency for the perceptual system that influences
spatial ability, an argument originally advanced by the Menninger Foundation group (Gardner et al., 1959). By this reasoning, correlation between mental ability and field articulation
cannot challenge field articulation as a construct, rather, personality must be proven irrelevant to both field articulation and
mental abilities.

versus feeling; (3) *social interaction* with self and others—introversion versus extraversion; and (4) interface with the *outer world*—judgment versus perception.

For both Jung and Myers, sensing, intuiting, thinking, and feeling are always present to various degrees in every individual, but one function tends to be dominant and the other subordinate. However, the functions of sensation, intuition, thinking, and feeling are less tightly organized in Jung's typology than in the Myers-Briggs scheme. For example, Jung does not refer to the "perceptive-judging" distinction directly, although he does refer to the function of feeling as "a kind of judging" (Jung, 1923).

The Myers-Briggs theory has been applied to a variety of fields; however, we focus our attention on findings regarding children in educational settings. According to Bargar and Hoover (1984), school children do not show an equal preference for the Myers-Briggs styles: Most children tending to be classified as extraverted and sensing (Lawrence, 1982; Myers, 1981). In this light, Lawrence (1982) recommends developing general teaching strategies for extraverted-sensing children, and more individualized approaches for other types of children. Extraversion, sensing, and feeling are also prominent among teachers, particularly elementary-school teachers (Myers, 1981). As we shall see shortly, the extent to which the styles of teachers and students are matched has been found to influence student learning and evaluation (Sternberg, 1994; Sternberg & Grigorenko, 1995).

Finally, perhaps one of the most influential theories of learning styles was proposed by Dunn and his associates (Dunn, 1988; Dunn, Beaudry, & Klavas, 1989; Dunn, Dunn, & Price, 1979), who define learning style as "a biologically and developmentally imposed set of personal characteristics that make the same teaching method effective for some and ineffective for others" (Dunn, Beaudry, & Klavas, 1989, p. 50). The *Dunn Learning Style Inventory* (Dunn, Dunn, & Price, 1979), developed to measure student learning styles, measures 18 aspects that affect student learning. These aspects are divided into four main categories: *environmental* (sound, light, temperature, design), *emotional* (motivation, persistence, responsibility, structure), *sociological* (peers, self, pair, team, adult, varied), and *physical* (perceptual, intake, time, mobility) (see Dunn & Dunn, 1978, for a detailed discussion). Yet despite its popularity among educators, and its admirable attempt to provide an overview of factors influencing student learning, the Dunns's definition of learning styles provides little rationale for the specific 18 aspects of their theory, or for

possible interactions among them. Furthermore, the theory focuses exclusively on the factors that affect children's ability to learn, and not on how they prefer to learn (Hyman & Rosoff, 1984).

Recently, learning styles have been linked to achievement in specific academic domains such as reading. For example, Corbo (1982, 1988) adapted Dunn and Dunn's (1978) learning styles inventory to develop the *Reading Styles Inventory* (RSI). Studies show that children's reading achievement improves when materials, teaching methods, and assessments are adapted to their preferred reading style, as identified by their individual RSI profile (Oglesby & Suter, 1995). As these results suggest, teachers can profit by adapting student learning activities to students' preferred learning styles. We now consider the learning activity aspect of learning styles in more detail.

Types of Learning Activity

In order to categorize important dimensions of *learning activities*, researchers have developed classifications of learners that differ from that of Myers-Briggs, but that are still loosely based on Jung's typology. For example, Kolb and his associates (Kolb, 1977; Kolb, Reuben, & McIntyre, 1979) designed the *Learning-Style Inventory* (LSI) (Kolb, 1978) to measure children's strengths and weaknesses as learners. The *Learning-Style Inventory* measures children's relative emphasis on four modes of learning: (1) thinking, or abstract conceptualization; (2) feeling, or concrete experience; (3) watching, or reflective observation; and (4) doing, or active experimentation. Based on the results of the *Learning-Style Inventory,* Kolb and his associates (1979) identified four dominant types of learning styles by crossing these dimensions: convergers (thinker-doers), divergers (feeler-watchers), assimilators (thinker-watchers), and accommodators (feeler-doers).

Convergers excel at abstract conceptualization and active experimentation. They prefer to focus on specific problems and to solve them through hypothetical-deductive reasoning. *Divergers* are people-oriented, tend to be imaginative and emotional, and are best at problems that require concrete experience and reflective observation. *Assimilators* are less people-oriented, and excel at abstract conceptualization and reflective observation; their greatest strength lies in the ability to use inductive reasoning to assimilate disparate observations into integrated theoretical models or explanations. Finally, *accommodators* excel at problems requiring concrete experience and active experimentation. They tend to take greater risks than do those with other learning styles. According to Kolb, children should become more effective learners by becoming aware of the consequences of their own learning style and of other possible learning styles.

In a theory that is virtually identical to Kolb's theory, Hagberg and Leider (1978) have crossed these same four dimensions to produce four learning styles: *practical* (thinker-actor), *imaginative* (feeler-observer), *logical* (thinker-observer), and *enthusiastic* (feeler-actor). As in the case of the Myers-Briggs scheme, the form and substance of both of these theories was influenced by Jung's typology, as shown by their systematic crossing of thinking versus feeling and of intuition versus systematic appraisal of information (Messick, 1994).

Interactions between Learning Styles and Learning Context

Learning context includes both teaching styles and general or specific classroom goals, all of which consistently shape how children engage in classroom learning activities. Although these consistent orientations are more situational (and thus less dispositional) than is typical in discussions of learning styles, they nevertheless lead to consistent patterns of student activity and hence are sometimes considered learning styles (Messick, 1994; Ramsden, 1992).

Like students, teachers also have cognitive styles that are reflected in their preferred teaching styles, and that are distinct from their methods of instruction. Although two teachers may use the same methods (e.g., lectures, audio-visual materials, discussion groups), they may differ in their teaching styles (Fischer & Fischer, 1979; Sternberg & Grigorenko, 1995). Teaching style interacts with subject matter being taught: "While the teacher's behavior is influenced by his understanding of the student—by his perception and diagnosis of the student's behavior—still the determining factor in the teacher's behavior is not his understanding of the student but his comprehension of the subject matter and the demands which clear instruction in the subject matter make upon him" (Smith, 1963, p. 296). Clearly, teachers need more than one approach if they are to achieve a "good fit" with subject material (Grigorenko & Sternberg, 1995; Oglesby & Suter, 1995). Nevertheless, teachers' roles in the learning process require an examination of how their cognitive styles (and concomitant teaching styles) affect classroom activities. We return to this topic shortly when discussing styles as forms of mental self-government.

Another current of research in educational psychology has focused on *classroom goals,* and has shown that classroom goals influence the types of learning goals adopted by students. Ames (1992; Ames & Archer, 1988) has shown that students' belief structures, or orientations toward learning depend on the reward structure set up in the classroom. Ames (1992) refers to *mastery orientation* as the aim to master the materials presented in class and to *performance orientation* as a concern with social evaluation by others of their own performance. Students who believed that classroom focus was on topic mastery reported using a greater number of more effective strategies than did those who believed that the class focused on performance. Students in mastery-oriented classrooms were also more positive about class, and were more likely to believe that improvement followed upon effort. Students in performance-oriented classes tended to have a more negative view of learning and to believe that their difficulties reflected low abilities.

Nicholls (1989) has also noted that many classroom goal structures (e.g., normative grading, ranking students, tying achievement to student worth) promote what he called ego involvement. Ego involvement links success at classroom activities relative to that of peers to feelings of being smart and having high ability, and links failure to feelings of having low ability. This stance toward learning tends to undermine effort when success is uncertain (as on novel tasks), because failure is taken as proof of low ability and must be avoided at all costs. A more positive approach toward instruction focuses on task involvement. Task involvement frames the point of school activities as mastering specific instructional material; task involvement rewards children for doing better than they did previously. Across 30 fifth-grade classrooms, work avoidance was more commonly reported in classes that fostered ego involvement than in classes that fostered task involvement. Students in the task-involved classes believed that success depended on interest, effort, and trying to learn, whereas students in ego-involved classes viewed success as due to one's being smarter than others. Academic satisfaction was higher in task-involved classrooms than in ego-involved classrooms (Duda & Nicholls, 1992; Nicholls, 1989). Furthermore, Nolen (1988) found that ego and task involvement led students to use different strategies when reading textbooks. Although all students endorsed and were observed to use surface level strategies (e.g., rereading whole passages), task-oriented students were more likely to endorse and to use deeper level strategies (e.g., reading for comprehension), suggesting that task orientation and use of higher level strategies may be linked.

Along similar lines, research has shown that students adapt their approach to learning to match the requirements of their classrooms (Ramsden, 1992). Biggs (1985), expanding upon work by Marton and Säljö (1976a, 1976b), has proposed three approaches to learning. A surface approach to learning is based on a guiding principle that is extrinsic to the real purpose of the task. It involves investing minimal effort to "satisfice" rather than satisfy task demands, and is often evidenced by rote learning of meaningless details. A deep approach is based on interest in the task; the focus is on the underlying meaning of the task and mastery of the material, not on its surface aspects. Data are commonly processed in terms of themes and principles, not just as unsupported specific facts. An achieving approach aims to organize time and work space effectively—through cue seeking, planning, and time allocation, for example—so as to maximize concordance between effort and task demands. Metalearning (knowledge about one's own learning process) is most likely to be associated with deep and achieving approaches because here one actively seeks to generate either meaning or successful performance (Biggs, 1985). The key point, however, is that students will adjust their orientation to learning to meet what they view to be the teacher's requirements for success (Ramsden, 1992). The type of classroom environment may thus be instrumental in developing children's theories of intelligence. These theories of intelligence seem to be instrumental in motivating children to continue to learn even under conditions of high risk or failure, as we saw earlier (Chiu et al., 1994; Dweck & Leggett, 1988).

Theories of styles originating in educational psychology have so far focused on the impact of different types of learners, learning activities, and learning contexts on actual achievement. Context has also been seen to interact with general and specific beliefs that learners have, both about themselves and about what they are trying to accomplish in the classroom. However, a key weakness in these and most of the models of cognitive styles discussed so far (with the exception of Royce's individuality theory) may be their lack of a clear guiding metaphor for determining dimensions along which individuals should differ as they acquire and use their mental abilities. One possible metaphor is that of an individual's preferred form of self-government, as is proposed by the theory of styles discussed next.

THE THEORY OF MENTAL SELF-GOVERNMENT

The theory of mental self-government (Sternberg, 1988c, 1990b, 1994)—in a reversal of sociocognitive theories based in the Vygotskian tradition—proposes that the various styles of government we see in the world are not there by coincidence, but rather are external reflections or mirrors of different cognitive styles. For example, governments may be monarchic, anarchic, hierarchic, or oligarchic; governments act legislatively, executively, or judicially, and at either a global or local level. Governments also address both internal (domestic) and external (foreign) affairs, and may have liberal or conservative leanings. Each of these aspects of social government suggests a parallel in terms of self-government. Furthermore, these different aspects of self-government have many obvious parallels to the cognitive and learning styles advanced in the different traditions of psychology discussed so far.

Mental Self-Government

Functions of Mental Self-Government

The mind carries out legislative, executive, and judicial functions, just as do governments. The legislative function of the mind is concerned with creating, formulating, imagining, and planning; the executive function of the mind is concerned with implementing and doing; and the judicial function of the mind is concerned with judging, evaluating, and comparing. Although any complex task typically involves all three functions of self-government, in most individuals, one of the functions tends to be dominant.

The *legislative style* characterizes individuals who enjoy creating, formulating, and planning problem solutions. Such individuals like to create their own rules and do things in their own way. They prefer problems that are not prestructured or prefabricated. For example, a student who must develop his own paper topic will benefit from having a legislative style. People with legislative styles will probably be accommodators in Kolb's theory.

Individuals with an *executive style* are implementers. Such individuals like to follow rules and to figure out which set of existing strategies would best get the job done; they prefer problems that are prefabricated or prestructured. Thus, individuals with an executive style prefer to be given a topic, and then to do the best possible job with it. Executive stylists resemble the assimilators in Kolb's theory.

The *judicial style* is seen in those people who like to judge rules and procedures, and who prefer problems in which one analyzes and evaluates existing things and ideas. As students, they will prefer analytical essays, such as ones in which they compare and contrast two points of view, or in which they evaluate a point of view. These individuals resemble convergers in Kolb's theory.

Forms of Mental Self-Government

Just as the functions of mental self-government resemble those of different branches of government, the forms of mental self-government resemble forms of government. At least four main forms of government can be identified: monarchic, hierarchic, oligarchic, and anarchic.

In the *monarchic* form, a single goal or way of doing things predominates. People with a monarchic style tend to focus single-mindedly on one goal or need at a time. They are either oblivious to obstacles or are able to set them aside. A student facing potential distractions who must turn in a paper by noon tomorrow, and is determined to do so, will benefit from a monarchic style. In this way, a monarchic form of self-government has obvious links to the ideas advanced by Kuhl (1985; see also Corno & Kanfer, 1993), in that this single-mindedness permits individuals to marshal the will they need to persevere at a task in the face of distractions. Monarchic individuals may also show low cognitive complexity.

The *hierarchic* form allows for many goals, each of which may have a different priority. People with a hierarchic style tend to enjoy dealing with multiple goals. They recognize that not all goals can be fulfilled equally well and that some goals are more important than others. They have a good sense of priorities and are systematic in their approach to solving problems. Such individuals should show a high level of cognitive integration, as subgoals are made subordinate to more general overarching goals. Thus, a hierarchic style requires a high level of cognitive complexity.

The *oligarchic* form allows for multiple goals, all of which are equally important. A student who has an oligarchic thinking style will do well in a course that includes several tests, each weighted equally, or that requires a major paper that will count just as much as the final exam. Oligarchic individuals relish dealing with multiple and often-competing goals of equal perceived importance. But competing goals may keep oligarchic individuals from completing tasks, because everything seems equally important to them. These individuals may show high levels of cognitive differentiation without integration, leading ultimately to less overall satisfaction with their accomplishments (Sheldon & Emmons, 1995).

For individuals with an *anarchic* style, rules, procedures, and guidelines are anathema. Students who have an anarchic thinking style tend to perform best when tasks and situations are unstructured, when there are no clear procedures to be followed, or when the problems they confront are most readily solved through insights that represent a departure from existing mindsets. People who have an anarchic style generally enjoy dealing with a potpourri of needs and goals that are often difficult to sort out. They tend to take a random approach to problem solving, often seem intolerant or unaware of the need for rules and regulations, and tend to resist authority.

Levels of Mental Self-Government

Government also functions at multiple levels (e.g., federal, state, county, and city). In general, one can distinguish between more global (broadly based) and more local (narrowly focused) levels. Corresponding to these levels are two aspects of mental self-government.

A person with a *global* style prefers to deal with relatively large and abstract issues and either to ignore details or to delegate them to someone else. A student with a global style will excel on assignments that require seeing the big picture (e.g., identifying the main themes of a novel), but will fare less well when required to deal with specific details (e.g., remembering the names of all of the characters of a novel). Oriented both toward a more abstract form of cognitive control (a dimension identified by Kolb and by Myers) and toward a more decontextualized approach (as is found in field-independent individuals), individuals with a global style thus span two main dimensions of other theories of styles.

The *local* style person tends to be pragmatically oriented, preferring more concrete detail-oriented problems. A student with a local style is more likely to enjoy a homework assignment consisting of numerous small problems than a conceptual essay that requires global analysis of a phenomenon. This person, metaphorically, tends to see the trees, but not always the forest of which they are part. Individuals who prefer this style tend to be both concrete and field dependent.

Scope of Mental Self-Government

Governments need to deal both with internal (domestic) affairs and with external (foreign) affairs. Similarly, mental self-governments need to deal with both internal and external issues. People who are more *internal* in style tend to be introverted, task-oriented, aloof, and interpersonally less aware than externalists. Such individuals will be highly subjective on the subjective-objective dimension proposed by Miller (1988), and introspective according to the Myers-Briggs typology. People who are more *external* in their style tend to be extroverted, people-oriented, outgoing, and more interpersonally aware than internalists. They will seek problems that either involve working with other people or that are about other people. These people will be more objective, according to Miller, and more extroverted, according to the Myers-Briggs scheme.

Leaning of Mental Self-Government

Governments can have various political leanings. Optimally, these leanings are represented on a continuum, but for present purposes, two major "regions" of leanings will be distinguished, conservative and liberal. Individuals with a predominantly *conservative* style like to adhere to existing rules and procedures, minimize change, and avoid ambiguous situations when possible. They prefer familiarity in life and work. A conservative style does not bar a simultaneously legislative one. A person may be both legislative and conservative if the person likes to come up with new ideas and ways of doing things that are essentially conservative in bent, drawing heavily upon what has been done in the past. A person with a *liberal* style likes to go beyond existing rules and procedures, to maximize change, and to find ambiguous and uncertain situations. This person becomes bored when things never seem to change. A person may be both executive and liberal, as in the case of an underling who supports and follows a very forward-moving point of view. This person likes the progressive stance, but follows rather than leads in it. One's preferred leaning has obvious parallels to the innovator-adaptor dimension proposed by Kirton (1976), as well as to tolerance for unrealistic experiences (Klein, 1958), or uncertainty (Sorrentino & Short, 1986).

The model of cognitive styles as different aspects or patterns of mental self-government seems to have potential to further the study of both human mental abilities and individual stylistic differences in performance. The theory may be especially important in its school-setting applications. Because various forms of school evaluation differentially benefit students with dissimilar style profiles, evaluation should be varied so as to avoid bias. The practical application of Sternberg's theory of mental self-government gives educators and psychologists an opportunity to understand how students use their intelligence. It may also help students to better develop and manage their own intelligence.

While the links to other theories indicated here are not meant to be exhaustive, they do show how a single underlying metaphor, such as the notion of mental self-government, provides a more unified view of cognitive styles than is commonly the case. Furthermore, this metaphor captures some of the most important stylistic dimensions identified by many previous theories of styles.

Testing the Theory of Mental Self-Government

Various kinds of testing instruments commonly used in academic settings (such as multiple-choice questions, essays, projects, interviews, etc.) will show a different degree of match to various patterns of mental self-government. Thus, effective testing will not use one testing format to the exclusion of all others but, rather, a combination of formats. Conventional multiple-choice tests have unfairly benefitted children with executive-local styles; but replacement of such tests with new, more "authentic" performance assessments will again benefit children with certain styles and not others. Testing, like any other kind of scientific assessment, is best when it uses converging operations (Sternberg, 1994).

In our own research, we have used several converging operations to measure thinking styles (Sternberg, 1994; Sternberg & Grigorenko, 1995; Sternberg & Wagner, 1991). One such measure is the *Thinking Styles Inventory.* In this inventory, subjects are given a series of statements measuring different styles, such as "If I work on a project, I like to plan what to do and how to do it" (which measures legislative style). Students are then asked to rate on a 1–9 scale how true the statement is of themselves. In one study, correlations between this inventory and both the *Myers-Briggs Type Indicator* (Myers & McCaulley, 1985) and the *Gregorc Style Delineator* (Gregorc, 1979) provided some construct validation of the theory. For the Myers-Briggs, about one quarter of the correlations (30 of 128) were statistically significant, whereas for the Gregorc, almost half (22 of 52) were significant, well above what would be expected by chance. This pattern of correlations suggests that the various style measures may partition a similar space of the intelligence-personality interface, but in different ways (Sternberg & Grigorenko, 1995).

We have also developed additional measures—such as the *Set of Thinking Styles Tasks for Students,* the *Thinking Styles Questionnaire for Teachers,* and the *Students' Thinking Styles Evaluated by Teachers*—to determine the relative importance of student and teacher thinking styles to student achievement (Sternberg & Grigorenko, 1995). No strong overall association was found between thinking styles and levels of academic success in school, although certain styles did match certain activities. For example, students with local and executive styles did better on multiple-choice tests than did either legislative or judicial ones. By contrast, evaluative essays favor students with a judicial style over those with legislative or executive styles (Sternberg & Grigorenko, 1995). Furthermore, pupils tended to match their teachers' style, consistent with the notion that styles are partially socialized. Students may unconsciously attempt to meet their teachers' expectations in order to get better grades, as was found in studies of orientations toward learning (Ramsden, 1992).

DEVELOPMENT OF COGNITIVE STYLES

Before concluding our discussion of cognitive styles, it is important to make at least brief mention of how cognitive styles may develop. Researchers have tried to understand how styles develop by studying cultural differences (Smith & Caplan, 1988); mother-child interaction and family environment (Caspi & Moffitt, 1995; Emory, 1983; Wise & Cramer, 1988); children's play (Saracho, 1992); concept formation (Lawson & Thompson, 1988); and genetic and environmental influences (Egorova, 1987; Grigorenko, LaBuda, & Carter, 1992; Tambs, 1987; Tellegen et al., 1988)—especially how differences in infant temperament influence the development of styles later in childhood (Block, 1993; Caspi, Henry, McGee, Moffitt, & Silva, 1995; Caspi & Silva, 1995; Kagan, 1989).

In general, these studies show that although some stylistic preference is inherited, stylistic inclination clearly develops through interaction with the environment. Early on, parents model and reward certain ways of interacting with the physical and social environment, and children tend to gravitate toward these ways of interacting. At the same time, children have built-in predispositions that constrain how effectively they can adopt these rewarded styles (Sternberg & Grigorenko, 1995). Since various situations reward different styles in different ways, children will moderate their styles depending on how they interpret a given situation and how others react to them (Mischel & Shoda, 1995). Furthermore, differences in temperament will influence the extent to which children actively engage their environment (Caspi & Moffitt, 1995).

For example, Saks (1988) observed 29- to 39-month-old infants perform three tasks: (1) choosing between large or small toy dowels, (2) navigating a maze at different speeds, and (3) spontaneously grouping toys. Mothers were also asked to complete a questionnaire about their children's ability to play alone. A preference for large dowels was found to correlate with broad categorization. Other studies have also shown that children as young as age four have "recognizable" cognitive styles, although styles in both infancy and childhood have sometimes also been correlated with social class (Gjerde, Block, & Block, 1985; Kalyan & Curry, 1987; Kogan, 1976; Saracho, 1992).

Studies of temperament have revealed links between behavioral styles in early childhood and adjustment problems in adolescence (Block, 1993; Thomas & Chess, 1986). More recently, Caspi, Silva, and their associates (Caspi et al., 1995; Caspi & Moffitt, 1995; Caspi & Silva, 1995) conducted a 12-year longitudinal study assessing the relations between early temperament and behavior problems in an unselected sample of over 800 children. Temperament measures (i.e., behavioral styles, or approach and response to novel situations) were abstracted from behavior ratings of children observed at ages 3, 5, 7, and 9. Factor analyses revealed three dimensions at each age: lack of control (which included ratings of emotional lability, restlessness, and negativism); approach (which included ratings of rapid adaptability, extreme friendliness, self-confidence, and self-reliance); and sluggishness (which included ratings of flat affect, passivity, and extreme malleability). Temperament dimensions at ages 3 and 5 were correlated with relevant behavior problems identified by teachers at ages 9 and 11, and by parents at ages 13 and 15. Children characterized by lack of control in early childhood, as adolescents, were more likely to experience internalizing problems and especially externalizing problems such as inattention and hyperactivity. They were also more likely to be overtly aggressive and antisocial (but not necessarily delinquent), compared to those who showed greater control in early childhood. Boys strong on the approach dimension in early childhood were less likely to suffer from anxiety and distress as adolescents, whereas no consistent effect was found for girls. Finally, long term effects of individual differences in sluggishness were more apparent in girls than in boys; although effect sizes were small, girls who scored high on this dimension as children were more likely to suffer from anxiety and distress and to experience attention problems in adolescence.

In further analyses of this data set, Caspi and Silva (1995) identified five clusters of behavioral styles at age three: (1) *undercontrolled* (irritable and distractible children who scored high on lack of control); (2) *inhibited* (high scores on both sluggishness and lack of control); (3) *confident* (high scores on approach); (4) *reserved* (high scores on sluggishness: these children were shy and fearful, but without the impulsiveness of those classified as inhibited); and (5) *well-adjusted* (average scores on all three dimensions). They found that these styles were significantly correlated with self-reports of preferred personality styles in late adolescence as assessed by the Multidimensional Personality Questionnaire (Tellegen, 1982). For example, children classified as undercontrolled as children described themselves as danger-seeking, impulsive, alienated, and prone to negative emotional responses to everyday events. Inhibited children at age three described themselves as restrained in their adult behavior and nonassertive in their interpersonal interactions. The three remaining clusters also showed continuity, but with less striking parallels to their infant behavioral styles (Caspi & Silva, 1995).

Finally, Sternberg and Grigorenko (1995) studied 53 twelve-year-old students at a private secondary school in Connecticut, assessing their thinking styles by using the *Set of Thinking Styles Tasks for Students*. However, whereas students were unable to evaluate their own styles using a second *Thinking Styles Inventory* questionnaire, their teachers were able to accurately describe their thinking styles using a third questionnaire called *Students' Thinking Styles Evaluated by Teachers*. Thus, by 12 years of age, thinking styles are evident to teachers but not to students themselves. Studies of children's theories of mind, mentioned earlier, suggest a promising avenue for future research into the youngest age at which children become aware of their own thinking styles (Chandler & Carpendale, in press; Flavell et al., 1995).

Environmental Influences on the Development of Cognitive Styles

At least four environmental influences are likely to affect the development of thinking styles (Sternberg, 1988c; Sternberg & Grigorenko, 1995).

Gender Role Expectations

Many studies have assessed gender variability in cognitive, learning, and teaching styles (Goldstein & Blackman, 1978). For example, females tend to be more judicial, conservative, and local, whereas males may tend to be more analytic, liberal, and global. Traditional gender role expectations influence patterns of style development, although

few studies have examined the extent to which gender differences in styles reflect biological, social, or cultural influences on development (Sternberg & Grigorenko, 1995).

Parenting Style

A child's cognitive style is likely to reflect what parents encourage and reward. Indeed, parents themselves exhibit styles which children may emulate. Parents who discipline their child in ways that address the larger rather than the smaller issues underlying actions will probably encourage a global style, whereas parents who focus on the details of the situation will probably encourage a local style. Thus, family environment, including parents' education and occupation, should play an important role in the development of children's thinking styles (Bornstein, 1996; Sternberg & Grigorenko, 1995).

Schooling (or Occupation)

Teachers and parents encourage their students to develop legislative, creative powers in the relatively unstructured and open environments of the home and preschool. Once children start elementary school, however, they are expected to become socialized into the largely conforming values of the school. Students who do not follow directions are viewed as undersocialized and even as misfits. Different schools and different occupations reward different styles and so will reinforce their development (Ramsden, 1992). For example, an art student is likely to be rewarded for being legislative and liberal, whereas a history student may be rewarded for demonstrating executive and conservative styles. Ironically, although some professions encourage a legislative style, schooling for such professions may not. For example, high school physics or history courses largely involve having students answer the teacher's questions, but physicists are expected to be more legislative and historians to be more judicial. Sadly, by the time they leave school students may have forgotten how!

Culture

Some cultures tend to reward certain styles more than others. For example, the North American emphasis on innovation may lead to relatively greater rewards for the legislative and liberal styles, at least among adults. Other nations, such as Japan, that emphasize conformity and tradition, may favor more executive and conservative styles (Bornstein, 1996). As mentioned earlier, cultures actively promote different categorization styles (Berry et al., 1986).

CONCLUSIONS AND FUTURE DIRECTIONS

What conclusions can be drawn from this whirlwind tour of the literatures on abilities and styles? One tempting conclusion is that no one knows what to make of either of these two concepts and that different researchers use the same words to mean very different things. A more hopeful conclusion would be to see the many different theories of abilities and styles as each approaching the questions of competence and performance from a variety of angles that are rarely mutually exclusive. In this final section, we conclude by (1) providing an integrative definition of abilities and styles and how they interact, and (2) addressing five key concerns in both the abilities and styles literatures: structure, function, context, development, and education.

Abilities and Styles and How They Are Related

Abilities

Abilities are hypothetical constructs proposed to explain how we adapt flexibly and effectively to different environments. Mental abilities are abilities that require cognitive representation and processing, and for which individual differences in sensory acuity and physical strength or agility generally constitute a small part of the total variance in performance (Jensen & Weng, 1994).

The four major approaches to the study of human mental abilities presented in this chapter—psychometric, information-processing, contextualist, and developmental—have all advanced our understanding of abilities. Within the *psychometric* tradition, measurements of human abilities are usually based on test performance, although some measurements involve judgments or ratings (self-ratings or other-ratings). Typically, tests of human mental abilities in this tradition involve tasks designed to measure a small number of cognitive abilities. Abilities are identified on the basis of correlations of performance across a range of tasks (e.g., tests of basic computational skill and numerical problem solving, to measure mathematical ability). Naturally, the abilities detected depend in part on the nature of the tests included in a given battery. Many ability tests are timed, leading to a possible confound between the speed at which one works and one's level of mastery in dealing with the material (Carroll, 1993; Sternberg, 1996).

Assessments of mental abilities within the *information-processing* tradition have involved three basic approaches: (a) the cognitive-correlates approach, which correlates performance on mental ability tests with theoretically-relevant information-processing tasks (e.g., to account for verbal ability, Hunt (1987) looked at processes such as those involved in recognizing that "A" and "a," despite their difference in physical appearance, represent the same letter); (b) the cognitive-components approach, which develops models of complex tasks by breaking them down into simpler component tasks, such as those involved in the study of verbal (Sternberg, 1987) or numeric (Schoenfeld, 1992) ability; and (c) the cognitive-contents approach, which compares expert and novice performance on some real-life task such as playing music (Ericsson, Krampe, & Tesch-Römer, 1993), reading (Wagner & Stanovich, 1996), or writing (Bryson, Bereiter, Scardamalia, & Jorum, 1991).

Assessments of mental abilities within the *contextualist* approach focus on measuring the impact of different contexts on how well individuals are able to use the same abilities on analogous tasks (Ceci, 1990). A variant of this approach is often used in cross-cultural research, for example, when investigators are examining cultural and contextual differences in classification and problem solving (Berry et al., 1986; Witkin & Goodenough, 1981).

Finally, reflecting a fourth approach to the study of abilities, some psychologists have engaged in a detailed analysis of how knowledge *develops* through the organism's construction of increasingly adaptive knowledge systems (Case, 1992; Fischer, 1980; Piaget, 1970/1983) or through internalizing culturally derived knowledge systems during personally meaningful activity (Bruner, 1996; Rogoff et al., 1993; Vygotsky, 1934/1986).

In order to clarify how abilities are measured within these four traditions, and to show how these measurements are related, consider the example of mathematical ability. From a *psychometric* point of view, mathematical ability is operationally defined in terms of performances requiring it (e.g., a math test). Generalizability can be established by having individuals perform a series of related tasks (e.g., calculating fractions and solving algebra problems) and examining the extent to which scores on different tests are correlated with each other. Highly correlated tasks are viewed as measuring the same, or similar abilities, whereas tasks that are uncorrelated are viewed as measuring different abilities. This procedure allows mathematical ability to be compared across children, and within different samples of children, such as those who differ in genetic makeup, age, sex, or grade level.

From an *information-processing* point of view, mathematical ability can be measured in terms of the availability, activation, and efficacy of component processes, knowledge, and strategies that lead to more or less successful performance (e.g., how actively one monitors problem solving, how well one understands mathematical concepts, or the procedures one uses), or in terms of how differences in prior knowledge affect performance (e.g., differences between mathematicians and individuals who have little training in math).

The *contextualist* approach examines the importance of context to performance (e.g., differences in measured mathematical ability of street vendors when selling their wares and when answering questions on a paper-and-pencil math test). Research has shown that these contextual differences have a marked impact on performance, over and above the covariance structures observed on psychometric tests (Ceci, 1990; Ceci & Roazzi, 1994).

Finally, from a *developmental* perspective, mathematical ability will naturally tend to develop through maturation, experience, and instruction (whether school instruction, apprenticeship, or peer interactions). Beyond these simple observations, however, some theorists postulate additional developmental mechanisms that regulate entire classes of performance. Increasingly, developmental theorists recognize that individuals are predisposed to attend to certain types of information, such as the basic numeric properties of collections of objects (Karmiloff-Smith, 1992; Spelke et al., 1992). These theorists argue that there are qualitative shifts during development; for example, infants in a normal environment become able to speak at about age 2, when no amount of practice would have allowed them to do so a year earlier.

Cognitive Styles

As we have seen, the concept of cognitive style has theoretical roots in many different literatures, making it difficult to provide a clear and concise definition of what exactly is meant by style. The approach to cognitive styles based in psychodynamic *ego psychology* examines how cognitive styles, originally called cognitive attitudes or cognitive controls, relate to other ego structures, such as defense mechanisms and motivational dynamics. In the approach to cognitive styles based in the tradition of *Gestalt psychology,* the key issue concerns stylistic consistency across perceptual or categorization tasks. Finally, in *educational psychology,* learning is influenced by different types of learners, different types of learning activities, and different types of learning context.

Advocates of each of these approaches agree that, in the broadest sense, a style is an integrative construct that relates personality to mental ability (Grigorenko & Sternberg,

1995; Royce & Powell, 1983; Sternberg, 1990a, 1994). Styles involve organizing and control mechanisms that cut across content domains, and express cognition and personality simultaneously. Sometimes these mechanisms are seen through consistent personal preference or ease in different forms of information processing, or in performing different sorts of actions; sometimes they are expressed through individual differences in the preferred structure of the cognitive system itself (e.g., cognitive complexity versus simplicity) (Grigorenko & Sternberg, 1995; Messick, 1987, 1994). In fact, styles may represent an important missing link integrating intelligence, personality, and real-world performance (Royce & Powell, 1983; Sternberg, 1994).

Styles are measured in terms of dominant, preferred, or typical performances. For example, children can use either broad or narrow categories when making perceptual judgments, so consistent use of one or the other is viewed as a difference in style. Styles are also measured in terms of contrasts between performances along a specific stylistic dimension. In this case, children are tested on both extremes of a particular dimension, and their style reflects the type of contrast in which they perform most effectively (Messick, 1994). For example, some children may be able to deal easily with tasks that require the use of broad perceptual categories, but find it quite difficult to use narrow categories. Thus, contrasted measures of performance also demonstrate children's stylistic mobility (Witkin & Goodenough, 1981), that is, the extent to which they can adapt flexibly along a particular stylistic dimension. Most commonly, measures of cognitive style include inventories of behavior (Sternberg, 1994; Sternberg & Grigorenko, 1995; Sternberg & Wagner, 1991), sorting or classification tasks (Kagan, Moss, & Sigel, 1963), or clinical perception tasks, such as identifying embedded figures (Witkin et al., 1971). In some cases, performance measures are used, such as asking children to write an essay on a given theme and then rating the essay for level of cognitive complexity (Suedfeld et al., 1992).

Relations between Abilities and Styles

Ability and style constructs are related in complex ways. Ability refers to the substance and level of performance, while style refers to its manner or form (Messick, 1994; Sternberg, 1994). Cognitive styles mediate and moderate the expression of particular abilities. Thus, styles are not "good" or "bad," but rather, in principle, each pole of a particular style has different adaptive implications. A "good" style facilitates task performance in some situations, but that same style may be a poor fit to others.

Children should find that tasks well-matched to their cognitive style are more intrinsically motivating and interesting than those that are not. Thus, given the same basic level of ability, children whose styles are mismatched to the task should perform less effectively than matched children, depending on how flexible they are in their stylistic preferences, and depending on how strongly motivated they are by contextual demands (Royce & Powell, 1983; Snow, 1994; Witkin & Goodenough, 1981). Children may value and prefer activities that do not make optimal use of their cognitive abilities, or they may not believe that they are capable of performances that they would be able to accomplish. Indeed, personal goals and capacity beliefs often result in consistent orientations in how abilities are used in context (Bandura, 1986, in press; Chiu et al., 1994) that are essentially indistinguishable from ways in which unconscious cognitive styles affect performance. For example, children who believe that they are unable to understand complex issues will consistently seek parsimonious, less differentiated explanations for events, and so will effectively have a less cognitively-complex style.

Certain styles of information processing appear to be favored by particular cultures, and socialization practices work to develop these styles in members of these societies (Berry et al., 1986; Witkin & Goodenough, 1981). After many years of training or schooling in tasks that require a particular style—judgment or analysis, for example—this orientation may become part of one's habitual cognitive style through the effect of repeated practice (Ericsson & Charness, 1994; Ericsson & Lehmann, 1996). Of course, children may deliberately seek out contexts that are well adapted to their temperament and abilities within a culture (Scarr, 1992).

Consider the earlier example of mathematical ability. If a student prefers very abstract and cognitively-complex tasks, she may excel at knot theory because her cognitive style will be well matched to a task that requires the use of mathematical ability to construct very complex mathematical objects. This same student, asked to solve simple equations designed to mirror concrete everyday experiences, may not excel in this context, for which she considers herself unsuited and toward which she is unmotivated. Over time, given the same initial aptitude, a child taught and evaluated in a way that did not match her cognitive style, and to which she was unable or unwilling to adjust, would not develop the same level of ability. The student in the context that matched her style would foster her abilities and become more capable; the mismatched student potentially would become less so.

In sum, mental abilities represent innate proclivities or learned capacities that are unidimensional and value-directional—the more you have of an ability, the better. Individual abilities are typically limited to a fairly specific domain of cognitive functioning or content, for example verbal, spatial, or reasoning ability. Abilities can be invoked deliberately or strategically in answer to the demands set by a particular type of task or according to one's own goals.

By contrast, styles reflect personal predispositions. Cognitive styles are typically bipolar and value-differentiated propensities that often cut across ability, personality, and interpersonal behavior domains. Styles are invoked spontaneously, without conscious strategic choice, in a wide variety of situations with similar information-processing or adaptive requirements, unless compelling situational cues incite one to act differently (Grigorenko & Sternberg, 1995; Messick, 1994).

How abilities are assessed (reaction times, multiple-choice questions, creative essays, verbal interviews, portfolios) may interact with styles to create consistent biases. For this reason, it is important to use different types of assessment when measuring an ability. By always using the same kinds of assessments, we are unwittingly benefiting people with styles that are well-suited to these assessments. In essence, we are confounding abilities with thinking styles which, in principle, are psychologically distinct from them (Sternberg, 1994).

Key Issues in the Study of Ability and Styles

Although abilities and styles have been studied within many different traditions, at least five key issues have been addressed in theory and research on both of these constructs: structure, function, context, development, and education.

Psychometric theories of both abilities and styles have focused on individual differences in how competence and performance are *structured*. Thus, abilities and styles are typically arranged in hierarchical structures of increasing generality. One might also examine the extent to which ability and personality are heritable. To our knowledge, little research has been conducted to determine the relative heritabilities of abilities and styles. These relative heritabilities might be an interesting avenue of research, if only to determine whether the specific predispositions one develops through interactions between ability and personality are as heritable as either ability or personality considered separately. For example, it may be the case that nonshared family environment is even more important in the development of cognitive styles than it is in the development of intellectual ability, or vice versa.

Research on how ability and styles *function* differently during problem solving has received a certain amount of attention in both ability and style literatures. More research needs to be done on the interactions between abilities and styles. It might be especially interesting to examine whether encouraging metacognitive reflection about task requirements, in tasks in which there are several equally valid approaches to problem solving, leads to the development of new strategies, or to an adaptation and modification of stylistic preferences.

The importance of *context* on the use of abilities has shown that ostensibly the same ability can be used more or less effectively, depending upon the specific context in which it is required. Similarly, styles or approaches to learning are also influenced by specific contexts, such as classroom goals, personal goals, and even task-specific appraisals of one's cognitive competence. There has been little research on the question of whether cognitive styles are consistent across contexts involving the same ability (for example, individuals' level of cognitive complexity in evaluating social judgments and in self-evaluation) and at tasks in which they have more or less expertise.

Perhaps one of the most interesting questions about the relationship between abilities and styles concerns their interactions during *development*. As pointed out in our discussion of the development of field articulation, in many cases one pole of a cognitive style (e.g., high levels of cognitive complexity or abstraction) becomes available over the course of development. An interesting topic for future research involves the interaction between the development of abilities and the development of stylistic preferences in different ability domains.

Finally, little research has examined the extent to which abilities and styles interact in *educational* settings. We have pointed out some research that examines the interactions between assessment and styles. It also would be interesting to explore the link between cognitive controls and self-regulation, especially when motivation and personal goals and beliefs have been found to influence self-regulation (Bouffard-Bouchard, Parent, & Larivée, 1991). Many studies have shown that making individuals aware of how to make learning and performance more effective leads people to adopt more efficient performance strategies, if they believe themselves to be personally capable of implementing such strategies. It remains to be seen to what extent these findings concerning specific task perfor-

mances are applicable to the general constructs of abilities and styles.

As mentioned earlier, contrasts between abilities and styles often involve specifying the differences between the content of performance and the manner in which a given performance is carried out. However, this original view of the distinction between abilities and styles is heavily steeped in the psychometric conception of these two concepts. When cognitive, contextual, and developmental views of abilities are taken into account, the old distinction between abilities and styles becomes much less clear. One important task, perhaps the most important, is to study ability and styles within a unified framework in which styles are viewed as pervasive moderators of performance. But styles also have to be understood in light of other powerful moderators, such as context, level of development, and level of expertise. Measurements need to be taken across a wide range of tasks assessing both types of ability (for example those proposed by the theory of multiple intelligences) and uses of ability (such as different profiles of mental self-government).

The development of a more integrated theory-based measurement of abilities and styles will lead to a more complete understanding of what determines performance in academic and real-world contexts. It thus will be of both theoretical and practical benefit. The theoretical benefit will be a better understanding of how competence and performance are influenced by biological proclivities, level of cognitive development, personal effort, and culture. The practical benefit of such knowledge will lie in improved assessment of ability that better predicts academic achievement and job performance under a range of conditions. Understanding how children develop as individuals requires new theories of intelligence that integrate children's mental abilities and styles into a unified framework, one that coordinates genetic and situation-specific influences on mental development. Armed with such theories, researchers can begin to acquire deeper insight into how and why some children develop to the best of their potential while, sadly, others do not.

REFERENCES

Aldhous, P. (1992). The promise and pitfalls of molecular genetics. *Science, 257,* 164–165.

Alexander, J. M., Carr, M., & Schwanenflugel, P. J. (1995). Development of metacognition in gifted children: Directions for future research. *Developmental Review, 15,* 1–37.

Alexander, J. M., & Schwanenflugel, P. J. (1994). Strategy regulation: The role of intelligence, metacognitive attributions, and knowledge base. *Developmental Psychology, 30,* 709–723.

Allport, G. W. (1937). *Personality, a psychological interpretation.* New York: Henry Holt.

Ames, C. (1992). Classrooms: Goals, structures, and student motivation. *Journal of Educational Psychology, 84,* 261–271.

Ames, C., & Archer, J. (1988). Achievement goals in the classroom: Students' learning strategies and motivation processes. *Journal of Educational Psychology, 80,* 260–267.

Anderson, J. R., & Thompson, R. (1989). Use of analogy in a production system architecture. In S. Vosniadou & A. Ortony (Eds.), *Similarity and analogical reasoning* (pp. 267–297). Cambridge, MA: Cambridge University Press.

Aristotle. (1984). In J. Barnes (Ed.), *The complete works of Aristotle: The revised Oxford translation* (Vol. 2, Bollingen series 71.2). Princeton, NJ: Princeton University Press. (Original work written circa ~300)

Bandura, A. (1986). *Social foundations of thought and action: A social cognitive theory.* Englewood Cliffs, NJ: Prentice-Hall.

Bandura, A. (in press). *Self-efficacy: The exercise of control.* New York: Freeman.

Bargar, R. R., & Hoover, R. L. (1984). Psychological type and the matching of cognitive styles. *Theory into Practice, 23*(1), 56–63.

Ben-Zeev, T. (1995). The nature and origin of rational errors in arithmetic thinking: Induction from examples and prior knowledge. *Cognitive Science, 19,* 341–376.

Berry, J. W., van de Koppel, J. M. H., Senechal, C., Annis, R. C., Bahuchet, S., Cavalli-Sforza, L. L., & Witkin, H. A. (1986). *On the edge of the forest: Cultural adaptation and cognitive development in Central Africa.* Lisse, The Netherlands: Swets & Zeitlinger.

Best, D. L., & Ornstein, P. A. (1986). Children's generation and communication of mnemonic organizational strategies. *Developmental Psychology, 22,* 845–853.

Biggs, J. G. (1985). The role of metalearning in study processes. *British Journal of Educational Psychology, 55,* 185–212.

Binet, A., & Simon, T. (1905). Methodes nouvelles pour le diagnostic du niveau intellectuel des anormaux. *L'Année Psychologique, 11,* 191–336.

Binet, A., & Simon, T. (1908). Le développement de l'intelligence chez les enfants (The development of intelligence in children). *L'Année Psychologique, 14,* 1–94.

Bisanz, J., Morrison, F. J., & Dunn, M. (1995). Effects of age and schooling on the acquisition of elementary quantitative skills. *Developmental Psychology, 31,* 221–236.

Block, J. (1993). Studying personality the long way. In D. Funder, R. D. Parke, & K. Widaman (Eds.), *Studying lives through time: Personality and development* (pp. 9–41). Washington, DC: American Psychological Association.

Boring, E. G. (1950). *A history of experimental psychology* (2nd ed.). New York: Appleton-Century-Crofts.

Borkowski, J. B., Carr, M., Rellinger, E., & Pressley, M. (1990). Self-regulated cognition: Independence of metacognition, attributions, and self-esteem. In B. F. Jones & L. Idol (Eds.), *Dimensions of thinking and cognitive instruction* (pp. 53–92). Hillsdale, NJ: Erlbaum.

Bornstein, M. (1996, March). *Some cross-cultural perspectives on parenting.* Invited address to the department of psychology at Yale University.

Bouchard, T. J., Jr., Lykken, D. T., McGue, M., Segal, N. L., & Tellegen, A. (1990). Sources of human psychological differences: The Minnesota study of twins reared apart. *Science, 250,* 223–228.

Bouchard, T. J., Jr., & McGue, M. (1981). Familial studies of intelligence: A review. *Science, 212,* 1055–1059.

Bouffard, T., Boisvert, J., Vezeau, C., & Larouche, C. (1995). The impact of goal orientation on self-regulation and performance among college students. *British Journal of Educational Psychology, 65,* 317–329.

Bouffard, T., & Vezeau, C. (in press). The development of the self-system and self-regulation among primary school children. In M. Ferrari & R. J. Sternberg (Eds.), *Self-awareness: Its nature and development.* New York: Guilford Press.

Bouffard-Bouchard, T., Parent, S., & Larivée, S. (1991). Influence of self-efficacy on self-regulation and performance among junior and senior high-school age students. *International Journal of Behavioral Development, 14,* 153–164.

Braine, M. (1990). The "natural-logic" approach to reasoning. In W. Overton (Ed.), *Reasoning, necessity and logic: Developmental perspectives.* Hillsdale, NJ: Erlbaum.

Briars, D., & Siegler, R. S. (1984). A featural analysis of preschooler's counting knowledge. *Developmental Psychology, 20,* 607–618.

Brewer, W., & Samarapungavan, A. (1991). Children's theories vs. scientific theories: Differences in reasoning or differences in knowledge? In R. Hoffman & D. Palermo (Eds.), *Cognition and the symbolic processes.* Hillsdale, NJ: Erlbaum.

Bronfenbrenner, U., & Ceci, S. J. (1993). Heredity, environment, and the question "how?": A first approximation. In R. Plomin & G. McClearn (Eds.), *Nature, nurture, and psychology* (pp. 313–325). Washington, DC: American Psychological Association.

Brown, A. L. (1978). Knowing when, where, and how to remember: A problem of metacognition. In R. Glaser (Ed.), *Advances in instructional psychology* (Vol. 1). Hillsdale, NJ: Erlbaum.

Brown, A. L. (1987). Metacognition, executive control, self-regulation, and other more mysterious mechanisms. In F. E. Weinert & R. H. Kluwe (Eds.), *Metacognition, motivation, and understanding* (pp. 65–116). Hillsdale, NJ: Erlbaum.

Bruner, J. (1996). *The culture of education.* Cambridge, MA: Harvard University Press.

Bryson, M., Bereiter, C., Scardamalia, M., & Jorum, E. (1991). Going beyond the problem as given: Problem solving in expert and novice writers. In R. J. Sternberg & P. A. Frensch (Eds.), *Complex problem solving: Principles and mechanisms* (pp. 61–84). Hillsdale, NJ: Erlbaum.

Burt, C. (1911). Experimental tests of higher mental processes and their relation to general intelligence. *Journal of Experimental Pedagogy, 1,* 93–112.

Burt, C. (1949). The structure of the mind: A review of the results of factor analysis. *British Journal of Educational Psychology, 19,* 100–111, 176–199.

Byrne, M. J. (1994). Reasoning, deductive. In R. J. Sternberg (Ed.), *Encyclopedia of human intelligence* (Vol. 1, pp. 930–935). New York: Macmillan.

Campbell, J. (1988). *Historical atlas of world mythology.* Perennial Library. New York: Harper & Row.

Cardon, L. R., & Fulker, D. W. (1993). The genetics of specific cognitive abilities. In R. Plomin & G. E. McClearn (Eds.), *Nature, nurture, and psychology* (pp. 99–120). Washington, DC: American Psychological Association.

Cardon, L. R., & Fulker, D. W. (1994). A model of developmental change in hierarchical phenotypes with application to specific cognitive abilities. *Behavior Genetics, 24,* 1–16.

Carey, S. (1985). *Conceptual change in childhood.* Cambridge, MA: MIT Press.

Carroll, J. B. (1993). *Human cognitive abilities: A survey of factor-analytic studies.* Cambridge, England: Cambridge University Press.

Carroll, J. B. (1996). Mathematical abilities: Some results from factor analysis. In R. J. Sternberg & T. Ben-Zeev (Eds.), *The nature of mathematical thinking* (pp. 3–25). Mahwah, NJ: Erlbaum.

Case, R. (1992). *The mind's staircase: Exploring the underpinnings of children's thought and knowledge.* Hillsdale, NJ: Erlbaum.

Case, R., & Okamoto, Y. (1996). The role of central conceptual structures in the development of children's literary, numerical, and spatial thought. *Monographs of the Society for Research in Child Development, 61*(1/2, Serial No. 246).

Caspi, A., Henry, B., McGee, R. O., Moffitt, T. E., & Silva, P. A. (1995). Temperamental origins and adolescent behavior problems: From age three to age fifteen. *Child Development, 66,* 55–68.

Caspi, A., & Moffitt, T. E. (1995). The continuity of maladaptive behavior. In D. Cicchetti & D. Cohen (Eds.), *Manual of developmental psychopathology: Vol. 2. Risk, disorder, and adaptation* (pp. 472–511). New York: Wiley.

Caspi, A., & Silva, P. A. (1995). Temperamental qualities at age three predict personality traits in young adulthood: Longitudinal evidence from a birth cohort. *Child Development, 66,* 486–498.

Cattell, R. B. (1943). The measurement of adult intelligence. *Psychological Bulletin, 40,* 153–193.

Cattell, R. B. (1987). *Abilities: Their structure, growth, and action* (Rev. ed.). Amsterdam, The Netherlands: North-Holland.

Ceci, S. J. (1990). *On intelligence . . . more or less: A bio-ecological treatise on intellectual development.* Englewood Cliffs, NJ: Prentice-Hall.

Ceci, S. J. (1994). Bioecological theory of intellectual development. In R. J. Sternberg (Ed.), *Encyclopedia of human intelligence* (Vol. 1, pp. 189–193). New York: Macmillan.

Ceci, S. J., & Bronfenbrenner, U. (1985). Don't forget to take the cupcakes out of the oven: Strategic time-monitoring, prospective memory and context. *Child Development, 56,* 175–190.

Ceci, S. J., & Liker, J. (1986). A day at the races: A study of IQ, cognitive complexity, and expertise. *Journal of Experimental Psychology: General, 115,* 255–266.

Ceci, S. J., & Roazzi, A. (1994). The effects of context on cognition: Postcards from Brazil. In R. J. Sternberg & R. K. Wagner (Eds.), *Mind in context* (pp. 74–99). New York: Cambridge University Press.

Chandler, M., & Carpendale, J. I. (in press). Inching toward a mature theory of mind. In M. Ferrari & R. J. Sternberg (Eds.), *Self-awareness: Its nature and development.* New York: Guilford Press.

Chen, C., & Stevenson, H. W. (1995). Motivation and mathematics achievement: A comparative study of Asian-American, Caucasian-American, and East Asian high school students. *Child Development, 66,* 1215–1234.

Cheng, P., & Holyoak, K. J. (1985). Pragmatic reasoning schemas. *Cognitive Psychology, 17,* 391–416.

Chi, M. T. H. (1992). Conceptual change within and across ontological categories: Examples from learning and discovery in science. In R. Giere (Ed.), *Cognitive models of science.* Minneapolis: University of Minnesota Press.

Chi, M. T. H. (1997). Creativity: Shifting across ontological categories flexibly. In T. B. Ward, S. M. Smith, & J. Vaid (Eds.), *Creative thought: An investigation of conceptual structures and processes* (pp. 209–234). Washington, DC: American Psychological Association.

Chi, M. T. H., Glaser, R., & Farr, M. J. (Eds.). (1988). *The nature of expertise.* Hillsdale, NJ: Erlbaum.

Chi, M. T. H., Hutchinson, J., & Robin, A. F. (1989). How inferences about novel domain-related concepts can be constrained by structured knowledge. *Merrill-Palmer Quarterly, 25*, 27–62.

Chi, M. T. H., & Koeske, R. D. (1983). Network representations of a child's dinosaur knowledge. *Developmental Psychology, 19*, 29–39.

Chipuer, H. M., Rovine, M. J., & Plomin, R. (1990). LISREL modeling: Genetic and environmental influences revisited. *Intelligence, 14*, 11–29.

Chiu, C., Hong, Y., & Dweck, C. S. (1994). Toward an integrative model of personality and intelligence: A general framework and some preliminary steps. In R. J. Sternberg & P. Ruzgis (Eds.), *Personality and intelligence* (pp. 104–134). New York: Cambridge University Press.

Corbo, M. (1982). *Reading style inventory (RSI)*. Roslyn Heights, New York: Learning Research Associates.

Corbo, M. (1988). *Reading style inventory manual.* Roslyn Heights, New York: Learning Research Associates.

Corno, L., & Kanfer, R. (1993). The role of volition in learning and performance. In L. Darling-Hammond (Ed.), *Review of research in education* (Vol. 19, pp. 301–341). Washington, DC: American Educational Research Association.

Cronbach, L. J., & Snow, R. E. (1977). *Aptitudes and instructional methods.* New York: Wiley.

Cross, S. E., & Markus, H. R. (1994). Self-schemas, possible selves, and competent performance. *Journal of Educational Psychology, 86*, 423–438.

Davis, J. K. (1991). Educational implications of field dependence-independence. In S. Wapner & J. Demick (Eds.), *Field dependence-independence: Cognitive styles across the lifespan* (pp. 149–176). Hillsdale, NJ: Erlbaum.

Davis, J. K., & Cochran, K. F. (1989). An information-processing view of field dependence-independence. *Early Child Development and Care, 51*, 31–47.

Deary, I. J. (1994). Sensory discrimination and intelligence: Postmortem or resurrection? *American Journal of Psychology, 107*, 95–115.

Deci, E. L., & Ryan, R. M. (1991). A motivational approach to self: Integration in personality. In R. A. Dienstbier (Ed.), *Perspectives on motivation: Nebraska Symposium on Motivation 1990* (Vol. 38, pp. 237–288). Hillsdale, NJ: Erlbaum.

DeFries, J. C., Plomin, R., & Fulker, D. W. (1994). *Nature and nurture during middle childhood.* Cambridge, MA: Blackwell.

Delclos, V. R., & Harrington, C. (1991). Effects of strategy monitoring and proactive instruction on children's problem-solving performance. *Journal of Educational Psychology, 83*, 35–42.

Dreyfus, T., & Eisenberg, T. (1996). On different facets of mathematical thinking. In R. Sternberg & T. Ben Zeev (Eds.), *The nature of mathematical thinking* (pp. 253–284). Mahwah, NJ: Erlbaum.

Duda, J. L., & Nicholls, J. G. (1992). Dimensions of achievement motivation in schoolwork and sport. *Journal of Education Psychology, 84*, 290–299.

Dunlosky, J., & Nelson, T. O. (1994). Does the sensitivity of judgments of learning (JOLs) to the effects of various study activities depend on when the JOLs occur? *Journal of Memory and Language, 33*, 545–565.

Dunn, R. (1988). Teaching students through their perceptual strengths or preferences. *Journal of Reading, 31*, 304–309.

Dunn, R., Beaudry, J. S., & Klavas, A. (1989). Survey of research on learning styles. *Educational Leadership, 46*, 50–58.

Dunn, R., & Dunn, K. (1978). *Teaching students through their individual learning styles: A practical approach.* Reston, VA: Reston.

Dunn, R., Dunn, K., & Price, K. (1979). *Learning Style Inventory (LSI) for students in grades 3–12.* Manual.

Dweck, C. S. (1986). Motivational processes affecting learning. *American Psychologist, 41*, 1040–1048.

Dweck, C. S. (1991). *Self-theories and goals: Their role in motivation, personality, and development. Nebraska Symposium on Motivation, 1990* (pp. 199–235). Lincoln: University of Nebraska Press.

Dweck, C. S., & Leggett, E. L. (1988). A social cognitive approach to motivation and personality. *Psychological Review, 95*, 256–273.

Efklides, A., Demetriou, A., & Metallidou, Y. (1994). The structure and development of propositional reasoning ability: Cognitive and metacognitive aspects. In A. Demetriou & A. Efklides (Eds.), *Intelligence, mind, and reasoning: Structure and development* (pp. 151–173). Amsterdam, The Netherlands: North-Holland.

Egorova, M. S. (1987). Genetic factors in interpersonal variance of field dependence-independence indicators. *Activatas Nervosa Superior, 29*(1), 19–22.

Emory, U. (1983). Maternal teaching styles, children's response patterns, and mother-child reflection-impulsivity. *Journal of Genetic Psychology, 142*, 315–316.

Ericsson, K. A., & Charness, N. (1994). Expert performance: Its structure and acquisition. *American Psychologist, 49*, 725–745.

Ericsson, K. A., Krampe, R. T., & Tesch-Römer, C. (1993). The role of deliberate practice in the acquisition of expert performance. *Psychological Review, 100*, 363–406.

Ericsson, K. A., & Lehmann, A. C. (1996). Expert and exceptional performance: Evidence of maximal adaptation to task constraints. *Annual Review of Psychology, 47,* 273–305.

Fayol, M., Abdi, H., & Gombert, J. E. (1987). Arithmetic problems formulation and working memory load. *Cognition and Instruction, 4,* 187–202.

Feldman, D. H. (1991). *Nature's gambit.* New York: Teachers College Press. (Original work published 1986)

Feldman, D. H. (1993). *Beyond universals in cognitive development* (2nd ed.). Norwood, NJ: ABLEX.

Ferrari, M., (1996). Observing the observer: Self-regulation in the observational learning of motor skills. *Developmental Review, 16,* 203–240.

Ferrari, M., & Sternberg, R. J. (Eds.) (in press). *Self-awareness: Its nature and development.* New York: Guilford Press.

Fischer, B. B., & Fischer, L. (1979). Styles in teaching and learning. *Educational Leadership, 36*(4), 245–254.

Fischer, K. W. (1980). A theory of cognitive development: The control and construction of hierarchies of skills. *Psychological Review, 87,* 477–531.

Flavell, J. H. (1976). Metacognitive aspects of problem solving. In L. B. Resnick (Ed.), *The nature of intelligence* (pp. 231–235). Hillsdale, NJ: Erlbaum.

Flavell, J. H., Green, F. L., & Flavell, E. R. (1993). Children's understanding of the stream of consciousness. *Child Development, 64,* 387–398.

Flavell, J. H., Green, F. L., & Flavell, E. R. (1995). Young children's knowledge about thinking. *Monographs of the Society for Research in Child Development, 60*(1, Serial No. 243).

Flynn, J. R. (1987). Massive IQ gains in 14 nations: What IQ tests really measure. *Psychological Bulletin, 101,* 171–191.

Fodor, J. A. (1983). *The modularity of mind.* Cambridge, MA: MIT Press.

Gaines, B. R., & Shaw, M. I. G. (1980). New directions in the analysis and interactive elicitation of personal construct systems. *International Journal of Man-Machine Studies, 13,* 81–116.

Gaines, B. R., & Shaw, M. I. G. (1992). Integrated knowledge acquisition architectures. *Journal for Intelligent Information Systems, 1*(1), 9–34.

Gallistel, C. R., & Gelman, R. (1992). Preverbal and verbal counting and computation. *Cognition, 44,* 43–74.

Galton, F. (1869). *Hereditary genius: An enquiry into its laws and consequences.* London: Collins.

Galton, F. (1883). *Inquiries into human faculty and its development.* London: Macmillan.

Gardner, H. (1993a). *Frames of mind* (10th anniversary ed.). New York: Basic Books.

Gardner, H. (1993b). *Multiple intelligences: The theory in practice.* New York: Basic Books.

Gardner, H. (1995). Reflections on multiple intelligences: Myths and messages. *Phi Delta Kappan, 77,* 200–209.

Gardner, H. (1997, April). *How are kids smart?* Third Horace Mann Lecture to the University of Pittsburgh School of Education, Pittsburgh.

Gardner, R. W., Holzman, P. S., Klein, G. S., Linton, H., & Spence, D. P. (1959). Cognitive control: A study of individual consistencies in cognitive behavior. *Psychological Issues, 1*(4).

Gardner, R. W., & Schoen, R. A. (1962). Differentiation and abstraction in concept formation. *Psychological Monographs, 76.*

Geary, D. C. (1993). Mathematical disabilities: Cognitive, neuropsychological, and genetic components. *Psychological Bulletin, 114,* 345–362.

Geary, D. C. (1996). Biology, culture, and cross-national differences in mathematical ability. In R. Sternberg & T. Ben Zeev (Eds.), *The nature of mathematical thinking* (pp. 145–171). Mahwah, NJ: Erlbaum.

Geary, D. C., Bow-Thomas, C. C., & Yao, Y. (1992). Counting knowledge and skill in cognitive addition: A comparison of normal and mathematically disabled children. *Journal of Experimental Child Psychology, 54,* 372–391.

Gelman, R., & Gallistel, C. R. (1978). *The child's understanding of number.* Cambridge, MA: Harvard University Press.

Gjerde, P. F., Block, J., & Block, J. H. (1985). Longitudinal consistency of Matching Familiar Figures Test performance from early childhood to preadolescence. *Developmental Psychology, 21,* 262–271.

Globerson, T., & Zelniker, T. (Eds.). (1989). *Cognitive style and cognitive development.* Norwood, NJ: ABLEX.

Goldsmith, H. H. (1993). Nature–nurture issues in the behavioral genetics context: Overcoming barriers to the communication. In R. Plomin & G. E. McClearn (Eds.), *Nature, nurture, and psychology* (pp. 325–339). Washington, DC: American Psychological Association.

Goldstein, K. M., & Blackman, S. (1978). *Cognitive style.* New York: Wiley.

Goodenough, D. R., Oltman, P. K., Snow, D., Cox, P. W., & Markowits, D. (1991). Field dependence–independence and embedded figures performance. In S. Wapner & J. Demick (Eds.), *Field dependence–independence: Cognitive styles across the lifespan* (pp. 131–148). Hillsdale, NJ: Erlbaum.

Gopnik, A., & Graf, P. (1988). Knowing how you know: Young children's ability to identify and remember the sources of their beliefs. *Child Development, 59,* 1366–1371.

Gottlieb, G. (1995). Some conceptual deficiencies in "developmental" behavior genetics. *Human Development, 38,* 131–141.

Graesser, A. C., & McMahen, C. L. (1993). Anomalous information triggers questions when adults solve quantitative problems and comprehend stories. *Journal of Educational Psychology, 85,* 136–151.

Granott, N., & Gardner, H. (1994). When minds meet: Interactions, coincidence, and development in domains of ability. In R. J. Sternberg & R. K. Wagner (Eds.), *Mind in context: Interactionist perspectives on human intelligence* (pp. 171–201). New York: Cambridge University Press.

Gregorc, A. F. (1979). Learning/teaching styles: Potent forces behind them. *Educational Leadership, 36*(4), 234–236.

Grigorenko, E., LaBuda, M. C., & Carter, A. S. (1992). Similarity in general cognitive ability, creativity, and cognitive styles in a sample of adolescent Russian twins. *Acta Geneticae Medicae Gemellollogiae, 41,* 65–72.

Grigorenko, E., & Sternberg, R. J. (1995). Thinking styles. In D. H. Saklofske & M. Zeidner (Eds.), *International handbook of personality and intelligence* (pp. 205–229). New York: Plenum Press.

Groen, G. J., & Parkman, J. M. (1972). A chronometric analysis of simple addition. *Psychological Review, 70,* 329–343.

Guilford, J. P. (1967). *The nature of human intelligence.* New York: McGraw-Hill.

Gustafsson, J. E. (1984). A unifying model for the structure of intellectual abilities. *Intelligence, 8,* 179–203.

Gustafsson, J. E. (1994). Hierarchical models of intelligence and educational achievement. In G. E. Stelmach & P. A. Vroon (Vol. Eds.) & A. Demetriou & A. Efklides (Eds.), *Advances in psychology 106. Intelligence, mind, and reasoning: Structure and development* (pp. 45–73). New York: Elsevier Science.

Hagberg, J. O., & Leider, R. J. (1978). *The inventurers: Excursions in life and career renewal.* Reading, MA: Addison-Wesley.

Hala, S., Chandler, M., & Fritz, A. S. (1991). Fledgling theories of mind: Deception as a marker of three-year-olds' understanding of false belief. *Child Development, 62,* 83–97.

Halford, G. S. (1982). *The development of thought.* Hillsdale, NJ: Erlbaum.

Harvey, O. J., Hunt, D. E., & Schroeder, H. M. (1961). *Conceptual systems and personality organization.* New York: Wiley.

Hegarty, M., Mayer, R. E., & Monk, C. A. (1995). Comprehension of arithmetic word problems. *Journal of Educational Psychology, 87,* 18–32.

Holland, J. H., Holyoak, K. L., Nisbett, R. E., & Thagard, P. R. (1986). *Induction: Processes of inference, learning, and discovery.* Cambridge, MA: MIT Press.

Holyoak, K. L., & Thagard, P. (1997). The analogical mind. *American Psychologist, 52,* 35–44.

Homer. (1990). *The Iliad* (R. Fagles, Trans.). New York: Viking. (Original work written ~800)

Horn, J. L. (1968). Organization of abilities and the development of intelligence. *Psychological Review, 79,* 242–259.

Horn, J. L. (1994). Theory of fluid and crystallized intelligence. In R. J. Sternberg (Ed.), *The encyclopedia of intelligence* (Vol. 1, pp. 443–451). New York: Macmillan.

Horn, J. L., & Cattell, R. B. (1966). Refinement and test of the theory of fluid and crystallized intelligence. *Journal of Educational Psychology, 57,* 253–270.

Horn, J. L., & Hofer, S. M. (1992). Major abilities and development in the adult period. In R. J. Sternberg & C. A. Berg (Eds.), *Intellectual development* (pp. 44–99). New York: Cambridge University Press.

Horn, J. L., & Stankov, L. (1982). Auditory and visual factors of intelligence. *Intelligence, 6,* 165–185.

Horowitz, F. D. (1993). The need for a comprehensive new environmentalism. In R. Plomin & G. E. McClearn (Eds.), *Nature, nurture, and psychology* (pp. 341–353). Washington, DC: American Psychological Association.

Hunt, E. B. (1987). The next word on verbal ability. In P. A. Vernon (Ed.), *Speed of information processing and intelligence* (pp. 347–392). Norwood, NJ: ABLEX.

Hyman, R., & Rosoff, B. (1984). Matching learning and teaching styles: The jug and what's in it. *Theory and Practice, 23*(1), 35–43.

Inhelder, B., & Cellérier, G. (in press). *Children's journeys to discovery* (T. Brown, E. Ackermann, & M. Ferrari, Trans.). Hillsdale, NJ: Erlbaum. (Original work published 1992)

Jensen, A. R. (1997). The puzzle of nongenetic variance. In R. J. Sternberg & E. L. Grigorenko (Eds.), *Intelligence, heredity and environment* (pp. 42–88). New York: Cambridge University Press.

Jensen, A. R., & Weng, L. (1994). What is good g. *Intelligence, 18,* 231–258.

Johnson, R. C., McClearn, G. E., Yuen, S., Nagoshi, C. T., Ahern, F. M., & Cole, R. E. (1985). Galton's data a century later. *American Psychologist, 40,* 875–892.

Johnson-Laird, P. N. (1983). *Mental models.* Cambridge, England: Cambridge University Press.

Johnson-Laird, P. N. (1993). *Human and machine thinking.* Hillsdale, NJ: Erlbaum.

Johnson-Laird, P. N., & Byrne, R. M. J. (1991). *Deduction.* Hillsdale, NJ: Erlbaum.

Johnson-Laird, P. N., Byrne, R. M. J., & Schaeken, W. (1992). Propositional reasoning by model. *Psychological Review, 99,* 418–439.

Jung, C. (1923). *Psychological types.* New York: Harcourt Brace.

Kagan, J. (1989). *Unstable ideas: Temperament, cognition, and self.* Cambridge, MA: Harvard University Press.

Kagan, J., & Kogan, N. (1970). Individual variation in cognitive processes. In P. A. Mussen (Ed.), *Carmichael's manual of child psychology* (Vol. 1). New York: Wiley.

Kagan, J., Moss, H. A., & Sigel, I. E. (1963). Psychological significance of types of conceptualization. *Monographs of the Society for Research in Child Development, 28*(2, Serial No. 86).

Kalyan, M. V., & Curry, E. (1987). Cognitive performance and cognitive style of young children. *Perceptual and Motor Skills, 65,* 571–579.

Karmiloff-Smith, A. (1992). *Beyond modularity: A developmental perspective on cognitive science.* Cambridge, MA: MIT Press.

Keil, F. C. (1989). *Concepts, kinds, and cognitive development.* Cambridge, MA: MIT Press.

Kelly, G. A. (1955). *The psychology of personal constructs* (2 vols.). New York: Norton.

Kihlstrom, J. (1987). The cognitive unconscious. *Science, 237,* 1445–1452.

Kirton, M. J. (1976). Adaptors and innovators: A description and measure. *Journal of Applied Psychology, 61,* 622–629.

Kirton, M. J. (1977). *Research edition: Kirton adaptation-innovation inventory [KAI].* London: National Federation for Educational Research.

Klein, G. S. (1954). Need and regulation. In M. R. Jones (Ed.), *Nebraska Symposium on Motivation.* Lincoln: University of Nebraska Press.

Klein, G. S. (1958). Cognitive control and motivation. In G. Linzay (Ed.), *Assessment of human motives* (pp. 87–118). New York: Holt, Rinehart and Winston.

Klein, G. S., & Schlesinger, H. J. (1949). Where is the perceiver in perceptual theory? *Journal of Personality, 18,* 32–57.

Kogan, N. (1976). *Cognitive styles in infancy and early childhood.* New York: Wiley.

Kogan, N. (1983). Stylistic variation in childhood and adolescence: Creativity, metaphor, and cognitive style. In P. H. Mussen (Series Ed.) & J. J. Flavell & E. M. Markman (Vol. Eds.), *Handbook of child psychology: Vol. 3. Cognitive development* (4th ed., pp. 630–706). New York: Wiley.

Kogan, N., & Block, J. (1991). Field dependence-independence from early childhood through adolescence: Personality and socialization aspects. In S. Wapner & J. Demick (Eds.), *Field dependence-independence: Cognitive styles across the lifespan* (pp. 177–208). Hillsdale, NJ: Erlbaum.

Kolb, D. A. (1977). *Learning style inventory: A self-description of preferred learning modes.* Boston: McBer.

Kolb, D. A. (1978). *Learning Style Inventory technical manual.* Boston: McBer.

Kolb, D. A., Reuben, I. M., & McIntyre, J. M. (1979). *Organizational psychology: An experimental approach* (3rd ed.). Englewood Cliffs, NJ: Prentice-Hall.

Kuhl, J. (1985). Volitional mediators of cognition-behavior consistency: Self-regulatory processes and action versus state orientation. In J. Kuhl & J. Beckmann (Eds.), *Action control: From action to behavior.* West Berlin: Springer-Verlag.

Kuhn, D., Garcia-Mila, M., Zohar, Z., & Andersen, C. (1995). Strategies of knowledge acquisition. *Monographs of the Society for Research in Child Development, 60*(4, Serial No. 245), 1–127.

Lawrence, G. W. (1982). *People type and tiger stripes.* Gainesville, FL: Center for the Application of Psychological Type.

Lawson, A. E., & Thompson, L. D. (1988). Formal reasoning ability and misconceptions concerning genetics and natural selection. *Journal of Research in Science Teaching, 25,* 733–746.

Leslie, S. (1994). Reasoning models and intellectual development. In A. Demetriou & A. Efklides (Eds.), *Intelligence, mind and reasoning: Structure and development* (pp. 173–190). New York: North-Holland.

Lewin, K. (1935). *A dynamic theory of personality.* New York: McGraw-Hill.

Lewis, A. B., & Mayer, R. E. (1987). Students' misconceptions of relational statements in arithmetic word problems. *Journal of Educational Psychology, 79,* 363–371.

Lewis, M. B., & Anderson, J. R. (1985). Discrimination of operator schemata in problem solving: Learning from examples. *Cognitive Psychology, 17,* 26–65.

Loehlin, J. C. (1994). Genetics, behavior. In R. J. Sternberg (Ed.), *Encyclopedia of human intelligence* (Vol. 1, pp. 475–483). New York: Macmillan.

Loehlin, J. C., & DeFries, J. C. (1987). Genotype-environment correlation and IQ. *Behavior Genetics, 17,* 263–277.

Loehlin, J. C., Horn, J. M., & Willerman, L. (1989). Modeling IQ change: Evidence from the Texas Adoption Project. *Child Development, 60,* 993–1004.

Lykken, D. T., McGue, M., Tellegen, A., & Bouchard, T. J. (1992). Emergenesis: Genetic traits that may not run in families. *American Psychologist, 47,* 1565–1577.

MacLeod, C. M., Jackson, R. A., & Palmer, J. (1986). On the relation between spatial ability and field dependence. *Intelligence, 10,* 141–151.

Markovits, H., & Nantel, G. (1989). The belief bias effect in the production and evaluation of logical syllogisms. *Memory and Cognition, 17,* 11–17.

Markovits, H., & Savary, F. (1992). Pragmatic schemas and the selection task: To reason or not to reason. *The Quarterly Journal of Experimental Psychology, 45A,* 133–148.

Marsh, H. W. (1992). Content specificity of relations between academic achievement and academic self-concept. *Journal of Educational Psychology, 84,* 35–42.

Marton, F., & Säljö, R. (1976a). On qualitative differences in learning: 1. Outcome and process. *British Journal of Educational Psychology, 46,* 4–11.

Marton, F., & Säljö, R. (1976b). On qualitative differences in learning: 2. Outcome as a function of the learner's conception of the task. *British Journal of Educational Psychology, 46,* 115–127.

Mayer, R. E., & Hegarty, M. (1996). The process of understanding mathematical problems. In R. Sternberg & T. Ben Zeev (Eds.), *The nature of mathematical thinking* (pp. 29–54). Mahwah, NJ: Erlbaum.

Mazzoni, G., & Nelson, T. O. (1995). Judgments of learning are affected by the kind of encoding in ways that cannot be attributed to the level of recall. *Journal of Experimental Psychology: Learning, Memory, and Cognition, 21,* 1263–1274.

McGue, M., Bouchard, T. J., Iacono, W. J., & Lykken, D. T. (1993). Behavioral genetics of cognitive ability: A life-span perspective. In R. Plomin & G. E. McClearn (Eds.), *Nature, nurture, and psychology* (pp. 59–76). Washington, DC: American Psychological Association.

Mead, A. D., & Drasgow, F. (1993). Equivalence of computerized and paper-and-pencil cognitive ability tests: A meta-analysis. *Psychological Bulletin, 114,* 449–458.

Messick, S. (1987). Structural relationships across cognition, personality, and style. In R. E. Snow & M. J. Farr (Eds.), *Aptitude, learning, and instruction: Vol. 3. Conative and affective process analysis* (pp. 35–75). Hillsdale, NJ: Erlbaum.

Messick, S. (1994). The matter of style: Manifestations of personality in cognition, learning, and teaching. *Educational Psychologist, 29,* 121–136.

Miller, A. (1988). Toward a typology of personality styles. *Canadian Psychology, 29,* 263–283.

Miller, K. F., & Parades, D. R. (1996). On the shoulders of giants: Cultural tools and mathematical development. In R. Sternberg & T. Ben Zeev (Eds.), *The nature of mathematical thinking* (pp. 83–118). Mahwah, NJ: Erlbaum.

Miller, K. F., Smith, C. M., Zhu, J., & Zhang, H. (1995). Preschool origins of cross-national differences in numerical competence: The role of number naming systems. *Psychological Science, 6,* 56–60.

Mischel, W., & Shoda, Y. (1995). A cognitive-affective system theory of personality: Reconceptualizing situations, dispositions, dynamics, and invariance in personality structure. *Psychological Review, 102,* 246–268.

Myers, I. B. (1981). *Gifts differing.* Gainesville, FL: Center for the Application of Psychological Type.

Myers, I. B., & McCaulley, M. H. (1985). *Manual: A guide to the development and use of the Myers-Briggs type indicator.* Palo Alto, CA: Consulting Psychological Press.

Neisser, U., Boodoo, G., Bouchard, T. J., Boykin, A. W., Brody, N., Ceci, S. J., Halpern, D. F., Loehlin, J. C., Perloff, R., Sternberg, R. J., & Urbina, S. (1996). Intelligence: Knowns and unknowns. *American Psychologist, 51,* 77–101.

Nelson, T. O. (1996). Consciousness and metacognition. *American Psychologist, 51,* 102–116.

Nelson, T. O., & Dunlosky, J. (1991). The delayed JOL effect: When delaying your judgments of learning can improve the accuracy of your metacognitive monitoring. *Psychological Science, 2,* 267–270.

Nelson, T. O., & Narens, L. (1994). Why investigate metacognition? In J. Metcalfe & A. Shimamura (Eds.), *Metacognition: Knowing about knowing* (pp. 1–25). Cambridge, MA: Bradford Books.

Nicholls, J. G. (1989). *The competitive ethos and democratic education.* Cambridge, MA: Harvard University Press.

Nolen, S. B. (1988). Reasons for studying: Motivational orientations and study strategies. *Cognition and Instruction, 5,* 269–287.

Oglesby, F., & Suter, W. N. (1995). Matching reading styles and reading instruction. *Research in the Schools, 2*(1), 11–15.

Okamoto, Y., Miura, I. T., & Tajika, H. (1995). *Children's intuitive understanding of number and formal mathematical training: A cross-national comparison.* Paper presented at the annual meeting of the American Educational Research Association, San Francisco.

Osherson, D., Smith, E. E., Wilkie, O., Lopez, A., & Shafir, E. (1990). Category-based induction. *Psychological Review, 97,* 185–200.

Otis, A. S. (1918). An absolute point scale for the group measurement of intelligence. *Journal of Educational Psychology, 9,* 238–261.

Pajares, F., & Miller, M. D. (1994). Role of self-efficacy and self-concept beliefs in mathematical problem solving: A path analysis. *Journal of Educational Psychology, 86,* 193–203.

Paris, S. G., & Winograd, P. (1990). How metacognition can promote academic learning and instruction. In B. F. Jones & L. Idol (Eds.), *Dimension of thinking and cognitive instruction* (pp. 15–51). Hillsdale, NJ: Erlbaum.

Parker, M., & Leinhardt, G. (1995). Percent: A privileged proportion. *Review of Educational Research, 65,* 421–481.

Pascual-Leone, J. (1988). Organismic processes for neo-Piagetian Theories: A dialectical causal account of cognitive development. In A. Demetriou (Ed.), *The neo-Piagetian theories of cognitive development: Toward an integration.* Amsterdam, The Netherlands: North-Holland.

Pascual-Leone, J. (1989). An organismic process model of Witkin's field dependence–independence. In T. Globerson & T. Zelniker (Eds.), *Cognitive style and cognitive development* (pp. 36–70). Norwood, NJ: ABLEX.

Pedersen, N. L., Plomin, R., & McClearn, G. E. (1994). Is there G beyond g? (Is there genetic influence on specific cognitive abilities independent of genetic influence on general cognitive ability?). *Intelligence, 18,* 133–143.

Pemberton, C. (1952). The closure factors related to temperament. *Journal of Personality, 21,* 159–175.

Piaget, J. (1974a). *La prise de conscience* (Consciousness' grasp). Paris: Presses Universitaires de France.

Piaget, J. (1974b). *Réussir et comprendre* (Success and understanding). Paris: Presses Universitaires de France.

Piaget, J. (1983). Piaget's theory. In P. H. Mussen (Series Ed.) & W. Kessen (Ed.), *Handbook of child psychology: Vol. 1. History, theory, and methods* (4th ed., pp. 103–128). New York: Wiley. (Originally published 1970)

Piaget, J., & Garcia, R. (1987). *Psychogenesis and the history of science* (H. Feider, Trans.). New York: Columbia University Press. (Original work published 1983)

Piaget, J., & Garcia, R. (1991). *Toward a logic of meanings.* New York: Erlbaum.

Pillow, B. H. (1989). The development of beliefs about selective attention. *Merrill-Palmer Quarterly, 35,* 421–443.

Pillow, B. H. (in press). Two trends in the development of conceptual perspective taking: An elaboration of the passive-active hypothesis. *International Journal of Behavioral Development.*

Pinard, A. (1992). Metaconscience et métacognition (Metaconsciousness and metacognition). *Canadian Psychology, 33,* 27–41.

Plato. (1961). Theatetus. In E. Hamilton & H. Cairns (Eds.), *Plato: The collected dialogues* (Bollingen series 71, pp. 845–919). Princeton, NJ: Princeton University Press. (Original work written circa ~300)

Plomin, R. (1988). The nature and nurture of cognitive abilities. In R. J. Sternberg (Ed.), *Advances in the psychology of human intelligence* (Vol. 4, pp. 1–33). Hillsdale, NJ: Erlbaum.

Plomin, R. (1993). Nature and nurture: Perspective and prospective. In R. Plomin & G. E. McClearn (Eds.), *Nature, nurture, and psychology* (pp. 459–485). Washington, DC: American Psychological Association.

Plomin, R., & McClearn, G. E. (Eds.). (1993). *Nature, nurture, and psychology.* Washington, DC: American Psychological Association.

Plomin, R., McClearn, G. E., Smith, D. L., Skuder, P., Vignetti, S., Chorney, M. J., Chorney, K., Kasarda, S., Thompson, L. A., Detterman, D. K., Petrill, S. A., Daniels, J., Owen, M. J., & McGuffin, P. (1995). Allelic associations between 100 DNA markers and high versus low IQ. *Intelligence, 21,* 31–48.

Plomin, R., McClearn, G. E., Smith, D. L., Vignetti, S., Chorney, M. J., Chorney, K., Venditti, C. P., Kasarda, S., Thompson, L. A., Detterman, D. K., Daniels, J., Owen, M., & McGuffin, P. (1994). DNA markers associated with high versus low IQ: The quantitative trait loci (QTL) project. *Behavior Genetics, 24,* 107–118.

Plomin, R., & Neiderhiser, J. M. (1991). Quantitative genetics, molecular genetics, and intelligence. *Intelligence, 15,* 369–387.

Poarth, M. (1992). Stage and structure in the development of children with various types of "giftedness." In R. Case (Ed.), *The mind's staircase* (pp. 303–317). Hillsdale, NJ: Erlbaum.

Ramsden, P. (1992). *Learning to teach in higher education.* New York: Routledge & Kegan Paul.

Reed, T. E., & Jensen, A. R. (1992). Conduction velocity in a brain nerve pathway of normal adults correlates with intelligence. *Intelligence, 16,* 259–272.

Riesbeck, C., & Schank, R. C. (1989). *Inside case-based reasoning.* Hillsdale, NJ: Erlbaum.

Rips, L. J. (1994). *The psychology of proof: Deductive reasoning in human thinking.* Cambridge, MA: MIT Press.

Robins, S., & Mayer, R. E. (1993). Schema training in analogical reasoning. *Journal of Educational Psychology, 85,* 529–538.

Robinson, D. N. (1994). Philosophical views of intelligence. In R. J. Sternberg (Ed.), *Encyclopedia of human intelligence* (Vol. 2, pp. 801–804). New York: Macmillan.

Rogoff, B., Mistry, J., Göncü, A., & Mosier, C. (1993). Guided participation in cultural activity by toddlers and caregivers. *Monograph of the Society for Research in Child Development, 58*(8, Serial No. 236).

Rowe, D. C., & Waldman, I. D. (1993). The question "how" reconsidered. In R. Plomin & G. E. McClearn (Eds.), *Nature, nurture, and psychology* (pp. 355–373). Washington, DC: American Psychological Association.

Royce, J. R. (1983). Personality integration: A synthesis of the parts and whole of individuality theory. *Journal of Personality, 51,* 683–706.

Royce, J. R., & Powell, A. (1983). *Theory of personality and individual differences: Factors, systems, and processes.* Englewood Cliffs, NJ: Prentice-Hall.

Rozin, P. (1996). Toward a psychology of food and eating: From motivation to module to model to marker, morality, meaning, and metaphor. *Current Directions in Psychological Science, 5,* 18–24.

Saks, M. (1988). Do two- and three-year-old children have cognitive styles? *Soviet Psychology, 26*(3), 84–102.

Saracho, O. N. (1992). Factors reflecting cognitive style in young children's play. *Learning and Individual Differences, 4*(1), 43–58.

Scarr, S. (1992). Developmental theories for the 1990s: Development and individual differences. *Child Development, 63,* 1–19.

Scarr, S. (1997). In R. J. Sternberg & E. L. Grigorenko (Eds.), *Intelligence, heredity, and environment* (pp. 3–41). New York: Cambridge University Press.

Scarr, S., & McCartney, K. (1983). How people make their own environments: A theory of genotype—environment effects. *Child Development, 54,* 424–435.

Schneider, W., & Korkel, J. (1989). Domain-specific knowledge and memory performance: A comparison of high- and low-aptitude children. *Journal of Educational Psychology, 81,* 306–312.

Schneider, W., & Sodian, B. (1991). A longitudinal study of young children's memory behavior and performance in a sort recall task. *Journal of Experimental Child Psychology, 51,* 14–29.

Schoenfeld, A. (1992). Learning to think mathematically: Problem-solving, metacognition, and sense making in mathematics. In D. A. Grouws (Ed.), *Handbook of research on mathematics teaching and learning* (pp. 334–370). New York: Macmillan.

Schraw, G., Dunkle, M. E., Bendixon, L. D., & DeBacker Roedel, T. (1995). Does a general monitoring skill exist? *Journal of Educational Psychology, 87,* 433–444.

Schroeder, H. M., Driver, M. J., & Streufert, S. (1967). *Human information processing.* New York: Holt, Rinehart and Winston.

Schunk, D. H., & Zimmerman, B. J. (1994). *Self-regulation of learning and performance: Issues and educational implications.* Hillsdale, NJ: Erlbaum.

Segal, N. L. (1986). Monozygotic and dizygotic twins: A comparative analysis of mental ability profiles. *Child Development, 56,* 1051–1058.

Sheldon, K. M., & Emmons, R. A. (1995). Comparing differentiation and integration within personal goal systems. *Personality and Individual Differences, 18,* 39–46.

Siegler, R. S., & Jenkins, E. (1989). *How children discover new strategies.* Hillsdale, NJ: Erlbaum.

Siegler, R. S., & Shrager, J. (1984). Strategy choices in addition and subtraction: How do children know what to do? In C. Sophian (Ed.), *Origins of cognitive skills* (pp. 229–293). Hillsdale, NJ: Erlbaum.

Skinner, E. A., Chapman, M., & Baltes, P. B. (1988). Control, means-ends, and agency beliefs: A new conceptualization and its measurement during childhood. *Journal of Personality and Social Psychology, 54,* 117–123.

Sloman, S. A. (1996). The empirical case for two systems of reasoning. *Psychological Bulletin, 119,* 3–22.

Smith, B. O. (1963). A conceptual analysis of instructional behavior. *The Journal of Teacher Education, 14,* 294–298.

Smith, J. D., & Caplan, J. (1988). Cultural differences in cognitive style development. *Developmental Psychology, 24,* 46–52.

Smolensky, P. (1988). On the proper treatment of connectionism. *Behavioral and Brain Sciences, 11,* 1–23.

Snow, R. E. (1994). A person-situation interaction theory of intelligence in outline. In G. E. Stelmach & P. A. Vroon (Series Eds.) & A. Demetriou & A. Efklides (Vol. Eds.), *Advances in psychology 106. Intelligence, mind, reasoning: Structure and development* (pp. 11–28). New York: North-Holland.

Sodian, B., & Schneider, W. (1990). Children's understanding of cognitive cueing: How to manipulate cues to fool a competitor. *Child Development, 61,* 697–704.

Sorrentino, R. M., Hewitt, E. C., & Rasco-Knott, P. A. (1992). Risk taking in games of chance and skill: Informational and affective influences in choice behavior. *Journal of Personality and Social Psychology, 62,* 522–533.

Sorrentino, R. M., & Short, J. C. (1986). Uncertainty orientation, motivation, and cognition. In R. M. Sorrentino & E. T. Higgins (Eds.), *The handbook of motivation and cognition: Foundations of social behavior* (pp. 379–403). New York: Guilford Press.

Spearman, C. (1904a). The proof and measurement of association between things. *American Journal of Psychology, 15,* 72–101.

Spearman, C. (1904b). General intelligence objectively determined and measured. *American Journal of Psychology, 15,* 210–293.

Spearman, C. (1981). *The abilities of man* (Rev. ed.). New York: AMS. (Original work published 1927)

Spelke, E. S., Breinlinger, K., Macomber, J., & Jacobsen (1992). Origins of knowledge. *Psychological Review, 99,* 605–632.

Sternberg, R. J. (1985). *Beyond IQ: A triarchic theory of human intelligence.* New York: Cambridge University Press.

Sternberg, R. J. (1987). The psychology of verbal comprehension. In R. Glaser (Ed.), *Advances in instructional psychology* (Vol. 3, pp. 97–151). Hillsdale, NJ: Erlbaum.

Sternberg, R. J. (1988a). *The triarchic mind: A new theory of human intelligence.* New York: Viking.

Sternberg, R. J. (1988b). Intelligence. In R. J. Sternberg & E. E. Smith (Eds.), *The psychology of human thought.* New York: Cambridge University Press.

Sternberg, R. J. (1988c). Mental self-government: A theory of intellectual styles and their development. *Human Development, 31,* 197–224.

Sternberg, R. J. (1990a). *Metaphors of mind: Conceptions of the nature of intelligence.* New York: Cambridge University Press.

Sternberg, R. J. (1990b). Intellectual styles: Theory and classroom implications. In B. Presseisen (Ed.), *Intellectual styles and interaction in the classroom* (pp. 18–42). West Orange, NJ: Leadership Library of America.

Sternberg, R. J. (1994). Thinking styles and testing: Bridging the gap between ability and personality assessment. In R. J. Sternberg & P. Ruzgis (Eds.), *Intelligence and personality.* New York: Cambridge University Press.

Sternberg, R. J. (1996). *Abilities are developing forms of expertise.* Manuscript submitted for publication, Yale University.

Sternberg, R. J., & Gardner, M. K. (1982). A componential interpretation of the general factor in human intelligence. In H. J. Eysenck (Ed.), *A model for intelligence* (pp. 231–254). Berlin: Springer-Verlag.

Sternberg, R. J., & Grigorenko, E. L. (1995). Styles of thinking in school. *European Journal of High Ability, 6*(2), 1–18.

Sternberg, R. J., & Wagner, R. K. (1991). *MSG Thinking Styles Inventory.* Manual.

Sternberg, R. J., & Wagner, R. K. (Eds.). (1994). *Mind in context.* New York: Cambridge University Press.

Sternberg, R. J., Wagner, R. K., Williams, W. M., & Horvath, J. A. (1995). Testing common sense. *American Psychologist, 50,* 912–927.

Suedfeld, P. (1994). Cognitive complexity. In R. J. Sternberg (Ed.), *Encyclopedia of human intelligence* (Vol. 1, pp. 286–291). New York: Macmillan.

Suedfeld, P., & Coren, S. (1992). Cognitive correlates of conceptual complexity. *Personality and Individual Differences, 13,* 1193–1199.

Suedfeld, P., Tetlock, P. E., & Streufert, S. (1992). Conceptual/integrative complexity. In C. P. Smith (Ed.), *Handbook of thematic analysis.* New York: Cambridge University Press.

Sweller, J. (1989). Cognitive load during problem solving: Effects on learning. *Cognitive Science, 21,* 257–285.

Tambs, K. (1987). No effect on variation in field dependence: A study of rod-and-frame scores in families of monozygotic twins. *Behavior Genetics, 17,* 493–502.

Tambs, K., Sundet, J. M., & Magnus, P. (1984). Heritability analysis of the WAIS subtests: A study of twins. *Intelligence, 8,* 283–293.

Tellegen, A. (1982). *Brief manual for the Multidimensional Personality Questionnaire.* Minneapolis: University of Minnesota.

Tellegen, A., Lykken, D. T., Bouchard, T. J., Wilcox, K. J., Segal, N. L., & Rich, S. (1988). Personality similarity in twins reared apart and together. *Journal of Personality and Social Psychology, 6,* 1031–1039.

Terman, L. M. (1916). *The measurement of intelligence: An explanation of and a complete guide for the use of the Stanford revision and extension of the Binet-Simon intelligence scale.* Boston: Houghton Mifflin.

Thomas, A., & Chess, S. (1986). The New York Longitudinal Study: From infancy to early adult life. In R. Plomin & J. Dunn (Eds.), *The study of temperament: Changes, continuities, and challenges* (pp. 39–52). Hillsdale, NJ: Erlbaum.

Thompson, V. A. (1995). Conditional reasoning: The necessary and sufficient conditions. *Canadian Journal of Experimental Psychology, 49,* 1–58.

Thurstone, L. L. (1938). Primary mental abilities. *Psychological Monographs, No. 1.*

Thurstone, L. L. (1944). A factorial study of perception. *Psychometric Monograph, No. 4.*

Thurstone, L. L., & Thurstone, T. C. (1941). *Factorial studies of intelligence.* Chicago: University of Chicago Press.

Torff, B., & Gardner, H. (in press). The vertical mind: The case for multiple intelligences. In M. Anderson (Ed.), *The development of intelligence.* London: University College Press.

Undheim, J. O., & Horn, J. L. (1977). Critical evaluation of Guilford's structure-of-intellect model. *Intelligence, 1,* 65–81.

Vandenberg, S. G. (1968). The nature and nurture of intelligence. In D. C. Glass (Ed.), *Genetics.* New York: Russell-Sage Foundation.

VanLehn, K. (1990). *Mind bugs: The origins of procedural misconceptions.* Cambridge, MA: MIT Press.

Vernon, P. A. (Ed.). (1993). *Biological approaches to the study of human intelligence.* Norwood, NJ: ABLEX.

Vernon, P. E. (1971). *The structure of human abilities.* London: Methuen.

Vygotsky, L. S. (1986). *Thought and speech.* Cambridge, MA: MIT Press. (Original work published 1934)

Wachs, T. D. (1993). The nature–nurture gap: What we have here is a failure to collaborate. In R. Plomin & G. E. McClearn (Eds.), *Nature, nurture, and psychology* (pp. 375–391). Washington, DC: American Psychological Association.

Wagner, R., & Stanovich, K. (1996). Developing expertise in reading. In K. A. Ericsson (Ed.), *The road to excellence: The acquisition of expert performance in the arts and sciences, sports and games.* Mahwah, NJ: Erlbaum.

Wapner, S., & Demick, J. (1991). *Field dependence–independence: Cognitive style across the life span.* Hillsdale, NJ: Erlbaum.

Wason, P. C. (1968). Reasoning about a rule. *Quarterly Journal of Experimental Psychology, 20,* 273–281.

Weiner, B. (1994). Ability versus effort revisited: The moral determinants of achievement evaluation and achievement as a moral system. *Educational Psychologist, 29,* 163–172.

White, K. R. (1982). The relation between socioeconomic status and academic achievement. *Psychological Bulletin, 91,* 461–481.

Williams, W. M. (in press). Are we raising smarter children today? School- and home-related influences on IQ. In U. Neisser (Ed.), *The rising curve: Long-term changes in IQ and related measures.* Washington, DC: American Psychological Association.

Wilson, R. S. (1983). The Louisville twin study: Developmental synchronies in behavior. *Child Development, 54,* 298–316.

Wise, P. S., & Cramer, S. H. (1988). Correlates of empathy and cognitive style in early adolescence. *Psychological Reports, 63,* 179–192.

Witkin, H. A., & Goodenough, D. R. (1981). *Cognitive styles: Essence and origins.* New York: International Universities Press.

Witkin, H. A., Lewis, H. B., Hertzman, M., Machover, K., Meissner, P. B., & Wapner, S. (1954). *Personality through perception.* New York: Harper.

Witkin, H. A., Oltman, P. K., Raskin, E., & Karp, S. A. (1971). *Embedded Figures Test, Children's Embedded Figures Test, Group Embedded Figures Test.* Manual. Palo Alto, CA: Consulting Psychologists Press.

Wozniak, R. H., & Fischer, K. W. (Eds.). (1993). *Development in context: Acting and thinking in specific environments.* Hillsdale, NJ: Erlbaum.

Wynn, K. (1992). Children's acquisition of the number words and the counting system. *Cognitive Psychology, 24,* 220–251.

CHAPTER 19

Cognitive Development beyond Childhood

DAVID MOSHMAN

Concluding this volume on children's cognition, this chapter addresses developmental changes in cognition that extend beyond childhood. I will not trace cognitive change across the entire span of adulthood (for lifespan accounts, see Cerella, Rybash, Hoyer, & Commons, 1993; Commons, Richards, & Armon, 1984; Craik & Salthouse, 1993; Holliday & Chandler, 1986; Hoyer & Rybash, 1994; Kausler, 1994; Lachman & Burack, 1993; Miller & Cook-Greuter, 1994; Rybash, Hoyer, & Roodin, 1986; Sinnott & Cavanaugh, 1991). Rather, I highlight changes associated with the second (and to a lesser extent the third) decade of life. The research reviewed suggests that developmental changes in cognition, at least in some individuals, continue at least through adolescence and early adulthood.

In the opening sections of the chapter, I address a variety of historical, theoretical, and methodological considerations regarding advanced cognitive development. I then argue that the central locus of developmental change in cognition beyond childhood is in reasoning—that is, in the deliberate application of epistemic constraints to one's own thinking. Three forms of reasoning—case-based, law-based, and dialectical—are distinguished and developmental research relevant to each is reviewed. Finally, I attempt to explain advanced cognitive development by proposing a metacognitive, constructivist, and pluralist conception of human rationality.

HISTORICAL CONCEPTIONS OF ADVANCED COGNITION

Formal Reasoning

Explicit conceptions about the nature of sophisticated reasoning and logic date back at least to Plato and Aristotle. The psychological study of advanced cognitive development can be traced to James Mark Baldwin (1895), who postulated a "hyper-logical" stage of mental development in which

> syllogistic forms come to have an independent or a priori force, and pure thought emerges—thought, that is, which thinks of anything or nothing. The subject of thought has fallen out, leaving the shell of form. (1930, p. 23; cited in Cairns, 1983)

In a similar vein, Piaget (1924/1972) presented early evidence that "formal reasoning" begins to be seen about the age of 11 or 12. By formal reasoning, Piaget meant "formal deduction," which

> consists in drawing conclusions, not from a fact given in immediate observation, nor from a judgment which one holds to be true without any qualifications (and thus incorporates into reality such as one conceives it), but in a judgment which one simply assumes, i.e. which one admits without believing it, just to see what it will lead to. (p. 69)

Piaget was clear that logical deduction could be seen in children as young as age 7 or 8, but insisted that such deduction "bears only upon the beliefs which the child has adopted himself" (p. 67). It is only at age 11 or 12, he suggested, that reasoning becomes "hypothetico-deductive" (p. 69). Formal reasoning, in Piaget's conception, enables the adolescent to reason strictly about hypotheses in a constructed realm of possibility that is explicitly distinguished from empirical reality. "To be formal," he proposed, "deduction must detach itself from reality and take up its stand upon the plane of the purely possible, which is by definition the domain of hypothesis" (p. 71).

Baldwin's theory and the early work of Piaget notwithstanding, the study of cognitive development beyond childhood remained relatively sparse and atheoretical. When Horrocks (1954) wrote what was intended as a comprehensive chapter on "The Adolescent" for the second edition of the present handbook, he devoted barely one page to "Intellectual Growth and Development." Drawing on a quantitative conception of intelligence associated with the psychometric tradition, Horrocks' review of adolescent cognitive development focused exclusively on the "rate of mental growth" and the age at which such growth ceased. His conclusion was that mental growth slows dramatically over the course of adolescence and that "in terms of mental ability or power the adolescent is nearing his peak" (p. 719).

Piaget's Theory of Formal Operations

The year after Horrocks' review, Inhelder and Piaget (1955/1958) published their classic *The Growth of Logical Thinking from Childhood to Adolescence,* the first full-length treatment of cognitive development beyond childhood. The book presented detailed accounts of performance by children and adolescents on a variety of ingenious tasks designed and administered by Inhelder and her associates; as well as an ambitious theoretical effort by Piaget to characterize and explain the observed developmental changes.

Methodologically, the 15 studies reported in *The Growth of Logical Thinking* each involved some sort of physical apparatus—flexible rods, a pendulum, an inclined plane, communicating vessels, a hydraulic press, or a balance scale. Children ranging in age from 5 through 16 were encouraged to manipulate the materials and to construct an understanding of the associated physical phenomena— for example, the effect of potentially relevant variables on the relative flexibility of the rods or on the rate of oscillation of the pendulum. They were interviewed individually about their experiments and conclusions. As in both prior (e.g., Piaget & Inhelder, 1951/1975) and subsequent (e.g., Piaget, 1987) research, responses were interpreted as revealing patterns of thinking that were common among adolescents, but rarely or never seen prior to age 11.

In many respects, Piaget's account of these results was continuous with his earliest theorizing about adolescent cognition. Formal thinking, he argued

> is essentially hypothetico-deductive. By this we mean that the deduction no longer refers directly to perceived realities but to hypothetical statements—*i.e.,* it refers to propositions which are formulations of hypotheses or which postulate facts or events independently of whether or not they actually occur. (p. 251)

The emphasis on the hypothetical involves a radical reconstruction of the perceived relation between realities and possibilities. That is,

> in formal thought, there is a reversal of the direction of thinking between *reality* and *possibility* in the subjects' method of approach. *Possibility* no longer appears merely as an extension of an empirical situation or of actions actually performed. Instead, it is *reality* that is now secondary to *possibility*. (p. 251, emphases in original)

Thus, Piaget continued to emphasize the importance of formal or hypothetico-deductive reasoning in adolescence. Such reasoning, he argued, is central to formulating a logically coherent realm of possibilities. The formulation of such a realm, in turn, was seen as central to a sophisticated understanding of reality. That is, reality can best be understood within the context of possibility. Formal understanding, moreover, involves "reflective thinking" (p. 342), including critical analysis of one's own thinking and the deliberate construction of theories that systematize one's ideas.

By 1955, however, Piaget was consolidating the most structural phase of his career. Having proposed a set of operational structures to explain the reasoning of middle childhood, he now saw the transition to adolescence as involving the construction of second-order, or formal, operations involving transformations of first-order, or concrete, operations. At a still more technical level, formal operations were characterized as an *ensemble des parties* or "structured whole" (p. xix, note 18), involving (a) a "complete combinatorial system" with the logico-mathematical properties of a lattice and (b) the coordination of two forms of reversibility—inversion and reciprocity—within the Identity-Negation-Reciprocity-Correlative (INRC) Group. In effect, Piaget postulated a version of propositional logic as the structure underlying formal operational reasoning (Smith, 1987). Although Piaget had earlier sketched a structural account of adolescent cognition as "formal operations" (1947/1960, pp. 147–150), *The Growth of Logical Thinking* was notable for a substantial elaboration of his structural theory. Thus, the theory of formal reasoning became the theory of formal operations (De Lisi, 1988).

Inhelder and Piaget's qualitative account of adolescent cognition as structurally distinct from childhood cognition revolutionized the study of adolescent cognitive development. By the 1970s, a substantial body of literature concerning Piaget's theory of formal operations had emerged. (For a classic Piagetian review, see Neimark, 1975; for an early critical review, see Keating, 1980; for more recent critiques and reformulations, see Braine & Rumain, 1983; Byrnes, 1988a, 1988b; Campbell & Bickhard, 1986; Gray, 1990; Halford, 1989; Keating, 1988, 1990; Smith, 1987.) In recent years, the literature on cognitive development in adolescence and beyond has increasingly transcended the theory of formal operations and branched off in multiple directions. The issues highlighted by Piaget, however, continue to set much of the agenda for research and theory.

DOES COGNITION DEVELOP BEYOND CHILDHOOD?

Piaget's theory claims that (a) developmental changes in cognition continue through early adolescence and (b) the cognitive structure associated with early adolescence, formal operations, is the final stage of development. Both claims are open to question. On one hand, extensive evidence of early cognitive competence (DeLoache, Miller, & Pierroutsakos, this volume; R. Gelman & Williams, this volume; S. Gelman & Wellman, this volume) raises the possibility that the most fundamental aspects of cognition emerge very early; later cognitive changes, it might be argued, are not developmental in nature. On the other hand, a number of theorists have proposed forms of advanced cognition that, they suggest, develop in late adolescence or adulthood (Commons et al., 1984; Miller & Cook-Greuter, 1994). Thus, Piaget's theory is challenged both by claims that cognitive development is limited to childhood, and by claims that it extends beyond adolescence.

In order to address the fundamental question of whether cognition develops beyond childhood, we must consider what we mean by development. Perhaps the paradigm case of a developmental change associated with adolescence is puberty, the transition to sexual maturity. It may be useful to consider what characteristics of this change lead us to construe it as developmental in nature. One obvious characteristic is that puberty is a long-term change. It occurs over a period of months or years, rather than minutes, hours, or days. Three additional characteristics appear worthy of note:

1. Puberty is a *qualitative* change. It involves a coordinated transformation of anatomical and physiological systems resulting in a structurally distinct state of maturity. In

contrast, increasing some number of inches in height is not a qualitative transformation. Mere growth is not a core example of *development.*

2. Puberty is a *progressive* change. It has a natural direction that constitutes progress toward a state of maturity. A transition involving a loss of reproductive capacity, by contrast, might be an equally important change, but would be less likely to be construed as prototypically developmental in nature.

3. Puberty is an *internally-directed* change. Although it requires environmental support (e.g., adequate nutrition), it is not caused or directed by the environment. On the contrary, the transition to sexual maturity is typically seen as genetically guided and universal across the species.

It is widely accepted among biologists that certain long-term anatomical and physiological changes, such as puberty, are qualitative, progressive, and internally-directed to a sufficient extent that such changes are usefully construed as falling into a category of change that may be labeled developmental change. Substantial evidence has led many psychological theorists to posit long-term cognitive changes that, like puberty, are sufficiently qualitative, progressive, and internally-directed to be usefully construed as developmental in nature (Case, Ch. 15, this Volume; Valsiner, Volume 1).

Even if cognition does develop, there remains the question of whether such development continues beyond childhood. A negative answer to that question would make this a very short chapter. I hope to demonstrate in this section the plausibility of a positive answer but raise the possibility that cognitive development beyond childhood differs in important ways from prototypical examples of development such as puberty.

Qualitative Change

At the historical and theoretical core of the theory of formal operations is the postulation of a qualitative shift to formal reasoning competence at about age 11 or 12 (De Lisi, 1988; Piaget, 1924/72). Research on hypothetico-deductive reasoning has provided substantial evidence for such a qualitative transformation at about this age (Markovits & Vachon, 1989; Moshman & Franks, 1986). A number of more recent theories also postulate qualitative changes in cognition beyond childhood. As we will see later in this chapter, there is substantial evidence for the existence of types, forms, or levels of cognition that are

common among adolescents and adults, but rarely seen much before the age of 11 (Basseches, 1980, 1984; Campbell & Bickhard, 1986; Case, Ch. 15, this Volume; Chandler & Boutilier, 1992; Commons et al., 1984; Dunbar & Klahr, 1989; Furby & Beyth-Marom, 1992; Inhelder & Piaget, 1958; King & Kitchener, 1994; Klahr, Fay, & Dunbar, 1993; Kohlberg, 1984; Kuhn, 1989; Kuhn, Amsel, & O'Loughlin, 1988; Lamborn, Fischer, & Pipp, 1994; Marini & Case, 1994; Markovits, 1993; Markovits, Schleifer, & Fortier, 1989; Markovits & Vachon, 1989, 1990; Moshman, 1990, 1993, 1995b; Moshman & Franks, 1986; O'Brien, 1987; Overton, 1990; Overton, Ward, Noveck, Black, & O'Brien, 1987; Ward & Overton, 1990).

It is far less clear whether there is a general and/or structural aspect to such change and, if so, how such generality and/or organization is best characterized. If change is general across domains, are qualitative shifts in multiple domains of cognition simultaneous, or at least highly correlated? Are there one or more abstract structures of cognition that can be applied, perhaps with a greater or lesser degree of success, to these domains?

The most influential candidate for a very general form of cognitive structure has been Piaget's conceptualization of formal operations. As we have seen, the theory of formal operations goes beyond Piaget's early postulation of a qualitative shift to formal reasoning by postulating a highly abstract logico-mathematical structure that forms the basis for a general stage of cognitive development. This proposal has been highly controversial (for diverse views, see Braine & Rumain, 1983; Byrnes, 1988a, 1988b; Campbell & Bickhard, 1986; Gray, 1990; Halford, 1989; Keating, 1980, 1988, 1990; Neimark, 1975; Smith, 1987). Even if the theory does provide an adequate account of some forms of reasoning, moreover, it is doubtful that it can fully account for the multiple forms of advanced cognition to be discussed in this chapter (Basseches, 1984; Broughton, 1977; Campbell & Bickhard, 1986; Chandler & Boutilier, 1992; Commons et al., 1984; Kitchener & Kitchener, 1981; Pieraut-Le Bonniec, 1980).

A central theoretical and methodological issue in efforts to identify and characterize structural transformation is the fact that qualitatively distinct forms of thought and knowledge routinely coexist in the same mind (Kuhn, Garcia-Mila, Zohar, & Andersen, 1995; Schauble, 1996; Wark & Krebs, 1996). It often seems reasonable to speak of a qualitative shift when an important new form of cognition appears, even if that form does not completely supplant earlier forms. The appropriate criteria for *structural* change, however, are much less clear. Some researchers attempt to address this problem via methodologies that high-light underlying competence (Overton, 1990) or optimal level of functioning (Lamborn et al., 1994) rather than typical behavior. Such methodologies often do yield evidence for general age-related limits on performance (Case, Ch. 15, this Volume; Marini & Case, 1994), but it remains unclear in what sense there might be general and/or structural change in later cognitive development (Wark & Krebs, 1996).

In sum, there do appear to be cognitive changes of a qualitative nature beyond childhood. The generality and organization of such changes, however, are matters of dispute.

Progressive Change

Another characteristic of developmental change is that it is progressive (R. Kitchener, 1986). With respect to puberty, it is fairly easy to specify a universally achieved state of sexual and reproductive maturity and to assess progress toward that state. With respect to cognition, a variety of formulations concerning the nature of maturity have been put forward. The best-known proposal concerning a state of cognitive maturity is Piaget's account of formal operations. Other theorists have proposed alternative general conceptions of cognitive maturity (Commons et al., 1984). Riegel (1973) and Basseches (1980, 1984), for example, proposed dialectical thinking as a general, post-formal, and final stage of cognitive development. Finally, some theorists have suggested domain-specific conceptions of cognitive maturity. Kohlberg (1984) posits a highest stage of moral development involving an ultimate level of abstract perspective taking. King and Kitchener (1994), to take another example, describe a highest stage in the development of reflective judgment, involving sophisticated conceptions of knowledge and justification.

Although the existence of a developmental endpoint would indicate the progressive nature of cognitive changes in the direction of that endpoint, the existence of such an endpoint is not a necessary condition for progressive change. Formal operational reasoning, for example, is a second-order structure that includes and transcends the first-order structure of concrete operations; the transition from concrete to formal operations can thereby be construed as progress, regardless of whether formal operations is a final stage. Similarly, the emergence of hypothetico-deductive reasoning may be seen as an expansion of the domain of deductive reasoning that constitutes progress, regardless of whether hypothetico-deductive reasoning is, or leads to, some sort of highest stage. Along the same lines, although stage theories such as those of Selman (1980), Kohlberg (1984), and King and Kitchener (1994) typically posit a highest stage, one can often make a strong case for each stage representing progress over the stage before without demonstrating that each stage increasingly approximates a mature state yet to come. Such a case might be made, for example, by showing that the later stage is more differentiated, integrated, organized, metacognitive, reflective, and/or adaptive (Campbell & Bickhard, 1986; Valsiner, Ch. 4, Volume 1).

Cross-sectional research suffices to demonstrate that some forms of cognition typically appear later than others. Longitudinal and cross-cultural evidence may strengthen the case that certain developmental sequences are invariant across individuals and cultures (Boyes & Walker, 1988; Kohlberg, 1984; Snarey, 1985). To make the case for cognitive progress, however, requires a demonstration that later cognitions are in some sense better, an epistemological claim that cannot be supported simply on the basis of empirical evidence. A key issue in the study of cognitive progress, then, is the theoretical coordination of empirical and epistemological considerations (R. Kitchener, 1986; Piaget, 1985; Smith, 1993).

As we will see throughout this chapter, a strong case can be made for progressive changes in cognition during adolescence and early adulthood. The existence of mature cognitive states, however, and the nature of any such developmental endpoints, remain matters of dispute.

Internally Directed Change

Finally, there is the question of whether cognitive transitions beyond childhood are internally directed. The most obvious sense in which a change may be internally directed is that it is guided by the genes. Many of the most important genetically guided changes with respect to anatomy and physiology are universal across the species.

Research on young children has led many theorists to the view that early cognitive development is to a large degree guided by innate constraints that are universal across individuals and cultures (Gelman & Williams, Ch. 12, this Volume; Karmiloff-Smith, 1992; Spelke & Newport, Ch. 6, Volume 1). Nevertheless, it does not follow that cognitive change is directed or determined by genes; any such conclusion would be especially dubious with respect to later cognitive transitions.

There is another sense, however, in which cognitive change might be said to be internally directed. A constructivist view of cognition posits an epistemic subject or rational agent actively constructing new knowledge and forms of thinking on the basis of his or her own perceptions and reasons. Although the constructive activities of such a subject are not genetically determined, they are nonetheless internal to the rational agent, rather than caused by the environment. Without positing either genetic determinism or universality across the species, a constructivist conception does suggest an important sense in which cognitive change is internally directed (Bidell, Lee, Bouchie, Ward, & Brass, 1994; Campbell & Bickhard, 1986; Karmiloff-Smith, 1992; R. Kitchener, 1986; Moshman, 1994, 1995a, 1995b; Piaget, 1985; Smith, 1993).

One useful approach to investigating the internally-directed nature of change is microgenetic research, in which subjects are observed over a period of time in a rich task environment to see how they construct and apply skills that are not directly taught (Schauble, 1990, 1996). Kuhn et al. (1995), for example, studied changes in the coordination of theories and evidence by children and adults over a series of ten sessions. They found progress in the ability to coordinate theories and evidence despite the absence of direct teaching, suggesting an inner-directed process of change. The fact that both children and adults made substantial progress in a relatively short period of time suggests a constructive process rather than a genetically based process of maturation.

Cross-cultural research provides another avenue for identifying changes that are not simply instilled by particular environments (Boyes & Walker, 1988; Snarey, 1985). Outside the realm of moral cognition, however, cross-cultural research on advanced cognitive development is rare.

As we will see, a strong theoretical and empirical case can be made for long-term cognitive changes that are internally directed. At advanced levels, however, there is no evidence that any such changes are genetically driven, and it is unclear what internally directed changes, if any, are universal across the species.

Conclusion

Throughout this chapter, we will see evidence for cognitive changes beyond childhood sufficiently like puberty to be labeled "developmental." Our core conception of development comes from the realm of biology, however, and may be misleading in the realm of cognition. We should not assume that everything we might call cognitive development has all those characteristics that lead us to construe puberty as a developmental change. As we will see, it appears that there

are indeed long-term changes in cognition that are qualitative, progressive, and internally directed; some such changes, moreover, continue into adolescence and beyond. It is doubtful that late cognitive changes are genetically driven, however. It remains unclear, moreover, in what respects, if any, advanced cognitive changes are structural, general across domains, aimed at one or more specific endpoints, or universal across persons and cultures (Hoyer & Rybash, 1994; Miller & Cook-Greuter, 1994; Rybash et al., 1986). These are questions to which we will return.

FROM INFERENCE TO REASONING

Cognition is generally construed to be inferential in that it routinely goes beyond the data at hand. In the present section, I will: (a) define thinking as an advanced form of inference; (b) define reasoning as an advanced form of thinking; (c) consider the specificity and generality of reasoning; and (d) suggest that reasoning is the primary locus of late developmental changes in cognition.

From Inference to Thinking

Inference may be defined as the generation of new cognitions from old. Inferential processing is central to most areas of human cognition and is typically automatic and unconscious. Reading, for example, routinely involves inferences that go beyond the text (Lea, O'Brien, Fisch, Noveck, & Braine, 1990). Similarly, effective social interaction involves an ongoing stream of inferences about the moods, meanings, and intentions of those with whom we interact (Hilton, 1995).

Thinking may be defined as the deliberate coordination of one's inferences to serve one's purposes (Moshman, 1995a). We think, for example, in order to solve a problem, make a decision, plan a project, justify a claim, or test a hypothesis. Thus defined, thinking is not limited to late development, nor does it ever replace elementary inference. Young children think, and adults continue to make automatic and unconscious inferences. Nevertheless, the emergence of thinking represents an important advance in the nature and use of inference. Research shows development at least through adolescence in problem solving (Foltz, Overton, & Ricco, 1995), decision making (Byrnes & McClenny, 1994; Furby & Beyth-Marom, 1992), planning (Lachman & Burack, 1993; Scholnick & Friedman, 1993), hypothesis testing (Kuhn et al., 1988), and other types of thinking.

From Thinking to Reasoning

Because thinking is purposeful, an act of thinking may be evaluated with respect to how well it serves the purposes of the thinker. Over the course of development, thinkers increasingly make such evaluations themselves and attempt to improve their inferential activities. Recognizing that some thought processes are more justifiable than others, they increasingly construct standards of rationality and apply these to their own thinking. To the extent that an individual attempts to constrain his or her thinking on the basis of a self-imposed standard of rationality, we may say the individual is engaged in reasoning. Reasoning, then, is epistemologically self-constrained thinking (Moshman, 1995a).

Consider, for example, developmental changes in decision making. At a primitive level, an individual might pursue a course of action on the basis of available information without any intent to select from two or more options or awareness of having done so. A psychologist studying this cognitive process might determine what inferences the individual made and might evaluate the adequacy of those inferences, but it would be misleading to say the individual has made a decision.

At a more advanced level, an individual understands that there are two or more options available, makes a series of inferences intended to determine the best option, and then consciously chooses that option. Such decision making may be usefully regarded as an act of thinking.

Research suggests that for at least some individuals, the quality of decision making continues to improve at least through adolescence (Byrnes & McClenny, 1994). A plausible explanation for this is: Over the course of development, individuals become increasingly successful in constraining their inferences to conform to increasingly justifiable norms. Some such norms may be specific to making decisions, whereas others may be applicable to multiple types of thinking.

At least three general forms of reasoning—to be discussed in the next three sections of this chapter—may play roles in decision making and other types of thinking. First, the decision maker may purposely choose the option most similar to one that has been successful in the past. This is analogical reasoning, a type of case-based reasoning. Second, the decision maker may deliberately constrain his or her inferences to conform to rules of logic or other epistemic laws. Such law-based reasoning is the focus of extensive developmental theory and research. Finally, the decision maker may move progressively toward a decision via some form of dialectical reflection or argumentation.

Developmental changes in problem solving may similarly reflect the emergence and application of epistemic self-constraints. Foltz et al. (1995), for example, assessed fifth and eighth graders on formal logical reasoning and presented each with a problem involving identification of a hidden figure. Formal reasoning competence was associated with the use of deductive proof construction strategies that enabled more efficient problem solving by avoiding the generation of redundant information.

This theoretical approach to thinking and reasoning has important methodological implications. Given the proposed definitions, an automatic inference is not an act of thinking and does not constitute reasoning, even if the inference conforms to logical, mathematical, or other epistemic norms. Correspondingly, a deliberate effort to constrain one's thinking on the basis of what one believes to be justifiable epistemic norms constitutes reasoning, even if the norms are not successfully applied or are demonstrably inappropriate. Bad reasoning, in this view, is still reasoning, whereas good inferences do not necessarily involve reasoning at all.

In assessing reasoning, then, it is not sufficient to present a task and see if subjects reach the logically or mathematically proper conclusion. Such an approach will overestimate reasoning competence in cases where automatic inferences suffice to reach the approved conclusion; it will underestimate reasoning competence in cases where deliberate efforts to constrain thinking do not suffice to generate the approved conclusion. As we will see, these are important considerations in attempting to reconcile the extensive literatures purporting to demonstrate logical, mathematical, and scientific reasoning in young children and the fundamental irrationality of adults (Hilton, 1995; Jones & Harris, 1982; Markovits, Schleifer, & Fortier, 1989; Moshman & Franks, 1986).

Specificity and Generality of Reasoning

An important issue in the study of cognition revolves around questions of specificity and generality. Rather than reduce this issue to a simplistic dichotomy of domain specificity versus generality, it will be useful to consider the various ways in which reasoning could be specific or general.

One way reasoning could be specific is with respect to domains of knowledge. Recent research with young children has suggested that they routinely construct knowledge within distinct domains such as physical causality, biological systems, social relations, and morality (Flavell & Miller, Ch. 17, this Volume; R. Gelman & Williams, Ch. 12, this Volume; S. Gelman & Wellman, Ch. 15, this Volume; Helwig, 1995b; Karmiloff-Smith, 1992; Maratsos, Ch. 9, this Volume; Spelke & Newport, Ch. 6, Volume 1). Such knowledge enables sophisticated patterns of inference within such domains. Domain-specific inferences undoubtedly play an important role in cognition at all ages. To the extent that people reflect on the epistemic properties of domain-specific inferences, they may construct forms of reasoning specific to particular inferential domains.

A second way reasoning could be specific is with respect to types of thinking. Problem solving, decision making, hypothesis testing, and planning, for example, might each involve distinct forms of epistemic constraint and thus constitute or generate distinct forms of reasoning.

A third possibility is that there are two or more distinct forms of reasoning applicable to multiple types of thinking and multiple domains of knowledge and inference. In the next three sections of this chapter, I suggest that three such forms of reasoning—case-based, law-based, and dialectical—can be distinguished and that each continues to develop long beyond childhood. Without denying the importance of domain-specific patterns of inference and distinct types of thinking, I suggest that each of these three forms of reasoning is applicable to various types of thinking and multiple domains of inference. With respect to specificity and generality, there are specific forms of reasoning, but each is general across types of thinking and domains of inference.

Finally, there remains the possibility that we can identify still broader generalities. Individuals may, for example, achieve levels of metacognitive understanding about the nature of inference that transcend domains of knowledge, types of thinking, and forms of reasoning. Research relevant to specificity and generality will be reviewed later in the chapter. First, in the next three sections, we consider three fundamental forms of reasoning.

CASE-BASED REASONING

Case-based reasoning is thinking constrained by attention to concrete manifestations (cases) that are deemed relevant to achieving a justifiable cognitive outcome in the case at hand. Two categories of case-based reasoning may be distinguished: analogical reasoning and precedent-based reasoning.

Analogical Reasoning

In analogical inference, a situation or issue is considered on the basis of other situations or exemplars. For example, one may approach a problem in a manner constrained by one's perception of how a relevantly similar problem has been solved or may categorize a phenomenon on the basis of its similarities to phenomena already categorized. Medin and Ross (1989) argue that problem solving and categorization often rely more on such use of concrete examples than on abstractions of any sort. Similarly, Halford (1992) notes that transitive inferences and understanding of class inclusion relations may involve use of analogy. Given that A is longer than B and B is longer than C, for example, a child may conclude that A is longer than C by analogy with the spatial relations of top, middle, and bottom. There is substantial evidence that detection, construction, and utilization of analogical relations is routine even in preschool children (DeLoache et al., Ch. 16, this Volume; Goswami, 1991).

The fact that young children make analogical inferences, however, does not show that they intended to make such inferences, that they have conscious control of those inferences, or that they understand the epistemic basis for such inferences. The emergence of analogical thinking may be identified when a child purposely seeks guidance from cases specifically deemed to be analogous. Such thinking may be identified as analogical reasoning, to the extent that the choice of analog and its application to the issue at hand are deemed justifiable by the thinker. Analogical reasoning, that is, is rooted in conceptual understanding about the epistemic advantages of using certain kinds of analogies in certain kinds of situations. Such (metacognitive) knowledge about analogy makes it possible for relevant similarities and differences to be deliberately assessed and coordinated.

The transition from inference to reasoning in the use of analogy has been examined via classical analogies of the form *a* is to *b* as *c* is to *d*. Full comprehension of such analogies requires not only simultaneous attention to two first-order relations (that of *a* to *b* and that of *c* to *d*), but explicit recognition of the asserted second-order relation of equality between the two first-order relations (*a* is to *b* as *c* is to *d*). Piaget's theory postulates that the second-order operations necessary for such comprehension do not develop until the emergence of formal operations at age 11.

Methodologically, identification of second-order relational reasoning requires evidence that the child explicitly compared the two first-order relations. Given the analogical question *Hand is to finger as foot is to what,* for example, a response of *toe* shows analogical reasoning only if there is evidence that the thinker explicitly considered the relation of finger to hand and deliberately sought a response that is related to foot in a similar way. At the very least, this requires evidence that *toe* would not be a spontaneous response to *foot* outside the context of the given analogy. A more stringent criterion is that the thinker can adequately justify his or her response and explain its superiority to alternative possibilities.

Research on classical analogy problems (carefully constructed to require systematic attention to the second-order relationship) indicates that analogical reasoning emerges long after simple analogical inferences, and continues to develop at least through adolescence (Goldman, Pellegrino, Parseghian, & Sallis, 1982; Sternberg & Nigro, 1980; Sternberg & Rifkin, 1979). Ability to explain and justify responses, moreover, is strongly correlated with the proportion of normatively correct conclusions (Goldman et al., 1982). Research and theory of the past decade, however, have focused more on the early development (Goswami, 1991) and pervasive nature (Halford, 1992) of analogical inference (DeLoache et al., Ch. 16, this Volume). Further research on the deliberate and reflective use of such inference—that is, on analogical reasoning—would be welcome. It is here that late developmental trends are likely to be found.

This does not necessarily mean a return to classical analogy problems, however. Two key limitations of such tasks is that they explicitly request analogical reasoning and highlight the relations to be considered. Future research might focus on how individuals (a) decide to seek or use an analogy, (b) consciously identify potentially analogous cases, and (c) deliberately assess the relevance of those cases via systematic consideration of similarities and differences. These are sophisticated competencies that likely develop in adolescence and beyond, but remain largely unexplored.

Precedent-Based Reasoning

Precedent-based reasoning resembles analogical reasoning in that analogous instances provide a basis for constraining one's thinking. In analogical reasoning, however, the analogous instances are merely heuristic. In precedent-based reasoning, on the other hand, application of the precedent forms a stricter constraint. Fidelity to precedent is considered mandatory; apparent deviations from precedent require specific justification. Precedent-based reasoning is important, for example, to certain kinds of legal thinking. In resolving a case, the previous resolution of a relevantly similar case is not merely an example of how the present case might be handled, but a fundamental constraint on the legitimacy of any solution (*Planned Parenthood v. Casey,* 1992; Rissland, 1991).

Research on precedent-based reasoning is sparse. It seems plausible, however, to posit a developmental trend from (a) implicit analogical inference with no differentiation of precedent from analogous instance to (b) explicit recognition of precedent as a distinct type of analogous instance that is to some degree binding, and later toward (c) increasing recognition of the role of current choices in setting new precedents and thus constraining future choices.

Consider, for example, a teacher's response to student behavior that is morally dubious but does not clearly violate any specific rule. Even a young child may see previous responses to such behavior as relevant to the current incident. A more advanced reasoner may explicitly recognize the moral force of precedent: Punishment of the current behavior is more clearly unfair, for example, if another child previously went unpunished for the same behavior. Still more advanced individuals may evaluate a teacher's response to ambiguous behavior with respect to the precedent that response sets for the future.

It seems likely, then, that development of case-based reasoning includes (a) a developmental trend from automatic analogical inference to increasingly self-conscious analogical reasoning and (b) in domains such as law and morality, an increasingly differentiated conception of binding precedents as distinct from heuristic analogies. Such developmental trends, which have received surprisingly little attention from researchers and theorists, almost surely continue into adolescence and beyond.

Legal Reasoning

Legal thinking may be defined as thinking aimed at determining what the law requires or forbids. It is often argued that legal education should be aimed at teaching a student how to "think like a lawyer," that is, to engage in legal reasoning. To refer to legal reasoning is to assume the existence of a particular form of epistemic constraint that is central and/or unique to legal thinking.

As already noted, precedent-based reasoning is important in many legal contexts. It is far from clear, however, that precedent-based reasoning is either central or unique to legal thinking. With respect to centrality, note that laws typically take the form of rules and that judicial decisions often apply and/or provide general principles; thus determination of what the law requires or forbids may involve rule-based or principled reasoning (to be discussed in the next section). With respect to uniqueness, it has already been noted that precedent-based reasoning is important to morality as well as law. If there is no form of reasoning central and/or unique to the domain of law, however, it may be misleading to speak of legal reasoning. Perhaps it would be more appropriate to focus on the application of general forms of reasoning (such as case-based, law-based, and dialectical reasoning) to specific domains of knowledge and action (such as law).

This is an issue to which we will return. First, however, there are other forms of reasoning to be considered.

LAW-BASED REASONING

Law-based reasoning is thinking constrained by the deliberate application of abstract laws that are construed by the individual as justifying his or her beliefs and/or actions. Two general categories of laws may be distinguished: rules and principles. I begin this section by considering logical reasoning, a form of rule-based reasoning that continues to develop well beyond childhood. I then turn to other types of rule-based reasoning. Next, I address principled reasoning as a form of reasoning that is law-based, but not rule-based. Finally, I raise the question of whether scientific thinking constitutes a distinct category of law-based reasoning.

Logical Reasoning

Knowing that a hidden ball is red or blue and that it is not red, 3-year-old Ellen concludes that the ball is blue. From an external perspective, we may theorize that Ellen has made an inference of the form *p or q; not p; therefore q.* Because the conclusion necessarily follows from the premises, we may designate this a deductive inference. Even if Ellen has indeed made this deductive inference, however, many questions remain: Did she intend to reach a conclusion? Did she construe the relevant portion of her knowledge as a set of premises? Does she know that she has made an inference? Does she know that her conclusion follows necessarily from her premises? Is the inference deductive from her point of view, or only from ours?

Children and adults routinely make inferences that can reasonably be construed as involving the application of logical rules (Braine, 1990; Braine & O'Brien, 1991; DeLoache et al., Ch. 16, this Volume; Falmagne & Gonsalves, 1995; Hawkins, Pea, Glick, & Scribner, 1984; Lea et al., 1990; O'Brien, 1987; Rips, 1994; Scholnick, 1990; Scholnick & Wing, 1995; Smith, Langston, & Nisbett, 1992). Logical inference gives rise to logical thinking as children become increasingly purposeful in the application and coordination of such rules. Logical thinking, in turn, gives rise to logical reasoning as individuals increasingly grasp the epistemic properties of logical rules (Keenan, Ruffman, & Olson, 1994). The transition from deductive inference to deductive reasoning, for example, involves increasingly explicit understanding about the logical necessity of deductions (Moshman, 1990).

Studies by Overton and his associates (reviewed in Overton, 1990) suggest that the emergence of logical reasoning from logical inference is an extended process that typically continues long beyond childhood. In one line of investigation, children and adolescents ranging from Grades 4 through 12 were presented with the four-card *selection task,* a much-studied conditional reasoning problem (Overton et al., 1987; Ward & Overton, 1990). The task involves a proposition of the form *if p then q* and four potential sources of information about the truth or falsity of that proposition. Specifically, the thinker may choose to investigate (a) whether a given *p* is associated with *q* or with *not-q;* (b) whether a given *not-p* is associated with *q* or with *not-q;* (c) whether a given *q* is associated with *p* or with *not-p;* and/or (d) whether a given *not-q* is associated with *p* or with *not-p.* Solution of the task requires the insight that only the combination *p and not-q* falsifies a proposition of the form *if p then q.* Thus investigations *a* and *d* are relevant to the truth of the conditional proposition because they could falsify it, whereas investigations *b* and *c* are unnecessary because no possible result of these investigations would disconfirm the conditional proposition. Although young children routinely make simple conditional inferences (Scholnick, 1990; Scholnick & Wing, 1995), the selection task is notoriously difficult even for college students (Evans, 1989; Newstead & Evans, 1995).

Part of the difficulty of the selection task is that the thinker must do more than simply generate a conclusion from premises using a conditional inference rule. Rather, the thinker must coordinate a variety of hypothetical conditional relations, including (a) the given conditional proposition, which the thinker knows may be true or false, and (b) the implications of each of the two possible results for each of the four potential investigations. Although some versions of the selection task are rarely solved by individuals of any age, Overton and his associates showed dramatic increases over the course of adolescence in the ability to solve meaningful variations of the task. The effects of content raise issues of generality that will be addressed later. The developmental trends, however, are consistent with a conception of conditional reasoning as a late-developing form of thinking involving deliberate coordination of conditional inferences on the basis of explicit understanding about the nature and justifiability of conditional inference rules.

In a more direct approach to assessing the development of understanding about the nature of logic, Moshman and Franks (1986) presented 197 individuals in Grades 4 (ages 9 to 10), 7 (ages 12 to 13), and college (ages 18 to 43) with a variety of logic-related tasks. Some of these simply required participants to make a correct inference from a set of premises. Performance on the simple inference tasks was nearly perfect at all ages across a variety of logical forms.

Other tasks involved the same logical forms, but required metalogical judgments about entire arguments. In a variety of conditions across three studies, participants were asked to sort, rank, and evaluate arguments varying with respect to: (a) form; (b) content; (c) empirical truth of the premises; (d) empirical truth of the conclusion; and (e) validity (i.e., whether the conclusion followed from the premises). Of central concern was whether participants would distinguish validity from truth, recognizing that (a) an argument in which the conclusion follows logically from the premises is valid even if the premises and/or conclusion are false, and (b) an argument in which the conclusion does not follow logically from the premises is not valid, even if the premises and/or conclusion are true.

As expected, truth was a salient consideration at all ages. In cases where truth status and validity were in conflict, even college students often had difficulty focusing on the latter. There were substantial age differences, however. Most college students clearly understood the metalogical distinction between valid and invalid arguments and applied this distinction spontaneously, albeit inconsistently. Seventh graders were usually less spontaneous in their application of the concept of validity but nevertheless, in supportive circumstances, most showed genuine understanding. Fourth graders, by contrast, generally failed to distinguish validity from truth, even in conditions where

they were provided with definitions, examples, and/or feedback concerning the nature of validity.

Related research by Markovits and his associates (Markovits & Bouffard-Bouchard, 1992; Markovits & Nantel, 1989; Markovits & Vachon, 1989; see also Efklides, Demetriou, & Metallidou, 1994) has shown that the ability to deduce conclusions from premises explicitly known to be hypothetical or false shows substantial development over the course of adolescence. Markovits and Bouffard-Bouchard (1992), moreover, found a positive relationship between (a) explicit knowledge about the distinction between inferential validity and empirical truth and (b) reasoning in accord with logical norms. Metalogical insight does not guarantee perfect reasoning, but may facilitate the application of logical rules to abstract content and the successful coordination of inferences on complex logical tasks.

Such findings are consistent with the core Piagetian claim that formal or hypothetico-deductive reasoning develops much later than competence in elementary logical inference. Without indicating a sudden transition at any particular age, developmental research on logical reasoning suggests that formal reasoning is common (albeit inconsistent) in adolescents and adults, but rarely seen much before the age of 11. This is not to say, however, that formal reasoning rests on formal operations. The transition from logical inference to logical reasoning may have less to do with logical structure than with the thinker's metacognitive attitude toward the propositions under consideration (Campbell & Bickhard, 1986).

Logical reasoning, then, seems to emerge long after logical inference. Although young children routinely make inferences in accord with rules of logic, only later in development do individuals increasingly think about such rules and understand their epistemic role in justifying connections among propositions. The construction of such metacognitive knowledge about logic may account for late developmental trends in the deliberate application and coordination of logical rules.

Rule-Based Reasoning

Although logical reasoning is the most researched form of rule-based reasoning, similar trends from rule-based inference to rule-based reasoning can be identified with respect to other systems of rules. In a classic investigation of the development of probabilistic concepts, Piaget and Inhelder (1951/1975) interviewed children and adolescents of ages

3 through 15 about chance phenomena involving balls, coins, cards, marbles, counters, toy men, and a spinner rigged with hidden magnets. Results showed developmental changes extending through early adolescence in conceptual knowledge about randomness, proportionality, normal distribution, the law of large numbers, and combinatorial possibilities. Unlike children under age 11, adolescents were frequently able to devise systems for generating all possible permutations, combinations, or other arrangements of a set of elements. Explicit knowledge of combinatorial possibilities, argued Piaget and Inhelder, provides the basis for insight into statistical regularities and thus for rule-based reasoning about patterns and distributions of chance events.

Research over the past several decades has shown that elementary laws of probability are implicit in the probabilistic inferences of children as young as age 4 (Huber & Huber, 1987). Consistent with Piaget and Inhelder's findings, however, it appears that probabilistic and proportional reasoning develop over a period extending well into adolescence (Ahl, Moore, & Dixon, 1992; Dixon & Moore, 1996; Kreitler & Kreitler, 1986; Moore, Dixon, & Haines, 1991). Sophisticated probabilistic concepts and associated forms of reasoning, in fact, remain elusive even in adults (Jones & Harris, 1982; Kosonen & Winne, 1995).

One area of probabilistic reasoning in which late developmental trends have received substantial attention is correlational reasoning. The standard methodological paradigm, devised by Inhelder and Piaget (1958), is to present children and/or adults with frequency data allowing judgments about the covariation of two dichotomous variables. For example, given information about the frequency of each of four potential combinations of hair color and eye color—dark hair/dark eyes; dark hair/light eyes; light hair/dark eyes; light hair/light eyes—it is possible to determine the direction and magnitude of the correlation, if any, between hair color and eye color. Although correlational inferences can be made from isolated bits of data, defensible conclusions about the existence and direction of a correlation require appropriate coordination of frequencies with respect to each of the four possible combinations. Research indicates that systematic application of sophisticated rules for assessing covariation in such data continues to develop at least through adolescence (Inhelder & Piaget, 1958), with substantial variation in adult performance (Shaklee, Holt, Elek, & Hall, 1988).

In many studies of logical and mathematical cognition, response patterns across carefully designed variations of standard tasks suggest the rule-based nature of subjects'

inferences and judgments. Through systematic application of this rule-assessment methodology, Siegler (1981) has demonstrated that even young children use rules in responding to a variety of tasks. His research has indicated developmental trends in multiple domains toward increasingly systematic coordination of such rules.

In addition to logical and mathematical rules, individuals may also apply a variety of social and moral rules. Although such rules may be identified in the ongoing social and moral inferences of young children, increasingly sophisticated conceptual knowledge regarding the nature and justification of such rules may underlie the long-term construction of social and moral reasoning through adolescence and, for many, well into adulthood (Moshman, 1995b).

Holyoak and Cheng (1995a, 1995b) have proposed that people often solve logical reasoning tasks by assimilating them to their knowledge of certain kinds of social, moral, and legal rules. Depending on content and context, for example, a conditional of the form *if p then q* might be construed as a deontic statement of permission or obligation (e.g., if you are at least 21 years old, then you may drink beer). This may activate a pragmatic reasoning schema that might suffice to solve the task in question. Research with variations of the selection task has indicated that pragmatic reasoning schemas may enable appropriate selections by adults (Holyoak & Cheng, 1995a, 1995b; Manktelow & Over, 1995) and by children as young as age 7 (Girotto, Blaye, & Farioli, 1989; Girotto, Gilly, Blaye, & Light, 1989; Light, Blaye, Gilly, & Girotto, 1989).

The work on pragmatic reasoning schemas suggests that rule-based inference and reasoning often rely on content-specific social and moral rules, rather than on more abstract logical rules. A more radical approach entirely rejects the assumption that people engage in rule-based inference or reasoning. Johnson-Laird and Byrne (1991; Johnson-Laird, Byrne, & Schaeken, 1992) have argued that reasoning involves the construction and manipulation of concrete mental models of potential states of affairs and is thus a semantic, rather than a formal or syntactic, process. Reasoning does not require the application of rules, at least none that can be designated as logical. Developmental changes in reasoning, in this view, reflect (a) emergence of the linguistic ability to comprehend logical terms in the premises (e.g., *all, some, none, if, and, or,* and *not*), and thus construct appropriate models of the premises, and (b) improvements in the manipulation of these models due to the growth of processing capacity (Johnson-Laird, 1990).

Although theorists generally agree that children and adults can and do use pragmatic reasoning schemas and mental models for a variety of cognitive purposes, including solving many kinds of logical problems, most argue that people also apply logical and other rules (Braine, 1990; Braine & O'Brien, 1991; DeLoache et al., Ch. 16, this Volume; Nisbett, Fong, Lehman, & Cheng, 1987; O'Brien, Braine, & Yang, 1994; Scholnick, 1990; Sloman, 1996; E. E. Smith et al., 1992; L. Smith, 1993). Consistent with the view that people use both rules and models, Markovits (1993; Markovits & Vachon, 1990) has proposed a theoretical integration of Piagetian and information-processing approaches to conditional reasoning in which developing conceptions of necessity and possibility (Piaget, 1987) are associated with qualitative transitions to increasingly abstract uses of mental models over the course of childhood and adolescence.

We may thus posit a category of rule-based reasoning including, but not limited to, logical and mathematical reasoning. Regardless of the specific rules involved, rule-based inference gives rise to rule-based thinking as children become increasingly purposeful in the application and coordination of rules (Zelazo, Reznick, & Piñon, 1995). Rule-based thinking, in turn, gives rise to rule-based reasoning as individuals increasingly grasp the epistemic properties of their rules (Keenan et al., 1994; Moshman, 1995a, 1995b).

Methodologically, then, a key criterion for demonstrating that an individual has engaged in rule-based reasoning is evidence that the individual is purposely applying what she or he deems to be epistemologically justifiable rules. Strict application of this criterion may be useful in resolving the apparent paradox that young children routinely make inferences in accord with logical, mathematical, and other norms (Braine, 1990; Hawkins et al., 1984; Huber & Huber, 1987; Scholnick, 1990; Scholnick & Wing, 1995), whereas adults routinely make inferences that deviate systematically from such norms (Evans, 1989; Newstead & Evans, 1995).

With respect to young children, task demands are often such that genuine reasoning is unnecessary. Hawkins et al. (1984), for example, showed that young children can reach correct conclusions from various sets of premises. Markovits et al. (1989) replicated these findings, but showed that removing the logical connections across premises made little difference in young children's responses, with increasing attention to logical form over the course of later childhood.

Tasks designed for adults, on the other hand, are often sufficiently complex that, depending on how a participant interprets the social context and task instructions, she or he may engage in sophisticated reasoning without reaching the conclusion indicated by the normative rules that the researcher intended to assess. Hilton (1995), for example, shows how conversational assumptions and attributions may account for reasonable but incorrect responses to a variety of reasoning tasks. Thus, early success on some logical tasks and adult failure on others may mask an underlying developmental transition from automatic rule-based inferences to self-consciously rule-based reasoning.

Principled Reasoning

Reflection on laws may generate a distinction between rules and principles. Rules are algorithms that yield a determinate answer—for example, laws of deduction, arithmetic, or probability. If two individuals are applying the same rule in the same circumstance, they must reach the same conclusion unless one of them makes a mistake. Principles, in contrast, are general guidelines whose application involves heuristic judgments. Reasonable people may differ about such judgments. Principled reasoning derives from commitment to some set of principles on the basis of a general metacognitive understanding about the nature and use of principles.

A variety of theorists have proposed principles implicit in everyday inference. Hilton (1995) and Politzer (1986), for example, discussed conversational principles that guide social interaction. Walton (1996) proposed a set of argumentation schemes that provide heuristic guidance in contexts where formal rules of logic are inadequate. Tversky and Kahneman (1974) identified several judgment heuristics routinely applied to probabilistic situations by children (Jacobs & Potenza, 1991) as well as adults.

In a study of mathematical reasoning, Dixon and Moore (1996) presented 116 students in Grades 2, 5, 8, 11, and college with tasks requiring them to predict the temperature that would result from adding one container of water to another. Patterns of judgment across tasks and verbal protocols were used to identify (a) intuitive principles concerning the effects of relative temperature and quantity on the direction and relative magnitude of temperature change and (b) mathematical strategies for calculating final temperature. Application of appropriate principles increased with age through adolescence and was a necessary, but not sufficient, condition for use of appropriate mathematical strategies.

Kohlberg (1984) suggested that principled reasoning is central to higher levels of moral development. The advanced moral reasoner construes morality as a matter of acting in accord with justifiable principles. Unlike moral rules, such principles do not dictate the one right solution to a moral dilemma. Rather, they constrain the range of acceptable solutions. Kohlberg's theory, especially in its later versions, sets stringent structural criteria for principled moral reasoning, with the result that such reasoning apparently fails to develop in most people and is rarely seen prior to late adolescence. Moshman (1995b) proposed a less stringent conception of moral principles in the form of metalaws justifying a variety of moral rules. Such principles, he suggested, are implicit in the understanding and use of moral rules by young children and increasingly become explicit objects of reflection over a period extending through adolescence.

Helwig (1995a, in press) and Dunkle (1993) specifically studied the development of principles related to freedoms of expression and religion. They found substantial improvement over the course of childhood and adolescence in the comprehension, application, justification, and coordination of such principles. Evidence for both early competence and late developmental change notwithstanding, it appears that adolescents and adults show forms of principled reasoning that are qualitatively superior to the rule-based inferences of young children (Moshman, 1993).

Available evidence is thus consistent with a general trend from the use of implicit principles to the deliberate application of explicit principles (Moshman, 1995b). One may thus posit a developmental trend from (a) undifferentiated law-based inferences toward (b) rule-based and principled reasoning.

Scientific Reasoning

Many theorists and researchers have been particularly interested in empirical inference, in which the thinker generalizes from what is construed as information about some aspect of reality. At a primitive level, an individual might simply make inductive inferences from available data without any intention to generate knowledge. At a more advanced level, the individual may intend to make inferences in such a way as to yield correct generalizations about specific empirical phenomena and may deliberately seek new evidence with this in mind. We may call this scientific *thinking*.

In attempting to reach the best generalizations, thinkers may constrain their inferences in accord with what they take to be appropriate norms. A major line of research initiated by Inhelder and Piaget (1958) has assumed that the

isolation of variables and corresponding rules of inference are fundamental norms of science. Such research indicates developmental trends extending into adolescence in the successful use of such rules (Kuhn & Brannock, 1977).

Others, however, have argued that scientific thinking cannot be reduced to some set of rules; rather, it relies heavily on heuristic principles. Principled scientific reasoning might, for example, involve general preferences for theories superior in parsimony, explanatory range, empirical adequacy, and internal consistency. Samarapungavan (1992) found that conformity to some such principles can be detected in the scientific thinking of children as young as age 7, but that there is improvement well beyond that age in the ability to provide explicit justifications based on principles of theory selection and in the application of such principles to theories inconsistent with one's own beliefs.

Theorists have also questioned the common assumption that scientific reasoning, at its core, involves seeking data that would disconfirm one's hypothesis. A number of theorists have proposed that confirmation bias—an allegedly irrational tendency to accumulate supportive evidence, rather than genuinely testing a hypothesis—may be better construed as a confirmation heuristic that serves a useful purpose in early phases of scientific inquiry (Tweney & Chitwood, 1995). Similarly, Koslowski and Maqueda (1993) argue that confirmation and disconfirmation are interrelated aspects of a defensible heuristic approach to testing and revising theories.

These considerations suggest that scientific thinking may improve with the development of rule-based and principled reasoning and raise the possibility that some sorts of law-based reasoning may be sufficiently central and unique to science as to be designated *scientific reasoning*. As we will see, however, questions about the existence and nature of scientific reasoning are complicated by indications that scientific thinking involves a complex dialectical coordination of theories, evidence, and methodologies (Chinn & Brewer, 1993; DeLoache et al., Ch. 16, this Volume; Dunbar & Klahr, 1989; Klahr et al., 1993; Kuhn et al., 1988, 1995; Kuhn, Schauble, & Garcia-Mila, 1992; Schauble, 1990, 1996). The present discussion of methodological rules and heuristics only begins our consideration of scientific reasoning. We will return to the topic shortly.

DIALECTICAL REASONING

Although the term *dialectic* is notably protean in its meanings, it generally refers to a developmental transformation.

Cognitive development is construed by many theorists as an intrinsically dialectical process. We may define dialectical thinking as the deliberate coordination of inferences for the purpose of making cognitive progress. Such thinking may be designated as *dialectical reasoning* to the extent that it rests on explicit knowledge about criteria for assessing such progress. Thus, the development of dialectical reasoning involves increasingly explicit knowledge about the nature of cognitive development and increasingly deliberate efforts to further that process.

Dialectical Reflection

In some cases, a thinker believes that a previous concrete case provides an appropriate constraint for resolving a current issue. I have defined the effort to apply a previous case to a current one as case-based reasoning. In other cases, a thinker believes that an abstract law provides the appropriate constraint. I have defined the application of such a law as law-based reasoning.

However, there are often a variety of potentially applicable cases and laws. It is not unusual, moreover, for these to point in different directions. With respect to a particular moral dilemma, for example, the thinker may perceive conflicts among applicable rules, principles, and precedents. Moreover, the moral obligations indicated by applicable rules, principles, and precedents may be construed as inconsistent with moral intuitions based on one's experience with analogous situations. Deliberate efforts to achieve coherence by reconstructing one's rules, principles, intuitions, and/or conceptions of precedent may be designated as *dialectical reflection*. More generally, dialectical reflection may be defined as a deliberate effort to make conceptual progress through active metacognition.

Basseches (1980, 1984), expanding on the work of Riegel (1973), formulated a set of 24 dialectical schemata—forms of thinking that apply sophisticated knowledge about structure, relations, context, perspective, contradiction, activity, change, and progress. He then interviewed nine first-year college students, nine seniors, and nine faculty members about the nature of education in order to get samples of reasoning about a complex issue. The dialectical schemata turned out to be well represented in the thinking of these research participants, and use of the schemata was positively correlated with educational level, consistent with the view that, at least among well-educated individuals, dialectical reflection continues to develop through late adolescence and early adulthood. Research by Chandler and Boutilier (1992) suggests that dialectical reasoning may be critical for understanding living, social, and other dynamic systems.

For reflection to be designated as dialectical reasoning, it must involve a deliberate effort to apply some criterion of progress. As already suggested, a common and important such criterion is increasing coherence. Thus, dialectical reflection may be construed broadly as encompassing what Moshman (1995a) called coherence-based reasoning. This would include both (a) reasoning aimed at achieving the temporal coherence of a narrative that unfolds across time (Feldman, Bruner, Kalmar, & Renderer, 1993), and (b) reasoning aimed at achieving more abstract forms of structural coherence (Fallon, 1987). Although an implicit preference for narrative or structural coherence may be characteristic even of young children's cognition (Piaget, 1985), the deliberate quest for coherence is usefully construed as a form of dialectical reasoning.

Argumentation

In many cases, dialectical reasoning is a profoundly social process. Kuhn (1991) investigated how adolescents and adults justify and defend their ideas in the face of alternative interpretations and viewpoints. Although participants were interviewed individually, they were challenged to provide arguments adequate to convince others and to respond to potential others who might hold different ideas.

The data showed argumentation skills to be far from perfect. People frequently failed to justify their own ideas and to evaluate alternatives on the basis of relevant considerations. Nevertheless, Kuhn provides a picture of reasoning as a collaborative process in which people formulate, communicate, criticize, justify, and revise their various ideas. Argumentation is usefully construed as a process of dialectical reasoning in which two or more individuals coordinate multiple cases and laws in a shared effort to make conceptual progress. That is, although arguments may be formulated and evaluated by individuals, argumentation is a fundamentally social process of collaborative reasoning. A number of studies suggest that, in some circumstances, reciprocal argumentation among two or more individuals may yield better results than individual reasoning (Dimant & Bearison, 1991).

Moshman and Geil (in press), for example, showed qualitatively superior performance in groups of college students reasoning about the original and most difficult version of the selection task (see earlier discussion under *Logical Reasoning*) than in individuals faced with the same task. Students solved the task either individually or in groups of 5 or 6. The groups were instructed to discuss the task with each other until reaching a consensus. Thus, in addition to the logical reasoning required in both conditions, the group condition involved a sustained process of argumentation. That is, group members engaged in a process of collaborative reasoning in which they proposed, justified, criticized, and defended a variety of potential solutions.

The difference between individual and group conditions was stark. Consistent with earlier research using this version of the task (Evans, 1989; Newstead & Evans, 1995), only 9% of students in the individual condition successfully tested the hypothesized conditional relation by systematically seeking evidence that could falsify it. In contrast, the correct falsification pattern was the consensus response for 75% of the 20 groups.

In half of the groups, individuals were asked to propose their own solutions prior to group discussion, thus enabling comparison of individual and group solutions. Of the 57 students in these 10 groups, 35 switched from incorrect to correct response patterns in the course of discussion, while only two showed the reverse transition. Moreover, these changes were not simply a matter of succumbing to peer pressure. The falsification response pattern was not initially the most common view in any group. Nevertheless, it was the pattern chosen by eight of these 10 groups. There were three groups, in fact, where not a single individual had initially selected the falsification pattern; all three of these groups, however, were among those that ultimately selected this pattern as the consensus solution.

These results support a conception of argumentation as a rational group process that may, in some circumstances, be superior to individual reasoning (Kobayashi, 1994). Such a conception, in turn, has important implications for our conception of reasoning. Reasoning is traditionally viewed as taking place within an individual. An alternative is to view reasoning as a fundamentally social process of group interchange, with individual reasoning a derivative phenomenon involving internalized aspects of the group process (Salmon & Zeitz, 1995). A middle-ground possibility is that individual and collaborative reasoning are partially distinct and equally fundamental, developing via a complex process of reciprocal influence.

Legal and Scientific Reasoning Revisited

As noted earlier, precedent often plays a central role in legal thinking. It would be too simple, however, to identify legal reasoning as a version of precedent-based reasoning. Fallon (1987), for example, proposes that constitutional interpretation not only involves consideration of (a) precedent, but also of (b) the literal meaning of specifically relevant provisions of the constitutional text; (c) historical considerations regarding the intended meaning of that text; (d) general considerations of constitutional theory; and (e) general ethical principles. Constitutional reasoning, in his view, properly involves a process of dialectical reflection that attempts to bring these five considerations into equilibrium. More generally, it appears that legal thinking involves a variety of forms of case-based, law-based, and dialectical reasoning.

Scientific thinking, it appears, is no less complex. Kuhn and her associates (1989; Kuhn et al., 1988, 1992, 1995; Schauble, 1990, 1996) have investigated scientific thinking as a dialectical process involving the coordination of theories and data. As noted earlier, scientific thinking can be construed more simply as a matter of following methodological rules, such as holding all variables but one constant or seeking data that would falsify one's hypothesis. Philosophers of science generally agree, however, that no set of methodological rules provides a direct path to scientific truth (R. Kitchener, 1986). Although acknowledging the role of methodological rules, Kuhn and her associates have found that (a) people's theories affect the collection and interpretation of data; (b) nevertheless, the resulting evidence sometimes leads to appropriate changes in those theories; and (c) the effort to coordinate theories and data sometimes leads to reflection on and reconstruction of strategies for knowledge acquisition. Research by Dunbar and Klahr (1989; Klahr et al., 1993) has yielded similar results (see also DeLoache et al., Ch. 16, this Volume).

In a broad-ranging review of the philosophical and psychological literatures on reflective theory change, Chinn and Brewer (1993) noted seven ways that individuals may respond to anomalous data.

1. The data may simply be ignored;
2. The data may be rejected as resulting from methodological error, random processes, or fraud;
3. The data may be excluded as outside the domain of the theory in question;
4. The data may be held in abeyance pending further articulation and development of the theory;
5. The data may be reinterpreted so as to render them consistent with the theory;

6. Peripheral aspects of the theory may be modified to accommodate the data; and,

7. There may be a change in core theoretical commitments.

What happens when one confronts anomalous data is a function of many factors, including (a) entrenchment of the relevant theory; (b) metatheoretical beliefs about theories and theory change; (c) other background knowledge; (d) availability of a plausible alternative theory; (e) quality of the alternative theory with respect to metatheoretical criteria such as scope, parsimony, empirical support, internal consistency, consistency with other theories, and fruitfulness in generating new research; (f) credibility, clarity, and scope of the anomalous data; and (g) the extent to which the individual reflects on the relevant theories and data.

Developmentally, the ability to distinguish generalizations from data and apply logical rules concerning the relation between these is typically present by age 6 (Ruffman, Perner, Olson, & Doherty, 1993; Sodian, Zaitchik, & Carey, 1991). The ability to construe such generalizations as hypotheses and evaluate potential sources of data, however, continues to develop at least through adolescence (Overton, 1990; Overton et al., 1987; Ward & Overton, 1990). The ongoing coordination of theories, data, and methodologies over a series of investigations, moreover, may require processes of dialectical reflection that continue to develop, for some, long beyond childhood (Dunbar & Klahr, 1989; Klahr et al., 1993; Kuhn, 1989; Kuhn et al., 1988, 1992, 1995; Schauble, 1990, 1996). Although demonstrably inadequate strategies and interpretations are common at all ages, these studies have shown developmental progress beyond childhood in the ability to deliberately coordinate theories, data, and methodologies so as to improve one's understanding. Scientific thinking, in other words, appears to become increasingly dialectical.

With these considerations in mind, we may return to the earlier questions about legal and scientific reasoning. Given that there does not appear to be any form of reasoning central and unique to thinking about law, it is not clear what it means to speak of legal reasoning. Similarly, given the lack of evidence for a particular form of reasoning central and unique to empirical investigation, it may be misleading to speak of scientific reasoning.

A direct comparison of legal and scientific thinking, however, suggests that they may indeed rest on distinguishable forms of rationality. Precedent often plays a key role in the justification of a legal claim, whereas in the scientific context, a comparable appeal to history or authority would likely be seen as fundamentally illegitimate. Correspondingly, scientific respect for empirical data arguably defines a form of rationality distinct from the precedent-based rationality of law. Such considerations suggest the possibility that various forms of case-based, law-based, and dialectical reasoning can be coordinated so as to produce new forms of reasoning unique to particular domains of knowledge (such as law) or types of thinking (such as hypothesis testing). Empirically and conceptually, however, we are a long way from knowing what those forms of reasoning might be.

THE RATIONAL BASIS OF REASONING

Reasoning, as defined earlier, involves constraining one's thinking on the basis of explicit knowledge about various mental actions and the justifiability of their results. By definition, reasoning is done by a rational agent, one who has reasons for his or her beliefs and behavior. In this section, I elaborate on the nature and development of rationality.

Metacognitive Understanding

Research already reviewed suggests that conceptual knowledge about cognition begins to emerge during childhood but, for most individuals, continues to develop at least into adolescence. A strong case can be made that the emergence of increasingly sophisticated metacognitive understanding is a central aspect of advanced cognitive development.

With respect to logical reasoning, for example, we have seen that even young children routinely make a variety of correct inferences (Braine, 1990; Hawkins et al., 1984; Scholnick, 1990; Scholnick & Wing, 1995). Metalogical understanding, however—conceptual knowledge about the nature of logic—is a later development. Although young children have intuitions of possibility, impossibility, necessity, and contingency, reflection on the logic of such intuitions generates higher levels of understanding about their significance and interrelations (Piaget, 1987; Piaget & Voyat, 1979; Pieraut-Le Bonniec, 1980). Recognizing logically necessary relations of hypothetical possibilities, for example, most adolescents and adults show an appreciation of inferential validity rarely seen in children much before age 11 (Markovits & Vachon, 1989; Moshman, 1990; Moshman & Franks, 1986).

Similarly, even young children are able to reach a conclusion about a hypothesis on the basis of evidence. Research suggests that children begin distinguishing generalizations from data as early as age 6 (Ruffman, et al., 1993; Sodian et al., 1991). The construction of metatheoretical understanding, however, appears to continue at least through adolescence. Developing individuals show increasing ability to construe generalizations as hypotheses, and to construe data as evidence bearing on those hypotheses. This may account for the long-term development of a deliberate orientation toward isolating variables, seeking falsifying evidence, and coordinating theories with evidence in ongoing investigations (Kuhn, 1989, 1991; Kuhn et al., 1988, 1995; Overton, 1990; Schauble, 1990, 1996). Thus, with development, the use of theories may become increasingly sophisticated because of the increasing ability to think *about* theories (Inhelder & Piaget, 1958).

These findings have important implications for our conception of the development of rationality. If we define rationality as correct inference, even young children are substantially rational and developmental trends in rationality are far from robust. If, on the other hand, we define rationality as involving some degree of metacognitive understanding about knowledge and thinking, a stronger case can be made that rationality develops over a period of time that, for many people, extends long beyond childhood (Moshman, 1994). Theoretical conceptions of cognitive development increasingly stress emergence of metacognitive understanding. Campbell and Bickhard (1986), for example, define higher stages as higher levels of reflection. Taking a somewhat different approach, Demetriou, Efklides, and Platsidou (1993) posit a "hypercognitive system," a developing "supersystem" that understands, organizes, and influences other aspects of cognition.

There remains the question of the relation of metacognitive understanding to reasoning. If metacognitive understanding were completely unrelated to normatively correct reasoning, one might wonder why it develops. Moshman (1994) suggests a conception of rationality as "metasubjective objectivity," involving defensible forms of reasoning that emerge via reflection on one's subjectivity. Correlational evidence indicates positive relationships between metacognitive understanding and normatively appropriate reasoning (Goldman et al., 1982; Kuhn, 1991; Markovits & Bouffard-Bouchard, 1992). Microgenetic research suggests that long-term reflection on reasoning leads not only to knowledge about reasoning, but to corresponding improvements in the quality of reasoning (Kuhn et al., 1992, 1995; Schauble, 1990, 1996).

Epistemic Cognition

Epistemic cognition is an aspect of metacognitive understanding involving knowledge about the nature and limits of knowledge, including knowledge about the justifiability of various cognitive processes and actions. A variety of theories and research programs have addressed the development of epistemic cognition (Baxter Magolda, 1992; Belenky, Clinchy, Goldberger, & Tarule, 1986; Broughton, 1978; Chandler, Boyes, & Ball, 1990; King & Kitchener, 1994; K. Kitchener, 1983; Kuhn, 1991; Orr & Luszcz, 1994; Perry, 1970; Reich, Oser, & Valentin, 1994; Schommer, 1994; Schommer & Walker, 1995; Schraw & Moshman, 1995).

Research into epistemic cognition typically involves interviewing children, adolescents, and/or adults about the justification of knowledge in general and/or about the epistemic properties of their own theories and reasoning. The most systematic approach to the assessment of epistemic cognition is the Reflective Judgment Interview (RJI) developed by King and Kitchener (1994). The RJI uses a semistructured format in which the interviewer presents a series of epistemic dilemmas. One such dilemma, for example, involves contradictory evidence regarding the safety of chemical additives in food. For each dilemma, the interviewee is asked about the origin and justification of his or her own viewpoint; whether this viewpoint could ever be proven correct; why people, including experts, disagree; and how such disagreements should be interpreted or resolved. Research with the RJI has provided substantial support for King and Kitchener's seven-stage model of the development of reflective judgment.

Although differing as to specifics and terminology, most theorists of epistemic cognition have postulated a developmental sequence from objectivist to subjectivist to rationalist conceptions of cognition over the course of adolescence and early adulthood, with substantial individual differences in the extent of progress through these levels. The objectivist construes knowledge as absolute and unproblematic. Justification, if considered at all, is simply a matter of appealing to direct observation or to the pronouncements of an authority. Such epistemic conceptions are typical of children and commonly seen in adolescents and adults as well.

Subjectivist conceptions of cognition involve relativist epistemologies. Knowledge is deemed to be uncertain, ambiguous, idiosyncratic, contextual, and/or subjective; justification in any strong or general sense is considered impossible. As one subject put it, "I wouldn't say that one person is wrong and another person is right. Each person, I think, has their own truth" (King & Kitchener, 1994, p. 64). Although some researchers have concluded that systematic subjectivism is rarely predominant before the college years (King & Kitchener, 1994), there is evidence that relativist conceptions of knowledge are common among adolescents (Chandler et al., 1990).

Finally, some individuals appear to make progress in late adolescence or beyond toward a more rationalist epistemology. Without returning to earlier notions of absolute and final truth or abandoning insights regarding context and subjectivity, the rationalist believes there are justifiable norms of inquiry such that, in some cases, some beliefs reasonably may be deemed to be better justified than others. Theory and research on epistemic cognition, then, are consistent with a view of rationality as metacognitive in nature and developing, at least in some cases, well into adulthood.

There is also evidence linking epistemic cognition to other aspects of cognition. Schommer (1994; Schommer & Walker, 1995) has identified epistemic beliefs that predict better comprehension and academic performance. Kuhn (1991) has shown a positive relationship between holding a rationalist epistemology and skill in argumentation. Chandler et al. (1990) provided evidence that advanced forms of epistemic cognition are positively associated with identity formation and negatively associated with psychopathology. Thus, epistemic cognition appears to be interconnected with learning, thinking, reasoning, and development.

Rational Identity

Although rationality is in part a cognitive phenomenon, the development of rationality should not be narrowly construed as the development of purely cognitive competencies. The ideally rational individual is one who spontaneously seeks relevant evidence and alternative views with the intent of altering his or her beliefs as appropriate. Such a person may be conceived as having a "critical spirit" (Siegel, 1988).

Critical spirit is more a matter of disposition than of ability. Perkins, Jay, and Tishman (1993) propose that good thinking includes dispositions to (a) be open-minded, flexible, and adventurous; (b) sustain intellectual curiosity; (c) clarify and seek understanding; (d) be planful and strategic; (e) be intellectually careful; (f) seek and evaluate reasons; and (g) be metacognitive. Although such dispositions would be of little use without associated cognitive abilities, those abilities may remain inert without the associated dispositions.

At a more global level, Cederblom (1989) suggests a developmental trend from (a) identifying oneself with one's beliefs toward (b) identifying oneself as a belief-forming process. To the extent that one identifies oneself with one's beliefs, any threat to those beliefs is likely to be seen as a threat to the self. Thus, even if one has the cognitive competence to change those beliefs appropriately, one is likely to resist evidence or arguments that suggest such change is necessary. To the extent that one identifies oneself as a belief-forming process, however, one is more likely to apply one's rational competencies. In this latter case, one construes the process of appropriately changing one's beliefs as confirming one's identity as a rational agent.

Rationality, then, transcends cognition to include motivational and dispositional considerations. The development of rationality is best construed as including the formation of a variety of intellectual dispositions and, more broadly, a critical spirit and a rational identity.

THE REFLECTIVE CONSTRUCTION OF RATIONALITY

I have proposed that advanced cognitive development is in large part the development of reasoning—that is, epistemologically self-constrained thinking. Reasoning, thus defined, is done by a rational agent—that is, an individual whose thinking is rooted in epistemic forms of metacognitive understanding. It follows that cognitive development beyond childhood consists largely of the development of rationality.

Now turn to questions of developmental process. In the present section, I present two approaches to accounting for the development of rationality—causal determinism and rational constructivism. Highlighting the latter, I conclude that rationality is best construed as a metacognitive phenomenon constructed through active processes of reflection.

Causal Determinism

A standard form of scientific explanation is to suggest that some event or process is caused by some other event or process. For example, if object A collides with stationary object B and the latter immediately begins to move, we are likely to explain the motion of B as caused by the impact of A. Causal explanations raise a variety of philosophical questions and become increasingly problematic as one moves from (a) physical interactions of macroscopic objects to (b) biological processes of anatomic and physiological development, then to (c) psychological processes of elementary behavioral development, and finally to (d) advanced cognitive development. In the present subsection, I consider three variations of the causal determinist approach and some limitations of each (Table 19.1).

The *universalist maturationist* approach makes the nativist assumption that cognitive development is an epigenetic process directed by genetic programs universal across the human species. Genes, in this view, not only play a role in cognitive development, but have primary responsibility for directing its course.

The proposition that genes influence cognitive development is not controversial. Characteristics of the human genome undoubtedly affect the course of cognitive development (Karmiloff-Smith, 1992; Spelke & Newport, Ch. 6, Volume 1) and influence the nature of advanced human cognition. A number of neo-Piagetian theories, moreover, have suggested age-related constraints on cognitive development, perhaps due to changes related to processing capacity (Case, Ch. 15, this Volume; Demetriou & Efklides, 1994; Demetriou et al., 1993; de Ribaupierre & Pascual-Leone, 1979; Halford, 1993; Johnson-Laird, 1990; Lamborn et al., 1994; Marini & Case, 1994). Although the explanation of such constraints is a matter of dispute, it seems plausible that they reflect genetically-based maturation of the nervous system.

Even if nervous system maturation plays a role in later cognitive development, however, there do not appear to be genetically based "critical periods" for such development (Kuhn et al., 1995). There is a fundamental difference, moreover, between the views that genes constrain development and that they determine its course. There is no evidence that the structure of advanced cognition is genetically determined. Substantial individual and cultural

differences with respect to advanced cognition, in fact, are difficult to reconcile with a universalist maturationist metatheory. No current theorist, to my knowledge, proposes that advanced cognitive development is a causal process directed by the genes.

The *relativist enculturationist* approach suggests that cultures differ in fundamental ways with respect to what is deemed to be advanced cognition. Changes in advanced cognition involve the inculcation of culturally valued skills and ideas and are unique to particular cultures. Indeed, from this perspective, there is no such thing as advanced cognition except within the context of a particular culture.

Culture and cognition are indeed intricately interrelated across the lifespan (Rogoff, 1990, Ch. 14, this Volume; Rogoff & Chavajay, 1995). Available evidence provides little or no support, however, for a determinist view that late cognitive changes are directly caused by forces unique to particular cultures. Even if environmental forces do exert some degree of causal influence, moreover, there are major conceptual difficulties for any suggestion that such changes constitute cognitive development.

An *interactionist contextualist* view would suggest that later changes in cognition are generated by complex ongoing interactions of genetic and environmental (including cultural) factors. One would therefore expect substantial variability in pathways of cognitive change. Such pathways, in fact, might be largely unique to particular individuals. Again, this casts considerable doubt on the existence of forms of cognition that are in some general sense advanced and raises questions about what changes in cognition, if any, are in some general sense developmental.

Interactionist contextualism is a more plausible and sophisticated perspective than either genetic or cultural determinism. The idea that genetic and environmental forces interact throughout the course of development, in fact, is fully consistent with a constructivist metatheory. The conceptual and empirical problems with construing genetic and environmental factors as causal forces that determine developmental change, however, are not resolved simply by recognizing the complex interactions of such factors. In particular, it is difficult to see how any causal determinist view can account for the sort of epistemic self-understanding that marks progress in rationality.

Rational Constructivism

A *rational constructivist* perspective emphasizes the active role of the developing individual in constructing advanced

TABLE 19.1 Theoretical Approaches to Advanced Cognitive Development

Developmental Paradigm	Basis for developmental change	Nature of developmental pathways
Universalist Maturationist	Genetic determinism	Psychologically universal
Relativist Enculturationist	Cultural determinism	Unique to each culture
Interactionist Contextualist	Interaction of genes and environment	Unique to each individual
Rational Constructivist	Reflective construction by rational agent	Epistemologically universal

forms of cognition that transcend less adequate earlier forms. The result is an ongoing progress toward higher levels of rationality. Theorists in this tradition typically postulate developmental sequences that are deemed to have epistemological validity across cultures. Because the construction of advanced cognition may be facilitated or hindered by a variety of individual and cultural factors, individual and cultural differences in the rate and extent of progress through these idealized stages are likely. Thus, although the stages have some degree of epistemic universality, psychological progress through them need not be universal.

Rational constructivism, by postulating a rational agent, may provide a more plausible account of progress in rationality than any version of the causal determinist perspective. Without denying the importance and interactive nature of genetic and environmental influences, rational constructivist theories emphasize the mediating role of the epistemic subject as an active force in its own development (R. Kitchener, 1986; Smith, 1993).

There remains, however, the problem of accounting for the origin of rational agency. A plausible developmental scenario is that an interaction of genetic and environmental forces produces an active biological agent, which transforms itself into an active cognitive agent, which increasingly constructs an ability to reflect on its own cognition, thus transforming itself into a rational agent that, to some extent, acts on the basis of its own reasons. Thus, a causal determinist view may be helpful in explaining the prenatal beginnings of developmental change. A constructivist worldview, with its emphasis on the active organism, becomes more and more relevant, however. With further development, moreover, the process of construction becomes increasingly cognitive and ultimately self-reflective, thus generating the sort of rational agent whose actions are best understood from a rational constructivist perspective.

For a rational constructivist, then, development occurs not as a result of genes, environment, or some interaction of the two, but as a result of active cognitive reflection (Berkowitz & Keller, 1994; Kitchener, 1986; Piaget, 1985; Smith, 1993). By reflecting on current cognition, the thinker may reconstruct his or her own cognitions in such a way as to render their implicit properties explicit (Campbell & Bickhard, 1986; Karmiloff-Smith, 1992). As we have seen, for example, reflection on the logical necessity implicit in one's deductive inferences may be central to the construction of deductive reasoning (Moshman, 1990).

Reflection is an inferential process, however, and at higher levels, is usefully construed as an act of reasoning. Rational constructivism thus directs our attention to reasoning as both a context for, and a process of, development.

Reasoning and Development

A rational constructivist perspective suggests that reasoning is not only a product of reflection, but also a context for further reflection and thus, further development. In the process of applying analogical relations, precedents, rules, and/or principles, one is likely to reflect on one's reasoning in such a way as to generate higher levels of epistemic understanding and, over the long run, better reasoning.

With respect to the role of reasoning in development, however, there is an important distinction to be made between (a) case-based and law-based reasoning and (b) dialectical reasoning. Although case-based and law-based reasoning may generate reflection and, in time, developmental change, they are not developmental processes per se. Dialectical reasoning, on the other hand, is usefully construed as a self-conscious form of the developmental process of reflection.

Consider, for example, an individual who applies a moral principle to resolve some dilemma. If the principle is merely implicit in his or her processing of information, this would be an example of inference, but not reasoning. If the individual understands the principle as a principle and deliberately applies it because it is perceived as morally relevant, this would be reasoning. Provided the dilemma is adequately resolved, however, there may be no further reflection on the principle.

If, however, the individual is motivated to engage in extended reflection on the principle, including its justifiability and its relation to other principles, this may lead to a qualitatively higher level of moral understanding and thus constitute a developmental transition. At the very least, we may suggest that such reflection involves an implicit dialectic. To the extent that the individual perceives difficulties with his or her current set of principles and intentionally coordinates and reconstructs them for the purpose of achieving a higher level of moral understanding, we may posit a process of dialectical reflection that is simultaneously a process of reasoning and a process of development.

Important developmental changes in cognition may also be generated by extended argumentation. Argumentation may not only be a context that encourages reflection, but may also enable the coconstruction of a collective rationality that serves as a particularly useful object of reflection. Peer discussion of a moral dilemma, for example, may generate a set of principles, including associated justifications, critiques, responses, and rejoinders, that constitute a collective structure of moral understanding none of the participants could have generated alone. Reflection on this structure may, for some of those participants, contribute to progress in moral understanding. A variety of theorists have emphasized the epistemic and developmental significance of argumentation among peers (Goldman, 1994; Habermas, 1990; Kuhn, 1991; Moshman, 1995a, 1995b; Piaget, 1924/1972; Salmon & Zeitz, 1995; Youniss & Damon, 1992), and there is substantial evidence for the role of peer interaction in developmental change (Dimant & Bearison, 1991; Kobayashi, 1994).

In a microgenetic study of combinatorial reasoning, for example, Dimant and Bearison (1991) had college students, over a series of six sessions, engage in incrementally more complex versions of a task in which they had to determine what combination of chemicals would generate a particular change in color. Some students worked on the task individually and others in dyads. All were pretested and posttested individually on a task requiring them to systematically generate all possible combinations of five candies.

For students in the dyadic condition, each speech act was coded using a system of categories designed to distinguish (a) collaborative engagement, in which individuals agree, disagree, ask questions, or supply explanations, from (b) speech acts not considered theoretically relevant to cognitive development. Collaborative engagement increased over the course of the six sessions. Pretest-posttest gains in combinatorial reasoning were greater for (a) students in dyads with above-average levels of collaborative engagement than for (b) students in dyads with below-average levels of collaborative engagement or (c) students who worked alone. The latter two groups did not differ, nor was there any effect for theoretically irrelevant speech acts. The developmental impact of peer interaction was apparently a function of the quality of argumentation.

In contrast to case-based and law-based reasoning, then, dialectical reasoning—including dialectical reflection and argumentation—is not only a context for developmental reflection, but a developmental force in itself. With the rise of dialectical forms of reasoning, the study of reasoning becomes indistinguishable from the study of development.

Dialectical reasoning is, in fact, usefully construed as an effort to take control of one's cognitive development.

TOWARD A PLURALIST RATIONAL CONSTRUCTIVISM

This rational constructivist metatheory, I suggest, is best able to account for the developing rationality that is central, in my view, to advanced cognitive development. The most familiar theoretical instantiation of the rational constructivist paradigm is Piaget's theory of cognitive development, which proposes the rational construction of structures that are general across domains and universal across persons and cultures, culminating in formal operations as the highest stage of cognitive development. Now consider evidence for cognitive variability that suggests a pluralist—rather than universalist—version of rational constructivism.

It should be emphasized that pluralist rational constructivism leaves open the possibility that there may be forms of advanced cognition that have a considerable degree of generality across cognitive domains and/or universality across individuals and cultures. There is substantial evidence for such generalities and universalities. Pluralist rational constructivism assumes, however, that there are also important forms of advanced cognition specific to particular domains, individuals, and/or cultures.

Specificity and Generality Revisited

Piaget proposed formal operations as a general structure of advanced cognition applicable to all domains of knowledge. It is possible, however, to construe logic as a domain and formal operations as the structure of advanced cognition within this domain, rather than as a general stage of development. Recent theories have proposed specific forms, structures, or processes of advanced cognition not only with respect to logic (Efklides et al., 1994; Markovits, 1993; Moshman, 1990), but in domains such as morality (Helwig, 1995b; Kohlberg, 1984), perspective taking (Selman, 1980), narrative interpretation (Feldman et al., 1993), and reflective judgment (King & Kitchener, 1994).

The domains potentially relevant to advanced cognitive development constitute a heterogeneous set that overlap each other in complex ways. Even if there are aspects of cognition specific to logic and other aspects specific to morality, for example, logic and morality do not appear to be domains in the same sense. Morality, for example, arguably involves a particular type of content, whereas logic is applicable to a variety of types of content, including morality. Whatever the evidence for domain specificity of cognition, it is doubtful that advanced cognitive development consists of independent developmental transitions in some finite number of distinct domains.

As suggested earlier, it is important to avoid a simplistic choice as to whether advanced cognition is domain specific or general across domains. Rather, I proposed a focus on reasoning and distinguished four ways in which reasoning could be specific or general.

1. There could be forms of reasoning unique to particular domains of knowledge and inference such as physical causality, biological systems, social relations, or morality;

2. There could be forms of reasoning unique to particular types of thinking, such as problem solving, decision making, or hypothesis testing, though these types of thinking may be applicable to multiple domains of knowledge and inference;

3. There could be two or more distinct forms of reasoning, each of which is applicable to multiple types of thinking and multiple domains of knowledge and inference; and

4. There could be generalities that transcend particular forms of reasoning.

To further complicate matters, it is important to distinguish epistemological from psychological considerations with respect to specificity and generality. In comparing two domains of knowledge, for example, we must distinguish (a) the epistemological question of whether it is possible to identify a form of reasoning applicable to both domains (epistemic generality) from (b) the psychological question of whether the development of that form of reasoning is general across domains (psychological generality). Even if a given form of reasoning is broadly applicable (epistemic generality), for instance, the application of such reasoning in multiple domains of knowledge may develop independently (psychological specificity). Without some conceptual basis for suggesting some sort of epistemic generality, however, psychological research on questions of generality may be meaningless. Inquiry into questions of specificity and generality, then, requires ongoing coordination of epistemological analysis concerning the nature and applicability of various forms of reasoning

and psychological research concerning synchronies and asynchronies in developmental change.

A number of researchers have addressed questions of specificity and generality with respect to reasoning about the physical and social worlds. Marini and Case (1994), for example, assessed levels of performance on (a) the Piagetian balance beam task (Inhelder & Piaget, 1958) and (b) a newly designed personality diagnosis task, requiring ability to identify abstract personality traits and use these to predict behavior. Four levels of complexity applicable to reasoning on both tasks were identified. Assessing 80 individuals ranging in age from 9 to 19, they found that most showed identical levels of performance on the two tasks, and almost all the rest differed by just one level. Without suggesting identical rates of development in the two domains, they concluded that a general potential for abstract reasoning typically develops about age 11 or 12 and can be observed in multiple domains under suitable experimental conditions.

The case for psychological and developmental generality is greatly strengthened by results from microgenetic research. In one such study, Kuhn et al. (1995) presented physical and social content to fourth graders and adults each week for a period of ten weeks. Participants generated and tested theories in their efforts to comprehend the causal relations in each domain. Developmental change in reasoning strategies was found for both age groups and, at each age, generalized across content. The authors concluded that both the children and the adults were constructing reasoning strategies applicable to both knowledge domains and were able to apply those strategies to a domain different than the domain in which they were constructed.

In still another approach to the generality of advanced cognition, Schraw, Dunkle, Bendixen, and Roedel (1995) assessed 269 college students in multiple domains with respect to both cognitive performance and several aspects of self-monitoring. The resulting pattern of correlations suggested that monitoring competence is neither entirely general nor entirely specific to domains. Acknowledging the importance of domain-specific knowledge, the authors concluded that monitoring within domains is in part a function of general metacognitive processes. In sum, studies differing greatly in design and focus provide converging evidence for the generality of advanced cognition across content. (For related research and theory, see Case, Ch. 15, this Volume; Chandler & Boutilier, 1992; Klahr et al., 1993; Kosonen & Winne, 1995; Kuhn, 1991; Kuhn et al.,

1992; Nisbett et al., 1987; Schauble, 1996; Schommer & Walker, 1995; Smith et al., 1992.)

Although research of this sort undercuts strong versions of domain specificity, it provides little reason to think that advanced cognitive development can be understood as progress along a single developmental pathway toward a general structural endpoint. I have already proposed that case-based, law-based, and dialectical reasoning constitute distinct forms of reasoning, each of which may include two or more distinct variants (e.g., analogical versus precedent-based forms of case-based reasoning). It is well-established, moreover, that even young children have richly structured domain-specific knowledge and there is substantial evidence that such domains remain important beyond childhood (Helwig, 1995b). Schauble (1996) provides detailed examples of the many ways specific knowledge affects the reasoning people use and the conclusions they reach. Pluralist rational constructivism does not assume that every identifiable domain constitutes its own form of rationality, thus generating its own form of reasoning, but neither does it rule out the possibility of domain-specific forms of rationality and reasoning. The earlier discussions concerning the nature and existence of legal and scientific reasoning illustrate the complexity of the theoretical and empirical questions that arise in this regard.

Whether the present analysis is seen as supportive of domain specificity or of domain generality depends on one's perspective. From the standpoint of Piaget's theory of formal operations, the present emphasis on several qualitatively distinct forms of reasoning may seem a move toward domain specificity, with each form of reasoning potentially constituting a distinct domain of development. On the other hand, the proposed forms of reasoning are applicable to multiple types of thinking and multiple domains of knowledge. Analogical reasoning, for example, can be used in solving problems, making decisions, and conceptualizing relationships with respect to a wide variety of physical, biological, social, and moral phenomena (DeLoache et al., Ch. 16, this Volume; Halford, 1992). From the standpoint of a theory emphasizing distinct types of thinking or distinct domains of knowledge, the present approach would seem domain general in its emphasis on broadly applicable forms of reasoning.

Evidence for distinct forms of reasoning applicable to multiple types of thinking and multiple domains of knowledge and inference, then, suggests a conception of advanced cognitive development more pluralist than that of Piaget, but nonetheless general in important ways. It

remains to be seen whether it will be possible to identify specific forms of reasoning, rooted in specific forms of rationality, that are unique and central to particular types of thinking and/or to particular domains of knowledge and inference.

Human Diversity and Universality

Cognitive variability may also be present or absent with respect to various biological and/or social groupings of individuals. Some studies, for example, have shown statistically significant differences between males and females in the prevalence of various forms of advanced cognition (Foltz et al., 1995; King & Kitchener, 1994; R. Orr & Luszcz, 1994; Shaklee et al., 1988; Walker, 1991; Wark & Krebs, 1996). Most theorists and researchers conclude from such differences that, in a given culture at a given point in its history, one gender may be somewhat more likely than the other to show certain forms of advanced cognition, due largely to differences in the socialization and experiences of males and females in that cultural context (Baxter Magolda, 1992).

Some theorists, however, have proposed that there are innate, fundamental, and/or essential differences between men and women such that certain developmental pathways and/or forms of advanced cognition may be considered prototypically masculine and others prototypically feminine (Labouvie-Vief, Orwoll, & Manion, 1995). It has been suggested, for example, that women use different logics than men (D. Orr, 1989), that they have different "ways of knowing" (Belenky et al., 1986), and that they typically construe moral issues in terms of care, compassion and relationships, whereas men focus on rights, justice, and autonomy (Gilligan, 1982).

Research has not supported the stronger claims of fundamental sex differences. With respect to morality, for example, it appears that both men and women are capable of both care and justice reasoning; how an individual thinks depends more on the nature of the moral dilemma than the gender of the thinker (Helwig, 1995a, in press; Jadack, Hyde, Moore, & Keller, 1995; Walker, 1991; Wark & Krebs, 1996). Similarly, research on logical reasoning, mathematical reasoning, epistemic cognition, and argumentation generally shows sex differences to be minimal, if they are found at all (Chandler et al., 1990; King & Kitchener, 1994; Kosonen & Winne, 1995; Kuhn, 1991; Moshman & Franks, 1986; R. Orr & Luszcz, 1994; Shaklee et al., 1988).

Overall, there is no evidence for any form of advanced cognition that is common among men but rare in women, or vice versa (Menssen, 1993). Correspondingly, there is little support for theories postulating qualitatively distinct pathways of late cognitive development for females and males. Even theorists who continue to highlight the role of gender in advanced cognition maintain complex and ambivalent positions on the question of sex differences (Baxter Magolda, 1992; Clinchy, 1995; Labouvie-Vief et al., 1995).

Culture may be a more important variable than gender with respect to advanced cognitive development (Rogoff, 1990; Rogoff & Chavajay, 1995). Two key questions about the relation of advanced cognition to culture are as follows: Are there forms of advanced cognition that are specific to particular cultures? Are there forms of advanced cognition that are common to diverse cultures? Each of these questions has a developmental counterpart: Are there developmental pathways specific to particular cultures? Are there developmental pathways traversed by individuals in many, and perhaps all, cultures?

The most systematic body of cross-cultural research on advanced cognitive development derives from Kohlberg's theory of moral development. It appears that the moral reasoning of individuals in a wide variety of cultures can be classified and understood with respect to Kohlberg's stages (Boyes & Walker, 1988; Snarey, 1985). The evidence is consistent with the view that these stages emerge in an invariant sequence, though strong tests of this are limited to a narrow range of cultures. There are substantial differences both within and across cultures in how far individuals progress.

Even within the domain of morality, however, there is evidence that certain forms of cognition are associated with certain cultures; we cannot rule out the possibility of developmental pathways specific to particular cultures or individuals (Campbell & Christopher, 1996; Moshman, 1995b). Given the paucity of cross-cultural evidence in other domains of advanced cognitive development, we must be cautious about any strong conclusions concerning the nature of human diversity and the extent of universality. Further research is likely to reveal both (a) forms of cognition appearing in adolescence or adulthood that are specific to particular individuals or cultures and (b) forms of cognition that may be deemed advanced in a general sense and that, even if not universal across individuals, are found in sufficiently developed individuals from a variety of cultures. Correspondingly, it continues to be a reason-

able working hypothesis that cognitive development beyond childhood includes: (a) progress along developmental pathways that are universal across cultures; (b) progress along pathways that are arguably developmental but specific to particular cultures; and (c) progress along pathways that are arguably developmental but specific to particular individuals.

With respect to universalities in advanced cognition, for example, some plausible candidates are: (a) hypothetico-deductive reasoning; (b) principled reasoning; (c) precedent-based reasoning; (d) deliberate coordination of theories with evidence; (e) systematic strategies for testing hypotheses; (f) dialectical argumentation; and (g) rationalist conceptions of knowledge. This is not to say such forms of advanced cognition are likely to be found to be the predominant modes of thinking in all adults in all cultures. On the contrary, as we have seen, there is already substantial evidence against this. It may turn out, however, that such forms of cognition exist in a variety of cultures among individuals who, according to epistemic criteria that transcend any particular culture, may be deemed advanced in their cognition. It may also turn out that those who achieve these or other forms of advanced cognition do so by progressing through the same sequence of stages, though again, the universality of the sequences may be more epistemological than psychological.

With respect to diversities, there may be some forms of advanced cognition specific to particular cultures or individuals. Constitutional reasoning, for example, may be a particular synthesis of rule-based, principled, and precedent-based reasoning constructed only within specialized contexts in cultures with a particular kind of legal system (Fallon, 1987). In some cases, an individual may progress through a unique series of conceptual revolutions to an advanced and novel form of understanding, as in the case of Darwin's construction of the theory of evolution through natural selection (Gruber, 1974). Individuals may construct their own domains of knowledge, and such domains may vary across cultures, thus adding another dimension to the issues of specificity and generality discussed earlier in this section (Campbell & Christopher, 1996; Moshman, 1995b; Rybash et al., 1986).

Universalist rational constructivism suggests that forms of cognition specific to particular individuals and cultures are special cases of more fundamental and universal forms of advanced cognition. This cannot be assumed in advance, however. Pluralist rational constructivism, without denying the existence and importance of universals, suggests that open-minded investigation of individuals and cultures may reveal advanced and fundamental forms of cognition undreamt of in our universalist psychologies (Campbell & Christopher, 1996; Miller & Cook-Greuter, 1994; Moshman, 1995b).

In sum, it is doubtful that late cognitive changes move exclusively toward or through formal operations, and unclear whether they approach any other general and universal endpoint. Current research and theory suggest the value of pluralist rational constructivism, a metatheoretical perspective within which active construction by rational agents is assumed, but generality across domains and universality across persons and cultures are open empirical and conceptual questions.

CONCLUSION

Does cognition develop beyond childhood? As we have seen, there is much evidence for long-term changes in cognition beyond childhood. Early in this chapter, I proposed that long-term changes are usefully construed as developmental if they are qualitative, progressive, and internally directed. I anticipated that some long-term changes in cognition beyond childhood are developmental in this sense, but that advanced cognitive development may not have other characteristics typically associated with developmental change. We now return to these issues.

Qualitative Change

Piaget's (1924/1972) theory of formal reasoning postulated the emergence of hypothetico-deductive reasoning at age 11 or 12. Hypothetico-deductive reasoning, for Piaget, was not a narrow technical skill but a self-conscious coordination of logic and hypothesis—or, in the language of Piaget (1987), of necessities and possibilities—that defined a new and final stage of cognitive development. The later theory of formal operations (Inhelder & Piaget, 1958; Piaget 1947/1960) proposed a logical structure central to this final stage.

The theory of formal operations—strictly construed as the logical model proposed by Inhelder and Piaget (1958)—no longer plays much role in the literature. A variety of neo-Piagetian theories posit the construction of cognitive structures, variously defined and characterized, and propose that such structures achieve higher levels of abstraction beginning age 11 or 12 (Case, Ch. 15, this Volume).

Other theorists, however, focus more on level of metacognitive reflection (Campbell & Bickhard, 1986; Kuhn, 1989, 1991; Moshman, 1990, 1994, 1995b). Although no one doubts that cognition is highly organized, the nature and breadth of advanced cognitive structures remains a matter of uncertainty and dispute.

I have suggested that three forms of reasoning—case-based, law-based, and dialectical—can be distinguished, with the possibility that these can be differentiated and/or coordinated to generate additional forms of reasoning. There is substantial evidence that some such forms of reasoning are general across domains of knowledge and inference (Kuhn et al., 1995; Marini & Case, 1994; Schauble, 1996), but this does not rule out the possibility that we will identify types of thinking or forms of reasoning specific to such domains. It appears that advanced cognition is both specific and general in multiple ways.

Although we have much to learn about matters of specificity, generality, and structure, the case for qualitative change in cognition beyond childhood is strong. Adolescents and adults show forms of reasoning and levels of understanding qualitatively different from the cognition of children (Basseches, 1984; Campbell & Bickhard, 1986; Case, Ch. 15, this Volume; Chandler & Boutilier, 1992; Commons et al., 1984; Inhelder & Piaget, 1958; King & Kitchener, 1994; Kohlberg, 1984; Kuhn, 1989; Markovits, 1993; Moshman, 1990, 1993, 1995b; O'Brien, 1987; Overton, 1990). In fact, there is surprisingly strong support for Piaget's 1924 proposal that formal or hypothetico-deductive reasoning—deliberate deduction from propositions consciously recognized as hypothetical—plays an important role in the thinking of adolescents and adults but is rarely seen much before the age of 11 or 12 (Markovits & Vachon, 1989; Moshman & Franks, 1986). The stronger support for the original theory of formal reasoning than for the structural theory of formal operations suggests that what emerges at about age 11 may not be a better logic, but a deeper level of reflection about the nature of logic, theory, and evidence (Campbell & Bickhard, 1986; Kuhn, 1989; Moshman, 1990).

Progressive Change

There appears to be a consensus that many of the qualitative changes in cognition beyond childhood observed in developmental research represent progress (R. Kitchener, 1986). The consensus may be due in part to the focus of so much research on aspects of logic or mathematics where the superiority of some cognitions to others seems clear.

The consensus may also be due in part, however, to the narrow range of cultures represented by most theorists and research participants. Pluralist rational constructivism suggests the need for more data on advanced cognition in multiple cultures and the corresponding need for more epistemological analysis of what constitutes advanced cognition and how progress in cognition can be identified in a manner that is not completely relative to culture.

The present analysis suggests ongoing transitions that are arguably progressive in a general sense. The emergence of thinking involves the deliberate coordination of inferences and thus represents a higher level of intentionality and complexity. The emergence of reasoning involves increasingly explicit knowledge about the epistemic properties of one's inferences, thus representing a higher level of reflection. It remains unclear toward what endpoints, if any, cognition tends, but such endpoints may not be necessary to identify cognitive progress.

Reflective Construction

I have suggested that advanced cognition is constructed via a process of dialectical reflection that coordinates multiple cognitions and renders their implicit properties explicit. It is in this sense that later cognitive changes, without being genetically determined, may be said to be internally directed and thus developmental. Pluralist rational constructivism suggests there may be forms of advanced cognition unique to individuals, forms associated with particular cultures, and forms universal across many or all cultures. Although some plausible universals have been proposed, evidence relevant to questions of universality and diversity is sparse and ambiguous.

Existing research and theory are sufficient, however, to suggest that advanced cognitions are not only constructed via reflection, but serve as a means of further reflection. Such reflection takes place in individuals, in groups, and in diverse cultural contexts. Our scientific efforts to understand cognition and development, moreover, are themselves reflective and constructive, generating theories of cognition that are themselves sophisticated forms of cognition.

It becomes increasingly difficult at higher levels to separate the application of cognition, the study of cognition, and the process of cognitive development. In both its universal and plural aspects, cognition develops beyond childhood via reflective processes that are simultaneously individual, social, and rational.

ACKNOWLEDGMENTS

I am grateful to Robert Campbell, Hemant Desai, Charles Helwig, Deanna Kuhn, Henry Markovits, and Edith Neimark for helpful comments on earlier versions of the manuscript.

REFERENCES

Ahl, V., Moore, C. F., & Dixon, J. A. (1992). Development of intuitive and numerical proportional reasoning. *Cognitive Development, 7,* 81–100.

Baldwin, J. M. (1895). *Mental development in the child and the race.* New York: Macmillan.

Baldwin, J. M. (1930). [Autobiography.] In C. Murchison (Ed.), *A history of psychology in autobiography* (Vol. 1). Worcester, MA: Clark University Press.

Basseches, M. (1980). Dialectical schemata: A framework for the empirical study of the development of dialectical thinking. *Human Development, 23,* 400–421.

Basseches, M. (1984). *Dialectical thinking and adult development.* Norwood, NJ: ABLEX.

Baxter Magolda, M. B. (1992). *Knowing and reasoning in college: Gender-related patterns in students' intellectual development.* San Francisco: Jossey-Bass.

Belenky, M. F., Clinchy, B. M., Goldberger, N. R., & Tarule, J. M. (1986). *Women's ways of knowing.* New York: Basic Books.

Berkowitz, M. W., & Keller, M. (1994). Transitional processes in social cognitive development: A longitudinal study. *International Journal of Behavioral Development, 17,* 447–467.

Bidell, T. R., Lee, E. M., Bouchie, N., Ward, C., & Brass, D. (1994). Developing conceptions of racism among young white adults in the context of cultural diversity course work. *Journal of Adult Development, 1,* 185–200.

Boyes, M. C., & Walker, L. J. (1988). Implications of cultural diversity for the universality claims of Kohlberg's theory of moral reasoning. *Human Development, 31,* 44–59.

Braine, M. D. S. (1990). The "natural logic" approach to reasoning. In W. F. Overton (Ed.), *Reasoning, necessity, and logic: Developmental perspectives* (pp. 133–157). Hillsdale, NJ: Erlbaum.

Braine, M. D. S., & O'Brien, D. P. (1991). A theory of *If:* A lexical entry, reasoning program, and pragmatic principles. *Psychological Review, 98,* 182–203.

Braine, M. D. S., & Rumain, B. (1983). Logical reasoning. In P. H. Mussen (Series Ed.) & J. H. Flavell & E. M. Markman (Eds.), *Handbook of child psychology: Vol. 3. Cognitive development* (pp. 263–340). New York: Wiley.

Broughton, J. (1977). "Beyond formal operations": Theoretical thought in adolescence. *Teachers College Record, 79,* 87–97.

Broughton, J. (1978). Development of concepts of self, mind, reality, and knowledge. In W. Damon (Ed.), *Social cognition* (pp. 75–100). San Francisco: Jossey-Bass.

Byrnes, J. P. (1988a). Formal operations: A systematic reformulation. *Developmental Review, 8,* 66–87.

Byrnes, J. P. (1988b). What's left is closer to right: A response to Keating. *Developmental Review, 8,* 385–392.

Byrnes, J. P., & McClenny, B. (1994). Decision-making in young adolescents and adults. *Journal of Experimental Child Psychology, 58,* 359–388.

Cairns, R. B. (1983). The emergence of developmental psychology. In P. H. Mussen (Series Ed.) & W. Kessen (Ed.), *Handbook of child psychology: Vol. 1. History, theory, and methods* (pp. 41–102). New York: Wiley.

Campbell, R. L., & Bickhard, M. H. (1986). *Knowing levels and developmental stages.* Basel, Switzerland: Karger.

Campbell, R. L., & Christopher, J. C. (1996). Moral development theory: A critique of its Kantian presuppositions. *Developmental Review, 16,* 1–47.

Cederblom, J. (1989). Willingness to reason and the identification of the self. In E. P. Maimon, B. F. Nodine, & F. W. O'Connor (Eds.), *Thinking, reasoning, and writing* (pp. 147–159). New York: Longman.

Cerella, J., Rybash, J., Hoyer, W., & Commons, M. L. (Eds.). (1993). *Adult information processing: Limits on loss.* New York: Academic Press.

Chandler, M., & Boutilier, R. G. (1992). The development of dynamic system reasoning. *Human Development, 35,* 121–137.

Chandler, M., Boyes, M., & Ball, L. (1990). Relativism and stations of epistemic doubt. *Journal of Experimental Child Psychology, 50,* 370–395.

Chinn, C. A., & Brewer, W. F. (1993). The role of anomalous data in knowledge acquisition: A theoretical framework and implications for science instruction. *Review of Educational Research, 63,* 1–49.

Clinchy, B. M. (1995). Commentary. *Human Development, 38,* 258–264.

Commons, M. L., Richards, F. A., & Armon, C. (1984). *Beyond formal operations: Late adolescent and adult cognitive development.* New York: Praeger.

Craik, F. I. M., & Salthouse, T. A. (Eds.). (1993). *Handbook of aging and cognition.* Hillsdale, NJ: Erlbaum.

De Lisi, R. (1988, June). *The concept of formal thought in Piaget's theory.* Paper presented at the meeting of the Jean Piaget Society, Philadelphia.

Demetriou, A., & Efklides, A. (1994). Structure, development, and dynamics of mind: A meta-Piagetian theory. In A. Demetriou & A. Efklides (Eds.), *Intelligence, mind, and reasoning: Structure and development* (pp. 75–109). Amsterdam, The Netherlands: North-Holland.

Demetriou, A., Efklides, A., & Platsidou, M. (1993). The architecture and dynamics of developing mind. *Monographs of the Society for Research in Child Development, 58*(Serial No. 234).

de Ribaupierre, A., & Pascual-Leone, J. (1979). Formal operations and *M* power: A neo-Piagetian investigation. In D. Kuhn (Ed.), *Intellectual development beyond childhood* (pp. 1–43). San Francisco: Jossey-Bass.

Dimant, R. J., & Bearison, D. J. (1991). Development of formal reasoning during successive peer interactions. *Developmental Psychology, 27,* 277–284.

Dixon, J. A., & Moore, C. F. (1996). The developmental role of intuitive principles in choosing mathematical strategies. *Developmental Psychology, 32,* 241–253.

Dunbar, K., & Klahr, D. (1989). Developmental differences in scientific discovery processes. In D. Klahr & K. Kotovsky (Eds.), *Complex information processing: The impact of Herbert A. Simon* (pp. 109–143). Hillsdale, NJ: Erlbaum.

Dunkle, M. E. (1993). The development of students' understanding of equal access. *Journal of Law and Education, 22,* 283–300.

Efklides, A., Demetriou, A., & Metallidou, Y. (1994). The structure and development of propositional reasoning ability: Cognitive and metacognitive aspects. In A. Demetriou & A. Efklides (Eds.), *Intelligence, mind, and reasoning: Structure and development* (pp. 151–172). Amsterdam, The Netherlands: North-Holland.

Evans, J. St. B. T. (1989). *Bias in human reasoning.* Hillsdale, NJ: Erlbaum.

Fallon, R. H. (1987). A constructivist coherence theory of constitutional interpretation. *Harvard Law Review, 100,* 1189–1286.

Falmagne, R. J., & Gonsalves, J. (1995). Deductive inference. *Annual Review of Psychology, 46,* 525–559.

Feldman, C., Bruner, J., Kalmar, D., & Renderer, B. (1993). Plot, plight, and dramatism: Interpretation at three ages. *Human Development, 36,* 327–342.

Foltz, C., Overton, W. F., & Ricco, R. B. (1995). Proof construction: Adolescent development from inductive to deductive problem-solving strategies. *Journal of Experimental Child Psychology, 59,* 179–195.

Furby, L., & Beyth-Marom, R. (1992). Risk taking in adolescence: A decision-making perspective. *Developmental Review, 12,* 1–44.

Gilligan, C. (1982). *In a different voice: Psychological theory and women's development.* Cambridge, MA: Harvard University Press.

Girotto, V., Blaye, A., & Farioli, F. (1989). A reason to reason: Pragmatic basis of children's search for counter examples. *European Bulletin of Cognitive Psychology, 9,* 297–321.

Girotto, V., Gilly, M., Blaye, A., & Light, P. (1989). Children's performance in the selection task: Plausibility and familiarity. *British Journal of Psychology, 80,* 79–95.

Goldman, A. I. (1994). Argumentation and social epistemology. *Journal of Philosophy, 91,* 27–49.

Goldman, S. R., Pellegrino, J. W., Parseghian, P., & Sallis, R. (1982). Developmental and individual differences in verbal analogical reasoning. *Child Development, 53,* 550–559.

Goswami, U. (1991). Analogical reasoning. What develops? A review of research and theory. *Child Development, 62,* 1–22.

Gray, W. M. (1990). Formal operational thought. In W. F. Overton (Ed.), *Reasoning, necessity, and logic: Developmental perspectives* (pp. 227–253). Hillsdale, NJ: Erlbaum.

Gruber, H. (1974). *Darwin on man.* New York: Dutton.

Habermas, J. (1990). *Moral consciousness and communicative action.* Cambridge, MA: MIT Press.

Halford, G. S. (1989). Reflections on 25 years of Piagetian cognitive developmental psychology, 1963–1988. *Human Development, 32,* 325–357.

Halford, G. S. (1992). Analogical reasoning and conceptual complexity in cognitive development. *Human Development, 35,* 193–217.

Halford, G. S. (1993). *Children's understanding: The development of mental models.* Hillsdale, NJ: Erlbaum.

Hawkins, J., Pea, R. D., Glick, J., & Scribner, S. (1984). "Merds that laugh don't like mushrooms": Evidence for deductive reasoning by preschoolers. *Developmental Psychology, 20,* 584–594.

Helwig, C. C. (1995a). Adolescents' and young adults' conceptions of civil liberties: Freedom of speech and religion. *Child Development, 66,* 152–166.

Helwig, C. C. (1995b). Social contexts in social cognition: Psychological harm and civil liberties. In M. Killen & D. Hart (Eds.), *Morality in everyday life: Developmental perspectives* (pp. 166–200). Cambridge, England: Cambridge University Press.

Helwig, C. C. (in press). The role of agent and social context in judgments of freedom of speech and religion. *Child Development.*

Hilton, D. J. (1995). The social context of reasoning: Conversational inference and rational judgment. *Psychological Bulletin, 118,* 248–271.

Holliday, S. G., & Chandler, M. J. (1986). *Wisdom: Explorations in adult competence.* Basel, Switzerland: Karger.

Holyoak, K. J., & Cheng, P. W. (1995a). Pragmatic reasoning about human voluntary action: Evidence from Wason's selection task. In S. E. Newstead & J. St. B. T. Evans (Eds.), *Perspectives on thinking and reasoning: Essays in honour of Peter Wason* (pp. 67–89). Hillsdale, NJ: Erlbaum.

Holyoak, K. J., & Cheng, P. W. (1995b). Pragmatic reasoning with a point of view. *Thinking & Reasoning, 1,* 289–313.

Horrocks, J. E. (1954). The adolescent. In L. Carmichael (Ed.), *Manual of child psychology* (2nd ed., pp. 697–734). New York: Wiley.

Hoyer, W. J., & Rybash, J. M. (1994). Characterizing adult cognitive development. *Journal of Adult Development, 1,* 7–12.

Huber, B. L., & Huber, O. (1987). Development of the concept of comparative subjective probability. *Journal of Experimental Child Psychology, 44,* 304–316.

Inhelder, B., & Piaget, J. (1958). *The growth of logical thinking from childhood to adolescence.* New York: Basic Books. (Original work published 1955)

Jacobs, J. E., & Potenza, M. (1991). The use of judgment heuristics to make social and object decisions: A developmental perspective. *Child Development, 62,* 166–178.

Jadack, R. A., Hyde, J. S., Moore, C. F., & Keller, M. L. (1995). Moral reasoning about sexually transmitted diseases. *Child Development, 66,* 167–177.

Johnson-Laird, P. N. (1990). The development of reasoning ability. In G. Butterworth & P. Bryant (Eds.), *Causes of development* (pp. 85–110). Hillsdale, NJ: Erlbaum.

Johnson-Laird, P. N., & Byrne, R. M. J. (1991). *Deduction.* Hillsdale, NJ: Erlbaum.

Johnson-Laird, P. N., Byrne, R. M. J., & Schaeken, W. (1992). Propositional reasoning by model. *Psychological Review, 99,* 418–439.

Jones, C. J., & Harris, P. L. (1982). Insight into the law of large numbers: A comparison of Piagetian and judgement theory. *Quarterly Journal of Experimental Psychology, 34A,* 479–488.

Karmiloff-Smith, A. (1992). *Beyond modularity: A developmental perspective on cognitive science.* Cambridge, MA: MIT Press.

Kausler, D. H. (1994). *Learning and memory in normal aging.* San Diego, CA: Academic Press.

Keating, D. P. (1980). Thinking processes in adolescence. In J. Adelson (Ed.), *Handbook of adolescent psychology* (pp. 211–246). New York: Wiley.

Keating, D. P. (1988). Byrnes' reformulation of Piaget's formal operations: Is what's left what's right? *Developmental Review, 8,* 376–384.

Keating, D. P. (1990). Structuralism, deconstruction, reconstruction: The limits of reasoning. In W. F. Overton (Ed.), *Reasoning, necessity, and logic: Developmental perspectives* (pp. 299–319). Hillsdale, NJ: Erlbaum.

Keenan, T., Ruffman, T., & Olson, D. R. (1994). When do children begin to understand logical inference as a source of knowledge? *Cognitive Development, 9,* 331–353.

King, P. M., & Kitchener, K. S. (1994). *Developing reflective judgment: Understanding and promoting intellectual growth and critical thinking in adolescents and adults.* San Francisco: Jossey-Bass.

Kitchener, K. S. (1983). Cognition, metacognition and epistemic cognition: A three-level model of cognitive processing. *Human Development, 26,* 222–232.

Kitchener, K. S., & Kitchener, R. F. (1981). The development of natural rationality: Can formal operations account for it? In J. A. Meacham & N. R. Santilli (Eds.), *Social development in youth: Structure and content* (pp. 160–181). Basel, Switzerland: Karger.

Kitchener, R. F. (1986). *Piaget's theory of knowledge: Genetic epistemology & scientific reason.* New Haven, CT: Yale University Press.

Klahr, D., Fay, A. L., & Dunbar, K. (1993). Heuristics for scientific experimentation: A developmental study. *Cognitive Psychology, 25,* 111–146.

Kobayashi, Y. (1994). Conceptual acquisition and change through social interaction. *Human Development, 37,* 233–241.

Kohlberg, L. (1984). *The psychology of moral development.* San Francisco: Harper & Row.

Koslowski, B., & Maqueda, M. (1993). What is confirmation bias and when do people actually have it? *Merrill-Palmer Quarterly, 39,* 104–130.

Kosonen, P., & Winne, P. H. (1995). Effects of teaching statistical laws on reasoning about everyday problems. *Journal of Educational Psychology, 87,* 33–46.

Kreitler, S., & Kreitler, H. (1986). Development of probability thinking in children 5- to 12-years-old. *Cognitive Development, 1,* 365–390.

Kuhn, D. (1989). Children and adults as intuitive scientists. *Psychological Review, 96,* 674–689.

Kuhn, D. (1991). *The skills of argument.* Cambridge, England: Cambridge University Press.

Kuhn, D., Amsel, E., & O'Loughlin, M. (1988). *The development of scientific reasoning skills.* New York: Academic Press.

Kuhn, D., & Brannock, J. (1977). Development of the isolation of variables scheme in experimental and "natural experiment" contexts. *Developmental Psychology, 13,* 9–14.

Kuhn, D., Garcia-Mila, M., Zohar, A., & Andersen, C. (1995). Strategies of knowledge acquisition. *Monographs of the Society for Research in Child Development, 60*(Serial No. 245).

Kuhn, D., Schauble, L., & Garcia-Mila, M. (1992). Cross-domain development of scientific reasoning. *Cognition and Instruction, 9,* 285–327.

Labouvie-Vief, G., Orwoll, L., & Manion, M. (1995). Narratives of mind, gender, and the life course. *Human Development, 38,* 239–257.

Lachman, M. E., & Burack, O. R. (1993). Planning and control processes across the life span: An overview. *International Journal of Behavioral Development, 16,* 131–143.

Lamborn, S. D., Fischer, K. W., & Pipp, S. (1994). Constructive criticism and social lies: A developmental sequence for understanding honesty and kindness in social interactions. *Developmental Psychology, 30,* 495–508.

Lea, R. B., O'Brien, D. P., Fisch, S. M., Noveck, I. A., & Braine, M. D. S. (1990). Predicting propositional logic inferences in text comprehension. *Journal of Memory and Language, 29,* 361–387.

Light, P., Blaye, A., Gilly, M., & Girotto, V. (1989). Pragmatic schemas and logical reasoning in 6- to 8-year-old children. *Cognitive Development, 4,* 49–64.

Manktelow, K. I., & Over, D. E. (1995). Deontic reasoning. In S. E. Newstead & J. St. B. T. Evans (Eds.), *Perspectives on thinking and reasoning: Essays in honour of Peter Wason* (pp. 91–114). Hillsdale, NJ: Erlbaum.

Marini, Z., & Case, R. (1994). The development of abstract reasoning about the physical and social world. *Child Development, 65,* 147–159.

Markovits, H. (1993). The development of conditional reasoning: A Piagetian reformulation of mental models theory. *Merrill-Palmer Quarterly, 39,* 131–158.

Markovits, H., & Bouffard-Bouchard, T. (1992). The belief-bias effect in reasoning: The development and activation of competence. *British Journal of Developmental Psychology, 10,* 269–284.

Markovits, H., & Nantel, G. (1989). The belief-bias effect in the production and evaluation of logical conclusions. *Memory and Cognition, 17,* 11–17.

Markovits, H., Schleifer, M., & Fortier, L. (1989). Development of elementary deductive reasoning in young children. *Developmental Psychology, 25,* 787–793.

Markovits, H., & Vachon, R. (1989). Reasoning with contrary-to-fact propositions. *Journal of Experimental Child Psychology, 47,* 398–412.

Markovits, H., & Vachon, R. (1990). Conditional reasoning, representation, and level of abstraction. *Developmental Psychology, 26,* 942–951.

Medin, D. L., & Ross, B. H. (1989). The specific character of abstract thought: Categorization, problem solving, and induction. In R. J. Sternberg (Ed.), *Advances in the psychology of human intelligence* (Vol. 5, pp. 189–223). Hillsdale, NJ: Erlbaum.

Menssen, S. (1993). Do women and men use different logics? A reply to Carol Gilligan and Deborah Orr. *Informal Logic, 15,* 123–138.

Miller, M. E., & Cook-Greuter, S. R. (1994). *Transcendence and mature thought in adulthood: The further reaches of adult development.* Lanham, MD: Rowman & Littlefield.

Moore, C. F., Dixon, J. A., & Haines, B. A. (1991). Components of understanding in proportional reasoning: A fuzzy set representation of developmental progression. *Child Development, 62,* 441–459.

Moshman, D. (1990). The development of metalogical understanding. In W. F. Overton (Ed.), *Reasoning, necessity, and logic: Developmental perspectives* (pp. 205–225). Hillsdale, NJ: Erlbaum.

Moshman, D. (1993). Adolescent reasoning and adolescent rights. *Human Development, 36,* 27–40.

Moshman, D. (1994). Reason, reasons, and reasoning: A constructivist account of human rationality. *Theory & Psychology, 4,* 245–260.

Moshman, D. (1995a). Reasoning as self-constrained thinking. *Human Development, 38,* 53–64.

Moshman, D. (1995b). The construction of moral rationality. *Human Development, 38,* 265–281.

Moshman, D., & Franks, B. F. (1986). Development of the concept of inferential validity. *Child Development, 57,* 153–165.

Moshman, D., & Geil, M. (in press). Collaborative reasoning: Evidence for collective rationality. *Thinking & Reasoning.*

Neimark, E. D. (1975). Intellectual development during adolescence. In F. D. Horowitz (Ed.), *Review of child development research* (Vol. 4, pp. 541–594). Chicago: University of Chicago Press.

Newstead, S. E., & Evans, J. St. B. T. (Eds.). (1995). *Perspectives on thinking and reasoning: Essays in honour of Peter Wason.* Hillsdale, NJ: Erlbaum.

Nisbett, R. E., Fong, G. T., Lehman, D. R., & Cheng, P. W. (1987). Teaching reasoning. *Science, 238,* 625–631.

O'Brien, D. P. (1987). The development of conditional reasoning: An iffy proposition. In H. W. Reese (Ed.), *Advances in child development and behavior* (Vol. 20, pp. 61–90). Orlando, FL: Academic Press.

O'Brien, D. P., Braine, M. D. S., & Yang, Y. (1994). Propositional reasoning by mental models? Simple to refute in principle and in practice. *Psychological Review, 101,* 711–724.

Orr, D. (1989). Just the facts Ma'am: Informal logic, gender, and pedagogy. *Informal Logic, 11,* 1–10.

Orr, R., & Luszcz, M. (1994). Rethinking women's ways of knowing: Gender commonalities and intersections with postformal thought. *Journal of Adult Development, 1,* 225–233.

Overton, W. F. (1990). Competence and procedures: Constraints on the development of logical reasoning. In W. F. Overton (Ed.), *Reasoning, necessity, and logic: Developmental perspectives* (pp. 1–32). Hillsdale, NJ: Erlbaum.

Overton, W. F., Ward, S. L., Noveck, I. A., Black, J., & O'Brien, D. P. (1987). Form and content in the development of deductive reasoning. *Developmental Psychology, 23,* 22–30.

Perkins, D. N., Jay, E., & Tishman, S. (1993). Beyond abilities: A dispositional theory of thinking. *Merrill-Palmer Quarterly, 39,* 1–21.

Perry, W. G., Jr. (1970). *Forms of intellectual and ethical development in the college years.* Troy, MO: Holt, Rinehart and Winston.

Piaget, J. (1960). *Psychology of intelligence.* Totowa, NJ: Littlefield, Adams. (Original work published 1947)

Piaget, J. (1972). *Judgment and reasoning in the child.* Totowa, NJ: Littlefield, Adams. (Original work published 1924)

Piaget, J. (1985). *The equilibration of cognitive structures.* Chicago: University of Chicago Press. (Original work published 1975)

Piaget, J. (1987). *Possibility and necessity* (2 volumes). Minneapolis: University of Minnesota Press. (Original work published 1981 & 1983)

Piaget, J., & Inhelder, B. (1975). *The origin of the idea of chance in children.* New York: Norton. (Original work published 1951)

Piaget, J., & Voyat, G. (1979). The possible, the impossible, and the necessary. In F. B. Murray (Ed.), *The impact of Piagetian theory on education, philosophy, psychiatry, and psychology* (pp. 65–85). Baltimore: University Park Press.

Pieraut-Le Bonniec, G. (1980). *The development of modal reasoning: Genesis of necessity and possibility notions.* New York: Academic Press.

Planned Parenthood *v.* Casey. 505 U.S. 833 (1992).

Politzer, G. (1986). Laws of language use and formal logic. *Journal of Psycholinguistic Research, 15,* 47–92.

Reich, K. H., Oser, F. K., & Valentin, P. (1994). Knowing why I now know better: Children's and youth's explanations of their world view changes. *Journal of Research on Adolescence, 4,* 151–173.

Riegel, K. F. (1973). Dialectic operations: The final period of cognitive development. *Human Development, 16,* 346–370.

Rips, L. J. (1994). *The psychology of proof: Deductive reasoning in human thinking.* Cambridge, MA: MIT Press.

Rissland, E. L. (1991). Example-based reasoning. In J. F. Voss, D. N. Perkins, & J. W. Segal (Eds.), *Informal reasoning and education* (pp. 187–208). Hillsdale, NJ: Erlbaum.

Rogoff, B. (1990). *Apprenticeship in thinking: Cognitive development in social context.* New York: Oxford University Press.

Rogoff, B., & Chavajay, P. (1995). What's become of research on the cultural basis of cognitive development? *American Psychologist, 50,* 859–877.

Ruffman, T., Perner, J., Olson, D. R., & Doherty, M. (1993). Reflecting on scientific thinking: Children's understanding of the hypothesis-evidence relation. *Child Development, 64,* 1617–1636.

Rybash, J. M., Hoyer, W. J., & Roodin, P. A. (1986). *Adult cognition and aging.* New York: Pergamon Press.

Salmon, M. H., & Zeitz, C. M. (1995). Analyzing conversational reasoning. *Informal Logic, 17,* 1–23.

Samarapungavan, A. (1992). Children's judgments in theory choice tasks: Scientific rationality in childhood. *Cognition, 45,* 1–32.

Schauble, L. (1990). Belief revision in children: The role of prior knowledge and strategies for generating evidence. *Journal of Experimental Child Psychology, 49,* 31–57.

Schauble, L. (1996). The development of scientific reasoning in knowledge-rich contexts. *Developmental Psychology, 32,* 102–119.

Scholnick, E. K. (1990). The three faces of If. In W. F. Overton (Ed.), *Reasoning, necessity, and logic: Developmental perspectives* (pp. 159–181). Hillsdale, NJ: Erlbaum.

Scholnick, E. K., & Friedman, S. L. (1993). Planning in context: Developmental and situational considerations. *International Journal of Behavioral Development, 16,* 145–167.

Scholnick, E. K., & Wing, C. S. (1995). Logic in conversation: Comparative studies of deduction in children and adults. *Cognitive Development, 10,* 319–345.

Schommer, M. (1994). Synthesizing epistemological belief research: Tentative understandings and provocative conclusions. *Educational Psychology Review, 6,* 293–319.

Schommer, M., & Walker, K. (1995). Are epistemological beliefs similar across domains? *Journal of Educational Psychology, 87,* 424–432.

Schraw, G., Dunkle, M. E., Bendixen, L. D., & Roedel, T. D. (1995). Does a general monitoring skill exist? *Journal of Educational Psychology, 87,* 433–444.

Schraw, G., & Moshman, D. (1995). Metacognitive theories. *Educational Psychology Review, 7,* 351–371.

Selman, R. L. (1980). *The growth of interpersonal understanding.* New York: Academic Press.

Shaklee, H., Holt, P., Elek, S., & Hall, L. (1988). Covariation judgment: Improving rule use among children, adolescents, and adults. *Child Development, 59,* 755–768.

Siegel, H. (1988). *Educating reason: Rationality, critical thinking, and education.* London: Routledge & Kegan Paul.

Siegler, R. S. (1981). Developmental sequences within and between concepts. *Monographs of the Society for Research in Child Development, 46*(Serial No. 189).

Sinnott, J. D., & Cavanaugh, J. (1991). (Eds.). *Bridging paradigms: Positive development in adulthood and cognitive aging.* New York: Praeger.

Sloman, S. A. (1996). The empirical case for two systems of reasoning. *Psychological Bulletin, 119,* 3–22.

Smith, E. E., Langston, C., & Nisbett, R. E. (1992). The case for rules in reasoning. *Cognitive Science, 16,* 1–40.

Smith, L. (1987). A constructivist interpretation of formal operations. *Human Development, 30,* 341–354.

Smith, L. (1993). *Necessary knowledge: Piagetian perspectives on constructivism.* Hillsdale, NJ: Erlbaum.

Snarey, J. (1985). Cross-cultural universality of social-moral development: A critical review of Kohlbergian research. *Psychological Bulletin, 97,* 202–232.

Sodian, B., Zaitchik, D., & Carey, S. (1991). Young children's differentiation of hypothetical beliefs from evidence. *Child Development, 62,* 753–766.

Sternberg, R. J., & Nigro, G. (1980). Developmental patterns in the solution of verbal analogies. *Child Development, 51,* 27–38.

Sternberg, R. J., & Rifkin, B. (1979). The development of analogical reasoning processes. *Journal of Experimental Child Psychology, 27,* 195–232.

Tversky, A., & Kahneman, D. (1974). Judgment under uncertainty: Heuristics and biases. *Science, 185,* 1124–1131.

Tweney, R. D., & Chitwood, S. T. (1995). Scientific reasoning. In S. E. Newstead & J. St. B. T. Evans (Eds.), *Perspectives on thinking and reasoning: Essays in honour of Peter Wason* (pp. 241–260). Hillsdale, NJ: Erlbaum.

Walker, L. J. (1991). Sex differences in moral reasoning. In W. M. Kurtines & J. L. Gewirtz (Eds.), *Handbook of moral behavior and development* (pp. 333–364). Hillsdale, NJ: Erlbaum.

Walton, D. N. (1996). *Argumentation schemes for presumptive reasoning.* Mahwah, NJ: Erlbaum.

Ward, S. L., & Overton, W. F. (1990). Semantic familiarity, relevance, and the development of deductive reasoning. *Developmental Psychology, 26,* 488–493.

Wark, G. R., & Krebs, D. L. (1996). Gender and dilemma differences in real-life moral judgment. *Developmental Psychology, 32,* 220–230.

Youniss, J., & Damon, W. (1992). Social construction in Piaget's theory. In H. Beilin & P. B. Pufall (Eds.), *Piaget's theory: Prospects and possibilities* (pp. 267–286). Hillsdale, NJ: Erlbaum.

Zelazo, P. D., Reznick, J. S., & Piñon, D. E. (1995). Response control and the execution of verbal rules. *Developmental Psychology, 31,* 508–517.

Afterword to Volume 2
Cognition, Perception, and Language

DEANNA KUHN

Editing a volume of this scope clearly stretches one. It affords an opportunity to read closely in areas that normally one would not, but even more valuable is exposure over a concentrated period to 19 different perspectives that beg for comparison and integration. The chapters in this volume offer strikingly diverse portrayals of the field, not only in the developmental phenomena their authors have singled out as most intriguing and worthy of their attention, but in the questions and issues identified as central to the field's continued progress. It had been my hope to represent this diversity of perspective at the editorial level as well, and that hope was well realized in having Bob Siegler as co-editor. The collaboration was a good one, and although we ended up agreeing more often than we disagreed, the different perspectives on the field that we brought to our task proved valuable.

As Bob indicates in his foreword, we asked authors to include some historical perspective in their treatment of their topics, and I was pleased that so many authors took this assignment very seriously. Indeed, many of them I suspect would have adopted a strong historical perspective without prompting from us. Increasingly, those of us who do research in developmental psychology have come to regard our undertakings in a narrative framework, that is, as one bit of plot development in an historical tale of how the field has approached its subject matter. Current approaches are best contemplated in the context of what has come before. It is this context that enables their relative strengths and weaknesses to be appreciated. In the present volume, an additional, more subtle sign of this historical awareness is the dissatisfaction with task-bound approaches expressed in several chapters, a concern Klahr and MacWhinney extend to the computer simulation models they examine. Task-driven programs of inquiry can keep researchers busy, but their generality and endurance will inevitably be limited.

Another fundamental topic we asked authors to address is *mechanisms of change*. It has by now been widely noted and agreed that explaining the process of change is the major challenge that faces developmentalists. In some topic areas, such as infant conceptual development, one can see a particularly striking shift in focus from the previous (1983) to the current (1997) edition, a shift away from defining the presence or absence of competencies and toward questions of process.

There is an irony, however, in the fact that just at the time that attention has finally been focused on process, it has become clear that the change that needs to be explained is a good deal more complicated than previously thought. As my own, Bob Siegler's, and a number of others' research has documented, development rarely if ever consists of a singular transition from a to b. Instead, an individual possesses a repertory of strategies that are applied variably even when the task remains constant. Development entails gradual shifts in the distribution of usage, that is, some strategies increase in frequency of usage while the frequencies of others decrease. An implication is that exclusion of the old is as important to development as acquisition of the new, a generalization that Johnson notes is as applicable to brain development as it is to behavioral development. Similarly as characteristic of brain development as behavioral development, Johnson claims, are the gradual rather than abrupt, and multidimensional rather than singular, nature of change. These are characteristics also noted by authors of other chapters with respect to phenomena ranging from early sensorimotor attainments to advanced kinds of reasoning and problem solving.

Further complicating this picture is the fact that even a single skill or strategy is not neatly classifiable as absent or present in an individual's repertory. As emphasized in this volume in chapters as disparate as those by Haith and

Benson and by Moshman, for most cognitive competencies there exists a continuum of attainment from implicit to explicit mastery. Development entails gradual progress along this continuum. We need to understand more about what such increases in conscious awareness, or what Karmiloff-Smith calls "representational redescriptions," consist of. Without a comprehensive picture of what is developing, we are unlikely to progress very far in explaining the process of development. For now, the broad implication is that we must approach development as involving multiple strands of gain and loss, probabilistic rather than absolute levels of performance (since which behaviors will appear on a particular occasion is never certain), and the states of "partial accomplishment" that Haith and Benson stress as most worthy of our investigation.

Examining the change process is complicated even further by two additional dimensions highlighted in the present volume. One is the subjective environment that Gelman and Williams emphasize is at least as important as the objective environment. Little doubt remains regarding the crucial role of environment in development. Yet, what comprises that environment is not constant across any two developing individuals. Because both children and adults select and shape the environment they attend to, as well as interpret it through their own subjective lens, it is never clear exactly what it is that they are experiencing. Yet it is this subjective environment that most directly influences development.

Compounding the difficulty in identifying the subjective environment is another dimension that can no longer be ignored—the social one that Rogoff's chapter highlights. The subjective meaning that individuals attribute to their experience develops in interaction with others. I make meaning from the selves others present to me, but, also, I come to know more fully what I mean by how others understand me. Although its social as well as subjective character complicates the researcher's efforts to examine the process of meaning-making, it has become increasingly clear that the topic of our investigations must be development as experienced, not as observed from the outside nor extracted from the social context in which it is embedded.

If the process of development is as multifaceted and complex as it now appears, it is not surprising that simplistic theories are increasingly likely to be rejected as inadequate to explain it. The present volume, relative to its 1983 predecessor, exhibits substantial evidence of the rejection of simple or unidimensional theories, in favor of explanations that invoke multiple mechanisms, dimensions, and

even pathways of development. Mandler, for example, proposes that multiple modalities of representation figure in development. Gelman and Williams invoke a particularly striking blend of multiple mechanisms that they claim play a role in development. A great many of their ideas reflect Piaget's influence. The influence of Piaget's ideas is evident as well in Wellman and Gelman's chapter and, even if in some cases less directly, in almost all of the other chapters. It is striking that in recent years Piaget has been shown wrong in so many ways and yet there exist today so many ways in which we recognize him to be right—a testament, perhaps, to the depth and richness of his contribution. Piaget's concept of accommodation as "doubly directed by assimilation" (in both directing its focus and registering its results), as just one example, seems alive and well in a number of chapters.

Yet Gelman and Williams find a prominent place for associative mechanisms, as well as information-processing principles and concepts, in their account—a state of affairs that reflects, I believe, the decline of exclusionary accounts of development, that is, ones claiming that development consists of this process rather than that one. In the 1960s and 1970s, the antithesis that opposed Piaget's constructivist thesis in North American developmental psychology was social learning theory. The rise of interest in Vygotsky's theory is one of the influences that has led to the demise of deceivingly simple polarities such as this one. A concept such as internalization, in the minds of Piagetians once firmly located on the opponent's turf, is now understood and made use of in much more subtle and sophisticated ways, as Rogoff's and others' chapters attest.

The present volume attests to a number of other deceptive polarities that have been put to rest, among them those associated with old heredity versus environment controversies. As Johnson notes, for example, the identification of brain involvement does not imply irrelevance of environment. Klahr and MacWhinney take on what recent theoretical developments have defined as a newer polarity—between connectionist and production-system explanations—and ask us to consider whether they really oppose one another.

What, then, is the future role of the "grand theories" of past decades? Case, Haith and Benson, and a number of other authors ask this inevitable question, one that Damon also broaches in his preface to this edition of the *Handbook*. Will promising newcomers, such as dynamic systems theory, assume the role of the earlier grand theories or are we more likely to see hybrid theories that incorporate multiple mechanisms and dimensions that stood alone in earlier theories? Is the unified model or "more integrated framework" that Case would like to achieve a realistic possibility, or are our own theoretical efforts destined to be characterized by the *bricoleur* metaphor that DeLoache and coauthors use to describe young theoreticians and reasoners?

The current era of predominantly "local" theories addressed to a limited range of phenomena is new enough that it is perhaps too soon to say what will follow. One prediction, however, is that we will demand of future theories that they account for more than a very narrow range of phenomena, particularly those tied to a specific task, even if they account for those phenomena quite well. We also can predict that future theories will be more inclusive than past ones, not only in incorporating multiple mechanisms as suggested earlier, but also in integrating multiple levels of explanation. At the moment, progress is being made in constructing accounts of cognitive development at the neurological level; at the level of action systems and perceptual systems; as well as at the various cognitive levels of representational systems, knowledge, strategies, information-processing mechanisms, and metacognitive awareness and control. Social systems represent yet another level of explanation. It is a misconception to treat these explanatory accounts as alternatives. We need not choose between knowledge and strategies, for example, to explain development—strategies constrain development of a knowledge base as much as knowledge constrains strategy use. Both constructs are needed to capture what is developing. More broadly, recognizing the coexistence of all of these different levels of explanation should remind us that it is in fact one individual who incorporates these systems— from the physical and molecular to the teleological and reflective— and that ultimately these levels of explanation must be integrated.

I conclude with two other predictions. One is that by the time of the next edition of the *Handbook,* we will see increased attention to what might develop, along with what routinely does. Many of the chapters in this volume quite reasonably are devoted to understanding the complexities that underlie the remarkable cognitive and linguistic achievements that occur routinely in the early years of life. But very soon—by age 3, 4, or certainly 5—differences among children in the cognitive competencies they have attained become enormous. Inter-individual variability is as much a fact of cognitive development as is intra-individual variability. And these differences amplify with each successive year, such that many of the higher order reasoning skills examined in the chapters by Moshman and by DeLoache and colleagues are likely to be ably demonstrated by some older children and adolescents and beyond the reach of many others. As developmental psychologists in a society whose young increasingly often are growing up in endangered circumstances, we would do well to devote attention to the kinds of development that may occur—to the competencies that our younger generation may be capable of attaining, given a favorable combination of circumstances, rather than only the universal cognitive achievements—impressive as they are—that occur even when circumstances are less favorable.

A second challenge that can be predicted to occupy developmentalists in the years from now until the next edition of this *Handbook* is also one with social implications. We must come to grips with what we mean by *development.* The blurring of the traditional distinction between development and learning has highlighted the question of how we are to define development. To define development as universally occurring structural change has proven too restrictive. Yet to equate development with any form of change is so inclusive as to leave us without a clear sense of our subject matter. Socioculturalists have done the dual service of focusing our attention on process and broadening our concern to encompass more diverse kinds of change than those associated with structural/universal definitions of development. At the same time, they have not yet tackled the question of what is to count as development. Can we, as Moshman asks, identify criteria (such as complexity or reflective awareness) that make it possible to specify developmental sequences or directions that have validity across cultures? And can we balance the valuing of developmental achievements with a genuine respect for diversity and multiple pathways? These are indeed questions for the 21st century.

Author Index

Subject Index